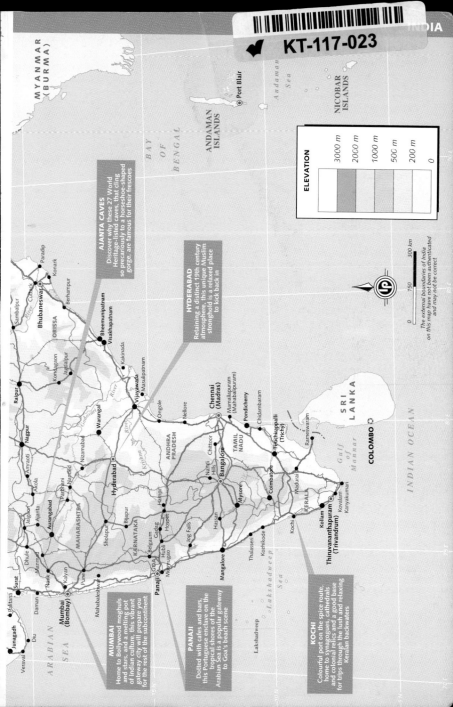

INDIA

KT-117-023

ELEVATION

3000 m
2000 m
1000 m
500 m
200 m
0

0   150   300 km

The external boundaries of India
on this map have not been authenticated
and may not be correct

AJANTA CAVES
Discover why these 27 World
Heritage-listed caves, that cling
so precariously to a horseshoe-shaped
gorge, are famous for their frescoes

HYDERABAD
Retaining a distinct 19th century
atmosphere, this unique Muslim
stronghold is a relaxed place
to kick back in

MUMBAI
Home to Bollywood moghuls
and stars, and a melting pot
of Indian culture, this vibrant
gateway city will prepare you
for the rest of the subcontinent

PANAJI
Dotted with cafes and bars,
this Portuguese enclave on the
tropical shores of the
Arabian Sea is a popular gateway
to Goa's beach scene

KOCHI
Colourful port on the spice route,
home to synagogues, cathedrals
and colonial relics and a good base
for trips through the lush and relaxing
Keralan backwaters

MYANMAR
(BURMA)

Port Blair

Andaman
Sea

ANDAMAN
ISLANDS

NICOBAR
ISLANDS

BAY

OF

BENGAL

Paradip
Konark
Cuttack
Sambalpur
Berhampur
Bhubaneswar
ORISSA
Bheemunipatnam
Konkagaon
Jagdalpur
Visakhapatnam
Kakinada
Raipur
Masulipatnam
Nagpur
Warangal
Vijayawada
Amraoti
Akola
Nizamabad
Ongole
Nellore
Bhusawal
Parbhani
Nagpad
Hyderabad
Chennai
(Madras)
Mamallapuram
(Mahabalipuram)
Jalgaon
Ajanta
ANDHRA
PRADESH
Pondicherry
Dhule
Aurangabad
MAHARASHTRA
Sholapur
Hampi
Chittoor
Chidambaram
Manmad
Bijapur
Nandi
Hills
TAMIL
NADU
Tiruchirappalli
(Trichy)
Nasik
Hospet
Belgaum
Jog Falls
Bangalore
Rameswaram
Kalyan
Pune
Hubli
KARNATAKA
Mysore
Coimbatore
Madurai
Gulf
of
Mannar
Mumbai
(Bombay)
Mahabaleshwar
Dharwad
Hassan
Kovalam
Mangalore
Kozhikode
KERALA
Kanyakumari
Surat
GOA
Panaji
Thalassery
Kochi
Kollam
Daman
Thiruvananthapuram
(Trivandrum)
Diu
Junagadh
Palitana
Veraval

ARABIAN

SEA

Lakshadweep

Lakshadweep
Sea

INDIAN OCEAN

SRI
LANKA

COLOMBO

India
8th edition – September 1999
First published – October 1981

Published by
Lonely Planet Publications Pty Ltd A.C.N. 005 607 983
192 Burwood Rd, Hawthorn, Victoria 3122, Australia

Lonely Planet Offices
Australia PO Box 617, Hawthorn, Victoria 3122
USA 150 Linden St, Oakland, CA 94607
UK 10a Spring Place, London NW5 3BH
France 1 rue du Dahomey, 75011 Paris

Photographs
All of the images in this guide are available for licensing from
Lonely Planet Images.
email: lpi@lonelyplanet.com.au

Front Cover Photograph
A holy cow in all its festival finery moves through the busy South Indian
traffic. (Eddie Gerald)

ISBN 0 86442 687 9

text & maps © Lonely Planet 1999
photos © photographers as indicated 1999

Printed by SNP Printing Pte Ltd, Singapore

Contents – Text

KERALA 1047

CHENNAI (MADRAS) 1103

TAMIL NADU 1124

ANDAMAN & NICOBAR ISLANDS 1201

LANGUAGE 1217

GLOSSARY 1221

ACKNOWLEDGEMENTS 1232

INDEX 1247

MAP LEGEND back page

METRIC CONVERSION inside back cover

Contents – Maps

NORTH-EASTERN REGION

RAJASTHAN

GUJARAT

MADHYA PRADESH

MUMBAI (BOMBAY)

MAHARASHTRA

GOA

KARNATAKA

ANDHRA PRADESH

MAP LEGEND   See Back Page

The Authors

Christine Niven

Christine set out from New Zealand for the big overseas experience at the age of 20 and never really settled down after that. Overlanding from Europe to India was her first long trip and was followed by journeys through China, Japan, South-East Asia and the Middle East. She continues to travel whenever the opportunity arises, probably in defiance of good sense.

Christine has also authored *South India* and *Sri Lanka* for Lonely Planet.

Teresa Cannon & Peter Davis

After too many years in a suffocating bureaucracy Teresa felt compelled to escape to the rarefied environment of the Himalaya. There she trekked through century-old rhododendron forests and traversed the peaks and passes of the western moonscape region. She succumbed to the continuing welcome *namaste*, which flowed like a mantra throughout the landscape. She wanted to stay. But visas run out and bank balances diminish.

Her love of travel led her to Asia several times where she gathered material and co-authored a book on Asian elephants which was published in 1995. A children's version was published by Cambridge University Press in April 1998. Teresa has also co-authored LP's *South India* and *Kerala* guides.

Following a brief stint as a cadet photographer on the Melbourne *Herald* Peter lost himself at University to study economics and politics followed by graduate studies in media. His first real job was selling fire extinguishers. He regards this as the beginning of his extinguished career.

He drifted into freelance journalism and photography. He has published hundreds of features and photographs from numerous locations around the world. Elephants play a big part in Peter's life. He is co-author and photographer of the book *Aliya – Stories of the Elephants of Sri Lanka*.

When he's not chasing a story or an elephant he lectures part time in professional writing at Deakin University and in photojournalism at Photography Studies College in Melbourne. Peter has also co-authored Lonely Planet's *South India* and *Kerala* guides.

David Collins

David was born in England but ran away as soon as he could. After graduating with the world's most obscure degree, he worked for a trade union, a leprosy colony, a magazine publisher and as a freelance journalist. Squandering the proceeds on a 'wouldn't it be nice to live here' world tour, David tried Santa Barbara, Sydney and Ouagoudougou on for size before signing on as Lonely Planet's Melbourne-based Web slave. He's also the author of Lonely Planet's *Mumbai* city guide.

9

Paul Harding

Born in Melbourne, Paul grew up mostly in country Victoria where he started working life as a reporter on a local newspaper. A three year overseas trip, including a stint as editor of a London travel magazine and travels through Europe and South-East Asia, forged his desire to mix travel and work.

In 1986 he joined Lonely Planet as an editor but, realising he was on the wrong side of the desk, swapped his red pen for a blue one and now works as a full-time writer. Paul has also contributed to Lonely Planet's *South-East Asia* guide.

Mark Honan

After a university degree in philosophy opened up a glittering career as an office clerk, Mark decided there was more to life than data entry. He set off on a two year trip round the world, armed with a backpack and an intent to sell travel stories and pictures upon his return. Astonishingly, this barely-formed plan succeeded and Mark has since contributed regularly to magazine travel pages.

He started writing for Lonely Planet in 1991 and has worked on Lonely Planet's *Austria, Switzerland, Mexico, Central America* and the *Solomon Islands* – next up is Switzerland again.

Bradley Mayhew

Bradley started travelling in South-West China, Tibet and northern Pakistan while studying Chinese at Oxford University. Upon graduation he fled to Central America for six months to forget his Chinese and then worked in Beijing in a futile attempt to get it back. Since then he has spent two months in the Silk Road cities of Bukhara and Khiva, two months trekking in Kyrgyzstan and has enjoyed extended trips to Iran, Eastern Turkey and Ladakh. He is also the co-author of LP's *Pakistan, Karakoram Highway, South-West China, Central Asia* and *Tibet* guides.

Bradley is also the co-author and photographer of the Odyssey Guide to Uzbekistan, and has lectured on Central Asia at the Royal Geographical Society. He splits his time between Sevenoaks in south-east England and Las Vegas, Nevada.

Richard Plunkett

Richard grew up on a farm in central Victoria. A week after his high school exams he arrived alone in Calcutta, and was never quite the same again. Between subsequent jaunts to Asia and the Middle East he worked as a journalist at *The Age* in Melbourne and the Australian edition of *The Big Issue*.

He eventually landed a job at Lonely Planet largely on the strength of knowing the capital of Burkina Faso. After 18 months of armchair travel, he took to the hills to research Ladakh, Garhwal, Sikkim and Arunachal Pradesh, as well as Lonely Planet's *Delhi* city guide.

Phillipa Saxton

The seed was sown for a life of penury as a travel writer during a childhood living in several countries and probably germinated after receiving a cheque for £5 as 'Encouragement Fee' for two travel stories published at the age of 14. Intervening years included studying to become the world's greatest forensic scientist (abandoned), marriage (terminated) and raising three wonderful children (completed). On becoming a full-time writer, the natural progression was to visit India, the ancestral home of five previous generations and the subject of many childhood stories. As with many visitors, India became her passion, and publishing a magazine, *Saffron Road*, was her attempt to repay India for the vast joy the association has given her.

The India experience has seen her sitting for 16 hours in a 3rd class compartment of a stationary train, staying at a Maharajah's palace and riding across the Himalaya on an Enfield motorcycle.

Sarina Singh

After completing a business degree in Melbourne, a deep passion for travel lured Sarina to India. There she did a marketing executive traineeship with Sheraton Hotels, but later drifted into journalism, working as a freelance journalist and foreign correspondent. Writing mainly about India, assignments also took her to Kenya, Zanzibar, the Middle East, Nepal and Pakistan where she interviewed a notorious Mujahedeen warlord at his clandestine headquarters near the Afghanistan border. After 3½ years in India, Sarina returned to Australia, did a post-graduate journalism course and wrote two television documentary scripts. Other Lonely Planet books she has worked on are *Rajasthan, Africa, Mauritius, Réunion & Seychelles, Sacred India* and *Out to Eat – Melbourne*.

FROM THE AUTHORS
Christine Niven

Thanks to all the people who slogged away at the research on this book, and to those who beat it into shape at the end.

Teresa Cannon & Peter Davis

We wish to thank Mr D Venkatesan for his assistance and quiet persistence; Mr Shankaran who, as well as being an excellent driver, worked as an interpreter, guide and tailor; Nalini Chettur for her ability to unearth yet another relevant tome; Mr MR Hari & Mr KV Ravisankar for their invaluable time and copious information; PJ Varghese whose knowledge of and passion for his country is infectious; Mr MS Venugopal who offered many good contacts and never shied from our constant questions. Also special thanks to Mr D Karunanidhi; Dr Venu; Mr Mani Madhavan; Mr Joseph Iype; and to all those people who helped further our appreciation of Indian food, culture and hospitality.

In Australia we wish to thank Christine Niven for her persistence and supportive emails; Adam, Lindsay, Sharan, Joyce, Monique, Thalia,

Maree *et al* at LP HQ; Dr Robyn Jeffrey for guidance and contacts; Isobel for minding our home and feeding the possums, cockatoos and kookaburras; and friends and family who never complained when we declined invitations with the excuse 'sorry, we're still working on the book'.

David Collins

Thanks to the resourceful Kamlesh Amin, patron saint of travellers; Homi Kaka and his crew for running a great hotel; Yasmin Poonegar Pouzet for being streets ahead of the competition; and Cedric for his best dressed man of the year poise.

Also thanks to Isaac Kehimkar of the Bombay Natural History Society, Nayan and Rima Marphatia for letting me raid their bookshelf; and Aravind Narasipur for supportive emails.

In Australia thanks to Joyce Connolly for a pain-free edit, Sharan Kaur for her patience and Cathy Thornton for not asking for the magic camera back. Special thanks to Anne Thornton for opening my eyes to Mumbai, and for almost making me redundant.

Paul Harding

Thanks to all those tourist officers (well, some of them), locals, guides and travellers who shared their knowledge and experience with me on this trip. In particular I would like to thank Mr GS Chahal of Madhya Pradesh Tourism in Bhopal; Mr RK Rai at MP Tourism's Hotel Sheesh Mahal in Orchha; Mr DM Yadav of the Government of India Tourist Office in Aurangabad for his professionalism, hospitality and paan; Mr UD Kamat of Goa's Department of Tourism in Panaji and his friend, Mr Mascarenhas. At home, thanks to Christine Niven and Michelle Coxall for a detailed and helpful brief, Douglas Streatfeild-James for (unwittingly) giving me a head start with his fine work on the *South India* guide, Sharan Kaur for her faith, Adam for not complaining about the maps, and Joyce for her fine work as co-ordinating editor.

Mark Honan

Much appreciation to everyone I met along the way who helped me get through my tough itinerary with spirit and bowels reasonably intact. Special thanks to Ed Simpson for insights into Mandvi and other locations in Gujarat, and to Mike I for sending the promised email update, and to Ramesh for simplifying Agra's complications, and to all the travellers who wrote in with useful tips.

Bradley Mayhew

Thanks to Mr Sah of Hotel Lake View for info and a lift to Naukuchiyatal and Mr Yogunda at Shimla HPTDC Ignace Pollet for trek notes.

Richard Plunkett

Big thanks to Linda and Elana in Ladakh, Nasir and friends in Leh, Franz and Trudi in the Nubra Valley, Jean-Claude and Martine in Zanskar, Mohammed Sadiq in Kargil, Gary and Pip in Badrinath, Avi and Steve in Rishikesh, Clay Youngkin and Ha-Jo in Sikkim, and Naved Chowdhury and Bina Lyngdoh in Meghalaya. Thanks also to the owners of Delhi's Hotel Namaskar, and to Sanjay Singh in Delhi and Asha in Sydney for their help with navigating Indian officialdom.

A very special thanks to Mr Chakraborty of Bandardewa for his help in getting me into Arunachal Pradesh. I'd probably still be at the checkpoint arguing with the border police if it weren't for you. Thanks also to the Buddhist community of Itanagar for being so helpful. Back in Melbourne, thanks to Hannah for letting me run away for so long, and to Geoff, Sue, Sharan and Adam at LP for the job.

Phillipa Saxton

My thanks to the Director and staff of the Government of India Tourist Office in Calcutta, especially Bidisha Sengupta; Diamond & Nimmie Oberoi at Hotel New Elgin, and all my other friends in Darjeeling, for their warm hospitality and friendship; Kanta Talukdar Stanchina, a good friend and an absolute font of information on Bengali culture and art; fellow travellers Peter Hunt (ferret extraordinaire) and Martin Bradshaw who walked his legs off on my behalf; Bryn Thomas without whose advice I would have been completely lost (and probably still be in India looking for facts and figures); Swosti Travels who introduced me to Orissa and saved me from many onerous bus trips; Warwick Blacker and Sue Larsen of Thai Airways in Sydney who dealt with perpetual excess luggage requests and changing itineraries; Michael Halstead a loyal and generous friend; Dee Davison; my sisters and family for their unstinting support; and Mike Ferris, who had to deal with calls home, general depression and the weeks of write-up on my return. At Lonely Planet I thank Joyce Connolly, Christine Niven, Lindsay Brown and Sharan Kaur who sent encouraging emails and made all sorts of allowances.

Sarina Singh

Special thanks to Amit, Swati & Parth Jhaveri in Mumbai; Arvind Singh Mewar in Udaipur and Sanjay Singh Badnor and his parents, Raghuraj and Lucky, in Ajmer – for always welcoming me warmly into their homes. I'm also grateful to Jitendra Singh Rathore in Udaipur for his assistance.

Thank you to Digvijay Singh Patan and his family for looking after me so well in Jaipur; Pushpendra (Bunty) Singh for making sure I got a look inside the Raj Mandir cinema; Sangeeta Singh for her wonderful company; Raju Singh for his offerings of cold beer after hot research trips in Jodhpur; to Sweety and family for their friendship; to the inimitable Dalvir Singh for keeping me incognito; Rattan Singh for helping me test out lassis and spices in Jodhpur; Laxmi Kant Jangid in Jhunjhunu for his enthusiasm; M.K Harshvardhan Singh (an advocate of the local weasel population!) for showing me around downtown Dungarpur; Mukesh Mehta in Bundi; the effervescent Himmat Singh in Pushkar; and R.S Shekhawat, assistant director at the Bikaner tourist office.

Thanks also to the fellow travellers I met on the way for their feedback: Paul Robinson (USA), Amber Ellington (UK), John and Amanda Black (USA), Jean-Marc Duvergé (France), Ellen Banks (Australia), Adam McIntyre (Australia), Evelyn Mayers (Germany), Alice Maguire (New Zealand) and Christophe Dubois (Switzerland).

A vote of thanks also to the hundreds of travellers who wrote into Lonely Planet – I read each and every letter. In Melbourne, warm thanks to my parents for their support and to my close friend, Robyn Anderson – for helping me see light at the end of the tunnel.

INDIA REGIONAL MAPS

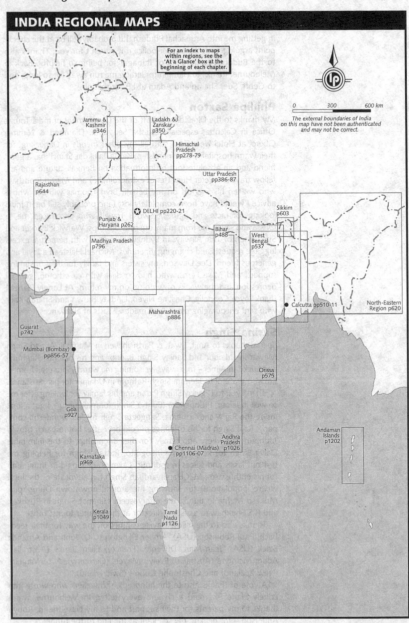

For an index to maps within regions, see the 'At a Glance' box at the beginning of each chapter.

0   300   600 km

The external boundaries of India on this map have not been authenticated and may not be correct.

Jammu & Kashmir p346

Ladakh & Zanskar p350

Himachal Pradesh pp278-79

Uttar Pradesh pp386-87

Rajasthan p644

DELHI pp220-21

Punjab & Haryana p262

Sikkim p603

Bihar p488

West Bengal p537

Madhya Pradesh p796

Calcutta pp510-11

North-Eastern Region p620

Maharashtra p886

Gujarat p742

Mumbai (Bombay) pp856-57

Orissa p575

Goa p927

Andhra Pradesh p1026

Andaman Islands p1202

Chennai (Madras) pp1106-07

Karnataka p969

Kerala p1049

Tamil Nadu p1126

This Book

When the first edition of this book emerged in 1981 it was the biggest, most complicated and most expensive project we'd tackled at Lonely Planet. It began with an exploratory trip to South India by Tony and Maureen – they returned the following year with Geoff Crowther and Prakash Raj to spend a combined total of about a year of more-or-less nonstop travel. The second, third and fourth editions were researched by Tony, Prakash, Geoff and Hugh Finlay. The fifth edition was researched by Hugh, Tony, Geoff and Bryn Thomas. The sixth edition was researched by Hugh, Tony, Bryn, Prakash, Michelle Coxall, Leanne Logan and Geert Cole. The seventh edition was researched and updated by Bryn, Christine Niven, David Collins, Rob Flynn, Sarina Singh and Dani Valent.

The first edition exceeded all our hopes and expectations: it instantly became our best-selling guide. In the UK it won the Thomas Cook Guidebook of the Year award and in India it became the most popular guide to the country – a book used even by Indians to explore their own country. It has continued to be one of Lonely Planet's most popular and successful guides.

For this eighth edition of India, Christine Niven coordinated the whole project. She also updated the introductory chapters, Jammu & Kashmir and the Sacred India colour section.

Teresa Cannon and Peter Davis updated Andhra Pradesh, Kerala, Chennai, Tamil Nadu and the Andaman & Nicobar Islands while David Collins updated Mumbai.

Richard Plunkett updated Delhi, Ladakh & Zanskar, Uttarakhand, Sikkim and North-Eastern Region and Mark Honan updated Punjab & Haryana, Gujarat and most of Uttar Pradesh. Bradley Mayhew took on Himachal Pradesh and parts of Uttar Pradesh, Sarina Singh updated Rajasthan, Paul Harding updated Madhya Pradesh, Maharashtra, Goa and Karnataka and Phillipa Saxton updated Bihar, Calcutta, Orissa and West Bengal.

From the Publisher

Joyce Connolly was the coordinating editor of this edition, while Maree 'tonsilectomy' Styles coordinated the maps and design. Brigitte Ellemor, Monique Choy, Thalia Kalkipsakis, Miriam Cannell, Michelle Coxall, Adam Ford, Sarah Mathers, Lara Morcombe, Darren Elder and Isabelle Young willingly helped Joyce.

Maree was assisted by Paul Piaia, Mark Germanchis, Sarah Sloane, Shahara Ahmed, Brett Moore, Hunor Csutoros, Csanad Csutoros, Mark Griffiths and Leanne Peake. Adriana Mammarella and Sharan Kaur provided invaluable support.

Quentin Frayne sorted out the language, the cover was designed by Simon Bracken & Guillame Roux and Simon Borg drew the illustrations.

THANKS
Many thanks to the travellers who used the last edition and wrote to us with helpful hints, advice and interesting anecdotes. Your names appear in the back of this book.

Foreword

ABOUT LONELY PLANET GUIDEBOOKS

The story begins with a classic travel adventure: Tony and Maureen Wheeler's 1972 journey across Europe and Asia to Australia. Useful information about the overland trail did not exist at that time, so Tony and Maureen published the first Lonely Planet guidebook to meet a growing need.

From a kitchen table, then from a tiny office in Melbourne (Australia), Lonely Planet has become the largest independent travel publisher in the world, an international company with offices in Melbourne, Oakland (USA), London (UK) and Paris (France).

Today Lonely Planet guidebooks cover the globe. There is an ever-growing list of books and there's information in a variety of forms and media. Some things haven't changed. The main aim is still to help make it possible for adventurous travellers to get out there – to explore and better understand the world.

At Lonely Planet we believe travellers can make a positive contribution to the countries they visit – if they respect their host communities and spend their money wisely. Since 1986 a percentage of the income from each book has been donated to aid projects and human rights campaigns.

Updates Lonely Planet thoroughly updates each guidebook as often as possible. This usually means there are around two years between editions, although for more unusual or more stable destinations the gap can be longer. Check the imprint page (following the colour map at the beginning of the book) for publication dates.

Between editions up-to-date information is available in two free newsletters – the paper *Planet Talk* and email *Comet* (to subscribe, contact any Lonely Planet office) – and on our Web site at www.lonelyplanet.com. The *Upgrades* section of the Web site covers a number of important and volatile destinations and is regularly updated by Lonely Planet authors. *Scoop* covers news and current affairs relevant to travellers. And, lastly, the *Thorn Tree* bulletin board and *Postcards* section of the site carry unverified, but fascinating, reports from travellers.

Correspondence The process of creating new editions begins with the letters, postcards and emails received from travellers. This correspondence often includes suggestions, criticisms and comments about the current editions. Interesting excerpts are immediately passed on via newsletters and the Web site, and everything goes to our authors to be verified when they're researching on the road. We're keen to get more feedback from organisations or individuals who represent communities visited by travellers.

> Lonely Planet gathers information for everyone who's curious about the planet – and especially for those who explore it first-hand. Through guidebooks, phrasebooks, activity guides, maps, literature, newsletters, image library, TV series and Web site we act as an information exchange for a worldwide community of travellers.

Research Authors aim to gather sufficient practical information to enable travellers to make informed choices and to make the mechanics of a journey run smoothly. They also research historical and cultural background to help enrich the travel experience and allow travellers to understand and respond appropriately to cultural and environmental issues.

Authors don't stay in every hotel because that would mean spending a couple of months in each medium-sized city and, no, they don't eat at every restaurant because that would mean stretching belts beyond capacity. They do visit hotels and restaurants to check standards and prices, but feedback based on readers' direct experiences can be very helpful.

Many of our authors work undercover, others aren't so secretive. None of them accept freebies in exchange for positive write-ups. And none of our guidebooks contain any advertising.

Production Authors submit their raw manuscripts and maps to offices in Australia, USA, UK or France. Editors and cartographers – all experienced travellers themselves – then begin the process of assembling the pieces. When the book finally hits the shops, some things are already out of date, we start getting feedback from readers and the process begins again …

WARNING & REQUEST

Things change – prices go up, schedules change, good places go bad and bad places go bankrupt – nothing stays the same. So, if you find things better or worse, recently opened or long since closed, please tell us and help make the next edition even more accurate and useful. We genuinely value all the feedback we receive. Julie Young coordinates a well travelled team that reads and acknowledges every letter, postcard and email and ensures that every morsel of information finds its way to the appropriate authors, editors and cartographers for verification.

Everyone who writes to us will find their name in the next edition of the appropriate guidebook. They will also receive the latest issue of *Planet Talk*, our quarterly printed newsletter, or *Comet*, our monthly email newsletter. Subscriptions to both newsletters are free. The very best contributions will be rewarded with a free guidebook.

Excerpts from your correspondence may appear in new editions of Lonely Planet guidebooks, the Lonely Planet Web site, *Planet Talk* or *Comet*, so please let us know if you *don't* want your letter published or your name acknowledged.

Send all correspondence to the Lonely Planet office closest to you:

Australia: PO Box 617, Hawthorn, Victoria 3122
USA: 150 Linden St, Oakland, CA 94607
UK: 10A Spring Place, London NW5 3BH
France: 1 rue du Dahomey, 75011 Paris

Or email us at: talk2us@lonelyplanet.com.au

For news, views and updates see our Web site: www.lonelyplanet.com

HOW TO USE A LONELY PLANET GUIDEBOOK

The best way to use a Lonely Planet guidebook is any way you choose. At Lonely Planet we believe the most memorable travel experiences are often those that are unexpected, and the finest discoveries are those you make yourself. Guidebooks are not intended to be used as if they provide a detailed set of infallible instructions!

Contents All Lonely Planet guidebooks follow roughly the same format. The Facts about the Destination chapters or sections give background information ranging from history to weather. Facts for the Visitor gives practical information on issues like visas and health. Getting There & Away gives a brief starting point for researching travel to and from the destination. Getting Around gives an overview of the transport options when you arrive.

The peculiar demands of each destination determine how subsequent chapters are broken up, but some things remain constant. We always start with background, then proceed to sights, places to stay, places to eat, entertainment, getting there and away, and getting around information – in that order.

Heading Hierarchy Lonely Planet headings are used in a strict hierarchical structure that can be visualised as a set of Russian dolls. Each heading (and its following text) is encompassed by any preceding heading that is higher on the hierarchical ladder.

Entry Points We do not assume guidebooks will be read from beginning to end, but that people will dip into them. The traditional entry points are the list of contents and the index. In addition, however, some books have a complete list of maps and an index map illustrating map coverage.

There may also be a colour map that shows highlights. These highlights are dealt with in greater detail in the Facts for the Visitor chapter, along with planning questions and suggested itineraries. Each chapter covering a geographical region usually begins with a locator map and another list of highlights. Once you find something of interest in a list of highlights, turn to the index.

Maps Maps play a crucial role in Lonely Planet guidebooks and include a huge amount of information. A legend is printed on the back page. We seek to have complete consistency between maps and text, and to have every important place in the text captured on a map. Map key numbers usually start in the top left corner.

Although inclusion in a guidebook usually implies a recommendation we cannot list every good place. Exclusion does not necessarily imply criticism. In fact there are a number of reasons why we might exclude a place – sometimes it is simply inappropriate to encourage an influx of travellers.

Introduction

India, it is often said, is not a country but a continent. From north to south and east to west, the people are different, the languages are different, the customs are different, the country is different.

There are few countries on earth with the enormous variety that India has to offer. It's a place that somehow gets into your blood.

Love it or hate it you can never ignore India. It's not an easy country to handle, and more than a few visitors are only too happy to finally get on to their flight and leave the place. Yet a year later they'll be hankering to get back.

It all comes back to India's amazing diversity – it's as vast as it is crowded, and as

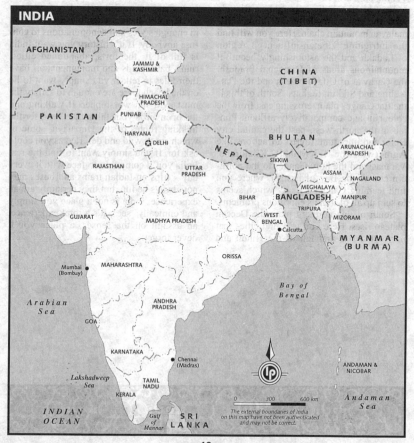

INDIA

AFGHANISTAN

JAMMU & KASHMIR

CHINA (TIBET)

HIMACHAL PRADESH

PAKISTAN   PUNJAB

HARYANA

✪ DELHI

BHUTAN

NEPAL

SIKKIM

ARUNACHAL PRADESH

RAJASTHAN   UTTAR PRADESH

ASSAM   NAGALAND

MEGHALAYA

BIHAR   BANGLADESH   MANIPUR

TRIPURA

GUJARAT   MADHYA PRADESH   WEST BENGAL   MIZORAM

● Calcutta

MYANMAR (BURMA)

ORISSA

Mumbai (Bombay) ●   MAHARASHTRA

Bay of Bengal

Arabian Sea   ANDHRA PRADESH

GOA

KARNATAKA

● Chennai (Madras)

ANDAMAN & NICOBAR

Lakshadweep Sea   TAMIL NADU

Andaman Sea

KERALA

INDIAN OCEAN

Gulf of Mannar   SRI LANKA

0   300   600 km

The external boundaries of India on this map have not been authenticated and may not be correct.

luxurious as it is squalid. The plains are as flat and featureless as the Himalaya are high and spectacular, the food as terrible as it can be magnificent, the transport as exhilarating as it can be boring and uncomfortable. Nothing is ever quite the way you expect it to be.

India is far from the easiest country in the world to travel around. It can be hard going, the poverty will get you down, Indian bureaucracy would try the patience of a saint, and the most experienced travellers find their tempers frayed at some point in India. Yet it's all worth it.

Very briefly, India is roughly a triangle with the top formed by the mighty Himalayan mountain chain. Here you will find the intriguing Tibetan-influenced region of Ladakh and the astonishingly beautiful mountainous areas of Himachal Pradesh, the Garhwal of Uttar Pradesh and the Darjeeling and Sikkim regions. South of this is the flat Ganges plain, crossing east from the colourful and comparatively affluent Punjab in the north-west, past the capital city Delhi and important tourist attractions like Agra (with the Taj Mahal), Khajuraho, Varanasi and the holy Ganges to the northern end of the Bay of Bengal, where you find teeming Calcutta, a city which seems to sum up all of India's enormous problems.

South of this northern plain the Deccan plateau rises. Here you will find cities that mirror the rise and fall of the Hindu and Muslim kingdoms, and the modern metropolis that their successors, the British, built at Mumbai (formally known as Bombay). India's story is one of many different kingdoms competing with each other, and this is never more clear than in places like Bijapur, Mandu, Golconda and other central Indian centres. Finally, there is the steamy south, where Muslim influence was fleeting. It's here that Hinduism was the least altered by outside influences and is at its most exuberant. The superbly colourful temple towns of the south are quite unlike those of the north.

Basically India is what you make of it and what you want it to be. If you want to see temples, there are temples in profusion in enough styles and denominations to confuse anybody. If it's history you want India is full of it; the forts, abandoned cities, ruins, battlefields and monuments all have their tales to tell. If you simply want to lie on the beach there are enough to satisfy the most avid sun worshipper. If walking and the open air is your thing then head for the trekking routes of the Himalaya, some of which are as wild and deserted as you could ask for. If you simply want to find the real India you'll come face to face with it every day – trips on Indian trains and buses may not always be fun, but they certainly are an experience. India is not a place you simply and clinically 'see'; it's a total experience, an assault on the senses, a place you'll never forget.

Facts about India

For at least 4000 years, India's social and religious structures have withstood invasions, famines, religious persecutions, political upheavals and many other cataclysms. Few other countries could claim to have a national identity with such a long history. To describe India as a land of contrasts is to state the obvious. Although there are many countries which would qualify for such a description in terms of their different ethnic groups, languages, religions, geography and traditions, few can match the vast scale and diversity found in India.

Change is inevitably taking place as modern technology is woven into the fabric of society, yet essentially rural India remains much the same as it has been for thousands of years. Even in the fast-paced modern cities like Delhi, Mumbai (formerly Bombay) and Bangalore, what appears to be a complete change of attitude and lifestyle is only surface gloss. Underneath, the age-old verities, loyalties and obligations still rule.

Possibly no other country has its religions so intertwined with every aspect of life. Coming to understand it can be a long process, particularly for those educated in the western liberal tradition with its basis in logic. For those people, 'Indian logic' can often seem bizarre, convoluted and even exasperating. Yet it encompasses a unique cosmology which is holistic and coherent as well as fascinating.

India was the birthplace of two of the world's great religions (Hinduism and Buddhism) and one of its smallest (Jainism). It's also home to one of the world's few remaining communities of Parsis, adherents of the faith of Zoroastrianism (see the Sacred India colour section).

The modern state itself is a relatively recent creation born out of a people's desire to throw off the yoke of colonialism. Even the mightiest of India's ancient civilisations could not encompass all of modern India,

and today it is still as much a country of diversities as of unities. Although there are many different Indias, sometimes hindering the development of a national conscience, it's worth remembering that India has remained the world's largest democracy for the last 50 years.

HISTORY
Indus Valley Civilisation
India's first major civilisation flourished around 2500 BC in the Indus River Valley, much of which lies within present day Pakistan. This civilisation, which lasted for 1000 years and is known as the Harappan culture, appears to have been the culmination of thousands of years of settlement. Excavation of different strata of Neolithic sites shows that the earliest inhabitants were nomadic tribesmen who began to cultivate the land and keep domestic animals. Considerable trade grew up, and by around 3500 BC an urban culture began to emerge. By 2500 BC the large cities of the Mature Harappa period were established.

The major cities such as Mohenjodaro and Harappa (discovered in the 1920s), and Lothal near Ahmedabad in India, were carefully laid out with precise street plans and even sewage facilities. Several sites had a separate acropolis pointing to a clear religious function, and the great tank at Mohenjodaro may well have been used for ritual bathing purposes. The major cities were sizeable – estimates of the population of Mohenjodaro are as high as 30,000 to 40,000.

By the middle of the 3rd millennium BC the Indus Valley culture was the equal of other great cultures emerging at the time. The Harappans traded with Mesopotamia, and developed a system of weights and measures, a script (which remains undeciphered), and a developed art in the form of terracotta and bronze figurines. Recovered relics include models of bullock carts and jewellery, demonstrating an already distinctively Indian culture. Clay figurines found at these sites suggest a Mother goddess (later personified as Kali) and a male three-faced god sitting in the attitude of a yogi attended by four animals (the prehistoric Shiva) were worshipped. Black stone pillars (associated with phallic worship of Shiva) and animal figures (the most prominent being the humped bull; later Shiva's mount) have also been discovered.

The decline of the culture, at the beginning of the 2nd millennium BC, was thought to have been caused by an Aryan invasion. Recently however, historians have suggested several intriguing alternatives, one theory being that the decline was caused by the flooding of the Indus Valley; another possibility is that climatic changes led to decreased rainfall and the subsequent failure of agriculture.

Early Invasions & the Rise of Religions

From around 1500 BC onwards, Aryan (from a Sanskrit word meaning noble) tribes from Afghanistan and Central Asia began to filter into north-west India. Despite their martial superiority, their progress was gradual, with successive tribes fighting over territory and new arrivals pushing farther east into the Ganges plain. Eventually these tribes controlled the whole of northern India as far as the Vindhya Hills, and many of the original inhabitants, the Dravidians, were pushed south.

The invaders brought with them their nature gods, among whom the gods of fire (Agni) and battle (Indra) were predominant, as well as cattle-raising and meat-eating traditions. It was during this period of transition (1500-1200 BC) that the Hindu sacred scriptures, the *Vedas*, were written, and that the caste system became formalised, distinguishing between the Aryans and the indigenous Indians who they were subduing. The *Vedas* justify caste (see Society & Conduct later in this chapter) by describing the natural creation of the system when the universe was formed:

When they divided Purusha, how many portions did they make?
What do they call his mouth, his arms? What do they call his thighs and feet?
The Brahman was his mouth, of both arms was the Rajanya Kshatriya made.
His thighs became the Vaishya, from his feet the Shudra was produced.

As the Aryan tribes spread out across the Ganges plain, in the late 7th century BC, many of them became grouped together into 16 major kingdoms. The *asvamedha* or horse sacrifice was one aspect of an increasingly formal system of rule that prevailed. In this ritual a horse was allowed to roam freely, followed by a band of soldiers. If the horse's progress was impeded the king would fight for the land in question. At the end of the prescribed period, the entire area over which the horse had wandered was taken to be the king's unchallenged territory, and the horse was sacrificed. This ritual was still being performed centuries later by dynasties such as the Chalukyas of Badami to assert their unchallenged right to territory, and to demonstrate the ruler's complete control of his kingdom.

Gradually the 16 major kingdoms were amalgamated into four large states, with Kosala and Magadha emerging to be the most powerful during the 5th century BC. After a series of dynastic changes, the Nanda dynasty came to power in 364 BC, ruling over a huge area of north India.

During this period, the heartland narrowly avoided two other invasions from the west. The first was by the Persian king, Darius (521-486 BC), who annexed the Punjab and Sind (on either side of the modern India-Pakistan border). Alexander the Great marched to India from Greece in 326 BC, but his troops refused to go beyond the Beas River, in Himachal Pradesh. It was the easternmost extent of the Persian empire he conquered, and he turned back without extending his power into India itself. His most lasting reminder in the east was the development of Gandharan art, an intriguing mix of Grecian artistic ideals and the new religious beliefs of Buddhism.

Buddhism and Jainism arose around 500 BC questioning the *Vedas* and condemning the caste system, though, unlike the Buddhists, the Jains never denied their Hindu heritage and their faith never extended beyond India.

Buddhism, on the other hand, drove a radical swathe through the spiritual and social body of Hinduism and enjoyed some spectacular growth after Emperor Ashoka embraced the faith in 262 BC and declared it the state religion. Nevertheless, it gradually lost touch with the masses and faded as Hinduism underwent a revival between 200 and 800 AD. Yet such was the appeal of Buddha that it could not be sidelined and forgotten. Buddha was therefore incorporated into the Hindu pantheon as yet another of the *avataars* (manifestations) of Vishnu; a prime example of the way in which Hinduism has absorbed spiritual competitors and heretical ideologies.

The Mauryas & Emperor Ashoka

Chandragupta Maurya, the founder of the first great Indian empire, came to power in 321 BC, having seized the Magadha throne from the Nandas. He soon expanded the empire to include a huge area of the Indus Valley previously conquered by Alexander. According to an eyewitness account by an ambassador to the Mauryan court, Megasthenes, Chandragupta's capital at Pataliputra (modern day Patna) was of an awesome size – 33.8km in circumference. If this is true, it would have been the largest city in the world at the time.

The Mauryan empire eventually spread across north India and as far south as modern day Karnataka. The Mauryas set up a well-organised kingdom with an efficient bureaucracy, organised tiers of local government and a well-defined social order consisting of a rigid caste system. Security was maintained by a huge standing army consisting, according to one account, of 9000 elephants, 30,000 cavalry and 600,000 infantry.

The empire reached its peak under Ashoka, who left pillars and rock-carved edicts which delineate the enormous span of his territory; these can be seen in Delhi, Gujarat, Orissa, Sarnath in Uttar Pradesh (on the spot where Buddha delivered his first sermon expounding the Noble Eightfold Path, or middle way to enlightenment) and Sanchi in Madhya Pradesh.

Ashoka also sent missions abroad, and he is revered in Sri Lanka because he sent his son to carry Buddhism to the island. The development of art and sculpture also flourished during his rule, and his standard, which topped many pillars, is now the seal of modern day India (four lions sitting back to back atop an abacus decorated with a frieze and the inscription 'truth alone triumphs'). The Republic of India, established on 26 January 1950, chose Emperor Ashoka's standard as its national emblem to reaffirm the ancient commitment to peace and goodwill. Under Ashoka, the Mauryan empire probably controlled more of India than any subsequent ruler prior to the Mughals or the British. Following Ashoka's death, in 232 BC, the empire rapidly disintegrated, finally collapsing in 184 BC.

An Interlude, Then the Guptas

A number of empires rose and fell following the collapse of the Mauryas. The Sungas ruled from 184 to 70 BC before being overcome by the short-lived Kanvas. In the north-west, the successors to Alexander's kingdoms expanded their power into the Punjab, before being overrun by a new wave of invaders from Central Asia, including the Shakas. The Shakas were later relieved of power in north India (but not in the north-west and south) by the Kushanas, who briefly ruled over a massive area of north India and Central Asia. In central India the powerful Shatavahanas ruled the roost, and throughout the subcontinent small tribes and kingdoms held varying amounts of territory and influence.

Despite the lack of a central power, this was a period of intense development. Trade with the Roman empire (both overland and by sea through the southern ports) became substantial during the 1st century AD, and there was also overland trade with China. Buddhism flourished, despite experiencing a doctrinal split between the *Hinayana* (lesser vehicle) and the *Mahayana* (greater vehicle) forms. Jainism's doctrine underwent a similar division, giving rise to the *Digambara* (sky clad) and *Svetambara* (white clad) sects.

In 319 AD, Chandragupta I, the third king of the little known Gupta tribe, came to prominence by a fortuitous marriage to the daughter of one of the most powerful tribes in the north, the Licchavis. The Gupta empire grew rapidly and under Chandragupta II (ruled 375 to 413 AD) it achieved its greatest extent. The Chinese pilgrim Fahsien, visiting India at the time, described what he found:

The people are rich and contented, the kings govern without recourse to capital punishment, but offenders are fined lightly or heavily according to the nature of their crime.

The arts flourished during this period, and some of the finest work was done at Ajanta, Ellora, Sanchi and Sarnath. Poetry and literature also experienced a golden age. Towards the end of the Gupta period, however, Buddhism and Jainism both began to decline and Hinduism began to rise in popularity once more.

The invasions of the Huns at the beginning of the 6th century signalled the end of this era of history, and in 510 AD the Gupta army was defeated by the Hun leader Toramana. Subsequently, north India broke up into a number of separate Hindu kingdoms and was not really unified again until the arrival of the Muslims.

Meanwhile in the South

Following the decline of the Mauryan empire in the early 2nd century BC, a number of powerful kingdoms arose in central and South India, among them the Shatavahanas, Kalingas and Vakatakas. In the far south, despite a slight influence from the Mauryas, the political developments of the north had little direct influence, and a completely separate set of kingdoms emerged, developing mainly from tribal territories on the fertile coastal plains. These subsequently grew into the great empires of the Cholas, Pandyas, Cheras, Chalukyas and Pallavas. The Chalukyas ruled mainly over the Deccan region of central India, although their power occasionally extended further north. With a capital at Badami in Karnataka, they ruled from 550 to 753 AD before falling to the Rashtrakutas. An eastern branch of the Chalukyas, with their capital at Kalyani rose and ruled again from 972 to 1190.

In the far south, the Pallavas pioneered Dravidian architecture with its exuberant, almost baroque, style. In 850, the Cholas rose to power and gradually superseded the Pallavas. They too were great builders who carried their power overseas and, under the reign of Raja Raja (985-1014), controlled almost the whole of South India, the Deccan plateau, Sri Lanka, and parts of the Malay peninsula and Sumatran-based Srivijaya kingdom.

The south's prosperity was based upon its long-established trading links with other civilisations. The Egyptians, and later the Romans, traded by sea with the South India. In return for spices, pearls, ivory and silk, the Indians received Roman gold. Indian merchants also extended their influence to South-East Asia.

While Buddhism and, to a lesser extent, Jainism were displacing Hinduism in the central and northern India, Hinduism continued to flourish in the south. For a time Buddhism, and later Hinduism, flourished in Indonesia, and the people of the region looked towards India as their cultural mentor. The *Ramayana*, that most famous of Hindu epics, is today told and retold in various forms in many South-East Asian countries. Another possible outside influence to South India during this period was St Thomas the Apostle, who is said to have arrived in Kerala in 52 AD. To this day, there is a strong Christian influence in the region.

First Muslim Invasions

During the period following the demise of the Guptas, north India, like the south, was controlled by a number of regional powers. Despite constant competition between the states a power balance was maintained. At the very beginning of the 11th century, however, a new enemy threatened India from the north-west.

Muslim power first made itself strongly felt on the subcontinent with the raids of Mahmud of Ghazni. Today, Ghazni is just a grubby little town between Kabul and Kandahar in Afghanistan, but in the early years of the 2nd millennium, Mahmud turned it into one of the world's most glorious capital cities. The funds for this development was plundered from his neighbours' territories; from 1001 to 1025 Mahmud conducted 17 raids into India including one on the famous Shiva temple at Somnath. A Hindu force of 70,000 died in fierce fighting trying to defend the temple which eventually fell in early 1026. In the aftermath of his victory Mahmud, unconcerned with acquiring territory, successfully transported a massive haul of gold and other booty back across the desert to his capital. These raids effectively shattered the balance of power in north India allowing subsequent invaders to claim the territory for themselves.

Following Mahmud's death in 1033, Ghazni was seized by the Seljuqs and subsequently fell to the Ghurs, who originated in western Afghanistan. Their style of warfare was brutal – having taken Ghazni in 1150, they are reported to have spent seven days sacking the city, a feat which they achieved so thoroughly that the Ghur general, Ala-ud-din was subsequently titled 'Burner of the World'.

In 1191, Mohammed of Ghur, who had been expanding his powers across the Punjab, advanced into India and fought a major battle against a confederacy of Hindu rulers. He was defeated, but returned the following year and routed his enemies. One of his generals, Qutb-ud-din, captured Delhi and was appointed governor, while another continued east carving out a separate empire in Bengal. Within a short time almost the whole of north India was under Ghur control and following Mohammed's death in 1206, Qutb-ud-din became the first of the sultans of Delhi. His successor, Iltutmish, brought Bengal back under central control and defended the empire from an attempted invasion by the Mongols.

After a brief interlude in which his succession was fought over, Ala-ud-din Khilji came to power in 1296. Through a series of phenomenal campaigns, he pushed the borders of the empire south, while simultaneously fending off further attacks by the Mongols.

After Ala-ud-din's death in 1320, Mohammed Tughlaq, having murdered his father, ascended the throne in 1324. During Mohammed's reign the empire achieved its greatest extent and also, due to Mohammed's overreaching ambition, began to disintegrate. Unlike his forebears (including great rulers such as Ashoka), Mohammed dreamed not only of extending his indirect influence over South India, but of controlling it directly as part of his empire. After a series of successful campaigns he decided to move the capital from Delhi to a more central location. The new capital was called Daulatabad and was near Aurangabad in Maharashtra. In order to populate the city he forced every single inhabitant out of Delhi and marched them southwards, with great loss of life. After only a short period, however, he realised that this left the north undefended and so the entire capital was moved north again. Raising revenue to finance his huge armies was another problem; an attempt to introduce copper coinage had disastrous results and wide counterfeiting soon buried the plan.

With the withdrawal from the south, several splinter kingdoms arose, including, in the Deccan, the Bahmani sultanate and the Hindu Vijayanagar empire. The last of the great sultans of Delhi, Firoz Shah, died in 1388 and the fate of the sultanate was sealed when Tamerlane (Timur) made a devastating raid from Samarkand into India in 1398. Tamerlane's sack of Delhi is supposed to have been truly merciless; some accounts say his soldiers slaughtered every Hindu inhabitant.

Meanwhile in the South (Again)

Once again, events in South India took a different path to those in the north, with the peninsula having largely escaped central rule from Delhi. Between 1000 and 1300, the Hoysala empire, which had centres at Belur, Halebid and Somnathpur, was at its peak (see Belur & Halebird in the Karnataka chapter). It eventually fell to a predatory raid by Mohammed Tughlaq in 1328, followed by the combined opposition of other Hindu states.

Two great kingdoms developed in the wake of Mohammed Tughlaq's withdrawal from central and South India. The Vijayanagar empire, with its capital at Hampi, was founded in 1336. In the following two centuries it became the strongest Hindu kingdom in India. The other, Vijayanagar's great rival to the north, the Muslim Bahmani sultanate, emerged in 1345 with its capital at Gulbarga then Bidar. At the end of the 15th century however, following much intrigue and plotting in the royal court, the sultanate disintegrated. As a result, five separate kingdoms, based on the major cities, were formed: Berar, Ahmednagar, Bijapur, Golconda and Ahmedabad.

While the five northern powers fought among themselves, Vijayanagar enjoyed a golden age of almost supreme power in the south, and in 1520 the Hindu king Krishnadevaraya even took Bijapur. In 1565, however, the northern Muslim states combined to destroy Vijayanagar power in the epic Battle of Talikota (see The Rise & Fall of the Vijayanagar Empire boxed text). Later, the Bahmani kingdoms were to fall to the Mughals.

The Mughals (1527-1757)

Back in the north, even as Vijayanagar was experiencing its last days, the next great Indian empire was being founded. Although

---

The Rise & Fall of the Vijayanagar Empire

Founded as an alliance of Hindu kingdoms banding together to counter the threat from the Muslims, the Vijayanagar empire rapidly grew into one of the wealthiest and greatest Hindu empires that India has ever seen. Under the rule of Bukka I (circa 1343-79) the majority of South India was brought under its control and its wealth, accrued through trade, began to flood in.

The kingdom and the Bahmani sultanate, which controlled much of the Deccan, had a fairly even balance of power creating an almost constant struggle and numerous bloody wars. The Vijayanagar armies occasionally got the upper hand, but generally the Bahmanis inflicted the worst defeats. Atrocities committed almost defy belief. In 1366, Bukka I responded to a perceived slight by capturing the Muslim stronghold of Mudkal and slaughtering every inhabitant bar one, who managed to escape and carry news of the attack to Mohammad Shah, the sultan. Mohammad swore that he would not rest until he had killed 100,000 Hindus, but he far exceeded even his own predictions. The Muslim historian Firishtah estimates that half a million 'infidels' were killed in the ensuing campaign.

Vijayanagar's fortunes improved considerably after 1482 when the Bahmani kingdom disintegrated. With little realistic opposition from the north, the Hindu empire reached its peak over the following years. The empire's heyday was also however, the start of its decline. A series of uprisings divided the kingdom fatally, just at a time when the Muslim sultanates were beginning to form a new alliance. In 1565 a Muslim coalition engaged the Hindu armies at the Battle of Talikota. The result was a complete rout of the Vijayanagar forces, and the devastation of Hampi. The last of the Vijayanagar line escaped, and the dynasty limped on for several years. In reality however, power in the region passed either to Muslim rulers, or local chiefs who had come to power as loyal followers of the Vijayanagar kings.

the Mughals' heyday was relatively brief, their empire was massive, covering, at its height, almost the entire subcontinent. Its significance was not only in its size, however. The Mughal emperors presided over a golden age of arts and literature and had a passion for building which resulted in some of the greatest architecture in India. In particular, Shah Jahan's magnificent Taj Mahal ranks as one of the wonders of the world. The six great Mughals and the length of their reigns were:

Babur	1527-1530
Humayun	1530-1556
Akbar	1556-1605
Jehangir	1605-1627
Shah Jahan	1627-1658
Aurangzeb	1658-1707

The founder of the Mughal line, Babur, was a descendant of both Genghis Khan and Tamerlane. In 1525 he marched into the Punjab from his capital at Kabul in Afghanistan. With revolutionary new knowledge of firearms, and consummate skill in employing artillery and cavalry together, Babur defeated the numerically superior armies of the Sultan of Delhi at the Battle of Panipat in 1526.

Despite this initial success, Babur's son, Humayun was defeated by a powerful ruler of eastern India, Sher Shah, in 1539 and forced to withdraw to Iran. Following Sher Shah's death in 1545, Humayun returned to claim his kingdom, eventually conquering Delhi in 1555. He died the following year and was succeeded by his young son Akbar who, during his 49 year reign, managed to extend and consolidate the empire until he ruled over a huge area.

Akbar was probably the greatest of the Mughals, for he not only had the military ability required of a ruler at that time, but was also a man of culture and wisdom with a sense of fairness. He saw, as previous Muslim rulers had not, that the number of Hindus in India was too great to subjugate. Instead, he integrated them into his empire and used them as advisers, generals and administrators. Akbar also had a deep interest in religious matters, and spent many hours in discussion with religious experts of all persuasions, including Christians and Parsis. He eventually formulated a religion, Deen Ilahi, which combined the best points of all those he had studied.

Jehangir ascended to the throne following Akbar's death in 1605. Despite several challenges to the authority of Jehangir himself, the empire remained in more or less the same form as Akbar had left it. In periods of stability Jehangir took the opportunity to spend time in his beloved Kashmir, eventually dying en route there in 1627. He was succeeded by his son, Shah Jahan, who secured his position as emperor by executing all male collateral relatives. During his reign, some of the most vivid and permanent reminders of the Mughals' glory were constructed.

The last of the great Mughals, Aurangzeb came to the throne in 1658, after a two year struggle against his brothers and having imprisoned his father (Shah Jahan). Aurangzeb devoted his resources to extending the empire's boundaries, and fell into much the same trap that Mohammed Tughlaq had some 300 years earlier. He, too, tried moving his capital south (to Aurangabad) and imposed heavy taxes to fund his military. A combination of decaying court life and dissatisfaction among the Hindu population at inflated taxes and religious intolerance, weakened the Mughal grip.

The empire was also facing serious challenges from the Marathas in central India and, more significantly, the British in Bengal (see Expansion of British Power later in this section). With Aurangzeb's death in 1707, the empire's fortunes rapidly declined, and the sack of Delhi by Persia's Nadir Shah in 1739 served to confirm the lack of real power. Mughal 'emperors' continued to rule right up to the Indian Uprising in 1857, but they were emperors without an empire. In sharp contrast to the magnificent tombs of his Mughal predecessors, Aurangzeb's tomb is a simple affair at Rauza, near Aurangabad.

The Rajputs & the Marathas

Throughout the Mughal period, there were still strong Hindu powers, most notably the Rajputs. Centred in Rajasthan, the Rajputs were a warrior caste with a strong and almost fanatical belief in the dictates of chivalry, both in battle and in the conduct of state affairs. Their place in Indian history is much like that of the knights of medieval Europe. The Rajputs opposed every foreign incursion into their territory, but were never united or sufficiently organised to be able to deal with superior forces on a long-term basis. Not only that, but when not battling foreign oppression they squandered their energies fighting each other. This eventually led to them becoming vassal states of the Mughal empire, but their prowess in battle was well recognised, and some of the best military men in the emperors' armies were Rajputs.

The Marathas first rose to prominence under their great leader Shivaji, who gathered popular support by championing the Hindu cause against the Muslim rulers. Between 1646 and 1680, Shivaji performed feats of arms and heroism across most of central India, and tales of his larger-than-life exploits are still popular with wandering storytellers today. He is a particular hero in Maharashtra, where many of his wildest adventures took place, but he is also revered for two other things: as a lower-caste Shudra, he showed that great leaders do not have to be *Kshatriyas* (soldiers or administrators); and he demonstrated great abilities in confronting the Mughals. At one time, Shivaji was captured by the Mughals and taken to Agra but, naturally, he managed to escape and continued his adventures.

Shivaji's son was captured, blinded and executed by Aurangzeb. His grandson was not made of the same sturdy stuff so the Maratha empire continued under the Peshwas, hereditary government ministers who became the real rulers. They gradually took over more and more of the weakening Mughal empire's powers, first by supplying troops and then actually taking control of Mughal land.

When Nadir Shah sacked Delhi in 1739, the declining Mughals were weakened farther. But the expansion of Maratha power came to an abrupt halt in 1761 at Panipat. There, where Babur had won the battle that established the Mughal empire over 200 years earlier, the Marathas were defeated by Ahmad Shah Durani from Afghanistan. Their expansion to the west was halted, but the Marathas consolidated their control over central India and the region known as Malwa. Soon, however, they were to fall to India's final imperial power, the British.

Expansion of British Power

The British were not the first European power to arrive in India, nor were they the last to leave – both those honours go to the Portuguese. In 1498, Vasco da Gama arrived on the coast of modern-day Kerala, having sailed around the Cape of Good Hope. Pioneering this route gave the Portuguese a century of uninterrupted monopoly over Indian and far eastern trade with Europe. In 1510, they captured Goa, the Indian enclave they controlled until 1961. In its heyday, the trade flowing through 'Golden Goa' was said to rival that passing through Lisbon. In the long term, however, the Portuguese did not have the resources to maintain a worldwide empire and they were quickly eclipsed after the arrival of the British, French and Dutch.

In 1600, Queen Elizabeth I granted a charter to a London trading company giving it a monopoly on British trade with India. In 1612, the East India Company's representatives established their first trading post at Surat in Gujarat. Further British trading posts, administered and governed by representatives of the Company, were established at Madras (now called Chennai) in 1640, Bengal in 1651 and Bombay (Mumbai) in 1668. Strange as it seems now, for nearly 250 years a commercial trading company and not the British government 'ruled' British India.

The British and Portuguese were not the only Europeans in India. The Danes and Dutch also had trading posts, and in 1672

Palaces & Forts

India's royal buildings and fortifications hold a certain mystique for travellers. During a tour round one of the many palaces, for example, it's easy to imagine the opulent, if somewhat insecure, lifestyle those at the top must have enjoyed. There were separate sections for the various tiers of royals, and those who attended them. Women invariably had their own quarters (usually known as a *zenana*) connected to the royal chambers by discreet tunnels. An interesting exception is Padmanabhapuram, palace of the maharajas of Tranvancore (now in Kerala). In this matrilineal society, the maharaja was expected to remain celibate so you'll find no secret tunnels here. In fact, although the maharaja's quarters are elevated above those of the other palace dwellers, they are smaller than those belonging to the matriarch.

One of the best examples of palace architecture is at the abandoned city of Fatehpur Sikri near Agra in Uttar Pradesh. Built by Akbar, the only emperor to stay there, the palace is divided into four main parts: the women's quarters; the emperor's quarters; a place for princes and nobles; and a weapons' magazine. There were also temples, a polo ground, numerous pavilions, gardens and audience areas. When it was in use, it would have been decorated with wall hangings and carpets.

The Rajputs, who absorbed Mughal aesthetic tastes during their required visits to the centre of power, adopted many of the decorative and architectural conventions of their rulers. Jai Singh I (1623-68) lived through the reigns of both Akbar and Shah Jahan, and borrowed major elements of their styles for his own courts.

India's fort builders exploited natural barriers where they could: water, such as lakes and the ocean, mountains and hills, forests and desert. Deforestation has deprived some forts of their obvious impregnability, but other impressive examples include the great fort at Jodhpur, which looms above the desert from an unassailable rocky base, and the romantic citadel of Jaisalmer. In the south, Vellor remains one of the best examples of a water fort, but it's Gingee which is one of the most impressive forts of any kind. Forming a triangle across three hills, its walls, gates and sheer size make it unforgettable. But perhaps the last word should be left for Shah Jahan, who gave the world the Taj Mahal and the Red Fort in Delhi – which happily married practical considerations with aesthetic appeal.

the French established themselves at Pondicherry, an enclave that they would hold even after the British had departed. The stage was set for more than a century of rivalry between the British and French for control of Indian trade. At one stage, under the guidance of a handful of talented and experienced commanders, the French appeared to hold the upper hand. In 1746, they took Madras (only to hand it back in 1749) and their success in placing their favoured candidate on the throne as Nizam (ruler) of Hyderabad augured well for the future. Serious French aspirations effectively ended, however in 1750 when the directors of the French East India Company decided their representatives were playing too much politics and doing too little trading. The key representatives were sacked and a settlement designed to end all ongoing political disputes was made with the British. Although the French Company's profits may have risen in the short term, the decision effectively removed France as a serious competitor for influence on the subcontinent. French interests remained strong enough, however, for them to continue supporting various local rulers in their struggles against the British.

The transformation of the British from traders to governors began almost by accident. Having been granted a licence to trade in

Bengal by the Great Mughal, and following the establishment of a new trading post (Calcutta) in 1690, business began to expand rapidly. Under the apprehensive gaze of the *nawab* (local ruler), British trading activities became extensive, and the 'factories' took on an increasingly permanent (and fortified) appearance. Eventually the nawab decided that British power had grown far enough. In June 1756 he attacked Calcutta and, having taken the city, locked his British prisoners in a tiny cell. The space was so cramped and airless that many were dead by the following morning, and the cell infamously became known as the 'Black Hole of Calcutta'.

Six months later, Robert Clive led a relief expedition to retake Calcutta and entered into an agreement with one of the nawab's generals to overthrow the nawab himself. This he did in June 1757 at the Battle of Plassey, and the general who had assisted him was placed on the throne. During the period that followed, with the British effectively in control of Bengal, the Company's agents engaged in a period of unbridled profiteering. When a subsequent nawab finally took up arms to protect his own interests, he was defeated at the Battle of Baksar in 1764. This victory confirmed the British as the paramount power in east India. The following year, Clive returned to Calcutta to sort out the administrative chaos and profiteering that was prevailing.

In 1771 one of the greatest figures of the time, Warren Hastings, was made governor in Bengal and during his tenure the Company greatly expanded its control. His astute statesmanship was aided by the fact that India at this time was in a state of flux – a power vacuum had been created by the disintegration of the Mughal empire. The Marathas were the only real Indian power to step into this gap and they themselves were divided. Hastings concluded a series of treaties with local rulers, including one with the main Maratha leader thus removing a major threat (at least for the time being).

In the south, where Mughal influence had never been great, the picture was confused by the strong British-French rivalry, as one ruler was played off against another. This was never clearer than in the series of Mysore wars where Hyder Ali and his son Tipu Sultan waged a brave and determined campaign against the British. In the Fourth Mysore War (1789-99) Tipu Sultan was killed at Srirangapatnam and British power took another step forward. The long-running struggle with the Marathas was finally concluded in 1803, leaving only the Punjab outside British control; it too finally fell in 1849 after the two Sikh wars.

It was during this time, following a brief series of battles between the British and the Gurkhas in 1814, that the borders of Nepal were delineated. The Gurkhas were initially victorious but, two years later, were forced to sue for peace as the British marched on Kathmandu. As part of the price for peace, the Nepalese were forced to cede the provinces of Kumaon and Shimla, but mutual respect for each others' military prowess prevented Nepal's incorporation into the Indian empire and led to the establishment of the Gurkha regiments that still exist in the British army today.

British India

By the early 19th century, India was effectively under British control. The country remained a patchwork of states, many nominally independent, and governed by their own rulers, the *maharajas* and nawabs. While these 'princely states' administered their own territories, a system of central government was developed. British organisation was replicated in the Indian government and civil service – a legacy which still exists today. A fearsome love of bureaucracy may be the downside to that, but the country reached Independence with a better organised, more efficient and less corrupt administrative system than most other ex-colonial countries. From 1784 onwards, the British government in London began to take a more direct role in supervising affairs in India, although the territory was still notionally administered by the East India Company until 1858.

An overwhelming interest in trade and profit resulted in far reaching changes. Iron and coal mining were developed and tea, coffee and cotton became key crops. A start was made on the vast rail network still in use today, irrigation projects were undertaken and the *zamindar* (landowner) system was encouraged. These absentee landlords eased the burden of administration and tax collection for the British, but contributed to an impoverished and landless peasantry – a problem which is still chronic in Bihar and West Bengal today.

The British also established English as the local language of administration. While this may have been useful in a country with so many different languages, and even today fulfils a very important function in nationwide communication, it did keep the new rulers at arm's length from the Indians.

The Indian Uprising

In 1857, half a century after having established firm control of India, the British suffered a serious setback. To this day, the causes of the Uprising (known at the time as the 'Indian Mutiny' and subsequently labelled by nationalist historians a 'War of Independence') are the subject of debate. The key factors included the influx of cheap goods, such as textiles, from Britain that destroyed many livelihoods, the dispossession of many rulers of their territories and taxes imposed on landowners.

The incident which is popularly held to have sparked the Uprising, however, took place at an army barracks in Meerut on 10 May 1857. A rumour leaked out that a new type of bullet was greased with animal fat. In Hindu circles the rumour held that it was cow fat, in Muslim company the grease came from pigs. Pigs, of course, are unclean to Muslims, and cows are sacred to Hindus. Since the procedure for loading a rifle involved biting the end off the waxed cartridge, there was considerable unrest.

In Meerut, the situation was handled with a singular lack of judgement. The commanding officer lined up his soldiers and ordered them to bite off the ends of their issued bullets. Those that refused were immediately marched off to prison. The following morning the soldiers of the garrison rebelled, shot their officers and marched to Delhi. Of the 74 Indian battalions of the Bengal army, seven (one of them Gurkhas) remained loyal, 20 were disarmed and the other 47 mutinied. The soldiers and peasants rallied around the ageing Great Mughal in Delhi, but there was never any clear idea of what they hoped to achieve. They held Delhi for four months and besieged the British Residency in Lucknow for five months, before they were finally suppressed leaving deep scars on both sides.

Almost immediately the East India Company was wound up and direct control of the country was assumed by the British government who announced their support of the existing rulers of the princely states, claiming they would not interfere in local matters as long as the states remained loyal to the British. A decision was also wisely taken that there should be no public search for scapegoats.

Road to Independence

Opposition to British rule began to increase at the turn of the 20th century. The Indian National Congress met for the first time in 1885 and soon began to push for a measure of participation in the government of the country. Progress was painfully slow, although there was movement after 1906 towards enfranchising a small proportion of Indian society. A highly unpopular attempt to partition Bengal in 1905 not only resulted in mass demonstrations, but also brought to light Hindu opposition to the division; the Muslim community formed its own league and campaigned for protected rights in any future political settlement. As pressure rose, a split emerged in Hindu circles between moderates and radicals, the latter resorting to violence to publicise their aims.

With the outbreak of WWI, the political situation eased. India contributed hugely to the war (over 1 million Indian volunteers were enlisted and sent overseas, suffering over 100,000 casualties). The contribution was sanctioned by Congress leaders, largely on the expectation that it would be rewarded after the war was over. Despite a number of hints and promises, no such rewards emerged and disillusion soon followed. Disturbances were particularly noticeable in the Punjab and in April 1919, following riots in Amritsar, a British army contingent was sent to quell the unrest. Under direct orders of the officer in charge they fired into a crowd of unarmed protesters attending a meeting. Firing continued for some 15 minutes, until there were well over 1000 casualties. News of the massacre spread rapidly throughout India and turned huge numbers of otherwise apolitical Indians into Congress supporters.

At this time, the Congress movement also found a new leader in Mohandas Gandhi. Gandhi, who subsequently became known as the Mahatma, or Great Soul, adopted a policy of passive resistance, known as *satyagraha*, to British rule. Not everyone involved in the struggle agreed with or followed Gandhi's policy of non-cooperation and nonviolence, yet the Congress Party and Gandhi remained at the forefront of the push for Independence.

As political power sharing began to look increasingly likely, and the mass movement led by Gandhi gained momentum, the Muslim reaction was to look to their own interests. The large Muslim minority had realised that an independent India would also be a Hindu-dominated India, and despite Gandhi's fair-minded approach, others in the Congress Party would not be so willing to share power. By the 1930s Muslims were raising the possibility of a separate Muslim state.

Political events were partially disrupted by WWII, when large numbers of Congress supporters were jailed to prevent disruption to the war effort. During this time, support grew among Muslims for an independent state of their own.

Independence

The Labour Party victory in the British, July 1945 elections brought a new breed of political leaders to power who realised that a solution to the Indian problem was imperative. Despite their willingness to grant Independence, there appeared to be no way to compromise between the wishes of the two major Indian parties. Mohammed Ali Jinnah, the leader of the Muslim League declared that he wished to have 'India divided or India destroyed'. Meanwhile the Congress Party, led by Jawaharlal Nehru, campaigned for an independent greater India. Gandhi, the father figure of Congress, urged reconciliation, but his voice was drowned out by others.

Each passing day increased the risks of intercommunity strife and bloodshed. In early 1946, a British mission failed to bring the two sides together and the country slid closer towards civil war. A 'Direct Action Day', called by the Muslim League in August 1946, led to the slaughter of Hindus in Calcutta, followed by reprisals against Muslims. Faced by a growing crisis, in February 1947, the British government made a momentous decision. The viceroy, Lord Wavell, would be replaced by Lord Louis Mountbatten and Independence would come by June 1948.

The new viceroy made a last-ditch attempt to convince the rival factions that a united India was a more sensible proposition, but they – Jinnah in particular – remained intransigent. The reluctant decision was then made to divide the country. Only Gandhi stood firmly against the division, preferring the possibility of a civil war to the chaos he so rightly expected. Faced with increasing civil violence, Mountbatten decided to follow a breakneck pace to Independence and announced that it would come on 14 August 1947. Once the decision had been made to divide the country, there were countless administrative decisions to be made, the most important being the actual location of the dividing line

Neatly slicing the country in two proved to be an impossible task. Although some areas were clearly Hindu or Muslim, others had evenly mixed populations, and there were isolated 'islands' of communities in

PETER DAVIS

RICHARD I'ANSON

RICHARD I'ANSON

PETER DAVIS

PETER DAVIS

EDDIE GERALD

Faces of India

A variety of faces and cultures will greet you, ranging from the mountain-dwelling Tibetan and Himalayan villagers to the island inhabitants of Andaman and Nicobar.

HIGHLIGHTS OF INDIAN HISTORY

Timeline: 2000 BC — 1500 BC — 1000 BC — 500 BC — 0 — 500 AD — 1000 AD — 1500 AD — 2000 AD

THE MUGHALS

This other great northern empire oversaw a golden age of arts, architecture and military advancement and the first religious integration before intolerance and harsh taxes weakened their power.

CHRIS MELLOR

THE CHOLAS

Great builders and traders, this southern power spread Hinduism to other parts of Asia.

EDDIE GERALD

THE GUPTAS

This northern empire encouraged the arts and Hinduism, leaving a legacy of elaborate temples.

MARK DAFFEY

VEDIC ARYAN PERIOD

The Aryans advanced from the north, drove the Dravidians south and formalised the caste system.

INDUS VALLEY CIVILISATION

This early civilisation developed trading, planned cities, advanced the arts, built sewerage systems and laid the foundations for the religions that predominate today.

ALEXANDER THE GREAT

Although his troops refused to march beyond Himachal Pradesh, Alexander left his mark on northern India spreading Buddhism and introducing some distinctive art styles.

THE MAURYAS

The first great Indian empire which controlled a large area marked by Ashokan pillars and edicts. It is also attributed with introducing bureaucracy and social order while consolidating the caste system.

MUSLIM POWER

Muslim raids left north India vulnerable to attack. This led to the rise of the Sultanate of Delhi which fought off Mongol invasions until their ambitious attempts to push south brought about their decline.

THE VIJAYANAGAR

This mighty southern alliance of Hindu kingdoms enjoyed a golden age in the south until their eventual defeat by the northern Muslim states at the Battle of Talikota.

KAREN TRIST

EUROPEAN COLONISATION

The Portuguese used 'Golden Goa' to gain a monopoly on far eastern trade, while under the British, under the guise of the East India Trading Co, effectively 'ruled' India for the 250 years prior to independence.

INDEPEN-DENCE

Although India is now the world's largest democracy, the road to independence was long, and despite Gandhi's campaign of passive resistance the resulting partition was bloody.

MARK HONAN

areas predominantly settled by other religions. Moreover, the two overwhelmingly Muslim regions were on opposite sides of the country and therefore Pakistan would inevitably have an eastern and western half divided by a hostile India. The instability of this arrangement was self-evident, but it took 25 years before the predestined split finally came and East Pakistan became Bangladesh.

Since a locally adjudicated dividing line was certain to bring recriminations from either side, an independent British referee was given the odious task of drawing the borders, knowing that the effects would be disastrous for countless people. Everywhere, the decisions were fraught with impossible dilemmas. In Bengal, Calcutta, with its Hindu majority, port facilities and jute mills, was divided from East Bengal, which had a Muslim majority, large-scale jute production, no mills and no port facilities. It has been estimated that one million Bengalis became refugees in the mass movement across the new border.

The problem was far worse in the Punjab, where intercommunity antagonisms were already running at fever pitch. The Punjab was one of the most fertile and affluent regions of the country, and had large Muslim, Hindu and Sikh communities. The Sikhs had already campaigned unsuccessfully for their own state, and now saw their homeland divided down the middle. The new border ran straight between the Punjab's two major cities – Lahore and Amritsar. Prior to Independence, Lahore's total population of 1.2 million included approximately 500,000 Hindus and 100,000 Sikhs. When the dust had finally settled, Lahore had a Hindu and Sikh population of only 1000.

It was clear that the Punjab contained all the ingredients for an epic disaster, but the resulting bloodshed was even worse than expected. Huge exchanges of population took place. Trains full of Muslims, fleeing westward, were held up and slaughtered by Hindu and Sikh mobs. Hindus and Sikhs fleeing to the east suffered the same fate. The army that was sent to maintain order

proved totally inadequate and, at times, all too ready to join the partisan carnage. By the time the Punjab chaos had run its course, over 10 million people had changed sides and even the most conservative estimates calculate that 250,000 people had been slaughtered. The true figure may well have been over half a million.

The provision of an independently adjudicated border between the two nations failed to prevent disputes. The issue was complicated largely by the fact that the 'princely states' in British India were nominally independent. As part of the settlement process, local rulers were asked which country they wished to belong to – in all but three cases the matter was solved relatively simply. Kashmir, however, was a predominantly Muslim state with a Hindu maharaja who, by October 1948, had still not opted for India or Pakistan when a rag-tag Pathan (Pakistani) army crossed the border, intent on racing to Srinagar and annexing Kashmir without provoking a real India-Pakistan conflict. Unfortunately for the Pakistanis, the Pathans, inspired to mount their invasion by the promise of plunder, did so much plundering en route that India had time to rush troops to Srinagar and prevent the town's capture. The indecisive maharaja finally opted for India, provoking the first, albeit brief, India-Pakistan war.

The UN eventually stepped in to keep the two sides apart, but the issue of Kashmir has remained a central cause for disagreement and conflict between the two countries ever since. With its overwhelming Muslim majority and its geographic links to Pakistan, many people were inclined to support Pakistan's claims to the region. To this day, India and Pakistan are divided in this region by a demarcation line (known as the Line of Actual Control), yet neither side agrees that this constitutes the official border.

The final stages of Independence had one last tragedy to be played out. On 30 January 1948, Mohandas Gandhi, deeply disheartened by Partition and the subsequent bloodshed, was assassinated by a Hindu fanatic. Throughout the events leading up to

Mahatma Gandhi

Mohandas Karamchand Gandhi was born on 2 October 1869 in Porbandar, a small principality in Gujarat where his father was chief minister. Married at the age of 13, his career path was largely decided by his family and in 1888 he left India to train as a barrister in London. He returned to India in 1891 to find the legal profession oversubscribed and his prospects poor so he accepted a contract to work in South Africa.

On arrival in South Africa he experienced first hand the discrimination directed at members of the Indian community. Overcoming his naturally quiet temperament, he quickly became the spokesman for the Indian community and fought for their rights. Despite his opposition to the government, Gandhi raised an ambulance unit and served as a stretcher bearer during the Boer War. He encouraged other Indians to follow his example, arguing that it was their duty to play an active role in their country's affairs. As soon as the war was over, however, he recommenced his political campaigning. During these years he developed the concept of satyagraha, mobilising the Indian workforce into mass protest and eventually forcing the South African government to concede to many of his demands.

Gandhi returned to India in 1915 with many of his policies and beliefs in place. Being from a religious family his background was one of faith, but he was also widely read and contemplative. The doctrine of *ahimsa* (nonviolence) was central to his beliefs, as was his devotion to a simple and disciplined lifestyle – typified in the two farming communities which he set up in South Africa. He also set up an ashram in Ahmedabad which was innovative for its admission of untouchables, and for its economic and social activities, such as community spinning and weaving.

Gandhi initially felt his way cautiously around the Indian political scene, but within a year saw his first victory, defending farmers in Bihar from exploitation. This was when he first received the title 'Mahatma' (Great Soul) from an admirer. The passage of the discriminatory Rowlatt Acts in 1919 spurred him to further action and he organised a national protest. In the days that followed this *hartal* (strike), feelings ran high throughout the country. In Amritsar, protesters at a peaceful meeting were massacred by soldiers and Gandhi, deeply shocked, called the movement off immediately.

By 1920 Gandhi was a key figure in the Indian National Congress, and he coordinated a national campaign of noncooperation. The effort was hugely successful in raising nationalist feelings, but once again led to violence. Again, Gandhi called off the satyagraha and was almost immediately imprisoned.

On his release in 1924, Gandhi appeared to many to be a spent political force, and throughout the mid-1920s kept a relatively low profile. He returned to the struggle in 1927, and three years later captured the imagination of the country, and the world, with his most successful act of defiance against the British government. In early 1930 he led a march of several thousand followers from Ahmedabad to Dandi on the coast of Gujarat. On arrival, Gandhi ceremoniously made salt by evaporating sea water, thus publicly defying the hated

Independence, he had stood almost alone in urging tolerance and the preservation of a single India. He argued that Jinnah should be given the leadership of a united India, if that was what it would take to prevent Partition. To some, whipped up by the events of the preceding months, this appeared to be tantamount to colluding with the enemy.

Independent India

Since Independence, India has faced many problems and made considerable progress.

Mahatma Gandhi

salt tax; once again he was imprisoned. He was released in 1931 in order to represent the Indian National Congress at the second Round Table Conference in London where, despite winning over the hearts of the British people, he failed to gain many real concessions from the government.

Jailed again on his return to India, Gandhi immediately began a hunger strike, aimed at forcing his fellow Indians to accept the rights of the Untouchables. The country was seized with apprehension, and as Gandhi grew weaker pressure on politicians mounted. Finally, just as it seemed that Gandhi was on the verge of death, an agreement was reached.

Emerging from jail, Gandhi found himself disillusioned with politics, believing the Congress leaders were ignoring his guidance on the correct course for India. In 1934, he resigned his seat in Congress, and began to follow a personal policy of rural education, living among the villagers and attempting to improve their lot. He returned to the fray very publicly in 1942, with the Quit India campaign, in which he urged the British to leave India immediately. Dur-

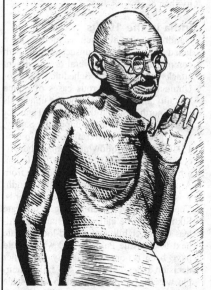

ing the tension of WWII his actions were deemed subversive and he and most of the Congress leadership were imprisoned.

In the frantic bargaining that followed the end of the war, Gandhi was largely left out of the equation, and watched helplessly as plans were made to partition the country, an outcome he regarded as nothing less than a tragedy. With no further chance of averting Partition, he took it upon himself to tour the trouble spots of the country, using his own influence to calm intercommunity tensions and promote peace. His actions and in particular his threats to fast to death met with spectacular successes in Calcutta and Delhi where, by force of personality, he prevented huge loss of life.

His work on behalf of members of all communities inevitably drew resentment from Hindu hardliners. In the end it was this that led to his death when, on his way to an evening prayer meeting on 30 January 1948, he was assassinated by a Hindu fanatic.

The fact that it has not, like so many developing countries, succumbed to dictatorships, military rule or wholesale foreign invasion is a testament to the basic strength of the country's government and institutions. Economically, it has made major steps in improving agricultural output and is one of the world's top 10 industrial powers.

Jawaharlal Nehru, India's first prime minister, tried to follow a strict policy of nonalignment. Yet, despite maintaining generally cordial relations with Britain and electing to join the Commonwealth, India moved towards the former USSR – partly because of conflicts with China and US support for its arch enemy Pakistan.

There were further clashes with Pakistan in 1965 and 1971, one over the intractable Kashmir dispute and another over Bangladesh. A border war with China in 1962 in the North-East Frontier Area (NEFA; now the North-Eastern Region) and Ladakh resulted in the loss of Aksai Chin (in Ladakh) and smaller NEFA areas. India continues to dispute sovereignty over these.

These outside events drew attention away from India's often serious internal problems, especially the failure to address rapid population growth.

Indira's India

Politically, India's major problem since Independence has been the personality cult that has developed around its leaders. There have only been three real prime ministers of stature – Nehru, his daughter Indira Gandhi (no relation to Mahatma Gandhi) and her son Rajiv Gandhi. Nehru personally led a series of five year plans to improve output and managed to keep India nonaligned, thereby receiving aid from the USSR, USA and Europe. He died in 1964 and in 1966 Indira was elected as prime minister, only to face serious opposition and unrest in 1975, which she countered by declaring a state of emergency – a situation that in many other countries might have become a dictatorship.

During the emergency, a mixed bag of good and bad policies were followed. Freed of many parliamentary constraints, Gandhi was able to control inflation remarkably well, boost the economy and decisively increase efficiency. On the negative side, political opponents often found themselves behind bars, India's judicial system was turned into a puppet theatre, the press was fettered and there was more than a hint of nepotism, particularly with her son, Sanjay. His disastrous program of forced sterilisations, in particular, caused much anger.

Despite murmurings of discontent, Gandhi decided the people were behind her and

in 1977 called a general election. Things did not go her way and her partially renamed Congress Party (Indira) was bundled out of power in favour of the Janata People's Party, a coalition formed with the sole purpose of defeating her. Once victorious, it quickly became obvious that Janata had no other cohesive policies. Its leader, Morarji Desai, seemed more interested in protecting cows, banning alcohol and getting his daily glass of urine than coming to grips with the country's problems. With inflation soaring, unrest rising and the economy faltering, nobody was surprised when Janata fell apart in late 1979. The 1980 election brought Indira Gandhi back to power with a larger majority than ever.

India in the 1980s

Gandhi's political touch seemed to have faded as she grappled unsuccessfully with communal unrest in several areas, violent attacks on Dalits (the Scheduled Caste or Untouchables), numerous cases of police brutality and corruption, and the upheavals in the north-east and the Punjab. Then her son and political heir, the unpopular Sanjay, was killed in a light aircraft accident in June 1980. In 1984, following a somewhat ill-considered decision to send in the Indian army to flush out armed Sikh radicals from Amritsar's Golden Temple, Mrs Gandhi was assassinated by her Sikh bodyguards. The radicals were demanding a separate Sikh state, to be called Khalistan. Regardless of the viability of a land-locked state next to a hostile Pakistan and what would have been a none-too-friendly India, her decision to desecrate the Sikhs' holiest temple was disasterous and led to large-scale riots, problems in the army (Sikhs form a significant part of the officer corps), and a legacy of hate and distrust in the Punjab.

Mrs Gandhi's son, Rajiv, a former Indian Airlines pilot, quickly become the next heir to the throne, and was swept into power with an overwhelming majority and enormous popular support.

Despite his previous lack of interest in politics, Rajiv Gandhi brought new and pragmatic policies to the country. Foreign investment and the use of modern technology were encouraged, import restrictions eased and many new industries established. They undoubtedly benefited the middle classes and provided many jobs for those displaced from the land and who had migrated to the cities in search of work, but whether these policies were necessarily in the long-term interests of India is open to question. They certainly projected India into the 1990s, woke the country from its partially self-induced isolationism, and broke its protectionist stance to world trade, but they didn't stimulate the rural sector.

Furthermore, Rajiv's administration continually failed to quell unrest in the Punjab or Kashmir and the Indian armed forces became bogged down in the civil war in neighbouring Sri Lanka, caused by Tamil secessionists in that country demanding an independent state. Support for militant Sri Lankan Tamil groups was clearly coming from Indian Tamils, and police activities in Tamil Nadu aimed at rooting out sympathisers and curtailing the flow of arms and equipment made Rajiv a marked man.

The Bofors scandal also dogged Rajiv's administration. Bribes were allegedly paid to members of the government to secure a contract to supply Swedish heavy artillery guns to the Indian army. It was even alleged that Rajiv, or at least his Italian-born wife, Sonia, were recipients of such bribes.

Following the November 1989 elections, Rajiv Gandhi's Congress Party, although the largest single party in parliament, was unable to form a government in its own right. The result was a new National Front Government, made up of five parties, including the Hindu fundamentalist Bharatiya Janata Party (BJP), were to form the next government. Like the previous attempt to cobble together a government of national unity from minority parties with radically different viewpoints, it didn't last long and fresh elections were announced.

During the election campaign, while on a tour of Tamil Nadu, Rajiv Gandhi, many of his aides and a number of bystanders were

Italian-born Sonia Gandhi shied away from politics following the assassination of her husband Rajiv. Recently however she has returned to the fray, seemingly disregarding her own personal safety and the critics who insist their leader should be Indian born.

killed by a bomb carried by a supporter of the Tamil Tigers (a Sri Lankan armed separatist group). Narasimha Rao assumed the leadership of the Congress Party and led it to victory at the polls. There were attempts, immediately after the assassination, to induce Rajiv's wife Sonia to assume the leadership, but she made it clear she had little interest in doing so. She continued to be a powerful, behind-the-scenes influence, and in 1997 became the party's president.

India in the 1990s

Narasimha Rao shared Rajiv's determination to drag India into the economic realities of the 1990s, particularly after the collapse of the USSR, India's long-term ally and benefactor. After some years of languishing behind tariff barriers and an unrealistic currency exchange rate, the economy was given an enormous boost in 1992. The finance minister, Manmohan Singh, made the momentous step of partially floating the rupee against a basket of 'hard' currencies and legalising the import of gold by non-resident Indians.

Rao inherited a number of intractable problems which tested the mettle of his government. His biggest headache, though, was the simmering issue of communalism – that potentially explosive conflict between different religious groups, particularly between Hindus and Muslims, for which Ayodhya became a focus.

This small town in central Uttar Pradesh is revered by Hindus as the birthplace of Rama. There are many Hindu temples here, but during Mughal times, the emperors razed several of them and constructed mosques on their sites. It was claimed that one of these mosques, the Babri Masjid, stood on the site of what was previously the Rama Temple. In December 1992 fundamentalist Hindus, egged on by the staunchly Hindu revivalist BJP (which controlled the UP state government), destroyed the mosque. Rioting followed in many cities across the north, extremists detonated bombs in Mumbai and Delhi and several hundred people died.

The practice of reserving government jobs and university places for members of so-called 'backward' classes, which generally means lower caste Hindus, has been used by all parties to buy votes, but has also caused further outbreaks of religious violence across the country. This system disaffects lower class Muslims because they don't qualify for places and has undone much of the work of people like Mahatma Gandhi, who worked tirelessly to improve the lot of the socially disadvantaged.

The early 1990s saw the Kashmir issue move to centre stage again, with demonstrations on both sides of the Line of Actual Control and an alarming increase in Jammu and Kashmir Liberation Front (JKLF) guerrilla activities in the Vale of Kashmir. Pakistan was almost certainly involved in encouraging, funding and supplying arms to the militants on the Indian side of the 'border' (which, of course, is denied), but reports suggest that the overzealous activities of the Indian army are also partially responsible for the upsurge in militancy. In 1995 the Charar-e-Sharif shrine and 1000 houses in the vicinity were burnt down, Kashmiris blamed the army. This led to riots in Srinagar. Incidents involving tourists in Kashmir are on the increase. Six westerners were kidnapped in 1995; the body of one was recovered and another escaped, but the fate of the others is unknown. In 1996 a family of Indian tourists were murdered on their Dal Lake houseboat.

The elections in September 1996, however, ushered in new hope. They ended direct rule from Delhi, installing Farooq Abdullah as chief minister. In Srinagar itself, the army presence seemed less intrusive and tourists cautiously returned – albeit in small numbers. But violence flared up again along the Pakistan border following the nuclear tests in early 1998. At the 10th South Asian Association for Regional Cooperation (SAARC) summit in Colombo, Sri Lanka, in August 1998, the Indian prime minister, Atal Bihari Vajpayee, and his Pakistani counterpart, Nawaz Sharif, met to discuss Kashmir. But there was no sight of a solution. At the time of writing, the situation had worsened when, after further nuclear testing by both sides, Pakistan shot down an Indian pilot that had crossed the Line of Control.

Another problem has been the growth of secessionist movements in several parts of the country, often involving violent clashes between the people and police. In 1996, the prime minister gave his backing to the creation of a new state, Uttarakhand, in northern Uttar Pradesh. This will no doubt lead other secessionist movements (Jharkhand in Bihar/West Bengal, Gorkhaland in the Darjeeling region, and Bodoland in Assam) to intensify their fight for Independence.

Developments in the Punjab have been encouraging. Elections were finally held under difficult circumstances in 1992 with Congress securing power at state level, although only 24% of the electorate voted after an Akalis boycot. The February 1997 elections saw a landslide victory for the Akali Dal-BJP alliance. The threat of terrorism has since waned considerably.

As Hindu fundamentalist parties such as the BJP and Shiv Sena have gained support in the last few years, the Congress Party has fallen out of favour with the people. In late 1994, they were dealt a severe blow with election routs in the states of Andhra Pradesh (Rao's home state) and Karnataka. It's hard to pinpoint the reasons for the voters' lack of confidence in the party, but there was definitely some backlash against corruption scandals and economic policies. The reduction of agricultural subsidies combined with high inflation (averaging 10%) made life even more difficult for millions of peasant farmers and labourers.

The 1996 general election was a disaster for the Congress Party, who were defeated by the BJP. The government formed by the BJP lasted less than two weeks, and was replaced by a coalition of 13 parties called the United Front – this didn't last either. Just nine months later, in April 1997, it was voted out of office after Congress withdrew its support. Then in 1998, the BJP and its allies emerged with the most seats of any single party causing Congress president Sitaram Kesri to step aside to make way for Sonia Gandhi. In late March, BJP leader Atal Behari Vajpayee put together a 13-party coalition. The BJP again won elections in October 1999.

In mid-1999, the Congress Party presidency belonged to Sonia Gandhi and some political observers were tipping her to be the next prime minister. Others, however believed it was essential that the country be led by an Indian-born prime minister and resigned in protest. Although this created turmoil within the party, Sonia emerged strong again and contested the 1999 elections as president.

In May 1998 India conducted five nuclear tests in the deserts of Rajasthan, with Pakistan following suit. The tests brought world-wide condemnation and the fallout for both countries has been economic as donor countries withheld nonhumanitarian aid.

GEOGRAPHY & GEOLOGY

India covers a total area of 3,287,263 sq km. This is divided into 25 states and seven directly administered union territories (including the capital, Delhi). The states are further subdivided into districts.

The Himalaya

The north of the country is decisively bordered by the long sweep of the Himalaya, the highest mountains on earth. They run from south-east to north-west, separating India from China and form one of the youngest mountain ranges in the world. The Himalaya evolution can be traced to the Jurassic era (80 million years ago) when the world's land masses were split into two: Laurasia in the northern hemisphere and Gondwanaland in the southern hemisphere. The land mass which is now India broke away from Gondwanaland and floated across the earth's surface, eventually colliding with Laurasia. The hard volcanic rocks of India were thrust against the soft sedimentary crust of Laurasia, forcing it upwards to create the Himalaya. This continental collision still continues with the mountains rising by up to 8mm each year.

The Himalaya are not a single mountain range but a series of ranges with beautiful valleys wedged between them. The Kullu Valley in Himachal Pradesh and the Vale of Kashmir in Jammu and Kashmir are both Himalayan valleys, as is the Kathmandu Valley in Nepal. Kanchenjunga (8598m) is the highest mountain in India, although until Sikkim (and Kanchenjunga) were absorbed into India that honour went to Nanda Devi (7817m). Beyond the Himalaya stretches the high, dry and barren Tibetan plateau; Ladakh is a small part of this plateau actually lying within India's boundaries.

The final southern range of the Himalaya, the Siwalik Hills, ends abruptly in the great northern plain of India.

The Northern Plain

In complete contrast to the soaring mountain peaks, the northern plain is flat and slopes so gradually that as it stretches east from Delhi to the Bay of Bengal it only drops a total of 200m. The mighty, holy Ganges River rises in Gangotri and drains a large part of the northern plain before merging with the Brahmaputra River. In the north-west, the Indus River starts flowing through Ladakh in India but soon diverts into Pakistan to become that country's most important river.

The North-East

The north-east boundary of India is defined by the foothills of the Himalaya, separating it from Myanmar (Burma). It's here that India bends almost entirely around Bangladesh almost meeting the sea on its eastern side.

Centre & South

South of the northern plains, the land rises up into the high plateau of the Deccan. The plateau is bordered on both sides by ranges of hills which parallel the coast to the east and west. Of these, the Western Ghats are higher and have a wider coastal strip than the eastern; the two ranges meet in the extreme south in the Nilgiri Hills. The major rivers of the south are the Godavari and the Krishna. Both rise on the eastern slope of the Western Ghats and flow across the Deccan into the sea on the eastern coast.

The West

On the western side, India is separated from Pakistan by three distinct regions. In the north, in the disputed area of Kashmir, the boundary is formed by the Himalaya which drop down to the plains of the Punjab, merging into the Great Thar Desert in the western part of Rajasthan. This is an area of great natural beauty and is extremely barren. It's hard to imagine that it was once covered by thick forests. Discoveries made by palaeontologists in 1996 suggest that the area was inhabited by dinosaurs and their ancestors as long as 300 million years ago.

Finally, the Indian state of Gujarat is separated from the Sind in Pakistan by the unusual marshland known as the Rann of Kutch (Katchchh). In the dry season (November to April), this marshland dries out, leaving many isolated salt islands perched on an expansive plain. In the wet season (June to August), the marshland floods to become a vast inland sea.

The Islands

Although politically part of India, the Andaman and Nicobar Islands, scattered along the eastern extremity of the Bay of Bengal, are in fact closer physically and geographically to Myanmar and Indonesia respectively, meanwhile the coral atolls known as Lakshadweep, some 300km west of the Malabar coast, are in effect a northern extension of the Maldives.

There are 300 Andaman Islands in total and the dense forests that once covered their hilly interiors are unfortunately now much sparser due to rampant logging. The coasts are fringed with coral and are deeply indented, providing natural harbours and tidal creeks. The 19 Nicobar Islands are largely flat and coral covered. An exception is Great Nicobar which reaches 642m and has numerous streams making it the only island in the group with plentiful fresh water. Lakshadweep consists of some two dozen islands covering a total land area of 22 sq km. All of the islands are coral atolls (theoretically formed around a submerged volcano) which slope towards the west, where low-lying lagoons protect the islands' inhabitants from the worst effects of the south-west monsoon.

CLIMATE

India is so vast that the climatic conditions in the far north have little relation to those of the extreme south. While the heat is building up to breaking point on the plains, the people of Ladakh, high in the Himalaya, will still be waiting for the snow to melt on the high passes.

India has a three-season year – the hot, the wet and the cool. Generally the best time to

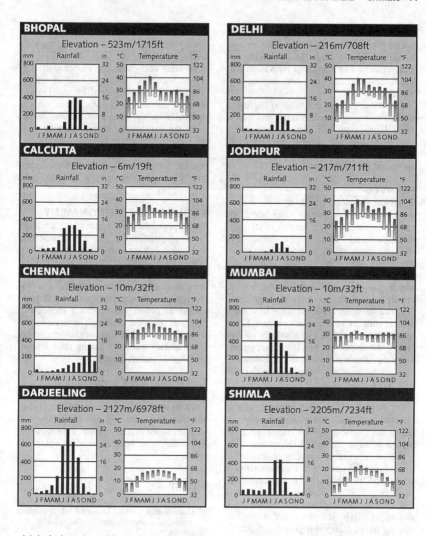

visit is during winter (November to February) although there are regional variations (see the 'At a Glance' tables at the start of each chapter for the best times to go to each area).

The Hot

The heat starts to build up on the northern plains of India from around February, and by April or May it becomes unbearable. In central India, temperatures of 45°C and above are commonplace – in the summer of 1994, Delhi had temperatures approaching 50°C! It's dry and dusty and everything is seen through a haze.

Later in May, the first signs of the monsoon are visible – high humidity, violent electrical storms, short rainstorms and dust storms that turn day into night. The hot and humid weather towards the end of the hot season can be like a hammer blow; you will feel listless and tired and your temper will run short.

The hot season is the time to leave the plains and retreat into the hills, and this is when Himalayan hill stations and states such as Sikkim are at their best. By early June, the snow on the passes into Ladakh melts and the roads reopen.

The Wet

When the monsoon finally arrives, it does not just suddenly appear. After some advance warning, the rain comes in steadily, starting around 1 June in the extreme south and sweeping north to cover the whole country by early July. The monsoon doesn't really cool things off; at first hot, dry, dusty weather is simply traded for hot, humid, muddy conditions. Even so, it's a great relief, not least for farmers who face their busiest time of year as they prepare fields for planting. It doesn't rain solidly all day during the monsoon, but it certainly rains every day; the water tends to come down in buckets for a while followed by the sun which is quite pleasant.

The main monsoon comes from the south-west, but the south-eastern coast is affected by the short and surprisingly wet north-east monsoon, which brings rain from mid-October to the end of December.

Although the monsoon brings life to India, it also brings its share of death. Almost every year there are destructive floods and thousands of people are made homeless. Rivers rise and sweep away road and railway lines and many flight schedules are disrupted, making travel during this period difficult.

The Cool

Finally, around October, the monsoon ends for most of the country, and this is probably the best time of year in India. Everything is still green and lush but you avoid a daily soaking. The temperatures are delightful, not too hot and not too cool. The air is clear

in the Himalaya, and the mountains are clearly visible, at least early in the day. Delhi and other northern cities become quite crisp at night in December and January. It becomes downright cold in the far north, but snow brings India's small skiing industry into action so a few places, such as the Kullu Valley, have a winter season too.

In the far south, where it never gets cool, the temperatures become comfortably warm rather than hot. Then, around February, the temperatures start to climb again, and before you know it you're back in the hot weather.

ECOLOGY & ENVIRONMENT

With a population fast approaching a billion, rapid industrialisation, ongoing deforestation and heavy reliance on chemical fertilisers, pesticides and herbicides, India's environment is under immense pressure. While there is no shortage of legislation designed to protect the environment, corruption and flagrant abuses of power can render it ineffective. Some of the most positive conservation efforts have emerged from within grassroots communities intent on saving their homes, livelihoods and traditions.

Conservation Contacts

The following organisations are working towards environmental protection and conservation in India and can offer information on conservation efforts countrywide. They may also be able to offer voluntary work.

Bombay Natural History Society
(☎ 022-284 3869, fax 283 7615) Hornbill House, Shaheed Bhagat Singh Rd, Mumbai, Maharashtra, 400023 – one of the more renowned environmental groups in India.

Equations
(email admin@equation.ilban.ernet.in) 198 2nd Cross, Church Rd, New Thippasandra, Bangalore 560075 – tourism pressure group helping indigenous people.

Himalayan Environment Trust
(☎ 011-621 5635, fax 686 2374) Legend Inn E-4 East of Kailash, New Delhi – nonprofit trust raising public awareness about increasing ecological threat to the Himalaya.

Madras Naturalists Society
 (☎ 044-450813) 36 IV Main Rd, RA Puram, Chennai 600028 – best people to contact in this part of Tamil Nadu.
Merlin Nature Club
 13 8th Cross, 30th Main, Sarakki ITI Layout, JP Nagar Phase, Bangalore 560078 – local ecological projects.
Mysore Amateur Naturalists
 (☎ 0821-541744) 571 9th Cross, Anikethana Rd, Kuvempu Nagar, Mysore – involved in Project Pelican.
Society for the Prevention of Cruelty to Animals
 (☎ 080-286 0205) Kasturba Rd, Bangalore 560001 – heavily involved in cruelty to animal issues.
TRAFFIC India (☎ 011-469 8578, fax 462 6837, email traffic@wwfind.ernet.in) 172-B Lodi Estate, New Delhi 110003 – campaigns against illegal wildlife trade. USA: (☎ 202-293 4800, fax 202-775 8287, email traffic.us@wwfus .org) 1250 24th St NW, Washington DC 20037, USA. UK: (☎ 01223-277 427, fax 277 237, email traffic@wcmc.org.uk) 219c Huntingdon Rd, Cambridge CB3 0DL, UK.
Wildlife Association of South India
 (☎ 080-578 379) 49 Richmond Rd, Bangalore 560025 – protects wildlife.
Wildlife Preservation Society of India
 7 Astley Hall, Dehra Dun, Garhwal, Uttar Pradesh – promotes conservation awareness.
Wildlife Protection Society of India
 (☎ 011-621 3864, fax 336 8729, email blue@ giasdlol.vsnl.net.in) Thapara House, 124 Janpath, Delhi – wildlife projects throughout the country.
World Wide Fund for Nature (WWF)
 Headquarters: (☎ 011-462 7586, fax 462 6837) 172-B Lodi Estate, Max Mueller Marg, New Delhi 110003
 Mumbai: (☎ 022-207 8105, fax 207 6037) National Insurance Bldg, 2nd floor, Dr DN Road, Mumbai, Maharashtra 400001
 Goa: (☎ 0832-226 020) Hill Side Apartments, Block B, Flat B-2, Ground Floor, Fontainhas, Panaji, Goa 403001
 Kerala: (☎ 0471-325 183) A/10 Tagore Nagar, TC No 15/989, Vazhutacaud, Thiruvananthapuram, Kerala 695014
 Bangalore: (☎ 080-286 3206, fax 286 6685) Kamala Mansion, 143 Infantry Rd, Bangalore 560001
 Tamil Nadu: (☎ 044-434 8064, fax 434 7967) 13 11th St, Nadanam Extension, Chennai, Tamil Nadu 600035
 Hyderabad: (☎ 040-334 0922) Block 2, Flat 4, Vijayanagar Colony, Hyderabad 500057

Deforestation

India has a long tradition of venerating forests and trees have always had their defenders. In the 18th century hundreds of men and women from the Bishnoi Jain sect in Rajasthan laid down their lives to save the sacred khejri trees – which the authorities wanted for burning lime. A temple at Khejarli still commemorates their sacrifice, which resulted in a royal ban on cutting any trees near a Bishnoi village. When the British commercialised forestry, protesters turned to Ghandian satyagraha to get their message across. In more recent times the Chipko movement has taken up the cause. Started as a localised protest in northern India in the mid-1970s it has evolved into a much larger and more powerful force with women playing a leading role. When the authorities closed in to clear the protesters, women embraced the trees and refused to move. 'Soil, water and oxygen – not timber' is the Chipko catch cry, one that's echoed the length and breadth of India as communities fight to save their forest.

India's first Five Year Plan in 1951 recognised the importance of forest cover for soil conservation, and the national forest policy supported the idea of increasing forest cover to at least 33%. But today just 11.7% of dense forest cover remains (although official sources claim it's closer to 19%) and despite laws to protect it, more is lost every year – since Independence, India has lost forest cover equivalent to the entire state of Punjab.

There are many reasons why this has happened. Fuel wood, upon which millions of people depend, is being taken out of the forests at a rate of about 250 million tonnes a year – only a quarter of this can be extracted without permanent damage. As grazing lands shrink, domestic animals increasingly move into the forests causing damage. Denotification, a process whereby states may relax the ban on commercial exploitation of protected areas, is another factor. States are supposed to earmark an equivalent area for reafforestation, but conservationists say this isn't always happening or the land set aside often isn't suitable.

Smuggling is another problem in some areas; the Western Ghats are regularly plundered for valuable sandalwood and rosewood. Forest rangers are ill-equipped to deal with armed-to-the-teeth tree poachers. Natural disasters such as a series of landslides in northern Uttar Pradesh in 1998 (which killed 400 people and destroyed 12 villages) also contribute to deforestation.

While plantation forest has increased in relative terms, critics point out that eucalyptus and other similarly exotic strands are no substitute for native forest.

In 1998 however, the government put forward a plan intended to increase re-afforestation, with an ultimate goal of having a third of the country under forest cover – 100 million hectares in all. The plan calls for action at village level, and improvements to the anti-poaching resources of forest officers.

Soil Degradation

Only 37% of India's land is free from soil degradation of some sort, causing a rethink

in the heavy use of chemicals encouraged during the Green Revolution of the 1960s when a quantum leap in agricultural output was achieved. India is the world's fourth largest consumer of fertilisers (69.6kg per hectare in 1998). But with some 18 million more mouths to feed every year, fertiliser will continue to be dumped on agricultural land; increasing by at least a third by 2000, according to some estimates. Much of this runs off into surface water and leaches into groundwater. The insecticides DDT and Benzene Hexachloride (BHC) were outlawed in 1992 and 1996 respectively. (Since Independence more than a million tonnes of DDT and BHC has been dumped on the land.)

Yet the demand for other chemicals seems unlikely to decline. Between 10 and 20% of annual produce is damaged by pests, a strong disincentive to cutting back on rat bait (see The Rat Catchers boxed text). Most of the damage, however, is caused by water erosion, which accounts for 80% of

The Rat Catchers

Floods, drought, fluctuating prices and land taxes are the bane of most farmer's lives. For rice farmers around Chennai in Tamil Nadu, rats are another devastating problem. These unwanted visitors contribute to the destruction of up to a quarter of crops. Modern pesticides help but they are very expensive and potentially harmful to delicate ecosystems.

Enter the Irula people. They are the indigenous inhabitants of the Chengalpattu district, 50km south-west of Chennai. They once lived a nomadic life as hunters and gatherers. Until the 1970s they supported themselves by catching snakes for the leather industry, but now that trade is outlawed they have turned their skills to rats.

About 100 Irulas have formed a cooperative which they call the Rat and Termite Squad (RATS). Their methods are highly labour intensive. They identify the rat burrows, crouch down at the entrance and listen carefully. When they hear a rat approaching they thrust an iron bar into the ground behind the burrow entrance, thus preventing the rat's escape back into it. Then they simply lift the protesting creature into a sack. If there is a large colony of rats, the Irulas might smoke them out using clay pots filled with straw.

In a scheme supported by the Department of Science and Technology, the Irulas are paid about Rs 2 for each rat they catch. A typical year will yield around 100,000 rodents. In what has become a commercially viable enterprise, some of the rats end up as dinner for the crocs at the Crocodile Bank near Mamalapuram. However, quite a few rats will be skinned, chopped, curried and consumed by the catchers. The Irulas claim that with rice the rats are particularly tasty and highly nutritious.

degraded land. Water and wind erosion are largely caused by the loss of tree cover (see Deforestation earlier in this section). Unfortunately, policies aimed at helping agriculturalists, such as providing subsidies on irrigation and pesticides, and bringing village water resources under government control, have added to the problem. But at local level some are trying to turn the tide. In October 1997, for example, farmers in the orchard-rich area of Dahanu near Mumbai, disillusioned with conventional techniques, welcomed a visit from Masanobu Fukuoka, Japanese natural-farming guru and author of the *One Straw Revolution*.

Water Resources

Arguably the biggest threat to public health in India is inadequate access to clean drinking water and proper sanitation; in 1993 a mere 3.5% of rural and 43% of urban dwellers were serviced to an acceptable standard. Agriculture, which uses 85% of water is expected to double its demand by 2025. Industry is similarly expected to double the amount it uses, and domestic use will triple. Already some parts of India, eg northern Gujarat, are suffering serious shortages. More than 40% of Gujarat's electricity is expended on powering bore wells. And big cities such as Chennai and Delhi cannot supply all their citizens' water needs; water tankers are a frequent sight in the suburbs that can afford them. Ground water (source of 85% of rural drinking water and 55% of urban drinking water) is suffering from uncontrolled extraction and is extremely vulnerable to contamination from leaching. In West Bengal (and Bangladesh) ever-deeper tube wells contaminated with arsenic (which occurs naturally in pyrite bedrock) are poisoning tens of thousands of villagers. In Tamil Nadu the water table is falling by more than 1m every year. Much pumped water trickles away from leaky pipes (some estimate that nationwide the loss amounts to at least half of all water piped). India's rivers too suffer from run off and industrial pollution as well as from sewage contamination with the Sabarmati and Ganges being the most polluted rivers in India.

Air Pollution

In 1970 there were fewer than two million vehicles in India; there are now more than 25 million. About 70% of them are two-stroke vehicles such as auto-rickshaws which, though economical to run and despite attempts to control their emissions, spew out pollutants. There's little incentive to move away from diesel, which is subsidised and relatively cheap. Diesel-run three-wheelers (*vikrams*) foul the air in cities such as Agra and Dehra Dun. In Delhi vehicles are the major source of the estimated 2000 metric tonnes of air pollutants discharged daily (see the Pollution Alert boxed text in the Delhi chapter). Industry too, despite laws aimed at curtailing toxic emissions, accounts for significant levels of pollution (about 44% of suspended particulate matter in Delhi alone).

Plastic Peril

According to a survey conducted in 1997, the Goan capital Panaji uses about 20 million printed plastic bags every year. And that's just those handed out by the city's 260 department stores. If all these bags were strewn over the town's open spaces, they would cover them entirely within 11 years. Everywhere in India plastic bags and bottles clog drains, litter city streets and beaches and, in the tourist centres like Shimla, Manali and Nainital, even stunt grass growth in the parks. The antiplastic lobby estimates that about 60% of the plastics used are discarded within a week; only 10% are recycled. Goa has introduced a scheme whereby newspapers are donated to charitable groups and orphanages to be made into bags which are sold to pharmacies and stores. On the whole, however, it's up to individuals (including travellers) to restrict their use of plastic, and responsibly recycle bottles and bags.

The worst disaster in India, indeed the worst industrial disaster in the world, is Bhopal (see The Bhopal Disaster – Curing an Outrage with Neglect boxed text in the Madhya Pradesh chapter).

Energy

Thermal plants account for 74% of India's total power generation with coal and lignite providing most commercial energy needs. The coal available in India is of poor quality; its high fly ash content contains toxic substances and causes respiratory diseases. In 1976 oil was discovered off the shores of Maharashtra. Crude production grew at about 10% a year until the mid-1980s when it declined due to aging fields and delays in finding new sources. The government has

Temples of Doom?

Nehru described dams as temples of modern India, capable of delivering potable water and power to millions. But there are many who refuse to pay homage. At Indore in Madhya Pradesh, the blue flags of the Narmada Bachao Andolan (Save the Narmada movement) flutter in the wind. Tea stalls and snack bars do a brisk trade. It seems the 25,000-plus crowd that's gathered to protest against yet another large dam are digging in for the long haul. This scene, in January 1998, has been repeated over and over at countless dam sites. And little wonder, given what's at stake.

This protest was one of many opposing the ambitious US$6 billion Narmada Valley Development Project that will see the creation of 30 major, 135 medium and 3000 small dams, flooding agricultural land, villages and prime forests to provide massive amounts of irrigation and electricity. Unfortunately it will also displace thousands upon thousands of people. Environmentalists have pointed out that it will also lead to the destruction of forests (5000 sq m have been flooded from 1500 large river valley projects), the waterlogging and salination of irrigation canals, the resurgence of malaria, the threat to animals and plants and the salination of drinking water in coastal states such as Kerala. Although there is legislation to ensure environmental considerations are taken into account before, and even during, dam construction, in practice they are often ineffective. Studies show that in up to 90% of cases, project authorities haven't complied with the conditions under which their projects were cleared. Solutions include clarifying environmental impact assessment guidelines, more community involvement in decision making, boosting the resources of environmental agencies, and coordinating the efforts and clearance procedures of such legislation as the Environment Protection Act and the Forest Conservation Act.

The Sardar Sarovar Dam in Maharashtra, part of this project, has become an international symbol of the negative effects of dams. Since the mid-1980s, thanks to dedicated activists the plight of the people and land affected has received wide publicity. In March 1993 the World Bank withdrew from the project, although this didn't halt production. However the Narmada Bachao Andolan has become a potent form of people power resulting in a Supreme Court order halting work on the dam until a complete review is completed. At the end of 1998, the Madhya Pradesh Government was considering a switch to rain-fed irrigation systems as an alternative to large-scale Narmada dam projects. Channelled monsoon water might also provide enough force for power generation, when coupled with biomass and solar energy systems.

Meantime, the work continues. In November 1998, after eight years of discussions, the state government and the Japanese Sumitomo Corporation struck a Rs 8.5 billion deal for the purchase of turbines and generators for a dam riverbed powerhouse.

been forced to turn to imports to meet domestic demand.

Far less important, but much more controversial, is hydro and nuclear power. The benefits of hydro dams (hydro generates 24% of total power) have been offset by environmental and social costs that critics claim cannot be justified in many cases (see the Temples of Doom? boxed text).

India has 10 nuclear power reactors operating at five sites around the country. The most recent, at Kakrapar 50km east of Surat in Gujarat, started production in 1991, although at the time of writing four reactors were in various stages of completion including one in the rainforests of Karnataka. However, nuclear power contributes less than 2000MW (about 2% of India's capacity), and the share of electricity produced is usually about 1%.

Biomass (cow dung, agricultural residues, wood) is important in the non-commercial sector, especially for cooking. About three-quarters is consumed as firewood. Although the share of biomass had fallen from 40% of total energy consumption in 1984 to 30% in 1993, the net consumption has risen by 15% since 1984. However, biomass can't power appliances or generate light, and the government has focused on electrification in the countryside. In 1970 only 20% of Indian villages were connected to the national grid. By 1993 this had grown to 85%.

Renewable energy installations include wind energy, solar and mini/micro hydro. Between 1990 and 1996 India became the world's third largest producer of wind energy. The subsequent sharp decline has been blamed on tax disincentives and over-optimistic projections by wind energy promoters. About 400,000 solar cookers were installed in 1997.

FLORA & FAUNA

There's a certain place on the Gulf of Kutch (Kachchh) in Gujarat where the desert merges with the sea. It's here the flamingos with their brilliant, pink plumage come in their thousands to build nest mounds from the salty mud, and raise their young. It's just

Healing Plants

When Rama's brother lay mortally wounded in Lanka, home of the evil king Ravana, Rama's loyal deputy Hanuman (the monkey god) flew to a sacred mountain in the Himalaya for lifesaving herbs. But when he got there he couldn't decide which plants to pick, so he lifted up the entire mountain and carried it back to Lanka. On the way there, and during the return journey, bits and pieces of earth dropped off, scattering plants over the Western Ghats in South India. This, so the story goes, is how plants used in traditional ayurvedic medicine came to grow in southern India.

Some 2000 plant species are described in ayurveda and at least 500 are in regular use. More than 90% are gathered from the wild, usually by Adivasis, but many are now under threat. The World Conservation Union's (IUCN) Red List has detailed 352 medicinal plants, of which 52 are critically threatened and 49 endangered. The *Rauwolfia serpentina* for example, used to treat blood pressure is found only in India. It's in worldwide demand but supply can't meet demand, with worrying consequences for the future of the species. In addition, there are questions arising over intellectual property rights to medicinal plants and the equitable distribution of the benefits of their commercial development.

one among many extraordinary sights in a country which can claim one of the world's richest natural heritages: 65,000 species of fauna, 350 of mammals (7.6% of the world's total), 408 of reptiles (6.2%), 197 of amphibians (4.4%), 1244 of birds (12.6%), 2546 of fish (11.7%) and 15,000 of flowering plants (6%).

India has some 16 major forest types which can be further subdivided into 221 minor types. Tropical forests are found in the Andaman and Nicobar Islands, the Western Ghats and the greater Assam region.

There are a few patches left in Orissa. The commercial value of the trees within these forests have opened them to exploitation; in the Western Ghats, for example, Indian rosewood *(Dalbergia Latifolia)*, Malabar kino *(Pterocarpus marsupium)* and teak have been virtually cleared from some areas. In the Himalaya alpine, temperate and subtropical vegetation can be found. Above the snowline hardy little plants like anemones, edelweiss and gentian can be found. Further down, in the monsoon-soaked foothills are mossy evergreen forests with cinnamon, chestnut, birch and plum. The subtropical vegetation of this region is referred to as *terai* and is usually dominated by a single species – Sal.

In the harsh extremes of India's hot deserts the khejri tree *(Prosopis Cineraria)* and various strains of acacia (scrubby, thorny plants well-adapted to the conditions) flourish. Any plant here needs to withstand temperatures of 50°C plus. Many have roots that can snake down deep into the soil to find water, and the leaves on most are small to minimise evaporation.

The Himalaya harbour a hardy range of creatures. Ladakh's freezing high-altitudes are home to the yak, a shaggy, horned wild ox weighing in at around one tonne, a wild sheep called the Ladakh urial, the Tibetan antelope and the bharal (blue sheep), the *kiang* (Tibetan wild ass), the Himalayan ibex and the Himalayan tahr. Other Himalayan inhabitants include black and brown bear (found in Kashmir), marmot, mouse-hare and musk deer – delicate creatures lacking antlers, but with hare-like ears and canines that in males look like tushes. This animal, not a true deer at all, has been hunted mercilessly for its musk, which is used in perfume.

When it comes to mystique, none of these animals matches the snow leopard. It's so elusive that many myths have grown up around it; some believe it can appear and disappear at will. There are fewer than 5000 snow leopards left in the world, and the number is dropping. Its beautiful light grey coat dotted with black rosettes provides the perfect camouflage in its rocky, snow covered habitat, but it has also, alas, put a price on the animal's head. The snow leopard is found in Sikkim and Arunachal Pradesh.

The endearing but very rare red panda inhabits the bamboo thickets of the eastern Himalaya where it feeds on bamboo shoots, fruit, leaves and insects. The lakes and marshes of Kashmir provide temporary homes to migrating waterbirds, geese and ducks, many of which fly all the way from Siberia to winter here. Some species exhibit an extraordinary affinity with high altitude travel; the red and yellow-billed crow-like choughs are capable of flying well above 5000m.

Down on the lowlands India teems with life, from the huge mangrove swamps of the Sunderbans in the east, to the burning sands of the Rann of Kutch in the west, and from the grasslands on the Nepalese border in the north to the gently eastward sloping Deccan plateau of the south. It is here that nature and humanity are locked in the most intense competition for land and livelihood, with nature on the run in many places.

The Ganges and Brahmaputra merge before twisting and turning their way for thousands of kilometres to empty into the Bay of Bengal, creating a delta of some 80,000 sq km. Within this delta are the swampy Sunderbans, home to smooth-coated otters, a surprisingly large population of tiger (possibly up to 700), cleverly adapted aquatic reptiles, fish of many species, crabs, wild boar, visiting sea turtles, snakes and spotted deer – which have adapted to the environment's saltiness by acquiring the ability to secrete salt from glands. In the freshwater reaches of the Ganga live Gangetic dolphins, Shiva's mythical messengers; crocodiles (mugger or marsh crocs, plus the narrow-snouted antediluvian-looking gharial), scavenger crabs and many species of fish.

The one-horned rhino and elephant can still (only just) be found in the northern grasslands (see Endangered Species later in this section).

The harsh deserts of Rajasthan and Gujarat are surprisingly well populated. The *chinkara* (Indian gazelle), the wild ass, the

Indian wolf and the black buck have all adapted to the heat, salty soils, and limited water resources of the region. Confined to a 1500 sq km protected area (the Gir Forest) on the edge of the Little Rann of Kutch (Kachchh) are the last of the Asiatic lions. There are fewer than 300 left and in 1998 there was talk of relocating some in a sanctuary in neighbouring Madhya Pradesh. These lions lack the impressive shaggy mane of their African relatives and they have an extra fold of skin on their bellies.

India's primates range from the extremely rare golden langur, found near the Bhutanese border, to more common species such as the bonnet macaque and its northern cousin, the rhesus macaque. The rainforests of the south also have rare lion-tailed macaques, glossy black Nilgiri langurs and the endangered slender loris (the slow loris is found in eastern India).

Distributed reasonably widely in peninsular India are *dhole* (wild dogs), jackal, and several species of deer and gazelle including the relatively common sambar. Barking deer and mouse deer are now quite rare. The snake-killing mongoose, immortalised by Kipling, is still hale and hearty.

Those averse to slithering creatures may prefer to ignore that India has 238 species of snakes, 50 of them (including 20 species of sea snakes) being poisonous. Found widely in India, the cobra, king of the snakes (at least mythologically), is the world's largest venomous snake (up to 5m in length). Its characteristic pose of arousal, hood spread, is an enduring image for anyone who's seen a snake charmer at work. Other poisonous snakes include the krait, Russel's viper and the saw-scaled viper. These four snakes together account for around 10,000 deaths each year, but on the whole it's rare for snakes and humans to come in contact. Harmless snakes include the rat snake, which looks disturbingly like a cobra, the bright green vine snake, the dark brown bronze-back tree snake, and the rock python.

The forests of the Western Ghats, which stretch all the way south from Mumbai to the tip of the peninsular, harbour a wealth of wildlife and plant life. Within their wet, relatively undisturbed confines can be found one of the rarest bats in the world, the little fruit-eating *Latidens salimalii*, flying lizards which can glide for up to 12m, sloth bear, leopard, jungle cat, hornbill and many other species of bird. Here too, on the mountains' rocky, misty slopes is the last remaining stronghold of the endangered Nilgiri tahr, or cloud goat.

Beyond the mainland, in the waters of the Bay of Bengal to the east and the Indian Ocean to the west, lie the Andaman and Nicobar Islands and Lakshadweep, respectively. Marine turtles, bottle-nosed dolphins, a hugely rich bird population (225 species and subspecies in the Andaman and Nicobar Islands alone), reptiles, amphibians, butterflies (hundreds of species), fish and coral are all found here. Also in the Andamans is a small population of elephant (some of which roam wild) brought over from the mainland by logging companies. These elephants are capable of swimming up to 3km between islands. Another oddity found in this part of the world is the coconut or robber crab, which (despite weighing up to 5kg) scuttles up coconut trees and tears open the fruit with its strong claws.

Endangered Species

Large animals, such as elephant, tiger and rhino, are often early and highly noticeable indicators of things going wrong with the ecosystem. By that measure, India's natural world is looking less than robust. All three species are in danger of extinction.

Wildlife sanctuaries have existed since ancient times, but after Independence many more were created; there are now 560 protected areas including 80 national parks. In 1972 the Wildlife Protection Act was introduced to stem the abuse of wildlife, followed by other conservation-orientated legislation such as the Forest Conservation Act and the Environment Protection Act. India is one of 143 signatories to the Convention on International Trade in Endangered Species of Fauna and Flora (CITES)

Major National Parks & Wildlife Sanctuaries

national park/ wildlife sanctuary	location	features	best time to visit
Valley of Flowers National Park	near Badrinath, Uttar Pradesh	3500m above sea level, flower-filled valley; trekking	Jun-Aug
Corbett Tiger Reserve	Uttar Pradesh	sal forest & river plains: tiger, chital, deer, elephant, leopard & sloth bear	Nov-May
Rajaji National Park	Uttar Pradesh	beautiful forested foothills: elephant, tiger, deer, sloth bear, tiger & leopard	Nov-Jun
Palamau Game Reserve	150km south of Ranchi, Bihar	tiger, leopard, elephant, gaur, sambar, muntjac, macaque, chital & langur	Feb-Mar
Sunderbans Wildlife Sanctuary	south-east of Calcutta, W Bengal	mangrove forests: tiger, fishing cats & great birdlife	Feb-Mar
Jaldhapara Wildlife Sanctuary	near Jaldhapara, West Bengal	forest & grasslands: Indian rhinoceros & elephant	Mar-May
Kaziranga National Park	Assam, North-Eastern Region	tall grasslands & swamp: rhino, elephant, tiger & birdlife	Feb-Mar
Sariska National Park	Rajasthan	plains: tiger, chinkara, sambar, nilgai & wild boar	Nov-Jun
Ranthambhore National Park	south of Jaipur, Rajasthan	set around crocodile-filled lake: crocodile & tiger	Oct-Apr
Keoladeo Ghana National Park	Rajasthan	heron, stork, crane, geese & deer	Sep-Feb
Sasan Gir National Park	Gujarat	oasis in desert: Asian lion, chowsingha & crocodile	Dec-Apr
Velavadar National Park	near Bhavnagar, Gujarat	grasslands in delta region: blackbuck	Oct-Jun
Little Rann of Kutch Wildlife Sanctuary	north-west Gujarat	desert region: Indian wild ass (khur), wolves & caracals	Oct-Jun

Major National Parks & Wildlife Sanctuaries

national park/ wildlife sanctuary	location	features	best time to visit
Madhav National Park	near Gwalior, Madhya Pradesh	open forests & lake: chinkara, chowsingha, nilgai, tiger & leopard	Feb-May
Kanha National Park	Madhya Pradesh	swamp deer, tiger, chital, gaur blackbuck, leopard & hyena	Mar-Apr
Bandhavgarh National Park	Madhya Pradesh	old fort on cliffs above plains: tiger	Nov-Apr
Navagaon National Park & Salim Ali Bird Sanctuary	140km east of Nagpur, Maharashtra	hilly forest & bamboo groves: tiger, leopard, sloth & migratory birds	Oct-Jun
Similipal National Park	Orissa	forest: tiger, elephant, leopard, sambar, muntjac & chevrotain	Nov-Jun
Sanjay Gandhi National Park	near Mumbai, Maharashtra	scenic area with waterbirds & butterflies	Oct-Apr & Aug-Nov
Periyar Wildlife Sanctuary	Kerala	langur, elephant, tortoise, wild dog, gaur, otter, kingfishers & fishing owl	Nov-Apr
Nilgiri Biosphere Reserve (Bandipur, Nagarhole, Wynaad & Mudumulai)	Karnataka, Tamil Nadu & Kerala	forest: elephant, leopard, gaur, sambar, chital, muntjac, chevrotain, bonnet macaque, giant squirrel & birds	Jan-Jun
Vedantangal Bird Sanctuary	near Chengalpattu, Tamil Nadu	cormorant, egret, heron, stork, ibis, spoonbill, grebe & pelican	Nov-Jan
Calimere Wildlife & Bird Sanctuary	near Thanjavur, Tamil Nadu	coastal wetland: water fowl, deer, blackbuck, flamingo & wild pig	Nov-Jan
Mundanthurai Tiger Sanctuary	Tamil Nadu	tiger (infrequent), chital, sambar & rare lion-tailed macaque	Jan-Mar
Indira Gandhi Wildlife Sanctuary	Tamil Nadu	elephant, gaur, tiger, panther, deer, boar, bear, porcupine & civet cat	Nov-Dec
Mahatma Gandhi National Marine Park	Andaman & Nicobar Islands	mangrove, rainforest & coral; diving & snorkelling	year-round

brought into force in 1975 to regulate the trade in endangered wildlife. But huge pressure from a growing population hungry for land, a massive demand for animal body parts from the insatiable Chinese medicine market, and a ready international market for skins and fur are proving to be a virtually insurmountable force.

India is one of 12 so-called megadiversity countries which together account for up to 70% of the world's biodiversity. It's the only country in the world that has both lions and tigers. But all across India many species are facing a perilous future. The World Conservation Union's 'Red List' of endangered plant species numbers 1236 for India (7.7% of the world's total) and its companion list of endangered animals includes 172 species (2.9% of the world's total).

But it's the tiger, India's national animal, that seems to personify the situation. In 1997 at least 63 tigers died at the hands of poachers; trapped, shot and poisoned. One was reported to have 'exploded' after eating bait. The WWF declared 1998 the year *for* the tiger and pledges were made to boost tiger protection. But critics claim that India's expenditure on wildlife (0.2% of GDP), and tiger conservation's portion of it, is not enough and that forest guards, armed only with *lathis* (bamboo batons) and sometimes lacking even basic essentials such as shoes and torches (flashlights), are no match for heavily armed poachers.

The one-horned rhinoceros' position is equally tenuous as it loses its natural grasslands habitat to sugar cane plantations and other cultivation. Now it's found only in small pockets near the Nepalese border. Its horn, actually matted hair, is sought for its supposed medicinal properties, as are its urine, flesh and blood.

At present there are about 2500 Indian elephants in the wild and, inspired by efforts to save the tiger, conservationists have launched a major effort to ensure their numbers stay relatively stable.

Project Elephant began in 1992 under the auspices of the Ministry of Environment & Forests, but with individual states contributing towards field costs and salaries. Eleven elephant reserves have been established, encompassing the four main elephant populations. These are in the north-west (Uttar Pradesh); central and east (Bihar, Orissa, West Bengal); north-east (Arunachal Pradesh, Assam, Meghalaya, Nagaland); and south (Karnataka, Kerala, Tamil Nadu, Andhra Pradesh). The project aims to: protect elephant habitats and corridors; protect elephants from poachers; minimise human-elephant conflicts; encourage humane treatment of captive elephants; improve the scientific management of elephant populations; and provide technical and financial assistance to the states.

So far the project has improved habitats and acquired land needed to keep elephant corridors open. It has boosted anti-poaching capacity, supplying radios, vehicles and arms to rangers, and establishing roads and camps in elephant country. Other strategies include building trenches and power fences, capturing problem animals and compensating villagers for damage inflicted by them.

Trade in plants, animals and insects, both dead and alive, is monitored by a WWF division called TRAFFIC (see the Conservation Contacts boxed text earlier in this chapter). TRAFFIC-India's 1996 campaign 'Don't Buy Trouble' targeted domestic consumers and overseas travellers in the hope of making them more aware of India's role in the insidious US$20 billion global wildlife market. Of particular concern is the trade in tiger bones, rhino horns, reptile skins, live mammals and reptiles, turtle shells and birds. A Delhi-based NGO called Friends of Butterflies has been instrumental in raising awareness of the trade in rare species, especially from the north-east (the 1972 Wildlife Protection Act specifically bans the trade in butterflies). The global butterfly trade is worth some US$200 million and rising, and the Himalaya mountains and foothills are the source of many rare species. Butterfly conservationists point out that the Atlas moth of the Khasi Hills is almost extinct due to poaching, an environmental catastrophe as it cross-pollinates many plants.

National Parks & Sanctuaries

National parks and other protected areas in India are administered at state level and are often promoted as part of each state's tourist attractions. To encourage more visitors, accommodation, road systems, transport and other facilities continue to be developed and upgraded.

Whenever possible, book in advance for transport and accommodation through the local tourist offices or state departments, and check if a permit is required, particularly in border areas. Various fees are charged for your visit (entrance, photography, etc) and these are usually included in advance arrangements. Meals may also be arranged when you book, but in some cases you must take your own food supplies and have them prepared for you.

Some parks offer modern guest houses with electricity, while others only have *dak*-style bungalows. Facilities usually include van and jeep transport, and at some parks you can take a boat trip to approach wildlife more discreetly. Watchtowers and hides are also often available, providing good opportunities to observe and photograph wildlife close up.

The national parks, wildlife sanctuaries and reserves listed in the Major National Parks & Sanctuaries table are included in more detail in the regional chapters.

GOVERNMENT & POLITICS

India is a constitutional democracy. There are 25 states and seven union territories and the constitution (which came into force on 26 January 1950) details the powers of the central and state governments as well as those powers that are shared. If the situation in a particular state is deemed to be unmanageable the central government has the controversial right to assume power there. Known as President's Rule, it has been enforced in recent years, either because the law and order situation has gotten out of hand – notably in Punjab from 1985 to 1992, Kashmir in 1990 and in Assam in 1991 – or because there is a political stalemate, such as occurred in Goa, Tamil Nadu,

Pondicherry, Haryana and Meghalaya in 1991, and Nagaland in 1992.

Parliament is bicameral; the lower house is known as the *Lok Sabha* (House of the People) and the upper house is known as the *Rajya Sabha* (Council of States).

The lower house has 544 members (excluding the speaker), and elections (using the first past the post system) are held every five years, unless the government calls an election earlier. All Indians over the age of 18 have the right to vote. Of the 544 seats, 125 are reserved for the Scheduled Castes and Tribes.

The upper house has 245 members; members are elected for six-year terms and a third of the house is elected every two years. The president appoints 12 members and the rest are elected by state assemblies using a regional quota system. The president (who's duties are largely ceremonial) is elected by both houses and the state legislatures (the election is held once every five years). The president must act on the advice of a council of ministers, chosen by the prime minister. The president may dissolve the lower house but not the upper.

At state level some legislatures are bicameral, and are run along the lines of the two houses of the national parliament. The chief minister is responsible to the legislature in the same way as the prime minister is responsible to parliament. Each state has a governor, who is appointed by the president and who may assume wide powers in times of crisis. At village level (where 74% of the population lives) there is renewed interest in reviving the *panchayat* system of village councils.

ECONOMY

In June 1991, India ended 40 years of central planning. Since Independence it had been so highly protectionist that its share of world trade had declined from 2% in the 1950s to under 0.5% in the 1980s. The reforms generated a huge increase in private investment, boosted exports and imports by some 20% (1993-96) and reduced the role of the public sector in many areas including heavy manufacturing, banking, telecommunications, power generation and distribution, ports and roads. The country's main exports are gems and jewellery, cotton yarn and fabrics, handicrafts, cereals, marine products, ready-made garments and transport equipment.

Agriculture

Agriculture contributes 29% of India's gross domestic product (GDP) and employs some 64% of the workforce. It is highly protected and subsidised. Less than 1% of the raw commodities produced (India is one of the world's most prolific producers of fruit, vegetables, milk, wheat and sugar) is processed and there are heavy restrictions on the import of processed foods. Foodgrains make up 63% of India's agricultural output (191 million tonnes in 1997), Uttar Pradesh is the leading state with 40% of total production. India is the world's second largest producer of paddy rice and the fourth largest wheat producer. It is the world's No 1 tea producer (762 tonnes in 1995-96) – the main growing regions being Assam, West Bengal, Kerala and Tamil Nadu – most is exported. Coffee is a smaller plantation crop; Karnataka is the major centre (53% of it is under coffee plantations). Arabica (49%) and Robusta (51%) are the main varieties. In 1995-96 coffee production stood at 0.23 million tonnes of which 0.17m tonnes were exported.

Rubber is an important crop domestically (India only imports about 5% of its needs). Kerala leads the country in rubber production, and together with Tamil Nadu accounts for 86% of the area given over to rubber plantation. India leads the world in the production of bananas, mangoes, coconuts and cashews, as well as potatoes, tomatoes, onions and green peas. It is among the top 10 producers of citrus, pineapples and apples. However, the top spot in terms of its contribution to the national economy goes to neither wheat nor rice, but milk.

In 1997 India became the world's No 1 milk producer (72 million tonnes, compared with the USA's 70.4 million tonnes). India's cattle population also leads the world, at some 193 million head.

Industry

The state and central governments own and operate many of the enterprises that supply other producers, eg fertiliser, machinery and chemicals. The private sector is made up of thousands of producers as well as a few large conglomerates (eg the Tata Iron and Steel Company). Of the big industry sectors, it's textile manufacturing – jute, cotton, wool, silk and synthetics – that employs the biggest workforce. But by far the biggest overall employers in the manufacturing sector are the millions of small handicraft businesses, some of which service only their own village.

In 1993-96, growth in India's industrial sector touched 9% per annum, but slowed to around 6.7% in 1996-97, a result it's claimed of the high cost of credit and infrastructure impediments. In its budget of 1 June 1998, the BJP-led government remained committed to privatisation in certain public sector industries and pledged a 35% increase in outlay for power, communications and energy.

Information Technology

In 1997-98 Indian software exports earned some US$1.75 billion, up 68% on the previous year. By 2000 some anticipate earnings will touch US$4 billion, with the number of companies exporting software tipped to exceed 800. Bangalore in Karnataka, dubbed India's silicon valley, currently accounts for at least a third of all India's exported software and services.

India's pool of highly skilled (and relatively inexpensive) labour has attracted many multinationals. These include Computer Vision (which does 80% of its research and development in Pune), Novel (Bangalore), Baan (Hyderabad), Boeing (Hyderabad), British Aerospace (Bangalore), Adobe (Delhi) and British Telecom (Pune). Other global giants investing in research and development schools in India include IBM and Silicon Graphics. In 1998

Microsoft announced it was setting up its first development centre outside of the US at Hyderabad in Andhra Pradesh. Karnataka has been particularly active in encouraging software industries, but other states have drafted information technology policies and are racing to set up software development cities. But the information superhighway within India is still relatively limited; there are only some 100,000 Internet connections. The government has sanctioned a budget of US$300 million to set up a high speed national telecom backbone.

Mining & Oil

Since about the 1970s Indian coal production has grown at about 4% per annum. There are more than 500 coal mines (mostly state-owned) and India produces a small surplus. However, the quality is low. India also has rich reserves of limestone, iron ore, bauxite and manganese. The country only produces about half the petroleum it needs; most of this comes from offshore fields near Mumbai, and from Gujarat and Assam.

Fishing & Forestry

Fishing takes place all along India's coastline and in the rivers and waterways of the interior. The commercial catch is between 1.4 and 1.6 million tonnes (sardines, Indian shad and whitebait account for about 30%). Most boats are non-mechanised, although mechanisation is increasing, causing a detrimental affect on local fishing communities and on the marine environment. Commercial forestry, though not a large industry in India, is found in the Western Ghats, the western Himalaya and hilly areas of central India.

POPULATION & PEOPLE

India has the world's second largest population in the world, exceeded only by that of China. Estimates for 1999 put the figure at about 980 million (16% of the world's population, occupying 2.4% of the world's land mass). And it's growing at about 2% per year. The 2001 national census (a census is held once every 10 years) is expected to reveal a population of one billion-plus. Within the first decades of the 21st century, India is tipped to claim the title as the world's most populous nation. The Indian people are not, however, a homogeneous group. It is quite easy to tell the difference between the shorter Bengalis of the east, the taller and lighter-skinned people who live in the centre and north, the Kashmiris with their distinctly Central Asian appearance, the Tibetan people of Ladakh, Sikkim and northern Himachal Pradesh, and the dark-skinned Tamils of the faiths in India, see the Sacred India colour section for details.

Despite India's many large cities, the nation is still overwhelmingly rural. It is estimated that about 74% of the population lives in the countryside (at the turn of the 20th century, it was nearly 90%). According to the 1991 census, Mumbai is India's biggest city, with an urban population of nearly 13 million; Calcutta comes second with 11 million and Delhi and Chennai third and fourth with 8 and 5 million respectively. The most densely populated parts of India (excluding Union Territories) are West Bengal with 767 people per square kilometre and Kerala with 749. At the other end of the spectrum is the remote north-east state of Arunachal Pradesh with 10. The national average is 273.

The bias against women continues (see Society & Conduct later in this chapter); more women die before the age of 35 than men and maternal mortality rates are high (forming 25% of the world's childbirth related deaths). The proportion of females to males has declined over the years (it was 972:1000 in 1901; the 1991 census figure was 927). A ratio of 950:1000 is considered favourable to females in India, and 11 states and Union Territories fall into this category. Chandigarh has the lowest proportion, with just 790 females for every 1000 males. Kerala is the only state where women outnumber men. Here there are 1036 females for every 1000 males. Male/female average life expectancy increased from 32/31 years in 1950 to 62/64 years in 1996.

Improving the living standards of the has been a priority for governments since

Adivasis

More than 50 million people belong to tribal communities. These Adivasis, as they are known in India, have origins which precede the Vedic Aryans and the Dravidians of the south. For thousands of years they have lived more or less undisturbed in the hills and densely wooded regions regarded as unattractive by agriculturalists. Many still speak tribal languages not understood by the politically dominant Hindus, and follow customs foreign to both Hindus and Muslims.

Although there has obviously been some contact between the Adivasis and the Hindu villagers on the plains, this has rarely led to friction since there was little or no competition for resources and land. All this has changed. In the past 50 years the vast majority of Adivasis have been dispossessed of their ancestral land and turned into impoverished labourers. The only region where this has not occurred, and where Adivasis continue to manage their own affairs, is Arunachal Pradesh in the extreme north-east.

Elsewhere in India, and especially in Madhya Pradesh, Andhra Pradesh, Bihar and the Andaman and Nicobar Islands, a shocking tale of exploitation, dispossession and widespread hunger has unfolded with the connivance and even encouragement of officialdom. It's a record the government would prefer to forget and which it vehemently denies. Instead it points to the millions of rupees said to have been sunk into schemes to improve the conditions of Adivasis. Although some of this has got through, corruption has claimed much of it.

It's unlikely that any genuine effort will be made to improve the lot of Adivasis in peninsular India, given the pressure for land. What is far more likely is that the erosion of the cultures and traditions will continue until they eventually 'disappear'.

Independence. However, poverty remains widespread. The gross national product (GNP) per capita is just US$350 per year and claims to have a quarter of the world's poor, the highest concentration anywhere. Of India's children, half are undernourished. Preventable diseases such as TB, malaria, blindness and leprosy account for half of all reported illnesses. HIV/AIDS is a major cause for concern; it's estimated that as many as 1% of the population may be infected with the HIV virus.

EDUCATION

Under the Indian constitution, education is compulsory and free for all up to the age of 14. There are 867,694 schools and colleges in India (590,421 primary schools alone) and 226 universities. Two-thirds of children are enrolled, including most children of primary school age (100 million enrolments in 1993). However, many don't attend school regularly and at least 33 million aren't enrolled at all. Only half the children in the 11

to 14 year age group are enrolled. Girls are under-represented, especially in higher education. Half of all students from rural areas drop out before completing school.

In addition to state schools, there are many private (usually English-language) schools, very often run by church organisations, and places in these exclusive institutions are highly coveted among those who can afford them. Much investment has gone into higher education, although critics say the quality has declined, with many liberal arts graduates unable to find work. India's brightest students frequently go abroad to undertake their higher degrees and many never return.

The state and union governments share responsibility for education, although the union government has been more active in promoting education for girls and other disadvantaged groups. Nevertheless, national literacy among those aged 15 and over is just 52% (for females, it is about 37.7%). Attempts to boost literacy among adults have met with mixed success. Operation Blackboard, launched in 1987 to bring literacy to 100 million adults in the 15-35 age group by 1997, failed mainly due to lack of funds.

SCIENCE & PHILOSOPHY

Philosophical systems in India can be classified into orthodox and unorthodox, with the former accepting the authority of the *Vedas* including the *Upanishads* (the oldest of which are deemed Vedic), which promote the notion of an all-pervading, universal One (see the Sacred India colour section.)

Unorthodox systems include Buddhism and Jainism (although they share with orthodox systems concepts of *karma*, justice for past deeds, and *moksha*, liberation). The distinction, however, isn't as cut and dried as it might appear. The *Vedas* are considered the ultimate authority as their origins are viewed as divine; all reasoning is considered subordinate.

Followers of the orthodox path however, though obliged to accept the authority of the *Vedas*, can introduce new points of view by writing commentaries, never openly claiming that they as individuals have seen the truth for the first time themselves. The six schools of orthodox Hinduism are:

- Sankhya of Ishvarakrishna
- Nyaya of Gotama
- Vaisheshika of Kanaka
- Yoga of Patanjali
- Mimamsa of Jaimini
- Vedanta of Badarayana

Of the six, the Vedanta school, which is based on the philosophical concepts found in the *Upanishads*, has been the most important interpreter of Hindu philosophy since about 700 AD. But the oldest known system of philosophy is the Sankhya and understanding its concepts is important for understanding Hinduism. Sankhya philosophy is commonly only associated with Ishvarakrishna, who wrote the oldest extant Sankhya text (2nd century AD), based on Kapila's teachings. According to this philosophy, all things arose from *prakriti* (primeval matter). Prakriti gave rise to *mahat* or *buddhi* (intelligence), from which arose *ahamkara* (ego sense), *manas* (mind), *tanmatras* (five senses), five sense organs, five organs of action and five gross elements (earth, air, ether, water, light). Matter is composed of three *gunas* (qualities) which are: *sattva* (light and pleasing), *rajas* (dynamism) and *tamas* (inertia). Suffering is said to be caused by ignorance of one's true nature (pure consciousness). Self is not matter, and realisation of this distinction releases one from suffering.

Challenges from Buddhism and Islam in India meant that by the 8th century some adherents felt the purity of the *Vedas* was being lost. Shankara (788-820), looking to turn the tide, cleaved to the notion of non-dualism and *jnana* (the importance of knowledge) as a means to salvation. His view was challenged by the Tamil Brahmin Ramanuja who, influenced by the southern *bhakti* cult (ie devotion to a personal god and the rejection of Brahminic ritual) promoted the notion that while knowledge was one path to salvation, it wasn't the only path or even the most effective one. In fact, he claimed giving oneself to God was a better option that didn't discriminate against lower castes or women (a Rajasthani princess, Mirabi, was an important contributor to the bhakti movement). *Karma yoga* (the path of action) was another approach promoted by those disillusioned with the orthodox ways. Its most important advocate Goraksha, originally a Buddhist, and his followers melded Shaivism (the cult of Shiva) and Buddhism laying the foundations for the development of *hatha yoga*. (Goraksha is the patron of Nepal, and the Ghurkhas are named after him.)

Buddhism and Jainism arose at a time when there was significant dissatisfaction with Brahminical Hinduism. Buddhism rejected the concept of *atman* (soul), although retained the notions of karma and moksha. Both Jainism and Buddhism recognised natural law, as opposed to Vedic law. (For more information on religion, see the Sacred India colour section.)

Sciences such as medicine, linguistics and mathematics in India have been traced back to the Vedic times when the rituals brought to India by Ayran invaders were anthologised. The study of linguistics was formalised by the Sanskrit grammarian Panini in his 4th century BC work *Ashtadhyayi*, claimed to represent the first scientific analysis of any single alphabet. The systematic study of mathematics emerges from the 5th century *Shulvasutras*, which lay down the geometric properties of plane figures such as the triangle, rectangle, rhombus and circle. A theory of numbers also developed about this time, and included the concept of zero and negative numbers and the use of simple algorithms using place-value notations. The concept of zero is in fact India's contribution to the world of mathematics and arrived in Europe via Arab traders.

About the same time as the *Shulvasutras* were being penned, the great mathematician Aryabhara also concluded that the earth's shadow was responsible for the waxing and waning of the moon and that the earth rotated on its own axis, while the moon rotated around Earth. Astronomy in India has traditionally been closely linked with the state, given that kings were viewed as divine and that the natural and social worlds worked as one. Some of India's most famous astronomers were therefore royal including most famously the Maharaja Sawai Jai Singh of Jaipur (1699-1743) who built five large observatories, at Jaipur, Delhi, Varanasi, Mathura and Ujjain.

The classic works on ayurvedic medicine, the *Charak Samhita* and the *Sushrita*, were written in the 6th century BC.

In 1930 Sir Chandrasekhar Venkata Raman (1888-1970) became the first Asian to win the Nobel prize for physics, acknowledging his achievements in the study of how light changes when passing through transparent bodies (the Raman Effect). In 1998, Amartya Sen (an Indian resident in the USA) won the Nobel prize for economics for his contribution to the field of welfare economics.

ARTS
Dance

In Hindu mythology it is Shiva, in his incarnation as Nataraja, who dances the world into existence and who dances again at its destruction. Encircled by flames, hair flying, Nataraja tramples the demon of ignorance as he paces out his cosmic steps. King of dance, he is also the patron of actors and dancers throughout India, and a temple at Chidambaram in Tamil Nadu is dedicated to his honour.

The oldest text (in Sanskrit) on dance and drama is the *Bharata Natya Shastra*. Its exact age is uncertain; scholars estimate it was written some time between the 2nd century BC and the 3rd century AD. No one can say for sure who the author was; Bharata is not necessarily always a name as such. Nevertheless, the knowledge contained within this work has been passed down through the centuries, albeit undergoing adaptations as times and fashions similarly changed. The traditional mode of transmission, from guru to disciple (a practise known as *gurukul*) survives, although these days students of dance may also learn their art at modern purpose-built schools.

The *Natya Shastra* divides dance into *margi* (that performed for the gods) and *desi* (that performed for the pleasure of people). Dance is further divided into *tandav* and *lasya*. Tandav (which mythology says was first danced by Nataraja and passed on to mortals via his disciple Tandu) is characterised by strength and vigour (generally deemed masculine qualities). Lasya is graceful and delicate, qualities associated with femininity. Lasya is said to have been passed on to mortals through Parvati, Shiva's consort.

Classical dance is made up of three components; *natya*, the dramatic element of the performance; *nritta*, often referred to as pure dance (the rhythmic movement of the body in dance); and *nritya*, the element that suggests *ras* (sentiment) and *bhava* (mood), conveyed through gestures and facial expressions. Natya and nritya employ four techniques collectively known as *abhinaya* (a Sanskrit word that loosely translates as 'a carrying to the spectators'). The techniques are: *angik* (gestures of the body); *vachik* (music, song and rhythm); *aharya* (make-up and costume); and *satvik* (physical manifestations of mental and emotional states).

There are four main schools of classical dance in India and two (*Orissi* and *Kuchipudi*) which are not considered sufficiently distinct from Bharata Natyam to be considered classical styles in their own rights.

Bharata Natyam Also known as *Dasi Attam* (or dance of the *devadasis* – the traditional southern temple dancers) this is lasya in character and as such, its exponents have generally been women. Despite its popularity today, the fortunes of Bharata Natyam once waned considerably along with those of the devadasis, who after the 16th century were associated with prostitution. The style seemed in danger of dying out, but was resurrected in the 19th century by four brothers from Thanjavur (Tamil Nadu) who returned to the dance's classical roots and helped restore its reputation.

Kathak Combines Hindu and Muslim influences and is both lasya and tandav (thus attracting male and female dancers). Kathak was particularly popular with the Mughals and dancers still wear costumes that hark back to the 17th century. Kathak also suffered a period of notoriety when it moved from the courts into houses where *nautch* (dancing) girls tantalised audiences with renditions of the Krishna and Radha love story. It was restored as a serious art form in the early 20th century.

Kathakali Unmistakably tandav Kathakali is, in its present form, a relative newcomer, having been commissioned by a 17th century Keralan royal. Dancers are traditionally male (although females occasionally take part), and stories are usually based on the epics (recited in Manipravalam, a Sanskritised form of Malayalam; see the Sacred India colour section). The open-air performances run through the night although superhuman concentration spans aren't expected from the audience; some doze through bits they find boring (and have a friend wake them for the exciting parts), wander out to buy snacks from the vendors who invariably attend such events, or chat. Kathakali has a rather pantomime quality about it; characters don't sing or talk, but at times shriek and groan

and the action may appear quite violent. But it's the make-up and costumes that leave a really lasting impression on the casual visitor. The hero, with his towering headpiece, glistening green make-up and billowing skirts, has become an enduring icon of Keralan culture (see the Kathakali boxed text in the Kerala chapter).

Manipuri Originating in the Assam Hills this dance came to the attention of the wider audience in the 1920s when Rabindranath Tagore invited one of its most revered exponents to teach at Shantiniketan, near Calcutta. Its slow, swaying rhythm makes Manipuri a distinctly lasya dance form, a counter to the accompanying drummer's energetic performance.

Kuchipudi A dance-drama created in the 17th century by a dance guru, this became the prerogative of Brahmin boys from the Andhra Pradesh village it takes its name from. The story centres on the jealous wife of Krishna and performances take place in the open air at night.

Odissi Claimed to be India's oldest classical dance form, this dance is a direct descendent of the Natya Shastra (many of Shastra's 108 dance units can be found in Odissi). Originally a temple art, Odissi was also performed at royal courts and although today it's performed mainly on the stage, it is still an act of devotion.

India has a wealth of folk dances ranging from the mysterious masked dances performed at festivals in the great Buddhist monasteries of Ladakh to the virile *Bhangra* dance of the Punjab, the theatrical dummy horse dances of Karnataka and Tamil Nadu and the graceful fishers' dance of Orissa.

Pioneers of modern dance forms in India include Uday Shankar, older brother of Sitar master Ravi, who once partnered Anna Pavlova. Uday was based in England for many years but eventually returned to India in 1938 to found the India Culture Centre at Almora in present-day Uttar Pradesh. His ballets were greeted enthusiastically, but a revival of interest in classical styles later fuelled criticism from purists. However, many of his students went on to have brilliant careers. The Bengali Rabindranath Tagore was another innovator who in 1901 set up a school near Calcutta that promoted the arts.

Classical Musical Instruments

CARNATIC INSTRUMENTS

A typical south Indian concert employs either a singer or a main melody instrument (usually a violin), a secondary melody instrument, a drone (eg the *tambura* – a four-stringed instrument, which provides the tonic note and its fifth thereby providing artists with a constant reference point) and one or two percussion instruments.

The tambura provides the drone.

Stringed The *vina* and the *chitravina* are arguably the most popular plucked instruments. The vina has 24 frets and seven strings. It's held like a sitar, the left hand pressing between the frets or pulling on the strings to produce ornamentations. The chitravina is fretless, has 21 strings and is played like a slide guitar. The guitar, the mandolin and the violin, adopted from the west, are also used, although tuning and playing techniques have been adapted to suit the Indian musical style. The most commonly used drone in Carnatic music is the tambura which is plucked throughout the concert.

The stringed vina.

Wind The *nagaswaram* (double-reed flute) and the *venu* (side-blown flute) are used but western instruments such as the clarinet and saxophone sometimes make an appearance.

A poet, playwright, philosopher, actor, painter and novelist, Tagore brought gurus from all over India to Shantiniketan, where a distinctive dance style evolved. Although this style was eventually criticised for its lack of technical precision, it is claimed the real achievement of the experiment lay in stimulating interest in dance within the wider public.

Music

Classical music in India traces its roots back to Vedic times, when religious poems chanted by priests were first collated in an anthology called the *Rig-Veda*. Over the millennia classical music has been shaped by many influences, and the legacy today is Carnatic (characteristic of South India) and Hindustani (the classical style of north India). With common origins, both share a number of features. Both use the *raga* (the melodic shape of the music) and *tala* (the rhythmic meter characterised by the number of beats). *Tintal* for example, is a tala of 16 beats. The audience follows the tala by clapping at the appropriate beat, which in tintal is at one, five and 13. There is no clap at the beat of nine since that is the *khali*

Classical Musical Instruments

Percussion Perhaps the most popular, the *mridangam* is a double-sided drum that produces tones of definite pitch. The more characteristically northern dual drum, the *tabla*, is sometimes used. Other instruments are the *ghatam* (clay pot with no covering), *thavil* (barrel-shaped double-ended drum) and *timila* (long, thin hour-glass shaped drum).

The tabla is used to keep the beat.

HINDUSTANI INSTRUMENTS

Instrumental music has gained increasing prominence in performances, with secondary melody instruments being employed during vocal music only.

Stringed Prominent among the melody instruments is the *sitar*, the rather larger *surbahar*, the shorter-necked, fretless *sarod*, and the bowed *sarangi*. The violin is also used in a manner similar to Carnatic. The *santoor* is of Persian origin and has over 100 strings divided into pairs and is struck with two wooden sticks. The violin and a plucked board zither called a *surmandal* may be used as secondary melody instruments when there is a singer. As in Carnatic music, the *tambura* remains the main drone instrument.

Wind Prominent melody instruments are the *bansuri*, a side-blown bamboo flute and the *shehnai*, which resembles an oboe.

Percussion The tabla, like the sitar, is well-known to western audiences and is the most popular percussive instrument. Others include the *bayan* and *pakhavaj*; the latter is similar to a large mridangam.

Keyboard The hand-pumped keyboard harmonium is used as a secondary melody instrument for vocal music.

The melodic sitar.

(empty section), indicated by a wave of the hand. Both the raga and the tala are used as a basis for composition and improvisation.

Both Carnatic and Hindustani are performed by small ensembles comprising about half a dozen musicians and both have many instruments in common. Neither style uses a change of key or harmonies; the drone establishes the raga's ground note (tonic) and usually its fifth as well. There is no fixed pitch (see the Classical Musical Instruments boxed text); but there are differences. Hindustani has been more heavily influenced by Persian musical conventions (a result of Mughal rule); Carnatic music, as it developed in South India, cleaves more closely to theory. But perhaps the most striking difference, at least for those relatively unfamiliar with India's classical forms, is Carnatic's greater use of voice; all composed pieces are mainly for the voice and possess lyrics; the most popular of these (devotional songs called *kriti*) having been created less than 200 years ago. Hindustani music has more purely instrumental compositions. The most common vocal forms in Hindustani music today are the *khyal* and the *thumri*, the latter is a light classical style based on devotional literature centred around the Krishna and Radha love story.

Classical music, however, is enjoyed by a relatively small section of society. Most people are more familiar with their own local, folk forms, popular during festivities and important village ceremonies – or with popular music. Musicians may be professional or semi-professional. But music is not the exclusive domain of those who call themselves musicians. Wandering magicians, snake charmers and storytellers may also use song to entertain their audiences; the storyteller often sings the tales from the great epics. Radio and cinema have played a large role in broadcasting popular music to the remote corners of India. Bollywood's latest musical offerings are never far away thanks to the proliferation of cassette players throughout the country.

Literature

India has a long tradition of Sanskrit literature, although works in the vernacular have contributed to a particularly rich legacy. In fact, it's claimed that there are as many literary traditions as there are written languages. For most visitors, only that written in (or translated into) English is accessible.

Prominent authors include: Mul Raj Anand whose work focuses on the downtrodden (eg *Cooli*, *Untouchable* – hailed as the first Dalit novel); novelist Raja Rao (*Kanthapura*, *The Serpent and the Rope*, *The Cat and Shakespeare*); Khushwant Singh (*Delhi*, *Train to Pakistan*); Nissam Ezekiel (one of post-Independence India's greatest poets); poets AK Ramanujan (*The Striders*, *Relations*) and Arun Kolatkar, who won the Commonwealth poetry prize in 1977 for *Jejuri*, a collection of 31 poems in English; Kamala Das (one of the best-known women poets); Vikram Seth (*A Suitable Boy*); and Shashi Tharoor, whose work, *The Great Indian Novel*, won the Commonwealth Award; and the widely translated novelist Amitav Ghosh whose work *The Circle of Reason* won the Prix Medici Estranger, one of France's top literary awards.

Keralan-born Arundhati Roy grabbed the headlines in 1997 by winning the Booker Prize for her novel *The God of Small Things*. The story, centring on the fate of seven-year-old twins, is set in Kerala which is evoked in beautiful, sensuous language.

One of India's best-known writers, RK Narayan, hails from Mysore and many of his stories centre on the fictitious South Indian town of Malgudi. His most well known works include: *Swami & His Friends*, *The Financial Expert*, *The Guide*, *Waiting for the Mahatma* and *Malgudi Days*.

Kushwant Singh is one of India's most published contemporary authors and journalists, although he seems to have as many detractors as fans. One of his more recent offerings is simply titled *Dehli*. This novel spans 600 years and brings to life various periods in Dehli's history through the eyes of poets, princes and emperors. Singh has also written the harrowing *Train to Pakistan* on the holocaust of Partition, the humorous *India – An Introduction*, and a collection of short stories, published in hardback.

Anita Desai has written widely on India, including *Cry*, *The Peacock*, *Fire on the Mountain*, and *In Custody* – which was filmed by Merchant-Ivory. Her daughter, Kiran, recently released her first novel *Hullabaloo in the Guava Orchard*, which centres on the fate of an aimless young man (described by one reviewer as Mr Bean-ji) who accidently becomes a guru.

A Matter of Time by Shashi Deshpande centres on the problems a middle class family faces when the husband walks out. Deshpande, from Bangalore herself, takes the reader back through several generations to demonstrate how inherited family traditions affect contemporary behaviour.

Sharanpanjara, or Cage of Arrows, by a Karnatakan author who simply calls herself Triveni is hailed as one of the great novels in the Kannada language (it's now available in English translation). The story centres on an upper-class Mysore woman facing the stigma of mental illness.

The Revised Kama Sutra by Richard Crasta takes an irreverant look at growing up in Mangalore in the 1960s and 1970s. It's a book that leaves you with a lasting insight into the local life of Mangalore and similar South Indian cities. More importantly it gives a first hand account of the tensions of growing up as an intelligent and well educated youngster with frustratingly few opportunities to shine.

Nectar in a Sieve by Kamala Markandaya is a harrowing, although at times uplifting, account of a woman's life in rural South India and the effect of industrialisation on traditional values and lifestyles.

Shobha De's racey novels have been heralded by some critics as being extremely significant in their representation of Indian female sexuality, although others have been critical of their content and style. She is the largest-selling Indian English-language author in India.

The Indian bookshop Crossword recently instigated a literary prize for the best English-language novel by an Indian writer. It was won in 1998 by I Allan Sealey for *Everest Hotel* (he has also written *The Trotter Nana*). Shortlisted novels were *Difficult Daughters*, *Tivolem*, *Across the Lake* and *The Madwoman of Jogare*.

Architecture

In ancient times Indian builders used wood (sometimes brick) to construct their temples. None has survived the vagaries of climate and today all that remains are Buddhist *stupas*. By the advent of the Guptas (4th to 6th centuries AD) of north India, sacred structures of a new type were being built, and these set the standard for temples for several hundred years (see the Sacred India colour section). One of the main distinguishing features between temples in north and south is the shikara. In the north, they are curvilinear topped with a grooved disk, on which sits a pot-shaped finial, and in the south they are stepped with the grooved disk being replaced with a solid dome (eg Temple of Brihadishwara in Thanjavur, Tamil Nadu).

Kerala's temple styles vary in deference to its climate, marked by heavy rainfall, and

typically have steeply sloping roofs of stone, that effectively drain the water away.

The Muslim invaders contributed their own architectural conventions; arched cloisters and domes among them. The Golgumbaz tomb in Bijapur, Karnataka, is one of the largest domes in existence. Under the Mughals, Persian, Indian and provincial styles were successfully melded to create works of great refinement and quality. They include the Persian influenced tomb of Humayun in Delhi, the great fort at Agra and the city of Fatehpur Sikri. But it's Shah Jahan (1627-58) who has made the most enduring mark on architectural history. He built the Red Fort in Delhi, but is better remembered for the Taj Mahal, the tomb for his queen Mumtaz Mahal.

Europeans left their mark in the churches of Goa (eg the Basilica of Bom Jesus, completed in 1605), in the neoclassical style buildings that were erected by the British in the 18th and 19th centuries (and of course the parliament complex of New Delhi), and in attempts to meld neo-Gothic and neo-Saracenic (Muslim) styles with local architectural traditions. Swiss architect Le Corbusier designed the entire city of Chandigarh in the Punjab in the early 1950s.

Painting

Some 1500 years ago artists covered the walls and ceilings of the Ajanta caves in western India with scenes from Buddha's life, lotus flowers, animals and birds. The freedom and grace with which the figures are endowed are unusual and in contrast to the next major style that emerged from this part of India in the 11th century. To attain spiritual merit, the Jain lay community – which flourished thanks to its stake in trade and local rulers sympathetic to the large community of Svetambara monks living in Gujarat – poured their money into lavish displays of temple building, until the Muslim conquest of Gujarat in 1299 after which they turned their attention to illustrated manuscripts, which could be hidden away and preserved. These manuscripts are the only form of Indian painting that managed to survive the Muslim conquest of north India. At first artists painted on palm leaves, but the availability of paper from the late 14th century allowed larger and more elaborate works, with gold-leaf script and lavish borders in blue, gold and red (complex designs and luxurious materials testified to the wealth of the patron). Unlike the flowing Ajanta paintings, the Jain style is angular, with deities and mortals depicted in profile, the eye projecting beyond the face.

The Indo-Persian style developed from Muslim royals, although the elongated eye is one convention that seems to have been retained from indigenous sources. The Persian influence flourished when artesans fled to India following the 1507 Uzbek attack on Herat, and with trade and gift-swapping between the Persian city of Shiraz, an established centre for miniature production, and Indian provincial sultans.

The 1526 victory by Babur at the Battle of Panipat ushered in the era of the Mughals in India. Although Babur and his son Humayun were both patrons of the arts, it was Humayun's son Akbar who is generally credited with developing the characteristically Mughal style. Akbar recruited artists from far and wide to create an atelier that was, initially anyway, under the control of Persian artists. Artistic endeavour at first centred on the production of illustrated manuscripts (topics varied from history and romance to myth and legend), but later broadened into portraiture and the glorification of everyday events.

Akbar took a personal interest in the artists' work and rewarded those who pleased him. Within the atelier there emerged a high division of labour, which meant more work could be turned out in less time. Skilled designers sketched the outlines of the work. Colourists applied layer upon layer of pigment, burnishing each to achieve an enamel-like finish. Painters used squirrel or camel-hair brushes to create the finest of lines. Artists of extraordinary talent, however, were allowed to do their own paintings and so display their mastery. European paintings influenced the artists, and occa-

sionally reveal themselves in experiments with motifs and perspective.

Akbar's son, Jahangir, also patronised painting, but his tastes and interests were different. He preferred portraiture and his fascination with natural science resulted in a rich legacy of paintings of birds, flowers and animals. Style also took a distinctive turn under Jahangir. Despite its richness, there is nothing frivolous or wasteful about the paintings turned out by his atelier. The more formal ordering of figures reflects a penchant for strict etiquette in courtly life. Jahangir also saw portraiture as a useful tool for sizing up foreign rivals; he desired such paintings to reveal personality and requested them so that he might judge the subject's characteristics. Under Jahangir's son Shah Jahan, the Mughal style became less fluid, and although the colouring was bright and eye-catching, the paintings lacked the life and vigour of before. It was a trend that continued, hastened by the disintegration of the Mughal court in the 18th century. Mughal painting as such ended with the reign of Shah Alam II (1759-1806).

By the 19th century painting was heavily influenced by western tastes (especially English watercolours), giving rise to what's been dubbed the Company School, which had its centre in Delhi.

In Rajasthan distinctive styles developed that were influenced by Mughal tastes and conventions, in part because local Rajput rulers were required to spend time at the Mughal court. But Rajasthani painting had its own characteristics, marked by a poetic imagery evident in such popular themes as the *ragamala*, a depiction of musical modes, and the *nayakanayikabheda*, a classification of ideal types of lovers. The romanticism and eroticism they depict are in stark contrast to the strict morality that pervaded Rajput society. Portraiture was influenced by Mughal trained artists recruited by Rajput rulers. But rather than the revealing pictures favoured by Jahangir, these portraits lean more towards ideal representations of individuals, whose weaknesses are well and truly disguised.

Top: The Khajuraho temples in Madhya Pradesh are famous for their abundance of erotic sculptures.
Bottom left: Mumbai's Victoria Terminus is adorned with carvings depicting peacocks, monkeys, elephants and British lions.
Bottom right: Mounted guard outside Parliament House, New Delhi.

Top: The fort at Gwalior surrounds several temples and ruined palaces. Since the 14th century this fort has been the scene of continual intrigue and clashes with neighbouring powers.
Bottom: Varanasi's ghats are steps that lead down to the River Ganges, one of the holiest places in India. To die here ensures release from the cycle of rebirths and an instant passport to heaven.

In the Himalayan foothills of north-west India a distinctive style of painting, dubbed Pahari, developed during the 17th and 18th centuries in a relatively small area (roughly between Jammu and Garhwal) which was divided into 35 kingdoms. Pahari painting can be divided into two main schools: the Basohli school preceded the Kangra, which eclipsed it in the late 18th century. Basholi art is robust, bold and colourful. Kangra art is more subdued and fluid, probably testament to the influence of Mughal court painters migrating into the area at the time. The Kangra school survived until the late 19th century, but its best works are usually dated to around the late 18th and early 19th centuries.

Sculpture

For about 1500 years after the demise of the Indus Valley civilisation sculpture in India seems to have vanished as an art form. Then, suddenly in the 3rd century BC, it reappeared in a new, technically accomplished style that flourished under the Mauryan rulers of central India.

It's a phenomenon that still puzzles scholars and art historians; some say Mauryan sculpture must have had its genesis abroad, possibly in Persia. But this has never been proved. The legacy of the Mauryan artists includes the burnished, sandstone columns erected by the Buddhist emperor Ashoka, the most famous of which, the lion-topped column at Sanchi, has become the state emblem of modern India.

Mid-way through the 2nd century BC a new format emerged, evident in the stupa railing of Bharut, Madhya Pradesh. Here can be seen the style and motifs that have since become an integral part of Indian sculpture. The ornamentation is symbolic of abundance (beauty and abundance are closely linked in Indian sculpture); the pot overflowing with flowers, the lotus, the trees, the elephants and the mythical *makara* (a protective crocodile-like creature). Here too are the *yakshas* and *yakshis*, male and female deities associated with ancient fertility cults and whose images provided the basis for Buddhist, Jain and Hindu iconography.

While there was an early reluctance to represent Buddha in more than symbolic form, yaksha figures gradually became Buddha-like in the succeeding centuries, albeit devoid of their elaborate dress and ornamentation (deemed inappropriate in the light of Buddhism's monastic traditions). The Sarnath Buddha, for example, has a robe characteristically thrown over the left shoulder, the right hand raised in a *mudra* (gesture) signifying freedom from fear, the left resting on the waist, but empty handed. By the Gupta period in north India (4th to 6th centuries AD) the rather earthy and robust yaksha-style Buddha icons had been transformed into models of serene contemplation, eyes lowered, as befitting the compassionate Master of the Law.

Hindu and Jain iconography also began to evolve their distinctive forms at this time. Images sprouted multiple arms and heads (distinguishing them from mere mortals), and eventually adopted the serene expressions which have become associated with calm contemplation.

From the 10th century, sculpture and architecture were generally inseparable; temples were lavishly decorated with religious sculpture designed to impress and instruct. The fantastic animal forms and towering *gopurams* (gateways) of the great temple complexes of South India (eg Meenakshi in Madurai, Tamil Nadu) took ornamentation and monumentalism to new levels.

Most, but not all, sculpture has left its legacy in stone. From South India comes a brilliant series of bronzes, created during the Chola dynasty of the 9th and 10th centuries. The lost wax technique artisans used to produce images of the most popular deities are still used in Tamil Nadu, but the brilliance of the Chola period has never quite been recaptured.

Pottery

The potter's craft is steeped in mythology. The first humans are said to have been shaped from clay by Brahma, the Creator, and indeed the name with which potters are most closely identified, prajapati, is one of Brahma's titles. Potters claim another link to the divine. When Shiva wished to marry Parvati it is said they lacked a necessary water pot, so Shiva created a man and a woman from two beads plucked from his necklace – the man created the pot and together the man and woman created a lineage of potters. Today potters are also known as *kumbhar* or *kumbar*, a name shared with the ubiquitous water pot *(kumbh)*.

Despite the intrusion of plastic into the marketplace, the potter's craft is evident in every household and at shrines throughout the country. Smooth, round terracotta water pots are arguably the most commonly used household utensils in India; the narrow neck prevents spillage as women carry the pots on their heads between the well and the home. Although plastic pots are also used these days, baked clay keeps the water pleasantly cool in a country where many households have no access to refrigeration. Potters also make a variety of cooking utensils; some say traditional dishes just don't taste the same prepared in metal pots and pans. And travellers will invariably come across the terracotta cups used by coffee vendors at train stations in the south and which, once emptied, are smashed on the tracks. In Tamil Nadu, it's traditional to smash one's old pots on the eve of the Pongal (harvest) festival, and replace them with new ones. This custom keeps potters all over the state busy.

Pots and storage jars of various kinds are created on the wheel (only men may use the wheel although women may decorate the pot after it has been removed); sometimes they are built up using slabs or coils. Plaster moulds are occasionally used.

The potter also applies their skill to making *chillums* (clay pipes), hookahs, beads and *jhanvan* (serrated palm-sized slabs) which can be used like pumice stone for smoothing rough skin on the feet.

Votive offerings, including terracotta horses and other creatures, idols of various descriptions, and sometimes replicas of parts of the human body (these are placed before a shrine by those hoping for a miraculous recovery), also have a place in the potter's repertoire. Occasionally the potter acts as an intermediary between the worshipper and the divine. For example, in Tamil Nadu, terracotta horses are made in honour of the protective deity Ayannar. The potter, requested to make the horses by villagers in times of dire need, also attends the associated ceremonial and, in a trance-like state, intercedes between the god and the community.

The Mughals manufactured coloured and patterned glazed-tiles with which they decorated their mosques, forts and palaces. Blue pottery (such as vases, plates, tiles and doorknobs), largely for export, is made in various places around India; the main centres being Jaipur and Khurja.

Cinema

When India's first (silent) epic-based feature film *Raja Harischandra* was released in 1913 few would have anticipated the enormous industry that would emerge in the following decades. The fruits of India's film-makers up to 1931 barely fill six video cassettes in the National Film Archives of India. But by the 1980s India's output had eclipsed Hollywood's, earning it the moniker Bollywood. But even Bollywood (or Mumbai by any other name) has found a challenger in the burgeoning southern cinema industry, fuelled by gigantic studios in Chennai and Hyderabad and a similarly huge demand from Tamil and Telugu-speaking audiences.

To date India has produced some 28,000 feature films and thousands more short films and documentaries. However, production fell slightly in 1996. One explanation is that cinema (commercial and art) is feeling the pressure from video and TV (cable and satellite), with art cinema especially, experiencing a difficult time finding distribution outlets. Nevertheless, the National Film Development Corporation has a major interest in expanding the national TV network. Tamil and Telugu directors especially, have been active in trying out new technology and storytelling techniques, looking to American cinema for inspiration. Mani Ratnam's 1993 film *Roja*, in which a young Tamil couple are posted to strife-torn Kashmir (a story therefore without a specifically regional bias), was dubbed into Hindi and proved a national success. Other southern films have since been similarly dubbed.

As India's film industry dates from the beginning of cinema itself and progresses through the days of the Raj, two world wars, world depression, Independence, Partition

My Life as an Extra

or What's a Jewish Boy from Melbourne Doing Dressed as a Catholic Priest in a Tamil Film?

'You look like an actor, you should go to the studios and try your luck.' These words were spoken to me by Mr Film News Anandan (yes that really is his name). I was interviewing the septuagenarian award-winning film historian about his collection of film stills from every Telugu and Tamil film ever made. I took his advice and ventured to MGR Film City in Chennai. Within one hour I was 'discovered': 'My name is Arjun, I'm an associate director and I've been observing you. I'd like to invite you to be in my film,' said the urbane gentleman dressed in white.

From that moment I was swept into the macho world of a swashbuckling Tamil blockbuster. First they gave me lunch, then a car and a driver. I was rushed to 'wardrobe' (a concrete cell somewhere in the bowels of Film City). Only then did I learn that I was to play a Catholic priest. The wardrobe department clearly wasn't geared up for western sizes. The search for white trousers that wouldn't render me a eunuch took many precious minutes. They put a white surplice (frock) over me, a crucifix around my neck, rosary beads in my right hand and a bible (in Tamil) in my left hand. Make-up consisted of a broken comb and an even more broken mirror. Then it was off to location – a paddock in the studio grounds where a mock grave had been dug and a black coffin was waiting to be lowered. My role was to preside over the burial of a young boy who had been shot by the villain.

Lighting technicians ran cables across wet grass (and issued warnings not to touch one light stand which had become 'live'). The camera crew prepared their lenses, and a large crowd of onlookers assembled. Three Indian tourists from Kerala requested my autograph and posed with me for their snaps. Into the mayhem came the cleanest car I had seen in Chennai and out stepped the denim clad, mobile phone wielding hero. The crowds deserted me. They rushed their hero for his autograph. He had come not to act, but to direct my scene (in Tamil films the hero is often allowed to direct some scenes).

Only when they yelled action and then 'rain' did I learn that the burial was to take place during the monsoonal downpour. Water from a fire hose gushed over me and my bible. As the coffin was slowly lowered, I muttered the mantra (what the hell am I doing here?), fondled my rosary and looked appropriately forlorn. Because it was a one camera shoot we had to do three takes from as many angles. Within two hours the shoot was over. Mr Arjun discreetly pressed my Rs 200 appearance fee into my hands and thanked me profusely. 'Call me when you're next in town,' he said.

The film is called *Thayin Mani Kodi*, a patriotic title loosely translated as Mother Country. And, surprisingly, it's about a hero who single-handedly defends his nation and wins the heart (and the body) of the heroine.

Peter Davis

and beyond, it provides an interesting window to social and cultural change during the 20th century as seen through the eyes of leading film makers of the day. Well-known to western audiences is Satyajit Ray's 1955 Bengali classic *Pather Panjali* (Song of the Road) where the protagonist, Apu, is torn between an individualistic urban existence and a yearning for the familiarity and security of traditional country ways, something evoked with nostalgic footage of the Bengali countryside. For 40 years Ray turned out consistently excellent work, and in 1992, shortly before he died, he was awarded an Oscar, which was presented to him at his bedside in Calcutta where he was seriously ill. Other good Ray films include *Pather Panchali, Apur Sansar, Ashani Sanket* and *Jana Aranya*.

Art cinema, which flourished first in Bengal before being taken up by film makers from Mumbai and Kerala, has dealt over the years with many topical issues including urbanisation, class conflict, caste and oppression. Despite pressure to churn out the money spinning confections commonly known as *masala* movies, the sense of alienation experienced by rapid urbanisation has been a constant theme in Indian cinema since the 1970s. An example of this is *Zanjeer*, in which a witness is killed on a Mumbai commuter train. Having said that, masala movies have had a tremendous influence on modern day culture, and in their favour can be said to be more than just song-and-dance spectacles, *Satyam* (1998) being an example of this. The three biggest masala movies of the past five years are *Kuch Kuch Hai* (1998), *Dil to Pagal, Hai* (1997), *Hum Appke Hai Kayn* (1994). In the 20th century there are arguably three major milestones in this genre: *Mother India* (1957), *Mughal-e-Azam* (1960) and *Sholay* (1980).

Shot on the streets of Mumbai is the excellent arthouse film *Salaam Bombay* by Mira Nair. It concentrates on the plight of the street children in Mumbai, and won the Golden Camera Prize at Cannes in 1989. Also directed by Mira Nair is *Kama Sutra*, released in 1997. Its theme of sensuality and

sexuality in 16th century India shocked the Bollywood establishment, which until very recently prohibited the depiction of even chaste kisses between romantic protagonists on celluloid. Another film which provoked controversy in India is *Bandit Queen*, directed by Shekhar Kapur, which is based on the life of the female *dacoit* (outlaw), Phoolan Devi.

Controversy certainly focused on Deepa Mehta's film *Fire* in 1998; the Shiv Sainaks smashed cinemas in Dehli and Mumbai where the film was being screened. Critics claimed it denigrated Indian culture while others supported it in the name of free speech. Most talked about film that year was *Satya*, a Hindi-language movie directed by Ram Gopal Verma which focused on the Mumbai underworld and the nexus of politics and organised crime.

Another popular film of 1998 was *Bombay Boys*, an English-language comedy centred on a group of nonresident Indians (NRIs) and how they dealt with local fraudsters.

Theatre

The oldest form of classical theatre in India, Sanskrit theatre, shares a common ancestry with dance. Details on both were laid down in the *Natya Shastra* in ancient times (see Dance earlier in this section). Sanskrit theatre, like dance, was divided into performances for the gods and those rendered for people's pleasure, and was further classified into naturalistic and stylised productions, notions reflected in the folk traditions of later times. This type of theatre thrived until about 1000 AD when it was eclipsed by folk theatre and today it lives only in the *kudiyattam* Sanskrit theatrical style of Kerala.

The many regions and languages of India provided fertile ground for folk theatre, which employs a few Sanskrit theatrical conventions (eg the opening prayer and the *vidushaka* (clown) – the hero's comic alter ego and the audience's ally). Folk theatre draws heavily from the epics (see the Sacred India colour section) but will also canvass current political and social issues. Performances always take place outdoors and actors are invariably from castes where the art is passed from father to son; in rare cases women may also act. Troupes may tour for several months at a time and the more popular theatrical forms (secular as opposed to religious in nature) enjoy a very healthy following.

Puppetry has also enjoyed a reasonably good following in India, although most people are only familiar with Rajasthani puppets *(kathputhilis)*; wooden creations, dressed in colourful costumes and manipulated by the puppeteers (always male) using strings. Less well known are the leather stick puppets of Andhra Pradesh (similar to the *wayang kulit* puppets of Indonesia) and the glove puppets of Kerala. Puppetry is losing its audience to competing attractions such as cinema and television and because of puppeteers' reluctance to challenge the epic-based repertoire.

Modern theatre had its inception in Bengal in the 18th century. Exposed to western theatrical and literary conventions earlier than most, Bengali artists combined western staging techniques with folk and Sanskrit conventions. Their plays soon became vehicles for social and political comment and opposition to British rule. The touring Bombay Parsi theatre companies that developed in the north and west of India in the 19th century also used western, classical and folk conventions to bring dramatic, lively entertainment in Hindi and Urdu to a wide audience.

Folk Art

India's folk arts represent a rich and vibrant tradition. Textiles have always played an important role in society and trade (the Romans had textiles made to order in India). A fabulous brocade wedding sari from the handlooms at Kanchipuram in Tamil Nadu is a prized possession. In Andhra Pradesh the custom of *kalamkari*, where designs are sketched out on cotton then painted in, still exists, although motifs are taken from the epics (in days gone by, courtly scenes were the vogue). Embroidery is a specialty in Gujarat, Rajasthan and parts of the Punjab. Jewellery of an apparent infinite variety is

Toda Shawls

Known as the *puthikuzhi*, the traditional Toda shawl assumes a significant role in Toda culture. Embroidered exclusively by the women, the shawls are made of thick white cotton about 2m by 1.5m. A large pocket is stitched into each shawl. According to anthropologists, Todas have never weaved their own cloth, instead purchasing plain cloth from the market and dedicating many hours to embroidering the distinctive black and red designs onto it. Although many Todas are now completely integrated into mainstream Indian society, this tradition of embroidering the cloth continues in Toda villages.

The shawls, worn by both men and women (though much less often by men), serve many purposes. A basic shawl is for everyday use around the village. The thickness of the cloth shields the morning and evening chill in the mountains. Sometimes the stripes are worn vertically, other times horizontally. On formal occasions, the shawl covers the head as well as the body. More intricate shawls are stitched for significant occasions such as weddings and births. However, the best quality shawls are reserved for funerals. During the complex rituals of a traditional Toda funeral the finest shawl is hung outside the hut where the corpse lies. Mourners touch the shawl with their forehead as they enter. At a certain point in the ceremony, the shawl is taken inside the hut. A handful of leaves is placed into the pocket. The shawl is then wrapped carefully around the corpse, offering protection and security in the next life.

made throughout India: semiprecious stones, gold, silver, enamelling – various techniques are used. Folk painting includes threshold designs (see the Kolams boxed text), and mural painting (which reached a high level of achievement under the patronage of wealthy merchant patrons in Shekhawati in Rajasthan in the 19th century). Devotional

Kolams

The rice flour designs or *kolams* that adorn thresholds in Tamil Nadu, especially during the Pongal (harvest) festival and the Hindu month of Markali (mid-December to mid-January) when the gods are deemed particularly accessible, are much more than mere decorations. Kolams (meaning play, form or beauty in the Tamil language) are auspicious and symbolic. Traditionally they are drawn at sunrise and are made of rice flour paste, which may be eaten by small creatures – symbolising a reverence for all life, even the most apparently insignificant. This gesture is doubly blessed; giving as one's first act of the day is viewed as extremely auspicious. Beneficial deities are deemed to be attracted to a beautiful kolam; the goddess Lakshmi, representing prosperity and good fortune, may thus be tempted to symbolically cross the threshold and bestow her beneficence on those who dwell within.

Kolams transmit all sorts of information to those who understand their nuances. They may signal to sadhus and holy men that they can expect food at a particular house or they may be a sign of the family's prosperity and hospitality generally. The absence of a kolam might signal ill fortune or a death in the household, or it might simply mean that the household has no women or that they are too busy working in the fields to make one. Some believe kolams protect against the evil eye, acting as a sort of deflector of ill intentions, envy and greed.

White and red are favoured colours in kolam design, although others such as blue may be used. Black is never used because of its association with dark and evil forces. Motifs vary. Some feature complex geometric shapes, others depict lotus flowers and sundry bird and animal creations. These days it is possible to buy bamboo or plastic tubes with holes punched into them. The tube is filled with chalk dust and rolled over a piece of moistened, hard-packed ground to make an attractive kolam design.

Tamil Nadu doesn't have a monopoly on kolams, also called *rangoli*. During the Onam festival in Kerala, for example, kolams are made with coloured dyes and flower petals.

---

art, such as the *thangkas* (paintings) of Ladakh, are now also turned out for the tourism market. Wooden toys, kites, beadwork, clay, lacquer and glass all have their traditions somewhere in India.

SOCIETY & CONDUCT
Marriage, Birth & Death

Known as *samskaras*, rites of passage ceremonies in Hindu culture have been simplified over the centuries. Most important today is the marriage ceremony which is generally elaborate and expensive. Marriages are usually arranged (see Women in Society later in this section). Discreet inquiries are made within the community. Desirable characteristics include a good job, a good position in society, a respectable family and reasonable looks and character. Where the community isn't as close-knit as it once was, advertisements may be placed in the local newspapers, something increasingly common within the growing urban middle class population. A family member will check the horoscopes of likely candidates and in some cases a chaperoned meeting will take place between the prospective bride and groom. Dowry, though illegal, is a key issue; the larger the dowry, the greater the chances of the bride's family securing a good match for their daughter, and families will often get into horrendous debt to raise the required cash and kind. An astrologer is consulted again when it comes to fixing a wedding date.

On the day of the wedding the bridegroom is escorted to his future in-law's home (usually accompanied by a very loud brass band and lots of friends and well-wishers) where offerings of roasted grain are tossed into the hearth fire. The ceremonies are officiated by a priest and the marriage is formalised when the bridegroom takes hold of his bride's hand and together they take seven steps around the fire. They are then escorted to their new home, the bride entering without touching the threshold.

Upon the birth of a child, tradition behoves the parents to undertake several ceremonies on the infant's behalf. These rituals centre on the casting of its first horoscope, name giving, feeding the first solid food and hair cutting, the latter performed on boys once they are about five years of age.

Divorce and remarriage are generally frowned upon. Among the higher castes, widows are not expected to remarry, but are admonished to wear white and live pious, celibate lives. Traditionally widows have been excluded from religious ceremonies and festivals, and they are generally regarded as harbingers of bad luck.

Hindus cremate their dead, and funeral ceremonies are designed to purify and console both the living and the deceased. An important aspect of the proceedings is the *sharadda*, or paying respect to one's ancestors by offering water and rice cakes. It's an observance that's repeated at each anniversary of the death. After the cremation the ashes are collected and 13 days after the death (when blood relatives are deemed ritually pure) a member of the family will scatter them in a holy river such as the Ganges, or in the ocean.

Pilgrimage

Every Hindu is expected to go on *tirtha yatra* (pilgrimages); at least once a year is considered desirable. Pilgrimages are undertaken for many reasons: to implore the gods to grant some wish, to take the ashes of a cremated relative to a holy river, to seek good health and fortune, or to gain spiritual merit. There are thousands upon thousands of holy sites in India to which pilgrims travel (the elderly often make Varanasi their final goal as to die here releases them from the cycle of rebirth).

Kumbh mela (religious fairs) are also a legitimate destination. Millions may attend these fairs which are held every three years in the holy cities of Nasik, Haridwar, Ujjain and Allahabad in the course of a cycle of 12 years. The most important of these is at Prayaga. Called the *tirthraja* (king of fairs), it attracted an estimated 20 million people in 1989 and was claimed to be the most auspicious event in 144 years.

The Caste System

The origins of the caste system are hazy, although Vedic hymns allude to its mythical origins. Brahmins or priests were said to have emerged from the mouth of Brahma at the moment of creation, Kshatriyas (warriors) were said to have come from his arms, the Vaishyas (merchants) from his thighs and Shudras (serfs) from his feet. A fifth class of people, known as Untouchables (now called Scheduled Castes or Dalits) remained outside this system. Their lives were the most menial of all, and even today sweepers and latrine cleaners are invariably drawn from their ranks. The first three *varnas* (as caste groups are called) are known as twice born *(dvija)*. They are born into the varna firstly through physical birth and a second time, for males, through initiation. Within the varnas are thousands of *jati*, social communities (sometimes but not always linked to occupation) into which individuals are born and which are ranked according to their ritual purity.

About a third of the Hindu population is, however, excluded from Brahminic practises, and many have converted to Buddhism or Christianity. While it is possible to move up the scale; the term 'sanskritisation' has been coined to describe the process by which lower castes emulate the observances (eg vegetarianism) of higher castes with the intention of eventually gaining acceptance – many are unable to completely shake off their old identities.

Today the caste system, although weakened, still wields some considerable power. The relationship between caste and politics is quite potent; those seeking power may look

Purity & Pollution

Ritual purity has over the millennia played a key role in Hindu culture. Caste distinctions have traditionally been more stringent in the south, and in the area now known as Kerala, Brahmins believed even the mere shadow of an Untouchable would pollute them. To the orthodox, travelling abroad can be defiling and requires elaborate cleansing rituals and possibly a ritual bath in the Ganges, to eradicate its effects. Some purifying rituals use the five products of the sacred cow (milk, curd, ghee, urine and faeces).

Death is polluting and a blood relative of the deceased is barred from normal duties such as cooking for 13 days after the death. Hindus are expected to rinse their mouths and wash their hands before prayers, before and after meals and after attending a funeral. Women are not allowed in the kitchen or a temple for the first three days of their menstrual cycle and are readmitted only after a ritually purifying bath. Ritual purification also takes place after the birth of a child.

Food that has come into contact with another person is considered unclean (and a cook should never taste food during preparation). Ideally all food should be offered to the gods before it is eaten. Food preparation itself falls into two main categories: *pukka* (deep fried) and *katcha* (raw, boiled, baked or lightly fried in ghee). Upper castes may accept pukka, but not katcha foods from lower castes.

to certain jatis as potential vote banks. The system also functions as an unofficial trade union, with strict rules to avoid demarcation disputes. Tensions between the upper castes and the Scheduled Castes sometimes erupt into violence. In an effort to improve the lot of the Scheduled Castes the government reserves huge numbers of public sector jobs, parliamentary seats and university places for them. With nearly 60% of the jobs reserved, many well-educated people are missing out on jobs they would get on merit. In 1994, some state governments (such as Karnataka) raised the reservation level even higher in an effort to win mass support. In 1991 and again in 1994, there were serious protests against the raising of the quotas. In 1991 at least 100 protesters immolated themselves.

Women in Society

Problems for Indian women often begin before birth. Such is the desire to have male children, that the government has had to pass legislation to prohibit the abortion of healthy foetuses, the modern equivalent of the age-old practise of female infanticide. 'Sex determination' clinics are also banned but abortions, following examinations in illegal ultrasound clinics, continue. Girls are often seen as a burden on the family, not only because they leave the family when married (traditionally boys remain in their parent's house even after marriage), but also because an adequate dowry must be supplied. Consequently, girls may get less food and their education is neglected.

Arranged marriages are still the norm rather than the exception. A village girl may well find herself married off while still in her early teens to a man she has never met. She then goes to live in his village, where she is expected not only to do manual labour (at perhaps half the wages that a man would receive for the same work), but also raise children and keep house. This might involve a daily trek of several kilometres to fetch water, as much again to gather firewood, and a similar amount again to gather fodder for domestic animals. She has no property rights if her husband owns land, and domestic violence is common; a man often feels it is his right to beat his wife. In many ways, her status is little better than that of a slave.

For the urban, middle-class woman, life is materially much more comfortable, but pressures still exist. She is much more likely to be given an education, but only because this will improve her marriage prospects. Once married, she is still expected to be mother and home maker above all else. Like her village counterpart, if she fails to live up to expectations – even if it is just not being able to give her in-laws a grandson – the consequences can be dire, as the practice of 'bride burning' is not uncommon. On a daily basis, newspaper report of women burning to death in kitchen fires, usually from 'spilt' kerosene. The majority of these cases, however, are either suicides – desperate women who could no longer cope with the pressure from their in-laws – or outright murders by parents-in-law who want their son to re-marry someone they consider to be a better prospect. It's claimed that for every reported case, 299 go unreported and that only 5% of the reported cases are actually pursued through the legal system.

A married woman faces even greater pressure if she wants to divorce her husband. Although the constitution allows for divorcees (and widows) to remarry, few are in a position to do so simply because they are considered outcasts from society – even her own family will turn their back on a woman who seeks divorce, and there is no social security net to provide for her. A marriage in India is not so much a union based on love between two individuals, as a social contract joining two people and their families. It is then the responsibility of the couple to make the marriage work, whatever the obstacles; if the marriage fails, both husband and wife are tainted, but the fall-out for the woman is far worse. Divorce rates are, not surprisingly, low.

While there is a downside to being a woman in India, the picture is not completely gloomy. In the past decade or so, the women's movement has had some successes in improving the status of women. Although the professions are still very much male dominated, women are making inroads – in 1993, the first women were inducted into the armed forces, and they account for around 10% of all parliamentarians.

For village women, it's much more difficult to get ahead, but groups such as Self Employed Women's Association (SEWA) in Ahmedabad have shown what's possible. Here, poor and low caste women, many of whom work on the fringes of the economy, have been organised into unions, offering at least some lobbying power against discriminatory and exploitative work practices. (See the SEWA boxed text in the Gujarat chapter.)

Although attitudes towards women are slowly changing, it will be a long time before they gain even a measure of equality with men. For the moment, their power lies in their considerable influence over family affairs and so remains largely invisible to outsiders.

Sati

When 18 year old Roop Kanwar burned to death on her husband's funeral pyre in 1987, she became *sati*, a goddess in the eyes not only of local villagers but among the wider community. Deorala, the small village in Rajasthan where the gruesome act took place, has thrived thanks to the thousands of people who make the pilgrimage to the shrine erected in her honour. Despite the prime minister of the day, Rajiv Gandhi, condemning the event as 'utterly reprehensible and barbaric', and legislation in December 1987 banning sati and outlining punishments for those glorifying it, sati remains a potent ideal. Women still pay homage at sati shrines, believing they have the power to cure infertility and terminal disease. Since Independence, 40 sati deaths have been officially recorded.

How or why the practice originated is unclear. It's not mentioned in the *Vedas*, India's ancient sacred texts, but it seems sati has been given a spurious religious sanction by mythology.

Birth Control

With a population tipped to exceed China's in the 21st century, birth control is a perennial matter for concern. Moves to introduce birth control gained notoriety in the 1970s especially during the 'Emergency' when sterilisation squads moved into the countryside and terrorised villagers. In the 1980s Prime Minister Rajiv Gandhi instituted an ambitious sterilisation target of 1.3 billion Indians by 2050. It's met with mixed success, especially in the countryside where children (especially male children) are regarded as security for one's old age. Widespread media coverage in support of birth control has promoted the ideal of the two-child family, and the use of contraceptives, especially condoms. It's estimated that 46% of couples use some form of contraception.

Indian Clothing

Brightly coloured, beaded, embroidered, painted and printed – Indian clothing in all its many variations has always held an exotic allure for foreigners. In Goa, traditional skirts sold by Lambadi women are snapped up by holiday-makers. In the bazaars of Rajasthan, brilliant mirror-work skirts and *zootis* (pointy-toed shoes) beckon. Most Indian women wear saris, and the fabulous silks from Varanasi and Kanchipuram with their jewel-like colours and gold brocade are a popular purchase among western women who, unlikely to actually wear a sari, make use of the fabric for other garments or home decoration. Simply going through the process of buying silk is an experience in itself. Invited to sit, shoeless, on a spotless, white cotton-covered mattress, you watch as the silk seller pulls out bolster after bolster of shiny fabrics, tossing them on the mattress where they roll out to reveal their colours and patterns. It's hard to say no.

Although not particularly practical for travellers, the sari is nonetheless a very economical garment. It comes in a single piece (between 5m and 9m long and 1m wide) and is cleverly tucked and pleated into place without the need for pins or buttons. Worn with the sari is a *choli* (tight-fitting, short-sleeved blouse) and a cotton draw-string petticoat. Muslim and young women tend to wear the *salwar kameez* (a loose tunic top) over draw-string pyjamas. For western women, this garment is particularly useful. It's comfortable, inexpensive and most of all, considered to be respectable attire (see Women Travellers in Facts for the Visitor). Worn with this costume is a scarf-like length of matching fabric called a *dupatta*. Usually this is draped across the neck at the front so that the two ends cascade down one's back. In strict Muslim areas it's used to cover the head. Occasionally women wear a variant of this, called a *churidar*, which is basically the same but tighter fitting at the hips, thighs and ankles. A collarless or mandarin-collared tunic called a *kurta* is sometimes worn over the top. Open-toed, low-heeled sandals are generally worn with both outfits.

Men generally wear western-style trousers and shirts, although the *dhoti* and (in the south) the *lungi* and the *mundu* are also commonly worn. The dhoti is a loose white garment pulled up between the legs. The lungi is more like a sarong, and is always coloured. It's usually sewn up like a tube; the wearer merely pleats it at the waist so that it fits snugly. The mundu worn in Kerala is like a lungi but is always white. Men frequently tuck the hems into the waist giving the garment a skirt-like appearance; a lungi or mundu should always be lowered when sitting down or entering someone's house.

Dos & Don'ts

Despite the hassles and hardships of travel in India you will generally be accorded great respect. In return you should be sensitive to local customs. While you are not expected to get everything right, you should at least exercise common sense and common courtesy. If in doubt about how you should behave, watch what the locals do (eg at a temple), or ask; people are generally happy to explain and delighted that you are taking an interest in their culture.

Religious Etiquette Take particular care when attending a religious place (such as a temple or shrine) or event. Dress and behave appropriately – don't wear shorts or sleeveless tops (this applies to men and women) and do not smoke or hold hands. Behave in a respectful manner; loud and intrusive behaviour isn't appreciated. Remove your shoes before entering a holy place (always take off your shoes with your left hand), and never touch a carving or statue of a deity. In some places, such as mosques, you will be required to cover your head. For religious reasons, do not touch locals on the head and similarly never direct the soles of your feet at a person, religious shrine, or image of a deity, as this may cause offence. Never touch someone with your feet. (See also each of the Etiquette for Visitors sections of the Sacred India colour section.)

Photographic Etiquette You should be sensitive about taking photos of people, especially women, who may find it offensive – always ask first. Taking photos at a funeral, a religious ceremony or of people bathing (in public baths or rivers) may cause offence. Don't use flash photography in prayer rooms in gompas (monasteries) or to take pictures of murals of any kind.

Guest & Food Etiquette Many Indians, especially urban middle-class people, are very westernised. However if you spend time with traditional or rural people there are some important things to remember. Don't touch food or cooking utensils that local people will use. You should use your right hand for all social interactions, whether passing money or food or any other item. Eat with your right hand only. If you are drinking from a shared water container, never touch the mouth of the container with your lips; hold the container a little above your mouth and pour. Similarly never touch someone else's food.

If you are invited to dine with a family, take off your shoes if they do and wash your hands before taking your meal. The hearth is the sacred centre of the home, so never approach it unless invited to do so.

Never enter the kitchen unless you have been invited to, and always take your shoes off before you go in. Similarly, never enter the area where drinking water is stored unless you are barefoot. Do not touch terracotta water vessels – you should always ask your host to serve you.

Bathing Nudity is completely unacceptable and a swimsuit must be worn even when bathing in a remote location. Indian women invariably wear saris when bathing in a river or any place where they are in public view and women should consider wearing a sarong rather than a bathing suit. (See also Women Travellers in the Facts for the Visitor chapter.)

Treatment of Animals
India's ancient reverence for the natural world manifests itself in numerous ways; in myths, beliefs and cults that are part of the cultural fabric. But in a country where millions live below the poverty line, survival often comes before sentiment. In addition, big money is involved in the trade of animal parts for Chinese medicine, which has been a major factor in bringing India's national animal, the tiger, to the brink of extinction.

The World Society for the Protection of Animals (WSPA) is working to raise awareness of cases of cruelty and exploitation, with a recent campaign centring on dancing bears. Endangered sloth bear cubs are captured from the wild, their muzzles are pierced so lead rope can be threaded through the hole, and their teeth are pulled out. The bears' nomadic handlers ply tourist traps in Karnataka, and more usually in Agra and Jaipur. WSPA urges visitors not to photograph the performances or give money.

A WSPA report on the conditions of domestic elephants was completed in 1999. Most domestic elephants are caught from the wild and the breaking-in process is extremely cruel. Elephants sometimes get their own back. In 1998 a court in Kerala ordered an elephant to appear before it after its keeper was accused of mistreating the animal.

Facts for the Visitor

HIGHLIGHTS

India can offer almost anything you want, whether it's beaches, forts, amazing travel experiences, fantastic spectacles or even a search for yourself. Listed here are just a few of those possibilities and where to start looking.

Beaches

People generally don't come all the way to India just to laze on a beach – but there are some superb beaches if you're in that mood. On the west coast, at the southern end of Kerala, there's Kovalam and Varkala; farther north, Goa has a whole collection of beautiful beaches complete with soft white sand, gentle lapping waves and swaying palms. If you find these a little overcommercialised then head for the tiny ex-Portuguese island of Diu off the southern coast of Saurashtra (Gujarat), or to southern Karnataka, where the ex-Goa crowd are now throwing down their bedrolls.

Over on the east coast you could try the beach at Mamallapuram in Tamil Nadu. In Orissa the beach at Gopalpur-on-Sea is clean and quiet. While they're not easily accessible, some of the beaches in the Andamans are straight out of a holiday brochure – white coral sand, gin-clear water and multi-coloured fish and coral. The beaches of Lakshadweep, a series of coral atolls off the west coast, are pristine, but alas only accessible to those with money to spare.

Time Out

Craving for some time out from the noise, the heat and the hassle? Well, you're in luck. India has numerous places where you can recharge, surrounded by like-minded souls. Goa's beaches are perennially popular for this purpose, but Hampi nearby is becoming increasingly popular for those who find Goa's beach life a little hectic. The holy lake of Pushkar in Rajasthan has a semi-permanent traveller population drawn by the spe-

cial atmosphere of this holy town. The technicolour Tibetan outlook on life (they've got a way with hotels and restaurants too) works well in Kathmandu, so why not in India – you'll find Dharamsala and Manali, both in Himachal Pradesh, also have longer term visitors. Finally, Puri (Orissa) and Mamallapuram (Tamil Nadu) both have temples and beaches, a sure-fire attraction.

Festivals & Special Events

India is a country of festivals and colourful events, and there are a number of places and times that are not to be missed (see Public Holidays & Special Events later in this chapter). They start with the Republic Day Festival in Delhi each January – elephants, a procession and military might with Indian princely splendour are the order of the day. Also early in the year is the Desert Festival in Jaisalmer, Rajasthan. In June/July the great Car Festival (Rath Yatra) in Puri is another superb spectacle as the gigantic temple car of Jagannath makes its annual journey, pulled by thousands of eager devotees. In Kerala, one of the big events of the year is the Nehru Cup Snake Boat Races on the backwaters at Alappuzha (Alleppey), which take place on the second Saturday of August (and again in December at Kochi for tourists). September/October is the time to head for the hills to see the delightful Festival of the Gods in Kullu. This is part of the Dussehra Festival, which is at its most spectacular in Mysore. November is the time for the huge and colourful Camel Festival at Pushkar in Rajasthan. Finally, at Christmas where else is there to be in India than Goa?

Deserted Cities

There are a number of places in crowded India where great cities of the past have been deserted. Fatehpur Sikri, near Agra, is the most famous. Akbar founded, built and left this impressive centre in less than 20 years. Hampi, the centre of the Vijayanagar empire, is equally impressive. Not too far from there are the ancient centres of Aihole and Badami. Some of the great forts that follow are also deserted cities.

Great Forts

India has more than its share of forts to tell of its tumultuous history. The Red Fort in Delhi is one of the most impressive, but Agra Fort is an equally massive reminder of Mughal power at its height. A short distance south is the huge, impregnable-looking Gwalior Fort. The Rajputs could build forts like nobody else and they've got them in all shapes and sizes and with every imaginable tale to tell. Chittorgarh is tragic, Bundi and Kota forts are whimsical, Jodhpur Fort is huge, Amber Fort simply beautiful and Jaisalmer the essence of romance. Way out west in Gujarat are the impressive forts of Junagadh and Bhuj built by the princely rulers of Saurashtra.

Further south there's Mandu, another fort impressive in its size and architecture but with a tragic tale to tell. Further south again at Daulatabad it's a tale of power, ambition and not all that much sense with another immense fort which was built and soon deserted. Important forts in the south include Bijapur and Golconda.

Naturally the European invaders had their forts too. You can see Portuguese forts in Goa, Bassein, Daman and Diu, the last being the most impressive. The British also built their share: Fort St George in Chennai (Madras) is open to the public and has a fascinating museum. Those built by the French, Dutch and Danes are, regrettably, largely in ruins, although the ruins also have a certain appeal.

Temples & Tombs

India is rich in reminders of its religious heritage and past rulers. Tamil Nadu has probably more Hindu temples than any other state – including Sri Meenakshi, Lepakshi, Nagore and Nataraja – although no part of the country is without some focus for worshippers. Other notable temples are Elephanta near Mumbai, Amritsar's Sikh

Golden Temple, the Sun Temple in Orissa and Dilwara in Rajasthan.

The Mughal rulers left a legacy of tombs, beautifully carved and embellished in marble, in the north. Most famous of all is the Taj Mahal (Agra), a mausoleum built by the emperor Shah Jahan for his favourite wife Mumtaz. Just as impressive are Humayun's Tomb and Nizam-Ud-Din's Shrine in Delhi.

Faded Touches of the Raj

Although the British left India more than 50 years ago, there are many places where you'd hardly know it. Much of India's government system, bureaucracy, communications, sports (the Indians are crazy over cricket) and media are British to the core, but you'll also find the British touch in more unusual, enjoyable and amusing ways.

Relax in true British style with afternoon tea at Glenary's tearooms in Darjeeling and later retire for a preprandial cocktail in front of the open fire in the lounge of the Windamere Hotel. There you can await the gong that summons you to dinner.

If you prefer your fading Edwardian splendour served southern-style, you can stay at the twee Home Counties rural atmosphere of the Woodlands Hotel or at the Fernhill Palace Hotel in Udhagamandalam (Ooty) which has has a very Raj feel. The Tollygunge Club in Calcutta is also a great place to stay.

Many of the schools and churches built by the British in the hill stations are a wonderful reminder of days gone by. The schools are still run very much the way they were 50 years ago, right down to the immaculate uniforms and strict rules. Most schools welcome visitors.

Other particularly British institutions include Victoria Terminus train station in Mumbai (Bombay), and the Lutyens-designed secretariat buildings in Delhi. In Uttar Pradesh, the Naini Tal Boat Club is an old British club with a lakeside ballroom which was once the preserve of only true-blue Brits (the famous British hunter, Jim Corbett, having been born in Nainital, was refused membership). The Gymkhana Club in Darjeeling still has its original snooker tables, Raj ghosts and cobwebs. Perhaps more nostalgic than all these is St Paul's Cathedral (Calcutta), which is stuffed with memorials to the Brits who didn't make it home, plus a Burne-Jones stained-glass window.

SUGGESTED ITINERARIES

With such a mind-boggling array of amazing things and places to see, it can be difficult deciding which ones to visit in the time you have available.

The following itineraries assume you have a month to spend in India. They take in the highlights of a region and hopefully will help you make the most of your time. They also assume that you don't want to spend the greater part of your time actually travelling between places – many first-time visitors to India make the mistake of trying to see too much in too short a period of time, and end up tired and frustrated.

Rajasthani Colour

Delhi – Agra – Bharatpur – Jaipur – Shekhawati – Bikaner – Jaisalmer – Jodhpur – Pushkar – Bundi – Chittorgarh – Udaipur – Aurangabad (Ajanta and Ellora caves) – Mumbai

This route gives you a taste of just about everything – Mughal architecture, including, of course, the Taj Mahal; wildlife; the desert; Hindu temples; hippie hang-outs; Rajput exuberance; unusual Islamic architecture; and the superb Buddhist paintings and sculptures of the Ajanta and Ellora caves. Mumbai and Delhi are both cities where you could happily spend a week, although a couple of days in each is usually all there's time for. Travel is by bus and train, except for the Udaipur-Aurangabad leg which can be flown.

Mughals, Jains & the Portuguese

Delhi – Agra – Jaipur – Pushkar – Jodhpur – Ranakpur – Udaipur – Bhuj – Rajkot – Junagadh – Sasan Gir – Diu – Palitana – Ahmedabad – Mumbai

Gujarat offers the chance to get off the usual tourist circuit and is well worth any time spent there. This route takes in not only Ra-jasthan but also the best of what Gujarat has to offer – the tribal cultures of the Rann of Kutch (Kachchh) in the far west of the state; the fortified town of Junagadh with some fine buildings; the magnificent Jain temples atop Girnar Hill; Sasan Gir Wildlife Sanctuary – the last home of the Asian lion; Diu – the old Portuguese enclave with its beaches; Palitana – another town with hilltop Jain temples; and Ahmedabad – the busy city which has, among other things, the Gandhi Ashram. Travel is by bus and train.

Hindu & Mughal Heartlands

Delhi – Jaipur – Agra – Varanasi – Khajuraho – Jhansi – Sanchi – Mandu – Aurangabad – Mumbai

Madhya Pradesh is another state that is largely untouristed but has enough places of interest to make a visit worthwhile. The Hindu temples at Khajuraho are the big attraction, but Sanchi and Mandu between them have fine examples of Buddhist, Hindu and Afghan architecture.

Varanasi, one of the holiest places in the country, Agra, with the incomparable Taj Mahal, and the caves of Ajanta and Ellora are other attractions on this route.

Hill Stations & the Himalaya

Delhi – Dalhousie – Dharamsala – Shimla – Manali – Leh – Delhi

Travel in this part of the country is generally by bus and, because of the terrain, is slow. This is a good route to follow if you're in India during the summer, when the heat on the plains becomes unbearable – in fact the road from Manali to Leh is only open for a couple of months a year when the snow melts.

The hill stations of Shimla and Dalhousie hark back to an era that is rapidly being consigned to history; Dharamsala is a fascinating cultural centre, being the home of the exiled Dalai Lama; Manali in the Kullu Valley is simply one of the most beautiful places in the country, while the two day bus trip from there to Leh, high on the Tibetan plateau, is incredibly rough but equally memorable – it's one of the highest motorable roads in the world. Leh is the capital of Ladakh and centre for another unique Himalayan culture. There are direct flights from Leh back to Delhi.

Trekkers and adventure seekers are well catered for at various places on this route. From Manali there are literally dozens of treks, ranging from a couple of days to a couple of weeks, into places such as the remote Zanskar Valley. Leh, too, is a centre for trekkers. Trekking agencies in Manali and Leh can arrange everything, or you can strike out on your own.

Palaces, Temples & Holy Cities

Delhi – Jaipur – Agra – Jhansi – Khajuraho – Jabalpur – Kanha – Varanasi – Calcutta

This route gives you a taste of Rajasthan and includes the Taj Mahal. Jhansi is the station for the bus journey to the famous temples of Khajuraho, but it's worth stopping at Orchha, 18km from Jhansi, to see this well-preserved old city of palaces and temples. From Khajuraho, a three hour bus journey brings you to Satna for trains to Jabalpur where a boat trip through the Marble Rocks is the main attraction. Next stop is Kanha National Park where the chances of seeing a tiger are good, and then it's back to Jabalpur to pick up a train to the holy city of Varanasi. There are direct trains from here to Calcutta, one of the most fascinating cities in the country.

Flight-Pass Route

Delhi – Agra – Khajuraho – Varanasi – Bhubaneswar – Calcutta – Andaman & Nicobar Islands – Darjeeling (Bagdogra) – Delhi

For US$500/750 for 15/21 days you can buy a 'Discover India' flight pass on Indian Airlines. Distance becomes no object and you can visit as many places as you like, within the time limit. This suggested itinerary links a number of the more exotic and distant places as well as 'musts' like the Taj. From Delhi fly to Agra, on to Khajuraho the next day and continue to Varanasi two days later. Next stop is the temple city of Bhubaneswar before taking the flight to Calcutta. An early-morning departure brings you to Port Blair, the capital of the Andaman & Nicobar Islands, for a few days at this rarely visited

tropical paradise. With a three week pass you could also nip up to Darjeeling (3½ hours by bus from the airport at Bagdogra), before changing planes in Calcutta, on the way back to Delhi.

Temples & Ancient Monuments

Chennai – Kanchipuram – Mamallapuram (Mahabalipuram) – Pondicherry – Kumbakonam – Thanjavur – Tiruchirappalli – Madurai – Kodaikanal – Udhagamandalam (Ooty) – Mysore – Bangalore – Belur/Halebid/ Sravanabelagola – Hampi – Badami – Bijapur – Mumbai

This route takes in a small slice of modern India, a popular travellers' beach resort, a glimpse of ex-French India, the experimental international community settlement of Auroville, and several days in the mountains bordering Tamil Nadu and Kerala. Transport is by train and bus plus the use of a one day Indian Tourism Development Corporation (ITDC) bus ex-Mysore or ex-Bangalore to the temple towns of Belur, Halebid and Sravanabelagola.

Temples & Beaches

Chennai – Mamallapuram – Pondicherry – Thanjavur – Tiruchirappalli – Madurai – Kanyakumari – Thiruvananthapuram – Kovalam Beach – Kollam – Alappuzha – Kochi – Bangalore and Mysore – Hampi – Bijapur – Mumbai

This route, a variation of the above, gives you a much broader perspective of southern India and takes you through the tropical paradise of Kerala with its beaches, backwaters, Kathakali dance-dramas and historical Indo-European associations. It also includes some of the major temple complexes of Tamil Nadu, the palaces of Mysore, the Vijayanagar ruins of Hampi and the Muslim splendour of Bijapur. Transport is by train, bus and boat. If time is getting short by the time you reach Bangalore, flights are available from there to Mumbai.

PLANNING

When to Go

Most foreign visitors visit India in the cooler winter months from November to March. For the Himalaya, it's too cold in winter;

April to September is the season here, although there are regional variations according to the onset and departure of the monsoon. For more information about when to go where, see Climate in the Facts about India chapter.

The timing of certain festivals and other special occasions may also influence when you want to go. Christmas, for example, is a magical time in Darjeeling with Christmas trees, log fires and strolling carol singers. Senior school students entertain hotel guests with beautiful Nepali versions of Silent Night and Come All Ye Faithful.

Maps

Lonely Planet's *India Travel Atlas* breaks the country down into over 100 pages of maps, and so gives unequalled coverage. It is fully indexed and the book format means it is easy to refer to, especially on buses and trains.

The Lascelles 1:4,000,000 map of *India, Pakistan, Nepal, Bangladesh & Sri Lanka* is probably the most useful general map of India; it was recently updated and expanded. The Bartholomews map is similar, and is widely available in India and overseas.

The Nelles Verlag series gives more detailed coverage, but you need to carry five maps to cover the whole country. They are excellent maps, but aren't widely available in India.

Locally, Nest & Wings produces a reasonable series of maps for Himalaya regions. The Survey of India has maps covering all of India available from its Delhi office. The maps are not all that useful since the government will not allow production of anything at a reasonable scale which shows India's sea or land borders, and many of them date back to the 1970s. It is illegal to take any Survey of India map of larger than 1:250,000 scale out of the country.

The Government of India tourist office has a number of excellent giveaway city maps and also a reasonable all-India map. State tourist offices do not have much in the way of maps, but the Himachal Pradesh office has three excellent trekking maps which cover the routes in that state.

Indian Maps

Getting maps of India 'right' is a real headache. In early 1995 imported atlases and copies of Encyclopaedia Britannica were banned in India because the Indian government didn't like the way they portrayed the country's borders. We have had the same problem with this book. The main problem is Kashmir where Pakistan and India both claim to own the lot. In reality there's a 'line of control' through the middle with Indian troops on one side and Pakistani troops on the other. Showing the actual line of control is not good enough; the whole lot has to be shown as part of India and even then a disclaimer has to be added to the map, presumably in case the government decides their border extends even further.

Lonely Planet used to put 'Government of India Statement – the external boundaries of India neither correct nor authenticated' on any potentially problematic maps with disputed borders, but midway through the life of one edition the government decided that this wasn't good enough. By saying it was a government statement perhaps it could be interpreted that only the government believed it. Lonely Planet had to reprint books for the Indian market with a new disclaimer. The absurdity of these rules is indicated by history books with disclaimers about the borders of India tagged onto maps of India under the rule of Emperor Ashoka two millennia ago. Turn on the BBC satellite TV news and you'll see maps the government can't put statements on; it's said the politicians just have to close their eyes or switch off the TV.

What to Bring

If you are only travelling to a single destination, eg Goa or Kerala, you can pretty much bring what you like. A suitcase is a good option. It's lockable, keeps your clothes flat and is less likely to get damaged by careless luggage handlers at the airport. Heavy luggage presents few problems if all you've got to do is get it into the taxi and to a hotel.

For others, a backpack is still the best carrying container. Many packs these days are lockable, otherwise you can make it a bit more thief-proof by sewing on tabs so you can padlock it shut. It's worth paying the money for a strong, good-quality pack as it's much more likely to withstand the rigours of Indian travel.

An alternative is a large, soft, zip bag with a wide shoulder strap. This is obviously not an option if you plan to do any trekking.

If you are undertaking a longer trip, whatever you carry your gear in, the usual budget travellers' rule applies – bring as little as possible.

If you are spending time in the hill stations, especially during the cool season, you will need a reasonably warm top or jacket for chilly nights.

Cultural considerations dictate the kind of clothing you should bring (see Society & Conduct in the Facts about India chapter). A reasonable list would include:

- underwear and swimming gear.
- one pair of cotton trousers.
- one pair of shorts (men only).
- one long cotton skirt (women).
- a few T-shirts or lightweight shirts.
- sweater for cool nights in the hills.
- one pair of sneakers or shoes.
- socks – useful for visiting temples, especially for traipsing over areas exposed to the sun.
- sandals.
- flip-flops (thongs) – handy to wear when showering.
- lightweight jacket or raincoat.
- a set of 'dress up' clothes.
- a hat – south Indians commonly use umbrellas instead of hats, which can be sweaty and uncomfortable. Umbrellas can be bought cheaply everywhere.

If you are going camping or trekking you will need to take:

- walking boots – these must give good ankle support and have a sole flexible enough to meet the anticipated walking conditions. Ensure your boots are well broken in beforehand.
- warm jacket.

- wool shirt or pullover.
- breeches or shorts – shorts are ideal but should not be worn in places where they may cause offence to locals.
- shirts – T-shirts are OK, but shirts with collars and sleeves will give added protection against the sun.
- socks – a sufficient supply of thick and thin pairs should be taken.
- a sunhat.
- a multi-fuel stove (optional).

Bedding A sleeping bag, although a hassle to carry, can come in handy. You can use it to spread over unsavoury-looking hotel bedding, as a cushion on hard train seats, and as a seat for long waits on railway platforms. If you are planning on camping or spending time in the hills (especially during the cool season) a sleeping bag is essential. A sheet sleeping bag will suffice if you are going to be spending all your time in hot, tropical places.

Toiletries Soap, toothpaste, shampoo and other toiletries are readily available. Conditioner can be hard to find; some brands combine shampoo and conditioner in one. If this doesn't appeal, bring your own supplies. A sink plug is worth having since few cheaper hotels have plugs. A nail brush or even something sturdier can be very useful for scrubbing the dirt and grit off your feet at the end of the day. For women, tampons are available in most major cities; sanitary pads are more widely available. Bring condoms with you, as the quality of locally made condoms may be suspect.

Men can safely leave their shaving gear at home. One of the pleasures of travelling in India is a shave in a barber shop every few days. With HIV/AIDS becoming more widespread in India, however, make sure you choose a barber's shop that looks clean, avoid roadside barbers, and make sure that a fresh blade is used. For just a few rupees you'll get the full treatment – lathering, followed by a shave, more lathering, another shave, and finally the hot, damp towel and sometimes talcum powder, or even a scalp massage.

Miscellaneous Items See the Health section later in this chapter for a medical kit check list. Some handy items to stow away in your pack could include the following:

- a padlock, especially for budget travellers – most cheap hotels and quite a number of mid-range places have doors locked by a flimsy latch and padlock. You'll find having your own sturdy lock on the door does wonders for your peace of mind.
- a knife (preferably Swiss Army) – it has a whole range of uses, such as peeling fruit etc.
- a mini electric element – to boil water in a cup.
- a sarong – can be used as a bed sheet, an item of clothing, an emergency towel and a pillow.
- insect repellent, a box of mosquito coils or an electric mosquito zapper – you can buy them in most places; try any medical store (remember, however, that many parts of India are subject to power cuts). A mosquito net can be very useful – bring tape with you if it doesn't come with a portable frame.
- a torch (flashlight) and/or candles – power cuts (euphemistically known as 'load shedding') are not uncommon and there's little street lighting at night.
- a voltage stabiliser – for those travellers who may be bringing sensitive electronic equipment.
- an inflatable pillow – available in India for Rs 50 to Rs 60.
- moisture-impregnated disposable tissues – for your hands and face.
- a spare set of glasses and your spectacle prescription. If your wear contact lenses, bring enough solution to last your trip.
- earplugs (to shut out the din in some hotels) and a sleeping mask.
- a sun hat and sunglasses – if you hate sweaty hats, buy an umbrella in India (it provides shade plus air circulation).
- a water bottle – it should always be by your side. Use water-purification tablets to avoid adding to India's growing plastic waste problem.
- high-factor sunscreen – though becoming more widely available in India it's *expensive*!
- lip balm – handy if you're planning to spend a lot of time on beaches or in the mountains.
- string – useful as a makeshift clothes line (double-strand nylon is good to secure your clothes if you have no pegs). You can buy small, inexpensive sachets of washing powder everywhere.
- a pair of binoculars – if you plan to be bird-watching and wildlife-spotting.
- a high-pitched whistle – some women carry them as a possible deterrent to would-be assailants.

If you are motorcycling remember that helmets are compulsory; bring a good one from home. Helmets are also compulsory for pillion passengers in Delhi (there is an exemption for Sikhs). You should also bring good wet-weather gear, strong waterproof boots and thermal underwear if you plan to ride the Himalaya (even in summer).

RESPONSIBLE TOURISM

Common sense and courtesy go a long way when you are travelling. Think about the impact you may be having on the environment and the people who inhabit it. One very simple way of minimising your impact is to reduce the amount of plastic you use. Buy terracotta cups at train stations rather than the plastic ones; recycle plastic bags; try and recycle plastic drinking bottles, or purify your water.

If you are planning on taking a camel safari in Rajasthan pay particular care to how you dispose of your rubbish; safaris operating out of Jaisalmer have left an alarming trail of trash through the desert. The same applies when trekking and mountaineering (see the Responsible Trekking boxed text).

Finally, as exotic and tempting as they may be, avoid buying products that further endanger threatened species and habitats. (See also the Responsible Diving boxed text in this section, and the Treatment of Animals boxed text in the Facts about India chapter.)

For information on environmental organisations working in India, see the Conservation Contacts entry in the Facts about India chapter.

Child Prostitution

Since 'Anglo India' Freddy Peat was convicted in 1996 of a number of horrific sex crimes against children in Goa, there has been increasing acceptance in that state that child prostitution is a problem that needs to be tackled. There is now greater vigilance by police and locals and the legal procedure is now in place to deal with paedophiles. Offenders face life imprisonment in an Indian jail if convicted. International watch-

Responsible Diving

The growing popularity of diving, especially in the Andaman Islands and Lakshadweep, makes it all the more important to observe a few simple rules to minimise your impact. Help preserve the ecology and beauty of India's reefs.

- Do not use anchors on reefs, and take care not to ground boats on coral. Encourage dive operators and regulatory bodies to establish permanent moorings at popular dive sites.

- Avoid touching living marine organisms with your body or dragging equipment across reefs. Polyps can be damaged by even the gentlest contact. Never stand on corals, even if they look solid and robust. If you must hold on to the reef, only touch exposed rock or dead coral.

- Be conscious of your fins. Even without contact the surge from heavy fin strokes near reefs can damage delicate organisms. When treading water in shallow reef areas, take care not to kick up clouds of sand. Settling sand can easily smother the delicate organisms of a reef.

- Practise and maintain proper buoyancy control. Major damage can be done by divers descending too fast and colliding with a reef. Make sure you are correctly weighted and that your weight belt is positioned so that you stay horizontal. If you have not dived for a while, have a practice dive in a pool before taking to the reef. Be aware that your buoyancy can change over the period of an extended dive trip: initially you may breathe harder and need more weight; a few days later you may breathe more easily and need less weight.

- Take great care in underwater caves. Spend as little time within them as possible as your air bubbles may be caught within the roof and thereby leave previously submerged organisms high and dry. Taking turns to inspect the interior of a small cave will lessen the chances of damaging contact.

- Resist the temptation to collect or buy coral or shells. Aside from the ecological damage, taking home marine souvenirs depletes the beauty of a site and spoils the enjoyment of others. The same goes for marine archaeological sites (mainly shipwrecks). Respect their integrity; some sites are even protected from looting by law.

- Ensure you take home all your rubbish and any litter you may find as well. Plastics in particular are a serious threat to marine life. Turtles can mistake plastic for jellyfish and eat it.

- Resist the temptation to feed fish. You may disturb their normal eating habits, encourage aggressive behaviour or feed them food that is detrimental to their health.

- Minimise your disturbance of marine animals. In particular, do not ride on the backs of turtles as this causes them great anxiety.

dog organisation End Child Prostitution, Pornography and Trafficking (ECPAT) included Goa in a series of research papers produced for the 1996 World Congress Against the Commercial Sexual Exploitation of Children.

The Indian Penal Code and India's Immoral Traffic Act impose penalties for kidnapping and prostitution. In addition, the international community has responded to what is essentially a global problem with laws that allow their nationals to be prosecuted for child sex offences upon their return home.

If you know, witness or suspect anyone engaged in these activities you should report it to police in the country you're in and again to the police when you get home.

Responsible Trekking

The popularity of trekking and mountaineering is placing great pressure on India's natural environment. Please consider the following tips when trekking and help preserve the ecology and beauty of the Himalaya and other mountain regions.

Rubbish

- Carry out all your rubbish. If you've carried it in you can carry it out. Don't overlook those easily forgotten items, such as aluminium foil, orange peel, cigarette butts and plastic wrappers. Empty packaging weighs very little anyway and should be stored in a dedicated rubbish bag. Make an effort to carry out rubbish left by others.

- Never bury your rubbish: digging disturbs soil and ground cover and encourages erosion. Buried rubbish will more than likely be dug up by animals, which may be injured or poisoned by it. It may also take years to decompose, especially at high altitudes.

- Minimise the waste you must carry out by taking minimal packaging and taking no more food than you will need. If you can't buy in bulk, unpack small-portion packages and combine their contents in one container before your trip. Take reusable containers or stuff sacks.

- Don't rely on bought water in plastic bottles. Disposal of these bottles is creating a major problem in India as in many developing countries. Use iodine drops or purification tablets instead.

- Sanitary napkins, tampons and condoms should also be carried out despite the inconvenience. They burn and decompose poorly.

Human Waste Disposal

- Contamination of water sources by human faeces can lead to the transmission of hepatitis, typhoid and intestinal parasites such as giardia, amoebas and roundworms. It can cause severe health risks not only to members of your party, but also to local residents and wildlife.

- Where there is a toilet, please use it.

- Where there is none, bury your waste. Dig a small hole 15cm deep and at least 100m from any watercourse. Consider carrying a lightweight trowel for this purpose. Cover the waste with soil and a rock. Use toilet paper sparingly and bury it with the waste. In snow, dig down to the soil; otherwise your waste will be exposed when the snow melts.

- If the area is inhabited, ask locals if they have any concerns about your chosen toilet site.

- Ensure that these guidelines are applied to a portable toilet tent if one is being used by a large trekking party. Encourage all party members, including porters, to use the site.

Washing

- Don't use detergents or toothpaste in or near watercourses, even if they are biodegradable.

- For personal washing, use biodegradable soap and a water container (or even a lightweight, portable basin) at least 50m away from the watercourse. Disperse the waste water widely to allow the soil to filter it fully before it finally makes it back to the watercourse.

- Wash cooking utensils 50m from watercourses using a scourer, sand or snow instead of detergent.

Responsible Trekking

Erosion

- Hillsides and mountain slopes, especially at high altitudes, are prone to erosion. It is important to stick to existing tracks and avoid short cuts that bypass a switchback. If you blaze a new trail straight down a slope, it will turn into a watercourse with the next heavy rainfall and eventually cause soil loss and deep scarring.

- If a well-used track passes through a mud patch, walk through the mud: walking around the edge will increase the size of the patch.

- Avoid removing the plant life that keeps topsoils in place.

Fires & Low-Impact Cooking

- Don't depend on open fires for cooking. Cutting wood in popular trekking areas can cause rapid deforestation. It's especially acute in the Himalaya. Use a lightweight kerosene, alcohol or Shellite (white gas) stove and avoid those powered by disposable butane gas canisters.

- If you're trekking with a hired guide and porters, supply stoves for the whole team. In alpine areas, ensure all members have enough clothing so fires are not necessary for warmth.

- If you use local accommodation, select places that don't use wood fires to heat water or cook.

- Fires may be acceptable below the tree line in areas that get very few visitors. If you light a fire, use an existing fireplace rather than creating a new one. Don't surround fires with rocks as this creates a visual scar. Use only dead, fallen wood. Remember the adage 'the bigger the fool, the bigger the fire' – use minimal wood, just what you need for cooking. In huts leave wood for the next person.

- Ensure that you fully extinguish a fire after use. Spread the embers and douse them with water. A fire is only truly safe to leave when you can comfortably place your hand in it.

Wildlife Conservation

- Do not engage in or encourage hunting. It's illegal in India's parks and sanctuaries, but even so you should refrain from killing, legal or not, any wild creatures.

- Don't assume animals in huts to be nonindigenous vermin and attempt to exterminate them. In wild places they are likely to be protected native animals.

- Discourage the presence of wildlife by not leaving food scraps behind you. Place gear out of reach and tie packs to rafters or trees.

- Don't feed wildlife; this can lead to animals becoming dependent on hand-outs and increases their risk of disease.

Trespassing

- Seek permission from landowners if you intend walking and/or camping on private property.

Park Regulations

- Take note of and observe any rules and regulations particular to the area you are visiting.

Trekking in Populated Areas

- Follow social and cultural considerations when interacting with the local community.

TOURIST OFFICES
Local Tourist Offices

In addition to the national (Government of India) tourist office, each state also maintains its own tourist office, and this can lead to some confusion. The state tourist offices vary widely in their efficiency and usefulness. Some are very good, some are hopeless.

In many states the tourism ministry also runs a chain of Tourist Bungalows which generally offer good accommodation at very reasonable prices. You can usually find the state tourist office in these bungalows.

The overlap between national and state tourist offices often causes wasteful duplication. Both might produce a brochure on place A, while neither has anything on place B.

To add to the confusion, in addition to the Government of India tourist office, in many places you will also find an office of the Indian Tourism Development Corporation (ITDC). The latter is more an actual 'doing' organisation than a 'telling' one. For example, the ITDC will actually operate the tour bus for which the tourist office sells tickets.

The ITDC also runs a series of hotels and travellers' lodges around the country under the Ashok name. States may also have a tourist transport operation equivalent to the national ITDC, so in some cities you might find that there's a national and a state tourist operator as well as a national and a state tourist office. Of course, this still doesn't guarantee that you'll be able to find the information you're after.

The Department of Tourism has a Web site (www.tourindia.com.tourism@x400 .nicgw.nic.in). For details see the Delhi and regional chapters.

Tourist Offices Abroad

The Government of India Department of Tourism maintains a string of tourist offices in other countries where you can get worthwhile brochures, leaflets and information. But not all foreign offices are as useful for obtaining information as those within India. There are also smaller 'promotion offices' in Osaka (Japan) and Dallas, Miami, San Francisco and Washington DC (USA).

Australia
(☎ 02-9264 4855, fax 9264 4860, email info@india.com.au) Level 2, Picadilly, 210 Pitt St, Sydney NSW 2000
Canada
(☎ 416-962 3787, fax 962 6279) 60 Bloor St West, Suite No 1003, Toronto, Ontario M4W 3B8
France
(☎ 01 45 23 30 45, fax 01 45 23 33 45, email info.fr@india-tourism.com) 8 Blvd de la Madeleine, 75008 Paris
Germany
(☎ 069-242 9490, fax 242 94977, email info@india-tourism.com) Baseler Strasse 48 60329, Frankfurt-am-Main
Italy
(☎ 02-805 3506, fax 7202 1681, email info.it@india-tourism.com) Via Albricci 9, 20122 Milan
Malaysia
(☎ 03-242 5285, fax 242 5301) Wisma HLA, Lot 203 Jalan Raja Chulan, 50200 Kuala Lumpur
Netherlands
(☎ 020-620 8991, fax 638 3059, email info.nl@india-tourism.com) Rokin 9-15, 1012 KK Amsterdam
Singapore
(☎ 0065-235 3800, fax 235 8677) United House, 20 Kramat Lane, Singapore 0922
Sweden
(☎ 08-215081, fax 210186, email info.se@India-Tourism.com) Sveavagen 9-11, S-III 57, Stockholm 11157
Thailand
(☎ 02-235 2585, fax 236 8411) KFC Bldg, 3rd floor, 62/5 Thaniya Rd, Bangkok 10500
UK
(☎ 020-7437 3677, fax 494 1048, 24 hour brochure line ☎ 01233-211999) 7 Cork St, London W1X 2LN
USA
(☎ 212-586 4901, fax 582 3274, Web site www.tourindia.com) 1270 Avenue of the Americas, Suite 1808, New York, NY 10020
(☎ 213-380 8855, fax 380 6111) 3550 Wilshire Blvd, Suite 204, Los Angeles, CA 90010

VISAS & DOCUMENTS
Passport

You must have a passport with you all of the time; it is the most basic travel document. Ensure that it will be valid for the entire period you intend to remain overseas. If your passport is lost or stolen, immediately contact your country's representative (see Embassies & Consulates later in this chapter).

Visas for India

Six month multiple-entry visas (valid from the date of issue) are now issued to most nationals regardless of whether you intend staying that long or re-entering the country. Visas cost A$55 for Australians, UK£19 for Britons, and FF200 for French passport holders. US passport holders may also apply for one year and 10 year multiple-entry visas, the latter, at the time of writing, only available from Indian embassies in the USA, Japan and Hong Kong. For US citizens, a six month multiple-entry visa costs US$50, a 12 month multiple-entry visa costs US$70, a 10 year multiple-entry visa costs US$120 and a transit visa costs US$25. Passport and visa forms for US citizens are available online from the San Francisco consulate's Web site at www.indianconsulate-sf.org).

If you prefer to get your visa en route to India you can pick it up in the following countries:

Nepal The Indian embassy in Kathmandu is open Monday to Friday from 9 am to 1 pm and 1.30 to 5.30 pm; visa applications are accepted Monday to Friday from 9.30 am to 12.30 pm and visas are available for collection between 4.45 and 5.30 pm – allow at least seven days for processing.

Pakistan The high commission in Islamabad is quite efficient, although if there is an Indian embassy in your home country they may have to fax there to check that you are not a thief, wanted by the police or in some other way undesirable. The process takes a few days, and of course you have to pay for the fax.

Sri Lanka The Indian High Commission in Colombo or the Assistant High Commission in Kandy, both in Sri Lanka, will also make you pay for a fax as well as the visa.

Thailand It usually takes four working days for non-Thai nationals to obtain an Indian visa.

Visa Extensions Fifteen-day extensions are available from Foreigners' Registration offices in the main Indian cities. You can only get another six months by leaving the country. Some travellers have reported difficulty getting another visa in Nepal.

Visas for Neighbouring Countries

Bhutan The Bhutan visa process is seemingly complicated, but actually straightforward once you understand the process. Visas are issued only when you arrive in the country, either at Paro airport or (if by road) at Phuentsholing. You must make an application in advance through a tour operator and receive approval before you travel to Bhutan. There is no point in applying for a Bhutan visa in India or anywhere else abroad unless you are on some sort of government or official project. All applications for tourist visas (a maximum of 15 days) and extensions (not exceeding six months) must be channelled through the tourism authority in Thimphu and no tour operator is allowed to entertain any visitor whose visa has been processed through other channels. For information on reputable tour operators and other aspects of travel relating to Bhutan, see Lonely Planet's *Bhutan*.

Myanmar (Burma) The embassy in Delhi is fast and efficient and issues four-week visas.

Nepal The Nepali embassy in Delhi is quite close to Connaught Place, not out at Chanakyapuri like most other embassies. You need one photo and passports are picked up the next day (except Friday, in which case they can be picked that afternoon between 2.30 pm and 3 pm). It is open Monday to Thursday from 9 am to noon and Friday from 10 to 11 am. Single entry, 15/30-day visas cost US$15/25, double-entry 30-day visas cost $40, and multiple-entry 60-day visas cost $60.

The consulate in Calcutta is open from 10 am to 1 pm and 2 to 4 pm. Visas are issued while you wait.

Sri Lanka Most western nationalities do not need a visa to visit Sri Lanka, but there is a high commission in New Delhi.

Thailand Most nationalities get a 30-day visa on arrival in Thailand. This visa-on-arrival can't be extended. A two-month visa from a Thai embassy costs US$12 and can be extended for one further month while in Thailand.

Restricted Area Permits

Even with a visa you are not allowed everywhere in India. Certain places require special additional permits. These are covered in more detail in the appropriate regional chapters.

Andaman Islands Foreigners need a permit to visit the Andaman Islands. The Nicobar Islands are off limits to all except Indian nationals engaged in research, government business or trade. The 30 day (maximum) permit allows foreigners to stay in South Andaman, Middle Andaman, Little Andaman (tribal reserves on these islands are out of bounds), Bharatang, North Passage, Neil, Havelock and Long islands. On North Andaman foreigners may stay only in Diglipur.

Day trips are permitted to Ross, Viper, Cinque, Narcondum, Interview, Brother and Sister islands, but currently there are only regular boats to Ross and Viper Islands. Boats may stop at Barren Island, but disembarkation is not allowed and, as yet, there are no regular services. All the islands of the Mahatma Gandhi National Marine Park are open except Boat, Hobday, Twin, Tarmugli, Malay and Pluto.

For air travellers, permits are issued on arrival in Port Blair. If you arrive with an unconfirmed return flight, you'll be given a permit of only 10 to 15 days, but this can be extended to allow a 30 day stay.

Travellers arriving by ship should obtain a permit before being issued with a ticket.

The permit is available from the Foreigners' Registration Office in either Chennai or Calcutta (allow five hours – more if the application is submitted late in the day), or from any Indian embassy overseas. On arrival, ship passengers must immediately report to the deputy superintendent of police in Port Blair (in Aberdeen Bazaar). If you fail to do this you could encounter problems when departing since it will be difficult to prove that you have not stayed longer than 30 days. Your permit will be stamped again when you depart.

Lakshadweep For bookings and permits for Lakshadweep contact the Society for the Promotion of Recreational Tourism & Sports in Lakshadweep (SPORTS) part of the main Lakshadweep Tourism organisation. Its office (☎ 0484-668387, fax 668155) is on IG Rd, Willingdon Island, Kochi, Kerala 682003. There are usually no problems in obtaining permits. The Lakshadweep tourist office in Delhi is useless for Bangaram bookings, but may be able to provide other information. Contact Mr Pukoya (☎ 011-338 6807, fax 378 2246), Liaison Office, UTF Lakshadweep, F306, Kusum Road Hostel, Kasturba Gandhi Marg, New Delhi, 110001.

North-Eastern Region No permits are needed for Assam, Meghalaya or Tripura. Permits for the other states must be approved by the Ministry of Home Affairs in Delhi, which can take forever if you don't have a travel agent, the state office or someone with good connections on your side. It usually takes three weeks to a month for a permit to be issued, though it can take longer.

Permits to Mizoram are granted to groups of four or more people fairly readily; the best places to apply are through the state representatives in Delhi and Calcutta.

To travel in Arunachal Pradesh you must be in a group of four and pay a minimum of US$50 a day just to be in the state. The government would prefer you spent US$150 a day on a package tour. Contact the state offices in Delhi or Calcutta, or approved travel agents (see the North-Eastern Region chapter).

Manipur and Nagaland are the most difficult states to acquire permits for. Currently foreigners are only allowed to enter Manipur by air on a tour arranged by the state tourism authority or a travel agent (again in a group of at least four). Nagaland can be entered by land but again you need to arrange travel for a group of at least four through a travel agent. The state representatives and emporia in Delhi and Calcutta are the best places to organise a permit.

Permits allow for a maximum 10 day stay in each state. In practice; you may only get five days in Manipur and Nagaland, but if you're willing to pay US$150 a day in Arunachal Pradesh your stay can be extended.

Sikkim A 15 day permit is issued either while you wait or within two or three hours (depending on where you apply for it) – see the Sikkim chapter for details.

Onward Tickets

Many Indian embassies and consulates will not issue a visa to enter India unless you hold an onward ticket, which is taken as sufficient evidence that you intend to leave the country.

Travel Insurance

A travel insurance policy to cover theft, loss and medical problems is a good idea. Some policies offer lower and higher medical expense options; the higher ones are chiefly for countries such as the USA, which have high medical costs. There is a wide variety of policies available, so check the small print.

Some policies specifically exclude 'dangerous activities', which can include scuba diving, motorcycling, or even trekking. A locally acquired motorcycle licence is not valid under some policies.

You may prefer a policy which pays doctors or hospitals directly rather than you having to pay on the spot and claim later. If you have to claim later make sure you keep all documentation. Some policies ask you to call back (reverse charges) to a centre in

your home country where an immediate assessment of your problem is made.

Check that the policy has ambulance and emergency flight home cover.

Driving Licence & Permits

If you are planning to drive in India, get an International Driving Licence from your national motoring organisation. In some centres, such as Delhi, it's possible to hire motorcycles. An International Driving Licence can also be used for other identification purposes, such as plain old bicycle hire.

Other Documents

A health certificate, while not necessary in India, may well be required for onward travel. Student cards are virtually useless these days – many student concessions have either been eliminated or replaced by 'youth fares' or similar age concessions. Similarly, a Youth Hostel (Hostelling International – HI) card is not generally required for India's many hostels, but you do pay slightly less at official youth hostels if you have one.

It's worth having a batch of passport photos for visa applications and for obtaining permits to remote regions. If you run out, Indian photo studios will do excellent portraits at pleasantly low prices.

Photocopies

All important documents (passport data page and visa page, credit cards, travel insurance policy, air/bus/train tickets, driving licence etc) should be photocopied before you leave home. Leave one copy with someone at home and keep another with you, separate from the originals.

EMBASSIES & CONSULATES
Indian Embassies

India's embassies, consulates and high commissions abroad are listed below (unless stated otherwise entries are for embassies):

Australia
  High Commission
  (☎ 02-6273 3999, fax 6273 3328, email hicanb@ozemail.com.au) 3-5 Moonah Place, Yarralumla, ACT 2600

Consulate General
(☎ 02-9223 9500, fax 9223 9246, email indianc@enternet.com.au) Level 27, 25 Bligh St, Sydney, NSW 2000
Honorary Consulates
(☎ 03-9384 0141) 15 Munro St, Coburg, Melbourne, VIC 3058
(☎ 08-9221 1485, fax 9221 1206, email india@vianet.net.au) 49 Bennett St, Perth, WA 6004

Austria
(☎ 01-505 8666, fax 505 9219, email indemb@eoivien.vienna.at) Kaerntnerring 2, A-1015 Vienna

Bangladesh
High Commission
(☎ 02-503606, fax 863662, email hcindia@bangla.net) 120 Road 2, Dhamondi, Residential Area, Dhaka
Assistant High Commission
(☎ 031-654201, fax 654147, email ahcindia@spnetctg.com) Bungalow 2, B-2, Road No 1, Kulsi, Chittagong

Belgium
(☎ 02-640 9802, fax 648 9638, email eoibru@skynet.be) 217 Chaussee de Vleugat, 1050 Brussels

Bhutan
(☎ 09752-22162, fax 23195) India House Estate, Thimpu

Canada
High Commission
(☎ 613-744 3751, fax 744 0913, email hicomind@ottawa.net) 10 Springfield Rd, Ottawa, Ontario K1M 1C9
Consulate Generals
(☎ 416-960 4831, fax 960 9812, email cgindia@pathcom.com)
Suite No 500, 2 Bloor St West, Toronto, Ontario M4W 3E2
(☎ 604-662 8811, fax 682 2471, email indiaadm@axionet.com) 325 How St, 2F, Vancouver, BC V6C 1Z7

China
(☎ 01-532 1908, fax 532 4684, email indembch@ublic3.bta.net.cn)
1 Ri Tan Dong Lu, Beijing 100 600
Consulate General
(☎ 21-275 8885, fax 275 8881, email cgisha@public.sta.net.cn) 1008 Shanghai International Trade Centre, 2200 Yan An (West) Rd, Shanghai 200335 (Web site www.shanghai-ed.com/india/)

Denmark
(☎ 045-3118 2888, fax 3927 0218, email indemb@euroconnect.dk) Vangehusvej 15, 2100 Copenhagen

France
(☎ 01 40 50 70 70, fax 01 40 50 09 96, email culture@indembparis.zee.net) 15 rue Alfred Dehodencq, 75016 Paris

Germany
(☎ 228-54050, fax 540 5153, email info-indembassy@csm.de) Adenauerallee 262-264, 53113 Bonn 1 & 11
(☎ 30-800178, fax 482 7034, email 106071.2115@compuserve.com) Majakowskiring 55, 13156 Berlin
Consulate General
(☎ 069-153 0050, fax 554 4125, email 100573.1322@compuserve.com) Mittelweg 49, 60318 Frankfurt

Ireland
(☎ 01-497 0483, fax 497 8074, email eoidublin@indigo.ie) 6 Leeson Park, Dublin 6

Israel
(☎ 03-510 1431, fax 510 1434, email indembtel@netvision.net.il) 4 Kaufman St, Sharbat House, Tel Aviv 68012

Italy
(☎ 06-488 4642, fax 481 9539, email ind.emb@flashnet.it) Via XX Settembre 5, 00187 Rome
Consulate General
(☎ 02-805 7691, fax 720 02226, email consolato.india@agora.stm.it) Via Larga 16 (5th & 6th floors), 20122 Milan

Japan
(☎ 03-3262 2391, fax 3234 4866, email indembjp@gol.com) 2-2-11 Kudan Minami, Chiyoda-ku, Tokyo 102

Myanmar (Burma)
(☎ 01-282550, fax 289562, email amb.indembygn@mtpt400.stems.com) 545-547 Merchant St, Yangon (Rangoon)

Nepal
(☎ 071-410900, fax 413132, email indemb@mos.com.np) Lain Chaur, PO Box 92, Kathmandu

The Netherlands
(☎ 070-346 9771, fax 361 7072, email fscom@indemb.nl) Buitenrustweg 2, 2517 KD, The Hague

New Zealand
High Commission
(☎ 04-473 6390, fax 499 0665, email hicomind@globe.co.nz) 180 Molesworth St, Wellington

Pakistan
High Commission
(☎ 051-814371, fax 820742, email hicomind@isb.compol.com) G5 Diplomatic Enclave, Islamabad

Consulate General
(☎ 021-522275, fax 568 0929) India House, 3 Fatima Jinnah Rd, Karachi

South Africa
High Commission
(☎ 012-342 5392, fax 345 1112, email eindia@computel.sk) Suite 208, Infotech Bldg, 1090 Arcadia St, GPO No 40216, Arcadia 0007, Pretoria

Sri Lanka
High Commission
(☎ 01-421605, fax 446403, email hicomind@sri.lanka.net) 36-38 Galle Rd, Colombo 3
Assistant High Commission
(☎ 08-24563, fax 32479) 31 Rajapihilla Mawatha, Kandy

Thailand
(☎ 02-258 0300, fax 258 4627, email indiaemb@mozart.inet.co.th) 46 Soi 23 (Prasarnmitr), Sukhumvit Rd, Bangkok
Consulate
(☎ 053-242491, fax 247879) 113 Bumruangrat Rd, Chiang Mai 50000

UK
High Commission
(☎ 020-7836 8484, fax 836 4331, email mailsoction@hicommind.domon.co.uk) India House, Aldwych, London WC2B 4NA
Consulate General
(☎ 021-212 2782, fax 212 2786, email cgi@congend.demon.co.uk) 20 Augusta St, Jewellery Quarters, Hockley, Birmingham B18 6JL

USA
(☎ 202-939 7000, fax 939 7027, email indembwash@indiagov.org) 2107 Massachusetts Ave NW, Washington, DC 20008
Consulates General
(☎ 212-774 0699, fax 861 3788, email indiacgny@aol.com) 3 East 64th St, Manhattan, New York, NY 10021-7097
(☎ 415-668 0662, fax 668 9764, email indiancon@best.com) 540 Arguello Blvd, San Francisco, CA 94118
(☎ 312-595 0405, inquiries hotline ☎ 595 0417, fax 595 0416, email congendia@aol.com) NBC Tower, 455 North Cityfront Plaza Drive, Suite No 850, Chicago, IL 60611

Embassies & Consulates in India

Most foreign diplomatic missions are in the nation's capital, Delhi, but there are also quite a few consulates in the other major cities of Mumbai, Calcutta and Chennai listed below.

As a tourist, it's important to realise what your embassy – the embassy of the country of which you are a citizen – can and can't do.

Generally speaking, it won't be much help in emergencies if the trouble you're in is remotely your own fault. Remember that you are bound by the laws of the country you are in. Your embassy will not be sympathetic if you end up in jail after committing a crime locally, even if such actions are legal in your own country.

In genuine emergencies you might get assistance, but only if other channels have been exhausted. For example if you need to get home urgently, a free ticket home is exceedingly unlikely – the embassy would expect you to have insurance. If you have all your money and documents stolen, it might assist with getting a new passport, but a loan for onward travel is out of the question.

Embassies used to keep letters for travellers or had a small reading room with home newspapers, but these days the mail holding service has been stopped and newspapers tend to be out of date.

Australia
(☎ 011-688 8223, fax 687 4126) 1/50-G Shantipath, Chanakyapuri, Delhi
(☎ 022-2181071)16th floor, Maker Tower, E Block, Cuffe Parade, Colaba, Mumbai
Austria
(☎ 011-688 9050, fax 688 6929) EP-13 Chandragupta Marg, Chanakyapuri, Delhi
Bangladesh
(☎ 011-683 4668, fax 683 9237) 56 Ring Rd, Lajpat Nagar III, Delhi
(☎ 033-247 5208) 9 Circus Ave, Calcutta
(☎ 0381-224807) Agartala, Tripura
Belgium
(☎ 011-688 9204, fax 688 5821) 50-N Shantipath, Chanakyapuri, Delhi
Bhutan
(☎ 011-688 9807, fax 687 6710) Chandragupta Marg, Chanakyapuri, Delhi
(☎ 033-241301) 48 Tivoli Court, Pramothesh Barua Sarani, Calcutta
Brazil
(☎ 011-301 7301, fax 379 3684) 8 Aurangzeb Rd, Delhi
Canada
(☎ 011-687 6500, fax 687 6579) 7/8 Shantipath, Chanakyapuri, Delhi

(☎ 022-2876028) 4th floor, Maker Chambers VI, J Bajaj Marg, Nariman Point, Mumbai

China
(☎ 011-687 1585, fax 688 5486) 50-D Shantipath, Chanakyapuri, Delhi

Denmark
(☎ 011-301 0900, fax 379 2019) 11 Aurangzeb Rd, Delhi
(☎ 033-248 7476, fax 248 8184) 3 Netaji Subhas Rd, Calcutta

Finland
(☎ 011-611 5258, fax 688 6713) E-3 Nyaya Marg, Chanakyapuri, Delhi

France
(☎ 011-611 8790, fax 687 2305) 2/50-E Shantipath, Chanakyapuri, Delhi
(☎ 033-229 2314, emergency ☎ 245 7300) 26 Park St, Calcutta
(☎ 044-827 0469) 16 Haddows Rd, Chennai
(☎ 022-4950918) 2nd floor, Datta Prasad Bldg, 10 NG Cross Rd, off N Gamadia Marg, Cumballa Hill, Mumbai
(☎ 0413-334058) Compagnie St, Pondicherry, Tamil Nadu

Germany
(☎ 011-687 1831, fax 687 3117) 6/50-G Shantipath, Chanakyapuri, Delhi
(☎ 033-479 1141, fax 479 3028) 1 Hastings Park Rd, Calcutta
(☎ 044-827 1747) 22 C-in-C Rd, Chennai
(☎ 022-2832422) 10th floor, Hoechst House, Vinayak K Shah Rd, Nariman Point, Mumbai

Iran
(☎ 011-332 9600, fax 332 5493) 5 Barakhamba Rd, Delhi

Ireland
(☎ 011-462 6733, fax 469 7053) 13 Jor Bagh Rd, Delhi
(☎ 022-2024607) 2nd floor, Royal Bombay Yacht Club, Shivaji Marg, Colaba, Mumbai

Israel
(☎ 011-301 3238, fax 301 4298) 3 Aurangzeb Rd, Delhi

Italy
(☎ 011-611 4355, fax 687 3889) 50-E Chandragupta Marg, Chanakyapuri, Delhi
(☎ 033-479 2426, fax 479 3872) 3 Raja Santosh Rd, Calcutta

Japan
(☎ 0111-687 6581, fax 688 5587) 4-5/50-G Shantipath, Chanakyapuri, Delhi
(☎ 033-282 2241) 12 Pretoria St, Calcutta
(☎ 044-827 1747) 22 C-in-C Rd, Chennai

Malaysia
(☎ 044-434 3048) 6 Sri Ram Nagar, Alwarpet, Chennai

Maldives
(☎ 033-248 5102) 7C Kiron Shankar Roy Rd, Calcutta

Myanmar (Burma)
(☎ 011-688 9007, fax 687 7942) 3/50-F Nyaya Marg, Chanakyapuri, Delhi

Nepal
(☎ 011-332 9969, fax 332 6857) Barakhamba Rd, Delhi
(☎ 479 1117/1224, fax 479 1410) 1 National Library Ave, Calcutta

The Netherlands
(☎ 011-688 4951, fax 688 4956) 6/50-F Shantipath, Chanakyapuri, Delhi

New Zealand
(☎ 011-688 3170, fax 687 2317) 50-N Nyaya Marg, Chanakyapuri, Delhi

Norway
(☎ 011-687 3532, fax 687 3814) 50-C Shantipath, Chanakyapuri, Delhi

Pakistan
(☎ 011-600603, fax 637 2339) 2/50-G Shantipath, Chanakyapuri, Delhi

Russia
(☎ 033-479 7006, fax 479 8889) Alipore Ave, Calcutta

Singapore
(☎ 044-827 3795/6393) Apex Plaza, 3 Nungambakkam High Rd, Chennai

South Africa
(☎ 011-614 9411, 614 3605) B 18 Vasant Marg, Vasant Vihar, Delhi

Spain
(☎ 011-379 2085, fax 379 3375) 12 Prithviraj Rd, Delhi

Sri Lanka
(☎ 033-248 5102) Nicco House, 2 Hare St, Calcutta
(☎ 044-827 0831, 826 3515) 9D Nawab Habibullah Rd, off Anderson Rd, Chennai
(☎ 022-2045861) Ground floor, Sri Lanka House, 34 Homi Modi St, Fort, Mumbai

Sweden
(☎ 011-687 5760, fax 688 5401) Nyaya Marg, Chanakyapuri, Delhi

Switzerland
(☎ 011-687 8372, fax 687 3093) Nyaya Marg, Chanakyapuri, Delhi

Thailand
(☎ 011-611 8103, fax 687 2029) 56-N Nyaya Marg, Chanakyapuri, Delhi
(☎ 033-440 7836, fax 440 6251) 18B Mandeville Gardens, Calcutta

UAE
(☎ 022-2183021) Jolly Makers Apartment No 1, Bungalow 7, Cuffe Parade, Colaba, Mumbai

UK
(☎ 011-687 2161, fax 687 2882) 50 Shantipath, Chanakyapuri, Delhi
(☎ 033-282 5171/75, 24 hour line ☎ 282 5172) 1 Ho Chi Monh Sarani, Calcutta
(☎ 044-827 3136/3137, fax 826 9004) 24 Anderson Rd, Chennai
(☎ 022-2830517) 2nd floor, Maker Chambers IV, J Bajaj Marg, Nariman Point, Mumbai
USA
(☎ 011-688 9033) Shantipath, Chanakyapuri, Delhi
(☎ 033-282 3611, fax 282 2335) 5/1 Ho Chi Minh Sarani, Calcutta
(☎ 044-827 3040) Gemini Circle, 220 Anna Salai, Chennai
(☎ 022-3633611) Lincoln House, 78 Bhulabhai Desai Rd, Cumballa Hill, Mumbai

CUSTOMS

The usual duty-free regulations apply for India; that is, one bottle of spirits and 200 cigarettes.

You're allowed to bring in all sorts of western technological wonders, but big items, such as video cameras, are likely to be entered on a 'Tourist Baggage Re-Export' form to ensure you take them out with you when you go. This also used to be the case with laptop computers, but some travellers have reported that it is no longer necessary. It's not necessary to declare still cameras, even if you have more than one.

Note that if you are entering India from Nepal you are not entitled to import anything free of duty.

MONEY
Currency

The rupee (Rs) is divided into 100 paise (p). There are coins of five, 10, 20, 25 and 50 paise, and Rs 1, 2 and 5, and Rs 10, 20, 50, 100 and 500 notes. In 1996, the Reserve Bank of India decided to stop printing Rs 1, 2 and 5 notes. There are plans to start printing a Rs 1000 note.

You are not allowed to bring Indian currency into or out of the country. You are allowed to bring in unlimited amounts of foreign currency or travellers cheques, but you are supposed to declare anything over US$1000 on arrival.

One of the most annoying things about India is that no one ever seems to have *any* change, and you'll find on numerous occasions that you'll be left waiting for five minutes while a shopkeeper hawks your Rs 100 note around other shops to secure change.

When changing money for the first time pay extra attention to the bills you are getting. Don't accept any ripped ones (staple holes are OK). Also Rs 10 can look very similar to Rs 50. Take your time and check each note even if the wad appears to have been stapled together.

Exchange Rates

country	unit		rupee
Australia	A$1	=	Rs 28
Canada	C$1	=	Rs 29
euro	€1	=	Rs 45
France	10FF	=	Rs 68
Germany	DM1	=	Rs 23
Japan	¥100	=	Rs 35
Nepal	NepRs 100	=	Rs 64
New Zealand	NZ$1	=	Rs 23
Pakistan	PakRs 100	=	Rs 83
Singapore	S$1	=	Rs 25
UK	UK£1	=	Rs 69
USA	US$1	=	Rs 43

Exchanging Money

Cash It pays to have some US$ or UK£ in cash for times when you can't change travellers cheques or use a credit card.

Travellers Cheques All major brands are accepted in India, with American Express and Thomas Cook being the most widely traded. Pounds sterling and US$ are the safest bet; Yen, DM and A$ can be changed in main cities, but not out of the way places. Not all places take all brands – which means it pays to carry more than one flavour. Charges for changing travellers cheques vary from place to place and bank to bank.

ATMs Mumbai, Calcutta, Bangalore, Chennai and Delhi, plus a few (but growing) number of smaller centres have ATMs. Any card with a PLUS or CIRRUS symbol is accepted at the following ATMs: Citibank, Hong Kong & Shanghai Bank, ANZ Grindlays Bank and Standard Chartered Bank.

Credit Cards Credit cards are accepted in most major tourist centres, but don't expect to be able to use a card in budget hotels and restaurants. MasterCard and Visa are the most widely accepted cards, and it might pay to bring both with you. You won't be able to use a credit card on the Andaman Islands. Cash advances on credit cards can be made at Thomas Cook, Bank of Baroda or the Central Bank of India at the Ashok Hotel in Delhi. (It is possible to get US$ from credit cards, debit cards, travellers cheques or money transfers.) Citibank account holders can access their accounts directly with their Citibank card. Bank of America account holders can do the same with their Verateller card and a cheque book. American Express will give a rupee advance on an American Express card.

International Transfers It's best not to run out of money in India, but if you do, you can have money transferred in no time at all via the Thomas Cook's Moneygram service (charges are relatively high as it's only considered an emergency service), or Western Union (via Sita Travels ☎ 011-331 1122, F-12 Connaught Place, Delhi, or DHL). If you are transferring sums of less than US$1000, Western Union is cheaper than Thomas Cook. Bring your passport when you come to pick up your money.

Black Market The rupee is a fully convertible currency; that is, the rate is set by the market not the government. For this reason there's not much of a black market, although you can get a couple of rupees more for your dollars or pounds cash. In the major tourist centres you will receive constant offers to change money. There's little risk involved although it is officially illegal.

Moneychangers Moneychangers are everywhere and open all hours. Their main advantage is their convenience. Of course a

caveat applies: always check the bank rates first, and check carefully the money you are given. Never accept very worn or dirty notes.

Security

The safest place for your money and your passport is next to your skin, either in a moneybelt around your waist or in a pouch under your shirt or T-shirt. Never, ever carry these things in your luggage. You are also asking for trouble if you walk around with your valuables in a shoulder bag. Bum bags have become quite popular in recent times, but be aware that this is virtually advertising the fact to all and sundry that you have something of value on your person; this could make you a target for a mugging. Never leave your valuable documents and travellers cheques in your hotel room. If the hotel is a reputable one, you should be able to use the hotel safe. It is wise to peel off a few hundred dollars and keep them stashed away separately from your main horde, just in case.

Costs

At rock bottom you can live on about US$7 a day. This means dormitories, travel in public buses and 3rd class trains, and basic local food (eg dhal and rice). The sky's the limit at the other extreme. In Rajasthan you can blow more than US$200 a night in a palace hotel, and of course there are plenty of things to buy and tours to take that will set you back even more. Most people will of course fall somewhere in the middle. If you want to stay in reasonable hotels, eat at regular restaurants occasionally splashing out on a meal at a fancy restaurant, and sometimes travel by auto-rickshaw or taxi, you're looking at an average of between US$15 and US$25 a day.

Tipping & Bargaining

In tourist restaurants or hotels, where service is usually tacked on in any case, the 10% figure usually applies. In smaller places, where tipping is optional, you need only tip a few rupees, not a percentage of the bill. Hotel porters expect Rs 5 to Rs 10;

Baksheesh

Baksheesh can be defined as a 'tip', but it is actually a lot more. Judicious baksheesh will open closed doors, find missing letters and perform other small miracles. It's not necessary for taxis nor for cheaper restaurants, but if you're going to be using a service repeatedly, an initial tip will ensure the standards are kept up.

Many westerners find this aspect of Indian travel the most trying – the constant demands for baksheesh and the expectations that because you're a foreigner you'll tip. However, from an Indian perspective, baksheesh is an integral part of the system. Take some time to observe how Indians (even those who are obviously not excessively wealthy) deal with baksheesh; they always give something, and it's expected and accepted by both sides.

Although most people think of baksheesh in terms of tipping, it also refers to giving alms to beggars. Wherever you turn in India you'll be confronted by beggars – many of them (often handicapped or hideously disfigured) genuinely in dire need, others, such as kids hassling for a rupee or a pen, obviously not.

All sorts of stories about where travellers' handouts end up do the rounds, many of them with little basis in fact. Stories such as rupee millionaire beggars, people (usually kids) being deliberately mutilated so they can beg, and a beggars' Mafia are common.

It's a matter of personal choice how you approach the issue of beggars and baksheesh. Some people feel it is best to give nothing to any beggar as it 'only encourages them', instead choosing to contribute by helping out at Mother Teresa's or a similar charitable institute; others give away loose change when they have it. Some insulate themselves entirely and give nothing in any way. It's up to you.

Whether or not you decide to give to beggars on the street, the 'one pen, one pen' brigade should be firmly discouraged.

other possible tipping levels are Rs 2 for bike-watching, Rs 10 or Rs 15 for train conductors or station porters performing miracles for you, and Rs 5 to Rs 15 for extra services from hotel staff.

While there are fixed price stores in major cities, in bazaars and at markets specifically geared to tourists, you are generally expected to bargain. The trick with bargaining is that you should have some idea of what you should be paying for any given article. You can find out by checking prices at fixed-price stores, asking other travellers what they have paid, and shopping around before settling on a particular vendor. Savvy shoppers have a good eye for quality and are able to make informed judgements. If all else fails, a general rule of thumb is to offer half the original asking price. You will generally end up paying around three-quarters of the original asking price. Bargaining is not a battle to the death; losing your temper and yelling will get you nowhere.

Taxes

Accommodation at star hotels in India, and food and beverages at the more upmarket restaurants usually come with a tax of some sort, sometimes more than one. It may be as little as 5%, but can be a lot more. It is always worthwhile asking before you check in whether you will be taxed, and by how much, just to save yourself from an unpleasant shock when you get the bill. The prices quoted in this book are *without* tax. For more information on which taxes apply in which states, see the regional chapters.

If you stay in India for more than 120 days you need a tax clearance certificate to leave the country. This supposedly proves that your time in India was financed with your own money, not by working in India or by selling things or playing the black market.

Basically all you have to do is find the foreign section of the Income Tax Department in Delhi, Calcutta, Chennai or Mumbai and turn up with your passport, visa extension form, any other similar paperwork and a handful of bank exchange receipts (to show you really have been changing foreign currency into rupees officially). You fill in a form and wait anything from 10 minutes to a couple of hours. You're then given your tax clearance certificate and away you go. We've never yet heard from anyone who has actually been asked for this document on departure.

Encashment Certificates

All money is supposed to be changed at official banks or moneychangers, and you are supposed to be given an encashment certificate for each transaction. In practice, some people surreptitiously bring rupees into the country with them – they can be bought at a discount price in places such as Singapore or Bangkok. Indian rupees can be brought in fairly openly from Nepal and again you can get a slightly better rate there.

Banks will usually give you an encashment certificate, but occasionally they don't bother. It is worth getting them, especially if you want to re-exchange excess rupees for hard currency when you depart India.

The other reason for saving encashment certificates is that if you stay in India longer than four months, you have to get a tas clearance certificate (see the previous entry). Some shipping agents may request these certificates.

POST & COMMUNICATIONS
Post

Indian postal and poste restante services are generally excellent. Expected letters are almost always there and letters you send almost invariably reach their destination, although they may take up to three weeks. American Express, in major city locations, offers an alternative to the poste restante system.

Postal Rates It costs Rs 6 to airmail a postcard and Rs 6.50 to send an aerogram anywhere in the world from India. A standard airmail letter (up to 20g) costs Rs 11. Post office-issued envelopes cost Rs 1 within India. The larger post offices have a speed post service. International rates are Rs 200 for the first 200g and Rs 60 for every additional 200g. Internal rates are Rs 20 for places within 500km and Rs 30 for places beyond 500km. You can buy stamps at larger hotels, saving a lot of queuing in crowded post offices.

Posting Parcels Most people discover how to do this the hard way, in which case it will take half a day. Go about it as described below and it should take up to an hour:

- Take the parcel to a tailor, or to a parcel-stitching-wallah (occasionally found just outside post offices) and ask for your parcel to be stitched up in cheap linen. Negotiate the price first.
- At the post office, ask for the necessary customs declaration forms. Fill them in and glue one to the parcel. The other will be stitched onto it. To avoid excise duty at the delivery end it's best to specify that the contents are a 'gift'.
- Be careful how much you declare the contents to be worth. If you specify over Rs 1000, your parcel will not be accepted without a bank clearance certificate, which is a hassle to get. State the value as less than Rs 1000.
- Have the parcel weighed and franked at the parcel counter.

Books or printed matter, can go by bookpost, which is considerably cheaper than parcel post, but the package must be wrapped a certain way: make sure that the package can either be opened for inspection along the way, or that it is wrapped in brown paper or cardboard and tied with string, with the two ends exposed so that the contents are visible. To protect the books, it might be worthwhile first wrapping them in clear plastic. No customs declaration form is necessary.

The maximum weight for a bookpost parcel is 5kg, which costs about Rs 1000 airmail and Rs 175 seamail. Parcels must be sent by 'open packet' mode, meaning they must be able to be easily opened and inspected. The packaging technique is best left to the professionals either at the post office or through one of the major bookshops. Beware of sending parcels COD; the cost may leap in quantum bounds by the time it reaches its destination. Rates for airmail bookpost range from Rs 45 for 200g to Rs 363 for 2000g.

Be cautious with places which offer to mail things to your home address after you have bought them. Government emporiums are usually OK. In most other places it pays to do the posting yourself.

Receiving Mail Have letters addressed to you with your surname in capitals and underlined, followed by poste restante, GPO, and the city or town in question. Many 'lost' letters are simply misfiled under given (first) names, so always check under both your names. Letters sent via poste restante are held for one month only, after which, if unclaimed, they are returned to the sender.

Having parcels sent to you in India is an extremely hit-and-miss affair. Don't count on anything bigger than a letter getting to you. And don't count on a letter getting to you if there's anything of market value inside it.

Telephone

Even in the smallest places, you'll find private STD/ISD call booths with direct local, interstate and international dialling. Usually found in shops or other businesses, they are easy to spot with large STD/ISD signs advertising the service. A digital meter lets you keep an eye on what the call is costing, and gives you a printout at the end. You then just pay the shop owner – quick, painless and a far cry from the not so distant past when a night spent at a telegraph office waiting for a line was not unusual. Direct international calls from these phones cost around Rs 100 per minute, depending on the country you are calling. To make an international call, you will need to dial the following:

00 (international access code from India) + country code (of the country you are calling) + area code + local number

In some centres, STD/ISD booths may offer a 'call back' service – you ring your folks or friends, give them the phone number of the booth and wait for them to call you back. The booth operator will charge about Rs 2 to Rs 3 per minute for this service, in addition to the cost of the preliminary call. Advise your caller how long you intend to wait at the booth in the event that they have trouble getting back to you. The number your caller dials will be as follows:

(caller's country international access code) + 91 (international country code for India) + area code + local number (booth number)

The central telegraph offices in major towns are usually reasonably efficient. Some are open 24 hours.

Also available is the home country direct service, which gives you access to the international operator in your home country. You can then make reverse charge (collect) or credit card calls, although this is not always easy. If you are calling from a hotel beware of exorbitant connection charges. You may also have trouble convincing the owner of the telephone you are using that they are not going to get charged for the call. The countries and numbers to dial are below.

country	no
Australia	0006117
Canada	000167
Germany	0004917
Italy	0003917
Japan	0008117
The Netherlands	0003117
New Zealand	0006417
Singapore	0006517
Spain	0003417
Taiwan	00088617
Thailand	0006617
UK	0004417
USA	000117

Fax

Fax rates at telegraph offices (usually found at or near the main post office) are Rs 60 per page for neighbouring countries, Rs 100 per page to other Asian destinations, Africa, Europe, Australia and New Zealand, and Rs 125 to the USA and Canada. Main telegraph offices are open 24 hours. Rates within India are Rs 15 per A4 sheet. It's also possible to receive faxes at telegraph offices.

Many of the STD/ISD booths also have a fax machine for public use but they cost between 5 and 30% more than government telegraph offices. If your fax doesn't go through you may still be liable for a fee. Private places will also usually accept incoming faxes for a small fee. However, many hotels turn off their machines and store them in cupboards when they're not sending faxes, making it somewhat difficult for incoming messages.

Email

There are bureaus where you can send and receive email in major cities (eg Chennai, Bangalore, Calcutta, Delhi, Mumbai, Jaipur), as well as a growing number of smaller places (all travellers' haunts, eg Dharamsala, have email facilities). While this is the cheapest way to send text (most charge around Rs 100 an hour), offices may charge more for receiving email than for receiving a fax. Some of the star-rated hotels have business centres with email facilities which, for a fee, are available to residents and nonresidents. Outside of the big cities email rarely exists.

INTERNET RESOURCES

The World Wide Web is a rich resource for travellers. You can research your trip, hunt down bargain air fares, book hotels, check on weather conditions or chat with locals and other travellers about the best places to visit (or avoid).

There's no better place to start your Web explorations than the Lonely Planet Web site (www.lonelyplanet.com). Here you'll find succinct summaries on travelling to most places on earth, postcards from other travellers and the Thorn Tree bulletin board, where you can ask questions before you go or dispense advice when you get back. You can

also find travel news and upgrades to many of our most popular guidebooks, and the sub-WWWay section links you to the most useful travel resources elsewhere on the Web.

BOOKS

India is one of the world's largest publishers of books in English. You'll find a great number of interesting, affordable books on India by Indian publishers, which are generally not available in the west. Recently published British and American books also reach Indian bookshops remarkably fast and with very low mark-ups. If a best seller in Europe or America has major appeal for India they'll often rush out a paperback in India to forestall possible pirates.

Most books are published in different editions by different publishers in different countries. As a result, a book might be a hardcover rarity in one country while it's readily available in paperback in another. Fortunately, bookshops and libraries search by title or author, so your local bookshop or library is best placed to advise you on the availability of the following recommendations.

Lonely Planet

It's pleasing to be able to say that for more information on India and its neighbours, and for travel beyond India, most of the best guides come from Lonely Planet!

Read This First: Asia & India, is essential reading for those tackling India for the first time – even those on a second, third or fourth trip will find it informative and detailed for planning itineraries, advice on budgeting and many more aspects of travel.

Lonely Planet's handy pocket-sized city guides to *Delhi* and *Mumbai* have more information on these major cities. The Himalaya is well covered, with *Indian Himalaya* and *Trekking in the Indian Himalaya*. The latter is by Garry Weare, who has spent years discovering the best trekking routes in the Himalaya, and his guide is full of practical descriptions and excellent maps. There are also Lonely Planet guides to *Kerala*, *Rajasthan*, *Goa* and *South India*. For all your language needs grab a copy of the *Hindi/Urdu phrasebook*.

In Rajasthan by Royina Grewal gives a fascinating insider's view of the people and places encountered in this state. The book is one of many titles in Lonely Planet's travel literature series, Journeys.

In 1998, Lonely Planet published *Chasing Rickshaws*, a tribute to cycle-powered vehicles and their drivers by photographer Richard I'Anson and Tony Wheeler. Tony and Richard chased cyclos, pedicabs and other hybrids through 12 Asian cities. Fellow traveller Michael Palin said that he hoped it was 'the first of many'. In 1999, Lonely Planet delivered the goods with *Sacred India*, another full-colour book with stunning images of India's diverse religious culture written by Lonely Planet staff and authors.

Other Guidebooks

Blue Guide's *Southern India* by George Michell provides very detailed information on the region's architecture, art, archaeology and history. The author has written numerous other books on the history and art of South India.

Window on Goa by Maurice Hall is a labour of love that took nearly 10 years to research and write. The author writes authoritatively about the churches, forts, and villages and much else besides. The book manages to be comprehensive while avoiding being purely academic. *Goa* by JM Richards is fairly easy to find in the bookshops of Panaji and Margao in Goa. It's less comprehensive than Hall's book, but is nonetheless an excellent overview.

From Here to Nirvana by Anne Cushman & Jerry Jones is an excellent guide to India's many and varied ashrams and gurus. It provides useful practical information which will help you figure out which place suits your particular needs and aspirations. It also provides useful tips on how to spot dodgy operators.

Many regional and local guidebooks are published in India. Some are excellent value and describe important sites (eg the Ajanta

and Ellora caves, Sanchi) in much greater detail than is possible in this book. The guides produced by the Archaeological Survey of India are particularly good. Another good guide, this time on the painted *havelis* (merchants' mansions) in Rajasthan is *The Painted Towns of Shekhawati* (Mapin Publishing), by Ilay Cooper, which comes complete with street maps.

If you're planning on trekking in Ladakh you'll find the detailed route descriptions and maps in *Trekking in Ladakh* (Trailblazer, 1999) very useful.

Railway buffs should enjoy *India by Rail* by Royston Ellis.

First published in 1859 *A Handbook for Travellers in India, Pakistan, Nepal, Bangladesh & Sri Lanka* by John Murray, is excellent on detail, especially if you are interested in Indian architecture.

For relatively cheap but excellently produced photo-essays of the subcontinent, try Insight Guides' *Rajasthan* and *India* by APA Productions. The Nelles Guides' *Northern India* and *Southern India* (Nelles Verlag) are similarly general guides with good photographs and text but skimpy hard information. In a similar vein is Odyssey Guides' *Delhi, Agra & Jaipur*.

Travel Writing

Robyn Davidson's *Desert Places* is an account of the author's journey by camel with the nomadic Rabari of Rajasthan. It gives a compelling insight into the plight of the nomads and the solo woman traveller.

Karma Cola by Gita Mehta is accurately subtitled 'the marketing of the mystic east'. It amusingly and cynically describes the unavoidable and hilarious collision between India looking to the west for technology and modern methods, and the west descending upon India in search of wisdom and enlightenment.

Subtitled A Year in Delhi, William Dalrymple's wonderful *City of Djinns* delves into this city's fascinating – and in many respects largely overlooked – history. Dalrymple turns up a few surprises in his wanderings around Delhi, and the book is written in a light style that makes it accessible to even hardened non-history readers. At the time of writing, his latest book is *The Age of Kali* (in some countries entitled At the Court of the Fish-Eyed Goddess). The six chapters contain observations and thoughts gleaned from 10 years of travelling a subcontinent experiencing enormous change and upheaval.

Slowly Down the Ganges by Eric Newby is an entertaining boat-trip tale, bordering, at times, on sheer masochism.

A Season in Heaven: True Tales from the Road to Kathmandu is an enticing and historic narrative from travellers who took the 'hippy trail' to India and Nepal in the 1960s and 1970s.

Bullet up the Grand Trunk Road by Jonathan Gregson is the author's account of his journey through northern India on a classic Enfield motorcycle. If you want to know what it's like, this is a good book to read.

India File by Trevor Fishlock (Rupa, Delhi) is a very readable collection of articles on India by the *Times* correspondent. The chapter on sex in India is often hilarious.

Ved Mehta has written a number of interesting personal views of India. *Walking the Indian Streets* is a slim and highly readable account of the culture shock he went through on returning to India after a long period abroad. *Portrait of India* is by the same author.

Ronald Segal's *The Crisis of India* is written by a South African Indian on the premise that spirituality is not always more important than a full stomach. *The Gunny Sack* by MG Vasanji explores a similar theme, this time from the point of view of a group of Gujarati families who migrated to East Africa in Raj times but retain their connections with India. It's a good read and has been dubbed 'Africa's answer to Midnight's Children' by some literary critics.

Frank Smyth's *Valley of Flowers* although written in 1938 is a worthwhile read for anyone interested in the western Himalaya's flora and fauna.

Dervla Murphy's classic, *On a Shoestring to Coorg*, is still one of the most comprehensive accounts of travelling in this part of South India, although much has changed in the ensuing decades. *Om – An Indian Pilgrimage* by Geoffrey Moorhouse provides a fascinating insight into the lives of a wide range of people in South India, from humble coir makers to royalty to holy men. His classic 1971 study Calcutta is also available as a Penguin paperback.

Chasing the Monsoon by Alexander Frater (Penguin India, 1990) is an Englishman's account of, as the title suggests, a journey north from Kovalam in Kerala all the way to one of the wettest places on earth (Cherrapunji in Meghalaya), all the while following the onset of the monsoon as it moves north across the country.

The Smile of Murugan by Michael Wood is an account of the author's time in Tamil Nadu in the mid-1990s and includes a description of a video bus pilgrimage that reveals why pilgrimage is still important in contemporary Indian society.

In *Where the Streets Lead* Sarayu Ahuja, an architect and town planner, takes the reader on a tour of several of India's major settlements and cities, offering insights into not just the structures, but the lives of the people who inhabit them.

In *Tranquebar* author Georgina Harding travels to this former Danish port on the Tamil Nadu coast with her young son. There is plenty of background that reveals a part of Indian history often overlooked.

Third Class Ticket by Heather Wood is a funny and at times poignant account of a 15,000km journey by a group of poor Bengali villagers across India.

Goddess in the Stones by Norman Lewis is an account of the author's travels through Bihar and the tribal villages of Orissa.

Rebels & Outcasts. A Journey through Christian India by Charlie Pye-Smith takes a look at the state of India's Christians in this predominantly Hindu nation.

Stars of India. Travels in Search of Astrologers & Fortune Tellers by Peter Holt is a *tour de force* of India's sooth-saying sector.

Finally, no survey of personal insights into India can ignore VS Naipaul's two controversial books *An Area of Darkness* and *India – A Wounded Civilisation*. Born in Trinidad but of Indian descent, Naipaul tells in the first book of how India, unseen and unvisited, haunted him and of the impact upon him when he eventually made the pilgrimage to the motherland. In the second book he writes of India's unsuccessful search for a new purpose and meaning for its civilisation. His *A Million Mutinies Now* is also excellent.

Novels
Rudyard Kipling, with books like *Kim* and *Plain Tales from the Hills*, is the Victorian English interpreter of India *par excellence*. In *A Passage to India*, EM Forster perfectly captures that collision of incomprehension between the English and the Indians. It's a very readable book.

Ruth Prawer Jhabwala's *Heat & Dust*, made into a film in the 1980s, wonderfully depicts the backpacker's India.

One of the most highly acclaimed Indian novels in recent times is Salman Rushdie's *Midnight's Children*, which won the Booker Prize. It tells of the children who were born, like modern India itself, at the stroke of midnight on that August night in 1947 and how the life of one particular midnight child is inextricably intertwined with events in India itself. Rushdie's follow-up, *Shame*, was set in modern Pakistan. His sardonic treatment of the post-Independence rulers of India and Pakistan in these novels upset a few over-inflated egos. *The Moor's Last Sigh* centres on a political party called Mumbai Axis.

Vikram Seth's epic novel about post-Independence India, *A Suitable Boy*, is set in the 1950s and centres on a Hindu mother's search for a suitable husband for her daughter. It touches on most aspects of Indian culture and important issues of the day.

Rohinton Mistry's *A Fine Balance* follows the experiences of four characters whose lives become intertwined in Mumbai during the Emergency.

Firdaus Kanga's book *Trying to Grow* is the story of a crippled homosexual Parsi boy growing up in Colaba.

Paul Scott's *The Raj Quartet* and *Staying On* are other important novels set in India. *Far Pavilions*, by MM Kaye, is a romantic novel that became a best seller.

William Sutcliffe's *Are You Experienced?* is a hilarious tale of a first-time backpacker who accompanies his best friend's girlfriend to India in an attempt to seduce her. The story follows him as he gets the girl, suffers Delhi-belly and 'experiences' India.

History
If you want a thorough introduction to Indian history generally then look for the two volume *A History of India*. In volume one Romila Thapar follows Indian history from 1000 BC to the coming of the Mughals in the 16th century. Volume two by Percival Spear follows the rise and fall of the Mughals to independent India. More cumbersome, but offering more detail, is the 900 page paperback *Oxford History of India* by Vincent Smith.

The Wonder That Was India by AL Basham gives detailed descriptions of the Indian civilisations, origins of the caste system and social customs, and detailed information on Hinduism, Buddhism and other religions in India. It is also very informative about art and architecture.

A History of South India From Prehistoric Times to the Fall of Vijayanagar by Nilakanta Sastri is the most comprehensive history of this region. At times heavy going, it nevertheless provides comprehensive and detailed coverage.

The Career and Legend of Vasco da Gama by Sanjay Subrahmanyam is one of the best recent investigations of the person who is credited with 'discovering' the sea route from Europe to India.

Christopher Hibbert's *The Great Mutiny – India* describes the often lurid events of this violent uprising. It is illustrated with contemporary photographs.

British historian Bamber Gascoigne's *The Mughals* is a happy mix of well-informed historical text and glossy pictures. *The Nehrus and the Gandhis* by Tariq Ali is a very readable account of the history of these families and hence of India in this century.

Plain Tales from the Raj edited by Charles Allen is the delightful book derived from the equally delightful radio series of the same name. It consists of a series of interviews with people who took part in British India on both sides of the table.

Robert Sewell's *A Forgotten Empire* is a classic on the Vijayanagar empire.

India – A Celebration of Independence 1947 to 1997, a photographic book, begins with an image of Mahatma Gandhi and ends more than 200 images later with a picture of chaos at Bombay port. Some of the world's leading photographers including Henry Cartier-Bresson, Mary Ellen Mark and Sebastiao Salgado are represented in this evocative photographic study.

Freedom at Midnight by Larry Collins and Dominique Lapierre is an enthralling account of events that led up to Independence in 1947. Former BBC correspondent Mark Tully has written widely on India's history and politics. His works include *Amritsar: Mrs Gandhi's Last Battle*, *From Raj to Rajiv*, a collection of short stories called *No Full Stops in India*, and *The Heart of India*.

Pavan K Varma's *The Great Indian Middle Class* is a powerful and often cutting social history of India's most influential socio-economic group, and its descent into cynicism and materialism.

Sanjoy's Assam, drawn from the diaries and writings of murdered activist Sanjay Ghose, offers keen insights into the problems of those parts of India weakened by corruption and militancy.

Architecture

The Archaeological Survey of India publishes a series of booklets on major sites and works (eg *Chola Temples*) which are inexpensive and widely available in India.

The History of Architecture in India: From the Dawn of Civilisation to the End of the Raj by Christopher Tadgell provides a good overview including important sites in South India and has plenty of illustrations.

Architecture and Art of Southern India by George Michell provides detail on the Vijayanagar empire and its successors, encompassing a period of some 400 years. Michell's *The Hindu Temple* is an excellent introduction to the symbolism and evolution of temple architecture.

Indian Art by Roy Craven is a succinct introduction to Indian art from earliest times to the Mughals. It is well illustrated. Basil Gray's *The Arts of India* is a more extensive survey of art forms with plenty of illustrations.

The Royal Palaces of India, with text by George Michell and photographs by Antonio Martinelli is a comprehensive guide to the forts and palaces of India. In addition to the photographs, there are some excellent archaeological maps.

Resorts of the Raj – Hill Stations of India by Vikram Bhatt (Mapin India) is a beautiful 192 page hardcover book that combines fact with anecdotes. The book is delightfully illustrated with a mixture of colour, black and white and sepia photographs and wonderful historical lithographs.

Ladakh – Crossroads of High Asia by Janet Rizvi analyses the economic and social changes that have occurred since the region opened up in 1974.

Arts & Crafts

Arts and Crafts of India by Ilay Cooper & John Gillow examines India's wealth of handicrafts and their manufacture and significance.

The Arts and Crafts of Tamilnadu by Nanitha Krishna with photography by VK Rajamani is a beautifully crafted volume that is much more than a coffee-table book. There is detailed information on a wide range of crafts including textiles, bronzes, terracotta, woodcraft, stone carving, basketry and painting. The text is supported by highly professional photography. Publication of this book was sponsored by the Indian giant, Ashok Leyland.

Woodcut Prints of Nineteenth Century Calcutta edited by Ashit Paul (Seagull Books Calcutta) is a collection of woodcut prints covering mythology, social scenes, book illustrations and advertising from 1816 to the early 20th century. Four essays focus on this short-lived but vital urban art form.

Religion

A Handbook of Living Religions edited by John R Hinnewls provides a succinct and readable summary of all the religions you will find in India, including Christianity and Judaism.

The English series of Penguin paperbacks are among the best and are generally available in India. In particular, *Hinduism* by KM Sen is brief and to the point. If you want to read the Hindu holy books these are available in translations: *The Upanishads* and *The Bhagavad Gita*. *Hindu Mythology*, edited by Wendy O'Flaherty, is an interesting annotated collection of extracts from the Hindu holy books.

A Classical Dictionary of Hindu Mythology & Religion by John Dowson (Rupa, Delhi, 1987) is an Indian paperback reprint of an old English hardback. As the name suggests, it is in dictionary form and is one of the best sources for unravelling who's who in Hinduism.

Travels Through Sacred India by Roger Housden provides a very readable account of popular and classical traditions and contains a gazetteer of sacred places plus a roundup of ashrams and retreats.

Am I a Hindu? is a Hinduism primer edited by Viswanathan which attempts to explore and explain the fundamental tenets of Hinduism through a discourse of questions and answers.

Why I am not a Hindu by Kancha Ilaiah is an insightful and provocative analysis of the caste system in modern India. Ilaiah is a reader in political science at Osmania University in Hyderabad. He is also a political activist with a long involvement in the movement for civil liberties and the rights of Dalits.

The Riddle of Ganesha by Rankorath Karunakaran is a beautifully illustrated and informative book that explains some of the nuances and complexities of the many sides of this popular elephant-headed god.

Hinduism, an Introduction by Shakunthala Jagannathan is a well-illustrated book that seeks to explain what Hinduism is all about. If you have no prior knowledge of the subject matter, this book is a good starting point.

The Marriage of East and West by Bede Griffiths is an attempt by the author (a monk who has lived in Tamil Nadu for many years) to distil the essence of eastern and western spiritual thought.

Indian Mythology by Veronica Ions is a comprehensive and well-illustrated book that covers the major religions in India.

Women

For an assessment of the position of women in Indian society, it is well worth getting hold of *May You Be the Mother of One Hundred Sons* by Elisabeth Bumiller. The author spent over three years in India in the late 1980s and interviewed Indian women from all walks of life. Her book offers some excellent insights into the plight of women in general and rural women in particular, especially with regard to arranged marriages, dowry deaths, *sati* and female infanticide.

A Princess Remembers (Rupa) by Gayatri Devi and Santha Rama Rau contains the memoirs of the maharani of Jaipur, Gayatri Devi, glamorous wife of the last maharaja, Man Singh. It's easy reading and provides a fascinating insight into the bygone days of India's royalty.

Author Anees Jung was born in Hyderabad and brought up in *purdah*. Her book *Unveiling India* touches on her own experiences and those of other women both rural and urban and explores various issues that affect women all over India today. *Difficult Daughters* by Manju Kapor, which is set at the time of Partition, provides an insight into the conflict between love and duty from the point of view of a young woman from Amritsar. *Caste as Woman* by Vrinda Nabar looks at what feminism really means in India in a variety of contexts.

An Indian Attachment by Sarah Lloyd is an unsentimental account of an Englishwoman's life in small villages in Punjab and Uttar Pradesh.

Tribal People

The Todas of South India – A New Look by Anthony R Walker is a comprehensive study of the Toda people of South India. Illustrated with drawings and some photography, it's an accessible read on one of the most documented Indian tribal groups.

The scholarly *Tribes of India – the Struggle for Survival* by Christoph von Fürer-Haimendorf documents the sometimes shocking treatment of India's tribal peoples.

Blue Mountains Revisited. Cultural Studies on the Nilgiri Hills edited by Paul Hockings is a collection of essays on culture, language and anthropology. It will appeal to the serious scholar with a particular interest in tribal customs and beliefs.

The Tribal World of Verrier Elwin is the remarkable autobiography of an Oxford graduate who became a follower of Gandhi, adopted Indian citizenship and later rose to become an influential force in tribal affairs.

Environment & Wildlife

The Book of Indian Animals by SH Prater was first written in 1948 but remains one of the best overviews of India wildlife and includes colour illustrations. Unfortunately it's hard to get outside of India. The Insight Guide *Indian Wildlife* provides solid background and plenty of colour illustrations. It's widely available.

The National Book Trust of India publishes a series of books on such topics as *Endangered Animals of India* by SM Nair, *Flowering Trees* by MS Randhawa, and *Our Environment* by Laeeq Futehally. Though they're mainly aimed at children the books are informative, illustrated cheap (Rs 35) and easy to find in India. The National Council for Science and Technology and the Bombay Natural History Society have jointly published a series of small books, all with black covers and priced at Rs 125. For a brief, readable overview of such topics as *Indian Elephants*, *Moths of India* and *Extinction is Forever* they are worth picking up.

Cheetal Walk: Living in the Wilderness by ERC Davidar describes the author's life among the elephants of the Nilgiri Hills and looks at how they can be saved from extinction.

This Fissured Land – An Ecological History of India by Madhav Gadgil & Ramachandra Guha provides an excellent overview of ecological issues.

Bird-watchers may find the *Collins Handguide to the Birds of the Indian Subcontinent* useful. It doesn't cover all the birds by any means but it does have the best illustrations and text.

Birds and Trees of Tolly is a wonderful book to have by your side if you are visiting the Tollygunge Club in Calcutta. Written by Kushal Mookherjee in collaboration with Anne and Robert (Bob) Wright (who ran the Tolly for several decades), it is available from the club.

The Delhi-based Centre for Science and Environment publishes highly detailed but readable studies of India's environmental problems. *Slow Murder – The Deadly Story of Vehicular Pollution in India* is recommended.

There are numerous glossy coffee-table books on Indian wildlife. Among the best are: *In Danger: Indian Wildlife & Habitat* by Paola Mandredi; *India's Wild Wonders* by Rajesh Bedi; *Through the Tiger's Eyes: A Chronicle of India's Wildlife* by Stanley Breeden & Belinda Wright; *In Search of Wild India* by Charlie Pye-Smith; and *Wild India: The Wildlife & Scenery of India and Nepal* by Cubitt & Mountfire and the WWF). The book from the BBC series of the same name, *Land of the Tiger*, by one of India's foremost wildlife experts, Valmik Thapar, is beautifully illustrated with plenty of interesting facts, figures and background.

WWF in Delhi has a bookshop that's a great source of anything on wildlife and the environment.

General

Autobiography of an Unknown Indian and *Thy Hand, Great Anarch!: India 1921-1952* are two autobiographical books by one of India's most prominent contemporary writers, Nirad Choudhuri. They are an excellent account of the history and culture of modern India. *An Indian Summer* by James Cameron is an autobiographical account of Independence and South India.

Everybody Loves a Good Drought by Mumbai-based journalist Palagummi Sainath is a collection of reports on the living conditions of the rural poor. This excellent book, researched in the mid-1990s, provides an unsentimental insight into how the poorest of India's people survive and how well-intentioned programs aimed at assisting them can lead to all sorts of absurdities. Many of the stories are from north and central India, but some centre on Tamil Nadu.

For a perceptive examination of India as it is today get hold of a copy of *The Idea of India* by Sunil Khilnani. It consists of a series of articles including 'Who is an Indian' and 'The Garb of Modernity'.

The Vintage Book of Indian Writing 1947-97 is a collection of essays and short stories edited by Salman Rushdie and Elizabeth West. It's one of the many books published in celebration of India's 50 years of independence and contains some excellent writing by such acclaimed authors as Jawaharlal Nehru, Nayantara Sahgal, Anita Desai, Vikram Seth and Arundhati Roy.

India! The Golden Jubilee (Granta 57) is a special edition marking India's 50th Independence anniversary which encompasses articles and extracts from some of the leading writers on India. The subject matter ranges from the 1996 election campaign in Kashmir to the fate of India's wilderness and an analysis of what drives the city of Mumbai.

In *In Light of India*, Paz Octavio, a poet and former Mexican ambassador to India, grapples with the complexity that is India – it's social conventions, its religions, languages and history.

The Garden of Life – An Introduction to the Healing Plants of India by Naveen Patnaik is a magnificently illustrated book on an intriguing subject. If you want to know the healing properties of such plants as basil, asparagus, hemp, coconut, lotus, mango, garlic, liquorice and many more,

this book will help. The text is interspersed with fine drawings and some highly evocative poetry. The author is a founding member of the India Trust for Art and Cultural Heritage.

Blue Mountains Revisited – Cultural Studies on the Nilgiri Hills edited by Paul Hockings is a fascinating collection of essays on culture, language and anthropology. It will appeal to the serious scholar with a particular interest in tribal customs and beliefs.

French anthropologist Chantal Boulanger has written a book about traditional sari styles in India called *The Art of Indian Drape* (Shakti Press International). For details on this book and others written by this author visit the Web site (www.devi.net).

South Indian Customs by PV Jagadisa Ayyar seeks to explain a range of practises from the smearing of cow dung outside the home to the formation of snake images beneath the banyan tree.

The Anger of Aubergines by Bubul Sharma is subtitled Stories of Women and Food. It's an amusing and unique culinary analysis of social relationships, interspersed with mouthwatering recipes.

The Remembered Village by MN Srinivas is an account of the author's field research during the late 1940s and early 1950s in a Karnataka village. Entertaining and revealing. Srinivas, one of India's most distinguished sociologists, has also written *Religion and Society Among the Coorgs of South India* and *Social Change in Modern India*.

Appreciating Carnatic Music (Ganesh & Co) by Chitravina Ravi Kiran is available in India for Rs 125 and is aimed at helping those more familiar with western music forms get to grips with this south Indian art. It's a compact little book with useful information including a question-and-answer section.

How to Speak Hindi Without Really Trying & The Essential Hindi Phrase Book by Haemish Kane builds from single words to short phrases and sentences. The first chapter is devoted to useful words such as 'go' (as in go away).

FILMS

The Indian film industry is the largest in the world in purely volume terms and boasts an enormous following – there are many thousands of cinemas. The vast proportion of what is produced are Bollywood 'masala movies' (see Cinema in the Facts about India chapter, as well as the Masala Movies boxed text in the Mumbai chapter).

A number of foreign films have been made about India over the years. Keep your eyes open for a showing of Louis Malle's two part film *Phantom India*. Running to about seven hours in all, this is a fascinating in-depth look at contemporary India. At times it's very self-indulgent and is now somewhat dated, but as an overall view it can't be beaten – it has been banned in India. The Australian ABC TV has produced two excellent documentary series on India, one titled *Journey into India*, the other *Journey into the Himalayas*. Both of them, but particularly the former, are worth seeing if you get a chance.

Of course the epic *Gandhi* was a major film, spawning a host of new and reprinted books on the Mahatma. *Heat & Dust* has also been made into an excellent film, as has *A Passage to India* and *Far Pavilions*. The film version of Lapierre's *City of Joy* was filmed in Calcutta in 1992 at a purpose-built slum. Directed by Roland Joffe (of *The Killing Fields*) with the principal character played by Patrick Swayze, it attracted a lot of flak from the West Bengal government which felt it was yet another condescending look at India's poor, but the critics, in general, felt otherwise.

CD ROM

The following CD ROMs are all available in India but only at major bookshops. *India: A Multimedia Journey* includes videos, slides, maps and travelling tips. *Karnataka* (very expensive at Rs 2500) includes a luscious coffee-table book about the state. *India Mystique* highlights Indian philosophy, history and religion. *Tarla Dalal's Desi Khana: The Best of Indian Vegetarian Cooking* provides a step-by-step guide to more than 140 recipes from all over India. *The Pleasure of Indian Cooking* (Ascent Interactive Multimedia Service) has 605 Indian recipes. *Indian Wildlife* has more than 650 pictures and slides as well as information on over 30 national parks. *Kerala: The Green Symphony* (Invis Media) has plenty of cultural, geographical and historical information, and lots of graphics. *Indian Cinema – Treasure 1* is the first Hindi cinema CD ROM to be released. It has information on 8000 films and includes 800 still shots, 40 video clips and 100 songs. It covers movies made between 1931 and 1997. It's produced by the National Film Development Corporation (Rs 1500). *India Festiva* (Rs 1595; Magic Software) includes information on India's numerous festivals. Magic Software also puts out *India Mystica*, an encyclopedia on Indian culture; *India Musica*, which explains Hindustani music; *Hindi Guru* and *Gujarati Guru* which explain these particular regional cultures; and *Yoga & Meditation*. Magic software has a Web site (www.magicsw.com). *Indian Classical Dance* (Rs 1450; Rizvie Software Consultancy) gives a rundown on major classical dance forms. *Himalayas – The Mountains Where God Lives* (www.synforest.com) is available in the USA for US$28.

NEWSPAPERS & MAGAZINES

English-language dailies include the *Times of India*, the *Hindustan Times*, the *Statesman*, and the *Indian Express*; many feel the *Express* is the best of the bunch. The *Economic Times* is a serious publication for those interested in business and economic analysis.

Weekly news magazines include *India Today*, *The Week*, *Sunday*, *Rashtriya Sahara*, *Outlook* and the *Illustrated Weekly of India*. They're widely available in bookshops and at train and bus stations.

There's a very wide range of general interest magazines published in English in India. They include: *Frontline*, a fortnightly magazine published by the Hindu newspaper group; *Gentleman,* for male yuppies; *Biznet*, a self-described cyber mag dedicated to Web surfers; and *Better Photography*, which contains good contacts within the Indian photographic scene. The *Indian Review of Books* is published monthly in Chennai.

Time and *Newsweek* are only available in the main cities, and anyway, once you've become used to Indian prices they seem very expensive. You can also find newspapers like the *Herald Tribune* and *Guardian* and magazines like *Der Spiegel* and its English, French and Italian clones in the major cities and at expensive hotels but, again, they're not cheap.

One thing you'll quickly find is that newspapers and magazines become public property on trains and buses. By your side you may have your virgin copy of *Time* magazine on which you have lashed out to help pass the time on a long train journey, and are just waiting for the right moment to start reading it. If a fellow passenger spots it, you'll be expected to hand it over, and it will then circulate until you go and collect it. If this annoys you, keep any reading matter out of sight until you are ready to use it.

TV & RADIO

Satellite TV runs 24 hours and offers up to 30 channels including BBC, CNN, Discovery, Star TV and Asianet. Various local channels broadcast in the vernacular. The national broadcaster is Doordashan; it has the news in English every evening. (Check the local newspapers for broadcast times.)

Radio programs can be heard on All India Radio (AIR) which provides the usual interviews, music and news features. There is also an FM band. Some programs are in English. Details on programs and frequencies are provided in the major English-language dailies.

PHOTOGRAPHY & VIDEO

The following are some handy hints for taking better photos:

- The quality of your photos depends on the quality of light you shoot under. Light is best when the sun is low in the sky – around sunrise and sunset.
- Don't buy cheap equipment, but don't load yourself down with expensive equipment you don't know how to use properly either.

- A good SLR camera is advisable, but be aware that the quality of your lenses is the most important thing. Zoom lenses are heavier than fixed focal length lenses and the quality isn't as good. An alternative to the zoom is a tele-converter which fits over your lens and doubles the focal length.
- Always carry a skylight or UV filter. A polarising filter can create dramatic effects and cut glare, but don't fit it over a UV filter.
- Take a tripod and faster film (at least 400ASA) rather than a flash. Flash creates harsh shadows. A cable release is useful for shooting with a tripod.
- Settle on a brand of film and know how it works *before* you head off.
- Keep your film in a cool dark place if possible, before and after exposure.
- Expose for the main component of a scene and fill the frame with what you are taking.
- Previsualise; it's one of the most important elements in photographic vision. You must 'see' your picture clearly before you take it.

Video in India uses the VHS format, although it is possible to convert to and from PAL and NTSC in the larger cities.

Film & Cartridges

Colour print film processing facilities are readily available in larger cities. Film is relatively cheap and the quality is usually (but not always) good. Kodak 100ASA colour print film costs around Rs 140 for a roll of 36. Always check the use-by date on local film stock. Heat and humidity can play havoc with film, even if the use-by date hasn't been exceeded. Developing costs are around Rs 25, plus Rs 5 per photo for printing. A tip: be wary of street hawkers. Some travellers report that old, useless film is loaded into new-looking canisters. The hapless tourist only discovers the trick when the film is developed back home. The best advice is to avoid street vendors and only buy film from reputable stores – and preferably film that's been refrigerated.

If you're taking slides bring the film with you. Colour slide film is only available in the major cities. Colour slides can be developed only in Delhi, and quality is not guaranteed – take your film home with you.

Kodachrome and other 'includes developing' film will have to be sent overseas.

Video users can readily get VHS, CVHS, Hi8, Betacam, Umatic (high and low) in Delhi, Mumbai, Bangalore, Chandigarh, Calcutta and Chennai.

Restrictions & Photographing People

Be careful what you photograph. India is touchy about places of military importance – this can include train stations, bridges, airports, military installations and sensitive border regions. Some temples prohibit photography in the *mandapa* (forechamber of a temple) and inner sanctum. If in doubt, ask. Some temples, and numerous forts and palaces, levy a fee to bring a still camera or video camera onto the premises. You have to pay up front – generally around Rs 25 for a still camera and Rs 50 for a video camera – and there's no refund if you decide not to take any pictures after all. Some people are more than happy to be photographed, but care should be taken in pointing cameras at women. Again, if in doubt, ask. A zoom is a less intrusive means of taking portraits – even when you've obtained permission to take a portrait, shoving a lens in your subject's face can be disconcerting. A reasonable distance between you and your subject will help to reduce your subject's discomfort, and will result in more natural shots.

Protecting Your Camera & Film

Film manufacturers warn that, once it's been exposed, film should be developed as quickly as possible; in practise the film seems to last, even in India's summer heat, without deterioration for months. Try to keep your film cool, and protect it in water and air-proof containers if you're travelling during the monsoon. Silica gel sachets distributed around your gear will help to absorb moisture.

It's worthwhile investing in a lead-lined bag, as repeated exposure to x-ray (even so-called 'film proof' x-ray) can damage film. *Never* put your film in baggage which will be placed in the cargo holds of aeroplanes.

It will probably be subjected to large doses of x-ray which will spoil or completely ruin it. Recently some airports (none in India yet) have installed super high-powered x-ray machines which will damage film, lead-shielded or otherwise. Some professional photographers *never* take film through any x-ray machine, but prefer to pack it in see-through plastic containers and carry them by hand through customs. But be aware that in some places customs officers may wish to open every single canister before you are allowed through.

Mahatta & Co (☎ 011-332 9769) M-Block Connaught Place, Delhi, is the sole Indian agent for Canon cameras and can safely repair them.

TIME

Indian Standard Time (IST) is 5½ hours ahead of GMT/UTC, 4½ hours behind Australian EST and 10½ hours ahead of American EST.

ELECTRICITY

The electric current is 230-240V AC, 50 cycles. Electricity is widely available in the main towns and cities and tourist destinations. Sockets are the three round-pin variety, similar (but not identical) to European sockets. European round-pin plugs will go into the sockets, but as the pins on Indian plugs are somewhat thicker, the fit is loose and connection is not always guaranteed.

You can buy small immersion elements, perfect for boiling water for tea or coffee, for Rs 50. For about Rs 70 you can buy electric mosquito zappers. These take chemical tablets that melt and give off deadly vapours (deadly for the mosquito, that is). There are many different brands and they are widely available – they come with quaint names such as Good Knight.

WEIGHTS & MEASURES

Although India is officially metricated, imperial weights and measures are still used in some areas of commerce. You will often hear people referring to *lakhs* (one lakh = 100,000) and *crore* (one crore = 10 million) of cars, apples or whatever. A metric conversion chart is included on the inside back cover of this book.

LAUNDRY

All of the top-end hotels, most of the mid-range hotels and some of the budget hotels and guesthouses offer a laundry service, and costs are minimal. Service is usually same-day. Be careful to sort coloured garments from white ones and specify that you want the white garments washed separately. Remember, your clothes will be washed at the dhobi ghats. If you don't think they will stand up to being beaten clean, then hand-wash them yourself. Washing powder can be bought very cheaply in small sachets anywhere in India, and guesthouses will usually be happy to lend you a bucket.

TOILETS

In five-star hotels and guesthouses geared mainly for foreign tourists, sitdown, flush toilets and toilet paper are invariably supplied. Off the beaten track, at train stations (and other public places) and in places that don't specifically cater for foreigners, it's squat toilets only. In such circumstances it's customary to use your left hand and water, not paper. A strategically placed tap (and usually a water container) is available in squat toilets. If you can't get used to the Indian method, bring your own paper (none is supplied, but is widely available to buy). But remember, that stuffing paper (and tampons) down the toilet is simply going to clog even further an already overloaded sewerage system. Sometimes a plastic bin is provided for the disposal of paper and tampons. If not, try to take paper with you to dispose of elsewhere.

HEALTH

Travel health depends on your predeparture preparations, your daily health care while travelling and how you handle any medical problem that does develop. While the potential dangers can seem quite frightening, in reality few travellers experience anything more than upset stomachs.

Predeparture Planning

Immunisations Plan ahead for getting your vaccinations: some of them require more than one injection, while some vaccinations should not be given together. It is recommended you seek medical advice at least six weeks before travel. Be aware that children and pregnant women are often at a greater risk from disease.

Record all vaccinations on an International Health Certificate, available from your doctor or government health department, and carry it with you.

Discuss your requirements with your doctor, but vaccinations you should consider for a trip to India include the following. For more details on the diseases themselves see the individual disease entries later in this section.

Hepatitis A This is the most common travel-acquired illness after diarrhoea. Hepatitis A vaccine (eg Havrix 1440 or VAQTA) provides long-term immunity (possibly more than 10 years) after an initial injection and a booster at six to 12 months.

An injection of gamma globulin (ready-made antibody collected from blood donations) also provides protection against hepatitis A. It is effective immediately, unlike the vaccine, but protection is short-lived – two to six months, depending on the dose given – and because it is a blood product there are concerns about its long-term safety.

A combined hepatitis A and hepatitis B vaccination, Twinrix, is also available. Three injections over a six month period are required.

Typhoid This is an important vaccination to have where hygiene is a problem. Available either as an injection or oral capsules.

Diphtheria & Tetanus Both these diseases occur worldwide and can be fatal. Everyone should have these vaccinations which are usually combined. After an initial course of three injections, boosters are necessary every 10 years.

Meningococcal Meningitis Vaccination is recommended for travellers to certain parts of India and Nepal. A single injection will give good protection for three years. Protection may be less effective in children under two years.

Hepatitis B Travellers who should consider a hepatitis B vaccination include those visiting countries (including India) where there are high levels of hepatitis B infection, where blood transfusions may not be adequately screened or where sexual contact or needle sharing is a possibility. It involves three injections, the quickest course being over three weeks with a booster at 12 months.

Polio Everyone should keep up to date with this vaccination, which is normally given in childhood. A booster every 10 years maintains immunity.

Rabies Vaccination should be considered by those who will spend a month or longer in the country, especially if they are cycling, handling animals, caving, travelling to remote areas, and for children (who may not report a bite). Pretravel rabies vaccination involves having three injections over 21 to 28 days. If someone who has been vaccinated is bitten or scratched by an infected animal they will require two booster injections of vaccine; those not vaccinated require more.

Japanese B Encephalitis Consider the vaccination if you are spending a month or longer in high risk areas in India, making repeated trips to a risk area or visiting while there's an epidemic. It involves three injections over 30 days. The vaccine is expensive and has been associated with serious allergic reactions so the decision to have it should be balanced against the risk of contracting the illness.

Tuberculosis TB risk to travellers is usually very low, unless you will be living with or closely associated with local people in high risk areas. Vaccination with the BCG vaccine is recommended for children and young adults living in these areas for three months or more.

Malaria Malaria occurs in most parts of India; malaria-free areas include Himachal Pradesh, Jammu & Kashmir and Sikkim. Antimalarial drugs do not prevent you from being infected but kill the malaria parasites during a stage in their development and significantly reduce the risk of becoming very ill or dying. Expert advice on medication should be sought, as there are many factors to consider including the area to be visited, the risk of exposure to malaria-carrying mosquitoes, the side effects of medication, your medical history and whether you are a child or adult or pregnant. Travellers to isolated areas in high risk countries may like to carry a treatment dose of medication for use if symptoms occur.

Health Insurance Make sure that you have adequate health insurance. See Visas & Documents earlier in this chapter.

Travel Health Guides If you are planning to be away or travelling in remote areas for a long period of time, you may like to consider taking a more detailed health guide.

Healthy Travel Asia & India, Dr Isabelle Young, Lonely Planet Publications, 2000. Covers it all from how to treat a nose bleed in Delhi to finding a doctor in Mumbai.

CDC's Complete Guide to Healthy Travel, Open Road Publishing, 1997. The US Centers for Disease Control & Prevention recommendations for international travel.

Staying Healthy in Asia, Africa & Latin America, Dirk Schroeder, Moon Publications, 1994. This guide is detailed and well organised.

Travellers' Health, Dr Richard Dawood, Oxford University Press, 1995. Comprehensive, easy to read, authoritative and highly recommended, although it's rather large to lug around.

Where There is No Doctor, David Werner, Macmillan, 1994. A very detailed guide intended for someone, such as a Peace Corps worker, going to work in an underdeveloped country.

Travel with Children, Maureen Wheeler, Lonely Planet Publications, 1995. Includes advice on travel health for younger children.

Medical Kit Check List

Following is a list of items you should consider including in your medical kit – consult your pharmacist for brands available in your country.

☐ **Aspirin** or **paracetamol** (acetaminophen in the US) – for pain or fever.

☐ **Antihistamine** – for allergies, eg hay fever; to ease the itch from insect bites or stings; and to prevent motion sickness.

☐ **Antibiotics** – consider including these if you're travelling well off the beaten track; see your doctor, as they must be prescribed, and carry the prescription with you.

☐ **Loperamide** or **diphenoxylate** – 'blockers' for diarrhoea; **prochlorperazine** or **metaclopramide** for nausea and vomiting.

☐ **Rehydration mixture** – to prevent dehydration, eg due to severe diarrhoea; particularly important when travelling with children.

☐ **Insect repellent, sunscreen, lip balm** and **eye drops**.

☐ **Calamine lotion, sting relief spray** or **aloe vera** – to ease irritation from sunburn and insect bites or stings.

☐ **Antifungal cream** or **powder** – for fungal skin infections and thrush.

☐ **Antiseptic** (such as povidone-iodine) – for cuts and grazes.

☐ **Bandages, Band-Aids (plasters)** and other wound dressings.

☐ **Water purification tablets** or **iodine**.

☐ **Scissors, tweezers** and a **thermometer** (note that mercury thermometers are prohibited by airlines).

☐ **Syringes** and **needles** – in case you need injections in a country with medical hygiene problems. Ask your doctor for a note explaining why you have them.

☐ **Cold** and **flu tablets, throat lozenges** and **nasal decongestant**.

☐ **Multivitamins** – consider for long trips, when dietary vitamin intake may be inadequate.

There are also a number of excellent travel health sites on the Internet. From the Lonely Planet Web site there are links (www.lonelyplanet.com/weblinks/wlprep.htm#heal) to the World Health Organization and the US Centers for Disease Control & Prevention.

Other Preparations Make sure you're healthy before you start travelling. If you are going on a long trip make sure your teeth are OK. If you wear glasses take a spare pair and your prescription.

If you require a particular medication take an adequate supply, as it may not be available locally. Take part of the packaging showing the generic name, rather than the brand, which will make getting replacements easier. It's a good idea to have a legible prescription or letter from your doctor to show that you legally use the medication to avoid any problems.

Basic Rules

Food There is an old colonial adage which says: 'If you can cook it, boil it or peel it you can eat it ... otherwise forget it'. Vegetables and fruit should be washed with purified water or peeled where possible. Beware of ice cream which is sold in the street or anywhere it might have been melted and refrozen; if there's any doubt (eg a power cut in the last day or two) steer well clear. Shellfish such as mussels, oysters and clams should be avoided as should undercooked meat, particularly in the form of mince. Steaming does not make shellfish safe for eating.

If a place looks clean and well run and the vendor also looks clean and healthy, then the food is probably safe. In general, places that are packed with travellers or locals will be fine, while empty restaurants are questionable. The food in busy restaurants is cooked and eaten quite quickly with little standing around and is probably not reheated.

Water The number-one rule is *be careful of the water* and especially ice. If you don't know for certain that the water is safe assume the worst. Reputable brands of bottled

Nutrition

If your food is poor or limited in availability, if you're travelling hard and fast and therefore missing meals, or if you simply lose your appetite, you can soon start to lose weight and place your health at risk.

Make sure your diet is well balanced. Cooked eggs, tofu, beans, lentils (dhal) and nuts are all safe ways to get protein. Fruit you can peel (eg bananas, oranges or mandarins) is usually safe (melons can harbour bacteria in their flesh and are best avoided) and a good source of vitamins. Try to eat plenty of grains (including rice) and bread. Remember that although food is generally safer if it is cooked well, overcooked food loses much of its nutritional value. If your diet isn't well balanced or if your food intake is insufficient, it's a good idea to take vitamin and iron pills.

In hot climates make sure you drink enough – don't rely on feeling thirsty to indicate when you should drink. Not needing to urinate or small amounts of very dark yellow urine is a danger sign of dehydration. Always carry a water bottle with you on long trips. Excessive sweating can lead to loss of salt and therefore muscle cramping. Salt tablets are not a good idea as a preventative, but in places where salt is not used much adding it to food can help.

water or soft drinks are generally fine, although in some places bottles may be refilled with tap water. Only use water from containers with a serrated seal – not tops or corks. Take care with fruit juice, particularly if water may have been added. Milk should be treated with suspicion as it is often unpasteurised, though boiled milk is fine if it is kept hygienically. Tea or coffee should also be OK, since the water should have been boiled.

Water Purification The simplest way of purifying water is to boil it thoroughly. Vigorous boiling should be satisfactory; however, at high altitude water boils at a lower temperature, so germs are less likely to be killed. Boil for longer in these environments.

Consider purchasing a water filter for a long trip. There are two main kinds of filter. Total filters take out all parasites, bacteria and viruses, and make water safe to drink. They are often expensive, but they can be more cost effective than buying bottled water. Simple filters (which can even be a nylon mesh bag) take out dirt and larger foreign bodies from the water so that chemical solutions work much more effectively; if water is dirty, chemical solutions may not

work at all. It's very important when buying a filter to read the specifications, so that you know exactly what it removes from the water and what it doesn't. Simple filtering will not remove all dangerous organisms, so if you cannot boil water it should be treated chemically. Chlorine tablets (eg Puritabs, Steritabs or other brands) will kill many pathogens, but not some parasites like giardia and amoebic cysts. Iodine is more effective in purifying water and is available in tablet form (such as Potable Aqua). Follow the directions carefully and remember that too much iodine can be harmful.

Medical Problems & Treatment

Self-diagnosis and treatment can be risky, so you should always seek medical help. An embassy, consulate or five-star hotel can usually recommend a local doctor or clinic. Although we do give drug dosages in this section, they are for emergency use only. Correct diagnosis is vital. Because drug brand names vary from country to country we have used their generic names throughout this section. Check with your pharmacist for brands available locally.

Antibiotics should ideally be administered only under medical supervision. Take only the recommended dose at the prescribed intervals and use the whole course, even if the illness seems to be cured earlier. Stop immediately if there are any serious reactions and don't use the antibiotic at all if you are unsure that you have the correct one. Some people are allergic to commonly prescribed antibiotics such as penicillin or sulpha drugs; carry this information (eg on a bracelet) when travelling.

Environmental Hazards

Altitude Sickness Areas of northern India form part of the Himalaya, therefore lack of oxygen at high altitudes (over 2500m) may affect some people. The effect may be mild or severe and occurs because less oxygen reaches the muscles and brain at high altitude, requiring the heart and lungs to compensate by working harder. Symptoms of acute mountain sickness (AMS) usually develop during the first 24 hours at altitude but may be delayed by up to three weeks. Mild symptoms include headache, lethargy, dizziness, difficulty sleeping and loss of appetite. AMS may become more severe without warning and can be fatal. Severe symptoms include breathlessness, a dry, ir-

ritative cough (which may progress to the production of pink, frothy sputum), severe headache, lack of coordination and balance, confusion, irrational behaviour, vomiting, drowsiness and unconsciousness. There is no hard-and-fast rule as to what is too high: AMS has been fatal at 3000m, although 3500m to 4500m is the usual range.

Treat mild symptoms by resting at the same altitude until recovery, usually a day or two. Paracetamol or aspirin can be taken for headaches. If symptoms persist or become worse, however, *immediate descent is necessary*; even 500m can help. Drug treatments should never be used to avoid descent or to enable further ascent.

The drugs acetazolamide (Diamox) and dexamethasone are recommended by some doctors for the prevention of AMS, however their use is controversial. They can reduce the symptoms, but they may also mask warning signs; severe and fatal AMS has occurred in people taking these drugs. In general we do not recommend them for travellers.

To prevent acute mountain sickness:

- Ascend slowly – have frequent rest days, spending two to three nights at each rise of 1000m. If you reach a high altitude by trekking, acclimatisation takes place gradually and you are less likely to be affected than if you fly directly to high altitude.
- It is always wise to sleep at a lower altitude than the greatest height reached during the day if possible. Also, once above 3000m, care should be taken not to increase the sleeping altitude by more than 300m per day.
- Drink extra fluids. The mountain air is dry and cold and moisture is lost as you breathe. Evaporation of sweat may occur unnoticed and result in dehydration.
- Eat light, high-carbohydrate meals for more energy.
- Avoid alcohol as it may increase the risk of dehydration.
- Avoid sedatives.

Everyday Health

Normal body temperature is 37°C or 98.6°F; more than 2°C (4°F) higher indicates a high fever. The normal adult pulse rate is 60 to 100 per minute (children 80 to 100, babies 100 to 140). As a general rule the pulse increases about 20 beats per minute for each 1°C (2°F) rise in fever.

Respiration (breathing) rate is also an indicator of illness. Count the number of breaths per minute: between 12 and 20 is normal for adults and older children (up to 30 for younger children, 40 for babies). People with a high fever or serious respiratory illness breathe more quickly than normal. More than 40 shallow breaths a minute may indicate pneumonia.

Heat Exhaustion Dehydration and salt deficiency can cause heat exhaustion. Take time to acclimatise to high temperatures, drink sufficient liquids and do not do anything too physically demanding.

Salt deficiency is characterised by fatigue, lethargy, headaches, giddiness and muscle cramps; salt tablets may help, but adding extra salt to your food is better.

Anhidrotic heat exhaustion is a rare form of heat exhaustion that is caused by an inability to sweat. It tends to affect people who have been in a hot climate for some time, rather than newcomers. It can progress to heatstroke. Treatment involves removal to a cooler climate.

Heatstroke This serious, occasionally fatal, condition can occur if the body's heat-regulating mechanism breaks down and the body temperature rises to dangerous levels. Long, continuous periods of exposure to high temperatures and insufficient fluids can leave you vulnerable to heatstroke.

The symptoms are feeling unwell, not sweating very much (or at all) and a high body temperature (39°C to 41°C or 102°F to 106°F). Where sweating has ceased the skin becomes flushed and red. Severe, throbbing headaches and lack of coordination will also occur, and the sufferer may be confused or aggressive. Eventually the victim will become delirious or convulse. Hospitalisation is essential, but in the interim get victims out of the sun, remove their clothing, cover them with a wet sheet or towel and then fan continually. Give fluids if they are conscious.

Hypothermia Too much cold can be just as dangerous as too much heat. If you are trekking at high altitudes or simply taking a long bus trip over mountains, particularly at night, be prepared. In some areas you should always be prepared for cold, wet or windy conditions even if you're just out walking or hitching.

Hypothermia occurs when the body loses heat faster than it can produce it and the core temperature of the body falls. It is surprisingly easy to progress from very cold to dangerously cold due to a combination of wind, wet clothing, fatigue and hunger, even if the air temperature is above freezing. It is best to dress in layers; silk, wool and some of the new artificial fibres are all good insulating materials. A hat is important, as a lot of heat is lost through the head. A strong, waterproof outer layer (and a 'space' blanket for emergencies) are essential. Carry basic supplies, including food containing simple sugars to generate heat quickly and fluid to drink.

Symptoms of hypothermia are exhaustion, numb skin (particularly toes and fingers), shivering, slurred speech, irrational or violent behaviour, lethargy, stumbling, dizzy spells, muscle cramps and violent bursts of energy. Irrationality may take the form of sufferers claiming they are warm and trying to take off their clothes.

To treat mild hypothermia, first get the person out of the wind and/or rain, remove their clothing if it's wet and replace it with dry, warm clothing. Give them hot liquids – not alcohol – and some high-kilojoule, easily digestible food. Do not rub victims, instead allow them to slowly warm themselves. This should be enough to treat the early stages of hypothermia. The early recognition and treatment of mild hypothermia is the only way to prevent severe hypothermia, which is a critical condition.

Jet Lag Jet lag is experienced when a person travels by air across more than three time zones (each time zone usually represents a one-hour time difference). It occurs because many of the functions of the human body (such as temperature, pulse rate and emptying of the bladder and bowels) are regulated by internal 24 hour cycles. When we travel long distances rapidly, our bodies take time to adjust to the 'new time' of our destination, and we may experience disorientation, insomnia, fatigue, impaired concentration, anxiety, and loss of appetite. These effects will usually be gone within three days of arrival, but to minimise the impact of jet lag:

- Rest for a couple of days prior to departure.
- Try to select flight schedules that minimise sleep deprivation; arriving late in the day means you can go to sleep soon after you arrive. For very long flights, try to organise a stopover.
- Avoid excessive eating (which bloats the stomach) and alcohol (which causes dehydration)

during the flight. Instead, drink plenty of non-carbonated, non-alcoholic drinks such as fruit juice or water.

- Avoid smoking.
- Make yourself comfortable by wearing loose-fitting clothes and perhaps bringing an eye mask and ear plugs to help you sleep.
- Try to sleep at the appropriate time for the time zone you are travelling to.

Motion Sickness Eating lightly before and during a trip will reduce the chances of motion sickness. If you are prone to motion sickness try to find a place that minimises movement – near the wing on aircraft, close to midships on boats, near the centre on buses. Fresh air usually helps; reading and cigarette smoke don't. Commercial motion-sickness preparations, which can cause drowsiness, have to be taken before the trip commences. Ginger (available in capsule form) and peppermint (including mint-flavoured sweets) are natural preventatives.

Prickly Heat Prickly heat is an itchy rash caused by excessive perspiration trapped under the skin. It usually strikes people who have just arrived in a hot climate. Keeping cool, bathing often, drying the skin or resorting to air-conditioning may help.

Sunburn In the tropics, the desert or at high altitude you can get sunburnt surprisingly quickly, even through cloud. Use a sunscreen, hat, and barrier cream for your nose and lips. Calamine lotion or a sting relief spray are good for mild sunburn. Protect your eyes with good-quality sunglasses, particularly if you will be near water, sand or snow.

Infectious Diseases

Diarrhoea Simple things like a change of water, food or climate can all cause a mild bout of diarrhoea, but a few rushed toilet trips with no other symptoms is not indicative of a major problem.

Dehydration is the main danger with any diarrhoea, particularly in children or the elderly as dehydration can occur quite quickly. Under all circumstances *fluid replacement* (at least equal to the volume being lost) is the most important thing to remember. Weak black tea with a little sugar, soda water, or soft drinks allowed to go flat and diluted 50% with clean water are all good. With severe diarrhoea a rehydrating solution is preferable to replace minerals and salts lost. Commercially available oral rehydration salts (ORS) are very useful; add them to boiled or bottled water. In an emergency you can make up a solution of six teaspoons of sugar and a half teaspoon of salt to a litre of boiled or bottled water. You need to drink at least the same volume of fluid that you are losing in bowel movements and vomiting. Urine is the best guide to the adequacy of replacement – if you have small amounts of concentrated urine, you need to drink more. Keep drinking small amounts often. Stick to a bland diet as you recover.

Gut-paralysing drugs such as loperamide or diphenoxylate can be used to bring relief from the symptoms, although they do not actually cure the problem. Only use these drugs if you do not have access to toilets, eg if you *must* travel. These drugs should not be used if the person has a high fever or is severely dehydrated, and are not recommended in children under 12 years.

In certain situations antibiotics may be required: diarrhoea with blood or mucus (dysentery), any diarrhoea with fever, profuse watery diarrhoea, persistent diarrhoea not improving after 48 hours, and severe diarrhoea. These suggest a more serious cause of diarrhoea and gut-paralysing drugs should be avoided.

In these situations, a stool test may be necessary to diagnose what bug is causing your diarrhoea, so you should seek medical help urgently. Where this is not possible the recommended drugs for bacterial diarrhoea (the most likely cause of severe diarrhoea in travellers) are norfloxacin 400mg twice daily for three days or ciprofloxacin 500mg twice daily for five days. These are not recommended for children or pregnant women. The drug of choice for children would be co-trimoxazole with dosage dependent on weight. A five day course is given.

Ampicillin or amoxycillin may be given in pregnancy, but medical care is necessary.

Two other causes of persistent diarrhoea in travellers are giardiasis and amoebic dysentery.

Giardiasis is caused by a common parasite, *Giardia lamblia*. Symptoms include stomach cramps, nausea, a bloated stomach, watery, foul-smelling diarrhoea and frequent gas. Giardiasis can appear several weeks after you have been exposed to the parasite. The symptoms may disappear for a few days and then return; this can go on for several weeks.

Amoebic dysentery, caused by the protozoon *Entamoeba histolytica*, is characterised by a gradual onset of low-grade diarrhoea, often with blood and mucus. Cramping abdominal pain and vomiting are less likely than in other types of diarrhoea, and fever may not be present. It will persist until treated and can recur and cause other health problems.

You should seek medical advice if you think you have giardiasis or amoebic dysentery, but where this is not possible, tinidazole, or metronidazole are the recommended drugs. Treatment is a 2g single dose of tinidazole or 250mg of metronidazole three times daily for five to 10 days.

Fungal Infections Fungal infections are more common in hot weather and are usually found on the scalp, between the toes (athlete's foot) or fingers, in the groin and on the body (ringworm). You get ringworm (which is a fungal infection, not a worm) from infected animals or other people. Moisture encourages these infections.

To prevent fungal infections wear loose, comfortable clothes, avoid artificial fibres, wash frequently and dry yourself carefully. If you do get an infection, wash the infected area at least daily with a disinfectant or medicated soap and water, and rinse and dry well. Apply an antifungal cream or powder like tolnaftate. Try to expose the infected area to air or sunlight as much as possible and wash all towels and underwear in hot water, change them often and let them dry in the sun.

Hepatitis Hepatitis is a general term for inflammation of the liver. It is a common disease in India, and worldwide. There are several different viruses that cause hepatitis, and they differ in the way that they are transmitted. The symptoms are similar in all forms of the illness, and include fever, chills, headache, fatigue, feelings of weakness and aches and pains, followed by loss of appetite, nausea, vomiting, abdominal pain, dark urine, light-coloured faeces, jaundiced (yellow) skin and yellowing of the whites of the eyes. People who have had hepatitis should avoid alcohol for some time after the illness, as the liver needs time to recover.

Hepatitis A is transmitted by contaminated food and drinking water. You should seek medical advice, but there is not much you can do apart from resting, drinking lots of fluids, eating lightly and avoiding fatty foods. Hepatitis E is transmitted in the same way as hepatitis A.

There are almost 300 million chronic carriers of **Hepatitis B** in the world. It is spread through contact with infected blood, blood products or body fluids, for example through sexual contact, unsterilised needles and blood transfusions, or contact with blood via small breaks in the skin. Other risk situations include having a shave, tattoo or your body pierced with contaminated equipment. The symptoms of hepatitis B may be more severe than type A and the disease can lead to long-term problems such as chronic liver damage, liver cancer or a long-term carrier state. Hepatitis C and D are spread in the same way as hepatitis B and can also lead to long-term complications.

There are vaccines against hepatitis A and B, but there are currently no vaccines against the other types of hepatitis. Following the basic rules about food and water (hepatitis A and E) and avoiding risk situations (hepatitis B, C and D) are important preventative measures.

HIV & AIDS Infection with the human immunodeficiency virus (HIV) may lead to the acquired immune deficiency syndrome

(AIDS), which is a fatal disease. Any exposure to blood, blood products or body fluids may put the individual at risk. The disease is often transmitted through sexual contact or dirty needles – vaccinations, acupuncture, tattooing and body piercing can be potentially as dangerous as intravenous drug use. HIV/AIDS can also be spread through infected blood transfusions.

If you do need an injection, ask to see the syringe unwrapped in front of you, or take a needle and syringe pack with you.

Fear of HIV infection should never preclude treatment for serious medical conditions.

Intestinal Worms These parasites are most common in rural, tropical areas. The different worms have different ways of infecting people. Some may be ingested with food such as undercooked meat (eg tapeworms) and some enter through your skin (eg hookworms). Infestations may not show up for some time, and although they are generally not serious, if left untreated some can cause severe health problems later. Consider having a stool test when you return home to check for these and determine the appropriate treatment.

Meningococcal Meningitis This serious disease can be fatal. There are recurring epidemics in northern India and Nepal.

A fever, severe headache, sensitivity to light and neck stiffness which prevents forward bending of the head are the first symptoms. There may also be purple patches on the skin. Death can occur within a few hours, so urgent medical treatment is required.

Trekkers to rural areas of Nepal should be particularly careful, as the disease is spread by close contact with people who carry it in their throats and noses and spread it through coughs and sneezes; they may not even be aware that they are carriers. Lodges in the hills where travellers spend the night are prime spots for the spread of infection.

Treatment is large doses of penicillin given intravenously, or chloramphenicol injections.

Sexually Transmitted Diseases HIV/AIDS and hepatitis B can be transmitted through sexual contact – see the relevant sections earlier for details. Gonorrhoea, herpes and syphilis are among these diseases; sores, discharges, blisters or rashes around the genitals or pain when urinating are common symptoms. In some STDs, such as wart virus or chlamydia, symptoms may be less marked or not observed at all, especially in women. Chlamydia infection can cause infertility in men and women before any symptoms are noticed. Syphilis symptoms eventually disappear completely but the disease continues and can cause severe problems in later years. While abstinence from sexual contact is the only 100% effective prevention, using condoms is also effective. The different sexually transmitted diseases each require specific antibiotic treatments.

Typhoid Typhoid fever is a dangerous gut infection caused by contaminated water and food. Medical help must be sought.

In its early stages sufferers may feel they have a bad cold or flu on the way, as early symptoms are a headache, body aches and a fever which rises a little each day until it is around 40°C (104°F) or more. The victim's pulse is often slow relative to the degree of fever present – unlike a normal fever where the pulse increases. There may also be vomiting, abdominal pain, diarrhoea or constipation.

In the second week the high fever and slow pulse continue and a few pink spots may appear on the body; trembling, delirium, weakness, weight loss and dehydration may occur. Complications such as pneumonia, perforated bowel or meningitis may occur.

Insect-Borne Diseases
Filariasis, leishmaniasis, Lyme disease, and typhus are all insect-borne diseases, but they do not pose a great risk to travellers. For more information on them see Less Common Diseases at the end of this section.

Malaria This serious and potentially fatal disease is spread by mosquito bites. If you are travelling in endemic areas it is extremely important to avoid mosquito bites and to take tablets to prevent this disease. Symptoms range from fever, chills and sweating, headache, diarrhoea and abdominal pains to a vague feeling of ill-health. Seek medical help immediately if malaria is suspected. Without treatment malaria can rapidly become more serious and can be fatal.

If medical care is not available, malaria tablets can be used for treatment. You need to use a malaria tablet which is different to the one you were taking when you contracted malaria. The standard treatment dose of mefloquine is two 250mg tablets and a further two six hours later. For Fansidar, it's a single dose of three tablets. If you were previously taking mefloquine and cannot obtain Fansidar, then other alternatives are Malarone (atovaquone-proguanil; four tablets once daily for three days), halofantrine (three doses of two 250mg tablets every six hours) or quinine sulphate (600mg every six hours). There is a greater risk of side effects with these dosages than in normal use if used with mefloquine, so medical advice is preferable. Be aware also that halofantrine is no longer recommended by the WHO as emergency stand-by treatment, because of side effects, and should only be used if no other drugs are available.

To prevent mosquito bites at all times:

- wear light-coloured clothing
- wear long trousers and long-sleeved shirts
- use mosquito repellents containing the compound DEET on exposed areas (prolonged overuse of DEET may be harmful, especially to children, but its use is considered preferable to being bitten by disease-transmitting mosquitoes)
- avoid perfumes or aftershave
- use a mosquito net impregnated with mosquito repellent (permethrin) – it may be worth taking your own
- impregnating clothes with permethrin effectively deters mosquitoes and other insects

Dengue Fever This viral disease is transmitted by mosquitoes and occurs mainly in tropical and subtropical areas of the world, including India. Generally, the risk to travellers is small except during epidemics, which are usually seasonal (during and just after the rainy season).

The *Aedes aegypti* mosquito which transmits the dengue virus is most active during the day, unlike the malaria mosquito, and is found mainly in urban areas, in and around human dwellings.

Signs and symptoms of dengue fever include a sudden onset of high fever, headache, joint and muscle pains (hence its old name, 'breakbone fever') and nausea and vomiting. A rash of small red spots appears three to four days after the onset of fever. Dengue is commonly mistaken for other infectious diseases, including influenza.

You should seek medical attention if you think you may be infected, although there is no specific treatment. Infection can be diagnosed by a blood test. Aspirin should be avoided, as it increases the risk of haemorrhaging. Recovery may be prolonged, with tiredness lasting for several weeks. Severe complications are rare in travellers, but include dengue haemorrhagic fever (DHF), which can be fatal without prompt medical treatment. DHF is thought to be a result of second infection due to a different strain (there are four major strains), and usually affects residents of the country rather than travellers.

There is no vaccine against dengue fever. The best prevention is to avoid mosquito bites at all times – see the Malaria section for more details.

If you have had dengue before, you are at higher risk of complications if you get infected again, so check with your doctor before you go.

Japanese B Encephalitis This viral infection of the brain is transmitted by mosquitoes. Most cases occur in rural areas as the virus exists in pigs and wading birds. Symptoms include fever, headache and alteration in consciousness. Hospitalisation is needed for correct diagnosis and treatment. There is a high mortality rate among those who have symptoms; of those who survive many are intellectually disabled.

Cuts, Bites & Stings
See Less Common Diseases for details of rabies, which is passed through animal bites.

Bedbugs & Lice Bedbugs live in various places, but particularly in dirty mattresses and bedding, evidenced by spots of blood on bedclothes or on the wall. Bedbugs leave itchy bites in neat rows. Calamine lotion or a sting relief spray may help.

All lice cause itching and discomfort. They make themselves at home in your hair (head lice), your clothing (body lice) or in your pubic hair (crabs). You catch lice through direct contact with infected people or by sharing combs, clothing and the like. Powder or shampoo treatment will kill the lice and infected clothing should then be washed in very hot, soapy water and left in the sun to dry.

Bites & Stings Bee and wasp stings are usually painful rather than dangerous. However in people who are allergic to them severe breathing difficulties may occur and require urgent medical care. Calamine lotion or a sting relief spray will ease the discomfort and ice packs will reduce the pain and swelling. There are some spiders with dangerous bites but antivenenes are usually available. Scorpion stings are notoriously painful and can actually be fatal. Scorpions often shelter in shoes or clothing.

There are various fish and other sea creatures which can sting or bite dangerously or which are dangerous to eat. Again, local advice is the best suggestion.

Cuts & Scratches Wash well and treat any cut with an antiseptic such as povidone-iodine. Where possible avoid bandages and Band-Aids, which can keep wounds wet. Coral cuts are notoriously slow to heal and if they are not adequately cleaned, small pieces of coral can become embedded in the wound.

Jellyfish Local advice is the best way of avoiding contact with these sea creatures which have stinging tentacles. Dousing in vinegar will deactivate any stingers which have not 'fired'.

Calamine lotion, antihistamines and analgesics may reduce the reaction and relieve the pain.

Leeches & Ticks Leeches may be present in damp rainforests; they attach themselves to your skin to suck your blood. Trekkers often get them on their legs or in their boots. Salt or a lighted cigarette end will make them fall off. Do not pull them off, as the bite is then more likely to become infected. Clean and apply pressure if the point of attachment is bleeding. An insect repellent may keep them away.

You should always check all over your body if you have been walking through a potentially tick-infested area as ticks can cause skin infections and other more serious diseases. If a tick is found attached, press down around the tick's head with tweezers, grab the head and gently pull upwards. Avoid pulling the rear of the body as this may squeeze the tick's gut contents through the attached mouth parts into the skin, increasing the risk of infection and disease. Smearing chemicals on the tick will not make it let go and is not recommended.

Snakes To minimise your chances of being bitten always wear boots, socks and long trousers when walking through undergrowth where snakes may be present. Don't put your hands into holes and crevices, and be careful when collecting firewood.

Snake bites do not cause instantaneous death and antivenenes are usually available. Immediately wrap the bitten limb tightly, as you would for a sprained ankle, and then attach a splint to immobilise it. Keep the victim still and seek medical help, if possible with the dead snake for identification. Don't attempt to catch the snake if there is a possibility of being bitten again. Tourniquets and sucking out the poison are now comprehensively discredited.

Women's Health

Gynaecological Problems Antibiotic use, synthetic underwear, sweating and contraceptive pills can lead to fungal vaginal infections, especially when travelling in hot climates. Fungal infections are characterised by a rash, itch and discharge, and can be treated with a vinegar or lemon-juice douche, or with yoghurt. Nystatin, miconazole or clotrimazole pessaries or vaginal cream are the usual treatment. Maintaining good personal hygiene, and wearing loose-fitting clothes and cotton underwear may help prevent these infections.

Sexually transmitted diseases are a major cause of vaginal problems. Symptoms include a smelly discharge, painful intercourse and sometimes a burning sensation when urinating. Medical attention should be sought and male sexual partners must also be treated. Remember that in addition to these diseases HIV or hepatitis B may also be acquired during exposure. Besides abstinence, the best thing is to practise safe sex using condoms.

Pregnancy It is not advisable to travel to some places while pregnant as some vaccinations normally used to prevent serious diseases are not advisable in pregnancy (eg yellow fever). In addition, some diseases are much more serious for the mother (and may increase the risk of a stillborn child) in pregnancy (eg malaria).

Most miscarriages occur during the first three months of pregnancy. Miscarriage is not uncommon, and can occasionally lead to severe bleeding. The last three months should also be spent within reasonable distance of good medical care. A baby born as early as 24 weeks stands a chance of survival, but only in a good modern hospital. Pregnant women should avoid all unnecessary medication, vaccinations and malarial prophylactics should still be taken where needed. Additional care should be taken to prevent illness and particular attention should be paid to diet and nutrition. Alcohol and nicotine, for example, should be avoided.

Less Common Diseases

The following diseases pose a small risk to travellers, and so are only mentioned in passing. Seek medical advice if you think you may have any of these diseases.

Cholera This is the worst watery diarrhoea and medical help should be sought. Cholera outbreaks are generally widely reported, so you can avoid problem areas. *Fluid replacement is the most vital treatment* – the risk of dehydration is severe as you may lose up to 20L a day. If there is a delay in getting to hospital then begin taking tetracycline. The adult dose is 250mg four times daily. It is not recommended for children under nine years nor for pregnant women. Tetracycline may help shorten the illness, but adequate fluid intake is required to save lives.

Filariasis This is a mosquito-transmitted parasitic infection found in India and other parts of Asia. Possible symptoms include fever, pain and swelling of the lymph glands; inflammation of lymph drainage areas; swelling of a limb or the scrotum; skin rashes and blindness. Treatment is available to eliminate the parasites from the body, but some of the damage already caused may not be reversible. Medical advice should be obtained promptly if the infection is suspected.

Leishmaniasis This is a group of parasitic diseases transmitted by the bite of sandflies which are found in India and other parts of the world. Cutaneous leishmaniasis affects the skin tissue causing ulceration and disfigurement and visceral leishmaniasis affects the internal organs. Seek medical advice as laboratory testing is required for diagnosis and correct treatment. Avoiding sandfly bites is the best precaution. Bites are usually painless, itchy and are yet another reason to cover up and apply repellent.

Lyme Disease This is a tick-transmitted infection which may be acquired in India. The illness usually begins with a spreading rash at the site of the tick bite and is accompanied by fever, headache, extreme fatigue, aching joints and muscle and mild neck stiffness. If untreated, these symptoms usually resolve over several weeks but over subsequent weeks or months disorders of the nervous system, heart and joints may develop. Treatment works best early in the illness. Medical help should be sought.

Rabies This fatal viral infection is found in many countries, including India. Many animals can be infected (eg dogs, cats, bats and monkeys) and it is their saliva which is infectious. Any bite, scratch or even lick from an animal should be cleaned immediately and thoroughly. Scrub with soap and running water, and then apply alcohol or iodine solution. Medical help should be sought promptly to receive a course of injections to prevent the onset of symptoms and death.

Tetanus This disease is caused by a germ which lives in soil and the faeces of horses and other animals. It enters the body via breaks in the skin. The first symptom may be discomfort in swallowing, or stiffening of the jaw and neck; this is followed by painful convulsions of the jaw and whole body. The disease can be fatal. It can be prevented by vaccination.

Tuberculosis (TB) TB is a bacterial infection transmitted from person to person by coughing but which may be transmitted through consumption of unpasteurised milk. Milk that has been boiled is safe to drink, and the souring of milk to make yoghurt or cheese also kills the bacilli. Travellers are usually not at great risk as close household contact with the infected person is usually required before the disease is passed on.

You may need to have a TB test before you travel as this can help diagnose the disease later if you become ill.

Typhus This disease is spread by ticks, mites or lice. It begins with fever, chills, headache and muscle pains followed a few days later by a body rash. There is often a large painful sore at the site of the bite and

nearby lymph nodes are swollen and painful. Typhus can be treated under medical supervision. Seek local advice on areas where ticks pose a danger and always check your skin carefully for them after .walking in a danger area such as a tropical forest. An insect repellent can help, and walkers in tick-infested areas should consider having their boots and trousers impregnated with benzyl benzoate and dibutylphthalate.

WOMEN TRAVELLERS

India is generally perfectly safe for women travellers, even for those travelling alone. An exception is the heavily touristed areas of Goa and Rajasthan. Here you are advised not to walk in isolated spots (down lonely alleys, along the beach) on your own – after dark especially. Two Swedish women were raped at Anjuna in 1997. If you are in doubt about whether it's safe or not, ask. Another place where one should exercise caution is Hampi; young travellers generally, are advised to be cautious about lingering in isolated, lonely spots at night. Cities are generally quite OK although if you are on your own, take reasonable care if you are out after dark. Staying safe is really a matter of common sense, although a few tips from those who have gone before always help. Below are some tips from a seasoned solo female traveller:

- Dress modestly. Long skirts are better than short shirts, slacks (loose-fitting) are better than jeans. Shorts, sleeveless blouses and tight-fitting clothing are frowned on.
- Walk confidently in the street, as though you were going somewhere, and answer men's glances with a haughty look.
- Treat service people (who are almost always men) impersonally. Don't invite their confidences. Ignore any personal remarks and report bad behaviour to the proper authorities, eg hotel and restaurant managers, the police, train conductors etc.
- Don't go home with people you meet on the street – you'll be asked frequently to visit family homes. Most of the time it will be safe, but why take chances?
- Lock your hotel room when you are in it. If you don't know who is knocking at your door,

phone down to the desk or ask who's there before opening it.

- Try to arrive in towns before nightfall. If you do arrive late, refuse to share a rickshaw or taxi with the driver's brother, cousin or friend.
- Take a book with you to restaurants. It keeps your eyes from roaming around too much and attracting attention from men who will be looking at you anyway. If a male approaches you, tell him to get lost or you will call the manager.
- If you are being followed, go to the nearest tourist hotel and wait for a few minutes. Most Indians (excluding businessmen) are discouraged from entering, and your follower will get tired of waiting and leave. Museums and other public sights are also good.
- Remember, Indians are basically modest and passers-by will be more than willing to help a woman being bothered. Ask anyone on the street who looks respectable – uniformed or suit-coated men are good.
- If you want to go out in the evening, try to arrange a rickshaw during the day to pick you up in the evening. Inform the hotel – even if it is only a hostel – where you are going and when you expect to return. If anything does happen they will know both who the driver is and where you went. Make sure that your driver understands he is to come and pick you up again.

Mary Anne Morel

Although you are unlikely to be at any physical risk, one of the wearying aspects of travelling in some parts of India, especially if you are alone, is the (unwanted) attention you will attract from young local men from time to time. If you don't want to be the constant object of what is euphemistically called 'Eve teasing' (harassment in various forms including public groping) then pay attention to the local norms of dress and behaviour. Dressing modestly helps. This means not wearing sleeveless tops, shorts or even jeans. Loose clothing that covers your legs and shoulders is best. The *salwar kameez* or traditional Punjabi shirt and pyjama combination is becoming increasingly popular among western women travellers because it's practical and cheap and, most of all, it's considered respectable attire. A cotton salwar kameez is also surprisingly cool in a hot climate and keeps the burning sun off your skin. A scarf (or the *dupatta* that is worn with

the salwar kameez) is handy if you intend travelling in Muslim areas (eg Kargil in Ladakh, or parts of Andhra Pradesh) where women invariably cover their heads.

Many places to eat have separate areas for women and families, usually called the 'family room'. If you are on your own and the main eating area is full of men, and you feel uncomfortable, head for the family room. The food is the same as 'outside' but sometimes you may be charged a little more. The service is generally very good.

On buses, the front section is usually deemed the area unofficially reserved for unaccompanied women, and families. If you are travelling alone you may feel more comfortable sitting in this part of the bus. Long-distance trains often have special carriages reserved for women and children. Having said that, they can be so noisy with small children you may wish you had opted for the ordinary carriage.

On the whole, a woman travelling alone is still very unusual in all but the most touristed areas, and much of the time you will find that there is great concern for your safety and welfare, and that people will go out of their way to assist you.

GAY & LESBIAN TRAVELLERS

While overt displays of affection between members of the opposite sex, such as cuddling and hand-holding, are frowned upon in India, it is not unusual to see Indian men holding hands with each other or engaged in other close affectionate behaviour. This does not necessarily suggest that they are gay. The gay movement in India is confined almost exclusively to larger cities and Mumbai is really the only place where there's a gay 'scene'. Since marriage is seen as very important, to be gay is a particular stigma – most gays stay in the closet or risk being disowned by their families.

As with relations between heterosexual western couples travelling in India – both married and unmarried – gay and lesbian travellers should exercise discretion and refrain from displaying overt affection towards each other in public.

Go for It

I have visited India many times before but never in a wheelchair as a disabled person. As India is so rewarding, it is worth the effort to see it despite the lack of facilities we are used to in the west.

I am 55 and have MS. I can walk two or three steps with support which does help but I was carried up and down steps very willingly where necessary. Even a car and driver for a few days isn't too expensive and Indians are expert at getting things like wheelchairs into boots of cars. It would, however, be almost impossible to do without a willing companion, not only for the pushing and pulling (pavements are never smooth) but to see if a restaurant, shop, hotel or temple is feasible. That saves a lot of time.

There is always plenty of people power available if they are shown what to do, and paying for it or tipping is obviously welcome. In the same way you can hire a nurse and the rate of exchange is such that it is very cheap to us. Bathrooms in the modest hotels are actually better than in the expensive ones. They are big, have western loos, marble or cement floors and shower taps come out of the wall about three feet from the ground with a tap at that level too. Loos out and about are the biggest problem. I solved it by taking a fold up stool with me and a 'slipper' potty which slots underneath so I could get into a loo (often it is the squat kind) and balance somewhat precariously.

Every disabled person is different and I find that thinking through every eventuality beforehand and taking whatever kit is essential is important. It would be difficult to buy things especially for the disabled but Indians are very good at making do and mending. You can then be prepared to be very surprised at how you can survive and how much you can enjoy a holiday in India.

Margaret Wilson

Legal Status

Homosexual relations for men are illegal in India. Section 377 of the national legislation forbids 'carnal intercourse against the order of nature' (that is, anal intercourse). The penalties for transgression can be up to life imprisonment. Because of this gay travellers could be the subject of blackmail – take care. There is no law against lesbian relations.

Publications & Groups

Bombay Dost is a gay and lesbian publication available from 105 Veena Beena Shopping Centre, Bandra (W) Mumbai; The People Tree, 8 Parliament St, New Delhi; and Classic Books, 10 Middleton St, Calcutta. Support groups include Bombay Dost (address above); Pravartak, Post Bag 10237, Calcutta, West Bengal 700019; Sakhi (Lesbian Group), PO Box 3526, Lajpat Nagar, New Delhi 110024; and Sneha Sangama, PO Box 3250, RT Nagar, Bangalore 560032.

DISABLED TRAVELLERS

Travelling in India can entail some fairly rigorous challenges, even for the able-bodied traveller – long bus trips in crowded vehicles between remote villages and endless queues in the scorching heat at bus and train stations can test even the hardiest traveller. If you can't walk, these challenges are increased many-fold. Few buildings have wheelchair access; toilets have certainly not been designed to accommodate wheelchairs; footpaths, where they exist (only in larger towns), are generally riddled with holes, littered with obstacles and packed with throngs of people, severely restricting mobility.

Nevertheless, many disabled travellers are taking on the challenge of travel in

India. Seeing the mobility impaired locals whizz through city traffic at breakneck speed in modified bicycles might even serve as inspiration! If your mobility is restricted you will need a strong, able-bodied companion to accompany you, and it would be well worth considering hiring a private vehicle and driver.

One organisation that may be able to assist with information on travel practicalities in India for disabled people is the Royal Association for Disability and Rehabilitation or RADAR (☎ 020-7250 3222, fax 250 0212, email radar@radar.org.uk) at 12 City Forum, 250 City Rd, London EC1V 8AF, UK. It also has a Web site (www.radar.org.uk).

SENIOR TRAVELLERS

Unless your mobility (see above) or your vision is impaired or you're in any other way incapacitated, and if you're in reasonable health, there is no reason why the senior traveller should not consider India as a potential holiday destination. It may be helpful to discuss your proposed trip with your local GP.

TRAVEL WITH CHILDREN

The numbers of intrepid souls travelling around India accompanied by one, or even two, young children, seems to be on the increase. Children can often enhance your encounters with local people, as they often possess little of the self-consciousness and sense of the cultural differences which can inhibit interaction between adults. Nevertheless, travelling with children can be hard work, and ideally the burden needs to be shared between two adults. For more information, see the Health section earlier in this chapter, and get hold of a copy of Lonely Planet's *Travel with Children* by Maureen Wheeler. A good Web site for a personal account of travelling in India with children is www.southwest.com.au/~lockley. Lonely Planet's Thorn Tree Web site (www.lonelyplanet.com.au) has a subdirectory on travelling with children.

DANGERS & ANNOYANCES

Common sense and reasonable caution are your best weapons against the risk of theft or worse. There's no need to be paranoid – talk to other travellers, and pay heed to what reliable staff at hotels and guesthouses tell you.

Theft

Never leave those most important valuables (passport, tickets, health certificates, money, travellers cheques) in your room; they should be with you at all times. Either have a stout leather passport wallet on your belt, a passport pouch under your shirt, or simply extra internal pockets in your clothing. On trains at night keep your gear near you; padlocking a bag to a luggage rack can be useful, and some of the newer trains have loops under the seats which you can chain

---

Carbon Monoxide Poisoning

! Lonely Planet recommends that travellers do not use fires as a means of heating in hotel rooms. The Indian police have confirmed that a number of deaths from carbon monoxide poisoning occur each year. The tragic story below explains why you should especially avoid burning charcoal or other fuels which give off toxic fumes.

On 25 January 1996 we had the heartbreaking news our precious son John and his beautiful girlfriend Lisa had been found dead in their hotel room in Darjeeling. Apparently the weather was freezing, and on asking for some heating they were brought a bucket of charcoal. Unfortunately, ventilation was almost nonexistent and they died from carbon monoxide poisoning.

Diane Stevens

things to. However some travellers report that padlocking your gear this way only serves to alert thieves to the fact that you have something worth stealing. Never walk around with valuables casually slung over your shoulder. Take extra care on crowded public transport.

Thieves are particularly prevalent on train routes where there are lots of tourists. The Delhi-Agra *Shatabdi Express* service is notorious; Delhi-Jaipur, Jaipur-Ajmer, Jodhpur-Jaisalmer, Varanasi-Calcutta, Delhi-Mumbai and Agra-Varanasi are other routes to take care on. Train departure time, when the confusion and crowds are at their worst, is the time to be most careful. Just as the train is about to leave, you are distracted by someone while their accomplice is stealing your bag from by your feet. Airports are another place to be careful, especially when international arrivals take place in the middle of the night, when you are unlikely to be at your most alert.

From time to time there are also drugging episodes. Travellers meet somebody on a train or bus or in a town, start talking and are then offered a *chai* or something similar. Hours later they wake up with a headache and all their gear gone, the tea having been full of sleeping pills. Don't accept drinks or food from strangers no matter how friendly they seem, particularly if you're on your own. This has even happened to people travelling in 1st class compartments who have fallen for a well-dressed, well-spoken con artist.

Beware also of your fellow travellers. Unhappily there are more than a few backpackers who make their money go a little bit further by helping themselves to other people's.

Remember that backpacks are very easy to rifle through. Don't leave valuables in them, especially during flights. Remember also that something may be of little or no value to a thief, but to lose it would be a real heartbreak to you – like film. Finally, a good travel insurance policy helps.

If you do have something stolen, you're going to have to report it to the police.

Diarrhoea with Your Meal, Sir?

Scams designed to part tourists from their money are many and varied. The nastiest scam of all involves poisoning diners to make money from subsequent medical treatment. There are variations on the same theme, but essentially it works like this: someone staying at a hotel is targeted, and when they eat at the restaurant their meal is deliberately adulterated. The victim becomes quickly and violently ill with a stomach complaint. The hotel then arranges for a 'doctor' to come round and/or for the victim to be sent to a private clinic. Either way, the victim pays for treatment and a tidy profit is made.

Usually, the poisoning scam is combined with a medical insurance fiddle, through which the clinic claims for expensive treatments under the victim's travel insurance, rather than getting the victim to pay directly. In this instance the clinic will insist the victim is hospitalised and undergo extensive (and perhaps unnecessary) treatment such as being hooked up to an intravenous drip in order to bump up the charge. Sometimes the insurance scam is offered all by itself: you will be encouraged to fraudulently sign for medical treatment even if you haven't been ill, perhaps in return for free lodging or a cash sum.

The poisoning scam became public knowledge in late 1998 when several victims complained to the authorities and two Irish backpackers allegedly died as a result of it. Now that the matter has been investigated by the police, it is to be hoped that the perpetrators will be scared off. Indeed, there have been no new reported cases at the time of writing. Nevertheless, it's wise to seek local advice from other travellers.

You'll also need a statement proving you have done so if you want to make an insurance claim.

Insurance companies, despite their rosy promises of full protection and speedy settlement of claims, are just as disbelieving as the Indian police and will often attempt every devious trick in the book to avoid paying out on a baggage claim.

Note that some policies specify that you must report an item stolen to the police within a certain amount of time after you observing that it is missing.

Travellers Cheques If you're unlucky enough to have things stolen, some precautions can ease the pain. All travellers cheques are replaceable, although this does you little immediate good if you have to go home and apply to your bank. What you want is instant replacement. Furthermore, what do you do if you lose your cheques and money and have a day or more to travel to the replacement office? The answer is to keep an emergency cash-stash in a totally separate place. In that same place you should keep a record of the cheque serial numbers, proof of purchase slips, encashment vouchers and your passport number.

American Express makes considerable noise about 'instant replacement' of their cheques but a lot of people find out, to their cost, that without a number of precautions 'instantly' can take longer than you think. If you don't have the receipt you were given when you bought the cheques, rapid replacement will be difficult. Obviously the receipt should be kept separate from the cheques, and a photocopy in yet another location doesn't hurt either. Chances are you'll be able to get a limited amount of funds on the spot, and the rest will be available when the bank has verified your initial purchase of the cheques. American Express has a 24 hour number in Delhi (☎ 011-687 5050) which you must ring within 24 hours of the theft.

Contaminated Food & Drink

Sometimes microbes aren't the sole, or main, risk when it comes to eating and drinking. In Rajasthan *bhang* lassis laced with marijuana can pack more of a punch than the hapless traveller would reasonably expect. Some people have become very sick indeed after drinking them. On a more serious note, a food scare broke out in northern India in 1998, principally in Agra and Varanasi, when numerous travellers became sick (a couple died) after eating at local establishments (see the Diarrhoea with Your Meal, Sir? boxed text).

Personal Safety

In the past few years more than a dozen foreigners have disappeared or been murdered in the Kullu region. See the Missing persons boxed text in the Himachal Pradesh chapter for details. Women should take care at the more touristy places in Goa, and all travellers should take care at Hampi. See also the Goa and Karnataka chapters and Women Travellers earlier in this chapter.

Border areas and particularly Jammu & Kashmir are subject to bombings and kidnappings. Although you will be bombarded by touts trying to get you to these areas, seek the latest advice from your embassy.

LEGAL MATTERS

If you find yourself in a sticky legal predicament, contact your embassy. You should carry your passport with you at all times.

In the Indian justice system it seems the burden of proof is on the accused, and proving one's innocence is virtually impossible. The police forces are often corrupt and will pay 'witnesses' to give evidence.

Drugs

For a long time India was a place where you could indulge in all sorts of illegal drugs (mostly grass and hashish) with relative ease – they were cheap, readily available and the risks were minimal. These days things have changed. Although dope is still widely available, penalties for possession, use and trafficking in illegal drugs are strictly enforced. If convicted on a drugs-related charge, sentences are long *(minimum* of 10 years), even for minor offences, and there is no remission or parole. In some cases it has taken three years just to get a court hearing.

In Goa the police have taken a tough, new anti-drugs line. A special court, the Narcotic Drugs and Psychotropic Substances Court, with its own judge, has been established expressly to try drug offences. It seems as though the prevailing attitude is 'if in doubt convict' on the basis that the accused can always appeal to a higher court if they wish to do so.

BUSINESS HOURS

Official business hours are 9.30 am to 5.30 pm (8.30 am to 5.30 pm in the Andaman Islands) Monday to Friday. Unofficially they tend to be more like 10 am to 5 pm. Government offices seem to have lengthy lunch hours, which are sacrosanct and can last from noon to 3 pm. Many public institutions such as museums, galleries and so on close at least one day during the week. Banks are open 10 am to 2 pm Monday to Friday, and 10 am to noon every second Saturday – there are variations, so it pays to check. Travellers cheque transactions usually cease 30 minutes before the official bank closing time. In some tourist centres there may be foreign exchange offices that stay open longer (eg Thomas Cook is open Monday to Saturday 9.30 am to 6 pm). In the state capitals, the main post office is open to 8 pm daily.

PUBLIC HOLIDAYS & SPECIAL EVENTS

Owing to its religious and regional variations, India has a great number of holidays and festivals. Most of them follow either the Indian lunar calendar (a highly complicated system determined chiefly by astrologers) or the Islamic calendar (which falls about 11 days earlier each year; 12 days earlier in leap years) and the dates therefore change from year to year according to the Gregorian calendar. The India-wide holidays and festivals listed below are arranged according to the Indian lunar (and Gregorian) calendar which starts in Chaitra (March/April) – local tourist offices should be able to provide specific dates. See the Festivals table at the start of each regional chapter for statewide and regional festivities.

Chaitra (Mar/Apr)

Mahavir Jayanti This Jain festival marks the birth of Mahavira, the founder of Jainism.

Ramanavami Hindu temples all over India celebrate the birth of Rama on this day. In the week leading up to Ramanavami, the *Ramayana* is widely read and performed.

Easter This Christian holiday marking the crucifixion and resurrection of Christ is most festive on Good Friday.

Vaishaka (Apr/May)

Muharram This 10 day Muslim festival commemorates the martyrdom of Mohammed's grandson, Imam Hussain (6 April 2000, 26 March 2001 and 15 March 2002).

Jyaistha (May/Jun)

Buddha Jayanti This 'triple blessed festival' falls on the full moon and celebrates Buddha's birth, enlightenment and attainment of nirvana. Processions of monks carrying sacred scriptures pass through the streets of Gangtok (Sikkim) and other towns.

Milad-un-Nabi This Muslim festival celebrates the birth of Mohammed (15 June 2000, 4 June 2001 and 25 May 2002).

Asadha (Jun/Jul)

Rath Yatra (Car Festival) Hindu Jagannath's great temple chariot makes its stately journey from his temple in Puri, Orissa, during this festival. Similar but far more grandiose festivals take place in other locations, particularly in the Dravidian south. Jagannath is one of Krishna's names, and the Puri procession celebrates his journey to Mathura to visit his aunt for a week! The images of his brother (Balarama) and sister (Subhadra) are also carried in the parade.

Sravana (Jul/Aug)

Naag Panchami This Hindu festival is dedicated to Ananta, the serpent upon whose coils Vishnu rested between universes. Offerings are made to snake images, and snake charmers do a roaring trade. Snakes are supposed to have power over the monsoon rainfall and keep evil from homes.

Raksha Bandhan (Narial Purnima) On the full-moon day girls fix amulets known as *rakhis* to their brothers' wrists to protect them in the coming year. The brothers reciprocate with gifts. Some people also worship the Vedic sea-god deity Varuna on this day.

Bhadra (Aug/Sep)

Independence Day This public holiday on 15 August celebrates the anniversary of India's independence from the UK in 1947. The prime minister delivers an address from the ramparts of Delhi's Red Fort.

Drukpa Teshi This festival celebrates the first teaching given by the Buddha. It is held on the fourth day of Bhadra.

Ganesh Chaturthi This festival, held on the fourth day of Bhadra, is dedicated to Ganesh. It is widely celebrated all over India, but with particular enthusiasm in Maharashtra. In every village, shrines are erected and a clay Ganesh idol is installed. Firecrackers explode at all hours, and each family buys a clay idol of Ganesh. On the day of the festival the idol is brought into the house, where it is kept and worshipped for a specified period before being ceremoniously immersed in a river, tank or the sea. As Ganesh is the god of wisdom and prosperity, Ganesh Chaturthi is considered to be the most auspicious day of the year. It is considered unlucky to look at the moon on this day.

Janmashtami The anniversary of Krishna's birth is celebrated with happy abandon in tune with Krishna's own mischievous moods. Although it is a national holiday, Agra, Bombay and Mathura (his birthplace) are the main centres of celebration. Devotees fast all day until midnight.

Shravan Purnima On this day of fasting, high-caste Hindus replace the sacred thread which they always wear looped over their left shoulder.

Asvina (Sep/Oct)

Dussehra The most popular of all festivals takes place over 10 days, beginning on the first day of Asvina. It celebrates Durga's victory over the buffalo-headed demon Mahishasura. In many places it culminates with the burning of huge images of the demon king Ravana and his accomplices, symbolic of the triumph of good over evil. In Delhi it is known as Ram Lila (Life story of Rama), with fireworks and re-enactments of the *Ramayana*, while in Mysore and Ahmedabad there are great processions. In West Bengal the festival is known as Durga Puja and in Gujarat it's Navratri (Festival of Nine Nights). In Kullu, in the north, the festival takes place a little later than elsewhere.

Gandhi Jayanti This public holiday is a solemn celebration of Gandhi's birthday on 2 October with prayer meetings at the Raj Ghat in Delhi where he was cremated.

Kartika (Oct/Nov)

Diwali (Deepavali) This is the happiest festival of the Hindu calendar, celebrated on the 15th day of Kartika. At night, countless oil lamps are lit to show Rama the way home from his period of exile. Today, the festival is also dedicated to Lakshmi (particularly in Mumbai) and to Kali in Calcutta. In all, the festival lasts five days. On the first day, houses are thoroughly cleaned and doorsteps are decorated with intricate *rangolis* (chalk designs). Day two is dedicated to Krishna's victory over Narakasura, a legendary tyrant. In the south on this day, a pre-dawn oil bath is followed by the donning of new clothes. Day three is spent in worshipping Lakshmi, the goddess of fortune. Traditionally, this is the beginning of the new financial year for companies. Day four commemorates the visit of the friendly demon Bali whom Vishnu put in his place. On the fifth day men visit their sisters to have a tika put on their forehead.

Diwali has also become the Festival of Sweets. Giving sweets has become as much a part of the tradition as the lighting of oil lamps and firecrackers. It is also celebrated by the Jains as their New Year's Day.

Govardhana Puja A Hindu festival dedicated to that holiest of animals, the cow.

Aghan (Nov/Dec)

Nanak Jayanti Celebration of the birthday of Guru Nanak, the founder of the Sikh religion.

Pausa (Dec/Jan)

Christmas Day The anniversary of the birth of Christ is an Indian public holiday.

Id-ul-Fitr This Muslim festival celebrates the end of Ramadan, the Muslim month of fasting which generally falls between December and January (8 January 2000, 27th December 2000, 16 December 2001 and 6 December 2002).

Magha (Jan/Feb)

Republic Day This public holiday on 26 January celebrates the anniversary of India's establishment as a republic in 1950; there are activities in all state capitals but most spectacularly in Delhi, where there is an enormously colourful military parade. As part of the same celebration, three days later a *Beating of the Retreat* ceremony takes place outside Rashtrapati Bhavan, the residence of the Indian president, in Delhi.

Pongal This Tamil festival marks the end of the harvest season. It is observed on the first day of the Tamil month of Thai, which is in the middle of January. The festivities last four days and include such activities as the boiling-over of a pot of *pongal* (a mixture of rice, sugar, dhal and milk), symbolic of prosperity and abundance. On the third day, cattle are washed, decorated and even painted, and then fed the pongal. In Andhra Pradesh the festival is known as *Makar Sankranti*.

Vasant Panchami It is traditional to dress in yellow to celebrate this Hindu spring festival, held on the 5th day of Magha. In some places, especially West Bengal, Saraswati, the goddess of learning, is honoured. Books, musical instruments and other objects related to the arts and scholarship are placed in front of the goddess to receive her blessing.

Phalguna (Feb/Mar)

Holi This is one of the most exuberant Hindu festivals, with people marking the end of winter by throwing coloured water and *gulal* (powder) at one another. In tourist places it might be seen as an opportunity to take liberties with foreigners; don't wear good clothes on this day, and be ready to duck. On the night before Holi, bonfires are built to symbolise the destruction of the evil demon Holika. It's mainly a northern festival; there is no real winter to end in the south so, it is as not widespread there. In Maharashtra, the festival is known as Rangapanchami and is celebrated with dancing and singing.

Shivaratri This day of Hindu fasting is dedicated to Shiva, who danced the *tandava* on this day. Temple processions are followed by the chanting of mantras and anointing of linga.

Id-ul-Zuhara This Muslim festival commemorates Abraham's attempt to sacrifice his son (8 March 2000, 25 February 2001, and 14 February 2002).

ACTIVITIES

There are plenty of activities for the adventurous and not-so-adventurous in India. The following list provides an overview of possibilities; for more information see the regional chapters.

Camel Safaris

It seems just about everyone in Rajasthan is offering camel safaris these days. An old favourite is in the environs of Jaisalmer, in western Rajasthan, where it's possible to

---

Warning

! While India has some world-class adventure activities on offer – and there are plenty of good, reputable and trustworthy operators around – it's worth noting that the level of experience and equipment available is not always up to scratch! When undertaking potentially dangerous sports and activities in India, whether it be paragliding in Himachal Pradesh or diving in Lakshadweep, you should always exercise good judgement (much the same as you would at home) and carefully scrutinise operators before committing yourself to their operation.

Over the years Lonely Planet has received numerous reports of dodgy operators taking naive tourists into dangerous situations, often resulting in serious injury and even death. Always check safety equipment before you set out and make sure it is included in the price quoted. If you're not comfortable with the operator's standards inform them; if they refuse to replace equipment or improve their standards refuse to use them and file a report with the local tourism authorities.

Once you have found an operator you are satisfied with, ensure you have adequate insurance should something go wrong; many travel insurance policies won't cover dangerous activities, including trekking!

The same common sense rules apply when swimming, Indian beaches can have dangerous rips and currents and many people drown on them each year. Some of the more popular beach destinations may have lifeguards or signs warning of dangers but many do not. Exercise caution and always check locally before swimming anywhere in the sea.

take a safari lasting from one day up to a week or more. There are other operators in Pushkar, Shekhawati and Bikaner.

Cycling & Motorcycling

There are few organised tours but it's not difficult or expensive to organise things for yourself. See the Bicycle and Motorcycle sections in the Getting Around chapter.

Diving

There are dive schools in Goa, Lakshadweep and the Andaman Islands (see the Responsible Diving boxed text earlier in this chapter).

Looking for Mr Good Guide

Some walks around the hills are no more than a two or three hour stroll and can be completed without a guide. Other walks are more difficult and can take a full day or even several days. These walks require experience as well as good local knowledge and are best undertaken with the help of a professional guide. The problem is, how do you know a good guide when you see one? There is no easy answer to this question. Some places in India are full of touts claiming to be professional guides. Some who offer themselves as guides clearly are highly professional and will make your experience worthwhile. Others may have little knowledge and will take you for a ride rather than a walk.

Have a firm idea of the type of walk you want to do as well as your capability. Are you looking for something easy or strenuous? Do you want to return before nightfall or are you looking to do a two or three day hike?

Seek specific recommendations from other travellers, and if you are engaged in negotiations with a potential guide don't be shy to ask the following questions:

- Do you have any written testimonials? (These of course are easy to fabricate but they can give you a sense of who you may be talking with.)
- Can you give us an idea of the route we'll take, including the distances, grades and the type of terrain involved?
- Can you identify any potential obstacles we may encounter: river crossings, wild animals, etc?
- If we are walking for more than a day, how many hours a day will we need to walk to complete the trek?
- If we are trekking into tribal areas do you speak the language? Know the customs?
- What time can we expect to return?
- Do you have a torch (flashlight) and first aid equipment? (Trekkers should always have their own but a good guide will also have some.)
- If the guide (or the booking company) is going to supply camping equipment, can we inspect the equipment before we agree to the deal?
- If the trek includes a cook, what's on the menu and who supplies the food?
- Will there be places along the way to replenish drinking water?
- Is the price quoted per person, group, day, hour or some combination of these? Does it include meals?

It is better to travel with even a small group rather than setting out alone with a guide, and of course you should ensure that you have adequate clothing (including footwear) for variable weather. It's also a good idea if you are taking a two or three day trek to let someone know where you will be and when you expect to return.

Horse Riding & Polo

Horses are available in many tourist areas, particularly the hill stations and Himalaya. There are a few specialist operators in Rajasthan who offer horse safaris. You can get polo lessons at the Dundlod Fort hotel in the tiny village of Dundlod at Shekhawati, Rajasthan.

Kayaking & River Rafting

The Mountaineering Institute & Allied Sports in Manali, Himachal Pradesh can arrange two-week kayaking trips on the Beas River in October and November.

River rafting expeditions are possible on the Beas River in Himachal Pradesh, on the Ganges and its tributaries in Uttarakhand (northern Uttar Pradesh), on the Indus and Zanskar rivers in Ladakh and Zanskar, and on the Teesta River in the West Bengal hills. Travel agencies in Gangtok (Sikkim) can also organise trips on the Teesta.

Mountaineering

Mountaineering expeditions interested in climbing peaks over 6000m need to obtain clearance from the Indian Mountaineering Foundation (IMF; ☎ 011-671211, fax 688 3412), Benito Juarez Rd, Anand Niketan, New Delhi 110021.

Gurus & Ashrams

Travellers who come to India on a spiritual quest are many and varied and India offers an equally varied array of gurus and ashrams. The word guru means dispeller of darkness or heavy with wisdom. An ashram is established when a guru stays in one place and disciples congregate round them. Any place of striving can be called an ashram, be it a commercial complex or someone's home. Some are more reputable than others; if possible attend one where the guru resides. Many ashrams have codes of conduct; most are vegetarian. On some you will be requested to wear white; others aren't so fussy.

Most ashrams don't require notice of your arrival, but if you are unsure, check in advance. Talk to locals and other travellers to see which ashram might best suit you. Be aware that gurus often move from place to place without much notice, so check first to avoid disappointment.

The atmosphere surrounding the ashram can have a profound and deeply moving effect on visitors. While this can be a rewarding experience, you should exercise common sense and discernment.

movement	location
Buddhism	Bodhghaya, Bihar
Krishna Consciousness	Vrindavan, Uttar Pradesh
	Krishnamurti Foundation Chennai, Tamil Nadu
Ma Maritanandamayi	Amritapuri, Kerala
Osho	Pune, Maharashtra
Raja Yoga	Mt Abu, Rajasthan
Ramakrishna	Calcutta, West Bengal
Ramana Maharishi	Tiruvannamalai, Tamil Nadu
Sai Baba	Puttaparthi, Andhra Pradesh
Sri Aurobindo	Pondicherry, Tamil Nadu
Theosophical Society	Chennai, Tamil Nadu
Tibetan Buddhism	Dharamsala, Himachal Pradesh
Various	Rishikesh, Uttar Pradesh

For information on mountaineering expeditions to less lofty heights in Uttar Pradesh, contact the Trekking & Mountaineering Division (☎ 01364-32648), Garhwal Mandal Vikas Nigam (GMVN), Lakshman Jhula Rd, Muni ki Reti, Rishikesh. Trekking and mountaineering equipment can be hired here. (See the Responsible Trekking boxed text earlier in this chapter.)

Skiing

India's premier ski resort is at Auli, near Joshimath in northern Uttar Pradesh. UP Tourism offers very competitive ski packages, which include ski hire, tows, lessons and accommodation. The Auli ski season extends from the beginning of January to the end of March.

There are also less developed resorts in Himachal Pradesh, at Solang Nullah, north of Manali, and near Shimla, at Kufri and Narkanda.

Trekking

With some of the highest mountains in the world, it's hardly surprising that India has some spectacular trekking regions, although the trekking industry is not as developed as it is in Nepal. The main areas are Ladakh, Himachal Pradesh, northern Uttar Pradesh, the Darjeeling area (West Bengal) and Sikkim. (See Lonely Planet's *Trekking in the Indian Himalaya* and the Responsible Trekking boxed text earlier in this chapter for more details.)

Wildlife Safaris

Elephant-back safaris are available at the larger wildlife sanctuaries and are highly recommended. They are usually very good value and the best way to get close to other animals.

Adventure Tour Operators

Local tour operators are listed in regional chapters. The following trek and tour outfits are all based in Delhi:

Amber Tours Pty Ltd
(☎ 011-331 2773, fax 331 2984) Flat 2, Dwarka Sadan, C-42 Connaught Place

– offers yoga and mystic tours, river rafting, trekking, fishing for mahseer, and private jet or helicopter flights over the Himalaya.
Himalayan River Runners
(☎ 011-615736) 188A Jor Bagh – offers a range of rafting expeditions in the western Himalaya.
Mercury Himalayan Explorations
(☎ 011-312008) Jeevan Tara Bldg, Parliament St – specialises in organised treks in the western Himalaya.
Shikhar Travels
(☎ 011-331 2444, fax 332 3660) S209 Competent House, 14 Middle Circle, Connaught Circus – specialises in trekking and mountaineering tours and can also organise mountaineering expeditions for beginners.
World Expeditions
(☎ 011-698 3358, fax 698 3357) Ground floor, MG Bhawan-1, 7 Local Shopping Centre, Madangir – has operated world-class Himalayan tours and treks since 1975.

COURSES

There are a wide range of courses available in India – the following is an overview. More details can be found in the regional chapters.

Language

The Landour Language School, near Mussoorie in northern Uttar Pradesh, offers three month beginners' courses in Hindi, as well as more advanced courses. At McLeod Ganj it's possible to learn Tibetan either at the Library of Tibetan Works & Archives or from private teachers. In Darjeeling, beginners' courses in Tibetan are available at the Manjushree Centre of Tibetan Culture.

Meditation, Yoga & Philosophy

Courses in aspects of Tibetan Buddhism and culture are offered in McLeod Ganj, Darjeeling, Choglamsar (near Leh) and Leh. Indian Hinayana Buddhism can also be studied in McLeod Ganj and Gaya.

Rishikesh has the biggest concentration of ashrams and yoga centres, although of course there are hundreds more places where you can learn meditation and philosophy including Karnataka, Kerala and Maharashtra. You can learn meditation or undertake a retreat at Bodhgaya in Bihar.

Cooking

There is a two week food tour and cooking course in Calcutta. During the course you get to see the city, sample Bengali culinary delights in some of the city's finest restaurants and learn to cook under the tutelage of local Bengali women. Contact Kali Travel Home Contacts (☎/fax 33-558 7980), 22/77 Raja Manindra Rd, Calcutta.

Dance, Art & Traditional Medicine

You can learn traditional Tibetan woodcarving at the Tibetan Refugee Self-Help Centre in Darjeeling. Contact the head office (☎ 0354-52346) at 65 Gandhi Rd. Kerala and Tamil Nadu are the places to learn traditional dance, traditional martial art and ayurvedic medicine in Kerala. The Kuchipudi Art Academy (☎ 044-493 7260), 105 Greenways Rd, Chennai, Tamil Nadu offers free teaching and accommodation to serious students of this traditional art form.

VOLUNTARY WORK

Numerous charities and international aid agencies have branches in India and, although they're mostly staffed by locals, there are some opportunities for foreigners. Though it may be possible to find temporary volunteer work when you are in India, you'll probably be of more use to the charity concerned if you write in advance and, if you're needed, if you stay for long enough to be of help. A week on a hospital ward may go a little way towards salving your own conscience, but you may actually do not much more than get in the way of the people who work there long term.

Some areas of voluntary work seem to be more attractive to volunteers than others. One traveller commented that there was no difficulty getting foreign volunteers to help with the babies in the orphanage where he was working but few came forward to work with the severely mentally disabled adults.

Overseas Aid Agencies

For information on specific charities in India, contact the main branches in your own country. For long-term posts, the following organisations may be able to help or offer advice and further contacts:

Australian Volunteers Abroad: Overseas Service Bureau Programme
(☎ 03-9279 1788, fax 9416 1619) PO Box 350, Fitzroy, VIC 3065, Australia
Coordinating Committee for International Voluntary Service
(☎ 01 45 68 27 31) c/o UNESCO, 1 rue Miollis, F-75015 Paris, France
Council of International Programs (CIP)
(☎ 703-527 1160) 1101 Wilson Blvd Ste 1708, Arlington VA 22209, USA
International Voluntary Service (IVS)
(☎ 0131-226 6722) St John's Church Centre, Edinburgh EH2 4BJ, UK
Peace Corps of the USA
(☎ 202-606 3970, fax 606 3110) 1990 K St NW, Washington, DC 20526, USA
Voluntary Service Overseas (VSO)
(☎ 020-8780 2266, fax 780 1326) 317 Putney Bridge Rd, London SW15 2PN, UK

Aid Programs in India

Following are some of the programs operating in India which may have opportunities for volunteers.

Mumbai Concern India Foundation (CIF; ☎ 022-202 9707, email concern@bom4 .vsnl.net.in), Ador House, 3rd floor, 6 K Dubash Marg, Kala Ghoda, Mumbai 400001, is a charitable trust that supports development-oriented organisations working with vulnerable members of the community. It doesn't engage in fieldwork; it's specialty is networking. It is happy to field requests from travellers who wish to offer their time and will try to match your skills or interests with particular projects.

Child Relief and You or CRY (☎ 022-306651, email crymum@bom3.vsnl.net.in), 189A Anand Estate, Sane Guruji Marg, is an independent trust organising fundraising for more than 300 projects India-wide, including a dozen projects in Mumbai helping deprived children.

Himachal Pradesh Long-term visitors at McLeod Ganj are always welcome to teach

English to newly arrived Tibetan refugees. Check at the Library of Tibetan Works & Archives in Gangchen Kyishong, near McLeod Ganj, as well as *Contact* magazine.

Ladakh Mahabodhi International Meditation Centre (PO Box 22, Leh, Ladakh, 194101 Jammu & Kashmir) operates a residential school for poor children and accepts volunteers to assist with teaching and secretarial work. Contact the centre at the above address, or through its head office (☎ 0812-260684, fax 260292) at 14 Kalidas Rd, Gandhinagar, Bangalore 560009.

If you have a particular interest in Ladakh and have some educational or agricultural experience, there are two organisations in Leh that may be able to use your experience and enthusiasm: the Ladakh Ecological Development Group (LEDeG), Leh, Ladakh, 194101 (☎ 01982-3746; fax 2484); and the Student's Educational & Cultural Movement of Ladakh or SECMOL (☎ 01982-3676), PO Box 4, Leh, Ladakh 194101.

Rajasthan SOS Worldwide runs over 30 programs across India. The society looks after orphaned, destitute and abandoned children, who are cared for by unmarried women, abandoned wives and widows. In Jaipur, SOS has a fine garden-surrounded property, and cares for more than 150 children and young adults. Volunteers are welcome at the centre to teach English, help the children with their homework and simply to join in their games. For more information contact SOS Children's Village (☎ 0141-202393; fax 200140), opposite Pital Factory, Jhotwara Rd, Jaipur 302016.

The Urmul Trust provides primary health care and education to the people of the remote villages in Rajasthan; raises awareness among the women of the desert of their rights and privileges in society; and promotes the handicrafts of rural artisans with profits going directly to artisans. There is volunteer work available in social welfare, teaching English, health care, and other projects. Even if you don't have skills in these areas, Urmul may have positions in implementation and overseeing of projects. Contact the secretary at the Urmul Trust (☎/fax 0151-523093), inside Urmul Dairy, Ganganagar Rd, Bikaner (next to the bus terminal).

Les Amis du Shekhawati is one of a number of charities whose aim is to safeguard and preserve India's crumbling architectural heritage – in this case the havelis and paintings of the Shekhawati region in Rajasthan. Ramesh Jangid is the president of the association. He welcomes volunteers keen to preserve the paintings of Shekhawati and can be contacted at the Ramesh Jangid's Tourist Pension (☎ 01594-24060, fax 24061) in Nawalgarh.

Help in Suffering (☎ 0141-550203, fax 548044), an animal hospital based in Jaipur, is doing excellent work. It's funded by the World Society for the Protection of Animals (WSPA) and Animaux Secours, Arthaz, France. Qualified vets interested in volunteering should write to: Help in Suffering, Maharani Farm, Durgapura, Jaipur, Rajasthan 302018.

West Bengal Mother Teresa's Missionaries of Charity headquarters, the 'Mother House', is at 54A Lower Circular Rd in Calcutta. For information about volunteering, contact the London branch: International Committee of Co-Workers (☎ 020-8574 1892), Missionaries of Charity, 41 Villiers Rd, Southall, Middlesex, UK.

Dr Graham's Homes & School (☎ 033-297211), Berkmyre Hostel, 4 Middleton Rd, Calcutta 700071) comprises a school for 1200 students, a farm, workshops, hospital, bakery and children's homes. Teachers are welcome to volunteer as well as nurses, child-care workers, carpenters, engineers, mechanics, and people with agricultural skills. Board and lodging is provided but volunteers need to make a minimum six month commitment.

In Darjeeling, the Nepali Girls' Social Service Centre may be able to offer voluntary work on an informal basis to travellers interested in teaching English, art or music. People interested in teaching English to

Tibetan refugees should contact the Tibetan Refugee Self-Help Centre in Darjeeling.

Also in Darjeeling, the Tibetan Self-Help Centre (☎ 0354-52346, 65 Gandhi Rd) has openings for volunteer teachers, medical staff, geriatric and child-care workers.

Hayden Hall is a Christian-based organisation that focuses on grass-roots programs. Volunteers should be prepared to work for at least six months. Contact Hayden Hall (email hayden@cal.vsnl.net.in) at 42 Laden La Rd, Darjeeling 734101.

St Alphonsus Social & Agricultural Centre or SASAC (☎ 0354-42059), Post Office Tung, District of Darjeeling, West Bengal, is a self-help organisation run by a Canadian Jesuit Priest. Improved crop and livestock management and a reduction of wood usage have been among the program's successes. Volunteers are welcome. You can also make a donation or purchase a tree for planting.

ACCOMMODATION

India has a very wide range of accommodation possibilities beyond straightforward hotels. Some hotels operate on a 24 hour system (ie, your time starts when you check in). Others have noon, or earlier, check-out times. It pays to check first. Some hotels request an upfront fee based on your estimated length of stay. If your expenses don't match the prepaid amount you will receive a refund at the time of checkout. If you have a credit card, you may be asked to sign a blank impression of your card which will be destroyed when you pay your bill at the end of your stay. The hotel may be acting with honest intent but such practises should not be encouraged. If they do insist on an impression of your card you should refuse to sign it. If they insist then write in an amount that will be less than your estimated expenditure.

Some of the very cheap, very basic places won't take foreigners because of the hassle of the foreign registration C forms (these have to be submitted to the local police station within 24 hours of the foreigner checking in).

Youth Hostels

Indian youth hostels (HI – Hostelling International) are generally very cheap and sometimes in excellent condition with superb facilities. They are, however, often some distance from the town centres. You are not usually required to be a YHA (HI) member (as in other countries) to use the hostels, although your YHA/HI card will generally get you a lower rate. The charge is typically Rs 15 for members, Rs 30 for nonmembers. Nor do the usual rules about arrival and departure times, lights-out or not using the hostel during the day apply.

There are also some state government youth hostels in main cities but they tend to be very badly run.

Government Accommodation

Back in the days of the British Raj, a whole string of government-run accommodation units were set up with labels like Rest Houses, Dak Bungalows, Circuit Houses, PWD (Public Works Department) Bungalows, Forest Rest Houses and so on. Today most of these are reserved for government officials, although in some places they may still be available for tourists, if there is room. In an approximate pecking order the Dak Bungalows are the most basic; they often have no electricity, the bare essential equipment and are in out-of-the-way places. Rest Houses are next up and at the top of the tree comes the Circuit Houses, which are strictly for travelling VIPs.

Tourist Bungalows

Usually run by the state government, tourist bungalows often serve as replacements for the older government-run accommodation. They are generally excellent value, although their facilities and level of service vary enormously.

They often have dorm beds as well as rooms. The rooms have a fan, two beds and bathroom; air-con rooms are often also available. Generally there's a restaurant or 'dining hall' and often a bar. The local branch of the state government tourist office is often at the tourist bungalow.

Almost every state has some towns where the tourist bungalow is definitely the best place to stay. Their biggest drawback is that, in common with state-run companies virtually anywhere, the staff may be less than 100% motivated – in some cases they are downright lazy and rude – and maintenance is not what it might be.

In tourist bungalows, as in many other government-run institutions in India, such as the railways you will find a curiously Indian institution: the 'complaints book'. In this you can write your complaints and periodically someone higher up the chain of command comes along, reads the terrible tales and the tourist bungalow manager gets his knuckles rapped. In disputes or other arguments, calling for the complaints book is the angry customer's best weapon; it's the one thing which minions seem to be genuinely afraid of. In many places the complaints book can provide interesting and amusing reading.

Railway Retiring Rooms

These are just like regular hotels or dormitories except they are at the train stations. To stay here you are generally supposed to have a railway ticket or Indrail Pass. The rooms are, of course, extremely convenient if you have an early train departure, although they can be noisy if it is a busy station. They are often very cheap and in some places they are also excellent value. Some stations have retiring rooms of definite Raj pretensions, with huge rooms and enough furniture to do up a flat or apartment back home. They are usually excellent value, if a little institutional in feel, and are let on a 24 hour basis. The main problem is getting a bed, as they are very popular and often full.

Railway Waiting Rooms

For emergency accommodation when all else fails or when you just need a few hours rest before your train departs at 2 am, waiting rooms are a free place to rest your weary head. The trick is to rest it in the (usually empty) 1st class waiting room and not the crowded 2nd class one. Officially

you need a 1st class ticket to be allowed to use the 1st class room and its superior facilities. In practice, luck, a 2nd class Indrail Pass or simply your foreign appearance may work. In some places your ticket will be checked.

Cheap Hotels

There are cheap hotels all over India, ranging from filthy, uninhabitable dives (but with prices at rock bottom) up to quite reasonable places in both standards and prices. Ceiling fans, mosquito nets on the beds, private toilets and bathrooms are all possibilities, even in doubles which cost Rs 200 or less per night.

Throughout India, hotels are defined as 'western' or 'Indian'. The differentiation is basically meaningless, although expensive hotels are always western, cheap ones Indian. 'Indian' hotels will be more simply and economically furnished but the acid test is the toilet. Western hotels have a sit-up-style toilet; Indian ones usually (but not always) have the traditional Asian squat style. You can find modern, well-equipped, clean places with Indian toilets and dirty, dismal dumps with western toilets. Some places even have the weird hybrid toilet, which is basically a western toilet with foot pads on the edge of the bowl.

Although prices are generally quoted in this book for singles and doubles, most hotels will put an extra bed in a room to make a triple for about an extra 25%. In some smaller hotels it's often possible to bargain a little if you really want to. On the other hand these places will often put their prices up if there's a shortage of accommodation.

Many hotels, and not only the cheap ones, operate on a 24 hour system. This can be convenient if you check in at 8 pm, as it gives you until 8 pm the following day to check out. Conversely, if you arrive at 8 am one day it can be a nuisance to have to be on the streets again by 8 am the next day. There are, however, considerable regional variations. Some hotels maintain a noon checkout; hill stations often operate on a 9 am (or even 7 am!) checkout. Make sure you know the checkout time at your hotel. Some hotels will offer a half-day rate if you want to stay a few extra hours.

Expensive Hotels

You won't find 'international standard' hotels throughout India. The big, air-con, swimming-pool places are generally confined to the major tourist centres and the large cities. There are a number of big hotel chains in India. The Taj Group has some of India's flashiest hotels, including the luxurious Taj Mahal Intercontinental in Mumbai, the romantic Rambagh Palace in Jaipur and the Lake Palace in Udaipur. Other interesting hotels are the Taj Coromandel in Chennai, the Fort Aguada Beach Resort in Goa and the Malabar Hotel in Kochi (Cochin). The Oberoi chain is as well known outside India as within. Clarks is a small chain with popular hotels in Varanasi and Agra, among other places. Other hotel chains include Welcomgroup (affiliated with Sheraton), Ritz, Casino, and the Air India-associated Centaur hotels.

In addition, there is the government-operated ITDC group which usually append the name 'Ashok' to their hotels. There's an Ashok hotel in virtually every town in India, so that test isn't foolproof, but the ITDC places include a number of smaller (but higher-standard) units in places like Sanchi or Konark where accommodation possibilities are limited. The ITDC has been under attack in India for some time about its overall inefficient operation, financial losses and poor standards. Privatisation was mooted at one stage as a way of raising capital and improving service, but this is still yet to happen and standards remain unchanged.

Most expensive hotels operate on a noon checkout basis.

You may be able to negotiate a discount on air-con rooms in December and January since air-con often isn't necessary then.

Homestays

Staying with an Indian family can be a real education. It's a change from dealing strictly with tourist-oriented people, and the differences and curiosities of everyday Indian life can be very interesting.

Homestay accommodation is organised on an official basis in Rajasthan. The cost is anything from Rs 50 upwards, depending on the level of facilities offered. The Rajasthan Tourism Development Corporation (RTDC) administers the scheme and main city offices have comprehensive lists of families offering this service. It's known as the Paying Guest House Scheme. Chennai and Mumbai have similar schemes, as do Calcutta and Chennai.

Other Possibilities

There are YMCAs and YWCAs in many of the big cities – some of these are modern, well equipped and cost about the same as a mid-range hotel (but are still good value). There are also a few Salvation Army Hostels – in particular in Mumbai, Calcutta and Chennai. There are a few camping places around India, but travellers with their own vehicles can almost always find hotels with gardens where they can park and camp.

Free accommodation is available at some Sikh *gurdwaras* (temples) where there is a tradition of hospitality to visitors. It can be interesting to try one, but please don't abuse this hospitality and spoil it for others.

At many pilgrimage sites there are *dharamsalas* and *choultries*, places which offer accommodation to pilgrims, and travellers are often welcome to use these. This particularly applies at isolated sites such as Ranakpur in Rajasthan. Jain dharamsalas usually don't allow leather articles inside.

Taxes & Service Charges

Most state governments impose a variety of taxes on hotel accommodation (and restaurants). At most rock-bottom hotels you won't have to pay any taxes. Once you get into the top end of budget places, and certainly for mid-range accommodation, you will have to pay something, and top-end places can really load on the tax. The tax varies from state to state – these are detailed in the regional chapters.

Another common tax, in addition to the above, is a service charge which is pegged at 10%. In some hotels, this is only levied on food, room service and use of telephones, not on the accommodation costs. At others, it's levied on the total bill. If you're trying to keep costs down, don't sign up meals or room service to your room bill and keep telephone use to a minimum if you know that a service charge is levied on the total bill.

Rates quoted in this book are the basic rate only unless otherwise indicated. Taxes and service charges are extra.

Seasonal Variations
In popular tourist places (hill stations, beaches and the Delhi-Agra-Rajasthan triangle), hoteliers raise their high season prices by two to three times the low-season price.

The definition of the high and low seasons obviously varies depending on location. For the beaches and the Delhi-Agra-Rajasthan triangle it's basically a month before and two months after Christmas. In the hill stations and Kashmir, it's usually April to July when the lowlands are unbearably hot. In some locations and at some hotels, there are even higher rates for the brief Christmas/New Year period, or over major festivals such as Diwali and Dussehra.

Conversely, in the low season(s), prices at even normally expensive hotels can be surprisingly reasonable.

Touts
Hordes of accommodation touts operate in many towns in India – Agra, Jaipur and Varanasi in particular – and at any international airport terminal. Very often they are the *rickshaw-wallahs* who meet you at the bus or train station. The technique is simple – they take you to hotel A and rake off a commission for taking you there rather than to hotel B. The problem with this procedure is that you may well end up not at the place you want to go to but at the place that pays the best commission. Some very good cheap hotels simply refuse to pay the touts and you'll then hear lots of stories about the hotel you want

being 'full', 'closed for repairs', 'no good any more' or even 'flooded'. Nine chances out of 10 they will be just that – stories.

Think twice before agreeing to stay in a hotel recommended by touts or rickshaw-wallahs, as some travellers have warned that they stayed in such hotels only to be subsequently badgered to take part in rip-off insurance and import schemes or to accept the sightseeing services of a particular taxi or rickshaw driver.

Touts do have a use though – if you arrive in a town when some big festival is on, or during peak season, finding a place to stay can be very difficult. Hop in a rickshaw, tell the driver in what price range you want a hotel, and off you go. The driver will know which places have rooms available and unless the search is a long one you shouldn't have to pay the driver too much. Remember that he will be getting a commission from the hotel too.

FOOD
Breads & Grains
Rice is, of course, the basic Indian staple, but although it is eaten throughout the country, it's all-important only in the south. The best Indian rice, it is generally agreed, is found in the north where Basmati rice grows in the Dehra Dun Valley. It has long grains, is yellowish and has a slightly sweetish or '*bas*' smell. In the north (where wheat is the staple) rice is supplemented by a whole range of breads known as *rotis* or *chapatis*. In the Punjab a roti is called *phulka*. Western-style white sliced bread is widely available, and it's generally pretty good.

Indian breads are varied but always delicious. Simplest is the chapati/roti, which is simply a mixture of flour and water cooked on a hotplate known as a *tawa*. Direct heat blows them up but how well that works depends on the gluten content of the wheat. Note that Hindus use their tawa concavely, Muslims convexly! A *paratha* is also cooked on the hotplate but ghee is used and the bread is rolled in a different way. There are also parathas that have been stuffed with peas or potato. Deep-fried bread which puffs up is known as a *puri* in the north and a *luchi* in the east. Bake the bread in a clay (tandoori) oven and you have *naan*. However you make them, Indian breads taste great. Use your chapati or paratha to mop or scoop up your curry.

Found all over India, but originating from the south, are *dosas*. These are basically paper-thin pancakes made from lentil and rice flour. Curried vegetables wrapped inside a dosa makes it a *masala dosa* – a terrific snack meal. An *idli* is a kind of south Indian rice dumpling, often served with a *dahin idli* (spicy curd sauce) or with spiced lentils and chutney; it is a popular breakfast dish in the south. *Papadams* are crispy deep-fried lentil-flour wafers often served with *thalis* or other meals. An *uttapam* is like a dosa.

Outside the Delhi Jama Masjid, you may see 'big' chapatis known as *rumali roti* (handkerchief bread).

Know Your Rice

Rice is a staple everywhere in India, in the south especially, where it is served with every meal. But rice isn't just rice. More than 200 varieties are grown in India, from the top-of-the range basmati to cheaper strains used for making rice flakes (poha or pawa) and rice flour. Rice is also very much a part of India's religious and cultural fabric. A new Hindu bride will kick over a small measure of rice as she crosses the threshold of her new home. By scattering the rice grains she brings good fortune with her. Roasted rice is tossed into the sacred fire by the bride and bridegroom during the marriage ceremony. And rice is showered upon wedding guests (much as rice is showered on newlyweds in the west). During the festival of otii bharan married women are presented with a handful of rice, a coconut and a length of fabric, to wish them a long, prosperous life. Rice (along with ghee, milk, curd and yoghurt, coconut, fruits and some vegetables) is considered a pure food, fit for religious feasts and for offering to the gods. It symbolises fertility and good fortune. Examples of Indian-grown rice include:

Basmati
This long-grained, fragrant rice cultivated mainly in the Himalayan foothills is considered the king of rice. Basmati improves with age; it can be kept up to 10 years given the right environment. The older it is, the fluffier (or less sticky) it is when cooked.

Patna
Also grown in north India, this long-grained, less translucent rice has a relatively mild, albeit pleasant, taste. Where basmati is used on special occasions, Patna rice is eaten on a daily basis. Because it is relatively inexpensive, it is also ground into flour.

Red Patna
This short-grained, red-husked rice is grown in central and west India and coastal regions. It is usually consumed locally, having been parboiled after harvesting to shorten its cooking time. It's nutty, chewy and very nutritious.

Ambemohar
This is a round-grained rice that's not usually available outside India. It's used in dishes where a fragrant rice such as basmati would also be suitable. While not in the same class as basmati, it's pleasant tasting, and a lot cheaper. It is therefore also used for making flour.

Curry & Spice

Believe it or not, there is no such thing as 'curry' in India. It's an English invention, an all-purpose term to cover the whole range of Indian food spicing. *Carhi*, incidentally, is a Gujarati dish, but never ask for it in Kumaon where it's a very rude word!

Although all Indian food is certainly not curry, this is the basis of Indian cuisine. Curry does not have to be hot enough to blow your head off, although it can if it's made that way. Curry most definitely is not something found in a packet of curry powder. Indian cooks have about 25 spices on their regular list and it is from these that they produce the curry flavour. Normally the spices are freshly ground in a mortar and pestle known as a *sil-vatta*. Spices are usually blended in certain combinations to produce *masalas* (mixes). *Garam masala* (hot mix), for example, is a combination of cloves, cinnamon, cardamom, coriander, cumin and peppercorns.

Popular spices include saffron, an expensive flavouring produced from the stamens of certain crocus flowers. This is used to give rice that yellow colouring and delicate fragrance. (It's an excellent buy in India, where a 1g packet costs around Rs 35 - you'll pay about 10 times more at home.) Turmeric also has a colouring property, acts as a preservative and has a distinctive smell and taste. Chillies are ground, dried or added whole to supply the heat. They come in red and green varieties but the green ones are the hottest. Ginger is supposed to be good for the digestion, while many masalas contain coriander because it is said to cool the body. Strongly aromatic cardamom is used in many desserts and in rich meat dishes. Other popular spices and flavourings include nutmeg, poppy seeds, caraway seeds, fenugreek, mace, garlic, cloves, bay leaves and curry leaves.

Basic Dishes

Curries can be vegetable, meat (usually chicken or lamb) or fish, and the all important spices will be fried in ghee (clarified butter) or vegetable oil to release their flavours and aromas. There are a number of dishes which aren't really curries but are close enough to them for western tastes. North or south, curries will be accompanied by rice, but in the north you can also choose from the range of breads.

aalu chhole – diced potatoes and spicy-sour chickpeas.
aalu dum – potato curry.
dhal – probably the most basic of Indian dishes. It is almost always there, whether as an accompaniment to a curry or as a very basic meal in itself with chapatis or rice. In the very small rural towns dhal and rice is just about all there is on the menu. The favourite dhal of Bengal and Gujarat is yellow *arhar*, whereas in Punjab it is *black urad*. The common green lentils are called *moong*; *rajmaa* (kidney beans) is the Heinz 57 variety of dhal!

dopiaza – literally means two onions and is a type of korma which uses onions at two stages in its preparation.
korma – rich, substantial dish prepared by braising (meat and vegetable). *Navratan korma* is a very tasty vegetable dish using nuts.
malai kofta – cheese-and-vegetable balls in a rich, cream-based sauce.
mattar paneer – peas and cheese in gravy.
palak paneer – spinach and cheese.
saag gosht – spinach and meat.
vindaloos – hot curry with vinegar marinade.
sambhar – a soup-like lentil and vegetable dish with a sour flavour

Vegetables include *paat gobi* (cabbage), *phuul gobi* (cauliflower), *baingan* (eggplant or brinjal) and *mattar* (peas).

Tandoori & Biryani

Tandoori food is a northern speciality and refers to the clay oven in which the food is cooked after first being marinated in a mixture of herbs and yoghurt. Tandoori chicken is a favourite. This food is not as hot as curry dishes and usually tastes terrific.

Biryani (again chicken is a popular biryani dish) is another northern Mughal dish. The meat is mixed with a deliciously flavoured, orange-coloured rice which is sometimes spiced with nuts or dried fruit. A Kashmiri biryani is basically fruit salad with rice.

A *pulao* is flavoured rice often with pulses and with or without meat. You will also find it in other Asian countries further west. Those who have the idea that Indian food is always curry and always fiery hot will be surprised by tandoori and biryani dishes.

Thalis

A thali is the all-purpose Indian dish. Although it is basically a product of South India, you will find restaurants serving thalis or 'plate meals' (veg or nonveg) all over India. Often the sign will simply announce 'Meals'. In addition, there are regional variations like the particularly sumptuous and sweet Gujarati thalis.

The name is taken from the 'thali' dish in which the meal is served. This consists of a metal plate with a number of small metal bowls known as *katoris* on it. Sometimes the small bowls will be replaced by simple indentations in the plate; in more basic places the 'plate' will be a big, fresh banana leaf. A thali consists of a variety of curry vegetable dishes, relishes, a couple of pappadams, puris or chapatis and a mountain of rice. A fancy thali may have a *pataa*, a rolled leaf stuffed with fruit and nuts. There'll probably be a bowl of curd and possibly even a small dessert or *paan*.

Thalis are consistently tasty and good food value, but they have two other unbeatable plus points for the budget traveller – they're cheap and they're usually 100% filling. Thalis can be as little as Rs 10 and will rarely cost much more than Rs 30 at the very most, though Gujarati thalis are the exception and you'll consistently be paying Rs 40 to Rs 50 for these at reasonable restaurants. Most are 100% filling because they're normally 'all you can eat'. When your plate starts to look empty they come round, add another mountain of rice and refill the katoris. Thalis are eaten with fingers, although

you may get a spoon for the curd or dhal. Always wash your hands before you eat one – a sink or other place to wash your hands is provided in a thali restaurant.

Regional Specialities

Rogan josh is straightforward lamb curry, always popular in the north and in Kashmir where it originated. *Gushtaba*, pounded and spiced meatballs cooked in a yoghurt sauce, is another Kashmiri speciality. Still in the north, *chicken makhanwala* is a rich dish cooked in a butter sauce.

Many coastal areas have excellent seafood, including Mumbai where the pomfret, a flounder-like fish, is popular; so is Bombay duck, which is not a duck at all but another fish dish. *Dhansaak* is a Parsi speciality found in Mumbai – lamb or chicken cooked with curried lentils and steamed rice. Further south, Goa has excellent fish and prawns; in Kerala, Kochi (Cochin) is famous for its prawns.

Another example of the central Asian influence on north Indian food is the popular kabab. You'll find them all across north India with a number of local variations and specialities. The two basic forms are *seekh* (skewered) or *shami* (wrapped). In Calcutta *kati kababs* are a local favourite. Another Bengali dish is *dahin maach* (curried fish in yoghurt sauce, flavoured with ginger and turmeric). Further south in Hyderabad you could try *haleen*, pounded wheat with a lightly spiced mutton gravy.

Lucknow is famous for its wide range of kababs and for *dum pukht* – the 'art' of steam pressure cooking, in which meat and vegetables are cooked in a sealed clay pot.

Side Dishes

Indian food generally has a number of side dishes to go with the main meal. Probably the most popular is *dahin* – curd or yoghurt. It has the useful ability of instantly cooling a fiery curry – either blend it into the curry or, if it's too late, you can administer it straight to your mouth. Curd is often used in the cooking of main meals, or as a dessert and also appears in the popular drink *lassi*.

Raita is another popular side dish consisting of curd mixed with cooked or raw vegetables, particularly cucumber (similar to Greek *tzatziki)* or tomato.

Sabzi is curried vegetables, and *baingan bharta* is a puréed eggplant dish. *Mulligatawny* is a soup-like dish which is really just a milder, more liquid curry. It's a dish adopted into the English menu by the Raj. Chutney is pickled fruit or vegetables and is the standard relish for a curry.

Street Food

One kind of Indian food that's impossible to copy at home is street food. From mouthwatering masala dosas made on the train platform in Mysore, to the fiery little vegetable curry served with a few puris in its own 'takeaway' container of a banana leaf and some twigs, the range of delicious foods that are whipped up out in the open and meant for immediate consumption is really amazing.

Vendors squat beside their karais (woklike vessels) full of bubbling oil, or tawas (hotplates), while the crowds jostle around and shout out their order for their bhajas (deep-fried crispy veg cakes), beguni (eggplant slices dipped in a besan (chickpea flour) batter and deep fried) or aloo bonda (round balls of spiced mashed potatoes covered in the same batter and deep fried). Lucknow loves its aloo tikki (flat potato cake with a lentil stuffing, served with a sweet & sour tamarind sauce and yoghurt), and some say bhelpuri is Mumbai's favourite snack: look out for the colourful wagons on Chowpatty Beach and join the queues for this irresistible nibble made from crunchy dhal and chickpeas, spices, chutney, potatoes, onions, mint, coriander, tomatoes and yoghurt.

The further north you go, the more you find roadside set-ups grilling lamb kebabs over hot coals, and serving them wrapped with yoghurt in warm bread. The flavour of *pakoras* (battered and deep fried veg), *samosas* (pastry triangle stuffed with spiced veg or meat) and bhajas, fresh from the boiling ghee of a vendor's karai, is so much better than in restaurants back home, that you might find yourself pining for them long after you've forgotten exactly how astonishing the Taj looked in the early-morning light.

Snacks

Chaat is the general term for snacks, while *namkin* is the name for the various spiced nibbles that are sold prepackaged – although one waiter referred to them as 'bitings'. *Channa* is spiced chickpeas *(gram)* served with small puris.

Western Food

Sometimes Indian food simply becomes too much and you want to escape to something familiar. The Indian-food blues are particularly prone to hit at breakfast time – somehow idlis never really hit the spot. Fortunately that's the meal where you'll find an approximation to the west most easily obtained. All those wonderful Indian varieties of eggs can be had – scrambled, half-fried, omelettes, you name it.

Toast and jam can almost always be found, and very often you can get cornflakes and hot milk, although these Indian cornflakes would definitely be rejects from the Kellogg's production line. The Scots must have visited India too, because porridge is often on the breakfast menu and is usually good.

Tiffin – the peculiar Raj-era term for a mid-morning snack still lives. Today tiffin means any sort of light meal or snack. One western dish which Indians seem to have come to terms with is chips (French fries). Unfortunately ordering chips is very much a hit and miss affair – sometimes they're excellent, and at other times truly dreadful. Some Indian cooks call chips 'Chinese potatoes' or 'finger chips'.

Other Cuisines

Other Asian foods, apart from Indian, are often available. There's still a small Chinese population in India, particularly in Calcutta and Mumbai. You can find Chinese food in the larger cities, and Mumbai and Bangalore in particular have excellent Chinese food.

Elsewhere, Chinese food (or Indian interpretations of it) features on most menus in mid-range or better restaurants. The results are highly unpredictable, but the food is usually rather bland and stodgy.

In the north, where many Tibetans settled following the Chinese invasion of Tibet, you'll find Tibetan restaurants in places such as Darjeeling, Dharamsala, Gangtok, Kalimpong and Manali.

In the big gateway cities, and other large cities such as Bangalore, restaurants featuring French, Thai, Japanese, Italian and other cuisines, are becoming more common. They are usually confined to the luxury hotels, and are therefore priced accordingly.

McDonald's, KFC and Domino's Pizza have arrived although they currently have only a handful of branches. Indian quality control standards seem to be slowing their advance. Politics has played a part, too. In 1996 Delhi's Hindu fundamentalist-controlled municipal council managed to get the first KFC branch closed down for low cleanliness standards. On this basis all restaurants throughout the capital would have to be closed down!

Desserts & Sweets

Indians have quite a sweet tooth and an amazing selection of desserts and sweets to satisfy it. The desserts are rice or milk-based, and often consist of nuts, or pastries dripping in sweet syrup.

Many Indian sweets are covered in a thin layer of silver, as are some of the desserts. It's just that: silver beaten paper-thin. Don't peel it off, it's quite edible. There are countless sweet shops with their goodies all lined up in glass showcases. These shops often sell curd, as well as sweet curd which makes a very pleasant dessert. Sweets include all sorts of unidentifiable goodies; try them and see.

barfi – made from *khoya* (thickened boiled-down milk) and available in flavours like coconut, pistachio, chocolate or almond.
gajar ka halva – translucent, vividly coloured sweet made from carrot, sweet spices and milk.

gulab jamuns – also made from khoya and flavoured with cardamom and rose water.
jalebis – orange-coloured squiggles with syrup inside made of flour coloured and flavoured with saffron.
kulfi – a delicious sweet similar to ice cream that is widely available. It comes in pistachio and other flavours. You can, of course, also get western-style ice cream all over India; a chain of upmarket ice-cream outlets was about to open at the time of writing in southern India. The major brands, such as Vadelal, Go Cool, Kwality (now in partnership with UK's Walls) and Havmor, are safe and very good.
ladu – yellow-coloured balls made from chickpea flour.
payasam – a sweet, southern drink made from coconut milk, mango pulp, cashews and spices.
ras gullas – sweet little balls of cream cheese flavoured with rose water (very popular Indian dessert).
sandesh – another milk sweet and a particular favourite in Calcutta.

Fruit

If your sweet tooth simply is not sweet enough to cope with too many Indian desserts, you'll be able to fall back on India's wide variety of fruit. It varies all the way from tropical delights in the south to apples, apricots and other temperate-region fruits in the north. Some local specialities include cherries and strawberries in Kashmir, and apricots in Ladakh and Himachal Pradesh. Apples are found all over this north-western region but particularly in the Kullu Valley of Himachal Pradesh.

Green coconuts are a fine thirst quencher when you're unsure about the water and fed up with soft drinks. There are coconut stalls on many city street corners, especially in the south. When you've drunk the milk the stall-holder will split the coconut open and cut you a slice from the outer shell with which to scoop the flesh out.

Mangoes are delicious and are widespread in summer. Bananas are also found virtually all over India, particularly in the south; pineapples are found in West Bengal and Kerala as well as elsewhere. You don't see oranges all over the place (lots in Kerala and throughout the Ganges plain though), but tangerines are widespread in central India, particularly during the hot season. You can go through an awful lot of them in a day.

Paan

An Indian meal should properly be finished with paan – the name given to the collection of spices and condiments chewed with betel nut. Found throughout eastern Asia, betel is a mildly intoxicating and addictive nut, but by itself it is quite inedible. After a meal you chew paan as a mild digestive.

Paan sellers have a whole collection of little trays, boxes and containers in which they mix either *saadha* 'plain' or *mithaa* 'sweet' paans. The ingredients may include, apart from the betel nut itself, lime paste (the ash not the fruit), the powder known as *catachu*, various spices and even a dash of opium in a pricey paan. The whole concoction is folded up in a piece of edible leaf which you pop in your mouth and chew. When finished you spit the leftovers out and add another red blotch to the pavement. Over a long period of time, indulgence in paan will turn your teeth red-black and even addict you to the betel nut. Trying one occasionally won't do you any harm.

DRINKS
Nonalcoholic Drinks

Tea & Coffee Indians make some of the most hideously over-sweetened, murkily milky excuses for tea (known as *chai*) that you'll ever see. Still, many travellers like it and it is cheap. At train stations it is often served in small clay pots, which you then smash on the ground when empty.

Better tea can be obtained if you ask for 'tray tea', which gives you the tea, the milk and the sugar separately and allows you to combine them as you see fit. Unless you specify otherwise, tea is 'mixed tea' or 'milk tea', which means it has been made by putting cold water, milk, sugar and tea into one pot and bringing the whole concoction to the boil, then letting it stew for a long time. The result can be imagined.

Tea is more popular in the north, while in the south coffee, which is generally good, is the number one drink. It's almost impossible to get a decent cup of coffee in the north. Even in an expensive restaurant instant coffee is almost always used. The Indian Coffee House chain is one of the few places with decent coffee.

Water In the big cities, the water is chlorinated and safe to drink, although if you've just arrived in India, the change from what you are used to drinking is in itself enough to bring on a mild dose of the shits.

Outside the cities you're on your own. Some travellers drink the water everywhere and never get sick, others are more careful and still get a bug. Basically, you should not drink the water in small towns unless you know it has been boiled, and definitely avoid the street vendors' carts everywhere. Even in the better class of hotel and restaurant, the water is usually only filtered and not boiled. The local water filters remove solids, but don't remove bacteria. Water is generally safer in the dry season than during the monsoon when it really can be dangerous.

Water-purifying tablets are available from pharmacies and camping shops in the west, but not in India. See the earlier Health section for more information.

Mineral Water Most travellers to India these days avoid tap water altogether and stick to mineral water. It is available virtually everywhere, and comes in 1L plastic bottles. Brand names include Bisleri, India King, Officer's Choice, Honeydew and Aqua Safe. However, virtually all the so-called mineral water available is actually treated tap water. A recent reliable survey found that 65% of the available mineral waters were less than totally pure, and in some cases were worse than what comes out of the tap! Generally, though, if you stick to bottled water, any gut problems you might have will be from other sources – food, dirty utensils, dirty hands etc (see Basic Rules in the Health section).

The best (real) mineral water is from Pondicherry, available in the south.

GREG ELMS

EDDIE GERALD

Top: Betel nut, a mild intoxicant, is sold wrapped in its own leaf with lime and spice. Be warned, it's addictive stuff that's so bitter it shouldn't be swallowed, which explains those bright red blotches lining the streets.

Middle: Coconut is the ubiquitous ingredient in southern Indian cuisine – its milk also makes a refreshing drink on those hot, sticky days.

Bottom: Corn chargrilled in its skin by the roadside makes a convenient and tasty snack.

EDDIE GERALD

Top: Indian breads are delicious dipped in pickles and chutneys.

2nd Row: Add spices to the humble chick pea and you have a hearty and tasty meal.

3rd Row: Flavoursome snacks like pakoras, samosas and bhajas can almost be a meal in themselves.

Bottom: Although not always hot, the blend of spices that go into Indian food can create some pretty vivid colours.

Top: Mainly served in katoris, specially designed metal bowls, in the north, you're more likely to see South Indian thalis being dished up on (disposable) banana leaves.

Middle: The Indian smorgasboard, thalis are delicious, nutritious and widely available from *dhabas* (hole-in-the-wall stalls) and restaurants.

Bottom: Got a sweet tooth? Combat the munchies with some Indian sweets.

Top: An abundance of fresh fruit, from the familiar to the slightly more exotic, makes for refreshing thirst quenchers.

Left: Developed a taste for Indian food? Stock up on some spices before you leave and you can impress your friends with genuine Indian-spiced cuisine when you get home.

Soft Drinks Soft drinks are a safe substitute for water although they tend to have a high sugar content. Coca-Cola got the boot from India a number of years back for not cooperating with the government, but both it and Pepsi Cola are back with a vengeance. There are many indigenous brands with names like Campa Cola, Thums Up, Limca, Gold Spot or Double Seven. They are reasonably priced, but are also sickly sweet.

Juices & Other Drinks One very pleasant escape from the sickly sweet soft drinks is

Beer

India's climate being what it is, there are few travellers who don't relish a wee drop of the amber nectar at the end of a hot, dusty day or as an accompaniment to the setting sun at a beach cafe. There is a plethora of brands, some of which are only brewed locally and others on a national basis.

In terms of taste, consistent quality, popularity and availability nationwide, the top five bottled beers would be Kingfisher, UB Export Lager, Kalyani Black Label, Black Knight and London Pilsner, which average around 5% alcohol content. Others which are usually only available locally but which are just as good include Goa Pilsner Dry, Hamburg Pils, Khajuraho and Haywards. Draught beer (usually Kingfisher or London Pilsner) is also becoming more common in the big cities. Occasionally you'll come across obscure local brands, and these vary from quite OK to totally undrinkable – 'like the dregs after a party, minus the cigarette butts' was one assessment.

Beers which purport to be strong or even super strong (around 8% v/v) with dangerous names like Bullet, Hit and Knock Out are definitely in the 'hangovers installed and serviced' category and should be imbibed in moderation.

Since most beers are lagers, they should always be drunk as cold as possible. This is often not a fact appreciated by bar owners, so feel the bottle first before allowing the waiter to pop the top. Some beers, especially the stronger varieties, are totally unpalatable served in any way other than ice-cold.

Beer and other alcoholic drinks have always been regarded in India as luxury items and are frowned on by the Hindu and Muslim elites alike. As a result, they're heavily taxed by most state governments (except in Pondicherry, Sikkim, and Goa) making the price of a bottle of beer three to four times the price of a thali meal.

Despite this disparity, brewing is a growth industry and bars proliferate, except in Gujarat and Andhra Pradesh where prohibition is in force. Prohibition was a common feature in many states during the 1960s and its legacy survives (especially in Tamil Nadu) in the form of 'permit rooms' which are so dark you can't even see the drink in front of you. The overall impression is that you ought not to be involved in such a nefarious activity as drinking beer. Other states have a much more enlightened attitude, so bars are well lit, there's contemporary music playing and they're often the centre of social activity. They do, however, maintain licensed hours – commonly 11 am to 3 pm and 5 to 11 pm unless you're also eating.

Pondicherry, Sikkim and Goa have never suffered from the approbation of rabid prohibitionists and there you'll find not only the cheapest beers but no licensed hours restrictions – only the barperson's willingness to stay awake.

The majority of nonveg restaurants these days also serve alcoholic drinks but you'll never find them in vegetarian restaurants – they remain the preserve of those who eschew such impurities.

apple juice, sold from the Himachal fruit stands at train stations. Also good are the small cardboard boxes of fruit juices, especially mango. These are excellent, if a little sweet.

Coconut water, straight from the young green coconut, is a popular drink, especially in the south. Another alternative to soft drinks is soda water – Bisleri, Spencer's and other brands are widely available. Not only does it come in a larger bottle, but it is also cheaper. With soda water you can get excellent, and safe, lemon squash sodas.

Falooda is a popular drink made with milk, nuts, cream and vermicelli strands. Finally there's lassi, that oh so cool, refreshing and delicious iced curd (yoghurt) drink.

Alcoholic Drinks

Alcohol is generally expensive, except in states such as Goa, Sikkim and Pondicherry. Indian beers have delightful names like Golden Eagle, Rosy Pelican, Cannon Extra Strong, Bullet, Black Label, Knock Out, Turbo, Kingfisher, Guru or Punjab. They're not too bad if you can find them cold, but most tend to be insipid. Avoid overindulgence or you'll wake up late in the morning feeling thoroughly disoriented with a thumping headache to boot. Preservatives (sulphur dioxide in the main) are lavishly used to combat the effects of climate on 'quality'.

Beer and other Indian interpretations of western alcoholic drinks are known as Indian Made Foreign Liquor (IMFL). They include imitations of Scotch and brandy under a plethora of different brand names. The taste varies from hospital disinfectant to passable imitation Scotch. Always buy the best brand. With the continuing freeing up of the economy, it is likely that in the near future well-known foreign brands of beer and spirits will be available. Fosters (from Australia) recently became available.

Local drinks are known as Country Liquor and include *toddy*, a mildly alcoholic extract from the coconut palm flower, and *feni*, a distilled liquor produced from fermented cashew nuts or coconuts. The two varieties taste quite different.

Arak is what the peasants drink to get blotto. It's a clear, distilled rice liquor and it creeps up on you without warning. Treat it with caution and only ever drink it from a bottle produced in a government-controlled distillery. *Never, ever* drink it otherwise – hundreds of people die or are blinded every year in India as a result of drinking arak produced in illicit stills. You can assume it contains some methyl alcohol (wood alcohol).

ENTERTAINMENT

When it comes to pubs and bars, nightclubs and other activities you may take for granted at home, India isn't a hive of activity. Major cities such as Bangalore, Mumbai and Delhi are about the nearest you'll come to finding these sorts of things. But one thing India is well endowed with is cinemas. There are many thousands of cinemas all over the country. Entry is inexpensive, and if you haven't seen a Bollywood blockbuster before, you should try to see one at least once during your trip.

Traditional music and dance performances are sometimes held at major hotels, but one of the best places to see these is at a festival – of which India has a great many. Kerala's famous Kathakali can be seen at Cochin and other venues.

SPECTATOR SPORT

India's national sport (obsession almost) is cricket. There's something about a game with as many idiosyncrasies and peculiarities as cricket which simply has to appeal to the Indian temperament. During the cricket season, if an international side is touring India and there is a test match on, you'll see crowds outside the many shops which have a TV, and people walking down the street with a pocket radio pressed to their ear. Test matches with Pakistan have a particularly strong following as the rivalry is intense. One thing you can count on is that most Indians will know the names of the entire touring cricket team and, if you come from the same country but don't know their names, then you may well be regarded as

Traditional Games

Kho-kho and *kabaddi* are two traditional sports that still enjoy a healthy following. Both are essentially games of tag. In kho-kho the defending team sends in players in batches of three. These players are chased along an oblong field towards the goal at the end by a member of the opposing team. Other members of the opposing team crouch in squares drawn along a centre line, and if they manage to touch one of those being chased with their open palm, that person is out. Championships are held at state and national level under the auspices of the Kho-Kho Federation of India. The game is open to both boys and girls.

Kabaddi (known as *hu-tu-tu* in South India) is also played in Sri Lanka, Nepal, Pakistan, Bangladesh and Japan. There are two teams of 12 players. The playing field is divided in two. One side sends a raider into the opponent's half. The raider must touch as many of the opposing team members as possible and return to the home side. But the trick is, this must be done in a single breath, chanting 'kabaddi kabaddi' all the way. If a raider runs out of breath before reaching the home side, or goes outside the boundary, they are out. There are local variations of this game. There is a Kabaddi Federation of India and an Asian Kabaddi Federation.

Board games also have a long tradition in India. Chess, for example, is thought to have originated in India in the 6th century AD. Carrom, although its origins are obscure, is today a popular pastime not only in India but in Sri Lanka as well. A maximum of four can play. Carrom centres on a square, wooden board. In the centre are nine back and nine white coins plus one pink coin called a queen. On each corner of the board are pockets and the goal is to use a striker to send the coins (black or white depending on which you have drawn) into one of the pockets.

mentally retarded. On the other hand, if you do have an interest in cricket, it can be a great way to start up conversations.

India is also one of the world leaders in hockey, and has several Olympic gold medals to its credit – although none since 1980. In the 1996 Olympics the country's only medal was a tennis bronze, won by Leander Paes.

Polo can be viewed at certain times of the year in Jaipur at the polo ground near the Rambagh Palace. The polo season extends over winter with the most important matches usually played in March.

Soccer has a keen following, particularly in Calcutta.

SHOPPING

India is packed with beautiful things to buy. The cardinal rule when purchasing handicrafts is to bargain and bargain hard. You can get a good idea of what is reasonable in quality and price by visiting the various state emporiums and the Central Cottage Industries Emporiums which can be found in Delhi, Calcutta, Mumbai, Chennai, Bangalore and Hyderabad. You can inspect items at these places from all over the country. Because prices are fixed, you will get an idea of how hard to bargain when you purchase similar items from regular dealers.

As with handicrafts in any country, don't buy until you have developed a little understanding and appreciation. Rushing in and buying the first thing you see will inevitably lead to later disappointment and a considerably reduced stash of travellers cheques. (See also the Shoppers' Delight colour section in the Uttar Pradesh chapter.)

Be careful when buying items which include delivery to your home country. You may be told that the price includes home delivery and all customs and handling charges. Inevitably this is not the case, and you may find yourself having to collect the item yourself from your country's main port or airport, pay customs charges (which could be as much as 20% of the item's value) and handling charges levied by the airline or shipping company (up to 10% of the value). If you can't collect the item promptly, or get someone to do it on your behalf, exorbitant storage charges may also be charged.

Carpets

It may not surprise you that India produces and exports more hand-crafted carpets than Iran, but it is probably more of a surprise that some of them are of virtually equal quality.

In Kashmir, where India's best carpets are produced, the carpet-making techniques and styles were brought from Persia even before the Mughal era. The art flourished under the Mughals and today Kashmir is packed with small carpet producers. Persian motifs have been much embellished on Kashmiri carpets, which come in a variety of sizes – 3ft x 5ft, 4ft x 6ft and so on. They are either made of pure wool, wool with a small percentage of silk to give a sheen (known as 'silk touch') or pure silk. The latter are more for decoration than hard wear. Expect to pay from Rs 7000 for a good-quality 4ft x 6ft carpet and don't be surprised if the price is more than twice as high.

Other carpet-making areas include Badhoi and Mirzapur in Uttar Pradesh or Warangal and Eluru in Andhra Pradesh. In Kashmir and Rajasthan, the coarsely woven woollen *numdas* are made. These are more primitive and folksy, and consequently cheaper, than the fine carpets. Around the Himalaya and Uttar Pradesh *dhurries*, flat-weave cotton warp-and-weft rugs are woven. In Kashmir *gabbas* are appliqué-like rugs. The numerous Tibetan refugees in India have brought their craft of making superbly colourful Tibetan rugs with them. A 3ft x 5ft Tibetan rug will be less than Rs 1000. Two of the best places to buy them are Darjeeling and Gangtok.

Unless you're an expert it is best to get advice or buy from a reputable dealer if you're spending large amounts of money on carpets. Check prices back home too; many western carpet dealers sell at prices you would have difficulty matching even at the source. Also look out for the Smiling Carpet label; this is a UN/NGO initiative to try and discourage the use of child labour in carpet manufacture.

Papier-Mâché

This is probably the most characteristic Kashmiri craft. The basic papier-mâché article is made in a mould, then painted and polished in successive layers until the final intricate design is produced. Prices depend upon the complexity and quality of the painted design and the amount of gold leaf used. Items include bowls, cups, containers, jewellery boxes, letter holders, tables, lamps, coasters, trays and so on. A cheap bowl might cost only Rs 25, a large, well-made item might approach Rs 1000.

Pottery

In Jaipur, Rajasthan, you can buy blue-glazed pottery which features floral and geometric motifs. Terracotta images of the gods and children's toys are made in Bihar. (See also Arts in the Facts about India chapter.)

Metalwork

Copper and brass items are popular throughout India. Candle-holders, trays, bowls, tankards and ashtrays are made in Mumbai and other centres. In Rajasthan and Uttar Pradesh the brass is inlaid with exquisite designs in red, green and blue enamel. *Bidri* is a craft of north-eastern Karnataka and Andhra Pradesh, where silver is inlaid into gunmetal (for more details see the Bidriware of Bidar boxed text in the Karnataka chapter). Hookah pipes, lamp bases and jewellery boxes are made in this manner.

Jewellery

Many Indian women put most of their wealth into jewellery, so it is no wonder that so much of it is available. For western tastes the heavy folk-art jewellery of Rajasthan has particular appeal. You'll find it all over the country, but particularly in Rajasthan. In the north you'll also find Tibetan jewellery, even chunkier and more folk-like than the Rajasthani variety.

If, on the other hand, you are looking for fine jewellery as opposed to folk jewellery, you may well find that much of what is produced in India is way over the top.

Leatherwork

Of course Indian leatherwork is not made from cow-hide but from buffalo-hide, camel, goat or some other substitute. *Chappals*,

A Warning

In touristy places, particularly Agra, Jaipur, Varanasi, Delhi and Calcutta, take extreme care with the commission merchants – these guys hang around waiting to pick you up and cart you off to their favourite dealers where whatever you pay will have a hefty margin built into it to pay their commission. Stories about 'my family's place', 'my brother's shop' and 'special deal at my friend's place' are just stories and nothing more.

Whatever you might be told, if you are taken by a rickshaw driver or tout to a place, be it a hotel, craft shop, market or even restaurant, the price you pay will be inflated. This can be by as much as 50%, so try to visit these places on your own. And don't underestimate the persistence of these guys. We heard of one ill traveller who virtually collapsed into a cycle-rickshaw in Agra and asked to be taken to a doctor only to end up at a marble workshop, with the rickshaw driver insisting that, yes, indeed a doctor did work there. The high pressure sales techniques of both the runners and the owners is the best in the world. Should you get up and leave without buying anything, the feigned anger is just that. Next time you turn up (alone), it will be all smiles – and the prices will have dropped dramatically.

Another trap which many foreigners fall into occurs when using a credit card. You may well be told that if you buy the goods, the merchant won't forward the credit slip for payment until you have received the goods, even if it is in three months' time – this is total bullshit. No trader will be sending you as much as a postcard until they have received the money, in full, for the goods you are buying. What you'll find in fact is that within 48 hours of you signing the credit slip, the merchant has telexed the bank in Delhi and the money will have been credited to their account.

Also beware of any shop which takes your credit card out the back and comes back with the slip for you to sign. Sometimes while out of sight, the vendor will imprint a few more forms, forge your signature, and you'll be billed for items you haven't purchased. Have the slip filled out right in front of you.

If you believe any stories about buying anything in India to sell at a profit elsewhere, you'll simply be proving (once again) that old adage about separating fools from their money. Precious stones and carpets are favourites for this game. Merchants will tell you that you can sell the items in Australia, Europe or the USA for several times the purchase price, and will even give you the (often imaginary) addresses of dealers who will buy them. You'll also be shown written statements, supposedly from other travellers, documenting the money they have supposedly made – it's all a scam. The stones or carpets you buy will be worth only a fraction of what you pay. Don't let greed cloud your judgement. It seems that with every edition of this book we make the warnings longer and more explicit, and yet we still get a steady trickle of letters from people with tales of woe and they usually concern scams we specifically warn of.

While it is certainly a minority of traders who are actually involved in dishonest schemes, virtually all are involved in the commission racket, so you need to shop with care – take your time, be firm and bargain hard. Good luck.

those basic sandals found all over India, are the most popular purchase. In craft shops in Delhi you can find well-made leather bags, handbags and other items. Kashmiri leather shoes and boots, often of quite good quality, are widely found, along with coats and jackets of often abysmally low quality.

In Rajasthan you can buy the traditional leather shoes called *jootis*; those for men often have curled up toes.

Kanpur in Uttar Pradesh is the country's major city for leatherwork.

Textiles

This is still India's major industry and 40% of the total production is at the village level where it is known as *khadi*. There are government khadi emporiums (known as Khadi Gramodyog) around the country, and these are good places to buy handmade items of homespun cloth, such as the popular 'Nehru jackets' and the *kurta pajama*. Bedspreads, tablecloths, cushion covers or material for clothes are other popular khadi purchases.

There is an amazing variety of cloth styles, types and techniques around the country including mirrorwork in Rajasthan and Gujarat and tie-dye work in Rajasthan and Kerala.

In Kashmir embroidered materials are made into shirts and dresses. Fine shawls and scarves of pashmina goats' wool are popular buys in the Kullu Valley. Phulkari bedspreads or wall hangings come from the Punjab. Another place which is famous for its embroidery is Barmer, near the Pakistani border and south-west of Jaisalmer in Rajasthan. Batik is a fairly recent introduction from Indonesia but already widespread; *kalamkari* cloth from Andhra Pradesh and Gujarat is an associated but far older craft.

Silks & Saris

Silk is cheap and the quality is often excellent. The 'silk capital' is Kanchipuram in Tamil Nadu, although Varanasi is also popular, especially for silk saris.

If you are buying a silk sari, it helps to know a bit about both the silk and the sari. Saris are 5.5m long, unless they have an attached blouse *(choli)*, in which case they are 6m. Sari silk is graded and sold by weight – in grams per metre.

Bronze Figures

In the south, delightful small images of the gods are made by the age-old lost-wax process. A wax figure is made, a mould is formed around it and the wax is melted and poured out. The molten metal is poured in and when it's solidified the mould is broken open. Figures of Shiva as dancing Nataraja are amongst the most popular.

Woodcarving

In the south, images of the gods are also carved out of sandalwood. Rosewood is used to carve animals – elephants in particular. Carved wooden furniture and other household items, either in natural finish or lacquered, are also made in various locations. In Kashmir, intricately carved wooden screens, tables, jewellery boxes and trays are carved from Indian walnut. They have a similar pattern to the decorative trim of houseboats.

Paintings

Reproductions of the beautiful old miniatures are painted in many places, but beware of paintings claimed to be antique – it's highly unlikely that they are. Also note that quality can vary widely; low prices often mean low quality, and if you buy before you've had a chance to look at a lot of miniatures and develop some appreciation you'll inevitably find you bought unwisely. Udaipur (Rajasthan) has some good shops specialising in modern reproductions.

In Kerala, and, to a lesser extent, Tamil Nadu, you'll come across vibrant miniature paintings on leaf skeletons enclosed on a printed card depicting domestic and rural scenes as well as gods and goddesses. In Andhra Pradesh you can buy paintings on cloth called kalamkari.

Antiques

Fort Cochin has a wonderful antique market – a highlight of a visit to this place.

However, the antiques don't come cheaply here. Articles over 100 years old are not allowed to be exported from India without an export clearance certificate. If you have doubts about any item and think it could be defined as an antique, you can check with branches of the Archaeological Survey of India.

Other Things to Buy

Marble inlay pieces from Agra are pleasant reminders of the beauty of the Taj. They come as either simple little pieces or larger items like jewellery boxes. Appliqué work is popular in many places, such as Orissa. Indian musical instruments always have an attraction for travellers.

Getting There & Away

AIR
Airports & Airlines

Mumbai (Bombay), Delhi, Calcutta and Chennai are the main gateways for international flights. At the time of writing a new international airport was to open near Kochi in Kerala, which would service direct flights to/from Europe and Asia. India's national airline is Air India.

Buying Tickets

The plane ticket will probably be the single most expensive item in your budget, and buying it can be an intimidating business. There is likely to be a multitude of airlines and travel agencies hoping to separate you from your money, and it is always worth putting aside a few hours to research the current state of the market.

Start early: some of the cheapest tickets have to be bought months in advance, and some popular flights sell out early. Talk to other recent travellers – they may be able to stop you making some of the same old mistakes. Look at the ads in newspapers and magazines (not forgetting the press of the ethnic group whose country you plan to visit), consult reference books and watch for special offers. Then phone around travel agencies for bargains. (Airlines can supply information on routes and timetables; however, except at times of inter-airline war, they do not supply the cheapest tickets.) Find out the fare, the route, the duration of the journey and any restrictions on the ticket. Then sit back and decide which is best for you.

You may discover that those impossibly cheap flights are 'fully booked, but we have another one that costs a bit more ...' Or the flight is on an airline notorious for its poor safety standards and leaves you in the world's worst airport in mid-journey for 14 hours. Or they claim only to have the last two seats available for that country for the whole of July, which they will hold for you for a maximum of two hours. Don't panic – keep ringing around.

Use the fares quoted in this book as a guide only. They are approximate and based on the rates advertised by travel agencies at the time of going to press. Quoted air fares do not necessarily constitute a recommendation for the carrier. If you are travelling from the UK or the USA, you will probably find that the cheapest flights are being advertised by obscure bucket shops whose names haven't yet reached the telephone directory. Many such firms are honest and solvent, but there are a few rogues who will take your money and disappear, to reopen elsewhere a month or two later under a new name. If you feel suspicious about a firm, don't give them all the money at once – leave a deposit of 20% or so and pay the balance when you get the ticket. If they insist on cash in advance, go somewhere else. And once you have the ticket, ring the airline to confirm that you are actually booked on the flight.

You may decide to pay more than the rock-bottom fare by opting for the safety of a better-known travel agency. Firms such as STA Travel, which has offices worldwide, Council Travel in the USA or Travel CUTS in Canada are not going to disappear overnight, leaving you clutching a receipt for a nonexistent ticket, but they do offer good prices to most destinations.

Round-the-World (RTW) fares are very competitive and are a popular way to travel to India (see the Air Travel Glossary boxed text for more information).

Once you have your ticket, write down its number, together with the flight number and other details, and keep the information somewhere separate. If the ticket is lost or stolen, this will help you get a replacement. It's sensible to buy travel insurance as early as possible. If you buy it the week before you fly, you may find, for example, that you're not covered for delays to your flight caused by industrial action.

Travellers with Special Needs

If you have special needs of any sort – you've broken a leg or you're vegetarian, travelling in a wheelchair, taking the baby, terrified of flying – you should let the airline know as soon as possible so that they can make arrangements accordingly. You should remind them when you reconfirm your booking (at least 72 hours before departure) and again when you check in at the airport. It may also be worth ringing round the airlines before you make your booking to find out how they can handle your particular needs.

Airports and airlines can be surprisingly helpful, but they do need advance warning. Most international airports will provide escorts from the check-in desk to the plane where needed, and there should be ramps, lifts, accessible toilets and reachable phones. Aircraft toilets, on the other hand, are likely to present a problem; travellers should discuss this with the airline at an early stage and, if necessary, with their doctor.

Guide dogs for the blind will often have to travel in a specially pressurised baggage compartment with other animals, away from their owner; smaller guide dogs may be admitted to the cabin. All guide dogs will be subject to the same quarantine laws (six months in isolation etc) as any other animal when entering or returning to countries currently free of rabies such as Australia.

Deaf travellers can ask for airport and inflight announcements to be written down for them.

Children under two travel for 10% of the standard fare (or free, on some airlines), as long as they don't occupy a seat. They don't get a baggage allowance either. 'Skycots' should be provided by the airline if requested in advance; these will take a child weighing up to about 10kg. Children between two and 12 can usually occupy a seat for half to two-thirds of the full fare and do get a baggage allowance. Push chairs can often be taken as hand luggage.

Departure Tax

Departure tax is Rs 500 which can be paid on purchase of some tickets or at the airport. There is a Rs 250 tax to neighbouring countries (Sri Lanka, Nepal, Pakistan and Bangladesh).

Cheap Tickets in India

Although you can get cheap tickets in Mumbai and Calcutta, it is in Delhi that the real wheeling and dealing goes on. There are a number of bucket shops around Connaught Place, but inquire with other travellers about their current trustworthiness. And if you use a bucket shop, double check with the airline itself that the booking has been made. Fares include:

Delhi-London	Rs 13,000-20,000
Delhi-New York	Rs 22,000-30,000
Delhi-Los Angeles	Rs 28,000-35,000
Delhi-Hong Kong	Rs 17,000-19,000

Air Travel Glossary

Baggage Allowance This will be written on your ticket and usually includes one 20kg item to go in the hold, plus one item of hand luggage.

Bucket Shops These are unbonded travel agencies specialising in discounted airline tickets.

Bumped Just because you have a confirmed seat doesn't mean you're going to get on the plane (see Overbooking).

Cancellation Penalties If you have to cancel or change a discounted ticket, there are often heavy penalties involved; insurance can sometimes be taken out against these penalties. Some airlines impose penalties on regular tickets as well, particularly against 'no-show' passengers.

Check-In Airlines ask you to check in a certain time ahead of the flight departure (usually one to two hours on international flights). If you fail to check in on time and the flight is overbooked, the airline can cancel your booking and give your seat to somebody else.

Confirmation Having a ticket written out with the flight and date you want doesn't mean you have a seat until the agent has checked with the airline that your status is 'OK' or confirmed. Meanwhile you could just be 'on request'.

Courier Fares Businesses often need to send urgent documents or freight securely and quickly. Courier companies hire people to accompany the package through customs and, in return, offer a discount ticket which is sometimes a phenomenal bargain. In effect, what the companies do is ship their freight as your luggage on regular commercial flights. This is a legitimate operation, but there are two shortcomings – the short turnaround time of the ticket (usually not longer than a month) and the limitation on your luggage allowance. You may have to surrender all your allowance and take only carry-on luggage.

Full Fares Airlines traditionally offer 1st class (coded F), business class (coded J) and economy class (coded Y) tickets. These days there are so many promotional and discounted fares available that few passengers pay full economy fare.

ITX An ITX, or 'independent inclusive tour excursion', is often available on tickets to popular holiday destinations. Officially it's a package deal combined with hotel accommodation, but many agents will sell you one of these for the flight only and give you phoney hotel vouchers in the unlikely event that you're challenged at the airport.

Lost Tickets If you lose your airline ticket an airline will usually treat it like a travellers cheque and, after inquiries, issue you with another one. Legally, however, an airline is entitled to treat it like cash and if you lose it then it's gone forever. Take good care of your tickets.

MCO An MCO, or 'miscellaneous charge order', is a voucher that looks like an airline ticket but carries no destination or date. It can be exchanged through any International Association of Travel Agents (IATA) airline for a ticket on a specific flight. It's a useful alternative to an onward ticket in those countries that demand one, and is more flexible than an ordinary ticket if you're unsure of your route.

No-Shows No-shows are passengers who fail to show up for their flight. Full-fare passengers who fail to turn up are sometimes entitled to travel on a later flight. Others may be penalised (see Cancellation Penalties).

On Request This is an unconfirmed booking for a flight.

Air Travel Glossary

Onward Tickets An entry requirement for many countries is that you have a ticket out of the country. If you're unsure of your next move, the easiest solution is to buy the cheapest onward ticket to a neighbouring country or a ticket from a reliable airline which can later be refunded if you do not use it.

Open Jaw Tickets These are return tickets where you fly out to one place but return from another. If available, this can save you backtracking to your arrival point.

Overbooking Airlines hate to fly empty seats and since every flight has some passengers who fail to show up, airlines often book more passengers than they have seats. Usually excess passengers make up for the no-shows, but occasionally somebody gets bumped. Guess who it is most likely to be? The passengers who check in late.

Point-to-Point Tickets These are discount tickets that can be bought on some routes in return for passengers waiving their rights to a stopover.

Promotional Fares These are officially discounted fares, available from travel agencies or direct from the airline.

Reconfirmation At least 72 hours prior to departure time of an onward or return flight, you must contact the airline and 'reconfirm' that you intend to be on the flight. If you don't do this the airline can delete your name from the passenger list and you could lose your seat.

Restrictions Discounted tickets often have various restrictions on them – such as needing to be paid for in advance and incurring a penalty to be altered. Others are restrictions on the minimum and maximum period you must be away, such as a minimum of 14 days or a maximum of one year.

Round-the-World Tickets RTW tickets give you a limited period (usually a year) in which to circumnavigate the globe. You can go anywhere the carrying airlines go, as long as you don't backtrack. The number of stopovers or total number of separate flights is decided before you set off and they usually cost a bit more than a basic return flight.

Stand-by This is a discounted ticket where you only fly if there is a seat free at the last moment. Stand-by fares are usually available only on domestic routes.

Transferred Tickets Airline tickets cannot be transferred from one person to another. Travellers sometimes try to sell the return half of their ticket, but officials can ask you to prove that you are the person named on the ticket. This is less likely to happen on domestic flights, but on an international flight tickets are compared with passports.

Travel Agencies Travel agencies vary widely and you should choose one that suits your needs. Some simply handle tours, while full-services agencies handle everything from tours and tickets to car rental and hotel bookings. If all you want is a ticket at the lowest possible price, then go to an agency specialising in discounted tickets.

Travel Periods Ticket prices vary with the time of year. There is a low (off-peak) season and a high (peak) season, and often a low-shoulder season and a high-shoulder season as well. Usually the fare depends on your outward flight - if you depart in the high season and return in the low season, you pay the high-season fare.

Delhi-Bangkok	Rs 12,000-13,575
Delhi-Lahore	US$100
Delhi-Karachi	US$180
Calcutta-Hong Kong	Rs 17,000-19,000
Calcutta-Bangkok	Rs 9500-9730
Calcutta-Rangoon	Rs 6160
Calcutta-Kathmandu	US$96

The USA

The *New York Times*, the *LA Times*, the *Chicago Tribune* and the *San Francisco Examiner* all produce weekly travel sections in which you'll find any number of travel agency ads. Council Travel and STA Travel have offices in major cities nationwide. The magazine *Travel Unlimited* (PO Box 1058, Allston, MA 02134) publishes details of the cheapest air fares and courier possibilities for destinations all over the world from the USA.

The high season for flights from the USA to India runs from June to August and again from December to January. Low season runs from March to around mid-May and from September to November.

High season fares from the east coast to Mumbai range from US$1650 (Air India via Delhi) to US$2300 (TWA/Air France via Paris). To Delhi, fares are US$1500 (Delta Air Lines via Frankfurt). To Chennai fares cost from US$2100 (Air India via Mumbai) to US$2700 (Air India via Amsterdam and Mumbai). Low season fares to Mumbai, Delhi and Chennai are: US$1500 (Alaska Airlines), US$1400 (Lufthansa), and US$1700 (Lufthansa via Frankfurt and Mumbai) respectively.

Aeroflot consistently offers the lowest fares: US$900 to Mumbai from either coast during the high season. Singapore Airlines also offers some very good deals.

Canada

Travel CUTS has offices in all major cities. The Toronto *Globe & Mail* and the *Vancouver Sun* carry travel agency ads. The magazine *Great Expeditions* (PO Box 8000-411, Abbotsford, BC V2S 6H1) is useful.

Vancouver to Mumbai fares are CA$1600 (Swissair or Lufthansa) in the low season and CA$1700 (Canadian Airlines via Chicago) in the high season. During the high season all flights from Vancouver are routed through the USA. Montreal to Mumbai flights cost CA$1600; with Swissair or Lufthansa in the low season and KLM/Northwest (via Amsterdam) or Lufthansa (via Frankfurt) during the high season.

Vancouver to Chennai costs CA$1900 (Cathay/Singapore Airlines via Hong Kong and Singapore) in the low season and CA$2000 in the high season (Cathay/Air India via Hong Kong and Singapore). Montreal to Chennai costs CA$2700 (Air Canada or British Airways via London and Mumbai) in the low season and CA$2600 (British Airways via London and Mumbai) in the high season.

Australia

STA Travel and Flight Centres International are major dealers in cheap air fares. Check the travel agency ads in the *Yellow Pages* and ring around.

The low season is 1 February to 21 November. Advance purchase tickets from the east coast of Australia to India range from A$1200 to A$1700 depending on the season and the destination in India. Fares are slightly cheaper from Darwin or Perth, and to Chennai and Calcutta rather than Mumbai or Delhi. Fares from Australia to the UK via India range from A$1950 to A$2250.

New Zealand

As in Australia, STA Travel and Flight Centres International are popular travel agencies. There are no direct flights between India and New Zealand so most airlines offer stopovers in Asia. Air fares to Delhi from Auckland with Malaysian Airlines cost from NZ$1745 return (NZ$1945 between November and January). There are a few cheaper combinations with Air India and Garuda.

The UK & Ireland

Various excursion fares are available from London to India, but you can get better prices through London's many cheap-ticket specialists. Trailfinders in west London produces a lavishly illustrated brochure which includes air fare details. STA Travel also has branches in the UK.

Look in the Sunday papers and *Exchange & Mart* for ads. Also look out for the free magazines widely available in London – start by looking outside the main train stations.

Most British travel agencies are registered with the Association of British Travel Agents (ABTA). If you have paid for your flight to an ABTA-registered agent which then goes out of business, ABTA will guarantee a refund or an alternative. Unregistered bucket shops are riskier but also sometimes cheaper.

The Globetrotters Club (BCM Roving, London WC1N 3XX) publishes a newsletter called *Globe*, which covers obscure destinations and can help in finding travelling companions.

From London to Delhi fares are approximately £290 to £380. KLM, Air India, Air Lanka and the Middle East airlines all offer very competitive fares. Lufthansa also offers good deals to Delhi, although you can't change your flight dates on the cheapest tickets.

London-Calcutta fares cost from £330 to £400, London-Mumbai from £300 to £400 and London-Chennai from £340 to £430.

Some companies offer packages to Goa and Kerala at competitive rates which include accommodation, breakfast and transfers. Check with travel agencies and travel page ads in newspapers and magazines. There are also a few packages including charter flights between London and Agra. If you want to stop in India en route to Australia expect to pay around £556 (although some tickets cost £900).

Fares from Belfast to Mumbai or Delhi cost from £439 and to Chennai (via Heathrow) £651. If you wish to stop over in Mumbai en route to Australia expect to pay £700.

Continental Europe

In Amsterdam, NBBS is a popular travel agency.

Paris to Mumbai or Delhi costs approximately 3600FF, and to Chennai 3850FF.

Africa

There are plenty of flights between East Africa and Mumbai due to the large Indian population in Kenya. Typical one-way fares from Mumbai to Nairobi are US$420.

Bangladesh

Bangladesh Biman and Indian Airlines fly between Calcutta and Dhaka (US$80) and between Calcutta and Chittagong (US$106) in Bangladesh.

Malaysia

The one-way economy fare from Kuala Lumpur to Delhi is US$435.

The Maldives

Thiruvananthapuram (Trivandrum) to Malé costs US$70 one way. It's cheaper to fly from Colombo in Sri Lanka.

Myanmar

There are no land crossing points between Myanmar and India (or between Myanmar and any other country), so your only choice from India is to fly there. Myanmar Airways flies Calcutta-Yangon (Rs 12,990); Bangladesh Biman flies Dhaka-Yangon.

Nepal

Royal Nepal Airlines Corporation (RNAC) and Indian Airlines share routes between India and Kathmandu. RNAC has two flights daily; Indian Airlines has one. Both airlines give a 25% discount to those under 30 years of age on flights between Kathmandu and India. No student card is needed. Delhi is the main departure point for flights between India and Kathmandu. RNAC has flights from Kathmandu to Delhi (US$142, one hour), Mumbai (US$257), Calcutta (US$96) and Varanasi (US$71). The flight from Varanasi is the last leg of the popular Delhi-Agra-Khajuraho-Varanasi-Kathmandu tourist flight. If you want to see the mountains as you fly into Kathmandu from Delhi or Varanasi, you must sit on the left side.

The Nepali airlines Necon Air recently started flying four times a week from Kathmandu to Patna (US$75), three times a week to Calcutta. Buddha Air was also, at the time of writing, planning to start flights between India and Nepal. Necon Air also flies out of Kathmandu with four flights per week to Patna (US$75) and three flights to Calcutta via Biratnagar (Nepal).

Pakistan

Pakistan International Airlines (PIA) and Air India operate flights from Karachi to Delhi for US$180 and Lahore to Delhi for US$100.

Singapore

The one-way economy fare from Singapore to Delhi is US$586.

Sri Lanka

There are flights between Colombo and Mumbai, Chennai, Tiruchirappalli or Thiruvananthapuram (Trivandrum). Fares from Chennai to Colombo are Rs 3655.

Thailand

Bangkok is a popular departure point from South-East Asia into Asia proper. Bangkok to Kathmandu with Thai International is 5240B one way, 8300B return for a ticket valid for three months and 9700B for a ticket valid for one year. Bangkok to Calcutta via Yangon (Myanmar) can by done for 10,060B by combing a Thai International ticket from Bangkok to Yangon with an Indian Airline ticket from Yangon to Calcutta (this ticket must be ordered three days in advance). Bangkok to Calcutta one way costs 5200B with Thai International.

LAND
Bangladesh

The situation with crossings between India and Bangladesh is vague. The main crossings are at Benapol/Haridispur (near Jessore, on the Calcutta route), Chilahati/Haldibari (in the far north, on the Siliguri-Darjeeling route) and more recently along the entire eastern border with India (eg at Tamabil/Dawki, in the north-east corner of the Shiloong route, and east of Brahmanbaria on the route to Agartala in the Tripura region). If officials tell you that you cannot cross elsewhere, be sceptical because we have letters to the contrary from travellers. In recent years travellers have crossed at Bhurungamari/Chengrabandha (in the north, well east of Chilahati, an alternate route to Siliguri and Darjeeling), Hili/Balurghat (north-west of Bogra) and Godagari/Lalgola (west of Rajshahi on the Padma River, an alternate route to Calcutta). It may also be possible to pass at Satkhira (south-west of Khulna).

The problem is that these lesser crossings witness so few westerners passing through (maybe only once or twice a year) that everyone assumes it's impossible. Getting the correct story from Indian and Bangladeshi officials is virtually impossible. The truth is probably that crossing at these lesser routes is simply more variable and never certain. If you do use one of the minor crossings, be sure you don't leave the border without a stamp in your passport, otherwise you're sure to run into problems when leaving the country.

No exit permit is required to leave Bangladesh. But if you enter Bangladesh by air and leave by land you do need a road permit, which can be obtained from the Passport & Immigration office, 2nd floor, 17/1 Segunbagicha Rd, Dhaka. It's open Thursday to Saturday 8 am to 1 pm. Two passport photos are required and the process takes about 24 hours; there is no fee. If you are driving from Bangladesh in your own vehicle, two permits are required: one from the Indian High Commission (☎ 504879), House 120, Road 2, Dhanmoni, Dhaka; and one from the Bangladesh Ministry of Foreign Affairs (☎ 883-260/261), Pioneer Rd, facing the Supreme Court in Segun Bagicha (in the city centre).

Dhaka to Calcutta The Dhaka to Calcutta route is the one used by the majority of land travellers between Bangladesh and India. Coming from Dhaka it's wise to book your seat on the bus at least a day in advance. The buses that operate overnight between Dhaka (departing between 8 and 11 pm) and the border are direct; they reach Benapol (the Bangladeshi border town) at dawn. From Benapol to the border, it's about 10 minutes by cycle-rickshaw (Tk 6). There are no daytime buses between the border and Benapol. Crossing the border takes an hour or so with the usual filling in and stamping of forms. From the border at Haridaspur (India) it's about 10km (Rs 17, 20 minutes by cycle-rickshaw, or Rs 90 by auto-rickshaw) to Bangaon. It's possible to change money at Bangaon where the rate is better than at the border.

Alternatively, you can take a Coaster (minibus) from Jessore to Benapol (Tk 14), from where you can proceed to the border and India.

Chilahati to Darjeeling The Bangladesh border point is at Chilahati, and this can be reached by train, although it's much quicker to take the bus. From Chilahati to Haldibari (the Indian border checkpoint), it's a 7km walk along a disused train line. The train trip from Haldibari to New Jalpaiguri takes two hours and costs Rs 11. From New Jalpaiguri to Darjeeling you can take the fast buses or the slower more picturesque toy train (if running). Note that changing money in Chilahati is virtually impossible. There are moneychangers at Haldibari.

Siliguri to Bhurungamari This northern border crossing is rarely used by travellers. Getting to the Indian border town of Chengrabandha from Siliguri is easy. There are buses every 45 minutes between 6 am and 1 pm. The 70km trip costs Rs 24 and takes 2½ hours. The Indian immigration office opens at 9 am. Outside you can change Indian rupees into taka. Bhurungamari is 1km from the border. It's a tiny village and if you're caught here for the night your only option may be to sleep on the floor of one of the bus offices. You can take buses direct to Rangpur (5½ hours), Bogra (eight hours) or Dhaka (15 hours).

Sylhet to Shillong It takes 2½ hours to get to Tamabil from Sylhet by bus from where it's a 15 minute hike to the border. It is then a further 1.5km walk to Dauki in India, from where buses run to Shillong (3½ hours).

Nepal
Political and weather conditions permitting, there are three main land entry points into Nepal. The most popular crossing points from India are Sunauli/Bhairawa (south of Pokhara), Raxaul Bazaar/Birganj (south of Kathmandu) and Kakarbhitta (near Siliguri and Darjeeling in the far east). If you are travelling to or from Delhi or elsewhere in western India the route through Sunauli/Bhairawa is the most convenient.

An ordinary bus to Sunauli from Varanasi costs Rs 105 (10 hours). There are bus/train packages to/from Agra. There are direct buses from Delhi, but these generally get bad reports from travellers. It's cheaper and more satisfactory to organise the trip yourself.

From Calcutta, Patna or most of eastern India, Raxaul Bazaar to Birganj is the best entry point. From Darjeeling it's easiest to go to Kakarbhitta. A 'through' bus from Varanasi to Kathmandu or Pokhara costs Rs 300, although remember that everyone has to change buses at the border.

You can also enter at Mahendranagar in the far west of Nepal, although this is a much more difficult route. When the Mahendra Highway is finally completed, the route will be open all year, but until then it is a dry-season-only proposition, and strictly for the hardy. There are daily buses from Delhi to Banbassa in Uttar Pradesh, the nearest Indian village to the border. The trip takes 11 hours. Banbassa is also connected by rail to Bareilly and by bus with the hill station Almora. There are direct buses from Mahendranagar to Kathmandu (2 pm) but they take a gruelling 22 hours. It's much better to do the whole trip during daylight and to break the journey at Nepalganj. There are plenty of night and day buses from Nepalganj to Kathmandu (14 hours).

Warning Many travellers have complained about scams involving ticket packages to India, especially out of Pokhara – bookings fail to materialise or are for lower quality services than were paid for. The package usually involves coordination between at least three different companies so the potential for an honest cock-up is at least as high as the potential for a deliberate rip-off.

Pakistan

At present, due to the continuing unstable political situation between India and Pakistan, there's only one border crossing open and that remains hostage to Pakistan-India relations. However, there have been signs that cross-border links will be strengthened with the introduction of a direct bus link between Delhi and Lahore – get current information before heading off.

Lahore to Amritsar The only legal overland crossing between India and Pakistan is at Wagah, just east of Lahore (Attari on the India side), by rail and road; you can also drive your own vehicle across here. On each side you clear immigration, customs and further security checks and walk across 100m of neutral territory. The border is open daily, 9 am to 3 pm (9.30 am to 3.30 pm India time). Daily express trains link Lahore with Amritsar in India. The *Amritsar Express* leaves Lahore City station at 11 am and reaches Amritsar about 3 pm. The return trip leaves Amritsar at 9.30 am, arriving at Lahore about 2 pm. Sometimes, however, border delays can make the trip much longer. There are also slower daily Lahore-Wagah trains. Buses are quicker and more frequent, though the trip still takes nearly half a day. There are no direct buses but plenty to and from the border on both sides.

A Lahore-Delhi bus service began in 1999. The route takes in Wagah, Attari, Amritsar and Sirhind. It runs four days a week but only for people with relatives on the other side.

Europe

A steady trickle of people drive their own motorcycles or vehicles overland from Europe. There are some interesting, though difficult, routes to the subcontinent through Eastern Europe and the republics that were once a part of the USSR. An international carnet is required. Many people combine travel to the subcontinent with the Middle East by flying from India or Pakistan to Amman in Jordan or one of the Gulf states. A number of the London-based overland companies operate bus or truck trips across Asia on a regular basis. See Organised Tours later in this chapter for companies that do overland trips.

For more detail on the Asian overland route see the Lonely Planet guides to Pakistan, Iran and Turkey.

South-East Asia

In contrast to the difficulties of travelling overland in central Asia, the South-East Asian overland trip is still wide open and as popular as ever. From Australia the first step is to Indonesia – Timor, Bali or Jakarta. Although most people fly from an east-coast city or Perth to Bali, there are also flights from Darwin and from Port Hedland in the north of Western Australia. The shortest route is the flight between Darwin and Kupang on the Indonesian island of Timor.

From Bali you head north through Java to Jakarta, from where you either travel by ship or fly to Singapore or continue north through Sumatra and then cross to Penang in Malaysia. After travelling around Malaysia you can fly from Penang to Chennai or, more popularly, continue north to Thailand and eventually fly out from Bangkok to India, perhaps with a stopover in Myanmar. Unfortunately, crossing by land from Myanmar to India (or indeed to any other country) is forbidden by the Myanmar government.

An interesting alternative route is to travel from Australia to Papua New Guinea and from there cross to Irian Jaya; then to Sulawesi in Indonesia. There are all sorts of travel variations possible in South-East Asia; the region is a delight to travel through, it's good value for money, the food is generally excellent and healthy, and all in all it's an area of the world not to be missed.

For full details see Lonely Planet's *South-East Asia on a shoestring*.

SEA

There is no longer a ferry service running between Rameswaram and Talaimannar in Sri Lanka. The service between Chennai and Penang (Malaysia) ended some years ago. The shipping services between Africa and India only carry freight (including vehicles), not passengers.

ORGANISED TOURS

In addition to companies that provide more standard tours, there are numerous foreign eco and adventure-travel companies which can provide unusual and interesting trips. There are too many to include them all here; check newspapers and travel magazines for ads, and journals such as *Earth Journal* (USA) for listings. The following are a few of the companies who organise tours to India.

USA

Adventure Center
  (☎ 800-227 8747, email tripinfo@
  adventure-center.com) 1311 63rd St,
  Suite 200, Emeryville, CA 94608
All Adventure Travel, Inc.
  (☎ 303-440 7924) PO Box 4307, Boulder,
  CO 80306
Asian Pacific Adventures
  (☎ 800-825 1680, email travelasia@earthlink
  .net) 826 Sierra Bonita Ave, Los Angeles,
  CA 90036
Geographic Expeditions
  (☎ 415-922 0448, fax 346 5535, email
  info@geoex.com) 2627 Lombard St,
  San Francisco, CA 94123
  (Web site www.geoex.com)

Australasia

One World Travel
  (☎ 03-650 3322, fax 650 4254) 3rd Floor,
227 Collins St, Melbourne, VIC 3000,
  Australia
One World Tours
  (☎ 08-8232 2727, email bwitty@ozemail
  .com.au) 99 Hay St, Subiaco, Perth, WA 6008,
  Australia
Peregrine Adventures
  (☎ 03-9663 8611) 258 Lonsdale St,
  Melbourne, VIC 3000, Australia
  (offices in Sydney, Brisbane, Adelaide, Perth
  and Hobart)
Venturetreks
  (☎ 09-379 9855, fax 09-377 0320) 164 Parnell
  Rd (PO Box 37610), Parnell, Auckland,
  New Zealand
Window to the World
  (☎/fax 612-6493 8595) 36 Fieldbuckets Rd,
  Quamma, NSW 2550, Australia
World Expeditions
  (☎ 02-9264 3366, fax 9261 1974) 3rd Floor,
  441 Kent St, Sydney, NSW 2000, Australia
  (☎ 03-9670 8400, fax 9670 7474) 1st Floor,
  393 Little Bourke St, Melbourne, VIC 3000,
  Australia

UK

Encounter Overland
  (☎ 020-7370 6845, fax 7244 9737, email
  adventure@encounter.co.uk) 267 Old
  Brompton Rd, London SW5 9JA
  (Web site www.encounter-overland.com)
Exodus Expeditions
  (☎ 020-8673 0859, fax 8673 0779, email
  sales@exodustravels.co.uk) 9 Weir Rd,
  London SW12 OLT (Web site
  www.exodustravels.co.uk)
Imaginative Traveller
  (☎ 020-8742 3113, fax 8742 3045,
  email info@imaginative-traveller.com)
  14 Barley Mow Passage, Chiswick,
  London W4 4PH (Web site
  www.imaginative-traveller.com)
Top Deck
  (☎ 020-7370 4555, fax 7373 6201) 131-135
  Earls Court Rd, London SW5 9RH
  (Web site www.topdecktravel.co.uk)

Getting Around

AIR
Domestic Air Services
India's major domestic airline, the government-run Indian Airlines, flies extensively throughout the nation and into neighbouring countries. Some services are operated by its subsidiary, Alliance Air. The country's international carrier, Air India, also operates domestic services, principally on the Mumbai (Bombay)-Delhi, Mumbai-Calcutta, Delhi-Calcutta and Mumbai-Chennai (Madras) routes. Jet Airways, one of the few private airlines still flying (and rated as the best airline in India), serves 26 cities across the country. There are also a handful of smaller regional airlines – Gujarat Airways, Sahara India, Archana Airways and Jagson Airlines.

Reservations
Indian Airlines has computerised booking at all but the smallest offices, so getting flight information and reservations is relatively simple – it's just getting to the head of the queue that takes the time.

The private operators are all reasonably efficient, and most have computerised booking.

For most airlines, tickets must be paid for with foreign currency or by credit card, or rupees backed up by encashment certificates. Change is given in rupees.

Infants up to two years old travel at 10% of the adult fare, but only one infant can travel at this fare per adult. Children two to 12 years old travel at 50% the adult fare. Indian nationals aged 65 and over also qualify for a 50% discount. There is a 25% reduction on the basic fare for foreign students with international student ID cards, and 25% off for those aged between 12 and 30. Refunds on adult tickets attract a charge of Rs 100 and can be made at any office. There are no refund charges on infant tickets. If a flight is delayed or cancelled, you cannot claim a refund. If you fail to show up 30 minutes before the flight, this is regarded as a 'no-show' and you forfeit the full value of the ticket.

Indian Airlines accepts no responsibility if you lose your tickets. They absolutely will not refund lost tickets, but at their discretion may issue replacements.

All domestic airlines require you reconfirm your flight 72 hours before departure.

Air Passes
Private airlines usually fly identical routes to Indian Airlines, although in some cases they can be much more expensive.

Indian Airlines has a Discover India pass, which costs US$500/750 for 15/21 days. This allows travel on its domestic routes with certain restrictions – no city can be transited more than once except on a connecting flight. It can be reasonable value if you have lots of long flights. There's also a 25% discount for foreign students.

The other flight pass is called the India Wonder Fare and costs US$300 for one week's unlimited travel between cities (except to Port Blair) within one of four regional groupings: north, west, south and east. Unless changing planes you may visit each place within the group only once. Cities included in the regional groupings are:

Northern Region
   Agra, Amritsar, Bhopal, Delhi, Chandigarh, Gwalior, Indore, Jaipur, Jammu, Jodhpur, Khajuraho, Leh, Lucknow, Raipur, Srinagar, Udaipur, Varanasi
Western Region
   Ahmedabad, Aurangabad, Bhavnagar, Bhuj, Goa, Indore, Jamnagar, Jodhpur, Kozhikode, Mangalore, Mumbai, Nagpur, Rajkot, Udaipur, Vadodara
Southern Region
   Bangalore, Chennai, Coimbatore, Goa, Hyderabad, Kochi, Kozhikode, Madurai, Nagpur, Pune, Thiruvananthapuram, Tiruchirappalli, Visakhapatnam
Eastern Region
   Agartala, Bhubaneswar, Calcutta, Dibrugarh, Dimapur, Guwahati, Imphal, Jorhat, Lucknow, Patna, Ranchi, Silchar, Tezpur, Vadodara, Varanasi, Visakhapatnam

Jet Airways operates a Visit India scheme with the same restrictions as the Discover India pass for US$500/750/900 for 15/21/30 days, but its network is not as comprehensive.

Check-In

Check-in time is one hour before departure. An extra 15 minutes is required on flights to and from Srinagar, Jammu and Leh.

Air India domestic flights leave from the international rather than the domestic terminals; check-in time is usually two hours.

The baggage allowance for domestic airlines is 20kg for economy seats and 30kg for business class.

As a security measure on some internal routes, you are required to identify your checked-in baggage on the tarmac immediately prior to boarding. Note that any batteries discovered by security guards in your hand luggage will be confiscated to prevent you from using them to detonate incendiary devices during the flight. Put all batteries (even cells used for camera flashguns) in checked baggage.

BUS

Travelling in India by train has such an overpowering image – the sights, sounds and smells of the stations, the romantic names and exotic old steam engines – that people forget there is also an extensive and well-developed bus system.

Classes

Buses vary widely from state to state, although generally bus travel is crowded, cramped, slow and uncomfortable, especially in the north. In some states there is a choice of buses on the main routes – ordinary, express, semi-luxe, deluxe, deluxe aircon and even deluxe sleeper!

Ordinary buses generally have five seats across – three on one side of the aisle, two on the other – although if there are only five people sitting in them consider yourself lucky! There are usually mounds of baggage in the aisles, chickens under seats, and in some more remote places there will be people travelling 'upper class' (ie on the roof).

These buses tend to be frustratingly slow, are usually in an advanced state of decrepitude and stop frequently – often for seemingly no reason – and for long periods, and can take forever. They're certainly colourful and can be an interesting way to travel on short journeys; on longer trips you'll probably wish you'd stayed at home.

Express buses are a big improvement in that they stop far less often. They're still crowded, but at least you feel like you're getting somewhere. The fare is usually a few rupees more than on an ordinary bus – well worth the extra.

Semi-luxe also have five seats across, but they have more padding and 'luxuries' such as tinted windows, and the buses stop infrequently. The fare is about 20% more than the ordinary fare, which discourages many of the locals who can only afford the cheapest mode of travel. The big difference between deluxe and semi-luxe is that deluxe buses have only four seats across and these usually recline.

There is generally a state-operated bus company in each state, and in most places this is backed up by privately operated buses – although they may only run on certain routes. Unlike state-operated bus companies, private operators are keen to maximise their profits and therefore maintenance is often less and speed more – a dangerous combination.

Despite the extra speed buses often offer, they become uncomfortable sooner than trains. If it's a long trip, particularly overnight, opt for a train if there's a choice.

The thing that foreigners find hardest to cope with on the buses is the music. Hindi pop music is usually played at maximum volume screeches on and on without end. Just as bad are the video machines found on many deluxe buses. These generally screen macho Bollywood garbage, also at full volume, for hours on end. If you're travelling overnight by bus, try to avoid video coaches.

Reservations

If there are two of you, work out a bus boarding plan where one of you can guard

Getting There is Half the Fun

A lot of travel in India can be indescribably dull, boring and uncomfortable. Trains take forever, buses fall apart and shake your fillings loose, even Indian Airlines sometimes manages to make your delay time far longer than your flying time.

Despite the hassles there are a fair number of trips where getting there is definitely half the fun. Trains, of course, are the key to Indian travel. The narrow-gauge line to Darjeeling is, alas, out of action at the moment, but other 'toy trains' include the run up to Matheran, just a couple of hours outside Mumbai; the 'rack train' which makes the climb to Ooty from Mettupalayam in Tamil Nadu; and the narrow-gauge line which connects the hill station of Shimla (Himachal Pradesh) with Kalka on the plains.

If boating is more to your liking, there is the delightful backwater trip through the waterways of Kerala between Kollam (Quilon) and Alappuzha (Alleppey) – not only is the trip fascinating, it's absurdly cheap.

Indian buses are generally a refined form of torture but the two day trip between Manali in Himachal Pradesh and Leh in Ladakh is too good to miss. The bus route from Darjeeling or Kalimpong to Gangtok in Sikkim is pretty good too, as is the climb up to Kodaikanal from Madurai in Tamil Nadu. Finally, flying into Leh you cross the full width (and height!) of the Himalaya – there could hardly be a more spectacular flight in the world.

trip	transportation	state
Neral to Matheran	toy train	Maharashtra
Mettupalayam to Udhagamandalam	rack train	Tamil Nadu
Kalka to Shimla	toy train	Himachal Pradesh
Alappuzha to Kollam	backwater boat	Kerala
Manali to Leh	bus or jeep	Himachal Pradesh/ Ladakh & Zanskar
Darjeeling to Gangtok	bus or jeep	West Bengal/Sikkim
Madurai to Kodaikanal	bus	Tamil Nadu
Delhi/Srinagar to Leh	air	Ladakh & Zanskar

the gear while the other storms the bus in search of a seat. The other accepted method is to pass a newspaper or article of clothing through the open window and place it on an empty seat, or ask a passenger to do it for you. Having made your 'reservation' you can then board the bus after things have simmered down. This method rarely fails.

The big advantage of buses over trains is that they go more frequently and getting one involves comparatively little predeparture hassle. You can, however, often make advance reservations for a small additional fee, but this usually only applies to express, semideluxe and deluxe services. Private buses should always be booked in advance.

At many bus stations there is a separate women's queue. You may not notice this because the relevant sign (where it exists at all) will not be in English and there may not be any women queuing. Usually the same ticket window will handle the male and the female queue, taking turns. What this means is that women can usually go straight to the front of the queue (beside the front of the male queue) and get almost immediate service.

Baggage

Baggage is generally carried for free on the roof, so it's an idea to take a few precautions. Make sure it's tied on properly and that nobody dumps a tin trunk on top of your gear. At times a tarpaulin will be tied across the baggage – make sure it covers your gear adequately.

Theft is sometimes a problem so keep an eye on your bags at chai stops. Having a large, heavy-duty bag into which your pack will fit can be a good idea, not only for bus travel but also for air travel.

If someone carries your bag onto the roof, you can expect to pay a few rupees for the service.

Toilet Stops

On long-distance bus trips, chai stops can be far too frequent or, conversely, agonisingly infrequent. Long-distance trips can be a real hassle for women travellers – toilet facilities are often hopelessly inadequate.

TRAIN

The Indian Railways system is the world's fourth largest, with a route length of over 60,000km. Every single day more than 7000 passenger trains run, carrying over 10.5 million passengers and connecting 7100 stations. It's also the world's largest single employer with a shade over 1.6 million employees!

During and shortly after the monsoon, rail services can be drastically affected by floods and high rivers, particularly in low-lying areas along the Ganges basin or where major rivers reach the sea, such as the coastal region of Andhra Pradesh.

India Railways' Web site has schedules and links to their fares (www.trainweb.com /indiarail/ttable.htm)

Timetables

The first step in coming to grips with Indian Railways is to get a timetable. *Trains at a Glance* is a handy, 100 page guide covering all the main routes and trains. It is usually available at major train stations, and sometimes on news stands in the larger cities.

If you can't find *Trains at a Glance*, a regional timetable provides much the same information, including more local train services and a pink section with timetables for

the major mail and express trains (the fast ones) throughout the country. Unfortunately, these are also often unavailable. *Southern Central Railway* is good for south Indian trains; you can find it at some train stations and bookshops.

There is also the 300 page *Indian Bradshaw*, which covers every train service throughout the country. It's more detailed than most people need and it can be frustratingly difficult to find things, but for serious exploring it's invaluable. Published monthly, it's not widely available but you can usually find it on the bookstalls at major city train stations. Thomas Cook's *Overseas Timetable* has good train timetables for India, although it's not available in India.

To calculate fares, see Costs, later in this section.

Train Types

What you want is a mail or express train. What you do not want is a passenger train. According to figures published by Indian Railways, express/mail trains average 47.1km/h, passenger trains 27.2km/h – if you had any ideas about going places in a hurry, you might as well forget it! Passenger trains are usually 2nd class only; 2nd class fares on passenger trains are less than on a mail or express train over the same route.

Air-con 'superfast' express services operate on certain main routes and, because of tighter scheduling and fewer stops, are much faster. India's top rail services are the *Rajdhani Express* trains, connecting most of the largest cities, and the *Shatabdi Express* trains, which tend to be even faster but don't usually operate overnight services. A separate fare structure applies to both these trains as meals are usually included. The *Rajdhani* and *Shatabdi* services are claimed to average around 130km/h.

Gauge There are three gauge types in India: broad, metre and narrow, and what you want nearly as much as a mail or express train is broad gauge. In broad gauge the rails are 1.676m apart; metre gauge is, as it says, 1m wide; narrow gauge is either

0.762m (two feet six inches) or 0.610m (two feet).

Broad gauge has a major advantage – it is much faster. It also gives a smoother ride. The carriages are much the same between broad gauge and metre gauge, but on narrow gauge they are much, much narrower and the accommodation very cramped. In areas where there are no broad-gauge lines it may be worth taking a bus, which will often be faster then the metre-gauge trains. A major engineering undertaking to convert metre-gauge to broad-gauge is now under way.

Classes

There are generally two classes – 1st and 2nd – but there are a number of subtle variations on this basic distinction. For a start there is 1st class and 1st class air-con. The air-con carriages only operate on the major trains and routes. The fare for 1st class air-con is considerably more than double normal 1st class. A slightly cheaper air-con alternative is the air-con two-tier sleeper, which costs about 25% more than 1st class. These carriages are a lot more common than 1st class air-con, but are still only found on the major routes.

Between 2nd and 1st class there are two more air-con options: air-con three-tier sleeper and air-con chair car. The former has three levels of berths rather than two, while the latter, as the name suggests, consists of carriages with aircraft-type layback seats. Once again, these carriages are only found on the major routes, and the latter only on day trains. The cost of air-con three-tier is about 70% of the 1st class fare; air-con chair is about 55% of the 1st class fare.

It's India for real on board the trains. In 2nd class, unreserved travel can be a nightmare since the trains are often hopelessly crowded, and not only with people. Combined with the crowds, the noise and the confusion there's the discomfort. Fans and lights have a nasty habit of failing at prolonged stops (of which there are many), just when there's no air moving through the carriage, and toilets can get more than a little rough towards the end of a long journey.

In 2nd class reserved it's a great deal better since, in theory, only four people share each bench, but there's inevitably the fifth, and sometimes even the sixth, person who gets the others to bunch up so they can get at least part of their bum on the seat. This normally doesn't happen at night or in 1st class, where there are either two or four people to a compartment and the compartment doors are lockable.

Sleepers There are 2nd class and 1st class sleepers, although by western standards even 1st class is not luxurious. Bedding is available, but only on certain 1st class and air-con two-tier services, and then only if they are arranged when booking your ticket. First class sleepers are generally private compartments with two or four berths in them, sometimes with a toilet as well. Usually the sleeping berths fold up to make a sitting compartment during the day. First class air-con sleepers are more luxurious, and much more expensive, than regular 1st class sleepers.

Second class sleepers are known as three-tier. They are arranged in doorless sections each with six berths. During the day the middle berth is lowered to make seats for six or eight. At night they are folded into position, everybody has to bed down at the same time, and a Travelling Ticket Examiner (TTE) ensures that nobody without a reservation gets into the carriage. Broad-gauge, three-tier sleeping carriages also have a row of narrow two-tier (upper and lower) berths along one side. These are not only narrower than the 'inside' berths, but are about 20cm shorter, so that for the average person stretching right out is not possible. When reserving 2nd class berths, always write 'inside' on the accommodation preference section of the booking form. Sleeping berths are only available from 9 pm to 6 am.

Reservations

The cost of reservations is nominal – it's the time it takes that hurts, although even this is generally getting better as computerised reservation becomes more widespread.

In Delhi, Mumbai, Calcutta and Chennai there are special tourist booking facilities at the main booking offices. These are for any foreign tourists and they make life much easier. The people at these offices are generally very knowledgeable and are often able to give you excellent advice – suggesting connections and routes that can save you a lot of time and effort.

At other major stations with computerised reservation offices, such as Ahmedabad and Jaipur, one ticket window will deal with foreign tourists and other minorities (such as 'Freedom Fighters'!). These windows are generally queue-free, so check to see if one exists.

Reservations can be made up to two months in advance and the further in advance you make them the better. Your reservation ticket will indicate which carriage and berth you have, and when the train arrives you will find a sheet of paper fixed to each carriage listing passenger names beside their appropriate berth number. Usually this information is also posted on notice boards on the platform. It is Indian rail efficiency at its best.

As at many bus stations, there are separate women's queues, usually with a sign saying 'Ladies' Queue'. Usually the same ticket window handles the male and female queue, serving one at a time. This means that women can go to the front of the queue, next to the first male at the window, and get almost immediate service.

Rail reservations incur a booking fee of Rs 15 to Rs 50, depending on the class. There are very rarely any 2nd class sitting compartments with reservations.

If the train you want is fully booked, it's often possible to get an RAC (Reservation Against Cancellation) ticket. This entitles you to board the train and have seating accommodation. Once the train is moving, the TTE will find a berth for you, but it may take an hour or more. This is different from a wait-listed ticket, which does not give you the right to actually board the train (should you be so cheeky you can be 'detrained and fined'). The hassle with RAC tickets is that

you will probably get split up if there are two or more of you.

If you've been unable to get a reservation, it's worth getting on the train in a reserved carriage anyway. Although there's the risk of a small fine for 'ticketless travel', most TTEs are sympathetic to foreign travellers. If there is a spare berth/seat they'll allot you one, and charge the normal fare plus the reservation fee. If all the berths/seats are already reserved you'll simply be banished to the crush and confusion in the unreserved carriages. This trick only works well for day travel. At night sleepers are generally booked out well in advance so if you can't get one (or an RAC ticket), then sitting up in 2nd class is your only choice.

If you plan your trip well ahead, you can avoid all the hassles by booking in advance from abroad. A good Indian travel agency will book and obtain tickets in advance and have them ready for you on arrival.

As an alternative to buying tickets as you go along, it's possible to buy a ticket from A to Z with all the stops along the way pre-booked. It might take a bit of time to sit down and work it out at the start, but if your time is limited and you can fix your schedule rigidly, this can be a good way to go.

For any sleeper reservation you should try to book at least several days ahead. There is usually a board in each station indicating what is available or how long before the next free berth/seat comes up on the various routes. At the major city stations this is usually computerised and TV screens give a continuous read-out. Once you've selected a particular train and date, you must fill in a reservation form. Do this before you get to the front of the queue. The forms are usually found in boxes around the reservation hall. The demand for 1st class sleepers is generally far less than for the 2nd class sleepers.

At most major stations there's usually a separate section or counter(s) in the booking hall (often called 'Tourist Cell'!) that deals with the tourist quota. Only foreigners and nonresident Indians are allowed to use this facility. Here you can make your reservations in relative comfort away from madding crowds *but* you must pay in foreign currency (cash or travellers cheques in US dollars or pounds sterling only) or with rupees backed up by exchange certificates, and any change will be given in rupees.

Women can ask about the Ladies' Compartments that many trains have and which are often a refuge from the crowds in other compartments.

Lastly, when deciding which train to take along any route, you may come up against that major source of bewilderment – the Indian custom of naming a train without indicating where it goes. On the timetable or state-of-reservation board at a station you could, for example, see the *Brindavan Express* or the *Cholan Express* etc. But where do they go to? It might be the train you want, but it might not. This is where your *Trains at a Glance* or *Indian Bradshaw* comes in. If you don't have one, you'll have to ask – and that's going to soak up time. Tourist offices can usually help by suggesting the best trains but there isn't always a tourist office. It's something you'll just have to come to terms with.

If you want a sleeper and there are none left then it's time to try to break into the quotas. Ask the stationmaster (often a helpful man who speaks English) if there is a tourist quota, station quota or a VIP quota. The last of these is often a good bet because VIPs rarely turn up to use their quotas.

If all that fails then you're going to be travelling unreserved and that can be no fun at all. To ease the pain get yourself some expert help. For, say, Rs 10 baksheesh you can get a porter who will absolutely ensure you get a seat if it's humanly possible. If it's a train starting from your station, the key to success is to be on the train before it arrives at the departure platform. Your porter will do just that, so when it rolls up you simply stroll on board and take the seat he has warmed for you. If it's a through train then it can be a real free-for-all, and you can be certain he'll be better at it than you are – he'll also not be encumbered with baggage or backpacks.

Costs

Fares operate on a distance basis. The timetables indicate the distance in kilometres between the stations and from this it is simple to calculate the cost between any two stations. If you have a ticket for at least 400km you can break your journey at the rate of one day per 200km so long as you travel at least 300km on the first sector. This can save a lot of hassle buying tickets and also, of course, results in a small saving.

The Indian Rail Fares table in this section indicates fares for set distances. Elsewhere in this book, unless otherwise indicated, fares are based on the faster ('express' rather than 'passenger') trains.

Refunds Booked tickets are refundable but cancellation fees apply. If you present the ticket more than one day in advance, a fee of Rs 10 to Rs 50 applies, depending on the class. Up to four hours before, you lose 25% of the ticket value; less than four hours before departure and between three and 12 hours after departure (depending on the distance of the ticketed journey) you lose 50%. Any later than that and you can keep the ticket as a souvenir.

Tickets for unreserved travel can be refunded up to three hours after the departure of the train, and the only penalty is a Rs 10 per passenger fee.

When refunding your ticket, you are officially entitled to go straight to the head of the queue (if there isn't a dedicated window for refunds), the rationale being that the spot you are surrendering may be just the one required by the next person in the queue.

Indrail Passes

Indrail Passes permit unlimited travel on Indian trains for the period of their validity, but they are expensive and not good value. To get the full value out of any of the passes you need to travel around 300km per day; with the speed of most Indian trains that's at least six hours' travelling!

Although the pass covers the cost of reservations, it doesn't get you to the front of the queue, so is of little help there, and

Indian Rail Fares in Rupees

distance (km)	1st class (air-con)	1st class	air-con chair	2nd class express	2nd class express (sleeper)	2nd class passenger (seat)
50	406	122	100	76	22	10
100	542	173	114	76	32	16
200	725	230	171	76	54	29
300	943	361	231	105	73	39
400	1156	455	277	129	90	48
500	1333	531	323	152	107	55
1000	2155	862	492	245	174	77
1500	2908	1156	658	311	219	94
2000	3616	1435	800	360	253	111

you join in the wait-list like everybody else if the train is fully booked. The only occasion when it's going to save you time is if you want to travel unreserved on a train, when you can simply hop on without queuing for a ticket. As these journeys are likely to be far fewer and shorter than those when you want to have a reserved berth, it's not much of a gain.

The average visitor to India might cover around 3000km in a month by rail. An aircon Indrail Pass for this would cost US$550; to buy the tickets as you go along would cost around US$100 to US$160, depending on the number and length of the journeys; even if you did 6000km, you still wouldn't come close to getting your money's worth. It's the same story with the other class passes: a 2nd class, one month pass costs US$125, the individual tickets for 3000km of travel would cost around US$12 to US$25. See the Indrail Pass table for the cost of these passes.

Children aged five to 12 years pay half fare. Indrail Passes can be bought overseas through some travel agencies or in India at certain major railway offices. Payment in India can be made only in either US dollars or pounds sterling, cash or travellers cheques, or in rupees backed up with exchange certificates. Second class passes are not available outside India. Indrail Passes

cover all reservation and berth costs at night, and they can be extended if you wish to keep on travelling. The main offices in India that handle Indrail Passes are:

Calcutta
  Railway Tourist Guide, Eastern Railway, Fairlie Place
  Central Reservation Office, South-Eastern Railway, Esplanade Mansion
Chennai
  Central Reservation Office, Southern Railway, Chennai Central
Delhi
  Railway Tourist Guide, New Delhi station
Mumbai
  Railway Tourist Guide, Western Railway Churchgate
  Railway Tourist Guide, Central Railway, Victoria Terminus

Special Trains

The special *Palace on Wheels* makes a regular circuit around Rajasthan – you not only travel by train, you stay in the 'fit for a maharaja' carriages. See the Rajasthan chapter for more details.

The *Royal Orient Express* is a similar luxury service that operates between Delhi and Ahmedabad via Rajasthan. See the Gujarat by Rail boxed text in the Gujarat chapter for details.

The English organisation, Butterfield's Indian Railway Tours, operates regular train

Indrail Pass Prices in US$

days	air-con	1st class	2nd class
7	300	150	80
15	370	185	90
21	440	220	100
30	550	275	125
60	800	400	185
90	1060	530	235

tours of India using a special carriage in which you travel, eat and sleep. The carriage is hooked onto regular trains and is left on the sidings of various towns you visit. The accommodation facilities are basic but you cover a lot of India, and using the railway in this way brings you into much closer contact with people than you'd get on a usual package tour staying in upmarket hotels. Tours from 16 to 29 days are available. For more information contact Butterfield's Railway Tours (☎ 01262-470230), Burton Fleming, Driffield, East Yorks YO25 0PQ, UK. Butterfield's can also be contacted through the Madras Hotel, Connaught Circus, Delhi.

Left Luggage

Most stations have a left-luggage facility (quaintly called a cloakroom) where backpacks can be left for Rs 2 per day. This is very useful if you're visiting (but not staying in) a town, or if you want to find a place to stay, unencumbered by gear. The regulations state that any luggage left in a cloakroom must be locked, although this is not strictly enforced.

CAR

Few people bring their own vehicles to India. If you do decide to bring a car or motorcycle to India it must be brought in under a carnet, a customs document guaranteeing its removal at the end of your stay. Failing to do so will be very expensive.

Rental

Self-drive car rental in India is not widespread, but it is possible. Both Budget and Hertz maintain offices in the major cities. Given India's crazy driving conditions it's far better, and much more straightforward, to hire a car and driver. By western standards the cost is quite low, certainly cheaper than a rent-a-car (without driver) in the west. Almost any local taxi will quite happily set off on a long-distance trip in India. Inquiring at a taxi rank is the easiest way to find a car – you can also ask your hotel to book one for you, although this will cost slightly more.

Trips are either 'one way' or the less expensive per-kilometre 'running trip'. The one-way fare is more expensive per kilometre because it is based on the assumption that the driver will return empty to the starting point. A running trip is based on a minimum of 250km a day with an additional charge per kilometre. There is no extra charge for overnight stops – your driver will stretch himself out on the back seat and be ready to go when you turn up for the return trip. An air-con car will cost about twice as much as a non air-con vehicle.

Long-distance car hire with driver is becoming an increasingly popular way to get around parts of India. Spread among say, four people, it's not overly expensive and you have the flexibility to go where you want when you want. An Ambassador car with driver hired from Delhi costs about Rs 1350 for up to 250km a day; after this it costs Rs 4.75 per kilometre. There is an additional tax of Rs 300 to Rs 400 for entry into other states. Car hire is more expensive in hill regions. Expect to pay Rs 700 for an eight hour day covering 80km; after this it costs Rs 5.5 per kilometre. You will be charged Rs 100 for an overnight stop.

Purchase

Buying a car is expensive and not worth the effort unless you intend to stay in India for months.

On the Road

Because of the extreme congestion in the cities and the narrow, bumpy roads in the country, driving is often a slow, stop-start

Indian Vehicles

In 1951 the number of motorised vehicles on India's roads totalled 300,000. The figure had climbed to 5.4 million by 1981 and shot to 26.5 million in 1996. India's metropolitan vehicle population has tripled since 1990 with dire results for the environment.

In the closed market following Independence the Indian motorist had to choose between a few license-built cast-offs from the west. When the Morris Oxford was replaced by a newer model in the UK in the mid-1950s, production shifted to Calcutta, where it has continued ever since as the Hindustan Ambassador. Variety was added in the early 1960s with an old version of the Fiat 1100D, renamed the Pal Padmini. Later the Fiat 124 was introduced. For a while the Triumph Herald was produced here, in a five door version known as the Standard Gazel. Hindustan bought the rights to a 1970s Vauxhall which has now become the Hindustan Contessa. Sipani Autos had a brief fling with Reliant, producing a four wheel version of the fibreglass three wheel Robin. They had similarly unsuccessful joint ventures with the Rover 2000 and the Austin Montego estate.

The big story, however, is the Maruti, a locally assembled Japanese Suzuki minicar, minivan and 4WD, put together in the Sanjay Gandhi 'people's car' factory near Delhi. They've swept the country and you now see them everywhere in surprisingly large numbers.

With this joint venture the floodgates opened and new arrivals on the Indian roads include the Ford Escort (complete with wood-effect dash and touted as a luxury vehicle), the Peugeot 309, Fiat Uno, Daewoo Cielo, Opel Astra, and the Mercedes 220 – all assembled in India. Soon to follow are Honda and Skoda.

Marutis start at around Rs 201,000 new. Ambassadors (now with safety belts!) start from around Rs 330,000. More expensive versions now have Isuzu engines and five-speed gearboxes. A Mercedes 220 will set you back Rs 2,250,436.

India's truck and bus industry is quite well developed, with companies like Tata and Ashok Leyland turning out sturdy trucks which you see all over India, and also in a number of other countries (Britain now imports Tata pick-ups). Here too there has been a Japanese onslaught, with the appearance of modern Japanese trucks. All Japanese vehicle builders in India must have at least 50% Indian ownership. The name thus becomes an Indo-Japanese hybrid, so you get Maruti-Suzuki, Hindustan-Isuzu, Allwyn-Nissan, Swaraj-Mazda and Honda-Kinetic.

The motorcycle and motor scooter industry has also experienced rapid growth. Motorcycles include the splendid Enfield India – a replica of the old British single-cylinder 350cc Royal Enfield Bullet of the 1950s. Enthusiasts for the old British singles will be delighted to see these vintage bikes still being made. Purists will be horrified by the diesel version. Motor scooters include Indian versions of both the Italian Lambretta and the Vespa. When production ceased in Italy, India bought the manufacturing plant from them lock, stock and barrel. The assembly of small Honda, Suzuki and Yamaha motorcycles is now widespread and they are a familiar a sight on the roads of India.

process – hard on you, the car and fuel economy. Service is so-so in India, parts and tyres are not always easy to obtain, though there are plenty of puncture-repair places. All in all, driving is no great pleasure except in rural areas where there's little traffic.

Petrol is expensive when compared to the cost of living in India – around Rs 24 per litre – but diesel is much cheaper at around Rs 10 per litre. Petrol is readily available in all larger towns and along main roads, so there is no need to carry spare fuel. You can now get unleaded petrol in Delhi, Mumbai, Calcutta and Chennai.

MOTORCYCLE

Travelling around India by motorcycle has become increasingly popular in recent years, and it certainly has its attractions – seeing small, untouristed villages and having the freedom to go when and where you like. You'll still get a sore bum, you'll have difficult and frustrating conversations and you'll get fed up with asking directions, receiving misleading answers, and getting lost, but you'll also have adventures not available to the visitor who relies on public transport.

This section is based largely on information originally contributed by intrepid Britons Ken Twyford and Gerald Smewing, with updates from Jim & Lucy Amos and Bill Keightley.

Equipment

An International Driving Licence is not mandatory, but is handy to have.

Helmets (required in the main cities) should definitely be brought with you. Although Indian helmets are cheap, it is often hard to find one that fits well, and the quality is rather suspect. You are not required by law to wear a helmet, but you'd be silly not to do so.

Leathers, gloves, boots, waterproofs and other protective gear should also be brought from your home country.

A few small bags will be a lot easier to carry than one large rucksack. A tent and sleeping bag are handy where accommodation is scarce.

Rental

Motorcycles can be rented from companies in several places in India (Delhi and Goa, for example) for a negotiable price, including insurance. Costs are around Rs 10,000 per month for a 500cc bike or Rs 8000 per month for a 350cc bike. Expect to pay about Rs 400 a day (including insurance). You'll have to leave a deposit (returnable) of cash and/or your return air ticket.

Some Indian Rules of the Road

Drive on the Left Theoretically vehicles are supposed to keep to the left in India – as in Japan, Britain, Australia and New Zealand. In practice, most vehicles keep to the middle of the road on the basis that there are fewer potholes in the middle than on the sides. When another vehicle is encountered the lesser vehicle should cower to the side. Misunderstandings as to the right of way of vehicles can have unfortunate consequences.

Overtaking In India it is not necessary to ascertain that there is space to complete the overtaking manoeuvre before pulling out. Overtaking can be attempted on blind corners, on the way up steep hills or in the face of oncoming traffic. Smaller vehicles unexpectedly encountered in mid-manoeuvre can be expected to swerve apologetically out of the way. If a larger vehicle is encountered it is to be hoped that the overtakee will slow, pull off or otherwise make room for the overtaker.

Use of Horn Although vehicles can be driven with bald tyres or nonexistent brakes, it is imperative that the horn be in superb working order. Surveys by Lonely Planet authors have revealed that the average driver uses the horn 10 to 20 times per kilometre, so a 100km trip can involve 2000 blasts of the horn. In any case the horn should be checked for its continued loud operation at least every 100m. Signs prohibiting use of horns are not to be taken seriously.

Purchase

India does not have used-vehicle dealers, motorcycle magazines or weekend newspapers with pages of motorcycle classified advertisements. To purchase a second-hand machine one simply needs to inquire. A good place to start is with mechanics. They are likely to know somebody who is selling a bike. In Delhi the area around Hari Singh Nalwa St in Karol Bagh is full of places buying, selling and renting motorcycles. One place that has been recommended by many travellers is Inder Motors (☎ 011-572 8579, fax 578 1052), 1744/55 Hari Singh Nalwa St. Others include Sharma Motorcycle Depot (☎ 011-752 1128), C-27 Double Story, Paharganj (deals in vintage bikes and spare parts), and Madaan Motors (☎ 011-573 5801, fax 723 5684), 1767/53 Naiwala St, Karol Bagh (new bikes but also stocks old Nortons and Matchless).

To buy a new bike, you'll have to have a local address and be a resident foreign national. However, unless the dealer you are buying from is totally devoid of imagination and contacts, this presents few problems. When buying second-hand, all you need to do is give an address.

New bikes are generally purchased through a showroom. Quoted new prices at the time of writing were:

Enfield 500cc	US$1500 (including ownership papers)
Enfield 350cc	Rs 54,000 (standard)
	Rs 58,000 (deluxe)
Rajdoot 175cc	US$800

Madaan can ship a bike for Rs 13,500 including the crate, packing and insurance. Second-hand bikes (two to three years old) cost about US$1000 for a 500cc. Transferring ownership costs Rs 1000 to Rs 1500. When buying second-hand it is best to engage the services of an 'auto consultant'. These people act as go-betweens to bring buyers and sellers together. They will usually be able to show you a number of machines to suit your price bracket. These agents may sometimes advertise on shopfronts.

The overall appearance of the bike doesn't seem to affect the price greatly. Dents and scratches don't reduce the cost much, and added extras don't increase it by much.

When the time comes to sell the bike, don't appear too anxious to get rid of it and don't hang around in one town too long as word gets around the auto consultants and the offers will get smaller as the days go by. If you get a reasonable offer, grab it. Regardless of which bike it is, you'll be told it's the 'least popular in India' and other such tales.

Ownership Papers A needless hint perhaps, but do not part with your money until you have the ownership papers, receipt and affidavit signed by a magistrate authorising the owner (as recorded in the ownership papers) to sell the machine – not to mention the keys to the bike and the bike itself!

Each state has a different set of ownership transfer formalities. Get assistance from the agent you're buying the machine through or from one of the many 'attorneys' hanging around under tin roofs by the Motor Vehicles Department. They will charge you a fee of up to Rs 300, which will consist largely of a bribe to expedite matters.

Alternatively, you could go to one of the many typing clerk services and ask them to type out the necessary forms, handling the matter cheaply yourself – but with no guarantee of a quick result.

Check that your name has been recorded in the ownership book and stamped and signed by the department head. If you intend to sell your motorcycle in another state then you will need a 'No Objections Certificate'. This confirms your ownership and is issued by the Motor Vehicles Department in the state of purchase, so get it immediately when transferring ownership papers to your name. The standard form can be typed up for a few rupees, or more speedily and expensively through one of the many attorneys.

Insurance & Tax As in most countries it is compulsory to have third-party insurance.

The New India Assurance Company or the National Insurance Company are just two of a number of companies who can provide it. The cost for comprehensive insurance is around Rs 1000 for 12 months, and this also covers you in Nepal.

Road tax is paid when the bike is bought new. This is valid for the life of the machine and is transferred to the new owner when the bike changes hands.

Which Bike? The big decision to make is whether to buy new or second-hand. Obviously, cost is the main factor, but remember that with a new bike you are less likely to get ripped off as the price is fixed and includes free servicing. Old bikes are obviously cheaper and you don't have to be a registered resident foreign national, but you are far more open to getting ripped off, either by paying too much or by getting a dud bike.

There is no single bike that suits everybody. The following is a rundown of what's readily available.

Mopeds These come with or without gears. As they are only 50cc capacity, they are really only useful around towns or for short distances.

Scooters There are the older design Bajaj and Vespa scooters, or the more modern Japanese designs by Honda-Kinetic and others. The older ones are 150cc while the Honda is 100cc and has no gears.

Several readers have written in praise of this form of transport. Scooters are economical to buy and run, are easy to ride, have a good resale value, and most have built-in lockable storage. The 150cc Bajaj Cheetak has plenty of power and acceleration for Indian road conditions. It's reliable as long as the spark plug is kept clean; newer models have electronic ignition so there's no need to adjust the points.

A big plus for the scooter is the spare tyre. I've experienced a puncture nearly every 1500km and believe me, pushing a dead motorcycle through the hot Indian sun is a pain. Wheel removal on a scooter is a breeze – five nuts and that's it. No

dirty chains to screw around with, no broken spokes to replace. Another inherent plus of this machine is the front end, which protects the rider from numerous surprise projections as well as mud and other flying excretions. Let someone else ride deafening Enfields with their greasy temperamental chains, no spare tyre and gas tank between their legs. I'll take a 'bulletproof' scooter any day!

Bill Keightley

100cc Motorcycles This is the area with the greatest choice. The four main Japanese companies – Honda, Suzuki, Kawasaki and Yamaha – all have 100cc, two-stroke machines, while Honda and Kawasaki also have four-stroke models.

There's little to differentiate between these bikes; all are lightweight, easy to ride, economical, reliable and have good resale value. They are suitable for intercity travel on reasonable roads but should not be laden down with too much gear. Spares and servicing are readily available.

If you're buying second-hand avoid the Rajdoot 175 XLT, which is based on a very old Polish model, and the Enfield Fury, which has a poor gearbox, spares that are hard to come by and a low resale value.

Bigger Bikes The Enfield Bullet is the classic machine and is the one most favoured among foreigners. Attractions are the traditional design, thumping engine sound and the price, which is not much more than the new 100cc Japanese bikes. It's a wonderfully durable bike, easy to maintain and economical to run, but mechanically a bit hit and miss, largely because of poorly engineered parts and inferior materials – valves and tappets are the main problem areas. Another drawback is the lack of an effective front brake – the small drum brake is a joke, totally inadequate for what is quite a heavy machine. The Bullet is also available in a 500cc single-cylinder version. It has a functional front brake and 12V electrics that are superior to the 350's 6V. If you opt for a 350cc, consider paying the Rs 5000 extra to have the 500cc front wheel fitted.

If you are buying a new Enfield with the intention of shipping it back home, it's definitely worth opting for the 500cc as it has features – such as folding rear footrest and longer exhaust pipe – that most other countries require. The emission control regulations in some places, such as the USA, are so strict that there is no way these bikes would be legal. As a result, they won't allow the vehicles to enter the country. You may be able to get around this by buying an older bike, as the regulations often only apply to new machines. Make sure you check all this out before you go lashing out on a new Enfield, only to find it unregisterable at home.

The Yezdi 250 Classic (or Monarch/Deluxe) is a cheap and basic bike. It's a rugged machine, and one that you often see in rural areas.

The Rajdoot 350 is an imported Yamaha 350cc. It's well engineered, fast and has good brakes. Disadvantages are that it's relatively uneconomical to run, and spares are hard to come by. These bikes are also showing their age badly as they haven't been made for some years now. The BMW F650 is available in India, but it's expensive.

On the Road

It must be said that, given the general road conditions, motorcycling is a reasonably hazardous endeavour, and one best undertaken by experienced riders only – you don't want to discover on the Grand Trunk Road with a lunatic in a Tata truck bearing down on you that you don't know how to take evasive action! Hazards range from families of pigs crossing the road to broken-down vehicles abandoned in the middle of the road.

Route-finding can be very tricky. It's certainly much easier to jump on a bus and leave the navigating to someone who knows the way. The directions people give you can be very interesting. It is invariably a 'straight road', although if pressed the person might also reveal that the said straight road actually involves taking two right turns, three left turns and the odd fork or two. Pronunciation can also cause problems, particularly in country areas.

On the whole people are very welcoming, and curious about how you are coping with the traffic conditions.

Generally you can park the bike and not have things stolen from it. The biggest annoyance is that people seem to treat parked motorcycles as public utilities – handy for sitting on, using the mirror to do their hair, fiddling with the switches – but they don't deliberately do any damage. You'll just have to turn all the switches off and readjust the mirrors when you get back on.

Run-ins with the law are not a major problem. The best policy is to give a smile and a friendly wave to any police officers, even if you are doing the opposite of what is signalled.

In the event of an accident, call the police straight away, and don't move anything until the police have seen exactly where and how everything ended up. One foreigner reported spending three days in jail on suspicion of being involved in an accident, when all he'd done was taken a child to hospital from the scene of an accident.

Don't try to cover too much territory in one day. As such a high level of concentration is needed to survive, long days are tiring and dangerous. On the busy national highways expect to average 50km/h without stops; on smaller roads, where driving conditions are worse, 10km/h is not an unrealistic average. On the whole you can expect to cover between 100km and 150km in a day on good roads.

Night driving should be avoided at all costs. If you think driving in daylight is difficult, imagine what it's like at night when there's the added hazard of half the vehicles being inadequately lit (or not lit at all), not to mention the breakdowns in the middle of the road.

Putting the bike on a train for really long hauls can be a convenient option. You'll pay about as much as the 2nd class passenger fare for the bike. It can be wrapped in straw for protection if you like; this is done at the parcels office at the station, which is also where you pay the bike fare. The petrol tank must be empty, and there should be a tag in

Road Safety

In India there are more than 70,000 road deaths each year – an astonishing total in relation to the number of vehicles on the road. The USA, for instance, has 43,000 road fatalities per year, but it also has more than 20 times the number of vehicles.

The reasons for the high road toll in India are numerous, and many of them fairly obvious. Firstly, there's road congestion and vehicle overcrowding – when a bus runs off the road there are plenty of people stuffed inside to get injured, and it's unlikely too many of them will be able to escape in a hurry.

Secondly, there is India's unwritten road law that vehicles always have the right of way over pedestrians and bigger vehicles always have the right of way over smaller ones. It's not surprising, then, that most fatalities are pedestrians involved in hit-and-run accidents. (The propensity to disappear after the incident is not wholly surprising, however, since lynch mobs can assemble remarkably quickly, even when the driver is not at fault!)

Most accidents are caused by trucks. Being the biggest, heaviest and mightiest vehicles on the road, you either get out of their way or get run down. Also, as with so many Indian vehicles they're likely to be grossly overloaded and not in the best of condition. Trucks are actually licensed and taxed to carry a load 25% more than the maximum recommended by the manufacturer. It's staggering to see the number of truck wrecks by the sides of the national highways, and these aren't old accidents, but ones that have obviously happened in the last 24 hours or so.

The karma theory of driving also helps to push up the statistics – it's not so much the vehicle that collides with you as the events of your previous life that caused the accident.

If you are driving, you need to be extremely vigilant at all times. At night there are unilluminated cars and ox carts, and in the daytime there are fearless bicycle riders and hordes of pedestrians. Day and night there are the crazy truck drivers to contend with. Indeed, at night, it's best to avoid driving at all along any major trunk route unless you're prepared to get off the road completely every time a truck is coming in the opposite direction! The other thing you have to contend with at night is the eccentric way in which headlights are used – a combination of full beam and totally off (dipped beams are virtually unheard of). A loud horn definitely helps since the normal driving technique is to put your hand firmly on the horn, close your eyes and plough through regardless.

an obvious place detailing name, destination, passport number and train details.

Repairs & Maintenance

Anyone who can handle a screwdriver and spanner in India can be called a mechanic, or *mistri*, so be careful. If you have any mechanical knowledge it may be better to buy your own tools and learn how to do your own repairs. This will save a lot of arguments over prices. If you are getting repairs done by someone, don't leave the premises while the work is being done or you may

find that good parts have been ripped off your bike and replaced with bodgy old ones.

Original spare parts bought from an 'authorised dealer' can be rather expensive compared to the copies available from your spare-parts wallah. If you're going up to Ladakh, take basic spares with you (valves, piston rings and rocker rods) as they are not easily available there.

If you buy an older machine you would do well to check and tighten all nuts and bolts every few days. Indian roads and engine vibration tend to work things loose, and constant checking could save you rupees and trouble. Check the engine and gearbox oil level regularly. With the quality of oil it is advisable to change it and clean the oil filter every couple of thousand kilometres.

Punctures Chances are you'll be requiring the services of a puncture-wallah *(punkucha wallah* in Hindi) at least once a week. They are found everywhere, often in the most surprising places, but it's advisable to at least have tools sufficient to remove your own wheel and take it to the puncture-wallah.

Given the hassles of constant flat tyres, it's worth lashing out on new tyres if you buy a second-hand bike with worn tyres. A new rear tyre for an Enfield costs around Rs 600.

Fuel Should you run out, try flagging down a passing car (not a truck or bus since they use diesel) and beg for some. Most Indians are willing to let you have some if you have a hose or siphon and a container. Alternatively, hitch a truck ride to the nearest petrol station. One route on which you will have to carry spare fuel (10L) is the Leh-Manali road.

Organised Motorcycle Tours

Classic Bike Adventure (☎ 0832-273351, fax 276124, 277343), Casa Tres Amigos, Socol Vado No 425, Assagao, Bardez, Goa, is a German company that organises bike tours on well-maintained Enfields with full insurance. Tours last two to three weeks and cover Rajasthan, the Himalaya between Kullu/Manali and Gangotri, and the south from Goa.

Ferris Wheels (☎/fax 02-9904 7419, email safari@ferriswheels.com.au), Box 743, Crows Nest, NSW 2065, Australia, also organises tours through the Himalaya and Rajasthan on classic Enfields. It has a Web site (www.ferriswheels.com.au).

Indian Motorcycle Adventures (☎ 09-372 7550, email gumby@ihug.co.nz), 40 O'Brien Rd, Rocky Bay, Waiheke Island, New Zealand, does 20-day tours of Rajasthan in November, January and February.

BICYCLE

Most of the following information comes from Ann Sorrel, with updates from various travellers.

Every day millions of Indians pedal along the country's roads. If they can do it so can you. India offers an immense array of challenges for a long-distance cyclist: there are high-altitude passes and rocky dirt tracks; smooth-surfaced, well-graded highways with roadside restaurants and lodges; coastal routes through coconut palms; and winding country roads through coffee plantations. There are city streets with all manner of animal and human-powered carts and vehicles and the spectacular bazaars. Hills, plains, plateaus, deserts – you name it, India's got it!

Nevertheless, long-distance cycling is not for the faint of heart or weak of knee. You'll need physical endurance to cope with the roads and the climate, plus you'll face cultural challenges – 'the people factor'.

Cycling in India is tough. Think how hard you want to travel before you go. But for all its chaos, dust and bumpy roads India is a beautiful country. The birds will thrill you, the animals and children will delight you and the warmth and generosity of the people will win you over. During one elevenses break a skinny old man appeared herding his cows. He immediately offered us his only bit of sugar cane. It made me feel very humble and it's typical of the Indians we met. It's a hard country to leave.

Ian & Allie Smith

Just how unusual is a cycle tourist in India? At a guess, currently 2000 foreign cyclists tour for a month or more each year somewhere on the subcontinent. That number appears to be growing rapidly. Perhaps 5000 Indians tour as well – mostly young men and college students. 'Kashmir to Kanyakumari' or a pilgrimage to holy places are their most common goals.

Before you set out, read some books on bicycle touring such as the Sierra Club's *The Bike Touring Manual* by Rob van de Plas (Bicycle Books, 1993). Cycling magazines provide useful information including

India by Enfield

Compared with the world's leading brands, Enfields are low-performance, heavy bikes. But they are ideal for Indian road conditions, as they are rugged and economical. On top of this is the thrill of riding a classic bike. We found that biking in India was the only way to travel.

There are plenty of 'great deals' around in the second-hand bike market (US$500 to US$600, or from local dealers Rs 20,000 to Rs 25,000). But unless you know a lot about bike mechanics, you are better off paying a little more. We met several travellers on oldies who were having severe problems and being given the runaround by local mechanics in out of the way places. In Delhi we paid Rs 30,000 for a 1992 500cc, plus Rs 6000 for carriers and other extras. This was considered a bargain by everyone we met, so you could expect to pay a little more, perhaps up to Rs 45,000. A brand new Bullet costs Rs 61,000.

Enfields need a lot of maintenance (usually easy enough to do). It's really important that you check the bike thoroughly every day before setting out. Things have a habit of shaking lose. Forget all the stories about spares for the 500cc being unobtainable. We easily got everything we needed. Get the preparation work done in Delhi and take spares. We looked all over Chennai for good-quality second-hand bikes but had no success. New bikes are readily available ex-factory in Chennai and there is a dealer on Vepery Rd who has some rear carriers. We ended up bringing our bikes down to Chennai from Delhi by train (Rs 950 – but well worth the money to save up to eight days of hard riding). You should get the bike packed before sending and remove all mirrors and loosen the handlebars. Inder Motors in Delhi does packing, or you can get it done at the train station parcel office (it shouldn't cost more than Rs 25). (Inder Motors in Delhi is still by far the best dealer and repairer of second-hand Enfields that we came across).

We strongly recommend having a twin lever front brake fitted. This costs about Rs 1200, but it means you have an effective front brake. The standard single lever is all but useless.

listings for bicycle tour operators and the addresses of spare-parts suppliers. They're also good places to look for a riding companion.

For a real feel of the adventure of bike touring in strange places, read Dervla Murphy's classic *Full Tilt – From Dunkirk to Delhi on a Bicycle*, Lloyd Sumner's *The Long Ride* or Bettina Selby's *Riding the Mountains Down* (subtitled 'A Journey by Bicycle to Kathmandu').

Your local cycling club may be able to help with information and advice. In the UK, the Cyclists Touring Club (☎ 01483-417217), 69 Meadrow, Godalming, Surrey GU7, has country touring sheets that are free to members. The International Bicycle Fund (☎ 206-628 9314), 4887 Columbia Drive South, Seattle, Washington 98108-1919, USA, has two useful publications: *Selecting and Preparing a Bike for Travel in Remote Areas* and *Flying with Your Bike*.

If you're a serious cyclist or amateur racer and want to contact counterparts while in India, there's the Cycle Federation of India; contact the Secretary, Yamun Velodrome, New Delhi.

Rental

Even in the smallest towns there will always be a shop that rents bikes. In tourist areas (such as hill stations) and places where foreigners are common (like Goa) you'll probably pay about double the normal rate.

If you're travelling with small children and would like to ride a lot, consider getting a bike seat made. If you find a shop making

India by Enfield

Driving goggles are essential, but we only saw them for sale in Delhi. Almost every helmet we saw for sale was of poor quality. We bought a couple of Rs 120 fibreglass numbers. But these would only be of use in a low-speed crash.

The paperwork is fairly complex. If you intend exporting the bike you will need a letter from your embassy. This process is best handled by an agent who should be able to transfer ownership smoothly. If you are renting or doing a buy-back, you will just need a rental agreement or a bill of sale. An International Driving Licence is recommended, though not essential. A permit from your home country will do.

On the road, give way to anything bigger than you; slow down, use your horn and try to ride around the other vehicle. It's extremely important to keep your speed down at all times. We have biked India several times and each time we've heard of young westerners dying on the roads when speeding. Trucks can be intimidating, but generally aren't aggressive, merely thoughtless. In South India between September and October beware of rice and millet laid out to dry on mats placed on the road. The trucks that run over the grain help thresh it, but it poses a real hazard to bikes.

Travelling the back roads is most rewarding. There is little traffic, but watch the potholes. We saw a van roll over after its wheel sank into a deep, water-filled pothole. Another thing to watch on the back roads is the cunningly disguised speed bumps at the entrances of many villages. And if you are biking in South India have someone write down the name of your destination in Tamil script; you will find this useful, as in many areas there are no signs in English.

Despite all this, getting off the beaten track is great. People are overwhelmingly friendly, wanting to help (and feed) you at every stop. The scenery is stunning. Expect to do a maximum of 300km on major highways and about 200km on back roads per day.

Steven Krzystyniak

cane furniture they'll make up a child's bicycle seat from a sketch. Get it made to fit on a standard-size rear carrier and it can be securely attached with a few lengths of cord.

Purchase

Finding an Indian bike for touring is no problem: every cycle town will have at least a couple of cycle shops. Shop around for prices and remember to bargain. Try to get a few extras – bell, stand, spare tube – thrown in. There are many brands of Indian clunkers – Hero, Atlas, BSA, Raleigh, Bajaj, Avon – but they all follow the same basic, sturdy design. A few mountain bike lookalikes have recently come on the market, but most have no gears. Raleigh is considered the finest quality, followed by BSA, which has a big line of models including some sporty

jobs. Hero and Atlas both claim to be the biggest seller. Look for the cheapest or the one with the snazziest plate label.

Once you've decided on a bike you have a choice of luggage carriers – mostly the rat-trap type varying only in size, price and strength. There's a wide range of saddles available but all are equally bum-breaking. A stand is certainly a useful addition and a bell or airhorn is a necessity. An advantage of buying a new bike is that the brakes actually work. Centre-pull and side-pull brakes are also available but at extra cost and may actually make the bike more difficult to sell. The average Indian will prefer the standard model.

Sportier 'mountain bike' styles with straight handlebars are popular in urban areas. In big cities and touristy areas it's also possible to find used touring bikes left by travellers. Also check with diplomatic community members for bikes.

Reselling is no problem. Count on getting about 70% of what you originally paid if it was a new bike. A local cycle-hire shop will probably be interested or you could ask the proprietor of your hotel if they know any prospective purchasers.

Using Your Own Bike

By all means consider bringing your own bike. Mountain bikes are especially suited to countries such as India. Their sturdier construction makes them more manoeuvrable, less prone to damage, and allows you to tackle rocky, muddy roads unsuitable for lighter machines.

There is a disadvantage however: your machine is likely to be a real curiosity and subject to much pushing, pulling and probing. If you can't tolerate people touching your bicycle, don't bring it to India.

Don't leave anything on your bike that can easily be removed when it's unattended – your pump and water bottle are particularly attractive to thieves.

However, don't be paranoid about theft – outside the major cities it would be well-nigh impossible for a thief to resell your bike as it would stand out too much. And not many folk understand quick-release levers on wheels. Your bike is probably safer in India than in western cities.

On the Road

The 'people factor' makes a bike ride in India both rewarding and frustrating. Those with Indian bikes are less likely to be mobbed by curious onlookers. A tea stop with an imported bike can attract a crowd of 50 men and boys eagerly commenting on the bike's operation – one points to the water-bottle saying 'petrol', another twists the shifter lever saying 'clutch', another squeezes a tyre saying 'tubeless' or 'airless', yet others nod knowingly as 'gear system', 'automatic' and 'racing bike' are mouthed. In some areas you'll even get 'disco bike'!

The worst scenario is stopping on a city street for a banana, looking up as you are pushing off to find rickshaws, cyclists and pedestrians all blocking your way! At times the crowd may be unruly – schoolboys especially. If the mob is too big, call over a *lathi*-wielding policeman. The boys will scatter pronto! Sometimes the hostile boys throw rocks. The best advice is to keep pedalling; don't turn around or stop, and don't leave your bike and chase them as this will only incite them further. Appeal to adults to discipline them. Children, especially boys seven to 13 years old, are unruly and dangerous in crowds. Avoid riding past a boys' school at recess.

Routes You can go anywhere on a bike that you would on trains and buses, with the added pleasure of seeing all the places in between.

Try to avoid the major highways up north like National Highway 1 through Haryana, and National Highway 2 – the Grand Trunk Rd – between Delhi and Calcutta. They're plagued by speeding buses and trucks. Other national highways can be pleasant – often lonely country roads well marked with a stone every kilometre. A basic knowledge of Hindi will help you to translate the signs, although at least one marker in five will be in English.

Another option is to follow canal and river paths. It's also possible in some areas to bike along railway tracks on maintenance roads. Do make inquiries before venturing off road.

Crossing international borders with a bicycle is relatively uncomplicated. India has border crossings with Pakistan, Nepal and Bangladesh. Unlike a car or motorcycle, papers need not be presented. Do not be surprised, however, if the bike is thoroughly inspected for contraband!

Asking Directions Asking directions can be a real frustration. Always ask three or four different people just to be certain, using traffic police only as a last resort. Try to be patient; be careful about 'left' and 'right' and be prepared for instructions like 'go straight and turn here and there'.

Distances If you've never cycled long distances, start with 20km to 40km a day and increase this as you gain stamina and confidence. Cycling long distances is 80% determination and 20% perspiration. Don't be ashamed to get off and push the bike up steep hills. For an eight hour pedal a serious cyclist and interested tourist will average 90km to 130km a day on undulating plains, or 70km to 100km in mountainous areas.

Food & Accommodation There's no need to bring a tent. Inexpensive lodges are widely available, and a tent pitched by the road would merely draw crowds. There's also no need to bring a stove and cooking kit (unless you cannot tolerate Indian food) as there are plenty of tea stalls and restaurants (called hotels). When you want to eat, ask for a hotel. When you want a room ask for a lodge. On major highways you can stop at *dhabas*, the Indian version of a truck stop. The one with the most trucks parked in front generally has the best food (or serves alcohol). Dhabas have *charpois* (string beds) to serve as tables and seats or as beds for weary cyclists. You should keep your bicycle next to you throughout the night. There will be no bathroom or toilet facilities but plenty of road noise. Dhabas are not recommended for single women riders.

Eating at dhabas is probably for the adventurous. We tried a couple but that was enough. The food was unpleasant and the water unsafe. So for lunch we opted for banana sandwiches eaten on a grassy verge. Bananas are cheap (Rs 6 per kilogram) and white (milk) bread is widely available. Sugar cane too was a great reviver and very juicy. We still got people coming up for a chat or just to stare but it wasn't as intimidating as in the dhabas.

Ian & Allie Smith

Transporting Your Bike Sometimes you may want to quit pedalling. For sports bikes, air travel is easy. With luck airline staff may not be familiar with procedures, so use this to your advantage. Tell them the bike doesn't need to be dismantled and that you've never had to pay for it. Remove all luggage and accessories and let the tyres down a bit.

Bus travel with a bike varies from state to state. Generally it goes for free on the roof. If it's a sports bike stress that it's lightweight. Secure it well to the roof rack, check it's in a place where it won't get damaged and take all your luggage inside.

Train travel is more complex – pedal up to the train station, buy a ticket and explain you want to book a cycle for the journey. You'll be directed to the luggage offices (or officer) where a triplicate form is prepared. Note down your bike's serial number and provide a good description of it. Again leave only the bike, not luggage or accessories. Your bike gets decorated with one copy of the form, usually pasted on the seat, you get another, and God only knows what happens to the third. Produce your copy of the form to claim the bicycle from the luggage van at your destination. If you change trains en route, *personally* ensure the cycle changes too!

Repairs & Maintenance

Indian Bikes As there are so many repair 'shops' (some consisting only of a puncture-wallah with his pump, a box of tools, a tube of rubber solution and a water pan under a tree), there is no need to carry spare parts, especially as you'll only own the bike for a few weeks or months. Just take a roll of tube-patch rubber, a tube of Dunlop patch glue, two tyre irons and the wonderful 'universal' Indian bike spanner, which fits all the nuts. Puncture-wallahs will patch tubes for a couple of rupees anyway, so chances are you won't have to fix a puncture yourself. Besides, Indian tyres are pretty heavy duty, so with luck you won't get too many flats.

Your Own Bike If you bring your own bicycle to India, you'll need to be prepared for the contingencies of part replacement or repair. Bring spare tyres, tubes, patch kits, chassis, cables, freewheels and spokes. Ensure you have a working knowledge of your machine. Bring all necessary tools with you as well as a compact bike manual with diagrams – Indian mechanics can work wonders and illustrations help overcome the language barrier. Roads don't have paved shoulders and are very dusty, so keep your chain lubricated.

Although India is officially metricated, tools and bike parts follow 'standard' or 'imperial' measurements. Don't expect to find tyres for 700cc rims, although 27 x 1¼ tyres are produced in India by Dunlop and Sawney. Some mountain bike tyres are available but the quality is dubious. Indian bicycle pumps cater to a tube valve different from the Presta and Schraeder valves commonly used in the west. If you're travelling with Presta valves (most high-pressure 27 x 1¼ tubes) bring a Schraeder (car type) adapter. In India you can buy a local pump adapter, which means you'll have an adapter on your adapter. Bring your own pump as well; most Indian pumps require two or three people to get air down the leaky cable.

In major cities Japanese tyres and parts (derailleurs, freewheels, chains) are available, but pricey – although so is postage, and transit time can be considerable. If you receive bike parts from abroad beware of exorbitant customs charges. Say you want the goods as 'in transit' to avoid these charges. They may list the parts in your passport!

For foreign parts try Metre Cycle, Kalba Devi Rd, Mumbai, or its branch in Thiruvananthapuram (Kerala); the cycle bazaar in the old city around Esplanade Rd, Delhi; Popular Cycle Importing Company on Popham's Broadway, Chennai; and Nundy & Company, Bentinck St, Calcutta. Alternatively, take your bicycle to a cycle market and ask around – someone will know which shop is likely to have things for your 'special' cycle. Beware of Taiwanese imitations and do watch out for tyres that may have been sitting collecting dust for years.

HITCHING

Hitching is never entirely safe in any country in the world, and we don't recommend it. Travellers who decide to hitch should understand that they are taking a small but potentially serious risk. People who do choose to hitch will be safer if they travel in pairs and let someone know where they are planning to go.

Hitching in India is not a realistic option. There are not that many private cars streaking across India so you are likely to be on board trucks. You are then stuck with the old quandaries of: 'Do they understand what I am doing?', 'Should I be paying for this?', 'Will the driver expect to be paid?', 'Will they be unhappy if I don't offer to pay?', 'Will they be unhappy if I offer or will they simply want too much?'.

It is a very bad idea for women to hitch. Remember India is a developing country with a patriarchal society far less sympathetic to rape victims than the west, and that's saying something. A woman in the cabin of a truck on a lonely road is perhaps tempting fate.

BOAT

Apart from ferries across rivers (of which there are many), the only real boating possibilities are the trips through the backwaters of Kerala – not to be missed (see the Kerala chapter for more details) and the ferries between Mumbai and Goa (see the Mumbai chapter).

The only other ferries connecting coastal ports are those from Calcutta and Chennai to the Andaman Islands (see Getting There & Away in the Port Blair section of the Andaman & Nicobar Islands chapter).

LOCAL TRANSPORT

Although there are comprehensive local bus networks in most major towns, unless you have time to familiarise yourself with the routes you're better off sticking to taxis, auto-rickshaws, cycle-rickshaws and hiring bicycles. The buses are often so hopelessly overcrowded that you can only really use them if you get on at the starting point and get off at the terminus.

A basic ground rule applies to any form of transport where the fare is not ticketed or fixed (unlike a bus or train), or calculated by a meter – agree on the fare beforehand. If you fail to do that you can expect enormous arguments and hassles when you get to your destination. And agree on the fare clearly – if there is more than one of you make sure it covers all of you. If you have baggage make sure there are no extra charges, or you may be asked for more at the end of the trip. If a driver refuses to use the meter, or insists on an extortionate rate, simply walk away – if he really wants the job the price will drop. If you can't agree on a reasonable fare, find another driver.

To/From the Airport

There are official buses, operated by the government, Indian Airlines or some local cooperative, to most airports in India. Where there aren't any, there will be taxis or auto-rickshaws. There are some airports close enough to town to get to by cycle-rickshaw.

When arriving at an airport anywhere in India, find out if there's a prepaid taxi booth inside the arrival hall. If there is, pay for one there. If you don't do this and simply walk outside to negotiate your own price, you'll invariably pay more. Taxi drivers are notorious for refusing to use the meter outside airport terminals. Confusingly, in some airports (Delhi in particular) there may be several prepaid taxi booths. The one with the lowest prices is the official one.

Taxi

There are taxis in most towns in India, and most of them (certainly in the major cities) are metered. Getting a metered fare is rather a different situation. First of all the meter may be 'broken'. Threatening to get another taxi will usually fix it immediately, except during rush hours.

Secondly the meter will almost certainly be out of date. Fares are adjusted upwards so much faster and more frequently than meters are recalibrated that drivers almost always have 'fare adjustment cards' indicating what you should pay compared to what the meter indicates. This is, of course, wide open to abuse. You have no idea if you're being shown the right card or if the

taxi's meter has actually been recalibrated and you're being shown the card anyway. In states where the numbers are written differently (such as Gujarat) it's not much use asking for the chart if you can't read it!

The only answer to all this is to try to get an idea of what the fare should be before departure (ask information desks at the airport or your hotel). You'll soon begin to develop a feel for what the meter says, what the cards say and what the two together should indicate.

Auto-Rickshaw

An auto-rickshaw is a noisy three-wheel device powered by a two-stroke motorcycle engine with a driver up front and seats for two (or sometimes more) passengers behind. They don't have doors (except in Goa) and have just a canvas top. They are also known as scooters or autos.

Although they are all made by Bajaj, it's amazing how the designs differ from town to town. Design seems to be unique to a particular town: in Chittorgarh in Rajasthan, for example, the auto-rickshaws are fitted with an extra seat facing backwards that enables them to carry four people (although they'll often carry eight or more!).

They're generally about half the price of a taxi, usually metered and follow the same ground rules as taxis.

Because of their size, auto-rickshaws are often faster than taxis for short trips and their drivers are decidedly nuttier – hair-raising near-misses are guaranteed and glancing-blow collisions are not infrequent; thrillseekers will love it!

In busy towns you'll find that, when stopped at traffic lights, the height you are sitting at is the same as most bus and truck exhaust pipes – copping dirty great lungfuls of diesel fumes is part of the fun of auto-rickshaw travel. Also, their small wheel size and rock-hard suspension makes them supremely uncomfortable; even the slightest bump will have you instantly airborne. The speed humps and huge potholes found everywhere are the bane of the rickshaw traveller – pity the poor drivers.

Tempo

Somewhat like a large auto-rickshaw, these ungainly looking three-wheel devices operate rather like minibuses or share taxis along fixed routes. Unless you are spending large amounts of time in one city, it is generally impractical to try to find out what the routes are. You'll find it much easier and more convenient to go by auto-rickshaw.

Cycle-Rickshaw

This is effectively a three-wheeler bicycle with a seat for two passengers behind the rider. Although they no longer operate in most of the big cities, except in the old part of Delhi and parts of Calcutta, you will find them in all the smaller cities and towns, where they're the basic means of transport.

Fares must always be agreed on in advance. Avoid situations where the driver says something like: 'As you like'. He's hoping you are not well acquainted with the correct fares and will overpay. Invariably, no matter what you pay in situations like this, it will be deemed too little and an unpleasant situation can develop quickly. This is especially the case in heavily touristed places, such as Agra and Jaipur. The best tactic is to settle on the price before you get moving.

It's quite feasible to hire a rickshaw-wallah by time, not just for a trip. Hiring one for a day or several days can make good financial sense.

Hassling over the fares is the biggest difficulty of cycle-rickshaw travel. They'll often go all out for a fare higher than it would cost you by taxi or auto-rickshaw. Nor does actually agreeing on a fare always make a big difference – there is a greater possibility of a post-travel fare disagreement when you travel by cycle-rickshaw than when you go by taxi or auto-rickshaw – whether they are metered or not.

Other Transport

In some places, tongas (horse-drawn two-wheelers) and victorias (horse-drawn carriages) still run.

Calcutta has a large tram network and India's first underground. Mumbai, Delhi and Chennai have suburban trains.

Once upon a time there used to be people-drawn rickshaws, but today these only exist in parts of Calcutta, although from January 1997 they were officially banned by the West Bengal government.

ORGANISED TOURS

At almost any place which is of tourist interest in India, and quite a few places which aren't, there will be tours operated either by the Government of India tourist office, the state tourist office or the local transport company – sometimes all three. Tours are usually excellent value, particularly in places where the sights are spread out. You probably couldn't get around Delhi on public transport as cheaply as you can on a tour.

These tours are not strictly for western tourists; you will almost always find yourself outnumbered by local tourists. Despite this, the tours are usually in English – possibly the only common language for middle-class Indian tourists in any case. These tours are an excellent place to meet Indians.

The big drawback is that many of them try to cram far too much into too short a period of time. If a tour looks too hectic, you're better off doing it yourself at a more appropriate pace or take the tour simply to find out which places you'd like to visit on your own.

SACRED
INDIA

Often painted over the doors of houses, the swastika is an ancient good luck symbol sacred to Hindus and Buddhists. The bent cross-bars symbolise motion. A swastika with cross-bars turning towards the right (clockwise) is associated with Ganesh and Vishnu, and is generally regarded as auspicious.

Heroes and demons, saints and saviours, ascetics and seekers; India, despite being a secular state, harbours arguably the world's richest heritage of spiritual and religious experience. India's major religion, Hinduism, is practised by approximately 80% of the population; more than 700 million people. It has the largest number of adherents of any religion in Asia – the only other Asian countries that are predominantly Hindu are Nepal, the Indonesian island of Bali and the Indian Ocean island of Mauritius. It is also (along with Buddhism, Jainism and Zoroastrianism) one of the oldest extant religions with firm roots extending back beyond 1000 BC. The Indus Valley civilisation seems to have developed a religion closely related to Hinduism, but it was the *Veda* scriptures that gave Hinduism its framework.

Buddhism and Jainism arose contemporaneously in the 6th century BC at a time of social and religious ferment. Both were reactions against the strictures of Brahminical Hinduism. Although more recent, Sikhism too has its roots in a protest movement, the *bhakti* (devotional) tradition of southern India. Islam swept into India from the north and was introduced to the south by Arab traders. Today it's the largest minority religion in the land. Christianity arrived in southern India with Syrian immigrants long before the first European ever dropped anchor in that part of the world, and today at least 18 million Indians belong to various Christian sects.

Title Page: Vibrant flower offerings can usually be found for sale in the streets leading to, and surrounding, temples.

Facing Page: Offerings to deities, made all over India each and every day of the year, can be given at temples, private homes or sacred sites, as seen in this river.

Right: There is a plethora of deities from all religious denominations worshipped and revered in India. Images of the more popular of these are available for sale throughout the country.

PAUL BEINSSEN

SACRED INDIA

EDDIE GERALD

HINDUISM

Hinduism defies attempts to define it in any specific sense. Some argue that it is more an association of religions. It has no founder, central authority or hierarchy. It is not a proselytising religion. You can't be converted; to be a Hindu you must be born one. The strictly orthodox maintain that only a person born in India of Hindu parents can truly claim to be Hindu.

To outsiders Hinduism often appears as a complex mix of contradictory beliefs and multiple gods. In theory it happily incorporates all forms of belief and worship. But for Hindus religious truth is ineffable; at its heart, Hinduism does not depend on the belief in the existence or otherwise of any individual or multiple gods. Essentially, all Hindus believe in Brahman, the One without a second, without attributes. Brahman is eternal, uncreated and infinite; everything that exists emanates from Brahman and will ultimately return to it. The multitude of gods and goddesses are merely manifestations – knowable aspects of this formless phenomenon – and one may freely pick and choose among them.

Although beliefs and practices vary widely from region to region, there are several unifying factors. These include common beliefs in reincarnation, *karma* (conduct or action) and *dharma* (appropriate behaviour for one's station in life), and in the caste system (see Society & Conduct in the Facts about India chapter).

Hindus believe earthly life is cyclical; you are born again and again (a process known as *samsara*), the quality of these rebirths being dependent upon your karma in previous lives. There is no escaping your

Facing Page: Most southern Indian temple architecture is based on Chalukyan temples, the ruins of which can still be seen in and around Badami in Karnataka.

Inset: Many pilgrims flock to Varanasi in Uttar Pradesh to bathe in the sacred waters of the holy River Ganges. Photo: Sarah-Jane Cleland

Right: Non-Hindus are only allowed into the outer courtyards of Tamil Nadu temples. However visitors should still be able to enjoy the colourful puja ceremonies that take place within temple grounds.

Far Right: Brahman priest at Kapaleeshwawar Temple in Chennai.

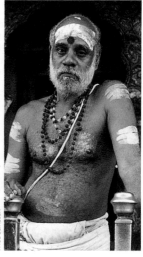

PAUL BEINSSEN

EDDIE GERALD

behaviour. Living a dharmic life and fulfilling your duty will enhance your chances of being born into a higher caste and better circumstances. Going the other way, rebirth may take animal form, but it's only as a human that you will gain sufficient self-knowledge to escape the cycle of reincarnation and achieve *moksha* (liberation). Traditionally, women are unable to attain moksha. The best they can do is fulfil their dharma and hope for a male incarnation next time round. For ordinary Hindus, fulfilling one's ritual and social duties is the main aim of worldly life. The *Bhagavad Gita* (see Sacred Texts later) is clear about this; doing your duty is more important than asserting your rights. That the householder and the renunciate may equally earn religious merit is a notion that was enshrined some 2000 years ago in the Brahmanic *ashrama* system. This kind of merit is only available to the upper three castes.

Essentially there are three stages in life recognised under the ashrama system: *brahmachari*, or chaste student; *grihastha*, the householder, who discharges their duty to their ancestors by having sons and making sacrifices to the gods; and *sanyasin*, the wandering ascetic who has renounced worldly things. The disinterested discharge of your ritual and social obligations is known as *karma-marga* and is one path to salvation. But there are others, including *jnana-marga*, or the way of knowledge (the study and practise of yoga and meditation), and *bhakti-marga*, devotion to a personal god. The latter path is open to women and *shudras* (caste of labourers).

Often written as 'om' and pronounced 'aum', this is an important mantra (sacred word or syllable) and one of Hinduism's most venerated signs. The '3' shape symbolises the creation, maintenance and destruction of the universe (and thus the trimurti). The inverted *chandra* (crescent or half moon) represents the discursive mind and the *bindu* (dot) within it, Brahman.

Sadhus

Wandering ascetics with ash-smeared bodies and matted hair are an enduring icon of the spiritual quest in India. Rejecting worldly attachments, sadhus, clad only in loincloths or saffron robes (the colour is said to symbolise the fertile blood of Parvati, Shiva's consort), travel light carrying little more than a begging bowl and a water pot (and sometimes a trident in deference to the greatest of all ascetics, Shiva).

Sadhus are famous for the austerities they practise: standing on one leg or holding an arm in the air for years at a time. These austerities, deemed necessary for those seriously committed to attaining enlightenment, are sometimes associated with the acquisition of *siddhis* (special powers such as levitation or the ability to appear and disappear at will).

The life of a sadhu can be the last stage in the ashrama cycle, however as dharma only offers men the opportunity for spiritual quest it is not an option available to women.

Left: Sadhus often relinquish all worldly possessions and although they rely almost exclusively on food donations from devotees, they rarely go hungry.
Photo: Peter Davis

Gods & Goddesses

The Hindu pantheon is prolific; some estimates put the total number of deities at 330 million. No beliefs or forms of worship are rejected by Hinduism. All are regarded as a manifestation of Brahman, and the particular object of veneration and supplication is often a matter of personal choice or tradition at a local or caste level. Brahman is often described as having three facets, the *trimurti:* Brahma, Vishnu and Shiva (also known as Mahesh).

RICHARD I'ANSON

Brahman The One; the ultimate reality. Brahman is formless, eternal and the source of all existence. Brahman is *nirguna* (without attributes), as opposed to all the other gods which are manifestations of Brahman and therefore *saguna* (with attributes).

Brahma Brahma only plays an active role during the creation of the universe. The rest of the time he is in meditation and is therefore regarded as an aloof figure, unlike the two other members of the trimurti, Shiva and Vishnu. His consort is Sarasvati, goddess of learning, and his vehicle is a swan. He is sometimes shown sitting on a lotus which rises from Vishnu's navel, symbolising the interdependence of the gods. He is generally depicted with four (crowned and bearded) heads, each turned towards the four points of the compass. And he usually holds the four books of the *Vedas*, one in each of his four hands.

Right: An image of the goddess Durga, whose victory over a buffalo-headed demon forms the basis for nationwide celebrations during the Dussehra festival in the Indian month of Asvina (September/October).

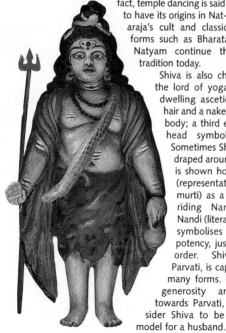

Vishnu The preserver or sustainer, Vishnu is associated with 'right action' and behaves as a lawful, devout Hindu. He protects and sustains all that is good in the world. He is usually depicted with four arms, each respectively holding: a lotus (whose petals are symbolic of the unfolding of the universe); a conch shell (as it can be blown like a trumpet it symbolises the cosmic vibration from which all existence emanates); a discus; and a mace (a reward for conquering Indra - the god of battle). His consort is Lakshmi, goddess of beauty and fortune. His vehicle is Garuda, a half bird/half beast creature, and he dwells in a heaven called Vaikuntha. The Ganges is said to flow from his feet.

Vishnu has 22 incarnations including Rama, Krishna and Buddha. He is alternatively known as Narayan (Lakshmi in turn is known as Mohini).

Shiva The destroyer, but without whom creation could not occur, Shiva is symbolised by the linga. With 1008 names Shiva takes many forms including Pashupati, champion of the animals, and Nataraja, lord of the *tandav* (dance), who paces out the creation and destruction of the cosmos. In fact, temple dancing is said to have its origins in Nataraja's cult and classic forms such as Bharata Natyam continue the tradition today.

Shiva is also characterised as the lord of yoga, a Himalaya-dwelling ascetic with matted hair and a naked, ash-smeared body; a third eye in his forehead symbolises wisdom. Sometimes Shiva has snakes draped around his neck and is shown holding a trident (representative of the trimurti) as a weapon while riding Nandi, his bull. Nandi (literally, enjoyment) symbolises power and potency, justice and moral order. Shiva's consort, Parvati, is capable of taking many forms. Because of his generosity and reverence towards Parvati, wom-en con-sider Shiva to be an ideal role model for a husband.

Top: Vishnu has descended from heaven several times to destroy evil and is expected to appear again sometime in the future in his incarnation as Kalki. Photo: Greg Elms

Left: Shiva is worshipped in many forms and can be the evil destroyer in one incarnation and creator of the universe and seed of life in another. Photo: Greg Elms

Ganesh Chubby and jolly, elephant-headed Ganesh is held in great affection and is especially popular in Maharashtra and Mumbai. He is the lord of beginnings, remover of obstacles and patron of scribes (the broken tusk he holds is the very one he used to write down later sections of the Mahabharata). In his other hands he holds an elephant goad, a noose and a bowl of sweetmeats. He is also often depicted with one hand raised in the gesture of fearlessness. The cobra round his waist and strands of matted hair hint at an association with Shiva, the ascetic. His animal mount is a rat-like creature, symbolic of Ganesh's light-hearted cunning (the rat is renowned for its slyness).

How Ganesh came to have the head of an elephant is a story with many variations. Generally it is said that Ganesh (created by Parvati) was asked by the goddess to guard the door while she bathed. When Shiva, her husband, arrived, Ganesh refused him entry. Angered by this Shiva lopped off Ganesh's head but repented once he realised who Ganesh was. To make amends he directed his attendants to bring back the head of the first creature they found. That creature was an elephant and thus restored, Ganesh was rewarded for his courage by being made guardian of entrances and lord of new ventures. Today his image graces the doors of homes and temples all over India.

Right: Instantly recognisable and hugely popular, images of the fearless Ganesh (like this one inside Sri Kodi Bhairava Swami Temple, Mysore, Karnataka) adorn temple entrances across the whole country. Ganesh came to worldwide prominence in 1995 when devotees discovered that his image was allegedly capable of drinking milk from a spoon – many Hindus believed this to be a divine message from the gods.
Photo: Eddie Gerald

Krishna An incarnation of Vishnu sent to earth to fight for good and combat evil. Krishna is tremendously popular. He is loyal and generous. His dalliances with the *gopis* (milkmaids) and his love for Radha (a married woman) have inspired countless paintings and songs. Krishna is depicted as being dark blue in colour and usually carries a flute.

Hanuman Hero of the *Ramayana* and loyal ally of Rama, Hanuman embodies the concept of *bhakti* (devotion). Images of Rama and Sita are said to be emblazoned upon his heart. He is king of the monkeys, therefore assuring them refuge at temples across the country, but he is capable of taking on any form he chooses.

Murugan Son of Shiva and brother of Skanda, god of war, Murugan is extremely popular in South India, especially Tamil Nadu. Some say Murugan and Skanda are one and the same. He is usually shown carrying a spear or trident.

Goddesses Within the Shaivite (followers of the Shiva cult) movement, Shakti – the goddess as mother and creator – is worshipped as a force in her own right. Those who follow her are known as shaktas.

The concept of Shakti is embodied in the ancient goddess Devi (mother and fierce destroyer). In Bengal she is known as Durga (a manifestation of Devi) and the Durga *puja* (blessing; commemorating Parvati's return to Shiva, Parvati being the benign aspect of Devi) is tremendously popular there. Durga's slaughter of the buffalo demon Mahishasura is a well-known Hindu myth and is frequently depicted in Hindu art as well as being the focus of the Dussehra festival held across India each September or October.

Kali, the 'black one' with the red tongue, is the most fearsome of the Hindu deities. She is often depicted dancing on Shiva's 'corpse' and garlanded with human heads. She is bloodthirsty, hankering after battle and carnage and, until its outlaw in the early 19th century, was appeased with human sacrifice.

In South India goddesses have always been especially potent and, at village level at least, are usually worshipped in their own right. They are fickle, bloodthirsty and earthy one moment, nurturing and creative the next.

Saraswati, goddess of learning, is the porcelain skinned consort of Brahma and is widely considered to be the most beautiful goddess.

New Deities New deities continue to emerge, for example Santoshi Mata, a figure created in the *Bollywood* film *Jai* (Hail). As she's claimed to descend from Shiva and Parvati, she has acquired a genealogy and has been absorbed into the pantheon as a bona fide goddess despite having no basis in the scriptures. Women appeal to her for success in the modern urban world; help with improving a husband's flagging career or the acquisition of a fridge or radio. Devotees fast on Friday in her honour. Established deities too fall in and out of fashion, but none is rejected out of hand.

Facing Page: Intricate images of deities can feature prominently on the exterior of temples. The riotously multi-coloured baroque Sri Meenakshi Temple, Madurai, Tamil Nadu is just one of many such examples.

Sacred Texts

Hindu sacred texts fall into two categories: those which are believed to be the word of god (*shruti*; meaning heard) and those produced by people (*smriti*; remembered).

The *Vedas*, introduced to the subcontinent by the conquering Aryan invaders, are regarded as shruti knowledge and are considered the authoritative basis for Hinduism. The oldest of the Veda texts, the *Rig-Veda*, was compiled more than 3000 years ago. Within its 1028 verses are prayers for prosperity and longevity as well as an explanation of the origins of the universe. The *Upanishads*, the last parts of the *Vedas*, reflect on the mystery of death and emphasise the oneness of the universe.

The oldest of the Vedic texts were written in Vedic Sanskrit, which is related to Old Persian. Later texts were composed in classical Sanskrit, but many have been translated into the vernacular.

The smriti texts comprise a large collection of literature spanning many centuries and include expositions on the proper performance of domestic ceremonies as well as proper pursuit of government, economics and religious law. Among the better known works contained within this body of literature are the *Karma Sutra*, *Ramayana*, *Mahabharata* and *Puranas*, which expand on the epics and promote the notion of the trimurti. Unlike the *Vedas*, the *Puranas* are not limited to initiated males of the higher castes and therefore have wider popular appeal. Also highly popular today are the *Mahabharata* and *Ramayana*, which drew an estimated audience of 80 million when it was serialised by Indian state television in the 1980s.

The *Mahabharata* The *Mahabharata* is thought to have been composed sometime around the 1st millennium BC and to have been the prerogative of the ruling and warrior classes, focusing as it did then on the exploits of their favourite deity, Krishna. By about 500 BC the *Mahabharata* had evolved into a far more complex creation, with substantial additions, including the *Bhagavad Gita* (where Krishna gives advice to Arjuna before a great battle). It is in fact the world's longest work of literature; eight times longer than the Greek epics the *Iliad* and the *Odyssey* combined.

The story centres on conflict between the gods – the heroes (Pandavas) and the demons (Kauravas). Overseeing events is Krishna (an incarnation of Vishnu) who has taken on human form. Krishna acts as charioteer for the Pandava hero, Arjuna, who eventually triumphs in a great battle with the Kauravas.

The *Ramayana* The *Ramayana* was composed around the 3rd or 2nd century BC and is believed to be largely the work of one person, the poet Valmiki. Like the *Mahabharata*, it centres on conflict between the gods and demons.

Basically, the story goes that the childless king of Ayodhya called upon the gods to provide him with a son. His wife duly gave birth to a boy. But this child, named Rama, was in fact an incarnation of Vishnu who had assumed human form to overthrow the demon king of Lanka, Ravana.

The adult Rama, who won the hand of the princess Sita in a competition, was chosen by his father to inherit his kingdom. But at the last minute Rama's stepmother intervened and demanded her son take Rama's place. Rama, Sita and Rama's brother, Lakshmana, were duly exiled and went off to the forests where Rama and Lakshmana battled demons and dark forces. Ravana's sister attempted to seduce Rama. She was rejected and in revenge, Ravana captured Sita and spirited her away to his palace in Lanka. Rama, assisted by an army of monkeys led by the loyal monkey god Hanuman, eventually found the palace, killed Ravana and rescued Sita. All returned victorious to Ayodhya where Rama was crowned king.

Bottom: Frescoes like these adorning the ceiling of the Brihadishwara Temple often bring to life scenes from the sacred texts.

BOTH PHOTOGRAPHS BY EDDIE GERALD

Sacred Places

The number seven has special significance in Hinduism. There are seven especially sacred cities which are major pilgrimage centres: Varanasi (associated with Shiva); Haridwar (where the Ganges enters the plains from the Himalaya); Ayodhya (birthplace of Rama); Mathura (birthplace of Krishna); Dwarka (legendary capital of Krishna thought to be off the Gujarat coast); Kanchipuram (the great Shiva temple); and Ujjain (site every 12 years of the Kumbha Mela). There are also seven sacred rivers: Ganges (Ganga); Sarasvati (thought to be underground); Yamuna; Indus; Narmada; Godavari; and Cauvery.

Of course there are thousands more sacred sites which can include groves, caves, mountains and other natural phenomena, or anything associated with the epics.

Puja

The ritual of puja allows worshippers to commune with the divine and can be conducted privately and simply at home or as a large, public and elaborate affair. Visitors to busy temple complexes may see several different pujas conducted before many shrines.

The rules governing puja are laid down in the sacred texts (the *shastras* and *agamas*) and the focal point is a deity whose image is treated as a special guest or royalty. In temples, puja is performed at sunrise and sunset and sometimes noon and midnight. Conducted by a priest, it begins with the reverential opening of the temple door. The god is woken by the din of temple musicians' drums and horns or by the priest's bell ringing and hand clapping. The god is then washed, anointed with oils and sandalwood paste, dressed and garlanded and may also be offered incense, food, perfume or a sacred thread. Visiting worshippers may be given a portion of *prasaad* (consecrated food). The priest presents devotees with the sacred flame, over which they pass their hands, thus receiving *darshana* (the blessing of the god). This is the climax of the ceremony when the fully clothed and alert deity is openly displayed to the worshippers.

Once the ceremony is over and the worshippers have left, the temple door is respectfully closed and the deity is left in peace until the next puja.

Left: Visitors to temples and sacred sites may be offered prasaad by temple caretakers or priests to use in puja ceremonies.

Temples

There is a saying that if the measurement of the temple is perfect, then there will be perfection in the universe. For Hindus the square is the perfect shape and complex rules govern the location, design and building of each temple, based on numerology, astrology, astronomy and religious law. These are so complicated and important that it's customary for each temple to harbour its own particular set of calculations as though they were religious texts.

Essentially, a temple is a map of the universe. At the centre there is an unadorned space, the *garbhagriha* (inner shrine), which is symbolic of the 'womb-cave' from which the universe emerged. This provides a residence for the deity to which the temple is dedicated. Above the shrine rises a superstructure known as a *vimana* in South India and a *shikara* in north India, which is representative of Mt Meru, the cosmic mountain that supports the heavens. Cave and mountain are linked by an axis that rises vertically from the shrine's icon to the finial atop the towering vimana.

As a temple provides a shelter for a deity it is sacred. Devotees acknowledge this by performing a *parkrama* (clockwise circumambulation) of it, a ritual that finds architectural expression in the passageways that track round the main shrine. Some temples also have *mandapas* (halls) connected to the sanctum by vestibules. These mandapas may also contain vimanas or shikaras.

Etiquette for Visitors Dress conservatively, remove your shoes before entering, and do not attempt to enter the inner shrine room if you are not a Hindu.

Bottom: The recently renovated Shri Meenakshi temple complex in the town of Madurai, Tamil Nadu is hugely popular with an estimated 10,000 visitors per day. Its 12 gopurams, ranging in height from 45 to 50m and covered in thousands of brightly coloured celestial and animal figures, are visible from almost every point in the city.

PETER DAVIS

SACRED INDIA

Holy Cows & Other Creatures

Animals, particularly snakes and cows, have been worshipped since ancient times in India. The cow represents fertility and nurturing, benign aspects of the mother goddess and is a symbol of Mother India. The bull is more aggressive but its association with Shiva (as his mount, Nandi) accords it enormous respect. Cows and large white bulls roam freely in India, even in cities where they repose beside busy roads (sometimes on traffic islands) seemingly unperturbed by the noisy, fume-belching vehicles surging around them.

Snakes, especially cobras, are also sacred and associated with fertility and welfare. *Naga* (snake) stones protect humans from snakes and are shrines to fertility. Some plants also have strong spiritual significance. The banyan tree *(Ficus benghalensis)* is so sacred that only in times of dire need would people pick its leaves or otherwise interfere with it. It symbolises the trimurti and a pilgrimage to a sacred banyan is equal to 12 years of sacrifice. Its ashes are said to have the power to eradicate sin. Mango trees *(Mangifera indica)* are symbolic of love; Shiva is believed to have married Parvati under a mango tree and so mango leaves are often used to decorate marriage *pandals* (marquees).

GREG ELMS

Left: In Tamil Nadu, on the third day of the Pongal (harvest) festival, sacred cows are washed, decorated and painted before being fed a mix of rice, sugar, dhal and milk. Also called pongal this dish ensures prosperity and abundance for the following year.

Folk Religion

Folk deities are frequently viewed as being more accessible to the ordinary person and more competent for dealing with everyday village life. Deities identified with mountains or forests may be represented simply by a pile of stones or tree branches, which devotees add to as they pass by. Others may have simple shrines erected in their honour to which devotees bring offerings of flowers, rice and fruit. Some are little known beyond a particular village. Others, such as the goddesses of pestilence (eg Mariyamma in South India), are widely recognised.

In South India folk deities are frequently female. A notable exception is Ayannar (ostensibly he is vegetarian and therefore ritually superior), who is worshipped in Tamil Nadu as a protective deity and for whom votive offerings, in the form of terracotta horses, are made in times of need.

Tribal Religion

Tribal religions have so merged with Hinduism and other mainstream religions that few are now clearly identifiable. But in the Nilgiri Hills of South India, the Toda people still cling to their own beliefs even though they have adopted some Hindu and Christian customs over the years. The vegetarian Toda venerate the buffalo upon which they depend for milk, butter and ghee. This relationship extends into the afterlife. When a Toda dies, a buffalo is killed to accompany them into the next world where it will continue to provide milk and its by-products for sustenance and for ritual purposes.

Bottom: Colourful and fragrant flower offerings for sale.

EDDIE GERALD

SACRED INDIA

ISLAM

More than 11% of India's population is Muslim, making it the largest minority religion in the country. Islam was introduced to the north by invading armies (in the 16th century the Mughal empire controlled much of north India) and to the south by Arab traders.

Islam as a religion was founded in Arabia by the Prophet Mohammed in the 7th century. The Arabic term *islam* means to surrender and believers (Muslims) undertake to surrender to the will of Allah (God). The will of Allah is revealed in the scriptures (*Quran*; Arabic for reading or recitation) and it was Mohammed to whom God revealed his will spurring him to act as his messenger.

Islam is monotheistic; God is unique and has no equal or partner. There is no concept of a trinity or trimurti as there is in Christianity and Hinduism. Everything is believed to be created by God and is deemed to have its own place and purpose within the universe. Only God is unlimited and self-sufficient. The purpose of all living things is submission to the divine will. Only humans have a choice: whether to obey or disobey. Humanity's weakness is its pride and sense of independence. Although God never speaks to Humankind directly, his word is conveyed through messengers (prophets – who are never themselves divine; Mohammed being the most recent prophet) who are charged with calling humanity back to God.

Facing Page: Nizam-ud-din's Tomb in Delhi is dedicated to the Sufi saint who followed a doctrine of renunciation and tolerance. In 1303 his prayers are reputed to have caused the withdrawal of Mughal invaders which made him enormously popular with all denominations.

Inset: Devotees at the Jama Masjid (literally Friday Mosque) in Old Delhi for prayers. Photo: Richard I'Anson

Right: Muslims firmly believe that cleanliness is next to godliness and will always perform ritual ablutions before attending prayers. Although they have no ritual significance devotees may use a prayer mat to avoid unclean surfaces.

In the years after Mohammed's death a succession dispute split the movement and the legacy today is the Sunnis and the Shi'ahs. The Sunnis, the majority, emphasise the 'well-trodden' path or the orthodox way. They look to tradition and the customs and views of the greater community. Shi'ahs believe that only *imams* (exemplary leaders) are able to reveal the hidden and true meaning of the Quran. The orthodox view is that there have been 12 imams, the last of them being Mohammed. However, since then *mujtahids* (divines) have interpreted

RICHARD I'ANSON

law and doctrine under the guidance of the imam, who will return at the end of time to spread truth and justice throughout the world.

All Muslims, however, share a belief in the five pillars of Islam: the *shahadah* (declaration of faith) 'there is no God but God; Mohammed is his prophet' (this must be recited aloud at least once in a believer's lifetime, with conviction and true understanding); prayer (five times a day and on one's own if one can't make it to a mosque); the *zakat* (tax) which today is usually a donation in the form of charity; fasting (during the month of Ramadan) for all except the sick, the very young, the elderly and those undertaking arduous journeys; the *haj* (pilgrimage) to Mecca, something a Muslim aspires to do at least once in their life.

One of the most striking differences between Hinduism and Islam is religious imagery. While Islamic art eschews any hint of idolatry or portrayal of god, it has evolved a rich heritage of abstract decorative motifs.

Most Muslims in India are Sunnis, although Kargil in western Ladakh has a Shi'ah majority. Kashmir is the only state in India with a Muslim majority.

Top Left: Unrolling prayer rugs for the morning devotions at the Jama Masjid in Delhi.

Bottom Left: Evening prayers at Tipu Sultan's Mosque, Calcutta.

RICHARD I'ANSON

Mosques

The basic elements of a typical mosque are essentially the same worldwide. A large space or hall is dedicated to communal prayer. In the hall is a *mihrab* (niche), which marks the direction of Mecca. Outside the hall there is usually some sort of courtyard which has places where devotees may wash their feet and hands before prayers. Minarets are placed at the cardinal points and it's from here that the faithful are called to prayer. The Jami Masjid in Fatehpur Sikri in Uttar Pradesh is said to be modelled on the mosque in Mecca.

Right: The great Jama Masjid of Old Delhi, completed in 1658, is the largest mosque in the country; its courtyard alone is capable of holding 25,000 people. It also represents the final architectural extravagance of Mughal emperor Shah Jahan, creator of the Taj Mahal in Agra.

Etiquette for Visitors Many mosques do not admit non-Muslims, and some don't admit women. Always inquire to see if you are allowed into a particular mosque. All who enter must remove their shoes and cover their legs. Women are required to cover their heads and to sit apart from the men.

CHRISTIANITY

When the Portuguese explorer Vasco da Gama dropped anchor at Calicut (in present day Kerala) in 1498 he claimed to be seeking Christians and spices. He found both.

Christianity is said to have arrived in South India (specifically the Malabar Coast) with the Apostle St Thomas in 52 AD. However scholars say that it's more likely Christianity arrived around the 4th century with a Syrian merchant, Thomas Cana, who set out for Kerala with 400 families to establish what later became a sect of the Syrian Orthodox church. This sect survives today; services are in a mixture of Aramaic and Malayalam, and the Patriarch of Baghdad is the sect's head.

Other eastern orthodox sects include the Jacobites, Canaanites and orthodox Syrians.

Catholicism established a strong presence in the wake of Vasco da Gama's visit and sects which have been active in the region include the Dominicans, Franciscans and Jesuits.

Protestantism arrived with the English, Dutch and Danish and their legacy lives on today in the Church of South India.

India has about 18 million Christians, around three-quarters of whom are South Indian.

Churches & Cathedrals

Churches in India reflect the fashions and trends of typically European ecclesiastical architecture. Gothic arches and flying buttresses, baroque ornamentation and elegant classical lines are all to be found in places like Goa, which has been heavily influenced by European style. Local artisans also left their imprint on these places, as a closer inspection of some of the embellishments and ornamentation reveals.

The Portuguese and others, far from home, made impressive attempts to replicate the great churches and cathedrals of their day. Old Goa's Church of the Lady of Divine Providence, for example, is a copy of St Peter's Basilica in Rome. Kerala, another Portugese enclave, also has many churches. One of the most significant from the point of view of historical importance, is St Francis Church at Fort Cochin. It was built in 1503 by Portuguese Franciscan friars and for 14 years housed the remains of the first recorded European to traverse the Indian Ocean, Vasco da Gama.

Facing Page: The Christmas star suspended above the Puttanpalli church in Thrissur, dominates the Keralan skyline. Although not always as festive as some other religious festivals, Christmas day is a public holiday in India.

Inset: A rich and dramatic carving inside Se Cathedral in Old Goa, the largest church in India.
Photo: Eddie Gerald

Etiquette for Visitors There are no requirements peculiar to churches in India, with the exception that you must remove your shoes (as for temples and mosques). As with other places of worship dress conservatively; women should wear a skirt or dress. When investigating plaques and other sights, do so quietly and discreetly. Ask before taking photographs and don't approach the altar unless you know it's OK to do so.

SIKHISM

There are some 16 million Sikhs in India, mostly from Punjab, where the Sikh religion was founded by Guru Nanak in the late 15th century. Sikhism had its inception in the Hindu bhakti movement that started in South India as a reaction against the caste system and Brahmin domination of ritual. It was conceived at a time of great social unrest and was an attempt to fuse the best of Islam and Hinduism. The Sikh's holy text, the *Adi Granth* or *Granth Sahib*, was completed by the fifth Sikh guru and declared by the 10th to be a guru in its own right, capable of providing leadership to the community.

Sikhs believe in one god and reject the worship of idols. Like Hindus and Buddhists, they accept samsara and karma, and believe that only a human birth offers the chance for salvation. Fundamental to Sikhs is the concept of *khalsa,* or belief in a chosen race of soldier-saints who abide by strict codes of moral conduct (abstaining from alcohol, tobacco and drugs) and engage in a crusade for *dharmayudha* (right-eousness). There is no ascetic or monastic tradition ending the eternal cycles of death and rebirth in Sikhism. There are five emblems associated with khalsa: *kesh* (a khalsa must not cut his hair); *kangha* (comb); *kacch* (drawers; worn by soldiers); *kirpan* (sabre); *kara* (steel bracelet usually worn on the right wrist). The kara is usually said to be a charm against evil; some claim it's to remind believers that they are shackled to god. One explanation for the rule against hair-cutting stems from a yogic practice for preserving vitality and drawing it upward.

Gurudwaras

Facing Page: The most sacred of Sikh temples, the Golden Temple in Amritsar is dramatically set within the waters of Amrit Sarowar, the tank from which the town derives its name.

Gurudwaras (Sikh temples) usually have a *nishan sahib* (flagpole) flying a triangular flag with the Sikh insignia. There is no special requirement for the design of the building. The Golden Temple in Amritsar is the holiest shrine of Sikhism.

Inset: Sikh men are instantly recognisable by their distinctive turban. Turbans are often given or exchanged by Sikhs as a symbolic gift of respect and friendship.
Photo: Greg Elms

Etiquette for Visitors Everyone is welcome to enter the temple but your shoes must be removed and heads should be covered.

Right: The inner sanctum of the Golden Temple contains sacred scriptures from which the priest reads during prayers.

RICHARD I'ANSON

BUDDHISM

Some six million people practise Buddhism in India, fewer than either Christianity or Sikhism. Buddha (the Awakened One) was an historical figure who is generally believed to have lived from about 563 to 483 BC. Formerly a prince (Sidhhartha Gautama) Buddha, aged 29, embarked on a quest for enlightenment and relief from the world of suffering. He finally achieved *nirvana* (the state of full awareness) aged 35 at Bodhgaya. His teachings were oral, but were eventually recorded by his disciples. Critical of the caste system, dependence upon Brahmin priests and the unthinking worship of gods, Buddha urged his disciples to seek truth within their own experiences.

Buddha taught that life is based on Four Noble Truths: life is rooted in *dukkha* (suffering); suffering is caused by *tanha* (craving) for worldly things; one can find release from suffering by eliminating craving; and the way to eliminate craving is by following the Noble Eight-Fold Path. This path consists of: right understanding; right intention; right speech; right action; right livelihood; right effort; right awareness; and right concentration. By successfully complying with these things one can attain nirvana.

Facing Page: Organising ceremonies like this one at the Dharma Wheel Gompa in Alchi, Ladakh is part of the *lamas* (monks) daily tasks. The rest of their time is spent training, making artefacts, attending puja and giving rites.

Inset: Festivals held at gompas across the Himalaya (see the festivals tables at the start of each chapter for details) offer lamas the opportunity to get dressed up in their traditional finery.
Photo: Richard I'Anson

Right: Young children serving as novices are a common sight in the gompas (literally solitary places) of the Himalaya.

RICHARD I'ANSON

BOTH PHOTOGRAPHS BY RICHARD I'ANSON

In the centuries after Buddha's death (allegedly from eating contaminated pork), Buddhism split into two groups: Theravada and Mahayana (known as the lesser and greater vehicles respectively). Theravadans stress the importance of austerity and monastic life; laypeople are therefore excluded from the means to salvation (and this is why it's called the lesser vehicle, because it offers the means of salvation only to a few). Mahayanans view Buddha as just one of many manifestations of the godhead and stress the compassionate role of Buddha as teacher. The ideal in the Mahayanan tradition is the Bodhisattva who sacrifices their own enlightenment in order to help others attain salvation. Laypeople are not excluded. However, women are; they must seek a male rebirth before they can attain enlightenment. Mahayana Buddhism is practised mainly in Tibet, China, Korea and Japan.

Buddhism had virtually died out in most of India by the turn of the 20th century. However, it enjoyed something of a revival among intellectuals disillusioned with Hinduism and later received a further boost with the influx of Tibetan refugees from the 1950s onward, and the inclusion (in 1975) of Sikkim within India. Ladakhi Buddhists follow traditions similar to those found in Tibet.

Top Left: Rumtek Gompa near Gangtok in Sikkim is renowned for its Tibetan-style religious murals.

Bottom Left: Novices studying at Pemayangtse (Perfect Sublime Lotus) Gompa in Sikkim – the head monastery of the Nyangma-pa sect.

Stupas

Stupas, which characterise Buddhist places of worship, essentially evolved from burial mounds. They were never designed to hold congregations, but were to serve as repositories for relics of the Buddha and, later, other venerated souls. A relatively recent innovation is the addition of a *chaitya* (hall) leading up to the stupa itself. Devotees circumambulate the stupa in a clockwise direction. Bodhgaya in Bihar, where the Buddha achieved enlightenment, is an important centre of pilgrimage. The Tibetan gompas found in Ladakh and Dharamsala are quite unlike anything else found on the subcontinent, embellished as they are with colourful, distinctly Tibetan motifs dedicated to the propagation of Mahayana Buddhist beliefs.

Bottom: Tibetan chortens (stupas), like this one near Rekong Peo in Himachal Pradesh, can be found all over the Himalaya and have often been erected in honour of Buddhist saints.

Etiquette for Visitors You should remove your shoes and hat (or furl your umbrella) before entering the precincts of a stupa. You should also cover your legs and shoulders. Always walk round a stupa in a clockwise direction and never turn your back on an image of Buddha.

GARRY WEARE

JAINISM

Jainism, which today has some three million followers in India, was founded in the 6th century BC by Mahavira, a contemporary of Buddha who was even born in the same region (the lower Ganges plain). Jains believe that only by achieving complete purity of the soul can one attain liberation. Purity means shedding all *karman*, matter generated by one's actions which binds itself to the soul.

By following various austerities (eg fasting, meditation, retreating to lonely places) one can shed karman and purify the soul. Right conduct is essential, and can really only be fully realised by monks as opposed to the laity. Fundamental to the right mode of conduct is *ahimsa* (non-violence) in thought and deed. The religious disciplines of the laity are less severe than those for monks. *Jinakalpins* (followers of the Svetambara sect), for example, go naked and use the palms of their hands as begging bowls. Slightly less ascetic are the *sthavirakalpins* who maintain a bare minimum of possessions including a broom, with which they sweep the path before them to avoid stepping on any living thing, and a piece of cloth which is tied over their mouths to prevent them accidentally inhaling insects.

Temples

From the outside Jain temples resemble Hindu temples. But inside, Jain temples are a riot of sculptural ornamentation, the very opposite of ascetic austerity. This is partly explained by the Jain notion that beauty is found within. Most Jain temples are aligned on an east-west axis.

Etiquette for Visitors You should remove your shoes and hat. Cover your legs and shoulders. Don't take photographs unless you have permission to do so.

Facing Page: Jainism was founded around 500 BC but most temples date from between 1000 and 1300 AD.

Inset: Jains are known for the decorative splendour of their temples, although most of the eleborate detail is found within the temple interiors. Photo: Richard I'Anson

Right: To visit the huge granite statue of Bahubali in Sravanabelagola, Karnataka you must first walk up 614 steps barefoot. The statue is the site of the Mahamastakabhisheka ceremony due to take place again in 2005.

PAUL HARDING

ZOROASTRIANISM

Zoroastrianism had its inception in Persia and was certainly known to the ancient Greeks. It influenced the evolution of Judaism and Christianity. Zoroaster (Zarathustra) himself was a priest about whom little is known except that he lived in eastern Persia. The religion that bears his name, however, became the state religion of the region now known as Iran and remained so for some 1200 years.

Zoroastrianism has a dualistic nature whereby good and evil are locked in continuous battle, with good always triumphing. While Zoroastrianism leans towards monotheism, it isn't quite: good and evil entities co-exist, although believers are enjoined to honour only the good. Humanity therefore has a choice; purity is achieved by avoiding contamination with dead matter and things pertaining to death. Unlike Christianity, there is no conflict between body and soul; both are united in the good versus evil struggle. Zoroastrianism therefore rejects such practices as fasting and celibacy except in purely ritualistic circumstances. Humanity, although mortal, has components such as the soul which are timeless. One's prospects for a pleasant afterlife depend on one's deeds, words, and thoughts during one's earthly existence. But not every lapse is entered on the balance sheet and the errant soul is not called to account on the day of judgement for each and every misdemeanour.

Zoroastrianism was eclipsed in Persia by the rise of Islam in the 7th century and its followers, many of whom openly resisted this, suffered persecution. In the 10th century some emigrated to India, where they became known as *Parsis* (Persians).

These Parsis settled in Gujarat, becoming farmers and adopting the Gujarati language.

When the British ruled India the Parsis moved into commerce and industry, forming a prosperous community in Mumbai (eg the Tata family). They adopted many British customs, including British dress, and banned the marriage of children.

Parsis worship in fire temples where eternal flames symbolise their god. This sacred fire and sacrifice (eg in the form of *haoma* or sacred liquor) still play a fundamental role in Zoroastrian ritual, but perhaps the most famous practice involves the tower of silence. The tower, a place of burial, is composed of three concentric circles (one each for men, women and children). The corpse is placed within, naked, and exposed to vultures, who pick the bones clean. The bones, once they have been dried by the sun, are swept into a central well. The fourth day of the burial rites is the most important for it is on this day that the deceased's soul reaches the next world and presents itself before the deities for judgement.

Parsis are endogamous, that is, they only marry within their group, but the 85,000 or so left in India remain economically and politically influential.

Inset: Figures from Zoroastrian mythology mark the entrance to a Parsi fire temple in Mumbai's Fort. Interestingly there is no specifically Zoroastrian religious art.
Photo: David Collins

Delhi

Delhi is the capital of India, its third-largest city and north India's industrial hub. Old Delhi was the capital of Muslim India between the 17th and 19th centuries. In Old Delhi you will find many mosques, monuments and forts relating to India's Muslim history. New Delhi was built as the imperial capital of India by the British. It is a spacious, open city and contains many embassies and government buildings. The newer, wealthy suburbs are mostly to the south of New Delhi, and an ever-growing belt of poorer suburbs and *jhuggies* (slums) stretches in all directions.

In addition to its historic interest and role as the government centre, Delhi is a major travel gateway. It is one of India's busiest entrance points for overseas airlines, the hub of the north Indian travel network, and a stop on the overland route across Asia. The city of Delhi covers most of the Delhi Union Territory, a federal district similar to Washington DC.

Not many travellers have a lot of good things to say about Delhi; the intense air pollution and persistent touts often make the city an unsettling experience for newcomers. It does, however, have a long and fascinating history and there are plenty of interesting things to see.

HISTORY

Delhi hasn't always been the capital of India, but it has played an important role in Indian history. The settlement of Indraprastha, which featured in the epic *Mahabharata* over 3000 years ago, was approximately on the site of present-day Delhi. Over 2000 years ago, Pataliputra (near modern-day Patna) was the capital of Ashoka's empire. The Mughal emperors made Agra the capital through the 16th and 17th centuries. Under the British, Calcutta was the capital until the inauguration of New Delhi in 1931.

There have been at least eight cities around modern Delhi, and the old saying

Delhi at a Glance

Population: 9.4 million
Area: 1483 sq km
Main Languages: Hindi, Urdu, English & Punjabi
Telephone Area Code: 011
Best Time to Go: October to March

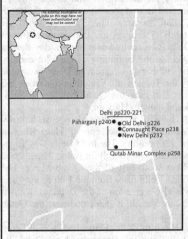

The external boundaries of India on this map have not been authenticated and may not be correct

Delhi pp220-221
Paharganj p240 ● ●Old Delhi p226
●Connaught Place p238
●New Delhi p232
Qutab Minar Complex p258

- **Red Fort** – wander at leisure around Delhi's massive Mughal-era fort

- **Qutab Minar** – a massive tower built to proclaim the arrival of Islam in India

- **Jama Masjid** – the largest mosque in India built by Shah Jahan, of Taj Mahal fame

- **Connaught Place** – the thriving heart of New Delhi

- **Humayun's Tomb** – a fine example of early Mughal architecture

- **Janpath** – visit the Central Cottage Industries Emporium, to peruse and purchase arts and crafts from across the country

Festivals of Delhi

festival	location	date	features
Republic Day	Rajpath	26 Jan	military parade
Independence Day	Red Fort	15 Aug	prime minister addresses the nation

that whoever founds a new city at Delhi will lose it has come true every time – most recently for the British who lasted only 16 years. The first four cities were to the south around the area where the Qutab Minar stands. Indraprastha, the earliest known Delhi, was centred near present-day Purana Qila. At the beginning of the 12th century the last Hindu kingdom of Delhi was ruled by the Tomara and Chauthan dynasties and was also near the Qutab Minar and Surajkund, now in Haryana.

This city was followed by Siri, built by Ala-ud-din near present-day Hauz Khas in the 12th century. The third Delhi was Tughlaqabad, now entirely in ruins, which stood 10km south-east of the Qutab Minar. The fourth Delhi dates from the 14th century and was also a creation of the Tughlaqs. Known as Jahanpanah, it also stood near the Qutab Minar.

The fifth Delhi, Ferozabad, was at Feroz Shah Kotla in present-day New Delhi. Its ruins include an Ashoka pillar, moved from elsewhere, and traces of a mosque where Tamerlane prayed during his attack on India.

Emperor Sher Shar created the sixth Delhi at Purana Qila, near India Gate in New Delhi today. Sher Shar was an Afghan ruler who defeated the Mughal Humayun and took control of Delhi. The Mughal emperor, Shah Jahan, constructed the seventh Delhi in the 17th century, thus shifting the Mughal capital from Agra to Delhi; his Shahjahanabad roughly corresponds to Old Delhi today and is largely preserved. His Delhi included the Red Fort and the majestic Jama Masjid (a *masjid* is a mosque). Finally, the eighth Delhi, New Delhi, was constructed by the British – the move from Calcutta was announced in 1911 but construction was not completed, and the city officially inaugurated, until 1931. In 1947, it became the capital of truncated India, and Hindu and Sikh refugees poured in from Pakistan.

Delhi has seen many invaders through the ages. Tamerlane plundered it in the 14th century; the Afghan Babur occupied it in the 16th century, and in 1739 the Persian emperor, Nadir Shah, sacked the city and carted the Kohinoor Diamond (now part of the British royal family's crown jewels) and the famous Peacock Throne off to Iran. The British captured Delhi in 1803, but during the Indian Uprising of 1857 it was a centre of resistance against the British. Prior to Partition, Delhi had a very large Muslim population and Urdu was the main language. Now Hindu Punjabis have replaced many of the Muslims, and Hindi predominates.

William Dalrymple's excellent *City of Djinns* is a wonderfully entertaining introduction to Delhi's past and present.

ORIENTATION

Delhi is a relatively easy city to find your way around although it is very spread out. The section of interest to visitors is on the west bank of the Yamuna River and is divided basically into two parts – the tightly packed streets of Old Delhi and the spacious, planned areas of New Delhi.

Old Delhi is the 17th century walled city of Shahjahanabad, with city gates, narrow alleys, constant traffic jams and terrible air pollution, the enormous Red Fort and Jama Masjid, temples, mosques, bazaars and the famous street known as Chandni Chowk. Here you will find the Delhi train station and, a little farther north, the main interstate bus station near Kashmiri Gate. Near New Delhi train station, and acting as a sort of buffer zone between the old and new cities, is the crowded market area of Paharganj. This has become the budget travellers' hang-out, and there are many popular cheap hotels and restaurants in this area.

New Delhi is a planned city of wide, tree-lined streets, parks and fountains, but still with the Indian touches of doe-eyed cows calmly ignoring the traffic and squatter hovels on waste land. It can be further subdivided into the business and residential areas around Connaught Place and the government areas around Rajpath to the south. At the eastern end of Rajpath is the India Gate memorial and at the west end is Rashtrapati Bhavan, the residence of the Indian president.

The hub of New Delhi is the great circle of Connaught Place and the streets that radiate from it. Here you will find most of the airline offices, banks, travel agents, state tourist offices and the national one, more budget accommodation and several of the big hotels. The Regal Cinema, at the south

---

Shoeshine Sir?

Thought you should hear about a scam being operated by shoeshine boys in Delhi at the moment.

They will pester you to shine your shoes. You decline as you happen to be wearing trainers or, in my case, suede. You look down to point this out and find a dollop of shit has found its way onto your shoe. You then agree to have this wiped off and a second boy arrives. They do a good job of cleaning your shoes and demand Rs 350 payment! They then become quite aggressive as you remonstrate. I ended up paying Rs 30. I saw several others caught in the same manner and was pestered again later on and found to my amazement another dollop of shit on my shoe. I guess they must have some kind of shitgun to get the stuff there so accurately!

Graeme Jackson

---

side of the circle, and the Plaza Cinema, at the north, are two important landmarks and are useful for telling taxi or auto-rickshaw drivers where you want to go.

Janpath, running off Connaught Place to the south, has the Government of India tourist office, the Student Travel Information Centre in the Imperial Hotel and a number of other useful addresses.

South of the New Delhi government areas are Delhi's more expensive residential areas, with names like Defence Colony, South Extension, Lodi Colony, Greater Kailash and Vasant Vihar. Many of the better (and more expensive) cinemas and shopping centres are found here. The Indira Gandhi international airport is to the southwest of the city, and about halfway between the airport and Connaught Place is Chanakyapuri, the diplomatic enclave. Most of Delhi's embassies (and the prime minister's house) are concentrated in this strikingly tidy area and there are several major hotels here.

Across the Jamuna River (heavily polluted for the nine months of the year when the monsoon is not flushing it) lie many new industrial and residential areas, as well as some of the grimmest slum areas.

The 250 page *Eicher City Map* (Rs 270) includes 174 area maps, and is a good reference if you are venturing further into the Delhi environs. It's available at most larger bookshops and modern fuel stations.

INFORMATION
Tourist Offices

The Government of India tourist office (☎ 332 0008) at 88 Janpath is open Monday to Friday, 9 am to 6 pm and Saturday, 9 am to 2 pm. The office has a lot of information and brochures on destinations all over India, but none of it is on display – you have to know what you want and ask for it. They have a good giveaway map of the city, and can also help you find accommodation. Some of the staff have been known to try to sell overpriced taxi tours.

In the arrivals hall at the international airport terminal there is a tourist counter

DELHI

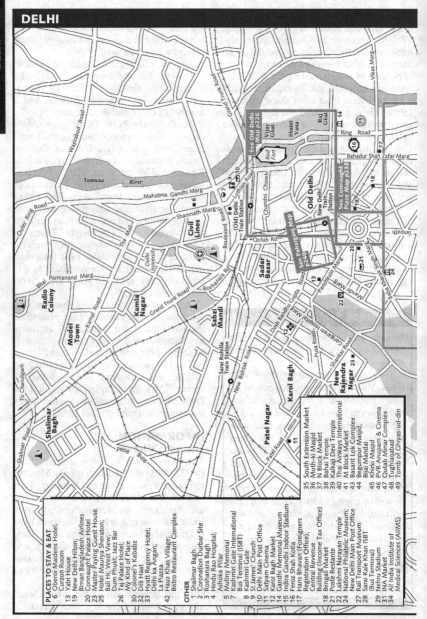

PLACES TO STAY & EAT
6 Oberoi Maidens Hotel;
   Curzon Room
13 Yatri House
19 New Delhi Hilton;
   Biman Bangladesh Airlines
20 Connaught Palace Hotel
23 Master Paying Guest House
25 Hotel Maurya Sheraton;
   Bali Hi; West View;
   Dum Phukt; Jazz Bar
26 Taj Palace Hotel;
   My Kind of Place
30 Colonel's Kababz
32 Dilli Haat
33 Hyatt Regency Hotel;
   Delhi ka Angan;
   La Piazza
42 Hauz Khas Village;
   Bistro Restaurant Complex

OTHER
1 Shalimar Bagh
2 Coronation Durbar Site
3 Roshanara Bagh
4 Hindu Rao Hospital;
   Ashoka Pillar
5 Mutiny Memorial
7 Kashmiri Gate International
   Bus Terminal (ISBT)
8 Kashmiri Gate
9 St James' Church
10 Delhi Main Post Office
11 Satyam Cinema
12 Carol Bagh Market
14 Gandhi Memorial Museum
15 Indira Gandhi Indoor Stadium
16 Feroz Shah Kotla
17 Hans Bhavan (Foreigners
   Registration Office);
   Central Revenue
   Building (Income Tax Office)
18 Bengali Market
21 Poste Restante
22 Lakshmi Narayan Temple
24 National Philatelic Museum
27 New Delhi Main Post Office
28 Rail Transport Museum
   Sarai Kale Khan ISBT
   (Bus Terminal)
29 Nehru Stadium
31 INA Market
34 All India Institute of
   Medical Sciences (AIIMS)
35 South Extension Market
36 Moth-ki Masjid
37 N Block Market
38 Bahai Temple
39 Kalkaji Devi Temple
40 Thai Airways International
41 M Block Market
43 Basant Lok Complex
44 Begumpur Masjid;
   Bijai Mandal
45 Khirki Masjid
46 PVR Anupam & Cinema
47 Qutab Minar Complex
48 Tughlaqabad
49 Tomb of Ghiyas-ud-din

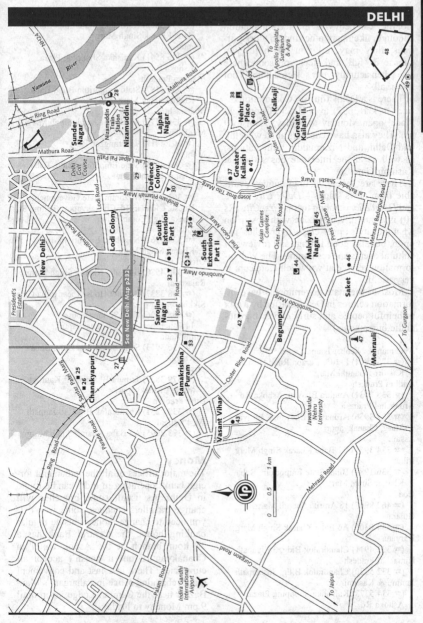

DELHI

DELHI

(☎ 569 1171) open around the clock. Here, too, they can help you find accommodation although, like many other Indian tourist offices, they may tell you the hotel you choose is 'full' and steer you somewhere else when actually your selected hotel is not full at all.

There is a Delhi Tourism Corporation office (☎ 331 3637) in N Block, Connaught Place, open Monday to Friday, 7 am to 9 pm. They also have counters at New Delhi, Old Delhi, and Nizamuddin train stations, as well as at the Interstate bus station at Kashmir Gate.

There are several listings guides available from news stands – *Delhi City Guide* and *Delhi Diary* among them. *First City* (Rs 30) is a monthly magazine with gossip on what the city's upper-class 'tiger ladies' are up to, but also good listings and reviews of cultural events and restaurants. The Web information service at www.delhigate.com is very useful.

Most of the state governments have information centres in Delhi, staffed by a mix of helpful people and surly *babus* (bureaucratic bureaucrats).

Andaman & Nicobar Islands
  (☎ 378 2904) F-105, Curzon Road Hostel, Kasturba Gandhi Marg
Andhra Pradesh
  (☎ 338 2031) Andhra Bhavan, Ashoka Rd
Arunachal Pradesh
  (☎ 301 3956) Arunachal Bhavan, Kautilya Marg, Chanakyapuri
Assam
  (☎ 334 3961) B1 Baba Kharak Singh Marg
Bihar
  (☎ 336 1987) Bihar State Emporium, Baba Kharak Singh Marg
Goa
  (☎ 462 9967) 18 Amrita Shergil Marg
Gujarat
  (☎ 334 0305) A6 Baba Kharak Singh Marg
Haryana
  (☎ 332 4911) Chandralok Bldg, 36 Janpath
Himachal Pradesh
  (☎ 332 5320) Chandralok Bldg, 36 Janpath
Jammu & Kashmir
  (☎ 334 5373) Kanishka Shopping Plaza, Ashoka Rd

Karnataka
  (☎ 336 3862) Karnataka State Emporium, Baba Kharak Singh Marg
Kerala
  (☎ 336 8541) Kanishka Shopping Plaza, Ashoka Rd
Madhya Pradesh
  (☎ 334 1187) State Emporium Bldg, Baba Kharak Singh Marg
Maharashtra
  (☎ 336 3773) A8 Baba Kharak Singh Marg
Meghalaya
  (☎ 301 4417) 9 Aurangzeb Rd
Manipur
  (☎ 334 4026) State Emporium Bldg, Baba Kharak Singh Marg
Mizoram
  (☎ 301 2331) Mizoram State Government House, Circular Rd, Chanakyapuri (behind Sri Lanka High Commission)
Nagaland
  (☎ 334 3161) Nagaland Emporium, Baba Kharak Singh Marg
Orissa
  (☎ 336 4580) B4 Baba Kharak Singh Marg
Rajasthan
  (☎ 338 3837) Bikaner House (near India Gate)
Sikkim
  (☎ 688 3026) New Sikkim House, 14 Panchsheel Marg, Chanakyapuri
Tamil Nadu
  (☎ 336 3913) State Emporium Bldg, Baba Kharak Singh Marg
Tripura
  (☎ 379 3827) Tripura Bhavan, off Kautilya Marg, Chanakyapuri
Uttar Pradesh
  (☎ 332 2251) Chandralok Bldg, 36 Janpath
West Bengal
  (☎ 373 2695) A2 Baba Kharak Singh Marg

Money

The major offices of all the Indian and foreign banks operating in India can be found in Delhi. As usual, some branches will change travellers cheques, some won't. If you need to change money outside regular banking hours, the Central Bank has a 24 hour branch at the Ashok Hotel in Chanakyapuri, but it doesn't accept all currencies. There is a fast and convenient moneychanging office in Paharganj's Main Bazaar near the Camran Lodge, open until 9 pm Monday to Friday.

Warning

Steer clear of touts leading you to the dozen or so 'tourist information centres' across the road from New Delhi train station. None of them are tourist offices as such, despite bold claims to the contrary; they are simply travel agencies, and many are simply out to fleece unsuspecting visitors – both foreign and Indian.

If you are going to make a booking at the foreign tourist booking office at the station you may well be approached by touts from these shops who will insist the office you want is closed and try to steer you to the shonky travel agencies and rake off a hefty commission. Don't be tempted by offers of cheap bus fares or hotels.

Many of the large international banks now have ATMs (open 24 hours) where you can use credit cards to get cash advances. You need to know your PIN. Without a PIN you can get cash advances over the counter during banking hours.

American Express (☎ 332 5221, fax 371 5352) has its office in A Block, Connaught Place, and although it's usually crowded, service is fast. You don't have to have American Express cheques to change money here. It's open every day, 9 am to 7 pm. If you want to replace lost American Express travellers cheques, you need a photocopy of the police report and one photo, as well as the proof-of-purchase slip and the numbers of the missing cheques. If you don't have the latter they will telex the place where you bought them. If you've had the lot stolen, American Express is empowered to give you limited funds while all this is going on. For lost or stolen cheques, they have a 24 hour number (☎ 614 5920) that you should contact as soon as possible. Other banks include:

ANZ Grindlays
  (☎ 372 1242) H10, Connaught Place
Bank of America
  (☎ 371 5565) Hansalya Bldg, Barakhamba Rd

Banque Nationale de Paris
  (☎ 331 3883) Hansalya Bldg, Barakhamba Rd
Citibank
  (☎ 371 2484) Jeevan Bharati Bldg, Outer Circle, Connaught Place
Deutsche Bank
  (☎ 371 2028) 15 Tolstoy House, Tolstoy Marg
Hongkong & Shanghai Bank
  (☎ 331 4355) 28 Kasturba Gandhi Marg
Standard Chartered Bank
  (☎ 336 0321) Allahabad Bank Bldg, 17 Sansad Marg
Thomas Cook
  (☎ 336 8359) Imperial Hotel, Janpath (moneygram transfers can also be arranged here)

Post & Communications

There is a small post office in A Block at Connaught Place but the main post office is on the roundabout on Baba Kharak Singh Marg, 500m south-west of Connaught Place. Poste restante mail can be collected from the Foreign Post Office on Market Rd (Bhai Vir Singh Marg). The poste restante office, around the back and up the stairs, is open Monday to Friday 9 am to 5 pm. Poste restante mail addressed to 'Delhi' will go to the inconveniently situated Old Delhi post office, so ask your correspondents to specify 'New Delhi'. Mail can be sent to the tourist office on Janpath or the Student Travel Information Centre.

Some reliable Internet/email cafes include the Calculus Cyber Centre on Connaught Circus in the Regal Cinema building, and the Internet office at the British Council on Kasturba Gandhi Marg. In Paharganj there's the E-Mail Centre near the Hotel Vishal. All charge Rs 100 per hour.

There are many private STD/ISD call offices around the city; many also have fax services and email.

Important Change Some telephone numbers in Delhi are changing. Numbers in this chapter that start with 752 are now 362 and those starting with 751 have become 361.

Foreign Embassies

For details on Foreign embassies and consulates in Delhi see Embassies & Consulates in the Facts for the Visitor chapter. See under Visas & Documents in the Facts for the Visitor chapter for details on obtaining visas in Delhi for other countries.

Visa Extensions & Other Permits

Hans Bhavan, near the Tilak Bridge train station, is where you will find the Foreigners' Regional Registration Office (FRRO) (☎ 331 9781). Come here to get permits for restricted areas such as Mizoram. The office is open Monday to Friday, 9.30 am to 1.30 pm and 2 to 4 pm.

The FRRO can issue 15 day visa extensions free if you just need a few extra days before you leave the country. To apply for a maximum one month longer on a six month visa is more complicated. First you have to collect the long-term visa extension form from the Ministry of Home Affairs at Lok Nayak Bhavan in Khan Market (☎ 467 7648), open Monday to Friday, 10 am to noon. It's a typical Indian government office, so be prepared to wait. Then take the form and four photos to the FRRO (about a Rs 20 rickshaw ride away). A one month extension costs Rs 775. When (and if) the extension is authorised, the authorisation has to be taken *back* to the Ministry of Home Affairs, where the actual visa extension is issued.

Since it's difficult to get an extension on a six month visa, you may be approached by people offering to forge your visa for a longer stay. Don't fall for this one, as the authorities will check your details carefully against their computer records when you leave India. There are heavy fines and you won't be allowed to visit India again.

If you need a tax clearance certificate before departure, the Foreign Section of the Income Tax Department (☎ 331 6161) is in the Central Revenue Building next to Hans Bhavan on Vikas Marg. Bring exchange certificates with you, though it's entirely likely nobody will ask for your clearance certificate when you leave the country. The office is closed 1 to 2 pm.

Export of any object over 100 years old requires a permit. If in doubt, contact the Director (☎ 301 7220), Antiquities, Archaeological Survey of India, Janpath, next to the National Museum.

Travel Agencies

In the Imperial Hotel, on Janpath, the Student Travel Information Centre (☎ 332 7582) is used by many travellers and is the place to renew or obtain student cards, although their tickets are not usually as cheap as elsewhere.

Some of the ticket discounters around Paharganj and Connaught Place are real fly-by-night operations, so take care. Those that have been recommended by readers include:

Aa Bee Travels
  (☎ 752 0117) Hare Rama Guest House, Paharganj
Cozy Travels
  (☎ 331 2873) BMC House, 1N Connaught Place
Don't Pass Me By Travels
  (☎ 335 2942) upstairs in the cafe of the same name, Ringo Guest House building
VINstring Holidays
  (☎ 336 8717) YWCA International Guest House, Sansad Marg
Vin Tours
  (☎ 334 8571) YWCA, Ashoka Rd
Y Tours & Travel
  (☎ 371 1662) YMCA, Ashoka Rd
Tan's Travel
  (☎ 332 1490) 72 Janpath

The Hotel Namaskar (☎ 752 1234), 917 Chandiwalan, just off Main Bazaar, Paharganj, and the travel agency at the Hotel Ajanta (☎ 752 0925), Arakashan Rd have also been recommended.

For more upmarket travel arrangements, both within India and for foreign travel, there are a number of places, mostly around Connaught Place. These include: Cox & Kings (☎ 332 0067), Sita World Travels (☎ 331 1133) and the Travel Corporation of India (☎ 331 5834).

Bookshops

There are a number of good bookshops around Connaught Place – a good place to look for interesting Indian books or to stock up with hefty paperbacks to while away those long train rides. Some of the better shops include:

The Bookshop
  Khan Market, Subramania Bharati Rd
Bookworm
  29B Radial Rd No 4, Connaught Place
English Book Depot
  17L Radial Road No 5, Connaught Place
New Book Depot
  18 B Block, Connaught Place
Piccadilly Book Store
  64 Shankar Market (just off Connaught Circus)
Oxford Book Shop
  Opposite N Block, Outer Circle, Connaught Place

Prabhu Book Service in Hauz Khas Village has an interesting selection of second-hand and rare books. Bookshops in deluxe hotels are more expensive but have a good selection of novels, glossy art books and historical works.

There are plenty of pavement stalls at various places around Connaught Place and on Sansad Marg, near the Kwality Restaurant. They have a good range of cheap paperbacks, and will often buy them back from you if they are returned in a reasonable condition. Almost next door to the Kwality Restaurant is People Tree, which sells books about the environment, and eco-friendly crafts.

The largest stockist of Lonely Planet guides is Bahri Sons, opposite the main gate at Khan Market.

Libraries & Cultural Centres
The India International Centre (☎ 461 9431), by the Lodi Tombs, has lectures each week on art, economics and other contemporary issues by Indian and foreign experts.

Sangeet Natak Akademi (☎ 338 7248), at 35 Feroz Shah Rd, Rabindra Bhavan is a major performing arts centre with substantial archive material. The academy of fine arts and sculpture, Lalit Laka Akademi and the literature academy, Sahitya Akademi, are also here in separate wings. All have galleries and there are souvenirs on sale.

World Wide Fund for Nature India (☎ 469 3744), 172B Lodi Estate, has excellent computerised environmental records, a good library, and an eco-shop selling handicrafts

and books. It's open Monday to Friday, 9.30 am to 5.30 pm.

The American Center (☎ 331 6841) is at 24 Kasturba Gandhi Marg and is open from 9.30 am to 6 pm. The British Council Library (☎ 371 0111), at 17 Kasturba Gandhi Marg, is open Tuesday to Saturday, 10 am to 6 pm. It's better than the US equivalent, but officially you have to join to get in.

Alliance Française (☎ 625 8128) can be found at D-13 South Extension Part II.

Film & Photography
There are lots of places around Connaught Place to buy and process film. The Delhi Photo Company, at 78 Janpath, close to the Government of India tourist office, processes both print and slide film competently.

Medical Services
The East West Medical Centre (☎ 462 3738/469 9229), near Delhi Golf Course, at 38 Golf Links Rd, has been recommended by many travellers, diplomats and expatriates. All rickshaw-wallahs know where it is. The Apollo Hospital (☎ 692 5858), Sarita Vihar, Mathura Rd, also has a good reputation.

Government hospitals include Dr Ram Manohar Lohia Hospital (☎ 336 5525), Baba Kharak Singh Marg; and the All India Institute of Medical Sciences, Ansari Nagar (☎ 656 1123). Embassies have lists of recommended doctors and dentists.

There is a 24 hour pharmacy at Super Bazaar in Connaught Place.

Aa ambulance service is available by calling ☎ 102.

Motorcycle Shops
If you are in the market for a new Enfield motorcycle, Karol Bagh is the place to look. Try Essaar on Jhandi Walan Extension and Nanna Motors at 112 Press Rd. For second-hand bikes and parts, try Madaan Motors at 1770/53 Naiwala Gali, Har Kishan Das Rd, and Chawla Motorcycles next door.

OLD DELHI
The old walled city of Shahjahanabad stands to the west of the Red Fort and was at one

time surrounded by a sturdy defensive wall, only fragments of which now exist. The **Kashmiri Gate**, at the northern end of the walled city, was the scene of desperate fighting when the British retook Delhi during the 1857 Uprising. West of here, near Sabzi Mandi, is the British-erected **Mutiny Memorial** to the soldiers who lost their lives during the Uprising. Near the monument is an **Ashoka pillar**, and like the one in Feroz Shah Kotla, it was brought here by Feroz Shah Tughlaq.

Red Fort

The red sandstone walls of Lal Qila, the Red Fort, extend for 2km and vary in height from 18m on the river side to 33m on the city side. Shah Jahan started construction of the massive fort in 1638 and it was completed in 1648. He never completely moved his capital from Agra to his new city of Shahjahanabad in Delhi because he was deposed and imprisoned in Agra Fort by his son Aurangzeb.

The Red Fort dates from the very peak of Mughal power. When the emperor rode out on elephant-back into the streets of Old Delhi it was a display of pomp and power at its most magnificent. The Mughal reign from Delhi was a short one, however: Aurangzeb was the first and last great Mughal emperor to rule from here.

Today, the fort is typically Indian, with would-be guides leaping forth to offer their services as soon as you enter. It's still a calm haven of peace if you've just left the frantic streets of Old Delhi, however. The city noise and confusion are light years away from the fort gardens and pavilions.

The Yamuna River used to flow right by the eastern edge of the fort, and filled the 10m deep moat. These days the river is over

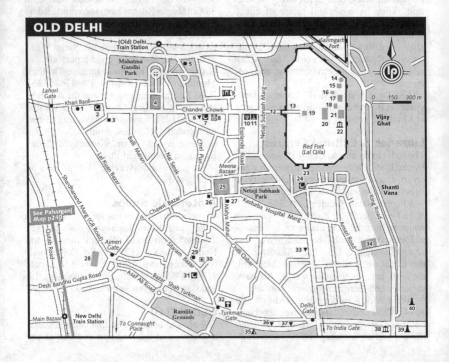

1km to the east and the moat remains empty. Entry to the fort is Rs 2 (free on Friday) from the kiosk opposite the main gate.

Lahore Gate The main gate to the fort takes its name from the fact that it faces towards Lahore, now in Pakistan. If one spot could be said to be the emotional and symbolic heart of the modern Indian nation, the Lahore Gate of the Red Fort is probably it. During the struggle for independence, one of the nationalists' declarations was that they would see the Indian flag flying over the Red Fort in Delhi. After independence, many important political speeches were given by Nehru and Indira Gandhi to the crowds amassed on the *maidan* (open place or square) outside, and on Independence Day (15 August) each year, the prime minister addresses a huge crowd from the gate.

You enter the fort here and immediately find yourself in a vaulted arcade, the **Chatta Chowk** (Covered Bazaar). The shops in this arcade used to sell the upmarket items that the royal household might fancy – silks, jewellery and gold. These days they cater to the tourist trade and the quality of the goods is certainly a little lower, although some still carry a royal price tag! This arcade of shops was also known as the Meena Bazaar, the shopping centre for ladies of the court. On Thursday the gates of the fort were closed to men; only women were allowed inside the citadel.

The arcade leads to the **Naubat Khana,** or Drum House, where musicians used to play for the emperor, and the arrival of princes and royalty was heralded from here. There's a dusty **Indian War Memorial museum** (free) upstairs. The open courtyard beyond the Drum House formerly had galleries along either side, but these were removed by the British army when the fort was used as its headquarters. Other reminders of the British presence are the monumentally ugly, three-storey barrack blocks that lie to the north of this courtyard.

Diwan-i-Am The Hall of Public Audiences was where the emperor would sit to hear complaints or disputes from his subjects. His alcove in the wall was marble-panelled and set with precious stones, many of which were looted following the 1857 Uprising. This elegant hall was restored as a result of a directive by Lord Curzon, the viceroy of India between 1898 and 1905.

Diwan-i-Khas The Hall of Private Audiences, constructed of white marble, was the luxurious chamber where the emperor would hold private meetings. The centrepiece (until Nadir Shah carted it off to Iran in 1739) was the magnificent Peacock

OLD DELHI

PLACES TO STAY		4	Town Hall	20	Diwan-i-Am
3	Bharat Hotel; Star Guest House	5	Delhi Public Library	21	Rang Mahal
		7	Sunehri Masjid	22	Mumtaz Mahal & Museum
26	Hotel New City Palace	8	Sisganj Gurdwara	23	Delhi Gate
27	Hotel Bombay Orient; Karim's	9	Begum Samru's Palace	24	Sunehri Masjid
35	Tourist Camp	10	Gauri Shankar Temple	25	Jama Masjid
		11	Digambara Jain Temple; Bird Hospital	28	Madrasah of Ghazi-ud-din
PLACES TO EAT				29	Bishan Swaroop Haveli
6	Ghantewala	12	Lahore Gate; Ticket Kiosk	30	Sultan Raziya's Tomb
33	Moti Mahal Restaurant	13	Chatta Chowk	31	Kalan Masjid
36	Hotel Broadway	14	Shahi Burj	32	Holy Trinity Church; Tomb of Hazrat Shah Turkman
37	Hotel President (Tandoor)	15	Hammams		
		16	Moti Masjid	34	Zinat-ul Masjid
OTHER		17	Diwan-i-Khas	38	Gandhi Memorial Museum
1	Gadodia Market	18	Khas Mahal	39	Gandhi Memorial
2	Fatehpuri Masjid	19	Naubat Khana	40	Raj Ghat

India's national bird, the peacock, is featured in many artworks, perhaps the most famous of which was the Peacock Throne.

surmounted by domes, with a fountain in the centre – one of which was set up as a sauna! The floors used to be inlaid with *pietra dura* work, and the rooms were illuminated through panels of coloured glass in the roof. The baths are closed to the public.

Shahi Burj This modest, three storey octagonal tower at the north-eastern edge of the fort was once Shah Jahan's private working area. From here water used to flow south through the Royal Baths, the Diwan-i-Khas, the Khas Mahal and the Rang Mahal. Like the baths, the tower is closed to the public.

Moti Masjid Built in 1659 by Aurangzeb for his own personal use and security, the small and totally enclosed Pearl Mosque, made of marble, is next to the baths. One curious feature of the mosque is that its outer walls are oriented exactly to be in symmetry with the rest of the fort, while the inner walls are slightly askew, so that the mosque has the correct orientation with Mecca.

Other Features The Khas Mahal, south of the Diwan-i-Khas, was the emperor's private palace, divided into rooms for worship, sleeping and living.

The **Rang Mahal** or Palace of Colour, farther south again, took its name from the painted interior, which is now gone. This was once the residence of the emperor's chief wife, and is where he ate. On the floor in the centre is a beautifully carved marble lotus, and the water flowing along the channel from the Shahi Burj used to end up here. Originally there was a fountain made of ivory in the centre.

There is a small Museum of Archaeology in the **Mumtaz Mahal**, still farther south along the eastern wall. It's well worth a look, although most visitors seem to rush through the Red Fort, bypassing the museum.

Another museum worth seeing is the **Svatantrata Sangrama Sangrahalaya** (Museum of the Independence Movement), to the left before the Naubat Khana, among the army buildings. The independence movement is charted with newspaper cuttings,

Throne. The solid gold throne had figures of peacocks standing behind it, their beautiful colours achieved with countless inlaid precious stones. Between them was a parrot carved out of a single emerald.

A masterpiece in precious metals, sapphires, rubies, emeralds and pearls was broken up, and the so-called Peacock Throne displayed in Tehran simply utilises various bits of the original. The marble pedestal on which the throne used to sit remains in place.

In 1760, the Marathas also removed the silver ceiling from the hall, so today it is a pale shadow of its former glory. Inscribed on the walls of the Diwan-i-Khas is that famous Persian couplet:

If there is a paradise on earth it is this, it is this, it is this.

Royal Baths Next to the Diwan-i-Khas are the *hammams* or baths – three large rooms letters, photos and several impressive dioramas. Did the Rani of Jhansi really ride into battle with a baby strapped to her back? There's no charge for entry.

Gardens Between these exquisite buildings were highly formal *charbaghs* (four-sectioned gardens), complete with fountains, pools and small pavilions. While the general outline and some pavilions are still in place, the gardens are not what they once were.

Sound-and-Light Show Each evening an interesting sound-and-light show recreates events of India's history, particularly those connected with the Red Fort. Shows are in English and Hindi, and tickets (Rs 20) are available from the fort. The English sessions start at 7.30 pm from November to January, 8.30 pm from February to April and September to October, and at 9 pm from May to August. It's well worth making the effort to see this show, but make sure you are well equipped with plenty of mosquito repellent.

Chandni Chowk

The main street of Old Delhi is the colourful shopping bazaar known as Chandni Chowk. It's hopelessly congested (and polluted) day and night, a very sharp contrast to the open, spacious streets of New Delhi. At the eastern (Red Fort) end of Chandni Chowk, there is a **Digambara Jain Gurdwara** (temple), with a small marble courtyard surrounded by a colonnade. Traditionally, Jain monks of the Digambara, or Sky Clad, sect, wore no garments. There's an interesting **bird hospital** here, run by the Jains; entry is free but donations are gratefully accepted.

Next to the *kotwali* (old police station) is the **Sunehri Masjid**. In 1739, Nadir Shah, the Persian invader who carried off the Peacock Throne, stood on the roof of this mosque and watched while his soldiers conducted a bloody massacre of Delhi's inhabitants.

The western end of Chandni Chowk is marked by the **Fatehpuri Masjid**, which was erected in 1650 by one of Shah Jahan's wives.

Jama Masjid

The great mosque of Old Delhi is both the largest in India and the final architectural extravagance of Shah Jahan. Begun in 1644, the mosque was not completed until 1658. It has three great gateways, four angle towers and two minarets standing 40m high and constructed of alternating vertical strips of red sandstone and white marble.

Broad flights of steps lead up to the imposing gateways. The eastern gateway was originally only opened for the emperor, and is now only open on Friday and Muslim festival days. The general public can enter by either the north or south gate (Rs 10). Shoes should be removed, and those people considered unsuitably dressed (bare legs for either men or women) can hire robes at the northern gate.

The courtyard of the mosque can hold 25,000 people. For Rs 5 (Rs 10 with a camera) it's possible to climb the southern minaret – if you're a man or you have one with you. The views in all directions are superb – Old Delhi, the Red Fort and the polluting factories beyond it across the river, and New Delhi to the south. You can also see one of the features that the architect Lutyens incorporated into his design of New Delhi – the Jama Masjid, Connaught Place and Sansad Bhavan (Parliament House) are in a direct line. There's also a fine view of the Red Fort from the east side of the mosque.

CORONATION DURBAR SITE

This is a sobering sight for people interested in the Raj. It's north of Old Delhi and is best reached by auto-rickshaw (about Rs 120 return from Paharganj) or taxi. In a desolate field stands a lone obelisk – this is where, in 1877 and 1903, the great theatrical durbars featuring the full set of Indian rulers paid homage to the British monarch.

It was also here in 1911 that King George V was declared emperor of India. If you look closely you can still see the old boy – a statue of him rises nearby in an unkempt walled park, where it was unceremoniously dumped after being removed from the canopy midway along Rajpath, between

India Gate and Rashtrapati Bhavan. Further inspection reveals other imperial dignitaries in the scrub, though mysteriously there are many more plinths these days than statues.

FEROZ SHAH KOTLA

Erected by Feroz Shah Tughlaq in 1354, the ruins of Ferozabad, the fifth city of Delhi, can be found at Feroz Shah Kotla, just off Bahadur Shah Zafar Marg between the old and new Delhis. In the fortress-palace is a 13m high sandstone **Ashoka pillar** inscribed with Ashoka's edicts (and a later inscription). The remains of an old mosque and a fine well can also be seen in the area, but most of the ruins of Ferozabad were used for the construction of later cities.

RAJ GHAT

North-east of Feroz Shah Kotla, on the banks of the Yamuna, a simple square platform of black marble marks the spot where Mahatma Gandhi was cremated following his assassination in 1948. A commemorative ceremony takes place each Friday, the day he was killed.

Jawaharlal Nehru, the first Indian prime minister, was cremated just to the north at Shanti Vana (Forest of Peace) in 1964. His daughter, Indira Gandhi, who was killed in 1984, and grandsons Sanjay (1980) and Rajiv (1991) were also cremated in this vicinity.

The Raj Ghat area is now a beautiful park. The **Gandhi Memorial Museum** here is well worth a visit; a macabre relic is the pistol with which Gandhi was assassinated. Entry is free; it's open Tuesday to Sunday, 9.30 am to 5.30 pm.

NEW DELHI
Connaught Place

At the northern end of New Delhi, Connaught Place is the business and tourist centre. It's a vast traffic circle with an architecturally uniform series of colonnaded buildings around the edge, mainly devoted to shops, banks, restaurants and airline offices. It's spacious but busy, and you're continually approached by people willing to provide you with everything imaginable,

from an airline ticket for Timbuktu to having your fortune read.

In 1995 the inner and outer circle were renamed Rajiv Chowk and Indira Chowk respectively (the son within the mother), but everyone still calls it CP (Connaught Place) despite the signs. The outer circle is known as Connaught Circus.

Jantar Mantar

Only a short stroll down Sansad Marg from Connaught Place, this strange collection of salmon-coloured structures is one of Maharaja Jai Singh II's observatories. The ruler from Jaipur constructed this observatory in 1725 and it is dominated by a huge sundial known as the Prince of Dials. Other instruments plot the course of heavenly bodies and predict eclipses.

Lakshmi Narayan Temple

Due west of Connaught Place, this garish modern temple was erected by the industrialist BD Birla in 1938. It's dedicated to Lakshmi, the goddess of prosperity and good fortune, and is commonly known as Birla Mandir (*mandir* means temple).

Rajpath

The Kingsway is another focus of Lutyens' New Delhi. It is immensely broad and is flanked on either side by ornamental ponds. The Republic Day parade is held here every 26 January, and millions of people gather to enjoy the spectacle.

At the eastern end of Rajpath lies the India Gate, while at the western end lies Rashtrapati Bhavan, now the president's residence, but built originally for the viceroy. It is flanked by the two large Secretariat buildings, and these three buildings sit upon a small rise, known as Raisina Hill.

India Gate

This 42m high stone arch of triumph stands at the eastern end of the Rajpath. It bears the names of 85,000 Indian army soldiers who died in the campaigns of WWI, the North-West Frontier operations of the same time and the 1919 Afghan fiasco.

Rashtrapati Bhavan

The official residence of the President of India stands at the opposite end of the Rajpath from India Gate. Completed in 1929, the palace-like building is an interesting blend of Mughal and western architectural styles, the most obvious Indian feature being the huge copper dome. To the west of the building is a Mughal garden that occupies 130 hectares. This garden is only open to the public in February and early March; book through the Government of India tourist office on Janpath.

Prior to Independence this was the viceroy's residence. At the time of Mountbatten, India's last viceroy, the number of servants needed to maintain the 340 rooms and its extensive gardens was enormous. There were 418 gardeners alone, 50 of them boys whose sole job was to chase away birds!

Secretariat Buildings

The north and south Secretariat buildings lie either side of Rajpath on Raisina Hill. These imposing buildings, topped with *chhatris* (small domes), now house the ministries of Finance and External Affairs respectively.

Sansad Bhavan

Although another large and imposing building, Sansad Bhavan, the Indian parliament building, stands almost hidden and virtually unnoticed at the end of Sansad Marg, just north of Rajpath. The building is a circular colonnaded structure 171m in diameter. Its relative physical insignificance in the grand scheme of New Delhi shows how the focus of power has shifted from the viceroy's residence, which was given pride of place during the time of the British Raj when New Delhi was conceived.

Permits to visit the parliament and sit in the public gallery are available from the reception office on Raisina Rd, but you'll need a letter of introduction from your embassy.

MUSEUMS & GALLERIES
National Museum

On Janpath, just south of Rajpath, the National Museum (☎ 301 9272) has a pretty good collection of Indian bronze, terracotta and wood sculptures dating back to the Mauryan period (2nd to 3rd century BC), exhibits from the Vijayanagar period in South India, miniature and mural paintings, and costumes of the various *Adivasis* (tribal peoples). The museum, open Tuesday to Sunday, 10 am to 5 pm, with free guided tours at 10.30 and 11.30 am, noon and 2 pm, is definitely worth visiting. Admission is Rs 0.50. There are film shows each afternoon.

Next door is the Archaeological Survey of India office. Publications available here cover all the main sites in India. Many of these are not available at the particular sites themselves. The office is open 9 am to 1 pm and 3.30 to 5 pm, Monday to Friday.

National Gallery of Modern Art

This gallery (☎ 338 2835) stands near India Gate at the eastern end of Rajpath, and was formerly the Delhi residence of the Maharaja of Jaipur. It houses an excellent collection of works by both Indian and colonial artists.

It is open Tuesday to Sunday, 10 am to 5 pm; admission is free.

Miniature paintings exhibited at the National Museum offer an insight into past traditions.

DELHI

NEW DELHI

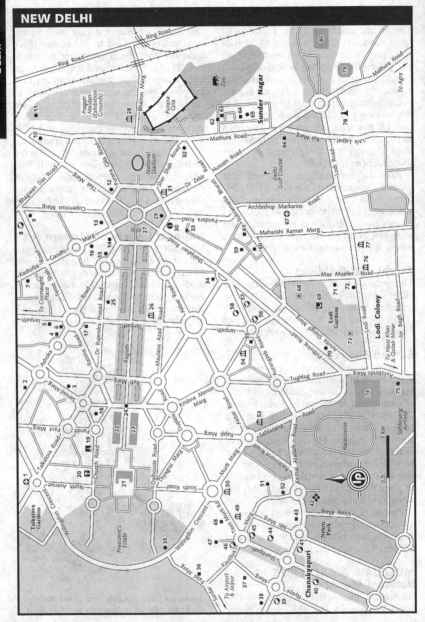

NEW DELHI

DELHI

Nehru Museum & Planetarium

On Teen Murti Rd near Chanakyapuri, the residence of Jawaharlal Nehru, Teen Murti Bhavan, has been converted into a museum. Photographs and newspaper clippings on display give a fascinating insight into the history of the independence movement. There's a planetarium in the grounds (shows at 11.30 am and 3 pm).

The museum is open from Tuesday to Sunday, between 9.30 am and 4.45 pm. Admission is free.

Rail Transport Museum

This museum (☎ 688 1816) at Chanakyapuri will be of great interest to anyone fascinated by India's exotic collection of railway engines. The exhibit includes an 1855 steam engine, still in working order, and a large number of oddities such as the skull of an elephant that charged a mail train in 1894, and lost.

The museum is open Tuesday to Sunday, between 9.30 am and 5 pm; admission costs Rs 5 (plus an extra Rs 10 for a camera).

Tibet House

This small museum (☎ 461 1515) has a fascinating collection of ceremonial items brought out of Tibet when the Dalai Lama fled following the Chinese occupation. Downstairs is a shop selling a wide range of Tibetan handicrafts. There are often lecture/discussion sessions. The museum is in the Institutional Area, Lodi Rd; it's open Monday to Saturday 10 am to 1 pm and 2 to 5 pm. Admission is Rs 1.

Crafts Museum

In the Aditi Pavilion at the Pragati Maidan Exhibition Grounds, Mathura Rd, this museum (☎ 337 1817) contains a collection of traditional Indian crafts in textiles, metal, wood and ceramics. The museum is part of a 'village life' complex where you can visit rural India without leaving Delhi. Opening hours are Tuesday to Sunday 9.30 am to 4.30 pm. Admission is free.

Indira Gandhi Memorial Museum

The former residence of Indira Gandhi at 1 Safdarjang Rd has also been converted into a museum (☎ 301 0094). On show are some of her personal effects, including the sari (complete with blood stains) she was wearing at the time of her assassination. Striking a somewhat macabre note is the crystal plaque in the garden, flanked constantly by two soldiers, which protects a few brown spots of Mrs Gandhi's blood on the spot where she actually fell after being shot by two of her Sikh bodyguards in December 1984. Opening hours are 9.30 am to 5 pm daily. Admission is free.

Other Museums

The **Museum of Natural History** (☎ 331 4849) is opposite the Nepalese embassy on Barakhamba Rd. Fronted by a large model dinosaur, it has a collection of fossils, stuffed animals and birds, and a 'hands-on' discovery room for children. It's open Tuesday to Sunday, 10 am to 5 pm.

The **National Philatelic Museum**, (☎ 371 0154) hidden in the post office at Dak Bhavan, Sardar Patel Chowk on Sansad Marg, has an extensive collection. It's closed on Saturday and Sunday.

In the Red Fort is the excellent **Svatantrata Sangrama Sangrahalaya** (Museum of the Independence Movement). See the Red Fort entry, earlier in this chapter.

PURANA QILA

Just south-east of India Gate and north of Humayun's tomb and Nizamuddin train station is the Purana Qila (Old Fort). This is the supposed site of Indraprastha, the original city of Delhi. The Afghan ruler, Sher Shar, who briefly interrupted the Mughal sovereignty by defeating Humayun, completed the fort during his reign from 1538 to 1545, before Humayun regained control of India. The fort has massive walls and three large gateways.

Entering from the south gate you'll see the small octagonal red sandstone tower, the Sher Mandal, later used by Humayun as a library. It was while descending the stairs of this tower one day in 1556 that he slipped, fell and received injuries from which he later died. Just beyond it is the Qila-i-Kuhran Mosque, or Mosque of Sher Shar, which, unlike the fort itself, is in a reasonable condition.

There's a small archaeological museum just inside the main gate, and there are good views of New Delhi from atop the gate. A sound and light show (through poor-quality loudspeakers) is held here. Timings and tickets (Rs 25) are available from the tourist office.

ZOO

The Delhi Zoo, on the south side of Purana Qila, is a peaceful retreat and not bad as far as zoos in the developing world go. There are white tigers and even an elephant who plays the harmonica (we're not making this up).

The zoo is open from Saturday to Thursday; it's extremely popular at weekends with Delhiites who seem to come here specifically to tease the animals. Admission costs Rs 40 for foreigners.

HUMAYUN'S TOMB

Built in the mid-16th century by Haji Begum, the Persian-born senior wife of Humayun, the second Mughal emperor, this is a wonderful early example of Mughal architecture. The elements in its design – a squat building, high arched entrances that let in light, topped by a bulbous dome and surrounded by formal gardens – were to be refined over the years to the magnificence of the Taj Mahal in Agra. This earlier tomb is thus of great interest for its relation to the later Taj. Haji Begum is also buried in the red-and-white sandstone and black-and-yellow marble tomb.

Other tombs in the classic Persian charbagh include that of Humayun's barber. The octagonal tomb of Isa Khan lies through a gate to the left of the entrance, and is a good example of Lodi architecture. Entry to Humayun's tomb is Rs 5 (and Rs 25 for video cameras) except on Friday when it is free. An excellent view can be obtained over the surrounding country from the terraces of the tomb.

NIZAM-UD-DIN'S SHRINE

Across the road from Humayun's tomb is the shrine of the Muslim Sufi saint, Nizam-ud-din Chishti, who died in 1325 aged 92. His shrine, with its large tank, is one of several interesting tombs here. The construction of Nizam-ud-din's tank caused a dispute between the saint and the constructor of Tughlaqabad, farther to the south of Delhi (see Tughlaqabad in the Greater Delhi section later in this chapter).

Other tombs include the later grave of Jahanara, the daughter of Shah Jahan, who stayed with her father during his imprisonment by Aurangzeb in Agra's Red Fort. Amir Khusru, a renowned Urdu poet, also has his tomb here, as does Atgah Khan, a favourite of Humayun and his son Akbar. Atgah Khan was murdered by Adham Khan in Agra. In turn Akbar had Adham Khan terminated and his grave is near the Qutab Minar.

It's worth visiting the shrine at around sunset on Thursday, as it is a popular time for worship, and *qawwali* (Sufi devotional singing) is performed after the evening prayers. This is one of Delhi's most important pilgrimage sites, so dress conservatively.

LODI GARDENS

About 3km to the west of Humayun's tomb and adjoining the India International Centre are the Lodi Gardens. In these well-kept gardens are the tombs of the Sayyid and Lodi rulers. Mohammed Shah's tomb (1450) was a prototype for the later Mughal-style tomb of Humayun, a design that would eventually develop into the Taj Mahal. Other tombs include those of his predecessor, Mubarak Shah (1433), Ibrahim Lodi (1526) and Sikander Lodi (1517). The Bara Gumbad Masjid is a fine example of its type of plaster decoration. An auto-rickshaw should cost about Rs 30 from Connaught Place one way.

SAFDARJANG'S TOMB

Beside the small Safdarjang airport, this tomb was built in 1753-54 by the Nawab of Avadh for his father, Safdarjang, and is one of the last examples of Mughal architecture before the final remnants of the great empire collapsed. The tomb stands on a high terrace surrounded by an extensive walled garden. It makes a pleasant retreat from the urban bustle. Entry is Rs 0.50; free on Friday. It's a short walk from Lodi Gardens.

HAUZ KHAS VILLAGE

Midway between Safdarjang's tomb and the Qutab Minar, this urban village surrounded by parkland was once the reservoir for the second city of Delhi – Siri – which lies slightly to the east. Interesting sights here include **Feroz Shah's tomb** (1398) and the remains of an ancient college. It was around this area that Tamerlane defeated the forces of Mohammed Shah Tughlaq in 1398. Hauz Khas is now one of the more chic places in Delhi; there are some excellent (if pricey) restaurants and shops here.

Also part of the old city of Siri is the **Moth-ki Masjid**, which lies some distance to the east of Hauz Khas. It is said to be the finest mosque in the Lodi style. Count on about Rs 60 for an auto-rickshaw from Connaught Place.

BAHAI TEMPLE

Lying to the east of Siri is this building shaped like a lotus flower. Completed in 1986, it is set among pools and gardens, and adherents of any faith are free to visit the temple and pray or meditate silently according to their own religion. It looks spectacular at dusk, particularly from the air, when it is floodlit, but is rather disappointing close up. The temple lies just inside the Outer Ring Road, 12km south-east of the city centre. A one-way auto-rickshaw fare should be around Rs 60.

ORGANISED TOURS

Delhi is very spread out, so taking a city tour makes a lot of sense. Two major organisations arrange Delhi tours – beware agents offering cut-price tours. The Indian Tourism Development Corporation (ITDC), operating under the name Ashok Travels & Tours (☎ 332 5035), has tours that include guides and a luxury coach. Their office is in L Block, Connaught Place, near Nirula's Hotel, but you can book at the Government of India tourist office on Janpath or at the major hotels. Delhi Tourism (☎ 331 3637), a branch of the city government, arranges similar tours and their office is in N Block, Middle Circle.

A five-hour morning tour of New Delhi costs Rs 125 with ITDC. Starting at 8 am, the tour includes the Qutab Minar, Humayun's tomb, India Gate, the Jantar Mantar and the Lakshmi Narayan Temple. The afternoon Old Delhi tour for Rs 100 starts at 2.15 pm and covers the Red Fort, Jama Masjid, Raj Ghat, Shanti Vana and Feroz Shah Kotla. If you take both tours on the same day (and a long day it will be) it costs Rs 200.

PLACES TO STAY

If Delhi is your first stop in India, you'd be well advised to phone or fax from abroad several days in advance to book your accommodation. The hotels that are reasonable value fill up quickly, leaving greenhorns easy prey to hotel touts. These guys will stop at nothing to earn their fat commissions by getting you into the rip-off joints.

During summer (May to August) discounts of up to 50% are often available and it's always worth asking for a discount if you intend staying for more than a couple of days.

Places to Stay – Budget

Delhi is no bargain when it comes to cheap hotels. You can easily pay Rs 200 for the most basic single room – a price that elsewhere in India will generally get you a double with bath.

There are basically two areas for cheap accommodation. Most travellers head for Paharganj near New Delhi train station – this is about midway between Old Delhi and New Delhi. There are legions of pushy touts and the air pollution is extreme when the electricity supply fails and the diesel generators crank up, but it does have a certain maddening charm.

The alternative area is around Janpath at the southern side of Connaught Place in New Delhi, but there's less choice (and lots of touts).

There are also a number of rock-bottom hotels in Old Delhi itself. They're colourful but generally noisy and too far away from New Delhi's agencies, offices, airlines and other facilities for most travellers, especially given the difficult transport situation.

Camping The *Tourist Camp* (☎ 327 2898) is deservedly popular. It's some way from Connaught Place but close to Old Delhi's sights. The camp is near Delhi Gate on Jawaharlal Nehru Marg, opposite the JP Narayan Hospital (Irwin Hospital), 2km from Connaught Place. You can set up your own tent (Rs 50) on the hard ground, or there are basic single/double rooms with shared bath for Rs 125/200, and doubles with air-cooler for Rs 250 (Rs 390 with bath). They're nothing flash and hot as hell in summer, but this place gets good recommendations from travellers. There's a basic restaurant and a left-luggage room.

Connaught Place & Janpath Area

There are a few cheap guesthouses near the Government of India tourist office. They're cramped but you meet lots of fellow travellers and there are dormitories.

Ringo Guest House (☎ 331 0605, 17 Scindia House), down a small side street near the tourist office, is an ageing travellers' institution and has its share of detractors as well as fans. Beds in crowded, 14-bed dorms are Rs 90; rooms with common bath are Rs 125/250 and doubles with private bath are Rs 350 to Rs 400. The rooms are very small but it's clean enough and the showers and toilets are well maintained. Meals are available in the rooftop courtyard. You can also store luggage for Rs 8 per item per day.

Sunny Guest House (☎ 331 2909, 152 Scindia House) is very similar to Ringo Guest House, and a few doors farther along the same side street. Dorm beds are Rs 90, singles/doubles with common bath are Rs 125/250, and it's Rs 280 to Rs 400 for a double with bath. Again, the rooms are small but the place has a sort of shabby charm, and this, along with the location, is what attracts so many people. The left-luggage facility is also Rs 8 per item per day.

Mr SC Jain's Guest House (☎ 332 3484, 7 Pratap Singh) seems to be in a prolonged decline. There are grubby rooms for Rs 150/300, all with common bath. Some say they find the owner an interesting guy to talk to, others say it's badly run.

Hotel Blue (☎ 332 9123, 126 M Block, Connaught Place), opposite Super Bazaar, has singles/doubles for Rs 200/400 with common bath, up to Rs 500/900 with bath. There's a pleasant sitting area on the balcony overlooking Connaught Place. It's reasonable value for this part of Delhi but nothing to write home about.

Hotel Palace Heights (☎ 332 1419, D Block, Connaught Place) is a moderately priced place close to Nirula's. It's on the 3rd floor of an office building and has a huge balcony. Rooms cost Rs 275/375 with air-cooler and common bath, or there are air-con doubles with bath for Rs 690. Some rooms are better than others; the same goes for the staff.

Paharganj Area

Directly opposite New Delhi train station's front entrance is the start of Main Bazaar, a narrow road that stretches due west for about 1km. Because of its proximity to the station it has become a major accommodation centre for Indians and foreigners alike. Virtually anything you'd care to name – from incense to washing machines – is sold in this bustling market, although a lot of shoddy goods (especially clothing) are passed off to the unwary. There are any number of cheap hotels along this road, offering varying degrees of comfort and quality.

Traveller Guest House Inn (☎ 354 4849, 4360 Main Bazaar) has clean rooms, though some are without windows. There are no singles; doubles with bath are Rs 180. A nice triple with TV and bath (hot water geyser) costs Rs 250.

Kailash Guest House (☎ 777 4993, 4469 Main Bazaar) is modern and clean enough, although many of the rooms face inwards and can be a bit stuffy; those with windows are fine. It's good value at Rs 110/160 with common bath, and Rs 225 for a double with bath (cold water only – Rs 5 for a bucket of the hot stuff).

Kiran Guest House (☎ 752 6104), next door, is virtually identical to the Kailash, and prices are similar at Rs 100/150 with common bath.

Hotel Bright Guest House (☎ 752 5852, 1089-90 Main Bazaar) is one of the cheapest places in Paharganj, and you get what you pay for. Rooms around a small courtyard cost Rs 80/100 with common bath, Rs 130 for a double with bath.

Hotel Star Palace (☎ 752 8584) is down the side lane to the left just before Hotel Bright. With clean but small rooms from Rs 250/325 with bath and TV, it's reasonably good. The rooftop restaurant is nice until the diesel generator starts up.

Hotel Down Town (☎ 355 5815) is down the same side lane as the Star Palace, but is a little bit quieter. They charge Rs 125/150 for good clean single/double rooms with shared bath, and Rs 150/200 with private bath.

CONNAUGHT PLACE

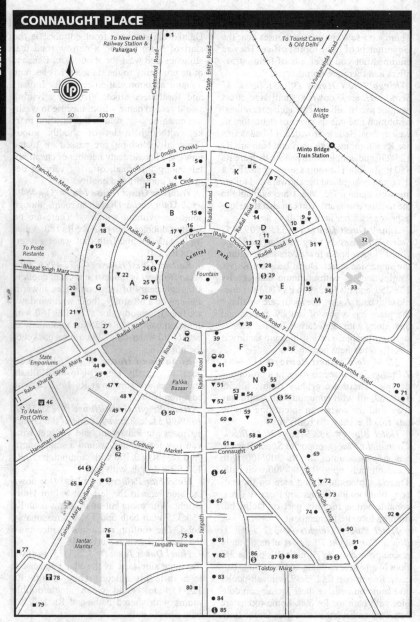

To New Delhi
Railway Station &
Paharganj

To Tourist Camp
& Old Delhi

Chelmsford Road

State Entry Road

Vivekananda Road

Minto
Bridge

Minto Bridge
Train Station

Panchkuin Marg

Connaught Circus

(Indira Chowk)

Middle Circle

Inner Circle — (Rajiv Chowk)

Radial Road 3

Radial Road 4

Radial Road 5

Radial Road 6

Central Park

Fountain

To Poste
Restante

Bhagat Singh Marg

Radial Road 2

Radial Road 1

Radial Road 8

Radial Road 7

Barakhamba Road

State Emporiums

Baba Kharak Singh Marg

Palika
Bazaar

To Main
Post Office

Hanuman Road

Clothing Market

Connaught Lane

Sansad Marg (Parliament Street)

Kasturba Gandhi Marg

Jantar
Mantar

Janpath

Janpath Lane

Tolstoy Marg

CONNAUGHT PLACE

PLACES TO STAY
3   Hotel 55
6   York Hotel
9   Nirula's Hotel
10 Jukaso Inn Down Town
11 Hotel Palace Heights
18 Hotel Marina
20 Hotel Alka; Vega
34 Hotel Blue
54 Hotel Central Court
58 Sunny Guest House
61 Ringo Guest House; Don't
     Pass Me By Café; Don't Pass
     Me By Travels
65 Park Hotel; Las Meninas;
     Someplace Else
76 Mr SC Jain's Guest House
77 YMCA Tourist Hotel; Y Tours
     & Travels
79 YWCA International Guest
     House; VINstring Holidays
80 Imperial Hotel; Spice Route;
     Tavern Restaurant; Garden
     Party; Thomas Cook; Student
     Travel Information Centre

PLACES TO EAT
8   Nirula's Restaurants; Pegasus
12 Embassy
13 Pizza Express
17 Cafe 100; Zen Restaurant
21 McDonald's
22 Fa Yian
23 Wenger's
25 El Rodeo
28 Kovil Pizza Hut
30 United Coffee House
31 Domino's Pizza
38 The Host
47 Gaylord
48 El Arab Restaurants; The
     Cellar

49 Kwality Restaurant; People
     Tree
51 Nirula's
52 Wimpy
59 Croissants Etc
72 Parikrama; Tarom
82 Sona Rupa Restaurant; Royal
     Nepal Airlines Corporation
     (RNAC)

OTHER
1   Railway Booking Office
2   ANZ Grindlays Bank
4   Cox & Kings
5   Plaza Cinema
7   English Book Depot
14 Odeon Cinema
15 Bookworm
16 New Book Depot
19 Gulf Air Jet Airways
24 American Express; Gulf Air;
     Singapore Airlines; Jet
     Airways
26 Post Office
27 Malaysia Airlines; Royal
     Jordanian
29 ANZ Grindlays Bank
32 Shankar Market (Piccadilly
     Book Store)
33 Super Bazaar
35 Singapore Airlines (SIA)
36 Aeroflot
37 Delhi Tourism
39 Sita World Travels
40 EATS Airport Bus
41 Indian Airlines
42 Prepaid Auto-Rickshaw Kiosk
43 Khadi Gramodyog Bhavan
44 Calculus Cyber Centre
45 Regal Cinema
46 Hanuman Mandir
50 Citibank; Air India

53 Blues Bar
55 Travel Corporation of India
56 Hongkong & Shanghai Bank
57 Air France
60 Oxford Book Shop
62 Bank of Baroda
63 British Airways; Swissair
64 Standard Chartered Bank;
     Allahabad Bank
66 Government of India Tourist
     Office; Delhi Photo Company
67 Tan's Travel
68 PIA
69 American Center
70 Emirates; Wheels Rent-a-Car
71 Kuwait Airways; Saudia
73 Air Canada
74 British Council
75 Map Sales Office
78 Free Church
81 Lufthansa Airlines
83 Central Cottage Industries
     Emporium
84 Japan Airlines
85 Chandralok Building
     (Haryana, Himachal Pradesh
     & Uttar Pradesh Tourist
     Offices; Delta Airlines; Druk
     Air; Japan Airlines; Lufthansa
     Airlines)
86 Deutsche Bank; Cathay
     Pacific Airlines
87 Deutsche Bank
88 Jagson Airlines
89 Credit Lyonnaise
90 Asian Airlines; Ethiopian
     Airlines
91 United; Sahara India;
     Scandinavian Airlines (SAS)
92 KLM; Northwest Airlines; El
     Al Israel Airline; Uzbekistan
     Airways

Not far beyond the Hotel Bright Guest House, *Hotel Namaskar* (☎ 752 1234, 917 Chandiwalan) is very friendly, quiet, and well managed by two brothers who go out of their way to help you. All rooms have windows and bath, and there's a geyser on each floor. Guest's luggage is stored free of charge if there is space. Rooms cost Rs 150/200, and three (Rs 300) and four (Rs 400) bed rooms are available. This place

has been recommended for bus tickets, plane tickets and car hire for extended trips.

Smyle Inn (☎ 355 9107, 916 Chandiwalan), next door also gets good reports; doubles with bath cost Rs 200.

Camran Lodge (☎ 352 6053, 1116 Main Bazaar) is a funky old place built into the side of the old mosque. It bills itself as a 'Trusted lodging house for distinguished people'. The rooms are small and grubby but

DELHI

PAHARGANJ

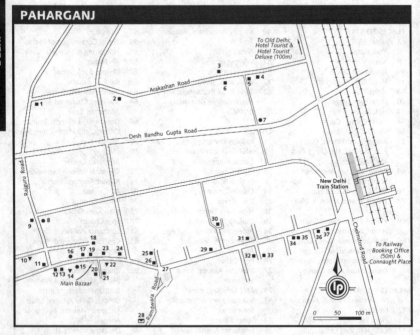

To Old Delhi;
Hotel Tourist &
Hotel Tourist
Deluxe (100m)

Arakashan Road

New Delhi
Train Station

Desh Bandhu Gupta Road

Rajguru Road

Chelmsford Road

To Railway
Booking Office
(50m) &
Connaught Place

Main Bazaar

Ramdwara Road

0   50   100 m

cheap at Rs 80/180 for a double without/with bath. Hot water by the bucket is free.

Hotel Navrang (☎ *753 1922, 6 Tooti Chowk*) is down a side street to the right off the vegetable market. It's a large and rather shabby cheapie with basic rooms on five floors: Rs 80/100 for rooms with common bath, Rs 100/120 with private bath.

Hotel Payal (☎ *352 0867, 1182 Main Bazaar*) has a flash marble lobby and rooms from Rs 150/200 with common bath, Rs 250/300 with bath.

Hotel Vivek (☎ *351 2900, 1534-50 Main Bazaar*) gets mixed reports these days. The rooms are pretty standard and smallish – Rs 200/250 with bath and hot water by the bucket, Rs 300/400 for rooms with hot showers, and air-con rooms for Rs 600/700.

Ajay Guest House (☎ *354 3125, 5084 Main Bazaar*) is down a side lane to the left. The rooms are fairly clean, the hot water system is

reliable, there's a pleasant rooftop and a German Bakery in the foyer (along with a shonky travel agent). All rooms have bath and cost Rs 160 to Rs 200 for singles and Rs 210 to Rs 250 for doubles. Checkout is 24 hours.

Hare Rama Guest House (☎ *352 9273*) is opposite the Ajay and just as popular, particularly with Israeli travellers. There are 65 rooms, some much nicer than others (not all have windows). They cost Rs 120/170 with common bath, Rs 210 and Rs 220 for doubles with bath. The restaurant is open 24 hours.

Ankush Guest House (☎ *751 9000, 1558 Main Bazaar*), is another place popular with travellers. Single rooms with common bath are Rs 100, or doubles/triples with bath are Rs 150/200.

Hotel Vishal (☎ *753 2079*), a little farther along, is similar, and has two good restaurants on the ground floor. Rooms cost Rs 160/250 with bath.

PAHARGANJ

PLACES TO STAY	20	Ajay Guest House; German	36	Traveller Guest House Inn
1 Hotel Diplomat Inn		Bakery	37	Hotel Gold Regency
2 Hotel Shiva Continental	21	Hare Rama Guest House; Aa		
3 Hotel Soma		Bee Travels		PLACES TO EAT
4 Hotel Ajanta	23	Ankush Guest House	10	Malhotra Restaurant
5 Hotel Syal	24	Hotel Vivek	14	Khosla Cafe
6 Tourist Inn; Swad Restaurant	25	Hotel Navrang	22	Diamond Cafe
9 Hotel Kelson	26	Hotel Payal		
11 Metropolis Tourist Home;	29	Camran Lodge; Money		OTHER
Metropolis Restaurant		Changer	7	Shiela Cinema
12 Hotel Star View	30	Hotel Namaskar; Smyle Inn	8	Imperial Cinema
13 Hotel Satyam	31	Hotel Bright Guest House	15	Book Exchange;
17 Hotel Vishal; Lords Cafe; Hare	32	Hotel Star Palace		Bicycle Hire
Krishna Guest House	33	Hotel Down Town	16	E-Mail Centre
18 Major's Den	34	Kiran Guest House	27	Vegetable Market
19 Anoop Hotel	35	Kailash Guest House	28	Paharganj Post Office

Hare Krishna Guest House (☎ 753 3017, 1572 Main Bazaar) has nice, clean doubles from Rs 190 to Rs 230, and there's a rooftop restaurant.

Anoop Hotel (☎ 352 9366, 1566 Main Bazaar) is good value for money. The rooms, which have bath and hot water, are a decent size and are marble-lined, which makes them cool, although a bit tomb-like. They cost Rs 180/250 (Rs 425 for an air-con double). The biggest attraction, however, is the rooftop terrace and snack bar. Checkout is 24 hours.

Hotel Satyam (☎ 352 5200) has clean rooms for Rs 200/250 with bath. The front rooms can be noisy, but that's true of all the places along Main Bazaar.

Hotel Kelson (☎ 752 2646, Rajguru Rd) is one of several similar hotels on this road, just off Main Bazaar. It's a clean and modern place, but the rooms are definitely on the small side, and many lack windows. They cost Rs 200/400 with TV and bath, or Rs 450 for a double with air-con.

Major's Den (☎ 752 9599, 2314 Lakshmi Naryan St), behind the Imperial Cinema, is clean, well run and a good place to stay. All rooms have 'bathrooms with modern gadgets' and cost from Rs 150/350 (larger doubles Rs 450). 'A small haven of peace' was how one traveller described this guesthouse.

Still in Paharganj, there's a whole group of places on Arakashan Rd, just north of New Delhi train station, past the Desh Bandhu Gupta Rd flyover. These are definitely at the top end of the budget category, but are mostly modern and well equipped.

Hotel Soma (☎ 752 1002, 33 Arakashan Rd) has clean and modern rooms of a decent size from Rs 295/375 to Rs 450/495.

Tourist Inn (☎ 777 7112, 8502 Arakashan Rd) is OK and cheaper than most in this area at Rs 350/400.

Old Delhi There's a group of hotels around the south-western corner of the Jama Masjid, and many more along Matya Mahal, the road that runs due south of the same mosque. These places are fine if you like the hustle and bustle, and if you don't mind being away from the business and restaurant centre of Connaught Place.

Hotel New City Palace (☎ 327 9548) is right behind the mosque. The front rooms have windows but also get the early-morning call from the mosque. It is clean and modern, and the management are friendly. Double rooms with bath and hot water cost Rs 300; with air-con it's Rs 400.

The **Hotel Bombay Orient** (☎ 328 6253, Matya Mahal), near the southern Jama Masjid gate, is also good, clean and well kept; rooms with shared bath are Rs 150/250, Rs 200/300 with private bath.

Bharat Hotel (☎ 395 5326) is at the west

end of Chandni Chowk, opposite the eastern gate of Fatehpuri Masjid. It's an old rambling place with a few small courtyards and quite a bit of atmosphere, though the rooms are a bit gloomy. Nevertheless, it's cheap and cheerful, with rooms for Rs 120/180.

The *Star Guest House (☎ 292 1127, 186 Katra Baryan)* is near the Bharat and is more modern. It has tolerably grubby rooms for Rs 100/160 with common bath.

Other Areas *Youth Hostel (☎ 301 6285, 5 Nyaya Marg, Chanakyapuri)* has dorm beds for Rs 30. With the inconvenient location, and the fact that this place takes members only, it's not really a great proposition.

Vishwa Yuvak Kendra – International Youth Centre (☎ 301 3631, Teen Murti Marg, Chanakyapuri) is not so hot either. Dorm beds are Rs 50, rooms Rs 650, but there is a good cheap canteen.

The *retiring rooms* at the airport can be useful; they're at both the domestic (Terminal I; ☎ 329 5126) and international (Terminal II; ☎ 545 2011) sections. You can use them if you have a confirmed departure within 24 hours of your arrival by plane, but officials often say they are full and eagerly suggest another hotel (where they get commission). Dorm beds cost Rs 80.

Places to Stay – Mid-Range

Again, there are few bargains in this price range in Delhi. There's currently a luxury tax of 10% on rooms over Rs 500 (not included in prices below), and some places also levy an additional service charge of 5 to 10%.

The Ys There are three YMCA or YWCA places, all of which take either sex. They're all very popular so you'll need to book ahead.

YMCA Tourist Hotel (☎ 336 1915, fax 374 6032, Jai Singh Rd) is near the Jantar Mantar. Although it has an institutional feel and is no great bargain, it's still popular with foreigners as it's well located, clean and has good facilities. There are gardens, a swimming pool, lounge and a restaurant with western, Indian and Mughlai cuisine. Despite what the touts may tell you, the hotel is open 24 hours, and credit cards are accepted. Rooms cost Rs 500/750 with common bath, Rs 950/1400 with air-con and bath. There's also an additional 5% service charge, a 10% luxury tax on rooms over Rs 500 and a temporary membership charge of Rs 10, valid for one month. Breakfast is included.

The *YWCA International Guest House (☎ 336 1517, fax 334 1763, 10 Sansad Marg)* has singles/doubles for Rs 550/850 (plus 10% service charge, and the 10% luxury tax on rooms over Rs 500); all rooms have bath and air-con and breakfast is included. It's conveniently located near Connaught Place and has a good restaurant, where a set breakfast is Rs 45. There's a good travel agency here.

YWCA Blue Triangle Family Hostel (☎ 336 0133, fax 336 0202, Ashoka Rd) is just off Sansad Marg. It's clean, well run and has a restaurant. Rates, including breakfast, are Rs 550/850 for an ordinary room, or Rs 750/1050 with air-con; all rooms have bath. There's also a temporary membership fee of Rs 10 but currently no service charge. It's only about a 10 minute walk from the heart of Connaught Place.

Connaught Place & Janpath Area There are several mid-range hotels around Janpath and Connaught Place.

ITDC Ashok Yatri Niwas (☎ 332 4511, intersection of Ashoka Rd and Janpath) is just a 10 minute walk from Connaught Place. Rooms in this high-rise, government-run hotel cost Rs 550/700/800 for singles/doubles/four-beds (plus 10% luxury tax) with bath. The rooms are a reasonable size and some have been renovated recently, but none has a phone, TV or room service. There's a self-service cafe and a restaurant. This place gets very mixed reviews – 'a managerial disaster that's been setting the standard for lousy service for some years now', say some – others think it's reasonable value for Delhi. It very much depends on the rooms available when you get there.

Hotel 55 (☎ 332 1244, fax 332 0769, 55 H Block, Connaught Circus) is well designed with air-con throughout. Rooms with balcony and bath are Rs 1000/1500.

Hotel Alka (☎ 344 4328, fax 373 2796, 16 P Block, Connaught Circus) has smallish air-con singles/doubles for Rs 1800/2900. As is typical of many places in this area, most of the rooms don't have windows. There's a very good vegetarian restaurant and a 24 hour coffee shop.

Hotel Central Court (☎ 331 5013, N Block, Connaught Place) has rooms from Rs 800/1150 with air-con and bath. It's nothing special, but there's a pleasant terrace and an astro-palmist is on call.

York Hotel (☎ 332 3769, fax 335 2419, K Block, Connaught Place) is clean but fairly characterless, and the rooms cost Rs 1600/2700. Those at the back are quieter.

Nirula's Hotel (☎ 332 2419, fax 335 3957, L Block, Connaught Place) is right beside the Nirula restaurants and snack bars. Singles/doubles are from Rs 1800/2900 in this small but good-standard hotel. Advance bookings are advisable.

Jukaso Inn Downtown (☎ 332 4451, fax 332 4448, L Block, Connaught Place) is similar in standard to nearby Nirula's. Rooms cost from Rs 1500/2000.

Paharganj Area *Hotel Star View* (☎ 355 6300, 5136 Main Bazaar) has a range of doubles from Rs 425 to Rs 675. All have windows, bath and TV.

Hotel Gold Regency (☎ 354 0101, fax 354 0202, 4350 Main Bazaar) is a new mid-range place with a good restaurant, an unreliable email centre and a noisy disco. The rooms, however, are large and clean, with possibly the biggest bathrooms in Paharganj. Doubles cost Rs 700 to Rs 900, and it's open 24 hours.

Metropolis Tourist Home (☎ 352 5492, fax 752 5600, 1634 Main Bazaar), is one of the top hotels in the area. Clean and comfortable air-con rooms with bath cost Rs 550/660, while suites costs Rs 1100. There's a good restaurant here.

The following places are on Arakashan Rd, parallel with and to the north of Main Bazaar.

Hotel Diplomat Inn (☎ 751 7881), at the western end of the street, is quite friendly and like lots of places in this area, quite willing to negotiate discounts. Singles/doubles with bath and TV start at Rs 695/895.

Hotel Shiva Continental (☎ 350 1493), situated where the street bends, is a decent mid-range place with air-cooled rooms from Rs 695/895 and air-con rooms from Rs 895/1195.

Hotel Tourist Lodge (☎ 732990) is spotlessly clean with striking chintzy decor and porcelain chandeliers. Air-cooled rooms are Rs 350/450, air-con rooms 500/650, and the deluxe rooms with their slightly raunchy honeymoon suite furnishings cost Rs 700.

Hotel Syal (☎ 751 0091) is fairly standard for the area, with rooms from Rs 500/650 and air-con rooms for Rs 945/995.

Hotel Ajanta (☎ 752 0925) gets generally good reviews, though some rooms are better than others. All rooms have bath with hot water, and the deluxe rooms have TV and phones. The charge is Rs 645/745 for deluxe, and Rs 745/845 for air-con. There's a restaurant, email centre and travel agency.

Hotel Tourist Deluxe (☎ 777 0985, Qutab Rd), north of Paharganj, is an older mid-range place with friendly staff. Clean air-con rooms with bathroom cost Rs 850/950, and rooms with a bathtub are Rs 950/1050.

Hotel Tourist (☎ 751 0334) is in the same compound but farther from Qutab Rd. It is a little shabbier and less friendly; air-cooled rooms cost Rs 425/645.

Sunder Nagar In a peaceful residential neighbourhood near the zoo are several small hotels set back from the main road. All rooms have bath, air-con and Star TV. Luxury tax (currently 10%) must be added to all prices below.

Maharani Guest House (☎ 469 3128, 3 Sunder Nagar) has a flashy foyer and comfortable rooms from Rs 1300/2000.

Kailash Inn (☎ 461 7401, 10 Sunder Nagar), is much smaller than the Maharani and around the corner on the square. It's a friendly place with good clean rooms from Rs 1400/1800.

La Sagrita Tourist Home (☎ 469 4541, 14 Sunder Nagar) is probably the best value of all these places. Rooms with nice soft beds are Rs 1595/3195 and there's a small garden.

Jukaso Inn (☎ 469 0308, 50 Sunder Nagar) should not be confused with the place of the same name on Connaught Place. It's a glitzy hotel with rooms from Rs 1400/2000, and is very popular with businesspeople.

Other Areas There are two excellent private guesthouses to the west of Connaught Place. The small inconvenience of being farther from the heart of things is compensated for by the friendly and relaxed atmosphere you find at these places. Advance bookings are advisable during the high season.

Master Paying Guest House (☎ 574 1089, 578 8914, R-500 New Rajendra Nagar) is a Rs 30 auto-rickshaw ride from Connaught Place, near the intersection of Shankar Rd and Gangaram Hospital Marg. This small and friendly place is in a quiet residential area and the helpful owner has worked hard to create a homelike atmosphere. It has large, airy and beautifully furnished doubles from Rs 350 to Rs 750. Light meals are available, there's a pleasant rooftop terrace, and car hire for extended trips can also be arranged.

Yatri House (☎ 752 5563, 3/4 Rani Jhansi Rd) is opposite the junction of Panchkuin Marg (Radial Rd No 3) and Mandir Marg, about 1km west of Connaught Place. It's calm, secure and there are trees, a lawn and a small courtyard at the back. The good-sized rooms cost from Rs 900, all with bath, and are kept spotlessly clean. For Rs 350 they'll meet you at the airport. There's car hire available for sightseeing trips, and air tickets can be arranged.

Places to Stay – Top End
Prices at Delhi's top hotels have increased dramatically over the past few years. To the prices below you can expect to add taxes of at least 20%.

Four-Star Hotels Unless otherwise stated, these hotels have no swimming pool.

Ambassador Hotel (☎ 463 2600, fax 463 2252) is a small hotel at Sujan Singh Park, a short distance south of India Gate. There are 81 rooms costing US$100/130. The hotel has a notable vegetarian restaurant, coffee shop and a bar.

Connaught Palace Hotel (☎ 346 4225, fax 334 0757, Bhagat Singh Marg) is due west of Connaught Place. It offers restaurants, 24 hour room service and car rental. Rooms cost from US$120/130 with breakfast.

Diplomat Hotel (☎ 301 0204, fax 301 8605, 9 Sardar Patel Marg), south-west of Rashtrapati Bhavan, is a smaller place with just 25 rooms from Rs 5000/5500, a restaurant and a bar.

Hotel Hans Plaza (☎ 331 6861, fax 331 4830, Tolstoy Marg) is conveniently central with rooms from US$175/190.

ITDC Hotel Janpath (☎ 332 0070, fax 332 7083, Janpath) has indifferent service but is in a good position. Rooms start at Rs 1800/2600.

ITDC Hotel Kanishka (☎ 332 4422, fax 332 4242, cnr Janpath and Ashoka Rds) is overpriced at US$120/150, but it's one of the few places to have a swimming pool.

Hotel Marina (☎ 332 4658, fax 332 8609, G Block, Connaught Place) is quite smart. The rooms, mostly with windows, are Rs 2600/3200 including buffet breakfast.

Oberoi Maidens Hotel (☎ 291 4841, fax 398 0771, 7 Shamnath Marg) is inconveniently located north of Old Delhi, but the building itself is a verandaed colonial relic and is very pleasant, as is the large garden. It has a swimming pool and the charming Cavalry Bar. Rooms start at US$110/135.

Five-Star Hotels If you're looking for a little more luxury, try one of the following.

Claridges Hotel (☎ 301 0211, fax 301 0625, 12 Aurangzeb Rd) is south of Rajpath in New Delhi. It's a very comfortable, older place, with four good restaurants, a swimming pool and a health club. It's probably the best-value five star hotel, with singles/doubles from US$175.

Imperial Hotel (☎ 332 5332, fax 332 4542, Janpath) is conveniently situated near the centre of the city. It's a pleasantly old-fashioned hotel with a pool and a big garden – wonderful for breakfast – and it's surprisingly quiet given its central location. Rooms are from US$200.

Park Hotel (☎ 373 2477, fax 373 2025, Sansad Marg) lacks character but is in a very central location only a block from Connaught Place. This hotel has a swimming pool, a superb Spanish restaurant and a business centre. Rooms are from US$250.

Centaur Hotel (☎ 565 2223, fax 565 2256, Gurgaon Rd) has rooms at US$150/170. It's 2km from the international terminal and 5km the domestic terminal.

Five-Star Deluxe Hotels *Radisson Hotel Delhi (☎ 613 7373)*, a flashy place just 3km from the airport's international terminal, has singles/doubles from US$350/450.

ITDC Ashok Hotel (☎ 611 0101, fax 687 3216, 50B Chanakyapuri) is the 563-room flagship of the ITDC hotel fleet. Need we say more? Singles/doubles cost from US$250/300.

New Delhi Hilton (☎ 332 0101, fax 332 5335) is a modern 445 room hotel that is very centrally located just off Barakhamba Rd, east of Connaught Place. It boasts every conceivable mod con, including an open-air swimming pool on a 3rd floor terrace. Standard singles/doubles cost US$335/360, and there are more expensive suites available.

Hyatt Regency (☎ 618 1234, fax 618 6633), with 518 rooms, is in the south of New Delhi, between Hauz Khas Village and Chanakyapuri. Facilities include a fitness centre, inhouse movies, restaurants, bar and coffee shop. For all this you pay US$350 for a double room.

Hotel Le Meridien (☎ 371 0101, fax 371 4545, corner of Janpath and Raisina Rds) is another very modern place with a stunning atrium. This 355 room hotel has a swimming pool, restaurants and a 24 hour coffee shop. The rates are US$325/350 for standard singles/doubles.

Hotel Oberoi New Delhi (☎ 436 3030, fax 436 0484) is south of New Delhi near the Purana Qila. Services include a 24 hour

business centre, travel desk, swimming pool and secretarial services. Rooms cost from US$350/400.

Hotel Maurya Sheraton (☎ 611 2233, fax 615 5555, Sardar Patel Marg) is west of Chanakyapuri on the road to the airport. Apart from a high level of comfort, the hotel boasts two excellent restaurants, a solar-heated swimming pool (the only one in Delhi) and a disco. It has 500 rooms costing from US$400.

Taj Mahal Hotel (☎ 301 6162, fax 301 7299, 1 Man Singh Rd) is a luxurious place that is fairly central but quiet. It has all the usual facilities including a swimming pool. Singles/doubles start at US$325/360.

Taj Palace Hotel (☎ 301 0404, fax 301 1252, Sardar Patel Marg) is near the Maurya Sheraton, and fairly convenient for the airport. Rooms are US$325/350.

PLACES TO EAT

Delhi has an excellent array of places to eat – from *dhabas* (snack bars) with dishes for less than Rs 15 up to top-of-the-range restaurants where a meal for two can top Rs 3500.

Janpath & Connaught Place

There are many Indian-style fast-food places in this area. Their plus point is that they have good food at reasonable prices and are clean and healthy. A minus point for some of them is they have no place to sit – it's stand, eat and run. They serve Indian food (from samosas to dosas) and western food (burgers to sandwiches).

Budget *Nirula's* does a wide variety of light snacks, both Indian and western. The ice cream parlour is amazingly busy, and is open 10 am to midnight. The main Nirula's is on L Block on the outer circle, and there are various other outlets dotted throughout suburban Delhi. Above the ice cream parlour is a sit-down restaurant called *Pot Pourri*, which is always busy. The smorgasbord salad bar is quite good value, other dishes less so. It's a good place for breakfast, which is served from 7.30 am. Also upstairs at Nirula's is the *Chinese Room*, with meals for two in the Rs 400 range. Downstairs there's the congenial British-style pub **Pegasus**.

Cafe 100 *(B Block, Connaught Place)* is a very popular semi self-service place that's giving Nirula's a run for its money. There are Indian snacks, burgers, a wide range of ice creams, and an excellent buffet upstairs (open noon to 3 pm, and 7 to 11 pm).

Croissants Etc *(Scindia House, Connaught Circus)* has an excellent range of filled croissants, rolls and cakes. You can either take them away or eat in and watch Channel V.

Wimpy, the well-named British hamburger chain, is on Janpath at N block. For hamburgers read lamb-burgers, and even as junk food goes it's ordinary. Touts tend to lurk here too.

Domino's Pizza opened in Connaught Place in 1997. It's the real thing but not cheap; medium-sized pizzas for around Rs 160. For free delivery phone ☎ 373 4876.

Pizza Hut and **Pizza Express** also have branches on Connaught Place, though the former seems to be more popular. Again they aren't cheap but the air-conditioning is great in summer. Both cost around Rs 400 per person for dinner.

McDonald's is in P Block, although their blanket advertising may give the impression they've taken over the whole area. Burger (not made of beef), fries and a drink cost Rs 95.

Sona Rupa Restaurant *(Janpath)* does good north and South Indian vegetarian food (excellent dosas) and has a bizarre self-service system (pay first, take the docket to the kitchen, then watch for the signal that your food is ready). It's great value at around Rs 80 per person.

Don't Pass Me By, in the same lane as the Ringo and Sunny guesthouses, is a popular, cheap little place that caters to international tastes. It's great for breakfast. There are some other cheap eateries along this lane.

Keventers *(corner of Connaught Place and Radial Rd No 3)* is a small milk bar around the corner from American Express that has good fresh milk.

Wenger's *(A Block, Connaught Place)* is a cake shop with a range of little cakes that they'll put in a cardboard box and tie up with a bow so you can self-consciously carry them back to your hotel room for private consumption.

Mid-Range & Top End The **Embassy** *(D Block, Connaught Place)* has excellent veg and nonveg food. It's popular among office workers; meals for two cost about Rs 350.

Kovil *(E Block, Connaught Place)* is one of the best places for South Indian vegetarian food, costing about Rs 150 per person.

Vega, at the Hotel Alka, specialises in vegetarian food cooked Delhi style (in pure ghee but without onion and garlic).

United Coffee House *(E Block, Connaught Place)* is quite plush with a very pleasantly relaxed atmosphere, good food and some of the best coffee in Delhi.

Kwality Restaurant *(Sansad Marg)* is clean and very efficient and the food's good value. The menu is the almost standard nonvegetarian menu you'll find at restaurants all over India. Main courses are around Rs 100. This is also a good place for non-Indian food if you want a break.

El Arab Restaurant *(corner of Sansad Marg and Outer Circle, Connaught Place)* has an interesting Middle Eastern menu with most dishes around Rs 100. Downstairs here is the more expensive **Cellar**.

Fa Yian *(A Block, Middle Circle, Connaught Place)* is owned and run by Chinese people, and is quite authentic. Dinner for two costs about Rs 400.

The Host *(F Block, Connaught Place)* serves excellent Indian and Chinese food. It's extremely popular with well-heeled Indians, but it ain't cheap.

Zen Restaurant *(B Block, Connaught Place)* has a focus on Chinese and Japanese food at similar prices to Fa Yian.

El Rodeo *(A Block, Connaught Place)* is a lively restaurant serving good Mexican and Italian (!) food near American Express; it's worth visiting just for the sight of waiters in cowboy suits! Dinner for two will set you back about Rs 400.

Gaylord (Connaught Circus) is one of the priciest, plushest restaurants on Connaught Place, with big mirrors, chandeliers and excellent Indian food. Main dishes are around Rs 200, but the high quality of the ingredients makes this a worthwhile splurge.

Parikrama (Kasturba Gandhi Marg), a revolving restaurant, is an interesting place to eat. Unlike many places of this ilk where the first class views are supposed to distract you from decidedly 2nd class food, the fare here is excellent but pricey. Main dishes are around Rs 150. It's open daily for lunch and dinner, and for drinks from 3 to 7 pm.

Yamu's Panchayat is where the wealthy go to round off their meal with some of the most pricey paan in the city. They range from Rs 5 to Rs 50 and some contain edible silver leaf.

Paharganj Area

In keeping with its role as a travellers' centre, Main Bazaar in Paharganj has a handful of cheap restaurants that cater almost exclusively to foreign travellers. Hotel rooftop restaurants are also good value, if not always as hygienic as you'd like. They are all up towards the western end of Main Bazaar.

German Bakery, in the foyer of the Hotel Ajay, does sandwiches, snacks and a wide range of sugar-laden cakes for about Rs 25 per piece.

Lords Cafe, in the Hotel Vishal, has passable cheap food.

Diamond Cafe, opposite the Hotel Vivek, is similar to Lords.

Khosla Cafe, near the Hotel Satyam, is a decent budget eatery.

Metropolis Restaurant, in the hotel of the same name just past Rajguru Rd, is a good place to eat, either in the ground floor restaurant or on the rooftop. With most main dishes around Rs 175, it's much more expensive than the other Main Bazaar cheapies.

Malhotra Restaurant has two branches in the street behind the Metropolis Tourist Home, one of which is air-conditioned. They both have large menus and get good reports.

On Arakashan Rd the restaurant in the *Hotel Ajanta* is reasonable if not terribly

exciting, while the *Swad Restaurant* at the Tourist Inn makes passable dosas for Rs 30.

Old Delhi

In Old Delhi there are many places to eat at the western end of Chandni Chowk.

Ghantewala (Chandni Chowk), near the Sisganj Gurdwara (Sikh temple), is reputed to have some of the best Indian sweets in Delhi. The stalls along the road in front of the Jama Masjid are very cheap.

ISBT Workers' Canteen, in the Interstate bus terminal, has good food at reasonable prices.

Karim's, down a lane across from the south gate of the Jama Masjid, is very well known for its excellent nonveg food. There's everything from kebabs to the richest Mughlai dishes in this large restaurant, and prices are reasonable.

Tandoor (Asaf Ali Rd) at the Hotel President, near the Tourist Camp, is an excellent place with the usual two-waiters-per-diner service and a sitar playing in the background. The tandoori kitchen can be seen through a glass panel.

Chor Bizaare (Asaf Ali Rd) is close by in the Hotel Broadway. They've certainly put some effort into decorating this place with an eclectic mix of bits and pieces collected from various markets – a four-poster bed, an old sports car (now used as a salad bar) and an old cello. The food is good but pricey; expect to pay Rs 800 for two.

Moti Mahal Restaurant (Netaji Subhash Marg, Daryaganj), around the corner, has been going for 50 years and is still noted for its tandoori dishes.

South Delhi

There are some good eating options in the area south of Connaught Place, but you'll need a taxi or transport to get to most of them.

At Pandara Market near Bikaner House are some good-value mid-range places such as *Ichiban*, *Pindi* and *Chicken Inn*, plus several others popular with middle class Delhiites. They all cost around Rs 300 to Rs 400 for two.

Khan Market also has some good restaurants, including **China Garden** and **China Fare**, for a little less than the Pandara Market places.

Basil & Thyme *(Chanakyapuri)*, in the swish Santushti Shopping Centre, is still quite hip. The continental food is good and the service excellent. Meals for two cost about Rs 500.

Dilli Haat *(Aurobindo Marg)*, opposite the INA Market, is a great place to sample food from all over India – many of the stalls devoted to particular states have restaurants and for around Rs 50 per person they offer cheap value too. This may be your one chance to try Naga or Mizo food. There is a Rs 5 entrance fee.

Defence Colony is one of the upmarket residential suburbs in south Delhi. The market here draws middle class Delhi-wallahs and their families in numbers in the evenings, especially on the weekends. **Colonel's Kababz** is a very popular stand-up kebab, tandoori and seafood place, although most diners remain in their cars and are served by scurrying waiters!

There are lots of restaurants in Hauz Khas Village, nearly all of them mid-range places that charge around Rs 250 per person. The Bistro Restaurant Complex includes the **Kowloon** (Chinese restaurant), **Mohalla** (curries in gravy) and **The Rooftop** (Indian barbecue plus live music); places here seem to change quite often.

Other Hauz Khas restaurants include **Baujee Ka Dhaba** (North-Western Frontier cuisine; a cooking style combining the Afghan, Central Asian and Indian influences from the North-Western Frontier Province of Pakistan), **Osaka** (Japanese and Chinese), **Naivedyam** (South Indian), **KC's** (Mughlai), **Thai Orchid**, **Khas Bagh** for tandoori and **Duke's Place**, which is a pleasant Italian place with live jazz music some nights. **Park Baluchi** is within the nearby Deep Park and specialises in Afghan cuisine.

Karim's *(Nizamuddin)* offers some of the best Mughlai cooking to be found in the city.

International Hotels

Many Delhi residents reckon the best food is at the major hotels.

Claridges
    The restaurants at this hotel are very good value and they're interesting places to eat. The **Dhaba** offers 'rugged roadside' cuisine, and is set up like a typical roadside cafe; the **Jade Garden** serves Chinese food in a bamboo grove setting; **Pickwicks** offers western food, and the decor is 19th century England; while outdoor **Corbetts** gets its inspiration from Jim Corbett of tiger hunting fame, complete with recorded jungle sounds. As might be expected, meat features prominently on the menu. All restaurants are moderately priced – most main dishes are under Rs 200.

Imperial Hotel
    This is a great place for an alfresco breakfast in the pleasant garden. **Spice Route** offers mainly Thai and Keralan dishes; it's very popular and very expensive (Rs 1800 for two). At the **Tavern Restaurant** main dishes are around Rs 200. Prices at the less formal **Garden Party** are 10% lower.

Ambassador Hotel
    There are upmarket thalis at the **Dasaprakash** vegetarian restaurant, and **Larry's China**.

Hyatt Regency
    Delhi Ka Angan specialises in very rich Punjabi and Mughlai food; **La Piazza** has Italian food and possibly Delhi's best Italian wine list. Both restaurants charge about Rs 1000 for two.

Park Hotel
    If you're staying nearby at one of the Ys, treat yourself to the all-you-can-eat buffet breakfast for Rs 234 including taxes. The dinner buffet costs Rs 411. There's also the Spanish restaurant, **Las Meninas**; the decor's very stylish (Rs 900 for two).

Le Meridien
    The rooftop **Le Belvedere** offers a range of mouth-watering western and Indian cuisine for about Rs 1200 for two. There's also an excellent Chinese restaurant, the **Golden Phoenix**, where meals costs around Rs 700 per person.

Oberoi New Delhi
    Baan Thai is probably the best Thai restaurant in Delhi. Count on Rs 1000 for two.

Oberoi Maidens
    The **Curzon Room** specialises in Anglo-Indian cuisine, and while expensive it's an authentic taste of the Raj. About Rs 800 for two.

Maurya Sheraton
    The **Bukhara** is one of the best restaurants in the city. It has many Central Asian specialities, including tandoori cooking and dishes from

the Peshawar region in north-west Pakistan. *Bali Hi* is their Chinese restaurant, and *West View* their European one. All these restaurants cost around Rs 1000 per person.

Another restaurant here is the *Dum Pukht*, named after the cuisine championed by the Nawabs of Avadh (Lucknow) around 300 years ago.

The dishes are covered by a pastry cap while cooking, so the food is steamed as much as anything else. It's quite distinctive and absolutely superb, and a little cheaper than the others at Rs 1200 for two.

Taj Mahal Hotel

The *House of Ming* is a popular Sichuan Chinese restaurant with main dishes around Rs 300, while *Captain's Cabin* is a seafood restaurant that does superb Goan dishes for Rs 2000 for two.

Haveli has live Indian classical music in the evenings. The best French restaurant in town is the *Longchamp*, at the top of this hotel, and possibly the most expensive as well (a mere Rs 3500 for two).

ENTERTAINMENT
Cultural Programs
Delhi is renowned for its dance and visual arts scene; check out *First City* magazine for what's going on. Major dance and live music venues include *Habitat World (☎ 469 1920, Lodhi Rd)* at the India Habitat Centre; the nearby *India International Centre (☎ 461 9431)*; *Kamani Auditorium (☎ 338 8084, Copernicus Marg)*; and the *Triveni Chamber Theatre (205 Tansen Marg)* at Triveni Kala Sangam, near Rabindra Bhavan. They give a mix of live theatre and dance.

Cinemas
For films there are a number of cinemas around Connaught Place, but the fare is typically Hindi mass-appeal movies; seats range from Rs 25 to Rs 50. For something a little more cerebral, the *British Council (☎ 371 0111, Kasturba Gandhi Marg)* often screens good foreign films.

The better cinemas are mostly in the southern suburbs, including the *Priya Cinema (☎ 614 0049, Basant Lok, Vasant Vihar)* and *PVR Anupam 4 (☎ 686 5999)*, in the Saket Community Centre, Saket.

The *Satyam Cineplex (☎ 579 7387, Patel Nagar)* is on Patel Road, west of Karol Bagh. These cinemas regularly show Hollywood blockbusters tame enough to sneak past the Indian censors. Habitat World also has a cinema concentrating on Indian documentaries and art-house films.

Bars & Nightclubs
Delhi's strict licensing laws are starting to be loosened to encourage people to drink beer in bars rather than knock down whisky at home. However, most bars and discos are at the five-star hotels and are fiercely expensive. The discos at these hotels are quite exclusive and entry is usually restricted to members and hotel guests; couples and women stand a better chance of being admitted than unaccompanied men.

El Rodeo, the bar-restaurant on Connaught Place (see Places to Eat), has a cover charge of Rs 200 after 7.30 pm if you only want to drink and not eat. Draught beer is Rs 80.

The *Blues Bar* on Connaught Circus and the *Pegasus Tavern* at Nirulas both have draught beer.

Jazz Bar at the Maurya Sheraton is good, with live jazz each evening, but drinks are expensive – over Rs 200 for a beer!

Someplace Else is a bar-disco at the Park Hotel. Entry is Rs 400 per couple; beer is Rs 250.

CJ's is a nightclub at Hotel Le Meridien. Entry is Rs 500 per couple.

My Kind of Place is at the Taj Palace Hotel. Entry is Rs 400 per couple.

SHOPPING
Good buys include silk products, precious stones, leather and woodwork, but the most important thing about Delhi is that you can find almost anything from anywhere in the whole country. If this is your first stop in India, and you intend to buy something while you are here, then it's a chance to compare what is available from all over the country. If this is your last stop and there was something you missed elsewhere in your travels, Delhi provides a chance to find it.

Two good places to start are in New Delhi, near Connaught Place. The **Central Cottage Industries Emporium** is on Janpath. In this building you will find items from all over India, generally of good quality and reasonably priced. Whether it's woodcarvings, brasswork, paintings, clothes, textiles or furniture, you'll find it here. Along Baba Kharak Singh Marg, two streets around (clockwise) from Janpath, are the **state emporiums** run by the state governments. Each of them displays and sells handicrafts from their state.

There are many other shops around **Connaught Place** and **Janpath**. By the Imperial Hotel are a number of stalls and small shops run by Tibetan refugees and rapacious Kashmiris selling carpets, jewellery and many (often instant) antiques.

In Old Delhi, **Chandni Chowk** is the famous shopping street. Here you will find carpets and jewellery, but you have to search the convoluted back alleys. In the narrow street called Cariba Kalan, perfumes are made as well.

Main Bazaar in Paharganj has a good range. You can find an interesting variety of perfumes, oils, soaps and incense at two places (both signposted), one near the Hotel Vivek and another near the Camran Lodge. Take advantage of all the free testers. Monday is the official weekly holiday for the shops in Main Bazaar, and many are closed on that day, although a surprising number remain open seven days a week.

In recent years the **Karol Bagh Market**, 3km west of Connaught Place along Panchkuin Marg (Radial Rd No 3), has become even more popular than Connaught Place or Main Bazaar.

Just south of the Purana Qila, beside Dr Zakir Hussain Rd, across from Hotel Oberoi New Delhi, is the **Sunder Nagar Market**, a collection of shops selling antiques and brassware. The prices may be high but you'll find fascinating and high-quality artefacts. Shops in the major international hotels often have high-quality items, at equally high prices.

Opposite the Ashok Hotel in Chanakyapuri is the **Santushti Shopping Centre**. There's a string of small upmarket boutiques here with a good range of crafts and high prices to match.

The **M Block Market** in Greater Kailash I is one of the biggest upper and middle class shopping centres. The **N Block Market** in Greater Kailash I has a similar collection of upmarket stores, including the famous clothing, fabric and furnishings store Fab India (younger Indian parliamentarians are sometimes referred to as the Fab India gang).

Hauz Khas Village in south Delhi has become a very interesting little shopping enclave, with an ever-changing collection of art galleries and boutiques catering for the upper end of the market.

GETTING THERE & AWAY

Delhi is a major international gateway to India; for details on arriving from overseas see the introductory Getting There & Away chapter. At certain times of the year international flights out of Delhi can be heavily booked so it's wise to make reservations as early as possible. This particularly applies to some of the heavily discounted airlines out of Europe – check and double-check your reservations and make sure you reconfirm your flight.

Delhi is also a major centre for domestic travel, with extensive bus, rail and air connections.

Air

The domestic terminals (Terminals IA and IB of the Indira Gandhi international airport) are 15km from the centre, and the international terminal (Terminal II) is a further 5km. There's a free IAAI bus between the two terminals, or you can use the Ex-Servicemen's Air Link Transport Service (EATS; see Getting Around later in this chapter).

If you're arriving at the airport from overseas, there's 24 hour State Bank of India and Thomas Cook foreign exchange counters in the arrivals hall, after you go through customs and immigration. Once you've left the arrivals hall you won't be allowed back in.

Several airlines now require you to have the baggage you're checking in x-rayed and sealed, so do this at the machines just inside the departure hall before you queue to check in. Nearly all airline tickets include the departure tax in the price; if it's not included, you must pay at the State Bank counter in the departures hall, also before check in.

Facilities at the international terminal include a dreadful snack bar, bookshop and banks. Once inside the departure lounge there are a few duty-free shops with the usual inflated prices, and another terrible snack bar where you have the privilege of paying in US dollars.

Indian Airlines Indian Airlines has a number of offices. The Malhotra Building office (☎ 331 0517) in F Block, Connaught Place, is probably the most convenient, though busy at most times. It's open daily except Saturday, 10 am to 5 pm.

There's another office in the PTI Building (☎ 371 9168) on Sansad Marg, open daily except Sunday, 10 am to 5 pm.

At Safdarjang airfield on Aurobindo Marg there's a 24 hour office (☎ 141), and this can be a quick place to make bookings.

Business class passengers can check in by telephone on ☎ 329 5166. For prerecorded flight departure information, ring ☎ 142.

Indian Airlines flights depart from Delhi to all the major Indian centres – see the Domestic Flights from Delhi boxed text. Check in at the airport is 75 minutes before departure. Note that if you have just arrived and have an

Warning

Many international flights arrive and depart at terrible hours of the morning. Take special care if this is your first foray into India and if you arrive exhausted and jetlagged. If you're leaving Delhi in the early hours of the morning, organise a taxi the afternoon before – it will be hard to find one in the night. There are retiring rooms at the airport – see Other Areas in the Places to Stay – Budget section earlier in this chapter.

onward connection to another city in India, it may be with Air India, the country's international carrier, rather than the domestic carrier, Indian Airlines. If that is the case, you must check in at the international terminal (Terminal II) rather than the domestic terminal.

Other Domestic Airlines As well as the offices listed below, private airlines have offices at the airport's domestic terminal.

Archana Airways
(☎ 684 2001/566 5768) 41A Friends Colony East, Mathura Rd
Jagson Airlines
(☎ 372 1593/4) 12E Vandana Bldg, 11 Tolstoy Marg
Jet Airways
(☎ 685 3700) Jetair House, 13 Community Centre, Yusuf Sarai
(☎ 332 0961) G12 Connaught Circus
Sahara India
(☎ 332 6851) Ambadeep Bldg, Kasturba Gandhi Marg

International Airlines Offices in Delhi include the following:

Aeroflot
(☎ 331 2843) BMC House, 1st Floor, 1N Connaught Place
Air Canada
(☎ 372 0014) Hindustan Times House, Kasturba Gandhi Marg
Air France
(☎ 331 2853) 7 Atma Ram Mansion, Connaught Circus
Air India
(☎ 331 1225) Jeevan Bharati Bldg, Outer Circle, Connaught Place
Air Lanka
(☎ 332 6843) Hotel Janpath
Asiana Airlines (Korea)
(☎ 331 5631) Ansal Bhavan, Kasturba Gandhi Marg
Biman Bangladesh Airlines
(☎ 335 4401) World Trade Centre, Babar Rd, Connaught Place
British Airways
(☎ 332 7428) DLF Bldg, Sansad Marg
Delta Airlines
(☎ 332 5222) Chandralok Bldg, 36 Janpath
Druk Air (Bhutan)
(☎ 331 0990) Chandralok Bldg, 36 Janpath

Domestic Flights from Delhi

destination	flight duration	flights per d[1]/w[2]	fare (US$)
Agra	35 min	1 d	50
Ahmedabad	1 h 25 min	4 d	120
Amritsar	1 h	6 w	90
Aurangabad	3 h 25 min	1 d	150
Bagdogra	1 h 55 min	10 w	185
Bangalore	2 h 30 min	7 d	230
Bhopal	1 h 5 min	1 d	105
Bhubaneswar	1 h 50 min	1 d	195
Calcutta	2 h	4 d	180
Chandigarh	40 min	2 w	65
Chennai	1 h 30 min	6 d	235
Dibrugarh	3 h 35 min	4 w	254
Goa	2 h 25 min	10 w	210
Guwahati	2 h 15 min	16 w	210
Gwalior	45 min	4 w	60
Hyderabad	2 h	3 d	185
Imphal	5 h 45 min	2 w	240
Indore	3 h	1 d	120
Jaipur	40 min	3 d	55
Jaisalmer	2 h 5 min	3 w	140
Jammu	1 h 10 min	3 d	105
Jodhpur	55 min	3 w	95
Khajuraho	1 h 45 min	2 d	90
Kochi	4 h	1 d	300
Kullu	1 h 20 min	2 d	150
Leh	1 h 15 min	4 w	105
Lucknow	55 min	25 w	80
Mumbai	1 h 55 min	23 d	155
Nagpur	2 h 55 min	1 d	135
Patna	1 h 25 min	14 w	130
Pune	2 h	2 d	185
Raipur	1 h 45 min	1 d	175
Ranchi	2 h 50 min	1 d	170
Srinagar	1 h 15 min	22 w	115
Thiruvananthapuram	4 h 25 min	1 d	325
Udaipur	1 h 50 min	14 w	95
Vadodara	1 h 25 min	1 d	135
Varanasi	1 h 10 min	24 w	110
Visakhapatnam	3 h 15 min	3 w	255

[1]daily, [2]weekly

El Al Israel Airlines
  (☎ 335 7965) Prakash Deep Bldg, 7 Tolstoy Marg
Emirates
  (☎ 332 4665) Kanchenjunga Bldg,
  18 Barakhamba Rd
Ethiopian Airlines
  (☎ 331 2302) Ansal Bhavan, Kasturba
  Gandhi Marg
Gulf Air
  (☎ 332 7814) G12, Connaught Circus
Iran Air
  (☎ 688 9123) Ashok Hotel, Chanakyapuri
Japan Airlines
  (☎ 332 7104) Chandralok Bldg, 36 Janpath
Kazakhstan Airlines
  (☎ 336 7889) Hotel Janpath
KLM-Royal Dutch Airlines
  (☎ 372 1141) Prakash Deep Bldg, 7 Tolstoy Marg
Kuwait Airways
  (☎ 331 4221) DCM Bldg, 16 Barakhamba Rd
Lufthansa Airlines
  (☎ 332 3310) 56 Janpath
Malaysia Airlines
  (☎ 332 4308) G55, Connaught Place
Northwest Airlines
  (☎ 372 1141) Prakash Deep Bldg, 7 Tolstoy
  Marg
Pakistan International Airlines (PIA)
  (☎ 331 3161) Kailash Bldg, Kasturba
  Gandhi Marg
Royal Jordanian
  (☎ 332 0635) G56 Connaught Place
Royal Nepal Airlines Corporation (RNAC)
  (☎ 332 1164) 44 Janpath
Scandinavian Airlines (SAS)
  (☎ 335 2299) Ambadeep Bldg, Kasturba
  Gandhi Marg
Saudia
  (☎ 331 0466) DCM Bldg, Kasturba
  Gandhi Marg
Singapore Airlines (SIA)
  (☎ 332 0145) G11, Connaught Circus
Swissair
  (☎ 332 5511) DLF Bldg, Sansad Marg
Tarom
  (☎ 335 4422) Antariksh Bhavan, Kasturba
  Gandhi Marg
Thai Airways International (THAI)
  (☎ 623 9988) Park Royal Hotel, America
  Plaza, Nehru Place
United Airlines
  (☎ 335 3377) Ambadeep Bldg, Kasturba
  Gandhi Marg
Uzbekistan Airways
  (☎ 335 8687) Prakash Deep Bldg, 7 Tolstoy
  Marg

Bus

All the main roads leading out of Delhi are heavily congested and not a little scary. It's best to leave early in the morning. The main bus station is the Interstate bus terminal (ISBT) at Kashmiri Gate, north of the (Old) Delhi train station. It has 24 hour left-luggage facilities, a State Bank of India branch, post office, pharmacy and restaurant. City buses depart from here to locations all around Delhi. State government bus companies (and the counter they operate from) are:

Delhi Transport Corporation (34)	☎ 335 4518
Haryana Roadways (35)	☎ 296 1262
Himachal Roadways (40)	☎ 296 6725
Punjab Roadways (37)	☎ 296 7842
Rajasthan Roadways (central block; bookings can also be made at Bikaner House, south of Rajpath)	☎ 296 1246
Uttar Pradesh Roadways (central block)	☎ 296 8709

Rajasthan Buses popular with travellers include the frequent and fast service to Jaipur (Rs 84, 5½ hours). Deluxe buses for Jaipur leave from Bikaner House, take five hours and cost Rs 150, or Rs 270 for the less frequent air-con services.

North of Delhi For Himalayan destinations buses are the only option, but it's more pleasant to take a train for the first part of the journey. Shimla is accessible by both train and bus; direct day buses are Rs 135 (10 hours), overnight deluxe buses are around Rs 350. Alternatively you could take the bus to Chandigarh (Rs 100, five hours) and the narrow-gauge train from there. There are also direct buses to Dharamsala (13 hours), Manali (16 hours), Dehra Dun (seven hours), Haridwar (eight hours), Nainital (nine hours) and Jammu (14 hours).

You can buy tickets for the private buses to these destinations at agencies in Connaught Place and Paharganj.

South of Delhi From the Sarai Kale Khan ISBT, close to Nizamuddin train station, there are frequent departures for Agra (Rs 75 to Rs 100 depending on class, five

hours), Mathura and Gwalior. It's generally quicker to go by train to all these places, though. There's a city bus link between this station and Kashmiri Gate ISBT.

Kathmandu Around Paharganj and the other travellers' hang-outs you'll see posters advertising direct buses to Kathmandu – these take around 36 hours and cost about Rs 600. Most travellers seem to find that it's a lot more comfortable and better value to do the trip by train to Gorakhpur (Uttar Pradesh), and then take buses from there.

A number of travellers have also entered Nepal at the border crossing just east of the northern Uttar Pradesh village of Banbassa. There are daily buses to this village from New Delhi. See the Uttar Pradesh chapter for more details.

Train

Delhi is an important rail centre and an excellent place to make bookings. The best place is the special foreign tourist booking office upstairs in New Delhi train station, open Monday to Saturday 7.30 am to 5 pm. Ignore the touts lurking around the station who will try to lead you astray. This is the place to go if you want a tourist-quota allocation, are the holder of an Indrail Pass or want to buy an Indrail Pass. It gets very busy, and it can take up to an hour to get served. If you make bookings here tickets must be paid with rupees backed up by bank exchange certificates, or in US dollars and pounds sterling with any change given in rupees.

The main ticket office is on Chelmsford Rd, between New Delhi train station and Connaught Place. This place is well organised, but it's also incredibly busy. Take a numbered ticket from the counter as you enter the building, and then wait at the allotted window.

It's best to arrive first thing in the morning, or when it reopens after lunch. The office is open Monday to Saturday, 7.45 am to 9 pm. On Sunday it's open until 1.50 pm only.

Remember that there are two main stations in Delhi – Delhi train station in Old

Delhi, and New Delhi train station at Paharganj. New Delhi is much closer to Connaught Place, and if you're departing from the Old Delhi train station you should allow adequate time (up to an hour in peak times) to wind your way through the traffic snarls of Old Delhi. Between the Old Delhi and New Delhi stations you can take the No 6 bus.

There's also the Nizamuddin train station south of the New Delhi area where some trains start or finish. It's worth getting off here if you are staying in Chanakyapuri or anywhere else south of Connaught Place.

Some trains between Delhi and Jaipur, Jodhpur and Udaipur operate to and from Sarai Rohilla station rather than Old Delhi – it's about 3.5km north-west of Connaught Place on Guru Govind Singh Marg. The one exception is the *Shatabdi Express* to Jaipur, which operates from New Delhi.

GETTING AROUND

Delhi is large, congested, and the buses get hopelessly crowded. The alternative is a taxi, an auto-rickshaw, or for the truly brave, a bicycle.

To/From the Airport

Although there are a number of options, airport-to-city transport is not as straightforward as it should be, due to predatory taxi and auto-rickshaw drivers who target unwary first-time visitors. See the Transport Scams in Delhi boxed text.

Bus The Ex-Servicemen's Air Link Transport Service (EATS; ☎ 331 6530) has a regular bus service between the airport (both terminals) and Connaught Place, operating between 4 am and 11 pm. The fare is Rs 30 plus Rs 5 per large piece of lug-

Major Trains from Delhi

destination	train no & name	departure time[1]	distance (km)	duration	fare (Rs) (2nd/1st)
Agra	2180 *Taj Exp*	7.15 am HN	199	4 h 35 min	49/223
	2002 *Shatabdi Exp*[2]	6.15 am ND		1 h 55 min	275/530
Bangalore	2430 *Rajdhani Exp*[2]	9.30 am HN	2444	35 h	1210/3850
	2628 *Karnataka Exp*	9.15 pm ND		41 h	342/1482
Calcutta	2302 *Rajdhani Exp*[2]	5.15 pm ND	1441	18 h	1015/2895
	2304 *Poorva Exp*	4.30 pm ND		24 h	270/995
Chennai	2622 *Tamil Nadu Exp*	10.30 pm ND	2194	33 h 20 min	324/1359
Gorakhpur	2554 *Vaishali Exp*	7.45 pm ND	758	13 h	186/642
Jaipur	2901 *Pink City Exp*	5.45 am SR[3]	308	6 h	72/318
	2002 *Shatabdi Exp*[2]	6.15 am ND		4 h 25 min	350/685
Jammu Tawi	4645 *Shalimar Exp*	4.10 pm ND	585	14 h	153/528
Lucknow	4230 *Lucknow Mail*	10.00 pm ND	487	9 h 15 min	134/464
	2004 *Shatabdi Exp*[2]	6.20 am ND		6 h 25 min	450/900
Mumbai	2952 *Rajdhani Exp*[2]	4.00 pm ND	1384	17 h	825/2835
	1038 *Punjab Mail*	6.00 am ND		26 h	263/965
Shimla	4095 *Himalayan Queen*	6.00 am ND	364	11 h	82/368
Udaipur	9617 *Garib Nawas Exp*	5.45 am SR[3]	739	17 h 45 min	181/632
Varanasi	2382 *Poorva Exp*	4.30 pm ND	764	12 h 20 min	186/649

[1] Abbreviations for train stations: ND – New Delhi, HN – Hazrat Nizamuddin, SR – Sarai Rohilla
[2] Air-con only; fare includes meals and drinks
[3] May revert to Old Delhi – check when you buy your ticket

gage, and they will drop you off at most of
the major hotels en route, and at the entrance to New Delhi train station (for Paharganj hotels). In Connaught Place the
service leaves from near the Indian Airlines
office, F Block, 4 am to 11.30 pm.

When leaving the international terminal,
the counter for the EATS bus is just to the
right as you exit the building. This is probably the best, although not the quickest,
way into the city if you arrive late at night
(see the warning about prepaid taxis in the
following entry).

Taxi What you want from the airport is not
just a prepaid taxi, but the right prepaid taxi.
Look for the Delhi Traffic Police Prepaid
Taxi Booth just outside the terminal, where
you'll get the lowest prices (Rs 170 to Paharganj). The others will try for much more
(after an 18 hour Air India jetlag special
one LP author didn't check the book and
paid Rs 450!). You'll be given a voucher
that you have to present at the booth just
outside the airport building.

We've had reports of a number of travellers who have been given the run around
by unofficial prepaid taxis in the middle of
the night; they get taken to a hotel, told it's
full, then on to another hotel (often in Karol
Bagh) and intimidated into staying there at
vastly inflated prices (up to US$150). This
seems to happen only after the driver has
established that the person hasn't been to
India before, and only in the middle of the
night when it's difficult to get your bearings
and there are few other vehicles about.

Bear in mind that if you do head into the
centre late at night, most budget hotels are
closed (and firmly locked) from around midnight until at least 6 am, so unless you have
arranged a late arrival in advance, your options are limited. If you do take a taxi from
the airport late at night, before getting into
the vehicle make an obvious point of noting
down the registration number, and try and
find a few companions in a similar predicament if you're on your own. Don't announce
the fact if this is your first visit to Delhi. If
the driver is not prepared to go where *you*

want to go, find another taxi. If it's your first
trip to India it is best to wait in the terminal
building until daylight when there is much
less risk of getting led astray (we all know
that the real baddies disappear at dawn).

At the domestic terminal, the taxi booking
desk is just inside the terminal and charges
Rs 170 to Paharganj, plus Rs 5 per bag. The
taxi-wallahs outside will try for much more.

Bus

Avoid buses during the rush hours. Whenever
possible try to board (and leave) at a starting
or finishing point, such as the Regal and
Plaza cinemas in Connaught Place, as there is
more chance of a seat. There are some seats
reserved for women on the left-hand side of
the bus. The Delhi Transport Corporation
runs some buses, others are privately owned,
but they all operate along the same set routes.
Western embassies generally advise their
staff not to take buses, but if you want to, the
White Line and Green Line buses are slightly
more expensive and thus a little less crowded.
Private buses and minibuses also run on these
routes. A short bus ride (like Connaught Place
to Red Fort) is only about Rs 2.

Useful buses include the following:

Bus No 505 – Super Bazaar or Janpath (from opposite the Imperial Hotel) to the Qutab Minar
Bus No 101 – Kashmiri Gate Interstate bus terminal to Connaught Place
Bus Nos 620 & 630 – Connaught Place (from outside the Jantar Mantar) to Chanakyapuri
Bus Nos 101, 104 & 139 – Regal Cinema bus
  stand to the Red Fort

Car

Given Delhi's mind-boggling traffic (six
road deaths per day on average), perhaps
it's best not to drive. If you must rent a car,
try Wheels Rent A Car (☎ 331 8695),
Kanchenjunga Building, 18 Barakhamba
Rd; or Hertz (☎ 687 7188), Ansal Chambers, Bhikaji Cama Place, next to the Hyatt
Regency on the Ring Road.

Taxi & Auto-Rickshaw

All taxis and auto-rickshaws are metered but
the meters are invariably out of date, allegedly

DELHI

Transport Scams in Delhi

While London cabbies catch the latest instalment of *EastEnders* and New York taxi drivers discuss the recent ball game, one imagines that Delhi taxi-wallahs spend their spare time concocting ever more devious scams to separate the dumb tourists from their money.

We all know that when the taxi-wallah or auto-rickshaw-wallah says the hotel you ask to be taken to is 'full' or 'closed', that it's probably not true and he only wants to suggest one that will pay him a fat commission. Nevertheless, this straightforward bit of trickery still ensnares a few first-timers. There are, however, far more subtle scams.

Delhi Riots Scam You arrive at the airport in the early hours of the morning, jetlagged and exhausted, and hop in a taxi for the city centre. You give the name of a hotel and off you go. After a few kilometres the driver suggests that it may not be such a great idea to go to that hotel because the 'road is closed'. You immediately recognise this as a scam along the lines of 'hotel full' and 'hotel burnt down' and insist on being taken there. After another few kilometres the driver says there are 'riots' in Delhi. Playing along you say that's no problem, you want to be dropped at the hotel you asked for. Suddenly the taxi is flagged down by a man in uniform – a policeman as far as you are concerned. There's a heated exchange in Hindi. The driver turns to you and says he doesn't want to go on as the rioting is very bad and many people have been killed. With the policeman there the picture looks altogether different to you. You let the driver take you to the hotel of his choice. It turns out to be rather more expensive than you'd expected, but you're safe. At breakfast a travel agent appears and sells you a trip to Rajasthan – leaving immediately. It would never happen to you? It has to more than a few foreign travellers.

The auto-rickshaw wallahs have a similar scam set up where they meet a bogus policeman down a side street, he says there are Hindu-Muslim riots in Paharganj and you land up in a rip-off hotel, usually in Karol Bagh.

Hotel Reservations Scam Coming out of the train station a cycle-rickshaw wallah meets you and says he'll take you to any hotel you want for Rs 5. After a few minutes the rickshaw wallah stops outside a travel agency. 'Check your room reservation for free', he says. You say there's no need but since it's free ... Inside they ask where you're staying, dial the number and pass the phone to you. The 'receptionist' answers, asks your name, and then says they're very sorry but they had to cancel your reservation as they'd double booked. What you don't know is that the 'receptionist' was actually in the room next door, you weren't speaking to the hotel at all. Naturally the travel agent is quick to suggest alternative accommodation.

'not working' or the drivers will simply refuse to use them.

If you're anywhere near Connaught Place and need an auto-rickshaw, pick one up from the very useful prepaid booth near Palika Bazaar. Otherwise, you'll need to negotiate a price before you set out and this will always be more than it should be.

At the end of a metered journey you will have to pay according to a perversely complicated scale of revised charges (there are separate charts for recalibrated and unrecalibrated meters). Drivers are supposed to carry conversion cards but if you demand to see one, strangely enough they won't be able to find it. The fare charts are, however, also printed in the *Delhi City Guide* (Rs 15, available from newsagents). If you have a chart, pay what you think is the right price and leave it at that. Rest assured that no one is going to be out of pocket, except yourself, despite hurt or angry protestations to the contrary.

Connaught Place to the Red Fort should cost around Rs 60 by taxi or Rs 30 by auto-rickshaw, although the traffic jams can make this a long trip. From Connaught Place to Paharganj should cost about Rs 8 according to the meter system, but Rs 15 seems to be the standard minimum fare for foreigners. About Rs 30 is fair for an auto-rickshaw from Connaught Place to Humayun's tomb.

From 11 pm to 5 am there is a 20% surcharge for auto-rickshaws and 25% for taxis. If you're on your own at night make a show of writing down the licence plate number before setting off.

Pollution Alert

The number of vehicles on Delhi's roads has tripled since 1990. Their uncontrolled emissions together with the foul smoke that belches from numerous factories around the city is poisoning the air. More than a third of the population is said to suffer from some kind of respiratory complaint. The level of carbon monoxide at traffic intersections can be as high as 5000mg per cubic metre, 50 times the WHO standard. On windless days it's especially bad and a dark veil hangs over the city.

Little is being done to save Delhi earning the title of world's most polluted city. Cars with black smoke pouring from their tail pipes carry stickers that read 'Pollution Under Control'. In 1997 the municipal council took the dramatic step of banning smoking in public places. Given that simply to breathe Delhi's foul air is equivalent to smoking 20 cigarettes a day (40 a day if you're in the thick of the traffic), this is unlikely to achieve a reduction in the growing number of deaths from respiratory diseases.

If you're asthmatic don't stay too long in Delhi.

You will no doubt be asked if you want to go shopping (the driver will insist that 'just looking' is OK), as drivers get paid (Rs 200 is standard) just for taking foreigners to stores – even if you don't purchase anything. You could arrange with your driver to make a show of looking around a few shops and in return get your sightseeing for free, although the hard-sell tactics at the shops can wear you down. To hire a taxi for eight hours should cost around Rs 450, though the driver will expect a tip (say Rs 100).

Bicycle & Cycle-Rickshaw

Although traffic and pollution are dreadful in Old Delhi and around Connaught Place, the bicycle is one way of getting around the sights to the south, though bicyclists are an oppressed caste on Delhi's roads. There are very few places to hire bikes, however. In Paharganj, there's a small cycle hire shop near Rajguru Rd.

Cycle-rickshaws are banned from the Connaught Place area and New Delhi itself, but they can be handy for travelling between Connaught Circus and Paharganj, for around Rs 10, and around Old Delhi.

Greater Delhi

KHIRKI MASJID & JAHANPANAH

This interesting mosque with its four open courts dates from 1380. The nearby village of Khirki also takes its name from the mosque.

Close to the mosque are remains of the fourth city of Delhi, Jahanpanah, including the high Bijai Mandal platform and the Begumpur Masjid with its multiplicity of domes.

TUGHLAQABAD

The massively strong walls of Tughlaqabad, the third city of Delhi, are east of the Qutab Minar. The walled city and fort with its 13 gateways was built by Ghiyas-ud-din Tughlaq. Its construction involved a legendary quarrel with the saint Nizam-ud-din – when the Tughlaq ruler took the workers whom

Nizam-ud-din wanted for work on his shrine, the saint cursed the king, warning that his city would be inhabited only by shepherds. Today that is indeed the situation.

The dispute between king and saint did not end with curse and counter-curse. When the king prepared to take vengeance on the saint, Nizam-ud-din calmly told his followers (in a saying that is just as current in India today): 'Delhi is a long way off'. Indeed it was, for the king was murdered on his way from Delhi in 1325.

The fort walls are constructed of massive blocks and outside the south wall of the city is an artificial lake with the king's tomb in its centre. A long causeway connects the tomb to the fort, both of which have walls that slope inward.

Getting There & Away
The easiest way to visit Tughlaqabad is to combine it with a visit to the Qutab Minar. It is a long trip by auto-rickshaw so a taxi is preferable.

QUTAB MINAR COMPLEX
The buildings in this complex, 15km south of Delhi, date from the onset of Muslim rule in India and are fine examples of early-Afghan architecture. It's open from sunrise to sunset; entry is Rs 2.

The Qutab Minar itself is a soaring tower of victory that was started in 1193, immediately after the defeat of the last Hindu kingdom in Delhi. It is nearly 73m high and tapers from a 15m diameter base to just 2.5m at the top.

The tower has five distinct storeys, each marked by a projecting balcony. The first three storeys are made of red sandstone, the fourth and fifth of marble and sandstone. Although Qutab-ud-din began construction of the tower, he only got to the first storey. His successors completed it and, in 1368, Feroz Shah Tughlaq rebuilt the top storeys and added a cupola. An earthquake brought the cupola down in 1803 and an Englishman replaced it with another in 1829. However, that dome was deemed inappropriate and was removed some years later.

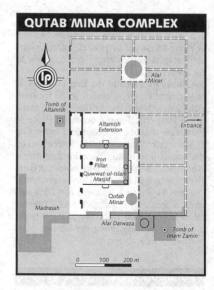

QUTAB MINAR COMPLEX

Today, this impressively ornate tower has a slight tilt, but otherwise has worn the centuries remarkably well. It is no longer possible to climb the tower.

Quwwat-ul-Islam Masjid
At the foot of the Qutab Minar stands the first mosque to be built in India, the Might of Islam Mosque. Qutab-ud-din began construction of the mosque in 1193, but it has had a number of additions and extensions over the centuries. The original mosque was built on the foundations of a Hindu temple, and an inscription over the east gate states that it was built with materials obtained from demolishing '27 idolatrous temples'. Many of the elements in the mosque's construction indicate their Hindu or Jain origins.

Altamish, Qutab-ud-din's son-in-law, surrounded the original mosque with a cloistered court built between 1210 and 1220. Ala-ud-din added a court to the east and the magnificent Alai Darwaza gateway in 1300.

Iron Pillar This 7m high pillar stands in the courtyard of the mosque and has been there since long before the mosque's construction. A six-line Sanskrit inscription indicates that it was initially erected outside a Vishnu temple, possibly in Bihar, and was raised in memory of the Gupta King Chandragupta Vikramaditya, who ruled from 375 to 413.

What the inscription does not tell is how it was made, for the iron in the pillar is of quite exceptional purity. Scientists have never discovered how this iron, which is of such purity that it has not rusted after 2000 years, could be cast with the technology of the time. It was said that if you can stand with your back to the pillar and encircle it with your arms your wish will be granted; however, the pillar is now protected by a fence.

Alai Minar

At the time Ala-ud-din made his additions to the mosque, he also conceived a far more ambitious construction program. He would build a second tower of victory, exactly like the Qutab Minar, except it would be twice as high! By the time of his death the tower had reached 27m and no one was willing to continue his overambitious project. The uncompleted tower stands to the north of the Qutab Minar and the mosque.

Other Features

Ala-ud-din's **Alai Darwaza** gateway is the main entrance to the whole complex. It was built of red sandstone in 1310 and stands just south-west of the Qutab Minar. The **tomb of Imam Zamin** stands beside the gateway, while the **tomb of Altamish**, who died in 1235, is by the north-western corner of the mosque. The largely ruined **madrasah of Ala-ud-din** stands at the rear of the complex.

A short distance west of the enclosure, in Mehrauli Village, is the **tomb of Adham Khan** who murdered his rival Atgah Khan, who like him was related to a wet nurse of the Emperor Akbar. (See Mandu in the Madhya Pradesh chapter.) When Akbar learned of the murder Adham Khan ended up being heaved off a terrace in the Agra Fort, not once but twice. Also in Mehrauli, a large new Shakti Pitha temple complex is under construction.

South of the enclosure is the Jain Ahimsa Sthal, and an impressive 4m statue in pink granite of Mahavir.

There are some summer palaces in the area and also the tombs of the last kings of Delhi, who succeeded the last Mughals. An empty space between two of the tombs was intended for the last king of Delhi, who died in exile in Yangon, Burma (Myanmar), in 1862, following his implication in the 1857 Indian Uprising.

Getting There & Away

You can get out to the Qutab Minar on a No 505 bus from the Ajmer Gate side of New Delhi train station, or from Janpath, opposite the Imperial Hotel. Hiring a taxi is more convenient.

Punjab & Haryana

The Punjab was probably the part of India that suffered the most destruction and damage at the time of Partition, yet today it is far and away the most affluent state in India. No natural resource or advantage gave the Punjabis this enviable position; it was sheer hard work.

Although the Punjab is predominantly an agricultural state, supplying a large proportion of India's rice and wheat requirements, it also has a number of thriving industries including Hero Bicycles at Ludhiana – India's (and the world's) biggest bicycle manufacturer.

From the traveller's point of view, each state has just one interesting destination – Amritsar in the Punjab and Chandigarh in Haryana. Apart from these, the states are mainly places of transit to and from Pakistan or the Indian Himalaya. Hotels don't add luxury tax in Chandigarh or Amritsar.

History

Prior to Partition the Punjab extended across both sides of what is now the India-Pakistan border, and what was its capital, Lahore, is now the capital of the Pakistani state of Punjab. The grim logic of Partition sliced the population of the Punjab into a Muslim region and a Sikh and Hindu region. As millions of Sikhs and Hindus fled eastward and equal numbers of Muslims fled west, there were innumerable atrocities and killings on both sides.

Punjab's major city is Amritsar, the holy city of the Sikhs, but it is so close to the Pakistani border that it was thought wise to build a safer capital farther within India. At first Shimla, the old imperial summer capital, was chosen, but Chandigarh, a new planned city, was conceived and built in the 1950s to serve as capital of the new state.

More recently, Sikh political demands have racked the state. Militants have demanded the creation of an independent Sikh state, to be called Khalistan (Land of the

Punjab & Haryana at a Glance

PUNJAB
Population: 21.4 million
Area: 50,362 sq km
Capital: Chandigarh
Main Language: Punjabi
Best Time to Go: October to March

HARYANA
Population: 17.8 million
Area: 44,212 sq km
Capital: Chandigarh
Main Language: Hindi
Best Time to Go: October to March

- **Amritsar** – home of the beautiful Golden Temple, Sikhism's most sacred site

- **Chandigarh** – Le Corbusier's planned city; visit the Rock Garden, where the city's discarded junk has been recycled into bizarre human and animal sculptures

Festivals of Punjab & Haryana			
festival	location	date	features
Crafts Mela	Surajkund	Feb	national crafts fair
Baisakhi	Punjab	13 Apr	Punjabi new year

Pure). In 1966, the Punjab underwent another split. This time it was divided along predominantly linguistic lines: the mostly Sikh, Punjabi-speaking state of Punjab and the majority Hindi-speaking state of Haryana.

But this further partition did not have the desired effect of appeasing the Sikh separatists. At the same time some of the northern parts of the Punjab were hived off to Himachal Pradesh. Chandigarh, on the border of Punjab and Haryana, remained the capital of both of the states. The separatist movement gained ground in 1973 when Sikh leaders listed their religious, political and economic demands in the Anandpur Sahib resolution. In 1984, extremists occupied the Golden Temple in Amritsar and were only evicted after a bloody battle with the Indian army.

In 1986 the government announced that Chandigarh would be handed over to Punjab in an attempt to placate the Sikhs. However, with the continued violence in Punjab this didn't take place, although eventually it will. In the meantime, Chandigarh remains the capital of the two states, yet is administered as a Union Territory from Delhi.

The terrorist activities of five extremist groups continued into the early 1990s, putting the Punjab firmly off limits to travellers. Support for these groups has dwindled, things are quiet now, and at the time of writing it was safe to visit.

Haryana

If you're going from Delhi to almost any major attraction in the north of India – Jaipur, Agra, Amritsar – you will need to go through Haryana. Except for Chandigarh, the state has no tourist attractions.

To make up for this, the Haryanans have built a series of 'service centres' along the main roads – motel-restaurant-service station complexes named after birds found in the state – that can make travelling through the area more enjoyable. Typically the complexes may have a camping site, camper huts (usually for around Rs 350) and rooms (in the Rs 450 to Rs 650 range if they have air-con, and cheaper without). Some places also have dormitories. All have restaurants, and some serve fast food. For details on the location, facilities and costs of service centres, pick up a pamphlet from the Haryana Government Tourist Bureau in Delhi (☎ 332 4910) Chanderlok Building, 36 Janpath or from the tourist office in Chandigarh (Sector 17B).

The **Suraj Kund Crafts Mela**, one of Haryana's highlights, takes place in the first two weeks of February. You buy direct from the craftspeople, quality is very high and prices lower than in the state emporiums. Suraj Kund is only 10km from Delhi.

CHANDIGARH
☎ 0172 • pop 750,000
Chandigarh was conceived and born in the 1950s and was the masterplan of the European modernist architect Le Corbusier. No other Indian city feels quite like this one. Indians are very proud of it and it's the cleanest and healthiest city in the country.

Orientation
Chandigarh is on the edge of the Siwalik Hills, the outermost edge of the Himalaya. Divided into 57 sectors, it's separated by broad avenues. Each sector is quartered into four zones, A-D, and each building within them has a unique number. Despite this logical breakdown, orientation can be tricky without a map, as only the broad separating avenues have street names. 'SCO' in business addresses, stands for 'shop-cum-office'. The bus station, modern shopping centre, and many of the restaurants are in Sector 17. As the train station is 8km out of Chandigarh, buses are much more convenient than trains.

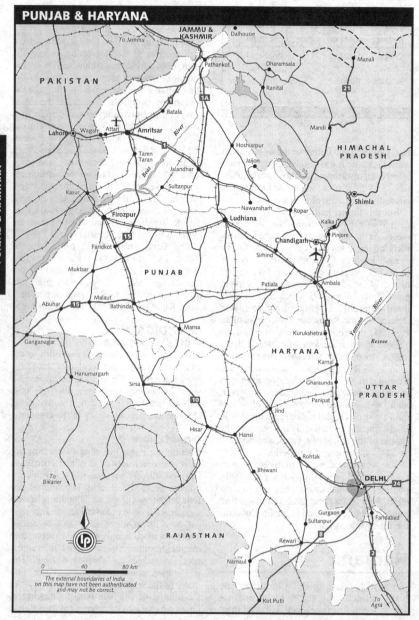

PUNJAB & HARYANA

Chandigarh – a Living City

Chandigarh is unlike any other city in India. On the positive side, it is orderly and regulated. It has a wonderful feeling of space, with modern concrete buildings broken up by broad boulevards and many open, green parks and lawns. It has an air of prosperity, with more private vehicles than one normally finds in India. Footpath dwellers, streetside cobblers and vendors, bedraggled beggars – all are mostly absent. Also – almost unique in India – there are no cows or other livestock roaming the streets. On the negative side, it is *too* spread out; some of the open stretches are rather barren, and it takes a long time to get anywhere, especially by cycle-rickshaw. The town seems to lack the life and colour of other Indian cities.

Most of these differences stem from the fact that it is a planned city. The government of Punjab appointed American town planner Albert Mayer and Polish architect Matthew Nowicki to create their new capital. But in the early days of the project Nowicki died in a plane crash (in 1950), prompting Mayer to withdraw.

The Swiss-born architect Le Corbusier was appointed to take over the project. Le Corbusier was known for his functional, concrete-and-steel buildings and he completely revised Nowicki and Mayer's plans. Le Corbusier wanted Chandigarh to fulfil four basic functions: living, working, circulation and care of body and spirit. He conceived of the city as a unified entity, like a living organism, with the administrative buildings in Sector 1 forming the head, the city centre (Sector 17) the heart, cultural institutions the intellect, and the roads the circulatory system.

Had Nowicki survived to complete his commission Chandigarh would undoubtedly have looked very different. Nowicki commented that the 'dream of some modern planners depends entirely on ... a way of life alien to that of India'. Did Le Corbusier take notice of these sentiments? Judge for yourself.

Information

Tourist Offices The Chandigarh tourist office (☎ 704614), upstairs in the bus station, is open 9 am to 5 pm Monday to Friday and 9 am to 1 pm Saturday. Next door is Himachal Tourism (☎ 708569). One floor up is Punjab Tourism (☎ 711878) and UP Tourism (☎ 707649). Haryana Tourism (☎ 702955) is in Sector 17B, SCO 17-19.

Money The major banks are in Sector 17B; the Bank of Baroda, SCO 62-63, does Visa cash advances and the State Bank of India, SCO 43, has a 24 hour ATM. Private money exchange bureaus are nearby.

Post & Communications The main post office, in Sector 17, is open Monday to Friday 9 am to 4 pm. STD/ISD booths with fax services can be found in sectors 17 and 22.

Email facilities are at Net Explosion (☎ 742470), Sector 9D; surfing costs Rs 30 for 15 minutes.

Government Buildings

The Secretariat and the Vidhan Sabha (Legislative Assembly) buildings are in Sector 1. The top of the Secretariat yields an excellent view over Chandigarh, but the building is less accessible since the chief minister of the Punjab was assassinated here in 1995. Ask the tourist office whether access is possible; likewise if the tours of the industrial-looking Vidhan Sabha have resumed. Nearby is a huge open hand sculpture, conceived as a symbol of unity, and the colourful High Court.

Rock Garden

Also in Sector 1, this strange and whimsical fantasy is Chandigarh's premier tourist attraction. Its a series of interconnected rocky grottoes, walkways and landscaped waterfalls. The most powerful aspect of the gardens is the thousands of animal or humanoid figures made out of discarded materials, which stand in rigid rows like silent, static

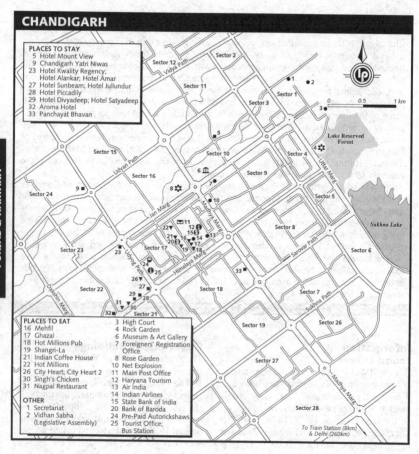

CHANDIGARH

PLACES TO STAY
5 Hotel Mount View
9 Chandigarh Yatri Niwas
23 Hotel Kwality Regency;
   Hotel Alankar; Hotel Amar
27 Hotel Sunbeam; Hotel Jullundur
28 Hotel Piccadily
29 Hotel Divyadeep; Hotel Satyadeep
32 Aroma Hotel
33 Panchayat Bhavan

PLACES TO EAT
16 Mehfil
17 Ghazal
18 Hot Millions Pub
19 Shangri-La
21 Indian Coffee House
22 Hot Millions
26 City Heart; City Heart 2
30 Singh's Chicken
31 Nagpal Restaurant

OTHER
1 Secretariat
2 Vidhan Sabha
   (Legislative Assembly)

3 High Court
4 Rock Garden
6 Museum & Art Gallery
7 Foreigners' Registration
   Office
8 Rose Garden
10 Net Explosion
11 Main Post Office
12 Haryana Tourism
13 Air India
14 Indian Airlines
15 State Bank of India
20 Bank of Baroda
24 Pre-Paid Autorickshaws
25 Tourist Office;
   Bus Station

armies. This fine example of 'outsider' art is
open 9 am to 1 pm and 3 to 7 pm from 1 April
to 30 September. The rest of the year it opens
and closes an hour earlier. Entry is Rs 1 (see
the Rock Garden – the Evolution of a Fantasy
Land boxed text). To the south-east is the artificial **Sukhna Lake**, where you can rent rowboats or stroll around its 2km perimeter.

Museums

Three museums are clustered in Sector 10C.
The **Museum & Art Gallery** contains a modest collection of Indian stone sculptures dating back to the Gandhara period, together
with some miniature paintings and modern
art (entry Rs 1). The adjacent **City Museum**
gives an excellent rundown of the planning,
development and architecture of Chandigarh.
The nearby **Science Museum** covers the evolution of life on earth, and displays fossils and
implements of prehistoric humans found in
India. The city and science museums are both
free. All three museums are open around 10
am to 4.30 or 5 pm, Tuesday to Sunday.

Rose Garden

The rose garden in Sector 16 is claimed to be the biggest in Asia and contains more than a thousand varieties of roses. It's open daily and entry is free.

Places to Stay – Budget

Chandigarh has scant budget accommodation, and hotels are often full. There are some cheap guesthouses but the government is trying to close these as they are located in residential streets. Currently you will be told that these places 'aren't registered to take foreigners'; this is being contested in court so the situation may change soon. There are a couple on the street behind Hotel Jullundur. Except for the railway retiring rooms, there is no accommodation by the train station or the airport.

Panchayat Bhavan (☎ 780701, Sector 18) is one of the least expensive options. However, it's an institutional block with a youth hostel atmosphere. Dorm beds cost Rs 15 or there are large, bare doubles with (hot) bath and TV for Rs 400.

Hotel Divyadeep (☎ 705191, Sector 22B, Himalaya Marg) has simple rooms with fan for Rs 200/250, Rs 300/350 with air-cooling and Rs 400/450 with air-con. They have bath, but hot water is by bucket.

Hotel Satyadeep (☎ 703103) is just along the road and gives an almost identical deal, except air-cooled and air-con rooms are Rs 50 cheaper. Both places have vegetarian restaurants.

Chandigarh Yatri Niwas (☎ 545904, Sector 24B) is rather anonymously hidden behind a block of flats. Clean, fresh rooms with bath cost Rs 600 with air-con or Rs 450 with air-cooling. There is a cheap restaurant here.

Places to Stay – Mid-Range

Hotel Jullundur (☎ 706777, Sector 22B) is opposite the bus station. Standard rooms (for one or two people) with TV, (hot) bath and air-con start at Rs 550.

About 500m north-west of the bus station there are a few hotels side by side on Udyog Path in Sector 22A.

PUNJAB & HARYANA

Rock Garden – the Evolution of a Fantasy Land

The Rock Garden is the creation of Nek Chand, who began the project in 1958 while working as a roads inspector for Chandigarh's engineering department. He would scour the streets and rubbish tips for discarded objects – broken ceramics, electrical wires and sockets, bits of machinery – with which to create his figures. He would take these to his garden which was hidden in what was then forest, far away from the embryonic city. Fearing the ridicule of his colleagues, Chand worked in secret – even his wife initially had no idea what he was up to. He spent around four hours per night on his project, often burning tyres to provide light to work by after dark.

In 1972 disaster loomed when Chand's garden was discovered by workmen clearing space for the expanding city. It had been built illegally on government land and was therefore slated for destruction. But the garden instantly became the talk of the city and prompted the authorities to relent. They did more than that – Chand was given a salary and a workforce in order to continue and extend his garden.

The Rock Garden has now expanded to cover 10 hectares, yet it is still not complete. Already some 5000 sculptures populate the garden, which are viewed by a similar number of daily visitors. In the meantime Chand has been acclaimed internationally as a key exponent of non-mainstream 'outsider' art.

Nek Chand is often to be found in the garden and is generally happy to speak to visitors. He comes across as self-effacing and rather modestly describes his work as 'engineering rather than art'.

Amar (☎ *703608)* charges Rs 500 for doubles (Rs 800 with air-con) with TV and bath; singles for Rs 350 are small and plain.

Alankar (☎ *708801)* has air-cooled singles/doubles with TV for Rs 425/525; air-con doubles are Rs 725.

Kwality Regency (☎ *720204)* is nearly top-end quality. It has 12 stylish 'designer rooms' from Rs 1295/1425.

The *Aroma Hotel* (☎ *700045, fax 700051, Sector 22C)* on Himalaya Marg is similarly swish. Rooms cost from Rs 1145/1395 and there's a restaurant and coffee shop.

Places to Stay – Top End
Hotel Sunbeam (☎ *708100, fax 708900, Udyog Path, Sector 22B)* is opposite the bus station. Pleasant air-con rooms cost from Rs 1095/1495.

Hotel Piccadilly (☎ *707571, fax 705692, Sector 22B)* is nearby on Himalaya Marg. It charges Rs 1190/1890 for singles/doubles and is popular with businesspeople.

Hotel Mount View (☎ *740544, fax 742220, Sector 10)* is set in peaceful gardens. It has air-con rooms for Rs 1950/2450, a restaurant and coffee shop, swimming pool and health club.

Places to Eat
Chandigarh has many places to eat and there's plenty of variety, from western-style fast food to Chinese and Indian regional dishes.

City Heart (Udyog Path), opposite the bus station, serves cheap Indian veg food. Nearby, *City Heart 2* is more expensive, nonveg, and serves beer.

Singh's Chicken (Sector 22, Himalaya Marg) has a good range of chicken dishes for about Rs 25 to Rs 50. Its sign makes the confusing claim that it's the 'Winner of Lonely Planet Book of UK World Tourism Guide'.

Along the road, *Nagpal Restaurant* is popular for Indian veg food dishes for less than Rs 40.

There are lots of places to eat in the Sector 17 shopping district.

Hot Millions (SCO 74-75, Sector 17D) serves fast food. Across the plaza, *Indian*

Coffee House serves very cheap Indian fare; it closes at 9.30 pm.

Shangri-La (SCO 94-95, Sector 17C), in the basement, is a Chinese restaurant serving big, tasty platefuls of veg/nonveg food for Rs 55 to Rs 90.

Mehfil (SCO 185, Sector 17C), and in the same street, *Ghazal (SCO 189-91)* are Chandigarh's top two restaurants. Their menus are the standard mix of continental, Chinese and Indian, with main courses around Rs 90. Mehfil has live music nightly, except Monday, and Ghazal has a bar.

Along the same street, the *Hot Millions Pub* is a good place for beers and Indian/western snacks and mains.

Shopping
Woollen sweaters and shawls from Punjab are good buys, especially in the various government emporiums. Most of these are in Sector 17, which probably has the most extensive range of shops in India.

Getting There & Away
Air Indian Airlines (☎ 704539), SCO 170, Sector 17C, is open 10 am to 5 pm. It has flights on Wednesday and Friday to both Delhi (US$65) and Amritsar (US$55) and one flight on Wednesday to Leh (US$70). Air India (☎ 703510) is at SCO 107, Sector 17B.

Bus Chandigarh has a huge and noisy bus station with good facilities and English timetables. Various private bus offices are in an arcade by the Hotel Piccadilly. To Delhi there are nearly 200 buses every day, departing around the clock. Destinations include:

Amritsar	Rs 90 express	6 hours
Dharamsala	Rs 117 ordinary	10 hours
Delhi	Rs 91/184 ordinary/deluxe	5 hours
Jaipur	Rs 372 deluxe	12 hours
Manali	Rs 155 ordinary	10 hours
Shimla	Rs 59/118 ordinary/deluxe	4 hours

Train The train station is inconveniently situated 8km south-east of the centre; however, reservations can be made at the office (☎ 708573) upstairs in the bus station. It's open 8 am to 8 pm.

It is 245km from Delhi to Chandigarh and the twice-daily *Shatabdi Express* does the journey in just three hours. The fare is Rs 400 in an air-con chair car, and Rs 790 in executive class.

There are four daily trains to Kalka (Rs 5), just 25km up the line, and from there it takes almost six hours to reach Shimla on the narrow-gauge mountain railway.

Getting Around
To/From the Airport The airport is 11km south of Sector 17. Fares are Rs 250 by taxi or Rs 57 by auto-rickshaw.

Local Transport Chandigarh is far too spread out to walk around. The extensive bus network is the cheapest option. Bus No 13 runs by the Aroma Hotel as far as the government buildings in Sector 1, and bus No 37 runs to the train station from the bus station.

If you're planning a longer trip across the city consider taking a blue auto-rickshaw. There is a prepaid auto-rickshaw stand behind the bus station – ask at the blue hut for the set fares. Rickshaw-wallahs may offer lower rates when business is slack. From the bus station it should cost Rs 34 to the train station or Rs 19 to the Rock Garden.

Bicycle is the best form of transport, but hire shops are hard to find; ask at your hotel.

AROUND CHANDIGARH
Pinjore
The **Yadavindra Gardens** at Pinjore were designed by Fidai Khan, Mughal ruler Aurangzeb's foster brother, who also designed the Badshahi Mosque in Lahore, Pakistan. Situated 20km from Chandigarh, near Kalka, the gardens include the Rajasthani Mughal-style **Shish Mahal** palace. Below it is the Rang Mahal and the cubical Jal Mahal. There is an otter house, and other animals can be seen in the mini-zoo near the gardens.

There are hourly buses from Chandigarh, which stop at the entrance to the gardens.

CHANDIGARH TO DELHI
There are many places of minor interest along the 260km route from Chandigarh to Delhi. The road, part of the Grand Trunk Road, is one of the busiest in India.

Karnal & Kurukshetra
Karnal is mentioned in the *Mahabharata*, and it was here that Nadir Shah, the Persian who took the Peacock Throne from Delhi, defeated the Mughal emperor Mohammed Shah, in 1739. The **Kurukshetra tank** has attracted as many as a million pilgrims during eclipses, when the water is believed to be especially purifying.

Gharaunda
The gateways of an old Mughal *serai* (resthouse) stand to the west of this village, 102km north of Delhi. Shah Jahan built *kos minars* (milestones) along the road from Delhi to Lahore and serais at longer intervals. Most of the kos minars still stand but there is little left of the various serais.

Panipat
Panipat, 92km north of Delhi, is reputed to be one of the most fly-infested places in India – due, it is said, to a Muslim saint buried here. He is supposed to have totally rid Panipat of flies, but when the people complained that he had done too good a job he gave them all the flies back, multiplied by a thousand.

Sultanpur
There are many birds, including flamingos, at Sultanpur's bird sanctuary, 46km southwest of Delhi. September to March is the best time to visit, and you can stay at Haryana Tourism's *Rosy Pelican* complex. To get there take a blue Haryana bus from Delhi to Gurgaon, and then take a Chandu bus to Sultanpur.

DELHI TO SIRSA
This route takes you north-west through Haryana towards the Punjab and Pakistan, south of the Delhi to Amritsar route. From Delhi the railway line runs 70km north-west through **Rohtak**, which was once a border town between the Sikhs' and Marathas' regions, and was the subject of frequent clashes.

PUNJAB & HARYANA

Hansi, north-west of Rohtak, was where Colonel Skinner died. (Skinner's Horse, the private cavalry regiment he founded in the 1790s, was responsible for the conquest of large areas of northern India for the East India Company.) Sirsa, 90km further north-west, is an ancient city but little remains apart from the city walls.

Punjab

AMRITSAR
☎ 0183 • pop 1 million

Founded in 1577 by Ram Das, the fourth guru of the Sikhs, Amritsar is both the centre of the Sikh religion and the major city of Punjab state. The name means Pool of Nectar, referring to the sacred tank around which the Sikhs' Golden Temple is built. Although Amritsar is just another dusty Indian city, the Golden Temple is an exceptionally beautiful and peaceful place.

The original site for the city was granted by the Mughal emperor, Akbar, but in 1761 Ahmad Shah Durani sacked the town and destroyed the temple. The temple was rebuilt in 1764, and in 1802 was roofed over with copper-gilded plates by Ranjit Singh and became known as the Golden Temple. During the turmoil of the partition of India in 1948, Amritsar was a flash point for the terrible events that shook the Punjab.

During unrest in the Punjab in the early 1980s the Golden Temple was occupied by Sikh extremists who were intent on expelling non-Sikhs from the state and creating a Sikh homeland. They were finally evicted, under the orders of Indira Gandhi, by the Indian army in 1984 in a military action that resulted in hundreds of Sikh deaths. Later that year Indira Gandhi was assassinated by her Sikh bodyguards. The temple was again occupied by extremists in 1986. The damage wrought on the Golden Temple by the tanks of the Indian army has now been repaired, and things are quiet again.

Sikhs are justifiably proud of their capital city and Golden Temple and they are known for their friendliness and helpfulness.

Orientation
The old city is south-east of the main train station and is surrounded by a circular road that used to contain the massive city walls. There are 18 gates still in existence but only the north gate, facing the Ram Bagh gardens, is original. The Golden Temple and the narrow alleys of the bazaar area are in the old city.

The more modern part of Amritsar is north of the train station, where you will find most of the hotels. The bus station is 2km east of the train station on the road to Delhi.

Information
Tourist Offices The tourist office (☎ 231452) is in the former youth hostel, 1km east of the bus station, and is fairly helpful. It's open Monday to Saturday 9 am to 5 pm. The information office at the Golden Temple is open daily 8 am to 1 pm and 2.30 to 8 pm, and staff are very helpful.

Money There are numerous moneychangers in Link Rd, opposite the train station; rates are marginally worse than at banks. There is a Bank of Punjab branch office at the Golden Temple that changes US dollars only. The State Bank of India in the old city changes dollars and sterling.

Post & Communications A post office at the Golden Temple sells stamps (open Monday to Saturday 9 am to 6.30 pm). The main post office is on Court Rd north-west of the train station (Monday to Saturday 9 am to 5 pm).

Golden Temple
The holiest shrine of the Sikh religion, also known as the Hari Mandir, is in the centre of the old part of Amritsar. The temple itself is surrounded by the pool Amrit Sarovar, which gave the town its name, and is reached by a causeway. Open to all, it's a beautiful place, especially early in the morning, though the weekends can get quite crowded.

Pilgrims and visitors to the Golden Temple must remove their shoes and cover their heads before entering the precincts. No

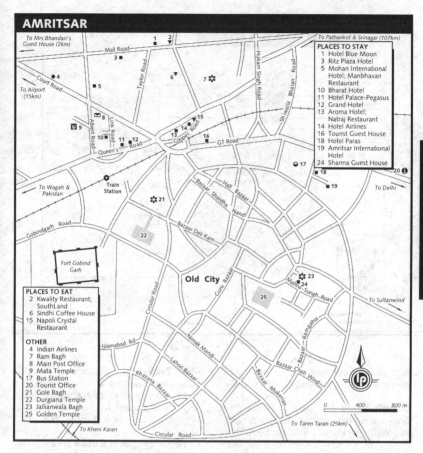

AMRITSAR

To Mrs Bhandari's Guest House (2km)

To Pathankot & Srinagar (107km)

Mall Road

Taylor Road

Hukam Singh Road

Shiwalla Bhaian Road

Court Road

To Airport (15km)

Albert Road

Link Road

Cooper Road

Queen's

Road

GT Road

To Wagah & Pakistan

Train Station

Bazaar Shardha

Hall Bazaar

Nandi

Gobindgarh Road

Bazaar Deli Kam

Fort Gobind Garh

Circular Road

Guru Bazaar

Old City

Mahna Singh Road

To Sultanwind

To Delhi

Islamabad Rd

Nimak Mandi

Ramgahia Bazaar

Lahori Bazaar

Bazaar Chati Wind

Khazana Bazaar

Bazaar Mukerian

To Kheri Karan

Circular Road

To Taren Taran (25km)

0   400   800 m

PLACES TO STAY
1 Hotel Blue Moon
3 Ritz Plaza Hotel
5 Mohan International Hotel; Manbhavan Restaurant
10 Bharat Hotel
11 Hotel Palace-Pegasus
12 Grand Hotel
13 Aroma Hotel; Natraj Restaurant
14 Hotel Airlines
16 Tourist Guest House
18 Hotel Paras
19 Amritsar International Hotel
24 Sharma Guest House

PLACES TO EAT
2 Kwality Restaurant; SouthLand
6 Sindhi Coffee House
15 Napoli Crystal Restaurant

OTHER
4 Indian Airlines
7 Ram Bagh
8 Main Post Office
9 Mata Temple
17 Bus Station
20 Tourist Office
21 Gole Bagh
22 Durgiana Temple
23 Jallianwala Bagh
25 Golden Temple

PUNJAB & HARYANA

smoking is allowed; photography is permitted from the Parkarma, the marble walkway that surrounds the sacred pool. An English-speaking guide is available at the information office near the clock tower that marks the temple's main entrance. The information office has a number of interesting free publications.

Hari Mandir Standing in the middle of the sacred pool, the Golden Temple is a two storey marble structure reached by a cause-

way known as the Gurus' bridge. The lower parts of the marble walls are decorated with inlaid flower and animal motifs in the *pietra dura* style of the Taj Mahal. Once inside the temple, pilgrims offer sweet doughy *prasaad* to the attendants, who take half to distribute to everyone as they leave the temple.

The architecture of the Golden Temple is a blend of Hindu and Muslim styles. The golden dome (said to be gilded with 100kg of pure gold) is supposed to represent an inverted lotus flower. It is inverted, turning

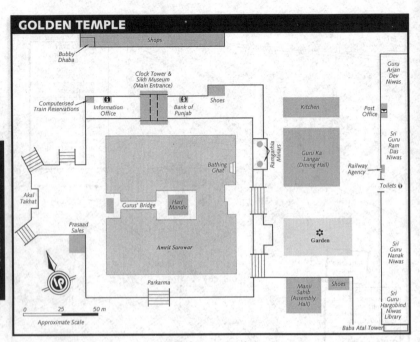

GOLDEN TEMPLE

Shops

Bubby
Dhaba

Clock Tower &
Sikh Museum
(Main Entrance)

Guru
Arjan
Dev
Niwas

Computerised
Train Reservations

Information
Office

Shoes

Bank of
Punjab

Kitchen

Post
Office

Sri
Guru
Ram
Das
Niwas

Ramgarhia
Minars

Guru Ka
Langar
(Dining Hall)

Railway
Agency

Toilets

Bathing
Ghat

Akal
Takhat

Gurus' Bridge

Hari
Mandir

Prasaad
Sales

Garden

Sri
Guru
Nanak
Niwas

Amrit Sarowar

Parkarma

Manji
Sahib
(Assembly
Hall)

Shoes

Sri
Guru
Hargobind
Niwas
Library

0   25   50 m
Approximate Scale

Baba Atal Tower

PUNJAB & HARYANA

back to the earth, to symbolise the Sikhs'
concern with the problems of this world.

Granth Sahib Four priests at key positions around the temple keep up a continuous reading in Punjabi from the Sikhs' holy
book. The reading is broadcast by loud-
speaker. The original copy of the Granth
Sahib is kept under a pink shroud in the
Golden Temple during the day and at
around 10 pm each day is ceremoniously returned to the Akal Takhat (Sikh Parliament)
building. The morning processional ceremony takes place at 4 am in summer, 5 am
in winter.

Sikh Museum The Central Sikh Museum
is upstairs in the clock tower and comprises
a gallery of often gruesome paintings telling
the story of the Sikhs and their martyrs. It's
open 7 am to 7 pm daily.

Akal Takhat The Shiromani Gurdwara
Parbandhak Committee, or Sikh Parliament,
traditionally meets in this building, which is
why it was a target for the Indian army in
1984. It has since been completely rebuilt.

Guru Ka Langar & Gurdwaras All Sikh
temples have a community kitchen, and in
this one volunteers prepare free meals for
around 30,000 people every day. The food
is very basic – chapatis and lentils – and is
prepared and dished out daily in an orderly
fashion. Nearby are the gurdwaras, offering
free accommodation to all. Pilgrims are
well provided for and there's a good library,
a post office, bank and railway booking
agent.

Other Buildings To the south-east of the
temple enclosure is the nine storey (30m)
Baba Atal Tower, which was built in 1784.

The tall **Ramgarhia Minars**, scarred by tank fire, stand outside the temple enclosure.

The Old City

A 15 minute walk from the Golden Temple through the narrow alleys of the old city brings you to the Hindu **Durgiana Temple**. This small temple, dedicated to the goddess Durga, dates back to the 16th century. A larger temple, built like the Golden Temple in the centre of a lake, is dedicated to the Hindu deities, Lakshmi and Narayan (Vishnu).

There are a number of mosques in the old city, including the mosque of **Mohammed Jan**, with three white domes and slender minarets.

Mata Temple

North-west of the train station, this Hindu temple commemorates a bespectacled 20th century female saint, Lal Devi. Women wishing to have children pray here. It's notable for a Disneyesque series of grottoes and shrines featuring Hindu deities (take the stairs on the left).

Jallianwala Bagh

This park commemorates the 2000 Indians who were killed or wounded here, shot indiscriminately by the British in 1919. This appalling massacre was one of the major events in India's struggle for independence and was movingly re-created in the film *Gandhi*.

The park is a five minute walk from the Golden Temple and is open 6 am to 7 pm in summer and 7 am to 6 pm in winter. A section of wall with visible bullet marks is preserved, as is the well that some people jumped into to escape; 120 bodies were recovered from the well. Portraits and potted histories of some of those involved appear in the **Martyrs' Gallery**, open 9 am to 5 pm in summer, 10 am to 4 pm in winter.

Ram Bagh

This park in the new part of town has a **museum** in the small palace built by the Sikh maharaja Ranjit Singh. The museum contains weapons dating back to Mughal times and some portraits of the ruling houses of

PUNJAB & HARYANA

Carnage at Jallianwala Bagh

Unrest in Amritsar was sparked by the *Rowlatt Act* (1919), which gave the British authorities emergency powers to imprison without trial Indians suspected of sedition. *Hartals* (one-day strikes) were organised in protest. The Lieutenant Governor of Punjab, Sir Michael O'Dwyer ('a reactionary with contempt for educated Indians', according to text in the Martyrs' Gallery) adopted a hard line, and an Indian leader was arrested. Further Indian protests followed, which escalated into rioting and looting after the British fired upon the protesters.

General Dyer was called upon to return order to the city. He and 150 troops arrived at a peaceful demonstration on 13 April 1919 in Jallianwala Bagh, attended by 20,000 Indians. Dyer ordered the crowd to disperse – tricky seeing that the meeting space was surrounded by high walls, and he and his men were ranged in front of the main entrance. Without further warning the British opened fire. Some six minutes later the toll of Indian deaths numbered 337 men, 41 boys and one baby. A further 1500 men and boys lay wounded. Some were shot as they tried to escape over the wall.

Although there was an international outcry over this massacre, O'Dwyer and Dyer were not considered culpable by the British; on the contrary, some thought them heroes. Meantime, in response, Gandhi instigated his program of civil disobedience and announced that 'co-operation in any shape or form with this satanic government is sinful'.

Dyer died in 1927 from a fall. O'Dwyer met his end in 1940, assassinated by a Sikh volunteer who had been serving water at the 1919 meeting.

the Punjab (entry Rs 5). It's open 10 am to 4.45 pm, Tuesday to Sunday.

Taren Taran

This is an important Sikh tank about 25km south of Amritsar. There's a temple, which predates Amritsar, and a tower on the eastern side of the tank, which was constructed by Ranjit Singh. It's said that any leper who can swim across the tank will be miraculously cured. Buses run hourly from Amritsar bus station.

Places to Stay – Budget

Rooms below have bath with hot water, unless indicated.

Hotel Palace-Pegasus (☎ *227111*) is conveniently opposite the train station. Variable singles/doubles cost from Rs 150/200, and Rs 400/600 with air-con. Prices may increase when the bathrooms are remodelled.

Bharat Hotel (☎ *227536*), just off Link Rd, is better value. This secure place has reasonable rooms for Rs 125/200 with TV.

Aroma Hotel (☎ *564079, Queen's Rd)* has big rooms with TV for Rs 150/250.

Hotel Paras (☎ *540208*) is the best value of the hotels opposite the bus station; rooms are only Rs 90.

Tourist Guest House (☎ *553830, GT Rd)*, east of the train station, has simple but good value singles/doubles for Rs 100/150 with common bath and Rs 200/250 with (hot) bath and TV. Beware of touts directing you to inferior similarly named substitutes.

Sharma Guest House (☎ *551757, Mahna Singh Rd)*, near the Golden Temple, is a small place with decent rooms with TV for Rs 300; those for Rs 200 aren't as good and may have common bath.

Hospitality to pilgrims is part of the Sikh faith, and the most interesting place to stay in Amritsar is at the Golden Temple itself. If you do stay here it is imperative that you respect the fact that this is a holy place – smoking, alcohol, drugs and any public display of familiarity between the sexes is grossly insulting to the Sikhs.

The gurdwaras *Sri Guru Ram Das Niwas* and *Sri Guru Nanak Niwas* are staffed by volunteers. Accommodation is free but you must pay a returnable deposit of Rs 50; you can stay for up to three days. There's a large dorm, bedding is provided and the toilets and shower block are in the centre of the courtyard. There's no pressure from any of the staff but a donation is expected – and you shouldn't forget to make one. Doubles with bath are sometimes available in the *Sri Guru Nanak Niwas*.

Nearby within the complex is the *Sri Guru Hargobind Niwas* (☎ *553997*), charging Rs 50 for rooms, and the newly built *Guru Arjan Dev Niwas*, which will have 100 beds.

Places to Stay – Mid-Range

Amritsar International Hotel (☎ *555991*), Punjab Tourism's centrally air-conditioned hotel, is a modern building near the bus station. Singles/doubles cost from Rs 475/550. It's the only place in this category that *doesn't* add a 10% service charge.

Hotel Airlines (☎ *564848, Cooper Rd)*, near the train station, has decent rooms from Rs 350/450 to Rs 600/850 with air-con. All have TV and there's a sun terrace and restaurant. Checkout is 24 hours.

Grand Hotel (☎ *562424, Queen's Rd)*, opposite the train station, has similar rooms for Rs 395/500, or Rs 600/700 with air-con. Rooms are built around a pleasant garden.

Hotel Blue Moon (☎ *220416, Mall Rd)* is cheaper (from Rs 330/400) but not quite as good.

Mrs Bhandari's Guest House (☎/fax *222390, 10 The Cantonment)* is a delightful place to stay, albeit pricey, and is set in a large peaceful garden with a swimming pool. Clean rooms are stuck in a now very fashionable 1950s time warp; they vary in size and cost Rs 600/700, or Rs 750/850 with air-con. Meals can be pre-ordered: breakfast is Rs 120, lunch and dinner cost Rs 200/250 veg/nonveg. People camping (with their own equipment) pay Rs 120 per person and Rs 50 to use the pool (open April to October).

Places to Stay – Top End

Ritz Plaza Hotel (☎ *566027, 45 Mall Rd, email ritz@del3vsnl.net.in)* has a gym and swimming pool, and good if overpriced air-con rooms from Rs 950/1250.

Mohan International Hotel (☎ 227801, fax 226520, Albert Rd) is Amritsar's top hotel, with rooms from Rs 1350/2400 with bathtubs. It has air-con, a swimming pool (Rs 75 for nonguests) and a good restaurant.

Places to Eat

It's interesting to join the pilgrims for a basic meal at the *Guru Ka Langar* at the Golden Temple; there's no charge but you should make a donation.

Opposite the Golden Temple information office are several cheap *dhabas* (snack bars). *Bubby Dhaba*, at the end of the group, does good *chana bhatura* (spiced chickpeas with fried Indian bread) for Rs 10.

Kwality Restaurant is near the Ram Bagh on Mall Rd. It has mid-price veg and nonveg dishes. Alongside is *South Land*, serving veg South Indian food for around Rs 20. *Sindhi Coffee House*, opposite Ram Bagh, is similar to Kwality, but slightly cheaper.

Queen's Rd has many options, starting with cheap *dhabas* opposite the train station.

Heading east, *Natraj*, in the Aroma Hotel, is inexpensive, and OK if you fancy a beer while you eat.

Further east are two restaurants with a good local reputation: *Napoli* and *Crystal*. Both serve a wide range of veg and nonveg dishes from Rs 60 to Rs 120.

At a similar price, but with a smarter ambience, alcohol, and live music in the evening, is the *Manbhavan Restaurant* in the Mohan International Hotel.

Shopping

Woollen blankets, shawls and sweaters are supposed to be cheaper in Amritsar than in other places in India, as they are locally manufactured. Katra Jaimal Singh, near the telephone exchange in the old city, is a good shopping area.

Getting There & Away

Air The Indian Airlines office (☎ 503780) is at 39A Court Rd. Amritsar is linked to Delhi (US$90) four times weekly.

Bus The bus journey to Delhi (Rs 160, 10 hours) is less comfortable than going by train. There's only one bus daily to Dehra Dun at 7 am (Rs 156, 10 hours), Dalhousie at 9.20 am (Rs 90) and Dharamsala at 11 am (Rs 156, 10 hours); you might find it easier to take a frequent bus to Pathankot (Rs 40, three hours) and take another bus from there. Regular buses also go to Chandigarh (Rs 90/180 ordinary/deluxe, six hours). For bus inquiries, call ☎ 551734.

There are private buses to Jammu (Rs 120) and Chandigarh (Rs 180) but these do not go from the bus station. Tickets must be bought in advance from the agencies near the train station.

Getting to Rajasthan is usually easier via Delhi, though direct buses go to Ganganagar (10 hours), about halfway to Bikaner.

Train There are direct rail links to Delhi (Rs 99/490 in 2nd/1st class, 447km) in eight to 10 hours, but the daily *Shatabdi Express* does the journey in only 5½ hours. Tickets are Rs 560/1110 in chair car/executive class. The *Amritsar-Howrah Mail* links Amritsar with Lucknow (850km, 17 hours), Varanasi (1251km, 23 hours) and Calcutta (1829km, 38 hours).

To/From Pakistan The rail crossing point is at Attari, 26km from Amritsar, and the 4607 *Indo-Pak Express* leaves Amritsar at 9.30 am, reaching Lahore in Pakistan at 1.35 pm. However, it only goes on Monday and Thursday and can be delayed for hours at the border.

The road crossing at Wagah, about 4km beyond Attari, is quicker. The border is open daily 9 am to 3.30 pm (winter) or 4 pm (summer), and most people walk across as vehicles are delayed. There are hourly buses till about 3 pm from Amritsar to Attari (Rs 13, one hour), but not all continue on to Wagah. It's easy to get a rickshaw between Attari and Wagah. Taxis from Amritsar cost Rs 300 to Rs 400, or look for minibuses by the train station (Rs 60).

Neem Chameli Tourist Complex (☎ 231452), operated by Punjab Tourism, at

Wagah, has dorm beds and cheap doubles, and there are cafes where you can eat or change money.

See the Getting There & Away chapter for further details on this border crossing.

Getting Around

The airport is 11km from the city centre. An auto-rickshaw should cost around Rs 80, a taxi Rs 170.

Auto-rickshaws charge Rs 25 from the train station to the Golden Temple. The same trip on a cycle-rickshaw will cost Rs 15.

PATHANKOT

☎ 0186 • pop 147,000

The town of Pathankot, in the extreme north of the Punjab, is important to travellers mainly as a railhead for trains to/from Delhi and as a bus station for departures up to Dalhousie and Dharamsala. It is a chaotic and uninspiring city, and you probably won't

Border Displays

Relations between India and Pakistan are rarely tranquil – each country seems determined to outdo the other at every opportunity, whether on the cricket pitch or, more worryingly, in the field of nuclear armaments. A harmless but entertaining manifestation of this long-standing rivalry can be witnessed every evening at the Wagah border, the only road crossing between the two countries.

About 30 minutes before sunset, the guards on each side assemble to parade and preen themselves in an immaculately turned out display of synchronised marching and bellowed military commands. The flag of each country is then lowered and the gates are slammed shut. Crowds congregate on each side of the border, with the Indians and Pakistanis cheering on the efforts of their own guards and deriding those of the opposition. Some make a special journey from Amritsar simply to witness the spectacle.

want to stay here for a moment longer than necessary.

Places to Stay & Eat

There are a number of fairly unsavoury lodgings to the right as you exit the main Pathankot train station. The *Green Hotel* has clean but noisy rooms for Rs 250 and the nearby *Hotel Darshan* (☎ 20660) has grim rooms with (cold) bath for Rs 100.

Further down the road is the much better *Hotel Tourist*, with a good variety of rooms set around a pleasant courtyard. Singles cost Rs 80, or Rs 130 with air-cooler and geyser. Air-cooled doubles range from Rs 175 to Rs 250, or Rs 350 with air-con.

Another good choice is the *Hotel Parag* (☎ 29867), a 300m walk to the right as you leave the bus station, or a five to 10 minute walk left out of the main train station. Comfortable air-cooled rooms with (hot) bath cost Rs 250.

All the hotels have decent restaurants, though the *Vatika Restaurant* at the Hotel Parag is the best.

Getting There & Away

The bus stand and the main train station are only about 400m apart. Chowkibank train station is 3km from Pathankot main station.

Overnight trains to Delhi are a popular option as they save time and a night's accommodation. Fares vary according to the train but are roughly Rs 150 for 2nd class sleeper, Rs 420 for air-con three tier sleeper and Rs 734 for air-con two tier sleeper. There are also several trains a day to Jammu (three hours).

There are buses to Dalhousie (Rs 39, 3½ hours) and Chamba (Rs 57, five hours) every 90 minutes or so from 6.40 am to 5 pm. There are also numerous buses to Dharamsala (Rs 39, 3½ hours) and a few morning buses continue to McLeod Ganj (Rs 47).

From Chowkibank to Pathankot main train and bus stations by cycle-rickshaw will cost Rs 25. There is a 24 hour taxi stand at Pathankot main station; to McLeod Ganj the fare is Rs 800 and to Dalhousie, Rs 820.

Major Trains from Pathankot

station	train no & name	departure time	duration	destination
Main station	1078 *Jhelum Exp*	12.25 am	10 h 30 min	New Delhi
	4034 *Pathankot Jammu Mail*	6.40 pm	12 h	New Delhi
	4646 *Shalimar Exp*	11.25 pm	12 h	Old Delhi
	4805 *Jammu-Jodhpur Exp*	11.00 am	19 h	Jodhpur
	3152 *Jammu-Sealdah Exp*	9.30 pm	13 h 30 min	Moradabad[1]
Chowkibank	2404 *Jammu-Delhi Exp*	8.40 pm	12 h	Old Delhi
	9368 *Malwa Exp*	10.40 am	8 h	New Delhi
	2472 *Swaraj Exp*	1.30 pm	8 h	New Delhi

[1] alight here for Corbett and Nainital

AMRITSAR TO DELHI

There are a few places of minor interest on the road and rail route from Amritsar to Delhi.

Only 80km south-east of Amritsar, **Jalandhar** was once the capital of an ancient Hindu kingdom. It survived a sacking by Mahmud of Ghazni nearly a thousand years ago and later became an important Mughal city. The town has a large serai built in 1857. There are places to stay a few minutes walk east of the bus stand.

Another 60km south-east is the textile centre of India, **Ludhiana**. It was the site of a great battle in the First Sikh War. The world's largest bicycle manufacturer, Hero Bicycles, which produces nearly three million bikes annually, is based here. There's little to see in Ludhiana, though a traveller reported that the archaic, bureaucratic muddle of the offices of the old law courts (the Purana Karcharia) is worth checking out.

Sirhind, 72km south-east of Ludhiana, was once a very important town and the capital of the Pathan Sur dynasty. In 1555, Humayun defeated Sikander Shah here and a year later his son, Akbar, completed the destruction of the Sur dynasty at Panipat. From then until 1709 Sirhind was a rich Mughal city, but clashes between the declining Mughal and rising Sikh powers led to the city's sacking in 1709 and complete destruction in 1763. The Pathan-style **tomb of Mir Miran** and the later Mughal **tomb of Pirbandi Nakshwala**, both ornamented with blue tiles, are worth seeing. The **Salabat Beg Haveli** is probably the largest private home remaining from the Mughal period. Southeast of the city is an important Mughal serai.

About 35km south of Sirhind is **Patiala**, which was once the capital of an independent Sikh state. There is a museum at the Motibagh Palace in the Baradari Gardens.

Punjab Tourism has *Tourist Complexes* in Jalandhar (☎ 0181-222250), Ludhiana (☎ 0161-741500, GT Rd) and Sirhind (☎ 01763-22170, GT Rd).

SOUTH-WEST PUNJAB

The railway line from Sirsa (Haryana) to Firozpur passes through **Bathinda**, which was an important town of the Pathan Sur dynasty.

Faridkot, 350km north-west of Delhi and close to the Pakistan border, was once the capital of a Sikh state of the same name and has a 700-year-old fort.

Firozpur, almost on the border, is 382km north-west of Delhi; before Partition, the railway line continued to Lahore, now in Pakistan.

Himachal Pradesh

Himachal Pradesh – the land of eternal snow peaks – takes in the transition zone from the plains to the high Himalaya and, in the trans-Himalayan region of Lahaul and Spiti, actually crosses that mighty barrier to the Tibetan plateau.

The Kullu Valley, with its developed and tourist-oriented economy, can be considered the backbone of the state. Off to the east is the Parbati Valley, popular with long-stay visitors. In the Chamba and Kangra regions can be found typical British hill stations and small but beautiful temple complexes. The residence of the Dalai Lama is in Upper Dharamsala, known as McLeod Ganj, which has become a centre for Buddhism, as well as the headquarters of the Tibetan Government in Exile. Shimla, the famous colonial hot-weather capital, remains Himachal's seat of government.

The bleak, high altitude regions of Lahaul, Spiti and Kinnaur were opened to foreigners in 1992 and bear a striking resemblance to Ladakh. Permits (easily obtained) are necessary to visit some parts. The predominant influence here is Tibetan Buddhism and there are some spectacular *gompas* (monasteries) here.

See Lonely Planet's *Trekking in the Indian Himalaya* and *Indian Himalaya* for details on trekking in this region.

History

The regions that today comprise Himachal were, in ancient times, crossed by trade routes to Tibet (over the Shipki La) and Central Asia (via the Baralacha La and Leh) and also commanded the Sach Pass that led to Kashmir. Rajas, Ranas and Thakurs ran their rival *rahuns* and *thakurais*, making Himachal a patchwork quilt of tiny states. Only Kangra and Kullu (and later Chamba) had the power to break out of the petty feuding system.

Several Himachal states had kings from Bengal, the best known of these is Mandi,

Himachal Pradesh at a Glance

Population: 6.13 million
Area: 55,673 sq km
Capital: Shimla
Main Languages: Hindi & Parhari
Best Time to Go: mid-May to mid-October (trekking); late December to March (winter sports)

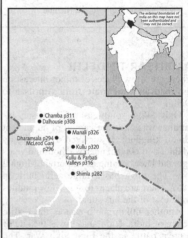

- **Shimla** – take a trip on the toy train to experience the decrepit grandeur of the Raj in this pleasant hill station

- **McLeod Ganj** – home of the Dalai Lama, this is the place to head for Tibetan culture (and chocolate cake)

- **Kullu Valley** – scenically pretty valley and an adventure playground

- **Chamba** – a beautiful town with ancient Hindu temples hidden in winding backstreets

- **Kinnaur** – grand mountain scenery and stunning views of Kinnaur Kailash from Kalpa

Festivals of Himachal Pradesh

festival	location	date	features
Losar (Tibetan New Year)	McLeod Ganj, Rewalsar Lake	Feb/Mar	teachings by Dalai Lama & Buddhist pilgrimages
Shivaratri	Mandi, Baijnath	Feb/Mar	Hindu processions & festivities
Holi	Paonta Sahib	Mar	Hindu pilgrimage & festivities
Baisakhi	Paonta Sahib	Mar	Hindu pilgrimage & festivities
Dussehra	Kullu	Mar/Apr	Hindu procession & dancing
Sui Mata	Chamba	Mar/Apr	Hindu procession, singing & dancing
Opera Festival	McLeod Ganj	Apr	music, folk dancing & theatre
Dhungri Festival	Dhungri Temple, Manali	May	Hindu sacrifices
Mashobra Fair	Mashobra	May	fair
TIPA Anniversary	McLeod Ganj; Baijnath	27 May	three day anniversary celebration
Chaam	Ki Gompa	Jun/Jul	Buddhist festival
Dalai Lama's birthday	McLeod Ganj	6 Jul	Buddhist celebrations
Ladarcha	near Kibber	Jul	Buddhist pilgrimage
Minjar	Chamba	Jul/Aug	colourful procession, Adavasi gatherings
Manimahesh Yatra	Brahmaur	Jul/Aug	Hindu fair & pilgrimage
Renuka	Renuka Lake	Nov	Hindu procession, bathing & dancing
Lavi Fair	Rampur	Nov	horse and local produce trading

which was founded in 1527. With the exception of the bigger states, most of the later hill states were founded by Rajput adventurers from the plains in the early medieval period.

The first westerners to visit the region were Jesuit missionaries in search of the legendary kingdom of Prester John. The British discovered Himachal after their wars with the Sikhs and the Gurkhas. And upon the subsequent discovery that Himachal was ideal for growing apples, an American missionary, the Reverend NS Stokes, developed the Kotgarh orchards (his family still runs them). Little bits of England were created at Shimla, Dalhousie and Dharamsala during the late 19th century. In the early part of the 20th century a railway was built to Shimla and another was laid through the Kangra Valley. In the interior, however, feudal conditions remained: men were forced to work without pay and women were regarded as *chattels*.

The state of Himachal Pradesh was formed in 1948. By 1966, the Pahari-speaking parts under Punjab administration, including Kangra, Kullu, Lahaul and Spiti, were added. Full statehood was achieved in 1971.

Geography

Himachal Pradesh is dominated by mountains and their associated rivers and valleys. The mountains include Leo Pargial (6791m), near Nako in Kinnaur; Deo Tibba (6001m), not far from Manali; and Kinnaur Kailash (6050m), which dominates the views from Rekong Peo and Kalpa in Kinnaur.

The passes, such as the Rohtang La (3978m), Baralacha La (4950m) and Kunzum La (4551m), are pivotal points between culturally distinct regions. ('La' is a Tibetan word meaning pass.) In winter, Lahaul and Spiti are completely isolated when these and other passes are blocked by snow.

Himachal Pradesh can be easily segregated by its valleys. Lahaul consists of the

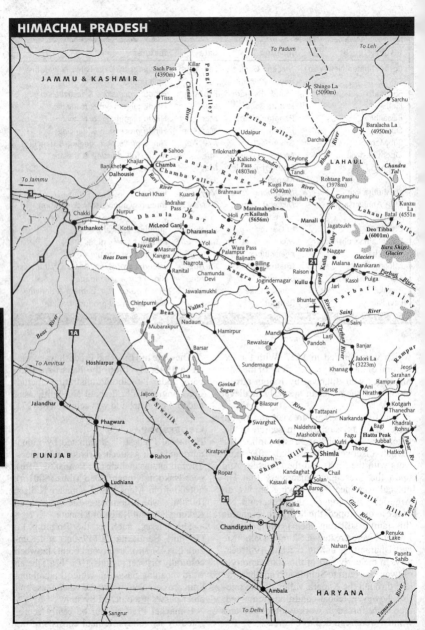

HIMACHAL PRADESH

To Padum
To Leh

JAMMU & KASHMIR

Sach Pass (4390m)
Killar
Pangi Valley
Shingo La (5090m)
Sarchu

Tissa
Chenab River
Pattan Valley
Baralacha La (4950m)

Udaipur
Darcha
Bhaga River
Chandra Tal

To Jammu
Pir Panjal Range
Sahoo
Trilokhath
Kalicho Pass (4803m)
Chandra
Keylong
LAHAUL

Banikhet
Khajiar
Chamba
Chamba Valley
Kugti Pass (5040m)
Tandi
Rohtang Pass (3978m)

Dalhousie
Ravi River
Kuarsi
Brahmaur
Solang Nullah
Gramphu
Kunzum La (4551m)

Chakki
Chauri Khas
Indrahar Pass
Holi
Manimahesh-Kailash (5656m)
Manali
Jagtsukh
Deo Tibba (6001m)
Batal
Lahaul Valley

Pathankot
Nurpur
Dhaula Dhar Range
McLeod Ganj
Dharamsala
Bara Shigri Glacier

Kotla
Gaggal
Yol
Waru Pass
Katrain
Naggar
Glaciers
Manikaran
Parbati River

Beas Dam
Jawali
Masrur
Kangra
Palampur
Baijnath
Billing
Bir
Raison
Malana
Pulga

Nagrota
Ranital
Chamunda Devi
Jogindernagar
Kullu
Jari
Kasol
Parbati Valley

Jawalamukhi
Beas
Valley
Bhuntar
Aut
Sainj
River

Chintpurni
Mubarakpur
Nadaun
Hamirpur
Mandi
Sainj

To Amritsar
Beas River
Barsar
Rewalsar
Pandoh
Banjar
Jalori La (3223m)
Rampur

Hoshiarpur
Una
Sundernagar
Khanag
Jeori
Sarahan

Jalandhar
Jaijon
Govind Sagar
Karsog
Ani
Nirath
Rampur

Phagwara
Siwalik Range
Bilaspur
Surej River
Tattapani
Narkanda
Kotgarh
Thanedhar
Khadrala
Rohru

Rahon
Swarghat
Naldehra
Mashobra
Fagu
Bagi
Hattu Peak
Jubbal
Pabar Rv

PUNJAB
Arki
Sutlej River
Kufri
Theog
Hatkoll

Ludhiana
Kiratpur
Nalagarh
Kandaghat
Shimla
Chail
Siwalik Hills
Tons Rv

Ropar
Kasauli
Solan
Barog
Giri River

Kalka
Pinjore

Chandigarh

Renuka Lake

Nahan
Paonta Sahib

Yamuna River

Ambala
HARYANA

Sangrur
To Delhi

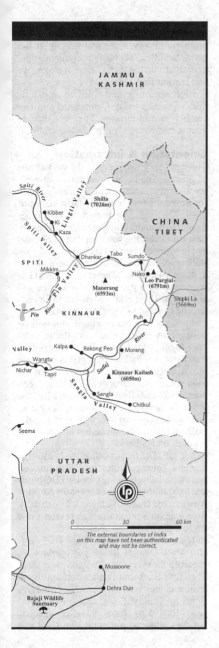

The external boundaries of India on this map have not been authenticated and may not be correct.

Chandra and Bhaga valleys. It is drained by the Chandra River, which turns into the Chenab River, before flowing west into Kashmir. Farther east, the Spiti River joins the Sutlej River in Kinnaur and flows all the way to the Punjab. The Kullu Valley is drained by the Beas River (pronounced 'bee-ahs') and stretches from Mandi to Manali. It is joined by the Parbati Valley from the east.

In the west, the beautiful Kangra Valley stretches from Mandi to Shahpur, near Pathankot. To the north of the Kangra Valley, on the other side of the Dhaula Dhar Range, is the Chamba Valley, which is separated from the remote Pattan Valley (upper Chenab River valley) by the Pir Panjal Range. The Ravi River flows through Chamba and on to Lahore in northern Pakistan.

Information

Tourist Offices The Himachal Pradesh Tourist Development Corporation (HPTDC) offers local information and maps, runs local tours and sometimes handles bookings for local airlines.

HPTDC manages about 50 hotels in Himachal Pradesh, most of them mid-range. All offer a 25% discount to single travellers staying in a double room. Some have cheap dorms. All HPTDC tourist offices and most HPTDC hotels can make bookings for another HPTDC hotel.

In season, HPTDC organises 'deluxe' buses for tourists between Shimla, Kullu and Manali, and links these places with Delhi and Chandigarh. HPTDC buses are more expensive than public buses but are quicker and far more comfortable. HPTDC also organises daily sightseeing tours out of Dharamsala, Shimla and Manali, which can be a useful way of visiting local areas.

HPTDC offices elsewhere in India can also provide worthwhile information:

Calcutta
    (☎ 033-271792) 2H, 2nd floor, Electronic
    Centre, 1-1A, BAC St, 700072
Chandigarh
    (☎ 0172-708569) Inter State Bus Terminal,
    Sector 17

HIMACHAL PRADESH

Delhi
(☎ 011-332 4764) Chandralok Bldg,
36 Janpath
Chennai
(☎ 044-827 2966) 28 Commander-in-Chief Rd
Mumbai (☎ 022-218 1123)
36 World Trade Centre, Cuffe Parade

Permits Inner line permits are required for some areas of Spiti and Kinnaur. However, regulations, and their implementation, have noticeably relaxed in the past year or so, and may relax further or even be abolished entirely. Check the current regulations with the relevant authorities and other travellers.

Foreigners can travel between Leh and Manali and between Leh/Manali and Kaza (the capital of the Spiti subdivision) without a permit. From Tabo to Rekong Peo you need a permit, but from Rekong Peo to Shimla, no permit is required.

Permits can be obtained from the district and subdivisional magistrates' offices in most regional centres but are most easily processed in Kaza or Rekong Peo. See the Inner Line Permits boxed text in the Kinnaur section for full details.

Shimla

☎ 0177 • pop 123,000

Shimla was once part of the Nepalese kingdom and called Shyamala, another name for the goddess Kali, but Shimla never gained any fame until it was 'discovered' by the British in 1819. Three years later, the first 'British' house was erected, and in 1864 Shimla became the summer capital of India. Every summer until 1939 the government of India would pack its bags and migrate almost 2000km from the sweltering heat of Calcutta or Delhi to the cool heights of Shimla. After the construction of the Kalka – Shimla railway line in 1903, Shimla really blossomed. Following Independence, Shimla was initially the capital of the Punjab, then became the capital of Himachal Pradesh in 1966.

Today, Shimla is a pleasant, sprawling town, set among cool pine-clad hills with plenty of crumbling colonial charm. Some travellers find the place too 'touristy' but nostalgic history buffs will love it. It has good facilities, although accommodation, particularly in the high season, is expensive and hard to find.

High season is mid-April to mid-July, mid-September to late October and mid-December to mid-January. The best time to visit is mid-September to late November.

Orientation & Information

There are only two roads in the central part of Shimla. The higher Mall runs east-west, reaching its highest point at Scandal Point (or Scandal Corner), the de facto centre of town. The mall area known as The Ridge runs from Scandal Point up to Christ Church. Cart Rd circles the southern part of Shimla, and is where the bus and taxi stands and train station are, from where everywhere else is a steep hike away. The rest of Shimla is connected by a mass of lively bazaars and alleyways. There is also a passenger lift connecting Cart Rd to The (eastern) Mall.

At the bus or train stations you will be besieged by porters who will offer to carry your luggage for Rs 4 to Rs 20, depending on weight and distance. A porter is not a bad idea, especially when you arrive. From the train station, for instance, it's a long, steep climb to The Mall or to somewhere like the Hotel Dreamland. Porters often double as hotel touts. Keep up with your porter, especially at night; after all he has all your possessions on his back!

The HPTDC tourist office (☎ 252561) at Scandal Point provides local information and maps, takes bookings for HPTDC buses and local tours and acts as agent for Archana Airways and Jagson Airlines. It's open daily from 8 am to 8 pm in the high season and 9 am to 6 pm in the low season.

The State Bank of India, along The (western) Mall, charges Rs 20 per transaction, plus Rs 3 for every travellers cheque cashed. The UCO Bank and Punjab National Bank change money with no fee. ANZ Grindlays Bank, at Scandal Point, charges an outrageous Rs 195 to change travellers cheques but does allow advances on Visa Card and

MasterCard, as does the Bank of Baroda, down on Cart Rd. If you are headed to Kinnaur it's worth changing extra money in Shimla as there are no exchange facilities at all in Kinnaur, Spiti or Lahaul.

The main post office, not far from Scandal Point, is open Monday to Saturday 10 am to 6 pm; Sunday and public holidays 10 am to 4 pm. There's a reliable poste restante service here. The central telegraph office (CTO; fax 202598), west of Scandal Point, is open 24 hours and is the cheapest place to make telephone calls and to send and receive faxes.

Himachal State Museum & Library

About 2.5km west of Scandal Point, the state museum has a good collection of statues, miniatures, coins, photos and other items from around Himachal Pradesh and is worth a visit. Entry to the museum is free and it's open daily 10 am to 5 pm (closed Monday and public holidays). Photography is strictly prohibited.

Viceregal Lodge & Botanical Gardens

The Viceregal Lodge, also known as Rashtrapati Niwas, was formerly the residence of the British Viceroy Lord Dufferin, and is where many decisions affecting the destiny of the subcontinent were made. Incredibly, every brick of the six storey building was transported by mule (the railway wasn't built at that stage). The lodge was eventually finished in 1888.

There's magnificent lawns, botanical gardens and a small cafe; the lodge also houses the Indian Institute of Advanced Study.

The lodge is a pleasant 2km walk west of the museum – about 4.5km from Scandal Point. It's open 9 am to 8.30 pm daily in summer, but closes a little earlier the rest of the year. A guided tour of the lodge (closed between 1 and 2 pm) costs Rs 6, while it's only Rs 3 to look around the gardens.

Next to the lodge is the Himalayan Aviary featuring, among others, the Monal pheasant (Himachal's state bird). The aviary is open 10 am to 5 pm daily (closed Monday). Entry

is Rs 5, but use of a still/video camera costs an extra Rs 25/100.

Christ Church & St Michael's Cathedral

The second oldest church in northern India (the oldest is in Ambala), Christ Church was built between 1846 and 1857. The clocks were added three years later, but none of them now work. The church is one of Shimla's major landmarks and is renowned for its stained glass windows. You can discreetly have a look inside the church, or attend English-language services every Sunday morning during the tourist season.

Jakhu Temple

Dedicated to the monkey god, Hanuman, Jakhu Temple is east of the town centre near the highest point of the Shimla ridge (2455m). It offers a fine view over the surrounding valleys out to the snow-capped peaks, and over Shimla itself. Appropriately, there are many monkeys around the temple. It's a steep 45 minute walk from Scandal Point. Take the footpath which heads east past the Hotel Dreamland. Sunrise is a good time to be there.

Bazaars

There are two main *mandi* (bazaar) areas in Shimla. Just below the western end of The (eastern) Mall, the bustling Sabzi Mandi (Vegetable Market), also known as Lower Bazaar, is a maze of steep, twisting lanes full of stalls selling food and just about everything imaginable. The kinetic chaos of the streets is a refreshing contrast to the genteel, British-influenced Mall.

Beyond The Ridge, the small, bustling Lakkar Bazaar is the place to buy souvenirs, although most shops seem to sell fairly tacky wooden stuff.

Hikes

In addition to a promenade along The Mall and the walk to the Jakhu Temple, there are a great number of interesting walks around Shimla. For information on places farther afield, see the Around Shimla section.

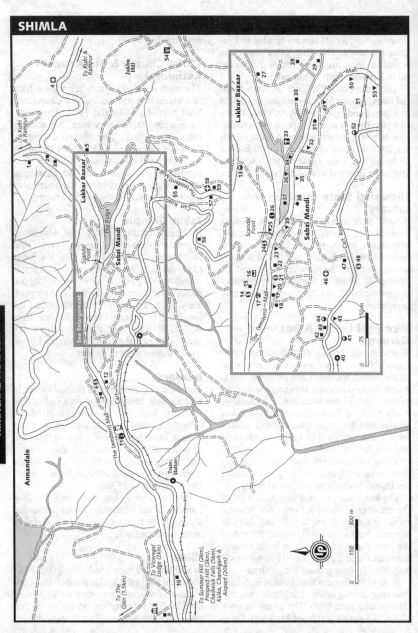

SHIMLA

PLACES TO STAY

1	Hotel Auckland
2	Hotel Chanakya; Hotel White
3	Hotel Diplomat
5	Hotel Uphar
7	Hotel Dalziel; Hotel Classic; Hotel Prakash
9	Spars Lodge
10	The Cecil
12	Hotel Gulmarg; Hotel Fontaine Bleau
15	YWCA
27	Hotel Dreamland
28	Hotel Mehman
29	Hotel Deogar
30	YMCA
42	Hotel Ranjan
43	Vikrant Hotel
47	Hotel Basant; Hotel Kohinoor
56	HPTDC Hotel Holiday Home
57	Oberoi Clarke's Hotel
59	Hotel Shingar; Hotel Sangeet

PLACES TO EAT

20	Indian Coffee House; Devicos Restaurant
23	Alfa Restaurant
25	Rendezvous Restaurant
32	Chung Fa Restaurant
34	Park Cafe
35	Himani's
36	Ashiana; Goofa; Quick Bite
39	Baljee's Restaurant; Fascination Restaurant
45	Local Dhabas
49	Sher-e-Punjab
50	Nilani's Restaurant; Krishna Bakers
53	Embassy Restaurant

OTHER

4	Indira Gandhi Hospital
6	State Bank of India
8	State Museum
11	HPTDC Tourist Information Centre (branch)
13	Rivoli Bus Station; Skating Rink
14	UCO Bank
16	Main Post Office
17	Central Telegraph Office
18	District Magistrate's Office
19	Himachal Emporium
21	Punjab National Bank; Span Tour & Travels
22	Kumar Studio Lab
24	ANZ Grindlays Bank
26	HPTDC Tourist Office (main)
31	Maria Brothers
33	Christ Church
37	Gaiety Theatre; Trishool's Bakery
38	Minerva Bookshop; Asia Book House
40	Branch Train Station
41	Inter State Bus Terminal (ISBT)
44	Kalka-Shimla Taxi Union Stand
46	Deen Dayal Upadhayay (Ripon) Hospital
48	Bank of Baroda
51	Passenger Lift
52	Vishal Himachal Taxi Operators' Union Stand
54	Jakhu Temple
55	Tibetan Refugee Handloom Shop
58	Kamla Nehru Hospital

HIMACHAL PRADESH

The Glen, about 4km west of Scandal Point, is one of the former playgrounds of rich British colonialists. The turn-off is on the way to the state museum and goes through **Annandale**, another lovely area. This was the site of a famous racecourse, and cricket and polo are still played there.

Summer Hill is 5km away, on the Shimla - Kalka railway line, and has pleasant, shady walks. It's also famous because Mahatma Gandhi once stayed at the Raj Kumari Amrit Kaur mansion here.

Chadwick Falls (67m high) are only really worth visiting during or just after the monsoons (July to October). The falls are 7km from Shimla and can be reached via Summer Hill.

Prospect Hill is about 5km west of Shimla, and a 15 minute climb from Boileauganj. The hill is a popular picnic spot with fine views over the surrounding country. The **Kamna Devi Temple** is nearby.

Sankat Mochan, 7km from Shimla, on the road to Chandigarh, has a Hanuman temple, and fine views of Shimla. It can also be reached by taxi.

Tara Devi Temple dedicated to Tara Devi, a Hindu version of the Tibetan goddess Drolma, is on a hilltop 10km from Shimla. Take a taxi from Shimla or walk the 3km from Tara Devi train station.

Organised Tours

HPTDC organises daily sightseeing tours in the high season. Buses leave from Rivoli bus stand at 10 am.

Kufri, Fagu, Mashobra & Naldehra (Rs 130)
Fagu and Theog & Narkanda (Rs 165)
Chail via Kufri (Rs 150)
Naldehra & Tattapani hot springs (Rs 150)

Taxi unions offer similar itineraries by private car.

Places to Stay

Accommodation in Shimla is expensive, particularly during the high season. But in the low season, or when business is quiet, prices drop substantially, sometimes by as much as half. Prices given below are for the high season.

Places to Stay – Budget

If you're on a low budget, the cheapest areas are around the main bus station, and along Cart Rd heading east from the bus station.

The **YMCA** (☎ 252375, fax 211016; for men and women) is probably the best budget choice in the high season, when it can be booked out (reservations are accepted by phone). Singles/doubles cost Rs 145/210 and include seven-day YMCA membership, breakfast and common hot water bathroom (7 pm to 9 am). Doubles with hot bath cost Rs 390, again with membership and breakfast. In the low season the YMCA doesn't drop its prices so you'll get a better deal at a private hotel. It's not far behind the Christ Church, up a laneway near a cinema.

The **YWCA** (☎ 203081), also for men and women, above the main post office, isn't quite as good value but it's a convenient, friendly old place, with great views. Small rooms with bath cost Rs 150/200 in high/low season, while larger 'suites' cost Rs 200/250. There is a Rs 20 temporary membership charge.

Hotel Ranjan (☎ 252818), near the bus station, has clean, large rooms for Rs 180 to Rs 200 with bath.

Vikrant Hotel (☎ 253602), nearby, has singles for about Rs 150 and doubles for Rs 303/413 with/without bath.

Hotel Basant (☎ 258341), farther east along busy Cart Rd, is quite basic and not great value in the low season. Singles with share bath cost Rs 110; doubles with bath from Rs 165 to Rs 220. Hot water comes by the bucket at Rs 5.

Hotel Kohinoor (☎ 202008), next door, is more expensive but much nicer. Rooms with bath and running hot water cost about Rs 325 (Rs 225 in the low season).

Around the Lakkar Bazaar area, a steep climb past The Ridge, are several reasonably priced places. **Hotel Dreamland** (☎ 206897) has rooms ranging from Rs 250/400 for a single/double to Rs 600 for a deluxe double.

The nearby **Hotel Uphar** (☎ 257670) is clean, friendly and used to backpackers. Doubles with hot shower are about Rs 275, or Rs 400 with a view and mini balcony.

Just downhill from the State Bank of India, at the western end of The Mall, the quaint, family-run **Hotel Fontaine Bleau** (☎ 23549) has rooms from Rs 175 to Rs 400 with share bath.

Hotel Gulmarg (☎ 253168), next door, has charmless, windowless rooms starting at Rs 250/350 a single/double with share bath or Rs 350/520 with private bath.

Places to Stay – Mid-Range

The majority of rooms in this range will usually include TV (often cable), and a bathroom with hot water. They are particularly good value in the low season, when a nice double room with cable TV and hot water costs about Rs 200.

Just off The (western) Mall, a short walk up from the train station, are three reasonable places. **Hotel Prakash** (☎ 213321) has some what overpriced rooms for Rs 400 and Rs 600. The friendly and comfortable **Hotel Classic** (☎ 253078) has nasty singles but decent doubles for Rs 400 to Rs 500 with good views. **Hotel Dalziel** is probably the best value with rooms from Rs 300 to Rs 500.

North of The Ridge, and around the Lakkar Bazaar area, are several good places, though they are a long hike from the bus or train stations.

Hotel Chanakya (☎ 254465) has clean and comfortable rooms from Rs 250 to Rs 480. **Hotel Diplomat** (☎ 257754), just a few doors away, is better, with doubles from Rs 500, or Rs 620 with a view.

Hotel White (☎ 255276), nearby, has comfortable doubles for Rs 425 and Rs 500 with good views. The more expensive the room, the better the view.

A couple of minutes' walk east of Christ Church is a sprinkling of newish places with a quiet, convenient location.

Hotel Deogar (☎ 208527) is a good choice, with flexibly priced doubles ranging from smallish 1st floor rooms for Rs 300 to the excellent rooftop suite which has fantastic views over Shimla at Rs 800.

The new *Hotel Mehman* (☎ *213692)* sports spotlessly clean carpets and bathrooms. Comfortable rooms range from Rs 550 to Rs 800, depending on the views, with a 50% discount in the low season.

There are two good places across from the Oberoi Clarke's Hotel, at the bottom end of The (eastern) Mall. *Hotel Shingar* (☎ *252881)* has rooms for Rs 700, or Rs 900 with a view. It's well run and good value. Nearby, the *Hotel Sangeet* (☎ *202506)* has good-value rooms at Rs 600.

The friendly HPTDC's *Hotel Holiday Home* (☎ *212890, Cart Rd)* is well set up with a bar and coffee shop, but is inconveniently located, and doesn't give low-season discounts. Rates range from Rs 500 for economy rooms to Rs 2300 for a luxury room.

For a quiet stay on the colonial edges of Shimla try the *Spars Lodge* (☎ *257908)*, 2km west of Shimla centre, near the state museum. Pleasant, homey rooms with clean, bright bathrooms and great food cost Rs 600/900 for singles/doubles.

Places to Stay – Top End
Woodville Palace Resort (☎ *223919)*, 2km south of the Oberoi Clarke's Hotel on The (eastern) Mall, is an ivy-covered building constructed in 1938 by Raja Rana Sir Bhagat Chandra, the ruler of the former princely state of Jubbal. It's a small place, set among very pleasant gardens. Double rooms are Rs 2000, and suites start at Rs 3000 – bookings are recommended.

Oberoi Clarke's Hotel (☎ *251010)*, down the far end of The (eastern) Mall, is one of Shimla's earliest hotels. The luxurious rooms start at US$108/120 (plus 10% tax), including the compulsory three meal 'American Plan'.

The Cecil (☎ *204848)*, at the western end of The Mall, is the classiest place in town. Rooms start at Rs 4700/6200 for a single/double in the low season, so bring a credit card.

Places to Eat
Indian Shimla has many places serving Indian food, primarily southern Indian.

Baljee's, along The (eastern) Mall, has a delicious range of Indian and western food, and the service is good. Prices can be a little high at around Rs 100 for a meat dish, but the seats are very comfortable. *Fascination*, the associated restaurant upstairs, is similarly priced and just as popular.

Alfa Restaurant, near Scandal Point, is about the same standard, price and popularity as Baljee's.

Himani's, at 49 The (eastern) Mall, does tasty southern Indian snacks and meals, and has a bar.

Rendezvous, right on Scandal Point, has Indian and Thai food at moderate prices but the service is slow.

Sher-e-Punjab, along The (eastern) Mall, is an excellent cheap option. The special *channa* is recommended at Rs 25.

Western & Chinese The self-serve *Embassy Restaurant*, not far from the top of the lift on The (eastern) Mall, has great individual pizzas and hamburgers, as well as Indian and Chinese food.

Devicos Restaurant, on The (western) Mall, near Scandal Point, is a clean, trendy place that does good, but a little overpriced, fast food.

Park Cafe, just down The (eastern) Mall and up some stairs is popular with backpackers. It's good for pizza (Rs 35 to Rs 50), milkshakes, breakfasts and laid-back late-evening music.

HPTDC has a building on The Ridge with three places to eat. The *Ashiana* is about the best (and most expensive) for decor and service. The *Goofa* downstairs is nowhere near as classy, but serves a reasonable (and early) breakfast. In the same complex, the *Quick Bite* has cheap pizzas and Indian food.

Oberoi Clarke's Hotel is good for a splurge in some luxurious surroundings; the set menu costs Rs 250 plus 8% tax.

Chung Fa, down some steps just off The Mall, is the best place for cheap Chinese

HIMACHAL PRADESH

food. It's run by an expat Chinese couple and there is a good range of noodles, dumplings and main dishes, all for less than Rs 40 a dish.

Bakeries *Trishool's*, next to the Gaiety Theatre, is recommended.

Baljee's has a bakery counter at the front, and is a great place for morning or afternoon teas.

Krishna Bakers, along The (eastern) Mall, does good burgers, cakes and pastries.

Entertainment

Probably the most popular, and best, entertainment is to stroll along The Mall and The Ridge (vehicle-free!) and watch everyone else watch everyone else. This is especially pleasant in the evenings when the views and lights are wonderful. An ice-skating rink is open in winter – follow the signs from Scandal Point.

The lovely old *Gaiety Theatre* often has some shows or recitals, particularly in summer.

The *Indian Coffee House*, along The (western) Mall, is where traditionally dressed waiters serve reasonably good coffee (but no tea) and southern Indian snacks.

Himani's has a bar. The *Rendezvous* on Scandal Point also has a bar, but it is dingy and unwelcoming. The expensive hotels usually serve alcohol.

Shopping

The Himachal Emporium on The (western) Mall has a reasonable collection of local handicrafts. The Tibetan Refugee Handloom Shop, at the other end of The Mall, is the showroom for a local development project and sells carpets, clothes and other Tibetan crafts.

Getting There & Away

Air Jagson Airlines flies daily 17-seat Otters to/from Delhi (US$105). Flights then continue on to Kullu (US$67). Archana Airways flies daily to/from Delhi only (US$105). Bookings can be made at the HPTDC office at Scandal Point or reliable agencies such as Span Tour & Travels

(☎ 206850), 4 The (western) Mall. Shimla's airport is 23km south at Jubbarhatti.

Bus The large and chaotic Inter State Bus Terminal (ISBT) on Cart Rd is set up on the reasonable assumption that most foreigners take the train or a tourist bus. However, there is a very handy private computer booking booth (counter 9), where the employees speak English, and you can book a ticket on any public bus up to a month ahead. There is a second booking office just next to the HPTDC office at Scandal Point.

Buses to destinations east of Shimla depart from the Rivoli bus station, on the northern side of the main ridge, below the HPTDC office.

For Tattapani, Kasauli and local destinations en route to Kalka or Narkanda such as Kufri and Theog, catch one of the regular local buses along Cart Rd.

To Manali (11 hours) there are two ordinary (Rs 106) and two semideluxe buses (Rs 139/174 daytime/overnight); all buses stop in Kullu (Rs 119 to Rs 149). One overnight semideluxe bus goes to Dharamsala (Rs 159, 10 hours). There are 10 buses a day to Mandi (Rs 83) or jump on any Manali-bound bus.

There is one overnight and one early-morning deluxe bus to Delhi (Rs 264, 10 hours), plus ordinary buses every hour (Rs 118). Ordinary buses to Chandigarh leave every half hour. Two buses depart every morning to Dehra Dun via Nahan (Rs 67), Paonta Sahib (Rs 90) and Haridwar (Rs 113, nine hours).

Rivoli bus station has seven buses between 4 am and 11.30 am to Rekong Peo (Rs 120, 10 hours) via Narkanda (Rs 32, three hours) and Rampur (Rs 60). There is one bus at 7.30 am to Sangla and a couple of buses around 9.30 am to Sarahan (Rs 87). There are also hourly buses to Naldehra.

Travel agencies along The Mall offer private overnight 'deluxe' buses to Manali (Rs 225) and Delhi (Rs 275). Prices and timings change according to demand and the season.

In the high season, HPTDC offers daily daytime buses to Manali (Rs 275, 10 hours)

and overnight buses to Delhi (Rs 290, 10 hours) via Chandigarh. HPTDC buses are best booked at the tourist office at Scandal Point but actually depart from the office at Victory Tunnel.

Train There are two train stations in Shimla. All trains arrive at and depart from the main station on the western edge of town; some trains also depart from the central branch station. The train reservation office (☎ 252915) at the main station can arrange bookings for the Kalka and Delhi line and, in theory, for other trips in northern India. It's open Monday to Saturday 10 am to 1.30 pm and 2 to 5 pm; Sunday 10 am to 2 pm.

The train journey to Shimla involves a change from broad to narrow gauge at Kalka, a little north of Chandigarh. There are three classes: 2nd class (Rs 14), chair car (Rs 114) and 1st class (Rs 169). During high season there is a special Rail Car service (Rs 216) offering luxury seats in a special glass-sided carriage. There are at least four daily trains each way between Shimla and Kalka (five hours), and usually three more in the high season. Ask at the station for details.

To travel from Delhi to Shimla by train in one trip, the best and most reliable way is to catch the *Himalayan Queen* from New Delhi station at 6 am, arriving in Kalka at 11.40 am. You then cross to another platform to take the noon toy train which arrives in Shimla at 5.20 pm. Reservations can be made all the way to Shimla and costs Rs 400 in air-con chair car (seats like an airplane). Some travellers have found their ticket or reservation is valid only to Kalka, so check this when you buy it.

The only way to do the reverse trip (Shimla-Delhi) in one day is to catch the 10.55 am train from Shimla, which connects with the *Himalayan Queen* at Kalka and arrives in New Delhi at 10.30 pm. The best overnight connection is the *Shivalik Express*, which leaves Shimla at 5.30 pm to connect with the *Kalka-Howrah Mail*, arriving in Delhi at 6.25 am. Fares are Rs 130/589 for 2nd class sleeper/air-con 2nd class sleeper.

Taxi There are two agencies with fixed-price taxis that are almost impossible to bargain down, even in the low season. They are the Kalka-Shimla Taxi Union (☎ 258225) on Cart Rd, near the ISBT bus station, and the Vishal Himachal Taxi Operators' Union (☎ 205164), at the bottom of the lift on Cart Rd. Both are about the same price. Taxis are either Gypsy jeeps or 'multivans' that take three passengers plus the driver; or the Ambassador taxi that takes four passengers and costs about 10% more than the prices that follow.

Examples of one-way taxi fares from Shimla are: Chandigarh (Rs 800 to Rs 1000), Kalka (Rs 700), Rampur (Rs 1200), Manali (Rs 2200), Kullu (Rs 1800 to Rs 2000), Dharamsala (Rs 2200), Rekong Peo/Kalpa (Rs 2500), Dehra Dun (Rs 2000 to Rs 2250) and Delhi (Rs 2500 to Rs 3000).

Both taxi companies also offer one day sightseeing tours to the following places:

- Narkanda via Fagu and Theog (Rs 760)
- Chail/Kufri (Rs 710)
- Naldehra via Mashobra (Rs 410)
- Tattapani via Mashobra and Naldehra (Rs 710)

Getting Around

To/From the Airport A fixed-price taxi costs Rs 400 from the airport to Shimla, but if you are staying anywhere along or near The Mall, you may have to walk the last bit yourself anyway. HPTDC runs a flaky airport bus service (Rs 50), otherwise local buses headed to Nalagarh go past the airport.

Passenger Lift At the eastern end of Cart Rd, next to the Vishal Himachal taxi stand, there is a lift which goes up to the eastern end of The Mall (Rs 3). It certainly does save a steep climb.

Around Shimla

There are a number of things to do around Shimla, including short walks near Kasauli, horse rides around the village of Kufri, golf at Naldehra and relaxing at the hot springs at Tattapani. For information on HPTDC and taxi tours to these places see the Shimla section.

SHIMLA TO KALKA

Solan is known as the home of the Mohan Meakan brewery, built in 1835, and is the capital of the Solan district. It pretends to be another hill station but does not have the scenery, facilities or charm of nearby Shimla.

Barog is not a bad place for a day trip by train from Shimla. There are nice walks nearby, including that to Churdhar Mountain (3647m). HPTDC's *Hotel Pinewood (☎ 38825)* has rooms, some with great views, for Rs 900 to Rs 1100 with hot water and TV. There are several other mid-range places from about Rs 250. The railway *retiring rooms* cost from Rs 50 to Rs 100.

The train from Shimla to Kalka stops in Solan and Barog, although it's probably easier to catch the buses which leave Shimla every 10 minutes or so.

Past the unexciting industrial town of Parwanoo, and just over the border into Haryana, **Kalka** is the start/finish for the toy train trip to/from Shimla. There is nothing to see or do, and nowhere to stay in Kalka, so get on the train to somewhere else.

About 5km south-west of Kalka, on the Chandigarh road, are the attractive Yadavindra (or Mughal) gardens at **Pinjore**.

KASAULI
☎ 01793
About 12km from the Shimla to Kalka road, Kasauli is a charming place and a popular side trip from Shimla, or an alternative to staying in Shimla.

There are numerous lovely walks around Kasauli, including one to **Sanawar**, another picturesque hill town, and the location of a famous colonial college.

The 4km walk to **Monkey Point** has great views, but unlike Shimla it has no monkeys. The area is owned by the Indian air force, so you'll have to obtain permission (at the gates) before you set out on the walk to Monkey Point.

Places to Stay
The *Alasia Hotel (☎ 72008)* costs from Rs 600; the *Maurice Hotel (☎ 72074)* has good-value singles/doubles from Rs 250/350; and the *Anchal Guest House (☎ 72052)* is OK at Rs 350 a room.

HPTDC's *Hotel Ros Common (☎ 72005)* has rooms with TV from Rs 750 to Rs 1000 and a pleasant location.

Getting There & Away
Regular local buses connect Shimla with Kasauli. By train, get off at the Dharampur station, and catch a local bus, or hitch a ride the 12km to Kasauli. A one-way/return taxi from Shimla to Kasauli costs about Rs 700/1000.

WILDFLOWER HALL
At **Charabra**, 13km from Shimla near Mashobra, Wildflower Hall was built as the residence of the then British commander-in-chief Lord Kitchener, specifically it seems to irritate his rival Viceroy Lord Curzon. Before it was severely damaged by fire in 1993, HPTDC ran the place as the *Wildflower Hall Hotel*. The hotel is being renovated and is due to open in the year 2000 as a top-end heritage hotel.

CHAIL
☎ 01792
Chail was created by the Maharaja of Patiala as a summer capital after his expulsion from Shimla. The town is built on three hills – one is topped by the Chail Palace, one by the village itself and the other by the Snowview mansion.

Three kilometres from the village is the world's highest **cricket ground** (2444m), built in 1893. There is also a **wildlife sanctuary** 3km from Chail with a limited number of deer and birds. This is also great hiking country.

Places to Stay & Eat
The HPTDC's *Palace Hotel (☎ 48141, fax 48142)* has a range of suites, cottages, log huts and rooms set among 70 acres of lawns. Modest luxury starts at Rs 800 for a log hut

or Rs 1000 for a regular room, and moves up to Rs 4700 for the four bed 'maharaja suite'. There is a top-class restaurant, cafe and bar.

HPTDC's *Hotel Himneel* (☎ 48337) has more modest rooms for Rs 600 a double.

Hotel Deodar (☎ 48318) has rooms from Rs 300 and the *Pine View Tourist Lodge* has rooms from Rs 100 to Rs 250.

Getting There & Away
Chail can be reached from the Shimla - Kalka road via Kandaghat or, more commonly, via the turn-off at Kufri. A return taxi from Shimla, via Kufri, costs Rs 700. There are occasional buses (more in the high season) to Chail from Shimla and Chandigarh.

NORTH OF SHIMLA
Mashobra
About 11km from Shimla, the small village of Mashobra has some pleasant walks, including one to Sipi, where there is a fair every May and a wooden **temple** dedicated to Shiva.

About 3km from Mashobra, along a lovely trail, is the resort of **Craignano**. You can book a room at the *Municipal Rest House* (☎ 224850) in Craignano through HPTDC in Shimla. The only other place to stay in or around Mashobra is the *Gables Resorts* (☎ 480171), which offers rural luxury from Rs 1600 upwards. The village has one or two *dhabas*.

Naldehra
Fifteen kilometres farther north, at an altitude of 2050m, Naldehra is a pleasant little village – so pleasant in fact that Lord Curzon named his youngest daughter after it. It is mostly famous for having one of the oldest and highest golf courses in India. There is even a temple, the **Mahunag Mandir**, in the middle of the course. Green fees are Rs 400 (Rs 100 for Indians) for 18 holes (twice around the course), plus Rs 100 to hire golf clubs and balls and Rs 50 for a caddy.

The *Hotel Golf Glade* (☎ 487739) has six luxurious log cabins from Rs 1000 to Rs 1500, and better value rooms from Rs 800 to Rs 1000.

Paradise Restaurant on the main road is the only reasonably good place to eat outside the hotel.

Tattapani
☎ 0117
Tattapani is famous only for its hot sulphurous springs. They are not as well developed or as nice as the ones in Vashisht, near Manali, or at Manikaran, along the Parbati Valley, but the setting is great and the village is small and relaxed. The hot water is piped from a section of the Sutlej River to the two guesthouses on the bank.

Places to Stay & Eat HPTDC's *Tourist Inn* (☎ 485949) has three run-down rooms from Rs 200 to Rs 350. Plush new baths (for guests only) at the back of the hotel should be open by 1999 but nonguests can use the old baths for Rs 10.

There are also some very basic *dorm rooms* for an unbeatable Rs 30 back at the entrance to town but you'd need your own bedding. They aren't easy to find; head about 100m up the lane to the left of the bridge before the village, turn sharp left again and look for a large wooden house.

Spring View Guest House (☎ 485958), down on the riverside, is friendly and relaxed, with rooms for Rs 100 or Rs 150. There's a decent restaurant and a free hot pool for guests.

Anupam Guest House, up in the village, has only two rooms but they are probably the best value in town. Prices are negotiable.

There are several reasonable places to eat by the bridge to Tattapani and both the riverside guesthouses have restaurants.

Getting There & Away Get off the bus just after the bridge over the Sutlej, about 10 minutes past Sunni. The guesthouses and springs are about 400m farther on, down by the river. The village itself is up the road to the left before the guesthouses. A local bus leaves Shimla every hour from Rivoli bus stand for Sunni, and normally continues to Tattapani. The last bus back to Shimla passes through Tattapani at around 6.30 pm.

HIMACHAL PRADESH

A return taxi from Shimla to Tattapani costs Rs 710, which includes some waiting time while you soak your weary limbs.

EAST OF SHIMLA
Kufri

Kufri (2510m) is a nondescript little village, but the nearby countryside offers some good hiking, including a hike to nearby Mahasu peak. Horses can be hired for trips around the valleys and hills.

The **Himalayan Nature Park** has a collection of animals and birds unique to Himachal Pradesh, but you won't see much unless you have your own vehicle or you're on a tour. There is a Rs 10 entrance fee, plus Rs 30 extra for a camera, it's open 10 am to 5 pm daily. Nearby, the **Indira Tourist Park** has great views, the HPTDC's *Cafe Lalit*, horse riding and a chance to have your photo taken standing next to a yak.

Kufri is promoted for its skiing (December to February) but the snow isn't reliable and the location isn't particularly good. Tobogganing is a popular and cheaper alternative.

Places to Stay & Eat The *Hotel Snow Shelter*, on the main road in the village, has cosy rooms, great views and hot water at a reasonable Rs 400.

Kufri Holiday Resorts (☎ 480341) has upmarket rooms from Rs 1150.

Atri Food Center and *Deluxe Food Corner*, on the main road, serve reasonable food.

Getting There & Away Kufri is a stop on any of the regular bus routes between Shimla, Narkanda and Rampur. A one-way taxi from Shimla to Kufri costs about Rs 400.

Fagu

Fagu is another unexciting village, but it serves as a good base for exploring the pleasant nearby countryside.

HPTDC's *Hotel Peach Blossom* (☎ 39522; bookings advisable) has enormous rooms with fireplaces. Doubles cost from Rs 275 to Rs 350 but you can expect prices to rise in the wake of recent renovations; check with HPTDC.

Narkanda
☎ 01782

Halfway between Shimla and Rampur, Narkanda is basically a truck stop town, but it is a popular place for skiing (in season) and hiking. The 3300m **Hattu peak**, 8km to the east, makes for a good day hike.

Skiing The ski season lasts from January to mid-April but Narkanda is not as well set up for skiing as Solang Nullah, north of Manali.

HPTDC's seven-day packages cost Rs 3500 including board, lodging, equipment and tuition. Better organised 15 day basic and intermediate packages with Manali's Directorate of Mountaineering & Allied Sports cost US$262. Unless you're in a group you'll have to join fixed date packages for both. Good opportunities for some cross-country skiing exist around Narkanda if you have the equipment and experience.

Places to Stay & Eat *Hotel Mahamaya* (☎ 8448) has lovely large rooms with hot water, balcony and views for Rs 400 to Rs 800. It should offer discounts in low season.

Hotel Snow View has dorm beds (in the lobby!) for Rs 38 or a ramshackle double with bathroom for Rs 220; amazing views and friendly staff make the place tolerable. Look for the sign from the village centre.

HPTDC's secluded *Hotel Hatu* (☎ 8430) is 250m up a track east of the main road (look for the sign). Good doubles cost Rs 750 or Rs 900 in the high season, Rs 525 or Rs 630 at other times.

There are many basic, friendly *dhabas* in the town centre. If you prefer eating with cutlery try the *restaurant* at the Hotel Hatu.

Getting There & Away Local buses travel in either direction along the main road at least every 30 minutes. A return taxi from Shimla will cost about Rs 750.

SUTLEJ VALLEY
Rampur
☎ 01782

Rampur was once on the ancient trade route between India and Tibet, and is a former centre of the mighty Bushahr empire, which spread deep into Kinnaur. Rampur is not a particularly exciting place to stay overnight, but there are one or two things to see if you do stop. The **Lavi Fair** is held in Rampur every year in the second week of November. People from the remote regions of Lahaul, Spiti and Kinnaur congregate in the town to trade local produce and horses.

The **Padam Palace**, built in 1925, is along the main road. You can't go inside, but there are lovely gardens, flanked by a Hindu temple, which you can wander around. Otherwise, the older part of town, by the river and below the palace, is the most interesting place to explore. It's a maze of tiny lanes full of shops and temples, such as the Hindu **Raghunath Temple** and the (Buddhist) **Sri Sat Nahan Temple**, built in 1926.

Places to Stay & Eat The *Narindera Hotel (☎ 33155)*, 150m north-east of the bus station, has decent doubles with hot water bathrooms from Rs 150 to Rs 250. Air-con rooms are Rs 500. There is a good restaurant here.

Hotel Bhagwati (☎ 33117), down in the old town (look for the huge sign on its roof), remains deservedly popular. Singles are Rs 75 and doubles Rs 125 or Rs 175, all with hot water bathrooms.

There are several cheaper dosshouses in town, but none are up to much.

HPTDC's *Cafe Sutlej* is worth the 1km walk from the palace towards Shimla for views and good food. The old town has plenty of *dhabas*, and several quite good bakeries.

Getting There & Away Rampur is a major transport hub, so is well connected by (normally full) buses. There are buses every 30 minutes (5.30 am to 4 pm) to Narkanda (Rs 33, two hours) and then on to Shimla (Rs 60, six hours). To Rekong Peo there are buses at 5, 5.30 and 8.30 am; the 5.30 am departure goes on to Kalpa. Buses to Sarahan depart every two hours or so until 6.30 pm. A one-way taxi from Shimla to Rampur will cost Rs 1200.

Sarahan
☎ 01782

Former summer capital of the Bushahr empire, Sarahan is a wonderful little village set high above the valley floor. It is definitely worth a visit – there are spectacular views of Srikhand Mahadev (5227m) to the north and hiking opportunities to nearby villages such as Ranwin and Bashal peak.

Bhimakali Temple This temple is one of the finest examples of Himachal architecture. There are some entry rules: you must wear a cap (which can be borrowed from inside the temple), no leather goods (belts, wallets etc) are allowed (they can be left with the guards), photography is only allowed outside the two main temples, and shoes must be removed.

As you pass through to the inner courtyard look out for the stunning silver doors. Stairs ascend (on your left) to the 2nd floor where the main statue of Bhimakali (a local version of Durga) is housed, surrounded by images of Parvati, Buddha and Annapurna, among others, all under a beautiful filigree silver canopy. Stairs descend to the 1st floor where there is a statue of Parvati, wife of Shiva.

In the far right of the courtyard is a small display of lamps and weapons. Next door is the **Lankra Vir Temple** where, up until the 19th century, human sacrifices were performed to appease Bhimakali. The dead bodies were subsequently thrown into the adjacent well.

There are a couple of other temples in the complex dedicated to Narsingh (Narasimha) and Raghunath.

Places to Stay & Eat The excellent *temple guesthouse*, inside the temple complex, is the best budget bet. It offers a handful of clean, quiet rooms with bath for Rs 150, Rs 200 or Rs 300.

Snow View Hotel (☎ 74260), near the bus stop, has ramshackle rooms for Rs 200. Its *Ajay Restaurant* is quite good.

HPTDC's *Hotel Shrikhand (☎ 74234)*, set at the edge of a bluff, has large, comfortable rooms with TV and hot water for Rs

550, Rs 600 or Rs 900. There are dorms for Rs 50 when available. The restaurant here is excellent.

There are a few *dhabas* in the village.

Getting There & Away Direct buses from Shimla (Rs 90), Narkanda (Rs 57) and Rampur run fairly regularly, but it's easier to get a through bus to the junction at Jeori and wait for a local bus (every hour or two) up the steep 17km road to Sarahan. A taxi from Rampur to Sarahan is pricey at around Rs 500 but will save a lot of time; from Jeori to Sarahan costs about Rs 200.

To get from Sarahan to Shimla in one day, take the 6.30 or 7.30 am daily bus. To reach Rekong Peo or Kalpa in one day, take the early Shimla or Rampur bus, get off at Jeori, and wait for one of the hopelessly crowded buses heading north-east.

Kangra Valley

The beautiful Kangra Valley starts near Mandi, runs north, then bends west and extends to Shahpur near Pathankot. To the north the valley is flanked by the Dhaula Dhar Range, to the side of which clings Dharamsala. There are a number of places of interest along the valley, including McLeod Ganj, home of the Dalai Lama and headquarters of the Tibetan Government in Exile.

The main Pathankot to Mandi road runs through the valley, and there is a narrow-gauge railway line from Pathankot as far as Jogindernagar. The Kangra school of painting developed in this valley.

BAIJNATH
☎ 01894
The small town of Baijnath, 46km south-east of Dharamsala, is an important pilgrimage place due to its ancient stone **Baidyanath Temple**, sacred to Siva as Lord of the Physicians. It is said to date from 804 AD, although according to tradition it was built by the Pandavas, the heroes of the *Mahabharata*. The temple features intricate carvings on the exterior walls, and the inner

sanctum enshrines one of India's 12 *jyoti linga* (linga of light). Large numbers of pilgrims make their way here for the **Shivaratri Festival** in late February/early March.

Baijnath itself is a chaotic and ramshackle town, although the Dhaula Dhar Range provides a fine backdrop.

Hotel Shanker View (☎ 63831), 300m out of town on the road to Mandi, has singles/doubles from Rs 125/150 to Rs 200/250. Deluxe rooms are overpriced at Rs 350.

The narrow-gauge railway passes through Baijnath on its way to Pathankot (six hours) and Jogindernagar (three hours). The station is at Paprola, 1km west of the main bus stand. A taxi from Dharamsala costs Rs 650 (Rs 850 return).

TASHIJONG GOMPA
This friendly gompa, 5km north-west of Baijnath, is the focus of a small Drukpa Kagyud community of 150 Tibetan monks and 400 refugees. The monastery complex has several halls you can visit and there's a carpet-making, *thangka*-painting and wood-carving cooperative here.

Tashijong village is a 2km walk north from the main Palampur to Baijnath road. Get off the bus at the bend in the road by the bridge.

It's possible to stay at the *Monastery Guesthouse*, where double rooms cost from Rs 100 to Rs 150. There is a second, cheaper *guesthouse* above the village clinic.

Two kilometres south of Tashijong, at Taragarh, is the extraordinary *Palace Hotel (☎ 01894-63034)*, the summer palace of Dr Karan Singh, the son of the last maharaja of Jammu and Kashmir. Portraits of the royal family are displayed throughout the hotel, which has the usual assortment of tiger skins and colonial furnishings. Doubles range from Rs 950; the beautifully furnished suites cost up to Rs 2300.

PALAMPUR
☎ 01894
A pleasant little town surrounded by tea plantations, Palampur is 30km south-east of Dharamsala and stands at 1260m. A four day

trek takes you from Palampur to **Holi** via the Waru La, or in a shorter walk you can visit the **Bundla chasm**, just outside of town, where a waterfall drops into the Bundla stream. If you are planning on trekking from Palampur to Holi bear in mind that there are no trekking agencies in Palampur so you must make the necessary arrangements in McLeod Ganj.

Places to Stay & Eat
HPTDC's *Hotel T-Bud (☎ 31298)*, 1km north of Main Bazaar, has doubles with bath from Rs 550 to Rs 800 (Rs 330 to Rs 450 in the low season).

Hotel Highland Regency (☎ 31222), just next to the new bus station, has pleasant rooms and clean bathrooms for Rs 275, Rs 400 or Rs 550. It also has a good restaurant.

Hotel Sawhney (☎ 30888), on the main road, has basic doubles for Rs 165, or Rs 250 with TV.

Pine's Hotel (☎ 32633), down near the old bus station, has singles from Rs 100 to Rs 125, and doubles from Rs 175 to Rs 250.

Joy Restaurant, near the hotel Sawhney, has cheap fare, including a very good egg chicken dosa for Rs 30. *Sapan Restaurant*, opposite the post office in Main Bazaar, serves Indian and Chinese cuisine.

Getting There & Away
The new bus station is 1km south of Main Bazaar; a taxi will charge Rs 15. Buses leave for Dharamsala (Rs 20, two hours); Mandi (Rs 45, four hours) and Pathankot (Rs 60, four hours; last bus at 1.30 pm). A taxi from Dharamsala costs Rs 425 (Rs 625 return).

Maranda, 2km west of Palampur, is on the narrow-gauge line between Pathankot and Jogindernagar. There are six trains daily between Maranda and Kangra to the west (for Dharamsala), or the end of the line at Jogindernagar, to the east.

CHAMUNDA DEVI TEMPLE
From Palampur the road passes through tea plantations before descending to the colourful Chamunda Devi Temple complex on the bank of the Baner River, 10km to the west.

Chamunda is a particularly wrathful form of Durga; the idol in the main temple is considered so sacred that it is completely hidden beneath a red cloth.

HPTDC's *Yatri Niwas (☎ 01892-36065)* has doubles for Rs 400 and Rs 550 and dorm beds for Rs 50.

The nearby *Chaumunda* and *Vatika* hotels both have rooms from Rs 300 to Rs 600.

Buses between Dharamsala and Palampur will drop you at the Chamunda Devi Temple.

DHARAMSALA
☎ 01892 • pop 19,200
While Dharamsala is synonymous with the Tibetan Government in Exile, the actual headquarters is about 4km above Dharamsala at Gangchen Kyishong, and most travellers hang out at McLeod Ganj, strung along a high ridge 10km above Dharamsala.

Dharamsala itself is of little interest to travellers, although Kotwali Bazaar, at the foot of the roads leading up to McLeod Ganj, is an interesting and colourful market, and you can visit the Kangra Art Museum.

Information
HPTDC's tourist office (☎ 24212) runs local tours (summer only) to Kangra, Jawalamukhi and Chamunda Devi (Rs 150) or to Palampur and Baijnath (Rs 150). It also runs luxury buses to Manali (Rs 250, 10 hours) in summer only. The office is open Monday to Saturday 9 am to 8 pm.

The main branch of the State Bank of India and the Punjab National Bank both accept major travellers cheques. The Bank of Baroda, nearby, can give cash advances on Visa cards within 24 hours.

Kangra Art Museum
This museum, a few minutes' walk south of the tourist office, has miniature paintings from the Kangra school of art, which flourished in the Kangra Valley during the 17th century; it also has elaborately embroidered costumes of Kangra people, woodcarvings and tribal jewellery. It's open Tuesday to Sunday 10 am to 5 pm. Entry is free.

HIMACHAL PRADESH

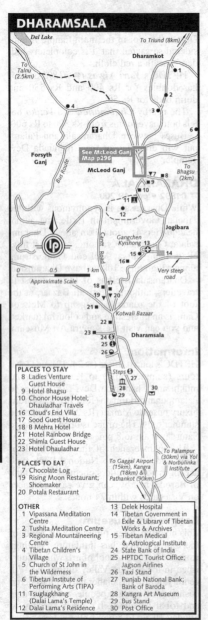

DHARAMSALA

Dal Lake

To Triund (8km)

Dharamkot

To Talnu (2.5km)

Forsyth Ganj

See McLeod Ganj Map p296

McLeod Ganj

To Bhagsu (2km)

Gangchen Kyishong

Jogibara

Very steep road

Kotwali Bazaar

Dharamsala

Steps

0   0.5   1 km
Approximate Scale

To Gaggal Airport (15km), Kangra (18km) & Pathankot (90km)

To Palampur (30km) via Yol & Norbulinka Institute

PLACES TO STAY
8 Ladies Venture Guest House
9 Hotel Bhagsu
10 Chonor House Hotel; Dhauladhar Travels
16 Cloud's End Villa
17 Sood Guest House
18 B Mehra Hotel
21 Hotel Rainbow Bridge
22 Shimla Guest House
23 Hotel Dhauladhar

PLACES TO EAT
7 Chocolate Log
19 Rising Moon Restaurant; Shoemaker
20 Potala Restaurant

OTHER
1 Vipassana Meditation Centre
2 Tushita Meditation Centre
3 Regional Mountaineering Centre
4 Tibetan Children's Village
5 Church of St John in the Wilderness
6 Tibetan Institute of Performing Arts (TIPA)
11 Tsuglagkhang (Dalai Lama's Temple)
12 Dalai Lama's Residence
13 Delek Hospital
14 Tibetan Government in Exile & Library of Tibetan Works & Archives
15 Tibetan Medical & Astrological Institute
24 State Bank of India
25 HPTDC Tourist Office; Jagson Airlines
26 Taxi Stand
27 Punjab National Bank; Bank of Baroda
28 Kangra Art Museum
29 Bus Stand
30 Post Office

Places to Stay & Eat

Sood Guest House, on Cantt Rd, Kotwali Bazaar, has doubles with bath for Rs 250 (Rs 100 in the low season) and bucket hot water for Rs 5.

B Mehra Hotel, a few doors up on the opposite side of the road, has scruffy doubles (with brilliant views!) for Rs 100 with hot bath. Singles with share bath are Rs 75.

Hotel Rainbow Bridge, just west of Kotwali Bazaar, is clean and quiet, with rooms from Rs 150 to Rs 400.

Shimla Guest House, down some steps off the main thoroughfare, is another decent choice. Rooms are spacious and clean for Rs 250 with hot water bath.

HPTDC's *Hotel Dhauladhar* (☎ 24926) has standard rooms for Rs 700/500 in high/low season and better value deluxe rooms for Rs 850/550. There's a restaurant and bar here with excellent sunset views.

Cloud's End Villa (☎ 24904) is the residence of the Raja of Lambagraon-Kangra. Although inconveniently located halfway between Dharamsala and Gangchen Kyishong, it's a great place for a splurge. The five rooms range from Rs 770 to Rs 1250 and have all the classic colonial trappings.

Rising Moon Restaurant, opposite the Sood Guest House, has continental breakfasts and Tibetan cuisine. It's run by a very friendly Tibetan man.

Potala Restaurant, up a narrow flight of stairs opposite, has good veg and nonveg Tibetan and Chinese cuisine.

Getting There & Away

Buses to McLeod Ganj (Rs 9, 30 minutes) depart every half hour. The easiest place to catch one is at the top (southern) end of Kotwali Bazaar. Cramped passenger jeeps also run a shuttle service for the same price. A Maruti van taxi, from the stand on the main thoroughfare, should cost Rs 80.

There are buses to Pathankot every hour or so between 5.45 am and 5 pm (Rs 39, 3½ hours); to Mandi at 4, 5 and 11 am and 6 pm (Rs 72, six hours); and to Manali (Rs 136, 12½ hours) at 5 and 11 am, and 5.30 and 8.30 pm via Kullu (Rs 110, 10 hours).

Ordinary buses to Shimla (Rs 160 to Rs 170, 10½ hours) leave at 6.40 and 8.30 am and 9.30 pm; semideluxe leave at noon and 7.45 pm.

To Delhi, there are ordinary services at 5 and 7.20 am and 1, 5 and 8 pm, a semideluxe service at 9.30 pm and a deluxe service at 6 and 8 pm (Rs 107 ordinary, Rs 145 semideluxe, Rs 204 deluxe, 13 hours).

To Dalhousie there's an 8.30 am private service (Rs 80, six hours) which continues to Chamba (Rs 113, eight hours). To Dehra Dun there's one service at 9 pm (Rs 225, 14 hours) and to Haridwar one service at 3 pm.

To the right of the bus terminal building is a steep staircase which leads up to the vegetable market at Kotwali Bazaar.

AROUND DHARAMSALA
Norbulinka Institute

This complex, 14km from McLeod Ganj and 4km from Dharamsala, is set amid Japanese-influenced gardens with shady paths, wooden bridges across small streams and tiny waterfalls. Norbulinka has been established to teach and preserve traditional Tibetan art, such as woodcarving, thangka painting, goldsmithing and embroidery.

Nearby is the **Dolmaling Nunnery**, where the Women's Higher Studies Institute is to be, offering nuns courses at advanced levels in Buddhist philosophy.

There is a *guesthouse* at Norbulinka with doubles/suites for Rs 550/850.

To get here, catch a Yol-bound bus and ask to be let off at Sidhpur, near the Sacred Heart School. At this crossroad is a signpost to Norbulinka, from where it is about a 20 minute walk. A taxi from McLeod will cost Rs 150.

MCLEOD GANJ
☎ 01892

Before Upper Dharamsala, or McLeod Ganj (named after the Lieutenant Governor of Punjab, David McLeod), was established in the mid-1850s as a British garrison, it was the home of the seminomadic Gaddi people. There is still a sizeable number of Gaddi families in the villages around McLeod Ganj. The British developed the settlement as an important administrative centre for the Kangra region but, following a major earthquake on 4 April 1905, moved the centre to Lower Dharamsala, 10km by road below McLeod Ganj.

Today McLeod Ganj is best known as the headquarters of the Tibetan Government in Exile and is the home of the His Holiness the 14th Dalai Lama, Tenzin Gyatso. Dalai, which means the embodiment of the ocean of wisdom, is a title that has been conferred on the rulers of Tibet since the 16th century.

In 1959, the Dalai Lama fled Tibet and was granted political asylum in India. In 1989, he was awarded the Nobel Peace Prize, presented to him primarily for his endeavours to find a peaceful solution in his struggles for the liberation of Tibet.

Today McLeod Ganj is one of the most popular Himalayan destinations for foreign tourists. Accommodation can be especially tight during Losar (Tibetan New Year), the Dalai Lama's birthday (6 July) and other Tibetan festivals.

Orientation

The heart of McLeod Ganj is the bus stand. From here roads radiate to various points around the township, including the main road back down to Dharamsala, which passes en route the church of St John in the Wilderness and the cantonment area of Forsyth Ganj. Other roads lead to the villages of Dharamkot and Bhagsu.

To the south, Temple Rd proceeds to the Tsuglagkhang Temple, about 800m to the south. From there it's possible to take a short cut down to the administrative area of Gangchen Kyishong, where after a walk of some 20 minutes you'll find the Library of Tibetan Works & Archives. The other road through the bazaar, Jogibara Rd, also wends its way down to Gangchen Kyishong via the village of Jogibara.

Information

Tourist Office The new HPTDC office, opposite Bookworm, is open daily from 10 am to 1.30 pm and 2 to 5 pm.

HIMACHAL PRADESH

Money The State Bank of India, near the post office, is open weekdays 10.30 am to 1.30 pm and Saturday 10.30 to 11.30 am. It changes American Express, Thomas Cook and Visa travellers cheques in US dollars and pounds sterling only.

Post The post office is on Jogibara Rd, just past the State Bank of India. To post parcels you need to complete a customs form (in triplicate!), which you can get at the Office of Tibetan Handicrafts, opposite the State Bank of India (Rs 3). This form is not required for book postage. There are several places which offer a parcel packing service, including a couple on Jogibara Rd. Letters sent c/o poste restante, GPO McLeod Ganj are held for one month.

Telephone & Fax The telecom office (fax 21528) is up a flight of stairs behind the bus stand. You can make international calls and send faxes at government rates. In theory you can also receive faxes here but be aware that they turn the machine off at night (when most overseas faxes will arrive) and at weekends. The office is open Monday to Saturday 10 am to 6 pm. Most hotels charge around Rs 3 per minute to receive incoming international calls.

Email & Internet Access McLeod Ganj has the best Internet facilities in the Himalaya. The Tibet Youth Congress Computer Section (email tyc@del2.vsnl.net.in) will send a one page email for Rs 40, including 20 minutes' typing time. Receiving emails costs Rs 5 per page. You can use the computer (offline) for Rs 50 per hour.

At the Green Cyber Cafe (email green@chi.vsnl.net.in) you can send/receive email for Rs 25/10 per page. Internet use (for accessing Hotmail accounts) costs Rs 140 per hour or Rs 35 for 15 minutes, though this is likely to drop soon. The Himalaya Cafe and Himachal Travels also offer a similarly good service.

Travel Agencies There are numerous travel agencies in McLeod Ganj. One reli-

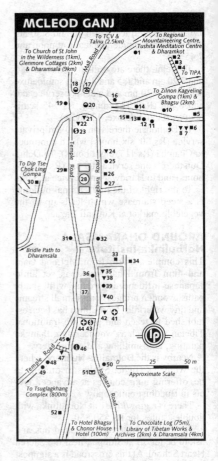

able outfit is Potala Tours & Travels (☎ 21378, fax 21427), opposite the Hotel Tibet. Potala can book air, train and bus tickets (see Getting There & Away), as well as arrange tours. Other reliable travel agencies include:

Dhauladhar Travels (☎ 21158, fax 21246) Temple Rd – arranges domestic and international air bookings.

Tibet Tours & Travels (☎ 21966, fax 21528), Temple Rd – is good for specialist and Buddhist tours as well as most other services.

MCLEOD GANJ

	PLACES TO STAY			
2	Paljor Gakyil Guest House	21	McLlo Restaurant	20	Bus Stand
3	Loselling Guest House	22	Friend's Corner	23	Punjab National Bank
4	Kalsang Guest House	24	Cafe Shambhala; Malabar	25	Video Hall
5	Tashi Khansar Guest House		Cafe	27	Tibetan Bookshop &
6	Green Hotel, Restaurant &	35	Snowland Restaurant		Information Centre
	Cyber Cafe	38	Gakyi Restaurant	28	Chorten & Prayer Wheels
13	Hotel India House	40	Aroma Restaurant	31	New Karyana Shop
15	Hotel Tibet; Take Out Bakery	42	Ashoka Restaurant; Tibetan		(Motorbike Hire)
26	Shangrila Guest House;		Handicrafts Cooperative	32	Charitrust Bookshop &
	Snowlion Guesthouse	47	Dreamland Restaurant		Handicraft Emporium
29	Kailash Hotel; Bhakto			36	Himachal Travels
	Restaurant		OTHER	37	Office of Tibetan
30	Om Guest House	1	Yeti Trekking		Handicrafts
33	Drepung Loseling Guest	9	Green Shop	39	Video Hall
	House	10	Tibetan Youth Congress	41	Dr Yeshi Dhonden's Clinic
34	Tibetan Ashoka Guest House	11	Branch Security & Tibetan	43	State Bank of India
52	Surya Resorts; Hotel Natraj;		Welfare Offices	44	Dr Lobsang Dolma Clinic
	Hotel Him Queen	12	Laundry	45	Bookworm
		14	Potala Tours & Travels	46	HPTDC Tourist Office
	PLACES TO EAT	16	Tara Herbal Gift Shop	48	Tibet Tours & Travels
7	Himalaya Cafe	17	Telecom Office	49	Youtse Bookshop
8	Nick's Italian Kitchen	18	Taxi Stand	50	Pema Youdon
		19	Nowrogee & Son Store	51	Post Office

Himachal Travels (☎ 21428, fax 21528, email katoch@vsnl.com), Jogibara Rd– is good for train and local and deluxe bus tickets. Will reconfirm international air tickets for Rs 100, or the cost of the telephone call plus Rs 50. They can book local bus tickets for a Rs 30 service charge. Internet connection is Rs 100 per hour.

Trekking Outfits Eagle Height Trekkers & Travellers can organise porters and guides, as well as arrange treks in the Kullu, Chamba, Lahaul and Spiti valleys and Ladakh from US$40 per day. At the time of writing they were in the process of moving offices so you will have to check on their location.

Yeti Trekking (☎ 21887, fax 21578) also arranges tailor-made treks to most areas, with accommodation en route in huts and houses. They can be found in a fine old building, reached through a gate off the Dharamkot road.

Regional Mountaineering Centre This centre (☎ 21787) is about 15 minutes' walk north of McLeod on the Dharamkot road. You can get advice here on treks and mountaineering in the Chamba and Kangra valleys, and there's a useful list of registered local guides and porters. It's a good idea to advise the centre if you are planning a treks.

Basic equipment can be hired, but only if it's not being used by a group. You can also purchase Survey of India trekking maps (Rs 15) and the paperback *Treks & Passes of Dhauladhar & Pir Panjal* (Rs 150) by SR Saini, the centre's director.

Bookshops There's an excellent selection of new books at Bookworm, up the road to the right of the State Bank of India. The Tibetan Bookshop & Information Centre on Jogibara Rd also has a comprehensive selection of books as well as government publications on the Tibetan struggle for independence and Tibetan Buddhism. The nearby Charitrust Bookshop has probably the town's best collection of books on Tibetan travel, history and Buddhism. Youtse Bookshop, on Temple Rd, is also worth a look.

Tibetan Organisations McLeod Ganj has numerous offices and organisations concerned with Tibetan affairs and the welfare of the refugee community. These include

HIMACHAL PRADESH

the Tibetan Welfare Office, the Refugee Reception Centre, Tibetan Youth Congress, Tibetan Children's Village (TCV) and the Tibetan Women's Association. Interested visitors are welcome at many of these.

All offices and institutions are open weekdays 9 am to 5 pm (closed for lunch 1 to 2 pm in summer, and noon to 1 pm in winter); all are closed on Tibetan holidays and three Indian national holidays (26 January, 15 August and 2 October).

Tibetan Publications *Contact* is a free local magazine which has a useful 'what's on' listing, plus information on local courses and volunteer work. Other journals published in McLeod include the *Tibetan Bulletin* and *Rangzen* (Freedom), published by the Tibetan Youth Congress.

Laundry Several laundries on the Bhagsu road, such as Sky Laundry and Quick Pick Laundry, offer a same-day service if you get your clothes to them before 10 am.

Medical Services Delek Hospital (☎ 22053) in Gangchen Kyishong often has volunteer western doctors on staff. For Tibetan medicine try Dr Yeshi Dhonden's clinic or the Dr Lobsang Dolma Khangsar Clinic, both near the State Bank of India.

Tsuglagkhang Complex

This complex, five minutes' walk south of McLeod Ganj, comprises the official residence of the Dalai Lama, as well as the Namgyal Monastery, bookshop and cafe and the Tsuglagkhang itself.

The **Tsuglagkhang**, or Central Chapel, is the exiled government's equivalent of the Jokhang Temple in Lhasa and as such is the most important Buddhist monument in McLeod Ganj. Although a relatively modest structure, it enshrines three magnificent images, including an enormous 3m-high gilt statue of Sakyamuni Buddha. To the left of this (and facing Tibet) are statues of Avalokitesvara (Tibetan: Chenresig), the Tibetan deity of compassion, of whom the Dalai Lama is considered an incarnation, and Pad-

masambhava (Tibetan: Guru Rinpoche), the Indian scholar who introduced Buddhism and Tantric teachings to Tibet in the 8th century. Inside the Avalokitesvara statue are several relics rescued from the Jokhang Temple during the Cultural Revolution.

Also housed in the temple is a collection of sacred texts known as the *Kangyur*, which are based on the teachings of the Buddha, as well as the *Tangyur*, which are translations of commentaries based on the Buddha's teachings. The mural to the side depicts the trio of ancient Tibetan kings who oversaw the introduction of Buddhism into Tibet.

Next to the Tsuglagkhang is the **Kalachakra Temple**, built in 1992, which houses a stunning mural of the Kalachakra (Wheel of Time) mandala. Sand mandalas are created here annually on the 5th day of the third Tibetan month. Photography is allowed in the Tsuglagkhang, but not the Kalachakra Temple.

The remaining buildings form the **Namgyal Gompa**, where it is possible to watch monks debate most afternoons, sealing points of logic with a great flourish and a clap of the hands.

Most Tibetan pilgrims make a *kora* (circuit) of the Tsuglagkhang complex. Take the road to the left, past the entrance to the temple, and after a few minutes a small path leads off to the right, eventually looping all the way around the Dalai Lama's residence back to the entrance to the temple. The path is flanked by colourful mani stones and prayer flags, and at one section there is a series of small prayer wheels. The kora should be made in a clockwise direction only.

Dip Tse-Chok Ling Gompa

This beautiful little gompa is at the bottom of a steep track, which leads off the lane past the Om Guest House. The main *dukhang* (prayer hall) houses an image of Sakyamuni, and two enormous goat-skin drums made by monks at the gompa. Also here are some superb butter sculptures, made during Losar and destroyed the following year. Fine and detailed sand mandalas are also made here.

An Audience with His Holiness the Dalai Lama

The Dalai Lama is so much in demand that a private audience is now very difficult to arrange. You're much more likely to be able to meet him face to face by attending a public audience. Contact the Branch Security Office in McLeod Ganj to find out when the next public audience is being held. You need to register your name two to three days in advance and your passport details are required. On the day of the audience, it's best to get to the temple about an hour in advance to get through the security checks. Cameras, bags and backpacks are strictly prohibited, and you should wear respectable dress and carry your passport.

Meeting this 14th incarnation of Chenresig, Tibetan Buddhism's deity of Universal Compassion, is no ordinary event. Not so much because of his title, nor even because of the high degree of reverence in which he is held by the Tibetan people; but more because of how it feels to be in his company. As an American friend put it: 'When you look at him, he is the size of a normal human being; but when you look away; you realise that his presence is filling the whole room'.

After waiting, strangely nervous, in the anteroom, we were ushered into the reception room for our audience with His Holiness, which seemed to speed by in a flash. However, several strong impressions remain, including the way in which he gives his whole attention to questions. He really listens, and pauses before replying, to give consideration to the subject matter. He responds rather than reacts to the issue under discussion. There is a wisdom in his thinking which comes through clearly in his words, filled as they are with common sense and realism.

I remember his direct and friendly gaze, his firm handshake, and an almost palpable sense of compassion. He also has a superb sense of humour, often remarked upon by those who meet him. He laughs often and easily – and what a laugh! He throws back his head to release a deep, thorough chuckle which rises from his abdomen and expresses pure mirth. It is kind laughter, and highly infectious.

As our audience came to a close, he accompanied us to the door. With each of us in turn, he took one of our hands in both of his. Bowing slightly over the joined hands, he looked up into our faces and beamed. Following this farewell, we seemed to be walking inches above the streets of McLeod Ganj. And we just couldn't stop smiling.

Vyvyan Cayley

Tibetan Institute of Performing Arts

This institute promotes the study and performance of the Tibetan performing arts to ensure the preservation of Tibet's traditional cultural heritage. The most important of the arts taught and practised at the institute is traditional *lhamo* (Tibetan opera). A small museum has recently opened at the site.

Library of Tibetan Works & Archives

The library, halfway between Dharamsala and McLeod at Gangchen Kyishong (take the short cut down past the Dalai Lama's temple, is the repository of Tibet's rich literary heritage. It contains about 40% of Tibet's original manuscripts, as well as an excellent general reference library, and is open to all.

There's also a **Tibetan Cultural Museum** on the 1st floor, with some excellent exhibits including fine statues, rare Tibetan stamps and a medal from the Younghusband mission to Lhasa. Entry costs Rs 5.

Also worth a visit near the library complex is the **Nechung Monastery**, home to the Tibetan state oracle.

Tibetan Medical & Astrological Institute

This institute is at Gangchen Kyishong, about five minutes' walk below the main entrance to the library area. There's a museum, library, research unit and a college at which Tibetan medicine and astrology is taught. It's possible to have a life horoscope prepared for US$30.

The museum (opened on request) has a well displayed exhibition of materials used in Tibetan medicines.

St John in the Wilderness

Dharamsala was originally a British hill resort, and one of the most poignant memories of that era is the pretty church of St John in the Wilderness. It's only a short distance north of McLeod on the main road to Dharamsala.

Hikes

There are many fine walks and even finer views around McLeod Ganj. The sheer rock wall of the Dhaula Dhar Range rises behind the township. Interesting walks include the 2km stroll east to **Bhagsu** and the 3km walk north-east to the little village of **Dharamkot**, where there are fine views. From Dharamkot, you can continue east down to Bhagsu and walk back to McLeod along the main Bhagsu road.

An 8km trek from McLeod Ganj will bring you to **Triund** (2827m) at the foot of the Dhaula Dhar. It's a steep but straightforward

ascent, with the path veering off to the right across scree just beyond Dharamkot. The views of the Dhaula Dhar from here are stunning. It's another 5km to the snow line at **Ilaqa** where there's a *Forest Rest House* (Rs 200). From Ilaqa, it's possible to continue over the Indrahar Pass to the Chamba Valley.

Courses
Buddhist Philosophy Courses About 20 minutes' walk above McLeod is the Tushita Meditation Centre. One path heads off to the right near a small white *chörten* just beyond the Regional Mountaineering Centre, another leads from Dharamkot village. The centre has facilities for retreats, as well as offering a monthly 11 day introductory course in Buddhist philosophy led by western and Tibetan teachers. There is a small library at Tushita, which is open to students and non-students, and there are books on Buddhism for sale. Tuition, food and accommodation costs around Rs 240 per day. The office (☎ 21866) is open Monday to Saturday 9.30 to 11.30 am and 1 to 4.30 pm.

Behind Tushita is the new Dhamma Sikhara Vipassana Meditation Centre (☎ 21309), which offers 10-day courses in Indian Hinayana Buddhism.

Down at the library (☎ 22467) in Gangchen Kyishong, classes in specific aspects of Buddhist philosophy are led by Tibetan lamas and translated into English. Subjects are divided into two-week chunks, as outlined in the prospectus available from reception. They take place weekdays between 9 and 11 am, and cost Rs 100 per month, plus Rs 50 registration. It's possible to attend the first class for free.

Tibetan Language Courses Pema Youdon is a friendly Tibetan woman who teaches Tibetan language from her home opposite the post office. The Kelsang Guest House offers private language tuition for Rs 80 per hour.

It's also possible to study Tibetan at the Library of Tibetan Works & Archives. Classes are held on weekdays and are divided into terms of three months. Beginner and advanced courses both cost Rs 200 per month, plus Rs 50 registration.

Voluntary Work

If you're interested in teaching English or computer skills to newly arrived refugees, check notice boards at the Library of Tibetan Works & Archives, as well as looking in *Contact* magazine.

Special Events

Each April TIPA convenes an **opera festival**, which includes folk dancing and contemporary and historical plays. There is also a three day **TIPA Anniversary Festival** from 27 May, celebrating the foundation of TIPA. Details of these and other performances are posted around McLeod Ganj.

Tibetan New Year (Losar) is a great time to be in McLeod Ganj, when the Dalai Lama gives week-long teachings.

Organised Tours

Local operators have devised the following fixed-rate taxi tours to points of interest around McLeod Ganj and in the Kangra Valley:

* Bhagsunath Temple, Tsuglagkhang, Dal Lake, St John's Church & Talnu (Rs 180, three hours)
* Norbulinka, Chinmaya ashram at Tapovan, Chamunda Devi, Kangra & Jawalamukhi temple (Rs 900, eight hours)
* Norbulinka, Tapovan, Chamunda Devi, Palampur & Baijnath (Rs 950, eight hours)

Places to Stay – Budget

Kalsang Guest House (☎ 21709), on the TIPA road, is very popular with travellers. There's a wide range of rooms: tiny singles/doubles with share bath are Rs 45/85; doubles with hot showers (but no external windows) are Rs 135 to Rs 180; and rooms with great views upstairs are Rs 275. You can get a hot shower in the share bathroom for Rs 10, but 30 minutes advance notice is required. It's possible to store bags here if you are going on a trek.

Loselling Guest House, just above the Kalsang, has small but clean doubles with bath for Rs 180 and singles with share bath for Rs 60 (a hot shower costs Rs 10).

Paljor Gakyil Guest House (☎ 21443), above the Loselling, has doubles with share bath for Rs 70, and doubles with bath from Rs 110 to Rs 132 (cold water) or Rs 155 to Rs 220 (hot water). Top floor rooms with a view cost Rs 275.

Green Hotel (☎ 21000), on the Bhagsu road, is a long-time favourite with travellers. Small spartan rooms with share bath cost Rs 55 to Rs 80, or Rs 150/250 with attached cold/hot bath. Deluxe rooms are overpriced at Rs 350. Some rooms have great valley views, and there's a good restaurant here.

Tashi Khansar Guest House, opposite the Green, has basic singles with common hot bath for Rs 70, and singles/doubles with bath for Rs 120/135, some with excellent views.

Kailash Hotel (☎ 21044), opposite the chörten, has doubles/triples for Rs 70/80, all with share bath (24 hour hot water). Rooms at the back have great views, but are pretty rustic.

Om Guest House (☎ 24313), on a path leading down from the bus stand behind the Kailash, has ground floor doubles with share bath for Rs 100, and nicer upper floor rooms for Rs 225 or Rs 250 with great valley views. There's a good restaurant but this means that the rooms can be noisy in the evening.

Shangrila Guest House, on the other side of the chörten, has doubles with share bath (bucket hot water) for Rs 55.

Snow Lion Guest House, next door, is friendly and has clean, well-maintained rooms with hot water bath for Rs 150, or Rs 200 with private balcony and good views.

Drepung Loselling Guest House (☎ 23187), down an alley off Jogbira Rd, is popular with long-term volunteers. It has doubles with cold/hot bath for Rs 150/190, or Rs 250 with hot bath and breakfast.

Tibetan Ashoka Guest House (☎ 21763), next door, has a range of dingy ground floor rooms from Rs 55 to Rs 162, and brighter top floor rooms for Rs 275 and Rs 330.

Ladies Venture (☎ 21559), down Jogibara Rd past the Chocolate Log (see Places to Eat), is a very quiet and friendly place.

Rooms with bath but no view are Rs 150/225; comfortable rooms with a view cost Rs 300 and Rs 400. Dorms cost Rs 50 but are often full.

It's possible to stay at the *Zilnon Kagyeling Nyingmapa Gompa Guesthouse*, about 1km from McLeod on the Bhagsu road. Rooms are Rs 60, and a hot shower is Rs 10. There is a rooftop cafe here.

Places to Stay – Mid-Range & Top End
Hotel Tibet (☎ 21587, fax 21327), a few steps from the bus stand on the Bhagsu road, has standard doubles for Rs 450, semideluxe doubles for Rs 500, and deluxe rooms for Rs 800. All rooms are carpeted and have cable TV and bath. There's a very good restaurant and bar here.

Hotel India House (☎ 21144) is bright, comfortable and a good option, though it lacks the Tibetan touch. Rooms cost Rs 800, Rs 1100 and Rs 1400 and most have a balcony with excellent views.

There are a few other large Indian-run hotels on the road past Bookworm. The *Hotel Natraj* (☎ 21574) has doubles for Rs 400 and Rs 600 without views. Deluxe rooms with good views are Rs 800. Farther along is the *Hotel Him Queen* (☎ 21184) and *Surya Resorts* (☎ 21418) which have rooms from Rs 750 to Rs 1200. You should be able to negotiate a good discount in the low season. HPTDC's *Hotel Bhagsu* (☎ 21091), at the end of this road, has a range of good doubles from Rs 600 to Rs 1500 (half this in low season).

Chonor House Hotel (☎ 21006, fax 21468) is a very stylish place owned by the Norbulinka Institute. Doubles range from Rs 1300 to Rs 1700 (with Rs 200 discount for singles) and are beautifully decorated with traditional Tibetan artefacts. There's also a good Tibetan restaurant and bakery here. Bookings are recommended.

About 2km above McLeod along a track which branches off the main Dharamsala road is *Glenmore Cottages* (☎ 21010), which has comfortable accommodation in five peacefully located cottages. Rates range from Rs 990 to Rs 2250 with hot bath and heating.

Places to Eat
Green Hotel has a very popular restaurant, with a range of excellent home-made cakes (the carrot cake is recommended), as well as vegetarian dishes like spinach quiche. It's also a good place for breakfast.

The nearby *Himalaya Cafe* also has good food and a wonderful rooftop balcony with views over the plains, though the service is very slow. You can get filter coffee here and refill your bottle with boiled and filtered water for Rs 5.

Nick's Italian Kitchen next door has good cakes, quiches and Italian food.

Hotel Tibet has one of the best restaurants in town and features Tibetan, Chinese and Indian cuisine. There's also a convivial bar here.

McLlo Restaurant, right above the bus stand, has an extensive menu, good food and a bar, though it's a little overpriced.

Friend's Corner, nearby, serves excellent Chinese food and prices are reasonable for the large portions.

Moving south, beneath the Kailash Hotel is the *Bhakto Restaurant*, which has cheap mutton *momos* and noodle soup at lunchtime only.

Malabar Cafe, on the opposite side of the chörten, is a pleasant little place serving good Indian, Chinese and continental cuisine. The nearby *Cafe Shambhala* is also popular.

Gakyi Restaurant, also on Jogibara Rd, serves the best special muesli in town (Rs 35) and has a good range of healthy vegetarian food such as tofu and brown rice. The nearby *Snowland Restaurant* is recommended for cheap and tasty Tibetan food.

Ashoka Restaurant, on Jogibara Rd, has the best Indian food in town. The tandoori chicken (Rs 70 for a half portion) and chicken Mughlai (Rs 100) are excellent and there are also continental dishes such as pizza (Rs 40) and spaghetti. Nearby is the *Aroma Restaurant* which offers cheap Israeli cuisine.

Another popular place is the restaurant at the *Om Guest House*. The vegie burger here is served with salad, a banana and chips, and is quite good. There's also a good sound system, plus spectacular sunset views.

Dreamland Restaurant, down a staircase to the right past Bookworm, has good salads and Tibetan and Chinese cuisine.

The restaurant at the *Hotel Bhagsu* is pricier but has very good food and cold beers. On sunny days, tables are set up in the gardens, and you can eat outside.

McLeod Ganj is a godsend for anyone with a longing for coffee and cake. The *Chocolate Log*, a few minutes' walk down past the post office on Jogibara Rd, is an old favourite serving western dishes such as pizza and various types of cakes.

Take Out is a place beneath the Hotel Tibet where you can buy freshly baked bread, cakes and doughnuts. The *Snow Lion Guest House* also serves great cakes and good Tibetan food.

Entertainment

There are several video halls in the town centre on Jogibara Rd. They show new releases and documentaries on Tibet all day and evening, with the program posted out the front. Tickets are Rs 5 to Rs 10.

Shopping

Tibetan textiles such as bags, *chubas* (dresses worn by Tibetan women), hats and trousers can be found at the Office of Tibetan Handicrafts, just north of the State Bank of India. Here you can have a chuba made to order with your own fabric (Rs 80), or with fabric supplied by the centre (Rs 350 to Rs 450).

Just opposite is the Tibetan Handicrafts Cooperative. The co-op employs about 145 people, many of them newly arrived refugees, in the weaving of Tibetan carpets. Fine New Zealand wool carpets, with 90 knots per sq inch cost Rs 4972 per sq m, while those of 48 knots per sq inch are Rs 2603 per sq m, depending on the design. The society can pack and post purchases home, and visitors are welcome to watch the carpet makers at work on traditional looms.

Cleaning Upper Dharamsala

This project is an innovation of the Welfare Office and a young Dutch man who helped raise money for the project. It consists of four 'green workers' – generally new arrivals from Tibet – who collect about 40 to 50kg of recyclable goods from homes and businesses around McLeod each day, including paper, glass, metals and plastics, which are then sold.

Another initiative under the Welfare Office is the Green Shop, on the Bhagsu road. This shop sells rechargeable batteries, hand-painted T-shirts, natural cosmetics and boiled and filtered water. In the low season, 25 to 30 bottles of water are sold each day. In the high season, this increases to 100 to 120 bottles per day. Posters on environmental issues, in Hindi, have been posted in villages around McLeod, and the project officers plan to work in cooperation with the Indian community.

Tourists can support the project and help promote a cleaner McLeod by having their mineral-water bottles refilled at the Green Shop, and by encouraging hotel owners to separate garbage and give it to the green workers, rather than throwing it on dumps.

Stitches of Time, farther downhill on Temple Rd, is run by the Tibetan Women's Association, and also makes chubas and other clothes to order.

Tara Herbal Gift Shop, near the bus stand, has traditional Tibetan herbal incense and books on Tibetan medicine. The Green Shop, on the Bhagsu road, has hand-painted T-shirts and recycled handmade paper.

Getting There & Away

Air Gaggal airport, 15km south of Dharamsala, currently has no flights but services might soon resume to Delhi, Kullu and/or Shimla, so check at travel agencies.

Bus The Himachal Roadways Transport Corporation (HRTC) booking office is at the bus stand. There's a daily bus to Manali at 5 am (Rs 100, 11 hours) and 6 pm (Rs 125) and to Dehra Dun at 7.30 pm (Rs 225, 12 hours). The deluxe service to Delhi leaves at 6 pm (Rs 300, 12 hours). Buses to Pathankot (Rs 47, four hours) leave at 9, 10 and 11 am and 4 pm. For other services you'll have to head down to Dharamsala.

Potala Tours & Travels, opposite the Hotel Tibet, has a deluxe service to Delhi, which leaves at 6 pm (Rs 350, 12 hours). Numerous other agencies offer deluxe buses. When booking a bus to Delhi take care to check that it goes to Connaught Place and/or Parharganj, not just the Inter State Bus Station at Kashmir Gate. Himachal Travels books buses to Manali (Rs 250) and Leh (Rs 1050). The Leh bus departs McLeod at 9 pm, arrives at Manali at 6 am, then departs Manali at 7 am, arriving at Leh the following evening (with an overnight stop en route) at 5 pm.

Himachal Travels can also book ordinary buses departing from Dharamsala, for a charge of around Rs 25 per ticket.

There are also buses for the 40 minute trip down to Dharamsala (Rs 9), departing every 30 minutes between 4.15 am and 8.30 pm. Cramped passenger jeeps also run when full for the same price.

Train Many travel agencies will book train tickets for services out of Pathankot, down on the plains in the Punjab (see Pathankot in the Punjab & Haryana chapter). It's worth booking as early as possible, preferably a week in advance. Generally, a Rs 75 booking fee is levied. There's a train booking office at the bus stand in Dharamsala, but it has only a tiny quota of tickets. It's only open between 10 and 11 am, and is closed on Sunday.

The closest train stations to McLeod are Kangra and Nagrota, both around 20km south of Dharamsala. Both are on the narrow-gauge line that connects Pathankot with the small settlement of Jogindernagar, 58km north-west of Mandi. It's a slow, five hour haul between Nagrota and Pathankot – the bus is much faster – but if you have the

time, it's worthwhile taking the scenic four hour trip east from Nagrota to Jogindernagar. There are six trains a day to Jogindernagar, passing through Palampur (one hour) and Baijnath (two hours).

Taxi McLeod's taxi stand (☎ 21034) is next to the bus station. A taxi to Pathankot is around Rs 800. To hire a taxi for the day, covering less than 80km, costs Rs 700.

Auto-Rickshaws to Bhagsu costs Rs 35. Taxis cost Rs 50 to Gangchen Kyishong, Rs 80 to Dharamsala's Kotwali Bazaar and Rs 90 to Dharamsala bus station.

AROUND MCLEOD GANJ
Dusallan
Many travellers planning to stay long-term, rent rooms from villagers in the settlements around McLeod Ganj. Between McLeod and Bhagsu, below the Bhagsu road (take the path beside the Green Hotel) is the tiny village of Dusallan. Several places rent rooms but you'll have to ask around. Rates are about Rs 40 per day, including a bucket of hot water, and some rooms have magnificent views down over the terraced fields.

Bhagsu
Two kilometres east of McLeod is the village of Bhagsu, or Bhagsunath, which has springs and a small Shiva temple built by the Raja of Kangra in the 16th century. There's also a waterfall here.

Hotel Triund (☎ 21122), on the left as you enter Bhagsu, has deluxe carpeted rooms with hot water for Rs 700, superdeluxe rooms for Rs 800 and VIP suites for Rs 995.

Hotel Meghavan is another big hotel catering largely to Indian tourists; rooms cost from Rs 600 to Rs 800.

Pink White Guest House nearby has good upper floor rooms with balcony and views for around Rs 150 to Rs 250.

If you take the path leading uphill from the main bus stop you come to three guesthouses aimed squarely at western backpackers. *Samgyal Guest House* has rooms with common/shared/bath for Rs 150/250 and the **Seven Seas Lodge** has clean and spacious marble-clad rooms for Rs 150 (ground floor) and Rs 200 (1st floor). Farther uphill is the **Omni Guest House**, with basic but pleasant rooms for Rs 80. There's a decent restaurant here and a free common hot shower.

Trimurti Restaurant has good, cheap vegetarian food and there's a notice board detailing local yoga and massage courses.

HPTDC's **Cafe Jaldhara** nearby offers southern Indian dishes. The **Shiva Cafe**, above the waterfall in Bhagsu, is a good spot for a chai.

SOUTH & WEST OF DHARAMSALA

Kangra
☎ 01892

There is little to see in this ancient town, 18km south of Dharamsala, but at one time it was a place of considerable importance as the seat of the Chand dynasty, which ruled over the princely state of Kangra. The famous **temple of Bajreshwari Devi** was of such legendary wealth that every invader worth their salt took time to sack it. Mahmud of Ghazni carted off a fabulous fortune in gold, silver and jewellery in 1009. In 1360 it was plundered once again by Tughlaq but it was still able to recover and, in Jehangir's reign, was paved in plates of pure silver. The temple is in the bazaar, at the end of a labyrinthine series of alleyways flanked with stalls selling *prasaad*.

The British took possession of the ancient fort of Kangra, 2.5km south of modern Kangra, and established a garrison. The disastrous earthquake that shook the valley in 1905 destroyed the fort and the temple, though the latter has since been rebuilt.

Nagar Kot, the ancient fort, is a beautiful place, perched high on a windswept ridge overlooking the confluence of the Manjhi and Baner rivers. It can be reached from Kangra by auto-rickshaw (Rs 35).

Places to Stay *Hotel Maurya* (☎ 65875), between the bus station and town centre, has singles for Rs 150, and doubles for Rs 250 and Rs 350, all with bath.

Jai Hotel (☎ 65568) is farther down Dharamsala Rd, and has rooms for Rs 100 and Rs 150.

Getting There & Away Kangra's bus stand is 1.5km north of the bazaar along Dharamsala Rd. There are buses to Dharamsala every 15 minutes (Rs 9, 45 minutes) and to Palampur every 20 minutes. Kangra has two train stations: Kangra station, 3km south of town, and Kangra Mandir station, 3km east and 500m from the nearest road. A taxi from McLeod Ganj to Kangra will cost Rs 300 (Rs 450 return).

Masrur

South-west of Dharamsala, via Gaggal, is the small settlement of Masrur, which has 15 Indo-Aryan style rock-cut temples which were hewn from the sandstone cliffs in the 10th century. They are partly ruined but still show their relationship to the better known and much larger temples at Ellora in Maharashtra. The temple area is a beautiful, peaceful place, fronted by a small artificial lake and a pleasant lawn compound. The sculptures are badly eroded, but three crude statues of Sita, Rama and Lakshmi can still be made out in the dimly lit sanctum of the central temple. Several more badly damaged sculptures can be seen leaning against the low wall by the lake in front of the temples.

There are buses to Masrur from Kangra, but from Dharamsala you'll probably have to change at Gaggal. A taxi from McLeod Ganj will charge around Rs 550 one way (Rs 700 return) and the road affords some magnificent views.

Jawalamukhi

Thirty-four kilometres south of Kangra is the temple of Jawalamukhi, the goddess of light. Pilgrims descend into a tiny square chamber where a priest, while intoning a blessing on their behalf, ignites natural gas emanating from a copper pipe, from which a blue flame, worshipped as the manifestation of the goddess, briefly flares. The temple is one of the most sacred sites in the Kangra Valley, and is topped by a golden dome and spire, the

HIMACHAL PRADESH

legacies of Ranjit Singh and the Mughal emperor Akbar.

HPTDC's **Hotel Jawalaji** (☎ 01970-22280) has doubles with bath from Rs 425 to Rs 850. Dorm beds are Rs 50. There's a 30% low-season discount.

Buses to Dharamsala (Rs 30) leave throughout the day from the stand below the road leading up to the temple.

Nurpur
Only 24km from Pathankot, on the Dharamsala road, this town was named by Jehangir in honour of his wife Nurjahan. Nurpur Fort is now in ruins, but still has some finely carved reliefs. A ruined temple dedicated to Krishna, also finely carved, stands within the fort, which looms over the main road.

There's a **PWD Rest House** (☎ 01893-2009) with large, very clean double rooms for Rs 100.

Chamba Valley

Separated from the Kangra Valley to the south by the high Dhaula Dhar Range and the remote Pattan Valley to the north by the Pir Panjal Range is the beautiful Chamba Valley, through which flows the Ravi River. For over 1000 years this region formed the princely state of Chamba, the most ancient state in northern India. Few travellers find their way here, and of those that do, even fewer continue down the valley beyond the hill station of Dalhousie. The valley is renowned for its fine *shikhara* temples, with excellent examples in the beautiful town of Chamba, 56km from Dalhousie, and at the ancient capital of Brahmaur, 65km farther down the valley to the southeast. Brahmaur is also the starting point for some fine treks, including that to the sacred lake of Manimahesh, 28km away.

DALHOUSIE
☎ 01899 • pop 10,100
Sprawling over five hills at around 2000m, Dalhousie was, in the British era, a sort of 'second string' hill station, mainly used by people who lived in Lahore. It was acquired from the Raja of Chamba by the British and was named after Lord Dalhousie, then viceroy of India, by David McLeod (after whom McLeod Ganj was named). Dalhousie is famous for its public schools.

Dalhousie is popular with Punjabi tourists and finding accommodation during the early summer and peak Indian holiday periods can be difficult. The high season runs from mid-April to mid-July, mid-September to mid-November and mid-December to early January.

Orientation
Dalhousie is quite spread out. Most of the shops are clustered around Gandhi Chowk, about a 15 minute walk up from the bus stand. Gandhi Chowk is connected to Subhash Chowk (also with a high concentration of hotels and restaurants) by The Mall – this is actually two roads, the highest of which is a pedestrian-only road locally known as Garam Sarak (Hot Rd) as it receives more sunshine than the other road, known as Thandi Sarak (Cold Rd). A road also connects the bus stand with Subhash Chowk, a steep five minute uphill walk.

Be careful when walking along Garam Sarak at night. It's badly lit with some parts in pitch darkness. Bring a torch (flashlight).

There are many registered porters around the bus stand. In the low season, they charge Rs 20 between the bus stand and Gandhi Chowk, and Rs 10 to Subhash Chowk. Expect to pay double in high season.

Information
Tourist Office The tourist office (☎ 42136) is on the top floor of the telegraph office, just below the bus stand. It's open Monday to Saturday 10 am to 5 pm; Sunday (during the tourist season) 10 am to 1 pm. During the season it runs full-day tours to points of interest around Dalhousie (including Khajiar and Chamba) for Rs 100.

Money The Punjab National Bank is about a five minute walk from Subhash Chowk, next to the Aroma-n-Claire Hotel. It's the only bank that exchanges travellers cheques, but there are no foreign transactions on Wednesday.

Travel Agencies Span Tours & Travels (☎ 40281, fax 40341) can book luxury coaches to Delhi, Manali and Dharamsala, and can also make train and air reservations. Trek-n-Travels (☎ 40277), nearby can arrange guides/porters for around Rs 200/125 per day and has some trekking gear for hire.

Newsagencies English-language newspapers are available at the bus stand, and at Dayal News Agency on Gandhi Chowk.

Emergency For police assistance call ☎ 42126; for medical attention call the Civil Hospital ☎ 42125.

Things to See & Do

With its dense forest, old British houses and thriving Tibetan community, Dalhousie can be a good place to spend a few days.

Midway along Garam Sarak, between Gandhi and Subhash chowks, you'll pass brightly painted low-relief pictures of Tibetan deities, including Padmasambhava and Avalokitesvara, as well as Tibetan script bearing the sacred mantra 'Om Mani Padmi Hum'.

Close to Gandhi Chowk is a rock painting of Tara Devi, and a little shrine has been constructed here.

There's a small **Tibetan market** just above the bus stand.

Kalatope Wildlife Sanctuary is 8.5km from Gandhi Chowk. The sanctuary is home to a variety of species including black bear and barking deer, as well as an abundant birdlife. There's a checkpoint at **Lakkar Mandi**, on the perimeter of the sanctuary, which has fine mountain views. It's possible to get a taxi here (Rs 150 return), and walk 3km into the sanctuary. To take a vehicle into the sanctuary, you require a permit from the district forest officer (DFO) in Chamba.

From April until November, Lakkar Mandi is home to an itinerant group of villagers who originally hail from Mandi, in the Kangra Valley. Their main source of income is derived from preparing charcoal, which they sell to the hotels in Dalhousie.

One leisurely stroll can take you from Subash Chowk down Court Rd, and back via Patryn Rd. En route you'll pass **DC Khanna & Sons**, a great old-fashioned store. A more rigorous walk is the Upper Bakrota Round, about 5km from Gandhi Chowk.

Places to Stay – Budget

Dalhousie has over 50 hotels, although a fair number of them have a run-down, left-by-the-Raj feel to them. Prices given below are for high season but remember that most give a 50% discount whenever business is quiet.

The *youth hostel* (☎ 42189), rather run-down but friendly, is a five minute walk from the bus stand. Rates remain constant all year. For Rs 20 (Rs 40 for nonmembers) you can get a bit of foam on the dorm floor, or there are doubles with bath for Rs 80 (Rs 100 for nonmembers). The hostel is closed between 10 am and 5 pm.

Hotel Satpushp (☎ 42346), near the bus stand, has cheap rooms from Rs 100 to Rs 200, all with hot bath.

Hotel Goher (☎ 42253), just off Subhash Chowk, has dingy singles with cold water bath for Rs 200, but nice bright doubles with hot water from Rs 400 to Rs 500. There's a 50% discount in the low season.

Hotel Crags (☎ 42124) is a five minute walk along Garam Sarak, just below the road. It has front-facing doubles for Rs 200 and huge doubles for Rs 400 to Rs 600, with a 50% discount most of the time. All rooms have hot water bath. It's a somewhat dilapidated place, but it's in a quiet location and has a nice sitting area with fine views.

Farther around Garam Sarak, near Ghandi Chowk, is a cluster of guesthouses including the *Arti*, *Jasmine* and *Monal* where you can get a comfortable room with good views for Rs 150 to Rs 250.

Places to Stay – Mid-Range

Aroma-n-Claire Hotel (☎ 42199) is an atmospheric hotel on Court Rd, about a five minutes walk south of Subhash Chowk.

HIMACHAL PRADESH

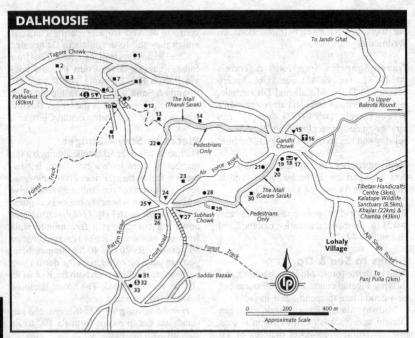

DALHOUSIE

It's slightly ramshackle, but has wonderful eclectic decorations and rooms of all shapes and sizes from Rs 600 to Rs 1200.

HPTDC's *Hotel Geetanjali* (☎ 42155), just off Thandi Sarak, is a lovely, if slightly run-down, old building. Enormous doubles with hot water bath cost Rs 500 to Rs 650.

Hotel Shangrila (☎ 42314), nearby, has a range of doubles from Rs 800 to Rs 1000 and singles for Rs 500. All rooms have views of the Pir Panjal and the staff are friendly and helpful.

Hotel Grand View (☎ 42623), just above the bus stand, has doubles for Rs 1000, and double suites for Rs 1300. This is a beautifully maintained place and better value than other hotels in the same price category.

Nearby, with less character, is the *Hotel Mount View* (☎ 42120), which has doubles for Rs 1000, Rs 1200 and Rs 1400. Both hotels offer a 30% low-season discount.

HPTDC's new *Hotel Manimahesh*, near the youth hostel, should open in 1999.

There's a *Forest Rest House* in the Kalatope Wildlife Sanctuary, to reserve a room you'll need to contact the district forest officer in Chamba (☎ 01899-42639).

Places to Eat

The *Restaurant Preet Palace,* on Subhash Chowk, features reasonably priced Mughlai, Kashmiri and Chinese cuisine. *Moti Mahal Restaurant*, nearby, serves southern Indian food and also has a bar.

Better value are the dhabas just off Subhash Chowk. Best of the lot is probably the *Amritsari Dhaba*, though the *Sher-e-Punjab* and *Alishan* dhabas are also worth checking out. Dalhousie's dhabas are a cut above the usual Indian dhaba.

Lovely Restaurant, at Gandhi Chowk, is open all year, and there's a sun terrace with

DALHOUSIE

PLACES TO STAY
2   Youth Hostel
3   Hotel Manimahesh
7   Hotel Mount View
8   Hotel Grand View
11 Hotel Satpushp
13 HPTDC Hotel Geetanjali
14 Hotel Shangrila
23 Hotel Goher
29 Hotel Crags
30 Monal; Jasmine Guest House;
    Arti Guest House
31 Aroma-n-Claire Hotel

PLACES TO EAT
5   Glory Restaurant
15 Kwality Restaurant

17 Lovely Restaurant
24 Restaurant Preet Palace
25 Moti Mahal Restaurant
27 Amritsari Dhaba;
    Sher-e-Punjab Dhaba;
    Alishan Dhaba

OTHER
1   English Cemetery
4   HPTDC Tourist Office;
    Telegraph Office
6   Dalhousie Club
9   Tibetan Market; Span
    Tours & Travels;
    Trek-n-Travels
10 Bus Stand;
    Taxi Stand

12 Cinema
16 St John's Church
18 Post Office
19 Tibetan Handicrafts Centre
    Showroom; Bengali Sweet
    Shop
20 Dayal News Agency
21 Tara Devi Shrine
22 Himachal Handloom
    Industry Emporium
26 St Francis Catholic
    Church
28 Tibetan Rock
    Paintings
32 Punjab National
    Bank
33 DC Khanna & Sons

outdoor seating. The menu features south
Indian and Chinese cuisine. Also at Gandhi
Chowk is the popular *Kwality Restaurant*
with an extensive menu.

The *Bengali Sweet Shop*, near the Tibetan Handicrafts Showroom at Gandhi
Chowk, has a range of sticky favourites
such as *ras malai* and *gulaab jamun*.

A tiny *Tibetan restaurant* in the Tibetan
Market above the bus stand serves fried
momos for Rs 10, and very cheap chow mein.

Glory Restaurant, near the bus stand, has
all-you-can-eat Gujarati *thalis* for Rs 60.

Shopping
Dalhousie is a good place to pick up a
woollen shawl. The Himachal Handloom
Industry Emporium on Thandi Sarak has a
good selection.

At the Tibetan Handicrafts Centre
(π 42119), 3km from Gandhi Chowk along
the Khajiar road, you can have Tibetan carpets made to order. There are over 180 traditional designs to choose from. You can
buy carpets, bags and purses from the Tibetan Handicrafts Centre Showroom, on
Garam Sarak. The shops nearby sell a range
of goods, including Kashmiri shawls.

Getting There & Away
The booking office at the bus stand is open
daily from 9 am to 2 pm and 3 to 5 pm.

There are buses every couple of hours to
Pathankot (Rs 39, four hours). For Dharamsala (Rs 80, six hours) there is one bus at
8.30 am but the service seems unreliable.
Another option is to take the Pathankot bus
and change at Chakki. There are two daily
services to Shimla (Rs 120, 12 hours) and
one to Manali.

Buses to Chamba leave at 9.30 am and
3.30 and 4.40 pm (Rs 30, three hours) and
most go via Khajiar (Rs 15, 1½ hours). Private tourist buses usually depart at 9.15 and
10.10 am for Khajiar, wait an hour or so,
and then continue to Chamba.

Rates quoted at the taxi stand (π 40220)
include Pathankot (Rs 820 one way),
Chamba (Rs 550 one way, Rs 820 return via
Khajiar), Khajiar (Rs 410 return), Brahmaur
(Rs 1300 one way), Kalatope (Rs 360 re-
turn) and Dharamsala (Rs 1350 one way).

Getting Around
From the bus stand to Gandhi Chowk, taxis
charge Rs 30, and to Subhash Chowk, Rs 36.

KHAJIAR
π 01899
This grassy *marg*, or meadow, is 22km from
Dalhousie towards Chamba, and you can
get here by bus (1½ hours) or on foot (a
day's walk). Over 1km long and nearly 1km
wide, it is ringed by pine trees with a pond

HIMACHAL PRADESH

in the middle. The 12th century **Khajjinag Temple** has fine woodcarving on the cornices, and some crude carvings of the five Pandavas, the heroes of the *Mahabharata*, which were installed in the temple by the Raja of Chamba in the 16th century.

It's possible to do a circuit of the marg on horseback (Rs 40).

Places to Stay & Eat

HPTDC's **Hotel Devdar** (☎ *36333)* has cottages right on the edge of the marg for Rs 450, doubles for Rs 550 and dorm beds for Rs 50. There are more dorm beds for Rs 50 in HPTDC's basic **Khajiar Cottage** on the north side of the marg.

Parul Guest House (☎ *36344)*, behind the temple, has pleasant rooms overlooking the marg for Rs 400; other rooms aren't half as nice.

Gautam Guest House (☎ *36355)*, a couple of minute's walk east of the marg, is the best budget choice. Clean and bright rooms with hot bath cost Rs 250 (Rs 150 in the low season) and there's a nice sitting area.

There are several *restaurants* on the marg.

Getting There & Away

Buses from Dalhousie to Khajiar (Rs 15, 1½ hours) leave at 9.30, 10.10 and 11.10 am and 4.30 pm. From Khajiar, they return at 8.30 am and 4 pm. To Chamba, they depart at noon, and 4.30 pm (Rs 15, 1½ hours). Tourist buses to Chamba stop at Khajiar for an hour – if you want more time then catch the 9.30 am bus from Dalhousie (if it's running) and continue to Chamba in the afternoon. A taxi from Khajiar to Chamba is around Rs 450.

CHAMBA
☎ 01899 • pop 19,000
It's a beautiful, if somewhat hair-raising 56km trip from Dalhousie to Chamba (43km via Khajiar). The views down over the terraced fields are spectacular, with tiny villages clinging to the sheer slopes of the valley.

Chamba lies in a valley at an altitude of 926m – quite a bit lower than Dalhousie, so it's warmer in the summer. Perched on a ledge flanking the Ravi river, it has often been compared to a medieval Italian village and is famed for its ancient temples.

For 1000 years prior to Independence, Chamba was the headquarters of a district of the same name, and was ruled by a single dynasty of maharajas. The town was founded by Raja Sahil Varman, who shifted the capital here from Brahmaur and named it after his daughter Champavati.

Chamba has a grassy promenade known as the Chowgan, which is the focus for the Minjar and Sui Mata festivals (see Special Events later in this section).

Information

The tourist office (☎ 22671) is in the Hotel Iravati on Court Rd, and there's a divisional tourism development office in the white building adjacent to the Iravati.

The State Bank of India will change Visa, American Express and Citicorp travellers cheques, as will the Punjab National Bank on Hospital Rd.

Mani Mahesh Travels (☎ 22507), close to the Lakshmi Narayan temple complex, can arrange porters/guides for Rs 150/250 per day, as well as all-inclusive treks. The owner's son can provide a commentary on Chamba's beautiful temples (Rs 200) and his daughter acts as a guide for female trekkers when required.

You can send/receive faxes at the telegraph office (fax 25333), hidden in the backstreets not far from the Rishi Hotel.

Lakshmi Narayan Temple Complex

The six temples in this complex, all featuring exquisite sculpture, are representative of the shikhara style, although they also share characteristics distinctive to the Chamba Valley. Three of the temples are dedicated to Vishnu, and three to Shiva. The largest (and oldest) temple in the group is that of Lakshmi Narayan (Vishnu) and is directly opposite the entrance to the complex. According to tradition, it was built during the reign of the founder of Chamba, Raja Sahil Varman, in the 10th century AD. It was extensively renovated in the 16th century by Raja Partap Singh Varna. The image of Lakshmi Narayan enshrined in the temple dates from the temple's foundation. Some of the fine sculptures around the temple include those of Vishnu and Lakshmi, Narsingh (Vishnu in his lion form), and Krishna with the *gopis* (milkmaids). A small niche at the back harbours a beautiful sculpture of a goddess churning the ocean with Sheshnag, the snake of Vishnu, to bring the poison up from the bottom.

The fourth temple on the right, the Gauri Shankar Temple, is dedicated to Shiva. Its stone carving of the Ganges and Yamuna rivers personified as goddesses on either side of the door frame is renowned.

The complex is open from 6 am to 12.30 pm and 2.30 to 8.30 pm.

Bajreshwari Devi Temple

A five minute walk through the old town north-east of the Lakshmi Naryan Temple complex leads you to the diminutive **Surara temples**. There's also a beautiful old **water**

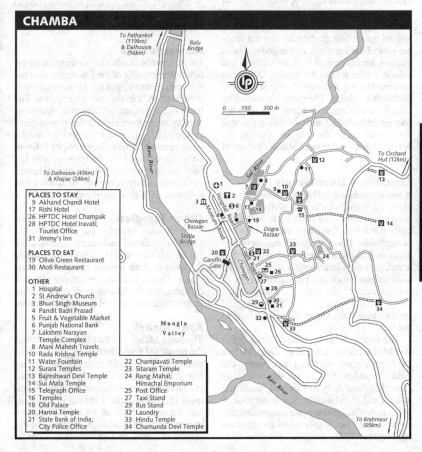

CHAMBA

To Pathankot (119km) & Dalhousie (56km)

Balu Bridge

0   150   300 m

Ravi River

Sal River

To Dalhousie (43km) & Khajiar (24km)

To Orchard Hut (12km)

Hospital Road

Museum Road

Chowgan Bazaar

Shitla Bridge

Dogra Bazaar

Court Road

Chowgan

Gandhi Gate

Mungla Valley

Ravi River

To Brahmaur (65km)

PLACES TO STAY
9 Akhand Chandi Hotel
17 Rishi Hotel
26 HPTDC Hotel Champak
28 HPTDC Hotel Iravati; Tourist Office
31 Jimmy's Inn

PLACES TO EAT
19 Olive Green Restaurant
30 Moti Restaurant

OTHER
1 Hospital
2 St Andrew's Church
3 Bhuri Singh Museum
4 Pandit Badri Prasad
5 Fruit & Vegetable Market
6 Punjab National Bank
7 Lakshmi Narayan Temple Complex
8 Mani Mahesh Travels
10 Rada Krishna Temple
11 Water Fountain
12 Surara Temples
13 Bajreshwari Devi Temple
14 Sui Mata Temple
15 Telegraph Office
16 Temples
18 Old Palace
20 Harirai Temple
21 State Bank of India; City Police Office
22 Champavati Temple
23 Sitaram Temple
24 Rang Mahal; Himachal Emporium
25 Post Office
27 Taxi Stand
29 Bus Stand
32 Laundry
33 Hindu Temple
34 Chamunda Devi Temple

HIMACHAL PRADESH

fountain nearby, more examples of which can be found in the Bhuri Singh Museum.

A further five minute walk leads up to the ancient Bajreshwari Devi Temple. The temple conforms to the shikhara style, and is topped by a wooden *amalaka* (fluted medallion-shaped flourish). The sanctum enshrines an image of Bajreshwari (a form of Durga), although it is difficult to make it out beneath its garlands of flowers. The entire surface of the temple is elaborately carved, featuring two friezes of rosettes at the lower levels. It is fronted by two stone columns with richly carved capitals and bases. A form of ancient script called *takri* can be seen crudely incised on the right column, and on other spots around the temple. In the niche on the western side of the temple is a damaged image of Undavi, the goddess of food, with a bowl and a ladle. At the rear of the temple, Durga can be seen slaying the giant Mahishasura and his buffalo vehicle. The giant is dwarfed by Durga, who is standing astride him with her foot on the buffalo. On either side of the door jambs, the rivers Yamuna and Ganges are personified as goddesses holding pitchers of water.

Chamunda Devi Temple

A terrace before this hilltop temple gives an excellent view of Chamba with its slate-roof houses (some of them up to 300 years old), the River Ravi and the surrounding countryside. It's a steep 30 minute climb along a path which begins above the bus stand, passing a small rock outcrop smeared with saffron which is revered as an image of the goddess of the forest, Banasti. When you reach the road, you can either proceed up the steep staircase, or follow the road to the left.

The temple is dedicated to Durga in her wrathful aspect as Chamunda Devi. Before the temple is her vehicle, a lion. Almost the entire wooden ceiling of the *mandapa* (forechamber) is richly carved, featuring animal and floral motifs, and depictions of various deities. From it are suspended numerous brass bells, offered to the goddess by devotees.

Just before the steps to the temple is a small pillar bearing the footprints of the goddess. Behind the temple is a very old, small shikhara-style temple dedicated to Shiva.

Sui Mata Temple

About a 10 minute walk from the Chamunda Devi Temple is a small modern temple dedicated to Sui Mata. Colourful paintings around the interior walls of the temple tell the story of Sui, a Chamba princess who gave her life for the inhabitants of Chamba. Women and children can be seen here laying wildflowers before the temple in devotion to Sui Mata. You can get here easily from the Bajreshwari Devi Temple.

Harirai Temple

This fine stone shikhara-style temple, on the north-western side of the Chowgan, near the fire station, dates from the 11th century. It is dedicated to Vishnu and enshrines a fine triple-headed image of Vaikuntha Vishnu reputedly made from eight different materials. In April 1971, the statue was stolen from the inner sanctum. It was discovered by Interpol on a ship destined for the USA seconds before the boat was to sail, and was returned to Chamba. At the rear of the temple is a fine sculpture of Vishnu astride six horses.

Other Temples

Several other temples lie hidden within Chamba's maze of backstreets; finding them can be half the fun. Places to dig out include the **Rada Krishna Temple**, also known as the Bhansi Gopal, the **Sitaram Temple**, devoted to Rama, and the **Champavati Temple**, dedicated to the daughter of Raja Sahil Varman.

Rang Mahal

The Rang Mahal, or Old Palace, now houses the **Himachal Emporium**. Here you can purchase *rumals* – small cloths featuring very fine embroidery in silk, a traditional craft executed by the women of Chamba for almost 1000 years. The stitching is very fine, and the reverse side of the cloth features a mirror image of the design – there is no evidence of knots or loose threads. Popular images portrayed on the cloths include Krishna and Radha, and those of Gaddi shepherds. A finely stitched rumal can take up to a month to complete, and costs from Rs 300 upwards.

You can also purchase repoussé brass plates and Chamba shawls here, and above the showroom is a workshop where you can see the shawls being made. An elaborately decorated shawl can take up to 45 days to make on a traditional wooden loom.

The emporium is open Monday to Friday, 10 am to 1 pm and 2 to 5 pm.

Bhuri Singh Museum

This museum has an interesting collection representing the art and culture of this region – particularly the miniature paintings of the Basohli and Kangra schools. It also houses some of the murals that were recovered from the Rang Mahal after it was damaged by fire. The museum is open Tuesday to Friday, every second Saturday, and Sunday from 10 am to 5 pm. Entry is free.

Gandhi Gate

This bright orange gateway on the southwestern side of the Chowgan was built in 1900 to welcome Viceroy Lord Curzon to the city. This was the main entrance into the city before the new road was built.

Special Events

The four day **Sui Mata Festival** is held in March/April on the Chowgan. Sui Mata, the daughter of an ancient raja, gave her life to save the inhabitants of her father's kingdom. She is particularly revered by Chamba women, who carry her image from the Old Palace up to her small shrine, accompanied by singing and dancing.

The **Minjar Festival** is celebrated in late July/early August. The origins of the fair are said to date back to 935 AD when the founder of Chamba, Raja Sahil Varman, returned to the town after defeating the Raja of Kangra. It more probably evolved from a harvest festival to celebrate the annual maize crop. *Minjars*, silk tassels worn by men and women and representing sheaves of maize,

are distributed during the festival. It culminates with a colourful procession and there are busy crowds of Gaddi, Churachi, Bhatti and Gujar people. An image of Raghuvira is carried aloft at the head of the procession and images of other gods and goddesses are borne in palanquins. The procession proceeds to the banks of the Ravi river, where the minjars are thrown into the water.

Places to Stay

HPTDC's *Hotel Iravati* (☎ 222671, fax 22565), a few minute's walk from the bus stand on Court Rd, has spotless doubles with bath from Rs 450 to Rs 800 (30% less in low season).

Hotel Champak (☎ 22774), behind the post office, is also run by HPTDC and has large doubles with common/private/bath for Rs 200/250. Dorm beds are Rs 50.

Jimmy's Inn (☎ 24748), opposite the bus stand, has small but clean rooms with cold bath for Rs 150. Larger and nicer doubles with TV cost Rs 250.

Rishi Hotel (☎ 24343), on Temple Rd, opposite the Lakshmi Narayan Temple complex, is popular with travellers. Doubles for Rs 150 and Rs 250 have hot water and unbeatable views out over the temples. Gloomy rooms at the back with common cold bath go for Rs 100. The dining hall here looks cheap but the food really isn't up to much.

Akhand Chandi Hotel (☎ 22371), in the shadow of the Rada Krishna Temple, is in a beautiful courtyard and has clean and carpeted rooms with hot water bath for Rs 200. At the time of research the hotel was in the process of changing hands and may close but it's worth checking out.

Orchard Hut (☎ 22607) is in a lovely tranquil spot in the Saal Valley, 12km from Chamba. Pitch your own tent, use one of theirs for Rs 100, or take a basic room for Rs 200 (Rs 350 with all meals). Check at Mani Mahesh Travels first, as getting there isn't easy.

Places to Eat

Chamba is known for its *chukh* – a chilli sauce consisting of red and green peppers,

HIMACHAL PRADESH

lemon juice, mustard oil and salt. You'll find jars in most of the provision stores in Dogra Bazaar for around Rs 25.

Olive Green Restaurant, upstairs on Temple Rd, is quiet and clean and serves good, reasonably priced veg and nonveg dishes. You can also sample the local dish *Chamba madhra* (kidney beans with curd and ghee).

Moti Restaurant near the bus stand serves up good standard Indian dishes.

Getting There & Away

There are six buses daily for the somewhat nerve-shattering trip to Brahmaur (Rs 32, 3½ hours). To Dharamsala there are buses at 11.30 am and 9.30 pm (Rs 113, 10 hours). To Khajiar, buses leave at 7.30 am and 2 pm (Rs 15, 1½ hours). To Dalhousie, they depart at 6, 7.30 and 11 am and 2 and 6 pm (Rs 30, three hours). There are nine buses daily to Pathankot (Rs 57, six hours). If there are no buses to Dalhousie at the time you want to leave, you could also take a Pathankot bus, and change to a local bus in Banikhet.

A taxi will cost Rs 400 to Khajiar and Rs 550 to Brahmaur.

BRAHMAUR
☎ 01090

Sixty-four kilometres south-east of Chamba is the ancient slate-roofed village of Brahmaur. It's a spectacular trip along a fairly precarious road up the Ravi river valley.

Before Raja Sahil Varman founded the new capital at Chamba in 920 AD, Brahmaur was the ancient capital of the princely state of Chamba for over 400 years. The Chaurasi temples are testament to the town's wealth. Dominating the group is the large shikhara-style **Manimahesh Temple**, dedicated to Shiva. Opposite is a smaller shikhara-style **temple** dedicated to Vishnu in his lion form as Narsingh. To its left is the **Dharmeshvar Temple**, sacred to Shiva.

Brahmaur is a centre for the seminomadic Gaddis, pastoralists who move their flocks up to alpine pastures during the summer, and descend to Kangra, Mandi and Bilaspur in winter.

There are some fine treks which commence from Brahmaur; see Lonely Planet's *Trekking in the Indian Himalaya* for details. The Mountaineering & Allied Sports Sub-Centre (☎ 25036) can arrange guides and porters.

In July/August pilgrims from all over northern India converge on Brahmaur for **Manimahesh Yatra** to commence the pilgrimage to the sacred lake of Manimahesh, 28km away and below the peak of Manimahesh Kailash (5656m). Parents blessed with a baby boy take the child on the pilgrimage, during which time the boy's hair is ceremonially cut. Prior to the pilgrimage, a seven day fair is held at Brahmaur, followed by wrestling competitions and folk dances by pilgrims from distant villages. Fifteen days after the commencement of the festival, the pilgrims are led by priests to Manimahesh. Here there is an ancient and very beautiful temple dedicated to Lakshmi Devi in her form as slayer of the buffalo demon (Mahishasuramardini). The image of the goddess enshrined in the inner sanctum dates from the 7th century AD.

Places to Stay

Chamunda Guest House (☎ 25056) is about a five minute walk up from the bus stand. Pleasant singles/doubles are Rs 100/200. Other cheap places include the *Krishna Lodge* and *Jamuna Lodge*.

Getting There & Away

There are frequent buses to Chamba between 6.30 am and 5.30 pm (Rs 32, 3½ hours).

Kullu & Parbati Valleys

The Kullu Valley and, to a lesser extent, the Parbati Valley, have always been a popular place to hang out and take in some mountain scenery. Recent tourist spillover from the political violence in Kashmir, however, has had a profound effect on the valley and Manali, in particular, has developed rapidly, threatening the valley's peaceful and un-hurried atmosphere.

Originally known as Kulanthapitha (End of the Habitable World), the first recorded inhabitants of the Kullu Valley date back to the 1st century. The capital was first at Jagatsukh, then moved to Naggar before the British moved it to Kullu town. The Kullu Valley, about 80km long and often less than 2km wide, rises northward from Mandi at 760m to the Rohtang La at 3980m, the gateway to Lahaul and Spiti.

The Kullu and Parbati valleys, from Mandi to Manali, are serviced by the airport at Bhuntar, 10km south of Kullu town.

The high season is mid-April to mid-June, mid-September to early November, Christmas and New Year.

MANDI
☎ 01905 • pop 26,000

Formerly an important junction on the salt route to Tibet, Mandi is the gateway to the Kullu Valley, and the junction of roads from Kullu, Kangra and Shimla. Mandi, which means market, is quite a good place to break the journey between Shimla and the Kullu Valley. There are some cheap hotels, you can dig out some of the 81 Hindu temples in the area or you can take a day trip to holy Rewalsar Lake. At less than 800m above sea level, Mandi is considerably warmer than other regional areas.

Orientation & Information

The centre of Mandi is the town square, dominated by a huge collection of shops called the Indira Market. Most of the hotels and places to eat are around or very near the square. Over the river, to the east, is the bus station, a 15 minute walk away.

The only place to change money is the Evening Plaza Hotel in the main square, which also changes American Express travellers cheques for a 1% commission. The Bank of Baroda does Visa cash advances.

Things to See & Do

For a cool respite from town, take an auto-rickshaw (about Rs 30 return) up the very

Shopping in the Kullu Valley

The road along the Kullu Valley, particularly from Bhuntar airport to Kullu town, is lined with shops selling Kullu shawls and other locally produced handicrafts. Once an important part of household and village life, the manufacture and sale of Kullu shawls and other goods is now a thriving local industry. It's worth having a look at some of these shops to see the weaving in action, or to visit a farm of pashmina goats or angora rabbits – although there will be some real pressure to buy.

Pattoos are thick woollen shawls worn by local women, and fastened with a gachi. Kullu caps are always colourful, and worth buying for trekking in cold climates. Other items available include a *gudma*, often used as a sort of blanket, and a *pullan*, a type of slipper worn in the home.

The shops between Bhuntar and Kullu cater more for the touristy crowds, and despite an obvious overabundance of places, they don't offer particularly competitive prices. The best places to buy Kullu gear are the market stalls and cooperatives along The Mall in Manali, and Akhara Bazaar in Kullu town.

steep 4 or 5km to **Tarna Hill**. At the summit, the Rani Amrit Kaur Park (opened by the Dalai Lama in 1957) has superb views and a nice cafe. In the park, the 17th century Hindu **Syamakali Temple**, also called the Tarna Devi Temple, is worth a look.

From the Bhutnath Temple you could head north into the cloth bazaar, down to the **Beas River** and its collection of riverside temples and ghats, including the impressive Triloknath and Panjvaktra temples.

Mandi's **Shivaratri Festival** is one of the most interesting held in Himachal Pradesh. Much of the activity takes place at the 16th century **Bhutnath Temple** in Moti Bazaar, west of the main square. Celebrations continue for weeks and deities from all over the district are carried into town.

KULLU & PARBATI VALLEYS

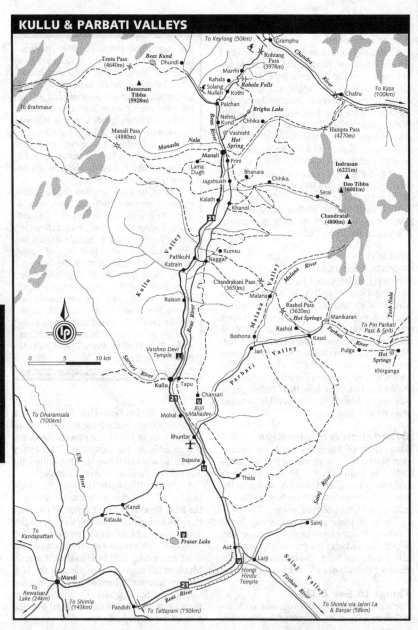

Places to Stay

The rambling *Raj Mahal* (☎ 22401), the former palace of the Raja of Mandi, oozes colonial time warp at budget prices. It's a decrepit building behind the grandstand at Indira Market, next to the district library. Comfortable singles/doubles with share bath cost Rs 98/127, while well-furnished rooms with private hot bath are worth the extra money at Rs 198/275.

HPTDC's *Hotel Mandav* (☎ 35503, fax 35551), up a lane behind the bus station, has quiet economy doubles in the old block with hot water bath and balcony for Rs 250. The more modern rooms are not as good value at Rs 500 (Rs 800 with air-con).

Around the town square are places of all types and prices. The popular *Standard Hotel* (☎ 22948) charges Rs 55 for a small single and Rs 100 to Rs 160 for a double with bath.

Hotel Shiva (☎ 24211) has noisy rooms from Rs 125 to Rs 275.

Evening Plaza (☎ 25123) and *Mayfair* are two mid-range places with rooms for around Rs 300 to Rs 400 (Rs 600 with air-con), but neither are especially good.

On the road across the bridge from the bus station are a number of cheap, noisy, places for about Rs 40/60. The better ones are: the *Hotel Anand* (☎ 22515), which is cramped but reasonably clean; the *Hotel Koyal* (☎ 22248); and the *Sangam Hotel* (☎ 22009), which offers some views.

Vyas Guest House is a five minute walk from the bus station (just follow the signs), not far from the Panjvaktra Temple. Clean, cool rooms range from Rs 100 to Rs 200 and there's a friendly atmosphere.

Places to Eat

Copacabana Bar & Restaurant at the Raj Mahal is a popular, open-air place where good food is served.

Hotel Mandav is worth the walk up for a good selection of mains, breakfasts and the bar (cold beer is Rs 60 a bottle). Dinner isn't served until 7 pm.

Treet Restaurant, on the ground floor of the Indira Ghandi Plaza, is probably the best

place in town and serves Chinese and southern Indian food in dark but clean surroundings. Prices are reasonable.

Hotel Standard has good, cheap food and there are plenty of *dhabas* around the main square.

Getting There & Away

As the junction for the Kangra and Kullu valleys, Mandi is well served by local public buses. The bus station – where you can make advance bookings – is across the river in the eastern part of town.

There are buses every hour or so until 1 pm to Shimla (Rs 80, six hours) via Bilaspur; until 12.30 pm for Dharamsala (Rs 72, six hours); and all day for Bhuntar, Kullu and Manali.

Taxis congregate outside the bus station, and at a stand on the eastern side of the town square. A one-way trip by taxi from Mandi to Kullu costs Rs 600.

AROUND MANDI
Rewalsar Lake
☎ 01905

Rewalsar Lake is high up in the hills, 24km south-west of Mandi and set beside the village of Rewalsar. It's a lovely area, with some pretty scenery, and is worth a day trip, or an overnight stay.

The small lake is revered by Buddhists because it is where Padmasambhava departed for Tibet. Every year, shortly after the Tibetan New Year (February/March), many Buddhists make a pilgrimage here, especially from Dharamsala.

Hindus also revere the lake because it was where the sage Rishi Lomas did his penance as a dedication to Shiva, who, in return, gave Rishi the seven lakes in the vicinity, including Rewalsar.

As you enter the lake area, the **Drigung Kagyud Gompa**, immediately on the right, has friendly monks who will show you around. The **Tso-Pema Ogyen Heru-kai Nyingmapa Gompa & Institute**, farther around the lake, is also worth a visit. Built in the 19th century, it has a little museum and some colourful murals.

Around the lake, there are three **Hindu temples** dedicated to Rishi Lomas, Shiva and Krishna.

The Sikhs have the huge **Guru Gobind Singh Gurdwara**. It was built in 1930 by Raja Joginder Sen, and dedicated to Gobind Singh, who stayed at the Rewalsar Lake for a month.

Places to Stay & Eat HPTDC's *Tourist Inn (☎ 80252)* has dorm beds for Rs 50, and nice doubles for Rs 200 or Rs 250. Triples/quads are Rs 300/400 and there's a decent restaurant.

The Drikung Kagyud Gompa offers cosy rooms in its *Peace Memorial Inn* for Rs 50/130 with common/private bath.

Tibet Hotel at the Ogyen Heru-kai Gompa has basic rooms on the lakeside for Rs 25/50 and deluxe rooms for Rs 100/150 with hot water bath.

The Zigar Gompa *guesthouse* has rooms with bath for Rs 40/80.

Tibetan Food Corner here has very good-value Tibetan and western food.

Getting There & Away Rewalsar isn't actually on the way to anywhere, so you will have to travel via Mandi. Buses from Mandi go to Rewalsar village, adjacent to the lake, every 30 or 40 minutes, making it an easy day trip along a pretty, but fairly rough, road (Rs 12, one hour). A return taxi from Mandi costs about Rs 300.

MANDI TO KULLU

Twenty kilometres from Mandi the road passes the huge **Pandoh Dam**, which diverts water from the Beas River through two 12km tunnels. Eight kilometres past the dam is the **Hongi Hindu Temple**, where your driver will probably offer thankful prayers for a safe passage.

A few kilometres farther is **Aut**, the turn-off for the undeveloped Sainj Valley. There's good trout fishing to be had at **Larji**, at the pretty junction of the Sainj and Tirthan rivers but you'll need a license from Kullu.

Fifteen kilometres south of Kullu in the village of Bajaura is the **Basheshar Ma-**hadev, the largest stone temple in the Kullu Valley. Built in the 8th century from carved stone blocks, the temple has fine carvings and sculptures. It's at the end of a 200m trail leading from the main road with a sign reading 'Indo Italian Fruit Dev'.

Bhuntar
☎ 01902

Bhuntar's dual claim to fame is its airport, which serves all of the Kullu Valley, and its position as the turn-off to the Parbati Valley on the other side of the Beas. Bhuntar is only 10km from Kullu but if you have an early departure or a late arrival, it might be handy to stay here.

Jagson Airlines (☎ 65222) has an office next to the airport and there are several travel agencies around the village.

Places to Stay & Eat Best of a bad bunch near the airport/bus station is the *Hotel Airport-End*, with clean but noisy rooms for a negotiable Rs 150 to Rs 450.

About 500m north of the airport, towards Kullu, are some mid-range places. All give a 50% discount in the low season. *Hotel Sunbeam (☎ 65790)* has singles and doubles for Rs 300, Rs 350 and Rs 450. *Hotel Amit (☎ 65123)*, next door, has doubles for Rs 400 and Rs 525.

Hotel Trans Shiva (☎ 65623), farther north, near the junction to the Parbati Valley, has rooms for Rs 250 to Rs 600.

Noble Guest House (☎ 65077), 400m east of the Trans Shiva, on the east bank of the Beas, is a good choice. Small but clean rooms with hot shower cost Rs 300 (Rs 150 when things are slow).

Around the bus station, several *dhabas* serve basic Indian and Chinese food; the *Malabar Restaurant* opposite the airport entrance is probably the best of the lot.

Lazeez Restaurant at the Sunbeam and the restaurant at the *Amit Hotel* have both good food and ambience.

Getting There & Away Bhuntar is well served by buses, which leave from outside the airport entrance. Most buses go to Kullu, where you may have to change for destinations farther north. All buses between Manali and anywhere south of Kullu stop at, or very near, Bhuntar.

Bhuntar has the valley's most frequent buses to Manikaran (and all places in between) from 7.30 am to 6.30 pm.

Sample taxi fares include Kullu (Rs 80), Manikaran (Rs 475) and Manali (Rs 600). Taxis hang around the bus station.

For details of flights from Bhuntar see Getting There & Away in Kullu.

KULLU
☎ 01902 • pop 16,000

At an altitude of 1200m, Kullu is the district headquarters of the valley but is not the main tourist centre – that honour goes to Manali. Kullu is reasonably set up with hotels and other facilities, and is not a bad place (especially around Dhalpur), but many visitors don't bother to stay long as there are nicer places around the valleys.

Orientation

Kullu is small enough to walk around. The *maidan* (field) area at Dhalpur, where Kullu's festivals are held, is the nicest part of town. The 'centre' of town is probably the area around the taxi stand. From there a busy footpath called Sarvari heads down (north) towards the bus station area (don't take the road if walking; it's longer). Sarvari is full of shops and cheap guesthouses. The road from the bus station then heads towards Manali through Akhara Bazaar, which is a good place to buy Kullu shawls and other handicrafts.

Information

The HPTDC tourist office (☎ 24605) is by the maidan at Dhalpur. It's open daily from 9 am to 7 pm in summer (10 am to 5 pm in winter) but is only really useful for booking HPTDC buses, which leave from outside the office.

The only place that changes money is the State Bank of Patiala, at the northern end of Akhara Bazaar, a five minute walk from the Central Hotel. It's open Monday to Friday,

10.45 am to 2 pm. This branch accepts most travellers cheques (except Citicorp) but doesn't change cash.

The main post office, up from the taxi stand, is open Monday to Saturday, 10 am to 5 pm, but service is a bit slow. You can send (and receive) faxes at government rates from the telegraph office (fax 22720) in Akhara Bazaar.

Temples

Raghunath Temple (1660 AD), in the north of town, is dedicated to the principal god in the valley. Although it's the most important temple in the area, it's not terribly interesting and is only open before 9 am and after 5 pm.

Three kilometres from Kullu, in the village of Bhekhli, is the **Jagannathi Devi Temple** (also known as the Bhekhli Temple). It's a stiff 1½ hour climb, but from the temple there are great views over Kullu. Take the path off the main road to Akhara Bazaar after crossing the bridge. Alternatively, take a one-way/return taxi for Rs 200/250, or an auto-rickshaw for far less. There are supposed to be two buses a day to Bhekhli at 8.30 am and 12.30 pm but don't count on it.

Special Events

Kullu holds one of the most colourful **Dussehra** festivals in India. During the festival Rama is worshipped in his form as Raghunath, whose image is borne through the streets on a wheeled *rath* (palanquin) pulled by pilgrims. Following the procession, villagers dance in traditional dress.

Organised Tours

The Kullu Taxi Operators' Union (☎ 22332), just north of the Dhalpur maidan, offers the following sightseeing tours:

- Bhekhli Temple, Vaishno Devi Temple, Raghunath Temple, shawl factory & Bajaura (Rs 500, five hours)
- Kasol & Manikaran (Rs 600, six hours)
- Larji fishing trip (Rs 550, five hours)
- Vaishno Devi Temple, Naggar Castle & Roerich Castle (Rs 500, five hours)
- Larji, Banjar & Jalori Pass (Rs 1500, eight hours)

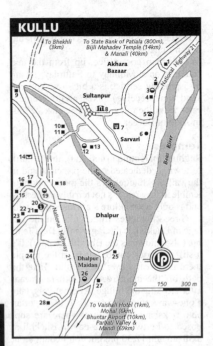

KULLU

PLACES TO STAY
1   Hotel Sidhartha
2   Central Hotel
4   Hotel Naman
9   Hotel Rock-n-River
10 Madhu Chandrika Guest House
11 Aaditya Guest House
13 The Nest
15 Hotel New Vikrant
16 Bhaga Sidh Guest House
17 Hotel Vimal
18 Hotel Shobla & Restaurant
21 Hotel Bijleshwar View
22 Hotel Aroma Classic
23 Hotel Daulat
24 Hotel Rohtang & Restaurant
25 Sa-Ba Tourist Home
27 Fancy Guest House
28 Hotel Sarvari & Restaurant

OTHER
3   Naggar Bus Stop
5   Telegraph Office
6   Himachal Emporium
7   Raghunath Temple
8   Palace
12 Main Bus Station
14 Main Post Office
19 Taxi Stand
20 HPTDC Tourist Office; Monal Cafe;
    Hotstuff Restaurant
26 Dhalpur Bus Stand

Places to Stay – Budget

Dhalpur The popular *Hotel Bijleshwar View* (☎ 22677), behind the tourist office, has rooms with hot bath from Rs 300 to Rs 500.

Hotel Rohtang (☎ 22303) is good value at Rs 200/450 for a double/four-bed room, but some are dark.

Hotel Daulat (☎ 22358) has slightly overpriced rooms with a balcony for Rs 200 to Rs 350.

Bhaga Sidh Guest House, up a lane at the back of the tourist office, has cheap singles/doubles in a family home for Rs 80/100. The *Hotel Vimal* has much the same for Rs 150.

Hotel New Vikrant (☎ 22756), farther up the road, has an excellent range of rooms from Rs 150 to Rs 375 and some nice communal sitting areas.

Across the other (eastern) side of the maidan are a couple of cheap places. *Fancy Guest House* (☎ 22681) isn't bad at Rs 100, Rs 125 and Rs 250 for rooms with hot water bath.

Sa-Ba Tourist Home is probably better value, with genuine single rooms for Rs 75 and doubles for Rs 150.

Hotel Rock-n-River (☎ 24214) has a somewhat inconvenient but pleasant location on the banks of the Sarvari River. Clean and bright rooms are good value at Rs 300 and Rs 400.

Bus Station Area *Aaditya Guest House* (☎ 24263), right by the river, has bright doubles with common/hot water bath for Rs 100/220. The nearby *Madhu Chandrika Guest House* is slightly more expensive.

Near the bus station, *The Nest* (☎ 22685)

HIMACHAL PRADESH

Trekking in the Himalayas is the best way to meet people and will make you appreciate the comfort of roads and rail. The enduring friendliness and good humour of these people is incomparable and will keep you going on those long and strenuous treks.

Whether in the Spiti district (top) or the Parbati Valley (bottom), expansive views and insights into the daily routines of the people who live in this region are rewards for the effort that mountain walking requires.

has enormous double rooms for Rs 250 and smaller ground floor rooms for Rs 150, all with bath. The location can be noisy.

Akhara Bazaar The *Hotel Naman* (☎ 22667) has musty singles for Rs 100 and Rs 150, and doubles for Rs 150 to Rs 300. The cheaper rooms can be gloomy and the more expensive rooms noisy, but it's not a bad place.

The friendly *Central Hotel* (☎ 22482) is the oldest in Kullu, with an almost infinite range of slightly threadbare rooms from Rs 30 to Rs 200.

Places to Stay – Mid-Range

The *Hotel Shobla* (☎ 22800), in the centre of town, has luxury rooms for Rs 550, Rs 770 and Rs 935, plus about Rs 360 for three meals.

HPTDC's *Hotel Sarvari* (☎ 22471) is a little south of the maidan, and a short walk off the main road. It's a well-run place with clean, bright doubles in the old block for Rs 400, rooms in the new block for Rs 700 or Rs 900, and dorm beds for Rs 45.

Hotel Aroma Classic (☎ 23075) is another well-run place with rooms for Rs 400, Rs 550 and Rs 675 and a good restaurant.

Hotel Sidhartha (☎ 24243) is the best hotel in Akhara Bazaar, with clean but small-ish rooms for Rs 400, Rs 500 and Rs 650.

Places to Eat

HPTDC's *Monal Cafe*, by the tourist office, serves good meals and snacks. *Hotstuff*, just opposite, is a great place for pizzas, soup and just about everything else.

Plenty of other cheap places around the bus stand, or the central taxi stand, serve basic Tibetan and Indian food.

Hotel Rohtang has nice views of Dhalpur maidan, a good food selection and reasonable prices; breakfast is good.

Hotel Aroma Classic looks expensive, but isn't – the setting, service and selection make it a good option.

Hotel Shobla has the best views, all the service you would expect and good food at fair prices (pizzas Rs 40; omelettes Rs 20).

Getting There & Away

Air Jagson Airlines flies between Kullu and Delhi (US$150) daily, with a stop in Shimla (US$67). Archana Airways has daily flights between Delhi and Bhuntar (US$150). The flights are in small aircraft, mainly 15 to 20 seaters.

Archana Airways (☎ 65630) has its office at Mohal, 6km south of Kullu; alternatively book at the Hotel Vaishali, about 1km south of Kullu (☎ 24225). Jagson Airlines has an office at the airport in Bhuntar. Tickets are most easily booked through travel agencies in Kullu.

Bus Kullu has a large, busy bus station; timetables are displayed in English, and there's an advance booking system (inquiries ☎ 23466). The bus stop at the Dhalpur maidan is only good if you're going to Bhuntar or the Parbati Valley, but these buses may be full by the time they get to Dhalpur from the main Kullu bus station.

There are several daily public buses to Mandi, or take any bus going to Shimla or Delhi. To Shimla there are four buses each day. To Manikaran, a bus leaves every 30 minutes or so, or take a bus to Bhuntar and change there. There is a bus every 15 or 20 minutes between Kullu and Manali (Rs 25, two hours). To Naggar, buses leave every few hours from a bus stop in Akhara Bazaar, 1km north of the main bus station. Alternatively, take a Manali-bound bus to Patlikuhl and change there.

There are three public buses every day (one overnight) to Dharamsala. To Bajaura, buses leave every hour or so. Regular daily express public buses go to Delhi via Chandigarh (Rs 180, 14 hours). Direct daily buses to Chandigarh also leave several times a day.

HPTDC buses from Manali stop at the tourist office in Kullu and bookings can be made in advance there. Buses run daily in season to Dharamsala (Rs 250), Shimla (Rs 250), Delhi (Rs 450; overnight) and Chandigarh (Rs 275).

Travel agencies in Kullu sell tickets for deluxe private buses 'from Kullu', but these are just really part of the trips from Manali

HIMACHAL PRADESH

organised by bus companies. In season, overnight buses to Delhi cost Rs 350; to Dharamsala, Rs 250; to Leh, with a connection in Manali, Rs 800; and to Shimla, Rs 250.

Taxi Taxis from Kullu to Manali cost Rs 500 via National Highway 21 (on the western side of the river), or Rs 650 if you take the slower, but more scenic route via Naggar.

Fixed taxi fares include Manikaran (Rs 500), Katrain (Rs 200), Mandi (Rs 600), Delhi (Rs 4400), Dharamsala (Rs 1900) and Shimla (Rs 1900). To Bhuntar airport, the set price is Rs 100.

Getting Around
An auto-rickshaw is handy to get around, particularly if you have heavy gear, or want to visit the nearby temples. From Dhalpur to the bus station should cost about Rs 15, or to the airport at Bhuntar, Rs 60.

JARI
Jari is halfway along the Parbati Valley – about 19km from Bhuntar. It has been developed to cater for the hippie crowd who have spilled over from Manikaran, or those who prefer Jari's peace and cheap rooms.

On the other side of the river from Jari, is the interesting Malana Valley. **Malana** (2652m) can be reached in a full day trek from Jari. There are about 500 people in Malana and they speak a peculiar dialect with strong Tibetan elements. It's an isolated village with its own system of government and a caste structure so rigid that it's forbidden for visitors to touch either the people or any of their possessions. It's very important to respect this custom; wait at the edge of the village for an invitation to enter.

Village Guest House, a 10 minute uphill hike from the village centre, is a peaceful, well-run place with decent rooms for Rs 50 or Rs 75.

Dharma Family Guest House has OK rooms for Rs 50, as does the *Om Shiva Guest House*. The *Roman Guest House* costs a little more at Rs 70 or Rs 100.

Golden Rays Hotel is the best bet on the main road, with clean, spacious doubles with common/private/bath for Rs 60/80. The toilets are the cleanest in the Parbati Valley.

Deepak Restaurant on the main road is the best, and most popular place for food. Om Shiva Guest House has the *Rooftop Cafe* with great views.

Parbati Valley buses stop in the centre of town if required. A one-way taxi from Kullu to Jari is around Rs 350.

KASOL
Kasol is another tiny village along the Parbati Valley road that has become a hang-out. It's in a lovely setting among pines, and streams with some trout. The village is actually divided into 'Old Kasol', on the Bhuntar side of the bridge, and 'New Kasol', on the Manikaran side.

Rainbow Cafe & Guest House in New Kasol has a few charmless rooms for Rs 100 (Rs 150 with bath), and serves basic food and eastern 'herbs' all day.

Old Kasol is generally a far nicer place to stay and there are plenty of guesthouses and cafes, some with nice gardens, which offer basic rooms for around Rs 50.

Yerpa's Guest House is the best of the bunch. Clean rooms with common hot bath go for Rs 100 and deluxe rooms with hot shower for Rs 250. There's a nice restaurant and a Tibetan-style sitting area (the owners are from Spiti).

MANIKARAN
☎ 01902
Famous for its hot springs, which are hot enough to boil rice and apparently cure anything from rheumatism to bronchitis, Manikaran is another place from which many foreigners have forgotten to leave. Manikaran means jewel from the ear in Sanskrit. According to the local legend, a giant snake took earrings from Parvati while she was bathing and then snorted them through its nose to create spaces where the hot springs spewed forth.

The town is split into two, over both sides of the roaring Parbati river. Almost all of the guesthouses, places to eat and temples are on the northern side, where no vehicles are allowed. The first bridge you see as you approach from Bhuntar is a footbridge which leads to the hot springs under the enormous Sikh gurdwara, and then continues into the village. The second bridge is at the end of the Parbati Valley road, where there is a taxi and bus stand. There is no place to change money in Manikaran; the nearest bank is in Kullu town.

The town is revered by both Hindus and Sikhs and is chock-a-block with sadhus, pilgrims and religious souvenir shops. The Hindu **Sri Ramchander Temple** is a quiet place where you can discreetly have a look around, while the Indian sadhus and western freaks huddle outside the temple trying to get some sun.

As you enter Manikaran, you cannot escape the extraordinary sight of the **Sri Guru Nanak Dev Ji** Sikh gurdwara.

There are three bathing options: the crowded but free hot baths (separate for men and women) under the Sikh temple; the Hotel Parvati, which charges Rs 25 for one person, or Rs 40 for two, for a 20 minute bath; or there are baths in most local guesthouses.

From Manikaran, a well defined trail leads 16km to the village of **Pulga** (four to five hours), where there are a couple of basic *guesthouses* and restaurants. The next stage (again four to five hours) continues on to the hot springs at **Khirganga**, where Shiva sat and meditated for 2000 years. Here there are a number of basic *teahouses* to spend the night before returning directly to Manikaran in one long stage. Porters and guides can be hired in Manikaran – ask at any guesthouse or restaurant.

Places to Stay
Like the rest of the region, prices vary according to demand.

HPTDC's *Hotel Parvati* (☎ 73735) has clean doubles at Rs 400 (Rs 200 in low season) which is not particularly good value around here.

Sharma Sadan (☎ 73703) has a fine location on the main square and has nice

rooms from Rs 100 (low season) to Rs 250 (June/July).

Sharma Guest House has decent doubles for Rs 50 to Rs 120. It is close to the first footbridge – follow the signs around the village.

Padha Family Guest House has a range of rooms around a courtyard cafe, many with a balcony overlooking the river, from Rs 50 to Rs 300.

Paradise Guest House, nearby, has damp doubles for Rs 50 and Rs 100.

Shivalik Hotel, on the darker, southern side of the river has damp but pleasant rooms for Rs 100, Rs 200 and Rs 300.

The nearby *PWD Guesthouse* is a bargain, with two doubles with hot bath for Rs 100 or Rs 200. You don't normally need a booking.

Places to Eat
Hot Spring Restaurant serves delicious pizzas. *O-Rest* does similar food, and is popular.

Holy Palace has reasonable Italian and Israeli food for around Rs 40 a dish.

Shiva Restaurant, near the gurdwara, is good but a little pricier than the competition.

Getting There & Away
Buses between Kullu and Manikaran leave every 30 minutes or so (Rs 23, 2½ hours). Alternatively, take a regular bus going to Bhuntar and catch another on to Manikaran (Rs 17, two hours). Buses link Manikaran with Manali six times a day (Rs 35, four hours). Another option is a day trip from Manali on a tourist bus for Rs 175, which stops at Kasol for a quick look on the way.

A return taxi from Manali to Manikaran will cost Rs 1100. A fixed-price taxi from the stand at the bus station in Manikaran will cost Rs 475 to Bhuntar (one way), and Rs 575 to Kullu (one way).

A six hour sightseeing return taxi trip from Kullu along the Parbati Valley road costs Rs 600.

KULLU TO MANALI
There are two roads between Kullu and Manali: the main highway runs along the west bank of the Beas, while the rougher

HIMACHAL PRADESH

Warning – Missing Persons

Between 1996 and 1998 over a dozen foreign tourists have disappeared from the Kullu Valley. Persons have been reported missing from the villages of Naggar, Malana, Manali, Manikaran and Kasol. During your travels you may well see posters for Ian Mogford, a student from Bristol who disappeared in 1996, and Ardeven Taherzadeh, a Canadian who disappeared in 1997. Though some relatives have found the local police less than cooperative, a concerted Israeli investigation into a missing airforce pilot eventually discovered he had been murdered in his sleeping bag. It is not known what has happened to the other disappeared but the region is a centre for *charas* (marijuana) production and the local drug mafia are suspected of being involved. It's possible that some disappeared while trekking alone through remote regions or have even lost themselves in some kind of spiritual search.

If going to the area we recommend you avoid trekking alone, be cautious of locals offering tea and other substances, register fully at guest houses and hotels, and be a little wary of befriending sadhus – not all of whom are holy men. A Foreign Missing Persons Bureau has been set up in Delhi and can be contacted through the British High Commission (☎ 011-687 2161).

but more scenic road goes along the east bank, through Naggar.

Raison, 13km from Kullu, is in a particularly wide and low part of the Kullu Valley. HPTDC's *Adventure Resort* (☎ 01902-40516) is right on the river. A hut with two bedrooms costs Rs 600/300 in high/low season, and a pretty camping spot is Rs 50.

Katrain, 6km north, has the HPTDC *Hotel Apple Blossom* (☎ 01902-40836), with doubles from Rs 250 to Rs 300, and a bed in a five bed dorm for Rs 50. The hotel has great views, but is looking a bit old and tired these days.

The cheap, family-run *Nangdraj Guest House* is the only other place worth staying in Katrain.

Patlikuhl is the largest village between Kullu and Manali, and almost exactly halfway between the two towns. Being so close to the lovely village of Naggar, just across the river, there seems little or no need to stay at Patlikuhl. There is a fisheries office at the northern edge of town where you can buy trout and get a fishing licence.

NAGGAR
☎ 01902

Naggar is a lovely little village set on a hill and surrounded by forests. It can be visited on a day trip from Manali or Kullu, but if you have time Naggar is worth stopping over for a night or two.

The Ragini, Snow View and Poonam Lodge hotels can help with trekking arrangements.

Naggar Castle

Naggar was capital of the Kullu Valley for nearly 1500 years. The castle, built about 500 years ago as the raja's headquarters, was converted to a hotel in 1978. The castle is built around a courtyard, and there are verandahs right around the castle's exterior, providing stupendous views over the valley. Inside the courtyard is the small **Jagtipath Temple** containing a slab of stone said to have been carried there by wild bees, and a small **museum**.

Naggar Castle is at the top of a steep 2km road, off the eastern Kullu to Manali road. To get to the castle, get off the bus at the village on the main road, and walk up, or take one of the auto-rickshaws milling around.

Temples

The grey sandstone Shiva **Temple of Gauri Shankar** is at the foot of the small bazaar below the castle and dates from the 11th or 12th century. Almost opposite the front of the castle is the curious little **Chatar Bhuj Temple** dedicated to Vishnu. Near the Snow View Guest House is the pagoda-like **Tripura Sundari Devi Temple**, with some ornate wooden carvings. High up on the ridge above Naggar, near the village of Thawa, is the **Murlidhar Krishna Temple**.

Roerich Gallery

One kilometre past the castle is the interesting Roerich Gallery, a fine old house displaying the artwork of both the eccentric Professor Nicholas Roerich, who died in Naggar in 1947, and his son, Svetoslav Roerich, who died in Bangalore in 1993. It's open daily, 9 am to 1 pm and 2 to 5 pm; entry is Rs 10. Leave your shoes at the front door.

Just uphill from the gallery is the **Urusvati Himalayan Folk & Art Museum** which houses a collection of embroidery and folk art. Upstairs is a modern art gallery, which sells postcards and copies of Roerich's paintings.

Places to Stay

The HPTDC *Castle Hotel* (☎ 47816), reputedly haunted, has a good range of accommodation. Basic rooms with share bath cost Rs 200 and Rs 300 or Rs 400 to Rs 1000 with private bath. Dorm beds for Rs 50 are often booked out, so try to book in advance.

Poonam Mountain Lodge & Restaurant is right behind the castle. Good singles/doubles with hot water cost Rs 150/200 and the helpful owner rents trekking gear.

Hotel Ragini (☎ 47793) is a mid-range place with nice wooden decor and excellent rooms for Rs 300, Rs 350 (with balcony) and Rs 500.

Sheetal Guest House (☎ 47719), next door, has tired-looking rooms from Rs 250 to Rs 650.

Closer to the Roerich Museum are two cheap guesthouses. The *Snow View Guest House* (☎ 47325), has dark but OK doubles from Rs 100 to Rs 200 and small singles for Rs 50 and Rs 70. The *Alliance Guest House* (☎ 47363) is a simple but clean, friendly and comfortable place run by an expat Frenchman. Rooms with common hot bath range from Rs 80 to Rs 150. There are a couple of rooms with bath for around Rs 300.

Places to Eat

The *Castle Hotel* provides the best views, certainly the best atmosphere in the village, and the food is pretty good, too.

Kailash Rooftop Restaurant at the Hotel Ragini and *Cinderella Restaurant* at the Sheetal Guest House are both worth a try.

Poonam Restaurant has vegetarian food and a great location in the shadow of the Vishnu Hotel.

La Purezza Italian Restaurant, in the village on the main road, at the start of the road up to the castle, serves authentic pasta dishes for around Rs 70.

Getting There & Away

Buses go directly between the village of Naggar (on the main road) and Manali six times a day (Rs 10, one hour).

Another option is to get the bus to Patlikuhl (there are more buses along the western side of the river) from either Manali or Kullu, then take a taxi (Rs 30) from Patlikuhl to Naggar Castle (you could walk, but it's a steep 7km).

A one-way/return taxi from Manali to Naggar Castle will cost Rs 300/400; a return taxi from Kullu is Rs 500. A Kullu to Manali taxi (Rs 500) will probably charge an extra Rs 150 for a quick stopover in Naggar. From Bhuntar airport, a taxi to Naggar Castle is Rs 450.

Manali

☎ 01902 • pop 4200

At the northern end of the Kullu Valley sits the ancient site, but modern town, of Manali. It lacks the colonial history or charm of Shimla, and the culture and spectacular setting common in Lahaul, Spiti and Kinnaur. But it's a pleasant, if overdeveloped, town with lovely forests and orchards nearby for hiking, and good facilities for visitors.

In the 1970s and 1980s, Manali was very much a 'scene'. In summer, the town would attract numerous western hippies and travellers drawn by the high quality marijuana that grows in the area. A lot of these people

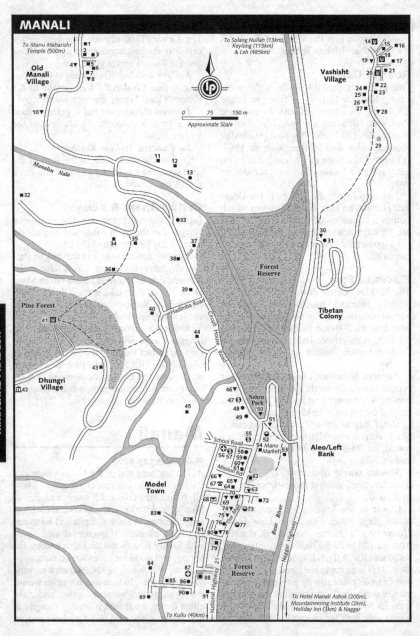

MANALI

To Manu Maharishi
Temple (500m)

Old
Manali
Village

To Solang Nullah (13km),
Keylong (115km)
& Leh (485km)

Vashisht
Village

Manalsu Nala

Forest
Reserve

Pine Forest

Hadimba Road

Circuit House Road

Tibetan
Colony

Dhungri
Village

Nehru Park

School Road

Manu
Market

Aleo/Left
Bank

Mission Rd

Model
Town

The Mall

Beas River

Naggar Highway

Forest
Reserve

National Highway 21

To Kullu (40km)

To Hotel Manali Ashok (200m),
Mountaineering Institute (2km),
Holiday Inn (3km) & Naggar

0   75   150 m
Approximate Scale

HIMACHAL PRADESH

MANALI

PLACES TO STAY			
1	Krishna Guest House	61	Hotel Renuka; Verma
2	Diplomat Guest House		Newsagency
3	Dragon Guest House	64	Sukhiran Guest House
5	Tourist Nest	79	Hotel Ibex;
6	Veer Paying Guest House		Tibetan Market
7	Kishoor Guest House	81	Premier Hotel; Mona Lisa
11	Hotel Riverbank; Hotel Him	82	Hotel Shishar; Lhasa Hotel
	View; Tibetan Kitchen	83	Mount View Hotel
	Restaurant	84	Potala Hotel
12	Rising Moon; Hema Guest	85	Hotel Sunflower
	House; Mamta Paying Guest	90	Hotel Snow Drop
	House; Jungle Bungalow	91	Samrat Hotel
15	Bodh Guest House		
16	New Dharma	PLACES TO EAT	
17	Amrit Guest House	4	Mount View Cafe
21	Kalptaru Guest House	8	Little Tibet Cafe; Shiva
22	Anand Guest House		Garden Cafe
23	Sonam Guest House	9	Ish Cafe
24	Janta Guest House	10	Moon Dance Garden
25	Surabhi Hotel	19	Superbake; Zodiac Cafe;
27	Hotel Bhrigu;		Ranu Rooftop Cafe
	Hotel Valley View	26	Freedom Cafe
32	HPTDC Log Huts	28	Rose Garden
34	Hotel New Highland	30	Phuntsok Coffee House
35	Hotel Kalpana	46	Johnson's Cafe
36	Hotel Chetna	50	Sa-Ba Restaurant
37	Pinewood Hotel	51	HPTDC Juniper Restaurant
38	Sunshine Guest House	60	Sher-e-Punjab Restaurant
39	John Banon's Hotel	63	Mona Lisa Restaurant
40	HPTDC Hotel Rohtang	65	Mayur Restaurant
	Manalsu	66	Swamiji's Madras Cafe;
43	Hotel Shrinagar		Sangam Restaurant
	Regency	69	Moc Restaurant
44	Hotel Tourist	70	Mahadev Food Corner
45	Hotel Hilltop	74	Mount View Restaurant;
53	HPTDC Hotel Beas		Chopsticks Restaurant
54	Hotel Kunzam; HPTDC	75	Kamal Dhaba;
	Tourist Offices		Himalaya Dhaba
		78	Gozy Restaurant

OTHER	
13	HPTDC Club House
14	Hindu Temple
18	Hindu Temple
20	Hindu Temple
29	HPTDC Hot Baths Complex
31	The Enfield Club
33	Nirvana Travels
41	Dhungri Temple
42	Museum of Traditional
	Himachal Culture;
	Utopia Complex
47	State Bank of India;
	Archana Airways
48	Himalayan Journeys
49	Jagson Airlines
52	Taxi Stand
55	UCO Bank; Parkash Studios
56	Mission Hospital
57	Solang Hotel Moneychangers
58	Himalayan Adventures
59	Charitrust Tibetan Handicraft
	Emporium
62	Himcoop
67	Central Telegraph Office
68	Main Post Office
71	Harrison Travel; Kullu-Kashmir
	Handicraft Coop
72	Bookworm
73	Bus Station
76	North Face Adventure Tours
77	Him-Aanchal Taxi Stand
80	Druk Expeditions
86	Inder Motors
87	Mentsikhang Clinic
88	Himalayan Nyingmapa
	Gompa
89	Gadhan Thekchokling
	Gompa

HIMACHAL PRADESH

have moved to the nearby villages of Dhungri and Vashisht, or to Manikaran and Pulga, along the Parbati Valley. Now the character of Manali has changed considerably; with literally hundreds of hotels and guesthouses, it's one of the most popular places in the country for honeymooning Indian couples.

Legend has it that Manu, Hinduism's Noah, stepped off a boat in Manali to recreate human life after floods had devastated the world – Manali means Home of Manu.

High season is mid-April to late June, mid-September to early November, Christmas and New Year.

Orientation
Manali is based around one street – The Mall, which is not nearly as charming as its namesake in Shimla. North-west of Manali centre is Old Manali, and east across the Beas River is the nearby village of Vashisht.

Information
Tourist Office For tourist information go to the HPTDC Tourist Reception Centre (☎ 52175), the small white hut under the Hotel Kunzam. Open 10 am to 5 pm in summer (fewer hours in winter), the Tourist Reception Centre should not be confused with

the far larger HPTDC Tourism Marketing Office (☎ 52360) next door, which sells bus tickets for HPTDC buses, arranges fishing permits and makes reservations for HPTDC skiing courses and hotels.

Money The State Bank of India (SBI) and UCO Bank, opposite the tourist offices, will only change Thomas Cook and American Express travellers cheques. A moneychanger at the Solang Hotel, on School Rd, keeps more convenient hours and will change all major brands of travellers cheques as well as cash. There's a Rs 50 commission for every US$100.

If you are headed north of Manali then change some extra money here as there are no exchange facilities in Lahaul, Spiti or Kinnaur.

Post & Communications The post office, in Model Town, is open Monday to Saturday, 9 am to 5 pm. The poste restante here is reliable. The central telegraph office (fax 52404), a block north, is very helpful and you can make international calls and send/receive faxes here at government rates.

Travel Agencies Of the many travel agencies in Manali, the following locally run places are reliable, long established and organise their own tours.

Antrek Tours
   (☎ 52292, fax 52786) Manu Market – trekking, porters, guides, trekking equipment hire and skiing.
Druk Expeditions
   (☎ 53135) Model Town – trekking and mountaineering.
Himalayan Adventures
   (☎ 52750, fax 52182) The Mall (next to the UCO Bank) – trekking, rafting, jeep safaris, jeep hire (US$45 per day) and trekking equipment hire. Fully inclusive local treks cost US$20 per person per day for a minimum of five persons, rising to US$35 per person for just two people.
Himalayan Journeys
   (☎ 52365, fax 53065, email himjourn@ del3.vsnl.net.in) The Mall – for just about anything.

North Face Adventure Tours
   (☎ 52441, fax 52694) The Mall (near Mount View Restaurant) – paragliding and skiing.

Bookshop Bookworm is at 16 NAC Markets, behind the bus station.

Dhungri Temple

The Dhungri or Hadimba Temple is a four storey wooden building in the middle of a lovely forested parkland, known as the Dhungri Van Vihar. Erected in 1553, the temple is dedicated to the goddess Hadimba and features intricate wooden carvings of dancers and characters from various Hindu stories; horns of bulls and other animals decorate the walls. Every May, there is a major festival at the temple, when sacrifices are carried out in honour of Hadimba.

A new road now goes all the way to the entrance of the park. It's a 20 minute walk or take a taxi or auto-rickshaw (Rs 20).

Museum of Traditional Himachal Culture

This small, privately funded museum near the Dhungri Temple is worth a quick visit. The curator has spent years collecting folk art and handicrafts from surrounding villages to protect the traditions of the Kullu Valley. The museum should keep the same opening hours as the nearby Utopia Complex. There's a reasonable entry fee of Rs 5.

Gadhan Thekchokling Gompa

Built by Tibetan refugees in the late 1960s, the gompa has some brightly coloured frescoes and a central statue of Sakyamuni Buddha. On the outside wall there is a list of Tibetan martyrs killed during the Chinese occupation from 1987 to 1989. The gompa, open from 6 am to 7 pm, dominates the Tibetan area at the bottom of The Mall.

Nearby is the **Himalayan Nyingmapa Gompa**, which is also worth a quick look.

Old Manali

The original settlement of Manali is about 2.5km north-west of 'new' Manali. It's a lovely (but rapidly developing) area of old guesthouses and orchards. The small **Manu Maharishi Temple** is where Manu meditated after he arrived in the area. To get to Old Manali, follow the signs and the road to the left at the top of The Mall – the village is across the bridge, and up the left-hand road.

Activities

The HPTDC Club House, near the bridge to Old Manali, offers one day temporary membership (Rs 5), allowing access to the nice, but pricey, bar and restaurant, and a library where you can read (but not borrow) English-language books. Table tennis and snooker can be played for a few extra rupees.

The Utopia Complex (☎ 53846) is a new leisure centre near the Dhungri Temple, which plans to offer a full size snooker table (Rs 100 per hour), steam bath, gymnasium (Rs 25 per session) and carom boards, as well as a restaurant and small museum.

Organised Tours

Tours are organised by the HPTDC Tourism Marketing Office and local private bus companies (see Getting There & Away later in this section). They may be touristy, but are often the cheapest and easiest way to visit local places, especially if you're on your own and you can't share the cost of a taxi. Each agency offers three identical day trips.

- Rohtang La (3978m), Nehru Kund (lake), Kothi, Rahala Falls & Marrhi viewpoints (Rs 150)
- Naggar Castle, Roerich art gallery & Jagatsukh temples (Rs 125)
- Parbati Valley, Vaishno Temple & Manikaran (Rs 175)

Places to Stay

Prices listed in hotel receptions are the authorised *maximum* price and most places will quickly offer a 'low-season discount' of up to 50%, even during high season if things are quiet. Prices quoted are for high season.

Places to Stay – Budget

While there aren't many cheap places in Manali itself, budget accommodation can be easily found in the nearby villages of Old Manali, Vashisht (see Around Manali) and Dhungri.

Manali *Sukhiran Guest House (☎ 52178)* behind The Mall is one of the best value places in Manali. Basic doubles are Rs 138 with share bath; dorms are Rs 25.

Hotel Renuka (☎ 52309) is central but can be noisy and rooms are nothing special at Rs 300/400 with hot water and balcony.

Mount View Hotel (☎ 52465), in Model Town, has decent doubles with TV for around Rs 400, plus good low-season discounts and recommended food.

Samrat Hotel (☎ 52356), on the main highway past the Hotel Ibex, has good value doubles in low season from Rs 250.

Hotel Snow Drop, in the Tibetan area, offers clean, airy rooms from Rs 100 to Rs 150, depending on the season.

Potala Hotel (☎ 53658), nearby, has clean and comfortable rooms for Rs 300 or Rs 425.

Sunflower (☎ 52419) is cheaper, with doubles for Rs 250 and Rs 350.

Old Manali The road to Old Manali starts to the left of the fork at the top of The Mall. At the bridge, just follow the signs advertising places to stay.

Near the HPTDC Club House are the *Rising Moon*, *Mamta Paying Guest House* and *Jungle Bungalow*, all of which have doubles for about Rs 100. More upmarket places include the *Hotel Riverbank*, *Hotel Him View* and the *Hema Guest House*, with rooms from around Rs 150 to Rs 400.

Tourist Nest (☎ 56520), in the village itself, is new with clean bright doubles with hot water bath for Rs 200 to Rs 250.

Dragon Guest House, opposite, is clean and modern with rooms for Rs 200 and Rs 250 and is surrounded by an apple orchard.

Nearby, the old wooden *Veer Paying Guest House* and the concrete *Kishoor Guest House* have nice settings and charge about Rs 125 for clean rooms with bath.

Farther uphill, the *Diplomat Guest House* and *Krishna Guest House* have rooms for around Rs 100.

Outdoor Activities in Manali

Fishing The hotel reservation counter at the HPTDC Tourism Marketing Office issues day fishing permits for Rs 100. You can also get permits at the fisheries office in Patlikhul. The best angling in the Kullu Valley is said to be at Larji, Katrain and Kasol.

Mountain Biking Himalayan Journeys will rent you a bike and helmet and drop you up at the Rohtang La for Rs 800 (minimum four people). They can also arrange biking tours.

Rafting Some basic rafting is available along the Beas River from May to mid-June, and, depending on the monsoon, from mid-September to mid-October. Trips generally start at Pirdi and continue 16km down to Jhiri. Prices depend on the number of passengers and your bargaining power but are around Rs 800 for the day, including transport, equipment, lunch and a guide. Contact Himalayan Adventures or Himalayan Journeys for more details.

Paragliding In summer, several travel agencies organise paragliding on the slopes of Solang Nullah, north of Manali. Himalayan Journeys and North Face Adventure Tours both offer two-minute tandem 'joy rides' for Rs 400, or 10 to 15 minute 'high rides' for Rs 1500. Both run a day beginners' course for Rs 700 per person and a week long course for Rs 3000 to Rs 4000. Prices include accommodation (if applicable), food, equipment and a guide, but not transport.

Skiing Skiing for beginners is possible at Solang Nullah from January to March – the later the better, because January is very cold. For details, see Solang Nullah in the Around Manali section. Skiing in summer (April to June) is possible at Rohtang La, north of Manali. North Face offers skiing day trips to Mahri, near the pass, for Rs 900.

Ski gear can be rented from the Mountaineering Institute, North Face Adventure Tours and Solang Nullah. All the gear you'll need for a day's skiing will cost around Rs 300.

For about US$850 a day you can try heli-skiing on any of the deep snowfields around the region. Himalayan Journeys can organise this if you have the money and experience.

Mountaineering & Kayaking The Mountaineering Institute & Allied Sports (☎ 52342) is about 3km south of The Mall, down a side road opposite the Ram Regency Honeymoon Hotel in Manali. It offers fixed date, single-sexed, 25 day basic (US$293) and 27 day advanced (US$329) mountaineering courses, and two weeks of kayaking on the Beas River in October/November for US$189. Prices include food, gear, training and (dormitory) accommodation, but not transport.

Hiking There are several good day hikes from Manali. The 12km hike up the western side of the Beas River to the Solang Valley is a nice alternative to the bus. Lama Dugh meadow is a 6km hike up the Manalsu Nala, west of Manali town and makes a nice day or overnight trip.

Dhungri A newer, grungy alternative to Old Manali and Vashisht, Dhungri village is an easy 2km walk from The Mall. Old village family homes have been converted to guesthouses with cheap rooms, share bathrooms, and, more often than not, a surplus of techno music and dope.

Places include the *Freedom Paying Guest House* and *Deodar Retreat*. New places are being built so it's best to just ask around.

Places to Stay – Mid-Range

A lot of the mid-range places are new concrete hotels all lined up in the charmless, uninspiring 'suburb' called Model Town, one block west of The Mall. Each hotel offers almost identical facilities – usually including TV and hot water – for an almost identical price of around Rs 450 for a double (high season). But this is a good area for low-season bargains, especially in summer – many places offer rooms at half the normal price. Of the dozens to choose from, some of the better hotels (close to the post office) are: *Mona Lisa* (☎ *52447*), *Hotel Shishar* (☎ *52745*), *Lhasa Hotel* (☎ *52134*) and *Premier Hotel* (☎ *52473*).

Most of the other places in this range are on the main road between Manali and Old Manali, catering mainly for the Indian family and honeymoon market. There are dozens of places, all of which offer TV, hot water and, often, some seclusion in lovely gardens.

John Banon's Hotel (☎ *52335*) is an old Raj-era building with clean, large rooms for Rs 1000-plus (not to be confused with the super swish, very expensive Banon Resorts nearby).

Sunshine Guest House (☎ *52320*) is another old-style place with a nice lawn and good rooms from Rs 350 to Rs 600.

Pinewood Hotel (☎ *52118*), at Rs 650 a double, is another good place run by the Banon family.

Hotel Chetna (☎ *52245*), farther west, has lovely views of the pine forest and rooms from Rs 250 to Rs 500.

Hotel Kalpana (☎ *52413*), nearby, has secluded doubles from Rs 300 to Rs 550.

Hotel New Highland (☎ *52399*), towards Old Manali, has rooms from Rs 650.

HPTDC runs several places. Bookings can be arranged at the HPTDC Tourism Marketing Office on The Mall.

Hotel Beas (*52832*), on the eastern side of The Mall, has great views of the river, and rooms from Rs 250 to Rs 550.

Hotel Rohtang Manalsu (☎ *52332*), on the road to the Dhungri Temple, is a pleasant place with good views across the valley. Doubles cost Rs 450 to Rs 650.

Places to Stay – Top End

Many of these places provide little extra in the way of service and facilities than the better places in the middle range.

Holiday Inn (☎ *52262, fax 52562*) has all the luxury you would expect, but is several kilometres south of town. Rooms, including meals, cost from Rs 2300.

Hotel Manali Ashok (☎ *52331*), halfway between the Holiday Inn and town, has luxurious rooms with views from Rs 1700 to Rs 2400.

Hotel Shrinagar Regency (☎ *52292*), en route to Dhungri village, has doubles from Rs 1650.

Hotel Ibex (☎ *52480, The Mall*) has rooms from Rs 600 to Rs 1000 in a handy location.

HPTDC's *Hotel Kunzam* (☎ *53197*), at the top of The Mall, has good rooms for Rs 900 and Rs 1150, 30% less in low season.

Places to Eat

Manali The *Sa-Ba* in Nehru Park, at the top of The Mall, has good western food such as hamburgers, pizzas and milkshakes.

HPTDC's *Juniper Restaurant*, right near the bridge, offers a vast selection in a good setting, but with higher prices.

Sher-e-Punjab, on The Mall, has a sterile setting, but its Indian food (as well as pizza and pasta) is recommended.

Gozy Restaurant, at the southern end of The Mall, has good service and a great selection of authentic Punjabi and Gujarati food at reasonable prices.

Mayur Restaurant, just off The Mall, has great vegetarian food and cosy decor.

Swamiji's Madras Cafe has large thalis for Rs 35. The nearby *Sangam* and *Neel Kamal* are also worth a try.

Mahadev Food Corner, a block south, has cheap Indian food and a nice sitting area next to a Hindu temple.

Mount View Restaurant and *Chopsticks,* next door, are cosy, friendly places where you can order authentic Chinese food, Tibetan momos or Japanese sukiyaki.

Moc Restaurant, near the Sukhiran Guest House, shares the same menu and kitchen as

HIMACHAL PRADESH

the Chopsticks but its prices are significantly lower.

Mona Lisa, opposite the bus station, is another congenial place that is popular for its Indian and western food at reasonable prices.

The *Kamal* and *Himalaya* dhabas offer good-value Indian food.

Johnson's Cafe is farther uphill and a bit more upmarket. The pleasant open air garden cafe serves good pasta and pizza (Rs 100), excellent desserts (creme caramel!) and cold beer.

Phuntsok Coffee House, at the junction of the Naggar Highway and the road to Vashisht, is a Tibetan-run place and the best in town. The apple, banana and walnut cakes/pies with custard all come highly recommended.

Old Manali The best places are over the bridge and up the road towards the village. There are several pleasant outdoor places which are great for taking an extended coffee break and swapping travellers' tales. All cater exclusively to westerners, so you'll be lucky to find any real Indian cuisine.

Moon Dance Garden, just over the bridge, is a typical laid-back, outdoor place with one of the many local 'German bakeries'.

Ish Cafe, farther up, is deservedly popular. Nearby, the *Little Tibet Cafe* serves wholesome, cheap Tibetan food.

Also nearby, the *Shiva Garden Cafe* has good Italian food, and serves Israeli cuisine. A bit farther up, the *Mount View Cafe* is worth a visit for its wonderful seclusion.

Back by the bridge, the *Tibet Kitchen* is the best bet, with an excellent range of hearty Tibetan noodles and western delicacies.

Shopping

There are plenty of places to buy clothes and souvenirs in Manali, particularly along The Mall. Prices are generally negotiable. Some of the better places are the Charitrust Tibetan Handicraft Emporium on The Mall, or any of the cooperatives run by local women, such as the Kullu-Kashmir Handicraft Co-op opposite the bus station. For a top quality pashmina shawl (pashmina is shorn from

the underbelly of the Ladakh snow goat), expect to pay upwards of Rs 10,000. Traditional pillbox-style hats (Afghan, Kullu and Kinnauri) are quite cheap.

The Tibetan Market, spread around the back of the Hotel Ibex, has a good range of thangkas and silver and turquoise jewellery but you'll find higher quality at the Tibetan and Nepalese shops near the post office.

For an indulgence, try some of the locally made pickles, jams and juices. Himco-op on The Mall is a good place to look. Natural oils for massages and shampoos are also available.

Getting There & Away

Air The nearest airport is Bhuntar, 52km south of Manali and 10km south of Kullu town. See Getting There & Away in Kullu for details on flights. There are no flights between Manali/Kullu (Bhuntar) and Leh. You can make bookings at the Jagson Airlines office (☎ 52843) in the north of Manali town (Visa cards accepted), and at most travel agencies. The official office for Archana Airways is Ambassador Travels (☎ 52110), next to the State Bank of India.

Bus There are two booths, open from 9 am to noon and 2 to 5 pm, which provide computerised booking services. You can book a ticket up to a month in advance.

Long-distance bus companies from Manali (and local sightseeing tour operators) are:

Enn Bee Tours & Travels
  (☎ 52650) The Mall (opposite the bus station)
Harison Travels
  (☎ 53319) The Mall
Ibex Travels
  (☎ 52480) Hotel Ibex, The Mall
Swagtam Tours
  (☎ 52390) Mission Rd

Leh Several daily deluxe and public buses connect Manali with Leh from about June to mid-September – private buses run a few weeks later according to the weather and demand. This long, truly spectacular ride takes two days, with a stopover in a tent.

HPTDC runs a daily bus (originating in Delhi) for Rs 1000, including an overnight camp at Sarchu, dinner and breakfast. Private agencies charge around Rs 800 without food or accommodation. Public buses cost from Rs 345 to Rs 525 and normally stop overnight at Keylong. Take some food, water and warm clothes and try not to sit at the back of the bus.

For details about the route, see Leh to Manali in the Ladakh & Zanskar chapter.

Kullu & Parbati Valleys Public buses shuttle between Manali and Kullu town every 15 minutes (Rs 25, two hours). Most buses travel via the quicker, western bank of the Beas. To Naggar (Rs 10, one hour) there are six daily buses from Manali, leaving every hour or so from 9.30 am.

Along the Parbati Valley, six public buses to Manikaran (Rs 35, 4 hours) leave Manali daily between 6.30 am and 1.30 pm. Alternatively get a bus to Bhuntar and change, as buses run from here to Manikaran until around 6 pm.

Other Places To Delhi (16 hours), there is one public 'deluxe' bus (Rs 345), one semideluxe (Rs 298), at least one overnight HPTDC bus (Rs 450) and usually several overnight private buses (about Rs 400). Private companies and HPTDC also run daily buses, in season, to Shimla (Rs 250 to Rs 275, 10 hours), Dharamsala (Rs 250 to Rs 275, 10 hours) and Chandigarh (Rs 300, 10 hours). You may find prices a little less in low season.

There are three daily public buses to Dharamsala (Rs 131, 10 hours); five to Delhi (Rs 298 semideluxe); four to Shimla (Rs 140 semideluxe); and five to Mandi (Rs 45, five hours). There are five early morning buses to Keylong (Rs 57, six hours). For Spiti catch the 4 am departure to Tabo (Rs 130, 14 hours) or the 6 am bus to Kaza (Rs 100, 12 hours).

Taxi Long-distance taxis are available from the two Him-Aanchal Taxi Operators' Union stands (☎ 52450) on The Mall. A one-way/return taxi from Manali to Kullu is Rs 500/700 (Rs 850 returning via Naggar). The fare to Naggar is Rs 300/400. Other one-way fares include Dharamsala (Rs 2500) and Leh (Rs 11,000, for three days, two nights).

Getting Around

To/From the Airport For buses between Bhuntar airport and Manali, take a regular Bhuntar to Kullu then a regular Kullu to Manali bus. A taxi between Manali and Bhuntar costs around Rs 600.

Motorcycle There are several places that hire motorcycles in old Manali and Vashisht, but only in summer. Nirvana Travels (☎ 53222), in north Manali, hires Enfields for Rs 275 per 24 hours, including third party insurance. For bike repairs or a tune-up before heading up to Leh, try Inder Motors in Manali's Tibetan area or The Enfield Club by the turn-off to Vashisht.

Auto-Rickshaw Known locally as three-wheelers, these can take you, and your heavy luggage, to Dhungri, Old Manali and Vashisht, but not much farther, for a negotiable Rs 30 to Rs 40.

AROUND MANALI
Vashisht

Vashisht is a lovely little village, about 4km by road up the hillside from The Mall. There are several decaying temples in the village dedicated to the sage Vashisht Muni and the god Rama.

The footpath and road to Vashisht go straight past the HPTDC Vashisht Hot Baths Complex, open every day from 8 am to 8 pm. A 30 minute soak in the regular baths costs Rs 40 for one person, Rs 50 for two; a splash-out in the deluxe baths costs Rs 100 for two people. The common public baths (separate areas for men and women) in Vashisht village are free, but don't look very hygienic. They are open daily from 5 am to 9 pm.

Places to Stay Vashisht remains a very popular place for long term budget travellers

HIMACHAL PRADESH

attracted by its cheap facilities, great setting and the availability of some locally grown 'horticultural products'.

New Dharma, *Bodh*, *Amrit* and *Kalptaru* guesthouses all offer very similar, no-frills rooms in the heart of the village, usually with a share bathroom, from about Rs 60 to Rs 100.

Anand Hotel has cleaner, spacious rooms with bath for Rs 100. It plans to open an Internet cafe here by 1999.

Surabhi Hotel is more expensive, but still good value, with nice rooms, great views and a *real* bath for Rs 250 or Rs 350.

Hotel Bhrigu (☎ 8240), and *Hotel Valley View* next door, offer good rooms and great views from Rs 300 to Rs 500.

Places to Eat The *cafe* at the HPTDC Hot Baths Complex serves hot and cold drinks, and a selection of good Chinese and Indian food.

Rose Garden Inn, next door, has pricey but delicious Italian and other 'continental' food.

Super Bake, in the village centre, serves wonderful baked goodies.

Ranu Rooftop Cafe and the *Zodiac Cafe* are both good places to hang out.

Freedom Cafe, just down the road, has a great outdoor setting and serves good western breakfasts and Israeli food, though it's a little more expensive than it used to be.

Hotel Valley View is more upmarket, with daily specials and good views.

Getting There & Away Vashisht is connected by a good road, so a three-wheeler can take you there for around Rs 40 (a good idea if you have loads of gear). On foot, it's quicker to take the unmarked trail which begins about 200m past the turn-off to Vashisht and goes all the way to the Hotel Valley View via the HPTDC Hot Baths Complex.

Solang Nullah
Some of Himachal Pradesh's best ski slopes are at Solang Nullah, about 13km north-west of Manali. There are 2.5km of runs, with black, red and blue routes mainly for begin-

ners, and one 300m ski lift. February and March are the best months to ski; January is bitterly cold, and Christmas can be busy with Indian tourists. But don't disregard Solang if it isn't snowing; the area is very pretty in spring and summer and offers great hikes.

Several options for skiing courses exist. Prices quoted are only a guide – final prices will depend upon the size of the group, type of accommodation and level of service.

HPTDC
  Organises seven-day skiing packages from Manali. Includes accommodation in Manali, food, lessons and some sightseeing for Rs 3500 per person. Some travellers have written complaining about poor tuition and service.
Antrek Tours
  Bookable through the Raju Paying Guest House, Manali, it offers seven to 10 day packages, including accommodation, all meals, porters and instruction, for around Rs 700 per day, plus Rs 200 extra per day for ski-gear hire.
North Face Adventure Tours
  Charges Rs 4660 for one week, Rs 3560 for three nights/four days and Rs 2860 for two nights/two days all-inclusive packages, with accommodation in Solang.
Himalayan Journeys
  Offers week-long courses from Rs 6000 (in a group of four) to Rs 7500 (individual tuition). A two week course is Rs 11,000. Prices include accommodation, guide and equipment.
Himalayan Adventures
  Runs a basic seven day course (minimum five persons) for Rs 3000.
Mountaineering Institute & Allied Sports
  Runs basic, intermediate and advanced all-inclusive 15-day courses for US$262, includes equipment, food and dorm accommodation near the slopes, but not transport.

Places to Stay & Eat The *Friendship Guest House* has large rooms for Rs 300 and smaller rooms with share bath for Rs 150.

Raju Paying Guest House has large doubles with attractive wood panelling for Rs 200, or four-bed rooms for Rs 300.

North Face offers a more basic, but still comfortable, alternative place to stay caters mainly for prearranged skiing packages.

Each hotel serves large plates of simple, hot, vegetarian food accompanied by loads of tea. There are several other good *restaurants* around the village catering for the tourist crowd, but these are usually closed in the low season.

Getting There & Away Buses leave Manali at 8 am and 1 and 4 pm every day for Solang Nullah (Rs 7). A nicer option is to take the bus to Palchan, the turn-off to Solang Nullah from the main road, and then walk for about an hour to Solang through gorgeous countryside. Taxis cost Rs 225/300 one way/return from Manali. Roads may be blocked by snow in January and February.

Lahaul & Spiti

Lahaul and Spiti, the largest district in Himachal Pradesh, is a vast area of high mountains and narrow valleys bounded by Ladakh to the north, Tibet to the east, Kinnaur to the south-east and the Kullu Valley to the south. Lahaul is often regarded as a midway point en route to Leh and the Indus Valley, but has more to offer travellers. Spiti has only recently been opened to foreign tourists attracted to its isolated Buddhist gompas and villages.

Most people in Spiti are Buddhists, and colourful gompas dominate the villages and village life. In Lahaul, about half of the population is Buddhist, while the other half is Hindu. In some Lahauli temples and homes it is not unusual to see idols from both religions side by side.

Due to the paucity of agricultural land, polyandry has traditionally been common, though this has changed recently. Farms, which are usually inherited by the eldest son, rely solely on natural springs or complicated irrigation systems for crop growth.

The main crops are barley *(no)*, wheat *(do)*, potatoes *(alu)*, feed for goats, sheep and yaks, and hops (Lahaul and Spiti is the only area in India where hops are grown). *Kuth*, a herb reputedly endowed with medicinal powers, is exported to Europe.

The main indigenous language of the area is Bhoti, which is very similar to Tibetan;

there are several distinct, but mutually comprehensible, dialects. The very handy word *jule*, which in Ladakh means hello, goodbye, please and thank you, is also used in Lahaul and Spiti.

Both Lahaul and Spiti are cut off from the Kullu Valley by heavy snow for up to eight months of the year. The Rohtang La to Lahaul is normally closed between mid-November and mid-June and the Kunzum La to Spiti is normally closed from mid-October to mid-July. A daily bus usually manages to run up the Sutlej Valley to Kaza year-round, except during periods of heavy snowfall in January and February. Beware of the power of the sun in this region – you can get burnt very easily even on cold days.

The best time to visit Lahaul is mid-June to late October, and Spiti is August to October.

History

In the 10th century, upper Lahaul was united with Spiti and Zanskar as part of the vast Guge kingdom of western Tibet. After Ladakh's defeat by the Mongol-Tibetan armies in the 18th century, Lahaul was split into two regions. Upper Lahaul came under the influence of the Kullu raja, while lower Lahaul, across to the district of Pangi, came under the influence of the courts of Chamba. The more geographically isolated Spiti remained part of Ladakh.

In 1847, Kullu and Lahaul came under British administration as a division of the Kangra state; Spiti was added two years later. In reality power rested with the Nonos, hereditary rulers of Spiti.

With the Chinese occupation of Tibet in 1949, the region's cultural links were severed. The exile of the Dalai Lama has, ironically, seen a resurgence in the cultural and religious life of Spiti. At the same time, improved communications have seen a rapid integration with the rest of India and a tentative entry into the modern world.

Permits

Inner line permits are not necessary for travel from Lahaul to Spiti and you are now permitted to go as far down valley as Tabo. A permit is only necessary if you're travelling between Tabo and Rekong Peo, the capital of Kinnaur. For more information, see the Inner Line Permits boxed text in the Kinnaur entry.

KAZA
☎ 01906
Kaza (3640m) is the administrative centre and transport hub of Spiti subdistrict.

Kaza's 'old town', around the new bus stand, is a maze of little shops, hotels and whitewashed houses. The 'new town', across the creek, is a collection of tin-roofed government buildings, including the subdivisional magistrate's office (look for the Indian flag). The State Bank of India doesn't change money, though some shopkeepers might exchange small US dollar notes.

It's an easy-going place to spend a few days – to rest from the arduous bus trips, to visit some stunning monasteries or to wait for your permit if you're heading on to Kinnaur.

Places to Stay & Eat
Mahabauda Guest House, on the main road at the top end of the old town, is a family-run place offering cosy rooms with share bath for Rs 100 or Rs 150.

Snow Lion Hotel and Restaurant, next door, is also friendly and good value with clean rooms for Rs 100 or Rs 130.

Milaraepa Guesthouse, across the creek, has good-value but scruffy singles/doubles for Rs 100/150.

Sakya's Abode (☎ 22254), next door, is a favourite of tour groups in a lovely garden. Good rooms cost Rs 200, Rs 300 and Rs 500, while gloomy singles cost Rs 100 and dorm beds are Rs 50. It has a great dining hall serving good Spitian food.

HPTDC's *Tourist Lodge*, in the new town, has five rooms with hot bath for Rs 300.

Layul Cafe serves huge bowls of excellent *kiyu* (square noodles, potato, tomato and onion stew) for Rs 25. Other places for food include the Tibetan-style *Ladakhi Hotel* and *Himalaya Hotel*.

Getting There & Away
The new bus stand is on the southern edge of town. A bus to Rekong Peo (Rs 105, 12 hours) leaves Kaza at 7 am. There are one or two daily buses to/from Manali (Rs 100, 12 hours) at 7 am and one to Kullu (Rs 120) at 4 am. There are also irregular buses between Kaza and Keylong (eight hours); otherwise take a Manali-bound bus to Gramphu (Rs 68) and change there. For Tabo (Rs 30, two hours) take any east-bound bus.

There's no official taxi stand or office, though minibuses often hang around the old town centre. Fares are high because of the lack of competition and petrol transportation costs. A taxi to Manali costs a pricey Rs 4000.

AROUND KAZA
Ki Gompa & Kibber
Ki (pronounced 'key'), the oldest and largest gompa in Spiti, has a spectacular location (4116m), 14km from Kaza. It was built by the famous Tibetan translator Ringchen Zangpo and belongs to the Gelukpa order. The gompa was invaded three times in the 19th century by Ladakhis, Dogras and Sikhs, and later partially destroyed by an earthquake in 1975.

Although being restored (donations are expected), the gompa is still famous for its priceless collection of ancient thangkas. No photos are allowed inside the gompa. Ki has a **chaam festival** in June/July.

About 11km from Ki village is the small village of **Kibber**, also known as Khyipur. Kibber was once part of the overland salt trade, and has a dramatic, if desolate location. At 4205m, it claims, somewhat dubiously, to be the highest village in the world (Gete, at 4270m, another village about 7km east of Ki, has a better claim to this honour). The **Ladarcha Festival**, held near Kibber each July, attracts Buddhists from all over the region.

Places to Stay & Eat It is normally possible to stay at Ki Gompa for a donation, otherwise the friendly *Samdup Tashi Khangsar Hotel & Restaurant* in Ki village has nice rooms for Rs 50.

Kibber has three small guesthouses. *Sargaung Guest House* and *Hotel Rainbow* rent out no-frills rooms for Rs 50 and offer basic food. *Resang Hotel & Restaurant*, at the entrance to the village, has carpeted rooms with bath for Rs 150.

Getting There & Away In summer, a bus leaves Kaza every day at 2 pm for Ki and Kibber (Rs 12). This will allow you time to see Ki Gompa while the bus continues on to Kibber, but you won't be able to see both Ki and Kibber in one day. A return taxi from Kaza to both Ki Gompa and Kibber village costs Rs 450 to Rs 500; to Ki only, Rs 250/300 one way/return.

Some travellers have attempted to walk to both Ki and Kibber from Kaza in one day, but it is a very long walk (about 22km from Kaza to Kibber). Perhaps a better option is to get the bus to Kibber, walk down to Ki and stay the night there.

Dhankar Gompa

Built nearly 1000 years ago, Dhankar Gompa has a spectacular rocky setting. Once the site of the capital of Spiti, and then a jail, the gompa still has some interesting sculptures and frescoes. A new monastery is being constructed 1km from the site and this is the place to look for a guide to show you around. Herbs growing here are claimed to cure lung and heart complaints.

From Kaza to Dhankar, take any bus headed down the valley and get off just before the village of *Sichling*, from where there is a steep 8km walk (including an altitude increase of about 600m). If you're lucky, there might be a daily bus between Sichling and Dhankar. A one-way/return taxi from Kaza to Dhankar Gompa costs Rs 600/700.

Pin Valley

The Pin Valley, south of Dhankar, has been declared a national park and is famous for its wildlife – tourist agencies refer to it as the 'land of ibex and snow leopard' – but you are unlikely to see anything bigger than a marmot. The beautiful valley holds Spiti's only concentration of Nyingmapa Buddhism. The

most important gompa in the valley is the 600-year-old **Kungri Gompa**, 2km off the main road near Gulling.

This is trekking and camping country. Accommodation is limited to the *Hotel Himalaya* at Gulling (Rs 120) and the *Ibex* and *Narzang* guesthouses at Sagnam (Rs 35 to Rs 50).

Public transport goes only to Mikkim, though a road is currently being built as far as Mud. A daily bus leaves Kaza at 9 am (Rs 22), or wait for it at Attargo, at the junction with the main road. A one-way taxi from Kaza to Mikkim costs Rs 700.

Tabo Gompa

Tabo Gompa is one of the most important monasteries in the Tibetan Buddhist world, and is planned as the place where the current Dalai Lama will retire. It was built in 996 AD by The Great Translator, Ringchen Zangpo, who brought artists from Kashmir to decorate the gompa. Along with Alchi in Ladakh and Tholing in western Tibet, Tabo has some of the best preserved examples of Indo-Tibetan art remaining in the world.

There are nine temples in the complex (collectively known as the *choskhor*), all at ground level and dating from the 10th to the 16th century. The main assembly hall of the **Tsuglhakhang** is surrounded by 33 raised Bodhisattva statues and houses a four-sided statue of Sarvarvid Vairocana, one of the five Dhyani Buddhas.

To the left of the Tsuglhakhang is the **Lhakang Chenmo**, featuring a central Sakyamuni Buddha and eight Medicine Buddhas. Farther left is the **Serkhang** (Golden Chapel). The statue of Tara is particularly beautiful, showing the same fluid lines and coloured *dhoti* as seen in Ladakh's Alchi Gompa.

Around the back of the main complex is the **Kyil Khor** (Mystic Mandala Temple), with some beautiful but faded mandalas. The last two chapels to the north are the **Dromton Lhakhang**, notable for its Kashmiri-influenced wooden door frame and the **Maitreya Chapel**, with a 6m statue of Maitreya (Jampa in Tibetan).

HIMACHAL PRADESH

On the other side of the road, opposite Tabo village, there are some **caves** known locally as Pho Gompa, with some faded ancient murals – bring a torch.

The excellent **library** in the monastery guesthouse is open to all and is an excellent place to learn about Tibetan Buddhism. There is also a **thangka painting school** nearby, founded by the Dalai Lama.

Places to Stay & Eat The *gompa guesthouse* has good rooms with share/private bath for Rs 150/250 and dorms for Rs 50.

Himalayan Ajanta Hotel has peaceful, carpeted rooms for Rs 150 and Rs 100.

The best food is at the *Tenzin Restaurant* and *Millennium Monastery Restaurant* at the back of the gompa guesthouse.

Getting There & Away From Kaza to Tabo (Rs 30, two hours), take the 7 am bus, which goes on to Rekong Peo. Buses returning to Kaza pass through Tabo in the afternoon. A bus to Kullu departs around 5.30 am daily. A taxi from Kaza costs Rs 1000.

KAZA TO KEYLONG

From Kaza, the first main village is Losar, about 60km away. It is a beautiful place with a couple of cheap guesthouses. A little farther on is the Kunzum La (4551m). From the pass, a 9km trail goes to the lovely **Chandratal** (Moon Lake), at about 4250m.

Batal is the starting point for treks to nearby **Bara Shigri** (Big Glacier), which is up to 10km long and 1km wide – one of the longest glaciers in the Himalaya. There are a couple of *dhabas* at Batal offering basic food.

Get off at Gramphu (or Keylong) if you want to continue on to Manali.

Khoksar is desolate and regarded as the coldest place in Himachal Pradesh. There's a police checkpoint here and you'll need to get out and sign the register. Single women travellers have reported harassment here so be on your toes, especially at night or if you smell alcohol on anyone's breath.

The road continues on to Gondhla, site of the seven storey **castle** of the Thakur of Gondhla and the starting point for a visit to

the **Guru Ghantal Gompa** at the village of Tupchiling, a steep 4km away. Founded about 800 years ago, but repaired extensively about 30 years ago, the gompa is linked to the one at Stakna, in Ladakh, and belongs to the Drukpa order. You can also hike to Tupchiling from **Tandi**, where the Bhaga and Chandra rivers join to form the Chenab.

KEYLONG
☎ 019002

In the fertile Bhaga valley, Keylong, the capital of Lahaul and Spiti, is a reasonable place to break up the journey from Leh to Manali (although you're almost at Manali anyway), or to base yourself for day trips to nearby gompas.

The bus station is on the main Manali to Leh road, from where it's a short walk down a series of steps to the town itself. There's a telegraph office in the north of town but nowhere to change money. Drilbu Adventures (☎ 22207), next to the Gyespa Hotel, is a new travel agency which can help arrange porters and transport to Leh.

Places to Stay & Eat
Lamayuru Hotel is a good budget bet; spacious, but damp rooms with hot water bathroom are Rs 125.

Gyespa Hotel has dreary singles/doubles for Rs 100/150 and is an emergency option only. However, it has a good restaurant.

Hotel Dubchen Keylong is better, with doubles for Rs 175 or Rs 250.

Hotel Snowland (☎ 22219), a two minute walk uphill from the Lamayaru, has comfortable rooms with nice bathrooms from Rs 300 to Rs 450.

HPTDC's *Tourist Bungalow (☎ 22247)* has a few overpriced doubles at Rs 350, and some dorm beds (six in a room) for Rs 50.

Hotel Dekyid (☎ 22217) and *Tashi Deleg* are mid-range places, with clean rooms for around Rs 300. Tashi Deleg has a good restaurant.

Getting There & Away
Six daily buses travel between Keylong and Manali (Rs 57, six hours); book your ticket

in advance at the ticket office. To Kaza sometimes there are direct buses; otherwise change at Gramphu.

From 15 July to 15 September the daily long-distance deluxe HPTDC buses between Leh and Manali stop in Keylong but it's very hard to get a confirmed seat. You may have to book the ticket from Manali to Leh and pay the full whack. The public bus costs about half the HPTDC price of Rs 600 and leaves Keylong at 4 am. Plenty of trucks ply the busy road and are a good alternative. (See the Leh to Manali section in the Ladakh & Zanskar chapter for more details.)

AROUND KEYLONG
Khardong Gompa
The 900-year-old gompa at Khardong, formerly a capital of Lahaul, lies directly across the Bhaga Valley from Keylong. This Drukpa Kagyud monastery is the largest in the area with about 30 lamas and *chomos* (nuns). There are excellent frescoes but you'll have to track down a nun to open the doors for you.

To get to the monastery, head through the bazaar, follow the stepped path down to the hospital, continue to the bridge over the Bhaga River and then hike up to Khardong.

Shashur Gompa
Three kilometres from Keylong is the Shashur Gompa. Dedicated to a Zanskari lama, it was built in the 16th century and is of the Gelukpa order. The 5m thangka is famous in the region. An annual **festival**, held every June or July (depending on the Tibetan calendar) is renowned for the mask dances performed by the lamas.

Kinnaur

☎ 01786
Kinnaur is a remote mountainous district between Shimla and the Tibetan border. The region was de-restricted in 1991 and travel to and around Kinnaur is now possible with easy-to-obtain permits.

Kinnaur is bound to the north by the formidable Zanskar Range, which forms the border with Tibet. The region is drained by the Sutlej River, which flows from close to Mt Kailash in Tibet. To the south, the Himalaya forms the backdrop of the region, with Kinnaur Kailash (6050m) one of its most spectacular peaks. South of Kinnaur Kailash is the popular Sangla Valley, which has been described as one of the most scenic in the entire Himalaya.

Because of regular references in ancient Hindu texts as 'celestial musicians', Kinnauris have always regarded themselves as a distinct people of the Aryan group. Most Kinnauris follow a mixture of Hinduism, which they gained from the area's ancient links with the rest of India, and Tibetan Buddhism. Particularly near the borders of Tibet, villages often have both Hindu and Buddhist temples, and lamas still influence village life. Kinnaur also has a rich spread of local gods, which live side by side with Hindu and Buddhist deities.

Probably the most distinctive part of the Kinnauris' dress is the grey woollen cap worn by men and women. It is curled up at one side, edged with red or green felt strips, and is called a *thepang*. Kinnauri shawls are famous for their quality and design.

Barley and wheat are the dominant crops, but peas, potatoes, apples, apricots and walnuts are often grown. Tradition forbids Kinnauris to consume chicken but they enjoy alcohol, such as *angoori* grape wine and *arak* made from fermented barley.

Kinnauri (often called Homskad) is the major indigenous language and it has about 12 different dialects. One of these is called Sangnaur, and is only spoken in the village of the same name, near Puh.

The roads in upper Kinnaur rank as some of the most spectacular in the Himalaya, passing through into the trans-Himalaya of upper Kinnaur and Spiti, without crossing a mountain pass.

Up a side road from the main highway through Kinnaur are the two main towns of Kalpa, the former capital, and Rekong Peo, the current capital of Kinnaur. Both places have the most stupendous settings in all of Himachal Pradesh – anywhere up the road will give you incredible views of mighty Kinnaur Kailash, among other mountains, at around 6000m.

The road up the Sutlej Valley – the Hindustan Tibet Highway – remains open for most of the year. The popular Sangla Valley is best either in spring (April to the end of May) or autumn (September and October).

PERMITS

From the Shimla region, you can get as far as Rekong Peo, Kalpa and the Sangla Valley without a permit. For travel to northern Kinnaur, past Jangi to Tabo in Spiti, you currently need an inner line permit. These can be easily obtained from the subdivisional magistrate's (SDM) office in Rekong Peo (see the Inner Line Permits boxed text).

REKONG PEO
☎ 01786

Rekong Peo has good facilities and transport connections, and is the place to apply for an inner line permit.

Orientation & Information

Rekong Peo is very small; everything is within a yak's spit of the bus stop in the centre of the village. The banks here do *not* change foreign currency. To get an inner line permit head for the SDM office at the bottom of town. There are several places to make photocopies of permits and passports, and stock up on some necessities (mineral water is hard to find outside of Peo). The Himachal Emporium, 100m past the Fairyland Hotel, sells Kinnauri caps, shawls etc.

Things to See

A lovely, brightly coloured gompa, the **Kinnaur Kalachakra Celestial Palace**, or Mahabodhi Gompa, is a 20 minute steep walk above the village, just behind the radio station. There is a huge outdoor Buddha statue nearby, facing Kinnaur Kailash. The setting alone is probably worth the trip to Kinnaur.

Places to Stay & Eat

Fairyland Guest House (☎ 22477), 200m from the bus stop, has decent rooms with hot water for Rs 200; an extra Rs 50 gives you fantastic views of Kinner Kailash without having to get out of bed. Its restaurant has a good selection of Indian food.

Hotel Snow View, in the centre of town; *Hotel Rangin*, along the path to the bus station; and the *Shambhala Hotel*, a 10 minute walk uphill from the bus station, all offer charmless but cheap rooms.

Shivling View Hotel & Restaurant (☎ 22421) is a five minute walk west of town on the road to Kalpa. Pleasant doubles with hot water cost Rs 220.

Manish Bhojnayla restaurant, in the centre of town, serves excellent Tibetan *thugpa*, momos and sweet tea.

Getting There & Away

Most arriving buses let passengers off in the centre of town but then actually depart from the new bus station, a five minute walk uphill from the centre (take the pathway as it's much quicker). Most buses are through buses, so departure times and seat bookings are a little unpredictable.

There are occasional buses uphill to Kalpa (via Pangi), but it's a lot quicker to get a taxi (Rs 100) or even hitch.

There are daily buses to Kaza (Rs 105, 12 hours) at 7.30 am, and to Sangla (Rs 25, 2½ hours) and Chitkul (Rs 35, 2¼ hours) at 9.30 am and 12.30, 1.30 and 4 pm. To Shimla, there are at least six buses a day starting from 4.30 am (Rs 120, 10 hours); there are also several private buses to Rampur.

KALPA

Known as Chini when it was the main town in Kinnaur, Kalpa is the legendary winter home of Shiva (during the winter, the god is said to retire to his Himalayan home here and indulge his passion for hashish). In the month of Magha (January/February), the gods of Kinnaur supposedly meet here for an annual conference with Shiva. Kalpa was also a favourite resting place for several high-level British colonialists, including Lord Dalhousie.

Kalpa is a tiny collection of narrow lanes, 7km and 600m above Rekong Peo. What it

Inner Line Permits

The Indo-Tibetan (Chinese) border is a touchy zone (the two countries were at war in 1962) and permits are currently needed for any travel within 40km of the Tibetan border. However, regulations have relaxed considerably in the last few years and these permits are now a mere formality; there is even talk of scrapping them entirely. For now you'll need an inner line permit for travel between Kinnaur and Spiti. You may also need a permit for certain treks – check before setting off. Indian nationals need no permit. You don't need a special permit to drive a car or motorcycle in the area – your biggest headache is finding fuel between Rekong Peo and Kaza.

In theory, permits can be obtained from district magistrates in Shimla, Rekong Peo, Keylong, Kullu and Chamba, or subdivisional magistrates in Kaza, Rampur and Nichar. In reality, Rekong Peo and Kaza are by far the easiest places to get a permit.

Officially you need a group of four people to apply, but this rule has been relaxed in Kaza and Rekong Peo, as it is often difficult to get a group together. You need three passport-sized photos, a photocopy of the front pages of your passport (with your personal details and photo), an application form from the magistrate's office and some patience – the whole process could take up to a day, assuming the official you need isn't 'out of station'.

In Shimla and Keylong you may also need a 'letter of introduction' from a travel agency. Most agencies will provide this for a small fee, or even arrange the whole permit for a little more.

Despite what may be written on the permit, you can stay in any village and camp anywhere along the main road between Kaza and Rekong Peo; you can travel on any form of public or private transport; and you can travel alone or in a group of any size. The form states you 'shall not resort to photography' – there is no restriction, but be careful around any sensitive or military areas (ie bridges, checkpoints). It also states that you cannot carry any 'maps' – you are allowed to do this, but most maps aren't very good anyway.

Checkpoints between Rekong Peo and Kaza are at Jangi, Chango and Sumdo. Never venture too close to the Tibetan border or too far from the main roads or you could end up lost – or worse.

lacks in facilities, Kalpa makes up with in atmosphere, charm, a couple of old wooden temples, a large chorten and some nice walks.

The walk between Kalpa and Rekong Peo is much shorter (45 minutes) if you follow the short cuts rather than the winding road. Don't even think about it uphill.

Places to Stay & Eat

HPTDC's *Hotel Kinner Kailash* has quite good rooms for Rs 500, Rs 600 and Rs 800. It's a stiff five minute walk above the village centre – look for the characteristic green roof.

Auktong Guest House (☎ 26019), set in a pleasant apple orchard a five minute walk

north-east of Kalpa village, is the best budget place. Pleasant rooms with share bath and nice views cost Rs 175.

Timberline Trekking Camps, on the outskirts of the village, offers luxury tents (with hot water) in a pleasant location for Rs 650. The whole place packs up and goes back to Delhi from October to May.

Getting There & Away

There are somewhat unreliable buses between Kalpa and Rekong Peo (Rs 5, one hour) at 6.30, 9, 10 and 10.30 am. Most continue on to other destinations, so if you are headed to Shimla or the Sangla Valley check first to see if there is a direct bus from

HIMACHAL PRADESH

Kalpa, otherwise head down to Rekong Peo. Taxis to Rekong Peo cost Rs 100/150 one way/return.

SANGLA VALLEY

The Sangla, or Baspa, Valley has been called 'the most beautiful valley in the Himalaya'. This is pushing it a bit, but the valley is graced with fine traditional wooden architecture, friendly people and spectacular mountains. The road into the valley must be one of the most hair-raising in the Himalaya. The Sangla Valley is mildly affected by the monsoon and can be wet and miserable in the summer.

Sangla

This village is the largest in the valley. From here you can hike 2km to **Kamru**, which has a five storey, wooden fort and a couple of temples. Kamru is a former capital of the Bushahr empire which once ruled Kinnaur.

Baspa Guesthouse (☎ 42206) has rooms for Rs 165, or Rs 220 with bath. *Highland* has basic rooms for Rs 150. *Kailash View*, just above the village, has good rooms with hot water for Rs 300 and dormitory beds for Rs 75. *Monal Restaurant* in the centre of town is a good place for Indian and Chinese food and breakfast.

There are several buses a day to Chitkul, Rampur and Rekong Peo.

Chitkul

The 44km valley road finishes at the pretty village of Chitkul, 1½ hours by bus from Sangla, where there are three 500-year-old **temples** and a small gompa. The friendly *Anwar House* offers rustic but pleasant doubles/triples for Rs 100/150 and will cook up basic food. Buses leave for Rekong Peo at 6.30 am and 2 pm.

REKONG PEO TO TABO

From Rekong Peo to Tabo in Spiti, there is private accommodation at Nako only. There are small gompas at Khanum, near Spillo, and at Morang.

Nako, 7km uphill from Yangthang, has a beautiful setting around a lovely small lake.

There is an 11th century **gompa** here, with four temples. The yellow *guesthouse* by the bus stop has rooms for Rs 100 and Rs 150. Buses head up to Nako from Yangthang at 1.30 and 6 pm and head back down at 6 am. It's an easy downhill walk. Nearby Milling is a blackspot for landslides. If you encounter one, you may have to walk across the slip and catch another bus or jeep on the other side.

Southern Himachal Pradesh

There are several areas of interest in the southern regions of the state, including the old settlement of Nahan, and picturesque Renuka Lake. If you're heading for the hill station of Mussoorie in northern Uttar Pradesh, you'll most likely travel via Paonta Sahib, on the border, which has an ancient Sikh gurdwara.

NAHAN
☎ 01702

The historical town of Nahan, founded in 1621, has an interesting bazaar, packed with crumbling temples and interesting backstreets. Few tourists make it here. It's a good place to break the trip between Shimla and Dehra Dun and is a springboard to nearby Renuka Lake.

Nahan hosts a festival called **Bhawan Dwadshi** at the end of the monsoon, when over 50 idols of Hindu gods are led through the streets and ceremonially bathed in picturesque Ranital (Rani Lake) in the centre of town.

Nahan is built on two levels, connected by the old town bazaar. The bus station is at the bottom, and the old palace (Raja Mahal; closed to visitors), football ground and Lytton Memorial building are at the top.

Places to Stay & Eat

Hotel Hill View, by the bus station, has decent rooms for Rs 100, Rs 200 or Rs 450.

Renuka Hotel (☎ 23306), at the top of town, opposite the football ground, has doubles with bath for Rs 100, Rs 125 and Rs 150, but the cheaper rooms are windowless and uninspiring.

Hotel Regency (☎ 23302) is the best hotel in town; good-value rooms with a nice balcony and hot bath are Rs 250. The *Milan Restaurant* here is the town's best.

Sirmaur Mahal Guest House (☎ 24378), in the bazaar's backstreets, has nice doubles for Rs 125 and Rs 150 and enjoys excellent views of the Raja Mahal.

Getting There & Away

There are hourly buses to Shimla (Rs 67, six hours) and Dehra Dun (Rs 41, three hours), with last buses leaving at 3 pm and 7 pm respectively. Buses leave for Delhi at 5 and 8 am (Rs 100). Every hour until 7 pm, crowded buses leave for Dadahu (Rs 17), near Renuka Lake, and others go to Paonta Sahib. You can get on buses at either Nahan bus station or outside the Renuka Hotel.

RENUKA LAKE

About an hour by bus from Nahan is lovely Renuka Lake (Renukaji). You can walk along the 3km circular track past the ashram and down to the **wildlife park**, which has Asiatic lions, barking deer and Himalayan black bear.

Alternatively, hire a pedal boat from the Hotel Renuka for Rs 30 per half hour, or take a tour in a motorboat, in season, for Rs 100.

Parshuramtal, the artificial lake next to Renukaji, has a small **temple** of the same name. If you're feeling more energetic, hike the 8km up to **Jamu peak** for great views.

The week-long **Renuka Mela** is held in November in honour of Renukaji. According to one of several local legends, Sahasarjuna killed Jamadagini and tried to take his wife, Renukaji. Preferring death to dishonour, Renukaji threw herself in the lake and drowned, but miraculously was brought back to life. During the celebrations, the image of the god Pashuram is carried down on a throne from Jamu peak to meet his mother, Renukaji, at the lake. Thousands of pilgrims join in the festivities, which include ritual bathing in the lake, dancing and general merrymaking.

Places to Stay & Eat

HPTDC's *Hotel Renuka (☎ 68339)* has spacious, comfortable rooms in secluded gardens from Rs 350 to Rs 650, all with hot water. There are also dorm beds for Rs 50, and a good restaurant.

Hotel Himlok, 4km away in the village of Dadahu, is the only other place to stay. Rooms cost Rs 200 to Rs 400.

Getting There & Away

A bus from Nahan goes to Dadahu roughly every hour, from where you can walk 40 minutes to the lake (though some buses do continue on to the lake). There are private buses from the lake direct to Paonta Sahib (Rs 25, two hours) at 7 and 10 am, noon and 4 pm.

PAONTA SAHIB
☎ 01704

On the Uttar Pradesh border is the uninteresting town of Paonta Sahib. Dedicated to the 10th Sikh guru, Gobind Singh, who lived there between the age of 16 and 20, the town's **gurdwara** is an impressive place, right on the river. During the Holi and Baisakhi festivals in March and April, the temple overflows with pilgrims.

Inside the temple is a small **museum** dedicated to Gobind Singh. Rules for entry are the same for all Sikh temples: bring a head covering (or borrow one from a counter on the right at the temple entrance), take off your shoes (leave them at a counter on the left at the temple entrance), and wash your feet before entering.

Places to Stay & Eat

HPTDC's *Hotel Yamuna (☎ 22341)*, on the riverside, about 100m from the entrance to the temple, is the best option. Nice doubles cost from Rs 350 to Rs 800, the latter with air-con, and there's a good restaurant and bar.

The few budget options are awful.

Getting There & Away

Hourly buses go to Shimla (Rs 90; till 1 pm), Dehra Dun (Rs 18, 1½ hours) and Nahan (Rs 23, two hours). There are four morning buses to Delhi (Rs 95, seven hours).

Jammu & Kashmir

The regions of Jammu and Kashmir (J&K for short) form part of a vast state which includes Ladakh. Srinagar is J&K's summer capital, while the city of Jammu, farther south on the plains, is the winter capital. Jammu and Kashmir (as distinct from Ladakh) have been subject to political unrest since the late 1980s. The following information is intended for background only; travellers are advised to contact their embassy in Delhi before travelling to these regions.

J&K is a state with wide cultural and geographical contrasts. The Kashmir Valley, or Vale of Kashmir, is a fertile, verdant region enclosed by the high snow-capped ridges of the Pir Panjal range to the west and south, and the main Himalaya range to the east. Its population is predominantly Muslim, with a rich Islamic history that can be traced back to the 14th century. South of the Kashmir Valley is the region of Jammu. It includes the city of Jammu, situated on the north Indian plains, a short distance from the rolling Siwalik Hills. North of the Siwaliks, the rest of the Jammu region is drained by the Chenab River whose vast catchment area includes several narrow valleys that extend deep into the high Himalaya. The region of Jammu is predominantly Hindu, although there are small Muslim communities in the vicinity of Banihal and Kishtwar immediately south of the Kashmir Valley.

The political violence in the Kashmir Valley since the late 1980s has discouraged most travellers from visiting the region. Until 1989, a stay on the famous houseboats of Dal Lake close to the city centre of Srinagar was considered a must for anyone visiting northern India, while the treks out of Gulmarg, Sonamarg and Pahalgam were among some of the most popular in the Himalaya. Before the outbreak of violence, more than 600,000 Indian tourists and 60,000 foreign tourists visited Kashmir throughout the summer season, from early June until mid-October.

Jammu & Kashmir at a Glance

Population: 8.8. million
Area: 222,236 sq km
Capital: Srinagar (summer), Jammu (winter)
Main Languages: Kashmiri, Dogri, Urdu & Ladakhi
Best Time to Go: May to September

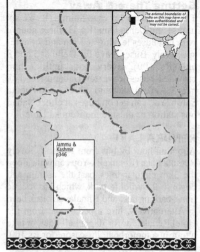

The external boundaries of India on this map have not been authenticated and may not be correct.

Jammu & Kashmir p346

HISTORY

J&K has always been a centre of conflict for independent India. When India and Pakistan became independent, there was much controversy over whether the region should be annexed to India or Pakistan. The population was predominantly Muslim but J&K was not a part of 'British India'. It was a 'princely state', ruled by a Hindu maharaja, in whose hands was left the decision of whether to merge with Muslim Pakistan or Hindu India. As told in *Freedom at Midnight*, by Larry Collins & Dominique Lapierre, the indecisive maharaja only made his decision when a Pathan (Pakistani)

Warning

! Lonely Planet strongly advises against travelling to Jammu and Kashmir. While the Indian government has not placed restrictions on visitors, it's foolhardy to go. There is a serious risk of kidnapping (four of the six westerners taken hostage in the Lidder Valley near Pahalgam in 1995 have never been accounted for). There have been bomb blasts in public places in Jammu and Srinagar (and buses and trains en route to Jammu have been bombed). Foreigners have been robbed at gunpoint. Areas near the Pakistani border (eg near Kargil heading west to Drass) are occasionally shelled. You are particularly urged to ignore touts in Delhi and other places who will try and convince you that everything is safe. It is not. Tensions, especially since the nuclear tests of early 1998, are still running high. If despite this you are still determined to go, you should definitely check with your embassy in Delhi to establish the current situation.

group from north-west Pakistan was already crossing his borders, and the inevitable result was the first India-Pakistani conflict.

Since that first conflict, in October 1948, Kashmir has remained a flash point between the two countries. A substantial part of the region is now Indian and the rest (Azad Kashmir) is administered by Pakistan; both countries claim all of it.

Since 1989, militant activity in Kashmir has increased substantially and it's estimated that as many as 20,000 Kashmiris have died in the fighting.

In 1990 the J&K state government was dissolved and the state was placed under direct rule from Delhi (President's Rule). In November 1995, the independent Election Commission rejected the Indian Government's request for elections in the province because J&K was too unstable. The Kashmiri opposition parties (and the Pakistan government, which assists the Muslim secessionists) planned to boycott the elections. However, the elections went ahead in September 1996 and were won by the National Conference Party (a pro-India, regional party), under the leadership of Farooq Abdullah. By October, Kashmir had its own elected government, ending the direct rule from Delhi, with Abdullah as chief minister. Hopes that this would signal a resolution have been dashed again and again. At the time of writing, the problem seemed as intractable as ever.

JAMMU REGION
Jammu
☎ 0191 • pop 257,000

Jammu is J&K's second-largest city and its winter capital. In summer it is a sweltering, uncomfortable contrast to the cool heights of Kashmir. From October onwards it becomes much more pleasant. Jammu is actually two towns. The old town sits on a hilltop overlooking the river, and several kilometres away across the river is the new town of Jammu Tawi.

Jammu to Srinagar

On the Jammu to Srinagar route are the hill resorts of Kud, Patnitop and Batote. The important Sudh Mahadev Shiva Temple is located 8km from Kud and Patnitop. Also on this route is Sanasar, a beautiful valley which is a centre for the Gujar shepherds each summer.

During the winter months, Srinagar was often completely cut off from the rest of India before the Jawarhar tunnel was completed. The 2.5km-long tunnel is 200km from Jammu and 93km from Srinagar and has two separate passages; inside it's very damp and full of vehicle-emission fumes. From Banihal, 17km south of the tunnel, the Kashmiri region begins and people speak Kashmiri as well as Dogri. At the northern end of the tunnel is the green, lush Vale of Kashmir.

JAMMU & KASHMIR

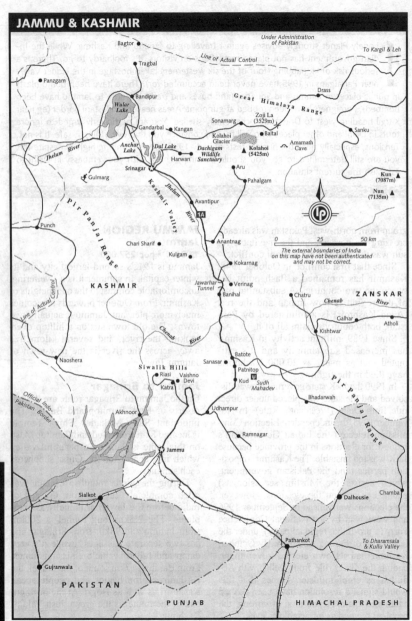

The external boundaries of India
on this map have not been authenticated
and may not be correct.

0   25   50 km

KASHMIR VALLEY
This is one of the most beautiful regions of India but since 1989 it has been racked by political violence.

The Mughal rulers of India were always happy to retreat from the heat of the plains to the cool green heights of Kashmir, and indeed Jehangir's last words, when he died en route to the 'happy valley', were a simple request for 'only Kashmir'. The Mughals developed their formal garden-style art to its greatest heights in Kashmir.

Among Kashmir's greatest attractions were the Dal Lake **houseboats**. During the Raj period Kashmir's ruler would not permit the British (who were as fond of Kashmir's cool climate as the Mughals) to own land here. So they adopted the solution of building houseboats – each one a little bit of England, afloat on Dal Lake. A visit to Kashmir, it was often said, was not complete until you had stayed on a houseboat.

Srinagar
☎ 0194 • pop 725,000
Srinagar, the summer capital of Kashmir, stands on Dal Lake and the picturesque Jhelum River.

It is a city with a distinctly Central Asian flavour. Indeed the people look different from those in the rest of India; and when you head south from Srinagar it is always referred to as 'returning to India'.

The old city is in the vicinity of Hari Parbat Hill and includes the labyrinth of alleyways, mosques and houses that constitute the commercial heart of the city. The more modern part of the city is farther up the Jhelum River (above its famous seven bridges), which sweeps through Srinagar.

East of the city is Dal Lake, much of it a maze of intricate waterways. Dal comprises a series of lakes, including Nagin Lake some 8km from the city centre. Most of the more modern houseboats are on these lakes. The famous Mughal gardens, including the Shalimar Bagh and Nishat Bagh, are on the far (east) side of Dal Lake.

Pahalgam
Pahalgam is about 95km east of Srinagar, at an altitude of 2130m. At the junction of the East and West Lidder rivers, Pahalgam was a popular trekking base before the present troubles. The Sri Amarnath *yatra* (pilgrimage) endures, however, and each year in July/August thousands of Hindu pilgrims approach the Amarnath cave from this area.

Gulmarg
The large meadow of Gulmarg is 52km south-west of Srinagar at 2730m. The name means Meadow of Flowers and in spring it's just that. Also once a popular trekking base, Gulmarg used to be India's premier skiing resort.

Srinagar to Kargil
Sonamarg, at 2740m, is the last major town before Ladakh, and until the terrorist activity began, it was an excellent base for trekking. Its name means Meadow of Gold.

Baltal, an army camp, is right at the foot of the Zoji La (3529m). **Zoji La** is the watershed between Kashmir and Ladakh – on one side you have the green, lush scenery of Kashmir while on the other side everything is barren and dry. **Drass** is the first main village after the pass. From here it's another 56km to Kargil (see the Ladakh & Zanskar chapter).

JAMMU & KASHMIR

Ladakh & Zanskar

Ladakh – the land of high passes – marks the boundary between the peaks of the western Himalaya and the vast Tibetan plateau. Opened up to tourism in 1974, Ladakh has been variously described as 'the Moonland', 'Little Tibet' and even 'the last Shangri La'. Whatever the description, it's one of the most remote regions of India.

The high culture of Ladakh is Buddhist, having close cultural and trading connections with Tibet. This is particularly evident in the most populated region of Leh and the Indus Valley, with its many whitewashed *gompas* (monasteries) and forts perched on top of sugarloaf mountains. Padum, the capital of the more remote Zanskar, shares this Buddhist heritage. Kargil and the Suru Valley, the third main region of Ladakh, is predominantly Shi'ah Muslim and shares a cultural affinity with Baltistan (in Pakistan since Indian Partition in 1947).

You do not need a permit to travel to Zanskar, Leh, or along the major routes to Srinagar and Manali. However, don't stray too close to sensitive border areas. The Kargil to Srinagar road was closed to foreigners for a time in 1998 because of Pakistani shelling.

History

Ladakh's earliest inhabitants were the Khampas, nomads who grazed their yaks on the high, windswept pastures. The first settlements, along the upper Indus, were established by Mons, Buddhist pilgrims on their way from India to Mt Kailash in Tibet. The Brokpa tribe (or Dards, as they are known in some areas), who today live downstream of Khalsi, are the last Indo-Iranian peoples to still follow Buddhism.

In the 9th century Ladakh's influence extended beyond the Indus Valley and during this time many forts and palaces, including Shey, were constructed. In the late 14th century a Tibetan pilgrim, Tsongkhapa, introduced to Ladakh a Buddhist order headed by the first Dalai Lama. The new order, known

Ladakh & Zanskar at a Glance

Population: 140,000
Area: approximately 96,701 sq km
Capitals: Leh & Kargil
Main Languages: Ladakhi, Purig, Tibetan & English
Best Time to Go: May to October

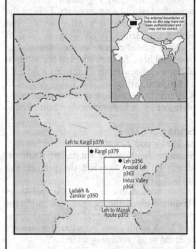

- **Activities** – a mecca for adventure sports, the region offers trekking, rafting, mountain climbing and mountain biking

- **Ladakh** – this 'Little Tibet' offers a Tibetan Buddhist experience without leaving India

- **Leh to Manali Route** – second highest motorable road in the world with some of the country's most spectacular scenery

- **Gompas** – visit one of the impressive Buddhist monasteries dotted throughout the region

Festivals of Ladakh's Gompas

gompa	date
Chemrey	Nov
Diskit	Feb
Hemis	Jun/Jul
Karsha	Jul
Leh	Feb
Likir	Feb
Losar	Dec
Matho	Feb/Mar
Phyang	Jul/Aug
Spituk	Jan
Stok	Feb/Mar
Taktok	Jul/Aug
Tikse	Oct/Nov

The New Year Festival is celebrated at all gompas.

as Gelugpa, flourished and led to the founding of gompas at Tikse, Likir and Spituk.

In the ensuing years, the Balti-Kashmiri armies launched various attacks against Ladakh which in the 16th century fell subject to the rule of Ali Mir of Baltistan. But its fortunes were revived under the rule of Singe Namgyal (1570-1642) who, in addition to territorial gains, established Leh as his capital and constructed a palace there. During the early 17th century, the Ladakhi royal family assisted Brokpa monks in establishing gompas at Hemis and Stakna.

Soon Ladakhi forces were called on to face a combined Mongol-Tibetan army and help was sought from the Kashmir governor. This involved symbolic tribute to the Mughal empire and the mosque in Leh's Main Bazaar was the price Aurangzeb extracted. After the conflict with Tibetan forces, trade relations resumed and Leh was able to re-establish its influence over Zanskar and farther south to Lahaul and Spiti.

Ladakh's fortunes changed again in the 1830s when the Dogra army from Jammu invaded Ladakh and exiled the king to Stok. The Dogras were led by the famous general Zorawar Singh, who was appointed by the first maharaja of Kashmir, Gulab Singh. Ladakh became an integral part of the maharaja's vast state in 1846 and remained under the control of Jammu & Kashmir after Independence until some administrative autonomy was granted in 1995.

Geography

Ladakh is bordered to the south-west by the main Himalaya Range, including the impressive snow-capped peaks of Nun (7135m) and Kun (7087m), the highest peaks in the Kashmir Himalaya. North and parallel to the Himalaya is the Zanskar Range, which is the main range between the Himalaya and the Indus Valley. The region is drained by the Zanskar River, which flows into the Indus River just below Leh,

Warning

Ladakh is still a sensitive area and its borders with both Pakistan and China have been disputed. India's war with China in 1962 exacerbated the problem and was one of the main reasons why Ladakh was closed to outsiders until 1974. While China and India are approaching accord on the border dispute, some heavy fighting continues between India and Pakistan on the Siachen Glacier (above 6000m in the eastern Karakoram region). This costly warfare – US$1 million a day since 1988 – ensures a significant military presence in Ladakh. Travellers are forbidden to go near the border area.

The Kargil to Srinagar road was closed to foreigners for a time in 1998 because of Pakistani shelling and Kargil itself has been shelled by the Pakistani army several times in recent years. During these times the town is declared off-limits.

LADAKH & ZANSKAR

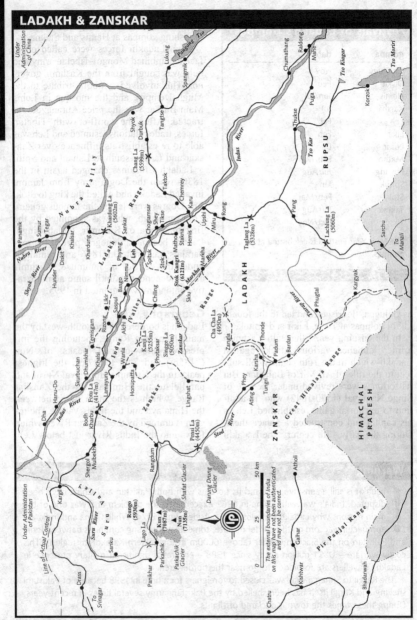

The external boundaries of India on this map have not been authenticated and may not be correct.

and the Suru River which flows into the Indus downstream of Kargil.

The Stok Range immediately south of Leh is an impressive outlier north of the Zanskar Range, while north of Leh is the snow-capped Ladakh Range. North of the Ladakh Range the Nubra and Shyok rivers drain the huge peaks of the eastern Karakoram including Rimo 1 (7385m) and Teram Kangri 1 (7464m), which define the northern border of Ladakh.

In the east of Ladakh are several scintillating lakes including the Pangong Tso (lake) forming the border with Tibet and Tso Moriri and Tso Kar set in a high-altitude desert characteristic of the Tibetan plateau.

Travel Tax

Travellers have reported that if they use a non-Ladakhi vehicle (ie a car with a Delhi or Manali number plate) to visit one of the gompas on the tourist circuit from Leh, they've been fined Rs 500 for not having a 'gompa ticket' (Rs 20) supposedly available from the taxi union in Leh. No one seemed to know anything about a 'gompa ticket' in Leh so, no doubt, this is just another devious scam to watch out for.

Special Events

Now that tourism is flourishing in the region, the annual Ladakh Festival has been extended and is now held in the first two weeks of September in a blatant attempt to prolong the tourist season. Nevertheless, the festival should not be missed. Regular large, colourful displays of dancing, sports, ceremonies and exhibitions are held throughout Ladakh, but Leh is the main venue.

The festival starts with a spectacular march through Leh's main streets. People from all over Ladakh, monks in yellow and orange robes, polo and archery troupes and Tibetan refugees from Choglamsar, walk proudly in traditional costume, wearing the tall, bright *perak* hats and the curled *papu* shoes. The march culminates in a day – long cultural display at Leh polo ground. (For the best view of the opening ceremonies, ig-

nore the march and get to the polo ground early to ensure a good seat.)

Other activities during the two weeks include mask dances, which are serious and hypnotic when performed by monks, or cheeky and frivolous when performed by small children. There are also archery and polo competitions, concerts and other cultural programs throughout Ladakh.

Apart from Leh, other smaller, associated festivals are held in Changspa, Tangtse (near Pangong Tso), Shey, Basgo, Korzok (on the shore of Tso Moriri) and Biama (in the Dha-Hanu region). In the Nubra Valley, Diskit and Sumur hold the biggest festival outside Leh, with camel races, 'warfare demonstrations' (not quite as violent as they sound), ibex and peacock dances, traditional marriage ceremonies, some sword dancing from Baltistan, flower displays and archery competitions.

There are individual festivals held at gompas throughout the region, see the Festivals of Ladakh's Gompas boxed text for the locations and dates of these.

Language

Ladakhi is the most common language used in Ladakh and Zanskar. Once similar to Tibetan, Ladakhi has now changed considerably. If you only remember one word, it will be the all-purpose *jule* (pronounced 'JOO-lay'), which means hello, goodbye, please and thank you.

Leh

☎ 01982 • pop 15,000

Leh is located in a side valley just to the north of the Indus Valley. Until 1947 it had close trading relations with Central Asia; yak trains would set off from the Leh Bazaar to complete the stages over the Karakoram Pass to Yarkand and Kashgar. Today Leh is an important strategic centre for India. The large military presence is a reminder that the region of Ladakh is situated along India's sensitive borders with both Pakistan and China.

Leh's character changed when Ladakh was opened up to foreign tourists in 1974. Since then, well over 100 hotels have been established and many of the shops in the main bazaar have been converted to sell arts and crafts. Leh is dominated by the dilapidated nine storey Leh Palace, home of the Ladakhi royal family before they were exiled to Stok in the 1830s. Above the palace at the top of Namgyal Hill is the Victory Fort, built to commemorate Ladakh's victory over the Balti-Kashmir armies in the early 16th century.

The old town of Leh, situated at the base of Namgyal Hill, is a labyrinth of alleyways and houses stacked with dry wood and dung, which is collected to use as fuel to withstand the long winter months. To the south of the old town is the polo ground (see the Spectator Sports section later). The mosque at the head of the Leh Bazaar was commissioned by the Mughal emperor Aurangzeb.

In Changspa, an outlying village of Leh, there are important Buddhist carvings dating back to the 8th and 9th centuries when Ladakh was converted to Buddhism. Close by is the village of Sankar, the site of a modern gompa which serves much of the Leh Valley. The gompa is attended by some 15 to 20 monks from the gompa at Spituk. Leh's main Buddhist place of worship is the Soma Gompa, close to the mosque.

Orientation

Leh is small enough to find your way around easily. The road from the airport goes past the new and old bus stands, then turns into the main street, Main Bazaar Rd, where there are plenty of shops and restaurants. South-west of the Leh Palace, around Fort Rd, is the most popular area for places to eat, sleep and spend money. About 2km north-west of town and out of Leh is the village of Changspa, with its many guesthouses and long-term visitors. A similar distance north-east, Sankar also has many family-run guesthouses.

Information

Tourist Offices The Tourist Reception Centre (☎ 52297) is 3km south of the town centre, on the road to the airport. For general inquiries the small counter in the same building as the foreign exchange on Fort Rd, is far handier. Both tourist offices are open 10 am to 4 pm daily except Sunday. There is a small tourist information counter at the airport, but this really just handles Foreigners' Registration Forms.

Permits Permits are not required for Leh. However, you must fill out a Foreigners' Registration Form at the airport, and again at your hotel. For permits to the newly opened regions of Ladakh, you can either pay Rs 100 for a travel agent to handle the bureaucratic formalities, or battle the red tape yourself at the District Magistrate's Office (☎ 52210), open normal business hours, just above the polo ground. For more details on permits, see the Ladakh Regions section later in the chapter.

Money Facilities are poor, to say the least, but Leh is the only place to change money between Manali and Kargil. The only bank which changes money is the State Bank of India's foreign exchange counter at the Tourist Information Centre on Fort Rd. In high season queuing can take four hours before reaching the one teller.

The Singge Palace and Khangri hotels also change money at slightly lower rates; the Jammu & Kashmir Bank on Old Leh Rd near the corner with Main Bazaar Rd may offer money-changing facilities in the future. Some travellers prefer to change US dollars cash at a slightly better rate with the shopkeepers on Fort Rd.

The foreign exchange is open from Monday to Friday, 10.30 am to 4 pm (but you'll need to be there by 1 pm in high season to be served); and on Saturday 10.30 am to noon. You must fill out two copies of a currency form, detailing the numbers on your travellers cheques or currency notes. Don't rely on credit cards in Ladakh, take cash or travellers cheques.

Post & Communications The main post office – open Monday to Saturday from 10 am

Top: An isolated hillside village in Lingshet, Ladakh.
Middle left: Ladakh's first inhabitants were nomadic graziers who tended yak on mountain pastures.
Middle right: Buddhist prayer flags carry prayers to heaven when the wind blows.
Bottom: Buddhist temples such as this have earned Ladakh the nickname 'The Last Shangri La'.

Top: Leh's Victory Fort, built to celebrate Ladakh's 16th century victory over the Balti-Kashmiri army.
Middle & Bottom: Zanskar consists of a number of small mountain-locked valleys. While road travel is impossible for most of the year, the snows begin to melt in June, and treks can be undertaken in relative safety until October.

to 1 pm and 2 to 5 pm – is hopelessly inconvenient, more than 3km south of the centre of Leh. The smaller post office on the corner of Fort and Main Bazaar roads is open 10 am to 4 pm, closed on Sunday. The poste restante at the main post office is not particularly reliable.

All around Leh are small phone booths with long-distance facilities. Calls within India cost Rs 30 to Rs 40 per minute; to Australia/New Zealand and Europe, Rs 85; and to USA/Canada, Rs 98. However, connections are poor, especially in the evening. Faxes are a more expensive and unreliable method of communication (Rs 3 per second for international faxes), but machines are available. You can send emails from the Gypsy's World office in the White House building on Fort Rd for Rs 100 per message, but you can't access the Internet. Receiving emails is free (email matin.chunka@gems.vsnl.net.in).

Travel Agencies Many travel agencies operate in Leh in the summer. Almost all agencies work on a commission basis, selling tickets for other agencies' buses and tours. The more reliable operators tend to be based at upmarket hotels, though you really should compare prices from several before deciding. Single women should take extra care when arranging a trip. Travel agencies recommended by readers include:

Explore Himalayas
  (☎ 52727) Main Bazaar Rd
Fantasy Trek & Tour
  White House Bldg, Fort Rd
Gypsy's World
  (☎ 52935) White House Bldg, Fort Rd
Paradise Trek & Tour
  (☎ 52818) Fort Rd
Rimo Expeditions
  (☎ 53348) near the police station

Equipment Hire Several travel agencies rent sleeping bags, tents and so on, but the gear can be of low quality and poorly maintained, plus they demand a hefty deposit for each item. Check the gear carefully before you take it. There are two places that rent gear, including mountaineering equipment;

the Traveller Shop (☎ 52248) in the White House building and Mero Expeditions across the road. Approximate rental prices per day are: two person tent, Rs 100; sleeping bag, Rs 70 and gas stove, Rs 30. A deposit on a tent can be as high as Rs 3000.

Rafting Agencies Several agencies in Leh offer white-water rafting trips on the Indus and Zanskar rivers. Rafting is not especially popular, as the rivers aren't particularly reliable, and the season only lasts from about early July to mid-September. A three hour, calm trip from Hemis to Choglamsar costs Rs 750 per person. Better rafting from Nimmu to Alchi or to Khalsi will cost Rs 1200 for the day. Longer, customised rafting trips for the adventurous cost about US$65 per day, including all transport, gear, food and a guide.

Two of the better travel agencies in Leh which handle rafting trips are Indus Himalayan Explorers (☎ 52735), opposite the taxi stand in Fort Rd and Rimo Expeditions (see Travel Agencies earlier).

Bookshops & Libraries Both the Artou Bookshop and Lost Horizon Books have great selections on Ladakh and Tibet, as well as novels. The Tibetan Handicraft Emporium, on Main Bazaar Rd, is also good for Tibetan literature. Bookworm, near the Hotel Ga-Ldan Continental on Old Fort Rd, has a selection of second-hand books (English, French, German, Japanese) and will buy back the books at half their selling price.

Next to the Hotel Bijoo, the small Leh District Library has (mainly old) books about Ladakh, recent issues of English-language newspapers and magazines. It is open Monday to Saturday, 10 am to 4 pm. The Ecology Centre (see The Ecology Centre, later in this section) runs a good library with books on local issues and ecological matters. For books on Buddhism and Tibet, try the Tibetan library in Choglamsar.

Newspapers & Magazines Daily Indian English language newspapers can be obtained at Parkash Booksellers, next to the German Bakery. The bilingual (English and

Ladakhi) quarterly magazine *Ladags Melong* (Rs 20) is an interesting source of information on Ladakhi culture, education, history and so on. It is sold at bookshops.

Film & Photography Several places along Fort and Main Bazaar roads sell print and slide film, but always check the expiry date. The Gemini Lab on Fort Rd, opposite the Hotel Yak Tail, does a pretty good job with developing print (not slide) film. You can also buy film and some wonderful prints of photos of old Ladakh from Syed Ali Shah's postcard shop.

Laundry Dzomsa is an environmentally friendly laundry which washes clothes away from streams to avoid contaminating the precious water supply. They charge Rs 15 for pants and Rs 10 for shirts, and do an excellent job. Dzomsa also refills water bottles with filtered water for Rs 7, which is not only cheap but spares Leh yet more plastic rubbish. Other laundries include one opposite the State Bank of India.

Medical Services Leh is at an altitude of 3505m, so it is important to acclimatise to avoid Acute Mountain Sickness (AMS). If you suspect you are suffering from the symptoms of AMS, medical advice is available (☎ 52014 from 10 am to 4 pm, ☎ 52360 from 4 pm to 10 am). For more information on AMS, see the Health section in the Facts for the Visitor chapter. Leh has several clinics and pharmacies which can dispense advice and medicines for low-level complaints, but for anything serious the public Sonam Norbu Memorial (SNM) Hospital (☎ 52014) is nearly 3km south of Leh. You can also contact a doctor through one of the upmarket hotels. The pharmacy near the mosque on Main Bazaar Rd sells western toiletries such as tampons.

Leh Palace
Looking for all the world like a miniature version of the Potala in Lhasa, Tibet, Leh Palace was built in the 17th century but is now deserted and dilapidated. Entry is Rs 10, including a look at the central prayer room. It's open 7 am to 9 pm, and watch out for holes in the floor.

Namgyal Tsemo Gompa
The Tsemo (Red) Gompa, built in 1430, contains a fine three storey-high Buddha image and ancient manuscripts and frescoes. It's usually open 7 to 9 am. The fort above the Tsemo Gompa is ruined, but the views of Leh from here are superb. The steep path starts from the road to the Leh Palace, or a taxi costs Rs 150 return.

Sankar Gompa
The Sankar Gompa is an easy couple of kilometres walk north of the town centre. The upstairs part of this interesting little gompa belonging to the Gelukpa order has an impressive representation of the Buddhist deity of compassion, Avalokiteshvara (or Chenresig), complete with 1000 arms and 1000 heads.

The gompa is only open between 7 and 10 am and 5 and 7 pm. A return taxi costs Rs 135.

Shanti Stupa
Looming impressively, especially at night when it is lit up, this *stupa* (Buddhist religious monument) was built by a Japanese order whose intention is to spread Buddhism by building temples throughout the world. With some financial assistance from the Japanese government, it was opened by the Dalai Lama in 1985.

From the top, there are great views. The stupa is located at the end of the road which goes through Changspa, about 3km from Fort Rd. If on foot, there is a very, very steep set of steps – not to be attempted if you have just arrived in Leh. By taxi (Rs 135 return) or with your own transport, a longish, winding (but less steep) road goes straight to the top.

The Ecology Centre (LEDeG)
Known as the Ecology Centre, Ladakh Ecological Development Group (LEDeG, founded 1983) initiates and promotes

'ecological and sustainable development which harmonises with and builds on the traditional culture'. This includes environmental and health education, strengthening the tradition of organic farming, and publishing books in the local language.

The video *Ancient Futures – Learning from Ladakh* is shown at the Ecology Centre; usually at 4.30 pm every second day except Sunday (ie one week it's Monday, Wednesday and Friday, and the following week it's Tuesday, Thursday and Saturday), if the demand is there. It's worth seeing for an insight into Ladakh, and the problems associated with tourism. An earnest discussion group follows the video. The small library is very good; and their handicraft shop has a good, if a little pricey (but it is non profit), selection of locally made goods. For further information, contact the Ladakh Project, 21 Victoria Sq, Clifton, Bristol, BS8 4ES, UK; or the Ladakh Project, PO Box 9475, Berkeley, CA 94709, USA.

Sauna & Massage
To help unwind after a trek, Thagang Sauna and Massage in Changspa opposite the Eagle Guest House offers a sauna for Rs 100 and a massage for Rs 300.

Courses
Buddhist study centres have been set up in both Leh and nearby Choglamsar. The Mahabodhi Meditation Centre on Changspa Lane (look for the sign on the way to the Shanti Stupa) has summer meditation sessions at 5 pm daily except Sunday. The centre also holds study camps taking upwards of five days.

Places to Stay
There is a huge choice of hotels and guesthouses in Leh, although most are only open during the high season (July to mid-September). Technically, prices are set by the local tourist authorities, but what you pay depends more on demand – prices can soar in the high season, especially after the arrival of a full flight. In low season, even a day or two after the high season ends,

prices can drop dramatically, sometimes by up to 50%. Prices quoted here are for the high season, but remember, the cost of a hotel will change from day to day. Many places will also charge an arbitrary 'service tax' of about 10%.

The electricity supply is spasmodic, so torches (flashlights) and candles may be needed. Before paying extra for hot water, inquire how regular it is; often it may only run for one or two hours a day. If you're staying for some time in Leh, it is worth checking into one place for the first night, then spending your first day, while acclimatising, finding a place that really suits.

Places to Stay – Budget
Budget accommodation can be found in three main areas: the old town, which is a little noisy and smelly, but has character; the 'newer', greener areas along, or within a short distance of, Fort Rd; and within the peaceful village of Changspa. Most other accommodation can be found in the newer parts of Leh.

Old Town Under the Leh Palace, along a quiet road to the Sankar Gompa, are several good places, and there are a couple of places with character in the old town. The water supply can be erratic, however.

Himalaya Hotel (☎ 52746) has a charming setting among brooks and willow trees. Small, rustic and family run, it has doubles with bath for Rs 300.

Khan Manzil Guest House (☎ 52681) near Syed Ali Shah's postcard shop, is a 200-year-old place built around a courtyard – the owner says he has avoided renovations to keep the character of the building. Rooms with common bath are Rs 80/100.

The *Old Ladakh Guest House (☎ 52951)* has doubles with common bath for Rs 180, and two charming doubles with bath for Rs 300 and Rs 250.

Tak Guest House nearby is a simple little place with shared baths – dark rooms downstairs for Rs 100 but a big airy double upstairs for Rs 150.

Changspa Changspa, about a 15 minute walk from the town centre, is a very popular place for travellers on a budget. Many of the older guesthouses around town are basic, with outside bathrooms, but they are usually very friendly and surrounded by some colourful gardens. Following are a few of the recommended places among the dozens to chose from, either in or on the way to Changspa.

Eagle Guest House (☎ 53074) has singles/doubles for Rs 150/200.

The *Tsavo Guest House* is a very basic, authentic Ladakhi home with doubles from Rs 100.

The *Stumpa Guest House* is another simple family home with rustic triple rooms for Rs 200.

The *Asia Guest House* (☎ 53403) is one of the nicer family-run places, with doubles for Rs 150 plus a terrace restaurant by a big garden.

The *Oriental Guest House* (☎ 53153), run by a very friendly family, has doubles

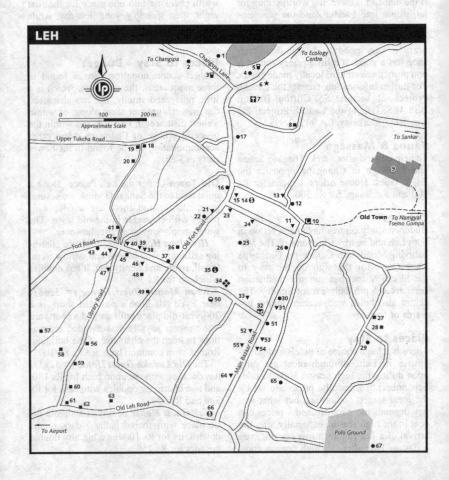

from around Rs 120 up to Rs 300 for a big double with a view.

Goba Guest House is a very peaceful farmhouse with simple but decent singles/doubles for 80/150.

The **Karzoo Guest House** (☎ 52324) has plain doubles with common bath for Rs 150, and there's a lovely garden.

Greenland Guest House (☎ 53156) is a pleasant family home with doubles for around Rs 150.

The friendly **Rainbow Guest House** (☎ 52211) has doubles with common bath for Rs 100 downstairs, Rs 120 upstairs. It is surrounded by fields and has a nice garden.

Other Areas Along the lane known as Library Rd (which the library isn't actually on) there are several good places. There are also a couple on or near Old Leh Rd.

Pangong Hotel is a little in the midrange, but has airy, bright singles/doubles with hot water for Rs 200/300.

The **Kang-La Hotel** is a cheery family-run hotel with creaky stairs and shared baths for Rs 150/200.

The **Hills View Hotel** (☎ 52058) has rooms for Rs 100/150 with slightly shabby common bath, Rs 250 for a double with bath.

The **Nezer View Guest House** has rooms from Rs 120 with common bath.

Up the lane beside the Penguin Bakery are several guesthouses. **Ti-Sei Guest House** (☎ 52404) has a nice garden and a traditional Ladakhi kitchen, with rooms for Rs 80/150.

The **Dehlex Hotel** (☎ 52755) is fairly rustic but it's central with a big garden; all rooms have common bath for Rs 80/150.

Jigmet Guest House (☎ 53563) not far away on Upper Tukcha Rd, is tidy and has large rooms for Rs 80/150 with common bath and Rs 300 with bath.

The **Streamview Guest House** (☎ 52745) next door has very pleasant rooms with common bath for Rs 100/150.

LEH

PLACES TO STAY					
8	Khan Manzil Guest House	11	Budshah Restaurant	6	Police Station
18	Jigmet Guest House;	13	Ladakhi Bakeries	7	Moravian Church
	Streamview Guest House	15	Tibetan Restaurant Devi	9	Leh Palace
19	Ti-Sei Guest House	21	Pumperknickel German	10	Jama Masjid
20	Dehlex House		Bakery	12	Syed Ali Shah's
27	Tak Guest House	23	La Terrasse		Postcard Shop
28	Old Ladakh Guest House	24	Banana Leaf Curry House	14	State Bank of India
36	Hotel Ga-Ldan Continental	31	Kokonov Tibetan Restaurant	16	Dzomsa Laundry & Water
41	Indus Guest House;	33	Tibetan Friends Corner		Refills
	Bimla Hotel		Restaurant	17	Artou Bookshop
45	Hotel Yak Tail	38	Narma Bar	22	Parkash Booksellers
48	Dreamland Hotel & Restaurant	39	Gezmo	25	Soma Gompa
49	Hotel Khangri	40	Poora Barba	26	Pharmacy
56	Hotel Bijoo	42	Penguin Bakery	29	Delite Cinema
57	Yasmin Guest House;	44	Tibetan Kitchen	30	Explore Himalayas Office
	Padma Guest House	46	Summer Harvest	32	Post Office
58	Hotel Choskor	47	Instyle German Bakery	34	Hotel Ibex Complex
59	Pangong Hotel	52	La Montessori	35	Tourist Office & Foreign
60	Kang-La Hotel	53	Wok Tibetan Kitchen		Exchange
61	Hotel Dragon	54	St Amdo II	37	HPTDC Bus Office
62	Nezer View Guest House	55	Amdo	43	White House Building
63	Singge Palace	64	Mughal Darbar	50	Taxi Stand 1 &
					Union Office
		OTHER		51	Lost Horizon Books
PLACES TO EAT		1	Moravian Mission School	65	Ladakh Art Palace
3	Mentokling Restaurant	2	Mahabodhi Meditation Centre	66	Jammu & Kashmir Bank
5	Mona Lisa Bar & Restaurant	4	Rimo Expeditions	67	District Magistrates Office

Places to Stay – Mid-Range

A few of the hotels which used to be in the budget range are a little overpriced despite improvements. These include several along the lane beside the Penguin Bakery.

The *Bimla Hotel* (☎ *52754)* is nicely decorated; prices range from Rs 100 for a single with shared bath up to Rs 500 for a big double with hot water and great views.

The *Indus Guest House* (☎ *52502)* close by has big clean doubles all with hot water for Rs 300 to Rs 400.

There are several options on or near Fort Rd. The *Dreamland Hotel* (☎ *52089)* is a very centrally located but reasonably quiet older hotel, with rooms for Rs 350/400.

Yasmin Guest House (☎ *52405)* has good doubles with hot water for Rs 300.

Padma Guest House (☎ *52630)* is deservedly popular; rooms range from doubles with shared bath in the old house for Rs 180 to larger doubles in a new wing with bath for Rs 700.

Hotel Choskor (☎ *52462)* is a rambling old place with big doubles for around Rs 300.

At the time of research *Hotel Sun-n-Sand* (☎ *52468)* and *Hotel Ri-Rab* (☎ *53108)*, both in Changspa, were willing to drop their rates from Rs 1400 to Rs 400.

On the way to Sankar the *Milarepa Deluxe Guest House* (☎ *53218)* has some beautiful double rooms for Rs 400 and Rs 500. Walk about 500m up the Sankar Rd from the Himalaya Hotel and then turn left down a lane for another 150m.

Places to Stay – Top End

Prices for these places are high, and offer little value; a room may have some form of heating or air-conditioning, and hot water, but no other extras. If not many tour groups paying full price have booked in, the prices are highly negotiable. Many places offer an 'American Plan', which includes three meals for an additional Rs 500 to Rs 600 per day. It may seem a reasonable deal, but there are also plenty of good cheap restaurants to eat in Leh, and why always eat at the same place?

The central *Hotel Khangri* (☎ *52311)*, the *K-Sar Palace* (☎ *52348)*, the *Singge*

Palace (☎ *53344)* and the quiet but isolated *Hotel Mandala* (☎ *52330)* are all top-end places charging Rs 1720/2070 for a single/double with all meals.

Centrally located around Fort Rd are the *Hotel Yak Tail* (☎ *52118)* from Rs 800/950, and the *Hotel Ga-Ldan Continental* (☎ *52436)* from Rs 1250/1500.

The *Hotel Bijoo* (☎ *52131)* on Library Rd has a nice garden and charges Rs 1500/1800 with all meals. Nearby is the superior *Hotel Dragon* (☎ *52139)*, charging Rs 1720/2070 with all meals.

The *Gypsy's Panorama Hotel* (☎ *52660)* at the foot of the Shanti Stupa hill boasts of being the first with central heating. In Changspa the *Hotel Omasila* (☎ *52119)* charges Rs 1720/2070.

Places to Stay – Winter

Almost every place to stay in Leh closes in winter, mainly because no one can get to the place. Prices at those places that remain open in the low season are still high because of a charge for room heating, which is certainly needed as the temperature in winter can plummet to about -35°C.

Some of the hotels which are reliably open in winter include the first and original *Old Ladakh Guest House*, which has remained open every day since 1974; the *Indus Guest House*; the *Hotel Khangri*; and the centrally heated *Gypsy's Panorama Hotel*.

Places to Eat

There is no shortage of places to eat in Leh (although supplies can be scarce), and it's a joy to sample various types of food from a multitude of good places. Almost all serve a range of cuisines. If you want to eat at a popular restaurant during the high season, you'll need to get there before 7 pm to get a table.

Indian Cuisine On Main Bazaar Rd *Mughal Darbar* is recommended. Although the servings are small, a great meal will only set you back about Rs 100 per person.

Poora Barba, opposite the Hotel Yak Tail on Fort Rd, is the place for no-frills, cheap

Indian food, such as filling plates of vegetable curries and rice.

Ibex Bar & Restaurant in the Hotel Ibex complex does terrific meals for about Rs 150 per person.

Banana Leaf Curry House, on the first floor of the Soma Gompa gateway, is a decent mid-range place.

The *Budshah Restaurant*, close to the mosque is also worth a visit; it specialises in Kashmiri cuisine.

Tibetan Cuisine Leh has a sizeable Tibetan refugee population, which naturally has influenced the cuisine and increased the number of Tibetan restaurants.

Along Main Bazaar Rd, mostly on the 2nd or 3rd floors, are several good, cheap (and well signed) places to try Tibetan specialities, including *Kokonor Tibetan Restaurant*, the *Wok Tibetan Kitchen* and the two *Amdo* cafes, which also serve reasonable western and Chinese food.

The *Tibetan Kitchen*, west of the centre of Fort Rd, is the best restaurant in town and charges accordingly, around Rs 250 for dinner. The varieties of Tibetan cuisine are explained on the menus for the uninitiated. It will do a famous *gyarhcee* (Tibetan hotpot) for at least four people with a day's notice.

The central *Dreamland Restaurant*, in the hotel of the same name, is popular for its Tibetan specialities, among other foods.

The unpretentious *Tibetan Restaurant Devi*, near the State Bank of India, has maintained its reputation for cheap, nourishing food.

La Montessori, on Main Bazaar Road, serves up big portions of very tasty Chinese, Tibetan and some western favourites.

The *Tibetan Friends Corner Restaurant*, near the taxi stand, is another established local favourite.

Western Cuisine The *Summer Harvest* on Fort Rd near the Hotel Yak Tail is very popular, and deservedly so.

Gezmo on Fort Rd is a popular place for breakfast and coffee and has a useful notice board.

La Terrasse, near the Soma Gompa, has a pleasant upstairs terrace with umbrellas, though it is better for breakfast or snacks than main meals.

Bakeries Though the fresh cinnamon rolls, croissants smothered in chocolate and other tasty cakes are generally very good for around Rs 30, the bakeries in Leh usually aren't so good at meals.

Instyle German Bakery on Fort Rd is a great place for getting a cup of coffee and a cake, sandwiches and breakfast, including some piping hot porridge. Their attempts at cooking dishes such as chow mein are dire, however.

Penguin Bakery, also on Fort Rd, is not a bad place for a snack.

The *Pumperknickel German Bakery* at the top of Old Fort Rd is very popular; specialities include lasagne and a big set-price breakfast (Rs 40).

Hot, fresh Indian and Tibetan-style bread can be bought in the early morning from the *Ladakhi bakeries* in the street just behind the mosque, near Syed Ali Shah's postcard shop. Get there very early to watch them make the bread. It is great with locally made jam.

Bars If you're desperate for a bottle of Turbo Extra Strong Lager, there are a couple of bars. Chang is hard to find; ask at your hotel if they can acquire some.

Namra Bar, a bit dark and seedy, is opposite the Hotel Yak Tail.

The open-air *Mona Lisa Bar & Restaurant*, near the Ecology Centre, is very relaxing and serves cans of beer for Rs 60, pizzas and Ladakhi bread with felafel for about the same price, and it has western popular music.

In Changspa the *Shelden Green Restaurant* serves beer rather more quickly than it serves the usual mix of western, Chinese and Indian meals, but the shady garden is pleasant. The *Mentokling Restaurant* near the Moravian Mission School is another open-air place selling beer.

There is a *shop* selling bottles of Indian beer and whisky at the Hotel Ibex complex, slightly ominously situated just across from the taxi stand where the drivers hang out.

Spectator Sports

Weekly polo matches are contested between Leh and the outlying villages of the Indus Valley at the polo ground to the south of Leh's old town. See also the Special Events information in the Nubra Valley section later in this chapter, for information on sport-oriented festivals.

Shopping

Prices in Leh are generally quite high; you may find exactly the same Tibetan-inspired item on sale at lower prices in Delhi, Dharamsala or Nepal. Remember to buy something only because you like it, not because it is unique, antique, sellable for a huge profit back home or any other standard selling spiel.

Some reasonable places for local goods are the Ladakh Art Palace in the old town, the Ecology Centre, or you can look around the shops in the old part of town behind Main Bazaar Rd. If you are around Leh at the time of the Ladakh Festival, there are good exhibitions and stalls selling local handicrafts and clothes.

Getting There & Away

Air Lots of travellers have a nightmarish time flying out of Leh in high season; going by road via Manali to Delhi is a more secure option at this time of year. From June to September Indian Airlines (IA) has at least four return flights a week between Leh and Delhi (US$105), and once a week via Chandigarh (US$70). There are direct flights once a week from Leh to Srinagar (US$55), and twice a week to Jammu (US$65). They can be a useful, indirect, way of getting out of Leh if the Leh to Delhi flights are overbooked. IA is currently the only airline flying to Leh, as compensation for the loss-making flights it must maintain during the winter.

From October to May IA generally still flies into Leh four times a week from Delhi, but this depends greatly on weather conditions. If flights from Leh are delayed, IA will pay for passengers' overnight accommodation in Leh.

IA warns passengers it cannot depart Leh with more than 70 to 80 passengers because of the altitude, climatic conditions and short runway. So, at peak periods, flights can be heavily over-booked. To avoid this, book well ahead but be prepared for disappointment. If you can't get a booking in economy class, it's worth trying for 1st class. Another answer is to get to the airport early on the day you want to go, because even if you are waitlisted up to number 100, there is still a chance you will get a flight, and an improvement in conditions may result in larger passenger load. Many people get caught out by booking their Delhi flight and flight home for the same day; you should extend your schedule to avoid this.

The chaotic Tushita Travels/Indian Airlines office (☎ 52076) is on the extension of Fort Rd, in a small white building, open 10 am to 5 pm Monday to Saturday – 10 am to noon on Sunday – with a lunch break from 1 to 2 pm. The competition for seats is savage during high season – some desperate people even resort to bribing the staff. It is worth getting to the office early.

Bus There are only two overland routes to Leh: the road from Srinagar, and the road from Manali in Himachal Pradesh. A complication when trying to leave Leh for Srinagar or Manali is that you may not be able to buy tickets on the local buses (or private buses at the end of the high season) until the evening before departure, because buses may not turn up from either of these places. Thus you can't be certain you will be leaving until the last moment. Try to book ahead, if possible, especially in the high season, at the new bus stand in Leh, from where the public buses leave.

Srinagar The Leh-Srinagar road is usually open from the beginning of June to October, but in practice the opening date can be variable. In 1998 the road from Kargil to Srinagar was closed to foreigners because of Pakistani shelling; check at the tourist of-

Polo & Archery

During the last century, polo games were played in the bazaar and main street of Leh. Nowadays, on Tuesdays and Saturdays in summer, they are often held at the Leh polo ground (although on Thursday the ground is reserved for a serious football game) with regular matches and competitions during the Ladakh Festival.

Historically, the game has always been more popular in the Muslim regions near Kargil than in Buddhist areas. In Leh, the two goals are placed about 100m apart, although in some villages over a dozen players in both teams may use fields over 350m long. Normally, a team consists of six men on horses (normally tough little Zanskari ponies), with one player defending the goal. One local rule stipulates that the team changes ends after each goal, so when a goal is scored defenders make an immediate dash to the opposite goals. The game is played at a frantic pace in 20-minute halves. (Beware, it can be hazardous sitting in the first row at the Leh polo ground!)

Archery competitions are usually held between two teams in the villages, or more often at the National Archery Stadium in Leh. A team with the most arrows closest to the target – often just a lump of sand with a painted round symbol – wins. Archery is not particularly exciting to watch, but it's a great excuse for local people to dress up in their finest traditional clothing. During a match, there is plenty of dancing, singing and drinking of *chang* – and some archery in between it all. Not surprisingly, the standard of archery is much higher in Kargil, where Islam forbids drinking.

fice for more information. The trip takes two days (about 12 hours travel each day), with an overnight halt at Kargil. There are two classes of public bus, but you may not get the class you want on the day you want. Jammu and Kashmir State Transport Corporation (J&KSTC) buses to Kargil/Srinagar cost: 'A Class' Rs 145/220; 'B Class' Rs 110/175. They leave from the new bus stand in Leh at 5.30 am every day, in high season.

At the time of research, deluxe/tourist buses, which used to connect Srinagar and Leh, were cancelled due to lack of demand.

Manali The Leh to Manali road is open for a shorter period, usually from July to mid-September, sometimes up to mid-October; again, the opening and closing dates can be variable depending on climatic conditions. There is a good selection of private and public buses for this route, indicating its popularity. (For more information on the buses, and the trip, refer to the Leh to Manali section later in this chapter.)

Jeep & Taxi These are an expensive, but useful alternative to the bus. 'Indian jeeps' take five passengers, while 'Japanese jeeps' and Ambassador taxis take four, plus driver. Fares are listed at stands in Leh and Kargil. Extra charges are Rs 250 if staying overnight; waiting for the second and third hours (the first is free) is Rs 115 per hour.

The two-day trip from Leh to Manali (including an overnight stop) will cost Rs 16,335. If hiring a jeep or taxi for a long trip, try to get a driver who speaks English and knows the area. This is not always possible because the next driver on the Taxi Union list gets the fare, regardless of his talents. Taxi drivers in Leh and Kargil are unionised; they must wear uniforms, and have to go through union checkpoints on all routes outside Leh.

While officially 'fixed', jeep and taxi fares for longer, more expensive trips are negotiable outside of high season.

Truck Trucks are a worthy, and acceptable, method of travelling to, or to places on the way to, Manali or Srinagar. Talk to drivers at the old bus stand in Leh the day before you want to travel.

Getting Around

To/From the Airport The bus service from the airport costs Rs 5 but it doesn't run regularly, if at all. Rates for jeeps and taxis are set at Rs 80 to Leh, or Rs 125 to Changspa.

Bus All public buses leave from the new bus stand, where it's difficult to secure information on schedules (because there is no real schedule). Both tourist offices have an updated, but often incomplete, timetable for public buses. To get to the new bus stand find the lane walk through the areas with the *chörtens* (Tibetan stupas), like everyone else; don't follow the long road.

Jeep & Taxi A taxi from the old and new bus stands to Fort Rd for those tired from a long journey and/or with loads of gear will cost about Rs 30. Day trips to nearby gompas cost: to Sankar, Spituk and Phyang Rs 580; to Shey, Tikse and Stok, Rs 685; or to just about every nearby gompa mentioned in the Around Leh section, Rs 1950.

Taxis in Leh congregate around three designated stands; they generally don't go around the streets looking for customers – you will have to approach them. Taxi drivers are unionised and accept only the union rate; fares are listed at the taxi stands.

Taxi stand No 1 (☎ 52723) is on Fort Rd, is open 7 am to 7 pm, but there are more taxis hanging around Fort Rd in the very early morning, waiting for fares to the airport or the new bus stand. Taxi stand No 2 is at the old bus stand, where a few old taxis loiter; and No 3 is at the new bus stand, but you may find it hard to get a taxi here.

Motorcycle Motorcycles are just about the perfect way of travelling around the area near Leh, but unfortunately local businesses don't seem to find it profitable to rent them out. Ask around and you may be able to hire a Vespa scooter for about Rs 500 per day, plus petrol. Ensure that you have comprehensive insurance that covers you in the event of an accident in which either yourself or a local person is injured.

Bicycle Bicycle rental is just catching on. Mountain bikes – a great way to visit the more accessible villages (but you may have to walk up to the gompas, anyway) – can be hired from Wisdom Travels on Fort Rd near the Hotel Yak Tail for Rs 200 per day.

AROUND LEH

There are many beautiful gompas and villages which make good day trips from Leh. The main places are described here; for more information refer to Lonely Planet's *Indian Himalaya*.

Choglamsar

This is an important centre for Tibetan Buddhism and the study of Tibetan culture and history. Around the refugee camp, off the main road from Leh, is a Tibetan library, medical centre, handicraft shops, study centre, bookshops, plenty of restaurants, and the Central Institute of Buddhist Studies.

Any bus heading south can drop you off at Choglamsar; or a one-way taxi costs Rs 130. There are a couple of crummy guesthouses along the very noisy main road.

Hemis Gompa

Also known as Chang-Chub-Sam-Ling (or the Lone Place of the Compassionate Person), Hemis Gompa, 45km south of Leh, belongs to the Brokpa order and was founded in the early 17th century. Now it is one of the most accessible, famous and, therefore, most visited gompas.

The gompa has an excellent library, well preserved frescoes showing some Kashmiri influence, and good Buddha figures. The largest *thangka* (Tibetan religious cloth painting) in Ladakh, over 12m long, is at Hemis, but is only exhibited every 12 years. It's next on display in 2004. To commemorate the birth of the renowned Indian sage, Padmasambhava, the famous annual **Hemis Festival** is held on the ninth to 11th days of the fifth Tibetan month, usually June/July.

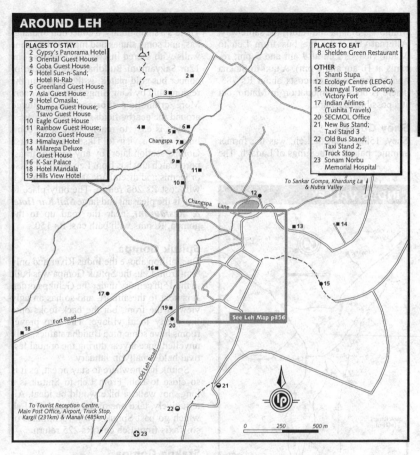

AROUND LEH

PLACES TO STAY
- 2 Gypsy's Panorama Hotel
- 3 Oriental Guest House
- 4 Goba Guest House
- 5 Hotel Sun-n-Sand;
  Hotel Ri-Rab
- 6 Greenland Guest House
- 7 Asia Guest House
- 9 Hotel Omasila;
  Stumpa Guest House;
  Tsavo Guest House
- 10 Eagle Guest House
- 11 Rainbow Guest House;
  Karzoo Guest House
- 13 Himalaya Hotel
- 14 Milarepa Deluxe
  Guest House
- 16 K-Sar Palace
- 18 Hotel Mandala
- 19 Hills View Hotel

PLACES TO EAT
- 8 Shelden Green Restaurant

OTHER
- 1 Shanti Stupa
- 12 Ecology Centre (LEDeG)
- 15 Namgyal Tsemo Gompa;
  Victory Fort
- 17 Indian Airlines
  (Tushita Travels)
- 20 SECMOL Office
- 21 New Bus Stand;
  Taxi Stand 3
- 22 Old Bus Stand;
  Taxi Stand 2;
  Truck Stop
- 23 Sonam Norbu
  Memorial Hospital

To Sankar Gompa, Khardung La & Nubra Valley

Changspa

Changspa Lane

See Leh Map p356

Fort Road

Old Leh Road

To Tourist Reception Centre,
Main Post Office, Airport, Truck Stop,
Kargil (231km) & Manali (485km)

0   250   500 m

There are no guesthouses near the gompa, but the *East West Guesthouse* in the village, a long walk away, has doubles for Rs 150. Several places near the gompa allow camping; you can set up your own tent next to the gompa for Rs 35, or rent a pre set two person tent for Rs 50. Book at the nice *outdoor restaurant*, next to the gompa entrance, which serves unexciting but welcome Chinese food, tea and beer. A daily bus leaves Leh for Hemis at 9.30 am and returns to Leh at 12.30 pm. The timings are not great, but allow you an hour or so to look around if you are on a day trip from Leh. Return taxis from Leh cost Rs 860.

Matho Gompa

Built in the 16th century, Matho holds an annual festival during which the monks and novices go into trances and self-inflict wounds which appear to leave no marks. The 5km road between Matho and Stakna Gompa is impassable for vehicles, but it's possible to walk. Take the bus to Hemis, get off at the sign to the Stakna Gompa, walk to Matho via Stakna and return the same way. Alternatively, take the bus from Leh to Matho (leaves Leh at 9 am and 5 pm; returns at 10 am and 6 pm). A taxi to Stakna and Matho from Leh costs about Rs 785. There is no accommodation in Matho, but it's possible to camp.

Shey Gompa

Shey, 15km south of Leh, was the former summer palace of the kings of Ladakh. The

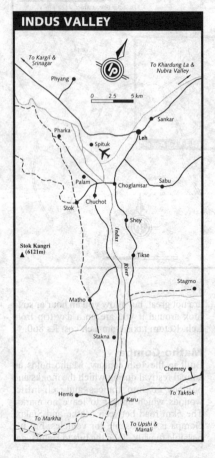

INDUS VALLEY

To Kargil &
Srinagar

Phyang

To Khardung La &
Nubra Valley

0   2.5   5 km

Sankar

Pharka

Spituk

Leh

Palam

Choglamsar

Sabu

Chuchot

Stok

Shey

Stok Kangri
▲(6121m)

Tikse

Stagmo

Matho

Stakna

Chemrey

Hemis

Karu

To Taktok

To Markha

To Upshi &
Manali

gompa, still partially used, is being restored. There's a small library, a collection of thangkas, and some stupas and **mani walls** (stone walls with sacred inscriptions) nearby. The 12m **Sakyamuni Buddha statue**, made of copper but gold plated, is the largest in the region, built by King Singge Namgyal's son. More crumbling **chörtens** are scattered around the nearby fields.

Shey is easy to reach and can be combined with a visit to Tikse (see the Tikse Gompa section later) by any form of transport. Catch any bus from Leh going to Tikse or Hemis and disembark at Shey; by taxi, it will cost Rs 265 return. The only place to stay is the pleasant and large *Shil Kar Hotel & Restaurant*, near the road up to the gompa. Rooms with bath cost Rs 150.

Spituk Gompa

On a hilltop above the Indus River and only 8km from Leh, the Spituk Gompa was built in the 15th century under the Gelukpa order. It is next to the airport, and so has an ugly view at the front, but the back looks onto the pretty local village. The two prayer rooms have some nice Buddha statues, only unveiled once a year during the annual festival held usually in January.

Spituk has nowhere to stay or eat, as it is so close to Leh. From Leh to Spituk is a long, hot walk; a bike would be ideal. Alternatively, take one of the buses from Leh which go past Spituk every 15 minutes or so. Taxis from Leh cost Rs 225 return.

Stakna Gompa

The gompa at Stakna – meaning Tiger's Nose – is another set spectacularly on the Hemis side of the Indus. Built by King Singge Namgyal's stepbrother, as part of the Brokpa order, it is accessible, and can be combined with a trip to Matho on the same day (see the earlier Matho Gompa entry).

To get there, take the Leh-Hemis bus and get off at the sign by the road to the gompa. Cross the bridge and walk for 30 minutes across the shadeless fields and up the steep path. A return taxi from Leh costs Rs 630. There is no guesthouse in the village, but it should be possible to camp back near the Indus.

Stok Gompa & Museum
Over the bridge from Choglamsar, the Stok Gompa is where the last king of Ladakh died in 1974. Built in 1814, it is a popular place because it is so easy to get to. There are over 80 rooms, only a few of which are open to the public.

The museum has a unique display of rare ornaments from the royal family plus thangkas, traditional clothing and jewellery. Entry is Rs 20 and it's open in summer 8 am to 7 pm. Photography is not permitted. The gompa, which has some fine masks and frescoes, is behind the museum.

The only nearby place to stay is the elegant *Hotel Highland* (☎ 3783), just under the museum, with doubles for Rs 600. There are other smaller places to stay towards the main road. Direct buses leave Leh at 7.30 am and 5 pm. Alternatively, try to get there by mountain bike or motorcycle. A return taxi from Leh will cost Rs 370.

Tikse Gompa
About 17km south of Leh, this gompa, part of the Gelukpa order, has an important collection of Tibetan books in its library, some excellent artwork and a new Maitreya Temple. It's a busy place, with almost incessant chanting and music, and there is a good chance to witness a *puja* (ritual offerings or prayers). Go to the roof for great views of the valleys and villages. There is even a small (and welcome) cafe and shop. The gompa is open daily 7.30 am to 6 pm. Permission is required to use video or movie cameras.

The only place to stay in Tikse is the *Skalzang Chamba Hotel* (☎ 47004), right at the start of the road leading to the gompa. It is a well run and pleasant place with a small garden, and costs Rs 200 per room, and there is a restaurant. Students (male only) of Buddhism, but not ordinary backpackers, may be able to stay at the gompa.

A bus from Leh to Tikse leaves about every hour or, alternatively, take the Hemis bus, which leaves Leh at 9.30 am. From the bus

stop, it is a fair walk up to the gompa, as usual. A return taxi from Leh will cost Rs 400.

Ladakh Regions

This section deals with areas which have been opened to travellers (with permits) by the Indian authorities.

Permits
Permits are required for all foreigners (including non-Ladakhi and non-Zanskari Indians) for the four restricted areas in Ladakh: the Nubra Valley, Pangong Tso, Tso Moriri and the Dha-Hanu region. Quite possibly the regulations for these new areas will be relaxed, or even abolished – although you are unlikely to ever get permission to go anywhere you want in the region, because it remains a sensitive part of India.

At the time of research, permits were valid for only seven days, and although four people must *apply* for a permit together, checkpoints do not require that you actually *travel* together. Take your permits with you at all times – there are several checkpoints along most roads. If you need a 'group', leave messages on noticeboards in Leh or let your travel agent organise things.

You will need to fill out the application form at your travel agency. List every place you may visit, within the permitted regions. You are allowed to travel to the regions by public or private transport or by taxi, alone or in a group of less than four, as long as there are four names and passport details on the permit. Travel agencies usually have old photocopies of other passports to help 'fill up' the required numbers for your 'group'.

It costs another Rs 100 per person for the travel agent to organise the permit, which includes a special 'fee' for speedy service at the District Magistrate's Office. This usually takes a day. Take a photocopy of the permit for yourself; permits must be shown at checkpoints, and hotels in the regions may also require details of your permit.

Don't even think about setting off without a permit, going to forbidden areas or overstaying your allotted seven days. If you get caught breaking the rules a visit to an Indian jail is not unlikely, and your travel agency will be severely penalised.

Climate

The average summer (June to September) and winter (October to May) temperatures for the four regions are:

region	max	min
Dha-Hanu region	29/15°C	-3/-15°C
Nubra Valley	28/15°C	-3/-15°C
Pangong Tso	18/5°C	-12/-25°C
Tso Moriri	17/6°C	-10/-22°C

What to Bring

For the two lake regions, Pangong Tso and Tso Moriri, there are no guesthouses, or shops to buy supplies (although this is likely to change soon). You must take all your own food, as well as sleeping and cooking equipment – which can be hired in Leh. In the more populated Dha-Hanu and Nubra Valley areas, there are a few guesthouses for accommodation and food, and small shops for basic supplies. To liven up a boring plate of *dhal* and rice or *thugpa* (Tibetan soup) or to please locals if you are willing to share, it's a good idea to bring some canned meat and fresh vegetables from Leh if visiting the remote villages in Dha-Hanu and Nubra.

At the height of summer, temperatures in some valleys can be extremely cold. A sleeping bag and warm clothes are vital in all areas. The days can be hot, causing dry skin and sunburn, so a hat, sunscreen and so on are important. Other items worth considering are torches (flashlights) and candles, as electricity, if there is any, is unreliable in all regions. Consider bringing binoculars to admire the wildlife, which is guaranteed to disappear when you get too close.

ORGANISED TOURS

Tours organised by reputable travel agencies in Leh are the easiest, most comfortable – but naturally most expensive – way to go. Make sure the tour is not just a local

taxi-driver-cum-guide because you can organise that yourself at the taxi-stand in Leh for far less. The quality of jeep, tent accommodation, food, destination and guide and the demand all affect the price of organised tours, but a rough idea of the sort of costs per day per person for an upmarket trip are: a five day package to the Nubra Valley for US$50; and to Tso Moriri for four days US$60.

NUBRA VALLEY

The Nubra Valley – *nubra* means green – used to be on the trading route connecting Tibet with Turkistan, and was the envy of Turkistan, which invaded it several times. Also known as the Valley of Flowers, Nubra has always been well cultivated and fertile, with the best climate in Ladakh, so grains and fruits, such as apples and apricots, have always been plentiful. The Nubra population is 90% Buddhist.

The valley is a wonderful area to visit, dominated by an incredible broad, empty valley between the Nubra and Shyok rivers. Camels are common near Hunder. There are pretty, small villages, dense forests and some wildlife, but inevitably the area is slowly becoming more affected by the increasing number of travellers who make the effort to visit. Remember that your permit only allows you to travel as far as Hunder along the southern valley, and to Panamik in the northern valley.

Special Events

The Nubra Valley isn't as crowded with gompas as the area around Leh, so festivals tend to be less religious and more sport oriented. As part of the annual **Ladakh Festival** in the first two weeks of September, there are many activities in the Nubra Valley which should not be missed, including a camel safari between Diskit and Hunder. Activities are generally centred in the main villages of Diskit and Sumur.

Leh to Khardung

The road to the Nubra Valley goes through the highest motorable pass in the world at

Khardung La (5602m). The pass is almost permanently covered in fog and snow, and is likely to be bitterly cold at the top regardless of the time of year. The pass is occupied by a grubby military camp and stacks of oil drums. In the summer, you may see one of the world's highest traffic jams of trucks and buses. The road between Leh and Khalsar is reasonable, except between the miserable road-building camps of South Pullu and North Pullu, just before and after Khardung La, where the road is atrocious. Near the pass, there are many places to stop for views, if you can, such as the intriguing-sounding **Siachen Taggler's Gate.**

The road then continues to Khardung Village, which has one very basic shop, and an unused Government Rest House. A small office may collect Rs 40 for 'wildlife' – perhaps to buy some.

Khalsar

The Nubra Valley really starts at the village of Khalsar, where there are several teahouses and a huge amount of discarded army equipment. The road then divides just before the village of Lughzhun – the left fork going to Hunder and beyond in the valley following the Shyok River, and the right heading north to Panamik and beyond, following the Nubra River.

Diskit

To Diskit, the road suddenly turns left, along an awesome, wide and dry riverbed for about 3km. Truck and bus drivers know where to turn off the riverbed (there are no signs), so if you have your own transport, ask and follow the other vehicles. Diskit is about 10km farther up the hill.

The **Diskit Gompa**, with about 70 monks, is the oldest – over 350 years old – and the biggest of its kind in the Nubra Valley.

Between Diskit and Hunder is an area of **sand dunes**, not unlike the Saharan region (if you can ignore the snow-capped Alps-like mountains in the background!).

Places to Stay & Eat About 50m from the Diskit Gompa is *Olthang Guest House and*

Camping. It has a nice garden, and costs Rs 300 per room, with a bath. The *Sun Rise Hotel*, on the main road near the Olthang, is OK for Rs 150 a room. The *Sand Dune Guest House* in the village centre has good singles/doubles for Rs 100/150.

Your hotel will rustle up something basic like dhal and rice, or try one of the little teahouses along the main street.

Hunder

Hunder is a pretty village, set among lots of trees and mingling streams. It is nicer than Diskit, but Diskit, the bigger village of the two, has slightly better facilities. From Diskit, it's about 7km to Hunder; some visitors enjoy the walk between the villages, either along the main road or across the sand dunes (but watch out for wild camels!).

The **gompa** at Hunder is about a 2km walk above the village, including a short, steep, rocky climb. It is completely deserted and quite eerie. There is only a small Buddha statue and some damaged frescoes, but the climb is worth it for the views and atmosphere. Don't wander too far up the road – there's a heavy military presence.

Places to Stay & Eat Hunder is a spread out village, like many others, full of cobbled streets, with no centre or street signs. There's no way of finding out the name and location of a guesthouse – they're often just a few rooms at the back of someone's home; so it's a matter of constantly asking directions.

One of the better places is the *Nerchung Pa Guesthouse*, owned by the local headmaster. It is friendly, set in a nice garden, costs Rs 150 per person including three meals, and is very hard to find – again, ask directions.

Sumur

Sumur, a major village along the Nubra River side of the valley, is a pretty place worth exploring.

The **Samstemling Gompa** at Sumur, over 150 years old, is a large complex with seven temples. Inaugurated by the Dalai Lama in 1962, it is a busy, friendly place with about

45 children busy chanting or cultivating apples and apricots. The prayer rooms that are open to the public house an impressive collection of thangkas and excellently restored frescoes.

By road, it is a fair distance from Sumur Village to the gompa: about 3km south towards the village of Tegar, from where a 3km road to the gompa starts. It's far quicker on foot, as you can go up the hill from the village and avoid the road, but you will have to ask directions. It can be confusing because the gompa near the start of the road to the Samstemling Gompa is actually the Tegar Gompa. The Samstemling Gompa is the more colourful one, and is situated closer to Sumur.

Places to Stay & Eat Along the main road in Sumur is the pretty dingy *Hotel Sumur* for rock-bottom price and comfort. The *Tsering Angchok Hotel* is another no-frills place but cheapish at Rs 100 per person – just follow the signs from the main road.

Farther up – ask for directions – is the *Stakray Guest House* (also owned by the local headmaster). For about Rs 200 per person with three meals, you get good, friendly service and mountain views.

Just opposite the road leading to the Samstemling Gompa, near the village of Tegar, is the upmarket *Hotel Yarab Tso*. For a rather overpriced Rs 600 per room, you get a large, clean room and immaculate bathroom with hot water.

You may be able to stay at the *Samstemling Gompa* if you are a serious (male) Buddhist student. There are some shops near the main road in Sumur with some limited supplies, and some tea stalls which serve basic food.

Panamik

Panamik is another small village, famous for centuries for its **hot springs**, and as the first or last stop along the ancient trade route between Ladakh and Central Asia. While Panamik may be a long way to come for some hot springs, they are worth visiting if you're already in the Nubra Valley.

The water, which is rumoured to cure rheumatism and other ailments, is pumped in by pipe from the Nubra River, about 2km from the village. It is usually common for men to have a bath or shower; unfortunately, women will have to be a bit more modest and careful about their attire. There are also a couple of craft shops in the village, where you can buy some weaving and woodcarvings.

The 250-year-old **Ensa Gompa** is a fair trek from the village – a couple of hours at least. It is farther than it seems and not really worth the effort; relax and enjoy the hot springs instead. If you do want to get to the gompa, walk about 5km to Hargam, then cross the bridge for some more walking. Some travellers have tried to cross the river by swimming or wading, and many have nearly come to a tragic end. Be sensible and take the bridge.

Places to Stay & Eat The only place to stay is the *Silk Route Guest House*, which costs Rs 200 for a big double room; dhal, rice and tea will cost more.

There are one or two small shops for supplies, but they offer little.

Getting There & Away

The road to the Nubra Valley (because of the very high Khardung La), and, therefore, the valley itself, is only open for three to four months of the year, from about June to September.

Bus Buses travel to both sides of the Nubra Valley from Leh every few days. The timetables are irregular, so check with local bus and tourist agencies. The buses are slow and crowded, as expected in this region, but are fun. Buses between Leh and Diskit travel on Friday (Rs 65, about six hours); they leave Leh at 6.30 am. Buses from Diskit to Panamik and back go on Monday and Wednesday. The bus will drop you off in the main street of Diskit, a little way off the main road. A bus to Sumur, and Panamik (Rs 79, about 10 hours), leaves Leh at 6.30 am on Monday and Wednesday.

Truck Lifts on trucks, even military ones – in fact, anything travelling along the roads to and around the Nubra Valley – is quite acceptable for tourists and locals alike. As usual, negotiate a fare (around the cost of the bus fare, ie Rs 65) the day before, and prepare yourself for a rough old ride.

Taxi Hiring jeeps or taxis may be the only alternative, and with a group it is often a good option. A one-way/return taxi to Diskit from Leh will cost Rs 3355/4425. A taxi from Leh to Panamik will cost Rs 3520, or Rs 4700 return. A return trip from Leh visiting Diskit, Hunder, Sumur and Panamik for three days will cost about Rs 8000 per taxi. If there are taxis around Diskit, they will offer full day tours around the area on the southern side of the valley for Rs 950; or Rs 1250 including both sides. From Diskit to Panamik, it will be Rs 1155/1490; from Diskit to Sumur, Rs 770/970.

RUPSU VALLEY

Known as 'mountain lake', Tso Moriri is located in the Rupsu Valley, only about 140km (but a rough-and-tumble six or so hours by jeep) from Leh. The lake is about 28km long, 8km at its widest and at an elevation of over 4000m. Surrounded by barren hills, which are backed by snow-covered mountains, Tso Moriri is not in a really spectacular setting, but it's a good place to relax, visit the nearby **gompas** and walk around the lake area. On the way from Leh to Tso Moriri is another brackish lake, the smaller Tso Kar, or 'white lake'.

This is an area of nomadic people, known as Khampas, who can often be seen taking advantage of the summer and moving herds of goats, cows and yaks from one grazing spot to another. Khampas live in large, movable family tents or in solid winterproof brick huts.

Another great aspect of this region is the amount of wildlife – the best (accessible) place in Ladakh for it. Commonly seen are wild asses (known as *kiangs*), foxes and cuddly marmots busy waking up from their last hibernation, or preparing for the next.

On the lakes, you may see large flocks of black-necked geese.

Tso Moriri

The small collection of huts on the shore of Tso Moriri is also called Tso Moriri. Here you must register and show your permit. You can pitch your tent here, but there is nothing stopping you from camping anywhere else. Tso Moriri Village has a toilet.

Korzok

A path at the back of the huts leads for a kilometre or so to the delightful village of Korzok, inhabited by friendly people. The **gompa** here is quite unusual because it is inhabited predominantly by about 30 women, who often spend their days making beautiful garments for themselves, but which are not for sale (or not yet). The gompa was built in about 1850, replacing one destroyed during a Dogra invasion.

Tso Kar

On Tso Kar, there is a small **gompa** at the village of Thukse, a collection of solid brick huts set up for the dramatic winters. You will have to find the monk to let you in. On a slight – and legal – detour off the track linking Tso Kar and Tso Moriri is the smaller lake of **Tso Kiagar**.

Places to Stay & Eat

In short, there is nowhere to stay in the region at all – though this may change as demand increases. You must bring your own tent and all equipment. There are pre set tents at the astronomical price of Rs 800 per two-person tent at Tso Moriri Village; these are set up for upmarket, organised tour groups. Some building was going on at Tso Moriri Village at the time of writing, so small shops selling limited supplies may be set up soon.

There is no place to eat in the region so, again, bring your own food and cooking equipment. This is a very fragile environment, so take out, and back to Leh, everything that you bring in – cans, bottles, papers, *everything*.

Getting There & Away

There are two ways that your 4WD jeep is physically able, and permitted, to enter or leave the region. The first route takes you over the Mahe bridge (near Raldong, at the eastern end of the Indus Valley road) through Puga, and then to one or both lakes. The other route is the road south from Upshi, over the Taglang La, then a detour off the road – look out for the yellow sign. Once you get off any main road, there are no signs (or maps) at all.

No public transport goes even remotely near the lakes. The area has no signposts, and quality maps of the area are nonexistent, so motorcycles are not recommended unless you have a guide (you could easily burn out the clutch in the sand drifts as well). There will be very few people around to give you directions, the marmots around here outnumber humans by about 50 to one!

Taxi A round trip from Leh to Tso Moriri over three days will cost about Rs 9000 via Tso Kar and Taglang La, or the shorter, more direct way is Rs 7500. From Leh, a two day round trip just to Tso Kar will be Rs 6500. Travel agencies in Leh can organise a three day 'jeep safari' from Rs 7500 to Rs 10,000 per vehicle, including meals and tent accommodation, depending which way you go.

DHA-HANU

Dha-Hanu consists of a handful of villages along the road leading north-west from Khalsi, while the main road continues to Kargil. The steep bare walls of the Indus give the terraced fields more light and heat than other parts of Ladakh, which combined with the lower altitude enables rich crops of vegetables and fruits (especially apricots).

The area is probably most famous for its inhabitants, known as Dards or Brokpas, 'people of the land', an ancient Indo-Iranian people. Despite their proximity to Pakistan and other Islamic regions, they are traditionally not Muslims (though there are a few mosques in the area) but retain their own Buddhist traditions and beliefs.

Places to Stay & Eat

There are a handful of basic guesthouses in the village of Dha; the *Skyababa Guesthouse* at the Leh end of the village has basic doubles for Rs 100, and the family is friendly.

In the heart of the village the *Chunu Guesthouse* has very rustic double rooms for Rs 60. The nearby *Lhariemo Shamo Guesthouse* is similar but charges RS 100 for a double.

There are recognised camping sites at the villages of Dhumkhar, Skurbuchan, Hanu-Do, Biama and Dha, and plenty of other legal, but unofficial, places along the way. The one or two shops at Dha and Skurbuchan offer little in the way of food, otherwise your guesthouse will provide something basic to eat; or bring your own supplies.

Getting There & Away

Buses from Leh to Dha leave every day at 9 am; and from Leh to Skurbuchan daily at 10 am. A taxi to Dha from Leh will cost Rs 2486, and Rs 3393 return over two days.

TREKS IN LADAKH

The following information is an overview for travellers wishing to experience a trek. Serious trekkers might consider buying Lonely Planet's *Trekking in the Indian Himalaya*. See Books in the Facts for the Visitor chapter for details.

Treks out of Leh and the Indus Valley include the popular trek from Spituk just below Leh to the Markha Valley and Hemis Gompa, and the trek from Lamayuru Gompa to Chiling Village alongside the Zanskar River. Treks can be completed from the end of June until the middle of October when the first of the winter snows settle on the high passes. Proper acclimatisation is also necessary as many of the passes are in the vicinity of 5000m. Indeed a few days resting in Leh (3505m) is recommended before commencing your trek.

There are many trekking agencies in Leh offering inclusive treks with a guide, pack horses, food and supplies for around US$50 per day. If you are making your own arrangements pack horses can be hired from Spituk or Lamayuru for around Rs 200 per horse per day. It is recommended that all camping gear including a sleeping bag and tent are brought with you even on *inclusive* treks, as the gear provided may not be adequate. Food supplies should also be carried with you from Leh as the village lodges and teahouses are not available on all stages of the treks.

Spituk to Markha Valley & Hemis via the Kongmaru La

The trek from Spituk Gompa follows the Jingchen Valley to the Ganda La (4920m). At least one rest day should be included before crossing the pass. Thereon, it is a steady descent to the Markha Valley and the village of Skiu. It is a further stage to Markha Village, before ascending to the yak grazing pastures at Nimaling. Above the camp is the impressive peak of Kangyaze (6400m). The Kongmaru La (5030m) is the highest pass on the trek and affords great views, south to the Zanskar Range and north to the Ladakh Range. After crossing the pass there is one further camp site at the village of Chogdo before reaching Hemis Gompa. From Hemis there is a daily bus back to Leh.

Stage 1	Spituk to Rumbak (6 to 7 hours)
Stage 2	Rumbak to Yurutse and camp (4 to 5 hours)
Stage 3	Yurutse to Skiu via the Ganda La (6 to 7 hours)
Stage 4	Skiu to Markha (7 to 8 hours)
Stage 5	Markha to Nimaling (7 to 8 hours)
Stage 6	Nimaling to Chogdo via Kongmaru La (6 hours)
Stage 7	Chogdo to Hemis (4 to 5 hours)

Lamayuru to Chiling via the Konze La & Dung Dung La

From Lamayuru the trek crosses the Prinkiti La (3750m) to the ancient gompa and village at Wanla. It is a further stage to the village of Hinju at the base of the Konze La (4950m) where an additional day is recommended for acclimatisation before crossing

the pass. From the Konze La there are impressive views of the East Karakoram Range before a short descent to the village of Sumdo Chinmu. The following day's climb to the Dung Dung La (4820m) is rewarded with views of the Zanskar Range and a bird's-eye view of the swirling Zanskar River before a long and tiring descent to the village of Chiling.

From Chiling you can either return to Leh or continue to the Markha Valley. The stage from Chiling to the village of Skiu in the Markha Valley can be completed in three hours. It's an interesting stage that includes crossing the Zanskar River by a pulley bridge which is maintained and operated by villagers from Chiling who charge Rs 100 per crossing.

Stage 1	Lamayuru to Wanla via Prinkiti La (3 to 4 hours)
Stage 2	Wanla to Hinju (4 to 5 hours)
Stage 3	Hinju to Sumdo Chinmu via Konze La (6 hours)
Stage 4	Sumdo Chinmu to Dung Dung La base camp (3 hours)
Stage 5	Base camp to Chiling via Dung Dung La (6 hours)

Likir to Temisgam

This trek can be completed in a day if you are fit! From Likir gompa the trail crosses a small pass to the village of Yantang a short distance from Rizong Gompa. Stage leads to the village of Hemis-Shukpachu. It is a further short stage over two minor passes to the roadhead at Temisgam. The trek can be completed throughout the year, horses can be hired from Likir while supplies and a tent must be brought from Leh. Road building will eventually render this trek obsolete. Until then there is a daily bus service to Likir, while there is a bus from Temisgam back to Leh each day around noon making it possible to complete the third stage of the trek and be back in Leh that evening.

Stage 1	Likir to Yangtang (4 to 5 hours)
Stage 2	Yangtang to Hemis-Shukpachu (3 hours)
Stage 3	Hemis-Shukpachu to Temisgam (3 to 4 hours)

Leh to Manali

Since opening to foreigners in 1989 this road has become a popular way into and out of Leh. The only other road to Leh goes through Kashmir and along a stretch between Drass and Kargil made more hazardous than usual by Pakistani artillery, and there is often difficulty in getting flights into and out of Leh. There is nothing to see along the road in the way of villages or gompas; it is the raw high altitude scenery which will certainly impress, and is reason enough for travelling this way.

The road to Manali is the world's second-highest motorable road, reaching 5328m at Taglang La. As only about half of the total distance of 485km between Leh and Manali is paved, it can be a rough journey. For much of the way the only inhabitants of the high plateaux are Khampa nomads, soldiers and teams of tar-covered workers from Bihar and Nepal struggling to keep this strategic road open. Whatever form of transport, it will take at least two days, with an overnight stop at a tent camp, probably in Sarchu.

Sudden changes in weather are common, even in the mid-summer month of August, causing delays of several days. It is worth having some cold and wet weather gear with you in the bus because the weather, especially around the highest passes, can be very cold and/or wet. The road is usually open between early June and mid-October.

LEH TO UPSHI

Leaving Leh, from the main road you will get your last glimpse (or your first, of course, if coming from Manali) of the magnificent gompas at Tikse, Shey and Stok. For an hour or so before Upshi, along a paved but dusty road, there are plenty of ugly military sites, such as at Karu, where there is the turn-off to the Pangong Tso area, and to the gompas at Taktok and Chemrey.

UPSHI

The first checkpoint of Upshi is the turn-off south to Manali. Although permits are not needed for this trip, foreigners have to register at the police hut. If travelling on a bus with plenty of other foreigners, there is lots of time for tea, a greasy 'omlate', or to stock up on supplies of chocolate and other goodies.

UPSHI TO TAGLANG LA

At Miru, there is a crumbling little **gompa** (worth a look) on the nearby hill and surrounded by chörtens. There is nowhere to stay or eat, but plenty of camping sites. Lato

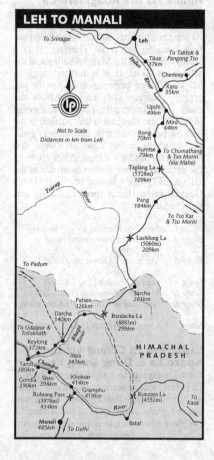

LEH TO MANALI

To Srinagar

Leh

To Taktok & Pangong Tso

Tikse 17km

Chemrey

Karu 35km

Upshi 49km

Miru 64km

Not to Scale
Distances in km from Leh

Rong 70km

Rumtse 79km — To Chumathang & Tso Moriri (via Mahe)

Taglang La (5328m) 109km

Tsarap River

Pang 184km

To Tso Kar & Tso Moriri

Lachlung La (5060m) 209km

To Padum

Sarchu 263km

Patseo 326km

Darcha 340km

Baralacha La (4883m) 299km

To Udaipur & Triloknath

Keylong 372km

Bhaga River

Jispa 347km

HIMACHAL PRADESH

Tandi 380km

Chandra

Gondla 390km

Sissu 398km

Khoksar 414km

Rohtang Pass (3978m) 434km

Gramphu 419km

Kunzum La (4551m)

To Kaza

Manali 485km

To Delhi

River

Batal

has a huge **chörten** on the side of the road, but there is no village to speak of. From here the road starts to climb for about three hours to Taglang La (5328m), where there's a little shrine, and possibly the world's highest 'Gents Urinal' and 'Ladies Urinal'. The bus will stop for a rest and a look around, but if coming from Manali and you haven't acclimatised to the altitude, take it easy.

TAGLANG LA TO LACHLUNG LA

Not long after Taglang La, the road surprisingly flattens out along the Morey plain, and becomes paved. This area is only occasionally inhabited by Khampa nomads. If going on to Tso Moriri or Tso Kar, you will have to look out for the sign. (Refer to Getting There & Away in the Rupsu Valley section, earlier in this chapter.) The road to Pang is good, through a windswept valley, then becomes hopelessly potholed. About 5km before Pang, the road descends through a dramatic **series of gorges** before reaching the teahouse settlement.

Pang, at the bottom of these gorges, has several **restaurants** in tents by the river where most buses stop for lunch. A plate of rice, dhal and vegetables costs about Rs 30, and you may be able to stock up on mineral water and biscuits. Most tents have a mattress where you can unroll your sleeping bag for around Rs 50 per night. There are some rather grim toilets nearby.

At 5060m, Lachlung La is the second-highest pass on the Leh to Manali road. Nearby, there is an incredible 20km of switchback roads, which includes the spine-tingling 21 Gata Loops, or hairpin bends, on one side of one mountain.

SARCHU

Sarchu is just inside Himachal Pradesh, and is where most buses stop overnight. It is just a collection of tents, dotted over a length of 15km or so, which are all packed up for eight months of the year (ie October to May). Just opposite the striped Himachal Pradesh Tourist Development Corporation (HPTDC) tent camps, you must register, again, with the police. Your bus driver may

collect passports and do it himself, but it still involves a lot of waiting.

HPTDC buses stop at HPTDC's own **tent camps**. They are the best of the lot: clean two-person tents with camp beds and lots of blankets are Rs 115 per person. A **tent kitchen** does passable dhal and rice for dinner, and omelettes for breakfast, for about Rs 40.

Public and other private bus drivers seem to have some sort of 'arrangement' with other tent site owners, so you may have little choice but to stay in a tent camp not even remotely as good as the HPTDC site, but for around the same price. Travellers on buses which arrive late at the camps suffer the most. Although the driver may try to dissuade you, you can sleep on the bus for free, where it will be warmer. There are plenty of places to put your own tent.

Just over the bridge from the HPTDC camp are several **tent restaurants** which serve dhal and rice, tea, omelettes, curried noodles, and, for those long cold evenings, a shot of whisky or chang (take it easy though; alcohol is more powerful at high altitude).

BARALACHA LA

It's only a short climb to this 4883m pass, which means 'crossroads pass' because it is a double pass linking both the upper Chandra and Bhaga valleys with the Lingti Valley and vast Lingti plains around Sarchu. About an hour further on is the police checkpoint at Patseo. Here the road begins to hug the Bhaga River to Tandi, where it meets the Chandra River.

DARCHA

Darcha is the other major tent site on this road. Faster buses from Leh, or slower ones from Manali, may stay here, depending on the time and the state of the road around Baralacha La, but Sarchu is more commonly used as a stopover. Like Sarchu, Darcha is just a temporary place, with some crummy tents for hire, and a few **tent restaurants** in the area. Shortly after Darcha, you pass through Jispa, where there is yet another large army camp.

Darcha is the start of a popular trekking option to get into Padum, and in winter it is the only way. From here, you can also trek into places such as Hemis (about 11 days). If you have your own transport, try to get to the little lake of **Deepak Tal** about 16km from Darcha. It is a great spot for camping and exploring.

KEYLONG TO MANALI

Keylong is the first town of any size on the journey from Leh to Manali, and the administrative centre of Lahaul and Spiti. From Keylong, it isn't far to the T-junction at Tandi. From here there is a road that goes sharply to the north-west along the Chenab River to the little-visited parts of Himachal Pradesh towards Udaipur and the famous temple site of Triloknath.

The road to Manali heads south-east, and climbs steadily past Gondla, Sissu and Khoksar. There are *PWD resthouses* which you may be able to use, in all three places, but nothing much else. At Sissu, there is a nice **waterfall** nearby, set under spectacular peaks. Farther on, at Gramphu, the road continues to climb along Lahaul and Spiti – get off at Gramphu or at Keylong if you want to continue to Kaza – or heads south to Manali.

Rohtang Pass (3978m) – not high, but treacherous all the same – starts the descent to Manali.

Refer to the Himachal Pradesh chapter for more details on the towns of Keylong and Manali.

GETTING THERE & AWAY
Bus

As the road goes up to 5328m at its highest point, most people suffer the effects of altitude (headaches, nausea), unless they have spent time acclimatising in Leh.

If you plan to fly one way, fly into Leh and take the bus out because the effects of the altitude on the Leh to Manali journey will not be so great as doing the journey in the other direction. Many people coming from Manali spend an uncomfortable night at Sarchu, where the altitude is around 4100m.

All buses leave Leh at about 6 am to get an early start for the long haul to the overnight stop. Make sure you know your bus number because at this early hour, in darkness, it can be quite confusing finding your bus, among several others.

There are three types of buses which travel between Leh and Manali, all of which generally run daily during the high season, more often if there is demand. Most bus services will not start until about early July and then cease in about mid-September, possibly later if there is demand and the weather holds. Late in the high season, the availability of buses from Leh depends on the demand for passengers travelling in the other direction, from Manali to Leh. From Manali, it is easy to get a connection on a deluxe bus almost straight away to Delhi for about Rs 400 or to many other places; less for the public bus.

HPTDC Bus The most comfortable bus is operated by the HPTDC. Bookings and departures are from the HPTDC office on Fort Rd in Leh, or the HPTDC Marketing Office (☎ 01902-2116) on The Mall, Manali. Tickets cost Rs 700 (Rs 600 from Leh to Keylong), or Rs 1000 including a tent, dinner and breakfast in Sarchu. This extra Rs 300 is not worth it, as you can stay in the same tent and order the same meals yourself in Sarchu for about half this. Try to book your bus ticket as far in advance as you can, especially if you intend travelling at the end of the season.

Private Bus Privately owned (mostly by travel agencies in Manali) buses offer an alternative. They all cost around the same: about Rs 800, plus accommodation and food in Sarchu or Darcha – but the price is subject to change according to demand. In Leh, you can buy your tickets from any travel agency, which means you probably won't know what bus you have a ticket for until you get on. In Manali, bookings can, and should be, made directly with the bus agencies themselves, or any of the travel agencies in Manali will sell you a ticket. See Getting There & Away under Manali in the Himachal Pradesh chapter for details.

Public Bus The third alternative is the less comfortable and generally slower, but certainly cheaper, public bus. They leave according to demand, every one or two days from Leh and Manali starting at about 4 am. 'Super Deluxe' (a bit of a misnomer) costs Rs 525, 'A Class' is Rs 500 and 'B Class' is Rs 345. Subtract about Rs 70 from the fare if you plan to get off at Keylong.

Truck

Trucks can often be quicker than buses, and should be cheaper. They may not stop at Sarchu, but instead drive through the night, which is not a great idea; or they may stop overnight anywhere alongside the road – also not much fun. Trucks are more comfortable if there are only a couple of people in the cabin. Plenty of trucks travel this route, in season. It is just a matter of organising a lift the day before where the trucks stop in Leh or Manali. Around Rs 300 is a reasonable price.

Taxi

An option – which is not outrageous if in a group – is a taxi between Leh and Manali for Rs 11,850. Discounts of up to 40% are possible outside the high season. This can be arranged at the Taxi Union on Fort Rd in Leh, or on The Mall, Manali. It will cost more for each day you take but it allows you to stop, take photos, visit villages and theoretically, have some control over your maniacal driver.

Motorcycle

Motorcycles are a popular means of travelling between Leh and Manali, and places beyond. This, of course, gives you the option of taking several days to admire the spectacular scenery.

It is worth remembering that there are no villages between Keylong and Leh, so you will have to take all your spare parts, particularly spare chains and tubes – and enough spare parts to get out of Leh, too, because Leh doesn't have much to offer either. Some tent sites may sell limited (and sometimes even diluted) petrol at twice the Leh or Man-

ali price; there are petrol stations at Tandi and Keylong, but nowhere else. At all times, it is advisable to wear cold and wet-weather gear throughout the trip, including boots, because the road is always substandard: muddy, wet and dusty in places.

Leh to Kargil

This section refers to places on, or near, the main road from Leh to Kargil. The places are listed in order of distance from Leh.

A number of buses ply the 231km road to Kargil. Trucks are also a good option for a lift between villages. Taxis may seem outrageous but with a group sharing the cost you can visit several gompas on the way to, say, Alchi or Lamayuru. A taxi from Leh to Alchi, stopping at Phyang, Basgo, Likir and Rizong, will cost about Rs 1200.

PHYANG

Not far past Spituk (refer to the earlier Around Leh section for details on Spituk), a long, roughish track off the main road leads to the pretty village of Phyang. **Mani walls** lead to the little-visited gompa, which was built around the 15th century by King Tashi Namgyal and now houses about 45 monks who belong to the Kagyupa order.

Direct buses from Leh leave daily at 7.30 am, 2 and 5 pm (Rs 9.50). Hitching is not really possible as very few vehicles make the detour to Phyang. Taxis from Leh cost Rs 495 return.

NIMMU

Nimmu is a pleasant place to stop for tea. About 8km east, towards Leh, is the junction of the differently coloured Indus and Zanskar rivers. If you can, get out and admire this really spectacular sight. To get to Nimmu, take any bus going from Leh beyond Nimmu, or a one-way/return taxi from Leh costs Rs 577/715.

BASGO

It's only 6km farther on to Basgo, which was the capital of lower Ladakh, before the

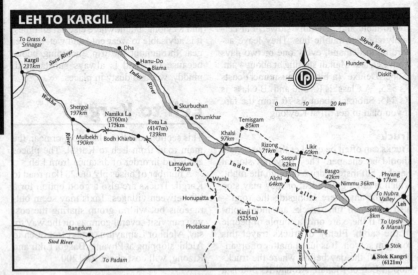

LEH TO KARGIL

Ladakh kingdom was united at Leh. The 400-year-old **gompa** is up some winding, steep tracks. It is often deserted, so ask around for one of the handful of monks in the village to open up. The prayer room in the **Ser Zung Temple** has great frescoes; another temple has an enormous gold and copper statue of the Maitreya Buddha (the coming Buddha), and some elaborate roof and wall frescoes. The views from the roof are wonderful.

The *Lagung Guest House*, next to the gompa, offers basic but reasonable accommodation. Daily buses from Leh go direct to Basgo at 1 and 4 pm (these times are changeable, so check at the tourist office in Leh for an update); or catch one of the daily buses to Alchi or beyond. A one-way/return taxi to Basgo from Leh costs Rs 660/825.

LIKIR

Located 5km north of the main road (turn off just before Saspul) is another magnificent gompa, overlooking the village of Likir. Known as the **Klu-kkhyil Gompa** (Klu-kkhyil means water spirits), it was founded in the 14th century, and was the first gompa in Ladakh known to have been built under the direction of Tibetan monks. The present gompa was rebuilt in the 18th century, rededicated to the Gelukpa order, and is now inhabited by almost 150 friendly monks, who offer free tea to visitors and are happy to show you around.

To stay in Likir, return to the village, about 30 minutes walk across the fields. The pleasant *Norboo Guest House* has a large, authentic Ladakhi kitchen. Rooms here, including all meals, are good value at Rs 150 per person. A bus to Likir Village, which continues to the gompa, leaves Leh every day at 3 pm. A one-way/return taxi from Leh costs Rs 795/890.

ALCHI

Alchi is a busy village with several good places to stay and eat, and masses of stalls selling handicrafts.

The **Alchi Gompa** is the only one in the Ladakhi region on flat ground, so no knee-breaking climb is involved. The gompa was founded in the 11th century by The Great

Translator, Ringchen Zangpo, on his return from India, which accounts for the Indian, and particularly Kashmiri, influences.

The three-storey **Dharma Wheel Gompa**, actually run by the gompa in Likir, is noted for its massive Buddha statues. Within the complex, there are other statues made of clay, lavish woodcarvings, the only examples of Kashmiri-style wall paintings in the area, and many chörtens around the village. Unfortunately, some of the frescoes showing the life of Buddha have been rather badly restored. But thanks to some help from German experts, all may not be lost or irrecoverable and restoration is continuing.

Places to Stay & Eat
In the village, a short walk from the temples, the family run **Choskor** offers good, simple doubles/triples for Rs 120/150, and basic meals in a nice garden. Closer to the temples, the **Zimskhang Guest House** has doubles for Rs 100 with shared bath, or Rs 200 for a double with bath.

Pota La Guest House has airy rooms with bath for Rs 150. It also has a restaurant and camping site. At a similar price and standard is the nearby **Samdup Ling Guest House**. The cheapest here is the **Lotsava**; it is simple, with shared bath, but good value for Rs 60/100. The **Alchi Resort** near the car park has two-room huts with bathroom and hot water set around a courtyard for a negotiable Rs 500.

Getting There & Away
There is one direct bus to Alchi every day, leaving Leh at 3 pm (Rs 30). Otherwise, take any of the other daily buses to places beyond Alchi, get off at the bridge about 2km past Saspul (tee it up with the bus conductor or driver). It is a fairly easy 3km walk from there (taking short cuts) to Alchi. A one-way/return taxi from Leh costs Rs 935/1155.

SASPUL
Saspul is a village on the main road, over the river from Alchi. Apparently there is a small **cave temple** nearby, but nobody seems to know much about it. While Saspul

is nice enough, Alchi has far more to offer. The **Chakzoth Guest House**, on the main road in Saspul, has small rooms for Rs 50. The **Hotel Duke** (☎ 194106-27021) is a decent new mid-range place painted with Ladakhi murals; it has comfortable doubles for Rs 500, and dinner for Rs 120.

RIZONG
About 6km along a steep, rocky track north of the main road is the start of the area containing the nunnery of Julichen and the gompa of Rizong.

There is no village at Rizong, but you may be able to stay at the gompa (men only) or the nunnery (women only); bring your own supplies. Alternatively, near the turn-off to Rizong, about 200m towards Alchi on the main road, is the pricey **Uley Tokpo Camping Ground** with mildly luxurious tents for Rs 800 for two, Rs 1650 with meals. The camp is set among apricot trees.

There is no direct bus to Rizong from Leh, so it is a matter of getting a bus bound for Lamayuru or beyond. If coming from Alchi, it is not difficult to hitch a ride on a truck or bus for 20 minutes between the turn-offs for Alchi and Rizong. As an alternative, a taxi one way from Leh to the bottom of the walk up to the gompa will set you back Rs 1330.

KHALSI
This is a major military area, where your passport will be checked regardless of where you are going, and your permit checked if you're going to the Dha-Hanu region.

LAMAYURU
After exploring other villages in the area, it comes as a surprise to find that Lamayuru is a scruffy little place. But it is completely overshadowed by one of the most famous and spectacularly set gompas in Ladakh.

The **gompa**, part of the Kagyupa order, is not as interesting as others; it's the location perched above a drained lake on an eroded crag overlooked by massive mountains, that makes it special. The oldest known gompa in Ladakh, dating back beyond the 10th century, it has been destroyed and restored several times over the centuries. There are renowned collections of carpets, thangkas and frescoes. Criminals were once granted asylum here (not any more, you'll be glad to know!) which explains one previous name for the gompa: Tharpa Ling or 'Place of Freedom'. Try to get there early to witness a mesmerising puja.

Several kilometres south of Lamayuru is the small **Wanla Gompa**, set on the popular trekking route to Padum in Zanskar.

Places to Stay & Eat
The options aren't so fantastic. The better places to stay are in the village, not on the main road. The *Hotel Shangri-La*, near the main road, has nice views and rooms for Rs 100. The slightly better option (no dirt floors) is the *Hotel Dragon* – just follow the ubiquitous signs – which has large rooms, with shared bath, for Rs 150 per room. Both hotels offer some food, but it's usually little more than dhal, rice or noodles. It's also possible to stay at the gompa's very basic lodgings for Rs 50 per person.

Getting There & Away
There are no buses from Leh or Kargil directly to Lamayuru, so take the Leh to Kargil/Srinagar bus and get off at the truck stop at the top of the village. A better option is a ride on one of the many trucks that stop there. Trucks leave Lamayuru early in the morning; ask at the truck stop for expected departure/arrival times. A one-way taxi in one long day from Leh costs Rs 1952. You can easily walk from the main road to the gompa, and to the village along a new road.

MULBEKH
From Lamayuru the road passes Fotu La (4147m), the highest pass on the route, then Namika La (3760m) before suddenly turning into a lovely green valley. Mulbekh is the last sign of Buddhism before you head into the Muslim-dominated regions near Kargil and beyond.

Mulbekh's main claim to fame is the impressive 8m **Maitreya statue**, an image of a future Buddha, cut into the rock face and

dating back to about 700 AD. Unfortunately, all buses stop for food and a rest at the village of Wakha, 2km from Mulbekh, so this gives you no opportunity to inspect the statue on the way, but you can see it from the bus window.

There are also two gompas, **Serdung** and **Gandentse**, which offer great views of the valley. As in other smaller villages, it is wise to inquire if the gompa is open before making the ascent.

The *Paradise Hotel and Restaurant*, right opposite the Chamba statue, costs Rs 80 per room. The *Namchung Hotel* is similar. Another option is the *Jammu & Kashmir Tourism Development Corporation (J&KTDC) Tourist Bungalow*, with rooms for Rs 40 per person.

From Leh, take the Kargil/Srinagar bus. Mulbekh makes a decent day trip from Kargil. A couple of buses leave Kargil for Mulbekh every day. A return taxi from Kargil plus an hour or so in Mulbekh will cost Rs 800.

SHERGOL
About 7km farther on towards Kargil, along a fertile valley, is the small village of Shergol. Meaning 'Lord of the Morning Star', Shergol is set on the opening of the Wakha River, and has a tiny **cave gompa** perched halfway up the steep, eastern slope of the mountain. It is almost deserted, and is really for those who can't get enough of gompas and stiff walks up mountains. The view, of course, is magnificent. Below the gompa is a **nunnery**.

Kargil & the Suru Valley

The valleys of Suru, Drass, Wakha and Bodkarbu lie midway between the alpine valleys of Kashmir and the fertile reaches of the Indus Valley and Ladakh. The region is politically part of India, ethnically part of Baltistan and geographically an integral part of Ladakh.

KARGIL
☎ 01985

Until 1947 Kargil was an important trading centre linking Ladakh with Gilgit (Pakistan) and the lower Indus Valley. There were also important trading links between the villages of the Suru Valley and the Zanskar Valley, and even 20 years ago it was not uncommon to see yak trains making their way from Padum all the way into the Kargil Bazaar.

Continuing political problems in Kashmir have seriously affected the number of visitors to Kargil and the hotels survive at present from the handful of visitors making their way from Leh to Padum and the Zanskar Valley.

The people of Kargil are mostly Shi'ah Muslims: Arabic script is found everywhere; women are rarely seen, and if so, are usually veiled; and mosques dominate the town. The town has been shelled by the Pakistani army several times; when artillery duels flare up, the town is declared off-limits.

Orientation & Information

Kargil, next to the roaring Suru River, is the second-largest town in Ladakh but is really little more than one long main road called Main Bazaar Rd, with lots of little lanes jutting off (watch out for wide trucks!). Along Main Bazaar Rd are plenty of places with long-distance/international telephone facilities, the post office and State Bank of India, open 10 am to 2 pm weekdays.

If you have time, walk up Hospital Rd for some decent views of the area. There are also nice fields and villages across the Qatilgah Bridge, at the end of Balti Bazaar Rd.

The Tourist Reception Centre, not to be confused with any similarly named government office, is next to the taxi stand, just off the main road. Open 10 am to 4 pm on

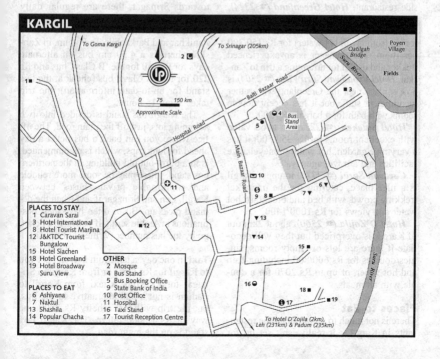

KARGIL

To Goma Kargil
To Srinagar (205km)
Qatilgah Bridge
Poyen Village
Suru River
Fields

0   75   150 km
Approximate Scale

Balti Bazaar Road

Hospital Road

Main Bazaar Road

Bus Stand Area

Suru River

To Hotel D'Zojila (2km), Leh (231km) & Padum (235km)

PLACES TO STAY
1 Caravan Sarai
3 Hotel International
8 Hotel Tourist Marjina
12 J&KTDC Tourist Bungalow
15 Hotel Siachen
18 Hotel Greenland
19 Hotel Broadway Suru View

PLACES TO EAT
6 Ashiyana
7 Naktul
13 Shashila
14 Popular Chacha

OTHER
2 Mosque
4 Bus Stand
5 Bus Booking Office
9 State Bank of India
10 Post Office
11 Hospital
16 Taxi Stand
17 Tourist Reception Centre

normal working days, it has no great information on local areas, or on Zanskar. It does however rent out trekking gear: tents Rs 40 per day, sleeping bags Rs 16 per day. The best place to arrange trekking and travel is through the Siachen and Greenland hotels.

Places to Stay

Kargil used to be full of grotty places for those travelling between Srinagar and Leh, or Zanskar. There's a few on Main Bazaar Rd, but they're awful – try to get somewhere without the bugs, mould and noise.

J&KTDC Tourist Bungalow (☎ 2348) has clean rooms, good views and is only Rs 40 per person, although it is a steep walk up from Main Bazaar Rd. The dilapidated *Hotel International* has passable rooms with cold shower for Rs 100/150.

Hotel Tourist Marjina (☎ 33085) has rather dark rooms with shared bath for Rs 100 set on a courtyard; you enter through a streetside restaurant. *Hotel Greenland* (☎ 2324), farther south near the taxi stand, has quiet rooms with a veranda, some with nice bathrooms (some with hot water) for Rs 150/200 per room. The manager is an experienced trekker and useful for arranging a trip to Zanskar. *Hotel Broadway Suru View* (☎ 2304) is a new place near the Greenland with rather incompetent staff, but it has decent double rooms with bath for a bargain Rs 200.

Hotel Siachen (☎ 2221), is good value with excellent rooms for Rs 350/500; it has a very nice garden, hot water moneychange facilities and a travel agency.

Caravan Sarai (☎ 2278) in upper Kargil is a nice place, catering for the upmarket trekking crowd, with bed and breakfast, hot water and wine for Rs 1000/1400.

Hotel D'Zojila (☎ 2360), about 2km out of Kargil, is overpriced but they will negotiate if there are lots of empty rooms; singles/doubles for Rs 600/800 including bath and hot water, or up to Rs 2070 for a double with all meals.

Places to Eat

There is not much to recommend the restaurants in Kargil – it really isn't set up for long-term visitors. Your hotel will probably do some bland Chinese dishes and some omelettes and bread for breakfast. On and near the Main Bazaar Rd are some bearable small restaurants – the *Naktul*, *Shashila* and *Popular Chacha* – all of which claim to 'Chine's' food. Also worth a try is the *Ashiyana*.

The *restaurants* at the Siachen and Greenland are quite adequate and they'll discreetly serve a bottle of beer for Rs 125 in the evening (alcohol is prohibited in Kargil, hence the price).

Getting There & Away

Bus The early morning daily bus from Kargil to Leh costs Rs 145 and leaves at 5 am; the bus to Srinagar costs Rs 145 and leaves at 4.30 am, though the road could be closed to foreigners because of Pakistani shelling. Towards Leh, there are also two daily buses to Mulbekh and one to Shergol; towards Srinagar, there are regular daily buses to Drass.

There are at least two a day to nearby Panikhar and Parkachik. To Padum, in Zanskar, there is a 4.30 am bus on alternate days for Rs 150 for the 'B Class' bus and Rs 220 for the 'A Class' bus (check at the bus stand for up-to-date information); the trip takes about 15 hours.

The Kargil bus stand is divided into two adjoining lots, just off the main road. The office where you can book a bus ticket a day ahead for long trips, which is recommended, is in a burnt-out old building in the northern bus stand. There may be some more reliable and comfortable private buses between Kargil, Leh and Srinagar if and when the demand picks up. Buses often have their destinations in Arabic script. If you have a ticket, go by the bus number (written in English).

Taxi In one day, a taxi from Leh can get you to Kargil for Rs 3355, or from Kargil to Srinagar for Rs 3100. A taxi from Kargil to Padum is not a bad alternative to the bus, but the trip will cost a hefty Rs 7000 one way or Rs 12,000 return. The Kargil taxi stand is on the main road.

KARGIL TO PADUM

Sanku

The road from Kargil heads south-west, away from Padum, following the Suru Valley and Suru River. It's still predominantly inhabited by Muslims, who converted to Islam in the 15th century; a **Muslim shrine**, dedicated to Sayed Mir Hashim, is located in Karpo-Khar near Sanku. Sanku can also be reached from Drass, west of Kargil on the road to Srinagar, on a two to three day trek.

There's a daily bus from Kargil to Sanku at 3 pm (Rs 18). Sanku accommodation is limited to the *Government Rest House* and *J&KTDC Tourist Bungalow*, which at the time of research was barely operational but charged only Rs 40 per person. One-way/return taxis from Kargil cost Rs 700/1050.

Panikhar

Farther down the Suru Valley, Panikhar and Parkachik are the places to get off and admire, or even get closer to, the twin mountains of **Nun** (7135m) and **Kun** (7087m). It is a lovely area in summer, often full of flowers. In Panikhar, the best accommodation option is a room at the comfortable *J&KTDC Tourist Bungalow*. At the time of research, with the lack of tourists in the area, it was a bargain Rs 40 per person.

Between Panikhar and Kargil, buses cost Rs 35, and leave twice a day in the morning; or take the Kargil to Padum bus which leaves on alternate days. One-way/return taxis cost Rs 1200/1800.

Rangdum

About halfway in time, but not distance, between Kargil and Padum, is Rangdum, where taxis and trucks (but not buses) may stop for the night. You can visit the 18th century **Rangdum Gompa** which serves as a base for about 35 monks and many novices. The *J&KTDC Tourist Complex* has basic facilities for Rs 40 per person. Several village *teahouses* offer unexciting food. From Rangdum, there is another good trek, east through the Kanji La (5255m) which links up to the Leh-Kargil road at Lamayuru.

The road from Rangdum heads in a more southerly direction and crosses the Pensi La (4450m). Farther on is Ating, from where you can visit the **Zongkul Gompa**. As you approach Padum, the valley becomes more populous, with plenty of small villages such as Tungri, Phey and Sani.

Zanskar

The isolated region of Zanskar is composed of a number of small mountain-locked valleys to the south of Ladakh. The valleys are bounded to the north by the Zanskar Range, and to the south by the main Himalaya. To the east and west, high ridges linking the Himalaya and Zanskar mountains ensure that there is no easy connection between Zanskar and the outside world.

Zanskar essentially comprises the Stod Valley in the west and the Lunak Valley in the east, which converge at Padum, the administrative centre of the region. The fertile region of Padum and its outlying villages and gompas form the nucleus of Zanskar. The area's uninterrupted Buddhist heritage has been principally due to its isolation.

PADUM

Padum is the administrative headquarters of the Zanskar region but was once an ancient capital. It is not a particularly attractive place, with incongruous government buildings that were constructed when the road from Kargil was completed in 1981. This has resulted in the town gaining a character similar to roadheads everywhere. Vehicles are repaired, diesel cans are discarded and much that is not used is disposed of here. The main camp site and the small hotel area is close to the newly constructed mosque (the only one in the Zanskar region) which serves the Sunni Muslim community. The only telephone office is at the Hotel Ibex.

Padum is also the starting point for a number of difficult long-distance treks.

Places to Stay & Eat

There's a limited choice of a few basic guesthouses and one more comfortable option.

Hotel Shapodok-la, in the centre of town, has cheap dorm beds. The *Hotel Haftal View*, by the bus stand, is a bit grubby with rooms for Rs 100/150. The *Hotel Chorala* nearby is somewhat better, also with doubles for Rs 150.

Hotel Snowland is one of the better choices, with a nice garden and singles/doubles for Rs 100/150. It is set in the fields about 100m behind the Hotel Chorala.

The *J&KTDC Tourist Bungalow* has fairly big rooms with bath (cold water only) for Rs 50 per person. *Hotel Ibex* (☎ 01983-45012) is the best in town, with decent doubles set around a sheltered courtyard for Rs 300 (no discount for singles).

There's not much to report on foodwise. The least worst place is the Hotel Ibex *restaurant*. The *Lhasa Tibetan restaurant* opposite the Ibex is OK, as is the *Hotel Chorala* and the *Tibetan restaurant* at the bus stand under the Campa Cola sign.

Getting There & Away
The trip between Kargil and Padum is spectacular, even impressing those jaded travellers who thought that they had seen it all along the Leh to Kargil road. But as usual in this part of the world, the road is also narrow, winding and slow. It is only open from July to early October and is completely impassable the rest of the year, effectively isolating the Zanskari people.

Bus In season, a bus runs between Padum and Kargil every alternate day (check with local bus stations for up-to-date information) departing at about 4.30 am. The cost of the bus between Kargil and Padum is Rs 150 for 'B Class' or Rs 220 for 'A Class' (it depends which bus shows up), and the trip usually takes about 15 hours, but can take a lot longer.

You can and should book your ticket the day before in Padum or Kargil. You can get off anywhere you want on the road between Kargil and Padum, but you may have to then wait a day or so for another bus, or rely on hitching a lift on an infrequently travelling truck.

Taxi By taxi, it costs Rs 7000 one way or Rs 12,000 return from Kargil to Padum, but with a group to cut costs, this is a great way to really admire the amazing scenery. This trip can be done in one long day with about 12 hours driving, or you can stop at Rangdum, Parkachik or Panikhar.

Truck Trucks occasionally ply this route, but not nearly as often as on the Kargil-Leh road, because so few people live in and around Zanskar. Nevertheless, hitching rides on a truck, if you can find one, is normal practice, and most drivers will take you for a fee, about the same as the bus.

Getting Around
Jeep & Taxi The Padum Taxi Union office opposite the Hotel Haftal View has exorbitant rates: Rs 650 return to Sani Gompa, Rs 800 return to Karsha Gompa, and Rs 5500/7000 to Rangdum. Not surprisingly, most visitors choose to trek.

TREKS IN ZANSKAR
Treks in the Zanskar area include the popular treks from Padum over the Shingo La (5090m) to Darcha and Manali, and over the Singge La (5050m) to Lamayuru and Leh. There is also a remote trek north over the Cha Cha La (4950m) and Rubrang La (5020m) to the Markha Valley and Leh.

These treks can be undertaken from the end of June – when the snows begin to melt on the high passes – to the middle of October before the first of the winter snows. There are of course exceptions to this as heavy storms blowing up from the Indian plains occasionally interrupt itineraries in August and September. River crossings are also a problem particularly on the trek from Padum to the Markha Valley and it is advisable not to undertake this trek until the middle of August when waters subside. It is also important to note that all of these treks involve high pass crossings of around 5000m so proper acclimatisation is essential.

If making your own arrangements, pack horses can be hired from Padum or Karsha for around Rs 200 a day although this can increase during the harvest period in late August to early September. A local guide is also a valuable asset particularly on the trek from Padum to the Markha Valley.

Camping gear including a tent and sleeping bag must be brought with you as there are a number of stages on these treks where there are no villages to stay. Food supplies must also be brought from Leh.

Padum to Darcha via Shingo La

This trek follows the well defined route up the Tsarap Valley for the first three stages before diverting to Phugtal Monastery, one of the oldest monasteries in Zanskar. The trek continues through a number of villages to the highest settlement at Kargyak. From here it is a further stage to the base of the Shingo La (5090m) before traversing the Great Himalaya Range. A final stage brings you to the roadhead at Darcha and your onward arrangements to Leh or Manali.

Stage 1	Padum to Mune (6 hours)
Stage 2	Mune to Purne (8 hours)
Stage 3	Purne to Phugtal monastery and Tetha (6 hours)
Stage 4	Tetha to Kargyak (7 hours)
Stage 5	Kargyak to Lakong (6 to 7 hours)
Stage 6	Lakong to Rumjak via the Shingo La (6 to 7 hours)
Stage 7	Rumjak to Darcha (6 to 7 hours)

Padum to Lamayuru via Singge La

This trek can start from either Padum or Karsha Monastery, the largest in the Zanskar region. It follows the true left bank of the Zanskar River for two stages before diverting towards the Hanuma La (4950m) and Lingshet Monastery. A further stage goes to the base of the Singge La (5050m) before crossing the Zanskar Range. The pass has dramatic views of the Zanskar gorges and the snow capped peaks of the Great Himalaya Range. The Singge La is not a particularly demanding pass crossing and the gradual descent to the village of Photaksar can be completed in one stage.

From Photaksar the trail crosses the Sisir La (4850m) to the village of Honupatta.

It is a further stage to the ancient monastery at Wanla before finally crossing the Prinkiti La (3750m) to Lamayuru Gompa and onward transport by bus or truck to Leh.

Stage 1	Padum to Karsha (2 hours)
Stage 2	Karsha to Pishu (4 to 5 hours)
Stage 3	Pishu to Hanumil (4 to 5 hours)
Stage 4	Hanumil to Snertse (5 hours)
Stage 5	Snertse to Lingshet via the Hanuma La (5 to 6 hours)
Stage 6	Lingshet to Singge La base camp (5 to 6 hours)
Stage 7	Singge La base camp to Photaksar via Singge La (5 to 6 hours)
Stage 8	Photaksar to Honupatta via the Sisir La (6 hours)
Stage 9	Honupatta to Wanla (5 hours)
Stage 10	Wanla to Lamayuru via Prinkiti La (3 to 4 hours)

Padum to Leh via Cha Cha La, Rubrang La & the Markha Valley

This challenging trek is followed by only a handful of trekkers each season. From Padum the trail heads north to the village of Zangla before diverting from the Zanskar Valley to the Cha Cha La (4950m). From the pass there are uninterrupted views south towards the Great Himalaya Range. Heading north the trail enters a series of dramatic gorges that support rare wildlife including brown bears, bharals and snow leopards. It takes a minimum of two stages to reach the Rubrang La (5020m) and the crest of the Zanskar Range before a steady descent to the villages of the Markha Valley. From Markha Village it takes a further three stages to cross the Kongmaru La (5030m) to Hemis Gompa and the Indus Valley.

Stage 1	Padum to Zangla (7 hours)
Stage 2	Zangla to Cha Cha La base camp (3 hours)
Stage 3	Base camp to Gorge camp via Cha Cha La (6 hours)
Stage 4	Gorge camp to Tilat Sumdo (6 hours)
Stage 5	Tilat Sumdo to Rubrang La base camp (5 to 6 hours)
Stage 6	Base camp to Markha via Rubrang La (6 hours)
Stage 7	Markha to Nimaling (7 to 8 hours)
Stage 8	Nimaling to Chogdo via Kongmaru La (6 hours)
Stage 9	Chogdo to Hemis (4 to 5 hours)

Uttar Pradesh

Often referred to as the cow belt or Hindi belt, Uttar Pradesh has been the most dominant state in Indian politics and culture since Independence, producing over half of India's prime ministers. This is partly because it's the nation's most populous state – it has as many inhabitants as Brazil – and partly because of the central role the region plays in the religious landscape of Hindus. The Ganges River, which forms the backbone of Uttar Pradesh, is the sacred river of Hinduism, and four of the religion's seven holy towns are in the state, including Varanasi, the holiest of them all. Uttar Pradesh is also a place of major importance to Buddhists, for it was at Sarnath, just outside Varanasi, that the Buddha first preached his message of the middle way.

Most of Uttar Pradesh consists of the vast Ganges plain, an area of awesome flatness which often floods dramatically during the monsoon. The people of this area are predominantly poorly educated farmers, whose unequal share in the wealth and resources enjoyed by the state's urbanites is a matter of social concern. In stark contrast to the plains, the scenic north-western corner has hill stations sprinkled along the foothills of the Himalaya, boasts excellent trekking and rises to form some of the highest mountains in India.

Except in the very cheapest hotels, you can expect a 5% luxury tax to be added to your hotel bill in Uttar Pradesh.

History

Over 2000 years ago the area that became Uttar Pradesh was part of Ashoka's great Buddhist empire. Muslim raids from the north-west began in the 11th century, and by the 16th century the region was part of the famed Mughal empire whose capital was for some time at Agra and Fatehpur Sikri.

Following the decline of the Mughal empire, the nawabs of Avadh rose to prominence in the central part of the region and were responsible for turning Lucknow into

Uttar Pradesh at a Glance

Population: 139 million
Area: 294,411 sq km
Capital: Lucknow
Main Language: Hindi
Best Time to Go: October to March

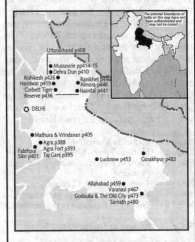

- **Agra** – the Taj Mahal at sunset and the deserted city of Fatehpur Sikri
- **Varanasi** – the peaceful ghats of India's holiest city
- **Rishikesh** – studying yoga in the mountains
- **Corbett Tiger Reserve** – tiger-spotting and high tea

a flourishing centre for the arts. When the British East India Company deposed the last nawab, the Uprising of 1857 began at Meerut, and its most tragic events took place in Lucknow and Kanpur. Agra was later merged with Avadh and the state became known as United Province. It was renamed Uttar Pradesh (Northern State) after Independence, and is often known simply as UP.

In recent times Uttar Pradesh has become the main focus for the Hindu fundamentalist Bharatiya Janata Party (BJP). The dispute at Ayodhya over the construction of a Hindu temple on the site of a mosque brought the state to flash point in 1992. It also led to riots and killings in other parts of India. Things have quietened since, but the anniversary of the Ayodhya dispute, 6 December, remains a potentially volatile time and security is tightened at key sites during this period.

In late 1996 the state was placed under direct rule from Delhi when elections resulted in a hung assembly. After five months of political stalemate the BJP, which won the most seats, formed a coalition government with the BSP, an anticaste, secular party at the opposite end of the political spectrum. The coalition has since been expanded to include the Congress Party. This uneasy alliance will be responsible for handling the central government's proposal to create Uttarakhand, a new state carved out of the Kumaon and Garhwal regions of northwestern Uttar Pradesh.

Tourist Offices

UP Tourism offices can be found in the major Indian cities.

Ahmedabad
(☎ 079-656 0752) 303 Ashwamedh House, 5 Smriti Kunj, Navrangpura
Calcutta
(☎ 033-220 7855) 12A Netaji Subashi Rd
Chandigarh
(☎ 0172-707649) SCO 1046-47, 1st Floor, Sector 22B
Chennai (Madras)
(☎ 044-828 3276) 28 Commander-in-Chief Rd
Delhi
(☎ 011-332-2251, fax 371-1296) Chandralok Bldg, 36 Janpath, Delhi
Lucknow
(☎ 0522-223-3632, fax 221 776, email up.tourism.luc@smt.sprintrpg.ems.vsnl.net.in) Chitrahar Bldg, 3 Naval Kishor Rd
Mumbai (Bombay)
(☎ 022-218-5458) 38 World Trade Centre, Cuffe Parade, Colaba

Agra Region

AGRA
☎ 0562 • pop 1,118,800

In the 16th and 17th centuries, Agra was the capital of India under the Mughals, and its superb monuments date from this era. They include a magnificent fort and the building which many people come to India solely to see – the Taj Mahal. Away from its handful of imposing monuments, there's little to distinguish Agra from any other northern Indian city: it has the usual dense *chowk*

Festivals of Uttar Pradesh

festival	location	date	features
Muharram	Lucknow	varies	Shi'ite celebrations
Magh Mela	Sangam, Haridwar	Magha (Jan/Feb)	Hindu bathing
Taj Mahotsav	Agra	Feb	music & dance
International Yoga Festival	Rishikesh	2-7 Feb	yoga & meditation
Buddha Purnima	Sarnath	May	Buddhist fair & procession
Holi	Barsana	Feb/Mar	coloured water fights
Krishna's birthday	Gokul	Jul/Aug	Hindu pilgrimage
Mahotsava	Lucknow	Nov/Dec	dancing, music, kite flying & tonga races
Id-ul-Fitr	Fatehpur Sikri	Dec/Jan	end of Muslim Ramadan celebrations

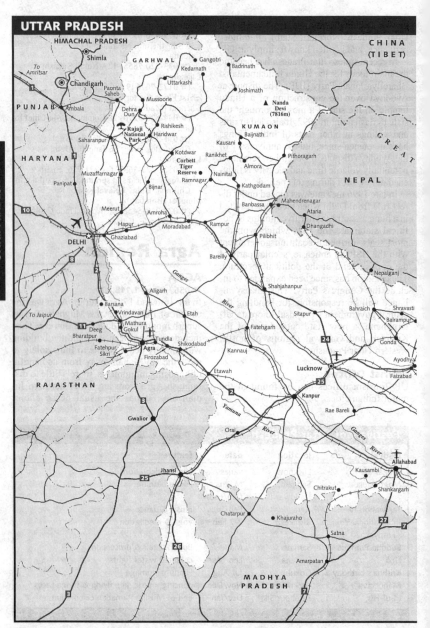

UTTAR PRADESH

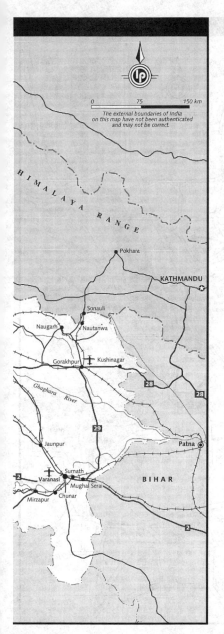

(market), a large cantonment, lots of predatory rickshaw-wallahs and highly polluted air. The Yamuna River, which flows through the city and is the backdrop to the Taj and Agra Fort, has become an open sewer – scientists recently declared it incapable of supporting any life form.

It's possible to day trip to Agra from Delhi, and there's an excellent train service making this eminently practicable. Many people do just that, as coping with Agra's touts, rickshaw-wallahs and numerous people who are determined to make a fast buck from your money can be very tiring. However, if you can cope with the hassles, Agra is worth more than a flying visit, particularly if you intend to see the nearby deserted city of Fatehpur Sikri. The Taj certainly deserves more than a single visit if you want to appreciate how its appearance changes under different light.

History

Badal Singh is credited with building a fort on the site of the present Agra Fort in 1475, but this didn't stop Sikander Lodi making his capital on the opposite bank of the Yamuna in 1501. Babur defeated the last Lodi sultan in 1526 at Panipat, 80km north of Delhi, and Agra then became the Mughal capital. The city reached the peak of its magnificence between the mid-16th and mid-17th centuries under the reigns of Akbar, Jehangir and Shah Jahan. It was during this period that the fort, Taj Mahal and Agra's major tombs were built. In 1638 Shah Jahan built a new city in Delhi, and Aurangzeb moved the capital there 10 years later.

In 1761 Agra fell to the Jats, who looted its monuments, including the Taj Mahal. It was taken by the Marathas in 1770, before the British wrested control in 1803. There was heavy fighting around the fort during the Uprising of 1857, and after the British regained control, they shifted the administration of the north-western provinces to Allahabad. Agra has since developed as an industrial centre.

Orientation

Agra is on the western bank of the Yamuna River, 204km south of Delhi. The old part

UTTAR PRADESH

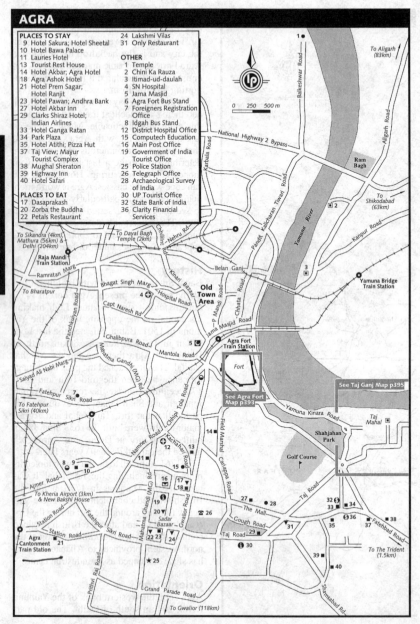

AGRA

PLACES TO STAY
9 Hotel Sakura; Hotel Sheetal
10 Hotel Bawa Palace
11 Lauries Hotel
13 Tourist Rest House
14 Hotel Akbar; Agra Hotel
18 Agra Ashok Hotel
21 Hotel Prem Sagar;
   Hotel Ranjit
23 Hotel Pawan; Andhra Bank
27 Hotel Akbar Inn
29 Clarks Shiraz Hotel;
   Indian Airlines
33 Hotel Ganga Ratan
34 Park Plaza
35 Hotel Atithi; Pizza Hut
37 Taj View; Mayur
   Tourist Complex
38 Mughal Sheraton
39 Highway Inn
40 Hotel Safari

PLACES TO EAT
17 Dasaprakash
20 Zorba the Buddha
22 Petals Restaurant

24 Lakshmi Vilas
31 Only Restaurant

OTHER
1 Temple
2 Chini Ka Rauza
3 Itimad-ud-daulah
4 SN Hospital
5 Jama Masjid
6 Agra Fort Bus Stand
7 Foreigners Registration
   Office
8 Idgah Bus Stand
12 District Hospital Office
15 Computech Education
16 Main Post Office
19 Government of India
   Tourist Office
25 Police Station
26 Telegraph Office
28 Archaeological Survey
   of India
30 UP Tourist Office
32 State Bank of India
36 Clarity Financial
   Services

of the city and the main marketplace (Kinari Bazaar) are north-west of the fort. The spacious British-built cantonment is to the south, and the main road running through it is called The Mall. The commercial centre of the cantonment is Sadar Bazaar.

The labourers and artisans who toiled on the Taj set up home immediately south of the mausoleum. This area of congested alleyways is known as Taj Ganj and today it contains most of Agra's budget hotels. The 'tourist class' hotels are predominantly in the area south of here.

Agra's main train station, Agra Cantonment (abbreviated as Agra Cantt), is west of Sadar Bazaar. The city's major bus stand, Idgah, is nearby. Agra's airport is 7km west of the city.

Information

The Government of India tourist office (☎ 363959), 191 The Mall, is open 9 am to 5.30 pm weekdays, 9 am to 1 pm Saturday. It has maps of Agra and a good brochure on Fatehpur Sikri. There's also a helpful UP tourist office (☎ 360517) at 64 Taj Rd, open daily (except Sunday and the 2nd Saturday in the month) 10 am to 5 pm. The tourist infor-mation counter (☎ 368598) at Agra Cantonment train station is open daily 8 am to 8 pm.

The State Bank of India south of Taj Ganj and the Andhra Bank in Sadar Bazaar (next to the Hotel Pawan) are the best banks to change money. Clarity Financial Services has slightly lower rates, but it's quick and open daily 9 am to 9 pm. You'll find the main post office, with its lax poste restante facility, on The Mall, opposite the Government of India tourist office. The post office is open Monday to Saturday 10 am to 6 pm.

If you're looking for reading material, the small bookshop in the Taj View Hotel carries stock in both English and French. Internet and email facilities are at Computech Education (☎ 253059), Kachahari Rd.

The Foreigners' Registration Office (☎ 269563) is at Police Lines, Fatehpur Sikri Rd. Some private clinics have been mixed up in medical insurance fraud (see Dangers & Annoyances in the Facts for the Visitor chapter), so stick with government hospitals: the District Hospital (☎ 363139) is at Mahatma Gandhi (MG) Rd; SN Hospital (☎ 361318) is at Hospital Rd.

The Archaeological Survey of India (☎ 363506) is at 22 The Mall. You need to

Agra Scams

In Agra, scams designed to part tourists from their money are many and varied. The nastiest scam of all involves poisoning diners in order to make money from subsequent medical treatment. (See the Diarrhoea with Your Meal Sir? boxed text in the Dangers & Annoyances section of the Facts for the Visitor chapter.) Various travellers have written to us and have named specific hotels and restaurants in Agra in connection with the poisoning/insurance scams. They were invariably in the Taj Ganj area. Although it's impossible to prove such complaints, we have ensured that places only appear in this edition if there has been no allegation of impropriety.

The food poisoning scam may be the most dangerous, but other scams proliferate in Agra as well. Familiar tricks are mentioned under Shopping in both this and the Facts for the Visitor chapter (the warning against not letting your credit card out of your sight during a transaction particularly applies in Agra). In addition to these, travellers have written in to inform us of new ploys to be wary of. One warned of being harassed (and pick-pocketed) by rickshaw-wallahs who boarded his bus, claiming he should alight as this was the closest point to the Taj; in fact they were only at the edge of town. Another said that a fake official in the train station had 'checked' his ticket and had returned a used one, meaning he had to buy another valid ticket and pay a fine when the real ticket inspector came around.

make a booking here if you want to stay at the Archaeological Survey Rest House when visiting Fatehpur Sikri.

Taj Mahal

Described as the most extravagant monument ever built for love, this poignant Mughal mausoleum has become the de facto tourist emblem of India. It was constructed by Emperor Shah Jahan in memory of his second wife, Mumtaz Mahal, whose death in childbirth in 1631 left the emperor so heartbroken that his hair is said to have turned grey overnight.

Construction of the Taj began in the same year and was not completed until 1653. In total, 20,000 people from India and Central Asia worked on the building (some later had their hands or thumbs amputated, to ensure that the perfection of the Taj could never be repeated). The main architect is believed to have been Isa Khan, who was from Shiraz in Iran. Experts were also brought from Europe – Austin of Bordeaux and Veroneo of Venice both had a hand in the Taj's decoration – which allowed the British to delude themselves for some time that such an exquisite building must certainly have been designed by a European.

The Taj is definitely worth more than a single visit (if you can afford it) as its character changes with the light during the day. Dawn is a magical time, and it's virtually deserted.

There are three entrances to the Taj (east, south and west); the main entrance is on the western side. The Taj is open 6 am to 7 pm daily except Monday. Entry fees rose substantially early in 2000. Earlier charges were Rs 15 during the day and Rs 105 at sunrise and sunset. Foreign visitors now pay Rs 505 at all times and Indian residents are charged Rs 15. There's no charge to visit the Taj on Friday but it tends to be impossibly crowded and not conducive to appreciating this most serene of monuments.

While this price hike is steep, if you've come this far you can't leave India without seeing the Taj! In winter, it's not really worth getting up early for the sunrise as it's invariably cold, hazy and foggy then. There are plans afoot to open the Taj for five evenings a month during the full moon, but the entry fee is likely to be exorbitant.

The grand red sandstone **gateway** on the south side of the interior forecourt is inscribed with verses from the Quran in Arabic. It would make a stunning entrance to the Taj, but unfortunately these days you only exit through here. The entrance is now through a small door to the right of the gate, where everyone has to undergo a security check. Food, tobacco, matches and other specified items (including, thankfully, the red-blotch forming *paan*) are not allowed to be taken inside. There's a cloakroom nearby for depositing things for safekeeping. Cameras are permitted, and there's no problem taking photos of the outside of the Taj, despite the ambiguously worded signs that state 'photography and trespassing on the lawn is not allowed'. However, guards will prevent you from taking photographs inside the mausoleum.

Paths leading from the gate to the Taj are divided by a long **watercourse** in which the Taj is reflected. The ornamental gardens through which the paths lead are set out along classical Mughal *charbagh* lines – a square quartered by watercourses. To the west is a small **museum** that's open 10 am to 5 pm daily except Monday and Friday. It houses original architectural drawings of the Taj, information on the semiprecious stones used in its construction, and some nifty celadon plates, said to split into pieces or change colour if the food served on them contains poison (handy for those dodgy Taj Ganj meals!). Entry to the museum is free.

The Taj Mahal itself stands on a raised marble platform, north of the ornamental gardens. Purely decorative white **minarets** grace each corner of the platform – as the Taj Mahal is not a mosque, nobody is called to prayer from them. Twin red sandstone buildings frame the Taj; the western one is a mosque, the identical eastern one is purely for symmetry. (It can't be used as a mosque because it faces in the wrong direction.)

Wear & Tear on the Face of Eternity

Although one of Akbar's court officials was moved to record that 'Agra is a great city having esteemed healthy air', this is no longer the case. The World Health Organization has classified Agra as a 'pollution intensive zone'. The city's coke-based industries and vehicle emissions are so befouling that visibility can be reduced to several hundred metres on a clear day. There is great concern that pollution is eroding the Taj, since sulphur dioxide, which settles on the mausoleum as sulphuric acid, is causing the marble to discolour and flake. The sheer volume of visitors doesn't help either – 10 million people view the Taj each year; each Friday between 100,000 and 200,000 pour in.

The political will to counter the effects of pollution was slow to develop, though new industries within a 10,000 sq km exclusion zone were banned. The Supreme Court has since ordered 260 coke-based industries in this area to either move out or switch over to gas. Meanwhile, the government has prevented vehicles from entering the precincts of the Taj, restricted parking within a 500m radius of the building, and planted thousands of trees in the Taj Protected Forest immediately east of the mausoleum in a bid to soak up harmful pollutants. Travellers can help these initiatives to save the Taj by not taking auto-rickshaws or taxis to or from the mausoleum.

The UP and federal governments are jointly spending US$140 million to clean up the environment, but critics argue that still not enough is being done. The amount of suspended particles in the air is said to be five times the maximum level the Taj can handle without sustaining damage. The Taj is now closed on Monday for cleaning.

Recently, numerous stickers have appeared around the city proclaiming 'Green Agra, Clean Agra'. Unfortunately, as yet, this is a statement of intent rather than fact.

The central Taj structure has four small domes surrounding the bulbous central dome. The **tombs** of Mumtaz Mahal and Shah Jahan are in a basement room. Above them in the main chamber are false tombs, a common practice in mausoleums of this type. Light is admitted into the central chamber by finely cut marble screens. The echo in this high-domed chamber is superb, and there is always somebody there to demonstrate it.

Ironically, the perfect symmetry of the Taj is disrupted only by the tomb of the man who built it. When Shah Jahan died in 1666, Aurangzeb placed his casket next to that of Mumtaz Mahal. His presence, which was never intended, unbalances the mausoleum's interior.

Although the Taj is amazingly graceful from almost any angle, it's the close-up detail which is really astounding. Semiprecious stones are inlaid into the marble in beautiful patterns using a process known as *pietra dura*. As many as 43 different gems were used for Mumtaz's tomb alone. The precision and care which went into the Taj Mahal's design and construction is just as impressive whether you view it from across the river or from arm's length.

Agra Fort

Construction of the massive red sandstone Agra Fort on the bank of the Yamuna River was begun by Emperor Akbar in 1565, though additions were made up until the rule of his grandson, Shah Jahan. In Akbar's time the fort was principally a military structure, but during Shah Jahan's reign it had partially become a palace.

The auricular fort's colossal double walls rise over 20m in height and measure 2.5km in circumference. They are encircled by a

Taj Tales

There are more apocryphal stories surrounding the Taj Mahal than there are coke-based industries. According to one tale, after 22 years of waiting, Shah Jahan was finally informed that his masterpiece had been completed. Keen to see it, he asked how long it would take to dismantle the scaffolding draping the mausoleum. 'At least several months', replied an official. Shah Jahan, understandably impatient, decreed that anyone who helped untie the scaffolding could keep the pieces for themselves. It took only a single day for the Taj to be whisked clean of building materials, and ready for the emperor's inspection.

Modern academic research indicates that the Taj was intended as more than an elaborate mausoleum. Analysis of the extensive passages from the Quran inscribed on the walls, and other factors, prompt some scholars to believe that the Taj was also designed to be a symbolic replica of the throne of God, and the formal gardens a representation of the gardens of paradise.

The most unusual story about the Taj is that there might well have been two of them. Shah Jahan, it is said, intended to build a second Taj as his own tomb in black marble, a negative image of the white Taj of Mumtaz Mahal, his wife. Preliminary excavations at the presumed site (across the Yamuna River) have actually uncovered Mughal gardens and building foundations that are in alignment with the Taj. However, a full replica of the Taj in black marble would have been prohibitively expensive, even for the vast treasuries of the Mughals. In any case, Shah Jahan was soon deposed by his son, Aurangzeb. He spent the rest of his life imprisoned in Agra Fort, looking out along the river to the final resting place of his wife.

fetid moat and contain a maze of buildings that form a small city within a city. Unfortunately not all buildings are open to visitors, including the white marble Moti Masjid (Pearl Mosque), regarded by some as the most beautiful mosque in India.

The Amar Singh Gate to the south is the sole entry point. It's open 6 am to 5.30 pm daily; admission is Rs 15 (free Friday). There's a lot to see in the fort, so you may find a guide useful.

Diwan-i-Am The Hall of Public Audiences was built by Shah Jahan and replaced an earlier wooden structure. His predecessors had a part in the hall's construction, but the throne room, with its typical inlaid mar-

ble work, indisputably bears Shah Jahan's stamp. This is where the emperor met officials and listened to petitioners. Beside the Diwan-i-Am is the small **Nagina Masjid** or Gem Mosque. A door leads from here into the **Ladies' Bazaar**, where female merchants came to sell goods to the ladies of the Mughal court. No males were allowed to enter the bazaar except Akbar, though according to one apocryphal story he still enjoyed visiting in female disguise.

Diwan-i-Khas The Hall of Private Audiences was also built by Shah Jahan, between 1636 and 1637. It's where the emperor received important dignitaries or foreign ambassadors. The hall consists of two rooms connected by three arches. The famous Peacock Throne was kept here before being moved to Delhi by Aurangzeb. It was later carted off to Iran and its remains are now in Tehran.

Musamman Burj The exquisite Musamman Burj (Octagonal Tower) stands close to the Diwan-i-Khas. Shah Jahan died here after seven years imprisonment in the fort. The tower looks out over the Yamuna and is traditionally considered to have one of the most poignant views of the Taj, but Agra's pollution is now so thick that it's hard to see. The Mina Masjid was Shah Jahan's private mosque during his imprisonment.

Jehangir's Palace Akbar is believed to have built this palace for his son. It was the largest private residence in the fort and indicates the changing emphasis from military to luxurious living quarters. The palace displays an interesting blend of Hindu and Central Asian architectural styles – a contrast to the unique Mughal style which had developed by the time of Shah Jahan.

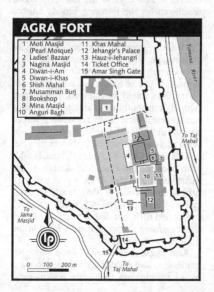

AGRA FORT

1	Moti Masjid
	(Pearl Mosque)
2	Ladies' Bazaar
3	Nagina Masjid
4	Diwan-i-Am
5	Diwan-i-Khas
6	Shish Mahal
7	Musamman Burj
8	Bookshop
9	Mina Masjid
10	Anguri Bagh
11	Khas Mahal
12	Jehangir's Palace
13	Hauz-i-Jehangri
14	Ticket Office
15	Amar Singh Gate

Yamuna River

To Taj Mahal

To Jama Masjid

0   100   200 m

To Taj Mahal

Other Buildings Shah Jahan's **Khas Mahal** is a beautiful white marble structure used as a private palace. The rooms underneath it were intended as a cool retreat from the summer heat. The **Shish Mahal** or Mirror Palace is reputed to have been the harem dressing room and its walls are inlaid with tiny mirrors. The **Anguri Bagh** or Grape Garden probably never had any grapevines but was simply a small, formal Mughal garden. It stood in front of the Khas Mahal.

In front of Jehangir's Palace is the **Hauz-i-Jehangri**, a huge bowl beautifully carved out of a single block of stone. According to one traditional story Jehangir's wife, Nur Jahan, made attar (perfumed essential oil) of roses in the bowl; it's also fabled to have been used for preparing bhang.

The **Amar Singh Gate** takes its name from a maharaja of Jodhpur who slew the imperial treasurer in the Diwan-i-Am in 1644 and, in a bid to escape, reputedly rode his horse over the fort wall near here. The unlucky horse perished, though it is now immortalised in stone. Amar Singh survived the fall but not Shah Jahan's wrath. Justice tended to be summary in those days; there is a shaft leading down to the river where those who made themselves unpopular with the great Mughals were hurled without further ado.

Jama Masjid

Across the train tracks from the Delhi Gate of Agra Fort is the Jama Masjid, built by Shah Jahan in 1648. An inscription over the main gate indicates that it was built in the name of Jahanara, Shah Jahan's favourite daughter, who was eventually imprisoned with Shah Jahan by Aurangzeb. The mosque has no minarets but its sandstone domes have striking marble patterning.

Itimad-ud-daulah

On the opposite bank of the Yamuna, north of the fort, is the exquisite Itimad-ud-daulah – the tomb of Mirza Ghiyas Beg. This Persian gentleman was Jehangir's *wazir*, or chief minister, and his beautiful daughter, Nur Jahan, later married the emperor. Nur

Jahan constructed the tomb between 1622 and 1628 in a style similar to the tomb she built for Jehangir near Lahore in Pakistan.

Interestingly, many of its design elements foreshadow the Taj, construction of which started only a few years later. The Itimad-ud-daulah was the first Mughal structure totally built from marble and the first to make extensive use of pietra dura, the marble inlay work which is so characteristic of the Taj. Though small and squat compared to its more famous cousin (it's known as the 'baby Taj'), its human scale is attractive. Extremely fine marble latticework passages admit light to the interior, and the beautifully patterned surface of the tomb is superb.

The Itimad-ud-daulah is open from around 6 am to 6 pm daily; admission is Rs 12 (free Friday).

Akbar's Mausoleum

The sandstone and marble tomb of Akbar, the greatest of the Mughal emperors, lies in the centre of a peaceful garden grazed by deer at Sikandra, 4km north-west of Agra. Akbar started its construction himself, blending Islamic, Hindu, Buddhist, Jain and Christian motifs and styles, much like the syncretic religious philosophy he developed called Deen Ilahi. When Akbar died, the mausoleum was completed by his son, Jehangir, who significantly modified the original plans. This accounts for its somewhat cluttered architectural lines.

Like Humayun's tomb in Delhi, it's an interesting place to study the gradual evolution in design that culminated in the Taj Mahal. Very tame langur monkeys hang out on the walkway waiting to be fed. The stunning southern gateway is the most impressive part of the complex. It has three-storey minarets at each corner and is built of red sandstone strikingly inlaid with white marble abstract patterns. The ticket office is located here, to the left of the arched entrance. The mausoleum is open from sunrise to sunset; entry is Rs 12 (free Friday). A video camera permit costs Rs 25.

Sikandra is named after Sikander Lodi, the Delhi sultan who ruled from 1488 to 1517, immediately preceding the rise of Mughal power on the subcontinent. He built the **Baradi Palace**, in the mausoleum gardens. Across the road from the mausoleum is the **Delhi Gate**. Between Sikandra and Agra are several tombs and two *kos minars*, or milestones.

Local buses heading to Sikandra run along MG Rd from the Agra Fort bus stand. They cost Rs 3. Auto-rickshaws charge around Rs 75 for the return trip with an hour's waiting time at the tomb.

Other Attractions

The alleyways of **Kinari Bazaar**, or old marketplace, start near the Jama Masjid. There are several distinct areas whose names are relics of the Mughal period, although they don't always bear relation to what is sold there today. The **Loha Mandi** (Iron Market) and **Sabji Mandi** (Vegetable Market) are still operational, but the **Nai ki Mandi** (Barber's Market) is now famous for textiles. Something entirely different is for sale in the **Malka Bazaar**, where women beckon to passing men from upstairs balconies. In the butcher's area next to the leather market, watch out for the festering bloody animal skins that are piled high in the streets.

The white marble **Dayal Bagh Temple** of the Radah Soami religion has been under construction since 1904 and is not expected to be completed until some time in the 21st century. If you're lucky, you may get to see pietra dura inlaid marblework in process. Although the building is architecturally unremarkable, the level of artisanship has to be admired. Dayal Bagh is 2km north of Agra and can be reached by bus or bicycle.

The squat **Chini Ka Rauza** (China Tomb), 1km north of the Itimad-ud-daulah, is the mausoleum of Afzal Khan, a poet and high official in the court of Shah Jahan. Its exterior was once covered in brightly coloured enamelled tiles, but due to years of neglect the remaining tile work merely hints at the building's former glory.

Ram Bagh, the earliest of India's Mughal gardens, is also forlorn. You'll need to use a lot of imagination to picture how it must have looked in 1528 when it was constructed by Babur. It's on the riverbank 500m north of the Chini Ka Rauza and is open 6 am to 5 pm daily; admission is Rs 2, free on Friday.

Swimming

The following hotels allow nonguests to use their pools for a fee: Agra Ashok Hotel (Rs 150), Lauries Hotel (Rs 150) Hotel Atithi (Rs 250), and the Clarks Shiraz Hotel (Rs 300). Ashok has the best pool.

Organised Tours

Guided tours depart from the Government of India tourist office at 9.30 am and proceed to Agra Cantonment train station to pick up passengers arriving from Delhi on the *Taj Express*, which pulls in at 9.47 am. The tours include the Taj Mahal, Agra Fort and a rather hasty visit to Fatehpur Sikri. They finish at 6 pm so day trippers can catch the *Taj Express* returning to Delhi at 6.35 pm. Buy tickets (Rs 175) from the tourist information counter at the train station (you can board the bus at the Government of India tourist office before buying).

Special Events

In February, the **Taj Mahotsav Festival** is held in Shilpgram, a crafts village and open-air emporium about a kilometre along the road running from the eastern gate of the Taj. The festival features live performances of music and dance.

Places to Stay – Budget

Agra's paying guest scheme enables you to stay with local families for between Rs 200 and Rs 500. Contact the tourist information counter at the train station when you arrive.

Unless stated otherwise, rooms mentioned have attached bathroom.

Taj Ganj Area There are plenty of surprisingly cheap hotels in this compact area immediately south of the Taj. Many of them boast views of the famous building, but often it's just wishful thinking. Shanti Lodge and Hotel Kamal have uninterrupted views from their rooftops, and the Taj Khema has

a decent view from a hummock in its garden. However, the government is currently struggling to stop hotels in Taj Ganj from 'encroaching' on the monument and ruining the skyline around it, so you may want to think twice about encouraging their skyward growth.

Hotel Host (☎ *331010*), not far from the Taj's western gate, has comfortable rooms with telephone, carpet, air-cooling and hot water. Singles/doubles are a bargain at Rs 80/100; doubles for Rs 150 have a TV. Checkout is 10 am.

Close by, *Hotel Sidhartha* (☎ *331238*) is a clean, friendly, spacious place built motel-style around a garden courtyard. Singles/doubles with bucket hot water cost Rs 100, or Rs 175/250 with hot water on tap.

Hotel Kamal (☎ *330126, email siit@del2.vsnl.net.in*) has helpful staff and OK singles/doubles for Rs 120/200. It has a

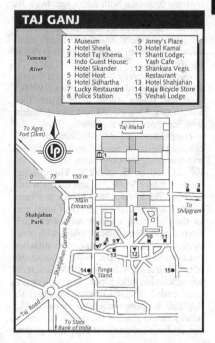

TAJ GANJ

1 Museum	9 Joney's Place
2 Hotel Sheela	10 Hotel Kamal
3 Hotel Taj Khema	11 Shanti Lodge;
4 Indo Guest House;	Yash Cafe
Hotel Sikander	12 Shankara Vegis
5 Hotel Host	Restaurant
6 Hotel Sidhartha	13 Hotel Shahjahan
7 Lucky Restaurant	14 Raja Bicycle Store
8 Police Station	15 Veshali Lodge

Yamuna River

To Agra Fort (2km)

Taj Mahal

0   75   150 m

Main Entrance

Shahjahan Park

Shahjahan Gardens Road

To Shilpgram

Tonga Stand

Taj Road

To State Bank of India

Warning: Food Poisoning Scam

Since mid-1998, we have received reports of a serious food poisoning scam in Agra. For further information, see Dangers & Annoyances in the Facts for the Visitor chapter.

prime view of the Taj from the sitting area on the roof and gets positive reviews from travellers. Checkout is 10 am.

Shanti Lodge (☎ 330900) gets mixed reviews, but it has a decent view of the Taj from its rooftop eating area. Cramped and slightly shabby rooms cost from Rs 80/100, or Rs 150 for doubles with 'views' of the Taj through a fly screen and a grubby window. Some rooms are definitely better than others.

Hotel Shahjahan (☎ 331159) in the heart of Taj Ganj has dorm beds for Rs 30, and reasonable rooms with hot water from Rs 50/100.

Indo Guest House, near the Taj's southern gate, is a clean, basic, family run affair where rooms with hot water are Rs 60/80 or Rs 100/120.

Hotel Sikander (☎ 330279) next door is a similar standard and charges Rs 60/100.

Veshali Lodge, 150m south of the Taj's eastern gate, has a garden, and average rooms with hot water from Rs 60/80.

Hotel Sheela (☎ 331194), near the Taj's eastern gate, is surrounded by a large garden and has singles/doubles with hot water for Rs 120/150 to Rs 200/250. The cheaper rooms are excellent value, and it's often full.

Hotel Taj Khema (☎ 330140) is a ramshackle, overpriced UP Tourism hotel east of the Taj, though prices reduce by 20% from April to September. Rooms with common bath cost Rs 250/300, with attached bath Rs 350/400 and with air-con Rs 650/750. Between October and March, tents are attached to toilet blocks and euphemistically called 'Swiss Cottages'. It costs Rs 300/350 to experience this delight. The hotel's saving grace is the excellent view of the Taj from the artificial hill in the garden.

South of Taj Ganj *Hotel Safari* (☎ 360110, Shamsabad Rd)* is popular, clean and good value. Air-cooled singles/doubles with hot water cost Rs 120/175. There are also air-con rooms for Rs 250/350. Some rooms have bathtubs and all are supplied with towel, soap and toilet roll.

Highway Inn (☎ 332758) nearby is popular with overlanders for its camping facilities which cost Rs 30 per person. Rooms are OK at Rs 75/150 with common bath and Rs 150/250 with attached bath. It puts on sitar/buffet evenings; inquire ahead.

Sadar Bazaar

Tourist Rest House (☎ 363961, Kachahari Rd, email trh@vsnl.com) is an excellent place to stay. It's managed by two benign brothers who make train/air reservations, provide good local information and also run tours to Rajasthan. Comfortable, spotless, air-cooled singles/doubles with hot water are Rs 65/85 to Rs 150/200, and toiletries and towels are provided. Checkout is 10 am. Decent vegetarian food is served in the candle-lit courtyard or in the rooftop restaurant. Don't confuse this place with the nearby (and inferior) Kapoor Tourist Rest House on Fatehpur Sikri Rd or the Tourist Guest House near Agra Fort bus stand.

Hotel Akbar Inn (☎ 363212, 21 The Mall) is midway between Sadar and Taj Ganj. It has tiny rooms with common bath from Rs 40/60 and better rooms with attached bath and hot water from Rs 80/100. You can also camp here for Rs 25 per tent. There are extensive lawns and a pleasant terrace.

Hotel Akbar (☎ 363312, 196 Field Marshal Cariappa Rd) has plain but OK singles/doubles with hot water for Rs 90/200, or only Rs 60 with cold water. There's a dorm for Rs 25, or you can camp for Rs 20 in the large, unkempt grounds. This place has big plans, which include a swimming pool. At the time of writing only the 'To the swimming pool' sign had been erected and this pointed at a large swampy sewer – still, you never know your luck.

Agra Hotel (☎ 363331) next door is a large, crumbling, dowdy place caught in a time warp. It's very friendly and peaceful and has a good range of rooms starting from Rs 150/200, all hot water and some amazing antediluvian plumbing. Air-cooling is Rs 50 extra and air-con doubles cost Rs 450.

The *Hotel Pawan (☎/fax 262442)*, also known as Hotel Jaiwal, is on the main drag of Sadar Bazaar close to shops and restaurants. Fine, bland air-cooled rooms with hot water cost between Rs 200/300 and Rs 300/400. Air-con rooms are Rs 400/500, and the management is helpful.

West of Sadar Bazaar Two good choices are 200m from the Idgah bus stand, on Ajmer Rd: *Hotel Sakura (☎ 369793)* and next-door *Hotel Sheetal (☎ 369420)*. Private buses to Rajasthan depart from outside. Both have friendly staff and variable rooms, so ask to see several. Singles/doubles start at Rs 125/150 in Sakura and Rs 100/125 in Sheetal. Both places serve veg/nonveg food, including on the rooftop in Sheetal.

Along the road, *Hotel Bawa Palace (☎ 265681)* is a step up. Carpeted rooms with TV are Rs 550/700, or Rs 800/1000 with air-con. Prices drop by 30% in the low season.

Hotel Prem Sagar (☎ 267408, 264 Station Rd), 300m east of Agra Cantonment train station, is friendly, but rooms with bucket hot water cost Rs 125/200 and are merely adequate.

Hotel Ranjit (☎ 364446), next door, is of a better standard and costs from Rs 245/400.

The *retiring rooms* at Agra Cantonment station have dorm beds for Rs 50, doubles for Rs 200 and air-con doubles for Rs 400.

Places to Stay – Mid-Range & Top End

Mayur Tourist Complex (☎ 332302, fax 332907, Fatehbad Rd) has pleasant cottage-style rooms arranged around a lawn with a swimming pool, but beware of mosquitoes. Air-cooled singles/doubles cost Rs 800/950 and air-con rooms are Rs 1000/1200. The hotel is efficiently run and it has a pretty good restaurant.

Hotel Atithi (☎ 330879, fax 330878, Fatehbad Rd) has good-sized, well-equipped air-con rooms from Rs 1050/1270, plus a swimming pool and restaurants. Rates are usually negotiable. Across the road, *Hotel Ganga Ratan (☎ 330329)* is a little less grand, but the rooms from Rs 900/1020 are almost as good.

Lauries Hotel (☎ 364536, MG Rd) is an established hotel where Queen Elizabeth II's party stayed on a visit to India in 1961. Any regal pretensions have long since faded, though it retains spacious arcaded corridors and extensive grounds. Large rooms cost Rs 650/800. You can also camp for Rs 50. Its swimming pool is open during the hotter months.

New Bakshi House (☎ 302176, fax 301448, 5 Laxman Nagar) is between the train station and the airport. It's effectively a private home, and you can use the family's lounge. Comfortable doubles in this clean place range from Rs 750 to Rs 1250, some with air-con. However, it's a bit pricey, especially as they add a 'tax' of 10% to 17.5%.

Places to Stay – Top End

All the top-end hotels are air-conditioned and have pools. Except for Agra Ashok and Clarks Shiraz Hotel, all are on Fatehbad Rd.

Agra Ashok Hotel (☎ 361223, fax 361620, 6B The Mall) is a well-managed, pleasant place to stay despite being part of the Indian Tourism Development Corporation chain. Room rates are Rs 1500/2500.

The Trident (☎ 331818, fax 331827) is a low-rise Mughal-style hotel with a garden and restaurant. Singles/doubles are excellent value at Rs 1195/2350 in summer, but from October to April prices soar to Rs 3550/3750 plus 10%. A visitor warned that a 'dreadful smell' drifts over from an abattoir if the wind's in the wrong direction.

Park Plaza (☎ 331870, fax 330408) is a new squeaky-clean hotel offering good rooms for US$45/75.

Clarks Shiraz Hotel (☎ 361421, fax 361428, email clarkraz@nda.vsnl.net.in) is a long-standing Agra landmark. Rooms for US$45/90 have the expected comforts, including a fridge.

Taj View (☎ 331841, fax 331860) is a five star member of the Taj Group of hotels.

UTTAR PRADESH

Rooms with a distant view of the Taj Mahal cost US$115/130; rooms without views are US$105/120.

The *Mughal Sheraton (☎ 331701, fax 331730)* is Agra's top hotel. It boasts all the usual luxuries (but no lift) and has standard rooms from US$130/140, or US$175/200 with a medium-range view of the Taj Mahal.

Places to Eat

Don't forget to try the local speciality, ultra-sweet candied pumpkin *peitha*.

Taj Ganj Area In the Taj Ganj area there are a huge number of makeshift eateries catering to budget travellers, many of them on rooftops or terraces. Their cooking facilities are minimal and hygiene is not always quite what it might be, though they still manage to produce extensive, multicuisine menus. Beer can be 'arranged' in most places and 'special' lassis are widely available. It only takes a few minutes to walk around this area and check out the latest 'in' places.

Joney's Place is tiny but it's one of the area's longest running establishments. It serves great western breakfasts, good Indian and Israeli food, and is justly famous for its banana lassis.

Shankara Vegis Restaurant has rooftop dining. It tries its hand at Indian vegetarian, Chinese, spaghetti and western breakfasts. Meals cost roughly Rs 30 to Rs 55. There are plenty of games available if you run out of conversation.

Lucky Restaurant has the usual have-a-go-at-everything menu but it's one of the more convivial places to hang out. Apart from the open-sided ground floor area, there are a few tables on the roof with views of the Taj.

Yash Cafe also has an enjoyable atmosphere, aided by western music, games, and comfy chairs. It has a wide menu of veg and nonveg food.

Elsewhere Although Agra has a fine tradition of Mughlai food, you would never know it from the food dished up in its cheaper restaurants. For quality Mughlai cuisine, you'll need to dip into the luxury hotels – and deep into your wallet.

Dasaprakash, in the Meher Cinema complex behind the Agra Ashok Hotel, serves tasty and highly regarded south Indian food in the Rs 45 to Rs 100 range.

Zorba the Buddha in Sadar Bazaar is a spotlessly clean, nonsmoking, Osho-run vegetarian restaurant. Excellent main dishes cost around Rs 70 to Rs 80, and you can polish one off with a nutty coffee flavoured with cinnamon and cashew nuts. It's very popular with travellers, so it can be hard to get a table in the evening. The restaurant is closed each year in May and June.

Lakshmi Vilas (Taj Rd) is a cheap south Indian veg restaurant nearby, recommended for its 23 varieties of *dosa* (lentil pancakes) from Rs 20.

Petals Restaurant (19A Taj Rd) is a newish, comfortable restaurant serving Indian, Chinese and continental food. Prices start at Rs 45 for veg and Rs 85 for nonveg.

For those craving western familiarity there's a *Pizza Hut* on Fatehbad Rd, next to Hotel Atithi, but it's rather pricey.

Only Restaurant, at the Taj Ganj end of The Mall, is highly rated by locals. Unfortunately the food (from Rs 55) is pretty bland, but at least there's live Indian music in the evening.

For top-end dining, try the restaurants in *Clarks Shiraz Hotel* and the *Mughal Sheraton*.

Shopping

Agra is well known for leather goods, jewellery, *dhurrie* (rug) weaving and marble items inlaid with coloured stones, similar to the pietra dura work on the Taj. Sadar Bazaar and the area south of Taj Ganj are full of emporiums of one kind or another, but prices here are more expensive than in the bazaars of the old part of the city. The best jewellery shops are around Pratapur, also in the old part of Agra, though you can still pick up precious stones cheaper in Jaipur.

About a kilometre along the road running from the eastern gate of the Taj is Shilpgram, a crafts village and open-air emporium. It has displays of crafts from all over the country. Prices are certainly on the high side, but the quality is good and the range hard to beat.

Read the warning boxed text under Shopping in the Facts for the Visitor chapter since quite a few tourists manage to get ripped off in Agra. The easiest way to avoid pitfalls is not to let rickshaw-wallahs persuade you to visit shops on the way to your destination – you'll pay inflated prices to cover the cost of commission. It's also best to avoid the cool young men on mopeds who claim to be students who want to learn about your country. An invitation to visit their home will inevitably lead you straight to a craft shop. Lastly, don't be tempted by the unconvincing scams which promise handsome profits in return for helping a shop export goods to your home country – somewhere along the line your credit card will take a beating.

Getting There & Away

Air The Indian Airlines office (☎ 360948) is at the Clarks Shiraz Hotel. It's open daily 10 am to 1.15 pm and 2 to 5 pm. Agra airport, 7km from town is on the popular daily tourist shuttle from Delhi to Agra, Khajuraho, Varanasi and back again. It's only a 40 minute flight from Delhi to Agra, leaving at 10 am. Fares from Agra are: Delhi US$50, Khajuraho US$70, and Varanasi US$95.

Bus Most buses leave from the Idgah bus stand. Buses to Delhi (Rs 70, five hours), Jaipur (Rs 93, six hours) and Mathura (Rs 21, 1½ hours) depart hourly. Buses to Fatehpur Sikri (Rs 13, 1½ hours) leave every 30 minutes. There's one bus to Khajuraho (Rs 120, 10 hours) at 5 am. Slower buses to Mathura (Rs 21, two hours) depart from the Agra Fort bus stand. Rajasthan government buses depart from a small booth outside Hotel Sheetal, close to the Idgah bus stand. Buses leave here every hour for Jaipur (Rs 112 deluxe, six hours), but you should book a day in advance.

Train Trains to/from Agra are very busy, especially those travelling between Delhi

and Varanasi. Try to reserve as far in advance as possible, especially if you want a sleeper.

Agra Cantonment station is on the main Delhi-Mumbai (Bombay) line. The fastest train to Delhi is the daily air-con *Shatabdi Express* (Rs 370 in air-con chair class, two hours). It leaves New Delhi at 6.15 am and departs from Agra for the return trip at 8.18 pm, making it ideal for day-tripping.

A much cheaper alternative is the daily *Taj Express* (Rs 53/258 in 2nd/1st class, 2½ hours). It leaves Delhi's Nizamuddin station at 7.15 am and departs from Agra for the return trip at 6.35 pm. This gives you less time in Agra but it conveniently connects with the organised tour (see Organised Tours earlier in this section). Plenty of other expresses operate between the two cities, most taking between three and 3½ hours. Take great care at New Delhi station; miscreants are aware that this is a popular tourist route and work overtime at parting unwary visitors from their valuables.

There are some direct trains to Mughal Serai (Rs 178/611 in sleeper/1st class, 12½ hours) near Varanasi, but most of the expresses running between Delhi and Calcutta do not stop at Agra. If you're heading to or from Varanasi (which is on this line), it may be more convenient to utilise Tundla or Firozabad stations, east of Agra, where most expresses stop. A bus between Firozabad and Agra takes 1½ hours and costs Rs 13; to Tundla it takes about an hour.

There are also direct trains to Mumbai (Rs 302/1102 in sleeper/1st class, 23 to 29 hours) Goa, Chennai (Madras) and Thiruvananthapuram (Trivandrum). If you're heading north towards the Himalaya there are trains through Agra which continue past Delhi – you don't have to stop and get another ticket.

Agra's train connections to cities in Rajasthan have been disrupted by Rajasthan's conversion from metre gauge to broad gauge. Currently, the only direct train to Jodhpur (via Jaipur) is the *Marudhar Express*, leaving Agra Fort station at 4.40 am and taking 14 hours.

Getting Around

To/From the Airport Agra's Kheria airport is 7km from the centre of town and 3km west of Idgah bus stand. From Taj Ganj, taxis charge around Rs 75 and autorickshaws Rs 40.

Taxi & Auto-Rickshaw Tempos (large three-wheelers) operate on set routes: from the Agra Fort bus stand to Taj Ganj it's just Rs 2. Taxis and auto-rickshaws are unmetered so be prepared to haggle.

Prepaid transport is available from Agra Cantonment train station to Taj Ganj (Rs 38/82 by rickshaw/taxi), Sadar Bazaar (Rs 17/35) and to the Taj Mahal and back with an hour's waiting time (Rs 65/125). Some travellers are now choosing not to take motorised transport to the Taj in an effort to reduce harmful pollutants in the mausoleum's vicinity (see the Wear & Tear on the Face of Eternity boxed text earlier in this section). A prepaid rickshaw for local sightseeing costs Rs 250 for a full day or Rs 135 for four hours; taxis cost Rs 400 for a full day locally, or Rs 550 if you also want to go to Fatehpur Sikri. Unfortunately, the prepaid rates aren't actually displayed, so if no one is in the booth, drivers may show their own falsely inflated fare charts. You should be able to beat the official prepaid fares if you bargain.

Cycle-Rickshaw Agra is very spread out and not conducive to walking since hordes of cycle-rickshaw wallahs pursue would-be pedestrians with unbelievable persistence. Many visitors get frustrated by this but the rickshaw-wallahs often speak English well and have a finely tuned sense of humour. They can also be useful sources of local information. Don't take any nonsense from rickshaw-wallahs who offer to take you from A to B via a few marble or jewellery shops.

From Taj Ganj to Sadar Bazaar is less than Rs 15, and to Agra Cantonment less than Rs 20, which is the most you should pay to get anywhere in Agra. Although cycle-rickshaws are the most environmentally friendly way to get around – certainly to the Taj – they are not particularly suited to Agra's diffuseness. If you're heading from the fort to the Taj, it's almost quicker to walk than catch a cycle-rickshaw since this stretch consists of a long, slow incline.

Bicycle The simple solution to Agra's transport problem is to hire a bicycle. The city is sufficiently traffic-free to make cycling an easy proposition and avoiding rickshaw-wallahs will increase your enjoyment of the city three-fold. Raja Bicycle Store, near the Taj Ganj tonga and rickshaw stand, hires bicycles for Rs 5 per hour, Rs 15 for half a day and Rs 30 for a full day; a new bike will cost Rs 10/25/50 to hire. Some hotels will also arrange bike hire.

FATEHPUR SIKRI
☎ 05619 • pop 29,280

This magnificent fortified ghost city was the capital of the Mughal empire between 1571 and 1585, during the reign of Emperor Akbar. Fatehpur Sikri was thereafter quickly abandoned, but thanks to the durable red sandstone and a lot of work by the Archaeological Survey of India it remains a perfectly preserved example of a Mughal city at the height of the empire's splendour.

Most people visit Fatehpur Sikri as a day trip from Agra, but it can be an atmospheric place to stay. Spending the night here would allow you to watch the impressive sunset over the ruins. The best viewpoint is from the top of the city walls, a 2km walk to the south.

The end of the festival of Ramadan is very lively in Fatehpur Sikri.

Orientation & Information

The deserted city lies along the top of a ridge, 40km west of Agra. The village, with its bus stand and train station, is at the bottom of the ridge's southern face. A Rs 4.50 fee per car is payable at Agra Gate, the eastern entrance to the village.

The historic enclosure is open 6 am to 5.30 pm; entry is Rs 5, free on Friday. A video camera permit is Rs 25. There's no entry fee to visit the Jama Masjid and the tomb of Shaikh Salim Chishti as they are outside the city enclosure. The function and

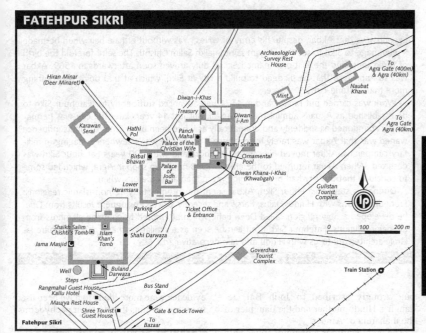

FATEHPUR SIKRI

Hiran Minar (Deer Minaret)

Archaeological Survey Rest House

To Agra Gate (400m) & Agra (40km)

Naubat Khana

Mint

Diwan-i-Khas

Treasury

Diwan-i-Am

Karawan Serai

Hathi Pol

Panch Mahal

Palace of the Christian Wife

Rumi Sultana

To Agra Gate Agra (40km)

Birbal Bhavan

Ornamental Pool

Palace of Jodh Bai

Diwan Khana-i-Khas (Khwabgah)

Lower Haramsara

Gulistan Tourist Complex

Parking

Ticket Office & Entrance

0   100   200 m

Shaikh Salim Chishti's Tomb

Islam Khan's Tomb

Shahi Darwaza

Jama Masjid

Goverdhan Tourist Complex

Well

Buland Darwaza

Steps

Train Station

Rangmahal Guest House

Kallu Hotel

Bus Stand

Maurya Rest House

Shree Tourist Guest House

Gate & Clock Tower

To Bazaar

Fatehpur Sikri

even the names of many buildings remain contentious so you may find it useful to hire a guide. Licensed guides cost around Rs 50 and loiter near the ticket office; unlicensed guides solicit tourists at the Buland Darwaza.

Jama Masjid

Fatehpur Sikri's beautiful mosque, known as Dargah Mosque, contains elements of Persian and Hindu design and is said to be a copy of the mosque at Mecca. The main entrance is through the impressive 54m high **Buland Darwaza**, the Gate of Victory, constructed to commemorate Akbar's victory in Gujarat. A Quran inscription inside its archway quotes Jesus saying: 'The world is a bridge, pass over it but build no house upon it. He who hopes for an hour may hope for eternity', which seems highly appropriate considering the fate of the city. Just outside the gateway is a deep well and,

when sufficient numbers of tourists assemble, local daredevils leap from the top of the entrance into the water.

In the northern part of the courtyard is the superb white marble *dargah* or **tomb of Shaikh Salim Chishti**, built in 1570. Just as Akbar came to the saint four centuries ago looking for a son, childless women visit his tomb today. The carved marble lattice screens (*jalis*) are probably the finest examples of such work you'll see anywhere in the country. The saint's grandson, Islam Khan, also has his tomb within the courtyard. The eastern gate of the mosque, known as the **Shahi Darwaza** (King's Gate), was the one used by Akbar.

Palace of Jodh Bai

North-east of the mosque is the ticket office and entrance to the old city. The first building inside the gate is a palace, commonly

The City of Akbar

Legend says that Akbar, despite his army of wives, was without a male heir when he made a pilgrimage to Sikri to see the Muslim saint Shaikh Salim Chishti. The saint foretold the birth of three sons, and the first one (named Salim) duly arrived soon afterwards in 1569. Akbar was so impressed that he pledged to build a city at Sikri, which at that point was nothing more than a stone-cutters' village.

Work was carried out rapidly and in 1571 had advanced sufficiently for Fatehpur Sikri to be established as Akbar's administrative capital. But just 14 years later the city was permanently abandoned as suddenly and dramatically as it had been built. One reason its influence waned was that Akbar was rarely in residence – usually he was elsewhere engaging in military campaigns. Akbar moved his capital to Lahore and within 20 years Fatehpur Sikri was deserted. When Akbar returned to the area in 1598 he set up shop in Agra, which led some to conclude that the city had been nothing more than an emperor's whim.

During his stay in Fatehpur Sikri, Akbar spent much time studying non-Islamic religions. From discussions with Hindus, Jains, Parsis and recently arrived Portuguese Jesuits from Goa, he developed a new religion called Deen Ilahi, which attempted to combine elements from all major religions. Fatehpur Sikri itself can be seen as a similar synthesis: a place where Islamic architecture fuses with Hindu and Jain decorative art.

but wrongly ascribed to Jodh Bai, Jehangir's Hindu mother and the daughter of the maharaja of Amber.

The architecture is a blend of styles with Hindu columns and Muslim cupolas. The **Hawa Mahal** (Palace of the Winds) is a projecting room whose walls are made entirely of stone latticework. The ladies of the court may have sat inside to keep an unobtrusive eye on events below.

Birbal Bhavan

Thought to have been built either by or for Akbar's favourite courtier, Raja Birbal, this elegant building provoked Victor Hugo, the 19th century French author, to comment that it was either a very small palace or a very large jewellery box. Birbal, who was a Hindu and noted for his wit and wisdom, unfortunately proved to be a hopeless soldier and lost his life, and most of his army, near Peshawar in 1586. The palace fronts onto the **Lower Haramsara**, which was once believed to be an enormous stable, with nearly 200 enclosures for elephants, horses and camels. This is now thought to be where the palace maids lived. The stone rings still in evidence were more likely to have been used to secure curtains than to fetter pachyderms.

Karawan Serai & Hiran Minar

The Karawan Serai or Caravanserai was a large courtyard surrounded by the hostels used by visiting merchants. Outside the fort grounds, The Hiran Minar (Deer Minaret) is said to have been erected over the grave of Akbar's favourite elephant. Stone elephant tusks protrude from the 21m tower from which Akbar is said to have shot at deer and other game which were driven in front of him. The flat expanse of land stretching away from the tower was once a lake and still occasionally floods today.

Palace of the Christian Wife

Close to the Jodh Bai Palace, this house was used by Akbar's Goan Christian wife, Maryam, and at one time was gilded throughout – giving it the name the Golden House.

Panch Mahal

This whimsical five storey palace was probably once used by the ladies of the court and originally had stone screens on the sides.

These have now been removed, making the open colonnades inside visible. Like a house of cards, each of the five storeys is stepped back from the previous one until the top floor consists of only a tiny kiosk. The lower floor has 84 columns, no two of which are exactly alike.

Treasury

For a long time this building was known as Ankh Micholi, which translates roughly as 'hide and seek' – a game the emperor is supposed to have played here with ladies of the harem. However, current thinking suggests that the building was the imperial treasury – an idea supported by the curious struts carved with sea monsters who are believed to protect the treasures of the deep. Near one corner is a small canopied enclosure known as the Astrologer's Seat, where Akbar's Hindu guru may have sat while instructing him. A more mundane explanation is that the court treasurer parked himself here to watch the dosh being counted.

Diwan-i-Khas

The Hall of Private Audiences, known as the Jewel House, is unique for its interior design. A carved stone column in the centre of the building flares to support a flat-topped 'throne' which is 6m high. Narrow stone bridges radiate from the corners of the room and meet at the throne. The function of the building is disputed: some think Akbar spent much time on the 'throne' (so to speak) discussing and debating with scholars of different religious persuasions; others believe it to be the perch from which he meted out justice. Another possibility is that this was where the emperor was weighed at the commencement of the Persian New Year.

Diwan-i-Am

Just inside the north-eastern gates of the deserted city is the Hall of Public Audiences, a large open courtyard surrounded by cloisters. Beside the Diwan-i-Am is the **Pachisi Courtyard**, set out like a gigantic game board. It is said that Akbar played the game pachisi here, using slave girls as the pieces.

Other Monuments

Musicians would play from the **Naubat Khana**, at one time the main entrance to the city, as processions passed beneath. The entrance road then ran between the mint and the treasury before reaching the Diwan-i-Am. The **Diwan Khana-i-Khas (Khwabgah)**, in front of the Daftar Khana (Record Office), was Akbar's own sleeping quarters. Beside the Khwabgah is the tiny but elaborately carved **Rumi Sultana** or Turkish Queen's House. Near the Karawan Serai, badly defaced elephants still guard the **Hathi Pol**, or Elephant Gate.

Outside the Jama Masjid are the remains of the small stone-cutters' mosque. Shaikh Salim Chishti's cave was supposedly at this site and the mosque predates Akbar's imperial city. There's also a **Hakim's House** (Doctor's House), and a fine **hammam**, or Turkish bath, beside it.

Places to Stay & Eat

The *Archaeological Survey Rest House* (☎ 882248) is the cheapest place to stay. It costs only Rs 9 but advance bookings must be made at the Archaeological Survey of India (☎ 0562-363506), 22 The Mall, Agra.

Maurya Rest House (☎ 882348), near the Buland Darwaza, is the most pleasant of the budget hotels in the village. There are basic singles/doubles with common bath for Rs 50/70 or Rs 90/120 with attached bath (free bucket of hot water). It's well run by a friendly family, and food is available in the small, shady courtyard or the rooftop restaurant. Two of the brothers play the sitar and tabla and there are occasional impromptu concerts in the evening.

Next door is *Rangmahal Guest House* (☎ 882219), offering rooms of a similar standard and price (checkout is 10 am), and *Kallu Hotel*, a basic restaurant serving *thalis* (vegetarian plate meals) for Rs 25.

Down the hill, *Shree Tourist Guest House* (☎ 882276) has six clean but spartan rooftop rooms from Rs 70/100.

Goverdhan Tourist Complex (☎ 882648) has a range of rooms, starting from Rs 60/100 with attached bath and bucket hot

UTTAR PRADESH

water. Dorm beds go for Rs 50, or camping on the lawn costs Rs 40 for two. Food is served from the garden terrace.

Gulistan Tourist Complex (☎ 882490) is a sympathetically designed upmarket UP Tourism operation with rooms from Rs 400/450 or from Rs 700/850 with air-con. It's a nice place to stay but not great value, though prices drop Rs 100 between March and September. It has a courtyard garden, a nonveg restaurant and a bar.

There are plenty of snack and soft-drink vendors around all the entrances to the enclosures. Fatehpur Sikri's speciality is *khataie*, the biscuits you'll see piled high in the bazaar.

Getting There & Away

Tour buses only stop for an hour or so at Fatehpur Sikri, so if you want to spend longer (which is recommended) it's worth catching a bus from Agra's Idgah bus terminal (Rs 13, 1½ hours). Buses depart every 30 minutes between 7 am and 7 pm. There are also four trains a day to Fatehpur Sikri from Agra Fort (Rs 8, one hour).

You can spend a day in Fatehpur Sikri and continue on to the world-renowned bird sanctuary at Bharatpur in the evening. Buses depart from Fatehpur Sikri's bus stand every hour until 4.30 pm (Rs 10).

Don't encourage the villagers along the Agra road who force dancing bears to stop the passing traffic.

MATHURA

☎ 0565 • pop 272,500

This area, popularly known as Brij Bhoomi, is a major pilgrimage place for Hindus. Krishna, the popular incarnation of Vishnu, is believed to have been born in Mathura (Muttra) and the area is closely linked with many episodes in his early life. Nearby is Vrindavan (Vrindaban) where Krishna 'sported' with his *gopis* (milkmaids) and where the Hare Krishnas have their headquarters.

Although Mathura has been an important centre for the arts, the region's significance is largely incorporeal. Its material attractions certainly pale in comparison to the rich associations drawn from Hindu mythology.

History

Mathura is an ancient cultural and religious centre. The Buddhist monasteries that were built here received considerable patronage from Ashoka, and Mathura was mentioned by Ptolemy and by the Chinese visitors Fahsien (who visited India from 401 to 410 AD) and Xuan Zhang (634-762 AD). By Xuan Zhang's visit, the population of Mathura's 20 monasteries had dropped from 3000 to 2000 as Buddhism in the region began to give way to Hinduism.

In 1017, Mahmud of Ghazni arrived on his rape, burn and pillage trip from Afghanistan, damaging the Hindu and remaining Buddhist shrines. Sikander Lodi continued the destruction in 1500 and the fanatical Aurangzeb flattened the Kesava Deo Temple, which had been built on the site of one of the most important Buddhist monasteries, and built a mosque in its place. The Afghan Ahmad Shah Abdali finished off what the others began by torching Mathura in 1757.

Information

The helpful tourist office (☎ 1913) at the old bus stand is open Monday to Saturday 10 am to 5 pm. Guided tours (Rs 45) depart from this bus stand at 6.30 am, visiting Vrindavan, Barsana, Nandgaon and Goverdhan. Note that many temples in the area are closed between about 11 am and 4 pm, siesta time for the deities and their attendants.

Shri Krishna Janmbhoomi

Among the foundations of the Kesava Deo Temple is a small room designed to look like a prison cell. Here pilgrims file past the stone slab on which Krishna is said to have been born 3500 years ago. He was obliged to make his entry into the world in these undignified surroundings because his parents had been imprisoned by the tyrannical King Kansa. Aurangzeb's mosque rises above the site and there's a more recent Hindu Temple beside it. Following the clashes between Hindus and Muslims in Ayodhya, there's now a heavy military presence; cameras must be deposited at the security checkpoint at the entrance. The temple is open 6 am to noon and 3 to 8 pm.

MATHURA & VRINDAVAN

Yamuna River

0   0.5   1 km

Vrindavan Train Station

Vrindavan

To Goverdhan (25km)

To Delhi (140km), Radha Ashok, Barsona & Nandgaon

PLACES TO STAY
8 ISKCON Guest House; Krishna Balaram Temple
16 Agra Hotel
19 Hotel Modern
21 Hotel Mansarovar Palace

OTHER
1 Nidhi Van Temple
2 Rangaji Temple
3 Bus Stand
4 Govind Dev Temple
5 Radha Ballabh Temple
6 Bankey Bihari Temple
7 Madan Mohan Temple
9 Pagal Baba Temple
10 Gita Mandir Temple
11 Shri Krishna Janmbhoomi; Aurangzeb's Mosque; International Guest House
12 Kans Qila Fort
13 Jama Masjid
14 Vishram Ghat; Sati Burj
15 Dwarkadheesh Temple
17 Archaeological Museum
18 New Bus Stand
20 Old Bus Stand; Tourist Office

To Gokul (10km) & Mahaban (12km)

To Hotel Madhuvan (2km) & Goverdhan

Mathura

Mathura Junction Train Station

Civil Lines

To Agra (47km)

Yamuna River

About 200m from the Shri Krishna Janmbhoomi there's an alternative Krishna birthplace, and nearby is the **Potara-Kund**, where baby Krishna's nappies (diapers) are supposed to have been washed.

Along the Yamuna River

The Yamuna River, which flows through Mathura, is lined with *ghats* (steps to a river). **Vishram Ghat** is the most important bathing ghat and is where Krishna is said to have rested after killing King Kansa. You can hire a boat for a spell on the river for Rs 20 for half an hour; turtles are often seen in the water here.

The **Sati Burj**, beside Vishram Ghat, is a four storey tower built by the son of Behari Mal of Jaipur in 1570 to commemorate his mother's *sati* (self-immolation). Aurangzeb knocked down the upper storeys, but they have since been rebuilt.

The ruined fort, **Kans Qila**, on the river-bank, was built by Raja Man Singh of Amber; Jai Singh of Jaipur built an observatory here, but it has since disappeared.

Set back from the river are the **Jama Masjid**, built by Abo-in Nabir Khan in 1661, and the **Dwarkadheesh Temple**. Built in 1814 by Seth Gokuldass, Dwarkadheesh is Mathura's main temple and is dedicated (surprise, surprise) to Krishna.

Archaeological Museum

The Archaeological Museum is well worth visiting to see its superb collection of the Mathura school of ancient Indian sculpture. This includes the famous and impressive 5th century standing Buddha found here. It's open daily except Monday 10.30 am to 4.30 pm. Admission is free.

Places to Stay & Eat

International Guest House (☎ 405888), next to Shri Krishna Janmbhoomi, is excellent value with singles/doubles with common bath costing Rs 30/50 and doubles with attached bath from Rs 75. It has a garden and a cheap vegetarian restaurant.

Agra Hotel (☎ 403318), overlooking the river on Bengali Ghat, has simple, air-cooled rooms with attached bath and hot water from Rs 100/200. Air-con doubles are Rs 450.

There are a few basic but acceptable places by the old bus stand. Of these, *Hotel Modern* (☎ 404747) has OK rooms with cold-water bath for Rs 125/200. Checkout is 24 hours, and there's a bar and nonveg restaurant.

Hotel Mansarovar Palace (☎ 408686) is more upmarket and has slightly ageing air-cooled rooms with attached bath and hot water for Rs 600/800 or Rs 700/800 for air-con. Its veg/nonveg restaurant is claimed to be run on 'scientific and hygienic principles'.

Hotel Madhuvan (☎ 420064, fax 420684) is a three star establishment, a Rs 15 cycle-rickshaw ride north-west from the new bus stand. Rooms are Rs 650/850 or Rs 700/850 with air-con. There's a swimming pool that nonguests can use for Rs 100, and also a restaurant and bar.

The top hotel in the area is Best Western's *Radha Ashok* (☎ 405557, fax 409557), 3km from town on the Delhi road. Good air-con rooms cost Rs 1575, and there's a restaurant and swimming pool.

Getting There & Away

Mathura is 47km north-west of Agra and 141km south of Delhi. From the new bus stand, there are half-hourly buses to Delhi's Sarai Kale Khan bus stand (Rs 50, 3½ hours) and to Agra (Rs 21, 1½ hours). The old bus stand serves local destinations, but also has two daily buses to Agra.

The fastest train to Delhi's Nizamuddin station is the *Taj Express*, which departs Mathura at 7.30 pm (Rs 42/213 in 2nd/1st class, 2¼ hours). Mathura also has direct trains to Agra (Rs 22/114, one hour), Bharatpur, Sawai Madhopur (for Ranthambhore) and Kota.

AROUND MATHURA
Vrindavan

This is where Krishna indulged in adolescent pranks like flirting with gopis in the forests and stealing their clothes while they bathed in the river. Little now remains of the legendary forests and the river has meandered away from most of Vrindavan's

bathing ghats, but this dusty town still attracts huge numbers of pilgrims.

The bulky red sandstone **Govind Dev Temple** is the most impressive building in Vrindavan. The name means Divine Cowherd – in other words Krishna. Architecturally it's one of the most advanced Hindu temples in northern India and was built in 1590 by Raja Man Singh of Amber. It was originally seven storeys high but Aurangzeb lopped off the top four floors. Venture inside to see its vaulted ceiling.

The **Rangaji Temple** dates from 1851 and is a bizarre mixture of architectural styles, including a Rajput entrance gate, a soaring south Indian *gopuram* (intricate gateway tower) and an Italianate colonnade. At the entrance are two amusing electronic puppet shows telling the stories of the *Ramayana* and the *Mahabharata*. Non-Hindus are not allowed in the middle enclosure of the temple where there's a 15m gold-plated pillar.

There are said to be 4000 other temples in Vrindavan, including the popular **Bankey Bihari**, **Radha Ballabh** (built in 1626), **Madan Mohan**, the 10 storey **Pagal Baba**, and the **Nidhi Van**.

The International Society of Krishna Consciousness (ISKCON) (☎ 442596) has its Indian base in Vrindavan. At its white marble **Krishna Balaram Temple** complex is a mausoleum dedicated to the sect's founder, Swami Prabhupada, who died in 1977. Every year several hundred westerners attend courses and seminars here. Phone the society for details.

Places to Stay & Eat *ISKCON Guest House* (☎ 442478) at the ISKCON complex has clean doubles with attached bath, bucket hot water and very hard beds for Rs 200. It's also possible to stay cheaply in some of Vrindavan's ashrams, such as *Maheswari* (☎ 442043). The restaurant at the ISKCON guesthouse is the best place to eat in this veg-only town. It serves thalis for Rs 40 and other meals for less than Rs 25.

Getting There & Away Tempos ply the 10km stretch between Mathura and Vrindavan. They depart from Mathura's new bus stand and Shri Krishna Janmbhoomi, and cost Rs 5 (though they try to charge foreigners more). The trip takes about 25 minutes and can get very squashy. Auto-rickshaws are more comfortable but charge around Rs 60 one way. Trains go from Mathura to Vrindavan at 7.10 and 9.40 am and 12.30, 6.05 and 8 pm; they return 15 minutes later.

Gokul & Mahaban

Krishna was secretly raised in Gokul, 16km south of Mathura. Hordes of pilgrims flock here during his birthday **festival** each July/August. It's best to get to Gokul by auto-rickshaw. It costs around Rs 150 return, including waiting time.

Mahaban, 18km south-east of Mathura, is where Krishna spent some of his youth.

Barsana & Goverdhan

Krishna's consort Radha was from Barsana, 50km north-west of Mathura. This is an interesting area to be during the festival of **Holi** when the women of Barsana attack the men of nearby Nandgaon with coloured water. Buses to Barsana depart from Mathura's new bus stand.

Krishna is said to have protected the inhabitants of Goverdhan from Indra's wrath (rain) by holding a hilltop, neatly balanced on top of his finger, over the town for seven days and nights. Goverdhan is 25km west of Mathura, on the road to Deeg.

MEERUT

☎ 0121 • pop 980,000

Only 70km north-east of Delhi, this is where the 1857 Uprising broke out, when Meerut was the largest garrison in northern India. There's little to remember that event by today – just the cemetery near St John's Church, which also has the grave of General Ochterlony, whose monument dominates the Maidan in Calcutta. The **Suraj Khund** is the most interesting Hindu temple in Meerut and there's a **Mughal mausoleum**, the Shahpir, near the old Shahpir Gate.

Meerut is a green revolution boom town and the new-found wealth, indicated by the many well-stocked stores, has led to communal tensions.

Sardhana, 18km north of Meerut, is the palace of Begum Samru. She converted to Catholicism and built the basilica here in 1809, which has an altar of white Jaipur marble. The begum's tomb is in the basilica.

There are several hotels in Meerut; the best is the ***Hotel Shaleen*** and there's also the cheaper ***Anand Hotel*** – both in the Begum Bridge area.

Uttarakhand

Uttarakhand, the Land of the North, is the name given to the northern part of Uttar Pradesh. It's an area of hills, mountains and lakes; the western half is known as Garhwal and the eastern part is Kumaon. There are moves under way in Delhi to make Uttarakhand into a new state called Uttaranchal, though this has become bogged down in disputes over the future of the plains areas at the foot of the mountains. The agitation for a new state was partly driven by the early 1990s issue of reservations for government jobs and places in educational institutions for backward castes; most of the people of Uttarakhand belong to middle and upper castes but are still poor.

The region has several popular hill stations, including Nainital and Mussoorie, and many trekking routes – most of them little known and even less used. Sensitive border areas previously closed to foreign trekkers and mountaineers are starting to open up. In the summer, pilgrims walk to the source of the holy Ganges near Gangotri, not far from the border with China. Gangotri is one of the four main Himalayan *yatra* (pilgrimage) destinations, the others being Badrinath, Kedarnath and Yamunotri – collectively known as the Char Dham. More accessible pilgrimage centres include Haridwar and Rishikesh, where the Ganges leaves the Himalaya and joins the plains for its long trip to the sea.

You can enter Nepal from northern Uttar Pradesh. See Banbassa at the end of this section for details.

UTTAR PRADESH

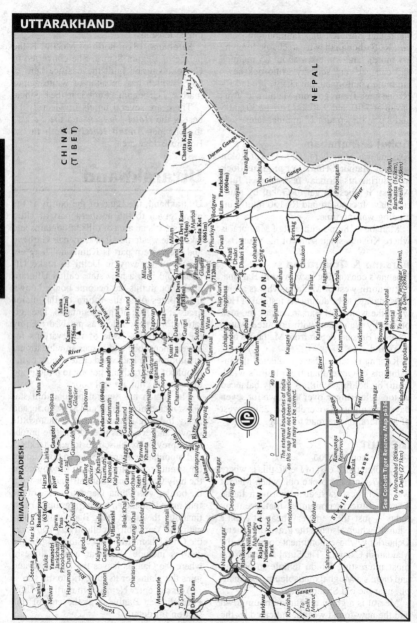

UTTARAKHAND

Tourist Offices

UP Tourism has offices in most major tourist centres (see the Information section at the beginning of this chapter). The Garhwal and Kumaon regions also have tourist organisations: Garhwal Mandal Vikas Nigam (GMVN), and Kumaon Mandal Vikas Nigam (KMVN), whose offices can be found in many larger towns. GMVN headquarters is in Dehra Dun, and a trekking and mountaineering division is in Rishikesh. There is a network of GMVN and KMVN tourist bungalows throughout Uttarakhand, with rates that vary according to the season.

Organised Tours

Five-day mountain cycling tours from Nainital and other centres in Kumaon are organised by UP Tourism. Contact its Delhi office for details.

The organisation also operates package tours during the yatra season (April to November) to the Char Dham temples of Garhwal. Packages from Delhi feature luxury buses and accommodation and an eight day tour to Badrinath and Kedarnath (Rs 4850); there's also a 12 day tour to the four temples (Rs 7100).

As well as its coach tours to the Char Dham during the yatra season, UP Tourism offers taxi packages. A seven day package departing from Delhi to Kedarnath and Badrinath is Rs 6300 per person for twin accommodation. Seven day taxi packages to Kedarnath and Badrinath from Delhi are Rs 10,000 per person.

DEHRA DUN
☎ 0135 • pop 424,500

This old centre of the Raj is situated in the broad Doon Valley between the Siwaliks and the front range of the Himalaya. The hill station Mussoorie can be seen, 34km away, on the high ranges above the valley.

Dehra Dun is at the centre of a forest area and the Forest Research Institute is here. The town is a major academic and research centre and a base for the Indian Military Academy and the Survey of India (which sells large-scale maps of many Indian cities).

There are also several prestigious boarding schools including the Doon School, India's most exclusive private school, where Rajiv Gandhi was educated. Quite a few of the larger houses around the town are home to retired army officers. On the way to Mussoorie there are several Tibetan Buddhist gompas and colleges.

Orientation

The clock tower is the hub of the town and most of the budget hotels are near it or close to the train station. The top-end hotels are in the area known as Astley Hall, north of the clock tower, and further north on Rajpur Rd. The main market is Paltan Bazaar; high quality basmati rice for which the Doon Valley is famous is sold here.

Information
Tourist Offices GMVN (☎ 654371) has offices at the Hotel Drona, near the Delhi bus stand at 45 Gandhi Rd. It's open Monday to Saturday 10 am to 5 pm (closed for lunch between 1 and 2 pm).

Money The State Bank of India is close to the clock tower, at 11A Rajpur Rd, in the Windlass Shopping Complex, beneath the Hotel Ambassador. Most travellers cheques are accepted, but *not* Visa. The Central Bank, Astley Hall area, on Rajpur Rd, is one of the few banks that will exchange Visa travellers cheques.

Travel Agencies BJ Travels (☎ 657888), about 200m north of the main post office at 15B Rajpur Rd, has a computerised reservation system and can provide instant confirmation on domestic and international flights. To arrange treks, contact Garhwal Tours & Trekking, 151 Araghar Rd (☎ 627769), or Trek Himalaya Tours (☎ 653005).

Bookshops Natraj Booksellers, at 17 Rajpur Rd, next to the Motel Himshri, has an extensive selection of books on environmental issues, with particular emphasis on the Indian Himalaya. There's also a hefty selection of Penguin titles. Around the corner

UTTAR PRADESH

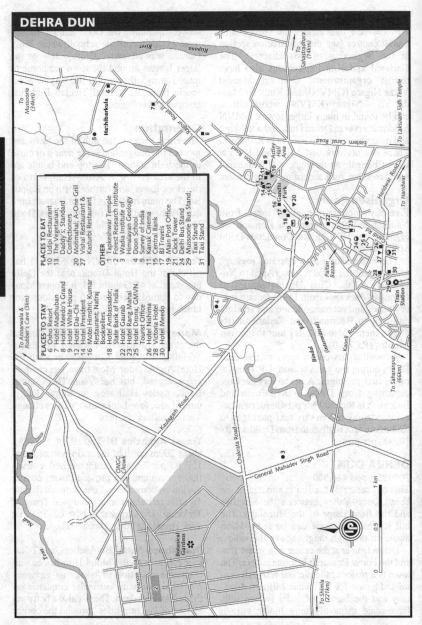

DEHRA DUN

To Sahastradhara (14km)

Kishana River

To Mussoorie (3km)

Hathibarkula

Rajpur Road

Eastern Canal Road

To Laksiam Sidh Temple

To Haridwar

To Amarwala & Robber's Cave (3km)

Lytton Road

Astley Hall Area

Gandhi Park

Kaulagarh Road

ONGC Chowk

Chakrata Road

Paltan Bazaar

Bindal Road

Binal (intermittent)

Kaonli Road

To Sahanpur (66km)

General Mahadev Singh Road

Pearson Road

Botanical Gardens

To Shimla (221km)

Tons

Nah

Grand Rd

Haridwar Rd

Train Station

PLACES TO EAT
10 Udipi Restaurant
13 The Vegetarian;
     Daddy's; Standard
     Confectioners
20 Motimahal; A-One Grill
27 Vishal Restaurant &
     Kasturbi Restaurant

OTHER
1   Tapkeshwar Temple
2   Forest Research Institute
3   Wadia Institute of
     Himalayan Geology
4   Doon School
5   Survey of India
11 Kanak Cinema
15 Central Bank
17 BJ Travels
19 Main Post Office
21 Clock Tower
24 Delhi Bus Stand
29 Mussoorie Bus Stand;
     Taxi Stand
31 Taxi Stand

PLACES TO STAY
6   Osho Resort
7   Hotel Madhuban
8   Hotel Meedo's Grand
9   Hotel White House
12 Hotel Dai-Chi
14 Hotel President
16 Motel Himshri; Kumar
     Restaurant; Natraj
     Booksellers
18 Hotel Ambassador;
     State Bank of India
22 Hotel Gaurab
23 Hotel Rang Mahal
25 Hotel Sona; GMVN
     Tourist Office
26 Hotel Nishima
28 Victoria Hotel
30 Hotel Meedo

1 km
0.5

at 15 Rajpur Rd, the English Book Depot also has an excellent range.

The Survey of India has its headquarters off Rajpur Rd, 4km from the clock tower, in an area called Hathibarkula. You can buy many maps of Indian states and regions from the map shop. It's open 10 am to 5 pm weekdays.

Film & Photography For photographic requirements, advice and excellent service, Harish Studio, in the Motel Himshri complex, is a good place to head.

Forest Research Institute

Established by the British early in the 20th century, the Forest Research Institute (FRI) is now reputedly one of the finest institutes of forest sciences in the world and houses an excellent museum. It's set in large botanical gardens, with the Himalaya providing a spectacular backdrop.

The institute is open Monday to Friday 10 am to 5 pm and entry is free. To get there take a six-seater Vikram (the local name for a tempo) from the clock tower to the institute gates.

Other Attractions

The **Wadia Institute of Himalayan Geology** has a museum (open Monday to Friday 10 am to 5 pm).

Tapkeshwar Temple is dedicated to Shiva. It's set beside a pretty little river in a damp cave, where water constantly drips onto the lingam. A small donation is asked. The cave is reached by a long set of steps leading down to the river, with several small shrines along the way. A large fair is held here on Shivaratri day (usually in March).

Other places to visit include the **Lakshman Sidh Temple**; the village of **Sahastradhara** (14km east of Dehra Dun) with cold sulphur springs and a *Tourist Rest House* (Rs 200 for double; book through the GMVN tourist office in Dehra Dun); and the **Robbers' Cave**, a popular picnic spot just beyond Anarwala Village, 8km from Dehra Dun. Take a local bus to Anarwala and walk the remaining 1.5km.

Organised Tours

GMVN runs sightseeing tours to sites around town for Rs 80, including to the Forest Research Institute and Tapkeshwar Temple, as well as day trips to Mussoorie (Rs 120) and Haridwar (Rs 160).

Places to Stay

Hotel Nishima (☎ 626640) is a simple budget place with singles/doubles for Rs 150/200, set off the street but close to the train and bus stations.

Hotel Meedo (☎ 627088) is a large place with rooms with attached bath from Rs 150 to Rs 350. Those at the back are quieter. There's a rather sleazy bar next door, but the Meedo itself is clean and friendly. (Don't confuse this place with the top-end Hotel Meedo's Grand.)

Hotel White House (☎ 652765) on Lytton Rd is a nice old villa (if a little run down) set in a quiet garden. It's popular locally for wedding receptions. Singles/doubles start at Rs 125/175; air-coolers are available for Rs 50 a day. Some of the rooms are enormous. A three-wheeler from the stations will cost about Rs 25; a Vikram Rs 4 (get off at Kanak Cinema).

Hotel Dai-Chi (☎ 658107), on Mahant Laxman Dass Rd, is also in a quiet part of town (quiet unless its sports day at St Joseph's Academy across the road). Large clean rooms with attached hot bath cost Rs 250/350, and there's a veg restaurant.

Most of Dehra Dun's more salubrious hotels can be found north of the town centre on Rajpur Rd.

The *Hotel Ambassador* (☎ 655831, fax 655830, 11A Rajpur Rd) on the top floors of the Windlass Shopping Centre, has air-cooled singles/doubles with colour TV from Rs 250/350.

Hotel Gaurab (☎ 654215) is a grand new hotel on Gandhi Rd. Pleasant rooms cost from Rs 270/370 to Rs 870 for a two room suite. The restaurant here is also good.

Motel Himshri (☎ 653880, fax 650177, 17 Rajpur Rd) has ordinary rooms from Rs 275/350; larger deluxe rooms cost Rs 425/525.

Hotel Drona (☎ 654371, 45 Gandhi Rd), next to the Delhi bus stand, is run by GMVN. Dorm beds (men only) cost Rs 60. Reasonably large rooms with attached hot bath cost Rs 375/500 or Rs 525/700 with air-con, but like so many government-run places it could be better. There's a restaurant and bar and a 10% mid/low season discount.

Hotel Meedo's Grand (☎ 747171, 28 Rajpur Rd), 3km from the train station, has comfortable rooms for Rs 400/500. There's a restaurant and bar.

The *President* (☎ 657082, fax 658883) at Astley Hall is a charming and tastefully decorated establishment. Air-cooled singles/doubles cost Rs 800/900, and there is a restaurant, bar and coffee shop.

Osho Resorts (☎ 749544, fax 748535, 111 Rajpur Rd) describes itself as a 'retreat with a waterfall'. It's certainly the most unusual place to stay in town. It's part of the organisation of the late Osho, the guru once known as the Bhagwan Rajneesh. Rooms range from Rs 390/490 up to Rs 1090/1290; there are also wooden huts. Videos of the late guru are available for viewing and there's a meditation centre as well as a vegetarian restaurant.

The most lavish hotel in town is the *Hotel Madhuban* (☎ 744307, fax 746496, 97 Rajpur Rd), north of Hotel Meedo's Grand. There is a mini golf course and air-con singles/doubles for Rs 1175/1800. The restaurants here are said to be the best in town.

Places to Eat

Kumar, on Rajpur Rd near Motel Himshri, serves up some of the best vegetarian food in town. Recommended are *gajar ka halwa*, *makki ki roti* and *saron ka saag* (corn roti with mustard-leaf spinach) with *lassi*.

A hundred metres south is another *Kumar* that serves nonveg and Chinese food.

Motimahal, one of the best in a string of eateries on the opposite side of Rajpur Rd, serves good veg and nonveg dishes.

The *A-One Grill* serves take-away tandoori chicken and kebabs from 8 pm until late.

Udipi Restaurant on Lytton Rd is a good south Indian place with air-con; *masala dosas* (curried vegie pancakes) cost Rs 80.

The *Vegetarian* by the Hotel President dishes up inexpensive (Rs 30 and under) but tasty meals.

Daddy's offers Mughlai, south Indian and Chinese food.

Standard Confectioners near the Vegetarian restaurant is one of several good bakeries in Dehra Dun.

Grand Bakers in Paltan Bazaar is another one, there are several good *sweet shops* near the clock tower.

Getting There & Away

Bus The Mussoorie bus stand, by the train station on Haridwar Rd, is for destinations in the hills. There are frequent departures to destinations in Garhwal:

Mussoorie	Rs 17	1½ hours
Nainital	Rs 125	11 hours
Uttarkashi	Rs 90	7 hours
Tehri	Rs 50	4 hours

The Delhi bus stand, beside the Hotel Drona, serves destinations on the plains. The seven hour trip to Delhi costs Rs 300 deluxe, Rs 240 semideluxe, Rs 150 ordinary. Deluxe buses leave hourly between 5.15 am and 10.30 pm; ordinary buses leave every 15 to 30 minutes.

Other destinations include: Rishikesh (Rs 15, 1½ hours); Lucknow (Rs 182, up to 16 hours) departing 1.30 and 6 pm; Shimla via the hills (Paonta Sahib, Solan and Kumar Hatti; Rs 108, seven hours, several departures in the morning) or via the plains (Saharanpur, Ambala and Chandigarh, Rs 130, nine hours, departing 7.25 and 9.15 am); Dharamsala (Rs 230, 15 hours, 12.30 pm); Kullu (Rs 215, 14 hours) and Manali (Rs 250, 16 hours), departing at 3.15 pm.

Train Services to Dehra Dun, the terminus of the Northern Railway, include the speedy *Shatabdi Express*, which leaves New Delhi at 7.10 am daily and reaches Haridwar at 11.15 am and Dehra Dun at 12.35 pm. A chair car seat costs Rs 485 to Dehra Dun.

The *Mussoorie Express* is an overnight train service from Delhi to Dehra Dun. It leaves Old Delhi station at 10.05 pm, arriving at Haridwar at 5.45 am and Dehra Dun at 8 am. On the return journey, it leaves Dehra Dun at 9.15 pm, Haridwar at 11 pm, arriving at Old Delhi at 7 am. There are also services to Lucknow, Varanasi and Mumbai.

Taxi There's a share-taxi stand in front of the Mussoorie bus stand on Haridwar Rd. Taxis leave for Mussoorie when full (five passengers required), and depart every hour or so between 6 am and 6 pm (Rs 60, 1¼ hours). You'll have more luck if you hang around the taxi stand when trains disgorge their passengers from Delhi. A second share-taxi stand is by the Hotel Prince, on Haridwar Rd. Taxis and jeeps depart when full for Rishikesh (Rs 20), Haridwar (Rs 20), and Paonta Sahib, just over the border in eastern Himachal Pradesh (Rs 18). The jeep stops 1km before the border, from where you can catch a rickshaw into Himachal Pradesh.

To reserve a whole taxi to Mussoorie will cost Rs 300; to other destinations expect to pay the following during the high season: Rishikesh (Rs 300), Haridwar (Rs 400), Uttarkashi (Rs 1200).

Getting Around
Six-seater tempos (Vikrams) belch diesel fumes all over the city, but are a cheap way to get around. They run on fixed routes for about half the price of an auto-rickshaw ride. Route No 1 runs from the clock tower along Rajpur Rd.

MUSSOORIE
☎ 0135 • pop 35,000
At an altitude of 2000m and 34km beyond Dehra Dun, Mussoorie has been a popular hill station with the British since it was visited in 1823 by a Captain Young. It has several rambling old Raj hotels and a couple of palaces which once belonged to Indian princes. Less formal than the Raj capital at Shimla, Mussoorie was known in British times as a place to have an affair; this tradition continues today in a more chaste form with Mussoorie being a popular honeymoon destination.

There are over 100 hotels jostling for the views across the Doon Valley to accommodate the hordes of tourists from Delhi in the hot season. It can be quite peaceful in the low season and there are good walks along the mountain ridges. The library (western) end of town is less congested than the Kulri Bazaar end.

Orientation
The Mall connects Gandhi Chowk with Kulri Bazaar, 2km away. Buses from Dehra Dun go to the library bus stand (Gandhi Chowk) or Picture Palace (Kulri Bazaar) but not both; make sure you get the one you want, as The Mall is closed to traffic during the high season.

Information
Tourist Offices There's a UP tourist office (☎ 632863) towards the Kulri Bazaar end of The Mall, near the ropeway station, and a GMVN tourist office (☎ 632984) at the Hotel Garhwal Terrace, about 500m further west along The Mall. There's a small GMVN booth (☎ 631281) at the library bus stand in Gandhi Chowk which runs tours to the touristy Kempty Falls (Rs 50, three hours) and full-day tours (Rs 200, October and November only) which include the picnic site of Dhanolti, set amid deodar forests and with excellent views of the Himalaya; and the Surkhanda Devi Temple, perched at

---

Warning

There is nowhere to change money in Garhwal other than at Rishikesh, Haridwar, Dehra Dun and Mussoorie. If you plan to head north into the mountains, ie to Badrinath or Gangotri, change all the money you will need (and then some) at one of these towns. Otherwise if you run short of money in the mountains the only option is to change money at highly unfavourable rates, perhaps two-thirds of the bank rate, with an unscrupulous hotel manager or travel agent.

UTTAR PRADESH

3050m and also affording magnificent views of a 300km long stretch of the Himalaya.

Money The State Bank of India at Kulri Bazaar will exchange American Express travellers cheques in US dollars only, and Thomas Cook and MasterCard cheques in US dollars and pounds sterling only. The only place it may be possible to change Visa travellers cheques is at the Trek Himalaya office (see the Trekking Outfits & Tour Operators section, following), although the rate won't be as good.

Travel Agencies at the Hotel Hill Queen, Ambic Travels (☎ 632238), Upper Mall Rd, The Mall (west) can book deluxe buses to Delhi, with air-con (Rs 270) or without (Rs 150). They also book air and train tickets. Hire cars can be arranged through Kulwant Travels (☎ 632717), at the Masonic Lodge bus stand, and Harry Tours & Travels (☎ 631747) at the same bus stand.

Trekking Outfits & Tour Operators A respected trek operator is Trek Himalaya Tours (☎ 630491, fax 631302) on Upper Mall just under the Ropeway. Neelu Badoni here can arrange treks in the Garhwal area, and jeep safaris to Kinnaur and Spiti, in Himachal Pradesh, and Ladakh, as well as sorting out the paperwork and necessary permits for these areas. Harry Tours & Travels (see the previous Travel Agencies section) can also organise treks.

Bookshops There's a good selection of books (including Penguins and regional guidebooks) and maps at Cambridge Booksellers and Chander Book Depot, both at Kulri Bazaar.

Medical Services You could try St Mary's Hospital (☎ 632845). James Chemist is a well-stocked dispensary near the Picture Palace; so too is A Kumar & Co, beneath the library at the western end of The Mall.

Gun Hill

A ropeway runs up to this hill (Rs 25 return), operating 9 am to 7 pm daily and until 10 pm between 15 May and 15 July. For early morn-

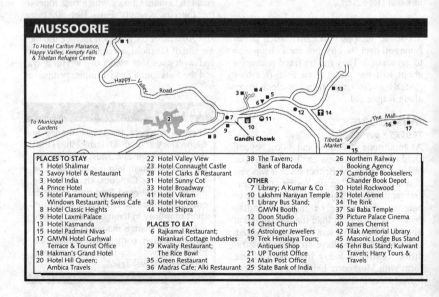

MUSSOORIE

To Hotel Carlton Plaisance, Happy Valley, Kempty Falls & Tibetan Refugee Centre

Happy—Valley Road

To Municipal Gardens

Gandhi Chowk

The Mall

Tibetan Market

PLACES TO STAY	22 Hotel Valley View	38 The Tavern;	26 Northern Railway
1 Hotel Shalimar	23 Hotel Connaught Castle	Bank of Baroda	Booking Agency
2 Savoy Hotel & Restaurant	28 Hotel Clarks & Restaurant		27 Cambridge Booksellers;
3 Hotel India	31 Hotel Sunny Cot	**OTHER**	Chander Book Depot
4 Prince Hotel	33 Hotel Broadway	7 Library; A Kumar & Co	30 Hotel Rockwood
5 Hotel Paramount; Whispering	41 Hotel Vikram	10 Lakshmi Narayan Temple	32 Hotel Avenel
Windows Restaurant; Swiss Cafe	43 Hotel Horizon	11 Library Bus Stand;	34 The Rink
8 Hotel Classic Heights	44 Hotel Shipra	GMVN Booth	37 Sai Baba Temple
9 Hotel Laxmi Palace		12 Doon Studio	39 Picture Palace Cinema
13 Hotel Kasmanda	**PLACES TO EAT**	14 Christ Church	40 James Chemist
16 Hotel Padmini Nivas	6 Rajkamal Restaurant;	19 Trek Himalaya Tours;	42 Tilak Memorial Library
17 GMVN Hotel Garhwal	Nirankari Cottage Industries	Antiques Shop	45 Masonic Lodge Bus Stand
Terrace & Tourist Office	29 Kwality Restaurant;	21 UP Tourist Office	46 Tehri Bus Stand; Kulwant
18 Hakman's Grand Hotel	The Rice Bowl	24 Main Post Office	Travels; Harry Tours &
20 Hotel Hill Queen;	35 Green Restaurant	25 State Bank of India	Travels
Ambica Travels	36 Madras Cafe; Alki Restaurant		

ing views of the Himalaya including Bandarpunch (6316m), you have to walk up. At the top, photo agencies will (if you like) dress you up in sequined Garhwali dress and take your photo for between Rs 30 and Rs 60.

Walks

The walks around Mussoorie offer great views. **Camel's Back Road** was built as a promenade and passes a rock formation that looks like a camel – hence the name. You can rent ponies or cycle-rickshaws (Rs 100). Another good walk takes you down to Happy Valley and the **Tibetan Refugee Centre** where there's a temple and a small shop selling hand-knitted sweaters. An enjoyable longer walk (5km) takes you through Landour Bazaar to **Childers Lodge** (Lal Tibba), the highest point in Mussoorie, and Sisters' Bazaar.

Language Courses

The Landour Language School (☎ 631487, fax 631917) in the attractively forested Landour area has introductory courses in Hindi, with most classes held in an old Methodist church. The school is open between 9 February and 11 December. Private lessons cost Rs 70 an hour and group lessons Rs 45 an hour. Contact the principal, Mr Chitranjan Datt, Landour Language School, Landour, Mussoorie, 248179.

Places to Stay

With so many hotels competing for your custom, prices vary enormously according to the season. Rates given here are for the mid-season (October and November) but you may be able to negotiate a further reduction at this time. Note that some hotels are closed in January and February. Prices are generally double those given here from May to July and finding anywhere to stay during the Hindu festivals of Dussehra or Diwali can be very difficult. Porters from either bus stand to any hotel expect Rs 30.

Places to Stay – Budget

Kulri Bazaar & The Mall (East End)
Hotel Broadway (☎ 632243) was a small English guesthouse run by a Miss Lee until 1954 when it was bought by the current

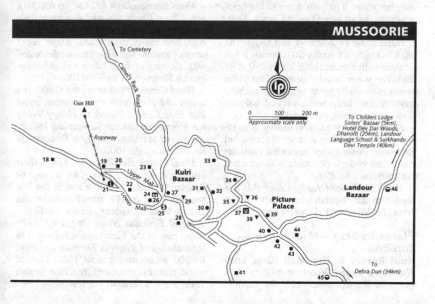

MUSSOORIE

To Cemetery

Camel's Back Road

Gun Hill ▲

Ropeway

0   100   200 m
Approximate scale only

To Childers Lodge
Sisters' Bazaar (5km),
Hotel Dev Dar Woods,
Dhanolti (25km), Landour
Language School & Surkhando
Devi Temple (40km)

Upper Mall

Kulri
Bazaar

Lower Mall

Landour
Bazaar

Picture
Palace

To
Dehra Dun (34km)

UTTAR PRADESH

owner, Mr Malik. It's a friendly, well-kept place with some nice views, and is deservedly popular. Doubles cost from Rs 125; there are a few singles for Rs 75.

Hotel Valley View (*☎ 632324*) on The Mall is a well-managed place with friendly staff; clean rooms go for Rs 200/450. There is a nonveg dining hall.

Hotel Clarks (*☎ 632393*) has plenty of Raj-era character and boasts a billiard room with a full-size table. The rooms themselves are a little shabby and range from Rs 200 to Rs 600.

Hotel Vikram (*☎ 632551*), near the Tilak Memorial Library, has doubles for Rs 200/300. Its a quiet place with decent rooms and great views over the Doon Valley.

Hotel Sunny Cot (*☎ 632789*) is a friendly family-run hotel with clean doubles for Rs 200. However, it's a little tricky to find. Take the path leading up to the Hotel Rockwood and turn left at the Hotel Avenel; it is at the top of the hill.

Library Area & The Mall (West End)

Hotel Laxmi Palace (*☎ 632774*) is a new place with clean, pleasant rooms and reliable hot water. The path down to the hotel is next to the arch on Gandhi Chowk. Doubles cost Rs 300.

Hotel India (*☎ 632359*), just above The Mall, is run by a friendly Sikh family. It has doubles with attached bath for Rs 250 to Rs 500. The water is solar heated. This place seems particularly prone to luggage raids by monkeys, so keep windows and balcony doors closed while you're gone!

Prince Hotel (*☎ 632674*) nearby, is an interesting old building with great views, but the rooms seem rather neglected (upstairs rooms are better). A double with attached hot bath costs Rs 250.

Hotel Shalimar (*Happy Valley Rd*) is a well-kept old British place about 600m from Gandhi Chowk. Doubles cost Rs 250.

Places to Stay – Mid-Range & Top End

Kulri Bazaar & The Mall (East End)

Hakman's Grand Hotel (*☎ 632959*) is a place for Raj-era nostalgia buffs; there is even a cash register in the lobby calibrated in *annas*. The large dark rooms, which may not be to everyone's taste, cost Rs 320 to Rs 560.

Hotel Shipra (*☎ 632662*), near the Masonic Lodge bus stand, has well-appointed rooms from Rs 1250 to Rs 1450, and a restaurant and bar.

Hotel Horizon (*☎ 631588*) is a very good small hotel opposite Hotel Shipra with thick pile carpets, satellite TV and views across the valley. Doubles cost Rs 1400; there's a 40% discount in the low season.

Hotel Connaught Castle (*☎ 632210*) is up a long driveway leading off the Upper Mall Rd. It's a stylish, modern place with marble corridors and luxurious rooms from Rs 1650.

Hotel Garhwal Terrace (*☎ 632682*) is a slightly shabby GMVN place. Rooms, all with satellite TV, cost Rs 500. Dorm beds cost Rs 80. There are two restaurants.

Library Area & The Mall (West End)

Hotel Paramount (*☎ 632352*), right on The Mall, is run by a friendly Sikh man. Rooms, although a little small, are reasonably airy and cost Rs 200 to Rs 500.

Hotel Kasmanda (*☎ 632424, fax 630007*), uphill from Christ Church, was formerly a palace of the maharaja of Kasmanda. It has been beautifully maintained. There are 3 acres of gardens and the rooms are decorated with pictures of tiger hunts and old lithographs. Rooms cost Rs 700/1100.

Hotel Carlton Plaisance (*☎ 632800*) is a lovely old place with a nice garden about 2km from Gandhi Chowk on Happy Valley Rd. Everest conqueror Sir Edmund Hillary left a letter of recommendation. Doubles are Rs 700, suites Rs 1000.

Hotel Classic Heights (*☎ 632514*), a short distance south of the library, has a range of doubles from Rs 795 (40% less in the low season). The hotel's travel counter can arrange trekking, fishing and horse riding.

Hotel Padmini Nivas (*☎/fax 632793*), 600m east of the library, once belonged to the maharaja of Rajpipla. Doubles start from Rs 500; an apartment is Rs 1500. The old world charm is enhanced by a rose garden There's also a Gujarati veg restaurant.

Savoy Hotel (☎ *632010, fax 632001*) is a vast British place covered with ivy and replete with faded touches of the Raj, including deer heads eaten down to the bone. It's so big it even has its own post office. On a foggy day it has a wonderfully Gothic atmosphere. Fittingly, it's said to have a resident ghost, one Lady Gore Ormsby, whose death allegedly provided inspiration for Agatha Christie's first novel *The Mysterious Affair at Styles*. Doubles (with three meals) start at Rs 1995, Rs 2795 for a suite.

Sisters' Bazaar The *Hotel Dev Dar Woods* (☎ *632644*) is in a lofty wooded location by Sisters' Bazaar. Popular with foreigners at the nearby language school, it's an interesting place to stay. Rooms cost Rs 300 including breakfast; three meals are included for the same price if you stay more than 15 days.

Places to Eat

Most of the better hotels have their own restaurants, and there are a lot of very good (and good-value) restaurants in the Kulri Bazaar area. Due to a steep hike in licensing fees, many restaurants no longer have bars. In the low season, restaurants generally close around 10 to 10.30 pm.

Kulri Bazaar & The Mall (East End)

The *Madras Cafe* specialises in south Indian food, with the menu featuring 24 different types of dosa (Rs 10 to Rs 30). There are also *idlis* (steamed rice cakes) with dhal, and *vadas* (deep fried veg doughnuts).

Alki Restaurant is a few doors down, with south Indian and Chinese dishes. Here a sweet *kulfi faluda* (kulfi ice cream with long chickpea-flour noodles) costs Rs 20.

Green Restaurant has good veg food; try the cheese *korma* (a curry-like braised dish, Rs 35).

The Tavern, near the Bank of Baroda, specialises in Mughlai and Chinese cuisine; the *reshmi kabab* (tender chicken kebab cooked in the tandoor) is excellent (Rs 90). There's live and recorded music here in the season, and this place remains open late throughout the year.

Kwality Restaurant in the heart of Kulri Bazaar has reasonable food but a spartan canteen atmosphere. Nonveg dishes are around Rs 50, with most veg dishes under Rs 40. Next door to Kwality is a fruit juice stand, where fresh juice is squeezed while you wait. The mango shakes are very good.

The Rice Bowl features Tibetan and Chinese cuisine, including good steamed mutton *momos* (dumplings, Rs 18) and special *thukpa* (noodle soup, Rs 22).

Clarks Restaurant, a short distance further along The Mall at the hotel of the same name, serves good cappuccino.

Library Area & The Mall (West End)

Whispering Windows, next to the Hotel Paramount, is a popular spot for watching the holiday-makers promenading along The Mall. During the season there's dancing to recorded music on the tiled floor.

The *Rajkamal Restaurant*, next door, has good cheap veg and nonveg food, and a dignified, ancient waiter resplendent in brass-buttoned livery.

Swiss Cafe next to the Hotel Paramount has Chinese and Indian food, as well as a selection of muffins and Danish pastries during the season.

Savoy Hotel meals are not cheap, with nonveg dishes around Rs 130, but you may be rewarded with a glimpse of the ghost of Lady Gore Ormsby (who probably expired at the sight of the bill). If you're feeling really magnanimous, you can shout your dining companions to a bottle of Moët et Chandon (Rs 2000). Beers are Rs 95. Advance reservations are essential.

Sisters' Bazaar Superb cheddar cheese (Rs 150 to Rs 175 per kg; not made during the monsoon) and home-made produce such as peanut butter, jams and chutneys can be found at *A Prakash & Co*, a long-established grocery store.

Shopping

Nirankari Cottage Industries, at the library end of The Mall, next to Rajkamal Restaurant, has carved wooden boxes, brass statues of Hindu deities and Buddhas, Tibetan prayer wheels, ceramic Chinese vases and hand-carved wooden walking sticks made from oak. Queen Mary, then the Princess of Wales, took the last of these walking sticks away with her as a souvenir of her visit to Mussoorie. There is an antiques shop next to the Trek Himalaya office with an interesting collection of furniture and mementos from old British homes – a good place to search for ancient editions of *Boys Own Adventure* books.

At the top of Gun Hill or at the Doon Studio, at the library end of The Mall, you can dress in traditional Garhwali garb and have your photo taken against a painted Himalayan backdrop (Rs 30 to Rs 60 for three postcard-sized prints; pictures ready in three to four days).

Pure pashmina wool shawls can be purchased at Jewellers – Astrologer, 5 The Mall (near the Hotel Garhwal Terrace), but they're not cheap, with prices starting at Rs 7000 and soaring to Rs 60,000 for antique Jamawar shawls produced on wooden looms and employing a method now lost.

Getting There & Away

Numerous buses leave from the Mussoorie bus stand (next to the train station) in Dehra Dun for Mussoorie between 6.30 am and 8.30 pm (Rs 18, 1½ hours). These go either to the library bus stand (Gandhi Chowk) or Kulri Bazaar (Masonic Lodge bus stand). When travelling to Mussoorie from the west or north (ie Jammu) by train, it is best to get off at Saharanpur and catch a bus from there to Dehra Dun or Mussoorie, if there's no convenient train connection.

Buses to Dehra Dun leave half-hourly to hourly from the library and Masonic Lodge stands (Rs 18). For Delhi, there's a deluxe overnight service from the library (Rs 160), and an ordinary express overnight service (Rs 130) from the Masonic Lodge stand.

Buses to Hanuman Chatti (for Yamunotri) originate in Dehra Dun and collect passengers in Mussoorie at 10 am at the library bus stand (Rs 90, seven hours).

The Tehri bus stand is for buses to Tehri (Rs 40, five hours) and connections to Ut-tarkashi and Gangotri. Although the trip can be rough, it does take in some marvellous mountain scenery.

With at least 24 hours notice, train tickets can be arranged through the Northern Railway booking agency (☎ 632846), at the Kulri Bazaar end of The Mall. There is only a small allocation of tickets. The office is open Monday to Saturday 10 am to 4 pm, and Sunday 8 am to 2 pm.

Reserve taxis from the library bus stand and the Masonic Lodge bus stand go to many destinations, including Rishikesh (Rs 700, 2½ hours), Haridwar (Rs 600, three hours), Sister's Bazaar (Rs 120 one way, Rs 180 return with a half-hour wait, 30 minutes), Delhi (Rs 1800, seven hours) and Ut-tarkashi, for Gangotri (Rs 1500, 5½ hours).

Getting Around

The Mall is closed to traffic for most of the year, so to traverse the 2km between Kulri Bazaar and the library area, you can either walk, rent a pony (officially Rs 20 per kilometre), or take a cycle-rickshaw. Expect to pay about Rs 20 to Rs 25 from the Ropeway to Gandhi Chowk.

HARIDWAR
☎ 0133 • pop 230,000

Haridwar's propitious location, at the point where the Ganges emerges from the Himalaya to begin its slow progress across the plains, makes it a particularly holy place. There are many ashrams here but you may find Rishikesh (24km to the north) more pleasant, especially if you wish to study meditation. Haridwar means Gateway to the Gods, but it seems like any other noisy town.

Every 12 years the Kumbh Mela (festival) attracts millions of pilgrims who bathe here. Kumbh Mela takes place every three years, consecutively at Allahabad, Nasik, Ujjain and Haridwar. It is next due to take place in Haridwar in 2010.

Orientation

Buses pull into the UP Roadways bus stand on Railway Rd at the south-western end of town. Railway Rd runs parallel to the Upper

Ganges Canal, connecting this end of town with Har ki Pairi (the main ghat), about 2.5km to the north-east. The train station is opposite the UP Roadways bus stand. The canal is traversed by the Laltarao Bridge, which you'll cross if you're coming from Rishikesh. The road over the bridge meets Railway Rd; the north-eastern section of Railway Rd (ie from Laltarao Bridge to Har ki Pairi) is known locally as Upper Rd. There are places to stay and eat scattered along the length of Railway Rd, with a lot of budget options in the area known as Shiv Murti, just to the north-east of the bus stand. Behind Har ki Pairi, running parallel to the canal, is the busy market area known as Bara Bazaar.

Information

Tourist Offices The GMVN tourist office (☎ 424240) is on Upper Rd, directly opposite the Laltarao Bridge. It's open Monday to

Saturday 10 am to 5 pm. You can book Char Dham (the four great pilgrimage sites) packages here, but the best source of local information is Sanjeev Mehta at Mohan's Fast Food, Railway Rd (see Places to Eat, later in this section). Sanjeev is a keen photographer, and spends most of his free time stalking through the jungle endeavouring to capture its inhabitants on film. UP Tourism's regional office (☎ 427370; open daily 10 am to 5 pm) is based at the Rahi Motel, further west down Railway Rd, past the UP Roadways bus stand.

Money The Bank of Baroda, next door to the Hotel Mansarovar International, exchanges American Express and Thomas Cook travellers cheques in US dollars and pounds sterling only. The State Bank of India on Sadhu Bela Marg also has foreign exchange facilities.

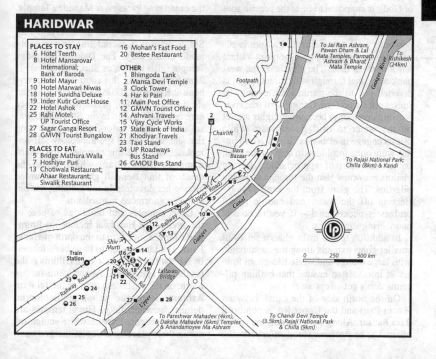

HARIDWAR

PLACES TO STAY
6 Hotel Teerth
8 Hotel Mansarovar International; Bank of Baroda
9 Hotel Mayur
10 Hotel Marwari Niwas
18 Hotel Suvidha Deluxe
19 Inder Kutir Guest House
22 Hotel Ashok
25 Rahi Motel; UP Tourist Office
27 Sagar Ganga Resort
28 GMVN Tourist Bungalow

PLACES TO EAT
5 Bridge Mathura Walla
7 Hoshiyar Puri
13 Chotiwala Restaurant; Ahaar Restaurant; Siwalik Restaurant

16 Mohan's Fast Food
20 Bestee Restaurant

OTHER
1 Bhimgoda Tank
2 Mansa Devi Temple
3 Clock Tower
4 Har ki Pairi
11 Main Post Office
12 GMVN Tourist Office
14 Ashvani Travels
15 Vijay Cycle Works
17 State Bank of India
21 Khodiyar Travels
23 Taxi Stand
24 UP Roadways Bus Stand
26 GMOU Bus Stand

To Jai Ram Ashram, Pawan Dham & Lal Mata Temples, Parmath Ashram & Bharat Mata Temple

To Rishikesh (24km)

Footpath

Chairlift

Bara Bazaar

To Rajaji National Park; Chilla (8km) & Kandi

Canal

Ganges

Railway Road (Upper Road)

Shiv Murti

Train Station

Jasaram Rd

Laltarao Bridge

Railway Road

0   250   500 km

To Pareshwar Mahadev (4km), & Daksha Mahadev (6km) Temples & Anandamoyee Ma Ashram

To Chandi Devi Temple (3.5km), Rajaji National Park & Chilla (9km)

Post & Communications The main post office is on Upper Rd (Railway Rd) about 200m north-west of Laltarao Bridge.

Trekking Outfits & Tour Operators Ashvani Travels (☎ 424581), at 3 Upper Rd, can organise trekking (including equipment), white-water rafting (September to March) and ski packages to Auli (January and February). They can also provide guides and porters to take visitors around the salient spots of Haridwar.

Things to See

Haridwar is a very old town, mentioned by the Chinese scholar/traveller Xuan Zhang in the 8th century AD, but its many temples were constructed comparatively recently, and are of little historical interest, although they do have many idols and illustrated scenes from the Hindi epics.

The main ghat, **Har ki Pairi** (The Footstep of God), is supposed to be at the precise spot where the Ganges leaves the mountains and enters the plains. Consequently, the river's power to wash away sins at this spot is superlative and endorsed by a footprint Vishnu left in a stone here. The ghat is on the west bank of a canal through which the Ganges is diverted just to the north. Each evening at sunset priests perform **Ganga Aarti** (the river worship ceremony) here, when lights are set on the water to drift downstream while priests engage in elaborate rituals. Non-Hindus were once forbidden to step on the ghat, but in a new spirit of rapprochement, foreign visitors may now join the throngs of Hindu pilgrims. The glare from the sun's rays reflecting off the water and marble paved bridges is phenomenal – if you're here at noon, bring sunglasses.

In addition to the main ghat, a series of smaller ghats extends along the canal bank, with large orange and white life-guard towers at intervals to ensure that bathing pilgrims don't get swept away.

On the north side of the canal, between Har ki Pairi and the Upper Rd, is colourful **Bara Bazaar**. Along with the religious paraphernalia, or *prasaad* (food offered to the gods, images of the deities, religious pamphlets etc) are scores of tiny stalls crammed along both sides of the bazaar selling an assortment of goods including *tiffins* (lunchtime snacks), shawls, ayurvedic medicines, brassware, glass bangles, wooden whistles, bamboo canes and cane baskets.

It is worth taking the chair lift (Rs 20 return) to the **Mansa Devi Temple** on the hill above the city. The lift is not exactly state of the art, but it's well maintained. It operates between 8 am and noon, and 2 and 5 pm. If you're feeling energetic, you can walk up (1.5km) and enjoy the view down over the city and the ghats at your leisure. Vendors sell colourfully packaged prasaad of coconuts, marigolds and other offerings to take up to the goddess. Mansa is one of the forms of Shakti Durga (The Inaccessible, one of the forms of Shiva's wife Devi. Photography is forbidden in the temple.

About 4km to the south of Haridwar is the brand new **Pareshwar Mahadev Temple**. The temple, which was inaugurated by the late former president of India, Gyani Zail Singh, houses a sacred lingam reputedly made of mercury. The **Daksha Mahadev Temple** (also known as Shri Dakheswar) is 2km further along this route, on the riverbank at Khankhal. Daksha, the father of Sati (Shiva's first wife), performed a sacrifice here but neglected to invite Shiva. Sati was so angry at this unforgivable indiscretion that she managed to spontaneously self-immolate! Opposite this temple is the **Anandamoyee Ma Ashram** which, since the death of this Bengali guru who counted among her devotees Indira Gandhi, has become an enormous mausoleum.

Other temples and buildings of note in the environs of Haridwar include the **Bhimgoda Tank**, about 1km to the north of Har ki Pairi. The tank is said to have been formed by a blow from Bhima's knee (Bhima is the brother of Hanuman). About 150m further north, on the Rishikesh road, is the **Jai Ram Ashram**. Here the usual multicoloured deities characteristic of Hindu temples are strangely absent. Pristine white sculptures are in their place, and depict the gods and the demons battling for the waters of humanity. Also here are electronically animated scenes from the Hindu epics.

About 500m further along this road, a turn-off to the right at a (usually) dry riverbed leads in a further 500m to the **Pawan Dham Temple**. This temple is famed for its fantastic glass and mirrorwork, and its elaborately garbed idols.

About 1km further along this road, on the left, is the extraordinary **Lal Mata Temple**, which was completed in 1994. This is a replica of the Vaishno Devi Temple in Kashmir, and it is completely faithful to the original – right down to the artificial hill on which the replica is situated. Adjacent is a perpetually frozen ice lingam, a replica of that in the Amarnath Cave in Kashmir.

Further along this road, which eventually rejoins the main Rishikesh road, is the **Parmath Ashram**, which has fine images of the goddess Durga. The road proceeds past the **Bharat Mata Temple**, looking like an apartment block with a central dome. It's eight storeys high and there's a lift to the top for lazy pilgrims. On the top floor is an image of Shankar (Shiva). Just before this route rejoins the main Rishikesh road is the **Sapt Rishi Ashram**, about 5km from Haridwar, named after the seven *rishis* (Hindu saints) who prayed here for the good of humanity. According to tradition, in order to please the seven rishis who were meditating in seven different locations, the Ganges split into seven streams here. Tempos (Vikrams) ply this route.

Chandi Devi, erected on Nhil Hill by a Kashmiri raja, Suchet Singh, in 1929, and a number of other temples in the hills are reached by an approximately 4km walk to the south-east. A ropeway cable car leads up to the temple.

You may see large **river turtles** on the banks of the Nildhara River, near Haridwar, which is over 2km broad during the monsoon.

Organised Tours

A nine day tour of the Char Dham is Rs 8000 (transport only). You may get more competitive rates from the travel agencies

on Jasharam Rd in the Shiv Murti area such as Shakti Wahini Travels (☎ 427002) or Khodiyar Travels (☎ 423560).

Places to Stay

Hotel Mayur (☎ 427586, Upper Rd), near the chair lift, has basic singles/doubles for Rs 170/220 in the low season, and Rs 300/500 in the high season (May and June). Rooms have attached baths, air-coolers and geysers, and those at the front are larger.

Hotel Marwari Niwas (☎ 427759) is down the laneway beside the Mayur, in the area known as Subzi Mandi. Air-cooled doubles are Rs 250, and rooms with air-con are Rs 450. Rooms are set around a well, and all have running hot water and satellite TV. Room service is available.

The *Hotel Mansarovar International* (☎ 426501), on Upper Rd, towards Bara Bazaar, is relatively new. Comfortable but drab singles/doubles cost Rs 550/750 with air-coolers, or Rs 750/900 with air-con. A 15% to 20% discount applies in the low season, and there's a good restaurant (the Swagat). Credit cards are accepted.

Hotel Teerth (☎ 425311), in the heart of Bara Bazaar, is set right on the river, with great views over Har ki Pairi. Doubles are Rs 500/800 with air-cooling/air-con. All rooms have balconies facing the river, the staff are friendly and helpful and there's a restaurant.

There's a cluster of budget and mid-range hotels in the area called Shiv Murti, just east of the bus stands and train station.

Hotel Kailash (☎ 427789, Jasharam Rd) has air-cooled doubles for Rs 300 and air-con doubles for Rs 650. Some of the rooms have balconies, and there's a restaurant.

Hotel Ashok (☎ 427328) has basic singles with attached cold bath for Rs 75. Doubles with common bath are Rs 165, or with attached hot bath, Rs 250. Air-cooled deluxe doubles are Rs 500. Rooms are spotless and there's a travel desk and dining hall.

Hotel Suvidha Deluxe (☎ 427423) is about five minutes' walk away, in a quiet location at Sharwan Nath Nagar. Pleasant doubles, all with colour TV, are Rs 600/1100 with air-cooler/air-con, and there's a restaurant.

Rahi Motel (☎ 426430) is handy to the bus stands, but in a quiet location. It's also the home of UP Tourism's regional tourist office. Air-cooled singles/doubles are Rs 400/450; with air-con, they're Rs 650/850. Rates include breakfast, and there is also a six bed dorm (Rs 70). All rooms have colour TV, and there's a restaurant.

Inder Kutir Guest House (☎ 426336) is a friendly, family-run place close to the Upper Ganges Canal. Air-cooled doubles cost Rs 150 and Rs 250, and there's a dining hall.

GMVN's *Tourist Bungalow* (☎ 426379) is in a peaceful location right on the river, outside the main part of town in Belwala. Singles/doubles are Rs 350/450. Dorm beds are Rs 100. There's no restaurant, but meals can be brought to your room.

Sagar Ganga Resort (☎ 422115) is a lovely Indo-Art Deco style lodge which once belonged to the King of Nepal, situated right on the river. Doubles cost Rs 750, and an enormous deluxe double costs Rs 1250.

Places to Eat

As a holy pilgrimage place, alcohol and meat are strictly prohibited; in fact, imbibing the one or consuming the other is a prosecutable offence. There is, however, a good selection of vegetarian restaurants.

Bestee Restaurant, in the Shiv Murti area, has good shakes (in season, try the delicious *cheiku* shake – cheiku is a small brown fruit similar in appearance to a potato, but sweet). There are also snacks such as vegie rolls and cutlets.

Hoshiyar Puri has been serving thalis for over 50 years, and they're still good value. The special thali features cheese korma, *mattar paneer* (peas and cheese in gravy) dhal and *kheer* (rice pud).

Bridge Mathura Walla sweet shop in the heart of the Bara Bazaar has a range of sticky temptations including *ras malai* – a milk and sugar based sweet served in a banana leaf plate, floating in sugar syrup and sprinkled with pistachio nuts; *rabri*, a similar milky confection; and wedges of cashew-nut-studded halwa.

Mohan's Fast Food, close to Shiv Murti, in the Chitra Cinema compound, Railway Rd, is deservedly popular. There are the usual offerings such as pizza and vegie burgers, with a few special Gujarati dishes thrown in for good measure, such as *batata vada* – four pakoras, green mint chutney and chilli (Rs 20), and *pao bhaji* – two buns with minced vegetables served in a thali with salad (Rs 20). There's also an astonishing range of ice creams and sundaes, and the friendly owner, Sanjeev Mehta, has a wealth of knowledge on sights around Haridwar, and on the Rajaji National Park.

Opposite the GMVN tourist office are three good upmarket dining places. *Ahaar Restaurant*, the pick of the bunch, specialises in Punjabi, south Indian and Chinese cuisine. It's downstairs next door to the *Ahaar* ice-cream parlour.

The long-running *Chotiwala*, a few doors down, has good dosas.

The *Siwalik*, on the corner, is a multicuisine restaurant that specialises in Gujarati dishes.

Getting There & Away

Bus The UP Roadways bus stand (☎ 427037) is at the south-western end of Railway Rd. Buses leave every 30 minutes for Rishikesh (Rs 10.50, one hour) and Dehra Dun (Rs 20, 1½ to two hours). For Mussoorie, you'll need to change at Dehra Dun. There are ordinary bus services every 30 minutes up to 11.30 pm to Delhi (Rs 68, eight hours), and early morning and late afternoon and evening services to Agra (Rs 114, 12 hours). Other destinations include:

Buses for Shimla leave at 6, 10 and 10.40 am, and 5, 7 and 9.30 pm (Rs 135, 14 hours); for Nainital at 6, 7 and 8 am, and 6.30 and 9.30 pm (Rs 107, seven hours); for Almora at 5 and 7 am, and 4 and 5 pm (Rs 128, 10 hours); for Ranikhet at 6 am and 4.30 pm (Rs 89, nine hours); Tehri (Rs 56, five hours) and for Uttarkashi (Rs 87, 10 hours) at 5.30, 6.30, 8.30 and 9.30 am.

For the Char Dham (Yamunotri, Gangotri, Badrinath and Kedarnath), you'll need to find your way to Rishikesh. As many of the buses to these pilgrimage sites leave in the wee hours, you'd do better to stay overnight in Rishikesh.

To get to Chilla (for Rajaji National Park), catch a Kandi-bound bus from the Garhwal Motor Owners' Union (GMOU) bus stand near the Rahi Motel. Buses leave at 7 and 9 am, and return at noon and 4 pm (Rs 9). See Getting There & Away in the Rajaji National Park section for information on catching share taxis or walking to Chilla.

Train See Getting There & Away in the Dehra Dun section for details of trains between Haridwar and Delhi. Other direct trains which connect to Haridwar are as follows (prices given are for air-con chair class):

Calcutta	1472km	35 hours	Rs 650
Mumbai	1649km	40 hours	Rs 700
Varanasi	894km	20 hours	Rs 580
Lucknow	493km	11 hours	Rs 325

Taxi The Haridwar Taxi Union (☎ 427338), open 24 hours, is directly opposite the bus stand. Posted rates are as follows:

Rishikesh	Rs 305
Dehra Dun	Rs 405
Mussoorie	Rs 705
Tehri	Rs 905
Uttarkashi	Rs 1200
Hanuman Chatti (for Yamunotri)	Rs 2000
Gangotri	Rs 2000
Delhi	Rs 1305
Chilla (for Rajaji National Park)	Rs 305
Ranikhet	Rs 2000
Almora	Rs 2000
Nainital	Rs 1800
Shimla	Rs 3000

Getting Around
You can get from the train station or UP Roadways bus stand to Har ki Pairi by cycle-rickshaw for Rs 10 or Vikram for Rs 5.

Low-tech rattle-you-senseless bicycles can be hired from Vijay Cycle Works, Railway Rd but for Rs 1.50 per hour, or Rs 10 per day, who's complaining?

RAJAJI NATIONAL PARK
This beautiful park, covering 820 sq km in the forested foothills east of Haridwar, is best known for its wild elephants, numbering around 150 in all. Unfortunately, their future is in question since human competition for land has severed their traditional migration route, which once stretched from here to the area which is now part of Corbett Tiger Reserve, 170km to the east (see the Corbett Tiger Reserve section, later in this chapter). Plans for a 'migration corridor' would involve moving several villages and have become bogged down in the usual bureaucracy. Nevertheless, increasing ecological awareness has brought about some advances, with large ducts having been constructed under the Chilla-Rishikesh road to enable the migrating animals to pass beneath. On a less happy note, there have been newspaper reports of well-connected Indians building lodges on the edge of the park and using it as a hunting reserve.

As well as elephants, the park contains some rarely seen tigers and leopards, chital (spotted deer), which can be seen in herds of up to 250 at one time, sambar (India's largest species of deer), wild boars, sloth bears, barking deer, porcupines, jungle fowls, hornbills and pythons. However, visitors report hardly any wildlife sightings at all.

Open from mid-November to mid-June, the entry fee is Rs 100 for up to three days, and Rs 50 for each additional day. Entry into the park is not permitted between sunset and sunrise. Photography fees are Rs 50 for a still camera, Rs 500 for a video camera.

The (rather unattractive) village of **Chilla**, 13km east of Haridwar, is the only area which currently has an infrastructure in place for visitors. Official hire rates for jeeps (available from Chilla) are Rs 30 per kilometre. The Forest Ranger's office is close to the tourist bungalow at Chilla; pay entry fees here.

About a kilometre beyond the entry gate is a *machaan* (hide), previously used by hunters, but now a vantage point from where visitors can unobtrusively view the park's inhabitants.

It may be possible to visit tribal villages in the park, where Gujars, who still live in their traditional clay huts and tend buffaloes, greet visitors with bowls of fresh, warm buffalo milk. Check at the Forest Ranger's bungalow in Chilla, or contact Sanjeev at Mohan's Fast Food, Railway Rd, Haridwar.

Places to Stay

The *Tourist Rest House* at Chilla is run by the GMVN. A standard double is Rs 450, an air-cooled double, Rs 550, and there are dorm beds for Rs 100; you may also be able to camp in the grounds.

Nine *Forest Rest Houses* are dotted around the park. Double rates at Beribara, Ranipur, Kansrao, Kunnao, Phandowala, Satyanarain and Asarodi are all Rs 250; at Motichur and Chilla, rates are Rs 450. At these places, other than at Chilla, you'll need to bring your own food. For bookings contact the Chief Forest Officer, Tilak Rd, Dehra Dun, or write to the Director, Rajaji National Park office, 5/1 Ansari Marg, Dehra Dun (☎ 621669).

Getting There & Away

Buses to Chilla leave from the Garhwal Motor Owners' Union (GMOU), Haridwar, close to the Rahi Motel, en route to Kandi. They depart at 7 and 9 am, and return at noon and 4 pm (Rs 9). If there are enough passengers, share taxis leave from the taxi stand opposite the UP Roadways bus stand (Rs 10). The official rate for a reserve taxi to Chilla from Haridwar is Rs 200 one way, Rs 300 return (although ensure that the driver knows how much time you plan to spend at the park). You could also cycle to Chilla; bikes are available for hire in Haridwar (see Haridwar's Getting Around section, earlier in this chapter).

To walk to Chilla from Haridwar, cross the Laltarao Bridge and walk to the roundabout, then turn left onto the Rishikesh road. Just before the cable bridge over the Ganges canal, turn right. After 100m you'll reach a dam; cross the dam and turn left, where a short walk will bring you to a small artificial lake. Here you'll see migratory birds, including Siberian cranes, ducks and other water fowl; in the evening wild animals, including elephants, come here to drink (although you should beware of wild elephants at dusk). The road flanking the lake leads to Chilla, 5km distant.

AROUND CHILLA

Situated 14km north-east of Chilla, 2km off the Chilla-Rishikesh road, is the small village of **Bindevasani**. Local buses ply between the village and both Chilla and Haridwar, with the section between Chilla and the turn-off to Bindevasani at a high elevation, affording good views out over the national park. There's a small temple sacred to Durga (Shiva's consort in her fierce form) a steep 15 to 20 minute walk above the village. The temple itself is not of great interest, but it commands an excellent position, overlooking the *sangam* (confluence) of the Bindedhara and Nildhara rivers.

About 14km north of Bindevasani is **Nilkantha**, with its Mahadev Temple dedicated to Shiva. From Nilkantha, it is possible to continue to **Lakshman Jhula** (see the Rishikesh section), the suspension bridge which traverses the Ganges to the north-east of Rishikesh. The trail follows the original pilgrim trail, which affords magnificent forest scenery – beware of wild elephants, especially at dusk.

There are *dharamsalas* (pilgrims' resthouses) at Nilkantha, but you'll need to be prepared to camp out (with your own provisions) at Bindevasani.

RISHIKESH

☎ 01364 • pop 82,000

In spite of its claim to being the 'Yoga Capital of the World', Rishikesh is a quieter and more easy-going place than Haridwar. Surrounded by hills on three sides, it lies at 356m. The holy Ganges (almost clear here) flows through the town. As in Haridwar, there are many ashrams along its banks and many bleary-eyed sadhus (holy men). This is a great place to stay and study yoga, meditation and other aspects of Hinduism, or just to unwind from the rigours of travel.

Back in the 60s Rishikesh gained instant fame as the place where the Beatles met their guru, the Maharishi Mahesh Yogi. Rishikesh is also the starting point for trips to Himalayan pilgrimage centres like Badrinath, Kedarnath and Gangotri.

Orientation

The main administrative and commercial sector is to the south of the (usually dry) Chandrabhaga River; the main and Yatra bus stands are here, as well as the main post office, banks and hotels. If you arrive by jeep you will probably be dropped on Haridwar Rd in this commercial area. The part of town between Haridwar Rd and the Ganges has many colourful old ashrams and temples, and is worth exploring.

The northern extension of Haridwar Rd is called Lakshman Jhula Rd. It goes past the GMVN tourist office to Shivanand Jhula; most of the temples and ashrams are to be found on either side of the river here. The Swarg Ashram area is filled with temples and sadhus and is blissfully free of traffic (scooters excepted). Lakshman Jhula (*jhula* means bridge) is 2km north. Here there are more ashrams and temples.

Information

Tourist Offices The UP tourist office (☎ 430209) is on Railway Station Rd. It's open Monday to Saturday 10 am to 5 pm (lunch is 1.30 to 2 pm). The helpful GMVN tourist office (☎ 430372) is in the area known as Muni ki Reti (open Monday to Saturday 10 am to 5 pm; closed for lunch between 2 and 3 pm). It's on Lakshman Jhula Rd, near Kailash Gate.

Money The State Bank of India is next to the Inderlok Hotel on Railway Station Rd. It exchanges most major travellers cheques, but *not* Visa or MasterCard. If you're carrying either of these, go to the Bank of Baroda, near the Yatra bus stand, which has a maddening policy of changing only US$100 per person per day. The only other place to change Visa travellers cheques is at the Hotel Ganga Kinare.

Travel Agencies Ajay Travels (☎ 32897), beneath the Hotel Neelkanth on Ghat Rd in the city centre, can arrange taxis and bus travel to the Char Dham and elsewhere. Similar services are offered by Blue Hills Travels (☎ 31865), in the Swarg Ashram area. In theory it's possible to send email from the Blue Hills office, but in practice the connections are very erratic.

Things to See

The **Triveni Ghat** is an interesting place to be at dawn, when people make offerings of milk to the river and feed the surprisingly large fish. After sunset, priests set floating lamps on the water in the Ganga Aarti (river worship) ceremony. Nearby is the **Bharat Mandir**, the oldest temple here.

The suspension bridge **Lakshman Jhula** was built in 1929 to replace a rope bridge. This is where Rama's brother Lakshmana is said to have crossed the river on a jute rope, and the old **Lakshman Temple** is on the west bank. Across the river are some turreted oddities, including the 13 storey **Kailashanand Mission Ashram.** There's a good view from the top. It's a pleasant 2km walk along this bank to the Shivanand Jhula.

Pilgrims take Ganga water to offer at **Nilkantha Mahadev**, a four hour walk from Lakshman Jhula on the east bank. There are fine views on the way up to the temple at 1700m but take something to drink and start early as it can get very hot. It's now possible to make the journey by bus.

There are also great views from **Kunjapuri**, in the hills north of Rishikesh. It's a 3km walk from Hindola Khal (45 minutes by bus from Rishikesh), which all buses to Tehri pass through.

Trekking

At the GMVN tourist office (☎ 30372) you can book Char Dham packages, and there's also a Trekking & Mountaineering division (☎ 32648) where you can hire tents, rucksacks, sleeping bags and mountaineering equipment, as well as book treks. Rates for treks start at Rs 1325 per day (minimum of three people required) and include transport

RISHIKESH

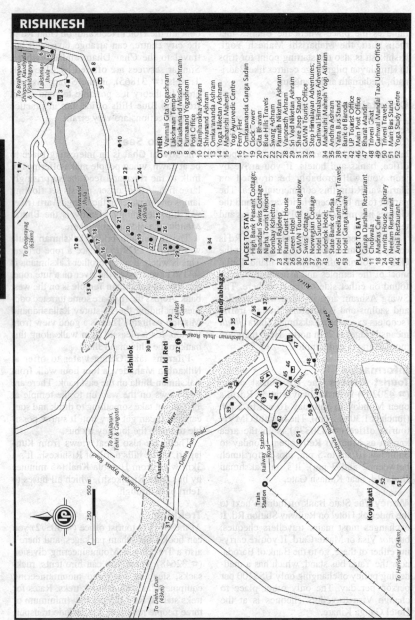

OTHER
1 Vanmali Gita Yogashram
2 Lakshman Temple
3 Kailashanand Mission Ashram
8 Purnanand Yogashram
9 Post Office
10 Ramjharokha Ashram
12 Shivanand Ashram
13 Omkaananda Ashram
14 Yoga Niketan Ashram
15 Maharishi Mahesh Yogi Ayurvedic Centre
16 Ferry Fier
17 Omkaaananda Ganga Sadan
19 Clock Tower
20 Gita Bhavan
21 Blue Hills Travels
22 Swarg Ashram
27 Parmath Niketan Ashram
28 Vanprasth Ashram
29 Sri Ved Niketan Ashram
31 Share Jeep Stand
32 GMVN Tourist Office
33 Step Himalayan Adventures; Garhwal Himalayas Adventures
35 Maharishi Mahesh Yogi Ashram
36 Andhi Ashram
38 Yatra Bis Stand
41 Bank of Baroda
42 UP Tourist Office
46 Main Post Office
47 Bharat Mandir
48 Triveni Jhat
49 Garhwal Mandal Taxi Union Office
50 Triveni Travels
51 Main Bus Stand
52 Yoga Study Centre

PLACES TO STAY
1 High Bank Peasant Cottage;
    Bhandari Swiss Cottage
7 Nigha Tourist Resort
23 Hotel Rajdeep
24 Rama Guest House
26 Green Hotel
30 GMVN Tourist Bungalow
36 Swiss Cottage
37 Norwegian Cottage
39 Hotel Suruchi
43 Inderlok Hotel;
    State Bank of India;
    State Bank Neelkanth; Ajay Travels
45 Hotel Ganga Kinare
53 Hotel Ganga Kinare

PLACES TO EAT
6 Ganga Darshan Restaurant
11 Chotiwala
18 Madras Cafe
24 Amrita House & Library
40 Neelam Restaurant
44 Anjali Restaurant

by deluxe coach or taxi, all meals, porters, guides and accommodation in tourist rest-houses or tents. Treks include a nine day Har ki Dun trek, a 10 day trek to the lake of Rup Kund, an eight day trek to the Valley of the Flowers, and a 14 day trek to the Khatling Glacier (all during the summer months only).

Rafting

Triveni Travels (☎ 433979, fax 432989) on Haridwar Rd can arrange rafting on the Ganges at Brahmpuri, 10km from Rishikesh, or through the more exhilarating rapids at Shivpuri, 18km from Rishikesh. It costs Rs 300 from Brahmpuri or Rs 400 from Shivpuri, including transport, lunch, life jackets and helmets. A minimum of five people is required.

From its camp at Kaudiyala near Rishikesh, UP Tourism offers rafting packages. Prices start at Rs 350 per day for rafting, Rs 150 for meals, and Rs 65 for share lodging (or Rs 100 for single occupancy).

Step Himalayan Adventures (☎ 432581, fax 431558) and Garhwal Himalayas Adventures (☎ 433478, fax 431654), both near Kailash Gate near the GMVN tourist office, also offer rafting at comparable rates.

Other Outdoor Activities

Triveni Travels (see previous section for address) also offers **caving expeditions** through the 200m long Vishitha Gufa, 16km from Rishikesh near Shivpuri (Rs 500), and half-day **elephant safaris** in the Rajaji National Park for four persons (Rs 750), as well as trekking and Char Dham packages. Triveni can also pick you up from Delhi airport and drive you straight to Rishikesh for Rs 1350 (phone or fax in advance with your flight number).

Step Himalayan Adventures and Garhwal Himalayas Adventures also offer wildlife tours and trekking (see previous section for addresses).

Meditation & Yoga Courses

There are many ashrams offering courses in meditation, yoga and Hindu philosophy. However many foreigners report difficulties

in finding one that satisfies them – some have extremely rigid rules, some only accept people for long-term study, and some see foreigners as the source of a quick buck. It is worth talking to other travellers first and going to a few lectures at different ashrams to find your guru, if you're looking for one. Some of the more reputable ashrams are included here, but ask around and you'll probably hear of others that are just as good. It is also possible to arrange for a yoga instructor to come to your hotel; it may not be as 'authentic' as an ashram but at least you know what you're getting.

Many westerners attend the hatha yoga and pranayama (a form of hatha yoga) meditation classes at **Sri Ved Niketan Ashram** in Swarg Ashram, founded by Shri Vishwaguruji Maharaj Yogasamrat. Lectures on various aspects of Hindu philosophy are also given here (in English). Courses cost Rs 300 for a week, and classes are held at 6.30 am and 6 pm. It is also possible to stay here (see Places to Stay, later in this section).

Shivanand Ashram (☎ 430040) was founded by Swami Shivananda and is under the auspices of the Divine Life Society. The ashram is on the west side of Lakshman Jhula Rd, opposite the Shivanand Jhula. There are lectures, discussion and meditation and yoga classes daily, with courses from three days to two months (all free). It is possible to stay at the ashram (for a limited period, by donation) but one month's notice is required: write to the Divine Life Society, PO Shivanandanagar, 249192, District Tehri, Garhwal, Uttar Pradesh.

Close by, reached along a path leading up from Lakshman Jhula Rd, and set in lovely gardens high above the Ganges, is the **Yoga Niketan Ashram** (☎ 430227). Classes on meditation and the pranayama form of hatha yoga are held throughout the year, although you must stay for a minimum of 15 days. It's possible to stay if you're attending classes (Rs 125 per day), and meals are available. Additional courses cost extra.

Above Yoga Niketan is the **Omkarananda Ashram** (☎ 430883), which runs courses (by donation) in a separate building called the

Omkarananda Ganga Sadan, back down on Lakshman Jhula Rd, near the Shivananda arch. If there are enough students (minimum 20 required), beginner courses are run in hatha yoga. Regular yoga courses are held daily (except Sunday) from 5.30 to 7 pm. Instruction in various forms of Indian classical dance is also given.

The **Yoga Study Centre** (☎ 431196) at Koyalgati runs three-week courses in the iyengar form of hatha yoga during February, April and September for beginners, intermediate and advanced students. Payment is by donation and accommodation can be arranged.

In the Lakshman Jhula area, on the right when approaching the bridge from the west side of the river, is the **Vanmali Gita Yogashram** (☎ 431316). The ashram was founded by Sri Swami Jayendra Saraswati Maharaj Jagadguru Sankaracharya; two-hour classes in yoga and meditation are held at 4 and 6.30 pm respectively.

Organised Tours

From Rishikesh, UP Tourism offers coach and taxi tours to the Char Dham. A four day bus tour to Badrinath is Rs 1695, including share accommodation. To Yamunotri and

---

Swami Alert

While many of Rishikesh's ashrams have charitable dispensaries and hospitals, providing invaluable service to India's sick and destitute, the sheer opulence of some suggests concerns with matters more earthly than spiritual, and the behaviour of some of their gurus leaves much to be desired. In 1995, one of these 'holy' men, Swami Rameshwarand Giriji Maharaj, fell from grace when he murdered the husband of a female devotee with whom he had enjoyed a less than spiritual alliance. He allegedly told the woman that she could attain spiritual salvation only through sexual relations with a person close to God like him!

Gangotri, a seven day tour departs each Friday during the yatra season (Rs 3200).

A 10 day taxi package to the Char Dham is Rs 8300 per person. The six day taxi package from Rishikesh to Kedarnath and Badrinath is Rs 5100 per person.

Special Events

The **International Yoga Festival**, arranged by UP Tourism, is held annually from 2 to 7 February. Yoga and meditation masters from around India converge on Rishikesh at this time to impart their wisdom. Seven-day packages including meals, hotel accommodation, transport from your hotel to venues, lectures and air-con deluxe coaches between Delhi and Rishikesh are US$500 per person. Bookings should be made at least two months in advance to the Director, UP Tourism, Chitrahar Building, 3 Naval Kishor Rd, Lucknow (☎ 0552-228349, fax 221776).

Places to Stay
City Centre, Chandrabhaga & Rishilok

While not as colourful or peaceful as the Swarg Ashram and Lakshman Jhula areas, there are some good choices in this area.

Inderlok Hotel (☎ 430555) on Ghat Rd has standard singles/doubles for Rs 500/600, Rs 770/880 with air-con. Rooms are cool and comfortable, all with colour TV. The hotel also has a travel desk.

Hotel Suruchi (☎ 432269), beside the Yatra bus stand, is built around a spacious atrium. Standard singles/doubles cost Rs 250/350; air-cooled rooms are Rs 350/450. Attached baths have cold water only, but bucket hot water is free. The restaurant here is very reasonably priced.

Hotel Ganga Kinare (☎/fax 431658) is a bit of a hike from the centre, about 2km south of Railway Station Rd at 16 Virbhadra Rd. However, it's in a lovely peaceful spot on the west bank of the Ganges, and rooms are very well appointed, some (the more expensive ones!) having beautiful river views. Air-con singles/doubles cost Rs 1350/1650, and there are suites for Rs 1800/2800. Free meditation classes are held on the terrace, and guests can use the hotel's rowing boats.

There's also a reference library on yoga, a travel desk which can arrange trekking, rafting, skiing, cycling and wildlife and cultural tours, and a reasonably priced restaurant. Evening prayers take place on the hotel's private ghat.

Swiss Cottage on the north side of the Chandrabhaga River is run by Swami Brahmananda, a disciple of Swami Shivananda. Rooms are set around a shady courtyard. Singles, doubles and triples are all Rs 50; some with attached bath. No meals are provided, but self-catering is OK. If this place is booked up, ask here for directions to the nearby *Norwegian Cottage*. It's equally as friendly, if not quite as atmospheric.

GMVN *Tourist Bungalow* (☎ 430373), in the area known as Rishilok, is a good place to stay and it is set in lovely grounds. Doubles with common/attached bath go for Rs 150/350. The restaurant is good, and you can store luggage for Rs 4 per bag per day.

Swarg Ashram Area There are a couple of guesthouses and a choice of two ashrams on the east side of the river, over the Shivanand Jhula.

Green Hotel (☎ 431242), down a quiet lane, has clean, if spartan, singles/doubles for Rs 75/125. Larger doubles with air-coolers are Rs 250, hot water is free by the bucket and there's a good restaurant.

Rama Guest House, behind the Green Hotel, has clean doubles with common bath for Rs 60 (there's one *tiny* single for Rs 40). The owner is very friendly, but there's no restaurant.

Hotel Rajdeep (☎ 432826, fax 433109) is a good mid-range place in the lanes east of the bridge, but easy to find if you follow the signs. Standard doubles cost Rs 225, air-cooled doubles Rs 325 and air-con deluxe rooms Rs 775. They can arrange trekking and rafting, there are yoga classes held here, and there's a nice rooftop area.

Vanprasth Ashram is right on the Ganges, at the southern end of Swarg Ashram, about a 10 minute walk from Shivanand Jhula. There are lovely flower gardens, and a resident yoga teacher, but you don't have to at-

tend classes if you don't want to. Doubles (facing the Ganges) and triples are Rs 100 with attached bath (cold water only), and there's a room which can accommodate up to six people (Rs 300). There's a canteen, but you can use the ashram's kitchen facilities (free). Foreigners can only stay between 1 November and 31 March.

Sri Ved Niketan Ashram next door to Vandprasth has an unmissable orange and turquoise edifice. There are daily yoga and meditation classes (see the Meditation & Yoga Courses section, earlier), but no pressure to attend. Large but very spartan singles/doubles with hard beds are Rs 30/70 with attached bath (cold water only; bucket hot water free). The upstairs rooms at the front have good views over the Ganges.

Lakshman Jhula Area The following places are farthest from the bus and train stations (at least 4km), but in a colourful and interesting area.

Bombay Kshettra is on the east side of the river. It's an atmospheric, colourful old building with rooms ranging from Rs 60 to Rs 80, depending on the size, all with common bath, and set around a pleasant courtyard.

Nigha Tourist Resort (☎ 434801) is a passable modern place with some rooms overlooking the Ganges. Doubles with attached bath cost Rs 150.

High Bank Peasants Cottage (☎ 431167) is set in beautiful flower gardens high above the Ganges. Take the road to the left, 1km before Lakshman Jhula; the cottage is about 500m up a track. Rooms are Rs 250/300 with attached bath (free bucket hot water), and the balcony has wicker chairs where you can sit and contemplate the Ganges. Discounts are offered for stays of over a week. Each morning Lisa, the family dog, brings the newspaper up from the front gate. Good Indian meals (not too spicy) using vegies from the garden are available, and you can arrange treks and river rafting here.

Bhandari Swiss Cottage (☎ 431534) is just above High Bank. Large, pleasant rooms cost Rs 150 for singles or doubles, slightly larger

UTTAR PRADESH

rooms cost Rs 250. Meals are available, and there are great views from the balcony.

Further up the track from High Bank, several villagers rent out rooms for long-term visitors, charging around Rs 150 per day.

Places to Eat

Rishikesh is a holy pilgrimage town, and is therefore strictly vegetarian.

Indrani at the Inderlok Hotel has a good range of Chinese cuisine (Cantonese and Manchurian), as well as specials such as *rajmah* – seasoned kidney beans (Rs 30) and *gajjar halwa* in season (Rs 20).

Anjali Restaurant, further down Railway Station Rd towards Triveni Ghat, has very cheap dishes (most under Rs 10) in its mirrored dining hall-cum-*dhaba* (hole-in-the wall restaurant).

Neelam Restaurant, run by the helpful Mr Singh, is a low-key place in a small lane just off Haridwar Rd. It's popular with westerners tempted here by dishes such as macaroni (Rs 30), spaghetti and good rice pud, as well as the standard Indian fare.

Madras Cafe, on the west side of Shivanand Jhula, has a good range of dosa, and if you don't like it hot, you can ask the cook to exercise restraint with the spices. There are also good lassis and cold coffee.

Amrita House & Library on the Swarg Ashram side is tricky to find but worth the search (locals seem accustomed to giving directions). It's a terrific little eatery with books for perusing while you tuck into your banana, raisin and curd pancakes. The owner also does excellent spaghetti and pizzas, made with home-made buffalo cheese.

Chotiwala, on the east side of the Shivanand Jhula, in Swarg Ashram, is a longtime favourite for rooftop dining. The filling special thali is Rs 30, and there's a good range of Kwality ice cream.

Tripti Restaurant at the Hotel Suruchi has excellent fare, including *dhal makhani* (black lentils and red kidney beans with cream and butter) and the sublime Suruchi sundae with hot chocolate sauce and nuts (Rs 15).

Ganga Darshan Restaurant, opposite the Bombay Kshettra, is set right on the river,

and has cheap, filling thalis for Rs 20, as well as south Indian food (dosa, idlis, etc).

Shopping

Rishikesh is a good place to pick up a *rudraksh mala*, the strings of beads used in *puja* (offerings) made from the nuts of the rudraksh tree. Prices start from around Rs 100, with beads of the smaller nuts commanding higher prices. Flanking the waterfront on the east side of the river, in the Swarg Ashram area, are dozens of stalls selling devotional accoutrements such as prasaad, scriptural booklets and cassettes, as well as shawls and ayurvedic medicines. There's also a good range of ayurvedic medicines made from herbs collected from the Himalaya at the Maharishi Mahesh Yogi Ayurvedic Centre, on Lakshman Jhula Rd, opposite the pathway up to Yoga Niketan Ashram.

Getting There & Away

Bus From the main bus stand (☎ 430066) there are buses to Haridwar every 30 minutes from 4.30 am to 10.30 pm (Rs 10.50, one hour), and numerous buses to Dehra Dun between 6.30 am and 8 pm (Rs 13.50, 1½ hours). Between 4.30 am and 10.30 pm there are hourly buses to Delhi. The trip takes six hours and costs Rs 78 for an ordinary seat, Rs 225 for semideluxe, or Rs 300 for super deluxe. There's one bus at 8.15 am to Ramnagar (Rs 85, six hours) which continues to Nainital (Rs 88, 8½ hours). To Shimla, you'll need to find your way to Dehra Dun, from where there are several services between 5.30 and 11.30 am (Rs 82, seven hours).

From the Yatra bus stand (☎ 432013) buses leave regularly during the pilgrimage season (April/October) for Badrinath between 3.30 and 5.30 am (Rs 118, 14 hours); Kedarnath at 3.45, 4.15 and 5 am, and 12.30 and 1 pm (Rs 92, 12 hours); Uttarkashi at 3.45, 5.30, 8, 10 and 11.30 am and 12.30 pm (Rs 60, seven hours); and Gangotri at 6, 6.30, 7 and 7.30 am (Rs 112, 12 hours). There are five buses to Hanuman Chatti, the roadhead for Yamunotri, from 5 to 8 am (Rs 96, 10 hours). Prices are 30% higher after 1 September.

Train Bookings can be made at the train station (☎ 131) from 10 am to 4 pm (closed for lunch 1.30 to 2 pm). The station has a small allocation of seats for Haridwar. There are trains to Haridwar at 6.40 and 9.15 am, 2.10, 3.15 and 6.40 pm (Rs 4). The 6.40 am service arrives at Delhi at 5.20 pm. The 6.40 pm train connects with the *Mussoorie Express* for Delhi and with overnight trains to Lucknow and Agra. The 2.10 pm train connects with the *Jammu Tawi* express to Pathankot and Jammu.

Taxi & Jeep Official, low-season reserve taxi rates are:

Delhi	Rs 1100
Dehra Dun	Rs 300
Mussoorie	Rs 550
Uttarkashi (for Gangotri)	Rs 850
Tehri	Rs 600
Haridwar	Rs 250
Ranikhet	Rs 1800

Expect to pay 20% to 50% more during summer. The main office for the Garhwal Mandal Taxi Union (☎ 430413) is on Haridwar Rd, just over Ghat Rd. Official rates for the Char Dham are Rs 7500, or for Badrinath and Kedarnath only, Rs 4200.

You can flag down share jeeps for Dehra Dun anywhere along the Dehra Dun Rd. The cost to Dehra Dun is Rs 20. You may be able to get a share taxi to Haridwar from the main bus stand (Rs 20). An alternative (and grubbier) proposition is to pick up a shared Vikram anywhere along the Haridwar Rd (Rs 10).

Share jeeps to Uttarkashi and Joshimath leave from the corner of Dehra Dun Rd and Dhalwala Bypass Rd. There's no timetable as such; jeeps leave when full (or to be more accurate, when overloaded) between 8 am and 2 pm. Seats cost Rs 110 to Uttarkashi and take about five hours, or Rs 200 to Joshimath (eight hours).

Getting Around
Vikrams run from Ghat Rd junction up to Shivanand Jhula (Rs 3) and Lakshman Jhula (Rs 5). Shivanand Jhula is a pedestrian-only bridge, so you'll have to lump your backpack across if you're planning to stay on the east side of the Ganges (ie in the Swarg Ashram area). On the east bank of the river, a seat in a jeep between Lakshman Jhula and Shivanand Jhula costs Rs 3.

For Rs 5 you can cross the river to Swarg Ashram between 8 am and 7 pm by boat (particularly auspicious).

UTTARAKHAND HIMALAYA
This northern district of Uttarakhand is best known for its four major pilgrimage centres: Gangotri, near the source of the Ganges, Yamunotri, by the source of the Yamuna, Badrinath and Kedarnath. See Lonely Planet's *Indian Himalaya* and *Trekking in the Indian Himalaya* for more details on this area.

Uttarkashi
☎ 01374
Uttarkashi is a regional centre 155km from Rishikesh and is the administrative headquarters of the district. Several trekking companies operate from here and the town is also the base for the Nehru Institute of Mountaineering, where Bachhendri Pal, the first Indian woman to climb to the summit of Mt Everest, was trained.

The town is pleasantly situated on the banks of the Bhagirathi River, drawing pilgrims to its **Vishwanatha Temple**, sacred to Shiva. It's possible that you'll wind up here looking for a bed before proceeding further north to Gangotri. You can stock up on supplies here if you're planning a trek further north, although the town has more to offer.

On the day of **Makar Sakranti**, which usually falls in January, the town hosts a colourful fair, when deities are borne aloft into the town on palanquins from outlying villages.

Accommodation in Uttarkashi includes the *Hotel Relax* (☎ 2893) up the main road from the noisy bus stand, where doubles cost from Rs 250 to Rs 400. Nearby, on the same road, the *Hotel Bhadari Annexe* (☎ 2384) is basic but clean with rooms for Rs 150/230. Buses depart in the morning for Gangotri (Rs 42) and Rishikesh (Rs 77).

UTTAR PRADESH

Yamunotri

Yamunotri is the source of the Yamuna River, the second-most sacred river in India after the Ganges. This was once the source of the Sarasvati River, one of the cradles of early Indian civilisation which, in ancient times, flowed through Rajasthan and Gujarat before geological upheavals diverted its course. It emerges from a frozen lake of ice and glaciers on the Kalinda Parvat mountain at an altitude of 4421m. The temple of the goddess Yamunotri is on the left bank of the river and, just below it, there are several hot springs where the priests warm themselves on a marble platform and cook potatoes in the scalding water. Buses go as far as Hanuman Chatti from Mussoorie or Rishikesh, although you may have to change buses at Barkot. From Hanuman Chatti, the trek to Yamunotri takes five to six hours, but there's a *Tourist Rest House* with doubles for Rs 250 just past the halfway point, at Jankichatti, and several basic *dharamsalas*. You can also stay at *dharamsalas* in Yamunotri.

TREKKING IN GARHWAL

There are many superb trekking opportunities in the Garhwal region of Uttarakhand. Traditionally, the region attracts many thousands of pilgrims to the important pilgrimage sites of Yamunotri and Gangotri, however only a handful of trekkers discover the delights of trekking further into the mountains.

The treks in the Garhwal Himalaya include those to the Har ki Dun Valley, Dodital and the trek to Gaumukh, the source of the Ganges. The best time to trek is either in the pre-monsoon period (mid-May to the end of June), or the post-monsoon season (mid-September to mid-October). In July and August the region is subject to heavy rainfall.

More detailed coverage of all the treks listed here can be found in Lonely Planet's *Trekking in the Indian Himalaya*, along with trail maps and safety information.

UP Tourism's regional subsidiary the Garhwal Mandal Vikas Nigam (GMVN) can organise all-inclusive treks, while there are a number of agencies in Uttarkashi, Rishikesh, Nainital and Mussoorie that can make similar arrangements. Budget for around US$40 to US$50 per day. If you're making your own arrangements, porters are normally available at the roadhead for around Rs 100 per day while guides rates vary from Rs 250 per day upwards. The GMVN at Rishikesh and Uttarkashi have stocks of sleeping bags and tents for hire, although supplies may be limited. As with most treks in the Indian Himalaya, experienced trekkers are advised to bring their own equipment.

Food supplies can be bought at Mussoorie or Uttarkashi before continuing on to the roadhead. On these treks there are many teahouses or Public Works Department (PWD) Rest Houses that provide both food and accommodation. However on some stages – for example if you're going beyond Har ki Dun to Ruinsara Lake, or beyond Dodital to Hanuman Chatti, or beyond Gaumukh to Tabovan – it is essential to bring your own supplies.

Har ki Dun Valley & Ruinsara Lake This trek follows a tributary of the Tons River to the beautiful meadow of Har ki Dun. The initial stages lead through well-established settlements to the highest village of Seema. It is a further stage to Har ki Dun where a day or two could be spent exploring the side valleys north of the Swargarohini Range. It is also possible to extend the trek by returning to the Dev Thach Valley above Seema Village and trekking to Ruinsara Lake with fine views of Swargarohini 1 (6525m).

Stage 1	Sankri to Taluka (3 hours)
Stage 2	Taluka to Seema (5 to 6 hours)
Stage 3	Seema Village to Har ki Dun (4 to 5 hours)
Stage 4	Har ki Dun to Dev Thach (3 hours)
Stage 5	Dev Thach to Ruinsara Lake and return (7 hours)
Stage 6	Dev Thach to Sankri (6 hours)

Uttarkashi to Hanuman Chatti via Dodital From Uttarkashi there is short bus ride to the roadhead at Sangam Chatti from where you trek up the well-defined trail to the village of Agoda. It takes a further stage to reach Dodital, an idyllic lake set in a forest of oak, pine, deodar and rhododendron.

From Dodital there is a short steep ascent to the Darwa Pass (4150m) before trekking along the alpine ridges to gain magnificent views of Bandarpunch (6316m). An intermediary camp is necessary at Seema camp before descending to the Hanuman Ganga and the pilgrim town of Hanuman Chatti from where there are regular buses to Uttarkashi or Mussoorie.

Stage 1   Sangam Chatti to Agoda (2 to 3 hours)
Stage 2   Agoda to Dodital (6 hours)
Stage 3   Dodital to Seema camp via Darwa Pass (6 to 7 hours)
Stage 4   Seema camp to Hanuman Chatti (4 hours)

Gangotri to Gaumukh & Tabovan The popular pilgrimage destination of Gangotri can be reached from Rishikesh by bus via Tehri and Uttarkashi, a 10 to 12 hour journey. The trek to the source of the holy Ganges starts from the bustling pilgrim village of Gangotri and follows a bridle trail along the true right of the Bhagirathi River. There are a number of established pilgrim rest stops with adequate shelter and food before reaching Gaumukh (3890m) and the 'Cows Mouth' and the true source of the Ganges. Beyond Gaumukh the going gets harder with a demanding stage across moraine to the meadow at Tabovan. From the camp there are inspiring views of Shivling (6543m) while the Bhagirathi peaks including Bhagirathi 1 (6856m) rise dramatically on the far side of the Gangotri Glacier.

Stage 1   Gangotri to Bhojbasa (6 to 7 hours)
Stage 2   Bhojbasa to Gaumukh (2 hours)
Stage 3   Gaumukh to Tabovan and return (5 to 6 hours)
Stage 4   Gaumukh to Gangotri (6 hours)

Trekking in Kumaon (Nanda Devi Region)

Treks in the vicinity of Nanda Devi (7816m), the highest peak wholly in India, are comparable with some of the spectacular treks in the Annapurna or Everest regions of Nepal, and yet they attract only a handful of trekkers each year.

Geographically, the summit of Nanda Devi is recognised as the northern border between the Uttarakhand regions of Garhwal and Kumaon. Treks to the west and south of Nanda Devi are included in the Garhwal region (see previous section) while treks to the east of Nanda Devi are included in the Kumaon region.

Treks on the western side of Nanda Devi include the famous Valley of the Flowers, the Kuari Pass trek and the trek to the mysterious lake of Rup Kund. South of Nanda Devi are the treks to the Pindari Glacier while to the east of Nanda Devi is the trek to the Milam Glacier. It should be noted that trekking in the Nanda Devi Sanctuary to the base of Nanda Devi (7816m) is still banned by the Indian government and at present there are no plans to lift this restriction.

The best time to trek in the Nanda Devi region is either in the pre-monsoon period (mid-May to the end of June), or the post-monsoon season (mid-September to mid-October). In July and August the region is subject to heavy rainfall, though this is the best time to appreciate the rich variety of wildflowers in the Valley of the Flowers or the nearby high alpine meadows or *bugyals*.

KMVN can organise all-inclusive treks. Budget for around US$40 to US$50 per day. If making your own arrangements, porters are normally available at the roadhead for around Rs 100 per day, while guides rates vary from Rs 250 per day upwards. The KMVN at Joshimath has stocks of sleeping bags and tents for hire, though supplies may be limited.

Food supplies can be bought at Almora or Joshimath before continuing on to the roadhead, while there are limited supplies of canned goods etc at Munsyari. On the trek to the Pindari Glacier there are many teahouses and PWD Rest Houses that provide both food and accommodation. On the other treks facilities are more limited and it is essential to bring your own supplies and equipment.

Valley of the Flowers National Park & Hem Kund The legendary Valley of the Flowers was first seen by a Brit when the

UTTAR PRADESH

mountaineer Frank Smythe arrived in the 1930s. Throughout the summer months (mid-June to mid-September) the valley is an enchanting sight with an impressive array of wildflowers while the snow-clad peaks including Nilgiri Parbat (6474m) stand in bold relief against the skyline. The valley is nearly 10km long and 2km wide, and is divided by the Pushpawati stream, into which several tiny streams and waterfalls merge. The valley has suffered the effects of large numbers of trekkers and shepherds in the past, leaving the authorities with little option but to create a national park. The current stipulation allows day walks into the valley but no overnight camping is permitted.

Many local buses operate between Joshimath and Govind Ghat, the starting point for the trek. From Govind Ghat there is a gradual ascent along a well-maintained pilgrim trail to the camp at Ghangaria – the base from where day walks can be made into the Valley of the Flowers. From Ghangaria, you can follow the Laxma Ganga to the lake at Hem Kund – quite a steep climb. In the Sikh holy book, the Granth Sahib, the Sikh Guru Gobind Singh recounts that in a previous life he meditated on the shores of a lake surrounded by seven snowcapped mountains now recognised as Hem Kund.

Stage 1	Govind Ghat to Ghangaria (7 hours)
Stage 2	Ghangaria to Valley of the Flowers and return (6 hours)
Stage 3	Ghangaria to Hem Kund and return (8 hours)
Stage 4	Ghangaria to Govind Ghat (5 hours)

Joshimath to Ghat via the Kuari Pass

Although the trek over the Kuari Pass is also known as the Curzon Trail (Lord Curzon was an enthusiastic Himalayan hiker) there is a bit of a misnomer here, for the Curzon party did not actually cross the pass, abandoning their attempt after being attacked by wild bees a few stages before the pass crossing.

From Joshimath there is a daily bus service to the village of Auli where you commence the trek. On the initial stages of the trek there are uninterrupted views up the Rishi Ganga to the Nanda Devi Sanctuary.

The trail then winds through a series of pastures and shepherd camps, with superb views of Dunagiri (7066m) and the Chaukhamba massif including Chaukhamba 1 (7138m) on the far side of Joshimath, to the first camp at Chitraganta. To gain the best views of Nanda Devi (7816m) requires a day walk along the ridge above the Kauri Pass.

From the Kauri Pass it is a steep descent to the meadow at Dakwani before continuing to the shepherd camp at Sutoli. It's a further two stages across the forested ridges and past small villages high above the Birthi Ganga to the village of Ramni. The final stage descends (steeply in places) to the roadhead at Ghat where jeeps and buses complete the 30km to Nandaprayag on the Joshimath-Rishikesh road.

Stage 1	Auli to Chitraganta (6 to 7 hours)
Stage 2	Chitraganta to Dakwani via the Kuari Pass (4 to 5 hours)
Stage 3	Dakwani to Ghangri (7 hours)
Stage 4	Ghangri to Ramni (5 to 6 hours)
Stage 5	Ramni to Ghat (5 hours)

Ghat to Mundoli via Rup Kund

Set beneath the towering summit of Trisul (7120m), Rup Kund is sometimes referred to as the 'mystery lake' on account of the many human skeletons found here. Every 12 years, thousands of devout pilgrims make an arduous trek when following the Raj Jay Yatra (pilgrimage) from Nauti Village, near Karnaprayag. The pilgrims are said to be led by a four-horned ram which takes them from here to Rup Kund. A golden idol of the goddess Nanda Devi is carried by the pilgrims in a silver palanquin.

The first stage of the trek climbs from Ghat to the village of Ramni before following a trail through mixed forests and traditional Hindu villages to the large village of Wan. The trail to Rup Kund then ascends through oak, pine and rhododendron forest to the alpine camp at Badni Bugyal. The views from this camp are among the finest in the western Himalaya. To the east are the peaks beyond Joshimath, while to the south-east the Great Himalaya Range extends as far as the eye can see across the western Garhwal. To the south the foothills descend to the

Ganges plains, while to the north Trisul (7120m) provides an impressive backdrop.

It's a further stage before you reach the camp at Bhogabasa. From here you can reach Rup Kund with time to return to Badni Bugyal the same day. From Badni Bugyal there are a number of short cuts across the bugyals and down to the trail between Wan and Mandoli. From Mandoli there are buses and jeeps to Debal and onward connections to Gwaldam and Nainital.

Stage 1	Ghat to Ramni (5 hours)
Stage 2	Ramni to Sutol (6 to 7 hours)
Stage 3	Sutol to Wan (5 hours)
Stage 4	Wan to Badni Bugyal (5 hours)
Stage 5	Badni Bugyal to Bhogabasa (4 to 5 hours)
Stage 6	Bhogabasa to Rup Kund and return to Badni Bugyal (6 to 7 hours)
Stage 7	Badni Bugyal to Mandoli(6 to 7 hours)

Song to the Pindari Glacier The Pindari Glacier flowing from Nanda Kot (6861m) and Nanda Khat (6611m) is on the southern rim of the Nanda Devi National Park.

From Almora there's an early morning bus to Song where the trek begins. The first stage (all uphill) is a tough one for a first time trekker. It follows a well-marked trail through forests of quercus oak and horse chestnut and across open meadows to Dhakri Khal (2830m). Views from the pass are impressive and take in Trisul (7120m) and Nanda Khat (6611m). The trail then winds down to the Pindari Valley and follows the river through luxuriant forest to the meadow at Phurkiya. It's another stage to the terminal moraine of the Pindari Glacier at Zero Point (3650m) beneath the impressive backdrop of Nanda Khat (6611m), Changuch (6322m) and Nanda Kot (6861m).

Stage 1	Song to Dhakri via Dhakri Khal (6 to 7 hours)
Stage 2	Dhakri to Dwali (6 to 7 hours)
Stage 3	Dwali to Phurkiya (3 hours)
Stage 4	Phurkiya to Zero Point at the Pindari Glacier and return to Dwali (7 to 8 hours)
Stage 5	Dwali to Dhakri (6 to 7 hours)
Stage 6	Dhakri to Song (5 to 6 hours)

Munsyari to the Milam Glacier The Milam Valley to the east of Nanda Devi is open to trekkers and although no special permits are needed to complete this trek, you will need to show your passport and register with the Indo-Tibet Border Police (ITBP) at Milam.

The trek includes magnificent views of Nanda Devi (7816m). The villages in the upper sections of the Milam Valley were the recruiting ground for the famous Pundits, the Indian explorers who mapped out much of Tibet in the later decades of the 19th century.

There is an early morning bus from Almora to the town of Munsyari where you commence the trek. The initial stages follow the course of the Gori Ganga past Hindu villages and mixed forests of chestnut and bamboo. The trail then enters impressive gorges where the Gori Ganga forges its way through the crest of the main Himalaya. It's a further stage to the village of Martoli and the turn-off for the trek to the base of Nanda Devi East. From Martoli it's an easy walk to Milam with views en route of the remarkable East Face of Nanda Devi.

Until 1962 Milam and the nearby villages maintained close trading ties with Tibet. Nowadays this is as far as villagers and trekkers are allowed to go, although you are normally permitted to continue for 3km to view the Milam Glacier and the peaks of Rishi Pahar (6992m), Hardeol (7151m) and Tirsuli (7074m).

Stage 1	Munsyari to Lilam (4 hours)
Stage 2	Lilam to Bodgwar (6 to 7 hours)
Stage 3	Bodgwar to Martoli (5 to 6 hours)
Stage 4	Martoli to Milam (4 hours)
Stage 5	Milam to Bodgwar (8 hours)
Stage 6	Bodgwar to Lilam (6 to 7 hours)
Stage 7	Lilam to Munsyari (4 hours)

AULI

This skiing resort, the best equipped in the country, boasts 5km-long slopes which drop from an altitude of 3049m to 2519m. There's also a 500m-long ski lift.

Open from January to March, Auli is 15km from Joshimath. GMVN operates the resort and has *Tourist Rest Houses* at Joshimath

(☎ 01389-2118) and Auli (☎ 013712-2226). Skis and boots can be hired here (Rs 200 per day) and seven or 14-day ski packages, including all meals, lodging, equipment, hire and lessons, are offered for Rs 1600/2800. To book, write in advance to the General Manager (☎ 0135-656817, fax 654408), GMVN, Survey Chowk, Lansdowne Marg, Dehra Dun, UP.

CORBETT TIGER RESERVE
☎ 05945

Established in 1936 as India's first national park, Corbett is famous for its wide variety of wildlife and its beautiful location in the foothills of the Himalaya by the Ramganga River. With the inclusion of the Sonanadi Wildlife Sanctuary to the west, Corbett has grown from 520 to 1318 sq km.

It may seem incongruous for a national park to be named after a famous British hunter (Jim Corbett is best known for his book *The Man-Eaters of Kumaon* and was greatly revered by local people for shooting tigers that had developed a liking for human flesh), but he was instrumental in setting up the reserve and eventually shot more wildlife with his camera than with his gun.

The Project Tiger program was inaugurated at Corbett National Park in 1973, and there are now 23 tiger reserves across India.

Seeing a tiger here is dependent on chance, since the animals are no longer baited or tracked (unlike at Kanha in Madhya Pradesh). Your best chance is to come late in the season (April to mid-June) and stay in the park for several days.

More commonly seen wildlife include wild elephants, langur monkeys (black face, long tail), rhesus macaques, peacocks, and several types of deer including chital (spotted deer), sambar, hog deer and barking

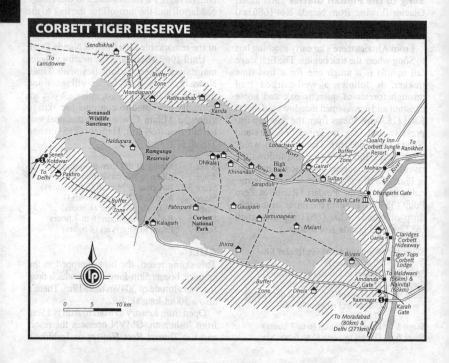

CORBETT TIGER RESERVE

deer. There are also mugger crocodiles, odd-looking gharials (thin-snouted, fish-eating crocodiles often spotted from High Bank), monitor lizards, wild boars and jackals. Leopards (referred to as panthers in India) are occasionally seen.

Corbett is also a bird-watcher's paradise, and since the creation of the Ramganga Reservoir on the Ramganga River, large numbers of waterfowl have been attracted here. The best time of year for sightings is from mid-December to the end of March.

Recent price hikes have made Corbett relatively expensive to visit. With the entrance fee, a jeep ride in and out and even the most basic accommodation, you are probably looking at around US$40 for a two day visit (though you can do it cheaper by sharing the jeep ride or by hitching).

The Tiger Reserve is open from mid-November to mid-June but you should avoid the crowded weekends. It's a good idea to bring mosquito repellent, mineral water and binoculars.

Orientation & Information

The Corbett Tiger Reserve encompasses both the original Corbett National Park, forming the eastern side of the reserve, and the Sonanadi Wildlife Sanctuary, forming the western side of the reserve.

The main reception centre is at Ramnagar (☎ 85489, fax 85376), outside the park on its south-eastern perimeter, and there is a second reception centre at Kotdwar (☎ 01382-23715), on the south-western edge of the park. The Ramnagar centre is open daily, including holidays, 8 am to 1 pm and 3 to 5 pm. Ramnagar is the nearest railhead and has several hotels as well as a State Bank of India which exchanges travellers cheques.

Dhikala, in the reserve, 51km north-west of Ramnagar, is the main accommodation centre and the place most travellers visit. Access is from the Dhangarhi Gate, about 20km to the north of Ramnagar. Day visitors are not allowed to visit Dhikala except through a trip booked at the Ramnagar visitors' centre (see Getting Around, later in this section). Otherwise, you will have to

Twenty-three tiger reserves have been set up in India under Project Tiger; sites with a wide variety of vegetation and terrain were chosen.

book accommodation at the Ramnagar visitors' centre and stay the night.

At Dhikala there's a library where interesting wildlife films are shown (free) in the evenings. The elephant rides at sunrise and sunset are not to be missed and cost Rs 100 each for four people for about two hours. During the day you can sit in one of the *machaan* (observation towers) to unobtrusively watch for animals.

At Bijrani is an interpretation centre and restaurant. It's sometimes possible to get elephant rides from here, although as there are only four elephants, priority is given to those staying overnight.

Permits Permits are normally bought at Dhangarhi Gate (for Dhikala) or Amdanda

Gate (for day trips to Bijrani). To stay at Dhikala you must first make an accommodation reservation at the park reception centre at Ramnagar. They will then give you a booking chit, which you must show at Dhangarhi Gate.

Charges listed here are for foreign nationals; Indians are charged about two-thirds less. At the gates you pay an entry fee of Rs 350 for a stay of up to three days, then Rs 175 per day There's no charge for a still camera but a video camera costs a whacking Rs 5000. To take a car into the park costs Rs 100, plus another Rs 200 (full day) or Rs 100 (half day) for a (compulsory) guide. If you hire a jeep you will have to pay these charges yourself.

Reserve Regulations

- No walking or trekking is allowed in the park at any time (introduced after a British ornithologist was killed by a tigress in 1985).
- Gates are closed at sunset and no night driving is permitted.
- An officially registered guide is required for all excursions, whether driving or walking.
- When leaving the park, visitors must obtain a clearance certificate (presumably to check you haven't stolen anything), which should be shown at the exit gate.

Organised Tours

UP Tourism in Delhi runs two/three-night fixed-departure tours to Dhikala from Delhi for Rs 3000/3500, including transport, accommodation, entrance fees, guide and one elephant ride.

Places to Stay & Eat

Most of the accommodation is at Dhikala, but there are Forest Rest Houses in both the national park and the Sonanadi Wildlife Sanctuary. Elephant rides are available at Dhikala and Bijrani, but bear in mind that if you stay outside these areas, your chances of spotting wildlife are reduced to sightings from the resthouses themselves, as venturing into the reserve on foot is prohibited.

Dhikala There is a wide range of accommodation in Dhikala, but the prices charged for foreigners mean that it is not good value.

The *Log Huts* have a very basic dormitory (like three-tier train sleepers!) for Rs 100. The *Tourist Hutment* has better value triples (Rs 500). An extra charge (Rs 25) is made for mattresses and sheets in both these places. *Cabins* are more comfortable – doubles are Rs 900 and come with attached bathroom. All three places can be booked at the reception centre at Ramnagar.

Doubles at the *Old Forest Rest House* (Rs 1500) or the *New Forest Rest House* (Rs 900) must be booked through the Chief Wildlife Warden in Lucknow (☎ 0522-283902).

There are also seven *annexe rooms* (Rs 900), which must be booked through UP Tourism in Delhi (☎ 011-332 2251).

There are two *restaurants*, one run by KMVN, and another run by a private operator.

Ramnagar The KMVN *Tourist Bungalow* (☎ 85225), next to the reception centre, has good doubles from Rs 300 to Rs 400. Dorm beds are Rs 60.

Hotel Everest (☎ 85099) has clean and comfortable rooms for Rs 100 to Rs 200 between 15 November and 15 June, and Rs 70 to Rs 125 at other times. Hot water is available in buckets for Rs 5, and room service is available. The hotel is in a side street opposite the bus station.

Hotel Govinda (☎ 85615), near the bus stand, has rooms with common bath for Rs 80 and Rs 100, and there's a good restaurant downstairs. The manager is friendly and the travellers' tips book is a good source of information.

Other Areas With your own transport and food, you can stay at the *Sultan Forest Rest House* and *Malani Forest Rest House* (doubles for Rs 450) in the Corbett National Park (ie the eastern end of the reserve). Also in this area are the resthouses at *Sarapduli* and *Gairal* (singles/doubles for Rs 500/900). There is no electricity at any of these places, although the resthouse at Sarapduli has its own generator. Bring a torch (flashlight). All these places can be accessed from the Dhangarhi Gate except Malani which is accessed from Amdanda Gate.

The resthouse at *Bijrani*, in the south-eastern corner of the reserve, has singles/doubles for Rs 500/900; access is via the Amdanda Gate.

There are also resthouses in the reserve buffer areas of *Dhela*, *Jhirna* and *Kalagarh*, on the southern perimeter of the reserve, and at *Lohachaur*, in the buffer zone to the north of the national park. Doubles at all of these cost Rs 300. You should bring a torch (flashlight) and your own food. Bookings for all these tourist resthouses must be made at the tourist reception centre at Ramnagar.

There are a number of resthouses in the Sonanadi Wildlife Sanctuary at the western end of the reserve, including those at *Sendhikhal*, *Mondiapani*, *Rathuadhab*, *Haldupara* and *Kanda* (actually just over the boundary in the Corbett National Park). Again, there is no electricity and you'll need to bring your own food. Double rates in all of these are Rs 300, and they must be booked through the reception office at Kotdwar.

Outside the Reserve There are several upmarket resorts strung along the Ramnagar-Ranikhet road, all outside the reserve precincts. All offer discounts of around 50% when the park is closed.

Tiger Tops Corbett Lodge (☎ *85279, Delhi 011-644 4016, fax 85278)*, 7km from Ramnagar, is a very luxurious place with prices to match: singles/doubles are US$170/230 for foreigners, Rs 2500/3500 for Indians. Prices include all meals and two day-visits to the reserve during the season. There are elephant rides, jeep trips, a pool and a wildlife slide show in the evenings. Despite the name, it's not part of the company that operates the famous resort in Chitwan (Nepal).

Claridges Corbett Hideaway (☎ *85959, Delhi 011-301 0211)* has accommodation in attractive ochre cottages set in an orchard of mango trees. Air-con doubles cost from Rs 4000 to Rs 4700, and rates include all meals. Staff can arrange bird-watching and nature-trail excursions, and mountain bikes are available for hire.

The *Quality Inn Corbett Jungle Resort* (☎/*fax 85230)*, in the Kumeria Forest Reserve, has attractive cottages high above the river for Rs 3850, including all meals. This place features its own in-house elephant (named Ramkali), so rides are assured.

Getting There & Away

Buses for Delhi depart Ramnagar approximately every hour, with the first service leaving at 5.30 am and the last at 8 pm (Rs 90, seven hours). Tickets can be booked at the Delhi Transport Corporation office or the main bus stand.

Services for other destinations in Kumaon are booked at the Kumaon Motor Owners' Union (KMOU) office, near the petrol pump on the Ranikhet road, on the opposite side to the reception centre. To Nainital, there are services at 7 am and 1 pm (Rs 24, 3½ hours), though it's probably quicker to get a more frequent bus to Haldwani and change there. The Ranikhet services depart at 7, 9.30 and 11.30 am, and 2 pm (Rs 50, 4½ hours); the 9.30 am bus continues to Almora (Rs 75, 6½ hours).

Ramnagar train station is 1.5km south of the reserve reception centre. The nightly *Ranikhet Express* leaves Ramnagar at 9.45 pm, arriving into Delhi at 4.45 am. For other destinations, change at Moradabad. It's worth making a reservation before you visit the reserve. The Hotel Govinda, near the bus stand, will arrange sleeper tickets for a Rs 20 commission.

Getting Around

There used to be a local bus service from Ramnagar to Dhikala which left at 4 pm (Rs 10, 2½ hours), returning to Ramnagar at 8 am the next day, but at the time of research it had been suspended.

Jeeps can usually only be rented at Ramnagar, and will cost about Rs 500 for a one-way drop to Dhikala, or Rs 1000 for a day safari, plus guide and car charges (see the Permits section earlier). Book through any hotel or deal directly with a driver.

The park reception centre in Ramnagar offers day trips by bus to Dhikala for Rs 1200, and Bijrani for Rs 600, including the entrance fee. This is the only way to visit

Dhikala on a day trip. Local jeep safaris sometimes operate from Dhikala, for around Rs 100 per person.

Safaris on foot are strictly prohibited. The only other mode of transport is the ubiquitous elephant.

NAINITAL
☎ 05942 • pop 35,7000

At 1938m, this attractive hill station was once the summer capital of Uttar Pradesh and is expected to become the future capital of the new state of Uttaranchal. The hotels and villas of this popular resort are set around the peaceful Naini lake or *tal*, hence the name.

Nainital is very much a green and pleasant land that immediately appealed to the homesick Brits, who were reminded of the Cumbrian Lake District. It became popular with the British Raj after a Mr Barron had his yacht carried up here in 1840. The Nainital Boat Club, whose wooden clubhouse still graces the edge of the lake, became the fashionable focus of the community. Disaster struck on 16 September 1880 when a major landslip occurred, burying 151 people and creating the recreation ground now known as the Flats.

This is certainly one of the most pleasant hill stations to visit and there are many interesting walks through the forests to points with superb views of the Himalaya.

The high season (when Nainital is packed and hotel prices double or triple) corresponds to school holidays. Avoid Christmas and the New Year, mid-April to mid-July and mid-September to the end of October.

Orientation

During the season, The Mall is closed to heavy vehicles for most of the day. Cycle-rickshaws take passengers along the 1.5km Mall between Tallital (Lake's Foot), at its southern end, and Mallital (Lake's Head), to the north-west. The bus stand is in Tallital. Hotels and guesthouses are found in Tallital, along the entire length of The Mall and in the Mallital area. Most of the top-end hotels are 10 to 15 minutes' walk to the west of Mallital in the area known as Sukhatal.

Information

There is a post office near the bus stand in Tallital and the main post office is in Mallital. The State Bank of India and Bank of Baroda in Mallital exchange all major travellers cheques. The friendly UP tourist office (☎ 35337) is towards the Mallital end of The Mall.

Bookshops There's a good selection of English-language books at Narains, on The Mall and Consul books in Mallital Bazaar. Narains has a special section on the Kumaon region. Books and magazines can be found at the Modern Book and General Store near the Hotel Alps.

Municipal Library The reading room here, right on the lake shore about halfway along The Mall between Mallital and Tallital, is a good place to escape the frenetic activity on The Mall, particularly in the late afternoon, when reflections from the lake create a lovely rippling effect on the walls and ceiling. Bibliophiles will appreciate the old wooden card files and hundreds of old volumes, and there are current newspapers for visitors' perusal. It's open 7.30 to 10.30 am and 5.30 to 8.30 pm in summer, and 8.30 to 10.30 am and 4 to 7 pm in winter.

Naini Lake

This attractive lake is said to be one of the emerald green eyes of Shiva's wife, Sati (*naina* is Sanskrit for eye). When Sati's father failed to invite Shiva to a family sacrifice, she burnt herself to death in protest. Shiva gathered the charred remains in his arms and proceeded to engage in a cosmic dance, which threatened to destroy the world. To terminate the dance, Vishnu chopped up the body into pieces, and the remains were scattered across India. The modern Naina Devi Temple at the northern end of the lake is built over the precise spot where the eye is believed to have fallen.

Boat operators will take you on a circuit of the lake for Rs 50 in a rowboat or you can hire a small yacht by the hour from the Nainital Boat Club (Rs 60). Alternatively,

NAINITAL

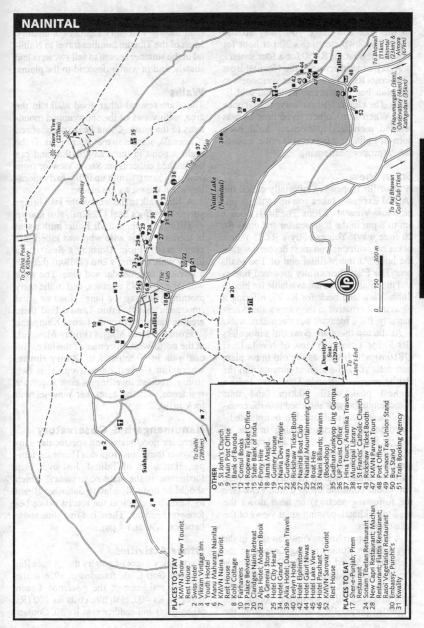

UTTAR PRADESH

PLACES TO STAY
1 KMVN Snow View Tourist Rest House
3 Swiss Hotel
4 Vikram Vintage Inn
5 Youth Hostel
6 Manu Maharani Nainital
7 KMVN Naina Tourist Rest House
8 Kohli Cottage
10 Fairhavens
13 Palace Belvedere
20 Claridges Naini Retreat
23 Alps Hotel; Modern Book & General Store
25 Hotel City Heart
34 Hotel Grand
39 Aika Hotel; Darshan Travels
40 Evelyn Hotel
42 Hotel Elphinstone
44 Hotel Gaj Niwas
46 Hotel Lake View
46 Hotel Prashant
52 KMVN Sarovar Tourist Rest House

PLACES TO EAT
17 Shere-e-Punjab; Prem Restaurant
24 Sonam Tibetan Restaurant
28 New Capri Restaurant; Machan Restaurant; Flattis Restaurant; Rasoi Vegetarian Restaurant
30 Embassy; Purohit's
31 Kwality

OTHER
5 St John's Church
9 Main Post Office
11 Bank of Baroda
12 Consul Books
14 Ropeway Ticket Office
15 State Bank of India
16 Pony Hire
18 Jama Masjid
19 Gurney House
21 Naina Devi Temple
22 Gurdwara
26 Rickshaw Ticket Booth
27 Nainital Boat Club
29 Nainital Mountaineering Club
32 Boat Hire
33 Naini Billiards; Narains (Bookshop)
35 Gadhan Kunkyop Ling Gompa
36 UP Tourist Office
37 Hina Tours; Anamika Travels
38 Municipal Library
41 St Francis' Catholic Church
43 Rickshaw Ticket Booth
47 KMVN Parvat Tours
48 Post Office
49 Kumaon Taxi Union Stand
50 Bus Stand
51 Train Booking Agency

you can join the small flotilla of pedal boats on the lake and make your way around under your own steam (Rs 30 per hour for a two-seat boat, or Rs 50 for a four seater).

A day's membership to the Nainital Boat Club costs Rs 50, which gives you access to the club bar, restaurant, ballroom and library. The club is less exclusive than it once was. When Jim Corbett lived here he was refused membership because he'd been born in India, and hence was not a *pukkah sahib* (proper gentleman).

Snow View

A chair lift (ropeway), officially called the 'Aerial Express', takes you up to the popular Snow View at 2270m. The lift is open 7 am to 8 pm in the high season and costs Rs 20 (one way). You can buy a Rs 35 return ticket but with this you must descend within the hour. At the Mallital end of The Mall, near The Flats, beautifully groomed horses and mountain ponies are available for hire to Snow View and back for Rs 75, offering a pleasant alternative to the steep walk. Alternatively, it's a pleasant but steep 2km walk.

At the top there are powerful binoculars (Rs 5) for a close-up view of Nanda Devi (7816m) which was, as the old brass plate here tells you, 'the highest mountain in the British empire'. Nanda Devi was India's highest peak until Sikkim (and thus Kanchenjunga) was absorbed into the country. There's a small marble temple dedicated to Dev Mundi housing images of Durga, Shiva, Sita, Rama, Lakshmana and Hanuman. From Snow View you can walk west to another viewpoint and then continue on to the main road to Kilbury. From here you could continue up to China Peak (see the following section) or head down the road to Sukhatal, passing great views of the lake en route.

A walk up to Snow View can take in the tiny **Gadhan Kunkyop Ling Gompa** of the Gelukpa order (of which the Dalai Lama is the spiritual leader). Take the road uphill from the Hotel City Heart, from where a path branches off towards the gompa (the colourful prayer flags are visible from the road). The gompa serves Nainital's small (and mostly itinerant) Tibetan community. Most of the Tibetan families travel to Nainital in the summer season to sell sweaters and shawls, and in winter descend to the plains.

Walks

There are several other good walks in the area, with views of the snowcapped mountains to the north. **China Peak** (pronounced 'Cheena'), also known as Naini Peak, is the highest point in the area (2610m) and can be reached either from Snow View or from Mallital (5km). Climb up in the early morning when the views are clearer.

A 4km walk to the west of the lake brings you to **Dorothy's Seat** (2292m), also known as Tiffin Top, where a Mr Kellet built a seat in memory of his wife who was killed in a plane crash. From Dorothy's Seat it's a lovely walk to **Land's End** (2118m) through a forest of oak, deodar and pine. The walk will take about 45 minutes, and in the early morning you may see jungle fowl or goral (mountain goats). From Land's End there are fine views out over the lake at Khurpatal.

From the Jama Masjid (Friday Mosque), at the north-western corner of the lake, you can walk in 30 minutes to **Gurney House**, where Jim Corbett once lived. This two storey wooden dwelling is now a private residence, but the caretaker may let you look inside.

Hanumangarh & Observatory

There are good views and spectacular sunsets over the plains from this Hanuman temple, 3km south of Tallital. Just over 1km further on is the state observatory, which should be open Monday to Saturday 10 am to 5 pm, but check at the tourist office before you head out. There is a free slide show between 1.30 and 4 pm.

Other Activities

If you fancy a spot of **golf** try the 18-hole Raj Bhawan Golf Club, founded in 1926 at the summer residence of the governor. Green fees cost Rs 400, club hire costs Rs 100 (Rs 50 half set) and caddies cost Rs 30. Contact the secretary SL Sah (☎ 36962) to arrange a pass, as the course lies in a military area.

The Nainital Mountaineering Club (☎ 35051), opposite the Hotel City Heart, runs **rock climbing** courses at nearby Bara Pattar for Rs 200 per day and can give advice on treks and expeditions in the area. Mr CL Sah at the club can help arrange guides and porters for around Rs 300 a day, or put you in touch with an English-speaking guide for nature walks in the Nainital area. The club also hires out tents and sleeping bags for around Rs 20 per day (plus Rs 3000 deposit).

At the Mallital end of The Mall is Naini Billiards. It's open daily, and costs Rs 40 per hour. Coaching is available for Rs 80 per hour.

Organised Tours

Almost every travel agency run tours to sights around Nainital and further afield in Kumaon. Agencies include Hina Tours (☎ 35860), Anamika Travels (☎ 35186) and Darshan Travels (☎ 35035, near the Alka Hotel), all on The Mall. Fewer tours run in the low season but these are often discounted. Tours include:

- Corbett Tiger Reserve
  includes park entry fees (Rs 650, day trip)
- Kausani, Almora, Ranikhet
  includes transport food & accommodation
  (Rs 250 to Rs 400, two days)
- Lakes tour
  Bhimtal,Naukuchiyatal, Sat-tal &
  Hanumangarh (Rs 80 to Rs 100, half day)
- Mukteshwar
  (Rs 150 to Rs 175, day trip)
- Ranikhet
  (Rs 150 to Rs 200, day trip)

Taxis are also available from the Kumaon Taxi Union Stand for these same tours. Prices are around Rs 600 for the Lakes tour and Rs 1800 for a two day Kausani itinerary.

Parvat Tours (% 35656), run by KMVN, is at the Tallital end of The Mall. It arranges the standard tours (see earlier) and also a four day tour to Badrinath (Rs 600) and a six day tour to Badrinath and Kedarnath (Rs 800) and a one/two day tour to Jageshwar in

summer only (Rs 150/225). Prices include dorm-itory accommodation, transfers and evening meals.

Parvat can also arrange high and low-altitude trekking for around US$20 per day from Bhageshwar. Luxury bus tickets to Delhi can also be booked here (see Getting There & Away later in this section).

Places to Stay

There are over 100 places to stay, from gloomy budget guesthouses to five-star hotels. During the high season, school holidays and during the festivals of Dussehra and Diwali, finding anywhere to stay can be a major hassle and prices can triple. Prices listed here are for the high season and may appear expensive but, unless otherwise stated, all hotels offer *at least* a 50% discount in the low season.

Places to Stay – Budget

Tallital & The Mall There are several good budget choices at the Tallital end of the lake on the road which runs above and parallel to The Mall at its southern end.

Hotel Lake View (☎ 35532, Ramji Rd), run by the gracious Mr and Mrs Shah, has doubles with attached bath from Rs 300 to Rs 600 in the high season (Rs 100 to Rs 300 in the low season). The more expensive rooms are at the front of the building with views over Tallital, across the lake and to Mallital.

Hotel Gauri Niwas, also on Ramji Rd, has double rooms with geysers and lake views from Rs 400 to Rs 600; gloomy windowless rooms at the back are Rs 250.

Hotel Prashant (☎ 35347) in the same area has doubles ranging from Rs 400 to Rs 700 with attached hot bath. The more expensive rooms have good views but the cheaper rooms are a bit shabby. There's a good dining hall.

Mallital & Sukhatal An excellent choice in the heart of Mallital, *Kohli Cottage (☎ 36368)* has doubles for Rs 300, Rs 400 and Rs 500, with attached bath and 24 hour hot water. Rooms are light, airy and clean and the manager is friendly and helpful. There are lovely views from the roof terrace.

Alps Hotel (☎ 35317) is a rather creaky centenarian, but has enormous doubles with basic attached bath for Rs 200. There's a lovely old broad balcony for watching the promenaders on The Mall.

The *Youth Hostel (☎ 36353)* is set in a peaceful wooded location, about 20 minutes' walk west of Mallital. Beds (with lockers) in the dorms cost Rs 22 for members, Rs 42 for nonmembers. Hot water is available in the mornings. There are also two doubles with common bath for the same rates. Filling vegetarian thalis (Rs 14) are available in the dining hall, and you can inquire about the Pindari Glacier and other treks here.

Places to Stay – Mid-Range & Top End
Tallital & The Mall KMVN *Sarovar Tourist Rest House (☎ 35570)* is close to the bus stand. From 1 April to 15 July, doubles/four-bed rooms are Rs 800/1500, and beds in dorm (with great lake views) are Rs 75. From 15 September to 15 November, rates are Rs 600/1000/60, and during the rest of the year, Rs 400/800/40. Rooms are comfortable, and some have good views.

Hotel Elphinstone (☎ 35534, The Mall) has a wide range of overpriced doubles from Rs 600. All rooms face the lake and have attached bath (bucket hot water). There's a pretty garden terrace.

Evelyn Hotel (☎ 35457) is a large building further north along The Mall. Doubles range from Rs 400 to Rs 900. To get to the cheapest rooms entails a strenuous climb up a seemingly endless series of stairs, but the views over the lake are excellent, and rooms are comfortable. There are several large and sunny roof terraces.

Alka Hotel (☎ 35220), also on The Mall, has overpriced doubles from Rs 1100 to Rs 1500 (Rs 700 to Rs 1000 in the low season). All rooms have running hot and cold water and piped music.

Mallital & Sukhatal Sukhatal has the bulk of the top-end places.

Hotel Grand (☎ 35406), at the Mallital end of The Mall, has singles/doubles for Rs 600/1000, and suites (with separate sitting area) for Rs 1200. There's running hot water in the morning only. The hotel is only open between 15 April and 15 November. There's a lovely wide shady balcony with potted geraniums, from where there are good lake views.

Fairhavens (☎ 36057, fax 36604), near the post office in Mallital, is one of the most stylish places to stay. Room rates are a reasonable Rs 1250, with a 30% low season discount.

Palace Belvedere (☎ 35082, fax 35493) was formerly the palace of the raja of Awagarh. Take the road which leads up behind the Bank of Baroda. Doubles start from Rs 1090, or with a separate sitting area, Rs 1180. Enormous doubles are Rs 1750. Some of the rooms have very good lake views, or you can look out over the lake from the wicker chairs on the shady verandah. There's a 30% low season discount. Credit cards are accepted.

Hotel City Heart (☎ 35228), directly opposite the Nainital Mountaineering Club, just off The Mall, is run by the effervescent Mr Pramod, a bass guitarist in an Indian rock band. Doubles are good value, with prices ranging from Rs 450 to Rs 1400. The cheaper rooms have no views, but are large, comfortable and spotless; the more expensive rooms have superlative views of the lake. There's a good roof terrace.

KMVN *Naina Tourist Rest House (☎ 36374)* is at Sukhatal, 1km from Mallital. Doubles range from Rs 550 to Rs 800 (high season); Rs 415 to Rs 600 (mid-season); and Rs 275 to Rs 400 (low season). Dorm beds cost around Rs 50.

KMVN *Snow View Tourist Rest House,* far from the madding crowd up at Snow View, has rooms for Rs 250/500 in low/high season.

Swiss Hotel (☎ 36013), set in pretty gardens about 10 minutes' walk west of Mallital, has comfortable, airy rooms, some with views over the garden. Doubles are Rs 1200, suites are Rs 1500 and four-bed rooms are

Rs 1800, all 25% less in the low season. Rates include breakfast and dinner. The owner's son can arrange bird and butterfly-spotting excursions around Nainital.

Vikram Vintage Inn (☎ 36177) is in a secluded location about 20 minutes' walk west of Mallital. Singles/doubles are Rs 2000/ 2500, including breakfast. Reception staff can arrange a private consultation with a palmist/numerologist (Rs 200 for 30 minutes).

Claridges Naini Retreat (☎ 35105, fax 35103) is in a quiet spot above Mallital and has luxury doubles for Rs 3250 including breakfast and one other meal.

Manu Maharani Nainital (☎ 36242, fax 37350, Grasmere Estate), about 10 minutes' walk north-west of Mallital, has luxuriously appointed rooms, most with lake views, for Rs 3500 to Rs 4800 (Rs 2500 to Rs 3500 in the low season) and is the best place in town.

Places to Eat

There's a wide range of eating establishments along the length of The Mall, and all of the top-end hotels have their own restaurants (visitors welcome).

Sher-e-Punjab and *Prem Restaurant* are cheap but good dhaba-style places in a small cul-de-sac in Mallital's main bazaar.

Sonam Tibetan Restaurant underneath the Alps Hotel has decent chicken momos (dumplings) and thukpa (noodle soup).

There's a *fresh fruit juice stall* by the rickshaw ticket office in Mallital that also does shakes and lassis.

New Capri Restaurant, at the Mallital end of The Mall, has Indian, Chinese and continental cuisine. It's popular, and often full at lunchtime. Nonveg dishes are around Rs 50.

Rasoi Vegetarian Restaurant, next door, has good thalis and pizza.

Flattis Restaurant, with prices similar to the Capri, is another popular eatery nearby which features mutton and chicken sizzlers.

Machan Restaurant, also nearby, serves excellent pizza (Rs 50) and tagliatelle (Rs 60), as well as Chinese and Indian standards.

Embassy is considered one of the best restaurants by locals. Main dishes are be-

tween Rs 65 and Rs 100. *Purohit's*, next door, serves vegetarian south Indian cuisine. There's alfresco dining with views across the lake, and filling thalis for Rs 32 and Rs 50.

Kwality, also at the Mallital end of The Mall, is set right on the water's edge. It's a bit rowdy at lunchtime, but prices are reasonable, with most veg dishes under Rs 50, nonveg a little more. There is also an ice-cream parlour here.

There are two restaurants at the Manu Maharani Nainital Hotel: the multicuisine *Kumaon*, and the *Lotus Garden*, serving Chinese cuisine. Main dishes in the restaurants cost between Rs 80 and Rs 140, with sweets (chocolate eclairs!) around Rs 40. If you're longing for a continental breakfast, the buffet breakfast (Rs 150) offers croissants, Danish pastries, cereals, scrambled eggs etc. The hotel also boasts Nainital's most stylish bar, the *Viceroy*, where a beer or cocktail costs Rs 100. It closes quite early at 10.45 pm.

Getting There & Away

Air The nearest airport is Pantnagar, 71km south, but it's not currently served by any scheduled flights.

Bus Buses (and shared jeeps) leave from the bus stand at Tallital every 30 minutes for the railhead at Kathgodam (Rs 30, 1½ hours). There's a deluxe (2x2) service to Delhi at 8.30 am (Rs 148, nine hours), a semideluxe (2x2) at 7.30 am (Rs 134) and an ordinary service (3x2) at 6 am and 6.30 pm (Rs 115). Many private agencies book overnight deluxe coach tickets to Delhi (Rs 350 air-con, Rs 250 deluxe) and Haridwar (Rs 250 deluxe).

Buses to Bhimtal leave hourly from 8 am to 6.30 pm (Rs 12, one hour). To Ramnagar, buses leave at 5 and 7 am (Rs 44, 3½ hours). To Almora there are services at 7 and 10 am and noon (Rs 33, three hours). Buses for Ranikhet leave at 8 am, 12.30 and 2.30 pm (Rs 31, 3½ hours). To Kausani there's one service at 7 am (Rs 60, five hours), otherwise change at Bhowali. There's also only one daily service to Pithoragarh at 7 am (Rs 88, nine hours). To Bareilly buses leave at 7.15 am, 1.30 and 2.30 pm (Rs 45, five hours). To Haridwar, ordinary buses depart at 5, 6, 7 and 8 am and 4.30 and 8 pm (Rs 132, eight hours) and there's a deluxe service at 8 pm (Rs 158).

There's only one direct service to Rishikesh, which leaves at 5 am (Rs 130, nine hours). To Dehra Dun, ordinary buses leave at 6 and 7 am and 4.30 pm (Rs 119, 10 hours), and there's a deluxe service at 8 pm (Rs 212).

A daily bus to Song (for the Pindari Glacier trek) leaves Bhowali, 11km from Nainital at the junction of the main routes to Ranikhet and Almora, at 6 am (six hours).

Train Kathgodam (35km south) is the nearest train station, and the train booking agency, near the bus stand, has a quota for trains to Delhi, Lucknow and Calcutta. The *Ranikhet Express* departs Old Delhi station at 11 pm, arriving into Kathgodam at 6.10 am. It departs Kathgodam at 10.45 pm, arriving into Old Delhi station at 4.45 am (Rs 139/567 in 2nd sleeper/2nd air-con class). Prices include the bus fare to Kathgodam. The office is open Monday to Saturday 9 am to noon, and 2 to 5 pm; Sunday 9 am to 2 pm.

Taxi & Jeep Share jeeps leave when full from the bus stand for the bazaar at Bhowali, 11km below Nainital (Rs 15, 30 minutes). Share taxis depart when full for Kathgodam and Haldwani (Rs 30).

Getting Around
The official rate for a rickshaw from Tallital to Mallital is Rs 4; tickets can be purchased at the booths at either end of The Mall.

RANIKHET
☎ 05966
North of Nainital and at an altitude of 1829m, this peaceful hill station offers excellent views of the snowcapped Himalaya, including Nanda Devi (7816m). It's an important army town and the headquarters of the Kumaon Regiment. There are a couple of churches that have been converted into tweed and shawl factories with hand-operated looms.

There are several good walks – to the **Jhula Devi Temple** (1km south of West View Hotel) and the orchards at **Chaubatia** (3km further on). The Kalika golf course, 4km away at **Upat**, has a 300km panoramic view of the Himalaya.

The tourist office (☎ 2227) is by the UP Roadways bus stand.

Places to Stay & Eat
There are several hotels in Sadar Bazaar between the bus stands. *Hotel Raj Deep* (☎ 2447) is the best of the cheap places, with a wide range of clean rooms from Rs 75 to Rs 250, and a communal sitting area.

Everest Hotel, nearby, has tatty but good-value rooms with squat toilets for Rs 85/100.

Tribhuvan Hotel (☎ 2524) has a range of rooms from Rs 200 to Rs 1000, most with

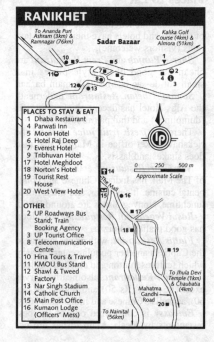

RANIKHET

To Ananda Puri Ashram (3km) & Ramnagar (76km)

Sadar Bazaar

Kalika Golf Course (4km) & Almora (51km)

PLACES TO STAY & EAT
1 Dhaba Restaurant
4 Parwati Inn
5 Moon Hotel
6 Hotel Raj Deep
7 Everest Hotel
9 Tribhuvan Hotel
17 Hotel Meghdoot
18 Norton's Hotel
19 Tourist Rest House
20 West View Hotel

OTHER
2 UP Roadways Bus Stand; Train Booking Agency
3 UP Tourist Office
8 Telecommunications Centre
10 Hina Tours & Travel
11 KMOU Bus Stand
12 Shawl & Tweed Factory
13 Nar Singh Stadium
14 Catholic Church
15 Main Post Office
16 Kumaon Lodge (Officers' Mess)

0   250   500 m
Approximate Scale

The Mall

To Jhula Devi Temple (1km) & Chaubatia (4km)

Mahatma Gandhi Road

To Nainital (56km)

nice balconies, but the bathrooms are pretty basic for the money and hot water only comes in buckets.

Moon Hotel has overpriced rooms from Rs 550 but the restaurant is quite good (main dishes cost around Rs 50).

Parwati Inn, once quite impressive, has rapidly deteriorated and, at Rs 350 for the cheapest rooms, is also overpriced.

The other places to stay are on The Mall, about 4km from Sadar Bazaar in a peaceful wooded location.

Hotel Meghdoot (☎ 2475) charges from Rs 200/300 for clean, carpeted singles/doubles with hot water, and has a good restaurant.

Nearby, *Norton's Hotel* (☎ 2377) is a Raj leftover with doubles for Rs 350 and Rs 400 (less in the low season) and dorm beds for Rs 65. There's a nice common sitting area and a good restaurant.

The quiet KMVN *Tourist Rest House* (☎ 2893) is a good place with rooms at Rs 550 and Rs 800 (50% less in low season), and dorm beds at Rs 60.

West View Hotel (☎ 2261) is another former Raj establishment. Large rooms with fireplaces start at Rs 1100. There's afternoon tea, and croquet on the lawn.

The dhaba-style *restaurant* next to the bus station serves up cheap and tasty Indian food.

Getting There & Away

Buses depart from both the UP Roadways and KMOU bus stands. There are several buses a day to:

Kathgodam	Rs 40	4 hours
Nainital	Rs 29	3 hours
Almora	Rs 27	3 hours
Kausani	Rs 31	4 hours
Ramnagar	Rs 47	4 hours
Delhi	Rs 165	12 hours
Haridwar	Rs 112-143	9 hours

Hina Tours and Travel operate deluxe overnight buses to Delhi (Rs 180), Haridwar (Rs 250) and, in season, daytime buses to Badrinath (Rs 250).

As with the other hill stations in the Kumaon region, Kathgodam is the nearest railhead. The train booking office has a tiny quota of tickets to Delhi.

ALMORA
☎ 05962 • pop 53,507

This picturesque hill station, at an altitude of 1650m, is one of the few not created by the British. Some 400 years ago it was the capital of the Chand rajas of Kumaon.

Almora is larger than Ranikhet and Kausani, and has good views of the mountains and some great walks. The 8km walk up to the **Kasar Devi Temple** is recommended – this is where Swami Vivekananda came to meditate. The area has the reputation of being something of a spiritual 'power centre' and some travellers rent houses and stay for months.

Attractions for tourists include the interesting **Lalal Bazaar**, with its coppersmiths, the **Nanda Devi Temple**, and the small **Pt GB Pant Museum**, with displays on local archaeology and ethnography. Several woollen mills have showrooms along The Mall.

Good views of the Himalaya (especially at sunset) can be had from a hilltop known as **Bright End Corner**, 2.5km south-west of the town centre.

Near the Hotel Savoy you'll find the UP tourist office (☎ 30180). The State Bank of India will change American Express travellers cheques only. High Adventure (☎ 32277) and Discover Himalaya (☎ 31470) can organise treks in the area.

Places to Stay & Eat

The huge *Hotel Shikhar* (☎ 30253) is the best, with a wide range of good rooms from Rs 150/245 with common/attached hot bath.

Just before the Hotel Shikhar, stairs lead down to the *Swagat Restaurant*. There's an extensive vegetarian menu, which features the sweet milk-based *rabri faluda*.

The *Madras Cafe*, just off The Mall near the Hotel Shikhar, is a no-frills, reasonably priced vegetarian restaurant with main dishes under Rs 25.

New Glory Restaurant, opposite, is recommended for vegetarian food. The popular Sikh-run *Soni Restaurant* is also good.

UTTAR PRADESH

ALMORA

PLACES TO STAY
4 Hotel Shikhar
13 Hotel Konark
15 Hotel Himsagar
19 Kailas Hotel
22 Hotel Surmool;
   Sunrise Restaurant
25 Hotel Savoy
26 KMVN Rest House

PLACES TO EAT
1 Madras Cafe
3 New Glory Restaurant
5 Swagat Restaurant;
   News Stand
8 Bansal Express
9 Soni Restaurant

OTHER
2 Nanda Devi Temple
6 Taxi Stand; Panchachauli
   Woolens
8 Dharanaula Bus Stand
10 Pt GB Pant Museum
11 State Bank of India
12 UP Roadways Bus Stand
14 Clock Tower
16 Kumaon Woolens
17 Gandhi Statue

18 High Adventure;
   Almora Book Depot
20 Discover Himalaya
21 Post Office; Central
   Telegraph Office
23 District Forestry Office
24 UP Tourist Office
27 Himalaya Woollen Mills

0   250   500 m

To Kasar Devi Temple (8km),
Katarmal (14km), Binsar (34km),
Jageshwar (34km)

The Mall

To Jageshwar
(34km) &
Pithoragarh
(122km)

Lalal
Bazaar

To Bright End
Corner (2.5km) &
Nainital (67km)

Upper Mall
Road

The extraordinary *Kailas Hotel* is certainly unique, and most travellers seem to enjoy the eccentricities of the guesthouse itself and its elderly proprietors, Mr and Mrs Shah. Mrs Shah's cooking is good (try the Kumaoni thali for Rs 35) and her herbal teas excellent. There are rooms from Rs 75/125 in summer, and dorm beds for Rs 40.

The peaceful *Hotel Savoy (☎ 30329, Upper Mall Rd)* is in the same area, with decent rooms from Rs 200, Rs 400 and Rs 500, all with attached bath. Prices are 25% less in the low season.

Hotel Surmool (☎ 22860), opposite the main post office, has good-value rooms with attached bath and geyser for Rs 400 (Rs 250 in low season); dorm beds are Rs 50. The *Sunrise Restaurant* here is also good value.

Hotel Konark (☎ 31217), on The Mall near the State Bank of India, has singles for Rs 150 or Rs 200 and doubles from Rs 150

to Rs 250. All rooms have attached bath. Staff are very friendly, and the rooms are spotless.

Hotel Himsagar (☎ 30711) is a good mid-range hotel with rooms from Rs 400 to Rs 600. The restaurant here is inexpensive and recommended.

If you are exploring the Lalal Bazaar, you could take a break (and a cappuccino, cold coffee or lassi) at the *Bansal Express*, just down one of the side streets.

Getting There & Away

Buses to the following destinations leave the UP Roadways bus stand on the Mall:

Delhi	Rs 138 (ordinary)	12 hours
Delhi	Rs 172 (semideluxe)	12 hours
Nainital	Rs 31	3 hours
Kausani	Rs 25	2 hours
Ranikhet	Rs 26	2 hours
Pithoragarh	Rs 62	5 hours
Song	Rs 52	5 hours
Banbassa	Rs 75	7 hours

Buses to Pithoragarh also depart from and arrive at the Dharanaula bus stand on the east side of Lalal Bazaar.

AROUND ALMORA
Katarmal & Jageshwar

There are a number of ancient temple sites in the area. At Katarmal (12km to Kosi and then a 2km walk west) is the 800-year-old Surya (Sun) Temple. A much larger group, dating back to the 7th century AD, is 34km away at Jageshwar in an attractive valley of deodars. There's a KMVN *Tourist Rest House* with rooms for Rs 250 and Rs 400 and dorms for Rs 50, and you can take a nice walk to old Jageshwar, 4km away. To get to Jageshwar take a Pithoragarh-bound bus to Artola and walk (or hitch) 3km north.

KAUSANI
☎ 059628

For an even closer view of the Himalaya, Kausani, 51km north of Almora, is the place to head for. There are fantastic views of Trisul (7120m), shaped like a trident, the twin peaks of Nanda Devi (7816m) and the

Panchchuli, or Five Chimneys (6904m) to the east. Gandhi stayed at the Anasakti Ashram in 1929 and was inspired by the superb Himalayan panorama.

Places to Stay & Eat

Uttarakhand Tourist Lodge (☎ 84112), at the top of the stairs leading up from the bus stand, has basic doubles with attached bath for Rs 100 (ground floor) or Rs 150 (1st floor). Good discounts are offered in the low season and all rooms face the snows.

Hotel Prashant, on Ashram Rd, five minutes' walk uphill from the centre, has a range of budget rooms from Rs 100 to Rs 300. Cheaper rooms may be gloomy, but this is a popular place, and a 50% discount applies in low season.

Anasakti Ashram has accommodation by donation. It has a good library that is open to all, and an indicator on the terrace that's useful for mountain identification.

The upmarket *Krishna Mount View* (☎ 45080), nearby, has comfortable doubles with Star TV and running hot water for Rs 850 to Rs 1500. All rooms face the snows and there's a good low-season discount. Its *Vaibhav Restaurant* features Mughlai and Gujarati cuisine. Main nonveg dishes are between Rs 60 and Rs 100, and there's a good range of sweets, including *sooji halwa*, a wheat and sugar-based dessert (Rs 30).

KMVN *Tourist Rest House* (☎ 45006) is a couple of kilometres beyond the village. It's very good value and has doubles from Rs 300 to Rs 800 with great views, balconies and hot water. There are dorm beds for Rs 60, and good low-season discounts.

Amar Holiday Home (☎ 45015, Ashram Rd) has rooms set in a beautiful garden and friendly owners. Unfortunately, recent construction work has killed many of the views. Doubles with attached bath (bucket hot water) are Rs 350, Rs 450 and Rs 650; singles are Rs 200 (50% less in the low season). There are several other mid-range places next door.

Halfway to the Prashant and Amar Holiday Home, the *Hill Queen* and *Sunrise* restaurants are popular places to eat.

Getting There & Away

Buses to Almora pass through town approximately every hour between 7 am and 3 pm (Rs 30, 2½ hours), continuing to Nainital (Rs 60, six hours). There are a couple of services to Ranikhet between 7 am and 2 pm (Rs 31, four hours).

For Karanprayag and destinations in the Garhwal, there's one direct bus at 7 am (Rs 53, three hours) or change at Gwaldam.

AROUND KAUSANI

The 12th century temples at **Baijnath**, 19km north of Kausani, are worth a trip. Buses leave every hour or so, or you can hike the 13km through the forest from Kausani. Don't follow the road, as it's 6km longer. Kausani's only taxi will charge around Rs 250 one way to Baijnath (Rs 400 return).

From Baijnath you could also visit the pilgrimage town of **Bhageshwar**, 41km from Kausani. The town has the large Baghnath Temple and smaller Baneshwar Mahadev Temple as well as some nice ghats and bazaar backstreets. There are several decent places to stay in Bhageshwar but it's easier to make a day trip. Buses leave every hour or so from Kausani for the 1½ hour trip or you can take a passenger jeep to Garur and another on to Bhageshwar. There are buses from Bhageshwar to Almora, Pithoragarh, Nainital, Ranikhet and Munsyari.

PITHORAGARH

☎ 05964 • pop 42,113

Situated at 1815m, Pithoragarh is the main town of a region that borders both Tibet and Nepal. It sits in a small valley that has been called 'Little Kashmir' and there are a number of picturesque walks in the area. You can climb up to **Chandak** (7km) for views of the Pithoragarh Valley and the Panchchuli (Five Chimneys) massif.

There's a tourist office (☎ 22527) and a KMVN *Tourist Lodge* here, with doubles for Rs 300 and dorm beds for Rs 50. There are several other hotels, including the *Uttranchal Deep* and *Samrat*. There are buses to Almora, Nainital, Haldwani, Delhi and Tanakpur (the railhead, 151km south).

BANBASSA

Banbassa is the closest Indian village to the Nepalese border post of Mahendrenagar, and it's possible to enter Nepal at this point. There are daily buses from Delhi (12 hours) and Banbassa is also connected by train to Bareilly. From Almora, a daily bus leaves at 7.30 am (Rs 75, seven hours).

From Banbassa, you can catch a rickshaw (20 minutes) to the border and across to Mahendrenagar. There are direct night buses from Mahendrenagar to Kathmandu, but they take a gruelling 25 hours. The countryside is beautiful and fascinating, so it's much better to travel during the day and to break the journey at Nepalganj. If you can't get a direct bus for the nine hour trip from Mahendrenagar to Nepalganj, take a bus to Ataria (at the junction for Dhangadhi) and from there to Nepalganj. There are plenty of buses from Nepalganj to Kathmandu (day and night journeys, 16 hours) and to Pokhara (night, 15 hours). Roads can sometimes be flooded in summer.

Central Uttar Pradesh

ALIGARH
• pop 562,330

Formerly known as Koil, this was the site of an important fort as far back as 1194. During the collapse of the Mughal empire, the region was fought for by the Afghans, Jats, Marathas and Rohillas – first one coming out on top, then another. Renamed Aligarh (High Fort) in 1776, it fell to the British in 1803 despite French support for its ruler Scindia. The **fort** is 3km north of the town, and in its present form dates from 1524.

Aligarh is best known today for the **Aligarh Muslim University** where the 'seeds of Pakistan were sown'. Muslim students from all over the Islamic world come here to study.

ETAWAH

This town rose to importance during the Mughal period, only to go through the usual series of rapid changes during the turmoil that followed the Mughals' decline. The Jama Masjid shows many similarities to the mosques of Jaunpur, and there are **bathing ghats** on the riverbank below the ruined fort.

KANNAUJ

Only a few dismal ruins indicate that this was the mighty Hindu capital of the region in the 7th century AD. It quickly fell into disrepair after Mahmud of Ghazni's raids. This was where Humayun was defeated by Sher Shar in 1540, and forced to temporarily flee India. There's not much to see now – just an archaeological museum, a mosque and the ruins of the fort.

KANPUR
☎ 0512 • pop 2,470,000

Although Lucknow is the capital of Uttar Pradesh, Kanpur is the state's largest city. It's a major industrial centre which attracts few tourists and has the unfortunate distinction of being one of the most polluted cities in the world.

Some of the most tragic events of the 1857 Uprising took place here when the city was known as Cawnpore. General Sir Hugh Wheeler defended a part of the cantonment for almost a month but, with supplies virtually exhausted, he surrendered to Nana Sahib, only to be massacred with most of his party at Sati Chaura Ghat. Over 100 women and children were taken hostage and imprisoned in a small room. Just before relief arrived, they were murdered and their dismembered bodies thrown down a well.

General Neill, their avenger, behaved just as sadistically. Some of the mutineers he captured were made to drink the English blood that still lay in a deep pool in the murder chamber. Before being executed, Hindus were force-fed beef and told they would be buried; Muslims got pork and the promise of cremation.

Things to See

There's not much to see in Kanpur, though you can visit the site of **General Wheeler's entrenchment**, just over 1km from Kanpur Central train station. Nearby is **All Souls' Memorial Church**, which has poignant reminders of the tragedy of the Uprising. There's a large zoo at Allen Park, a few kilometres north-west of The Mall.

The main shopping centre, **Navin Market**, is famous for its locally produced cotton goods. Kanpur is a good place to find cheap leather shoes and bags.

Places to Stay & Eat

Kanpur has a string of overpriced hotels along The Mall, which is where you'll probably have to stay since the city's budget hotels, located around the train station, do not accept non-Indians. It is a Rs 8 cycle-rickshaw ride from Kanpur Central train station to The Mall. All the hotels listed here provide room service.

The *retiring rooms* at Kanpur Central train station are a useful option in the circumstances and have certainly improved since travel writers Eric and Wanda Newby spent a sleepless night here on their way down the Ganges in 1963. Dorm beds cost Rs 100, doubles Rs 250 and air-con doubles Rs 400 for 24 hours. Rates are roughly two-thirds this if you stay less than 12 hours.

Meera Inn (☎ 319972, 37/19 The Mall) has good air-cooled singles/doubles with attached bath and hot water from Rs 450/550.

The Attic (☎ 311691, 15/198 Vikramajit Singh Rd), just north of The Mall, is a Raj-era bungalow in a pleasant garden with a good restaurant. Air-con rooms cost Rs 500/600 which, for Kanpur, is good value. Both places add a 10% 'amenities' charge.

Hotel Meghdoot (☎ 311999, fax 310209, The Mall), 100m from Meera Inn, has air-con singles/doubles from Rs 1200/1800. It has two expensive restaurants, a bar, and a rooftop swimming pool, but is rather run-down nowadays.

Getting There & Away

Kanpur has plenty of connections to Delhi (Rs 99/490 in 2nd/1st class, around six hours) and Calcutta (Rs 262/885 in sleeper/1st class, 16 to 25 hours). There are also trains to Mumbai (Rs 302/1102, around 24 hours), Allahabad (Rs 53/259 2nd/1st class, three hours), Varanasi (Rs 79/388, seven

hours), Agra (Rs 66/322, five hours) and Lucknow (Rs 28/149, 1½ hours).

The Chunniganj bus stand, 3km west of The Mall, services destinations to the west. The Collectorganj bus stand, 300m from the train station (exit from the side opposite the retiring rooms), covers points east, and has plenty of buses to Lucknow (Rs 28, two hours).

JHANSI

Jhansi is a major transport hub for the north of Madhya Pradesh and is the most popular transit point for Khajuraho. Though it's actually in Uttar Pradesh, it's included in the Madhya Pradesh chapter of this book (see that chapter for details).

LUCKNOW

☎ 0522 • pop 1,917,000

The capital of Uttar Pradesh rose to prominence as the centre of the nawabs of Avadh. These decadent Muslim rulers, also known as the nawabs of Oudh, controlled a region of north-central India for about a century after the decline of the Mughal empire. Most of the interesting monuments in Lucknow date from this period. The nawabs were:

Burhan-ul-mulk	1724-1739
Safdar Jang	1739-1753
Shuja-ud-Daula	1753-1775
Asaf-ud-Daula	1775-1797
Sa'adat Ali Khan	1798-1814
Ghazi-ud-din Haidar	1814-1827
Nasir-ud-din Haidar	1827-1837
Mohammad Ali Shah	1837-1842
Amjad Ali Shah	1842-1847
Wajid Ali Shah	1847-1856

The capital of Avadh was moved from Faizabad to Lucknow during the reign of Asaf-ud-Daula. After Sa'adat Ali Khan, the rest of the Avadh nawabs were uniformly hopeless at running affairs of state. Wajid Ali Shah was so extravagant and indolent that to this day his name is regarded by many in India as synonymous with lavishness. However, the nawabs were great patrons of the arts, especially dance and music, and Lucknow's reputation as a city of culture and gracious living stems from this time.

In 1856 the British annexed Avadh, exiling the incompetent Wajid Ali Shah to a palace in Calcutta with an annual pension of UK£120,000. The annexation was one of the sparks that ignited the Indian Uprising in 1857. Lucknow became the scene for some of the most dramatic events of the Uprising. The British residents of the city held out in the Residency for 87 harrowing days, only to be besieged again for a further two months after being relieved.

Despite its rich cultural associations, Lucknow is not a particularly attractive city and it suffers from high levels of pollution. However, the huge crumbling mausoleums of the nawabs and the pock-marked ruins of the Residency make it an interesting place to visit. Lucknow has recently become popular with western followers of the octogenarian guru, Poonjaji, who died in 1997. If you're interested in visiting his nearby ashram, inquire at the Carlton Hotel.

Orientation

Lucknow is very spread out. The historic monuments are mainly in the north-western part of the old city, near the Gomti River. The narrow alleys of Aminabad are the main shopping area. Hazratganj is the modern, fashionable district where you'll find most of the budget and mid-range hotels.

Information

Tourist information is available at the Hotel Gomti from UP Tours (☎ 212659), a branch of UP Tourism.

The regional tourist office (☎ 226205) is hidden down an alley off Station Rd. It's open Monday to Saturday, 10 am to 5 pm, but it's pretty hopeless. There's a useful information booth at Charbagh train station, open 7 am to 6 pm daily. All the offices sell maps of the city for Rs 2.

The State Bank of India on Ashok Marg is a convenient place to change money in Hazratganj. There's a British Council library (☎ 222144) in Hazratganj, open 10.30 am to 6.30 pm Tuesday to Saturday. Next door on one side is Mayfair Travels, the American Express Travel Service representative; on the other side is Ram Advani, an excellent bookshop. Round the corner is Fast Business Centre (FBC), where you can send and receive email for Rs 40.

Bara Imambara

The Bara or Great Imambara (an *imambara* is the tomb of a Shi'ite Muslim holy man) was built in 1784 by Asaf-ud-Daula as a famine relief project. The central hall of the Imambara, at 50m long and 15m high, is one of the largest vaulted galleries in the world. An external stairway leads to an upper floor laid out as an amazing labyrinth known as the **bhulbhulaiya**; a guide may be useful since the dark passages stop abruptly at openings which drop straight to the courtyard below. Guides claim that tunnels extend as far as Jaipur, Delhi and Mumbai! The labyrinth entry fee of Rs 10 includes entry to a picture gallery.

There's a mosque with two tall minarets in the courtyard complex but non-Muslims are not allowed in. To the right of this is a 'bottomless' well. The Imambara complex is open from sunrise to sunset.

Beside the Bara Imambara, and also built by Asaf-ud-Daula, is the imposing **Rumi Darwaza**, a replica of an entrance gate built in Istanbul. 'Rumi' (relating to Rome) is the term Muslims applied to Istanbul when it was still Byzantium, the capital of the eastern Roman empire.

Lakshman Tila, the high ground on the southern bank of the Gomti River nearby, was the original site of the town which became known as Lucknau in the 15th century. Aurangzeb's mosque now stands on this site.

Hussainabad Imambara

Also known as the Chhota, or Small Imambara, this was built by Mohammed Ali Shah in 1837 as his own mausoleum. Thousands of labourers worked on the project to gain famine relief. The large courtyard encloses a raised rectangular tank with small imitations of the Taj Mahal on each side.

LUCKNOW

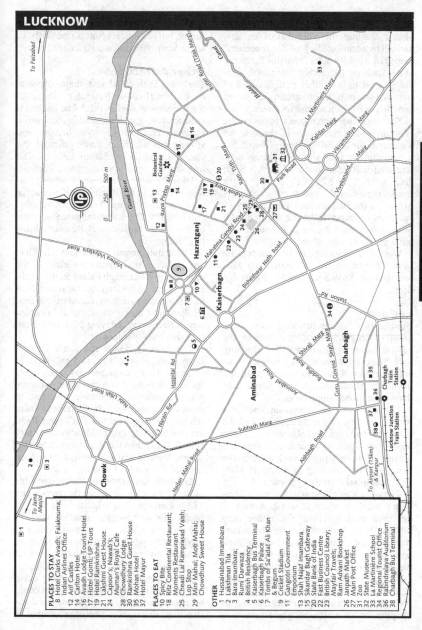

UTTAR PRADESH

PLACES TO STAY
8 Hotel Clarks Avadh; Falaknuma;
    Indian Airlines Office
12 Arif Castles
14 Carlton Hotel
16 Avadh Lodge Tourist Hotel
17 Hotel Gomti; UP Tours
19 Hotel Ramkrishna
21 Lakshmi Guest House
24 Capoor's; Nawab's;
    Muman's Royal Cafe
28 Chowdhury Lodge
30 Ramkrishna Guest House
35 Mohan Hotel
37 Hotel Mayur

PLACES TO EAT
10 Spicy Bite
18 Ritz Continental Restaurant;
    Moments Restaurant
25 Cheadi Lal Ramprasad Vaish;
    Lalla Stop
29 Mini Mahal; Moti Mahal;
    Chowdhury Sweet House

OTHER
1 Hussainabad Imambara
2 Lakshman Tila
3 Bara Imambara;
    Rumi Darwaza
4 British Residency
5 Kaiserbagh Bus Terminal
6 Kaiserbagh Palace
7 Tombs of Sa'adat Ali Khan
    & Begum
11 Cricket Stadium
13 Gangotri Government
    Emporium
14 Shah Najaf Imambara
15 Sikandar Bagh Gateway
20 State Bank of India
22 Fast Business Centre
23 British Council Library;
    Mayfair Travels;
    Ram Advani Bookshop
26 Janpath Market
27 Main Post Office
31 Zoo
32 State Museum
33 La Martinière School
34 Regional Tourist Office
36 Rabindralaya Auditorium
38 Charbagh Bus Terminal

One of them is the tomb of Mohammed Ali Shah's daughter, the other that of her husband. The main building of the imambara, topped by a golden dome, contains the tombs of Ali Shah and his mother. The nawab's silver-covered throne, other paraphernalia of state and lots of tacky chandeliers are stored here. It's open from sunrise to sunset.

The decaying **watchtower** opposite the Hussainabad Imambara is known as Satkhanda, or the Seven Storey Tower, but it actually has four storeys because construction was abandoned when Ali Shah died in 1840. A 67m-high defunct **clock tower**, reputedly the tallest in the country, overlooks the Hussainabad Tank nearby. A *baradari* or **summer house**, built by Ali Shah, fronts onto the tank. It houses portraits of the nawabs of Avadh.

West of the Hussainabad Imambara is the **Jama Masjid** which was started by Mohammed Ali Shah and completed after his death.

Residency

Built in 1800 for the British Resident, this group of buildings became the stage for the most dramatic events of the 1857 Uprising – the Siege of Lucknow. The red-brick ruins are peaceful nowadays, surrounded by lawns and flowerbeds, but thousands died during the months-long siege.

The Residency has been maintained as it was at the time of the final relief, and the shattered walls are still scarred by cannon shot. Even since Independence, little has changed. The only major work done on the place was the unveiling of an **Indian Martyrs' Memorial** directly opposite.

There's a **model room** in the main Residency building which is worth visiting to get your bearings from the rather tatty model. Downstairs you can see the cellars where many of the women and children lived throughout the siege. The **cemetery** at the nearby ruined church has the graves of 2000 men, women and children, including that of Sir Henry Lawrence, 'who tried to do his duty' according to the famous inscription on his weathered gravestone.

The Residency is open from sunrise to sunset, but the model room is open only 10 am to 5 pm. Admission is Rs 2 (free Friday).

Other Attractions

The plain **Shah Najaf Imambara**, opposite the Carlton Hotel, is the tomb of Ghazi-ud-din Haidar who died in 1827. The interior is used to store garish chandeliers and *tazia*, elaborate creations of wood, bamboo and silver paper which are carried through the streets during the Muharram Festival. The imambara is open from sunrise to sunset.

Sikandar Bagh, the scene of pitched battles in 1857, is a partially fortified garden with a modest gateway bearing the nawabs' fish emblem. The **botanical gardens**, home of the National Botanical Research Institute, are nearby.

The stately **tombs** of Sa'adat Ali Khan and his wife (the begum) are close to the remnants of **Kaiserbagh Palace** on the southeastern edge of the large double roundabout near the cricket stadium. Cannons mounted on the tombs during the siege of Lucknow were effective in delaying Havelock from relieving the Residency.

The dusty Lucknow **zoo** in the Banarsi Bagh (Park) is open 8 am to 5 pm (6 pm in summer) daily except Monday; entry costs Rs 5. Within the zoo is the **state museum**, which contains an impressive collection of stone sculptures, especially from the Mathura school (1st to 6th centuries). It's open 10.30 am to 4 pm daily except Monday, and entry is Rs 2. Don't miss the British-era statues (of Queen Victoria and others) that have been dumped in a garden round the back.

La Martinière School on the eastern edge of the city was designed by the Frenchman Major-General Claude Martin as a palatial home. His architectural abilities were, to say the least, a little confused – Gothic gargoyles were piled merrily atop Corinthian columns to produce a finished product which a British marquess sarcastically pronounced was inspired by a wedding cake. Martin died in 1800 before his home could be completed, but left the money and instructions that it should become a school. It

The Siege of Lucknow

The Uprising of 1857 is known to some as the 1857 Mutiny and to others as the First War of Independence, or the First Freedom Struggle.

Upon the outbreak of the Uprising the British inhabitants of the city all took refuge with Sir Henry Lawrence in the Residency. In total there were 2994 people crammed into the Residency's grounds: 740 British soldiers, 700 pro-British Indian troops, 130 British and Indian officers, 150 European volunteers, 27 non-combatant European men, 237 women, 260 children, 50 La Martinière schoolboys and 700 Indian servants. The Residency was technically indefensible, but those seeking shelter expected relief to arrive in a matter of days.

In fact it was 87 days before a small force under Sir Henry Havelock broke through the besiegers to the remaining half-starved defenders. But once Havelock and his troops were within the Residency, the siege immediately recommenced. It continued unabated from 25 September to 17 November, when relief finally arrived with Sir Colin Campbell. Only 980 of the original inhabitants survived the ordeal. Many who did not die from bullet wounds succumbed to cholera, typhoid or smallpox.

The published accounts of the siege of Lucknow combine tales of derring-do with traces of domestic comedy wrung from the British contingent's struggle to maintain a stiff upper lip in the face of adversity.

Several accounts were written by women, some of whom at first seemed more troubled by the shortage of good domestic help than by being surrounded by tens of thousands of bloodthirsty mutineers. This changed during the drawn-out months of the siege, by the end of which they were said to be able to judge the weight of shot being fired into the compound better than the men.

In *The Siege of Lucknow*, Julia Inglis (whose husband took command on the death of Sir Henry Lawrence) flatly records the day-to-day horrors of life in the Residency:

July 1st – Poor Miss Palmer had her leg taken off by a round shot to-day, she, with some other
ladies, having remained in the second storey of the Residency house, though warned it was
not safe...
July 4th – Poor Sir Henry (Lawrence) died to-day, after suffering fearful pain...
July 8th – Mr Polehampton, one of our chaplains, was shot through the body to-day whilst shaving...
October 1st – I was with Mrs Couper nearly all day, watching her baby dying...

duly became one of India's premier private schools (the school in Rudyard Kipling's story *Kim* is modelled on La Martinière). The school can be visited with permission from the principal (☎ 223863).

Organised Tours

UP Tours (☎ 212659) runs worthwhile half-day sightseeing tours of Lucknow (Rs 50, reserve ahead). Tours pick up people from the train station (8.30 am) and various hotels, including the Hotel Gomti (9.45 am).

Special Events

The spirit of the nawabs returns during the **Lucknow Mahotsava** between late November and early December. During the 10 day festival of nostalgia there are processions, plays, *kathak* dancing (an energetic style of traditional dancing, performed in striking costumes), *ghazal* and sitar recitals, kite flying and tonga races.

Lucknow is a good place to see the **Shi'ite Muharram** celebrations (dates vary from year to year) as it has been the principal

Indian Shi'ite city since the nawabs arrived. The activity during Muharram, which centres on the Bara Imambara, can get intense as penitents scourge themselves with whips; keep a low profile.

Places to Stay – Budget

There are plenty of hotels in Lucknow but good budget accommodation is in fairly short supply. Most travellers head for the Hazratganj area. Rooms mentioned here have attached bath.

Chowdhury Lodge (☎ 221911), down an alley opposite the main post office, has singles/doubles, some without windows, from Rs 125/170 and air-cooled rooms for Rs 250. Rates include bed tea which is provided at a distressingly early hour. The lodge has 24 hour checkout and charges extra for sheets, blankets and buckets of hot water.

Hotel Ramkrishna (☎ 280380, Ashok Marg) is a standard Indian hotel with clean air-cooled singles/doubles/triples with hot water for Rs 180/230/350, and air-con rooms for Rs 620. It also has a restaurant. Checkout is 24 hours.

Ramkrishna Guest House (☎ 272472, 4A Park Rd) has fairly good air-cooled doubles from Rs 200 and air-con doubles with TV for Rs 550.

Avadh Lodge Tourist Hotel (☎ 282861, 1 Ram Mohan Rai Marg), near Sikandar Bagh, is a tatty, atmospheric place with the feel of a fusty old natural history museum. Large quantities of the local fauna, including the now-rare gharial (fish-eating crocodile), decorate the walls. Varied singles/doubles/triples with hot water cost Rs 200/300/375; air-con is Rs 180 extra.

Lakshmi Guest House (☎ 228661, 5 Shahnajaf Rd) is a new place with decent rooms with hot water and TV for Rs 350/450, or Rs 450/550 with air-cooling and Rs 550/650 with air-con.

There are a few options in the noisy area near the train stations. The best option is *Hotel Mayur* (☎ 451824, Subhash Marg), which has rooms with bucket hot water for Rs 175/200, or Rs 300 with TV and hot-water geyser.

The train station *retiring rooms* offer dorm beds (Rs 30), doubles (Rs 250) and air-con rooms (Rs 450) for a 24 hour period.

Mohan Hotel (☎ 454216, Buddha Rd) is fine but generally overpriced. Dorm beds are Rs 100 and rooms start from Rs 300/400. Checkout is 24 hours.

Places to Stay – Mid-Range & Top End

Carlton Hotel (☎ 224021, fax 229793) was once a palace and is still an impressive building with a musty air of decaying elegance. Large rooms with character cost Rs 500/600, or Rs 800/1100 with air-con and TV. Extensive gardens make it a relaxing place to stay.

Capoor's (☎ 223958, Mahatma Gandhi (MG) Rd) is a long-established hotel in the heart of Hazratganj, but it's only so-so value and beds are rather hard. Most rooms are air-con (Rs 700), though there are a few tatty air-cooled rooms for Rs 400.

Hotel Gomti (☎ 220624, 6 Sapru Marg) is a UP Tourism operation with overpriced but good air-cooled rooms with TV for Rs 500/600 and air-con rooms for Rs 1050/1150. The hotel has a restaurant, coffee shop and a popular bar.

Arif Castles (☎ 211313, fax 211360, 4 Rana Pratap Marg) is a modern hotel with small but pleasant rooms from Rs 850/950.

Hotel Clarks Avadh (☎ 216500, fax 216507, 8 MG Rd) has rooms with good views and the expected luxury fittings from Rs 2200/2500. There's a restaurant, coffee shop and bar, but no pool.

Places to Eat

The refined palates of the nawabs have left Lucknow with a reputation for rich Mughlai cuisine. The city is famous for its wide range of kebabs and for *dum pukht* – the 'art' of steam pressure cooking, in which meat and vegetables are cooked in a sealed clay pot. Huge paper-thin chapatis *(rumali roti)* are served in many small Muslim restaurants in the old city. They arrive folded up and should be eaten with a goat or lamb curry like *bhuna ghosht* or *roghan josh*. The popular dessert *kulfi faluda* (ice cream with cornflour noodles) is served in several places in Aminabad. The sweet orange-coloured rice dish known as *zarda* is also popular. In the hot months of May and June, Lucknow has some of the world's finest mangoes, particularly the wonderful *dashhari* variety grown in the village of Malihabad, west of the city.

Hazratganj's Mahatma Gandhi (MG) Rd is lined with restaurants, snack bars and western-style fast-food joints.

Nawab's, in Capoor's hotel, serves decent veg/nonveg fare from Rs 40, and has live Indian music in the evenings. Nawab's *khas* dishes have a good, rich sauce.

Muman's Royal Cafe, next to Capoor's, is also good, also with live music. It has veg/nonveg Indian and Chinese food, prompt service, and a civilised ambience. The excellent *chaat* (snack) stall outside does a roaring trade in tasty snacks costing only Rs 15.

Cheadi Lal Ramprasad Vaish (MG Rd) has great coffee, juices and ice cream, which are consumed by customers standing on the pavement outside. It's poorly marked, but next to the Lop Stop fast-food joint.

Mini Mahal nearby has a good selection of Indian sweets and pastries, and Chinese fast food. *Moti Mahal* next door is similar, but has Indian food.

Also close by, *Chowdhury Sweet House* is an atmospheric place for coffee or tea.

Ritz Continental (Sapru Marg) is a fairly upmarket vegetarian restaurant, serving good snacks, Indian and Chinese food, and pizzas (Rs 35 to Rs 50).

Next door, *Moments Restaurant* is inexpensive, and good for kebabs and chicken.

Spicy Bite, in the Tulsi Theatre building, is rated highly by locals. Acceptable pizzas cost from Rs 50 and burgers Rs 32, though it mostly specialises in Chinese food.

Falaknuma, in Hotel Clarks Avadh, is one of the best places to try Lucknow cuisine. Main courses are expensive but the food is good and the restaurant has great views across the city.

Entertainment

Lucknow has a strong tradition in the performing arts. The Rabindralaya auditorium

(☎ 455670), opposite the train stations, hosts classical music, dance and theatrical performances.

Shopping

The bazaars of Aminabad and Chowk are interesting to wander through, even if you're not buying. In the narrow lanes of Aminabad you can buy *attar* – pure essential oils extracted from flowers in the traditional manner. In Chowk, you'll find a bird-sellers' district known as Nakkhas – pigeon-keeping and cockfighting have been popular in Lucknow since the time of the nawabs.

The Gangotri government emporium in Hazratganj sells local handicrafts, including the hand-woven embroidered cloth known as *chikan* for which Lucknow is famous.

Getting There & Away

Air The airport is 14km from town. Indian Airlines office (☎ 220927) is at the Hotel Clarks Avadh. Indian Airlines operates daily flights to Delhi (US$80), and flights to Patna (US$90) and Calcutta (US$140) four times weekly.

Sahara India Airlines (☎ 377675) has daily flights to Delhi (US$80) and Mumbai (US$225). Jet Airways (☎ 202026) also has flights to Delhi and Mumbai.

Bus There are two bus terminals: Charbagh, near the train stations, and Kaiserbagh. From Charbagh there are regular departures to Kanpur (Rs 28, two hours) and Allahabad (Rs 66, five hours), and early-morning and evening buses to Varanasi (Rs 94, 8½ hours) and Agra (Rs 130, 10 hours). From Kaiserbagh there are buses to Delhi (Rs 168, 12 hours), Gorakhpur (Rs 89, 7½ hours) and Faizabad (Rs 46, three hours).

Train The two main stations, Charbagh and Lucknow Junction, are side by side; Northern Railway trains run to both, North Eastern Railway trains only to the latter. Essentially, Charbagh handles all trains between New Delhi and Calcutta, while Lucknow Junction handles many of the trains heading to cities in the south.

Shatabdi Express runs between Lucknow and Delhi (Rs 595 in air-con chair class, 6½ hours) via Kanpur (Rs 190, 1½ hours). There are also plenty of regular expresses to both Delhi (Rs 107/531 in 2nd/1st class, eight to nine hours) and Calcutta (Rs 262/885 in sleeper/1st class, around 23 hours).

Other express trains (fares in 2nd/1st class) from Lucknow are:

Allahabad	Rs 57/272	4 hours
Varanasi	Rs 79/388	5-6 hours
Faizabad	Rs 39/196	3 hours
Gorakhpur	Rs 70/341	5-6 hours

The train to Mumbai costs Rs 311/1156 in sleeper/1st class (27 hours) and to Agra Rs 81/115/398 in 2nd/sleeper/1st class (five to six hours).

Getting Around

To/From the Airport Amausi airport is 15km south-west of Lucknow. Taxis charge around Rs 200 for the trip; if you don't have much baggage catch a tempo from Charbagh train station for Rs 6.

Local Transport There are no auto-rickshaws. Instead, tempos run along fixed routes, connecting Charbagh train station with the main post office (Hazratganj), Sikandar Bagh, Kaiserbagh (for the bus terminal) and Chowk (for the imambaras). Most journeys cost around Rs 3.

A cycle-rickshaw between the train stations and Hazratganj costs locals Rs 5 but foreigners can expect to pay Rs 10 to Rs 15. From Hazratganj to the imambaras costs Rs 15; sightseeing is around Rs 25 per hour.

ALLAHABAD

☎ 0532 • pop 2,000,000

The city of Allahabad is 135km west of Varanasi at the confluence of two of India's most important rivers – the Ganges and the Yamuna (Jumna). The mythical Sarasvati River, the River of Enlightenment, is also believed to join them here. The confluence, known as the *sangam*, is considered to have great soul-cleansing powers and all pious Hindus hope to bathe here at least once in their lifetime. Hundreds of thousands bathe here every January/February in the Magh Mela, and once every 12 years the Kumbh Mela, the world's largest gathering of pilgrims, draws millions to the confluence for a holy dip.

Allahabad has a fort built by Akbar, which overlooks the confluence of the rivers, and also the Nehru family home, Anand Bhavan. Not many foreign travellers pause in this friendly city, but it's an interesting, relaxing and worthwhile stop, especially if you're partial to Indian-style espressos and sidewalk cafes.

History

Built on a very ancient site, Allahabad was known in Aryan times as Prayag, and Brahma himself is said to have performed a sacrifice here. The Chinese pilgrim Xuan Zhang described visiting the city in 634 AD, and it acquired its present name in 1584, under Akbar. Later Allahabad was taken by the Marathas, sacked by the Pathans and finally ceded to the British in 1801 by the nawab of Avadh.

It was in Allahabad that the East India Company officially handed over control of India to the British government in 1858, following the Uprising. The city was a centre of the Indian National Congress and at the conference here in 1920, Mahatma Gandhi proposed his program of nonviolent resistance to achieve independence.

Orientation & Information

Allahabad's Civil Lines is an area of broad avenues, Raj-era bungalows, modern shops and some outdoor eating stalls. The main bus terminal is also here. It's divided from the dense, older part of town, known as Chowk, by Allahabad Junction train station.

There's a UP tourist office (☎ 601873) in the Tourist Bungalow hotel on Mahatma Gandhi (MG) Marg. It's open 10 am to 5 pm, daily except Sunday and the second Saturday in the month. The main branch of the State Bank of India in Police Lines is

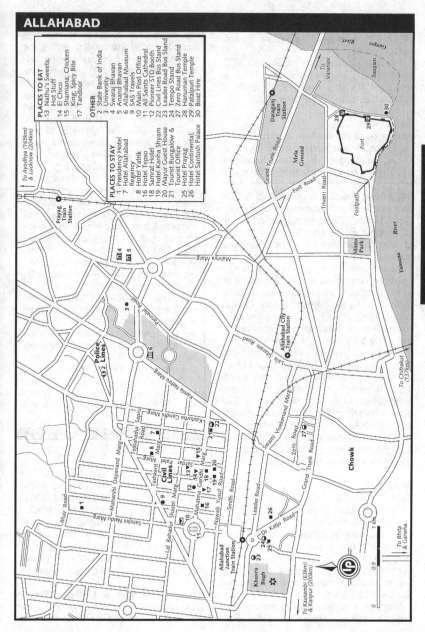

ALLAHABAD

PLACES TO EAT
13 Nathu's Sweets;
   Hot Stuff
14 El Chico
15 Shamiana; Chicken
   King; Spicy Bite
17 Tandoor

OTHER
2 State Bank of India
3 University
4 Swaraj Bhavan
5 Anand Bhavan
6 Allahabad Museum
9 SAS Travels
10 Main Post Office
11 All Saints Cathedral
12 Pioneer STD Booth
22 Civil Lines Bus Stand
23 Leader Road Bus Stand
24 Tempo Stand
27 Zero Road Bus Stand
28 Hanuman Temple
29 Patalpuri Temple
30 Boat Hire

PLACES TO STAY
1 Presidency Hotel
7 Hotel Allahabad
   Regency
8 Hotel Yatrik
16 Hotel Tepso
18 Samrat Hotel
19 Hotel Kanha Shyam
20 Mayur Guest House
21 Tourist Bungalow &
   Tourist Office
25 Hotel Prayag
26 Hotel Continental;
   Hotel Santosh Palace

UTTAR PRADESH

the place to change money. SAS Travels (☎ 623598) is an agent for Sahara, Jet and Indian Airlines.

For Internet access, try the Pioneer STD booth on MG Marg, opposite the Tandoor restaurant. It's open 9 am to 9.30 pm daily; browsing costs Rs 25 per 10 minutes.

Sangam

At this point the shallow, muddy Ganges meets the clearer, deeper, green Yamuna. During the month of Magha (mid-January to mid-February) pilgrims come to bathe at this holy confluence for the festival known as the **Magh Mela**. Astrologers calculate the holiest time to enter the water and draw up a 'Holy Dip Schedule'. The most propitious time of all happens only every 12 years when the massive **Kumbh Mela** takes place. There's a half-mela (Ardh Mela) every six years.

An enormous temporary township springs up on the vacant land on the Allahabad side of the river and elaborate precautions have to be taken for the pilgrims' safety – in the early 1950s, 350 people were killed in a stampede to the water (an incident recreated in Vikram Seth's novel, *A Suitable Boy*).

Sunrise and sunset can be spectacular here. Boats out to the confluence are a bit of a tourist trap and what you pay very much depends on how many other people are around. Next to the fort you should be able hire a whole boat for Rs 50 to Rs 60, though you'll probably be asked Rs 200 initially. It's more interesting sharing with Indians on a pilgrimage since you'll then appreciate the spot's religious significance.

Fort

Built by Akbar in 1583, the fort stands on the northern bank of the Yamuna, near the confluence with the Ganges. It has massive walls and three gateways flanked by high towers. It's most impressive when viewed from the river, so if you don't catch a boat out to the sangam it's worth walking along the riverbank footpath which skirts the fort's southern wall.

The fort is in the hands of the army so prior permission is required for a visit. Pas-

Kumbh Mela

According to Hindu creation myths, the gods and demons once fought a great battle for a *kumbh* (pitcher) containing the nectar of immortality. Vishnu got his hands on the container and spirited it away, but during his flight four drops of nectar spilt on the earth – at Allahabad, Haridwar, Nasik and Ujjain. The fight lasted 12 days but the gods finally triumphed and got to quaff the nectar – a scene often portrayed in illustrations of Hindu mythology.

A huge *mela* (fair) is held at each of the four places the sacred nectar fell once every 12 years (since one day in the life of the gods equates to 12 years in the life of mortals). It is next due to take place in Allahabad in 2001. The Allahabad Kumbh Mela is the largest and holiest mela of them all – some say the largest religious gathering that takes place anywhere on earth. Unsubstantiated estimates of the numbers who came to bathe in the Ganges and Yamuna during Allahabad's last Kumbh Mela in 1989 ran as high as 20 million, though it was probably lower than this. The event is noted for the huge number of Hindu holy men it attracts, especially the naked sadhus or *nagas* of militant Hindu monastic orders.

Mark Tully's *No Full Stops in India* has a fascinating chapter on the politics, logistics and significance of Allahabad's last Kumbh Mela.

ses can be obtained from the Defence Ministry Security Officer, though these are hard to get and are only usually granted to VIPs. In any case, there's nothing very much to see. Apart from one Mughal building, the only item of antiquity in the restricted area is an **Ashoka pillar** dating from 232 BC. Its inscription eulogises the victories of Samudragupta and contains the usual edicts.

Patalpuri Temple & Undying Tree A small door in the fort's eastern wall leads to the one portion of the fort you can visit without permission – the underground Patalpuri Temple which is home to the 'Undying Banyan Tree'. Also known as Akshai Veta, this tree is mentioned by Xuan Zhang, who tells of pilgrims sacrificing their lives by leaping to their deaths from it in order to seek salvation. This would be difficult now as there's not much of it left.

Hanuman Temple This popular temple, open to non-Hindus, is unusual because the Hanuman idol is reclining rather than upright. It's said that each year during the floods the Ganges rises to touch the feet of the sleeping Hanuman before receding.

Anand Bhavan
This shrine to the Nehru family must be the best kept museum in the country, indicating the high regard in which this famous dynasty is held in India. The family home was donated to the Indian government by Indira Gandhi in 1970. The exhibits in the house show how this well-off family became involved in the struggle for Indian independence and produced four generations of astute politicians – Motilal Nehru, Jawaharlal Nehru, Indira Gandhi and Rajiv Gandhi.

Visitors walk around the verandahs of the two storey mansion looking through glass panels into the rooms. You can see Nehru's bedroom and study, the room where Mahatma Gandhi used to stay during his visits and Indira Gandhi's room, as well as many personal items connected with the Nehru family. A quick look at the extensive bookshelves (full of Marx and Lenin) indicate where India's post-Independence faith in socialism sprang from. The house is open daily, except holidays and Monday, between 9.30 am and 5.30 pm. It's free to see the ground floor but costs Rs 2 to go upstairs. Last entry is at 5 pm, and no tickets are sold 12.45 to 1.30 pm.

In the manicured garden is an outbuilding housing a pictorial display of Jawaharlal Nehru's life. A **planetarium**, built in the grounds in 1979, has hourly shows between 11 am and 4 pm; tickets cost Rs 10.

Next door is **Swaraj Bhavan**, where Motilal Nehru lived until 1930 and where Indira

Gandhi was born. It houses a museum featuring dimly lit rooms and an audio-visual presentation 'The Story of Independence'. Unfortunately, commentary is only in Hindi. It is open daily except Monday 10 am to 1.30 pm and 2 to 4.15 pm and entry costs Rs 5.

Other Attractions
Close to the Allahabad Junction train station is **Khusru Bagh**, a scrappy walled garden which contains the tomb of Prince Khusru, son of Jehangir, who sought to wrest power from his father and was executed by his brother Shah Jahan. Nearby is the unoccupied tomb intended for his sister and the tomb of his Rajput mother, who was said to have poisoned herself in despair at Khusru's opposition to his father.

All Saints Cathedral was designed by Sir William Emerson, the architect of the Victoria Memorial in Calcutta. Its brass memorial plaques show that even for the sons and daughters of the Raj, life was not all high teas and pink gins. The inscriptions morbidly record the causes of death: 'died of blood poisoning', 'died in a polo accident' and, probably even more likely today, 'died in a motor accident on the road to Nainital'. It is open 8 to 10 am and has services in English on Sunday.

Allahabad Museum has galleries devoted to local archaeological finds, including terracotta figurines from Kausambi. It also has natural history exhibits, an art gallery and a large room of artefacts donated by the Nehru family. In the latter are all sorts of wonderful and ridiculous items presented to Nehru while he was prime minister. The museum is open 10 am to 5 pm daily except Monday and holidays. Admission is Rs 5. Not far away, opposite the university, is the house where Rudyard Kipling lived, but it isn't open to the public.

Minto Park, near the Yamuna, is where Lord Canning read out the declaration by which Britain took over control of India from the East India Company in 1858. The **Nag Basuki Temple** is mentioned in the *Puranas* and is on the bank of the Ganges, north of the railway bridge.

Places to Stay – Budget

Budget hotels can be found in the peaceful Civil Lines area though many are immediately south of Allahabad Junction train station. Rooms have attached bath unless otherwise stated.

The **Tourist Bungalow** (☎ 601440, fax 611374, 35 MG Marg) is a clean UP Tourism operation set back from the road in a well-tended garden, with a restaurant. Good, fairly spacious singles/doubles cost Rs 225/275. Air-cooled rooms for Rs 350/400 and air-con rooms for Rs 550/600 have a TV. It's good value if you can put up with the noise that filters through from the adjacent bus stand.

Mayur Guest House (☎ 420250, 10 Sardar Patel Marg), just off MG Marg, has acceptable, smallish air-cooled rooms with hot water and TV from Rs 250/325 and air-con rooms for Rs 425/550.

Hotel Tepso (☎ 623635, MG Marg) has a dilapidated reception area but the rooms are OK, and reasonably quiet. Singles/doubles are Rs 250/350.

Hotel Prayag (☎ 656416, fax 609633, 73 Noorullah Rd), south of Allahabad Junction train station, is a typical good budget hotel. It has rooms (most with TV) from Rs 125/160 to Rs 450/500 with air-con.

There are numerous places to stay in the same price bracket along Dr Katju Rd, the next street east, including **Hotel Continental** (☎ 652629), which operates on the 24 hour checkout system. The new **Hotel Santosh Palace** (☎ 654773, fax 653976, 100 Dr Katju Rd) offers a generally higher standard. Modern rooms with TV, new fittings and air-cooling start from Rs 200/300, or from Rs 600/700 with air-con. Some rooms are very spacious and checkout is 24 hours.

The **retiring rooms** at Allahabad Junction train station cost Rs 135 for a double and Rs 50 in a dorm. Rates are for 24 hours; the tariff is roughly two-thirds this if you stay less than 12 hours.

Places to Stay – Mid-Range & Top End

All the mid-range and top-end hotels are in the Civil Lines area.

Samrat Hotel (☎ 420780, fax 420785), in an alley off MG Marg, has clean rooms with TV for Rs 475/675 with air-cooling and Rs 550/900 with air-con. Luggage storage is available.

Hotel Allahabad Regency (☎ 601519, fax 611110, 16 Tashkent Marg, email tglalld@hotmail.com) is a tranquil two-star place with air-con rooms from Rs 850/950, including breakfast. It has a nice pool (open April to September), garden and a gym.

Hotel Yatrik (☎ 601713, fax 601434, 33 Sardar Patel Marg) is a smart, modern establishment. Air-con rooms are a slightly higher standard and cost Rs 900/1100. It has a lovely garden and a good pool (open late April to September). Checkout is 24 hours.

The **Presidency Hotel** (☎ 623308, fax 623897, Sarojini Naidu Marg) is in a quiet residential area a little north of Civil Lines. Modern, neat, air-con rooms cost from Rs 850/875. It also has a garden, and a pool (open March to October).

The classiest hotel is the modern, newly built high-rise **Hotel Kanha Shyam** (☎ 420281, fax 622164, email info@kanhashyam.com) just off MG Marg. Prices start at Rs 1250/1400 and there's a coffee shop, restaurant and bar. They're also building a pool and a health club.

Places to Eat

Outdoor eating is all the rage in Allahabad. Many semipermanent stalls set up tables and chairs on the footpath of MG Marg in the evening, making it a popular, atmospheric and cheap area to eat. There's a good sidewalk **coffee stall** in front of Hotel Tepso, one of many in the area boasting an espresso machine.

Shamiana is one of the few established food stalls on MG Marg open all day. It dishes up excellent chow mein for Rs 16/28 a half/full plate and OK masala dosa for Rs 14. A little further east, **Chicken King** and neighbouring **Spicy Bite** are stalls serving cheap and tasty veg/nonveg and Chinese food.

There's nothing much to distinguish between Allahabad's handful of proper restaurants, which try to cover every possible base by offering veg/nonveg Indian, Chinese and continental fare. They're rather bland compared to the outdoor stalls, and none serve alcohol.

El Chico is arguably the best of the bunch, though meals are not cheap at Rs 60 to Rs 125. It also has a good pastry and sweet shop. The *potato chaat stand* directly in front of El Chico serves fantastic snacks for Rs 5. *Tandoor* focuses more closely on Indian food; main dishes are Rs 50 to Rs 80. These places are all on MG Marg.

Nathu's Sweets (18B Sardar Patel Marg) is a newly opened vegetarian place with pizza, south Indian dishes and a wide selection of sweets downstairs. A few doors along is *Hot Stuff*, a western-style fast-food joint with pizzas from Rs 45, burgers, Indian and Chinese food, and a good range of ice cream.

There are many basic restaurants in the old town, plus several *dhaba* places close to the train station along Dr Katju Rd. The bar in the *Tourist Bungalow* in Civil Lines is a cosy place to sink a beer.

Getting There & Away
Allahabad is a good place from which to travel to Khajuraho, since there are numerous express trains to Satna (Rs 52/245, 3½ hours). The *Patna-Kurla Express* leaves at 8.30 am, leaving plenty of time to catch a bus from Satna to Khajuraho (four hours). Buses from Allahabad to Satna take several hours longer than express trains.

At the time of research there were no flights to Allahabad, though in 1999 Sahara should be starting limited services, including a thrice-weekly flight to Delhi.

Bus From the Civil Lines bus stand, beside the Tourist Bungalow, there are regular buses to Varanasi (Rs 41, three hours), Lucknow (Rs 66 normal, Rs 111 super-deluxe, five hours), Faizabad (Rs 56, five hours) and Gorakhpur (Rs 98, 9½ hours) via Jaunpur. There are four buses to Sonauli (Rs 112, 13 hours) if you're heading to Nepal.

Train The main train station is Allahabad Junction, in the centre of the city. There are connections to Varanasi (Rs 36/189 in 2nd/1st class, three hours) and Lucknow (Rs 53/258, four hours). There are also expresses to Delhi (Rs 191/679 in sleeper/1st class, 10 hours), Calcutta (Rs 214/766, 15 hours) and Mumbai (Rs 289/1049, 24 hours).

Getting Around
There are plenty of cycle-rickshaws for hire but few auto-rickshaws. Use the back exit at Allahabad Junction train station to reach Civil Lines. A cycle-rickshaw from the train station to the Civil Lines bus stand costs no more than Rs 5. It's a Rs 20 cycle-rickshaw ride from the train station to the fort and Rs 10 from MG Marg to Anand Bhavan. Tempos go from Allahabad Junction train station to Daraganj train station, which is 800m north of the fort.

AROUND ALLAHABAD
Bhita
Excavations at this site on the Yamuna River, 18km south of Allahabad, have revealed the remains of an ancient fortified city. Layers of occupation dating from the Gupta period (320 to 510 AD) back to the Mauryan period (321 to 184 BC) and perhaps even earlier have been uncovered. There's a museum with stone and metal seals, coins and terracotta statues. It's best to get here from Allahabad by taxi.

Garwha
The ruined temples in this walled enclosure are about 50km south-west of Allahabad, 8km from Shankargarh – the last 3km have to be completed on foot.

The major temple has 16 beautifully carved stone pillars, and inscriptions reveal that the temples date back to the Gupta period at the very least. Some of the better sculptures from Garwha are now on display in the state museum in Lucknow. Transport connections to Shankargarh are not good, so consider hiring a taxi in Allahabad.

Kausambi
This ancient Buddhist centre, once known as Kosam, is 63km south-west of Allahabad on

the way to Chitrakut. It was the capital of King Udaya, a contemporary of the Buddha, and the Enlightened One is said to have preached several sermons here. There's a huge **fortress** near the village which contains the broken remains of an **Ashoka pillar**, minus any pre-Gupta period inscriptions. Buses depart irregularly from Allahabad's Leader Rd bus stand.

Chitrakut

It was here that Brahma, Vishnu and Shiva are believed to have been 'born' and taken on their incarnations, which makes this town a popular Hindu pilgrimage place. **Bathing ghats** line the Mandakini River and there are over 30 temples in the town. UP Tourism has a *Tourist Bungalow* here, and there are a number of other cheap hotels and basic restaurants. The town is close to the border with Madhya Pradesh, 132km from Allahabad and 195km from Khajuraho. Buses depart from Allahabad's Zero Rd bus stand.

FAIZABAD

☎ 05278 • pop 350,000

Faizabad was once the capital of Avadh but rapidly declined after the death of Bahu Begum, the wife of Nawab Shuja-ud-Daula. Most of the Islamic buildings in Faizabad were built at her behest, and her mausoleum is said to be the finest of its type in Uttar Pradesh. Her husband also has an impressive mausoleum. There are three large mosques in the market (chowk) area and pleasant gardens in Guptar Park, where the temple from which Rama is supposed to have disappeared stands. The town makes a convenient base for visiting nearby Ayodhya.

Places to Stay & Eat

There are a couple of good hotels in the Civil Lines area, about 1.5km west of the chowk, but both are on the main Lucknow-Gorakhpur Rd so avoid the front rooms. If your pack isn't too heavy you can walk to the hotels from the bus stand, which is on the same road; the train station is a Rs 5 cycle-rickshaw ride away.

Hotel Shane-Avadh (☎ 23586) is a clean, efficiently run place with a lift. Singles/doubles with attached hot bath cost from Rs 130/160 and air-con rooms with TV are Rs 450/550. Its *Mezban* restaurant turns out decent veg/nonveg and Chinese fare in big portions (from Rs 30), and has coffee so frothy you could mistake it for a cappuccino if you've been in India long enough.

Hotel Tirupati (☎ 23231) next door is also good value and has helpful staff. Rooms with attached bath, hot water and TV cost from Rs 120/150, or Rs 450/550 with air-con. It also has a restaurant, with a similar range and prices to the Mezban restaurant.

Abha Hotel (☎ 22550) is the best of several places on a side street near the Majestic Cinema in the chowk area. It has acceptable rooms with attached bath and TV from Rs 125/165, and a veg/nonveg restaurant. It's a Rs 10 cycle-rickshaw ride from the train station and Rs 8 from the bus stand.

The recently opened *Hotel Krishna Palace* (☎ 21367, fax 21371), a few minutes walk from the train station, is Faizabad's top hotel, though there's no lift. It has a range of modern, comfortable rooms starting at Rs 250/300, or Rs 500/600 with air-con. The *Caveri Restaurant* serves good Indian, Chinese and continental food.

Getting There & Away

Faizabad has fairly good train connections, including expresses to Lucknow (Rs 40/205 in 2nd/1st class, three hours) and Varanasi (Rs 54/266, four to six hours).

There are numerous buses from the quiet bus stand on the Lucknow-Gorakhpur Rd, 750m west of Hotel Shane-Avadh. Connections include Gorakhpur (Rs 48, four hours), Lucknow (Rs 43, three hours), Allahabad (Rs 56, five hours), Sonauli (Rs 80) and Ayodhya (Rs 3). Tempos to Ayodhya (Rs 6) depart from the main road, about 80m north of the clock tower in the chowk area.

AYODHYA

☎ 05278 • pop 75,000

Ayodhya, 6km from Faizabad, is one of Hinduism's seven holy cities. It's a major

SHOPPERS' DELIGHT

All across India, from trekking routes in the Himalaya to Goan beaches you'll find local traders and artisans plying their wares, many using skills that have been handed down from generation to generation. The intricate detail and range of the goods available is truly awesome.

Serious shoppers should consider carrying out a bit of research. Most of the major cities have a government cooperative or emporium which displays regional crafts – these will give you a rough idea of the quality available as well as the prices you should be bargaining for. Fellow travellers can also be a good source of 'reasonable' prices you can expect to pay. Whatever your approach, deciding on the perfect souvenir is going to be difficult. Choices range from the dazzling mirrorwork of Rajasthan and the papier-mâché jewellery boxes of Kashmir to tie dyed t-shirts and basketware. In fact the only factor limiting your options will be the size of your backpack or suitcase.

Even those strong-willed (and tight-budgeted) folk who can resist the urge to shop will enjoy watching traders and artisans as they go about their work, especially as they often provide an interesting alternative (or addition) to checking out temples and forts. (See also Shopping in the Facts for the Visitor chapter.)

Inset: Indian clothing is a perennial favourite and skilful tailors can copy a designer garment as easily as they can whip up a *salwar kameez*.
Photo: Peter Davis

Bottom: Free enterprise abounds in India with plenty of artisans taking to the streets to ply their wares.

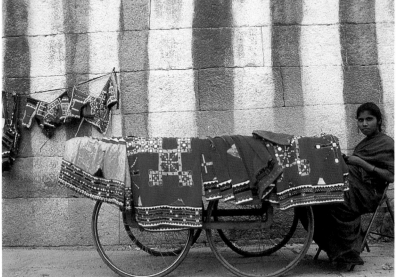

EDDIE GERALD

Top: Those on a tight budget, or with an extended family back home, will appreciate the fantastic choice of cheap and funky jewellery available from street stalls.

Far left: Indian potters are believed to be direct descendants of Parvati. Today pots still play a vital role in everyday Indian life; keeping water cool and providing storage.

Left: These puppets, traditionally used in storytelling, have extra strings which allow them to perform an impressive range of acrobatics.

Right: Varanasi and Kanchipuram are the main Indian silk weaving centres and are the places to go for quality fabrics. One way of ascertaining whether silk is genuine or not is the flame test – silk burns whereas synthetic material melts. Ask the vendor for a cut-off sample before taking it outside for testing.

Bottom: Varanasi in particular is known for the quality and range of its silk brocades so there's plenty of choice when it comes to choosing a suitable pattern for a sari.

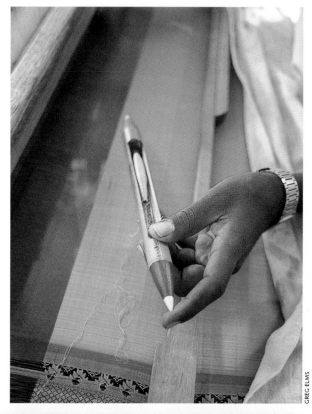

GREG ELMS

SARA-JANE CLELAND

CHRIS MELLOR

Left: Indian produced garments are generally much more comfortable and practical than the clothes brought from home. Cotton shirts and skirts widely available from bazaars adhere to Indian dress standards and will keep you nice and cool during the hot summer months.

Bottom; When haggling over a few rupees bear in mind the amount of intricate work and detail that will have gone into creating your souvenir.

RICHARD I'ANSON

pilgrimage centre since it is not only the birthplace of Rama, it's also connected with many events in the *Ramayana*. Unfortunately, its name has become synonymous with rising Hindu fanaticism since the fateful day on 6 December 1992 when a Hindu mob destroyed a mosque they believed had been built on the site of a temple marking Rama's birthplace. The event sent shock waves throughout India and threatened the nation's secular framework.

The Atharvaveda described Ayodhya as 'a city built by gods and being as prosperous as paradise itself' although today it's just a small, dusty town with an amazing abundance of temples and monkeys. It sees few foreigners, and anyone intending to visit should keep an eye on the latest developments in the temple-mosque saga. Give the town a wide berth if there's rioting. Be particularly careful on the 6 December anniversary.

Babri Masjid – Ram Janam Bhumi
The **Babri Masjid** was constructed by the Mughals in the 15th century on what was reputed to be the site of Rama's birth. The mosque was little used and was eventually closed to Muslims by the civil authorities and limited Hindu *puja* was permitted inside.

By 1990, Rama had been appropriated by Hindu fundamentalists to justify their calls for a Hindu India. Their plans to build a temple to Rama (the Ram Mandir) in place of the mosque led to outbreaks of violence between local Hindus and Muslims. A fragile court order called for the maintenance of the status quo and armed guards surrounded the mosque and attempted to keep the two communities apart.

In late 1992, a Hindu mob stormed the site and destroyed the Babri Masjid, erecting a small Hindu shrine known as **Ram Janam Bhumi** (also known as Ram Janmabhoomi) in its place. The destruction sparked riots across India and caused unrest in neighbouring Muslim countries.

The government, which owns the site, has promised to build a temple here if it is decided a temple was here before the mosque.

In late 1994 the Indian High Court wisely refused to adjudicate on the issue, after which the matter moved on to the Allahabad High Court. A final resolution has yet to be reached, though orders were passed requiring the union government to maintain the status quo as it existed on 7 January 1993.

There is a massive security presence at the temple/mosque site, since it's the country's most volatile flash point. You will be thoroughly (and rather over-zealously) searched. Cameras are prohibited, and you cannot safely deposit them. In fact you can't take any bags in with you – even pens are taken away. Carry your passport. Once through the checks, you pass through a long narrow caged path lined by police, and you will probably be escorted all the way to and from the shrine.

Although the palpable tension in the air makes a visit memorable, as a tourist spectacle it's eminently forgettable; all you see is a small shrine protected by a tent-like structure. The site is open three hours in the morning and three hours in the afternoon. The exact hours change periodically; at the time of research they were 7.30 to 10.30 am and 2 to 5 pm.

From Faizabad, take the small road that turns left off the main Faizabad-Ayodhya road next to the Hanumangadhi (Hanuman Temple). If you arrive by tempo, ask the driver to drop you at the Hanuman Temple, from where it's about 10 minutes' walk.

Other Attractions
The **Hanumangadhi** is dedicated to Hanuman, who is believed to have lived in a cave here while guarding the Janam Bhumi. It was built within the thick white walls of a fortress. There are good views from the ramparts, and real monkeys scampering around the Hanuman images. There are more than 100 other temples in Ayodhya, including the **Kanak Mandir** and several **Jain shrines.**

Places to Stay
The UP *Tourist Bungalow* (☎ *32435*), also known locally as the Saket Hotel, is near the train station and is the only acceptable place to stay in Ayodhya. Singles/doubles with

attached bath cost from Rs 150/175, air-con rooms are Rs 300/341 and a bed in the dorm costs Rs 50. There's a lacklustre veg restaurant and a tourist office.

Getting There & Away

There are regular tempos shuttling along the main road between Ayodhya and Faizabad for Rs 6, or you can take a bus for Rs 3. Ayodhya bus station is about 300m from the Hanumangadhi in the direction of Faizabad.

SHRAVASTI

The extensive ruins of this ancient city and Jetavana Monastery are near the villages of Saheth-Maheth. Here the Buddha performed the miracle of sitting on a 1000-petalled lotus and multiplying himself a million times while fire and water came from his body. Ashoka was an early pilgrim and left a couple of pillars to commemorate his visit.

The site can be reached from Gonda, 50km north-west of Ayodhya. The nearest train station is Gainjahwa, on the Gonda-Naugarh-Gorakhpur loop. The nearest large town is 20km away at Balrampur.

Varanasi Region

VARANASI

☎ 0542 • pop 2,000,000

The city of Shiva on the bank of the sacred Ganges is one of the holiest places in India. Hindu pilgrims come to bathe in the waters of the Ganges, a ritual which washes away all sins. The city, also known as Benares (or Banaras), is an auspicious place to die, since expiring here ensures release from the cycle of rebirths and an instant passport to heaven. It's a magical city where the most intimate rituals of life and death take place in public on the city's famous ghats (steps which lead down to the river). It's this accessibility to the practices of an ancient religious tradition that captivates so many visitors.

In the past, the city has been known as Kashi and Benares, but its present name is a restoration of an ancient name meaning the city between two rivers – the Varuna and Assi.

It has been a centre of learning and civilisation for over 2000 years, and claims to be one of the oldest living cities in the world. Mark Twain obviously thought it looked the part when he dropped by on a lecture tour, since he told the world that 'Benares is older than history, older than tradition, older even than legend, and looks twice as old as all of them put together'. The old city does have an antique feel but few buildings are more than a couple of hundred years old thanks to marauding Muslim invaders and Aurangzeb's destructive tendencies.

Orientation

The old city of Varanasi is situated along the western bank of the Ganges and extends back from the riverbank ghats in a labyrinth of alleyways too narrow for traffic. Godaulia is just outside the old city, and Lahurabir is to the north-east, separated from the cantonment by the train line.

One of the best ways to get your bearings in Varanasi is to remember the positions of the ghats, particularly important ones like Dasaswamedh Ghat. The alleyways of the old city can be disorienting, but the hotels here are well signposted. The big international hotels and the Government of India tourist office are in the cantonment north of Varanasi Junction train station. The TV tower is the most obvious landmark in this area.

Information

Tourist Offices There's a helpful UP tourist information booth (☎ 346370) at Varanasi Junction train station that has city and train information. It's usually open 6 am to 8 pm, though weekend hours may be

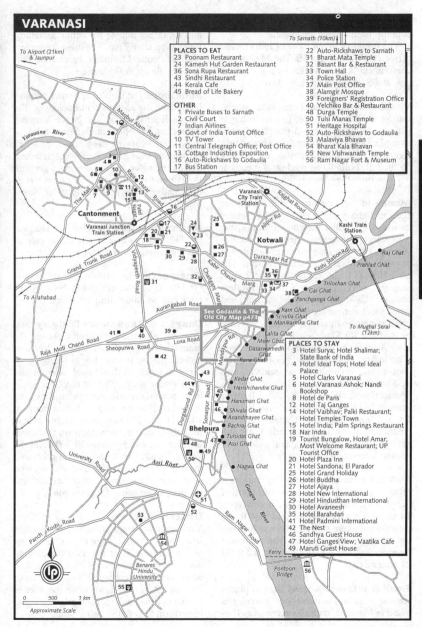

VARANASI

To Sarnath (10km)

UTTAR PRADESH

PLACES TO EAT
23 Poonam Restaurant
24 Kamesh Hut Garden Restaurant
36 Sona Rupa Restaurant
43 Sindhi Restaurant
44 Kerala Cafe
45 Bread of Life Bakery

OTHER
1 Private Buses to Sarnath
2 Civil Court
7 Indian Airlines
9 Govt of India Tourist Office
10 TV Tower
11 Central Telegraph Office; Post Office
13 Cottage Industries Exposition
16 Auto-Rickshaws to Godaulia
17 Bus Station

22 Auto-Rickshaws to Sarnath
31 Bharat Mata Temple
32 Basant Bar & Restaurant
33 Town Hall
34 Police Station
37 Main Post Office
38 Alamgir Mosque
39 Foreigners' Registration Office
40 Yelchiko Bar & Restaurant
48 Durga Temple
50 Tulsi Manas Temple
51 Heritage Hospital
52 Auto-Rickshaws to Godaulia
53 Malaviya Bhavan
54 Bharat Kala Bhavan
55 New Vishwanath Temple
56 Ram Nagar Fort & Museum

PLACES TO STAY
3 Hotel Surya; Hotel Shalimar; State Bank of India
4 Hotel Ideal Tops; Hotel Ideal Palace
5 Hotel Clarks Varanasi
6 Hotel Varanasi Ashok; Nandi Bookshop
8 Hotel de Paris
12 Hotel Taj Ganges
14 Hotel Vaibhav; Palki Restaurant; Hotel Temples Town
15 Hotel India; Palm Springs Restaurant
18 Nar Indra
19 Tourist Bungalow, Hotel Amar; Most Welcome Restaurant; UP Tourist Office
20 Hotel Plaza Inn
21 Hotel Sandona; El Parador
25 Hotel Grand Holiday
26 Hotel Buddha
27 Hotel Ajaya
28 Hotel New International
29 Hotel Hindusthan International
30 Hotel Avaneesh
35 Hotel Barahdari
41 Hotel Padmini International
42 The Nest
46 Sandhya Guest House
47 Hotel Ganges View; Vaatika Cafe
49 Maruti Guest House

To Airport (21km) & Jaunpur

Maqbul Alam Road

Varauana River

Raja Bazar Road

The Mall

Patel Nagar

Cantonment

Varanasi Junction Train Station

Grand Trunk Road

To Allahabad

Vidyapeeth Road

Varanasi City Train Station

Raighat Road

Alpur Rd

Kotwali

Daranagar Rd

Kabir Chaura

Chaitganj Marg

Marg

Aurangabad Road

Kashi Train Station

Kashi Station Rd

Raj Ghat

Prahlad Ghat

Trilochan Ghat

Gai Ghat

Panchganga Ghat

See Godaulia & The Old City Map p473

Ram Ghat
Scindia Ghat
Manikarnika Ghat
Lalita Ghat
Meer Ghat
Dasaswamedh Ghat
Rana Ghat

To Mughal Serai (12km)

Raja Moti Chand Road

Sheopurwa Road

Luxar Road

Mandir Road

Sonarpur Road

Kedar Ghat
Harishchandra Ghat
Hanuman Ghat
Shivala Ghat
Anandmayee Ghat
Bachraj Ghat
Tulsidas Ghat
Assi Ghat

University Road

Durgakund Rd

Bhelpura

Assi River

Nagwa Ghat

Ganges River

Ram Nagar Road

Panch Koshi Road

Benares Hindu University

Ferry

Pontoon Bridge

0   500   1 km
Approximate Scale

shorter. Another UP tourist office (☎ 341162) is in the Tourist Bungalow hotel.

The friendly Government of India tourist office (☎ 343744) at 15B The Mall in the cantonment is open weekdays 9 am to 5.30 pm, and Saturday 9 am to 4.30 pm.

Visa Extensions The Foreigners' Registration Office (☎ 351968) is in Srinagar Colony, Siddgiri Bagh, Sigra. Head west along Luxa Rd away from the river and turn right just before the Theosophical Society on the left. Follow this road until it ends at a T-junction; the office is 50m to the right.

Money In the cantonment area, the State Bank of India near the Hotel Surya changes cash and US dollar travellers cheques, but won't accept travellers cheques in pounds sterling. There are also exchange facilities in several upmarket cantonment hotels. The State Bank of India near Dasaswamedh Ghat changes only Thomas Cook travellers cheques (US dollar or pounds sterling) and won't touch currencies. The most convenient place to change money is Radiant Services, on the Luxa Rd, Godaulia. Rates are slightly lower than in the banks but it is quick, open 8 am to 8 pm daily, and changes all travellers cheques and 36 currencies. Branches are also at Shanti Guest House, Radiant YMCA Tourist Hostel, and above the Union Bank of India in The Mall, Cantonment. The Bank of Baroda (near the Hotel Ganges) and the Andhra Bank on Dasaswamedh Ghat Rd, next to Yelchiko Restaurant, provide cash advances on major credit cards.

Post & Communications The main post office is a short cycle-rickshaw ride north of the old city. The poste restante here is open 10 am to 6 pm Monday to Saturday. In the cantonment, there's a post office at the central telegraph office (CTO). You can make international and STD calls from the CTO 24 hours a day.

Email & Internet Access Lots of places provide this, but as no service provider is based in Varanasi, it can be expensive. Typ-ical prices are Rs 30/25 to send/collect email and Rs 18 per minute for online searching. Rates drop after 7 pm. The most convenient place is Fontac Computer, behind the Garden Restaurant in Godaulia.

Bookshops The Universal Book Company in Godaulia is an excellent bookshop. The Nandi Bookshop in the Hotel Varanasi Ashok has lots of old and unusual titles.

Benares: City of Light by Diana Eck (Princeton University Press) has information on each ghat and temple, and a good introduction to Hinduism. The *Pioneer* is an informative local English-language newspaper.

Medical Services The Heritage Hospital (☎ 313977) is close to the main gate of Benares Hindu University.

Emergency The closest police station (☎ 330653) to the old city is between the town hall and the main post office.

Dangers & Annoyances Predatory rickshaw-wallahs and persistent touts are the main hassles. Varanasi suffers frequent power cuts, so if you stay in the old city, carry a torch to find your way in the labyrinthine alleys. The old city is also said to be potentially dangerous after dark, and many hotels in this area lock their doors at 10 or 11 pm. The Ganges is far from clean (at Tulsi Ghat the faecal coliform count was measured at a staggering 250,000 times the World Health Organization safe permitted maximum!) so avoid ghat chai-wallahs who rinse their glasses in the river. See also the warning at the start of this section.

Ghats

Varanasi's principal attraction is the long string of ghats which line the western bank of the Ganges. Most are used for bathing but there are also several 'burning ghats' where bodies are cremated. The best time to visit the ghats is at dawn when the river is bathed in a magical light and pilgrims come to perform puja to the rising sun.

UTTAR PRADESH

There are around 100 ghats in Varanasi, but Dasaswamedh Ghat is probably the most convenient starting point. A short boat trip from Dasaswamedh to Manikarnika Ghat can be an interesting introduction to the river (see Activities, later in this section, for more information). Alternatively, if the water level is low, you can simply walk from one ghat to the next. This way you're among the throng of people who come to the edge of the Ganges not only for a ritual bath, but to do yoga, offer blessings, buy paan, sell flowers, get a massage, play cricket, have a swim, get a shave, and improve their karma by giving money to beggars.

The city extends from Raj Ghat, near the major road and rail bridge, to Assi Ghat, near the university. The **Assi Ghat** is one of the five special ghats which pilgrims are supposed to bathe at in sequence during the ritual route called Panchatirthi Yatra. The order is Assi, Dasaswamedh, Adi Keshava, Panchganga and finally Manikarnika.

Much of the **Tulsi Ghat** has fallen down towards the river. The **Bachraj Ghat** is Jain and there are three riverbank Jain temples. Many of the ghats are owned by maharajas or other princely rulers, such as the very fine **Shivala Ghat** owned by the maharaja of Varanasi. The **Dandi Ghat** is the ghat of ascetics known as Dandi Panths, and nearby is the very popular **Hanuman Ghat**.

The **Harishchandra** or Smashan Ghat is a secondary burning ghat. It's one of the oldest ghats in the city. Above it, the crowded **Kedar Ghat** is a shrine popular with Bengalis and south Indians. **Mansarowar Ghat** was built by Raja Man Singh of Amber and named after the Tibetan lake at the foot of Mt Kailash, Shiva's Himalayan home. **Someswar** or Lord of the Moon Ghat is said to be able to heal diseases. The **Munshi Ghat** is very picturesque, while **Ahalya Bai's Ghat** is named after the female Maratha ruler of Indore.

The name of **Dasaswamedh Ghat** indicates that Brahma sacrificed (*medh*) 10 (*das*) horses (*aswa*) here. Conveniently central, it's one of the most important and busiest ghats and therefore is a good place to linger and

Sadhus give up all their material possessions to enter the fourth stage of the ideal Hindu life: that of the wandering ascetic.

soak up the atmosphere. Note its statues and the shrine of Sitala, goddess of smallpox.

Raja Man Singh's **Man Mandir Ghat** was built in 1600 but was poorly restored in the 19th century. The northern corner of the ghat has a fine stone balcony and Raja Jai Singh of Jaipur erected one of his unusual observatories on this ghat in 1710.

The **Meer Ghat** leads to the Nepalese Temple, which has erotic sculptures. The **Jalsain Ghat**, where cremations take place, virtually adjoins **Manikarnika Ghat**, one of the oldest and most sacred in Varanasi. Manikarnika is the main burning ghat and one of the most auspicious places that a Hindu can be cremated. Bodies are handled by outcasts known as *doms*, and they are carried through the alleyways of the old city to the holy Ganges on a bamboo stretcher swathed in cloth. The corpse is doused in the Ganges prior to cremation. You'll see huge piles of firewood stacked along the top of the ghat, each log carefully weighed on giant scales so that the price of cremation can be calculated. There are no problems watching cremations, since at Manikarnika death is simply business as usual, but don't take photos and keep your camera well hidden.

Above the steps here is a tank known as the **Manikarnika Well**; Parvati is said to have dropped her earring here and Shiva dug the tank to recover it, filling the depression with his sweat. The **Charanpaduka**, a slab of stone between the well and the ghat, bears footprints made by Vishnu. Privileged VIPs are cremated at the Charanpaduka. There is also a temple dedicated to Ganesh on the ghat.

Dattatreya Ghat bears the footprint of the Brahmin saint of that name in a small temple nearby. **Scindia Ghat** was originally built in 1830 but was so huge and magnificent that it collapsed into the river and had to be rebuilt. The **Ram Ghat** was built by the raja of Jaipur. The **Panchganga Ghat**, as its name indicates, is where five rivers are supposed to meet. Dominating the ghat is Aurangzeb's smaller mosque, also known as the **Alamgir Mosque**, which he built on the site of a large Vishnu Temple erected by the Maratha chieftain Beni Madhav Rao Scindia. The **Gai Ghat** has a figure of a cow made of stone upon it. The **Trilochan Ghat** has two turrets emerging from the river, and the water between them is especially holy. **Raj Ghat** was the ferry pier until the road and rail bridge was completed here.

Vishwanath Temple

The Vishwanath Temple, or Golden Temple, is the most sacred temple in Varanasi and is dedicated to Vishveswara – Shiva as lord of the universe. The current temple was built in 1776 by Ahalya Bai of Indore, and the 800kg of gold plating on the towers, which gives the temple its colloquial name, was provided by Maharaja Ranjit Singh of Lahore some 50 years later. It's located in the narrow alleys of the old city. Non-Hindus are not allowed into the temple but can view it from the upper floor of a house across the street.

There has been a succession of Shiva temples in the vicinity for at least the past 1500 years, but they were routinely destroyed by Muslim invaders. Aurangzeb continued this tradition, knocking down the previous temple and building his **Great Mosque** over it. Armed guards protect the mosque since the BJP has declared that, after Ayodhya, the mosques at Varanasi and Mathura are its next targets. Be discreet if taking photographs in this area as the soldiers sometimes disapprove.

Next to the Vishwanath Temple is the **Gyan Kupor Well** (Well of Knowledge). The faithful believe drinking its water leads to a higher spiritual plane, though they are prevented from doing so by both tradition and a strong security screen. The well is said to contain the Shiva lingam removed from the previous temple and hidden to protect it from Aurangzeb.

Durga Temple

The Durga Temple is commonly known as the Monkey Temple due to the many frisky monkeys that have made it their home. Located about 2km south of the old city, this small temple was built in the 18th century by a Bengali maharani and is stained red with ochre. It's in north Indian Nagara style with a multi-tiered *shikhara* (spire). Durga is the 'terrible' form of Shiva's consort Parvati, so at festivals there are often sacrifices of goats. Non-Hindus can enter the courtyard but not the inner sanctum.

Tulsi Manas Temple

Only 150m south of the Durga Temple is the modern marble shikhara-style Tulsi Manas Temple, built in 1964. Its two-tier walls are engraved with verses and scenes from the *Ram Charit Manas*, the Hindi version of the *Ramayana*. Its author, poet Tulsi Das, lived here while writing it.

You can watch figures performing scenes from Hindu mythology on the 2nd floor for Rs 1. The temple is open 6 to 11.30 am and 3 to 9 pm.

Benares Hindu University

Varanasi has long been a centre of learning and that tradition is continued today at the Benares Hindu University (BHU), built in 1917. It was founded by the great nationalist Pandit Malaviya as a centre for education in Indian art, music, culture and philosophy, and for the study of Sanskrit. The five sq km campus houses the **Bharat Kala Bhavan** which has a fine collection of miniature paintings, sculptures from the 1st to 15th centuries and old photographs of Varanasi. It's open Monday to Saturday 11 am to 4.30 pm (7.30 am to 12.30 pm May/June). To visit all sections costs Rs 40, or Rs 10 for Indian nationals. BHU is a 20 minute walk or a short rickshaw ride from the Durga Temple.

New Vishwanath Temple

It's about a 30 minute walk from the gates of the university to the New Vishwanath Temple, which was planned by Pandit Malaviya and built by the wealthy Birla family of industrialists. Pandit Malaviya wished to see Hinduism revived without its caste distinctions and prejudices – accordingly, unlike many temples in Varanasi, this temple is open to all, irrespective of caste or religion. The interior has a Shiva lingam and verses from Hindu scriptures inscribed on the walls. The temple is supposed to be a replica of the earlier Vishwanath Temple destroyed by Aurangzeb. It's open 5 am to noon and 1.30 to 9 pm. From Godaulia it costs around Rs 15 by cycle-rickshaw or Rs 30 by auto-rickshaw to reach the temple.

Ram Nagar Fort & Museum

On the opposite bank of the river, this 17th century fort is the home of the former maharaja of Benares. It looks most impressive from the river, though the decrepit planking of the pontoon bridge you cross to reach it is somewhat of a distraction. During the monsoon, access is by ferry. The interesting museum here contains old silver and brocade palanquins for the ladies of the court, gold-plated elephant howdahs (seats for carrying people on an elephant's back), an astrological clock, macabre elephant traps and an armoury of swords and old guns. The fort is open daily 9 am to noon and 2 to 5 pm; entry is Rs 4.

Bharat Mata Temple

Dedicated to 'Mother India', this unadorned temple has a marble relief map of India instead of the usual images of gods and goddesses. The map is said to be perfectly in scale, both vertically and horizontally. It's open daily 7 am to 5 pm; entry is free though photography costs Rs 5 (Rs 10 for videos). The temple was opened by Mahatma Gandhi.

Activities

River Trips A boat ride on the Ganges has become one of the must-dos of a visit to Varanasi, but be prepared to see the odd corpse floating down the river. It's customary to do the trip early in the morning when the light is particularly atmospheric. Even if you're not staying near the river, it's easy to organise a boat for sunrise as rickshaw-wallahs are keen to get a pre-dawn rendezvous arranged for the trip to the river. Get the rickshaw-wallah to take you to a large ghat such as Dasaswamedh, since there will be a number of boats to choose from. Travellers have reported being taken to smaller ghats where there was only one boat, placing them in a poor bargaining position.

The government rate for hiring a boat capable of holding up to four people is supposedly set at Rs 50 per hour; for a boat that can seat up to 10 people it's Rs 75 per hour. You'll undoubtedly have to remind boatmen of these rates since tourists frequently pay much more. Be sure to agree on a price before getting into a boat.

Swimming If the sight of pilgrims bathing in the Ganges makes you want to have a splash yourself, the following hotels permit nonguests to use their pools: Hotel Varanasi Ashok (Rs 150), Hotel Hindusthan International (Rs 200), and Hotel Clarks Varanasi (Rs 200). Clarks has the best pool.

Yoga The Malaviya Bhavan (☎ 310291, fax 312059) at Benares Hindu University offers courses in yoga and Hindu philosophy, such as a four-week certificate course or a four-month part-time diploma. For the less committed, the Shanti Guest House runs morning and evening yoga classes which cost Rs 50. Various places in the old city alleys also offer yoga instruction.

Steam Baths & Massage The Hotel Surya offers steam baths for just Rs 35, and body massages for Rs 150. You can get a vigorous head, neck and back massage at Dasaswamedh Ghat from about Rs 10.

Organised Tours

Government guides hired via the Government of India tourist office cost Rs 230/345 for a half/full day, or you can pay more to include road and/or boat transport. A three-hour tour including taxi/auto rickshaw would cost about Rs 500/350. You can choose from their set itineraries or construct your own.

Places to Stay

There are three main accommodation areas in Varanasi: the old city, Lahurabir and the cantonment. Wherever you intend to stay in Varanasi, be firm when giving instructions to your rickshaw-wallah when you first arrive. Since they get paid high commissions, they are keen to direct new arrivals to specific hotels. Don't listen to any nonsense about the hotel of your choice being 'closed', 'full up', 'burnt down' or 'flooded'. For places in the old city, it's better to just ask the rickshaw-wallah for Dasaswamedh Ghat and walk to the hotel from there, since rickshaws won't be able to negotiate the alleyways anyway.

Contact the Government of India tourist office about Varanasi's paying guest accommodation, which enables you to stay with a local family. *The Nest* (☎ 360137, B21/122 A2, Kamachha), near Baijnath Mandir, is one of the cheapest of such places and charges Rs 100 for two people.

Note that most hotels drop their rates by up to 50% in the low season (April to July).

Places to Stay – Budget & Mid-Range

Old City & Ghats Area The old city is the place to look for budget hotels if you don't mind living in cramped conditions. The area is certainly the city's most atmospheric and there are several good lodges right on the river with superb views along the ghats. Nearly all the hotels have rooftop terraces to relax on. However, there are very few options

above the budget level. Monkeys scampering along the rooftops of the riverside places can be entertaining, but also a nuisance.

Vishnu Rest House (☎ 329206, Panday Ghat) is a popular riverside place with terraces offering great views. Fine singles/doubles with bath start at Rs 70/90 and dorm beds are Rs 35. Bucket hot water is free. Don't confuse it with the Real Vishnu Guest House or various other similarly named lodges which deliberately try to feed off its success. Phone ahead as it's generally full.

Close by, *Ajay Guest House* (☎ 327970, Ranamahal Ghat) has received unfavourable hygiene reports, particularly in its restaurant, and is not recommended.

Shiva Guest House (Munshi Ghat) is a small, simple place with rooms for Rs 40/60 with common bath, or Rs 80 with attached bath, all with bucket hot water.

Ganpathi Guest House (☎ 327110, Meer Ghat), north of Dasaswamedh Ghat, has wonderful views from its terrace restaurant. Rooms with common hot bath are Rs 60/100. Doubles with attached bath range from Rs 175 to Rs 400 (with colour TV and a view).

Alka Hotel (☎ 328445, fax 328445, Meer Ghat, hotelalka@hotmail.com) is a new hotel and slightly more upmarket than other riverside places in the area. There's hot water, a pleasant terrace restaurant, and they're planning to install TVs in rooms. Prices range from Rs 110/150 with common bath up to Rs 750 for air-con rooms with a balcony.

Scindhia Guest House (☎ 320319, Scindia Ghat), a little way north, has clean rooms, some with superb river views. It charges Rs 75/100 with common bath and Rs 125/125 for rooms with attached cold bath. Doubles with attached hot bath, a balcony and air-cooling go for Rs 250. The management is not keen on drug use.

You don't need a river view to enjoy the old city and many travellers prefer the places in the alleys set back from the ghats.

Yogi Lodge (☎ 392588, Kalika Gali) has long been a favourite with budget travellers and it's efficiently run by a friendly family. Dorm beds cost from Rs 40, and small rooms with common bath cost from Rs 80/100.

Sheets and blankets are Rs 5 extra. Like many other popular hotels in the old city, its success has spawned countless similarly named, inferior places.

Close by, *Golden Lodge* (☎ 323832) is a quiet place with basic rooms for Rs 60/80 with common bath (hot water) or Rs 100/150 with attached bath. Checkout is 10.30 am.

Sri Venkateswar Lodge (☎ 392357), behind the Shiva temple on Dasaswamedh Ghat Rd, is a quiet place with hot water and rooms round a courtyard. It charges Rs

60/90 with common bath and from Rs 160 for doubles with attached bath. The management is helpful and not overly keen on noxious substances.

The popular *Trimurti Guest House* (☎ 393554), near the Vishwanath Temple, has dorm beds for Rs 30, singles/doubles with common bath for Rs 50/80 and doubles with attached hot bath for Rs 120.

Shanti Guest House (☎ 392568) is just off an alleyway leading to Manikarnika Ghat. It's very popular and has a 24 hour

UTTAR PRADESH

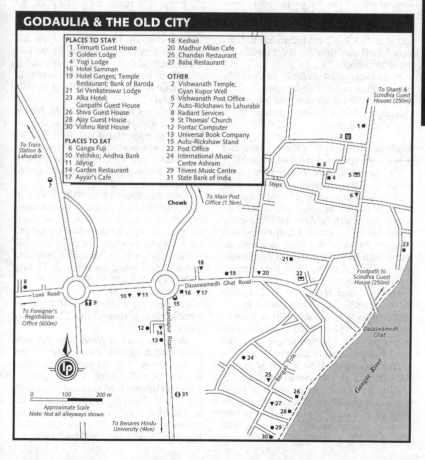

GODAULIA & THE OLD CITY

PLACES TO STAY
1 Trimurti Guest House
3 Golden Lodge
4 Yogi Lodge
16 Hotel Samman
19 Hotel Ganges; Temple Restaurant; Bank of Baroda
21 Sri Venkateswar Lodge
23 Alka Hotel; Ganpathi Guest House
26 Shiva Guest House
28 Ajay Guest House
30 Vishnu Rest House

PLACES TO EAT
6 Ganga Fuji
10 Yelchiko; Andhra Bank
11 Jalyog
14 Garden Restaurant
17 Ayyar's Cafe

18 Keshari
20 Madhur Milan Cafe
25 Chandan Restaurant
27 Baba Restaurant

OTHER
2 Vishwanath Temple; Gyan Kupor Well
5 Vishwanath Post Office
7 Auto-Rickshaws to Lahurabir
8 Radiant Services
9 St Thomas' Church
12 Fontac Computer
13 Universal Book Company
15 Auto-Rickshaw Stand
22 Post Office
24 International Music Centre Ashram
29 Triveni Music Centre
31 State Bank of India

To Shanti & Scindhia Guest Houses (250m)

To Train Station & Lahurabir

Chowk

To Main Post Office (1.5km)

Steps

To Luxa Road

To Foreigner's Registration Office (600m)

Dasaswamedh Ghat Road

Mandapur Road

Bengal Tola

Footpath to Scindhia Guest House (250m)

Dasaswamedh Ghat

Ganges River

0   100   200 m
Approximate Scale
Note: Not all alleyways shown

To Benares Hindu University (4km)

rooftop restaurant that has great views of the old city and the river. Spartan rooms with common bath start from a mere Rs 30/50. Rooms with attached bath and lukewarm water start from Rs 80/100. Unfortunately, the place has few outward facing windows and the slightest noise reverberates through the building – you'll certainly know about it when your neighbour decides to go for a dawn boat ride or suddenly gets the runs.

There are a couple of decent choices on Dasaswamedh Ghat Rd in Godaulia. they're a bit more spacious than those in the alleyways of the old city but try to avoid rooms that front onto the noisy main road.

Hotel Samman (☎ 322241) is good value and often full. Basic but fine rooms with attached bath start from Rs 100/150. Checkout is 24 hours.

Hotel Ganges (☎ 321097) has variable rooms with attached bath from Rs 175/225, to Rs 400/500 with air-con. Add 5% service charge. There's a business centre and a restaurant on site.

Bhelpura This area is by the river, midway between the old town and the university.

The *Sandhya Guest House (☎ 313292, Sonarpur Rd)* is a few minutes' walk from Shivala Ghat. It's run by a friendly, helpful manager and has an eating area on the roof where you can chow down on home-made soups and brown bread. Clean rooms with common bath cost Rs 70/90 and with attached bath Rs 90/120. You can sleep on the roof on a bedroll for Rs 15 or 'whatever you feel like paying'.

Maruti Guest House (☎ 312261, Assi Rd) is a friendly, family-run place with singles/doubles from just Rs 40/70, or from Rs 80 with attached bath. Interesting conversation is provided by the doctor-owner, who gives free yoga and meditation lessons.

Hotel Ganges View (☎ 313218, fax 313965) is a stylish, cultured place overlooking Assi Ghat. There are lots of paintings and ornaments on display, and excellent vegetarian meals are available in the evening. Singles/doubles start at Rs 300/350, or Rs 800 with air-con.

Lahurabir & Chetganj While these areas offer nothing of particular interest, they may be to your liking if you want to keep out of the crush of the old city, or need to be close to transport options.

Hotel Ajaya (☎ 343707, Kabir Chaura Marg) is good value. It has clean, pleasant rooms with attached bath and colour TV for Rs 150/200 and air-con rooms for Rs 450/500. Checkout is on the 24 hour system.

Hotel Buddha (☎ 343686) is one of the best low-budget hotels in the area. It's behind the Hotel Ajaya, off the main street, so it's quieter. The rooms are a little plain, but they're mostly spacious with high ceilings. Singles/doubles with attached hot bath cost from Rs 150/220. There are also a few tiny rooms with common bath for Rs 90/130. The hotel food is pretty good and sensibly priced, and served on a verandah overlooking a narrow garden. The staff are friendly and helpful.

Hotel Grand Holiday (☎ 343791, Narain Villa) is in a quiet residential street, and has variable rooms with hot bath from Rs 250, or Rs 500 with air-con. The best thing about this place is the garden and the friendly, family atmosphere. Checkout is 24 hours. Call ahead for free pick-up.

Hotel Barahdari (☎ 330040) is east of Lahurabir, not far from the main post office and within walking distance of the ghats. It's well run by a friendly Jain family and has a vegetarian restaurant and a peaceful garden. Comfortable, smallish, air-cooled rooms with attached hot bath and TV cost Rs 300/450, or Rs 500/550 with air-con.

Hotel Avaneesh (☎ 350730, Station Rd) is a modern place offering small but comfortable air-con rooms with TV from Rs 450/550.

Along the road is *Hotel New International (☎/fax 350805)* with a range of new rooms from Rs 350/450 with TV and other facilities. A 10% service charge is added.

Hotel Padmini International (☎ 220079, fax 220972, Sigra Rd) is good value if a little out of the way. Good rooms with attached hot bath and TV are Rs 350/400, or Rs 475/575 with air-con. Most rooms are airy, with a marble floor, and there's a good restaurant.

Train Station Area There are lots of cheap hotels close to Varanasi Junction train station if you need to be close to transport options. Most supply bucket hot water during the cool season.

The *Tourist Bungalow (☎ 343413, Parade Kothi)* is quite popular since it has a pleasant garden. There's also a veg/nonveg restaurant and a bar. Dorm beds cost Rs 50. Singles/doubles with attached bath go for Rs 150/200, deluxe air-cooled rooms with TV for Rs 275/350 and air-con rooms for Rs 475/550.

Across the road is *Hotel Plaza Inn (☎ 348210, fax 340504)*, a newly built hotel with comfortable, air-con rooms with all amenities. Prices start at Rs 750/950.

The other places in this street are very basic, but at least at *Hotel Amar (☎ 343509)* there's hot water (Rs 5 a bucket) and all rooms have a TV. Singles/doubles are Rs 110/150 with bath or Rs 70/110 without.

Hotel Sandona (☎ 346555), near the bus station, has clean, spartan singles/doubles with attached bath for Rs 100/150; deluxe rooms with TV are Rs 200. Checkout is after 24 hours.

Nar Indra (☎ 343586) is one of several hotels lining the noisy Grand Trunk Rd, right outside the train station. Clean, simple rooms with TV cost Rs 150/200 with common bath, Rs 200/225 with attached bath and Rs 300/350 with air-con. It has 24 hour checkout and a veg/nonveg restaurant.

The *retiring rooms* at Varanasi Junction train station have dorm beds (Rs 50), rooms (Rs 150/200) and air-con doubles (Rs 350).

Cantonment Area This area, on the northern side of Varanasi Junction station, contains a sprinkling of budget hotels and most of the city's upmarket accommodation. It's the place to retreat to when the claustrophobia of the old city gets to you. If you stay here, you'll depend on hotel restaurants for sustenance since there are few independent eating places in the area.

Hotel Surya (☎ 343014, fax 348330, The Mall) is a great place to stay if you need to wind down from the rigours of being on the road. It's set around a pleasant garden and has singles/doubles with bath and hot water for Rs 200/250, or Rs 500/650 with air-con. The hotel is popular with overlanders, and you can camp on the lawn for Rs 50.

Hotel Shalimar (☎ 346227) is next door; it's a similar standard but lacks the garden. The rooms for Rs 200/300 are fine, but the air-con rooms for Rs 600/700 aren't such good value, despite having colour TV. Prices are discounted in the low season.

There's a group of hotels on Patel Nagar, the street that runs north from the train station into the cantonment.

Hotel Temples Town (☎ 346582, 53 Patel Nagar) is clean and basic and operates on the 24 hour checkout system. Singles/doubles/triples with attached bath but no outward-facing window cost Rs 150/200/260.

Hotel Vaibhav (☎ 345056, fax 346466, 56 Patel Nagar) is clean, well run and has a bar and a good restaurant. Comfortable rooms with attached bath, hot water and TV cost Rs 350/450 and air-con rooms Rs 600/700. Rooms in the new wing (from Rs 750/850) are very pleasant.

Hotel India (☎ 342912, fax 348327, 59 Patel Nagar) feels slightly more upmarket. A few rooms with attached bath and hot water go for Rs 300/400. Air-con rooms with bathtubs start from Rs 500/600 and rise to Rs 850/1100 in the semiluxurious modern wing. The hotel has an excellent restaurant, a cellar bar and a scrappy rooftop eating area.

Places to Stay – Top End

Nearly all the top-end hotels are in the cantonment.

Hotel Clarks Varanasi (☎ 348501, fax 348186, The Mall) is the oldest hotel in the city. It dates back to the British era, though it now has a large modern extension. It boasts the usual range of facilities plus a good swimming pool. Air-con singles/doubles cost US$48/90.

Hotel Taj Ganges (☎ 345100, fax 348067, Nadesar Palace) is equally upmarket and has the most luxurious rooms in town, costing from US$105/120. It has a swimming pool, tennis court, jogging track and other amenities.

Hotel Ideal Tops (☎ 348091, fax 348685, The Mall), near Clarks, is a modern three star hotel with well-appointed air-con rooms for Rs 1195/1695. If you want some luxury at an affordable price and don't need a pool, this is an excellent place to stay. The brand-new hotel new door, *Hotel Ideal Palace*, has the same prices and ownership.

The *Hotel Varanasi Ashok* (☎ 346020, fax 348089, The Mall), on the other side of Clarks, is a four star establishment with air-con rooms with balconies for Rs 1500/2500 (Rs 1400/2000 April to September). It has a swimming pool, restaurant, a bar and a quiet atmosphere.

Hotel de Paris (☎ 346601, fax 348520, 15 The Mall) is in a large rambling building in a spacious garden. This old-fashioned three-star place is a little run-down. Huge, simple rooms with big windows and (usually) air-con are perhaps overpriced at US$25/35.

The *Hotel Hindusthan International* (☎ 351484, fax 350931, Maldahiya) is the only luxury hotel outside the cantonment. It's a modern four star concrete block in the centre of the city offering air-con rooms for US$34/68. Facilities include a swimming pool, a massage centre, a snug bar and a restaurant with rather overdone decor.

Places to Eat

Godaulia & the Old City The food in the old city is pretty uninspiring and standards of hygiene are not all that they might be. Cafes offer a standard travellers' menu consisting of western breakfasts and snacks that mostly involve giving their jaffle machine a serious work out. Indian food tends to be oily and there are plenty of restaurants where no matter what you order, every dish that comes out of the kitchen looks exactly the same. On the other hand, Varanasi is well known for its sweets and high-quality paan. The alleyways of the old city are full of shops offering ample opportunity to indulge in either. Places in the old city are not

supposed to serve alcohol, though in one or two places you can get beer: it's served discretely in a teapot! If you arrive during mango season, try the locally grown variety known as Langda Aam.

Shanti Guest House, *Yogi Lodge*, *Trimurti Guest House* and *Vishnu Rest House* all have restaurants popular with travellers. Shanti and Vishnu both have excellent views, though the food at Shanti gets mixed reports.

Ganga Fuji, not far from the Vishwanath Temple, is a snug place offering western breakfasts and Indian, Chinese and Japanese meals for between Rs 25 and Rs 40, including nonveg. There's live classical Indian music in the evenings, starting 7.30 pm.

Garden Restaurant is a relaxing little rooftop eatery with the usual travellers' menu. It also has veg/nonveg Indian food for between Rs 25 and Rs 60, though portions are quite small.

There's a number of eateries along Dasaswamedh Ghat Rd offering Indian food.

Yelchiko by the main roundabout in Godaulia is a basement restaurant serving standard Indian-Chinese-continental fare for between Rs 25 and Rs 45. The food is merely adequate, but you can get special 'tea' here for Rs 75.

Next door, *Jalyog* has Indian-style breakfasts of puris and vegetables, known as *kachauri*. It's small, simple, and the entry sign is mainly in Hindi. Samosas are only Rs 2.

Ayyar's Cafe is a modest veg eatery on Dasaswamedh Ghat Rd serving good masala dosas for less than Rs 18, and full thalis for Rs 30.

Keshari, down a small alley opposite, is a clean, popular veg restaurant providing an extensive menu of meals and snacks. Main dishes are around Rs 25 to Rs 40.

Temple Restaurant in the Hotel Ganges offers a 1st floor view of the hustle and bustle of Dasaswamedh Ghat Rd. It serves good veg/nonveg Indian fare, Chinese food and western breakfasts. Main dishes (which are 'very pleasing' according to the menu) are between Rs 20 and Rs 70, and there's live Indian classical music in the evenings.

A little way east is *Madhur Milan Cafe*, a small but busy vegetarian restaurant with cheap dosas, samosas and thalis.

Traveller-style restaurants on Begali Tola, an alley south of Dasaswamedh Ghat Rd, include *Chandan Restaurant* and *Baba Restaurant*.

Bhelupura *Sindhi Restaurant*, by the Lalita Cinema, prepares a range of good south Indian vegetarian food for less than Rs 40.

Even more popular is the *Kerala Cafe (Mandapur Rd)*, across the junction, which mostly specialises in dosas for only Rs 10 to Rs 16.

Bread of Life Bakery (Sonarpur Rd) is a haven for western-style breads and biscuits. It also has a restaurant section with western meals for Rs 95, plus breakfasts and baked potatoes. It's open 8 am to 9 pm, closed Monday.

Vaatika Cafe, next to the Hotel Ganges View and overlooking Assi Ghat, serves reasonable versions of pizza and spaghetti for Rs 30 to Rs 45.

Train Station & Lahurabir There are several places to choose from in these areas. In addition to the places listed here, the restaurants in the hotels Buddha, Padmini International and Plaza Inn are worth visiting (see the Places to Stay section, earlier).

Most Welcome Restaurant, near the Tourist Bungalow, is a cute little eatery with cheap veg/nonveg fare and western breakfasts. Prices are between Rs 15 and Rs 30. It claims to be recommended by all the guide books of the world, which is pretty good for a place no bigger than the average western kitchen.

Fairly close by and next to Hotel Sandona is *El Parador*, with an eclectic menu offering Greek, Mexican and Italian dishes, and a relaxed 'traveller' ambience. However, reports on the food are mixed, and it's pricey, with meals costing around Rs 90 to Rs 100.

The *Poonam Restaurant* in the Pradeep Hotel, Jagatganj, has good service and decent Indian, Chinese and continental dishes. Mains start from Rs 70/95 for veg/nonveg.

Around the corner is the *Kamesh Hut Garden Restaurant*. It has a pleasant garden setting, attentive service, and excellent food for the price. Indian, Chinese and continental dishes start at Rs 25 for veg and Rs 45 for nonveg.

Opposite the main post office is *Sona Rupa Restaurant*, serving Indian vegetarian dishes. The dosas for around Rs 20 are popular. There's also a bakery on site.

Cantonment Area Hotel restaurants are the best bet in this area. *Canton Restaurant* at the Hotel Surya serves good veg/nonveg fare, western stand-bys and, despite its name, more Indian than Chinese dishes. The restaurant overlooks the hotel garden and a lazy breakfast on the lawn makes a great start to the day. The staff are friendly and efficient. Mains are between Rs 35 and Rs 70; beer is a tad pricey at Rs 80.

Palm Springs in the Hotel India has excellent Indian cuisine. Dishes cost around Rs 100 but they're worth it. If you can order the Huggy Buggy without laughing you should win a prize. *Palki Restaurant* in the next-door Hotel Vaibhav is equally good.

Hotel Clarks and the *Hotel Taj Ganges* are the places to go if you want to dine in style. Each has a choice of restaurants.

Entertainment

Varanasi is not renowned for its nightlife. About the only choice, other than the cinemas showing Bollywood fare, are the Indian classical music recitals. These are mostly held at music teaching centres, such as at the International Music Centre Ashram, south of Dasaswamedh Ghat Rd (at 8 pm on Wednesday and Saturday) and the Triveni Music Centre, near Panday Ghat (Monday at 7 pm and Thursday at 9 pm). Major classical concerts are also occasionally held at Nagari Natak Mandali. Check the *Pioneer* for details.

The *Temple* and *Ganja Fuji* restaurants (see the Places to Eat section, earlier) also have music in the evenings.

Bars are few and far between in Varanasi. Two to try are *Yelchiko Bar & Restaurant*

(Vidyapeeth Rd), open 11 am to 10.30 pm, and **Basant Bar & Restaurant** *(Chaitganj Marg)*. A bottle of beer starts at Rs 65.

Shopping

Varanasi is famous throughout India for silk brocades and beautiful Benares saris. However, there are lots of rip-off merchants and commission people at work. Invitations to 'come to my home for tea' will inevitably mean to somebody's silk showroom, where you will be pressured into buying things. See the UP Tourism city map (free from the tourist offices) for addresses of government emporiums and 'recognised' souvenir shops.

There's a market west of the main post office called Golghar where the makers of silk brocades sell directly to local shops. You can get cheaper silk brocade in this area than in the big stores in the chowk area, but you must be careful about the quality. Mixtures of silk and cotton can look very like pure silk to the untrained eye. Pilikothi, a Muslim area north-east of the main post office, also has good silk.

Varanasi is also renowned for its ingenious toys, musical instruments and expensive Bhadohi carpets. There's a range of local and national products in the fixed-price Cottage Industries Exposition in the cantonment, opposite the Hotel Taj Ganges. Its prices are high but a visit will give you an idea of the relative costs of various items.

Getting There & Away

Air Varanasi is on the popular daily tourist shuttle route linking Khajuraho (US$70), Agra (US$95) and Delhi (US$110). There are also daily Indian Airlines flights to Mumbai (US$210). The Indian Airlines office (☎ 345959) is in the cantonment near the Hotel de Paris. Office hours are 10 am to 1 pm and 2 to 5 pm.

Sahara India Airlines (☎ 343094) has four flights a week to Mumbai and Lucknow and three flights a week to Delhi.

Bus Varanasi's bus station is a few hundred metres north-east of Varanasi Junction train station. It's a fairly sleepy depot and there's no timetable information in English. Buses lined up on the street out front are mostly faster, private buses. There are frequent express buses to Jaunpur (Rs 21, 1½ hours), Allahabad (Rs 42, three hours), Lucknow (Rs 94, 8½ hours), Faizabad (Rs 70, seven hours) and Gorakhpur (Rs 73, seven hours).

No buses run direct to Khajuraho so take a train to Satna and a bus to Khajuraho (four hours) from there.

Train Varanasi Junction (also known as Varanasi Cantonment) is the main station. There is a separate reservation centre building on the left as you approach the station, but foreign tourist quota tickets must be purchased at the Foreign Tourist Assistance Bureau by the UP Tourism information booth in the main station building. This office is open daily except Sunday between 8 am and 8 pm.

Not all trains between Delhi and Calcutta stop at Varanasi Junction but most halt at Mughal Serai, 12km south of Varanasi. This is a 45 minute ride by bus (Rs 5), tempo (Rs 10) or auto-rickshaw (Rs 70) along a congested stretch of the Grand Trunk Rd. You can make reservations at Varanasi Junction train station for trains leaving from Mughal Serai.

Travellers should keep a close eye on their baggage while on trains heading to Varanasi. The tourist information booth at Varanasi Junction reckons hardly a day goes by without a traveller arriving on the platform without their backpack.

Nepal There are regular ordinary buses from Varanasi's bus stand to Sonauli (Rs 105, 10 hours). Plenty of travel agents and lodges offer 'through' tickets to Kathmandu and Pokhara (Rs 300). This involves spending a night in spartan accommodation in Sonauli and a change of buses at the border. Doing it yourself is not only cheaper but gives you a choice of accommodation and buses at the border.

It's not worth catching a train to the border since the line from Gorakhpur to Sonauli is metre gauge, though you could

Major Trains from Varanasi

destination	train number & name	departure time[1]	distance (km)	duration (hours)	fare (Rs) (2nd/1st)
Calcutta	2382 *Poorva Exp*	5.00 am V	678	11.00	135/679
	3010 *Doon Exp*	4.15 pm V	678	15.00	135/679
Chennai (Madras)	6040 *Ganga Kaveri Exp*	5.50 pm V	2144	41.00	264/1545
Delhi	2301 or 2305 *Rajdhani Exp* [2]	12.50 am MS	764	9.00	920/2625
	2381 *Poorva Exp*	8.00 pm V	792	12.00	152/766
	4257 *Kashi Vishwanath Exp*	2.00 pm V		16.30	152/766
Gorakhpur	5104 *Intercity Exp*	5.50 am V	231	5.00	62/298
Lucknow	4227 *Varuna Exp*	5.15 am V	302	4.30	77/370
Mumbai (Bombay)	1094 *Mahanagri Exp*	11.30 am V	1509	24.30	223/1209
New Jalpaiguri	5622 *N E Exp*	6.15 pm MS	848	15.30	59/767
Patna	3484 *Farrakka Exp*	3.15 pm V	228	5.30	61/294
Puri	8476 *Neelachal Exp*	8.05 pm V	1061	23.00	186/916
Satna	5218 *Kurla Exp*	11.30 pm V	236	7.00	62/298

All trains run daily except:
Ganga Kaveri 6040 only Mon/Wed   Rajdhani 2301 only Tue/Wed/Fri/Sat/Sun
Poorva 2382 only Mon/Tue/Fri   Rajdhani 2305 only Mon/Thur
Poorva 2381 only Wed/Thur/Sun   Neelachal 8476 only Tue/Fri/Sun

[1]Abbreviations for train stations: V – Varanasi Junction, MS – Mughal Serai
[2]Air-con only; fare includes meals and drinks

catch an express train to Gorakhpur and pick up a bus to Sonauli from there.

Indian Airlines has a daily flight to Kathmandu (US$71 plus US$4 tax), but it can be difficult getting a seat. If you can't get on the plane and don't want to experience the long bus journey, travel agents can arrange a car for about Rs 4.25 per kilometre; the 620km to Kathmandu should take about 12 hours.

Getting Around
To/From the Airport
Babatpur airport is 22km north-west of the city. A bus runs from the Hotel Vaibhav in the cantonment at 10.30 am and 2.30 pm, going via the Government of India tourist office and the Indian Airlines office. The fare is Rs 25 and it takes around 45 minutes. If you bargain hard you should get an auto-rickshaw to the airport for around Rs 100 to Rs 120. In the opposite direction, rickshaw-wallahs may charge much less since they assume they'll pick up a commission at the hotel where they drop you. Taxis will try to charge well over Rs 200 to the airport, though the pre-paid rate is Rs 186.

Bus Local buses are very crowded unless you can get on at the starting point. They cost Rs 2 to Rs 5, but they're irregular and you need to beware of pickpockets. A useful bus goes from Varanasi Junction train station to Lanka, which is close to Benares Hindu University.

Taxis & Auto-Rickshaws For 'private' trips by taxi or auto-rickshaw you'll have to agree a price since they do not have meters.

You'll have a hard time trying to get a decent rate, but the task has been made easier by the recent introduction of prepaid booths on the south side of Varanasi Junction train station. In theory, the booths should be staffed 24 hours. Some of the displayed prepaid taxi rates from there are: Dasaswamedh Ghat Rs 50, Assi Ghat Rs 64, Benares Hindu University or Sarnath Rs 78, Mughal Serai Rs 136. Some prepaid auto-rickshaw rates are: Godaulia Rs 25, Benares Hindu University Rs 30, Sarnath Rs 40 and Mughal Serai Rs 70.

Shared Auto-Rickshaw & Tempo These operate along set routes with fixed prices (Rs 3 to Rs 5). They can be the best way to get around the city cheaply, although not when you have hefty baggage. From the stand outside the northern entrance of Varanasi Junction train station it's Rs 5 to the cantonment TV tower. There's a stand outside the southern entrance for destinations including Lahurabir (Rs 5).

Cycle-Rickshaw & Bicycle It won't take long walking the streets before you start perceiving yourself as transport bait for cycle-rickshaw-wallahs. Figures quoted for trips usually start five times the price instead of just double, and some rickshaw-wallahs in the cantonment are cheeky enough to quote prices in US dollars. In theory, a trip between the train station and Godaulia should cost about Rs 10; from the cantonment hotels to Godaulia should be around Rs 15 and to Lahurabir around Rs 10. However, these prices are what Indians would pay, and it is generally accepted locally that foreigners should pay more. Unless you want to spend half your visit haggling, expect to pay double these rates.

SARNATH
☎ 0542

The Buddha came to this hamlet, 10km north-east of Varanasi, to preach his message of the 'middle way' to nirvana after he achieved enlightenment at Bodhgaya. Later, the great Buddhist emperor Ashoka erected magnificent stupas and monasteries here.

Sarnath was at its peak when the indefatigable Chinese traveller Fahsien visited the site early in the 5th century AD. When Xuan Zhang, another Chinese traveller, dropped by in 640 AD, Sarnath had 1500 priests, a stupa nearly 100m high, Ashoka's mighty stone pillar and many other wonders. The city was known as the Deer Park, after the Buddha's famous first sermon, *The Sermon in the Deer Park*.

Soon after, Buddhism went into decline and when Muslim invaders destroyed and desecrated the city's buildings, Sarnath became little more than a shell. It was not until 1835 when British archaeologists started excavations that Sarnath regained some of its past glory. It's now a major Buddhist centre.

Most of Sarnath's monuments are set in landscaped gardens, making it a pleasant place to spend half a day. During the **Buddha Purnima Festival** in May, Sarnath cele-

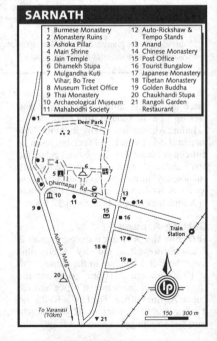

SARNATH

1 Burmese Monastery	12 Auto-Rickshaw &
2 Monastery Ruins	Tempo Stands
3 Ashoka Pillar	13 Anand
4 Main Shrine	14 Chinese Monastery
5 Jain Temple	15 Post Office
6 Dhamekh Stupa	16 Tourist Bungalow
7 Mulgandha Kuti	17 Japanese Monastery
Vihar; Bo Tree	18 Tibetan Monastery
8 Museum Ticket Office	19 Golden Buddha
9 Thai Monastery	20 Chaukhandi Stupa
10 Archaeological Museum	21 Rangoli Garden
11 Mahabodhi Society	Restaurant

brates the birth of the Buddha with a big fair and a procession. Although you may be able to arrange to stay in some of Sarnath's monasteries, you'd be better off going to Bodhgaya or Dharamsala if you're interested in studying Buddhism.

Dhamekh Stupa

This 34m stupa dominates the site and is believed to mark the spot where the Buddha preached his famous sermon. In its present form it dates from around 500 AD but was probably rebuilt a number of times. The geometrical and floral patterns on the stupa are typical of the Gupta period, but excavations have revealed brickwork from the Mauryan period – around 200 BC. Originally there was a second stupa, Dharmarajika Stupa, but this was reduced to rubble by 19th century treasure seekers.

The nearby **Jain Temple**, built in 1824, is thought to mark the birthplace of the 11th Jain tirthankar, Shreyanshnath.

Main Shrine & Ashoka Pillar

Ashoka is said to have meditated in the building known as the 'main shrine'. The foundations are all that can now be seen, and to the north of it are the extensive ruins of the monasteries.

Standing in front of the main shrine are the remains of Ashoka's pillar. At one time this stood over 20m high, but the capital is now in the Archaeological Museum, significantly shortening the column. An edict issued by Ashoka is engraved on the remaining portion of the column.

Entry is free on Friday, otherwise you need to buy the Archaeological Museum ticket to get in.

Archaeological Museum

The main attraction at this excellent museum is the superb capital from the Ashokan pillar. It has the Ashokan symbol of four back-to-back lions which has been adopted as the state emblem of modern India. Below this are representations of a lion, elephant, horse and bull. The lion represents bravery, the elephant symbolises the dream Buddha's

mother had before his birth, and the horse recalls that Buddha left his home on horseback in search of enlightenment.

Other finds from the site include figures and sculptures from Sarnath's Mauryan, Kushana and Gupta periods. Among them is the (very fine) earliest Buddha image found at Sarnath and many images of Hindu gods dating from the 9th to 12th centuries. The museum is open 10 am to 5 pm daily except Friday; entry is Rs 2. Buy tickets from the booth across the road.

Mulgandha Kuti Vihar

This modern Mahabodhi Society temple has a series of frescoes by the Japanese artist Kosetsu Nosi in the interior. A bodi tree growing here was transplanted in 1931 from the tree in Anuradhapura, Sri Lanka, which in turn is said to be an offspring of the original tree under which the Buddha attained enlightenment. There's a group of statues here showing the Buddha giving his first sermon to his five disciples. The temple is closed between 11.30 am and 1.30 pm.

Other Temples & Deer Park

You can visit the modern temples in the Thai, Chinese, Tibetan, Burmese and Japanese monasteries.

The **Chaukhandi Stupa** dates from the Gupta period. There's a good view from the Moghul tower, which was built by Akbar.

North of the Mulgandha Kuti Vihar is the deer park, where the deer inmates are accompanied by some Indian birds and waterfowl.

Places to Stay & Eat

The UP *Tourist Bungalow* (☎ 386965) has rooms with hot bath for Rs 240, or Rs 475 with air-con. There's also a basic dorm costing Rs 50 per bed, and a restaurant serving the standard tourist bungalow fare.

The new *Golden Buddah* (☎ 311030) has rooms with bath for Rs 200/300, and a garden.

Anand is a small, inexpensive restaurant serving Indian and Chinese food. *Rangoli Garden Restaurant* is a larger place with inside or garden seating. Meals start at Rs 25 for veg and Rs 50 for nonveg.

UTTAR PRADESH

Getting There & Away

Most visitors day trip from Varanasi. An auto-rickshaw for the 20 minute journey costs Rs 40 (prepaid rate). Local buses depart frequently from the south side of Varanasi Junction train station (Rs 4, 45 minutes); they call at the Civil Court (Rs 3) in the cantonment but they'll be full by then. Only a few local trains stop at Sarnath.

JAUNPUR
☎ 05452 • pop 160,000

This bustling town 58km north-west of Varanasi sees few travellers but is of interest to architectural historians for its mosques, which are built in a unique style that is part Islamic, part Hindu and part Jain.

Founded by Firoz Shah Tughlaq in 1360 on an ancient site, Jaunpur became the capital of the independent Muslim Sharqui kingdom. The most impressive mosques were constructed between 1394 and 1478. They were built on the ruins of Hindu, Buddhist and Jain temples and shrines, and are notable for their odd mixture of architectural styles, their two storey arcades and large gateways, and their unusual minarets. Jaunpur was sacked by Sikander Lodi, who left only the mosques undamaged. The Mughals took over in 1530.

The bus stand is south of the Gomti River, a Rs 8 cycle-rickshaw ride from the 16th century stone **Akbari Bridge**, which crosses to the northern part of town where most of the mosques and the train station are located. The sights are spread out over two or three sq km so a cycle-rickshaw can be useful, and the wallahs can also act as guides.

The modest but well-maintained **Jaunpur Fort**, built by Firoz Shah in 1360, overlooks the Gomti River. Continue 500m north to see the **Atala Masjid**, built in 1408 on the site of a Hindu temple dedicated to Atala Devi. Another 500m north-west is the most impressive of the mosques, the **Jama Masjid**, built between 1438 and 1478.

Other places to see include the Jhanjhri Masjid, the tombs of the Sharqui sultans, the Char Ungli Masjid and the Lal Darwaza Masjid.

Places to Stay & Eat

The few travellers who come here tend to day-trip from Varanasi, though there are several inexpensive hotels along the 600m-long road between the bus station and the town centre.

The *Hotel Amber* (☎ 63201), near the fort, has basic but acceptable singles/doubles with attached bath for Rs 80/100.

The small *dhabas* near Jaunpur Junction train station and in the bazaars are as fancy as the eating opportunities get.

Getting There & Away

There are regular buses to and from Varanasi (Rs 21, 1½ hours). A few express trains connect Jaunpur Junction with Varanasi (Rs 25, 1½ hours), Faizabad (Rs 43, three hours) and Lucknow (Rs 61, six hours).

GORAKHPUR
☎ 0551 • pop 575,000

Most travellers happily pass straight through Gorakhpur on their way to or from Nepal. This is hardly surprising since the city is infamous for its annual plagues of flies and mosquitoes and even the local tourist office candidly tells visitors 'there are no sights in Gorakhpur'. The city is, however, the headquarters of the North Eastern Railway and is a useful train junction.

Gorakhpur is named after the sage, Yogi Gorakhnath. The **Gorakhnath Temple** is a couple of kilometres north-west of the city centre and is worth visiting if you have time to fill in between transport connections. The city is also home to well-known Hindu religious publishers Geeta Press. A visit to their office will result in a pile of invaluable English-language books being offered to you with titles like 'How to lead a household life'. These make excellent presents to friends back home with a sense of humour.

Information

Tourist offices are at the train station and on Park Rd (☎ 335450). They're open Monday to Saturday 10 am to 5 pm and give out a useful map of Gorakhpur and Kushinagar. The State Bank of India on Bank Rd exchanges only cash and American Express travellers cheques (US dollar or pounds sterling).

Places to Stay

The best places to stay in Gorakhpur are in the central Golghar district, close to the few decent restaurants in the city, but none are particularly inspiring and all have bucket hot water. Checkout is typically 24 hours. It costs under Rs 10 to reach them by cycle-rickshaw from the train station.

Hotel Yark-Inn (☎ *338233*) has a range of rooms with attached bath and (usually) TV. Prices go from Rs 100/175 a single/double up to Rs 400 for a large air-con double.

Hotel Marina (☎ *337630*) has big, clean rooms from Rs 140/195 with attached bath and TV, and air-con doubles from Rs 400.

Hotel President (☎ *337654*), in front of Hotel Marina, has a lift but is not as good value at Rs 225/350 for rooms with attached bath and TV or Rs 550 with air-con.

The hotels opposite the train station are the closest to the bus stand – handy for those early buses to Sonauli. Unfortunately, the area can be so noisy that you may not need to set your alarm.

Hotel Elora (☎ *200647*) is the best of this bunch. Rooms at the back have balconies overlooking a large playing field and are sheltered from the worst of the noise. Singles/doubles cost from Rs 90/150 with attached bath and TV and Rs 250/350 for air-con.

Standard Hotel (☎ *201439*) has pleasant singles/doubles/triples with bath for Rs 115/175/225. The mosquito nets over beds are useful, but they do make sleeping hot from late March onwards.

The *retiring rooms* at the train station cost Rs 90/140 with attached bath, and Rs 175/300 with air-con. Dorm beds for Rs 50.

Places to Eat

There aren't many places in Gorakhpur catering to visitors so you could do worse than try the small outdoor eateries near the train station.

The busy *Bobi's* at the Ambar Hotel in the city centre has decent veg/nonveg fare and serves pastries and ice cream.

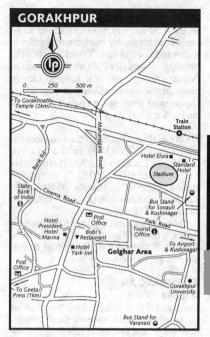

Queen's Restaurant in the Hotel President is also good. It's inexpensive, and has the added advantage of staying open until 11 pm – long after the rest of the city is safely tucked up in bed. Like Bobi's, it serves Indian and Chinese food.

Getting There & Away

Bus There are frequent buses from the same bus stand to Lucknow (Rs 89, 7½ hours) and Faizabad (Rs 48, four hours). Buses to Kushinagar (Rs 19, 1½ hours) depart every 30 minutes.

Buses to Varanasi (Rs 73, seven hours) depart regularly from the Katchari bus stand, a Rs 5 cycle-rickshaw ride south-east of the city centre.

Nepal There are regular departures for the border at Sonauli (Rs 33, three hours) from 4.30 am onwards from the bus stand just south of the train station. You'll need to be on the 4.30 am bus from Gorakhpur to be sure of catching a day bus from the border to Kathmandu or Pokhara. Travel agents offer 'through' tickets (Rs 250) to Kathmandu or Pokhara though you still have to change buses at the border. Doing it yourself is cheaper and gives you a choice of buses at the border.

Train Gorakhpur has direct train connections with Varanasi (Rs 67/332 in 2nd/1st class, five hours); Lucknow (Rs 70/341, five to six hours); Delhi (Rs 223/752 in sleeper/1st class, 15 hours); Calcutta (Rs 245/862, 18 to 22 hours); and Mumbai (Rs 337/1278, 30 to 34 hours, 1690km).

There are also metre-gauge trains to Nautanwa, which is 8km short of the border at Sonauli. It's much faster and more convenient to get to Sonauli by bus.

KUSHINAGAR
☎ 05564

The Buddha is reputed to have breathed his last words, 'Decay is inherent in all component things' and expired at Kushinagar. Now pilgrims come in large numbers to see the remains of his brick **cremation stupa**, the reclining Buddha figure in the **Mahaparinirvana Temple**, the modern **IndoJapan-Sri Lanka Buddhist Centre** and the numerous Buddhist monasteries here. The tourist office opposite the Myanmar monastery is helpful and open Monday to Saturday 10 am to 5 pm, and sometimes Sunday.

Places to Stay & Eat

Budget accommodation, either by donation or for a set fee, is provided at the Chinese, Myanmar, Thai and Tibetan monasteries.

The new *International Cultural Guest House* (☎ 72164), opposite the Buddhist Centre, charges Rs 100 for bare, clean doubles.

Pathik Nivas (☎ 71038), the UP Tourist Bungalow, is in a garden setting and has good but overpriced singles/doubles with attached hot bath from Rs 400/500 to Rs 1100/1200 (with air-con). Its pricey restaurant charges Rs 30 for a bottle of water.

Lotus Nikko Hotel (☎/fax 71139) is a new three star establishment popular with Japanese visitors touring India's Buddhist sites. Per person rates, including three meals a day, are US$90 for huge rooms or US$40 in the cheaper annexe. It boasts a Japanese restaurant and a Japanese bathhouse.

Yama Kwality Cafe, by the Chinese temple, provides inexpensive veg/nonveg fare.

Getting There & Away

Kushinagar is 55km east of Gorakhpur and there are frequent buses (Rs 19, 1½ hours) between the two towns (the last at around 6 pm). The Kushinagar bus stand is several kilometres from the temples and monasteries, so get off/on by the Kushinagar Police Post, and walk down the southwards turn-off for the temples.

SONAULI
☎ 05522

This sleepy village straddling the Nepalese border is little more than a bus stop, a couple of hotels, a few shops and a 24 hour border post. There's a much greater range of facilities on the Nepalese side, where the atmosphere is decidedly more upbeat. Indians and Nepalese are free to wander back and forth between the two parts of Sonauli without going through any formalities. Foreigners, however, must officially exit one country and acquire the requisite visa for the other.

The Nepalese border post is actually called Belhiya but everyone refers to it as Sonauli. Nepalese visas are available 24 hours (so they claim!) from the immigration office in 10 minutes. Visas cost US$15 for 15 days or US$25 for 30 days, payable in US dollars or Nepalese rupees but not in travellers cheques. Make sure you have an encashment certificate if you intend to pay in Nepalese rupees.

The easy-to-miss Indian immigration checkpoint is on the right-hand side of the road heading towards Nepal, about 200m from the border post.

The State Bank of India in Sonauli does not change money, but there are numerous foreign exchange offices on the Nepalese side offering competitive rates. Note that you can pay for bus tickets and just about anything else in Indian rupees on the Nepalese side of the border.

Places to Stay & Eat

Hotel Niranjana (☎ 38201), one of UP Tourism's establishments, is a clean and friendly place with a garden, 600m from the border. It has singles/doubles with attached bath, hot water and air cooling for Rs 200/240, some air-con rooms with TV for Rs 342/394 and a dorm for Rs 40. The restaurant serves unexciting but acceptable fare.

Baba Restaurant & Lodge (☎ 38366), by the bus stand, is a new place with cheap veg/nonveg food. Rooms are Rs 225 with attached bath, Rs 125 without. Dorm beds cost Rs 35.

Sanju Lodge (☎ 38355) is round the corner from the Indian immigration post. It's fairly rudimentary but has pleasant common areas and a hard bed in a clean but crowded dorm costs only Rs 25. Rooms cost Rs 50/80 with common bath and Rs 125/150 with attached bath and hot water.

There are several good, cheap hotels, plenty of open-air restaurants and a sudden blitz of beer advertisements on the Nepalese side of the border, where most travellers prefer to stay.

Getting There & Away

Bus Buses to Indian cities depart from the Sonauli bus stand on the edge of town, about 800m from the border post. There are plenty of buses to and from Gorakhpur (Rs 33, three hours) and direct buses to Varanasi

(Rs 105 to Rs 120, 10 hours) and Delhi (Rs 292, 24 hours), via Lucknow (12 hours).

If you're entering India at Sonauli, be wary of touts offering onward combined bus/rail tickets, since these are not 100% reliable. It's easy enough to arrange onward train travel yourself at the Gorakhpur or Varanasi train stations.

Nepal Private buses leave from the Nepalese side of the border for Kathmandu (Nep Rs 240, nine hours) or Pokhara (Nep Rs 230, nine hours), roughly every hour between 6 and 10 am and between 6 and 8 pm. Travelling during the day is preferable – at night it not only takes longer, you also miss the great views on the journey. You should get a ticket in advance; there's a booking office at the Nepalese bus stand. Travel agents on either side of the border also sell bus tickets, or can arrange a taxi (about Nep Rs 800, six hours).

Government 'Sajha' buses leave for Kathmandu from Bhairawa, 4km north of Sonauli, at 6.45 and 8 am, and at 6.30 and 7 pm. They're very popular as they're cheaper (around Nep Rs 180) and bookings should be made a day in advance. Tickets are sold from a kiosk near the Hotel Yeti in Bhairawa, on the main road from Sonauli. A cycle-rickshaw from the border to Bhairawa costs only Nep Rs 3. There are no government buses to Pokhara.

Numerous buses ply the 22km stretch between Bhairawa and Lumbini, the birthplace of the Buddha. They depart from the bus stand, which is about 1km north of the Hotel Yeti.

Bihar

Despite having areas of great beauty and historic religious links, Bihar is India's poorest state and is notorious for political uprisings and Naxalite bandit activity. Bordering Nepal, Uttar Pradesh, West Bengal, Orissa and Madhya Pradesh, the River Ganges flows west to east across it.

Today the Buddha's predictions continue to come true. The rivers periodically flood, causing disastrous problems for Bihar's dense population, which scratches a bare living from the soil. Per capita income is low, yet the Chotanagpur plateau in the south produces 40% of India's mineral wealth. Bihar's literacy rate is one of the lowest in the country, the state is considered to have the most widespread corruption and the state government is chronically short of money. Strikes and demonstrations are the order of the day and 'feud and fire' take the form of outbreaks of inter-caste warfare and violence - *dacoity* (banditry) is still widespread in Bihar.

Because of the lawlessness, political instability and lack of tourism infrastructure in the state, few travellers spend much time in Bihar, most just passing through Patna on their way to Calcutta or Kathmandu. This is a pity because there is much to see. In addition to the Buddhist sites, there are areas of natural beauty such as lakes, waterfalls and hot springs. Also worth seeing are the wildlife sanctuaries such as Betla in the south west and Valmiki Nagar in the far north-west, adjacent to the Royal Chitwan National Park in Nepal (but without the facilities). Unfortunately they are both in areas infested with Naxalite activity, so you must take an escort.

Bodhgaya is an excellent place to visit if you want to study Buddhism, and Rajgir, Sasaram and especially Nalanda are some of the most fascinating places you'll find off the usual tourist trail.

Other than in Bodhgaya, there are few Western tourists seen in Bihar, so be pre-

Bihar at a Glance

Population: 86.3 million
Area: 173,877 sq km
Capital: Patna
Main Language: Hindi
Best Time to Go: October to March

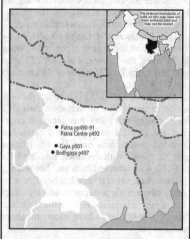

- **Bodhgaya** – soak up the Buddhist vibes under the sacred bodhi tree
- **Patna Museum** – a little oasis of knowledge and peace
- **Nalanda University** – enjoy the peaceful, serenity and ambience at the ruins of this ancient seat of learning
- **Sonepur Fair** – check out everything from chickens to elephants at India's largest livestock fair

pared to attract a lot of attention. If you happen to be on your own, female and a smoker, the interest will grow exponentially on each count!

Festivals of Bihar

festival	location	date	features
Rajgir Mahotsava	Rajgir	24-26 Oct	classical performing arts
Sonepur Fair	Sonepur	Oct/Nov	cattle fair
Pataliputra Mahotsava	Patna	Mar	parades, sport, dance & music
Saurath Sabha	Saurath village, District Madhubani	Jun	marriage market

History

The name Bihar is derived from the word *vihara*, meaning monastery. Bihar was a great religious centre for Jains, Hindus and, most importantly, Buddhists. It was at Bodhgaya that the Buddha attained enlightenment. A descendant of the original tree still flourishes there today. Nearby Nalanda was a world-famous Buddhist university in the 5th century AD, while Rajgir was associated with both the Buddha and the Jain apostle Mahavira.

Buddha prophesied that, although a great city would arise in Bihar, it would always be in danger from 'feud, fire and flood'. From the 6th century BC to the 5th century AD, Bihar was coveted by a succession of rulers and major empires. Ajatshatru, the second Magadha king, ruled his empire from Rajgir. Over 250 years later, in the 3rd century BC, the first of Buddha's predictions was seen with Chandragupta Maurya ruling from the great city of Pataliputra (now Patna). His grandson, Emperor Ashoka succeeded him. It's hard to imagine this city, the capital of one of the most backward states in the country, was then the largest city in the world and capital of India's greatest empire.

The Magadha dynasty rose to glory again during the reign of the Guptas (4th and 5th centuries). The dynasty was followed by the Palas of Bengal, who ruled until 1197.

Muslim rule which lasted from the 12th to the 17th century, also left an indelible mark on the region. Though there is little evidence to suggest it, the British acquired Bihar in 1764 following the Battle of Buxar, and ruled here until India's Independence in 1947.

Warning

The extreme poverty in Bihar makes tourist buses and private hire cars targets for dacoits. There have been several incidents where tourists have been robbed and assaulted by armed criminals who use road blocks, mock accidents and road works to force vehicles to stop. To reduce the danger, the Bihar government promised armed escorts to all foreign travellers. However, these are not automatic and a certain amount of perseverance is required to induce them to provide the service.

Chances are you won't encounter any trouble. However, it's not a bad idea to split up your valuables if making long journeys by road in Bihar and *never* travel after dusk.

PATNA
☎ 0612 • pop 1,285,470

As you would expect of one of India's poorest and most densely populated states, Bihar's capital is incredibly noisy, dirty and polluted, but strangely not as chaotic as many other cities. It is on the southern bank of the Ganges, which at this point is very wide, having been joined by three major tributaries between Varanasi and Patna. The Mahatma Gandhi Seti, one of the longest bridges in the world at 7.5km, crosses the Ganges 5km west of the city centre.

Every March Patna comes alive with the **Pataliputra Mahotsava** featuring parades, sports, dancing and music.

BIHAR

BIHAR

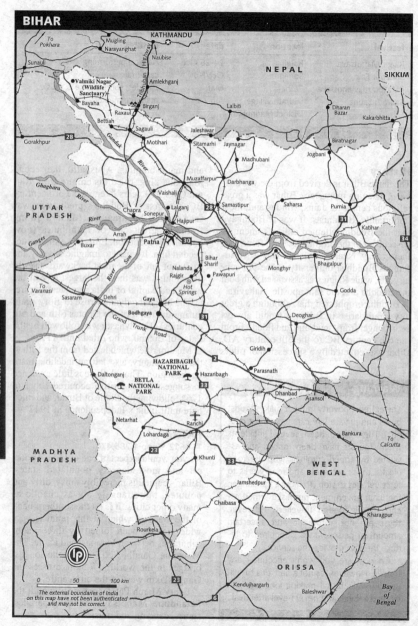

BIHAR

To Pokhara

KATHMANDU

Sunauli

Mugling
Narayanghat

Naubise

NEPAL

SIKKIM

Valmiki Nagar
(Wildlife
Sanctuary)

Amlekhganj

Bayaha

Birganj

Lalbiti

Dharan
Bazar

Kakarbhitta

Raxaul

Bettiah

Sagauli

Jaleshwar

Gorakhpur

28

Motihari

Sitamarhi

Jaynagar

Biratnagar

Ghaghara River

River

Muzaffarpur

Madhubani

Jogbani

Darbhanga

UTTAR
PRADESH

Chapra

Vaishali

Lalganj

28

Samastipur

Saharsa

Purnia

31

River

Sonepur

Hajipur

Katihar

Ganges

Arrah

Patna

30

Buxar

River Son

Nalanda
Rajgir

Bihar
Sharif

Pawapuri

Monghyr

Bhagalpur

34

To Varanasi

Sasaram

Dehri

Gaya

Hot
Springs

Godda

Bodhgaya

Grand Trunk Road

31

Deoghar

Giridih

Daltonganj

HAZARIBAGH
NATIONAL
PARK

2

BETLA
NATIONAL
PARK

Hazaribagh

Parasnath

33

Netarhat

Dhanbad

Asansol

Lohardaga

Ranchi

Bankura

To Calcutta

MADHYA
PRADESH

23

Khunti

33

WEST
BENGAL

Jamshedpur

Chaibasa

Rourkela

Kharagpur

ORISSA

Bay
of
Bengal

0   50   100 km

*The external boundaries of India
on this map have not been authenticated
and may not be correct.*

Kendujhargarh

6

Baleshwar

History

Early in the 5th century BC, Ajatasatru shifted his capital of the Magadha empire from Rajgir to Patna, fulfilling Buddha's prophecy that a great city would arise here. The remains of his ancient city of Pataliputra can still be seen in Kumrahar, a southern district of Patna. The capital of a huge empire spanning most of ancient India – Chandragupta Maurya and Ashoka ruled from here – for almost 1000 years it was one of the most important cities on the subcontinent.

Renamed Azimabad, the city regained its political importance in the mid-16th century AD when Sher Shar made it his capital after defeating Humayun. In 1764, after the Battle of Buxar, it passed to the British.

Orientation

The city stretches along the southern bank of the Ganges for about 15km. The hotels, main train station and airport are in the western half of Patna, known as Bankipur, while the older and more traditional area is to the east, in Patna City. The 'hub' of the new Patna is at Gandhi Maidan. The main market area is Ashok Raj Path, which starts from Gandhi Maidan.

Near the train station, Fraser and Exhibition Rds have officially had their names changed to Muzharul Haque Path and Braj Kishore Path respectively, and Boring Rd has become Jal Prakash Rd, but everyone still uses the old names. Gardiner Rd however, is now nearly always referred to as Birchand Patel Path.

Information

The state tourist office (BSTO; ☎ 210219, fax 236218) is in spacious new premises at Jaiprakash Loknayak Bawan on the corner of Dak Bungalow and Fraser Rds. There are also counters at the train station and the airport, but don't expect much from them. There's a Government of India tourist office (☎ 345776), inconveniently located south of the railway line.

Trade Wings, behind the Maurya Patna hotel, is a good place to change foreign currency and travellers cheques, or to get credit card advances. The State Bank at Gandhi Maidan has an ATM.

There are a couple of quite reasonable bookshops on Fraser Rd near the Satkar International Hotel, and a British Library (☎ 224198) on Bank Rd near the Biscomaun Bhavan by Gandhi Maidan.

There are no email or Internet facilities in Bihar and, with the exception of the top-end hotels, almost nobody accepts credit cards.

Golghar

This huge beehive-shaped building overlooking the maidan, was constructed as a granary. It was built by Captain John Garstin in 1786 at the instigation of the British administrator, Warren Hastings. Although the Bihar government is making use of it now, it has never been filled. Standing about 25m high, with steps winding around the outside to the top, when there is a break in the smog the Golghar provides fine views over the town and the Ganges. The park in which it rests is filthy, waterlogged and strewn with litter, and the disused fountain and high ground are used for drying washing.

Patna Museum

This excellent, albeit somewhat dog-eared museum contains badly labelled metal and stone sculptures dating back to the Maurya and Gupta periods, terracotta figures and archaeological finds from sites in Bihar such as Nalanda. It also houses the world's longest fossilised tree – 16m and 200 million years old. Stuffed wildlife includes the usual (tiger, deer) and the unusual (a kid with three ears and eight legs). There is a fine collection of Chinese paintings and *thangkas* (Tibetan cloth paintings), but unfortunately this collection is frequently closed. The museum is open 10.30 am to 4.30 pm; Tuesday to Sunday. Entry costs Rs 2 and cameras are allowed.

Kumrahar Excavations

The remains of Pataliputra, as well as the ancient capital of Ajatasatru (491-459 BC), Chandragupta (321-297 BC) and Ashoka (274-237 BC), have been uncovered in

Kumrahar, south of Patna. A few large pillars from the assembly hall, dating back to the Mauryan period, and the foundations of the brick Buddhist monastery known as Anand Bihar are all that remain. There's a small display of clay figures and wooden beams which were discovered here.

The Kumrahar excavations are fairly esoteric and are likely to attract only those with a keen interest in archaeology and India's ancient history. They are set in a pleasant park and open Tuesday to Sunday 9 am to 5 pm; entry costs Rs 5.

Har Mandir

At the eastern end of the city, in the Chowk area of old Patna, stands one of the holiest Sikh shrines. Built of white marble by Ranjit Singh, it marks the place where Gobind Singh, the 10th and last of the Sikh gurus, was born in 1660.

You must be barefoot within the temple precincts and your head must be covered. They lend cloths for this purpose at the entrance.

Qila House

Built on the foundations of Sher Shar's fort, Qila House (also known as Jalan Museum) contains an impressive private collection of antiques, including a dinner service that once belonged to George III, Marie Antoinette's Sèvres porcelain, Napoleon's four-poster bed, Chinese jade and Mughal silver filigree. Phone ahead ☎ 642354 for permission to visit.

Khuda Baksh Oriental Library

Founded in 1900, this library has a renowned collection of very rare Arabic and Persian manuscripts, Mughal and Rajput paintings and oddities like the Quran inscribed in a

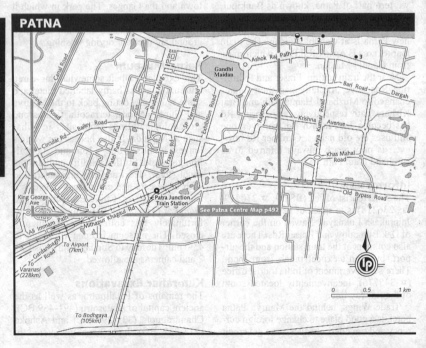

book only 25mm wide. The library also contains the only books to survive the sacking of the Moorish University of Cordoba in Spain.

Other Attractions

Non-Hindus are welcome at the modern **Mahavir Mandir**, dedicated to the popular god, Hanuman. At night this place is lit up in garish pink and green neon – you can't possibly miss it as you leave the main train station.

The heavy, domed **Sher Shahi**, built by the Afghan ruler Sher Shar in 1545, is the oldest mosque in Patna. Other mosques include the squat **Pathar ki Masjid** and the riverbank **Madrassa.**

Gulzarbagh, to the east of the city, was the site of the East India Company's infamous **opium warehouse**. The building is currently occupied by a state government print works.

Organised Tours

The state tourist office operates a day trip which includes Patna, Rajgir, Nalanda and Pawapuri. It runs on Saturday and Sunday, and the cost is Rs 125. For departure times, contact the tourist office or the Kautilya Vihar Tourist Bungalow. Car hire and organised tours can also be arranged through City Tours (☎ 224265/225411, fax 229235).

Places to Stay – Budget

Fraser Rd is Patna's hub and a lot of the cheaper hotels are tucked away in lanes off the main street.

The *Youth Hostel (SP Verma Rd)* south of the Maurya Patna, has clean, spartan dorms and rooms. Single members/non-members rates are Rs 20/40, double are Rs 40/80.

Hotel Swayam Sidhi (☎ 655312) has clean, spacious singles/doubles with bath for Rs 200/350.

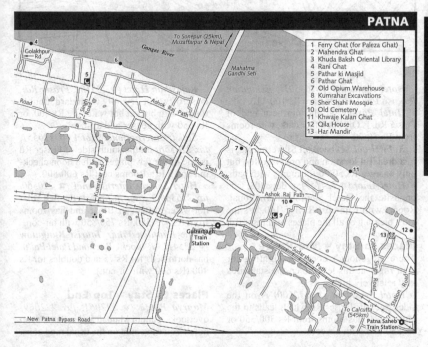

PATNA

1 Ferry Ghat (for Paleza Ghat)
2 Mahendra Ghat
3 Khuda Baksh Oriental Library
4 Rani Ghat
5 Pathar ki Masjid
6 Pathar Ghat
7 Old Opium Warehouse
8 Kumrahar Excavations
9 Sher Shahi Mosque
10 Old Cemetery
11 Khwaje Kalan Ghat
12 Qila House
13 Har Mandir

BIHAR

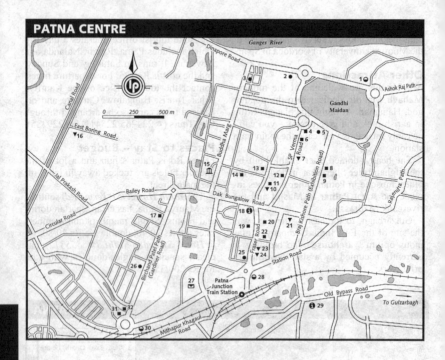

PATNA CENTRE

Hotel Rajkumar (☎ 655011, Exhibition Rd), isn't bad. Rooms are Rs 100/110.

Hotel Parker, at the northern end of Fraser Rd, is OK but rather dark, with rooms from Rs 50/70.

Ruby Hotel, set back off SP Verma Rd, is in a dreadful location and pretty grotty, but only charges Rs 50/70 for rooms with bath.

Hotel Amar (☎ 224157), is down the lane opposite the Hotel Samrat International. Rooms with bath cost Rs 125/140. It's the most pleasant of all the places off Fraser Rd.

Places to Stay – Mid-Range

There are enough operators fighting for your rupee at this level to ensure standards stay relatively high.

Hotel President (☎ 220600) is on the side street off Fraser Rd which leads to the museum. It has rooms from Rs 300/350 or Rs 550/650 with air-con.

Rajasthan Hotel (☎ 225102, Fraser Rd), is scruffy but friendly. Standard double rooms with bucket hot water are Rs 400, or Rs 650 with geyser and air-con.

Satkar International Hotel (☎ 220551, fax 220556) on the south side of Fraser Rd is one of the few places with a noon check-out and a lift. Rooms cost Rs 600/800.

Hotel Samrat International (☎ 220560, fax 226386, Fraser Rd) boasts the first solar hot-water system in Bihar and has rooms from Rs 475/550, Rs 750/850 with air-con.

The *Kautilya Vihar Tourist Bungalow (☎ 225411, 'R-block', Birchand Patel Path)*, has dorm beds for Rs 75 and doubles for Rs 400 (Rs 600 with air-con).

Places to Stay – Top End

Maurya Patna (☎ 222061, fax 222069) overlooks Gandhi Maidan and is Patna's top hotel. You can count on the usual mod cons,

PATNA CENTRE

PLACES TO STAY		32	Kautilya Vihar Tourist	2	Golghar
4	Maurya Patna; Trade Wings		Bungalow	3	British Library
6	YHA		PLACES TO EAT	5	Indian Airlines
8	Hotel Swayam Sidhi	7	Hot Breads	15	Patna Museum
9	Hotel Rajkumar	10	Ashoka Restaurant;	18	Bihar State Tourist Office
11	Rajasthan Hotel		Silveroak Bar & Restaurant	25	Jail
12	Ruby Hotel	16	Ruyi Family Restaurant;	26	Water Tower
13	Hotel Parker		Hot Breads	27	Main Post Office
14	Hotel President	21	Sri Krishna Sandwich Bar	28	Auto-Rickshaw
17	Hotel Pataliputra Ashok	23	Mayfair Icecream Parlour		Stand for Gulzarbagh
19	Hotel Samrat International	24	Mamta Restaurant	29	Government of India
20	Satkar International Hotel				Tourist Office
22	Hotel Amar		OTHER	30	Main Bus Terminal
31	Hotel Chanakya	1	Gandhi Maidan Bus Stand		

including a pool. Rooms start at Rs 1700/2500 with breakfast.

Hotel Pataliputra Ashok (☎ 226270) is similar at Rs 1500/2000.

Hotel Chanakya (☎ 220591, fax 220598), near Kautilya Vihar Tourist Bungalow, is a centrally air-conditioned three star place that charges Rs 1800/2200 for singles/doubles.

Places to Eat

Patna has plenty of places to eat, many of them along Fraser Rd. *Mayfair Icecream Parlour* is a clean and very popular place with good *masala dosas* and other snacks, as well as 16-odd ice-cream flavours.

Mamta Restaurant has main dishes for Rs 35 and beer costs Rs 55.

Ashoka Restaurant, further up Fraser Rd, is rather dark but the non vegetarian food (Chinese, tandoori) is good.

Rajasthan Hotel, not far from the Ashoka, has a good vegetarian restaurant. It's not cheap, but the food is excellent and they have a good range of ice cream.

Gaurav's Restaurant at Hotel Swayam Sidhi is another good vegetarian restaurant.

Sri Krishna Sandwich Bar, round the corner on Dak Bungalow Rd, has good pizzas, sandwiches and sweets.

Silveroak Bar & Restaurant on Fraser Rd next to the Ashoka Restaurant, serves Indian and Chinese meals. It is clean, comfortable and affordable

Hot Breads sells excellent freshly baked breads, pastries and cakes and has two outlets, one on SP Verma Rd and one, which also sells ice cream, on East Boring Rd.

The *Ruyi Family Restaurant* next to Hot Breads on East Boring Rd is the only restaurant in Bihar specialising in Chinese cuisine. While being quite expensive, it is well decorated, clean, friendly, nonsmoking and the service is first class.

Getting There & Away

Air Indian Airlines (☎ 226433) has daily flights between Patna and Delhi (US$130), Calcutta (US$90) and Ranchi (US$60). Three flights a week connect Patna with Lucknow (US$90) and you can book tickets at the Indian Airlines office near Gandhi Maidan. Sahara Air has one flight a day to Varanasi (US$40) and Delhi. Necon Air flies four times a week between Kathmandu and Patna (US$75).

Bus The main bus terminal is at Harding Park, just west of Patna Junction train station. It's a large place with departure gates spread out along the road. Buses from Gate 7 include:

Gaya	Rs 45	4 hours
Rajgir	Rs 26	3 hours
Ranchi	Rs 110 & Rs 150	9 hours
Sasaram	Rs 75	6 hours
Siliguri	Rs 145	12 hours

BIHAR

The Gandhi Maidan bus stand is used by government buses going to many places in Bihar. There are night buses to Ranchi and a deluxe bus to Siliguri (Rs 155, 3 pm).

Nepal Buses for Raxaul, on the Nepalese border go from the main bus terminal (Gate 6; Rs 70, seven hours). There are hourly morning departures and less frequent afternoon services. A deluxe night bus also leaves the Gandhi Maidan bus stand (Rs 90, seven hours) at 10 pm. Buses from Birganj (on the Nepalese side of the border) to Kathmandu cost Rs 82 (Nep Rs 114).

Train Patna Junction is the main train station. The train booking office is a joke – it's absolutely chaotic. Unless you have several hours to spare you might be better off paying a small commission to a tour company to buy tickets for you.

The fastest trains on the Calcutta to Delhi line take 12 hours to Delhi (Rs 229/797 in 2nd/1st class, 992km) and 7 hours to Calcutta (Rs 187/642, 545km). There are a number of direct trains daily to Varanasi (228km, five hours); Gaya (Rs 88/294, two hours, 92km); Ranchi (Rs 30/161, 10 hours, 591km); and Mumbai (Rs 176/611) and a weekly service to Chennai.

If you're heading to Darjeeling or the North-Eastern Region, the fast *North East Express* from Delhi leaves Patna at 10 pm, arriving in New Jalpaiguri (Siliguri) at 7 am (Rs 190/700 in 2nd/2nd class air-con, 636km).

There are no direct trains from Patna to the border town of Raxaul (you have to change at Muzaffarpur) so buses are faster.

Getting Around

To/From the Airport The airport is 7km west of the city centre. It is ridiculously chaotic and informal. There is a massive free-for-all for Immigration and Customs, and the security staff appear to double as porters. Indian Airlines runs a bus service from their office by the Gandhi Maidan, cycle-rickshaws cost approximately Rs 50 and taxis should charge about Rs 120. However, the latest scam is for the driver to agree on one price and then, as soon as the car has left the airport, say you will have to pay extra if your hotel won't pay their commission!

Auto-Rickshaw Shared auto-rickshaws shuttle back and forth between the main Patna Junction train station and Gulzarbagh (Rs 5). The other main route is from the Patna Junction train station to Gandhi Maidan bus stand (Rs 3).

Northern Bihar

SONEPUR
☎ 06654

Sonepur Fair a two week cattle fair is held in October/November here. It takes place around the full moon of Kartika Purnima, the most auspicious time to bathe at the confluence of the Ganges and Gandak rivers. Four times the size of Pushkar Fair, it's probably the largest animal fair in Asia. Not only cattle are traded here, at Haathi Bazaar, elephants change hands for anything from Rs 10,000 to Rs 100,000, depending on their age and condition. If you're considering purchasing an alternative form of transport, Mark Shand's *Travels on my Elephant* is essential reading for the modern-day *mahout* (elephant trainer).

The Bihar State Tourist Development Corporation (BSTDC) operates a tourist village during the fair. Double cottages cost Rs 500 (no single rates). There is also a 20-bed dorm for Rs 75 a head and several temporary huts, decorated with traditional Mithila paintings. The cost of the huts varies according to demand! For bookings contact BSTDC or City Tours in Patna (☎ 0612-225411/210219).

VAISHALI
☎ 06225

As long ago as the 6th century BC, Vaishali was the capital of a republic. Mahavira, one of the Jain *tirthankars* (apostles) was born here, and Buddha preached his last sermon here. There's little to see – an **Ashoka pillar** (with its lion capital intact), a few dilapi-

Mithila Paintings

Bihar's unique and most famous folk art is its *Mithila* or *Madhubani* paintings. Traditionally, wives from Madhubani and surounding villages in the Mithila district started creating strong line drawings on the walls of their homes from the day of their marriage. Using pigments from natural products such as spices, minerals, charcoal and vegetable matter, the women painted local deities and scenes from mythology. Special events and aspects of everyday life were often incorporated with the images of gods and goddesses.

These paintings, both in black and white and strong primary colours, are now being professionally produced on paper, canvas and textiles for commercial purposes and are available throughout Bihar.

Examples of the original wall paintings can still be seen in homes around Madhubani (aproximately 160km north-east of Patna, five to six hours by bus) and also in the Bihar Government Tourist Village huts at the Sonepur Fair.

Each June, the Saurath Sabha is held in a mango grove in Saurath village. It is a unique gathering of Mithila Brahmins from all over India, who come for the biggest marriage market in the country. Parents of marriageable children come armed with horoscopes in the hopes of negotiating suitable marriages for their offspring.

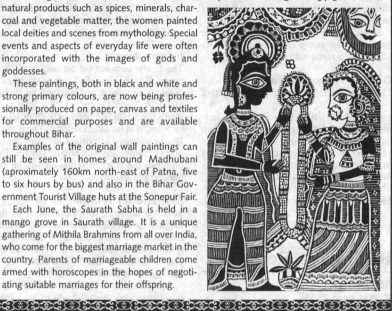

dated **stupas** (one contains an eighth of Buddha's ashes) and a small **museum**. There are guided tours from Patna or buses from Lalganj and Muzaffarpur. An inexpensive *BSTDC Tourist Youth Hostel & Tourist Bungalow* has rooms for Rs 150/180.

MUZAFFARPUR
☎ 0621 • pop 282,120

Apart from being a bus-transit point en route to the Nepal border, Muzaffarpur is a poverty-stricken, agriculturally backward area of limited interest.

If you have to stay the night, *Hotel Deepak* has reasonable food and spartan single rooms for Rs 100. Better air-con doubles are Rs 300/450.

Hotel Elite is near the train station on Saraiya Gunj and offers double rooms for Rs 300/400.

MOTIHARI
North of Muzaffarpur, the area becomes even poorer. Motihari, where George Orwell was born, is a small provincial town which is also the district headquarters.

RAXAUL
☎ 06255

Raxaul is virtually a twin town with Birganj, just across the border in Nepal. Both are crowded and dirty. Cycle-rickshaws take 20 minutes (Rs 20) from the border (open 4 am to midnight) to the bus stand in

BIHAR

Birganj. Nepalese visas are available at the border for US$25. Be warned that US currency *only* is accepted as payment for visas at this border.

Neither Raxaul or Birganj are places to stick around, but if you're stuck *Hotel Kaveri* has rooms for Rs 85/110.

Hotel Ajanta is better. It's down a side road near the bus stand and charges Rs 80/100 for a room with shared bath.

Getting There & Away

There are several buses a day from Raxaul to Patna (Rs 70, seven hours) and even more to Muzaffarpur. Beware of touts selling combined bus/train tickets: it's much more reliable to organise things yourself.

From Birganj morning and evening buses to Kathmandu take around 12 hours (Rs 80); Pokhara buses take 10 hours (Rs 60). Most Kathmandu buses take the much longer road via Narayanghat and Mugling, rather than the dramatically scenic Tribhuvan Highway via Naubise.

Bodhgaya Region

BODHGAYA

☎ 0631 • pop 25,585

The four most holy places associated with Buddha are Lumbini, in Nepal, where he was born; Sarnath, near Varanasi, where he first preached his message; Kushinagar, near Gorakhpur, where he died; and Bodhgaya, where he attained enlightenment. For the traveller, Bodhgaya is probably the most interesting of the four, being much more of a working Buddhist centre than an archaeological site. It's also the most important Buddhist pilgrimage site in the world.

The focal point is the Mahabodhi Temple which marks the spot where Buddha gained enlightenment and set out on his life of preaching.

Buddhists from all over the world flock to Bodhgaya, along with non-Buddhists who come to learn about Buddhism and meditation. Bodhgaya is small and quiet, but growing rapidly and accumulating all the usual 'tourism' paraphernalia. However, it is still a pleasant place to stay a few days. The best time to visit is during winter when Tibetan pilgrims come down from Dharamsala. The Dalai Lama often spends December here. When the Tibetans leave in mid-February they seem to take some of the atmosphere with them.

Information

The tourist complex on the corner of Bodhgaya Rd and Temple St consists of two hotels, a restaurant, gardens and an 'Information & Media Centre' which is little more than a fancy building open daily, from 10 am to 5 pm, it is less than helpful. There are a few brochures and posters for sale, but no maps or information on hotels. The BSTDC promises the scant information will be expanded and improved.

Mahabodhi Temple

Standing adjacent to a descendent of the original bodhi tree under which Buddha meditated on the excesses of life and the formulated his philosophy of a balanced approach to it, this temple is a place of pilgrimage for all Buddhists.

A sapling from the original bodhi tree was carried to Anuradhapura in Sri Lanka by Sanghamitta (the Emperor Ashoka's daughter). That tree now flourishes there and, in turn, a cutting from it was carried back to Bodhgaya when the original tree died. A red sandstone slab under the tree is said to be the Vajrasan, or diamond throne, on which Buddha sat.

The Mahabodhi Temple stands on the site of a temple erected by Ashoka in the 3rd century BC. Topped by a 50m pyramidal spire, the ornate structure houses a large gilded image of Buddha. The current temple was restored in the 11th century, and again in 1882. The stone railing around the temple, parts of which still stand, is considered to be from the Sunga period (around 184-172 BC). The carved and sculptured railing has been restored, although parts of it now stand in the museum in Calcutta and in the Victoria & Albert Museum in London.

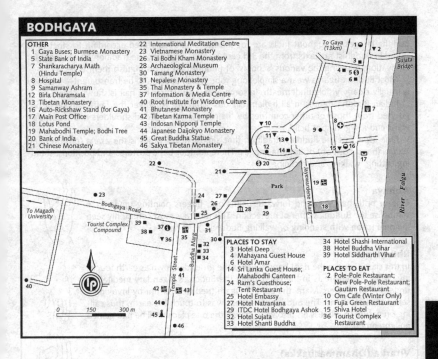

BODHGAYA

OTHER
1 Gaya Buses; Burmese Monastery
5 State Bank of India
7 Shankaracharya Math (Hindu Temple)
8 Hospital
9 Samanway Ashram
12 Birla Dharamsala
13 Tibetan Monastery
16 Auto-Rickshaw Stand (for Gaya)
17 Main Post Office
18 Lotus Pond
19 Mahabodhi Temple; Bodhi Tree
20 Bank of India
21 Chinese Monastery

22 International Meditation Centre
23 Vietnamese Monastery
26 Tai Bodhi Kham Monastery
28 Archaeological Museum
30 Tamang Monastery
31 Nepalese Monastery
35 Thai Monastery & Temple
37 Information & Media Centre
40 Root Institute for Wisdom Culture
41 Bhutanese Monastery
42 Tibetan Karma Temple
43 Indosan Nipponji Temple
44 Japanese Daijokyo Monastery
45 Great Buddha Statue
46 Sakya Tibetan Monastery

PLACES TO STAY
3 Hotel Deep
4 Mahayana Guest House
6 Hotel Amar
14 Sri Lanka Guest House; Mahabodhi Canteen
24 Ram's Guesthouse; Tent Restaurant
25 Hotel Embassy
27 Hotel Natranjana
29 ITDC Hotel Bodhgaya Ashok
32 Hotel Sujata
33 Hotel Shanti Buddha

34 Hotel Shashi International
38 Hotel Buddha Vihar
39 Hotel Siddharth Vihar

PLACES TO EAT
2 Pole-Pole Restaurant; New Pole-Pole Restaurant; Gautam Restaurant
10 Om Cafe (Winter Only)
11 Fujia Green Restaurant
15 Shiva Hotel
36 Tourist Complex Restaurant

Stone stupas, erected by visiting pilgrims, dot the temple courtyard.

There is a great sense of peace and serenity within the temple compound. Pilgrims and visitors from all walks of life and religions come here to worship or just admire. Entry to the temple grounds, which are open 6 am to noon and 2 to 6.30 pm, is free, but there is a Rs 5 charge for cameras. For more information on Buddhism and Buddha's life, see the Sacred India colour section earlier in the book.

Monasteries

Most countries with a large Buddhist population have a temple or monastery here, usually built in a representative architectural style. Thus the Thai temple looks very much like the colourful *wats* you see in Thailand. The Tibetan temple and monastery were built in 1934 and contain a large prayer wheel.

The Burmese, who led the campaign to restore the Mahabodhi Temple in the 19th century, built their present monastery in 1936. The Japanese temple (Indosan Nipponji) has a very beautiful image of Buddha brought from Japan – across the road is the Daijokyo Temple. There are also Chinese, Sri Lankan, Bhutanese, Vietnamese, Nepalese, Korean, Taiwanese and Bangladeshi monasteries. The Tai Bodhi Kham Monastery was built by Buddhist tribes from Assam and Arunachal Pradesh.

Other Attractions

The archaeological museum (10 am to 5 pm Saturday to Thursday) has a small collection of Buddha figures and pillars found in the area. The Hindu Shankaracharya Math has a temple, and there's a sculpture gallery in the grounds. Across the river are the Dungeshwari and Suraya temples.

Sculptural Symbolism

Buddha images throughout India are for the most part sculptured according to strict rules found in Buddhist art texts from the 3rd century AD. However, the tradition leaves room for innovation, allowing the various 'schools' of Buddhist art to distinguish themselves.

Most Buddha figures wear a simple long robe which appears to be transparent – the body is usually clearly visible underneath. In some earlier sculptures his hair is shown coiled.

Indian Buddha figures in all Indian religious sculpture whatever the faith, can be distinguished from those of other countries by their body type – broad shoulders and chest, slim waist and a slightly pot belly.

One aspect of the Buddhist tradition that almost never varies is the *asana* (posture) and *mudra* (hand position) of Buddha images. There are four basic postures and positions: standing, sitting, walking and reclining.

Abhaya

One or both hands extend forward, palms out, fingers pointing upward, to symbolise the Buddha's offer of protection. This mudra is most commonly seen in conjunction with standing or walking Buddhas.

Bhumisparsa

In this classic mudra the right hand touches the ground, known as earth touching, while the left rests in the lap. During the Buddha's legendary meditation under the Bodhi tree, Mara, the Lord of Death tried to interrupt by invoking a series of distractions. The Buddha's response was to touch the earth, thus calling on nature to witness his resolve to stay in the one place until he had gained enlightenment.

Vitarka (Dhammachakka)

When the thumb and forefinger of one hand (vitarka) or both hands (dhammachakka) form a circle with the other fingers curving outward the mudra evokes the first public discourse on Buddhist doctrine.

Dhyana

Both hands rest palms up on the Buddha's lap, with the right hand on top, signifying meditation.

The 25m **Great Buddha Statue** in the Japanese Kamakura style was unveiled by the Dalai Lama in 1989. There's a plan to build a Maitreya Buddha statue over 100m high in Bodhgaya as a symbol of world peace.

Meditation Courses

Courses and retreats take place in the winter, mainly from November to early February.

Some of the most accessible courses are run by the Root Institute for Wisdom Culture (☎ 400714). They run basic five day meditation courses and hold retreats in a peaceful location on the edge of Bodhgaya. Travellers who have spent some time here seem impressed, not only with the courses but by the way the Institute is working to put something back into the local community with health, agricultural and educational projects.

Courses are also run by the International Meditation Centre (☎ 400707) near the Magadh University (5km from Bodhgaya), and another centre closer to town. The annual insight meditation *(Vipassana)* and spiritual inquiry retreats, which have places for 130 people, take place from 7th to 17th January, 17th to 27th January, and 28th January to 4th February at the Thai Monastery. For information and bookings write to Gaia House (☎ 01803-813188), West Ogwell, Near Newton Abbot, Devon TQ12 6EN, UK or (from mid-October) to Thomas Jost, Bodhgaya Post Office, Gaya District, Bihar 824231. Meditation courses are also offered at the Burmese and Tibetan monasteries, and at the Dhammabodhi Vipassana Meditation Centre (☎ 400437), near Magadh University. Other courses are advertised on the noticeboard in the Om Cafe.

If you're interested in working on social development projects in the area, contact the Samanway Ashram.

Places to Stay – Budget

Prices given here are for the high season (October to March), when room rates can be almost double the low-season rates.

Hotel Deep (☎ 400913/400463) on the road to Gaya, near the Pole-Pole Restaurant and next to the Burmese Monastery comes highly recommended. The shared western-style bathrooms are clean and have copious hot water. Singles cost Rs 100 to Rs 300, doubles Rs 150 to Rs 350.

Hotel Amar close by on the same road, is a basic little place with doubles for around Rs 100.

Sri Lanka Guest House, a Mahabodhi Society place, is popular and well run. They accept donations of around Rs 75 for rooms with bath.

Ram's Guesthouse (☎ 400644), set back from the road behind the Hotel Embassy is a friendly family-run place which has recently been extended. Double rooms with bath and lots of hot water are Rs 400. Doubles with clean, shared bathrooms are Rs 200.

Tourist Bungalows No 1 and No 2 are next door to each other and are also known

as more imaginative names: the *Hotel Buddha Vihar* (☎ 400445) has very comfortable dormitory accommodation. Beds with common/private bath are Rs 50/75. *Hotel Siddharth Vihar* (☎ 400445) offers compact doubles with bath for Rs 300.

If you're planning a longer stay or don't mind roughing it a little, behaving in a dignified manner and abiding by some simple rules, it's possible to stay at some of the monasteries.

The *Burmese Monastery* has a peaceful garden, and is particularly popular with westerners for its study courses. The rooms are extremely basic and you're expected to make a donation of Rs 50 per night.

Unfortunately at the *Japanese Monastery,* western visitors have made themselves unpopular by breaking rules and they may not be keen to let them in. It's clean and comfortable but usually full of Japanese tour groups in high season.

The *Bhutanese Monastery* is a good place where rooms cost between Rs 30 and Rs 50.

The *Tibetan Monastery* is a bit more spartan and cheaper. Other places you could try include the *Sakya Tibetan Monastery* and the *Thai* and *Nepalese* monasteries.

Places to Stay – Mid-Range & Top End

The continuing spate of building in this range ensures competitive prices and plenty of rooms.

Mahayana Guest House (☎ 400744) adjacent to the State Bank of India, is a bit of a misnomer. Run by the Tibetan Monastery, this brand new, large hotel with impressive marble lobby, was the host hotel for the 1998 visit by the Dalai Lama. With its internal courtyards and comfortable, spacious rooms, it is the best value of the mid-range hotels. Doubles cost Rs 500/750 with common/private bath.

Hotel Natranjana (☎ 400475) has spotless doubles with bath and TV cost Rs 600 to Rs 900.

Hotel Embassy (☎ 400711) with its rooftop seating passes the white-glove test. Rooms with TV and bath are Rs 500/800.

The *ITDC Hotel Bodhgaya Ashok* (☎ *400700/790, fax 400788)* has rooms for Rs 1000/1500 (singles/doubles), or with air-con Rs 1600/2400. Overpriced dorm beds are Rs 400.

Hotel Sujata (☎ *400761/481, fax 400515)* in Buddha Marg is an upmarket place with 24 hour room service, foreign exchange and restaurant. There is a *hammam* (Japanese-style bathroom) and prayer hall. Doubles cost Rs 1200/1500.

Hotel Shanti Buddha (☎ *400534)* is a rather grim place next door. The staff are nice, but the rooms are overpriced. Singles are Rs 700, doubles are Rs 800 on the ground floor and Rs 1000 with carpet (a dubious extra) on the top floor.

Next door, *Hotel Shashi International* (☎ *400459, fax 400483)* a new place on the site of a former little guest house, has small but spotless doubles at Rs 1000/1200.

Places to Eat

The standard of food here is pretty low out of season and surprisingly high during winter, when the pilgrims arrive.

Mahabodi Canteen at the Sri Lanka Guest House is a reliable place serving quite reasonable Chinese food.

Shiva Hotel, attempts to cater to western tastes, with mixed results.

Ram's Guesthouse has a friendly and cheap tent restaurant with a good selection of Sri Lankan, Japanese, Chinese, Tibetan and western food.

Other tent-restaurants which offer great value include *Pole-Pole*, *New Pole-Pole* and the *Gautam* opposite the Burmese monastery. All have varied menus, good tape collections and are popular. The Gautam also has a bakery in winter.

There are also several Tibetan-run restaurants behind the Tibetan Monastery. Most operate in tents and only open during winter, but there are some perennial places which you can try.

Om Cafe is well established, and is a popular meeting place.

Fujia Green serves Tibetan and Chinese grub year-round.

Getting There & Away

Bodhgaya is 13km from Gaya, and share auto-rickshaws shuttle back and forth between the two. They're phenomenally overloaded: a total of up to 15 people (plus animals, goods and so on) travel on a vehicle intended for three! The fare is Rs 7 (or up to Rs 100 for the whole auto-rickshaw).

There are frequent buses to Gaya (Rs 6), and are also very crowded. They leave regularly from outside the Burmese monastery. Direct buses to or from Varanasi cost Rs 65.

GAYA
☎ 0631 • pop 373,120

Gaya is about 100km south of Patna. Just as nearby Bodhgaya is a major centre for Buddhist pilgrims, Gaya is a centre for Hindu pilgrims. Vishnu is said to have given Gaya the power to absolve sinners. Pilgrims offer *pindas* (funeral cakes) at the ghats along the river here, and perform a lengthy circuit of the holy places around Gaya, to free their ancestors from bondage to the earth.

There's a BSTO at the train station. The nearest foreign exchange is in Bodhgaya.

Things to See & Do

In the crowded central part of the old town, the *sikhara*-style Visnupad Temple was constructed in 1787 by Queen Ahalya Bai of Indore on the banks of the River Falgu. Inside the temple the 40cm 'footprint' of Vishnu is imprinted in solid rock and surrounded by a silver-plated basin. Note that Non-Hindus are not permitted to enter.

During the monsoon, the river carries a great deal of water here but it dries up completely in winter. You can see cremations taking place on the riverbanks.

A flight of 1000 stone steps leads to the top of the **Brahmajuni Hill**, 1km south-west of the Vishnupad Temple. There's a good view over the town from the top. Gaya also has a small **archaeological museum** (open Tuesday to Sunday) near the tank.

A **temple of Surya**, the sun god, stands 20km to the north at Deos. The **Barabar Caves**, (200 BC), are 36km north of Gaya. These are the 'Marabar' caves of EM

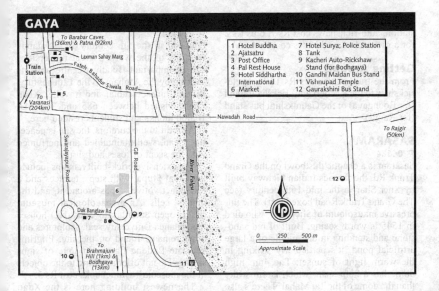

GAYA

1	Hotel Buddha	7	Hotel Surya; Police Station
2	Ajatsatru	8	Tank
3	Post Office	9	Kacheri Auto-Rickshaw
4	Pal Rest House		Stand (for Bodhgaya)
5	Hotel Siddhartha	10	Gandhi Maidan Bus Stand
	International	11	Vishnupad Temple
6	Market	12	Gaurakshini Bus Stand

Forster's *A Passage to India*. Two of the caves contain Ashokan inscriptions. To get there take the train to Betla, grab a tonga from there for 10km of potholes and it's then an arduous 5km walk to the two groups of caves. Although well worth visiting, it is advisable not to travel on your own. Take an armed guard as the caves are in the heart of Naxalite bandit country.

Places to Stay & Eat
There's many options around the station, most are spartan but OK for a short pause.

Hotel Buddha (☎ 23428) is down the lane opposite the train station. There is a roof garden and rooms are Rs 140/175.

Pal Rest House (☎ 436753), set back from the road, is quiet and cheap. Singles with bath cost Rs 60/80, doubles Rs 110.

At *Ajatsatru* (☎ 21514), rooms vary greatly; some are small, some dark, some have balconies and some are spacious and light. Singles are Rs 150, doubles are Rs 175 to Rs 295, or Rs 595 with air-con.

Hotel Surya (☎ 24004), adjacent to the police station on the main road through town, is a Rs 5 cycle-rickshaw ride from the train station. It has doubles for Rs 140 with bath, or Rs 190 with geyser and air-cooler.

Hotel Siddhartha International (☎ 21254) is rather overpriced and caters to upmarket pilgrims. Singles/doubles cost US$45/60 and breakfast/dinner is US$6/9.

All over Bihar you will see stalls selling the popular puff-pastry sweet known as *khaja*, which originated in a village between Gaya and Rajgir. Catch them as they come out of the oil – the flies are as partial to them as the Biharis are.

Getting There & Away
Buses to Patna (Rs 35, four hours) and Ranchi (Rs 80 to Rs 110, seven hours) leave from Gandhi Maidan bus stand. Buses to Rajgir (Rs 22, three hours) leave from Gaurakshini bus stand, across the river.

Gaya is on the main Delhi-Calcutta railway line and there are direct trains to Delhi, Calcutta, Varanasi, Puri and Patna.

Auto-rickshaws from the train station to Bodhgaya (13km) should cost Rs 75 but they'll try for twice as much. From the

BIHAR

Kacheri stand, a 25 minute walk from the station, auto-richshaws cost Rs 7, plus Rs 2 for a rucksack. Local buses cost Rs 6.

Getting Around

From the train station it's Rs 10 by cycle-rickshaw to the Kacheri auto-rickshaw stand (for Bodhgaya) or the Gaurakshini bus stand (for Rajgir).

SASARAM
☎ 06184

Sasaram is a chaotic dustbowl on the Grand Trunk Rd, the famous Indian highway built by Sher Shar in the mid-16th century (see The Grand Trunk Road boxed text). The impressive **mausoleum of Sher Shar**, who died in 1545 is worth seeing. Built of red sandstone and standing in the middle of a large artificial pond, it's particularly striking in the warm light of sunset. The 46m high dome has a 22m span, which is 4m wider than the dome of the Taj Mahal. There's also the **tomb of Hassan Khan** (Sher Shar's father) and several other Muslim monuments.

There are more Muslim tombs at **Maner**. At **Dehri**, 17km from Sasaram, the railway and the Grand Trunk Rd cross the River Son on a 3km-long bridge. The hill fort of **Rohtas** is 38km from here.

Places to Stay

The *Shershah Tourist Lodge* is the best place to stay. Turn left onto the Grand Trunk Rd outside the train station and it's by the second petrol station, 15 minutes walk away. Doubles are Rs 100, or Rs 150/350 with bath/aircon. Dorm beds cost Rs 50.

Getting There & Away

There are frequent buses for Patna (Rs 75, five hours).

For Varanasi and Gaya it's better to take a train as buses start at Dehri, 17km away, and few stop here. There are only two trains direct from Varanasi, but it's possible to take a local bus from outside Varanasi train station to Mughal Serai (Rs 8, 17km), from where there are frequent trains to Sasaram (Rs 23, three hours).

NALANDA
☎ 061194

Founded in the 5th century BC, Nalanda was one of the world's great universities and an important Buddhist centre until its sacking by the Afghans in the 12th century. When Chinese scholar and traveller Xuan Zhang visited between 685 and 762 AD, 10,000 monks and students resided here.

A credit to the curators, the site is peaceful, clean, well-maintained and perfumed with the scent of roses and shrubs.

The extensive brick-built remains include the **Great Stupa**, with steps, terraces and a few intact votive stupas around it, and the monks' cells. An **archaeological museum** (Rs 1, open Saturday to Thursday) houses the Nalanda University seal, sculptures and other remains found on the site. Pilgrims venerate Buddha figures in spite of signs saying 'Do not offer anything to the objects in the museum'! Guidebooks cost Rs 3.

The newest building here is the **Xuan Zhang Memorial Hall**, built as a peace pagoda by the Chinese. Xuan Zhang spent five years here as both student and teacher.

There's also an international centre for the study of Buddhism, established in 1951. You can stay at the Burmese, Japanese or Jain *dharamsalas* (pilgrims' resthouses) at Nalanda as well as the PWD Rest House.

Getting There & Away

Shared Trekkers (jeeps) cost Rs 7 from Rajgir to Nalanda Village, from there it's Rs 8 for the 10 minute ride on a shared tonga to the university site. Take another jeep (Rs 5) from Nalanda Village to Bihar Sharif, north of Nalanda, for buses to Patna (Rs 26, 3½ hours).

RAJGIR
☎ 06119

This was the capital of the Magadha empire until Ajatasatru moved to Pataliputra (Patna) in the 5th century BC. Today, Rajgir, 19km south of Nalanda, is a minor Indian holiday centre. In winter, visitors are drawn by the hot springs and healthy climate.

Rajgir is an important Buddhist pilgrimage site since Buddha spent 12 years here,

BIHAR

The Grand Trunk Road

India's Grand Trunk Road (GTR) runs the breadth of the country, from the Pakistan border near Amritsar to Calcutta. It has been in existence for many centuries, and is by far the busiest road in the country. Rudyard Kipling described it as a 'river of life', and many of the events in his novel *Kim* take place along it.

During the time of Ashoka's rule, pillars of edicts were placed along the road. In Mughal times it was *kos minars* (milestones) which were placed by the roadside, as the royal *kos* was the base unit for measuring long distances. Also of great importance were the *serais* (rest houses), established by many rulers over time but particularly during the Mughal era. These evolved from basic postal relay stations into establishments which became the focal point for commerce in many areas, and housed government officials; some were more grandiose constructions which even the emperor himself used when he passed through.

One of the rulers with greatest influence over the appearance of the GTR was the emperor Jehangir, who planted avenues of *khayabans* trees to provide shade for travellers. So pleasant was the road that it became known as 'the Long Walk' among European travellers in the 17th century. Unfortunately the decline of the Mughal empire also saw maintenance cease and a decline in the trees.

The only significant realignment of the road was under the British, when the East India Company sought a more direct route between Calcutta and Varanasi. This route – the one that exists today – was completed in 1838 and is still a vital part of the Indian road network. Sit at a roadside *dhaba* somewhere in rural India and observe the passing parade, and you will witness a vivid picture of Indians on the move – oil tankers from Assam, Tata trucks from Punjab; garish and battered buses, all with horns blaring; barefoot sadhus on a Ganga pilgrimage; farmers steering overloaded ox-carts; wayward cows; schoolkids on bicycles; and women on foot. You'll probably also suffer industrial deafness from the racket.

and the first Buddhist council after Buddha attained nirvana was held here. It's also an important place for Jains, as Mahavira spent some time in Rajgir and the hills are topped with Digambara (the 'sky-clad' Jain sect) shrines. A mention in the *Mahabharata* also ensures that there is a good supply of Hindu pilgrims.

Orientation & Information

The main road with the train station, bus stand a number of hotels is about 0.5km west of town. There's a tourist complex by the hot springs, about 1km south of town along the main road.

The **Rajgir Mahotsava** (Indian Classical Performing Arts Festival) is held 24-26 October every year. The festival includes performances of folk dance, ballet, opera, devotional song and instrumental music.

Things to See

Most people rent a tonga for half a day to see the sites, as they're spread out over several kilometres. This costs about Rs 50, but, with the brutal way these horses are treated, you might prefer to take a taxi.

Main sites include parts of the ruined city, caves and places associated with Ajatasatru and his father Bhimbisara, whom he imprisoned and murdered. The pink building by the crowded hot springs is the **Lakshmi Narayan Temple**.

There's also a Burmese temple, an interesting **Jain exhibition** (Rs 5) and a modern Japanese temple. On the top of Ratnagiri Hill, 3km south of the hot springs, is the **Japanese Shanti Stupa**, reached by a chairlift (10 am to 5 pm daily; Rs 15 return). Apparently the tourism department has recently replaced the old cable and they are

BIHAR

'systematically replacing the missing safety bars on the chairs'.

Places to Stay & Eat

Accommodation prices have escalated out of sight. High season (October to March) rates are given, but up to 50% discount applies out of season or if occupancy is low.

Hotel Anand, near the bus stand, is one of the cheaper places. Gloomy rooms cost Rs 75/150. The Jain restaurant is strictly vegan and serves no eggs, onions or garlic.

Hotel Mamata (☎ 25044) close by is bright and cheap. Room rates range from Rs 110 for a double, to Rs 150 for four.

Hotel Siddharth (☎ 25216), south of town near the hot springs, is recently refurbished within a pleasant walled courtyard, it is known for its excellent food and friendly staff. Rooms are Rs 250/450 with bath.

The *Hotel Rajgir (☎ 25266)* is an old-fashioned Indian style hotel with a garden. The basic rooms with bath are a staggering Rs 205/305 plus Rs 5 for bucket hot water.

The BSTDC has three properties in Rajgir, the all-dorm *Ajatshatru (☎ 25027)* is Rs 45/50 with shared/private bath. *Gautam (☎ 25273)*, has dorm beds for Rs 50 and double rooms from Rs 200 to Rs 400 with air-con. *Tathagat Vihar (☎ 25176)*, has double rooms at Rs 250 to Rs 300, or Rs 500 with air-con.

Hotel Centaur Hokke (☎ 25245), 3km west of the hot springs, is Rajgir's top hotel. It's a very pleasant, Japanese-designed place with in-house communal bathhouse and temple. Rooms, in either Japanese or western-style, are US$86/124 plus a service charge (meals are an extra US$43 per person per day). The restaurant at the hotel, which serves Indian and Japanese food, is moderately expensive.

Getting There & Away

Rajgir is on a branch line, with daily trains to Patna, but the buses are faster (Rs 24, four hours). You may need to change at Bihar Sharif. There are also buses to Gaya (Rs 22, three hours) and Pawapuri. For Nalanda take a shared jeep for Rs 7.

PAWPURI

Mahavira, the final tirthankar and founder of Jainism, died and was cremated here in about 500 BC. It is said the demand for his sacred ashes was so great that a large amount of soil was removed around the funeral pyre, creating the lotus-filled tank. A marble temple, the Jalmandir, was later built in the middle of the tank and is now a major pilgrimage spot for Jains. You can get here by bus from Rajgir or Bihar Sharif.

Southern Bihar

RANCHI
☎ 0651

At 652m, Ranchi doesn't really deserve its title of hill station, especially since it has now lost most of its tree cover. In British times it was Bihar's summer capital, with a reputation as a health resort.

An interesting things to see here is the Jagannath Temple, a small version of the great Jagannath Temple at Puri. It's 6km southwest of Ranchi and visitors are welcome.

There are many beautiful waterfalls in the area, the most spectacular, especially at the end of the monsoon, are the Hundru Falls 45km north-east of Ranchi.

About the same distance away to the north-west is Macluskiganj, a basically deserted hill station, once a holiday haven for Anglo-Indians. There is not a lot to see, but it does offer some pleasant walks through woods, gardens and orchards and the opportunity to view some of the old, albeit dilapidated, Victorian buildings.

There are a number of hills on the edges of Ranchi offering sunset views over the rocky landscape. There's also a Tribal Research Institute with a museum of anthropology.

There are BSTDC offices at the train station and airport.

Places to Stay & Eat

There are many hotels around the bus stand. *Hotel Konark (☎ 307840)*, the best small place, is friendly with clean singles/doubles for Rs 125/175 and a good restaurant.

Hotel Paradise, with rooms at Rs 100/180, is another good place.

Tourist Bungalow Birsa Vihar (☎ 314826) has dorms for Rs 60 and rooms for 150/200.

Hotel Yuvraj (☎ 300403), 'a house of respectable living', is 15 minutes from the train station with rooms from Rs 300/400.

Hotel Yuvraj Palace (☎ 300805), nearby, is centrally air-conditioned with rooms from Rs 1000/1400. This is Ranchi's best hotel.

Getting There & Away

Ranchi has good air, bus and train connections. The train station is 500m from the bus stand. There are buses to Gaya (Rs 110, seven hours), Hazaribagh (Rs 30, three hours) and Netarhat (Rs 45, four hours). A direct bus to Puri takes 15 hours.

HAZARIBAGH
☎ 06546

This pleasant leafy town lies 107km north of Ranchi, at an altitude of 615m. About the only reason for coming here would be to visit **Betla National Park**, 19km to the north. Permission to enter the park must be procured from the District Forest Officer in Betla (see the following entry), and although there are *machaans* for viewing the animals, wildlife is sparse since the government drove a major road through the area.

Hotel Upkar (☎ 2246) is the best hotel in Hazaribagh, and good value with singles/doubles for Rs 150/250.

The *Tourist Lodge* or *Forest Rest House* are the places to stay in the park itself.

The train station, Hazaribagh Rd, is 67km away! Private minibuses to Gaya (Rs 45, four hours) leave from the bus terminal.

BETLA (PALAMAU) NATIONAL PARK

Known as both Palamau and Betla, this park, 140km west of Ranchi, is part of Project Tiger and is one of the best places to see wild elephants. When the waterholes begin to dry up in March/ April, Palamau's 100 elephants are easy to spot. Jeep safaris can be organised in Betla, the park's access point. Expect to pay around Rs 8 per kilo-

metre for spins around the park's 250 sq km. There are also tree-top and ground-level hideaways where you can watch the animals without being seen.

Accommodation is mostly in Betla, but you can also stay further afield in Daltonganj (24km away). In Betla, the *Forest Rest House* or *Tourist Lodge* (built as a three star ITDC hotel), are reasonable places to stay.

Betla is accessible by road from Ranchi and Gaya (both Rs 50, 4 to 5 hours).

Unfortunately, it is the same old bandit warning story – before going into the area it is imperative to seek security advice and/or an escort from the local police.

PARASNATH
☎ 0653232

Just inside the Bihar state boundary with West Bengal, and only a bit north of the Grand Trunk Rd, Parasnath is the railhead for Sikayi the major Jain pilgrimage centre in the east of India (Madhuban is the main town). Sikayi at 1450m is the highest point in Bihar and, like so many other pilgrimage centres, it is reached by a stiff climb on foot. Rich pilgrims from Calcutta are carried up in palanquins by porters.

The 24 temples, representing the Jain tirthankars, stand at an altitude of 1366m. Parasnath, the 23rd tirthankar, achieved nirvana here 100 years after his birth.

An internationally famous yoga school at Munger (☎ 06344-22430), known as the Bihar Yoga School, the University of Yoga and the Bihar Yog Vidyalaya has courses.

Places to Stay

There are a number of *dharamsalas* in Sikayi, but they are strictly vegan and, like those in Bodhgaya, there are strict rules of conduct. There is also a *Tourist Bungalow*, built by the BSTDC and given to the Jain community at Madhuban, but it has no fixed rate.

Getting There & Away

Trains run to Patna and Calcutta, and Maruti vans and mini-buses run between the train station and Madhuban.

BIHAR

Calcutta

Densely populated and frequently polluted, Calcutta can be an ugly and desperate place. Yet, don't let first impressions put you off this city. Calcutta has long been acknowledged as the cultural capital of India, and has some scenes of rare beauty.

Certainly, Calcutta has suffered economically and the effects have taken their toll. It has been plagued by chronic labour unrest resulting in a decline in productivity. Massive trade union rallies frequently block traffic in the city centre for hours at a time and the port has been silting up, limiting the size of ships that can use it. The Farakka Barrage (250km north of Calcutta), designed to improve the river flow through the city, has been the subject of dispute between India and Bangladesh because it will affect the flow of the Ganges through Bangladesh.

The Marxist government of West Bengal has come in for much criticism over the chaos existing in Calcutta but, as it is also pointed out, its apparent neglect and mismanagement of the city is combined with considerable improvement in the rural environment. Threats of flood or famine in the countryside no longer send hordes of refugees streaming into the city as in the past.

Despite its problems, Calcutta is a city with a soul, and its residents and many visitors, are inordinately fond of it. Bengali humour is renowned throughout India and the Bengalis, so ready to raise arms against political wrongdoings, are also the poets and artists of India. Calcutta was the birthplace and/or home of many famous men and women including the Bengali poet Rabindranath Tagore (see the Tagore House section later in this chapter), the novelist William Thackeray and the actress Merle Oberon. Oberon appeared in films such as *The Scarlet Pimpernel* and the house she lived in is on Lindsay St near New Market.

The contrast between the Mumbai and Calcutta movie industries more or less sums up the city's strengths. While Mumbai, the

Calcutta at a Glance

Population: 12 million
Main Language: Bengali
Telephone Area Code: 033
Best Time to Go: November to March

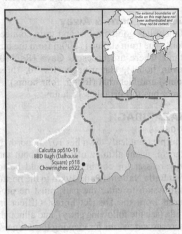

Calcutta pp510-11
BBD Bagh (Dalhousie Square) p518
Chowringhee p522

- **Victoria Memorial** – standing guard over the Maidan (Calcutta's lungs), this magnificent and proud memorial exemplifies fine British colonial architecture

- **Howrah Bridge** – the grey bulk against the ethereal expanse of the Hooghly River and the bustle of puja-flower sellers below offer a fascinating spectacle

- **Maidan** – visit during early morning and late afternoon and watch Calcutta residents walk their dogs, ride their horses and exercise their bodies

- **Botanical Gardens** – a wonderful haven from the furore of the city featuring an enormous and spectacular banyan tree

CALCUTTA

Festivals of Calcutta

festival	date	features
Book Fair	Jan/Feb	Asia's largest book fair
Calcutta Festival	Jan	ethnic food and cultural events

Hollywood of India, churns out movies of tinsel banality, the smaller number of movie makers in Calcutta make noncommercial gems that stand up to anything produced for sophisticated western audiences.

Some books worth reading while you're here include Geoffrey Moorhouse's classic 1971 study *Calcutta*, available as a Penguin paperback. VS Naipaul has some interesting chapters on Calcutta in his *India – A Million Mutinies Now*. Dominique Lapierre's *City of Joy* is *de rigueur* reading among travellers to Calcutta and is available in paperback (pirated or otherwise) at almost every bookshop. There is a plethora of books published about the life of Mother Teresa.

Amid the squalor and confusion, Calcutta has its moments of sheer magic: flower sellers beside the misty, ethereal Hooghly River; the majestic sweep of the Maidan; and the grand beauty of the Victoria Memorial – they're all part of this amazing city.

History

Calcutta isn't an ancient city like Delhi, with its impressive relics of the past. In fact, it's largely a British creation that dates back only some 300 years and was the capital of British India until the beginning of this century.

In 1686 the British abandoned Hooghly, their trading post 38km up the Hooghly River from present-day Calcutta, and moved downriver to three small villages – Sutanati, Govindpur and Kalikata. Calcutta takes its name from the last of those three tiny settlements. Job Charnock, an English merchant who later married a Brahmin's widow whom he dissuaded from becoming a *sati*, was the leader of the British mer-

chants who made this move. At first the post was not a great success and was abandoned on a number of occasions, but in 1696 a fort was laid out near present-day BBD Bagh (Dalhousie Square) and in 1698, Aurangzeb's grandson gave the British official permission to occupy the villages.

Calcutta then grew steadily until 1756, when Siraj-ud-daula, the Nawab of Murshidabad, attacked the town. Most of the British inhabitants escaped, but those captured were packed into an underground cellar where, during the night, most of them suffocated in what became known as 'the black hole of Calcutta'.

Early in 1757, the British, under Clive of India, retook Calcutta and made peace with the nawab. Later the same year, however, Siraj-ud-daula sided with the French and was defeated at the Battle of Plassey, a turning point in British-Indian history. A much stronger fort was built in Calcutta and the town became the capital of British India.

Much of Calcutta's most enduring development took place between 1780 and 1820. Later in the 19th century, Bengal became an important centre in the struggle for Indian independence, and this was a major reason for the decision to transfer the capital to Delhi in 1911. Loss of political power did not alter Calcutta's economic control, and the city continued to prosper until after WWII.

Partition affected Calcutta more than any other major Indian city. Bengal and the Punjab were the two areas of India with mixed Hindu and Muslim populations and the dividing line was drawn through them. The result in Bengal was that Calcutta, the jute-producing and export centre of India, became a city without a hinterland, while across the border in East Pakistan (now Bangladesh), the jute (a plant fibre used in making sacking and mats) was grown without anywhere to process or export it. Furthermore, West Bengal and Calcutta were disrupted by tens of thousands of refugees fleeing from East Bengal, although fortunately without the communal violence and bloodshed that Partition brought to the Punjab.

CALCUTTA

The massive influx of refugees, combined with India's own postwar population explosion, led to Calcutta becoming an international urban horror story. The mere name was enough to conjure up visions of squalor, starvation, disease and death. The work of Mother Teresa's Calcutta mission also focused worldwide attention on Calcutta's festering problems. In 1971, the India-Pakistan conflict and the creation of Bangladesh led to another flood of refugees, and Calcutta's already chaotic condition further deteriorated.

Orientation

Calcutta sprawls north-south along the eastern bank of the Hooghly River, which divides it from Howrah on the western bank. If you arrive from anywhere west of Calcutta by rail, you'll come into the immense Howrah train station and have to cross the Howrah Bridge into Calcutta proper.

For visitors, the more relevant parts of Calcutta are south of the bridge in the areas around BBD Bagh and Chowringhee. BBD Bagh, formerly Dalhousie Square, is the hub of the central business district (CBD). Here you will find the main post office, the international telephone office, the West Bengal tourist office, the American Express office and various railway booking offices.

South of BBD Bagh is the open expanse of the Maidan along the river, and east from here is the area known as Chowringhee. Most of the budget and mid-range hotels are concentrated here, together with many of the banks, airline offices, restaurants, travel agencies and the Indian Museum. At the southern end of Chowringhee you'll find the Government of India tourist office and the British Council (and library) on Shakespeare Sarani, and, nearby, the Birla Planetarium and Victoria Memorial.

There are a number of landmarks in Calcutta and a couple of important streets to remember. The Ochterlony Monument at the northern end of the Maidan is one of the most visible landmarks – it's a tall column rising from the flat expanse of the Maidan. Sudder St runs off Chowringhee Rd and is the core of the Calcutta travellers' scene. Most of the popular cheap hotels are along Sudder St so the area is well known to any taxi or rickshaw-wallah. The Indian Museum is on the corner of Sudder St and Chowringhee Rd.

Farther south down Chowringhee Rd, which runs alongside the eastern edge of the Maidan, is Park St, with a great number of more upmarket restaurants and shops. The newest landmark is the cable bridge (Vidyasagar Setu) over the Hooghly, finished in 1994. Although it was supposed to relieve the crush on the old Howrah Bridge, the new bridge is now almost as chaotic itself.

Street Names Getting around Calcutta is slightly confused by the renaming of city streets, particularly those with Raj-era connotations. However, many street signs still display the old names. Some maps show old names and others show new ones, but taxi-wallahs inevitably only know the old names.

Adding to the confusion, in an attempt to ease traffic problems, Calcutta has introduced 'timed' one-way streets which flow in different directions depending on the time of day. For example, in morning rush hour a street might flow east to west, in the afternoon rush hour it will flow west to east, and in the middle of the day it might take two-way traffic! This makes things very convenient for unscrupulous taxi drivers who can take you on long (unnecessary) detours 'to avoid the congestion' or because 'the road doesn't go that way at this time of day'.

Information

Tourist Offices The Government of India tourist office (☎ 282 5813, fax 282 3521), 4 Shakespeare Sarani, is very helpful; staff can give you (somewhat dated) computerised printouts of any destination in India.

The West Bengal tourist office (☎ 248 8271), 3/2 BBD Bagh (on the opposite side to the post office), is open Monday to Friday 10.30 am to 5.30 pm, but don't expect to find many brochures or much useful information. Both the state and national tourist offices have counters at the airport (☎ 511 8299), and West Bengal has an office at Howrah station (☎ 660 2518) open 7 am to 1 pm daily.

Some other states have tourist offices here including the more obscure North-Eastern Region states, Sikkim, and the Andaman & Nicobar Islands. They are as follows:

Andaman & Nicobar Islands
(☎ 247 5084/2604) 3A Auckland Place
Arunachal Pradesh
(☎ 228 6500) 4B Chowringhee Place
Assam
(☎ 295094) 8 Russel St
Bihar
(☎ 280 3304) 26B Camac St
Himachal Pradesh
(☎ 033-271792) 2H, 2nd floor, Electronic Centre, 1-1A, BAC St, 700072
Madhya Pradesh
(☎ 247 5855) 6th floor, Chitrakoot Bldg, 230A AJC Bose Rd
Manipur
(☎ 747075, 747087) 26 Roland Rd
Meghalaya
(☎ 290797, 291775) 9 Russel St
Mizoram
(☎ 247 7034) 24 Old Ballygunge Rd
Nagaland
(☎ 242 5269) 11 Shakespeare Sarani
Orissa
(☎ 244 3653) 55 Lenin Sarani
Sikkim
(☎ 226 8983/6717) 5/2 Russel St
Tripura
(☎ 282 2801/5703) 1 Pretoria St

To find out exactly what's happening on the cultural front, get hold of a free copy of the leaflet *Calcutta This Fortnight* from any tourist office.

Money American Express (☎ 282 0623, fax 248 8896) is at 21 Old Court House St. The Thomas Cook office (☎ 247 4560, fax 247 5854) is in the Chitrakoot Bldg, 230 AJC Bose Rd.

Calcutta is embracing the world of electronic banking and most city banks have, or are in the process of installing, ATMs.

On Chowringhee Rd there are branches of Citibank, the State Bank of India, Standard Chartered and ANZ Grindlays (near Park St metro station). ANZ Grindlays has another branch on Shakespeare Sarani. All these banks have ATMs with 24 hour access, in

Calcutta's Renamed Roads

old name	new name
Ballygunge Rd	Gurusday Rd
Bowbazar St	Bepin Behary Ganguly
Buckland Rd	Bankim Ch Rd
Chowringhee Rd	Jawaharlal Nehru Rd
Free School St	Mirza Ghalib St
Harrington St	Ho Chi Minh Sarani
Harrison Rd	Mahatma Gandhi Rd
Kyd St	Dr M Ishaque Rd
Lansdowne Rd	Sarat Bose Rd
Lindsay St	Neille Sengupta Sarani
Lower Chitpur Rd	Rabindra Sarani
Lower Circular Rd	Acharya Jagadish Chandra (AJC) Bose Rd
Machuabazar St	Madan Mohan St & Keshab Sen St
Mirzapore St	Suryya Sen St
Theatre Rd	Shakespeare Sarani
Wellesley St	Rafi Ahmed Kidwai Rd
Wellington St	Nirmal Chunder St

which you can use credit, Giro and Cirrus cards. ANZ Grindlays and Standard Chartered branches near the main post office have ATMs, as does the Hong Kong Bank on the corner of Hare and West Court House Sts, and the Reserve Bank of India, which changes torn notes.

The Banque National de Paris has a branch at BBD Bagh, next to the West Bengal tourist office. Next door again, in the crumbling Stephen Building, is RN Dutt, a licensed private moneychanger who deals in just about any currency.

On Sudder St there are a few licensed moneychangers. Travellers' Express Club, at 20 Mirza Ghalib (Free School) St, is one of the few places you can change money on a Sunday.

The State Bank of India has a 24 hour counter in the new terminal building at the airport.

CALCUTTA

CALCUTTA

CALCUTTA

PLACES TO STAY
16 Yatri Niwas
31 YMCA
37 (Royal) Calcutta
 Guest House
40 Motherhouse
 Taj Bengal Hotel
55 Tollygunge Club

PLACES TO EAT
19 Indian Coffee House
53 The Rice Bowl

OTHER
1 Dakshineswar Kali
 Temple
2 Belur Math
3 Belur Math Ghat
5 Digambara Jain Temple
8 Kasi Mitra Ghat
10 Nimtala Ghat
11 Pareshnath Jain
 Temple
13 Tagore House
14 Marble Palace
17 Nakhoda Mosque
18 Calcutta University
21 BBD Bagh
22 Chandpal Ghat
25 Babu Ghat
26 Outram Ghat
27 Botanical Gardens
28 Takta Ghat
29 Kidderpore Docks
32 Mother Teresa's Mission

34 Victoria Memorial
35 Calcutta Racecourse
36 Bangladeshi Consulate
41 Nepalese Consulate
42 National Library
43 German Consulate
45 Birla Industrial
 & Technological Museum
46 Thai Consulate
48 Kali Temple
49 Italian Consulate
51 Birla Academy of Art
 & Culture
52 Ramakrishna Mission
 Institute of Culture

METRO STATIONS
4 Dum Dum
6 Belgachia
7 Shyam Bazaar
9 Shoba Bazaar
12 Girish Park
15 MG Rd
20 Central
23 Chandni Chowk
24 Esplanade
30 Park Street
33 Maidan
38 Rabindra Sadan
44 Bhawanipore
47 Jatindas Park
50 Kalighat
54 Rabindra Sarobar
56 Tollygunge

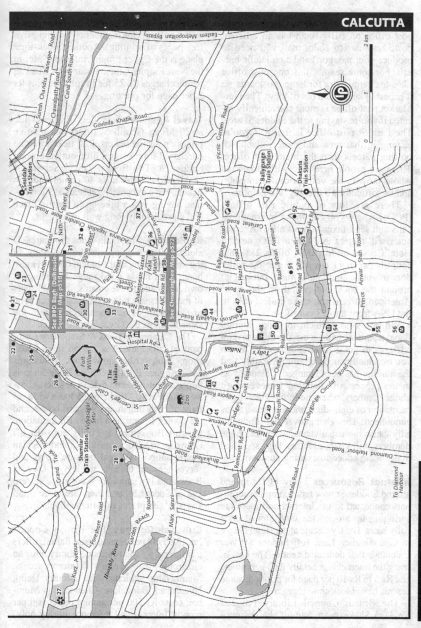

CALCUTTA

Post & Communications Calcutta's main post office on BBD Bagh has an efficient poste restante (to claim mail you need to produce your passport) and a philatelic bureau. For some reason, this one post office likes to charge extra for larger postcards, so it is best to keep them out of view. The New Market post office is more conveniently located if you're staying in the Sudder St area. The Park St post office is useful if you're staying in that area and more reliable for posting parcels than the main post office. There are people here who will handle the whole process for you (prices negotiable) and the officials are friendly and helpful.

There are lots of public call offices (PCOs) where you can make international calls and send faxes, almost all with 'computerised' meters. A 24 hour PCO, next to Hotel Crystal on Mirza St, offers 25% discount between 11 pm and 6 am; the roller door might be shut late at night, but just go around the back and pound on the door! American citizens can make collect calls to the USA from the US consulate.

While it's no problem to make international telephone calls, it usually takes several attempts to get a local call through. When you eventually succeed, you invariably find the number has been changed. Calcutta was in the process of changing to seven-digit phone numbers, when the India-wide implementation of eight-digit phone numbers was announced. This changeover will undoubtedly cause the usual chaos, as entire phone numbers will change, rather than specified digits being added to existing numbers.

Internet Resources Many PCOs in and around Sudder St now have computer terminals connected to the Internet and more are springing up around the city, almost on a daily basis. The Cybercafe at the Hotel Palace in Chowringhee Lane (off Sudder St) was Calcutta's first dedicated centre. The cost of using the Internet is generally Rs 3 per minute and Rs 5 to Rs 10 per page for printing; some centres have block-time charges.

The British Council Library (☎ 282 5944), 5 Shakespeare Sarani, charges non-members Rs 100 for half an hour (minimum) or Rs 50 for members (including five free pages of printing). Another block-time place is the Cyber Empire Internet Cafe, in the New Empire Cinema near New Market, which charges Rs 25 for 15 minutes plus Rs 2 per page for printing.

Travel Agencies Travellers' Express Club at 20 Mirza Ghalib St offers competitive prices on airline tickets. Rail tickets can be purchased from several little outlets around Sudder St. The Bengal Travel Service, 4 Sudder St, charges a Rs 40 commission on tickets, but can usually get seats at short notice, saving you a hike up to Fairlie Place and a predictably long wait in a queue.

Bookshops The main bookshop area is along College St, opposite the university. In the same building as the Indian Coffee House here, Rupa has a good range including its own publications. Newman's, the publishers of the Bradshaw railway timetable, runs one of Calcutta's oldest bookshops. It's in the same block as the Great Eastern Hotel.

The Cambridge Book & Stationery Company at 20D Park St is a good small bookshop. A bit farther down Park St towards Chowringhee Rd, the Oxford Book Shop is larger and also has an extensive stock. Classic Books, at 10 Middleton St, has a wide variety of both Indian and western books, and the owner, Bharat, is a mine of information. Seagull Bookstore & Publishers, just off Chowringhee Rd, opposite Rabindra Sadan metro station, is a real treasure trove, and serves tea and biscuits while you browse. Booklands is a small bookstall at the eastern end of Sudder St, and there are more small swap 'n' sell places on Mirza Ghalib St.

Cultural Centres The British Council (☎ 282 5944) on Shakespeare Sarani, offers a full lending and reference library, plus an electronic media centre with Internet access. Membership, which covers Calcutta, Delhi, Hyderabad, Bangalore, Chennai and Mumbai, costs Rs 500 per annum or Rs 100 per month (Internet and reference library only)

– a worthwhile investment if you're a longer term visitor to India. Photocopying costs Rs 1 per sheet (as opposed to Rs 5 to Rs 10 elsewhere). There is a garden cafe that serves light meals and nonalcoholic drinks. The library is open Tuesday to Friday 10.30 am to 10 pm, Saturday to 6 pm.

Medical Services Dr Paes at Vital Medical Services (☎ 282 5664, fax 282 5656), 6 Ho Chi Minh Sarani, is open 9.30 to 11 am. The Wockhardt Medical Centre (☎ 475 4320/4096) at 2/7 Sarat Bose (Lansdowne) Rd is open 11.30 am to 2 pm. Alternatively, medical queries should be directed to any of the large hospitals.

Indian Museum

This museum, built in 1874, is a beautiful colonial building with an impressive facade. Its huge galleries display India's finest collection of treasures.

The entrance hall is dominated by an original Mauryan Lion Capitol, India's national symbol, and the archaeological gallery houses the Barhut Gateway (2nd century BC), a massive structure decorated with a bas-relief depicting the life of Buddha. It has the best collection of Pala statues in the country and the art collection has many fine pieces from Orissan and other temples. It also has superb examples of Buddhist Gandharan art – an interesting meeting point between Greek artistry and Buddhist ideals that produced Buddha images and other sculptures of great beauty. The art and textile galleries are definitely worthy of attention. Unfortunately, the natural history collection, while being vast, is disintegrating fast with exhibits coated in dust and birds falling off their perches. The museum is open Tuesday to Sunday, 10 am to 5 pm. Between December and February it closes half an hour earlier. Entry is Rs 5.

Asiatic Society

Founded on 15 February 1784, at the instigation of scholar and visionary Sir William Jones, the Asiatic Society was formed to preserve the science, civilisation and culture of India. The society established the first Asian modern museum in 1814 in Calcutta, but due to a chronic lack of space and facilities, most of the priceless exhibits were eventually transferred to the Indian Museum on its completion in 1875. However, a small collection of valuable art and antiquities was retained and is now on display at the society's museum in Park St. Among the fabulous collection of paintings, *thangkas*, object d'art and botanical specimens, the Barhut Ashokan Rock Edict (circa 250 BC, from Orissa) is unquestionably the most important piece, representing India's most famous and revered Emperor and his conversion to Buddhism. Of great interest to scholars, is the library which contains over 200,000 books, journals and manuscripts of rare antiquity.

Library hours are Monday to Friday, 10.30 am to 7 pm; Saturday, 11 am to 5 pm. Entry is free. The museum is open Monday to Friday, noon to 5 pm. A small but informative publication, *The Asiatic Society*, is sold (Rs 15) at the society's offices.

Maidan & Fort William

After the events of 1756, when Siraj-ud-daula sacked the town, the British set out to replace the original Fort William, in the Maidan, with a massive and impregnable new fort. First they 'cleared out' the inhabitants of the village of Govindpur and in 1758 laid the foundations of a fort. By the time it was completed in 1781, the fort had cost the awesome total, for those days, of £2 million. Around the fort a huge expanse of jungle was cut down to give the cannons a clear line of fire but, as often happened, the fort has never fired a single shot in aggression.

The fort is still in use today and visitors are only allowed inside with special permission (rarely granted). Even the trenches and deep fortifications surrounding the fort's massive walls seem to be out of bounds.

The area cleared around Fort William became the Maidan, the 'lungs' of modern Calcutta. This huge green expanse stretches 3km north to south and is over 1km wide. It is bounded by Strand Rd along the river to

CALCUTTA

the west, and by Chowringhee Rd, lined with shops, offices, hotels and eating places, to the east. The stream known as Tolly's Nullah forms its southern boundary, and here you will find a racecourse and the Victoria Memorial. In the north-west corner of the Maidan is Eden Gardens, while Raj Bhavan overlooks it from the north.

Within the gardens are cricket and football fields, tennis courts, ponds, trees and even musical fountains. Cows graze, political discussions are held, people stroll across the grounds or come for early morning yoga sessions.

Ochterlony Monument Now officially renamed the Shahid (Martyr's) Minar, this 48m column towers over the northern end of the Maidan. It was erected in 1828 and named after Sir David Ochterlony, who is credited with winning the Nepal War (1814-16). The column is an intriguing combination of Turkish, Egyptian and Syrian architectural elements.

There's a fine view from the top of the column, but it's only open Monday to Friday for the middle two weeks of the month. Permission to ascend must be obtained from police headquarters on Lal Bazaar St; simply ask for a 'monument pass' at the assistant commissioner's office on the 2nd floor. Cameras (and umbrellas!) are not allowed.

Eden Gardens In the north-west corner of the Maidan are the small and pleasantly laid out Eden Gardens. A tiny Burmese pagoda was brought here from Prome, Myanmar (Burma) in 1856; it's set in a small lake and is extraordinarily picturesque. The gardens were named after the sister of Lord Auckland, the former governor general. The Calcutta Cricket Ground (Ranji Stadium), where international Test and one-day matches are held, is also within the gardens.

Near the gardens you can take a pleasant **walk** along the banks of the Hooghly River. Ferries run across the river from several ghats and there are plenty of boat operators around offering to take you out on the water for a short **cruise**.

In the corner of the gardens near the old Government House or Raj Bhavan (where a diagonal pathway joins the road), there is a colony of small, virtually tame, **'sacred' rats** that live in underground burrows. If you don't have an aversion to these cute, furry creatures, you can join the people who come here to feed them in the morning and late afternoon.

Victoria Memorial

At the southern end of the Maidan stands the Victoria Memorial, possibly the most impressive reminder of the Raj to be found in India.

This huge white-marble museum houses a vast collection of memorabilia from the days of the British empire. There are portraits, statues and busts of almost all the main participants in British-Indian history. Scenes from military conflicts and the events of the Indian Uprising are illustrated. There are some superb watercolours of Indian landscapes and buildings that were executed by travelling Victorian artists. There's also a piano Queen Victoria played as a young girl and a huge painting depicting King Edward VII entering Jaipur in a regal procession in 1876. French guns captured at the Battle of Plassey are on show along with the black stone throne of the nawab defeated by Clive.

The **Calcutta Gallery**, opened in 1992, exhibits many early pictures of Calcutta and a model of Fort William. There is a good view over the Maidan from the balcony above the entrance.

The memorial is open daily except Monday from 10 am to 3.30 pm, and until 4.30 pm in summer. Entry costs Rs 5. The informative sound-and-light show runs daily except Monday from November to May. The English-language program starts at 7.15 pm. Tickets are Rs 10 (Rs 5 for children).

The booklet *A Brief Guide to the Victoria Memorial* is available in the building.

Birla Planetarium

This planetarium, near the Government of India tourist office, is one of the largest in the world. For Rs 10 you'll get a much better view of the stars in here than in the polluted atmosphere outside. There are shows in English every day, but as times vary, check in advance (☎ 223 1516). Beware of pickpockets, especially in the queue outside.

Other Museums & Galleries

Calcutta has a number of other interesting museums apart from the magnificent Indian Museum and the Victoria Memorial. The **Asutosh Museum** at Calcutta University has a collection of art objects with emphasis on Bengali folk art. It's open Monday to Friday, 10.30 am to 4.30 pm; Saturday 10.30 am to 3 pm; admission is free.

The small **Nehru Children's Museum**, 94/1 Chowringhee Rd, is worth visiting for its models depicting the Hindu epics, the *Ramayana* and the *Mahabharata*. It's open daily except Monday from 11.30 am to 8.30 pm; admission is Rs 10.

At 19A Gurusday Rd is the **Birla Industrial & Technological Museum**, open daily except Monday, 10 am to 5 pm (admission is Rs 5). The philanthropic (and very wealthy) Birlas have also provided the **Birla Academy of Art & Culture** at 109 Southern Ave, open daily except Monday from 4 to 8 pm (admission Rs 5). It has a good collection of sculpture and modern art.

Also in the same area of Ballygunge, is the **Cima Gallery** at Sunny Towers, 43 Ashutesh Chowdhauri Ave. The gallery displays contemporary art and is open Tuesday to Sunday, 4 pm to 8 pm.

The **Academy of Fine Arts**, on Cathedral Rd in Chowringhee, has a permanent exhibition and runs an artists' studio. There are cultural shows in the evening. The academy is open daily except Monday from 3 to 8 pm; entry is Rs 5.

Next door to the main post office on BBD Bagh there's a small **postal museum**.

St Paul's Cathedral

Built between 1839 and 1847, St Paul's Cathedral is one of the first important churches in India. It stands at the southern end of the Maidan, just east of the Victoria Memorial. The steeple fell during an earthquake in 1897 and, following further damage in a 1934 quake, was redesigned and rebuilt. Inside, there's some impressive stained glass, including the great west window by Sir Edward Burne-Jones. It's open to visitors 9 am to noon and 3 to 6 pm daily. Sunday services are at 7.30 and 8.30 am, and 6 pm.

Kali Temple

Rebuilt in 1809 on the site of a much older temple, Kalighat (as it is also known) is the actual temple from which Kalikata (anglicised to Calcutta) takes its name. According to legend, when Shiva's wife's corpse was cut up, one of her fingers fell here. Since then it has been an important pilgrimage site and is always extremely busy.

Kali represents the destructive side of Shiva's consort and demands daily sacrifices. In the morning goats are slaughtered to satisfy the goddess' bloodlust. During the day many poor people come here for a free feed. You'll be latched on to by temple 'priests' who whisk you around and ask for a donation of anything from Rs 100 to Rs 1000 for a small bag of rice.

Mother Teresa's **Hospital for the Dying Destitute** is right next door to the temple and volunteers and travellers are welcome to visit.

The temple is 2km south of St Paul's Cathedral and is easily accessible by metro (Kalighat station).

Howrah Bridge

Until 1943, the Hooghly River was crossed by a pontoon bridge that opened to let river traffic through. To alleviate fears that the building of a new bridge would affect river currents and cause silting problems, the Howrah Bridge was constructed to cross the river in a single 450m span – there are no pylons at all on the riverbed.

This amazing feat of engineering, also known as Rabindra Setu, is similar in size to Australia's Sydney Harbour Bridge, but with a daily stream of close to 100,000 vehicles and pedestrians too numerous to count, it is easily the busiest bridge in the world. It's intriguing to stand at one end of

Mother Teresa

Mother Teresa, the 'Saint of the Gutters', came to epitomise selflessness for her dedication to the destitute, the suffering and the dying. Born Agnes Gonxha Bojaxhiu in Serbia in 1910 to Albanian parents, she joined the Irish Order of Loreto nuns in 1929 and was sent to Darjeeling as a teacher. Moving to a school in Calcutta in 1937, she was horrified at the number of poor people left to die on the streets of the city because there was nowhere else for them to go. She began to feel that behind the secure walls of the nunnery she was too far removed from the people she wanted to help.

The Missionaries of Charity was Mother Teresa's new order, formed in 1950. Among their vows was the promise 'to give wholehearted and free service to the poorest of the poor'. This vow was put into action with the setting up of several homes including Nirmal Hriday (the Home for the Dying), Shanti Nagar (for lepers) and Nirmala Shishu Bhavan (the children's home). There are now homes in many other places around the world including Kalimpong in the West Bengal hills.

For all her saintliness, Mother Teresa was not without her critics. Germaine Greer, for example, accused her of being a religious imperialist, although anyone who has spent some time with the nuns and seen them at work could hardly call them Bible-bashing evangelists. Mother Teresa herself said that hers was contemplative work. Her inspiration was spiritual and Christian, but put into practice mainly by ministering to physical needs; she never sought to convert anyone. In 1979 her work achieved world recognition when she was awarded the Nobel Peace Prize.

On 5 September 1997, a few days after her 87th birthday, and the day of Princess Diana's funeral, Mother Teresa went to join her God. Not one to tolerate the restrictions of a hospital, she died surrounded by the sisters in her beloved Motherhouse in Calcutta.

For one week her body lay in a glass case, draped with the Indian flag, in St Thomas' Church. Thousands of people, from the poorest of the poor to dignitaries from around the world, came to pay their last respects. The outpouring of grief was seen not only in Calcutta, but throughout India and the world.

the bridge at morning rush hour and watch the procession of double-decker buses come across, heeled over like yachts in a heavy wind from the weight of passengers hanging onto the sides. In between the buses are lumbering bullock carts, push carts, hordes of bicycles and even the odd car. During rush hour it can take 45 minutes to get across. The ferries running from below Howrah train station are a more convenient way to cross the river and also give you a good view of the bridge. However, if you are not too encumbered, walking is often the easiest way of crossing.

A second bridge, the Vidyasagar Setu, a Golden Gate Bridge lookalike, 2km downriver, was completed in 1994. Unfortunately it is not making the big difference that was envisaged, as the approaches are too narrow to handle the amount of traffic that uses the bridge, and plans for widening the roads are slow in implementation.

BBD Bagh (Dalhousie Square)

When Calcutta was the administrative centre for British India, BBD Bagh was the centre of power. On the north side stands the huge **Writers' Building**, dating from 1880 (when clerical workers were known as writers). The East India Company's writers have now been replaced by modern-day West Bengal state government employees, and this is where the quintuplicate forms, carbon copies and red ink come from.

Mother Teresa

The government honoured Mother Teresa with a state funeral, her coffin carried on a gun carriage that once bore the bodies of India's greatest statesmen, Mahatma Gandhi and Jawaharlal Nehru. The funeral service, attended by 12,000, was held in Calcutta's largest indoor stadium. Under grey monsoon skies and drizzling rain, the procession passed thousands of mourners as it wound its solemn way from the church to the stadium, and from there to the Motherhouse. Hundreds of thousands of mourners watched on television – the government had even requested that schools and other government buildings with TVs open their doors to the public.

Mother Teresa's coffin now rests under a plain tombstone in the Motherhouse; its only embellishment a small marble tombstone inscribed with her name and the legend, 'Love one another as I have loved you'.

Early in 1997, Mother Teresa had resigned her position at the Missionaries due to bad health, and had named Sister Nirmala as her replacement. While Sister Nirmala says she must walk in her own shoes, the order intends to carry on as before, following its unique vow of giving wholehearted free service to the poorest of the poor.

A pictorial presentation of Mother Teresa's work can be found in the Victoria Memorial.

If you are considering undertaking volunteer work in India, see the Volunteer Work boxed text in this chapter or the Volunteer Work section in the Facts for the Visitor chapter.

Until it was abandoned in 1757, the original Fort William stood on the site of the present-day post office. It stretched from there down to the river, which has since changed its course. Brass markers by the post office indicate where the fort walls used to be. Calcutta's famous black hole stood at the north-east corner of the post office, but since Independence all indications of its position have been removed.

The **black hole** was actually a tiny guardroom in the fort and, according to the British version of the story, 146 people were forced into it on that fateful night when the city fell to Siraj-ud-daula. Next morning, only 23 were still alive. Historians now suggest the numbers of prisoners and fatalities were exaggerated in a propaganda exercise; there were probably only half as many incarcerated and half as many deaths. Whatever the numbers, death by suffocation on a humid Calcutta night must have been a horrific way to go.

Other British Buildings

Raj Bhavan, the old British Government House, built between 1799 and 1805 at the north end of the Maidan, is now occupied by the governor of West Bengal and entry is restricted. Next to Raj Bhavan is the Doric-style **town hall**, and next to that the **High Court**, which was copied from the Staadhaus at Ypres, Belgium, and completed in 1872. It has a 55m tower.

CALCUTTA

BBD BAGH (DALHOUSIE SQUARE)

PLACES TO STAY
20 Great Eastern Hotel; Newman's Bookshop
21 Hotel Embassy
22 Broadway Hotel
26 Central Guest House
35 Heera Hotel

PLACES TO EAT
24 Chung Wah Restaurant
25 Anand Restaurant
27 Indian Coffee House; Rupa Bookshop
28 Amber Hotel
30 KC Das
32 Paris Bar & Restaurant
37 Indra Mahal
40 Nizam's

OTHER
1 Fairlie Ghat
2 Railway Booking Office (Tourist Quota)
3 ANZ Grindlays Bank
4 Standard Chartered Bank
5 Writers' Building
6 Police Headquarters
7 Postal Museum
8 Main Post Office
9 Railway Booking Office
10 Shipping Corporation of India
11 Banque Nationale de Paris
12 West Bengal Tourist Office
13 Hong Kong Bank
14 Central Telegraph Office
15 Church of St John
16 High Court
17 Town Hall
18 Raj Bhavan
19 American Express
23 Indian Airlines
29 Income Tax Office
31 Tipu Sultan's Mosque
33 Metro Cinema
34 Cottage Industries Emporium
36 Calcutta Mounted Police
38 Esplanade Metro Station
39 Ochterlony Monument (Shahid Minar)

Hooghly River

Fairlie Place
Lyons Range
Strand Road South
Kalighat Street
Bankshall Street
Hare Street
Church Lane
BBD Bagh (Dalhousie Square)
Lal Bazaar Street
K. Sankar Roy Road
Red Cross Place
Old Court House Street
Weston Street
Ganesh Chandra Avenue
Princep Street
Chittaranjan Avenue
Esplanade West
West Council House Street
Waterloo Street
East Esplanade
Dacres Lane
Bentinck Street
Chandni Chowk Street
Grant Street
Hospital Street
Lenin Sarani
Eden Gardens
Tram Terminus
Esplanade Bus Station
Madan Street
Surendra Nath Banerji Road
Chowringhee Road
Nehru Road (Chowringhee Road)
Newmarket Street
New Market
Lindsay Street

0   150   300 m

See Chowringhee Map p522

Just south of the zoo in Alipore is the **National Library**, the biggest in India, which is housed in Belvedere House, the former residence of the lieutenant-governor of Bengal.

South Park St Cemetery has been restored and shows the high price paid by the early settlers from England. There are marvellous tombs and inscriptions at this peaceful site. The more famous occupants include Colonel Kyd, founder of the botanical gardens, and Rose Aylmer, remembered only because her unfortunate death was supposed to have been caused by an addiction to pineapples! The lighting and ambience are wonderful in the early morning.

Church of St John

A little south of BBD Bagh is the Church of St John, which dates from 1787. The overgrown graveyard here has a number of interesting monuments, including the octagonal mausoleum of Job Charnock, founder of Calcutta, who died in 1692. Admiral Watson, who supported Clive in retaking Calcutta from Siraj-ud-daula, is also buried here. The obelisk commemorating the black hole was moved from near the main post office to a corner of this graveyard.

Marble Palace

On Muktaram Babu St, a narrow lane off Chittaranjan Ave, this private mansion was built in 1835 by a Bengali *zamindar* (feudal landowner). The palace houses an incongruous collection of curios standing alongside significant statues and paintings (including works of Rubens and Sir Joshua Reynolds). There's a private zoo here too, but the inhabitants are only slightly more animated than the marble lions gracing the palace lawns. It's open daily except Monday and Thursday, 10 am to 4 pm, and entry is free with a permit from the Government of India tourist office.

Tagore House

The rambling old Tagore House is a centre for Indian dance, drama, music and other arts. This is the birthplace of Rabindranath Tagore, India's greatest modern poet, and his final resting place. It's just off Rabindra Sarani, north of BBD Bagh, and is open Monday to Friday 10 am to 5 pm, Saturday to 2 pm (closed Sunday). There is a daily Bengali sound-and-light show at 6 and 7 pm.

Pareshnath Jain Temple

This temple, in the north-east of the city, was built in 1867 and dedicated to Sheetalnathji, the 10th of the 24 Jain *tirthankars*. The temple is an ornate mass of mirrors, coloured stones and glass mosaics. It overlooks a garden, and is open 6 to 11.30 am and 3 to 7 pm daily.

Nakhoda Mosque

North of BBD Bagh, this is Calcutta's principal Muslim place of worship. Built in 1926, the huge Nakhoda Mosque is said to accommodate 10,000 people and was modelled on Akbar's tomb at Sikandra near Agra. The red-sandstone mosque has two 46m minarets and a brightly painted onion-shaped dome. Outside the mosque, every day except Sunday, you can buy *attar*, perfume made from essential oils and flower fragrances.

Belur Math

North of the city, on the west bank of the Hooghly River, is the headquarters of the Ramakrishna Mission, Belur Math. Ramakrishna, an Indian philosopher, preached the unity of all religions. He died in 1886, and his follower Swami Vivekananda founded the Ramakrishna Mission in 1897. There are now branches all over India. Belur Math, the movement's international headquarters, was founded in 1899. It is supposed to represent a church, a mosque and a temple, depending on how you look at it. Belur Math is open 6.30 to 11 am and 3.30 to 7 pm daily; admission is free.

The Mission's **Institute of Culture**, which has a library, reading rooms and lecture halls, is in the south of the city near Dhakuria train station.

Dakshineswar Kali Temple

Across the river and north of Belur Math is this Kali temple where Ramakrishna was a priest, and where he reached his spiritual vision of the unity of all religions. The temple was built in 1847 and is surrounded by 12 other temples dedicated to Shiva.

Zoo & Horticultural Gardens

South of the Maidan, Calcutta's 16 hectare zoo was opened in 1875. Some animals are displayed in near natural environments, others in pitiful conditions characteristic of Third World zoos. It's open from sunrise to sunset; admission is Rs 10.

Just south of the zoo on Alipore Rd are the pleasant and quiet horticultural gardens. They're open daily from 8 am to 5 pm; admission is Rs 5.

Botanical Gardens

The extensive Botanical Gardens, on the west bank of the Hooghly River, stretch for over 1km along the river and occupy 109 hectares. The gardens were originally founded in 1786 and administered by Colonel Kyd. It was from these gardens that the tea now grown in Assam and Darjeeling was first developed.

The gardens' prime attraction is the 200-year-old **banyan tree**, claimed to have the second largest canopy in the world (the largest is in Andhra Pradesh). It covers an area of ground nearly 400m in circumference and continues to flourish despite having its central trunk removed in 1925 due to fungus damage. The **palm house** in the centre of the gardens is also well worth a visit.

The gardens are over the Howrah Bridge, 19km by bus from Chowringhee (on the way to Sibpur). However, it's much more pleasant if you can catch a ferry. When running, they leave from Chandpal or Babu Ghats, but they run on a casual basis at sporadic times. The fare should be Rs 3 or Rs 5, but you may have to pay a little more. The gardens are open from sunrise to sunset, and although they tend to be very crowded on Sunday, on other days they are peaceful and make a pleasant escape from the hassles and crowds of Calcutta.

Activities

Horse Riding The Tollygunge Club has well-bred horses and ponies that can be hired by guests and club members (Rs 70 per hour) to use on the bridleway around the perimeter of the club.

The Riding School Officers Institute and Fort William both offer horse riding and tuition.

Golf The magnificent Royal Calcutta Golf Club at Tollygunge, is the oldest golf club in the world outside Great Britain. Established in 1829, the club was originally near the airport, but moved to Tollygunge in 1910. The title 'Royal' was conferred upon it by King George V and Queen Mary in 1911.

Organised Tours

The Government of India tourist office (☎ 282 5813), 4 Shakespeare Sarani, has a full-day tour for Rs 100, departing at 8 am daily (except Monday) from its office. It covers Belur Math, Dakshineswar Temple, the Jain temple, the Victoria Memorial, the Indian Museum, the Nehru Children's Museum and the zoo.

The West Bengal tourist office (☎ 248 8271) at 3/2 BBD Bagh has a similar tour for Rs 75 or a second tour that crams in even more for Rs 100. One of the problems with sightseeing in Calcutta is that an awful lot of time is spent just sitting in traffic jams.

Bus tours are also conducted for the various festivals and pujas around the state – consult *Calcutta This Fortnight* or a tourist office for details.

West Bengal Tourism operates weekly trips to the Sunderbans Wildlife Sanctuary from October to March. See the Sunderbans section in the West Bengal chapter for more information.

Walking Tours Fascinating and informative walking tours of BBD Bagh and north Calcutta (including Tagore House and areas off the tourist circuit) are conducted by architect and conservationist, Manish Chakraborti. They leave from the Great Eastern Hotel and cover historic buildings, heritage sites and general history. For more information contact Footsteps, AA171A Salt Lake, Calcutta 700 064 (☎ 337 5757).

Volunteer Work

There are quite a number of charity organisations in Calcutta and West Bengal that accept volunteers. The best known of these is the Missionaries of Charity, the order started by Mother Teresa. Volunteers can work in any or all of the homes in Calcutta; Nirmal Hriday (Home for the Dying), Prem Dan (for the sick and mentally ill), Nirmala Shishu Bhavan (the children's home) and Shanti Nagar (for lepers, six hours from Calcutta). Although untrained helpers are accepted at some of the centres for periods of time, from one day to a year or more, it is the long-term volunteers who are of most use and are most sought after by the organisations.

Most volunteers stay at one of the many cheap lodgings around Sudder St (Rs 100 to Rs 250 per day). Inquiries can be directed to the Motherhouse, 54 AJC Bose Rd, Calcutta 700016, or just visit the Motherhouse on arrival in Calcutta.

There are also opportunities to work with the sisters in rural areas or at the Gandhi Welfare Centre which incorporates a nursery, dispensary, food distribution program and preschool. Inquire at the Motherhouse.

For those with the time to give a medium to long-term commitment, especially if you have any medical background, try Calcutta Rescue. Started in 1979 by Dr J Preger, and now encompassing several different clinics including a mobile unit, Dr Jack's, as it affectionately known, caters to the medical, nutritional and educational needs of the destitute and socially disadvantaged of Calcutta and rural West Bengal. Postal inquiries should be directed to Calcutta Rescue, PO Box 9253, Middleton Row PO, Calcutta 700071. In Calcutta, you can call in person to the administrative office at 85 Collins St (☎/fax 244 5675, 246 1520, email calres@cal.vsnl.net.in).

Other Tours For those with time on their hands, there is a two-week **Calcutta Food Tour**, where you see the city, sample Bengali culinary delights in some of the city's finest restaurants and learn to cook the cuisine under the tutelage of local Bengali women, actually in their homes. For more details contact David Rowe or Martin Brown, Kali Travel Home, c/o KL Gosh (☎ 556 1443, email ganesh@giascl01.vsnl.net.in).

Kali Travel Home also conducts three-week **sketching and drawing tours** of Calcutta, and three-week Darjeeling walking tours.

Special Events

For 10 days at the end of January the largest **book fair** in Asia is held on the Maidan. It costs a whole Rs 2 to enter, and it is just as well the fee is so low because you can lose yourself for days in here. And, unlike in other countries, drinks and snacks within the expo cost exactly the same, or less, than out on the street. A 10% discount applies to all books bought at the fair. Also held in January on the Maidan, the lively Calcutta Festival features ethnic food stalls and cultural events.

Places to Stay – Budget

Calcutta suffers from a shortage of good cheap places to stay. Budget travellers' accommodation is centred on Sudder St, running off Chowringhee Rd beside the Indian Museum. You should aim to arrive in Calcutta before noon or you may have great difficulty in finding a cheap bed.

CALCUTTA

CHOWRINGHEE

See BBD Bagh (Dalhousie Square) Map p518

Newmarket Street

New Market

Lindsay Street

Sudder Street

Chowringhee Lane

Dr M Ishaque Road (Kyd Street)

Marquis Street

Outram Road

The
Maidan

Park Street

Ripon Street

Royd Street

Rafi Ahmed Kidwai Road

Park Lane

Middleton Row

Jawaharlal Nehru Road (Chowringhee Road)

Russel Street

Mirza Ghalib Street (Free School Street)

Market Street

Hartford Lane

Park Street

0   100   200 m

Queen's Way

Middleton Street

Short Street

Little Russel Street

Ho Chi Minh Sarani

Wood Street

Loudon Street

Shakespeare Sarani

Victoria
Memorial

Cathedral Road

Lord Sinha Road

Pretoria Street

Camac Street

Hungerford Street

Moira Street

Rawdon Street

AJC Bose Road

CALCUTTA

CHOWRINGHEE

PLACES TO STAY		12	Khalsa Restaurant	49	Japan Airlines
1	Oberoi Grand Hotel	15	Zaranj Restaurant	52	French Consulate
6	Centrepoint Guest House;	18	Blue Sky Cafe; Curd Corner	55	Park St Post Office
	Hotel Diplomat;	19	Zurich's	57	State Bank of India
	Hotel Astoria;	22	Khwaja	58	American Center
	Travellers' Express Club	24	JoJo's Restaurant	59	British Airways; RNAC;
7	Hotel Plaza; Astoria	28	Abdul Khalique Hotel		Air France
8	Fairlawn Hotel	30	Princess Restaurant & Bar	60	Cathay Pacific; KLM
10	Hotel Lindsay; Gujral Lodge	31	Hong Kong Restaurant	62	British High Commission
11	CKT Inn	42	Mocambo's; Armenian	63	US Consulate
13	Lytton Hotel		College	64	Vital Medical Services
14	YMCA		(Thackery's Birthplace)	65	ANZ Grindlays Bank
17	Salvation Army Guest House	43	Peiping Restaurant	67	British Council & Library
20	Hotel Maria; Titrupati's	46	Kwality Restaurant	68	AC Market
21	Shilton Hotel	47	Bar BQ	70	Swissair
25	Modern Lodge	48	Junior Brothers	71	Birla Planetarium
26	Hotel Paragon; Hotel Galaxy	50	Flury's	72	Government of India
27	Hotel Palace; Cybercafe	51	Golden Dragon Restaurant		Tourist Office
29	Timestar Hotel	53	Peter Cat	73	St Paul's Cathedral;
32	Sonali Guest House	56	Waldorf Restaurant		Academy of Fine Arts
34	Neelam Hotel	76	Hare Krishna Bakery; ISKCON	74	Air India
35	Hotel Crystal;			75	Japanese Consulate
	PCO (Telephone	**OTHER**		78	Thai Airways
39	East End Hotel	2	New Empire Cinema;		International
40	Classic Hotel		Lighthouse Bar & Restaurant	79	Thomas Cook
41	Hotel VIP International;	3	Merle Oberon's House	81	Singapore Airlines
	Gupta Restaurant	4	New Market Post Office	82	Foreigners' Registration
45	Park Hotel; Trinca's Restaurant	9	Treasure Island Market;		Office
54	YWCA		City Express Supermarket	83	Aeroflot
66	Astor Hotel	16	Indian Museum	84	Nehru Children's
69	Kenilworth Hotel	23	English Wine Shop		Museum
77	Motherhouse	33	Off Cum On Rambo Bar	85	Rabindra Sadan
80	Hotel Hindustan International	37	Bangladesh Biman Airlines;		
			Lufthansa	**METRO STATIONS**	
PLACES TO EAT		38	Asiatic Society	36	Park St
5	Kathleen's Confectioners;	44	Standard Chartered Bank;	61	Maidan
	Princess Restaurant & Bars		ANZ Grindlays Bank	86	Rabindra Sadan

The **Salvation Army Guest House** (☎ 245 0599, 2 Sudder St) is popular with volunteers working for Mother Teresa's mission. It has dorm beds for Rs 60 and private doubles from Rs 100 to a staggering Rs 700. The guesthouse is clean and well kept, has a good atmosphere and its cheaper rooms are great value.

Hotel Maria (☎ 245 0860), farther down Sudder St, is equally popular, with dorm beds for Rs 70. There are also singles/doubles for Rs 150/180 with common bath, Rs 200/250 with attached bath. It has a nice rooftop meeting area, its own PCO and a strict 'no drugs, no alcohol' policy.

Hotel Hilson (☎ 249 0864, 4 Sudder St) has clean singles with common bath for Rs 150, doubles with bath from Rs 350 and triples at Rs 450.

Shilton Hotel (☎ 245 1512), farther on, has singles/doubles with attached bath for Rs 150/275.

Hotel Paragon (☎ 244 2445, 2 Stuart Lane), once a favourite, now suffers reports of being very unfriendly. It has dorm beds at Rs 60 (upstairs), tiny rooms with common bath for Rs 130/140 and doubles with bath from Rs 350. The ground floor rooms are rather gloomy but there's a pleasant courtyard upstairs. **Hotel Galaxy** (☎ 246 4565),

CALCUTTA

next door, has only four rooms at Rs 400, all with TV, phone and hot water.

Modern Lodge (☎ *243 4690, 1 Stuart Lane)*, is one of Calcutta's most popular budget establishments, especially with long-term volunteers. The rooftop area is a popular meeting place in the evening, and tea and soft drinks are available. Singles with bath are Rs 70 and Rs100 and doubles Rs 350.

Times Guest House (☎ *245 1796)* is a friendly Sikh-run place near the Blue Sky Cafe. Doubles are Rs 200/250 with common/attached bath.

Centrepoint Guest House (☎ *244 8184, 20 Mirza Ghalib St)* is a bustling, popular place. Clean dorm beds on the top floor are Rs 70. Double rooms are Rs 200, or Rs 450 with air-con, and there's a lounge with TV.

Sonali Guest House (☎ *245 1844)*, farther south on Mirza Ghalib St, is small and friendly with a nice roof area. Singles cost Rs 150 and doubles are Rs 300, or Rs 350 with TV and phone.

Hotel Palace (☎ *244 6214)*, down Chowringhee Lane, has singles from Rs 175 to Rs 200 with attached bath, and doubles from Rs 350 to Rs 400 with TV and air-con.

Capital Guest House (☎ *245 0598)*, also on Chowringhee Lane, is in a quiet courtyard away from the noise of Sudder St. Singles/doubles cost Rs 200/300 to Rs 350.

Timestar Hotel (☎ *245 0028)* in Tottee Lane, next to 4 Sudder St, is popular with Japanese travellers. Single/doubles are Rs 150/225.

East End Hotel (☎ *229 2673)* is south of Sudder St, on Dr M Ishaque Rd (Kyd St). This is an old, well-maintained place run by friendly people. Singles/doubles with attached bath cost from Rs 200/300 to Rs 250/350. *Neelam Hotel* (☎ *226 9198)*, opposite, has singles/doubles for Rs 175/250 and rooms with air-con for Rs 400.

Classic Hotel (☎ *229 7390)*, down an alley off Mirza Ghalib St, has singles with common bath for Rs 150. Doubles with bath are Rs 260, or Rs 550 with air-con. Hot water is available free by the bucket.

Gujral Lodge (☎ *244 0620)* in the same building as Hotel Lindsay, but off to the side

on the 2nd floor, has spacious rooms at Rs 240/650 with attached bath.

YMCA (☎ *249 2192, 25 Chowringhee Rd)* is a big, gloomy, dilapidated building. All accommodation includes early morning tea, breakfast and dinner; the rooms have attached baths. There are dorm beds for Rs 220 and singles/doubles for Rs 325/460, or Rs 560/730 with air-con.

There's another *YMCA* (☎ *244 3814, 42 Surendra Nath Banerji Rd)* with simple rooms starting at Rs 100.

The *YWCA* (☎ *297033, 1 Middleton Row)* is airy and spotless with a beautiful tennis court. Room rates include all meals. Singles/doubles are Rs 300/500 with common bath, or Rs 550/750 with attached bath.

Central Guest House (☎ *274876)* is a recommended hotel. Good-value, clean singles/doubles with attached bath go for Rs 190/250. The hotel fronts onto Chittaranjan (CR) Ave, but the entrance is around the corner at 18 Prafulla Sarkar St.

There are also *retiring rooms* at Howrah and Sealdah train stations (Rs 130 for doubles with bath). For transit passengers, there are also rooms at Calcutta airport. Check at the reservations desk at the terminal.

Yatri Nivas (☎ *660 1742)*, in the new building next door to Howrah station, has dorm beds for Rs 85 and doubles with bath for Rs 300, Rs 450 with air-con. You can only stay here if you have a train ticket for 200km plus, and then only for three nights.

For devotees of Hare Krishna there is a temple, library and *guesthouse* at 3C Albert Rd (☎ *247 6075)*. Rooms range in size and price, from Rs 150 for a single room, up to Rs 700 for a large room.

Places to Stay – Mid-Range
There's a bunch of mid-range places within easy walking distance of BBD Bagh. Air-con rooms are subject to tax.

Hotel Embassy (☎ *279040)* is the old place on nearby Princep St. Singles/doubles with bath, TV and phone are Rs 350/400. Air-con doubles cost from Rs 800.

Broadway Hotel (☎ *263930, fax 264151)* is a popular place one block east. There's a

Safety Warning

There is a practice among budget hotels and bottom-end to mid-range properties to install 'safety' gates across the entrance to the hotel or, worse, at each individual floor. Locked at night with a padlock, they are designed to keep out undesirables. Unfortunately, they also keep the guests in – not good in case of fire.

Although the management will undoubtedly kick up a big fuss and say you can always ring reception if you should need to get out ('There's always someone on duty'), insist on being given a copy of the key. Alternatively, you can insist on the gates being left unlocked and have a *chowkidar* (nightwatchman) sleep on each floor.

range of rooms from Rs 310 for a single to Rs 410/510 for doubles/triples with TV and phone.

You willll also find some moderately priced hotels around Chowringhee and Sudder St.

Hotel Crystal (☎ 226 6400, fax 246 5019, 11 Dr M Ishaque Rd) is a good-value place close to the action. Singles/doubles with TV and phone cost Rs 300/425, or Rs 750 with air-con. There's a PCO in the courtyard.

Hotel VIP International (☎ 290345, fax 293715, 51 Mirza Ghalib St) is clean but quite tatty once you go beyond reception. All rooms have air-con. Doubles range from Rs 1095 to Rs 1500.

Hotel Lindsay (☎ 244 1039, fax 245 0310, 8A Lindsay St) is a rather scruffy rabbit warren with small singles/doubles from Rs 600/700, or Rs 900/1000 with air-con.

CKT Inn (☎ 244 0047, 12A Lindsay St) is a small friendly place with rooms for Rs 700/1100, including TV, air-con, bath and all taxes and service charges.

Hotel Plaza (☎ 244 6411, 10 Sudder St) has boxy windowless rooms for Rs 375 with bath, Rs 475 with air-con. Next door, with the

same owners, **Hotel Diplomat** (☎ 246 8434), has rooms from Rs 175 to Rs 495.

Hotel Astoria (☎ 2454 9679, fax 244 8589, 6/2 Sudder St), is all air-con. Huge rooms with bath, colour TV and telephone are Rs 770/895.

Heera Hotel (☎ 228 0663, 28 Grant St), north of New Market, is clean, modern and friendly with room service, air-con and the world's smallest lift! Good rooms are Rs 400/500 or Rs 650/750 with air-con.

(Royal) Calcutta Guest House (☎ 280 0377, 124 Karaya Rd), away from the central district (look for the preschool sign), is quiet and good for long-term stays. All the spacious, bright, double rooms are arranged in pairs with a common lounge and kitchen in between. Singles/doubles are Rs 400/450, or Rs 650/750 with air-con.

Places to Stay – Top End
If you can afford it, there are some terrific luxury hotels in Calcutta. Taxes are extra, but they do take credit cards.

The **Tollygunge Club** (☎ 473 2316, fax 473 1903) is set on 44 hectares on the southern edge of Calcutta. It's not only a wonderfully relaxing place to stay, but is also home to the oldest golf club outside Great Britain and just the place to get an idea how the other half lived and played in the days of the Raj. For decades it was run by Englishman, Bob Wright, who now lives in retirement on the property.

'Tolly' is the playground of the city's elite and business community. As well as the famous championship golf course, there are indoor and outdoor pools, grass and clay tennis courts, squash courts, a croquet lawn, billiards room, badminton and table tennis rooms, and a stable of horses and ponies. As a foreign visitor, so long as you telephone, fax or write in advance (120 DP Sasmal Rd, Calcutta 700033), you may stay here and have temporary membership allowing you to use the facilities. Guests are expected to maintain the decorum of the club and be reasonably tidy, but jackets and ties are not necessary. The cheapest rooms are in 'Hastings' cost Rs 950/1000, with air-con and

CALCUTTA

bath. The 'Grandstand' cottages cost Rs 2000/2400 and have small sitting areas overlooking the golf course. Most rooms in Tolly Towers or Tolly Terrace are similarly priced. The club is a 10 minute walk from Tollygunge metro station and next to a tram stop.

Great Eastern Hotel (☎ 248 2311, fax 248 0289, 1-3 Old Court House St) is a rambling, old Raj-style hotel south of BBD Bagh. Originally named The Auckland when it was built in 1840, the 200 spacious rooms and public areas are undergoing a two-year renovation and refurbishment program – be prepared to find variations in the condition of rooms and in the rates quoted here. Basic singles/doubles are Rs 550/850 and air-con doubles are Rs 2180 to Rs 3630. There are several restaurants, and a coffee shop.

Fairlawn Hotel (☎ 245 1510, fax 244 1835, 13A Sudder St) is a piece of Calcutta where the Raj still lives, albeit in a decidedly eccentric manner. Edmund Smith and his Armenian wife, Violet, still run the hotel more than 50 years after Independence. The hotel is crammed with memorabilia, chintz and prewar furnishings. Also, it is very green – you enter through a courtyard and beer garden surrounded by lush greenery, and then everything, from the walls to the ashtrays, is painted a different shade of green. Most of the rooms have air-con, TV and phone. The bathrooms are old fashioned, some with deep baths standing on ball and claw feet. Singles/doubles cost US$40/50. The tariff includes three meals (set menu), plus afternoon tea in the garden. A 20% discount is offered from April to September. The hotel has its own well and water filtration equipment. Outside guests can drink and dine here.

Lytton Hotel (☎ 249 1872, fax 249 1747, 14 Sudder St), though clean and modern is a little lacking in character (the bars aren't too bad). Centrally air-con singles/doubles are Rs 1400/2000.

Astor Hotel (☎ 242 9957, fax 242 5136, 15 Shakespeare Sarani) is in a good location and has roomy air-con singles/doubles from Rs 1100/1300. The hotel has a very pleasant garden and there are daily barbecues.

The *Kenilworth Hotel (☎ 282 8394, fax 282 5136, 1-2 Little Russel St)* has old and new wings but all rooms are air-con with fridge, TV and attached bath. Basic rates are US$85/95.

The modern *ITDC Airport Ashok (☎ 552 9111, fax 552 9137)*, at the airport, is convenient for passengers in transit. Singles/doubles with air-con start at US$70/80.

Hotel Hindustan International (☎ 247 2394, fax 247 2824, 235 AJC Bose Rd), has 212 rooms and all the facilities you would expect of a five-star hotel: health club, shopping arcade, restaurants, bars, conference rooms and swimming pool. Singles/doubles start at US$165/185.

There are also three hotels which fall into the truly international luxury category. All have pools, health clubs, top restaurants, state-of-the-art business centres and in-room communication systems.

Park Hotel (☎ 249 3121, fax 249 7343, 17 Park St) is a member of the Small Luxury Hotels of the World group. While being a relatively large property, it has all the ambience of a boutique hotel. Rooms start at US$220/250 for air-con singles/doubles.

Oberoi Grand Hotel (☎ 249 2323, fax 249 1217, 15 Chowringhee Rd) is a member of the Leading Hotels of the World group. It has long been acknowledged as Calcutta's best hotel and one of the jewels in the Oberoi crown. Rooms start at US$220/245.

Taj Bengal (☎ 223 3939, fax 223 1766), at the southern end of the Maidan, is a plush competitor for gold-card clientele. It has an opulent atrium with a waterfall, all the mod cons you'd expect and excellent, attentive service. Rooms start at US$235/255 for singles/doubles.

Places to Eat

Sudder St Area Finding good food at reasonable prices is no problem here. Always packed, *Blue Sky Cafe*, just off Sudder St, does quite good breakfasts and snacks. It is trading on its reputation a bit, and seems to think it *de rigueur* to have rude staff. *Curd Corner*, next door on Sudder St, serves some of the best curd and lassis in town.

Zurich's close by on Sudder St, has become immensely popular. It serves excellent rice and noodle dishes and does a good job of lemon and banana pancakes, omelettes and porridge.

Titrupati's is a great little street stall outside Hotel Maria, much patronised by volunteers. It serves excellent meals for Rs 10 to Rs 20.

Khwaja is opposite Booklands on Sudder St and is owned by the same family. It's a little more expensive than other cheapies in the area, but it serves good food and is an excellent place to sit, eat, read/write and escape the furore of the street.

Khalsa Restaurant, just off Sudder St in the street opposite the Salvation Army Guest House, has been popular with locals and travellers for many years. Food is plentiful and good, the service excellent and it is a nonsmoking restaurant.

JoJo's Restaurant, a popular spot with tourists and locals, is down the lane opposite Hotel Maria. It's open for breakfast, lunch and dinner, is air-con and spotless.

Jharokha is a rooftop restaurant 10 floors above the Hotel Lindsay. It offers sweeping views over Calcutta and is a great for takinng photos (it also has an immaculate loo). You can eat outside, or inside in air-con. The meals, at an average of Rs 50, are very generous. It's open 7 am to 10 pm.

Still within reach of the Sudder St area is *Nizam's*, around the corner from the Elite Cinema. It's very popular among Calcuttans for mutton and chicken rolls, kebabs and Muslim food.

A bit farther north, on Chowringhee Rd, *Indra Mahal* is a great place to try Bengali sweets. Specialities include *Mughal paratha* and *misthi dhoi* (curd with jaggery).

The *Fairlawn Hotel*, is an expensive, English-style eating option on Sudder St. The set-menu lunches and dinners can be fun and are certainly different, announced by a gong and served by uniformed waiters. The food varies but is generally OK (check the day's menu posted at reception). Breakfast costs Rs 100, lunch Rs 120 and dinner Rs 150. The garden in front of the hotel is

an excellent place for afternoon tea or a beer in the evening, although the mosquitoes are very friendly, the drinks dry up at 8 pm *sharp* and the service can be haphazard.

Zaranj Restaurant, also on Sudder St, is as expensive as its decor with most dishes costing around Rs 140; despite this it is generally packed.

Mirza Ghalib St *Gupta Restaurant,* next to Hotel VIP International, serves excellent food. A shared meal of three or four dishes between two will cost from Rs 50 to Rs 60 per person.

Mocambo is quite upmarket. It has a grand piano, is licensed and serves good Indian dishes from Rs 70 to Rs100.

Princess Restaurant & Bar has mains at around Rs 80.

Cheaper meals can be had at *How Hua* where northern Chinese dishes such as *jiaozi* (a bit like Tibetan *momos*), is served.

Golden Dragon and *Hong Kong,* at opposite ends of Mirza Ghalib St, are also both quite reasonable in terms of food and price.

Prince Restaurant, on the corner of Mirza Ghalib and Marquis Sts, specialises in Bengali cuisine. Try the fish curry.

Kathleen Confectioners has a good selection of pastries and lots of wonderful, calorie-filled cakes and sweets. There are outlets on Mirza Ghalib St, Russel St and AJC Bose Rd.

Park St Area *Bar BQ* on Park St, despite its name, is one of the most popular Chinese and Indian restaurants in the area and there is usually a queue after 7.30 pm. The service is excellent and the atmosphere buzzes. Dishes are around Rs 35.

Waldorf Restaurant, also on Park St, has a Chinese chef, but also turns a hand to Thai food.

Junior Brothers is a comfortable, cheap Indian restaurant tucked in among the many ritzy options on Park St.

Kwality Restaurant at 17 Park St, beside the Park Hotel, has a small menu, with main dishes around Rs 65, but it's quite a good place to eat.

Doggie Bags

Meal portions in Calcutta are generally extremely generous and lead to frequent leftovers. One suggestion is to ask for a doggie-bag, a concept well-understood at even the most basic *dhaba*. The leftover, *untouched* food, can then be offered to beggars in the street. This practice has two benefits, firstly it alleviates waste in a city where so many people are going hungry, and secondly, it sorts the genuine beggars out from the 'organised' beggars. If the offering is refused, the beggar is probably working for a 'master' and isn't hungry at all.

Many beggars, especially in the Sudder St area, are quite well paid as evidenced by the sighting behind New Market of one well-known (sad) face from Sudder St, laughing with friends and counting her morning takings – hundreds of rupees.

Trinca's Restaurant, on the corner of the Park Hotel building, has good but quite expensive food; you'll have to pay a surcharge if, as is usual, there's a band playing.

Peter Cat, off Park St on Middleton Row, near the YWCA, is good for a meal or just a few drinks (though drinks are expensive). The menu includes excellent kababs.

Flury's, on Park St, is a great place for a peaceful tea and cake session.

If money is no object, there are excellent restaurants at the Oberoi Grand (the *Baan Thai* and *Gharana*), The Park (the *Zen* and *Saffron*) and the *Taj Bengal*, famous for its poolside barbeques and Bengali restaurant.

Chittaranjan Ave Area *Chung Wah Chinese Restaurant*, on Chittaranjan Ave, with private wooden booths, looks like something out of Shanghai in the 1930s. Mains are around Rs 50; they also have value set lunches at another branch around the corner.

Anand Restaurant, also on Chittaranjan Ave, is probably the best vegetarian restaurant in the city. It's a smart place but main dishes are good value at Rs 35.

Amber Hotel (☎ 248 6520) is right in the centre of town at 11 Waterloo St (the narrow street that runs by the Great Eastern Hotel). The food is excellent and it is often voted by residents of Calcutta as the best place to eat in the city. Prices are very reasonable, with most dishes at around Rs 50, and the tandoori items are very good. Phone to reserve a table.

The *Indian Coffee House*, near Calcutta University, is an institution. For years it was the meeting place of the city's intellectuals. Nowadays it's popular with young undergraduates. There's a more central branch on Chittaranjan Ave, with a sign warning that the management 'reserves the right to maintain the dignity of the coffee shop'.

Elsewhere *Amina Restaurant*, (6A Surendra Nath Banerjee Rd), serves authentic Mughlai food. It is a big fast-food joint (along the lines of an Asian food hall) with an open kitchen. Meals cost around Rs 35, and they do takeaways.

Hare Krishna Bakery, on the corner of Middleton and Russel Sts, is the place for good bread and takeaway snacks. Go early for the excellent brown bread.

The Rice Bowl, opposite the Calcutta Rowing Club at Rabindra Sarobar (the lakes), is reputedly one of the city's best Chinese restaurants.

Suruchi, on Elliot Rd, by the Mallik Bazaar bus stop, specialises in Bengali food but is only open for lunch.

Gangaur Sweets on Russel St, *Krishan Sweets* and *Upper Crust* on Carmac St and *KC Das* on Lenin Sarani (near the corner of Bentinck St), are terrific sweet shops.

Entertainment

Pubs/Bars Thursday is a 'dry' day in Calcutta and the only places where you can get alcoholic drinks are in the four and five-star hotels, although some places seem to disregard this ruling.

In the Sudder St area, the *Sun Set Bar* at the Lytton Hotel is a good place for a drink. It's friendly and there's a good music system. Similar is the open-air bar in the forecourt of the *Fairlawn Hotel* where there's always an interesting crowd.

Paris Bar & Restaurant, on Surendra Nath Banerji Rd, is an interesting combination of Indian pub and nightclub. Open from noon to 11 pm, it has singers, live bands and sells all the really mind-altering beers like Thunderbolt and Haward's Turbo 5000. This large cavern of a place has a good atmosphere.

Astor Hotel, on Shakespeare Sarani, has a pleasant garden that's good for a relaxing drink (beers are Rs 60) or a barbecue (daily between 6 and 11 pm). On Saturday evenings there's live music.

Another good place popular with the locals is the *Lighthouse Bar & Restaurant* in the New Empire Cinema complex near New Market.

The *Off Cum On Rambo Bar* on Mirza Ghalib St, is an absolute dive, probably best avoided by women on their own, but it does sell beer till late.

Discos Quite a few of the larger hotels have discos which go on until early morning. The *Pink Elephant* at the Oberoi Grand Hotel operates on Wednesday, Friday and Saturday nights and Sunday afternoon. Entry is Rs 150 for solo cruisers, or Rs 250 for a couple.

Someplace Else at the Park Hotel is another favourite spot with a great atmosphere. Early in the evening, before it hots up, it's also a good place to meet for a quiet drink.

If you don't mind going a little further afield, or are staying in north Calcutta, there are a couple of other upmarket discos; *Anticlock* can be found at the Hotel Hindustan and *Incognito* is at the Taj Bengal.

Dance & Theatre Calcutta is famous for its culture – film, poetry, music, art and dance all have their devotees here. Programs are listed in the daily newspapers or in the leaflet *Calcutta This Fortnight*, available free from tourist offices.

A dance-drama performance, Bengali poetry reading or a similar event takes place on most nights at the *Rabindra Sadan* (☎ 247 2413, Cathedral Rd).

There are often drama performances in English at the *Kala Mandir* (☎ 247 9086, 48 Shakespeare Sarani), and musical programs at the *Sisir Mancha* (☎ 248 1451, 1/1 AJC Bose Rd).

Every Saturday and Sunday at 5.30 pm the *Hotel Hindustan International* has a 'Dances of India' show. Entry is free.

The Government of India also holds dance performances (5.50 pm, Monday to Friday) by the Academy of Oriental Dance at its Shakespeare Sarani premises.

Cinema Foreign films and retrospectives are shown at the Nandan complex near Cathedral Rd; many Chowringhee cinemas show recent-release US movies.

Shopping

Many interesting shops line Chowringhee Rd selling everything from carpets to handicrafts. The Central Cottage Industries Emporium at 7 Chowringhee Rd is quite good. The shops along the entrance arcade to the Oberoi Grand Hotel are interesting but not as entertaining as Chowringhee's amazing variety of pavement vendors who sell everything from water pistols to dancing dolls. Calcutta's administration is trying to move the street hawkers to (as yet unbuilt) underground markets in an attempt to clear the footpaths, but the unionised street merchants have so far resisted attempts to budge them.

New Market, formerly Hogg Market, is Calcutta's premier place for bargain shopping. Here you can find a little of almost everything, and it is always worth an hour or so of wandering around. A particularly good bargain, if you're flying straight home from Calcutta, is caneware. This is very cheap compared to prices in the west and is, of course, very light if rather bulky.

Between Sudder St and New Market is the Treasure Island air-con market. In the basement is City Express Supermarket with fully computerised checkouts and at least one supermarket helper per customer. The AC Market on Shakespeare Sarani specialises in imported foodstuffs. You can find Diet Coke, Marmite and sometimes even Vegemite here.

Opposite New Market, behind the Oberoi Grand Hotel, is a shopping mall, complete with air-con, atrium, fountains and glass lift. The shops mostly sell clothes, electrical goods, jewellery and toys.

The area around Park, Carmac and Russel Sts is awash with upmarket boutiques, jewellery stores and designer label outlets.

There's a good street market (mainly clothes) along Lenin Sarani in the evenings.

Getting There & Away

Air Most airline offices are around Chowringhee. Indian Airlines is on Chittaranjan Ave, and it also has an office in the Great Eastern Hotel. Other airline offices are:

Aeroflot
    (☎ 282 9831/3765) 58 Chowringhee Rd
Air France
    (☎ 226 6161) 41 Chowringhee Rd;
    enter from Middleton St
Air India
    (☎ 282 2356) 50 Chowringhee Rd
Bangladesh Biman
    (☎ 229 2844) 30C Chowringhee Rd
British Airways
    (☎ 226 3450/3454) 41 Chowringhee Rd;
    enter from Middleton St
Cathay Pacific
    (☎ 240 3312/3211) 1 Middleton St
Gulf Air
    (☎ 247 7783/5576) 230A AJC Bose Rd
Indian Airlines
    (☎ 262548, 264433) 39 Chittaranjan Ave
Japan Airlines
    (☎ 246 8370/8371) 35A Chowringhee Rd
Jet Airways
    (☎ 229 2813/2660) 18 Park St
KLM – Royal Dutch Airlines
    (☎ 240 3135/1636) 1 Middleton St
Lufthansa Airlines
    (☎ 229 9365) 30A/B Chowringhee Rd
Necon Air (GSA)
    (☎ 229 2471/4340) DG Links,
    22 Palace Court, Dr M Ishaque Rd
Royal Nepal Airlines (RNAC)
    (☎ 246 8534) 41 Chowringhee Rd;
    enter from Middleton St
Sahara India Airlines
    (☎ 282 9067) 2A Shakespeare Sarani
Scandinavian Airlines (SAS)
    (☎ 475 0226/0240) 2/7 Sarat Bose Rd
Singapore Airlines
    (☎ 280 9898/8586) 1 Lee Rd; off AJC Bose Rd
Swissair
    (☎ 282 4643) 46C Chowringhee Rd
Tarom (Romania)
    (☎ 240 5196) 228A AJC Bose Rd
Thai Airways International
    (☎ 280 1630/1635) 229 AJC Bose Rd

Calcutta is good for competitive air fares to other parts of Asia, Europe and the US east coast. Flights are usually with Air India, Indian Airlines, Thai Airways International, Royal Nepal Airlines, Aeroflot, Bangladesh Biman, Royal Brunei or Tarom. Ridiculously low fares that bear no resemblance to any quoted 'special' fare can sometimes be found. The best way to find the best deals is by word of mouth from other travellers and frequent checks with agencies and airlines.

Calcutta's Indian Airlines office (☎ 262548) is open 24 hours seven days a week. There's a tourist counter which rarely has a queue so it's very quick. Even refunds or a change of flight date are no hassle.

As well as its domestic routes (see the Flights from Calcutta table), Indian Airlines also flies four international routes: to Dhaka (Rs 2380, US$43, five times weekly), Bangkok (Rs 9730, four times weekly) and Kathmandu (US$192, six times weekly). Youth concessions are available.

Bus It's generally better to travel from Calcutta by train, though there are several useful bus routes to other towns in West Bengal.

The only buses that travellers use with any regularity are those from Calcutta to Siliguri and New Jalpaiguri (for Darjeeling). The 'Rocket Service' (!) costs Rs 160 and leaves Calcutta at 8 pm, arriving the next morning. It's much rougher than going by train and only a Rs 30 saving.

Buses generally depart from the Esplanade bus station area at the northern end of the Maidan, near Chowringhee Rd, but there are a number of private companies that have their own stands. Buses to and from the south generally use the bus stand near Fort William at Babu Ghat.

Train Calcutta has two major train stations, both of them frenetic. Howrah, on the west

Flights from Calcutta

destination	direct flight duration	flights per d/w[1]	fare (US$)
Agartala (Bangladesh)	50 min	11 w	50
Ahmedabad	2 h 30 min	6 w	50
Aizawl	55 min	2 w	90
Bagdogra	50 min	7 w	80
Bangalore	2 h 20 min	10 w	240
Bhubaneswar	50 min	5 w	75
Chennai	2 h	10 w	200
Delhi	2 h	32 w	180
Dibrugarh	1 h 30 min	4 w	95
Dimapur	2 h 10 min	4 w	90
Guwahati	1 h 10 min	24 w	70
Hyderabad	2 h	2 d	120
Imphal	2 h 10 min	9 w	80
Jaipur	2 h 25 min	3 w	200
Jorhat	1 h 20 min	4 w	90
Lucknow	2 h 20 min	4 w	115
Mumbai	2 h 30 min	40 w	205
Nagpur	1 h 30 min	2 w	150
Patna	50 min	4 w	90
Port Blair	2 h	4 w	195
Pune	4 h	3 w	250
Ranchi	50 min	2 w	70
Silchar	1 h	6 w	75
Tezpur	1 h 15 min	2 w	80
Visakhapatnam	1 h 20 min	3 w	130

[1]d-daily, w-weekly

bank of the Hooghly River, handles most trains into the city, but trains going north to Darjeeling or the North-Eastern Region leave from Sealdah station on the east side of the Hooghly. Beware of pickpockets at both stations. At Howrah station, platforms 1 to 16 are in the old main building, platforms 17 to 22 are in the new annexe next door. Bearers (porters) should only charge Rs 5 to Rs 10 per bag, but will try for Rs 20 or Rs 50. Even if you are exhausted, pick up your own bag and the fee will drop automatically.

The tourist railway booking office is on the 1st floor at 6 Fairlie Place near BBD Bagh. It's fully computerised and has a tourist quota, but can be very crowded. It's open Monday to Saturday, 9 am to 1 pm and 1.30 to 4 pm, and Sunday 9 am to 2 pm. There's another booking office nearby, at 14 Strand Rd South, where you can buy advance tickets on routes into and out of Delhi, Chennai and Mumbai. Get a form and join the correct queue; the tourist quota isn't accessible from this office. Bookings can be made up to 60 days before departure for all trains apart from the *Shatabdi Express*, for which bookings are only open within 15 days of departure.

Both these places attract long queues and the staff at Fairlie Place office demand to see exchange certificates if you pay in rupees. There are other computerised booking offices that may be better for buying advance tickets out of Calcutta. The office at Tollygunge metro station is easy to get to and never seems to be very busy. For a small fee (about Rs 40), agents in and around Sudder St can get tickets for you, often at short notice. The agents' offices are well posted and other travellers tend to know who offers the best service.

If you have just flown into Calcutta, it might be worth checking the rail reservation desk at the airport as they have an air-travellers' quota for same-day or next-day travel on the main expresses.

Note that there are five classes of rail travel between 2nd class and 1st class. As many travellers prefer 2nd class sleeper in preference to ordinary 2nd class, these fares have also been included in the Major Trains from Calcutta table.

Boat See the Andaman & Nicobar Islands chapter for details on the shipping services from Calcutta.

Getting Around
To/From the Airport The airport is 17km north-east of the city centre. A public minibus (No S10) runs from BBD Bagh to the airport for Rs 8. Bus No L33 goes from

Major Trains from Calcutta

destination	train no & name	departure time[1]	distance (km)	duration (hours)	fare (RS) (2nd/1st)
Chennai	2841 *Coromandel Exp*	2.50 pm H	1636	27 h 30 min	223/1209
Delhi	2305 *Rajdhani Exp*[2]	1.45 pm H	1441	18 h	2190/3825
	2303 *Poorva Exp*	9.15 am H	1441	24 h	1719/3189
Mumbai VT	2860 *Gitanjali Exp*	12.30 pm H	1960	33 h	253/1435
New Jalpaiguri	3143 *Darjeeling Mail*	7.15 pm S	573	11 h 45 min	120/598
Patna	2381 *Poorva Exp*	9.15 am H	545	8 h	117/574
	3005 *Amritsar Mail*	7.20 pm H		9 h 40 min	117/574
Puri	8007 *Puri Exp*	10.15 pm H	500	10 h	108/531
Varanasi	2303 *Poorva Exp*	9.15 am H	670	10 h 30 min	135/672

[1] Abbreviations for train stations: H – Howrah, S – Sealdah
[2] Air-con only; fare includes meals and drinks

the Esplanade bus station to the airport also for Rs 8. There's also an airport minibus from Babu Ghat bus stand. The metro line to Dum Dum stops 5km short of the airport; a bus from there will cost Rs 5 (a taxi Rs 40).

If you want to take a taxi from the airport, it's cheaper to go to the prepaid kiosk where you'll be assigned one. It costs Rs 130 to Sudder St or the Oberoi Grand Hotel. In the opposite direction expect to pay at least 25% more, though shared between four people it's not so expensive.

Incidentally, Calcutta's airport takes its name, Dum Dum airport, from the fact that this was the site of the Dum Dum Barracks, where the explosive dumdum bullet, banned after the Boer War, was once made.

Bus Calcutta's bus system is hopelessly crowded. Fares start at Rs 1.50. Take a No S7 or S27 bus between Howrah station and Sudder St; ask for the Indian Museum. There is a secondary private minibus service, which is rather faster and slightly more expensive, with fares starting at Rs 1.75.

Beware of pickpockets on any of Calcutta's public transport.

Tram Calcutta has a public tram service, but the amazingly dilapidated trams are like sar-

dine tins in rush hour. They may be pollution-free but since they're a major cause of traffic jams, there's pressure to abolish them. Tram enthusiasts, including a sister society in Melbourne, Australia, have been campaigning to retain the trams and it looks like they've succeeded – for now. Local politicians are under pressure (especially in the wallet area) from bus companies to pull up the tracks and start pumping more diesel into Calcutta's 'air'. Fares start at Rs 1.20. Out of rush hour they are a relatively fast, cheap way to get to areas outside the city centre.

Metro India's first underground railway system is being built at minimum cost and in maximum time, almost totally by hand. Calcutta's soggy soil makes digging holes by hand no fun at all – after each monsoon it took half the time until the next monsoon simply to drain out what had already been dug. Nevertheless, the northern and southern sectors are open, and work is to proceed on an extension further to the south.

The southern sector, from Chandni Chowk to Tollygunge station and the north sector to the west of BBD Bagh, are most useful. There are two stations near Sudder St; to the north (almost opposite the Oberoi Grand) and to the south (opposite Dr M Ishaque Rd).

The metro is clean and efficient, although still chokingly crowded during peak hours. Movies are shown on platform TVs and the stations are air-conditioned and well decorated (Rabindra Sadan has Tagore's poems on the walls). Trains run from 8.15 am to 9.15 pm, Monday to Saturday and from 3 to 9.15 pm on Sunday. Tickets cost from Rs 3 (one sector) to Rs 7 (to the end of the line).

Taxi The first thing to understand about taxi fares in Calcutta is that the final cost of travel is the meter reading *plus 100%*, as the meters are out of date.

Officially, taxi fares start at Rs 5 and go up by Rs 0.50 increments, but that can be more theory than practice. In reality, a third of drivers are willing to use the meter, another third can be talked into it and a belligerent third are as likely to use the meter as they are to offer you a free ride and a picnic in the Maidan! Also, some drivers will point-blank refuse to take a fare for a short distance; others will agree on a price and then change it 500m down the road. If you argue, they will often just stop and tell you to get out, or

try to talk one of their colleagues into taking you. Frustrating as it is, there are plenty of taxis, so shop around for a metered ride or a reasonable negotiated price.

At Howrah station there's a prepaid taxi rank outside, and from here it will cost you Rs 39 to Sudder St, although it can take 15 minutes or more to get to the front of the queue. If you want to avoid the queue, other sharks will offer to take you for between Rs 100 and Rs 120.

Rickshaw Calcutta is the last bastion of the human-powered rickshaw, apart from at resorts like Mussoorie where they're just for the tourists. Calcutta's rickshaw-wallahs would not accept the new-fangled cycle-rickshaws when they were introduced elsewhere in India. After all, who could afford a bicycle? Most can't even afford to buy their own rickshaw and have to rent from someone who takes the lion's share of the fares.

You may find it morally unacceptable to have a man pulling you around in a carriage – these men are usually very thin, unhealthy and die early – but Calcutta's citizens are

Local Buses

Local buses in Calcutta, like most parts of India, are unbelievably crowded, dilapidated and travel everywhere at break-neck speed; except when they are stuck in traffic. Little time is given for disembarkation and there are daily reports of injury and death caused by buses. However, these phenomena are easily explained when one understands how the bus system – state and private – works.

Bus drivers are paid by the number of passengers they carry, and fined for each minute they are late. Naturally, this leads to dangerous and excessive competition among bus drivers. The drivers who are caught for dangerous driving are given bail and return immediately to work, happy in the knowledge that their case won't come to court for years; by that time any witnesses have disappeared or have little memory of the incident. According to the newspaper reports, four out of five drivers are simply fined.

Many drivers freely admit they are 'forced' to adopt 'techniques' such as purposely blocking the way of rival buses, or scrambling to overtake them; with the result that lives are put at risk and the buses look like they have come from a wreckers yard. Drivers say, in off-peak times they drive slowly to pick up the maximum number of passengers, then put on a burst of speed towards the end of the journey to make up time and avoid a fine. The moral is, when crossing a road, don't step out in front of an oncoming bus or weave through a group of buses at a stop – another, faster moving bus may be obscured by the first one!

quite happy to use them. The only compensation is that they wouldn't have a job if people didn't use them and, as a tourist, you naturally pay more than local people. Calcutta's administration wants to completely ban the rickshaws, as part of a short-sighted traffic-management plan that equates slow-moving transport with slow-moving traffic. As it is, Calcutta's narrow lanes and poor drainage mean that, aside from walking, jumping in a rickshaw is often the only way to get somewhere.

These sort of rickshaws only exist in small parts of central Calcutta and they are restricted to the smaller roads. Across the river in Howrah or in the suburbs, there are auto and cycle-rickshaws.

Ferry The ferries can be a quicker and a more pleasant way to get across the river than the congested Howrah Bridge. From Howrah to Chandpal Ghat or Fairlie Ghat there are several crossings an hour between 8 am and 8 pm. Ferries to the botanical gardens go from Chandpal Ghat or Babu Ghat, but they are a 'casual' service on negotiation and not at any designated times. The fares are minimal, from about Rs 3 to Rs 5.

West Bengal

The cradle of Indian renaissance and the national freedom movement, Bengal has long been considered by many as the cultural centre of India. After Partition, the state was split into East and West Bengal. East Bengal eventually became Bangladesh and West Bengal, a state of India with Calcutta as its capital. The state is long and narrow, running from the delta of the Ganges River system in the Bay of Bengal to the south, up through the Ganges plain, to the heights of the Himalaya and Darjeeling in the north.

A land of aesthetes and political activists, West Bengal is famous for its many eminent writers, poets, artists, spiritualists, social reformers, freedom fighters and revolutionaries.

Apart from Calcutta, with its bewildering maelstrom of noise, beauty, culture, confusion and squalor, and Darjeeling, which is congested yet somehow still serene, West Bengal is relatively untouched by commercialism and tourism.

South of Calcutta on the Bay of Bengal is the area known as the Sunderbans, one of the largest deltas in the world, and home to the elusive Royal Bengal tiger. To the north lie the flourishing mango plantations and jute fields of the fertile river plains. Farther north again in the Himalayan foothills are the world famous Darjeeling tea plantations.

Everywhere you look you will find historic sites and some interesting aspect of Bengali culture. Yet, foreign tourists have been slow to visit the ruined mosques of Malda, the palaces of Murshidabad, the living arts museum and university of Shantiniketan, the temples of Vishnupur or even the Sunderbans Wildlife Sanctuary. If you do, the friendly Bengalis will make you feel all the more welcome for being an exception to the rule.

History

Referred to as Vanga in the *Mahabharata*, this area has a long history that predates the Aryan invasions of India. It was part of the

West Bengal at a Glance

Population: 74.5 million
Area: 87,853 sq km
Capital: Calcutta
Main Language: Bengali
Best Time to Go: October to March

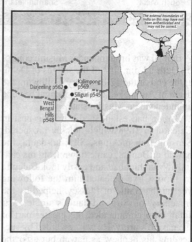

- **Darjeeling** – the quaint Britishness of this archetypal hill station

- **Sunderbans Wildlife Sanctuary** – search for the prolific wildlife in this World Heritage listed park within the world's largest river delta

- **Tea Plantations** – visit a plantation to savour a 'real' cuppa

Mauryan empire in the 3rd century before being overrun by the Guptas. For three centuries from around the 9th century AD, the Pala dynasty controlled a large area based in Bengal and including parts of Orissa, Bihar and modern Bangladesh.

Festivals of West Bengal

festival	location	date	features
Bathing Festival	Sagar Island	Jan	bathing
Magh Mela	Shantiniketan	6-8 Feb	anniversary & fair
Vasantotsava	Shantiniketan	20 Mar	spring festival
Rath Yatra	Mahesh	Jun/Jul	fair
Jhapan Festival	Vishnupur	Aug	snake worship/charmers
Flower Festival	Kalimpong	Oct	floriade
Teesta Tea & Tourism Festival	Darjeeling	14-20 Nov	cutural events
Poush Mela	Shantiniketan	Dec	annual fair

Bengal was brought under Muslim control by Qutb-ud-din, first of the sultans of Delhi, at the end of the 12th century. Following the death of Aurangzeb in 1707, Bengal became an independent Muslim state.

Britain had established a trading post in Calcutta in 1698 which quickly prospered. Sensing rich pickings, Siraj-ud-daula, the nawab of Bengal, came down from his capital at Murshidabad and easily took Calcutta in 1756. Clive defeated him the following year at the Battle of Plassey, helped by the treachery of Siraj-ud-daula's uncle, Mir Jafar, who commanded the greater part of the nawab's army. He was rewarded by succeeding his nephew as nawab but after the Battle of Buxar in 1764, the British took full control of Bengal. For entertaining background reading on this period as seen through the eyes of a modern-day traveller, Peter Holt's book *In Clive's Footsteps* is recommended. The author is the five times removed great-grandson of Clive.

Permits

Permission is necessary if you wish to visit the Sunderbans Wildlife Sanctuary. For Sajnekhali and the Project Tiger areas, permits are available free of charge while you wait (and wait...) at the Forest Department (G Block, 6th floor) in the Writers' Building, Calcutta. You must bring your passport. For other Sunderbans areas go to the Divisional Forest Officer (☎ 033-245 1037), 24 Parganas, 35 Gopalnagar Rd, Calcutta.

South of Calcutta

DOWN THE HOOGHLY

The Hooghly River is very difficult to navigate due to constantly shifting shoals and sandbanks. River pilots have to stay in touch with it to keep track of its frequent course changes. When the Howrah Bridge was built, it was feared it would affect the river's flow patterns.

Tides rise and fall 3.5m at Calcutta and there is a bore, 2m high, during rising tides. As a result of this and the silting up of the Hooghly, Calcutta is losing its importance as a port.

Falta, 43km downriver, was the site of a Dutch factory. The British retreated here in 1756 when Calcutta was captured by Siraj-ud-daula. It's also from here that Clive recaptured Calcutta. Below Falta the Damodar River joins the Hooghly.

The Rupnarain River also joins the Hooghly nearby and a little up this river is **Tamluk**, an important Buddhist centre over 1000 years ago. The James & Mary Shoal, the most dangerous on the Hooghly, is just above the point where the Rupnarain River enters. Its name comes from a ship wrecked here in 1694.

DIAMOND HARBOUR
☎ 03174
A resort 51km south of Calcutta by road, Diamond Harbour is at the point where the

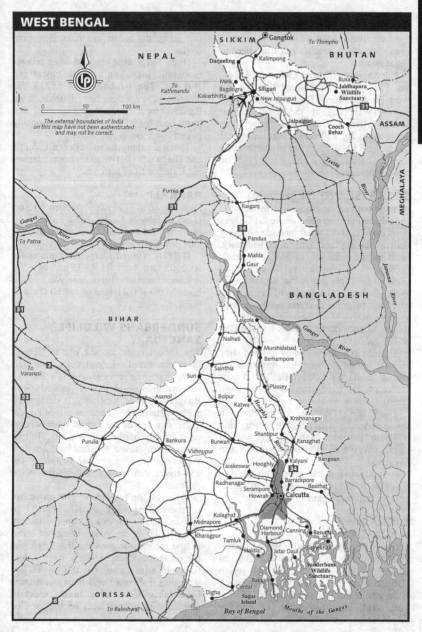

WEST BENGAL

The external boundaries of India on this map have not been authenticated and may not be correct.

Hooghly turns south and flows into the open sea. It can be reached by bus or train from Calcutta. Launches run from here to Sagar Island.

The *Sagarika Tourist Lodge (☎ 55246, fax 55246)* can be booked through the West Bengal Tourist Development Corporation (WBTDC) or the West Bengal Tourist Office in Calcutta. Double rooms range from Rs 260 to Rs 600, basement rooms are Rs 100, and a bed in a dorm costs Rs 30. There is also a restaurant, cafeteria and bar here.

SAGAR ISLAND (Sagardwip)
At the mouth of the Hooghly, this island is considered to be the point where the Ganges joins the sea, and a great three-day bathing festival takes place here in mid-January. Held on the occasion of Maker Sankrati (mid-January), the festival is called the Gangasagar Mela and is the largest fair in West Bengal. Hundreds of thousands of Hindu pilgrims descend on the area to visit the Kapil Muni Temple and bathe in the confluence of the Ganges and the Bay of Bengal.

Sagardwip is accessible by bus and ferry from Diamond Harbour. For further information contact the West Bengal Tourist Office (☎ 248 5917/5168), 3/2 BBD Bagh (East).

There are a number of ashrams in the area where it is possible to stay and a Youth Hostel which can be booked through West Bengal Tourist Office (Youth Services).

A lighthouse marks the south-western tip of the island but navigation is still difficult for a further 65km south.

DIGHA
☎ 03220
Close to the border with Orissa, 185km south-west of Calcutta on the Bay of Bengal, Digha is another self-styled 'Brighton of the East'. The 7km beach is very wide but if a beach holiday is what you want, carry on south to Puri or Gopalpur-on-Sea.

The Chandaneshwar Siva Temple is just across the border in Orissa, 8km from Digha.

Digha has a wide range of other accommodation, including a *youth hostel* and *WBTDC Tourist Lodge (☎ 66255, fax 66256)*. The lodge has doubles from Rs 250 (from Rs 500 with air-con) and dorm beds for Rs 75. Meals are reasonably priced and there is also a bar.

There are daily buses between Calcutta and Digha (Rs 60, five to six hours) departing Calcutta from 6.15 am.

BAKKALI
Also known as Fraserganj, this beach resort is not as busy as Digha, and a bit less polluted. It's 132km from Calcutta, on the east side of the Hooghly.

WBTDC Tourist Lodge has doubles for Rs 250, dorm beds for Rs 75 and there's a restaurant and bar. From here you can get boats to the small island of **Jambu Dwip** to the south-west.

SUNDERBANS WILDLIFE SANCTUARY
The innumerable mouths of the Ganges form the world's largest delta, and part of this vast mangrove swamp is a 2585 sq km wildlife reserve that extends into Bangladesh. The sanctuary is designated a World Heritage Site and, as part of Project Tiger, has one of the largest tiger populations of any of the Indian parks. Tourist agencies capitalise on this fact, but few visitors get even a glimpse of one of the 250 tigers that remain well-hidden in the sanctuary.

You wouldn't want to get too close to these dangerous animals. Partial to human flesh, they kill approximately 20 people each year, lying in wait beside the narrow channels that crisscross the estuarine forest. Since a tiger is less likely to attack you if it thinks you are watching, fishermen and honey collectors have taken to wearing masks cleverly painted with human faces on the back of their heads.

Winter and spring are the best time to visit the wildlife sanctuary. Other wildlife in the sanctuary includes spotted deer, wild pigs and monkeys. The journey here, by local boat and cycle-rickshaw through small traditional Bengali villages, can be fun. The whole area is teeming with birdlife and is wonderfully peaceful after frenetic Calcutta.

There's a **heron sanctuary** (best between July and September) near Sajnekhali.

At the **Sajnekhali visitors' centre** there's a crocodile enclosure, shark pond, turtle hatchery and an interesting Mangrove Interpretation Centre. From here **boats** are available for excursions through the mangroves. Trips cost around Rs 500 per person for the whole day, or Rs 350 for four hours, and you need a guide and boat permits. There are watchtowers at several points around the park.

South of the Sunderbans are **Lothian** and **Halliday** islands, reached from Namkhana (three hours by bus from Calcutta).

Permission is required to visit the Sunderbans; see Permits at the start of this chapter. There's also a small entry fee to visit the reserve, payable at Sajnekhali.

Organised Tours

From October to March, the WBTDC organises weekly boat tours, including food and accommodation (on board or in the Tourist Lodge). A two or three day trip costs from Rs 800 for basic accommodation, to Rs 2350 for a two berth cabin. If you're expecting 'adventure at every corner', as one brochure suggests, forget it. One reader said 'More like a totally uneventful three-day picnic on the water'.

Places to Stay

Sajnekhali Tourist Lodge (☎ *03463-52699, fax 52398)* at Sajnekhali has doubles from Rs 250, air-con doubles from Rs 525 and dorm beds for Rs 180. Rates include one major meal and breakfast. The signs say 'Movement prohibited after evening' and they mean it. In 1991 a couple of tigers jumped over the fence and spent the night sniffing around the doors of the rooms where tourists were sleeping!

Getting There & Away

Travelling independently is more complicated than the WBTDC boat tour (see Organised Tours earlier) but could be more fun. From Calcutta (Babu Ghat) it's quickest to get a bus to Basunti/Sonakhali (three hours). Alternatively take a train to Canning (Rs 15, 1¼ hours), cross the river to Dok Kart (Rs 2) by *bodbooti* (small ferry) and then head to Sonakhali by shared autorickshaw (Rs 8) or bus (Rs 5, 50 minutes).

Continuing from Basunti/Sonakhali the next step is a boat to Gosava (Rs 8, 1¼ hours). From there get a cycle-rickshaw (no seats, just a wooden platform!) for the 40 minute ride to Pakhirala (Rs 18) then a boat across the river to Sajnekhali.

There's also a direct boat (Rs 8) leaving Gosava at 1 pm to reach Sajnekhali at 3.30 pm. It departs from Sajnekhali at 8.30 am for Gosava.

A private boat to Sajnekhali costs Rs 800 or Rs 400 from Canning or Sonakhali/Basunti. If you go via Canning you may be able to get a ride directly to Sajnekhali with one of the tour boats.

North of Calcutta

SERAMPORE & BARRACKPORE

On the Hooghly River, 25km from Calcutta, Serampore was a Danish centre until Denmark's holdings in India were transferred to the East India Company in 1845. The old **Danish church** and **cemetery** still stand. The missionaries Ward, Marshman and Carey operated from here in the early 19th century.

Across the river is Barrackpore. A few dilapidated buildings are all that are left of the East India Company's cantonment here. There are also some gardens and a memorial to Gandhi by the river.

Mahesh, 3km from Serampore, has a large and very old Jagannath temple. In July each year the **Mahesh Rath Yatra (Car Festival)** takes place here. It is second in size only to the great Car Festival of Jagannath at Puri, Orissa.

CHANDARNAGAR

Also known as Chandernagore, this was one of the French enclaves in India that were handed over at the same time as Pondicherry in 1951. On the banks of the Hooghly, 39km north of Calcutta, it has several crumbling buildings dating from the French era. The first French settlers arrived here in 1673 and the place later became an important trading post, although it was taken by the British during conflicts with the French.

HOOGHLY & SATGAON

The historic town of Hooghly is 41km north of Calcutta and very close to two other interesting sites – Chinsura and Bandel (see the following section). Hooghly was an important trading port long before Calcutta rose to prominence. In 1537 the Portuguese set up a factory here; before that time Satgaon, 10km further north, had been the main port of Bengal but was abandoned because the river silted up. There are still a few traces of Satgaon's former grandeur, including a ruined mosque.

After a lengthy siege, the Portuguese were expelled from Hooghly in 1632 by Shah Jahan, but were allowed to return a year later. The British East India Company also established a factory here in 1651. The imambara, built in 1836, with its gateway flanked by lofty minarets, is the main sight. Across the road is an older imambara, dating from 1776-67.

CHINSURA

Only 1km or so south of Hooghly, Chinsura was exchanged by the Dutch for the British-held Indonesian island of Sumatra in 1825. There is a fort and the Dutch cemetery, with many old tombs, 1km to the west.

BANDEL

A couple of kilometres north of Hooghly, and 43km from Calcutta, Bandel is the site of a Portuguese church and monastery built here in 1599. Destroyed by Shah Jahan in 1640, they were later rebuilt.

To get there, take the train to Naihati and then the hourly shuttle across the river.

BANSBERIA

Four kilometres north of Bandel, Bansberia has the Vasudev Temple, with interesting terracotta wall carvings, and the Hanseswari Temple.

VISHNUPUR

☎ 03244

Also spelt Bishnupur, this interesting town of terracotta temples is a famous cultural centre. It flourished as the capital of the Malla kings from the 16th to the early 19th centuries. The Mallas were great patrons of the arts.

Since there is no stone found in the area, the traditional building material for important buildings was brick. The facades of the dozen or so temples here are covered with ornate terracotta tiles depicting lively scenes from the Hindu epics. The main temples to see are the highly decorated Jor Bangla, the large Madan Mohan, the pyramidal Ras Mancha and the Shyam Rai, built in 1643.

Vishnupur is in Bankura district, famous for its pottery (particularly the stylised Bankura horse) and silk. In the markets here you can also find metalwork, tussar silk and Baluchari saris, *ganjifa* (circular playing cards for a game long forgotten) and conch shell jewellery.

In August, the Jhapan Festival draws snake charmers to honour the goddess Manasa who is the central figure to the cult of snake worship.

Places to Stay

Accommodation is limited. The *Tourist Lodge* (☎ 52013), about 3km from the train station, is good. Dorm beds go for Rs 79 and doubles from Rs 289, Rs 460 with aircon. *Vishnupur Lodge* (☎ 53173) and other cheap hotels are found around the market.

Getting There & Away

There are buses from Calcutta (Rs 37, 4½ hours). The *Purulia Express*, from Howrah, is the fastest train, taking 3½ hours.

JAIRAMBATI & KAMARPUKUR

Ramakrishna was born in Kamarpukur, 143km north-west of Calcutta, and there is a Ramakrishna Mission ashram here. Ramakrishna was a 19th century Hindu saint who did much to rejuvenate Hinduism when it was going through a period of decline during British rule. Jairambati, 5km away, is another important point for Ramakrishna devotees.

SHANTINIKETAN

The town of Shantiniketan is 3km from Bolpur and takes its name from two Bengali words: *shanti*, meaning peaceful and *niketan*, meaning abode.

The brilliant and prolific poet, writer, artist and nationalist Rabindranath Tagore (1861-1941) founded a school here in 1901. It later developed into the Visvabharati University with an emphasis on humanity's relationship with nature – many classes are conducted in the open air. Tagore went on to win the Nobel Prize for literature in 1913 and is credited with introducing India's historical and cultural greatness to the modern world. In 1915 Tagore was awarded a knighthood by the British, but he surrendered it in 1919 as a protest against the Amritsar massacre.

There are colleges of science, teacher training, Sanskrit, Sino-Indian studies, philosophy, arts and crafts, and music and dance. The university also runs community-based programs for the advancement of agriculture, cottage industries and historic reconstruction. **Sriniketan**, 4km away, was started to revitalise traditional crafts: *kantha* embroidery, weaving, batik and pottery.

It is worth noting that it is necessary to obtain permission from the public relations officer for taking photographs within the university campus.

Shantiniketan is a very peaceful place and certainly worthy of a visit if you have a specific interest in art, culture, the humanities and the life and works of Tagore. Of particular interest are the famous **Shantiniketan Murals** – Seagull Books publishes a magnificently illustrated book, *The Shantiniketan Murals* by Jayanta Chakrabarti, R Siva Kumar & Arun K Nag.

There's a **museum** and **art gallery** within the Uttarayan complex where Tagore lived.

They are open from 10.30 am to 1 pm and 2 to 4.30 pm Thursday to Monday (mornings only on Tuesday). The university is open to visitors in the afternoons (mornings only on Tuesday and during vacations). It is closed on Wednesday, the day the university was founded.

There are several **festivals** held at Shantiniketan each year. The Varsha-Mangal (Festival of Rains), Foundation Day Ceremony and Paush Mela (Annual Fair) held 22-25 December, Magh Mela (Anniversary of Shantiniketan and Fair) held in February and Vasantotsava (Spring Festival).

Places to Stay

The *International Guest House*, run by the university, has cheap accommodation and meals. If you're planning a long stay there are also *university guesthouses*.

The *retiring rooms* at Bolpur train station are good value.

Shantiniketan Tourist Lodge (☎ 526999), run by WBTDC, has good singles/doubles for Rs 250/300 or air-con doubles for Rs 600 to Rs 800. Dorm beds are Rs 75.

Chhuti Holiday Resort (☎ 52692, 241 Charupalli) is the top place in town. Air-cooled singles/doubles are Rs 650/800, Rs 900/1100 with air-con; all rooms have bathrooms.

Getting There & Away

The 3015 *Shantiniketan Express* leaves Howrah daily at 9.55 am, reaching Bolpur at 12.25 pm. It departs from Bolpur at 1 pm for Howrah. For Darjeeling, there is the nightly *Darjeeling Mail* at 10.30 pm. Many other trains stop in Shantiniketan.

NABADWIP & MAYAPUR

Also known as Nadia, Nabadwip is an ancient centre of the Sanskrit culture, 114km north of Calcutta. The last Hindu king of Bengal, Lakshman Sen, moved his capital here from Gaur. There are many temples at this important pilgrimage centre.

Across the river from Nabadwip, Mayapur is a centre for the ISKCON (Hare Krishna) movement. There's a large, white temple and gardens, and cheap accommodation is available in the *ISKCON Guest House*. A bus tour is run from Calcutta on Sunday (daily during the winter). Details are available from ISKCON (☎ 033-247 6075) at 3C Albert Rd, Calcutta.

PALASHI

In 1757 Clive defeated Siraj-ud-daula and his French supporters at Plassey (now Palashi), a turning point in British influence in India. Palashi is 172km north of Calcutta. There's nothing to see here apart from the 15m-high memorial a few kilometres west.

BERHAMPORE

Eleven kilometres south of Murshidabad is this large town, a notable centre for silk production. The **Government Silk Research Centre** is interesting to visit. In the old bazaar area of Khagra, in the northern part of Berhampore, the dilapidated mansions of European traders are quietly subsiding into the river.

Places to Stay & Eat

The *WBTDC Tourist Lodge* is good value and the best place to eat. Doubles are Rs 275, Rs 500 with air-con. Beds in the four-bed dorm are Rs 75. It's about 15 minutes from Berhampore Court train station by cycle-rickshaw and close to the bus stand.

The *retiring rooms* at the train station have a four-bed dorm.

Getting There & Away

On this branch line between Sealdah and Lalgola, there are several trains a day from Calcutta (Rs 29, four to six hours, 186km). There's a bus from Calcutta (five hours) leaving at 6.30 am, and other buses to Malda (3½ hours), Bolpur (four hours) and Siliguri (seven hours).

Across the river is Khagraghat Road station which is on the Howrah-Azimganj line.

MURSHIDABAD

☎ 03482 • pop 34,100
When Siraj-ud-daula was nawab of Bengal, this was his capital, and it was here that he

was assassinated after the defeat at Plassey (Palashi). Murshidabad was also the major trading town between inland India and the port of Calcutta, 221km south. Today it's an insignificant, but peaceful town on the banks of the Bhagirathi River; a chance to see typical rural Bengali life.

Cycle-rickshaw-wallahs offer you guided tours of all the sites for around Rs 60 for a half day. This is a good idea as everything's fairly spread out.

Hazarduari

This classical-style Palace of a Thousand Doors was built for the nawabs in 1837. In the renovated throne room a vast chandelier, a gift from Queen Victoria, is suspended above the nawab's silver throne. In the armoury downstairs is a cannon used at Plassey. At present, only 25% of the collection is displayed; the remainder is stored or undergoing restoration. The palace is open 10 am to 4.30 pm Saturday to Thursday. Entry is Rs 5; cameras are strictly prohibited.

The **library** houses 10,000 books, 3000 manuscripts and a collection of magnificently illuminated Qurans. Though closed to the public, permission to view or use the collection is available from the Assistant Superintending Archaeologist (☎ 70334), Archaeological Survey of India, Hazarduari Palace Museum, Murshidabad.

Other Attractions

Across the grass from the palace is the deteriorating **Great Imambara**. Murshid Quli Khan, who moved the capital here in 1705, is buried beside the impressive ruins of the **Katra Mosque**. Siraj-ud-daula was assassinated at the **Nimak Haram Deohri** (Traitor's Gate). The Jain **Parswanath Temple** is at Kathgola, and south of the train station there's the **Moti Jhil**, or Pearl Lake, a fine place to view the sunset. It's worth taking a boat across the river to visit Siraj's **tomb** at Khusbagh, the Garden of Happiness.

Places to Stay

Near the palace, *Hotel Manjusha* (☎ 70321) is the pick of the bunch. On the banks of the river, with great views and lovely gardens, this spotless, quiet and atmospheric place has friendly staff, a pet dog and a resident mongoose. Bright singles/doubles with mosquito nets cost Rs 125/200. There is also an al fresco restaurant and gazebo where you can sit and sip tea while the river flows by.

Netaji Abas – Murshidabad Municipal Guest House (☎ *70232, Netaji Rd*) is OK with singles/doubles for Rs 125 and Rs 200/Rs 175 and Rs 300 with mosquito nets; there's a reasonable restaurant and garden.

Ekenta Appan nearby, is dark and pokey with a small garden, 24 hour checkout and meals. Singles/doubles are Rs 75/125.

If you're after a bargain, the *retiring rooms* at the train station are Rs 50 for a double with bath.

Getting There & Away
Murshidabad is also on the Sealdah-Lalgola line and there are several daily trains from Calcutta (Rs 29, four to six hours, 197km). For long-distance buses you must go to Berhampore (11km). Auto-rickshaws, taxis, private hire cars and buses regularly ply this route and a private taxi will cost approximately Rs 500 for the day; a bus costs Rs 5 each way.

West Bengal Hills

MALDA & ENGLISH BAZAAR
☎ 03512
On the route to Darjeeling, 349km north of Calcutta, Malda is the base for visiting the ruined cities of Gaur and Pandua (see the following entries), although it's probably more famous now for its large Fajli mangoes. Gaur is delightful – incredibly peaceful and beautiful. Malda's not particularly interesting, but it has a small **museum**.

English Bazaar, also transliterated as Ingraj Bazar, is now a suburb of Malda. An English factory was established here in 1771. **Old Malda** is nearby, at the junction of the Kalindi and Mahananda rivers. It was once an important port for the former Muslim capital of Pandua.

Places to Stay & Eat
There are *retiring rooms* and a good refreshment room at the train station.

Malda Tourist Lodge (☎ *66123*) is reasonable with an attractive garden. A double with share/private bath is Rs 150/300, Rs 450 with air-con. The tourist office is here. A rickshaw from the train station is Rs 7.

Hotel Samrat, opposite, and *Hotel Natraj*, on the road to the bus stand, are similarly priced.

Hotel Purbanchal, with rooms from Rs 150/180 to Rs 500/700 with air-con, is the top place in town. It's 20 minutes from the station by rickshaw.

Getting There & Away
Malda is on the main railway line to Calcutta (seven hours, 344km) and New Jalpaiguri (five hours, 233km). There are buses to Siliguri (six hours) for Darjeeling, Berhampore (three hours) Murshidabad and Calcutta (eight hours).

GAUR
Twelve kilometres south of Malda and right on the border with Bangladesh, Gaur was first the capital of the Buddhist Pala dynasty, then it became the seat of the Hindu Sena dynasty, and finally the capital of the Muslim nawabs. The ruins of the extensive fortifications and several large mosques are all that remain. (There are also some ruins on the other side of the ill-defined border.) Most impressive are the **Bara Sona Mosque** and the nearby brick **Dakhil Darwajah** built in 1425. **Qadam Rasul Mosque** enshrines a footprint of the Mohammed but it looks as if he was wearing thongs when he made it! Fath Khan's tomb is nearby and a sign informs you that he 'vomited blood and died on this spot'. There are still some colourful enamelled tiles on the **Gumti Gate** and **Lattan Mosque** but few left on the **Firoz Minar**, which you can climb for a good view.

Getting There & Away
The monuments are very spread out and not all easy to find. Some determined cycle-rickshaw-wallahs offer half-day trips from

Malda for anything up to Rs 180. Taxis cost about Rs 500 and include Pandua.

PANDUA

Gaur once alternated with Pandua as the seat of power. The main place of interest is the vast **Adina Mosque**, built by Sikander Shah in the 14th century. Built over a Hindu temple, traces of which are still evident, it was one of the largest mosques in India but is now in ruins. Nearby is the **Eklakhi mausoleum**, so called because it cost Rs 1 lakh (Rs 100,000) to build. There are also several smaller mosques. The dusty deer park, 2.5km across the highway in the 'forest', is not worth going to.

Getting There & Away

Pandua is on main highway (National Highway 34), 18km north of Malda, and there are many buses that can drop you here. The main sites are at Adina, 2km north of the village of Pandua, and right by the highway.

SILIGURI & NEW JALPAIGURI

☎ 0353 • pop 257,500

Siliguri lies 8km north of the main railway junction of New Jalpaiguri (known throughout the district as NJP), though there's effectively no break between the two places. This crowded sprawl is the departure point and major trade centre for Darjeeling, Kalimpong, Sikkim, the North-Eastern Region and eastern Nepal. As a consequence, it is packed with trucks, buses and 40,000 bicycle-rickshaws!

It may not be the most pleasant place to stay, but it does have a wonderful climate in winter, is central to the main attractions in the region and is only one hour from Paniktanki – opposite the Nepal border town of Kakarbhitta.

Orientation & Information

The towns of Siliguri and New Jalpaiguri essentially have just one north-south main road – Tenzing Norgay Rd (also known as Hillcart Rd). It's about 4km from NJP train station to Siliguri Town train station, and a further 4km from there to Siliguri Junction

train station, behind the Tenzing Norgay central bus terminal. You can catch the toy train (if it's running) from any of these train stations. Bagdogra, 12km west of Siliguri, is the airport serving this northern region.

The West Bengal tourist office (☎ 431974) is up a flight of stairs on Tenzing Norgay Rd, on the south side of the river. Here, it's possible to book accommodation in the Jaldhapara Wildlife Sanctuary (see the following entry). There are also tourist counters at the airport and train stations.

The State Bank of India exchanges American Express travellers cheques in US dollars and pounds sterling only.

Permits Permits for Sikkim are available from Sikkim Tourism (☎ 432646) at the Sikkim Nationalised Transport (SNT) office, diagonally opposite the bus terminal. Sikkim Tourism is open Monday to Saturday, 10 am to 4 pm.

Places to Stay

There are dozens of hotels in town, many opposite the Tenzing Norgay central bus terminal.

In a quiet spot next door to SNT is the *Siliguri Lodge*. There's a pleasant garden fronting the lodge, and rooms are very clean and airy. Doubles range from Rs 155 (ground floor) to Rs 250 (upstairs). Beds in the four-bed dorm are Rs 45.

About 750m to the north on Tenzing Norgay Rd is *WBTDC Mainak Tourist Lodge* (☎ 430986). Rooms are Rs 600/700, or Rs 850/1250 with air-con and there are foreign exchange facilities and a restaurant.

A good budget choice is the friendly, Tibetan-run *Hotel Chancellor* (☎ 432360, corner of Sevoke and Tenzing Norgay Rds). Small but comfortable singles are Rs 190, and doubles are Rs 200 or Rs 215 with balcony. Three/four-bed rooms are Rs 255/350. Fresh towels and mosquito zappers are provided. The front rooms are a little noisy. There's a pleasant rooftop patio.

The *Hotel Vinayak* (☎ 431130, LM Moulik Complex, Tenzing Norgay Rd) is a good mid-range choice. Rooms are spotless

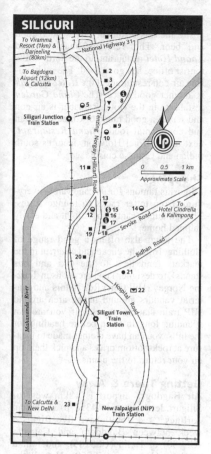

SILIGURI

PLACES TO STAY
1   Hotel Sinclairs
2   WBTDC Mainak Tourist Lodge; Indian Airlines
3   Ganga Hotel
6   Hotel Mount View
9   Siliguri Lodge
11   Hotel Rajdarbar
16   Hotel Blue Star
18   Hotel Chancellor
19   Hotel Vinayak; Jet Airways
20   Ranjit Hotel & Lodge
23   Hotel Holydon; Hotel Baydanath;
     Miami Restaurant

PLACES TO EAT
7   Shere Punjab Hotel Restaurant
13   Anand Hotel Restaurant

OTHER
4   Mallaguri Garage
5   Tenzing Norgay Central Bus Terminal;
     Share Jeeps
8   Assam Tourist Office
10   Sikkim Nationalised Transport
     (SNT) Terminal; Sikkim Tourism
12   Taxi Stand
14   Share Jeep Stand
15   State Bank of India
17   West Bengal Tourist Office
21   Railway Booking Office
22   Main Post Office

and well appointed with bathrooms. Singles/doubles range from Rs 200/300 up to Rs 600/950 (air-con). There's good room service and a restaurant.

Friendly *Hotel Rajdarbar* (☎ *534316, Tenzing Norgay Rd*) has singles/doubles with bathrooms, phone and TV starting at Rs 250/300, or Rs 450/550 with air-con.

The *Hotel Blue Star* (☎ *431550),* north of the West Bengal tourist office on Tenzing Norgay Rd, takes credit cards. Singles/doubles start at Rs 250/350.

Farther north on the same side of the road, but set back, is the *Ganga Hotel*. Though a bit grubby, it's cheap, the bedding is clean, mozzie nets are provided and the management's really friendly. Singles/doubles cost Rs 80/150. The rooms at the front of the hotel are brighter but noisier than those at the back.

Opposite the Tenzing Norgay bus terminal, the *Hotel Mount View* (☎ *425919)* is friendly, clean and also set back from the road. Singles range from Rs 175 to Rs 250, and doubles from Rs 250 to Rs 350. There's a decent restaurant.

Another good place is the *Hotel Air View* (☎ *431542, Hill Cart Rd).* Large doubles with bath and mozzie nets cost Rs 300; cheaper rooms are Rs 180. There's also an excellent, cheap restaurant.

The three-star *Hotel Sinclairs* (☎ *22674, fax 432743, Tenzing Norgay Rd)* is 2km north of Tenzing Norgay Central bus terminal. Doubles are Rs 725 and Rs 880, or Rs 1035 and Rs 1330 with air-con. There's a foreign-exchange facility, a swimming pool, bar and restaurant.

A couple of hotels outside Siliguri stand out. *Hotel Cindrella* (☎ *547136/544130, fax 531173, 3rd Mile, Sevoke Rd, email cin drella@gokulmail.com)* is very quiet and has a swimming pool, gym, health club and billiards room. It also offers Internet facilities, foreign exchange and an excellent travel desk and tour agency. Spacious singles/doubles are Rs 900/1000, or Rs 1200/1400 with air-con. The hotel also has a Web site (www.cindrellahotels.com).

Viramma Resort (☎ *26222, fax 432497)* is about 1km beyond the National Highway overpass on the road to Darjeeling. It offers two swimming pools, a health club, jogging track, extensive lawns and gardens, a small boating lake, business centre, foreign exchange, a restaurant and bar. Standard singles/doubles (with bed tea) are Rs 450/550, or Rs 750/875 with air-con. Deluxe doubles are Rs 980.

The closest place to the airport is the *Hotel Marina* (☎ *450371)*, which has comfortable rooms with bath for Rs 250/300. It's quiet, has a restaurant, bar and provides free bed tea.

There are a couple of places within walking distance of NJP train station. The *Hotel Holydon* (☎ *23558)* has singles with shared bath for Rs 125 and doubles with bathroom (hot water) for Rs 225 and Rs 300. The more expensive rooms at the front are bright and airy. There's a small restaurant. Next door is the *Hotel Baydanath* with very good singles/doubles with bathroom and running hot and cold water for Rs 225/300.

Places to Eat
The *Oriental Room* at Hotel Sinclairs, serves good Chinese and Mughlai cuisine, but service is excruciatingly slow. The best vegan restaurant in Siliguri, the *Amrapali*, is a fair way out of town at Hotel Cindrella.

The budget priced *Shere Punjab Hotel*, opposite the bus terminal, serves good food and beer. The very reasonably priced *Anand Hotel* restaurant, to the north of the tourist office, has good food. The multicuisine air-con restaurant at the *Hotel Vinayak* is another good place. The *China Garden* restaurant in the Hotel Rajdabar is air-con and serves a good range of Chinese, Indian and continental food. *Miami Restaurant*, next to the Hotel Holydon, features south Indian and Chinese cuisine.

Shopping
Siliguri is famous for its caneware – everything from letter racks to lounge suites. Though bulky, caneware is light and easily shipped home.

The town also offers a good range of clothing, from the cheap and cheerful in the markets (and next to the taxi and bus stands), to designer label creations in Tenzing Norgay (Hill Cart) Rd. Tailors and material vendors abound in the area around NJP train station, so even if you are not spending long in town before heading for the hills, you can have clothes made to measure at rock-bottom prices and pick them up on your return to the plains.

Getting There & Away
Air Bagdogra airport is 12km west of Siliguri. Jet Airways (☎ 435876) and Indian Airlines (☎ 431509) have five flights a week between Bagdogra and Calcutta (US$80) or Delhi (US$185), and four a week to Guwahati (US$50). Not all the flights to Delhi are direct, some backtrack to Guwahati first. Skyline NEPC also has three flights a week to Calcutta.

Bus Most North Bengal State Transport Corporation (NBSTC) buses leave from the Tenzing Norgay central bus terminal. Private buses with services to hill regions (Darjeeling, Gangtok etc) also have counters at the terminal. Note that if you are travelling to Jorethang in West Sikkim, you will require a trekking permit. See the Permits section in the Sikkim chapter for details.

NBSTC buses for Darjeeling (Rs 28, three hours), depart between 6.30 and 11.30 am. There's a bus at 7 am for Kalimpong (Rs 45, three hours), and services at 7.30 am and 2.30 pm for Mirik (Rs 25, 2½ hours).

The 'Rocket' services to Calcutta leave at 6, 7 and 8 pm (Rs 160, 12 hours). Other destinations include Malda (Rs 49, six hours), Berhampore (Rs 95, eight hours) and Patna (Rs 145, 12 hours). The bus to Patna leaves from Mallaguri Garage, a 10 minute walk north up Tenzing Norgay Rd.

For Guwahati, there's a NBSTC Rocket service from Tenzing Norgay terminal at 5 pm (Rs 165, 12 hours), and an ordinary service from Mallaguri Garage at 7.30 am (Rs 140).

Sikkim Nationalised Transport (SNT) buses to Gangtok (Rs 47, five hours) leave the SNT terminal every hour between 7 am and 4 pm. There's also a deluxe bus (Rs 80) at 7 am and 1 pm.

To/From Nepal For Nepal, local buses leave from in front of the Tenzing Norgay central bus terminal for Paniktanki (Rs 7, one hour) which is opposite the Nepal border town of Kakarbhitta. See the Darjeeling Getting There & Away section for more details.

Train The *Darjeeling Mail* leaves Sealdah (Calcutta) at 7 pm (12 hours, 570km). Tickets are Rs 120/598 in 2nd/1st class. The return trip leaves NJP train station at 6.45 pm, reaching Sealdah at 8.30 am.

The *North East Express* is the fastest train to Delhi (33 hours, 1628km). It departs at 5.25 pm, travelling via Patna (16 hours, 636km). In the other direction this train continues to Guwahati (10 hours, 423km).

There's a train booking office on Bidhan Rd, just off Tenzing Norgay Rd. It's open Monday to Saturday, 8 am to 8 pm; Sunday and holidays, 8 am to 2 pm.

Bangladesh To reach Bangladesh you can take a train from NJP to Haldibari, the Indian border checkpoint (Rs 15, two hours). From here it's a 7km walk along a disused railway line to the Bangladesh border point at Chiliharti, where there's a train station.

Toy Train If the toy train from Siliguri/New Jalpaiguri to Darjeeling is running (which it hasn't been for a couple of years due to a major landslide), tickets can be purchased from NJP, Siliguri Town or Siliguri Junction train stations. As there are no advance reservations, it may be easier during the busy high season (May to mid-July) to pick up tickets at NJP, where the train originates. When in operation, a daily service leaves at 9 am (also at 7.15 am during high season). The journey takes an interminable nine hours to cover the 80km up to the hill station, or four hours to Kurseong, 30km short of Darjeeling. For more details see the Darjeeling Getting There & Away section.

Taxi & Jeep The fastest and most comfortable way of getting around the hills is by share jeep. There are a number of taxi stands, including one on Sevoke Rd and one outside Tenzing Norgay terminal, where you can get share jeeps to destinations in the West Bengal Hills and Sikkim including: Darjeeling (Rs 47, 2½ hours), Kalimpong (Rs 50, 2½ hours), Kurseong (Rs 26, two hours), Mirik (Rs 35, 2½ hours) and Gangtok (Rs 80, 4½ hours).

Posted rates for a private taxi are: Darjeeling, Rs 750; Kalimpong, Rs 750; Mirik, Rs 600; and Gawahati, Rs 4000.

Getting Around

From Tenzing Norgay central bus terminal to NJP train station a taxi/auto-rickshaw will cost about Rs 150/75. Cycle-rickshaw cost about Rs 20 for the 40 minute trip from NJP to Siliguri Junction, or Rs 20 to Tenzing Norgay bus terminal. There are infrequent bus services along this route (Rs 4).

If you are flying out of Bagdogra airport, you may be able to get a lift from Siliguri to the airport with airline staff. Check at the Jet Airways or Indian Airlines offices in Siliguri. A taxi between the airport and Siliguri costs Rs 150. A less expensive option is to take a taxi to Bagdogra bazaar (Rs 50, 3km), and get a local bus from there into Siliguri (Rs 4, 9km).

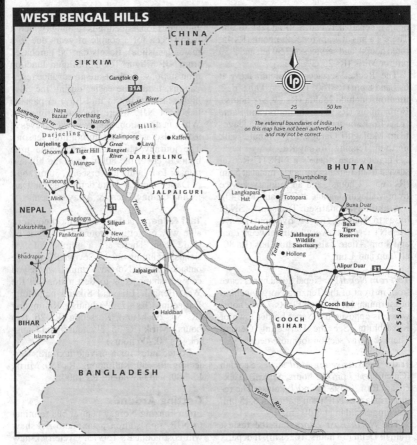

WEST BENGAL HILLS

JALDHAPARA WILDLIFE SANCTUARY

Although most visitors are keen to head for the hills after the chaotic strip of mayhem that is Siliguri, it's worth making the 135km trip east to this rarely visited sanctuary. It protects 100 sq km of lush forests and grasslands, is cut by the wide Torsa River and is also a refuge for the Indian one-horned rhinoceros *(Rhinoceros unicornis)*, whose numbers have come under serious threat from poachers.

The best time to visit is from October to May, particularly in March/April when wild animals are attracted by the growth of new grasses. Apart from about 35 rhinos, other animals found in the park environs are tigers (rarely seen), wild elephants, and various deer. You can take elephant safaris from Hollong, inside the park. Cost is Rs 70 for Indians, Rs 80 for foreigners and Rs 65 for students. The park entry fee is Rs 10 per person, and Rs 10 per light vehicle. Still camera charges are Rs 5 per day.

Places to Stay & Eat

Within the park itself is the *Hollong Forest Lodge* with doubles for Indians/foreigners at Rs 425/850, plus Rs 120/125 per person (compulsory) for breakfast, dinner and bed tea. Outside the park precincts at Madarihat is the *Jaldhapara Tourist Lodge*. Doubles are Rs 850 and dorm beds Rs 190, including all meals. Both of these places must be booked in advance through the Sub-Regional Tourist Office (☎ 0353-431974) in Siliguri, or the Government of West Bengal Tourist Office (☎ 033-248 8271), 3/2 BBD Bagh East, Calcutta, 700001. West Bengal Tourism has packages including accommodation, all meals, and an hour elephant safari.

Getting There & Away

From Tenzing Norgay central bus terminal in Siliguri, buses ply the route to Madarihat, 9km from Jaldhapara (Rs 27, three hours). From here, a taxi to Hollong, inside the park, is Rs 150. To hire a taxi from Siliguri to Jaldhapara will cost about Rs 950. In theory, a train leaves Siliguri at 11.30 am, arriving Madarihat at 4 pm, but the service is erratic.

MIRIK
☎ 0354

Being promoted as a 'new' hill station, Mirik (at an altitude of 1767m) is about 50km from both Siliguri and Darjeeling. The artificial lake is the main attraction here; there's a 3.5km path which meanders around it. The main tourist area lies to the south of the lake, in the area known as Krishnanagar.

While this is certainly a pretty spot surrounded by tea estates, orange orchards and cardamom plantations (the views from the top of the hill are stunning), attempts to 'develop' the area for tourism are already threatening to spoil the tranquil ambience. Swimming in the lake is strongly inadvisable as there is no sewage system in Mirikas and so it is highly polluted.

Mirik is the only place in India where the dog population appears to outweigh the human population. All the dogs are nocturnal and extremely vociferous! Take earplugs if you plan to sleep at night.

The post office is in the lane opposite the State Bank of India. The bank doesn't exchange travellers cheques; the only foreign exchange facilities are at Hotel Jagdeet (US dollars only).

Things to See & Do

Perched high above the town is the **Bokar Gompa**, a small and very brightly coloured gompa whose 70 monks are Mahayana Buddhists. It can be reached in about 10 minutes via a path leading up from the southern end of the main road. On the west side of the lake, about a 10 minute walk from the taxi stand and set among banana trees, are three small **Hindu temples** sacred to Hanuman, Kalamata (Durga as the Mother of Time) and Shiva.

Two/four seater **Boats** can be hired on the east side of the lake for Rs 32/42 per 30 minutes.

A good way to see the sights is by **pony ride**. Half-day (three hours) hire costs Rs 200 to Rs 300 (check the condition of the saddle padding before you leave!). A trip around the lake costs Rs 50, or Rs 60 to the Swiss Cottages at the top of the hill. Unfortunately, you will have trouble stopping the pony-wallahs (who insist on accompanying you) from whipping your poor beast to make it go faster. They have no understanding of people who treat animals gently and who do not want to go 'too much fast'.

Places to Stay & Eat

Down a small lane opposite the State Bank of India is the *Lodge Ashirvad* (☎ 43272). Downstairs doubles with shared bath are Rs 130; upstairs doubles with private bath start from Rs 200. There are separate kitchen facilities here for people who wish to self-cater.

Next door, *Lodge Panchashil* (☎ 43284) has tiny but light and airy singles/doubles with bathroom for Rs 120/150, or larger doubles/triples for Rs 150/200. The manager is friendly and helpful, and there's a pleasant rooftop terrace.

Hotel Mhelung (☎ 43300, *Samendu Complex*) is light and spotlessly clean. All rooms have polished timber floors, room

Mirik to Kurseong Day Trek

If you do not have time for a longer trek, or just want a taste of Himalayan village life in the West Bengal Hills, the trek from Mirik to Kurseong (seven to eight hours) may be your cup of tea.

Note, however, that a guide is essential owing to the myriad trails in the last part of the walk. Guides can be arranged for around Rs 500 at the DGHC Tourist Lodge in Mirik. Guides can also be arranged through the DGHC office or a trekking agency in Darjeeling.

The trail starts at the Genesis English School just past the Tourist Lodge. Heading out of town you will pass a number of schools. There are good views of Kanchenjunga 1km from Mirik. Continuing, you will pass through a number of small villages, stands of pine and bamboo, and orange groves, finally entering Murmah Tea Estate.

Walk through the tea estate, heading downhill, roughly following the ropeway (used to carry tea and supplies to and from the estate). A few villages later you will reach the river. Only ford the river if the water level is low, and only with an experienced guide. It is better to cross the bridge that is visible 1km upstream and then backtrack.

After crossing the river, head up the tributary for 500m, then up the steep hill on the right-hand side. Stop for a 'Darjeeling' chai and biscuits in the village of Khomara atop the hill. From the teahouse you have excellent views back across the valley you have just traversed.

There are a two main routes to Kurseong from here. The right-hand track is shorter but takes you through less villages. We took the left-hand trail. Again, you walk through a number of tea estates interspersed with villages and pockets of forest. From the Singell Tea Estate follow the jeep track, taking short cuts when you can, and you will emerge on the main Darjeeling-Kurseong road. Turn right for Kurseong (roughly 1km away) or left for Darjeeling. You may be lucky and catch a jeep or minibus to Kurseong or even back to Darjeeling.

Martin Bradshaw

---

heaters, phones and cable TV. Doubles are Rs 400/500.

The *Quality Restaurant & Sweet Parlour*, opposite, offers low-priced meals and a good selection of local sweets, packet chocolate, biscuits and drinks. The restaurant is fresh, bright and clean.

Hotel Jagdeet (☎ 43359), on the main road, has doubles with bathroom and geyser from Rs 550 to Rs 850; a family room is Rs 1000. All rooms are carpeted, and room service is available. There is a popular restaurant and bar next door. They take credit cards and will handle foreign exchange (US$) at a push.

Slightly further afield, but within easy walking distance of the lake, is the Darjeeling Gorkha Hill Council (DGHC) *Mirik Tourist Lodge* (☎ 42237). Doubles with heaters are Rs 300 and Rs 350; dorm beds are Rs 30.

Mirik (Swiss) Cottages (☎ 43270), run by DGHC, are perched on the top of the hill. The property affords stunning, panoramic views of the township and surrounding countryside including Khanchenjunga. Two-storey cottages contain a lounge/dining room and kitchen downstairs, and a large double bedroom, accommodating four people, upstairs. Rates are Rs 750 for two people, Rs 1000 with kitchen equipment.

Getting There & Away

Buses to Darjeeling leave at 11.30 am, 1.15, 1.45 and 2.15 pm (Rs 20, three hours). There are buses to Kurseong (Rs 28, three hours) and Siliguri (Rs 30, 2½ hours). Tickets can be purchased from the wooden

Helping Hands

St Alphonsus Social & Agricultural Centre (SASAC) just outside Kurseong, is a self-help organisation run by a Canadian Jesuit priest, Father Abraham. Over the years, the centre has helped to raise the local subsistence farmers' productivity through improved crop and livestock management. Father Abraham set up a model teaching farm, assisted in the building of new homes, and established a viable sales channel for excess farm produce.

One of his most recent successes is in the reduction of wood usage – an enormous problem in the hills. Using small, interest-free loans through a co-operative savings scheme, families have been able to purchase stoves and gas cylinders for cooking, thereby reducing deforestation. When their tiny loan is repaid, he then encourages the women to buy a pressure cooker, which increases the nutritional value of cooked foods and reduces gas usage by 25%. SASAC also has established a plantation and a reforestation scheme.

Anyone wishing to undertake volunteer work at SASAC, make a donation or purchase a tree for the plantation should contact Father Abraham (☎ 0354-42059), SASAC, Post Office Tung, District of Darjeeling, West Bengal.

For more information on voluntary work see the Facts for the Visitor chapter.

---

shack next to the Restaurant Liberty, near the lake shore.

There are no share taxis to Darjeeling. A private taxi to Darjeeling or Siliguri will cost Rs 600.

KURSEONG
☎ 03554 • pop 18,000
Kurseong is 51km north of Siliguri and 30km south of Darjeeling. The name is said to be derived from the Lepcha word, *kursonrip*, a reference to the small white orchid prolific in this area.

Because of its elevation (1458m), Kurseong enjoys a mild climate throughout the year – warmer than Darjeeling in the winter, cooler than the plains in summer. It's a good place to break the journey en route to or from Darjeeling. It has a wonderfully peaceful atmosphere and no real tourist infrastructure, so it offers the chance to really get to know the (predominantly Nepalese) mountain people.

Next to Hotel Delhi is Kumai Studio, a combined photographic studio, music shop, gift store and bookshop. Sujan Kumai, the English-speaking owner, is a mine of information about treks and places of interest in the district.

There are several good **walks**, including one to Eagle's Crag that affords fine views down over the Teesta and the southern plains, and a four-hour walk along the ridge and through unspoilt forest to Ghoom. The toy train to and from Darjeeling stops right in the heart of the town.

Places to Stay & Eat
The *Tourist Lodge* (☎ 44409) is undoubtedly the best place in town. It has large rooms with superb views, heaters and excellent bedding (rooms in the old block also have balconies). Doubles are Rs 525 in the new annexe, and Rs 550 in the original building. There's a restaurant and bar, and discounts are offered in the low season.

Hotel Amarjeet Restaurant & Bar (☎ 44669, Hill Cart Rd), west of the taxi stand, has doubles with hot water for Rs 300, and there's a bar here. The *Shyam Hotel* (☎ 44240, Dr Kumar Rd), has doubles and triples for Rs 300. *Luxury Hotel* (☎ 44321), east of the station, has singles/doubles for Rs 150/200 and a restaurant. *Maya Guest House* (☎ 44783), directly opposite the station, is one of the oldest guesthouses in Kurseong. Run by a Tibetan family, they serve excellent *momos*. Very basic singles/doubles are

Rs 80/150. *Kurseong Palace,* close to the jeep stand, has singles/doubles with hot water and TV for Rs 250/300.

Hotel Delhi Durbar & Restaurant (☎ *44084),* on the main road to Darjeeling, offers singles with shared bath for Rs 70 and doubles with hot water bathroom for Rs 150 or Rs 250. There are great views from the back rooms.

Getting There & Away

Regular buses run to Darjeeling (Rs 20, 1½ hours), Siliguri (Rs 26, 2½ hours), and Mirik (Rs 28, three hours). The toy train from Siliguri to Kurseong (when it is running) takes four hours.

DARJEELING

☎ 0354 • pop 83,000

Straddling a ridge at 2134m and surrounded by tea plantations, Darjeeling has been a popular hill station since the British established it as an R&R centre for their troops in the mid-1800s. People come here now, as they did then, to escape the heat, humidity and hassle of the north Indian plain. You get an indication of how popular Darjeeling is from the 100 or so hotels recognised by the tourist office and the scores of others which don't come up to its requirements. Here you will find yourself surrounded by mountain people from all over the eastern Himalaya who have come to work, to trade or – in the case of the Tibetans – as refugees.

Outside the monsoon (June to September), the views over the mountains to the snowy peaks of Kanchenjunga are magnificent.

Darjeeling is a fascinating place where you can see Buddhist monasteries, visit a tea plantation, go for a ride on the chairlift, spend days hunting for bargains in colourful markets and handicraft shops, or go trekking to high-altitude spots for closer views of Kanchenjunga.

Like many places in the Himalaya, getting there can be half the fun and Darjeeling is no exception. For generations, Darjeeling's famous toy train has been looping its way up the steep mountainsides from the plains. Unfortunately, its progress has been frequently halted, sometimes for years, by savage landslides which wipe out the tracks, or make the ground unstable even for this tiny train.

History

Until the beginning of the 18th century the whole of the area between the present borders of Sikkim and the plains of Bengal, including Darjeeling and Kalimpong, belonged to the rajas of Sikkim. In 1706 they lost Kalimpong to the Bhutanese, and control of the remainder was wrested from them by the Gurkhas who invaded Sikkim in 1780, following consolidation of the latter's rule in Nepal.

These annexations by the Gurkhas, however, brought them into conflict with the British East India Company. A series of battles were fought between the two parties, eventually leading to the defeat of the Gurkhas and the ceding of all the land they had taken from the Sikkimese to the East India Company. Part of this territory was restored to the rajas of Sikkim and the country's sovereignty guaranteed by the British in return for British control over any disputes which arose with neighbouring states.

One dispute in 1828 led to the dispatch of two British officers to this area, and it was during their fact-finding tour that they spent some time at Darjeeling (then called Dorje Ling – Place of the Thunderbolt – after the lama who founded the monastery which once stood on Observatory Hill). The officers were quick to appreciate Darjeeling's value as a site for a sanatorium and hill station, and as the key to a pass into Nepal and Tibet. The officers' observations were reported to the authorities in Calcutta and a pretext was eventually found to pressure the raja into granting the site to the British in return for an annual stipend of Rs 3000 (raised to Rs 6000 in 1846).

When the British arrived in Darjeeling it was almost completely forested and virtually uninhabited, though before the wars with Bhutan and Nepal it had been a sizeable village. Development was rapid and by 1840 a road had been built, along with many houses, a sanatorium and a hotel. By 1857, it had a population of some 10,000.

The population increase was due mainly to the recruitment of Nepalese labourers to work the tea plantations established in the early 1840s by the British. Even today, the vast majority of people speak Nepali as a first language and the name Darjeeling continues to be synonymous with tea.

The immigration of Nepali-speaking peoples, mainly Gurkhas, into the mountainous areas of West Bengal eventually led to political problems in the mid-1980s. Resentment had been growing among the Gurkhas over what they felt was discrimination against them by the government of West Bengal. Their language was not recognised by the Indian constitution and government jobs were thus only open to those who could speak Bengali.

The tensions finally came to a head in widespread riots throughout the hill country which continued for two years, and in which hundreds of people lost their lives and thousands were made homeless. Tourism ground to a halt and the Indian army was sent in to maintain some semblance of order. The riots were orchestrated by the Gurkha National Liberation Front (GNLF), led by Subash Ghising, which demanded a separate state to be known as Gorkhaland. The Communist Party of India (Marxist) was also responsible for a good deal of the violence since it was afraid of losing the support it had once enjoyed among the hill peoples.

A compromise was eventually hammered out in late 1988 whereby the Darjeeling Gorkha Hill Council (DGHC) was given a large measure of autonomy from the state government and fresh elections to the council were held. Darjeeling remains part of West Bengal, but now has greater control over its own affairs.

Following the prime minister's declaration in 1996 that the hill region of Uttar Pradesh would become a separate state (Uttarakhand), there were renewed demands for a separate Gorkhaland in the Darjeeling region. However, it now has a certain amount of autonomy, and the general consensus is that a separate homeland will eventually be negotiated; things have settled down.

Climate

For mountain views, the best time to visit has always been mid-September to mid-December. However, this appears to be changing, with warm sunny days and crystal clear skies continuing after Christmas (the nights can still be bitterly cold). The season resumes around mid-March and continues to mid-June but as the haze builds the views become unclear. During the monsoon (June/September), clouds obscure the mountains and the rain is often so heavy that whole sections of the road from the plains are washed away, though the town is rarely cut off for more than a few days at a time.

Orientation

Darjeeling sprawls over a west-facing ridge, spilling down the hillside in a complicated series of interconnecting roads and flights of steps. Hill Cart Rd is the main road through the lower part of the town, and the train station and the bus and taxi stand are all on it. It was officially renamed Tenzing Norgay Rd, even though Darjeeling already has another road by the same name, but this is rarely used. The most important route connecting Hill Cart Rd with Chowrasta (the town square) at the top of the ridge is via Laden La and Nehru Rds. (Nehru Rd is another renamed road, and is still generally referred to as The Mall.)

Running more or less parallel to, and above, Laden La, and connected to it by staircases at intervals, is Gandhi Rd, with several mid-range places to stay along its length. Laden La and Gandhi Rds converge at a major junction known as Clubside. Robertson Rd and Nehru Rd run off Clubside to the north. Nehru Rd (The Mall) meets Chowrasta at its northern end. Along its length are a number of mid-range hotels, photographic supply shops, curio shops and restaurants.

The youth hostel and a number of budget guesthouses are on or near Dr Zakir Hussain Rd, which extends along the top of the ridge about 600m above the bus stand. It can be reached via Rockville Rd, above Gandhi Rd and, once you know the area, also via a myriad pathways.

Tea Plantations, Darjeeling

Tea is, of course, Darjeeling's most famous export. From its gardens, employing over 40,000 people, it produces the bulk of West Bengal's crop, which is almost a quarter of India's total.

The tea from some of these estates is of very high quality. The world record for the highest price paid for tea is held by some fine leaves from the Castleton Estate in Darjeeling, for which a Japanese bidder paid US$220 per kg!

Although the area has just the right climatic conditions for producing fine tea bushes, the final result is dependent on a complex drying process. After picking, the fresh green leaves are placed 15cm to 25cm deep in a 'withering trough' where the moisture content is reduced from 70% or 80% down to 30% or 40% using high-velocity fans. When this is completed, the withered leaves are rolled and pressed to break the cell walls and express their juices onto the surface of the leaves. Normally, two rollings at different pressures are undertaken, and in between rolls the leaves are sifted to separate the coarse from the fine. The leaves, coated with their juices, are then allowed to ferment on racks in a high-humidity room, a process which develops their characteristic aroma and flavour. This fermentation must be controlled carefully since either over or under-fermentation will ruin the tea.

This process is stopped by passing the leaves through a dry air chamber at 115°C to 120°C on a conveyer belt to further reduce the moisture content to around 2% or 3%.

The last process is the sorting of the tea into grades. In order of value they are: Golden Flowery Orange Pekoe (unbroken leaves), Golden Broken Orange Pekoe, Orange Fannings and Dust (the latter three consisting of broken leaves).

Margaret's Hope plantation on the road to Kurseong produces the tea which eventually finds its way to Buckingham Palace. The plantation's name came about from a rather sad story. An English tea planter took his daughter to England to be educated, but she was not happy there. Her one wish was to return to Darjeeling and the mountains, but she died before she could ever return. In her memory, her father named his property Margaret's Hope.

While most plantations, including Margaret's Hope, welcome visitors, the most convenient one to visit is the Happy Valley Tea Estate 2km from the centre of Darjeeling. Here, tea is still produced by the 'orthodox' method as opposed to the 'curling, tearing and crushing' (CTC) method adopted on the plains. However, it's only worth going when plucking is in progress (April to November) because it's only then that the processing takes place. It's open daily from 8 am to noon and 1 to 4.30 pm, except on Monday and Sunday afternoon. An employee might latch on to you, whisk you around the factory and then demand some outrageous sum for his trouble; about Rs 15 per person is appropriate.

The bulk of the top-end hotels are clustered around Observatory Hill beyond Chowrasta. There are many mid-range hotels along Dr Zakir Hussain and AJC Bose Rds.

Information

Tourist Office The tourist office (☎ 54050) is below the Bellevue Hotel, Chowrasta. Staff are helpful and have reasonably up-to-date pamphlets and a map of Darjeeling.

You can buy tickets (Rs 75) in advance here for the bus to Bagdogra airport. The office is open Monday to Friday, 10 am to 4.30 pm. When it's closed, tickets for the airport bus are available from the DGHC Tourism Office (☎ 54214) in the Silver Fir building opposite Hotel Alice Villa.

Permits The Foreigners' Registration Office is on Laden La Rd. To get a 15 day permit for Sikkim you must first visit the Deputy Commissioner's Office, otherwise known as the DM (District Magistrate). Then get an endorsement from the Foreigners' Registration Office and return to the DM to collect your permit. The DM's office is open for permit applications 11 am to 1 pm and 2 to 4 pm Monday to Friday. The whole process takes about an hour. If you want to enter western Sikkim direct from Darjeeling (rather than first going to Gangtok), make sure that Naya Bazaar is one of the places listed on the permit.

Money ANZ Grindlays and the State Bank of India are both on Laden La Rd, to the north of the post office, and are open 10 am to 3 pm. The ANZ Bank only changes travellers cheques Monday to Friday from 10 am to 1 pm, and charges Rs 100. The State Bank of India has no charge, but often has long queues. Both banks will change most foreign currency. If you want a cash advance on your credit card, you will save money by collecting the cash the following day. The same-day encashment charge is Rs 250, next day is Rs 50!

Post & Communications The post office is central on Laden La Rd. There's a handy parcel posting office next door.

Internet Resources Email and Internet facilities are springing up all over Darjeeling; costs are the same as Calcutta (Rs 3 per minute). However, using the Internet or email in this town can be very frustrating as the lines frequently drop out.

The Cyber Cafe (☎ 53950, 53551, email udayan@cal2.vsnl.net.in), on the 1st floor of the Hotel Red Rose, was the first such facility in Darjeeling and is still the best. It offers multiple terminals, Web site development, a photocopying service and is also a PCO, so you can phone home, send a fax and email in one visit.

The Compuset Centre (☎ 54636), one minute from the clock tower next to the Hotel Fairmont, is a friendly place where you can arrange to pick up email if you

don't have your own email address (compuset@cal.vsnl.net.in); it's closed Sunday.

Trekking Outfits & Tour Operators
There are many trekking and tour agencies in Darjeeling, including:

Clubside Tours & Travels
　(☎ 54646), JP Sharma Rd (off Laden La Rd) – arranges treks and tours in North Bengal, Sikkim and Assam. It specialises in wildlife tours and can arrange trips to Manas and Kaziranga wildlife reserves in Assam, and Jaldhapara Wildlife Sanctuary.
Diamond Tours & Travels
　Super Market complex, Hill Cart Rd – has been operating for 11 years and can book treks in Sikkim, hotels and luxury bus trips.
Dorjee 'Ling' Tours & Travels
　(☎ 55099, fax 54717, email tashi@cal.vsnl.net.in), at Hotel Seven Seventeen on HD Lama Rd – offers some good local sightseeing tours, as well as longer tours, treks and vehicle rental. They can also arrange instant hotel bookings in Darjeeling, Sikkim, Bhutan and Nepal.
Himalayan Adventures
　(☎ 54004/90, fax 54237, email dastrek@ozemail.com.au) – in the same premises as Das Studios on Nehru Rd (The Mall), specialise in trekking and tours of the entire Himalaya region. It's run by Sheila Pradhan, a real character who can organise some unique experiences.
Himalayan Tours & Travels
　(☎ 54544), Ghandi Rd – has 20 years' experience booking treks in Darjeeling and Sikkim, and also leads mountaineering expeditions.
Himali Treks & Tours
　Super Market complex near the Bazaar bus stand on Hill Cart Rd – books treks, hires equipment and can arrange rafting on the Teesta river.
Kasturi Tours & Travels
　Super Market complex, (Hill Cart Rd) – organises tours to Kathmandu, Gangtok and Bhutan.
Tenzing Himalayan Expeditions
　(☎ 54778, fax 52392) – operated by Tenzing Norgay's eldest daughter, Pem Pem Tshering, can organise just about anything, from a ride to Gangtok to private climbing instruction and mountaineering expeditions to Kanchenjunga.
Trek-Mate Tours & Pineridge Travels
　(☎ 53912), next to Pineridge Hotel in Chowrasta – tailors treks in Sikkim and Darjeeling, arranges guides and porters, and has equipment for hire. The modern and computerised Pineridge Travels is the general sales agent (GSA) for Jet Air, Necon Air and Bengal Air.

Trekking gear can be hired from the youth hostel, but you must leave a deposit to cover the value of the articles you borrow (deposits returnable, less hire charges, on return of the equipment). Typical charges per day are Rs 25 for a sleeping bag, Rs 15 for a rucksack, and Rs 25 for a down jacket. There's a good visitors' book here with useful trekking notes.

The DGHC Lowis Jubilee Complex on Dr SK Pal Rd, also hires equipment at minimal charges (a few rupees a day, plus a refundable deposit), as does Himali Treks & Tours and Trek-Mate Tours.

Bookshops The Oxford Book & Stationery Company on Chowrasta (☎ 54325) is the best bookshop here. It's open until well into the evening so there's plenty of time for browsing after the sun has gone down. It has a comprehensive selection of books specialising in Tibet, Nepal, Sikkim, Bhutan and the Himalaya. It has a good, reliable mailing system which allows your purchases to be packed and shipped home by sea or air.

Photography Das Studios, on Nehru Rd, is a good place to head for advice regarding matters photographic. They stock up to 400ASA print and slide film but, as yet, there is no provision for slide processing in Darjeeling. This friendly shop is a good place to browse as it also sells CDs, books, magazines, greeting cards and gifts.

Medical Services Puri & Co has a well stocked dispensary on The Mall (Nehru Rd), just up from Keventer's Snack Bar. If you need a doctor, inquire here.

Opposite the post office at 7 Laden La Rd is the Economic Pharmacy. The Tibetan Medical & Astro Institute is beneath the Hotel Seven Seventeen, at 26 HD Lama Rd; it's open Monday to Friday 9 am to noon and 2 to 4 pm.

As an alternative to the state hospital, the Mariam Nursing Home (☎ 54327/54328) comes well recommended by an English psychotherapist who had occasion to avail

himself of its diagnostic services. This small private hospital is down the hill from the Gymkhana Club, well hidden behind shops and buildings. It boasts a small operating department, various consultancy disciplines and an efficient pathology/diagnostics lab. A consultation costs Rs 80, and tests range from Rs 40 to Rs 100.

Tiger Hill

The highest spot in the area (2590m) is Tiger Hill, 11km from Darjeeling near Ghoom. The hill affords magnificent dawn views over Kangchenjunga and other eastern Himalayan peaks.

Every day a large convoy of battered jeeps leaves Darjeeling for Tiger Hill at 4.30 am, which means that in the smaller lodges you get woken up at this time every day, whether you like it or not. The return trip costs Rs 50. It can be very cold and very crowded at the top, but coffee is available.

The early start and discomfort are justified by the spectacular vision of a 250km stretch of the Himalayan massifs, with, from left to right, Lhotse (8501m) flanked by Everest (8848m) and Makalu (8475m), then an apparent gap before the craggy Kokang (5505m), flanked by Janu (7710m), Rathong (6630m), the apparently flat summit of Kabru (7338m), Kangchenjunga (8598m), Pandim (6691m), Simvo (6811m) and the cone-like Siniolchu (5780m).

There's a view tower and entry costs Rs 2 for the top or Rs 7 for the warmer VIP lounge. Halfway down the hill a temple priest causes a massive traffic jam by anointing the steering wheel of each vehicle on the return trip!

Many take the jeep one way (Rs 30) and then walk back, a very pleasant two hour trip. Tickets can be purchased at the tourist office beneath the Bellevue Hotel. For those who have just trekked in, or don't want to get up too horribly early to watch the sunrise, there's a four-bed and an eight-bed dormitory at *Tiger Hill Tourist Lodge*. Beds cost Rs 75.

Close by is **Senchal Lake** which, at a height of 2448m, supplies Darjeeling with its domestic water. It's a particularly scenic area and popular as a picnic spot with Indian holiday-makers.

Kanchenjunga Views
At 8598m, this is the world's third highest mountain. From Darjeeling, the best uninterrupted views of it are from Bhan Bhakta Sarani. From Chowrasta, take the road to the right-hand side of the Windamere Hotel and continue about 300m; you can then wander around Observatory Hill. If you happen to be staying up on the ridge at, or near, the youth hostel, all you have to do is go outside onto a little knoll to see early morning views almost rivalling those from Tiger Hill. However, as the weather in the mountains can be fickle, nobody should go to Darjeeling just for the views, haze can conceal them for days on end.

The name Kanchenjunga is derived from the Tibetan *khang* (snow), *chen* (big), *dzong* (fortress or treasury) *nga* (five) – big five-peaked snow fortress, or big five-peaked treasury of the snow (depending on whom you ask).

Observatory Hill
Above the Windamere Hotel, this viewpoint is sacred to both Hindus and Buddhists. There's a Kali shrine here and the multicoloured prayer flags double as trapezes for the monkeys. Watch out for them as they can be aggressive.

Bhutia Busty Gompa
Not far from Chowrasta is this colourful monastery, with Kanchenjunga providing a spectacular backdrop. Originally a branch of the Nyingmapa sect's Phodang Monastery in Sikkim, it was transferred to Darjeeling in 1879. The shrine here originally stood on Observatory Hill. There's a library of Buddhist texts upstairs which houses the original copy of the *Tibetan Book of the Dead*.

Ghoom Gompa
More correctly known as Yogachoeling Gompa, this is probably the most famous monastery in Darjeeling and is about 8km south of town, just below Hill Cart Rd and the train station near Ghoom. It enshrines an image of the Maitreya Buddha (the coming Buddha). Foreigners are allowed to enter the shrine and take photographs. A small donation is customary and the monks are very friendly. As Ghoom is frequently swathed in mists, and the monastery is old and dark, it is often affectionately called Gloom Monastery.

Other Gompas
There are three other gompas in Ghoom: the very large but relatively uninteresting **Samdenchoeling**, the nearby and smaller **Sakyachoeling**, and the **Phin Sotholing**.

Nearer Darjeeling, on Tenzing Norgay Rd, **Aloobari Monastery** welcomes visitors. The monks often sell Tibetan and Sikkimese handicrafts and religious objects (usually hand bells). If the monastery is closed ask at the cottage next door and they'll let you in.

Halfway between Ghoom and Darjeeling is the **Thupten Sangachoeling Gompa** at Dali. Westerners interested in Tibetan Buddhism often study here. A little closer to Darjeeling on the same road is the opulent **Sonada Gompa**.

Dhirdham Temple
The most conspicuous Hindu temple in Darjeeling, this is just below the train station and is modelled on the famous Pashupatinath Temple in Kathmandu.

Bengal Natural History Museum
Established in 1903, a comprehensive but dilapidated collection of Himalayan and Bengali fauna is packed into this little museum. Among the 4300 specimens is the estuarine crocodile, the animal responsible for the greatest loss of human life in Asia. The museum is open 10 am to 4 pm Friday to Wednesday. Entry is Rs 2.

Padmaja Naidu Himalayan Zoological Park
This zoo was established in 1958 with the objectives of study, conservation and preservation of Himalayan fauna. The animals are

well cared for by dedicated keepers (some of whom have worked with the same animals for 20 years). However, it is still a zoo, and visitors must realise that any zoo is a compromise. To protect and breed the dwindling stocks of wild animals, to educate the public and instil in them a sense of the worth of these wonderful creatures, it is necessary to keep them in pseudo-natural habitats.

The zoo houses India's only collection of (massive) Siberian tigers, and some rare species, such as the red panda and the Tibetan wolf. There has been enormous success in breeding the Tibetan wolf at the zoo, and recent success in breeding the red panda.

The zoo is a 30 minute walk from Chowrasta on Jawahar Rd West. It's open 8 am to 4 pm Friday to Wednesday. Entry is Rs 6, and Rs 5 for a 'steel' camera.

Snow Leopard Breeding Program

The snow leopards (*Panthera uncia*) were originally housed in the main zoo complex but, due to the disturbance of visitors and the proximity of other animals, breeding was largely unsuccessful. Pairs of these rare and beautiful animals are now moved to a large separate enclosure on the way to the ropeway (about 15 minutes' walk beyond the zoo) and this has made all the difference.

Kiran Moktan at the centre welcomes interested visitors between 9 and 11 am, and 2 to 3.30 pm; it's better to visit in the afternoon when the leopards are more active, but you should not make too much noise. During the mating season, entry is prohibited. The centre is open Friday to Wednesday; entry is Rs 10.

Himalayan Mountaineering Institute (HMI)

India's most prestigious mountaineering institute, founded in 1954, lies about 2km from the town centre on a hilltop known as Birch Hill Park. It is entered through the zoo, on Jawahar Rd West. The **Mountaineering Museum** has a collection of historic mountaineering equipment, specimens of Himalayan flora and fauna and a relief model of the Himalaya showing the principal peaks. There is a display of badges and pins from mountaineering clubs around the world, and of the traditional dress of the hill tribes of the Himalaya. The **Everest Museum** next door traces the history of attempts on the great peak, with photographs and biographies of all the summiteers.

Sherpa Tenzing Norgay, who conquered Everest with Edmund Hillary in 1953, lived in Darjeeling and was the director of the institute for many years. He died in 1986 and his statue now stands beside his cremation spot just above the institute.

The institute is open daily from 9 am to 1 pm and 2 to 5 pm (4 pm in winter). There's a reasonable veg restaurant and refreshment and chai shop by Sherpa Tenzing's statue.

Passenger Ropeway

At North Point, about 3km north of the town, is India's oldest passenger ropeway (cable car). It is 5km long and connects Darjeeling with Singla Bazaar on the Little Rangeet River at the bottom of the valley. A return trip (including insurance) is Rs 45 and takes about an hour. Cars leave every 30 minutes between 8 am and 3.30 pm (closed Sunday and holidays during the low season). It's a popular trip and you must book a day in advance in person at the ropeway station. However, you can phone first to check it's running (☎ 52731).

Lloyd Botanical Gardens

Below the bus and taxi stand near the market, these gardens contain a representative collection of Himalayan plants, flowers and orchids. The hothouses are well worth a visit. The gardens are open between 6 am and 5 pm; entry is free.

Tibetan Refugee Centre

A 20 to 30 minute walk from Chowrasta through leafy glades and tea plantations, brings you down to the Tibetan Refugee Centre. Established in 1959, the centre comprises a home for the aged, an orphanage, school, clinic/hospital (☎ 53122), gompa and craft workshops that produce carpets of

Fight for Survival

The beautiful Snow Leopard can be found across the entire Indian Himalaya, from Kashmir in the west to Bhutan beyond Sikkim's eastern borders. To the north they are found in Tibet, Central Asia and the Altais, but due to the inaccessibility of the terrain and the high altitudes (over 3600m) of their habitats. It is almost impossible to be accurate about numbers in the wild, but it estimated to be between four and five thousand. However, although the snow leopard is a highly endangered and protected species, the smuggling of its pelts continues, which must result in a decline in these numbers.

To ensure the survival of the species, the International Snow Leopard Trust, which controls all breeding programmes, was founded in the early 1970s. The Snow Leopard Breeding Program in Darjeeling commenced in 1986 with two leopards brought from Switzerland. The centre had nine cats in 1999, six of which were born at the zoo. The latest arrival, from the Nubra Valley, is a great addition to the gene pool.

In captivity, snow leopards live approximately 14 years, female snow leopards have two breeding cycles per year, but are more likely to conceive in the winter cycle. The gestation period is from 92 to 100 days and there are usually two cubs per litter, though this can be up to five in the wild.

While it is distressing to see these magnificent animals behind wire enclosures, it's a sad fact that it is programs such as these which enhance the snow leopard's prospects for survival as a species. Certainly, the cats are in wonderful condition in Darjeeling and the dedication of the staff here has to be applauded. Much credit for the program's success in India must be given to its director, Kiran Moktan. To watch him playing with, and talking about his charges is a delight.

For further information contact: The Conservation Education Director (206-632 2421, fax 632 3967, email islt@serv.net), International Snow Leopard Trust, 4649 Sunnyside Ave Nth, Seattle, Washington 98103, USA.

pure Ladakhi wool, woodcarving, leatherwork and wool items. The craftwork and Tibetan curios, coins, banknotes, jewellery etc, are available for sale in the centre's showroom (☎ 52552). Prices are on a par with those in the curio shops of Chowrasta and Nehru Rd, but the proceeds go straight back to the Tibetan community.

You can wander at leisure through the workshops and watch the work in progress, but the centre is closed on Sunday. The weaving and dyeing shops and the woodcarving shop are particularly interesting, and the people are friendly and welcoming. As the centre is self-funding, and a registered charity, donations are always welcome. (See also Volunteer Work later in this section.)

Gymkhana Club
Membership of the Darjeeling Gymkhana Club costs just Rs 30 per day, but the activities here are not just equestrian. The word gymkhana is actually derived from the Hindi *gendkhana* (ball house). Games on

offer include tennis, squash and badminton (court hire from 6 am to noon, Rs 35 per hour per person including equipment); roller-skating (10 am to 1 pm and 3 to 5 pm, Rs 5 per hour); table tennis (Rs 5 per hour); and billiards (Rs 15 per person per hour).

Pony Rides

Beware of the pony-wallahs who congregate on Chowrasta. They come along with you as a guide and at the end you'll find you're paying for a second pony and for their guiding time! The usual charge is Rs 60 an hour. You can organise with one of the pony-wallahs to hire by the day or week for pony treks. The cost is negotiable, usually around Rs 200 to Rs 300 per day (plus guide).

Courses

Three month Tibetan-language courses for beginners are conducted at the Manjushree Centre of Tibetan Culture (☎ 54159), 8 Burdwan Rd. There are also more advanced six and nine month courses. The centre can also arrange Buddhist study courses for groups of six or more, and can organise talks and seminars on Tibetan culture. For details, contact Norbu at Dekevas Restaurant, who has worked at the centre as a volunteer for the last seven years.

You can learn traditional Tibetan woodcarving at the Tibetan Refugee Self-Help Centre (☎ 54686, fax 54237). Contact the head office (☎ 734101) at 65 Gandhi Rd.

Reiki (Universal Life) is the Japanese Usui Tradition of Natural Healing. Short courses and treatments are available in Darjeeling. For details contact Frans & Bronwyn Stiene (email bronwyn@hotmail.com), Reiki House, 1 Nehru Rd, Darjeeling, West Bengal.

Volunteer Work

The Nepali Girls' Social Service Centre (☎ 2985), Gandhi Rd, undertakes projects that promote the empowerment of women, child survival and development, and environmental protection. Volunteers would be welcome on an informal basis to teach English, art, or music. Contact the centre for details.

Carbon Monoxide Poisoning

Fires – charcoal burners in particular – are not recommended as a means of heating in hotel rooms. The Indian police have confirmed that a number of deaths from carbon monoxide poisoning occur each year.

If you're cold, and are unsure of the ventilation in the room, take a tip from trekkers who fill their drinking bottles with boiling water at night to use as a hot-water bottle (covered with a sock to prevent burning). In the morning, the water can be drunk since it's been purified through boiling. More upmarket hotels usually provide proper hot-water bottles. At all costs, never allow charcoal burners to be used.

Hayden Hall is a Christian-based organisation which can arrange volunteer work in medicine, teaching, handicrafts and counselling. Volunteers must be prepared to commit themselves for a period of not less than six months. For more information contact Father EP Burns or Noreen Dunne (email hayden@cal.vsnl.net.in), Hayden Hall (near the ANZ Grindlays Bank), 42 Laden La Rd, Darjeeling 734101.

The Tibetan Refugee Self-Help Centre (☎ 52346) has openings for volunteer teachers (of children and adults), medical staff and geriatric and child care workers. For more information contact the office at 65 Gandhi Rd.

Organised Tours

Between mid-September and mid-December, the DGHC Tourism Office offers a sunrise trip to Tiger Hill which leaves daily at 4 am. Tickets are Rs 50 and must be booked in advance. Most people go with the independent operators who charge a little less; some operators even send a runner to your hotel to make sure you get up! Depending on demand, the tourist office also organises a local sightseeing tour, a trip to Mirik and a two-day tour to Kalimpong and Gangtok.

Himali Treks & Tours has a half-day mountain-bike tour which leaves from

Chowrasta, taking in the Aloobari Gompa and Senchal Lake. Other outdoor companies also offer local sightseeing tours, see the Trekking & Tour Operators section earlier.

Special Events
In 1998, the **Teesta, Tea & Tourism Festival** was launched in a joint undertaking by the tourist regions of Dooars, Sikkim and Darjeeling. It will be held each year from 14-20 November. Targeted as much to local people as foreigners, it will focus on regional events and cultural exchange. As well as cultural displays, there will be tea garden visits and stays, organised tours, treks and walks through the regions.

Places to Stay
As there is such a great number of places to stay, only a limited selection follows. Prices vary widely with the season; those listed are for the high season (15 March to 15 July and 15 September to 15 November). In the low season prices drop by 50% to 75%, less for bottom-end places; discounts are negotiable.

Accommodation touts are paid up to 30% commission for finding guests, and you will ultimately pay for this if you follow them. However, telling them 'No' doesn't always work as they will often follow you to your hotel and then demand payment from the manager saying they brought you. If you are followed, be sure to inform the manager immediately that the tout was in no way responsible for your choice of hotel.

Note that Darjeeling suffers from chronic power and water shortages and that not all hotels have backup generators.

Places to Stay – Budget
Many travellers head for the area around the youth hostel and TV tower, on or near Dr Zakir Hussain Rd. It's about a 25 to 45 minute walk (600m uphill) from the train station.

The *Tenzing Norgay Youth Hostel* is reasonable value, if a little characterless. It is perched on a ridge at the top of the town, is spotlessly clean and undoubtedly has some of the best views in Darjeeling. There's no need to get up early to go to Tiger Hill to watch the sunrise on Mt Kanchenjunga – cling to your bed for an extra 90 minutes and just wander out onto the balcony. There's a good travellers' comment book here, and the staff are informative about treks in the area. Dorm beds cost Rs 40 and doubles Rs 120; there are no low-season discounts.

Virtually opposite is the *Triveni Guest House & Restaurant* (☎ 53878/144). Dorm beds are Rs 40, and there are singles/doubles with shared bath for Rs 40/80, or Rs 60/80 with bathroom. There is a rooftop terrace, an in-house PCO, cable TV and a terrific, cheap restaurant.

Nearby the very popular *Aliment Restaurant & Hotel* (☎ 55068) has singles/doubles from Rs 50/150, and dorm beds for Rs 30. There's a secure storeroom, laundry service, rooftop terrace, good borrowing library (with games and magazines) and a great little restaurant. It's run by a charming and knowledgeable ex-British Gurkha who can organise local tours and a stay at the family-owned orange and cardamom gardens in Mirik.

Also near the Triveni is *Ratna's*, which has four charming and cosy doubles for Rs 80, and a comfortable sitting room. This is a great place and rooms are very good value.

An excellent place is the very friendly, Sherpa-run *Hotel Tshering Denzongpa* (☎ 56061, 6 JP Sharma Rd). Doubles range from Rs 250 to Rs 600. The more expensive rooms have better views.

Hotel Springburn (☎ 52054), past the clock tower and next to Hotel Fairmont on Gandhi Rd, has basic clean rooms for Rs 385. Rooms at the back of the hotel have Khanchenjunga views.

Places to Stay – Mid-Range
An old favourite found in this price bracket is the two star *Bellevue Hotel* (☎ 54075), a charming old hotel right on Chowrasta. Fine wood-panelled doubles range from Rs 550 to Rs 800, and all rooms have bathrooms (hot water mornings only). Room 49 has the best views and a separate sitting room. For long-term guests there are huge, but rather characterless rooms at the back of

WEST BENGAL

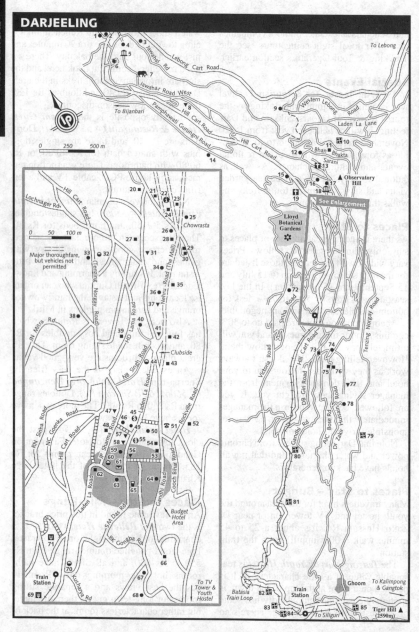

DARJEELING

To Lebong

Jawahar Rd
Lebong Cart Road

Jawahar Road West

To Bijanbari

Pamphawati Gunungni Road

Hill Cart Road West

Hill Cart Road

Western Lebong Road

Laden La Lane

Bhan Bhakta Sarani

Observatory Hill

See Enlargement

Lloyd Botanical Gardens

Sinha Road

Victoria Road

Hill Cart Road

DB Giri Road

Gandhi Rd

AJC Bose Rd

Dr Zakir Hussain Road

Tenzing Norgay Road

0   250   500 m

Lochnager Rd

Hill Cart Road

Major thoroughfare, but vehicles not permitted

0   50   100 m

JN Mitra Rd

RN Sinha Road

NC Goenka Road

Hill Cart Road

Laden La Road

(Tenzing Norgay Road)

HD Lama Road

NB Singh Road

Laden La Road

Nehru Road (The Mall)

Chowrasta

Clubside

Rockville Road

Cooch Bihar Road

JP Sharma Road

SM Das Rd

BK Goenka Rd

Gandhi Road

Budget Hotel Area

Kutchery Rd

Train Station

To TV Tower & Youth Hostel

To Kalimpong & Gangtok

Ghoom

Batasia Train Loop

Train Station

Tiger Hill (2590m)

To Siliguri

PLACES TO STAY		
11	Sailung Hotel	
20	New Elgin Hotel; Kanchen Restaurant	
21	Hotel Alice Villa	
23	Windamere Hotel	
24	Hotel Sunflower	
27	Hotel Mohit	
28	Pineridge Hotel; Trek-Mate Tours	
29	Bellevue Hotel; Tourist Office; Indian Airlines	
30	Main Bellevue Hotel	
35	Hotel Shangrila	
39	Hotel Seven Seventeen; Tibetan Medical & Astro Institute	
42	Planters' Club	
43	Hotel Dekeling; Dekevas Restaurant	
48	Hotel Tshering Denzongpa	
52	Hotels Valentino; Embassy Restaurant	
53	Hotel Fairmont	
54	Hotel Springburn	
62	Hotel Red Rose; Cyber Café	
66	Sinclairs	
73	Hotel Silver Cascade	
75	Triveni Guest House & Restaurant; Aliment Restaurant & Hotel	
76	Tenzing Norgay Youth Hostel	

PLACES TO EAT		
8	Hot Stimulating Cafe	
31	Great Punjab Restaurant	
37	Glenary's	
41	Kev's (Keventer's Snack Bar)	
47	New Dish Restaurant	

56	Tibetan Restaurants	
57	Jain Jaika Restaurant; Park Restaurant; Hayden Hall	
58	Golden Dragon Restaurant & Bar	
77	Hotel Tower View	

OTHER		
1	North Point	
2	St Joseph's School	
3	Shrubbery	
4	Ropeway Station	
5	Himalayan Mountaineering Institute	
6	Snow Leopard Enclosure	
7	Zoo	
8	Tibetan Refugee Centre	
9	Bhutia Busty Gompa	
12	Raj Bhavan (Government House)	
13	Gymkhana Club; St Andrew's Church	
14	Happy Valley Tea Estate	
15	Deputy Commissioner's Office	
18	Bengal Natural History Museum	
19	Loreto Convent & Catholic Church	
22	Darjeeling Gorkha Hill Council (DGHC) Tourism Office	
25	Pony Stand	
26	Oxford Book & Stationery Company	
32	Buses, Jeeps & Taxis to Kalimpong, Siliguri & Sikkim	
33	Super Market	
34	Curio Shops	

36	Das Studios; Himalayan Adventures	
38	Market	
40	Manjushree Centre of Tibetan Culture	
44	Clubside Taxi Stand	
45	ANZ Grindlays Bank	
46	Clubside Tours & Travels	
49	Foreigners' Registration Office	
50	Clock Tower	
51	Telegraph Office	
55	State Bank of India	
59	Nathmull's Tea Merchants	
60	Buses to Sikkim (Darjeeling Motor Service Co)	
61	Main Post Office	
63	Economic Pharmacy	
64	Himalayan Tours & Travels	
65	Joey's Pub	
67	Tibetan Refugee Self-Help Centre (Head Office)	
68	Nepali Girls' Social Service Centre	
69	Dhirdham Temple	
70	Taxis to Ghoom	
71	Maa Singha Temple	
72	DGHC Lowis Jubilee Complex	
74	TV Tower	
78	St Paul's School	
79	Aloobari Gompa	
80	Sonada Gompa	
81	Thupten Sangacholeing Gompa	
82	Samdenchoeling Gompa	
83	Ghoom (Yogachoeling) Gompa	
84	Sakyacholeing Gompa	
85	Phin Sotholing Gompa	

the property (some with kitchens). For guests only, there's a rooftop terrace, a private Buddhist prayer room and cafe with excellent views out over Chowrasta.

Away from the noise and bustle of the town centre, on the north side of Observatory Rd (a continuation of Nehru Rd) is the **Sailung Hotel** (*☎/fax 56289*). As a corporate holiday home, it only has four guest rooms available to the public (down a mountainside of stairs), but they all have uninterrupted views of Khanchenjunga. Rates are Rs 500 for a double.

Behind the Bellevue is the **Main Bellevue Hotel** (*☎ 54178*), a lovely old Raj-era building with doubles/triples for Rs 300/700, and a special double with Kangchenjunga views for Rs 800. The hotel is set in a lovely established garden. It has a slightly shabby, yesteryear atmosphere, and a gracious and attentive manager.

Opposite the Bellevue Hotel on Nehru Rd is the huge old **Pineridge Hotel** (*☎ 54074*). The miles of corridors are painted 'institution green' which gives it a rather oppressive feel, but the rooms are big and bright, if a little shabby. Doubles are Rs 550/700, and the deluxe rooms with polished wooden floors cost from Rs 850. All rooms have fireplaces, are simply furnished and some have bay windows. Extensive renovations are planned, hopefully leaving the gracious old-world character intact.

Farther down Nehru Rd, *Hotel Shangrila* (☎ 54149) has enormous, light, airy rooms with polished wooden floors and pine ceilings for Rs 750 (Rs 500 in low season) plus tax. It's a friendly place, but the downstairs restaurant is disappointing.

A short distance north of Chowrasta is the *Hotel Alice Villa* (☎ 54181, 41 HD Lama Rd). Doubles/triples are Rs 990/1450. Rooms in the original building are charming, but those in the ugly new annexe are a bit disappointing. Rates include breakfast and one other meal.

Darjeeling Club (☎ 54349, fax 54348, above Nehru Rd) is a real ghost of the Raj era. Also known as the Planters Club, downstairs doubles for Rs 1200 are shabby, gloomy and chilly, but there are plans to renovate. Upstairs doubles cost Rs 1400 to Rs 1800. There's a billiard room, a musty library, plenty of memorabilia and lots of nice seating areas including a broad terrace. Temporary membership is Rs 50 per day.

The *Hotel Dekeling* (☎ 54159, fax 53298, 51 Gandhi Rd, email compuset.@cal.vsnl. net.in), is above the Dekevas Restaurant and owned by the same Tibetan family. It's popular with travellers, and probably the best value in town, if you don't mind walking up hundreds of stairs. Doubles with bathroom are Rs 500 and Rs 800, Rs 800 and Rs 1050 with fantastic Khanchenjunga views. The pleasant wood-panelled attic rooms have desks and open onto a friendly sitting area. They cost Rs 400 to Rs 600 with shared bath. Hot-water bottles and kerosene heaters are the norm in winter and there are plenty of cosy common areas. Like most places, a 50% discount is offered in the low season.

Hotel Sunflower (☎ 54391, fax 54390, Nehru Rd (The Mall), email sunflower@ shivanet.com), has a PCO. Doubles with phone and TV are Rs 1200 and Rs 1500,

with a 60% discount for singles. They have a safe deposit and accept credit cards.

The *Ivanhoe* (☎/fax 56082, 4 Franklin Prestage Rd) is a heritage hotel nestled in a quiet area below the Mayfair Resort on The Mall. It was once one of a group of five English manors known collectively as Panch Kothi. They were built by an English lady, Mrs Makie (the proprietor of Kokrung Tea Estate), for her five daughters. Huge singles/doubles are Rs 1350/1650.

Hotel Fairmont (☎ 53646, fax 53647, 10 Gandhi Rd) is just past the clock tower. All rooms have great views, TV, phone and hot water, and there is a restaurant. Rates for doubles/triples/quads are Rs 1050/1500/2000.

Hotel Seven Seventeen (☎ 54717, fax 54717, email tashi@cal.vsnl.net.in) is the best of several hotels on HD Lama Rd. It is Tibetan-run, warm and welcoming with four star service and facilities at two-star prices. Singles/doubles are Rs 650/700. There's a restaurant (which serves traditional Tibetan meals on request), a cosy bar and Dorjee 'Ling' Tours & Travels.

Hotel Mohit (☎ 54351, Mount Pleasant Rd), is a popular three star property with singles/doubles for Rs 700/900 to Rs 1500. The restaurant has a good selection of multicuisine, and the bar carries imported wines and spirits. There is also a billiard room. The hotel accepts all major credit cards, has foreign exchange facilities, safe deposit, car park and can arrange trekking, tours and vehicle hire.

Close to the train station, *Hotel Red Rose* (☎ 56062, fax 52615, 37 Laden La Rd, email udayan@cal2.vsnl.net.in) houses the Cyber Cafe and Udayan Communications and PCO. It's a nice hotel, despite its rather noisy location, and all rooms have a TV, intercom and bathroom with running hot water. Doubles range from Rs 500 to Rs 1250.

Hotel Silver Cascade (☎ 52026, 9 Cooch Bihar Rd) is up towards the top of the ridge near Hotel Aliment. This place is light, bright and spotless with two restaurants and good singles/doubles for Rs 1000/1400. All rooms have TV, intercom, balcony, heater and 24 hour hot water.

Hotel Valentino (☎ *52228, 6 Rockville Rd*) has singles/doubles for Rs 750/950 and deluxe rooms for Rs 1000/1250. Rates include breakfast, and heaters are provided free in winter. The hotel has an Oriental ambience and an excellent Chinese restaurant.

Places to Stay – Top End

The *New Elgin* (☎ *54114, fax 54267, email newelgin@cal.vsnl.net.in*), off Robertson Rd, to the north of Chowrasta, but one road lower, is one of the town's oldest. It's been completely, tastefully and stylishly renovated, but retains the ambience of its colonial past. Elegantly furnished singles/doubles are Rs 1800/2200 – most with open fires, marble bathrooms and hot-water bottles. There's 24 hour room service, a fully stocked bar, a very good restaurant, laundry/valet service and lovely gardens with a gazebo to relax and enjoy afternoon tea.

The *Windamere Hotel* (☎ *54041, fax 54043*) is a veritable institution among Raj relic aficionados, with Tibetan maids in starched frilly aprons, high tea served in the drawing room to the strains of a string quartet, and a magnificent old bar where the silence is broken only by an old pendulum clock. The hotel, which is now completely nonsmoking (despite the odd smokey fire in the rooms) has been owned since the 1920s by Mrs Tenduf-la, a Tibetan lady of advancing years. The rooms are cosy and comfortable, and TVs are conspicuously (and deliberately) absent. Singles/doubles are US$70/110, including all meals. There is also a double suite for US$140.

Mayfair Hill Resort (☎ *56376, fax 52674, email mayfair@cal2.vsnl.net.in*) on the lower Mall opposite the Raj Bhavan (Government House), is the most recent addition to Darjeeling's top-end hotels. Originally a heritage property (the summer palace of a maharaja), it has been so extensively renovated that its origins are no longer apparent. It does however, offer luxury in beautiful surroundings, and with fabulous views. The 21 large guest rooms and 10 cottages are beautifully appointed (complete with hair driers), tastefully furnished and boast working fireplaces.

There is a restaurant, bar, lounge, marble-decked terraces and gardens. Single/double rates for rooms and cottages are US$82/110.

Places to Eat

There are so many places to eat in Darjeeling it would fill a book. The following is a small sample. *Kev's* (Keventer's Snack Bar), on Nehru Rd, is still the best place to head for a bacon sandwich. The deli downstairs has sausages, cheeses, ham and other goods.

Supersoft Ice Cream Parlour, virtually next door, has a wonderful selection of tasty treats. A short walk up The Mall brings you to *Glenary's*, which offers continental dishes, as well as tandoori and Chinese dishes in its upstairs restaurant. However, service is appallingly slow. The bakery downstairs sells excellent brown bread, a range of calorie-laden cakes, great pastries and superb home-made chocolates.

On the lower end of Nehru Rd, under Hotel Dekling, is the popular *Deveka's Restaurant*, famous for its pizzas.

The best Chinese food in Darjeeling can be found at the Hotel Valentino's *Embassy* restaurant (open until 8 pm) and the Chinese-run *New Dish* restaurant (a large airy place with great sunset views) on JP Sharma Rd.

The *Great Punjab Restaurant*, Robertson Rd has, as the name suggests, excellent Punjabi food.

Nonguests are welcome to dine at the *Windamere Hotel* for lunch or dinner, but advance notice is required, and meal times are extremely strict. Afternoon tea is an institution here.

Nonguests are also welcome at the *Kanchen Restaurant* at the New Elgin, also with advance notice.

Opposite the State Bank of India on Laden La Rd is the *Jain Jaika Restaurant* with pure vegetarian cuisine. Upstairs is the *Park* restaurant, with a pleasant outlook over Darjeeling.

A few doors away is the *Golden Dragon Restaurant & Bar*, with rainbow-painted walls and a seedy 1920s ambience. It's a smoky little den with a very basic menu – beer's the main attraction here. Further down Laden La Rd, close to the main post office, are a series of tiny *cheap eateries* generally serving Tibetan cuisine.

Most of the guesthouses in the TV tower area have their own dining rooms and can rustle up traditional dishes as well as western favourites such as banana pancakes, jaffles etc. Favourite places are the *Tower View*, *Ratna*, *Aliment* and the *Triveni*.

One different place is the tiny *Hot Stimulating Cafe*, perched out over the mountainside on the road down to the zoo. You can't see Khanchenjunga from here, but the views over the hills and valleys are beautiful. The Nepalese owners make great food (especially momos) and serve excellent chai and coffee. can tell you where to get tongba.

Shopping

Curios Most curio shops are on Chowrasta and along Nehru Rd. All things Himalayan are sold here – *thangkas*, brass statues, religious objects, jewellery, woodcarvings, woven fabrics, carpets etc – but if you're looking for bargains you have to shop judiciously and be prepared to spend plenty of time looking. Thangkas in particular may look impressive at first sight, but you will find in the cheaper ones that little care has been taken over the finer detail.

If you're looking for bronze statues, the real goodies are kept under the counter and cost in multiples of US$100! Woodcarvings tend to be excellent value for money. Most of the shops accept international credit cards.

West Bengal's Manjusha Emporium, on Nehru Rd, is a fixed-price shop selling Himalayan handicrafts, silk and handwoven products.

There's also a market off Hill Cart Rd next to the bus and taxi stands. Here you can find excellent and relatively cheap patterned woollen sweaters and an incredible selection of second-hand western clothes that have been donated to Tibetan refugee projects and, as there is always a surplus, have been sold to make money. If you need an umbrella these can be bought cheaply. Some, made out of bamboo, are collectors' items themselves!

Tibetan Carpets For Tibetan carpets, one of the cheapest places in the area is at Hayden Hall, opposite the State Bank of India on Laden La Rd. This women's co-operative sells *casemillon* (wool/synthetic mix) shawls, woollen hats, socks and mufflers.

Virtually next door to Hayden Hall is the Third Eye, an all-women enterprise run by Dechen Wangdi. It gives free training to women weavers and guarantees work at the

---

Tongba – Nectar of the Gods

Only made in the eastern Himalaya, Tongba is the 'beer' of the region. Millet is mixed with water and 'special' yeast and cooked for two hours, then stored in an airtight container for at least 24 hours. (A good tongba is kept much longer.)

Tongba is served in a bamboo container, hot water is added and, after waiting a few minutes for the juices to flow, it is sipped through a bamboo straw.

Note that there is a definite etiquette to be followed. First, always let your tongba sit before drinking. Second, observe others and don't suck through the wrong end of the straw. Third, it is definitely bad form to stir your tongba with the straw. Tongba is refreshed simply by adding more water.

The taste? Well, it's just like warm fermented millet. Very nice in fact – not very strong and the locals will tell you, 'good for health'. It's a great drink after a hard day's walking through the mountains, but watch out, you may feel a little wobbly after three or four bamboos!

Martin Bradshaw

end of their training. Shipping of carpets can be arranged.

Darjeeling Tea Tea is a popular souvenir. First Flush Super Fine Tippy Golden Flowery Orange Pekoe I is the top quality. The price varies enormously – anything from Rs 200 to Rs 3000 per kg! To test it, take a small handful in your closed fist, breathe on it through your fingers, open your hand and smell the aromas released. At least it'll look as if you know what you're doing even if you don't have a clue! Avoid the tea in fancy boxes as it's usually blend-ed and from Calcutta. A good supplier is Nathmull's Tea Merchants, near the post office on Laden La Rd. Mr Vijay Sarda enthralls as he waxes lyrical over the virtues of teas.

Getting There & Away

Air The nearest airport is 90km away at Bagdogra, down on the plains 12km from Siliguri. There's a direct bus to Darjeeling from the airport (Rs 75, 3½ hours) which connects with flights. Taxi drivers will try to convince you that it doesn't exist, instead trying to charge you the Rs 850 to Darjeerling.

The agents for Jet Airways are Clubside Tours & Travels (☎ 54646) on JP Sharma Rd (off Laden La Rd), and Pineridge Travels (☎ 53912) on Chowrasta.

The Indian Airlines office (☎ 54230) is beneath the Bellevue Hotel on Chowrasta. It's open 10 am to 1 pm and 2 to 5 pm daily. Tickets for the airport bus to Bagdogra can be purchased at the tourist office, next door.

Bus Most of the buses from Darjeeling leave from the Bazaar bus stand on Hill Cart Rd. These include the following:

- Gangtok (Rs 75, 5 h) at 7.30, 8 am, 1.15 and 1.30 pm
- Kalimpong (Rs 37, 3 h 30 min) at 8 am
- Mirik (Rs 26, 3 h) every 40 min from 8.30 am to 3.15 pm
- Siliguri (Rs 38, 3 h) every 20 min from 6.20 am to 5.30 pm

The agent for Sikkim Nationalised Transport (SNT) is the Darjeeling Motor Service

Co (☎ 52101), 32 Laden La Rd, open 10 am to 1 pm daily. There is one daily bus to Gangtok which leaves from opposite the office at 1 pm (Rs 65, five hours).

Nepal A number of companies offer daily buses between Darjeeling and Kathmandu, but none of them are direct; you have to change buses at Siliguri.

The usual arrangement is that agents will sell you a ticket as far as Siliguri, but guarantee you a seat on the connecting bus with the same agency. You arrive at the border around 3 pm (Kakarbhitta is the town on the Nepalese side), leave again at around 4 pm and arrive in Kathmandu at around 9 or 10 am the next day.

Most travellers prefer to do the whole cross-border trip independently, although it involves four changes – bus from Darjeeling to Siliguri (Rs 38), bus (Rs 10) or jeep (Rs 30) from Siliguri to Paniktanki on the border, rickshaw across the border to Kakarbhitta (Rs 10), and bus from Kakarbhitta to Kathmandu (Nepalese Rs 280, 17 hours). This is cheaper than the package deal, and you get a choice of buses from the border, plus you have the option of travelling during the day and staying over at places along the way. There are day buses from Kakarbhitta that stop at a number of other towns on the *terai* (Nepalese plains), including Janakpur, and night buses direct to Pokhara.

The nearest Nepalese consulate is in Calcutta, but visas are available at Paniktanki on the Indian side of the border for US$25 (which must be paid in cash); these can be extended in Kathmandu.

Taxi & Jeep Most travel agencies book private jeeps and/or Maruti vans. Quoted rates are:

Gangtok	Rs 1200	5 h
Jorethang	Rs 800	2 h 30 min
Kalimpong	Rs 600	3 h
Pemayangtse	Rs 2500	4 h 30 min
Siliguri	Rs 500	3 h
Yuksom	Rs 2800	5 h

The section between Darjeeling and Naya Bazaar (21km) is very steep, and during the monsoon it is subject to landslides. If the road is closed, a detour is taken via Teesta Bridge which costs an additional Rs 500.

There is a share jeep stand for Sikkim to the right of the bus ticket office at the bus stand on Hill Cart Rd. Rates (Rs 5 cheaper in the back of the jeep) are: Kurseong (Rs 30, 45 minutes), Kalimpong (Rs 55, 2½ hours), Gangtok (Rs 110, five hours) and Jorethang (Rs 60, two to three hours).

Buses from Jorethang to Yuksom – road-head for the Dzongri trail – leave at 8 and 9.30 am (Rs 33, three hours). You will require a trekking permit to visit Yuksom. See Permits in the Sikkim chapter for details.

The share jeep office for Kalimpong is at the southern end of the taxi rank, beneath the staircase to the first level of the Super Market.

Train Siliguri/New Jalpaiguri is the railhead for all trains other than the narrow-gauge toy train. (See the Siliguri Getting There & Away section earlier in this chapter for details.) Reservations for major trains out of New Jalpaiguri can be made at the Darjeeling train station (the toy train terminus) between 10 am and 1 pm and 2 and 4 pm daily.

Toy Train The toy train service has been washed out by monsoon rains and a major landslide, but is slated to resume service. If running, it should leave Siliguri/New Jalpaiguri at 9 am daily, arriving in Darjeeling at 5.30 pm. During high season, another service leaves Siliguri at 7.15 am. The returning train leaves at 7 and 10 am.

Whether runningto Siliguri or not, the toy train still goes to Kurseong (four hours, 34km) or Ghoom (45 minutes, 8km). From Ghoom, you can return via a very pleasant ridge track. Trains leave Darjeeling at *approximately* 10 am (check with the station or DGHC or West Bengal tourist offices).

KALIMPONG
☎ 03552 • pop 46,500
Though still relatively small, Kalimpong is a bustling and rapidly expanding bazaar town set among the rolling foothills and deep valleys of the Himalaya at an altitude of 1250m. Until the beginning of the 18th century it was part of the lands belonging to the rajas of Sikkim, when it was taken from them by the Bhutanese. In the 19th century it passed into the hands of the British and thus became part of West Bengal. It became a centre for Scottish missionary activity in the late 19th century, and Dr Graham's orphanage and school is still running today.

Kalimpong's attractions include its peaceful ambience, three monasteries, a couple of lovely old churches, an excellent private library for the study of Tibetan and Himalayan language and culture, a sericulture (silkworm) centre, orchid nurseries and fine views over the surrounding countryside. Although not many travellers bother to visit Kalimpong, there's enough here to keep you occupied for a couple of days, and for the energetic there's some good trekking, and rafting in nearby Teesta Bazaar (see the following Around Kalimpong entry).

The trip to Kalimpong passes through forests, crosses the Teesta River bridge and affords fabulous views of the confluence of the Teesta and Rangeet rivers. If you have no permit for Sikkim then the town is worth visiting for the journey alone.

There's a **flower festival** held in Kalimpong in October.

Orientation & Information
Though much smaller than Darjeeling, Kalimpong follows a similar kind of layout, straddling a ridge and made up of a series of interconnected streets and steps.

Life centres around the sports ground and market. The bus stand and Chowrasta is also busy, and where you'll find most of the cheap cafes and hotels. The Central Bank of India, at the northern end of Main Rd, has a very efficient and speedy foreign exchange service, and accepts most major travellers cheques. There's an email and Internet facility on Rishi Rd, opposite the post office.

For bookings on trains out of Siliguri/New Jalpaiguri, there's an agency (☎ 55643) on Mani Rd, a tiny lane below Rishi Rd.

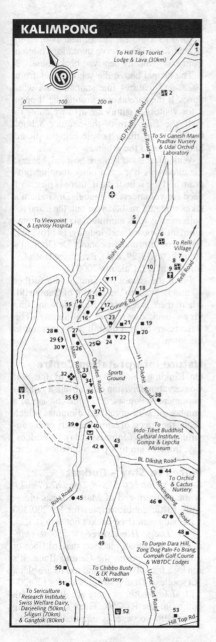

KALIMPONG

KALIMPONG

PLACES TO STAY
3   Deki Lodge
5   Bethlehem Lodge
18 China Garden Lodge
19 Chimnoy Lodge
20 Crown Lodge
21 Panchvati Lodge; Classic Hotel
23 Janakee Lodge
24 Cozy Nook Lodge
27 Lodge Himalshree
28 Gompu's Hotel & Restaurant
43 Hotel Silver Oaks
44 Hotel Chimal
48 Kalimpong Park Hotel
49 Himalayan Hotel
50 Sood's Guest House
53 Gurudongma House & Travels

PLACES TO EAT
11 Glenary's
13 Lark's Provisions
17 Annapurna Restuarant
22 Kalsang Restaurant
30 Ritu's Fast Food
34 Glenary's
37 Ferrazzini's Bakery

OTHER
1   Dr Graham's Home
2   Tharpa Choeling Gompa
4   Hospital
6   Thongsa Monastery
7   Mother Teresa's Home
8   Mangal Dham Krishna Temple
9   St Teresa's (Oriental) Catholic Church
10 Market
12 Railway Booking Office
14 Bhutia Shop
15 Arts & Crafts Co-op
16 Kashi Nath Booksellers
25 Bus & Jeep Stand
26 SNT (Sikkim) Bus Office
29 Central Bank of India
31 Thakurbari Temple
32 Shopping Complex
33 Mintri Transport
35 State Bank of India
36 Speedways Travel Agency
38 Hill Crafts Institute
39 Email & Internet Centre
40 Foreigners' Registration Office
41 Sub Post Office
42 Town Hall
45 Cinema
46 Nature Interpretation Centre
47 Rishi Bankim Park
51 Universal Flower Nursery
52 Kali Mandir

WEST BENGAL

Gompas

Established in 1922, the **Tharpa Choeling Gompa** belongs to the Yellow Hat (Gelukpa) sect of Tibetan Buddhism. This sect, founded in Tibet in the 14th century, is the one to which the Dalai Lama belongs. It's a 40 minute walk (uphill) from town; take the path to the right off KD Pradhan Rd, just before the Milk Collection and Extension Wing Building.

Lower down the hill, the **Tongsa Gompa**, or Bhutanese Monastery, is the oldest monastery in the area and was founded in 1692. The present building isn't so old – the original was destroyed by the Gurkhas in their rampage across Sikkim before the arrival of the British.

Zong Dog Palri Fo-Brang Gompa, 5km south of the town centre at the end of the ridge, was built in the mid-1970s at Durpin Dara Hill and was consecrated by the Dalai Lama. There are impressive wall paintings in the prayer room, and a rare three dimensional mandala upstairs. Mountain views are good from Durpin Dara Hill. This area is a big military camp, but you're free to walk or drive through it.

Flower Nurseries

Kalimpong produces 80% of India's gladioli and is an important orchid-growing area – flowers are exported from here to many cities in northern India. The Sri Ganesh Moni Pradhan Nursery and the Udai Mani Pradhan Nursery are among the most important in the area. The Standard and the Universal Nurseries also specialise in cacti.

Sericulture Research Institute

Silkworms are bred and silk is produced here, as well as herbs and plants. It's on the road to Darjeeling and can be visited between 9.30 am and 4 pm.

Dr Graham's Home

It takes less than an hour to walk from the town centre up through stands of bamboo to Dr Graham's Home, which was founded in 1900 on the lower slopes of Deolo Hill. The school was established to educate the children of tea garden workers and there are now about 1300 students. Enrolment is open to all, but there is a reserve quota for children from economically deprived backgrounds.

The chapel above the school dates from 1925, and features fine stained-glass windows. If the caretaker is around, he'll open it for visitors. Visitors are also welcome to visit the fine turn-of-the-century school building, and many people bring a picnic lunch to eat in the grounds.

With a farm, workshops, hospital, bakery, the children's homes, a nurse training program and the school itself, there is plenty of need for volunteers. Although Dr Graham's takes students on their year out, the usual requirement is for a minimum six month commitment – board and lodging is provided. For more information contact Dr Graham's Homes (☎ 033-297211), Berkmyre Hostel, 4 Middleton Rd, Calcutta 700071.

From the school building, it is a further 40 minute walk to the summit of **Deolo Hill**, where there is a *Tourist Bungalow* and fine views back down over Kalimpong. The three reservoirs on the hill provide water to the town.

Nature Interpretation Centre

On Rinkingpong Rd, and run by the Soil Conservation Division of the Ministry of Environment & Forests, the centre consists of a number of well-organised dioramas which depict the effects of human activity on the environment. The centre is Friday to Wednesday, from 10 am to 4 pm; admission is free.

Places to Stay – Budget

Gompu's Hotel (☎ 55818, Dambar Chowk), at the northern end of Main Rd, has pleasantly rustic doubles/triples for Rs 200/300 with bathroom (free bucket hot water).

The *Lodge Himalshree (☎ 55070, Ongden Rd)* is a small place on the 3rd floor of a building opposite the Central Bank. It's run by a friendly family and rooms are plain, but spotless. Doubles/triples are Rs 120/200 with shared bath, or there are doubles with bathroom for Rs 250. There's no running water here, so water is supplied in buckets.

One of the most popular places to stay with travellers is the **Deki Lodge** (☎ 55095, fax 55290, Tripai Rd). It's off Rishi Rd, about a 10 minute walk north of the bus stand. Singles/doubles range from Rs 100 to Rs 550, most with common 24 hour hot showers. There's also a triple room with bathroom and geyser for Rs 450. This rambling, happy place has a great atmosphere and is always full of pets. It is run by a friendly family who are a good source of information on treks in the area, and there is secure parking for a couple of cars or several motorcycles.

Janakee Lodge (☎ 55479) has spartan but clean rooms that vary in price according to which floor they on; the 1st floor is cheapest. Single/double/triple rooms range from Rs 130 to Rs 260 with shared bath, to Rs 180 to Rs 360 with bathroom.

Panchvati Lodge (☎ 56165) is a tiny place with a rooftop terrace, homey atmosphere and a pleasant owner. Doubles are Rs 150/200 with bathroom; the three-bed room costs Rs 250.

In a small cul-de-sac around the corner from the Janakee is the **Classic Hotel** (☎ 56335), with singles/doubles for Rs 150/250 with bathroom. Rooms are small, but some have good valley views. There's an extensive Chinese and Indian menu in the downstairs restaurant.

China Garden Lodge (☎ 55945) has good clean doubles with bathroom for Rs 350. There's also a rooftop 'suite' with balcony and terrace (and Indian loo) for the same price.

Crown Lodge (☎ 55846, Murgihatta Rd), off HL Dikshit Rd, is quiet, spacious and clean and has singles/double rooms for Rs 250/350 with bathroom with geysers (hot water in the morning only). Towels and soap are provided and there's free bed tea. Some of the rooms have pleasant views out over the sports ground.

Down a few steps from the Crown, **Chimnoy Lodge** (☎ 56264/55557, email heavy. scene@delta.gokulnet.com) is bright and tidy with pleasant hill views. Singles/doubles/triples start at Rs 150/250/350. An extra Rs 50 gives you a TV and views. All rooms have bathroom with 24 hour hot water and the helpful owner can organise tours and transport.

If you want to get out of town, **Sood's Guest House** (☎ 55297, 56207) is a nice little place in a garden setting 0.5km from town on the main road to Darjeeling. Singles/doubles are Rs 400/600; self-contained cottages Rs 650.

Hotel Chimal (☎ 55776) is also a little out of town on Rinkingpong Rd. It offers good doubles with cable TV at Rs 225 to Rs 300.

Places to Stay – Mid-Range

The few mid-range places are all south of the town centre along Rinkingpong Rd. Pick of the bunch is the **Kalimpong Park Hotel** (☎ 55304) with singles/doubles with hot water bathroom for Rs 1150/1170. The double deluxe rooms are in the original building, once the summer residence of the maharaja of Dinajpur; room No 5 has beautiful views of Kangchenjunga and Deolo Hill. Most of the other rooms are in the 20-year-old annexe behind the hotel, which is quite comfortable, although not as sumptuous.

A lovely quiet option is **Gurudongma House** (☎ 55204, Hill Top Rd) 2km from the centre of Kalimpong. General Jimmy Singh will pick up guests from the town centre. Singles/doubles are Rs 600/800; beds in three and four person dorms are Rs 210. There's a lovely garden, and rooms are in private cottages with pine trimmings and Japanese futon-style beds. Rooms inside the main house and meals are also available.

The best hotel views in West Bengal must surely be from the WBTDC **Hill Top Tourist Lodge** (☎ 55654) high above Dr Graham's Home. This unbelievably sited hotel stands sentinel over the surrounding countryside and has panoramic views of the hills, valleys and perpetual snows of the Himalaya. There is one double (Rs 750), six three-bed rooms (Rs 1000), and a 16-bed dorm (Rs 250 per bed).

WBTDC has two places farther out along the same road. They are old colonial bungalows with nice gardens and views, but can be a hassle to get to without your own transport. The nicer of the two is the *Morgan House Tourist Lodge* (☎ 55384), about 3km from the town centre. Singles/doubles start at Rs 650/1100. All rooms have bathrooms with hot showers, and rates include meals and bed tea. The hotel is wonderfully perched on the top of a ridge with valleys falling away on either side. Above the hotel is Gouripur House, where Rabindranath Tagore lived and wrote a number of his poems.

A cobblestone path through a magnificent flower garden leads from Morgan House to the adjacent WBTDC *Tashiding Tourist Lodge* (☎ 55929). Singles/doubles are Rs 600/1150, including all meals. The rooms have a lovely outlook but are fairly basic.

Places to Stay – Top End
If you have the money, there's no better place to stay in Kalimpong than the beautiful old *Himalayan Hotel* (☎ 55248; fax 55122, Upper Cart Rd) about 300m up the hill past the post office. The hotel is surrounded by superb gardens featuring camellias, azaleas, orchids and poinsettias, and there are views across to the snow-covered peaks of Kangchenjunga. Room-only rates are Rs 1650/2700 plus 10% tax, and there are also more expensive full-board rates.

Hotel Silver Oaks (☎ 55296, Rinkingpong Rd) is about 100m uphill from the post office. Once the home of a British jute family, the original eight-bedroom building has been extended to a 20-room hotel with delightful gardens and its own bakery. There's 24 hour room service, foreign-exchange facilities and bar.

All the spacious, sunny rooms (singles/doubles are US$80/92) have views of either the valley or Kangchenjunga, and are furnished in an old-world style with heavy bureaus, dressers and floral chintz drapery.

Places to Eat
Kalimpong cheese is a local speciality introduced by the Jesuits who established the Swiss dairy here. The dairy has now closed but cheese is still produced in the area. Similar to a slightly tart cheddar, it's very moreish and available at several shops including *Lark's Provisions* on Rishi Rd. It costs Rs 120 per kg.

Kalimpong lollipops are another speciality introduced by the sweet-toothed Jesuits, and shops still sell them.

Glenary's has opened two coffee shops and bakeries in Kalimpong, one on Rishi Rd, just beyond the train booking office, and one on Ongden Rd. They serve cakes, pastries, tea and even Nescafe.

Most places to eat close early in Kalimpong, and you'll have trouble getting a bite to eat after 9 pm, particularly in the low season.

The popular, but slightly pricey, bar and restaurant at *Gompu's Hotel* close at 8 pm.

New Restaurant is a tiny little eatery at the northern end of Main Rd. The *Kalsang Restaurant*, Link Rd, is a lovely rustic little place run by friendly Tibetans, who serve butter tea and pork *ghaytuk*.

The *Annapurna Restaurant,* upstairs on the corner of Gurung Rd, near the Kashi Nath bookshop, is cheap, clean, friendly and serves all sorts of alcohol and spirits (beer, rum, whisky). However, the service is unbelievably slow, and you have to ignore the malodorous stairway.

One of the best places to eat in town is the *Mandarin Restaurant* at the bus stand. The speciality is Mandarin fish, but you'll need to order it two hours in advance. Other tasty dishes include fried chicken balls and Chinese roast pork.

Nonguests are welcome to dine at the *Himalayan Hotel* and *Silver Oaks*, but advance notice is required.

Shopping
Open Wednesday and Saturday, the market is definitely worth visiting, especially if you want to meet the locals.

The Bhutia Shop, Dambar Chowk, stocks traditional Bhutia crafts such as woodcarvings, as well as pastel paintings, embroidered bags and other items.

Kalimpong tapestry bags and purses, copperware, scrolls and paintings from Dr Graham's Home are sold at the Kalimpong Arts

& Crafts Co-operative. Shops selling Tibetan jewellery and artefacts can be found in the streets to the east of Dambar Chowk.

Getting There & Away

There are frequent jeeps for the trip to Darjeeling (Rs 37, three hours). The buses are less frequent, slower and more uncomfortable. All transport, other than taxis, leaves from the Bazaar bus stand.

Buses for Siliguri cost Rs 45 (three hours) and should be booked in advance from one of the offices around the bus stand. A share jeep costs Rs 50. The road to Siliguri follows the Teesta River after the bridge, so it's much cheaper and quicker than going via Darjeeling. The views are magnificent.

Sikkim Nationalised Transport (SNT) has two buses daily to Gangtok (Rs 36, 4½ hours), at 8 am and 3 pm. These should be booked in advance at the SNT office near the bus stand. There are also private buses and jeeps on this route.

Mintri Transport operates one bus daily to Siliguri and Bagdogra airport at 7 am (Rs 90, three hours) from its office (also the Indian Airlines office; ☎ 55241) on Main Rd. Mintri Transport can also book flights, including those with Royal Nepal Airlines.

Bhutan From Kalimpong it is possible to visit Phuntsholing, just over the Bhutanese border, without a visa.

There's a daily bus to Jaigaon, on the Indian side of the border, which leaves at 8.30 am (Rs 49, six hours). There are hotels and guesthouses available at Phuntsholing, but not Jaigaon.

AROUND KALIMPONG
Teesta Bazaar

Sixteen kilometres from Kalimpong where the road divides for Darjeeling and Siliguri, Teesta Bazaar is becoming a centre for white-water rafting. It's possible to tackle the rapids between 15 November and 15 February. Contact DGHC Tourism, Teesta, Kalimpong (☎ 03552-62261); DGHC, Silver Fir Bldg, The Mall, Darjeeling (☎ 0354-54879/214), or Johnny Gurkha (☎ 03592-55374).

Lava & Kaffer

At 2353m and about 30km east of Kalim-pong, Lava is a small village with a Kagyupa **gompa**. Tuesday is market day, and a good time to visit. The summit of Kangchenjunga can be seen from Kaffer (1555m) and is best viewed at sunrise. There are *Forest Rest Houses* at both Lava and Kaffer (Rs 450 for doubles; Rs 50 for a dorm bed). Also at Kaffer is the *Yankee Resort*, with singles/doubles for Rs 180/300. Buses and jeeps ply regularly between Kalimpong and Lava.

Samco Ropeway

Thrill seekers should head for this chair lift installed by the Swedish as part of an aid program to help villagers cross the Teesta River. If the idea of dangling from a piece of wire 30m above the water doesn't entice, give this a miss – it's definitely not for vertigo sufferers! The ropeway is on the main Siliguri-Gangtok road, at a place known locally as 27th Mile. Catch any Siliguri bus from Kalimpong (1½ hours).

Orissa

The tropical state of Orissa lies along the eastern seaboard of India, on the Bay of Bengal. Its main attractions are the temples of the capital Bhubaneswar, the long sandy beach at Puri and the great Sun Temple at Konark. These sites make a convenient and compact triangle, and Bhubaneswar is on the main Calcutta-Chennai (Madras) train route.

Orissa is predominantly rural, with fertile green coastal plains rising to the hills of the Eastern Ghats. Largely based on agriculture, Orissa's economy is often destabilised by natural disasters, including floods, droughts and cyclones. A devastating cyclone lashed the state's coastal areas in November 1999, leaving more than 10,000 people dead and a million homeless. Much of the state's infrastructure was affected. However, flooding in the Mahanadi Delta, which used to occur regularly, has been much reduced by the building of the Hirakud Dam. The state is mineral rich and is a big exporter of iron ore.

Few visitors venture outside the Konark-Puri-Bhubaneswar triangle, but this is changing. Travelling in Orissa can be rewarding, with so many places of historic interest and areas of immense natural beauty. The Oriyas, 25% of whom are indigenous peoples *(adivasis)*, are very friendly and hospitable, and the atmosphere of the state is generally relaxed.

History

Although known throughout the ancient world as a formidable maritime empire, with trading routes stretching to Bali, Sumatra and Java, the history of Orissa (once called 'Kalinga') is a little hazy until the demise of the Kalinga dynasty in 260 BC. Near modern Bhubaneswar, Kalinga was conquered in a bloody battle by the great Indian emperor Ashoka. Shocked at the carnage, Ashoka foreswore violence and converted to Buddhism, which he subsequently assisted in spreading to Sri Lanka and East Asia.

Around the 1st century BC, under the rule of Kharavela, the third Chedi king, Buddhism

Orissa at a Glance

Population: 34.2 million
Area: 155,707 sq km
Capital: Bhubaneswar
Main Language: Oriya
Best Time to Go: November to March

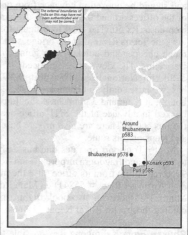

The external boundaries of India on this map have not been authenticated and may not be correct.

Around Bhubaneswar p583

Bhubaneswar p578

Konark p593

Puri p586

- **Konark** – the architraves and erotic carvings of the mysterious Sun Temple

- **Similipal National Park** – elephants, tigers and waterfalls in beautiful forests

- **Puri** – the colourful spectacle of the Rath Yatra festival

- **Bhitar Kanika Wildlife Sanctuary** – waterways, mangroves and beaches alive with turtles, birds and crocodiles

declined and Jainism was restored as the faith of the people. During this period the monastery caves were created and the twin hills, Udayagiri and Khandagiri (8km from Bhubaneswar) were important Jain centres.

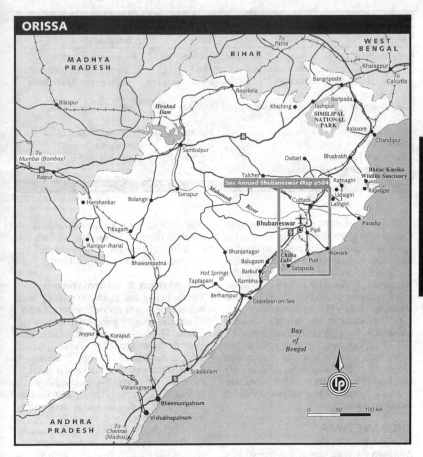

ORISSA

By the 7th century AD, Hinduism had, in turn, supplanted Jainism. Under the Kesari and Ganga kings, trade and commerce increased and Orissan culture flourished – countless temples from that classical period stand today. The Oriyas defied the Muslim rulers in Delhi until the region finally fell to the Mughals during the 16th century, when many of Bhubaneswar's temples were destroyed. Since then Orissa has been successively ruled by Afghans, Marathas and the British (from 1803 to Independence).

Shopping

Orissa has a very wide and distinctive selection of handicrafts. Best known is the gorgeous appliqué work of Pipli. Brightly coloured patches of fabric, cut into animal and flower shapes, have been sewn onto bed covers, cushions and beach umbrellas. The village of Raghurajpur is famous for its *patachitra*, or paintings on specially prepared cloth. Cuttack is known for its horn and brass crafts, and exquisitely delicate silver filigree jewellery and ornaments.

Festivals of Orissa

festival	location	date	features
Makar Mela	Kalijai Is, Lake Chilka	2nd week Jan	Hindu festival to Kalijai
Adivasi Mela	Bhubaneswar	26-31 Jan	folk art, dances, handicrafts
Magha Saptami (Sun Festival)	Konark	late Jan/early Feb	Hindu festival/fair to Surya
Ashokashtami (Lingaraj Mandir)	Bhubaneswar	Mar/Apr	Hindu chariot festival
Chaitra Parba	Baripada	mid April	Chhou dances
Rath Yatra	Puri	Jun/Jul	Hindu 'car festival'
Puri Beach Festival	Puri	5-9 Nov	beach festival
Konark Dance Festival	Konark	Dec	open-air dance festival

ORISSA

More than 300,000 Orissans work as handloom weavers, producing numerous types of uniquely Orissan fabrics in silk and cotton. Sambalpur is the centre of the area specialising in tie-dye and *ikat* fabrics. The complex ikat process involves tie-dying the thread before it is woven to produce material with an attractive, slightly blurred, pattern.

In Puri you can buy brightly coloured carved wooden replicas of Jagannath and his two siblings. Across the state you can find horoscopes, religious texts and also intricate images from the *Kama Sutra* painstakingly inscribed or painted on palm leaves. At Balasore, lacquered children's toys and wooden masks are manufactured.

BHUBANESWAR
☎ 0674 • pop 528,390

Although the state capital was moved here from overcrowded Cuttack in 1950, the city's history goes back over 2000 years.

Bhubaneswar is a rural Indian capital city with a delightful juxtaposition of modern buildings and ancient temples which rise in sepulchral splendour above new hotels, office blocks and industrial complexes.

With its many temples, dating from the 8th to the 13th century AD, Bhubaneswar is known as Temple Town. It is said that at one time the Bindu Sagar tank alone had over 7000 temples around it. Today, tour guides tell you there are only 500, but even this seems an exaggeration. The most significant temple is the great Lingaraj Mandir. It's one of the most important temples in India, but unfortunately is closed to non-Hindus.

Orientation & Information

The sprawling and rapidly expanding town of Bhubaneswar is divided by the train line, which runs roughly north-south through the middle. The main (new) bus terminal is 5km away on the western edge of town – farther out than the airport! The temples are mainly in the south-east and the closest hotel to them, the Panthanivas Tourist Bungalow, run by the Orissa Tourism Development Corporation (OTDC), is well within comfortable walking distance.

OTDC (☎ 431299) is down the lane by the Panthanivas Tourist Bungalow and has branches at the airport and the train station (☎ 404715, open 24 hours). You will also find a Government of India tourist office (☎ 432202) not far from the museum.

Major banks (ie the State Bank of India and ANZ Grindlays) and hotels in which you are staying should exchange travellers cheques and foreign currency.

The Modern Book Depot has a good selection of maps and English books.

Lingaraj Mandir

Surrounded by a high wall, the great temple of Bhubaneswar is closed to non-Hindus.

However, a viewing platform allows visitors to see over the wall. You'll be asked for a donation at the platform and shown a book to 'prove' that some people give over Rs 1000. How much you give is up to you, but a few rupees is more than enough.

The temple itself is dedicated to Tribhuvaneswar, or lord of the three worlds, also known as Bhubaneswar. Its present form dates from 1090 to 1104, although parts of it are over 1400 years old. The granite block, representing Tribhuvaneswar, is said to be bathed daily with water, milk and *bhang* (marijuana). The temple compound is about 150m square and is dominated by the 40m high temple tower. More than 50 smaller temples and shrines crowd the enclosure. In the north-east corner, a small temple to Parvati is particularly interesting.

There is an annual **chariot festival** in the temple in April.

Bindu Sagar

The Bindu Sagar (Ocean Drop Tank), just north of the Lingaraj Mandir, is said to contain water from every holy stream, pool and tank in India – obviously a good place to wash away sin. There are a number of temples and shrines scattered around the tank, several with towers in imitation of the ones at the Lingaraj Mandir. In the centre of the tank is a water pavilion where, once a year, the Lingaraj Mandir's deity is brought for ritual bathing.

Vaital Mandir

Close to the Bindu Sagar, this temple has a double-storey 'wagon roof', an influence from Buddhist cave architecture. It dates from the 8th century and was a centre of Tantric worship. You can see the presiding deity Chamunda (Kali) in the dingy interior, although her necklace of skulls and the corpse on which she sits are usually hidden beneath her temple robes.

Parsurameswar Mandir

Close to the main Bhubaneswar-Puri road, on the same side as the Lingaraj Mandir, the Grove of the Perfect Beings is a cluster of about 20 smaller temples, including some of the most important in Bhubaneswar. The best preserved of the early temples is the Parsurameswar, a Shiva temple built about 650 AD. It has lively bas-reliefs of elephant and horse processions, lattice windows and Shiva images.

Mukteswar, Siddheswar & Kedargauri Mandirs

Not far from the Parsurameswar is the small 10th century Mukteswar Mandir, one of the most ornate temples in Bhubaneswar. The

ORISSA

Orissan Temple Architecture

Orissan temples – whether the mighty Lingaraj in Bhubaneswar, the Jagannath in Puri, the Sun Temple at Konark or the many smaller temples – all follow a similar pattern. Basically there are two structures, the *jagamohan*, or assembly hall, and the *deul*, where the image of the temple deity is kept and above which the temple tower rises. The design is complicated in larger temples by the addition of other entrance halls in front of the jagamohan. These are the *bhoga-mandapa*, or hall of offering, and the *natamandir*, or dancing hall.

The whole structure may be enclosed by an outer wall, and within the enclosure there may be smaller, subsidiary temples and shrines. The most notable aspects of the temple design are the soaring tower and the intricate carvings that cover every surface. These may be figures of gods, men and women, plants and trees, flowers, animals and every other aspect of everyday life, but to many visitors it is the erotic carvings which create the greatest interest. They reach their artistic and explicit peak at Konark, where the close-up detail is every bit as interesting as the temple's sheer size.

BHUBANESWAR

To Nandankanan Zoo (25km)
& Calcutta (437km)

To Cuttack
(35km)

National Highway No 5

Sachivalaya Marg

Orissa Truck Rd.

Maharishi College Road

Bhubaneswar Road

Vidyut Marg

Azad Marg

Janpath

Mahatma Gandhi Marg

See Enlargement

To Berhampur (160km)
& Chennai

Raj Path

Train
Station

Ekamra Marg

Forest
Park

Gangua Nala

Daya Canal

Puri Cuttack Road

Airport

Mahatma Gandhi Marg

Janpath

Train
Station

Raj Path

Bhubaneswar Rd.

Bindu
Sagar

Mahatab Road

To Chennai
(1232km)

To Puri (60km)
& Konark (64km)

0   0.5   1 km

0   1.5   3 km

---

finely detailed carvings show a mixture of
Buddhist, Jain and Hindu styles, but unfortu-
nately some of the figures have been defaced.
The ceiling carvings are particularly striking.

In front of the temple is a beautiful arched
torana (architrave) clearly showing a Buddhist influence.

The later Siddheswar Mandir in the same
compound, is plainer than the Mukteswar,
but boasts a fine standing Ganesh figure.

Also by the road, across the path from the
Mukteswar, the Kedargauri Mandir is one

of the older temples in Bhubaneswar, although it has been substantially rebuilt.

Raj Rani Mandir

This temple (circa 1100 AD), surrounded by
well-maintained gardens, is famous for its
ornate *deul* (sanctuary). Around the compass points are pairs of statues representing
the eight *dikpalas* (temple guardians), who
protect the temple. Between them, nymphs,
embracing couples, elephants and lions fill
the niches and decorate the pillars. As it's no

BHUBANESWAR

PLACES TO STAY		29	Hotel Kalinga Ashok	9	Indian Airlines
1	Oberoi Hotel	30	Hotel Oddisi High	10	Capital (Old) Bus Stand
3	Imperial Guesthouse	31	Venus Inn; Swagat Inn;	17	Post Office
7	Park View Guest House		Hotel Rajdhani	19	Modern Book Depot
11	Hotel Prachi	34	Panthanivas Tourist Bungalow	22	Market
12	Yatri Nivas			32	Orissa State Museum
13	Hotel Swagat	PLACES TO EAT		33	Tourist Office
14	Hotel Richi	18	Hare Krishna Restaurant	35	Orissa Tourism
15	Hotel Keshari	20	Shanti Restaurant	36	Vaital Mandir
16	Hotel Swosti	27	South Indian Hotel	37	Parsurameswar Mandir
21	Bhubaneswar Hotel			38	Siddheswar
23	Central Lodge	OTHER			& Mukteswar
24	Tourist Guest House	2	Planetarium	39	Raj Rani Mandir
25	Hotels Bhagat Nivas;	4	Tribal Research Centre	40	Kedargauri Mandir
	Hotel Pushpak; Hotel Padma	5	New Bus Station	41	Lingaraj Mandir
26	Hotel Sishmo	6	Udayagiri Caves & Khandagiri	42	Brahmeswar Mandir
28	Hotel Janpath	8	State Bank of India	43	Sisuphal Garh

ORISSA

longer used for worship you are free to wander at will.

Brahmeswar Mandir

About a kilometre east of the main road, the Brahmeswar Mandir stands in a courtyard flanked by four smaller structures. It's notable for its finely detailed sculptures with erotic and sometimes amusing elements. The temple dates from the 9th century.

Orissa State Museum

Better laid out and brighter than the Indian Museum in Calcutta, this museum is really worth a visit. Opposite the Hotel Kalinga Ashok, it boasts a rich collection of rare palm-leaf manuscripts, traditional and folk musical instruments, bronze-age tools, an armory and an interesting display of Orissan tribal anthropology.

The natural history collection is better than most, with the exhibits still retaining their fur and feathers. The magnificent collection of Buddhist and Jain sculptures, which are displayed in chronological order, constitutes the most important antiquities in the museum.

The museum, which also has a brilliant gallery displaying the works of contemporary Orissan artists, is open 10 am to 5 pm daily, except Monday; entry is Rs 2.

Tribal Research Centre

Although the Tribal Research Centre (or Museum of Man) is primarily an anthropological research centre, visitors are welcome. There's an outdoor display of houses of Orissan adivasis, including the Santal, Juang, Gadaba, Saora and Kondh. It's open 10 am to 5 pm daily except Sunday; admission is free. Buses between the new bus station and centre of town pass by the museum.

Udayagiri & Khandagiri Caves

A couple of kilometres south of the new bus terminal in Bhubaneswar, these two hills facing each other across the road are riddled with caves, many of which are ornately carved. Most are thought to have been chiselled out for Jain ascetics in the 1st century BC.

See the Udayagiri & Khandagiri Caves Tour boxed text for descriptions. The caves are open 8 am to 6 pm; entry is Rs 5. A government restaurant and chai shops are nearby.

No buses go specifically to the caves, but there are plenty passing the nearby junction on the main Calcutta-Chennai highway. It's about Rs 5 from town, or you can take an auto-rickshaw for about Rs 80.

Other Attractions

The partly excavated ruins at Sisuphal Garh are thought to be the remains of an Ashokan city. In the north of the city, the **botanical gardens** and **regional plant reserve** have a large collection of plants, including many cacti and an extensive rose garden. The city's **planetarium** has shows every hour from 2 to 5 pm (4 pm in English) daily except Monday; tickets cost Rs 5.

Courses

Art Vision conducts one-month in-house courses in Oddisi and Chhau dance in Bhubaneswar. The cost, including lodging, is US$200. There is also a special intensive workshop from 15 December to 15 January (US$300). For more information check out Art Vision's Web site: www.kalinga.net/ileana or contact Dr Ileana Citaristi (☎/fax 433779, email ileana5@hotmail.com), Art

Vision, 1965 Bindu Sagar, Old Town, Bhubaneswar, 751002.

Organised Tours

During the high season, tours operate daily except Monday from the Panthanivas Tourist Bungalow (☎ 431515, 431314). If you're pressed for time, you can take a day tour through Pipli to Puri and Konark for Rs 100 (Rs 150 by air-con bus). By taxi this tour would cost upwards of Rs 650.

Other possible day tours stay in and around Bhubaneswar, taking in the Nandankanan zoo, the Udayagiri and Khandagiri caves and Dhauli (Rs 95, or Rs 120 air-con). However, these tours tend to linger at the zoo, and whiz through the caves and temples, so you might prefer to organise private transport.

Places to Stay – Budget

There's a wide choice of budget accommodation in Bhubaneswar. If you arrive by train, no matter what porters or rickshawwallahs tell you, there is an exit on the eastern side of the station, open 24 hours a day, only a few minutes' walk from the majority of the budget hotels.

Throughout Orissa, hotel rates (including some OTDC properties) drop 20% to 50% during the monsoon and times of low occupancy. It always pays to ask for a discount.

Hotel Bhagat Nivas (☎ 411545) is a recommended place, with singles from Rs 80 to Rs 150 and doubles with TV and bath from Rs 170 to Rs 250. Prices for air-con doubles start at Rs 400. It's clean and friendly.

Hotel Pushpak (☎ 415545) is close by and boasts a nonsmoking bar. Double rooms are Rs 150, or Rs 350 with air-con.

The *Hotel Padma* (☎ 416626, 67 Budha Nagar), has single rooms at Rs 60 and double rooms from Rs 160 to Rs 200.

Venus Inn (☎ 401738), with a good south Indian restaurant, *Swagat Inn* (☎ 408486) with its fast-food restaurant, and *Hotel Rajdhani* are all clustered together nearby. Singles/doubles start from Rs 150/300. Air-con doubles start from Rs 450.

Bhubaneswar Hotel (☎ 416977, Cuttack Rd), is a popular place. Despite its rather

---

Adivasi Area Tours

Although there is some controversy regarding the advisability and morality of visiting adivasi (tribal) areas, tourism does bring much-needed funds to these already developing regions and organised tours are becoming increasingly popular.

Although many of the areas are still virtually off limits to tourists, others (mostly in the south-west) are becoming less restricted. Tribe Tours and Heritage Tours in Puri can arrange cars and interpreters for tours to this region. Swosti Travel, one of the first to design sympathetic itineraries into the adivasi zones, has a fleet of cars and modern air-con buses, and can arrange both individual and group tours. Because of the remoteness of the areas, a minimum of seven days is advised for any trip into these fascinating regions.

For more information on visiting the region, or to get a list of other recommended tour companies, contact OTDC in Bhubaneswar (☎ 0674-432177). To learn more about adivasi people, visit the Tribal Research Centre in Bhubaneswar. See the Organised Tours in Similipal National Park section for other information on this area.

Udayagiri & Khandagiri Caves Tour

Udayagiri, or Sunrise Hill, to the north of the approach road, has the more interesting caves, which are found at various levels up the hill and all are numbered.

At the base of the hill, around to the right, is the two-storey Rani ka Naur or Queen's Palace Cave (cave 1). Both levels have eight entrances and the cave is extensively carved.

Return to the road via the Chota Hathi Gumpha (cave 3), with its carvings of elephants coming out from behind a tree. The Jaya Vijaya Cave (5) is double-storeyed and a bodhi tree is carved in the central compartment.

Back at the entrance, ascend the hill to cave 9, the Swargapuri, and cave 14, the Hathi Gumpha or Elephant Cave. The latter is plain, but a 117-line inscription relates the exploits of its builder, King Kharaveli of Kalinga, who ruled from 168 to 153 BC.

Around the hill to the right, is the single-storeyed Ganesh Gumpha (cave 10), which is almost directly above the Rani ka Naur. The carvings tell the same tale as in the lower level cave but are better made. Retrace your steps to cave 14, then on to the Pavana Gumpha, or Cave of Purification, and the small Sarpa Gumpha or Serpent Cave, where the tiny door is surmounted by a three-headed cobra. Only 15m or so from this is the Bagh Gumpha (cave 12) or Tiger Cave, entered through the mouth of the beast.

Across the road, Khandagiri offers a fine view back over Bhubaneswar from its summit. The steep path divides about a third of the way up the hill. The right path goes to the Ananta Cave (3), with its carved figures of athletes, women, elephants and geese carrying flowers. Further along is a series of Jain temples and, at the top, another Jain temple from the 18th century.

ORISSA

flashy appearance and roof garden, this hotel offers good rates. Rooms with bath are Rs 125/300, or rooms with air-con are Rs 550.

Hotel Swagat (☎ 416686, 425879) farther north on Cuttack Rd, down a lane between the Ambica Restaurant and Orissa Plastics, has 24 hour checkout and friendly management. Singles/doubles with hot bucket water cost Rs 150/250.

Yatri Nivas (☎ 475839), even farther north, is a friendly place, very much like a youth hostel. Dorm beds start from Rs 50 and there's a cheap restaurant.

There are several new hotels springing up on the western side of the train tracks. These places qualify as mid-range places to stay but also offer good budget rooms.

Hotel Janpath (☎ 405547, 29 Bapuji Nagar, off Janpath), is a modern hotel with reasonable rates. Singles are Rs 110 to Rs 450 with air-con and doubles are Rs 135 to Rs 550 with air-con.

The *Central Lodge* (☎ 533803), in a row of el cheapo lodges on Raj Path, has rooms with bath for Rs 100. A sign at reception warns 'deceased persons are not allowed in the lodge'.

Places to Stay – Mid-Range

If you can pay a little extra, there are some lovely places to stay.

Hotel Richi (☎ 506619, 506639, New Station Square), is close to the station behind Hotel Swosti on the western side. Singles with bath start from Rs 200 and doubles from Rs 300 (Rs 650 with air-con). All rates include bed tea.

Tourist Guest House (☎ 500857) is a pleasant little place well deserving of its popularity. Clean, comfortable rooms are Rs 350 to Rs 450 with bath. Meals are available. If it's full, the same owner has two other guesthouses which are just as welcoming but not so well located.

Park View Guest House (☎ 400664, Ekamra Marg, Forest Park) is north of the airport and has doubles from Rs 600 to Rs 750, all with TV.

Imperial Guesthouse (☎ 415010), closer to town, has rooms from Rs 450.

Hotel Oddisi High (☎ 417084) is a spotless hotel with rooms from Rs 300/400.

Rooms at *Panthanivas Tourist Bungalow* (☎ 432515, 432314) aren't great value, and it has a nightmare checkout time (8 am). But it's close to the temples and has comfortable doubles for Rs 375, or Rs 700 with air-con.

Places to Stay – Top End

Bhubaneswar also caters for those who crave comfort, carpet and coddling.

Hotel Keshari (☎ 501095, fax 511553, 113 Station Square), has all the top inclusions and a multicuisine restaurant which also specialises in Orissan food. Singles are Rs 675 to Rs 1300, doubles Rs 775 to Rs 1450. Family rooms and suites are Rs 1800 to Rs 2800.

Hotel Kalinga Ashok (☎ 431055, fax 432001) is almost opposite the museum. Singles/doubles cost from Rs 1700/2000.

Hotel Sishmo (☎ 433600, fax 433351), which used to be the Kenilworth, has a good reproduction of a Konark chariot wheel outside and is recommended for its position and facilities. Air-con rooms are Rs 1950/2450. There is a swimming pool here (closed 10 am to 4 pm) that nonguests can use for Rs 100, a pastry shop, bookshop and resident masseur. Indian classical music recitals are held from 7 pm to 9 pm each evening.

Hotel Prachi (☎ 502328, fax 503287) is a good air-con place with rooms at Rs 1300/1850. Facilities include the 'Wim Bul Don' (a tennis court) and a pool that nonguests can use for Rs 75.

Hotel Swosti (☎ 508526, fax 518261, 103 Janpath), not far from the train station, is a good four star hotel with pleasant service and spacious rooms. Single rooms start from Rs 1950, doubles from Rs 2525 including breakfast.

Oberoi Hotel (☎ 440890, fax 440898), on the outskirts of town, is at the top of the pile. Mimicking Orissan temple layout and design, it charges US$100/120 for singles/doubles. It has the all mod cons, including swimming pool, floodlit tennis courts, health club and jogging track.

Places to Eat

There are many good, cheap south Indian places around the junction of Raj Path and Janpath, and in the laneways behind Hotel Swosti there are some terrific Indian fast-food outlets.

Hare Krishna Restaurant, run by the organisation itself, is the best vegetarian eatery in Bhubaneswar. It's a smart place with powerful air-con and excellent, though pricey, food.

Panthanivas Tourist Bungalow has two restaurants, but both serve the same baffling attempts at Chinese and continental dishes.

Sangam Restaurant at the Hotel Sishmo is a recommended place for an evening out. During the dry season there are barbecues on the roof terrace.

Executive Restaurant and the more up-market *Exclusive Restaurant* at the Hotel Swosti offer great service and excellent menus. Both will make Orissan food with eight hours' notice.

There are many vegetarian places in the temple area if you are down that way at lunchtime.

Aahar Restaurant near the Parsurameswar Mandir serves a wide range of Bengali and Orissan dishes.

Shopping

Orissan handicrafts, including appliqué and ikat work, can be bought at the market off Raj Path. There are a number of shops, including the Orissa State Handloom Cooperative or Utkalika, located in the market building near Hotel Swosti.

There's also the Orissa State Handicrafts Emporium, not far from the temples.

Getting There & Away

Air Indian Airlines (☎ 400533, 400544) has five flights a week between Bhubaneswar and Calcutta (US$75), daily flights to Delhi (US$195), two flights a week to Chennai (US$180), three to Hyderabad (US$145) and six to Chennai (US$225). There are also four flights a week from Varanasi to Bhubaneswar but nothing in the opposite direction.

Bus The impressive bus station (which looks more like an airport terminal) is on the main highway (National Highway 5), 5km west of town. Buses to Cuttack, Puri and Konark still stop at the old Capital bus stand, much more conveniently located in the centre of town. The trip to Puri takes a little over an hour and costs Rs 15. Direct buses to Konark are Rs 15. Otherwise, take a Puri bus and change at Pipli, where the Konark road branches off.

From the new bus terminal there are three afternoon departures to Calcutta (Rs 150, overnight). Regular buses go to Cuttack (Rs 5, one hour) and Berhampur (Rs 45, five hours). There is one morning and one evening service for Sambalpur (Rs 100, nine hours). Private coaches run to Baripada (Rs 80, seven hours).

Train Bhubaneswar is on the main Calcutta-Chennai train line, so there are plenty of trains to these places. Many services from the north terminate at Puri. The *Rajdhani Express* departs from Calcutta at 10.45 am every Saturday and arrives in Bhubaneswar just over seven hours later (Rs 181/498 in sleeper/three-tier air-con, 437km). This train leaves Bhubaneswar every Sunday at 8.50 am for the return journey to Calcutta and goes on to Delhi (24 hours, 2077km).

There are also direct rail connections to Berhampur (Rs 48/233, 2½ hours, 166km), Chennai (Rs 200/1004, 24 hours, 1226km), Varanasi (Rs 174/862, 20 hours, 998km) and Agra (Rs 249/1874, 39 hours, 1874km).

Getting Around

The airport is very close to the town. There's no bus service and a taxi costs Rs 65 to Panthanivas Tourist Bungalow or Rs 100 to the Oberoi. A cycle-rickshaw costs only Rs 20, but you have to walk the last 500m between the terminal and the airport entrance.

Between the new bus station and the town centre you're up for Rs 40 by autorickshaw, or there are city buses to the old Capital bus stand for Rs 3.

Cycle-rickshaws offer 'five temple' tours for around Rs 50, which cover the main temples; shorter journeys are around Rs 10.

Taxis have set rates which are available from the tourist office. They may be unwilling to drive you for those rates, but it's worth a try.

AROUND BHUBANESWAR
Dhauli

Around 260 BC, King Ashoka had his famous edicts carved onto a large rock halfway up a hill at Dhauli, 8km south of Bhubaneswar just off the Puri road. After murdering several members of his family to gain power, then hundreds of thousands on the battlefield as he enlarged his empire, Ashoka finally 'saw the light' and converted to Buddhism.

Given his past record, Ashoka was wise to choose a pen name for his edicts, referring to himself as King Piyadasi (meaning He Who Looks on Everything with Kindness). In the edicts he tells his subjects,

ORISSA

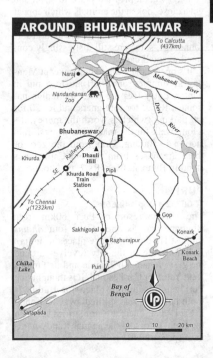

AROUND BHUBANESWAR

'Meritorious is abstention from killing living creatures, meritorious is abstention from reviling the unorthodox ...'.

At the top of the hill is a dazzling white peace pagoda built by the Japanese in the 1970s. Older Buddha figures are set into the modern structure.

You can get to the turn-off from the main road on any Puri or Konark bus for Rs 4. From there it's a 3km walk to Dhauli. By auto-rickshaw the trip costs about Rs 100.

Nandankanan Zoo

Famous for its white tigers, and touted as 'the best zoo in India', Nandankanan is 25km north of Bhubaneswar. As well as the usual animal enclosures, there are elephant rides, a cable car, toy train, boating on the large and beautiful lake and also lion and tiger safari parks which you can tour in 'armoured' buses.

The zoo is a pleasant place to stroll and get a close look at the animals which appear to be healthy. However, although many are housed in large compounds and natural surroundings, some are still distressingly confined in small cages.

It's open daily 7 am to 6 pm except Monday in summer, and 7.30 am to 5 pm in winter. Entry fees are Rs 3 for Indian nationals, Rs 20 for foreigners and Rs 20 for car parking (which is worth the money, it's a long walk for the road). The nearest train station is Barang, 2km from the zoo, or there are buses from the old Capital bus stand in Bhubaneswar (Rs 7, two hours).

PURI

☎ 06752 • pop 142,665

The seaside resort of Puri, 60km from Bhubaneswar, is one of the four *dhams* (holiest Hindu pilgrimage places in India). Religious life in the city revolves around the great Jagannath Temple and its famous Rath Yatra, or Car Festival. It is thought that Puri was the hiding place for Buddha's tooth before it was spirited away to Kandy in Sri Lanka. There are similarities between the Rath Yatra and the annual Kandy *perahera* (procession).

Puri's other great attraction has been its long sandy beach. Unfortunately, these days much of it is heavily polluted and decorated with a disgusting array of human excreta, dead sea creatures and fish. However, Puri still draws large numbers of visitors, especially between October and January and, as a result, parts of the beachfront are getting very built up. Whatever the drawbacks, it's a friendly place with a relaxed atmosphere. In fact, many people who visit Puri end up suffering from a local disorder known as 'Puri paralysis'. Once there, they fall into a state of inertia and find it difficult to leave!

Orientation

Grand Rd, a wide highway built to accommodate the hundreds of thousands of pilgrims who come to Puri for the Rath Yatra festival, runs from the Jagannath Temple to the Gundicha Mandir. The Bhubaneswar bus stand is at the eastern end of this road, but the train station is more central. Most hotels are along the seafront, but there are two distinct beach areas – Indians to the west, foreign travellers to the east.

Information

The tourist office (☎ 22664) is on Station Rd and there's a counter at the train station (☎ 23536).

The State Bank of India offers the usual slow service for foreign exchange. The Andhra Bank near the post office handles credit card cash advances.

The Hotel Ghandara (open 8 am to 8 pm daily) changes cash and travellers cheques and will advance cash on credit cards, but charges 3% for the service. South-Eastern Railway Hotel and Trade Wings opposite Z Hotel (open 9 am to 6 pm daily) also change travellers cheques and foreign currency.

Email facilities are found at Harry's Cafe on Chakra Tirtha (CT) Rd (Rs 6 per minute, STD rates).

The Loknath Bookshop on CT Rd is a good place to rent or buy second-hand books.

Opposite the bookshop, a ladies' massage parlour, The Face Beauty Parlour, is open 8.30 am to 9 pm. The proprietor, Kuni, offers a whole range of massage and beauty treatments including Ayurvedic facials for Rs 150 per hour and a full body massage for Rs 200. Shoulder and neck massages only are available for men.

Jagannath Temple

This famous and distinctive temple makes Puri one of the four dhams, or cardinal centres of pilgrimage, the others being Dwarka in Gujarat (west), Badrinath in Uttar Pradesh (north) and Rameswaram in Tamil Nadu (south). Its considerable popularity among Hindus is partly due to the lack of caste distinctions – all are welcome. Well, almost all – Indira Gandhi was barred from entering because she married a non-Hindu.

The temple is dedicated to Jagannath, lord of the universe, who is an incarnation of Vishnu. It was built in its present form in 1198 and is protected by two surrounding walls. The conical tower of the temple is

58m high and is topped by the flag and wheel of Vishnu, visible from far out to sea.

The temple is closed to non-Hindus, but nonbelievers can observe from the roof of the library opposite which is open 9 am to noon and 4 to 8 pm – a 'donation' is compulsory. There's a good collection of ancient palm-leaf manuscripts in the library, but another 'donation' is required to see them.

In front of the main entrance is a beautiful pillar, topped by an image of the Garuda, which originally stood in front of the temple at Konark. Guarded by two stone lions, the entrance is known as the Lion Gate, and is the gate used in the chariot procession. The southern, eastern and northern gates are guarded by statues of men on horseback, tigers and elephants respectively.

In the central *jagamohan*, or assembly hall (see the Orissan Temple Architecture boxed text earlier in this chapter), pilgrims can see the images of Jagannath, his brother

ORISSA

Rath Yatra (Car Festival)

One of India's greatest annual events takes place in Puri each June or July, when the fantastic festival of the cars sets forth from the Jagannath Temple. It commemorates the journey of Krishna from Gokul to Mathura. The images of Jagannath, his brother and his sister are brought out from the temple and dragged in huge 'cars', known as *raths*, down the wide Grand Rd to the Gundicha Mandir (Garden House), over 1km away.

The main car of Jagannath stands 14m high, over 10m sq, and rides on 16 wheels, each over 2m in diameter. It is from these colossal cars that our word 'juggernaut' is derived and, in centuries past, devotees were known to have thrown themselves beneath the wheels of the juggernaut in order to die in the god's sight. To haul the cars takes over 4000 professional car pullers, all employees of the temple. Hundreds of thousands of pilgrims (and tourists) flock from all over India to witness this stupendous scene. The huge and unwieldy cars take an enormous effort to pull, are virtually impossible to turn and, once moving, are nearly unstoppable.

Once they reach the Gundicha Mandir (Garden House, or Aunt's House) at the other end of the road, the gods take a week-long summer break before being reloaded onto the cars and returned to the Jagannath Temple, in a virtual repeat of the previous week's procession. Following the festival, the cars are broken up and used for firewood in the communal kitchens inside the temple, or for funeral-pyre fuel. New cars are constructed each year. At intervals of 8, 11 or 19 years (or combinations of those numbers depending on various astrological occurrences), the gods themselves are also disposed of and new images made. In the past 150 years there have been new images in 1863, 1893, 1931, 1950, 1969, 1977 and 1996. The old ones are buried at a site near the northern gate.

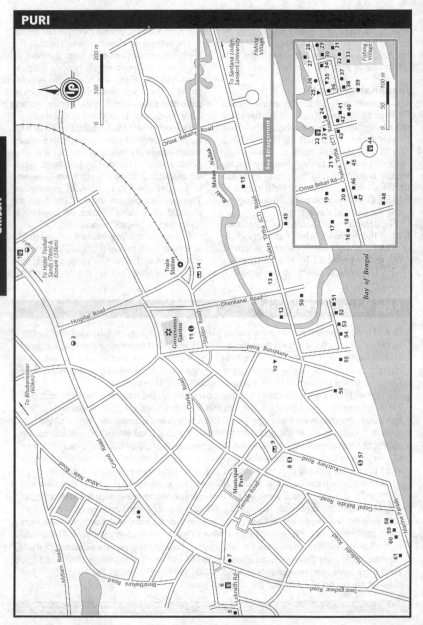

PURI

See Enlargement

To Santana Lodge,
Sanskrit University

Fishing
Village

Orissa Bekari
Road

Bhati Mohan Nullah

Chakra Tirtha (CT) Road

Bay of Bengal

Fishing
Village

Chakra Tirtha (CT) Road

Orissa Bekari Rd

To Hotel Toshali
Sands (7km) &
Konark (33km)

Train
Station

To Bhubaneswar
(60km)

Hospital Road

Dhenkanal Road

Government
Garden

Station Road

Armstrong Road

Clarke Road

Grand Road

Athar Nala Road

Kutchery Road

Municipal
Park

Temple Road

Gopal Ballabh Road

Marine Parade

Hudsahi Road

Bisarbhakura Road

Mithani Road

Loknath Rd

Swargadwar Road

PURI

PLACES TO STAY		46	Hotel Tanuja;		35	Raju's
12	Hotel Sealand		Tanuja Tribe Tours		45	Peace Restaurant
13	South-Eastern Railway Hotel	47	Holiday House			
15	Bay View Hotel	48	Hotel Shankar International		**OTHER**	
16	Hotel Love & Life	49	Hotel Holiday Resort		1	Gundicha Mandir
17	Hotel Dreamland	50	Youth Hostel		2	Bus Station
18	Hotel Ghandara	51	Hotel Samudra		3	Bhubaneswar Bus Stand
19	Hotel Sea 'n Sand	52	Hotel Vijoya International		4	Government Bhang Shop
20	Sun Row Cottages	53	Mayfair Beach Resort		5	Government Bhang Shop
27	Lodge Happy Haunt	54	Hotel Repose		6	Jagannath Temple
28	Hotel Sri Balajee	55	Panthanivas		7	Library
30	Hotel Akash International		Tourist Bungalow		8	Andhra Bank
31	Dalmia Atithi Vihar	56	Hotel Nilachal Ashok		9	Main Post Office
32	Krishna Lodge	58	Puri Hotel		11	Tourist Office
33	Lodge Sagar Saikate	59	Victoria Club		14	Post Office
34	Monali Lodge	60	Panthabhavan		22	Temple
37	Hotel Beach Hut	61	The Seagull		24	Unique Travel
38	Hotel Sapphire International					(Bike Hire)
39	Pink House		**PLACES TO EAT**		26	The Face Beauty Parlour
40	Hotel Nilambu	10	Lee Garden Restaurant		29	Government Bhang Shop
41	Hotel Derby	21	Harry's Cafe		36	Loknath Bookshop
42	Z Hotel	23	Mickey Mouse; Xanadu		44	Temple
43	Travellers' Inn; Tribe Tours	25	The Dolphin		57	State Bank of India

ORISSA

Balbhadra and sister Subhadra. If you're not Hindu, you're not, of course, able to see them but the many stalls outside the temple sell small wooden replicas. The curious images are carved from tree trunks, in a child-like caricature of a human face. The brothers have arms but the smaller Subhadra, does not. All three are garlanded and dressed for ceremonies and the various seasons.

The temple employs 6000 men to perform the temple functions and the complicated rituals involved in caring for the gods. It has been estimated that in all, 20,000 people are dependent on Jagannath for their livelihood and all are classed as the god's attendants – divided into 36 orders and 97 classes!

The best food in Puri is the magnificent *prasaad* cooked and blessed in the Jagannath Temple. You might not be able to enter the temple to get some yourself, but there's no prohibition against partaking of prasaad if someone will go inside and buy it for you.

Gundicha Mandir

The Garden House (also known as the Aunt's House), in which the images of the gods reside for the seven days of Rath Yatra, is off limits to non-Hindus. The walls enclose a garden where the temple is built. Puri has a number of other temples, but most of these are also off limits to non-Hindus.

Beach

Puri has a stretch of dirty sand where Indian pilgrims bathe in their customary fully attired manner. Don't come here expecting a tropical paradise. The beach is very wide and exposed and there's not a scrap of shade to be found.

Orissan fishermen and hotel 'lifeguards', wearing conical straw hats (designed, apparently, to break the surface tension of the water and stop the wearer from being stunned by giant waves and high swell), guide bathers out through the surf. As there have been several reports of drownings, and an eyewitness report of a lifeguard turning back and leaving a person to disappear under the water, they are unlikely to be much help should trouble arise.

Past the travellers' beach to the east is the local fishing village. As with many Indian

Warning

! Currents can be treacherous, so don't go out of your depth unless you're a very strong swimmer. Also, muggings and attacks on women have been reported. The best advice is: do not swim alone, go to the beach on your own or wander close to the fishing village after dusk.

beaches, this one doubles as a public lavatory, automatically flushed twice daily by the sea. Many of Puri's fishing families come from Andhra Pradesh. It's worth getting up before sunrise to watch them head out to sea. For a little baksheesh they may take you with them – one traveller said, 'It was the highlight of my trip witnessing the dawn over the sea'. The crude construction of the boats is unusual – they're made of solid tree trunks and are enormously heavy – buoyancy is achieved purely from the bulk of the wood. Around the fishing village is the worst part, and it really can stink here in the afternoon when the catch is being gutted. A 15 minute walk past the fishing village, will take you to an empty beach which extends for miles.

Organised Tours

Tours operate out of Puri daily, except Monday, to Konark, Pipli, Dhauli, Bhubaneswar, Nandankanan zoo and the Udayagiri and Khandagiri caves. They depart at 6.30 am from the Panthabhavan Hotel at Sea Beach, and return at 6.30 pm (Rs 110). Pick-up can also be arranged from Panthanivas Tourist Bungalow. There's also a daily tour to Chilka Lake (Rs 85, see Chilka Lake, later).

Tribe Tours (☎ 24246, fax 24907), next to the Travellers' Inn, can organise a car and interpreter for visits to adivasis areas in the south of Orissa. Tanuja Tribe Tours, purported to be the first tour company in Purti, is owned and run by the lovely family who run Hotel Tanuja and is recommended, as is Heritage Tours.

Places to Stay

Puri's rickshaw-wallahs are notorious for telling tales about hotels – 'it's closed down', 'it's changed its name', 'it's very expensive' and 'it's full' – so they can take you to the place that pays the best commission. Insist on going to the hotel of your choice and check it out yourself.

Prices quoted are for high season (October to February), but healthy discounts can be negotiated outside this period. Watch for checkout times, some are as early as 7 am!

Although most hotels provide mosquito coils or nets, the mosquitoes in Puri are voracious, so arm yourself with repellent.

It is possible to rent long-term accommodation, but the only way to find places is by word-of-mouth.

The eastern end of the beach is a low-key collection of mostly low-rise properties that straddle CT Rd and spill down onto the beach. The western end resembles a European seaside resort with a fairground, some souvenir and food stalls and lots of big hotels on the inland side of a beach promenade.

Places to Stay – Budget

Most budget hotels are at the eastern end of the beach towards the fishing village, along or off Chakra Tirtha Rd (known as CT Rd). Unless otherwise stated all rates are for rooms with bathroom.

Bay View Hotel, in a scruffy English villa, is quiet and pleasant. Rooms start from Rs 80 (most with bath).

Hotel Dreamland (☎ 24122) is a small, recommended place with singles/doubles for Rs 50/80 and a friendly manager. It's set back from the road in a secluded garden.

Hotel Love & Life (☎ 24433, fax 26093) is friendly, with dorm beds for Rs 35, singles/doubles from Rs 80/100 to Rs 100/215, and cottages for Rs 200/250. There is a small library plus TV and video rental.

Hotel Ghandara (☎ 24623, fax 25909) is more modern. Dorm beds are Rs 30; rooms cost from Rs 110 to Rs 350 or Rs 750 air-con.

Hotel Sea 'n Sand (☎ 23107), nearby, is a clean place with doubles for Rs 150, or Rs 250 with bath.

ORISSA

Sun Row Cottages (☎ 23259), back on CT Rd, has rooms, all with balconies, set well back from the road in a flower-filled garden. Doubles range from Rs 100 to Rs 140, less for long-term stays, and there is 24 hour checkout.

Lodge Happy Haunt (☎ 22355), is a cute place run by good people. It has a spacious but bare courtyard and plenty of undercover parking. Downstairs doubles are Rs 75 to Rs 100. Upstairs, two rooms share a common rooftop terrace and one also has a large balcony (Rs 125 and Rs 250 respectively).

Hotel Sri Balajee (☎ 23388) is a good family-run place back on CT Rd. It's Rs 60/100 for standard singles/doubles, Rs 100/200 with bath, and Rs 350 for a double with a TV, air-cooler and phone. Each room has a verandah with table and chairs. There is an undercover veg restaurant and you can also order food on the roof top terrace. The hotel boasts its own mini-mart, public call office (PCO), library, plus TV, video, car and motorcycle rental. Be very clear about what you're paying, including taxes, before you book in.

Hotel Akash International (☎ 24204) is opposite. Rooms are Rs 150/250.

Krishna Lodge (☎ 24354) is closer to the beach. Bright clean doubles are Rs 80.

Lodge Sagar Saikate (☎ 23253) is an old place right on the beach and looks like a small yellow castle (it was a fortified English villa). It has a great roof area, perfect for undisturbed sunbathing, and big rooms with high ceilings. Singles/doubles are Rs 150/250, or Rs 60/80 with common bath.

Monali Lodge (CT Rd) is a little more expensive. Singles with common/attached bath are Rs 60/150, doubles are Rs 120/200.

Hotel Beach Hut (☎ 25704) on the beach near Pink House, has singles for Rs 100 and doubles from Rs 200 to Rs 350. It has a garden, restaurant, rooftop terrace and beer bar.

Hotel Sapphire International also on the beach, has singles at Rs 70/100 and doubles at Rs 100/200, up to Rs 600 with air-con.

Pink House (☎ 22253) is a popular choice on the beach. Basic rooms cost Rs 150/250, or Rs 40/60 for singles/doubles with a common bath.

Hotel Nilambu is another cheap place on the way up to CT Rd.

Hotel Derby (☎ 23961), close by, has doubles/triples for Rs 200/300. There's a delightful garden and snack bar. Moped and motorcycle hire is also available.

Z Hotel, that's Zed not Zee!, (☎ 22554) is an excellent place popular with travellers. Formerly the palace of a minor maharaja, it's an old, rambling building with large, airy rooms, many of them facing the sea. The management is easy-going, the hotel peaceful and the restaurant serves good seafood. There's a female-only dorm with beds for Rs 50. Singles/doubles with common bath cost Rs 150/250, while huge rooms with bath and balcony are Rs 400. There are plenty of common areas, a lovely garden and a roof terrace for sunbathing.

Travellers' Inn (☎ 23592) is a basic lodge beside Z Hotel. Rooms are Rs 150/200, or Rs 70/100 with common bath.

Hotel Tanuja (☎ 24823) is a discreet family-run hotel with friendly resident Doberman and a pleasant manicured garden. Rooms go for Rs 70/125.

Holiday House (☎ 23782, fax 24363) is immaculate; good doubles (with towels!) from Rs 200 to Rs 300, or Rs 250 to Rs 350 with sea views.

The **Youth Hostel** (☎ 22424) is set in a pleasant garden and is ridiculously cheap. (You can ignore its proximity to the sewage works – they don't smell.) Dormitory beds for members/nonmembers are Rs 20/40. The restaurant is recommended for its excellent Orissan-style *thalis*, but the hostel is governed by the usual strict youth hostel rules including a 10 pm curfew.

Santana Lodge (☎ 23491) is set back from the sea, at the eastern end of CT Rd in the fishing village area known as Pentakota. It's run by a friendly and helpful manager who speaks fluent Japanese. His brother owns the Santana Restaurant in Osaka. Singles/doubles are Rs 40/60 with common bath. Doubles with bath are Rs 100. There's a library with a comprehensive selection of

ORISSA

Japanese-language books. Ask to see the visitors' books which stretch back over 20 years. They have motorcycles and mopeds for hire. The hotel is a Rs 15 to Rs 20 cycle-rickshaw ride from the train station and if the rickshaw-wallahs say they don't know where this hotel is – it's not true!

At the western end of the beach, along Marine Parade, many other hotels patron-ised almost exclusively by Indian pilgrims.

Puri Hotel (☎ 22114, fax 22744) is very popular, with rooms from Rs 150/170. It has 24 hour checkout and a free bus service to the station.

Victoria Club (☎ 22005) has doubles for Rs 200/400 (Indian nationals only).

Places to Stay – Mid-Range & Top End

Hotel Sealand (☎ 23705) is a group of pleasant but rather cramped cottages near the lagoon on CT Rd. Doubles are Rs 450 or Rs 880 with air-con.

South-Eastern Railway Hotel (☎ 22063, fax 23005) is the only heritage hotel in Orissa. Full of old-world character, sin-gles/doubles start from Rs 400/650. More modern air-con rooms start at Rs 650/900 up to Rs 1500. All meals can be included for an extra Rs 200 per person. The hotel has a pleasant lounge, bar, dining room, bil-liards room and an immaculate stretch of lawn. It also offers 24 hour checkout.

Dalmia Atithi Vihar is a pleasant new re-sort on the beach off CT Rd. It has a good vegetarian restaurant and nice gardens. Rooms are Rs 800 and Rs 900 on the 1st floor with views of the beach.

Hotel Shankar International (☎ 23637) is a good beachfront hotel on spacious grounds. Rooms start at Rs 350/450, and huge sea-facing four-bed rooms with a bal-cony are Rs 550. There are six cottages with TV, hot water and fridge, for Rs 700.

The *Hotel Holiday Resort* (☎ 22440, fax 24370) is a big lug of a place. Doubles with balconies overlooking the sea are Rs 550, or Rs 830 with air-con. Cottage 'suites' are Rs 1080. For those with private air transport, there is a helipad!

Hotel Samudra (☎ 22705) is right on the beach; most rooms have a balcony facing the sea and cost from Rs 350. Beware of the 7 am checkout.

Hotel Vijoya International (☎ 22702, fax 22881) is a modern block with double rooms at Rs 500, Rs 900 with air-con.

Mayfair Beach Resort (☎ 24041, fax 24242) is a very upmarket and discreet place set in lush gardens. Comfortable, spacious air-con rooms with terrace start at Rs 1800 and private garden cottages go for Rs 2050. There is a delightful 'Raj' style open restau-rant – all white cane, blue and white linen, hanging plants and a good menu. This place has a pool, but it's only open to guests. The semi-private beach is patrolled and main-tained by the hotel.

Panthanivas Tourist Bungalow (☎ 22562) has an enormous garden with access di-rectly to the beach. Doubles start from Rs 350 or Rs 550 with a sea view.

The adjacent *Hotel Repose* (☎ 23376) has all sea-facing doubles with balconies, costing Rs 350 and Rs 450, or Rs 550 with air-con.

Hotel Nilachal Ashok (☎ 23639, fax 23676) is set in huge grounds adjacent to the Raj Bhavan (Governor's House) on VIP Rd. Pleasant enough, but lacking character in the public areas. Air-con rooms, many newly renovated, range from Rs 1300 to Rs 2000. Barbecues are held in the garden on the beachfront.

Panthabhavan (☎ 23526, Marine Pa-rade), is a rather gloomy converted palace. Doubles are Rs 450.

The Seagull (☎ 23618, Sea Beach, Marine Parade), is a brand new, good-value place with very flexible 'season' rates. Rooms start from Rs 450 to Rs 780.

The *Hotel Toshali Sands* (☎ 22888, fax 23899), 7km from Puri on the road to Konark, is a very secluded 'ethnic village re-sort'. Cottages cost US$33/43. It's a 3km walk through the Balukhand Forest and Tur-tle Reserve to the private beach, but the hotel also has a pool, which nonguests can use for Rs 100. The food is very good, but it's not cheap.

Places to Eat

You can get some excellent seafood in Puri including tuna steaks and occasionally lobster.

Western menus can cause some amusement and occasionally consternation. Look out for 'custrod', 'our special teat', 'water-poached and water-fried eggs', 'wainer snighal', and the warning 'dishes subject to availability of increment'!

Harry's Cafe, *Mickey Mouse* and *Xanadu* cater almost exclusively to travellers. They're all in a group near Z Hotel. They serve western-style dishes – and service is typically very slow.

The Dolphin, which gets the morning sun, and *Raju's* which gets the afternoon sun, are opposite each other at the top end of CT Rd near the fishing village.

Pink House, on the beach, has a popular open-air restaurant recommended for its view. However, there have been reports of ill effects from eating here, so check with other travellers.

Z Hotel is the best of the restaurants in the budget hotels, the food is very good and the surroundings are pleasant.

Peace Restaurant is one of the most popular places to eat. The indoor section is a bit ordinary, but the garden is delightful and makes a good meeting place. The menu is extensive and the food excellent, especially the tuna steaks and fried vegetables. The menu states, 'All good things are worth waiting for'. They are not kidding, the service is abysmally slow. If you are in a hurry, make sure you tell them – it works.

The *South-Eastern Railway Hotel's* set dinners can be good for an evening out. The food is authentically Raj (often including puddings like trifle) and served in style by attentive uniformed waiters. It costs Rs 150 for five courses plus coffee, and you need to make a reservation.

Mayfair Beach Resort's restaurant is good but expensive.

The dining room at the *Hotel Toshali Sands* is very good, but is really only convenient if you are staying there or have transport.

There are also a number of cafes at the western end of the beach, and in the old town there are countless vegetarian places.

Shopping

Being a holy place, Puri is one of those delightfully eccentric Indian towns where the use of ganja is not only legal, but the government provides special bhang shops. The quality, however, is dubious.

There are stalls along the western end of the beach selling crafts, fabric, beads, shells and bamboo work. The eastern end of town has more Kashmiri and Tibetan shops.

Near the Jagannath Temple, on Temple and Swargadwar Rds, there are numerous places selling palm-leaf paintings and engravings, handicrafts and Orissan hand-woven ikat fabric which you can buy in lengths, or as ready-made garments. The Sudarshan Workshop nearby, is where stone masons and sculptors carve religious icons.

The bazaar areas near the main post office sell the usual assortment of 'bizarre' things – clothing, pots and pans, luggage and Puri handicrafts. While most people go home with at least one Jagannath image – carved, sculpted or painted – other popular souvenirs are the palm-leaf paintings and inscriptions and exquisite silk-screen printed postcards which cost only Rs 5.

Getting There & Away

Bus Puri's bus stand is beside the Gundicha Mandir, though some of the private buses depart from around the nearby junction of Grand and Hospital Rds. Minibuses to Bhubaneswar (Rs 15, one hour) are much quicker than the big buses.

Between 6 am and 4.30 pm there are frequent bus departures for Konark (Rs 8, one hour). Early-morning services for Berhampur (Rs 50, 5½ hours) and Taptapani (Rs 75, eight hours), late afternoon departures for Sambalpur (Rs 90, nine hours) and one morning and one afternoon bus to Calcutta.

Train There are two overnight trains each way between Puri and Calcutta (Rs 152/531 in sleeper/1st class, 500km) and three daily departures to Delhi (Rs 369/1490, about 36 hours, 2140km). There are several trains between Puri and Bhubaneswar (Rs 19, two hours) but the buses are quicker.

If you're travelling to or from Chennai (1207km) or other stations in the south, you don't have to go via Bhubaneswar. Khurda Road train station, 44km from Puri, is a convenient junction that all trains pass through. The *Coromandel Express* to Chennai departs at 10 pm and arrives at 5.30 pm the following day (Rs 196/992).

The train booking office is computerised and is open Monday to Saturday 8 am to noon and 12.30 to 3 pm. On Sunday, it's only open in the morning. It's advisable to book ahead during the pilgrim season when trains to Chennai and Calcutta are booked out five to 10 days ahead. For guests, reservations can be made at the South-Eastern Railway Hotel which has its own quotas.

Getting Around

A cycle-rickshaw from the bus stand or train station to the main hotel areas costs around Rs 10 to Rs 15. Buses shuttle between the Jagannath Temple and the bus stand and between the train station and the bus stand for Rs 3.

A good way to get around is by bicycle, and there are several places at the eastern end of the beach where you can rent one for Rs 15 to Rs 20 per day. You can also hire motorcycles. An Enfield Bullet costs Rs 250 to Rs 350 per day, or a less impressive 100cc Rajdoot or Yamaha motorcycle, scooter or moped costs Rs 125 to Rs 200. Unique Travels on CT Rd (☎ 23961, 24246), near Z Hotel, specialises in motorcycle, scooter and bicycle hire. Hotels Derby, Sri Balajee and Santana Lodge also rent motorcycles.

AROUND PURI
Raghurajpur

Famous for its patachitra painting, this artists' village, 10km from Puri, makes an interesting excursion. The paintings are done on cotton cloth that's been coated with a mixture of gum and chalk and then polished before natural colours are applied.

The best way to get to the village is by taxi or bike. From Puri, take the Bhubaneswar road for 9km, almost to Chandipur. Turn right before the bridge, cross the train line, then follow the right fork through the coconut plantation for 1km until you come to Raghurajpur.

Pipli

At the junction of the Konark, Bhubaneswar, Puri roads, 23km from Puri, this small village is notable for its brilliant appliqué craft. The colourful materials are used to make bedspreads, temple umbrellas and wall hangings.

KONARK
☎ 06758 • pop 12,681

Konark consists of little more than the Sun Temple and a handful of stalls, a few places to stay and a tourist office in the Yatri Nivas. Although it's a day trip from Puri or Bhubaneswar, it's also a peaceful place to spend a few days – the temple has more atmosphere once the day-trippers have all gone. There isn't much accommodation, and hopefully never will be. So far all requests for planning permission have been denied on environmental grounds. Konark is protected as a United Nations Educational, Scientific and Cultural Organization (UNESCO) World Heritage Site.

Sun Temple

The great Sun Temple of Konark (also known as Konarak) is 3km from the coast, 36km from Puri and 64km from Bhubaneswar. Konark was constructed in the mid-13th century, but remarkably little is known about its early history. It's thought to have been built by Orissan king Narashimhadev I, to celebrate his military victory over the Muslims. It is believed to have fallen into disuse in the early 17th century after being desecrated by one of Jehangir's envoys.

Originally nearer the coast (the sea has receded), Konark was visible from far out at sea and was known as the 'Black Pagoda' by sailors, in contrast to the whitewashed temples of Puri.

As the temple history is a complicated amalgam of fact and legend, it is worth hiring a guide (about Rs 60 an hour). The stories they tell are fascinating and they can show you features and sculptures which you might otherwise overlook – such as the dancer with high-heeled shoes, a giraffe (the first recorded sighting in India) and even a man treating himself for venereal disease! Be sure the guide is registered; unlicensed guides abound but are unreliable.

The main entrance is guarded by two stone lions crushing elephants. Steps, flanked by straining horses, rise to the main entrance. The jagamohan – or assembly hall – still stands, but the deul (temple sanctuary) behind it, in which the temple deity was kept, has collapsed. The three impressive chlorite images of Surya have been restored to their positions, aligned to catch the sun at dawn, noon and sunset. Between the main steps to the jagamohan and the entrance enclosure is an intricately carved dancing hall. To the north is a group of elephants and to the south a group of horses rearing and trampling men.

The image of the deity which resided here is thought to have been moved to the Jagannath Temple in Puri in the 17th century.

The temple looks particularly impressive in the evening as it is illuminated between 6 and 9 pm.

Nine Planets' Shrine

The 6m chlorite slab, once the architrave above the main entrance of the jagamohan, is now the centrepiece of a small shrine just outside the temple walls. The carved seated figures represent Surya (the sun), Chandra (the moon), Mars, Mercury, Jupiter, Venus, Saturn, Rahu and Ketu.

Archaeological Museum

Outside the temple enclosure is a museum containing many sculptures and carvings found during the temple excavation. It's open 10 am to 5 pm, closed Friday. Some of the small pieces (the statue of Agni, the fire god, for example) are particularly good. For more information, purchase a copy of the Archaeological Survey of India's Konark.

ORISSA

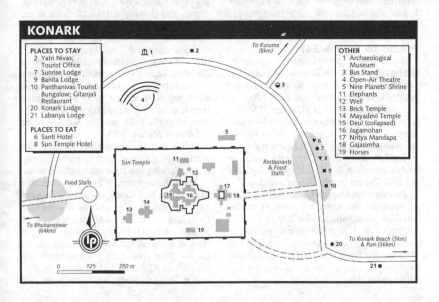

KONARK

PLACES TO STAY
2 Yatri Nivas; Tourist Office
7 Sunrise Lodge
9 Banita Lodge
10 Panthanivas Tourist Bungalow; Gitanjali Restaurant
20 Konark Lodge
21 Labanya Lodge

PLACES TO EAT
6 Santi Hotel
8 Sun Temple Hotel

OTHER
1 Archaeological Museum
3 Bus Stand
4 Open-Air Theatre
5 Nine Planets' Shrine
11 Elephants
12 Well
13 Brick Temple
14 Mayadevi Temple
15 Deul (collapsed)
16 Jagamohan
17 Nritya Mandapa
18 Gajasimha
19 Horses

To Kuruma (8km)

Sun Temple

Food Stalls

Restaurants & Food Stalls

To Bhubaneswar (64km)

To Konark Beach (3km) & Puri (36km)

0   125   250 m

Konark Beach

The sea is 3km from the temple; you can walk there or hire a bicycle (Rs 20 per day from Yatri Nivas) or take a cycle-rickshaw. This part of the beach is much quieter and cleaner than Puri, but beware of the strong current. A number of stalls sell drinks, snacks and souvenirs. If you don't like the tourist atmosphere, you can always move along the beach a bit. In fact, if you have your own transport, stop somewhere along the tea-tree zone approaching Konark and walk across the sand dunes to miles of deserted beach. If you want to be alone, try to conceal your vehicle. If you fail to do so, tourist buses, assuming there is some interesting attraction, will stop and disgorge passengers!

Special Events

An open-air theatre has been built near the Sun Temple and the **Konark Dance Festival** is staged here in early December.

The much bigger **Magha Saptami** (Sun Festival) is held in January/February on the seventh day (saptami) of the bright half of the month of Magha. During this happy festival and fair, pilgrims bathe at the beach before sunrise then proceed to the temple to worship.

Places to Stay & Eat

The cheapest accommodation is just south of the bus stand. The basic *Sunrise Lodge* has doubles with bath from Rs 60. *Banita Lodge*, nearby, is similar with rooms for Rs 70.

Labanya Lodge (☎ 35824, fax 35860) is a friendly, popular place in a quiet location. Singles are Rs 60, doubles Rs 80 or Rs 125 upstairs, and there's a nice roof terrace.

Yatri Nivas (☎ 35820) is government run and quite reasonable. Doubles with bath are Rs 110. The restaurant is best avoided.

Panthanivas Tourist Bungalow (☎ 35831) is opposite the temple's main entrance. Doubles with bath are Rs 200 or Rs 350 with air-con. It's well kept and pleasantly located. Many people taking day trips from Puri use the Bungalow's *Gitanjali Restaurant* for meals; the food is OK, but the service can be slow.

There are numerous *chai shops* outside the temple entrance and a few more down by the beach.

Santi Hotel near Sunrise Lodge has meals for Rs 15 to Rs 35. *Sun Temple Hotel* is similarly priced. Try their chutney, it's delicious.

Getting There & Away

Dilapidated buses and overcrowded minibuses run along the coastal road between Puri and Konark (Rs 8, one hour). There's an early-morning bus from Puri and a late bus back (or on to Bhubaneswar) in the afternoon, which will give you plenty of time to have a look at the temple. As it is a good flat road, some people even cycle the 36km from Puri and stay the night at Konark. John Murray's *Handbook to India* (1953) offers another option, 'The shore route along the beach takes 10-12 hours by bullock cart, by night'. Pass.

CHILKA LAKE

South-west of Puri, Chilka Lake, Asia's largest lagoon, is dotted with islands and is noted for the many migratory birds (including osprey, grey-legged geese, herons, cranes and flamingoes) which flock to the nesting sanctuary in winter. The shallow lake, about 70km long and averaging 15km wide, is separated from the sea by a long, low sand bar. Wildlife abounds on some of the larger islands and surrounding foreshore.

Other than the bird sanctuaries, one of the most popular sites is a small island with a temple dedicated to the goddess Kalijai. Indian pilgrims flock here in January when the **Makar Mela** is held.

Unfortunately, environmental problems such as silting and commercial prawn fishing, are threatening this important wetland area.

There are commercial boat trips available to the main bird sanctuary and for dolphin viewing, and the dolphins can also be seen from the shore. Kayaks/launches can be hired from the OTDC Panthanivas hotels at Barkul, Rambha and Satapada from around Rs 50/350 per hour for a seven-seater. Be warned, as it takes three to four hours to go to the bird sanctuary, negotiate a set rate based on two hours. You can also try to join a boat with a spare seat or talk the fishermen into taking you out.

Places to Stay

Most of the accommodation around the lake is owned by the OTDC, but there are private hotels at Balugaon and Satapada. The lakeside hotels all have a really laid-back, holiday atmosphere.

Senapati Lodge at Balugaon has singles/doubles for Rs 50/70. Coming from the ferry, it is on the right after you cross the main road. Close by, on the main road, is the more upmarket *Hotel Ashok* which has single/double rooms for Rs 150/350.

Barkul Panthanivas (☎ 06756-20488) 6km south of Balugaon, has doubles for Rs 350 or Rs 700 for air-con rooms. The toilet here is remarkable, it must be the most 'commodious' in all India!

Rambha Panthanivas (☎ 06810-87346) in Rambha (130km from Bhubaneswar) is pleasantly located and a friendly place to stay. Doubles with bath and balconies overlooking the lake are Rs 250 or Rs 500 with air-con. There's a good restaurant which serves up crab and prawns from the lake. A launch is available for hire here or the fishermen will take you out for Rs 50 per hour.

Satapada Panthanivas (☎/fax 0674-432177) is a new place on the lake shore at Satapada (50km south of Puri). Doubles with bath, balcony and comfortable, clean beds are only Rs 150. In hot weather, ask for a room with windows on both sides for cross-ventilation. There is a good restaurant which serves seafood.

There's another nice, family-run place just before Panthanivas with rooms for Rs 100.

Getting There & Away

Buses and trains run from Bhubaneswar to Balugaon on the west side of the lake. If you are heading south from Puri, there is no need to return to Bhubaneswar, a local bus goes to Satapada (Rs 12) on the south arm of the lake, where you can catch a ferry to Balugaon. In good weather the trip across the lake takes 3½ hours. Ferries leave Satapada at noon. From the other side, ferries leave Balugaon at 7 am. The trip from Puri to Satapada takes you past peaceful rural scenes, picturesque rice paddies, teeming prawn and fish farms, extensive lagoons and sleepy villages with traditionally decorated Orissan huts.

The main highway and train line run along the inland edge of the lake. There are train stations at Balugaon, Barkul and Rambha.

GOPALPUR-ON-SEA
☎ 0680

Gopalpur is a delightful, peaceful little seaside resort, 18km south-east of Berhampur. The beach is attractive and far less polluted than Puri. There's very little to do but laze around and go for walks – a great place to chill out.

Places to Stay & Eat

Prices vary according to season and demand. Prices quoted below are for the high season (November to January), but you can get hefty discounts out of season and if there aren't many people about.

'Dining out' can be quite an experience, as few places are geared up for itinerant guests. If you don't plan to eat where you are staying, it pays to give the restaurant three to four hours notice. Many kitchens will willingly cook the seafood you can buy fresh in the market or on the beach or, given 24 hours' notice, most kitchens will endeavour to acquire your chosen seafood delicacy for you.

Hotel Sea Side Breeze (☎ 282075), at the far end of Beach Rd, is in a great location right on the beach. It has roomy ground floor doubles facing the ocean for Rs 250 and 1st floor doubles for Rs 350.

Motel Mermaid (☎ 282050), at the same end of the road, is much flashier, but does not have sea views. Single rooms cost from Rs 500 to Rs 550, doubles from Rs 600 to Rs 650, all with balconies, and rates include all meals. Nonguests can eat here with advance notice.

Hotel Sea Pearl on the beach at the corner of the car park was opened at the end of 1997. The spotless doubles with large balconies are Rs 600.

ORISSA

Hotel Kalinga (☎ 282067), by the beach next to Sea Pearl, has a lovely family atmosphere. Doubles, many with views of the sea, are Rs 200/250, all with bath. There's a restaurant here.

Hotel Holiday Home (☎ 282049), on the corner of Beach Rd, has doubles from Rs 250.

Hotel Rosalin (☎ 282071) is opposite the **Seashell** fast-food stand by the beach. Rooms are Rs 80 and or Rs 100 with attached bath (less for long-term stays).

Hotel Song of the Sea (☎ 282347), near the lighthouse, is a quiet place with good views. Doubles with sparkling bathrooms are Rs 600.

Oberoi Palm Beach Hotel (☎ 282021, fax 282300) is a luxurious low-key retreat in a coconut grove right by the sea. It holds a place in history as the first hotel bought (without partners) by MS Oberoi, founder of the famous Oberoi group. It boasts its own fruit and veg garden, a tiny children's 'zoo' (deer, rabbit, birds), jogging track and a semi-private beach with lifesavers. Rooms are from US$110/170 for singles/doubles, including all meals. Delicious à la carte or fixed-priced dining is available to nonguests at reasonable rates.

Hotel Sagar (☎ 282327) on the main road into town has ground floor rooms for Rs 100/150. Upstairs rooms with balcony go for Rs 200, or Rs 400/500 with air-con. There are plans for a large restaurant and swimming pool.

Hotel Rohini (☎ 282309), also on the main road, has rooms for Rs 150 and a good-value tandoor restaurant.

The **Youth Hostel** is down the street beside Rohini's. It's run-down but has beds for Rs 40. **Holiday Inn Lodge** close by has singles/doubles for Rs 60/80 with bath. It's possible to cook your own food here.

Getting There & Away
The only buses from Gopalpur are to Berhampur (Rs 5, 45 minutes) which is on the main Calcutta-Chennai train line. A cycle-rickshaw for the 3km between the train station and the Berhampur bus stand costs Rs 10. From the bus stand there are regular departures to Bhubaneswar (Rs 45, five hours), overnight buses to Jeypur (Rs 100) and regular buses to Taptapani (Rs 12, two hours).

TAPTAPANI
☎ 06814
Apart from the small hot springs in this peaceful place in the hills west of Gopalpur, there's not much else to see. However, for a great winter splurge book one of the two rooms at the **Panthanivas Tourist Bungalow** (☎ 47531), which has hot spring water channelled directly to the vast tubs in its Roman-style bathrooms. Hot-spring doubles cost Rs 650 and standard doubles Rs 350.

Near **Chandragiri**, 36km away, there's a Tibetan refugee community and a temple. The Tibetans support themselves by breeding Tibetan Lhasa Apso dogs and weaving carpets, which you can buy here.

CUTTACK
☎ 0671 • pop 500,915
Only 35km north of Bhubaneswar, on the banks of the Mahanadi, Devi and Kathajuri rivers, Cuttack is one of Orissa's oldest cities and was the capital until 1950. Today it's a chaotic and largely uninteresting place, but the shopping is great. Silk and cotton textiles, horn and brass wares are manufactured here along with the exquisite, delicate silver filigree work for which Cuttack is famous.

For those who enjoy history, the 14th century **Barabati Fort** is here, but only a gateway and the moat remain. The stone retaining wall on the Kathajuri River, which protects the city from seasonal floods, dates from the 11th century. The **Kadam Rasul** in the centre of the city is sacred to Hindus as well as Muslims. The 18th century shrine contains the footprint of the Prophet Mohammad.

Paradip, 90km east of Cuttack, is a major port and minor beach resort.

Places to Stay & Eat
Most visitors to Cuttack just make a day trip from Bhubaneswar, but there are a number of comfortable hotels here.

Pigeon Post

In this age of hi-tech communications, pigeons are, incredibly, still used to great effect by the police force in Orissa. When the British left India in 1947, they left behind a breeding flock of carrier, or homing pigeons. The force now has a stock of over 900 pigeons trained to fly on three courses – static, mobile and boomerang. Messages written on a small sheet of paper are inserted into a cylinder and attached to the pigeon's leg. To increase delivery success rate, usually two birds carrying the same message are released simultaneously.

The Orissa Police has achieved some fantastic results in times of emergency, riots and when dealing with remote regions. There are pigeon post stations in Cuttack, Chatrapur, Kendrapara, Sambalpur and Dhenkanal.

The *Panthanivas Tourist Bungalow* (☎ 621867) in Buxi Bazaar, has doubles for Rs 250 or Rs 400 to Rs 575 with air-con.

Hotel Dwaraka (☎ 622220, fax 624332, BK Rd) has singles for Rs 450, or Rs 900 with air-con. Doubles are Rs 600, or Rs 950 to Rs 1100 with air-con.

Hotel Neeladri (☎ 614221, Mangala Bagh) has singles/doubles from Rs 160/250.

Hotel Akbari Continental (☎ 622342, Haripur Rd) has air-con doubles from Rs 825 to Rs 1400, and there's also a restaurant.

Hotel Ashoka (☎ 613508, College Square), takes credit cards. Singles cost from Rs 200 (Rs 525 with air-con), and doubles from Rs 260 (Rs 625 with air-con).

Bombay Hotel (☎ 613828), also on College Rd, has singles from Rs 180 to Rs 375 and doubles from Rs 250 to Rs 475.

Hotel Adarsh (☎ 619898, fax 617738, Banwararilal Moda Market) is a budget hotel with reasonable facilities. Singles cost Rs 60, doubles are from Rs 100 to Rs 350. *Hotel Puspanjali* in Malgodown has singles/doubles for Rs 60/80.

Getting There & Away

Cuttack is on the main Calcutta-Chennai train line, so there are plenty of interstate and local trains. Buses to Bhubaneswar (Rs 15, one hour) and Puri (Rs 20, three hours) leave regularly throughout the day. There is a morning and afternoon bus to Rajnagar on the outskirts of the Bhitar Kanika Wildlife Sanctuary (Rs 24, four hours) and Sambalpur (Rs 70, seven hours).

Cycle-rickshaws between the train station and bus depot will cost about Rs 15.

LALITGIRI, UDAIGIRI & RATNAGIRI

Buddhist relics and ruins can be found at these three hilltop complexes, north-east of Cuttack about 100km from Bhubaneswar.

A gold casket, thought to contain **relics of the Buddha**, was discovered at Lalitgiri. Excavations are continuing. Udaigiri, 8km away, has its own **monastery complex** and a brick stupa.

The Ratnagiri site, 5km beyond Udaigiri, has the most interesting and extensive **ruins** and is well worth a visit. The two large monasteries here flourished from the 6th to the 12th centuries AD. There are beautifully carved doorways, a large stupa and enormous Buddha figures.

From Cuttack there are buses to Lalitgiri only. Direct travel to Ratnagiri and Udaigiri entails an expensive taxi ride from Cuttack, or a rickshaw from near the Lalitgiri turn off.

The *Panthasala Tourist Bungalow*, in Patharajpur village below the Lalitgiri hill, is the nearest accommodation. Rooms cost Rs 100 and can be booked through the tourist office in Cuttack (☎ 0671-612225).

BHITAR KANIKA WILDLIFE SANCTUARY

This sanctuary on the coast of the Bay of Bengal, between Paradip and Chandipur, was proclaimed largely to protect the nesting habitat of more than one million olive Ridley marine turtles which come to nest near the mouth of the Brahmani River in the Gahirmatha (Marine) Wildlife Sanctuary. Also within its protective environs and extensive waterways is a very successful breeding and conservation program for saltwater crocodiles and an enormous waterbird rookery.

The sanctuary is home to more than 170 recorded species of resident and migratory birds. A large heronry on Bagagaham Island sees the colonial nesting of herons and other waterbirds. The birds start to arrive in early June and nesting finishes in November.

For naturalists, another interesting feature of the sanctuary is the mangroves. Out of 70 species of mangroves found in the world, 62 are represented in Bhitar Kanika.

The wildlife reserve is also the seat of several internationally recognised scientific research projects, protection and conservation schemes.

As yet there is little in the way of facilities. There is accommodation at the *Forest Rest House* in Chandbali, which you can get to from the main highway at Bhadrakh and deep within the sanctuary are other resthouses at Dangmal (suites and dorm) and Gupti (dorm only). Ekakula (suites and dorm) and Habalikhati (dorm) are on the beach in the marine park. Suites are Rs 75/150 for Indian/foreigners; all dorm beds Rs 25.

Most of the attractions and resthouses can only be reached by boat, so advance bookings and permission to enter the sanctuary must be obtained beforehand from the Divisional Forest Officer in Rajnagar (☎ 06729-8460), or from the Conservator of Forests (☎ 0674-515840), Mayur Bhawan, Sahid Nagar, Bhubaneswar, 751004.

Entrance fees for Indians/foreigners are Rs 1/10 per day. A small fee is charged for cameras (and a maximum of Rs 500 for professional video/film). All food and bottled water must be carried into the reserve.

BALASORE & CHANDIPUR
☎ 06782
Balasore is the first major town in north Orissa on the train line from Calcutta. It was once an important trading centre with Dutch, Danish, English and French factories. In 1634 it had the first British East India Company factory in Bengal. **Remina**,

8km away, has the Gopinath Temple, an important pilgrimage centre.

Chandipur, 16km away on the coast, is a beach resort where the beach extends 5km at low tide and the sea can be very shallow. There are several buses a day from Balasore.

As a district headquarters town, Balasore has a number of hotels including *Deepak Lodging*, which is pleasant and reasonably priced. Walk from the train station to the main road, turn left and it's on the right-hand side, two blocks from the corner and across the street from the cinema. *Panthanivas Tourist Bungalow (☎ 72251)*, in Chandipur, has dorm beds for Rs 70 and doubles for Rs 300 (Rs 625 with air-con).

SIMILIPAL NATIONAL PARK
☎ 06792
In the north-east of the state, 250km from Calcutta and 320km from Bhubaneswar, Similipal is one of India's little secrets. It covers 2750 sq km and is part of Project Tiger. The park has abundant wildlife including tigers (around 80), elephants, deer and crocodiles. The scenery is beautiful and varied, with hills, waterfalls and undisturbed forest in which the wildlife manages to remain well hidden. The park is open 1 November to 15 June, but is a bit of a pain to visit. Tourist facilities within the park are not well developed and you must arrange your own transport and bring your own food (which a *chowkidar*, or caretaker, can cook for you).

Orientation & Information
Entrances to the park are at Jashipur on the western side, or more conveniently at Pithibata near Baripada. Your first stop must be the Similipal park office (☎ 06792-52593) at Baripada, to arrange permits and confirm accommodation.

It is essential to stay in the park for early morning and evening animal viewing. You must book in person at least 10 days in advance or in writing not less than 30 days in advance. Applications are made to the Field Director, (☎ 52593), Similipal Tiger Reserve, Baripada 757002, Mayurbhunj District, Orissa. Applications (accompanied by payment) must show your name, sex, nationality, passport and visa numbers, the dates of your visit (three consecutive nights only) and names of the lodges in which you wish to stay. Cash payments can be made at the counter or, for postal reservation, with a bank draft from the State Bank of India, made out to the Field Director, Similipal Tiger Reserve. Foreign currency, travellers cheques and credit cards are not accepted.

Entry permits are obtained from The Assistant Conservator of Forests, National Park, NH-6, Jashipur, 757091 or the Range Officer, Pithabata Check Gate. Entry fees for Indians/foreigners are Rs 10/100 (Rs 5/50 for students). Camera fees (per day) are Rs 20/100 (35mm); Rs 200/1000 (video). Professional film or video camera operators are slugged a whopping Rs 1000/10,000 per day.

Organised Tours

If you want to avoid all the hassles of arranging a visit, the best option is to go on an organised tour. With their contacts and quotas, tour companies can make all the necessary arrangements at short notice, including transport and guide. Tribe Tours (☎ 06752-24246) and Heritage Tours (☎ 06752-23656) in Puri and Swosti Travel, in Bhubaneswar (☎ 0674-508526, fax 520796, email swosti@cal.vsnl.in) which also has branches in Calcutta and Delhi, are all reliable and reasonably priced.

Places to Stay

There are several hotels in Baripada and six Forest Rest Houses dotted around the park. Doubles cost Rs 400 to Rs 800 (50% discount for Indian nationals).

Barheipani, near a 450m waterfall, offers impressive views. *Gudugudia* is good for bird-watching. *Chahala*, a former maharaja's hunting lodge near a salt lick, is brilliant in the evenings. Both *Newana*, which can get pretty cold at night, and *Joranda* are good for wildlife viewing and natural attractions.

Aranya Niwas Tourist Lodge at Lulung, about 10km inside the park (35km from Baripada), is the only lodge not *necessarily* requiring permission. Double rooms (with

solar electricity) cost Rs 400, or there is cheaper dorm accommodation.

Jashipur is accessible by bus (or train and bus via Bangriposhi) from Baripada. *Tourist Lodge* in Jashipur is run by Mr Roy, who charges Rs 80 for a double. You can arrange to hire a jeep (Rs 5.50 per kilometre).

SAMBALPUR
☎ 0663 • pop 1,490,000

In the west, near the border with Madhya Pradesh, is the large town of Sambalpur, famous for its ikat weaving. You can buy fabric, also known as *sambalpuri*, in the main Gole Bazaar and in government cooperative shops.

Only 10km from the town is the 24km-long **Hirakud Dam**. Built to control monsoon floods in the Mahanadi delta around Bhubaneswar, it drains an area twice the size of Sri Lanka and is purported to be the largest artificial lake in Asia.

Sonapur, 80km south, is another textile centre, which also has Tantric temples.

The OTDC maintains tourist offices at the train station and the Panthanivas Tourist Bungalow.

Places to Stay & Eat

Chances are you won't be in Sambalpur for long, but there are a few decent places clustered together on Veer Surendra Sai (VSS) Marg. All have attached bathrooms.

Hotel Sujata (☎ 400403, fax 400662) is a modern hotel with singles/doubles from Rs 150/350.

Hotel Uphar (☎ 21308) is a good place. Singles/doubles are Rs 250/350, or Rs 450 with air-con, although a 20% discount seems to be standard. The restaurant is not great.

Hotel Uphar Palace not to be confused with the above, has rooms from Rs 225 to Rs 450. The restaurant is a little more salubrious.

Panthanivas Tourist Bungalow (☎ 21482) is on top of a small hill at the end of the main street and has good views from some rooms. A double with bath costs Rs 225, and Rs 400 with air-con.

More basic accommodation can be found near the bus stand. *Indhrapuri Guest House*

ORISSA

(☎ 21712) has small rooms for Rs 60 or Rs 90. *Rani Lodge*, about five minutes' walk away on the main street, is similar.

All the major hotels have restaurants serving Indian, Chinese and continental cuisine. For Chinese only try the *Hong Kong Restaurant* and *Hotel Sujata* on VSS Marg.

Central Hotel, opposite the Indhrapuri Guest House, is a good place for cheap meals. *Town Hotel* at Gole Bazaar and *Probhat Hotel* near the municipal council building, are good for typical Indian food.

Getting There & Away
Bus The bus stand is in the centre of town. There are three afternoon buses to Puri (Rs 85, nine hours), but as these arrive quite late, it's better to catch a morning bus for Cuttack (Rs 70, seven hours) and another onwards to Puri.

Deluxe video coaches from the main street (night only) leave for Puri (Rs 100), Bhubaneswar (Rs 110) and Ranipur (Rs 75). The state bus company also has a deluxe night bus to Bhubaneswar (Rs 100). Book in advance at the bus stand.

Train The train station is only about 3km from the town centre, but auto-rickshaws charge Rs 30 to Rs 50. There are direct trains to Bilaspur, Jhansi, Calcutta, Bhubaneswar (17 hours, via Vizianagram in Andhra Pradesh), Delhi and Chennai. Most of these trains also stop at Sambalpur Road train station, which is a little closer to the centre.

OTHER ATTRACTIONS
In the north of Orissa, 50km south-west of Jashipur, **Khiching** was once an ancient capital and has a number of ancient temples (some in ruins) and a small museum. Farther inland is the important industrial city of **Rourkela**. A little north-west of Cuttack is the Shiva temple of **Kapilas**.

Bronze-casting is done in the **Bolangir** area in the west of the state. **Harishankar**, west of Bolangir, has a number of temples and a waterfall. The twin villages of **Ranipur-Jharial** are 30km from Titlagarh and are noted for their extensive collection of temples on a rock outcrop. These include a circular 64-*yogini* temple which, like the one at Khajuraho, once had 64 cells for figures of yoginis who attended to the goddess Kali.

Gupteswar Cave, 85km west of Koraput in Orissa's large southern district, is in an area inhabited by several adivasi groups, including the Bonda people.

Sikkim

For many years, Sikkim was regarded as one of the last Himalayan 'Shangri-las' because of its remoteness, spectacular mountain terrain, varied flora and fauna and ancient Buddhist monasteries. It was never easy to visit and, even now, you need a permit to enter, though this is easy to obtain (see the Tourist & Trekking Permits entry later in this chapter). All the same, access to the northern and eastern parts of Sikkim along the Tibetan border remain restricted, and trekking to the base of Kanchenjunga has to be organised through a recognised travel agency.

Until 1975 Sikkim was an independent kingdom, albeit under a treaty which allowed the Indian government to control Sikkim's foreign affairs and defence. However, following a period of political crises and riots in the capital, Gangtok, India annexed the country and Sikkim became the 22nd Indian state.

The move sparked widespread criticism, but tensions have now cooled. The central government has been spending relatively large sums of money to subsidise Sikkim's road building, electrification, water supply and agricultural and industrial development. Much of this activity was no doubt motivated by India's fear of Chinese military designs on the Himalayan region. Sikkim certainly now seems a more affluent place than neighbouring West Bengal, and being a tax-free zone no doubt helps further.

If you've ever visited Nepal you'll feel on familiar turf here: 75% of the population is Nepali and that's now Sikkim's main language.

History

The country was originally home to the Lepchas, a tribal people thought to have migrated from the hills of Assam, or possibly even from South-East Asia, around the 13th century. The Lepchas were peaceful forest foragers and small-crop cultivators who worshipped nature spirits. They still constitute

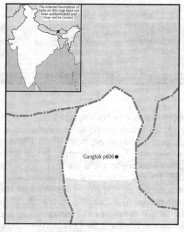

Sikkim at a Glance

Population: 406,457
Area: 7096 sq km
Capital: Gangtok
Main Language: Nepali
Best Time to Go: March to August

The external boundaries of India on this map have not been authenticated and may not be correct.

Gangtok p606

- **Rumtek Gompa** – the monks at this Tibetan Buddhist monastery are very welcoming – join them in a butter tea as they go about their daily business

- **Kanchenjunga** – hike to this, the third highest mountain in the world (8598m)

some 18% of the total population of Sikkim – the Lepcha homeland is the restricted Dzongu region in the centre of the state.

Tibetans began immigrating into Sikkim during the 15th century to escape religious strife between various Buddhist orders. In Tibet itself, the Gelukpa order (of which the Dalai Lama is the head) gradually gained the

Festivals of Sikkim

festival	location	date	features
Bumchu	Tashiding Gompa	Jan	Buddhist festival
Chaam	Enchey Gompa	Jan/Feb	dancing
Kagyat Dance	Gangtok, Pemayangtse & Phodong	monthly	mask dancing
Chaam	Rumtek	Feb/Mar	Buddhist dance
Losar	Pemayangtse & Rumtek	Feb/Mar	Tibetan new year
Tse Chu	Rumtek	May	Buddhist dancing
Saga Dawa	Gangtok	May	Buddha's first teaching
Drukpa Teshi	statewide	Jul	Buddha's first teaching
Phang Lhabsol	statewide	Aug	mask dance
Dasain	statewide	Sep/Oct	gift swapping & animal sacrifice

upper hand. The Nyingmapa order was introduced in Sikkim by three Tibetan lamas, Lhatsun Chempo, Kathok Rikzin Chempo and Ngadak Sempa Chempo. It was these lamas who consecrated the first *chogyal* or king, Phuntsog Namgyal, at Yuksom, which became the capital of the kingdom (it was later moved to Rabdentse, near Pelling). In the face of the waves of Tibetan immigrants (known as Bhutias), the Lepchas retreated to remote regions. A blood brotherhood was eventually forged between their leader, Thekong Tek, and the Bhutia leader, Khye-Bumsa, and spiritual and temporal authority was imposed on the Lepchas.

When the kingdom of Sikkim was founded, the country included the area encompassed by the present state as well as part of eastern Nepal, the Chumbi Valley (Tibet), Ha Valley (Bhutan) and the Terai foothills down to the plains of India, including Darjeeling and Kalimpong.

In 1835, the British, seeking a hill station as a rest and recreation centre for their troops and officials, persuaded the chogyal to cede the Darjeeling area in return for an annual stipend. The Tibetans objected to this transfer of territory. They continued to regard Sikkim as a vassal state, and Darjeel-

ing's rapid growth as a trade centre began to make a considerable impact on the fortunes of Sikkim's leading lamas and merchants.

Tensions rose and, in 1849, a high-ranking British official and a botanist, who were exploring the Lachen regions with the permission of both the Sikkim chogyal and the British government, were arrested. Although the two prisoners were unconditionally released a month later following threats of intervention, the British annexed the entire area between the present Sikkimese border and the Ganges plains and withdrew the chogyal's stipend.

Further British interference in the affairs of this area lead to the declaration of a protectorate over Sikkim in 1861 and the delineation of its borders. The Tibetans, however, continued to regard these actions as illegal and, in 1886, invaded Sikkim to reassert their authority. The attack was repulsed by the British, who sent a punitive military expedition to Lhasa in 1888 in retaliation. The powers of the chogyal were further reduced.

Keen to develop Sikkim, the British encouraged emigration from Nepal, as they had done in Darjeeling, and a considerable amount of land was brought under rice and cardamom cultivation. This influx of labour

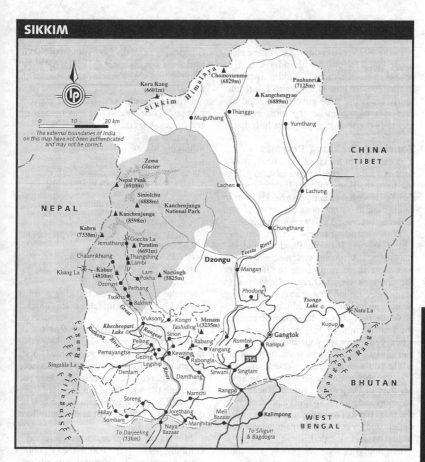

continued right up until the 1960s, when the chogyal was constrained to prohibit further immigration.

The British treaties with Sikkim passed to India at Independence. Demands within Sikkim for a democratic form of government as opposed to rule by the chogyal were growing. The Indian government supported these moves – it didn't want to be seen to be propping up an autocratic regime while doing its best to sweep away the last traces of princely rule in India itself.

The last chogyal, Palden Thondup Namgyal, came to the throne in 1963 and struggled to live up to the revered memory of his father, Tashi Namgyal. The Nepali majority pushed for a greater say in government, and impoverished Nepali farmers began attacking the larger landowning monasteries. The chogyal resisted demands for a change in the method of government until demonstrations threatened to get out of control. He was eventually forced to ask India to take over the country's administration, and his

American-born wife Hope Cook returned to New York.

In the 1975 referendum, 97% of the electorate voted for union with India. China, of course, refuses to accept Sikkim as part of India. The Sikkim Democratic Front currently leads the state government, and has earned a reputation as the most environmentally conscious government in India.

Tourist & Trekking Permits

You can stay in Sikkim for 15 days, with a further 15 day extension available in Gangtok from the Home Office (Tashiling Secretariat). However, re-entry into Sikkim within three months is not possible, even if you leave before your 15-day permit expires.

With a standard tourist permit you may visit Gangtok, Rumtek, Phodong and Pemayangtse. A special endorsement (available from the permit office in Gangtok or the Gangtok Home Office) allows you to visit areas around Pemayangtse, including Khecheopari Lake and Tashiding.

While permits can be obtained through the Indian embassy in your home country when you apply for your Indian visa, they can also be obtained in India itself, either while you wait or within a few hours. It is considerably easier to get a permit in Siliguri than in Darjeeling. You will need your passport and one photo, plus a photocopy of the front page of your passport (with expiry details and so on), and the page where your Indian visa is stamped; there's no charge. When applying for your permit, you must specify your date of entry into Sikkim.

Permits for Tsongo Lake (valid for a day visit only) and Yumthang (in North Sikkim; a nonextendable five day/four night permit) can only be obtained from the permit office in Gangtok, but as you must join a tour (minimum of four) to visit these two places, it's best to let the travel agency sort out the paperwork for you.

The main trekking area in Sikkim is the Dzongri area of West Sikkim, which has put undue pressure on the environment there. New trekking routes in West Sikkim and North Sikkim are opening. Trekking permits are in addition to the normal tourist permit and are issued at the permit office in Gangtok, or from the Government of Sikkim Resident Commissioner in Delhi (see below). Gangtok trekking agencies take care of the formalities.

Permits are checked and your passport stamped when entering or leaving Sikkim, and at Legship and Yuksom.

Permits can be obtained from any of the following places:

Foreigners' Regional Registration Offices
    Delhi, Mumbai, Calcutta & Darjeeling
Resident Commissioner
    (☎ 011-6115346) Government of Sikkim,
    14 Panchsheel Marg, Chanakyapuri, Delhi
Sikkim Tourism Information Centre
    (☎ 033-2499935) 4C Poonam, 5/2 Russel St,
    Calcutta
    (☎ 0353-432646) SNT Bus Compound,
    Tenzing Norgay Rd, Siliguri

For more information on trekking permits, see Trekking in Sikkim later in this chapter.

Kanchenjunga National Park

Access to the heart of Kanchenjunga National Park, including the vast Zemu Glacier, is generally only permitted to mountaineering expeditions or experienced trekking parties using the services of a recognised travel agency. Gangtok travel agencies are best acquainted with the system and usually have the best contacts.

Mountaineering expeditions interested in climbing peaks over 6000m need to obtain clearance at least six months in advance from the Indian Mountaineering Foundation (☎ 011-4671211, fax 688 3412), Benito Juarez Rd, Anand Niketan, Delhi 110021. Many peaks are off limits because they are regarded as sacred; climbers have always stopped short of the very top of Kangchenjunga for this reason.

East Sikkim

Owing to its proximity to the Tibetan border, entry to most of East Sikkim by foreigners is prohibited. However, this region does encompass the capital, Gangtok, which is included on the standard tourist permit. Within the city and its immediate environs are some fascinating places to visit, including Rumtek Gompa, 24km to the west, the head of the Kagyupa order of Tibetan Buddhism.

GANGTOK
☎ 03592 • pop 90,000
The capital of Sikkim, Gangtok (which means 'hilltop'), sprawls down the west side of a long ridge flanking the Ranipul River. The scenery is spectacular and there are excellent views of the entire Kanchenjunga Range from many points in the environs of the city.

Many people expect Gangtok to be a smaller version of Kathmandu. It's not, but it is not a bad place to spend a couple of days. Gangtok only became the capital in the mid-19th century (previous capitals were at Yuksom and Rabdentse) and the town has undergone a rapid and rather unattractive modernisation in recent years.

Gangtok has also become something of a hill station resort for holidaying Bengalis. The influx peaks during the 10-day Durga Puja holiday period at the end of September or early October, when Bengalis converge on the town en masse to enjoy the fresh air and cheap booze. It's a good time to give Gangtok a miss, as prices rise – especially for accommodation and local transport – and finding a room at *any* price can be a major headache.

Orientation
To the north is Enchey Gompa and the telecommunications tower. The palace of the former chogyal and the impressive Royal Chapel (the Tsuk-La-Khang) are lower down along the ridge. Nearby is the huge Tashiling Secretariat complex, and below it, the relatively recently built Legislative Assembly, both executed in a traditional architectural style.

On a continuation of this ridge but much lower is the Namgyal Institute of Tibetology, an Orchid Sanctuary and, not far beyond the institute, a large *chörten* (Tibetan stupa) and adjoining gompa.

All the main facilities – hotels, cafes, bazaars, bus stand, post office, tourist office and the Foreigners' Registration Office – are either on, or very near, the main Darjeeling road (National Highway 31A).

Information
Tourist Office The helpful tourist office (☎ 22064) is at the top (north) end of MG Marg. In high season it's open daily, including holidays, 9 am to 7 pm. Between June and August it's open Monday to Saturday 10 am to 4 pm.

Money There's nowhere to cash Visa travellers cheques, but most other brands can be exchanged at the State Bank of India near the tourist office.

Post & Communications The main post office is open Monday to Saturday. Faxes and telephone calls can be made from any number of telephone offices around town. At the time of research email access wasn't really possible because the only link was via radio, and thus exceedingly slow.

Permits Trekking permits for West Sikkim (ie north of Yuksom) can be obtained from the permit office in the same building as the tourist office. It's open Monday to Saturday 10 am to 4 pm. To visit Tsongo Lake or North Sikkim, you need to be in a group of four and book a package through a travel agency; which will arrange permits. Apply for extensions at the Home Office, Government of Sikkim, Tashiling Secretariat.

For more information on permits for Sikkim, see the Tourist & Trekking Permits section earlier in this chapter.

Tours Local tours operate on a point system – points referring to sites of interest around Gangtok. A seven point sightseeing trip taking in Enchey and Rumtek gompas, and the Namgyal Institute of Tibetology, among other places, takes four to five hours and costs Rs 150. Half-day tours also cover

GANGTOK

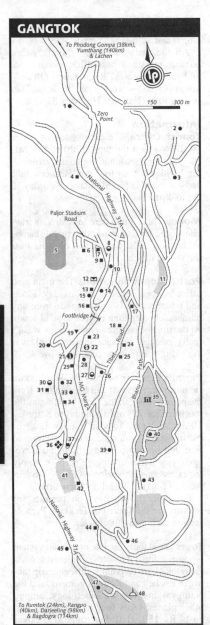

GANGTOK

PLACES TO STAY

4	Hotel Superview Himalchuli; Yak & Yeti Travels
6	Nor-Khill Hotel
7	Hotel Mount View
9	Hotel Lakhar
13	Hotel Tibet
16	Blue Heaven Lodge
17	Netuk House
18	Hotel Sonam Delek
23	Gangtok Lodge; New Kho-Chi Restaurant
24	Modern Central Lodge
25	Hotel Lhakpa
29	Green Hotel
31	Sunny Guest House
34	Hotel Orchid
37	Denzong Inn
42	Hotel Tashi Delek
44	Pine Ridge Hotel

PLACE TO EAT

19	Metro Fast Food

OTHER

1	Cottage Industries Emporium
2	Telecommunications Tower
3	Enchey Gompa
5	Stadium
8	SNT Bus Stand
10	Yoksum Tours & Travels
11	Ridge Park; Flower Exhibition Centre; White Hall
12	Main Post Office; Telegraph Office
14	Siniolchu; Potala Tours & Travels
15	Tibetan Curio Store
20	Sikkim Tours & Travels
21	Tourist Office; Permit Office
22	State Bank of India
26	Indian Airlines
27	Children's Park Taxi Stand
28	Chiranjilal Lalchand Dispensary
30	Private Bus & Taxi Stands
32	Tashila Tours & Travels
33	Rural Artisans' Marketing Centre
35	Palace
36	Super Market Complex; Sikkim Trekking & Travel Services; Mahayana Tours & Travels; Kikis Garden Restaurant
38	Lall Market Taxi Stand
39	Foreigners' Registration Office
40	Tsuk-La-Khang (Royal Chapel)
41	Lall Market
43	Tashiling Secretariat Complex (Home Office)
45	Forest Secretariat
46	Legislative Assembly
47	Namgyal Institute of Tibetology; Orchid Sanctuary
48	Cörten & Gompa

SIKKIM

Rumtek but don't give you much time, and you'd be better off doing this yourself.

Emergency Useful emergency contacts include the police (☎ 22033) and the hospital (☎ 22944).

Namgyal Institute of Tibetology
Established in 1958 and built in traditional style, this unique institute promotes research into Mahayana Buddhism and the language and traditions of Tibet. It has one of the world's largest collections of books and rare manuscripts on Mahayana Buddhism, many religious works of art and a collection of beautiful, finely embroidered silk *thangkas* (Tibetan cloth religious paintings). There are also relics of monks from the time of Ashoka, examples of Lepcha script, masks, and ceremonial and sacred objects, such as the *kapali*, a bowl made from a human skull, and a *varku*, a flute made from a thigh bone.

The institute sells a number of religious art and craft works and books on Tibetan Buddhism. The person who runs the publications shop is very interesting to talk to.

It's open Monday to Friday and every second Saturday 10 am to 4 pm; entry is Rs 2. This is a sacred place, and footwear should be removed before entering.

Orchid Sanctuaries
Surrounding the institute, and itself enclosed by a peaceful forest, is the **Orchid Sanctuary**, where you can see many of the 454 species of orchid found in Sikkim. The best times to visit the sanctuary are March to early May and the end of September to the beginning of December.

There is another, much larger, orchid sanctuary, called the **Orchidarium**, off the main road to Rangpo alongside the Rani Khola, a tributary of the Teesta. It is accessible by public bus and is also usually included on tours to Rumtek Gompa.

On top of the ridge, near White Hall, is a **Flower Exhibition Centre**, featuring orchids, seasonal flowers and bonsai. It's open April to June and September until late November, 10 am to 6 pm daily; entry is Rs 2.

Chörten & Gompa
The gold apex of this huge white chörten, surrounded by prayer flags, is visible from many points in Gangtok. Next to the chörten, about 500m beyond the Namgyal Institute, is a gompa for young lamas with a shrine containing huge images of Padmasambhava and his manifestation, Guru Snang-Sid Zilzon. As at other Buddhist gompas, the chörten is surrounded by prayer wheels.

Tsuk-La-Khang
The Tsuk-La-Khang, or Royal Chapel, is the Buddhists' principal place of worship and assembly, and the repository of a large collection of scriptures. It's a beautiful and impressive building, and its interior is covered with murals. Lavishly decorated altars hold images of the Buddha, Bodhisattvas and Tantric deities, and there are also a great many fine woodcarvings. The only time it's definitely open to visitors is during Losar, the Tibetan New Year – which usually falls in February (6 February 2000) – when the famous dance portraying the triumph of good over evil is performed. It's also worth asking at the gate whether you can see the building.

Enchey Gompa
Near the telecommunications tower, about 2km from the centre of town, Enchey Monastery is worth a visit, particularly if you're in Gangtok when religious dances are performed in January or February (18th and 19th days of the 12th Tibetan month). In 2000 the festival falls around 23 January.

Built in 1909, it's a relatively small place and not as impressive as other monasteries in Sikkim, but it does sit on a spectacular ridge overlooking Gangtok, and there are views across to Kanchenjunga. It is home to about 100 monks from the Nyingmapa order.

Trekking Outfits & Tour Operators
You'll need the services of a recognised tour operator and at least four people in your trekking party if you want to travel to North Sikkim or do the Dzongri trek (Kanchenjunga). Operators in Gangtok charge between

US$25 and US$60 per person per day, and also offer bird watching tours, gompa tours, and white-water rafting. Equipment hire (sleeping bags etc) is available from some operators.

Mahayana Tours & Travels
(☎ 23885, fax 22707 attention 'Mahayana') Room 23, Super Market Complex – offers a range of treks, including gompa treks and an eight day rhododendron trek from Yuksom to Bakhim, Dzongri, Phodong and Tsokha.

Potala Tours & Travels
(☎ 22041) Paljor Stadium Rd – offers the usual range of treks at attractive prices.

Sikkim Tours & Travels
(☎ 22188, fax 22707 attention 'Sikkim Tours') Church Rd, near the private bus stand – Lukendra (Luke) here is a keen photographer, and can also organise tailor-made photography and bird-watching tours.

Sikkim Trekking & Travel Services
(☎ 23638, fax 22707 attention 'Sikkim Trekking') Room No 1, Super Market Complex – not the cheapest, but it's very professional and was the first outfit established in Sikkim; can also organise visits to Bhutan and the North-Eastern Region.

Siniolchu Tours & Travels
(☎ 24457, fax 22707 attention 'Siniolchu') Paljor Stadium Rd – also offers a wide range of tours, including a four-day cultural tour of the gompas of Sikkim – US$120 per person with accommodation in tents.

Tashila Tours & Travels
(☎ 23546, fax 22155) National Highway 31A, opposite the private bus stand – managed by Alok Raj Pradhan, who can also arrange special-interest tours such as high-altitude rhododendron and primula tours (the primulas are at their best in May and June).

Vajra Adventure Tours
(☎ 22446, fax 22707 attention 'Vajra') Kyitsel House, Arithang Rd, Gangtok – mid-range, good quality outfit, with skilled guides and their own lodge and camp sites on the Goecha La trek.

Yak & Yeti Travels
(☎ 22714, fax 24643) Hotel Superview Himalchuli, NH 31A, Zero point – good value and run by the enthusiastic Satish Bardewa, who also has mountaineering experience.

Yoksum Tours & Travels
(☎ 23473, fax 22707 attention 'Yoksum') National Highway 31A – organises treks to West Sikkim and tours to North Sikkim.

Places to Stay

In the winter it's important to inquire about hot water and heating. A bucket of hot water for showering is available at most places (sometimes for a small extra charge), but heating is a rarity. Where an electric heater is available it will definitely cost you more. Few places have single rooms, and there's often no discount for single occupancy of a double room. Top-end hotels add a 10% service charge.

Ask about low-season discounts. They vary between 15 and 30%, usually around January to March, and in July and August.

Places to Stay – Budget

Hotel Lhakpa (☎ 23002, Tibet Rd) above MG Marg, has very basic four-bed rooms with common bath for Rs 350, doubles with bath for Rs 300, and with geyser, Rs 400. There's a little bar downstairs with a good sound system.

Modern Central Lodge (☎ 24670, Tibet Rd) is popular but some travellers have reported that the management can be belligerent at times (around cocktail hour!). Normally they are very helpful. There is a very useful travellers' comment book, plus free maps with handy transport information. Dorm beds are Rs 30, singles are Rs 60, doubles with toilet are Rs 80 (these rooms are a little dark) or Rs 100 with good views. With bath, rooms cost from Rs 100/120 to Rs 180/200, the most expensive rooms having the best views and geysers in the bathrooms. There's a TV room, snooker room, restaurant, and roof terrace.

Green Hotel (☎ 23354) is on MG Marg, by the tourist office. There's a range of rooms, from Rs 120/150 with bath and hot water in buckets to Rs 200/250 for rooms with bath and geyser. The cheaper rooms are in the old block, and some are a little dark. There's a popular bar and restaurant.

Hotel Lakhar (☎ 22198) is right opposite the SNT bus stand. Rooms with common bath cost Rs 100/200 and doubles with bath and geyser are Rs 300. This is a pleasant place, run by a friendly Tibetan couple, with basic, but spotless rooms.

Blue Heaven Lodge (☎ 23827, Paljor Stadium Rd) is clean and friendly. All rooms have bathroom and constant hot water. Some rooms even have 'honeymoon' beds (just standard double beds but something of a rarity here). Rooms are from Rs 150/200 to Rs 275/350 – the more expensive ones come with a view.

Sunny Guest House (☎ 22179) is at the private bus stand. Doubles with common bath are Rs 300; doubles with bath are Rs 400 and Rs 500, the latter with a balcony and good views.

Hotel Orchid (☎ 23151) on the highway near the private bus stand is another reasonable, basic option, although the manager could be more cheerful. Singles/doubles with shared bath are Rs 100/200, Doubles with bath are Rs 300, four-bed rooms with bathroom are Rs 400.

Places to Stay – Mid-Range
Most mid-range places add an additional 10% service charge to the bill.

Gangtok Lodge (☎ 24670), diagonally opposite the tourist office on MG Marg, is friendly and central. Doubles are Rs 450 with bath (cold water, but there's a geyser in the common bathroom), or with a view, Rs 500. Good discounts are offered in the low season.

Pine Ridge Hotel (☎ 24958), near the Legislative Assembly, is run by the owners of Modern Central Lodge. All rooms have bathrooms and cost Rs 325/450, Rs 525 for a deluxe double. It's a good place but the cheaper rooms are quite small.

Hotel Sonam Delek (☎ 22566, Tibet Rd), is pleasant. Doubles with common bath are Rs 500 to Rs 800 (with possibly the best views you'll get in Gangtok). A 40% discount is offered in the low season, and there's a good restaurant here.

Hotel Superview Himalchuli (☎ 22714) is a pleasant hotel with excellent views and very helpful staff. It's set just out of the main part of town towards Zero Point, in a less congested and more pleasant area. Doubles/triples with bath are Rs 675/775, and there's also dormitory accommodation for Rs 75. There are good low-season discounts,

a groovy Sixties-style bar, a garden restaurant, and a telescope for mountain viewing. Yak & Yeti Travels have their office here.

Hotel Mount View (☎ 23647, Paljor Stadium Rd) has doubles from Rs 400 to Rs 900. All are well appointed, and have baths with 24 hour hot water, and colour TVs.

Denzong Inn (☎ 22692) is in the Denzong Cinema complex, just outside Lall Market. Rooms with bath and geyser are Rs 400/600, and there's an enormous suite for Rs 2000 which could comfortably accommodate four people. The cheaper rooms are nothing special, but some open onto a roof terrace with great Kanchenjunga views.

Places to Stay – Top End
Hotel Tashi Delek (☎ 22991, fax 22362) is centrally located on MG Marg. The tiny ornate doorway opens onto an opulent lobby with Tibetan woodcarving and *objets d'art*. Singles/doubles are Rs 2000/2100, double suites are Rs 4000; add Rs 700 to include all meals included. The double deluxe suites have great mountain views; the less-expensive rooms are comfortable, but the views are of the grimy walls of neighbouring hotels. There's a nice terrace restaurant with great views of Kanchenjunga.

Hotel Tibet (☎ 22523, fax 22707) is a popular choice. You'll be welcomed by a doorman in full traditional Tibetan dress. Rooms range from Rs 760/1020 to Rs 1760/2350. There's 24 hour room service, foreign exchange facilities, a travel desk and a small bookshop with books on Tibetan issues. The cheaper rooms are on the road side, and are rather small, as are the mid-range rooms on the valley side. The more expensive rooms are very plush, with traditional Tibetan decor.

Netuk House (☎ 22374, fax 24802) is the home of an old Sikkimese family, the Denzongpas, and part of the 'Heritage Houses of the Himalayas' association. It is comfortable, quiet and there are fine views from the terrace. Rates are Rs 1650/2700 with all meals.

Nor-Khill Hotel (☎ 25637, fax 23187), above the stadium, was once the royal guesthouse. It's now a beautiful hotel with

SIKKIM

singles/doubles for Rs 4500/3500 including all meals. There's a travel desk, gift shop and foreign exchange, and the hotel is set in attractive gardens.

Places to Eat

Most of the hotels in Gangtok have their own restaurants and some of them are very good.

Modern Central Lodge, *Hotel Lhakpa*, *Hotel Lakhar* and *Green Hotel* have restaurants which are popular with travellers. All offer cheap and tasty meals in a variety of cuisines – usually Tibetan, Chinese and Indian – with some western alternatives such as pancakes. Chicken fried rice will set you back about Rs 25 at these places, *tsampa* (Tibetan staple of roast barley flour) is around Rs 15.

Oyster Restaurant, at the Hotel Sonam Delek, is a bit more upmarket. There are continental favourites such as French toast and banana pancakes, as well as Chinese, Indian and Tibetan cuisine.

New Kho-Chi Restaurant & Bar is in a handy location beneath the Gangtok Lodge on MG Marg. There's an extensive Chinese and Indian menu, most dishes under Rs 50.

Metro Fast Food is a cheap South Indian snack bar opposite Gangtok Lodge.

Kikis Garden Restaurant is on the top floor of the Super Market complex. During high season there's a buffet here featuring Sikkimese cuisine.

Blue Poppy Restaurant is at the Hotel Tashi Delek. They do good Sikkimese cuisine but it must be ordered 12 hours in advance. Veg dishes start at Rs 50, and non-veg dishes are around Rs 100. The terrace restaurant is a nice place to relax over lunch.

Snow Lion Restaurant, at the Hotel Tibet, is expensive and the servings aren't very big but the atmosphere compensates. There's Tibetan cuisine, some Japanese and seafood dishes and good Indian food from their tandoor.

There are numerous seedy little bars with refreshingly cheap prices after West Bengal. A beer is about Rs 30. Full-moon and new-moon days are 'dry' days in Sikkim. Try *chang* from a shop in the market – a large bamboo mug full of fermenting millet.

Shopping

The Cottage Industries Emporium specialises in hand-woven carpets, blankets, shawls, Lepcha weaves, patterned decorative paper and Choktse tables, exquisitely carved in relief. It's open daily during the high season; in the low season, it's open daily except Sunday and every second Saturday, 9 am to 3.30 pm. There are numerous other shops selling Tibetan handicrafts.

Getting There & Away

Air Bagdogra near Siliguri is the nearest airport. Indian Airlines (☎ 23099) has an agency on Tibet Rd.

Bus Sikkim Nationalised Transport (SNT) is the main bus operator to Gangtok, and they have plenty of services from their well-organised bus stand on Paljor Stadium Rd. Book as far in advance as possible, particularly during the Durga Puja holiday period. The booking office is open 9 am to noon and 1 to 2 pm.

There are daily buses to Siliguri (Rs 47, five hours), Darjeeling (Rs 83, seven hours) Kalimpong (Rs 50, three hours), and Bagdogra (Rs 60, 4½ hours).

In addition to the SNT buses, there are private buses which run from the private bus stand (adjacent to Sunny Guest House) to Siliguri, Darjeeling and Kalimpong. To Siliguri there are at least 10 buses daily (mostly in the afternoon), and to Darjeeling and Kalimpong at least two daily. They cost much the same as the SNT buses, and should be booked in advance at the private bus stand.

SNT buses for destinations within Sikkim leave for Gezing (for Pemayangtse) at 7 am (Rs 52, 4½ hours) – buses travel via Singtam, Rablongla, Kewzing and Legship (for connections to Tashiding and Yuksom); Rumtek at 4 pm (Rs 15, 1½ hours); Phodong at 8 am, 9 am and 4 pm (Rs 20, 2½ hours); and Jorethang at 2 pm (Rs 40, four hours).

Train There's a train reservation counter at the SNT bus stand on Paljor Stadium Rd, but it has only a meagre allocation of tickets.

Taxi & Jeep Share jeeps are a faster alternative to buses, which may not make you feel any safer on the mountain roads.

At the private bus stand you can get share jeeps to Siliguri (Rs 80, 3½ hours), Darjeeling (Rs 90, four hours) and Kalimpong (Rs 80, 2½ hours).

From Children's Park taxi stand, jeeps leave for destinations in West Sikkim such as Jorethang (Rs 55, three hours), Gezing (Rs 90, 5½ hours) and on to Pelling (Rs 120, six hours from Gangtok); and in North Sikkim to Phodong (Rs 35, two hours).

From Lall Market, you can get share jeeps to Rumtek and Tsongo Lake. During the high season, share jeeps for Rumtek leave when full between 2 and 4 pm (Rs 25, one hour), and return between 6 am and 4 pm. In the low season, they leave between 11 am and 3 pm, and return between 6 and 8 am. Share jeeps for Tsongo Lake leave in the high season only at 9 am and 2 pm (Rs 150, two hours), and return between noon and 2 pm.

Getting Around

The new city bus service, bitterly opposed by the taxi-wallahs, should now be running along National Highway 31A.

All the taxis are new or near-new Maruti vans. Rs 50 will get you just about anywhere around town. To Rumtek you're looking at about Rs 400 return, including about an hour at the gompa.

AROUND GANGTOK
Rumtek Gompa
☎ 03592

Rumtek, on the other side of the Ranipul Valley, is visible from Gangtok though it's 24km away by road. This huge and wealthy monastery is the seat of the Gyalwa Karmapa, the head of the Kagyupa order of Tibetan Buddhism. The order was founded in the 11th century by Lama Marpa, the disciple of the Indian guru Naropa, and later split into several subsects, the most important of which are Drukpa, Kagyupa and Karmapa. Since 1992 there has been a bitter and sometimes violent dispute over the successor to the 16th Gyalwa Karmapa who died in 1981, with the factions led by two Rumtek abbots, Samar Rinpoche and Situ Rinpoche. The Dalai Lama chose Situ Rinpoche after performing the Kalachakra (Wheel of Time) ceremony in 1993, however they're still struggling for power. There are police stationed at Rumtek to keep the situation under control.

The main monastery is a recent structure, built by the 16th Gyalwa Karmapa in strict accordance with the traditional designs of his monastery in Tibet. Visitors are welcome and there's no objection to you sitting in on the prayer and chanting sessions. They'll even bring you a cup of salted butter tea when it's served to the monks. The mural work here is not as refined as some of Sikkim's older gompas. Behind the main monastery is the lavishly decorated Nalanda Institute of Buddhist Studies. In the building opposite the entrance to the institute is a small hall featuring a beautiful jewel-studded chörten, which contains the ashes and bones of the 16th Gyalwa Karmapa.

The *chaam*, or religious dance, known as Tse Chu, is performed on the 10th day of the fifth lunar month (May), and depicts events in Guru Rinpoche's life. A chaam, presenting the battle between good and evil, takes place two days before the Tibetan New Year (around late February/early March).

Much activity takes place in late afternoon, but the gompa is open for visitors 8 am to 5 pm in summer, and 10 am to 5 pm in winter.

If you follow the tarmac road for 3km beyond Rumtek you'll find another interesting, but smaller, monastery which was restored in 1983. Opposite is an old and run-down monastery with leather prayer wheels.

Places to Stay & Eat The *Sangay Hotel*, 100m down the motor road from the monastery, is a friendly little place. It's basic but clean, and blankets are provided. Rooms cost Rs 75/150 with common bath and hot water by the bucket. Cheap and basic meals are available.

Hotel Kunga Delek, where there are small but clean doubles with bath and hot water are Rs 150, is opposite the main entrance.

Martam Resort (☎ *23314*) is 5km from Rumtek, in the village of Martam. Rooms cost Rs 1650/2700 with all meals. It's in a beautiful location in the middle of a paddy field, and staff here can arrange horse riding and treks in the surrounding area.

Getting There & Away There are buses and share jeeps to Rumtek from Gangtok. See Getting There & Away in the Gangtok section for details. If you feel like a bit of exercise, it's a very pleasant 12km hike (downhill) to the National Highway, from where it's easy to get a ride for the 12km (uphill!) trip to Gangtok.

Tsongo Lake

Foreigners have recently been permitted to visit this lake (also known as Changu Lake), which is 35km north-east of Gangtok; technically you should be in a group of four, and need to join a tour (US$12). Permits are valid for a day visit only. Numerous agencies in Gangtok offer tours to the lake, and can arrange the requisite permit.

North Sikkim

Previously foreigners were only permitted to travel as far north as Phodong, 38km by road to the north of Gangtok and accessible on the standard tourist permit. However, it is now possible to visit Yumthang, 102km farther north via the villages of Mangan and Chungthang. It is necessary to make arrangements through a travel agency in Gangtok and join a tour with a minimum of four people, costing US$45 per day. During the monsoon the roads are often cut off by landslides.

PHODONG

Phodong Gompa, north of Gangtok along a winding but largely tarmac road, belongs to the same order (Kagyupa) as Rumtek, but is much smaller and less ornate than that gompa. After the 16th Karmapa fled from Tibet and before he established himself in Rumtek in 1959, Phodong was the most im-

portant of Sikkim's three Kagyupa gompas (the third is Ralang Gompa). The gompa sits high up above the main road to Mangan and there are tremendous views down into the valley below.

Phodong is a fairly recent structure, although the original gompa here was founded, like Rumtek, in 1740. The gompa has a community of about 60 monks, many of them born in India after the Chinese occupation of Tibet. They're very friendly and are happy to show you around.

Opposite the gompa is a small community of nuns who belong to the same order. **Labrang Gompa**, 4km farther uphill beyond Phodong Gompa, was established in 1844, and belongs to the Nyingmapa order. Beware of leeches when walking up here.

Places to Stay & Eat

The village of Phodong straddles the main Gangtok to Mangan road, and is about 1km north of the turn-off to the gompas towards Mangan. There are a couple of basic places to stay here.

Yak & Yeti Lodge has clean rooms with common bath for Rs 80/120, and doubles with bath for Rs 150.

Northway Lodge has doubles with common bath for Rs 120, some with good views, and you can also get basic meals here.

Getting There & Away

See Getting There & Away in the Gangtok section for details of local buses and taxis to Phodong.

YUMTHANG VALLEY

The Yumthang Valley lies 140km north of Gangtok, at an elevation of 3564m. This region has recently been opened to foreigners, but trekking is still prohibited. The best time to visit is in April and May, when the rhododendrons are in full bloom. There are **hot springs**, covered by a wooden shelter. To get here, you'll need to join a tour and the travel agency will arrange the permit. The road from Gangtok follows the Teesta River, crossing a spectacular **gorge** over the Rang Rang suspension bridge.

West Sikkim

This area of Sikkim is attracting more and more visitors. Its main attractions, other than trekking up to Dzongri at the base of Kanchenjunga, are the two old monasteries of Pemayangtse and Tashiding, and hikes in the Pemayangtse area.

JORETHANG
☎ 03595

Set in the forested Rangeet Valley, the pleasant market town of Jorethang lies 30km north of Darjeeling. Across the river in West Bengal is Naya Bazaar.

Hotel Rangeet Valley (☎ 57263) opposite the bus stand, has rooms with bath, nets and fans for Rs 130.

Hotel Namgyal, just past the bus stand towards the bridge, is the best place to stay. Singles/doubles/triples with bath are Rs 150/300/450, and are spotless.

From Jorethang, there are direct buses to Yuksom at 8 and 9.30 am (Rs 30, three hours), and to Legship at 11.30 am and 4.30 pm (one hour), continuing through to Gezing (Rs 19, 2½ hours). There are share jeeps to Darjeeling (Rs 60, three hours), Gangtok (three hours), Siliguri (3½ hours), Gezing (2½ hours) and Legship (one hour).

LEGSHIP

Legship lies 100km west of Gangtok, and 27km north of Jorethang, on the banks of the Rangeet River. It's a chaotic place on a major road junction but it has a certain ramshackle appeal, with the colourful produce of fruit and vegie sellers piled in pyramids in wooden shacks flanking the main road. There's a police checkpoint where passports are stamped. The *Hotel Trishna* near the main intersection has rooms with bath and geyser for Rs 200/250.

GEZING
☎ 03595

The road from Legship leaves the river and ascends high up above the village for 15km to Gezing. On Friday, villagers from outlying regions bring their produce into town and a colourful and busy market dominates the main square. Travellers cheques can be exchanged at the Central Bank of India, down a lane behind the town square.

Places to Stay

There are half a dozen hotels around the town square, all very basic. The *Hotel Attri (☎ 50602)* is the best, uphill from the main square with the police station on the ground floor. Rooms cost Rs 450 with bath and constant hot water, and there are good views from the roof terrace.

Getting There & Away

There are SNT buses to Gangtok at 9 am and 1 pm (Rs 48, 4½ hours); and to Pelling (Rs 6, 30 minutes) at 8.30 am, 1 and 2 pm (many more buses on Friday). To Yuksom, buses leave at 1 and 2 pm (Rs 25, four hours); there are also buses to Tashiding, Jorethang and Siliguri. To get to Kalimpong, change buses at either Meli Bazaar or Teesta Bazaar; for Darjeeling change at Jorethang.

There are numerous share jeeps to Pelling (Rs 15), and also to Gangtok via Jorethang or Rablongla (both Rs 90, 4½ hours). There is one share jeep daily for Tashiding and Yuksom (Rs 60). A taxi from the town square will charge Rs 150 to Pelling.

PELLING
☎ 03593

Pelling is perched high on a ridge, 2.5km from Pemayangtse Gompa, and is rapidly developing into a Bengali hill resort. There are great views north to Kanchenjunga and also to the south when the weather is clear. The town has a post office, but no foreign exchange facilities. In Lower Pelling, the Cottage Industries Training Centre sells pullovers, hats and scarves.

Things to See & Do

Standing at a height of 2085m and framed on two sides by snowcapped mountains, Pemayangtse (Perfect Sublime Lotus) is one of the state's oldest and most important gompas. It has been reconstructed several times and belongs to the Nyingmapa order, which was established by Padmasambhava in the 8th century. All the order's monasteries are characterised by a prominent image of this teacher, together with two female consorts, and this monastery is the head of all others in Sikkim. You can recognise followers of the order by their red caps.

The monastery is a three storey structure filled with wall paintings and sculptures. On the third floor you'll find **Zandog palri**, an amazing seven-tiered painted wooden model of the abode of Guru Rinpoche, complete with rainbows, angels and the whole panoply of Buddhas and Bodhisattvas on the third floor. The model was built single-handedly by the late Dungzin Rinpoche in five years.

In February each year the chaam, or masked dance, is performed by the monks. The exact dates are the 28th and 29th days of the 12th lunar month.

You can walk here from Pelling in about 40 minutes. SNT buses between Gezing and Pelling pass by the turn-off for Pemayangtse, from where it's a 10 minute walk.

It's excellent hiking territory around here – despite the leeches!

A 45 minute walk west from Pelling through the forest (go left across the open, flat 'helipad' to find the track) brings you to **Sangachoeling Gompa**. The monastery pre-dates Pemayangtse by some 10 years and is the second oldest in Sikkim, and has a magical position high on a ridge. As at Pemayangtse, the interior walls are highly decorated with paintings.

The **ruins** of Rabdentse, Sikkim's second capital, are easy to get lost in but it's an interesting place to explore. Walk about 6km along the road to Legship, turn left and walk across an archery field. At the far end of the field is the start of a 2km winding track through the forest, passing through a small set of ruins and eventually on to the ruins of the palace, with chörtens nearby. It's fairly easy to find your way down from here downhill to the Legship to Pelling road.

Farther afield are the **Sangay Waterfalls**, about 10km from Pelling along the road to Dentam.

Places to Stay & Eat

There is a lot of building going on in Pelling. Lower Pelling has many new hotels, though some of them prefer only large Indian groups.

Ladakh Guesthouse, close to the Hotel Garuda towards the helipad, is a rustic Sikkimese house with five rooms, all sharing the bathroom (with geyser). Doubles/triples are 250/350.

Hotel Garuda (☎ 50614) is in the centre where the buses stop. It's a popular travellers haunt with excellent trekking information. You can also store excess gear here while you trek. Dorm beds cost Rs 80, or there are basic rooms for Rs 100/200 with common bath, doubles with bath for Rs 400. It can get noisy. The food is cheap and occasionally tasty but the service is memorably inept.

Hotel View Point (☎ 50614) is a more modern, well-run hotel in a quiet location on the right side of the helipad in Upper Pelling. Doubles/triples with bath and geyser cost Rs 300/450.

Hotel Kabur (☎ 50685), in Upper Pelling towards Pemayangtse, is a bit overpriced but the family are friendly. Doubles/triples are Rs 550/600 with bath. There's also a slightly pricey restaurant here.

Sikkim Tourist Centre (☎ 50788) is a good mid-range hotel that's popular with tour groups. The rooms (all doubles) have hot bath and cost Rs 500 (Rs 600 with a view). There's a good restaurant on the top floor and they can organise tours around Sikkim

Hotel Mt Pandim (☎ 50756), known locally as the tourist lodge, is 2km outside Pelling, at the foot of the road leading up to Pemayangtse. It's a hulking, slightly run-down place run by Sikkim Tourism with a vaguely Soviet-era atmosphere. At least the views from the garden are superb. Rooms with bath cost Rs 550/650 or Rs 750/850 for deluxe rooms with a view of Kanchenjunga. There's also a restaurant.

Getting There & Away

Although a number of buses pass through Pelling, the choice is far greater from Gezing. It's a 50 minute steep downhill walk to Gezing.

Jeeps leave for Gangtok at 6 am and noon (Rs 100) and for Siliguri at 6 am (Rs 100). Tickets should be booked the day before at the *paan* stall between the Sikkim Tourist Centre and the Hotel Garuda. To charter a taxi to Khecheopari Lake and Yuksom costs Rs 650 and 700 respectively.

There are numerous share jeeps down to Gezing on market day (Friday) in the morning (Rs 15).

KHECHEOPARI LAKE

Pronounced 'catch a perry', and sometimes spelt Khechepari, Khecheopalri or Khech-upherei, this place is a popular objective for trekkers. The sacred lake lies in a depression surrounded by prayer flags and forested hills. Resist the temptation to swim, as it's a holy place. If you feel like a dip, you can swim in the river downhill from Pelling en route to the lake. Take care!

By the lakeshore is the small Lepcha village of Tsojo, and about 1.5km above the lake is the Khecheopari Gompa.

There is a *trekkers' hut* and a *Rest House* at the lake. The trekkers' hut is grimy and dark – not very salubrious. A bed at the Rest House will cost around Rs 80. There are several *chai* (tea) shops at the lake. It gets very cold here at night, so bring warm gear with you.

By road the lake is about 27km from Pelling; the hiking trail is shorter, but much steeper, and will take about 4½ hours. See Trekking in Sikkim later in this chapter for details.

From Khecheopari it is possible to continue on foot to Yuksom. The short cut is confusing, so ask for advice whenever you meet anyone en route. It should take three hours to get between the lake and Yuksom.

There's one bus daily between Pelling and Khecheopari, leaving Pelling at 3 pm (two hours), and returning at 7 am.

TASHIDING

The friendly little town of Tashiding is becoming popular with trekkers. Technically you should have your permit endorsed in Gangtok to come here but there's currently no checkpoint.

Tashiding Gompa

Founded around 1716, Tashiding Monastery is perched atop a conical hill between the Rangeet and Rathong rivers, a 45 minute slog on foot from Tashiding Village. In Sikkim, only Pemayangtse Monastery is more sacred. The Bumchu festival is held here on the 15th day of the first Tibetan month (during January).

Places to Stay & Eat

Blue Bird Hotel is a simple but welcoming little place with rooms for Rs 40 and good *dhal bhat* in the restaurant.

Hotel Laxmi also has a restaurant and rooms for Rs 50/100.

Siniolchu Guest House charges Rs 100 for a good room. Meals are served with the family.

Getting There & Away

There is one bus daily to Yuksom (3 pm), and it passes through at 8 am in the morning on the return journey to Legship and Gezing. Share jeeps that pass through Tashiding are often full.

YUKSOM

Yuksom (also spelt Yoksum and Yuksam), 35km by road from Pemayangtse, is the farthest north you can get by road in West Sikkim and is the trailhead for those intending to trek to Dzongri. It's a very peaceful village surrounded by cardamom plantations on a wide shelf above the valley of the Rathong. It was here that the three lamas of the Nyingmapa order arrived to establish Buddhism in Sikkim; the coronation of the first chogyal of Sikkim took place here. The stone throne is next to a big chörten in a small hall not far from the Hotel Tashi Gang.

Dubdi Gompa, an hour's walk uphill from Yuksom, was the first capital of Sikkim, and was where the first monarch of Sikkim was crowned in 1641. It's worth a visit (if you can brave the leeches), but there are no monks here and it's only opened during special Buddhist festivals. The police check permits at the start of the Dzongri to Goecha La trek, so don't try setting off without one. See Trekking in Sikkim for details.

Places to Stay & Eat

Hotel Arpan has a few singles and doubles for Rs 80/100, and serves basic meals. It's about 800m from the centre of town on the main road, near the school.

Hotel Wild Orchid has clean rooms for Rs 75/100.

Hotel Dzongrila has basic rooms for Rs 50/100, as well as good food, beer and chang. It's run by a friendly family who speak English.

Hotel Demazong is a clean, well-run place with dorm beds for Rs 60, doubles with shared bath for Rs 200, and doubles with bath and geyser for Rs 400.

There are also two *trekkers huts* and a *Forest Rest House*, which must be booked in Gangtok.

Hotel Tashi Gang is Yuksom's only up-market hotel, in an unmissable location on a hill. The charming timber-floored rooms have fine views. Singles/doubles/suites cost Rs 500/700/1200. There's also a good restaurant and a pleasant garden terrace where a bottle of Dansberg beer costs Rs 50.

Getting There & Away

There is one bus daily (at 7 am) to Gezing (Rs 22) via Tashiding and Legship and also share jeeps to Gezing and Jorethang leaving at 6.30 am for Rs 50.

TREKKING
Pelling-Legship Circuit Trek

Linking some interesting villages together in West Sikkim it's possible to do a four day trek. You don't need a trekking permit for this but you should get your Sikkim permit endorsed in Gangtok to allow you to visit the area around Pemayangtse, including Khecheopari Lake and Tashiding Gompa.

The first stage takes you to the lake. For the second stage, if you go via a short cut to Yuksom it takes only three hours, heading downhill for the first stage, and then for the last two hours, ascending gradually to Yuksom. From Yuksom to Tashiding you can follow the road, taking some of the obvious short cuts. Then it's an easy one hour walk along the road to Legship. Bring snacks as there's not much on offer along the way, and check with locals and other travellers for the best short cuts.

Stage 1	Pelling to Khecheopari	4 hours
Stage 2	Khecheopari to Yuksom	3 hours
Stage 3	Yuksom to Tashiding	6 hours
Stage 4	Tashiding to Legship	1 hour

Yuksom-Dzongri-Goecha La Trek

The most popular trek in Sikkim is from Yuksom to Dzongri and Goecha La has superb views of Kanchenjunga. To undertake this trek you must get together a group of at least four people and make arrangements through a recognised travel agency in Gangtok; they'll arrange your trekking permit. They usually charge from US$25 to US$60 per person per day, including food, yaks and porters. Make sure everyone is clear about exactly what will be provided – particularly the food. At overnight stops there are trekkers' huts which are the best bet if it's cold. At the height of the season there's not enough space in the huts and your trekking company will need to provide tents. Whatever the option it is imperative not to trek too high too quickly. See the Health section in the Facts for the Visitor chapter for advice about preventing and treating altitude sickness.

From Yuksom (1630m) the trail follows the Rathong Valley through unspoilt forests to Baktim (2740m) where there's a *forest rest house*. From Baktim there is a steep ascent to the village of Tsokha (3050m), where a couple of *lodges* provide overnight accommodation. Above Tsokha the trail enters magnificent rhododendron forests to an intermediary camp at Pethang (3760m). It's a wise idea to either bring tents and spend a night here or spend two nights at Tsokha to acclimatise. A further stage brings you to Dzongri (4025m) where there are *trekkers' huts*. From Dablakang, 200m above Dzongri there are excellent mountain views. You should spend two nights at Dzongri to acclimatise; walk up to Dzongri La (4 hours return, 4415m) for great views of Kabru and Dome.

From Dzongri the trail drops steeply down to the river where there's a new *trekkers' hut*; you follow the river to Thangshing (3840m) where there's another *trekkers' hut*. The final stop is at the *trekkers' hut* at Samiti Lake (4200m) from which an early morning assault is made up to the head-spinning

Goecha La (4940m) for the best views of Kanchenjunga. Then it's down to Thangshing for the night and back to Yuksom two days later.

Stage 1	Yuksom to Tsokha	7 hours
Stage 2	Tsokha to Pethang	3 hours
Stage 3	Acclimatisation Day	
Stage 4	Pethang to Dzongri	2-3 hours
Stage 5	Acclimatisation Day	
Stage 6	Dzongri to Samiti Lake	7 hours
Stage 7	Samiti Lake to Goecha La	
	& down to Thangshing	9-10 hours
Stage 8	Thangshing to Tsokha	6-7 hours

North-Eastern Region

The North-Eastern Region is the most varied yet the least visited part of India. Before Independence this beautiful area of rolling forested hills and lush green fields was known as Assam province, but it has since been gradually broken up into seven separate states. Nowadays Assam consists mostly of the plains around the Brahmaputra and Barak rivers, while the other states (excluding Tripura) occupy the hills.

The north-east is the country's chief tribal area, with many different languages and dialects – in Arunachal Pradesh alone over 50 distinct languages are spoken! These tribal people have many similarities to the hill tribes, who live across an arc that stretches from the eastern end of the Himalaya through Myanmar (Burma) and Thailand into Laos.

Mizoram, Meghalaya and Nagaland are the only states with a Christian majority.

India has always been touchy about the north-east, although the permit requirement for foreign tourists visiting Assam, Meghalaya and Tripura was lifted in 1995. Encompassing a sensitive border zone where India meets Bhutan, China, Myanmar and Bangladesh, the region is remote – only the narrow Siliguri corridor connects it to the rest of India; before Independence the route to Assam would have been through Bangladesh. Today, it involves making a long loop north and then east.

As well as the perceived threat from their neighbours, some of the states in the North-Eastern Region have been wreaked by insurgencies and ethnic violence. The reasons for this unrest include a feeling of neglect from the central government (poor transport links and lack of industrial development were the main complaints). Very little of the oil wealth from Assam, for example, found its way back for the state's industrial development. The whole region remains overwhelmingly agricultural.

But economic neglect and exploitation was only a minor issue. The main issue was

North-Eastern Region at a Glance

ASSAM	**TRIPURA**
Pop: 26 million	**Pop:** 3.1 million
Area: 78,438 sq km	**Area:** 10,486 sq km
Capital: Dispur	**Capital:** Agartala
MANIPUR	**NAGALAND**
Pop: 2 million	**Pop:** 1.4 million
Area: 22,327 sq km	**Area:** 16,579 sq km
Capital: Imphal	**Capital:** Kohima
MEGHALAYA	**MIZORAM**
Pop: 2 million	**Pop:** 820,000
Area: 22,429 sq km	**Area:** 21,081 sq km
Capital: Shillong	**Capital:** Aizawl

ARUNACHAL PRADESH
Pop: 950,000
Area: 83,743 sq km
Capital: Itanagar

- **Majuli** – Vaishnavaite monasteries on the world's biggest river island
- **Shillong** – pseudo Scottish hill station

Festivals of the North-Eastern Region

festival	location	date	features
Ambuchi Festival	Guwahati	Jul	end of earth's menstrual cycle
Karchi Puja	Old Agartala	Jul	Hindu festival
Diwala	Udaipur	Oct/Nov	large fair

about the inflow of 'foreigners' into the region. The poverty in crowded Bangladesh and the oppression of that country's Hindu minority has created a never-ending flow of Bangladeshis to the north-east. This has been so great that, in the case of Tripura, the immigrants have overwhelmed the tribal population. There has also been a significant migration of Nepalis to the hill states.

Matters have been complicated by the demands of various ethnic minorities within the states. In Assam, for example, the Bodos are demanding a homeland separate from the rest of the state. In Manipur, there is bitter fighting between rival tribes, especially the Kukis and Nagas. In some states, like Tripura, insurgency has simply become a way of life, with good money to be made from kidnapping and extortion. Several hundred local people die each year in the north-east as a result of the troubles; and the situation does not seem to be improving.

Permits

Permits are no longer required for Assam, Meghalaya or Tripura, but check with locals to establish whether it's safe to go.

For the other four states – Arunachal Pradesh, Mizoram, Manipur and Nagaland – foreigners must travel in a group of four tourists on a tour arranged through an approved travel agent, and obtain a Restricted

Warning

Because of terrorist activity in the region, you are strongly advised to check the current situation before visiting this area.

Area Permit from the Foreigners' Regional Registration Offices in Chennai (Madras), Delhi, Mumbai (Bombay) and Calcutta, or from the following state government offices.

Arunachal Pradesh
(☎ 011-301 3915) Arunachal Bhawan, Kautilya Marg, Chanakyapuri, New Delhi
(☎ 033-248 6500) Arunachal Bhawan, 4B Chowringee Place, Calcutta
Manipur
(☎ 011-301 3009) Manipur Bhawan, 2 Sardar Patel Marg, Chanakyapuri, New Delhi
(☎ 033-350 4412) Manipur Bhawan, 25 Ashutosh Shastri Rd, Calcutta
Mizoram
(☎ 011-301 5951) Mizoram Bhawan, Circular Rd, Chanakyapuri, New Delhi
(☎ 033-247 7034) Mizoram House, 4 Old Ballygunge Rd, Calcutta
Nagaland
(☎ 011-379 3019) Nagaland House, 29 Aurangzeb Rd, New Delhi
(☎ 033-242 5247) Nagaland House, 13 Shakespeare Sarani, Calcutta

Permits for foreigners are valid for 10 days, and you need separate permits for each state.

If your patience knows no bounds and you want to try your luck at getting into these states without going through a travel agent, you'll either need a very good excuse for visiting (eg a relative buried in the war graves in Kohima) or friends in high places. Permits can be applied for at any overseas Indian consular office, or at the Ministry of Home Affairs, Foreigners' Division, Lok Nayak Bhavan, Khan Market, New Delhi 110003, where you can expect a bureaucratic nightmare. Apply at least a month in advance, and be prepared for several visits and many hours spent in the waiting room.

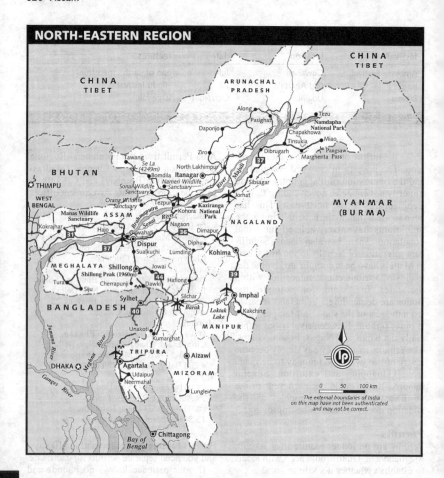

NORTH-EASTERN REGION

The external boundaries of India on this map have not been authenticated and may not be correct.

It's worth contacting someone at the state tourist offices for advice before applying; a letter from them or from the state representatives will raise your chances.

Even in the states that are now wide open to tourists, red tape is alive and well. When arriving by plane, you'll be checked in (and out) by the police at the airport. Not only do hotels have to lodge the usual 'C' form with police stations but they also have to make photocopies of the information pages of your passport.

Assam

The largest and most accessible of the north-east states, Assam grows 60% of India's tea and produces a large proportion of India's oil. The main attraction is Kaziranga National Park, home of India's rare one-horned rhinoceros.

History

Early Assamese history includes some semi-mythical Hindu rulers such as the great

Narakasura, mentioned in the *Mahabharata*, who ruled from Pragjyotishpura (modern-day Guwahati). Branches of Hinduism based on *shakti* (power) worship and mystic-erotic Tantric cults are though to have emerged in Assam and these traditions continue at temples such as Kamakhya in Guwahati today.

The Chinese traveller Hiuen Tsang visited the court of King Bhaskar Barman, an ally of the Gupta dynasty, in 640. In the 13th century, the Ahoms, a Shan tribe from Myanmar (Burma), conquered Assam, adopted Hinduism and established a dynasty which lasted until 1826 and repulsed some 17 invasion by the Mughals, allowing Assam's Hindu culture to blossom in relative peace. The dynasty reached its peak under Rudra Singha (1696-1714), who built trade links with Tibet and won renown as a military strategist. During the late 16th century, the philosopher-saint Sankardeva began a Vaishnavite movement which rejected the Hindu caste system and the rituals of Tantric Hinduism. Instead a Hinduism based on community prayer, was spread by *satras* or monasteries which became centres for arts such as dance, manuscript painting and music. The monks also played a major role in reclaiming the wetlands of the Brahmaputra valley for rice cultivation.

The Ahom dynasty gradually decayed until a Burmese invasion in 1817 which lasted five years and killed one in every three people finished it off. The British drove out the Burmese and annexed the Ahom kingdom.

The British developed the tea industry, but found the locals unwilling to be labourers, and so by 1900 there were hundreds of thousands of tribal people from Bihar and Orissa (the `tea tribes' of today) contracted to work on the plantations.

In the lead-up to Independence it took delicate manoeuvring, and the separation of the Muslim-majority Sylhet district to join East Pakistan to keep Assam in India. After Independence the old rivalries between hill and plain, Hindu and Muslim, tribal and non-tribal rose and Assam gradually separated into the seven states of today.

For the last 20 years Assam has been subject to the militant actions of a number of groups. The United Liberation Front of Asom (ULFA) is pledged to the independence of Assam through armed struggle. Its military wing enjoyed a great deal of initial success and kept the Indian army on the run for many years, operating from bases deep in the jungle and Bangladesh. Unwilling to countenance the loss of Assam, the Indian government was finally forced to mount a series of massive military operations to flush out the guerrillas. The much publicised Operation Rhino, in 1991, had some success, but in the following years the ULFA regrouped and the bombings, kidnappings and killings have continued.

While the ULFA demands an independent Assam, the Bodo ethnic minority has been campaigning for a state stretching along the border with Bhutan. There are now several Bodo groups, the most militant being the Bodo Liberation Tiger Force (BLTF) and the National Democratic Front of Bodoland (NDFB), which often fight among themselves. Since 1993 about 300 non-Bodos have been killed by the militants. The BLTF has bombed bridges and trains around Kokrajhar.

The national government's Unified Command counter insurgency operation is now in operation, and the army has a high profile. Although the rebels tend to operate in isolated rural areas, you are strongly advised to check on the current situation before visiting Assam.

GUWAHATI (Gauhati)
☎ 0361 • pop 580,000

Beside the impressively wide Brahmaputra River, fast-growing Guwahati is Assam's biggest city. The state government is based in the drab outlying town of Dispur, about 8km away. Once known as Pragjyotishpura (the Eastern City of Light) and mentioned in the *Mahabharata*, Guwahati has long been the region's most important city. It's now the service centre for the oil industry and tea plantations; the world's largest tea auctions are held here.

Guwahati has some pleasant neighbourhoods but there is tension, mostly between the Assamese and the Bangladeshi immigrants. There are numerous ancient Hindu temples in and around the town and a fine zoo, but its main importance is as the gateway to the North-Eastern Region.

Orientation

Guwahati is split into two towns on either side of the river, with most places of interest and offices in the southern section, simply known as Guwahati (the northern section is North Guwahati).

Most long-distance buses leave from busy Paltan Bazaar, just south of the train station. The busiest shopping areas are Fancy Bazaar and Pan Bazaar, both about 1km west of the train station. The area north of the railway lines is the more pleasant part of town.

Information

The Assam Tourism's office (☎ 544475), at the Tourist Lodge on Station Rd, is open

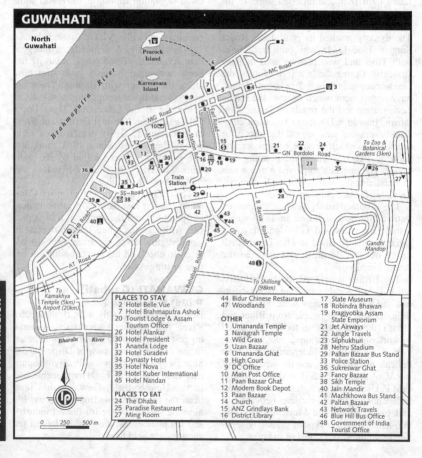

GUWAHATI

North Guwahati

Peacock Island

Karmanasa Island

Brahmaputra River

MC Road

MG Road

East Road

Station Rd

MN Road

NN Road

To Zoo & Botanical Gardens (3km)

GN Bordoloi Road

Train Station

SS Road

JB Road

AT Road

B Barua Road

Rehabari Road

GS Road

Gandhi Mandop

To Kamakhya Temple (5km) & Airport (20km)

Bharalu River

To Shillong (98km)

LP

0   250   500 m

PLACES TO STAY
2 Hotel Belle Vue
7 Hotel Brahmaputra Ashok
20 Tourist Lodge & Assam Tourism Office
26 Hotel Alankar
30 Hotel President
31 Ananda Lodge
32 Hotel Suradevi
34 Dynasty Hotel
35 Hotel Nova
39 Hotel Kuber International
45 Hotel Nandan

PLACES TO EAT
24 The Dhaba
25 Paradise Restaurant
27 Ming Room

44 Bidur Chinese Restaurant
47 Woodlands

OTHER
1 Umananda Temple
3 Navagrah Temple
5 Uzan Bazaar
6 Umananda Ghat
8 High Court
9 DC Office
10 Main Post Office
11 Paan Bazaar Ghat
12 Modern Book Depot
13 Paan Bazaar
14 Church
15 ANZ Grindlays Bank
16 District Library

17 State Museum
18 Robindra Bhawan
19 Pragjyotika Assam State Emporium
21 Jet Airways
22 Jungle Travels
23 Silphukhri
28 Nehru Stadium
29 Paltan Bazaar Bus Stand
33 Police Station
36 Sukreswar Ghat
37 Fancy Bazaar
38 Sikh Temple
40 Jain Mandir
41 Machkhowa Bus Stand
42 Paltan Bazaar
43 Network Travels
46 Blue Hill Bus Office
48 Government of India Tourist Office

Monday to Friday 10 am to 5 pm, and Saturday until 1 pm. There's also a Government of India tourist office (☎ 547407) on BK Kakoti Rd. Meghalaya Tourism has a little office at the bus station.

Assam Tourism runs a city tour on Wednesday and Sunday from 9 am to 3 pm; tickets cost Rs 70.

ANZ Grindlays Bank on GN Bordoloi Rd is a good place to change money, but the foreign exchange rates usually don't arrive until 11 am (sometimes later). It's open Monday to Friday 10 am to 3 pm. The foreign exchange office at the Hotel Brahmaputra Ashok is another option.

It may be possible to send email from the Hotel Brahmaputra Ashok.

Network Travels (☎ 512700), GS Rd, books and runs tours in the region. Jungle Travels (☎ 547862, fax 540630), GN Bordoloi Rd, is the American Express agent; it has package trips to Kaziranga. Destination North East (☎ 511565, fax 540376), Dighalipukhuri (East) and also runs package trips to Kaziranga, Meghalaya and Arunachal Pradesh. Wild Grass (☎ 546827, fax 541186), Baruah Bhawan, 107 MC Rd, is helpful and knowledgeable and runs an excellent resort at Kaziranga, plus tours to neighbouring states.

Modern Book Depot, HB Rd, has a good range of books on the North-Eastern region.

Guwahati Medical College Hospital (☎ 562159) is 5km south, off GS Rd.

Umananda Temple

The most interesting thing about this Shiva temple is its location, on Peacock Island in the middle of the river. Ferries usually leave Umananda Ghat from 7 am to 5 pm. A return trip is Rs 8, although the departure point changes with the height of the river.

Navagrah Temple

On Chitrachal Hill to the east of the town, Navagrah Temple (Temple of the Nine Planets) has long been known as a centre of astrology and astronomy. The nine planets are represented by nine linga inside the main temple.

Kamakhya Temple

Guwahati's best-known temple is the Kamakhya Temple on Nilachal Hill, 8km west of the city. It is the centre for Shakti worship and Tantric Hinduism because it's believed that when Shiva sorrowfully carried away the corpse of his first wife, Shakti, her body disintegrated and her *yoni* (vagina) fell here.

Rebuilt in 1665, after being destroyed by Muslim invaders, the temple's origins are much older than that. It was probably an ancient Khasi sacrificial site, and daily goat sacrifices are still very much part of worship here.

It attracts pilgrims from all over India, especially during the Ambuchi Festival, a celebration of the end of the earth's menstrual cycle, which usually falls around June or July.

Leave your shoes at the entrance. Non-Hindus are usually allowed into the inner sanctum, but no photographs are permitted. Inside it's dark and quite eerie, and the floor is sticky with the blood of sacrificial goats.

You can get here by taking bus No 15 from Paltan Bazaar in the town centre.

Assam State Museum

This archaeological, ethnographic and natural history museum has recently been enlarged and is well worth a visit. Particularly interesting are the dioramas of Assamese tribal villages – in one you walk right through the reconstructed huts. There are also good displays of weavings, musical instruments and an impressive sculpture gallery.

The museum is open Tuesday to Sunday, from 10 am to 4.15 pm (5 pm in summer). It's closed on Sunday afternoon and the second and fourth Saturday of each month. Entry is Rs 2.

Assam State Zoo & Botanical Gardens

The zoo and botanical gardens are about 5km east of the train station. The zoo is spacious and well managed, and has tigers, leopards, and, of course, Assam's famous rhinos – plus the African two-horned variety for comparison. They're open Saturday to Thursday; entry is Rs 3.

Places to Stay

Prices of hotels listed here do not include tax, which is currently 10% on hotels costing Rs 100 to Rs 199, 15% for Rs 200 to Rs 299, and 20% on Rs 300 and above. Some hotels also add a 10% service charge.

Places to Stay – Budget

Hotel Alankar (☎ 543819, GN Bordoloi Rd), about 3km from the station, is good value and run by friendly people. Dorm beds are Rs 25 and singles/doubles with bathroom are Rs 75/120. The rooms in the annexe at the back are quietest.

Ananda Lodge (☎ 544832, MN Rd) is nothing special but there's a pleasant courtyard. Doubles cost from Rs 60, or Rs 95 with bathroom.

Tourist Lodge (☎ 544475, Station Rd), is run by Assam Tourism which has an office here. Very close to the station, the lodge is sadly shabby and may not be suitable for solo women travellers. There are dorm beds for Rs 40 and doubles from Rs 170 which they'll occasionally rent as singles for Rs 100. All rooms have bathrooms, and bucket hot water.

Hotel Suradevi (☎ 545050, MN Rd) is a large budget place with basic, clean rooms for Rs 95/150 and dorm beds for Rs 60. The managers may baulk at letting foreigners stay because of the red tape involved, so it pays to persist a little.

Places to Stay – Mid-Range

Hotel Kuber International (☎ 520807, HB Rd), is a well-known hotel in Fancy Bazaar. It's a little rundown but fine, and all rooms have bathrooms; they cost Rs 200/300, or Rs 325/425 with air-con. The restaurant is quite good.

Hotel Nova (☎ 523464, SS Rd), is in busy Fancy Bazaar, about 1.5km west of the bus and train stations. It's a good place with helpful staff. Rooms with bathroom cost Rs 440/590 to Rs 615/765 (air-con), and they all have satellite TV.

Hotel President (☎ 544979, GN Bordoloi Rd), is a reasonable place with rooms from Rs 275/400, Rs 500/600 with air-con. It's also quite central near Paan Bazaar.

Hotel Nandan (☎ 540855, GS Rd) is a comfortable three star place conveniently near the train station. There are rooms from Rs 500/700, Rs 725/950 with air-con. There's an excellent restaurant, a bar and all rooms have bathrooms and satellite TV.

Places to Stay – Top End

Hotel Belle Vue (☎ 540847, fax 540848), 'where the chirping of birds provides the wake-up call', is 3km from the train station in a very peaceful, elevated location with views over the Brahmaputra. The rooms are large with a bathroom and TV. Ordinary rooms cost Rs 750/950, deluxe rooms are Rs 1000/1150.

Hotel Brahmaputra Ashok (☎ 541064, fax 540870, MG Rd), is in an excellent location right by the river. Rooms are large and airy and some have wonderful river views, so you can watch the dramatic sunset from the comfort of your bed. Singles/doubles are Rs 1500/2400. There's a restaurant, bar, email and money changing facilities.

Dynasty Hotel (☎ 510496, fax 522112, SS Rd), right in the centre of town, is a favourite with businesspeople. The comfortable rooms all have air-con, bathroom and Star (satellite) TV; prices range from Rs 1150/1650 to Rs 4500 (for a suite).

Places to Eat

Fish is a big feature of Guwahati menus and can be very good. The most common fish are known locally as *rahu*, *elish*, *puthi* and *chital*; in cheap restaurants they range from Rs 10 to Rs 25 per plate.

All but the cheapest restaurants add 8% sales tax to the bill, and some also add a 10% service charge. No alcohol is available anywhere on the first day of each month – pay day.

Paradise Restaurant (GN Bordoloi Rd) is the place to go to try local cuisine. Assamese thalis cost Rs 55/60 for veg/nonveg and the waiters will explain the dishes. It's open daily 10 am to 3.30 pm and 6 to 9.30 pm. Beer costs Rs 55 in the bar upstairs (closes at 7.30 pm).

The Dhaba (GN Bordoloi Rd), not far from Paradise Restaurant, is an open-air north Indian place. It's clean and good value – chicken mughlai is Rs 35, *mattar paneer* is Rs 20.

Ming Room is hidden under the flyover off GN Bordoloi Rd. As the name suggests it's a Chinese restaurant, currently the best in Guwahati. Most nonveg dishes are around Rs 100.

Bidur Chinese Restaurant (GS Rd), is cheap and does some Tibetan dishes. It closes at 7.30 pm.

Woodlands (GS Rd), is a well-known South Indian vegetarian restaurant, offering a filling thali for Rs 60. The food's good and the restaurant is air-con.

Utsav, at the Hotel Nandan, is an excellent upmarket north Indian restaurant that does very good tandooris and *naan*.

Dynasty Hotel has Chinese and Indian restaurants, but they also do some western dishes including roast pork and apple sauce for Rs 100.

Shopping
The best places to buy Assam's *muga* silk and local crafts are the shops on GN Bordoloi Rd, including Pragjyotika Assam State Emporium.

Getting There & Away
Air Borjhav airport is 23km west of Guwahati. Indian Airlines (☎ 564420) has flights to/from Calcutta (US$70, daily), Delhi (US$210, five per week), Agartala (US$45, three per week), Aizawl (US$75, three per week) and Imphal (US$50, two per week). Jet Airways (☎ 522396) has daily flights to Bagdogra (US$50), Calcutta (US$71) and Delhi (US$211).

Bus The Paltan Bazaar bus stand is by the southern exit of the train station. It's well organised and all the state transport companies are based here. The offices for private bus companies are also in this area and along GS Rd; the most reliable companies seem to be Blue Hills and Green Valley. It's worth paying extra for a modern bus with decent suspension, as Assam's roads are some of the worst in India! There's also a second bus station known as Machkhowa bus stand with departures to surrounding towns including Hajo.

There are buses to Shillong (Rs 50, 3½ hours) every 30 minutes between 6 am and 5 pm; overnight buses to Siliguri in West Bengal (Rs 225, 13 hours), Bomdila (Rs 205, 18 hours), and Itanagar (Rs 160, 12 hours), among many others.

Within Assam, there are frequent departures for Nagaon, (Rs 40, four hours), Tezpur (Rs 70, five hours), Kaziranga (Rs 90, 5½ hours), Jorhat (Rs 115, seven hours), Haflong (Rs 175, nine hours) and Sibsagar (Rs 130, eight hours). There are overnight buses to Silchar (Rs 195, 12 hours). Green Valley has an air-con bus to Kaziranga for Rs 180.

Train The most convenient points from which to get to Guwahati are Calcutta and New Jalpaiguri.

From Calcutta (Howrah), it's 993km and about 24 hours to Guwahati on the *Kamrup Express* or 22 hours on the *Kanchenjunga Express* (Sealdah) at a cost of Rs 245/849 in 2nd/1st class. These trains pass through New Jalpaiguri station at 5.30 am and 6.10 pm, respectively. There is also the *North East Express* which comes from New Delhi and passes through New Jalpaiguri at 9.40 am. The 422km journey from here to Guwahati takes about eight hours and costs Rs 135/471 in 2nd/1st class.

Faster and more expensive is the *Rajdhani Express* which leaves Delhi on Monday, Wednesday and Saturday at 5 pm, passing through New Jalpaiguri at 1.50 pm the following day, reaching Guwahati at 8.30 pm. From Delhi it costs Rs 1650/4920 in three-tier air-con sleeper/1st class (Rs 685/1690 from New Jalpaiguri).

The *Brahmaputra Mail* and *Kamrup Express* continue east to Dibrugarh (18 hours). This line passes briefly through Nagaland with a stop at Dimapur, where you are not allowed to disembark without a permit. The line from Lumding to Silchar is metre gauge.

NORTH-EASTERN REGION

Getting Around
There's an irregular airport bus (Rs 25) but most passengers share taxis for the 23km journey into town (Rs 300 per taxi).

There's no shortage of auto-rickshaws, taxis and cycle-rickshaws, and the bus service is a cheap and easy way to get around.

If you want to get out on the river there are frequent ferry crossings from Pan Bazaar Ghat to North Guwahati (Rs 1).

AROUND GUWAHATI
On the north bank of the Brahmaputra 28km from Guwahati, Hajo is an important pilgrimage centre for Hindus, Buddhists and Muslims. Some Buddhists believe that Buddha attained nirvana here, Hindus worship at the Hayagriba Madhab Temple. For Muslims, the Pao Mecca Mosque is considered to have one-quarter *(pao)* the sanctity of the great mosque at Mecca. Numerous buses link Guwahati's Machkhowa bus stand with Hajo in a little over an hour. Assam Tourism runs tours here on Sundays for Rs 100.

About 32km south of the city towards Shillong, Sualkuchi is a famous silk weaving centre best known for its muga silk which is naturally golden-coloured, not dyed. *Endi* and *pat* silks are also woven here, and prices are lower than in Guwahati (around Rs 300 per metre for muga and Rs 150 for pat). There is a regular ferry across the river and a bus several times daily.

A popular picnic spot with small temples and a waterfall, **Basistha** is where the *rishi* or sage, Basistha, once lived. It's 12km from Guwahati and reached by one of the numerous city buses from GN Bordoloi Rd.

The beautiful natural lagoon at **Chandubi** is 64km from Guwahati. **Barpeta**, with a monastery and the shrine of a Vaishnavaite reformer, is 145km north-west of Guwahati.

TEZPUR
☎ 03712
On the north bank of the Brahmaputra, 198km from Guwahati, Tezpur is a centre for the **tea** industry. The town still has a colonial feel to it and there's an old church by the *maidan* (open grassed area).

There are several ancient temples including the **Mahabhairava Temple**, and ancient Gupta sculptures at the ruins of **Da-Parbatia Temple**, 5km west of Tezpur. In **Cole Park**, opposite the Tourist Lodge in town, are 9th century sculptures and excavated sections of the palace of a former king. At sunset there is a superb view of the river from **Agnigarh Hill**.

Places to Stay & Eat
Tourist Lodge, opposite Cole Park, is quite good and has a very friendly and helpful manager. Rooms are Rs 100/170 with bathroom and mosquito nets; dorm beds are Rs 40.

Hotel Meghdoot (KK Rd) is 500m from the bus stand. Rooms are Rs 75/100 and it's not bad.

Hotel Luit (☎ 21220), near the bus stand, is the top hotel in town. There are air-con rooms for Rs 325/450, and a good restaurant.

Getting There & Away
Indian Airlines (☎ 20083) has two flights a week from Saloni airport (16km away) to Calcutta (US$80).

Since Tezpur is on a branch line, buses are more useful than trains. There are frequent departures for Guwahati (Rs 70, six hours) and Kaziranga (Rs 28, two hours). There are also buses to Itanagar (Rs 90, six hours) and Tawang (Rs 150, 24 hours).

NAMERI WILDLIFE SANCTUARY
Straddling the border between Assam and Arunachal Pradesh, the Nameri Wildlife Sanctuary protects 137 sq km of forest and wetlands along the Jia Bharali river. About 38km north of Tezpur lies the *Eco Camp*, offering eco-friendly fishing (tag the fish and throw them back), bird-watching, rafting and elephant rides. A double tent with meals costs Rs 400/800 per day for Indians/foreigners; boats cost Rs 300/600 per day.

The Eco Camp can be booked through the Assam Anglers Association in Tezpur (☎ 03712-20004, fax 21583) or in Guwahati (☎/fax 0361-545847), who can also help you get a fishing licence from the Forest Department. Wild Grass in Guwahati can also arrange for you to stay here. The best time to fish is October and November.

KAZIRANGA NATIONAL PARK

North-east of Guwahati, on the swampy banks of the Brahmaputra river, is the Kaziranga National Park, famous as the last major home of *Rhinoceros unicornis*. The 430 sq km park is thought to have a rhino population approaching 1500, although in 1904 they were on the verge of extinction. The park became a game sanctuary in 1926, and by 1966 rhino numbers had risen to about 400. They are still threatened by poachers and floods.

The park has gaur (Indian bison), deer, elephant, tiger, bear and water bird species which breed here. The best way to see the wildlife is from elephant-back; the rhino are used to camera-toting tourists.

Manas, the other main park, is in the heartland of the Bodo insurgency and was off limits at the time of research. There are two smaller parks at **Orang** and **Sonai**.

Information

The park is open from November to April and the best time to see birdlife is December/January. The main gate is at Kohora. There's a tourist information centre (☎ 036776-62423) at Bonani Tourist Lodge, where you're required to sign in. At the park headquarters here you can reserve accommodation, and book jeeps and elephant rides. Prices for Indians/non-Indians are Rs 10/175 to enter the park, Rs 50/150 to bring a vehicle into the park, Rs 10/175 for a camera (plus Rs 50 if you have a telephoto lens), and Rs 750/150 for an hour-long elephant ride. To rent a jeep for up to nine people costs Rs 800 for 1½ hours.

Avoid organised tours to Kaziranga from Guwahati since they're too short (two days) and you'll spend most of that time on the bus (some nine hours in all) and have only one game drive. It's best to have at least three nights and four days in Kaziranga.

Places to Stay & Eat

There is a variety of accommodation around the park.

Forest Lodges must be reserved at the tourist office or park HQ. A bed costs Rs 85 at *Bonashree* while a dorm bed is Rs 30 at *Kunjaban*. Singles/doubles are Rs 350/450 at *Bonani*, which also has a restaurant; and at *Aranya*, the best of the Forest Lodges, there are air-con rooms for Rs 450/550 with bathroom and balcony, Rs 350/450 without air-con. There's a good restaurant here.

Wild Grass Resort (☎ 036776-62437) is an excellent, eco-friendly private resort about 5km from Kohora. Accommodation is either in luxury tents or a lodge. Doubles are Rs 750 (no singles). Their Jungle Plan for Rs 2100 per person per day includes accommodation, meals and trips into the park

Rhinoceros Unicornis

Assam is famous for its rare one-horned Great Indian Rhinoceros – when Marco Polo first saw one he thought he'd found the legendary unicorn. Once widely distributed across the northern floodplains of the subcontinent, the rhino has been hunted and displaced by humans and is now restricted to only a handful of wildlife reserves. In India, the greatest numbers are found in Kaziranga National Park.

Although its cause is less well publicised than that of the tiger, its numbers are even fewer – barely 1500 – and the majority of these are in just one area. Large and formidable, the rhino has few natural predators, but a naturally slow population growth makes them especially vulnerable to hunting. The rhino's preferred habitat often coincides with human habitation and is increasingly sought for agriculture. As in Africa, political turmoil has provided a cover for poachers, and there is an ever-present market for rhino products. Powdered rhino horn is highly valued as a medicine in the east and can fetch up to almost US$40,000 a kilo. In India and Nepal there is little of a rhino's anatomy that is not prized for its aphrodisiac, medicinal or spiritual attributes.

on elephant. For bookings contact the Guwahati office (☎ 0361-546827, fax 541186),
Bharuah Bhawan, 107 MC Rd.

Getting There & Away
The nearest airport is at Jorhat, 84km from
the park. Buses from Guwahati (233km)
bound for Jorhat, Sibsagar and Dibrugarh all
pass Kohora gate (Rs 85, 5½ hours). There's
also an air-con bus (Rs 180) run by Green
Valley, and Assam Tourism runs a daily bus
from the Tourist Lodge in Guwahati.

UPPER ASSAM
Jorhat
☎ 03666
Jorhat is the gateway to Upper Assam. You
may need to spend the night here on the
way to or from Majuli. as it's not really
feasible to do a day trip to Majuli from
Jorhat.

Assam Tourism is at the Tourist Lodge.
The State Bank of India on AT Rd cashes
travellers cheques.

There's a reasonable choice of accommodation near the bus station. The *Tourist
Lodge* (☎ 321579) has good singles/doubles
with bathroom for Rs 100/170; *Dipti Hotel*
has clean rooms for Rs 120/190; and *Hotel
Paradise* (☎ 321521, Solicitor's Rd) is the
best choice with rooms for Rs 300/450.

There are four flights a week between
Jorhat and Calcutta (US$90) on Indian Air-
lines (☎ 320011) and Jet Airways (☎325652).
There are numerous buses to Guwahati (Rs
100, seven hours), Sibsagar (Rs 13, 1½
hours), and Kaziranga (Rs 23, 2½ hours), as
well as many other destinations in the
north-east. Trains are less convenient as
Jorhat is on a branch line.

Majuli
Majuli is famous as the world's biggest
(though rapidly eroding) river island, but it's
really most interesting for its 22 *satras*,
Hindu Vaishnavaite monasteries that also
function as centres for Assamese arts. The
institution of the satra was founded in the
15th century by the Assamese poet, composer and philosopher Sankardeva. At the

Majuli satras, Vishnu is worshipped through
dance dramas re-enacting the stories of the
Mahabharata, and with music and poetry.
Sankardeva saw Vishnu as the pre-eminent
deity, without form, a concept that marks
Assamese Hinduism apart from the other
traditions.

The main satras are at Kamalabari, Natun
Kamalabari, Garamur, Samaguri, Auniati,
Dakhinpat and Bengenaati. They're all
about 5km apart; taxis and auto-rickshaws
are available. It's possible to stay at some
satras but you should make a donation. The
other alternatives are the *Circuit House* in
Garamur, or lodgings with villagers.

There are ferries in the morning and afternoon from Neamati Ghat, 13km north of
Jorhat. From the landing stage on Majuli
there's usually a bus for the 8km journey to
the island's capital, Garamur. To visit the
satras you can hire a auto-rickshaw/taxi in
Garamur for about Rs 300/600 per day.

Sibsagar
☎ 03772
Sibsagar, 55km north-east of Jorhat, was the
old capital of the Ahom dynasty, who ruled
Assam for 600 years. It's now an important
centre for the tea and oil industries. The
area's tea gardens employ the 'tea tribes', including Santhals and Oraons brought here
from central India by the British.

The huge artificial lake, created by
Queen Madambika in 1734, lies at the centre of the town. Beside the tank stands the
Shivadol temple, at 33m the tallest Shiva
temple in the country. About 6km from the
centre are the ruins of the 18th century
palaces of Kareng Ghar and Talatal Ghar;
13km to the east is Gargaon Palace. About
12km along the road to Jorhat is the Gau-
risagar tank and three more temples. The
tombs of the Ahom kings lie at Charaideo
Hill, about 28km east of town.

There is the excellent *Tourist Lodge*
(☎ 21814) by the tank, with rooms with
bathroom for Rs 100/170. Assam Tourism's
office is here. *Kareng Hotel* (☎ 22713,
Temple Rd) is good value at Rs 70/120 and
has a reasonable restaurant. *Hotel Brinda-*

van (☎ 22974, AT Rd) has air-con doubles from Rs 600.

Simaluguri, the mainline train station, is 20km from Sibsagar, but there are lots of buses – Guwahati (Rs 130, 8½ hours), Jorhat (Rs 15, 1½ hours).

SOUTH ASSAM

Assam's southern finger links the Brahmaputra and Barak valleys, with the multitribal North Cachar Hill District in between. The state extends down as far as Tripura and Mizoram, and also has borders with Bangladesh and Manipur.

Haflong

This is Assam's only hill station, 85km north of Silchar. It's a friendly little place with a mixed population of Hmar, Mizo and Naga people. The area is best known for Jatinga, 9km south of Haflong, where flocks of birds are said to come to commit suicide on misty September nights. What actually happens is that migrating birds passing this way are attracted to lights set up by the villagers; the birds land and end up in the villagers' cooking pots.

There's a *Tourist Lodge* in Haflong with rooms for Rs 100/170, and several other budget choices. The best lodgings and restaurant in town is at the *Hotel Elite*, just above the market.

There are two very slow buses a day to/from Silchar (four hours). From the station at Lower Haflong there are three trains a day to Lumding (5 hours), one to Kumarghat in Tripura (12 hours) and two to Silchar (6 hours).

Silchar

Silchar, located on the Barak River in the far south region of the state, is a significant transport hub.

If you need to spend the night here there's the *Tourist Lodge* on Park Rd, with rooms for Rs 100/170.

There are several buses a day that travel to Agartala (Rs 150), Aizawl (Rs 100) and Guwahati (Rs 195). There are two trains a day that ride the metre gauge up to Lower

Haflong and further on to Lumding (11 hours).

Meghalaya

Created in 1972, Meghalaya (The Abode of Clouds) is the home of the Khasi, Jaintia and Garo tribespeople, notable for their matrilineal society – property and wealth are passed through the female rather than the male line. Great stone monoliths erected to the old tribal kings can be found in the Khasi and Jaintia hills, as well as sacred forest groves. The gently rolling hills of the state are noted for growing fruit and betel nut, which the locals chew an awful lot of.

The hill station of Shillong is the state capital, while Cherrapunji, 58km south, was until recently said to be the wettest place on earth, with an average annual rainfall of 1150cm – nearly 40 feet! In one year 26.5m of rain fell. (Nearby Mawsynram recently took the title from Cherrapunji.)

History

Khasi and Jaintia tribes are closely related and are thought to have originally emigrated from South-East Asia, while the Garo came from Tibet. The Khasi and Jaintia trace their descent back to the Ri Hinniew Trep, or Seven Families. In the beginning legend has it there were 16 families, nine in heaven and seven on earth, connected by a golden vine ladder, but when sin poisoned the earth the link was severed.

Garo traditionally practice shifting *jhumming* (slash-and-burn agriculture), though in recent years population pressure has encouraged a change to wet rice cultivation. In the forested Garo regions men would stand guard in treetop *borangs* (watchtowers).

Warring chiefs ruled the area before the arrival of the British, who established control by the 1820s by playing the tribes off against each other. Missionaries were permitted to work among the tribes, and nowadays more than half the population is Christian. Shillong's gentle rainy climate made it a favoured retreat from the plains for the British tea planters and administrators of the region, and the town was once described as `mini London'. The state separated from Assam in 1972, and has been a political and economic backwater since.

SHILLONG
☎ 0364 • pop 260,000

From 1874 until 1972 Shillong was the capital of Assam and known as the Scotland of the East. Surrounded by pine trees and veiled in clouds, you can quite understand why it reminded the Brits so strongly of home. Standing at an altitude of 1496m it provided a welcome relief from the heat of the plains. They built a championship golf course (the world's wettest), and a polo ground, and soon the surrounding hills were dotted with neat Victorian bungalows and churches. English is widely spoken, and western music like the Eagles and Creedence Clearwater Revival is more popular Hindi pop.

The centre of Shillong is becoming congested with traffic snarls, and a multitude of ugly concrete buildings have sprung up. Nevertheless, there are good walks in the area, and interesting markets that attract tribespeople from outlying villages. Shillong does have communal tensions, however, which regularly turn nasty during major Hindu festivals.

Orientation
Shillong is spread over several rolling hills. Ward's Lake, the botanical gardens and the polo ground (all to the north) were formerly the European area; this is still a peaceful part of Shillong, and you'll find some of the upmarket hotels here. Police Bazaar is at the centre of the town and the government bus stand, restaurants, more upmarket shops and many of the budget and mid-range hotels are here. About 1.5km to the west is crowded Bara Bazaar and the private bus stand.

Information
The Meghalaya Tourism office (☎ 226220) is on Jail Rd in Police Bazaar. It's open Monday to Saturday 7.30 am to 5 pm (until 11 am on Sunday). If there's enough inter-est it runs local tours (8.30 am to 2 pm, Rs 75) and trips to Cherrapunji (8 am to 4.30 pm, Rs 100). There's a Government of India tourist office (☎ 225632) nearby on GS Rd.

Travellers cheques can be cashed at the State Bank of India opposite Shillong Club.

Parks & Waterfalls
East of Police Bazaar, **Ward's Lake** was the focus of the European settlement. It's said that its construction was initiated by a bored Khasi prisoner who'd requested any kind of work to get him out of his cell. He was set to digging holes and filling them in again. When he hit a spring in this spot the civic engineer decided that a lake and gardens should be created; it was named after Sir William Ward, the Chief Commissioner. It's still quite an attractive place and there's boating on the lake.

About 1.5km south of Police Bazaar is **Lady Hydari Park**, which blooms in April and October. There's also a mini-zoo here; entry is Rs 2.

There are more gardens and a swimming pool nearby at the **Crinolene Falls**. As you might expect in a place so wet, there are numerous other waterfalls and pretty spots around Shillong.

Museums
The **State Museum** gives dusty coverage to the flora, fauna, culture and anthropology of the state. It's closed on Sunday and the second and fourth Saturday of each month. More interesting is the **Butterfly Museum**, on Jaiaw Rd, 1.5km north of Police Bazaar, run by Wankhar & Co who breed butterflies and supply conservation organisations around the world. It's open Monday to Friday 10 am to 4 pm, and on Saturday until noon.

Other Attractions
In the **Anglican graveyard** the gravestones show that even for the privileged Brits, life could be short and death not always peaceful. There are a few gory inscriptions such as 'killed in the great earthquake' or 'murdered by headhunters'. If the graveyard's

SHILLONG

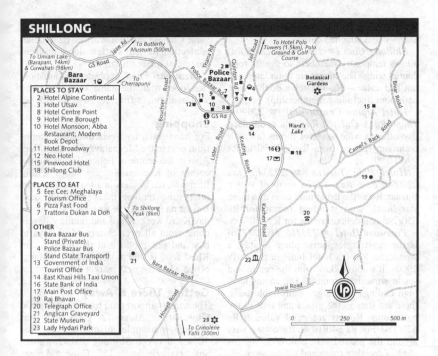

PLACES TO STAY
- 2 Hotel Alpine Continental
- 3 Hotel Utsav
- 8 Hotel Centre Point
- 9 Hotel Pine Borough
- 10 Hotel Monsoon; Abba Restaurant; Modern Book Depot
- 11 Hotel Broadway
- 12 Neo Hotel
- 15 Pinewood Hotel
- 18 Shillong Club

PLACES TO EAT
- 5 Eee Cee; Meghalaya Tourism Office
- 6 Pizza Fast Food
- 7 Trattoria Dukan Ja Doh

OTHER
- 1 Bara Bazaar Bus Stand (Private)
- 4 Police Bazaar Bus Stand (State Transport)
- 13 Government of India Tourist Office
- 14 East Khasi Hills Taxi Union
- 16 State Bank of India
- 17 Main Post Office
- 19 Raj Bhavan
- 20 Telegraph Office
- 21 Anglican Graveyard
- 22 State Museum
- 23 Lady Hydari Park

locked, get the key from the adjoining gate-keeper's house.

The town takes its name from the 1960m **Shillong Peak**, from where there are fine views. It's 10km from the centre, and a path winds up to the summit.

Umiam Lake (Barapani), a popular place for fishing and boating, lies 16km north on the road to Guwahati.

Places to Stay – Budget

There are numerous cheap hotels (all fairly similar) in Police Bazaar, many on or around GS Rd.

Neo Hotel (☎ 224363, *GS Rd*) is conveniently located. There are basic singles/doubles for Rs 100/200 with shared bath, Rs 200/350 with private bath.

Hotel Broadway (☎ 226996, *GS Rd*), is good but a bit pricey. Clean rooms are Rs 200/300 with shared bath, Rs 290/390 with

private bath. There's a busy restaurant downstairs.

Hotel Monsoon (☎ 223316, *GS Rd*), is a decent place nest to Abba Restaurant. Singles/doubles with bathroom are Rs 250/450.

Hotel Pine Borough (☎ 220698) is down the lane beside Hotel Centre Point. It's quite popular with businesspeople on a tight budget and has rooms from Rs 180/300 to Rs 850 for the executive suite. All have TV and bathroom and there's a restaurant and travel agent.

Places to Stay – Mid-Range & Top End

Government tax will currently add 10% to these prices, and some hotels also add a 5% to 10% service charge.

The *Hotel Centre Point* (☎ 225210, *fax 225239, GS Rd*), a landmark in the centre of Police Bazaar, has good rooms from

NORTH-EASTERN REGION

Rs 495/595 to Rs 845/995. All rooms have Star TV and attached baths.

Shillong Club (☎ 226938, Kacheri Rd) allows temporary members to use its residential wing. The rooms are quite large and not bad value – Rs 425 for a double with bathroom (including membership).

Hotel Alpine Continental (☎ 220991, Thana Rd & Quinton Rd), is a good place that offers a wide range of rooms (all with bathroom) priced from Rs 550/690 to Rs 990/1,290.

Hotel Polo Towers (☎ 222340, fax 220090, Polo Rd), 1.5km north of Police Bazaar. It has the usual mod cons of a three star hotel, with standard rooms for Rs 650/795 and deluxe rooms for Rs 850/995.

Pinewood Hotel (☎ 223116, fax 224176) is the most atmospheric place to stay, a wonderful Raj-era hotel built in the early 1900s. It's about 2km from the centre and set in attractive grounds. The rooms have high ceilings and large comfortable beds, there are fires in the grates and tubs in the bathrooms. Rooms are good value at Rs 520/780. For Rs 840/1090, the cottages set around the grounds are enormous and include a dressing room and sitting room.

Places to Eat

Some of the best restaurants are in the hotels. Try *La Galerie* at the Hotel Centre Point for Indian and Chinese dishes, and the *Pinewood Hotel* for Raj cuisine. The Pinewood serves the sorts of meals that must have been set before crusty Scottish tea planters 70 years ago, and orders are taken by the 'butler'. There's a good range of restaurants in the Police Bazaar area.

Trattoria Dukan Ja Doh, down the small side road beside Hotel Centre Point, is a simple cafe where you can try Khasi fare. There's no menu but the delicacies include pig's brains with ginger and Khasi fried rice (sometimes flavoured with pig's blood!).

Abba (GS Rd), is a small but excellent Chinese/Tibetan place. *Palace Restaurant* (Hotel Centre Point) serves Indian fastfood. *Samosas* (Rs 3), *dosas* (Rs 15) and *chana bhatura* (spiced chick peas) (Rs 15).

Eee Cee is a busy restaurant with good value Chinese and Indian dishes (and Indian confectioneries). It's a few doors up from the tourist office on Jail Rd.

Pizza Fast Food, opposite the tourist office, does what the name says, and quite well, with prices from Rs 50 to Rs 125.

Shopping

For handicrafts try Porbashree, the emporium next to the Meghalaya Tourism office. Also in the centre of Police Bazaar, on the corner of Kacheri Rd, are shops selling finely-woven baskets in all sizes. The most interesting market takes place in Bara Bazaar on Iewduh, the first day of the eight-day Khasi week. Khasi and Jaintia villagers come from all over eastern Meghalaya to buy and sell produce at the market, and Khasi food is sold at stalls. Ask the tourist office when the next market day is.

Getting There & Away

The nearest airport (and train station) are at Guwahati in Assam. A good road runs through pineapple plantations for the 100km between Shillong and Guwahati; share taxis charge Rs 155. Those and buses are sometimes available direct to Shillong from Guwahati airport.

From Shillong there are state transport buses from the Police Bazaar stand every half hour to Guwahati (Rs 40/50 for ordinary/deluxe, 3½ hours) and overnight buses to Silchar (Rs 93, 8½ hours) and Tura (Rs 125, 12 hours). Private companies such as Green Valley Travels have offices in Police Bazaar but their buses operate from the Bara Bazaar bus stand. A deluxe private bus to Agartala (18 hours) costs Rs 250. Local buses depart from Bara Bazaar. Other bus services are intermittent and usually very crowded. Hiring a taxi is the best option – budget travel isn't so easy here.

The East Khasi Hills Taxi Union (☎ 223895) charges Rs 625 one way to Guwahati, Rs 800 return to Jowai and Rs 350 return to Shillong Peak. Taxis can also be hired through the Meghalaya Tourism office for around Rs 100/800 per hour/day.

AROUND SHILLONG

There are daily buses to **Cherrapunji**, 58km south of Shillong, from where there are superb views from the escarpment over Bangladesh. The rains blow in from the Bay of Bengal between June and October, mostly at night. The town is rather drab but there are some traditional Khasi homes in the area, built with curved walls and a sturdy arching roof to withstand the storms. Krem Mawmluh is a 4.5km-long cave near Cherrapunji. Meghalaya Tourism runs tours from Shillong.

The border post with Bangladesh is 1.5km from **Dawki**, 70km from Shillong and linked by a bus service. There's no Bangladesh embassy in Shillong; the nearest is in Agartala.

Mawsynram, which recently took the title of wettest place on earth from Cherrapunji, is 55km south-west of Shillong. Mawjymbuin Cave features a giant stalagmite worshipped as a Shiva lingam by Hindu pilgrims. There are hot springs at **Jakrem**, 66km from Shillong.

In the Jaintia Hills, near the pleasant market town of Jowai, is Krem Um Lawan, which at 6.5km is India's longest cave. At **Nartiang**, about 12km north of Jowai, lies the atmospheric remnants of the ancient capital of the Jaintia kingdom, and there are monoliths here as tall as 8m.

GARO HILLS

There are numerous deep caves in the Garo Hills around Siju, 50km from the district capital of Tura. One accommodation possibility is the *Orchid Lodge*, run by Meghalaya Tourism (☎ 0364-2224933), 3km out of Tura. Buses to Tura (Rs 125, 12 hours) from Shillong go via Guwahati.

The untouched 220 sq km **Balpakram National Park** south of Tura features the canyon of the Mahadeo River, with fauna including tiger, elephant, barking deer and gaur. The park is also known for its medicinal herbs. The valley has been left untouched partly because of a Garo myth that souls linger here for a while after death. Balpakram isn't easy to get to; Orchid Lodge at Tura is the best place to organise a visit.

There has been ethnic violence in the Garo Hills, so check on the current situation before coming here.

Tripura

The tiny state of Tripura is the second smallest in the country with a population of a mere three million, and is almost surrounded by Bangladesh. Tripura was once part of a large Hindu kingdom conquered by the Mughals in 1733. It was taken over by the British in 1808, became a union territory of India in 1956 and a full state in 1972.

Over half the state is forested, and the largest industry is handloom weaving. Although there are 19 tribes in Tripura, the majority of the population is Bengali.

Visitors should heed local advice as to where it's currently safe to go. For the past few years Tripura's government has been trying to bring the several insurgent groups that terrorise the state under its control. The security situation worsened in 1998.

History

Tripura emerged as a distinct entity at the end of the 14th century under the Manikya dynasty, former Indo-Mongolian tribal chieftains who adopted Hinduism. Tribal customs such as leaving parasols over ponds to commemorate the dead can still be seen in rural areas, and official visitors to villages have bamboo arches built in their honour (the state has a vast array of caneware products).

Under the British Raj the Maharajas led a self-ruling princely state, though each ruler had to be firstly approved by the colonial overlords. At Independence the Regent Maharani took the state into India, while Sylhet district to the north joined East Pakistan (now Bangladesh). Like West Bengal the communist CPI (ML) has dominated state politics in recent decades.

AGARTALA

☎ 0381 • pop 175,500

Tripura's sleepy capital was moved to its present site in 1850 by Maharaja Radha

Krishna Kishore Manikya Bahadur. The town is dominated by the Ujjayanta Palace, built in Indo-Saracenic style in 1901. It's a pleasant enough place and the locals are very welcoming (few speak English), but there's not a lot to see.

Agartala is just 2km from the border with Bangladesh. Visas are easily available at the embassy here.

Orientation & Information

The town is arranged on a grid plan so orientation is easy. The airport is 12km to the north, and Airport Rd brings you into the town by the Ujjayanta Palace. The main shopping street is HGB Rd, where the State Bank of India, museum and post office are.

Tripura Tourism (☎ 225930), in the eastern wing of the palace, can be very helpful. They also organise tours around Agartala, to Neermahal and other sites around the state, depending on demand and the security situation. There's a Bangladesh tourist office at the Bangladesh embassy (☎ 224807), 1.5km north of Agartala just off Airport Rd. Ask for Circuit House and it's down the lane beside Green Travels (opposite Assam Rifles). It's open for visa applications Monday to Friday 10 am to noon; you need to bring two photos and fill out an application form, then go to the State Bank of India on HGB Rd to deposit the visa fee in the embassy's account. Visas are ready for collection the following day between 3 and 4.30 pm; for an extra fee same-day visas are possible.

Things to See & Do

Standing before a small lake, **Ujjayanta Palace** was built by Maharaja Radhakishore Manikya in 1901 in a mixed European-Mughal style and is surrounded by 28 hectares of parkland. Since the building now houses the state legislative assembly it's not usually open to the public. However, if you go to the front gate between 3 and 4 pm (Monday to Saturday) they may give you an entry pass. In the grounds and open to all are the **Ummaneshwar Temple** and the **Jagannath Temple**, both painted a striking ochre colour. At the **Buddha Vihar** on Air-

port Rd north of the city, there are Burmese statues of the Buddha. There's a **mosque** near the motor stand.

The **State Museum** is at the roundabout on HGB Rd. It's worth a visit, the results of excavations within the state are on display, and there are old coins and ethnographic displays. It's open Monday to Saturday from 10 am to 5 pm; entry is free.

Old Agartala, the former capital, is 5km to the east. **The Temple of Fourteen Deities** here draws thousands of devotees in July for the Karchi Puja.

Places to Stay & Eat

Hotels in Tripura are all fairly basic but some have air-con rooms. Hotel tax is currently 10%; some places also add an additional 10% service charge.

Agartala Rest House (Motor Stand Rd) has some of the cheapest rooms in town – around Rs 40 for an extremely basic single with shared bath.

Hotel Minakshi (☎ 223430, Hawkers' Corner Rd), has basic rooms with bathroom for Rs 55/95, and deluxe rooms with hot water and TV for Rs 90/150. It's good value.

Hotel Ambar (☎ 223587, Sakuntala Rd), is also good and has similar prices to Hotel Minakshi.

Hotel Moonlight & Restaurant (LNB Rd), is better known as a place to eat but also has some basic rooms for Rs 80/100.

Deep Hotel (☎ 227482, LNB Rd), is clean and popular. Rooms with bathroom cost Rs 150/250.

Royal Guest House (☎ 225652, Royal Compound) has good rooms from Rs 150/300 with attached bath, and Rs 300/400 with air-con. Although there's nothing royal about it, apart from the location, it's a friendly place. There's also a good restaurant.

Hotel Rajdhani (☎ 223387, BK Rd), says it is the first hotel in Tripura to have a lift installed. Ordinary rooms cost Rs 170/250 with bathroom. There are also air-con rooms for Rs 290/450. Rooms are clean and come with mosquito nets.

Hotel Gujrat is a good cheap place to eat, and there are veg and nonveg dishes.

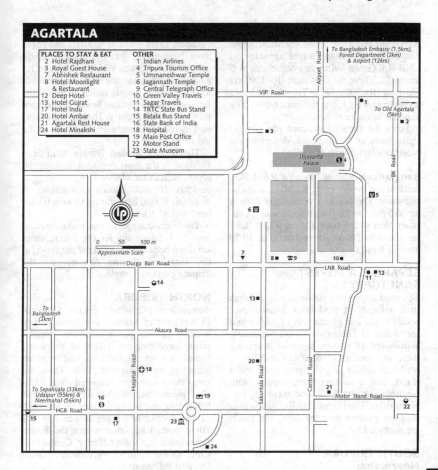

AGARTALA

PLACES TO STAY & EAT
2 Hotel Rajdhani
3 Royal Guest House
7 Abhishek Restaurant
8 Hotel Moonlight
 & Restaurant
12 Deep Hotel
13 Hotel Gujrat
17 Hotel Indu
20 Hotel Ambar
21 Agartala Rest House
24 Hotel Minakshi

OTHER
1 Indian Airlines
4 Tripura Tourism Office
5 Ummaneshwar Temple
6 Jagannath Temple
9 Central Telegraph Office
10 Green Valley Travels
11 Sagar Travels
14 TRTC State Bus Stand
15 Batala Bus Stand
16 State Bank of India
18 Hospital
19 Main Post Office
22 Motor Stand
23 State Museum

To Bangladesh Embassy (1.5km),
Forest Department (2km)
& Airport (12km)

To Old Agartala
(5km)

VIP Road

Airport Road

BK Road

Ujjayanta
Palace

Durga Bari Road

LNB Road

To
Bangladesh
(2km)

Akaura Road

Hospital Road

Sakuntala Road

Central Road

Motor Stand Road

To Sepahijala (33km),
Udaipur (55km) &
Neermahal (56km)

HGB Road

0   50   100 m
Approximate Scale

Hotel Indu (HGB Rd) is the place to go for
a cheap meal. Rice is just Rs 2, dhal Rs 1, or
you could splash out on fish curry for Rs 12.

Abhishek Restaurant (LNB Rd) has tables under umbrellas in the garden and
small veg and nonveg rooms inside. It's
moderately priced.

Getting There & Away

Air Indian Airlines (☎ 225470) has daily
flights to/from Calcutta (US$50) and three
flights a week to/from Guwahati (US$45).

From the airport (12km), the taxis/auto-
rickshaws cost Rs 150/75.

Bus & Share Jeep There are three bus
stands. From the TRTC stand on Hospital
Rd, there's a bus to Guwahati (Rs 300, 25
hours) via Shillong at 4 pm, Monday to Saturday. There are buses for Silchar, Udaipur,
Melaghar and Unakoti. All buses between
Tellamura and Kumarghat have army escorts in case of attack from insurgents.
Check the current situation before going.

Private buses leave from the chaotic Batala bus stand and the Motor Stand; some can be booked at the travel agencies on LNB Rd. Green Valley has departures at 6 am and 2.30 pm for Guwahati (Rs 350) via Shillong (Rs 300). Sagar Travels has buses to Silchar for Rs 150 at the same times; they can also book air tickets.

From the Batala bus stand you can get share jeeps to Udaipur and Melaghar (for Neermahal), for around Rs 20.

Bangladesh Follow Akaura Rd 1.5km west to the border post; Rs 10 in a cycle-rickshaw. The border's open daily from 8 am to 5 pm. On the Bangladeshi side it's another 5km to the train station where there are trains to Dhaka (three hours) at 10.30 am and 6 pm.

SEPAHIJALA FOREST SANCTUARY

The road south from Agartala runs through little villages of mud brick houses, past paddy fields and plantations of rubber and tea, 33km to Sepahijala Forest Sanctuary. Within the 18 sq km, some of it fenced, there are species of deer and monkey, a well-kept mini-zoo with tigers, bears and a rhino, and a boating lake popular with birdlife. Entry is Rs 3, and there are elephant rides. The Forest Dak Bungalow is in pleasant gardens near the lake, and meals are provided.

SOUTH TRIPURA
Neermahal

South of Sepahijala one road continues 22km to Melaghar, 1km from **Rudrasagar Lake**. On an island in the lake is Tripura's top attraction, the **Water Palace of Neermahal**. The palace was built by a British firm in the 1920s, but is now starting to fall into ruin. It's a beautifully peaceful place that attracts migrating birds in winter.

On the lake shore, Tripura Tourism's *Sagarmahal Tourist Lodge* has doubles with bath for Rs 80, and dorm beds for Rs 30. Make a reservation at the tourist office in Agartala.

Udaipur

Udaipur, 55km south of Agartala and 25km from Neermahal, was the ancient Hindu capital. At the centre of Udaipur is the Jagannath Digthi tank, and on its banks the ruined Jagannath Temple which once held the famous Jagannath statue brought here from Puri in the 16th century. There are also several temples to Vishnu and the ruins of the old royal palace.

The **Tripura Sundari Temple**, 4km from Udaipur, is the most famous temple in the south, built in the classic Bengali-hut style in 1501. It's also known as Matabari. A large fair is held here during Diwala (October/November).

There are share jeeps that make frequent runs to Udaipur for Rs 60, where there are dorm beds for Rs 30 (three per room) at the *Matabari Pantha Niwas*, near the Tripura Sundari Temple.

NORTH TRIPURA

An ancient pilgrimage centre, **Unakoti**, 180km north of Agartala, is believed to date back to the 8th century. Several impressively large rock-cut images of Shiva and Ganesh are set into the hills, and there are attractive waterfalls and pools. There are many other sculptures scattered about – Unakoti means 'one less than a crore'. Legend has it that one sculptor, divinely inspired, carved 9,999,999 images in one day. It's 10km from Kailasahar where the Forest Department has a *Rest House*. Contact the Chief Conservator of Forests in advance (Airport Rd, Agartala).

There are two buses a day to Kailasahar from Agartala (Rs 50, eight hours).

Other States in the North-East

The only way into these states is on a group tour of at least four people, which can be organised through a recognised travel agent; or with an personal invitation from a friend.

ARUNACHAL PRADESH
• pop 1.01 million

One of the most remote regions in India, Arunachal Pradesh borders Bhutan, China and Myanmar. The state comprises valleys separated by the ridges of the eastern Himalaya, and 80% of the land is still forested. There are 66 or so tribes (though the 1971 census counted as many as 115), ranging from slash-and-burn animists to the Tibetan Buddhist Monpa villages in the west and a Thai people, the Khampti, in the east. The largest groups are the Adi, in the Along area, the Mishmi in the ranges north-east of Pasighat, and the Nishi around Itanagar.

A stable and reasonably effective administration has helped Arunachal avoid the ethnic violence of neighbouring states. The central government kept Arunachal essentially off limits until very recently, when a policy of gradually opening up the state without swamping the traditional cultures was introduced.

The roads are much better in Arunachal than in Assam, a sign of its strategic importance. Foreigners are currently permitted to visit Tawang in the west, Itanagar, the road from Ziro through Daporijo and Along to Pasighat, and Namdapha National Park. The state government charges US$50 per day just to be in the state, or US$150 for an all-inclusive package tour, although at the time of research there were suggestions that this would change to a simple US$50 fee for a 10 day permit. Check with the state government offices listed under Permits at the start of the chapter for current regulations.

History

Of all the north-eastern states Arunachal has the least documented history. The Ahom dynasty in Assam had a policy of not interfering with the hill tribes, except for retaliatory raids. The British continued this policy and after declaring it off-limits in 1873 ignored the place until the eve of WWII. After Independence Nehru supported the policies of Verrier Elwin, a British-born anthropologist who adopted Indian citizenship, to gradually prepare the tribes for the impact of the modern world. Firstly village democracy was introduced, in preparation for a statewide legislature. Development was stepped up after China invaded Tawang in 1962 (this Buddhist mountain valley had until the late 1940s been claimed by Tibet). China inexplicably advanced as far as Tezpur in Assam and then withdrew, and India moved quickly to build roads and military bases along the border. In 1972 Arunachal became a Union Territory, and in 1987 a state. During the tenure of Chief Minister Gegong Apang (1979-1999) the state's forests were increasingly overexploited, until a court ban on logging in 1997 came into force. Like many of the region's hill tribes, the Arunachalese are increasingly turning to Christianity to build social bonds as the tribal systems of mutual obligation break down in the modern cash economy. Since the ban on logging the state has been in a deep economic slump, which is partly why tourism is opening up.

Itanagar
☎ 0360 • pop 17,700

The capital, Itanagar, is new and not especially interesting, although you do meet a cross-section of Arunachal's peoples. Traditional huts are scattered among modern houses. The **Buddha Vihar** on the hill near the Hotel Arun Subansiri is about all there is to see in the way of monuments. About 6km from Itanagar, **Ganga Lake** lies at the end of a rugged road and a short but steep track. The surrounding forests are quite beautiful.

The **Jawaharlal Nehru Museum** near the Secretariat covers the state's many tribes with dioramas and collections of wood carvings, textiles, musical instruments and an incredible variety of headwear. On the first floor are exhibits from archaeological sites such as Ita Fort and Malinithan. It's open Tuesday to Sunday, 10 am to 5 pm.

In Ganga Market the **Hotel Blue Pine** (☎ 212042) is a good mid-range option, with singles/doubles with attached bathroom for Rs 290/500. **Hotel Arun Subansiri** (☎ 212677, Zero Point) has some very comfortable rooms for Rs 600/800. **Hotel Donyi**

Polo Ashok (☎ 212626) is the top hotel with air-con rooms for a negotiable Rs 800/1200.

In Naharlagun, Itanagar's twin town 10km away, the *Hotel Arunachal (☎ 244960)*, has rooms for Rs 300/400; Rs 500/700 with air-con.

The nearest airport is 216km away at Tezpur in Assam. Green Valley and Blue Hills are reliable operators with several buses to Guwahati (Rs 160, 12 hours).

West Arunachal Pradesh

In the far north-west, **Tawang Gompa** is in a superb location at 3400m, near the border with Bhutan. Dating from the mid 17th century, this is the most important monastery in the north-east. The sixth Dalai Lama was born here. It has an interesting collection of *thangkas* (Tibetan painting on cloth) and a large gilded statue of Sakyamuni (the historical Buddha) in the prayer hall. The monastery is beautifully situated on a spur about 2km from the heart of town.

The *Tourist Lodge* is a bit decrepit but OK, with doubles from Rs 400 to Rs 700. The *Inspection Bungalow* uphill from the bus stand is better and much cheaper at Rs 80 per bed. The *Hotel Paradise* in the main market has doubles from Rs 200 to Rs 500 for a 'suite'.

There is a handicrafts centre at the lower end of Tawang town near the hospital.

Getting to Tawang is no picnic – it's 350km from the nearest airport at Tezpur in Assam and you have to cross the 4249m Se La. By local bus from Tezpur it takes about 24 hours and costs Rs 150, and around 12 hours by share jeep.

About halfway between Tezpur and Tawang is the attractive town of **Bomdila**, where there are a couple of Buddhist *gompas*. The friendly *Hotel Siphiyang Phong (03782-22373)* has decent rooms from Rs 400/650.

At Tipi, a few kilometres from the state border with Assam at Bhalukpong, there is an **Orchid Research Centre**, best visited in April or May.

Central Arunachal Pradesh

Ziro is the home of the Apatani people, who are not slash-and-burn farmers like the neigh-

bouring Nishi and Hill Miri tribes, but grow rice on terraces on the 26 sq km Apatani Plateau. You can stay at the *Blue Pine Lodge*, which has good doubles for Rs 300 and a few singles for Rs 200, or at the *Inspection Bungalow*, where beds are Rs 80 per person.

Daporijo is an overgrown village on the Subansiri River; there's not much to do but look at and be looked at by the local Tagin and Hill Miri tribespeople. The *Circuit House* where beds are Rs 80 per person is the best option.

Along is the next stop; a quiet town mostly inhabited by Adi people, where there is a *Circuit House* (Rs 80 per person). **Pasighat** is a larger Adi town on the banks of the Brahmaputra River (known locally as the Siang). Here the river widens out onto the plains of Assam. There are some local emporiums selling handicrafts, a few basic hotels and the *Circuit House* (Rs 80 per person), the best place to stay.

Namdapha National Park

In the remote far east of the state bordering Myanmar, this vast reserve covers 1850 sq km, ranging from the plains up to 4500m. It is unique in being home to four big cats; tiger, leopard, clouded leopard and snow leopard. There aren't many treks or trails into the park; it is still largely wilderness.

Accommodation is available at Deban though it must be booked at the office of the Namdapha National Park Field Director in Miao. The *Forest Rest House* and the two *Tourist Bungalows* are simple but pleasant; doubles cost Rs 95. The cooks are good but you may want to bring extra snacks. Entry to the park is Rs 10/50 for Indians/foreigners.

Deban is 28km east of the market town of Miao, where there is an *Inspection Bungalow* and a couple of basic hotels. The Tibetan refugee settlement of Choephelling, where Tibetan carpets are sold, is 3km from Miao on the Deban road.

MIZORAM
• pop 750,000

This finger-like extension in the extreme south-east of the region pokes between

Myanmar and Bangladesh. The name means Hill People's Land – from Mizo, 'man of the hill', and 'ram', Land. It's a picturesque place where the population is both predominantly tribal and overwhelmingly Christian. Many people speak English. Under the British, the area was known as the Lushai Hills, a name that persisted until 1972 when it became a Union Territory. For 20 years the Mizo National Front agitated for independence from Delhi, but in 1986 the Mizoram Peace Accord was signed and the region gained a measure of self government as a state in its own right. Happily and unusually for the north-east, Mizoram has been peaceful since achieving statehood.

If you can get a permit for Mizoram it's an interesting place to visit, more for the people than for any particular sight. The Mizos have the second highest literacy rate in India and many speak English.

History

The Mizo people are believed to have settled here some 300 years ago, perhaps coming from China. Under the British the Lushai Hills as they were called were among the few areas where missionaries were encouraged to operate, and today almost 95% of the entire Mizo population is Christian. Some groups have even identified themselves as the lost tribes of Israel and converted to Judaism. Social cohesion is boosted by large volunteer groups such as the Young Mizo Association (YMA), which has recruited as high as 60% of people between 15 and 25. Buddhist and animist tribes such as the Chakmas and Reangs have been discriminated against, even forced out of the state.

A natural crisis called *mautam* began the Mizo rebellion which wreaked the state for more than 20 years. Every 50 years the great bamboo forests burst into flower, in which turn attracts a plague of rats which devour the rice fields and vegetable gardens. This happened in 1959. The two-year famine which followed inspired a bank clerk named Laldinga to turn his Mizo Famine Front into the Mizo National Front, which fought for

independence from what they saw as the inept and uncaring Indian administration. During the conflict Mizo were herded from their tiny villages into new towns under Indian army control. I 1987, after years of bitter fighting a peace deal which included statehood was made with Rajiv Gandhi.

Aizawl

☎ 0389 • pop 160,000

Mizoram's capital clings to the sides of a central ridge at an altitude of 1130m. The staff at Mizoram Tourism (☎ 21227), Chandmary, are friendly and helpful.

The **Bara Bazaar**, in the centre of town, is an interesting market. Good places for weavings and bags are the **Weaving Centre** and **Solomon's Cave**. Bamboo items are a good buy. The **Mizoram State Museum**, at Babu Tlang, has a good collection of traditional Mizo dress and implements. There's also a mini-zoo.

Luangmual is a small ridge-top village 7km from Aizawl. Apart from the pleasant views and budget accommodation at the *Yatri Niwas*, there's a good handicrafts centre.

Places to stay in Aizawl include the *Hotel Embassy* (☎ 22570), near the tourist office, with rooms for around Rs 200/250 and a good restaurant; and the similarly-priced *tourist lodge* at Chatlang, further from the centre. In Bara Bazaar, the *Hotel Ritz* is a little cheaper and has been recommended.

There are currently no flights into Mizoram and no railway lines. Road transport comes via Silchar, 175km north of Aizawl (6 hours, Rs 150). There are day and night buses for the six hour journey. Capital Travels, at the bus station, has a daily bus to Guwahati (Rs 345, 22 hours).

MANIPUR

• pop 2 million

South of Nagaland, Manipur (Jewelled Land) borders Myanmar and is a 'dry' state. The state is inhabited by over two dozen tribes. Manipuri dancing is one of the great classical dance forms, which involves acrobatics on the part of the male dancers and slow graceful movements from the female dancers. The main sport is polo, and along with several other places in Asia, Manipur claims to have invented the game. Agriculture and weaving form the basis of the economy.

In the course of Manipur's long history there have been several invasions from Myanmar and numerous clashes with the Nagas. During WWII it was occupied by the Japanese. For the last 15 years there have been violent disturbances not only by separatist groups, but also between the Naga and Kuki tribes, especially in the hilly south. An estimated 50 different guerilla armies have been operating in the state in the last decade. Hundreds have been killed, thousands left homeless.

At the time of writing, foreigners were only permitted to visit the central valley of the state, going to and from Imphal by air.

History

The Imphal valley of Manipur (actually more of a highland plateau) has a unique Hindu culture, fostered in the security of the hills. The Hinduised tribe of the Imphal valley, the Meitei, were championed by Rabindranath Tagore for their dances and music. After a war against the Burmese, Manipur aligned itself with the British and signed the Treaty of Yandabo in 1826, becoming a princely state within the Raj. The Maharajas ruled with little interference, but their power began to erode after a popular leader and relative of the royal family embraced communism. During WWII most of the state was occupied by the Japanese. The Indian National Army, recruited from Indian prisoners of war, fought against British India. At Independence the Maharaja ceded his state to India. A movement to disown Vaishnavite Hinduism and the Bengali script grew among the Meitei in the 1960s, looking back 200 years to the time before Hinduism had been adopted. Numerous rebel movements and the state's isolation have so hampered its development that when Japanese veterans returned after 40 years they remarked that it looked almost exactly the same.

The Naga and Kuki tribes of the hills surrounding the valley are predominantly Christian. The hill districts have been the site of bitter ethnic violence. Some accuse the Indian security forces of promoting ethnic rivalry to split the pro-independence forces.

Imphal
☎ 0385 • pop 210,000

The capital lies at an elevation of 790m, with wooded hills in the distance and lakes nearby. The Vaishnavaite **Shri Govindaji Temple** has two gold domes; ceremonial dances are often held here. Next to the temple are the ruins of the **Old Palace**. The **Khwairamband Bazaar** is probably the most interesting thing to see here and a great place to buy Manipuri wickerwork, basketry and weavings, as well as provisions, fruit and vegetables. It's one of the biggest women's markets in India. There are also **war cemeteries** and a very interesting **state museum**.

There's a range of accommodation, including air-con rooms at the government-run *Hotel Imphal (☎ 220459)*. Manipur Tourism is based here.

Imphal is linked by daily flights to Calcutta (US$80) and twice weekly flights to Delhi (US$240) on Indian Airlines (☎ 220999) and NEPC Airlines. There are two flights a week to Guwahati (US$50) and three per week to Silchar (US$25). Kohima is 125km north of Imphal, Silchar 160km west; there are buses to both these places and also to Guwahati (Rs 315, 20 hours).

Loktak Lake

Loktak Lake is the largest freshwater lake in the north-east, and much of it falls within the Keibul Lamjao National Park. Large areas of the lake are covered with thick matted weeds, and the local fishing people and some rare species including the *sangai*, or Manipur dancing deer, live on this unique floating habitat. There's a *tourist lodge* here.

NAGALAND
• pop 1.55 million

South of Arunachal Pradesh and north of Manipur, the remote and hilly state of Nagaland is bordered by Myanmar. Getting a permit to visit is difficult owing to the political instability in the state. However in 1998 one faction of the Naga guerillas signed a peace deal, and in the aftermath Indian tourists have been allowed to visit the state; foreigners are restricted to the vicinity of Kohima.

History

The 16 tribes of Nagaland were once head-hunters dreaded by the neighbouring Assamese. Naga warriors collected heads during raids and stored them in the *morung*, the boys' dormitory and ceremonial house at the core of traditional Naga villages. The custom was linked to the beliefs that the soul can only be released when the head is severed and in the magic ability of the gruesome trophies to ensure the village harvest. After first encountering the Nagas in 1832 the British finally managed to crush them with considerable difficulty in 1879 at the stone-walled village redoubt of Khonoma, an event which became a symbol for Naga nationalism. Naga leaders campaigned for outright independence before the British left, but were unwillingly absorbed into India. Almost immediately a rebellion began, which has continued through many factional splits and failed peace deals until the present day.

As with Mizoram the main religion is Christianity, and churches are the centre of communities in place of the morung. English is spoken in preference to Hindi, another sign of the Naga's rejection of India.

The Nagas

Animists until the arrival of the Christian missionaries, they were duly converted – over 90% are now Christians.

The Nagas' fighting spirit remains; a party of Naga women are famously said to have bared their backsides to Nehru after he landed in the state on a prime ministerial visit. There are 16 Naga tribes, including

the Angamis, Rengmas, Aos, Konyaks, Wanchus, Semas and Lothas.

Kohima

☎ 03866 • pop 54,000

The capital of Nagaland, Kohima was where the Japanese advance into India was halted in April 1944. The well-maintained **war cemetery** is the main tourist sight; there's also an interesting **state museum** with anthropological displays of the Naga tribes, including a log drum, statues and woodcarvings. On the hill above Kohima is **Bara Basti** (Kohima Village) the original Naga settlement. You can still find a few old traditional houses with crossed horns on their gables. The 20th century has caught up with Kohima, and you need to get out into the hill villages to see traditional Naga ways of life.

Nagaland Tourism has rooms at the *Tourist Lodge* (☎ 22417) for Rs 85/100 and the *Yatri Niwas* for Rs 60/80. The top hotel is the *Hotel Japfu* (☎ 22721) with rooms for Rs 600/900. The best hotel is the *Japfu Ashok* (☎ 22721) on PR Hill, with spacious heated rooms for Rs 900/1300.

The nearest airport and railhead are at Dimapur, four hours by road to the north. There are state buses from Guwahati (Rs 255, 16 hours).

Dimapur

☎ 03862

Nagaland's gateway is also its commercial centre. Near the border with Assam, in the 13th century it was the capital of the Kachari tribal kingdom. Their huge decorative phallic symbols can still be seen. There's a range of accommodation including a *Tourist Lodge* (☎ 21416) with rooms from Rs 85/100, and the *Hotel Tragopan*, Circular Rd, with rooms from Rs 600/900 with air-con; there's a good restaurant here.

Dimapur is an important air, bus, and train transportation hub. Indian Airlines (☎ 20114) flies to Calcutta four times a week for US$90.

NORTH-EASTERN REGION

Rajasthan

Rajasthan, the Land of the Kings, is India at its exotic and colourful best with its battle-scarred forts, its palaces of breathtaking grandeur and whimsical charm, its riotous colours and even its romantic sense of pride and honour.

The state is diagonally divided into the hilly and rugged south-eastern region and the barren north-western Thar Desert, which extends across the border into Pakistan. There are plenty of historic cities, incredible fortresses awash with legends, and rare gems of impressionistic beauty, such as Udaipur. There are also a number of centres which attract travellers from far and wide, such as Pushkar with its holy lake, and the desert city of Jaisalmer which resembles a fantasy from *The Thousand & One Nights*.

At the time of writing, the government of Rajasthan was phasing out the sale of beer from restaurants and beer bars. However beer is still available in hotel bars and it is quite possible that the ban on beer could be temporary – check the situation out locally.

Rajasthan is one of India's prime tourist destinations. Nobody leaves here without priceless memories, a bundle of souvenirs, and an address book full of friends.

History

This diverse state is the home of the Rajputs, a group of warrior clans who have controlled this part of India for 1000 years according to a code of chivalry and honour akin to that of the medieval European knights. While temporary alliances and marriages of convenience were the order of the day, pride and independence were always paramount. The Rajputs were therefore never able to present a united front against a common aggressor. Indeed, much of their energy was spent squabbling among themselves and the resultant weakness eventually led to their becoming vassal states of the Mughal empire. Nevertheless, the Rajputs' bravery and sense of honour were unparalleled.

Rajasthan at a Glance

Population: 49.7 million
Area: 342,239 sq km
Capital: Jaipur
Main Languages: Hindi, Rajasthani
Best Time to Go: mid-October to mid-March

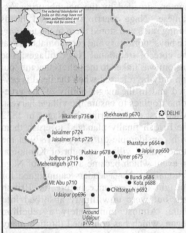

The external boundaries of India on this map have not been authenticated and may not be correct.

Bikaner p736 •   Shekhawati p670 •   DELHI

Jaisalmer p724
Jaisalmer Fort p725

Bharatpur p664 •
Pushkar p678 •   • Jaipur pp650
Jodhpur p716 •   • Ajmer p675
Meherangarh p717

• Bundi p686
• Mt Abu p710   • Kota p688
• Chittorgarh p692
Udaipur pp696

Around Udaipur p705

- **Jaisalmer** – stunning medieval fort rising from a stark desert landscape

- **Pushkar** – beautiful temple town around a lake, home to the Camel Fair

- **Udaipur** – whitewashed temples and grand palaces surround a lake and the gorgeous Lake Palace

- **Keoladeo Ghana National Park** – World Heritage-listed bird sanctuary

- **Ranthambhore & Sariska** – tiger and other wildlife in wilderness regions

- **Shekhawati** – Rajasthan's 'open-air gallery' with scores of ornately painted *havelis*, or mansions

- **Dilwara Temples** – exquisitely sculptured ancient Jain temple complex at Mt Abu

Festivals of Rajasthan

festival	location	1999	2000	2001	2002
Camel Festival	Bikaner	1-2 Jan	20-21 Jan	8-9 Jan	27-28 Jan
Nagaur Cattle Fair	Nagaur	24-27 Jan	12-15 Feb	31 Jan-3 Feb	19-22 Feb
Baneshwar Fair	Dungarpur	27-31 Jan	16-19 Feb	4-8 Feb	23-27 Feb
Desert Festival	Jaisalmer	29-31 Jan	17-19 Feb	6-8 Feb	25-27 Feb
Elephant Festival	Jaipur	1 Mar	19 Mar	9 Mar	28 Mar
Gangaur Fair	statewide	20-21 Mar	7-8 Apr	28-29 Mar	15-16 Apr
Mewar Festival	Udaipur	20-21 Mar	7-8 Apr	28-29 Mar	15-16 Apr
Summer Festival	Mt Abu	1-3 Jun	1-3 Jun	1-3 Jun	1-3 Jun
Teej Fair	Jaipur	14-15 Aug	2-3 Aug	23-24 Jul	11-12 Aug
Dussehra Mela	Kota	17-19 Oct	5-7 Oct	24-26 Oct	13-15 Oct
Marwar Festival	Jodhpur	23-24 Oct	12-13 Oct	31 Oct-1 Nov	19-20 Oct
Camel Fair	Pushkar	20-23 Nov	9-11 Nov	27-30 Nov	16-19 Nov
Chandrabhaga Fair	Jhalrapatan	22-24 Nov	10-12 Nov	29 Nov-1 Dec	18-20 Nov

Rajput warriors would fight against all odds and, when no hope was left, chivalry demanded that *jauhar* take place. In this grim ritual, the women and children committed suicide by immolating themselves on a huge funeral pyre, while the men donned saffron robes and rode out to confront the enemy and certain death. In some of the larger battles, tens of thousands of Rajput warriors lost their lives in this way. Three times in Chittorgarh's long history, the women consigned themselves to the flames while the men rode out to their martyrdom. The same tragic fate befell many other forts around the state. It's hardly surprising that Akbar persuaded Rajputs to lead his army, nor that subsequent Mughal emperors had such difficulty controlling this part of their empire.

With the decline of the Mughal empire, the Rajputs gradually clawed back their independence through a series of spectacular victories, but then a new force appeared on the scene in the form of the British. As the Raj inexorably expanded, most Rajput states signed articles of alliance with the British which allowed them to continue as independent states, each with its own maharaja (or similarly titled leader), subject to certain political and economic constraints. The British, after all, were not there for humanitarian reasons, but to establish an empire and gain a controlling interest in the economy of the subcontinent in the same way as the Mughals had done.

These alliances proved to be the beginning of the end for the Rajput rulers. Indulgence and extravagance soon replaced chivalry and honour so that by the early 1900s, many of the maharajas spent much of their time travelling the world with scores of concubines and retainers, playing polo, racing horses, and occupying whole floors of the most expensive hotels in Europe and America. While it suited the British to indulge them in this respect, their profligate waste of the resources of Rajputana (the land of the Rajputs) was economically and socially detrimental. When India gained its independence, Rajasthan had one of the subcontinent's lowest rates of life expectancy and literacy.

At Independence, India's ruling Congress Party was forced to make a deal with the nominally independent Rajput states in order to secure their agreement to join the new India. The rulers were allowed to keep their titles, their property holdings were

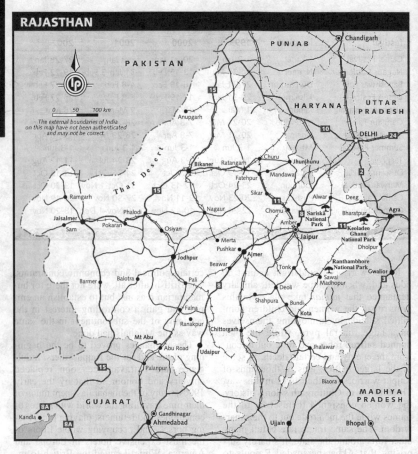

RAJASTHAN

secured and they were paid an annual stipend commensurate with their status. It couldn't last forever, given India's socialist persuasion, and the crunch came in the early 1970s when Indira Gandhi abolished both the titles and the stipends and severely sequestered their property rights.

While some of the rulers have survived this by converting their palaces into luxury hotels, many have fallen by the wayside, unable to cope with the financial and managerial demands of the late 20th century.

Art & Architecture

Rajasthan has various schools of miniature painting, largely derived from the Mughal style but with some clear differences – in particular, the palace and hunting scenes are complemented by religious themes, particularly relating to the Krishna legends.

Most of Rajasthan's early architecture was damaged or destroyed by the first waves of Muslim invaders. Fragments remaining from that period include the Adhai-din-ka-Jhonpra in Ajmer. There are many buildings dating from the 10th to 15th centuries, including the superb Jain temples at Ranakpur and Mt Abu. Most of the great forts date, in their present form, from the Mughal period.

Money

Most major towns change money, but it's a good idea to carry adequate rupees with you to smaller places, such as to the villages of Shekhawati. Banks are open Monday to Friday 10 am to 2 pm, and 10 am to noon on Saturday.

Special Events

Rajasthan has all the usual Hindu and Muslim festivals, some celebrated with special local fervour, as well as a number of festivals of its own. Rajasthan is perhaps best known for the flamboyant Pushkar Camel Fair, held annually in October/November. (See the Pushkar section for details.)

Exclusive to Rajasthan is the Gangaur Fair, which celebrates the love between Shiva and Gauri (Parvati). Unmarried women pray to Gauri for a good husband, and married women pray for their husbands' health and longevity. Jaipur, Bikaner, Jodhpur, Nathdwara and Jaisalmer all celebrate colourful fairs of Gangaur.

The dates of the fairs and festivals are determined by the lunar calendar. See the Festivals of Rajasthan table for details.

Accommodation

Palaces, Forts & Castles Rajasthan is famous for its superb palace hotels. The bulk of Rajasthan's maharajas have had to turn their palaces into hotels to make ends meet. The most renowned are Udaipur's beautiful Lake Palace Hotel and Shiv Niwas Palace Hotel, Jaipur's Rambagh Palace, and the Umaid Bhawan Palace in Jodhpur.

You don't have to spend a fortune to stay in a palace – there are plenty of other former royal abodes which are more moderately priced. Many of these are known as Heritage Hotels, and they include *havelis* (traditional mansions), forts and hunting lodges. Many tourist offices have a brochure listing Heritage Hotels. For more information contact

the Heritage Hotels Association of India (☎ 0141-374112, fax 372084 in Jaipur).

Hotel Tariffs Most hotel tariffs will have risen by the time you read this (the increase can be anything from 5% to 50%).

Many hotels whack an additional tax (usually about 10%) on top of their advertised room rates. This extra charge goes by various names including: luxury tax, service tax, sales tax, extra tax or jusst plain old 'tax'. On the plus side, many places offer discounts of 25% to 40% in the low season (May to August).

Tourist Bungalows The Rajasthan Tourism Development Corporation (RTDC) operates a network of hotels called 'tourist bungalows' around the state. Once upon a time they were top value, but those days have long gone – the fabric and services of most have severely deteriorated. On the plus side, for shoestringers, many offer cheap dormitory accommodation. The local tourist office (usually called the Tourist Reception Centre) is often in the RTDC's hotel premises.

Home-Stay Accommodation Staying with an Indian family can be an enriching education, and Rajasthan's home-stay accommodation (known as the Paying Guest House Scheme) gives you the opportunity to do just that. The scheme, which is administered by the RTDC, operates in most major towns. The price varies depending on the level of facilities offered (it's primarily aimed at the budget end of the market). The tourist offices have comprehensive lists of the participating families.

Getting Around

Air You're strongly advised to make flight reservations well in advance, especially in the busy tourist season. Indian Airlines offers a 25% discount for passengers under 30 years of age (foreigners only). Note that airline prices are expected to increase by around 10% in late 1999.

Bus Rajasthan has an extensive and reasonably good state bus system. On most sectors

Warning

Although rarely printed in menus, many restaurants in Rajasthan serve *bhang lassi*, a yoghurt and iced-water beverage laced with bhang, a derivative of marijuana. Usually called 'special lassi', this often potent concoction does not agree with everyone. Some travellers have been stuck in bed for several miserable days after drinking it; others have been robbed while lying in a state of delirium.

there is a choice of ordinary and express buses. You're advised to stick to expresses since the ordinary buses make a lot of frustrating detours, take a long time to get anywhere and are generally decrepit vehicles.

If you're taking a bus from a major bus stand, it's worth buying a ticket from the ticket office rather than on board the bus. It guarantees (or at least comes closer to guaranteeing) a seat, and you're also more likely to get on the right bus since the ticket clerk usually writes the bus registration number on your ticket. This can be an important consideration because timetables at bus stations are invariably in Hindi. A number of private bus companies run luxury buses between the major towns; however, be aware that their schedules can be changed with little notice or even cancelled.

If you're travelling overnight by bus, try to avoid video coaches, which usually have the soundtrack pumped up at full volume.

For long journeys make sure you go to the toilet beforehand, as stops can be infrequent and in less than desirable places (especially for women).

Train Travelling by train in Rajasthan used to be a slow process because much of the track was metre gauge and narrower than the broad gauge used in the rest of the country. As part of the national 'uni-gauge' drive, some of the lines have now been converted and most of the rest are expected to be upgraded by 2001. This means that you're

likely to find some parts of the rail system in Rajasthan out of action during your visit.

Train fares and schedules constantly change in Rajasthan, so double-check details. Seats can fill up fast, so book ahead.

The *Palace on Wheels*, one of India's most famous railway experiences, runs through Jaipur, Chittorgarh, Udaipur, Ranthambhore National Park, Jaisalmer, Jodhpur, Bharatpur and Agra. This train, a mobile hotel, is fitted out to look like a traditional maharaja's state carriage, and is an expensive but luxurious way to travel. For more information, see the *Palace on Wheels* boxed text.

Eastern Rajasthan

JAIPUR
☎ 0141 • pop 1.8 million

Jaipur, the vibrant capital of Rajasthan, is popularly known as the 'pink city' because of the pink-coloured buildings in its old city. It sits on a dry lake bed in a somewhat arid landscape, surrounded by barren hills surmounted by forts and crenellated walls. This buzzing metropolis is certainly a place of wild contrasts and a feast for the eyes. Vegetable-laden camel carts thread their way through streets jam-packed with cars, rickshaws, bicycles, tempos, motorcycles and pedestrians frantically dodging the crazy traffic. Traditionally dressed Rajput men sporting bright turbans and swashbuckling moustaches discuss village politics outside restaurants serving spaghetti bolognese and American ice-cream sodas. Ramshackle roadside stalls selling *jootis* (traditional Rajasthani shoes) stand beside kitsch shops flogging a mishmash of modern trinkets.

Jaipur has long outstripped the confines of its city wall and is today among the most tumultuous and polluted places in Rajasthan. Despite this, it seldom disappoints the first-time visitor.

History
The city owes its name, its foundation and its careful planning to the great warrior-as-

tronomer Maharaja Jai Singh II (1693-1743). His predecessors had enjoyed good relations with the Mughals and Jai Singh was careful to preserve this alliance.

In 1727, with Mughal power on the wane, Jai Singh decided the time was ripe to move down from his somewhat cramped hillside fort at nearby Amber to a new site on the plains. He laid out the city, with its surrounding walls and rectangular blocks, according to principles set down in the *Shilpa-Shastra*, an ancient Hindu treatise on architecture. In 1728, he built the remarkable observatory (Jantar Mantar) which is still one of Jaipur's main attractions.

Orientation

The walled old city is in the north-east of Jaipur, the new parts spread to the south and west. The main tourist attractions are in the old city. The principal shopping centre in the old city is Johari Bazaar, the jewellers' market. Unlike most other shopping centres in narrow alleys in India and elsewhere in Asia, this one is broad and open.

There are three main interconnecting roads in the new part of town – Mirza Ismail Rd (MI Rd), Station Rd and Sansar Chandra Marg. Along or just off these roads are most of the budget and mid-range hotels and restaurants, the main train and bus stations, many of the banks and the modern shopping centre.

Information

Tourist Offices The Tourist Reception Centre (☎ 365256) is in the RTDC's Tourist Hotel compound on MI Rd and is open daily except Sunday, 10 am to 5 pm. It has a range of literature and the staff are quite helpful, especially Madan Singh. There's another tourist office (☎ 315714) on platform No 1 at the train station. It's open daily, 7 am to 6 pm. The Government of India tourist office (☎ 372200) is in the Hotel Khasa Kothi, but it's of limited use.

Money You can change money at Thomas Cook (☎ 360940) on the 1st floor of Jaipur Towers on MI Rd. It's open daily except

Palace on Wheels

The RTDC *Palace on Wheels* is a special tourist train service that operates weekly tours of Rajasthan, departing from Delhi every Wednesday from September to the end of April. The itinerary takes in Jaipur, Chittorgarh, Udaipur, Sawai Madhopur (for Ranthambhore National Park), Jaisalmer, Jodhpur, Bharatpur (for the Keoladeo Ghana National Park) and Agra. It's a hell of a lot of ground to cover in a week, but most of the travelling is done at night.

Originally this train used carriages which once belonged to various maharajas, but these became so ancient that new carriages were refurbished to look like the originals. They were also fitted with air-conditioning. The result is a very luxurious mobile hotel and it can be a memorable way to travel if you have limited time and limitless resources. The train comes equipped with two dining cars and a well stocked bar. Each coach, which is attended by a splendidly costumed catain and attendant, contains four coupes (double or twin share) with bathrooms.

The cost includes tours, entry fees, accommodation on the train plus all meals. Rates per person per day from October to March are US$260 for triple occupancy (the third person sleeps on a fold-away bed), US$325 for double occupancy and US$460 for single occupancy. In the months of September and April the tariff is lower: US$215/270/370. It's a very popular service and bookings must be made in advance at the RTDC's Tourist Reception Centre (☎ 011-338 1884, fax 3381884), Bikaner House, Pandara Rd, New Delhi 110011, or at the RTDC's Hotel Swagatam Campus (☎ 0141-203531, fax 201045, Web site www.palaceonwheels.net), Near Train Station, Jaipur 302006.

Adivasis of Rajasthan

The main tribal, or *adivasi*, groups of Rajasthan are the Bhils and the Minas, who were the original inhabitants of the area now called Rajasthan, but who were forced into the Aravalli Range by the Aryan invasion. Smaller groups of adivasis include the Sahariyas, Damariyas, Garasias and the Gaduliya Lohars.

Bhils The Bhils traditionally inhabited the south-eastern corner of the state – the area around Udaipur, Chittorgarh and Dungarpur – although the largest concentrations of them are found in neighbouring Madhya Pradesh.

Legend has it that the Bhils were fine archers, hence their name, which can be traced to the Tamil word *vil*, meaning bow. Bhil bowmen are mentioned in both the *Mahabharata* and the *Ramayana*. They were highly regarded as warriors, and the Rajput rulers relied heavily on them to thwart the invading Marathas and Mughals. In fact, some scholars suggest that the Rajputs owe their warrior propensities to their exposure to the Bhils, whom they emulated. The British formed a Mewar Bhil Corps in the 1820s in recognition of the Bhils' martial tradition.

Although originally food gatherers, the Bhils these days have taken up small-scale agriculture, or have abandoned the land altogether and taken up city residence and employment. The literacy rate of the Bhils, particularly the women, used to be one of the lowest of any group in the country which made them prime targets for exploitation and bonded labour. This trend is now being reversed, and the fortunes of the Bhils are improving accordingly. Several Bhils have even entered state parliament, becoming MLAs, including, in one instance, a Bhil woman.

Those Bhils who can afford it engage in polygamy. Marriages of love, as opposed to arranged marriages which are the norm in India, are condoned.

The Baneshwar Fair is a Bhil festival held near Dungarpur in January/February each year, and large numbers of Bhils gather for several days of singing, dancing and worship. Holi is another important time for the Bhils.

Witchcraft, magic and superstition are deeply rooted aspects of Bhil culture.

Minas The Minas are the second largest adivasi group in the state after the Bhils, and are the most widely spread. They live in the regions of Shekhawati and eastern Rajasthan. Scholars still disagree as to whether the Minas are indigenous, or whether they migrated to the region from Central Asia.

The name Mina is derived from *meen*, or fish, and the Minas claim descent from the fish incarnation of Vishnu. Originally they were a ruling tribe, but their downfall was a long, drawn-out affair. It began with the Rajputs and was completed when the British government

Sunday, 9.30 am to 6 pm. The tiny Bank of Rajasthan (☎ 381416) in the Rambagh Palace changes money and is conveniently open 7 am to 8 pm daily.

The Andhra Bank (☎ 369606), MI Rd, does cash advances on MasterCard, Visa and JCB (Japanese Credit Bureau) cards. The Central Bank of India (☎ 317419), Anand Building, Sansar Chandra Marg, is-

sues cash advances on MasterCard and Visa (minimum US$100).

Post & Communications The main post office (☎ 368740) on MI Rd is quite efficient and there's a man at the entrance who sews up parcels, sealing them with wax.

DHL Worldwide Express (☎ 362826) is in a lane off MI Rd at C-scheme, G-7A declared them a criminal tribe in 1924, mainly to stop them trying to regain their territory from the Rajputs. In their skirmishes with the Rajputs, the Minas resorted to various unorthodox means such as demanding 'protection money' from villagers to curtail their dacoit activities.

Following Independence, their ignominious status as a 'criminal tribe' was lifted. However, their culture was by this time more or less totally destroyed, and they have been given protection as a Scheduled Tribe.

With the withdrawal of the Criminal Tribes Act, the Minas took to agriculture. As is the case with the Bhils, the literacy rate among the Minas was very low, but is improving.

Marriage is generally within the tribe. This is arranged by the parents and most marriages take place when the children are quite young.

Gaduliya Lohars The Gaduliya Lohars were originally martial Rajput adivasis, but these days are nomadic blacksmiths. Their traditional territory was Mewar (Udaipur) and they fought with the maharana against the Mughals. With typical Rajput chivalry, they made a vow to the maharana that they would only enter his fort at Chittorgarh after he had overcome the Mughals. As he died without achieving this, the clan was forced to become nomadic. When Nehru was in power he led a group of Gaduliya Lohars into Chittorgarh, with the hope that they would then resettle in their former lands, but they preferred to remain nomadic.

Garasias The Garasias are a small Rajput adivasi group found in the Abu Road area of southern Rajasthan. It is thought that they intermingled with the Bhils to some extent, which is supported by the fact that bows and arrows are widely used.

The marriage ceremony is curious in that the couple elope, and a sum of money is paid to the father of the bride. If the marriage fails, the bride returns home, with a small sum of money to give to the father. Widows are not entitled to a share of their husband's property, and so generally remarry.

Sahariyas The Sahariyas are thought to be of Bhil origin, and live in the areas of Kota, Dungarpur and Sawai Madhopur in the south-east of the state. They are one of the least educated of the adivasi groups in the country, with a literacy rate of only 5% and, as unskilled labourers, have been cruelly exploited.

As all members of the clan are considered to be related, marriages are arranged beyond the tribe. Their food and worship traditions are closely related to Hindu customs.

Vinobha Marg. It operates air freight around the world.

There are scores of round-the-clock local/long-distance telephone booths in Jaipur, and their charges are generally cheaper than the hotels.

Internet Resources Internet outlets are rapidly mushrooming in Jaipur, so by the time you read this there should be plenty more. One good fairly central place where you can snack and surf is the Mewar Cyber Café & Communication (☎ 206172, email mewar@jp1.dot.net.in), near the main bus station on Station Rd.

Bookshops If you're on the hunt for reading material, there's a wide range of

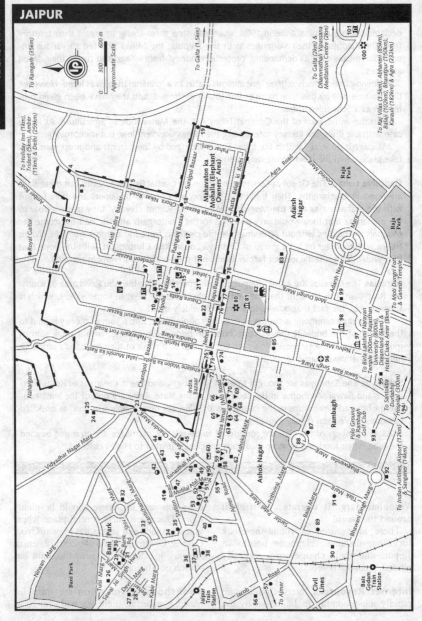

JAIPUR

JAIPUR

PLACES TO STAY
3 Samode Haveli
16 Hotel Kailash
22 Hotel Sweet Dream
24 Hotel Bissau Palace
25 Hotel Khetri House
26 Hotel Meghniwas
27 Tirupati Guest House
28 Shapura House
29 Madhuban;
   Madhavanand Ashram
30 Umaid Bhawan Guest House;
   Sajjan Niwas Guest House
31 Pipalda House
32 Jaipur Inn
33 Hotel Jaipur Ashok
34 RTDC's Hotel Teej
36 RTDC's Hotel Swagatam
37 Rajputana Palace Sheraton
39 Hotel Khasa Kothi;
   Government of India
   Tourist Office
40 RTDC's Hotel Gangaur
43 Jai Mangal Palace
44 Alsisar Haveli
45 Hotel Arya Niwas
46 Hotel Mangal
48 Mansingh Hotel;
   Central Bank of India
49 Hotel Neelam; Karni Niwas
52 Atithi Guest House;
   Aangan Guest House
56 Jai Mahal Palace Hotel
58 RTDC's Tourist Hotel;
   Tourist Reception Centre
62 Evergreen Guest House;
   Hotel Pink Sun;
   Ashiyana Guest House
83 Nana-ki-Haveli
86 Hotel Diggi Palace
90 Rajmahal Palace
92 Youth Hostel
93 Rambagh Palace; Bank of
   Rajasthan; Rajasthan Tours

95 Narain Niwas Palace Hotel
99 Rajasthan Palace Hotel

PLACES TO EAT
20 Royal's
21 LMB Hotel & Restaurant
50 Ganpati Plaza; Swaad; Pizza
   Hut; Celebrations; Baskin 31
   Robbins; Hot Breads;
   Rajasthan Travel Service;
   Air India
55 Rainbow Restaurant
59 Copper Chimney
61 Handi Restaurant
65 Chanakya Restaurant
66 Lassiwala; Goyal Colour Lab;
   Charmica
69 Golden Dragon Restaurant;
   Bake Hut
70 Niro's; Surya Mahal;
   Jal Mahal; Natraj Restaurant
73 Indian Coffee House

OTHER
1 Samrat Gate
2 Zorawar Gate
4 Gangapol (Gate)
5 Char Darwaja (Gate)
6 Govind Devji Temple
7 Jantar Mantar (Observatory)
8 City Palace & Maharaja Sawai
   Mansingh II Museum;
   Foreigners Registration Office
9 Choti Chaupar
10 Iswari Minar Swarga Sal
11 Dr Vinod Shastri (Astrologer)
12 Tripolia Gate
13 Hawa Mahal
14 Gopalji ka Rasta
15 Jama Masjid
17 Haldio ka Rasta
18 Ramganj Chaupar
19 Surajpol (Gate)
23 Chandpol (Gate)

35 Sita World Travels
38 Aravali Safari & Tours
41 Mewar Cyber Café &
   Communication
42 Main Bus Terminal
47 Polo Victory Cinema
51 Cathay Pacific
53 British Airways
54 Jaipur Towers (Thomas Cook
   & Airline Agents)
57 Soma
60 Main Post Office;
   Philatelic Museum
63 DHL Worldwide Express
64 Andhra Bank
67 Books Corner
68 Raj Mandir Cinema
71 Books & News Mart
72 Singhpol (Gate)
74 Rajasthali Emporium;
   Rajasthan Handloom House
75 Ajmeri Gate
76 New Gate
77 Lufthansa; Singapore Airlines
78 Sanganeri Gate
79 Ghat Gate
80 Ram Niwas Public Gardens
81 Ravindra Rangmanch
   Art Gallery
82 Zoo
84 Central Museum
   (Albert Hall)
85 Maharaja College
87 Birla Planetarium
88 Statue Circle
89 Registhan Tours
91 Anokhi Showroom
94 Rambagh Circle
96 Sawai Mansingh Hospital
97 Dolls Museum
98 Museum of Indology
100 Vidyadharji ka Bagh
101 Sisodia Rani Palace
   & Gardens

English-language books as well as magazines and maps at Books Corner, MI Rd (near Niro's restaurant). You can pick up a copy of the informative *Jaipur Vision* here, which contains useful information about the city. A good range of titles can also be found in the bookshops at the Rambagh Palace, Rajputana Palace Sheraton and at the Bissau Palace hotel.

Medical Services Should you need medical attention, the Sawai Mansingh Hospital (☎ 560291) is on Sawai Ram Singh Marg and you'll find the Santokba Durlabhji Hospital (☎ 566251) on Bhawani Singh Marg. Most hotels can arrange a private doctor.

Emergency Emergency numbers are: police ☎100; fire ☎101; and ambulance ☎102.

Old City (Pink City)

In 1876, Maharaja Ram Singh had the entire old city painted pink, traditionally a colour associated with hospitality, to welcome the Prince of Wales (later King Edward VII), a tradition which has been maintained. The old city is partially encircled by a crenellated wall with a number of gates – the major gates are Chandpol, Ajmeri and Sanganeri. Broad avenues, over 30m wide, divide the pink city into neat rectangles. In the evening light, the pink and orange buildings have a magical glow which is complemented by the brightly clothed Rajasthanis.

The major landmark in this part of town is the **Iswari Minar Swarga Sal** (Heaven Piercing Minaret), near the Tripolia Gate, which was built to overlook the city.

The main **bazaars** in the old city include Johari Bazaar, Tripolia Bazaar, Bapu Bazaar and Chandpol Bazaar.

Hawa Mahal Constructed in 1799, the Hawa Mahal, or Palace of the Winds, is one of Jaipur's major landmarks, although it is actually little more than a facade. This five storey building, which overlooks the main street of the bustling old city, is a stunning example of Rajput artistry with its pink, delicately honeycombed sandstone windows. It was originally built to enable ladies of the royal household to watch the everyday life and processions of the city. You can climb to the top of the Hawa Mahal for a fine view over the city. The palace was built by Maharaja Sawaj Pratap Singh and is part of the City Palace complex. There's a small **archaeological museum** (closed Saturday) on the same site.

Entrance to the Hawa Mahal is from the rear of the building. To get there, go back to the intersection on your left as you face the Hawa Mahal, turn right and then take the first right again through an archway. It's open daily 9 am to 4.30 pm and entry costs Rs 2. A still camera costs Rs 10/30 for Indians/foreigners, and a video camera is Rs 20/70.

City Palace Complex In the heart of the old city, the City Palace occupies a large area divided into a series of courtyards, gardens and buildings. The outer wall was built by Jai Singh, but other additions are much more recent, some dating from the start of this century. Today, the palace is a blend of Rajasthani and Mughal architecture. The son of the last maharaja and his family still reside in part of the palace.

Before the palace proper you'll see the **Mubarak Mahal**, or Welcome Palace, which was built in the late 19th century by Maharaja Sawai Madho Singh II as a reception centre for visiting dignitaries. It now forms part of the **Maharaja Sawai Mansingh II Museum**, containing a collection of royal costumes and superb shawls including Kashmiri *pashmina* (goats' wool) shawls. One remarkable exhibit is a set of the voluminous clothing of Sawai Madho Singh I, who was a stately 2m tall, 1.2m wide and weighed 250kg!

Other points of interest in the palace include the **Diwan-i-Am**, or the Hall of Public Audience, with its intricate decorations and manuscripts in Persian and Sanskrit, the **Diwan-i-Khas**, or Hall of Private Audience, with a marble-paved gallery, and the exquisite **Peacock Gate** in the Chandra Mahal courtyard.

Outside the buildings, you can see enormous silver vessels in which a former maharaja used to take holy Ganges water to England. Being a devout Hindu, he preferred not to risk the English water!

The palace and museum are open daily between 9.30 am and 4.45 pm. Entry is Rs 35/110 for Indians/foreigners (this includes entry to Jaigarh – see the Around Jaipur section – and the ticket is valid for two days). Photography opportunities are severely limited because it is prohibited inside the museums. If you're still interested, a video camera costs Rs 100 for everyone, but a Rs 50 camera fee is only levied on Indians! There are guides for hire inside the palace complex for Rs 150.

Jantar Mantar Next to the entrance to the City Palace is the Jantar Mantar, or Observatory, begun by Jai Singh in 1728. Jai

Singh's passion for astronomy was even more notable than his prowess as a warrior and, before commencing construction, he sent scholars abroad to study foreign observatories. The Jaipur observatory is the largest and the best preserved of the five he built, and was restored in 1901. Others are in Delhi (the oldest, dating from 1724), Varanasi and Ujjain. The fifth, the Muttra observatory, is gone.

At first glance, Jantar Mantar appears to be just a curious collection of sculptures but in fact each construction has a specific purpose, such as measuring the positions of stars, altitudes and azimuths, and calculating eclipses. The most striking instrument is the sundial with its 27m-high gnomon. The shadow this casts moves up to 4m an hour.

The observatory is open 9 am to 4.30 pm daily and admission is Rs 4 (free on Monday). Photography is Rs 20/50 for Indians/foreigners; Rs 50/100 for videos.

Royalty at play: an 18th century ivory door panel.

Central Museum

This somewhat dusty collection is housed in the architecturally impressive Albert Hall in the Ram Niwas Public Gardens, south of the old city. Exhibits include a natural history collection, models of yogis adopting various positions, tribal ware, dioramas depicting Rajasthani dances and sections on decorative arts, costumes, drawings and musical instruments. The museum is open daily except Friday, 10 am to 4.30 pm. Entry is Rs 5/30 for Indians/foreigners (free on Monday). Photography is prohibited.

Other Attractions

The Ram Niwas Public Gardens also has a **zoo** with unhappy looking animals (open daily except Tuesday 8 am to 5 pm; entry is Rs 2). Nearby an old theatre houses Jaipur's **Modern Art Gallery**, on the 1st floor of the Ravindra Rangmanch Building (free entry, closed Sunday). For excellent contemporary paintings, go to the **Juneja Art Gallery** (for more details, see the Shopping section).

The rather ramshackle **Museum of Indology** is an extraordinary private collection of folk art objects and other bits and

pieces of interest – there's everything from a map of India painted on a rice grain, to manuscripts (one written by Aurangzeb), tribal ornaments, fossils, old currency notes, clocks and much more. The museum is actually a private house (although the living quarters seem to have been swallowed up by the collection), and is signposted off J Nehru Marg, south of the Central Museum. It's open 8 am to 6 pm daily. Entry is Rs 40 (including a guide). Cameras and videos are not allowed. For stamp enthusiasts, there's a small **Philatelic Museum** at the main post office (free; closed Sunday).

Farther south down J Nehru Marg, looming above the road to the left, is the small fort of **Moti Dungri** (closed to the public). At the foot of this fort is the large modern **Birla Lakshmi Narayan Temple**. There is a small **museum** next to the temple, which is open daily 8 am to noon and 4 to 8 pm (free). Nearby is a **Ganesh temple**, which is also worth a look.

About 3km south-west of the old city is the **Rambagh Palace**, now one of India's most renowned hotels. Gayatri Devi, the glamorous third wife of the last maharaja of Jaipur, resides in part of this gracious palace.

Meditation & Yoga

The Dhammathali Vipassana Meditation Centre (☎ 641520) at Galta (see the Around Jaipur section) runs meditation courses for a donation.

Yoga courses are available at the Prakaritic Chikitsalya (☎ 510590), Bapu Nagar (near the Rajasthan University campus), and also at the Madhavanand Ashram (☎ 200317), C-19 Behari Marg, Bani Park.

Astrology

Dr Vinod Shastri (☎ 663338, 551117, email vshastri@jp1.dot.net.in) is the General Secretary of the Rajasthan Astrological Council & Research Institute and works from his shop near the City Palace on Chandani Chowk, Tripolia Gate. It costs Rs 300 for a 20 minute consultation and you will need to have your exact time of birth in order to get a computerised horoscope drawn up. A five year prediction costs Rs 900 and a 30 year prediction costs a whopping Rs 3000. It's advisable to make an advance appointment.

These days, many hotels are cashing in on foreigners' interest in fortune telling.

Organised Tours

Jaipur City The RTDC offers half and full-day tours of Jaipur and its environs. A full-day tour (9 am to 6 pm) costs Rs 115; there's a lunch break at Nahargarh. Half-day tours are a little rushed but otherwise OK. They cost Rs 75; timings are 8 am to 1 pm, 11.30 am to 4.30 pm and 1.30 to 6.30 pm. Entrance fees to monuments are extra. Tours depart daily from the train station (according to demand), but you can also arrange to be collected from any of the RTDC hotels. Contact the Tourist Reception Centre or tourist office at the train station for details (see Information, earlier).

Other Tours There are RTDC tours (minimum 10 people) to Nahargarh (see Around Jaipur) for Rs 150 including dinner. There are also tours to Chokhi Dhani, a rather contrived restaurant near the airport, which has evening traditional folk performances and Rajasthani cuisine (Rs 125).

If you want a taste of rural Rajasthan, the Hotel Bissau Palace organises tours to its former hunting pavilion, The Retreat (where Prince Charles and Princess Diana once visited). It is about 27km from Jaipur. From here you are whisked away by camel cart to several nearby villages. It costs Rs 500 per person (for a minimum of six people) or Rs 750 per person (for groups of five or less). This includes transport, the village tour and lunch. Book in advance at the Hotel Bissau Palace (☎ 304391, fax 304628).

Special Events

Teej, also known as the Festival of Swings (a reference to the flower-bedecked swings which are erected at this time), celebrates the onset of the monsoon and is held in honour of the marriage of Shiva and Parvati. It is celebrated with particular fervour in Jaipur. For dates, see the Festivals of Rajasthan table at the start of this chapter.

Places to Stay

Getting to the hotel of your choice in Jaipur can be a headache. Auto-rickshaw drivers besiege most travellers who arrive by train (less so if you come by bus). Their persistence can drive you nuts, but just keep your cool. If you don't want to go to a hotel of their choice, they'll either refuse to take you or they'll demand at least double the normal fare. If you do go to the hotel of their choice, you'll pay through the nose for accommodation because the manager will be paying them a commission of at least 30% of what you are charged for a bed (and the charge won't go down for subsequent nights). To get around this, go straight to the prepaid auto-rickshaw stands which have been set up at both the bus and train stations, where rates are set by the government.

If you wish to stay with an Indian family, contact the Tourist Reception Centre, which has details of Jaipur's Paying Guest House Scheme. They sell a handy booklet listing all paying guesthouses in Rajasthan (Rs 5).

Places to Stay – Budget

Jaipur Inn (☎ *201121, fax 204796, B-17 Shiv Marg, Bani Park, email jaipurinn@ hotmail.com)* is an old-time favourite with travellers. Run by retired Wing Commander RN Bhargava and his son, this place is certainly geared up for travellers. Rooms range from spartan singles/doubles with common bath for Rs 200/250 to Rs 500/700 for better rooms with attached bath. Beds in the rather cramped dorm cost Rs 100, and you can even camp on the lawn (Rs 50 per person) if you have your own tent. Mozzie nets can be hired for Rs 15 per day, and bike hire is Rs 25 per day. Meals are available and the rooftop terrace commands sensational views.

Hotel Diggi Palace (☎ *373091, fax 370359)*, just off Sawai Ram Singh Marg, less than 1km south of Ajmeri Gate, is another popular hang-out with budget travellers. Formerly the residence of the *thakur* (similar to a lord or baron) of Diggi, it has a lovely lawn area and relaxing ambience. Bare doubles with common bath (free bucket hot water) cost Rs 100 and Rs 125. With attached bath and geyser, they're Rs 250; better air-cooled/air-con rooms are Rs 400/750. Good meals are available in the restaurant.

Karni Niwas (☎ *365433, fax 375034, C-5 Motilal Atal Marg, email karniniwas@ hotmail.com)*, in a lane behind the Hotel Neelam, is a down-to-earth place run by an amiable family. Clean singles/doubles with attached bath range from Rs 275/325 to Rs 650/700. Many rooms have a balcony and meals are available.

Atithi Guest House (☎ *378679, fax 379496, 1 Park House Scheme Rd, email tanmay@jp1.dot.net.in)*, opposite All India Radio, between MI and Station Rds, is a well-kept place run by the helpful Shukla family. Fresh, squeaky clean singles/doubles with private bath range from Rs 300/350 to Rs 600/650. Veg meals are available and there's a pleasant rooftop terrace. Next door is the similarly priced *Aangan Guest House* (☎ *373449, fax 364596)* is reasonably good.

The *Hotel Arya Niwas* (☎ *372456, fax 364376, email aryahotl@jp1.dot.net.in)*, just off Sansar Chandra Marg, is another very popular choice. This large but well maintained hotel has singles/doubles with attached bath from Rs 300/400. There's a nice front lawn and a self-service veg restaurant.

Evergreen Guest House (☎ *363446, fax 204234)* is a rambling hotel just off MI Rd in the area known as Chameliwala Market. It's a good place to meet other backpackers, although the cleanliness and service are variable. Facilities include a small swimming pool and restaurant. Singles/doubles with bath start at Rs 150/175 (free bucket hot water). Checkout is an ungenerous 10 am.

Ashiyana Guest House (☎ *375414)* is nearby if you find the Evergreen too much of a scene. The cheapest rooms (with common bath and bucket hot water for Rs 10) go for Rs 70/150 a single/double. No meals are available. In the same area is the slightly cheaper but less impressive *Hotel Pink Sun* (☎ *370385)*.

Devi Niwas (☎ *363727, Dhuleshwar Bagh, Sadar Patel Marg)* is an unpretentious little place with just a handful of rooms with bath (Rs 300).

Hotel Sweet Dream (☎ *314409)*, in the old city, has average singles/doubles with attached bath from Rs 230/300. There's a veg restaurant on the rooftop.

Pipalda House (☎ *201925, D-240A Bank Rd, Bani Park)* has basic singles/doubles with bath from Rs 150/250.

Hotel Kailash (☎ *565372, fax 566195)*, opposite the Jama Masjid, is one of the few places to stay within the old city. It's basic but friendly. Small singles/doubles cost Rs 150/175 with common bath, Rs 215/240 with private bath.

RTDC's Hotel Swagatam (☎ *200595)*, near the train station, has a rather institutional feel. Dorm beds are Rs 50; rooms with bath start at Rs 275/350 (including breakfast). Other RTDC budget hotels are the *Tourist Hotel* (☎ *360238)* and the *Hotel Teej* (☎ *205482)*, which is actually a mid-range place but also has dorm beds (Rs 50).

Retiring rooms at the train station are handy if you're catching an early-morning train. Singles/doubles with common bath are Rs 100/250, or Rs 400 with bath and air-con.

Places to Stay – Mid-Range

Alsisar Haveli (☎/*fax 368290, Sansar Chandra Marg*) is a gracious 19th century mansion set in well-manicured gardens. Although more pricey than other mid-range places, it's still a marvellous choice, with quaintly furnished rooms for Rs 1195/1550.

The *Madhuban* (☎ *200033, fax 202344, D-237 Behari Marg, Bani Park, email madhuban@usa.net*) is heartily recommended if you crave a homey ambience with no hassles whatsoever. Run by the helpful 'Dicky' and his family, singles/doubles range from Rs 400/500 to Rs 850/950. The more expensive rooms have fine antique furnishings. They offer free pick-ups from the bus and train stations (ring ahead). There's an indoor restaurant, or you can eat out in the pleasant garden. For dessert, try the delicious Rajasthani *maalpuas*.

The *Hotel Meghniwas* (☎ *202034, fax 201425, C-9 Sawai Jai Singh Hwy, Bani Park*) is another excellent choice. This place is kept in tiptop condition by the charming owner, Mrs Indu Singh. Air-con singles/doubles start at Rs 950/1000. Room Nos 201 and 209 are like mini-apartments and are ideal for long-term guests (Rs 1495). There's a swimming pool, lawn area and good restaurant.

The *Umaid Bhawan Guest House* (☎ *206426, D1-2A Bani Park*), behind the Collectorate via Bank Rd, has good singles/doubles from Rs 350/450. A Regal suite costs Rs 1500.

Sajjan Niwas Guest House (☎ *311544, fax 201494, D1-2B Bani Park*) is great value with spacious, airy singles/doubles from Rs 300/400.

Shapura House (☎ *202293, fax 201494, D-257 Devi Marg, Bani Park*) has doubles from Rs 600 to Rs 1000.

Nana-ki-Haveli (☎ *665502, fax 605481*), on Fateh Tiba, off Moti Dungri Marg, is a delightful place with a homey touch. Rooms are Rs 1095/1195 and meals are available.

Chirmi Palace Hotel (☎ *365063, fax 364462, Dhuleshwar Bagh, Sadar Patel Marg*) has decent singles/doubles for Rs 1050/1195; some rooms are better than others. There's a cute restaurant and local sightseeing trips can be arranged (Rs 190/310 for two/four hours).

LMB Hotel (☎ *565844, fax 562176*) is right in the heart of the old city in Johari Bazaar, above the well-known restaurant of the same name. Ordinary singles/doubles are Rs 975/1275.

Hotel Neelam (☎ *372215, fax 367808, A-3 Motilal Atal Marg*), near the Polo Victory Cinema, has comfortable, if somewhat dank, rooms from Rs 750/900 a single/double. There's a veg restaurant.

Hotel Bissau Palace (☎ *304391, fax 304628, email sanjai@jp1.dot.net.in*), north of Chandpol, was built by the *rawal* (nobleman) of Bissau. The cheapest singles/doubles are Rs 600/750; some rooms have more character than others. There are two restaurants (one on the rooftop with fine views), a swimming pool and an interesting library. They can also arrange good village tours at their country estate, The Retreat – see Organised Tours earlier in this section.

Narain Niwas Palace Hotel (☎ *561291, fax 561045*), on Narain Singh Rd, is another royal building, although it's looking a little faded around the edges these days. Singles/doubles start at Rs 1195/1750. There's a pool and nice garden. The owners also operate the *Royal Castle Kanota*, 14km south-east of Jaipur.

RTDC's Hotel Teej (☎ *205482*), Bani Park, has slightly musty rooms from Rs 450/550. Just off MI Rd, *RTDC's Hotel Gangaur* (☎ *361233*) , is similarly priced.

Places to Stay – Top End

Raj Vilas (☎ *640101, fax 640202, email reservations@rajvilas.com*), about 8km from the city centre on Goner Rd, is the most upmarket hotel in Jaipur, if not Rajasthan. Run by the Oberoi Group, this sophisticated boutique hotel has 71 rooms yet still manages to retain a personal touch. Set on over 12 hectares, all rooms are immaculate and tastefully decorated. Deluxe singles/doubles are US$260/280, luxury tents are US$300 and villas (each with their own pool) range from US$600 to US$1000.

Ayurvedic treatments are available in the health centre.

Rambagh Palace (☎ 381919, fax 381098, Bhawani Singh Marg) was once the maharaja of Jaipur's residence, but is now a stylish hotel operated by the Taj Group. Standard singles/doubles are US$185/205, superior rooms cost US$220/240, the 'maharaja suite' is US$475, and the 'royal suite' is US$675. If you're going to splurge, take one of the more expensive rooms, which are more sumptuous. If you can't afford to stay, at least treat yourself to an evening drink at the Polo Bar (see Places to Eat).

Jai Mahal Palace Hotel (☎ 371616, fax 365237) is on the corner of Jacob and Ajmer Rds. Also run by the Taj Group, this property has rooms beginning at US$155/175. In the evening you can consult the astrologer (Rs 200).

Rajmahal Palace (☎ 381625, fax 381887, Sadar Patel Marg) is also run by the Taj Group, but is more modest than the Rambagh or Jai Mahal. It is the former British Residency and offers standard singles/doubles for US$70/80. There's a pool and good restaurant. The huge forecourt is popular for wedding receptions.

Samode Haveli (☎ 632370, fax 632407, Ganga Pol) is one of the most interesting top-end places to stay. This 200-year-old building was once the town house of the rawal (nobleman) of Samode, who was also prime minister of Jaipur. There's an impressive dining room, and a couple of breathtaking suites – including one totally covered with original mirrorwork. Doubles range from Rs 2200 to Rs 2395.

Trident (☎ 630101, fax 630303), north of the city (opposite Jal Mahal – the Water Palace; see Around Jaipur), is run by the Oberoi Group. Attractive rooms cost Rs 3600/3900.

Mansingh Hotel (☎ 378771, fax 377582), off Sansar Chandra Marg in the centre of town, has rooms from Rs 1995/3000. Amenities include a pool, health club and two restaurants.

Rajputana Palace Sheraton (☎ 360011, fax 367848) is between Station and Palace

Rds. Run by Welcomgroup, it's not a palace as the name suggests, but rather a modern hotel built around a swimming pool. Standard singles/doubles cost US$130/140. There's a coffee shop, bar, two restaurants, a disco and a health club.

The ***Hotel Clarks Amer*** (☎ 550616, fax 550013) is less expensive but inconveniently located about 10km south of the city centre. Other top-end hotels in Jaipur include the ***Holiday Inn*** (☎ 635000, fax 635608, Amber Rd), with rooms from Rs 2000/3200 (including a buffet breakfast), and the less exciting ***Hotel Jaipur Ashok*** (☎ 204491, fax 202099, Bani Park).

Places to Eat

Niro's (MI Rd) was established in 1949 and is a favourite with Indians and westerners alike. It fills up fast (especially on weekends) but you can book ahead (☎ 374493). There's an extensive menu offering excellent veg and nonveg Indian, Chinese and continental food. Chicken pepper steak is Rs 130 and an American ice-cream soda will set you back a cool Rs 60. The nearby ***Surya Mahal*** serves good Indian food.

Natraj Restaurant, near Niro's, is a very good veg place that's also popular for its Indian sweets and spicy nibbles. Their north Indian food is tasty; the vegetable bomb curry (Rs 70) is a blast.

Golden Dragon Restaurant, down the side street next to Niro's, specialises in Chinese cuisine, but also serves some Indian dishes. The food is OK but not exceptional; Singapore noodles are Rs 70.

Bake Hut, nearby, offers a selection of sweet treats including chocolate donuts (Rs 8) and little lemon tarts (Rs 10). They can bake birthday cakes to order (☎ 369840). ***Venus Bakery*** (Subhash Marg), just off MI Rd, also sells pastries. But the biggest and best selection of fresh breads and pastries can be found at ***Hot Breads***, in the Ganpati Plaza complex on MI Rd.

Lassiwala, opposite Niro's, has its name up in brass and is the place to go for a thick, creamy lassi which will set you back Rs 10/20 for a small/jumbo cup.

Chanakya Restaurant, on the north side of MI Rd, is highly recommended. The attentive staff are happy to explain the various pure veg menu items; continental dishes range from Rs 65 to Rs 150, and Indian food costs from Rs 45 to Rs 130.

Handi Restaurant, opposite the main post office, is tucked away at the back of the Maya Mansions building. It's nothing flash as far as decor goes, but it offers scrumptious barbecue dishes at reasonable prices. In the evenings, you can get take-away kebabs at the entrance to the restaurant.

Copper Chimney, nearby, offers veg and nonveg Indian, continental and Chinese food in a pleasant setting. A main veg course ranges from Rs 50 to Rs 100, and between Rs 85 and Rs 200 for nonveg. Try the Rajasthani dish *lal maas* (mutton in a thick spicy gravy) for Rs 85.

Swaad (Ganpati Plaza, MI Rd) is recommended for a minor splurge. It has interesting Indian, continental and Chinese cuisine; travellers' favourites include *subz malaai kofta-palak* (cottage cheese and herbs in spinach gravy) for Rs 60 and the sizzlers (Rs 95 to Rs 165). Go downstairs for a beer. Desserts start at Rs 45, up to Rs 105 for the baked Alaska. In the same complex is the swanky, but less popular, *Celebrations*, which serves pure veg food.

Pizza Hut, also in the Ganpati Plaza, is the place to come if you're craving *real* pizza. There are traditional western-style pizzas, as well as 'fusion' creations, such as chicken tikka pizza. You can eat in, take away, or opt for the free delivery service (☎ 388627). Also in the Ganpati Plaza is *Baskin 31 Robbins*, where you can indulge in ice creams with evocative names such as 'kiss me nut'.

Four Seasons (D-43A Subhash Marg, C-Scheme) is not that centrally located, but the food is great. This multicuisine veg restaurant has moderately priced fare served in pleasant surroundings. A speciality is the *rava dosa* (Rs 35), which is a ground rice and semolina pancake with coconut, chilli, carrot and onion.

LMB (Laxmi Mishthan Bhandar), in Johari Bazaar, has been going strong since 1954, but the food and service are not as good as they once were. Main dishes range from Rs 35 to Rs 80. Out the front, a counter serves snacks and colourful Indian sweets.

Indian Coffee House (MI Rd), off the street, next to Arrow men's wear, is rather seedy inside, but good if you are craving a decent cup of coffee. Cheap south Indian food is also available.

Jaipur Inn (see Places to Stay) boasts one of the city's only rooftop restaurants, with superlative views over Jaipur. The Indian veg buffet dinner costs Rs 100 (nonresidents should book in advance).

Polo Bar, at the Rambagh Palace, is Jaipur's most atmospheric watering hole; a bottle of beer is Rs 150, cocktails are around Rs 250. Limited snacks are available.

Entertainment

Entertainment in the capital is limited, although many hotels put on some sort of evening music, dance or puppet show.

Raj Mandir Cinema (☎ 379372), just off MI Rd, is *the* place to go if you're planning to take in at least one Hindi film while you're in India. This opulent cinema is a Jaipur tourist attraction in its own right and is usually full, despite its immense size. Bookings can be made one day in advance (between 4 and 5 pm) and this is your best chance of securing a seat. Tickets range from Rs 15 to Rs 46; avoid the cheaper tickets, which are very close to the screen.

Bowling alleys seem to be the latest rage with Jaipurians. The best alley is at *Dreamland (☎ 546608)*, somewhat inconveniently located in Malviya Nagar at Gaurav Tower, Bardiya Shopping Centre. This complex also has video games, the New Yorker veg fast-food eatery, and the Space Station disco. The bowling alley at *Kin Pin (☎ 623029)*, on the 3rd floor of Centre Point in Raja Park, is not as good – there's a *Wimpy* hamburger joint downstairs.

Rambagh Golf Club (☎ 384482), near the Rambagh Palace, charges Rs 100/600 for Indians/foreigners per day, plus Rs 100 for equipment and Rs 50 for a caddie. For tennis, there's the *Jai Club (☎ 362052)*, off

MI Rd, which charges Rs 200 per couple per hour (advance bookings essential).

Shopping

Jaipur is *the* place to shop until you drop! It has a plethora of handicrafts ranging from grimacing papier-mâché puppets to exquisitely carved furniture. You'll have to bargain hard though – this city is accustomed to tourists with lots of money and little time to spend it. Shops around the tourist traps, such as the City Palace and Hawa Mahal, tend to be more expensive.

Jaipur is especially well known for precious stones, which seem cheaper here than elsewhere in India, and is even better known for semiprecious gems. There are many shops which offer bargain prices, but you do need to know your gems. Marble statues, costume jewellery and textile prints are other Jaipur specialities.

The Rajasthali emporium on MI Rd, near Ajmeri Gate, sells an interesting range of handicrafts from around the state. Rajasthan Handloom House is next door, with a range of textiles. Another highly recommended place for textiles is the Anokhi showroom, at 2 Tilak Marg, near the Secretariat. It has high quality products such as block-printed fabrics, tablecloths, bed covers and cosmetic bags. Soma, out at 5 Jacob Rd in Civil Lines, sells similar fare.

Kripal Kumbh, B-18A Shiva Marg in Bani Park, is a great place to see Jaipur's famous blue pottery. There's also Neerja (closed Sunday), S-19 Bhawani Singh Rd at C-Scheme. For good quality jootis (traditional Rajasthani shoes), go to Charmica (opposite the Natraj restaurant) on MI Rd; a pair of jootis ranges from Rs 150 to Rs 350.

The Juneja Art Gallery, Lakshmi Complex on MI Rd (not far from the main post office), has a fabulous range of contemporary paintings by predominantly Rajasthani artists. Prices range from Rs 100 to Rs 50,000.

Many rickshaw-wallahs are right into the commission business and it's almost guaranteed that they'll be getting a hefty cut from any shop they take you to. Many unwary visitors get talked into buying things for resale at inflated prices. Beware of these 'buy now to sell at a profit later' scams – see the warning under Shopping in the Facts for the Visitor chapter for more details.

Getting There & Away

Air Numerous international airlines are conveniently based in the Jaipur Towers building on MI Rd, including Ansett Australia, Air New Zealand, Air Canada, United Airlines and Air France.

You can book all domestic flights at a travel agent, such as Satyam Travels & Tours (☎ 378794, fax 375426), on the ground floor of the Jaipur Towers building. The office is open Monday to Saturday 10 am to 6 pm. The Indian Airlines office (☎ 514500) is a little out of town on Tonk Rd, the southern extension of Sawai Ram Singh Marg. Indian Airlines operates flights between Delhi and Jaipur (US$55) daily, and most flights continue to Mumbai (Bombay) (US$140), Udaipur (US$70), or Aurangabad (US$125). There are several weekly flights between Jaipur and Mumbai, (US$140), Ahmedabad (US$95), Calcutta (US$200) and Jaisalmer (US$110). Private airlines sometimes put on extra flights during the tourist season (check with a travel agent).

Bus Rajasthan State Transport Corporation (RSTC) buses all leave from the main bus station on Station Rd, picking up passengers at Narain Singh Circle. Some services are deluxe (essentially nonstop). There is a left-luggage office at the main terminal (Rs 5 per bag for 12 hours), as well as a prepaid auto-rickshaw stand. The deluxe buses all leave from platform No 3, which is tucked away in the right-hand corner of the bus station. These buses should be booked in advance, and the reservation office is also at platform 3. For express bus inquiries call ☎ 206143; ☎ 205621 for deluxe bus.

There are deluxe buses to many destinations including Delhi (Rs 190), Jodhpur (Rs 160), Kota (Rs 120), Ajmer (Rs 63), Udaipur (Rs 200), Bikaner (Rs 168), Bharatpur (Rs 87), Bundi (Rs 111), Mt Abu (Rs 246),

Jaisalmer (Rs 286), Chittorgarh (Rs 152) and Jhunjhunu (Rs 87).

Numerous private travel agencies in Jaipur book services to major cities. There's a cluster along Motilal Atal Marg, near the Polo Victory Cinema.

Train The reasonably efficient computerised railway reservation office (☎ 201401) is in the building to your right as you exit the main train station. It's open (for advance reservations only) Monday to Saturday 8 am to 2 pm and 2.15 to 8 pm; Sunday 8 am to 2 pm. Join the queue for 'Freedom Fighters and Foreign Tourists' (counter 769). For same-day travel, you'll need to buy your ticket at the train station. For metre-gauge trains, the booking office is on platform No 6. For railway inquiries call ☎ 131.

Many of the lines into Jaipur have been converted to broad gauge. As other parts of the state's railway are converted expect disruptions to services.

Car Cars and drivers can be hired through numerous travel agencies, including Sita World Travels (☎ 203626) on Station Rd. Costs at Sita are Rs 4.50 per kilometre (minimum 250km per day) for a non air-con car, or Rs 7.50 for an air-con car; the overnight charge is an extra Rs 75 per day. Competition between tour operators is high, so it's worth bargaining.

If you're game, self-drive rental cars can be hired at Hertz (☎ 635000, fax 609090), which has a desk at the Holiday Inn on Amber Rd. It costs about Rs 2000 per day.

Getting Around

To/From the Airport There is currently no scheduled bus service between the airport and the city. An auto-rickshaw/taxi will cost at least Rs 150/200 for the 15km journey into the city centre. Cut costs by sharing.

Auto-Rickshaw There are prepaid auto-rickshaw stands at the bus and train stations. Rates are fixed by the government, so there's no need to haggle. If you want to hire an auto-rickshaw for local sightseeing it should cost about Rs 200/300 for a half/full day (including a visit to Amber). Prices are often inflated for tourists, so be prepared to bargain. Cycle-rickshaws are a cheaper option.

Bicycle Bicycles can be hired from most bike shops, including the one to the right as you exit the main train station, a few steps past the reservation office (Rs 2/24 per hour/day). Some hotels can also arrange bike hire.

AROUND JAIPUR

There are some interesting attractions around Jaipur and you can get to most of these places by bus. Alternatively there are

Major Trains from Jaipur

destination	train no & name	departs	arrives	fare (Rs) 2nd/1st class
Agra	2308 *Howrah Jodhpur Exp*	11.20 pm	6.35 am	160/672
Abu Road	9106 *Ahmedabad Mail*	4.40 am	12.55 pm	161/725
Bikaner	4737 *Bikaner Exp*	9.05 pm	7.00 am	83/477
Jodhpur	2465 *Intercity Exp*	5.30 pm	10 00 pm	104/292
Jodhpur	2461 *Mandore Express*	2.45 am	7.55 am	153/628
New Delhi	2015 *Shatabdi Exp*	5.55 pm	10.15 pm	465/910
New Delhi	2414 *Delhi-Jaipur Superfast*	4.30 pm	9.50 pm	102/–
Udaipur	9615 *Chetak Exp*	10.10 pm	10.25 am	161/515

organised tours (see Organised Tours earlier in this section).

Amber

About 11km north of Jaipur, on the Delhi-Jaipur road, is Amber, the ancient capital of Jaipur state. Construction of the fort-palace was begun in 1592 by Maharaja Man Singh, the Rajput commander of Akbar's army. It was later extended and completed by the Jai Singhs before the move to Jaipur on the plains below. The fort is a superb example of Rajput architecture, stunningly situated on a hillside and overlooking a lake which reflects its terraces and ramparts.

You can climb up to the fort from the road in about 10 minutes, and cold drinks are available within the palace if the climb is a hot one. A seat in a jeep up to the fort costs Rs 15 return. Riding up on elephants is popular, though daylight robbery at Rs 400 per elephant return (each can carry up to four people).

An imposing stairway leads to the **Diwan-i-Am**, or Hall of Public Audience, with a double row of columns and latticed galleries above. Steps to the right lead to the small **Kali Temple**.

The maharaja's apartments are on the higher terrace – you enter through a gateway decorated with mosaics and sculptures. The **Jai Mandir**, or Hall of Victory, is noted for its inlaid panels and glittering mirror ceiling. Regrettably, much of this was allowed to deteriorate during the 1970s and 1980s but restoration proceeds. Opposite the Jai Mandir is the **Sukh Niwas**, or Hall of Pleasure, with an ivory-inlaid sandalwood door, and a channel running right through the room which once carried cooling water. From the Jai Mandir you can take in the fine views from the palace ramparts over the lake below.

Amber Palace is open daily 9 am to 4.30 pm and entry costs Rs 4. A camera costs Rs 20/50 for Indians/foreigners, Rs 50/100 for a video. Guides can be hired at the tourist office (at the fort entrance) for Rs 75/230/345 for 1½ hours/half day/full day (maximum four people).

There are frequent buses to Amber from near the Hawa Mahal and from the train station in Jaipur (Rs 4, 25 minutes).

Nahargarh

Nahargarh, also known as the Tiger Fort, overlooks the city from a sheer ridge to the north, and is floodlit at night. The fort was built in 1734 and extended in 1868. An 8km road runs up through the hills from Jaipur, and the fort can be reached along a zigzagging 2km path. The glorious views fully justify the effort. Entry is Rs 2, and a camera/video costs Rs 30/70.

There's a small restaurant on the top (with a toilet). You can even stay at the fort, although there's only one basic double room which costs a hefty Rs 500 – reservations should be made at the Tourist Reception Centre (☎ 0141-365256) in Jaipur.

Jaigarh

The imposing Jaigarh, built in 1726 by Jai Singh, was opened to the public in mid-1983. The fort was never captured and so has survived virtually intact through the centuries. It's within walking distance of Amber and offers a great view over the plains from the Diwa Burj watchtower. The fort, with its water reservoirs, residential areas, puppet theatre and the cannon, Jaya Vana, is open 9 am to 5 pm daily. Entry is Rs 15, plus Rs 50 per car, Rs 20 for a camera and Rs 100 for a video camera. (Note that you can also enter Jaigarh on the same entry ticket you used for Jaipur's City Palace, as long as it is within two days of purchase; car entry and cameras are extra.)

Royal Gaitor

The **cenotaphs** of the royal family are at Gaitor, just outside the city walls. The cenotaph of Maharaja Jai Singh II is particularly impressive. Entry is free, but there's a charge of Rs 10/20 for a camera/video.

The cenotaphs of the maharanis of Jaipur are on Amber Rd, midway between Jaipur and Amber. Nearby is the **Jal Mahal** (Water Palace), in the middle of a lake and reached by a causeway.

Sisodia Rani Palace & Gardens & Vidyadharji ka Bagh

Six kilometres from the city on Agra Rd (leave Jaipur by the Ghat Gate), and surrounded by terraced gardens, this palace was built for Maharaja Jai Singh's second wife, the Sisodia princess. The outer walls are decorated with murals depicting hunting scenes and the Krishna legend.

Vidyadharji ka Bagh, a garden built in honour of Jai Singh's chief architect and town planner, Vidyadhar, is about 200m before Sisodia Rani Palace on Agra Rd.

Both gardens are open 8 am to 6 pm daily and there's a small entry fee (no video cameras allowed).

Galta

The temple of the sun god at Galta is 100m above Jaipur to the east, a 2.5km climb from Surajpol. A deep, temple-studded gorge stands behind the temple and there are good views over the surrounding plains.

Sanganer & Bagru

The small town of Sanganer is 16km south of Jaipur and is entered through the ruins of two *tripolias*, or triple gateways. In addition to its ruined palace, Sanganer has a group of Jain temples with fine carvings to which entry is restricted. The town is noted for handmade paper and block printing (most shops can be found on, or just off, Stadium Rd). Salim's Paper on Gramodyog Rd is the largest handmade paper factory in India. Here you can see the paper production process and they also sell a beautiful range of paper products. For block-printed fabrics, there are a number of shops, including Sakshi, which also has excellent blue pottery (downstairs).

About 20km west of Sanganer is the village of Bagru, also known for its block printing (but it's less obvious than in Sanganer).

A bus from Jaipur to Sanganer takes 30 minutes and costs Rs 5.50. To Bagru it takes 45 minutes and is Rs 7.

Samode

This small village is nestled among rugged hills about 50km north of Jaipur. The only reason to visit it is if you can afford to stay in the beautiful Samode Palace (although strictly speaking it's not actually a palace, as it wasn't owned by a ruler but by a nobleman). Like the Samode Haveli in Jaipur, this building was owned by the rawal of Samode. The highlight of the building is the exquisite Diwan-i-Khas, which is covered with original paintings and mirrorwork.

Samode Palace (☎ 01423-4114, fax 4123, reservations ☎ 0141-632370, fax 632407) has pleasant doubles costing from Rs 2750 to Rs 3750. Breakfast/lunch/dinner is Rs 250/375/425. Entry to the palace for nonguests is Rs 100 (deducted if you have a set meal). Similarly priced luxurious tent accommodation is available 3km away at *Samode Bagh*, where there's a lovely garden and pool.

There are four daily direct buses from Jaipur's main bus station to Samode (Rs 13.50, 1½ hours).

Ramgarh

This green oasis, about 35km from Jaipur, has a picturesque lake (boating available), polo ground (call Jaipur ☎ 0141-374791 to find out when matches are being played) and an ancient Durga temple.

Ramgarh Lodge (☎ 01426-552217, fax 381098), a former royal hunting lodge overlooking Ramgarh Lake, is the best place to stay (Rs 1600/2300 a single/double). Inside the lodge, there are a number of stuffed beasts, including a tacky elephant's trunk pot plant holder.

RTDC's Jheel Tourist Village (☎ 01426-52370), farther away from the lake, is cheaper at Rs 300/350 with attached bath.

Buses travel daily between Jaipur and Ramgarh (Rs 9, one hour).

Abhaneri

About 95km from Jaipur on the Agra road, this little village has one of Rajasthan's most awesome *baolis* (step-wells). Flanking the baoli is a small, crumbling palace, now inhabited by pigeons and bats.

From Jaipur, catch a bus to Sikandra, from where you can hire a jeep for the 10km trip to Abhaneri (Rs 200 return, including a 30 minute stop). Alternatively, from Jaipur get a bus to Gular, from where it's a 5km walk to Abhaneri.

Balaji

The Hindu exorcism temple of Balaji is about 43km from Abhaneri, about 1.5km off the Jaipur-Agra road. The exorcisms are sometimes very violent and many being exorcised don't hesitate to discuss their experiences. Most exorcisms take place on Tuesday and Saturday (go upstairs). Remove your shoes before entering the temple. Photography is prohibited.

From Jaipur there are numerous local buses to Balaji (Rs 26, 2½ hours).

Karauli

Located 182km south-east of Jaipur, Karauli was founded in 1348 and has some important Krishna temples.

Bhanwar Vilas Palace (☎ 07464-20024, reservations ☎ 0141-211532, fax 210512) is a country retreat with rooms from US$29/32. They can organise excursions to nearby points of interest, including the old city palace.

Buses between Jaipur and Karauli take five hours and cost Rs 45.

BHARATPUR
☎ 05644 • pop 1,646,500

Bharatpur is renowned for its World Heritage-listed bird sanctuary, the Keoladeo Ghana National Park. This is one bird sanctuary which even non-ornithologists should visit. In fact, many travellers rate it as a highlight of their visit to India.

In the 17th and 18th centuries, the town was an important Jat stronghold. Before the arrival of the Rajputs, the Jats inhabited this area and were able to retain a high degree of autonomy, both because of their prowess in battle and because of their chiefs' marriage alliances with Rajput nobility. They successfully opposed the Mughals on more than one occasion and their fort at Bharatpur, constructed in the 18th century, withstood an attack by the British in 1805 and a long

siege in 1825. This siege eventually led to the signing of the first treaty of friendship between the Indian states of north-west India and the East India Company.

The town itself, which was once surrounded by an 11km wall (now demolished), is of little interest. Bring mosquito repellent with you, as the mozzies can be bothersome.

Orientation & Information

The Keoladeo National Park lies 5km to the south of the city centre, and is easily accessed by cycle-rickshaw.

The very helpful Tourist Reception Centre (☎ 22542) is at the RTDC's Hotel Saras, about 700m from the park entrance (although the office may have shifted across the road from the RTDC by now). It's open daily (except Sunday and every second Saturday of the month) from 10 am to 5 pm. A guidebook including a map is available at the park entrance. It contains a short history of the park and a seemingly endless list of bird species, but is otherwise of little help to anyone without an understanding of ornithology. Books on birdlife are also available at a bookshop inside the park, about 1.5km from the main gate.

You can change money at the State Bank of Bikaner & Jaipur, near the Binarayan Gate.

Keoladeo Ghana National Park

The best time to visit the sanctuary is from October to late February when many migratory birds can be seen, including the highly endangered Siberian crane. According to recent reports, around 354 species of birds have been identified at the beautiful Keoladeo sanctuary. The sanctuary was formerly a vast semi-arid region, filling with water during the monsoon season only to rapidly dry up afterwards. To prevent this, the maharaja of Bharatpur diverted water from a nearby irrigation canal and, within a few years, birds began to settle in vast numbers. The maharaja was compelled not by conservationist motives, but by the desire to have a ready supply of waterfowl, affording fine shooting (and dining) possibilities. Indeed,

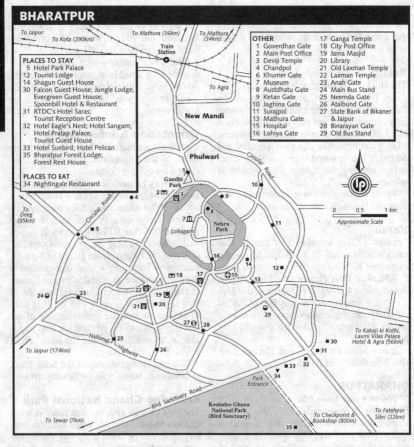

BHARATPUR

To Jaipur
To Kota (290km)
To Mathura (36km)
To Mathura (34km)
Train Station
To Agra

PLACES TO STAY
5 Hotel Park Palace
12 Tourist Lodge
14 Shagun Guest House
30 Falcon Guest House; Jungle Lodge;
    Evergreen Guest House;
    Spoonbill Hotel & Restaurant
31 RTDC's Hotel Saras;
    Tourist Reception Centre
32 Hotel Eagle's Nest; Hotel Sangam;
    Hotel Pratap Palace;
    Tourist Guest House
33 Hotel Sunbird; Hotel Pelican
35 Bharatpur Forest Lodge;
    Forest Rest House

PLACES TO EAT
34 Nightingale Restaurant

OTHER
1 Goverdhan Gate
2 Main Post Office
3 Deviji Temple
4 Chandpol
6 Khumer Gate
7 Museum
8 Austdhatu Gate
9 Ketan Gate
10 Jaghina Gate
11 Surajpol
13 Mathura Gate
15 Hospital
16 Lohiya Gate
17 Ganga Temple
18 City Post Office
19 Jama Masjid
20 Library
21 Old Laxman Temple
22 Laxman Temple
23 Anah Gate
24 Main Bus Stand
25 Neemda Gate
26 Atalbund Gate
27 State Bank of Bikaner
    & Jaipur
28 Binarayan Gate
29 Old Bus Stand

New Mandi

Phulwari

Circular Road

Gandhi Park

Lohagarh

Nehru Park

To Deeg (35km)

0   0.5   1 km
Approximate Scale

Circular Road

To Kakaji ki Kothi,
Laxmi Vilas Palace
Hotel & Agra (56km)

To Jaipur (174km)

National Highway

To Sewar (7km)

Bird Sanctuary Road

Park Entrance

Keoladeo Ghana
National Park
(Bird Sanctuary)

To Checkpoint &
Bookshop (800m)

To Fatehpur
Sikri (22km)

Keoladeo continued to supply the maharajas' tables until as late as 1965. An inscription on a pillar near the small temple in the park bears testimony to the maharajas' penchant for hunting. It reveals that on one day alone, over 5000 ducks were shot!

The park is open 6 am to 6 pm daily. Entry is Rs 20/100 for Indians/foreigners, which entitles you to enter the park as many times as you wish in one day. A still camera is free, but there's a whopping Rs 200 video charge. There's also an entry fee for

bicycles (Rs 3) and cycle-rickshaws (Rs 5). A horse-drawn tonga costs Rs 60 per hour (maximum six people). Motorised vehicles are prohibited beyond the checkpoint, so the only way of getting around is by foot, bicycle or cycle-rickshaw.

Only those cycle-rickshaws authorised by the government (recognisable by the yellow plate bolted onto the front) are allowed inside the park – beware of anyone who tells you otherwise! Although you don't pay entry fees for the drivers of these cycle-rickshaws, you'll be up for Rs 30 per hour if you take one and they'll expect a tip on top of that. Some of the drivers actually know a lot about the birds you'll see and can be very helpful. If you wish to hire an experienced ornithologist guide, this will cost around Rs 35 per hour (maximum five people), Rs 75 (more than five people). Guides can be hired at the park entrance.

An excellent way to see the park is to hire a bicycle. There are bikes for hire at the park entrance for Rs 20 per day. Some hotels rent bicycles as well. This allows you to easily avoid the bottlenecks which inevitably occur at the nesting sites of the larger birds. It's just about the only way you'll be able to watch the numerous kingfishers at close quarters – noise or human activity frightens them away. A bicycle also enables you to avoid clocking up a large bill with a rickshaw driver. If you plan to visit the sanctuary at dawn (one of the best times to see the birds), you should hire your bicycle the day before. The southern reaches of the park are virtually devoid of *humanus touristicus*, and so are much better than the northern part for serious bird-watching.

Boats can be hired for Rs 80 per hour (maximum four people). They are a very good way of getting close to the wildlife.

A small display of photos, stuffed birds, nests and aquatic species found in the park's lakes is at the main entrance to the park (free entry). There's a small snack bar about halfway through the park, next to the Keoladeo Temple.

Lohagarh

Lohagarh, or Iron Fort, was built in the early 18th century and took its name from its supposedly impregnable defences. Maharaja Suraj Mahl, the fort's constructor and founder of Bharatpur, built two towers within the ramparts, the Jawahar Burj and Fateh Burj, to commemorate his victories over the Mughals and the British.

The fort occupies the entire small artificial island in the centre of the town, and the three palaces within its precincts are in an advanced state of decay. One of the palaces

houses a museum exhibiting sculptures, paintings, weapons and dusty animal trophies. The museum is open daily except Friday 10 am to 4.30 pm. Entry is Rs 3 (free on Monday), and an additional Rs 10/20 for a camera/video.

Places to Stay & Eat

The Paying Guest House Scheme operates in Bharatpur (contact the Tourist Reception Centre). Many hotels have bicycles and binoculars for hire and can organise a packed lunch for you to take into the bird park. The commission system has reared its ugly head in Bharatpur – don't be pressured by touts at the train station or bus stand.

Park Precincts The following places are all within easy walking distance of the main entrance to the bird sanctuary, making them the most popular with travellers.

RTDC's Hotel Saras (☎ 23700) is at the junction of Fatehpur Sikri and Bird Sanctuary Rds. Rather shabby singles/doubles start at Rs 300/350, while a bed in the musty dorm is Rs 50. There's a restaurant; chicken biryani is Rs 70.

Spoonbill Hotel & Restaurant (☎ 23571), just behind the RTDC's Hotel Saras, is a popular choice with travellers. It has good singles/doubles with bath for Rs 150/200 and dorm beds for Rs 50. There's a restaurant and in the winter there's a campfire. They hire out a bird spotter's guide for Rs 20 per day.

Falcon Guest House (☎ 23815), in the same area, is run by Mrs Rajni Singh and is a well kept and homey place to stay. Good sized singles/doubles go for Rs 150/200 with bath; Rs 350/400 gets you a bigger room with a softer mattress and private balcony. There's a little garden restaurant; a veg thali is Rs 60. Nearby is another cheapie, the *Evergreen Guest House* (☎ 25917).

Jungle Lodge (☎ 25622), also nearby, has small but comfortable rooms with attached bath from Rs 100/200. There's a lending library and a nice garden.

Hotel Sangam (☎ 25616), directly opposite the RTDC's Hotel Saras, has rooms with bath from Rs 150/200. The restaurant serves veg and nonveg fare, including banana *paratha* (Rs 12).

Hotel Eagle's Nest (☎ 25144, fax 23170), nearby, has clean and comfortable rooms from Rs 250/350 with bath. Meals are available.

Hotel Pratap Palace (☎ 24245, fax 25093), also on Bird Sanctuary Rd, has rooms with common bath for Rs 100/150, or Rs 200/300 with attached bath.

Hotel Sunbird (☎ 25701) is farther along the road, and the rooms in this popular place fill up fast. Decent singles/doubles with attached bath start at Rs 150/250. The restaurant has a good range of dishes.

Hotel Pelican (☎ 24221), nearby, is another popular budget place. Tiny but airy rooms with common bath go for Rs 40/75; larger rooms are Rs 100/125 with bath.

The *Nightingale Restaurant* (☎ 27022, fax 24351), in a eucalyptus grove, offers small two-person tents for Rs 80 and larger tents for Rs 200 (available from around mid-October to mid-February). The restaurant has cheap eats such as *palak paneer* (Rs 30). Come armed with mozzie repellent, as the little bloodsuckers here can be tenacious.

Bharatpur Forest Lodge (☎ 22760, fax 22864), run by the ITDC, is inside the park, 1km beyond the park entrance gate. It's comfortable enough, but is looking a little faded these days. Standard singles/doubles cost Rs 1700/2500. The restaurant is open to nonresidents; the buffet lunch or dinner is Rs 250, or you can opt for a light snack. Not far away, there's the *Forest Rest House* (☎ 22777), which sometimes rents out simple double rooms for Rs 600, including meals.

Bharatpur Tourist Lodge (☎ 23742), near Mathura Gate, is an unpretentious little budget place. Small singles/doubles with common bath go for Rs 50/80, or from Rs 75/100 with bath attached. Meals are available.

Shagun Guest House (☎ 29202), down a laneway just inside Mathura Gate, is very basic but great if you're strapped for cash. The owner, Rajeev, is a friendly guy and has

a wealth of knowledge on the bird park. Primitive grass huts cost just Rs 44/66, singles/doubles with common bath are Rs 56/76, and rooms with bath cost Rs 68/86.

Laxmi Vilas Palace Hotel (☎ 23523, fax 25259), Kakaji ki Kothi, on the old Agra road, is an upmarket hotel with singles/doubles from Rs 1195/1250.

Hotel Park Palace (☎ 23783) is not far from Khumer Gate. There are budget rooms with bath for Rs 200/250. Better rooms range from Rs 350/400 to Rs 800/875. This place is handy for catching early-morning buses, but some rooms cop a lot of traffic noise.

Getting There & Away

Bus There are buses to a number of destinations including Agra (Rs 22, 1½ hours), Fatehpur Sikri (Rs 10, one hour), Jaipur (Rs 70, 4½ hours) and Deeg (Rs 15, one hour).

Train The *Firozpur Janta Express* leaves New Delhi station at 2 pm and arrives in Bharatpur at 6.15 pm. The 175km trip costs Rs 96/245 in 2nd/1st class. It leaves Bharatpur at 8 am, arriving in the capital at 12.30 pm. There are also rail connections to Sawai Madhopur (Rs 96/258, 182km), which continue to Kota (Rs 72/361, 290km) and Mumbai (Rs 200/1004, 1210km). There's also a passenger train to Agra which takes 1½ hours and costs Rs 11.

Getting Around

Bharatpur has auto-rickshaws, cycle-rickshaws and tongas. A fantastic way of zipping around is by bicycle, which costs Rs 20 to Rs 50 per day (the more expensive ones are in better condition).

DEEG

☎ 05641 • pop 40,000

Very few travellers ever make it to Deeg, about 36km north of Bharatpur. This is a pity because this small town with its massive fortifications, stunning palace and busy market is actually more interesting than Bharatpur itself (apart from the bird sanctuary, of course). It's an easy day trip from Bharatpur, Agra or Mathura.

Built by Suraj Mahl in the mid-18th century, Deeg was formerly the second capital of Bharatpur state and the site of a famous battle in which the maharaja's forces successfully withstood a combined Mughal and Maratha army of some 80,000 men. Eight years later, the maharaja even had the temerity to attack the Red Fort in Delhi! The booty he carried off included an entire marble building which can still be seen.

Suraj Mahl's Palace

Suraj Mahl's Palace (Gopal Bhavan) has to be one of India's most beautiful and delicately proportioned buildings. It's also in an excellent state of repair and, as it was used by the maharajas until the early 1970s, most of the rooms still contain their original furnishings.

Built in a combination of Rajput and Mughal architectural styles, the 18th century palace fronts onto a tank, the Gopal Sagar, and is flanked by two exquisite pavilions. The tank and palace are surrounded by well-maintained gardens which also contain the Keshav Bhavan, or Summer Pavilion, with its hundreds of fountains, many of which are still functional but usually only turned on for local festivals.

The palace is open 8 am to 5 pm daily (free entry).

Deeg's massive **walls** (up to 28m high) and 12 bastions, some with their cannons still in place, are also worth exploring.

Place to Stay

Currently there is only one decent place to stay in Deeg. The *RTDC's Motel Deeg* (☎ 21000), not far from the bus stand, has just three rooms with private bath for Rs 250/300 a single/double. If you have a tent, they'll let you pitch in their compound for Rs 30 per person (includes use of bathroom). Meals are available; a veg thali is Rs 55.

Getting There & Away

There are frequent buses between Deeg and Alwar; the 2½ hour trip costs Rs 22/28 by local/express bus. Buses for Bharatpur leave every 30 minutes and the one hour journey

costs Rs 12/15 for a local/express bus. There is one daily direct bus to Agra (Rs 45).

ALWAR

☎ 0144 • pop 250,000

Alwar was once an important Rajput state. It emerged in the 18th century under Pratap Singh, who pushed back the rulers of Jaipur to the south and the Jats of Bharatpur to the east, and who successfully resisted the Marathas. It was one of the first Rajput states to ally itself with the fledgling British empire, although British interference in Alwar's internal affairs meant that this partnership was not always amicable.

The Tourist Reception Centre (☎ 21868) is not far from the train station and is open Monday to Saturday 10 am to 1.30 pm and 2 to 5 pm. You can change foreign currency at the State Bank of Bikaner & Jaipur, near the bus stand.

Bala Quila

This imposing fort, with its 5km of ramparts, stands 300m above the city. Predating the time of Pratap Singh, it's one of the few forts in Rajasthan built before the rise of the Mughals. Unfortunately, the fort now houses a radio transmitter station and the inside can only be visited with special permission from the superintendent of police (☎ 337453).

Palace Complex

Below the fort sprawls the huge city palace complex, its massive gates and tank lined by a beautifully symmetrical chain of *ghats* and pavilions. Today, most of the complex is occupied by government offices, but there's an interesting **government museum** housed in the former City Palace. It's open daily except Friday 10 am to 4.30 pm and entry is Rs 3 (free on Monday). Photography is prohibited. Some of the museum's exhibits include stunning weapons, royal ivory slippers, and old musical instruments.

Places to Stay & Eat

For details about Alwar's paying guest accommodation, contact the Tourist Reception Centre.

Ankur (☎ *333025*), *New Alankar* (☎ *20027*), *Atlantic* (☎ *21581*), *Akash Deep* (☎ *22912*) and the *Ashoka* (☎ *21780*) are a cluster of cheap hotels which all face each other around a central courtyard, about 500m east of the bus stand, set back from Manu Marg. The five hotels are each owned by one of five brothers, and each hotel begins with the letter 'A'! Without wishing to upset any of the brothers, the Ashoka seems to be the best of the lot, with singles/doubles with attached bath (Rs 3 for bucket hot water) for Rs 100/150 and Rs 200/250 with geyser. However, there's really not much difference between them, and prices are comparable at all the hotels.

Hotel Aravali (☎ *332883, fax 332011*), near the train station, is run by the Kakkar family (the owner's son, Achal and his wife, Anika, are helpful). Dorm beds cost Rs 100; singles/doubles with private bath start from Rs 200/250 (request a quiet room). There's a restaurant, bar and pool (summer only).

RTDC's Hotel Meenal (☎ *22852*) is a respectable mid-range place, charging from Rs 350/450 for tidy singles/doubles. There's a little dining hall; a veg/nonveg thali costs Rs 55/68.

Alwar Hotel (☎ *20012, fax 332250, 26 Manu Marg*), set in a leafy garden, has decent rooms from Rs 300/450 with bath. There's a good restaurant.

Retiring rooms at the train station have beds for Rs 40 per person.

Narula's, near the Ganesh Talkies, whips up Indian, Chinese and continental cuisine. This pleasant restaurant, which is down a stairway, offers a good choice of dishes, including veg sizzlers (Rs 45) and strawberry milkshakes (Rs 25).

Getting There & Away
From Alwar, there are frequent local and express buses to Sariska (Rs 8/13 local/express, one hour), Bharatpur (Rs 45, 3½ hours express; Rs 29, 4½ hours local), Deeg (Rs 23/30 local/express, 2½ hours), Jaipur (Rs 45/61 local/express, four hours).

There are also rail links with Jaipur and Delhi.

Getting Around
There are cycle-rickshaws, auto-rickshaws, tempos and some tongas. A cycle-rickshaw from the train station to the town centre should cost Rs 10. Bicycles can be hired near the train station (Rs 20 per day).

AROUND ALWAR
Siliserh
At Siliserh, 20km south-west of Alwar, *RTDC's Hotel Lake Palace* (☎ *0144-86322*) is a fairly modest palace built by the Alwar Maharaja Vinaya Singh. It is in a dramatic location, overlooking a picturesque lake, and has rooms from Rs 200/300 with private bath. This property is beautiful, but unfortunately the cleanliness and service is variable.

Kesroli
Twelve kilometres from Alwar in Kesroli village, *Hill Fort Kesroli* (☎ *0144-81312, reservations 011-4616145, fax 4621112*) is run by the Neemrana Fort people (see the following section). Double rooms in the 14th century fort range from Rs 1500 to Rs 4000. The buffet lunch/dinner is Rs 150/200.

Neemrana
About 75km north of Alwar is the restored fort *Neemrana Fort Palace* (☎/fax 01494-46005, 011-4616145, fax 4621112 for Delhi bookings, email neemrana@fwacziarg.com). Dating from the 15th century, the Rajput king Prithviraj Chauhan III reigned from here. Rooms are suitably luxurious and start from Rs 1500/2500 (some rooms are better than others). Nonguests can visit for Rs 100 (free if you eat at the restaurant).

SARISKA NATIONAL PARK
☎ 0144
Located 107km from Jaipur and 200km from Delhi, the sanctuary is in a wooded valley surrounded by barren mountains. It covers 800 sq km (including a core area of 498 sq km) and has sambar, spotted deer, wild boar and, above all, tigers. Project Tiger has been in charge of the sanctuary since 1979.

As at Ranthambhore National Park, also in Rajasthan, this park contains ruined temples, as well as a fort and pavilions built by the maharajas of Alwar. The sanctuary can be visited year-round, although during July and August your chance of spotting wildlife is minimal. The best time is between November and June. You'll see most wildlife in the evening, although tiger sightings are becoming more common during the day.

The park is open in winter (October to the end of February) from 7 am to 4 pm, and during the rest of the year from 6.30 am to 5 pm. The best way to visit the park is by jeep and these can be arranged at the Forest Reception Office (☎ 41333) on Jaipur Rd, directly opposite the Hotel Sariska Palace. Diesel/petrol jeeps cost Rs 500/600 per jeep (maximum five people). There's an entry fee of Rs 125 per jeep and an admission fee of Rs 20/100 for Indians/foreigners. Entry for Indians is free on Tuesday and Saturday (from 8 am to 3 pm), so try to avoid visiting on these days as the park can get busy. Using a still camera is free but a video camera will cost you Rs 200. Guides are available for Rs 50 per hour.

Places to Stay & Eat

Hotel Sariska Palace (☎ 41322, fax 41323), near the park entrance, is the imposing former hunting lodge of the maharajas of Alwar. It's a very pleasant place to stay with rooms from Rs 2000/3000. There's a small lending library, restaurant (lunch or dinner is Rs 350), and jeeps for hire.

RTDC's Hotel Tiger Den (☎ 41342) is cheaper and has a lovely garden, although the rooms are a bit run-down. Dorm beds are Rs 50, air-cooled singles/doubles with bath are Rs 550/600, air-con rooms are Rs 700/825. Some travellers recommend bringing a mozzie net/repellent. A veg thali costs Rs 65.

Getting There & Away

Sariska is 35km from Alwar, which is a convenient town from which to approach the sanctuary. Though some people attempt to visit Sariska on a day trip from Jaipur, this option is expensive and largely a waste of time. Frequent buses travel between Sariska and Alwar (Rs 14, one hour). It takes about three hours to Jaipur (Rs 48). Buses stop out the front of the Forest Reception Office.

SHEKHAWATI

The semidesert Shekhawati region lies in the triangular area between Delhi, Jaipur and Bikaner. Starting around the 14th century, a number of Muslim clans moved into the area and the towns which developed in the region became important trading posts on the caravan routes emanating from the ports of Gujarat.

Although the towns have long since lost any importance they may once have had, what they have not lost is the beautiful painted havelis (mansions) constructed by the merchants of the region. Most of the buildings date from the 18th century to early this century, and the entire area has been dubbed by some as the 'open air gallery of Rajasthan'. There are also forts, a couple of minor castles, baolis (stepwells), *chhatris*, and a handful of mosques.

The major towns of interest in the region are Fatehpur, Nawalgarh, Mandawa, Ramgarh and Jhunjhunu, although virtually every town has at least a few surviving havelis.

Guidebooks

Lonely Planet's *Rajasthan* guidebook has a substantially more detailed chapter devoted to Shekhawati. For a full rundown of the history, people, towns and buildings of the area, it's worth investing in a copy of *The Guide to the Painted Towns of Shekhawati* by Ilay Cooper. The book gives details of the buildings of interest in each town, along with fine sketch maps of the larger towns in the area.

Lakshmangarh

Dominating this town is the 19th century **fort**, built by Lakshman Singh, the raja of Sikar. It has fine views down to the town which was laid out, like Jaipur, along a grid pattern. Some of the most interesting **havelis** here include the Char Chowk Haveli, the Rathi Family Haveli and the Shyonarayan Kyal Haveli.

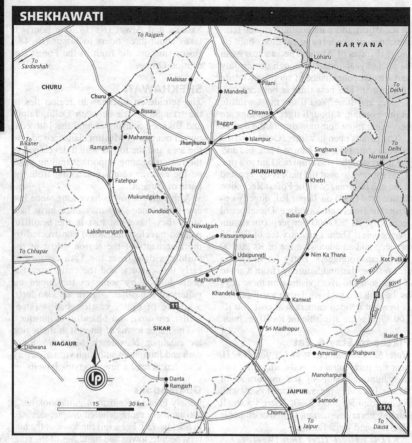

SHEKHAWATI

To Rajgarh

HARYANA

To
Sardarshah

Loharu

To
Delhi

CHURU

Malsisar

Pilani

Mandrela

Churu

Bissau

Chirawa

Baggar

To
Bikaner

Mahansar

Ramgarh

Islampur

Jhunjhunu

Singhana

To
Delhi

Narnaul

Mandawa

JHUNJHUNU

Fatehpur

Khetri

Mukundgarh

Dundlod

Babai

Lakshmangarh

Nawalgarh

To Chhapar

Parsurampura

Udaipurvati

Nim Ka Thana

Kot Putli

Raghunathgarh

Sota River

River

Sikar

Khandela

Kanwat

Jhili

SIKAR

Sri Madhopur

Bairat

NAGAUR

Didwana

Amarsar

Shahpura

Manoharpur

Danta
Ramgarh

JAIPUR

Samode

11A

Chomu

To
Jaipur

To
Dausa

0   15   30 km

Ramgarh

The town of Ramgarh was founded by the powerful Poddar merchant family in 1791, after they had left the village of Churu following a disagreement with the thakur. It had its heyday in the mid-19th century and was one of the richest towns of the area.

The **Ram Gopal Poddar Chhatri** near the bus stand, and the **Poddar Havelis**, near the Churu Gate, are both worth checking out. This town is also known for its local handicrafts.

Fatehpur

Fatehpur was established in 1451 as a capital for Muslim nawabs but was taken by the Shekhawat Rajputs in the 18th century.

Some of the main **havelis** of interest are the Mahavir Prasad Goenka Haveli, the Geori Shankar Haveli, the Nand Lal Devra Haveli and the Harikrishnan Das Sarogi Haveli.

Near the private bus stand are the remains of a large 17th century **baoli**. Sadly it is half-full with rubbish, and is in a pitiful state of decay.

RTDC's Hotel Haveli (☎ 01571-20293), about 500m south of the bus stand, has dorm beds for Rs 50, and singles/doubles with bath from Rs 300/400. There's a dining hall; chicken curry is Rs 48, a curd lassi is Rs 13.

Mandawa

The compact and busy little market town of Mandawa was settled in the 18th century, and was fortified by the dominant merchant families. It is becoming increasingly popular with tourists, which would account for the mushrooming antique shops and commercial ambience.

Of the havelis, the **Binsidhar Newatia Haveli** has some curious paintings on its outer eastern wall – a boy using a telephone, and a European woman in a car driven by a chauffeur. The haveli is in the compound of the State Bank of Bikaner & Jaipur. The **Gulab Rai Ladia Haveli** has some defaced erotic images.

Places to Stay *Hotel Castle Mandawa* (☎ 01592-23124, fax 23171) is one of the most upmarket, yet most impersonal, places to stay in Shekhawati. It's a large hotel, with tastefully designed rooms ranging from Rs 1300/1600 to Rs 1995/3995. Some rooms

Havelis

With large amounts of money coming from trade, the merchants of Shekhawati were keen to build mansions on a grand scale as a testimony to their new wealth. The popular design was a building that, from the outside, was relatively unremarkable – the focus was, instead, on one or more internal courtyards. This provided security and privacy for the women of the household, as well as offering some relief from the fierce heat which grips the area in summer.

The main entrance is usually a large wooden gate leading into a small courtyard, which in turn leads into another courtyard. The largest mansions had as many as four courtyards and were up to six storeys high.

Having built a house of grand proportions, the families then had them decorated with murals, and it is these which are the major attraction today. The major themes found are Hindu mythology, history, folk tales, eroticism (many now defaced or destroyed), and – one of the most curious – foreigners and their modern inventions, such as planes and gramophones.

Many of the artists and masons were commissioned from beyond Shekhawati – particularly from Jaipur. Originally the colours used in the murals were all ochre-based, but in the 1860s artificial pigments were introduced from Germany. The predominant colours are blue and maroon, but other colours such as yellow, green and indigo are also featured.

Many of the havelis these days are not inhabited by the owners, who find that the small rural towns in outback Rajasthan have little appeal. Many are occupied by a single *chowki-dar* (caretaker), while others may be home to a local family. Not many are open as museums or for display, and consequently quite a few are either totally or partially locked.

While the locals seem fairly tolerant of strangers wandering into their front courtyard, be aware that these are private abodes, so tact and discretion should be used – don't just blunder in as though you own the place. Local custom dictates that shoes should be removed when entering the inner courtyard of a haveli.

One unfortunate aspect of the tourist trade is also beginning to manifest itself here – the desire for antiques. A couple of towns have antique shops chock-a-block with items ripped from the havelis – particularly doors and window frames, but anything that can be carted away is fair game. Investing in these antiques is tantamount to condoning this desecration.

have more charm than others, so try to look at a few first. Their similarly priced *Desert Resort* (☎ 01592-23245) is not as centrally placed, but is in a peaceful setting with pleasant rooms and a swimming pool.

Hotel Heritage Mandawa (☎ 01592-23243), near the Subhash Chowk bus stand, is an old haveli and is a great budget choice. It has clean singles/doubles with bath for Rs 300/400. Lunch/dinner is Rs 75/100 (open to nonresidents).

Gayatri Niwas (☎ 01592-23065) has basic but very cheap rooms in a 142-year-old haveli. Singles/doubles with common bath are Rs 100/200 (free bucket hot water). This place can be tough to find – get directions from Kalyan Singh or Madhusudan Khemani at the Gayatri Art Gallery, opposite the State Bank of Bikaner & Jaipur, near the Hotel Castle Mandawa.

Dundlod

Dundlod is a tiny village right in the heart of the Shekhawati region. The **fort** here dates back to 1750, though much of it is more recent. The Diwan-i-Khas is still in very good condition and has stained-glass windows.

Other attractions in Dundlod include the **Tuganram Goenka Haveli**, the **Jagathia Haveli** and the **Satyanarayan Temple**.

Dundlod Fort (☎ 01594-52519, 0141-211276 in Jaipur), at the fort, offers good rooms for Rs 1195/1350 a single/double. Breakfast/lunch/dinner is Rs 150/250/300. Horse, camel and jeep safaris are available, and they can even teach you polo!

Nawalgarh

The main building in this town is the **fort**, founded in 1737 but today largely disfigured by modern accretions. It houses two banks and some government offices. **Havelis** of interest include the Anandi Lal Poddar Haveli, built in the 1920s (entry is Rs 15), the **Aath Havelis**, the Hem Raj Kulwal Haveli, the Bhagton ki Haveli and the Khedwal Bhavan.

Places to Stay & Eat *Ramesh Jangid's Tourist Pension* (☎ 01594-24060, fax 24061), near the Maur Hospital, offers cheap

and cheerful accommodation in a homey atmosphere. The owner, Ramesh Jangid, and his son, Rajesh, are very friendly and have a wealth of knowledge about Shekhawati. Clean singles/doubles with attached bath (bucket hot water) range from Rs 150/180 to Rs 250/280. Veg meals are available. They can arrange guided tours and bicycle hire.

Apani Dhani (☎ 01594-22239, fax 24061), or Eco Farm, is Ramesh's second place to stay, located near the TV tower on the west side of the main Jaipur road. Rooms are decorated in traditional style and have thatched roofs and mud plaster. Alternative energy is used wherever possible. Rooms cost Rs 600/750.

Roop Niwas Palace (☎ 01594-22008, fax 23388), 1km from the fort, is the most luxurious place to stay. Rooms cost Rs 950/1150; try to look at a few rooms first as some are much nicer than others. There's a restaurant and swimming pool.

Parsurampura

Located 20km south-east of Nawalgarh, this little village has among the best preserved and oldest paintings in Shekhawati. The paintings of the interior of the dome of the **Chhatri of Thakur Sardul Singh** date from the mid-18th century and are worth a look. There's also the **Shamji Sharaf Haveli** and the small **Gopinathji Mandir**, an 18th century temple constructed by Sardul Singh.

Jhunjhunu

Jhunjhunu is one of the largest towns of Shekhawati and is the district headquarters. The town was founded by the Kaimkhani nawabs in the mid-15th century, and stayed under their control until it was taken by the Rajput ruler Sardul Singh in 1730.

It was in Jhunjhunu that the British based their Shekhawati Brigade, a troop raised locally in the 1830s to try to halt the activities of the *dacoits* (bandits), who were largely local petty rulers who had decided it was easier to become wealthy by pinching other peoples' money than by earning their own.

The Tourist Reception Centre (☎ 01592-32909) is out of the town centre at the Churu bypass, Mandawa Circle. It's open Monday to Friday and every second Saturday 10 am to 5 pm.

Things to See The main item of interest here is the **Khetri Mahal**, a minor palace dating from around 1770. It's one of the most sophisticated buildings in the region, although it's not in the greatest condition. From the top, there are sensational views of the whole town. The **Bihariji Temple** is from a similar period and contains some fine murals, although these too have suffered over the years. The **Modi Havelis** and the **Kaniram Narsinghdas Tibrewala Haveli**, both in the main bazaar, are covered with murals.

Places to Stay & Eat *Hotel Shiv Shekhawati* (☎ 01592-32651, fax 32603), east of the town centre, is the most popular hotel with travellers and deservedly so. Squeaky clean rooms cost Rs 300/400 with attached bath, and Rs 700/800 with air-con. Meals are available and the owner, Mr Laxmi Kant Jangid, is very knowledgeable about the Shekhawati area.

Hotel Jamuna Resort (☎ 01592-32871, fax 32603), 1km away, is also owned by Mr Jangid. It only has a few rooms and there's a swimming pool (which nonguests can use for Rs 50). Singles/doubles cost Rs 700/800, and some rooms are decorated with mirrorwork. The vibrant 'painted room' is Rs 1500. There's a relaxing outdoor dining area also open to nonresidents; a set veg/nonveg meal is Rs 150/200.

Hotel Sangam (☎ 01592-32544), near the bus stand, has singles/doubles with attached bath (bucket hot water) from Rs 100/200. The rooms aren't great, but are convenient if you're catching an early morning bus. Nearby is the less impressive *Hotel Naveen* (☎ 01592-32527), which has rooms from Rs 60/100.

Hotel Shekhawati Heritage (☎ 01592-35757, fax 35378), nearby, has rooms from Rs 300/400 with bath. There's also the similarly priced *Hotel Shalimar* (☎ 01592-34505, fax 35225). An RTDC hotel near the Tourist Reception Centre is planned.

Mahansar

Although this sleepy little village does not have a great deal of painted havelis, it oozes old-world charm. Attractions include the mid-19th century Raghunath temple, the Sona ki Dukan Haveli and the Sahaj Ram Poddar Chhatri.

Narayan Niwas Castle (☎ 01595-64322), in the old fort, is an authentic castle (without the commercial flavour of many of Rajasthan's royal hotels). This creaky castle is run by the down-to-earth Thakur of Mahansar and his wife, an elderly couple who have some interesting stories about days long gone. Singles/doubles start at Rs 700/900 – see a few rooms first, as some have more atmosphere than others. The thakur's nephew has some cheaper rooms in a separate portion of the castle.

Getting There & Away

Access to the Shekhawati region is easiest from Jaipur or Bikaner. The towns of Sikar (gateway to the region, but with no notable havelis) and Fatehpur are on the main Jaipur-Bikaner road and are served by many buses.

Churu is on the main Delhi-Bikaner railway line, while Sikar, Nawalgarh and Jhunjhunu have several daily passenger train links with Jaipur and Delhi.

Getting Around

The Shekhawati region is crisscrossed by narrow bitumen roads, and all towns are well served by government or private buses. The local services to the smaller towns can get very crowded and riding 'upper class' (on the roof!) is quite acceptable – and often necessary.

If you have a group of four or five people, it's worth hiring a taxi for the day to take you around the area. It's usually easy to arrange in the towns which have accommodation, although finding a driver who speaks English can be a challenge. The official taxi rate is Rs 4 per kilometre with a minimum of 300km per day. Alternatively, you could opt for a camel or horse safari; ask at your hotel.

AJMER

☎ 0145 • pop 477,000

Just over 130km south-west of Jaipur is Ajmer, a burgeoning town on the shore of the Ana Sagar, flanked by barren hills. Historically, Ajmer had considerable strategic importance and was sacked by Mohammed of Ghori on one of his periodic forays from Afghanistan. Later, it became a favourite residence of the mighty Mughals. One of the first contacts between the Mughals and the British occurred in Ajmer, when Sir Thomas Roe met with Jehangir here in 1616.

The city was subsequently taken by the Scindias and, in 1818, it was handed over to the British, becoming one of the few places in Rajasthan controlled directly by the British rather than being part of a princely state. The British chose Ajmer as the site for Mayo College, a prestigious school opened in 1875 exclusively for the Indian princes, but today open to all those who can afford the fees. Ajmer is a major centre for Muslim pilgrims during the fast of Ramadan, and has some impressive Muslim architecture. However for most travellers, Ajmer is essentially just a stepping stone to nearby Pushkar. It can make a convenient base if you can't get accommodation in Pushkar during the Camel Fair.

Orientation & Information

The main bus stand is close to the RTDC's Hotel Khadim on the east side of town. The train station and most of the hotels are on the west side of town.

The tourist office (☎ 52426) is in the RTDC's Hotel Khadim compound and is open daily except Sunday 8 am to noon and 3 to 6 pm. There's also a small tourist information counter at the train station (closed Sunday). The State Bank of India, opposite the Collectorate, changes travellers cheques and currency. The Bank of Baroda on Prithviraj Marg, opposite the main post office, only changes travellers cheques, but also issues cash advances on MasterCard and Visa.

Ana Sagar

This artificial lake was created in the 12th century by damming the River Luni. On its bank is a pleasant park, the **Dault Bagh**, containing a series of marble pavilions erected in 1637 by Shah Jahan. There are fine views from the hill beside the Dault Bagh. At the Ana Sagar jetty, paddle boats can be hired for Rs 40 (30 minutes).

The lake tends to dry up if the monsoon is poor, so the city's water supply is taken from **Foy Sagar**, 3km farther up the valley.

Dargah

At the foot of a desolate hill in the old part of town, this is one of India's most important places for Muslim pilgrims. The Dargah is the tomb of a Sufi saint, Khwaja Muin-ud-din Chishti, who came to Ajmer from Persia in 1192. Construction of the shrine was completed by Humayun and the gate was added by the nizam of Hyderabad. Akbar used to make the pilgrimage to the Dargah from Agra once a year.

You have to cover your head in certain areas so don't forget to take a scarf or cap – you can buy one at the bazaar leading to the shrine.

As you enter the courtyard, removing your shoes at the gateway, a mosque constructed by Akbar is on the right. The large iron cauldrons are for offerings which are customarily shared by families involved in the shrine's upkeep. In an inner court, there is another mosque built by Shah Jahan. Constructed of white marble, it has 11 arches and a Persian inscription running the full length of the building.

The saint's tomb is in the centre of the second court. It has a marble dome and the actual tomb inside is surrounded by a silver platform. The horseshoes nailed to the shrine doors are offerings from successful horse dealers! Beware of 'guides' pestering for donations around the Dargah using the standard fake donation books or 'visitor registers' – you'll have to pay a generous donation if you sign up.

The tomb attracts hundreds of thousands of pilgrims every year on the anniversary of the saint's death, the Urs, in the seventh month of the lunar calendar (the dates are variable so check with the tourist office).

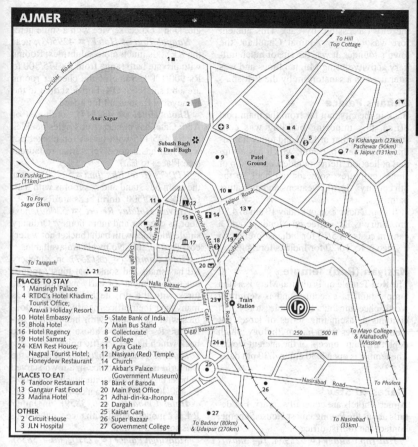

AJMER

To Hill Top Cottage

Circular Road

1 ■

2 ■

Ana Sagar

3 ●

Subash Bagh & Dault Bagh

4 ●

5 ●

To Kishangarh (27km), Pachewar (90km) & Jaipur (131km)

7 ●

9 ●

Patel Ground

8 ●

6 ▼

To Pushkar (11km)

To Foy Sagar (3km)

Jaipur Road

10 ■

11 ● 12 ■

15 ● 14 ■ 13 ▼

Railway Colony

16 ●

17 ■

18 ● 19 ●

Kutchery Road

Prithviraj Marg

Anna Bazaar

Dargah Bazaar

To Taragarh

21 ..

20 ●

Nalla Bazaar

22 ●

23 ▼ Train Station

Station Road

Madar Gate

Diggi Bazaar

24 ■

25 ●

26 ●

27 ●

To Mayo College & Mahabodhi Mission

To Phulera

Nasirabad Road

To Nasirabad (33km)

To Badnor (80km) & Udaipur (270km)

0 250 500 m

PLACES TO STAY
1 Mansingh Palace
4 RTDC's Hotel Khadim; Tourist Office; Aravali Holiday Resort
10 Hotel Embassy
15 Bhola Hotel
16 Hotel Regency
19 Hotel Samrat
24 KEM Rest House; Nagpal Tourist Hotel; Honeydew Restaurant

PLACES TO EAT
6 Tandoor Restaurant
13 Gangaur Fast Food
23 Madina Hotel

OTHER
2 Circuit House
3 JLN Hospital

5 State Bank of India
7 Main Bus Stand
8 Collectorate
9 College
11 Agra Gate
12 Nasiyan (Red) Temple
14 Church
17 Akbar's Palace (Government Museum)
18 Bank of Baroda
20 Main Post Office
21 Adhai-din-ka-Jhonpra
22 Dargah
25 Kaisar Ganj
26 Super Bazaar
27 Government College

It's an interesting festival, but the crowds can be suffocating. As well as the pilgrims, sufis from all over India converge on Ajmer.

Adhai-din-ka-Jhonpra & Taragarh

Beyond the Dargah, on the very outskirts of town, are the ruins of the Adhai-din-ka-Jhonpra mosque. According to legend, its construction, in 1153, took 2½ days, as its name indicates. Others say it was named after a festival lasting 2½ days. It was ori-

ginally built as a Sanskrit college, but in 1198 Mohammed of Ghori seized Ajmer and converted the building into a mosque by adding a seven-arched wall in front of the pillared hall.

Although the mosque is now in need of restoration, it is a particularly fine piece of architecture – the pillars are all different and the arched 'screen', with its damaged minarets, is noteworthy.

Three kilometres and a steep 1½ hour climb beyond the mosque, the Taragarh, or

Star Fort, commands a superb view over the city (accessible by car). This ancient fort was built by Ajaipal Chauhan, the town's founder. It was the site of much military activity during Mughal times and was later used as a sanatorium by the British.

Akbar's Palace

Back in the city, not far from the main post office, this imposing building was constructed by Akbar in 1570 and today houses the government museum, which has a limited collection. Items include a collection of stone sculptures, some dating back to the 8th century AD, old weapons and miniature paintings.

It's open daily except Friday 10 am to 4.30 pm. Entry is Rs 3 (free on Monday), and a camera costs Rs 5/10 for Indians/foreigners; a video is Rs 10/20 for Indians/foreigners.

Nasiyan (Red) Temple

The Red Temple on Prithviraj Marg is a Jain temple built last century and is definitely worth checking out. Its double storey hall contains a fascinating series of large, gilt wooden figures from Jain mythology which depict the Jain concept of the ancient world. The temple is open 8.30 am to 4.30 pm daily (Rs 3).

Places to Stay

Ajmer's hotels are generally dreary. For details about the Paying Guest House Scheme, contact the tourist office.

Hill Top Cottage (☎ 623984, 164 Shastri Nagar), behind the shopping centre, is one of the most homey places to stay in Ajmer. Far removed from the crowds and dust, it's not a cottage as the name suggests, but a family-run house on an elevated site (the rooftop has panoramic views). Clean singles/doubles/triples with bath go for Rs 400/500/600. There are also cheaper, but smaller, rooms for Rs 300/400. Breakfast is Rs 30 and a veg lunch/dinner is Rs 50.

King Edward Memorial Rest House (☎ 429936), known locally as KEM, is to the left as you exit the train station. This poorly maintained flophouse has rooms with bath starting at Rs 65 for a '2nd class' single. Don't expect service with a smile here.

Nagpal Tourist Hotel (☎ 429503), near the KEM, is much more salubrious. Rooms with private bath range from Rs 175/300 to Rs 900/1200. Some of the cheaper rooms are a bit small but OK. Pop next door to the Honeydew Restaurant for a feed.

Bhola Hotel (☎ 432844), south-east of Agra Gate, has nondescript singles/doubles for Rs 125/175 with bath (free bucket hot water). It has a good vegetarian restaurant (see Places to Eat).

RTDC's Hotel Khadim (☎ 52490) is near the main bus stand and has rooms with bath from Rs 320/500; dorm beds are Rs 50.

Aravali Holiday Resort (☎ 52089), next door, is cheaper and more homey. Ordinary singles/doubles with bath (bucket hot water) cost Rs 150/200. No meals are available.

Hotel Samrat (☎ 621257) on Kutchery Rd has small and somewhat musty rooms, but is convenient for early-morning departures with the private bus companies, as many have their offices nearby. Singles/doubles with bath (some with Indian-style toilet) are Rs 180/300. Choose a room at the back which has less traffic noise.

Hotel Regency (☎ 620296), close to the Dargarh, is a good choice in a town starved of hotel talent. Rooms with attached bath cost Rs 380/400 and there's a nice veg restaurant.

Hotel Embassy (☎ 623859), on Jaipur Rd, is a modern hotel with nice singles/doubles for Rs 500/800.

Mansingh Palace (☎ 425702, fax 425858), on Circular Rd overlooking Ana Sagar, is Ajmer's only top-end hotel. Although it's comfortable enough, there is lack of attention to detail, and it's not good value at Rs 1995/3000. There's a bar and restaurant here (see Places to Eat).

Places to Eat

Bhola Hotel has a very good veg restaurant at the top of a seedy staircase. Tasty thalis cost Rs 35, and there's also a variety of other dishes such as paneer kofta (Rs 40).

Honeydew Restaurant, next to the KEM Rest House, has a good selection of veg and nonveg Indian, Chinese and continental food. There are hot dogs (Rs 18), pizzas (around Rs 40), and for the adventurous, brain pakoras (Rs 40). Their banana lassi (Rs 20) is refreshing. You can chow down indoors or out in the garden.

Tandoor Restaurant, a little out of town on Jaipur Rd, offers an assortment of Indian veg and nonveg fare; a tandoori chicken costs Rs 90.

Sheesh Mahal, at the Mansingh Palace, is worth considering for a minor splurge. It serves Indian, Chinese and continental cuisine including chicken tikka masala (Rs 160).

Madina Hotel is handy if you're waiting for a train (the station is directly opposite). This simple eatery cooks up cheap veg and nonveg fare.

Getting There & Away

Bus There are buses from Jaipur to Ajmer every 30 minutes, some nonstop (Rs 52, 2½ hours). The nine hour trip to Delhi costs Rs 152. The Roadways inquiry number is ☎ 429398.

State transport buses go to many destinations including Jodhpur (Rs 80, 210km), Udaipur (Rs 132, 303km), Bundi (Rs 65, 165km), Bharatpur (Rs 122, 305km), Bikaner (Rs 108, 277km), and Jaisalmer (Rs 175, 490km). Also available are private buses – most of the companies have offices on Kutchery Rd. If you book your ticket to one of these destinations through an agency in Pushkar, they should provide a free jeep transfer to Ajmer to commence your journey. There are frequent buses from Ajmer to Pushkar (Rs 5, 30 minutes).

Train Ajmer is on the Delhi-Jaipur-Marwar-Ahmedabad-Mumbai line and most of the trains on this line stop at Ajmer. The comfortable *Shatabdi Express* travels daily, except Sunday, between Ajmer and Delhi (the fare is Rs 580/1125 in ordinary/executive class) via Jaipur (Rs 290/555). This train leaves Delhi at 6.15 am and arrives in Ajmer at 12.40 pm. Going in the other direction, it leaves Ajmer at 3.30 pm and arrives in Delhi at 10.15 pm.

The *Jaipur-Bandra Express* travels between Ajmer and Mumbai (Rs 245). The fastest train to Udaipur takes 7½ hours (Rs 370/564 in 2nd/1st class).

Getting Around

There are plenty of auto-rickshaws as well as some cycle-rickshaws and tongas. To travel anywhere in town by auto-rickshaw should cost you around Rs 15.

AROUND AJMER
Kishangarh

Located 27km north-east of Ajmer, the small town of Kishangarh was founded by Kishan Singh in the early 17th century. Kishangarh is famous for its unique style of miniature painting, first produced in the 18th century.

Roopangarh Fort (☎ 01497-20217, fax 42001, 011-6220031, fax 6220032 in Delhi), about 25km out of town, is a 17th century fort which has been converted into a hotel by the maharaja and maharani of Kishangarh. The smaller rooms are Rs 750, while bigger rooms cost Rs 1190/1575, or Rs 2500 for a suite. Room No 7 has an awesome bed. The rooftop is the place to be at sunset.

Phool Mahal Palace, in Kishangarh, should be up and running as an upmarket hotel by the time you read this. Contact Roopangarh Fort for details.

PUSHKAR
☎ 0145 • pop 13,000

Despite having a distinct touristy flavour these days, Pushkar is still a bewitching little town. It is right on the edge of the desert and is only 11km from Ajmer but separated from it by Nag Pahar, the Snake Mountain.

This traveller-friendly town clings to the side of the small Pushkar Lake with its many bathing ghats and temples. For Hindus, Pushkar is a very important pilgrimage centre and you'll see plenty of sadhus (individuals on a spiritual search).

Pushkar is perhaps best known for its Camel Fair which takes place here each October/November. This massive congregation of camels, cattle, livestock traders, pilgrims, tourists and film-makers is one of

RAJASTHAN

the planet's most incredible events. If you are anywhere within striking distance at the time, it's an event not to be missed.

Being a holy place, alcohol, meat and even eggs are banned.

Information

There is no tourist office in Pushkar, but there are lots of travel agents and it's easy to find your way around. At the time of writing the State Bank of Bikaner & Jaipur only changed travellers cheques (not currency) – the wait can be long and the staff brusque. Currency (and travellers cheques) can be changed at moneychangers scattered along Sadar Bazaar Rd. On the same road are a number of places offering Internet services.

Temples

Pushkar boasts temples, though few are as ancient as you might expect at such an im-

portant pilgrimage site, since many were desecrated by Aurangzeb and subsequently rebuilt. The most famous is the **Brahma Temple**, said to be one of the few temples in the world dedicated to this deity. It's marked by a red spire, and over the entrance gateway is the *hans*, or goose symbol, of Brahma, who is said to have personally chosen Pushkar as its site.

The one hour trek up to the hilltop **Savitri Temple** overlooking the lake is best made early in the morning; the view is magical.

Ghats

Numerous ghats run down to the lake, and pilgrims are constantly bathing in the lake's sacred waters. If you wish to join them, do it with respect, remember this is a holy place. Remove your shoes, don't smoke, refrain from kidding around and do not take photographs.

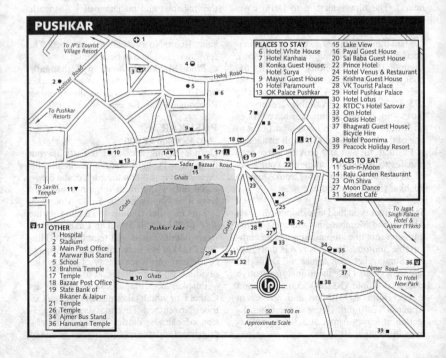

PUSHKAR

PLACES TO STAY
6 Hotel White House
7 Hotel Kanhaia
8 Konika Guest House;
   Hotel Surya
9 Mayur Guest House
10 Hotel Paramount
13 OK Palace Pushkar
15 Lake View
16 Payal Guest House
20 Sai Baba Guest House
22 Prince Hotel
24 Hotel Venus & Restaurant
25 Krishna Guest House
28 VK Tourist Palace
29 Hotel Pushkar Palace
30 Hotel Lotus
32 RTDC's Hotel Sarovar
33 Om Hotel
35 Oasis Hotel
37 Bhagwati Guest House;
   Bicycle Hire
38 Hotel Poornima
39 Peacock Holiday Resort

PLACES TO EAT
11 Sun-n-Moon
14 Raju Garden Restaurant
23 Om Shiva
27 Moon Dance
31 Sunset Café

OTHER
1 Hospital
2 Stadium
3 Main Post Office
4 Marwar Bus Stand
5 School
12 Brahma Temple
17 Temple
18 Bazaar Post Office
19 State Bank of
   Bikaner & Jaipur
21 Temple
26 Temple
34 Ajmer Bus Stand
36 Hanuman Temple

To JP's Tourist Village Resort

Heloj Road

Motisar Road

To Pushkar Resorts

To Savitri Temple

Sadar Bazaar Road

Ghats

Pushkar Lake

Ghats

Ghats

To Jagat Singh Palace Hotel & Ajmer (11km)

Ajmer Road

To Hotel New Park

0   50   100 m
Approximate Scale

Camel Fair

The exact date on which the Camel Fair is held depends on the lunar calendar but, in Hindu chronology, it falls on the full moon of Kartik Purnima, when devotees cleanse away their sins by bathing in the holy lake. Each year, up to 200,000 people flock to Pushkar for the Camel Fair, bringing with them some 50,000 camels and cattle for several days of pilgrimage, livestock trading, horse dealing and spirited festivities. There are camel races, street theatre and a variety of stalls selling interesting handicrafts. The place becomes a flurry of activity with musicians, mystics, comedians, tourists, traders, animals and devotees all converging on the small town. It's truly a feast for the eyes, so don't forget to bring your camera.

It's strongly recommended that you get to the fair several days prior to the official commencement date in order to see the camel and cattle trading at its peak. Although the place assumes a carnival atmosphere, the Camel Fair is taken very seriously by livestock owners, who come from all over the country with the sole intent of trading. A good camel can fetch tens of thousands of rupees and is a vital source of income for many villagers.

This fair is the only one of its kind in the world and has featured in numerous magazines, travel shows and films. It can get noisy at night so if you're a light sleeper, bring earplugs. Carry appropriate allergy medication if you are affected by dust and/or animal hair.

See the Festivals of Rajasthan table at the beginning of this chapter for forthcoming dates.

Places to Stay

Most hotels in Pushkar are nothing fancy, but they're generally clean and freshly whitewashed. You should ask to see a few rooms before deciding, as many have a cell-like atmosphere owing to the tiny or nonexistent windows. Be warned that most hotel tariffs blow sky high during the Camel Fair, when demand for rooms is exceptionally high.

Pushkar Town *Hotel Pushkar Palace* (☎ 72001, fax 72226), near the lake, is the most popular place to stay and highly recommended. Once belonging to the maharaja of Kishangarh, the cheapest rooms cost Rs 150/200 with common bath. These are cramped but right by the lake. Better rooms with bath range from Rs 550/600 to Rs 1100/1195. The most expensive rooms have superlative lake views. There's a good restaurant (see Places to Eat).

RTDC's Hotel Sarovar (☎ 72040) is next to the Hotel Pushkar Palace but approached from a different entrance. Set in its own spacious grounds at the far end of the lake and with a restaurant, it has more character than most other RTDC places, although

some travellers have complained about the poor levels of cleanliness. Singles/doubles with common bath cost Rs 125/200, Rs 250/300 with attached bath. Lake view rooms cost Rs 325/500. There are also dorm beds for Rs 50.

VK Tourist Palace (☎ 72174), also in this area, is a popular cheapie with acceptable rooms from Rs 75/150 with common bath, Rs 150/250 with private bath. There's a good rooftop restaurant.

Hotel Venus (☎ 72323), nearby, offers singles/doubles with bath for Rs 100/150. Set in a shady garden, there's also a popular restaurant upstairs. The owner, Himmat Singh, is a helpful chap who will enthusiastically answer any questions you may have about Pushkar. *Krishna Guest House* (☎ 72091) and *Om Hotel* (☎ 72672) are other cheap options in this area.

Hotel Poornima (☎ 72254), near the Ajmer bus stand, has rooms with attached bath for Rs 60/100.

Bhagwati Guest House (☎ 72423), nearby, is very cheap, with small singles/doubles going for Rs 40/60 with common bath. Larger doubles with bath range from

Pushkar Passports

You can tell a traveller who's been to the ghats in Pushkar by the red ribbon (the 'Pushkar Passport') tied around their wrist. Getting one can be an expensive procedure if you allow yourself to be bullied into a more generous donation than you might otherwise have wanted to give. Priests, some genuine, some not, will approach you near the ghats and offer to do a *puja*. At some point during the prayers they'll ask you to tell Brahma how much you're going to give him, Rs 100 to Rs 400 being the suggested figure (although some travellers have even been asked for US dollars!). Don't fall for this emotional blackmail – if you want to give just Rs 10, that's fine, although the 'priest' will probably tell you it's not enough and doesn't even cover the cost of his 'materials'. It's best to tell him in advance how much you will give to avert a scene later. Many visitors have copped verbal abuse if they do not shell out the cash demanded by the priest. Some clever travellers now wear a red ribbon prior to visiting the lake in order to avoid being approached by a priest.

A current 'scam' involves 'priests' giving a traveller a flower. Once you take it, you are then asked to throw it into the holy lake – for a price! To avoid a scene, it's best to not take any flowers offered to you at all.

Unfortunately more and more travellers are reporting problems with some pushy priests at Pushkar. If you feel strongly about it, try lodging a written complaint with the tourist office in nearby Ajmer.

Rs 80 to Rs 125. The owner, Chandu, and the restaurant, are both great.

Oasis Hotel (☎ 72100), across the road, is a big place with rooms from Rs 125/150 with private bath. There's a pool and restaurant.

Peacock Holiday Resort (☎ 72093, fax 72516), on the outskirts of town, is in a pleasant setting but gets mixed reports from travellers. There's a shady courtyard and a swimming pool with a slide. Standard singles/doubles cost Rs 300/450.

Hotel New Park (☎ 72464, fax 72244), also in this area, is more peaceful and good value for money. Well-kept singles/doubles start from Rs 100/150 with private bath. There's also a restaurant and pool.

Prince Hotel (☎ 72674), closer to the lake, is quite primitive but undeniably cheap. It has rooms for Rs 50/80 with common bath, Rs 100 for a double with bath.

Sai Baba Guest House (*no phone*) nearby, is very mellow and ideal if you're low on cash. Somewhat gloomy rooms are just Rs 40/70 with common bath. Close by is the *Konika Guest House* (*no phone*), which has five clean doubles with bath from Rs 100.

Hotel Kanhaia (☎ 72146), also in this area, has clean doubles without/with attached bath for Rs 100/200.

Hotel White House (☎ 72147), north of the lake, is an appealing place with fine views from the rooftop restaurant. Rooms cost Rs 80/150 with common bath and Rs 200/300 with private bath. Their mango tea is refreshing.

Mayur Guest House (☎ 72302), closer to the lake, is an unpretentious place with rooms for Rs 40/60 with common bath; Rs 80/100 with bath. Only breakfast is available.

Payal Guest House (☎ 72163), right in the middle of the main bazaar, is a travellers' favourite. It's a relaxed and homey place with rooms from Rs 50/100 with common bath, or Rs 100/150 with private bath. There's a banana tree shaded courtyard and a resident rabbit. Meals are available and there's even a small bakery.

Lake View (☎ 72106) is across the road and has some rooms with good views of the lake. Double rooms are Rs 100/150 with common/attached bath.

Hotel Paramount (☎ 72428) has fine views over the lake. Doubles with common bath are Rs 100. The best rooms (Nos 106, 108, 109 and 111) have private baths and a balcony (around Rs 450).

Nearby is the *OK Palace Pushkar* (☎ 72868) – good if you're suffering a cash crunch. Singles/doubles with common bath go for Rs 40/80, or doubles with bath cost Rs 100.

Jagat Singh Palace Hotel (☎ 72953, fax 72952), a little out of the main town area, is one of the most upmarket places in Pushkar. Designed like a fort, well-furnished singles/doubles cost around Rs 1500/1700. There's a large garden, restaurant and a pool is planned.

Pushkar Resorts (☎ 72017, fax 72946, email pushkar@pushkarresorts.com), 5km out of town, is also suitably luxurious. There are 40 modern cottages which are comfortable but a little lacking in character. All have air-con and TV and cost Rs 1695/1995 a single/double. There's a dining hall (residents only), a swimming pool and two telescopes for stargazing.

JP's Tourist Village Resort (☎ 72067, fax 72026) is also a little out of town, but is a peaceful place to stay. Comfortable doubles with attached bath range from Rs 400 to Rs 750. It costs Rs 150 per person to inhabit the treehouse. There's also a swimming pool and restaurant.

Tourist Village During the Camel Fair, the RTDC and many private operators set up a sea of tents near the *mela* (fair) ground. It can get quite cold at night, so bring something warm to wear. A torch (flashlight) may also be useful. Demand for tents is high so you're strongly advised to book well ahead.

RTDC's Tourist Village (☎ 72074) has dormitory tents for US$7 per person, and standard single/double tents with common bath for US$69/84, including all meals. There are also more upmarket tents with attached bath for US$105/119 and deluxe huts for US$119/132, including meals. These huts are open all year round, and are significantly cheaper outside fair time. To book, contact the General Manager, Central Reservations (☎ 0141-202586, fax 201045), RTDC's Hotel Swagatam Campus, Near Railway Station, Jaipur. Full payment must be received 45 days in advance if you want to be sure of accommodation.

Royal Tents, owned by the maharaja of Jodhpur, seem to be the most luxurious tents, but you'll pay for this privilege. They cost US$175/225 a single/double with private bath (bucket hot water), including all meals. Reservations should be made in advance at the Umaid Bhawan Palace in Jodhpur (☎ 0291-433316, fax 635373).

Royal Desert Camp, farther away from the fairground, is another good option with tents for US$90/100 with bath and running showers. There are also some cheaper tents with shared bathroom. The price includes all meals and a 'camel shuttle service' to and from the fair. Book well ahead through the Hotel Pushkar Palace in Pushkar (☎ 72001, fax 72226).

Places to Eat

Pushkar has plenty of reasonably priced eating places. Strict vegetarianism that forbids even eggs rather limits the range of ingredients, but the cooks make up for this with imagination. You can even get an eggless omelette in some places!

Buffet meals are popular, with many places offering all-you-can-eat meals for Rs 25 to Rs 40. German bakeries seem to be all the rage.

Hotel Pushkar Palace is a good place to dine, and you can eat in the restaurant or out in the relaxing garden. Palak paneer is Rs 60, mango lassi is Rs 25 and the buffet lunch is Rs 100. There's also a small bakery here; a croissant costs Rs 10.

Sunset Café, nearby, has long been a popular hang-out with travellers – a good place to swap stories about Goa, Kathmandu and beyond. This simple cafe offers the usual have-a-go-at-anything menu, and includes dosas (Rs 20) and sizzlers (from Rs 50 to Rs 75). There's a German bakery too. The location by the lake shore is pleasant, especially at sunset, however the service can be sluggish.

Om Shiva, near the State Bank of Bikaner & Jaipur, offers reasonably priced and tasty buffets (Rs 40), but the service is variable.

Venus Restaurant, at the Hotel Venus, has a multicuisine restaurant on the rooftop, which is a great place to kick back and watch the world go by. A veg thali is Rs 30 and a banana lassi is Rs 10.

Moon Dance has tables in a laid-back garden and serves a wide range of food, including good Indian, Mexican, Italian and even Thai dishes; a spinach and mushroom enchilada is Rs 45 and a cup of soothing cinnamon tea is Rs 5.

Raju Garden Restaurant serves a mishmash of western, Chinese and Indian fare. The prices are a little high, but the selection is good. If your tummy is screaming for something simple, try the baked potatoes (Rs 45). Birthday cakes can be ordered here (with advance notice); they range from a meek Rs 65 to a mind-blowing Rs 1000!

Sun-n-Moon, not far from the Brahma Temple, has tables around a bodi tree, and is a peaceful place to eat. It offers a variety of western and Indian food such as Kashmiri burgers (Rs 45).

Shopping

Pushkar's main bazaar is a tangle of narrow lanes lined with an assortment of interesting little shops – ideal for picking up gifts for friends back home. It's especially good for costume jewellery and embroidered fabrics such as wall hangings and groovy shoulder bags. A lot of what is stocked here actually comes from the Barmer district south of Jaisalmer and other tribal areas of Rajasthan. You'll have to haggle over prices, as Pushkar has long been exposed to tourists with money to burn and not much time to burn it. There's the usual nonsense about 'last price' quotes which aren't negotiable – take your time and visit a few shops. In between these shops are the inevitable clothing shops catering to styles which were in vogue at the end of the 1960s. You may find occasional timeless items, but much of it is pretty clichéd.

The music shops, on the other hand, are well worth a visit if you're keen to pick up some traditional, contemporary or fusion music.

There are a number of bookshops in the main bazaar selling a tremendous range of second-hand novels in various languages, and they'll usually buy them back for around 50% of what you pay.

Getting There & Away

To Pushkar, buses depart Ajmer frequently for Rs 5 (although it's only Rs 4 when going from Pushkar to Ajmer – because of the road toll; for cars the toll is Rs 25). It's a spectacular climb up and over the hills and you never know quite what to expect around each turn.

There are some travel agencies in Pushkar offering tickets for private buses to various destinations – shop around for the best price. These buses generally leave from Ajmer, but the agents should provide you with free transport to Ajmer in time for the departures. See the Ajmer section for destinations. For around Rs 50, some agents will book rail tickets for services ex-Ajmer (including a free jeep transfer to Ajmer).

Getting Around

Fortunately there are no auto-rickshaws in the town centre, but it's a breeze to get around by foot. Another good option is to hire a bicycle (Rs 4/25 per hour/day). A wallah can carry your luggage on a hand-drawn cart to or from the bus stand for around Rs 10.

RANTHAMBHORE NATIONAL PARK
☎ 07462

Near the town of **Sawai Madhopur**, midway between Bharatpur and Kota, Ranthambhore National Park is one of the prime examples of Project Tiger's conservation efforts in Rajasthan. Sadly, it also demonstrates the program's overall failure, for it was in this park that government officials were implicated in the poaching of tigers for the Chinese folk medicine trade. According to the 1996 census, the park has a total of 28 tigers (several cubs have apparently been born since then).

There's a reasonable chance of seeing one, but you should plan on two or three safaris. Other wildlife, especially the larger and smaller herbivores, are more numerous, and there's also a considerable bird population here. Even if you don't see a tiger, it's worth the effort for the scenery alone: in India it's not often you get the chance to visit such a large area of virgin bush.

The park itself covers some 1334 sq km and its scenery is very beautiful. A system of lakes and rivers is hemmed in by steep, high crags and on top of one of these is the Ranthambhore Fort, built in the 10th century. The lower ground alternates between open bushland and fairly dense forest and is peppered with ruined pavilions, chhatris and 'hides' – the area was formerly a hunting preserve of the maharajas.

Orientation & Information

It's 10km from Sawai Madhopur to the first park gate, where you pay the entry fees, and a farther 3km to the main gate and the Ranthambhore Fort. The accommodation is strung out all the way along the road from the town to the park.

The Tourist Reception Centre (☎ 20808) is in the grounds of the RTDC's Vinayak Tourist Complex. It's open daily except Sunday 10 am to 1.30 pm and 2 to 5 pm. You can change travellers cheques (not currency) at the State Bank of Bikaner & Jaipur, in Sawai Madhopur.

The Project Tiger office (☎ 20223) is 500m from the train station; however, at the time of writing, there were plans to shift it to the Tourist Reception Centre.

Wildlife Safaris

The best time to visit the park is between October and April, and the park is closed during the monsoon from 1 July to 1 October. Early morning and late afternoon are generally the best times for spotting wildlife.

There are four trails within the park, and on each safari two or three jeeps take each trail. There are also large trucks (open-topped), called canters, which seat 20 people, but they're limited to only two of the

trails. If you've ever been on safari in Africa, you might think this is an unduly risky venture, but the tigers appear unconcerned by jeep loads of garrulous tourists touting cameras only metres away from where they're lying. No one has been mauled or devoured – yet!

If you are taking photos, it's worthwhile bringing some 400ASA or 800ASA film, as the undergrowth is dense and surprisingly dark in places.

There's a Rs 20/100 park entry fee for Indians/foreigners, plus Rs 200 for a video camera. You'll also have to pay the entry fee of Rs 125 per jeep (the entry fee for canters is included in the ticket price). A seat in a canter costs Rs 80, and you can arrange to be picked up if your hotel is on the road between the town and the park. Jeeps cost Rs 600 per trip, and this can be shared by up to five people. A guide is compulsory and is included in the ticket price for a canter, but will cost an extra Rs 100 if you go by jeep.

In winter (October to February), both canters and jeeps leave at 7 am and 2.30 pm; the safari takes three hours. In summer (March to June), they leave at 6.30 am and 3.30 pm. Jeeps and canters must be booked at the Project Tiger office. Bookings for morning trips can be made between 4 and 5 pm on the day before, and between 11 am and noon for the afternoon safari. Jeeps fill up fast, but can be booked up to one month in advance.

Places to Stay & Eat

The best places to stay are on Ranthambhore Rd, but shoestringers will find the cheapest lodgings in Sawai Madhopur. Many places offer a hefty low-season discount (between May and September).

Ranthambhore Rd The *Sawai Madhopur Lodge* (☎ 20541, fax 20718), 3km from the train station, once belonged to the maharaja of Jaipur. Run by the Taj Group, it's suitably luxurious with a pool (open to nonresidents for Rs 300), bar, restaurant, library and lovely gardens. Rooms are Rs 2500/3500, and upmarket tented accommodation (with private bath) is Rs 2800 a double.

Ankur Resort (☎ 20792, fax 20697), not far away, is a popular choice with clean rooms with private bath for Rs 400/550. Cottages are Rs 600/750.

Hotel Anurag Resort (☎/fax 20451), next door, has singles/doubles from Rs 400/500. Dorm beds are Rs 75, and it's possible to camp (in your own tent) for Rs 100.

RTDC's Castle Jhoomar Baori (☎ 20495) is a former royal hunting lodge stunningly located on a hillside, about 7km from the train station. The rooms are not really luxurious, but they do have character. Standard singles/doubles cost Rs 700/800. A Panther suite is Rs 900/1100, while a Tiger or Leopard suite is Rs 1200/1500.

Hammir Wildlife Resort (☎ 20562, fax 20697) has rather neglected rooms with bath for Rs 450/550, and cottages for Rs 750.

RTDC's Vinayak Tourist Complex (☎ 21333), farther along the road, has decent rooms for Rs 550/650. There's a nice lawn area and a campfire is lit in the winter.

Tiger Moon Resort (☎ 022-6433622, fax 6406399 in Mumbai, or ☎/fax 52042 in Sawai Madhopur), 11km from the train station, has an appealing jungle ambience with its cottages scattered under a canopy of trees. Rates are US$54 per person, including breakfast. Their 'Jungle Plan' includes accommodation, meals and a morning and evening safari (US$92 per person). There's a good restaurant and swimming pool.

Sawai Madhopur The *Hotel Chinkara* (☎ 20340, 13 Indira Colony, Civil Lines) has large rooms for Rs 200/300 with attached bath. A few doors away is the similarly priced *Rajeev Resort* (☎ 21067).

Vishal Hotel (☎ 20504), in the main bazaar, offers OK singles/doubles with attached bath (free bucket hot water) for Rs 50/80. The nearby, rather seedy, *Hotel Swagat* (☎ 20601) is similarly priced but not nearly as good.

Hotel Pink Palace (☎ 20722, plot A1, Bal Mandir Colony) has basic rooms with bath (free bucket hot water) for Rs 125/150. Next door is the simple *Hotel Mayur* (☎ 20909), with rooms for Rs 125/200.

Retiring rooms at the train station have doubles with attached bath for Rs 110, and dorm beds for Rs 35.

Getting There & Away
There are buses to a number of places including Jaipur (Rs 45, 4½ hours) and Kota (Rs 45, four hours).

Sawai Madhopur has rail connections to a wide range of destinations including Agra, Kota and Jaipur.

Getting Around
Bicycle hire is available at the shops just outside the main entrance to the train station, and at the eastern end of the main bazaar (around Rs 15 per day).

DHOLPUR
Although the town of Dholpur is in Rajasthan, this place can be more easily reached from Madhya Pradesh. Hence, details are given in that chapter.

Southern Rajasthan

BUNDI
☎ 0747 • pop 77,000
Bundi, 39km north-west of Kota, has a good deal of panache and rustic charm. It was the capital of a major princely state during the heyday of the Rajputs. Although its importance dwindled with the rise of Kota during Mughal times, it kept its independence until its incorporation into the state of Rajasthan in 1947. Kota itself was part of Bundi until its separation in 1624 at the instigation of the Mughal emperor, Jehangir. The town's Rajput legacy is well preserved in the massive fort, which broods over the town in the narrow valley below, and the imposing palace which stands beneath it. In this palace are the famous Bundi murals.

Bundi has a lot of interesting historic sites, but sadly many are in a state of disrepair.

Information
There's a small tourist office (☎ 22697) in the grounds of the Circuit House. It's open

Monday to Saturday 10 am to 1.30 pm and 2 to 5 pm. The Bank of Baroda, which is opposite Raniji-ki-Baori, will change travellers cheques. The Haveli Braj Bhushanjee (see Places to Stay) is planning to offer an email service.

If you're feeling a little off colour, there's an Ayurvedic Hospital (☎ 22708) at Balchand Pada (opposite the Haveli Braj Bhushanjee), which prescribes natural remedies.

Taragarh

The rather neglected Taragarh, or Star Fort, was built in 1354 and is a great place to ramble around at leisure. It is reached by a steep road leading up the hillside to its enormous gateway, topped by rampant elephants. Inside are huge reservoirs carved out of solid rock and the Bhim Burj, the largest of the battlements, on which is mounted a famous cannon. Views over the town and surrounding countryside are magical, especially at sunset. It's a shame that the national broadcaster, Doordarshan, decided to build an ugly concrete transmission tower right next to the fort – it's a real eyesore.

Bundi Palace

The palace is reached from the north-western end of the bazaar, through a huge wooden gateway and up a steep cobbled ramp. Only one portion of the outer perimeter of the palace, the Chittra Shala, is officially open to the public. To see the best Bundi murals in the closed sections, you could try contacting the secretary of the maharaja of Bundi (☎ 32812), or ask at your hotel.

Baolis & Water Tanks

Bundi has scores of impressive baolis (step-wells), many right in the centre of town. The noteworthy Raniji-ki-Baoli is 46m deep and has some fine carving. It is one of the largest of its kind, built in 1699 by Rani Nathavatji. The Nagar Sagar Kund is a pair of matching step-wells just outside the Chogan Gate to the old city, right in the centre of town.

Visible from the fort is the square artificial lake of Nawal Sagar. In the centre is a temple to Varuna, the Aryan god of water.

Also worth a look are the Bhora-ji-ka-Kund and Dhabhai Kund.

Other Attractions

Take a stroll through the old city to soak in the medieval ambience of this town. It's worth visiting the colourful sabzi (vegetable) market situated between Raniji-ki-Baori and Nagar Sagar Kund (take along your camera).

Bundi's other attractions are all out of town and are difficult to reach without transport. The modern palace, known as the Phool Sagar Palace, has a beautiful artificial tank and gardens, and is several kilometres out of town on the Ajmer road. It was closed to the public, mainly due to a dispute between the current maharaja and his sister. The maharaja sold this palace to the Oberoi hotel chain, but his sister is now claiming her share of the proceeds. Unless the dispute is settled the palace will remain closed.

There's another palace, the smaller Sukh Mahal, closer to town on the edge of the beautiful Jait Sagar. It's now the Irrigation Rest House. The nearby, rather neglected, Sar Bagh has a number of royal cenotaphs, some with terrific carvings. Shikar Burj is a small former royal hunting lodge on the road which runs along the north side of the Jait Sagar. South of town is the stunning 84 Pillared Cenotaph, set in gardens and definitely worth a visit, especially at night when it is lit up.

About 32km from Bundi at the village of Garardha, you can see some ancient rock paintings. Found on some of the boulders flanking the river, these are believed to be about 15,000 years old. There's a curious depiction of a man riding a huge bird as well as some hunting scenes. It's best to come here with a guide who is familiar with the area – contact Mukesh Mehta at the Haveli Braj Bhushanjee (see Places to Stay) for more information.

Places to Stay & Eat

The commission racket operates in Bundi. Beware of auto-rickshaw drivers who may try to dump you at a hotel where they get commission (usually not the best places).

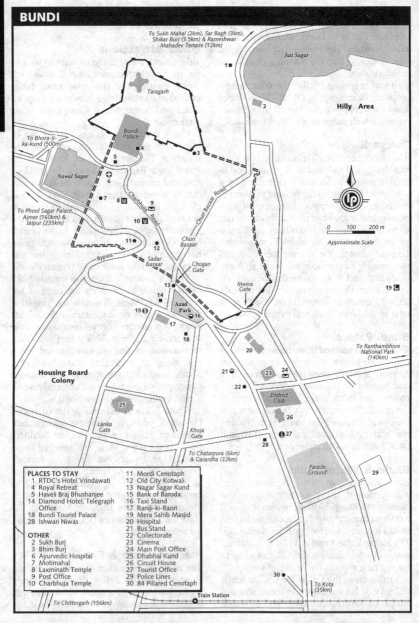

BUNDI

To Sukh Mahal (2km), Sar Bagh (3km),
Shikar Burj (3.5km) & Rameshwar
Mahadev Temple (12km)

Jait Sagar

Hilly   Area

Taragarh

Bundi
Palace

To Bhora-ji-
ka-kund (500m)

Nawal Sagar

To Phool Sagar Palace,
Ajmer (160km) &
Jaipur (235km)

Charbhuja Road

Churi Bazaar Road

Churi
Bazaar

Bypass

Sadar Bazaar

Chogan
Gate

Meera
Gate

Azad
Park

Housing Board
Colony

Lanka
Gate

Khoja
Gate

To Chatarpura (6km)
& Garardha (32km)

District
Club

Parade
Ground

To Ranthambhore
National Park
(140km)

To Kota
(35km)

0   100   200 m

Approximate Scale

PLACES TO STAY	11 Mordi Cenotaph
1 RTDC's Hotel Vrindawati	12 Old City Kotwali
4 Royal Retreat	13 Nagar Sagar Kund
5 Haveli Braj Bhushanjee	15 Bank of Baroda
14 Diamond Hotel; Telegraph	16 Taxi Stand
Office	17 Raniji-ki-Baori
18 Bundi Tourist Palace	19 Mera Sahib Masjid
28 Ishwari Niwas	20 Hospital
	21 Bus Stand
OTHER	22 Collectorate
2 Sukh Burj	23 Cinema
3 Bhim Burj	24 Main Post Office
6 Ayurvedic Hospital	25 Dhabhai Kund
7 Motimahal	26 Circuit House
8 Laxminath Temple	27 Tourist Office
9 Post Office	29 Police Lines
10 Charbhuja Temple	30 84 Pillared Cenotaph

Train Station

To Chittorgarh (156km)

The tourist office has a list of Bundi's paying guesthouses (these are particularly good if you're seeking budget accommodation).

Haveli Braj Bhushanjee (☎ 32322, fax 32142), opposite the Ayurvedic Hospital, just below the palace, is the most popular place with travellers and deservedly so. The views from the rooftop terrace are magical. Quaint rooms with private bath start at Rs 250/300. There are wholesome, but expensive, set veg meals (Rs 250). They do free pick-ups from the bus stand and train station (advance notice appreciated). If you arrive after hours, just ring the doorbell. Ask to see their photos of the Bundi murals which were taken inside the closed part of the palace.

Royal Retreat (☎ 34426), ideally situated in the palace compound, is also a very pleasant place set around a quiet, open-air courtyard. There are two small double rooms with common bath for Rs 250, and several larger rooms with bath for Rs 550/750. There's a reasonably priced veg restaurant (open to nonresidents) and an interesting collection of handicrafts for sale in their shop.

Ishwari Niwas (☎ 32414, fax 32486, 1 Civil Lines), opposite the tourist office, has royal associations and is good, if pricey, compared to other hotels. Rooms are set around a lovely courtyard and begin at Rs 600/1200. The owners seem helpful and keen to help.

Bundi Tourist Palace (☎ 32650), opposite Azad Park, is ideal if you're low on dough. There are six rooms with common bath for Rs 60/120; hot water costs Rs 5 per bucket. The rooms are tiny but OK. No meals are available.

Diamond Hotel (☎ 22656), in the noisy bazaar area, has somewhat grimy singles/doubles with bath from Rs 75/150. The restaurant serves veg dishes at nominal prices.

RTDC's Hotel Vrindawati (☎ 32473) out by Jait Sagar, has seven rooms with bath ranging from Rs 275/350 to Rs 325/400. The cheaper rooms are better value. There's a small dining hall.

Getting There & Away
There are express buses to Ajmer (Rs 60, five hours), Kota (Rs 15, 50 minutes), Sawai Madhopur (Rs 50, 4½ hours), Udaipur (Rs 120, 8½ hours) and Jaipur (Rs 80, five hours).

There are rail connections between Bundi and Agra, Chittor, Kota and onwards.

Getting Around
The bus stand is at the Kota (south-east) end of town. Auto-rickshaw drivers will quote Rs 50 per hour for local sightseeing. Alternatively, bikes are a great way to buzz around and can be rented near the old city *kotwali* (police station) for Rs 10 per day.

KOTA
☎ 0744 • pop 640,000
Following the Rajput conquest of this area of Rajasthan in the 12th century, Bundi was chosen as the capital, with Kota as the land grant of the ruler's eldest son. This situation continued until 1624 when Kota became a separate state, remaining so until it was integrated into Rajasthan after Independence.

Building of the city began in 1264 following the defeat of the Bhil chieftains, but Kota didn't reach its present size until well into the 17th century, when Rao Madho Singh, a son of the ruler of Bundi, was made ruler of Kota by the Mughal emperor, Jehangir. Subsequent rulers have all added to the fort and palaces which stand here now.

Today, Kota serves as an army headquarters. It's also Rajasthan's industrial centre (mainly chemicals), powered by the hydroelectric plants on the Chambal River – the only permanent river in the state – and the nearby nuclear plant. The latter made headlines in 1992 when it was revealed that levels of radioactivity in the area were way above 'safe' levels. Most travellers prefer to visit Kota on a day trip from Bundi.

Orientation & Information
Kota is strung out along the east bank of the Chambal River. The train station is well to the north; a number of other hotels and the bus stand are in the centre.

The Tourist Reception Centre (☎ 327695) is in the grounds of the RTDC's Hotel Chambal. It's open Monday to Saturday 10 am to 5 pm. The State Bank of Bikaner &

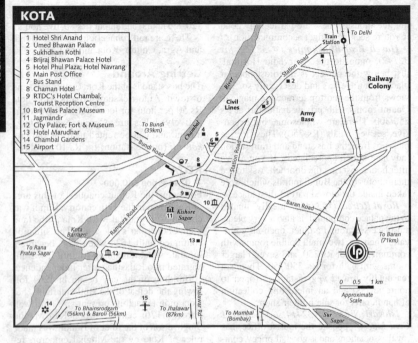

KOTA

1 Hotel Shri Anand
2 Umed Bhawan Palace
3 Sukhdham Kothi
4 Brijraj Bhawan Palace Hotel
5 Hotel Phul Plaza; Hotel Navrang
6 Main Post Office
7 Bus Stand
8 Chaman Hotel
9 RTDC's Hotel Chambal;
   Tourist Reception Centre
10 Brij Vilas Palace Museum
11 Jagmandir
12 City Palace; Fort & Museum
13 Hotel Marudhar
14 Chambal Gardens
15 Airport

Jaipur, at Industrial Estate (opposite Rajasthan Patrika), changes travellers cheques and currency.

City Palace & Fort

Beside the Kota Barrage, overlooking the Chambal River, the City Palace and fort is one of the largest such complexes in Rajasthan. Some of its buildings are now occupied by schools, but most of the complex is open to the public. Entry is from the south side through the **Naya Darwaza**, or New Gate.

The **Rao Madho Singh Museum**, in the City Palace, is excellent. It's on the right-hand side of the complex's huge central courtyard and is entered through a gateway topped by rampant elephants. Inside, you'll find well displayed weapons, old costumes, stuffed beasts, and some of the best preserved murals in the state. The museum is

open daily except Friday 10 am to 4.30 pm. Entry is Rs 7/50 for Indians/foreigners, plus Rs 50/75 for a camera/video.

Jagmandir

Between the City Palace and the RTDC's Hotel Chambal is the picturesque artificial tank of Kishore Sagar, constructed in 1346. In the middle of the tank, on a small island, is the enchanting little palace of Jagmandir. Built in 1740 by one of the maharanis of Kota, it's best seen early in the morning but is exquisite at any time of day. It's not currently open to the public, but you can take a close look at it by taking a boat (daily except Monday 10 am to 5 pm). The cost is Rs 60 per boat for a 15 minute ride.

Brij Vilas Palace Museum

Near the Kishore Sagar, this small government museum is not as good as the City

Palace museum. It has a collection of stone idols and other sculptural fragments, mainly from the archaeological sites at Baroli and Jhalawar. It's open daily except Friday 10 am to 4.30 pm; entry is Rs 3 (free on Monday). Photography is prohibited.

Gardens

Kota has several well maintained gardens – a sight for sore eyes in this industrial town. On the banks of the Chambal River, south of the fort, are the **Chambal Gardens**. The centrepiece is a murky pond stocked with crocodiles. Once common all along the river, by the middle of the 20th century crocodiles had been virtually exterminated through hunting. There are also some rare gharials (thin-snouted fish-eating crocodiles).

Beside the RTDC's Hotel Chambal are the **Chhattar Bilas Gardens**, a curious collection of somewhat neglected but impressive royal cenotaphs.

Special Events

The celebration of **Dussehra Mela** to commemorate the victory of Rama over Ravana has a special significance in Kota, where festivities take the form of a large *mela*, or fair. See the Festivals of Rajasthan table at the start of the chapter for dates.

Places to Stay & Eat

Budget accommodation is limited and lacklustre. On the footpath outside the main post office, omelette and snack stalls set up in the early evening, and this can be a cheap way to eat.

Hotel Navrang (☎ 323294, fax 450044), near the main post office, in Nayapura, is one of the best places to stay. Don't be deceived by the front of the hotel which looks rather run-down. Singles/doubles are set around an inner courtyard and start at Rs 350/400 with bath (some rooms have more character than others). There's a veg restaurant.

The *Hotel Phul Plaza (☎ 329350, fax 322614)*, next door, offers a range of rooms, all with attached bath, from Rs 275/350. There's a good veg restaurant with most dishes under Rs 40.

RTDC's Hotel Chambal (☎ 326527), near Kishore Sagar, has bland rooms with bath from Rs 300/350. A veg thali costs Rs 55.

Chaman Hotel (☎ 323377), closer to the bus stand, on Station Rd, is one of the cheapest (and grubbiest) places in Kota. Dingy rooms cost Rs 80/120. Single female travellers may feel uncomfortable staying at this seedy flophouse.

Hotel Shri Anand (☎ 441157), a fairyfloss pink building 100m along the street opposite the train station, is useful if you're catching an early-morning train. The rooms are tiny and could be cleaner, but are cheap at Rs 150/200 with bath. Veg meals are available.

Hotel Marudhar (☎ 326186, fax 324415) is between the fort and Kishore Sagar and also has a pink paint job. Small rooms with bath cost Rs 225/250. This hotel fronts a busy road, so ask for a quiet room.

Brijraj Bhawan Palace Hotel (☎ 450529, fax 450057), on an elevated site overlooking the Chambal River, is Kota's most interesting hotel. Named after the current maharao of Kota, Brijraj Singh (who still lives here), this serene place has attractive rooms for Rs 1050/1450, or Rs 1800 for a capacious suite. Unlike most palaces, this one is more homey than grand. There's a cosy dining room; the set lunch or dinner is Rs 240 (residents only).

Umed Bhawan Palace (☎ 325262, fax 451110), in Civil Lines, is a more grandiose palace but frankly, the rooms and service are mediocre. Run by Welcomgroup, this gracious building is set in cool gardens and has standard singles/doubles for Rs 1190/1790.

Sukhdham Kothi (☎ 320081, fax 327781) has comfortable rooms for Rs 950/1195. Set in nice grounds in Civil Lines, this building is over 100 years old. They can organise jeep safaris to places of interest around Kota.

Getting There & Away

There are express buses to Ajmer (Rs 75, six hours), Chittorgarh (Rs 73, six hours), Jaipur (Rs 95, six hours), Udaipur (Rs 90, six hours), Jodhpur (Rs 175, 11 hours) and Bikaner (Rs 175, 12 hours). Buses leave for Bundi every half hour (Rs 15, 50 minutes).

Kota is on the main broad-gauge Mumbai-Delhi line via Sawai Madhopur, so there are plenty of trains to choose from. For Sawai Madhopur, the 108km journey takes just over two hours (Rs 76/112 in 2nd/1st class). To Agra Fort it's 343km (Rs 105/361). There's a line linking Kota with Chittorgarh via Bundi; the daily train departs at 6.30 am, arriving in Bundi at 8 am (Rs 8) and in Chittorgarh at 11.30 am (Rs 51). To Jaipur the trip takes about five hours (Rs 90/313 in 2nd/1st class). The 10 hour trip to Delhi costs Rs 160/546.

Getting Around

Minibuses link the train station and bus stand (Rs 2). An auto-rickshaw should cost Rs 15 for this journey. Cycle-rickshaws are a cheaper option.

AROUND KOTA
Baroli

One of Rajasthan's oldest temple complexes is at Baroli, 56km south-west of Kota on the way to Rana Pratap Sagar. Many of the temples were vandalised by Muslim armies but much remains. Some of the sculptures from these 9th century temples are displayed in the government museum in Kota.

There are hourly buses to Baroli from Kota (Rs 15, 1½ hours).

JHALAWAR
☎ 07432

Located 87km south of Kota, at the centre of an opium producing region, Jhalawar was the capital of a small princely state created in 1838. This little archaeological town is well off the beaten track and sees very few travellers. In the centre of town is the run-down Jhalawar Fort which today houses government offices. There's also a small government museum which houses a collection of 8th century sculptures, gold coins and old weapons. It is open daily except Friday 10 am to 4.30 pm (free entry).

In October/November the Chandrabhaga Fair is held on the banks of the Chandrabhaga River, just outside Jhalrapatan (see Around Jhalawar). On the last day of this fair, thousands of devotees take a holy dip.

The tourist office (☎ 30081) is in the RTDC's Hotel Chandrawati, but it's not very helpful. It's open daily except Sunday, 10 am to 5 pm. Bring enough rupees with you for your stay, as there is nowhere to change money in Jhalawar.

Places to Stay & Eat

Purvaj Hotel (☎ 30951), on Mangalpura, near the clock tower, has basic rooms, and the owner, Dileep Singh Jhala, is nice. This old haveli has dorm beds for Rs 50 and rooms with attached bath (free bucket hot water) for Rs 100/200. Better rooms with a view cost Rs 300. There's a bike hire place nearby (Rs 10 per day).

Hotel Dwarika (☎ 22626), on Hospital Rd, has rooms with bath from Rs 170/190. The similarly priced (but not as good) *RTDC's Hotel Chandrawati* (☎ 30015) is on Jhalrapatan Rd.

Getting There & Away

There are buses to various major towns in Rajasthan, including Kota (Rs 34, 2½ hours) and Ajmer (Rs 100, 6½ hours).

AROUND JHALAWAR

At Jhalrapatan (City of Temple Bells), 7km south of Jhalawar, are the ruins of a huge 10th century Surya temple which has impressive sculptures as well as one of the best preserved idols of Surya (the sun god) in India. The 12th century Shantinath Jain Temple is also worth visiting, as is the imposing Gagron Fort, 10km from Jhalawar. About 90km from Jhalawar near Kolvi town are ancient Buddhist caves atop a desolate hill. These extraordinary, but poorly preserved, caves are believed to date from the 5th century. It's a short climb to the top, where you'll find large stupas, bat-filled meditation chambers and weathered sculptures of Buddha.

CHITTORGARH (Chittor)
☎ 01472 • pop 84,500

The sprawling hilltop fort of Chittorgarh epitomises the whole romantic, doomed ideal of Rajput chivalry. Three times in its long history, Chittor was sacked by a stronger enemy and, on each occasion, the end came in textbook Rajput fashion as jauhar was declared in the face of impossible odds. The men donned the saffron robes of martyrdom and rode out from the fort to certain death, while the women and children immolated themselves on a huge funeral pyre. Honour was always more important than death.

Despite the fort's impressive location and colourful history, Chittor is off the main tourist circuit and sees surprisingly few visitors (which accounts for the lacklustre accommodation options). It's well worth the detour – if you're pressed for time you could squeeze in a day trip to Chittor from Udaipur.

History

Chittor's first defeat occurred in 1303 when Ala-ud-din Khilji, the Pathan king of Delhi, besieged the fort in order to capture the beautiful Padmini, wife of the Rana's uncle, Bhim Singh. When defeat was inevitable, the Rajput noblewomen, including Padmini, committed jauhar and Bhim Singh led the orange-clad noblemen out to their deaths.

In 1535 it was Bahadur Shah, the sultan of Gujarat, who besieged the fort and, once again, the medieval dictates of chivalry determined the outcome. This time, the carnage was immense. It is said that 13,000 Rajput women and 32,000 Rajput warriors died following the declaration of jauhar.

The final sacking of Chittor came just 33 years later, in 1568, when the Mughal emperor, Akbar, took the town. Once again, the fort was defended heroically but, once again, the odds were overwhelming and the women performed jauhar, the fort gates were flung open and 8000 orange-robed warriors rode out to their deaths. On this occasion, Maharana Udai Singh II fled to Udaipur where he re-established his capital. In 1616, Jehangir returned Chittor to the Rajputs but there was no attempt at resettlement.

Orientation & Information

The fort stands on a 280 hectare site on top of a 180m-high hill, which rises abruptly

from the surrounding plain. Until 1568, the town of Chittor was also on the hilltop within the fort walls but today's modern town, known as Lower Town, sprawls to the west of the hill. A river separates it from the bus stand, railway line and the rest of the town.

The Tourist Reception Centre (☎ 41089) is near the train station and is open Monday to Saturday 10 am to 5 pm (closed for lunch 1 to 2 pm). You can change money at the State Bank of Bikaner & Jaipur.

Fort

According to legend, Bhim, one of the Pandava heroes of the *Mahabharata*, is credited with the fort's original construction. All of Chittor's attractions are within the fort. A zigzag ascent of over 1km leads through seven gateways to the main gate on the western side, the Rampol.

On the climb, you pass two chhatris, memorials marking spots where Jaimal and Kalla, heroes of the 1568 siege, fell during the struggle against Akbar. The main gate on the eastern side of the fort is known as the Surajpol. Within the fort, a circular road runs around the ruins and there's a deer park at the southern end. From the western end of the fort, there are fine views over the town and across the surrounding countryside, as well as a less-than charming view of an enormous cement factory.

Today, the fort of Chittor is a virtually deserted ruin, but impressive reminders of its grandeur still stand. The main sites can all be seen in half a day (assuming you're not walking – see under Getting Around) but, if you like the atmosphere of ancient sites, then it's worth spending longer as this is a very mellow place. Entry to the fort is Rs 2/50 for Indians/foreigners; there's a Rs 25 video camera charge for the Tower of Victory. Car entry is free, but if there is just one passenger there is a Rs 25 charge. Guides are available in the fort, usually at the Rana Kumbha Palace; they charge around Rs 200.

Rana Kumbha Palace After entering the fort and turning right, you come almost immediately to the ruins of this palace. It has

RAJASTHAN

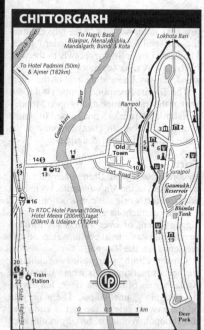

CHITTORGARH

(map labels)

To Nagri, Bassi,
Bijaipur, Menal, Bijolia,
Mandalgarh, Bundi & Kota

Lokhota Bari

Beach River

To Hotel Padmini (50m)
& Ajmer (182km)

River

Rampol

Gambheri

Old
Town

Fort Road

Surajpol

11

14

15

13 12

Gaumukh
Reservoir

Bhimlat
Tank

17 16

To RTDC Hotel Panna (100m),
Hotel Meera (200m), Jagat
(20km) & Udaipur (112km)

18

19

20
21
22 Train
Station

State Highway

0   0.5   1 km

Deer
Park

LP

CHITTORGARH

PLACES TO STAY
11 Bhagwati Hotel
13 Natraj Tourist Hotel
16 Hotel Pratap Palace
21 Shalimar Hotel
22 Hotel Chetak

OTHER
1   Mahavir Temple; Tower of Fame
2   Fateh Prakash Palace
3   Archaeological Museum & Office
4   Rana Kumbha Palace
5   Chhatris of Jaimal & Kalla
6   Kumbha Shyam Temple; Meera Temple
7   Temple of Neelkanth Mahadev
8   Tower of Victory
9   Mahasati Temple; Sammidheshwar Temple
10 Rawat Bagh Singh Memorial
12 Bus Stand
14 State Bank of India
15 State Bank of Bikaner & Jaipur
17 Main Post Office
18 Kalika Mata Temple
19 Padmini's Palace
20 Tourist Reception Centre

elephant and horse stables and a Shiva temple. One of the jauhars is said to have taken place in a vaulted cellar. Across from the palace is the archaeological office and museum, and the treasury building or Nau Lakha Bhandar. The **Singa Chowri Temple** is nearby.

Fateh Prakash Palace Just beyond the Rana Kumbha Palace, this palace is much more modern (Maharana Fateh Singh died in 1930). It houses a small **museum**, and the rest of the building is closed. The museum is open daily except Friday 10.30 am to 4.30 pm. Entry is Rs 3 (free on Monday).

Tower of Victory Continuing anticlockwise around the fort, you come to the Jaya Stambh, or Tower of Victory. Erected by Rana Kumbha to commemorate his victory over Mahmud Khilji of Malwa in 1440, the

tower was constructed between 1458 and 1468. It rises 37m in nine storeys and you can climb the narrow stairs to the eighth storey. Watch your head on the lintels! Entry is Rs 3 (free on Friday).

Hindu sculptures adorn the outside of the tower, but the dome was damaged by lightning and repaired during the last century. Close to the tower is the Mahasati, an area where the ranas were cremated during Chittorgarh's period as the Mewar capital. (Mewar is the area encompassing Chittorgarh and Udaipur.) There are many *sati* stones here, commemorating women who burned on their husbands' funeral pyres. The **Sammidheshwar Temple** stands in the same area.

Gaumukh Reservoir Walk down beyond the temple and, at the very edge of the cliff, you'll see this deep tank. A spring feeds the tank from a carved cow's mouth in the cliffside – from which the reservoir got its name. The opening here leads to the cave in which Padmini and her compatriots are said to have committed jauhar.

Padmini's Palace Continuing south, you come to Padmini's Palace, built beside a large pool with a pavilion in its centre. Legend relates that, as Padmini sat in this pavilion, Ala-ud-din was permitted to see her reflection in a mirror in the palace. This glimpse was the spark that convinced him to destroy Chittor in order to possess her. The bronze gates in this pavilion were carried off by Akbar and can now be seen in the fort at Agra.

Continuing around the circular road, you pass the deer park, the Bhimlat Tank, the Surajpol and the Temple of Neelkanth Mahadev, before reaching the Tower of Fame.

Tower of Fame Chittor's other famous tower, the 22m-high Kirti Stambha, or Tower of Fame, is older (probably built around the 12th century) and smaller than the Tower of Victory. Built by a Jain merchant, it is dedicated to Adinath, the first Jain *tirthankar* (revered Jain teacher), and is decorated with naked figures of the various tirthankars, thus indicating that it is a Digambara, or Sky Clad, monument. A narrow stairway leads through the seven storeys to the top.

Other Buildings Close to the Fateh Prakash Palace is the **Meera Temple**, built during the reign of Rana Kumbha in the ornate Indo-Aryan style and associated with the mystic-poetess Meerabai. The larger temple which is in this same compound is the **Kumbha Shyam Temple**, or Temple of Varah.

Across from Padmini's Palace is the **Kalika Mata Temple**, an 8th century Surya temple. It was later converted to a temple to the goddess Kali. At the northern tip of the fort is another gate, the **Lokhota Bari**, while at the southern end is a small opening from which criminals and traitors were hurled into the abyss.

Places to Stay & Eat

Overall, hotels in Chittor are disappointing; the cleanliness and service is below average and many of the cheaper places have rather grotty bathrooms. The Paying Guest House Scheme operates in Chittor (ask at the Tourist Reception Centre).

Shalimar Hotel (☎ 40842), opposite the train station, has dreary singles/doubles for Rs 80/100 with common bath, or Rs 125/200 with bath attached.

Hotel Chetak (☎ 41588), nearby, is a somewhat better choice. Rooms start at Rs 150/250 with bath. There's also a good restaurant.

Hotel Meera (☎ 40266), also near the train station, is a more salubrious choice, with singles/doubles from Rs 300/350 with bath.

Natraj Tourist Hotel (☎ 41009), by the bus stand, is very basic but dirt cheap. Small rooms cost just Rs 40/60 with common bath, Rs 60/100 with bath; but you'll probably have to get them to change the sheets.

Bhagwati Hotel (☎ 46226), just over the river, is better, and has rooms for Rs 60/80 with bath (bucket hot water). Some rooms can be noisy.

RTDC's Hotel Panna (☎ 41238), closer to the (new) town centre, has dorm beds for Rs 50, singles/doubles with bath ranging from Rs 175/225 to Rs 475/575. The rooms are nothing special.

Hotel Pratap Palace (☎ 40099, fax 41042), between the bus stand and the RTDC's Hotel Panna, is popular with travellers. Rooms with attached bath start at Rs 200/250. A half tandoori chicken in the restaurant costs Rs 80. Village safaris can be arranged, as well as visits to their castle in Bijaipur (see Around Chittorgarh).

Hotel Padmini (☎/fax 41718), a little out of town by the Bearch River, is the most upmarket place in Chittor, with rooms from Rs 400/500. The vegetarian restaurant is good value; palak paneer is Rs 35.

Retiring rooms at the train station cost Rs 100 per double; Rs 200 with air-con. They sell simple veg thalis (Rs 16).

Getting There & Away

Chittor is on the main bus and rail routes. By road, it's 182km from Ajmer, 158km from Bundi and 112km from Udaipur. There are frequent connections to these places. All the Kota buses go via Bundi (a slow 4½ hour trip).

It's possible to take an early bus from Udaipur to Chittorgarh (Rs 44, three hours), spend about three hours visiting the fort, and then catch a late afternoon bus to Ajmer, but this is definitely pushing it.

Chittorgarh has rail links with Ahmedabad, Ajmer, Udaipur, Jaipur, Kota and Delhi.

Getting Around

It's about 6km from the train station to the fort, less from the bus stand, and 7km around the fort itself, not including the long southern loop out to the deer park. To tour the fort, auto-rickshaws charge around Rs 100, which includes waiting time at the various sites. Bicycles can also be rented near the train station (Rs 30 per day), allowing you to explore the fort at leisure. As Indian bicycles rarely have gears, you may have to push the machine to the top – still, they're great once you get to the top, and for the journey back down – but check the brakes first!

AROUND CHITTORGARH

In **Bijaipur**, 40km from Chittor, *Castle Bijaipur* is a converted 16th century palace with pleasant rooms from Rs 800/850 to Rs 1350/1500. The friendly owners can organise horse and jeep safaris to nearby villages. Reservations can be made through the Hotel Pratap Palace in Chittor (☎ 01472-40099, fax 41042). There are frequent daily buses from Chittor to Bijaipur (Rs 20, 1½ hours).

Lying on the Bundi-Chittorgarh road, 48km from Bundi, **Menal** is a complex of Shiva temples built during the Gupta period. After a good monsoon, there's an impressive waterfall in this area.

Bijolia, 16km from Menal, was once a group of 100 temples. Today, only three are left standing, one of which has a huge figure of Ganesh.

A detour between Menal and Bijolia takes you to **Mandalgarh**. This is the third fort of Mewar built by Rana Kumbha – the others are the great fort of Chittorgarh and the fort at Kumbhalgarh.

One of the oldest towns in Rajasthan, **Nagri** is 17km north of Chittor. Hindu and Buddhist remains from the Mauryan to the Gupta periods have been found here.

At the small town of **Jagat**, 20km south of the Udaipur-Chittorgarh road, is a small 10th century Durga temple. There are some fine sculptures, including a couple of small erotic carvings, which have inspired some people to call the town the Khajuraho of Rajasthan (total nonsense!).

UDAIPUR

☎ 0294 • pop 366,000

Possibly no city in Rajasthan is quite as romantic as Udaipur. The French Impressionist painters, let alone the Brothers Grimm, would have loved this place, and it's not without justification that Udaipur has been called the Venice of the East.

Founded in 1568 by Maharana Udai Singh II following the final sacking of Chittorgarh by the Mughal emperor, Akbar, Udaipur rivals any of the world-famous creations of the Mughals with its Rajput love of the whimsical and its superbly crafted elegance. The Lake Palace is certainly the best late example of this unique cultural explosion, but Udaipur is full of palaces, temples and havelis ranging from the modest to the extravagant. It's also proud of its heritage as a centre for the performing arts, painting and crafts.

Until recent times, the higher uninhabited parts of the city were covered in forests but, as elsewhere in India, most of these have inevitably been turned into firewood. There is, however, a movement afoot to reverse this process.

The city was once surrounded by a wall and, although the gates and much of the wall over the higher crags remain, a great deal of it has disappeared. The old city is, however, still a jumble of tangled streets.

In common with most Indian cities, Udaipur's urban and industrial sprawl goes beyond the city's original boundaries, and pollution of various kinds can be discouraging. This will be your first impression of Udaipur if you arrive at the train or bus stations. Ignore it and head for the old city where a different world awaits.

Orientation

The old city, bounded by the remains of a city wall, is on the east side of Lake Pichola. The train station and bus stand are both just outside the city wall to the south east.

Information

Tourist Offices The Tourist Reception Centre (☎ 411535) is in the Fateh Memorial Building near Surajpol, less than a kilometre from the bus stand. The office is open Monday to Saturday 10 am to 1.30 pm and 2 to 5 pm. There are also smaller tourist information counters at the train station, airport and at the southern end of the City Palace complex.

Money You can change money at a number of places including the Vijaya Bank and Thomas Cook, both in the City Palace complex. At Chetak Circle, the State Bank of Bikaner & Jaipur changes money. There's also the Bank of Baroda, the Bank of Rajasthan and the Punjab National Bank, all in Bapu Bazaar.

Post & Communications The main post office is directly north of the old city, at Chetak Circle, but poste restante is at the post office at Shastri Circle. There's also a small post office in the quadrant outside the City Palace Museum. The DHL Worldwide Express office (☎ 414388) is at 380 Ashok Nagar, Shree Niketan Building (near Ayer Bridge).

Internet Resources At the time of writing, the Hotel Raj Palace (see Places to Stay) and Comfort Travels & Tours, in the courtyard outside the City Palace Museum, were the only places with email facilities.

Lake Pichola

Placid Lake Pichola was enlarged by Maharana Udai Singh II after he founded the city. He built a masonry dam, known as the Badipol, and the lake is now 4km in length and 3km wide. Nevertheless, it remains fairly shallow and can actually dry up in severe droughts. Fortunately, this doesn't happen often. The City Palace extends a considerable distance along the east bank of the lake. North of the palace, you can wander along the lake shore, where there are some interesting bathing and *dhobi* (laundry) ghats. Unfortunately the lake can sometimes get choked with water hyacinth.

Out in the lake are two islands – Jagniwas and Jagmandir. **Boat rides**, which leave regularly from the City Palace jetty (known as Bansi Ghat), are popular. These cost Rs 75 for half an hour, Rs 150 for one hour (the latter includes a visit to Jagmandir Island).

Jagniwas Island Jagniwas, the Lake Palace island, is about 1.5 hectares in size. The palace was built by Maharana Jagat Singh II in 1754 and covers the whole island. Formerly the royal summer palace, today it is the ultimate in luxury hotels, with shady courtyards, lotus ponds and even a small mango tree-shaded swimming pool. Yes, this is the perfect place to fall in love, but casual visitors are not really encouraged. Nonguests can only come over for lunch or dinner – and then only if the hotel is not full, which it often is. Hotel launches cross to the island from the City Palace jetty. The Lake Palace, along with the Shiv Niwas Palace and Monsoon Palace in Udaipur, were used as sets in the James Bond movie, *Octopussy*.

Behind Jagniwas is a much smaller island called **Arsi Vilas**, which has been used in recent times as a helipad.

Jagmandir Island The other island palace, Jagmandir, was commenced by Maharana Karan Singh, but takes its name from Maharana Jagat Singh (1628-52) who made a number of additions to it. It is said that the Mughal emperor, Shah Jahan, derived some of his inspiration for the Taj Mahal from this palace after staying here in 1623-24 while leading a revolt against his father, Jehangir. Flanked by a row of enormous stone elephants, the island has an impressive chhatri carved from grey-blue stone. The view across the lake, to the city and its glorious golden palace, is a scene of rare beauty.

RAJASTHAN

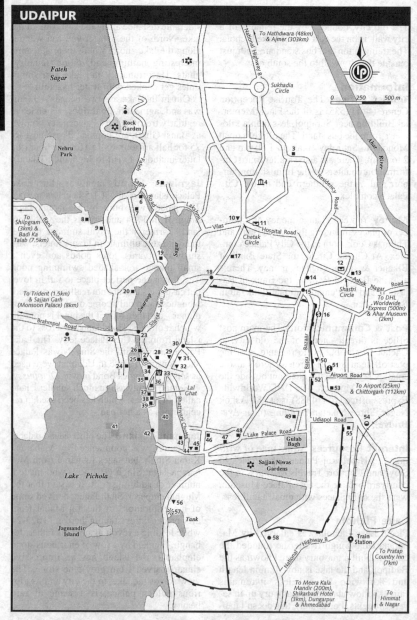

UDAIPUR

To Nathdwara (48km)
& Ajmer (303km)

National Highway 8

Sukhadia
Circle

0   250   500 m

Fateh
Sagar

1 ✿

2 ■
Rock
Garden

Nehru
Park

3 ■

Fateh Sagar Road

5 ■

🏛 4

Residency Road

6 ■
7 ■

8 ■
9 ■

Lakshmi Vilas

10 ▼
11 ✉

Chetak
Circle

Hospital Road

To
Shilpgram
(3km) &
Badi Ka
Talab (7.5km)

Rani Road

Sagar

19 ■

17 ■

18 ●

12 ■
13 ■
Ashok Nagar Road

14 ●

Shastri
Circle

To DHL
Worldwide
Express (500m)
& Ahar Museum
(2km)

To Trident (1.5km)
& Sajjan Garh
(Monsoon Palace) (8km)

Swaroop Sagar Rd

20 ●

15 ●

Brahmpol Road

Silvat Vari Rd

16 🏦

Bapu Bazaar

21 ●

22 ●

23 ●

30 ●
▼ 31
▼ 32

26 ●
27 ■
25 ■

28 ■
29 ■

34 ■
33 ■
36 ■
35 ■

24 ●

37 ■
38 ■
39 ■

Lal
Ghat

Bhattiyani Chotta

40 ■

50 ●
51 ●
Airport Road

▼ 52
53 ■

To Airport (25km)
& Chittorgarh (112km)

41 ■

49 ●

48 ●
46 ●
47 ●

43 ■
44 ▼
45 ●

Lake Palace Road

Gulab
Bagh

Udaipol Road

54 ●
55 ■

Sajjan Niwas
Gardens

Lake   Pichola

▼ 56
✿ 57
Tank

Jagmandir
Island

58 ●

National Highway 8

Train
Station

To Pratap
Country Inn
(7km)

To Meera Kala
Mandir (200m),
Shikarbadi Hotel
(3km), Dungarpur
& Ahmedabad

To
Himmat
& Nagar

UDAIPUR

PLACES TO STAY
3   Mewar Inn
5   Laxmi Vilas Palace Hotel;
    Hotel Anand Bhawan
6   Hotel Gulab Niwas
7   Hotel Hilltop Palace
8   Hotel Lakend
9   Hotel Ram Pratap Palace
13 RTDC's Hotel Kajri
17 Ajanta Hotel
19 Pahadi Palace
20 Hotel Natural
24 Wonder View Palace; Lake
    Pichola Hotel; Lake Shore
    Hotel; Udai Kothi; Ambrai
25 Jheel Guest House
26 Nukkad Guest House
27 Hotel Gangaur Palace
28 Hotel Badi Haveli & Heera
    Cycle Store;
    Lehar Guest House;
    Anjani Hotel
34 Jag Niwas Guest House
35 Hotel Caravanserai; Lalghat
    Guest House; Evergreen
    Guest House & Restaurant
    Natural View
36 Lake Ghat Guest House;
    Ratan Palace Guest House

37 Kankarwa Haveli; Jagat
    Niwas Palace Hotel; Rainbow
    Guest House
38 Hotel Sai-Niwas;
    Shiva Guest House
39 Lake Corner Soni Paying
    Guest House
41 Jagniwas Island (Lake Palace
    Hotel)
43 Hotel Raj Palace
45 Rang Niwas Palace Hotel
46 Ranjit Niwas Hotel
47 Hotel Mahendra Prakash;
    Hotel Shambhu Vilas
48 Haveli Hotel
49 Hotel Vishnupriya
    (Quality Inn)
53 Apsara Hotel
55 Hotel Welcome

PLACES TO EAT
10 Berry's Restaurant
29 Maxim's Café
31 Anna Restaurant
32 Mayur Café
44 Roof Garden Café
50 Park View
52 16 Chef Restaurant; Surajpol
56 Café Hill Park

OTHER
1   Saheliyon ki Bari
2   Pratap Smarak (Moti Magri)
4   Bhartiya Lok Kala Museum
11 Main Post Office
12 Poste Restante
14 Indian Airlines
15 Delhi Gate
16 Bank of Baroda;
    Punjab National Bank;
    Bank of Rajasthan
18 Hathipol
21 Brahmpol
22 Ambapol
23 Chandpol
30 Clock Tower
33 Jagdish Temple
40 City Palace; Museums; WWF;
    Banks; Comfort Travels &
    Tours; Shiv Niwas Palace
    Hotel; Fateh Prakash Palace
    Hotel; Sunset View Terrace;
    Samor Bagh
42 Bansi Ghat
    (City Palace Jetty)
51 Tourist Reception Centre
54 Bus Stand
57 Sunset Point
58 Kishanpol

City Palace & Museums

The imposing City Palace, towering over the lake, is the largest palace complex in Rajasthan. Actually a conglomeration of buildings added by various maharanas, it still manages to retain a surprising uniformity of design. Building was started by Maharana Udai Singh II, the city's founder. The palace is surmounted by balconies, towers and cupolas and there are fine views over the lake and the city from the upper terraces.

The palace is entered through the Baripol (built 1600) and the Tripolia Gate (1725), with its eight carved marble arches. It was once a custom for maharanas to be weighed under the gate and their weight in gold or silver distributed to the populace.

The main part of the palace is now preserved as a museum. It includes the **Mor Chowk** with its beautiful mosaics of peacocks, the favourite Rajasthani bird. The **Manak (or Ruby) Mahal** has glass and mirrorwork, while **Krishna Vilas** has a remarkable collection of miniatures (no photography allowed). In the **Bari Mahal**, there is a pleasant central garden. The **Moti Mahal** has beautiful mirrorwork and the **Chini Mahal** is covered in ornamental tiles. There's an armoury section downstairs. More paintings can be seen in the **Zenana Mahal**. There's a large tiger-catching cage near the Zenana Mahal entrance, and a tiny WWF shop nearby.

The museum is open daily 9.30 am to 4.30 pm and admission is Rs 25, or a hefty Rs 75 if you enter from the Lake Palace side. It costs Rs 50 for a camera, and a whopping Rs 300 for a video camera. A guide (Rs 95) is worthwhile; the knowledgeable Kishan Das speaks French, English and Hindi, and is currently learning Spanish.

There's also a **government museum** (Rs 3; free Monday) within the palace complex. Exhibits include a stuffed kangaroo, a freaky monkey holding a small lamp and Siamese-twin deer. There's also more serious stuff like sculptures and paintings. In the large courtyard outside the City Palace Museum are a number of pricey handicraft shops, a money-exchange facility, a kiosk and places to buy film.

The other part of the palace is against the lake shore and has been partly converted into two luxury hotels: Shiv Niwas Palace and the Fateh Prakash Palace – see Places to Stay.

There's a stunning **Crystal Gallery** at the Fateh Prakash Palace Hotel in the City Palace complex. This rare collection of Osler's crystal was ordered from England by Maharana Sajjan Singh in 1877. Items include crystal chairs, tables and even beds! It's open daily 10 am to 1 pm and 3 to 8 pm; entry (Rs 200) includes a soft drink, coffee or tea. No photography is allowed.

The Crystal Gallery overlooks the grandiose **Durbar Hall** with its massive chandeliers and striking portraits of former maharanas of Mewar. Many palaces in India have a durbar hall, or hall of audience. Historically, the durbar hall was used by India's rulers for official occasions such as state banquets. It was also used to hold formal or informal meetings. However this is undoubtedly one of India's most impressive, with a lavish interior boasting some of the largest chandeliers in the country. The walls display royal weapons and striking portraits of former maharanas of Mewar (a most distinguished looking lot). The illustrious Mewar rulers come from what is believed to be the oldest ruling dynasty in the world, spanning 76 generations.

The foundation stone of the durbar hall was laid in 1909 by Lord Minto, the viceroy of India, during the reign of Maharana Fateh Singh. As a mark of honour to Lord Minto, it was originally named the Minto Hall. The top floor of this high-ceilinged hall is surrounded by viewing galleries, where ladies of the palace could watch in veiled seclusion what was happening below.

Today, the durbar hall in Udaipur is open to visitors. It still has the capacity to hold hundreds of people and can even be hired for special functions, such as conferences or social gatherings – contact the Fateh Prakash Palace Hotel (☎ 528016, fax 528006). Entry to the durbar hall is Rs 50 (free for residents of the Fateh Prakash Palace and Shiv Niwas Palace hotels).

Jagdish Temple

Only 150m north of the entrance to the City Palace, this fine Indo-Aryan temple was built by Maharana Jagat Singh in 1651 and enshrines a black stone image of Vishnu as Jagannath, lord of the universe. A brass image of the Garuda is in a shrine in front of the temple. The temple is open daily 5 am to 2 pm and 4 to 10 pm.

Fateh Sagar

North of Lake Pichola, this lake is overlooked by a number of hills and is a hangout for young lovers. It was originally built in 1678 by Maharana Jai Singh but, after heavy rains destroyed the dam, it was reconstructed by Maharana Fateh Singh. In the middle of the lake is Nehru Park, a popular garden island with a boat-shaped cafe. You can get there by boat from near the bottom of Moti Magri for Rs 5. Pedal boats (Rs 40 for 30 minutes) are also available. An auto-rickshaw from the old city should cost around Rs 20 (one way).

Moti Magri

Atop the Moti Magri, or Pearl Hill, overlooking Fateh Sagar, is a **statue** of the Rajput hero Maharana Pratap, who frequently defied the Mughals. The path to the top traverses elegant **gardens**, including a Japanese rock garden. The park is open daily 7.30 am to 7 pm and admission is Rs 10. To get there, take a bicycle/scooter for Rs 1/3 or a rickshaw/car for Rs 5/15.

Bhartiya Lok Kala Museum

Exhibits at this small museum, which is also a foundation for the preservation and promotion of local folk arts, include dolls, masks, musical instruments, paintings and – the high point of the exhibits – puppets. It is open 9 am to 6 pm daily and entry is Rs 10, plus Rs 10/50 for a camera/video. Regular free 15 minute puppet shows are staged daily. Longer puppet and cultural shows are held daily 6 to 7 pm (Rs 30). Call ☎ 529296 for details.

Saheliyon ki Bari

The Saheliyon ki Bari, or Garden of the Maids of Honour, is in the north of the city. This small ornamental garden, with its fountains, kiosks, marble elephants and delightful lotus pool, is open 9 am to 6 pm daily. Entry is Rs 2, plus Rs 2 to turn the fountains on.

Shilpgram

Shilpgram, a crafts village 3km west of Fateh Sagar, has displays of traditional houses from Rajasthan, Gujarat, Goa and Maharashtra. There are also demonstrations by musicians, dancers, or artisans from these states. Although it's much more animated during festival times (usually in early December, but check with the Tourist Reception Centre), there's usually something happening. It's open 11 am to 7 pm daily; entry is Rs 5/10 for Indians/foreigners.

Next to the site, the *Shilpi Restaurant* serves up good Indian, continental and Chinese food. It also has a swimming pool (Rs 100), open daily 11 am to 4 pm. Not far away is the rather less impressive *Woodland Restaurant*.

A return auto-rickshaw trip (including a 30 minute stop) between the old city and Shilpgram is Rs 80.

Ahar Museum

About 2km east of Udaipur are the remains of an ancient city. The small collection at the museum here includes some very old earthen pottery. It's open daily except Friday 10 am to 4.30 pm; entry is Rs 3 (free Monday). No photography is allowed.

Nearby is an impressive cluster of **cenotaphs** of the maharanas of Mewar, which have been recently restored.

Monsoon Palace

On a distant mountain range, this neglected palace was constructed by Maharana Sajjan Singh in the late 19th century. It is now owned by the government, and is closed to the public (although a little baksheesh to the caretaker may open doors). The main reason to come here is to take in the absolutely breathtaking views. The palace is illuminated at night and from a distance looks like something out of a fairy tale. The round trip takes about one hour by car. The return trip by auto-rickshaw should cost Rs 100 (including 30 minutes at the site).

Other Attractions

The **Sajjan Niwas Gardens** have pleasant lawns and a zoo – beware of unfriendly dogs here. Beside it is the Rose Garden, or **Gulab Bagh**. Don't confuse the **Nehru Park** opposite Bapu Bazaar with the island park of the same name in Fateh Sagar. **Sunset Point**, not far from the Café Hill Park, is indeed lovely at sunset (entry Rs 5). There's a musical fountain here, which plays each evening.

The **Madan Mohan Malvai Ayurvedic College & Hospital** at Ambamata Scheme, near Fateh Sagar, prescribes natural medicines and conducts courses in ayurvedia.

Almost 5km beyond Shilpgram is **Badi ka Talab**, also referred to as Tiger Lake. This mammoth artificial lake, flanked by hills, is a pleasant picnic spot. Crocodiles apparently lurk in parts of the lake, so swimmers beware!

Organised Tours

Five-hour city tours leave daily at 8 am from the RTDC's Hotel Kajri. Cost is Rs 50 (excluding entry to sites). Depending on demand, an afternoon tour (2 to 7 pm) goes out to Eklingji, Haldighati and Nathdwara and costs Rs 80. Contact the Tourist Reception Centre for details. For information on boat tours, see Lake Pichola earlier in this section.

Places to Stay – Budget

Udaipur pioneered the Paying Guest House Scheme in Rajasthan, and there are now over 75 families participating. Expect to pay Rs 100 to Rs 600 per night; contact the Tourist Reception Centre for details.

Hotels around the Jagdish Temple are definitely preferable to the others. Next best are those between the City Palace and the bus stand, along Lake Palace Rd and Bhattiyani Chotta. Lake-view rooms are usually a bit more expensive and should be requested when booking.

The commission system is notorious here and many travellers are bullied by autorickshaw drivers into staying at a hotel where they get commission (see Getting Around, later in this section).

Jagdish Temple Area You'll pay a little more for a hotel in this area, but there is hardly any traffic noise, most places have views over the lake, and the central location is ideal.

Hotel Gangaur Palace (☎ 422303, 3 Gangaur Ghat) is a fabulous choice in this area. Singles/doubles with common bath are Rs 60/80. Large doubles with bath range from Rs 150 to Rs 350 for lake view rooms. There's a rooftop restaurant serving Indian and continental cuisine.

Hotel Badi Haveli (☎ 412588, 85 Gangaur Ghat Rd) is a popular place with fine views over the lake and old city. Plain but neat singles/doubles with common bath are Rs 100/150, doubles with bath are Rs 180, and the best room with a view is Rs 250. Veg meals are available; a thali is Rs 51. Nearby is the *Anjani Hotel (☎ 421770)* with rooms with bath from Rs 100.

Lalghat Guest House (☎ 525301, fax 418508, 33 Lalghat) has a rooftop with great views over the water. It's another travellers' favourite, with dorm beds for Rs 50, small rooms with common bath for Rs 75/100 and rooms with attached bath from Rs 250 to Rs 350. There is a small kitchen for self-caterers, and a shop.

Evergreen Guest House (☎ 421585, 32 Lalghat), next door, has rooms around a small courtyard. Doubles with common/attached bath are Rs 100/150; the best room is Rs 250.

Jag Niwas Guest House (☎ 422067, 21 Gangaur Rd) is a little place with rooms for

Rs 80/150 with bath. The rooftop sports a veg restaurant.

Lake Ghat Guest House (☎ 521636, fax 520023), across the road from the Lalghat Guest House, is another popular cheapie. Singles/doubles/triples with bath start from Rs 150/200/250. There's also a good restaurant and terrace area.

Lake Corner Soni Paying Guest House (no phone), in the Lal Ghat area, is nothing fancy but is owned by a sweet elderly couple. Doubles without/with bath are Rs 100/150 (many rooms with Indian-style toilets). The rooftop affords terrific views.

Jheel Guest House (☎ 421352, 56 Gangaur Ghat) is right at the bottom of the hill, by the ghat. Housed in an old haveli, rooms with common bath are around Rs 80/150. The newer annexe across the road has better (more expensive) rooms and a rooftop restaurant overlooking the lake. In the same area is the friendly *Lehar Guest House (☎ 417651, 86 Gangaur Ghat Rd)* with doubles with bath from Rs 80.

Nukkad Guest House (no phone, 56 Ganesh Ghati), run by a friendly couple, has very basic but affordable rooms. Doubles without/with bath cost Rs 60/80.

Lake Palace Rd Area This area is central but farther away from Lake Pichola. *Hotel Mahendra Prakash (☎ 522993, Lake Palace Rd)* has doubles with attached bath ranging from Rs 150 to Rs 600. There's also a sparkling clean swimming pool, a restaurant and a rooftop with views of the City Palace.

Hotel Shambhu Vilas (☎ 421921), a few doors away, has singles/doubles from Rs 200/350. Nearby is the rather dishevelled *Haveli Hotel (☎ 421351)*.

Ranjit Niwas Hotel (☎ 525774), not too far away, is nothing flash but quite cheap. Dorm beds are Rs 50, basic rooms with common bath are Rs 100/150. With attached bath they're Rs 150/250.

Bus Stand Area For people catching an early-morning bus, there are several mundane options in this uninspiring area.

Apsara Hotel (☎ *420400*), north of the bus stand, is a huge place set back from the road. The rooms front onto an internal courtyard making them relatively quiet. Dorm beds are Rs 50 and rooms with bath start at Rs 75/200.

Hotel Welcome (☎ *485375*), opposite the bus stand, has rooms with bath from Rs 95/125.

Elsewhere If you don't mind staying away from the heart of the old city, there are some decent budget options.

Lake Shore Hotel (*no phone*), south of Chandpol, across from the City Palace on the opposite side of Lake Pichola, is a mellow place and has a terrace with marvellous views over the water. Basic but neat singles/doubles with common bath are Rs 100/200. There are more expensive rooms with bath and lake views. The restaurant here is very good; baked potatoes with garlic cheese costs Rs 40.

Hotel Natural (☎ *527879, 55 Rang Sagar*) is farther away from Lake Pichola but good if you want to escape the hustle and bustle. Basic doubles with bath start from Rs 150 (some rooms have Indian-style toilets). There's good veg food cooked with tender loving care.

Pahadi Palace (☎ *420099, 18 Ambargarh, Swaroop Sagar*), not far away, has spotlessly clean rooms and is good value for money. Well-kept doubles with bath range from Rs 100 to Rs 750. This pleasant place is run by the affable Ansar Ahmed.

Mewar Inn (☎ *522090, 42 Residency Rd*), is not in a very thrilling location at all, but may be worth considering if you're really strapped for cash. Basic singles/doubles with common bath are Rs 30/40. Rooms with bath start at Rs 69/79. A discount is given to YHA members. There's a rooftop veg restaurant and bicycles for hire (Rs 15 per day).

Pratap Country Inn (☎ *583138, fax 583058*) is a serene and secluded retreat at Titaradi village, about 7km outside Udaipur. Run by the charming Maharaj Narendra Singh, doubles with attached bath range from Rs 200 to Rs 1200. Horse riding is

available and they also organise longer safaris – from US$100 per person per day. It can be tough getting a rickshaw out here (Rs 50). The hotel can pick you up from Udaipur with advance notice.

Places to Stay – Mid-Range
Jagdish Temple Area *Kankarwa Haveli* (☎ *411457, fax 521403, 26 Lalghat*), run by the helpful Janardan Singh, is an excellent family-run haveli. Squeaky clean doubles range from Rs 400 to Rs 1200. The more expensive rooms overlook Lake Pichola. Book well ahead as this place fills up fast.

Jagat Niwas Palace Hotel (☎ *420133, fax 520023, 25 Lalghat*), on the lake shore, has long been popular with travellers. This converted haveli has a very good restaurant which boasts tremendous lake views. Double rooms range from Rs 350 to Rs 1400.

Hotel Sai-Niwas (☎*/fax 524909, 75 Navghat Marg*), just down the hill towards the ghat from the City Palace entrance, is also heartily recommended. The seven double rooms are imaginatively decorated and range from Rs 800 to Rs 1000. There's a good restaurant; lentil soup is Rs 40.

Ratan Palace Guest House (☎ *561153, 21 Lalghat*) is also popular. Double rooms cost from Rs 250 to Rs 450. The terrace has lake views and meals are available.

Hotel Caravanserai (☎ *411103, fax 521252, 14 Lalghat*) is a modern place that offers nice rooms from Rs 300 to Rs 1195. The food at the rooftop restaurant is average, but it has good lake views and live Indian classical music in the evening.

Lake Palace Rd Area This area is central but farther away from Lake Pichola than the hotels in the Jagdish Temple area.

Rang Niwas Palace Hotel (☎ *523890, fax 527884*) is one of the best mid-range options. In shady gardens, with a swimming pool, it's relaxed and friendly. There's accommodation in the old building, formerly a royal guesthouse, and also comfortable rooms in the new building. Doubles range from Rs 500 to Rs 2000. There are also two budget rooms with common bath (Rs 350).

The *Hotel Raj Palace* (☎ *527092, fax 410395, 103 Bhattiyani Chotta*) is also a good place to stay. There's a small dorm (Rs 75), and double rooms from Rs 250 to Rs 950. There's also a lush courtyard restaurant that serves excellent food.

The *Hotel Vishnupriya (Quality Inn)* (☎ *421313, fax 420314, 9 Garden Rd*), near Gulab Bagh, has rooms from Rs 995/1495.

Fateh Sagar Area There are hotels around Udaipur's other major lake, Fateh Sagar, however these are a little inconveniently located away from the old city. Although they lack the panache of the hotels around Lake Pichola, they are away from the hustle and bustle. Options include the *Hotel Lakend* (☎ *415100, fax 523898*), *Hotel Ram Pratap Palace* (☎ *528701, fax 528700, 5B Alkapuri*), *Hotel Anand Bhawan* (☎ *523256, fax 523247*) and *Hotel Gulab Niwas* (☎/*fax 523644*).

Elsewhere Both of the hotels below are across from the City Palace, on the opposite side of Lake Pichola.

Wonder View Palace (☎ *522996*), a little out of town south of Chandpol, has average rooms from Rs 400/500.

Udai Kothi (☎ *524002*), nearby, was being built at the time of writing and will boast Udaipur's *only* rooftop swimming pool. Doubles are expected to cost from Rs 600 to Rs 800.

Places to Stay – Top End

The *Lake Pichola Hotel* (☎ *421197, fax 410575*), out of the old city, south of Chandpol, is the best of the lower priced top-range hotels. It's in a superb location with stunning views of the ghats and City Palace (go up to the rooftop terrace to really soak in the view). Singles/doubles cost Rs 975/1000, but it's worth spending Rs 1150/1195, which gets you a balcony and lake view.

Trident (☎ *419393, fax 419494*) is a bit inconveniently located beyond Chandpol, but is Udaipur's slickest hotel. Hidden in the hills, it is part of the Oberoi Group, and offers singles/doubles from US$125/140.

The multicuisine restaurant is excellent and even has frothy cappuccinos. Don't miss the wild boar feeding frenzy.

Laxmi Vilas Palace Hotel (☎ *529711, fax 526273*) is between Swaroop Sagar and Fateh Sagar, up on the hill. It's a pleasant four star ITDC place where air-con rooms cost US$115/130. There's a bar, restaurant and swimming pool.

Hotel Hilltop Palace (☎ *521997, fax 525106*), in the same area, is a modern hotel boasting a remarkable 360° view of Udaipur. Rooms start at Rs 1350/2100; although well kept, this place has a somewhat sterile ambience.

Shikarbadi Hotel (☎ *583201, fax 584841*), 3km out of town on the Ahmedabad road, is the perfect place to go for serenity and fresh air. Once a royal hunting lodge, it's set in beautiful grounds and has a pool. Smart singles/doubles cost Rs 1195/2395. A stud farm on the premises offers short horse rides as well as longer safaris. Sip tea while you watch the wild boar feeding (4 pm each day).

Lake Palace Hotel (☎ *527961, fax 527974*), which appears to be floating in the middle of Lake Pichola, is one of the world's most spectacular hotels. It's the very image of what a maharaja's palace should be like and most people with sufficient money would not pass up an opportunity to stay here. This swanky white palace has a bar, restaurant, little shopping arcade, open air courtyards, lotus ponds, and a small swimming pool. The cheapest doubles are US$210 (no lake view); US$245 gets you a lake view. Sumptuous suites cost US$325 to US$550. Needless to say, you need to book well in advance.

Shiv Niwas Palace Hotel (☎ *528016, fax 528006, email resv@hrhindia.com*) is part of the City Palace complex, and is another atmospheric palace/hotel. The cheapest rooms (US$100) aren't really great value. It's better to get a room around the pool which start from US$250 a double (room 16 has fine views over the lake). There's a good restaurant, bar, holistic health centre, and marble pool (open to nonresidents for Rs

240 including towel). A small bagpipe (!) band strikes up a merry tune each evening. It's wise to also book well ahead here, as demand for rooms is high.

Fateh Prakash Palace Hotel (☎ *528016, fax 528006*), also in the City Palace complex, was built in the early 20th century during the reign of Maharana Fateh Singh. The cheapest rooms are US$100, but these are not in the main palace. More ornate rooms furnished with traditional palace pieces cost US$200/250 a single/double (some with a lake view). The intimate Gallery Restaurant has brilliant views across the lake.

Places to Eat

Udaipur has scores of rooftop cafes catering to budget travellers, as well as fine dining at the top-end hotels. Many of the budget restaurants try to lure customers by putting on a nightly screening of the James Bond movie *Octopussy*, which was partly filmed in Udaipur. These days, contemporary cult movies are also screened.

Sunset View Terrace, ideally situated on a terrace overlooking Lake Pichola, is *the* place to be at sunset. Part of the Fateh Prakash Palace Hotel, this place is worth visiting for the views alone (don't forget your camera). Live Indian classical music is played in the late afternoon and the menu offers a range of snacks such as pizzas (Rs 110), burgers (Rs 90) and milk shakes (Rs 50).

Ambrai is worth visiting purely for the superb location – unlike other restaurants, it sits at water level. It is just beyond the Lake Pichola Hotel at Chandpol. It serves Indian, Chinese and continental cuisine and is also a great place to kick back with a beer.

El Parador, out in the Fateh Sagar area (oppiste the Ayurvedic College & Hospital on Ambamata Rd), is highly recommended. This is one of the only places in Rajasthan which makes *real* percolated coffee (Rs 60 per heavenly pot)! It's run by a friendly family who whips up a range of moderately priced Italian, Greek, Mexican and French cuisine.

Mayur Café, by the Jagdish Temple, has long been popular, although travellers give mixed reports about the food and service. There are south Indian dishes as well as western alternatives; spaghetti with cheese is Rs 30.

Maxim's Café, nearby, is better value and not as indifferent to travellers as the Mayur Café. Menu items include *paneer tikka* (Rs 20) and Rajasthani pizza (Rs 22). Not far away is the *Anna Restaurant*, which is also good for a cheap chow down.

Samor Bagh, at the Lake Palace Rd entrance to the City Palace, has Indian, Chinese and continental food. Their speciality is *paneer pasanda* (Rs 50). You can sit in the large 'hut' or out in the garden.

Restaurant Natural View, on the rooftop of the Evergreen Guest House, has lovely lake views but is a bit overpriced. It serves Indian, Chinese and continental fare; chicken palak is Rs 55.

Roof Garden Café, around the corner from the Rang Niwas Palace Hotel, facing the City Palace, looks like the Hanging Gardens of Babylon. The setting is more exciting than the food; chicken curry is Rs 45.

Café Hill Park, south-west of the Sajjan Niwas Gardens on a hill overlooking Lake Pichola, is worth a visit just for the views. This rather ramshackle cafe offers Indian, continental and Chinese fare.

Park View is opposite the park in the main part of town but there's absolutely no view. This dimly lit place is particularly good for its north Indian cuisine and is often packed with middle-class Indian families. Prices are reasonable.

16 Chef Restaurant (*16 Gyan Marg*), inside Surajpol, is a possibility if you're short of cash. It has cheap vegetarian Indian, Chinese and some continental dishes (most below Rs 35).

Berry's Restaurant (*Chetak Circle*) has a sterile ambience but cooks up pretty good Indian dishes – the butter chicken is a hot seller.

Jagat Niwas Palace Hotel has a restaurant with superlative lake views and is recommended for a minor splurge. Their western dishes are rather pricey, but the Indian food is cheaper; palak paneer is Rs 50.

It's wise to book ahead for dinner, as the place can fill up fast (call ☎ 420133).

Shiv Niwas Palace Hotel is highly recommended for an unforgettable dining experience. There's seating indoors or in the pleasant open-air courtyard by the pool. Their Indian food is best – try the *aloo chutneywale*, potatoes stuffed with Indian cottage cheese in a mango and mint chutney – for Rs 75. Indian classical music is performed each evening by the poolside, creating a magical ambience. Nonresidents are welcome, but it's a good idea to book ahead (especially for dinner). Check out the plush bar while you're here.

Gallery Restaurant, at the Fateh Prakash Palace Hotel, serves a set continental lunch/dinner for Rs 500/600. Although the food is nothing to write home about, this elegant little restaurant has beguiling views across Lake Pichola. For a really romantic evening, come here at sunset for a drink, then enjoy the live Indian classical music while you dine. For a minor splurge, afternoon tea is served daily 3 to 5 pm. A 'full cream tea' costs Rs 125.

Lake Palace Hotel is, of course, the ultimate dining experience, although there's no guarantee you'll get in, since it is usually only possible to get a table when the hotel is not full. The buffet lunch/dinner costs Rs 500/600 (including the boat crossing) and before your meal, you can take a drink at the pleasant bar. Reservations are essential, and reasonably tidy dress is expected. For something different, ask about their tiny *floating pontoon*, which arranges lunch/dinner for US$40 (maximum four people).

Hotel Natural (see Places to Stay) has good veg food and also bakes delicious home-made birthday cakes for Rs 100. Ring Ritu (☎ 529573) to place your order.

Entertainment

Meera Kala Mandir (☎ *583176, Sector 11, Hiran Magari*), near the Pars Theatre, has one hour Rajasthani folk dance and music performances daily except Sunday at 7 pm from August to April. It costs Rs 60 per person. An auto-rickshaw from the City Palace area costs Rs 25.

Many hotels stage their own entertainment for guests – usually puppet shows or Rajasthani music/dance performances.

Shopping

Udaipur has oodles of little shops selling a jumble of things, from funky western clothing to traditional antique jewellery. The town is popular for its local crafts, particularly miniature paintings in the Rajput-Mughal style. There's a good cluster of shops selling these on Lake Palace Rd, next to the Rang Niwas Palace Hotel, and others around the Jagdish Temple. Be prepared to bargain hard, as most places have ridiculously inflated prices for tourists.

Getting There & Away

Air The Indian Airlines office (☎ 410999) at Delhi Gate is open Monday to Saturday, 10 am to 1 pm and 2 to 5 pm and Sunday, 10 am to 2 pm.Indian Airlines operates flights to Delhi (US$95), Jaipur (US$70), Aurangabad (US$105), Jodhpur (US$55) and Mumbai (US$110).

Bus Destinations served by deluxe buses include Jaipur (Rs 200, nine hours), Ajmer (Rs 110, six hours), Kota/Bundi (Rs 100, six hours), Jodhpur (Rs 110, eight hours) and Chittorgarh (Rs 50, three hours).

There are quite a few private bus companies which operate to such places as Ahmedabad (Rs 80, six hours), Vadodara (Rs 120, eight hours), Mumbai (Rs 200, 16 hours), Delhi (Rs 200, 14 hours), Indore (Rs 150, 10 hours) and Mt Abu (Rs 70, five hours).

Train Lines into Udaipur are currently metre gauge only, but are scheduled to be converted to broad gauge – nobody is really sure when this will happen. It's quicker in most cases to catch a bus.

The *Chetak Express* takes 20 hours to get to Delhi and costs Rs 233/718 in 2nd/1st class. This train goes via Chittorgarh (Rs 76/184 in 2nd/1st class), Ajmer (Rs 125/370) and Jaipur (Rs 161/515). The *Mewar Fast Express* also does the trip to Chittor (Rs 36/184).

Taxi There are plenty of taxis willing to take you to places around Udaipur. Many drivers will show you a list of 'official' rates to places like Mt Abu, Chittor and Jodhpur. Shop around, as you can often barter for better rates. For travel out of town, remember that taxis generally charge return trip fares even if you're only going one way.

Getting Around

To/From the Airport The airport is 25km from the city. There's no airport bus; an auto-rickshaw/taxi will cost at least Rs 150/190.

Auto-Rickshaw These are unmetered so you should agree on a fare before setting off. The standard fare for tourists anywhere within the city appears to be around Rs 20. It costs Rs 130 to hire an auto-rickshaw for half a day of local sightseeing.

The commission system is in place with a vengeance, so most rickshaw drivers will desperately try to drag you to a place of their choice rather than yours, especially if you want to go to the Lal Ghat area. If that's the case, just ask for the Jagdish Temple, as all the guesthouses in that area are within easy walking distance of the temple. Some drivers will insist that the hotel of your choice has burnt down, suddenly closed, or the owner died in a freak accident! Don't be fooled by these far-fetched stories.

Bicycle You can hire bicycles all over town for around Rs 25 per day. Heera Cycle Store (☎ 523525), near the Hotel Badi Haveli in the old city, rents out bicycles/mopeds/motorcycles for Rs 25/150/300 per day.

AROUND UDAIPUR
Eklingji & Nagda

The little village of Eklingji, with a number of ancient temples, is only 22km north of Udaipur. The **Shiva temple** in the village itself was originally built in 734, although its present form dates from the rule of Maharana Raimal, between 1473 and 1509. The walled complex includes an elaborately pillared hall under a large pyramidal roof and features a four faced Shiva image of black

marble. The temple is open 4.15 to 6.45 am, 10.30 am to 1.30 pm and 5.15 to 7.45 pm (double-check times, in case they have changed). Photography is not allowed. Avoid the temple on Monday (an auspicious day for devotees), as it can get very crowded. The maharana of Udaipur pays a visit on Monday evening.

At Nagda, about 1km off the road and 1km before Eklingji, are three old temples. The Jain temple of **Adbudji** is essentially ruined, but its architecture is quite interesting.

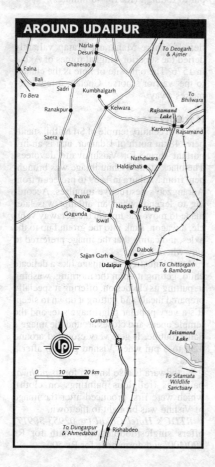

AROUND UDAIPUR

Narlai
Desuri
Ghanerao
Falna
Bali
Sadri
To Bera
Ranakpur
Saera
Kumbhalgarh
Kelwara
Rajsamand Lake
Kankroli
Rajsamand
Nathdwara
Haldighati
Jharoli
Nagda
Eklingji
Gogunda
Iswal
Dabok
Sajjan Garh
Udaipur
To Chittorgarh & Bambora
Guman
Jaisamand Lake
To Sitamata Wildlife Sanctuary
To Dungarpur & Ahmedabad
Rishabdeo

To Deogarh & Ajmer
To Bhilwara

0   10   20 km

The nearby **Sas Bahu**, or Mother and Daughter-in-Law, group has intricate architecture and carvings, including some erotic figures. You can reach these temples most conveniently by hiring a bicycle in Eklingji.

Heritage Resorts (☎ 0294-440382, fax 527549), at Lake Bagela in Nagda, is set in delightful, quiet grounds. Singles/doubles are Rs 1540/2900 and there's a small pool, restaurant (non-guests welcome) and some good walks in the surrounding countryside.

There are hourly local buses from Udaipur to Eklingji (Rs 15, 40 minutes).

Haldighati

This site, 40km north of Udaipur, is the battlefield where Maharana Pratap valiantly defied the superior Mughal forces of Akbar in 1576. The only site of note is the chhatri to the warrior's horse, Chetak, a few kilometres away.

Nathdwara

The 18th century temple of **Sri Nathji** stands here, 48km north of Udaipur, and is an important shrine for Vaishnavaite devotees. The black stone Vishnu image was brought here from Mathura in 1669 to protect it from Aurangzeb's destructive impulses. According to legend, when an attempt was later made to move the image, the getaway vehicle, a wagon, sank into the ground up to the axles, indicating that the image preferred to stay where it was!

Attendants treat the image like a delicate child, getting it up in the morning, washing it, putting its clothes on, offering it specially prepared meals and putting it down to sleep. It's a very popular pilgrimage site, and the temple opens and closes around the image's daily routine. It gets very crowded around 4.30 to 5 pm when Vishnu gets up after a siesta.

Nathdwara is also known for its *pichwai* paintings (religious paintings on cloth), which were first produced after the image of Vishnu was brought to the town.

RTDC's Hotel Gokul (☎ 02953-30917) offers singles/doubles with bath for Rs 300/400, and dorm beds for Rs 50.

RSTC buses leave from Udaipur to Nathdwara every hour (Rs 20, 1½ hours).

Kankroli & Rajsamand Lake

Farther north at Kankroli, Dwarkadhish (an incarnation of Vishnu) has a **temple** similar to the temple at Nathdwara and opening hours here are similarly erratic.

Nearby is a lake created by the dam constructed in 1660 by Maharana Raj Singh. There are many ornamental arches and chhatris along the huge *bund* (embankment).

There are hourly RSTC buses from Udaipur (Rs 30, 2½ hours).

Kumbhalgarh

Eighty-four kilometres north of Udaipur, this is the most important fort in the Mewar region after Chittorgarh. It's a secluded place, built by Maharana Kumbha in the 15th century and, owing to its inaccessibility on top of the Aravalli range at 1100m, it was taken only once in its history. Even then, it took the combined armies of the Mughal emperor, Akbar, and those of Amber and Marwar to breach its defences. It was here that the rulers of Mewar retreated in times of danger. The walls of the fort stretch some 36km and enclose many temples, palaces, gardens and water storage facilities.

There's also a big **wildlife sanctuary** here, known for its wolves. The scarcity of waterholes between March and June makes this the best time to see animals. Other wildlife includes *chowsingha* (four-horned antelope), leopards and sloth bears. You need permission from the forest department in nearby Kelwara to enter the reserve, or from the Deputy Chief Wildlife Warden in Udaipur (☎ 0294-421361). There's an entry charge.

Aodhi Hotel (☎ 02954-4222, reservations ☎ 0294-528016, fax 528006) is by far the best place to stay. Rooms in this blissfully tranquil hotel cost Rs 1195/2395. There's a little bar, a restaurant (open to nonresidents) and an inviting pool. Horse/jeep safaris can be arranged. This is a wonderful place to rejuvenate yourself. Nearby is the similarly priced **Kumbhalgarh Fort Hotel** (☎ 02954-42372, fax 525106).

Hotel Ratnadeep (☎ *02954-42217)*, at nearby Kelwara, is farther away from the fort, but has cheap doubles for Rs 400 with bath (most with Indian-style toilets). A dorm bed is Rs 100.

There are several daily RSTC buses from Udaipur (Rs 28, 3½ hours) and one express bus each morning (Rs 35).

Ranakpur

The exceptionally beautiful Ranakpur complex, 60km north of Udaipur, is one of the largest and most important Jain temples in India. It is tucked away in a remote valley of the Aravalli range and is certainly worth seeing.

The main temple is the **Chaumukha Temple**, or Four-Faced Temple, dedicated to Adinath. Built in 1439, this huge, superbly crafted and well-kept marble temple has 29 halls supported by 1444 pillars, no two alike. Within the complex are two other Jain temples to **Neminath** and **Parasnath** and, a little distance away, a **Sun Temple**. One kilometre from the main complex is the **Amba Mata Temple**.

The temple complex is open daily to Jains from 6 am to 8.30 pm and to non-Jains from 11 am to 5 pm. Shoes and all leather articles must be left at the entrance. Admission is free but there's a Rs 25/125 camera/video charge.

Places to Stay & Eat *Maharani Bagh Orchard Retreat* (☎ *02934-85151, reservations* ☎ *0291-433316, fax 635373)* is 4km from Ranakpur and the best place to stay. Set in a lush mango orchard, it offers accommodation in cottages for Rs 1190/2100. Hearty buffet meals are available; lunch or dinner costs Rs 300 (nonresidents are welcome).

RTDC's Hotel Shilpi (☎ *02934-85074)* is conveniently located near the temple complex and has rooms with bath from Rs 200/250. For the cash conscious, there's a dorm for Rs 50. A veg thali in the dining room is Rs 55.

The Castle (☎ *02934-85133)* is set in large grounds and offers singles/doubles for Rs 600/700.

Dharamsala (☎ *02934-85019)* (pilgrims' lodgings) within the temple complex has very basic accommodation for a donation. A veg thali is Rs 12.

Roopam Restaurant (☎ *02934-3921)* has a few nice rooms for Rs 550/650 with bath. The restaurant offers a buffet (Rs 150) or à la carte dining (Rs 35 to Rs 60 for a main dish). A bottle of beer is Rs 80.

Getting There & Away From Udaipur there are frequent express buses (Rs 35, three hours).

Narlai & Ghanerao

Not too far from Ranakpur, Narlai can make an ideal base for exploration of the various attractions around Udaipur.

Rawla Narlai (*bookings through Ajit Bhawan* ☎ *0291-437410, fax 637774 in Jodhpur)* has attractive rooms for Rs 1190/ 1795. Meals are available. Not far from the hotel are some old temples and a fine baoli (step-well).

Deluxe buses from Udaipur take about 3½ hours (Rs 70).

About 7km from Narlai is the town of Ghanerao. The *Ghanerao Royal Castle* (☎ *02934-84035)*, has rooms for Rs 1250/ 1500. There's a nice restaurant with breakfast/lunch/dinner for Rs 125/200/250, and jeep excursions can be organised.

An RSTC bus from Udaipur to Ghanerao takes about four hours (Rs 50).

Deogarh

The atmospheric little town of Deogarh (pronounced 'Dev-gar') is 135km north of Udaipur and has a wonderful castle that has been converted into a hotel. It makes an ideal stopover between Udaipur and Jodhpur, Ajmer or Jaipur and is a great place to catch up on some serious relaxation. While you're here, check out the **Anjaneshwar Mahadev**, an extraordinary cave temple believed to be around 2000 years old.

Deogarh Castle (☎ *02904-52777, fax 52555, email deogarh@hotmail.com)* is a family-run hotel with character-filled doubles from Rs 2050 to Rs 3500. This well-managed castle has a good restaurant – request the rarely found *palak ka halwa*, a dessert made from spinach which sounds awful, looks awful, but tastes great (kind of like semi-burnt toffee). You can go on a 'rural ramble' jeep excursion for Rs 350 per person, including refreshments. A deluxe bus from Udaipur takes about three hours and costs Rs 60. There are also railway connections between Udaipur and Deogarh (Rs 24/150 in 2nd/1st class).

Jaisamand Lake

Located 48km south-east of Udaipur, this stunningly located artificial lake, created by damming the Gomti River, was built by Maharana Jai Singh in the 17th century. It's one of the largest artificial lakes in Asia, and there are beautiful marble chhatris around the embankment. The summer palaces of the Udaipur queens are also here and there's a wildlife sanctuary nearby.

Jaisamand Island Resort (☎ 02906-2222, *reservations* ☎ 0294-415100, fax 523898) is a modern hotel in a secluded position 20 minutes by boat across the lake. Rooms start at Rs 1150/2700.

There are frequent RSTC buses from Udaipur (Rs 15, 1½ hours).

Bambora

About 45km south-east of Udaipur, this sleepy little village has a 250-year-old fort that has been converted into an impressive hotel.

Karni Fort (☎ 0291-432220, fax 433495 *in Jodhpur*) has smart singles/double from Rs 2000/2500. The best room (on the 2nd floor) has a blissfully soft round bed with panoramic views over the countryside; it costs Rs 3750. There's a restaurant, secret tunnel and a gorgeous pool with four water-spurting marble elephants.

Dungarpur

About 110km south of Udaipur, Dungarpur, the City of Hills, was founded in the 13th century. Points of interest include the **government museum,** with pieces dating from the 6th century, and the beautifully carved

12th century **Deo Somnath Temple**, about 25km out of town.

Udai Bilas Palace (☎ 02964-30808, fax 31008) is ideally located on the banks of a lake which attracts a variety of birdlife. Pleasant rooms cost Rs 1450/1900 and capacious suites go for Rs 2600. A feature is the intricately carved Ek Thambia Mahal (one pillared palace). Meals are taken at the long dining room table with stuffed beasts watching your every bite. The hotel can arrange a visit to **Juna Mahal**, a deserted old palace built in stages between the 13th and 18th centuries and filled with old frescoes, paintings and colourful glass inlay work.

Hotel Pratibha Palace (☎ 02964-30775), Shastri Colony, is good for shoestringers; tiny singles/doubles with bath start from Rs 50/100.

Frequent RSTC buses travel to Dungarpur from Udaipur (Rs 35, three hours). There's also a slow train to Dungarpur (Rs 78/184 in 2nd/1st class).

Baneshwar

Each January/February the **Baneshwar Fair** is held at the Baneshwar Temple, about 80km from Dungarpur, attracting thousands of Bhil adivasis. Tents can be arranged through Fort Dhariyawad (see Sitamata Wildlife Sanctuary Area, later). The tents are comfortable, with attached bathroom but a minimum of 10 tents is required; the cost is Rs 5500 a double including all meals.

Bera

About 145km from Udaipur, Bera is an ideal place for leopard and other wildlife spotting.

Leopards Lair (☎/fax 02933-43479) has comfortable modern cottages for Rs 4000/4500 a single/double. The price includes all meals and two wildlife safaris with the amicable thakur of Bera, Devi Singh.

Sitamata Wildlife Sanctuary Area

Located 65km south-east of Udaipur, the Sitamata Wildlife Sanctuary covers 423 sq km of mainly deciduous forest. Wildlife includes deer, sambar, caracal and wild boar.

Teekhi Magri Resort (☎ *0141-212235 in Jaipur*) is highly recommended if you're craving a secluded jungle retreat. There are just three brick-clay cottages which cost Rs 1100 a double (lighting is by lantern). Meals are available and the star-gazing is superb. This remote resort is run by Thakur Digvijay Singh and his son Brijraj, who accompany guests on village safaris and other excursions, in their 1945 American jeep. There are some rock carvings down a dry creek bed (wear strong shoes), believed to date back to the Mesolithic era (10,000 to 5000 years BC). You can also visit the owners' 17th century castle at Dhamotra, 22km away.

Advance bookings are essential. Contact Dhamotar House, 21 Surendra Pal Colony, New Sanganer Rd, Jaipur.

Fort Dhariyawad (☎ *02950-20050, reservations* ☎ *0141-201180*) does not have the same jungle appeal but offers comfortable modern lodgings for Rs 1100 a double.

MT ABU
☎ 02974 • pop 18,000

Mt Abu, sprawling along a 1200m high plateau in the south of the state, close to the Gujarat border, is Rajasthan's only hill station. It's a pleasant hot-season retreat from the plains of both Rajasthan and Gujarat. Mt Abu's pace is easy-going, although it can get ridiculously crowded with people and traffic during the summer months.

Mt Abu has a number of important temples, particularly the breathtaking Dilwara group of Jain temples, 5km away. This is an important pilgrimage centre for Jains and boasts some of the finest marble carvings in all of Rajasthan, if not India. Also, like some other hill stations in India, Mt Abu has its own lake, which is the centre of activity.

Orientation & Information

Mt Abu is on a hilly plateau about 22km long by 6km wide, 27km from the nearest train station (Abu Road). The main part of the town extends along the road in from Abu Road, down to Nakki Lake.

The Tourist Reception Centre (☎ 43151) is opposite the main bus stand and is open

Monday to Saturday 10 am to 1.30 pm and 2 to 5 pm. Money can be changed at the State Bank of Bikaner & Jaipur.

Nakki Lake

Nakki Lake is virtually in the heart of Mt Abu and is a big attraction with tourists. The lake takes its name from the legend that it was scooped out by a god, using only his nails, or *nakh*. It's a pleasant stroll around the lake – look for the strange **rock formations**. The best known, Toad Rock, looks just like a toad about to hop into the lake. Others, like Nun Rock, Nandi Rock or Camel Rock, require more imagination. The 14th century **Raghunath temple** stands beside the lake. You can hire your own boat (Rs 25 for 30 minutes).

On the lake is a dilapidated concrete boat-shaped snack bar (only serving tea and coffee).

Viewpoints

Of the various viewpoints around town, **Sunset Point** is the most popular. Hordes stroll out here every evening to catch the setting sun. Other popular spots include **Honeymoon Point**, which also offers a view of the sunset, **The Crags** and **Robert's Spur**. You can follow the white arrows along a path up to the summit of **Shanti Shikhar**, west of Adhar Devi Temple, where there are panoramic views.

For a good view over the lake, the best point is probably the terrace of the maharaja of Jaipur's former **summer palace**. No one seems to mind if you climb up here for the view and a photo.

Brahma Kumaris Spiritual University & Museum

The Brahma Kumaris teach that all religions lead to God and so are equally valid, and the principles of each should be studied. The university's stated aim is the establishment of universal peace through 'the impartation of spiritual knowledge and training of easy raja yoga meditation'. There are over 4500 branches in 70 countries around the world; to do a residential course at the university,

RAJASTHAN

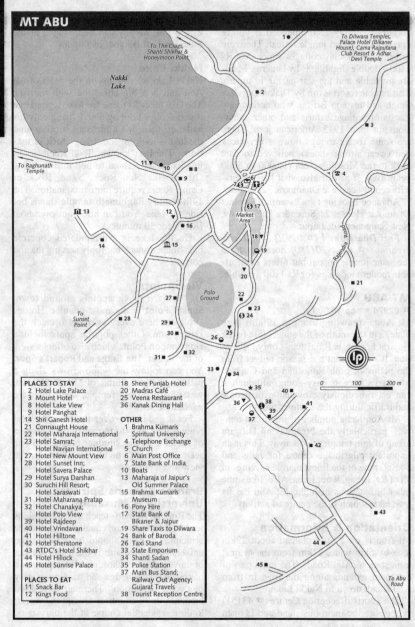

MT ABU

Nakki Lake

To The Crags, Shanti Shikhar & Honeymoon Point

To Dilwara Temples, Palace Hotel (Bikaner House), Cama Rajputana Club Resort & Adhar Devi Temple

To Raghunath Temple

To Sunset Point

Market Area

Polo Ground

Rajendra Road

To Abu Road

0   100   200 m

PLACES TO STAY
2   Hotel Lake Palace
3   Mount Hotel
8   Hotel Lake View
9   Hotel Panghat
14   Shri Ganesh Hotel
21   Connaught House
22   Hotel Maharaja International
23   Hotel Samrat;
     Hotel Navijan International
27   Hotel New Mount View
28   Hotel Sunset Inn;
     Hotel Savera Palace
29   Hotel Surya Darshan
30   Suruchi Hill Resort;
     Hotel Saraswati
31   Hotel Maharana Pratap
32   Hotel Chanakya;
     Hotel Polo View
39   Hotel Rajdeep
40   Hotel Vrindavan
41   Hotel Hilltone
42   Hotel Sheraton
43   RTDC's Hotel Shikhar
44   Hotel Hillock
45   Hotel Sunrise Palace

PLACES TO EAT
11   Snack Bar
12   Kings Food

18   Shere Punjab Hotel
20   Madras Café
25   Veena Restaurant
36   Kanak Dining Hall

OTHER
1   Brahma Kumaris
     Spiritual University
4   Telephone Exchange
5   Church
6   Main Post Office
7   State Bank of India
10   Boats
13   Maharaja of Jaipur's
     Old Summer Palace
15   Brahma Kumaris
     Museum
16   Pony Hire
17   State Bank of
     Bikaner & Jaipur
19   Share Taxis to Dilwara
24   Bank of Baroda
26   Taxi Stand
33   State Emporium
34   Shanti Sadan
35   Police Station
37   Main Bus Stand;
     Railway Out Agency;
     Gujarat Travels
38   Tourist Reception Centre

you need to contact your local branch. You can, however, attend an introductory course (seven lessons) while you're in Mt Abu; this would take a minimum of three days. There's no charge – the organisation is entirely supported by donations.

There's a museum (free) in the town outlining the university's teachings and offering meditation sessions. It's open daily 8 am to 8 pm.

Adhar Devi Temple
Three kilometres north of town, some 365 steps lead to this Durga temple built in a natural cleft in the rock. You have to stoop to get through the low entrance to the temple. There are fine views over Mt Abu from up here.

Dilwara Temples
These remarkable Jain temples are Mt Abu's main attraction and among the finest examples of Jain architecture in India. The complex includes two temples in which the art of carving marble reached unsurpassed heights.

The older of the temples is the **Vimal Vasahi**, built in 1031 and dedicated to the first tirthankar, Adinath. The central shrine has an image of Adinath, while around the courtyard are 52 identical cells, each with a Buddha-like cross-legged image. Forty-eight elegantly carved pillars form the entrance to the courtyard. In front of the temple stands the **House of Elephants,** with figures of elephants marching in procession to the temple entrance.

The later **Tejpal Temple** is dedicated to Neminath, the 22nd tirthankar, and was built in 1230 by the brothers Tejpal and Vastupal. Like Vimal, they were ministers in the government of the ruler of Gujarat. Although the Tejpal Temple is important as an extremely old and complete example of a Jain temple, its most notable feature is the brilliant intricacy and delicacy of the marble carving. The carving is so fine that, in places, the marble becomes almost transparent. In particular, the lotus flower which hangs from the centre of the dome is an astonishing piece of work. It's difficult to believe that this huge lace-like filigree actually

started as a solid block of marble. The temple employs several full-time stone carvers to maintain and restore the work. There are three other temples in the enclosure, but they all pale beside the Tejpal and Vimal Vasahi. There's a festival here in June (dates vary according to the lunar calendar).

The complex is open from noon to 6 pm (Jains can visit from sunrise to sunset). Photography is not allowed. As at other Jain temples, all articles of leather (belts as well as shoes) have to be left at the entrance. You can stroll out to Dilwara from the town in less than an hour, or take a share taxi for Rs 3 from opposite the Madras Cafe in the centre of town.

Organised Tours
The RTDC has five-hour tours of all the main sites, leaving from the main bus stand at 8.30 am and 1.30 pm (later in summer). The tours cost Rs 35 plus all entry and camera fees. The afternoon tour finishes at Sunset Point.

Places to Stay
There is a plethora of hotels in Mt Abu. The high season is from mid-April to mid-November. As most hotel owners raise prices to whatever the market will bear at this time, Mt Abu can be an expensive place to stay. During Diwali (October/November), rooms are virtually unobtainable without advance booking and the tariffs are exorbitant.

In the low season (with the exception of Christmas and New Year), discounts of up to 50% are available and mid-range accommodation can be an absolute bargain. Negotiate a deal with hotel staff. The hotels usually have an ungenerous 9 am checkout time and many also levy a 10% tax.

At all times of the year there are plenty of touts working the bus and taxi stands. In the low season you can safely ignore them; at peak times they can save you a lot of legwork as they'll know exactly where the last available room is.

Paying Guest House accommodation is available in Mt Abu. Contact the Tourist Reception Centre for details.

Places to Stay – Budget

Hotel Lake View (☎ 38659) overlooks picturesque Nakki Lake and, although the views are certainly good, it's really only an average hotel. In winter, doubles start from Rs 200 with bath (hot water is available between 7 and 11 am).

Hotel Panghat (☎ 38886), nearby, is better value. There are rooms with lake views, TV and attached bath (hot water 7 to 10 am) from Rs 150.

Shri Ganesh Hotel (☎ 43591), up the hill towards the maharaja of Jaipur's old summer palace, is a popular place with travellers. It's in a quiet location and the rooms are not bad considering the price. Doubles with bath are Rs 100 in the low season. As this place is a little farther from the centre of things, the high season rates tend to be a little more sensible than elsewhere (Rs 350 a double), and bargaining is possible. Only breakfast is available.

RTDC's Hotel Shikhar (☎ 38944), back from the main road and up a steepish path, is a huge place with ordinary singles/doubles from Rs 200/275 with bath. A dorm bed is Rs 50.

Hotel Chanakya (☎ 43438) charges Rs 450 in the low season for a comfortable double with attached bath and constant hot water. In the high season the price shoots up to Rs 950.

Hotel Saraswati (☎ 38887, fax 38337), nearby, is good value. There are well-kept doubles for Rs 100, and a range of other rooms from Rs 150 to Rs 350. The vegetarian restaurant serves tasty Gujarati thalis (Rs 40).

Hotel Polo View (☎ 43487), *Hotel Surya Darshan* (☎ 43165) and *Hotel New Mount View* (☎ 38279), also in this area, all charge around Rs 250 for a room with bath.

Places to Stay – Mid-Range

Mount Hotel (☎ 43150) is a homey place in a tranquil location along the road to the Dilwara Temples. It once belonged to a British army officer and has changed little since those days. The rooms are a bit worn and weary, but the owner, Jimmy and his dog, Spots, are friendly and you'll have no hassles here whatsoever. Doubles range from Rs 400 to Rs 600. Vegetarian meals (Rs 90) are available with advance notice. Jimmy can organise horse safaris.

Hotel Lake Palace (☎ 43254), across from the lake, has singles/doubles/triples for Rs 600/750/900 in the high season; bargain hard in the low season and you should be able to slash at least 30% off these prices.

Hotel Sunset Inn (☎ 43194, fax 43515), on the western edge of Mt Abu, is a modern hotel with good doubles for Rs 650 and a 30% discount in the low season. The restaurant serves satisfying meals. The nearby *Hotel Savera Palace* (☎ 43354) is not as good value for money.

Suruchi Hill Resort (☎ 43577), at the bottom end of the polo ground, has doubles for Rs 690 in the high season, and there's a 50% low-season discount.

Hotel Maharana Pratap (☎ 38667, fax 38900), nearby, is a smart place with decent rooms from Rs 500 in the low season. The restaurant serves Indian, Chinese and continental food.

Hotel Vrindavan (☎ 43147), near the main bus stand, is a bit cheaper than other places in this category. Acceptable rooms range from Rs 250 to Rs 450 in the low season.

Hotel Sheratone (☎ 43544), in the same area, has airy doubles from Rs 400 to Rs 750 in the low season; Rs 900 to Rs 1250 in the high season.

Hotel Samrat (☎ 43153) and *Hotel Navijan International* (☎ 43173), on the main road, are basically the same hotel although they appear to be separate. Low-season rates in the Samrat are from Rs 550 for a double; the Navijan is a touch cheaper but less impressive.

Hotel Maharaja International (☎ 38114), directly opposite, is a little more upmarket, with doubles from Rs 590 (low season).

Places to Stay – Top End

Palace Hotel (Bikaner House) (☎ 38673, fax 38674), not far from the Dilwara temples, is the most atmospheric hotel in Mt Abu. It is a great place to chill out, replete with shady gardens, a private lake, tennis courts and a restaurant (see Places to Eat). Once the summer residence of the maharaja of Bikaner, it is now run by the maharaja's amiable son-in-law). Singles/doubles are a very reasonable Rs 1095/1350.

Cama Rajputana Club Resort (☎ 38205, fax 38412), nearby, is a large place with comfortable doubles from Rs 1800. There's also a good restaurant.

Connaught House (☎ 38560, reservations ☎ 0291-433316, fax 635373), just east of the town, has an English cottage feel and is a homey place to stay. Owned by the maharaja of Jodhpur, it's set in its own pleasant gardens – the perfect place to sit back with a good book. The rooms in the old building are Rs 1190/1950 and have more character than those in the new wing, which cost Rs 1190/1750. Meals are available (order in advance).

Hotel Sunrise Palace (☎ 43573, fax 38775), at the southern end of Mt Abu, is yet another former summer residence of a Rajput maharaja (this time the maharaja of Bharatpur). It lacks the panache of the above two places but is still comfortable enough. Rooms range from Rs 650 to Rs 1450.

Hotel Hillock (☎ 38463, fax 38467), in the same area, is a flash place – large, spotlessly clean and well decorated, (although the outside of the building is quite ugly). Its tariff ranges from a healthy Rs 1790 to Rs 3790 (30% discount in the low season). There's a restaurant, bar and pool.

Hotel Hilltone (☎ 38391, fax 38395) is closer to town and has a swimming pool, restaurant, bar and sauna. It's a modern place with 68 comfortable doubles from Rs 1300 to Rs 2400 and cottages for Rs 2800; there's a 30% discount in the low season. *Kesar Bhavan Palace* (☎ 38647) was under construction at the time of writing. Rooms are expected to cost Rs 900 to Rs 1150.

Places to Eat

Kanak Dining Hall, near the main bus stand, is a popular. The all-you-can-eat Gujarati thalis are perhaps the best in Mt Abu (Rs 45); there's seating indoors and outdoors.

Veena Restaurant is farther uphill, next to the junction at the bottom end of the polo ground. Its Gujarati thalis (Rs 40) are also excellent.

Shere Punjab Hotel, in the bazaar area, has reasonably priced Punjabi and Chinese food. They take delight in their brain preparations (brain pakora is Rs 30). There are also some more conventional creations.

Madras Café, also in this area, is a pure veg place with an assortment of Indian and western fare. There are even Jain pizzas (no garlic, onion or cheese) for Rs 30. Meat eaters are catered for upstairs.

Kings Food, on the road leading down to the lake, has the usual have-a-go-at-anything menu and is good for a light bite.

Palace Hotel (Bikaner House) is the best place to go for a special meal. The set lunch or dinner costs Rs 235 (veg), Rs 295 (non-veg). It's a good idea to make an advance reservation.

Shopping

There are numerous shops and stalls selling all sorts of cheap souvenirs around Nakki Lake. In the evening, the town really comes to life and this is an enjoyable time to do some leisurely browsing.

Getting There & Away

As you enter Mt Abu, there's a toll gate where bus and car passengers are charged Rs 5, plus Rs 5 for a car. If you're travelling by bus, this is an irksome hold-up, as you have to wait until the collector painstakingly gathers the toll from each and every passenger (keep small change handy).

Bus From 6 am onwards, regular buses make the 27km climb from Abu Road station up to Mt Abu (Rs 15, one hour). Some RSTC buses go all the way to Mt Abu, while others terminate at Abu Road, so make sure you get the one you want.

The bus schedule from Mt Abu is extensive, and for many destinations you will find a direct bus faster and more convenient than going down to Abu Road station and waiting for a train. Deluxe buses go to Jaipur (Rs

130, 11 hours), Ajmer (Rs 120, eight hours), Udaipur (Rs 70, five hours), Jodhpur (Rs 100, eight hours), Ahmedabad (R 100, six hours) and Surat (Rs 180, 10 hours).

Train Abu Road, the railhead for Mt Abu, is on the broad-gauge line between Delhi and Mumbai via Ahmedabad.

In Mt Abu there's a Railway Out Agency near the main bus stand (opposite the police station) which has quotas on most of the express trains out of Abu Road. It's open daily 10 am to 1 pm and 2 to 4 pm (only until noon on Sunday).

From Abu Road, direct trains run to various destinations including Ajmer, Jodhpur, Jaipur, Ahmedabad and Agra. For Bhuj and the rest of the Kathiawar peninsula in Gujarat, change trains at Palanpur, 53km south of Abu Road.

Taxi A taxi, which you can share with up to five people, costs about Rs 200 from Abu Road. To hire a jeep for local sightseeing costs around Rs 800 per day (bargain hard and you may just bring it down).

Getting Around

Buses from the bus stand go to the various sites in Mt Abu, but it takes a little planning to get out and back without too much hanging around. For Dilwara it's easier to take a share taxi. These leave when full from opposite the Madras Café in the centre of town; the fare is Rs 3 per person.

There are no auto-rickshaws in Mt Abu, but it's relatively easy to get around on foot. Porters with trolleys can be hired for a small charge to transport your luggage – weary travellers can even be transported on the trolley!

AROUND MT ABU
Achalgarh

The Shiva temple of **Achaleshwar Mahandeva**, 11km north of Mt Abu, has a number of interesting features, including a toe of Shiva, a brass Nandi and, where the Shiva lingam would normally be, a deep hole said to extend all the way to the underworld.

Outside, by the car park, three stone buffaloes stand around a tank while the figure of a king shoots at them with a bow and arrows. A legend states that the tank was once filled with ghee, but demons in the form of buffaloes came down and polluted the ghee – until the king shot them. A path leads up the hillside to a group of colourful **Jain temples** with fine views out over the plains.

Guru Shikhar

At the end of the plateau, 15km from Mt Abu, is Guru Shikhar, the highest point in Rajasthan at 1721m. A road goes almost all the way to the summit. At the top is the **Atri Rishi Temple**, complete with a priest and good views all around.

Mt Abu Wildlife Sanctuary

This 290 sq km sanctuary, 8km north-east of Mt Abu, is home to panthers, sambar, foxes, wild boar and bears. It's open 8 am to 5 pm daily. Admission is Rs 5/40 for Indians/foreigners. Vehicle entry is Rs 125, or Rs 15 for a motorcycle.

Gaumukh Temple

Down on the Abu Road side of Mt Abu, a small stream flows from the mouth of a marble cow, giving the shrine its name. There is also a marble figure of Nandi, Shiva's vehicle. The tank here, **Agni Kund**, is said to be the site of the sacrificial fire made by the sage Vasishta, from which four of the great Rajput clans were born. An image of Vasishta is flanked by figures of Rama and Krishna.

ABU ROAD

This station down on the plains is the rail junction for Mt Abu. The train station and bus stand are right next to each other on the edge of town. Although there are RSTC buses from Abu Road to other cities such as Jodhpur, Jaipur, Udaipur and Ahmedabad, there's little point in catching them here as they're all available from Mt Abu.

Retiring rooms at the train station are convenient if you're catching an early-morning train. They go for Rs 120 a double; a veg thali is Rs 35.

Western Rajasthan

JODHPUR

☎ 0291 • pop 770,000

Jodhpur is at the edge of the Thar Desert and is the largest city in Rajasthan after Jaipur. The city is dominated by a massive fort, topping a sheer rocky ridge right in the middle of the town. Jodhpur was founded in 1459 by Rao Jodha, a chief of the Rajput clan known as the Rathores. His descendants ruled not only Jodhpur, but also other Rajput princely states. The Rathore kingdom was once known as Marwar, the Land of Death.

The old city of Jodhpur is surrounded by a 10km-long wall, built about a century after the city was founded. From the fort, you can clearly see where the old city ends and the new begins. It's fascinating to wander around the jumble of winding streets in the old city, out of which eight gates lead. Part of the film *Rudyard Kipling's Jungle Book*, starring Sam Neill and John Cleese, was shot in Jodhpur and yes, it was from here that those baggy-tight horse-riding trousers, jodhpurs, took their name.

As one of the closest major Indian cities to the border with Pakistan, Jodhpur has a large defence contingent. Don't dive for cover when you hear booming jet fighter planes above – Jodhpur is not under siege; the air force is simply undergoing its routine training exercise.

Orientation

The Tourist Reception Centre, train stations and bus stand are all outside the old city. High Court Rd runs from the Raika Bagh train station, past the Umaid gardens, the RTDC's Hotel Ghoomar, and round beside the city wall towards the main station.

Information

Tourist Office The Tourist Reception Centre (☎ 545083) is in the RTDC's Hotel Ghoomar compound and is open Monday to Saturday 8 am to 7 pm.

There's an International Tourists Bureau (☎ 439052) at the main train station which provides information, has comfortable armchairs, a shower and a toilet.

Money The State Bank of India (High Court Rd branch) changes currency and travellers cheques. The Bank of Baroda, near the Hotel Arun, changes travellers cheques.

Meherangarh

Still run by the maharaja of Jodhpur, Meherangarh, the Majestic Fort, is just that. Sprawled across a 125m-high hill, this is the most formidable fort in fort-studded Rajasthan. A winding road leads up to the entrance from the city, 5km below. The second gate is still scarred by cannon ball hits, indicating that this was a fort which earned its keep. The gates, of which there are seven, include the **Jayapol**, built by Maharaja Man Singh in 1806 following his victory over the armies of Jaipur and Bikaner, and the **Fatehpol**, or Victory Gate, erected by Maharaja Ajit Singh to commemorate his defeat of the Mughals.

Jodhpur's Got the Blues

Hats off to the people of Rajasthan for converting their stark landscape into a mosaic of vivid colours. Apart from the Rajasthanis themselves, adorned in wildly colourful garments, a number of Rajasthan's major towns have adopted colourful identities – there's the pink city of Jaipur, the golden city of Jaisalmer and the blue city of Jodhpur.

Jodhpur is affectionately referred to as the 'blue city' because of the indigo-coloured houses in the old town. These can best be seen from the ramparts of the mighty Meherangarh, which looms high above the buzzing city.

Traditionally, blue signified the home of a Brahmin, but these days, non-Brahmins have also taken on the practice. Apart from looking fresh and lively, it is believed that the colour works as an effective mosquito repellent.

RAJASTHAN

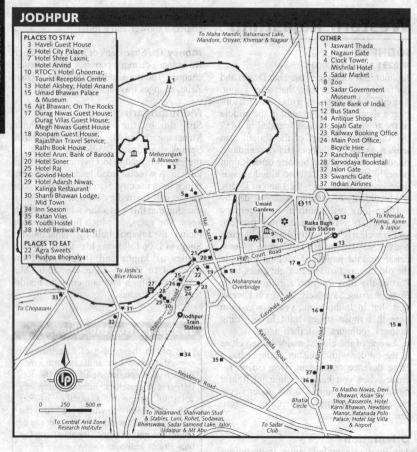

JODHPUR

PLACES TO STAY
3   Haveli Guest House
6   Hotel City Palace
7   Hotel Shree Laxmi;
    Hotel Arvind
10 RTDC's Hotel Ghoomar;
    Tourist Reception Centre
13 Hotel Akshey; Hotel Anand
15 Umaid Bhawan Palace
    & Museum
16 Ajit Bhawan; On The Rocks
17 Durag Niwas Guest House;
    Durag Villas Guest House;
    Megh Niwas Guest House
18 Roopam Guest House;
    Rajasthan Travel Service;
    Rathi Book House
19 Hotel Arun; Bank of Baroda
20 Hotel Soner
25 Hotel Raj
26 Govind Hotel
29 Hotel Adarsh Niwas;
    Kalinga Restaurant
30 Shanti Bhawan Lodge;
    Mid Town
34 Inn Season
35 Ratan Vilas
36 Youth Hostel
38 Hotel Beniwal Palace

PLACES TO EAT
22 Agra Sweets
31 Pushpa Bhojnalya

OTHER
1   Jaswant Thada
2   Nagaur Gate
4   Clock Tower;
    Mishrilal Hotel
5   Sadar Market
8   Zoo
9   Sadar Government
    Museum
11 State Bank of India
12 Bus Stand
14 Antique Shops
21 Sojati Gate
23 Railway Booking Office
24 Main Post Office;
    Bicycle Hire
27 Ranchodji Temple
28 Sarvodaya Bookstall
32 Jalori Gate
33 Siwanchi Gate
37 Indian Airlines

To Maha Mandir, Balsamand Lake,
Mandore, Osiyan, Khimsar & Nagaur

Meherangarh & Museum

To Kherjala,
Nimaj, Ajmer
& Jaipur

Umaid
Gardens

Raika Bagh
Train Station

Nai Sarak

High Court Road

To Joshi's
Blue House

Mohanpura
Overbridge

Gaushala Road

Ratanada Road

Airport Road

Station Road

To Chopasani

Jodhpur
Train
Station

To Madho Niwas, Devi
Bhawan, Asian Sky
Shop, Kasserole, Hotel
Karni Bhawan, Newtons
Manor, Ratanada Polo
Palace, Hotel Jag Villa
& Airport

Residency Road

Bhatia
Circle

To Sadar
Club

To Jhalamand, Shalivahan Stud
& Stables, Luni, Rohet, Sodawas,
Bhenswara, Sadar Samand Lake, Jalor,
Udaipur & Mt Abu

To Central Arid Zone
Research Institute

0   250   500 m

The final gate is the **Lohapol**, or Iron Gate, beside which are 15 hand prints, the sati (self-immolation) marks of Maharaja Man Singh's widows who threw themselves upon his funeral pyre in 1843. They still attract devotional attention and are usually covered in red powder.

Inside the fort, there is a series of courtyards and palaces. The **palace apartments** have evocative names like the Sukh Mahal, or Pleasure Palace, and the Phool Mahal, or Flower Palace. They house a splendid col-

lection of the trappings of Indian royalty, including an amazing collection of elephant howdahs (used when the maharajas rode their elephants in glittering procession through their capitals), miniature paintings from a variety of schools and the inevitable Rajput armoury, palanquins, furniture and costumes. In one room, there's even an exhibit of rocking cradles.

At the southern end of the fort, old cannons look out from the ramparts over the sheer drop to the old town beneath. You can clearly hear voices and city sounds swept up by the air currents from the houses far below. The views from these ramparts are nothing less than magical. From here, you can also see the many houses painted blue – see the Jodhpur's Got the Blues boxed text. The **Chamunda Devi Temple**, dedicated to Durga, stands at this end of the fort.

The fort is open daily 9 am to 1 pm and 2 to 5 pm. Entry costs Rs 10/50 for Indians/foreigners and there's a Rs 50/100 camera/video charge. Guides are available for around Rs 100. For weary travellers, an elevator will take you right up to the top of the fort for Rs 10. There is an astrologer, Mr Sharma, at the fort (☎ 548992) who charges Rs 100 for a short consultation. He is available daily 9 am to 1 pm and 2 to 5 pm.

Jaswant Thada

This white marble memorial to Maharaja Jaswant Singh II is a short distance from the fort, just off the fort road. The cenotaph, built in 1899, was followed by the royal crematorium and three other cenotaphs which stand nearby. There is some beautiful marble *jali* (lattice) work and fine views from the terrace in front of the cenotaph. Entry is Rs 5/10 for Indians/foreigners.

Clock Tower & Markets

The clock tower is a popular landmark in the old city. The vibrant Sardar Market is close to the tower, and narrow alleys lead from here to bazaars selling vegetables, spices (see Shopping), Indian sweets, textiles, silver and handicrafts. It's a great place to ramble around at leisure.

Umaid Bhawan Palace & Museum

Built of marble and pink sandstone, this immense palace is also known as the Chhittar Palace because of the local Chhittar sandstone used. Begun in 1929, it was designed by the president of the British Royal Institute of Architects for Maharaja Umaid Singh, and took 15 years to complete.

Probably the most surprising thing about this grandiose palace is that it was built so close to Independence, after which the maharajas, princely states and the grand extravagances common to this class would soon be a thing of the past. It is said that the palace was built as a royal job-creation program to provide employment for thousands of local people during a time of severe drought.

Maharaja Umaid Singh died in 1947; his successor still lives in part of the building. The rest has been turned into a hotel – and what a hotel! While it lacks the charm of Udaipur's palace hotels, it certainly makes up for it in spacious grandeur. There are even Hollywood hit movies screened each evening (for hotel guests) in the palace's home theatre, the Ali Akbar auditorium.

The palace (not including the museum) is closed to nonguests, unless you want to pay the fee of Rs 330, which is deducted from any food or drink you might purchase.

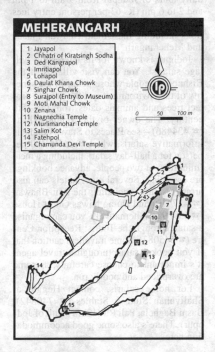

MEHERANGARH

1 Jayapol
2 Chhatri of Kiratsingh Sodha
3 Ded Kangrapol
4 Imritiapol
5 Lohapol
6 Daulat Khana Chowk
7 Singhar Chowk
8 Surajpol (Entry to Museum)
9 Moti Mahal Chowk
10 Zenana
11 Nagnechia Temple
12 Murlimanohar Temple
13 Salim Kot
14 Fatehpol
15 Chamunda Devi Temple

0   50   100 m

The very good **museum** is well worth a visit. On display is an amazing array of items belonging to the maharaja – weapons, fascinating antique clocks, dainty crockery, and hunting trophies. Entry is Rs 10/50 for Indians/foreigners.

Umaid Gardens & Sadar Government Museum
The pleasant Umaid gardens contain the Sadar Government Museum, the library and the zoo (entry is Rs 1). The museum's exhibits include moth-eaten stuffed animals, old weapons and sculptures; unfortunately the pieces are not labelled. It's open daily except Friday from 10 am to 4.30 pm and entry costs Rs 3.

Organised Tours & Village Safaris
The Tourist Reception Centre conducts daily tours of Jodhpur from 9 am to 1 pm and 2 to 6 pm (Rs 63 per person; entry fees are extra). These take in all the local attractions including the Umaid Bhawan Palace and Meherangarh.

Jodhpur is known for its interesting 'village safaris'. You can visit villages of the Bishnoi, a people whose belief in the sanctity of the environment and the need to protect trees and animals dates from the 15th century. The owner of the Madho Niwas (☎ 434486) – see Places to Stay – conducts informative safaris, which cost Rs 400 per person for a half-day safari, including a meal (minimum of two people; advance bookings are essential). Several other hotels can also arrange safaris, including the Ajit Bhawan (☎ 437410) and Durag Niwas Guest House (☎ 639092). Alternatively, you can organise a safari through the Tourist Reception Centre (☎ 545083). Some travellers caution that if you book a safari through a travel agent it's important to choose carefully, as some are overpriced and poorly run.

For horse safaris, contact Heggie at Shalivahan Stud & Stables (☎ 740842), Basni Baghela, Pali Rd (12km south of Jodhpur). There's also some good accommodation here.

Places to Stay – Budget
Jodhpur operates the Paying Guest House Scheme with prices ranging from Rs 90 to Rs 800. Contact the Tourist Reception Centre for details.

Haveli Guest House (☎ 614615) is inside the walled city at Makrana Mohalla. It is excellent value for money and has plenty of character. Doubles with attached bath are Rs 200. The rooftop veg restaurant boasts stunning views of the fort, Jaswant Thada and the blue city. The family who run this place are friendly and helpful.

Madho Niwas (Bhenswara House) (☎/fax 434486, New Airport Rd, Ratanada) is run by Dalvir Singh and is a homey place to stay with a quiet lawn area. Singles/doubles with private bath start at Rs 350/400. Meals are available; the Marwari-style barbecue chicken with a squeeze of lemon is delicious. Good village safaris or a sojourn at **Ravla Bhenswara** (see the Around Jodhpur section) can be arranged.

Durag Niwas Guest House (☎ 639092, 1 Old Public Park), another family-run place, has decent doubles with bath from Rs 250 to Rs 500.

Durag Villas Guest House (☎ 621300), next door, is good value, with doubles with bath starting at Rs 150. Just around the corner you'll find the **Megh Niwas Guest House** (☎ 640530, 30 Umed Club Rd) which has rooms from Rs 300/350.

Roopam Guest House (☎ 627374, 7 Jagannath Building, Mohanpura Overbridge) is run by retired Major TS Rathore. It has one room with common bath for Rs 200/250, and three rooms with bath for Rs 400/500.

Joshi's Blue House (☎ 612066, Novechokiya Rd, Brahm Puri, Chuna ki Choki) is an atmospheric little place in the old city. This family-run blue-coloured house is said to be 500 years old and is pretty authentic (don't expect modern gadgets). Simple singles/doubles with common bath start at Rs 60/90 (free bucket hot water). Go to the rooftop for a fine view.

RTDC's Hotel Ghoomar (☎ 548010, High Court Rd) has acceptable singles/doubles with bath from Rs 300/375 and dorm beds for Rs 50.

Govind Hotel (☎ 622758), opposite the main post office, is just five minutes' walk from the train station – great if you've got an early-morning train departure. Run by the helpful Jagdish Sadarangani, this is a very traveller-friendly place. The rooms are basic but cheap. Dorm beds go for Rs 50, small singles with common bath for Rs 60, and singles/doubles with attached bath for Rs 150/175. The rooftop restaurant has wonderful views of the palace and fort.

Hotel Arvind (☎ 547159, fax 547423, 135 Nai Sarak) offers OK rooms for a low Rs 90/150 with common bath, or Rs 165/200 with bath (Indian-style toilet).

Shanti Bhawan Lodge (☎ 637001), in the street opposite the train station, has rooms with common bath for Rs 70/100, and doubles with attached bath from Rs 150 to Rs 600. Some of the cheaper rooms are spartan and the bathrooms could be cleaner.

Hotel Akshey (☎ 437327), opposite the Raika Bagh train station, has dorm beds for Rs 50 and rooms with bath from Rs 175/225. The cleanliness and service is variable.

Retiring rooms at the main train station cost Rs 100 for a double with bath; Rs 300 with air-con.

Places to Stay – Mid-Range

Devi Bhawan (☎/fax 434215, 1 Ratanada Area) is highly recommended and great value for money. Run by a charming couple, you'll have no hassles here whatsoever. This green oasis has fresh rooms for Rs 700/750 a single/double, and cottages for Rs 850. There's a good restaurant and the garden would have to be one of the best in Jodhpur.

Ratan Vilas (☎/fax 614418, Loco Shed Rd, Ratanada) is another well-kept family villa set in a nice garden. Comfortable rooms cost Rs 600 and meals are available.

Newtons Manor (☎ 430686, fax 610603, 86 Jawahar Colony, Ratanada) also has a beautiful homey atmosphere. There are just five rooms ranging from Rs 895 to Rs 1100. Scrumptious home-cooked meals are also available here.

Hotel Adarsh Niwas (☎ 627338, fax 627314) is convenient if you want to be close to the main train station. Dull but comfortable rooms begin at Rs 650/850.

Hotel City Palace (☎ 431933, fax 639033, 32 Nai Sarak) has singles/doubles from Rs 790/990 and the Gossip veg restaurant.

There are some more upmarket and expensive hotels in the mid-range category that are recommended.

Ajit Bhawan (☎ 437410, fax 637774, Airport Rd) has long been popular with travellers. It has a series of modern stone cottages arranged around a relaxing garden for Rs 1550/1800. There's a restaurant, sensational swimming pool (nonguests Rs 250) and village safaris are available. The setting is delightful, but the staff can be rather indifferent.

Hotel Karni Bhawan (☎ 432220, fax 433495) is a modern place with traditional touches on Palace Rd. Set in well-manicured gardens and with a pool, comfortable singles/doubles start at Rs 1175/1425 (the rooms in the new building are best). The restaurant is excellent and you can eat indoors or under the stars. They have a country retreat at Sodawas, 90km south of Jodhpur.

Inn Season (☎/fax 616400), opposite the PWD office, is a homey place with well-kept rooms from Rs 1200. Check out the funky old German record player with an equally funky collection of records, including Louis Armstrong and Ella Fitzgerald.

Places to Stay – Top End

Umaid Bhawan Palace (☎ 433316, fax 635373) is the place to stay if you have a passion for pure luxury. This very elegant palace has an indoor swimming pool, tennis court, billiard room, lush lawns and several restaurants (see Places to Eat). Standard rooms cost US$195/220, and suites range from US$350 to a phenomenal US$990. If you can possibly afford it, opt for a suite, as the cheaper rooms are suitably comfortable, but hardly palatial.

The **Ratanada Polo Palace** (☎ 431910, fax 433118, Residency Rd) is in its own spacious grounds, but is a little lacking in character. It has a pool, restaurant and rooms for Rs 1800/2400.

Another top-end hotel, under construction at the time of writing, is the *Taj Hari Mahal Palace* (☎ 022-2025515, fax 2846683 in Mumbai).

Places to Eat

While you're in Jodhpur, try a glass of *makhania lassi*, a filling saffron-flavoured variety of that most refreshing of drinks.

Mishrilal Hotel, at the clock tower, is nothing fancy to look at, but whips up the best lassis in town. A delicious glass of creamy special makhania lassi is Rs 10.

Agra Sweets, opposite Sojati Gate, also sells good lassis (Rs 10), as well as tasty Jodhpur dessert specialities such as *mawa ladoo* (Rs 5) and the baklava-like *mawa kachori* (Rs 9).

Kalinga Restaurant at the Hotel Adarsh Niwas, near the train station, is a pleasant place to eat. It has tasty veg and nonveg Indian, Chinese and continental food; chicken curry is Rs 65. It's open 7 am to 10.30 pm daily. *Mid Town*, nearby, is a bit overpriced but not bad. Most mains cost between Rs 40 and Rs 65 and there are some Rajasthani specialities such as *chakki-ka-sagh* (Rs 55) and Rajasthani thalis (Rs 60).

Kasserole, not far from the Hotel Karni Bhawan, is the place to go for a Chinese chow down. The Buddhist chef whips up dishes like shredded lamb in hot garlic sauce (Rs 50) and sweet and sour vegies (Rs 30). This unpretentious restaurant is on the top floor of a house and is only open for dinner.

On the Rocks at the Ajit Bhawan hotel is very popular, especially with locals. It serves tasty Indian cuisine outdoors; veg biryani is Rs 50. The service can be sluggish, especially when it's busy. In the same compound, there's a bar and an excellent bakery.

Umaid Bhawan Palace has four restaurants, including the very grand *Marwar Hall* (however, the buffet here is lacklustre). Overlooking the back lawn is *The Pillars*, a breezy informal eatery recommended for a light bite; the *Risala*, which is more upmarket; and *Kebab Konner*, an open-air restaurant which specialises in moderately priced barbecue Indian food (dinner only). Or, you may just like to have a drop of amber fluid at the *Trophy Bar*.

The *refreshment room* on the 1st floor of the main train station is surprisingly good. There's veg and nonveg food to munch on while waiting for your train; a veg/nonveg thali is just Rs 16/22.

Shopping

The usual Rajasthani handicrafts are available here, but Jodhpur particularly specialises in antiques. The greatest number of antique shops is along the road connecting the Ajit Bhawan with the Umaid Bhawan Palace. These shops are well known to western antique dealers who come here with wallets stuffed with plastic cards. As a result, you'll be hard pressed to find any bargains. Many places also sell cheaper replicas based on original antique designs. The trade in antique architectural fixtures is contributing to the desecration of India's cultural heritage and is not condoned by Lonely Planet.

For excellent Indian spices, check out Mohanlal Verhomal (☎/fax 615846), shop 209B at the sabzi (vegetable) market, very close to the clock tower. There is a tantalizing array of spices including a 'winter tonic' to enhance sexual stamina (Rs 175). The owner has a deep love of spices and will happily answer any questions you may have about them.

Getting There & Away

Air Indian Airlines (☎ 636757) is south of the centre on Airport Rd (open daily 10 am to 1.15 pm and 2 to 4.30 pm). It operates flights to Delhi (US$95), Udaipur (US$55), Jaisalmer (US$60), Jaipur (US$70) and Mumbai (US$135).

Bus There are buses to various places such as Udaipur (Rs 70, eight hours), Jaipur (Rs 80, seven hours), Ajmer (Rs 70, four hours), Jaisalmer (Rs 70, five hours), Ahmedabad (R 130, 10 hours) and Delhi (Rs 160, 12½ hours).

Train There are rail connections to Jaisalmer, Jaipur, Kota, Bikaner, Ahmedabad and Delhi. The booking office is on Station Rd, between the train station and Sojati Gate. There's a tourist quota and the office is open Monday to Saturday 8 am to 8 pm (to 1.45 pm Sunday).

Getting Around

To/From the Airport The airport is only 5km from the city centre. It costs about Rs 50/110 in an auto-rickshaw/taxi.

Taxi & Auto-Rickshaw There's a taxi stand near the main train station. Most auto-rickshaw journeys in town should cost no more than Rs 25.

Bicycle You can hire a bike from several places near the Kalinga Restaurant, not far from the main post office. The usual charge is about Rs 2/15 per hour/day.

AROUND JODHPUR
Jhalamand

Hotel Jhalamand Garh (☎ *0291-740481, fax 741125)*, 10km south of Jodhpur, is a tranquil 18th century royal abode with singles/doubles from Rs 1000/1100. It's ideal if you want to stay a stone's throw away from the hustle and bustle of Jodhpur.

Maha Mandir & Balsamand Lake

About 4km north-east of the city is the Maha Mandir (Great Temple). It's built around a 100-pillared Shiva temple but is nothing to write home about. Five kilometres farther north is the picturesque Balsamand Lake.

Balsamand Palace (☎ *0291-433316, fax 635373 in Jodhpur)* is a comfortable and serene hotel. Singles/doubles are US$60/75, and suites range from US$125 to US$325. Around sunset, numerous bats swoop into the lake for a drink – creepy, yet fascinating.

Mandore

Situated 9km north of Jodhpur, Mandore was the capital of Marwar prior to the foundation of Jodhpur. Today, its extensive **gardens** with high rock terraces make it a

popular local attraction. The gardens also contain the cenotaphs of Jodhpur rulers, including the soaring memorial to Maharaja Dhiraj Ajit Singh.

The **Hall of Heroes** contains 15 figures carved out of a rock wall. The brightly painted figures represent Hindu deities, and local heroes on horseback. The Shrine of 33 Crore (330 million) Gods is painted with figures of deities and spirits.

Mandore Guest House (☎ *0291-545620, fax 546959)* has delightful accommodation in a leafy garden. It's great value with singles/doubles with bath costing Rs 350/500.

Sardar Samand Lake

The route to this wildlife centre, 66km southeast of Jodhpur, passes through a number of colourful little villages. Some of the wildlife to be seen at the lake includes blackbuck, chinkara and a variety of birdlife.

Sardar Samand Palace (☎ *0291-433316, fax 635373 in Jodhpur)*, formerly the maharaja of Jodhpur's summer palace, has now been converted into a hotel, with rooms for US$60/75. There's a restaurant and a stylish lakeside swimming pool. This place is a world away from the clamour of Jodhpur.

Bhenswara

Ravla Bhenswara (☎ *02978-22080, or ☎/fax 0291-434486 in Jodhpur)* is a simple rural manor that is perfect if you want some respite from the rigours of travelling in India. Located 130km south of Jodhpur, it is run by a friendly young couple, Shiv Pratap Singh and Uma Kumari, who give this place a homey appeal. The quaint rooms start at Rs 800/950 a single/double. There's a pool, village safaris are available and they can arrange a visit to the nearby **Jalor Fort**. Don't miss the evening parakeet invasion at nearby **Madho Bagh**.

Rohet

Rohet Garh (☎ *02936-68231)* is a heritage hotel in this small village, 40km south of Jodhpur, where Bruce Chatwin wrote *The Songlines* and William Dalrymple began *City of Djinns*. Good rooms start at

Rs 1100/1700, meals are available and there's a fantastic swimming pool. They can also organise village safaris.

Luni

Fort Chanwa (☎/fax 0291-432460 in Jodhpur), not too far from Rohet, offers tasteful accommodation in a red sandstone fort. Rooms cost Rs 1550/1800. There's a pool, restaurant and some interesting walks in the area. Village safaris are available.

Osiyan

The ancient Thar Desert town of Osiyan, 65km north of Jodhpur, was a great trading centre between the 8th and 12th centuries when it was dominated by the Jains. The wealth of Osiyan's medieval inhabitants allowed them to build lavish and exquisitely sculptured temples, most of which have withstood the ravages of time. The sculptural detail on the Osiyan temples rivals that of the Hoysala temples of Karnataka and the Sun Temple of Konark in Orissa.

The Camel Camp (☎/fax 0291-437023 in Jodhpur) offers a range of tented accommodation in a magical location – atop a secluded sand dune overlooking Osiyan. Double occupancy tents with common bath are Rs 300. More luxurious tents with attached bath (and shower) are also available. There's a breezy bar with views of the temples, and camel safaris can be arranged. The owner, Reggie, is here most of the time. Advance bookings are essential. Contact The Safari Club, High Court Colony, Jodhpur.

For cheaper accommodation, contact Bhanu Prakash Sharma, a Brahmin priest with a very basic *guesthouse (☎ 02922-74232)* for Rs 200 per room (maximum five people).

There are regular buses from Jodhpur to Osiyan (Rs 20, 1½ hours).

Khimsar

Khimsar Fort (☎ 01585-62345, fax 62228), 75km north of Jodhpur, dates from 1523. Pleasant rooms go for US$85/135 and there is also a pool, plus a restaurant and nice gardens.

Nagaur

Nagaur, 135km north-east of Jodhpur, has the historic **Ahhichatragarh**, an ancient fort which is currently being restored (entry costs Rs 5/15 for Indians/foreigners, plus Rs 25/50 for a camera/video). Nagaur also sports a smaller version of Pushkar's Camel Fair; the **Nagaur Cattle Fair** in January/February attracts thousands of rural people from far and wide.

Royal Tents are available for US$175/225 a single/double at fair time. These luxurious tents must be booked in advance through the Umaid Bhawan Palace in Jodhpur *(☎ 0291-433316, fax 635373)*.

RTDC's Kurjan Nagaur (no phone) has good rooms for Rs 250/300 with bath (US$40/53 during the fair). For more details contact the General Manager, Central Reservations (☎ 0141-202586, fax 201045), RTDC's Hotel Swagatam Campus, Near Railway Station, Jaipur. Other hotels in Nagaur include the *Hotel Bhaskar (☎ 01582-22100)*, with rooms from Rs 100/250, and the slightly more expensive *Hotel Mahaveer International (☎ 01582-43158)*.

Khejarla

Fort Khejarla (☎ 02930-58311), 85km east of Jodhpur en route to Ajmer, is not as swanky as most other fort hotels, but it has a certain rustic charm. Singles/doubles at this 400-year-old fort are Rs 850/950 (bucket hot water).

Village safaris can be arranged, as well as a visit to an old step-well (ask Dalip Singh about the ghost).

JAISALMER
☎ 02992 • pop 46,500

Nothing else in India is remotely similar to Jaisalmer. This captivating sandy outpost has been dubbed the Golden City because of the honey colour imparted to its stone ramparts by the setting sun. Its desert fort, which resembles a gigantic sandcastle, is straight out of *The Thousand and One Nights*.

Centuries ago, Jaisalmer's strategic position on the camel train routes between India and Central Asia brought it great wealth.

The merchants and townspeople built magnificent houses and mansions, all exquisitely carved from wood and golden sandstone. These havelis can be found elsewhere in Rajasthan, but nowhere are they quite as exquisite as in Jaisalmer. Even the humblest shops and houses display something of the Rajput love of the decorative arts.

The rise of shipping trade and the port of Mumbai (Bombay) saw the decline of Jaisalmer. At Independence, Partition and the cutting of the trade routes through to Pakistan seemingly sealed the city's fate, and water shortages could have pronounced the death sentence. However, the 1965 and 1971 India-Pakistan wars revealed Jaisalmer's strategic importance, and the Indira Gandhi Canal, to the north, is beginning to restore life to the desert.

Today, tourism rivals the military base as the pillar of the city's economy. The presence of the Border Security Force hardly impinges at all on the life of the old city and only the occasional sound of war planes ever disturbs the tranquility of this desert gem.

It hasn't always been so, as forts have rarely been constructed for aesthetic reasons and medieval desert chieftains weren't known for their pacific temperaments. Chivalric rivalry and ferocity between various Rajput clans were the order of the day, and the Bhatti Rajputs of Jaisalmer were regarded as a formidable force throughout the region. While Jaisal-mer largely escaped direct conquest by the Muslim rulers of Delhi, it did experience its share of sieges and sackings with the inevitable jauhar (collective sacrifice) being declared in the face of certain defeat. There is perhaps no other city in which you can more easily conjure up the spirit of those times.

However, there is a down side to Jaisalmer becoming one of Rajasthan's most popular tourist destinations. The number of hotels in the fort has significantly increased over the years and a major concern is that the poor plumbing and open drains have saturated the foundations, causing subsidence and collapse in buildings. The old open drains were created to take a limited amount of water and waste, and cannot cope with the pressure being placed upon them today.

For more information on the initiatives being taken to preserve Jaisalmer, contact Jaisalmer Conservation Initiative, 71 Lodi Estate, New Delhi 110 003 (☎ 011-463 1818, fax 461 1290) or the British-registered charity Jaisalmer in Jeopardy (☎/fax 0171-460 8592, email jaisalmer@lineone.net) 20E Redcliffe Gardens, London SW10 9EX.

Orientation

Jaisalmer is a great place to simply wander. The streets within the old city walls are a tangled maze, but the city is small enough for this not to matter. You simply head off in what seems like the right direction and you'll get somewhere eventually.

The old city was once completely surrounded by an extensive wall, much of which has sadly been ripped away in recent times for building material. Some of it remains, however, including the city gates and, inside them, the massive fort which rises above the city and is the essence of Jaisalmer. The fort itself is a warren of narrow, paved streets complete with Jain temples and the old palace of the former ruler.

The main market area is directly below the hill, while the banks, the new palace and several other shops and offices are near the Amar Sagar Gate to the west.

Information

Tourist Offices The Tourist Reception Centre (☎ 52406) is on Gadi Sagar Rd, 2km south-east of the First Fort Gate. It's open Monday to Saturday 10 am to 5 pm. There's also a small tourist counter at the train station.

Money The Bank of Baroda at Gandhi Chowk changes travellers cheques and issues cash advances on Visa and MasterCard. The State Bank of Bikaner & Jaipur, opposite the Hotel Neeraj, changes travellers cheques and major currencies.

Jaisalmer Fort

Jaisalmer Fort is the most alive of any museum, fort or palace that you're likely to

RAJASTHAN

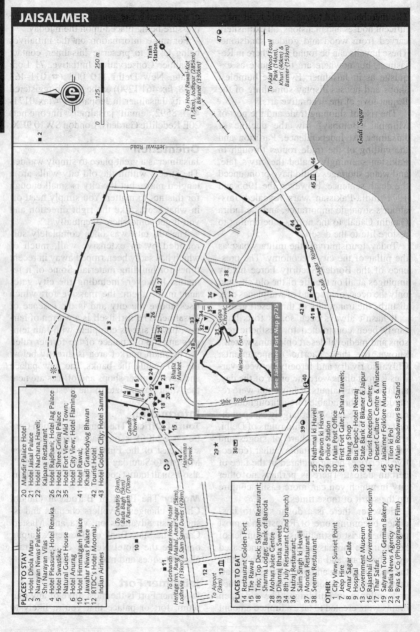

JAISALMER

To Akal Wood Fossil
Park (14km),
Khuri (40km) &
Barmer (153km)

To Hotel Rawal-Kot
(1.5km), Jodhpur (285km)
& Bikaner (330km)

Train
Station

Jethwai Road

Gadi Sagar

0   125   250 m

See Jaisalmer Fort Map p725

Jaisalmer Fort

Gopa
Chowk

Bhatia
Market.

Shiv Road

Gandhi
Chowk

Hanuman
Chowk

To Chhatris (2km),
Bada Bagh (5km)
& Ramgarh (70km)

To Gorbandh Palace Hotel, Hotel
Heritage Inn, Rang Mahal, Amar Sagar (5km),
Lodhruva (13km) & Sam Sand Dunes (42km)

To Airport
(3km)

PLACES TO STAY
2   Hotel Dhola Maru
3   Hotel Jaisal Palace
4   Narayan Niwas Palace;
    Shri Narayan Vilas
5   Hotel Pleasure; Hotel Renuka
6   Hotel Swastika;
    Natural Guest House
10 Hotel Anurag
11 Hotel Himmatgarh Palace
12 Jawahar Niwas Palace

20 Mandir Palace Hotel
21 Hotel Jaisal Palace
22 Hotel Nachana Haveli;
    Kalpana Restaurant
26 Hotel Rajdhani; Hotel Jag Palace
32 Hotel Shree Giriraj Palace
35 Hotel Fort View; Mid Town;
    Hotel City View; Hotel Flamingo
41 Hotel Rawal;
    Khadi Gramodyog Bhavan
42 Tourist Hotel
43 RTDC's Hotel Moomal;
    Indian Airlines

45 Hotel Golden City; Hotel Samrat

PLACES TO EAT
14 Restaurant Golden Fort
15 The Rawal
16 Trio; Top Deck; Skyroom Restaurant;
    Sharma Lodge; Bank of Baroda
28 Mohan Juice Centre
34 Dhanraj Bhatia Sweets
36 8th July Restaurant (2nd branch)
36 Natraj Restaurant;
    Salim Singh ki Haveli
37 Monica Restaurant
38 Seema Restaurant

OTHER
1   City View; Sunset Point
7   Jeep Hire
8   Amar Sagar Gate
9   Hospital
13 Government Museum
13 Rajasthali (Government Emporium)
17 Thar Safari
19 Satyam Tours; German Bakery
23 Bhatia News Agency
24 Byas & Co (Photographic Film)

25 Nathmal ki Haveli
27 Patwon ki Haveli
29 Police Station
30 Main Post Office
31 First Fort Gate; Sahara Travels;
    Bhang Shop
39 Bus Depot; Hotel Neeraj
40 State Bank of Bikaner & Jaipur
44 Tourist Reception Centre;
    Desert Culture Centre & Museum
45 Jaisalmer Folklore Museum
46 Tilon ki Pol
47 Main Roadways Bus Stand

JAISALMER FORT

PLACES TO STAY
1 Hotel Simla
3 Ishar Palace
9 Hotel Chandra Niwas;
   Hotel Laxmi Niwas (Old)
10 Deepak Rest House
11 Hotel Castle Paying Guest House
14 Hotel Jaisal Castle
16 Hotel Suraj; Hotel Temple View
18 Hotel Shreenath Palace
19 Jay Laxmi Paying Guest House
22 Hotel Paradise
23 Student (Suraja) Paying Guest House
24 Hotel Laxmi Niwas (New)
25 Killa Bhawan Resort

PLACES TO EAT
12 Vyas Meal Service
20 8th July Restaurant
21 Refreshing Point Rooftop Restaurant

OTHER
2 Ganesh Gate
4 Laxminath Temple
5 Hawa Gate
6 Surya Gate
7 First Fort Gate (Main Entrance)
8 Rajmahal (Maharaja's Palace & Museum)
13 Jain Temples
15 Post Office
17 Light of the East

0   50   100 m

visit in India. There are homes and hotels hidden in the laneways, and shops and stalls swaddled in the kaleidoscopic mirrors and embroideries of brilliant Rajasthani cloth. And yet it's so quiet that even the ubiquitous challenge issued by the wandering jewellery sellers – 'yes madam, sir, you buy' – can't dispel the magic air of peace and protection afforded by the massive and beautiful enclosure.

Built in 1156 by the Rajput ruler Jaisala, and reinforced by subsequent rulers, the fort crowns the 80m-high Trikuta Hill. About a quarter of the old city's population resides within the fort walls, which have 99 bastions around their circumference.

The fort is entered through a forbidding series of massive gates leading to a large courtyard. The former maharaja's seven storey palace fronts onto this. The square was formerly used to review troops, hear petitions and present extravagant entertainment for important visitors. Part of the palace is open to the public, but there's little to see inside. It's open daily 8 am to 5 pm; entry is Rs 10, plus Rs 20/50 for a camera/video.

Jain Temples Within the fort walls are a group of beautifully carved Jain temples built between the 12th and 15th centuries. They're dedicated to Rikhabdev and Sambhavanth.

The temples are open daily 7 am to noon. Entry is free but it costs Rs 40 for a camera, Rs 70 for a video.

Havelis

The impressive mansions built by the wealthy merchants of Jaisalmer are known as havelis, and several of these fine sandstone buildings are still in good condition.

Patwon ki Haveli This most elaborate and magnificent of all the Jaisalmer havelis stands in a narrow lane. It's divided into six apartments, two owned by the Archaeological Survey of India, two by families who operate craftshops here, and two private homes. There are remnants of paintings on some of the inside walls as well as some mirrorwork. To enter costs Rs 2.

Salim Singh ki Haveli This haveli was built about 300 years ago and part of it is still occupied. Salim Singh was the prime minister when Jaisalmer was the capital of a princely state, and his mansion has a beautifully arched roof with superb carved brackets in the form of peacocks. The mansion is just below the hill and, it is said, once had two additional wooden storeys in an attempt to make it as high as the maharaja's palace, but the maharaja had the upper storeys torn down! There's a Rs 15 entry charge at this haveli and it's open daily between 8 am and 6 pm.

Nathmal ki Haveli This late 19th century haveli was also a prime minister's house. The left and right wings of the building were carved by brothers and are very similar, but not identical. Yellow sandstone elephants guard the building, and even the front door is a work of art.

Gadi Sagar
This tank, south of the city walls, was once the water supply of the city and there are many small temples and shrines around it. A wide variety of waterfowl flock here in winter.

The attractive gateway which arches across the road down to the tank is said to have been built by a famous prostitute. When she offered to pay to have this gateway constructed, the maharaja refused permission on the grounds that he would have to pass under it to go down to the tank, and he felt that this would be beneath his dignity. While he was away, she built the gate anyway, adding a Krishna temple on top so the king could not tear it down.

Museums
Next to the Tourist Reception Centre is the **Desert Culture Centre & Museum**, which has textiles, old coins, fossils and traditional Rajasthani instruments among other things. Its aim is to preserve Rajasthan's cultural heritage and conduct research on local history. It's open 9 am to 8 pm daily. Entry costs Rs 5/10 for Indians/foreigners, which includes entry to the **Jaisalmer Folklore Museum** – on the road leading down to the

lake (open 8 am to 7 pm daily). The hill near this museum is a fabulous place to soak in the sunset.

Close to the RTDC's Hotel Moomal is the small **government museum**, which has a limited but well-captioned collection of fossils, some which date back to the Jurassic era (160 to 180 million years ago!). Other artefacts include a stuffed great Indian bustard, the state bird of Rajasthan, which thrives in the Thar Desert but is declining in numbers elsewhere. The museum is open daily except Friday 10 am to 4.30 pm. Entry costs Rs 3 (Rs 1 for students), free for everyone on Monday. Photography is not permitted.

Organised Tours
Few travellers visit Jaisalmer without taking a camel safari into the desert. For details, see the Camel Safaris Around Jaisalmer boxed text later in this section.

The Tourist Reception Centre offers a morning and evening city sightseeing tour (Rs 60 per person), and a sunset tour to the Sam sand dunes (Rs 100 per person). On request, tours to Sam can stop at Kanoi, 5km before the dunes, from where it's possible to get a camel to the dunes in time for sunset (about Rs 50).

The Hotel Fort View (see Places to Stay) has a travel counter (☎ 50740; ask for Om Vyas) which operates very reasonably priced excursions. These include a three hour city sightseeing trip (Rs 30 per person), and a full-day trip which also incorporates attractions in the environs of Jaisalmer (Rs 200 per person including lunch). Both these tours require a minimum of four people. They can also arrange camel safaris.

Special Events
In January/February, the (rather contrived) **Jaisalmer Desert Festival** has camel races, dances, folk music, desert ballads and puppeteers. See the Festivals of Rajasthan table at the start of this chapter for exact dates.

Places to Stay
Jaisalmer is a major tourist trap, and many hotels, both cheap and not so cheap, have

sprung up to meet the demand. The touting situation has reached such proportions that the district magistrate has set up a mobile Tourist Protection Force to keep the touts at a distance. Their aims are laudable – but they can only do so much. If you do encounter pressure from touts, especially around the bus station, keep in mind that some of them are less than honest about the service they provide – don't believe *anyone* who offers to take you 'anywhere you like' for a few rupees, and take with a grain of salt claims that the hotel you want to stay in is 'full', 'closed', 'no good any more' or has suffered some other inglorious fate. They'll only lead you to a succession of hotels, where of course they get commission if you stay.

Another word of advice – check that you have in fact been taken to the hotel you asked for, as some cunning rickshaw drivers will hurry you into a different hotel where they get their commission and disappear in a flash. To overcome this problem, many of the popular budget hotels send their own vehicles to meet the bus or train.

Unfortunately, quite a few of the cheap places are really into the high-pressure selling of camel safaris. Some places can get quite ugly if you book a safari through someone else. Not only will they refuse to hold your baggage, but in many cases they'll actually evict you from the hotel! Before you check in, stress that you will only stay if you don't have to do a safari – if they hassle you, simply move on to another hotel.

As is so often the case in Rajasthani towns, if there's a festival on, prices skyrocket and accommodation of any kind can be hard to get. Many places offer a lowseason discounts between April and August – but you'd be crazy to come here during this time, as Jaisalmer becomes hellishly hot.

Places to Stay – Budget
Town Area There's a good choice of budget hotels along the two streets that run parallel to each other north of the Trio restaurant. Many have bucket hot water and Indian-style toilets.

Hotel Swastika (☎ 52483) is a popular hang-out with travellers and deservedly so. It's friendly and there are great views from the rooftop. Singles/doubles with common bath go for Rs 100/150 and rooms with bath are from Rs 150/220. A dorm bed is Rs 60. It even throws in a free cup of tea in the morning.

Natural Guest House (no phone) has three rooms with common bath for a low Rs 50/80, and one double with bath for Rs 100.

Hotel Anurag (☎ 50276) is good if you're strapped for cash, offering singles/doubles with common bath for a mere Rs 30/40, or Rs 40/50 with attached bath (including a free cup of tea).

Hotel Pleasure (☎ 52323) has good rooms with common bath for Rs 60/80, and rooms with bath for Rs 100/120.

Hotel Renuka (☎ 52757), nearby, is a pleasant family-run place with fabulous rooftop views. Rooms with common bath range from Rs 40 to Rs 100 (Rs 100 to Rs 180 with attached bath). The best room with a balcony costs Rs 200. Meals are available.

Hotel Fort View (☎ 52214) is another popular cheapie and is close to the entrance to the fort, although some of the rooms are tiny. Singles/doubles with attached bath start at Rs 66/88. A large room with a view of the fort is Rs 350. There's a nice restaurant on the top floor.

Hotel Shree Giriraj Palace (☎ 52268), also in this area, is cheap and cheerful, with rooms from Rs 50/80 with common bath and Rs 80/120 with attached bath. There's a rooftop restaurant.

Hotel Rajdhani (☎ 52746), not far from the Patwon ki Haveli, has small, spartan but clean rooms with common bath for Rs 60/100 (Rs 150/200 with attached bath). The rooftop restaurant has fine fort views.

Hotel Jag Palace (☎ 50438) has tidy rooms with bath for Rs 150/200. Vegetarian meals are available on the roof terrace.

Hotel Samrat (☎ 51498), out in the southern section of the walled city, just off Gadi Sagar Rd, is a possibility if you're going through a cash crunch. A dorm bed is a mere Rs 10 and clean singles/doubles start at Rs 30/40 with common bath, or Rs 40/50 with attached bath. Not far away is another very good budget choice, the *Hotel Golden City* (☎ 51664).

Retiring rooms at the train station are Rs 100 for doubles with bath. There are also a cluster of thatched huts for the same price. No meals are available.

Fort The *Hotel Simla* (☎ 53061) is a terrific choice and you'll have no troubles here whatsoever. Rooms with common bath are Rs 60/100 and Rs 150/200. With attached bath they're Rs 250/350, and a pretty room with an alcove and balcony is Rs 300/450. There's also a small tent on the roof (Rs 50 a double), or you can sleep on the roof (Rs 25), which includes mattresses and blankets. You're welcomed with a free cup of tea.

Deepak Rest House (☎ 52665, fax 52070) is actually part of the fort wall and offers stunning views from its rooftop. However, travellers have mixed reports about the cleanliness and service here. Basic rooms are Rs 40/60 with common bath. Rooms with bath start at Rs 60/80. Room No 9 (Rs 300/350) is the best. There's also a rather tatty dorm for Rs 20.

Hotel Chandra Niwas (no phone) is a relaxing place to stay with just four well-maintained rooms from Rs 70 (common bath) to Rs 200 (attached bath).

Hotel Laxmi Niwas (☎ 52758) has tiny rooms for Rs 50/100 with common bath (the common shower is a bit primitive). It also has a new annexe on the other side of the fort with better rooms from Rs 200/250.

Hotel Paradise (☎ 52674) is on the far side of the main square from the palace as you come through the last gate into the fort. This popular place is a kind of haveli, with 23 rooms arranged around a leafy courtyard and sensational views from the roof. Singles/doubles with common bath are Rs 60/150, or from Rs 350 to Rs 650 with attached bath. You can sleep on the roof for Rs 30, which includes a blanket and mattress.

Hotel Castle Paying Guest House (☎ 52988) has just a few shabby but OK double rooms from Rs 100 to Rs 250.

Hotel Temple View (☎ 52832) has small but acceptable rooms for Rs 60/100 with common bath, and Rs 250 with bath. The owner, Sunny, is very helpful.

Places to Stay – Mid-Range

Town Area The *Hotel Jaisal Palace* (☎ 52717, fax 50257), not far from the Amar Sagar Gate, is a well-maintained place. All rooms have attached hot bath and are Rs 500/600/900 a single/double/triple (the best rooms are Nos 107,108 and 109). The rooftop veg restaurant boasts fine views – there's a chair swing on the very top.

Hotel Nachana Haveli (☎ 52110, fax 52778, Gandhi Chowk) is a charming old haveli with rooms around a courtyard. Singles/doubles range from Rs 650/750 to Rs 950/1150. Meals are available with advance notice.

RTDC's Hotel Moomal (☎ 52392) has a more impressive exterior than interior. Situated out of the walled city, it has thatched huts for Rs 750, or conventional rooms from Rs 450/500. A dorm bed is Rs 50. There's a restaurant and a beer shop.

Hotel Neeraj (☎ 52442, fax 52545) is even farther away from the centre, and fronts a busy road. Overpriced singles/doubles start at Rs 700/800.

Mandir Palace Hotel (☎ 52788, fax 51158) has royal associations but is overpriced for what it offers. Rooms begin at Rs 850/1350.

Shri Narayan Vilas (☎ 52283) is inside the town walls, to the north of the fort. Somewhat run-down rooms start from Rs 525/625.

Fort The *Hotel Suraj* (☎ 51623), near the Jain temples, is an interesting old haveli with rooms ranging from Rs 300/350 to Rs 550/650, all with private bath. Veg meals are available; lunch/dinner costs Rs 50/75. In their building opposite are some slightly cheaper rooms.

Hotel Shreenath Palace (☎ 52907) is another atmospheric old haveli. Rooms (all doubles) cost Rs 350 with common bath (free bucket hot water). Room No 4 is lovely.

Hotel Jaisal Castle (☎ 52362, fax 52101) is a restored haveli in the south-west corner of the fort. Its biggest attraction is its position high on the ramparts looking out over the desert. The cheapest rooms are Rs 500/650. The staff can be a bit indifferent here.

Killa Bhawan Resort (☎ 51204) is more expensive, and offers comfortable but small-ish doubles with common bath from Rs 1000 to Rs 1250.

Places to Stay – Top End

Rang Mahal (☎ 50907, fax 51305), 2.5km west of the fort, is a dramatic building with marvellous rooms from Rs 1500/1850. The deluxe suites (Rs 3800) are dreamy. At the time of writing a pool was being planned.

Gorbandh Palace Hotel (☎ 51511, fax 52749), nearby, is another upmarket modern hotel with traditional design elements. Built of local sandstone, the friezes around the hotel were sculpted by local artisans. Standard rooms in a fairly nondescript block behind the main building cost Rs 1195/2395 and there's a coffee shop, bar, restaurant, travel desk and superb pool. The *Hotel Heritage Inn* (☎ 52769, fax 51638), next door, has rooms for Rs 1190/1950.

Jawahar Niwas Palace (☎ 52208, fax 52611), 1km west of the fort, is a stunning palace, standing in its own sandy grounds. At the time of writing it was undergoing vigorous renovations, but it should be ready by now and is worth checking out. Rates are expected to be Rs 2495/2995.

Narayan Niwas Palace (☎ 52408, fax 52101) is north of the fort. The rooms aren't very exciting, but are comfortable enough at Rs 1175/1800, or Rs 2050 for a suite. There's a gloomy indoor swimming pool, and great views of the fort from the rooftop.

Other good top-end hotels include *Hotel Himmatgarh Palace* (☎ 52002, fax 52005), the *Hotel Rawal-Kot* (☎ 51874, fax 50444) and the *Hotel Dhola Maru* (☎ 52863, fax 53124).

Places to Eat

Like all travellers' centres, Jaisalmer's budget restaurants attract their own cliques of long-time stayers. Hygiene is variable, though, and prices steadily rise in line with tourist numbers.

Town Area Not far from the First Fort Gate, *Monica Restaurant* is popular with travellers and has an extensive menu offering Indian, continental and Chinese food. There's also a selection of Rajasthani cuisine – to sample a variety of dishes try the filling Rajasthani thali (Rs 70).

Natraj Restaurant, not far away, has a fine view of the upper part of the Salim Singh ki Haveli next door. The food is good and the prices are fairly reasonable; chicken Mughlai is Rs 50 and fried ice cream is Rs 30. Nearby is the *Seema Restaurant*, which offers veg and nonveg fare.

Mid Town, also near the fort gate, has packed tables and average food. A Rajasthani special thali costs Rs 40.

Trio, near the Amar Sagar Gate, is one of Jaisalmer's longest running restaurants. Although pricier than its neighbours, the food is great and well presented. The *saagwala mutton* (Rs 80) is tasty. The nearby *Skyroom Restaurant* has a more limited menu.

Kalpana Restaurant, in the same area, is nothing special, but is a good place to watch the world go by while sipping on a banana lassi (Rs 14).

Top Deck, nearby, is popular and offers reasonably priced Indian, continental and Chinese cuisine. Their fruit lassi (Rs 15) is refreshing.

Bhang Shop, outside the First Fort Gate, not far from Sahara Travels, is a government-authorised bhang shop! Lassis are Rs 25 per glass and bhang cookies can be baked with advance notice. Bhang does not agree with everyone – see the Warning boxed text at the beginning of this chapter.

Dhanraj Bhatia Sweets (Sadar Bazaar, Bhatia Market), opposite the 8th July Restaurant's outside the fort, has been churning out sweet treats for the past 10 generations. It is renowned in Jaisalmer and beyond for its speciality sweets, such as *ghotua* and *panchadhari ladoos* (Rs 4.50 each). This simple little place is worth visiting just to watch the sweetmakers ply their trade.

The Rawal whips up interesting Indian dishes such as a tandoori thali (Rs 150), as well as continental and Chinese fare. Their mixed fruit lassi (Rs 22) is positively divine. There are fine fort views. Nearby is the *Restaurant Golden Fort*, which also has panoramic views, but a more limited menu.

Fort The *8th July Restaurant*, above the main square, is certainly conveniently located, but the food and service could be better. The menu is purely vegetarian and largely caters to western tastes. Vegemite-deprived Aussies can get the black wonder-spread here (Rs 30 for three slices of toast). There's another branch outside the fort but it's not as atmospheric.

Refreshing Point Rooftop Restaurant, nearby, is so popular that you may have to wait for a table. There's a phenomenal menu offering Indian, continental, Italian, Mexican, Tibetan, Chinese and even Greek cuisine. Moussaka is Rs 40 and sizzlers are Rs 65. They serve hearty breakfasts as well. There's also a small German bakery selling goodies such as choco-banana croissants (Rs 20).

Vyas Meal Service, near the Jain temples in the fort, is an excellent place to get home-cooked veg food. Their thalis are popular and they also do good masala tea.

Shopping

Jaisalmer is renowned for embroidery, Rajasthani mirrorwork, rugs, blankets, old stonework and antiques. Tie-dye and other fabrics are made at the Khadi Gramodyog Bhavan (Seemagram), not too far from the fort. One traveller warns that you should watch out for silver items bought in Jaisalmer as the metal may be adulterated with bronze.

In the fort, on the laneway leading up to the Jain temples, is a fascinating shop called the Light of the East. It sells crystals and rare mineral specimens. Ask to have a look at the huge apophyllite piece which is kept in a closed box – don't set your heart on it – it's not for sale.

Getting There & Away

Air Indian Airlines operates flights between Jaisalmer and Jodhpur (US$60), Jaipur (US$110), Mumbai (US$175) and Delhi (US$140). The Indian Airlines office (☎ 51912) is in the grounds of the RTDC's Hotel Moomal and is open daily 9.30 am to 1 pm and 2 to 5.30 pm.

Bus You'll find the main Roadways bus stand (☎ 51541) some distance from the centre of town, near the train station. Fortunately, all buses start from a bus depot just behind the Hotel Neeraj, which is more conveniently located.

To Jodhpur there are frequent daily deluxe buses (Rs 60, 5½ hours). There is one daily deluxe bus direct to Jaipur (Rs 130, 13 hours) and several daily direct deluxe buses to Bikaner (Rs 100, seven hours).

It's possible to book luxury buses through most of the travel agencies. Quoted rates were: Udaipur, Rs 150; Jaipur, Rs 150; Delhi, Rs 250; Ajmer, Rs 140; Bikaner, Rs 110; and Jodhpur, Rs 75. The trip to Udaipur requires a change of bus at Jodhpur. Others may also require a change en route.

Train The reservations office at the train station is open 8 am to 8 pm daily.

The *IJPJ* leaves Jaisalmer daily at 7.15 am, arriving in Jodhpur at 3.30 pm (Rs 44/340 in 2nd/1st class). The *Jodhpur Express* leaves Jaisalmer at 10.30 pm and arrives in Jodhpur at 5.20 am (Rs 124/568 in 2nd/1st class).

Jeep You can hire a jeep from the stand on Gandhi Chowk. To Khuri or Sam, expect to pay Rs 300 return with a one hour wait. Share with people to split the cost.

Getting Around

Auto-Rickshaw An auto-rickshaw to Gadi Sagar costs about Rs 15 one way from the fort entrance. Rickshaw drivers can be rapacious in this touristy town – bargain hard.

Bicycle A good way to zip around is by bicycle. There are a number of hire places, including a cheap one at Gandhi Chowk in the lane opposite the Skyroom Restaurant (Rs 3/15 per hour/day), and another just outside the main gate of the fort (which is more expensive).

AROUND JAISALMER

There are some fascinating places to see in the area around Jaisalmer, although it soon fades out into a barren sand dune desert which stretches across the lonely border into Pakistan.

Due to alleged arms smuggling across the border from Pakistan, most of Rajasthan, west of National Highway No 15, is a restricted area. Special permission is required from the District Collector's Office in Jaisalmer (☎ 02992-52201) if you want to go there, and this is only issued in exceptional circumstances. Places exempted are Amar Sagar, Bada Bagh, Lodhruva, Kuldhara, Akal, Sam, Ramkund, Khuri and Mool Sagar.

Bada Bagh & Chhatris

About 7km north of Jaisalmer, Bada Bagh is a fertile oasis with a huge old dam. Above the gardens are royal chhatris with finely carved ceilings and equestrian statues of former rulers. Entry is Rs 10.

Amar Sagar

Seven kilometres north-west of Jaisalmer, this once-pleasant formal garden has now fallen into ruin. The lake here dries up several months into the dry season. Nearby is a beautifully carved **Jain temple**. It's free to enter the temple, but there's a Rs 25/50 camera/video charge.

Lodhruva

Farther out beyond Amar Sagar, 15km north-west of Jaisalmer, are the deserted ruins of this town which was the ancient capital before the move to Jaisalmer. The **Jain temples**, rebuilt in the late 1970s, are the only reminders of the city's former magnificence. The main temple has an image of Parasnath, the 23rd tirthankar. In the temple is a hole from which a cobra is said to

emerge every evening – it is considered auspicious to see it. Entry to the temple is free, but there's a Rs 40/70 camera/video charge.

Mool Sagar

Nine kilometres west of Jaisalmer, this is another pleasant, but somewhat neglected, small garden and tank. It belongs to the royal family of Jaisalmer. Admission is Rs 5.

Sam Sand Dunes

A desert national park has been established in the Thar Desert near Sam village. One of the most popular excursions is to the sand dunes on the edge of the park, 42km from Jaisalmer. This is Jaisalmer's nearest real Sahara-like desert. It's best to be here at sunrise or sunset, and many camel safaris spend a night at the dunes. Just before sunset jeep loads of trippers arrive from Jaisalmer to be chased across the sands by young boys selling soft drinks and by tenacious camel owners offering short rides. Yes, this place has become a massive tourist attraction, so don't set your heart on a solitary desert sunset experience. If you want less touristy sand dunes, Khuri is a good alternative (see following section).

One tragic consequence of the rising tourist numbers is the discarded rubbish – please don't contribute to the problem. Encourage locals to keep the dunes clean. There's a small entry charge to visit the dunes.

RTDC's Hotel Sam Dhani (no phone) is the only place to stay here. Doubles with bath go for Rs 300, and dorm beds are Rs 50. There is no power, but lanterns are provided. Veg meals are available. Bookings can be made at the RTDC's Hotel Moomal (☎ 02992-52392) in Jaisalmer.

There are just a few daily buses between Sam and Jaisalmer (Rs 15, 1½ hours).

Khuri

Khuri is a village 40km south-west of Jaisalmer, out among the sand dunes (minus the tourist hype of those at Sam). It's a peaceful place with houses of mud and straw decorated like the patterns on Persian carpets.

RAJASTHAN

Camel Safaris Around Jaisalmer

The most interesting means of exploring the desert around Jaisalmer is by camel safari and virtually everyone who comes here goes on one. October to February is the best time.

Competition between safari organisers is cut-throat and standards vary considerably. This has resulted in many complaints when promises have been made and not kept. Touts will begin to hassle you even before you get off the bus or train; and, at the budget end of the market, hotel rooms can be as little as Rs 20 – providing you take the hotel's safari. Try to talk to other travellers for feedback on who is currently offering good, reliable and honest service, and don't be pressured by agents who tell you that if you don't go on the trip leaving tomorrow there won't be another until next week. Naturally they all offer *the* best safari and spare no invective in pouring scorn on their rivals.

The truth is more mundane. None of the hotels have their own camels – these are all independently owned – so the hoteliers and the travel agents are just go-betweens, though the hotels often organise the food and drink supplies. You need to consider a few things before jumping at what appears to be a bargain. Hotel owners typically pay the camel drivers around Rs 100 per camel per day to hire them, so if you're offered a safari at Rs 140 per day, this leaves only a small margin for food and the agent's profit. It's obvious that you can't possibly expect three reasonable meals a day on these margins, but this is frequently what is promised. As a result, a lot of travellers feel they've been ripped off when the food isn't what was offered.

The realistic minimum price for a basic safari is about Rs 350 per person per day. For this you can expect a breakfast of porridge, tea and toast, and a lunch and dinner of rice, dhal and chapatis – pretty unexciting stuff. Blankets are also supplied. You must bring your own mineral water. Of course you can pay more for greater levels of comfort – tents, stretcher beds, better food, beer etc.

There are several independent camel safari agents (not linked to any hotels) that have been recommended. Sahara Travels (☎ 52609), by the First Fort Gate, is run by Mr Bissa, alias Mr Desert. If you think you've seen his face before it's because he's India's Marlboro Man – the rugged model in the Jaisalmer cigarette ads. His basic tours cost Rs 350 a day for two to four days (you get your own camel). Tented safaris start at Rs 500.

Other options include Satyam Tours (☎ 50773), at Gandhi Chowk, which also charges Rs 350 per person for a basic safari (but you share your camel), and the nearby Thar Safari (☎/fax 52722), which has safaris from Rs 450. Whoever you book your safari through, insist that all rubbish is carried back to Jaisalmer, and not left at the Sam sand dunes or in remote villages where the wind will carry it across the desert.

However much you decide to spend, make sure you know exactly what is being provided and make sure it's there before you leave Jaisalmer. Ensure you know where they're going to take you. Attempting to get a refund for services not provided is a waste of time.

Most safaris last three to four days and, if you want to get to the most interesting places, this is a bare minimum. Bring something comfortable to sit on – many travellers fail to do this and come back with very sore legs and/or backsides! A wide-brimmed hat (or Rajput-style turban), long trousers, toilet paper, sun cream and a personal water bottle (with a strap so you can secure it easily) are also recommended. It can get very cold at night, so if you have a sleeping bag bring it along even if you're told that lots of blankets will be supplied. Women should consider wearing a sports bra, as the trotting momentum of the camels can cause some discomfort after even just a few hours.

Camel Safaris Around Jaisalmer

If you're on your own it's worth getting a group of at least four people together before looking for a safari. Organisers will make up groups but four days is a long time to spend with people you might not get on with. Usually each person is assigned their own camel, but check this, as some agencies might try to save money by hiring fewer camels, meaning you'll find yourself sharing your camel with a camel driver or cook, which is not nearly as much fun. The reins are fastened to the camel's nose peg, so the animals are easily steered. At resting points, the camels are completely unsaddled and hobbled. They limp away to browse on nearby shrubs while the cameleers brew sweet chai or prepare food. The whole crew rests in the shade of thorn trees by a tank or well.

A camel safari is a great way to see the desert, which is surprisingly well populated and sprinkled with ruins. You often come across tiny fields of millet, girls picking berries or boys herding flocks of sheep or goats. The latter are usually fitted with tinkling neck bells and, in the desert silence, it's music to the ears. Unfortunately the same cannot be said for the noises emitted by the notoriously flatulent camels!

Camping out at night, huddling around a tiny fire beneath the stars and listening to the camel drivers' yarns can be quite romantic. The camel drivers will expect a tip or gift at the end of the trip. Don't neglect to do this.

Take care of your possessions, particularly on the return journey. A recent scam involves the drivers suggesting that you walk to some nearby ruins while they stay with the camels and keep an eye on your bags. The police station in Jaisalmer receives numerous reports of items missing from luggage but seems unwilling to help.

The usual circuit takes in such places as Amar Sagar, Lodhruva, Mool Sagar, Bada Bagh and Sam, as well as various abandoned villages along the way. It's not possible to ride by camel to the Sam sand dunes in one day; in 1½ days you could get a jeep to Sam, stay there overnight, and take a camel from there to either Kuldahra (then a jeep back to Jaisalmer) or to Kanoi (and catch a jeep from there to Jaisalmer). If you're really pressed for time, you could opt for a half-day camel safari (which involves jeep transfers).

In 2½ days you could travel by camel to Lodhruva, spend the second night at the Sam sand dunes, and return the following day to Jaisalmer by jeep. If you have more time, obviously you can travel at a more leisurely pace through these regions and forgo the jeep component.

Places to stay in Khuri are pretty basic with *charpois* (Indian rope beds) and bucket hot water. Most can arrange camel safaris.

Khuri Guest House (☎ 02992-75444), near the bus stand, is run by a friendly fellow and has rooms with common bath for Rs 75/100, as well as huts with common bath for Rs 100/125.

The *Mama's Guest House (☎ 02992-92675423)* consists of various attractive, but rather pricey, clusters of thatched huts. The cheapest with shared bath costs Rs 350, including meals.

The *Sodha Guest House (☎ 02992-92675403)* has doubles with common bath for Rs 150. Huts are also available at *Gangaur Guest House (☎ 02992-92675464)*.

There are several daily buses between Jaisalmer and Khuri (Rs 13, two hours).

Akal Wood Fossil Park

Three kilometres off the road to Barmer, 16km from Jaisalmer, are the fossilised remains of a 180 million-year-old forest. To the untrained eye it's not particularly interesting. Entry is Rs 5/20 for Indians/foreigners, plus Rs 10 per vehicle. The park is open 8 am to 5 pm daily (closed for lunch 1 to 2 pm).

Barmer

Barmer is a centre for woodcarving, carpets, embroidery, block printing and other handicrafts, and its products are famous throughout Rajasthan. Otherwise, this desert town, 153km south of Jaisalmer, isn't very interesting. There are two annual fairs in Barmer: the **Barmer Thar Festival** in early March and the **Barmer Cattle Fair** (held at nearby Tilwara) in March/April. For details, contact the Tourist Reception Centre in Jaisalmer.

RTDC's Khartal (☎ 02982-22956) has neat singles/doubles with attached bath for Rs 225/350. Other options include the *Hotel Krishna (☎ 02982-20785)*, with rooms from Rs 100/200 (with common bath) and the even cheaper *Kailash Sarover Hotel (☎ 02982-20730)*.

From Barmer there are frequent daily express buses to Jaisalmer and Jodhpur.

Pokaran

At the junction of the Jaisalmer, Jodhpur and Bikaner roads, 110km from Jaisalmer, is the site of another fort – but it's not as dramatic as those of Jaisalmer or Jodhpur. The Pokaran Fort rises from the desert and shelters a tangle of narrow streets lined by balconied houses. The fort is open daily 7 am to 7 pm. Entry costs Rs 20 and it costs Rs 10 to bring a camera or video with you.

It was in Pokaran in May 1998 that India detonated five nuclear devices, heightening tension between India and neighbouring Pakistan. While world leaders vehemently condemned India's nuclear tests, hundreds of thousands of Hindu loyalists celebrated the Prime Minister Atal Behari Vajpayee's controversial decision. Pakistan's swift response was to detonate its own nuclear devices, igniting global concern about a nuclear arms race in south Asia.

A stop at Pokaran breaks the long journey between Jodhpur and Jaisalmer. However, accommodation is lacklustre, so most travellers prefer to stop here for lunch rather than overnight.

RTDC's Motel Godavan (☎ 02994-22275) conveniently rents out rooms with attached bath for six hours (Rs 200), or per night (Rs 300). There are also more expensive cottages. An Indian veg lunch or dinner is Rs 135 (nonveg Rs 165).

Fort Pokaran (☎ 02994-22274, fax 22279), within the fort itself, is more upmarket, but is in need of a facelift. Singles/doubles with bath are rather overpriced at Rs 950/1100. Lunch/dinner costs Rs 225.

There are frequent RSTC buses to Jaisalmer which take about 2½ hours and cost Rs 30. There are also daily rail services to Jaisalmer (Rs 15) and Jodhpur (Rs 25).

Khichan

This small village lies a few kilometres from the large town of Phalodi, between Jodhpur and Jaisalmer. It has not yet been listed as a wildlife sanctuary, but is a must for bird lovers. From late August/early September to the end of March, it's possible to witness the spectacular sight of hundreds of demoiselle cranes descending on the fields around the village.

BIKANER
☎ 0151 • pop 493,000

This desert town in the north of the state was founded in 1488 by Rao Bika, a descendant of Jodha, the founder of Jodhpur. Like many others in Rajasthan, the old city is surrounded by a high crenellated wall and, like Jaisalmer, it was once an important staging post on the great caravan trade routes. The Ganga Canal, built between 1925 and 1927, irrigates a large area of previously arid land around Bikaner.

As the tourist hype in Jaisalmer heightens, Bikaner is becoming more and more popular with travellers. It's easy to see why – Bikaner has a superb fort, camel safaris, and 30km to the south is the extraordinary Karni Mata Temple where thousands of holy rats are worshipped.

Orientation & Information

The old city is encircled by a 7km-long city wall with five entrance gates, constructed in the 18th century. The fort and palace, built of the same reddish-pink sandstone as Jaipur's famous buildings, are outside the city walls.

The helpful Tourist Reception Centre (☎ 544125) is in the grounds of RTDC's Hotel Dhola Maru. It's open daily except Sunday 10 am to 5 pm.

You can change money at the State Bank of Bikaner & Jaipur, near the Thar Hotel, and at its public park branch (near Junagarh). At the time of writing, no banks in Bikaner issued cash advances on credit cards.

Junagarh

Constructed between 1588 and 1593 by Raja Rai Singh – a general in the army of the Mughal emperor, Akbar – this most impressive fort has a 986m-long wall with 37 bastions, a moat and two entrances. The Surajpol, or Sun Gate, is the main entrance to the fort. The palaces within the fort are on the southern side and make a picturesque ensemble of courtyards, balconies, kiosks, towers

and windows. A major feature of this fort and its palaces is the magnificent stone carving.

Highlights include: the Diwan-i-Khas; the Phool Mahal (Flower Palace), which is decorated with paintings and carved marble panels; and the Hawa Mahal, Badal Mahal and Anup Mahal. Items of interest include an unusual Rajput weapon collection, and an old WWI biplane presented to Maharaja Ganga Singh by the British. This is one of only two models of this plane in the world.

The fort is open 10 am to 4.30 pm daily. Entry is Rs 10/50 for Indians/foreigners and there's a Rs 30/50 camera/video charge. A guide is included in the ticket price.

Lalgarh Palace

Three kilometres north of the city centre, this red sandstone palace was built by Maharaja Ganga Singh (1881-1942) in memory of his father Maharaja Lal Singh. Although it's an imposing building with overhanging balconies and delicate latticework, it's not the most beautiful of Rajasthani royal residences.

The **Sri Sadul Museum** covers the entire 1st floor of the palace. It has an assortment of exhibits, including old photos depicting royal hunts, and an extraordinary collection of the former maharaja's personal possessions – golf tees, sneakers, earplugs and even his electric toothbrush! There's also the usual depressing exhibition of Indian beasts, shot and stuffed. The museum is open daily except Wednesday 10 am to 5 pm; entry is Rs 5. Photography is not allowed. In front of the palace is a carriage from the maharaja's royal train.

Other Attractions

The narrow streets of the old city conceal a number of old havelis and a couple of notable **Jain temples**. The Bhandasar and Sandeshwar temples date from around the 15th century. The temples have colourful wall paintings and some intricate carving.

The **Ganga Golden Jubilee Museum** houses an interesting collection of sculptures, terracotta ware, paintings and also musical instruments. It's open daily

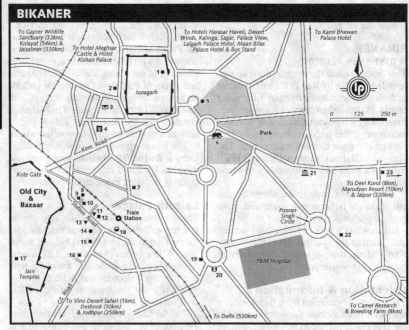

BIKANER

PLACES TO STAY			
2	Bhairon Vilas	17	Hotel Bhanwar Niwas
7	Hotel Jaswant Bhawan	19	Thar Hotel
8	Hotel Akashdeep;	22	RTDC's Hotel Dhola
	Hotel Amit		Maru; Tourist Reception
9	Hotel Deluxe		Centre
10	Evergreen Hotel	23	Hotel Padmini Niwas
12	Hotel Joshi; Kwality		
15	Hotel Shri Shanti Niwas	**PLACES TO EAT**	
16	Indre Lodge;	11	Chhotu Motu Joshi
	Hotel Marudhar Heritage		Sweet Shop
		13	Amber Restaurant

OTHER	
1	Abhivyakti (Urmul Trust Shop)
3	Main Post Office
4	Ratan Behari Temple & Garden
5	Courts
6	Zoo
14	Bike Hire
18	Taxi Stand; Clock Tower
20	State Bank of Bikaner & Jaipur
21	Ganga Golden Jubilee
	Museum

except Friday 10 am to 4.30 pm and there's a small entry fee (video cameras are prohibited).

There's a **Camel Festival** held in Bikaner each January (see the Festivals of Rajasthan table earlier in this chapter for the exact dates).

Organised Tours

The Tourist Reception Centre can arrange English-speaking guides (Rs 75 for two hours).

If you wanted to take a camel safari in Jaisalmer but didn't because it was too much of a scene, Bikaner is an excellent alterna-

Top: Amber Fort is one of the spectacular sights of Jaipur, with its ornate inlay stonework. One of its main features is a small Kali Temple, where daily goat sacrifices were performed until 1980.
Bottom left: In Jaipur, a carpet maker goes about her daily work.
Bottom right: A Rajasthani boy from a nearby village.

JOHN HAY

RICHARD I'ANSON

MICHELLE COXALL

RICHARD I'ANSON

Top: The Samode Palace boasts a range of audience halls covered in paintings and mirrorwork.
Middle: A snake charmer plies his trade in the streets of Jaipur.
Bottom left: A camel starts its life near a breeding farm outside Bikaner.
Bottom right: All over Rajasthan, women can be seen carrying out the daily task of fetching water.

tive. One good camel safari operator is Vino Desert Safari (☎ 204445, fax 525150), opposite the Gopeshwar Temple, which is run by the amiable Vinod Bhojak. Camel treks (minimum of two days) cost Rs 400 per person per day, including meals and blankets (you sleep under the stars). More expensive safaris in tented accommodation are also available. If you're looking for more upmarket camel safaris, try Rajasthan Safaris & Treks (☎ 543738); prices begin at Rs 1200 per person per day (minimum of six people).

Places to Stay – Budget

There are numerous budget options near the train station. Station Rd is an amazingly busy thoroughfare so the noise level in any room fronting it can be diabolical – choose carefully. Many places in the rock-bottom bracket have Indian-style toilets.

The Tourist Reception Centre has a list of Bikaner's paying guesthouses.

Hotel Meghsar Castle (☎ 527315, fax 522041, 9 Gajner Rd) is popular with travellers and has clean, spacious rooms with attached bath from Rs 250/300. The front rooms can cop a bit of traffic noise. Next door is the *Hotel Kishan Palace* (☎ 527762), with a cottage for Rs 100/150 with bath, and regular rooms from Rs 200/300.

Hotel Desert Winds (☎ 542202), near the Karni Singh Stadium, has singles/doubles with bath from Rs 200/250.

Evergreen Hotel (☎ 542061), on Station Rd, is not a bad choice, although some of the rooms can be noisy. Singles/doubles with common bath cost Rs 80/125, or Rs 125/175 with attached bath. Hot water is by the bucket (Rs 5). There's a restaurant downstairs. Nearby is the similarly priced but less impressive *Hotel Deluxe* (☎ 528127).

Hotel Akashdeep (☎ 543745), behind the Hotel Deluxe, has rather tatty rooms with bath for Rs 100/150 (free bucket hot water). Single women travellers may feel uncomfortable here.

Hotel Shri Shanti Niwas (☎ 521925) is on the road directly opposite the train station. Basic but quite clean rooms are Rs 75/125 with attached bath.

Indre Lodge (☎ 524813) is about 10m farther along this road, down a laneway that leads to the right, and is quieter than most other hotels in this area. Simple singles/doubles with bath go for Rs 70/150 (Rs 4 for bucket hot water). Better rooms are Rs 125/220. No meals are available.

Hotel Marudhar Heritage (☎ 522524), nearby, offers more luxurious rooms with bath for Rs 225/300, Rs 350/450 with air-cooling and Rs 750 for an air-con double.

RTDC's Hotel Dhola Maru (☎ 529621) is near Pooran Singh Circle, 1km from the centre of the city. Bland rooms with bath begin at Rs 175/225.

Retiring rooms at the train station cost Rs 75/115 with bath; Rs 150/200 with air-con. The dorm costs Rs 35/50 for 12/24 hours.

Places to Stay – Mid-Range

Bhairon Vilas (☎/fax 544751), near Junagarh, opposite the main post office, is the funkiest place to stay in Bikaner, managed by the equally funky Harshvardhan Singh. Quaint doubles range from Rs 500 to Rs 1600 – request a quiet room. Meals are available with advance notice in the dining room.

Hotel Harasar Haveli (☎ 209891, fax 525150), near the Karni Singh Stadium, is another great place to stay, with clean singles/doubles for Rs 450/650. The owner, Visvajeet Singh, can organise traditional fire dance performances at his farmhouse in Khara village, 20km from Bikaner (Rs 400 per person, minimum of five people).

Hotel Palace View (☎ 543625, fax 522741) is the closest hotel to the Lalgarh Palace and is a good place to stay. Clean rooms are Rs 750/850, or smaller rooms are Rs 400/500. Nearby is the pink *Hotel Sagar* (☎ 520677), with rooms from Rs 750/850.

Hotel Kalinga (☎ 209751), in the Lalgarh Palace campus area, has spartan singles/doubles for Rs 300/400.

Hotel Padmini Niwas (☎ 522794, 148 Sadul Ganj) has clean singles/doubles from Rs 425/550, up to Rs 650/750 with air-con. There's a restaurant and nice lawn area.

Hotel Joshi (☎ 527700, fax 521213), near the train station, has singles/doubles from Rs 300/375 and there's a veg restaurant here. Good ice cream is available next door at Kwality.

Thar Hotel (☎ *543050, fax 525150*), near the hospital, has mundane rooms from Rs 511/660. There's a nonveg restaurant here.

Hotel Jaswant Bhawan (☎/*fax 521834*), is an unchecked option not far from the train station on Alakh Sagar Rd. Singles/doubles are Rs 450/500. If you do end up staying here, let us know how it was.

Marudyan Resort (☎ *86945, fax 544107*), 10km out of Bikaner on the Jaipur road, has modern cottage-style accommodation for Rs 950/1150.

Places to Stay – Top End

Hotel Bhanwar Niwas (☎ *201043, fax 200880*), in the Rampuri Haveli, near the kotwali (police station) in the old city, is an excellent choice. This attractive pink sandstone building has rooms around a courtyard for Rs 2000/2900. In the foyer is a stunning blue 1927 Buick with a silver horn in the shape of a dragon.

Lalgarh Palace Hotel (☎ *540201, fax 522253*), 3km north of the city centre, is part of the maharaja's modern palace and has well-appointed singles/doubles for US$85/ 135. There's a bar, restaurant, billiard room, indoor pool and resident astrologer. In the same compound you'll find the smaller ***Maan Bilas Palace Hotel*** (☎ *524711*), with nine rooms going for Rs 1195/1675 a single/double.

Karni Bhawan Palace Hotel (☎ *524701, fax 522408*), in Gandhi Colony, near the Lalgarh Palace Hotel, is ugly but peaceful and comfortable. Art Deco-style rooms cost Rs 1195/2395, or Rs 3500 for a huge suite. Good meals are available in the restaurant.

Places to Eat

Bikaner is noted for the spicy snacks known as namkin, sold in the shops along Station Rd, among other places.

Deluxe Restaurant, at the hotel of the same name on Station Rd, features a limited selection of cheap veg south Indian and Chinese dishes. All dishes are under Rs 30. There's an extensive ice cream menu.

Amber Restaurant, diagonally opposite the Deluxe, is also popular for veg fare. Most dishes are under Rs 40 and there are some continental dishes such as baked macaroni (Rs 36). The Indian sweets are good.

Hotel Bhanwar Niwas welcomes nonguests to their vegetarian dining hall (with advance reservation). The set lunch/dinner is Rs 250/275, or you can just come here for a drink in the courtyard.

Lalgarh Palace Hotel is good for a treat; the set lunch/dinner costs US$10/11, or you can opt for à la carte dining.

Chhotu Motu Joshi Sweet Shop on Station Rd is Bikaner's most loved sweet stop, with an assortment of Indian treats.

Shopping

On the right-hand side as you enter the fort is a small craftshop, Abhivyakti, run by the Urmul Trust. Items sold here are of high quality and made by people from surrounding villages. Proceeds go directly to improve health and education projects in these villages. You can browse here without the usual constant hassles to buy.

Go to Usta St in the old city to see the making of traditional *usta* (camel leather) products.

Getting There & Away

The bus stand is 3km north of the city centre, almost opposite the road leading to the Lalgarh Palace Hotel (if your bus is coming from the south and you want to get down in the town centre, ask the driver – you may be lucky!). There are frequent express buses to a variety of destinations including Udaipur (Rs 213), Ajmer (Rs 105), Jaipur (Rs 137), Jodhpur (Rs 101), Jaisalmer (Rs 133), Jhunjhunu (Rs 90) and Kota (Rs 186).

There are several trains to Jaipur, Jodhpur and Delhi – the Tourist Reception Centre has a useful chart with details.

Getting Around

An auto-rickshaw from the train station to the palace should cost Rs 20, but you'll probably be asked for more. Bicycles can be hired at the Dau Cycle Shop, opposite the police station on Station Rd (Rs 2/10 per hour/day).

AROUND BIKANER
Devi Kund
Eight kilometres east of Bikaner, this is the site of the royal chhatris of many of the Bika dynasty rulers. The white marble chhatri of Maharaja Surat Singh is very imposing.

Camel Research & Breeding Farm
This government-managed camel research and breeding station, 8km from Bikaner, is probably unique in Asia. The British army had a camel corps drawn from Bikaner during WWI. As this is essentially a research centre and not a tourist site, there's frankly not a great deal to see here other than camels (which may appeal to those who didn't get to Jaisalmer).

The farm is open Monday to Friday and every second Saturday 3 to 5 pm (free entry). Cameras are theoretically prohibited, but this doesn't seem to be policed.

Gajner Wildlife Sanctuary
The lake and forested hills of this reserve, 32km from Bikaner on the Jaisalmer road, are inhabited by wildfowl and a number of deer and antelopes. Imperial sand grouse migrate here in winter. The reserve is only accessible by Gajner Palace Hotel vehicles (Rs 1000 per jeep, maximum six people).

Gajner Palace Hotel (☎ *01534-55065, fax 55060, reservations* ☎ *0151-524701, fax 522408)* is the former royal winter palace and is ideally situated on the banks of a lake. It's an impressive building made of red sandstone and is set in serene surroundings. Standard rooms are Rs 1195/2395 (the Gulab Niwas garden rooms are best). Old-fashioned suites (all with a lake view) are in the main palace and cost Rs 3500.

Kolayat
This small temple town set around a lake, 22km south of Gajner, is often referred to as a mini-Pushkar. It lacks the vibrant character of Pushkar, but is far less touristy. There's a fair here around the same time as the Pushkar Camel Fair (minus the camels and cattle, but with plenty of sadhus).

Deshnok
A visit to the fascinating **Karni Mata Temple** at this village 30km south of Bikaner, is not for the squeamish. The thousands of rats that inhabit the temple are considered incarnations of mystics, and the holy rodents run riot over the temple complex.

Once you've admired the silver doors and marble carvings donated by Maharaja Ganga Singh, you plunge into the rats' domain, hoping that some will scamper over your feet – most auspicious. Keep your eyes peeled for a rare white rat – it's considered good fortune if you spot one. Eating *prasaad* (holy food offering) that has been salivated over by these holy rats also apparently brings good luck, but is not recommended for the usual wimpish western constitution.

The temple is open 6 am to 9.30 pm daily and there's a Rs 20 camera charge, Rs 50 for a video. And remember, this is a place of worship, so don't conveniently forget to remove your shoes!

There are buses every hour from Bikaner to Deshnok (Rs 12, 40 minutes).

Gujarat

The west coast state of Gujarat is not one of India's busiest tourist destinations and although it is quite easy to slot Gujarat in between a visit to Mumbai (Bombay) and the cities of Rajasthan, few people pause to explore this interesting state.

Gujarat has always been a major centre for the Jains, and some of its most interesting sights are Jain temple centres like those at Palitana, and at Girnar Hill, near Junagadh. The Jains are an influential and energetic group and, as a result, Gujarat is one of India's wealthier states, with a number of important industries (particularly textiles and electronics) and the dubious distinction of having the largest petrochemical complex in the country.

Apart from its Jain temples, Gujarat's major attractions include the last Asian lions (in the Gir Forest) and the fascinating Indo-Saracenic architecture of Ahmedabad. The colourful tribal villages of Kutch (Kachchh) are well worth the effort of making your way out to this barren region. For more hedonistic pleasures, there are the pristine beaches at Diu, off Gujarat's southern coast, and at Mandvi, 60km south-west of Bhuj, in Kutch.

Geographically, Gujarat can be divided into three areas. The eastern (mainland) region includes the major cities of Ahmedabad, Surat and Vadodara (Baroda). The Gulf of Cambay divides the mainland strip from the flat, often barren, plain of the Kathiawar peninsula, also known as Saurashtra.

Gujarat is the former home of a surprisingly large proportion of India's emigrants, particularly to the UK and USA. Around 40% of the Indians in the New York area are Gujaratis; there, the common Gujarati surname 'Patel' has come to be commonly identified as Indian.

Except in the very cheapest hotels, in Gujarat you can usually expect a 15% luxury tax to be added to your accommodation bill. In top-end places this soars to 30%.

HISTORY

If you want to go beyond history into the realm of legend, then Gujarat's Temple of Somnath was actually there to witness the

Festivals of Gujarat

festival	location	date	features
Makar	Ahmedabad	15 Jan	kite flying, folk music & dance
Bhavnath Fair	Girnar Hill, Junagadh	Jan/Feb	folk music & dance
Dang Durbar	The Dangs	Feb/Mar	Adivasi festival
Rann Festival	Bhuj, Kutch	Feb/Mar	craft, culture, tours
Madhavrai Fair	Madhavpur	Mar/Apr	Krishna's elopement with Rukmini
Makakali, Champaner	Pavagadh Hill	Mar/Apr	honours goddess Makakali
Tarnetar	Trineteshwar	Aug/Sep	honours Shiva
Janmashtami	Dwarka	Aug/Sep	Krishna's birthday
Shrad Purnima	Dakor	Oct/Nov	Krishna
Kartika Purnima	Somnath	Nov/Dec	full moon night of month of Kartik

GUJARAT

creation of the universe! Along the south coast are the sites where many of the great events in Krishna's life took place.

On firmer historic footing, Lothal was the site of a Harappan or Indus Valley civilisation more than 4000 years ago. The main sites of this very ancient culture are now in Pakistan, but it is thought that Lothal may have survived the great cities of the Sindh by as much as 500 years. Gujarat featured in the exploits of the mighty Buddhist emperor, Ashoka, and one of his rock edicts can be seen near Junagadh.

Later, Gujarat suffered Muslim incursions from Mahmud of Ghazni and subsequent Mughal rulers, and was a battlefield between the Mughals and the Marathas. It was also an early point of contact with the west and the first British commercial outpost was established at Surat. Daman and Diu survived as Portuguese enclaves within the borders of Gujarat until 1961.

Saurashtra was never incorporated into British India, but survived in the form of more than 200 princely states right up to Independence. In 1956, they were amalgamated into the state of Mumbai but in 1960, Mumbai was in turn split, on linguistic grounds, into Maharashtra and Gujarat.

Gujarat also had close ties with the life of the father of modern India, Mahatma Gandhi. It was in Gujarat that Gandhi was born and spent his early years, and it was to

Ahmedabad, the main city of Gujarat, that he returned to wage his long struggle with the British for independence.

The Gulf of Kutch divides Saurashtra from Kutch, which is virtually an island, cut off from the rest of Gujarat to the east and Pakistan to the north by the low-lying *ranns* (deserts) of Kutch.

Eastern Gujarat

AHMEDABAD
☎ 079 • pop 5.49 million

Gujarat's principal city is Ahmedabad (also known as Amdavad), a major industrial city in India. Although it retains little evidence of the Raj, it's been called the 'Manchester of the East' due to its textile industries and smokestacks. It's a noisy and polluted city.

Visitors in the hot season should bear in mind the derisive title given to Ahmedabad by the Mughal emperor, Jehangir: Gardabad, the City of Dust. Nevertheless, this comparatively infrequently visited city has a number of attractions for travellers, and is one of the best places to study the blend of Hindu and Islamic architectural styles known as the Indo-Saracenic.

The new capital of Gujarat, Gandhinagar, is 32km from Ahmedabad.

Over the centuries Ahmedabad has had several periods of grandeur, each followed by

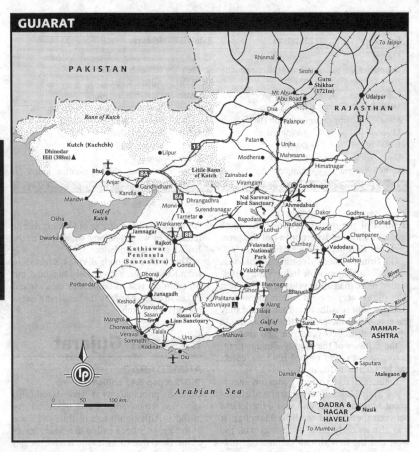

decline. It was founded in 1411 by Ahmed Shah (from whom the city takes its name) and in the 17th century was thought to be one of the finest cities in India. In 1615, the noted English ambassador, Sir Thomas Roe, judged it to be 'a goodly city, as large as London' but in the 18th century it went through a period of decline. Its industrial strength once again raised the city up, and from 1915 it became famous as the site of Gandhi's ashram and the place where he launched his celebrated march against the Salt Law.

Makar Sakranti is the time to see an extravaganza of kite flying in what has become an international festival.

Orientation

The city straddles the Sabarmati River which dries to a mere trickle in the hot season. On the eastern bank, two main roads run east from the river to the train station, about 3km away. They are Mahatma Gandhi Rd and the very congested and chaotic Relief Rd. The busy road flanking the western bank of the

Sabarmati is Sri RC Rd. This is the main road to the Gandhi Ashram and is called Ashram Rd at its northern end, although most locals refer to the entire road as Ashram Rd. The airport is off to the north-east of the city. Ramanlal Rd with places to stay along it is also known as Salapose Rd. Virtually all the old city walls are now demolished, but some of the gates remain.

Information

Gujarat Tourism publishes a range of free brochures and maps. It has current information on forthcoming events and performances in Ahmedabad. The Ahmedabad edition of the *Times of India* has up-to-the-minute flight and rail information on page two.

Tourist Office The helpful state tourist office Gujarat Tourism (☎ 658 9683, email tcgl.ahd@rmt.sprintrpg.ems.vsnl.net.in) is just off Ashram Rd, across the river from the town centre. Opening hours are 10.30 am to 1.30 pm and 2 to 6 pm (closed Sunday and the second and fourth Saturday in the month). The office has good maps of Ahmedabad and Gujarat state, and can also arrange tours and car hire. Ask rickshaw drivers for HK House on Ashram Rd (the tourist office is in this building, down the laneway near the South Indian Bank) or the BATA showroom (a more commonly known landmark).

Money The State Bank of India branch near Lal Darwaja (the local bus stand) and the Bank of Baroda, at the west end of Relief Rd, have moneychanging facilities. For quicker moneychanging, try Forexchange, opposite Sidi Saiyad's Mosque, open Monday to Friday, 10 am to 6 pm, Saturday 10 am to 3 pm. The Bank of Baroda on Ashram Rd can give cash advances on Visa cards.

Visa Extensions The Foreigners' Registration Office (☎ 562 0990) is in the office of the Commissioner of Police in Shahibaug, north of the town centre on Balvantrai Mehta Rd.

Post & Communications The main post office is central, just off Relief Rd. The central telegraph office is just south of Sidi Saiyad's Mosque.

Internet access, at Random@ccess, Ambawadi Rd, open daily 8 am to midnight, costs Rs 50/90 for 30/60 minutes.

Bookshops There are a number of good bookshops at the Nehru Bridge end of Relief Rd. Sastu Kitab Ghar, opposite the Relief Cinema has a good selection. Crossword, in the Shree Krishna complex at Mithakali Six Rds, has a wide range of books, plus CDs, maps and a coffee shop. It's open daily from 10.30 am to 8.30 pm.

Libraries & Cultural Centres The British Library (☎ 656 4693) is at Bhaikaka Hall, west of the river. Informative lectures on topical issues are sometimes held here; check listings in the *Times of India*. About 400m east is the Alliance Française (☎ 644 1551). The centre has information on French films which are sometimes screened in the city.

Things to Buy

With its busy modern textile works, it's not surprising that Gujarat offers a number of interesting buys in this line. Extremely fine, and often extremely expensive, patola silk saris are still made by a handful of master craftspeople in Patan. From Surat comes the zari, or gold-thread embroidery work. Surat is also a centre for silk saris. Less opulent, but still beautiful, are the block prints of Ahmedabad.

Jamnagar is famous for its tie-dye work, which you'll see throughout Saurashtra. Brightly coloured embroideries and beadwork are also found in Saurashtra, along with woollen shawls, blankets and rugs. Brass-covered wooden chests are manufactured in Bhavnagar, and Kutch is the centre for exquisite, fine embroidery. Most Gujarati handicrafts are on display at Gurjari or Handloom House, both on Ashram Rd, Ahmedabad.

GUJARAT

The Darpana Academy (☎ 644 5189), about 1km north of Gujarat Tourism on Ashram Rd, has regular cultural programs.

Medical Services The Civil Hospital (☎ 212 3721) is around 2.5km north of the train station.

Bhadra Fort & Teen Darwaja

Bhadra Fort was built by the city's founder, Ahmed Shah, in 1411 and later named after the goddess Bhadra, an incarnation of Kali. It now houses government offices, where you can ask for access to the roof for views of the surrounding streets. There is a post office in the former Palace of Azam Khan, within the fort. To the east of the fort stands the Teen Darwaja (triple gateway), from

---

Gujarat – by Rail & in Style

If you want to explore Gujarat quickly and in pure luxury, you should consider *The Royal Orient*, a special tourist train service which visits various destinations predominantly in Gujarat. Run by the Tourism Corporation of Gujarat and Indian Railways, it's a similar concept to the luxurious RTDC *Palace On Wheels* train that tours Rajasthan. *The Royal Orient* also visits several popular tourist spots in Rajasthan.

The seven day trip leaves Delhi on Wednesday and travels to Chittorgarh, Udaipur, Junagadh, Veraval, Sasan Gir, Delwada, Palitana, Sarkhej, Ahmedabad and Jaipur.

Rates per person per day are US$175/ 200/350 for triple/double/single occupancy. Children between five and 12 years are charged half price (free for kids under five), and all fares are reduced 25% in April and September. Prices include tours, entry fees, accommodation on the train plus all meals. Bookings must be made in advance at HK House, Ashram Rd, Ahmedabad (☎ 079-685 9172, fax 658 2183, email tcogl@adi.vsnl.net.in), or via India-specialist travel agents worldwide.

---

which sultans watched processions from the palace to the Jama Masjid.

Jama Masjid

The Jama Masjid, built in 1423 by Ahmed Shah, is beside Mahatma Gandhi Rd, to the east of the Teen Darwaja. Although 260 columns support the roof, the two 'shaking' minarets lost half their height in the great earthquake of 1819, and another tremor in 1957 completed their demolition.

Much of this early Ahmedabad mosque was built using items salvaged from the demolished Hindu and Jain temples. It is said that a large black slab by the main arch is actually the base of a Jain idol, buried upside down for the Muslim faithful to tread on.

Tombs of Ahmed Shah & his Queens

The tomb of Ahmed Shah stands just outside the east gate of the Jama Masjid. It was built shortly after his death in 1442. His son and grandson, also have their cenotaphs in this tomb. Women are not allowed into the central chamber. Across the street on a raised platform is the tomb of his queens, now a market and in very poor shape compared to his own tomb.

Sidi Saiyad's Mosque

This small mosque is close to the river end of Relief Rd. It was constructed in 1573 by Sidi Saiyad, a slave of Ahmed Shah, and has beautiful carved stone windows depicting the intricate intertwining of the branches of a tree. These can be viewed from outside (women can't enter).

Ahmed Shah's Mosque

Dating from 1414, this was one of the earliest mosques in the city and was probably built on the site of a Hindu temple, using parts of that temple in its construction. It is to the south-west of the Bhadra Fort. The front of the mosque is now a garden.

Rani Rupmati's Mosque

A little north of the city centre, Rani Rupmati's Mosque was built between 1430 and

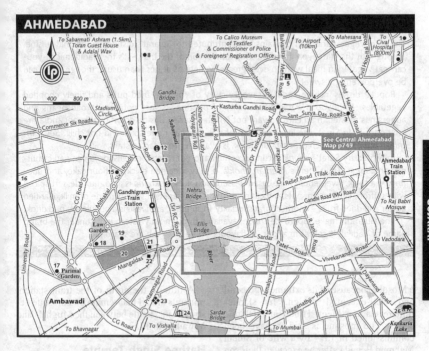

AHMEDABAD

PLACES TO STAY
21 Inder Residency
22 Hotel Westend

PLACES TO EAT
9 Mirch Masala
11 Sankalp Restaurant;
   Punjab Travels (Embassy
   Market)

OTHER
1 Mata Bhavani's Well
2 Dada Hari Wav (Stepwell)

3 Prem Gate
4 Dariapur Gate
5 Hathee Singh Temple
6 Delhi Gate
7 Rani Rupmati's Mosque
8 Darpana Academy
10 High Court
12 Gujarat Tourism
13 Gurjari (State Crafts
   Emporium)
14 Bank of Baroda
15 Crossword Bookshop;
   Shree Krishna Complex

16 Institute of Indology
17 Random@ccess
   (Cyber Cafe)
18 British Library
19 Alliance Française
20 Gujarat College
23 Punjab & Bonny Travels
   (Shefali Shopping Centre)
24 NC Mehta Museum
   of Miniatures
25 Jamalpur Gate
26 Zoo

1440 and named after the sultan's Hindu wife. The minarets were partially brought down by the great earthquake of 1819. Note the way the dome is elevated to allow light in around its base. As with so many of Ahmedabad's early mosques, this one displays elements of both Hindu and Islamic design.

Rani Sipri's Mosque

This small mosque south-east of the city is also known as the Masjid-e-Nagira (Jewel of

Gujarati Food

The strict vegetarianism of the Jains has contributed to Gujarat's distinctive regional cuisine. Throughout the state, you'll find the Gujarati version of the thali – it's the traditional all-you-can-eat vegetarian meal with an even greater variety of dishes than usual, though some can be overpoweringly sweet.

Popular dishes include *kadhi*, a savoury curry of yoghurt, fried puffs and finely chopped vegetables. *Undhyoo* is a winter speciality of potatoes, sweet potatoes, broad beans and aubergines roasted in an earthenware pot which is buried upside down (*undhyoo*) and a fire built on top. In Surat, the local variation of this dish has more spice and hot chilli. *Sev ganthia*, a crunchy fried chickpea-flour snack, is available from *farsan* stalls.

In winter, try Surat's *paunk*, a curious combination of roasted cereals; or *jowar*, garlic chutney and sugar. Then there's *khaman dhokla*, a salty, steamed chickpea flour cake, and *doodhpak*, a thick, sweetened, milk-based dessert with nuts. *Srikhand* is a yoghurt dessert spiced with saffron, cardamom, nuts and candied fruit. *Gharis* are rich sweets made of milk, clarified butter and dried fruits – another Surat speciality. In summer, *aam rasis* is a popular mango drink.

The Gujaratis make superb ice cream, available throughout western India under the brand name of Vadilal. It comes in about 20 flavours, some of which are seasonal.

a Mosque) because of its extremely graceful and well-executed design. Its slender minarets again blend Hindu and Islamic styles. The mosque is said to have been commissioned in 1514 by a wife of Sultan Mahmud Begada after he executed their son for some minor misdemeanour, and she is in fact buried here.

Sidi Bashir's Mosque & Shaking Minarets

Just south of the train station, outside the Sarangpur Gate, the Sidi Bashir Mosque is famed for its shaking minarets, or jhulta minars. When one minaret is shaken, the other rocks in sympathy. This is said to be protection against earthquake damage. It's a fairly fanciful proposition, and one which you'll be unable to verify, unless of course you happen to be here during an earthquake.

Raj Babri Mosque

The Raj Babri Mosque, south-east of the train station in the suburb of Gomtipur, also had shaking minarets, one of which was partially dismantled by an inquisitive Englishman in an unsuccessful attempt to find out how it worked.

A little to the north of the train station, minarets are all that remain of a mosque destroyed in a battle between the Mughals and Marathas in 1753.

Hathee Singh Temple

Just outside the Delhi Gate, to the north of the old city, this temple, as with so many Jain temples, is made of white marble. Built in 1848, it is dedicated to Dharamanath, the 15th Jain *tirthankar* (teacher).

Other Mosques & Temples

There's no shortage of mosques in Ahmedabad. If your enthusiasm for them is limited, don't go further than Sidi Saiyad's Mosque and the Jama Masjid. If you have real endurance, you could visit **Dastur Khan's Mosque** near the Rani Sipri Mosque; also, the mosques of Haibat Khan, Saiyad Alam, Shuja'at Khan and Shaikh Hasan Mohammed Chisti.

For a complete change, you could plunge into the narrow streets of the old part of town and seek out the brightly-painted, wood-carved **Swami Narayan Temple**. Enclosed in a large courtyard, it dates from 1850. To the south of this Hindu temple are the nine tombs known as the Nau Gaz Pir (Nine Yard Saints).

Step-Wells

Step-wells *(wavs* or *baolis)* are strange constructions, unique to northern India, and **Dada Hari Wav** is one of the best. Built in 1501 by a woman of Sultan Begara's harem, it has a series of steps leading down to lower platforms terminating at a small, octagonal well. The depths of the well are cool, even on the hottest day, and it must once have been quite beautiful. Today, it is completely neglected and often bone dry, but it's a fascinatingly eerie place with galleries above the well and a small portico at ground level.

The best time to visit and photograph the well is between 10 and 11 am; at other times the sun doesn't penetrate to the various levels. Entry is free. Behind the well is the equally neglected mosque and *rauza* (tomb) of Dada Hari. The mosque has a tree motif like the one on the windows of Sidi Saiyad's Mosque. Bus No 111 (Rs 2.50) to Asarwa goes nearby.

Mata Bhavani's Well is about 200m north of Dada Hari's. Ask children to show you the way. Thought to be several hundred years older, it is much less ornate and is now used as a simple Hindu temple.

Kankaria Lake

South-east of the city, this artificial lake, complete with an island summer palace, was constructed in 1451 and has 34 sides, each 60m long. Once frequented by Emperor Jehangir and Empress Nur Jahan, it is now a local picnic spot. There's a huge **zoo** and children's park by the lake, and the Ghattamendal pavilion in the centre houses an **aquarium**. The Balvatika waterpark, with a sauna and a restaurant, should open here by 2001. To get there, take bus No 32, 42, 60, 152 or 153 from the Lal Darwaja (Rs 2.50).

Museums

The excellent **Calico Museum of Textiles** (☎ 786 8172) exhibits antique and modern textiles including rare tapestries, wall hang-

ings and costumes. Also on display are various old weaving machines. The museum is in Sarabhai House, a former *haveli* (mansion), in the Shahi Bagh Gardens. You can only enter on a free guided tour. Tours depart at 10.30 am and 2.45 pm, and the museum is closed on Wednesday. As in some other museums, photography is not allowed. To get there, take bus No 101, 102 or 105 (Rs 2.50) out through the Delhi Gate.

The **Institute of Indology** beyond Gujarat College, near the Gujarat University campus, has an important collection of illustrated manuscripts and miniatures and one of the finest collections relating to Jainism in India. It's free and open from 11 am to 5.30 pm (closed Sunday).

The **NC Mehta Museum of Miniatures** west of Sardar Bridge has excellent examples of the various schools of Indian miniature painting. It's open Monday to Saturday from 10 am to 1.30 pm and 2 to 5.30 pm. The building was designed by Swiss-born architect Le Corbusier who also planned the city of Chandigarh, the capital of Punjab and Haryana states.

The **Shreyas Folk Museum**, about 2.5km west of the Sabarmati in the suburb of Ambavadi, displays the folk arts and crafts of Gujarat, particularly textiles and clothing. It's open 9 am to noon and 3 to 5 pm Thursday to Tuesday. Take bus No 34 or 200 (Rs 3). There is also the **National Institute of Design**, the **Tribal Research & Training Institute Museum**, and the **Philatelic Museum**.

The **Utensils Museum** in the compound of the Vishalla restaurant (see Places to Eat) has a collection of receptacles, nutcrackers, locks and other diverse utensils. It is open daily from 10 am to 10 pm and entry costs Rs 3.

Sabarmati Ashram

About 5km from the centre of town, on the west bank of the Sabarmati River, this ashram was Gandhi's headquarters during the long struggle for Indian independence. His ashram was founded in 1915 and still makes handicrafts, handmade paper and spinning wheels. Gandhi's spartan living quarters are preserved as a small museum and there is a pictorial record of the major events in his life. There's also a bookshop selling books by and about the Mahatma.

The ashram is open from 8.30 am to 6.30 pm (7 pm between April and September). Admission is free. There is a sound-and-light show for a small charge at 6.30 pm (in Gujarati) and 8.30 pm (in English on Sunday, Wednesday and Friday; in Hindi on other nights). Bus No 81, 83/1 or 84/1 (Rs 3) will take you there. An auto-rickshaw will cost about Rs 25.

Other Attractions

In many streets, there are Jain bird-feeding places known as *parabdis*. Children catch and release pigeons for the fun of it. The older parts of the city are divided into totally separate areas known as *pols*. It's easy to get lost.

The pleasant **Victoria Gardens** are at the east end of the Ellis Bridge. The **Law Gardens** on the west bank are also worth a visit, particularly towards sunset when textile stallholders set up their wares around the edge of the gardens.

On the sandy banks of the Sabarmati River, traditional block-printed fabrics are still stretched out to dry, despite the city's 70-plus large textile mills.

Other places of interest in and around town include the ruined **Tomb of Darya Khan**, 1.5km north-west of the Hathee Singh Temple. Built in 1453, the tomb has a particularly large dome. Nearby, across the railway line, is the **Chhota Shahi Bagh**. Ladies of the harem used to live in the *chhota* (small) garden. In Saraspur, about 1km east of the railway line, the **Temple of Chintaman** is a Jain temple originally constructed in 1638 and converted into a mosque by Aurangzeb.

Organised Tours

The municipal corporation (☎ 535 2911) runs city tours from Lal Darwaja daily at 8 am and 1.30 pm. They take four hours, and commentaries are given in English (Rs 60 per person). All-day tours include Gandhinagar (from Rs 100; book ahead).

Places to Stay – Budget

Lots of cheap hotels are scattered along or close to Relief Rd. The real cheapies are opposite the train station, but most are assailed by Ahmedabad's horrendous noise and air pollution and are probably best avoided unless you have a very early morning departure. The area around Sidi Saiyad's Mosque at the western end of Relief Rd is better, although it's still far from serene. Many hotels have 24 hour checkout and a 15% luxury tax on top of their advertised room rates, though top-end hotels add a whopping 30% tax – and often have a stingy 9 am checkout. Rooms mentioned below have bathroom, unless indicated.

A-One Hotel (☎ 214 9823) is opposite the train station. Singles/doubles for Rs 175/200 are OK, but those with shared bathroom (Rs 90/140) are small and dingy. Dorm beds (men only) are Rs 60.

Hotel Naigra (☎ 384977), just off Relief Rd, has fairly quiet, though small rooms from Rs 150/200, or Rs 90 with shared bathroom.

Hotel Natraj (☎ 550 6048) near Lal Darwaja, has good-sized if grubby rooms for Rs 120/200 with free bucket hot water. Ask for a room facing the pleasant gardens of Ahmed Shah's Mosque. Don't confuse this place with the more upmarket Hotel Natraj on the west side of the Sabarmati River.

Hotel Roopalee (☎ 550 6397, Dr Tankaria Rd), near Sidi Saiyad's Mosque, is not a bad choice. Simple but pleasant rooms with bucket hot water and TV are Rs 100/190, or there's a dorm for Rs 55.

Across the alley is **Hotel Gulmarg** (☎ 550 6204), with a range of rooms from Rs 150/250, also with TV and hot water.

Hotel Mehul (☎ 550 7862, Hanuman Lane) off Relief Rd, has rooms with hot water for Rs 165/200. Rooms are large, beds are hard, TVs are B&W.

Hotel Ashiana (☎ 535 1114, Ramanlal Sheth Rd) has spartan, small singles/doubles with hot water for Rs 125/170, or Rs 100/150 with shared bathroom.

Hotel Relax (☎ 550 7301) is down a quiet lane opposite the Advance Cinema.

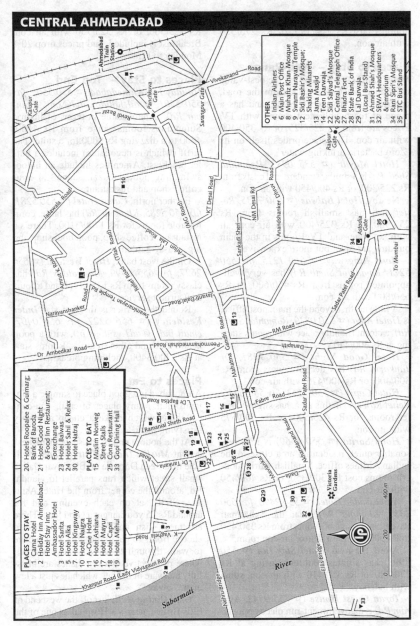

CENTRAL AHMEDABAD

PLACES TO STAY
1 Cama Hotel
2 Holiday Inn Ahmedabad;
  Hotel Stay Inn;
  Ambassador Hotel
3 Hotel Sarita
5 Hotel Alka
7 Hotel Kingsway
10 Hotel Naigra
11 A-One Hotel
16 Hotel Ashiana
17 Hotel Mayur
18 Hotel Capri
19 Hotel Mehul
20 Hotels Roopalee & Gulmarg;
   Bank of Baroda
21 Hotel Good Night
   & Food Inn Restaurant;
   Forexchange
23 Hotel Balwas
24 Hotels Sahil & Relax
30 Hotel Natraj

PLACES TO EAT
15 Muslim Nonveg
   Street Stalls
25 Cona Restaurant
33 Gopi Dining Hall

OTHER
4 Indian Airlines
6 Main Post Office
8 Muhafiz Khan Mosque
9 Swami Narayan Temple
12 Sidi Bashir's Mosque;
   Shaking Minarets
13 Jama Masjid
14 Teen Darwaja
22 Sidi Saiyad's Mosque
26 Central Telegraph Office
27 Bhadra Fort
28 State Bank of India
29 Lal Darwaja
   (Local Bus Stand)
31 Ahmed Shah's Mosque
32 SEWA Headquarters
   & Emporium
34 Rani Sipri's Mosque
35 STC Bus Stand

GUJARAT

Tiny, windowless but fairly clean singles/doubles cost Rs 125/195, or Rs 275/350 with air-con.

Places to Stay – Mid-Range

Hotel Sahil (☎ 550 6265) is the best-value mid-range place. It's back from the road, opposite the Advance Cinema, and has a range of reasonably neat rooms with TV. Prices are from Rs 225/325, or Rs 350/400 with air-con. This place prides itself on its 'Zero bacteria drinking water'.

Hotel Mayur (☎ 535 0933, *Ramanlal Sheth Rd)* is a similar standard and costs from Rs 225/300, or Rs 400/450 with air-con.

Nearby, *Hotel Balwas* (☎ 550 7135, *Relief Rd)* has smallish rooms from Rs 250/350, or Rs 325/400 with air-con, all with hot water and TV. Rooms in the main building are nicer but more expensive.

Hotel Kingsway (☎ 550 1215, fax 550 5271, *Ramanlal Sheth Rd)* has very well-appointed rooms from Rs 450/600, or Rs 650/800 with air-con.

A little north, beyond the main post office, is *Hotel Alka* (☎ 550 0830, *Ramanlal Sheth Rd)*, a clean, friendly place with rooms starting at Rs 300/440.

Hotel Good Night (☎ 550 7181, *Dr Tankaria Rd)* has decent rooms from Rs 300/400, or Rs 400/475 with air-con.

Hotel Capri (☎ 550 7143, fax 550 6646, *Relief Rd)*, also in this area, has slightly better rooms for Rs 425/500, or Rs 500/575 with air-con.

Hotel Sarita (☎ 550 1569) is in a reasonably quiet, residential area close to the Indian Airlines office. Smallish, fairly modern rooms cost Rs 300/350, or Rs 400/450 with air-con.

Ambassador Hotel (☎ 550 2490, fax 550 2327, *Khanpur Rd)*, near the Sabarmati River, has a range of rooms from Rs 350/450 to Rs 500/600 for a deluxe air-con room.

Along the road, *Hotel Stay Inn* (☎ 550 3993) has singles/doubles starting at Rs 270/320, or Rs 350/410 with air-con, some with balcony.

Toran Guest House (☎ 755 9342, *Ashram Rd)* is a government-run place opposite the Gandhi Ashram. Very clean rooms cost Rs 325/500, or Rs 525/750 with air-con. Breakfast is included, and prices drop 20% Monday to Friday.

Places to Stay – Top End

Holiday Inn Ahmedabad (☎ 550 5505, fax 550 5501, email holiday.ahd@sml, *Khanpur Rd)*, is unbeatable in terms of luxury. Sumptuous rooms range from Rs 4100/4600 to a dizzying Rs 9000 for a suite. The tariff (which is negotiable) includes a buffet breakfast. Amenities include an indoor swimming pool, jacuzzi, sauna, 24 hour coffee shop and restaurant.

Further north, *Cama Hotel* (☎ 550 5281, fax 550 5285, *Khanpur Rd)* has large, comfortable rooms for Rs 1700/3100. There's a restaurant, coffee shop, pool, bookshop and big, grassy garden.

On the west bank, *Hotel Westend* (☎ 656 2627, fax 655 0999, *Mangaldas Rd)* has classy rooms from Rs 1350/1750 and a courtesy airport service.

Round the corner is the five star *Inder Residency* (☎ 656 5222, fax 656 0407, email inder@ad1.vsnl.net.in), with a pool, health club and other luxuries. Rooms start at Rs 2700/3400, including breakfast.

Places to Eat

Ahmedabad is a good place to sample a Gujarati thali. Many places offer all-you-can-eat thalis which make a cheap and very satisfying meal.

At the bottom end of the scale there's excellent *Muslim (nonveg) street food* available near Teen Darwaja on Bhathiyar Gali, a small street which runs parallel to Gandhi Rd, around the corner from the Hotel Ashiana. Stalls set up each evening and for around Rs 25 you can get a good feed. There are meat, fish and vegetarian dishes to choose from. To get to this area, you'll have to walk through the live poultry market, where prospective chicken dishes are blissfully unaware of the fate which lies just a few metres away.

Gopi Dining Hall, just off the west end of Ellis Bridge, near VS Hospital, is one of the most popular thali places. Excellent all-you-can-eat Gujarati thalis are Rs 45 (lunch) or Rs 55 (dinner).

Cona Restaurant, opposite the Advance Cinema, is a good place for cheap vegetarian food.

The *Food Inn* of Hotel Good Night has Chinese and Indian cuisine for about Rs 20 to Rs 50, including 'choiceable chicken' and 'eatEble mutton'. The standard is good and the place gets busy.

Sankalp Restaurant, off Ashram Rd near Dinesh Hall in the Embassy Market area, is worth a visit. This air-con restaurant boasts one of the longest dosas in India – 4ft long! (Rs 301). The Rs 40 South Indian thalis also make a pleasant change from the sweet Gujarati cuisine.

Vishalla (☎ 403357), on the southern edge of town in Vasana, is a 'theme' dining experience that evokes the atmosphere of a Gujarat village. You eat in Indian fashion, seated on the floor in rustic wooden huts, and within the complex there are craft stalls, a puppet display and the Utensils Museum (see Museums earlier in this section). Lunch (11 am to 2 pm) costs Rs 125; dinner (7.30 to 11 pm) is Rs 188 and is accompanied by music and dance performances. The food is a set, veg-only all-you-can-eat meal, though dessert costs extra! Bus No 31 will get you within walking distance; an auto-rickshaw from the centre of town will cost Rs 30, but expect to pay about Rs 50 for the return trip.

Mirch Masala (CG Rd) evokes a Gujarat village with the aid of colourful murals. Veg/nonveg dishes start at Rs 75/90 and it's so popular you may have to queue in the evening.

For a splurge, head to the top hotels. Holiday Inn's *Waterfall Restaurant* is plush but affordable (main courses from Rs 95); Cama Hotel's *Aabodaana Restaurant* is slightly cheaper and has a different style of live music each night.

Shopping

On Ashram Rd, just to the south of the tourist office, is the Gujarat state crafts emporium, Gurjari. For some hand-printed fabrics and other textiles, the Self-Employed Women's Association (SEWA; see the SEWA boxed text) has two retail outlets: 8 Chandan Complex, near Mirch Masala Restaurant, and at the eastern end of Ellis Bridge, opposite the Victoria Gardens (open 10 am to 6.30 pm, closed Sunday). The headquarters is adjacent to the latter, and visitors are welcome.

Getting There & Away

Air Ahmedabad airport has international and domestic services. Air India (☎ 658 5644), Premchand House, near the High Court building on Ashram Rd, has direct flights to the UK and the USA.

Indian Airlines (☎ 550 3061) is on Relief Rd, near the Nehru Bridge. It has flights from Ahmedabad to Mumbai at least daily (US$75); connections to Goa twice a week), and twice-daily flights to Delhi (US$120). Other destinations are Bangalore (US$200, three times weekly) and Chennai (Madras; US$220, three times weekly).

Jet Airways (☎ 754 3304), Ashram Rd, has flights twice daily to Mumbai (US$75) and once daily to Delhi (US$120).

Bus Buses to Gandhinagar (Rs 9) depart every 15 minutes from Lal Darwaja or one of the numerous stops on Ashram Rd.

Plenty of buses operate around Gujarat that also travel to neighbouring states. The Gujarat State Transport Corporation (STC; ☎ 214 4764) buses are a bit battered, but reasonably reliable. Destinations include Vadodara (Rs 30, 2½ hours), Palitana (five hours), Jamnagar (eight hours) and Rajkot (6½ hours). STC buses leave from the station near the Rani Sipri's mosque.

If you're travelling long distance, private minibuses are a more expensive but much quicker alternative; many of their offices are just east of the STC bus stand. Punjab Travels (☎ 658 9200), Embassy Market, just off Ashram Rd and near Gujarat Tourism, has a number of intercity services, including: Ajmer (Rs 160, 13 hours) and Jaipur (Rs 160, 16 hours) at 5.30 pm; Mumbai at 8 pm (Rs 150, 15 hours); Mt Abu at 8 am and 10

SEWA

The Self-Employed Women's Association, more commonly known by its acronym, SEWA, is Gujarat's single largest union, comprising 211,000 members in India – 159,000 in Gujarat alone. Established in 1972, SEWA identifies three types of self-employed workers: hawkers and vendors, who sell their wares from carts, baskets or small shops; home-based workers such as weavers, potters and bidi rollers; and manual labourers and service providers such as agricultural labourers, contract labourers, construction workers, and laundry and domestic workers. More than 94% of women and 93% of all workers in India fall into one of these 'unorganised' fields of labour.

Adhering to a Gandhian philosophy of change through non-violent means, SEWA embodies three movements: the labour movement; the co-operative movement; and the women's movement. The aim of the organisation is to enable women to actively participate in the mainstream economy and to attain empowerment through financial autonomy. Self-employment is the keystone of the organisation and SEWA aims to assist its members by raising the profile of women in the social and political arenas. SEWA assists self-employed workers to organise into unions and cooperatives, so they can ultimately control the fruits of their own labours. Policies and programs are implemented in an endeavour to reflect the experience, needs and realities of the self-employed.

SEWA has also set up a bank, giving many poor women their first access to a savings or lending body, since conventional banks are often unwilling to deal with people of such limited means.

The two main goals of the movement are full employment and self-reliance, and their fulfilment is based on policies focusing on areas such as health and child care, literacy, appropriate housing and self-sufficiency. Membership costs Rs 5 per annum, and SEWA is active in the campaign for a needs-based minimum wage of Rs 125 per day.

pm (Rs 120, seven hours); and Udaipur at 9.30 pm (Rs 100, eight hours).

Punjab Travels has another office in the Shefali Shopping Centre, 2.5km to the south on Pritamnagar Rd. In the same centre Bonny Travels (☎ 657 6712), serves Jamnagar (Rs 95) and Rajkot (Rs 70).

Train There is a computerised booking office to the left as you exit Ahmedabad train station. It's open Monday to Saturday 8 am to 8 pm, Sunday 8 am to 2 pm. Window No 6 handles the foreign tourist quota.

Getting Around

To/From the Airport The airport is 10km north of town; an auto-rickshaw costs about Rs 90. A cheaper option is a local bus from Lal Darwaja (Rs 5, bus No 102 or 105).

Local Transport Ahmedabad's traffic is even more chaotic than most other Indian cities. Most auto-rickshaw drivers are willing to use the meter (it's the dial by their left knee); make sure they set it to zero at the outset. On arrival, ask to see the fare adjustment card; as this is in Gujarati it pays to learn the Gujarati numbers. At the time of research, 100 units on the dial equalled Rs 20. Travelling from Ahmedabad train station to Sidi Saiyad's mosque costs about Rs 10, though drivers will quote much more.

The local bus stand is known as Lal Darwaja, and it's just west of Bhadra Fort. Details of the routes, destinations and fares are all posted in Gujarati; for inquiries call ☎ 533 2911. Routes may change if the proposed ring roads are introduced.

Major Trains from Ahmedabad

destination	train no & name	departure time	distance (km)	duration	fare (Rs) (2nd/1st)
Vadodara (Baroda)	2010 *Shatabdi Exp*	2.45 pm	100	1 h 30 min	200/400
Bhavnagar	9910 *Shetrunji Exp*	5.10 pm	299	5 h 30 min	73/361
Gandhidham (for Bhuj)	9031 *Kutch Exp*	2.00 am	300	6 h 25 min	73/361
Dwarka	9005 *Saurashtra Mai*	6.15 am	453	10 h	102/500
Delhi	9105 *Delhi Mail*	10.00 am	938	19 h 20 min	169/821
Mumbai	2902 *Gujarat Mail*	10.00 pm	92	8 h 50 min	107/531
Udaipur	9944 *Sarai Rohila Exp*	11.00 pm	297	9 h 5 min	73/361

GUJARAT

AROUND AHMEDABAD

Sarkhej

The suburb of Sarkhej, 8km south-west of Ahmedabad, is noted for its elegant group of buildings, including the **Mausoleum of Azam & Mu'assam**, built in 1457 by the brothers responsible for Sarkhej's architecture. The architecture is interesting because the style is almost purely Hindu, with little of the Saracenic influence so evident in Ahmedabad.

As you enter Sarkhej, you pass the **Mausoleum of Mahmud Begara** and, beside the tank and connected to his tomb, that of his queen, Rajabai (1461). Also by the tank is the **Tomb of Ahmad Khattu Ganj Buksh**, a renowned Muslim saint and spiritual adviser to Ahmed Shah. The saint is said to have died in 1445 at the age of 111. Next to this is a fine mosque. Like the other buildings, it is notable for the complete absence of arches, a usual feature of Muslim architecture. The palace, with pavilions and a harem, is also around the tank.

The Dutch established a factory in Sarkhej in 1620 to process the indigo that is grown here.

To get to Sarkhej from Ahmedabad, take bus No 31 from Lal Dawaja.

Batwa

Ten kilometres south-east of Ahmedabad (take bus No 14), the suburb of Batwa has tombs of a noted Muslim saint (himself the son of another saint) and the saint's son. Batwa also has an important mosque.

Adalaj Wav

Nineteen kilometres north of Ahmedabad, Adalaj Wav is one of the finest of the Gujarati step-wells, with carvings depicting intricate motifs of flowers and birds. Built by Queen Rudabai in 1499 it provided a cool and secluded retreat during the hot summer months. The Ahmedabad-Gandhinagar bus will get you within walking distance (ask the conductor where to get off).

Nal Sarovar Bird Sanctuary

Between November and February, this 116 sq km lake, 60km south-west of Ahmedabad, is home to flocks of indigenous and migratory birds. Ducks, geese, pelicans and flamingos are best seen early in morning and in the evening; the sanctuary is best visited as a day excursion by taxi, as buses are infrequent and there is no convenient accommodation. One visitor had the following advice.

You can hire a boat on Nal Sarovar with someone to punt you to the areas where the flamingos and pelicans are; but please avoid going too close and try to restrain the boatman from scaring the birds, as this causes them to fly away. One of the main reasons for the decline in population of some birds is excessive human disturbance. If possible, avoid weekends and holidays when it gets quite crowded.

Krys Kazmierczak, UK

GUJARAT

Lothal

About 85km south-west of Ahmedabad, and towards Bhavnagar, this important archaeological site was discovered in 1954. The city that stood here 4500 years ago is clearly related to the Indus Valley cities of Mohenjodaro and Harappa, both in Pakistan. It has the same neatly laid-out street pattern, the same carefully assembled brickwork and the same scientific drainage system.

The name Lothal actually means Mound of the Dead in Gujarati, as does Mohenjodaro in Sindhi. Excavations have revealed a dockyard – at its peak, this was probably one of the most important ports on the subcontinent. Seals discovered at the site suggest that trade may have been conducted with the civilisations of Mesopotamia, Egypt and Persia.

The **archaeological museum** at the site displays jewellery, pots and other finds (open 10 am to 5 pm, closed Sunday).

Accommodation is a problem in Lothal, though there is the expensive *Utelia Palace*, 7km from the archaeological site, by the Bhugavo River.

Lothal is a long day trip from Ahmedabad (at least three hours travel each way). You can reach it by rail, disembarking at Bhurkhi on the Ahmedabad to Bhavnagar railway line, from where you can take a bus.

Mehesena

Two hours and 68km north of Ahmedabad by rail, Mehesana is of interest merely as a possible base for visiting sites like Modhera and Patan (buses every 30 minutes). There are a few cheap hotels around the bus stand and the train station, including *Hotel Apsara* and *Hotel Natraj*.

Modhera

The beautiful and partially ruined **Sun Temple of Modhera** was built by King Bhimdev I (1026-27) and bears some resemblance to the later, and far better known, Sun Temple of Konark in the state of Orissa, which it predates by some 200 years. Like that temple, it was designed so that the dawn sun shone on the image of Surya, the sun god,

at the time of the equinoxes. The main hall and shrine are reached through a pillared porch and the temple exterior is intricately and delicately carved. As with the Temple of Somnath, this fine temple was ruined by Mahmud of Ghazni. The temple is open daily from 8 am to 6 pm.

Accommodation can pose a real problem here. There are a few cheap rest houses but foreigners often find it difficult to get a bed at them.

Modhera is 102km north-west of Ahmedabad. There are direct buses (Rs 30, 3½ hours), or you can take the train to Mehesana and then catch a bus for the 26km trip to Modhera.

Unjha & Sidhpur

A little north of Mahesana and a base for those visiting the Modhera Temple, the town of Unjha is known for the marriage customs of the Kadwakanbis who live in this region. Marriages occur only once every 11 years and, on that day, every unmarried girl over 40 days old must be wed. If no husband can be found, a proxy wedding takes place and the bride immediately becomes a 'widow'. She later remarries when a suitable husband shows up.

There are a number of private guest houses at Unjha.

About 10km north of Unjha is Sidhpur where you'll find the very fragmented ruins of an ancient temple. This region was an important centre for growing opium poppies.

Patan

About 130km north-west of Ahmedabad, this was an ancient Hindu capital before it was sacked by Mahmud of Ghazni in 1024. Now a pale shadow of its former self, it still has more than 100 **Jain temples** and is famous for its beautifully designed patola **silk saris**. There's also the renovated **Rani-ki-Vav**, a step-well which boasts some of Gujarat's finest carvings. It's very impressive and certainly warrants a visit if you're in this area.

Try looking for cheap accommodation near the bus stand and the train station.

Patan is 25km north-west of Mahesana. Buses from Ahmedabad take 3½ hours and cost Rs 40.

GANDHINAGAR
☎ 82 from Ahmedabad, ☎ 02712 from elsewhere • pop 380,000

Although Ahmedabad became the capital of Gujarat state when the old state of Mumbai was split, a new capital was planned 32km north-east on the west bank of the Sabarmati River. Named Gandhinagar after Gujarat-born Mahatma Gandhi, it is India's second planned city after Chandigarh and, like that city, is laid out in rather dull, numbered sectors. Le Corbusier designed Chandigarh and also had a hand in the construction of Gandhinagar, which commenced in 1965. The secretariat was moved here in 1970.

Gandhinagar's sole tourist sight is the splendid **Akshardham Temple** of the Hindu Swaminarayan sect, constructed out of 6000 tonnes of pink sandstone. It's on Ja Rd in Sector 20.

The *Youth Hostel (☎ 22364, Sector 16)*, has Rs 40 beds and offers cheap meals.

Hotel Haveli (☎ 23905, fax 24057, Sector 11) is a more upmarket option. Rooms are from Rs 1250 to Rs 2000, and there's a good restaurant here. Checkout is noon.

Getting There & Away
Buses from Ahmedabad cost Rs 9 (1 hour). They leave from Lal Darwaja, or from one of the numerous stops along Ashram Rd.

VADODARA (Baroda)
☎ 0265 • pop 1.8 million

Baroda was the capital of the princely Gaekwad state prior to Independence. Today Vadodara (or Baroda, as it is still generally known) is a pleasant, medium-sized city with some interesting museums and art galleries and a fine park. The city's Fine Arts College attracts students from around the country and abroad.

Orientation & Information
The train station, bus stand and a cluster of cheaper hotels are all on the west side of the Vishwarmurti River, which bisects the city. The state tourist office, Gujarat Tourism (☎ 427489) is on the ground floor of Narmada Bhavan, on Jail Rd. It's open daily from 10.30 am to 6 pm Monday to Saturday. There's also a Municipal Tourist Office (☎ 794456) opposite the train station, open 9.30 am to 6 pm daily. Pick up the useful *Know Vadodara* booklet here (Rs 25). Tilak Rd connects the station with the main part of town. The State Bank of India on Tilak Rd changes money, and the Bank of Baroda on RC Dutt Rd (west of the station) gives Visa cash advances.

Sayaji Bagh
This extensive park, encircled by a mini-railway, is a popular spot for an evening stroll. Within the park are several attractions. The most important is the **Baroda Museum & Art Gallery**, open daily from 10 am to 5 pm (Rs 1). The museum has some good Indian statues and carvings, but there's also zoology exhibits and an Egyptian room; the gallery has Mughal miniatures and a mediocre collection of European masters. The **planetarium** gives demonstrations at 5 pm (English) and 6 pm (Hindi); it's open Friday to Wednesday and entry costs Rs 5. The small **zoo** is open 9 am to 5 pm Friday to Wednesday (Rs 5). There's also a health museum (free).

Maharaja Fateh Singh Museum
South of the centre, this royal art collection includes copies of European works by Raphael, Titian and Murillo and examples of Greco-Roman, Chinese and Japanese art, as well as Indian exhibits. The museum, in the palace grounds, is open Tuesday to Sunday from 10.30 am to 5.30 pm. Entry costs Rs 10.

Other Attractions
The **Laxmi Vilas Palace** has a large collection of armour and sculptures and although not normally open to the public, foreigners can usually visit by making an advance booking (☎ 431819) and paying the whopping Rs 100 entry fee. The **Naulakhi Well**, a fine baoli, is 50m north of the palace.

GUJARAT

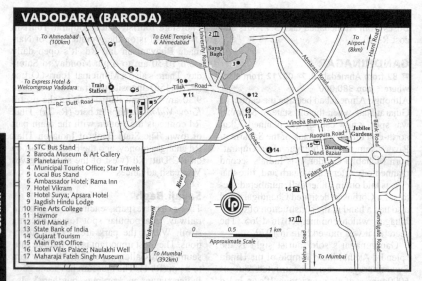

VADODARA (BARODA)

To Ahmedabad (100km)

To EME Temple & Ahmedabad

To Airport (8km)

To Express Hotel & Welcomgroup Vadodara

Train Station

Tilak Road

RC Dutt Road

Sayaji Bagh

University Road

Harni Road

Atmaram Road

Vinoba Bhave Road

Raopura Road

Jubilee Gardens

Bank Road

Jail Road

Dandi Bazaar

Sursagar

Palace Road

River Vishwamitri

To Mumbai (392km)

Nehru Road

Gendigate Road

To Mumbai

0   0.5   1 km
Approximate Scale

1 STC Bus Stand
2 Baroda Museum & Art Gallery
3 Planetarium
4 Municipal Tourist Office; Star Travels
5 Local Bus Stand
6 Ambassador Hotel; Rama Inn
7 Hotel Vikram
8 Hotel Surya; Apsara Hotel
9 Jagdish Hindu Lodge
10 Fine Arts College
11 Havmor
12 Kirti Mandir
13 State Bank of India
14 Gujarat Tourism
15 Main Post Office
16 Laxmi Vilas Palace; Naulakhi Well
17 Maharaja Fateh Singh Museum

About 5km north of the town centre is the unusual **EME Temple**, a Hindu temple with an aluminium domed roof.

Organised Tours

The Municipal Tourist Office conducts city tours every Tuesday, Wednesday and Friday from 2 to 6 pm (Rs 25; book in advance). Ask at Gujarat Tourism about day trips that include the surrounding region.

Places to Stay – Budget

Vadodara has limited budget options.

Jagdish Hindu Lodge (☎ 361495) is in the Sayaji Gunj district near the train station. It has fairly gloomy rooms arranged around a scruffy courtyard. Singles/doubles with bathroom cost Rs 60/85.

Hotel Vikram (☎ 361918) is in the same street but a notch upmarket. It offers rooms with private cold-water bath for Rs 165/250, or Rs 220/350 with air-con.

Apsara Hotel (☎ 362345) is in the next street west. It's a well-maintained place with rooms for Rs 180/240 with bathroom (bucket hot water).

Places to Stay – Mid-Range & Top End

All rooms in this class have colour TV, bathroom and hot water.

Ambassador Hotel (☎ 362726) is opposite the Apsara. There are large, quiet singles/doubles from Rs 200/330, or Rs 455/555 with air-con.

Next door, *Rama Inn* (☎ 362381) underwent extensive renovations in 1998. It has rooms for Rs 550/725, or Rs 775/1100 with air-con. There's also a swimming pool and restaurant.

Hotel Surya (☎ 361361) opposite, has less in the way of facilities but offers a courtesy coach to the airport. Rooms (including breakfast) go for Rs 425/650, or Rs 650/900 with air-con.

Express Hotel (☎ 337001, RC Dutt Rd), about 1.5km west of the train station, has air-con rooms for Rs 950/1250. There's a coffee shop and two restaurants.

Just along the road, *Welcomgroup Vadodara* (☎ 330033, fax 330050) is the most luxurious hotel in town. Well-appointed singles/doubles start from Rs 2000/3300, all rooms have air-con. There's also a travel counter, swimming pool, 24 hour coffee shop and excellent Indian restaurant.

Places to Eat

Havmor (*Tilak Rd*), near the river, offers reasonable Indian, Continental and Chinese food. Veg/nonveg main courses are Rs 55 to Rs 125. This road also has ice cream parlours.

Hotel Surya has two restaurants: *Vega*, where help-yourself buffets cost Rs 75, and *Myra* where excellent and filling Gujarati thalis also cost Rs 75.

Ruchika at the Welcomgroup Vadodara hotel, is recommended for a special treat. It serves scrumptious veg and nonveg Indian cuisine in pleasant surroundings. Be prepared to fork out a couple of hundred rupees to dine here. Otherwise try its coffee shop where the fare is cheaper.

Getting There & Away

Air The airport is 8km north-east of the train station. Indian Airlines (☎ 794747) has daily flights from Vadodara to Mumbai (US$70) and Delhi (US$135). Jet Airways (☎ 343441) has daily flights to Mumbai, while Gujarat Airways (☎ 330864) services Mumbai (three times a week), Pune (daily except Sunday) and Ahmedabad (three times a week).

Bus The long-distance bus stand is 400m north of the train station, and there are STC buses to many destinations in Gujarat, western Madhya Pradesh and northern Maharashtra. Buses to Ahmedabad leave at least every 30 minutes (Rs 30, 2½ hours).

Private companies have offices nearby.

Train Vadodara is 100km south of Ahmedabad (Rs 32/173 in 2nd/1st class, two hours) and 392km north of Mumbai (Rs 90/455, six hours). Because this is a main route there are plenty of trains to choose from. Travel agents opposite the station (eg Star Travels) will reserve train tickets for a small fee.

Between Vadodara and Ahmedabad you pass through **Anand**, noted for its dairy produce. At the station, hordes of vendors selling bottles of cold milk often besiege passing trains.

AROUND VADODARA
Champaner (Pavagadh)

This city, 47km north-east of Vadodara, was taken by Sultan Mahmud Begara in 1484, and he renamed it Muhammadabad. The **Jama Masjid** here is one of the finest mosques in Gujarat and is similar in style to the Jama Masjid of Ahmedabad.

The **Hill of Pavagadh**, with its ruined fort, rises beside Champaner in three levels. In 1553 the Mughals, led by Humayun himself, scaled the fort walls using iron spikes driven into the rocks, and captured both the fort and its city. Parts of the massive fort walls still stand. According to Hindu legend, the hill is actually a chunk of the Himalayan mountainside which the monkey god Hanuman carted off to Lanka in an episode of the *Ramayana*, hence the name Pavagadh, which means Quarter of a Hill.

In the month of Chaitra (March/April), a major festival takes place at the foot of Pavagadh Hill, honouring the goddess Mahakali.

Hotel Champaner (☎ 02676-45641) is run by Gujarat Tourism. Dorm beds cost Rs 75 per person and singles/doubles are Rs 100/150, or Rs 400/450 with air-con.

The trip from Vadodara takes 1½ hours: take a frequent bus to Halol then a minibus to Champaner.

Dabhoi

The 13th century walled town of Dabhoi is 29km south-east of Vadodara (buses every 15 minutes from the STC bus stand). A fine example of Hindu military architecture, it is notable for the design of its four gateways – particularly the Hira, or Diamond Gate.

Dakor

Equidistant from Vadodara and Ahmedabad, the Temple of Ranchodrai in Dakor is sacred to Krishna and is a major centre for the Sharad Purnima festival in October/November.

Buses run from Ahmedabad (Rs 26, 2½ hours).

GUJARAT

BHARUCH (Broach)
• pop 213,000

This very old town was mentioned in historical records nearly 2000 years ago. It's on the main rail line between Vadodara and Surat, about one hour from each place. The **fort** overlooks the wide Narmada River from a hilltop and at its base is the **Jama Masjid**. On the riverbank, east of the city, is the **Temple of Bhrigu Rishi**, from which the city took its name, Bhrigukachba, later shortened to Bharuch. There are places to stay near the train station.

The Narmada River has featured in the news both locally and internationally due to the construction of a large dam, the Sardar Sarovar, upstream of Bharuch near the village of Manibeli (see the Temples of Doom boxed text in the Facts about India chapter).

SURAT
☎ 0261 • pop 2.3 million

Surat stands on the banks of the Tapti River and was once one of western India's major ports and trading towns. Parsis first settled in Surat in the 12th century. In 1573 Surat fell to Akbar after a prolonged siege. It then became an important Mughal trading port and also the point of departure for Mecca-bound Muslim pilgrims.

Surat soon became a wealthy city. In 1612, the British established a trading factory, followed by the Dutch in 1616 and the French in 1664.

Surat is no longer an important port, though it is a major industrial centre, especially for the manufacture of textiles and chemicals, and the processing and finishing of diamonds. But the city is probably best known these days as the site of an outbreak of pneumonic plague in 1994; at this time it was rated as the filthiest city in India.

Since then it has apparently transformed itself into India's second cleanest and healthiest city (after Chandigarh). However, a brief acquaintance with the horrific noise, pollution and chaos of the traffic around the train station will make you question this statistic.

Despite its industrial importance Surat is of little interest to travellers.

Things to See & Do

Built in 1546 by the Sultan of Gujarat, the **castle** is on the riverbank, beside the Tapti Bridge. Since most of it has been given over to offices it is no longer of great interest, but there is a good view over the city and river from its bastions. To get there, ask for the Tapti Bridge.

The now very run-down, overgrown and neglected **English cemetery** is just beyond the Kataragama Gate, to the right of the main road. About 500m after the Kataragama Gate, you'll find the **Dutch cemetery**. There's a massive mausoleum of Baron Adriaan van Reede, who died in 1691. Adjoining the Dutch cemetery is the **Armenian cemetery**.

Surat has a number of mosques and Jain, Hindu and Parsi temples.

Places to Stay – Budget

Immediately to the left of the train station are various noisy, fairly grotty hotels.

Rupali Guest House (☎ 423874) is in the rock-bottom bracket and is very basic. It has dorm beds for Rs 40, doubles with bathroom for Rs 150 and singles with shared bath for Rs 80.

Simla Guest House (☎ 442339) is better but still unremarkable. It has doubles with bath for Rs 200 and singles with shared bath for Rs 100.

Sarvajanik Hotel (☎ 426159) is at the top end of this category, with singles/doubles with bath for Rs 185/275.

Places to Stay – Mid-Range & Top End

Hotel Central Excellency (☎ 425325, fax 441271) is opposite the train station. It has rooms with private bath and TV from Rs 550/700, with air-con from Rs 850/1050. There's also a restaurant.

Hotel Yuvraj (☎ 413001, Station Rd) nearby is another mid-range place with two vegetarian restaurants. Rooms have air-con and start at Rs 850/1050. More expensive rooms come with a car for free sightseeing. **Embassy Hotel** (☎ 443170, fax 443173, Station Rd) next door is newer and slightly pricier.

Rates at the above three places include breakfast.

Holiday Inn Hotel (☎ *226565, fax 227294*), near Bharti Park in Athwa Lines, 6km from the city centre, is Surat's finest hotel. Air-con rooms with plenty of buttons and switches are Rs 3275/4300. Facilities include a swimming pool, health club, coffee shop and restaurant.

Places to Eat

Sher-e-Punjab, next to the Hotel Central Excellency, offers good veg/nonveg Punjabi and Chinese dishes from around Rs 30.

Holiday Inn Hotel has a fine restaurant serving delicious (though pricey) Indian food. For something cheaper there's also a coffee shop in this hotel that serves a buffet dinner for Rs 250.

Getting There & Away

Surat is on the main Mumbai to Ahmedabad railway line. The 263km trip to Mumbai takes between 4½ and 6½ hours and costs Rs 66/322 in 2nd/1st class. To Ahmedabad, the 229km trip takes from 3½ to 4½ hours and costs Rs 61/286.

AROUND SURAT

There are a number of beaches near Surat. Only 16km away, **Dumas** is a popular resort with locals. **Hajira** is 28km from the city and **Ubhrat** is 42km out, while **Tithal** is 108km away and only 5km from Valsad on the Mumbai-Vadodara train line.

Twenty-nine kilometres south of Surat, **Navsari** has been a headquarters for the Parsi community since the earliest days of their settlement in India. **Udvada**, only 10km north of Vapi, the station for Daman, has the oldest Parsi sacred fire in India. It is said that the fire was brought from Persia to Diu, on the opposite coast of the Gulf of Cambay, in 700 AD. **Sanjan**, in the extreme south of the state, is the small port where the Parsis first landed. A pillar marks the spot.

In the week preceding Holi (February/March), the Adivasi have a major festival in the forested region called The Dangs, east of Surat near the Maharashtra border – it's known as the Dang Durbar.

Holiday Homes abound on the coast, so if you want to stay overnight, ask around.

DAMAN
☎ 02638 • pop 90,000

Right in the south of Gujarat, the 56 sq km enclave of Daman was, along with Diu and Goa, taken from the Portuguese in 1961. For a time, Daman and Diu were governed from Goa but both now constitute the Union Territory of Daman and Diu, which is governed from Delhi. Daman (population 40,000) is a laid back little town with a somewhat tropical flavour, although its beaches are rather drab and dirty.

Daman's main role now seems to be as a place to buy alcohol, since the surrounding state of Gujarat is completely 'dry'. The streets of Daman are lined with bars selling beer, 'Finest Scotch Whisky – Made in India' and various other spirits such as *feni* (distilled from fermented cashew nuts or coconuts). You are forbidden to take alcohol out of Daman into Gujarat unless you obtain a permit. There are police checks as you leave Daman and alcohol without a permit will be confiscated.

The Portuguese seized Daman in 1531 and were officially ceded the region by Bahadur Shah, the last major Gujarati sultan, in 1559. There's still a lingering Portuguese flavour to the town, with its fine old forts and churches, but it's definitely not a smaller version of Goa. The town is divided by the Daman Ganga River. The northern section is known as Nani Daman, or Little Daman, with hotels, restaurants, bars and so on. In the southern part, known as Moti Daman, or Big Daman, government buildings and churches are enclosed within an imposing wall.

Information

The tourist office (☎ 55104) near the bus stand is open Monday to Friday from 9.30 am to 1.30 pm and 2.30 to 6 pm.

No bank changes money, but Executive Travels & Tours, in the arcade below Hotel

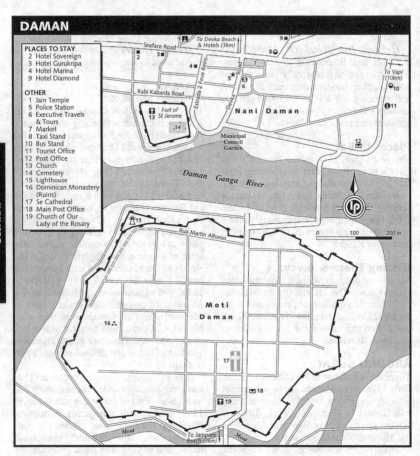

DAMAN

PLACES TO STAY
2 Hotel Sovereign
3 Hotel Gurukripa
4 Hotel Marina
9 Hotel Diamond

OTHER
1 Jain Temple
5 Police Station
6 Executive Travels & Tours
7 Market
8 Taxi Stand
10 Bus Stand
11 Tourist Office
12 Post Office
13 Church
14 Cemetery
15 Lighthouse
16 Dominican Monastery (Ruins)
17 Se Cathedral
18 Main Post Office
19 Church of Our Lady of the Rosary

Maharaja, changes travellers cheques at only 50 paise below the bank rate. The main post office is south of the river in Moti Daman, but there's a more convenient branch in Nani Daman near the bridge.

Nani Daman

You can walk around the ramparts of the **Nani Daman Fort** (Fort of St Jerome). They're a good place from which to watch the fish market and small fishing fleet which anchors alongside.

To the north is a **Jain temple**. If you inquire in the temple office, a caretaker should be able to show you around. The walls inside are completely covered with glassed-over 18th century murals depicting the life of Mahavira, who lived around 500 BC.

Moti Daman

It's quite pleasant to wander around the wide streets within the fortified walls. The place has a sleepy atmosphere, and the views across the river to Nani Daman from the ramparts just near the lighthouse are not bad.

The **Se Cathedral** dates from the 17th century and is totally Iberian. It has recently been renovated and looks quite impressive. The **Church of Our Lady of the Rosary**, across the overgrown square, has ancient Portuguese tombstones set into its cool, damp floor. The altar is a masterpiece of intricately carved, gold-painted wood. Light filters through the dusty windows, illuminating wooden panels painted with scenes of Christ and the apostles. If it's closed, check with the vicar of the Se Cathedral for the key.

Beaches

About 3km north of Nani Daman, the rocky shores of Devka beach are none too clean, and nobody swims there. But the ambience of the place is easy-going, and there's a 'tourist complex' containing landscaped walkways and a children's playground. The beach at Jampore is better (but still not that special), about 3km south of Moti Daman. An auto-rickshaw from town to either beach will cost about Rs 25 each way.

Places to Stay

Town Area Most of the cheaper hotels are on Seaface Rd. They are generally pretty basic and uninspiring.

Hotel Marina (☎ 54420), just off Seaface Rd, is one of the few surviving Portuguese-style houses and it's good value. Rooms with bathroom cost Rs 150/175, or Rs 175/200 for deluxe rooms. There's a bar and restaurant downstairs.

Hotel Diamond (☎ 55135), near the taxi stand, is a bit better. Decent rooms with bath cost Rs 200/250, and air-con rooms go for Rs 350/400. There's also a bar and restaurant.

Hotel Gurukripa (☎ 55046, Seaface Rd) has good, if slightly musty, air-con rooms with TV for Rs 475/575. There's a good restaurant here.

Nearby, *Hotel Sovereign* (☎ 55023, fax 54433, Seaface Rd) has been extensively renovated and has good air-con rooms for Rs 550/650.

Beach Area There are lots of decent mid-range places to stay at Devka Beach; these stretch for 1.5km along the main road. All have a restaurant.

Nearest Daman, *Hotel Shilton* (☎ 54558) has a range of rooms starting at Rs 500, or Rs 600 with air-con. There's a garden and prices drop 25% in low season. Next door *Hotel Ashoka Palace* (☎ 54239) charges from Rs 450 and also has negotiable prices.

Hotel Miramar (☎ 54471, fax 54934) is right on the beach. The rooms (all with air-con) start from Rs 700, while a sea-facing cottage costs Rs 1700.

Sandy Resort (☎/fax 54644) is one of the best options. It's a friendly place which boasts a pool, restaurant and disco. Comfortable rooms start from Rs 575, all have air-con.

There's just one place to stay in Jampore Beach: *Hotel China Town* (☎ 54920) has rooms with bathroom and TV for Rs 250/350, or Rs 350/450 with air-con. Its restaurant serves good food.

Places to Eat

The best eating places are in the hotels. In February, Daman is noted for *papri*, boiled and salted sweet peas served wrapped in newspaper. Crab and lobster are in season in October. *Tari* palm wine is a popular drink sold in earthenware pots.

Hotel Gurukripa has a popular air-con restaurant that offers tasty veg and nonveg fare. Most dishes cost above Rs 50.

A Kingfisher beer will set you back only Rs 25 at any of Daman's bars, but most hotels charge Rs 35 or more. If you fancy a drop of port wine, most bars charge about Rs 100 for a bottle.

Getting There & Away

Vapi station, on the main railway line, is the access point for Daman. Vapi is about 170km from Mumbai and 90km from Surat. It's about 10km from Vapi to Daman. Plenty of share taxis (Rs 10 per person) wait outside the train station and leave frequently for Daman. The trip takes about 20 minutes. Also available are some ramshackle buses (Rs 5).

The road from Daman to Surat would have to be one of the most congested in India so expect some delays. It's the major route for trucks travelling between Mumbai and Ahmedabad.

SAPUTARA

This cool hill resort in the south-east corner of the state is at an altitude of 1000m. It's a popular base for excursions to **Mahal Bardipara Forest Wildlife Sanctuary** (60km) or the **Gira Waterfalls** (52km). Saputara means Abode of Serpents and there is a sacred snake image on the banks of the River Sarpagana.

Toran Hill Resort (☎ 02631-37226) offers dorm beds for Rs 50, ordinary rooms for Rs 550, valley-view rooms for Rs 800, and mountain-view rooms for Rs 1600.

State buses run here from Surat.

Saurashtra

The often bleak plains of Saurashtra on the Kathiawar peninsula are inhabited by friendly but reserved people. Those in the country are distinctively dressed – the men wear white turbans, pleated jackets (short-waisted and long-sleeved) and jodhpurs (baggy seat and drainpipe legs) and often sport golden stud earrings. The women are nearly as colourful as the women of Rajasthan and wear embroidered backless cholis, which are known by various names but most commonly as *kanjeri*.

The peninsula took its name from the Kathi tribespeople who used to roam the area at night stealing whatever was not locked into the many *kots* (village forts). Around Kathiawar, you may notice long lines of memorial stones known as *palias* – men are usually depicted riding on large horses while women ride on wheels, showing that they were in carriages.

Although somewhat off the main tourist routes, Saurashtra is pleasant to travel around with very interesting – sometimes spectacular – temple sites and cities to explore, not to mention some beautiful beaches and the Sasan Gir Lion Sanctuary. Bus journeys tend to be slow as many roads are poorly maintained.

BHAVNAGAR
☎ 0278 • pop 750,000

Founded in 1743, Bhavnagar is still an important trading post for cotton goods manufactured in Gujarat. The Bhavnagar lock gate keeps ships afloat in the port at low tide. On the surface, it isn't the most exciting place to visit and few travellers get here. It does, however, have an interesting bazaar area with overhanging wooden balconies, countless little shops, lots of local colour and rarely a tourist in sight.

Orientation & Information

Bhavnagar is a sprawling city with distinctly separate old and new sections. The bus stand is in the new part of town and the train station is at the far end of the old town, around 2.5km away. To complicate matters, private bus companies usually have their own depots; sometimes a long way from the bus stand.

There are a few cheap hotels in the old town, but none around the bus stand. Bank of India in the old town changes cash. Darbargadh is the town centre with shops, banks and hotels.

Things to See

Takhteshwar Temple sits on a small hillock, which is nevertheless high enough to provide good views over the city and out into the Gulf of Cambay. The temple itself is of minor interest.

North-east, by the clock tower, is the **Gandhi Smriti Museum**, with a moderate collection of Gandhi memorabilia and religious statues (free; closed Sunday and the second and fourth Saturday in the month).

For local colour, wander the atmospheric shopping streets in the old town, near the Bank of India.

Places to Stay – Budget

The only cheap hotels in Bhavnagar are in the old bazaar area and there's very little

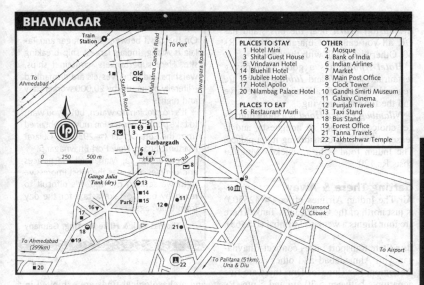

BHAVNAGAR

PLACES TO STAY	OTHER
1 Hotel Mini	2 Mosque
3 Shital Guest House	4 Bank of India
5 Vrindavan Hotel	6 Indian Airlines
14 Bluehill Hotel	7 Market
15 Jubilee Hotel	8 Main Post Office
17 Hotel Apollo	9 Clock Tower
20 Nilambag Palace Hotel	10 Gandhi Smriti Museum
	11 Galaxy Cinema
PLACES TO EAT	12 Punjab Travels
16 Restaurant Murli	13 Taxi Stand
	18 Bus Stand
	19 Forest Office
	21 Tanna Travels
	22 Takhteshwar Temple

GUJARAT

choice. Note that many places add a 10% service tax on their room rates.

Shital Guest House (☎ 428360, Amba Chowk, Mali Tekra), in the middle of the bazaar area, is not a bad choice. Enter through the rear of the building. Simple singles/doubles with shared bathroom cost Rs 65/100, doubles with bathroom cost Rs 120; the best rooms have a balcony. Checkout is 9 am.

Vrindavan Hotel (☎ 518928, Darbargadh), not far from the Shital, is well signposted. Entry is through an archway, then the reception stairs are on the right, and the restaurant on the left. This large, old place has basic but clean singles/doubles with bathroom for Rs 100/150, or there are dorm beds from Rs 35.

The **Hotel Mini** (☎ 24415, Station Rd), located in the Old City, close to the train station, is one of the better of the budget hotels. It's clean and quiet and has single or double rooms from Rs 100/175 with bathroom. The hotel staff are very friendly and there's even a dining hall. Meals need to be pre-ordered.

Places to Stay – Mid-Range & Top End

Hotel Apollo (☎ 245251), directly opposite the bus stand, is the best mid-price deal. It has good rooms with TV for Rs 450/600, or Rs 620/800 with air-con. There are money-changing facilities and the hotel has a good restaurant.

Bluehill Hotel (☎ 426951), down a quiet road from the taxi stand, is well appointed with air-con from Rs 900/1350. There are two veg restaurants.

Jubilee Hotel (☎ 430045) next door is rather rundown nowadays. Sizeable air-con rooms start at Rs 500/700, but don't expect everything to work. Upper storeys have good views of the park opposite.

The **Nilambag Palace Hotel** (☎ 424241, fax 428072), west of the bus stand on the Ahmedabad road. An interesting place to stay – if you can afford it. This former maharaja's palace is not as swish as some other palace hotels, but it's still quite luxurious. Rooms are Rs 1990/3200 in the palace or Rs 1000/1500 in the 'royal cottage'. There's also a swimming pool and restaurant.

Places to Eat

Restaurant Murli near the bus stand has OK all-you-can-eat Gujarati thalis for Rs 60. Otherwise, stick with the hotels.

Hotel Apollo has a good veg/nonveg restaurant; *Bluehill* and *Jubilee Hotels* are veg only. They are all fairly inexpensive and the food is satisfying.

Nilambag Palace Hotel is a more upmarket choice. It's open to nonguests, and is reasonably priced considering it's a palace. The Indian food is best; chicken Mughlai costs Rs 120.

Getting There & Away

Air The Indian Airlines office (☎ 426503) is just north of the Ganga Jalia Tank. There are four flights a week to Mumbai (US$65).

Bus State transport buses connect Bhavnagar with Ahmedabad and other centres in the region. For Una (for Diu) there are five departures between 5.30 am and 5 pm (Rs 50, five hours). To Palitana there are buses every hour from 5 am (Rs 12, 1½ hours). The timetable at the state bus stand in Bhavnagar is entirely in Gujarati.

Private bus companies include Punjab Travels (☎ 424582), opposite the Galaxy Cinema, and Tanna Travels (☎ 420477), nearby. Both offer regular deluxe buses to Ahmedabad (Rs 70, four hours) and one daily bus to Mumbai (Rs 275, 13 hours).

Train Bhavnagar is 299km by rail from Ahmedabad. There are four direct trains daily (5½ hours) and the fare is Rs 97/332 in 2nd/1st class. To Palitana there are three daily trains which cover the 51km in 1½ hours (Rs 10).

Getting Around

An auto-rickshaw to the airport costs around Rs 60.

AROUND BHAVNAGAR
Valabhipur

About 42km north-west of Bhavnagar, this ancient city was once the capital of this part of India. Extensive ruins have been located

---

Alang

On the coast between Bhavnagar and Talaja is Alang, India's largest ship-breaking site. Here supertankers, container ships, warships and other vessels are dismantled – literally by hand – by 20,000 workers day and night.

It's no problem to watch, but if you want to take photos, permission must be obtained from the Port Officer (☎ 293020), Gujarat Maritime Board, New Port Bhavnagar 5.

Despite the Taj Mahal, all the palaces and temples, this was the most impressive sight we saw on our trip. It's difficult to reach by bus, so take a taxi for the day from Bhavnagar.

Thomas Tolk & Hilke Rensing, Germany

---

and archaeological finds are exhibited in a museum, but there's little to see apart from scattered stones.

Velavadar National Park

This park, 65km north of Bhavnagar, is well known for its blackbucks protected within a sanctuary. Blackbucks sport impressive spiralling horns which can be as long as 60cm in mature males. The best time to visit is from October to June. If you want to go there, ask about current regulations at the Forest Office (☎ 0278-426425) near Bhavnagar's bus stand.

Getting there by bus from Bhavagnar is possible (change at Valabhipur), but to visit on a day trip you would need to hire a taxi (no more than Rs 700).

PALITANA
☎ 02848 • pop 46,830

The town of Palitana, 51km south-west of Bhavnagar, is little more than a gateway to Shatrunjaya.

Shatrunjaya

Strewn with 863 temples, the hilltop complex of Shatrunjaya (the Place of Victory) is one of Jainism's holiest pilgrimage sites. The temples were built over a period of 900 years on a hilltop dedicated entirely to the gods; at dusk, even the priests depart from the temples, leaving them deserted.

Almost all the temples are Jain, and this hill demonstrates their belief that merit is derived from constructing temples. The hilltops are bounded by sturdy walls and the temples are grouped into nine *tunks* (enclosures) – each with a central temple with many minor ones clustered around. Some of the earliest temples here were built in the 11th century but were destroyed by Muslims in the 14th and 15th centuries; the current temples date from the 16th century onwards.

The hilltop affords a very fine view in all directions; on a clear day you can see the Gulf of Cambay beyond Bhavnagar. The most notable of the temples is dedicated to **Shri Adishwara**, the first Jain *tirthankar*. Note the frieze of dragons around this temple. Adjacent is the Muslim shrine of **Angar Pir**. Women who want children make offerings of miniature cradles at this shrine.

Built in 1618 by a wealthy Jain merchant, the **Chaumukh**, or Four-Faced shrine, has images of Adinath facing out in the four cardinal directions. Other important temples are those dedicated to Kumar Pal, Sampriti Raj and Vimal Shah.

The temples are open from 6.30 am to 5.30 pm. A photography permit can be purchased for Rs 25 just inside the main entrance. (There are two entrances – the main one is reached by taking the left-hand fork as you near the top of the hill and the other by the right-hand fork.) Shoes should be removed at the entrance to the compound, and leather items, including belts and bags, should not be brought onto the site.

A horse cart to the base of the hill costs Rs 20, or you can walk from the Palitana bus stand in about 30 minutes. The heat can be extreme by late morning, so it's a good idea to start early for the ascent. Water (not bottled) can be bought at intervals, and you can buy refreshing curd in pottery bowls outside the temple compound for Rs 10.

The 600m ascent from the base of the hill to the summit is 2km, up more than 3000 steps. At a moderate pace, the ascent will take about 1½ hours. You can be carried up the hill in a *doli* (rope chair) which costs from Rs 200 to Rs 700 dependent on comfort (the choice of quite a few affluent and obese pilgrims). The most conspicuous sight on first entering the temple compound is that of exhausted doli bearers resting in the shade.

Places to Stay & Eat

Palitana has scores of dharamsalas (pilgrims' rest houses) but unless you're a Jain, you're unlikely to be allowed to stay at any of them.

Gujarat Tourism's *Hotel Sumeru* (☎ 2327, *Station Rd*), 200m towards the train station from the bus stand, is the best choice. Rooms are Rs 350/500, or Rs 525/750 with air-con, and dorm beds are Rs 50. Prices approximately halve from 15 June to 15 September. Its veg restaurant serves Gujarati thalis (Rs 45) as well as Punjabi and Continental dishes.

Hotel Shravak (☎ 2428) opposite the bus stand, has basic singles (shared bath)/doubles/triples (with bathroom) for Rs 200/400/600. Dorm beds (men only) are a pricey Rs 100. Checkout is 24 hours for rooms, 9 am for the dorm.

Across the alley, *Jagruti Restaurant* is a wildly busy 24 hour snack place offering puris, sabzi, curd, roasted peppers and *ganthia* (varieties of fried dough).

Havmor is a popular ice cream parlour on the right as you approach the base of Shatrunjaya.

Getting There & Away

Bus STC buses make the 1½ hour trip to/from Bhavnagar hourly (Rs 10). There are also regular departures for Ahmedabad (Rs 55, five hours).

Infrequent buses go to Talaja, where you can switch to a bus to Una or Diu. The total journey takes about six hours; it's a trip from hell, along bumpy village roads in dilapidated old rattletraps.

Train Sleepy Palitana station is only 800m from the bus stand, heading away from

Shatrunjaya. It only receives trains to/from Bhavagnar (though they stop at Sihor, which has connections to Ahmedabad). They depart Palitana at 9 am, 6.05 pm and 8.30 pm, and depart Bhavnagar at 6.30 am, 2.45 pm and 18.45 pm (Rs 10, 1½ hours).

DIU
☎ 02875 • pop 64,000

Like Daman and Goa, Diu was a Portuguese colony until it was taken over by India in 1961. Along with Daman, it is still governed from Delhi as a Union Territory rather than as part of Gujarat. The former colony includes the island of Diu, about 13km long by 3km wide, separated from the coast by a narrow channel. There are also two tiny mainland enclaves. One of these, where the village of Ghoghla stands, is the entry point to Diu from Una.

Diu's crowning glory in sightseeing terms is its huge fort. The northern side of the island, facing Gujarat, is tidal marsh and saltpans while the southern coast alternates between limestone cliffs, rocky coves and sandy beaches.

The somewhat windswept and arid island is riddled with quarries from which the Portuguese removed vast quantities of limestone to build the fort, city walls, monuments and buildings.

The rocky and sandy interior reaches a maximum height of just 29m, so agriculture is limited although there are extensive stands of coconut and other palms. Branching palms (*Hyphaene* species) are very much a feature of the island and were originally introduced from Africa by the Portuguese.

The island's main industry would have to be fishing, followed by booze and salt. Kalpana Distillery at Malala produces rum from sugar cane. Diu town has many bars where visitors from the 'dry' mainland can enjoy a beer (or stronger IMFL – Indian Made Foreign Liquor).

Diu is a popular hang-out with travellers and you'll probably see more foreigners here than anywhere else in Gujarat. Although the beaches are nothing compared to Goa's, it is still a great place to let your hair down and watch the world drift by. It's well worth the long trek to get here.

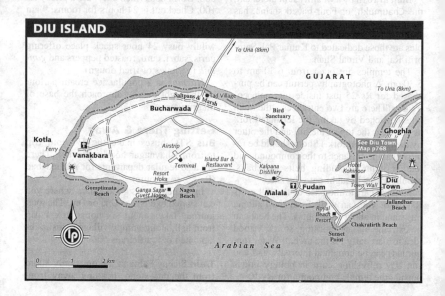

DIU ISLAND

History

Between the 14th and 16th centuries, Diu was an important trading post and naval base from which the Ottoman Turks controlled the shipping routes in the northern part of the Arabian Sea.

Portugal made an unsuccessful attempt to capture the island in 1531, during which Bahadur Shah, the Sultan of Gujarat, was assisted by the Turkish navy. Yet the Portuguese finally secured control in 1535 by taking advantage of a quarrel between the sultan and the Mughal emperor, Humayun. Humayun had defeated Bahadur Shah the previous year and had forced him into exile in Malwa, but while he was distracted by clashes with the Afghan Sher Khan, Bahadur was able to return.

With pressure still being exerted by both the Portuguese and the Mughals, Bahadur concluded a peace treaty with the Portuguese, effectively giving them control over the port at Diu. The treaty was soon cast to the wind and, although both Bahadur Shah and his successor, Sultan Mahmud III, attempted to contest the issue, the peace treaty that was eventually signed in 1539 ceded the island of Diu and the mainland enclave of Ghoghla to Portugal. Soon after the signing of this treaty, the Portuguese began constructing their fort.

The Indian government appears to have an official policy of playing down the Portuguese era. Seven Rajput soldiers (six of them Singhs) and a few civilians were killed in Operation Vijay, which ended Portuguese rule in 1961. After the Indian Air Force unnecessarily bombed the airstrip and terminal near Nagoa, it remained derelict until the late 1980s. The old church in Diu Fort was also bombed and is now a roofless ruin. It's said that the Portuguese blew up Government House to stop it falling into 'enemy' hands.

Orientation & Information

The tourist office (☎ 52212) is on Bunder Rd, the main road that runs through Diu Town parallel to the waterfront. It has transport information and simple (free) maps. The office is open Monday to Friday from 9.30 am to 1.30 pm and 2.30 to 6 pm, and (usually) Saturday from 9.30 am to 1.30 pm.

You can change money at the State Bank of Saurashtra near the town square, but at slightly lower rates than on the mainland. The main post office is on the town square (1st floor, above shops), and there's another post office at Ghoghla.

The Jethibai bus stand, for intercity buses, is just outside the city walls, near the bridge to Ghoghla.

Diu Town

Laid-back Dui Town (population 37,000) was the first landing point for the Parsis when they fled from Persia, although they stayed only three years.

The town is sandwiched between the massive fort to the east and a huge city wall to the west. The main **Zampa Gateway** in the wall has carvings of lions, angels and a priest, while just inside the gate is a miniature chapel with an icon, dating from 1702. Just to the south, outside the wall, is the **Zampa Waterfall**, a strange artificial creation that is lit up at night.

St Paul's is the only church in town still fulfilling its original function. (It's said that there are now only about 15 Christian families left on the whole island.) Though showing signs of neglect, it has fine statues and wooden altars.

Nearby is St Thomas' Church, which houses the **Diu Museum** (free). There's an interesting collection of Catholic statues, including a somewhat disturbing statue of Christ prostrate on a bier, flanked by two angels. If you thought the Hindu pantheon was confusing, take a look at the bewildering collection of Christian saints. The third church is **St Francis of Assisi**, which has been converted into a hospital.

Unlike Daman, the buildings in Diu show a some significant Portuguese influence. The town is a maze of narrow, winding streets and many of the houses are well ornamented and brightly painted. Further away from this tightly packed residential quarter, the streets turn into meandering and often leafy lanes.

GUJARAT

In a small park on the esplanade, between the square and the police station, the **Marwar Memorial**, topped by a griffin, commemorates the liberation of the island from the Portuguese.

Completed in 1541, the massive Portuguese fort with its double moat (one tidal) must once have been virtually impregnable, but sea erosion and neglect are leading to a slow but inevitable collapse. Piles of cannon balls litter the place and the ramparts have a superb array of cannons, many old yet in good condition. A small chapel holds engraved tombstone fragments.

The fort also serves as the island's jail, and it's open daily from 7 am to 6 pm. Entry is free. Photography is allowed.

Around the Island

Beaches Temple and fort-satiated travellers used to head to **Nagoa** to catch up on some serious relaxation. But though it's still a pleasant palm-fringed beach and safe for swimming, it's quite busy nowadays, and western women tend to get unwanted attention from the numerous young, Indian men

hanging around. **Gomptimata**, to the west, is a sandy beach that still is deserted, and gets big waves. Beaches within easy reach of Diu Town include, from east to west, **Jallandhar**, **Chakratirth** and stunning **Sunset Point**.

Fudam Close to Diu Town, the village of Fudam has a huge church, Our Lady of Remedies, that's now used as a guest house. A large, old, carved wooden altar with Madonna and child remains inside.

Vanakbara At the extreme west of the island, Vanakbara has a church (Our Lady of Mercy), fort, lighthouse, small bazaar, post office and fishing fleet. This little fishing village is worth a visit – wander through the town to the port area where you can see the locals mending nets and repairing their colourful fishing boats.

Places to Stay

Most hotels offer a discount in the low season, but it's worth bargaining at any time of the year, as places will slash prices if they are not full. Prices given are for the peak

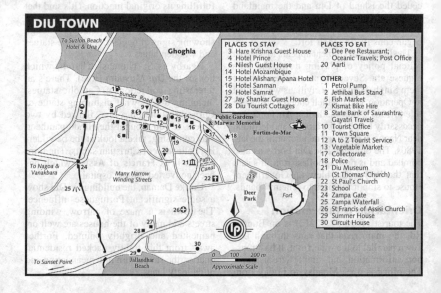

DIU TOWN

To Suzlon Beach, Hotel & Una

Ghoghla

Bunder Road

Public Gardens & Marwar Memorial

Fortim-do-Mar

To Nagoa & Vanakbara

Many Narrow Winding Streets

Path Canal

Deer Park

Fort

To Sunset Point

Jallandhar Beach

0   100   200 m
Approximate Scale

PLACES TO STAY
3   Hare Krishna Guest House
4   Hotel Prince
6   Nilesh Guest House
14 Hotel Mozambique
15 Hotel Alishan; Apana Hotel
16 Hotel Sanman
19 Hotel Samrat
27 Jay Shankar Guest House
28 Diu Tourist Cottages

PLACES TO EAT
9   Dee Pee Restaurant;
     Oceanic Travels; Post Office
20 Aarti

OTHER
1   Petrol Pump
2   Jethibai Bus Stand
5   Fish Market
7   Kismat Bike Hire
8   State Bank of Saurashtra;
     Gayatri Travels
10 Tourist Office
11 Town Square
12 A to Z Tourist Service
13 Vegetable Market
17 Collectorate
18 Police
21 Diu Museum
     (St Thomas' Church)
22 St Paul's Church
23 School
24 Zampa Gate
25 Zampa Waterfall
26 St Francis of Assisi Church
29 Summer House
30 Circuit House

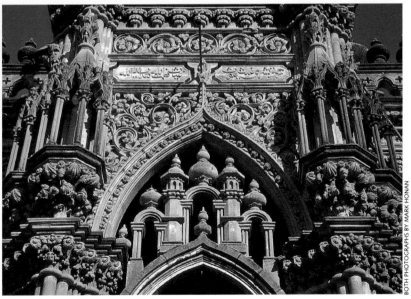

Gujarati Architecture
Top: Detail of the Christian Portuguese-built Diu Fort, which was completed in 1541.
Bottom: The traditional spires and minarets of Mahabat Maqbara, the mausoleum of one of the Muslim nawabs of Junagadh.

BOTH PHOTOGRAPHS BY MARK HONAN

Top: Shatrunjaya, in Saurashtra, translates as 'the place of victory', and is one of Jainism's holiest pilgrimage sites. Over eight hundred temples, most of them Jain, can be found here.
Bottom: Fishing is Diu Island's main industry; closely followed by the local rum distillery, which makes for a fairly laid-back attitude among islanders and tourists alike!

season, which runs roughly from October to June. Rooms mentioned have a bathroom, unless stated otherwise.

Diu Town On the west side of town is *Hare Krishna Guest House* (☎ 52213). This small place has simple singles/doubles/triples (cold water) for only Rs 75/100/150.

Hotel Prince (☎ 52265), nearby and close to the fish market, is slightly overpriced at Rs 350/500 with/without bathroom, though hefty discounts may be offered. Rooms have a balcony and there's also a beer bar and restaurant.

Round the corner, *Nilesh Guest House* (☎ 52319) also may slash prices. It has singles/doubles with shared bath for Rs 160/200, and doubles/triples with bathroom for Rs 500/600. Bucket hot water is free. Room size and ambience depends on which part of the building they're in, but they're clean, staff are friendly, and the restaurant has both a downstairs and a rooftop section.

Hotel Mozambique (☎ 52223), by the vegetable market, is cheap enough (from Rs 100/175 in low/high season), but is also fairly grubby and has a seedy bar.

Hotel Samrat (☎ 52354), a couple of blocks south of the town square, has double rooms from Rs 250/400 in low/high season (Rs 600/800 with air-con), and there are four-bed rooms for Rs 400. Rooms are well appointed, all with balconies and TV, and room service is available. There's a good restaurant and bar and if the kitchen is not busy, for about Rs 50 the chef will cook fish bought by guests at the fish market.

Hotel Sanman (☎ 52342, Bunder Rd) is an old Portuguese villa midway between the town square and fort. This popular little place is often booked out. In previous incarnations it has been known as the Baron's Inn, the totally misleading Fun Club, and Pensâo BeiraMar! Large, basic doubles (cold water) cost Rs 150/200 in low/high season. Staff are friendly, and there's an atmospheric rooftop restaurant and bar.

Apana Hotel (☎ 52112, Bunder Rd) nearby, has smallish, modern rooms with hot water and TV starting from Rs 550, or

Rs 950 with air-con. There's a good nonveg restaurant.

Hotel Alishan (☎ 52340, Bunder Rd) next door, has decent rooms with TV and balcony. Double rooms cost Rs 700, or Rs 800 with a sea view. Big discounts are offered if it isn't busy. There's a restaurant and bar.

Jallandhar Beach Just out of Diu Town, *Diu Tourist Cottages* (☎ 52654) offers cottages with double or twin beds for Rs 700. There are also four-person rooms (the second double bed is in a loft) for Rs 1100 with air-con. Many rooms have sea views, and its Pelican Bar & Restaurant is not bad. If you don't mind being a little out of town, this is a very laid-back place. The same family has opened the new *Royal Beach Resort* (☎ 52654) at Sunset Point, charging from Rs 400 a double.

Jay Shankar Guest House (☎ 52424), near Diu Tourist Cottages, has doubles from Rs 80 up to Rs 200 (with balcony and sea view). It's good value, but some people have complained recently that the management is unhelpful.

Fudam to Nagoa Beach On the road to Fudam is the new *Hotel Kohinoor* (☎ 52209, fax 52372), with attractive, well-equipped villas grouped round a swimming pool. Rooms cost from Rs 800, or Rs 1250 with air-con, and there's a good restaurant.

Estrella Do Mar (☎ 52966) at the Fudam church has double rooms for about Rs 150 with cold water. There's no restaurant, but guests can use the kitchen.

Island Bar & Restaurant (☎ 52473), on the Fudam to Nagoa Beach road, has built some white villas with rooms for Rs 500. The 'restaurant' only serves snacks, and the extensive grounds look a bit derelict.

Ganga Sagar Guest House (☎ 52249) is right on Nagoa Beach. Small singles/doubles round a beachside garden cost Rs 150/300 (bucket hot water).

Close by, on the main road, is the new *Resort Hoka* (☎ 53036). Doubles go for Rs 350 and the management seems eager to please.

Ghoghla *Suzlon Beach Hotel* (☎ 52212) is in the village of Ghoghla on the mainland (where there's a good beach). This is the first building in Diu after you come through the barrier that marks the border with Gujarat. Renovated air-con doubles cost Rs 1000. There's a pleasant restaurant and bar overlooking the sea.

Places to Eat
Beer and drinks are blissfully cheap in Diu – from Rs 30 for a Kingfisher. Unfortunately, food is mostly average at best.

Hotel Sanman has a relaxing rooftop restaurant that's a popular hang-out with travellers, especially in the evening. It has great sea views and is a wonderful place to sit back and chat over a drink. There's reasonably priced Indian and Chinese food; prawns masala costs Rs 50. The food is nothing to write home about, but the atmosphere is terrific.

Nilkanth Restaurant in the Jay Shankar Guest House serves beer and is another popular place to spend some time. However, the inexpensive food gets reports ranging from 'great' to 'terrible'.

Hotel Samrat, Hotel Apana and *Nilesh Guest House* also have decent restaurants.

Aarti is a relaxed traveller restaurant, with wall hangings and western music. Pizzas (from Rs 50) are excellent and there are usually good fish specialities.

For cheap Indian vegetarian food, try *Dee Pee*, opposite the tourist office.

There are a couple of places at Nagoa Beach. *Ganga Sagar Restaurant* (beside the basic snack bar) has the usual range of moderately-priced Chinese and Indian food. So does *Dub-Chichk Bar & Restaurant*, which is next door on the 1st floor and gets sea breezes; Kingfisher is Rs 35.

Gomptimata Beach has no cafes, so bring food with you.

Getting There & Away
Air Gujarat Airways has at least one daily flight to Mumbai (US$95). The Gujarat Airways agent is Oceanic Travels (☎ 52180), on the town square near the post office.

Bus Una is the access point for Diu, and there are direct buses there from Bhavnagar, Veraval, Talaja and elsewhere. Once in Una, you have to get yourself the 10km or so to Ghoghla and Diu. Buses depart every 30 minutes from Una bus stand between 7.30 am and 8 pm (Rs 7, 40 minutes). Outside these hours, walk 1km to Tower Chowk in Una (ask directions), from where crowded share rickshaws go to Ghoghla or Diu for about the same as the bus fare. An auto-rickshaw from Una costs about Rs 100.

Some Gujarat STC buses run all the way to Diu, but there are only one to three departures a day from Diu to Ahmedabad, Veraval (Rs 22, 2½ hours), Junagadh (Rs 40, five hours) and Jamnagar (Rs 63). Rajkot is best served, with about six daily departures (Rs 60, seven hours). Early morning buses start from outside the tourist office, calling at the Jethibai bus stand.

Private minibuses currently go to Mumbai at 10 am (Rs 300, 22 hours) and to Ahmedabad at 7 pm (Rs 120, 10½ hours). Book in advance from Gayatri Travels (☎ 52346) or elsewhere.

Train Delwada, between Una and Ghoghla and only about 8km from Diu, is the nearest railhead. A share auto-rickshaw from there to Ghoghla costs about Rs 5. There's a direct train at 6 am from Delwada to Veraval (Rs 32/173, 96km). There is also a daily service to Junagadh (Rs 48/233, 164km) via Sasan Gir.

Ferry A ferry crosses from Vanakbara to Kotla village on the mainland and you can get a bus from there to Kodinar

Getting Around
Auto-rickshaw drivers will demand Rs 100 to Una, and generally want high prices. To travel anywhere within the town of Diu should cost no more than Rs 10. To Nagoa Beach, pay about Rs 30, and to Sunset Point, Rs 20. Share rickshaws to Ghoghla cost Rs 3 per person.

Cycling is ideal for getting around Diu Town, though for longer trips a moped is affordable and a great way to travel, especially as the roads are relatively deserted and in good condition. There are various rental places in Diu Town; the going rate per day is Rs 15 for a cycle or Rs 100 for a moped (plus fuel). Try Kismat (☎ 52971) at the back of the town square for cycles and mopeds, or A to Z Tourist Service, by the vegetable market, for mopeds.

Local buses from Diu Town to Nagoa Beach and Vanakbara leave from the Jethibal bus stand at 7 and 11 am and 4 pm. From Nagoa, they depart for Diu Town from near the police post at 1, 5.30 and 7 pm (Rs 4).

VERAVAL
☎ 02876 • pop 130,000
On the south coast of Saurashtra, Veraval was the major seaport for Mecca pilgrims before the rise of Surat. It still has some importance as one of India's major fishing ports (more than 1000 boats work from here), and as the base for a visit to Somnath Temple, 6km to the east.

Wooden *dhows* of all sizes, from fishing dinghies right up to ocean-going vessels, are still built totally by hand. The largest dhows still make the journey from here to Dubai and other Middle Eastern destinations, and you may see some of them loading or discharging cargo.

It's well worth a wander around the **port** area, although photography is supposedly prohibited. If you're on a bicycle heading for Somnath, you can take a shortcut through the port area. You can change money at the State Bank of India and at the State Bank of Saurashtra. Despite its size, and apart from the port, there's not a lot to see in Veraval.

Places to Stay
There are plenty of hotels along ST Rd between the bus stand and the clock tower.

Chetna Rest House (☎ 20688), opposite the bus stand, has clean, simple singles/doubles for Rs 60/110 with attached cold bath, Rs 50/95 without. Dorm beds for men are only Rs 30.

Hotel Satkar (☎ 20120), round the corner, has a phone and TV in most rooms and staff

are obliging. Rates are from Rs 100/175 or Rs 400/475 with air-con. All rooms have bathroom with hot water (mornings only).

Toran Tourist Bungalow (☎ 20488), not far from the lighthouse, is in a rather inconvenient location. Singles/doubles are Rs 225/350, or Rs 275/450 for a bigger room with TV. Prices nearly halve from January to March and in July and September. Good points include the garden, veg restaurant and views of the nearby old nawab's palace (now a college); a bad point is the chemical smell from the nearby factory.

Chandrani Guest House (☎ 20356), opposite the train station, has very basic, cell-like singles/doubles with bathroom for Rs 50/100. There are cheap *Retiring Rooms* in the train station.

Places to Eat
Food World (ST Rd) serves good bottomless Gujarati thalis for Rs 35. There's a similar place across the road.

Fast Food Restaurant, near the clock tower on the road to the station, has simple vegetarian food for around Rs 25.

Getting There & Away
Bus STC buses to Junagadh depart half-hourly from the bus stand from 5.45 am (Rs 22, two hours); to Porbandar from 6 am (Rs 25, three hours); and to Rajkot from 6 am (Rs 40, five hours). There are regular departures for Sasan Gir (Rs 12, 1½ hours). The trip to Diu takes three hours (Rs 22) but departures are more frequent if you change at Una.

There are agents for the private bus companies opposite the bus stand.

Train It's 431km from Ahmedabad to Veraval. Fares for the 11½ hour trip are Rs 99/490 in 2nd/1st class. There are also trains for Sasan Gir at 9 am and 2.15 pm (Rs 10, two hours). A daily passenger service to Delwada (for Diu) leaves at 9 am with a change at Talala, arriving at 12.45 pm, or there's a direct train at 3.45 pm, arriving at 7.50 pm (Rs 31/161 in 2nd/1st class).

There is a daily train at 11.30 am to Rajkot, arriving at 4.40 pm (Rs 53/258, 186km).

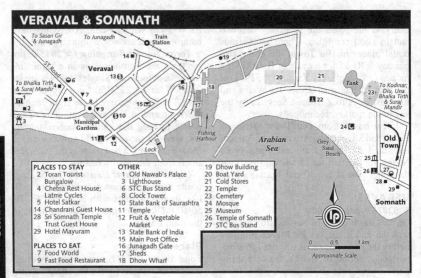

VERAVAL & SOMNATH

PLACES TO STAY
2 Toran Tourist Bungalow
4 Chetna Rest House; Latme Cycles
5 Hotel Satkar
14 Chandrani Guest House
28 Sri Somnath Temple Trust Guest House
29 Hotel Mayuram

PLACES TO EAT
7 Food World
9 Fast Food Restaurant

OTHER
1 Old Nawab's Palace
3 Lighthouse
6 STC Bus Stand
8 Clock Tower
10 State Bank of Saurashtra
11 Temple
12 Fruit & Vegetable Market
13 State Bank of India
15 Main Post Office
16 Junagadh Gate
17 Sheds
18 Dhow Wharf
19 Dhow Building
20 Boat Yard
21 Cold Stores
22 Temple
23 Cemetery
24 Mosque
25 Museum
26 Temple of Somnath
27 STC Bus Stand

Getting Around

Bicycles can be hired opposite the bus stand from Latme Cycles (the sign is in Gujarati only), for Rs 3 per hour, or Rs 20 per day.

An auto-rickshaw to Somnath, 6km away, will cost you about Rs 30. There are local buses to Somnath for Rs 3.50. The local bus stand is near the long-distance STC stand, on the same road.

SOMNATH

Somnath has a large fair at the full moon of Kartika Purnima in November/December.

Temple of Somnath

This temple, at Somnath near Veraval and about 80km from Junagadh, has an extremely chequered past. Its earliest history fades into legend – it is said to have originally been built out of gold by Somraj, the moon god, only to be rebuilt by Rawana in silver, then by Krishna in wood and Bhimdev in stone. A description of the temple by Al Biruni, an Arab traveller, was so glowing that it prompted a visit in 1024 by a most unwelcome tourist – Mahmud of Ghazni. At

that time, the temple was so wealthy that it had 300 musicians, 500 dancing girls and even 300 barbers just to shave the heads of visiting pilgrims.

Mahmud of Ghazni, whose raids on the riches of India are legendary, descended on Somnath from his Afghan kingdom and, after a two day battle, took the town and the temple. Having looted its fabulous wealth, he destroyed it for good measure. So began a pattern of Muslim destruction and Hindu rebuilding that continued for centuries. The temple was again razed in 1297, 1394 and finally in 1706 by Aurangzeb, the notorious Mughal fundamentalist.

After the 1706 demolition, the temple was not rebuilt until 1950. Outside, opposite the entrance, is a statue of SV Patel (1875-1950), who was responsible for the reconstruction.

The current temple was built to traditional designs on the original site by the sea. It contains one of the 12 sacred Shiva shrines known as *jyoti linga*. Photography is prohibited inside the temple, and you must leave your camera at the luggage-check hut outside. The grey-sand beach outside the temple is OK for a swim, although there's no shade.

Museum

Down the lane from the temple is a museum, open from 8.30 am to 12.15 pm and 2.30 to 6 pm (closed Wednesdays, holidays and every second and fourth Saturday). There's a small entry fee. Remains of the temple can be seen here as a jumble of old carved stones littering a courtyard. There are pottery shards, a seashell collection and a (strange) glass case of water bottles containing samples from the Danube, Nile, St Lawrence, Tigris, River Plate and even the Murray in Australia, as well as seawater from Tasmania and New Zealand.

Other Sites

The town of Somnath is entered from Veraval by the **Junagadh Gate**. This is the very ancient triple gate Mahmud finally broke through to take the town. Close to the second gate is an old **mosque** dating from Mahmud's time. The **Jama Masjid**, reached through the town's busy **bazaar**, was constructed using parts of a Hindu temple and has interesting bodhi tree carvings at all four corners. It is now a museum with a collection from many of these temples.

About 1km before the Junagadh Gate, coming from Veraval, the finely carved **Mai Puri** was once a Temple of the Sun. This Hindu temple was converted into a mosque during Mahmud's time and is surrounded by thousands of tombs and palias (memorial stones). Two old tombs are close by and, on the shore, the **Bhidiyo Pagoda** probably dates from the 14th century.

To the east of the town is the **Bhalka Tirth** where Krishna was mistaken for a deer and wounded by an arrow while sleeping in a deerskin. The legendary spot is at the confluence of three rivers. You get to it through the small *sangam* (confluence gate), which is simply known as the Nana, or Small Gate. North of this sacred spot is the **Suraj Mandir**, or Temple of the Sun, which Mahmud also had a go at knocking down. This very old

temple, with a frieze of lions with elephant trunks around its walls, probably dates from the same time as the original Somnath Temple. Back inside the small gate is a temple which Ahalya Bai of Indore built as a replacement for the Somnath Temple.

Places to Stay & Eat

Sri Somnath Temple Trust Guest House (☎ 02876-20212) is rather dilapidated; its name is written in Gujarati. Go to the booking office first, directly opposite the bus stand. The cheaper rooms are a bit dingy and cost Rs 60/100 for a double/triple. The best rooms cost Rs 350, or Rs 550 with air-con.

Hotel Mayuram (☎ 02876-20286) is just down the road, heading away from the temple. It has doubles/triples with bathroom (cold water) for Rs 200/300.

SASAN GIR NATIONAL PARK

The last home of the Asiatic lion *(Panthera leo lersica)* is 59km from Junagadh via Visavadar. The 1400 sq km sanctuary was set up to protect the lion and its habitat: since 1980 numbers have increased from less than 200 to an estimated 286 in 1997. However, while the lions have been the winners, the local *maaldharis* (herders) have lost valuable grazing land for their cattle. The Madhya Pradesh government has proposed moving 200 lions to the Pulpur Kuno sanctuary in Madhya Pradesh, but thus far the move has been blocked by the Gujarat government.

Although the lions seem remarkably tame, in recent years they have reportedly been wandering well outside the limits of the sanctuary in search of easy game – namely calves – which in earlier times was found within the park. The problem is compounded by the declining areas of forest outside the sanctuary, forcing villagers to forage for fuel within the sanctuary precincts, reducing the habitat of the lions.

The best time to visit the sanctuary is from December to April, and it is closed from 16 June to 15 October and even later if there has been a heavy monsoon.

Apart from lions there are more than 30 species of other animals, including panthers,

GUJARAT

hyenas, foxes, wild boars and a number of deer and antelope. The deer include the largest Indian antelope (the nilgai), the graceful chinkara gazelle, the chowsingha and the barking deer. You may also see parrots, peacocks and monkeys.

The lions are elusive but you'd be unlucky not to see at least one on a safari, although if you're determined to spot one allow for a couple of trips. Morning safaris are generally a better bet than those in the afternoon. Unfortunately the local guides are poorly trained and speak little English.

Private vehicles can not be used to tour the sanctuary. Whatever else you do, take a jeep and not a minibus. While the latter stick to the main tracks, the jeeps can take the small trails where you're much more likely to come across lions.

Before you can go on safari, you must get a permit. These are issued on the spot at the Sinh Sadan Forest Lodge office (see Places to Stay & Eat) and cost Rs 15 per person for the first day (every additional day costs Rs 7.50), plus Rs 35 for a camera and Rs 75 for a video. Jeep tours taking up to six people cost upwards of Rs 150. There are three main tracks in the park, so you'll cover 25 to 35km in about three hours, depending on the track your jeep is assigned to.

The guide's fee for a group is set at Rs 20 for Indians and Rs 70 for foreigners, and if your guide's been keen and searched hard then a tip is certainly justified, otherwise it's up to you. Jeeps can be hired from the lodge office every day from 8 to 11 am and 3 to 5 pm during winter (October to February) and from 7 am during summer (March to June).

Twelve kilometres from Sasan village at Devalia within the sanctuary precincts, is the **Gir Interpretation Zone**. The 4.12 sq km zone has a cross section of the wildlife in Gir, so you'd be certain to see a lion here if you've been unlucky in the main sanctuary. The cost to enter the zone, including a minibus mini-safari, permit and guide, is around Rs 100 per person, though you'd have to add on your jeep costs to and from the zone.

There are 25 species of reptiles in the sanctuary. A **crocodile-rearing centre** has been established next to Sinh Sadan Forest Lodge, where hatchlings are reared and then released into their natural habitat.

Places to Stay & Eat

There are only a few places to stay at Sasan Gir village. It's a good idea to make an advance booking, as rooms can suddenly fill up.

Sinh Sadan Forest Lodge (☎ 02877-85540) is about a 10 minute walk from the train station. It's a pleasant place to stay, although the staff are sometimes a little indifferent. A very aged film about the park is screened here most evenings at 7 pm. Comfortable doubles with private bath cost Rs 150, or Rs 450 with air-con. Dorms are Rs 50. There's a restaurant (guests only, who must order in advance) which serves thalis (Rs 25).

Gir Lodge (☎ 02877-85521, fax 85528) down by the river about 200m from the Sinh Sadan Forest Lodge, is an upmarket hotel surrounded by well-maintained gardens and operated by the Taj Group. Well-appointed singles/doubles including three meals cost Rs 2257/3920, or Rs 2829/4436 with air-con. Checkout is noon. The restaurant is open to nonguests, but only if they pre-order and pay a deposit.

Getting There & Away

STC and express buses travel between Junagadh and Veraval via Sasan Gir regularly throughout the day. The 45km trip to Veraval takes 1½ hours (Rs 14). To Junagadh, the 59km trip takes around two hours (Rs 18). Trains run to Veraval (Rs 10, two hours) twice daily, to Delwada (for Diu) once daily at 8.50 am, and to Junagadh once a day (Rs 15, 2½ hours).

JUNAGADH

☎ 0285 • pop 225,000

Junagadh is at the base of the temple-studded Girnar Hill and is the departure point for visits to the Gir Forest. This interesting and unspoilt town has some exotic old buildings, and is a fascinating place to explore, although few tourists come here.

The city takes its name from the fort that enclosed the old city (*jirna* means old). Dating from 250 BC, the Ashokan edicts near the town testify to the great antiquity of this site. At the time of Partition, the Nawab of Junagadh opted to take his tiny state into Pakistan. However, the inhabitants were predominantly Hindu and the nawab soon found himself in exile, which perhaps explains the sorry state of his former palace and fort.

Information

The best source of information is Mr Sorathia, the manager of the Hotel Relief – the town's unofficial tourist centre. The State Bank of India, near Diwan Chowk, has moneychanging facilities. Other banks are close by.

Junagadh's main post office is inconveniently south of the city centre at Gandhigram. There's a branch in a small street off MG Rd near the local bus stand. The telegraph office is on Jhalorapa Rd, near Ajanta Talkies.

Uperkot Fort

This very old fort stands on the eastern side of Junagadh. It is believed to have been built in 319 BC by Chandragupta, though it has been rebuilt and extended many times over the centuries. In places, the walls are 20m high and an ornate triple gateway forms the entrance to the fort. It's said that the fort was once besieged for a full 12 year period. In all, it was besieged 16 times. It is also said that the fort was abandoned from the 7th to 10th centuries and, when rediscovered, it was completely overgrown by jungle. The plateau-like area formed by the top of the old fort is covered in lantana scrub. The fort is open daily from 7 am to 6.30 pm; entry is Rs 1.

GUJARAT

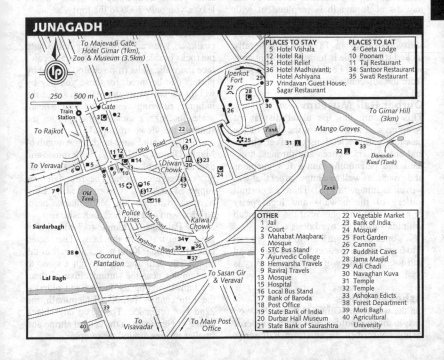

JUNAGADH

To Majevadi Gate;
Hotel Girnar (1km),
Zoo & Museum (3.5km)

0   250   500 m

Gate
Train Station

To Rajkot

To Veraval

Dhal Road

Diwan Chowk

Old Tank

Police Lines

MG Road

Sardarbagh

Jayshree Road

Coconut Plantation

Lal Bagh

To Visavadar

To Main Post Office

To Sasan Gir & Veraval

Uperkot Fort

Tank

Kalwa Chowk

Mango Groves

To Girnar Hill (3km)

Damodar Kund (Tank)

Tank

PLACES TO STAY
5 Hotel Vishala
12 Hotel Raj
14 Hotel Relief
36 Hotel Madhuvanti;
   Hotel Ashiyana
37 Vrindavan Guest House;
   Sagar Restaurant

PLACES TO EAT
4 Geeta Lodge
10 Poonam
11 Taj Restaurant
34 Santoor Restaurant
35 Swati Restaurant

OTHER
1 Jail
2 Court
3 Mahabat Maqbara;
   Mosque
6 STC Bus Stand
7 Ayurvedic College
8 Hemvarsha Travels
9 Raviraj Travels
13 Mosque
15 Hospital
16 Local Bus Stand
17 Bank of Baroda
18 Post Office
19 State Bank of India
20 Durbar Hall Museum
21 State Bank of Saurashtra
22 Vegetable Market
23 Bank of India
24 Mosque
25 Fort Garden
26 Cannon
27 Buddhist Caves
28 Jama Masjid
29 Adi Chadi
30 Navaghan Kuva
31 Temple
32 Temple
33 Ashokan Edicts
38 Forest Department
39 Moti Bagh
40 Agricultural
   University

The **Jama Masjid**, the mosque inside the fort, was built from a demolished Hindu temple. Other points of interest include the **Tomb of Nuri Shah** and two fine baolis (stepwells) known as the **Adi Chadi** and the **Navaghan Kuva**. The Adi Chadi is named after two of the slave girls who use to fetch water from it. The Navaghan Kuva is reached by a magnificent winding staircase cut into the rock.

Cut into the hillside close to the mosque are some ancient **Buddhist caves** which are thought to be at least 1500 years old. These eerie double-storey caves have six pillars with weathered carvings. The soft rock on which Junagadh is built encouraged the construction of caves and wells, and there are several other caves, including some thought to date from the time of Ashoka.

Mahabat Maqbara

This stunning mausoleum of one of the nawabs of Junagadh is resplendent with silver doors and intricate architecture, including minarets encircled by spiralling stairways. Built in 1892, it is generally locked (the outside is more interesting anyway) but you may be able to obtain the keys from the adjacent mosque.

Durbar Hall Museum

This museum has the usual display of weapons and armour from the days of the nawabs, with collections of silver chains and chandeliers, settees and thrones, howdahs and palanquins, and a few cushions and gowns, as well as a huge carpet that was woven in Junagadh's jail. There's a portrait gallery of the nawabs and local petty princes, including photos of the last nawab with his various beloved dogs.

It's open daily from 9 am to 12.15 pm and 3 to 6 pm (closed Wednesday and the second and fourth Saturday of the month), entry is Rs 1.

Ashokan Edicts

On the way to the Girnar Hill temples, you pass a huge boulder on which Emperor Ashoka inscribed 14 edicts in Pali script around 250 BC. Later Sanskrit inscriptions were added around 150 AD by Emperor Rudradama and in about 450 AD by Skandagupta, the last emperor of the Mauryas. The 14 edicts are moral lectures, while the other inscriptions refer mainly to recurring floods destroying the embankments of a nearby lake, the Sudershan, which no longer exists. The boulder is actually housed in a small roadside building, on the right towards Girnar.

Girnar Hill

The climb up the 10,000 stone steps to the summit of Girnar is best begun early in the morning, preferably at dawn. The steps are well built and maintained and were constructed between 1889 and 1908 from the proceeds of a lottery. The start of the climb is in scrubby teak forest, 1 to 2km beyond the Damodar Kund, and the road actually takes you to around step No 3000 – which leaves you only 7000 to the top!

There are several refreshment stalls on the 2½ hour ascent, which sometimes sell chalk, so you can graffiti your name onto the rocks beside the path! If you really can't face the walk, dolis (rope chairs) carried by porters can be hired; for these you pay by weight so, before setting off, you suffer the indignity of being weighed on a huge beam scale, just like a sack of grain. From the summit, the views are superb.

The Bhavnath Fair is held in the month of Magha (January/February). Folk music and dancing takes place and lots of naked sadhus converge on town. The first fair was supposed to have been organised by Lord Krishna to honour the Mahabharata hero, Arjuna, who had reached Saurashtra.

Like Palitana, the temple-topped hill is of great significance to the Jains. The sacred tank of **Damodar Kund** marks the start of the climb. The path ascends through a wood to the temples near the summit. Five of them are Jain, including the largest and oldest – the 12th century **Temple of Neminath**, the 22nd Jain tirthankar. There is a large black image of Neminath in the central shrine and smaller images around the temple.

The nearby triple **Temple of Mallinath**, the 9th tirthankar, was erected in 1177 by two brothers. During festivals, this temple is a favourite gathering place for sadhus and a great fair is held here during the Kartika Purnima festival. On top of the peak is the **Temple of Amba Mata**, where newlyweds are supposed to worship at the shrine of the goddess in order to ensure a happy marriage.

A No 3 or 4 bus from the local bus stand will take you to Girnar Taleti at the base of the hill. Buses run about once an hour from 6 am (Rs 2) and pass by the Ashokan edicts. An auto-rickshaw from town costs about Rs 30.

Other Attractions

If you are unable to visit the Sasan Gir National Park, Junagadh's **zoo** at Sakar Bagh, 3.5km from the town centre on the Rajkot road, has Gir lions. The zoo was set up by the nawab in 1863 specifically to save the lion from extinction and is surprisingly good with lions, tigers and leopards being the main attractions. The zoo is open from 9 am to 6 pm and entry costs Rs 3. There is also a fine **museum** at the zoo with paintings, manuscripts, archaeological finds and various other exhibits including a natural history section. It's open daily (closed Wednesday and the second and fourth Saturday of each month) from 9 am to noon and 3 to 6 pm. Take a No 6 bus (Rs 2), or walk there by the old Majevadi Gate north of the jail.

The **Ayurvedic College** at Sardarbagh on the western edge of town is housed in one of the former nawab's palaces, and has a small museum devoted to ayurvedic medicine. The staff are knowledgeable and it's a good place for information on this ancient traditional medicine. It is open daily from 9 am to 6 pm.

Other old constructions include the gate opposite the train station on Dhal Rd, the clock tower near the central post office and the building opposite the Durbar Hall museum.

Places to Stay

Rooms are equipped with bathrooms, unless indicated otherwise.

Hotel Relief (☎ 620280, Dhal Rd), is a popular hang-out for travellers. Singles/doubles cost Rs 100/200, or Rs 500 for air-con rooms. Staff are friendly and helpful, and good meals are available for guests. Check-out is 10 am.

Hotel Raj (☎ 623961, Dhal Rd) nearby, has small, reasonably clean rooms for only Rs 75/100 – take care of your valuables here.

Hotel Vishala (☎ 631599), opposite the bus stand, has a range of rooms for a range of prices, but they're generally good value. Singles/doubles start at Rs 75/175 (bucket hot water), or Rs 275/400 with air-con. There's also dorm beds for Rs 50.

Hotel Girnar (☎ 621201, Majewadi Darwaja) is a Gujarat Tourism hotel about 2km out of town. It offers singles/doubles for Rs 225/400, or Rs 425/650 with air-con. Most rooms are spacious and have a balcony (try to get one of these). Prices drop 40% from 15 June to 15 September, and the restaurant serves Gujarati thalis for Rs 40.

Retiring Rooms at the train station are Rs 50/100; dorm beds are Rs 30.

There are a number of hotels around Kalwa Chowk, one of the two main squares in Junagadh, though some are pretty grotty. It's convenient for restaurants, but less so for the tourist sights.

The *Vrindavan Guest House* (☎ 622777, Jayshree Rd) is basic but reasonably welcoming. Small rooms with hot water cost only Rs 60/110.

Opposite are two hotels in the same building. *Hotel Madhuvanti* (☎ 620087, Jayshree Rd) on the 1st floor has big, clean rooms for Rs 150/250 round an enclosed courtyard. *Hotel Ashiyana* (☎ 620706, Jayshree Rd) on the 2nd floor has decent rooms with TV from Rs 200/350.

Places to Eat

Geeta Lodge, close to the train station, has all-you-can-eat thalis for Rs 35.

Santoor Restaurant (MG Rd), has quick service, good veg food (Rs 20 to Rs 40) and good lassis. This air-con restaurant is a pleasant surprise at the top of a fairly seedy-looking staircase.

Swati Restaurant and *Sagar Restaurant*, both on Jayshree Rd, are of a similar standard and price to Santoor.

Meat eaters have little choice in this town. You could try *Taj Restaurant (Dhal Rd)* but it gets mixed reports.

Poonam, down a side road opposite Taj Restaurant, is another veg place, with thalis for Rs 25. It's above an STD phone place (its sign is in Gujarati).

Junagadh is famous for its fruit, especially *kesar* mangoes and *chiku* (sapodilla) which are popular in milkshakes in November/December.

Getting There & Away

Bus The timetable at the STC stand is entirely in Gujarati. Buses leave hourly for Rajkot (Rs 27, two hours) and for Sasan Gir (Rs 18, two hours), and there are regular departures to other centres in the state. To Porbandar there's ordinary (Rs 29) or nonstop (Rs 30, two hours) state buses.

Various private bus offices are nearby on Dhal Road, near the rail tracks. Raviraj Travels (☎ 626988), has deluxe minibuses to Rajkot every 30 minutes (Rs 25, two hours), and numerous departures to Ahmedabad (Rs 90, seven hours). Hemvarsha Travels (☎ 622746) with a sign in Gujarati, has buses to Veraval (Rs 25, two hours), Una (Rs 45, four hours), Janmagar (Rs 35, three hours) and elsewhere.

Train Coming from Veraval, the *Somnath Mail* departs Junagadh at 7.05 pm, arriving in Ahmedabad at 4.25 am. The *Girnar Express* departs at 9.13 pm, arriving in Ahmedabad at 6.05 am (377km, Rs 88/434 in 2nd/1st class) trip.

To Veraval (Rs 30/159, two hours) there are additional services at 5 and 9.05 am, and 2.25 and 6.20 pm. At 6.20 am a train to Sasan Gir (Rs 15, 2½ hours) continues to Delwada (for Una and Diu) arriving at 12.50 pm (Rs 27 in 2nd class only). The *Veraval-Rajkot Mail* runs between Rajkot (Rs 40/205 in 2nd/1st class, 3½ hours, 131km) and Veraval via Junagadh, departing Junagadh from 11.15 am to 1.30 pm.

PORBANDAR

☎ 0286 • pop 183,000

On the south-east coast, about midway between Veraval and Dwarka, modern-day Porbandar is chiefly noted as the birthplace of Mahatma Gandhi. In ancient times, the city was called Sudamapuri after Sudama, a compatriot of Krishna, and there was once a flourishing trade from here to Africa and the Persian Gulf. The Africa connection is apparent in the number of Indianised blacks, called Siddis, who form a virtually separate caste of *Dalits*.

Porbandar has several cement and chemical factories and a textile mill. Dhows are still built, and fish-drying is an important activity, lending a certain aroma to the town!

Swimming at rocky Chowpatty Beach is not recommended. This beach is used as a local latrine and there is a factory drain outlet by the Hazur Palace. Swimming is said to be OK a few kilometres down the coast towards Veraval.

The State Bank of India opposite the Hotel Flamingo has moneychanging facilities.

Along the coast at Madhavpur near Porbandar, the Madhavrai Fair is held in the month of Chaitra (March/April) to celebrate Krishna's elopement with Rukmini.

Kirti Mandir

This memorial to Gandhi was built in 1950. There's a small bookshop and (take the stairs by the entrance) an exhibit of photographs, some with English captions. Next door is Gandhi's actual birthplace – a three storey, 300 year-old house. It's mostly empty but the guide will show you around (free, but expect to pay baksheesh).

Nehru Planetarium & Bharat Mandir

These are 2km from town centre. The route crosses a creek, home to flocks of flamingos. Men and women enter the Nehru planetarium from the veranda by separate doors whose panels celebrate Indian nonalignment, showing Shastri with Kosygin on one side and Nehru with JFK on the other! The planetarium has afternoon sessions in Gujarati.

The large Bharat Mandir hall is in a garden opposite the planetarium. On the floor is a huge relief map of India and the building's pillars are painted with bas-reliefs of more than 100 religious figures and personages from Hindu epics (entry Rs 1).

Places to Stay

Rajkamal Guest House (☎ 242674, MG Rd) is very cheap at Rs 50/70 with bathroom (cold water), and is no worse than any of the other budget places.

Nilam Guest House (☎ 244503, ST Rd), near the Municipal Gardens, has dusty rooms from Rs 100 with bucket hot water. Avoid the darker rooms where windows face into the hall.

Nilesh Guest House (☎ 246905, MG Rd) has dorms for Rs 40 and doubles with bathroom, hot water and TV for Rs 150.

Hotel Flamingo (☎ 247123, MG Rd) opposite, is a friendly place with a good restaurant. Singles/doubles cost from Rs 100/150, or Rs 250/300 with air-con. Most

GUJARAT

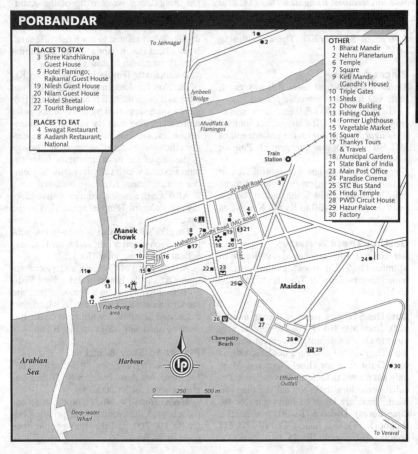

PORBANDAR

PLACES TO STAY
3 Shree Kandhlikrupa Guest House
5 Hotel Flamingo; Rajkamal Guest House
19 Nilesh Guest House
20 Nilam Guest House
22 Hotel Sheetal
27 Tourist Bungalow

PLACES TO EAT
4 Swagat Restaurant
8 Aadarsh Restaurant; National

OTHER
1 Bharat Mandir
2 Nehru Planetarium
6 Temple
7 Square
9 Kirti Mandir (Gandhi's House)
10 Triple Gates
11 Sheds
12 Dhow Building
13 Fishing Quays
14 Former Lighthouse
15 Vegetable Market
16 Square
17 Thankys Tours & Travels
18 Municipal Gardens
21 State Bank of India
23 Main Post Office
24 Paradise Cinema
25 STC Bus Stand
26 Hindu Temple
28 PWD Circuit House
29 Hazur Palace
30 Factory

To Jamnagar

Jynbeeli Bridge

Mudflats & Flamingos

Train Station

SV-Patel Road

Manek Chowk

Mahatma Gandhi Road (MG Road)

ST Road

Maidan

Fish-drying area

Arabian Sea

Harbour

0   250   500 m

Chowpatty Beach

Effluent Outfall

Deep-water Wharf

To Veraval

GUJARAT

are sizeable but some have no external windows. Checkout is 10 am.

Hotel Sheetal (☎ 241821), opposite the main post office, is a slightly better standard. Rooms have TV, hot water and often unusual furnishings. Prices start at Rs 250/300, or Rs 400/450 with air-con.

The *Shree Kandhlikrupa Guest House (☎ 246655, SV Patel Rd)*, on the corner near the train station, offers good rooms with bath for Rs 100/200, Rs 400 with air-con. Some rooms have TV.

If you want to be near the sea, Gujarat Tourism's *Tourist Bungalow (☎ 245476)* at Chowpatty Beach. It looks very rundown on the outside, but the rooms are fine and cost about Rs 150/200. There's a dining hall.

Places to Eat

Aadarsh Restaurant (MG Rd) has good, basic veg food at reasonable prices.

The *National (MG Rd)* next door, serves only nonveg dishes. It's simple but not bad.

Swagat Restaurant on the eastern end of MG Rd is a popular place, with Punjabi food from Rs 20.

Hotel Flamingo has a delightful air-con restaurant which offers a wide range of Punjabi, Chinese and South Indian food; a main dish costs Rs 30 to Rs 60. Nonguests are welcome.

Getting There & Away

Air Gujarat Airways has daily flights to Mumbai (US$125). Bookings can be made with Thankys Tours & Travels (☎ 245128) on MG Rd.

Bus The STC bus stand is a four minute walk from MG Rd. There are regular services to Dwarka, Jamnagar, Veraval and Rajkot. The private bus companies have offices on MG Rd, near the Hotel Flamingo. Most only have signs in Gujarati so you'll need to enlist some local help to find the one you want. There are buses to Jamnagar (Rs 40, three hours), Dwarka (Rs 30, two hours), Rajkot (Rs 50, four hours), Diu (Rs 60, 6½ hours) and Junagadh (Rs 25, two hours).

Train Porbandar is the terminus of a railway line. The main service is the *Saurashtra Express* to and from Mumbai (Rs 170/836 in 2nd/1st class, 959km, 23 hours), via Rajkot (Rs 61/286, 4½ hours) and Ahmedabad (Rs 104/510, 10 hours).

Getting Around

An auto-rickshaw to the airport costs about Rs 30.

DWARKA
☎ 02892 • pop 52,000

On the extreme western tip of the Kathiawar peninsula, Dwarka is one of the four most holy Hindu pilgrimage sites in India and is closely related to the Krishna legend. It was here that Krishna set up his capital after fleeing from Mathura.

Dwarkanath Temple is dedicated to Krishna. Non-Hindus can enter after filling out a form, though the exterior, with its tall five storey spire supported by 60 columns, is far more interesting than the interior. Archaeological excavations have revealed five earlier cities at the site, all submerged. Dwarka is the site of the most important Janmashtami Festival which falls in August/September and celebrates Krishna's birthday.

Also worth a look are the evocative carvings of **Rukmini Temple**, about 1km to the east.

Dwarka's **lighthouse** is open to the public between 4 and 6 pm, and affords an excellent panoramic view (Rs 1.50).

A little north of Dwarka, a ferry crosses from Okha to the **Island of Bet**, where Vishnu is said to have slain a demon. There are modern Krishna temples on the island, and a deserted beach on the northern coast. Beware of unfriendly dogs on this island.

Places to Stay & Eat

Toran Tourist Bungalow (☎ 34013), a state-run place, has dorm beds for Rs 50 and singles/doubles for Rs 200/300.

Meera Hotel (☎ 34031), on the main approach road, has rooms with private bath for Rs 100/200, and the dining room does good thalis for Rs 25.

Maruti Guest House (☎ 34722) is just a few minutes from Teen Bati Chowk. Simple singles/doubles are Rs 75/150, though some have no windows.

If you don't fancy feeding from the street stalls, nearby **Shetty's Fast Food** is one of the cheapest restaurants in town.

Getting There & Away
There is a railway line between Dwarka and Jamnagar (Rs 40, 132km), and there are trains to Mumbai (Rs 170/836, 945km) via Rajkot (Rs 58/272, 207km) and Ahmedabad (Rs 102/500, 453km).

STC buses run to all points in Saurashtra and Ahmedabad.

JAMNAGAR
☎ 0288 • pop 614,000
Prior to independence, the princely state of Jamnagar was ruled by the Jadeja Rajputs. The city was built around the small Ranmal Lake, in the centre of which is a small palace, reached by a causeway.

Jamnagar has a long history of pearl fishing and *bandhani* (a time-consuming knotting and dyeing process; see The Kutch – a Unique Region in Gujarat boxed text), but today is equally known for having the only Ayurvedic university in India and a temple listed in the *Guinness Book of Records* (see Bala Hanuman Temple entry).

The old part of town known as Chandni Chowk, has a number of interesting and impressive old buildings, such as the Mandvi Tower, and is very colourful. The centre of the old town is known as Darbar Gadh, a semicircular gathering place where the former Maharaja of Nawanagar once held public audiences.

Orientation & Information
The STC bus stand and the new train station are several kilometres apart and both are a long way from the city centre, so you'll need to take an auto-rickshaw. Most places to stay are in or near Teen Batti Chowk, though there are a couple of options by the bus stand.

English-language dailies can be found at the newsstand near the Hotel Swati.

The Corporation Bank, by Bedi Gate, exchanges travellers cheques Monday to Friday between 11 am and 3 pm. You may have to remind them to give you an encashment certificate.

Lakhota Palace
This diminutive palace once belonged to the Maharaja of Nawanagar. Today it houses a small museum with displays from local archaeological sites. The **museum** is reached by a short causeway from the northern side of Ranmal Lake, and is open daily from 10.30 am to 1 pm and 3 to 5.30 pm (closed Wednesday and the second and fourth Saturday in the month). Entry costs Rs 0.50.

Bala Hanuman Temple
The Bala Hanuman Temple is on the southeastern side of Ranmal Lake, and here, 24 hours a day since 1 August 1964, there's been continuous chanting of the invocation 'Shri Ram, Jai Ram, Jai Jai Ram'. This devotion has earned the temple a place in the *Guinness Book of Records*. Early evening is a particularly good time to visit as it's fairly animated then. In fact this whole area on the south-eastern edge of the lake becomes very lively around sunset when people come to promenade, and the usual *chai* and *kulfi* stalls set up and ply their trade.

Jain Temples
Two Jain temples, Shantinath Mandir and Adinath Mandir, in front of the main post office in Darbar Gadh, are very colourful with fine murals and domes.

Cremation Park
You don't require a morbid disposition to visit Jamnagar's cremation park, only 10 minutes north of the city centre by autorickshaw. There are statues of saints, deities, and scenes from the *Ramayana*. This is an interesting place to visit, and the atmosphere is anything but depressing.

Places to Stay
Getting accommodation here can be difficult. Jamnagar has a burgeoning industrial

GUJARAT

GUJARAT

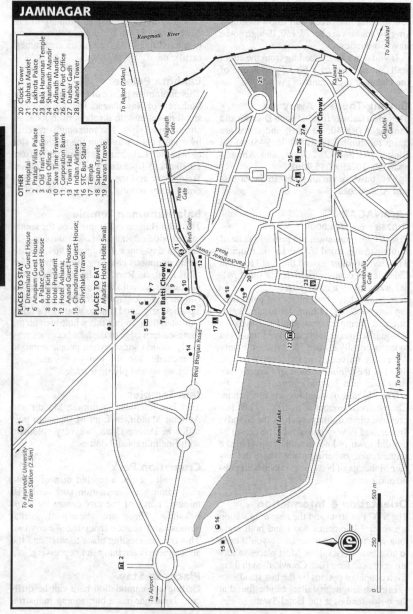

JAMNAGAR

PLACES TO STAY
4 Dreamland Guest House
6 Anupam Guest House
& Palace Guest House
8 Hotel Kirti
9 Hotel President
12 Hotel Ashiana;
Anand Guest House
15 Chandramauli Guest House;
Shivshakti Travels

PLACES TO EAT
7 Madras Hotel; Hotel Swati

OTHER
1 Hospital
2 Pratap Villas Palace
3 Old Train Station
5 Post Office
10 Save Time Travels
11 Corporation Bank
13 Town Hall
14 Indian Airlines
16 STC Bus Stand
17 Temple
18 Sapan Travels
19 Paavan Travels
20 Clock Tower
21 Subhas Market
22 Lakhota Palace
23 Bala Hanuman Temple
24 Shantinath Mandir
25 Adinath Mandir
26 Main Post Office
27 Darbar Gadh
28 Mandvi Tower

Rangmati   River

To Kalavad

Kalawat Gate

Ghalachi Gate

Chandni Chowk

Khambhalia Gate

To Porbandar

Khambhalia Gate

Ranmal Lake

To Rajkot (75km)

Nagnath Gate

Three Gate

Bedi Gate

Panchleshwar Tower

Panchleshwar Road

Teen Batti Chowk

Bhid Bhanjan Road

To Ayurvedic University
& Train Station (2.5km)

To Airport

0   250   500 m

sector and hordes of business travellers constantly converge on the town so it's a good idea to book ahead.

Anupam and *Palace* guest houses, in Teen Batti Chowk, have singles/doubles for Rs 100/150 and Rs 125/150 respectively. However, they're depressing dosshouses so if you can afford somewhere better, go there.

Dreamland Guest House (☎ *670436*), also in this area, is set back from the road and reasonably quiet. Double rooms with bathroom cost from Rs 200 (ordinary) up to Rs 800 (deluxe air-con).

Hotel Ashiana (☎ *550583*) a vast, rambling place on the top floor of the New Super Market complex, has a range of rooms with bathroom and TV from Rs 200/300, or Rs 500/600 with air-con. Beware of those rooms with thin plywood walls. There's a veg restaurant here.

Anand Guest House, (☎ *678983*) in the same complex, has seedy rooms for Rs 75/100 with cold water.

Hotel Kirti (☎ *557121*), off Teen Batti Chowk, has clean rooms with TV and hot water, and sometimes balcony. Singles/doubles go for Rs 350/450, or Rs 500/60 with air-con.

Chandramauli Guest House (☎ *672111*) is opposite the bus stand, on the 2nd floor. Rooms with hot water and (usually) TV are Rs 200/300, or Rs 500 with air-con. It's the best value of several nearby places.

Hotel President (☎ *557491, fax 558491*), Teen Batti Chowk, is Jamnagar's best hotel. Singles/doubles with private bath, hot water and TV are Rs 450/560, or Rs 650/790 with air-con. They're the best rooms in town in this range. There's a restaurant and moneychanging facilities.

Places to Eat

For cheap snack food in the evening try the stalls set up near Bala Hanuman Temple. In the centre of town in the Teen Batti Chowk area, there are plenty of small eating places.

Around Mandvi Tower in the heart of the old town there's an extraordinary array of 'sweetmeat' shops selling a wide variety of sweet and sticky creations.

Hotel Swati is a vegetarian place with an extensive range of South Indian, Jain and Punjabi dishes for Rs 30 to Rs 60.

Madras Hotel, nearby, specialises in vegetarian South Indian and Punjabi cuisine, as well as pizzas (Rs 35).

7 Seas Restaurant at the Hotel President offers good food, which includes continental choices; veg/nonveg dishes start at Rs 40/60.

Getting There & Away

Air Indian Airlines (☎ 550211) has five flights a week to Mumbai (US$95); its on Bhid Bhanjan Rd, open daily from 10 am to 5 pm. Bookings can also be made with Save Time Travels (☎ 553137), between Bedi Gate and the town hall.

Bus STC buses go hourly to Rajkot (Rs 26) and every 30 minutes to Junagadh (Rs 34); other buses go to Dwarka, Porbandar, Bhuj and Ahmedabad.

There are various private bus companies. Shivshakti Travels (☎ 670091) in the basement of the building opposite the bus stand, has departures every 20 minutes to Rajkot (Rs 25, two hours), as well as services to Junagadh (Rs 35, three hours) and Porbandar (Rs 40, three hours). Most of the other offices are in the town centre, on a road leading west from the clock tower. These include Sapan Travels (☎ 558558), with buses to Rajkot and Ahmedabad (six hours, Rs 90), and Paavan Travels (☎ 552002), with four departures to Ahmedabad, and one at 3 pm to Mumbai (Rs 270, 20 hours).

Train There are direct trains from Mumbai and Ahmedabad (via Rajkot). The fare for the 321km trip to Ahmedabad is Rs 79/388, or Rs 320 for a three tier sleeper. The 813km trip to Mumbai costs Rs 156/766.

To Dwarka, the 132km journey takes three hours by express train, or a tedious 5½ hours on the daily 'fast passenger' service (Rs 40).

Getting Around

There is no minibus service to the airport, which is a long way out. Auto-rickshaw drivers demand at least Rs 100. A rickshaw from the bus stand to the Bedi Gate area costs about Rs 10. From Teen Batti Chowk to the new train station, about 4km north of the city centre, expect to pay about Rs 25.

RAJKOT
☎ 0281 • pop 1.13 million

This bustling town was once the capital of the princely state of Saurashtra and is also a former British government headquarters. Mahatma Gandhi spent the early years of his life here and the school he attended is marked with a statue.

The prestigious Rajkumar College dates back to the second half of last century and is regarded as one of the best private schools in the country. It was one of five schools set up by the British for the education of the sons of nobility (*rajkumar* means prince).

Information

Rajkot has very a helpful tourist office (☎ 234507), but it's hidden away behind the old State Bank of Saurashtra building on Jawahar Rd, almost opposite the Galaxy Hotel. It's open Monday to Friday and the first and third Saturday of the month, from 10.30 am to 1.30 pm and 2 to 6 pm. Ask here about Motel, a new 'theme' village on Kalawad Rd, with a restaurant and expensive cottage accommodation.

The State Bank of India, to the north of the Jubilee Gardens, has moneychanging facilities. Entry is from the rear of the building.

Watson Museum & Library

The Watson Museum and Library in the Jubilee Gardens commemorates Colonel John Watson, Political Agent from 1886-89.

The entrance is flanked by two imperial lions. Among the exhibits are copies of artefacts from Mohenjodaro, 13th century carvings, temple statues, natural history exhibits and dioramas of local Adivasi costumes and housing styles.

Perhaps the most startling piece is a huge marble statue of Queen Victoria seated on a throne, decidedly not amused. The museum is open Thursday to Tuesday from 9 am to 1 pm and 2 to 6 pm; entry costs Rs 0.50.

Kaba Gandhi No Delo

This is the house where Gandhi grew up, and it now holds a permanent exhibition of Gandhi items. It's within the old city on Ghee Kanta Rd, and entry is free. Opening hours are flexible, around 9 am to noon and 3 to 5.30 pm, Monday to Saturday. The old city itself is an atmospheric place to wander around in.

Places to Stay – Budget

Rajkot has a good range of accommodation. Kanak Rd, on the east side of the STC bus stand, has a number of hotels.

Milan Guest House (☎ 235878), right by the bus stand, is OK, with small singles from Rs 60, and doubles with bathroom for Rs 100.

Jayshree Guest House (☎ 227954, *Kanak Rd*), a little north, has plain rooms for Rs 70/120, or Rs 85/150 with bathroom. Deluxe rooms for Rs 180/225 are much better, and have a TV.

Jyoti Guest House (☎ 225271, *Kanak Rd*) is a little further from the bus stand, so is a fraction quieter. Doubles with bath are Rs 125, and dorm beds are Rs 30.

Hotel Yash (☎ 227052, *Dhebar Rd*), a five minute walk from the bus stand, is new and has clean, attractively furnished rooms with TV, telephone and bath. It's good value at Rs 150/200, or Rs 295/395 with air-con.

Vijay Guest House (☎ 236550) nearby, is simpler but also a good deal, charging from Rs 70/130 with bath.

Places to Stay – Mid-Range & Top End

Hotel Samrat International (☎ 222269, *37 Karanpara Rd*), south of the bus stand, has well-appointed rooms for Rs 260/400, or from Rs 450/650 with air-con; there's a veg restaurant here.

Hotel Tulsi (☎ 231731, fax 231735), on the middle of the three adjoining roads heading south, is a good choice, with comfortable and clean rooms for Rs 260/400, or Rs 400/550 with air-con.

Galaxy Hotel (☎ 222904, fax 227053), on the 3rd floor of the Galaxy Commercial

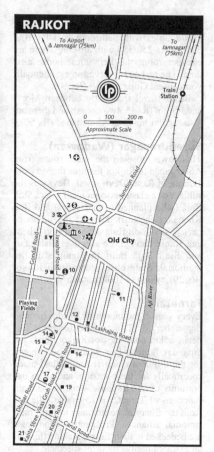

RAJKOT

PLACES TO STAY
9   Galaxy Hotel
14 Hotel Yash & Indian Airlines
15 Vijay Guest House
16 Jyoti Guest House & Woodland Restaurant
18 Jayshree Guest House
19 Milan Guest House
20 Hotel Samrat International
21 Hotel Tulsi

PLACES TO EAT
8   Havmor
13 Rainbow Restaurant

OTHER
1   Government Hospital
2   State Bank of India
3   Telegraph Office
4   Hospital
5   Gandhi School & Statue
6   Watson Museum & Library
7   Jubilee Gardens
10 Tourist Office
11 Kaba Gandhi No Delo
12 Library
17 STC Bus Stand

GUJARAT

Centre on Jawahar Rd, has a slightly classier ambience, with rooms from Rs 400/600, or Rs 600/900 with air-con. The hotel has moneychanging facilities for guests, but no restaurant.

Places to Eat
Rainbow Restaurant (Lakhajiraj Rd) has tasty and cheap South Indian cuisine. There's an air-con section upstairs. This place has an impressive selection of ice cream: see if you can resist 'Nuts in Love'!

Havmor, up near the Jubilee Gardens, serves Indian, Chinese and western food from Rs 40 (veg and nonveg).

The quality and ambience of the *Woodland Restaurant (Kanak Rd)* in the Hotel Kavery makes it feel like an upmarket place, but the prices are very reasonable. Vegetarian dishes start at Rs 22; Gujarati thalis are Rs 65.

Getting There & Away
Air The Indian Airlines office (☎ 227916) is on Dhebar Rd. Indian Airlines has four direct flights a week between Rajkot and Mumbai (US$75).

Bus STC buses connect Rajkot with Jamnagar, Junagadh, Porbandar, Veraval and Ahmedabad. The trip to Veraval (Rs 40, five hours) is via Junagadh (Rs 25, two hours).

There are a number of private buses which operate to such places as Ahmedabad, Bhuj, Bhavnagar, Una (for Diu), Mt Abu, Udaipur and Mumbai. These companies' offices are on Kanak Rd, by the bus stand.

Train A number of broad-gauge express trains connect Rajkot with Ahmedabad (Rs 62/313, 5½ hours, 246km). Trains also go to/from Jamnagar (Rs 28/149, 75km), Porbandar (Rs 61/294, 221km), and Mumbai (Rs 145/726, 738km). There's a metre-gauge service to Veraval (Rs 53/258, 186km).

Getting Around

A rickshaw to the airport from the city centre costs about Rs 50; to the train station expect to pay Rs 15.

AROUND RAJKOT
Wankaner

This tiny town is about 38km north of Rajkot, and has a striking **palace** (☎ 02828-20000) that looks like something straight out of a fairytale. It was built in 1907 and is a curious Greco-Roman Gothic Indo Scottish baronial extravagance.

As the royal family still lives in the palace, guests are accommodated a couple of kilometres away. *Oasis House* is an original Art Deco building complete with indoor swimming pool. While hardly palatial, the rooms are comfortable, and meals are taken at the palace with the family. The charge is Rs 1650 per person, including meals.

There are regular buses to Rajkot every half hour, and Wankaner Junction is on the main railway line to Ahmedabad (Rs 58/272, 205km).

Morvi

About 65km north of Rajkot is Morvi, a friendly little town that's well off the main tourist track. There's an amazing 'swinging bridge' here that's definitely worth checking out if you're in the area. The suspended 19th century wooden bridge connects the old palace with the new palace, and yes, it actually shakes, creaks and rocks as you make your way across. The bridge overlooks a murky river (no crocodiles!) and has good views of the palace (closed to the public) and town. The swinging bridge is open daily from 7 am to 7 pm and there's an entry fee.

Thakar Lodge (☎ 02822-31578) about 1km from the bus stand and near the veg-etable market, is the best place to stay. Singles/doubles with bathroom cost Rs 100/330, or Rs 250/555 with air-con. There are cheaper rooms at their guest house next door. The restaurant serves an excellent all-you-can-eat Gujarati thali (Rs 60).

Buses travel frequently between Morvi and Rajkot (Rs 15, two hours), and there are also regular buses to Ahmedabad (Rs 50).

Surendranagar (Wadhwan)

This town close to the main route from Ahmedabad to Rajkot features the very old **Temple of Ranik Devi**. Ranik Devi was the subject of a clash between local rulers Sidh Raja (who planned to marry her) and Rao Khengar (who carried her off and did marry her). When Sidh Raja defeated Rao Khengar, Ranik Devi chose *sati* over dishonour and Sidh Raja built the temple as her memorial. State buses go to/from Rajkot (Rs 29), which is 100km south-west.

Tarnetar

Every year in the month of Bhadra (around September), the Trineteshwar Temple at Tarnetar, 65km north-east of Rajkot, hosts the three day **Tarnetar Fair**, which is best known for the different *chhatris* (umbrellas) made specifically for the occasion, and as an opportunity to find a spouse – one of the main functions of Tarnetar is to enable villagers from the Bharwad community to form matrimonial alliances. Prospective candidates are bedecked in their finery, making this fair an extraordinarily colourful spectacle.

According to legend, Arjuna once danced at this site, and the River Ganges flows into the tank here once a year.

Special state buses go to/from Rajkot during the fair.

Gondal

On the Rajkot to Junagadh road, 39km south of Rajkot on the River Gondali, is the town of Gondal. Once the centre of a former prosperous princely state, it still has some impressive buildings. The **Naulakaha Darbargadh palace** (named after the nine lakhs it cost to build) is well worth a look.

Riverside Palace (☎ *02825-20002)* is an interesting place to stay in Gondal. It costs Rs 1975 per person including all meals and local sightseeing. The present royal family still has the Maharaja's collection of 30 or so vintage cars, and in the palace railway yard are two royal rail carriages. One of these carriages has been restored to its former glory; sleeping here costs Rs 2200, including meals.

There are regular state buses to Gondal from Rajkot (Rs 12, one hour).

Kutch (Kachchh)

The westernmost part of Gujarat is virtually an island; during the monsoon period from May onwards, it really is an island. The Gulf of Kutch divides Kutch (also known as Kachchh) from the Kathiawar peninsula. To the north, it is separated from the Sind region of Pakistan by the Great Rann of Kutch.

The salt in the soil makes this low-lying marsh area almost completely barren. Only on scattered 'islands' above the salt level is there vegetation. During the dry season, the Rann is a vast expanse of hard, dried mud. Then, with the start of the monsoon in May, it is flooded first by sea water, then by the fresh river water. Kutch is also separated from the rest of Gujarat to the east by the Little Rann of Kutch.

During the winter, the Gulf of Kutch is a breeding ground for flamingos and pelicans. Few tourists make it to this remote part of India.

BHUJ
☎ 02832 • pop 200,000

Bhuj, the major town of Kutch, is an old walled city – in the past the city gates were locked each night from dusk to dawn. You can lose yourself for hours in the intricate maze of streets and alleys of this fascinating town. There are walls within walls, attractive crenellated gateways, old palaces with intricately carved wooden pavilions, and striking, brightly decorated Hindu temples.

The large Hamirsar Tank adjoins the old town to the west (this will be dry if there's been no monsoon). It is named after Maharao Hamir who established Bhuj in 1510. In 1549 Rao Khengarji I selected Bhuj as his capital, and in 1723 the city walls were built – some sections of which are still standing.

Bhuj resembles much of India before the tourist invasion, and you're much more likely to come across that disarming hospitality which was once the hallmark of rural India.

It also hosts the annual Rann Utsav Festival in February/March. There are craft demonstrations, cultural programs and tours to places of interest in the region. Also known as the Deseert Festival, it usually coincides with the full moon of Shivaratri.

Information

The tourist office (☎ 20004), housed in the Aina Mahal, is staffed by Mr PJ Jethi, who is a mine of information on anything to do with Bhuj and Kutch. It's possible to arrange a guide (Rs 350 per day) and car (Rs 750) through the tourist office, though you can get cheaper rates by asking around the taxi stands. The tourist office is open daily from 9 am to noon, and 3 to 6 pm Sunday to Friday. It sells city and Kutch maps for Rs 5, and postcards and books on Kutch.

The State Bank of India on Station Rd offers moneychanging facilities, but only accepts Thomas Cook travellers cheques. The Hotel Prince will change money for anyone, at acceptable rates. Or there's Globex Travels & Exchange, Sahar Rd, which changes many currencies (no commission) and travellers cheques (Rs 50 commission). It's open 10 am to 9 pm, Monday to Saturday.

If you feel like taking a refreshing dip, there's a swimming pool at Hotel Lakeview, at the south end of the lake. Opening times vary, and it costs Rs 10 for 45 minutes.

The main post office is about a five minute walk from the STC bus stand. There is also a branch opposite the City Guest House.

Mr Thacker runs a helpful STD office in front of the bus station (1st floor), and plans to install email facilities.

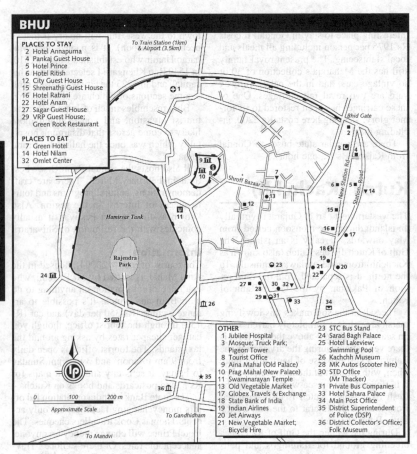

BHUJ

PLACES TO STAY
2 Hotel Annapurna
4 Pankaj Guest House
5 Hotel Prince
6 Hotel Ritish
12 City Guest House
15 Shreenathji Guest House
16 Hotel Ratrani
22 Hotel Anam
27 Sagar Guest House
29 VRP Guest House;
    Green Rock Restaurant

PLACES TO EAT
7 Green Hotel
14 Hotel Nilam
32 Omlet Center

To Train Station (1km)
& Airport (3.5km)

Bhid Gate

Shroff Bazaar

New Station Rd
Station Road

Hamirsar Tank

Rajendra
Park

To Gandhidham

To Mandvi

0   100   200 m
Approximate Scale

★ 35

36

OTHER
1 Jubilee Hospital
3 Mosque; Truck Park;
    Pigeon Tower
8 Tourist Office
9 Aina Mahal (Old Palace)
10 Prag Mahal (New Palace)
11 Swaminarayan Temple
13 Old Vegetable Market
17 Globex Travels & Exchange
18 State Bank of India
19 Indian Airlines
20 Jet Airways
21 New Vegetable Market;
    Bicycle Hire
23 STC Bus Stand
24 Sarad Bagh Palace
25 Hotel Lakeview;
    Swimming Pool
26 Kachchh Museum
28 MK Autos (scooter hire)
30 STD Office
    (Mr Thacker)
31 Private Bus Companies
33 Hotel Sahara Palace
34 Main Post Office
35 District Superintendent
    of Police (DSP)
36 District Collector's Office;
    Folk Museum

Curiocity in Gujarat (☎ 53408) runs tours in Kutch, including camel safaris.

Permits To visit the villages north of Kutch, including Khavda, Bhirandiara and Dumaro, permission is required from the District Collector. First you need to present yourself (in person) at the District Superintendent of Police (DSP) office, where you have to complete a form advising which villages you wish to visit, with dates. Bring your passport, and two photocopies of your passport and visa details. It's open Monday to Saturday from 10.30 to 6 pm. Then take the documentation to the District Collector's office (about three minutes walk; open weekdays from 11 am to 2 pm and 4 to 6 pm) where the form will be authorised. The whole procedure should take no more than 1½ hours, and there is no fee.

Aina Mahal (Old Palace)

Maharao Lakhpatji's old palace, built in traditional Kutchi style, is in a small fortified courtyard in the old part of the city. It's a beautifully presented museum and is one of the highlights of a visit to Bhuj. The entrance to the palace houses the tourist office, and this is also the site of the **Maharao Madansinhji Museum**, which has a varied collection of paintings, photos, ornaments and embroideries. There's a 15m-long scroll depicting the Royal Procession of Maharao Shri Pragmalji Bahadur (1838-75). Check out the expression on the last blue-turbaned figure in this epic painting – he looks quite peeved at having to ignobly bring up the rear of the procession!

The real attraction here, though, is the **Hall of Mirrors**, created by the master artisan, Ram Singh Malam, under the patronage of his poet-ruler, Maharao Shri Lakhpatji around the middle of the 18th century. A blend of Indian and European artistry (Ram Singh acquired his skills in Europe), the walls of the great hall are of white marble covered by mirrors separated by gilded ornaments. Light is provided by elaborate candelabra, with shades of Venetian glass. Another remarkable feature is the **pleasure pool**, in the middle of which rises a square platform where the maharao composed his poems and gave encouragement to the classical arts of dancing girls, bards and musicians. Upstairs, note the massive elephant earrings.

This palace is well worth a two hour visit, and is open Sunday to Friday from 9 am to noon and 3 to 6 pm. Entry is Rs 5 and photography is prohibited.

Prag Mahal (New Palace)

Across the courtyard from the Aina Mahal is the new palace, an ornate marble and sandstone building that was constructed in the latter part of the 19th century. Parts of it are now government offices but sections are open to the public. **Durbar Hall** is a kitsch unfurnished hall bearing portraits of past maharaos, and the remnants of big game driven to the verge of extinction in the name of pleasure. The **clock tower** provides a good view of the town. Combined entry is Rs 5, Rs 15 a camera and Rs 50 for a video.

Kachchh Museum

This was originally known as the Fergusson Museum after its founder, Sir James Fergusson, a governor of Mumbai under the Raj. Built in 1877, it's the oldest museum in Gujarat and has an excellent collection. The well-maintained exhibits (labelled in English and Gujarati) include a picture gallery, an anthropological section, archaeological finds, textiles, weapons, unique regional musical instruments, a shipping section and, of course, stuffed beasts. The museum is open daily except Wednesday and the second and fourth Saturday of each month, from 9 am to noon and 3 to 6 pm. Entry is Rs 0.50.

Sarad Bagh Palace

The last maharao died in the UK in 1991 and his palace to the west of the lake has been turned into a small museum. Set in spacious and beautifully tended gardens, the palace itself, built in 1867, is of very modest proportions, with just a drawing room downstairs and bedroom upstairs (closed). The dining room is in a separate building and on display here are a number of the maharao's personal possessions, including his video player. Also on display is his coffin, in which his body was brought back from the UK for cremation.

The palace is open from 9 am to noon and 3 to 6 pm Saturday to Thursday; entry is Rs 5. There's also a Rs 15 camera charge, Rs 50 for a video.

Other Attractions

A huge old wall stretches around the hills overlooking the city. Unfortunately, you can't explore; it's a restricted military area.

The very colourful and richly decorated **Swaminarayan Temple** is near the Aina Mahal. It's open to the public from around 7 to 11 am and 4 to 7 pm.

The **Bhartiya Sanscruti Darshan Kachchh** (Folk Museum) houses a private collection of beautiful textiles and artefacts, and also has reconstructions of typical village habitats. It's open 9 am to noon and 3 to 6 pm, Tuesday to Sunday, and entry costs Rs 5.

Places to Stay – Budget

There's a good range of cheap accommodation in Bhuj. Unless stated, rooms mentioned have bathroom.

Hotel Annapurna (☎ 20831), by Bhid Gate, is a good choice. It has rooms from Rs 60/100, or Rs 50/70 with shared bathroom. There's a restaurant, and the hosts are helpful and friendly.

The *City Guest House* (☎ 21067) is between the old vegetable market and the palace, in the middle of the old walled city. This traveller-friendly hotel has a courtyard area and views from the rooftop. Small but clean doubles go for Rs 170; singles/doubles with shared bath are Rs 60/130. There is free bucket hot water, and checkout is 24 hours.

Shreenathji Guest House (☎ 22388, New Station Rd) is just east of Shroff Bazaar. Singles/doubles with hot water cost Rs 60/100. The restaurant serves Gujarati thalis at lunch for Rs 25.

Hotel Ritish (☎ 24117, New Station Rd) is 50m north and has clean, large rooms with hot water in the mornings only for Rs 75/110. There are also rooms with shared bath for Rs 55/85 and dorm beds for Rs 30.

A little further north is *Pankaj Guest House* (☎ 21867). It's great value (rooms for Rs 50/75) but the tourist office warns about locals gambling and drinking here.

Sagar Guest House (☎ 21479), near the bus stand, has tiny singles with shared bath for Rs 50, and singles/doubles/triples with bathroom for Rs 75/100/155. Dorm beds are a mere Rs 30. The rooms are right above the street, so they can get a bit noisy.

VRP Guest House (☎ 21388), around the corner, has clean and fairly quiet rooms with shared bath for Rs 50/80, and with private bathroom for Rs 55/100.

Places to Stay – Mid-Range & Top End

Hotel Anam (☎/fax 53397, Station Rd) has a range of clean, reasonably-sized rooms, all with hot water and TV. Prices are Rs 200/400, or Rs 550/700 with air-con. There's a good veg restaurant here.

Hotel Prince (☎ 20370, fax 50373, Station Rd) is a noticeable step up in furnishings, facilities and ambience. Singles/doubles cost Rs 400/550, or from Rs 850/1100 with air-con. There are several restaurants, a craft shop and moneychanging facilities.

Places to Eat

Omlet Center, in the line of shops outside the bus stand, is good for a cheap breakfast from 8 am.

Hotel Anam is the place to go for a really serious feed. The restaurant limits itself to tasty all-you-can-eat Gujarati thalis for Rs 50. An afternoon nap is recommended for those who over-indulge!

Green Rock restaurant in the same building as the VRP Guest House also serves excellent refillable thalis (Rs 50), and has Indian and Chinese veg dishes.

Hotel Prince has both veg and nonveg restaurants, and also offers open-air dining in the atmospheric courtyard. Most dishes are above Rs 60.

Hotel Nilam, opposite the Hotel Prince, is a popular vegetarian restaurant specialising in Punjabi and Chinese cuisine (from Rs 35).

Green Hotel, down a small alley opposite the old vegetable market, offers cheap veg meals and snacks.

Shopping

If you are genuinely interested in the embroidery from villages in the Kutch region, get in touch with Mr AA Wazir (☎ 24187). He has a priceless collection of more than 4000 pieces, many of them very old. Some pieces are for sale (with prices starting at around Rs 500). Remember, this is not a museum or shop, so don't expect the owner to show you each and every piece.

In the bustling Shroff Bazaar there are a range of reasonably priced shops, including some good embroidery and fabric places. Many places are not willing to bargain.

Getting There & Away

Air The Indian Airlines office (☎ 21433) is open daily from 10 am to 5 pm. There are four flights weekly to Mumbai (US$100).

Jet Airways (☎ 53671) charges US$102 to Mumbai, but flights are daily. As the Indian Air Force has a base at the airport, there is tight security there.

Bus The private company offices are in the bus stand area. They have services to Rajkot (Rs 65, six hours), Ahmedabad (Rs 110 for a seat, or Rs 160 for a berth – yes, sleeper coaches for this seven hour trip!), and in summer only to Mumbai (Rs 450, 18 hours). Patel Tours, Sahjanand Tours and Hemal Travels all book sleeper coaches.

STC buses run to Jaisalmer in Rajasthan via Rathapur and Tarada (Rs 170, 15 hours). For other places in Rajasthan, such as Abu Rd, Ajmer and Jaipur, you'll need to get a bus to Palanpur (Rs 85, at 11 am only), and a second bus from there.

There are regular departures to the villages of Kutch; see Around Bhuj for details.

Train New Bhuj train station is 1km north of town down a little back road from the Sarpat (North) gate of the old town. Palanpur (Rs 90/455, 391km, 12 hours, departure at 8.20 pm) is the gateway to various points in Rajasthan. It's possible to travel to Ahmedabad via Palanpur but it's quicker to get a train or bus to Gandhidham (Rs 15, 1½ hours), which has connections to Rajkot, Ahmedabad, Vadodara, Mumbai and elsewhere.

To book a ticket, you don't have to face the hassle of going out to the train station. For Rs 25, some travel agents will make the reservation for you. One place that offers this service is Hemal Travels (☎ 52491), near the STC bus stand.

Share Taxi A share taxi to Mandvi or Gandhidham is Rs 25; these leave from the side road by the Hotel Sahara Palace.

Taxis to Kutch villages leave from near the STC stand; they usually have to be hired on a private basis (Rs 3 per kilometre) though sometimes you can find shared taxis.

Getting Around
An auto-rickshaw to the train station costs Rs 20, and to the airport, at least Rs 30.

Auto-rickshaws can't negotiate the crowded streets of the bazaar area.

There's only one (hard to find) place renting bicycles: it's behind Shankar Lodge east of the bus stand (Rs 4 per hour, Rs 30 per day, closed Sunday). Pricey scooters can be hired from MK Autos (☎ 22242), west of the STC bus stand. Prices per day are Rs 250 (Bajaj) or Rs 250 (Honda Hero).

AROUND BHUJ
Gandhidham
☎ 02836 • pop 335,000
The new town of Gandhidham, near Kandla, was established to take refugees from the Sind following Partition. The town has nothing of interest, but there are plenty of hotels if you are stuck here for a night.

Hotel Natraj (☎ 21955), opposite the bus stand, is a good choice. this comfortable place has rooms with bathroom for Rs 287/460, or Rs 375/575 with air-con. There's a veg restaurant.

The bus stand is about 200m diagonally to your right as you leave the train station. Buses to Bhuj leave every 30 minutes (Rs 15, 1½ hours).

Kutch Villages
The villages of the Kutch region each specialise in a different form of handicraft, and it would be easy to spend a week visiting some of them using Bhuj as a base. Due to their proximity to the Pakistan border, you will require a permit signed by the Bhuj District Collector (see Permits in the Bhuj section for details) to visit the villages north of Bhuj. Bhuj tourist office's map indicates which villages you can visit with or without permission. When visiting these villages, be sensitive to local customs and sensibilities, eg wear clothes that cover your knees, and ask before photographing people.

Some of the more important villages, (and the crafts they specialise in) include **Bhujjodi** (wool and cotton weaving), **Padhar** and **Dhaneti** (Ahir embroidery), **Dhamanka** (block printing), **Lilpur** (embroidery) and **Anjar** (nut-crackers, block printing and tie-dyeing). Several travellers warn of the children in Padhar and Dhaneti, who some-times throw stones. But generally people are friendly and welcoming, and you might be invited into their homes (remove your shoes before entering).

Dholavira is a little village on a small 'is-land' north-east of Bhuj. Here, archaeolo-gists have unearthed a city belonging to the Harappan (Indus Valley) civilisation.

For more information, contact Mr Jethi at the tourist office in the Aina Mahal, Bhuj. He also gives details of the meditation cen-tre at Bada, near Mandvi, offering free 10-day courses (donation requested).

Places to Stay & Eat Accommodation in the villages is predictably limited.

Gandhi Ashram at Lilpur offers rooms for around Rs 100 including meals. Anjar also has some very basic guesthouses.

Getting There & Away There are buses to Anjar (Rs 10) every 30 minutes from the bus stand in Bhuj. To Lilpur, there are three daily buses (Rs 30), or take one of the many buses to Rapar and get another bus from there. Alternatively, ask the driver on the bus to Rapar to drop you off at the turn-off to Lilpur, and walk the 3km to the village.

The Kutch – a Unique Region in Gujarat

The Kutch is a fascinating, isolated region of India that well rewards the few travellers who take time to explore its many villages. Local women wear colourful, distinctive costumes that are often augmented by elaborate earrings or nosepieces. Tattooing is also common among unmarried women and men.

There are several different tribes that populate the Kutch, including the Jats, Ahirs and Hari-jans. The Rabaris are the largest group. They are traditionally seminomadic; the men spend up to 10 months of the year seeking new grazing pastures with their livestock (sheep, goats or camels), while the women and children stay in the village. Milk and milk products are their main source of income, though Rabari women also excel at embroidery work.

Kutch handicrafts encompass a range of products and skills, including engraved silver jew-ellery, intricate leather and fabric embroidery, and wood carvings. Usually different tribes spe-cialise in different skills. The best-known method of preparing cloth or other fabrics is a tie-dye process called *badhani*, believed to have been used in the area for up to 5000 years. It's a very time-consuming process of tying thousands of tiny knots in a piece of fabric that has first been folded upon itself a number of times. This is then dyed in several stages using dif-ferent colours. The knots are then pulled apart and the fabric unfolded, to reveal a repeating pattern in a variety of hues. The process is used for saris, shirts, shawls and other items.

If you're interested in buying Kutch handicrafts, but want to ensure that the craftspeople get a fair cut of the profits, consider buying through the Qasab stall in the Hotel Prince, Bhuj. Qasab handicrafts are produced by Kutch Mahila Vikas Sangathan (KMVS; ☎ 02832-22124), an organisation comprising 4000 rural women that pays members a dividend of the profits and invests money at village level to meet social needs. Look out also for Shrujan, a charita-ble trust that runs training programs in various handicrafts skills for rural women and pro-vides a marketing infrastructure for 2000 artisans.

Although many aspects of Kutchi culture are thriving, some of its unique folk musical tra-ditions are dying out. Surando is an unusual stringed instrument that is very hard to manu-facture and master. Currently only one person in Gujarat is able to play it, and nobody is able to make one! Anyone with a special interest in Kutch music should contact Mr Jadia in the Kachchh Museum in Bhuj.

Than Monastery

About 60km from Bhuj, at the base of Dhin-odar Hill, the Than Monastery is a good place to trek to. It's a community of sadhus founded by Dharamnath (see the Dharamnath boxed text). Permission to visit this area is required from the District Collector in Bhuj.

Dharamsala has extremely basic accommodation (by donation). It's considerate to try to limit your stay here to just a night or two, because this place is really for pilgrims, not tourists.

There are three daily buses from Bhuj to Than (Rs 10). Alternatively, you could take an hourly bus to Nakatrana (Rs 10), west of Bhuj, and then another bus to Than (Rs 10). You will have to walk the last 3km to the monastery, which is at the end of the road.

MANDVI

☎ 02834 • pop 40,670

Sixty kilometres south-west of Bhuj, Mandvi is being promoted as a beach resort, and the beach is good, long and clean. The town has a long history of shipbuilding, and fishing boats and larger cargo vessels are still built in the port. Mandvi is a pleasant and unspoilt seaside town, with friendly people and no hassles, but not many travellers venture out here.

Places to Stay & Eat

The Jain *Dharamsala* near the bus stand has rooms for only Rs 30, though you'll need to respect the pilgrims' beliefs (no smoking or alcohol).

Shital Guest House (☎ 21160) has very basic rooms with shared bath for Rs 50/70 and dorm beds for a mere Rs 20.

Newer and nicer is *Maitri Guest House* (☎ 20183, Bunder Rd), with clean singles/doubles with bathroom (hot water) for Rs 150/200.

Sahara Guest House (☎ 20272), in the town centre, is also good. Rooms for Rs 175/250 come with hot water and TV.

An eccentric but enjoyable place to stay is the new *Rukmavati Guest House* (☎ 20558). It's a converted hospital, still with hospital-style beds and the owner uses the ambulance to conduct tours! Singles/doubles are Rs 150/200 (bucket hot water), dorms are Rs 50, and checkout is 24 hours.

Vijay Villas Guest House (☎ 20043) within the Vijay Villas Palace compound, is 8km west of Mandvi and 10 minutes from a good beach. There are just a few double rooms with bathroom from Rs 300, and meals can be ordered.

Zorba the Buddha, in the heart of the city, is a good place for cheap thalis (Rs 30). *Krishna Hotel* (*Bhed Bazaar*) and *Nayna Hotel* (*Azad Chowk*) are also good for veg food.

Getting There & Away

Buses leave for Mandvi from the bus stand in Bhuj every 30 minutes (Rs 20). A share taxi from Bhuj to Mandvi costs Rs 25.

Mandvi-Mumbai and Mandvi-Jamnagar ferry services have been talked about for years. They might actually happen very soon.

LITTLE RANN OF KUTCH

The Little Rann of Kutch, the barren expanse of 'desert' (actually salt plains) which divides Gujarat's western region of Kutch from the rest of Gujarat, is the home of the last remaining population of *khur* (Asiatic wild ass) in India. There's also a large bird population, particularly of lesser flamingos. Both are protected in the 5000 sq km Little Rann sanctuary, which is approached from Dhrangadhra; get permission to enter from the sanctuary superintendent's office in Dhrangadhra. But consider the following traveller's advice.

The Rann can be treacherously difficult to explore as the desert consists of salt deposited at a time when the area formed part of the delta of the River Indus. This means that rain can quickly turn parts of the desert into a sea of mud, and what to the untrained eye looks like solid ground may in fact be a thin crust of dry silt with soft mud underneath. Hence it is essential to have someone along who is familiar with local conditions.

Krys Kazmierczak, UK

The small town of **Zainabad**, 105km north-west of Ahmedabad, is very close to the

Dharamanath

Indian saints and sadhus are renowned for the lengths to which they will go in their quests to attain spiritual salvation. From standing on nails to sealing themselves in caves for decades, acts of self-mortification seem limited only by the practitioner's imagination.

One of these spiritual warriors was Dharamanath, who journeyed to Kutch in the 12th century to find a tranquil spot in which to practise penance. He settled himself under a tree near Raipur and, while focusing on matters spiritual, depended on the people of Raipur to attend to his material needs. However, the Raipurians were not exactly forthcoming so, in a fit of rage, Dharamanath invoked a curse upon them. The city became desolate and its inhabitants hastily removed themselves to Mandvi. Dharamanath, overcome by remorse, resolved to climb the highest hill he could find, in order to engage in a penance commensurate with his vengeful act. After being rejected by two hills, which refused to carry the burden of his guilt, he climbed *backwards* up a third hill – Dhinodar – and there proceeded to stand on his head – for 12 years. The gods, concerned at this excess, pleaded with Dharamanath to cease his penance. Dharamanath acceded – on condition that wherever his gaze fell, that region should become barren. Casting his gaze before him, the seas receded, leaving a barren, desolate wasteland – the Great Rann of Kutch.

On the highest peak of Dhinodar, a shrine dedicated to Dharamanath contains a red be-smeared stone, which allegedly bore the head of the inverted ascetic during his extraordinary act of penance.

Dharamanath founded the community of sadhus at Than, know as the *Kanphata* (split eared), because they had to split open their ears upon joining. This is still done today with a heavy ring.

Little Rann of Kutch. Desert Coursers (☎/fax 02757-41333) is a family-run tour company that organises interesting safari and cultural tours on the Rann. Prices are about Rs 1900 per day.

The same family runs Camp Zainabad, offering kooba (traditional thatch-roofed huts) with bathrooms in a peaceful setting. It costs about Rs 800 per person per night, including breakfast and dinner. Advance booking is advised. The self-contained huts are basic but comfortable.

Dhrangadhra is on the Gandhidham-Ahmedabad rail route 170km (3½ hours) from Gandhidham, and 130km (three hours) from Ahmedabad.

To get to Zainabad from Ahmedabad, you can take a bus to Dasada, 12km north-east of Zainabad (Rs 23, 2½ hours). From here Desert Coursers does free pick-ups, or you can use are local buses instead. There are also direct buses from Rajkot. Desert Coursers can arrange taxis for around Rs 2.50 per kilometre.

Madhya Pradesh

Madhya Pradesh is India's largest state and the geographical heartland of the country. Most of the state is a high plateau and in summer it can be very dry and hot, but it also has the highest percentage of forest in India, sheltering a wide variety of wildlife including 22% of the world's tiger population. Virtually all phases of Indian history have left their mark on Madhya Pradesh, historically known as Malwa. There are still many pre-Aryan Gond and Bhil *adivasis* (tribal people) in the state, but Madhya Pradesh is overwhelmingly Indo-Aryan.

Some of Madhya Pradesh's attractions are remote and isolated: Khajuraho, in the north of the state, is a long way from anywhere and most easily visited when travelling between Agra and Varanasi; Jabalpur, with its marble rocks, is in the centre of the state; Kanha National Park, famous for its tigers, is 160km south-east of Jabalpur.

Most of the state's other attractions are on or near the main Delhi to Mumbai railway line. From Agra, just outside the state to the north, you can head south through Gwalior (with its magnificent fort), Sanchi, Bhopal, Ujjain, Indore and Mandu.

Madhya Pradesh is part of what is known as the Hindi belt, a region of northern India inhabited predominantly by Hindus. However, tense state assembly elections in November 1998 saw the Hindu fundamentalist BJP ousted by the Congress Party.

History

Although signs of habitation date back some 12,000 years with the rock cave paintings at Bhimbetka, near Bhopal, Madhya Pradesh's history can be traced back to the 3rd century BC when the great Buddhist emperor Ashoka controlled the Maurya empire in Malwa.

At Sanchi you can see the Buddhist centre founded by Ashoka, the most important reminder of him in India today. The Mauryans were followed by the Sungas and then by the

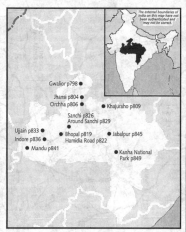

Madhya Pradesh at a Glance

Population: 66.1 million
Area: 443,446 sq km
Capital: Bhopal
Main Language: Hindi
Best Time to Go: September to February

- **Khajuraho** – exquisite temples, India's visual *Kamasutra*, depicting love and daily life a millennium ago

- **Orchha** – fortified palaces on a river island and magnificent temples

- **Sanchi** – entangled in jungle for centuries, Sanchi, with its ancient stupas, reveals Buddhism's Indian origins

- **Bhimbetka** – 12,000-year-old cave paintings depicting prehistoric India

- **Mandu** – vast fortress complex: perfect for cycle explorations

- **Kanha & Bandhavgarh National Parks** – better-than-average tiger-spotting opportunities

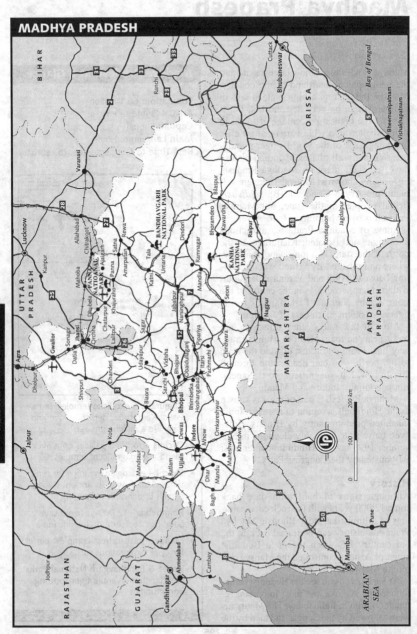

Festivals of Madhya Pradesh

festival	location	date	features
Khajuraho Festival of Dance	Khajuraho	Mar	classical dance & music
Jhansi Festival	Jhansi	Feb/Mar	local music arts & dance
Sivaratri Mela	Pachmarhi	Feb/Mar	symbolic tridents celebrating Shiva
Navratri (Dussehra)	Ujjain	Sept/Oct	lively Hindu festival
Feast of St Jude	Jhansi	Oct/Nov	pleading to patron saint of lost causes
Chethiyagiri Vihara Festival	Sanchi	end Nov	Buddhists view relics of two Buddhas
Tansen Music Festival	Tansen	Oct/Nov	musicians, singers & stage performances

Guptas, before the Huns swept across the state. Around a thousand years ago the Parmaras ruled in south-west Madhya Pradesh – they're chiefly remembered for Raja Bhoj, who gave his name to the city of Bhopal and also ruled over Indore and Mandu.

From 950 to 1050 AD the Chandelas constructed the fantastic series of temples at Khajuraho in the north of the state.

Between the 12th and 16th centuries, the region saw continuing struggles between Hindu and Muslim rulers or invaders. The fortified city of Mandu in the south-west was frequently the scene for these battles, but finally the Mughals overcame Hindu resistance and controlled the region. The Mughals, however, met their fate at the hands of the Marathas who, in turn, fell to the British.

Northern Madhya Pradesh

GWALIOR
☎ 0751 • pop 830,720

Just a few hours from Agra by train or road, Gwalior is famous for its old and very large fort. Within the fort walls are several interesting temples and ruined palaces. The dramatic and colourful history of the great fort goes back over 1000 years.

History
Gwalior's legendary beginning stems from a meeting between Suraj Sen and the hermit Gwalipa, who lived on the hilltop where the fort stands. The hermit cured Suraj Sen of leprosy with a drink of water from the Suraj Kund, which still remains in the fort. He then gave him a new name, Suhan Pal, and said his descendants would remain in power so long as they kept the name Pal. His next 83 descendants did just that, but number 84 changed his name to Tej Karan and – you guessed it – goodbye kingdom.

What is more certain is that in 1398 the Tomar dynasty came to power in Gwalior and, over the next several centuries, Gwalior Fort was the scene of continual intrigue and clashes with neighbouring powers. Man Singh, who came to power in 1486, was the greatest of these Tomar rulers. In 1505 he repelled an assault on the fort by Sikandar Lodi of Delhi, but in 1516 the fort was besieged by Ibrahim Lodi. Man Singh died early in the siege, but his son held out for a year before capitulating. Later the Mughals, under Babur, took the fort and held it until 1754 when the Marathas captured it.

For the next 50 years the fort changed hands on several occasions, including twice to the British. It finally passed into the hands of the Scindias. At the time of the Indian Uprising in 1857, the maharaja remained loyal to the British but his troops didn't, and in mid-1858 the fort was the scene for some of the final, and most dramatic, events of the Uprising. It was near here that the British finally defeated Tantia Topi and it was in the final assault on the fort that the rani of Jhansi was killed (see Jhansi entry).

MADHYA PRADESH

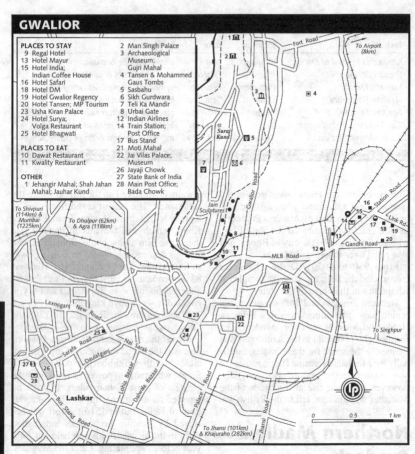

GWALIOR

PLACES TO STAY
9 Regal Hotel
13 Hotel Mayur
15 Hotel India;
 Indian Coffee House
16 Hotel Safari
18 Hotel DM
19 Hotel Gwalior Regency
20 Hotel Tansen; MP Tourism
23 Usha Kiran Palace
24 Hotel Surya;
 Volga Restaurant
25 Hotel Bhagwati

PLACES TO EAT
10 Dawat Restaurant
11 Kwality Restaurant

OTHER
1 Jehangir Mahal; Shah Jahan
 Mahal; Jauhar Kund

2 Man Singh Palace
3 Archaeological
 Museum;
 Gujri Mahal
4 Tansen & Mohammed
 Gaus Tombs
5 Sasbahu
6 Sikh Gurdwara
7 Teli Ka Mandir
8 Urbai Gate
12 Indian Airlines
14 Train Station;
 Post Office
17 Bus Stand
21 Moti Mahal
22 Jai Vilas Palace;
 Museum
26 Jayaji Chowk
27 State Bank of India
28 Main Post Office;
 Bada Chowk

To Shivpuri (114km) & Mumbai (1225km)
To Dholpur (62km) & Agra (118km)
To Airport (8km)

Fort Road
Suraj Kund
Gwalior Road
Jain Sculptures
MLB Road
Station Road
Link Rd
Gandhi Road
To Singhpur
Laxmiganj New Road
Sarafa Road
Nai Sarak
Daulatganj
Lohia Bazaar
Dalwala Bazaar
Palace Road
Jhansi Road
Bus Stand Road
Lashkar

To Jhansi (101km) & Khajuraho (282km)

0   0.5   1 km

The area around Gwalior, particularly be-tween Agra and Gwalior, was until recent years well known for the *dacoits* (armed robbers) who terrorised travellers and villagers. In the Chambal river valley region you still see men walking along the roads carrying rifles.

Orientation & Information

Gwalior is dominated by its fort, or *kila*, which tops the long hill to the north of Lashkar, the new town. The old town clings to the hill, north-east of the fort. The main market area, Jayaji Chowk, is Lashkar's hub, and nearby is Bada Chowk, where you'll find the post office and the State Bank of India, where you can change money.

The tourist office (☎ 340370, fax 340371) is in the Hotel Tansen, which you'll find about 500m south-east of the train station. There's another tourist office in the train station, open 9 am to 1 pm and 5 to 9 pm.

Fort

Rising 100m above the town, the fort hill is about 3km in length. Its width varies from nearly 1km to less than 200m. The walls, which encircle almost the entire hilltop, are 10m high and imposingly solid. Beneath them, the hill face is a sheer drop away to the plains. On a clear day the view from the fort walls is superb.

You can approach the fort from the south or the north-east. The north-eastern path starts from the archaeological museum and follows a wide, winding slope to the doors of the Man Singh Palace. The southern entrance, via Urbai Gate, is a long, gradual ascent by road, past cliff-face Jain sculptures.

An atmospheric sound-and-light show is held every evening at the open-air amphitheatre outside the Man Singh Palace. The English version is at 7.30 pm (the 6.30 pm showing is in Hindi); tickets are Rs 50.

There are several things to see in and around the fort, although most of the enclosed area is simply open space, fields and the grounds occupied by the prestigious private Scindia School. Admission to the fort is Rs 0.20, plus Rs 25 for a video camera. Guides can be hired at the gate from around Rs 100 for two or three hours.

Jain Sculptures The long ascent on the southern side climbs up through a ravine to the fort gate. Along the rock faces flanking this road are many Jain sculptures, some impressively big. Originally cut into the cliff faces in the mid-15th century, they were defaced by the forces of Babur in 1527 but were later repaired.

The images are in five main groups and are numbered. In the Arwahi group, image 20 is a 17m-high standing sculpture of the first Jain *tirthankar* (revered teacher or saint), Adinath, while image 22 is a 10m-high seated figure of Nemnath, the 22nd Jain tirthankar. The south-eastern group is the most important and covers nearly 1km of the cliff face with more than 20 images.

Teli Ka Mandir This temple probably dates from the 9th century but has been restored.

Its peculiar design incorporates a Dravidian roof with Indo-Aryan decorations (the whole temple is covered with sculptures). A Garuda tops the 10m-high doorway.

Between the Teli Ka Mandir and the Sasbahu temples is an impressive gleaming white **Sikh gurdwara**, or temple.

Sasbahu Temples The Sasbahu, or Mother-in-Law and Daughter-in-Law temples, stand close to the eastern wall about midway along that side of the fort. The two temples are similar in style, and date from the 9th to 11th centuries. The larger temple has an ornately carved base and figures of Vishnu over the entrances, and four huge pillars carry the heavy roof. Entry is Rs 2.

Man Singh Palace The palace, a delightfully whimsical building, is also known as the Chit Mandir, or Painted Palace, because of the tiled and painted decorations of ducks, elephants and peacocks. Painted blue, with hints of green and gold, it still looks very impressive today.

The palace was built by Man Singh between 1486 and 1516, and was repaired in 1881. It has four levels, two of them underground and all of them now deserted. The subterranean ones were used as prison cells during the Mughal period. The Emperor Aurangzeb had his brother Murad imprisoned and executed here. The east face of the palace, with its six towers topped by domed cupolas, stands over the fort entrance path.

There's a small **museum** next to the Man Singh Palace housing sculpture and carvings from around the fort. It's open daily except Friday 10 am to 5 pm (free).

Other Palaces There are other palaces clustered within the fort walls at the northern end, though none as interesting or as well preserved as the Man Singh Palace. The **Karan Palace**, or Kirti Mandir, is a long, narrow two storey building on the western side of the fort. At the northern end are the **Jehangir Mahal** and **Shah Jahan Mahal** with a very large and deep tank, the **Jauhar Kund**. It was here that the Rajput women of the harem committed mass *sati*, or self-immolation, after the raja was defeated in battle in 1232.

North-East Entrance There is a whole series of gates as you descend the worn steps of the path to the archaeological museum. The sixth gate, the **Hawa Gate**, originally stood within the palace but has been removed. The fifth gate, the **Hathiya Paur**, or Elephant Gate, is the entrance to the palace.

Descending, you pass a Vishnu shrine dating from 876 AD known as the **Chatarbhuj Mandir**, or Temple of the Four-Armed. A tomb nearby is that of a nobleman killed in an assault on this gate in 1518. From here a series of steps lead to rock-cut Jain and Hindu **sculptures**.

The interesting fourth gate was built in the 15th century and named after the elephant-headed god, Ganesh. There is a small pigeon house, or **Kabutar Khana**, here, as well as a small four-pillared **Hindu temple** to the hermit Gwalipa, after whom the fort and town were named.

The third gate is known as the **Badalgarh**, after Badal Singh, Man Singh's uncle. The second gate, the Bansur, or Archer's Gate, has disappeared. The first gate is the **Alamgiri Gate**, dating from 1660.

Archaeological Museum The museum is within the **Gujri Mahal**. Built in the 15th century by Man Singh for his favourite queen, Mrignayni, the palace is now in a rather deteriorated condition. There's a large collection of Hindu and Jain sculptures and copies of the Bagh Caves frescoes. It's open daily except Monday from 10 am to 5 pm (Rs 2 plus Rs 2 for a camera).

Jai Vilas Palace & Scindia Museum

Although the current maharaja still lives in the palace of the Scindia family, 35 rooms are now a museum. It's full of the bizarre items Hollywood maharajas are supposed to collect, such as Belgian cut-glass furniture (including a rocking chair), and what looks like half the tiger population of India, all shot, stuffed and moth-eaten. Modes of transport range from a Rolls Royce on rails to a German bubble car. Then there's a little room full of erotica, including a life-sized marble statue of Leda having her way with a swan. But the *pièce de résistance* is a model railway that carried brandy and cigars around the dining table after dinner.

The main durbar hall is impressive. The gold paint used around the room is said to weigh 58kg, and the two giant chandeliers are incredible; they each hold 248 candles, are 12.5m high and weigh 3.5 tonnes apiece – so heavy that before they were installed, elephants were suspended from the ceiling to check that it could take the weight.

If you go there by auto-rickshaw, ask for the museum, which is not at the palace entrance. It is open daily except Monday 9.30 am to 5 pm. Admission is a ridiculously royal Rs 160 plus a Rs 20/50 camera/video fee.

Old Town

The old town of Gwalior lies to the north and north-east of the fort hill. The 1661 **Jama Masjid** is a fine old building, constructed of sandstone quarried from the fort hill. On the eastern side of town is the **tomb of Mohammed Gaus**, a Muslim saint who played a key role in Babur's acquisition of the fort. A good example of early Mughal architecture, it has hexagonal towers at its four corners and a dome that was once covered with glazed blue tiles.

Nearby is the smaller **tomb of Tansen**, a singer much admired by Akbar. Chewing the leaves of the tamarind tree near his grave is supposed to do wonders for your voice. It is a place of pilgrimage for musicians during October/November, when the tree tends to look unseasonally autumnal, stripped by visiting enthusiasts. To find it, follow the Fort Rd from the north-eastern gate for about 15 minutes and turn right onto a small road.

The **Moti Mahal** is an imposing edifice. It was formerly a palace, but these days it's government offices.

Special Events

The **Tansen Music Festival** is held around October/November each year and attracts classical musicians and vocalists from all over India. Free performances are usually staged at Tansen's tomb in the old town.

Places to Stay – Budget

A few budget hotels can be found within walking distance of the train station and there are a couple of seedy cheap places across town near Jayaji Chowk, Lashkar.

Hotel Mayur (☎ 325559, Padav) is the best of the cheap places and is in a good location down a quiet alley just a few minutes' walk from the train station. A bed in the roomy, air-cooled dorm (no bunks) costs Rs 55. The dorm has two bathrooms, and there are lockers under each bed. Spotless air-cooled singles/doubles with bath start from Rs 120/150, up to Rs 300/350 with air-con.

Hotel Safari (☎ 340638, Station Rd) is above shops on a busy road but it's not bad value. Reasonably clean fan-cooled rooms with bath are Rs 130/165 and deluxe rooms with TV and hot water are Rs 190/225.

Hotel DM (☎ 342083, Link Rd) is a peaceful, friendly place away from the hustle and bustle but close to the bus stand. It was getting a fresh coat of paint when we visited. Singles/doubles with bath are good value at Rs 150/205, or bigger rooms with TV are Rs 185/250. There's a restaurant.

Hotel Bhagwati (☎ 310319, Nai Sarak) is one of several cheap but unappealing places near the Jayaji Chowk area. Cell-like singles with common bath are Rs 50 and better (but dingy) doubles with bath are Rs 125.

Regal Hotel (☎ 22599, MLB Rd) has nothing to recommend it other than its proximity to the fort – and even then it's not really within easy walking distance. Pokey rooms with bath are Rs 150/200 and the deluxe rooms aren't much better. Air-con rooms are Rs 350/400. The restaurant is pretty gloomy but it serves cold beer.

Places to Stay – Mid-Range & Top End

Most of the mid-range places are near the train station.

Hotel Tansen (☎ 340370, fax 340371, 6A Gandhi Rd), an MP Tourism place, is pleasantly situated in a shady area about 1km south-east of the station. Rooms are spacious but not great value at Rs 350/450 (plus Rs 50 for an air-cooler), or Rs 590/690 with air-con. Checkout is noon and there's a restaurant and bar.

Hotel Surya (☎ 331183, fax 310083, Jayendra Ganj, Lashkar) has plain but comfortable air-cooled rooms for Rs 275/350 and air-con rooms for Rs 375/450.

Hotel Gwalior Regency (☎ 340670, fax 343520, Link Rd) has stylish, centrally air-conditioned rooms from Rs 475/675. There's a range of facilities including a health club and swimming pool.

Usha Kiran Palace (☎ 323993, fax 321103, Jayendra Ganj, Lashkar) is the town's top hotel. This serene former maharaja's palace is great for a splurge with opulent furnishings and huge rooms starting from US$50/90 for the standard singles/doubles to US$105/110 for the suite, plus 20% tax.

Places to Eat

The *Indian Coffee House* below the Hotel India is a good cheap place, with *masala dosas* for Rs 15 and other vegetarian snacks. It's staffed by the usual attentive waiters in fan-shaped headgear.

Kwality Restaurant is an air-con haven not far from the southern fort gate on MLB Rd. The food is fresh, the service is good and prices are reasonable with mains from around Rs 40.

Dawat Restaurant, nearby on the same main road, is classier than Kwality with slightly higher prices to match.

Volga Restaurant is at the Hotel Surya. There's nothing Russian about it, but very good Indian food is served.

The *Usha Kiran Palace* restaurant is the place to eat out in style. The Mughlai food is excellent and they occasionally have a buffet as well as a la carte with mains from around Rs 110.

Getting There & Away

Air Indian Airlines (☎ 326872), MLB Rd, has a 'hopping' flight from Delhi (US$60) through Gwalior to Bhopal (US$70), Indore (US$95) and Mumbai (US$145). It flies from Delhi on Monday, Wednesday and Friday, and returns via the same route on Monday, Tuesday, Thursday and Saturday.

Bus From the government bus stand on Link Rd there are regular services to Agra (Rs 43, three hours), Jhansi (Rs 34, three hours) and Shivpuri (Rs 38, 2½ hours), and a few departures for Ujjain, Indore, Bhopal and Jabalpur. There are two buses a day at 7.30 and 8.30 am to Khajuraho (Rs 89, nine hours), but it's better to take the train to Jhansi and a bus from there.

Train Gwalior is on the main Delhi to Mumbai railway line. The superfast *Shatabdi Express* links Gwalior with Delhi (Rs 465/910 in 2nd/1st class, 3¼ hours), Agra (Rs 225/440, 1¼ hours), Jhansi (Rs 200/400, one hour) and Bhopal (Rs 505/1010, 4½ hours). If you've got the money but not the time you could use this reliable service for a day trip to Gwalior from Agra.

On other express trains it's five hours to Delhi (Rs 79/377 in 2nd/1st, 317km), two hours to Agra (Rs 36/189, 118km), 12 hours to Indore (Rs 190/662 sleeper/1st class, 652km) and 24 hours to Mumbai (Rs 280/992, 1225km).

Slow passenger trains are useful if you want to get off at Sonagir or Datia on the way to Jhansi, or Dholpur on the way to Agra.

Getting Around

To/From the Airport Auto-rickshaws charge around Rs 80 for the 8km trip to the airport. A taxi costs around Rs 200.

Local Transport Gwalior is spread out and congested with traffic so finding your way around on foot can prove futile. Auto-rickshaws are plentiful but the meters are just fashion accessories; Rs 10 should cover short trips. A ride from the train station to Bada Chowk, the main square in Lashkar, will cost Rs 20 – but you'll have to bargain. The frightening-looking *tempos* are useful and cheap if you can work out where they're going. They

run fixed routes around the city; the fare is Rs 5 from the station to Bada Chowk.

AROUND GWALIOR
Shivpuri
☎ 07492
The old summer capital of the Scindias was at Shivpuri, 114km south-west of Gwalior and 94km west of Jhansi. Set in formal gardens, the **chhatris** (tombs) are the main attraction here. With Mughal pavilions and *sikhara* spires, these beautiful memorials to the Scindia rulers are inlaid in *pietra dura* style, like the Taj Mahal. The chhatri of Madho Rao Scindia faces his mother's chhatri across the tank.

Nearby is **Madhav National Park**, essentially a deer park. On the edge of the park is the Sakhya Sagar lake. Swimming from the old boat club pier here might not be wise as there are crocodiles in the lake.

Places to Stay Most of the accommodation is in MP Tourism lodges, but there are a couple of private options.

Chinkara Motel (☎ 31297) is MP Tourism's place in Shivpuri. Singles/doubles are Rs 350/450.

Tourist Village (☎ 33760) is near Bhadaiya Kund, only a few kilometres from Madhav National Park. It has comfortable rooms in attractive cottages for Rs 390/490, or Rs 590/690 with air-con.

Getting There & Away There are frequent buses to/from Gwalior (Rs 38, 2½ hours) and Jhansi (Rs 31, four hours).

Dholpur
Between Gwalior and Agra, actually in a part of Rajasthan that separates Madhya Pradesh and Uttar Pradesh, Dholpur was the scene of a pitched battle between Aurangzeb's sons to determine who would succeed him as emperor of the rapidly declining Mughal empire. The **Shergarh Fort** in Dholpur is very old and is now in ruins.

West of Dholpur near Bari is the **Khanpur Mahal**, a pavilioned palace built for Shah Jahan but never occupied.

Slow passenger trains between Agra and Gwalior stop at Dholpur.

CHANDERI

At the time of Mandu's greatest power, Chanderi was an important place, as indicated by the many ruined palaces, *serais* (inns), mosques and tombs – all in a Pathan style similar to that of Mandu. The **Koshak Mahal** is a ruined Muslim palace that is still being maintained.

Today the town is chiefly known for its gold brocades and saris. Accommodation in the town includes a ***Circuit House*** and the ***Rest House*** near the bus stand. Chanderi is 33km west of Lalitpur, which is 90km south of Jhansi on the main railway line.

JHANSI

☎ 0517 • pop 456,895

Jhansi, 101km south of Gwalior, is actually just across the border in Uttar Pradesh, but for convenience we've included it here. Although Jhansi has played a colourful role in Indian history, for most visitors it's simply a convenient transit point for Khajuraho, and increasingly for Orchha, only 18km away.

Jhansi was an important centre under Raja Bir Singh Deo around the 17th century. In 1803 the British East India Company got a foot in the door and gradually assumed control over the state. The last of a string of rajas died in 1853 and the British, who had recently passed a law letting them take over any princely state under their patronage if the ruler died without a male heir, pensioned the rani off and took full control.

The rani (Rani Lakshmibai), however, was unhappy about being forcibly retired by the British in 1853, so when the Indian Uprising burst into flame four years later, she was in the forefront of the rebellion at Jhansi. The British contingent in Jhansi were all massacred, but the following year the rebel forces were still quarrelling among themselves and the British retook Jhansi. The rani fled to Gwalior and, in a valiant last stand, she rode out against the British, disguised as a man, and was killed. She has since become a heroine of the Indian independence movement.

Orientation & Information

The old city is behind the fort, 3km from the train station. The town is quite spread out so you'll need to use auto-rickshaws to get around.

The Uttar Pradesh and Madhya Pradesh state governments have tourist booths at the train station, though neither of them is particularly good. There's a helpful UP tourist office (☎ 441267) at the Hotel Veerangana.

The State Bank of India accepts only American Express travellers cheques (in US dollars). Try Hotel Sita or the Jhansi Hotel for cash exchange.

Jhansi Fort

Once used by the Indian army, the fort was built in 1613 by Maharaja Bir Singh Deo of Orchha. The British ceded the fort to the maharaja of Scindia in 1858, but later exchanged it for Gwalior in 1866. There's nothing much to see, apart from the excellent views from the ramparts. Guides (around Rs 50) are on hand to show you around and tell some colourful tales. Watch out for the band of aggressive monkeys by the temples here. The fort is open sunrise to sunset daily (Rs 0.25, free Friday).

Just below the walls as you approach the fort is a bizarre blood-and-guts diorama of the battle in which the rani of Jhansi died.

Rani Mahal

The former palace of Rani Lakshmibai, consisting of arched chambers around an open courtyard, was built in the 18th century. In a famous incident at the palace, British troops stormed the building through a rear stable and massacred 50 of the rani's bodyguards. The palace is now a museum containing hundreds of 9th to 12th century sculptures. The durbar hall on the 2nd floor features an original painted wood-panelled ceiling.

The Rani Mahal is open daily 9.30 am to 5.30 pm (Rs 2, free Friday). Photography is not permitted.

Government Museum

On the road leading up to the fort is the large but the largely empty government

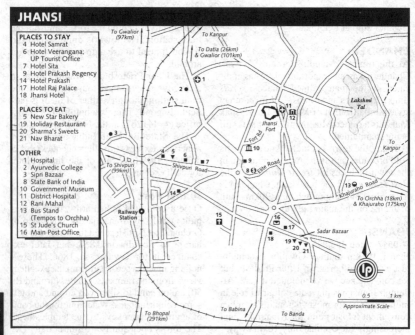

JHANSI

PLACES TO STAY
4 Hotel Samrat
6 Hotel Veerangana;
   UP Tourist Office
7 Hotel Sita
9 Hotel Prakash Regency
14 Hotel Prakash
17 Hotel Raj Palace
18 Jhansi Hotel

PLACES TO EAT
5 New Star Bakery
19 Holiday Restaurant
20 Sharma's Sweets
21 Nav Bharat

OTHER
1 Hospital
2 Ayurvedic College
3 Sipri Bazaar
8 State Bank of India
10 Government Museum
11 District Hospital
12 Rani Mahal
13 Bus Stand
   (Tempos to Orchha)
15 St Jude's Church
16 Main Post Office

museum. Its four galleries house an interesting collection of prehistoric tools; terracottas dating from the 4th century BC; and sculptures, costumes and weapons from the Chandela dynasty. It's open daily except Monday and every second Saturday from 10.30 am to 4.30 pm (free).

Special Events
The **Jhansi Festival** is a lively arts and cultural event held in February/March. A recent introduction to Madhya Pradesh's festival calendar, it is a locally organised program of music, arts and dance. Jhansi is also known for the **Feast of St Jude** on 28 October when thousands of desperate Christian pilgrims converge on St Jude's Church to plead their case to the patron saint of lost causes. The big day is preceded by a 10 day novena. The church is said to contain a relic of St Jude.

Places to Stay
Jhansi has a range of accommodation, much of it strung along Shivpuri Rd. A dorm bed at the train station *retiring rooms* is Rs 30.

Hotel Veerangana (☎ 442402, *Shivpuri Rd*) is a UP Tourism place with singles/doubles from Rs 175/225, up to Rs 450/500 with air-con. Though it's a bit run-down, it's a large place with a garden and a good restaurant.

Hotel Samrat (☎ 444943, *Shivpuri Rd*) is pretty good value, with rooms from Rs 150/200 with bath or Rs 175/225 with air-cooler and TV as well. There's 24 hour checkout here.

Hotel Prakash (☎ 448822, *Station Rd*) isn't far from the train station. It's dilapidated but welcoming with small singles/doubles for Rs 150/200. The deluxe rooms are much better at Rs 250/300 and air-con doubles are Rs 450.

Hotel Prakash Regency (☎ 330133, 360 Sardari Lal Market) lives up to the 'regency' tag with a fancy lobby and winding staircase, but the cheap air-cooled rooms are disappointing at Rs 250. The air-con double rooms (no single rates) at Rs 425 are much nicer. There's a pool and health club.

Jhansi Hotel (☎ 470360, Shastri Marg) is one of the best in town for old-fashioned charm. It was a hotel in British times and touches of the Raj are still evident. Huge doubles with colonial furniture are Rs 475/575. The restaurant here is very good, and the bar is open all day.

Hotel Raj Palace (☎ 470554, Shastri Marg) is a nondescript modern place with air-cooled rooms from Rs 200/220, or Rs 225/245 with hot water. Air-con rooms are Rs 350/380.

Hotel Sita (☎ 442956, fax 444691, Shivpuri Rd) is the place to head if you like your creature comforts. Rooms in this clean and well-maintained three star place have TV, phone and hot water. Singles/doubles are Rs 500/550, or Rs 750/800 with air-con.

Places to Eat

Most of the hotels have restaurants (those in the *Jhansi Hotel, Prakash Regency* and *Veerangana* are recommended) and there are more casual options.

Holiday Restaurant, in the Sadar Bazaar near the Jhansi Hotel, is deservedly popular with a good range of north Indian and Chinese dishes, and tea served in fine china. *Nav Bharat* runs a creditable second and there are a number of good ice cream parlours near here too.

New Star Bakery (Shivpuri Rd) conjures up excellent sweets which you can enjoy with a coffee from the espresso machine set up on the road out the front.

Getting There & Away

Bus Deluxe buses to Khajuraho (Shatabdi Link) leave from the train station at 6, 7 and 11 am (Rs 85, 4½ hours). Local buses (Rs 72, 5½ hours) leave more frequently from the bus stand east of town. Head to this bus stand for services to many other places including Gwalior (Rs 33, three hours), Shivpuri (Rs 31, four hours) and Datia (Rs 10, one hour). For Orchha, the tempos from here are better. They cost Rs 10 for the 40 minute journey and leave when (very) full. Buses to Orchha cost Rs 7.

Train Jhansi is on the main Delhi-Agra-Bhopal-Mumbai railway line. Tickets on the crack *Shatabdi Express* cost Rs 525/1045 in 2nd/1st class for Delhi, Rs 295/615 for Agra, Rs 200/400 for Gwalior and Rs 450/865 for Bhopal. It departs at 10.47 am for Bhopal and 5.55 pm for Delhi.

Other expresses connect Jhansi with Delhi (Rs 93/460, 414km), Agra (Rs 61/272, 215km, three hours), Gwalior (Rs 32/173, 97km, 1½ hours), Bhopal (Rs 103/347 for sleeper/1st class, 291km, 4½ hours), Indore (Rs 119/584, 555km, 10 hours) and Mumbai (Rs 280/992 sleeper/1st class, 1158km, 22 hours). There are also direct trains from Jhansi to Bangalore, Lucknow, Chennai, Pune and Varanasi.

Getting Around

The forecourt outside the train station is filled with predatory auto-rickshaw drivers. They charge around Rs 20 for the trip to the bus stand; crowded tempos will drop you there for Rs 5.

AROUND JHANSI
Sonagir

To the west of the railway line, 61km south of Gwalior, a large group of white **Jain temples** is scattered along a hill. It's one of those strange, dream-like apparitions that so often seem simply to materialise in India. Slow trains between Gwalior and Jhansi stop at Sonagir, not far from the temples.

Datia

Only 26km north of Jhansi, Datia makes an interesting side-trip. The main attraction is the deserted seven storey **palace** of Raj Bir Singh Deo, an impressive building with some rooms still containing murals. The town is surrounded by a stone wall and the palace is to the west.

The best way to get there is on one of the frequent buses from Jhansi (Rs 10, one hour), or hop on a passenger train heading towards Gwalior.

ORCHHA
☎ 07680

Once the capital city of the Bundelas, Orchha (hidden place) is now just a village, set among a wonderful complex of well-preserved palaces and temples. The main palaces were protected inside fortified walls on an island in the Betwa River. It's definitely worth a visit and a lot of travellers are beginning to discover Orchha's peaceful beauty. Tour groups do it in a couple of hours but it's a very relaxing place to stay, and you can even get a room in part of the palace here.

History

Orchha was founded in 1531 and remained the capital of a powerful Rajput kingdom until 1783, when nearby Tikamgarh became the new capital. Bir Singh Deo ruled from Orchha between 1605 and 1627 and built the Jhansi Fort. A favourite of the Mughal Prince Salim, he feuded with Akbar and in 1602 narrowly escaped the emperor's displeasure; his kingdom was all but ruined by Akbar's forces. Then in 1605 Prince Salim became Emperor Jehangir, and for the next 22 years Bir Singh was a powerful figure. In 1627, Shah Jahan became emperor and Bir Singh once again found himself out of favour; his attempt at revolt was put down by the 13-year-old Aurangzeb.

Orchha's golden age was during the first half of the 17th century. When Jehangir visited the city in 1606, a special palace, the Jehangir Mahal, was constructed for him. Later, both Shah Jahan and Aurangzeb raided the city.

Information

The helpful MP Tourism office is at the Hotel Sheesh Mahal. Cash and travellers cheques can be changed at the Canara Bank on the main road, open Monday to Friday 10 am to 2 pm and Saturday 10 am to noon.

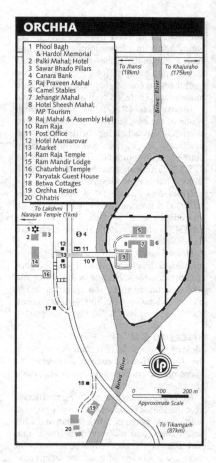

ORCHHA

1 Phool Bagh & Hardol Memorial
2 Palki Mahal; Hotel
3 Sawar Bhado Pillars
4 Canara Bank
5 Raj Praveen Mahal
6 Camel Stables
7 Jehangir Mahal
8 Hotel Sheesh Mahal; MP Tourism
9 Raj Mahal & Assembly Hall
10 Ram Raja
11 Post Office
12 Hotel Mansarovar
13 Market
14 Ram Raja Temple
15 Ram Mandir Lodge
16 Chaturbhuj Temple
17 Paryatak Guest House
18 Betwa Cottages
19 Orchha Resort
20 Chhatris

To Jhansi (18km)
To Khajuraho (175km)
Betwa River
To Lakshmi Narayan Temple (1km)
To Tikamgarh (87km)
0   100   200 m
Approximate Scale

Palaces

Crossing the bridge over the Betwa River to the fortified island brings you to three 17th century palaces. The **Jehangir Mahal** is an impressive, rambling complex with good views of the countryside from the upper levels. There's a small **archaeological museum** on the ground floor. The **Raj Mahal** nearby has superb murals. Below the Jehangir Mahal is the smaller **Raj Praveen Mahal**, a palace built near a garden. The *hammam* (baths) and camel stables are nearby. Go-ahead MP Tourism has an excellent personal headset tour; you follow the arrows painted on the floor of the palaces in sync with the commentary. The English narration, sound effects and backing music really bring the empty rooms to life. It costs Rs 50 plus a Rs 500 deposit.

On the other side of the village, **Dinman Hardol's Palace** (also called **Palki Mahal**), next to the Ram Raja Temple, is also interesting, as is his story. The son of Bir Singh Deo, he committed suicide (or was poisoned) to 'prove his innocence' over an affair with his brother's wife achieving the status of a folklore hero through his martyrdom.

Temples

Orchha's impressive temples date back to the 16th century. They're still in use today and are visited regularly by thousands of devotees. In the centre of the modern village is the **Ram Raja Temple** with its soaring spires. Originally a palace, it was turned into a temple when an image of Rama, temporarily installed, proved impossible to move. It now seems to have somehow made its way into the nearby **Chaturbhuj Temple**, where it is hidden behind silver doors. The **Lakshmi Narayan Temple** is linked to Ram Raja by a 1km-long path; it's worth the walk to see the well-preserved murals.

Other Attractions

The walled **Phool Bagh** gardens, a cool summer retreat beside the Palki Mahal, are a memorial to Dinman Hardol. Also worth seeing are the impressive **chhatris** (cenotaphs) to Orchha's rulers, down by the Betwa River, about 500m south of the village.

Places to Stay

Orchha has a couple of very cheap places, and the wonderful Hotel Sheesh Mahal.

Hotel Mansarovar (☎ 52628, Main Market), run by the Special Area Development Authority (SADA), looks shabby but has clean rooms for Rs 50/75 with common bath.

Palki Mahal Hotel, another SADA place (check in at Hotel Mansarovar), is atmospherically set in part of the former palace of Dinman Hardol – though the rooms are anything but palatial. Simple doubles with common bath are Rs 90 or a dorm bed is Rs 25. It's popular with backpackers hanging out for a few days. The third SADA place, *Paryatak Guest House*, is strictly a last resort – creepy cells are Rs 40/75 without/with bath.

Ram Mandir Lodge, opposite Mansarovar, has basic but clean rooms with common bath for Rs 75/90 and a balcony which overlooks the main street.

MP Tourism runs two places in Orchha, both fairly upmarket.

Betwa Cottages (☎ 52618), in a peaceful location by the river about 500m from the village, is set in a spacious, well-tended garden with good views to the palace and the chhatris. Singles/doubles are Rs 490/590, or Rs 690/790 with air-con.

Hotel Sheesh Mahal (☎ 52624), in a converted wing of the Jehangir Mahal, must be the most romantic place to stay in Madhya Pradesh. There's one single for Rs 190 and the ordinary rooms, with large bathrooms, colonial furniture and views into the palace courtyard, are Rs 490/590 plus tax. The real luxury is found in the Royal Apartment (Rs 2990), with its own porch and dining area, huge marble bathroom and superb views over Orchha, or the equally luxurious room below it (Rs 1990). It's worth booking ahead if you want to stay here.

Orchha Resort (☎ 0517-452759) is a new low-level five-star hotel that's been plonked right in front of the ancient chhatris. The place does nothing for Orchha's character, but if you want ultramodern luxury it's Rs 1195/2350.

Places to Eat

The restaurant at the *Hotel Sheesh Mahal* is the best place to eat in Orchha and is a good spot for breakfast before exploring the palaces. Excellent buffet dinners with traditional entertainment are occasionally held on the upstairs terrace.

There are a few veg restaurants in the village on the road running between the Jehangir Mahal and the market. *Ram Raja*, near the bridge, is the pick of the bunch.

Getting There & Away

There are regular buses (Rs 7) and tempos (Rs 10) from the Jhansi bus stand for the 18km journey to Orchha. An auto-rickshaw will cost around Rs 100.

KHAJURAHO

☎ 07686 • pop 7665

Close behind the Taj and up there with Varanasi, Jaipur and Delhi, the temples of Khajuraho are one of India's major attractions. Once a great Chandela capital, Khajuraho is now a quiet village. In spite of all the tourist attention it's still a mellow place to spend a few days, though the attention from hawkers immediately outside the western temple enclosure can be irritating.

Large numbers of visitors come to Khajuraho in March for the spectacular dance festival (see Special Events).

Orientation

The modern village of Khajuraho is a cluster of hotels, restaurants, shops and stalls near the western group of temples. About 1km east of the bus stand is the old village of Khajuraho. Around it are the temples of the eastern group and to the south are two further groups of temples.

Information

Tourist Offices The Government of India tourist office (☎ 42347), opposite the western group of temples, is the best place for information. There's also an office at the airport. The MP Tourism office (☎ 44051) is hardly worth visiting; it's hidden away at the Chandela Cultural Centre.

Guides Government of India approved guides can be organised at tourist offices or at Raja's Café and cost Rs 200/300 a half/full day for up to four people. Multilingual guides are an extra Rs 100. MP Tourism also has a novel headset tour of the western group of temples for Rs 50 plus Rs 500 deposit. The narration is informative and easy to follow.

Money As well as the usual opening hours, the State Bank of India is open for foreign currency transactions Monday to Friday 4 to 6 pm and Saturday 2.30 to 3.30 pm.

The Canara Bank down behind the bus stand is less busy than the State Bank of India and there are a few private money-changers in the village offering lower rates than the banks.

Temples

Khajuraho's temples were built during the Chandela period, a dynasty that survived for five centuries before falling to the Mughal onslaught. Most date from one century-long burst of creative genius from 950 to 1050 AD. Almost as intriguing as the sheer beauty and size of the temples is the question of why and how they were built here. Khajuraho is a long way from anywhere and was probably just as far off the beaten track a thousand years ago as it is today. There is nothing of great interest or beauty to recommend it as a building site, there is no great population centre here and during the hot season Khajuraho is very hot and dry.

Having chosen such a strange site, how did the Chandelas manage to recruit the labour to turn their awesome dreams into stone? To build so many temples of such monumental size in just 100 years must have required a huge amount of human labour. Whatever their reasons, we can be thankful they built Khajuraho where they did, because its very remoteness helped preserve it from the desecration Muslim invaders were only too ready to inflict on 'idolatrous' temples elsewhere in India.

The temples are superb examples of Indo-Aryan architecture, but it's the decorations with which they are so liberally embellished that have made Khajuraho famous. Around the temples are bands of exceedingly artistic stonework showing many aspects of Indian life a millennium ago – gods and goddesses, warriors and musicians, real and mythological animals.

But two elements appear over and over again and in greater detail than anything else – women and sex. Stone figures of *apsaras*, or celestial maidens, appear on every temple. They pout and pose for all the world

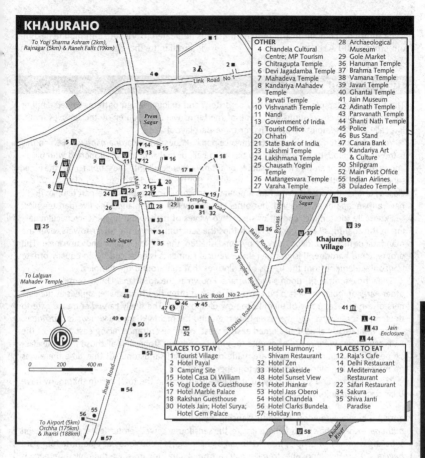

KHAJURAHO

To Yogi Sharma Ashram (2km),
Rajnagar (5km) & Raneh Falls (19km)

Link Road No 1

Prem
Sagar

Main Road

Jain Temples Road

Jain Temples
Road

Narora
Sagar

Bypass Road

Basti Road

Narora
Sagar

Khajuraho
Village

Shiv Sagar

To Lalguan
Mahadev Temple

Link Road No 2

Bypass Road

Jhansi Road

Jain
Enclosure

To Airport (5km)
Orchha (175km)
& Jhansi (188km)

0   200   400 m

Khodar River

OTHER
4 Chandela Cultural Centre; MP Tourism
5 Chitragupta Temple
6 Devi Jagadamba Temple
7 Mahadeva Temple
8 Kandariya Mahadev Temple
9 Parvati Temple
10 Vishvanath Temple
11 Nandi
13 Government of India Tourist Office
20 Chhatri
21 State Bank of India
23 Lakshmi Temple
24 Lakshmana Temple
25 Chausath Yogini Temple
26 Matangesvara Temple
27 Varaha Temple
28 Archaeological Museum
29 Gole Market
36 Hanuman Temple
37 Brahma Temple
38 Vamana Temple
39 Javari Temple
40 Ghantai Temple
41 Jain Museum
42 Adinath Temple
43 Parsvanath Temple
44 Shanti Nath Temple
45 Police
46 Bus Stand
47 Canara Bank
49 Kandariya Art & Culture
50 Shilpgram
52 Main Post Office
55 Indian Airlines
58 Duladeo Temple

PLACES TO STAY
1 Tourist Village
2 Hotel Payal
3 Camping Site
15 Hotel Casa Di William
16 Yogi Lodge & Guesthouse
17 Hotel Marble Palace
18 Rakshan Guesthouse
30 Hotels Jain; Hotel Surya; Hotel Gem Palace
31 Hotel Harmony; Shivam Restaurant
32 Hotel Zen
33 Hotel Lakeside
48 Hotel Sunset View
51 Hotel Jhankar
53 Hotel Jass Oberoi
54 Hotel Chandela
56 Hotel Clarks Bundela
57 Holiday Inn

PLACES TO EAT
12 Raja's Cafe
14 Delhi Restaurant
19 Mediterraneo Restaurant
22 Safari Restaurant
34 Sakura
35 Shiva Janti Paradise

MADHYA PRADESH

like pin-up models posing for the camera. In between are the *mithuna*, erotic figures, running through a whole *Kamasutra* of positions and possibilities.

Western Group The main temples are in the western group, most contained within a fenced enclosure that is very well maintained as a park. The enclosure is open sunrise to sunset (Rs 5). This includes entry to the archaeological museum across the road, so don't lose your ticket. Admission is free

on Friday. Ask at the ticket office about the excellent Archaeological Survey of India guidebook to Khajuraho. It's often out of stock, but worth buying if available (Rs 20).

The temples are described here in a clockwise direction.

Lakshmi & Varaha Facing the large Lakshmana Temple are these two small shrines. The Varaha Temple, dedicated to Vishnu's boar incarnation or Varaha *avataar*, faces the Matangesvara Temple. Inside this small, open shrine is a huge, solid and intricately carved figure of the boar incarnation, dating from around 900 AD.

Lakshmana The large Lakshmana Temple is dedicated to Vishnu, although in design it is similar to the Kandariya Mahadev and

Temple Terminology

The Khajuraho temples follow a fairly consistent and unique design pattern. Understanding the architectural conventions and some of the terms will help you enjoy the temples more. Basically all the temples follow a five or three-part layout.

You enter the temples through an entrance porch, known as the *ardhamandapa*. Behind this is the hall or *mandapa*. This leads into the main hall, or *mahamandapa*, supported with pillars and with a corridor around it. A vestibule or *antarala* then leads into the *garbhagriha*, the inner sanctum, where the image of the god to which the temple is dedicated is displayed. An enclosed corridor, the *pradakshina*, runs around this sanctum. The simpler three-part temples don't have a mandapa or pradakshina, but otherwise follow the same plan as the five-part temples.

Externally the temples consist of successive waves of higher and higher towers culminating in the soaring *sikhara* (spire), which tops the sanctum. While the lower towers, over the mandapa or mahamandapa, may be pyramid-shaped, the sikhara is taller and curvilinear. The ornate, even baroque, design of all these vertical elements is balanced by an equally ornate horizontal element from the bands of sculptures that run around the temples.

The whole temple sits upon a high terrace, known as the *adisthana*. Unlike temples in most other parts of India, these had no enclosing wall but often had four smaller shrines at the corners of the terrace; many of them have now disappeared. The finely carved entrance gate to the temple is a *torana*, and the lesser towers around the main sikhara are known as *urusringas*.

The temples are almost all aligned east to west, with the entrance facing east. Some of the earliest temples were made of granite, or granite and sandstone, but all those from the classic period of Khajuraho's history are made completely of sandstone. At that time there was no mortar, so the blocks were fitted together.

The sculptures and statues play such an important part in the total design that many have their own terminology:

apsara – heavenly nymph, beautiful dancing woman.
mithuna – Khajuraho's most famous image, the sensuously carved, erotic figures that have been shocking a variety of people, from Victorian archaeologists to busloads of blue-rinse tourists.
nayika – it's really impossible to tell a nayika from a surasundari, since the only difference is that the surasundari is supposed to be a heavenly creature while a nayika is human.
salabhanjika – female figure with tree, which together act as supporting brackets in the inner chambers of the temple. Apsaras also perform this bracket function.
surasundari – when a surasundari is dancing she is an apsara. Otherwise she attends the gods and goddesses by carrying flowers, water, ornaments, mirrors or other offerings. She also engages in everyday activities like washing her hair, applying make-up, taking a thorn out of her foot, fondling herself, playing with pets and babies, writing letters, playing musical instruments or posing seductively.
sardula – a mythical beast, part lion, part some other animal or even human. Sardulas usually carry armed men on their backs, and can be seen on many of the temples. They all look like lions but the faces are often different.

Vishvanath temples. It is one of the earliest of the western enclosure temples, dating from around 930 to 950 AD, and is also one of the best preserved, with a full five-part floor plan and four subsidiary shrines. Around the temple are two bands of sculpture instead of the usual three; the lower one has fine figures of apsaras and some erotic scenes. Inside are excellent examples of apsaras acting as supporting brackets.

On the subsidiary shrine at the south-west corner is an architect working with his students – it is thought this may be the temple's designer including himself in the grand plan. Around the base of the temple is a continuous frieze with scenes of battles, hunting and processions. The first metre or two consists of a highly energetic orgy, including one gentleman proving that a horse can be a person's best friend, while a stunned group of women look away in shock.

The temple platform gives you a good view of the Matangesvara Temple (see later in this section).

Kandariya Mahadev The first of the temples on the common platform at the back of the western enclosure is not only the largest, it is also artistically and architecturally the most perfect. Built 1025-50, it represents Chandela art at its finest. Although the four subsidiary shrines that once stood around the main temple are long gone, the central shrine is in superb condition and shows the typical five-part design of Khajuraho temples.

The main spire is 31m high, and the temple is lavishly carved. The English archaeologist Cunningham counted 226 statues inside the temple and a further 646 outside – 872 in total with most of them nearly 1m high. The statues are carved around the temple in three bands and include gods, goddesses, beautiful women, musicians and, of course, some of the famed erotic groups. The mithuna on the Kandariya Mahadev include some of the most energetic eroticism to be seen at Khajuraho.

Mahadeva This small and mainly ruined temple stands on the same base as the Kandariya Mahadev and the Devi Jagadamba. Although small and insignificant compared to its mighty neighbours, it houses one of Khajuraho's best sculptures – a fine sardula figure caressing a lion.

Devi Jagadamba The third temple on the common platform is slightly older than the Kandariya Mahadev and of a simpler, three-part design. It was probably originally dedicated to Vishnu, but later dedicated to Parvati and then Kali. Some students believe it may still be a Parvati temple and that the Kali image (or Jagadamba) is actually an image of Parvati, painted black. The sculptures around the temple are again in three bands. Many of the two lower band images are of Vishnu with sardulas in the inner recesses. But on the third and uppermost band the mithuna again come out to play.

Chitragupta The fourth temple at the back of the western enclosure does not share the common platform with the other three. Similar in design to the Devi Jagadamba, this temple is probably slightly newer and is unique at Khajuraho in being dedicated to Surya, the sun god.

Attempts have obviously been made at restoration, but it is not in as good condition as other temples. Nevertheless it has some very fine sculptures, which include processions, dancing girls, elephant fights and hunting scenes. In the inner sanctum, Surya can be seen driving his chariot and seven horses, while on the central niche in the south facade you can see an 11-headed statue of Vishnu. The central head is that of Vishnu himself; the 10 others are of his incarnations.

Parvati Continuing around the enclosure, you come to the Parvati Temple on your right. The name is probably incorrect since this small and not so interesting temple was originally dedicated to Vishnu and now has an image of Ganga riding on the back of a crocodile.

Vishvanath & Nandi Believed to have been built in 1002, this temple has the

MADHYA PRADESH

complete five-part design of the larger Kandariya Mahadev Temple, but two of its four subsidiary shrines still stand. The large image of Shiva's vehicle, the bull Nandi, faces the temple from the other end of the common platform. Steps lead up to this high terrace, flanked by lions on the northern side and elephants on the southern side.

The sculptures around the temple include the usual Khajuraho scenes, but the sculptures of women are particularly notable here. They write letters, fondle a baby, play music and, perhaps more so than at any other temple, languish in provocative poses.

Matangesvara Standing next to the Lakshmana Temple, this temple is not within the fenced enclosure because it is still in everyday use, unlike all the other old Khajuraho temples. It may be the plainest temple here (suggesting that it was one of the first built) but inside it sports a polished lingam, 2.5m high.

Early in the morning, flower-sellers do a brisk trade in garlands for the statue of Ganesh outside. People drape them round the elephant-headed statue, say a prayer and as they walk away the sellers whip the flowers off to resell!

Chausath Yogini & Lalguan Mahadev Standing beyond the tank, some distance from the other western group temples, this ruined temple is probably the oldest at Khajuraho, dating from 900 AD or earlier. It is also the only temple constructed entirely of granite and the only one not aligned east to west. Chausath means 64 – the temple once had 64 cells for figures of the 64 *yoginis* who attended the goddess Kali. A 65th cell sheltered Kali herself.

A farther 500m west is the Lalguan Mahadev Temple, a small, ruined shrine dedicated to Shiva and constructed of granite and sandstone.

Eastern Group The eastern group of temples can be subdivided into two groups. The first is made up of interesting Jain temples in the walled enclosure. The other four tem-

ples are scattered through the old village of Khajuraho (as distinct from the modern village near the western temples).

Jain Museum Outside the Jain enclosure is this modern circular gallery, filled with statues of the 24 tirthankars. It's open 8 am to 5 pm (closed Sunday); entry is Rs 2.

Parsvanath The largest of the Jain temples in the walled enclosure is also one of the finest at Khajuraho. Although it does not approach the western enclosure temples in size, and does not attempt to compete in the sexual activity stakes, it is notable for the exceptional skill and precision of its construction, and for the beauty of its sculptures. Some of the best known figures at Khajuraho can be seen here, including the classic figure of a woman removing a thorn from her foot and another of a woman applying eye make-up. Although it was originally dedicated to Adinath, an image of Parsvanath was substituted about a century ago; the temple takes its name from this newer image.

Adinath Adjacent to the Parsvanath Temple, the smaller Adinath has been partially restored over the centuries. It has fine carvings on its three bands of sculptures and, like the Parsvanath, is very similar to the Hindu temples of Khajuraho. Only the striking black image in the inner sanctum indicates that it is Jain rather than Hindu.

Shanti Nath This temple is a relatively modern one built about a century ago, but it contains many components from older temples around Khajuraho. The 4.5m-high statue of Adinath is said to have been sculpted in 1028. Groups of Digambara (Sky-clad, or naked) Jain pilgrims occasionally stay at the *dharamsala* (pilgrims' lodging) here.

Ghantai Walking from the eastern Jain temple group towards Khajuraho village, you come to this small, ruined Jain temple. Only its pillared shell remains, but it is interesting for the delicate columns with their bell-and-chain decoration and for the figure of a Jain goddess astride a Garuda that marks the entrance.

Javari Walk through the village, a typical small Indian settlement, to this temple. Dating from around 1075 to 1100 AD, it is dedicated to Vishnu and is a particularly fine example of Khajuraho architecture on a small scale. The exterior has more of Khajuraho's maidens.

Vamana About 200m north of the Javari Temple, this temple is dedicated to Vamana, the dwarf incarnation of Vishnu. Slightly older than the Javari Temple, the Vamana Temple stands out in a field all by itself. It's notable for the relatively simple design of its sikhara. The bands of sculpture around the temple are, as usual, very fine with numerous celestial maidens adopting interesting poses.

Brahma & Hanuman Turning back (west) towards the modern village, you pass a granite and sandstone temple, one of the oldest at Khajuraho. It was actually dedicated to Vishnu and the definition of it as a Brahma temple is incorrect.

Taking the road directly from the modern village to the Jain enclosure, you pass a Hanuman Temple containing a large image of the monkey god. This 2.5m statue has on it the oldest inscription here – 922 AD.

Southern Group There are only two temples in the southern group.

Duladeo A dirt track runs to this isolated temple, about 1km south of the Jain enclosure. This is a later temple, and experts say that at this time the skill of Khajuraho's temple builders had passed its peak and the sculptures are more 'wooden' and 'stereotyped' than on earlier temples. Nevertheless, it's a fine and graceful temple with figures of women in a variety of pin-up poses and a number of mithuna couples.

Chaturbhuja South of the river, about 3km from the village and a healthy hike down a dirt road, this ruined temple has a fine 3m-high image of Vishnu.

Archaeological Museum
Close to the western enclosure, this small museum has a fine collection of statues and sculptures rescued from around Khajuraho. Admission is included in the western enclosure entrance fee (so hang on to your ticket) and it's open daily except Friday 10 am to 5 pm.

Special Events
The **Khajuraho Festival of Dance** is a week-long event held every year in February/March. It attracts the cream of Indian classical dancers who perform amid the temples in the western enclosure. In 2000 the festival will take place from 2 to 8 March, marking the end of Khajuraho's year-long millennium celebrations. Performances are open-air, with the floodlit temples as a backdrop. MP Tourism's Web site (www.mptourism.com) is the best place to find a program.

Places to Stay
Khajuraho has a plethora of accommodation. MP Tourism has several hotels, which are good value at the height of the season but overpriced at other times when private hotels reduce their prices. On your arrival at the bus stand you'll be besieged by the usual rickshaw-wallahs offering Rs 5 rides – these are commission agents and you'll find bargaining for a room difficult if they take you to a hotel.

The cheapest places are in the centre of the new village, close to the western group of temples.

Places to Stay – Budget
Yogi Lodge & Guesthouse (☎ *44158*), the most popular budget place; has singles/doubles with bath and hot water from Rs 80/120. For real tranquillity ask here about *Yogi Sharma Ashram Lodge*, a large house with a garden about 2km north of the village. It has bright rooms for Rs 80/100 or dorm beds for Rs 30, all with common bath, plus free meditation classes every morning with the Yogi Ramprakash Sharma.

MADHYA PRADESH

Khajuraho's Erotica

The most frequently asked question by visitors to Khajuraho is why all the sex? One theory has it that the erotic posturing was a kind of *Kamasutra* in stone, a how-to-do-it manual for adolescent Brahmin boys growing up segregated from the world in special temple schools. Another claims that the figures were thought to prevent the temples being struck by lightning, by appeasing the rain god Indra. This old lecher is supposedly a keen voyeur who wouldn't want the source of his pleasure damaged.

Rather more convincing is the explanation that these are Tantric images. According to this cult, gratification of the baser instincts is one way to blot out the evils of the world and achieve final deliverance. *Bhoga* (physical enjoyment) and *yoga* (spiritual exercise) are seen as equally valid in this quest for nirvana.

Probably the most accurate theory is that the Khajuraho sculptors were simply representing life as it was viewed by their society, unhampered by *Old Testament* morality. In spite of the fact that modern visitors are drawn as much for reasons of prurience as for cultural appreciation, this is not pornography. Although there are certainly large numbers of erotic images here, many other day-to-day scenes are also shown. The carvings should be seen as a joyous celebration of all aspects of life.

There's a string of very good budget places side by side on Jain Temples Rd. *Hotel Gem Palace* (☎ 44100) has small singles/doubles for Rs 100/150, or bigger rooms for Rs 150/200, all with bath and running hot water. *Hotel Harmony* (☎ 44135) is also good value. Comfortable rooms with bath are Rs 150/250. The small walled garden is bright and immaculate.

Hotel Surya (☎ 44145), next door, has a large garden with fruit trees and free yoga classes at dawn. Good rooms with bath are Rs 150/200; rooms with balcony are Rs 250/350. *Hotel Jain* (☎ 42352) is a family-run place and an old favourite with travellers. There's a range of rooms from Rs 80/100 upwards, some with balconies.

Hotel Lakeside (☎ 44120, Main Rd) faces the lake and has clean rooms set around a central area. Rooms with bath and cooler cost from Rs 150/200.

Hotel Sunset View (☎ 44077, Main Rd) is lower on the budget scale. It's not the cleanest place around but has good-sized rooms with bath for Rs 75/100 or Rs 100/150. It's on the main Jhansi road.

MP Tourism's *Tourist Village* (☎ 44128) is a somewhat shabby collection of cottages decorated with local carpets and furnishings for Rs 250 and there's an open-air restaurant. It's quiet and north of the village.

Places to Stay – Mid-Range

Hotel Marble Palace (☎ 44353) is a private hotel that lives up to its name with its marble floors and winding staircase. Spacious, comfortable rooms with bathtubs are very nice but a little overpriced for Khajuraho at Rs 550/650, and Rs 850 with air-con.

Hotel Zen (☎ 44228, fax 44341, Jain Temples Rd) is a compact, immaculate place with a pleasant courtyard garden. Double rooms start at Rs 200, or Rs 400 with bathtub and balcony facing the garden.

Hotel Casa Di William (☎ 44244, fax 44192), on a side road just past the tourist office, has touches of the Mediterranean with its marble floors and whitewashed railings. Comfortable rooms with hot water are Rs 300/400, or Rs 550/650 with air-con. There's a good restaurant serving Indian and Italian specialities.

Rakshan Guest House is a new place (*no phone*) in its own little space just east of the village. Large, very clean singles/doubles start at Rs 150/200 and the friendly management has big plans for the rooftop terrace and garden.

Hotel Payal (☎ *440644*), up near the Tourist Village, is a dilapidated place with a sprawling garden and singles/doubles for Rs 340/390, or Rs 590/690 with air-con. It's clean and rooms have hot water and TV.

Hotel Jhankar (☎ *44063, fax 44194*), south of the village, is MP Tourism's flagship here. Slightly ageing rooms cost Rs 340/390, or Rs 590/690 for air-con, all with bathrooms and hot water. There's a restaurant and cold beer.

Places to Stay – Top End

Most deluxe hotels attempt to outdo one another and are south of the modern village.

Hotel Jass Oberoi (☎ *42344, fax 42345*) has singles/doubles for US$40/75 and a certain charm despite its box-like exterior. The hotel's pool is open to nonguests for Rs 150. The Oberoi has entertainment most evenings, open to all. From August to April there is a folk dance (Rs 150). Year-round there is a nightly puppet show, and a sitar and tabla recital (both free).

Hotel Chandela (☎ *42355, fax 42366, Jhansi Rd*) has air-con rooms for US$38/70, with comfortable beds, and bathtubs. Diversions for 'templed-out' guests include tennis, yoga, archery, croquet and badminton. There's a good bookshop, two excellent restaurants and a coffee shop.

Hotel Clarks Bundela (☎ *42386, fax 42385, Jhansi Rd*), south of the Hotel Chandela, charges US$45/85 and has a swimming pool. Discounts of up to 50% are available in the low season.

Holiday Inn (☎ *42301, fax 42304, Jhansi Rd*), farther south again, has a cavernous lobby, tastefully furnished rooms (US$40/75) and helpful staff. It's probably the most luxurious of the five stars and has a pool, bar and two restaurants.

Places to Eat

Raja's Cafe has been here almost 20 years and so has the Swiss woman who runs it. The large shady tree makes the restaurant's courtyard a popular gathering spot and there

are good views to the temples from the terrace above. Tourist information and guides are also available here.

Delhi Restaurant, on the other side of the tourist office, is a friendly place serving very good Indian food.

The hole-in-the-wall *Shivam Restaurant* (*Jain Temples Rd*) has plain *thalis* for Rs 15 and very good Gujarati thalis for Rs 30.

Safari Restaurant, opposite the archaeological museum, is good for reasonably priced breakfasts.

Mediterraneo Restaurant (*Jain Temples Rd*) is one of several popular places specialising in Italian food.

There's a string of decent restaurants on Main Rd with terraces overlooking the small Shiv Sagar – a good place to be in the early evening as the sun sets. *Sakura* features Japanese dishes on its extensive menu. *Shiva Janti* and *Paradise* are also reasonable.

The top-end hotels all have good restaurants – expect to pay around Rs 200 per person, excluding drinks.

Entertainment

There are two traditional dance programs, opposite each other on Main Rd south of the village, which compete for evening entertainment business.

Shilpgram, on the left-hand side coming from the village, is a government operation with nightly performances in an atmospheric open-air theatre. The changing program features folk dance troupes from different states of India. It runs from 7 to 9 pm and costs Rs 50.

Kandariya Art & Culture is a private setup with a similar program performed in a comfortable indoor theatre. One-hour shows start at 6.30 and 8.30 pm and cost Rs 150.

The *Hotel Jass Oberoi* hosts various cultural and musical performances. There's also a pool open to nonguests. See Places to Stay.

Getting There & Away

Khajuraho is on the way from nowhere to nowhere, and while many travellers slot it in between Varanasi and Agra, it involves a lot of slow bus travel over small country roads.

This will change if the rumoured rail line connecting Jhansi and Satna becomes reality. If affordable, flying is a good alternative.

Air Indian Airlines (☎ 2035) has a daily Delhi-Agra-Khajuraho-Varanasi flight that returns by the same route to Delhi. It's probably the most popular tourist flight in India and can often be booked solid for days by tour groups. It leaves Khajuraho at 2.40 pm for Delhi (US$90) and Agra (US$70), and at 12.15 pm for Varanasi (US$70). At the time of writing a new triangular Mumbai-Khajuraho-Varanasi-Mumbai flight was being introduced (Tuesday and Saturday only). The fare to Mumbai is US$245.

Indian Airlines, next to the Hotel Clarks Bundela, is open daily 10 am to 5 pm.

Bus & Train Jhansi (Rs 75/90 ordinary/deluxe, 4½ to six hours) is the nearest approach to Khajuraho on the main Delhi to Mumbai railway line, and there are half a dozen buses a day on this popular route. There are also direct Agra-Gwalior buses.

There is no direct route to Varanasi from Khajuraho. Satna (Rs 29, four hours) is the nearest reliable railhead for travellers from Varanasi and the east. It's on the Mumbai to Allahabad line so there are plenty of connections. There are five buses daily from Satna to Khajuraho (Rs 40, four hours). However, it may not be possible to get from Varanasi to Khajuraho in one day as the last bus from Satna leaves at 3.30 pm. A good option is to take the overnight *Varanasi Kurla Express* at 11.30 pm, which gets you into Satna at 6.30 am.

You can also get to Khajuraho from Varanasi by taking a train to Mahoba, 60km north of Khajuraho, then a bus from there.

There's a 7.30 am daily bus to Jabalpur (11 hours), but the train from Satna is more comfortable. Regular buses run to Panna (Rs 15, one hour) via Madla for Panna National Park.

Getting Around
To/From the Airport Taxis to the airport charge Rs 80 for this short journey; cycle-rickshaws will pedal the 3km for Rs 40.

Local Transport The best way to get around Khajuraho is by bicycle, since it's flat and pleasantly traffic-free. Bicycles cost Rs 30 per day from several places in the new village. Cycle-rickshaws are generally a rip-off, but if you don't want to hire a bicycle, it's a long walk to the eastern group of temples.

A cycle-rickshaw should cost around Rs 100 for a half-day trip – make sure it includes stops at the southern temples and waiting time.

AROUND KHAJURAHO
Panna National Park
The road to Satna passes through this 543 sq km park along the River Ken, 32km from Khajuraho. It has large areas of unspoilt forest and a variety of wildlife including leopards, chittal (spotted deer), langur monkeys and sambar. There are about 22 tigers in the park but since they're not tracked (as at Kanha) you'd be very lucky to spot one.

Entry to the park is Rs 100 (Rs 10 for Indians) plus Rs 10/100 for a camera/video. Transport within the park is in petrol-driven 'Gypsys' only; they can be hired at the park's entrance in Madla, or Khajuraho – see Getting There & Away later in this entry.

The cooler months are the best time to visit; in summer it can be hotter than a furnace. The park is closed June to October.

Day trips from Khajuraho (48km) often also take in a visit to the **diamond mines** at Majhgawan, the **Rajgarh Palace**, **Ranah Falls** and the **temples** of Panna town.

Places to Stay *Giles Tree House*, on the Ken River 3km from the park entrance, is the best place to stay. It's literally a platform built in a tree with a few huts down by the river. Basic huts are Rs 300, rooms are Rs 500 and rooms by the river with bath are Rs 800. Book at Raja's Cafe in Khajuraho.

The *Forest Rest House* in Madla provides basic accommodation for Rs 250 per person. It can be booked at the office by the park entrance or through the director in Panna village (☎ 07732-52135). You'll need to bring your own food here. There's another *Forest Rest House* (same booking details) on the opposite side of the park at Hinouta, about 50km from Khajuraho.

Getting There & Away Regular local buses run from Khajuraho to Panna (Rs 15, one hour) via Madla (45 minutes) – get off at Madla for the park.

Day trips (in six-seater Gypsys only) can be organised through travel agents in Khajuraho or at Raja's Cafe. They cost around Rs 2000 excluding entry and guide fees.

Ajaigarh & Kalinjar Forts

At Ajaigarh, 80km from Khajuraho, is a large isolated hilltop fort. It was built by the Chandelas when their influence in the area was on the decline. Kalinjar Fort, 25km north (just inside Uttar Pradesh) is much older, built during the Gupta period and mentioned by Ptolemy in the 2nd century AD. It was a stronghold of the Chandelas from the 9th to 15th centuries before being conquered by Akbar in 1569.

The forts can be reached on long day trips from Khajuraho if you hire a car for around Rs 1500. It's possible to get to Kalinjar by public bus (change at Panna), but not as a day trip. A closer access point is Chitrakoot in Uttar Pradesh.

SATNA
☎ 07672

You may find it convenient or necessary to stay overnight here on your way to or from Khajuraho. There's an MP Tourism office at the train station.

Places to Stay & Eat

The choice is basically between proximity to the bus stand or the train station.

Hotel India (☎ 22482, Rewa Rd) is a good place behind (east of) the bus stand. Reasonably clean rooms are Rs 95/126 with bath; there's a good cheap restaurant downstairs, part of the *Indian Coffee House* chain.

Nearby, *Padam Lodge* (☎ 22076, Semariya Chowk), is basic but cheap. Dorm beds are Rs 30, a single is Rs 50 and singles/doubles with bath are Rs 80/90.

Hotel Park (☎ 23017, Rewa Rd), on the other side of the bus stand is quieter and clean with rooms for Rs 100/160, Rs 450/500 with air-con. It has a veg restaurant.

Hotel Chanakya (☎ 25026, Station Rd), about 500m from the train station, has large, clean rooms with TV for Rs 200/300, or with air-con for Rs 350/450. There is a restaurant here.

Hotel Khajuraho (☎ 23330), behind the road leading from the train station, has air-cooled rooms at Rs 250/300.

Saloni Restaurant (Rewa Rd) is a clean air-con vegetarian place opposite the bus stand. There are plenty of *food stalls* in the market around the bus stand.

Getting There & Away

Four buses to Khajuraho (Rs 40, four hours) leave from 6.30 am to 2.30 pm. For Bandhavgarh National Park a state-run Gogri bus to Tala leaves daily at 8 am (Rs 50, five hours). Otherwise, you can take a bus to tiny Gorsari for tea and samosas with the locals while waiting for the bus from Rewa which continues to Tala.

The train station and the bus stand are about 2km apart; cycle-rickshaws charge Rs 5, auto-rickshaws Rs 10. There are direct trains from Satna to Varanasi (Rs 113/377 in sleeper/1st class, 316km, eight hours) and Jabalpur (Rs 76/258, 189km, three hours). Other direct expresses connect with Allahabad, Calcutta, Mumbai and Chennai.

Central Madhya Pradesh

BHOPAL
☎ 0755 • pop 1,278,030

The capital of Madhya Pradesh, Bhopal was built on the site of the 11th century city of Bhojapal. It was founded by the legendary Raja Bhoj who is credited with having constructed the lakes around which the city is built. The present city was laid out by the Afghan chief Dost Mohammed Khan, who was in charge of Bhopal during Aurangzeb's reign, but took advantage of the confusion following Aurangzeb's death in 1707 to carve out his own small kingdom.

Today, Bhopal has a multifaceted profile. There is the old city with its crowded market-places, huge old mosques, and the palaces of the former begums who ruled over the city from 1819 to 1926. To the north sprawl the huge industrial suburbs and the slums that these developments in India inevitably give rise to. The new city with its broad avenues, high-rise offices and leafy residential areas lies to the south. In the centre of Bhopal are two lakes that, while providing recreational facilities, are also the source of its plagues of mosquitoes.

Bhopal is hardly on every traveller's itinerary, but it has a relaxed feel for a state capital, a number of cultural attractions and is a good base for some excellent excursions.

The city is also famous as the site of the world's worst industrial disaster. See The Bhopal Disaster – Curing an Outrage with Neglect boxed text later in this chapter for more information.

Orientation

Both the train station and bus stand are within easy walking distance of the main hotel area along Hamidia Rd in Old Bhopal. When arriving by train, leave the station by platform No 4 or 5 to reach Hamidia Rd.

The new part of the city, which encompasses TT Nagar, site of most of the major banks and the tourist office, is a long way from either of the transport terminals so you'll have to take an auto-rickshaw or taxi. Old and New Bhopal are effectively separated by the Upper and Lower lakes.

Information

Shops in New Bhopal close on Monday, and in Old Bhopal on Sunday. Businesses such as airlines and banks close at noon on Saturday and are also closed all day Sunday.

Tourist Offices There are helpful and efficient tourist information counters at both the train station and airport. The headquarters of MP Tourism (☎ 778383, fax 774289,

email mail@mptourism.com) is in the Gangotri Complex, 4th floor, TT Nagar, in the new town, and there's a regional tourist office (☎ 553006) at the Hotel Palash. MP Tourism can book its hotels throughout the state (it's best to book five days in advance). Their Web site is at www.mptourism.com.

MP Tourism can organise a car and driver from Rs 3.50 per kilometre or Rs 400 per day.

Money You have to head over to TT Nagar to change travellers cheques or cash. The State Bank of India (near the Rangmahal Talkies cinema), the State Bank of Indore (beneath the Hotel Panchanan) or the Allahabad Bank, Bhadbhada Rd, will do the requisite transactions.

Post & Communications The main post office is on Sultania Rd, Old Bhopal, near the Taj-ul-Masjid. Poste restante letters should be marked 'Bhopal GPO', or they will be directed to the central post office in TT Nagar. They appear to be held for collection until they have completely disintegrated.

The British Council Library (see Cultural Centres) has Internet access for Rs 50 per half hour.

Bookshops Bhadbhada Rd, between the State Bank of India and MP Tourism in TT Nagar, has a couple of bookshops with a small English-language range. Variety Book House has the best selection (you can also get maps here), and Books World stocks a lot of second-hand titles.

Cultural Centres The Alliance Française (☎ 566595) is in Arera Colony. Officially services are for members only, but French visitors who are not members may be able to have a look at their French newspapers and journals. The British Council Library (☎ 553767), GTB Complex, TT Nagar, has a well-stocked reading room and is open Tuesday to Saturday 11 am to 7 pm.

Medical Services Hamidia Hospital (☎ 511446), Royal Market St, presiding over Old Bhopal is the city's best public hospital.

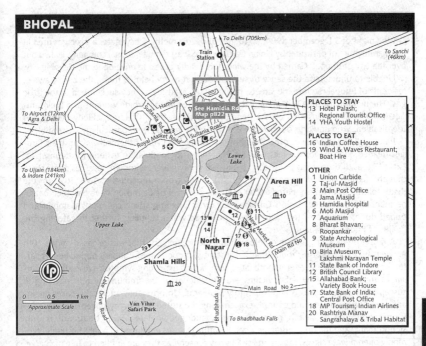

BHOPAL

To Delhi (705km)

Train Station

To Sanchi (46km)

Hamidia Road

To Airport (12km) Agra & Delhi

See Hamidia Rd Map p822

Sultania Rd

Royal Market Road

Sultania Road

Sultania Road

To Ujjain (184km) & Indore (241km)

Lower Lake

Arera Hill

Kamla Park Road

Upper Lake

New Market Rd

North TT Nagar

Main Rd No 1

Shamla Hills

Lake Drive Road

Bhadbhada Road

Main Road No 2

Van Vihar Safari Park

To Bhadbhada Falls

0   0.5   1 km
Approximate Scale

PLACES TO STAY
13 Hotel Palash;
     Regional Tourist Office
14 YHA Youth Hostel

PLACES TO EAT
16 Indian Coffee House
19 Wind & Waves Restaurant;
     Boat Hire

OTHER
1   Union Carbide
2   Taj-ul-Masjid
3   Main Post Office
4   Jama Masjid
5   Hamidia Hospital
6   Moti Masjid
7   Aquarium
8   Bharat Bhavan;
     Roopankar
9   State Archaeological
     Museum
10 Birla Museum;
     Lakshmi Narayan Temple
11 State Bank of Indore
12 British Council Library
15 Allahabad Bank;
     Variety Book House
17 State Bank of India;
     Central Post Office
18 MP Tourism; Indian Airlines
20 Rashtriya Manav
     Sangrahalaya & Tribal Habitat

MADHYA PRADESH

Taj-ul-Masjid

Commenced by Shah Jahan Begum (1868-1901) but never really completed – construction recommenced in 1971 – the Taj-ul-Masjid is one of the largest mosques in India. It's a huge pink mosque with two massive white-domed minarets and three white domes over the main building. The entrance to the mosque is not on Sultania Rd, despite the huge staircase here; go around the corner and enter from busy Royal Market Rd. It's closed to nonmuslims on Friday.

Other Mosques

The **Jama Masjid**, built in 1837 by Qudsia Begum, is surrounded by the bazaar and has very squat minarets. The **Moti Masjid** was built by Qudsia Begum's daughter, Sikander Jahan Begum, in 1860. Similar in style to the Jama Masjid in Delhi, it is a smaller

mosque with two dark-red minarets crowned by golden spikes.

Lakes

The larger Upper Lake covers 6 sq km and a bridge separates it from the smaller Lower Lake. A veritable flotilla of boats is available for hire on the Upper Lake, including rowboats (Rs 50 for 30 minutes), pedal boats (Rs 60 per hour), sailboats (Rs 100 per hour) and motorboats (Rs 30 for five minutes). There's a booking office at the bottom of the driveway leading to the Wind & Waves Restaurant.

There's a fairly dull **aquarium** near the Lower Lake, open daily except Monday. 3 to 8 pm (Rs 1).

Lakshmi Narayan Temple & Birla Museum

There are good views over the lakes to the old town from the Lakshmi Narayan Temple,

The Bhopal Disaster – Curing an Outrage with Neglect

On the night of 3 December 1984, 40 tonnes of deadly methyl icocyanate, a toxic gas used in the manufacture of pesticides by Union Carbide, a US-based multinational company, leaked out over the city of Bhopal. Carried by the wind, this deadly gas soon enveloped the sleeping city.

Unable to understand the sense of suffocation that overwhelmed them, the barely awake residents of Bhopal ran into the streets, falling by the roadside as they succumbed to the toxic gas. The majority of the 6000 immediate victims were Union Carbide workers and their families living in slums clustered on the perimeters of the factory. Children, elderly people and the disabled, who couldn't outdistance the spreading fumes, were particularly susceptible.

Panic and chaos ensued; officials intent on saving the lives of themselves and their families headed, literally, for the hills, leaving the bulk of the population to fend for themselves. Exact figures of those who perished in the disaster may never be known; local residents claim that the figures quoted by government officials are grossly unrepresentative. To date, the death toll stands at an estimated 16,000 people, and over half a million have had their health permanently destroyed. Union Carbide's legacy is ongoing: toxic chemicals dumped and buried during the life of the factory have poisoned water supplies, further threatening the health of Bhopal's residents.

A report prepared by a team of international medical experts that was released on the 10th anniversary of the disaster found that 'a substantial proportion of Bhopal's population' is suffering from 'genuine long-term morbidity', with victims exhibiting symptoms disturbingly similar to those suffered by AIDS victims – a breakdown of the immune system resulting in susceptibility to tuberculosis and respiratory problems. Unfortunately, medical services are inadequate, underfunded and corrupt, exacerbating the suffering of many patients. Since long-term monitoring of health problems was abandoned in late 1994, treatment is only symptomatic, and the drugs used are often harmful. Doctors employed in public hospitals commonly open private clinics, forcing the sick to pay for services they are entitled to free of charge.

Soon after the disaster, the Indian government demanded US$3 billion in compensation, but was persuaded to accept US$470 million or have the case drawn out for at least a decade. All criminal charges were dropped, Union Carbide renounced any liability for the accident, and the money was paid to the government. It was not until seven years after the disaster and after another 2000 people had died that a tiny portion of this money began to trickle down. The compensation funds continue to filter their way through various pockets on the slow flow down to the victims.

Today Bhopal is a pleasant, cosmopolitan city, and residents are understandably reluctant to talk about the horror that suddenly enveloped their lives over a decade ago. Outside the now-closed factory, which lies just north of Hamidia Rd, a memorial statue to the dead is the only testimony to the tragedy of Bhopal.

Union Carbide (also operating as Everyday Industries) is a profitable business once more, and batteries produced by this company are available throughout the country. Read the small print when buying batteries in India.

also known as the Birla Mandir. Beside it on Arera Hill is an excellent museum, containing a small but very selective collection of local sculptures dating mainly from the Paramana period. The stone sculptures are mainly of Vishnu, Shiva and their respective consorts and incarnations. The museum is open daily except Monday, 10 am to 5 pm (Rs 3).

State Archaeological Museum

Near the Lower Lake, this museum contains a small collection of 6th to 10th century Hindu sculptures, bronzes, prehistoric exhibits and copies of paintings from the Bagh caves. It's open daily except Monday 10 am to 6 pm (free).

Bharat Bhavan

Bharat Bhavan (☎ 540353) is a complex for the verbal, visual and performing arts, designed by the well-known architect Charles Correa and opened in 1982. It's now regarded as one of the most important centres in the country for the preservation of traditional folk art. As well as the workshops and theatres here, there's the two-part **Roopankar Gallery**. To the right of the entrance is a superb exhibition of tribal folk art paintings, sculptures and carvings produced by previously unknown adivasi (tribal) artists. Among the most striking exhibits are the colourful murals depicting animals and village life. Across the central courtyard, the second gallery provides a contrast with some of India's finest contemporary urban photographs and sculptures.

Bharat Bhavan is open daily except Monday, 2 to 8 pm (Rs 1).

Rashtriya Manav Sangrahalaya

This 40 hectare complex in the hills overlooking the Upper Lake is an ambitious attempt to showcase the lives, culture, art and religion of a fraction of India's 450 plus adivasis. The complex started with **Tribal Habitat (Museum of Man)**, an open-air exhibition of some 25 tribal dwellings in authentic village-like settings. The buildings, from all over India, were constructed using genuine materials by members of the tribes themselves, many of whom continue to maintain the site. The three newer elements to the park, **Coastal Village** (which runs along the eastern edge of the lake), **Desert Village** and **Rock Heritage** are designed along similar lines and there are prehistoric rock art sites scattered around the park. A huge indoor museum and gallery is under construction and will contain adivasi costumes, jewellery, ornaments, a multimedia display and an information database.

The complex is very much an educational project: there are two visitor information centres, as well as craft and pottery demonstrations, and film shows on Saturday at 4 pm (one hour). Admission to the exhibits and the film are free. The display is open daily (except Monday) 10.30 am to 5 pm. You can walk between the exhibits (there's a sealed road) but it makes for a tiring visit. A bicycle would be the answer but there doesn't seem to be anywhere in Bhopal to hire one. An auto-rickshaw costs around Rs 100 to take you up there, including waiting time.

Van Vihar Safari Park

This 445 hectare park is more of a zoo than a safari park, despite the promise of 'natural surroundings'. But if you're in the north during the monsoon, when all the national parks are closed, it's good to know you don't have to completely miss out on tigers, lions, leopards and crocodiles. The park is open every day except Tuesday 7 to 11 am and 3 to 5.30 pm (Rs 30). A spin around Van Vihar in a rickshaw (from the city centre) should cost around Rs 120.

Places to Stay

Hamidia Rd in Old Bhopal is where most of the city's hotels are clustered. Although it can be difficult to find good cheap accommodation in Bhopal (many hotels don't bother with the 'C' forms for foreigner registration), there are some excellent reasonably priced mid-range hotels.

Places to Stay – Budget

Most of the following places have rooms with bathrooms.

The *YHA Youth Hostel (☎ 553670, TT Nagar)*, near Hotel Palash, is dirt cheap but a bit of a disgrace by YHA standards. Members pay Rs 20 for a bed in a grimy dorm, Rs 60 for a double room. Nonmembers pay double.

Hotel Ranjit (☎ 533511, 3 Hamidia Rd) is Bhopal's most popular moderately priced hotel. Very clean air-cooled singles/doubles are Rs 150/200, or Rs 325/375 with air-con.

MADHYA PRADESH

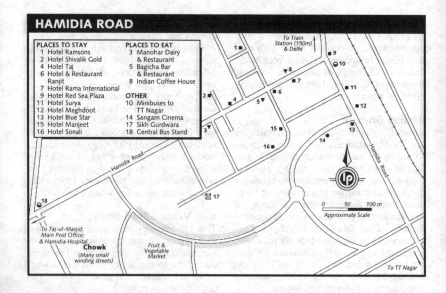

HAMIDIA ROAD

PLACES TO STAY
1 Hotel Ramsons
2 Hotel Shivalik Gold
4 Hotel Taj
6 Hotel & Restaurant
  Ranjit
7 Hotel Rama International
9 Hotel Red Sea Plaza
11 Hotel Surya
12 Hotel Meghdoot
13 Hotel Blue Star
15 Hotel Manjeet
16 Hotel Sonali

PLACES TO EAT
3 Manohar Dairy
  & Restaurant
5 Bagicha Bar
  & Restaurant
8 Indian Coffee House

OTHER
10 Minibuses to
  TT Nagar
14 Sangam Cinema
17 Sikh Gurdwara
18 Central Bus Stand

To Train Station (150m) & Delhi

Hamidia Road

Approximate Scale
0   50   100 m

To Taj-ul-Masjid;
Main Post Office;
& Hamidia Hospital

Chowk
(Many small winding streets)

Fruit & Vegetable Market

To TT Nagar

Hotel Rama International (☎ 535542, *Hamidia Rd*), nearby, is spacious, if a little shabby. Rooms are Rs 150/200, or Rs 250/300 with air-con.

Hotel Meghdoot (☎ 511375) has rooms from Rs 100/140 or Rs 150/200 for better deluxe rooms.

Hotel Manjeet (☎ 536168), just off Hamidia Rd near the Ranjit, has smallish but very clean singles/doubles from Rs 175/220, better rooms at Rs 190/250 and air-con rooms for Rs 400/450.

Hotel Red Sea Plaza (☎ 535518) looms over the main Hamidia Rd junction. Rooms are from Rs 135/190, or Rs 360/410 with air-con. A deposit of Rs 500 is demanded on check-in!

Places to Stay – Mid-Range
Hotel Sonali (☎ 533880, fax 510337, *Radha Talkies Rd*), hidden just off busy Hamidia Rd, is possibly Bhopal's best-value hotel. The cheapest rooms are definitely mid-range standard and a bargain at Rs 185/250 with hot water shower, room service and balcony. There are also deluxe

rooms for Rs 250/325 and air-con from Rs 400/475.

Hotel Taj (☎ 533162, *52 Hamidia Rd*) is a big old hotel with a central courtyard. The cheap rooms are OK at Rs 150/300, or Rs 450/600 with air-con (plus 20% tax). There's a restaurant, but no bar.

Hotel Shivalik Gold (☎ 536000, fax 710224, *40 Hamidia Rd*), behind the Taj, is a worn place with comfortable rooms from Rs 200/275, or Rs 400/500 with air-con.

Hotel Ramsons (☎ 535298) is in the backstreets off Hamidia Rd. Staff are friendly but it's gloomy and cavernous compared to its modern neighbours – reminiscent of the Overlook Hotel from the movie *The Shining* (apart from the management, of course). Big old rooms are Rs 240/310, or Rs 450/550 with air-con.

Hotel Surya (☎ 536925, *Hamidia Rd*) is modern and well run with standard rooms from Rs 200/250, air-con at Rs 450/550 and a good restaurant. Checkout is noon.

Hotel Palash (☎ 553006, *TT Nagar*), MP Tourism's hotel, is convenient if you want to stay in New Market and it's handy for the lake area. Rooms are not cheap, however, starting at Rs 550/650, or Rs 790/890 with air-con.

Places to Stay – Top End

Those who can afford it head for the hills.

Residency Hotel (☎ 556002, 208 Zone 1, MP Nagar) is a three star hotel with a swimming pool and health club. Standard rooms are Rs 1140/1940 and deluxe rooms are Rs 1595/2500, plus a whopping 25% tax.

Hotel Lake View Ashok (☎ 541600, fax 541606) is a well-appointed hotel in the Shamla Hills with an excellent restaurant. All rooms have private balconies, and there are good views over the lake. Comfortable rooms are Rs 1400/2000, deluxe doubles are Rs 2600 (plus 10% tax).

Jehan Numa Palace (☎ 540100, fax 540720), only a stone's throw away, was formerly a palace, built in the late 19th century and is Bhopal's stand-out hotel. Rooms are from Rs 1999/2499, or Rs 3899 for deluxe doubles, all with 10% tax; there's a restaurant and bar.

Places to Eat

The cheapest places to eat are the street stalls surrounding the bus and train stations. Many of the hotels around Hamidia Rd have good restaurants/bars.

The *Indian Coffee House* is a good cheap place; there are outlets in both Old and New Bhopal.

Hotel Ranjit has an excellent (and well-deserved) reputation. Most dishes on the huge menu (there is even an 'everything' heading!) are around Rs 40, and ice-cold beer is Rs 50.

Bagicha Bar & Restaurant, a few doors down, also prepares a good range of food in a quieter, open-air setting. It's set a little way back from the cacophony of Hamidia Rd.

Manohar Dairy & Restaurant has lots of gooey favourites such as *gulab jamun*, as well as an astonishing variety of ice cream. Dosas, *idlis* and veg burgers are also available. This place is very popular with locals.

Kwality Restaurant (New Market Rd, TT Nagar), opposite the State Bank of Indore,

does reasonable fast food, pizzas and Chinese and has an outdoor eating area.

Shahnama Restaurant at the Jehan Numa Palace is the place for a splurge. It's not cheap, with main dishes from Rs 100, but the food is excellent.

Wind & Waves Restaurant is a (fairly ordinary) snack shop, but you can enjoy a cold drink here (including beer) overlooking the Upper Lake.

Shopping

Bhopal's two main shopping areas are the new market area, in New Bhopal, and the old market area, or *chowk*, in Old Bhopal. While similar items can be found in both markets, prices are much more reasonable in the atmospheric chowk, just off Hamidia Rd near the bus stand. The labyrinthine streets and alleys here make this a fascinating area to wander around – but count on getting totally lost! Here you'll find fine gold and silver jewellery, beautifully woven saris and hand-embroidered appliqué skirts at reasonable prices.

Mrignayni is the registered trade name for MP state handicraft merchandise – many retail shops carry Mrignayni products.

Getting There & Away

Air Indian Airlines (☎ 770480) has daily flights to Mumbai (US$115), Indore (US$50) and Delhi (US$105), and four flights weekly to Gwalior (US$70). The office is in TT Nagar, adjacent to MP Tourism.

Bus From the bus stand on Hamidia Rd there are numerous daily buses to Sanchi (Rs 14, 1½ hours; via Raisen, Rs 16); Vidisha (Rs 18, 2½ hours); Indore (Rs 58/73/87 ordinary/express/deluxe, five to six hours); Ujjain (Rs 58, five hours); Pachmarhi (Rs 71, seven hours, three daily) and Jabalpur (Rs 115, 12 hours).

There's an overnight service to Khajuraho, but it's better to go by train to Jhansi and connect by bus from there.

A computerised reservation system operates from 11 am to 8 pm for all deluxe and long-distance buses.

MP Tourism operates a deluxe bus to Indore (Rs 160, 4½ hours). It departs from the train station at 2.30 pm (meeting the *Shatabdi Express* from Delhi). It also has a daily minibus to Pachmarhi at 8 am (Rs 100, 4½ hours), departing from Hotel Palash – a better option than the local buses.

Train There's an efficient air-con reservation hall on the left as you exit the main terminal, and a separate counter for the *Shatabdi Express* within the terminal building itself. There's a 24 hour left-luggage facility at the train station.

Bhopal is on one of the two main Delhi to Mumbai railway lines. It's the terminus for the daily *Shatabdi Express*, which leaves New Delhi station at 6.15 am, reaching Bhopal at 2 pm and returning to New Delhi after a stop here of 40 minutes. Cheapest fares from Bhopal (air-con chair class) are Rs 450 for Jhansi (three hours), Rs 505 for Gwalior (4¼ hours), Rs 595 for Agra (5½ hours) and Rs 780 for Delhi (7¾ hours).

Other express trains connect Bhopal with Delhi (Rs 196/687 in sleeper/1st class, 705km, 10 to 12 hours), Mumbai (Rs 223/767, 837km, 12 to 15 hours), Agra (Rs 137/469, 506km, 8½ hours), Gwalior (Rs 152/531, 388km, 6½ hours), Jhansi (Rs 103/347, 291km, 4½ hours) and Ujjain (Rs 76/258, 188km, three hours). Express trains leave for Sanchi (Rs 22, 46km, one hour) at 8 am and 2.40 pm; there are numerous slower passenger trains to Sanchi and Vidisha.

Getting Around

To/From the Airport The airport is 12km from Old Bhopal. Fixed rates operate for both taxis (Rs 180) and rickshaws (Rs 100).

Local Transport Auto-rickshaw drivers almost always use their meters (sheer luxury), except at night when you'll have to negotiate the fare. Hopelessly crowded minibuses for TT Nagar (Nos 2, 3 or 9) depart about every two minutes from Hamidia Rd near Hotel Red Sea Plaza (Rs 2). A rickshaw costs about Rs 25.

AROUND BHOPAL
Bhojpur

The legendary Raja Bhoj (1010-53) not only built the lakes at Bhopal but also built another one, estimated at 400 sq km, in Bhojpur, 28km south-east of the state capital. History records that the lake was held back by massive earthen dams faced on both sides with huge blocks of sandstone set without mortar.

Unfortunately, the lake no longer exists, having been destroyed by Hoshang Shah, the ruler of Mandu, in a fit of destructive passion in the early 15th century. What does survive here is the huge, partially completed **Bhojeshwar Temple**, which originally overlooked the lake. Dedicated to Shiva, it has some very unusual design features and sports a massive lingam, 2.3m high and 5.3m in circumference. The earthen rampart used to raise stones for the construction of the dome still remains. Nearby is another incomplete monolithic temple, this time a **Jain shrine** containing a colossal statue of Mahavira, over 6m tall.

A few local buses run to Bhojpur from Bhopal's bus stand, or take any Hoshangabad-bound bus (Rs 10) and get off at the turn-off to Bhojpur from where you should be able to pick up a tempo (Rs 2).

Bhimbetka

Like the Aboriginal rock paintings in the outback of Australia, the cave paintings of the Bushmen in the Kalahari Desert in Africa or the Palaeolithic Lascaux caves of France, the Bhimbetka caves are a must-see. Among forests of teak and sal in the craggy cliffs of an almost African setting 45km south of Bhopal, some thousand rock shelters have been discovered. Almost half contain ancient paintings depicting the life and times of the different people who lived here.

Because of the natural red and white pigments used by the painters, the colours have been remarkably well preserved and it's obvious in certain caves that the same surface has been used by different people at different times. There's everything from figures of wild buffalo (gaur), rhinoceros, bears and tigers, to hunting scenes, initiation ceremonies, childbirth, communal dancing and drinking scenes, religious rites and burials.

The extent and archaeological importance of the site was only recently realised and dating is still not complete. The oldest paintings are believed to be up to 12,000 years old, whereas some of the crude, geometric figures probably date from as recently as the medieval period.

The caves themselves are not difficult to find; 15 are accessible and signposted, and linked by a concrete path. A local guide can be useful for pointing out some of the more obscure paintings and explaining their significance. The **Zoo Rock Shelter** is one of the first you come to, famous for its variety of animal paintings. Rock shelter No 15 features a huge red bison attacking a helpless stick figure. There's nothing here other than the caves, so bring water.

Getting There & Away From Bhopal, 45km away, take any bus to Hoshangabad or Itarsi (Rs 15) via Obaidullaganj, 50 minutes south of Bhopal. Get off 6.5km after Obaidullaganj by the sign pointing right with '3.2' and some Hindi on it (ask the driver). Follow this sign, crossing the railway line for the 3km walk to the hills in front of you. To get back you can flag down a truck or bus on the main road. If you don't fancy the walk, pick up a rickshaw in Obaidullaganj. If you want to visit both Bhimbetka and Bhojpur it's worth springing for a taxi. You can hire a car and driver through MP Tourism in Bhopal for around Rs 400 a day (see Tourist Offices in the Bhopal section).

Other Places

Neori, only 6km from Bhopal, has an 11th century Shiva Temple and is a popular picnic spot. **Islamnagar**, 11km from Bhopal on the Berasia Rd, is a hilltop palace built by Dost Mohammed Khan in the 18th century. In the palace's formal gardens, a highly decorated pavilion combines elements of the Afghan rulers' Islamic art and the local Hindus' decorative style. Any Berasia bus will drop you off here. At **Ashapuri**, 6km north of Bhopal, there are ruined temples and Jain palaces with statues scattered on the ground. **Hathaikheda**, 10km out of Bhopal on the Raisen Rd, is a peaceful fishing spot. Also on the Raisen Rd, **Samardha**, 26km from Bhopal, has forest clearings just begging for a picnic blanket. **Chiklod**, 45km out, has a palace in a peaceful sylvan setting.

SANCHI
☎ 07482

Beside the main railway line, 46km northeast of Bhopal, a hill rises from the plain. It's topped by some of the oldest and most interesting Buddhist structures in India. This site had no direct connection with the life of Buddha. It was the great Emperor Ashoka, Buddhism's most famous convert, who built the first stupas here in the 3rd century BC, and a great number of stupas and other religious structures were added over the succeeding centuries.

As Buddhism was gradually absorbed back into Hinduism in its land of origin, the site decayed and was eventually completely forgotten. In 1818 a British officer rediscovered the site, and in the following years amateur archaeologists and greedy treasure hunters did immense damage to Sanchi before a proper restoration was commenced in 1881. Finally, between 1912 and 1919, the structures were carefully repaired and restored to their present condition by Sir John Marshall.

Sanchi is a very special place and is not to be missed if you're anywhere within striking distance. The site is also a good base for a number of interesting bicycle excursions.

Orientation & Information

Sanchi is little more than a small village at the foot of the hill on which the site is located. The site is open daily from dawn to dusk and tickets are available from the kiosk outside the museum. Entry costs Rs 5 (free on Friday), which covers both the site and the museum (if you plan on going up for the superb sunrise, you'll need to buy a ticket the day before). It's worth getting a copy of the *Sanchi* guidebook (Rs 12), published by the Archaeological Survey of India. There's also a museum guidebook on sale here.

It's sometimes possible to visit the silk-worm farm (Sericulture Centre). Ask at the MP Travellers' Lodge, next door.

The quickest way up to the site is via the stone steps off to the right of the tarmac road. There's a drink stall by the modern *vihara* (monastery) on Sanchi hill, and Buddhist publications are for sale in the vihara. Following is a brief description of the buildings at the site; the *Sanchi* guidebook de-scribes all these buildings, and many others, in much greater detail.

Archaeological Museum

This museum has a small collection of sculpture from the site. The most interesting pieces are the lion capital from the Ashoka pillar, a *yakshi* (maiden) hanging from a mango tree and a beautiful Buddha figure in red sandstone. It's open 10 am to 5 pm daily except Friday.

Great Stupa

Stupa 1, as it is listed on the site, is the main structure on the hill. Originally constructed by Ashoka in the 3rd century BC, it was later enlarged and the original brick stupa enclosed within a stone one. In its present form it stands 16m high and is 37m in diameter. A railing encircles the stupa and there are four entrances through magnificently carved gateways, or *toranas*. These toranas are the finest works of art at Sanchi and among the finest examples of Buddhist art in India.

Toranas The four gateways were erected around 35 BC and had all fallen down at the time of the stupa's restoration. The scenes carved onto the pillars and their triple architraves are mainly tales from the Jatakas, the episodes of the Buddha's various lives. At this stage in Buddhist art the Buddha was never represented directly – his presence was always alluded to through symbols. The lotus stands for his birth, the bo tree represents his enlightenment, the wheel his teachings and the footprint and throne symbolise his presence. Even a stupa itself is a symbol of the Buddha.

Walk around the stupa clockwise, as one should around all Buddhist monuments.

Northern Gateway The northern gateway, topped by a broken wheel of law, is the best-preserved of the toranas. Scenes include a monkey offering a bowl of honey to the Buddha, whose presence is indicated by a bo tree. In another panel he ascends a road into the air (again represented by a bo tree) in the Miracle of Sravasti. This is just one

SANCHI

Train Station
Jaiswal Lodge
Sri Lanka Mahabodhi Society Guest House
To Vidisha (10km) & Udaigiri Caves (14km)
Bike Hire
Mrignayni Emporium
Food Stalls & Bike Hire
Bus Stand
Health Centre
Tourist Cafeteria
Sericulture Centre
Travellers' Lodge
Ticket Office
Archaeological Museum
PWD Circuit House (VIPs only)
Post Office
To Bhopal (46km)
Gate
To Sanchi Village
Tank
Steps
Vihara
Stupa 4
Stupa 2
Stupa 1
Stupa 3 Temple 31
Monastery 51
Stupa 5
Pillar 10 (Ashoka)
Building 43
Temple 18
Temple 40
To Monasteries 45 & 47
0 100 200 m

of several miraculous feats he performs on the northern gateway – all of which leave his spectators stunned. Elephants, facing in four directions, support the architraves above the columns, while horses with riders and more elephants fill the gaps between the architraves.

Eastern Gateway One pillar on this gateway includes scenes of the Buddha's entry to nirvana. Across the front of the middle architrave is the Great Departure, where the Buddha (symbolised by a riderless horse) renounces the sensual life and sets out to find enlightenment. Maya's dream of an elephant standing on the moon, which she had when she conceived the Buddha, is also shown on one of the columns. The figure of a yakshi, hanging out from one of the architraves, is one of the best known images of Sanchi.

Southern Gateway The oldest of the gateways, this includes scenes of the Buddha's birth and also events from Ashoka's life as a Buddhist. At the rear of the top architrave there is another representation of the Great Departure. As on the western gateway, the tale of the Chhaddanta Jataka features on this gateway.

Western Gateway The western gateway, with the architraves supported by dwarfs, has some of the most interesting scenes at the site. The rear face of one of the pillars shows the Buddha undergoing the Temptation of Mara, while demons flee and angels cheer his resistance. The top front architrave shows the Buddha in seven different incarnations, but since he could not, at the time, be represented directly, he appears three times as a stupa and four times as a tree.

The colourful events of the Chhaddanta Jataka are related on the front face of the bottom architrave. In this tale the Buddha, in a lower incarnation, took the form of a six-tusked elephant, but one of his two wives became jealous; she managed to reincarnate as a queen and then arranged to have the six-tusked elephant hunted and killed. The sight of his tusks, sawn off by the hunter, was sufficient for the queen to die of remorse! Pot-bellied dwarfs support the architraves on this gateway.

Other Stupas

There are many other stupas on the hill, some of them tiny votive ones less than 1m high. Eight were built by Ashoka but only three remain, including the Great Stupa. **Stupa 2**, one of the most interesting of the lesser stupas, is halfway down the hill to the west. If you come up from the town by the main route you can walk back down via stupa 2. There are no gateways to this stupa, but the 'medallions' that decorate the surrounding wall are of great interest. Their design is almost childlike, but full of energy and imagination. Flowers, animals and people – some mythological – are found all around the stupa.

Stupa 3 stands north-east of the main stupa and is similar in design, though smaller in size. It has only one gateway and is thought to have been constructed soon after the completion of the Great Stupa. Stupa 3 once contained relics of two important disciples of the Buddha. They were removed and taken to London in 1853 but returned to Sanchi in 1953 and are now housed in the modern vihara.

Now almost totally destroyed, the 2nd century BC stupa 4 stands right behind stupa 3. Between stupa 1 (the Great Stupa) and stupa 3 is stupa 5, which is unusual in that it once had an image of the Buddha, now displayed in the museum.

Pillars

Scattered around the site are pillars and the remains of pillars. The most important is **pillar 10**, which was erected by Ashoka and stands close to the southern entrance to the Great Stupa. Only the base of this beautifully proportioned and executed shaft now stands, but the fine capital can be seen in the museum. The four back-to-back lions that once topped the column are an excellent example of the Greco-Buddhist art of that era. They now form the state emblem of India and can be seen on every banknote.

MADHYA PRADESH

Pillar 25, dating from the Sunga period (2nd century BC) and **pillar 35**, dating from the 5th century AD, are not as fine as the earlier Ashoka pillar.

Temples

Immediately south of stupa 1 is **temple 18**, a *chaitya* that is remarkably similar in style to classical Greek-columned buildings. It dates from around the 7th century AD, but traces of earlier wooden buildings have been discovered beneath it. Beside this temple is the small **temple 17**, also Greek-like in style. The large **temple 40**, slightly south-east of these two temples, in part dates back to the Ashokan period.

Temple 31, built originally during the 6th or 7th centuries but reconstructed during either the 10th or 11th centuries, is adjacent to stupa 5. This flat-roofed rectangular temple contains a well-executed image of the Buddha. This appears to have been moved here from another temple during the reconstruction of temple 31, as it does not exactly fit the pedestal on which it is mounted.

Monasteries

The earliest monasteries on the site were made of wood and are long gone. The usual plan is of a central courtyard surrounded by monastic cells. **Monasteries 45** and **47** stand on the higher, eastern edge of the hilltop. They date from the later period of building at Sanchi, a time of transition from Buddhism to Hinduism, and show strong Hindu elements in their design. There is a good view of the village of Sanchi below and Vidisha in the distance from this side of the hill.

Monastery 51 is partway down the hill on the western side toward stupa 2. Nearby is the **Great Bowl** in which food and offerings were placed for distribution to the monks. It was carved out of a huge boulder. The modern **vihara** on the hill was built to house the returned relics from stupa 3. The design is a poor shadow of the former artistry of Sanchi.

Special Events

In late November each year, the **Chethiyagiri Vihara Festival** attracts hundreds of Buddhist monks and pilgrims to see the relics of two of Buddha's early disciples, Sari Puttha and Maha Moggallana. The relics, originally discovered in stupa 3 in 1853, are now kept in the vihara and brought out for display during the festival.

Places to Stay & Eat

It's possible to take in all that Sanchi has to offer in just two or three hours. However, this is such a peaceful place that it's really worth spending the night here.

The *Sri Lanka Mahabodhi Society Guest House* (☎ 62739) is where the visiting monks stay and the best budget option in Sanchi. Spartan rooms are in a tranquil garden setting and cost Rs 40 with shared bath (cold water only). *The Jaiswal Lodge* (☎ 63908), over the road, has five rooms available for Rs 50.

MP Tourism runs two places in Sanchi, both with restaurants serving standard fare. *Tourist Cafeteria* (☎ 62743) has clean rooms with bath for Rs 200/290. Rooms have ceiling fans, or there's a Rs 50 surcharge to use the air-cooler. *Travellers' Lodge* (☎ 62723), on the main road to Bhopal about 250m from the crossroads, is a better hotel, but it's not as close to the stupas. Rooms cost Rs 250/300, or Rs 350/450 for the deluxe rooms. Don't forget the air-cooler surcharge.

The market area around the bus stand has a variety of fruit and food *stalls*, as well as a couple of basic *restaurants*.

Getting There & Away

Bus Local buses connect Bhopal with Sanchi (and other towns and villages in the area) about every hour from dawn to dusk, but there are two possible routes. The longer route (main road) goes via Raisen (see the Around Sanchi section later), costs Rs 16 and takes three hours for the 68km trip. The shorter route follows the railway line to Bhopal, costs Rs 14 and takes 1½ hours.

To Vidisha, buses depart from the Sanchi bus stand about every 30 minutes (Rs 4). A rickshaw to Vidisha can be bargained down to about Rs 20.

Train Sanchi is on the main Delhi to Mumbai railway line, 46km north of Bhopal. Slow passenger trains (Rs 10) can take over two hours to get to Bhopal, but there are two express trains each day (Rs 22, one hour). The expresses depart Bhopal at 8 am and 2.40 pm, and depart Sanchi at 10.18 am and 4 pm, so it's possible to visit Sanchi in a day trip.

Getting Around
In Sanchi itself everything is within easy walking distance. For excursions to places nearby, like Vidisha (10km) and the Udaigiri caves (14km), you can rent bikes in Sanchi's market for about Rs 15 a day.

AROUND SANCHI
Within cycling distance of Sanchi are more Buddhist sites, although none are of the scale or as well preserved as those at Sanchi. **Sonari**, 10km south-west of Sanchi, has eight stupas, two of them important. At **Satdhara**, west of Sanchi on the bank of the Beas River, are two stupas, one 30m in diameter. Another 8km to the south-east is **Andher**, where there are three small but well-preserved stupas. These stupas were all discovered in 1851, after the discovery of Sanchi.

Vidisha
• **pop 109,695**
Vidisha was important in Ashoka's time and it was from here that his wife came. Then it was known as Besnagar and was the largest town in the area. The ruins of the 2nd century BC Brahmanical shrine here show traces of lime mortar – the earliest use of cement in India. Finds from the site are displayed in the **museum** near the train station.

From the 6th century AD the city was deserted for three centuries. It was renamed Bhilsa by the Muslims who built the now-ruined Bija Mandal, a mosque constructed from the remains of Hindu temples. From Sanchi you can reach Vidisha by bike (see the Udaigiri Caves entry for directions), bus (Rs 4, every 30 minutes), train (Rs 15), or rickshaw (Rs 30).

Heliodorus Pillar (Khamb Baba)
Between Vidisha and Udaigiri, 1km north of the Udaigiri caves turn-off, is this inscribed pillar, known locally as the Khamb Baba pillar. Erected in about 140 BC by Heliodorus, a Greek ambassador to the city from Taxila (now in Pakistan), the pillar celebrates his conversion to Hinduism. It's dedicated to Vishnu and worshipped by local fishers.

Udaigiri Caves
Cut into the sandstone hill, 5km from Vidisha, are about 20 Gupta cave shrines dating from 320 to 606 AD; two are Jain, the other 18 Hindu. In cave 5 there is a superb image of Vishnu in his boar incarnation. Cave 7 was cut out for the personal use of King Chandragupta II. Cave 20 is particularly interesting, with detailed Jain carvings. On the top of the hill are the ruins of a 6th century Gupta temple.

Getting There & Away
From Bhopal or Sanchi take a bus or train to Vidisha, and from there take a tonga or auto-rickshaw to the caves. To reach the caves by bike from

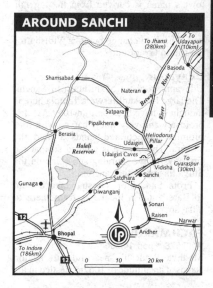

AROUND SANCHI

MADHYA PRADESH

Sanchi, cycle towards Vidisha until you cross the river (6km). Turn left 1km farther on (or carry straight on if you want to visit Vidisha first). After 3km you'll reach a junction in the colourful bazaar – turn left again. One kilometer farther is another left turn. Take this road for the caves (3.5km) or continue for 1km for the Heliodorus Pillar.

Raisen

On the alternate road to Bhopal, 23km south of Sanchi, the huge and colourful hilltop **fort** of Raisen has temples, cannons, three palaces, 40 wells and a large tank. This Malwa fort was built around 1200 AD, and although initially the centre of an independent kingdom, it later came under the control of Mandu. There are also ancient paintings in the caves in this area. There are local buses to Raisen hourly from Sanchi (Rs 10), and regular departures from Bhopal's bus stand (Rs 12).

Gyaraspur

There are tanks, temples and a fort dating from the 9th and 10th centuries AD at this town, 51km north-east of Sanchi. The town's name is derived from the big fair that used to be held here in the 11th month, sometimes known as Gyaras. From Sanchi you'll have to change buses at Vidisha for the trip to Gyaraspur.

Udayapur

Udayapur is about 65km north of Sanchi. The large **Neelkantheswara Temple** here is thought to have been built in 1059 AD. It's profusely and very finely carved with four prominent, decorated bands around the sikhara. The temple is aligned so that the first rays of the morning sun shine on the Shiva lingam in the sanctum.

From Sanchi or Vidisha, take a train to Bareth and a local bus from there to Udayapur.

PACHMARHI

☎ 07578 • pop 14,700

Madhya Pradesh's peaceful hill station stands at an altitude of 1067m, nestled in the Satpura Ranges National Park 210km southeast of Bhopal. It was 'discovered' by a Captain Forsyth who realised the potential of the saucer-shaped valley as a health resort in 1857, when he first saw it from the viewpoint that originally bore his name, but is now known as Priyadarshini.

Although nothing like a Himalayan hill station, Pachmarhi is a very attractive, relaxing place rarely visited by foreign tourists. The area draws quite a few artists, and gurus occasionally hold retreats up here.

There are fine views out over the surrounding red sandstone hills, pools and waterfalls to bathe in, ancient **cave paintings** and some interesting walks through the sal forests.

Orientation & Information

The bus stand is at the north end of the small village. The main road continues south from here for about 3km to the seven-way junction called Jaistambha, which makes an excellent landmark for walks. Accommodation is spread over a wide area, so you'll need to use a taxi unless you're staying in the village itself.

There is a tourist information kiosk (☎ 52029) at the bus stand, and a regional tourist office (☎ 52100) next to the Hotel Amaltas. They can provide brochures, fairly ordinary maps and arrange guides. There's no foreign exchange facilities in Pachmarhi.

Things to See & Do

Built by Captain Forsyth in 1862, **Bison Lodge** was Pachmarhi's first forest lodge and is now a museum covering the history of the area and the flora and fauna of the Satpura region. A free wildlife film is shown in the open-air theatre here nightly (except Monday) at 6 pm.

There are a number of interesting short **walks** around Pachmarhi, as well as longer treks for which you'll probably need a guide. **Jatashankar** is a revered cave temple in a gorge less than 2km from the bus stand. The small Shiva shrine is hidden under a huge overhanging rock formation.

Bee Falls is the most accessible of several waterfalls in the district – the drawback is the Rs 100 national park entry fee (Rs 10 for Indians) to get there. From the main road about 1km south of Jaistambha a trail leads down to the park entrance, then steps continue down to the falls. About 2km east of Jaistambha, the **Pandav Caves** are five 1000-year-old rock-cut caves overlooking an attractive garden. Legend has it the Pandavas lived here during their 12 year exile.

A recommended long day walk is to the hilltop shrine of **Chauragarh**, 4km from Mahadeo. You can see the cave paintings at **Mahadeo** on the way.

Special Events
Every February/March up to 100,000 Shaivite pilgrims, sadhus and adivasis attend the **Shivaratri Mela** celebrations at Mahadeo Temple, 10km south of Pachmarhi. The festival commemorates Lord Shiva and participants bring symbolic tridents and plant them on top of nearby Chauragarh hill.

Places to Stay
Most of the accommodation in Pachmarhi is run by MP Tourism or SADA, but there are a few private places in the village that are only really good value in the low season when they drop their prices. High season is April to July and December/January.

Places to Stay – Budget
Hotel Pachmarhi (☎ 52170, Patel Marg), in the village, has reasonable doubles from Rs 200 and Rs 250, with a 40% low-season discount.

Hotel Utkarsh (☎ 52162), a short walk south of the bus stand just off the main road, has doubles with bath and hot water for Rs 200, or Rs 100 in the low season.

Holiday Homes (☎ 52099) is the MP Tourism budget choice, and a pretty good one. Clean double rooms with bath, TV and hot water are Rs 290. It's about 1km from the bus stand back towards Piparya.

New Hotel (☎ 52017, Mahadeo Rd) is a large place operated by SADA, about 4km from the village. There's a wide range of

rooms from Rs 100 to Rs 250 (with TV), and a 25% low-season discount.

Nandanvan Cottages (☎ 52018) are well placed near Jaistambha, and are at the top of the budget range at Rs 385 a double.

Places to Stay – Mid-Range & Top End
The following are MP Tourism places, except Nilamber (SADA).

Amaltas (☎ 52098) is a rambling old former colonial bungalow. Nondescript double rooms with bath are Rs 550, deluxe rooms are Rs 690.

Satpura Retreat (☎ 52097) is another old Raj bungalow but much more atmospheric with a large veranda, comfortable rooms and vast bathrooms. It's in a quiet (isolated) location along the Mahadeo road. Standard doubles are Rs 690, but the good rooms are Rs 1390.

Nilamber Cottages (☎ 52039) are excellent. Perched up on a small hill about 3km south of the village, there's great east-west views from the verandas. Doubles with bath, hot water and TV are worth the Rs 550.

Rock End Manor (☎ 52079), just below Nilamber Cottages, is the swankiest address in Pachmarhi. It used to be the local maharaja's golf retreat, but has been converted into an elegant heritage hotel. Double rooms with panoramic views and all mod cons are Rs 1590, or Rs 1990 with air-con.

Places to Eat
The best places to eat are the hotel restaurants, especially the *China Bowl* at Panchavati Huts & Cottages and *The Club* at Rock End Manor, but there are a few decent independent places and numerous cheap cafes in the bazaar area around the bus stand.

Mahfil Restaurant, near the bus stand, has cheap dosas and good veg burgers. *Khalsa Restaurant* has a pleasant outdoor setting by the lake and a range of good veg and nonveg food.

Getting There & Away
From the bus stand there are two services to Bhopal (Rs 71, seven hours) and the direct

MP Tourism minibus at 2.30 pm (Rs 100, five hours). There are departures every couple of hours to Pipariya (Rs 18, 1½ hours). Jeeps also ply this route for Rs 25 per person (if full).

Getting Around
Plenty of jeeps hang around the bus stand looking for passengers to take to Pachmarhi's viewpoints. A half-day trip costs at least Rs 400. They're also the local taxis (Rs 20 for a short trip). Bicycles can be hired from the shop just north of the bazaar for Rs 25 a day and are a good way to get to the various trailheads and viewpoints.

PIPARIYA
☎ 07576
Pipariya is the nearest road/rail junction to Pachmarhi, 47km away. It's on the railway line that runs from Mumbai to Jabalpur. If you get stuck here there's the MP Tourism *Tourist Motel* (☎ 22299) with doubles at Rs 150 (share bathroom) and a restaurant. It's about 200m from the train station.

Local buses and jeeps leave from the bus stand behind the train station regularly for Pachmarhi. A local bus to/from Bhopal costs Rs 60 and takes six hours.

Western Madhya Pradesh

UJJAIN
☎ 0734 • pop 433,465
Only 56km from Indore, ancient Ujjain is one of India's holiest cities for Hindus. It gets its sanctity from a mythological tale about the churning of the oceans by the gods and demons in search of the nectar of immortality. When the coveted vessel of nectar was finally found, there followed a mad scramble across the skies with the demons pursuing the gods in an attempt to take the nectar from them. Four drops were spilt and they fell at Haridwar, Nasik, Ujjain and Prayag (Allahabad). As a result, Ujjain is one of the sites of the Kumbh Mela,

which takes place here every 12 years. The 1992 Kumbh Mela drew millions to bathe in the Shipra river.

Despite its relative obscurity today, Ujjain ranks equal as a great religious centre with such places as Varanasi, Gaya and Kanchipuram. The city really comes alive during Navratri (September/October). For non-Hindus, though, it can be a pretty dull place once you've explored the temples and ghats.

History
On an ancient trade route, Ujjain has a distinguished history whose origins are lost in the mists of time. It was an important city under Ashoka's father, when it was known as Avantika. Later Chandragupta II (380-414 AD) ruled from here rather than from his actual capital, Pataliputra. It was at his court that Kalidasa, one of Hinduism's most revered poets, wrote the *Meghdoot*, with its famous lyrical description of the city and its people.

With the passing of the Guptas and the rise of the Parmaras, Ujjain became the centre of a struggle for control of the Malwa region. The last of the Parmaras, Siladitya, was captured by the Muslim sultans of Mandu, and Ujjain thus passed into the hands of Mughal vassals.

An invasion by Altamish in 1234 resulted in the wholesale desecration of many of the temples, but that was halted during the reign of Baz Bahadur of Mandu. Bahadur himself was eventually overthrown by the Mughal emperor, Akbar. Later, under Aurangzeb, grants were provided to fund temple reconstruction.

Following the demise of the Mughals, Maharaja Jai Singh (of Jaipur fame) became the governor of Malwa, and during his rule the observatory and several new temples were constructed at Ujjain. With his passing, Ujjain experienced another period of turmoil at the hands of the Marathas until it was finally taken by the Scindias in 1750. When the Scindia capital was moved to Gwalior in 1810, Ujjain's commercial importance declined rapidly.

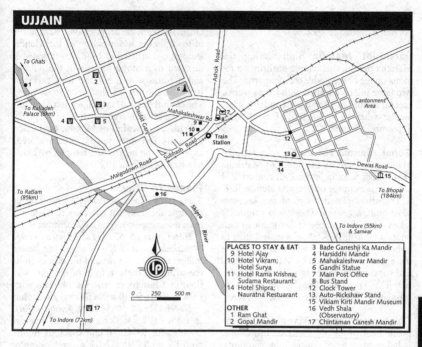

UJJAIN

To Ghats
To Kaliadeh Palace (8km)
Ashok Road
Daulat Ganj
Mahakaleshwar Rd
Subhash Road
Train Station
Malgodown Road
To Ratlam (85km)
Shipra River
Cantonment Area
Dewas Road
To Bhopal (184km)
To Indore (55km) & Sanwar
To Indore (72km)

0   250   500 m

PLACES TO STAY & EAT	
9 Hotel Ajay	3 Bade Ganeshji Ka Mandir
10 Hotel Vikram;	4 Harsiddhi Mandir
Hotel Surya	5 Mahakaleshwar Mandir
11 Hotel Rama Krishna;	6 Gandhi Statue
Sudama Restaurant	7 Main Post Office
14 Hotel Shipra;	8 Bus Stand
Nauratna Restuarant	12 Clock Tower
	13 Auto-Rickshaw Stand
OTHER	15 Vikiam Kirti Mandir Museum
1 Ram Ghat	16 Vedh Shala
2 Gopal Mandir	(Observatory)
	17 Chintaman Ganesh Mandir

MADHYA PRADESH

Orientation & Information

The railway line divides the city: the old section, including the bazaar and most of the temples and ghats, are to the north-west of the city, and the new section is on the south-east side. The cheap hotels are in front of the train station. Tourist information is available at the Hotel Shipra. There's nowhere to change money in Ujjain – Indore and Bhopal are the closest places.

Temples

Mahakaleshwar Mandir The most important temple in Ujjain, the Mahakaleshwar Mandir is dedicated to Shiva. The temple enshrines one of India's 12 *jyothirlingam* – naturally occurring lingam believed to derive currents of power (*shakti*) from within themselves as opposed to lingam ritually invested with *mantra-shakti* by the priests.

The myth of the jyothirlingam (the lingam of light) stems from a long dispute for primacy between Brahma and Vishnu. During the dispute, according to legend, the earth split apart to reveal an incandescent column of light. To find the source of this column, Vishnu became a boar and burrowed underground while Brahma took to the sky in the form of an eagle. After 1000 years of fruitless searching, Shiva emerged from the lingam of light and both Brahma and Vishnu acknowledged that he was the greatest of the gods.

The temple was destroyed by Altamish of Delhi in 1235 but restored by the Scindias in the 19th century. Non-Hindus are welcome to make the busy, jostling round of the many mini-temples in this evocative complex, and you may find yourself on the receiving end of a puja.

Above the tank near the Mahakaleshwar Mandir, the large ornate statue of Ganesh here makes **Bade Ganeshji Ka Mandir** a popular pilgrimage spot.

Harsiddhi Mandir Built during the Maratha period, this temple enshrines a famous image of the goddess Annapurna. The two large pillars adorned with lamps were a special feature of Maratha art and are spectacular when lit at Navratri (Dussehra) in September/October.

Gopal Mandir The marble-spired Gopal Mandir was built by the queen of Maharaja Daulat Rao Scindia in the 19th century and is an great example of Maratha architecture.

The silver-plated doors of the sanctum have quite a history. They were originally taken from the temple at Somnath in Gujarat to Ghazni in Afghanistan and then to Lahore by Mohammed Shah Abdati. From there they were rescued by Mahadji Scindia and shortly afterwards installed in the temple. This is a large temple but is easy to miss as it's buried in the bazaar.

Chintaman Ganesh Mandir On the opposite bank of the Shipra River, this temple is believed to be of considerable antiquity. The artistically carved pillars of the assembly hall date back to the Parmara period.

Ghats

Since most of the temples are of relatively recent construction you may find more of interest on the ghats, especially at dawn and dusk when the locals frame their days with prayer. The largest is Ram Ghat, fairly close to the Harsiddhi Mandir. The others are some considerable distance north of the centre.

Vedh Shala (Observatory)

Since the 4th century BC, Ujjain has been India's Greenwich (as far as Indian geographers were concerned), with the first meridian of longitude passing through it. Maharaja Jai Singh built one of his quirky observatories here between 1725 and 1730. Astrologers can purchase the complete year's astronomical ephemeris in both English and Hindi at the observatory.

Kaliadeh Palace

On an island in the Shipra River, 8km north of town, is the water palace of the Mandu sultans, constructed in 1458. River water is diverted over stone screens in the palace, and the bridge to the island uses carvings from the sun temple that once stood here. The central dome of the palace is a good example of Persian architecture.

With the downfall of Mandu, the palace gradually fell into ruin but was restored, along with the nearby sun temple, by Madhav Rao Scindia in 1920.

Places to Stay

There's a few cheap and cheerless hotels right opposite the train station. They're basic but even the cheapest rooms have bathrooms.

Hotel Ajay (☎ 551354, 12 Dewas Gate, Mahakaleshwar Rd) is one of the better budget choices. It's around the corner from the string of hotels in front of the train station, and has rooms for Rs 143/165 with bath or Rs 165/240 with TV and air-cooler.

Hotel Vikram (☎ 562220, Subhash Rd), in front of the station, has small singles/doubles for Rs 60/80 and spacious rooms with TV for Rs 100/120. It's a pretty grubby place – avoid the grotty cells with shared bathrooms.

Hotel Surya (☎ 560747), next door, has better rooms for Rs 85/100, or Rs 135/160 with TV. All rooms have running hot water.

Hotel Rama Krishna (☎ 557012, Subhash Rd) charges Rs 125/150, or Rs 250/350 with air-con.

Retiring rooms at the train station have dorm beds for Rs 30.

MP Tourism's *Hotel Shipra* (☎ 551495), down a quiet road in a very pleasant setting, has an impressive marble foyer, but is generally gloomy. Rooms are from Rs 350/390, up to Rs 690/790 with air-con, plus tax. The restaurant here is quite good, and there's a bar. To get to the Shipra from the train station, exit at platform 7.

Places to Eat

There are a number of places to eat opposite the station.

Sudama Restaurant has good vegetarian dishes for under Rs 30 but the breakfasts are spooky.

Nauratna Restaurant in the Hotel Shipra serves good food, although the servings are a little modest.

Getting There & Away

Bus There are buses roughly every 20 minutes for the bone-shaking trip to Indore (Rs 18, two hours), which are generally faster than the train. Buses to Bhopal (Rs 55/70 ordinary/deluxe, four hours) go via Dewas. For Mandu you have to change at Indore. An early-morning bus connects Ujjain with Kota in Rajasthan (Rs 75, 256km).

Train The *Malwa Express*, departing at 2.45 pm, is the fastest link with Delhi. It takes 17½ hours (Rs 162/797 in sleeper/1st class 885km), via Bhopal (Rs 76/255, 184km, four hours), Jhansi (Rs 148/510, 475km, nine hours), Gwalior (Rs 174/604, 572km, 10½ hours) and Agra (Rs 196/687, 690km, 13 hours).

The *Narmada Express* connects Ujjain with Indore (Rs 76/150, 2¼ hours) and, heading east: Bhopal, Jabalpur (Rs 167/574, 540km, 12½ hours) and Bilaspur (Rs 235/805, 929km, 25 hours).

The 5.20 pm *Awantika Express* is the only direct service to Mumbai but it terminates at Bandra at 6.40 am (Rs 143/706). Alternatively, you can catch a passenger train to Nagda (1½ hours), to connect with the overnight *Golden Temple Mail*, which departs at 6.20 pm.

The *Bhopal-Rajkot Express* to Ahmedabad departs at 11.15 pm and arrives at 8.50 am (Rs 146/500).

There is an efficient reservation hall to the left as you leave the station.

Getting Around

Many of Ujjain's sights are a long way from the centre of town so you'll probably use quite a few auto-rickshaws or the more romantic horse-drawn tongas. There are registration booths at both the bus and train stations that auto-rickshaw drivers are obliged to use if you request it. The normal system of bargaining should work though – from the train station to the Mahakaleshwar Mandir costs around Rs 10 (Rs 20 for a tonga).

INDORE
☎ 0731 • pop 1,278,690

Indore is not of great interest, but it's a good base for visiting Mandu. The city is a major textile-producing centre and at Pithampur, 35km away, Hindustan Motors, Kinetic Honda, Bajaj Tempo and Eischer all have factories. Indians call Pithampur the Detroit of India, and Indore is its gateway.

Although the city is on an ancient pilgrimage route to Ujjain, nothing much happened here until the 18th century. From 1733, it was ruled by the Holkar dynasty who were firm supporters of the British, even during the Uprising.

Orientation & Information

The older part of town is on the western side of the railway line, the newer part on the east. If arriving by train, leave the station by platform No 1 for the east side of town and by platform No 4 for the west side.

The tourist office (☎ 528653) is by the Tourist Bungalow at the back of the RN Tagore Natya Griha Hall, RN Tagore Rd. It's open from 10 am to 5 pm.

Cash and travellers cheques can be changed at the main branch of the State Bank of India, near the main post office.

Internet and email facilities are available at Indore Telecom's flash multimedia centre (Central Telegraph Building) in Nehru Park. You have to remove your shoes to enter the spotless air-con room. Rates are reasonable at Rs 20 per 15 minutes but the connections are slow. It's open daily except Sunday 10 am to 6 pm.

There's a good selection of reading material at Badshah Book Shop, in the City Centre shopping complex on MG Rd.

Rajwada

In the old part of town, the multistorey gateway of the Rajwada or Old Palace looks out

MADHYA PRADESH

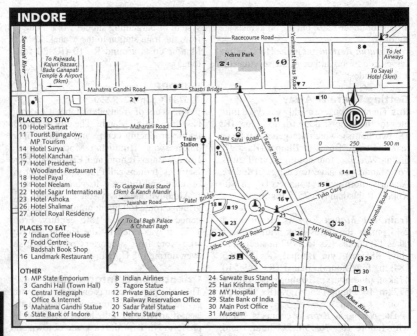

INDORE

PLACES TO STAY
10 Hotel Samrat
11 Tourist Bungalow;
   MP Tourism
14 Hotel Surya
15 Hotel Kanchan
17 Hotel President;
   Woodlands Restaurant
18 Hotel Payal
19 Hotel Neelam
22 Hotel Sagar International
23 Hotel Ashoka
26 Hotel Shalimar
27 Hotel Royal Residency

PLACES TO EAT
2 Indian Coffee House
7 Food Centre;
   Badshah Book Shop
16 Landmark Restaurant

OTHER
1 MP State Emporium
3 Gandhi Hall (Town Hall)
4 Central Telegraph
   Office & Internet
5 Mahatma Gandhi Statue
6 State Bank of Indore
8 Indian Airlines
9 Tagore Statue
12 Private Bus Companies
13 Railway Reservation Office
20 Sadar Patel Statue
21 Nehru Statue
24 Sarwate Bus Stand
25 Hari Krishna Temple
28 MY Hospital
29 State Bank of India
30 Main Post Office
31 Museum

onto the palm-lined main square in the crowded streets of the Kajuri Bazaar. A mixture of French, Mughal and Maratha styles, the palace has been up in flames three times in its 200-year history. After a very serious conflagration in 1984, it's now not much more than a facade.

Kanch Mandir

On Jawahar Rd, not far from the Rajwada, is the Kanch Mandir or Seth Hukanchand Temple. This Jain temple is very plain externally, but inside is completely mirrored with pictures of sinners being tortured in the afterlife.

Museum

The museum, near the main post office, has one of the best collections of medieval and pre-medieval Hindu sculpture in Madhya Pradesh. Most are from Hinglajgarh in the Mandasaur district of western Madhya Pradesh and range from early Gupta to Paramana times.

The museum is open daily except Sunday 10 am to 5 pm (free).

Lal Bagh Palace

In the south-west of the city, surrounded by gardens, lies the grand Lal Bagh Palace, built 1886-1921. It has all the usual over-the-top touches like entrance gates that are replicas of those at Buckingham Palace, a wooden ballroom floor mounted on springs, marble columns, chandeliers, stained-glass windows and stuffed tigers. It's open daily except Monday 10 am to 5 pm (Rs 5).

Other Attractions

The magnificent **Gandhi Hall** (town hall) is open to visitors daily 10 am to 5 pm. Exhibitions are sometimes held here.

The chhatris, or memorial tombs, of the region's former rulers are now neglected and forgotten. They stand in the **Chhatri Bagh**. The cenotaph of Malhar Rao Holkar I, founder of the Holkar dynasty, is the most impressive.

At the western end of MG Rd, the **Bada Ganapati Temple** contains an 8m-high bright-orange statue of Ganesh – reputed to be the world's largest.

The busy streets of the **Kajuri Bazaar** are a good place to take a stroll.

Organised Tours

MP Tourism operates day tours to Mandu from July to September only (Rs 180), as the monsoon is the high season for local tourists. It's a similar story for tours to Maheshwar and Omkareshwar (Rs 180). These tours include lunch and afternoon tea and a minimum of 10 passengers is required.

Places to Stay – Budget

The train station and the Sarwate bus stand are about five minutes walk apart, and it's in this lively, polluted area that you'll find the budget hotels. The following places have rooms with bathrooms and 24 hour checkout.

Hotel Ashoka (☎ 65991, 14 Nasia Rd) is the closest to the bus stand (directly behind it). The cheapest rooms are way up on the 4th floor (no lift), but they're not bad at Rs 140/190 with running hot water. For a shorter walk you pay Rs 175/225, or Rs 300/350 with air-con. Checkout is 24 hours.

Hotel Payal (☎ 463202, Patel Bridge) is a small, friendly place with reasonably priced singles/doubles for Rs 110/150. Free bucket hot water is available.

Hotel Neelam (☎ 466001, 33/2 Patel Bridge Corner), just around the corner, is a much smarter hotel and good value with singles/doubles from Rs 140/185 to Rs 260/310 (with air-con), all with TV and hot water. The rooms are spotless but the white tile decor is like sleeping in someone's bathroom.

Hotel Sagar International (☎ 462630, 6 Kibe Compound) has large carpeted rooms with TV and hot-water bath for a reasonable Rs 125/175, up to Rs 300/400 with air-con.

Hotel Shalimar (☎ 462481, 224 RN Tagore Rd), hidden behind the flash new Hotel Royal Residency, couldn't be called clean but it's dirt cheap with tiny rooms at Rs 45/85.

Places to Stay – Mid-Range & Top End

Indore has a good selection of comfortable mid-price hotels, as befits a business city of this size.

The *Tourist Bungalow* (☎ 541818, RN Tagore Rd) is at the back of the Tagore Natya Griha Hall. Comfortable rooms are Rs 300/350, or Rs 390/490 with air-con.

Hotel Royal Residency (☎ 764633, fax 465377, 225 RN Tagore Rd) was only a few days old when we visited, so 'immaculate' is an understatement. Well-appointed standard rooms are great value at Rs 450/600. Air-con starts at Rs 650/800, up to suites from Rs 950/1100. Checkout is 9 am.

Hotel Kanchan (☎ 527932, fax 517054, Kanchan Bagh) is a small place with clean and comfortable rooms for Rs 350/450 and air-con for Rs 450/600. There's a bar and restaurant.

Hotel Samrat (☎ 433889, MG Rd), a large modern hotel, has comfortable rooms with TV for Rs 325/425, or Rs 425/525 with air-con. The restaurant here has a good reputation and there's a bar. Checkout is 24 hours.

Hotel Surya (☎ 517701, 5/5 Nath Mandir Rd) is another good choice. Standard rooms are Rs 550/750 and air-con rooms are Rs 670/870.

Hotel President (☎ 528866, fax 512230, RN Tagore Rd) has a health club and sauna for guests. Well-appointed rooms start at Rs 875/1075, all with air-con and including breakfast. Checkout is 9 am.

Sayaji Hotel (☎ 552121, fax 553131, Vijay Nagar), 4km east of the town centre, is a huge place and Indore's top hotel. It's got a swimming pool, bowling alley, tennis and squash courts, health club and luxurious rooms for Rs 1450/1800.

Places to Eat
Indore is famous for its variety of *namkin* – Prakash brand is the best. If you're here during one of the festivals watch out for the *bhang gota* – samosas with added spice!

The **Indian Coffee House** is always a good, cheap choice. There's a branch on MG Rd, near Gandhi Hall.

Food Centre is a busy cafeteria serving tasty south Indian food in the City Centre shopping complex on MG Rd.

Landmark Restaurant, next to the Hotel President on RN Tagore Rd is a very good continental-style place doing things rarely seen in India like Waldorf salad and roast lamb. The service is good and prices are reasonable.

Most of the top hotels have restaurants and bars. **Woodlands Restaurant** at the Hotel President is an excellent choice, and meals are very reasonably priced. *Hotel Surya's* restaurant is another great place for a splurge.

Shopping
The Kajuri Bazaar is only one of a number of colourful and lively bazaars in the vicinity of the Rajwada, specialising in gold and silverwork, cloth, leather work and traditional garments.

Getting There & Away
Air Indian Airlines (☎ 431595), on Racecourse Rd, has daily evening flights to Mumbai (US$80). There are also daily morning flights to Delhi (US$120), via Bhopal (US$50) and Gwalior (US$95).

Jet Airways (☎ 544590), Vidyapati Complex, 7 Racecourse Rd, has daily flights to Mumbai (US$85) at 8.40 am.

Bus There are departures from the Sarwate bus stand every half hour to Ujjain (Rs 18, 1½ hours) and Bhopal (Rs 58/73/87 ordinary/express/deluxe, five hours). For Mandu, take a bus to Dhar (Rs 20, two hours) and another to Mandu from there (Rs 12, 1½ hours). From Sarwate there are buses to Dhar at 5, 6, 7, 8 and 9 am. From Gangwal bus stand, about 3km west along Jawahar

Rd, there are departures to Dhar every 30 minutes. There are direct buses to Omkareshwar (Rs 25, three hours), most departing before 11 am.

There are two services to Aurangabad (for the Ajanta and Ellora caves) at 5 am and 9 pm (Rs 163, 13 hours); the morning service stops at Ajanta but the overnight bus is direct to Aurangabad. There's one daily bus for Mumbai (Rs 204, 16 hours) at 5 am or 5 pm (alternate days).

There are a number of private bus companies between the bus and train stations and RN Tagore Rd. Fares are higher than state buses but they're more comfortable for the long hauls. Destinations include Mumbai, Pune, Nagpur, Jaipur, Gwalior, Aurangabad and Ahmedabad.

MP Tourism has a luxury service to Bhopal. It departs from the tourist office at 8 am, takes four to five hours, and costs Rs 130, or Rs 180 for air-con.

Train Indore is connected to the main broad-gauge lines between Delhi and Mumbai by tracks from Nagda via Ujjain in the west and Bhopal in the east. The daily *Malwa Express* leaves Indore at 1 pm for New Delhi (Rs 240/836 in sleeper/1st, 969km, 19 hours), via Ujjain (Rs 29/150, 80km, 1½ hours), Bhopal (Rs 66/322, 264km, 5½ hours), Jhansi (Rs 169/584, 555km, 10½ hours), Gwalior (Rs 190/662, 652km, 12½ hours) and Agra (Rs 213/752, 770km, 14 hours).

For Mumbai, the *Awantika Express* leaves Indore at 3.45 pm and arrives in Bandra Terminus at 6.40 am (Rs 220/766 in sleeper/1st class).

The other broad-gauge line runs from Indore to Bilaspur via Ujjain, Bhopal and Jabalpur. The *Narmada Express* departs Indore at 3 pm, reaching Jabalpur (Rs 178/611, 600km, 15 hours) at dawn. There's also the Indore-Bhopal *Intercity Express* on this line departing at 6 am (4½ hours).

There is also a metre-gauge line through Indore. Services on this line run from Jaipur in Rajasthan to Indore (Rs 186/632, 610km, 16 hours), and on to Khandwa and Purna.

The reservation office is in an ugly pink and yellow building 30m along the small street directly opposite the train station, open 8 am to 8 pm (8 am to 2 pm on Sunday). There's 24 hour left luggage in the main station building.

Car An alternative to the slow public transport to Mandu, Omkareshwar and Maheshwar is a taxi or hired car and driver. MP Tourism (☎ 528653) can organise a car for Rs 3.50/km (minimum 250km per day). An overnight stay – essential if you want to visit all three places – costs an extra day, which makes it a bit costly. It's better to scout around outside the train station or bus stand where you should find a reliable operator offering around Rs 3 per kilometre and no additional overnight charge.

Getting Around
To/From the Airport The airport is 9km from the city. Auto-rickshaws charge Rs 70 and taxis Rs 200.

Local Transport Indore's auto-rickshaws are cheap (most journeys are under Rs 10) and drivers will generally use their meters. Tempos operate along set routes and cost Rs 3 from point to point. The main stands are in front of the train station and at Gandhi Hall.

AROUND INDORE
Omkareshwar
This island at the confluence of the Narmada and Kaveri rivers has drawn Hindu pilgrims for centuries on account of its jyothirlingam, one of the 12 throughout India, at the Shiva **temple of Shri Omkar Mandhata**. (For an explanation of the myth of the jyothirlingam see the Mahakaleshwar Mandir section under Ujjain earlier in this chapter.)

The temple is constructed from local soft stone that has enabled its artisans to achieve a rare degree of detailed work, particularly in the friezes on the upper parts of the structure.

The setting here is stunning. From the village on the banks of the Narmada, the island seems to loom out of the river, crowned by a former palace. A high footbridge connects the village with the island, or you can descend to the ghats and take a motorboat across the Narmada (Rs 5). The path up to the temple is lined with the usual colourful pilgrim paraphernalia – garlands of marigolds, coconuts, strings of beads and tacky souvenirs. Crowds gather for the puja that is performed in the temple three times a day.

There are other temples on this island including the **Siddhnath**, a good example of early medieval Brahminic architecture, and a cluster of other Hindu and Jain temples. Though damaged by Muslim invaders in the time of Mohammed of Ghazni (11th century), these temples and those on the nearby riverbanks remain essentially intact. The island temples present a very picturesque sight and are well worth visiting.

Places to Stay Many *dharamsalas* offer basic accommodation in the village, but they're mainly for Hindu pilgrims.

Hotel Aishwarya (☎ 07280-71325) is a new concrete block place and easily the most comfortable hotel in the village. Clean rooms with bath and running hot water are Rs 200/250, or Rs 250/300 with air-cooler and bathtub. The hotel is on the other side of the village from the bus stand and is well-signposted from the main road.

Holkar Guesthouse is a bit difficult to find – it's the faded yellow building perched on a rocky outcrop with good views across to Omkareshwar Island. Ask for directions in the marketplace. Basic doubles with shared bath are Rs 100.

Yatrika Guest House, right near the bus stand, has simple but clean rooms with bath for Rs 150.

Getting There & Away There are seven direct buses daily to Indore (Rs 25, three hours). Coming from Indore, buses depart from Sarwate bus stand at regular intervals until about 11 am. There are a few direct buses – on atrocious roads – to Maheshwar (Rs 20, 2½ hours), or you can take one of the regular buses to Barwaha and change there.

Local trains run from Indore to Omkareshwar Road station but it's inconvenient as Omkareshwar itself is 12km from here by road.

Maheshwar

Maheshwar was an important cultural and political centre at the dawn of Hindu civilisation and was mentioned in the *Ramayana* and *Mahabharata* under its former name of Mahishmati. It languished in obscurity for many centuries after that until revived by the Holkar queen, Rani Ahilyabai of Indore, in the late 18th century. It's from these times that most of the temples and the fort complex date.

The principal sights are the **fort**, which is now a museum displaying heirlooms and relics of the Holkar dynasty, the three **ghats** lining the banks of the Narmada River, and the many-tiered **temples**, distinguished by their overhanging balconies and intricately worked doorways.

Maheshwar saris are famous throughout the country for their unique weave and beautifully complex patterns. The Rewa Society, inside the fort, runs a **sari weaving factory** where you can see the weavers at work on handlooms. Saris are on sale here (around Rs 1000 for silk, Rs 500 for cotton), or you can shop around for them in the market.

Places to Stay Maheshwar is easily fitted in between Omkareshwar and Mandu, and the choice of accommodation is slim. *Akashdeep Rest House*, on the road up to the fort, has very simple double rooms with common bath for Rs 50, or try the *Ahilya Trust Guesthouse*, also near the fort.

Getting There & Away There is an afternoon bus from Indore (four hours). Otherwise, regular local buses run to Maheshwar from Barwaha and Dhar, both of which are easily reached by local bus from Indore.

Dhar

Founded by Raja Bhoj, the legendary founder of Bhopal and Mandu, this was the capital of Malwa until Mandu rose to power.

There are good views from the ramparts of Dhar's well-preserved **fort**. Dhar also has the large stone **Bhojashala Mosque** with ancient Sanskrit inscriptions, and the adjoining **tomb** of the Muslim saint Kamal Maula.

Dhar is best visited en route to or from Mandu, 33km away.

MANDU
☎ 07292

The extensive and now mainly deserted hilltop fort of Mandu is one of the most evocative sights in central India. It's on an isolated outcrop separated from the tableland to the north by a deep and wide valley, over which a natural causeway runs to the main city gate. To the south of Mandu the land drops steeply away to the plains far below and the view is superb. Deep ravines cut into the sides of the 20 sq km plateau occupied by the fort.

Although it's possible to make a long day trip from Indore, Mandu is worth at least a night. In winter, Mandu is quite popular with foreign visitors but the local tourist season is during the monsoon, when the place turns verdant green and the buildings are mirrored in the lakes.

History

Mandu, known as the city of joy, has had a chequered history. Founded as a fortress and retreat in the 10th century by Raja Bhoj, it was conquered by the Muslim rulers of Delhi in 1304. When the Mughals invaded and took Delhi in 1401, the Afghan Dilawar Khan, Governor of Malwa, set up his own little kingdom and Mandu embarked on its golden age.

Although Dilawar Khan first established Mandu as an independent kingdom, it was his son, Hoshang Shah, who shifted the capital from Dhar to Mandu and raised it to its greatest splendour.

Hoshang's son ruled for only a year before being poisoned by Mohammed Shah, who became king himself and ruled for 33 years. During his reign Mandu was in frequent and often bitter dispute with neighbouring powers.

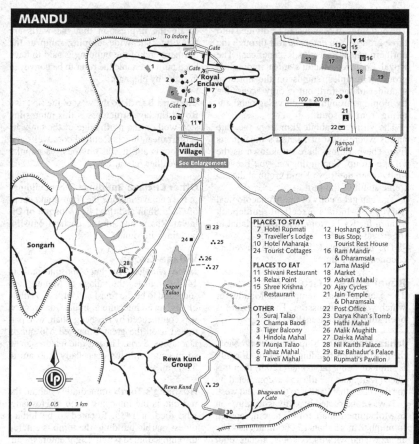

MANDU

To Indore

Gate
Gate
Royal
Enclave

Mandu
Village
See Enlargement

0   100   200 m

Rampol
(Gate)

Songarh

Sagar
Talao

Rewa Kund
Group

Rewa Kund

Bhagwanla
Gate

0   0.5   1 km

PLACES TO STAY
7 Hotel Rupmati
9 Traveller's Lodge
10 Hotel Maharaja
24 Tourist Cottages

PLACES TO EAT
11 Shivani Restaurant
14 Relax Point
15 Shree Krishna
   Restaurant

OTHER
1 Suraj Talao
2 Champa Baodi
3 Tiger Balcony
4 Hindola Mahal
5 Munja Talao
6 Jahaz Mahal
8 Taveli Mahal

12 Hoshang's Tomb
13 Bus Stop;
   Tourist Rest House
16 Ram Mandir
   & Dharamsala
17 Jama Masjid
18 Market
19 Ashrafi Mahal
20 Ajay Cycles
21 Jain Temple
   & Dharamsala
22 Post Office
23 Darya Khan's Tomb
25 Hathi Mahal
26 Malik Mughith
27 Dai-ka Mahal
28 Nil Kanth Palace
29 Baz Bahadur's Palace
30 Rupmati's Pavilion

MADHYA PRADESH

In 1469, Ghiyas-ud-din, Mohammed Shah's son, ascended the throne and spent the next 31 years devoting himself to women and song, before being poisoned at the age of 80 by his son, Nasir-ud-din. The son lived only another 10 years before dying, some say of guilt. In turn his son, Mohammed, had an unhappy reign. Finally, in 1526, Bahadur Shah of Gujarat conquered Mandu.

In 1534 the Mughal Humayun defeated Bahadur Shah, but as soon as Humayun turned his back an officer of the former dynasty took over. Several more changes of fortune eventually led to Baz Bahadur taking power in 1554. In 1561 he fled Mandu rather than face Akbar's advancing troops.

Even after it was added to the Mughal empire by Akbar, it kept a considerable degree of independence, until taken by the Marathas. The capital of Malwa was shifted back to Dhar, and Mandu became a ghost town. For a ghost town, however, it's very grandiose and impressive, and has one of the best collections of Afghan architecture in India.

Orientation & Information

The buildings of Mandu can be divided into three groups. You enter the fort through the northern gates (Rs 1 plus Rs 5 per car). The Royal Enclave, Mandu's most impressive group of temples, stands on the northern shoulder of the fort, but is only accessible by looping through Mandu village and entering from the south.

The village is about 2km from the gate and is where most of Mandu's inhabitants live. The buildings here are known as the village group. Continuing on, you'll eventually reach the Rewa Kund group at the extreme south of the fort.

You can get a copy of the Archaeological Survey of India's excellent guidebook *Mandu* for Rs 11 from the Taveli Mahal in the Royal Enclave.

The nearest bank for cashing travellers cheques is in Indore.

Royal Enclave Group

These are the only temples at Mandu for which you pay admission. The enclosure is open sunrise to sunset (Rs 2).

Jahaz Mahal The Ship Palace is probably the most famous building in Mandu. It really is shiplike, being far longer (120m) than it is wide (15m), and the illusion is completed by the two lakes that flank it to the east and west.

It was constructed by Ghiyas-ud-din, son of Mohammed Shah, for his harem, reputed to number more than 15,000 maidens. The Jahaz Mahal with its lookouts, arches, cool rooms and beautiful pool was their playground.

Taveli Mahal Just south of the Jahaz Mahal this palace is now the Archaeological Survey of India's Antiquity Gallery. This small museum is open daily 9.30 am to 5.30 pm except Friday (free). Exhibits include fragments of utensils and vessels found at the site, and some stone images.

Hindola Mahal Just north of Ghiyas' stately pleasure dome, this churchlike hall is known as the Swing Palace because the inward slope of the walls is supposed to create the impression that the walls are swaying. The wide, sloping ramp at the northern end of the building is said to have been built to enable the ruler to be conveyed upstairs by elephant.

Champa Baodi To the west of the first two Royal Enclave structures is this interesting step-well on the north edge of the tank. Its subterranean levels featured cool wells and bathrooms and it was obviously a popular hot-weather retreat.

Other Enclave Buildings Other buildings in the enclave include the 'house and shop' of Gada Shah and the 1405 **Mosque of Dilawar Khan**, one of the earliest Muslim buildings in Mandu.

Village Group

Jama Masjid This huge mosque built in 1454 dominates the village of Mandu. It is supposed to be the finest and largest example of Afghan architecture in India. Construction was commenced by Hoshang Shah, who patterned it on the great Omayyed Mosque in Damascus, Syria. The mosque features an 80 sq m courtyard. It's open daily 8.30 am to 5.30 pm.

Hoshang's Tomb Immediately behind the mosque is the imposing tomb of Hoshang, who died in 1435. Reputed to be India's oldest marble building, the tomb is entered through a domed porch. Light enters the interior through stone *jali* (carved marble lattice screens), typical of the Hindu influence on the tomb's fine design. It has a double arch and a squat, central dome surrounded by four smaller domes. It is said that Shah Jahan sent his architects to Mandu to study this tomb before they embarked upon the design of the Taj Mahal.

To one side of the tomb enclosure is a long, low colonnade with its width divided into three by rows of pillars. Behind is a long, narrow hall with a typically Muslim barrel-vaulted ceiling, intended as a shelter for visiting pilgrims.

Ashrafi Mahal The ruin of this building stands directly across the road from the Jama Masjid. Originally built as a *madrasah* (religious college), it was later extended by its builder, Mohammed Shah, to become his tomb. The design was simply too ambitious for its builders' abilities and it later collapsed. The seven storey circular tower of victory, which Mohammed Shah erected, has also fallen. A great stairway still leads up to the entrance to the empty shell of the building.

Jain Temple There are numerous buildings in this modern and ever-developing temple complex. The temples are richly decorated and feature tirthankars in marble, silver and gold, some with glinting jade eyes. Towards the back of the compound is a theme-park style Jain **museum**, which includes a walk-on replica of Shatrunjaya, the hilltop temple complex at Palitana, Gujarat, and a mural of colourful kitschy Jain homilies. One particularly explicit panel shows the terrible consequences of drinking and meat-eating: a drunk carnivore lies on the street with dogs pissing on him.

Rewa Kund Group
About 3km south of the village group, past the large Sagar Talao, is the Rewa Kund group.

Baz Bahadur's Palace Baz Bahadur was the last independent ruler of Mandu. His palace, constructed around 1509, is beside the Rewa Kund and there was a water lift at the northern end of the tank to supply water to the palace. A curious mix of Rajasthani and Mughal styles, it was actually built well before Baz Bahadur came to power.

Rupmati's Pavilion At the very edge of the fort, perched on the hillside overlooking the plains below, is the pavilion of Rupmati. The Malwa legends relate that she was a beautiful Hindu singer, and that Baz Bahadur persuaded her to leave her home on the plains by building her this pavilion. From its terrace and domed pavilions Rup-

mati could gaze down on the Narmada River, which is now dammed but which once wound across the plains far below.

It's a romantic building, the perfect setting for a fairytale romance – but one with an unhappy ending. Akbar, it is said, was prompted to conquer Mandu partly due to Rupmati's beauty. And when Akbar marched on the fort Baz Bahadur fled, leaving Rupmati to poison herself.

For maximum romantic effect come here in the late afternoon to watch the sunset, or at night when the moon is full. Bring a torch (flashlight) as there's no lighting on the road back.

Darya Khan's Tomb & Hathi Mahal
To the east of the road, between the Rewa Kund and the village, are these two buildings. The Hathi Mahal, or Elephant Palace, is so named because the pillars supporting the dome are of massive proportions – like elephant legs. Nearby is the tomb of Darya Khan, which was once decorated with intricate patterns of mosaic tiles.

Nil Kanth Palace
This palace, at the end of one of the ravines that cuts into the fort, is actually below the level of the hilltop and is reached by a flight of steps going down the hillside. At one time it was a Shiva shrine, as the name – God with the Blue Throat – suggests. Under the Mughals it became a pleasant water palace with a cascade running down the middle.

At the top of the steps, villagers sell the seeds of the baobab tree; Mandu is one of the few places in India where the baobab is found. It's difficult to miss – it's the tubby grey tree that looks as if it has been planted upside down with its roots in the air.

Organised Tours
Tours to Mandu are run from Indore, July to September only. See Organised Tours under Indore earlier in this chapter. Local guides loiter around the bus stand offering their services.

Places to Stay

Hotel Maharaja (☎ 63280, Jahaz Mahal Rd), in a quiet location between the village and the Royal Enclave, is the best budget option. Basic doubles with bath are Rs 100/150 (Rs 150/200 in the monsoon season). There's a simple restaurant and friendly staff.

Tourist Rest House is a dull SADA place right opposite the Jama Masjid. Rooms with bath are dingy at Rs 125, plus they ask for a Rs 200 deposit.

The following MP Tourism places should be booked at the tourist office in Indore (☎ 0731-528653) if you want to ensure a bed. *Traveller's Lodge (☎ 63221)* looks a little shabby compared to the Rupmati next door, but it's comfortable enough with rooms at Rs 290/390 with bath and hot water. *Tourist Cottages (☎ 63235)* are in a very pleasant location overlooking the Sagar Talao. Rooms cost Rs 350/450, or Rs 750/850 with air-con. Breakfast and dinner are served in the outdoor restaurant and nonguests are welcome.

Hotel Rupmati (☎ 63270) is the top hotel in Mandu. Its 10 spacious rooms have fine views over the gorge from back patios. The modern, comfortable rooms cost Rs 300/375. Air-con doubles are Rs 750. There's a pleasant terrace restaurant.

If you're stuck for a place to stay, there are two *dharamsalas* at the Jain temple and Shree Ram Mandir, but neither was accepting foreign tourists at the time of writing.

Places to Eat

The restaurants at Hotel Rupmati and the MP Tourism hotels are the best places to eat, but there are a few cheap independent places in the village. Look out for the green, hard-shelled seed of the baobab tree in the market. The locals love it, but it's a bit like eating sweet and sour chalk dust.

Relax Point has drinks and a shop but doesn't seem to cook food. You may be able to coax a menu out of *Shree Krishna Restaurant* next door. Regular thalis are Rs 22, or the intriguing 'Special Buffalo Thali', Rs 35.

Shivani Restaurant, farther north, serves up good, reasonably priced veg food and breakfasts.

Getting There & Away

There are six daily buses direct from Mandu to Indore (via Dhar, Rs 32, 3½ hours), but coming the other way you must change at Dhar. There's one bus to Maheshwar at 7.30 am (Rs 20, 2½ hours).

For Bhopal, take the 5.30 am bus to Indore where you can connect with a bus or train to Bhopal. The buses stop near the Jama Masjid in the village.

The alternative is hiring a car; see Getting There & Away in the previous Indore section.

Getting Around

You can hire bikes from Ajay Cycles, south of the Jama Masjid, or from the market for Rs 3 an hour or Rs 25 a day (24 hours). This is the best way to get around as the sights are quite far apart, and the terrain is relatively flat. This is also a fine area for walking.

There's just one auto-rickshaw in Mandu, which is available (of course) for a three to four hour tour of Mandu's sights (Rs 150). It costs Rs 20 return from the village to Rupmati's Pavilion.

BAGH CAVES

The Bagh Caves are 7km from the village of Bagh and 3km off the main road. Bagh is about 50km west of Mandu, on the road between Indore and Vadodara in Gujarat. The Buddhist caves date from 400 to 700 AD and all were in extremely bad shape before restoration work began some years ago. There's a *PWD Dak Bungalow* in Bagh village and an *Archaeological Survey Rest House* closer to the caves.

Eastern Madhya Pradesh

JABALPUR

☎ 0761 • pop 1,065,025

Almost due south of Khajuraho and east of Bhopal, the large city of Jabalpur is principally famous today for the gorge on the Narmada River known as the Marble Rocks. It's also the departure point for a visit to the national parks of Kanha (160km) and Bandhavgarh (197km).

Jabalpur is a major administrative and educational centre and the army headquarters for the states of Orissa and Madhya Pradesh. It was close to the epicentre of a destructive earthquake in May 1997 that shook the foundations of many villages in the district, killing dozens of people.

History

The original settlement in this area was ancient Tripuri and the rulers of this city, the Hayahaya, are mentioned in the *Mahabharata*. It passed successively into Mauryan and then Gupta control until, in 875 AD, it was taken by the Kalchuri rulers. In the 13th century it was overrun by the Gonds and by the early 16th century it had become the powerful state of Gondwana.

Though besieged by Mughal armies from time to time, Gondwana survived until 1789 when it was conquered by the Marathas. Their rule was unpopular, due largely to the increased activities of the *thuggees*, ritual murderers and bandits from whom the word thug is derived. The Marathas were defeated in 1817 and the thuggees subdued by the British who developed the town in the mid-19th century.

Information

The tourist office (☎ 322111) is at the train station, and is open daily 6 am to 10 pm. They can book MP Tourism accommodation for you at Kanha National Park (payment in full required) and Marble Rocks, and this is the place to book the minibus to Kanha.

Money can be changed at the main branch of the State Bank of India (opposite Hotel Rishi Regency) and at Jackson's Hotel.

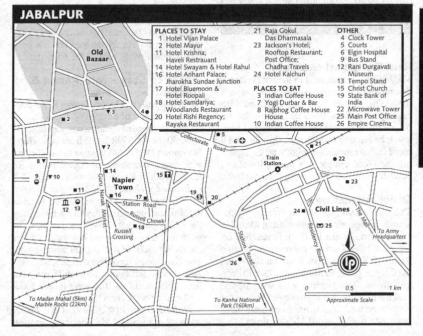

JABALPUR

PLACES TO STAY
1 Hotel Vijan Palace
2 Hotel Mayur
11 Hotel Krishna;
   Haveli Restrauant
14 Hotel Swayam & Hotel Rahul
16 Hotel Arihant Palace;
   Jharokha Sundae Junction
17 Hotel Bluemoon &
   Hotel Roopali
18 Hotel Samdariya;
   Woodlands Restaurant
20 Hotel Rishi Regency;
   Rayaka Restaurant

21 Raja Gokul
   Das Dharmasala
23 Jackson's Hotel;
   Rooftop Restaurant;
   Post Office;
   Chadha Travels
24 Hotel Kalchuri

PLACES TO EAT
3 Indian Coffee House
7 Yogi Durbar & Bar
8 Rajbhog Coffee House
   House
10 Indian Coffee House

OTHER
4 Clock Tower
5 Courts
6 Elgin Hospital
9 Bus Stand
12 Rani Durgavati
   Museum
13 Tempo Stand
15 Christ Church
19 State Bank of
   India
22 Microwave Tower
25 Main Post Office
26 Empire Cinema

Old Bazaar

Collectorate Road

Train Station

Napier Town

Station Road

Russell Chowk

Guru Nanak Market

Russell Crossing

Civil Lines

The Mall

Residency Road

Station Road

To Army Headquarters

To Madan Mahal (5km) & Marble Rocks (22km)

To Kanha National Park (160km)

0   0.5   1 km

Approximate Scale

MADHYA PRADESH

Thugs

It was from Narsinghpur in the early 19th century that Colonel Sleeman waged his war against the bizarre Hindu *thuggee* cult that claimed as many as a million lives over about 500 years. From as early as the 14th century, followers had roamed the main highways of India engaging in the ritual murder of travellers, strangling their victims with a yellow silk scarf in order to please the bloodthirsty goddess Kali.

Bizarre thuggee rites included sugar sacrifices and axe-worshipping ceremonies and they resisted infiltration by using secret signs and developing their own jargon.

It was largely due to Sleeman's efforts that the thuggee (from which the word 'thug' is derived) were wiped out. His campaign during the 1830s was sanctioned by the British governor-general Lord Bentinck and saw more than 400 thugs hanged and about 3000 imprisoned or banished, ensuring the virtual eradication of these scarf-wielding nasties.

Rani Durgavati Museum

South of the bazaar, next to the tempo stand, this museum's diverse collection is worth a look. The ground floor has 10th and 11th century sculptures from temples in the Jabalpur district. Upstairs are letters and photographs relating to Mahatma Gandhi, and a room full of models and photographs depicting the Gond people. It's open Monday to Saturday from 10 am to 5 pm (entry is free).

Other Attractions

The old **bazaar** has Indian smells, sights, sounds and goods for sale. **Madan Mahal**, a Gond fortress built in 1116, is perched on top of a huge boulder en route to Marble Rocks. It's about 5km from Jabalpur and the tempos going to Marble Rocks will drop you there. The Gonds, who worshipped snakes, lived in this region even before the Aryans arrived, and maintained their independence right up until Mughal times.

Places to Stay – Budget

The cheapest places to stay are almost all down near the bus stand, about 3km from the train station. The commission racket for rickshaw-wallahs is alive and well in Jabalpur – if you're taken to a hotel (even one of your choice) you'll almost certainly pay for it at check-in with 'applicable taxes'.

Hotel Mayur (☎ 310035, Malviya Chowk) is cheap, clean and only a few minutes' walk from the bus stand. Economy singles/doubles are Rs 100/200 and the better 'deluxe' rooms are Rs 150/250, all with bath.

Hotel Vijan Palace (☎ 310972, 313 Vijan Market) is a reasonable choice in the heart of the bazaar. Basic rooms with bath are Rs 150/170 and air-con rooms are Rs 300/400.

Swayam Hotel (☎ 325377, Guru Nanak Market) is grubby but cheap at Rs 50/90.

Hotel Rahul (☎ 325525), next door, is only slightly better with rooms at Rs 90/120, or Rs 140/165 with TV and hot water.

Raja Gokul Das Dharmasala is a traditional pilgrim's lodge and the cheapest place in town. An impressive building from the outside, it has the most basic of rooms (common bath) for Rs 24 per person. It's only five minutes' walk east of the train station.

Places to Stay – Mid-Range & Top End

Hotel Roopali (☎ 325566, Station Rd) is popular and the best of a bunch of places on Station Rd. A range of clean rooms start from Rs 300/350, or Rs 550/650 with air-con. *Hotel Bluemoon* (☎ 325146, Station Rd) is cheaper with small, charmless air-cooled rooms for Rs 170/200, or Rs 350/460 with air-con.

Jackson's Hotel (☎ 322320, fax 322066, Civil Lines) must have been the best hotel in town at one time; these days it's a bit shabby but still popular with travellers. Large, well-worn rooms with bath and hot-water shower are Rs 350/400, or Rs 500/600 with air-con. You can change travellers cheques, and baggage can be left here safely while you visit Kanha National Park. Jackson's is only about a 10 minute walk from the train station.

Hotel Kalchuri (☎ 321491, Civil Lines) is a well-maintained MP Tourism operation close to the train station. Hot water rooms are Rs 390/490, Rs 690/790 with air-con.

Hotel Arihant Palace (☎ 372311, fax 392114, Russell Crossing) is new, central and reasonable; rooms cost Rs 300/375.

The Hotel Samdariya (☎ 316800, fax 316354, Russell Chowk), a very modern place in a quiet location, has a swimming pool and a health club. The cheapest rooms are great value at Rs 450/650, including a buffet breakfast, and air-con rooms start from Rs 1000/1300.

Hotel Rishi Regency (☎/fax 321804, Civil Lines) is a three star place near the State Bank of India. It's Rs 495/695, or Rs 895/1095 with air-con.

Places to Eat
Most of the hotels have restaurants.

Rooftop Restaurant at Jackson's Hotel has a wide range of decent food, comfy seating and cold beer. *Haveli Restaurant* in the Hotel Krishna is another good place, though a little more expensive. *Woodlands Restaurant* at the Samdariya is recommended.

Zayaka Restaurant at the Rishi Regency serves good Indian food, and there's a barbecue restaurant next door.

Rajbhog Coffee House, near the bus stand, is good for a snack. The waiters have fan-shaped headgear and cummerbunds. The *Indian Coffee House* is similar.

Yogi Durbar & Bar is a popular place though it's a dimly lit cave inside. Good food is reasonably priced – where else can you get a full tandoori chicken for Rs 70? Most mains are Rs 20 to Rs 30.

Jharokha Sundae Junction, next to the Hotel Arihant Palace, is good for ice cream.

Getting There & Away
Bus There are buses to Jabalpur from Allahabad, Khajuraho, Varanasi, Bhopal, Nagpur and other main centres. For overnight journeys the private buses are better – MP state transport buses are mostly in an advanced state of decay. The bus agents are situated near the bus stand (across the road or nearby) and the private buses leave from outside the agent. There's one bus a day to Khajuraho

(Rs 95, 11 hours) leaving at 9 am but it's more comfortable to take the train to Satna from where there are regular bone-shattering buses to Khajuraho (Rs 40, four hours).

See Kanha National Park, later, for details on getting there from Jabalpur.

Train There are direct connections between Jabalpur and Satna (Rs 76/258 in sleeper/1st class, 189km, three hours), Varanasi (Rs 152/531, 505km, 13 hours) and Bhopal (Rs 115/398, 336km, 7½ hours).

For the Ajanta and Ellora caves, catch a train on the Mumbai line to Bhusaval (all the trains stop here) and another to Jalgaon. There are buses to the caves from there.

Getting Around
You'll be besieged by rickshaw-wallahs at the train station and bus stand offering cheap rides (to a hotel) – agree on a fare and a destination before getting in. If arriving by bus, most of the budget and mid-range hotels are within 10 minutes' walk of the city bus stand.

Tempos trundle around town but the only time you're likely to use one is to get to Marble Rocks (Rs 7). The tempo stand is near the bus stand (opposite Hotel Krishna).

AROUND JABALPUR
Marble Rocks
Known locally as Bhedaghat (after the nearby village), this gorge on the Narmada River is 22km from Jabalpur. The gleaming white (and sometimes pink, brown and black) cliffs rise sheer from the clear water and are a very impressive sight, especially by moonlight. On weekends and full moon nights the place is invariably packed with local tourists.

The trip up the 2km-long gorge is made in a shared rowboat – Rs 10 per person on a 20 seat boat. These go all day every day October to June from the jetty at the bottom of the gorge and leave when full. The first 500m is pretty dull, but as you glide upstream with the massive, naturally sculpted marble crags crowding in around you, it's difficult not to be impressed. The guides on the boat point out various formations (in

Hindi). When the river level is high, the boats may not go all the way to the head of the gorge. The cliffs are floodlit at night.

A worthwhile 1km walk from the jetty is the **Dhuandhar** or Smoke Cascade waterfall. Around the falls are hundreds of stalls selling marble carvings, mostly fairly clichéd, but you can find some nice pieces if you shop around. Along the way is the **Chausath Yogini** or Madanpur Temple. The circular temple has damaged ancient images of the 64 yoginis, or attendants of the goddess Kali.

Places to Stay & Eat The *Motel Marble Rocks* (☎ *0761-83424*) is a very pleasant MP Tourism place overlooking the foot of the gorge. It has a well-kept garden and an excellent restaurant. The motel is a comfortable ex-colonial bungalow with only four double rooms for Rs 450. Bookings can be made at the Jabalpur tourist office. There are plenty of cheap cafes in the village.

Getting There & Away Tempos run to the Marble Rocks from the city tempo stand near the museum in Jabalpur for Rs 7.

Narsinghpur

Narsinghpur, 84km west of Jabalpur, is just a sleepy town but worth a stop if you're interested in the Sleeman trail (see the Thugs boxed text earlier). There's a fascinating account of Sleeman's anti-thug detective work in Sir Francis Tuker's *The Yellow Scarf.*

Narsingh Mandir is an old temple with a honeycomb of tunnels beneath it. The caretaker may show you the room where Sleeman trapped some of the thuggee leaders.

Lunawat Inn (☎ *0792-30034*) has singles/doubles with bath for Rs 60/100 or doubles with TV for Rs 150. It's about 100m from the train station (turn right at the exit).

Narsinghpur is on the main Jabalpur-Mumbai/Bhopal rail line and a handful of expresses stop here.

KANHA NATIONAL PARK
☎ 07649

Kanha, 160km south-east of Jabalpur, is one of India's largest national parks, covering 1945 sq km including a 'core zone' of 940 sq km. The setting for Kipling's *Jungle Book*, it's a beautiful area of sal forest and lightly wooded grassland with many rivers and streams, that supports excellent wildlife. It is also part of Project Tiger.

Wildlife was first given limited protection here as early as 1933 but it wasn't until 1955 that the area was declared a national park. A policy of wildlife management over the past 30 years has seen a steady increase in the numbers of tigers and leopards, as well as sambar, chital (spotted deer), barasingha (swamp deer) and gaur (Indian bison). At the last census (1997) the tiger population was 114 and leopards numbered 86.

There's a good chance of sighting tigers, gaur and herbivores, and this is one of the best places in the state for bird-watching.

Orientation & Information

Kanha is completely closed from 1 July to 31 October, owing to the monsoons. Although it's possible to see wildlife can be seen throughout the season, sightings increase as the weather gets hotter in March and April and the animals move out of the tree cover in search of water. The hottest months are May and June, when the temperature can reach 42°C in the afternoon. December and January are the coolest months and, although it's warm during the day, as soon as the sun sets the temperature quickly plunges to zero and below.

Khatia village, at the western entrance to Kanha, is the best place to base yourself for visits to the park. Kisli, 3km farther in, is the main gate where you pay the entry (Rs 100) and camera fees (Rs 10/100 for video/still camera).

There are no facilities for changing money here, but there's a telephone, small shop and petrol pump at Kisli. You'll need fast film (400 ASA or higher) because of the low light during the early-morning and evening excursions.

The local market at **Sarekha** on Friday draws the colourful Baiga adivasis and is worth going to. A closer market is at **Mocha**, 5km back from Khatia, held on Wednesday.

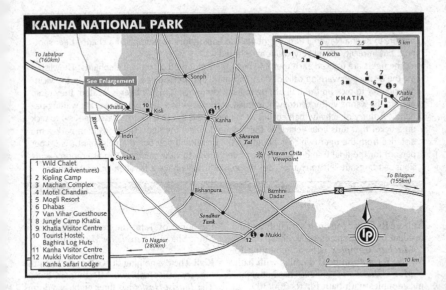

KANHA NATIONAL PARK

To Jabalpur (160km)

See Enlargement

Sonph

Khatia

Kisli

Kanha

Indri

Sarekha

River Banjar

Mocha

KHATIA

Khatia Gate

Shravan Tal

Shravan Chita Viewpoint

Bishanpura

Bamhni Dadar

Sondhar Tank

To Nagpur (280km)

Mukki

To Bilaspur (155km)

26

0   2.5   5 km

0   5   10 km

1 Wild Chalet (Indian Adventures)
2 Kipling Camp
3 Machan Complex
4 Motel Chandan
5 Mogli Resort
6 Dhabas
7 Van Vihar Guesthouse
8 Jungle Camp Khatia
9 Khatia Visitor Centre
10 Tourist Hostel; Baghira Log Huts
11 Kanha Visitor Centre
12 Mukki Visitor Centre; Kanha Safari Lodge

Visitor Centres There are three excellent visitor centres at Kanha (within the park), Khatia and Mukki with high-standard interpretive displays. The Kanha display is the most impressive, with five galleries and a research hall. There's a novel sound-and-light show 'Encounters in the Dark'.

A number of books and postcards are also sold. The centres are open 7 to 11 am and 3 to 6 pm daily, and a free outdoor film is shown each evening at the Khatia centre.

Wildlife Safaris

Excursions into the park are made in the early morning and evening; no night driving is allowed. Jeeps can be arranged by most of the accommodation places (which gives you a better chance of splitting the cost with others) and the cost is calculated on a per kilometre basis. Expect to pay around Rs 500 (which can be shared by up to six people), plus Rs 100 for a compulsory guide. Park entry fees are extra but only need to be paid once a day. At the height of the season there may not be enough jeeps to go around so book as soon as you arrive.

Park gates open sunrise to noon and 3 pm to sunset from 1 November to 15 February; sunrise to noon and 4 pm to sunset from 16 February to 30 April; and sunrise to 11 am and 5 pm to sunset from 1 May-30 June.

You may need warm clothes for early-morning outings; choose your safari outfit carefully – a sign in the Khatia visitor centre warns: 'Avoid wearing colours that jar. Violaters are liable to be prosecuted'!

Places to Stay & Eat

Accommodation is strung out over a distance of about 6.5km along the road from Jabalpur, so it's important that you get off the bus at the right place. Most accommodation is around Khatia, ranging from cheap guesthouses to the high-priced lodges operating on all-inclusive 'jungle plans'. Apart from the lodge restaurants, there are a couple of basic *dhabas* (snack and chai shacks) serving veg food just outside Khatia Gate.

Khatia *Van Vihar Guesthouse*, the pink building, 400m from the road at Khatia Gate, is the best budget place. Basic doubles with

MADHYA PRADESH

On the Tiger Trail

Visitors to Kanha National Park might well be hoping for the triumph of a chance tiger spotting, but in reality it's all very well orchestrated.

The tigers are tracked each morning by rangers mounted on trained elephants. They listen for the distinctive warning calls of deer and monkeys that indicate a predator is in the vicinity, then try to pick up the trail of pug marks (footprints). Once a tiger is located, they radio back to the Kanha visitor centre where most of the jeeps and their passengers are waiting patiently. A flurry of activity then ensues as the jeep drivers race back to a base (eg Kisli) to pick up a ticket that puts your vehicle in the 'queue' to view the tiger. The jeeps then park some distance from the tiger (which is hopefully still there) and you board an elephant (Rs 50 per person) for the final tramp through the undergrowth to view the tiger. On afternoon excursions sightings are left to chance, but the guides usually have a fair idea where to look.

bath are Rs 50 per person. It's friendly and the resident family prepares good, cheap food.

Machan Complex is basic, charging Rs 50/200 for a dorm beds/doubles with bath.

Motel Chandan (☎ 77220) has better singles/doubles with bath for Rs 200/300 and large deluxe rooms for Rs 400/500. There's a good restaurant here with Rs 25 thalis.

Mogli Resort (☎ 77228) is a newly built-modern place with little jungle character but clean and comfortable rooms. Singles/doubles with balcony and bath are Rs 300/500 and attractive cottages with air-con and bathtub are Rs 1100/1400. There's also a smaller cottage for Rs 500/750.

Wild Chalet (☎ 77203), about 5km from Khatia, is by the river and very peaceful with friendly and knowledgeable staff. Double chalets with bath are US$80 per person (single occupancy is 30% more) including meals and transport into the park (plus two game drives per day). Staff also organise nature trails and bird-watching trips. Book with Indian Adventures (☎ 022-642 8244), 257 SV Rd, Bandra, Mumbai 400050.

Kipling Camp (☎/fax 77219) is the best place. Staffed by enthusiastic Brits, it's run by Bob Wright, who can be contacted through the Tollygunge Club (☎ 033-473 4539, fax 473 1903), 120 DP Sasmal Rd, Calcutta 700033. Make advance bookings; it's not cheap at an all-inclusive Rs 3700 per day (less for three nights or more). It's also

the home of Tara, the central character in Mark Shand's *Travels on My Elephant*.

Kisli There's nothing at Kisli apart from the forestry office and two MP Tourism hotels. The *Tourist Hostel* has three eight-bed dorms at an overpriced Rs 267 a bed including all meals (vegetarian only) and hot showers.

Baghira Log Huts has reasonable air-cooled singles/doubles for Rs 590/640, and a restaurant and bar. Advance bookings can be made at the following MP Tourism offices, but full payment up front is required:

Bhopal
   (☎ 0755-778383) 4th floor, Gangotri, TT Nagar
Calcutta
   (☎ 033-247 8543) 6th floor, Chitrakoot Bldg, 230A, AJC Bose Rd,
Delhi
   (☎ 011-334 1187) 2nd floor, Kanishka Shopping Plaza, 19 Ashok Rd
Mumbai
   (☎ 022-218 7603) 74 World Trade Centre, Cuffe Parade, Colaba

Bookings less than five days in advance must be made through the tourist office (☎ 0761-322111) at the train station in Jabalpur.

Mukki The *Kanha Safari Lodge* is another MP Tourism place in a pleasant but isolated location 36km from Khatia. It's worth trying if you're coming from Bilaspur or Kawardha but otherwise you're better off in Khatia. Doubles cost Rs 490, or Rs 690 with air-con and there's a restaurant. See the earlier Kisli section for booking information.

Getting There & Away

The best way to reach Kanha from Jabalpur is on MP Tourism's minibus (Rs 100, 3½ hours). It leaves Jabalpur train station at 8 am daily, stopping at Khatia (and other lodges on request) and terminating at Kisli. It leaves Kanha for Jabalpur at 2.30 pm. Book through the tourist office in Jabalpur (☎ 0761-322111) at least a day in advance.

Otherwise, there are dilapidated state transport buses from the city bus stand in Jabalpur to Kisli Gate twice daily at 7 am (six hours) and 11 am (seven hours), which cost Rs 50. The same buses depart from Kisli at around 8 am and 12.30 pm. These buses are crowded and agonisingly slow.

There's one bus a day from Jabalpur to Malakhand, which passes through Mukki (Rs 65, six hours).

BANDHAVGARH NATIONAL PARK

This national park is 197km north-east of Jabalpur in the Vindhyan mountain range. It's much smaller than Kanha but claims to have the highest density tiger population in India with between 46 and 52 tigers. There are also 27 leopards.

The park area is 448 sq km, of which 105 sq km is the 'core area' – the remaining area can't be designated as national park until six small villages of some 2000 people are relocated.

Bandhavgarh's setting is impressive. It's named after the ancient fort built on 800m-high cliffs. There's a temple at the fort that can be visited by jeep and below it are numerous rock-cut cave shrines.

The core area of the park has a fragile ecology, but it supports a variety of wildlife such as nilgai, wild boar, jackals, gaur, sambar and porcupines as well as many species of birds. The ramparts of the fort provide a home for vultures, blue rock thrushes and crag martins. Bandhavgarh receives fewer visitors than Kanha and

there's a good chance of spotting a tiger here.

Orientation & Information

The village of Tala is the access point for the park and the best place to stay. MP Tourism has an office at the White Tiger Forest Lodge (see Places to Stay) and there's a small visitor centre at the park gate. There's nowhere to change money in Tala.

Like Kanha, entry to the park is restricted to morning and evening visits in hired jeeps. The park entry fee is Rs 100 (Rs 10 for Indians), Rs 10 for a camera or Rs 100 for a video camera. To hire a jeep (with up to six passengers) costs around Rs 550, including guide. Bandhavgarh is closed from 1 July to 31 October. The telephone area code for Tala is ☎ 07653.

Bhaghela Museum

Attached to the Bandhavgarh Safari Camp in Tala, this museum is part of the private collection of the maharaja of Rewa. As well as the stuffed white tiger, Mohan, exhibits include the usual military and hunting paraphernalia, a carved ivory and silver chess set, and an extravagant swing bench made of Belgian cut glass and silver. It's open 10 am to 3 pm and 5 to 8 pm daily (Rs 8).

Elephant Rides

Unlike at Kanha, elephants are still used for leisurely late afternoon rides through the park. The cost is Rs 200 per hour (maximum of four) and can be arranged at the forestry office near the gate on Umaria Rd.

Places to Stay & Eat

Most of the accommodation is along Umaria Rd through Tala.

Tiger Lodge, right where the bus stops, is the cheapest around. Simple double rooms with grotty shared bathroom are Rs 150. The *dhaba* downstairs does good thalis for Rs 20 and basic breakfasts.

Kum Kum Home (☎ 65324) is a good budget option. There are four clean doubles with large bathrooms (hot water geyser) for Rs 200.

V Patel (☎ *65323*) is a good choice if you want a bit more comfort at a reasonable price. Set well back from Umaria Rd, it offers pleasant singles/doubles (room only) for Rs 300/400, or US$65/120 including all meals, transport and park fees.

White Tiger Forest Lodge (☎ *65308*) is a good MP Tourism place, with pleasant cottages overlooking the river where the elephants bathe. Singles/doubles with bath cost Rs 590/690, or rooms set back from the river with air-con are Rs 790/890 (plus 10% tax). There's a good restaurant and a bar. Advance booking is advisable.

Bandhavgarh Safari Camp (☎ *65322*) is the former palace of the maharaja of Rewa. Spacious old-fashioned rooms with typically cavernous bathrooms are pricey at Rs 1000.

Bandhavgarh Jungle Lodge (☎ *65317*) steps right up the price scale, operating on 'jungle plan' where all meals, park fees and safaris are included. It's hidden away near the park entrance where rustic thatched cottages of mud, dung and straw cost US$125 per night. Bookings are through Tiger Resorts (☎ 033-6853760, fax 6865212, T-Resorts @indiantiger.com), suite 206, Rakeesh Deep, 11 Commercial Complex, Gulmohar Enclave, New Delhi.

Getting There & Away

Umaria, 32km away on the Katni to Bilaspur line, is the nearest railhead. Local buses run from there to Tala (Rs 12, one hour). Jeeps are also available from Tala to Umaria if demand is high enough. From Satna there is one direct bus to Tala at 8 am (Rs 60), or inconvenient services via Rewa.

Heading west, the only useful train service from Umaria is the 3.30 pm *Bilaspur-Indore Express* through Katni, Jabalpur and Bhopal.

BHORAMDEO & KAWARDHA

At Bhoramdeo, 125km east of Kisli (Kanha), is a small and interesting 11th century **Shiva temple** built in the style of the temples of Khajuraho. Carvings cover virtually every external surface, with deities indulging in the usual range of activities including the famil-

iar sexual acrobatics. The temple is still very much in use today – a cobra lives inside and is fed by the priests. A few kilometres away there are two other temples, the **Mandwa Mahal** and the **Madanmanjari Mahal**, which date from the same period.

Places to Stay & Eat

Well off the tourist trail, 20km south of Bhoramdeo, the maharaja of Kawardha has opened part of his palace to guests.

Palace Kawardha (☎ *07741-32085, fax 32088*) is a delightfully peaceful place and you're made to feel very welcome here. As far as palaces go it's neither enormous nor particularly old (it was built in 1939), but it does have the touches you'd expect in a maharaja's palace – Italian marble floors, stuffed tigers and ancient English bathroom fittings. It costs US$108 per person (with reductions for stays of more than one night), including all meals, taken with the charming ex-maharaja and his family, and outings in the jeep. Open 1 October to 30 April, reservations must be made in advance. Write to Margaret Watts-Carter, Palace Kawardha, Kawardha, District Rajnandgaon, Madhya Pradesh 491995.

BILASPUR

☎ 07752 • pop 282,230

Bilaspur is a bustling city in the far east of Madhya Pradesh. It has no 'attractions' to speak of, but you may find it convenient to stop here if heading from Kanha National Park to Puri in Orissa.

Natraj Hotel (☎ *45451, Link Rd*), near the bus stand is well located on the main street, and has rooms from Rs 200/250.

Hotel Centrepoint (☎ *24004, Anand Marg*) is a better quality choice with rooms from Rs 300/350.

The bus stand, in the centre of town, has regular departures for Kawardha, Nagpur, Raipur and Mukki (for Kanha National Park).

Bilaspur has rail connections with Jabalpur, Raipur, Bhopal, Sambalpur, Puri, Calcutta and Delhi. The train station is 3km from the town centre.

Mumbai (Bombay)

Mumbai is an exhilarating city fuelled by entrepreneurial energy, determination and dreams. It's the economic powerhouse of the nation and compared to the torpor of the rest of India, it can seem like a foreign country.

It's India's finance centre, the capital of the Hindi film industry, and the industrial hub of everything from textiles to petrochemicals. But while it has aspirations to become another Singapore, it's also a magnet to the rural poor. It's these new migrants who continually re-shape the city in their own image, making sure Mumbai keeps one foot in its hinterland and the other in the global marketplace.

To many visitors, Mumbai is the glamour of Bollywood cinema, cricket on the *maidans* on weekends, *bhelpuri* on the beach at Chowpatty and red double-decker buses. It is also the infamous red-light district of Kamathipura, Asia's largest slums, communalist politics and powerful underworld dons. This tug-of-war for the city's soul is played out against a stately Victorian townscape more reminiscent of a prosperous 19th century English industrial city than anything you'd expect to find on the edge of the Arabian Sea.

Most travellers miss out on Mumbai, tending to stick around long enough only to organise transport to Goa, but it's an exciting, charismatic city that fully rewards exploration. It has vital streetlife, great nightlife, more bazaars than you could ever explore, and personality by the bucketload.

History

The islands that now form Mumbai were first home to the Koli fisherfolk whose shanties occupy parts of the city shoreline today. The islands were ruled by a succession of Hindu dynasties, invaded by Muslims in the 14th century and then ceded to Portugal by the sultan of Gujarat in 1534. The Portuguese did little to develop them before the major island of the group was in-

cluded in Catherine of Braganza's dowry when she married England's Charles II in 1661. The British government took possession of the islands in 1665 but leased them three years later to the East India Company for a meagre annual rent of UK£10.

Festivals of Mumbai

festival	location	dates	features
Elephanta	Elephanta Island	18-19 Feb	classical dance and music
Banganga	Walkeshwar	8-9 Jan	music festival
Gudi Padava	statewide	Mar/Apr	Maharashtrian new year
Dr Ambedkar's Birthday	statewide	14 Apr	public holiday
Maharashtra day	statewide	1 May	public holiday
Nariyal Poornima	Colaba & Versova	Aug	start of fishing season
Parsi New Year	citywide	Aug/Sep	feasting
Ganesh Chaturthi	Chowpatty Beach	Aug/Sep (10 days)	Ganesh's birthday
Bandra Feast	Basilica of Mt Mary	8 Sep	feast day
Diwali	Banganga Tank	Oct/Nov	raucous festivities
Ramadan	Mohammed Ali & Merchant Rds	Dec/Jan	Muslim daylight fasting
Kala Ghoda Fair	K Dubash Marg	every Sunday Nov-Jan	performing arts

Then called Bombay, the area soon developed as a trading port, thanks to its fine harbour, and merchants were attracted from other parts of India by the British promise of religious freedom and land grants. Migrants included sizeable communities of Parsis, plus Gujarati Banias, and south Indian Hindus fleeing Portuguese persecution in Goa. Their arrival, and that of later immigrant groups, laid the basis for Bombay's celebrated multicultural society. Within 20 years the presidency of the East India Company was transferred to Bombay from Surat and, thanks to the vision of Governor Gerald Aungier, it became the trading headquarters for the whole west coast of India.

Bombay's fort was built in the 1720s, and land reclamation projects began the century-long process of joining the original seven islands into a single land mass. Although Bombay grew steadily during the 18th century, it remained isolated from its hinterland until the British defeated the Marathas and annexed substantial portions of western India in 1818. Growth was spurred by the arrival of steam ships and the construction of the first railway in Asia from Bombay to Thana in 1853. The first cotton mill was built in the city the following year, and the American Civil War – which temporarily dried up Britain's supply of cotton – sparked Bombay's cotton boom.

The fort walls were dismantled in 1864 and the city embarked on a major building spree as it sought to construct a townscape commensurate with its new-found wealth. The opening of the Suez Canal in 1869 and the massive expansion of Bombay's docks cemented the city's future as India's primary port.

Bombay played a formative role in the struggle for Independence, hosting the first Indian National Congress in 1885 and the launch of the 'Quit India' campaign in 1942. After Independence the city became capital of the Bombay Presidency, but this was divided on linguistic grounds into Maharashtra and Gujarat in 1960; Bombay then became the capital of Marathi-speaking Maharashtra.

Marathi-speakers accounted for around 40% of the city's population but they tended to be at the bottom of the economic hierarchy. This gave rise to a pro-Maratha regionalist movement, spearheaded by the Shiv Sena, which broke the city's multicultural mould by actively discriminating against non-Maharashtrians and Muslims.

The Shiv Sena won power in the city's municipal elections in 1985. Communalist tensions increased and the city's cosmopolitan self-image took a battering when nearly 800 people died in riots that followed the destruction of the Babri Masjid in Ayodhya in December 1992 and January 1993. They were followed by a dozen bombings on 12 March 1993 which killed more than 300 people and damaged landmarks like the Bombay Stock Exchange and the Air India Building.

The Shiv Sena was blamed for orchestrating the second phase of rioting, while the city's underworld picked up the tab for the bombings – though the dividing line between the political establishment and organised crime has become extremely hard to define of late.

In 1996 the Shiv Sena officially renamed the city Mumbai, the Marathi name for Bombay. While it skilfully addressed some symbolic issues, the Sena was much less effective in tackling social problems like the shortage of adequate housing, access to safe drinking water and the deteriorating urban environment.

In late 1998 a spate of murders and police shoot-outs dominated the news as underworld extortion began to take its toll on the city's growing middle class. Despite the economic downturn and the fact that many companies have begun to choose less problematic environments in which to conduct business, Mumbai remains buoyant and resilient, and is slated to soon become the second largest city in the world (after Tokyo).

Orientation

Mumbai is an island connected by bridges to the mainland. The principal part of the city is concentrated at the southern claw-shaped end of the island known as South Mumbai. The southernmost peninsula is known as Colaba and this is where most travellers gravitate since it has a decent range of hotels and restaurants and two of the city's best known landmarks: the Gateway of India and the Taj Mahal Hotel.

Directly north of Colaba is the congested commercial area known as the Fort, since this is where the old British fort once stood. On the northern and western fringes of this area are most of the city's impressive colonial buildings, including Victoria Terminus (VT) and the main post office. It's bordered on the west by a series of interconnected grass areas known as maidans. Beyond the maidans is Churchgate train station and the poorly planned modern high-rise business centre of Nariman Point. Marine Drive sweeps around Back Bay, connecting Nariman Point with Chowpatty Beach and the classy residential peninsula of Malabar Hill.

South Mumbai ends around Crawford Market. North of here, and in complete contrast, are the congested central bazaars of Kalbadevi. The island's eastern seaboard is dominated by the city's docks, which are off limits. Farther north, across Mahim Creek, on what was once the separate island of Salsette, are the suburbs of Greater Mumbai and the international and domestic airports. The satellite city of New Bombay is taking shape on the mainland east of Mumbai.

Street Names The city's name change from Bombay to Mumbai is hardly surprising, since street names in the city have been changing regularly since Independence.

Some of the 'new' official names have been popularly adopted while others are ignored by everyone except municipal cartographers. Since half the streets in the city seem to have two names, you can make your life a lot easier by picking up the free Maharashtra Tourism Development Corporation (MTDC) *Bombay Tourist Map* which lists all the important changes. You then just have to figure out which ones are in currency and which ones aren't. In this chapter, we've stuck to the names the locals use.

Information

Tourist Offices The efficient Government of India tourist office (☎ 203 3144, fax 201 4496) at 123 Maharshi Karve Rd, opposite Churchgate train station, is open weekdays 8.30 am to 6 pm, and Saturday 8.30 am to

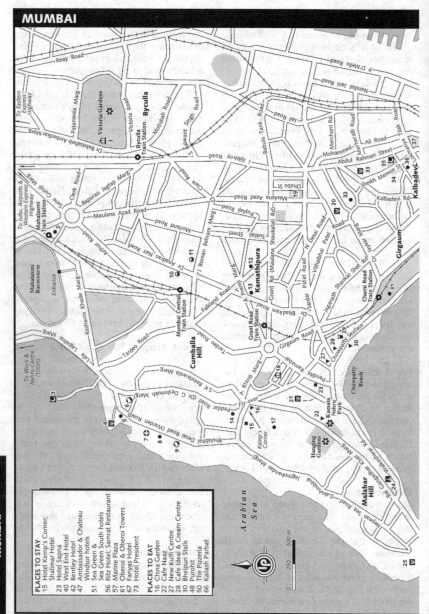

MUMBAI

PLACES TO STAY
15 Hotel Kemp's Corner;
    Shalimar Hotel
23 Hotel Sapna
40 West End Hotel
42 Bentley Hotel
47 Ambassador & Chateau
    Windsor hotels
51 Sea Green &
    Sea Green South hotels
56 Ritz Hotel; Samrat Restaurant
57 Marine Plaza
61 Oberoi & Oberoi Towers
67 Fariyas Hotel
73 Hotel President

PLACES TO EAT
16 China Garden
22 Cafe Naaz
27 New Kulfi Centre
28 Cafe Ideal & Cream Centre
30 Bhelpuri Stalls
48 Purohit
50 The Pizzeria
66 Kailash Parbat

MUMBAI

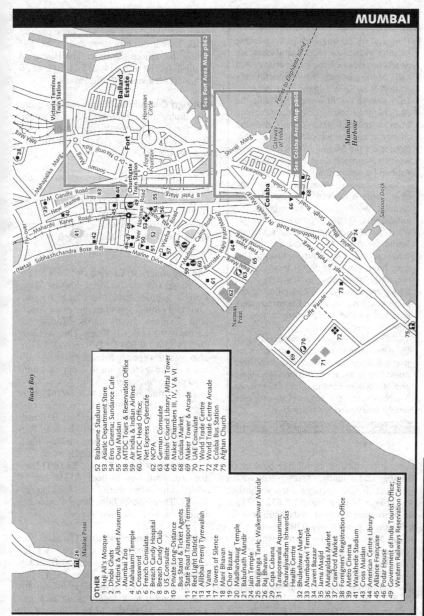

Victoria Terminus Train Station

See Fort Area Map p862

Ballard Estate

Horniman Circle

Ferries to Elephanta Island

Fort

Gateway of India

Flora Fountain

Churchgate Train Station

Mumbai Harbour

See Colaba Area Map p868

Colaba

Sassoon Dock

Marine Drive

Nariman Point

Cuffe Parade

Back Bay

Malabar Point

MUMBAI

OTHER
1 Haji Ali's Mosque
2 Dhobi Ghats
3 Victoria & Albert Museum;
   Mumbai Zoo
4 Mahalaxmi Temple
5 Crossroads
6 French Consulate
7 Breach Candy Hospital
8 Breach Candy Club
9 US Consulate
10 Private Long-Distance
   Bus Stand & Ticket Agents
11 State Road Transport Terminal
12 Red Light District
13 Allibhai Premji Tyrewallah
14 Vama
17 Towers of Silence
18 Mani Bhavan
19 Chor Bazaar
20 Madhavbaug Temple
21 Babulnath Mandir
24 Jain Temple
25 Banganga Tank; Walkeshwar Mandir
26 Raj Bhavan
29 Copa Cabana
31 Taraporewala Aquarium;
   Chaivalvadham Ishwardas
   Health Centre
32 Bhuleshwar Market
33 Mumbadevi Temple
34 Zaveri Bazaar
35 Jama Masjid
36 Mangaldas Market
37 Crawford Market
38 Foreigners' Registration Office
39 Metro Cinema
41 Wankhede Stadium
43 Cross Maidan
44 American Centre Library
45 Alliance Française
46 Podar House
49 Government of India Tourist Office;
   Western Railways Reservation Centre

52 Brabourne Stadium
53 Asiatic Department Store
54 Eros Cinema; Sundance Cafe
55 Oval Maidan
58 MTDC Tours & Reservation Office
59 Air India & Indian Airlines
60 MTDC Head Office;
   Net Express Cybercafe
62 NCPA
63 German Consulate
64 British Council Library; Mittal Tower
65 Maker Chambers III, IV, V & VI
68 Colaba Market
69 Maker Tower & Arcade
70 UAE Consulate
71 World Trade Centre
72 World Trade Centre Arcade
74 Colaba Bus Station
75 Afghan Church

What's in a Name?

The city of Bombay officially became Mumbai in January 1996. Many locals are clearly in favour of the name change – it had been part of the democratically elected Shiv Sena's agenda for decades. They believe the new name reclaims the city's heritage and signifies its emergence from a colonial past. Others see the change as an assertion of Maratha identity (Mumbai is the Maratha name for the city) which is inappropriate in a city built and inhabited by people from all over India.

Supporters of 'Mumbai' believe the city's name is derived from the goddess Mumba, worshipped by the original Koli inhabitants at the Mumbadevi Temple which stood on the present site of Victoria Terminus. When the Portuguese arrived they called the harbour Bombaim. This may have stemmed from 'buan bahia', meaning 'good bay' in Portuguese, or (much more likely) is a corruption of the original Koli name. When the islands were donated to the British, they anglicised Bombaim into Bombay.

Although the political implications of the name change are significant, locals are pretty relaxed about it all and you'll hear one name as much as the other. The media and officialdom tend to refer to the city as Mumbai, while the English-speaking elite nearly always stick with Bombay.

2 pm. It produces a useful free booklet on Mumbai and a modest fortnightly 'what's on' sheet. It also operates a tourist hotline (☎ 1913), a 24 hour booth (☎ 832 5331) at the international airport, and a counter at the domestic airport (☎ 614 9200).

The Maharashtra Tourism Development Corporation (MTDC) head office (☎ 202 4482, fax 202 4521) on the 9th floor, Express Towers, Nariman Point, has limited information on Mumbai and Maharashtra. Nearby is its more practical Tours Division & Reservation Office (☎ 202 6713, fax 285 2182) at CDO Hutments, Madame Cama Rd, Nariman Point, where bookings can be made for various city tours and for MTDC hotels throughout the state. The Himachal Pradesh tourist office (☎ 218 1123) is at 36 World Trade Centre, Cuffe Parade.

Foreign Consulates Many countries maintain diplomatic representation in Mumbai. See the Facts for the Visitor chapter for a list. The local *Yellow Pages* has a comprehensive list.

Visa Extensions The Foreigners' Registration Office (☎ 262 0111 ext 266) is in Annexe Building No 2, CID, 3rd floor, Say-ed Badruddin Rd, near the Police Commissioner's Office. If you're walking north along Dr D Naoroji Rd, turn left into the laneway near the footbridge to VT.

Money American Express (☎ 204 8291) in the Regal Cinema Building, Shivaji Marg, Colaba, handles foreign exchange transactions and provides cash advances on American Express credit cards Monday to Saturday 9.30 am to 6.30 pm. Thomas Cook (☎ 204 8556) at 324 Dr D Naoroji Rd, Fort, also provides speedy foreign exchange. It's open weekdays 9.30 am to 7 pm, and until 6.30 pm on Saturday.

ANZ Grindlays Bank (☎ 267 0162) at 90 Mahatma Gandhi (MG) Rd, Fort, offers cash advances on Visa and MasterCard. Bobcards (☎ 202 0630) on the 1st floor, Bank of Baroda, Colaba Causeway, provides a similar service but charges a 1% commission.

Citibank (☎ 823 2484) at 293 Dr D Naoroji Rd, Fort, has 24 hour ATMs, one of which is linked to international banking networks. There are 24 hour foreign exchange bureaus at both Mumbai airports.

Post & Communications The main post office is an imposing building near VT. It's open 10 am to 8 pm Monday to Saturday. Poste restante is at counter Nos 2 and 3 (not No 93 as indicated on the signs inside). It's open Monday to Saturday 9 am to 6 pm. Letters sent there should be addressed c/o

Poste Restante, Mumbai GPO, Mumbai 400 001. You'll need to bring your passport to collect mail. The parcel post office is in a separate building behind the main post office, accessible from a driveway off P D'Mello Rd. It's open Monday to Saturday 11 am to 4 pm (closed 1 to 1.30 pm). There's a useful post office in Colaba on Henry Rd.

Private phone/fax centres in Colaba and the Fort are convenient for STD and international calls. The international telecommunications centre run by VSNL (☎ 262 4020, fax 262 4027) is on Bhaurao Patil Marg in the fort area. It's most useful for home country direct, collect call and callback services. It's open 8 am to 8 pm daily.

To send air freight parcels out of India, try DHL Worldwide Express (☎ 283 7187) in the Sea Green South Hotel, 145A Marine Drive. It can get packages to most countries in three days. If you require local expertise in customs clearance, contact Perfect Cargo Movers (☎ 283 1457) on the 4th floor of 56 Abdullabhia Currimjee Building, Ghoga St (Janmabhoomi Marg), Fort.

Internet Resources C-39 The Cybercafe in Colaba's Cafe de la Plaz (see Places to Eat later in this chapter) has a couple of terminals with Internet access. It's open daily except Sunday 9.45 am to 9 pm and charges Rs 50 for 15 minutes. The NetExpress Cybercafe (☎ 202 2627 ext 402) on the ground floor, Express Towers, Nariman Point, is open daily 8.30 am to 10.30 pm and charges roughly the same price. The British Council Library (see Libraries & Cultural Centres later in this chapter) is the cheapest option at Rs 50 for 30 minutes.

Travel Agencies For personal service and discounted tickets it's hard to get much better than Transway International (☎ 262 6066, email transkam.etn@smt.sprintrpg .ems.vsnl.net.in) on the 2nd floor of Pantaky House, 8 Maruti Cross Lane, off Maruti St, Fort. It can be a challenge to find but the service is worth the hunt. Ask for the old Handloom House (now burnt down); Maruti St is behind it. Note that Transway can provide

advice on bus and rail travel but does not issue tickets for either, and don't be fooled by the decoy Transunique agency operating on the same floor.

Other reliable options in the Fort include Space Travels (☎ 266 3258) at Nanabhay Mansion, Sir P Mehta Rd, and Thomas Cook (see the Money section for details). Magnum Leisure Holidays (☎ 283 8628) at 10 Henry Rd is handy for those staying in Colaba.

Bookshops The best bookshop in the city is Crossword (☎ 492 0253) on the 1st floor at 22 Bhulabhai Desai Rd, Breach Candy. The Strand Book Stall (☎ 266 1994), just off Sir P Mehta Rd, Fort, offers the most generous discounts. The Nalanda Bookshop in the Taj Mahal Hotel, Colaba, has the best selection of international magazines.

Shankar Book Stall, outside Cafe Mondegar on Colaba Causeway, has an assortment of paperbacks, maps and guidebooks. A motley selection of bookstalls line Veer Nariman Rd, just west of Flora Fountain at the edge of the Fort.

Lonely Planet publishes *Mumbai*, the only in-depth travel guide to the city. *City of Gold: the Biography of Bombay* (Rs 125) by Gillian Tindall is the standard historical work. Mumbai is the backdrop to much Indian literature written in English, including Rohinton Mistry's *A Fine Balance* and much of Salman Rushdie's *The Moor's Last Sigh*.

Newspapers & Magazines The *Times of India* and the *Indian Express* both have Mumbai editions; local English-language papers include *Mid-Day* and the *Afternoon Despatch & Courier*. India's only gay magazine is called *Bombay Dost* (Rs 50).

Film & Photography Modern digital processing, print and slide film, video cartridges and camera accessories are available from Colour Vision (☎ 261 2468), Image House, W Hirachand Marg, Fort. The Asiatic Department Store on Veer Nariman Rd also offers reliable developing and has a passport photo booth. A 36-exposure colour print film costs Rs 105, and around Rs 200 to develop.

MUMBAI

Libraries & Cultural Centres The British Council Library (☎ 282 3560) at Mittal Tower A Wing, 1st floor, Barrister Rajni Patel Marg, Nariman Point, has an extensive collection of books, British newspapers and Internet access. It's open Tuesday to Saturday 10 am to 5.45 pm. It costs Rs 20 for a casual visit (Rs 50 on Saturday).

The United States Information Service (USIS) (☎ 262 4590) hosts the American Centre Library on the 3rd floor, 4 New Marine Lines, Churchgate. The library is open 10 am to 6 pm, closed Wednesday and Sunday. It costs Rs 10 for a casual visit.

You can read the French papers for free at Alliance Française (☎ 203 6187) at 40 New Marine Lines on weekdays 9.30 am to 5.30 pm and on Saturday until 1 pm. German speakers can do the same at Max Mueller Bhavan (☎ 202 7542) on K Dubash Marg, Fort between 11 am and 6 pm Tuesday to Saturday.

Medical Services In an emergency, phone ☎ 102 for an ambulance. Breach Candy Hospital (☎ 363 2657) is at 60 Bhulabhai Desai Rd, Breach Candy. Apollo Pharmacy (☎ 284 2683), 18 K Dubash Marg, Fort, is a central 24 hour chemist.

Gateway of India

The Gateway of India is an exaggerated colonial marker conceived following the visit of King George V in 1911. The yellow basalt arch of triumph, derived from the Muslim styles of 16th century Gujarat, is located on the shore of Mumbai Harbour at the tip of Apollo Bunder in Colaba. Officially opened in 1924, it was redundant just 24 years later when the last British regiment ceremoniously departed India through its archway.

The Gateway has become a popular emblem of the city and is a favourite gathering spot for locals in the evening and on weekends. Boats depart from the Gateway's wharfs for Elephanta Island, and touts, balloon sellers, photographers and snake charmers give the area the hubbub of a bazaar. Nearby are statues of the religious reformer Swami Vivekananda, and of the Maratha leader Shivaji astride his horse.

Taj Mahal Hotel

The majestic **Taj Mahal Hotel** overlooks Apollo Bunder and has good views of the Gateway from its top-floor Apollo Bar. This Mumbai institution was built in 1903 by the Parsi industrialist JN Tata, supposedly after he was refused entry to one of the European hotels on account of being 'a native'. It's a beautiful hotel and it's worth seeing the grand central stairway in the hotel's old wing. Nearby is the august **Royal Bombay Yacht Club**, where the clock seems to have stopped in the late 19th century.

Colaba

This vibrant fashionable suburb occupying the city's southernmost peninsula is the travellers' centre. **Colaba Causeway** (Shahid Bhagat Singh Marg) is the busy commercial thoroughfare which runs the length of much of the promontory; most budget hotels are located in the backstreets between the causeway and the Taj.

The causeway passes close to **Sassoon Dock**, a scene of intense and pungent activity at dawn when colourfully clad Koli fisherwomen sort the catch unloaded from fishing boats at the quay. The fish drying in the sun are *bombil*, which are deep fried to make Bombay Duck. Photography at the dock is forbidden without permission from the Mumbai Port Trust.

If you're interested in colonial history, the steepled Church of St John the Evangelist, also known as the **Afghan Church**, is near the southern end of the causeway. It was built in 1847 and is dedicated to the soldiers who died in the Sind campaign of 1838 and the First Afghan War of 1843.

Prince of Wales Museum

The Prince of Wales Museum (☎ 284 4519) was built to commemorate King George V's first visit to India in 1905 (while he was still Prince of Wales), though it did not open until 1923. Designed by George Wittet in grand Indo-Saracenic style, it is set in an ornamental garden and boasts a galleried central hall topped by a huge dome, said to have been inspired by the Golgumbaz in Bijapur.

Its collection includes impressive sculptures from Elephanta Island, Gujarat and Karnataka, terracotta figurines from the Indus Valley, Gandharan Buddhas, miniature paintings, porcelain and weaponry. There's a natural history section and a collection of second-rate European paintings, including a Gainsborough and three small Constables.

The museum is between Colaba and the Fort and is open Tuesday to Sunday 10.15 am to 6 pm. Entry costs Rs 5; a photography permit is Rs 30 and a video permit Rs 200. Bags must be left at the entrance gate cloakroom.

National Gallery of Modern Art & Jehangir Art Gallery

The National Gallery of Modern Art (☎ 285 2457) in the Sir Cowasji Jehangir Public Hall on MG Rd is a dramatic exhibition space showcasing quality Indian modern art. The gallery is open daily except Monday 11 am to 6 pm; entry is free. Bags must be left at the cloakroom.

The Jehangir Art Gallery (☎ 284 3989) at 161B MG Rd used to be the city's principal exhibition space and still hosts interesting weekly shows by contemporary Indian artists. It's open 11 am to 7 pm daily and has a pleasant cafe. Entry is free.

Opposite the Jehangir are a number of significant Victorian buildings, including the decrepit old **Watson's Hotel** where the city's love affair with cinema began with the screening of the Lumiere Brothers' *Cinematographe* in 1896.

Bombay University & High Court

Many of Mumbai's impressive Victorian buildings were constructed on the edge of Oval Maidan during the building boom of the 1860s and 70s which was sparked by the dismantling of the fort walls. The maidans were on the seafront in those days, and a series of grandiose structures, including the Secretariat, Bombay University, the High Court and the Western Railway Building, faced directly onto the Arabian Sea.

The most impressive of these is Bombay University, designed by Gilbert Scott of St Pancras Station fame. It looks like a 15th century Italian masterpiece dropped into the middle of an Indian metropolis. It consists of the exquisite **University Library**, **Convocation Hall** and the 80m high **Rajabai Tower**, whose clock used to play *God Save the Queen* and *Home Sweet Home* to mark the hour.

The neighbouring High Court was obviously designed to dispel any doubts about the weightiness and authority of the justice dispensed inside. Local stone carvers, who often worked independently, presumably saw things differently: they carved a one-eyed monkey holding the scales of justice on one of its pillars.

Flora Fountain

This cherished but undistinguished fountain stands at the established business centre of Mumbai. Though named after the Roman goddess of abundance, it was erected in 1869 in honour of Sir Bartle Frere, the governor of Bombay who was responsible for dismantling the fort and shaping much of modern Mumbai.

The goddess now shares her diminished area with a monument honouring those who died fighting to carve the state of Maharashtra out of the Bombay Presidency: hence the area's new name, Hutatma Chowk or Martyr's Square.

Dr D Naoroji Rd, named after the first Indian to become a British MP, heads northeast from the fountain towards VT. It's lined with the grand 19th century edifices of British commercial firms, although the street's elegant arcades are now clogged by hawkers' stalls – a favourite local metaphor for the Indianisation of British Bombay.

Horniman Circle

This stately arcaded circle of buildings, laid out in the 1860s around the sole surviving section of Bombay's original Cotton Green, was the result of a British attempt to stamp some discipline on the disorder of the Fort.

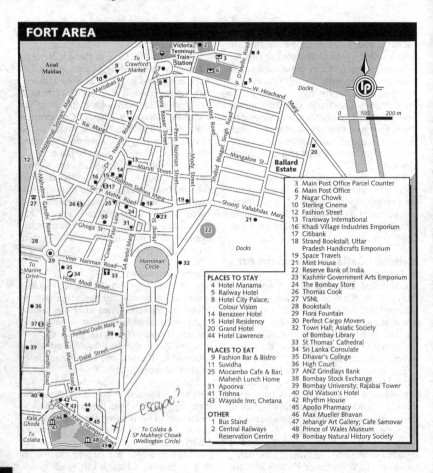

FORT AREA

PLACES TO STAY
4 Hotel Manama
5 Railway Hotel
8 Hotel City Palace;
   Colour Vision
14 Benazeer Hotel
15 Hotel Residency
20 Grand Hotel
44 Hotel Lawrence

PLACES TO EAT
9 Fashion Bar & Bistro
11 Suvidha
25 Mocambo Cafe & Bar;
   Mahesh Lunch Home
31 Apoorva
41 Trishna
43 Wayside Inn; Chetana

OTHER
1 Bus Stand
2 Central Railways
   Reservation Centre
3 Main Post Office Parcel Counter
6 Main Post Office
7 Nagar Chowk
10 Sterling Cinema
12 Fashion Street
13 Transway International
16 Khadi Village Industries Emporium
17 Citibank
18 Strand Bookstall; Uttar
   Pradesh Handicrafts Emporium
19 Space Travels
21 Mint House
22 Reserve Bank of India
23 Kashmir Government Arts Emporium
24 The Bombay Store
26 Thomas Cook
27 VSNL
28 Bookstalls
29 Flora Fountain
30 Perfect Cargo Movers
32 Town Hall; Asiatic Society
   of Bombay Library
33 St Thomas' Cathedral
34 Sri Lanka Consulate
35 Dhavar's College
36 High Court
37 ANZ Grindlays Bank
38 Bombay Stock Exchange
39 Bombay University; Rajabai Tower
40 Old Watson's Hotel
42 Rhythm House
45 Apollo Pharmacy
46 Max Mueller Bhavan
47 Jehangir Art Gallery; Cafe Samovar
48 Prince of Wales Museum
49 Bombay Natural History Society

The circle is overlooked from the east by the neoclassical **town hall**, which contains the august members-only Asiatic Society of Bombay library (☎ 266 0956) and Mumbai's State Central Library. Behind the town hall, in the inaccessible dockland, are the **Mint** and the remains of the original **Bombay Castle**.

The peaceful park in the centre of Horniman Circle still contains the banyan tree under which stockbrokers gathered to trade shares in the early days of the Bombay Stock Exchange. The modern **stock exchange**, India's largest, is housed in the inappropriate high rise just to the south; vociferous trading of shares still takes place on the street in nearby Ambalal Doshi Marg when the stock exchange closes around 2 pm.

The pretty **St Thomas' Cathedral** nearby is the oldest English building standing in Mumbai. Construction began in 1672 but remained unfinished until 1718. Its airy whitewashed interior is full of poignant colonial memorials, including one to Henry

Robertson Bower, lieutenant of the Royal Indian Marine, 'who lost his life returning from the South Pole with Scott'.

Victoria Terminus (VT)

The city's most exuberant Gothic building looks more like a lavishly decorated palace or cathedral than anything as mundane as a transport depot. It was designed by Frederick Stevens as the headquarters of the Great Indian Peninsular Railway Company and was completed in 1887, 34 years after the first train in India left this site on its way to nearby Thana. Carvings of peacocks, gargoyles, monkeys and British lions are mixed up among the buttresses, domes, turrets, spires and stained-glass windows. Topping it all is a 4m-high image of 'Progress' – though the rest of the building looks more like a celebration of pandemonium. VT is also known as Chhatrapati Shivaji Terminus (CST); don't wait until you have to catch a train to see it.

Marine Drive

Built on land reclaimed from Back Bay in 1920, Marine Drive (Netaji Subhashchandra Bose Rd) runs along the shore of the Arabian Sea from Nariman Point past Chowpatty Beach to the foot of Malabar Hill. It's a grand sweeping affair that's poorly landscaped and lined by Art Deco apartments in need of a good lick of paint; plans to smarten up the area and allow it to take its rightful place alongside the world's great seafront boulevards remain on the drawing board.

This is one of Mumbai's most popular promenades and sunset-watching spots but beware, during Diwali a barrage of firecrackers turns it into a war zone.

Tourist brochures are fond of dubbing Marine Drive the Queen's Necklace, because of the dramatic curve of its streetlights at night – best seen from Kamala Nehru Park or the upper floors of the Ambassador and Oberoi Towers hotels.

Chowpatty Beach

In a bid to clean up Mumbai's famous beach and to rid the area of unsavoury elements, the authorities have dispersed the Koli fishing community, and the roundabouts, Ferris wheels, shooting galleries and card games which gave Chowpatty so much of its charm at night.

Fortunately it's still a favourite evening spot for courting couples, political rallies and to enjoy the fresh air. Eating *bhelpuri* at the collection of stalls on the edge of the beach at night is an essential part of the Mumbai experience (see Places to Eat), so is getting a vigorous head rub from a *malish-wallah* (Rs 10). Forget about visiting during the day for a sunbathe or a dip.

The highlight of the year at Chowpatty is during **Ganesh Chaturthi** (August/September) when huge crowds gather to watch images of the elephant god Ganesh paraded through the city streets and immersed in the sea. Its current form as a mass procession began in 1893, when nationalists sought to harness the appeal of a Hindu festival. In recent years, the Shiv Sena has been accused of using the festival to promote its particular brand of Hindu chauvinism.

The uninspiring **Taraporewala Aquarium** is nearby on Marine Drive. **Babulnath Mandir**, one of Mumbai's most popular Hindu temples, is a short walk away, at the foot of Malabar Hill.

Malabar Hill

On the northern promontory of Back Bay is the expensive residential area of Malabar Hill, favoured for its cool breezes and fine views. The colonial bungalows that peppered the hillside in the 18th century have now been replaced by the apartment blocks of Mumbai's nouveau riche.

On the main road climbing Malabar Hill is a gaudy **Jain temple**, built in 1904, dedicated to the first Jain *tirthankar* (teacher), Adinath.

The formal **Hanging Gardens** (Pherozeshah Mehta Gardens) on top of the hill are a reasonable place for a stroll, though it's the smaller **Kamala Nehru Park** opposite which has views of Chowpatty Beach, Marine Drive and the city.

Beside the Hanging Gardens, but carefully shielded from view, are the Parsi **Towers of**

Silence. Parsis hold fire, earth and water sacred so do not cremate or bury their dead. Instead the corpses are laid out within the towers to be picked clean by vultures. Elaborate precautions are taken to keep ghoulish sightseers out so don't come here expecting to see anything.

Towards the southern end of the promontory is the sacred precinct of **Banganga Tank**. Bathing pilgrims, picturesque old dharamsalas, a dozen temples and scores of curious kids make this neighbourhood an oasis from the intrusive apartment blocks towering above.

The tank is steeped in legend dating back to the *Ramayana* and during Diwali traditional lamps float on its waters. The **Banganga Festival**, a music festival held by the MTDC, is also held here.

The most important temple in the area is the **Walkeshwar Mandir** (Sand Lord Temple), on the tank's western flank. Rama is said to have constructed a lingam of sand at the site while on his way to Lanka to rescue Sita. The original temple was possibly built 1000 years ago; the current unimpressive structure dates only to the 1950s.

At the end of the promontory is the inaccessible **Raj Bhavan**, once the British governor's house and now home to the governor of Maharashtra.

Mani Bhavan

The building where Mahatma Gandhi stayed during his visits to Bombay 1917-34 is a small museum. Gandhi's simple room remains untouched and there are a library and photographic exhibits of Gandhi's life. Mani Bhavan (☎ 380 5864) is at 19 Laburnum Rd, near August Kranti Maidan where the campaign to persuade the British to 'Quit India' was launched in 1942. It's open daily 9.30 am to 6 pm; entry is free.

Haji Ali's Mosque

Situated at the end of a long causeway poking into the Arabian Sea is a whitewashed fairy-tale mosque containing the tomb of the Muslim saint Haji Ali. The saint is believed to have been a wealthy local busi-

---

Mahalaxmi Temple

An ancient temple dedicated to Mahalaxmi is known to have stood on a headland of Malabar Hill until it was destroyed by Muslim invaders. According to local legend, the Muslims threw an icon of the goddess into the sea. When the British were constructing a sea wall joining Malabar Hill and Worli Island at the end of the 18th century, the local Hindu contractor claimed the goddess appeared to him in a dream. She told him that while several previous attempts to build a dike had failed, his construction would be successful if he promised to rebuild the temple.

Amazingly, a statue of the goddess was unearthed during construction of the wall. Upon the wall's completion, the contractor was granted land nearby where he built the temple to Mahalaxmi which stands today. Since Mahalaxmi is the goddess of wealth, the temple is one of the most popular in Mumbai. It's an interesting place to visit and the street approaching the temple is lined with beautiful flower stalls.

---

nessman who renounced the material world and meditated on a nearby headland after a pilgrimage to Mecca. The mosque and tomb were built by devotees in the early 19th century. Alternative versions say Haji Ali died while on a pilgrimage to Mecca and his casket miraculously floated back to Mumbai and landed at this spot.

The mosque becomes an island at high tide, but is accessible at other times via a causeway lined with beggars. It's a sobering walk but there's nothing sombre about the building's cool courtyard, full of chattering families and refreshment stalls. The rocks exposed at low tide behind the mosque are a favourite spot to catch sea breezes.

Crawford Market

This colourful market (officially called Mahatma Phule Market) is the last outpost of British Bombay before the tumult of the central bazaars begins. It used to be the city's wholesale produce market before this was strategically moved to New Bombay, but it still sells some excellent fruit and vegetables.

Bas-reliefs by Rudyard Kipling's father, Lockwood Kipling, adorn the Norman-Gothic exterior, and a gaudy fountain he designed stands buried beneath old fruit boxes in the market's central courtyard. The animal market at the rear sells everything from sausage dogs to cockatoos, most kept in cruelly small cages. The meat market is for the brave only, being one of the few places you can expect to be accosted and asked to buy a bloody goat's head. The fish market is just across MRA Marg.

South of the market, on the opposite side of Dr D Naoroji Rd, is the **JJ School of Art**, an important institution in the development of Indian art. Rudyard Kipling was born here in 1865; his birthplace is now the Dean's residence.

Kalbadevi & Bhuleshwar

No visit to Mumbai is complete without a foray into the bazaars of Kalbadevi and Bhuleshwar, north of Crawford Market. The narrow lanes of this area are in complete contrast to the relative orderliness of South Mumbai, and a seething mass of people bring Mumbai's traffic to a standstill.

Highlights include **Mangaldas Market**, **Zaveri Bazaar**, **Bhuleshwar Market** and **Chor Bazaar** (see Shopping later in this chapter). You'll also find the **Jama Masjid** and the interesting **Mumbadevi Temple**, dedicated to the patron goddess of the island's original Koli inhabitants.

If you've taken a shine to some of the cute-looking cows in India, the precincts of the **Madhavbaug Temple** contain a shelter where you can feed, pat and scratch the holy beasts to your heart's content.

It's best to venture into this area without a clear destination in mind and wander aimlessly; when you've had enough and need to get your bearings, head east until you hit the main thoroughfare of Mohammed Ali Rd. Catch bus Nos 1, 3 or 21 from Colaba or Flora Fountain.

Victoria Gardens

These gardens contain the **Victoria & Albert Museum** (Dr Bhau Daji Lad Museum) and the city **zoo**. The museum houses a hotchpotch of unexciting exhibits; the best are old maps of Bombay and a model of a Parsi Tower of Silence.

Just outside the museum is the large stone elephant removed from Elephanta Island (see the Around Mumbai section later). Nearby is a row of decaying statues of colonial worthies removed from their pedestals in the city and unceremoniously parked here after Independence.

The garden, which has officially been renamed Veermata Jijabai Bhonsle Udyan, is in Byculla, north of the city centre. It's open daily except Wednesday, 9 am to 6 pm. The museum is open Thursday to Tuesday, 10.30 am to 4.30 pm. Entry to the museum costs Rs 2 (free Thursday); the zoo costs Rs 4.

Catch bus No 3 from Colaba or Flora Fountain, or take a train to Byculla train station from VT.

Juhu

A decade ago the luxury hotels fronting Juhu Beach were the height of glamour for Mumbai's film crowd. The allure is a little jaded these days but Juhu's reputation is still strong enough to make it a must-do for all Indian tourists visiting Mumbai.

It's a pleasant enough beach if you're not expecting a sunbathe or a swim, and on weekend afternoons and evenings it develops a carnival atmosphere as crowds of locals and tourists paddle in the sea, play cricket and enjoy the fresh air. There are heaps of snack stands and fruit vendors, fairground rides, toy sellers, fortune tellers, and every other type of Indian beach entertainment.

The Hare Krishna **ISKCON** complex is nearby, and is worth a peek when the temple is open (7.15 am to 1 pm and 4 to 9 pm).

Juhu is 25km north of the city centre, not far from Mumbai's airports. Catch bus No 231 from Santa Cruz train station or an auto-rickshaw from Vile Parle train station.

MUMBAI

Dhobi Ghats

Ever wondered what happens to your dirty laundry when you hand it over at your hotel? Take a look at Mumbai's municipal laundry or *dhobi ghat* at Mahalaxmi, where some 5000 men use rows of open-air troughs to beat the dirt out of the thousands of kilograms of soiled clothes brought from all over the city each day. The best view is from the bridge across the railway tracks near Mahalaxmi train station; Mahalaxmi is five stops north of Churchgate train station.

Organised Tours

The Maharashtra Tourist Development Corporation (MTDC) operates uninspiring daily city (Rs 75) and suburban (Rs 130) tours. It also has short open-deck bus tours of the city's illuminated heritage buildings on weekend evenings (Rs 50) and a similar tour by horse-drawn buggy (a pricey Rs 500/person). All can be booked at the MTDC office on Madame Cama Rd.

The Government of India tourist office can arrange multilingual personal guides if you wish to explore Mumbai at your own pace. They cost Rs 230/345 for a half/full day.

Activities

Swimming Mumbai is hot and sticky year-round, but if you want to swim and you aren't staying at a luxury hotel, you are limited to a tiny pool at the Fariyas Hotel in Colaba (Rs 330) or the Breach Candy Club (☎ 367 4381) on Bhulabhai Desai Rd. The latter has a pool built in the shape of India. Day tickets cost Rs 200 on weekdays, Rs 300 on Saturday and Rs 500 on Sunday.

Hindi Classes Dhavar's College (☎ 204 2007), 3rd floor, Jehangir Building, Flora Fountain, offers Hindi language classes suitable for beginners.

Yoga It costs Rs 130 for four yoga classes at the Khaivalyadham Ishwardas Health Centre (☎ 612 2185), Marine Drive, Chowpatty. The Hare Krishna ISKCON complex (☎ 620 6860) at Juhu Beach also runs occasional classes and workshops.

Dhaba-Wallahs

If you're near VT or Churchgate train stations around midday, look out for the crowds of dhaba-wallahs dressed in white and wearing Nehru caps who wait for suburban trains to deliver home-cooked lunches prepared for office workers.

These meals are packed into metal tiffin boxes, collected from suburban street corners all over the city, sorted according to destination, put onto trains, and then collected at stations such as Churchgate and VT and delivered to the desks of downtown office workers.

Mumbai has 5000 dhaba-wallahs and they deliver around 175,000 meals a day. This massive distribution system works without hiccup thanks to colour-coded delivery notations on the tiffin lids that enable the often illiterate dhaba-wallahs to sort the lunches correctly.

Places to Stay

Mumbai is India's most expensive city to stay in, and pressure for accommodation can be intense during the Christmas season. If you know where you want to stay, it's smart to plan ahead.

Most travellers gravitate towards Colaba, which has plenty of budget and mid-range hotels. It has a few of the usual disadvantages of places where travellers congregate in large numbers. If you want to pick up on the daytime buzz of Mumbai it's better to stay in the Fort, where everyone is far too busy going about their business to take any notice of foreigners. To stay with a local family, contact the Government of India tourist office for a list of homes participating in Mumbai's paying guest scheme.

Places to Stay – Budget

Colaba The *Salvation Army Red Shield Hostel* (☎ 284 1824, 30 Mereweather Rd) is the cheapest place to stay in Colaba. A bed in a separate-sex dorm costs Rs 100 including breakfast or Rs 150 with full board. It's a little institutional and some travellers report problems with bed bugs, but it's great value for those on a tight budget. Full board in a double with attached bath costs Rs 400, including tax. Dorms beds are leased on a first-come first-served basis. The maximum stay is one week and checkout time is 9 am. Lockers are available.

Hotel Volga II (☎ 282 4755, *Rustam Manzil, 1st floor, Nawroji F Rd)*, just near Leopold Cafe and Bar, has doubles/triples with common bath for Rs 350/400, doubles with attached bath for Rs 400 or Rs 600 with air-con (including tax). Rooms consist of little more than a bed, but they're clean and acceptably priced.

Carlton Hotel (☎ 202 0642, *12 Mereweather Rd)* has basic singles/doubles/triples with common bath and TV for Rs 275/400/600; air-con doubles with attached bath are not such great value at Rs 950 including tax. It has a pleasant balcony, though the view may not be what you bargained for.

Apollo Guest House (☎ 204 5540, *43/45 Mathuradas Estate Building, 1st floor, Colaba Causeway)* has clean but cramped singles/doubles with common bath for Rs 330/440, and tidy air-con doubles with attached bath for Rs 800 including tax.

Maria Lodge (☎ 285 4081, *5/2 Grants Building, Arthur Bunder Rd)* has small but neat doubles with attached shower for Rs 350 and air-con doubles for Rs 500 including tax.

Sea Shore Hotel (☎ 287 4237, *1/39 Kamal Mansion, 4th floor, Arthur Bunder Rd)* has spartan, windowless rooms with TV and common bath for Rs 300/400, or better rooms with small harbour views for Rs 400/450, plus 4% tax. Triples with harbour views cost Rs 550.

India Guest House (☎ 283 3769, *1/39 Kamal Mansion, 3rd floor, Arthur Bunder Rd)* has rudimentary rooms with share bath and hardboard partitions that don't reach the ceiling for Rs 250/350, and doubles with water views for Rs 400, plus 4% tax.

Hotel Prosser's (☎ 284 1715, *2 Henry Rd)*, close to the harbour, has adequate singles/doubles with common bath for Rs 300/350, and more spacious rooms for Rs 450/500 including tax.

Bentley's Hotel (☎ 288 2890, *17 Oliver Rd, email bentleyshotel@hotmail.com)* is a successful, friendly hotel. Doubles range from Rs 650 to Rs 970, including TV, breakfast and tax. The more expensive rooms are spacious and excellent value. Air-con costs Rs 175 to Rs 200 extra. Reservations are recommended.

Hotel Whalley's (☎ 282 1802, *41 Mereweather Rd)* has a range of rooms starting from Rs 500/650 for common bath and rising to Rs 750/1100 for air-con and attached bath; tax and breakfast are included in the room rate.

The *YWCA International Centre* (☎ 202 5053, *2nd floor, 18 Madame Cama Rd)* accepts both women and men. Singles/doubles/triples in spacious, institutional rooms with attached bath cost Rs 570/1102/1603. The tariff includes breakfast, dinner and taxes. Temporary membership costs Rs 60 and a hefty deposit is required.

Fort Area *Hotel Lawrence* (☎ 928 43618, *3rd floor, Rope Walk Lane)* is a good value budget hotel with clean, plain singles/doubles/triples with common bath for Rs 300/400/600 including taxes. Book three weeks in advance.

Hotel Residency (☎ 262 5525, *fax 261 9164, 26 Rustom Sidhwa Marg)* is one of the few comfortable options in the heart of the Fort. It has spotless air-con singles/doubles with attached bath and TV from Rs 990/1090. Bookings are recommended.

Benazeer Hotel (☎ 261 1725, *fax 261 7798, 16 Rustom Sidhwa Marg)* has adequate air-con rooms with attached bath and TV from Rs 700 to Rs 932 including tax.

Hotel City Palace (☎ 261 5515, *fax 267 6897, 121 City Terrace, W Hirachand Marg)* has a range of compact, clean singles/doubles/triples with bathroom and TV for Rs 700/850/1050, plus 4% tax. Air-con costs an extra Rs 350. A few air-con broom closets with common bath go for Rs 450/650. It's opposite VT and a good place to stay if you are only in Mumbai a short time.

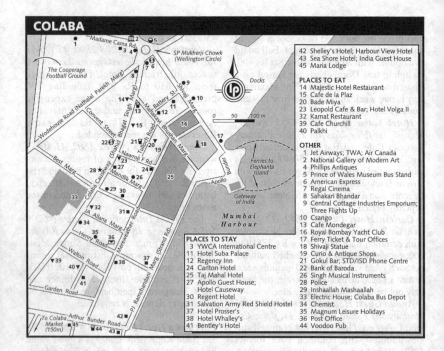

COLABA

PLACES TO STAY
3 YWCA International Centre
11 Hotel Suba Palace
12 Regency Inn
24 Carlton Hotel
25 Taj Mahal Hotel
27 Apollo Guest House;
   Hotel Causeway
30 Regent Hotel
31 Salvation Army Red Shield Hostel
37 Hotel Prosser's
38 Hotel Whalley's
41 Bentley's Hotel
42 Shelley's Hotel; Harbour View Hotel
43 Sea Shore Hotel; India Guest House
45 Maria Lodge

PLACES TO EAT
14 Majestic Hotel Restaurant
15 Cafe de la Plaz
20 Bade Miya
23 Leopold Cafe & Bar; Hotel Volga II
32 Kamat Restaurant
39 Cafe Churchill
40 Palkhi

OTHER
1 Jet Airways; TWA; Air Canada
2 National Gallery of Modern Art
4 Phillips Antiques
5 Prince of Wales Museum Bus Stand
6 American Express
7 Regal Cinema
8 Sahakari Bhandar
9 Central Cottage Industries Emporium;
   Three Flights Up
10 Csango
13 Cafe Mondegar
16 Royal Bombay Yacht Club
17 Ferry Ticket & Tour Offices
18 Shivaji Statue
19 Curio & Antique Shops
21 Gokul Bar; STD/ISD Phone Centre
22 Bank of Baroda
26 Singh Musical Instruments
28 Police
29 Inshaallah Mashaallah
33 Electric House; Colaba Bus Depot
34 Chemist
35 Magnum Leisure Holidays
36 Post Office
44 Voodoo Pub

Hotel Manama (☎ 261 3412, fax 261 3860, 221/225 P D'Mello Rd) has average doubles with TV for Rs 400/550 with common/attached bath, or Rs 700 with air-con, including tax. It makes a good budget option close to VT.

Railway Hotel (☎ 261 6705, fax 265 8049, 249 P D'Mello Rd) is a clean, adequate place on a noisy intersection close to VT. Singles/doubles cost from Rs 750/1000 with attached bath, TV and fridge or Rs 1050/1350 with air-con, plus 4% tax.

Retiring rooms (1st floor, Victoria Terminus) at VT train station cost Rs 180 for a dorm bed and Rs 600 for a double for 24 hours.

Airport Area There are a couple of budget hotels in Vile Parle (pronounced 'Veelay Parlay'), a middle-class suburb adjoining the domestic airport.

Shangri-La (☎ 612 8983, Nanda Patkar Rd, Vile Parle East) is the cheapest budget hotel close to Santa Cruz domestic airport. It has no-frills doubles with attached bath and TV for Rs 350 including tax. Air-con doubles cost Rs 676. Head west on Nehru Rd at the crossroads outside the airport, and take the second left-hand turn into Nanda Patkar Rd. It's a 10 minute walk from the terminal or a Rs 7.50 auto-rickshaw ride.

Hotel Aircraft International (☎ 612 1419, fax 618 2942, 179 Dayaldas Rd, off Western Express Highway, Vile Parle East) is opposite the domestic airport entrance. It has budget air-con singles/doubles with bath and TV for Rs 850/950, plus 4% tax. Checkout time is 24 hours after check in.

Elsewhere **Bentley Hotel** (☎ 281 5244, Krishna Mahal, 3rd floor, corner of Marine Drive and D Rd) is the only budget hotel on

491-22
764

Back Bay. It offers no-frills B&B in a variety of box-like singles/doubles with common bath for Rs 430/550 plus 4% tax. It's not bad value. Checkout time is 24 hours after check in.

Hotel Kemp's Corner (☎ 363 4646, 131 August Kranti Marg, Kemp's Corner) has compact air-con singles/doubles with attached bath and TV for Rs 975/1100, plus 9% tax. It's good value for an upmarket area. Book two weeks in advance.

Retiring rooms (3rd floor, Mumbai Central) at Mumbai Central train station cost Rs 180 for a dorm and Rs 600 for a double for 24 hours.

Places to Stay – Mid-Range

Unless otherwise indicated all mid-range hotels offer air-con rooms with attached bathroom, TV and fridge.

Colaba *Shelleys Hotel* (☎ 284 0229, fax 284 0385, 30 PJ Ramchandani Marg) overlooks the waters of Mumbai Harbour. It's an excellent place with a slight hint of the Raj about it. Doubles start from Rs 1415 and rise to Rs 1900 with water views, including tax.

Harbour View Hotel (☎ 282 1089, 4th floor, 25 PJ Ramchandani Marg, email parkview@bom3.vsnl.net.in) is a tastefully refurbished hotel with spotless doubles from Rs 1500, rising to Rs 1990 for rooms with water views, plus 14% tax. Its rooftop restaurant is a major plus. 25 · 3n·

Regency Inn (☎ 202 0292, fax 285 5226, 18 Lansdowne House, Mahakavi Bhushan Marg) has compact rooms with common bath for Rs 750, and spacious rooms with attached bath for Rs 1200/1490 including tax. It's good value.

Hotel Suba Palace (☎ 202 0636, Battery St, email subapalace@hotmail.com) has comfortable, modern singles/doubles for Rs 1195/1800, plus 14% tax. It gets positive reviews from travellers. Reservations are recommended.

The *Regent Hotel* (☎ 287 1854, fax 202 0363, 8 Best Marg) has decent single/double/triple rooms for Rs 1976/2080/2184, including tax.

Hotel Causeway (☎ 281 7777, fax 281 0999, 43/45 Mathuradas Estate Building, 3rd floor, Colaba Causeway) has adequate rooms from Rs 1000/1500 including tax.

Near the Fort *Grand Hotel* (☎ 261 8211, email grandh@bom3.vsnl.net.in, 17 Shri Shiv Sagar Ramgulam Marg, Ballard Estate) fails to live up to its name, but it has clean, spacious, single/double rooms with dowdy furniture for Rs 1980/2392 including tax (no fridge).

West End Hotel (☎ 203 9121, 45 New Marine Lines, email west.hotel@gems.vsnl.net.in) has huge, spotless, old-fashioned singles/doubles/triples for Rs 2160/2394/3591, including tax (no fridge).

Ritz Hotel (☎ 285 0500, fax 285 0494, 5 J Tata Rd, Churchgate) has some comfortable rooms but few amenities. Singles/doubles start from a pricey Rs 4000/4800, plus 31% tax.

Marine Drive *Chateau Windsor Hotel* (☎ 204 3376, fax 202 6459, 5th floor, 86 Veer Nariman Rd, Churchgate) is well run and has spotless fan-cooled rooms with common bath for Rs 750/970 and singles/doubles/triples with attached bath for Rs 970/1190/1690, plus 4% tax (no fridge). Air-con rooms go for Rs 1190/1690/1910.

Sea Green Hotel (☎ 282 2294, fax 283 6158, 145 Marine Drive) and the *Sea Green South Hotel* (☎ 282 1613, fax 283 6303, 145A Marine Drive) are identical hotels offering spacious but spartan rooms for Rs 1250/1550, plus 14% tax. Ask for a sea view.

Chowpatty & Kemp's Corner *Hotel Sapna* (☎ 367 0041, fax 361 9115, Pandita Ramabai Marg, Chowpatty), opposite Bharatiya Vidhya Bhavan, is a clean serviceable place with rooms from Rs 1395/1645, plus 20% tax.

Shalimar Hotel (☎ 363 1311, August Kranti Marg, email shalimar@giasbm01.vsnl.net.in) has decent but pricey air-con singles/doubles from US$70/105, plus 20% tax.

Airport Area There are about half a dozen mid-range hotels clustered on Nehru Rd Extension close to the entrance to the domestic airport. They're twice the price of equivalent rooms in the city. Bookings are recommended; most offer courtesy airport pick-up.

Hotel Bawa International (☎ 611 3636, fax 610 7096, Nehru Rd Extension, Vile Parle East) is a pleasant, functional hotel with rooms for Rs 3300/3800, plus 20% tax.

Hotel Atithi (☎ 618 7941, fax 611 1998, 77 A-B Nehru Rd Extension, Vile Parle East) has clean, basic doubles for Rs 2495, including tax (no fridge).

Kumaria Presidency (☎ 835 2601, fax 837 3850, Anderhi-Kurla Rd), facing Sahar international airport, has acceptable rooms for Rs 1700/1950, plus 10% tax; not bad value for the area.

Juhu Beach *Juhu Hotel* (☎ 618 4012, fax 619 2578, Juhu Tara Rd) is a small single-storey beachfront hotel with rooms for Rs 1150/1800 plus 4% tax (no fridge). It attracts a fashionable young crowd and has a popular nightclub.

ISKCON (☎ 620 6860, fax 620 5214, Hare Krishna Land) has good-value, fan-cooled singles/doubles with attached bath for Rs 960/1150; air-con costs Rs 1050/1440, plus 4% tax (no TV, no fridge). Bookings recommended.

Places to Stay – Top End

Colaba *The Taj Mahal Hotel* (☎ 202 3366, fax 287 2711, Apollo Bunder), next to the Gateway of India, is one of the best hotels in the country. Singles/doubles in the superb old wing cost from US$295/325, rising to US$325/365 with a harbour view, plus 20% tax. Rooms in the modern wing are 20% cheaper. The Taj is a second home to Mumbai's elite and has every conceivable facility, including three quality restaurants, several bars, a coffee shop, swimming pool, gymnasium and nightclub.

Fariyas Hotel (☎ 204 2911, 25 Justice Devshanker V Vijas Marg, email fariyas@ bom3.vsnl.net.in) is a comfortable, modern

four star establishment offering quality rooms from US$125. It has a tiny pool, a restaurant and popular bar.

Hotel President (☎ 215 0808, fax 215 1201, 90 Cuffe Parade) is a dated five star hotel used by tour groups and businesspeople. Singles/doubles are US$234/252, including tax.

Marine Drive *The Oberoi* (☎ 202 5757, email reservations@oberoi-mumbai.com, Marine Drive, Nariman Point) competes with the Taj Mahal in a bid to be Mumbai's most opulent hostelry. It's a modern, service-oriented, luxury business hotel overlooking the Arabian Sea. It has rooms for US$325/355, rising to US$360/ 380 with a sea view, plus 20% tax. It has a pool, a gymnasium, three good restaurants and a bar.

The Oberoi Towers (☎ 202 4343, fax 204 3282, Marine Drive, Nariman Point) attracts upmarket travellers, businesspeople and airline crews, many of them drawn by the fantastic views of Back Bay and the city from the upper floors. Rooms start from US$260/285. The hotel has an ordinary pool, a gymnasium, two gauche restaurants and a bar. It's connected to the Oberoi, and guests can make use of both hotels' facilities.

Marine Plaza (☎ 285 1212, fax 282 8585, 29 Marine Drive, Nariman Point) is a modern boutique five star hotel with Art Deco flourishes. It has stylish rooms starting from US$230 with sea views, plus 20% tax. Facilities include a gymnasium, restaurant, coffee shop and popular bar. An ambitious glass-bottomed rooftop pool was not functional at the time of writing.

Ambassador Hotel (☎ 204 1131, email ambhotel@bom3.vsnl.net.in, Veer Nariman Rd, Churchgate) is a modern four-star establishment with comfortable rooms from US$135/190, plus 20% tax. It's an acceptable hotel (with a revolving restaurant) but it has few luxury facilities and no pool.

Airport Area *Leela Kempinski* (☎ 836 3636, email leela.bom@leela.sprintrpg.ems .vsnl.net.in) is opposite Sahar international airport, Andheri. It's the only five star hotel in Mumbai that can compete with the Oberoi and the Taj. Comfortable singles/doubles start from US$315/340, plus 20% tax.

The Orchid (☎ 610 0707, email info@ orchidhotel.com), off Nehru Rd Extension in Vile Parle East, is a stylish new five star hotel next to the domestic airport. It's the first certified eco-friendly hotel in Asia and deserves all the support it can get. Excellent rooms start from US$225, plus 20% tax.

Juhu Beach The *Holiday Inn (☎ 620 4444, Balraj Sahani Marg, email reserve@ holidayinn.sprintsmx.ems.vsnl.net.in)* has a beachfront location, a decent pool and a relaxing ambience. Fine rooms cost from US$220, plus 20% tax.

Ramada Hotel Palm Grove (☎ 611 2323, Juhu Tara Rd, email palmgrov@giasbm01 .vsnl.net.in) is a beachfront establishment with a pretty good pool and singles/doubles for Rs 6000/7000, plus 20% tax.

Places to Eat

Mumbai has the best selection of restaurants in India. You could trace the cultural history of the metropolis by trawling through the variety of food available: from Parsi *dhansaak* (meat with curried lentils and rice), Gujarati thalis and Muslim kababs to Goan vindaloos and Mangalorean seafood. The city's delicious seafood is safe to eat – even during the monsoon months. If you've just been to Chowpatty and looked at the water, it's best to pretend that the fish came from the kitchen rather than the ocean. Be sure to try Mumbai's famous bhelpuri – a tasty snack of crisp vermicelli, puffed rice, spiced vegetables, chutney and chillies. During the summer mango season don't miss the delicious Alphonsoes grown in nearby Ratnagiri. During the Muslim holy month of Ramadan, fantastic night food markets line Mohammed Ali and Merchant roads.

Most budget restaurants and cafes open daily from breakfast to around 11 pm. Smarter restaurants tend to open only for lunch and dinner; they generally accept credit cards. A tip of 5% (up to a maximum of Rs 25) is appropriate for good service.

A 24 hour telephone information service (☎ 888 8888) can provide additional information on Mumbai's restaurants.

Colaba If you're self-catering, the Colaba market on Lala Nigam St has plenty of fresh fruit.

Leopold Cafe & Bar (☎ 202 0131) at the corner of Colaba Causeway and Nawroji F Rd, is a Mumbai institution dating back to 1871. Travellers arriving in the city from less salubrious parts of India traditionally make it their first port of call. It has an extensive Chinese, continental and Indian menu, an excellent juice bar, and consistently good food.

Cafe Churchill (☎ 284 4689, 103B Colaba Causeway) serves some of the best comfort food in the neighbourhood. It's a tiny place, but it makes ace sandwiches (Rs 50) good meals and delicious brownies. It opens at 11 am.

Bade Miya (☎ 284 1649) on Tulloch Rd, is an evening street stall with a city-wide reputation. It serves excellent kababs, tikkas and rotis (around Rs 30) to customers milling on the street or seated at tables on the roadside.

Kailash Parbat, (☎ 287 4823, 5 Sheela Mahal, 1st Pasta Lane) is a Mumbai legend thanks to its inexpensive Sindhi-influenced pure veg snacks (Rs 15) and its mouthwatering sweets (around Rs 17 each).

Kamat Restaurant (☎ 287 4734) opposite Electric House on Colaba Causeway serves respectable north and south Indian veg fare, such as *masala dosas* (curried vegetables inside a rice-flour pancake) for Rs 18 and thalis for Rs 25.

Majestic Hotel (☎ 202 1585), opposite Cafe Mondegar on Colaba Causeway, is a no-nonsense dining hall where you can pick up a tasty thali for just Rs 20.

Cafe de la Plaz (☎ 204 5807, 1st floor, Metro Plaza, Colaba Causeway) is an outdoor terrace cafe serving set western breakfasts (Rs 40), sandwiches and pizzas. There's a small cybercafe inside. It's closed Sunday.

Palkhi (☎ 284 0053, 15 Walton Rd) specialises in Mughlai and north Indian cuisine,

MUMBAI

including a succulent assortment of kababs (Rs 150). It's a very swanky place that makes a great alternative to dining in an upmarket hotel.

Tanjore (☎ *202 3366, Apollo Bunder*), the poster-child of the Taj Mahal Hotel, offers a select menu of khad cuisine (cooked and served in mud pots) and north Indian, south Indian and Mumbai thalis (Rs 385 to Rs 485). Indian music and dance performances accompany dinner. Dress smartly.

Fort *Cafe Samovar* (☎ *284800, Jehangir Art Gallery, 161B MG Rd*) serves light meals and snacks (Rs 25 to Rs 40) on a makeshift jungly veranda. It's open daily except Sunday 11 am to 7 pm.

Wayside Inn (☎ *284 4324, 38 K Dubash Marg*) is a comfortable historic spot to hang out in central Mumbai. Dr Ambedkar must have felt that way, since he wrote parts of the draft of the Indian constitution here. It serves nostalgic Raj fare and meals cost around Rs 70. It's open daily except Sunday 9 am to 7 pm.

Chetana (☎ *284 4968, 34 K Dubash Marg*) opened the year before Independence and played a key role in the development of Indian contemporary art. It's a great place to deconstruct the mysteries of the north Indian thali (Rs 150).

Mocambo Cafe & Bar (☎ *287 0458, 23A Sir P Mehta Rd*) has an open street frontage that lets you absorb the atmosphere of the Fort. It's a convenient spot for breakfast, sandwiches and cold beer.

Suvidha (☎ *207 2131, National Insurance Building, 204 Dr D Naoroji Rd*) has decent south Indian veg and Punjabi food for under Rs 30. Expect a queue at lunchtime.

Mahesh Lunch Home (☎ *287 0938, 8B Cawasji Patel St*) is the place to try Mangalore seafood. Renowned for its ladyfish, pomfret (Rs 70) and crabs (Rs 170, the *rawas tikka* and pomfret tandoor are superb.

Apoorva Restaurant and Bar (☎ *287 0335, Noble Chambers, SA Brelvi Rd*) is an excellent Mangalorean seafood specialist whose mouthwatering crabs and prawn *gassis* are known throughout South Mumbai.

Seafood dishes start from Rs 45 and rise to Rs 250.

Trishna (☎ *267 2176, 7 Rope Walk Lane*) is the rage among the city's foodies. The quality of seafood is superb; most substantial dishes are in the Rs 200 range. Bookings are advisable.

Churchgate *The Pizzeria* (☎ *285 6115, Soona Mahal, 143 Marine Drive*) has decent pizzas and fine views of Back Bay and the lights of Malabar Hill at night. Pizzas with the usual western toppings, plus local variations, like 'Bombay Masala', start from Rs 90.

Purohit (☎ *204 9231, Veer Nariman Rd*) looks new but has been serving veg food for over 60 years. It knows a thing or two about Gujarati thalis (Rs 120) and has an extensive a la carte menu (around Rs 80).

Sundance Cafe (☎ *282 1286, Eros Cinema Building, 42 Maharshi Karve Rd*) is a handy meeting spot for a pre-movie munch. It serves decent salads, sandwiches (Rs 50), pizzas (Rs 65) and sizzlers (Rs 110).

Samrat Restaurant (☎ *282 0942, Prem Court, J Tata Rd*) is an upmarket pure veg restaurant dishing up quality Gujarati thalis (Rs 95).

Chowpatty Beach & Malabar Hill The **stalls** on Chowpatty Beach in the evening are atmospheric spots to snack on bhelpuri (Rs 10), panipuri and ice cream.

Cafe Ideal (☎ *363 0943, Fulchand Niwas, Chowpatty Seaface*) is a bustling Irani-style cafe with a CD jukebox and a Chinese and continental menu. Most dishes cost around Rs 35; beer is more popular at Rs 60.

New Kulfi Centre (*corner of Chowpatty Seaface and Sardar V Patel Rd*) makes some of the most delicious kulfi (Rs 12 to Rs 25) in Mumbai. It's weighed into 100g slabs, cut into cubes, and served to customers clustered on the pavement.

Cream Centre (☎ *369 2025, Chowpatty Seaface*) is an iconic veg snack bar and ice-cream parlour that's been on the Chowpatty must-do list for over 40 years. It serves delicious puris, *parathas*, samosas and sand-

MUMBAI

wiches (Rs 50), plus ready-made and create-your-own sundaes (around Rs 60).

Cafe Naaz (☎ 367 2969), opposite Hanging Gardens in Malabar Hill, is a multitiered terrace cafe on the edge of Kamala Nehru Park. The food is no great shakes but it has fine views of Back Bay and Chowpatty Beach.

China Garden (☎ 363 0841, Om Chambers, Kemp's Corner) specialises in Cantonese and Szechuan cuisine. It's a classy place and locals unanimously agree that it has the best Chinese food in the city. Most dishes cost between Rs 150 and Rs 200; bookings are essential.

Entertainment

The Thursday edition of *Mid-Day* incorporates *The List*, a weekly guide to Mumbai entertainment. Newspapers have information on mainstream events and film screenings.

Bars & Nightclubs Compared to most Indian cities Mumbai has a relaxed attitude to alcohol and a good nightlife, though at the time of writing authorities had imposed a closing time of midnight. Hopefully this is temporary and, when lifted, clubs should stay open until 3 am. In some clubs entry is restricted to couples or women; sober, appropriately dressed foreigners may find it possible to circumnavigate these rules.

Cafe Mondegar (☎ 202 0591, Metro House, 5A Colaba Causeway) is a cramped cafe-bar with a CD jukebox that's popular with travellers. It's open daily from 8 am.

Gokul Bar (☎ 284 8428) on Tulloch Rd in Colaba, is a serious, 100% male, Indian drinking den. It can get pretty lively. Beer is cheap. It's open from 11 am daily.

Voodoo Pub (☎ 284 1959, 2/5 Kamal Mansion, Arthur Bunder Rd, Colaba) is a dark, clubby grunge bar recommended by gay travellers. The graffiti claims 'Adam was made for Steve not Eve', but a bevy of bar girls do their best to contradict this. It's open nightly from 7.30 pm and there's a Rs 120 cover charge after 8.30 pm.

The Tavern (☎ 204 2911, Fariyas Hotel, 25 Justice Devshanker V Vijas Marg, Co-laba), an English-style air-con tavern, is quite popular with 30-something Indians of both genders thanks to its singalong mainstream western music. It's open nightly at 6.30 pm.

Three Flights Up (☎ 282 9934, Narang House, 1st floor, 34 Shivaji Marg, Colaba) is a stylish club above the Cottage Industries Emporium. It's a converted warehouse space and boasts the longest bar in India. It's open nightly; gents pay Rs 150 weekdays and Rs 300 on Friday and Saturday.

The Garden Bar (☎ 204 1131, 14th floor, Ambassador Hotel, Veer Nariman Rd, Churchgate) is an under-utilised space but it's worth a visit for the superb 360 degree panorama of the bay and city. It's open nightly at 6.30 pm.

Fashion Bar (☎ 207 7270, 1st floor, Dhiraj Chambers Annex, 16 Marzaban Rd, Fort) is the hippest spot in town and it's packed with glam young things. There's a cover charge of Rs 200 per person (Rs 300 on Friday and Saturday) which is redeemable at the bar. It's open daily from 7 pm; couples only.

Copa Cabana (☎ 368 0274, Darya Vihar, Chowpatty Seaface) is a small, buzzing, Latin-flavoured club/bar with decent music, fine margaritas and no elbow room. It's open daily from 7 pm. There's usually an entry fee; women and couples only.

Cinema There are well over one hundred cinemas in Mumbai. *The Regal* (☎ 202 1017, Colaba Causeway) and *Sterling* (☎ 207 5187, Marzaban Rd) in the Fort show first-run English-language movies (Rs 40 to Rs 80). To check out a Bollywood blockbuster, try *Eros* (☎ 282 2335) opposite Churchgate train station or *Metro* on MG Rd (Rs 20 to Rs 75). You'll need to reserve tickets in advance, especially for weekend screenings. Tickets go on sale two days before films are screened.

Music, Dance & Theatre The *NCPA* (☎ 283 3737), located at the tip of Nariman Point, is the hub of Mumbai's music, theatre and dance scene. In any given week, it

Masala Movies

Mumbai is the centre of India's huge Hindi film industry, though falling production means it now produces about 120 feature films a year (compared to around 200 a decade ago). Much of the glamour associated with the city stems from its pivotal position as the dream factory of the nation.

The local film industry is known as Bollywood and the films it produces tend to be spectacular melodramatic fantasies, known disparagingly as 'masala movies' because they're made to an established formula that mixes a variety of ingredients – action, violence, music, dance, romance and moralising – into one outrageous blend.

While plenty of thought-provoking 'artistic' Indian films are appreciated in the west, Hindi popular cinema is viewed with contempt largely because it's unpalatable to audiences used to realistic narratives and because it doesn't subscribe to the same aesthetic values dominant in the West.

The trick to appreciating Hindi films is to view them on their own terms, since popular Indian cinema owes more to the Hindu epics and Sanskrit theatre than it does to the conventions of classical Hollywood cinema.

Although most Hindi films are dismissed as escapist, they frequently address important social issues such as communalism, caste and modernisation. Since Independence, Hindi-language cinema has also been a potent force in shaping Indian ideas of nationhood – no mean feat in such a multicultural, multilingual and multireligious environment.

That said, Bollywood movies remain exuberant, spectacle-driven entertainment and the success of a film is determined by its stars, film score, choreography and playback singers (all songs are dubbed) not by its message.

A major film can cost Rs 50 million to produce, and less than 20% of Hindi films make a return on their investment. Reliable figures on film financing are difficult to find, partly because black money has been a primary source of funding for decades.

The largest export market for Hindi films is in the Gulf, but there are significant returns in countries such as Russia, Indonesia and the UK (where the 1998 Bollywood hit *Kuch Kuch Hota Hai* was in the top 10 grossing movies of the year).

Unfortunately, there are no organised tours of Mumbai's film studios, but permission to visit sets may be possible if you contact the public relations officers of Film City (☎ 840 1533) in Goregaon East or RK Studio (☎ 556 3252) in Chembur-Sion. Otherwise you'll have to do what locals do: flick through the pages of filmzines like *Cineblitz*, check out the latest offerings on TV channels like Zee Cinema or pay a visit to a downtown cinema.

might host Marathi theatre, dance troupes from Bihar, ensembles from Europe, and Indian classical music. It also contains the *Tata Theatre* (which occasionally has English-language plays) and the *Experimental Theatre*.

Most of the cultural centres (see the Libraries & Cultural Centres section earlier in this chapter) host regular music, dance and theatre performances.

You can see regional artists perform on K Dubash Marg every Sunday evening during the Kala Ghoda Fair which takes place on Sunday from November to January.

English-language plays are performed at the *Nehru Centre* (☎ 492 8086), Dr Annie Besant Rd, Worli. The *Privthi Theatre* (☎ 614 9546) at Juhu Beach is a good place at which to see both English-language and Hindi theatre.

Spectator Sports

The *Times of India* lists the day's sporting events in a handy box-out on its back page.

Cricket The cricket season runs from October to February. Test matches are played at Wankhede Stadium (☎ 281 1795), just off Marine Drive. Ticket prices start at Rs 150.

Horse Racing Mumbai's horse racing season runs from November to April. Races are held on Sunday and Wednesday afternoons at Mahalaxmi Racecourse (☎ 307 1401). The big races are major social occasions. Entry costs around Rs 12 in the public enclosure.

Football The Cooperage Football Ground (☎ 202 4020), Maharshi Karve Rd, Colaba hosts soccer matches between November and February. Tickets cost around Rs 25.

Shopping

Mumbai is India's great marketplace and many people consider it to have the best shopping in the country. Every Sunday from November to January K Dubash Marg hosts the Kala Ghoda Fair – a celebration of arts and crafts with performing arts, and food and handicraft stalls.

Markets You can buy just about anything in the dense bazaars north of the Fort. The main areas are Crawford Market (fruit and veg), Mangaldas Market (silk and cloth), Zaveri Bazaar (jewellery), Bhuleshwar Market (fruit and veg) and Chor Bazaar (Mumbai's 'thieves' market').

Specialist streets worth checking out in Kalbadevi include Shamsheth Lane, two streets north of the Jama Masjid, for lace; and Dhabu St in Chor Bazaar, which is still worth a peek for leather goods. Mutton St in Chor Bazaar specialises in antiques, ingenious reproductions and miscellaneous junk.

Don't place too much faith in the authenticity or lifespan of objects with mechanical parts.

Handicrafts & Gifts You can pick up handicrafts made all over the country from various state government emporiums in the World Trade Centre Arcade near Cuffe Parade; there's more on Sir P Mehta Rd, Fort. The Central Cottage Industries Emporium (☎ 202 7537) on Shivaji Marg, Colaba, has the biggest selection of mass produced trinkets, and is a convenient place to buy gifts.

If you're looking for something that won't look incredibly tacky the moment you take it home, try the Bombay Store (☎ 288 5048) on Sir P Mehta Rd, Fort. It sells rugs, textiles, home furnishings and bric-a-brac.

Antiques & Curios Small antique and curio shops line Mereweather Rd behind the Taj Mahal Hotel. Prices aren't cheap but the quality is definitely a step up from government emporiums. If you prefer Raj-era bric-a-brac, head to Chor Bazaar (see Markets) or Phillips Antiques (☎ 202 0564), opposite the Regal Cinema, Colaba, specialising in silverware, porcelain and Victoriana.

Clothes & Department Stores You can save a small fortune by buying your backpacking wardrobe at 'Fashion Street', the stalls lining MG Rd between Cross and Azad maidans. Colaba Causeway shops sell cheap and decent western-style clothes. Vama Department Store (☎ 387 1450), 72 Peddar Rd, Kemp's Corner, has western labels ie Bennetton, Levi's and Nike.

For something hip, you're better off checking the cluster of boutiques at Kemp's Corner, between the flyover and the junction with Nepean Sea Rd. Pieces by Indian designers sell here for half the price of off-the-shelf gear back home.

Ready-made traditional Indian clothing can be picked up at the Khadi Village Industries Emporium (☎ 207 3280) at 286 Dr D Naoroji Rd, Fort, where time seems to have stopped somewhere in the 1940s.

Sahakari Bhandar (☎ 202 2248), opposite the Regal Cinema, Colaba, is an indoor market with a pharmacy. It's useful for purchasing practical stuff for travelling like sheets and towels. The Asiatic Department Store (☎ 287 2815) on Veer Nariman Rd, Churchgate, is a handy shop with a

MUMBAI

pharmacy, photo developing lab and Internet terminals.

Miscellaneous Csango (☎ 202 4309), Dhanraj Mahal, Shivaji Marg, Colaba, has quality high-priced leather bags, jackets, wallets and belts. With a bit of sifting, you can pick up decent belts and wallets from the stalls on Dr D Naoroji Rd. It is still worth trawling declining Dhabu St in Kalbadevi but the cheapest leather goods are now found in Dharavi.

Inshaallah Mashaallah (☎ 204 9495) on Best Marg, Colaba, has a vast range of perfumes and helpful staff to guide you through the olfactory chaos.

Rhythm House (☎ 284 2835), near the Jehangir Art Gallery, has a huge selection of Hindi film and Indian classical music. Cassettes/CDs start from Rs 30/275. Crossword and Nalanda (see the Bookshop section earlier) also stock CDs. Singh Musical Instruments (☎ 284 1373) at Ram-Nimi, Mandlik

Marg, Colaba, sells tablas, sitars and guitars, and has handy self-instruction manuals.

Getting There & Away

Air Mumbai is the main international gateway to India. It also has the busiest network of domestic flights. The international terminal (Sahar) is about 4km away from the domestic terminal (Santa Cruz). They are 30km and 26km respectively north of Nariman Point in downtown Mumbai.

Facilities in Sahar's arrival hall include a duty-free shop, several foreign exchange counters offering acceptable rates, a Government of India tourist office (☎ 832 5331), a hotel reservation counter (☎ 615 5239, email yez.patel@usa.net) and a prepaid taxi booth – all open 24 hours. There's a left-luggage shed in the car park, about 200m left of the arrivals hall exit.

If you're leaving India from Mumbai be sure to reconfirm your ticket three days before departure. Passengers are advised to check in three hours before international flights depart. Leftover rupees backed by encashment certificates can be exchanged for a range of hard currencies at foreign exchange bureaus opposite the check-in desks. There are duty-free shops and eateries in the lounges beyond immigration.

Mumbai's Santa Cruz domestic airport has two terminals, a couple of minutes' walk apart. Terminal A handles Indian Airlines flights, while terminal B caters to Jet Airways, Sahara and Gujarat Airways. Planes start departing and arriving around dawn and stop around midnight. You're advised to check in one hour before departure.

Both terminals have foreign exchange bureaus, ticketing counters and a restaurant-bar. The 24 hour left-luggage facility is midway between the two terminals. Note that flights on domestic sectors of Air India routes depart from the international airport.

Domestic Airlines Addresses of domestic carriers that service Mumbai include:

Gujarat Airways
    (☎ 617 7063) Santa Cruz Airport

Arriving Late at Night

Most long-haul international flights to Mumbai arrive in the middle of the night. Many travellers, wary of tramping around an unfamiliar city in the early hours of the morning, either wait until dawn before heading into the city or book expensive rooms in hotels close to the airport. This is unnecessary and can be avoided by reserving a room in advance and informing the hotel of your arrival time or calling a hotel yourself from the airport. Alternatives are to ask the 24 hour Government of India tourist office or the hotel reservation counter in the airport arrivals hall to book a room for you.

Mumbai is not a dangerous city for foreign travellers and the taxi ride from the airport is a damn sight quicker at night than during morning rush hour. Virtually all hotels claim to have 24 hour reception, though in some budget places this still means you'll have to wake the security guard or bang on a few doors to gain entrance.

Indian Airlines
(☎ 202 3031) Air India Bldg, Nariman Point
Jet Airways
(☎ 838 6111) Amarchand Mansion,
Madame Cama Rd
Sahara India Airlines
(☎ 283 5671), 7 Tulsiani Chambers,
Free Press Journal Marg, Nariman Point

Domestic Flights from Mumbai There
are flights to more than 30 Indian cities, including daily flights to Bangalore (US$125
one way), Calcutta (US$205), Chennai
(US$145), Delhi (US$155), Goa (US$75 to
US$90; one hour) and Varanasi (US$210).
Travellers under 30 years old can take advantage of youth fares, which are 25%
cheaper on all airlines except Gujarati.

International Airlines Most international
airline offices are in or close to Nariman
Point (see the Getting There & Away chapter for more details on international routes).
These include:

Aeroflot
(☎ 281 0969) 9 Tulsiani Chambers, Ground
floor, Free Press Journal Marg, Nariman Point
Air Canada
(☎ 202 1111) Amarchand Mansion,
Madame Cama Rd
Air France
(☎ 202 5021) 1st floor, Maker Chambers VI,
J Bajaj Marg, Nariman Point
Air India
(☎ 282 5994) Air India Bldg, Nariman Point
Air Lanka
(☎ 282 3288) 12D Raheja Centre, Ground
floor, Free Press Journal Marg, Nariman Point
Air New Zealand
(☎ 284 2681) Podar House, 10 Marine Drive
Alitalia
(☎ 204 5023) Industrial Assurance Bldg,
Veer Nariman Rd, Churchgate
Biman Bangladesh Airlines
(☎ 282 4659) 199 J Tata Rd, Churchgate
British Airways
(☎ 282 0888) Valcan Insurance Bldg,
202B Veer Nariman Rd, Churchgate
Cathay Pacific Airways
(☎ 202 9112) Taj Mahal Hotel,
Apollo Bunder, Colaba
Delta
(☎ 288 5659) Taj Mahal Hotel, Apollo
Bunder, Colaba

Druk Air
(☎ 287 4936) Ground floor, 2 Raheja Centre,
Free Press Journal Marg, Nariman Point
Emirates
(☎ 287 1645) Ground floor, Mittal Chambers,
Nariman Point
Gulf Air
(☎ 202 1626) Ground floor, Maker
Chambers V, J Bajaj Marg, Nariman Point
Japan Airlines
(☎ 287 4936) Ground floor, 2 Raheja Centre,
Free Press Journal Marg, Nariman Point
Kenya Airways
(☎ 282 0064) 199 J Tata Rd, Churchgate
KLM
(☎ 283 3338) Khaitan Bhavan,
198 J Tata Rd, Churchgate
Kuwait Airways
(☎ 204 5351) Chateau Windsor,
86 Veer Nariman Rd, Churchgate
Lufthansa
(☎ 202 3430) Ground floor,
Express Towers, Nariman Point
Malaysian Airlines
(☎ 218 1431) GSA Stic Travels & Tours,
6 Maker Arcade, Cuffe Parade
Pakistan International Airlines
(☎ 202 1373) 4th floor, B Wing, Mittal Towers,
Free Press Journal Marg, Nariman Point
Qantas
(☎ 202 9297) 4th floor, 42 Sakhar Bhavan,
Nariman Point
Royal Nepal Airlines
(☎ 283 6197) 2nd floor, Maker Chambers V,
J Bajaj Marg, Nariman Point
SAS
(☎ 202 7083) Podar House, 10 Marine Drive
Singapore Airlines
(☎ 202 2747) Taj Mahal Hotel,
Apollo Bunder, Colaba
South African Airways
(☎ 282 3450) Podar House, 10 Marine Drive
Swissair
(☎ 287 2210) Ground floor, Maker Chambers
VI, J Bajaj Marg, Nariman Point
Thai Airways International
(☎ 215 5301) 15 World Trade Centre Arcade,
Cuffe Parade
TWA
(☎ 282 3080) Amarchand Mansion,
Madame Cama Rd
United Airlines
(☎ 204 7027) Podar House, 10 Marine Drive

Bus Numerous private operators and state
governments run long-distance buses to and
from Mumbai. Private operators provide

faster service, better comfort and simpler booking procedures.

Private long-distance buses depart for all points from Dr Anadrao Nair Rd, near Mumbai Central train station. Buses to Goa also depart roughly every 30 minutes between 2 and 6 pm (Rs 150/300 for upright/reclining seat or Rs 350/400 air-con; 15 hours) from MG Rd, just south of the Metro cinema. Some buses to South India depart from MRA Marg at the rear of Crawford Market. It's best to purchase tickets directly from agents clustered in either of these areas.

Long-distance buses run by various state governments depart from the state road transport terminal close to Mumbai Central train station. Buses service major towns in Maharashtra and neighbouring states, but are best avoided unless there's no privately run alternative. The booking office (☎ 307 4272; inquiries only) is on the 1st floor, and is open 8 am to 8 pm daily.

The MTDC reservation office on Madame Cama Rd has buses to Mahabaleshwar (Rs 180), Ganpatipule (Rs 200) and Shirdi (Rs 225 return), and takes bookings for sleepers to Aurangabad (Rs 500, 11 hours).

Train Two train systems operate out of Mumbai. Central Railways handles services

Major Trains from Mumbai

destination	train no & name	departure time[1]	distance (km)	duration	fare (Rs) (2nd/1st)[2]
Agra	2137 Punjab Mail	7.10 pm VT	1344	21 h 30 min	295/792
Ahmedabad	2009 Shatabdi[3,4]	6.25 am MC	492	7 h	570/1150
	2901 Gujarat Mail	9.50 pm MC	492	9 h	151/419
Aurangabad	1003 Devagiri Exp	9.20 pm VT	374	7 h 30 min	125/347
	7617 Tapovan Exp	6.05 am VT	374	7 h 30 min	
Bangalore	6529 Udyan Exp	7.55 am VT	1210	24 h 30 min	280/750
Calcutta	2859 Gitanjali Exp	6.00 am VT	1968	33 h 30 min	355/1006
	8001 Howrah Mail	8.15 pm VT	1968	36 h	355/1006
Delhi	2951 Rajdhani Exp[3,5]	4.55 pm MC	1384	17 h	1095/1320
	2925 Paschim Exp	11.35 am MC	1384	23 h	300/806
Goa	0111 Madgaon Exp	10.30 pm VT	588	12 h	230/744
	6635 Netravati Exp	4.40 pm K	588	10 h 30 min	230/744
	2619 Kurla-Mangalore Exp	3.15 pm K	588	11 h	230/744
Hyderabad	7001 Hussainsagar Exp	9.55 pm VT	790	15 h	213/577
Jaipur	2955 Jaipur Exp	7.05 pm MC	1200	17 h 30 min	280/750
Kochi	6635 Netravati Exp	4.40 pm K	1300	28 h	350/1000
Madras	1063 Chennai Exp	7.50 pm D	1279	24 h	288/773
Pune	2123 Deccan Queen	5.10 pm VT	191	3 h 30 min	53/258
	1007 Deccan Exp	6.35 am VT	191	4 h 30 min	53/258
Varanasi	1065 Kurla-Varanasi Exp[6]	5.20 am K	1500	26 h 30 min	311/853

[1]Abbreviations: VT – Victoria Terminus, MC – Mumbai Central, K – Kurla, D – Dadar
[2]Fares are for sleeper/air-con 3-tier sleeper on overnight journeys
[3]Air-con only; fare includes meals and drinks
[4]Daily (except Friday)
[5]Daily (except Monday)
[6]Monday, Wednesday & Thursday only

to the east and south, plus a few trains to the north. It operates from Victoria Terminus (VT), which is also known as Chhatrapati Shivaji Terminus (CST). The reservation centre at VT is open Monday to Saturday 8 am to 8 pm, and until 2 pm on Sunday. Tourist-quota tickets (which can be fully booked several weeks in advance during the high season) and Indrail passes can be bought at counter No 7 Monday to Saturday 9 am to 1 pm and 1.30 to 4 pm.

A few Central Railways trains depart from Dadar (D), half a dozen stations north of VT or Churchgate. They include the *Chennai Express*, the fastest train to Chennai. Another handful of useful expresses depart from Kurla (K), 16km north of VT on VT's suburban main line. You can book tickets for all these trains at VT.

The other train system is Western Railways, which has services to the north from Mumbai Central (MC) train station (still usually called Bombay Central). The easiest place to make bookings for Western Railways trains is at the reservation centre opposite Churchgate train station. There's a reservation centre adjacent to Mumbai Central, but it doesn't sell tourist-quota tickets.

The Churchgate reservation centre is open Monday to Saturday 8 am to 8 pm, and until 2 pm on Sunday. Tourist-quota tickets are issued only 24 hours before train departures; they're sold from a desk on the 1st floor on weekdays 9.30 am to 4.30 pm, and until 2 pm Saturday.

See the Major trains from Mumbai table for a selection of trains.

Getting Around
To/From the International Airport
There's a prepaid taxi booth at the international airport with set fares to various cities. To Colaba, the Fort and Marine Drive costs Rs 242 during the day and Rs 282 between midnight and 5 am; it's an extra Rs 5 for each bag. The journey takes about one hour at night and 1½ to two hours during the day.

Don't try to catch an auto-rickshaw from the airport to the city: they're prohibited from entering downtown Mumbai and will drop you a few kilometres down the road at Mahim Creek. Taxis loitering there will take maximum advantage of your predicament.

Bus No 13 shuttles between the international airport and VT every 20 minutes between 8 am and 8.45 pm daily. The journey takes between 1½ and two hours and costs Rs 12. Heading to the airport, you'll need to board the bus at Dr D Naoroji Rd, outside the Bombay Municipal Corporation Building. Allow plenty of time for delays and cancellations.

An alternative is to catch an auto-rickshaw (around Rs 25) to Andheri train station and catch a suburban train (Rs 5, 45 minutes) to Churchgate or VT. It's unlikely that you'll be up for this after a long-haul flight; don't attempt it during rush hours or if weighed down with luggage.

Minibuses outside the arrival hall offer free shuttle services to the airport and Juhu hotels. There's also a free Air India shuttle service between the international and domestic airports.

A taxi from the city centre to the international airport costs around Rs 200 on the meter, plus extra for baggage; taxi drivers in Colaba always ask for Rs 300. Be prepared to pay about 30% more between midnight and 5 am.

To/From the Domestic Airport
Taxis and auto-rickshaws queue up outside both domestic terminals. There's no prepaid taxi counter so make sure that drivers use the meter. A taxi takes between one and 1½ hours to reach the city centre and costs around Rs 180, plus extra for baggage. Auto-rickshaws are not allowed into the city centre (see the previous section)

If you don't have too much luggage, bus No 2 stops on nearby Nehru Rd, opposite the junction to Nanda Patkar Rd, and terminates at the Prince of Wales Museum (Rs 9.50). It stops on the highway opposite the airport when heading out of the city.

Another alternative is to catch an auto-rickshaw between the airport and Vile Parle train station (Rs 10), and catch a suburban train between Vile Parle and Churchgate or

VT (Rs 5, 45 minutes). Don't attempt this during rush hour. Note that Santa Cruz train station is not the closest station to Santa Cruz airport.

Most airport and Juhu hotels offer free airport pick-up. Airport hotels are within easy walking distance if you're not weighed down by luggage; to reach Juhu independently, catch an auto-rickshaw (around Rs 25).

Bus Despite popular myth Mumbai's red single and double-decker buses are one of the best ways to travel short distances in the city, though it *is* best to avoid them during rush hours. Fares around South Mumbai cost less than Rs 5 so make sure you have some small change available; pay the conductor once you're aboard.

Route numbers and destinations on the front of buses are written in Marathi and English signs are on the side. Position yourself at the bus stop so you can read the English signs as the bus pulls to a stop. Some destinations and bus numbers are as follows (all these buses depart from Colaba Causeway and pass Flora Fountain):

destination	bus no
Breach Candy	132
Churchgate	132
Chowpatty	103, 106, 107, 123
Haji Ali	83, 124, 132
Hanging Gardens	106
Mani Bhavan	123
Metro Cinema	103, 124
Mohammed Ali Rd	1, 3, 21,
Mumbai Central Station	124
Mumbai Zoo	3
VT & Crawford Market	1, 3, 21, 103, 124
Walkeshwar	103, 106, 107

Note that bus stops can have up to three stands for various buses operating along the route; some stands list the buses that stop there, others don't. Colaba-bound buses may have signs reading 'Colaba Bus Station', 'Church' or 'Navy Nagar'; they all rumble down Colaba Causeway.

Train Mumbai has an efficient but overcrowded suburban train network, and it's virtually the only place in India where it's worth taking trains for intracity travel.

There are only three main lines, making it easy to navigate. The most useful operates from Churchgate heading north to stations like Charni Rd (for Chowpatty Beach), Mumbai Central, Mahalaxmi (Dhobi Ghats), Vile Parle (Santa Cruz airport), Andheri (Sahar International) and Borivali (Sanjay Gandhi National Park). A couple of other suburban lines operate from VT. Trains begin operating just after 4 am and run until almost 1 am. From Churchgate, 2nd/1st class fares cost Rs 3/30 to Mumbai Central, Rs 5/53 to Santa Cruz airport and Rs 8/82 to Borivali.

Travellers should avoid rush hours when trains are jam-packed. Women should take advantage of the ladies-only carriages. Trains stop at suburban train stations for about 10 seconds so don't hang around. Take the usual precautions with valuables.

Taxi & Auto-Rickshaw Mumbai has a huge fleet of metered black-and-yellow taxis and they're the most convenient way to get around the city; auto-rickshaws are confined to the suburbs north of Mahim Creek.

Taxi meters are out of date, so the fare is calculated using a conversion chart which all drivers carry – ask to see it at the end of the journey. The rough conversion rate during the day is around 11 times the meter reading. The minimum fare is Rs 11 for the first 1.6km and Rs 6.50 per kilometre after this. It's about 25% more expensive between midnight and 6 am.

Cool Cabs (☎ 613 1111) operates correctly-metered, blue, air-con taxis. They're about 33% more expensive than regular cabs and can be booked by telephone.

If you're north of Mahim Creek and not heading into the city, it's best to catch auto-rickshaws. They're metered but also use a conversion chart. The fare is roughly 7.5 times the meter reading. The minimum fare is Rs 7.50 for the first kilometre and Rs 3.80 per kilometre after this.

Car Cars are generally hired for an eight hour day and with a maximum of 80km; additional charges rack up if you exceed these limits.

Mumbai Safari (☎ 282 0139) at the Apollo Bunder ticket booths near the Gateway of India, can arrange a non air-con Maruti with driver for Rs 600. With some heavy negotiating, regular taxi drivers accept a similar price; Cool Cabs (☎ 613 1111) charges Rs 975.

The Hertz-affiliated Autoriders International (☎ 492 1838), 139 Autoworld, Tardeo Rd, Tardeo, offers self-drive air-con Marutis for Rs 850 per day or Rs 1650 with driver.

Motorcycle Allibhai Premji Tyrewallah (☎ 309 9313, email premjis@bom3.vsnl .net.in) at 205 Lamington Rd, Opera House, is the place to rent or purchase a motorcycle. Hire costs between Rs 1500 and Rs 2000 per week, depending on the model. It's possible to buy a bike and pre-arrange to sell it back to the store after a specific period. The buy-back price after three months on a second-hand Enfield is around Rs 18,000 less than the original price. Note that Mumbai is no place to learn how to ride a motorcycle.

Boat Ferries shuttle between the Gateway of India and Elephanta Island (see the Around Mumbai section), and between the Gateway and Mandwa on the mainland. The latter is useful to access Chaul and Murud-Janjira (see the Maharashtra chapter) by bus.

AROUND MUMBAI
Elephanta Island

The rock-cut temples on Elephanta Island, 9km north-east of the Gateway of India, are Mumbai's major tourist attraction. Little is known about their origins, but they are thought to have been created between 450 and 750 AD, when the island was known as Gharapuri (Place of Caves). The Portuguese renamed it Elephanta because of a large stone elephant near the shore. This statue collapsed in 1814 and the British moved and reassembled the remaining pieces at the Vic-

toria Gardens, where it stands today. Unfortunately, the Portuguese did considerable damage to the sculptures, but their size, beauty and power remain impressive.

There is one main cave with a number of large sculptured panels, all relating to Shiva. The most famous of the panels is the Trimurti, or triple-headed Shiva, where the god is depicted as destroyer, preserver and creator. The central bust of Shiva, its eyes closed in eternal contemplation, may be the most serene sight you witness in India.

There are also figures of Shiva dancing the Tandava, the marriage of Shiva and Parvati, Ravana shaking Kailasa, a scary carving of Shiva killing the demon Andhaka, and one in which Shiva appears as Ardhanari, uniting both sexes in one body.

The caves are open daily except Monday 9 am to 5.30 pm. It costs Rs 5 to enter; a video camera permit costs Rs 25. It's worth making use of the free English-language guide service offered to travellers with deluxe launch tickets. Tours depart every hour on the half hour from the ticket booth. If you prefer to explore independently, pick up Pramod Chandra's *A Guide to the Elephanta Caves* (Rs 40) from the stalls lining the stairway. The best time to visit Elephanta is during the week; weekends are not conducive to calm contemplation of the temple. The MTDC holds the **Elephanta Festival**, an annual celebration of classical music and dance, in front of the cave temple here.

The tree-top terrace of the MTDC's *Chalukya Restaurant & Beer Bar (☎ 284 8323),* at the top of the stairway, is a fine spot to sit back and take in the expansive views of Mumbai Harbour.

The state government has been criticised for its failure to maintain both the monument and the island's environment. Travellers can help initiatives to improve this sorry state of affairs by carrying rubbish they generate with them back on the boat to Mumbai.

Getting There & Away Launches head to Elephanta Island from the Gateway of India. Small economy boats cost Rs 50 return and

MUMBAI

more spacious deluxe launches, Rs 70 return. Tickets are sold by touts at the Gateway and booths nearby. Economy boats leave from the wharf near the ticket booths; deluxe launches moor next to the Gateway.

Boats depart every half hour from around 9 am to 2.30 pm between Tuesday and Sunday. The voyage takes go for an hour and, though not particularly picturesque, does give an indication of the size of Mumbai Harbour.

The caves are at the top of a gentle stairway, which begins almost immediately where the ferry wharf hits dry land. It's lined with handicraft stalls and patrolled by pesky monkeys. Palanquins are available for those who need to be carried.

If you have a deluxe ticket, you can return on any boat; if you have an economy ticket, you can return on any economy boat. The last boat leaves Elephanta around 5.30 pm. During the monsoon, economy boats are suspended. For inquiries phone ☎ 202 6364.

Sanjay Gandhi National Park

This 104 sq km protected area of forested hills on the city's northern fringe, formerly called the Borivali National Park, has interesting flora, birdlife and butterflies, and boasts a small population of tigers. It's a fantastic asset to have within the city limits but it's under serious threat from urban encroachment. The Bombay Natural History Society runs a **Conservation Education Centre** (☎ 842 1174) close to the park's southern entrance. The park is open daily and entry costs Rs 2. The best time to see birds is October to April; the best time to see butterflies is August to November.

The park contains the 109 **Kanheri Caves**, which line the side of a rocky ravine 5km from the northern park entrance. They were used by Buddhist monks between the 2nd and 9th centuries as *viharas* (monasteries) and *chaityas* (temples). The most impressive is cave 3, the Great Chaitya cave, which is flanked by two huge Buddhas and has a long colonnade of decorated pillars and a 5m high *dagoba* at the back. Several interesting caves are nearby but most others

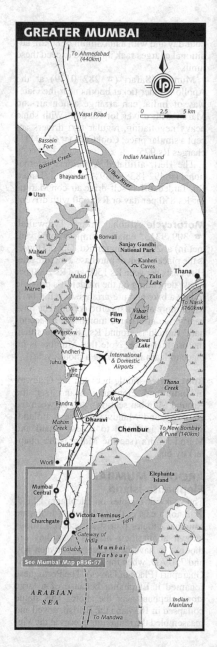

GREATER MUMBAI

are little more than cells carved into the rock. The caves are open 9.30 am to 5.30 pm daily; entry costs Rs 2.

There's a **Lion Safari** and **Tiger Safari** 1km inside the northern entrance. Trips in enclosed vehicles run every 20 minutes from 9 am to 1 pm and 2.20 to 5.20 pm from Tuesday to Sunday; entry to each costs Rs 15.

Getting There & Away Take the train from Churchgate to Borivali train station (Rs 8, one hour). From the station, you can either walk (10 minutes), take an auto-rickshaw or catch bus No 188 to the park entrance. It's a further 10-minute walk from the entrance to the safari parks.

Auto-rickshaws are not allowed into the park, so to reach Kanheri Caves you'll need to catch bus No 188, either from Borivali train station or from just inside the park entrance (Rs 5). Expect a long queue at the caves for the bus back to Borivali on weekends. The safaris and the caves can also be visited on the MTDC's suburban tour. See the Organised Tours section earlier in this chapter.

Bassein Fort

The atmospheric remains of the Portuguese fortified city of Bassein are on the northern side of Bassein Creek, the river which separates Greater Mumbai from the Indian mainland. After securing the area in 1534, the Portuguese built a city of such pomp and splendour that it came to be known as the Court of the North. In 1739 the Marathas besieged the city and the Portuguese surrendered after appalling losses. The city walls are still standing and you can explore the ruins of the Cathedral of St Joseph.

To reach Bassein catch a train from Churchgate to Vasai Road (Rs 11, 75 minutes) and then an auto-rickshaw (Rs 8 per person) for the 20 minute trip to the fort.

Maharashtra

Maharashtra is a large, populous and economically important state. From Mumbai most travellers head south to the beaches of Goa, south-east to Pune and its famous ashram, or north-east to the World Heritage-listed cave temples of Ajanta and Ellora.

The Western Ghats run parallel with the coast; the rest of the state stands on the high Deccan plateau, stretching some 800km east.

History

Mughal power dominated much of central and southern India in the 16th century until the Deccan became the epicentre of the Maratha empire in the 17th century. With a relatively small army, Shivaji established a base at Pune and later Raigad. From the early 18th century the Maratha empire was controlled by the Peshwas who retained power until they upset the British in 1817.

Maharashtra also has strong links with Gandhi and India's Independence. Gandhi was interned by the British in Pune for two years after the Quit India declaration, and his ashram is at Sevagram in the state's far east. After Independence, western Maharashtra and Gujarat were joined to form Bombay state. Today's state, with Mumbai as capital, was formed in 1960 when the Marathi and Gujarati-speaking areas were again separated.

The state's politics are dominated by the right-wing Shiv Sena, though its popularity is waning. In 1996 Sena partnered the BJP in the 'saffron alliance' – an uneasy state government coalition.

Southern Maharashtra

THE KONKAN COAST

Maharashtra's Konkan Coast – the narrow strip between the Western Ghats and Arabian Sea – is a region of deserted beaches, abandoned forts and isolated fishing communities. It is well known for its fresh produce, especially pomfret (a fish), avocados and delicious Alphonso mangoes.

The opening of the Konkan Railway in 1998 theoretically made the area more

Maharashtra at a Glance

Population: 78.9 million
Area: 307,690 sq km
Capital: Mumbai
Main Language: Marathi
Best Time to Go: September to April (coast); September to mid-June (hills)

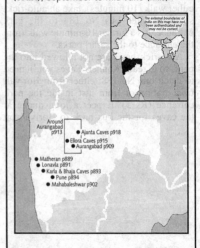

The external boundaries of India on this map have not been authenticated and may not be correct

Around Aurangabad p913
● Ajanta Caves p918
● Ellora Caves p915
● Aurangabad p909
● Matheran p889
● Lonavla p891
● Karla & Bhaja Caves p893
● Pune p894
● Mahabaleshwar p902

- **Matheran** – take the toy-train ride up to the hill station

- **Ellora** – the hand-carved extravagance of the Kailasa Temple

- **Sevagram Ashram** – meditating under Gandhi's pipal tree

- **Mahabaleshwar** – dining on berries and cream

Festivals of Maharashtra

festival	location	date	features
Paithan Fair	Paithan	Mar/Apr	10-day celebration for St Eknath Matharaj
Naag Panchami (snake festival)	Kolhapur, Pune	Aug	snake worship
Ganesh Chaturthi/ Pune Festival	Pune	Aug/Sep	dance, music, cart races & wrestling
Ellora Festival	Kailasa Temple, Ellora	Dec	classical dance & music
Kumbh Mela	Trimbakeshwar Temple, Nasik	every 12 years (next 2003)	Hindu pilgrimage

accessible to visitors but so far it has meant most travellers make a quicker dash for Goa.

Chaul

This Portuguese trading settlement on the north shore of the Roha River estuary was once second in importance only to Bassein. The Portuguese came here in 1522, building a fortified city with numerous churches, factories and a governor's house, but eventually relinquished it to the Marathas. The easiest way to reach Chaul is to catch a ferry from Mumbai's Gateway of India to Mandwa (Rs 40 to Rs 80, one hour); the ferry ticket includes a free bus ride to nearby Alibag. Buses shuttle between Alibag and Chaul (Rs 5, 30 minutes) roughly every half hour.

Murud-Janjira & Kashid

Just off the coast 160km south of Mumbai is the majestic island fortress of Janjira, the 16th century capital of the Siddis of Janjira, descendants of sailor-traders from the Horn of Africa. It is one of Maharashtra's most commanding coastal forts, stretched along an island a short distance off the tranquil fishing town of Murud and only accessible by local boat (20 minutes).

The fort's 12m high walls made it impregnable to everyone, even the Marathas – Shivaji tried to conquer it by sea and his son, Sambhaji, even attempted to tunnel to it!

The *MTDC Holiday Resort* (☎ 021447-4078) offers basic accommodation on the beach at Murud, 5km north of the fort. There's a variety of rooms available from Rs 400 to Rs 600 a double. Cottages sleeping four are Rs 1200.

About 20km north is the resort of Kashid, which boasts a clean 3km sweep of beach with good swimming.

Buses from Mumbai Central take around four hours to Kashid and a further hour to Murud. There are also two express Asiad buses daily (3½ hours to Murud). The nearest railhead on the Konkan Railway is Indapur.

Ganpatipule

Ganpatipule, on the coast 375km south of Mumbai, has another of Maharashtra's pristine beaches, but is better known for its **Swayambhu Ganpati** or 'naturally formed' monolithic Ganesh, which attracts thousands of pilgrims from all over India.

Another 19km south is **Ratnagiri**, the largest town on the state's south coast and the main transport hub. It was the birthplace of freedom fighter Lokmanya Tilak and the place where the British interned the last Burmese king, Thibaw, from 1886 until his death in 1916.

Places to Stay The MTDC Holiday Resort (☎ 02357-35248), on the beach at Ganpatipule, has a range of pricey rooms from Rs 400/800 for doubles with/without aircon up to Rs 1800 for the air-con 'sea view

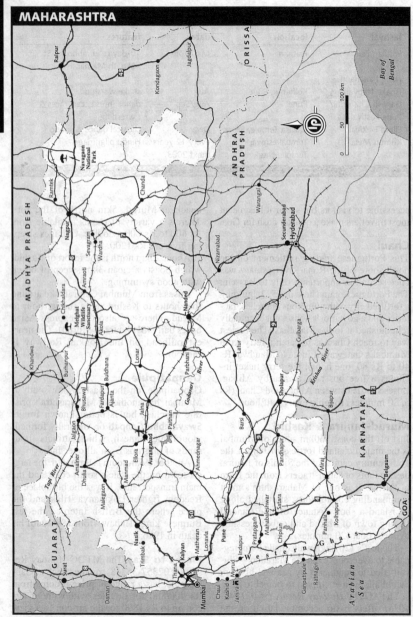

Maharashtran Cave Architecture

Maharashtra's famous rock-cut caves have several distinct design elements. The Buddhist caves, which are generally the older ones, are either *chaityas* (temples) or *viharas* (monasteries). Chaityas are usually deep and narrow with a *stupa* (Buddhist monument containing relics) at the end of the cave. There may be a row of columns down both sides of the cave and around the stupa.

The viharas are usually not as deep and narrow as the chaityas. Viharas were normally intended to be living quarters for the monks and usually have rows of cells along both sides. In the back there is often a small shrine containing an image of the Buddha. At Ajanta, the cliff face into which the caves are cut is very steep and there is often a small verandah or entrance porch in front of the main cave. At Ellora, the rock face is more sloping and the verandah or porch element generally becomes a separate courtyard.

Cave architecture reached the peak of its complexity and design in the Hindu temples at Ellora, and particularly in the magnificent Kailasa Temple. These can hardly be called 'caves', for each temple is open to the sky. In design they are much like other temples of that era – except that instead of being built up from the bottom they were cut from the living rock from the top down.

---

cottages'. It also has a Tent Resort (☎ 2357-35348) with two/four-bed tents at Rs 250/350. All rates are 30% less in the low season.

Getting There & Away The MTDC has an overnight bus direct from Mumbai to Ganpatipule departing at 8.30 pm from its office in Nariman point. It's not the height of luxury for Rs 200 (one way) but none of the private bus companies run on this route. The bus returns from Ganpatipule at 7.30 pm.

The Konkan Railway is the best way to reach Ratnagiri, though the only express currently departing from Mumbai Chhatrapati Shivaaji Terminus (CST) is the *Madgaon Express* at 10.30 pm (Rs 118/410 in sleeper/1st class, seven hours). From Goa, there are at least five express trains from Margao to Ratnagiri daily (Rs 90/298, four hours); local buses run from Ratnagiri station to Ganpatipule.

MATHERAN
☎ 02148 • pop 5500

Matheran, which means jungle topped, is the nearest hill station to Mumbai. It's an undulating hilltop (800m) cloaked in shady trees and ringed by walking tracks leading to lookouts that drop sheer to the plains. On a clear day the views are fantastic and it's possible to see (and supposedly even hear) Mumbai from Hart point.

Hugh Malet, climbing the path known as Shivaji's Ladder, is credited with the 'discovery' of Matheran in 1850 and it soon became a popular hill station during the days of the Raj.

Matheran owes its tranquillity to a complete ban on motor vehicles (and bicycles), but on the weekends the town is overrun by day-trippers and the pleasant trails are clogged with people.

In theory the high seasons in Matheran run from November to February and April to June, but accommodation is packed out (and overpriced) usually only in the peak holiday periods of April/May, Diwali and Christmas. During the monsoon (mid-June to early-October) the village virtually closes up and the dirt walking trails and roads become very muddy.

Getting to Matheran is half the fun; from Neral Junction you take a narrow-gauge toy train up the 21km route to the heart of the hill station. It's a very scenic two hour

The Konkan Railway

The British may have scratched a spider web of railway lines across the surface of India but they left one blank space: the Konkan Coast from Bombay to Goa and on through Karnataka to Mangalore. Hills, ravines, rivers, flood plains and swamps made railway construction an intimidating prospect and as a result connections down the coast have always been slow-going and hard work.

But the Rs 25 billion Konkan Railway project – the biggest railway construction in South Asia this century – has bridged this important gap. The 760km railway, officially opened in December 1996 but not completed until January 1998, is the fastest railway line in India, capable of handling trains travelling at up to 160km an hour! Rail travel time between Mumbai and Goa (Margao) has been cut from 20 hours to 12. The trip from Goa to Mangalore takes around four hours, but as of the end of 1998 there were still no direct expresses connecting Mumbai and Mangalore.

The Konkan Railway is a formidable engineering undertaking, crossing 140 major rivers with 2137 bridges and using 83km of tunnels. The 2km Kundakika Bridge over the Saravati River is the longest on the route. The highest viaduct (64m) is at Panvel in Maharashtra and the Karbude tunnel is the longest, at 6.5km. Communications along the line are handled by state-of-the-art fibre optic cabling.

ascent as the train winds its way around the steep slopes and, at one point, passes through 'one kiss tunnel', much to the delight of any schoolchildren who might be on board. See Getting There & Away for more information about this trip.

Information

Entry to Matheran costs Rs 7 (Rs 4 for children), which you pay on arrival at the train station or at the Dasturi car park.

There are a couple of tourist information kiosks along Mahatma Gandhi (MG) Rd, the main road through town, where you can pick up a basic map of Matheran but not much else. The Union Bank of India, also on MG Rd, changes travellers cheques. Few of the paths around town are lit at night – a torch may come in handy.

Walks & Views

Louisa point (Sunset View), Panorama point and Little Chouk point have the finest views. You can reach the valley below One Tree Hill down the path known as **Shivaji's Ladder**, so called because the Maratha leader is said to have used it.

Places to Stay

There are a few budget places close to the train station but most of the mid-range and expensive 'resort' accommodation is a 10 to 20 minute walk away. Many of these resort hotels offer only full-board rates, especially in the high season. As with most hill stations, the checkout time can be as early as 7 am. Unless otherwise stated, rates quoted here are outside high season (Christmas, Diwali etc). If you're mad enough to come then, expect to pay between 30% and 200% more.

Places to Stay – Budget

Hotel Prasanna (☎ 30258) is directly opposite the train station. It has plain but clean rooms with attached bath for Rs 200/500 in the low/high season; hot water is available in the morning.

Hanjar House (☎ 30536), on the same side as the station, is a new family-run place with spotless doubles with attached bath for Rs 200.

Janata Happy Home (☎ 30229, *Kasturba Rd*), is a popular place with 24 hour hot water and 9 am checkout. Singles/doubles are Rs 300/600 including all meals.

Hope Hall Hotel (☎ 30193), a rambling, welcoming lodge on MG Rd, has large clean doubles set on a pleasant garden for Rs 200.

Khan's Hotel (☎ 30240), a slightly run-down place with a long list of rules and regulations, has a tiny single with running water (but no bathroom as such) for Rs 100, and doubles with attached bath for Rs 200. There's a veg and non-veg restaurant here, as well as 'Chinese Corner'.

MTDC Tourist Camp (☎ 30277) is next to the Dasturi car park, 2.5km north-east of

town. Dorm beds are Rs 60 and doubles range from Rs 400 to Rs 650. There's a restaurant, and beer is available.

Places to Stay – Mid-Range & Top End

Royal Hotel Matheran (☎ 30247) is a garishly coloured two-star 'resort' popular with Indian families. Rates are Rs 320 per person (full board) in the low season, and Rs 1100 or Rs 1600 with air-con in high season. There's a bar, a children's park and a veg restaurant.

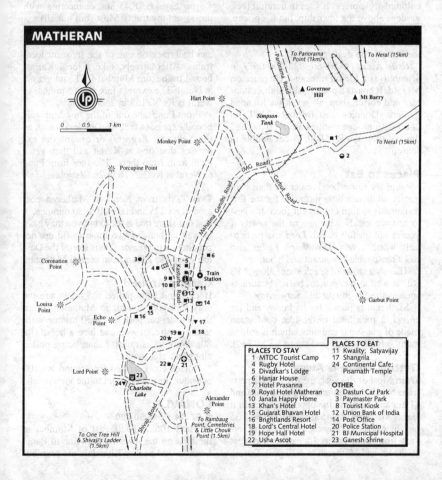

MATHERAN

To Panorama Point (1km)

To Neral (15km)

Hart Point

Governor Hill

Mt Barry

Simpson Tank

Monkey Point

To Neral (15km)

Porcupine Point

(MG Road)

Garbut Road

0   0.5   1 km

Mahatma Gandhi Road

Coronation Point

3

4

Kasturba Road

6

Train Station

Garbut Point

5

7

8

9

11

10

12

Louisa Point

13

14

Echo Point

15

16

17

18

Lord Point

19

20

21

22

24

23

Charlotte Lake

Alexander Point

To Rambaug Point, Cemeteries & Little Chouk Point (1.5km)

Shivaji Road

To One Tree Hill & Shivaji's Ladder (1.5km)

PLACES TO STAY
1 MTDC Tourist Camp
4 Rugby Hotel
5 Divadkar's Lodge
6 Hanjar House
7 Hotel Prasanna
9 Royal Hotel Matheran
10 Janata Happy Home
13 Khan's Hotel
15 Gujarat Bhavan Hotel
16 Brightlands Resort
18 Lord's Central Hotel
19 Hope Hall Hotel
22 Usha Ascot

PLACES TO EAT
11 Kwality; Satyavijay
17 Shangrila
24 Continental Cafe;
    Pisarnath Temple

OTHER
2 Dasturi Car Park
3 Paymaster Park
8 Tourist Kiosk
12 Union Bank of India
14 Post Office
20 Police Station
21 BJ Municipal Hospital
23 Ganesh Shrine

MAHARASHTRA

Lord's Central Hotel (☎ 30228, 022-386 7776 in Mumbai), presided over by the genial Mr Lord, is one of the most charming places to stay in Matheran. High season rates, including full board, are Rs 850 per person in the regular rooms, or Rs 1100 to Rs 1400 in the 'valley view' rooms. The low season discount is 20%. There's a bar and a dining room renowned for its generously served, delicious home-cooked meals.

Rugby Hotel (☎ 30291, 022-282 1721 in Mumbai, Vithal Rao Kotwal Rd), is another colonial-style place. It's set in tranquil rock gardens above the township, but it's pricey. Bungalow-style doubles range from Rs 2400 to Rs 3100 in the low season, though there are some deals available.

Usha Ascot (☎ 30360, 022-200 0671 in Mumbai) is a Mediterranean-style place on MG Rd. It boasts a pool, health club, restaurant and coffee shop, all set in well-tended gardens. Doubles start from Rs 2200 (Rs 2800 with air-con), suites are Rs 5200 and duplex villas are Rs 5800. Prices double in season.

Places to Eat

Most of the resort hotels cater for their own guests, so there's little incentive for the few restaurants to turn out decent food. It's best to arrange meals with one of the hotels if you're not on full board. *Lord's* is particularly worth a visit. *Divadkar's Lodge* also has a reasonable restaurant and a bar.

There's a string of snack shops along MG Rd, as well as a couple of basic restaurants such as the *Shangrila* and *Satyavijay*.

Matheran is famed for its honey and for *chikki*, a rock-hard toffee-like confection made of gur sugar and nuts which is sold at many 'chikki marts' and shops on MG Rd.

Getting There & Away

Train Most of the year, the toy train departs from Neral Junction train station at 8.40 and 11 am and 5 pm; in the opposite direction it leaves Matheran at 5.45 am and 1.10 and 2.35 pm. In April and May there's one extra service from both points (departing Neral at 10.20 am and Matheran at 4.10 pm). During the monsoon there is only one train per day – it departs Neral at 8.40 am and Matheran at 1.10 pm. The fares are Rs 24/145 in 2nd/1st class. The toy train can only be booked in advance from Mumbai or Pune which is a good idea in the high season (no reservations are accepted at Neral or Matheran but tickets go on sale 45 minutes before departure).

From Mumbai CST, only a few of the Pune expresses stop at Neral Junction, including the *Deccan Express* (6.40 am, connecting with the 8.40 am toy train) and the *Koyna Express* (8.45 am, connecting with the 11 am toy train). Most (but not all) expresses from Mumbai stop at Karjat further down the line from Neral, from where you can backtrack on one of the frequent local trains. Alternatively, take a local Karjat-bound train from Mumbai CST and get off at Neral. The express fare from Mumbai to Neral is Rs 30/159 in 2nd/1st class.

From Pune take one of the few Mumbai-bound expresses that stop at Neral (such as the *Sahyadri Express*) or one of the expresses that stop at Karjat and then get a local train from there. The fare from Pune to Neral is Rs 23/176 in 2nd/1st class.

Taxi Taxis from Neral to Matheran cost around Rs 225 and take 20 to 30 minutes. A seat in a share taxi is Rs 45 but you may have to wait an hour or two for it to fill up, depending on the season. Taxis stop at the Dasturi car park, 2.5km from central Matheran.

Getting Around

Horses and hand-pulled rickshaws are the only transport options in Matheran. From the Dasturi car park, it's a 30 minute walk to the centre, or you can hire a horse (Rs 80). Walking is quicker than being pulled along in a rickshaw.

Horses can be hired for around Rs 100 per hour for trots around to the viewpoints.

LONAVLA

☎ 02114 • pop 50,000

Situated 106km south-east of Mumbai in the hills on the main railway line to Pune, Lonavla and nearby Khandala are twin hill resorts catering for weekenders and conference groups from Mumbai. There is little of interest in the towns themselves – for most travellers Lonavla is simply the most convenient base from which to visit the Karla and Bhaja caves.

The MTDC (☎ 82230) organises rock climbing at the Duke's Nose and other locations in the Karla hills.

Orientation & Information

Most of the places of interest to travellers – hotels, restaurants and the main road to the caves – are north of the train station (exit from platform one), but most of Lonavla town, including the market, is south of the station.

It's best to change money at Mumbai or Pune – the Canara Bank in Lonavla will only change money for guests staying at the Kaivalyadhama ashram.

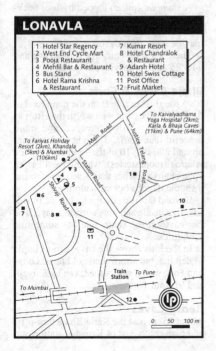

LONAVLA

1 Hotel Star Regency
2 West End Cycle Mart
3 Pooja Restaurant
4 Mehfil Bar & Restaurant
5 Bus Stand
6 Hotel Rama Krishna & Restaurant
7 Kumar Resort
8 Hotel Chandralok & Restaurant
9 Adarsh Hotel
10 Hotel Swiss Cottage
11 Post Office
12 Fruit Market

To Kaivalyadhama Yoga Hospital (2km); Karla & Bhaja Caves (11km) & Pune (64km)

To Fariyas Holiday Resort (2km), Khandala (5km) & Mumbai (106km)

To Mumbai

Train Station To Pune

0   50   100 m

Kaivalyadhama Yoga Hospital

About 2km from Lonavla on the road to the Karla and Bhaja caves, this ashram has long been popular with Indians seeking yogic healing but is attracting an increasing number of westerners. It was founded in 1924 by Swami Kuvalayanandji and combines yoga courses with a yoga research centre and a training college. Even if you don't want to stay here, it's worth asking if you can have a look around the interesting 'scientific research department'.

The ashram is open to people who just want to learn yoga (rather than be cured by it). The minimum course is eight days and the all-inclusive cost is US$10/15 per day in a single with common/attached bath or US$12/20 in a double. Indians pay a little less. Bookings are advised (☎ 73039, fax 71983).

Places to Stay

Hotel Chandralok (☎ 72921) is a clean, friendly place not far from the station. Singles/doubles start from Rs 275/375; air-con doubles are Rs 700 (all year). All rooms have attached hot bath.

Adarsh Hotel (☎ 72353), across the road, is another reasonable choice, though it backs onto the bus stand so avoid the rooms on that side. On weekdays, doubles start from Rs 275 (Rs 550 with TV); air-con suites are Rs 800. Rates increase 20% on weekends.

Hotel Swiss Cottage (☎ 71320) is tucked away on quiet Wadekar Bungalow Rd, a short walk from the station. It's a big, old place with singles/doubles for Rs 250/500 or Rs 400/700 with air-con. There's a 30% low-season discount.

Hotel Star Regency (☎ 73331, 022-618 3708 in Mumbai) is on Justice Telang Rd, a quiet, leafy lane. Doubles go from Rs 810 to Rs 1440 and suites for Rs 1800. There's a two night package for Rs 3150 a double including breakfast, dinner and taxes. Low season is 15% less.

Kumar Resort (☎ 73091, 022-604 5669 in Mumbai) has a range of large, air-con rooms from Rs 1190 to Rs 2490, plus a wave pool and a bar.

Fariyas Holiday Resort (☎ *022-73852, 265 5317 in Mumbai*) offers five-star luxury on a quiet hill on the western outskirts of town. It has an indoor swimming pool, health club, two restaurants and extensive gardens. Rooms are Rs 3400.

Places to Eat
The best places to eat are at the hotel restaurants. The *Hotel Rama Krishna* and the *Kumar Resort*, on the main Mumbai-Pune road, have excellent open-air restaurants. Check out the *Chandralok* for its superb bottomless Gujarati thali (Rs 60).

Mehfil Bar & Restaurant is a clean air-con place with an extensive menu of Indian and Chinese dishes. Mains are around Rs 80.

Pooja Restaurant is cheaper, with Rs 20 thalis and a range of north and south Indian food.

There's an excellent *fruit market* in the bazaar, south of the train station and Lonavla is famous for chikki – every second shop is a chikki mart.

Getting There & Away
Most of the MSRTC buses are pretty rough and, as they take up to four hours to get to Mumbai, you're better off using the trains. There are frequent buses to Pune (Rs 36, two hours).

All express trains from Mumbai to Pune stop at Lonavla. The trip to Mumbai (three hours, 128km) costs Rs 39/196 in 2nd/1st class. To Pune (64km) there are express trains (one hour, Rs 26/129) and hourly shuttle trains (two hours).

Getting Around
See the following section for details on getting to/from the caves. Regular buses shuttle between Lonavla and Khandala (Rs 2). Bicycles can be hired from West End Cycle Mart, on the main road, for Rs 4 an hour.

KARLA & BHAJA CAVES
Dating from around the 2nd century BC, the rock-cut caves in the hills near Lonavla are among the oldest and finest examples of Hinayana Buddhist rock temple art in India.

It's possible to visit the caves in a day trip from either Mumbai or Pune if you hire an auto-rickshaw from Lonavla for the day.

Karla Cave
A steep 20 minute climb from the car park brings you to the Karla cave, the largest Hinayana Buddhist *chaitya* (temple) in India. Completed in 80 BC, the chaitya is around 40m long and 15m high, carved by monks and artisans from the rock in imitation of more familiar wooden architecture.

A semicircular 'sun window' filters light in towards the cave's representation of Buddha – a *dagoba*, or stupa, protected by a carved wooden umbrella. The 37 pillars which form the aisles are each topped by kneeling elephants carrying seated figures. The roof of the cave is ribbed with teak beams said to be original. On the sides of the vestibule are carved elephant heads which once had ivory tusks.

A *stambha* (pillar) topped by four back-to-back lions, an image usually associated with Ashoka, stands outside the cave and may be older than the cave itself.

There's a Rs 2 entry fee to the cave and a Rs 25 charge for video cameras.

Bhaja Caves & Forts
It's a rough 3km ride from the main road to the Bhaja caves, but well worth the effort as the setting is lusher, greener, and more peaceful than Karla. Thought to date from around 200 BC, 10 of the 18 caves here are *viharas* (monasteries), while cave 12 is an open chaitya, earlier than Karla, containing a simple dagoba but no sculpture.

Beyond this is a strange huddle of 14 stupas, five inside and nine outside a cave. The last cave on the south side has some fine sculptures.

In the hills above the caves are a couple of derelict, but atmospheric old forts; **Lohagad Fort**, which was twice taken by Shivaji, and **Visapur Fort**.

Bedsa Caves
About 15km past the Karla/Bhaja turn-offs, and 6km south-east of Kamshet station, are

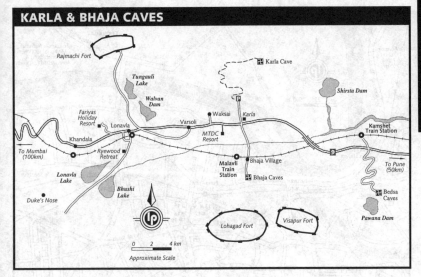

KARLA & BHAJA CAVES

the Bedsa caves. These caves see very few visitors, partly because of the 3km walk from Bedsa village to reach them and partly because the main cave – a chaitya thought to be later than Karla – is much poorer in design and execution.

Places to Stay & Eat
The *MTDC Resort (☎ 82230)* is just off the Mumbai-Pune road near the turn-off to the caves and has doubles for Rs 300 and Rs 400, plus suites and cottages for Rs 650 to Rs 1400, some with air-con. Low-season prices are about 20% less. There's a bar and a good restaurant.

Getting There & Away
Local buses are scheduled to run about a dozen times a day between Lonavla and Karla (Rs 5, 12km) but may be less frequent.

With a bit of walking you can get around comfortably in a day for about Rs 20. First, catch the 8 or 9 am bus from Lonavla to Karla cave, walk to Bhaja (1½ hours, 5km), then walk back to Malavli station (one hour, 3km) and catch a local train back to Lon-

avla. You can cut out the long walk by taking an auto-rickshaw from Karla to Bhaja for around Rs 60.

Auto-rickshaws are plentiful and the price usually includes waiting time at the sites. A return trip from Lonavla to the Karla and Bhaja caves will cost around Rs 300, a little more if you include Bedsa.

PUNE
☎ 0212 • pop 2.8 million
Shivaji, the great Maratha leader, was raised in Pune, which was granted to his grandfather in 1599. Later it became the seat of power for the Brahmin Peshwa family until 1817 when it fell to the British and became their alternative capital during the monsoon. Pune (pronounced and often spelt 'Poona') has a rather more pleasant climate than muggy Mumbai.

With fast (but full) express commuter trains connecting Pune to Mumbai in less than four hours, many people who can't afford the sky-high prices of accommodation in Mumbai commute daily between the two cities. As a result, the big-city influence has

MAHARASHTRA

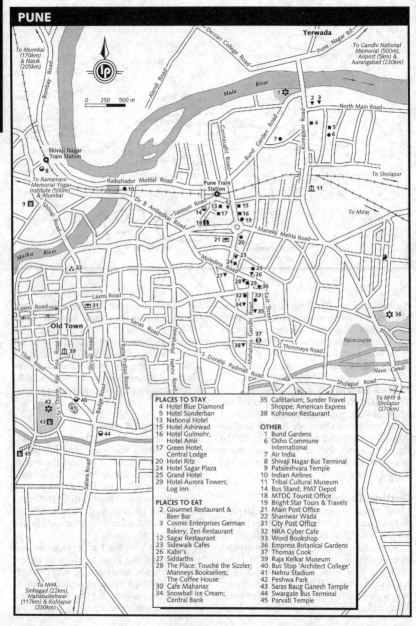

PUNE

Yerwada

To Mumbai
(170km)
& Nasik
(205km)

To Gandhi National
Memorial (500m),
Airport (5km) &
Aurangabad (230km)

Deccan College Road

Pune Nagar Rd

Mula River

North Main Road

Shivaji Nagar
Train Station

0   250   500 m

Bombay Road

Alandi Road

Connaught Road

Bund Garden Road

Koregaon Road

To Sholapur

To Ramamani
Memorial Yoga
Institute (500m)
& Mumbai

Raibahadur Motilal Road

Pune Train
Station

Shivaji Road

Dr B Ambedkar Road

Sassoon Road

Manekji Mehta Road

To Miraj

Mutha River

Moledina Road

Laxmi Road

Sanas Road

Laxmi Road

East Street

Old Town

Tilak Road

Raja Road

Shivaji Road

Rana Pratap Road

Badge Road

Sri Thorle

Nehru Road

Purushwarwadi

Mahatma Gandhi Road

S Dorabji Padmali Road

G Thimmaya Road

Racecourse

Nava Canal

Sholapur Road

To NH9 &
Sholapur
(270km)

To NH4,
Sinhagad (22km),
Mahabaleshwar
(117km) & Kohlapur
(230km)

PLACES TO STAY
4 Hotel Blue Diamond
5 Hotel Sunderban
13 National Hotel
15 Hotel Ashirwad
16 Hotel Gulmohr;
   Hotel Amir
17 Green Hotel;
   Central Lodge
20 Hotel Ritz
24 Hotel Sagar Plaza
25 Grand Hotel
29 Hotel Aurora Towers;
   Log Inn

PLACES TO EAT
2 Gourmet Restaurant &
   Beer Bar
3 Cosmic Enterprises German
   Bakery; Zen Restaurant
12 Sagar Restaurant
23 Sidewalk Cafes
26 Kabir's
27 Siddarths
28 The Place: Touché the Sizzler;
   Manneys Booksellers;
   The Coffee House
30 Cafe Mahanaz
34 Snowball Ice Cream;
   Central Bank

35 Cafétarium; Sunder Travel
   Shoppe; American Express
38 Kohinoor Restaurant

OTHER
1 Bund Gardens
6 Osho Commune
   International
7 Air India
8 Shivaji Nagar Bus Terminal
9 Pat004aleshvara Temple
10 Indian Airlines
11 Tribal Cultural Museum
14 Bus Stand; PMT Depot
18 MTDC Tourist Office
19 Bright Star Tours & Travels
21 Main Post Office
22 Shaniwar Wada
31 City Post Office
32 NRA Cyber Cafe
33 Word Bookshop
36 Empress Botanical Gardens
37 Thomas Cook
39 Raja Kelkar Museum
40 Bus Stop 'Architect College'
41 Nehru Stadium
42 Peshwa Park
43 Saras Baug Ganesh Temple
44 Swargate Bus Terminal
45 Parvati Temple

rubbed off on Pune, and fashion shops and fast-food outlets are constantly springing up. Pune boasts a prestigious university (styling itself as the 'Oxford of the East'), and is a major industrial centre.

For many western visitors, the city's major attraction is the Osho Commune International, better known as the ashram of Bhagwan Rajneesh.

Orientation
The city is at the confluence of the Mutha and Mula rivers. Mahatma Gandhi (MG) Rd is the main street and is lined with banks, restaurants and shops. South-west of here, the streets narrow and take on the atmosphere of a traditional bazaar town.

Information
Tourist Office The MTDC tourist office (☎ 668867), buried in the government buildings a short walk south of the train station, stocks a colourful map of Pune (Rs 5) but nothing else.

Money There are several efficient foreign exchange offices in Pune. American Express (☎ 631848), at the Sunder Travel Shoppe on MG Rd, is open Monday to Friday 9 am to 6 pm; Saturday 9 am to 4 pm. Thomas Cook (☎ 648188), 13 Thacker House, 2418 G Thimmaya Rd (between East St and MG Rd) is open Monday to Saturday, 10 am to 5 pm. Both charge a Rs 30 encashment fee, but there's a small exchange office around the corner from Thomas Cook in East St that gives the same rate with no fee.

The Central Bank on MG Rd gives credit card cash advances but closes at 2 pm.

Post & Communications The main post office on Connaught Rd is open Monday to Saturday, 10 am to 6 pm, but the parcel office closes at 4 pm.

Pune is cyberjunkie's heaven, with a glut of Internet cafes around MG Rd charging around Rs 50 an hour and several claiming to stay open 24 hours. Try Log Inn, in the Hotel Aurora Towers building on MG Rd; Crystal Cyber Cafe in the Amba Complex, 320 MG

Rd; or NRA Cyber Cafe on the ground floor of the Ashok Vijay Complex, 326 MG Rd, which offers access for Rs 30 an hour.

Travel Agencies One of the best travel agents in town for flights and tours is Sunder Travel Shoppe (☎ 631848, fax 631534, Sunder Plaza, 19 MG Rd).

Bookshops The best bookshop is Manneys Booksellers, Clover Centre, 7 Moledina Rd (near the junction with MG Rd); open Monday to Saturday, 9 am to 1 pm and 4 to 8 pm. The Word Bookshop, downstairs at the Kumar Plaza in MG Rd, is also very good.

Osho Commune International
The Bhagwan Rajneesh's famous ashram (☎ 628562, fax 624181, commune@osho. net, 17 Koregaon Park) is in a leafy northern suburb of Pune. Styling itself as a 'spiritual health club', it has continued to prosper since the Bhagwan's death in 1990 and attracts thousands of visitors each year. Facilities include a swimming pool, sauna, tennis and basketball courts, massage and beauty parlour, bistro, bookshop and a five hectare Zen garden known as **Osho Teerth**, open to the public from 6 to 9 am and 4 to 7 pm daily. The main centres for meditation or spiritual dance are the Buddha Hall (where the 'White Robe Brotherhood' gathers every evening) and the Osho Samadhi, where the guru's ashes are kept.

The commune is big business – its 'Multiversity' runs a plethora of (expensive) courses in traditional meditation as well as New Age techniques, all with computerised booking facilities. Those wishing to meditate at the commune must fill out an application form (complete with two passport photographs), prove HIV-negative to an on-the-spot test given at the centre (Rs 125) and purchase three tunics (two maroon and one white). Meditation is then Rs 100 per day (Rs 35 for Indians) and you can come and go as you please. You must also arrange your own accommodation, outside the ashram.

Casual visitors can take a one hour tour and video presentation (Rs 70, including some Osho literature) at 10.30 am and 2.30 pm daily. Even if you don't decide to enter the ashram, it's worthwhile just to see hundreds of maroon-clad soul-searchers being individuals together – though there are just as many wandering around outside the ashram. It's advisable to book ahead.

Ramamani Iyengar Memorial Yoga Institute

Despite the pulling power of the Osho Commune, many visitors are drawn to Pune for the more serious study of hatha yoga under the watchful eye of the legendary BKS Iyengar.

In many ways Iyengar, author of the book *Light on Yoga*, revolutionised yoga in the 1950s with his vigorous physical therapies. The institute (☎ 356134) is about 5km west of the centre, just off Ganesh Khind Rd in Model Colony. Fees are US$200 a month with six classes a week. Accommodation must be arranged outside the institute.

Raja Kelkar Museum

This fascinating museum is one of Pune's real delights. The exhibits are the personal collection of Sri Dinkar Gangadhar (aka Kaka Kelkar) who died in 1990. Among the 17,000 or so artworks and curios he collected

Osho, the Bhagwan

Bhagwan Shree Rajneesh (1931-90), or Osho as he preferred to be called, was one of India's most popular and flamboyant 'export gurus' and without doubt the most controversial. He followed no particular religion, tradition or philosophy and his often acerbic criticism and dismissal of various religious and political leaders made him many enemies the world over. What particularly outraged his Indian critics was his advocacy of sex as a path to enlightenment, an approach which earned him the epithet 'sex guru' from the Indian press.

Rajneesh used a curious blend of Californian pop psychology and Indian mysticism to motivate his followers. His last technique, tagged The Mystic Rose, involved following a regime of laughing for three hours a day for one week, crying for three hours a day the next week, followed by becoming a 'watcher on the hill' (ie sitting) for three hours a day for another week. The Bhagwan felt that it was 'the most important breakthrough in meditation since Buddha's *vipassana*, created 25 centuries ago'. Indeed, he began to lean heavily towards Zen Buddhism in the years before his death and at one point, even declared himself to be the Buddha.

In 1981, Rajneesh went to the USA and set up the agricultural commune and ashram of Rajneeshpuram in Oregon. It was here that he drew the attention of the international media, and the ashram's notoriety (along with its highly publicised fleet of Rolls Royces) grew and grew. Eventually, with rumours and local paranoia about the ashram's activities running wild, the Bhagwan was charged with immigration fraud, fined US$400,000 and deported to India in November 1985.

In January 1987, Rajneesh took up residence again at the Pune ashram, and soon thousands of foreigners (mostly from Germany, Italy and Japan) were flocking to attend his nightly discourses and meditation courses. From early 1989 until his death, Rajneesh reverted to silence as he had done so once in America.

Before his death, the orange clothes and the *mala* (the string of beads and photograph of the Bhagwan worn around the neck), which used to be the distinctive mark of Bhagwan followers, had been discarded. This was done so that his followers could (according to the ashram press office) 'avoid harassment and molestation by the authorities'. These days there seems to be no such discrimination against the followers (who now get around in maroon).

over 70 years are Peshwa and other miniatures, a bizarre collection of musical instruments, carved doors and windows, hookah pipes, strange locks, oil lamps and a superb collection of betel-nut cutters, adorned brass foot scrubbers, carved wooden noodle makers and hair-drying combs.

The museum is open 8.30 am to 6 pm daily (Rs 40, Rs 5 for Indians); photography is not permitted.

Shaniwar Wada

The ruins of this fortress-like palace stand in the old part of the city. Built in 1736, the palace of the Peshwa rulers burnt down in 1828, but the massive walls remain. Today there's an unkempt two hectare garden inside and not a lot to see. There's a small gallery above the main entrance. The sturdy palace doors are studded with spikes designed to dissuade enemies from leaning too heavily against the entrance, and in a nearby street the Peshwa rulers executed offenders by having elephants trample them. The palace is open 8 am to 6.30 pm daily (Rs 2, free on Friday).

Pataleshvara Temple

Just across the river on Jangali Maharaj Rd is the wonderful rock-cut Pataleshvara Temple (aka Panchalesvara cave), a small 8th century temple similar in style to the much grander rock temple at Elephanta but never completed. More importantly, it's an active temple. In front of the excavation is a circular Nandi *mandapam* (pavilion). Adjacent is the Jangali Maharaj (Lord of the Jungle) temple, dedicated to a Hindu ascetic who died here in 1818.

Tribal Cultural Museum

About 1.5km east of the Pune train station at 28 Queens Gardens, this excellent museum documents the cultures of Maharashtran adivasi communities, particularly those from the Sahyadri and Gondwana regions. It's open 10 am to 5 pm daily (entry is free).

Gardens

The Empress Botanical Gardens have fine tropical trees and a there's a small zoo nearby. The moated Saras Baug Ganesh Temple is in Peshwa Park and has dozens of food stalls at night. The Bund Gardens, on the banks of the Mula River, are popular for an evening stroll. The bridge here crosses to Yerwada and the Gandhi National Memorial.

Gandhi National Memorial

Across the river in Yerwada is this fine memorial set in 6.5 hectares of gardens. Built by Imamsultan Muhammad Sha Aga Khan III in 1892, it was the Aga Khan's palace until 1956 after which it became a school. In 1969 it was donated to India by the Aga Khan IV.

After Mahatma Gandhi delivered his momentous Quit India resolution in Bombay in 1942, the British interned him and other leaders of India's independence movement here for nearly two years. Both Kasturba Gandhi, the Mahatma's wife, and Mahadoebhai Desai, his secretary for 35 years, died here during this period of imprisonment. Their ashes are kept in memorial tombs *(samadhis)* in the gardens.

A photographic exhibition details some of the highlights of Gandhi's long career, but it is the simple personal effects (including a pair of sandals and a thermos) and the personal tragedies of the Mahatma during this period that leave the deepest impression. Film buffs will recognise the building from the movie *Gandhi*.

The memorial is open from 9 am to 5.45 pm daily (entry is Rs 2).

Organised Tours

All-day city bus tours of Pune leave the Pune Municipal Transport (PMT) depot near the train station at 9 am daily (Rs 70). They cover all the main sights and are reasonable value if you're in a hurry. Book at the PMT office or inquire at the tourist office.

Special Events

While Ganesh Chaturthi is celebrated all over India, the festival is most extravagant at Mumbai and Pune. Traditionally a household affair, it was converted into a public celebration a century ago when the freedom fighter, Lokmanya Tilak, used it to unite the masses for the freedom struggle. Ganesh (or Ganpati as he's often affectionately called) is, after all, the remover of obstacles.

At the end of the 11 day festival, plaster and clay images of Ganesh, some of them 6m high, are taken from homes and street *mandals* (shrines) and carried in huge processions to be immersed in the river.

The procession of Ganesh is the climax of the very popular **Pune Festival,** which features classical dance and music concerts, folk dance and a village festival including bullock cart races and wrestling. The opening ceremony presents some of the country's best musicians and dancers, and is usually held around late August or early September.

Places to Stay

There are plenty of hotels in Pune, but it's difficult to find a decent cheap place. If you're planning on staying a while to hang out at the Osho Commune, ask around at the cafes and restaurants near the ashram – rooms in homes or apartments are usually available for rent on a monthly basis.

Places to Stay – Budget

Most of the cheapies close to the train station are fleapits, but there are some reasonable places in the area known as Wilson Gardens, directly opposite the station and behind the National Hotel. There are good *retiring rooms* at the train station.

Green Hotel (☎ 625229, 16 Wilson Gardens) is a Georgian building with a touch of character. Rooms are Rs 175/250 without/with bath or Rs 300 for a larger double.

Central Lodge (☎ 621313, 13 Wilson Gardens) has passably clean doubles/triples with common bath for Rs 125/150, or dorm beds for Rs 50.

The *National Hotel (☎ 625054, 14 Sassoon Rd)*, opposite the train station, is a good choice in this range. Bahai-run, it is a ramshackle old mansion with verandas and high ceilings. There are singles with common bath for Rs 150 and doubles with attached bath for Rs 350, or nice little cottages for Rs 300. The rooms are in varying condition, so ask to see a few; there's hot water in the morning only.

Grand Hotel (☎ 668728) is a crumbling old place in private grounds on MG Rd. Single 'cabins' (beds separated by partition walls) cost Rs 100 with common bath. Double rooms with attached bath go for Rs 320. The hotel has its own beer bar, patio and restaurant.

Places to Stay – Mid-Range

Add between 5% and 20% tax to prices quoted for the mid-range and top-end hotels.

Hotel Gulmohr (☎ 622773, 15A/1 Connaught Rd) is within easy walking distance of the train station. Rooms start at Rs 300/480 or Rs 580/790 with air-con, some with a small balcony. There's 24 hour hot water.

The *Hotel Ashirwad (☎ 628585, 16 Connaught Rd)* is also close to the station and offers spacious rooms with balcony from Rs 750/900 or Rs 1000/1300 with air-con. Rooms have direct-dial phones and Star TV. There's a restaurant with good vegetarian food but no bar.

Hotel Amir (☎ 621841, 15 Connaught Rd) is seemingly modelled on a prison cell block and some rooms are shabby. Facilities include a bar, restaurants and a dreary shopping arcade. Rooms start at Rs 795/1045, or Rs 995/1245 with air-con.

Hotel Ritz (☎ 626161, 6 Sadhu Vaswani Path), opposite the post office, is a renovated heritage hotel with more character than most. Comfortable singles/doubles cost Rs 950/1100 or Rs 1199/1550 with air-con. There's a pleasant garden restaurant and a speciality restaurant serving legendary Gujarati thalis (Rs 80).

Hotel Sunderban (☎ 624949, fax 623535, 19 Koregaon Park), next to the ashram, is well kept and the obvious choice if you're visiting Osho. There's a wide variety of rooms available from US$18 including taxes.

Places to Stay – Top End

Hotel Sagar Plaza (☎ 622622, fax 622633, 1 Bund Garden Rd), off Moledina Rd, has well-appointed air-con rooms from Rs 2700/3100 including a buffet breakfast.

There's a bar, coffee shop, restaurant, small swimming pool and bookshop.

Hotel Aurora Towers (☎ *631818, fax 631826, 9 Moledina Rd*), at the junction of MG Rd, has air-con economy singles/doubles for Rs 1850/2350 and deluxe doubles for Rs 3350; suites start at Rs 3500. Facilities include a shopping arcade, rooftop swimming pool with city views, a bar, two restaurants and a 24 hour coffee shop.

The *Hotel Blue Diamond* (☎ *625555, fax 627755, 11 Koregaon Rd*) is a five-star hotel just 10 minutes walk from the Osho ashram. Rooms start from Rs 4100/4500.

Places to Eat

Cafe Mahanaz, opposite Aurora Towers on MG Rd is a busy, no-nonsense cafe and bakery. It's a good place for breakfast (great toast) and there's nothing over Rs 15 on the menu.

The *sidewalk cafes* just south of the post office are a good place to go in the evening for a cheap meal. They offer a variety of food and cold drinks.

The Place: Touché the Sizzler, just down the street, is a popular two tier air-con restaurant specialising in sizzlers from Rs 110 but also offers cheaper Indian, tandoori and continental dishes. The home-made ice creams (Rs 35 to Rs 55) are delicious. It's open for lunch and dinner.

The part open-air *Kabir's*, opposite, offers cheaper Indian, Mughlai and tandoori dishes, as well as vegetarian pizzas and burgers. Both The Place and Kabir's serve cold beer.

The *Coffee House*, also on Moledina Rd, is a trendy hang-out with slick waiters.

Cafétarium, in the atrium of the Sunder Plaza on MG Rd, is another spot for coffee and even a plate of pasta or a burger. It's open 11 am to 11 pm.

Kohinoor Restaurant, a little further south on MG Rd, is always busy at lunchtime, serving thalis and a range of other delicious veg meals.

Cosmic Enterprises German Bakery (a place you'll end up at sooner or later if you're visiting Osho) churns out coffee, cakes and lassis and has become a bit too popular for its own good. *Zen Restaurant* is right behind – just the ticket after a long day of *zazen*. There's always an interesting international crowd of Osho *sanyasins* (seekers) at these places.

The *Gourmet Restaurant & Beer Bar*, next to the bakery, is quieter but serves reasonable Indian and Chinese dishes from Rs 45. There's another cluster of restaurants further east along North Main Rd.

Getting There & Away

Air The Indian Airlines office (☎ 140 or 141) is at 39 Dr B Ambedkar Rd, the main road to Mumbai. Air India (☎ 628190) is at 4 Hermeskunj Mangaldas Rd. Jet Airways (☎ 637181) has a city office at 243 Century Arcade, Naurangi Baug Rd.

Indian Airlines flies every day to Delhi (US$185), four times a week to Bangalore (US$130) and three times to Chennai (US$155). Jet Airways has two to three flights daily to Mumbai (US$75), and daily flights to Bangalore (US$130) and Delhi (US$185). Gujarat Airways (☎ 691538) flies direct to Goa on Monday, Wednesday and Friday at 10.30 am (US$90).

Bus Pune has three bus terminals: Pune train station terminal for points south – including Goa, Belgaum, Kolhapur, Mahabaleshwar and Panchgani; Shivaji Nagar terminal for points north and north-east – Ahmednagar, Aurangabad, Lonavla and Nasik; and Swargate terminal – for Sinhagad, Bangalore, Mangalore and Mumbai. Deluxe buses also shuttle from the train station bus stand to Dadar every 15 minutes (Rs 90).

The MSRTC buses are pretty rough and most travellers prefer to use the trains. There are plenty of private deluxe buses to most centres including Goa (Rs 250, 12 hours), Nasik (Rs 100, five hours) and Aurangabad (Rs 100, six hours), but beware of going through agencies as you may find yourself dumped on a regular MSRTC bus. Try Bright Star Tours & Travels (☎ 625916, Sadhu Waswani Square), the office is not signposted – it's inside the petrol station.

Train Pune is one of the Deccan's most important train stations and all express and mail trains stop here. The computerised booking hall is upstairs in the building to the left of the station as you face the entrance.

The *Deccan Queen* and *Pragati Express* are fast commuter trains to Mumbai and are heavily subscribed. Other expresses take four to five hours.

For Matheran, the only express train stopping at Neral is the *Sahyadri Express*, which leaves at 7.55 am. See the Matheran section, earlier in this chapter, for further details.

Taxi Long-distance share taxis (four passengers) connect Pune with Dadar in Mumbai around the clock. They leave from the taxi stand in front of Pune train station (Rs 200, four hours). A similar service operates from Shivaji Nagar train station to Nasik (Rs 200) and Aurangabad (Rs 220).

Getting Around

To/From the Airport The airport is 8km north-east of the city. An airport bus departs from Hotel Amir (Rs 20). An auto-rickshaw will cost Rs 60, a taxi Rs 150.

Bus The most useful local bus is the No 4, which runs from the PMT terminal beside Pune train station to Swargate via the Shivaji Nagar bus terminal. The Marathi number '4' looks like an '8' with a gap at the top.

Auto-Rickshaws Auto-rickshaws are plentiful and the best option for most trips around town. Official rates are Rs 5.50 for the first kilometre and Rs 3.50 per kilometre after that (or around four times the rate shown on the out-of-date meters). Before getting in, ensure that the driver will use not only his meter but also the official tariff conversion card. If you're going to be around for a few days, you can pick up a conversion card from some shops and newsstands. After dark you'll probably have to negotiate a fare.

Bicycle Many of Pune's students get around by bicycle, but be warned – Pune has some of the most maniacal drivers in India. Getting around the Koregaon Park area is a breeze though. Bikes can be rented from most of the bicycle shops around town or from the stall near the entrance to the National Hotel.

AROUND PUNE
Sinhagad

Sinhagad, the Lion Fort, is 24km south-west of Pune and makes an excellent day trip. The nearly ruined fort stands on top of a steep hill, where there are also a number of old bungalows; including one where Gandhi met with the freedom fighter Tilak in 1915.

In 1670 Shivaji's general, Tanaji Malusre, led a force who scaled the steep hillside in

Train Services from Pune

destination	train no & name	departure time	distance (km)	duration	fare (Rs) (sleeper/1st)
Bangalore	6529 *Udyan Exp*	12.20 pm	1019	33.00h	262/885
Chennai	6011 *Mumbai-Chennai Exp*	6.40 pm	1088	20.00h	267/930
	1063 *Chennai Exp*	11.55 pm	1088	20.10h/min	267/930
Delhi	1077 *Jhelum Exp*	5.35 pm	1595	27.45h/min	317/1209
Hyderabad	7031 *Hyderabad Exp*	5.15 pm	600	13.15h/min	155/528
Mumbai CST	2124 *Deccan Queen*	7.15 am	191	3.25h/min	125/611
	2028 *Shatabdi Exp*	5.35 pm	191	3.20h/min	330/645[1]

[1] fares are for air-con chair/executive class

the dark and defeated the unprepared forces of Bijapur. Legends about this dramatic attack relate that the Maratha forces used trained lizards to carry ropes up the hillside!

A road winds up to the fort, but if you come by local bus it's a sweaty 1½ to two hour walk to the top. It's a good idea to bring water and food with you. The Pune city bus No 50 runs frequently to Sinhagad Village (from where you must walk) from 5.25 am until evening. It leaves from the 'Architect College' bus stop opposite Nehru Stadium (Rs 10, 45 minutes).

MAHABALESHWAR
☎ 02168 • pop 12,000

The terraced hills and fertile valleys of Maharashtra's most popular hill station at 1372m, are a welcome escape from the noise and fumes of Mumbai and Pune. Mahabaleshwar has pleasant walks and panoramic lookouts, and the area has strong historical connections with Shivaji. Founded in 1828 by Sir John 'Boy' Malcolm, it was the summer capital of the Bombay presidency during the days of the Raj.

Like most hill stations, Mahabaleshwar closes up for the monsoon (mid-June to mid-September) when an unbelievable 6m of rain falls. Local buildings are clad with *kulum* grass to prevent damage from the torrential downpour. As with Matheran, Mahabaleshwar is hopelessly crowded during the peak periods of April/May, Christmas and Diwali, and is best avoided then.

Orientation & Information

Most of the action is in the main bazaar (Main Rd, also called Dr Sabane Rd) – a 200m strip of ice cream and chikki parlours, video games, flashing lights and tacky stalls, with the bus stand at the western end. A Rs 5 entry fee is payable on arrival and private vehicles also pay a Rs 2 per day parking fee.

You can get a reasonable map of the district (Rs 20) from most hotels or from the small tourist office near the bus stand.

The Bank of Maharashtra, in the main bazaar, changes cash and travellers cheques at lower than average rates.

Things to See & Do

Some faded traces of the Raj persist in Mahabaleshwar in the many preserved and dilapidated buildings dotted around the town. The most evocative is **Mount Malcolm**, built as government house and residence of 'Boy' Malcolm in 1829. Once a magnificent country residence, it's now derelict and overgrown.

Faring better after Independence is the **Sir BD Petit Library** near the bus stand. Inside (apart from a lot of books) is a full-size billiard table that you can use for Rs 32 per half hour. Also worth a detour is **Morarji Castle**, where Mahatma Gandhi lived during 1945.

Elphinstone, Babington, Bombay and Kate's points offer fine **views** from the wooded plateau to the plains below. Arthur's Seat, 12km from Mahabaleshwar, looks out over a sheer drop of 600m to the Konkan coastal strip. There are pleasant **waterfalls** around Mahabaleshwar, such as Chinaman's, Dhobi's and Lingmala falls.

In the village of **Old Mahabaleshwar** there are two ancient temples worth visiting. The Krishnabai, or Panchganga (Five Streams) Mandir is said to contain the springs of five rivers, including the sacred Krishna River which issues from the mouth of a sculpted cow suckling a calf. The Mahabaleshwar Mandir is of interest for its naturally occurring lingam.

Organised Tours

In the high season, the MTDC organises separate tours of Mahabaleshwar, Pratapgarh Fort and Panchgani, each costing Rs 70 per person. These can be booked at the tourist kiosk or the MTDC Resort. At other times taxi drivers will fall over themselves to get you on their 14-point tour of Mahabaleshwar's sights for around Rs 200. This amounts to a ride out to Arthur's Seat and back with a stop at Old Mahabaleshwar along the way.

Places to Stay

Accommodation prices are all about supply and demand in Mahabaleshwar – prices rocket during the high season of Christmas,

MAHARASHTRA

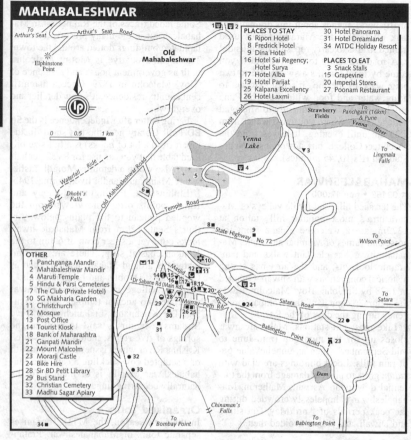

MAHABALESHWAR

To Arthur's Seat

Arthur's Seat Road

Old Mahabaleshwar

Elphinstone Point

0   0.5   1 km

Waterfall Ride

Dhobi's Falls

Dhobi

Old Mahabaleshwar Road

Petit Road

Temple Road

Venna Lake

Strawberry Fields

Panchgani (16km) & Pune

Venna River

To Lingmala Falls

State Highway No 72

To Wilson Point

Masjid Road

Dr Sabane Rd (Main Rd)

Murray–Peth Rd

Satara Road

To Satara

Babington Point Road

Chinaman's Falls

Dam

To Bombay Point

To Babington Point

PLACES TO STAY
6 Ripon Hotel
8 Fredrick Hotel
9 Dina Hotel
16 Hotel Sai Regency; Hotel Surya
17 Hotel Alba
19 Hotel Parijat
25 Kalpana Excellency
26 Hotel Laxmi
30 Hotel Panorama
31 Hotel Dreamland
34 MTDC Holiday Resort

PLACES TO EAT
3 Snack Stalls
15 Grapevine
20 Imperial Stores
27 Poonam Restaurant

OTHER
1 Panchganga Mandir
2 Mahabaleshwar Mandir
4 Maruti Temple
5 Hindu & Parsi Cemeteries
7 The Club (Private Hotel)
10 SG Makharia Garden
11 Christchurch
12 Mosque
13 Post Office
14 Tourist Kiosk
18 Bank of Maharashtra
21 Ganpati Mandir
22 Mount Malcolm
23 Morarji Castle
24 Bike Hire
28 Sir BD Petit Library
29 Bus Stand
32 Christian Cemetery
33 Madhu Sagar Apiary

Diwali and April/June (school holidays). Outside these times (low season) some of the cheaper lodges are good value. It's difficult to find a place offering a single occupancy rate – the rationale being that no one should come to Mahabaleshwar alone! Most of the budget places are around the main bazaar near the bus stand.

Hotel Surya (☎ 60966, 48 Main Rd), hidden along a laneway connecting Main Rd and Masjid Rd, has clean doubles with TV and hot shower for Rs 150 and Rs 200 in the low season, rising to a ludicrous Rs 1200 in the high season.

Hotel Sai Regency (☎ 60157, Main Rd) is good value as the rooms are better than most in this price range. Spotless doubles cost Rs 225 (Rs 950 in high season).

Hotel Parijat (☎ 60196, 85 Main Rd) is friendly and clean with doubles from Rs 150 to Rs 220 in the low season.

Kalpana Excellency (☎ 60419) is a recently renovated place and by far the best of a string of hotels along Murray Peth Rd.

Well-appointed rooms around a Mediter-ranean-style courtyard cost Rs 400/1200 in the low/high season.

The *MTDC Holiday Resort* (☎ 60318), 2km south-west of the centre, has dorm beds for Rs 50 per person, good doubles for Rs 200 to Rs 300, and cottages and suites (three to four people) for Rs 400 to Rs 750. Prices rise by about a third in season. A taxi from the bus stand costs Rs 30.

Hotel Dreamland (☎ 60228, fax 60063), behind the bus stand, is set in spacious gardens with an open-air restaurant and pool. It offers a range of bungalow-style accommodation from Rs 800, including excellent veg meals.

Hotel Panorama (☎ 60404, fax 61234) has all the mod cons as well as a pool that features its own waterfall and paddle boats. Well-appointed rooms are Rs 800 to Rs 1950 (50% more in season).

More expensive resort-style hotels include the *Regal Hotel* (☎ 60001), the *Dina Hotel* (☎ 60246) and the *Fredrick Hotel* (☎ 60240). These places generally quote all-inclusive prices of around Rs 1000 per person in the low season and Rs 1500 to Rs 2000 in the high season.

Places to Eat

There are plenty of cafes and fast-food places lining the bazaar, and most hotels have attached restaurants.

The *Imperial Stores* at the far end of Main Rd was once victualler to the Raj and now turns out pizza, toasted sandwiches, burgers and other snacks. The *Poonam* at the Shere Punjab Hotel on Main Rd has good non-veg food, and the *Nukkad* next door is also popular.

The *Grapevine*, on Masjid Rd, is a classy little place with various romantic seating arrangements. It has a reasonable go at Thai and continental dishes (around Rs 80), and draught beer is available.

Mahabaleshwar is famous for its amazing variety of berries, which you can buy fresh (in season) or in juice, ice cream and jams. Chikki, that rock-hard conglomeration of nuts and gur sugar, is also popular here.

Getting There & Away

Mahabaleshwar is 117km south-west of Pune via Panchgani. Frequent buses run to Satara (Rs 22, two hours) and Panchgani (Rs 5) and there are several daily to Kolhapur (Rs 60, five hours) and Pune (Rs 50/70, four hours). There are two buses to Mumbai daily at 9 am (Rs 100 semideluxe) and 1 pm (Rs 120 deluxe), and two expensive MTDC luxury buses at 9.30 am and 12.30 pm (Rs 180, seven hours). Going to Mahabaleshwar, the MTDC buses leave from Nariman Point in Mumbai at 6.30 am and 11 pm.

There are plenty of private bus booking agents in the bazaar for luxury buses to destinations within Maharashtra or to Goa (via Surul). They all quote similar prices and timings, but it pays to find out exactly where they intend to drop you at your destination.

Getting Around

Mahabaleshwar has no auto-rickshaws but there are plenty of taxis and Maruti vans hanging around near the bus station to take you around the main viewpoints or to Panchgani (see Organised Tours, earlier).

Strawberry Fields Forever

Mahabaleshwar and Panchgani are famous for producing some of India's finest strawberries, as well as raspberries, mulberries and gooseberries.

Along the road between the two hill stations stretches some 5km of strawberry fields producing varieties such as Californian, Australian and Sweet Chandler. Planting begins soon after the monsoon and fruits are harvested from late November to June with the best crops coming around February. You can visit the farms and buy direct, or get them from the berry vendors who sit cross-legged in Mahabaleshwar's bazaar presiding over neat pyramids of strawberries, raspberries and mulberries. There's also a big industry in fruit drinks, sweets, fudges and jams – the main processor, Mapro, has its plant near Panchgani.

Cycling is a good option; there's little traffic, though the narrow lanes have many blind corners and require extra care if you're planning to ride to the viewpoints. Reasonable bikes can be hired from a shop at the eastern end of Main Rd for Rs 5 an hour.

AROUND MAHABALESHWAR
Panchgani

Panchgani (Five Hills), 19km east of Mahabaleshwar and just 38m lower, is splendidly located with some fine viewpoints, but is overshadowed by its better-known neighbour.

There are quite a few hotels in Panchgani and they're generally cheaper than in Mahabaleshwar.

The *Hotel Simla* (☎ 40235), about 100m from the bus stand on the road to Mahabaleshwar, has pleasant bungalow-style singles/doubles set around a garden for Rs 150/220. Prices double in the high season.

Pan Hill Hotel (☎ 40444), opposite the bus stand on Main Rd, has reasonable rooms for Rs 250 per person.

Hotel Prospect (☎ 40236) is a charming colonial hotel perched on a hill 1km from the bus stand. Large and comfortable three-bed rooms are Rs 700/900 in low/high season.

Pratapgarh & Raigad Forts

Further afield are two impressive hill forts associated with Shivaji.

Built in 1656, Pratapgarh Fort dominates a high ridge 24km west of Mahabaleshwar and has spectacular views. Regular buses from Mahabaleshwar take about one hour to get to the fort, which is then reached by a 500-step climb.

Raigad (or Raigarh) Fort, 80km northwest of Mahabaleshwar, also has wonderful views from its isolated hilltop location, reached by a long, steep ascent. It was here that Shivaji was crowned in 1648 and where he died in 1680.

Basic *MTDC accommodation* (☎ 02145-22898) is available, with dorm space (no beds) for Rs 25; doubles are Rs 125. Day trips to both forts leave in the high season (see Organised Tours in the Mahabaleshwar section).

Satara

Satara has a number of relics of the Maratha leader Shivaji. A building near the new palace contains his sword, the coat he wore when he met Afzal Khan and the *waghnakh* (tiger's claws) with which he killed him. The **Shivaji Maharaj Museum** is opposite the bus terminal.

Wasota Fort in the south of the town has a colourful and bloody history, including being captured from the Marathas in 1699 by the forces of Aurangzeb, only to be recaptured in 1705 by means of a Brahmin who befriended the fort's defenders, then let in a band of Marathas.

There are buses from Satara to Pune (Rs 40, three hours), Mahabaleshwar (Rs 22, two hours) and Kolhapur (Rs 30, two hours). Express trains between Mumbai and Kolhapur stop at Satara Rd station, 15km away.

KOLHAPUR
☎ 0231 • pop 480,200

Kolhapur was once the capital of an important Maratha state. It's an interesting little town and worth exploring for a day or two if you're passing through.

Pratapgarh Protagonists

Outnumbered by the forces of Bijapur, Shivaji arranged to meet with the opposing General Afzal Khan. Neither was supposed to carry any weapon or wear armour. Neither, it turned out, could be trusted.

When they met, Afzal Khan pulled out a dagger and stabbed Shivaji, but the Maratha leader had worn a shirt of mail under his white robe, and concealed in his left hand was a *waghnakh*, a deadly set of 'tiger's claws'. This nasty weapon consisted of a series of rings to which long, sharpened metal claws were attached. Shivaji drove these claws into Khan and disembowelled him. Today a tomb marks where the encounter took place, and a tower was erected over the Khan's head. There is a statue of Shivaji in the ruined Pratapgarh Fort.

You can pick up a city map (Rs 15) from the MTDC tourist office (☎ 652935), next to the Hotel Tourist on Station Rd. It's open weekdays from 10 am to 6 pm and weekends from 8.30 am to noon and 4 to 6 pm.

For foreign exchange, the State Bank of India is a Rs 10 auto-rickshaw ride southwest of the train station near Hutatma Park.

Maharaja's Palace

The maharaja's 'new' palace, completed in 1881, houses the **Shahaji Chhatrapati Museum**, one of the most bizarre collections of memorabilia in the country. The building was designed by 'Mad' Charles Mant, the British architect who fashioned the Indo-Saracenic style of colonial architecture (he practised the style on several colonial buildings in Kolhapur) and is a cross between a Victorian train station (clock tower included) and the Addams Family mansion.

The palace contains a weird and wonderful array of the old maharaja's possessions including his clothes, old hunting photos, silver peacock-shaped elephant saddles and the memorial silver spade he used to 'turn the first sod of the Kolhapur State Railway' in 1888.

But dominating every room in the palace are reminders of the maharaja's macabre passion: killing wild animals to decorate his palace. Skins cover floors and furniture, trophy heads stare blankly from the walls, ashtrays and coffee tables are made from tiger and elephant feet, lamp stands from ostrich legs and zebra hoofs. The variety of stuffed animals includes black bear, rhino, pangolin, panther and an entire family of tigers in a forest diorama.

The palace is a few kilometres north of the centre. Rent a bicycle, or take an auto-rickshaw (Rs 15). Entry is Rs 10.

Other Attractions

The **Mahalakshmi Temple**, dedicated to the goddess Amba Bai, dominates the old town. Of particular interest is the carved ceiling of the columned mandapam. Nearby, the **Old Palace** still accommodates members of the maharaja's family, but in its cool atrium

(open 10 am to 6 pm daily) you're more likely to find students poring over books.

An alley leads from the front of the palace to Kolhapur's famous **wrestling ground**, which resembles an enormous sandpit. Kolhapur has produced several Indian national wrestling champions, and you can see them training most days in the early morning or evening at one of the local wrestling clubs. Ask around for the *kusti akhada*.

The town hall, built by Mant in 1872-76, is now a small but satisfying **museum**, housing pottery and bronze artefacts found during archaeological excavations on nearby Brahmapuri Hill.

For a respite from the city's bustle, head down to the sacred **ghats** on the Panchganga River or to **Lake Rankala**, 5km from the train station.

Places to Stay

The main hotel and restaurant area is around the square opposite the bus stand, 10 to 15 minutes walk from the centre of town and the train station.

City Lodge, above the shops on the western side of the square, is a clean budget place. Dorm beds are Rs 60 and rooms with bath are Rs 150/190. There's hot water and a 24 hour checkout.

Hotel Maharaja (☎ 652140, Station Rd) is quite good and the better rooms are often full. Singles/doubles with common bath cost Rs 75/150 or Rs 150/250 with attached bath and hot water (mornings only).

Hotel Tourist (☎ 650421), a few minutes walk east of the bus station, is a much more pleasant place. Comfortable singles/doubles with bath, TV and phone are good value at Rs 250/290. Air-con rooms start from Rs 350/400. There's a reasonable restaurant and a bar.

Further along Station Rd are a couple of upmarket mid-range places. Rooms near the front can be noisy. The *Hotel International* (☎ 652442, fax 652445) has rooms from Rs 300/400 to Rs 350/450 or Rs 600/675 with air-con, all with TV and phone. The *Hotel Panchsil* (☎ 650517, fax 659322) is more comfortable and pricier, with rooms for Rs

575/625 or Rs 725/775 with air-con; suites are Rs 900.

Hotel Shalini Palace (☎ 620401, fax 620407), at Lake Rankala, is the top place to stay in Kolhapur. Situated on the lake 5km south-west of the bus stand or train station, this is the maharaja's old summer palace. It dates back only to the 1930s but has plenty of regal grandeur with huge rooms, marble balconies and four-poster beds. Standard rooms are Rs 800/1150, and the suites range from Rs 1450 to Rs 2100.

Places to Eat
The restaurants are also clustered around the bus station square. The *Subraya Restaurant* has north Indian veg and nonveg dishes, and regulation thalis. *Hotel Sahyadri*, opposite, also has a very busy veg restaurant downstairs.

For a better class of food, the restaurants at the *Hotel International* and *Hotel Panchsil* are worth trying.

In the evening dozens of *snack stalls* set up opposite the bus stand.

Getting There & Away
Bus There are daily departures for Mumbai (Rs 135, nine hours), Pune (Rs 70, five hours) via Satara, and Mahabaleshwar (Rs 60, four hours), as well as direct services to Belgaum, Ratnagiri and Bijapur. There are plenty of private bus companies around the square offering luxury coach services to Goa, Mumbai and other destinations.

Train The train station is 10 minutes walk west of the bus station, towards the centre of town. The broad-gauge line connects Kolhapur via Miraj with Pune (eight hours) and Mumbai (13 hours) – take the daily *Koyna Express* or the overnight *Sahyadri Express* or *Mahalaxmi Express*.

AROUND KOLHAPUR
Panhala
Panhala, a little-visited hill station (altitude 975m) 18km north-west of Kolhapur, makes an interesting excursion. Originally the stronghold of Raja Bhoj II in 1192, the hill-

top fort was captured by both the Mughals and the Marathas and was finally taken by the British in 1844. The **Pawala caves** can be found nearby, as well as a couple of Buddhist cave temples.

The *MTDC Tourist Resort (☎ 02328-35048)* is the place to go if you want to stay the night here. Singles/doubles cost Rs 250/350.

Regular local buses go from the bus stand in Kolhapur to Panhala (Rs 7).

Northern Maharashtra

NASIK
☎ 0253 • pop 834,000
This interesting town with hundreds of temples and colourful bathing ghats stands on the Godavari River, one of the holiest rivers of the Deccan.

Nasik has a particularly devotional and untouristed feel that makes it a worthwhile detour on the way to or from Aurangabad.

Orientation & Information
MG Rd, a couple of blocks north of the central bus stand, is Nasik's hub. The Godavari River, lined with temples and bathing ghats, flows through town just east of here.

The MTDC tourist office (☎ 570059) is opposite the Golf Club Rest House, 1km south of the bus stand. It has a map of Nasik and staff can help with most queries. The State Bank of India, less than 100m from the bus stand on Old Agra Rd, changes cash and travellers cheques (eventually).

Ramkund
This holy bathing tank, 1km east of the town centre, is the focus for pilgrims filing into Nasik. Surrounded by ghats and the riverside market, it's a lively and interesting area to explore.

The Ramkund is said to have been used by Rama and Sita during their exile in the epic *Ramayana*. Its holy water is believed to provide *moksha*, or liberation of the soul, to those whose ashes are immersed here – Indira Gandhi and Jawaharlal Nehru are among those to have had this treatment.

Kala Rama Mandir
A short walk east of the Ramkund, the Kala Rama, or Black Rama, is the city's holiest temple. The black stone temple is in a 96-arched enclosure and contains icons of Rama, Sita and Laxman as well as a huge bell which can be heard from 5km away.

Other Attractions
Near Kala Rama is the **Sita Gupta cave**. According to the *Ramayana* it was from here that Sita, the deity of agriculture and wife of Rama, was carried off to the island of Lanka by the evil king Ravana. For a small donation you can join the queue crawling through the narrow opening, but there's not much to see.

Among the many temples in Nasik, the **Sundar Narayan Temple** at the western end of Victoria Bridge is worth a visit.

The **Muktidham Temple**, near the train station about 7km south-east of the city, is a modern and strikingly white marble structure. The walls of its vast interior are lined with the 18 chapters of the *Bhagavad Gita*.

Kumbh Mela
The Kumbh Mela, supposedly the largest celebration of any kind on earth, alternates between Nasik, Allahabad, Ujjain and Haridwar with each city hosting it once every 12 years. *Kumbh* means 'pot' or 'pitcher', and in Hindu mythology four drops of the nectar of immortality fell to earth, one in each of these places. In Nasik much of the celebration is centred on the Trimbakeshwar Temple, 33km away. The next Kumbh Mela in Nasik will be in 2003. For more details about this extraordinary pilgrimage, see the Kumbh Mela boxed text in the Allahabad section of the Uttar Pradesh chapter.

Organised Tours
An all-day sightseeing tour of Nasik, including Trimbak and Pandu Lena, departs daily at 7.30 am from the central bus stand (Rs 60). The guide speaks Marathi only but if you want to see a few of Nasik's estimated 2000 temples, it's as good a way as any.

Places to Stay & Eat
Hotel Panchavati (☎ 575771, 430 Vakilwadi), just off MG Rd, is one of the best value places in Nasik with modern, clean single/double rooms for Rs 490/690; the cheaper annexe at the back has rooms for Rs 390/540. The complex includes a couple of very good restaurants, an ice cream parlour and a bar.

Hotel Padma (☎ 576837, Sharanpur Rd), opposite the central bus stand, has simple, clean rooms with attached bath from Rs 250/350.

Hotel Samrat (☎ 577211, Old Agra Rd), 50m further south, has better rooms for Rs 345/490 or Rs 530/590 with air-con. Its restaurant serves good Gujarati thalis and there's a bar.

There are a few budget hotels around the Dwarka Circle, the junction of the main roads to Mumbai and Pune, a couple of kilometres south of the town centre. *Sun Moon Guest House* (☎ 596748) has a grubby dorm with beds at Rs 30, small doubles for Rs 120 or clean rooms with hot private bath and TV for Rs 150/200.

Hotel Sunflower (☎ 75944), opposite, has much nicer rooms with hot water at Rs 300/350 or air-con doubles at Rs 450.

Anand Fast Food & Juice Centre (MG Rd) is a small, clean place serving cheap Chinese food, sandwiches, milkshakes and juices. The *Tandoor*, opposite the bus stand on Shivaji Rd, has also been recommended.

Getting There & Away
The Nasik Rd train station is 8km from the town centre but there's a useful railway reservation office in a small lane near MG Rd (open Monday to Saturday 8 am to 2 pm and 4.15 pm to 8 pm, Sunday 8 am to 2 pm). The fastest train to Mumbai is the *Panchvati Express* which takes four hours, leaving at 7.09 am (Rs 76/258 sleeper/1st class, 188km). The *Tapovan Express* is the only convenient direct train to Aurangabad, departing at 10.05 am and taking 3½ hours.

There are frequent buses to Mumbai (Rs 76), but they're slower than the train as they get caught up in Mumbai's traffic chaos. Regular buses also go to Aurangabad (Rs 80, five hours) and Pune (Rs 86, five hours). There are private bus agents near the bus stand.

Getting Around

Local buses ply between the Nasik Rd train station and the bus stand (Rs 3). An auto-rickshaw costs about Rs 40.

AROUND NASIK
Pandu Lena

About 8km south of Nasik, close to the Mumbai road, is a group of 24 Hinayana Buddhist caves dating from around the 1st century BC to the 2nd century AD. Cave 3 is a large *vihara* (monastery) with some interesting sculptures. Cave 10 is also a vihara and is almost identical in design to cave 3, although it is much older and finer in its detail. Cave 18 is a well-sculpted *chaitya* (temple) and its elaborate facade is particularly noteworthy.

Buses run to the caves from the second stop north of the central bus stand on Old Agra Rd. A return auto-rickshaw ride (including waiting time) costs around Rs 100.

Trimbak

From a spring high on a steep hill above Trimbak, 33km west of Nasik, the source of the Godavari River dribbles into the **Gangasagar bathing tank** whose waters are reputed to wash away sins. From this tiny start the Godavari eventually flows down to the Bay of Bengal, clear across India.

The **Trimbakeshwar Temple** is one of India's most sacred, containing one of the 12 *jyotirlinga* (naturally occurring linga) of Shiva. The temple is open to Hindus only, but it's possible to see into the courtyard to the shrine from a convenient vantage point.

The **MTDC Resort** has dorm beds at Rs 40 and singles/doubles for Rs 250/300. Book at the tourist office in Nasik.

Regular buses run from the central bus stand in Nasik to Trimbak (Rs 15).

AURANGABAD
☎ 0240 • pop 682,000

Aurangabad has a number of attractions and could easily stand on its own were it not overshadowed by the famous Ellora and Ajanta caves nearby. The city was originally founded in 1610 on the site of a village called Khirki, by Malik Ambar, prime minister of the Murtaza Nizam Shah II. Ambar's son, Fateh Khan, succeeded the throne in 1626, renaming the city Fatehpur, before Aurangzeb moved in and made it his capital in 1653. The city is named after him.

Aurangabad is remarkably uncrowded and quiet for a city of its size.

Orientation

The train station, tourist office and a variety of cheaper hotels and restaurants are clustered in the south of the town. The bus stand is 1.5km to the north along Station Rd. North-east of here is the crowded old town with its narrow streets and distinct Muslim quarter.

Information

Tourist Offices The Government of India tourist office (☎ 331217) on Station Rd West has a decent range of brochures and will try to answer almost any query. It's open Monday to Friday 8.30 am to 6 pm and until 1.30 pm on Saturday. The state tourist office (☎ 331513) in the MTDC Holiday Resort, Station Rd East, is open 7 am to 7 pm and is the place to book tours. There are also information counters at the airport and train station.

Money The best place to change cash and travellers cheques is Trade Wings Foreign Exchange (open daily from 8 am to 7 pm), opposite Hotel Printravel on Station Rd West. The Bank of Baroda, near the Paithan Gate on Pattan Darwaza Rd, gives cash advances on Visa and MasterCard, but only between 1 and 2.30 pm Monday to Friday, and 10.30 am and 12.30 pm Saturday.

Post & Communications Poste restante can be collected from the busy main post

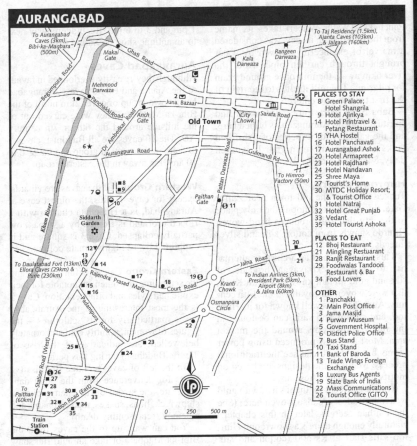

AURANGABAD

To Aurangabad
Caves (3km),
Bibi-ka-Maqbara
(500m)

To Taj Residency (1.5km),
Ajanta Caves (103km)
& Jalgaon (160km)

Makai
Gate

Ghati Road

Kala
Darwaza

Rangeen
Darwaza

Mehmood
Darwaza

Begumpura Road

Panchakki Road

Dr. Ambedkar Road

Anch
Gate

Juna Bazaar

Old Town

City
Chowk

Sarafa Road

Aurangpura Road

Gulmandi Rd

Pattan Darwaza Road

To Himroo
Factory (50m)

Kham River

Siddarth
Garden

Paithan
Gate

Jalna Road

To Daulatabad Fort (13km),
Ellora Caves (29km) &
Pune (230km)

Dr. Rajendra Prasad Marg

Court Road

Kranti
Chowk

To Indian Airlines (3km),
President Park (5km),
Airport (8km)
& Jalna (60km)

Padampura Road

Osmanpura
Circle

Station Road (West)

To
Paithan
(60km)

Station Road (East)

Train
Station

0   250   500 m

PLACES TO STAY
8 Green Palace;
   Hotel Shangrila
9 Hotel Ajinkya
14 Hotel Printravel &
   Petang Restaurant
15 YHA Hostel
16 Hotel Panchavati
17 Aurangabad Ashok
20 Hotel Armapreet
23 Hotel Rajdhani
24 Hotel Nandavan
25 Shree Maya
27 Tourist's Home
30 MTDC Holiday Resort;
   & Tourist Office
31 Hotel Natraj
32 Hotel Great Punjab
33 Vedant
35 Hotel Tourist Ashoka

PLACES TO EAT
12 Bhoj Restaurant
21 Mingling Restuarant
28 Ranjit Restaurant
29 Foodwalas Tandoori
   Restaurant & Bar
34 Food Lovers

OTHER
1 Panchakki
2 Main Post Office
3 Jama Masjid
4 Purwar Museum
5 Government Hospital
6 District Police Office
7 Bus Stand
10 Taxi Stand
11 Bank of Baroda
13 Trade Wings Foreign
   Exchange
18 Luxury Bus Agents
19 State Bank of India
22 Mass Communications
26 Tourist Office (GITO)

office at Juna Bazaar Monday to Saturday, 10 am to 5 pm.

For Internet access, Mass Communications on Osmanpura Circle at the end of Station Rd East charges Rs 150 per hour, while Hotel Printravel (see Places to Stay, later) also offers access at Rs 120 per hour.

Bibi-ka-Maqbara

The so-called 'poor-man's Taj Mahal' was built in 1679 as a mausoleum for Aurangzeb's wife, Rabia-ud-Daurani. It's a cheap imitation of the Taj in both design and execution – it simply looks awkward compared with the elegance and symmetry of the Taj; and where the Taj has gleaming marble, this tomb has flaking plaster (though substantial restoration work is under way). It's still worth a visit and is most atmospheric at night, when floodlit.

The building is open from sunrise to 10 pm (Rs 2). There's a very small archaeological museum behind the Bibi-ka-Maqbara.

Panchakki

Panchakki (Water Wheel) takes its name from the mill that, in its day, was considered a marvel of engineering. Driven by water brought through earthen pipes from the river 6km away, the mill once ground grain for pilgrims. The mill itself is to the right of the first tank as you enter.

Baba Shah Muzaffar, a Sufi saint and spiritual guide to Aurangzeb, is buried here, and the garden with its series of fish-filled tanks serves as his memorial. It is open daily, 8 am to 8 pm (Rs 2).

Himroo Factory

Tucked away in the old town near Zaffar Gate, this small workshop is the only place in the city that still produces hand-woven Himroo shawls from cotton, silk and silver threads.

This art developed as a cheaper alternative to the more extravagant brocades of silk and gold thread, known as Kam Khab, that were woven for royalty in the 14th century. Aurangabad is well known for its Himroo, and shawls and saris can be found in the many showrooms around the market area. Most are mass produced using power looms but here you can see the traditional process. Many of the designs are based on motifs in the Ajanta frescoes.

The magnificent Paithani saris, with gold weave brocades, are also woven here. (See the Paithan section, later in this chapter.) Naturally enough there's a showroom; Himroo saris start at Rs 500 (cotton and silk blend) and Paithani saris range from Rs 6000 to Rs 80,000. The factory is open 10 am to 5 pm daily.

Purwar Museum

This tiny two-room museum contains the fascinating personal collection of a retired doctor. Among the exhibits are a 500-year-old chain mail suit, a copy of the Koran handwritten by Aurangzeb and an 800-year-old Paithani sari.

At the time of writing Mr Purwar was planning another larger museum dedicated to the Maratha ruler Shivaji. The Purwar

Museum (☎ 350166) is open daily, 10 am to 1 pm and 3 to 6 pm. It's hidden away next to an antique shop on Sarafa Rd.

Aurangabad Caves

Although they're easily overlooked in favour of the Ajanta and Ellora caves, Aurangabad has its own group of caves 2km north of the Bibi-ka-Maqbara. They were carved out of the hillside around the 6th or 7th century AD. The 10 caves are all Buddhist; caves 1 to 5 are in the western group and caves 6 to 10 are 1km away in the eastern group.

Western Group All the caves are viharas, except for cave 4. This, the oldest cave at Aurangabad, is a Hinayana chaitya with a ribbed roof and is fronted by a stupa, now partially collapsed. Cave 3 is square and is supported by 12 highly ornate columns.

Eastern Group Cave 6 is fairly intact and the sculptures of women are notable for their exotic hairstyles and ornamentation. Cave 7 is the most interesting of the Aurangabad caves, particularly for its sculptures – the figures of women, scantily clad and ornately bejewelled, are indicative of the rise of Tantric Buddhism during this period.

To the left of cave 7 a huge Bodhisattva prays for deliverance from the eight dangers: fire, the sword of the enemy, chains, shipwreck, lions, snakes, mad elephants and a demon (representing death).

You can walk up to the caves from the Bibi-ka-Maqbara or take an auto-rickshaw up to the eastern group, walk back down the road to the western group and then cut straight back across country to the Bibi-ka-Maqbara.

Organised Tours

The MTDC (☎ 331513) and the MSRTC (☎ 331647) run almost identical daily tours to the Ajanta and Ellora caves. These include an accompanying guide. In each case the Ellora tour also includes the major Aurangabad sites – Daulatabad Fort, Grishneshwar Temple, Aurangzeb's Tomb, Bibi-ka-Maqbara and Panchakki – which is way too much to cover adequately in a single day.

MTDC tours start and finish at the MTDC Holiday Resort and the MSRTC tours at the central bus stand.

Ellora	departs	returns	cost
MTDC	9.30 am	5.30 pm	Rs 115
MSRTC	8.00 am	6.00 pm	Rs 57

Ajanta	departs	returns	cost
MTDC	8.00 am	6.00 pm	Rs 150

Places to Stay – Budget

There are *retiring rooms* at the train station with dorm beds for Rs 30.

The *YHA Hostel (☎ 334892, cnr Padampura Rd and Station Rd West)*, is clean, friendly and secure. Separate-sex dorms cost Rs 40 per person (Rs 20 for YHA members) and double rooms are Rs 100. The rooms are basic but it's a well-kept place with a lounge and common room. There's a 10 pm curfew and 9 am checkout, hot water in the morning and cheap meals are available.

There's a string of cheap but fairly dismal places on Station Rd East near the train station with rooms from Rs 125/150, but the places north of the train station along Station Rd West are a better bet.

Hotel Natraj (☎ 324260) is a typical family-run boarding house with singles/doubles/triples around a courtyard for Rs 80/100/150 with bath.

Tourist's Home (☎ 337212) has basic but very clean and spacious rooms at Rs 90/150 with bath.

Hotel Panchavati (☎ 328755, Padampura St), next to the youth hostel, has good-value rooms with bath for Rs 100/150 (hot water in the mornings). It's basic but the staff are amicable and there's a good restaurant and bar.

Shree Maya (☎ 333093, Bansilal Nagar), off Station Rd West, is well kept and friendly with rooms for Rs 140/195 and air-con doubles for Rs 350. Each room has a TV and hot water.

The popular *Hotel Printravel (☎ 329707)*, 600m south of the bus stand, has rooms with bath for Rs 175/275.

For the best places close to the bus stand, walk down the small road directly opposite and turn left into Nehru Place. *Green Palace (☎ 335501)* is certainly no palace, but the rooms are in a reasonable state and it's friendly. Singles/doubles with attached bath and hot water shower are Rs 175/300.

Hotel Shangrila (☎ 336481), next door, has small singles/doubles with common bath for Rs 50/80 and basic rooms with bath for Rs 80/125. Better rooms cost Rs 180 and Rs 250; all rooms have TV.

Hotel Ajinkya (☎ 335601), also in Nehru Place, has the nicest rooms of the three, starting at Rs 160/210 or Rs 450/550 with air-con.

Places to Stay – Mid-Range

MTDC Holiday Resort (☎ 331513, Station Rd East), is set in its own shady grounds. Singles/doubles with bath are Rs 225/275 in the 'Ellora' section or Rs 300/350 in the better 'Ajanta' suite. Air-con rooms are Rs 400/550. Mosquito nets are provided and there's a restaurant and bar. Checkout is 8 am.

Hotel Great Punjab (☎ 336482) is at the bottom end of this range with reasonable rooms at Rs 195/275.

Hotel Nandavan (☎ 336314), 1km from the train station, is good value at Rs 190/250 with bath, 24 hour hot water and TV, or Rs 300/350 with air-con.

Hotel Rajdhani Executive (☎ 326103, fax 336553) has been recently renovated and its immaculate carpeted rooms are good value at Rs 400/450 or Rs 550/600 with air-con. It also has a good restaurant and bar.

Places to Stay – Top End

Aurangabad Ashok (☎ 332492, fax 313328, Dr Rajendra Prasad Marg) has air-con rooms for Rs 1195/2300. It has all the usual Ashok amenities but has seen better days.

Vedant (☎ 350701, fax 350700, Station Rd East), is a modern Quality Inn hotel with two restaurants, bar, central air-con and swimming pool. Rooms cost Rs 1330/2430 including breakfast, direct-dial phone and TV.

President Park (☎ *486201, fax 484823*) is a very classy three-star a little further out towards the airport and is excellent value at Rs 1195/1800. The best feature of this hotel is its semicircular swimming pool set in gardens with a poolside bar. It also has a travel desk, gym, multicuisine restaurant and coffee shop.

Taj Residency (☎ *381106, fax 381053, Ajanta Rd*) is a gleaming oasis in the northern fringes of Aurangabad. The hotel sweeps around an immaculate garden and swimming pool. Well-appointed rooms start at Rs 1800/2100.

Places to Eat

There's a clutch of rock-bottom restaurants along Station Rd East, including the *Tirupati*, *Bharthi* and *The Kitchen*, which specialise in cheap South Indian meals. The *food stalls* around the bus stand do great omelettes.

Food Lovers is a garden restaurant near the train station and has the best ambience in town – earthen floor, thatched walls and an ingenious cooling system on hot days. The Punjabi and Chinese food is delicious. It's open until midnight.

Foodwalas Tandoori Restaurant & Bar is further up Station Rd East and offers reasonable tandoori dishes.

Bhoj (Dr Ambedkar Rd), is a popular 2nd floor restaurant serving expensive but excellent south Indian veg dishes. It opens for breakfast from 7 am.

Ranjit Restaurant (Station Rd West), near the tourist office, is a spotless place serving good north Indian food.

Mingling (Jalna Rd), has a reputation for tasty and even imaginative Chinese and Indian food.

Getting There & Away

Air The airport is 10km east of town on the Jalna road. En route you'll find the Indian Airlines office (☎ 485421). The Jet Airways office (☎ 487092) is almost opposite Indian Airlines.

Indian Airlines has a daily morning flight to Mumbai (US$65) and an evening flight to Udaipur (US$105), which continues to Jaipur (US$125) and Delhi (US$150). Jet Airways flies daily to Mumbai (US$69).

Bus There are regular MSRTC buses from Aurangabad to Pune (Rs 80, six hours) and Nasik (Rs 78, five hours), as well as overnight services to Indore and Mumbai (Rs 168, 388km via Manmad, 400km via Pune). The MSRTC and MTDC also offer deluxe overnight buses to Mumbai (Rs 225, 12 hours). The luxury bus agents congregate around the corner where Dr Rajendra Prasad Marg becomes Court Rd and there are a few closer to the bus stand on Station Rd.

To Ellora & Ajanta Caves Unless you're planning to take an organised tour from Aurangabad to Ajanta, you may find it more convenient to stay at Ajanta than to rely on local transport there and back.

There are local buses to Ellora every half hour (Rs 15, 45 minutes), four morning buses direct to Ajanta (Rs 45, three hours) and hourly services to Jalgaon (Rs 65, 4½ hours). Not all the Aurangabad-Jalgaon buses go right to Ajanta, so if it's the caves you specifically want and not Fardapur (the nearest village), make sure you get on the right bus.

Train Aurangabad is not on a main line but there are two direct trains daily to/from Mumbai (375km) which are often heavily booked. The *Tapovan Express* departs at 2.55 pm and costs Rs 126/434 in sleeper/1st class but it gets you into Mumbai CST at 10.50 pm. The overnight *Devgiri Express* departs from Aurangabad at 9.40 pm and arrives at Mumbai CST at 5.40 am. Coming from Mumbai, the same train leaves at 9.20 pm and arrives at Aurangabad at 4.55 am.

Alternatively, you can get a bus or a local train to the nearest main line train station, Manmad, 113km north-west of Aurangabad, from where there are more frequent express trains to Mumbai.

To Hyderabad (Secunderabad), the daily *Devgiri Express* departs from Aurangabad at 4.45 am and the journey takes 14 hours, or the *Aurangabad-Kacheguda Express* departs at 7.30 pm and arrives at Secunderabad at 8.45 am.

Getting Around

There are plenty of auto-rickshaws in Aurangabad and the drivers double as excellent tour guides.

The taxi stand is next to the bus stand; share jeeps also depart from here for destinations around Aurangabad, including Ellora and Daulatabad.

A bicycle is a good way to get around to some of the city sights and they can be hired from stalls near the bus stand.

AROUND AURANGABAD
Daulatabad

Halfway (13km) between Aurangabad and the Ellora caves is the magnificent hilltop fortress of Daulatabad. The **fort** is surrounded by 5km of sturdy walls, while the central bastion tops a 200m high hill, which was originally known as Devagiri, the Hill of the Gods.

In the 14th century it was renamed Daulatabad, the City of Fortune, by Mohammed Tughlaq. This somewhat unbalanced Sultan of Delhi conceived the crazy plan of not only building himself a new capital here, but marching the entire population of Delhi 1100km south to populate it. His unhappy subjects proceeded to drop dead like flies on this forced march, and 17 years later he turned round and marched them all back to Delhi.

Climb to the top for the superb views over the surrounding countryside. Along the way you'll pass through a complicated and ingenious series of defences, including multiple doorways to prevent elephant charges, and spike-studded doors just in case. A magnificent tower of victory, known as the **Chand Minar** (Tower of the Moon), built in 1435, soars 60m.

Higher up is the blue-tiled **Chini Mahal** where the last king of Golconda was imprisoned for 13 years until his death. Finally, you climb the central fort to a 6m **cannon**, cast from five different metals and engraved with Aurangzeb's name.

The final ascent to the top goes through a pitch black spiralling tunnel, down which the fort's defenders could hurl burning coals at invaders. Of course your guide may tell you that the fort was once successfully conquered despite all these elaborate precautions – by simply bribing the guard at the gate.

If you take one of the MTDC bus tours to Daulatabad and Ellora, you won't have time to climb to the summit. The fort is open until 6 pm (Rs 2).

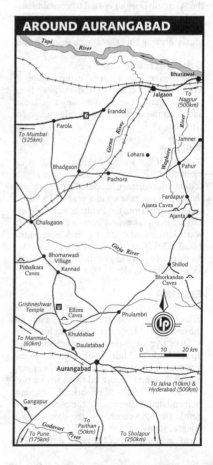

AROUND AURANGABAD

Khuldabad

Khuldabad, the Heavenly Abode, is a walled town just 3km from Ellora. It is the Karbala (holy shrine) of Deccan Muslims. A number of historical figures are buried here, including Aurangzeb, the last great Mughal emperor. His final resting place is a simple affair of bare earth in a courtyard of the **Alamgir Dargah** at the centre of the town.

Within the building there is supposed to be a robe worn by the prophet Mohammed; it is only shown to the faithful once each year. Another shrine across the road from the Alamgir Dargah is said to contain hairs of the prophet's beard and lumps of silver from a tree of solid silver which miraculously grew at this site after a saint's death.

Grishneshwar

Close to the Ellora caves in the village of Verul, the 18th century Grishneshwar Temple has one of the 12 *jyotirlinga* in India, and is an important place of pilgrimage for Hindus.

Paithan

Paithan, 56km south of Aurangabad, is famous for its Paithani silk saris. These highly sought after saris are brocaded with pure gold thread and can take up to a year and a half to weave. Apart from the Paithani weaving centre, the main attraction here is the Gyaneshwar Gardens, the largest in Maharashtra. Local MSRTC buses go to Paithan from Aurangabad, or you can join the MTDC half-day tour on Monday (Rs 115).

ELLORA

The World Heritage-listed cave temples of Ellora, about 30km from Aurangabad, are the pinnacle of Deccan rock-cut architecture.

Over five centuries, generations of Buddhist, Hindu and Jain monks carved monasteries, chapels and temples from a 2km long escarpment and decorated them with a profusion of sculptures of remarkable imagination and detail. Because of the escarpment's gentle slope, in contrast to the sheer drop at Ajanta, many of the caves have elaborate courtyards in front of the main shrines. The

Not on Monday

As with an increasing number of India's heritage monuments, the Ajanta and Ellora caves are closed on Monday. This allows staff to clean up a bit after the weekend crowds.

caves run north-south and take on a golden radiance in the late-afternoon sun.

In all there are 34 caves at Ellora: 12 Buddhist (600-800 AD), 17 Hindu (600-900 AD) and five Jain (800-1000 AD). Ellora represents the renaissance of Hinduism under the Chalukya and Rashtrakuta dynasties, the subsequent decline of Indian Buddhism, and a brief resurgence of Jainism under official patronage. The sculptural work at Ellora shows the increasing influence of Tantric elements in India's three great religions, and their coexistence at one site indicates a prolonged period of religious tolerance.

The masterpiece of Ellora is the astonishing Kailasa Temple (cave 16). Dedicated to Shiva, it is the world's largest monolithic sculpture, hewn from the rock by 7000 labourers over a 150 year period. (See Kailasa – Temple of the Gods boxed text later in this chapter for more information.) For four days in December the Kailasa Temple is the venue of the annual **Ellora Dance & Music Festival**.

Entry to Ellora is free, except to the Kailasa Temple which costs Rs 5, plus Rs 25 for a video camera. Allow at least half a day to visit Ellora; many visitors prefer to begin with the earlier Buddhist and Hindu caves (caves 1 to 15) as a prelude to Kailasa. The caves are closed on Monday.

Official guides can be hired at the ticket office in front of the Kailasa Temple for Rs 100. Most of them speak English reasonably well and all have a sound knowledge of the cave architecture. Otherwise, you will also find a selection of guidebooks available at the site.

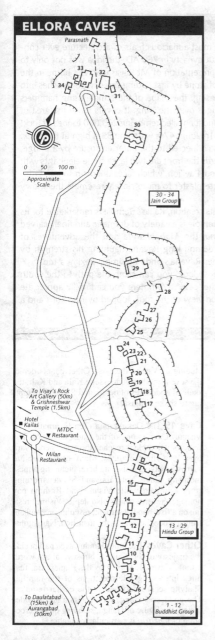

ELLORA CAVES

Parasnath

33
32
34
31

30

0   50   100 m
Approximate
Scale

30 - 34
Jain Group

29

28

27
26
25

24
23 22
21
20
19
18
17

To Vijay's Rock
Art Gallery (50m)
& Grishneshwar
Temple (1.5km)

Hotel
Kailas

MTDC
Restaurant

Milan
Restaurant

16

15

14

13

12

13 - 29
Hindu Group

11
10
9
8
7
6

To Daulatabad
(15km) &
Aurangabad
(30km)

1 2 3 4 5

1 - 12
Buddhist Group

Buddhist Caves

The southernmost 12 caves are all Buddhist viharas, except cave 10 which is a chaitya. While the earliest caves are quite simple, caves 11 and 12 are much more ambitious, probably in an attempt to compete with the more impressive Hindu temples.

Caves 1 to 4 Cave 1 is the simplest vihara and may have been a granary. Cave 2 is notable for its ornate pillars and its imposing seated Buddha facing the setting sun, his huge feet planted solidly on the earth. Caves 3 and 4 are earlier, simpler and less well preserved.

Cave 5 This is the largest vihara in this group, 18m wide and 36m long; the rows of stone benches indicate that it may have been an assembly or dining hall.

Caves 6 & 9 As well as the large seated Buddha in the shrine room, this ornate vihara also has wonderful images of Tara (on the left), consort of the Bodhisattva Avalokiteshvara, and of the Buddhist goddess of learning, Mahamayuri, looking remarkably similar to her Hindu equivalent, Saraswati. Cave 9 is notable for its wonderfully carved facade.

Cave 10 The Viswakarma or Carpenter's Cave is the only chaitya in the Buddhist group, and one of the finest in India. It takes its name from the ribs carved into the roof, in imitation of wooden beams; steps from the left of the courtyard lead to the balcony and upper gallery for a closer view of the ceiling and a frieze depicting amorous couples. A small, decorative window gently illuminates an enormous teaching Buddha.

Cave 11 The Do Thal (Two Storey) Cave is entered through its third, basement level, not discovered until 1876. Like cave 12 it probably owes its size to competition with the more impressive Hindu caves of the same period. The upper level is the most interesting and is reached by stairs on the left.

Cave 12 The enormous Tin Thal (Three Storey) Cave is entered through a courtyard. The (locked) shrine on the top floor contains a large seated Buddha flanked by his seven previous incarnations. The walls are carved with relief pictures, as in the Hindu caves.

Hindu Caves

Where calm and contemplation infuses the Buddhist caves, drama and dynamic energy

Kailasa – Temple of the Gods

Ellora's Kailasa Temple (cave 16) is one of the most audacious feats of architecture ever conceived. Built by King Krishna I of the Rashtrakut dynasty in 760 AD, the idea was not only to build an enormous and fantastically carved representation of Mt Kailasa, Shiva's home in the Himalaya, but to create it from a single piece of stone by first cutting three huge trenches into the rock of the Ellora cliff face and then 'releasing' the shape of the temple using hammers and chisels. The sheer scale of the undertaking is overwhelming. It covers twice the area of the Parthenon in Athens, is 1½ times as high, and it entailed removing 200,000 tonnes of rock!

The temple consists of a huge courtyard, 81m long, 47m wide and 33m high at the back. In the centre, the main temple rises up and is connected to the outer enclosure by a bridge. Around the enclosure are galleries, while towards the front are two large stone elephants with two massive stone 'flagstaffs' flanking the Nandi Pavilion, which faces the main shrine. Originally the entire structure was covered in white plaster to more closely resemble the snowy peak of Mt Kailasa.

Apart from the technical genius evident in its creation, Kailasa Temple is remarkable for its prodigious sculptural decoration. Around the temple is a variety of dramatic and finely carved panels, depicting scenes from the *Ramayana*, the *Mahabharata* and the adventures of Krishna. The most superb panel depicts the demon king Ravana flaunting his strength by shaking Mt Kailasa. Unimpressed, Shiva crushes Ravana's pride by simply flexing a toe.

Before entering the Kailasa Temple for a close look, you can climb the path to the south and walk right around the top perimeter of the 'cave'. From here you can really appreciate the massive scale of the temple and get a good view of the roof, topped by four lions and a pyramidal tower.

characterise those of the Hindu group (caves 13 to 29) in the middle of the escarpment. In terms of scale, creative vision and skill of execution, these are in a totally different league to the neighbouring Buddhist and Jain caves.

All these temples were cut from the top down, so that it was never necessary to use scaffolding – the builders began with the roof and moved down to the floor. The planning and coordination required over several generations must have been unbelievably precise – there was no way of adding a panel or a pillar if things didn't work out as expected.

Cave 14 The Ravana Ki Khai Cave is a Buddhist vihara converted to a temple dedicated to Shiva some time in the 7th century. Familiar scenes include Shiva dancing the *tandava*, a victory dance over the demon Mahisa; Shiva playing chess with his wife Parvati; and Durga defeating the buffalo demon. Vishnu makes several appearances, in-

cluding as Varaha the boar. Other panels depict the seven 'mother goddesses'; Kala and Kali, the skeletal goddesses of death; and Ravana attempting to shake Kailasa.

Cave 15 The Das Avatara (Ten Incarnations of Vishnu) Cave is one of the finest at Ellora. The two storey temple is reached through its courtyard by a long flight of steps. Many of the familiar scenes involving Shiva are here, including a mesmerising Shiva Nataraja, and Shiva emerging from a lingam while Vishnu and Brahma pay homage. Several panels also depict Vishnu: resting on a five-hooded serpent; rescuing an elephant from a crocodile; and as the man-lion, Narasimha.

Other Caves The other Hindu caves pall beside the majesty of the Kailasa, but several are worth a look. Cave 21, known as the Ramesvara, features interesting interpretations of the familiar Shaivite scenes depicted in the earlier temples. The goddesses Ganga and Yamuna are also depicted; the figure of Ganga, standing on her crocodile or *makara*, is particularly notable.

The very large cave 29, the Dumar Lena, is thought to be a transitional model between the simpler hollowed-out caves and the fully developed temples exemplified by the Kailasa. It has a wonderfully peaceful outlook over the nearby waterfall and it's possible to walk under the waterfall to cave 28 or vice versa.

Jain Caves

The Jain caves mark the final phase of Ellora. They do not have the drama and high-voltage energy of the best Hindu temples nor are they as ambitious in size, but they balance this with their exceptionally detailed work. There are only five Jain temples, and they're 1km north of the last Hindu temple (cave 29) at the end of the bitumen road.

Cave 30 The Chota Kailasa or Little Kailasa is a poor imitation of the great Kailasa Temple and was never completed. It stands by itself some distance from the other Jain temples.

Cave 32 The Indra Sabha (Assembly Hall of Indra) is the finest of the Jain temples. Its ground-floor plan is similar to that of the Kailasa, but the upstairs area, reached by a stairway, is as ornate and richly decorated as downstairs is plain. There are images of the Jain *tirthankars* Parasnath and Gomateshvara, the latter surrounded by vegetation and wildlife. Inside the shrine is a seated figure of Mahavira, the 24th and last tirthankar, and founder of the Jain religion.

Other Caves Cave 31 is really an extension of 32. Cave 33, the Jagannath Sabha, is similar in plan to 32 and has some particularly well-preserved sculptures. The final temple, the small cave 34, also has interesting sculptures. On the hilltop over the Jain temples, a 5m-high image of Parasnath looks down on Ellora.

Places to Stay & Eat

Hotel Kailas (☎ 02437-41043), close to the caves, is Ellora's only real hotel. Attractive rooms with bath in cottages range from Rs 400/500 to Rs 600/700 or Rs 1000 with air-con. The more expensive rooms have a view of the caves. There's also a budget annexe where basic singles/doubles are Rs 150/200. The restaurant has Indian and Chinese fare, and is cheaper than the nearby *MTDC restaurant*.

Vijay's Rock Art Gallery, a short walk further along the road past the Kailas, is the place for creative minds. Resident artist Vijay Kulkarni has set up a 'retreat for artists, writers and thinkers' behind his gallery and studio. Very basic rooms with bath range from Rs 150 to Rs 400. Vijay's passion and life's work is reproducing the cave paintings of Ajanta.

The *Milan Restaurant* across the road from the Hotel Kailas is good value for inexpensive snacks.

Getting There & Away

There are regular buses to Aurangabad from Ellora (Rs 15); the last returns from Ellora at around 7 pm. There are also shared jeeps which leave when jam-packed and stop at the bus stand in Aurangabad (Rs 15). An auto-rickshaw tour to Ellora with stops en route costs around Rs 250.

AJANTA

The Buddhist caves of Ajanta – 166km north-east of Aurangabad, or about 60km south of Jalgaon – date from around 200 BC to 650 AD, predating those at Ellora. As Ellora developed and Buddhism gradually declined, the Ajanta caves were abandoned and eventually forgotten. But in 1819 a British hunting party stumbled upon them, and their remote beauty was soon unveiled. Their isolation contributed to the fine state of preservation in which some of their remarkable paintings remain to this day. Ajanta is listed as a World Heritage Site by the United Nations Educational, Scientific and Cultural Organization (UNESCO).

Information

The caves open Tuesday to Sunday 9 am to 5.30 pm. Entry is Rs 5 plus a Rs 5 lighting fee and Rs 25 for a video camera. Flash photography is prohibited in many of the caves.

Many of the caves are dark and a torch comes in useful; if you're not on a tour you'll still need to buy a lighting ticket to gain entry to four of the main caves.

If possible, avoid coming here on weekends or public holidays when Ajanta seems

AJANTA CAVES

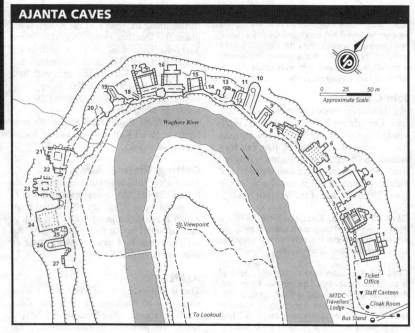

Waghore River

0   25   50 m
Approximate Scale

Viewpoint

To Lookout

Ticket Office
Staff Canteen
MTDC Travellers' Lodge
Cloak Room
Bus Stand

to attract half the population of India. The hawkers at Ajanta are persistent too – if you don't want to buy, don't accept 'gifts' or make promises to 'just look'.

There's a 'cloakroom' near the entrance where you can safely leave gear (Rs 2), so it is possible to arrive on a morning bus from Jalgaon, look around the caves, and continue to Aurangabad in the evening, or vice versa. If you want to visit Ajanta and Ellora in chronological order, visit Ajanta first.

Guides Government of India tourist office guides can be hired from the ticket office for around Rs 100. It's worth at least having a guide for the main caves as they really bring the frescoes to life and can explain the complex stories behind them. Guides are included with tours but the groups are often quite large.

Books There are a couple of good books available from the stalls at the caves. *Ajanta – A World Heritage Monument* (Rs 30) is an excellent introduction, while *Ajanta & Ellora* (Rs 300) contains some wonderful photography – including frescoes which you won't be able to photograph yourself.

The Caves

The 30 caves are cut into the steep face of a horseshoe-shaped rock gorge on the Waghore River. They are sequentially numbered from one end of the gorge to the other but do not follow a chronological order; the oldest are mainly in the middle and the newer ones are close to each end.

Five of the caves are chaityas while the other 25 are viharas. Caves 8, 9, 10, 12 and 13 are older Hinayana caves, while the others are Mahayana (dated from around the 5th century AD). In the simpler, more austere

Hinayana school Buddha was never represented directly – his presence was always alluded to by a symbol such as the footprint or wheel of law.

Cave 1 This Mahayana vihara is one of the latest excavated and is the most beautifully decorated of the Ajanta caves. If you prefer building to a climax, leave this cave till last.

A veranda at the front leads to a large congregation hall with elaborate sculptures and narrative murals, surrounded by several smaller cells. Of particular interest is the use of perspective in the paintings and the details of dress and daily life which are depicted. Many of the facial expressions are also wonderfully executed. The colours in the paintings were created from local minerals, with the exception of the vibrant blue made from Central Asian lapis lazuli.

There are several fine paintings of women, some remarkably similar to the paintings at Sigiriya in Sri Lanka. Other paintings include scenes from the Jatakas, and portraits of the Bodhisattvas Padmapani (holding a lotus flower) and Vajrapani. Among the interesting sculptures is one of four deer sharing a common head.

Don't leave cave 1 without seeing the three aspects of Buddha (you'll need to ask an attendant to move the spotlight): a large statue of Buddha preaching in the deer park is illuminated from each side and then from below to reveal distinct facial expressions of solemnity, joy and serenity.

Cave 2 This is also a late Mahayana vihara with deliriously ornamented columns and capitals and some fine paintings, though some are badly damaged. As well as murals, the ceiling is decorated with geometric and floral patterns. The mural scenes include a number of Jatakas and events surrounding Buddha's birth, including his mother's dream of the six-tusked elephant which heralded Buddha's conception. Details depict Gautama being held by his mother and taking his first steps, and the miracle of 1000 Buddhas.

Cave 4 This is the largest vihara at Ajanta and is supported by 28 pillars. Although never completed, the cave has some fine sculptures, including scenes of people fleeing from the 'eight great dangers' to the protection of Buddha's disciple Avalokiteshvara. Caves 3 and 5 were never completed.

Cave 6 This is the only two storey vihara at Ajanta, but parts of the lower storey have collapsed. Inside is a seated Buddha figure with an intricately carved door to the shrine. Upstairs the hall is surrounded by cells with fine paintings on the doorways.

The 'Frescoes' of Ajanta

The famous Ajanta 'frescoes' are technically not frescoes at all. A fresco is a painting done on a wet surface that absorbs the colour. The Ajanta paintings are more correctly *tempera*, since they were painted on a dry surface. The rough-hewn rock walls were coated with a 1cm thick layer of clay and cow dung mixed with rice husks. A final coat of lime was applied to produce the finished surface on which the artist painted. This was then polished to produce a high gloss. The colours were obtained from a variety of minerals and ochres – the striking blue comes from the semiprecious lapis lazuli.

The paintings initially suffered some deterioration after their rediscovery, and some heavy-handed restoration also caused damage, but between 1920 and 1922, two Italian art experts conducted a meticulous restoration process, and the paintings have been carefully preserved ever since.

Early attempts to record the paintings also ended in disaster. A Major Robert Gill spent 27 years at the site from 1844, meticulously recording the paintings. They were displayed at the Crystal Palace in London but were lost in December 1866 when the Crystal Palace burnt to the ground. Gill returned to Ajanta to recommence his labours, but died only a year later. In 1872, John Griffiths of the Bombay School of Art arrived at the site and spent 13 years recording the paintings. Tragically his work was also lost in a fire at the Victoria and Albert Museum in London.

Cave 7 This cave is of unusual design in that the veranda does not lead into a hall with cells down the sides and a shrine room at the rear. Here there are porches before the veranda, which leads directly to the four cells and the elaborately sculptured shrine.

Cave 9 This is one of the earliest chaityas at Ajanta. Although it dates from the Hinayana period, the two Buddha figures flanking the entrance door were probably later Mahayana additions. Columns run down both sides of the cave and around the 3m-high dagoba at the far end. At the front there's a horseshoe-shaped window above the entrance, and the vaulted roof has traces of wooden ribs.

Cave 10 This is thought to be the oldest cave (200 BC) and was the one first spotted by the British soldiers who rediscovered Ajanta. It is the largest chaitya and is similar in design to cave 9. The facade has collapsed and the paintings inside have been damaged, in some cases by graffiti dating from soon after the caves' rediscovery. The indentations in the floor near the left-hand wall were used for mixing paint pigments.

Cave 16 Some of Ajanta's finest paintings can be seen in this, one of the later vihara caves. It is thought that cave 16 may have been the original entrance to the entire complex, and there is a fine view of the river from the front of the cave. The best known of these paintings is the 'dying princess' – Sundari, wife of Buddha's half-brother Nanda, is said to have fainted at the news that her husband was renouncing the material life (and her) in order to become a monk. Nanda features in several other paintings, including one of his conversion by Buddha.

Carved figures appear to support the ceiling in imitation of wooden architectural details, and there's a statue of Buddha seated on a lion throne teaching the eight-fold path.

Cave 17 This cave has the finest paintings at Ajanta. Not only are they in the best condition, they are also the most numerous and varied. They include beautiful women flying overhead on the roof while carved dwarfs support the pillars. One of Ajanta's best known images shows a princess, surrounded by attendants, applying make-up. In one there is a royal procession, while in another an amorous prince plies his lover with wine. In yet another panel, Buddha returns from his enlightenment to his own home to beg from his wife and astonished son.

A detailed panel tells the story of Prince Simhala's expedition to Sri Lanka. With his 500 companions he is shipwrecked on an island where ogresses appear as beautiful women, only to seize and devour their victims. Simhala escapes on a flying horse and returns to conquer the island.

Cave 19 The facade of this magnificent chaitya is remarkably detailed and includes an impressive horseshoe-shaped window as its dominant feature. Two fine standing Buddha figures flank the entrance. Inside is a three tiered dagoba with a figure of Buddha on the front.

One of the most striking sculptures is outside the cave to the west, where there is an image of the Naga king with seven cobra hoods around his head. His wife, hooded by a single cobra, is seated beside him.

Cave 24 This would have been the largest vihara at Ajanta if it had been finished, and shows how the caves were constructed – long galleries were cut into the rock, and then the rock between them was broken through.

Caves 26 & 27 The fourth chaitya's facade has fallen and almost every trace of its paintings has disappeared. Nevertheless, there are some fine sculptures remaining. On the left wall is a huge figure of the 'reclining Buddha', lying back as he prepares to enter nirvana. Other scenes include a lengthy depiction of Buddha's temptation by Mara. Cave 27 is virtually a vihara connected to the cave 26 chaitya. There's a great pool in a box canyon 200m upstream from the cave.

Viewpoints

There are two lookouts from where you can get a good view of the whole horseshoe-shaped gorge from which the Ajanta caves were carved. The first is an easy 10 minute walk beyond the river crossing below cave 27 (a path leads down from cave 16 through a small park to the concrete bridge). A further 20 minute uphill walk from here leads to the lookout from where the British party first spotted the caves. It's also possible to take a taxi up to this viewpoint from the car park outside the caves.

Places to Stay & Eat

It's a long day trip to Ajanta and many visitors prefer to stay close by.

The *MTDC Travellers' Lodge* (☎ 02438-4226) is right by the entrance to the caves.

Rooms with common bath cost Rs 150/250. Checkout is 9 am. The food in the restaurant is reasonably good.

The *MTDC Holiday Resort (☎ 02438-4230)* at Fardapur, 5km from the caves, is more popular with some as it's quieter and away from the stalls and hawkers. Large, clean doubles along a pleasant veranda are Rs 250/350 with hot shower. Each room has clean sheets and a fan. Dorm beds are Rs 40. The attached *Vihara Restaurant* serves uninspiring thalis, nonveg food and cold beer.

Near the ticket window at the caves themselves, the *staff canteen* is open to all (the name seems to be a bit of a gimmick) and serves good cheap thalis and other veg snacks as well as cold drinks.

Getting There & Away

For information on buses from Aurangabad or Jalgaon, see those sections. Buses pull up right in front of the entrance to the caves and there's a timetable posted in the MTDC Travellers' Lodge. The last bus back to Aurangabad is at 5.45 pm and the last one to Jalgaon at 5.35 pm.

The caves are 4km off the main road from Aurangabad to Jalgaon and Fardapur is 1km farther down the main road towards Jalgaon. Regular buses shuttle between Fardapur and Ajanta (Rs 5).

Shared taxis operate between the caves, Fardapur and Jalgaon. Prices are negotiable, but expect to pay around Rs 15 from Ajanta to Fardapur and Rs 450 for the whole taxi to Jalgaon.

Coming from Mumbai, it's best to get an express train to Jalgaon and a local bus from there.

JALGAON
☎ 0257

Jalgaon is on the main railway line from Mumbai to the country's north-east, and is a convenient overnight stop en route to the Ajanta caves, 60km to the south.

Places to Stay

The *retiring rooms* at the station aren't bad value with dorm beds for Rs 40 and doubles at Rs 60 per person, but Jalgaon is blessed with some very decent hotels right in front of the train station.

Hotel Plaza (☎ 227354), about 150m up from the station on the left-hand side, has spotless rooms with white tiled floors, attached bath and TV for Rs 170/220, or one economy single for Rs 150. The manager is friendly and helpful.

The *Anjali Guest House (☎ 225079)*, on the right past the auto-rickshaw stand, is also a very clean, newly renovated place with rooms from Rs 200/250 to Rs 250/300. There's a good veg restaurant downstairs.

Hotel Amar Prem (☎ 226601) is cheaper but acceptable at Rs 100/140 for rooms with common bath or Rs 140/190 with attached bath.

Hotel Galaxy (☎ 23578, Jilha Rd) is next to the bus stand, about 2km from the train station. Rooms with TV cost Rs 150/250 and air-con doubles are Rs 450.

Getting There & Away

Several express trains between Mumbai and Delhi or Calcutta stop briefly in Jalgaon. The trip to Mumbai (eight hours, 420km) costs Rs 135/471 in sleeper/1st class. Departing Mumbai at 9.10 pm, the *Mumbai-Howrah Mail* gets into Jalgaon at 4.04 am.

From Jalgaon there are frequent buses to Fardapur (Rs 25, two hours), some of which continue to Ajanta and then on to Aurangabad. The train and bus stations are about 2km apart (Rs 10 by auto-rickshaw). There are plenty of luxury bus offices on Station Rd.

LONAR METEORITE CRATER

At the small village of Lonar, three hours by bus north-east of Jalna or 4½ hours south-east of Ajanta, is a huge meteorite crater. Believed to be about 50,000 years old, the crater is 2km in diameter and 170m deep, with a shallow lake at the bottom. A plaque at the rim states that it is 'the only natural hypervelocity impact crater in basaltic rock in the world'. Scientists suspect that the meteor is still embedded about 600m below the south-eastern rim of the crater.

There are several **Hindu temples** on the crater floor, and langur monkeys, peacocks and gazelles inhabit the bushes by the lake. The crater is about 15 minutes walk from the bus stand – ask for directions to Lonar Tank.

Places to Stay & Eat

The *PWD Resthouse* is right on the rim of the crater, 1km from the village. It has four simple but comfortable single rooms with bath for Rs 50. Meals can be arranged, or there are basic *dhabas* in the village.

Getting There & Away

Change at Buldhana for buses to Fardapur (for Ajanta), a total of Rs 50. Heading south there are direct buses to Jalna, from where there are trains and buses to Aurangabad, a total journey of about five hours. There's also one direct bus to Lonar from Aurangabad (Rs 50) around midday.

Lonar can be visited in a day trip from Aurangabad if you hire a car and driver. Classic Travels (☎ 337788), based at the MTDC office in Aurangabad, is a reliable operator with cars for around Rs 1200, or shop around for taxis outside the bus stand.

NAGPUR

☎ 0712 • pop 1.8 million

Situated on the River Nag, Nagpur is India's orange-growing capital. It was once the capital of the central province, but was later incorporated into Maharashtra. Long ago it was a centre for the aboriginal Gond tribes who remained in power until the early 18th century; many Gonds still live in the region.

On 18 October each year the town hosts thousands of Buddhists celebrating the anniversary of Dr Ambedkar's conversion to Buddhism in 1956. Dr Ambedkar, a low-caste Hindu, was an important figure during the fight for Independence, and was Law Minister and Scheduled Castes leader. An estimated three million low-caste Hindus followed him in converting to Buddhism.

There is little of interest to attract travellers, except those heading for Gandhi's ashram at Sevagram or taking a break on the long journey across the subcontinent.

Information

There's an MTDC office (☎ 533325) at Sanskritik Bachat Bhava, Sitabuldi, which has little information on Nagpur.

The easiest place to change money is Trade Wings Foreign Exchange, A/410 Lokmat Bhavan. It's open Monday to Friday, 9.30 am to 5.30 pm, Saturday 9.30 am to 1 pm and Sunday 10.30 am to 1 pm. The State Bank of India is on Kingsway, 250m north of the train station.

If you're heading up to Madhya Pradesh, a useful MP Tourism office (☎ 523374) is on the same floor as the Trade Wings office at Lokmat Bhavan.

Places to Stay

If you arrive by train there's a number of budget and mid-range places to stay within walking distance. Turn right as you leave the station concourse, then right again across the bridge over the railway tracks into Central Ave. A 10 minute walk brings you to a string of hotels.

The station's *retiring rooms* cost Rs 50 for dorm beds including coupons for a free newspaper, morning tea and a boot polish!

Hotel New Central (☎ 726235, 4 Central Ave) is pretty grubby but a cheap option at Rs 50/90 for singles/doubles with common bath or Rs 65/110 with attached bath. Bucket hot water is available.

Hotel Blue Diamond (☎ 727461, 113 Central Ave, Dosar Chowk) is a reasonable choice. Single singles/doubles are Rs 80/120 with common bath, Rs 130/200 with attached bath and Rs 350/450 with air-con. Air coolers and TVs are available for an extra charge and the hotel has a restaurant and bar.

Hotel Rajdhani (☎ 728773, Central Ave), is classier. Comfortable rooms range from Rs 250/350 to Rs 550/600 with air-con, all with TV, phone and 14% tax.

Hotel Pal Palace (☎ 724725, 25 Central Ave) is clean, quiet and comfortable with singles/doubles from Rs 250/350 to Rs 550/650 (air-con); suites are Rs 1200 (all plus tax). There's a good restaurant here and a foreign exchange desk for guests.

Places to Eat

Most of the hotels have reasonable restaurants and there are a couple of good south Indian places among the budget hotels on Central Ave.

Krishnum has cheap dosas, samosas, pastries and ice creams served in spotless surroundings. The *bakery* and sweet shop downstairs also has a good selection.

Getting There & Away

Air Indian Airlines (☎ 533962), on RN Tagore, Civil Lines, has two daily flights to Mumbai (US$115), one to Delhi (US$135), and flights on Wednesday and Sunday to Hyderabad (US$95) and Calcutta (US$150). Gujarat Airways (☎ 560141) also flies three times a week to Pune.

Bus The main MSRTC bus stand is 2km south of the train station and hotel area. There are regular departures for Wardha/Sevagram (Rs 25, two hours) and Ramtek (Rs 20, one hour) and morning buses to Jalgaon (Rs 152, 10 hours) and Hyderabad (Rs 200, 12 hours). Buses to Madhya Pradesh operate from a separate stand 1km away, including Bhopal (Rs 140, 12 hours) and Jabalpur (Rs 96, seven hours).

Train Nagpur Junction train station is centrally located and has good connections to Bangalore, Mumbai, Calcutta, Delhi and Hyderabad, as well as Sevagram and Jalgaon.

RAMTEK

About 40km north-east of Nagpur, Ramtek has a number of picturesque 600-year-old **temples** surmounting the Hill of Rama. The old British cantonment of Kemtee is nearby, and a **memorial** to the Sanskrit dramatist Kalidasa is just along the road from the MTDC holiday resort, which has a spectacular view of the town.

The *MTDC Holiday Resort* (☎ 07114-55620) has dorm beds and a few basic rooms for Rs 150.

Buses regularly make the one hour trip between Ramtek and the MSRTC bus stand in Nagpur.

SEVAGRAM

If you are at all interested in the life and philosophy of Mahatma Gandhi, it's well worth making the long trek to the heart of India to visit Sevagram, the Village of Service, where Gandhi established his ashram in 1933. For the 15 years from then until India achieved Independence, Gandhi's headquarters was in some ways the alternative capital of India – the British considered it important enough to install a telephone box here with a hotline to Delhi. For more historical information on Gandhi, see the boxed text Mohandas Gandhi in the Facts About India chapter.

The ashram encompasses 100 acres of farmland, as well as residences and research centres, though the central complex itself is quite small. The original adobe huts of the ashram are still preserved, as are the Mahatma's personal effects, including his famous spinning wheel and spectacles.

There's an interesting photo exhibition following the events in Gandhi's life across the road from the ashram. Unfortunately, not all of the exhibits and photos are labelled in English but the attendant may be able to help with translations.

Nondenominational prayer services are held daily at 4.45 am and 6 pm under the pipal tree planted by Gandhi in 1936. Ashramites follow a strict daily routine and while visitors aren't required to work, they are encouraged to participate in half an hour of spinning each day, and to be on time for meals. At other times, life at Sevagram is extremely leisurely.

Hand-spun cloth *(khadi)* is for sale at the ashram, as well as volumes of Gandhi's writings.

Places to Stay & Eat

Accommodation at the ashram is basic but clean and naturally very cheap.

Rustam Bhavan consists of four double rooms with bath for Rs 25 per person. *Yatri Nivas*, across the road, is similar but often caters for groups. The ashram can be contacted on ☎ 07152-43526/40527 to check availability of accommodation. Vegetarian meals are served communally in the dining hall for a nominal sum.

The *MTDC Holiday Resort* (☎ 07152-43872) in Wardha offers less interesting but more comfortable rooms for Rs 150/220. Turn right as you exit the train station and it's a five minute walk, across the road from the bus stand.

Getting There & Away

The ashram can be reached from Wardha or Sevagram train stations, both on the Central Railway. Express trains from Nagpur to Sevagram (76km) take a little over an hour. Express MSRTC buses run frequently between Nagpur and Wardha (Rs 25, two hours).

From Sevagram station an auto-rickshaw costs around Rs 20. There are regular local buses to the ashram from Wardha (Rs 3, 20 minutes), or an auto-rickshaw will cost Rs 30 for the 8km trip.

AROUND SEVAGRAM
Paunar

At Paunar, just 3km from Sevagram on the road to Nagpur, is the ashram of Vinoba Bhave, Gandhi's disciple. This persistent soul walked through India encouraging rich landlords to hand over tracts of land for redistribution to the landless and poor – he managed to persuade them to hand over a total of four million acres.

The ashram, run almost entirely by women, is dedicated to *swarajya*, or rural self-sufficiency. It is an interesting working ashram, operated on a social system of consensus with no central management. Basic accommodation at a nominal cost is available at the ashram and, while women are preferred, it is open to all.

An auto-rickshaw from Sevagram will cost around Rs 25, or catch any bus heading from Wardha to Nagpur.

Goa

The former Portuguese enclave of Goa, one of India's gems, has enjoyed a prominent place in the travellers' lexicon for many years with its magnificent palm-fringed beaches and renowned 'travellers' scene'.

Yet it offers much more than just the hedonism of sun, sand and sea. Goa has a character quite distinct from the rest of India. Despite four decades of 'liberation' from Portuguese colonial rule, Roman Catholicism remains a major religion in Goa, skirts far outnumber saris, and the people display an easy-going tropical indulgence, humour and civility.

Gleaming, Portuguese-style whitewashed churches, paddy fields, dense coconut palm groves, and crumbling forts guarding rocky capes make up the Goan landscape. Markets are lively, colourful affairs, and siesta is widely observed during the hot afternoons. Carnival explodes onto the streets over four riotous days and nights prior to Lent. The original reason was to celebrate the arrival of spring, which was observed within the Catholic community as three days of partying before the start of Lent (February/March). Carnival is now really just one big party.

Farming, fishing, tourism and iron-ore mining form the basis of the economy, although the last two sources of income are sometimes incompatible with the former. Mining has caused damage to paddy fields, and the five-star tourist resorts, with their swimming pools, have placed a heavy strain on water supplies.

History

Goa's history stretches back to the 3rd century BC when it formed part of the Mauryan empire. Later, at the beginning of the Christian era, it was ruled by the Satavahanas of Kolhapur and eventually passed to the Chalukyans of Badami control from 580 to 750 AD.

Goa fell to the Muslims for the first time in 1312, but the invaders were forced out in

Goa at a Glance

Population: 1.3 million
Area: 3701 sq km
Capital: Panaji
Main Languages: Konkani, Marathi, English & Hindi
Best Time to Go: October to May – but April & May are very hot

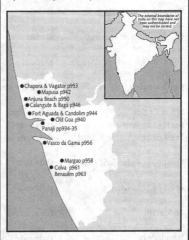

The external boundaries of India on this map have not been authenticated and may not be correct.

- Chapora & Vagator p953
- Mapusa p942
- Anjuna Beach p950
- Calangute & Baga p946
- Fort Aguada & Candolim p944
- Old Goa p940
- Panaji pp934-35
- Vasco da Gama p956
- Margao p958
- Colva p961
- Benaulim p963

- **Panaji** – sip *feni* in the old Portuguese quarter of Goa's capital

- **Old Goa** – explore Old Goa's magnificent Portuguese cathedrals

- **Anjuna Beach** – check out Anjuna's famous Wednesday flea market and full-moon raves

- **Palolem Beach** – chill out under the coconut palms at one of Goa's least-developed beaches

- **Calangute & Baga** – sample some of India's best seafood at Goa's busiest resorts

GOA

Festivals of Goa

festival	location	date	features
Feast of the Three Kings	Reis Magos, Cansaulim & Chandor	6 Jan	Christian re-enactments
Feast of Our Lady of Candelaria	Pomburpa	2 Feb	Christian feast day
Pop, Beat & Jazz Music	Kala Academy, Panaji	Feb	two days of music
Shigmotsav (Shigmo)	statewide	Feb/Mar	Goa's version of Holi
Carnival	statewide	start of Lent (Feb/Mar)	3 day party
Sabado Gordo	Panaji	Saturday before Lent	Christian float processions
Procession of All Saints	Old Goa	5th Monday in Lent	Christian parades
Feast of Jesus of Nazareth	Sindao	1st Sunday after Easter	Christian feast day
Feast of Our Lady of Miracles	Mapusa	16 days after Easter	Hindu & Christian feast day
Beach Bonanza	Colva & Calangute	Apr	music, dance & entertainment
Igitun Chalne	Sirigao Temple	May	fire-walking
Feast of St Anthony	statewide	13 Jun	Christian feast day
Feast of St John the Baptist	statewide	24 Jun	Christian monsoon thanksgiving
Feast of St Peter & St Paul	statewide	29 Jun	Christian monsoon celebration
Feast of St Lawrence	statewide	Aug	Christian feast day & monsoon celebration
Bonderam	Divar Island	4th Saturday of Aug	Processions & mock battles
Navidades	statewide	24 Aug	offerings to head of state
Fama de Menino Jesus	Colva	2nd Monday of Oct	feast day
Marathi Drama Festival	Kala Academy, Panaji	Nov/Dec	drama & arts
Food & Cultural Festival	Miramar Beach	Nov/Dec	5 days of food & entertainment
Konkani Drama Festival	Kala Academy, Panaji	Nov/Dec	arts performances
Feast of Our Lady of the Rosary	Navelim	Nov	Christian feast day
Tiatr Festival	Kala Academy, Panaji	Nov	arts
State Art Exhibition	statewide	Dec	arts & crafts
Feast of St Francis Xavier	Old Goa	3 Dec	feast day, processions & services
Feast of Our Lady of Immaculate Conception	Panaji & Margao	Dec	feast day & large fair

GOA

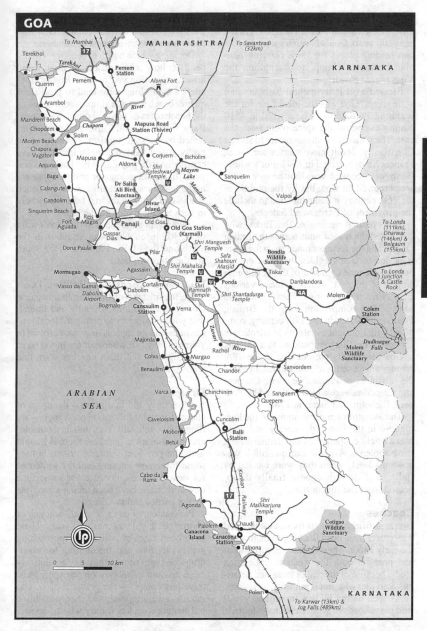

GOA

1370 by Harihara I of the Vijayanagar empire, whose capital was at Hampi. Over the next 100 years Goa's harbours were important landing places for ships carrying Arabian horses to Hampi to strengthen the Vijayanagar cavalry.

Blessed as it is by natural harbours and wide rivers, Goa was the ideal base for the seafaring Portuguese, who arrived in 1510 aiming to control the spice route from the east. They also had a strong desire to spread Christianity. Jesuit missionaries led by St Francis Xavier arrived in 1542. For a while, Portuguese control was limited to a small area around Old Goa, but by the middle of the 16th century it had expanded to include the provinces of Bardez and Salcete.

The eventual ousting of the Turks, who controlled the trade routes across the Indian Ocean, and the fortunes made from the spice trade led to Goa's golden age. The colony became the viceregal seat of the Portuguese empire of the east, which included various East African port cities, East Timor and Macau. But competition from the British, French and Dutch in the 17th century, combined with Portugal's inability to adequately service its far-flung empire, led to a decline.

Goa reached its present size in the 18th century after a series of annexations. In 1763, the provinces of Ponda, Sanguem, Quepem and Canacona were added, followed by Pednem, Bicholim and Satari in 1788.

The Marathas almost vanquished the Portuguese in the late 18th century and there was a brief occupation by the British during the Napoleonic Wars in Europe. But it was not until 1961, when they were ejected by India, that the Portuguese finally disappeared from the subcontinent.

Beaches

Goa is justifiably famous for its beaches, and westerners have been flocking to them since the early 1960s. They sometimes suffer from bad press in both the western and Indian media because of the real or imagined nefarious activities of a small minority of visitors.

As well as the budget travellers, you'll find plane-loads of western package tourists in the burgeoning major resorts, particularly Calangute. Indians from outside Goa also come here in ever-increasing numbers.

Deciding which beach to head for will depend on how long you intend to stay and how much action you're after. Budget travellers staying long term tend to head for a quieter beach to rent a simple room at one of the beach cafes or private homes. Calangute, Baga, Candolim and Colva tend to be dominated by package tourism, so they can be pretty lively. Anjuna, the traditional rave centre, is still popular with backpackers, while the smaller Vagator and Chapora are more laid-back. Benaulim, with its beach shacks and low-key resorts, falls somewhere in between the hype and the hip.

If you want a quiet beach (but don't want to be Robinson Crusoe), Arambol in the north and the idyllic Palolem in the south are the places to head.

Nudism & Local Sensibilities Don't make the mistake of thinking that because Goa is so welcoming, friendly and liberal, that you're at liberty to disregard local sensibilities and go topless or prance around in your birthday suit whenever the mood takes you. Signs on the main beaches warn that nudism is illegal.

Drugs

Acid, ecstasy and marijuana – the drugs of choice for many full-moon partygoers – are illegal (though still very much available) and any attempt to purchase them is fraught with danger. Fort Aguada prison houses some foreigners serving lengthy sentences for drug offences, because for some time now authorities have been taking a hard line on the parties and the drugs.

Possession of even a small amount of *charas* (hashish) can mean 10 years. There have been cases of policemen approaching hapless tourists and threatening to 'plant' drugs on them unless they pay a relatively large amount of money on the spot. Most travellers comply – the prospect of several months awaiting trial, and then possibly a jail sentence, makes it only wise to do so.

Water Conservation

Take great care to use water as sparingly as possible because Goa's supplies are severely limited. Tourism in general has placed a heavy strain on the state's water resources, but the upmarket hotels carry most of the blame. In some areas, guests languish beside Olympic-sized swimming pools while just outside the gates the water supply is limited to a few hours a day. Some of the bigger hotels have drilled deep tube wells to syphon off their own supplies, but the effect has been to lower the water table in the area. Wells have dried up in some villages and have been polluted with salt water in others.

Don't leave taps running. Even if your hotel has a bathtub in the bathroom, use the shower instead. If you're on a package tour or choosing an upmarket hotel to stay at, consider whether you want to condone the use of a swimming pool. Who needs a pool anyway when the Arabian Sea is just a short walk away?

Probably the best way to deal with the problem should it happen to you is to try persuasion, but if that fails, pay the baksheesh. While doing this, make a mental note of every distinguishing feature of the policeman you are paying. Immediately after the incident, write a letter describing exactly what happened, with as much detail as possible.

Copies of the letter should go to the Government of India tourist office in Panaji (not the Goan Tourist Department), any one (or all) of the three daily English-language newspapers in Goa, and the Government of India tourist office in your own country.

Special Events

There is a strong Christian influence in Goa and this is reflected in the number of feast days and festivals that follow the religious calendar. As well as the more popular Christian holidays (ie Christmas, Easter etc) Goans use feast days to celebrate events such

as the arrival of the monsoon. Igitun Chalne, held at Sirigao Temple in Bicholim *taluka* (province) in May is one of Goa's most distinctive festivals. Meaning fire-walking; the high point of the festival comes when devotees of the goddess Lairaya walk across burning coals to prove their devotion.

The Feast of St Anthony in June, has also taken on local significance. It is said that if the monsoon has not arrived by the time of this feast day, a statue of the saint should be lowered into the family well to hasten the arrival of the rain. The Feast of St John in June is a thanksgiving for the arrival of the monsoon. Wells start to fill up again, and to mark the event young men jump into the water. Since each well owner by tradition has to supply *feni* to the swimmers, the feast day is marked by increasingly high spirits. Another celebration of the monsoon takes place during the Feast of St Peter & St Paul. During this time, the fishing community, particularly in Bardez *taluka* use boats to form rafts which serve as stages.

Medical Services

If you're unlucky enough to be injured in a motorcycle accident – relatively common in Goa – the best bone specialist in Goa is Dr Bhale (☎ 0832-217053), who runs a 24 hour x-ray clinic at Porvorim, 6km north of Panaji on the NH17 road to Mapusa.

Accommodation

Accommodation prices in Goa are based on high, middle and low seasons. High season is mid-December to late January, the middle (shoulder) period is from October to mid-December and February to June, and the low season from July to September. Unless otherwise stated, prices quoted in this chapter are high-season rates. If you're in Goa during the rest of the year, then expect discounts of about 25%/60% in mid/low season. Prices may rise again, sometimes to ridiculous heights, over the peak Christmas period from around 22 December to 3 January. This usually applies to short-term stays.

Year round, there's a 5%/10%/15% luxury tax on rooms over Rs 100/500/800. For most

Security

Goa's booming tourist industry has brought with it inevitable problems, crime being one of them. The temptation to get hold of tourist dollars has proved too strong in some cases, and there has been a spate of robberies and muggings in recent years. Much more disturbing has been a number of attacks on women travellers – many organisers of beach parties now strongly advise women not to wander off on their own.

The Goans are understandably concerned by the recent developments, and blame the incidents on criminals from neighbouring states. Some measures have been taken to discourage further attacks, although realistically their effectiveness is doubtful. Limited street lighting has been installed, and there are now security patrols on some beaches.

To put all this into context, Goa is still fairly safe compared to many places one could think of, and most visitors will have no problems whatsoever. It pays, however, to be wary. Don't walk alone along the beach at night, or go unaccompanied along dark, unlit village lanes if you can help it. The unlit back lanes in Benaulim have been the scene of several muggings, in some of which chilli powder has been thrown into the eyes of the victims before their bags were snatched. If you are staying in a reasonable hotel or family house where there is a safe or similar facility, it is worth leaving your passport etc there rather than carrying it with you all the time. Women travellers should not walk alone in deserted areas at night.

Finally, if you're here in the low season avoid staying in isolated accommodation near the beach. During high season beach huts are fine because there are other travellers around, but there have been several cases of thieves targeting foreigners staying on their own.

budget places, the prices quoted include tax, but in mid - range and top - end hotels you can expect tax to be added to the bill.

There are no accommodation agents as such in Goa, but Goa Tourism produces a pretty good booklet listing the main hotels and guesthouses as well as some private homes.

Food & Drink

Scottish missionary Edward Aitken wrote of the people of Goa in 1889, 'while they carry through the world patronymics which breathe of conquest and discovery, they devote their energies rather to the violin and the art of cookery'.

Goans are passionate about their food and there are several local specialities, including the popular pork vindaloo. Other pork specialities include the *chourisso* (Goan sausage), and the pig's liver dish known as *sorpotel*. *Xacutí* is a chicken or meat dish; *bangra* is Goan mackerel; *sanna* are rice 'cupcakes' soaked in palm toddy before

cooking; *dodol* and *bebinca* are special Christmas sweets; and *Moira kela* are cooking plantains (banana-like fruit) from Moira village in Bardez. The plaintains were probably introduced from Africa and can be found in the vegetable market close to the Indian Airlines office in Panaji.

Although the ready availability (and low price) of commercially produced alcohol contrasts markedly with most other parts of India, the Goans also brew their own local varieties. Most common of these is *feni*, a spirit made from coconut or cashews (the fruit, not the nut itself). A bottle bought from a liquor shop costs only slightly more than a bottle of beer bought at a restaurant. Reasonably palatable wines are also being turned out. The dry white is not bad; the red is basically a port. As always, the quality depends on the price you pay.

Getting There & Away

Air Goa's international airport, Dabolim, is 29km from Panaji, on the coast near Vasco da Gama. Most of India's domestic airlines operate services here, as well as several direct charter companies that fly into Goa from the UK and Germany.

There are numerous flights between Goa and Mumbai. Indian Airlines flies daily (with two flights on Monday and Thursday) for US$75, and Jet Airways has two flights daily (three on Wednesday, Thursday and Saturday) for US$90. Sahara Airlines also flies to Mumbai (US$90) and Delhi (US$210).

Indian Airlines has daily direct flights to Delhi (US$210) and Cochin (US$110), and four flights a week to Bangalore (US$95) and Chennai (US$125). Gujarat Airways flies direct to Pune (US$90) on Monday, Wednesday and Friday.

Bus See the Panaji Getting There & Away entry for details of long-distance bus travel.

Train The completion of the 760km Konkan Railway linking Mangalore to Mumbai in 1998 has opened Goa up. (See The Konkan Railway boxed text in the Maharashtra chapter for more on this monumental project.)

At the time of writing there was only one direct express between Margao and Mumbai CST (11½ hours) and five between Margao and Mangalore or Kankanadi (5½ hours). Numerous passenger trains depart from Kurla (16km from Mumbai).

With the conversion to broad gauge also complete, long-haul journeys are faster. Trains to Bangalore (via Londa, 689km) take about 15 hours and cost Rs 191/679 in sleeper/1st class, or Rs 953 for air-con two-tier sleeper. Mumbai (720km) costs Rs 202/706. Getting to Delhi from Goa (2200km) takes about 44 hours and the fare is Rs 376/1545 in sleeper/1st class, and Rs 1939 for air-con two-tier sleeper.

Goa's two main stations are at Margao (Madgaon) and Vasco da Gama. Seats and sleepers can be booked at either of these, or at the train reservation office in Panaji's Kadamba bus stand. Other useful stations on the Konkan route are Mapusa Road (Thivim) for Mapusa and Old Goa (Karmali) for Panaji.

Taxi It takes 14 hours to drive the 600km from Mumbai to Goa, but this can be done over two days. You'll have to pay for the taxi's return trip, so the cost will be around Rs 6000 (Rs 5 per kilometre). Shop around for the taxi that offers the lowest rate.

Boat The catamaran service between Mumbai and Panaji, operated by Frank Shipping, has been a bit erratic in recent years due to breakdowns. In theory it sails between October and May. From Goa it sails every Monday, Wednesday, Friday, Saturday and Sunday, departing at 10 am and arriving in Mumbai at 5.30 pm. Going the other way, it departs Mumbai on Tuesday and Thursday at 10 am, arriving in Panaji at 5.30 pm; on Friday, Saturday and Sunday, it leaves Mumbai at 10.30 pm, arriving at 6.30 am. Bookings can be made through travel agencies or at the company's offices in Mumbai (☎ 022-283 8904) and Panaji (☎ 0832-228711).

It's not cheap at Rs 1600/1800 for economy/business class and apart from the half-hour cruise up the Mandovi River, the trip is pretty dull as the catamaran is obliged to stay at least 15km from the coast to avoid fishing fleets.

Getting Around

Bus The state-run Kadamba bus company is the main operator, although there are also many private companies. Local buses are cheap, services are frequent and they run to just about everywhere. Destination signs at the bus stands are in English, so there are no worries about finding the bus you want. They are, however, fairly slow because they make frequent stops.

Car Rental Self-drive car rental is available in Goa, although it's expensive. Several companies have counters at the airport. Hertz (☎ 0832-423998) charges from Rs 1750 per day for a small Maruti-Suzuki, with reductions for longer rentals. Budget (☎ 0832-217755) also has an office at the airport. It's often cheaper, however, to rent a taxi for a specific trip.

Motorcycle Rental Hiring a motorcycle in Goa is easy, and popular with many travellers. The machines that are available are old Enfields, more modern Yamaha 100s and the gearless Kinetic Honda scooters. Obviously what you pay for, with some exceptions, is what you get, and prices also vary according to season. In high season, on a daily basis, you're looking at up to Rs 300 for a scooter, Rs 400 for the small bikes and Rs 500 for an Enfield. Some places need your passport and a sizeable deposit before they'll let you go; others just want to know where you're staying.

Out of town, Classic Bike Adventure (fax 0832-262076), Casa Tres Amigos, Assagao, deals mainly with organised two to three-week tours on well-maintained Enfields, but will sometimes also rent bikes.

While most bikes will have some sort of insurance, if you're involved in an accident you'll probably be required to pay for the damage to the rental bike, at the very least.

You should be aware that India has the worst record for road accidents in the world. Although Goan lanes are probably a little safer than the Grand Trunk Road, inexperienced, helmetless foreigners on motorcycles are extremely vulnerable. Each season, more than a few tourists travel home in a box via the state mortuary in Panaji. Never forget that the Highway Code in India can be reduced to one essential truth – 'might is right' – and on a motorcycle, you're pretty low on the hierarchy. Also make sure that the machine you rent is in a reasonable state of repair (with working horn, indicators and brakes).

Make sure that you carry the necessary paperwork (licence, registration and insurance) at all times because licence checks on foreigners are a lucrative source of baksheesh for the police. They may try for anything up to Rs 1000, but can usually be bargained down. Places to avoid are the towns (particularly Panaji, Margao and Mapusa) and Anjuna on market day (Wednesday) – although you'll melt into the hundreds of other motorcyclists at Anjuna! British licences are valid in Goa, otherwise you should carry an International Driving Permit.

Motorcycle Taxi Goa is the one place in India where motorcycles are a licensed form of taxi. They are much cheaper than other transport, and backpacks are no problem. Licensed motorcycles are common and can be identified by a yellow front mudguard.

Bicycle Rental There are plenty of places to hire bicycles in all the major towns and beach resorts – around Rs 40 for a full day.

Boat One of the joys of travelling around Goa is the combined passenger/vehicle ferries that cross the small state's many rivers. There are, however, bridges being built over several rivers that will eventually put the ferries out of business. The main ferries are:

Siolim-Chopdem
   For Arambol and places north. Every half hour from 6.30 am until 10 pm; the 10 minute crossing costs Rs 0.75/3 for passengers/motorcycles.
Querim-Terekhol
   Accesses Terekhol Fort, in the far north of the state. Services run approx every half hour.
Dona Paula-Mormugao
   Runs frequent but erratic crossings between September and May (till around 5 pm). At certain times of the day, you could find yourself waiting two hours. The crossing takes 30 to 45 minutes; buses wait on either side. This is a passenger ferry only, but it's a pleasant way of getting from Panaji to Vasco da Gama.
Old Goa-Divar Island
   Half hour service.
Other Ferries
   Approximately 20 other ferry services operate throughout the state. These include: Panaji-Betim; Aldona-Corjuem; Pomburpa-Chorao; and Ribandar-Chorao.

North Goa

Goa neatly splits into two districts: North and South Goa. North Goa has the state capital, Panaji; the former capital of Old Goa, with its interesting churches and cathedrals; and a string of beaches running right up the coast to Maharashtra.

PANAJI (Panjim)
☎ 0832 • pop 93,000

Panaji is one of India's smallest and most pleasant state capitals. Built on the south bank of the wide Mandovi River, it officially became the capital of Goa in 1843 when Old Goa was finally abandoned.

Each year on Sabado Gordo (Fat Saturday), **Carnival** centres around a procession of colourful floats. The event is opened by the arrival of King Momo, who orders his subjects to forget their worries and have a good time.

Most travellers pass through Panaji on their way to the beaches or to Old Goa, but the town is well worth a visit.

Information
Tourist Offices The Goan Tourist Development Corporation (GTDC, also known as Goa Tourism) tourist office (☎ 225715) is in the government-run Patto Tourist Home between the Kadamba bus stand and the Ourem River. Good maps of Goa and Panaji are available (Rs 12). There's also a useful tourist counter at the Kadamba bus stand. A third counter at the airport is open for incoming flights.

The Government of India tourist office (☎ 223412) in the Communidade Building, Church Square, is helpful for onward travel plans, on the same square is a Karnataka state tourist office (☎ 224110).

Money There are plenty of efficient foreign exchange places in Panaji. Thomas Cook is open Monday to Saturday 9.30 am to 6 pm, and Sunday (October to March only) 10 am to 5 pm. The American Express representative is Menezes Travel (☎ 230704), Ourem St, but there's no currency exchange here. The Bank of Baroda, on the Azad Maidan, will provide Visa and MasterCard advances (Rs 100 fee plus 1% commission) 10 am to 1 pm Monday to Friday and 10 to 11 am on Saturday.

Post & Communications The efficient poste restante at the main post office is open Monday to Saturday 9 am to 5 pm.

You can send and receive email or access the Internet at Shruti Communications on 31st January Rd for Rs 75 per hour. It's bound to be busy since it's right below Hotel Venite. Another place is Classic Business Centre, just off MG Rd (Rs 100 per hour).

Visa Extensions Visa extensions are not granted as a matter of course in Panaji – officially they're not granted at all on tourist visas – but if your appearance and attitude are right, your application is more likely to be viewed favourably. If you're unsuccessful here, Mumbai and Bangalore are the nearest alternatives. The Foreigners' Registration Office, in the police headquarters in the centre of Panaji, is open Monday to Friday 9.30 am to 1 pm.

Travel Agencies Reputable travel agencies include Aero Mundial (☎ 224831) at the Hotel Mandovi; Georgeson & Georgeson (☎ 223742), opposite the main post office (1st floor); and MGM International Travels (☎ 225150), Mamai Camotin Building, near the Secretariat (they also have branches at Calangute and Anjuna).

Bookshops & Libraries The Mandovi and Fidalgo hotels have good bookshops that stock international magazines. Panaji Central Library is on the west side of the Azad Maidan, next to the police headquarters.

Our Lady of the Immaculate Conception
This striking edifice is Panaji's main church. It stands above the square in the main part of town, reached by several intersecting flights of stairs. The original construction was consecrated in 1541. Panaji was the first port of call for voyages from Lisbon, so Portuguese sailors would visit this church to give thanks for a safe crossing before continuing to Old Goa. Mass is held here daily in English, Konkani and Portuguese.

Goa State Museum
Opened in 1996, this modern, well-laid out museum has several galleries featuring

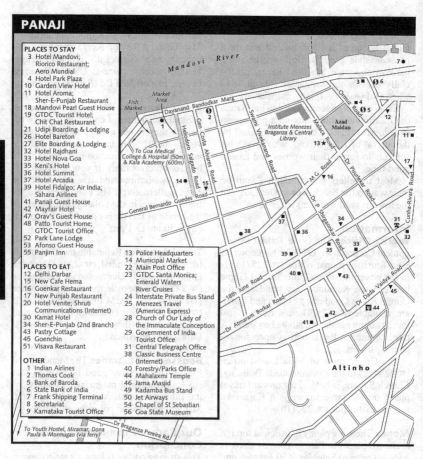

PANAJI

PLACES TO STAY
3 Hotel Mandovi;
  Riorico Restaurant;
  Aero Mundial
4 Hotel Park Plaza
10 Garden View Hotel
11 Hotel Aroma;
  Sher-E-Punjab Restaurant
18 Mandovi Pearl Guest House
19 GTDC Tourist Hotel;
  Chit Chat Restaurant
21 Udipi Boarding & Lodging
26 Hotel Bareton
27 Elite Boarding & Lodging
32 Hotel Rajdhani
33 Hotel Nova Goa
35 Keni's Hotel
36 Hotel Summit
37 Hotel Arcadia
39 Hotel Fidalgo; Air India;
  Sahara Airlines
41 Panaji Guest House
42 Mayfair Hotel
47 Orav's Guest House
48 Patto Tourist Home;
  GTDC Tourist Office
52 Park Lane Lodge
53 Afonso Guest House
55 Panjim Inn

PLACES TO EAT
12 Delhi Darbar
15 New Cafe Hema
16 Goenkar Restaurant
17 New Punjab Restaurant
20 Hotel Venite; Shruti
  Communications (Internet)
30 Kamat Hotel
34 Sher-E-Punjab (2nd Branch)
43 Pastry Cottage
45 Goenchin
51 Visava Restaurant

OTHER
1 Indian Airlines
2 Thomas Cook
5 Bank of Baroda
6 State Bank of India
7 Frank Shipping Terminal
8 Secretariat
9 Karnataka Tourist Office

13 Police Headquarters
14 Municipal Market
22 Main Post Office
23 GTDC Santa Monica;
  Emerald Waters
  River Cruises
24 Interstate Private Bus Stand
25 Menezes Travel
  (American Express)
28 Church of Our Lady of
  the Immaculate Conception
29 Government of India
  Tourist Office
31 Central Telegraph Office
38 Classic Business Centre
  (Internet)
40 Forestry/Parks Office
44 Mahalaxmi Temple
46 Jama Masjid
49 Kadamba Bus Stand
50 Jet Airways
54 Chapel of St Sebastian
56 Goa State Museum

Christian art, Hindu and Jain sculpture and bronzes, and paintings from all over India. The museum is still being developed so the present collection is small, but worthwhile. It is near the bus stand, open Monday to Friday 9 am to 1.15 pm and 2 to 5.30 pm (free).

Fontainhas & Sao Tomé

Just west of the Ourem River, these old Portuguese districts are Panaji's most interesting areas. The narrow cobbled streets, tiled buildings, shuttered windows and tiny overhanging balconies present an atmosphere more reminiscent of the Mediterranean than of India. Local men sip *feni* in tiny bars and some of Panaji's best guesthouses are in this quarter.

The **Chapel of St Sebastian** stands at the end of a picturesque street in Fontainhas. Although it dates only from the 1880s, it contains a number of interesting features, in particular a striking crucifix that originally stood in the Palace of the Inquisition in Old Goa.

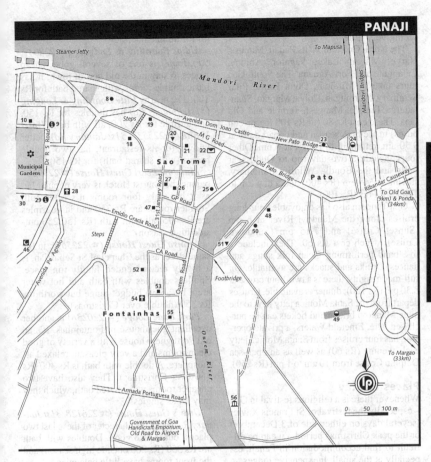

Other Attractions

The **Secretariat** building is interesting. Dating from the 16th century, it was originally the palace of Adil Shah, ruler of the Adil Shahi dynasty of Bijapur, and in 1759 it became the viceroy's official residence. The bizarre **statue** of a man apparently about to strangle a woman nearby is of Abbé Faria, a famous hypnotist, and his assistant. Born in Candolim in 1756, he emigrated to France, where he became a celebrated hypnotic medium.

The modern **Mahalaxmi Temple** is a reminder that there's a thriving Hindu community in Panaji. For good views over the town, walk up to the **Altinho** district. You can get there by walking south from Fontainhas or following the road up past Our Lady of the Immaculate Conception church.

Organised Tours

A variety of tours are offered by Goa Tourism (book at the tourist office in Panaji) and private agencies. Some of the day tours pack too much in, so you end up seeing very little.

The North Goa tour visits Panaji, Mapusa, Narve, Mayem Lake, Vagator, Anjuna, Calangute and Fort Aguada. The South Goa tours take in Miramar, Dona Paula, Pilar Seminary, Mormugao, Colva, Margao, Shantadurga Temple, Mangesh Temple and Old Goa. These cost Rs 80 (or Rs 100 for air-con buses) in the high season and depart daily at 9.30 am, returning to Panaji at 6 pm. Other tours include a two day trip to Dudhsagar Falls and the Bondla Wildlife Sanctuary, staying at Molem (Rs 400) and a day trip to Terekhol Fort (Rs 100).

Goa Tourism also has enjoyable hour-long cruises along the Mandovi River at 6 pm (Sunset Cruise) and 7.15 pm (Sundown Cruise), which cost Rs 60. They include a live band performing Goan folk songs and dances. Drinks and snacks are available. On full-moon nights, there is a two-hour cruise at 8.30 pm (Rs 100); dinner is available. Cruises depart from the Santa Monica jetty next to the huge Mandovi bridge and tickets can be purchased here. Emerald Waters, a private operator, has four cruises from Santa Monica jetty each evening (Rs 60) as well as an open-sea Dolphin Cruise from 10 am to 1 pm (Rs 250).

Places to Stay

Whenever there is a religious festival in Goa – especially the festival of St Francis Xavier (several days on either side of 3 December) or the peak Christmas period – it can be difficult to find accommodation in Panaji, especially at the small, inexpensive lodges.

Places to Stay – Budget

Patto Tourist Home (☎ 227972), in a complex that includes the tourist office, is by the Ourem River, between the Kadamba bus stand and the town centre. Dormitory beds (Rs 50) aren't easy to get since management won't let foreigners share with Indians. Triple rooms are Rs 350.

The *Youth Hostel* (☎ 225433) is at Miramar, 3km west of Panaji, in a shady she-oak garden by the water. It has an institutional air, is inconveniently located and there's an

8 am checkout. Dorm beds cost Rs 20 (Rs 40 for nonmembers).

Udipi Boarding & Lodging (☎ 228047, Sao Tomé) is one of several good, cheap places to stay in the old part of town. It has basic double rooms with shared bath for Rs 100. The nearby *Elite Boarding & Lodging* (*31st January Rd*) has doubles for Rs 150, and a triple for Rs 200, all with bath. *Hotel Venite* (☎ 225537, 31st January Rd), better known for its restaurant, has two double rooms (with shared bath) for Rs 150.

Mandovi Pearl Guest House (☎ 223928), behind the Tourist Hotel, is very popular but as it has only four rooms it's often full. Smaller rooms are Rs 350 and large triples are Rs 475, all with bath (Rs 150/250 outside high season).

Afonso Guest House (☎ 222359), in the same street as the Chapel of St Sebastian, is a highly recommended family-run place. Spotless doubles with bath and hot water are a bit above budget range but worth the Rs 350 (double over Christmas).

Park Lane Lodge (☎ 220238) is another excellent guesthouse in Fontainhas. It's an old Portuguese house with a variety of good clean rooms and a very pleasant relaxed atmosphere. A double with bath is Rs 300 (Rs 450 over Christmas). They also have two cheaper rooms with shared bath, which they may let as singles.

Orav's Guest House (☎ 226128, 31st January Rd) lacks the character of these last two places, but is also good. Doubles with bath are Rs 350 (Rs 200 outside high season) and the front rooms have little balconies.

Panaji Guest House (☎ 228511, Swami Vivekanand Rd) is a cheap option if there's nothing else around. Dorm beds are Rs 60 and basic doubles are Rs 150.

Places to Stay – Mid-Range

The *GTDC Tourist Hotel* (☎ 227103, MG Rd) is an unremarkable place on a busy road but it's popular with travellers. Doubles cost Rs 450, with Rs 700 for air-con. Prices drop by only Rs 50 in the low season. There's a terrace restaurant, bar, bookshop and a handicraft shop on the ground floor.

Garden View Hotel (☎ 227844, Diogo de Couto Rd) is in a pleasant spot overlooking the municipal gardens. Plain but decent-sized single/doubles cost Rs 350/450.

Hotel Aroma (☎ 43519, Cunha-Rivara Rd) is a modern place that fronts onto the Municipal gardens. The clean, airy double rooms with bath are relatively good value at Rs 500 (Rs 350 mid-season). The tandoori restaurant on the 1st floor is one of the best in Panaji.

Hotel Bareton (☎ 226405, Luis Menezes Rd) is a small place with singles/doubles from Rs 450/600. There's 24 hour hot water and an 8.30 am checkout.

Mayfair Hotel (☎ 223317, Dr Dada Vaidya Rd) is pleasant and comfortable but overpriced with standard/deluxe rooms for Rs 600/800, (Rs 380/490 mid-season); they also let them as singles for Rs 280.

Hotel Arcadia (☎ 226721, MG Rd) is in the same league as the Mayfair but cheaper. Clean, pleasant rooms are Rs 300, or Rs 400 with air-con (more for a room with balcony).

Hotel Summit (☎ 426736, fax 229487, Menezes Braganza Rd) is similar but more expensive at Rs 600/800 (Rs 500/600 mid-season). All rooms have air-con.

Keni's Hotel (☎ 224581, fax 235227, 18th June Rd) is fairly good value. Singles/doubles cost Rs 400/550; air-con doubles cost Rs 650 with bathroom, hot water and colour TV. There's a bar, restaurant and shopping arcade.

Panjim Inn (☎ 226523, 31st January Rd) is by far the nicest (albeit expensive) place to stay in this range. It's a beautiful 300-year-old mansion with a large 1st floor veranda and leafy garden. Rooms cost Rs 495/630 (plus 15% tax) or Rs 630/720 from 21 December to 10 January. Try to see a few rooms – some are definitely better than others. There's a TV lounge, and a good restaurant.

Hotel Rajdhani (☎ 225362, Dr Atmaram Borkar Rd) is a good clean place in the centre of town. It charges Rs 750 for a double (Rs 850 for air-con) and there's a popular vegetarian restaurant downstairs.

Hotel Park Plaza (☎ 422601, fax 225635, Azad Maidan) is centrally located and reasonably modern. The cheapest rooms are Rs 795/1000 (Rs 600/795 outside Christmas).

Places to Stay – Top End

Hotel Mandovi (☎ 224405, fax 225451, Dayanand Bandodkar Marg) is the best of the top-end places. Rooms in this colonial hotel start at Rs 1300/1900. There's a good restaurant on the 1st floor and a pleasant bar on the balcony.

Hotel Nova Goa (☎ 226231, fax 224958, Dr Atmaram Borkar Rd) is the best of the modern hotels. Singles/doubles cost from Rs 1200/1800 (Rs 2600 for doubles over Christmas). There are also more-expensive suites, and a shaded pool.

Hotel Fidalgo (☎ 226291, fax 225061, 18th June Rd) is a big old place, also with a swimming pool, but is rather run-down. Rooms start at Rs 800/1000 (Rs 1100 in high season).

Places to Eat

Hotel Venite (31st January Rd, Sao Tomé) has long been popular with travellers. With its tiny balconies hanging over the street and rustic Portuguese decor it has bags of atmosphere. The Goan dishes and seafood are excellent, though not cheap by local standards. *Chourisso*, chicken cafrial and tiger prawns are among the specialities. It's also a great spot for a cold beer or two during siesta. The Venite is open for breakfast, lunch and dinner Monday to Saturday.

Udipi Boarding & Lodging, one street east of the Venite, also has a 1st floor restaurant with a balcony overlooking the street. Although it doesn't attract many foreigners, it's always crowded with Goans, and serves cheap, basic but tasty food.

The *New Cafe Hema (General Bernado Guedes Rd)* is a cheap, clean place near the municipal market serving a superb fish, curry and rice *thali* for Rs 15 and cheap veg snacks for Rs 5.

Chit Chat Restaurant, upstairs at the Tourist Hotel, has a pleasant veranda overlooking the Mandovi River. It's a popular place for breakfast, and is open for lunch and dinner (though servings are a bit small).

GOA

Kamat Hotel, on the south side of the municipal gardens, is part of the excellent chain of vegetarian restaurants.

Visava Restaurant is a very pleasant semi open-air place on the east bank of the Ourem River (at the end of the footbridge). It serves reasonably priced Goan dishes, as well as Chinese and vegetarian food.

Sher-E-Punjab, at the Hotel Aroma, is a flash place serving arguably the best tandoori in town. There's a second branch on 18th June Rd.

Delhi Darbar (MG Rd) is another recommended tandoori place, though it's a little more expensive than the Sher-E-Punjab. It's one of the most popular restaurants in town and is often fully booked in the later part of the evening.

Goenchin, just off Dr Dada Vaidya Rd, is an excellent Chinese restaurant but it's a splurge option with main dishes from Rs 90, and specials from Rs 100 to Rs 150.

Riorico, at the Hotel Mandovi, is supposedly the best restaurant for Goan cuisine, but the menu is limited and the service is slow. Prawn vindaloo is Rs 125, lobster balchao is Rs 650 and *bebinca* (a tasty Goan dessert) is Rs 40. There's a pleasant balcony overlooking the Mandovi River.

There are several pastry shops in Panaji: the best is probably the *Pastry Cottage*, near the Hotel Nova Goa.

Entertainment

The *Kala Academy* (☎ 224293, *Dayanand Bandodkar Marg*), on the west side of the city, has a cultural program of dance, music and art exhibitions throughout the year.

Getting There & Away

Air Indian Airlines (☎ 223831) is at Dempo Building, Dayanand Bandodkar Marg. Air India (☎ 231101) is next to the Hotel Fidalgo, on 18th June Rd. Other airlines with offices in Panaji include Jet Airways (☎ 221472), Shop 789, Sesa Ghor, Patto Plaza, and Sahara Airlines (☎ 230237) in the Hotel Fidalgo.

See Getting There & Away at the start of this chapter for flights to Dabolim (29km).

Bus Goa, Maharashtra and Karnataka state road transport corporations all operate services out of Panaji's Kadamba bus stand. Typical fares and timings include: Mumbai (Rs 205, 15 to 18 hours), Mangalore (Rs 141, 11 hours), Bangalore (Rs 223, 14 hours), Mysore (Rs 198, 16 hours), Hospet (Rs 102, nine hours) and Pune (Rs 138, 12 hours).

There are also services to Londa (where you can get a daily direct railway connection to Mysore every day), Hubli (a railway junction on the main Mumbai to Bangalore line, where you can also get trains to Gadag for both Bijapur and Badami, and Hospet and Hampi) and Belgaum.

Many private operators have offices outside the entrance to the bus stand, with luxury and air-con buses to Mumbai, Bangalore, Hampi and other destinations. Most private interstate buses arrive and depart from a separate bus stand next to the Mandovi Bridge. Paulo Tours & Travel (☎ 223736) has nightly sleeper coaches to Hampi (Rs 350), Mumbai (Rs 600) and Bangalore (Rs 400), which are popular but the comfort factor gets mixed reports from travellers. Luxury buses can also be booked through agents in Margao, Mapusa and the beach resorts.

For journeys within Goa, some of the more popular routes from Panaji include:

Vasco da Gama & Mormugao
You can either go via the ferry from Dona Paula to Mormugao, or by road via Agassaim and Cortalim. Unless you know there will be a ferry waiting for you on arrival at Dona Paula, the route via Agassaim and Cortalim is the quicker of the two. Both cost Rs 8 and take one hour.

Margao
Direct ordinary/express buses to Margao cost Rs 8/12 (about one hour). Buses via Ponda take about two hours. Change at Margao for the beaches of the south.

Old Goa
Frequent buses go straight to Old Goa or take any bus going to Ponda (Rs 3, 25 minutes).

Calangute
There are frequent services throughout the day and evening (Rs 4, 35 minutes).

Mapusa
Frequent buses run to Mapusa (pronounced 'Mapsa') and there's a separate ticket kiosk at the Kadamba bus stand for express services (Rs 4, 25 minutes). Change at Mapusa for Chapora.

Train The train is a better option than the bus for Mumbai and Mangalore – see Getting There & Away at the start of this chapter. The nearest train station to Panaji is Karmali, 11km to the east near Old Goa, but it's not yet clear which expresses will stop here. There's a railway reservation office upstairs in Panaji's Kadamba bus stand, open Monday to Saturday 9 to 11.30 am and 1.30 to 5 pm and Sunday 9 am to 2 pm.

Boat See the Getting There & Away section at the start of this chapter for details of the daily catamaran service to Mumbai.

Getting Around

To/From the Airport There is no bus from Panaji to Dabolim airport. A taxi costs Rs 350 and takes about 40 minutes, or you can take a taxi to Vasco da Gama and get a bus from there.

Taxi & Auto-Rickshaw Getting drivers to use their meters is extremely difficult. Negotiate the fare before heading off. Typical taxi fares from Panaji include Rs 175/325 to Calangute/Colva.

Motorcycle It's easy enough to rent a motorcycle or scooter in Panaji and you'll generally pay a little less than at the busy beach resorts in high season. There are no hire shops as such – ask at your guesthouse or head to the cluster of bikes opposite the main post office on MG Rd. See the Getting Around section at the start of this chapter.

AROUND PANAJI

Miramar, 3km west of Panaji, is the nearest beach to the capital, but it's neither particularly attractive nor a good place to swim.

Four kilometres farther along is **Dona Paula**, a small town with several resorts that has grown up around a fishing village.

Frequent buses to Miramar and Dona Paula leave Panaji's Kadamba bus stand.

OLD GOA

Just 9km east of Panaji, half a dozen imposing churches and cathedrals (among the largest in Asia) are all that remain of the Portuguese capital that was once said to rival Lisbon in magnificence. Some of the old buildings have become museums maintained by the Archaeological Survey of India – a maintenance that is very necessary because unless the lime plaster that protects the laterite structures is renewed frequently, the monsoons will reduce the buildings to ruin.

The **Procession of All Saints**, on the fifth Monday in Lent, is the only procession of its sort outside Rome. Thirty statues of saints are brought out from storage and paraded around Old Goa's neighbouring villages.

History

Even before the arrival of the Portuguese, Old Goa was a thriving and prosperous city, and the second capital of the Adil Shahi dynasty of Bijapur. At that time, it was a fortress surrounded by walls, towers and a moat, and contained temples, mosques and the large palace of Adil Shah. Today, none of these structures remain except for a fragment of the palace gateway.

Under the Portuguese, the city grew rapidly in size and splendour, despite an epidemic in 1543 that wiped out a large part of the population. Old Goa's splendour was short-lived, however, because by the end of the 16th century, Portuguese supremacy on the seas had been replaced by that of the British, Dutch and French. The city's decline was accelerated by the Inquisition and another devastating epidemic that struck in 1635. Indeed, if it hadn't been for the treaty between the British and the Portuguese, Goa would probably have either passed to the Dutch or been absorbed into British India. In 1843 the capital shifted to Panaji.

Information

The Archaeological Survey of India publishes the excellent booklet *Old Goa* by S Rajagopalan (Rs 10). It's available from the archaeological museum in Old Goa.

Se Cathedral

The largest of the churches in Old Goa, Se Cathedral was begun in 1562 during the

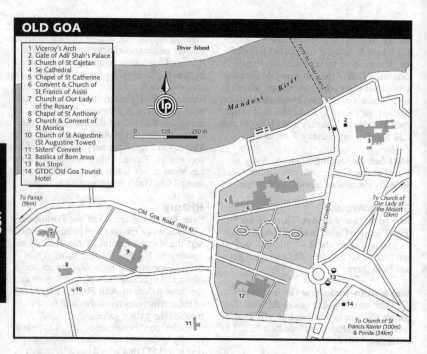

OLD GOA

1 Viceroy's Arch
2 Gate of Adil Shah's Palace
3 Church of St Cajetan
4 Se Cathedral
5 Chapel of St Catherine
6 Convent & Church of
   St Francis of Assisi
7 Church of Our Lady
   of the Rosary
8 Chapel of St Anthony
9 Church & Convent of
   St Monica
10 Church of St Augustine
   (St Augustine Tower)
11 Sisters' Convent
12 Basilica of Bom Jesus
13 Bus Stops
14 GTDC Old Goa Tourist
   Hotel

Divar Island

Ferry to Divar Island

Mandovi River

To Panaji
(9km)

Old Goa Road (NH 4)

Rua Direita

To Church of
Our Lady of
the Mount
(2km)

To Church of St
Francis Xavier (100m)
& Ponda (24km)

0   125   250 m

reign of King Dom Sebastião (1557-58). It was substantially completed by 1619, though the altars were not finished until 1652. The cathedral was built for the Dominicans and paid for by the royal treasury out of the proceeds of the sale of crown property.

The building's style is Portuguese-Gothic with a Tuscan exterior and Corinthian interior. The remaining tower houses a famous bell, one of the largest in Goa, often called the Golden Bell because of its rich sound. The main altar is dedicated to St Catherine of Alexandria, and paintings on either side of it depict scenes from her life and martyrdom.

Convent & Church of St Francis of Assisi

This is one of the most interesting buildings in Old Goa. It contains gilded and carved woodwork, old murals depicting scenes from the life of St Francis, and a floor sub-stantially made of carved gravestones – complete with family coats of arms dating back to the early 16th century. The church was built by eight Franciscan friars who ar-rived here in 1517 and constructed a small chapel consisting of three altars and a choir. This was later pulled down and the present building was built on the same spot in 1661.

A convent behind this church is now the **archaeological museum** (open Saturday to Thursday, 10 am to 5 pm; free). It houses por-traits of the Portuguese viceroys, most of them inexpertly restored; sculpture fragments from Hindu temple sites; stone Vetal images from the animist cult that flourished in this part of India centuries ago; and a model of a Portuguese caravel, minus the rigging.

Basilica of Bom Jesus

The Basilica of Bom Jesus is famous throughout the Roman Catholic world. It contains the tomb and mortal remains of St Francis Xavier who, in 1541, was given the task of spreading Christianity among the subjects of the Portuguese colonies in the east.

A former pupil of St Ignatius Loyola, the founder of the Jesuit Order, St Francis Xavier's missionary voyages became legendary and, considering the state of transport at the time, were nothing short of miraculous.

Apart from the richly gilded altars, the interior of the church is remarkable for its simplicity. This is the only church that is not plastered on the outside (although it was originally). Construction began in 1594 and it was completed in 1605. The focus of the church is, of course, the tomb of St Francis.

The construction of which was underwritten by the duke of Tuscany and executed by the Florentine sculptor Giovanni Batista Foggini. It took 10 years to build and was completed in 1698. The remains of the body are housed in a silver casket, which at one time was covered in jewels. On the walls surrounding it are murals depicting scenes from the saint's journeys, and one of his death on Sancian Island.

The **Professed House**, next door to the basilica, is a two storey laterite building covered with lime plaster. It was completed in 1585, despite much opposition to the Jesuits. Part of the building burned down in 1633 and was partially rebuilt in 1783. There is a modern **art gallery** attached to the basilica.

The Incorrupt Body of St Francis Xavier

Goa's patron saint, Francis Xavier, had spent 10 years as a tireless missionary in South-East Asia when he died on 2 December 1552, but it was through his death that his greatest power in the region was released.

He died on the island of Sancian, off the coast of China. A servant is said to have emptied four sacks of quicklime into his coffin to consume his flesh in case the order came to return the remains to Goa. Two months later, the body was transferred to Malacca, where it was observed to be still in perfect condition – refusing to rot despite the quicklime. The following year, it was returned to Goa, where the people were declaring the preservation a miracle.

The Church was slower to acknowledge it, requiring a medical examination to establish that the body had not been embalmed. This was performed, in 1556, by the viceroy's physician, who declared that all internal organs were still intact and that no preservative agents had been used. He noticed a small wound in the chest and asked two Jesuits to put their fingers into it. He noted, 'When they withdrew them, they were covered with blood which I smelt and found to be absolutely untainted'.

In comparison to 16th and 17th century church bureaucracy, modern Indian bureaucracy seems positively streamlined, for it was not until 1622 that canonisation took place. By then, holy relic hunters had started work on the 'incorrupt body'. In 1614, the right arm was removed and divided between Jesuits in Japan and Rome, and by 1636, parts of one shoulder blade and all the internal organs had been scattered through South-East Asia. By the end of the 17th century, the body was in an advanced state of desiccation, and the miracle appeared to be over. The Jesuits decided to enclose the corpse in a glass coffin out of view, and it was not until the mid-19th century that the current cycle of 10 yearly expositions began. During the 54 days of the 1994-95 exposition, over one million pilgrims filed past the ghoulish remains.

The next exposition is not until November 2004, but if you're anywhere in the area on 3 December the annual celebration of the saint's day is well worth attending.

Church of St Cajetan

Modelled on the original design of St Peter's in Rome, this church was built by Italian friars of the Order of Theatines, who were sent by Pope Urban III to preach Christianity in the kingdom of Golconda (near Hyderabad). The friars were not permitted to work in Golconda, so settled at Old Goa in 1640. The construction of the church began in 1655. Historically, it's of much less interest than the other churches.

Church of St Augustine Ruins

All that is really left of this church is the enormous 46m tower that served as a belfry and formed part of the facade of the church. It was constructed in 1602 by Augustinian friars who arrived at in 1587.

It was abandoned in 1835 due to the repressive policies of the Portuguese government, resulting in the eviction of many religious orders from Goa. The church fell into neglect and the vault collapsed in 1842. In 1931, the facade and half the tower fell down, more sections followed in 1938.

Church & Convent of St Monica

This huge three storey laterite building was completed in 1627, only to burn down nine years later. Reconstruction started the following year, and it's from this time that the buildings date. Once known as the Royal Monastery, due to the royal patronage that it enjoyed, the building is now used by the Mater Dei Institute as a nunnery and it was inaugurated in 1964. Reasonably attired Visitors are allowed inside.

Other Buildings

Other monuments of minor interest in Old Goa are the Viceroy's Arch, Gate of Adil Shah's Palace, Chapel of St Anthony, Chapel of St Catherine, and the Church of Our Lady of the Rosary.

Places to Stay

Most people visit Old Goa as a day trip, but there is one hotel. The **GTDC Old Goa Tourist Hotel** (☎ 0832-286127) has basic doubles for Rs 260 (Rs 160 in low season).

Getting There & Away

Frequent buses to Old Goa leave the bus stand at Panaji (Rs 3, 25 minutes) and stop on the east side of the main roundabout.

MAPUSA

☎ 0832 • pop 34,800

Mapusa (pronounced 'Mapsa') is the main population centre in the northern *talukas* (provinces) of Goa and the main town for supplies if you are staying at Anjuna or Chapora. There's not much to see in Mapusa, though the Friday market (8 am to 2 pm) is worth a visit.

Places to Stay & Eat

Accommodation at the nearby beaches of Anjuna, Vagator and Chapora is far preferable to that on offer in Mapusa.

Hotel Vilena (☎ 263115, Feira Baixa) is a good, clean place with doubles with shared bath for Rs 200, or Rs 300 with bath.

Hotel Suhas (☎ 262700) is a cheap option; dorm beds are Rs 60 and doubles with bath are Rs 99, but in high season the doubles become four-bed rooms at Rs 320.

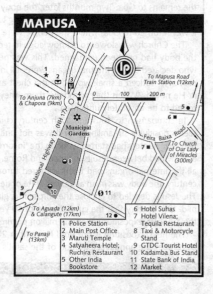

MAPUSA

To Mapusa Road Train Station (12km)

To Anjuna (7km) & Chapora (9km)

0   100   200 m

Municipal Gardens

Feira Baixa Road

To Church of Our Lady of Miracles (300m)

National Highway 17 (NH 17)

To Aguada (12km) & Calangute (17km)

To Panaji (13km)

1 Police Station	6 Hotel Suhas
2 Main Post Office	7 Hotel Vilena;
3 Maruti Temple	Tequila Restaurant
4 Satyaheera Hotel;	8 Taxi & Motorcycle
Ruchira Restaurant	Stand
5 Other India	9 GTDC Tourist Hotel
Bookstore	10 Kadamba Bus Stand
	11 State Bank of India
	12 Market

GTDC Tourist Hotel (☎ *262794*), on the southern roundabout, is popular and has doubles for Rs 280, four-bed rooms for Rs 350. The air-con doubles (Rs 400) have water heaters. There's an unremarkable restaurant on the 1st floor.

Satyaheera Hotel (☎ *262849*), near the Maruti Temple on the northern roundabout, is the best Mapusa has to offer. Doubles are Rs 300 (Rs 600 with air-con), all with bath. The *Ruchira*, reputed to be one of the best restaurants in Mapusa, is on the top floor. Main dishes are Rs 30 to Rs 50.

Getting There & Away

If you're coming from Mumbai, Mapusa is the jumping off point for the northern beaches. From the Kadamba bus stand, there are afternoon and evening buses to Mumbai (Rs 207 for a 'luxury' bus, 17 hours), as well as Pune, Hubli and Belgaum. Private operators have kiosks by the taxi and auto rickshaw stand.

There are frequent local buses to Panaji (Rs 4, 25 minutes), and half-hourly buses to Calangute and Anjuna (both Rs 4). Other buses go to Margao (Rs 18 by private express service), Chapora, Candolim and Arambol. A motorcycle to Anjuna or Calangute costs Rs 50 and takes about 15 minutes. Auto rickshaws/taxis charge around Rs 70/100.

Mapusa Road (Thivim), about 12km north-east of town, is the nearest train station on the Konkan Railway. Rickshaw/taxi drivers want about Rs 80/120 – and it's not yet clear which expresses will stop here.

FORT AGUADA & CANDOLIM
☎ 0832

The beaches of North Goa extend from Fort Aguada in an almost uninterrupted 30km sandy stretch to the border with Maharashtra. Sinquerim, the beach below the fort, and Candolim are popular with package tourists – there's not much for those on a very tight budget. These beaches tend to be much quieter than Calangute.

Guarding the mouth of the Mandovi River, **Fort Aguada** was built by the Portuguese in 1612. It's worth visiting the moated ruins on the hilltop for the views, which are particularly good from the old lighthouse. You can also visit the dungeons. Nearby, the new **lighthouse** can be visited from 4 to 5.30 pm; photography from it is forbidden.

To the east is **Aguada Jail**; most inmates (including westerners) are in on drug charges. They're only allowed one visit a month, so although they usually appreciate visits from other foreigners, you need to make sure you won't be denying them the visit of someone they're expecting. You'll also need to contact your embassy for a list of names.

Goan Banana and the Taj Holiday Village operate water sports, including parasailing and jet skis at the southern end of Sinqerem Beach, so this is not a great spot for swimming. It's much quieter further up along Candolim Beach.

Places to Stay

Moving south from Calangute, the hotels become progressively more expensive. Prices listed below are for doubles with bathrooms in the high season when some hotels are taken over entirely by package groups.

There's a clutch of places from Rs 400 to Rs 700 in an excellent position very close to the beach. These include *Dona Florina Beach Resort*, *D'Mello's* (rooms with balconies upstairs) and *Shanu Holiday Home*. There are even sea views from some of these places.

There are some cheaper, good value places in this area, with doubles from around Rs 250, including *Manuel Guest House* (☎ *277729*), *Ave Maria* (☎ *276904*) and the cheaper *Moonlight Bar & Restaurant* (☎ *279249*). *Pretty Petal Guest House* (☎ *276184*) is a nice place, with rooms for Rs 300, Rs 400 and Rs 500.

Tropicano Beach Resort (☎ *277732*) is an excellent choice with pleasant doubles for Rs 350 (Rs 450 with breakfast). There's a nice garden and the doors have traditional Goan glazing – seashells!

Sea Side Rendezvous (☎ *276323*) has a good restaurant, a small pool and expensive

FORT AGUADA & CANDOLIM

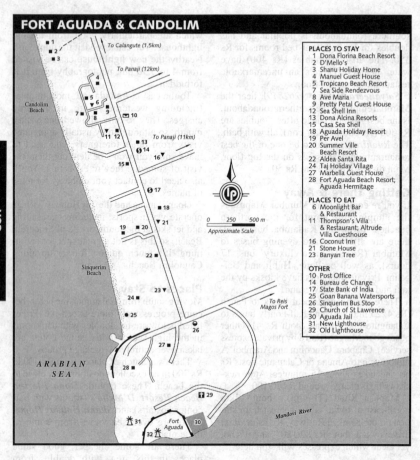

To Calangute (1.5km)

To Panaji (12km)

Candolim
Beach

To Panaji (11km)

Sinquerim
Beach

*ARABIAN
SEA*

To Reis
Magos Fort

Mandovi River

Fort
Aguada

0   250   500 m
Approximate Scale

PLACES TO STAY
1 Dona Florina Beach Resort
2 D'Mello's
3 Shanu Holiday Home
4 Manuel Guest House
5 Tropicano Beach Resort
7 Sea Side Rendezvous
8 Ave Maria
9 Pretty Petal Guest House
12 Sea Shell Inn
13 Dona Alcina Resorts
15 Casa Sea Shell
18 Aguada Holiday Resort
19 Per Avel
20 Summer Ville
    Beach Resort
22 Aldea Santa Rita
24 Taj Holiday Village
27 Marbella Guest House
28 Fort Aguada Beach Resort;
    Aguada Hermitage

PLACES TO EAT
6 Moonlight Bar
   & Restaurant
11 Thompson's Villa
   & Restaurant; Altrude
   Villa Guesthouse
16 Coconut Inn
21 Stone House
23 Banyan Tree

OTHER
10 Post Office
14 Bureau de Change
17 State Bank of India
25 Goan Banana Watersports
26 Sinquerim Bus Stop
29 Church of St Lawrence
30 Aguada Jail
31 New Lighthouse
32 Old Lighthouse

rooms at Rs 1395/1795. It's also a base for a water sports outfit.

Altrude Villa Guesthouse (☎ 277703) has reasonable doubles with hot-water shower for Rs 500.

Moving south, but still in the Rs 500 to Rs 750 price range, *Sea Shell Inn* (☎ 276131), on the main road, has comfortable rooms in an old colonial house. *Casa Sea Shell* (☎ 277879), the homely *Per Avel* (☎ 277074) and the spotless *Summer Ville Beach Resort* (☎ 277075) are also worth looking into.

Hotels (with pools) in the Rs 1000 to Rs 1500 range include the Portuguese-style villas of the *Aldea Santa Rita* (☎ 276868), and the *Aguada Holiday Resort* (☎ 276071). The *Dona Alcina Resorts* (☎ 277453) is more expensive still at Rs 2000 in the high season.

Marbella Guest House (fax 276509) is one of the nicest places in the whole area. It's a beautifully restored Portuguese villa hidden away down a quiet lane behind the Fort Aguada Beach Resort. The six airy rooms, each superbly decorated in a differ-

BRADLEY MAYHEW

TERESA CANNON

RICHARD I'ANSON

Festivals

Wherever you stay in India, from Himalayan gompas to the beaches of Goa, you're going to encounter some kind of festival or celebration. A part of everyday Indian life, and often linked to religion, they usually involve elaborate, colourful and riotous processions.

Kawachot Festival
Varanasi, on the banks of the Ganges, is one of seven sacred Hindu sites. The ghats fill to overflowing as women congregate to pray for their husbands' wellbeing during the Kawachot festival.

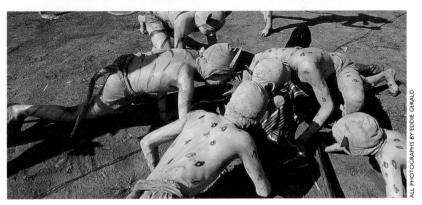

Top: A woman decorates her doorstep during the Pongal festival, a four-day celebration of the new rice harvest.
Middle: Colourfully decorated elephants are an important part of festivals throughout India.
Bottom: Revellers dress as tigers and imitate the animal's behaviour.

RICHARD I'ANSON

MICHELLE COXALL

RICHARD I'ANSON

Top: Festivals and celebrations always attract large crowds of Indians.
Bottom left: During the Holi festival, no one escapes the barrage of coloured water and powder.
Bottom right: Dusshera, called Durga Puja in Calcutta, celebrates Durga's victory over the buffalo-headed demon Mahishasura.

ent style, cost Rs 950 to Rs 1800 (Rs 800 to Rs 1500 mid-season). It's highly recommended, but in the high season you'll need to book in advance.

The Taj Group (☎ *276201, fax 276044*) operates a complex of three five-star deluxe hotels beside Sinquerim Beach, to the south of Candolim. The beachside *Taj Holiday Village* charges US$210 and has a watersports centre. Within the outer walls of the old fort, the *Fort Aguada Beach Resort* has rooms for US$225. Above it are the luxurious villas of the *Aguada Hermitage*, which have northern views and singles/doubles are US$465/585.

Places to Eat

Most hotels have restaurants, and down on the beach are dozens more places to try, all serving excellent seafood, snacks and cold drinks.

Coconut Inn is one of the more established places in the area and is a pleasant, open-air, upmarket place to eat.

Stone House is a mellower place, with tables laid out in a raised garden, nonstop Marley and Dylan on the sound system, and suitably relaxed service.

The restaurant at the *Sea Shell Inn* is very popular for dinner, with excellent seafood and sizzlers in an open-air setting.

Thompson's Villa & Restaurant, down a quiet lane back from the beach, is a good inexpensive place to try.

Banyan Tree, in the grounds of the Taj Holiday Village, is one of the best restaurants in the area. It's an open-sided affair serving excellent Thai and Chinese cuisine. Main dishes are from Rs 150.

Getting There & Away

Buses run from Panaji to Sinquerim (14km) and continue north to Calangute. A prepaid taxi from the airport costs Rs 460.

CALANGUTE & BAGA
☎ 0832

Calangute's heyday as the Mecca of all expatriate hippies has passed. The local people, who used to rent out rooms in their houses for a pittance, have moved on to more profitable things, and Calangute is now the centre of Goa's rapidly expanding package tourist market. Hotels and guesthouses stretch almost without a break from Calangute to Baga.

The beach isn't one of the best in Goa and many people will find it far too crowded – dotted, as it is, with sunbeds, deck chairs and slowly burning bodies. There is, however, plenty going on, and lots of good places to stay and eat. The beach at Baga is better, the landscape more interesting, and it's handy for those wanting to commute to the nightlife at Anjuna and Vagator.

Orientation & Information

Most of the information services are clustered around a single street where you'll find the market and bus stand.

Limited tourist information is available from the GTDC Calangute Tourist Resort (☎ 276024). Rama Bookshop offers a great range of books in many lages. MGM International Travels is a reputable travel agency nearby.

The Bank of Baroda, on the main Anjuna road near the market, gives MasterCard or Visa advances, and there are many exchange offices nearby that will change cash or travellers cheques.

Email and Internet can be accessed at several places in Calangute for around Rs 2 per minute, including Computer Spot, Edson's Travel & Communications and Cyberdyne, at the Albenjoh guesthouse on Baga Rd.

Goan Banana operates water sports about halfway along the beach between Calangute and Baga. Parasailing is Rs 900, banana boat rides Rs 200, water-skiing Rs 550 and dolphin trips Rs 300.

Kerkar Art Complex

This complex in South Calangute has a gallery with paintings on sale by local artists and twice-weekly concerts of Indian classical music and dance (see Entertainment).

Places to Stay

Prices quoted here are for a doubles with bath during high season. Singles are limited.

GOA

GOA

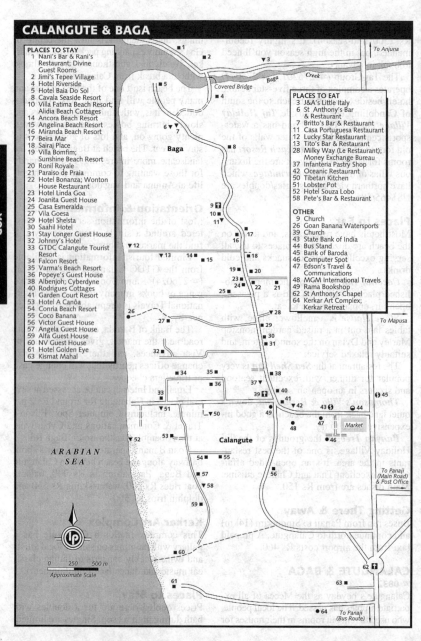

CALANGUTE & BAGA

PLACES TO STAY
1 Nani's Bar & Rani's
  Restaurant; Divine
  Guest Rooms
2 Jimi's Tepee Village
4 Hotel Riverside
5 Hotel Baia Do Sol
8 Cavala Seaside Resort
10 Villa Fatima Beach Resort;
  Alidia Beach Cottages
14 Ancora Beach Resort
15 Angelina Beach Resort
16 Miranda Beach Resort
17 Beira Mar
18 Sairaj Place
19 Villa Bomfim;
  Sunshine Beach Resort
20 Ronil Royale
21 Paraiso de Praia
22 Hotel Bonanza; Wonton
  House Restaurant
23 Hotel Linda Goa
24 Joanita Guest House
25 Casa Esmeralda
27 Vila Goesa
29 Hotel Shelsta
30 Saahil Hotel
31 Stay Longer Guest House
32 Johnny's Hotel
33 GTDC Calangute Tourist
  Resort
34 Falcon Resort
35 Varma's Beach Resort
36 Popeye's Guest House
38 Albenjoh; Cyberdyne
40 Rodrigues Cottages
41 Garden Court Resort
51 Hotel A Canôa
54 Conria Beach Resort
55 Coco Banana
56 Victor Guest House
57 Angela Guest House
59 Alfa Guest House
60 NIV Guest House
61 Hotel Golden Eye
63 Kismat Mahal

PLACES TO EAT
3 J&A's Little Italy
6 St Anthony's Bar
  & Restaurant
7 Britto's Bar & Restaurant
11 Casa Portuguesa Restaurant
13 Lucky Star Restaurant
13 Tito's Bar & Restaurant
28 Milky Way (Le Restaurant);
  Money Exchange Bureau
37 Infanteria Pastry Shop
42 Oceanic Restaurant
50 Tibetan Kitchen
51 Lobster Pot
52 Hotel Souza Lobo
58 Pete's Bar & Restaurant

OTHER
9 Church
26 Goan Banana Watersports
39 Church
43 State Bank of India
44 Bus Stand
45 Bank of Baroda
46 Computer Spot
47 Edson's Travel &
  Communications
48 MGM International Travels
49 Rama Bookshop
62 St Anthony's Chapel
64 Kerkar Art Complex;
  Kerkar Retreat

To Anjuna

Baga Creek

Covered Bridge

Baga

Calangute

ARABIAN
SEA

Market

To Mapusa

To Panaji
(Main Road)
& Post Office

To Panaji
(Bus Route)

0   250   500 m
Approximate Scale

Central Calangute In the centre of Calangute are a number of popular budget options.

Angela Guest House (☎ 277269) offers basic doubles for Rs 150. It's popular and staff are friendly. If it's full, there are several other places nearby. The *Conria Beach Resort* (☎ 277354) has rooms for Rs 250.

Hotel A Canôa (☎ 276082) has some nice rooms with sea views, and is great value at Rs 100/150 for singles/doubles or Rs 250 for larger doubles; unfortunately it's often full.

Alfa Guest House is set back from the beach, with rooms for Rs 300 (Rs 150 outside high season).

Victor Guest House (☎ 276966), also away from the beach, is a pleasant family home with just four doubles (with hot water) for Rs 300.

Coco Banana (☎ 276478), near Angela Guest House, is very popular. Rooms in this mid-range establishment surround a quiet courtyard and are spotless and secure. The beds are comfortable, and the owners are friendly and helpful. Prices jump to Rs 850 in mid-December, but are more reasonable once the rush is over.

The ugly *GTDC Calangute Tourist Resort* (☎ 276024) dominates the beach. Double rooms cost Rs 260 to Rs 350, or Rs 450 for a triple, all with fan. There's also a dormitory further up the road for Rs 60 (Rs 50 in low season).

Falcon Resort (☎ 277033) is one of a few upmarket places nearby. Clean doubles are Rs 600, deluxe doubles are Rs 1000 and aircon is Rs 1200. Rates halve in low season.

Varma's Beach Resort (☎ 276077) is secure and peaceful, but rather exclusive, with rooms set around a leafy courtyard. At Christmas, doubles cost Rs 1400 (Rs 1600 with air-con), although prices drop to Rs 450 in low season.

Popeye's Guest House (☎ 279296), opposite, is cheaper with doubles for Rs 450.

Albenjoh (☎ 276422, *Calangute-Baga Rd*) is a very clean good choice, with rooms from Rs 300 to Rs 600, all with hot water. More expensive rooms have balconies. There's also a cyber cafe here.

Rodrigues Cottages (☎ 276458), nearby, has a few rooms at Rs 150 (Rs 100 in low season).

Garden Court Resort (☎ 276054), next door, has reasonable doubles for Rs 500 and the owners run an unofficial tourist information service.

South Calangute There are a few cheap places left in this area, but they're in the minority. *NV Guest House* (☎ 279749), in an excellent location, is the best of the lot. Run by a friendly family, there's a variety of rooms. New ones are Rs 500 with hot water, while older rooms are Rs 250 and Rs 150 – it has unique rates fixed all year! The restaurant, only a few metres from the beach, serves fresh seafood.

For other budget options search around the back lanes leading towards the beach.

Kismat Mahal (☎ 276067), near St Anthony's Chapel, is a friendly family-run place with downstairs/upstairs doubles for Rs 300/400.

In the Rs 500 to Rs 1000 range, there's a group of small hotels notable only for their position near the beach. The *Hotel Golden Eye* (☎ 277308) also has a good restaurant.

The *Kerkar Retreat* (☎ 276017) is a brand new upmarket place opened by the owners of the Kerkar Complex. Stylish rooms with air-con are Rs 1500 to Rs 2000.

Calangute to Baga Many hotels in this area have been tarted up to pull in the package tourists, so it's no surprise that prices are relatively high.

Johnny's Hotel (☎ 277458) is a modern brick building close to the beach. Rooms here go for Rs 500 during the high season and meals are available.

Stay Longer Guest House (☎ 277460) is the best of the smaller places to be found back on the main road heading north. It's run by a very friendly family and cheap at Rs 200/300 for singles doubles. The nearby *Saahil Hotel* charges Rs 300.

Hotel Shelsta (☎ 276069) is a bit more upmarket, with a pleasant garden and singles/doubles for Rs 400/600.

Vila Goesa (☎ 277535) is an upmarket hotel in an attractive garden near the beach. Rooms are Rs 1450, or Rs 1650 with air-con.

Casa Esmeralda (☎ 277194) is a good bet outside high season when rooms are Rs 500. Rates double over Christmas and it's closed from May to September.

Joanita Guest House (☎ 277166), set back from the road near Casa Esmeralda, has good rooms facing a pleasant, shady garden for Rs 500.

Hotel Linda Goa (☎ 276066) is one of a number of package tour hotels on the main road that have upped their prices in recent years. Rooms are Rs 1800, or Rs 2000 with air-con.

In the same area, with pools and rooms costing from Rs 900 to Rs 1200, is the *Sunshine Beach Resort* (☎ 276003), *Paraiso de Praia* (☎ 276768), *Villa Bomfim* (☎ 276105), *Ronil Royale* (☎ 276183) and the *Beira Mar* (☎ 276246). This last place doubles its prices over Christmas.

Ancora Beach Resort (☎ 276096), down the next side lane (lined with persistent Kashmiri traders), is overpriced in high season. Rooms without/with balcony are Rs 800/1200. There's a restaurant and bar. Also down this lane is the *Angelina Beach Resort* (☎ 279268), with rooms for Rs 800.

Hotel Hacienda (☎ 277348) has some good rooms with hot water for Rs 500; it's back on the main road.

Hotel Bonanza (☎ 276010), across the road, is Rs 550.

Miranda Beach Resort (☎ 276092) has doubles for Rs 350.

Sairaj Place (☎ 277659), down a small alley, is quiet and there's a good chance of getting a room here in the high season. Doubles are Rs 500 (Rs 250 in the low season).

Baga If you're looking for a room or house to rent ask at any of the restaurants on the main road in Baga. There are also a number of houses and cottages for rent across the river, but they're often occupied by long-term visitors.

Villa Fatima Beach Resort (☎ 277418), set back from the road amid the coconut palm groves, is a good hotel. It's a popular place to stay, run by a lovely family. Double rooms with bath cost from Rs 150/200 for a courtyard room up to Rs 600 for a room facing the sea. There's a restaurant and TV area, and you can rent a safety deposit box for Rs 50.

Alidia Beach Cottages (☎ 276835) is another good place to stay. Over the Christmas fortnight, the very pleasant rooms here go for around Rs 800, dropping as low as Rs 150 in the low season.

Hotel Riverside (☎ 276062) has pleasant rooms in a quiet area for Rs 800, or Rs 1100 with air-con.

Hotel Baia Do Sol (☎ 276084), in an attractive flower garden, charges around Rs 1000 but is closer to the beach.

The *Cavala Seaside Resort* (☎ 276090) has an English manor house style about it and a pleasant garden. Doubles with veranda and bathroom cost Rs 1700 in the high season, dropping to Rs 700 from mid-January.

Divine Guest House (☎ 279546), north of the river (cross through the extraordinarily ugly covered bridge), is a good value family place. Clean doubles are Rs 200, or Rs 300 for the new 1st floor rooms. Low-season rates are Rs 120/200. There's a good restaurant and a balcony terrace.

Further around this road, *Nani's Bar & Rani's Restaurant* (☎ 276313), has a few basic doubles with shared bath for Rs 100, or Rs 300 with private bath.

Jimi's Tepee Village (fax 276124, goa@ bay-watch.com) is by far the most unusual place to stay in Goa. Six sturdy tepees, specially made in Mumbai, have been erected on the hillside opposite the bridge. The tepees contain mattresses, fans, lights and power points, and each has a strongbox set into the floor. They range in size and cost from Rs 150 to Rs 350, and there's a great treehouse with its own shower and kitchen for Rs 500. The whole place is run by the genial Jimi.

Places to Eat

There are literally hundreds of small restaurants crammed into every available bit of space in Calangute, Baga and along the beach between the two. The bamboo beach shacks are a great place to watch the sun go down with a cold beer and, as you might expect, seafood features prominently on the menus.

Infanteria Pastry Shop is your first stop for breakfast. It's an excellent place for a croissant and coffee. There's also a good range of bread and cakes, and a few meals.

Hotel Souza Lobo is an established favourite – so popular that the owners are planning to close the accommodation part to concentrate on meals. It's a perfect place to watch the sunset or relax in the early afternoon. Pepper steak is Rs 50, whole grilled kingfish Rs 125, and tiger prawns Rs 350.

Pete's Bar & Restaurant, beside the Angela Guest House, is another good place to eat or sit around with a few cold beers. It's much more of a travellers' place than the Souza Lobo.

The **Tibetan Kitchen** offers *momos* and other Tibetan food in a relaxed setting, with magazines and board games available to encourage long stays. It's a good place to meet other travellers.

Lobster Pot, opposite Calangute Tourist Resort, is a pleasant circular place with reasonably priced seafood and speedy service.

The **Oceanic Restaurant**, near the State Bank of India, does excellent seafood. Tandoori shark is Rs 100, most other main dishes are Rs 60 to Rs 100.

The **Milky Way** serves ice cream, milk shakes and snacks. In the evening this turns into the upmarket **Le Restaurant**, where main dishes are around Rs 150.

Tito's Bar & Restaurant is the major nightspot. It boasts a high-powered sound system and a large terrace that is usually packed by about 11 pm. Prices are more than you'd pay in other restaurants in Calangute and Baga (see Entertainment).

Casa Portuguesa Restaurant, set within the walled grounds of an old villa, has a unique old-world charm. Among the specialities here are roast wild boar. It's a good place for a splurge.

Britto's and **St Anthony's** are probably the longest running of the beach bars, but there are many others. **Lucky Star**, a beach shack at the end of the road past Tito's, has been recommended for its seafood.

J&A's Little Italy, further along the road to Anjuna, serves good, authentic Italian food but it's definitely not cheap. Gourmet pizzas are Rs 135 to Rs 175, pasta dishes are around Rs 170. Wine is Rs 35 by the glass. It's in a pleasant spot by Baga Creek.

Entertainment

The **Kerkar Art Complex** (☎ 276017) hosts concerts of Indian classical music and dance on Tuesday and Saturday at 6.45 pm. Tickets cost Rs 250.

At **Tito's Bar & Restaurant** (see Places to Eat), it's Rs 100 to get into the small disco (open till 3 am). We've had reports of trouble in this area late at night – solo travellers should take care.

Shopping

Calangute and Baga have been swamped by Kashmiri traders eager to cash in on the tourist boom. Their incessant hassling and pressure selling can become tedious. There is, however, a good range of things to buy: Kashmiri carpets, embroideries, and papier mâché boxes, as well as genuine and reproduction Tibetan and Rajasthani crafts.

Most things are well made but nothing is cheap. If you're going to buy, bargain hard and don't be afraid to offer a price far below the first price suggested.

Getting There & Away

There are frequent buses to Panaji (Rs 4, 35 minutes) and Mapusa (Rs 4) from Calangute. A taxi from Calangute or Baga to Panaji costs Rs 150 and takes about 20 minutes.

On Wednesday, boats leave regularly from Baga Beach for the Anjuna flea market (Rs 50).

Getting Around

Most of the buses from Panaji terminate at Calangute; few continue on to Baga. Bicycles and motorcycles can be hired at many places in Calangute and Baga (see Getting Around at the start of this chapter) and touts

GOA

cruise up and down looking for customers for their motorcycles.

ANJUNA
☎ 0832

Famous throughout Goa for its Wednesday flea market, this is the beach that everyone went to when Calangute had been filmed, recorded and reported into the sand.

It's still a popular meeting point for travellers but times are changing, and comfy hotels and package tourism are beginning to make their mark. The full-moon parties and the rave scene are still here though, and it's a more relaxing place to stay than Calangute, Baga or Colva. Local outrage and official concern about the excesses of a certain minority has led to periodic clampdowns and an exodus to more remote beaches like Arambol to the north and Gokarna, south of the border in Karnataka.

Information

You can have mail sent to Anjuna post office. There are numerous travel agencies where you can make onward travel bookings and get flights confirmed. MGM International Travels, on the main road, and Kwick Travels at the Manali Guest House are both good. True to its status as a long-term travellers hang-out, Anjuna has a few Internet outlets – Manali Guest House charges Rs 2.50 per minute, or try Mama Janet's Cafe.

The retail needs of the expatriate community are served by the Oxford Stores and the Orchard Stores, which stand opposite each other, and there's the newer Oxford Arcade, closer to the beach. Here you can get everything from a loaf of bread to a Christmas turkey, and the shelves are piled high with 'exotic' goodies – Vegemite, Heinz baked beans etc. You can change money here and at several other places around the village.

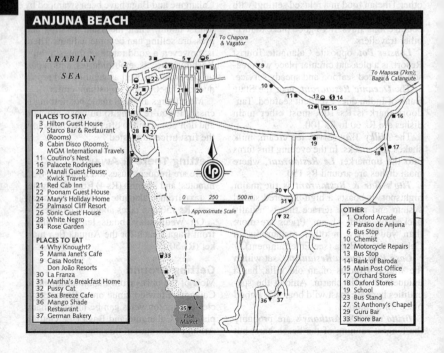

ANJUNA BEACH

ARABIAN SEA

To Chapora & Vagator

To Mapusa (7km); Baga & Calangute

Approximate Scale
0   250   500 m

Flea Market

PLACES TO STAY
3 Hilton Guest House
7 Starco Bar & Restaurant (Rooms)
8 Cabin Disco (Rooms); MGM International Travels
11 Coutino's Nest
16 Palacete Rodrigues
20 Manali Guest House; Kwick Travels
21 Red Cab Inn
22 Poonam Guest House
24 Mary's Holiday Home
25 Palmasol Cliff Resort
26 Sonic Guest House
28 White Negro
34 Rose Garden

PLACES TO EAT
4 Why Knought?
5 Mama Janet's Cafe
9 Casa Nostra; Don João Resorts
30 La Franza
31 Martha's Breakfast Home
32 Pussy Cat
35 Sea Breeze Cafe
36 Mango Shade Restaurant
37 German Bakery

OTHER
1 Oxford Arcade
2 Paraiso de Anjuna
6 Bus Stop
10 Chemist
12 Motorcycle Repairs
13 Bus Stop
14 Bank of Baroda
15 Main Post Office
17 Orchard Stores
18 Oxford Stores
19 School
23 Bus Stand
27 St Anthony's Chapel
29 Guru Bar
33 Shore Bar

Take great care of your possessions in Anjuna, particularly on party nights, as theft is a big problem. The Bank of Baroda has safety deposit boxes that you can use. It charges Rs 100 per month, but you have to pay it every time you open the safe to remove your valuables. This bank also gives cash advances on MasterCard and Visa.

Anjuna Flea Market

The Wednesday flea market at Anjuna is a major attraction for people from all the Goan beaches. It's a wonderful blend of Tibetan and Kashmiri traders, colourful Gujarati tribal women and blissed-out 1960s-style hippies. It's quite a scene. Whatever you need, from a used paperback to a haircut, you'll find it here – along with hundreds of stalls selling jewellery, carvings, T-shirts, sarongs, chillums, spices and everything else you can think of. You have to bargain hard to get a reasonable deal as plenty of well-heeled tourists also make their way here and the traders start high with their prices.

There's also lots of good Indian and western food available, as well as a couple of bars, and when it all gets too much you can wander down to a makeshift chill-out tent on the beach. Traditional-style fishing boats are available for transport to the market from Baga Beach – you'll see notices advertising this in Baga's restaurants.

The market is a great meeting place and though some visitors have described it as little more than an overhyped freak show, Anjuna and its market is the Goa experience in concentrated form – a syrup of hippies, ravers, handicrafts, hard-sell and sunshine, undiluted by the harsh realities of rural India.

The market starts in the morning but does not hot up until mid-afternoon and continues until the crowds drift away after sunset.

Places to Stay

There are plenty of guesthouses around the village, and even a couple of hotels, but finding a place to stay during the high season can still be a problem. If you're planning to stay long term look out for 'To Let' signs on houses – there are plenty along the back

lanes leading to the German Bakery. You may have to settle for something a bit more expensive until a cheap place comes up.

Prices given are for the high season from mid-December to mid-January. In November and February, they drop about 30 to 50% .

Poonam Guest House (☎ 273247) is an attractive place built around a garden. The rooms, all with bathrooms, are much in demand in high season, and are priced accordingly: Rs 600 for a double with a sea view, Rs 500 for a room without the view. Rates halve in the low season.

Mary's Holiday Home (☎ 273216), near the bus stand, is cheaper; doubles with bath go for Rs 300 and smaller rooms are Rs 250.

Sonic Guest House, down by the rocky seafront, charges Rs 300 for a double.

Guru Bar (☎ 273319), further along, has 10 doubles with bath for a budget Rs 150.

Palmasol Cliff Resort (☎ 273258) has better rooms with bath and hot water for Rs 410.

White Negro (☎ 273326), nearby, is a stylish renovated place. The new rooms with bath and hot water are Rs 600. There may be some cheaper rooms available too.

Red Cab Inn (☎ 274427) is a bit flash for any self-respecting backpacker, but great if you can afford it. Doubles are Rs 550. There's a free program of Indian classical dance and music here on Monday night.

Cabin Disco (☎ 273254), back on the Mapusa road, charges Rs 200/300 without/with bath.

Starco Bar & Restaurant, nearby, is better value; the five double rooms, all with bath, go for Rs 250.

Manali Guest House (☎ 273477) has rooms for Rs 125/250 without/with bath.

Coutino's Nest (☎ 274386) is a clean place with rooms for Rs 200 with shared bath (hot shower). It's run by a friendly family and there's a pleasant terrace.

Hilton Guest House (☎ 274432) is another good family home closer to the beach. Comfy doubles with bath are Rs 300.

Rose Garden Motel (☎ 273362) is right down on the beach, close to the Shore Bar and market area. There are eight fairly basic rooms with bath behind the restaurant. Larger rooms are Rs 350.

Palacete Rodrigues (☎ 273358), on the outskirts of Anjuna, is an old colonial house built around a courtyard. Singles/doubles are great value at a fixed Rs 500/600, or Rs 700 for the suite.

Don João Resorts (☎ 274325) is a characterless package hotel. If they have a room free in high season (unlikely) they charge around Rs 1500.

Places to Eat

Anjuna doesn't have beach shacks like Calangute, but there are a few beachside restaurants and some refreshingly different places to eat.

The *German Bakery* serves herbal teas and espresso coffee and all manner of other goodies. It's a great place to relax and read a book or meet with friends.

Mango Shade Restaurant is another popular place behind the flea market site.

Motel Rose Garden, right on the beach, has excellent seafood and cold beer.

Sea Breeze Cafe has reasonable food but is mainly patronised on market day.

White Negro is a popular bar and restaurant with good, well-presented food. Main dishes are around Rs 50 to Rs 60.

Martha's Breakfast Home is a good place to start the day. The breakfasts aren't particularly cheap but they're excellent and served in a pleasant, shady garden. It also has a few rooms to rent. *La Franza*, nearby, is another popular place serving huge portions, while *Pussy Cat* does lassis, ice cream, fruit juice and milk shakes.

There is a string of good but unremarkable cafes and restaurants around the crossroads in the main part of the village and along the road leading to Mapusa. *Why Knought?* isn't bad for seafood sizzlers, and *Casa Nostra* turns out pretty good Italian fare. Pasta dishes are around Rs 80 and you can wash it down with a red wine.

Entertainment

The *Shore Bar* is still a popular spot to sink a few beers and watch the sun go down. It can get very crowded on market day, and the powerful sound system keeps people here until long after dark.

Back towards the village, the *Guru Bar* and *Sonic* attract a few patrons, but a lot of the night-time action has moved over to Vagator and Chapora (see the following entry). Anjuna's latest hot spot is *Paraiso de Anjuna* (known to all as 'Paradiso' – eventually they may actually change the name to that!). It's perched in an ideal spot overlooking the beach and stays open till the early hours on selected nights pumping out house music.

The legendary parties are usually held on full-moon nights, and Christmas and New Year's Eve, but there's also often something going on after the flea market. The motorcycle taxi-wallahs are often good sources of party information.

Getting There & Away

There are buses every hour or so to Anjuna and Chapora from Mapusa. They can be very crowded, so it's usually a lot easier to take a motorcycle taxi (about Rs 50) or to get a group together and hire a taxi.

Getting Around

Licence and insurance checks on foreigners who rent motorcycles are becoming more common, particularly on market day. See the warning under Getting Around at the start of this chapter for more details. It is, however, very easy to hire a bike here and it's most people's preferred method of transport. In the high season it can be difficult to hire one for less than a week.

CHAPORA & VAGATOR
☎ 0832

This is one of the most beautiful and interesting parts of Goa's coastline. Much of the inhabited area nestles under a canopy of dense coconut palms, and Chapora Village is dominated by a rocky hill on top of which sits an old Portuguese fort. The views from its ramparts are excellent.

Secluded, sandy coves are found all the way around the northern side of this rocky outcrop, though Vagator's main beaches

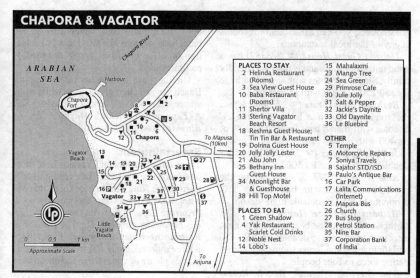

CHAPORA & VAGATOR

PLACES TO STAY
2 Helinda Restaurant (Rooms)
3 Sea View Guest House
10 Baba Restaurant (Rooms)
11 Shertor Villa
13 Sterling Vagator Beach Resort
18 Reshma Guest House; Tin Tin Bar & Restaurant
19 Dolrina Guest House
20 Jolly Jolly Lester
21 Abu John
25 Bethany Inn Guest House
34 Moonlight Bar & Guesthouse
38 Hill Top Motel

PLACES TO EAT
1 Green Shadow
4 Yak Restaurant; Scarlet Cold Drinks
12 Noble Nest
14 Lobo's
15 Mahalaxmi
23 Mango Tree
24 Sea Green
29 Primrose Cafe
30 Julie Jolly
31 Salt & Pepper
32 Jackie's Daynite
33 Old Daynite
36 Le Bluebird

OTHER
5 Temple
6 Motorcycle Repairs
7 Soniya Travels
8 Sajator STD/ISD
9 Paulo's Antique Bar
16 Car Park
17 Lalita Communications (Internet)
22 Mapusa Bus
26 Church
27 Bus Stop
28 Petrol Station
35 Nine Bar
37 Corporation Bank of India

ARABIAN SEA

Chapora River

Harbour

Chapora Fort

Chapora

To Mapusa (10km)

Vagator Beach

Vagator

Little Vagator Beach

To Anjuna

0   0.5   1 km
Approximate Scale

GOA

---

face west towards the Arabian Sea. Little Vagator, the beach to the south, is very popular with travellers.

Many westerners stay here on a long-term basis, but it's not a tourist ghetto. The local people remain friendly and it's much more laid back than even Anjuna, particularly at Chapora.

Information

Despite the absence of upscale tourism, Chapora and Vagator are not without their services for travellers. There are STD/ISD phone places in the main street of Chapora as well as a small bookstall. Soniya Travels (☎ 273344) in Chapora is a good agency for transport bookings, foreign exchange and Internet access (Rs 150 per hour). In Vagator, you'll find Internet access at Lalita Communications.

Places to Stay

Most people who come here tend to stay a long time in cheap rooms. Initially, you'll have to take whatever is available and ask around, or stay at Calangute or Baga and 'commute' until you've found something. There should be no problem if you arrive before the height of the season.

Chapora *Shertor Villa* is popular but the basic rooms are nothing to get excited about. There are about 20 rooms at Rs 150 for a double with shared bath (reductions for long stays). If there's no one here, check over the road at Noble Nest restaurant.

Baba Restaurant (☎ 273339) has six rooms with shared bath for Rs 200 over Christmas, dropping to Rs 150 in January.

Sea View Guest House (☎ 273565) has some very basic rooms (little more than a mattress on the floor) from Rs 70 to Rs 100. They prefer long-termers here.

Helinda Restaurant (☎ 274345) has some of the best rooms in Chapora. It's clean, friendly and easy-going, but is often booked solid; doubles without/with bath are Rs 250/300 and there's a single with shared bath for Rs 150.

Look around for 'To Let' signs for rooms in private houses and expect to pay around Rs 50 per night.

Vagator As well as trying the following guesthouses, you can ask around for rooms at any of the local restaurants.

Dolrina Guest House (☎ 273382) has a good range of rooms and is run by a friendly family. Singles/doubles with shared bath are Rs 150/250, Rs 300 with private bath.

Reshma Guest House (☎ 272568), across the road and down a lane, has singles/doubles with shared bath for Rs 150/200, or Rs 400 with private bath.

Jolly Jolly Lester (☎ 273620) has better doubles with bath at Rs 500.

Abu John (☎ 273757), further up the road, has cottages with bath for Rs 350, dropping to Rs 150 outside high season.

Bethany Inn Guest House (☎ 273731), further back from the beach, is fairly new. Spacious and spotless doubles cost Rs 450 and there are some larger rooms accommodating three to four people.

The *Sterling Vagator Beach Resort* (☎ 273277, *Vagator Beach*) is the most up-market place in the area and gets good reports from travellers who like to spend a bit more. There's a restaurant, bar and cottages in a shady garden. Doubles cost Rs 2100.

Hill Top Motel (☎ 273665) is set back a fair distance from Little Vagator Beach and has doubles with shared bath for Rs 150. Nearer the beach, several of the houses around Jackie's Daynite restaurant have rooms to let.

Moonlight Bar has five double rooms for Rs 200/300 without/with bath.

Le Bluebird (☎ 273695) has simple but comfortable rooms from Rs 150 to Rs 250 and a nice little French-style restaurant.

Places to Eat

There are numerous restaurants along the main street of Chapora Village.

Scarlet Cold Drinks, *Green Shadow* and *Helinda* are all popular. *Yak Restaurant*, opposite Soniya Travel, serves up a range of excellent food including Italian, continental, burgers and seafood. The prawn goulash with herbal noodles (Rs 60) is a classic.

Lobo's and *Mahalaxmi* are among several busy restaurants just above Vagator Beach.

Sea Green serves up tasty Chinese food on a shady patio area, covered by an old parachute. *Mango Tee* also has a fair selection on offer and *Jaws*, across the road, is recommended.

On the lane leading to Little Vagator Beach is a selection of places to while away a lazy afternoon or evening, including *Salt & Pepper* and *Jackie's Daynite*. Try *Le Bluebird* for French cuisine.

Entertainment

These days Chapora and Vagator have more of a scene than Anjuna. The evening usually starts at the *Nine Bar* overlooking Little Vagator Beach. By 11 pm the party is up at *Primrose Cafe*. In between there are numerous bars to be sampled. The *Tin Tin Bar & Restaurant* occasionally has live music, while *Paulo's Antique Bar* in Chapora is tiny but has plenty of atmosphere and cheap beer.

Getting There & Away

Fairly frequent buses run to both Chapora and Vagator from Mapusa throughout the day. Many go via Anjuna. There are also occasional direct buses from Panaji that follow the coast instead of going via Mapusa. The bus stop is near the road junction in Chapora Village. It's often easier and much quicker to rent a motorcycle from Mapusa or to get a group together and hire a taxi. Ask at hotels and restaurants about renting a motorcycle.

It takes about 45 minutes to walk from Vagator to Anjuna, but it's not a great idea to do this alone at night – you may be a target for theft or, as one traveller reported, there's a chance of being stopped by police angling for baksheesh.

CHAPORA TO ARAMBOL

The ride up the coast between Chapora and Arambol offers the opportunity to detour to some picturesque and peaceful beaches. **Morjim Beach**, just north of Chapora, has a handful of beach shacks and a couple of hotels at its northern end. **Mandrem Beach** is not quite as idyllic to look at but is a great place to get away from it all. There are rooms to let in the village behind the dunes.

ARAMBOL (Harmal)

One of Goa's more remote beaches, Arambol stills draws plenty of people but is far from being developed.

The seashore is beautiful and the village quiet and friendly, with just a few hundred locals, mostly fishing people. Accommodation is basic but there are enough facilities here to keep travellers going.

Buses from Mapusa stop at the modern part of Arambol, on the main road, where there's a church, a few shops, but no bank. From here, a side road leads 1km down to the village, and the beach is about 500m further on. This main beach is a good place to swim but to the north are several much more attractive bays – follow the path over the headland. There are some chalets on the hillside of the first bay. Behind the second bay is a small freshwater pool that's very pleasant to lie about in.

There are a few stores in the village and travel agencies that will change cash and travellers cheques.

If you can drag yourself away from doing nothing, you can paraglide off nearby cliffs. Tandem flights (20 minutes) are Rs 1200, a four day certified course is Rs 7000. Contact the Relax Inn on the beach at Arambol for information.

Places to Stay & Eat

Long-term visitors rent rooms from the villagers. The most basic places are often no more than four walls and a roof. You can rent mattresses, cookers and all the rest from the shops at the village.

The most pleasant accommodation is in the little *chalets* on the next bay to the north. They're basic – outside toilets and water from a spring – but the sea views are superb. At the height of the season these places are in demand, and rooms are Rs 250 to Rs 275.

Villa Oceanic, in the village, is a private house with several immaculate rooms, and a friendly atmosphere. All rooms are doubles with shared bath, and cost Rs 150. The house is just back from the southern end of the beach, and is accessible from the road by a path that's difficult to follow – ask directions.

Laxmi Niwas, 500m back from the beach and above Ganesh Stores, has dingy, basic rooms with shared bath for Rs 100. *Ganga Travels* (☎ 297784), across the road, has doubles for Rs 100 and a large room with kitchen.

Mrs Naik Home is much more pleasant, and is consequently usually fully booked. It's on the road to the beach, and has doubles with bath for Rs 250 to Rs 300.

There are several bars and shacks lining the main beach, in which all the usual fare is available. *Namaste Beer Bar* and *Relax Inn* are good. Set back from the beach, the *Garden of Meals* is open every evening and usually has a different set special each night.

Getting There & Away

There are buses from Mapusa to Arambol every couple of hours (about one hour). Alternatively, get a group together and hire a taxi, but you'll have to pay the fare both ways since the driver is unlikely to be able to pick up passengers for the return journey.

Boats every Wednesday to the Anjuna flea market are Rs 75/150 one way/return.

TEREKHOL FORT

At Terekhol (Tiracol), on the north bank of the river of the same name, is a small Portuguese fort with a little church within its walls. It's now a hotel, the *Hotel Tiracol Fort Heritage* (☎ 2366-68248), and is an interesting, if slightly isolated, place to stay. There's little else here but the setting is spectacular, and the rooms in the old fort are unique. Singles/doubles are Rs 800/850, and the deluxe suites (complete with a huge circular tub) cost Rs 1750.

The fort makes a good outing on a motorcycle, and you could stop for a swim on deserted Querim Beach, but there's very little to see or do at the fort itself, apart from admire the views.

There are occasional buses from Mapusa or Pernem to Querim, on the south bank of the river, opposite Terekhol, and also between Arambol and Querim. The ferry between Querim and Terekhol runs every half hour from 6 am to 9.30 pm.

South Goa

South Goa's beaches include travellers' centres like Colva and Benaulim, and a sprinkling of upmarket resorts, but there's generally less tourist development here than in the north. Margao is both the capital of the region and the transport hub. Goa's Dabolim airport is near Vasco da Gama.

VASCO DA GAMA
☎ 0834

Close to Mormugao Harbour and 3km from Dabolim airport, Vasco da Gama is the terminus of the railway line into Goa. With the new station at Margao taking over as the main rail hub, however, few travellers bother to venture up to this unexciting town. If you fly into Goa, it's possible you may need to stay overnight in Vasco unless you're prepared to take a taxi further afield.

Places to Stay
Twiga Lodge (☎ 512682), near the main bus stand, is the best budget option. The old Portuguese house run by Tony and Iva Pereira. Theres just one single and four doubles for Rs 80/100; they're often full in high season.

Hotel Westend (☎ 511575, Panday Rd) has clean doubles for Rs 170.

The *GTDC Tourist Hotel* (☎ 510829) is good and central. Rooms are Rs 200/280 (Rs 150/240 in low season); there are also some four-bed rooms and air-con rooms.

Kamakshi Hotel (☎ 512403, FL Gomes Rd), down a small alley, has reasonable doubles at Rs 140 (fixed all year) and 24 hour checkout.

The Citadel (☎ 512097, Pe José Vaz Rd) near the Tourist Hotel, is more upmarket, but reasonable value – Rs 500 (Rs 350 in low season), or Rs 850 for air-con rooms.

Hotel La Paz Gardens (☎ 512121, fax 513302) is the top hotel, with rooms from Rs 900/1200 to deluxe suites at Rs 1750/2500 all with air-con (plus 25% tax).

Places to Eat
Nanking Chinese Restaurant, near Hotel La Paz Gardens, is a friendly place with good food. Szechuan chicken is Rs 40.

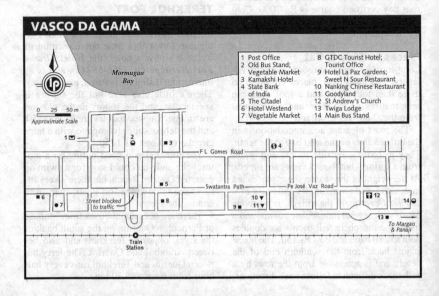

VASCO DA GAMA

Mormugao Bay

0 25 50 m
Approximate Scale

1 Post Office
2 Old Bus Stand; Vegetable Market
3 Kamakshi Hotel
4 State Bank of India
5 The Citadel
6 Hotel Westend
7 Vegetable Market
8 GTDC Tourist Hotel; Tourist Office
9 Hotel La Paz Gardens; Sweet N Sour Restaurant
10 Nanking Chinese Restaurant
11 Goodyland
12 St Andrew's Church
13 Twiga Lodge
14 Main Bus Stand

F L Gomes Road
Swatantra Path
Pe José Vaz Road
Street blocked to traffic
Train Station
To Margao & Panaji

Goodyland is a fast-food joint and bakery near the Nanking, serving excellent pizzas (Rs 45), sausage rolls and ice cream.

Sweet N Sour, in the Hotel La Paz Gardens, is a more expensive Chinese place with an excellent reputation.

Getting There & Away

There are frequent buses to Margao and Panaji (Rs 8, one hour). Change at Panaji for Mapusa and the beaches of North Goa. Long-distance private buses can be booked at the kiosks outside the train station, and there are buses to Mumbai and Bangalore from the main bus stand.

See Getting There & Away at the start of this chapter for trains from Vasco.

A taxi to the airport costs Rs 80, an auto-rickshaw Rs 50.

BOGMALO

Bogmalo, 8km from Vasco and 4km from the airport, is a small, sandy cove dominated by the five-star Park Plaza Resort, which evaded the restriction requiring all hotels to be built at least 500m from the beach.

There's little here apart from a pleasant beach with several expensive cafes, water sports facilities and the small village of Bogmalo.

Park Plaza Resort (☎ 513291, fax 512510) has rooms from US$45/95 plus taxes (US$150 for a double over Christmas). There's a pool and all the usual trimmings you'd expect in a hotel of this calibre.

Petite Guest House (☎ 555035), in the village, not far from the beach, has singles/doubles for Rs 1100/1500.

Saritas Guest House (☎ 555965), on the beach, has clean but unremarkable rooms for Rs 550 (Rs 1100 over Christmas).

Joets Guest House (☎ 555036), further down the beach, has doubles for Rs 450 but is usually booked up by package companies. It's the base for diving and other water sports at Bogmalo.

Frequent buses run between Bogmalo and Vasco da Gama, from where you can pick up buses to Margao and Panaji.

MARGAO (Madgaon)
☎ 0834 • pop 79,800

The capital of Salcete province, Margao is the main population centre of South Goa and is a busy provincial town that still displays reminders of its Portuguese past.

Though not really of great interest to travellers, Margao's richly decorated **Church of the Holy Spirit** is worth a visit, and the **covered market** is the best of its kind in Goa. Margao is the service and transport centre for people staying at Colva and Benaulim beaches.

Orientation & Information

The main (Kadamba) bus stand is about 2km north of the town centre, on the road to Panaji, while Margao's flash new train station is 1.5km east.

The tourist office (☎ 722513) is in the GTDC Tourist Hostel, in the centre of town. The State Bank of India is opposite the Municipal gardens. You can get Visa or MasterCard advances at the Bank of Baroda near the covered market.

Paramount Travels (☎ 731150) can arrange tickets for the Frank Shipping catamaran to Mumbai. Menezes Travel Agency (☎ 720401), behind the Secretariat, is an Indian Airlines agent.

The main post office is on the north side of the Municipal gardens, but the poste restante (open 8.30 to 10.30 am and 3 to 4.30 pm) has its own office, 300m south-west of the post office. Cyber Inn, in the Kalika Chambers, is open from 9 am to 1 pm and 2 to 6 pm. Internet access is available for Rs 3 per minute.

Places to Stay

Rukrish Hotel (☎ 721709) is one of an unappealing range of cheapies. Reasonably clean singles with small balconies overlooking the street are Rs 75; doubles with tiny bathrooms are Rs 189. Checkout is 24 hours.

Hotel Greenview (☎ 720151), across the road from the old train station, is better but still basic with doubles for Rs 115/150 with bath.

The *GTDC Tourist Hostel (☎ 721966)*, near the market in the middle of town, is a reasonable place with doubles for Rs 280 (Rs 40 less in the low season). It's of a similar standard to the Tourist Hotel in Panaji.

Hotel La Flor (☎ 731402, fax 731382, Erasmo Carvalho St) is well run and friendly. Deluxe rooms with TV and bath cost from Rs 350/450.

Hotel Saaj (☎ 711757, Miguel Loyola Furtado Rd) is also a good mid-range option. Modern rooms are Rs 390/450, or Rs 490/550 with air-con, and there's a single for Rs 280.

Woodlands Hotel (☎ 720310, fax 738732, Miguel Loyola Furtado Rd) is one of Margao's best hotels, but the wide range of rooms means anyone can afford to stay here. Basic rooms with bath and TV are Rs 180/250, air-con suites are Rs 600/650. There's a bar and restaurant.

Places to Eat

Bombay Cafe is a popular vegetarian place with cheap snacks. **Tato**, to the east of the Municipal gardens, is the best vegetarian

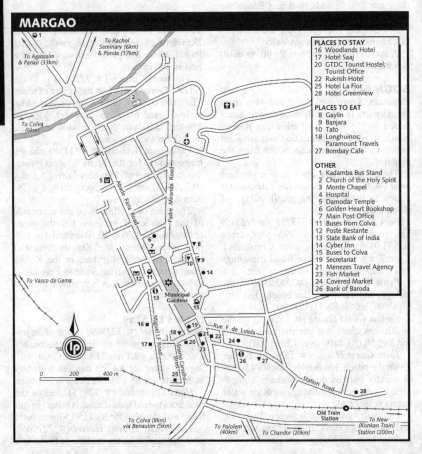

MARGAO

To Rachol Seminary (6km) & Ponda (17km)

To Agassaim & Panaji (33km)

To Colva (6km)

Abade Faria Road

Padre Miranda Road

To Vasco da Gama

Municipal Gardens

Miguel L F Road

Erasmo Carvalho Street

To Colva (8km) via Benaulim (5km)

To Palolem (40km)

To Chandor (20km)

Station Road

Old Train Station

To New (Konkan Train) Station (200m)

0   200   400 m

PLACES TO STAY
16 Woodlands Hotel
17 Hotel Saaj
20 GTDC Tourist Hostel; Tourist Office
22 Rukrish Hotel
25 Hotel La Flor
28 Hotel Greenview

PLACES TO EAT
8 Gaylin
9 Banjara
10 Tato
18 Longhuinos; Paramount Travels
27 Bombay Cafe

OTHER
1 Kadamba Bus Stand
2 Church of the Holy Spirit
3 Monte Chapel
4 Hospital
5 Damodar Temple
6 Golden Heart Bookshop
7 Main Post Office
11 Buses from Colva
12 Poste Restante
13 State Bank of India
14 Cyber Inn
15 Buses to Colva
19 Secretariat
21 Menezes Travel Agency
23 Fish Market
24 Covered Market
26 Bank of Baroda

restaurant in Margao. A thali costs Rs 20, and the place is spotlessly clean.

Longhuinos, opposite the tourist office, is recommended for Goan cuisine such as chourisso (Rs 25). They also do pastries, sweets and good tandoori dishes, and there's a busy bar serving draught beer.

Woodlands Hotel has a good value restaurant – fish curry rice is Rs 25, fried chicken is Rs 35.

Banjara is a subterranean restaurant near Tato that has excellent north Indian food in very civilised air-con surroundings. Main dishes are Rs 70 to Rs 80.

Gaylin is an excellent and popular Chinese restaurant just north of Banjara.

Getting There & Away

Bus From the Kadamba bus stand there are deluxe daily buses to Mumbai (Rs 319, 16 hours), Bangalore (Rs 225, 14 hours), Pune (Rs 265, 15 hours), Hubli (Rs 45, six hours) and Belgaum (Rs 42, five hours). There are numerous buses to Karwar, all of which stop at Chaudi, near Palolem.

There are plenty of private bus agents in the town centre near the Tourist Hostel.

The Kadamba bus stand has good connections with beaches and other towns in Goa:

Colva Beach
    Buses (Rs 4, 20 minutes – some via Benaulim) also run from the Municipal gardens (east side), approximately every hour (7.30 am to 7 pm).
Panaji
    Buses (Rs 8/12 by public/express bus, one hour) depart about every 15 minutes from 6 am to 9.15 pm. It's a picturesque journey, with old, white-washed churches and monasteries. The alternative route via Ponda takes at least an hour longer.
Chaudi (Rs 12)
Rachol (Rs 6)
Vasco da Gama (Rs 8)
Majorda (Rs 3)

Train Margao's new station is about 1.5km east of the town centre; access is via the road south of the train line, not Station Rd (which leads to the now closed old station). If you're walking there, however, you can cross the tracks at the old station. There's a reservation hall within the main building.

For inquires phone ☎ 712790. See Getting There & Away at the start of this chapter for train information.

Taxi To get to Colva, you can take a motorcycle taxi for about Rs 35 (no objection to backpacks), auto-rickshaw (around Rs 50) or taxi (about Rs 70).

AROUND MARGAO
Rachol Seminary & Church

Rachol Seminary and Church is 6km from Margao, near the village of Raia. The **Museum of Christian Art** here has some interesting displays including textiles, some of the silver once used in the churches of Old Goa, a magnificent 17th century silver monstrance in the shape of a swan, and a mobile mass kit (complete with candlesticks) – standard issue for missionaries out in the jungle. The museum is open Tuesday to Sunday 9.30 am to 12.30 pm and 2.30 to 5 pm.

The church dates from 1610 and the seminary has interesting architecture, a decaying library and paintings of Christian characters done in Indian styles. This is not a tourist site, so you should ask before wandering around.

There are buses from Margao, but make sure you get on one to Rachol Seminary, not Illa de Rachol.

Braganza House

Twenty kilometres east of Margao, in the village of Chandor, are several interesting colonial mansions. One of the grandest, the Braganza House, is open to the public. The house has two wings, each owned by different sides of the Braganza family (it was originally built by two brothers in the 17th century). The west wing, or **Menezes Braganza House**, has been lovingly renovated and the rooms are furnished with antiques, hung with chandeliers, and the windows are glazed with stained glass. The east wing, or **Braganza Pereira House**, is a fascinating jumble of antiques, ancient furniture and unpolished silver. It has an air of living antiquity and grandeur with its ballroom and baroque private chapel. The family even

GOA

keeps a relic of St Francis Xavier (a fingernail) hidden in the house.

The families are happy to show you around and, while there's no entry fee, they request a donation towards renovations.

On 6 January, Chandor (along with Reis Magos and Cansaulim villages) celebrate the **Feast of the Three Kings** with local boys re-enacting the three kings arriving with gifts for Christ.

There are frequent buses to Chandor from Margao.

COLVA & BENAULIM
☎ 0834

Twenty years ago, precious little disturbed Colva, except the local fishing people who pulled their catch in by hand each morning, and a few of the more intrepid hippies who had forsaken the obligatory sex, drugs and rock and roll of Calangute for the soothing tranquility of this paradise. Since there were only a couple of cottages for rent, most people stayed either on the beach itself or in palm-leaf shelters, which they constructed themselves.

Those days are gone forever. The property developers moved in swiftly, and you can see the results of their efforts – air-con resort complexes, close-packed ranks of tourist cottages, trinket stalls and drink stands. You'll be lucky if you see a fisherman around the main area; most now have motorised trawlers standing anchored in a line offshore. Likewise, you won't come across anyone sleeping out on the beach these days or throwing up a palm-leaf shelter.

The development is contained within relatively small areas. The dozen or so resort complexes that have sprung up along this 30km coastline are, for the most part, widely spaced and self contained. Colva itself has suffered, but much of the development here is in the small area around the end of the road from Margao. Walk 2km in either direction, and you'll get close to what it used to be like before the cement mixers began chugging away. The area still has a long way to go before it gets as developed as Calangute.

With fewer people than the northern beaches and quiet, unlit back lanes, occasional robberies have been reported in Benaulim – avoid walking back from the beach alone at night if possible.

The **Beach Bonanza** held on successive Sundays From mid-April features live music, dancing and entertainment. **Fama de Menino Jesus** on the second Monday of October, held at the Church of Our Lady of Mercy, celebrates the 'miraculous' favours granted by the 'Menino Jesus'.

Information
The nearest post office is in Colva Village, where letters can be sent poste restante; you'll need to take your passport or similar proof of identity to collect mail. There's a small Bank of Baroda next to the church, and a couple of travel agencies in both Colva and Benaulim that will change cash and travellers cheques. Thomas Cook has a mobile exchange van that parks outside Goa Tourism's Colva Cottages daily (in season) 3 to 5 pm, and gives the best rates of all.

Sanatan's, on the road leading back to Margao in Colva Village, has Internet and email facilities.

Organised Tours
If you're not planning to stay at any of the northern beaches, it's worth making the day trip to the Wednesday flea market at Anjuna. Trips are advertised at the beach bars and cost about Rs 75 (try Dominick's in Colva). They take the best part of a day, but are worth it, because tackling this trip by public transport involves umpteen bus changes. Over Christmas, buses are also organised to get you to the big parties and bring you back the next morning!

Places to Stay
Prices below are for the high season: mid-December to late January.

It's possible to rent houses long term in Colva and Benaulim – just ask around in the restaurants and shops. Most houses are a 20 minute walk from the beach. As well as the places listed here, there are a string of

COLVA

To Majorda

ARABIAN SEA

Cafes

Colva Village

To Margao (6km)

Cafes & Bars

0   250   500 m
Approximate Scale

See Benaulim Map p963

COLVA

PLACES TO STAY
1   Sam's Beach Resort
2   Lucky Star Restaurant (Rooms)
3   Longhuinos Beach Resort
4   Fishermen's Cottages
5   Hotel Tourist Nest
6   Hotel Colmar; Pasta Hut
7   Sea Pearl Hotel
8   Joema Tourist Home; Garden Cottages
9   GTDC Colva Cottages
11   Skylark Cottages
12   Colva Beach Resort
13   Blue Diamond Cottages
22   Vailankanni Cottages; Rice Bowl
23   William's Resort
24   Resort La Ben
25   Silver Sands Hotel
26   Jymi's Cottages
28   'C' Roque Resort;
     Splash; Ziggy's

PLACES TO EAT
14   Johnny Cool
21   Convite Restaurant; A Concha Resort
27   Munchies

OTHER
10   Bus Stand
15   Meeting Point Travel
16   Bank of Baroda
17   Church
18   Sanatan's (Internet)
19   Police Post
20   Post Office

guesthouses and homes along the road between Colva and Benaulim.

Colva There's a wide choice of short-term accommodation in Colva. At the cheaper end are the places strung out along the roads behind the beach, north of the main area.

Hotel Tourist Nest (☎ 723944) is a rambling old Portuguese house set in a peaceful location among the palm groves. Doubles are Rs 100/150 without/with bath.

Joema Tourist Home, nearby, is also good value. Basic rooms with bath and mosquito nets range from Rs 150 to Rs 200 in high season. The *Garden Cottages*, next door, is similar.

Lucky Star Restaurant (☎ 730069) is close to the beach and has sea-facing doubles with bath for Rs 200.

Fishermen's Cottages is also close to the beach. Prices during high season range from Rs 150 to Rs 200 for a double with bath, though it's not the cleanest place in Colva.

Vailankanni Cottages (☎ 737747) is one of several places right in the thick of things on the main street. Popular with travellers for the friendly atmosphere, doubles cost from Rs 200 with bath.

Blue Diamond Cottages is another good choice. This older place offers good, clean rooms for Rs 280 with bath.

Jymi's Cottages (☎ 712502) is run by a friendly family and is close to the beach just south of the main drag. Doubles (with bath) are clean but basic at Rs 350.

GTDC Colva Cottages (☎ 722287) is a two storey terrace of rooms facing the sea (each with its own balcony), a separate

GOA

block of cottages, a restaurant, bar, reception area and garden. Doubles cost Rs 340 with fan and bathroom, or Rs 500 with air-con. There's also dorm beds for Rs 60.

Hotel Colmar (☎ 721253) is popular, although not cheap over Christmas. Standard doubles with bath are Rs 500. The hotel has its own restaurant, bar and moneychanging facilities, and is used by overland tour groups.

Sea Pearl Hotel (☎ 730070) offers spotlessly clean doubles with/without balcony for Rs 210/315. Its restaurant is popular for its excellent seafood.

Sam's Beach Resort (☎ 735304), about 500m further along the same road, is another good bet. Spacious doubles with bath are Rs 300.

Resort La Ben (☎ 722009) is a fairly characterless building on the main road. The rooms are clean and comfortable but the Rs 475 price tag is probably a bit much.

'C' Roque Resort (☎ 738199), midway between Colva and Benaulim, is a good choice if you want to stay right on the beach. The clean, simple doubles, all with bath, are good value at Rs 300. There's no road access so you'll have to get down to the seafront at Colva or Benaulim and walk along the beach (about 10 minutes).

Skylark Cottages (☎ 723669) is clean and reasonable. Doubles with hot-water shower cost Rs 420.

Colva Beach Resort (☎ 721975) is on the main road to the beach. There are doubles for Rs 800 and air-con doubles for Rs 950; prices drop significantly mid-season.

William's Resort (☎ 721077) is a superior place charging Rs 750 for a double or Rs 1200 with air-con (plus tax). Nonguests can use the pool for Rs 25 per hour.

A Concha Resort (☎ 723593), at the junction of the road to Benaulim, is pretty good value. Clean singles/doubles with hot water cost Rs 425/550 and there's an excellent Chinese restaurant.

Silver Sands Hotel (☎ 721645, fax 735816) is in the centre of Colva. Singles/doubles cost from Rs 850/900 (Rs 1500 over Christmas), plus tax. There's a swimming pool, health club, water sports

and indoor games, an excellent bar and restaurant, live bands in the high season, and a travel counter.

Longhuinos Beach Resort (☎ 731645, fax 737588) is in an excellent location near the beach. The rooms are simply furnished but most have balconies and sea views. High-season rates are from Rs 875/1000 with hot water and satellite TV. Breakfast is included and there's a small garden with beach access.

Benaulim Less than 2km from Colva, Benaulim is much more peaceful.

Furtado's Beach House (☎ 720776) is right on the beach; rooms with bath cost Rs 300.

Xavier's Bar (☎ 730780), nearby, has slightly cheaper rooms at Rs 200.

L'Amour Beach Resort (☎ 223720) is a semi-upmarket place that has reasonable rooms with bath from Rs 250 and Rs 500.

O Palmar Beach Cottages (☎ 722901), opposite, is more basic. Doubles are Rs 368 with fan and bath. Neither of these places has much in the way of shade or gardens, but they're both very close to the beach and are often full in the high season.

Most other places are scattered around the village of Benaulim, about 1km from the beach, where accommodation is generally cheaper.

Rosario's Inn (☎ 734167) is a big place run by a charming family. It's very popular and has rooms with veranda and bath for Rs 200. There are also cheaper rooms with shared bath.

Savio Rest House (☎ 735954) is a cheap and basic option, behind a decrepit-looking building. Doubles are Rs 70/90 without/with bath, and there's an upstairs balcony room for Rs 95. *Jacinta Moraes Tourist House (☎ 722706)*, nearby, has very good doubles with bath for just Rs 100, and it's run by a friendly family.

Kenkre Tourist Cottages, nearby, is excellent value at Rs 80 for a double with bath.

Caroline Guest House (☎ 739649), on the road to the beach, is a pleasant family home with good doubles with bath for Rs 150.

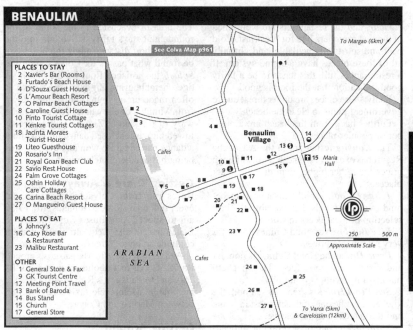

BENAULIM

See Colva Map p961

To Margao (6km)

Benaulim
Village

Maria
Hall

Cafes

ARABIAN
SEA

Cafes

0   250   500 m
Approximate Scale

To Varca (5km)
& Cavelossim (12km)

GOA

PLACES TO STAY
2 Xavier's Bar (Rooms)
3 Furtado's Beach House
4 D'Souza Guest House
6 L'Amour Beach Resort
7 O Palmar Beach Cottages
8 Caroline Guest House
10 Pinto Tourist Cottage
11 Kenkre Tourist Cottages
18 Jacinta Moraes
   Tourist House
19 Liteo Guesthouse
20 Rosario's Inn
21 Royal Goan Beach Club
22 Savio Rest House
24 Palm Grove Cottages
25 Oshin Holiday
   Care Cottages
26 Carina Beach Resort
27 O Mangueiro Guest House

PLACES TO EAT
5 Johncy's
16 Cacy Rose Bar
   & Restaurant
23 Malibu Restaurant

OTHER
1 General Store & Fax
9 GK Tourist Centre
12 Meeting Point Travel
13 Bank of Baroda
14 Bus Stand
15 Church
17 General Store

Liteo Guesthouse (☎ 721173) offers reasonable doubles with bath for Rs 300.

D'Souza Guest House (☎ 734364), a short distance north along the road to Colva, is a small, excellent, upmarket guesthouse in a Goan bungalow with an extensive garden. Spotless rooms are Rs 375 (half this outside high season). Also on this road is the *Pinto Tourist Cottage* (☎ 710744), which has a few doubles for Rs 125.

Palm Grove Cottages (☎ 722533) further south, is excellent, with a leafy, peaceful garden and outdoor restaurant. There's a wide range of rooms (Rs 175 to Rs 750).

O Mangueiro Guest House (☎ 734164) has rooms in the family house (with shared bath) for Rs 200 – cheaper long-term rates – and a newly-built section where spotless doubles with bath are Rs 400. They are planning further improvements including air-con and TVs in rooms.

Oshin Holiday Care Cottages (☎ 722707) are in a very peaceful area, set back from the road. Singles/doubles with bath are Rs 175/275. There's also a double with shared bath for Rs 150.

Carina Beach Resort (☎ 734166) is one of the top hotels in Benaulim. It's low-key with a garden and swimming pool. Rooms are Rs 1050 to Rs 1200, dropping to Rs 800 in the low season. It's closed from June to September.

Royal Goan Beach Club, just recently opened, is the flashest place and the first step towards upmarket tourism.

Places to Eat

Colva The most popular places to eat (and drink) around Colva are the string of open-air, wooden restaurants lining the beach either side of where the road ends. They're all individually owned and the standard of food

GOA

is pretty high. Seafood is, of course, *de rigueur*, and the restaurants are well tuned in to what travellers like for breakfast. Cold beer and spirits are available, and virtually all of these places have a sound system. If a restaurant is full, this tends to be a fairly good indication that the food is good.

Sadly, these places are under threat due to government plans to clear the beach.

Further back from the beach are a number of popular places.

The *Convite* restaurant in the A Concha Resort has excellent Chinese food, although prices are rather higher than those in other places.

Johnny Cool, rapidly disappearing behind two new hotels, has possibly the best selection of local beers in Colva.

Rice Bowl serves good Chinese food for very reasonable prices.

Pasta Hut at the Hotel Colmar is popular and serves very good food. The spaghetti marinara is excellent (naturally).

Sea Pearl Hotel is great for seafood; the kitchen must be one of the cleanest in India, and the selection is impressive.

Munchies is one of several cheap open-air restaurants among the group of shops and souvenir stalls near the roundabout. It is hidden away on the beachside of the other places, and serves a selection of Indian and western food.

Benaulim Almost all the beach shacks serve excellent seafood and cold beer but, as in Colva, their future existence is in question.

L'Amour Beach Resort produces excellent tandoori food.

Johncy's, down on the beach, is a perennial favourite and a popular meeting place, though the food is nothing to write home about.

The restaurant at the *Palm Grove Cottages* is popular with foreigners, as is the nearby *Malibu Restaurant*.

Cacy Rose Bar & Restaurant in the Benaulim Village is a friendly family-run spot, and it is also a good place to ask around for accommodation.

Entertainment

The area of beachside to the south of the roundabout stays fairly active late into the night. A short distance along the beach can be found what passes for Colva's nightlife. *Splash* has a dance floor by the beach, as does neighbouring *Ziggy's*. The crowd is often made up of young Indian men down from Mumbai or elsewhere. The owners are wary of this and at Ziggy's you're not allowed into the enclosed dance floor without a dance partner. Solo women have reported being hassled here late at night.

Getting There & Away

Buses run from Colva to Margao about every half hour (Rs 4, 20 minutes) from 7.30 am to about 7 pm. Buses from Margao to Benaulim are also frequent; some of them continue south to Varca and Cavelossim.

A taxi from Colva to Margao costs around Rs 70. Colva to Dabolim airport costs Rs 250, and to Panaji, it's Rs 325. All fares are negotiable. Motorcycle taxis charge Rs 35 between Margao and Colva.

Getting Around

There are plenty of places renting bicycles, mopeds, 100cc motorcycles and Enfields. At low tide, you can cycle 15km along the beach to Mobor, at the southern end. It's possible to get a boat across the estuary to Betul and then cycle back via Margao.

VARCA & CAVELOSSIM
☎ 0834

The 10km strip of pristine beach south of Benaulim has become Goa's upmarket resort beach, with at least half a dozen hotels of varying degrees of luxury. As far as resorts go, some of them are quite good, and they are certainly isolated from anything that might disturb the peace. Access is along the main road south from Benaulim. Varca is 5km south of Benaulim, and Cavelossim is 7km further on.

Places to Stay

Varca The *Resorte de Goa* (☎ 745066, fax 745310) is quite small with rooms and villas set around a swimming pool. The beach is a short walk away and this place is very quiet. The cheapest rooms are Rs 2150 but the villas (Rs 2500) are better.

Goa Renaissance Resort (☎ 745208, fax 745225), 500m beyond Resorte de Goa, is a true five star establishment. All rooms (starting at US$210) have a balcony facing the sea, there's a pool, beachside bar, and even a six-hole golf course. There's a couple of restaurants, and water sports are available.

Cavelossim *Gaffino's Beach Resort (☎ 746385)* is a guesthouse with rooms for Rs 350/400 (Rs 300/350 outside high season). It's good, clean and perfect if all you want to do is get away from India and rub shoulders with package tourists.

Holiday Inn Resort (☎ 746303, fax 746333) has rooms around a pool, just back from the beach. Doubles and singles alike go for Rs 4000 plus 15% tax.

Leela Beach Resort (☎ 746363, fax 746352) is at the end of the road at Mobor, near the mouth of a small estuary. This well-designed five-star deluxe complex is built around an artificial lagoon. Rooms cost from US$225/350. Leisure facilities include tennis and squash courts, gym, pool and health spa, plus a full range of water sports.

MOBOR TO PALOLEM

There are a few pleasant and quiet beaches along the coast between Mobor and Palolem. The fishing village of **Betul** can be reached either by boat or by bus from Margao (Rs 4, 45 minutes) via Chinchinim or Cuncolim. North of the village, near the harbour, is the peaceful *Oceanic Tourist Hotel (☎ 0834-760301)*. It's a small place with double rooms with bath from Rs 175. It takes about an hour to walk to Betul Beach from the hotel, so it's better to take a boat across the estuary to Mobor.

The road from Betul to Agonda winds over hills, past the old Portuguese fort of **Cabo de Rama**. There are now several places to stay in **Agonda**, a little village by an empty 2km stretch of sand. They're about 1km past the village, along the beach road. *Dunhill*

Bar and Restaurant (☎ 0834-647328) has simple doubles with shared bath for Rs 200, and a shady bar and restaurant. Nearby is *Dersy Bar (☎ 0834-647503)* with doubles for Rs 200/300 without/with bath.

PALOLEM
☎ 0834

Palolem is probably Goa's most beautiful and idyllic beach. The sweeping crescent of white sand is fringed by a shady rim of coconut palms and the whole beach is hemmed in at either end by rocky crags.

Palolem is hardly undiscovered; lots of day-trippers come down from Colva and Cavelossim and many travellers drift down from the northern beaches to spend days, weeks or even months chilling out here; there is very little development and it's extremely laid-back. Most accommodation is in simple, rickety beach huts or villagers' homes, with a handful of more solid guesthouses scattered around.

Palolem Village is nestled in the palms back from the beach. Few facilities are here, but it's not far to Chaudi, the nearest town.

Places to Stay & Eat

Along the edge of the beach are several groups of palm thatch or bamboo huts available for about Rs 150 in high season. Rooms in village homes are also available for Rs 100 to Rs 120.

Cocohuts, at the southern end of the beach, is interesting. Sturdy double huts with a fan, light and mattress built up on stilts cost Rs 400. It's open from October to May.

Ciaran's Camp (☎ 643477), about halfway along the beach, has decent bamboo huts with power for Rs 250 and rooms in a house (with bath) for Rs 400.

La Allegro (☎ 643550) is a solid old place on the beach where doubles with bath go for Rs 300.

Palolem Beach Resort (☎ 643054) is more upmarket but still low-key. Doubles with bath are Rs 400, cottages are Rs 250, or you can rent a tent for Rs 200. There's a restaurant and you can change cash and travellers cheques here (even if you're not a guest).

There are several guesthouses in the village. *D'Mello Tourist Home* (☎ 643057) has doubles without/with bath from Rs 100/250.

There are the usual cafes as well as a few restaurants near the beach. *Classic German Restaurant & Bar*, in a quiet spot on the road towards Cocohuts, has an interesting selection of health foods, cakes, rolls and drinks.

Getting There & Away

Buses run from Margao to Chaudi, from where an auto-rickshaw costs about Rs 35. There are two direct buses a day from Palolem to Margao. A better way is to take a train on the Konkan Railway to Canacona – rickshaws wait here to meet trains. Motorcycles can be hired in Palolem Village.

PONDA

Although the central, inland town of Ponda is of no great interest, it does boast an old mosque. The surrounding area has a number of unique Hindu temples rebuilt from originals destroyed by the Portuguese – their lamp towers are a distinctive Goan feature.

Five of Goa's most important Hindu temples are on the inland route between Panaji and Margao. The Shiva temple of **Shri Manguesh** is at Priol-Ponda Taluka, about 22km from Panaji. This tiny 18th century hilltop temple, with its white tower, is a local landmark. Less than 2km further down the road is **Shri Mahalsa**, a Vishnu temple.

About 5km from Ponda are the **Shri Ramnath** and **Shri Manguesh** temples, and nearby is the **Shri Shantadurga Temple**. Dedicated to Shantadurga, the goddess of peace, this temple sports an unusual, almost pagoda-like, structure with a roof made from long slabs of stone. Further south are the temples of **Shri Chandreshwar**, east of Betul; and **Shri Mallikarjuna**, east of Chaudi.

The oldest mosque remaining in Goa is the **Safa Shahouri Masjid** at Ponda, built by Ali Adilshah in 1560.

Getting There & Away

There are regular buses from Panaji and Margao, but to get to the temples it's best to have your own transport.

BONDLA WILDLIFE SANCTUARY

Up in the lush foothills of the Western Ghats, Bondla is the smallest of the Goan wildlife sanctuaries (8 sq km) but the easiest to reach. It's 52km from Panaji and 38km from Margao.

There's a botanical garden, fenced deer park and a zoo that is better than most, with reasonably spacious enclosures. Fauna here includes gaur and sambar but unless you're prepared to spend a few days and put in the time on an observation platform, you're unlikely to see much.

Bookings for chalet accommodation should be made in advance at the office of the Department of Forestry in Panaji, they are very good value at under Rs 50 per person.

To get to Bondla, take any bus heading east out of Goa along the NH4A, and ask to be let down at Usgao Tisk. From there catch a motorcycle taxi to the park (Rs 50).

DUDHSAGAR FALLS

On the eastern border with Karnataka are Goa's most impressive waterfalls. Providing the South Central Railway line is fully operational, Dudhsagar is best reached by train from Margao. You can catch a morning train up and spend several hours at the falls – there are pools to swim in – before taking an afternoon train back. Check timetables at Margao station.

MOLEM & COTIGAO WILDLIFE SANCTUARIES

These wildlife sanctuaries are larger than Bondla but you will need your own transport to get to them. There's a tree-top watchtower in Cotigao but the animals (including gaur, sambar, leopards, spotted deer and snakes) manage to remain well hidden, so you won't see a lot.

Accommodation is available at Molem in the *Tourist Resort* (☎ 0834-600238). rooms cost Rs 170/220, and meals are available if booked in advance. There's no accommodation in the Cotigao sanctuary, although you can stay in the *Forest Rest House*, nearby, if you get permission from the Department of Forestry in Panaji.

Karnataka

The Kannada-speaking state of Karnataka, formerly known as Mysore, has a finely balanced mix of natural attractions and superb historic architecture. It appeals equally to temple lovers, wildlife enthusiasts, trekkers and beach bums, yet much of the state sees few travellers compared to neighbouring Goa, Kerala and Tamil Nadu.

The state consists of a narrow coastal strip backed by the monsoon-drenched Western Ghats and a drier, cooler interior plateau that turns arid in the far north. It's a major producer of coffee, spices and betel nut, and supplies 60% of the country's silk. The capital, Bangalore, is the centre of India's science and technology industry and is one of the fastest growing cities in Asia.

History

A multitude of religions, cultures and kingdoms have unrolled across the terrain of Karnataka, beginning in the 3rd century BC when Chandragupta Maurya, India's first great emperor, retreated to Sravanabelagola after he renounced worldly ways and embraced Jainism. In the 6th century, the Chalukyans built some of the earliest Hindu temples in India near Badami. All later south Indian temple architecture stemmed from their designs, and from those by the Pallavas at Kanchipuram and Mahabalipuram in Tamil Nadu.

Other important Indian dynasties, such as the Cholas and the Gangas, have also played their part in Karnataka's history, but it was the Hoysalas, who ruled between the 11th and 14th centuries, who left the most vivid evidence of their presence. The beautiful Hoysala temples at Somnathpur, Halebid and Belur are gems of Indian architecture, with intricate and detailed sculptures rivalling anything to be found at Khajuraho (Madhya Pradesh) or Konark (Orissa).

In 1327, Halebid fell to the Muslim army of Mohammed Tughlaq, but his triumph was brief and in 1346 it was annexed by the

Karnataka at a Glance

Population: 44.9 million
Area: 191,791 sq km
Capital: Bangalore
Main Language: Kannada
Best Time to Go: September to February

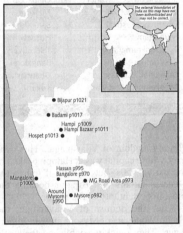

- **Hampi** – Karnataka's pre-eminent ancient site: explore the haunting ruins of the Vijayanagar empire capital

- **Badami** – here, and at nearby Aihole and Pattadakal, are some of India's finest examples of Dravidian temples and rock-cut caves

- **Belur & Halebid** – exquisitely sculpted temples rivalling the famous Khajuraho temples in detail and execution

- **Sravanabelagola** – site of the 17m-high Jain statue of Bahubali, possibly the tallest monolithic statue in the world

- **Gokarna** – a string of laid-back beaches on which to chill out and revive

- **Mysore** – another great place to chill out or join in the Dusshera festivities

Festivals of Karnataka

festival	location	date	features
Udipi	Udipi	Jan (biennial)	7 day Hindu festival
Classical Dance Festival	Pattadakal	Jan	dance
Banashankari Fair	Banashankari	Jan	7 day fair
Ranganathaswamy Festival	Srirangapatnam	Jan	1 day festival
Siddheshwara Festival	Bijapur	Jan/Feb	8 day festival
Virupakshaswamy Festival	Hampi	Feb	4 day festival
Shivaratri	Gokarna	Feb/Mar	chariot processions
Sharana Baseveshvara Festival	Gulbarga	Mar	15 day festival
Vairamudi Festival	Melkote	Mar/Apr	5 day Hindu festival
Dharmaya Festival	Bangalore	Apr	1 day festival
Muharram	Hospet	May/Jun	Islamic commemorations
Tula Sankramana	Telecauvery	Oct	festival of rebirth
Basavanna	Bangalore	Nov	1 day festival
Manjunatheshwara	Dharmastala	Nov	3 day festival
Mookambika Festival	Kollur	Nov	10 day festival

Hindu kingdom of Vijayanagar. This dynasty, whose capital was at Hampi, peaked in the early 1550s, but in 1565 it fell to the Deccan sultans and Bijapur became the most important city of the region.

After the demise of Vijayanagar, the Hindu Wodeyars of Mysore grew in importance. They quickly established their rule over a large part of southern India, including all of the old Mysore state and parts of Tamil Nadu, with their capital at Srirangapatnam. Their power remained more or less unchallenged until 1761 when Hyder Ali (one of their generals) deposed them.

The French helped Hyder Ali and his son, Tipu Sultan, to consolidate their hold over the area in return for support in fighting the British. In 1799 the British defeated Tipu Sultan, annexed part of his kingdom, and put the Wodeyars back on Mysore's throne.

The Wodeyars continued to rule Mysore state until Independence when they were pensioned off. They were enlightened and progressive rulers, so popular with their subjects that the maharaja became the first governor of the post-Independence state. The boundaries of Mysore state were re-drawn on linguistic grounds in 1956 and the extended Kannada-speaking state of Greater Mysore was established. This was renamed Karnataka in 1972.

Southern Karnataka

BANGALORE
☎ 080 • pop 5.2 million

The capital of Karnataka state is a thriving modern business centre – dubbed the 'Silicon Valley' of India – whose gracious garrison-town features are being remodelled in the image of India's mall-loving middle class.

The pace of life, like the intellectual and political climate, is brisk. Hardly a day goes by without a new controversy boiling over across the front pages or onto the streets. It's also regarded as one of India's most progressive and liberal cities as far as social attitudes go. Its stark contrast with the rest of the state is most evident in the MG Rd area, where fast-food joints, yuppie theme bars and glitzy malls are all the rage.

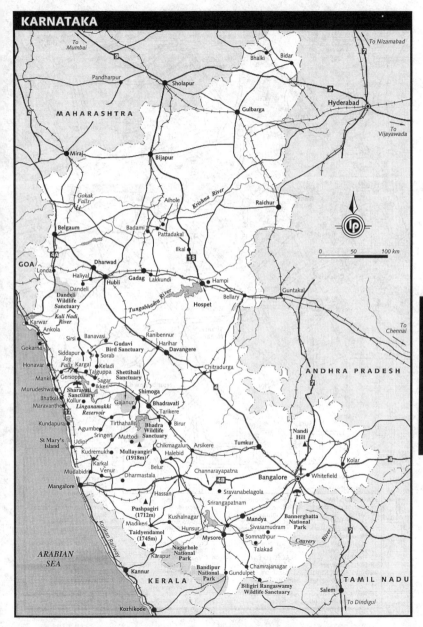

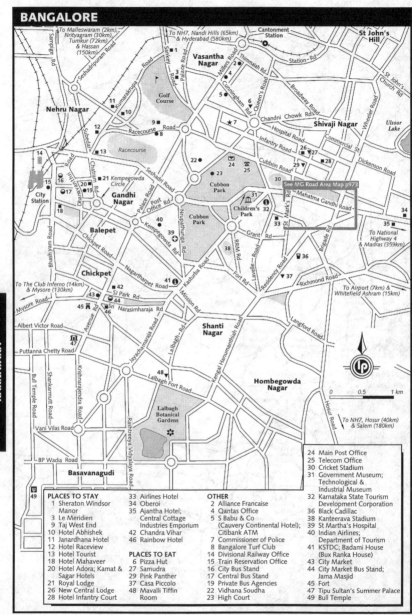

BANGALORE

To Malleswaram (2km);
Nrityagram (30km);
Tumkur (72km)
& Hassan
(150km)

To NH7, Nandi Hills (65km)
& Hyderabad (580km)

Cantonment
Station

St John's
Hill

Sampige Rd

Seshadripuram Road

Sankey Rd

Palace Road

Vasantha
Nagar

Miller's Road

Thimmaiah Rd

Station Rd

St John's Church Rd

Kumarakrupa Road

Cunningham Rd

Queen's Road

Broadway Road

Wheeler Road

Nehru Nagar

11
10

Golf
Course

5

6

Chandni Chowk Rd

Shivaji Nagar

Commercial St

Ulsoor
Lake

12

9
8

Racecourse Road

7

Hospital Road

Infantry Road

26
27

29
28

Dickenson Road

13

Racecourse

Kempegowda
Circle

21

Seshadri Road

22

24
25

23

Cubbon
Park

30

See MG Road Area Map p973

Mahatma Gandhi Road

City
Station

15
16
20 19
17

Gandhi
Nagar

Post Office Rd

Nrupathunga Road

31

Children's
Park

32

St Mark's Rd

Brigade Rd

34

18

40

Cubbon
Park

33

35

To National
Highway 4
& Madras (359km)

Balepet

39

Grant Rd

RRM Rd

Lavelle Road

To The Club Inferno (14km)
& Mysore (130km)

Chickpet

Nagartharpet Road

41

38

Fort Rd

Kasturba Rd

Residency Road

36

37

Richmond Road

To Airport (7km) &
Whitefield Ashram (15km)

42

SJ Park Rd

43
44
45
46

Sri
Narasimharaja Rd

Mission Road

Shanti
Nagar

Kempegowda Rd

Langford Road

Albert Victor Road

Puttanna Chetty Road

Avenue Rd

Jayachamaraja Rd

Lalbagh Rd

Kenpal Hanumanthiah Rd

Hombegowda
Nagar

Mysore Road

Bhashyam Road

47

Krishnarajendra Road

Rashtreeya Vidyalaya Road

48

Lalbagh Fort Road

Lalbagh
Botanical
Gardens

To NH7, Hosur (40km)
& Salem (180km)

Hosur Road

0   0.5   1 km

Bull Temple Road

Shankarmutt Road

Vani Vilas Road

BP Wadia Road

Basavanagudi

49

PLACES TO STAY	33 Airlines Hotel	**OTHER**
1 Sheraton Windsor Manor	34 Oberoi	2 Alliance Francaise
	35 Ajantha Hotel; Central Cottage Industries Emporium	4 Qantas Office
9 Taj West End		5 S Babu & Co (Cauvery Continental Hotel); Citibank ATM
10 Hotel Abhishek	42 Chandra Vihar	
11 Janardhana Hotel	46 Rainbow Hotel	7 Commissioner of Police
12 Hotel Raceview		8 Bangalore Turf Club
13 Hotel Tourist	**PLACES TO EAT**	14 Divisional Railway Office
18 Hotel Mahaveer	6 Pizza Hut	15 Train Reservation Office
20 Hotel Adora; Kamat & Sagar Hotels	27 Samudra	16 City Bus Stand
	29 Pink Panther	17 Central Bus Stand
21 Royal Lodge	37 Casa Piccolo	19 Private Bus Agencies
26 New Central Lodge	48 Mavalli Tiffin Room	22 Vidhana Soudha
28 Hotel Infantry Court		23 High Court

24 Main Post Office
25 Telecom Office
30 Cricket Stadium
31 Government Museum; Technological & Industrial Museum
32 Karnataka State Tourism Development Corporation
36 Black Cadillac
38 Kanteerava Stadium
39 St Martha's Hospital
40 Indian Airlines; Department of Tourism
41 KSTDC; Badami House (Bux Ranka House)
43 City Market
44 City Market Bus Stand; Jama Masjid
45 Fort
47 Tipu Sultan's Summer Palace
49 Bull Temple

Tourist brochures call this the 'Garden City', and while it boasts some pleasant parks and gardens, Bangalore is generally busy, traffic-clogged and fairly light on 'attractions'. However, it has good transport connections, is a useful place to arrange trips to Karnataka's national parks and wildlife sanctuaries, and is worth exploring for a couple of days in its own right.

History

Bangalore is said to have received its name after an old woman living near here served a humble dish of boiled beans to a lost Hoysala king. The 'town of boiled beans' was formally founded by Kempegowda in the early 16th century. He built a mud fort and mapped out the extent of the city he envisioned with four watchtowers (all now swallowed by the city's urban sprawl). Two centuries later, Bangalore became an important fortress city under Hyder Ali and Tipu Sultan, though little remains from this period except the Lalbagh botanical gardens and a small palace. The British moved their regional administrative headquarters from Srirangapatnam to Bangalore in 1831 and the town began to take on the familiar ordered look of a British cantonment.

Bangalore's rapid growth began in the 1960s when the government located key defence and telecommunications research establishments here. Over the following decades it became the science and technology centre of India, and home to many multinational companies.

Orientation

Bangalore is a sprawling, disorienting city, but travellers usually only need to concentrate on fathoming two areas: Gandhi Nagar in the west and the Mahatma Gandhi (MG) Rd area 4km to the east.

The Central bus stand and the City train station are on the edge of Gandhi Nagar. The crowded streets in this lively but unprepossessing part of town are crammed with shops, cinemas and budget hotels. The area bounded by MG, Brigade, St Marks and Residency Rds is the retail, entertainment and social hub for the city's more affluent citizenry and for its student population. Here you'll find a mixture of budget and luxury hotels, fast-food joints, cybercafes, bars, bookshops and craft shops.

Bangalore's few remaining historical relics are all south of the City Market in the old part of town.

Information

Tourist Offices The helpful Government of India tourist office (☎ 558 5417), in the KFC Building at 48 Church St, is open Monday to Friday 9.30 am to 6 pm and Saturday 9 am to 1 pm.

The Karnataka State Tourism Development Corporation (KSTDC) has its head office (☎ 221 2901) on the 2nd floor of Mitra Towers, 10/4 Kasturba Rd, Queen's Circle. It's open 10 am to 5.30 pm daily except Sunday. There are also KSTDC operations at Badami House (☎ 227 5869) and at the City train station and the airport.

The Government of Karnataka Department of Tourism (☎ 221 5489) is on the 1st floor of F block, Cauvery Bhavan, Kempegowda (KG) Rd, behind the Indian Airlines office.

All the tourist offices have decent free maps of Bangalore. You can also buy good city maps from bookshops on MG Rd.

The handy what's-on guide, *Bangalore This Fortnight*, is free at tourist offices and hotels. The *Deccan Herald*, Bangalore's major newspaper, is a lively read and carries advertisements for most local events.

Money Thomas Cook at 55 MG Rd is an efficient place for foreign exchange but there's a Rs 30 commission charge on travellers cheques other than their own. For Amex cheques try Weizman Foreign Exchange on Residency Rd. The Bank of Baroda at 72 MG Rd provides cash advances on MasterCard and Visa credit cards, as does the Canara Bank nearby at No 8.

Citibank has several 24 hour ATMs that accept most international cards. The head office is at the Prestige Meridian on MG Rd, but there's a more convenient machine

KARNATAKA

India's Silicon Valley

Bangalore's meteoric recent growth is founded on an aspect of modern India that is seen in few other places in the country – world-class technological excellence. During the last 20 years the city has become home to a number of businesses including, in particular, India's booming computer software industry.

It all began in 1958 when Texas Instruments set up a successful design centre in Bangalore, paving the way for other multinational IT companies to set up here. By the mid-1990s India was the world's largest software exporter after the USA, and Bangalore accounted for a third of this US$2 billion software development industry. Multinationals have piled into the country to take advantage of the large pool of expertly trained talent that is being turned out of South India's technical training colleges. Recently a Bangalore entrepreneur was bought out by Microsoft, and every day Indian companies are proving that they are at the cutting edge of the industry.

The growth rate in this industry has been phenomenal – about 60% a year – which has spawned the development of 'Electronic City' and various IT 'parks' outside the city boundaries to provide space for offices, plants and housing for employees. The latest development is the Technology Information Centre at Whitefield, about 20km east of Bangalore.

Companies based in Bangalore include Motorola, Compaq, AT&T and Nexus – although Microsoft chose Hyderabad as its base in India.

outside Nilgiri's department store on Brigade Rd. There's another north of the centre on Cunningham Rd.

Post The main post office on Cubbon Rd is open Monday to Saturday 8 am to 7 pm and Sunday 10.30 am to 1.30 pm. The efficient poste restante service is at counter No 22, open Monday to Saturday 10 am to 6 pm. There's a sub post office on Brigade Rd.

Telephone & Fax From the modern telegraph office next to the main post office, you can send international faxes and make telephone calls 24 hours a day.

Email & Internet Access There are more cybercafes in the MG Rd area alone than in the rest of Karnataka put together. This is the hi-tech student hang-out where you'll find Cyber Alley, Cyber Club and Cyber Space all vying for your online time. Le Web, on the 2nd floor of the Shrungar Shopping Centre (enter from Church St), is not usually too busy and is one of the cheapest around at Rs 50 per hour.

Coffee Day Cyber Cafe at 13-15 Brigade Rd is one of the originals – it's always busy and more expensive at Rs 60 per half hour but the coffee is certainly good.

Visa Extensions Apply for visa extensions at the office of the Commissioner of Police (☎ 225 6242 ext 513) on Infantry Rd, a five minute walk from the post office. It's open Monday to Saturday 10 am to 5.30 pm. The process usually takes two to three days.

Bookshops There are several excellent bookshops in town. One of the best is the Premier Bookshop, around the corner from Berrys Hotel. Books on every conceivable subject are piled from floor to ceiling. Gangarams Book Bureau at 72 MG Rd is also good. There's a Higginbothams at No 68.

Cultural Centres The British Library (☎ 221 3485) on St Mark's Rd has British newspapers and magazines. It's open Tuesday to Saturday 10.30 am to 6.30 pm.

Alliance Française (☎ 225 8762), on Thimmaiah Rd near Cantonment train station, has a library with French papers and magazines, and is open Monday to Friday 9 am to 1 pm and 3 to 7 pm; Saturday 9 am to 1 pm. It also hosts exhibitions, cultural activities and has French-language courses.

Medical Services In an emergency, call ☎ 102. For less urgent medical attention, try St Martha's Hospital (☎ 227 5081), Nrupathunga Rd.

National Parks To arrange accommodation in Bandipur National Park, contact the Chief Wildlife Warden (☎ 334 1993), Aranya Bhavan, 18th Cross, Malleswaram, Bangalore. This can also be done in Mysore (see that section). It's also possible to make bookings in Bangalore for Nagarhole National Park, but it's better to do this at Hunsur. See the Nagarhole National Park section later in this chapter.

Jungle Lodges & Resorts Ltd (☎ 559 7025, fax 558 6163), in the Shrungar Shopping Centre on MG Rd, arranges excellent private accommodation at Nagarhole National Park and several other reserves around the state.

Vidhana Soudha
At the north-western end of Cubbon Park, this massive, granite, neo-Dravidian style building is one of Bangalore's most imposing. Built in 1954, it houses the Secretariat and the State Legislature. It's floodlit on weekend evenings but isn't open to the public.

Cubbon Park & Museums
Laid out in 1864, this 120 hectare park is one of the main 'lungs' of the city. It's not the most beautiful of gardens but it's a pleasant escape from the surrounding urban chaos.

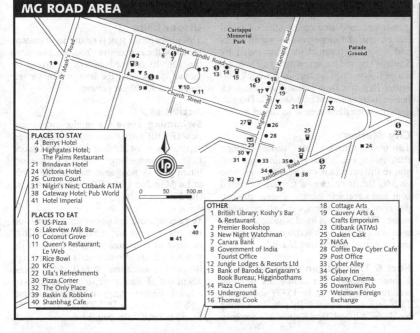

MG ROAD AREA

KARNATAKA

PLACES TO STAY
4 Berrys Hotel
9 Highgates Hotel;
  The Palms Restaurant
21 Brindavan Hotel
24 Victoria Hotel
26 Curzon Court
31 Nilgiri's Nest; Citibank ATM
38 Gateway Hotel; Pub World
41 Hotel Imperial

PLACES TO EAT
5 US Pizza
6 Lakeview Milk Bar
10 Coconut Grove
11 Queen's Restaurant;
   Le Web
17 Rice Bowl
20 KFC
22 Ulla's Refreshments
30 Pizza Corner
32 The Only Place
39 Baskin & Robbins
40 Shanbhag Cafe

OTHER
1 British Library; Koshy's Bar
  & Restaurant
2 Premier Bookshop
3 New Night Watchman
7 Canara Bank
8 Government of India
  Tourist Office
12 Jungle Lodges & Resorts Ltd
13 Bank of Baroda; Gangaram's
   Book Bureau; Higginbothams
14 Plaza Cinema
15 Underground
16 Thomas Cook
18 Cottage Arts
19 Cauvery Arts &
   Crafts Emporium
23 Citibank (ATMs)
25 Oaken Cask
27 NASA
28 Coffee Day Cyber Cafe
29 Post Office
33 Cyber Alley
34 Cyber Inn
35 Galaxy Cinema
36 Downtown Pub
37 Weizman Foreign
   Exchange

On its fringes are the superbly restored neo-classical High Court, the grand Public Library, two municipal museums and a dull aquarium. Also in the gardens is a huge **children's park**, which adults are wisely not allowed into unless accompanied by a minor.

The **Government Museum**, one of the oldest in India, was established in 1886 and houses a poorly presented collection of stone carvings, pottery, weapons, paintings, and some good pieces from Halebid. It's open daily except Monday 10 am to 5 pm (Rs 1).

The **Visvesvaraya Technological & Industrial Museum** is usually full of school children pressing buttons on exhibits that reflect India's technological progress. It's open daily 10 am to 6 pm (Rs 10).

Lalbagh Botanical Gardens

This pleasant 96 hectare park in the southern suburbs of Bangalore was laid out in the 18th century by Hyder Ali and his son Tipu Sultan. It contains many labelled centuries-old trees, one of India's largest collections of rare tropical and subtropical plants, a glasshouse modelled on London's Crystal Palace, one of Kempegowda's watchtowers and a surreal lawn clock surrounded by Snow White and the seven dwarfs. There are major flower displays here in the week preceding Republic Day (January) and the week before Independence Day (August). The gardens are open daily sunrise to sunset.

City Market

This bustling market south-west of Cubbon Park is all you need to remind you that you're still in India if you've spent your time on MG Rd. It contains a tarpaulin-covered fruit and vegetable bazaar, a spice market, plenty of garland sellers, cloth shops and an entire colourful street lined with hole-in-the-wall tailor shops. Also in this bustling area is the imposing, white **Jama Masjid**.

Fort & Tipu Sultan's Palace

Kempegowda built a mud-brick defence structure on this site in 1537, and in the 18th century it was solidly rebuilt in stone by Hyder Ali and Tipu Sultan. It's a sturdy little fort, though much of it was destroyed during the wars with the British. It's worth a quick visit if you're exploring the City Market.

Tipu Sultan's modest palace is notable for its elegant teak pillars. It was begun by Hyder Ali, and completed by Tipu in 1791. The palace is a five minute walk south-west of the City Market. Entry is Rs 5 and Rs 25 for a video camera.

Bull Temple

Situated on Bugle Hill at the southern end of Bull Temple Rd, this is one of Bangalore's oldest temples. Built by Kempegowda in the Dravidian style in the 16th century, it contains a huge granite monolith of Nandi. Non-Hindus are allowed to enter the temple and the priests are friendly. It's especially interesting on weekends, when there are often musicians, wedding processions and even *pujas* to bless new motor cars. Bus Nos 31, 31E, 35 or 49 from the City bus stand will get you to Bull Temple.

Ulsoor Lake

This pretty picnic spot is on the north-eastern fringe of the city centre. You can hire row-boats for Rs 60 per half hour or have a 10 minute spin around the lake in a motorised dinghy for Rs 10 per person.

Activities

Swimming There's a public swimming pool (Rs 10), with some carefully regulated separate-sex swimming hours, at Ulsoor Lake. For something more fancy (at exorbitant prices), nonguests can use the pools at Le Meridien (Rs 350) or Taj West End (Rs 500).

Yoga Bangalore has numerous ashrams and schools for yoga and meditation. The Government of India tourist office can provide you with a list. Vivekananda Kentra Yoga Research Foundation (☎ 660 8645), about 35km out of Bangalore, is a huge modern ashram offering a range of courses at around US$10 per class, or US$300 per month. Bus No 35 bus will take you there.

Atma Darshan Yoga Ashram (☎ 663 9490), 589 10th Cross, Jayanagar, has five-day evening courses for Rs 300. Shri Shri Ravi Shankar's Art of Living Foundation has three-day residential courses at its ashram about 21km from the city for Rs 800, and more advanced courses. Contact the ashram on ☎ 843 2273, or the city office on ☎ 664 5106.

Adventure Activities For activities such as trekking, rafting, caving and rock-climbing, contact the General Thimmaiah National Academy for Adventure (☎ 221 0454), State Youth Centre, Nrupathunga Rd, Bangalore.

Organised Tours
The KSTDC offers a huge range of tours, which can be booked at any of its offices. They all start at Badami House (aka Bux Ranka House). The city sightseeing tour runs twice daily at 7.30 am and 2 pm (Rs 85). It quickly covers the city's main attractions with an obligatory stop at a government-owned silk and handicraft emporium – not bad value if you really want to see everything, but it's a bit dull. There's also a tour to Srirangapatnam, Mysore and Brindavan gardens departing daily at 7.15 am and returning at 11 pm (Rs 220, including entrance fees); tours to Nandi Hill (Rs 150); to Belur, Halebid and Sravanabelagola (Rs 300); and a weekend tour to Hampi (Rs 675).

Maharaja Tours (☎ 333 4442) offers cultural tours that include introductions to Indian arts, a visit to a temple, a yoga demonstration, a concert and dance, and a visit to an Indian home. They depart at 3 pm, return at 9 pm and cost Rs 900 per person, including a vegetarian dinner (minimum five people).

Places to Stay – Budget
Bus Stand Area A dozen or more budget hotels line Subedar Chatram Rd (SC Rd) in the heart of Gandhi Nagar, just east of the bus stands.

Royal Lodge (☎ 226 6575, 251 SC Rd) is one of the cheapest, largest and oldest. It has clean singles/doubles with common bath for Rs 100/140 and doubles with bath and hot water in the morning for Rs 205 (Rs 253 with TV).

Hotel Adora (☎ 220 0324, 47 SC Rd), almost opposite, has decent rooms with bath for Rs 150/253.

Hotel Mahaveer (☎ 287 3670, Tank Bund Rd), immediately south of the City train station, is a spotless, modern budget hotel. Small rooms with TV, bath and hot water in the morning cost Rs 225/320 and air-con doubles cost Rs 610.

Hotel Tourist (☎ 226 2381, 5 Racecourse Rd) is a little further afield. It's reasonable value at Rs 80/160 for rooms with bath and hot water in the morning.

MG Rd Area *Hotel Ajantha* (☎ 558 4321, MG Rd) is a good value budget hotel, slightly removed from the main hubbub. Clean rooms cost Rs 168/330.

New Central Lodge (☎ 559 2395, 56 Infantry Rd) is a very average place with basic and overpriced singles/doubles with common bath for Rs 130/270, or with attached bath for Rs 320/350. There's hot water from 6 to 9 am.

Hotel Imperial (☎ 558 5473, 93-94 Residency Rd) has singles/doubles with bath for Rs 170/300. It's in a noisy area and staff are a bit offhand.

Airlines Hotel (☎ 227 3783, 4 Madras Bank Rd) is set back from the road in its own leafy grounds and has a range of facilities including a garden restaurant, a supermarket and a bakery. Singles/doubles with bath and hot water in the morning cost from Rs 125/250, or Rs 330/450 for deluxe rooms (with TV). Unfortunately it's so popular that you need to make a reservation 10 to 15 days in advance.

Brindavan Hotel (☎ 558 4000, 108 MG Rd) has decent rooms with bath from Rs 160/280 and air-con rooms for Rs 425/850. The hotel is fairly quiet since it's set back from the road, but it's also often full – book a week ahead.

City Market Area This is the place to stay if you enjoy being in the thick of the noise, bustle and atmosphere of the bazaar. It's a 25 minute walk south from the City train station.

Chandra Vihar (☎ 222 4146, *Avenue Rd*) charges Rs 168/303 for clean, decent-sized rooms with bath and hot water in the morning, or Rs 145 for a smaller single. There are great views of the market from some rooms.

Rainbow Hotel (☎ 6702235, *Sri Narasimharaja Rd*), opposite the City Market bus stand and the Jama Masjid, is OK value at Rs 125/250 for singles/doubles with bath, though it's pretty dingy.

Places to Stay – Mid-Range

Most of the hotels in this price range are in the MG Rd area but there are a few near the racecourse, a relatively dull area that's a short auto-rickshaw ride from the City train station and Central bus stand.

MG Rd Area The *Victoria Hotel* (☎ 558 4076, fax 558 4945, 47-48 Residency Rd) is a classy, established hotel set in grounds filled with huge shady trees. It's full of Raj-era charm and there are not many rooms so you need to make an advance reservation. They've upped their room prices so it's not the best value these days anyway. Singles/doubles are Rs 400/1050, and a suite costs Rs 1150, plus 22.5% tax. There's a bar and restaurant with indoor and garden dining.

Curzon Court (☎ 558 2997, fax 558 2278, 10 Brigade Rd) offers comfortable air-con rooms with TV and hot shower from Rs 900/1000, to Rs 1150/1400 for the suite.

Nilgiri's Nest (☎ 558 8401, fax 558 5348, 171 Brigade Rd) is right in the thick of things on the 3rd floor above a supermarket of the same name. It has clean, spacious, airy rooms with TV and bath for Rs 700/950, or Rs 900/1150 with air-con, but it's nothing special for these prices. Checkout is 24 hours.

Berrys Hotel (☎ 558 7211, 46/1 Church St) is a large, standard, mid-range establishment that's rarely full, but it is well located. Decent rooms with TV and hot water cost Rs 500/550, or Rs 550/600 for the suite.

Highgates Hotel (☎ 559 7172, fax 559 7799, 33 Church St) is a tasteful, modern, three-star hotel at the top of this price range.

Comfortable air-con rooms with TV, fridge and bath cost Rs 1195/1600. It has a restaurant, a lobby coffee shop and a patio. Reservations are recommended.

Hotel Infantry Court (☎ 559 1800, fax 559 2276, 66 Infantry Rd) is part of the Comfort Inn chain and is a very comfortable new hotel without the top-end prices. Modern air-con rooms are Rs 1330/1696 including breakfast.

Racecourse Area *Hotel Raceview* (☎ 220 3401, 25 Racecourse Rd) has doubles (no singles) for Rs 450. Keen punters may be interested to know that some of the more expensive rooms have a good view of the racetrack.

Hotel Abhishek (☎ 226 2713, fax 226 8953, 19/2 Kumarakrupa Rd) has singles/doubles with TV and bath for Rs 810/900, or Rs 900/990 with air-con.

Places to Stay – Top End

Bangalore's importance as an industrial and business centre has resulted in a plethora of swanky hotels, most of them around MG Rd or in the more peaceful northern part of town, close to the golf and racecourse. The Oberoi and the Taj West End vie for the title of best hotel in town.

Gateway Hotel (☎ 558 4545, fax 558 4030, 66 Residency Rd) is a four-star member of the Taj Group. It has excellent singles/doubles from US$85/95, including breakfast. Facilities include a swimming pool and a restaurant specialising in Malabar Coast cuisine.

Le Meridien (☎ 226 2233, fax 226 7676, 28 Sankey Rd) has rooms from US$145/165.

Sheraton Windsor Manor (☎ 226 9898, fax 226 4941, 25 Sankey Rd) occupies a beautiful old manor house where rooms cost from US$130/140.

Oberoi (☎ 558 5858, fax 558 5960, 37-39 MG Rd) has luxurious rooms that open onto an immense tranquil garden for US$225/255. There's a swimming pool and all the usual five-star amenities.

Taj West End (☎ 225 5055, fax 220 0010, Racecourse Rd) is a classy five-star hotel occupying a carefully restored 19th century mansion and several villas set in a beautiful eight hectare garden. Rooms start from US$195/215.

Places to Eat

MG Rd Area There are a huge number of places to eat around MG Rd, though most are expensive and mediocre imitations of western fast-food or pizza joints. Their attractiveness will probably be determined by how long you've been in India.

Ulla's Refreshments, on the 1st floor of General Hall, MG Rd, is a local favourite and a great spot for snacks and south Indian vegetarian dishes. It has an indoor area and a big, convivial terrace.

US Pizza (Church St) makes reasonable pizzas from around Rs 80, and it has a pleasant veranda dining area.

Pizza Corner is a newer and more popular pizza chain with a branch on Brigade Rd. Pizzas are around Rs 105 and it offers free delivery (☎ 344 6111).

Coconut Grove (Church St) is a friendly, semi open-air restaurant with a mouthwatering array of Keralan, Goan and Coorg regional dishes. The bamboo screens, attentive service and tranquil dining area add to the experience here. Main courses cost Rs 85 to Rs 100.

Rice Bowl (Brigade Rd) is a cosy Chinese joint run by Tibetans. The food is average but it comes in hearty proportions.

Shanbhag Cafe (Residency Rd) dishes up decent south Indian *thalis* for Rs 23, and a more luxurious north Indian variety for Rs 61.

Victoria Hotel (47-48 Residency Rd) has a nice shady garden restaurant and an old-fashioned dining hall that are both interesting eating places if you have the patience to handle the lacklustre service.

Casa Piccolo (131 Residency Rd) receives enthusiastic raves from travellers. It's yet another western-style eatery, but it has a good atmosphere and prices are sensible.

The Only Place (Royal Arcade, Brigade Rd) is a good place for a steak with a decent plate of vegetables. Mains are around Rs 100.

Queen's Restaurant (Church St) has an earthy atmosphere with mud walls, tribal decorations and cane furniture. It's very popular and serves reasonably priced Indian and Chinese food.

Lakeview Milk Bar (38 MG Rd) and *Baskin & Robbins (Residency Rd)* are the places to go for ice cream.

Elsewhere The *Kamat Hotel* and *Sagar Hotel* are the two best options in Subedar Chatram Rd in Gandhi Nagar. The former dishes up south Indian vegetarian fare, and the latter Andhra-style cuisine.

Samudra (25 Lady Curzon Rd) has delicious north Indian fare and more impressive fish tanks than Bangalore's aquarium. Main dishes cost Rs 50 to Rs 60. It's a 10 minute walk north of MG Rd. Also in this area is *Pink Panther*, a bright, westernised restaurant and cafe with an interesting menu.

Mavalli Tiffin Room, near Lalbagh botanical gardens, may not look much, but it's a legendary *dosa* and snack joint with excellent lassis.

Paradise Island at the Taj West End is the most interesting of the five-star hotel restaurants. Set in a beautiful garden pavilion, it serves excellent Thai and Chinese cuisine.

Entertainment

Bars Bangalore's affluence has bred a pub culture that wouldn't be out of place in any western country but that comes as a complete culture shock in India. Flashy bars, well-lit discos and draught beers are all the rage with well-heeled young people and office workers.

The MG Rd area has a bizarre collection of male-dominated theme bars, with deafening music and carefully structured seating arrangements that prevent too much social interaction between strangers; women are often quarantined in 'family only' areas.

Bars are open during lunchtime and from 5 to 11 pm. Draught beer costs around Rs 35 for a small mug, Rs 70 for a large mug and Rs 175 for a pitcher. Nearly all bars serve snacks.

Pub World, next to the Gateway Hotel, is symptomatic of Bangalore's restless mimicry of the west. It manages to squeeze a British pub, German beer hall, Wild West saloon and Manhattan cocktail bar into one room, though you may have trouble realising which one you're meant to be in.

NASA (Church St) is decked out like a spaceship and has laser shows, a young crowd, bar staff in flight uniform, MTV and mega-decibel music. If you like this place, you'll also like the *Underground (MG Rd)*, which is modelled like a London tube station.

New Night Watchman, near Berrys Hotel, has a nifty cubist park bench arrangement but thankfully no theme decor, and is a good place for a beer.

Oaken Cask, just around the corner from Residency Rd, is another British-style pub that's quieter than most.

Black Cadillac (50 Residency Rd) has quieter music, more expensive drinks and a cover charge on Friday and Saturday night. Friday night is popular with Bangalore's expat community.

Downtown Pub, opposite the Gateway Hotel, has good music, a relaxed atmosphere and a couple of pool tables.

The two nicest places for a beer have nothing to do with Bangalore's pub culture: try the veranda of the *Victoria Hotel* and the old fashioned tea-room ambience of *Koshy's Bar & Restaurant (St Mark's Rd)*.

Nightclubs Bangalore's trend-conscious nightclub scene is constantly changing. *The Club Inferno*, on the Mysore road, about 14km from the city centre, is popular.

Cinema The *Plaza (MG Rd)* and the *Galaxy (Residency Rd)* both show first-run English-language films. Regional films are best watched at one of the many cinemas along KG Rd in Gandhi Nagar.

Spectator Sports

Horse Racing Bangalore's winter race season runs from November to February and its summer season from May to July. Races are generally held on either Friday or weekends and can be a lot of fun. Contact the Bangalore Turf Club (☎ 226 2391) for details.

Cricket If you want to see India's sporting passion up close, Bangalore's Chinnaswami Stadium hosts occasional international matches and regular domestic matches. Contact the Karnataka Cricket Association (☎ 286 4487) for information.

Shopping

Bangalore is a good place to purchase silk, sandalwood and rosewood items, and Lambani tribal jewellery.

The most pleasant shopping experience is to be found on Commercial St, north of MG Rd, home to many silk, handicraft and clothes shops. Stunning, hand-embroidered saris are reasonably priced and fabric is cheaper here than in the silk emporiums lining MG Rd.

There are plenty of handicraft shops on MG Rd. Cauvery Arts & Crafts Emporium at No 23 stocks the same range of statues, jewellery, ceramics, carpets and *agarbathi* (incense) that you've seen in a thousand other tourist towns across the country. Cottage Arts at No 52 and Central Cottage Industries Emporium at No 144 also stock the usual range of artefacts.

There are a number of shops around MG Rd selling cheap new release CDs and tapes of western and Hindi music. The tapes are a bargain at around Rs 100.

Getting There & Away

Air The Indian Airlines office (☎ 221 1914) is in the Housing Board Buildings, Kempegowda (KG) Rd. Other operators include Jet Airways (☎ 555 0856) and Sahara (☎ 558 6976).

There are daily connections to Mumbai (Bombay, four flights a day, US$125), Calcutta (US$240), Delhi (US$230), Hyderabad (US$95), Chennai (Madras, US$65), plus numerous flights to Ahmedabad (US$200), Goa (US$95), Kochi (US$70), Mangalore (US$70), Pune (US$130) and Thiruvananthapuram (US$105).

The only direct international flights from Bangalore are to Muscat, Sharjah and Singapore, but there are numerous international connecting flights via Mumbai, including flights to the Gulf States, Paris, London, New York and Singapore. The advantage is that you can go through customs and immigration in relative peace at Bangalore airport.

International airlines with offices in Bangalore include:

Air France
　(☎ 558 9397) Sunrise Chambers, 22 Ulsoor Rd
Air India
　(☎ 227 7747) Unity Bldgs, Jayachamaraja Rd
British Airways
　(☎ 227 1205) 7 St Mark's Rd
KLM
　(☎ 226 8703) West End Hotel, Racecourse Rd
Lufthansa
　(☎ 558 8791) 44/2 Dickenson Rd
Qantas
　(☎ 225 6611) Westminster Bldg, Cunningham Rd
Singapore Airlines
　(☎ 221 3833) 51 Richmond Rd

Bus Bangalore's huge and well-organised Central bus stand is directly in front of the City train station. All the regular buses within the state are operated by the Karnataka State Road Transport Corporation (KSRTC, ☎ 287 3377). Interstate buses are operated by KSRTC as well as the state transport corporation of Andhra Pradesh (APSRTC, ☎ 287 3915, platform 15), Tamil Nadu's JJTC (☎ 287 6974, platform 14) and Goa's Kadamba Transport Corporation. Computerised advance booking is available for all KSRTC superdeluxe and express buses as well as for the bus companies of neighbouring states, and all have booths in the main reservations office. It's advisable to book in advance for long-distance journeys.

KSRTC operates horrifyingly fast buses to Mysore every 15 minutes from 5 am to midnight (Rs 36/48 ordinary/deluxe, three hours, platforms 17 & 18). It also has six daily departures to Ernakulam (16 hours), 12 to Hospet (nine hours), four to Jog Falls (eight hours), 10 to Chennai (eight hours), three to Mumbai (24 hours), three to Ooty (eight hours) and two to Panaji (15 hours). The KSTDC has a deluxe bus to Hospet (for Hampi), departing every morning from Badami House.

Kadamba buses depart for Margao at 5.30 pm (Rs 221) and Panaji at 6 pm (Rs 223, 13 hours). The APSRTC has plenty of buses to Hyderabad (Rs 233, 12 hours); one departs at 7.45 am and the rest leave in the evening. JJTC has frequent departures to Madurai (10 hours) and Coimbatore (11 hours), plus seven daily buses to Chennai (Rs 108, eight hours).

In addition to the various state buses, numerous private companies offer more comfortable and only slightly more expensive buses between Bangalore and the other major cities in central and southern India. You'll find private operators lining the street facing the Central bus stand. Most private buses depart in the evening.

Train There are two train stations in Bangalore. The main one, the City train station, is the place to make reservations. Cantonment train station is a useful spot to disembark if you're arriving in Bangalore and heading for the MG Rd area.

Rail reservations in Bangalore are computerised but there are no tourist quotas and bookings are heavy on most routes. However, it's usually possible for travellers to get into the emergency quota. First you have to buy a ticket (waitlisted), then fill out a form at the Divisional Office building immediately north of the City train station. You find out about six hours before departure whether you're on (a good chance) and if not, the ticket is refunded. The reservation and inquiry office is on the left as you're facing the station and is open Monday to Saturday 8 am to 8 pm, Sunday 8 am to 2 pm. Luggage can be left at the City train station.

Bangalore is connected by direct daily express trains with all the main cities in southern and central India. The only line disrupted by conversion from metre to broad gauge at the time of writing was the stretch between Hassan and Mangalore.

To get to Goa, catch the daily *Ranichannamma Express* at 8 pm and change trains at Londa. The journey takes 12 hours.

See the table for a selection of major trains from Bangalore.

KARNATAKA

Major Trains from Bangalore

destination	train no & name	departure time	distance (km)	duration	fare (Rs) (sleeper/1st)
Calcutta	5625 Guwahati Exp	11.30 pm Thur & Fri	2025	38 h	360/1435
Ernakulam	6526 Kanniya Kumari Exp	9.00 pm	638	13 h	187/650
Hospet	6592 Hampi Exp	9.55 pm	491	10 h	151/531
Hyderabad	7686 Secunderabad Exp	5.05 pm	790	16 h 30 min	214/766
Chennai	2608 Lalbagh Exp	6.30 am	361	5 h 20 min	120/415
	2640 Brindavan Exp	2.30 pm			
	2008 Shatabdi Exp[1]	4.20 pm		4 h 55 min	495/980
Mumbai	6530 Udyan Exp	8.30 pm	1211	24 h	369/1490
Mysore	6222 Kaveri Exp	7.15 am	139	2 h 30 min	41/207
	6206 Tipu Exp	2.25 pm			
	6216 Chamundi Exp	6.15 pm			
	2007 Shatabdi Exp[1]	10.55 am		2 h	250/490
Delhi	2627 Karnataka Exp	6.25 pm	2444	41 h 45 min	392/1648
	2429 Rajdhani Exp[2]	6.45 am Wed & Fri		33 h 43 min	1920/5565
Thiruvanan-thapuram	6526 Kanniya Kumari Exp	9.00 pm	851	18 h 15 min	224/767

[1] Air-con only; fare includes meals and drinks; Wednesday to Monday
[2] Air-con only

Getting Around

To/From the Airport The airport is 13km east of the City train station and about 9km east of the MG Rd area. There are prepaid taxis from the airport to the city (Rs 170); in the other direction you'll probably have to haggle for a price – count on around Rs 130 for a taxi or Rs 50 for an auto-rickshaw. Bus Nos 13 and 333 go from the City bus stand to the airport for around Rs 7.50.

Bus Bangalore has a comprehensive local bus network. Most local buses (light blue) run from the City bus stand next to the Central bus stand; a few operate from the City Market bus stand to the south.

To get from the City train station to the MG Rd area, catch any bus from platform 17 at the City bus stand. For the City mar-ket, take bus No 31, 31E, 35 or 49 from platform 8.

Car There are plenty of places around Bangalore to hire a car with driver or (if you're brave enough) self-drive. Europcar (☎ 221 9502), 85 Richmond Rd, has self-drive Maruti 800s for Rs 825 per day (up to 150km) or Rs 625 for eight hours with driver. Dial-a-Car (☎ 526 1737) is also good value and has an office in the Airlines Hotel complex. KSTDC rates are Rs 3.50 per kilometre for a minimum of 250km per day, plus Rs 100 allowance for the driver.

Auto-Rickshaw The city's auto-rickshaw drivers are required by law to use their meters (which are properly calibrated), and locals will *insist* on them being used. Do likewise! After dark you may have to bargain, or pay 50% above the metered rate.

Flagfall is Rs 7 and then Rs 3.60 for each extra kilometre. Expect to pay about Rs 20 from the train station to MG Rd – more if you have a lot of luggage.

AROUND BANGALORE
Whitefield Ashram

About 20km east of Bangalore is the summer ashram of Sri Sathya Sai Baba, where he is usually in residence in March and April and June and July. His main ashram, Puttaparthi, is in neighbouring Andhra Pradesh (see that chapter for details).

Transport to both ashrams can be arranged in Bangalore at S Babu & Co (☎ 226 1351) travel agency in the Cauvery Continental Hotel, 11 Cunningham Rd. Between March and May, half-day tours to Whitefield for either morning or evening *darshan* (audience with the guru) cost Rs 350. You can also get to Whitefield on bus No 333-E or 334 from platform 17 at the City bus stand, but make sure Sai Baba is in residence before you head out there.

Bannerghatta National Park

This modest national park, 21km south of Bangalore, is home to a small population of leopards. There's also a staged 'safari' where you can see lions, tigers and elephants in a fenced-in area, plus a crocodile and snake farm. It's open daily except Tuesday; catch bus No 365 from platform 15 at the City bus stand.

Nrityagram

This dance village, 30km north-west of Bangalore, was established in the early 1990s to revive Indian classical dance. Under the auspices of well-known Odissi dancer, Protima Gauri, it offers the long-term study of classical dance and its allied subjects, such as choreography, philosophy, music, mythology and painting. The village, designed by award-winning Goan architect, Gerard Da Cunha, welcomes visitors and accommodates guests. Contact Nrityagram's Bangalore office (☎ 846 6314).

Nandi Hill
☎ 08156

Nandi Hill (1615m), 68km north of Bangalore, is one of the most majestic places in the region and is well worth a visit. It was a popular summer retreat even in Tipu Sultan's days. **Tipu's Drop**, a 600m-high cliff face, not only provided a good view over the surrounding country, it was also a convenient place to dispose of enemies. There are two notable Chola temples here.

Entry is Rs 2 and it's open daily during daylight hours. Avoid Sunday when the day-tripping crowds are out in force.

Places to Stay & Eat *Nehru Nilaya Guest House* (☎ 78621) has clean double rooms for Rs 150 or a quaint cottage for Rs 200.

KSTDC's Hotel Mayura Pine Top (☎ 78624) has only two rooms so booking is essential – either directly with the hotel or at the KSTDC office in Bangalore. Singles/doubles cost Rs 190/220. Both these places have restaurants.

Getting There & Away There are KSRTC buses to Nandi Hill (Rs 18, two hours) from Bangalore's Central bus stand. Alternatively, you can visit on a KSTDC tour; see Organised Tours in the Bangalore section.

MYSORE
☎ 0821 • pop 735,000

This charming, easy-going city has long been a favourite with travellers – it's a manageable size, enjoys a good climate and has chosen to retain and promote its heritage rather than replace it. The city is famous for its silk and is also a thriving sandalwood and incense centre, though don't expect the air to be any more fragrant than that of the next town.

Until Independence, Mysore was the seat of the maharajas of Mysore, a princely state covering about a third of present-day Karnataka. The maharajas' walled palace is a major attraction.

History

Mysore has been named after the mythical Mahisuru, where the goddess Chamundi

KARNATAKA

MYSORE

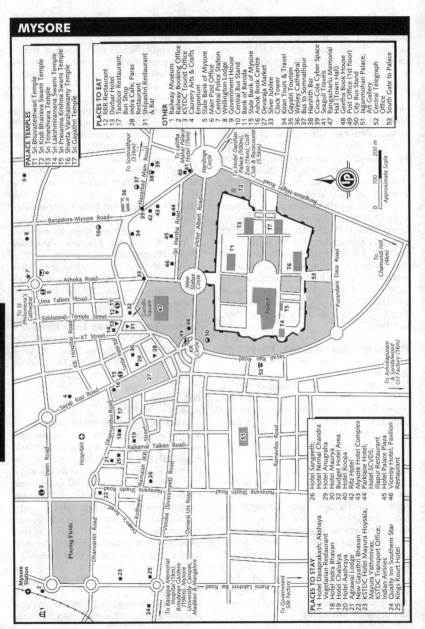

PALACE TEMPLES
T1 Sri Bhuvaneshwari Temple
T2 Sri Kodi Bhairava Swami Temple
T3 Sri Trineshvara Temple
T4 Sri Lakshmiramana Swami Temple
T5 Sri Prasanna Krishna Swami Temple
T6 Shweta Varahaswamy Temple
T7 Sri Gayathri Temple

PLACES TO EAT
12 RRR Restaurant
13 Durbar Hotel
17 Durbar Restaurant;
      Bun Shop
28 Indra Cafe; Paras
      Restaurant
31 Shipashri Restaurant
      & Bar

OTHER
1   Railway Museum
2   Railway Booking Office
3   KSTDC Tourist Office
4   Cauvery Arts & Crafts
      Emporium
5   State Bank of Mysore
6   Main Post Office
7   Central Police Station
8   Wellington Lodge
9   Government House
10 Central Bus Stand
15 State Bank of Mysore
16 Bank of Baroda
27 Devaraja Market
33 Ashok Book Centre
      Silver Jubilee
      Clock Tower
34 Kiran Tours & Travel
35 Gayatri Tourism
36 Wesley Cathedral
37 Bus to Somnathpur
38 Harshith Bar
39 Coca-Cola Cyber Space
41 Seagull Travels
47 Rangacharlu Memorial
      Hall (Town Hall)
48 Geetha Book House
49 Post Office (1st floor)
50 City Bus Stand
51 Jaganmohan Palace;
      Art Gallery
52 Central Telegraph
      Office
53 South Gate to Palace

PLACES TO STAY
14 Hotel Dasaprakash; Akshaya
      Vegetarian Restaurant
18 Hotel Indra Bhavan
19 Hotel Chalukya
20 Hotel Aashraya
21 Agrawal Lodge
22 New Gayathri Bhavan
23 KSTDC Hotel Mayura Hoysala;
      Mayura Yathrinivas;
      KSTC Transport Office;
      Indian Airlines
24 Quality Inn Southern Star
25 Kings Kourt Hotel
26 Hotel Sangeeth;
      Hotel Nirmal Chandra
29 Hotel Anugraha
30 Hotel Maurya
32 Budget Hotel Area
40 Hotel Roopa
42 Ritz Hotel
44 Mysore Hotel Complex
      Parklane Hotel;
      Suruchi VDS;
      Illapur Restaurant
45 Hotel Palace Plaza
46 Viceroy Hotel; Pavilion
      Restaurant

slew the demon Mahishasura. The Mysore dynasty was founded in 1399, but up until the middle of the 16th century its rulers, the Wodeyars, were in the service of the Vijayanagar emperor. With the fall of the empire in 1565 the Mysore rulers were among the first to declare their independence.

Apart from a brief period in the late 18th century when Hyder Ali and Tipu Sultan usurped the throne, the Wodeyars continued to rule until Independence in 1947. In 1956, when the new state was formed, the former maharaja was elected governor.

Orientation

The train station is on the north-western fringe of the city centre, about 1km from the main shopping street, Sayaji Rao Rd. The Central bus stand is on the Bangalore-Mysore road, on the north-eastern fringe of the city centre. Mysore Palace occupies the entire south-eastern sector of the city centre. Chamundi Hill is an ever visible landmark to the south.

Information

Tourist Office The KSTDC tourist office (☎ 442096, fax 441833) is in the Old Exhibition Building on Irwin Rd and is open Monday to Saturday 10 am to 5.30 pm. There are also counters at the train station (☎ 522976), the Central bus stand (☎ 54497) and a transport office (☎ 423652) next to the Hotel Mayura Hoysala.

Money The State Bank of Mysore, on the corner of Irwin and Ashoka Rds, has efficient foreign exchange facilities, as does its branch office on Sayaji Rao Rd. The Bank of Baroda on Gandhi Square gives cash advances on MasterCard and Visa credit cards.

Post & Communications The main post office is on the corner of Irwin and Ashoka Rds. It's open 10 am to 6 pm, though the poste restante facility is only open until 4 pm. There's a handy local post office on the 1st floor of a building fronting KR Circle.

The central telegraph office is on the western side of the palace and is open 24 hours.

There are a couple of cybercafes: Coca-Cola Cyber Space on Nazarbad Main Rd is central and open 9 am to 10 pm daily. Rates for Internet access are Rs 100 per hour (minimum 30 minutes).

Bookshops Geetha Book House, on KR Circle, is the best bookstore in Mysore. The Ashok Book Centre, on Dhanvanthri Rd, is also worth checking out.

Medical Services The Basappa Memorial Hospital (☎ 512401), on Hunsur Rd about 2km west of the city, is considered the best hospital in Mysore.

National Parks Accommodation and transport for Bandipur National Park (80km south of Mysore) should be booked with the Field Director (☎ 480901), Project Tiger, Ashokapuram, Mysore. Take an auto-rickshaw or a No 61 bus from the City bus stand.

Mysore Palace

The beautiful profile of this walled Indo-Saracenic palace, the seat of the maharajas of Mysore, graces the city's skyline. An earlier palace burnt down in 1897 and the present one, designed by English architect Henry Irwin, was completed in 1912 at a cost of Rs 4.2 million. The former maharaja is still in residence at the back of the palace.

Inside it's a kaleidoscope of stained glass, mirrors, gilt and gaudy colours. Some of it is undoubtedly over the top but there are also beautiful carved wooden doors and mosaic floors, as well as a whole series of mediocre, though historically interesting, paintings depicting life in Mysore during the Edwardian Raj. The palace even has a selection of Hindu temples within its grounds, including the Shweta Varahaswamy Temple whose *gopuram* (Dravidian gateway tower) influenced the style of the later Sri Chamundeswari Temple on Chamundi Hill.

The main rooms of the palace are open to the public daily 10.30 am to 5.30 pm, and the crowds can sometimes rival those in the departure lounge of a major international airport. The Rs 10 entry fee is paid at the southern gate of the palace grounds, though you need to retain the ticket to enter the palace building itself. Cameras must be deposited at the entrance gate (free); visitors can only take pictures of the outside of the buildings. Shoes are left at the shoe deposit counter near the palace entrance. There's a Mysore Palace guidebook available (Rs 10), but the kiosk selling it is where you exit the palace rooms – walk around behind the shoe deposit counter and ask the attendants if you can purchase one before going inside. There is also an Archaeological Survey of India storeroom in the palace grounds, full of books (available for sale) on various historical sites.

The **Residential Museum**, incorporating some of the palace's living quarters and an array of personal effects belonging to the maharaja's family, costs an extra Rs 15 and is rather dull after the magnificence of the palace itself.

On Sunday night and during the entire Dussehra Festival, there's a carnival atmosphere around the palace as 97,000 light bulbs spectacularly illuminate the building from 7 to 8 pm.

Chamundi Hill

Overlooking Mysore from the 1062m summit of Chamundi Hill, the **Sri Chamundeswari Temple** makes a pleasant half-day excursion. Pilgrims are supposed to climb the 1000-plus steps to the top; those not needing to improve their karma will find descending easier on the leg muscles. There's a road to the top; bus No 201 departs from the City bus stand in Mysore for the summit every 40 minutes (Rs 3). A taxi to the top from Mysore will cost around Rs 175.

Before exploring the temple, visit the free **Godly Museum** near the car park where you can ponder the price of various sins.

The Chamundeswari Temple is dominated by a towering seven storey, 40m-high gopuram. The statue in the car park is of the demon Mahishasura, who was one of the goddess Chamundi's victims. The goddess was the family deity of the maharajas and Mysore derived its name from Mahishasura.

One of the largest Nandi bull statues in India sits on Chamundi Hill.

The temple is open 6 am to 2 pm, 3.30 to 6.30 pm and 7.30 to 9 pm. If the queues look unmanageable, you can jump them by paying Rs 10 at the 'Demand Tickets Special Entrance'.

After visiting the temple start back to the car park and look for the top of the stairway, behind the Mahishasura statue, marked by a sign proclaiming 'Way to Big Bull'. It's a pleasant descent and the views over the city and surrounding countryside are superb.

Two-thirds of the way down you come to the famous 5m-high **Nandi** (Shiva's bull vehicle), carved out of solid rock in 1659. It's one of the largest in India and is visited by hordes of pilgrims offering *prasaad* to the priest in attendance there.

You'll probably have rubbery legs by the time you reach the bottom of the hill and it's still a couple of kilometres back into the centre of Mysore. Fortunately there are usually auto-rickshaws waiting to ferry pedestrians back to town for around Rs 35.

Devaraja Fruit & Vegetable Market

The Devaraja Market, stretching along the western side of Sayaji Rao Rd, south of Dhanvanthri Rd, is one of the most colourful in India and provides excellent subject material for photographers.

Jaganmohan Palace & Art Gallery

The Jayachamarajendra Art Gallery in the Jaganmohan Palace, just west of Mysore

Palace, has a collection of kitsch objects and memorabilia from the Wodeyars (former rulers of Mysore state), including weird and wonderful musical machines, rare instruments and paintings by Raja Ravi Varma. The palace was built in 1861 and served as a royal auditorium. It's open daily (Rs 5).

Mysore Zoo
Mysore has one of India's better kept zoos. It's set in parched but pretty gardens on the eastern edge of the city centre. Among the attractions are a couple of white tigers and several Bengal tigers, as well as the usual range of primates, elephants, bears, birds and rhinos. Come in the morning or evening if you want to see the tigers roaming in their enclosures rather than in the depressing cages. The zoo is open daily except Tuesday (Rs 10).

Rail Museum
Mysore's paltry rail museum boasts a maharani's saloon carriage, complete with royal toilet, dating from around 1899. It's east of the train station, just across the railway track, and is open daily, though closed for lunch 1 to 2 pm (Rs 2).

Folklore Museum
This small museum (☎ 51554) is in the Mysore University Campus, north-east of the city centre. Among the exhibits is a superb collection of carved wooden figures from Karnatakan villages, decorative masks and ceremonial head wear, and a display of leather shadow puppets (thogalu bomba) used to perform stories from the Ramayana and Mahabharata – similar to the wayang kulit of Java in Indonesia. There are also wooden puppets, including one of a 10-headed demon Ravana. The museum is open daily except Sunday (and every second Saturday) from 10 am to 1.30 pm and 2.30 to 5.30 pm (free). It's in the building behind the university canteen.

Other Attractions
Mysore has several fine buildings and monuments in a variety of architectural styles.

Dating from 1805, **Government House**, formerly the British Residency, is a 'Tuscan Doric' building set in 20 hectares of gardens. West of Government House is **Wellington Lodge**, where Arthur Wellesley (later the Duke of Wellington) lived after the defeat of Tipu Sultan.

In front of the north gate of Mysore Palace, a 1920 **statue** of Maharaja Chamarajendar Wodeyar stands in the New Statue Circle, facing the 1927 **Silver Jubilee Clock Tower**. If he glanced sideways he'd see the imposing town hall, the **Rangacharlu Memorial Hall** of 1884. The next traffic circle west is the 1950s **Krishnaraja Circle** (KR Circle), graced by a statue of Maharaja Krishnaraja Wodeyar.

Towering **St Philomena's Cathedral**, built 1933 to 1941 in neo-Gothic style, is one of the largest in India. Beneath the altar a subterranean chapel contains a relic of St Philsomena, a 3rd century martyr said to have performed several miracles after her death.

The Royal City by TP Issar (INTACH, Mysore, 1991), available from Mysore bookshops, is a comprehensive survey of the city's architecture.

Yoga
Mr K Pattabhi Jois runs the Ashtang Yoga School (☎ 25558). The shortest of the available courses is three months and costs US$400 per month.

Organised Tours
The KSTDC's Mysore city tour covers the city sights plus Chamundi Hill, the Keshava Temple at Somnathpur, Srirangapatnam and Brindavan gardens. The tour starts daily at 7.30 am, ends at 8.30 pm and costs Rs 100. It's quite good, though some of the sights are a bit rushed.

The KSTDC also runs a Belur, Halebid and Sravanabelagola tour every Tuesday, Wednesday, Friday and Sunday (daily in the high season), at 7.30 am, ending at 9 pm. (Rs 180). This is an excellent tour if your time is limited. There's also a tour to Ooty on Monday, Thursday and Saturday (daily in season) departing at 7 am (Rs 180).

KARNATAKA

Dussehra Festival

This 10-day festival in the first two weeks of October is a wonderful time to visit Mysore. The palace is illuminated every night and on the last day the former maharaja leads one of India's most colourful processions. Richly caparisoned elephants, liveried retainers, cavalry, and the gaudy and flower-bedecked images of deities make their way through the streets to the sound of jazz and brass bands and inevitable clouds of incense.

Places to Stay

Accommodation can be hard to find during the Dussehra Festival, so if you're arriving in October book ahead.

Places to Stay – Budget

Mysore has plenty of budget hotels. The main areas are around Gandhi Square and in the area between Dhanvanthri and Vinoba Rds.

Parklane Hotel (☎ 434340, fax 428424, 2720 Sri Harsha Rd) is the most popular budget hotel in the city. It's a travellers hang-out with decent rooms with bath for Rs 100/125 on the ground floor and Rs 125/149 on the 1st floor. There's a courtyard bar and restaurant downstairs. You'll need to make a reservation days in advance. There have been some complaints from women travellers: be cautious.

Hotel Maurya (☎ 26677, Hanumantha Rao St II) is well run and excellent value. Clean singles/doubles/triples with bath and bucket shower cost Rs 105/195/280 and open onto a bright, airy courtyard.

Hotel Dasaprakash (☎ 442444, Gandhi Square) is part of a south Indian hotel chain. It's a huge, airy place built around a central courtyard with basic but acceptable rooms with bath from Rs 125/250 to Rs 215/335. Checkout is 24 hours. There's an excellent vegetarian restaurant, an ice cream parlour, a travel agency and, for emergencies, an astro-palmist on call.

Hotel Anugraha (☎ 430768, Sayaji Rao Rd), in the centre of town near the junction with Sardar Patel Rd, is a standard Indian hotel facing a noisy street. Basic rooms with bath cost Rs 100/150. Checkout is 24 hours.

There's a string of hotels in the Dhanvanthri Rd area with not much to distinguish between them.

New Gayathri Bhavan (☎ 421224, Dhanvanthri Rd) is handy for the train station. It's a cheap, friendly, large place with a wide variety of rooms starting from Rs 60/125 with common bath and Rs 90/185 with bath.

Hotel Sangeeth (☎ 424693, 1966 Narayana Shastri Rd) is a very clean, no-frills place with doubles for Rs 175.

Hotel Nirmal Chandra (☎ 432238, 58 Kothwal Ramaiah St), nearby, is a very pleasant lodge with doubles/triples for Rs 175/225.

Hotel Chalukya (☎ 427374, Rajkamal Talkies Rd) has ordinary rooms with bath for Rs 90/175, and larger deluxe doubles for Rs 300.

Hotel Indra Bhavan (☎ 423933, Dhanvanthri Rd) is relatively clean but a bit worn. Singles/doubles with bath cost Rs 140/160, or better doubles are Rs 190. There's a 'meals' hall downstairs.

Places to Stay – Mid-Range

Ritz Hotel (☎ 422668, Bangalore-Nilgiri Rd), a few hundred metres from the Central bus stand, is the best choice in this range if you can get in. It has loads of colonial charm and huge rooms with four-poster beds. There are only four rooms: spacious doubles with mosquito nets and 24 hour hot water are Rs 300, and a four bed room costs Rs 400. Book in advance. There's a restaurant and bar downstairs and a comfortable guests' dining area upstairs.

The *KSTDC Hotel Mayura Hoysala (☎ 425349, 2 Jhansi Lakshmi Bai Rd)* is a good place on the opposite side of the city centre. It has a relaxing ambience with its own quiet gardens and offers decent rooms with enormous bathroom for Rs 250/300. There's a bar and restaurant here.

The *Hotel Palace Plaza (☎ 430034, fax 421070, Sri Harsha Rd)* is a recommended modern hotel offering a variety of rooms ranging from Rs 400/500 with TV and bath to Rs 700 with air-con, circular beds, fantasy curtains and mirrored ceilings!

The **Viceroy Hotel** (☎ 428001, fax 433391, Sri Harsha Rd), nearby, is a newer place catering to a business clientele, where you can be pampered without spending a fortune. Very nice rooms are Rs 525/575, or Rs 775/875 with air-con.

Hotel SCVDS (☎ 421379, fax 426297, Sri Harsha Rd), next to the Parklane Hotel, has modern doubles with mosquito nets, TV and bath from Rs 350, or Rs 650 with air-con. It's keen to attract foreign travellers, so offers discounts on these rates.

There are a couple of modern but uninspiring hotels, popular with Indian tourists, south of the Central bus stand.

Mysore Hotel Complex (☎ 426217, Bangalore-Nilgiri Rd) has characterless doubles with bath from Rs 275, or with air-con for a pricey Rs 800.

Hotel Roopa (☎ 443770, Bangalore-Nilgiri Rd) is better value but still nothing special. Average doubles cost from Rs 240, or Rs 500 with air-con.

Places to Stay – Top End

Kings Kourt Hotel (☎ 421142, fax 438384, Jhansi Lakshmi Bai Rd) is a large, modern establishment opposite the old Hotel Metropole. It charges from Rs 1390/1690 for air-con rooms, though at slack periods you may get a good discount.

Quality Inn Southern Star (☎ 438141, fax 421689, 13-14 Vinoba Rd) is a plush, modern hotel. It boasts a swimming pool, health club, poolside barbecue, restaurant and coffee shop. Centrally air-conditioned rooms cost Rs 2100/2900 including breakfast.

Lalitha Mahal Palace Hotel (☎ 571265, fax 571770), 7km from the city centre, is Mysore's most luxurious hotel and was once one of the maharaja's palaces. Standard rooms cost US$140/160, though there are some cramped 'turret' rooms for US$60/70, all plus 25% tax. The rooms in the older part of the building have the most character, but they can be gloomy and lack balconies. Facilities include a rather ordinary swimming pool, a tennis court, and a large bar with reputedly the best billiard table in India.

Places to Eat

Shilpashri Restaurant & Bar (Gandhi Square) is very popular with travellers, and for good reason. The food is very good, the prices are reasonable and the rooftop is a lovely place to dine in the evening. It serves western breakfasts and Indian, Chinese and continental mains from Rs 40 to Rs 60.

If it's full, the **Durbar Hotel** also has a roof bar but it's a relatively scruffy place.

Akshaya Vegetarian Restaurant in the Dasaprakash Hotel has excellent meals from Rs 20. There's also a good ice cream parlour in the courtyard.

RRR Restaurant (Gandhi Square) is a typical vegetarian place and travellers rave about their all-you-can-eat thalis.

Parklane Hotel (Sri Harsha Rd) has a convivial courtyard restaurant that's long been a travellers' favourite, and it's often full. It serves everything from tandoori chicken and chop suey to sandwiches and beer.

Paras Restaurant (Sayaji Rao Rd) is a popular local eatery serving south (Rs 22) and north Indian (Rs 45) thalis at lunch.

Tandoor Restaurant (Dhanvanthri Rd) is a hole-in-the-wall eatery serving Punjabi fare and cheap western breakfasts. The nearby **Bun Shop** sells tasty potato buns that make a fine light lunch for just Rs 3.

Pavilion Restaurant in the Viceroy is a smart air-con place with mains from Rs 55.

Lalitha Mahal Palace Hotel offers the city's most sumptuous dining experience, though some find the over-refined atmosphere and the baby-blue Wedgwood-style decor in the grand dining hall unsettling to the digestion. Dinner for two here costs around Rs 600, excluding drinks. The food is superb and there's live Indian classical music. The a la carte menu is replaced by a buffet outside the busy tourist season.

Entertainment

Relaxing places for a beer include the **Parklane Hotel**, **Shilpashri** (15 varieties), or the gentleman's club-style bar at the **Lalitha Mahal Palace Hotel** (expensive). **Harshith Bar** is a small but popular drinking hole on Nazarbad Main Rd.

KARNATAKA

There are plenty of cinemas showing Hindi and English-language films in the area between the Central bus stand and Gandhi Square.

Shopping

Mysore is famous for carved sandalwood, inlay work, silk saris and wooden toys. The best place to see the whole range is at the Cauvery Arts & Crafts Emporium on Sayaji Rao Rd, although it's not cheap. Open daily 10 am to 1.30 pm and 3 to 7.30 pm, it accepts credit cards, foreign currency or travellers cheques and will arrange packing and export. There are a number of other souvenir and handicraft shops in the precincts of the Jaganmohan Palace and along Dhanvanthri Rd. Silk shops can be found along Devaraj Urs Rd.

You can buy silk and see weavers at work at the Government Silk Factory on Jhansi Lakshmi Bai Rd. The factory is open to visitors from 10.30 am to noon and 2.30 to 4 pm and you need to get a permit from just inside the front gate. Mysore is one of India's major incense manufacturing centres, and scores of small, family-owned *agarbathi* (incense) factories around town export their products all over the world.

Usually handmade by women and children – a good worker can turn out at least 10,000 a day – they are made with thin slivers of bamboo, dyed red or green at one end, onto which is rolled a sandalwood putty base. The sticks are then dipped into small piles of powdered perfume and laid out to harden in the shade. You can also visit a sandalwood oil extracting plant in the suburb of Ashokapuram, about 2km southeast of Mysore Palace, and purchase oil and scented incense sticks here.

Getting There & Away

Air There are no flights to Mysore but Indian Airlines (☎ 421846) has an office next to the Hotel Mayura Hoysala, open Monday to Saturday 10 am to 1.30 pm and 2.15 to 5 pm.

Bus The Central bus stand handles all of the KSRTC long-distance buses. Reservations can be made six days in advance. The City bus stand, on KR Circle, is for city, Srirangapatnam and Chamundi Hill buses. Private long-distance bus agencies are clustered around the road junction near the Wesley Cathedral.

Nonstop KSRTC buses hurtle off to Bangalore (Rs 36/44 ordinary/semi-deluxe, three hours) every 15 minutes. If you're heading for Belur, Halebid or Sravanabelagola, the usual gateway is Hassan (Rs 31, three hours). Buses depart every 30 minutes. There's only one direct bus at 12.30 pm to Sravanabelagola (Rs 23, 2½ hours), but buses depart every 30 minutes to Channarayapatna, 10km from Sravanabelagola; you can pick up a local bus from there. There are two buses to Hospet (Rs 120, 12 hours), where you change for Hampi. Ten buses a day head to Ooty (Rs 45, five hours) via Bandipur National Park. There are plenty of buses to Mangalore (Rs 68, seven hours) and three buses to Ernakulam (Rs 171, 12 hours). One bus heads to Gokarna (Rs 200, 14 hours) at 6 am and one goes to Chennai (Rs 123, 10 hours) at 5 pm.

In addition to the KSRTC buses, there are a number of private bus companies that run to such places as Bangalore, Mumbai, Goa, Hyderabad, Chennai, Mangalore, Ooty and Pune. Fares on these buses are higher than the KSRTC buses but they are definitely more comfortable. To book tickets, try Gayatri Tourism, opposite the Ritz Hotel, and nearby Kiran Tours & Travel.

Train The booking office at the Mysore train station is computerised and rarely has long queues, but there's no tourist quota. The office is open Monday to Saturday 8 am to 2 pm and 2.15 to 8 pm, Sunday 8 am to 2 pm. There are four daily express trains to Bangalore (Rs 41 in 2nd class, three hours), plus the air-con high-speed *Shatabdi Express* (Rs 250, two hours), which departs at 2.10 pm daily except Tuesday. The *Shatabdi* continues on to Chennai (Rs 570, seven hours).

At the time of writing, conversion from metre to broad gauge was limiting other services. There were two passenger trains to Arsikere and Hassan, and one express to Mumbai via Arsikere on Friday only at 6 am.

Passenger services between Mysore and Bangalore stop in Srirangapatnam, an alternative to catching the bus.

From the City bus stand, bus Nos 150, 303 and 304 go to Brindavan gardens (Rs 4.25), departing every 30 minutes. Bus Nos 125 and 313 leave every 40 minutes for Srirangapatnam (Rs 4). A direct private bus to Somnathpur (1½ hours) runs along Nazarabad Main Rd at around 11.45 am (Rs 12), but there are plenty of similar buses on this stretch heading to T Narsipur or Bannur, where you can change to another bus for Somnathpur.

Getting Around
Bus From the City bus stand, bus No 201 travels to Chamundi Hill (Rs 3) every 40 minutes.

Car If you intend to explore the many sights around Mysore in a car, KSTDC recommended rates for car and driver hire are Rs 3.50 per kilometre for a minimum of 250km per day, plus Rs 100 for the driver.

Taxi & Auto-Rickshaw There are plenty of auto-rickshaws, and drivers are usually willing to use the meter. Flagfall is Rs 7 and then around Rs 3 per kilometre. Taxis are considerably more expensive and do not have meters so fares must be negotiated.

AROUND MYSORE
Somnathpur
☎ 08227

The **Keshava Temple** stands at the edge of the tranquil village of Somnathpur, 33km east of Mysore. Built in 1268 during the heyday of the Hoysala kings, it's an astonishingly beautiful, unspoilt building. It's also complete, unlike the larger Hoysala temples at Belur and Halebid. For more details on Hoysala architecture, see the boxed text under Belur & Halebid later in this chapter.

The walls of this star-shaped temple are covered with superb sculptures in stone depicting various scenes from the *Ramayana,*

Mahabharata and *Bhagavad Gita* and the life and times of the Hoysala kings. No two friezes are alike. The carved frieze, which goes around the temple, has six strips, starting with elephants at the bottom, followed by horses, a floral strip, scenes, crocodiles or lions and, finally, geese.

The temple is open daily 9 am to 5.30 pm (Rs 2). Somnathpur is just a few kilometres south of Bannur and 10km north of T Narsipur. It's easily visited as a day trip from Mysore – see the earlier Mysore Getting There & Away section for details on public transport.

Talakad & Sivasamudram
The remains of the capital of the 4th to 5th century Ganga dynasty, built on a bank of the Cauvery River at Talakad, are now largely buried by sand. A few buildings, including a 12th century Hoysala temple, still poke through the surface. Once every 12 years this surreal temple is dug out for the performance of Panchalinga Darshan, although it doesn't take long for it to be smothered once again by the sand. Talakad is 50km south-east of Mysore.

A further 25km downstream, the Cauvery suddenly drops more than 50m at the twin waterfalls at Sivasamudram, best seen immediately after the monsoon.

Srirangapatnam
On the Bangalore road 16km from Mysore stand the ruins of Hyder Ali's and Tipu Sultan's capital, from which they ruled much of southern India during the 18th century. In 1799, the British finally conquered them with the help of disgruntled local leaders. Tipu's defeat marked the real beginning of British territorial expansion in southern India.

Srirangapatnam was built on a long island in the Cauvery River. There isn't much left of it since the British did a good job of demolishing the place, but **ramparts** and battlements and some of the gates still stand.

The dungeon where Tipu held a number of British officers has been preserved. Inside the fortress walls there's a mosque and the **Sri Ranganathaswamy Temple.**

KARNATAKA

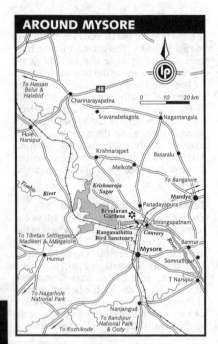

AROUND MYSORE

To Hassan
Belur &
Halebid

Channarayapatna

0   10   20 km

Sravanabelagola

Nagamangala

Hole
Narsipur

Krishnarajpet

Basaralu

Melkote

Krishnaraja
Sagar

To Bangalore

Timbis River

Mandya

Panadayapura

Brindavan
Gardens

Srirangapatnam

To Tibetan Settlements
Madikeri & Mangalore

Ranganathittu
Bird Sanctuary

Cauvery

Bannur

Mysore

Hunsur

Somnathpur

T Narsipur

To Nagarhole
National Park

Nanjangud

To Bandipur
National Park
& Ooty

To Kozhikode

One kilometre east of the fort, set in ornamental gardens, is Tipu's summer palace, known as the **Daria Daulat Bagh**. After Tipu's defeat, it was temporarily the home of Colonel Arthur Wellesley (later the Duke of Wellington). Its highly decorated interior now houses a **museum** with a motley collection of family memorabilia and paintings depicting Tipu's campaigns against the British. The museum is open daily except Friday (Rs 2).

Two kilometres further east is the impressive onion-domed **Gumbaz**, or mausoleum, of Tipu and his father, Hyder Ali.

Places to Stay The best place to stay is the *KSTDC Hotel Mayura River View* (☎ 08236-52114), peacefully located beside the Cauvery River, a few kilometres from the bus stand and train station. It has well-kept double cottages from Rs 450 (no singles) plus an indoor/outdoor restaurant-bar.

You can arrange a coracle (a saucer-shaped raft) ride with a local, but don't go for a dip unless you want to be crocodile bait.

Getting There & Away Scores of buses ply the Mysore to Bangalore road. It's also possible to get to Srirangapatnam on Mysore to Bangalore passenger trains. See the earlier Mysore Getting There & Away section for details.

Getting Around The points of interest are very spread out so the best plan is to hire a bicycle on the main street in the fort, about 500m from the bus stand. All the sites are signposted so it's not difficult to find your way around. There are also tongas and auto-rickshaws for hire.

Ranganathittu Bird Sanctuary

This sanctuary is on one of three islands in the Cauvery River, 3km upstream from Sriranga-patnam. It's a good place to see storks, ibis, egrets, darters, spoonbills and cormorants.

The sanctuary is open 8.30 am to 6 pm daily, but you should try to get there in the early morning or late afternoon to see the most birdlife. There's a foreigners' entry fee of Rs 100. It's open all year round but the best time to visit is June to November. Access is by a motorable road and boats are available for hire inside the sanctuary.

Brindavan Gardens

These tranquil ornamental gardens, laid out below the immense Krishnaraja Sagar dam, look like they belong in a tidy central European spa resort rather than the south of India. The gardens are a popular picnic spot and crowds come each night to see the illuminated fountains.

The gardens are illuminated Monday to Friday 6.30 to 7.25 pm (7 to 7.55 pm in summer) and on weekends until 8.25 pm (to 8.55 pm in summer). Entry is Rs 5, plus Rs 15 for a camera permit. If you arrive by car after 4.30 pm or without a hotel booking, you'll have to walk the pleasant 1.5km stretch from the main gate, across the top of the dam, to the gardens as the road is closed to cars then.

Places to Stay The *Hotel Mayura Cauvery* (☎ 08236-57252) is the only place to stay here. Clean, basic rooms with bath and partial views of the garden cost Rs 135/160. It has a restaurant with a limited menu.

Getting There & Away The gardens are 19km north-west of Mysore, and one of the KSTDC tours stops here briefly. See the earlier Mysore Getting There & Away section for details on public transport.

Tibetan Settlements

There are many Tibetan refugee settlements in the low, rolling hills west of Mysore, in the area between Hunsur and Madikeri. The Tibetans are extremely friendly and generally very hospitable towards the few travellers who visit.

Bylakuppe is one of the main areas of settlements, with nearly 20 villages, and the largest Tibetan population in India. The villages are spread out, so it's a good idea to have your own transport or to spend a couple of days and wander at your leisure. One of the villages, **Sera Je**, is the site of the Sera Je Monastic University, one of the three largest Tibetan Monasteries in exile. About 8km from the main road, the settlement has a guesthouse and an enormous, newly completed monastery. There are several handicrafts operations in the area, including carpet factories (where you can get Tibetan carpets made to your own design), an incense factory and various social organisations.

The *Siddhartha Guest House* (☎ 08276-74981) has clean doubles with bath for Rs 125, and there's a good restaurant downstairs. Few travellers make it here, but the atmosphere is very friendly and welcoming.

Mandya District

There are several beautiful Hoysala temples in the Mandya district, which stretches north and east of Mysore. The Cheluvarayaswami Temple at **Melkote**, approximately 50km north of Mysore via the town of Pandayapura, was built in the 12th century and later came under the patronage of the Mysore maharajas and even of Tipu Sultan. It's an important religious centre and there's a festival (Vairamudi) each year during March/April, when the temple image is adorned with jewels belonging to the former maharajas of Mysore.

North of Melkote is **Nagamangala**, which was an important town even in the days of the Hoysalas. Its principal attraction is the Saumyakeshava Temple, which was built in the 12th century and later added to by the Vijayanagar kings.

About 20km west of Melkote, near Krishnarajpet, is the village of **Hosaholalu**. Here you'll find the Lakshminarayana Temple, a superb example of 13th century Hoysala temple architecture that rivals in artistry the temples at Belur and Halebid.

The village of **Basaralu**, some 25km north of Mandya, is home to the exquisite 12th century Mallikarjuna Temple, executed in early Hoysala style. It's adorned with beautiful sculptures, including a 16-armed Shiva dancing on Andhakasura's head, and Ravana lifting Mt Kailash.

Getting to any of these towns involves the use of numerous local buses; you'll have to ask around to find the right ones as the timetables are all in Kannada. Mysore is your best base for all of them except Basaralu, for which Mandya might be better. There's a range of modest accommodation in Mandya.

BANDIPUR NATIONAL PARK

Eighty kilometres south of Mysore on the Mysore to Udhagamandalam (Ooty) road, this wildlife sanctuary covers 865 sq km and is part of a larger national park that also includes the neighbouring wildlife sanctuaries of Mudumalai in Tamil Nadu and Wynad in Kerala. This was once the Mysore maharajas' private game reserve.

The sanctuary is one of 15 selected in India for Project Tiger, a scheme launched in 1973 by the World Wide Fund for Nature (WWF) to save the tiger and its habitat. It's noted for herds of gaur (Indian bison), chital (spotted deer), elephants, sambar, sloth bears and langur. There are also supposed to be 75 tigers, but they are rarely seen.

Information

The best time to see wildlife is March to April, but the most comfortable time to visit is winter (November to February). If there is a drought, the park may not be worth visiting because the animals migrate to the adjoining Mudumalai park for water. Bandipur was completely closed for more than a year during 1997/98 due to smuggling and poaching activities, but it had just reopened at the time of writing.

The park entry fee is Rs 150 per day (for foreigners) plus Rs 10 for a camera or Rs 100 for a video camera. The only way to tour the park is in the Forest Department's bus, which leaves hourly every day 6 to 9 am, and 4 to 6 pm (Rs 15, one hour), or on elephant rides (Rs 20 per person, minimum four). Private vehicles are not allowed to tour the park. Try to avoid coming on weekends (especially Sunday), when hordes of tourists from Mysore and Ooty shatter the serenity.

Bus tours and Forest Department accommodation should be booked in advance. For reservations, contact either the Chief Wildlife Warden (☎ 080-334 1993), Aranya Bhavan, 18th Cross, Malleswaram in Bangalore or the Field Director (☎ 0821-480901), Project Tiger, Ashokapuram, Mysore.

Places to Stay & Eat

The Forest Department's huge deluxe *bungalows* have bathroom and hot water (if there's no water shortage) and cost Rs 75 to Rs 150, or dormitory beds are Rs 20. The caretaker can prepare meals if notified in advance. The bungalows must be booked at the Department's wildlife offices in Mysore or Bangalore.

The *KSTDC's Hotel Mayura Prakruti* (☎ 08229-7301) is on the Mysore road, 3km outside the park. Double rooms or pleasant cottages cost Rs 275/375 for singles/doubles. You can book direct or at the tourist offices in Mysore or Bangalore.

Bush Betta is a private resort about 4km from the Bandipur reception centre, off the road to Mudumalai. It has singles/doubles for US$85/155, including all meals, an elephant ride and a jeep safari. Bookings must be made in advance at the resort's Bangalore office (☎ 080-551 2631, fax 559 3451) at Gainnet, Raheja Plaza, Ground Floor, Richmond Rd. Resort guests are picked up at the Bandipur reception centre.

Tusker Trails resort is on the eastern edge of the park near Mangala village. It is run by a maharaja's daughter and consists of six twin-bed cottages and a swimming pool. Doubles are US$72 including food and wildlife trips into the forest. Bookings should be made in advance at Hospital Cottage, Bangalore Palace, Bangalore (☎ 080-334 2862).

Tiger Ranch is another 'ecotourist' resort with bamboo cottages at the reasonable rate of Rs 940. Book through Ranch Colorado Resorts (☎ 080-337 4558, fax 337 3508).

Getting There & Away

All buses between Mysore (2½ hours) and Ooty (three hours) will drop you at Bandipur, Gundulpet or Hotel Mayura Prakruti. For other resorts you'll have to arrange private transport.

NAGARHOLE NATIONAL PARK

This 643 sq km wildlife sanctuary (also known as Rajiv Gandhi National Park) is in an isolated pocket of the Kodagu (Coorg) region, 93km south-west of Mysore. Until a few years ago, it was one of the country's finest deciduous forests. Unfortunately, some of the forest was destroyed by fire in 1992 when tensions between officials involved in anti-poaching activities and local graziers and farmers erupted in a frenzy of arson. The destruction is no longer obvious and the forest has regenerated. There are currently 55 to 60 tigers as well as leopards and elephants, but you're more likely to see gaur, muntjac (barking deer), wild dogs, bonnet macaques and common langur.

The park has seen few visitors in recent years and facilities are still minimal. As with Bandipur, foreigners pay a Rs 150 per day fee to enter the park and the only way around for day visitors is on the bus tour (included in the fee). The best time to view wildlife is the hot months (April to May), but winter is a much more pleasant time (November to February).

Places to Stay & Eat

In Nagarhole, there are two Forest Department *dormitories* (Rs 20 per bed), and rustic but charming *bungalows* (Rs 75 to Rs 150 per double). Don't turn up without reserving in advance. All inquiries and bookings should be directed to the Deputy Conservator of the Forest & Wildlife Division (☎ 08222-52041) at Hunsur, and bookings should be made 15 days in advance.

Kabini River Lodge, near Karapur on the Mysore to Mananthavadi road, is a former maharaja's hunting lodge. It costs US$110 per person twin share, including full board and wildlife safaris. The lodge is on the southern fringe of the park, about 65km from the sanctuary's reception centre, and has access to far more of the park than the Forest Department accommodation. Bookings should be made with Jungle Lodges & Resorts Ltd (☎ 080-559 7025, fax 558 6163) in the Shrungar Shopping Centre, MG Rd, Bangalore.

Getting There & Away

Direct buses to Nagarhole leave from Mysore's Central bus stand at 7 am and 1.30 pm and take four hours to reach the park. Jungle Lodges & Resorts Ltd can arrange private transportation to Kabini River Lodge.

MADIKERI (Mercara)

☎ 08272 • pop 31,200

The elevated market town of Madikeri is the capital of the Kodagu (Coorg) region, a cool green mountainous area in the southwest of Karnataka, which is one of the most underrated scenic areas of India. Madikeri itself is not a particularly pretty town, but it has a pleasant climate, is a good base for organising treks and is surrounded by picturesque hills where the roads are lined with hedgerows, flowering trees, spice plantations and coffee estates.

If it seems a world apart from the rest of Karnataka, that's because Kodagu was a mini-state in its own right until 1956. Even today, there are still calls for an independent Kodagu homeland.

Orientation & Information

Madikeri is spread out along a series of ridges and, as with most hill towns, many of the streets are connected by steps. The bus stand and most of the hotels and restaurants are in a compact area in the centre.

There's a small tourist office (☎ 28580) in the poorly signed PWD Bungalow beside the first roundabout on the Mysore road. It is open 10 am to 5.30 pm daily except Sunday, but it's useless for information. See the Trekking in the Kodagu section for better sources of local trekking information. The Canara Bank on Gandhi Chowk changes cash and travellers cheques.

Things to See

Madikeri has a modest **fort**, containing the old palace of the Kodava kings, which is now the district's municipal headquarters. Also within the fort walls **St Mark's Church** is the unlikely site of a small museum with a collection of weaponry and Hindu and Jain sculptures. The austere **Omkareshwara Temple**, just below the fort and accessible via steps going down past the police station, is an interesting blend of Keralan and Islamic architectural styles. The view from **Raja's Seat**, the garden and lookout close to Madikeri's KSTDC hotel, is superb and will give you some idea of what to expect when trekking. The scenic **Abbi Falls** are about 8km from the town centre. You can hike there and visit **Raja's Tombs** on the way, or an auto-rickshaw will cost about Rs 130 for the return trip.

Trekking

The Kodagu region has superb trekking opportunities which travellers are only just beginning to take advantage of. Facilities are limited and there are no detailed maps, but there are several people in Madikeri who can arrange guides, food, transport and accommodation. Most treks last two to three days, but longer treks of up to 10 days are possible. Overnight accommodation is

KARNATAKA

usually in local houses or schools, though on one trek you can bunk down in an old palace.

The trekking season lasts from November to March. A guide is essential since you will easily get lost in the labyrinth of forest tracks without one. Trekking some obscure routes requires prior permission from the Forestry Department, which generally takes locals two days to procure. The most popular treks – to the 1700m high peaks of Tadiyendamol and Pushpagiri, and to smaller Kotebetta – do not require permission.

The man to contact in Madikeri is Mr Raja Shekhar, Project Coordinator of the YHA. He can be found at Friends Tours & Travels (☎ 29974) on College Rd, or (if he's away trekking) contact the owner of Sri Ganesh Automobile just up the road. He arranges one to three day treks with guides costing around Rs 150 per day per person (minimum two), plus accommodation and food (around Rs 100). Short treks take only a day or two to prepare. Alternatively, Mr Ganesh Aiyana at the Hotel Cauvery arranges all inclusive treks for around Rs 500 per day, but you need to make arrangements two weeks in advance. The Tadiyendamol trek can also be arranged through Apparanda Prakesh Poovana, Palace Estate, Kakkabe (☎ 08272-38346).

Another good place to arrange treks is the Coorg Tourist Travel Agency (☎ 25817) at the Vinayaka Lodge.

For more information see Lonely Planet's *South India*.

Places to Stay

Hotel Cauvery (☎ 25492, School Rd) is clean, friendly and good value. Singles/doubles with bath cost Rs 150/300, and there's hot water in the morning. It's central, near the main bus stand, and the owner arranges treks and visits to local homes.

Vinayaka Lodge (☎ 29830) is virtually right next to the main bus stand and is a reasonable budget option. Basic rooms with bath cost Rs 120/250.

Hotel Chitra (☎ 25191, School Rd), near the Cauvery, is a more upmarket place with large, clean rooms for Rs 250/350 (Rs 300/350 with TV) plus tax.

KSTDC'S Hotel Mayura Valley View (☎ 28387, MG Rd) is a 20 minute walk from the town centre near Raja's Seat. Rundown rooms with bath cost too much at Rs 300/400, dropping to Rs 275/330 in the low season (mid-June to mid-September). It has a restaurant and great views.

Capitol Village Resort (☎ 25929, Chettali-Siddapur Rd), 8km from Madikeri, is a charming lodge, beautifully located among paddy fields and coffee, cardamom, pepper and citrus plantations. Modern cottages with bath cost Rs 600 for a double and full board is available. You can get there by hourly buses from Madikeri, or by auto-rickshaw (Rs 35), but call ahead as it may be full (or you can book at the Hotel Cauvery).

Hotel Rajdarshan (☎ 29142, 116/2 MG Rd), on the way up to Raja's Seat, is a modern hotel and the best in town. Comfortable rooms cost Rs 475/575, suites are Rs 950.

Places to Eat

Hotel Veglands, near the fort, is the most popular veg restaurant in town. The restaurant at *Hotel East End* is a bit out of town but the food gets plenty of praise from locals.

Chitra Lodge and *Hotel Mayura Valley View* have standard hotel restaurants (and bars) – the terrace of the Mayura, overlooking the valley, is a great place for breakfast.

Redfern Bar & Restaurant is one of the few independent places in town. It serves Indian and Chinese food and cold beer in a pleasant setting, but prices are a little high.

Ganesh Coffee on School Rd is the place to buy local Coorg coffee. A 250g bag of pure coffee is Rs 30, chicory mix is Rs 25. You can sample a brew next door at the *Shri Krishna Bhavan Restaurant*.

Getting There & Away

The KSRTC bus stand is close to the centre of town and handles public buses to destinations outside Kodagu. There are frequent buses (roughly every 30 minutes) to Bangalore (Rs 83/99 semi/superdeluxe, six hours) and Mysore (Rs 38/46, three hours) from

6.30 am until 11 pm. Regular buses also go to Mangalore (Rs 44/53, four hours), Hassan (Rs 30, 3½ hours) and Shimoga (Rs 68).

The chaotic private bus stand is predominantly for local buses within the Kodagu region.

HASSAN
☎ 08172 • pop 121,000

Traditionally, Hassan has been the most convenient base from which to explore Belur (38km), Halebid (33km) and Sravanabelagola (48km), since it's the nearest railhead to all three sights. However, rail services to Mysore and Mangalore have been disrupted for several years due to line conversion work; see Getting There & Away at the end of the Hassan section.

There are ample bus connections to compensate for the rail disruption, so you'll still almost certainly pass through here, but apart from a few reasonable hotels, Hassan has nothing to offer.

Information
The tourist office (☎ 68862), on the Bangalore to Mangalore road, is open 10 am to 5.30 pm. For foreign exchange, go to the State Bank of Mysore.

Places to Stay
Vaishnavi Lodging (☎ 67413, Harsha Mahal Rd), a one minute walk from the bus stand, is good value at Rs 100/160 for clean singles/doubles with bath.

Hotel Lakshmi Prasanna (☎ 68391, Subhas Square), in the centre of town, has decent cheap rooms with bath and bucket hot water for Rs 85/130.

Hotel Palika (☎ 67349, Racecourse Rd) has undergone renovations and offers comfortable economy rooms with bath from Rs 148/198, and carpeted deluxe rooms with TV and balcony for Rs 200/300.

Hotel Hassan Ashok (☎ 68731, fax 68324, Bangalore-Mangalore Rd) is the best hotel in town and is popular with tour groups. Well-appointed rooms cost Rs 1200/1500, or Rs 1600/2300 with air-con and there's a good restaurant.

Places to Eat
Hotel Sanman and *Lakshmi Prasanna* have very popular vegetarian restaurants serving thalis for Rs 12.

Hotel Soumya has separate veg and nonveg sections, is reasonably priced and is popular with travellers.

Palika Paradise Restaurant, in the Hotel Palika, has a more upmarket atmosphere and serves decent veg/nonveg fare.

Getting There & Away
Bus If you intend visiting Belur and Halebid on the same day from Hassan, go to Halebid first as there are more buses from Belur to Hassan and they run until much later.

There are hourly buses from Hassan to Halebid (Rs 8, one hour). The first bus departs at 6 am, and the last bus back to Hassan leaves Halebid at 5.30 pm. There are also lots of buses from Hassan to Belur

HASSAN

1 Vaishnavi Lodging
2 Bus Stand
3 Hotel Soumya
4 Post Office
5 Hotel Palika; Palika Paradise Restaurant
6 State Bank of Mysore
7 Hotel Lakshmi Prasanna; Hotel Sanman
8 Hotel Hassan Ashok
9 Tourist Office

To Halebid (33km)
Harsha Mahal Road
Bus Stand Road
Racecourse Road
Municipal Office Road
Bangalore-Mangalore Road (NH48)
To Belur (38km)
Gandhi Road
To Train Station (2km) & Sravanabelagola (48km)
To Mysore (105km)

0   50   100 m

KARNATAKA

(Rs 10, 1½ hours). The first leaves Hassan at 5.45 am and there are buses from Belur to Hassan until late in the evening.

There are four direct buses to Sravanabelagola (Rs 14, 1½ hours), but the first one doesn't leave until 12.45 pm. To get an early start, catch a bus to Channarayapatna (Rs 11, one hour) and catch one of the many local buses to Sravanabelagola from there.

There are frequent buses to Mysore (Rs 31, three hours) and Bangalore (Rs 48, four hours). The first bus to both cities leaves at 5.15 am and the last at 7.45 pm.

Train The train station is about 2km east of town; Rs 10 by auto-rickshaw. The line to Mysore reopened in 1998 and at the time of writing there were two passenger trains from Hassan at 5.45 am and 6.30 pm. Express services won't resume, however, until the line is completed to Mangalore (possibly by 2000). There is also one train to Arsikere at 3 pm, continuing on to Bangalore.

Taxi Throngs of taxi drivers hang out on the road just north of the bus stand so it's easy to negotiate a good fare for a tour of Belur and Halebid. Expect to pay around Rs 500 for the day. A taxi to Sravanabelogola costs about Rs 300.

BELUR & HALEBID
☎ 08177
The Hoysala temples at Halebid (Halebeed, Halebidu) and Belur, along with the one at Somnathpur, east of Mysore, are the cream of one of the most artistically exuberant periods of Hindu cultural development. Their sculptural decoration rivals that of Khajuraho (Madhya Pradesh) and Konark (Orissa), or the best of European Gothic art.

Belur
The **Channekeshava Temple** at Belur is the only one at the three major Hoysala sites still in daily use – try to be there for the daily ceremonies at around 10 am and 7 pm. Begun in 1116 to commemorate the Hoysala's victory over the Cholas at Talakad, it was worked on for over a century.

Its exterior is not, in the lower friezes, as extensively sculptured as the other Hoysala temples, but the work higher up on the walls is unsurpassed in detail and artistry. Particularly interesting are angled bracket figures depicting female figures dancing or in ritual poses. Much decorative work can also be found on the internal supporting pillars and lintels. It is said that every major deity in the Hindu pantheon is represented on the Chennekeshava Temple at Belur.

The temple, enclosed in a paved compound, includes a well and bathing tank. The temple's 14th century seven storey gopuram has some sensual sculptures explicitly portraying the après-temple activities of dancing girls.

Open daily from sunrise to sunset (free). Non-Hindus are allowed inside but not into the inner sanctum. Guides can be hired for Rs 50 and are very helpful in explaining the significance of the detailed sculptural work.

The other, lesser, Hoysala temples at Belur are the **Chennigaraya** and the **Viranarayana**.

Halebid
Construction of the **Hoysaleswara Temple** at Halebid began around 1121. Despite more than 80 years of labour, it was never completed. Nevertheless, it is easily the most outstanding example of Hoysala art. Every inch of the outside walls and much of the interior is covered with an endless variety of Hindu deities, sages, stylised animals and birds, and friezes depicting the life of the Hoysala rulers.

The temple is set in a well-tended garden, and there's a small **museum** adjacent to it housing a collection of sculptures. The temple is open daily from sunrise to sunset (free). The museum is open daily except Friday 10 am to 5 pm.

Halebid also has a smaller temple known as **Kedareswara** and a little-visited enclosure containing three **Jain temples** (*bastis*), which also have fine carvings.

Places to Stay & Eat
Belur The *KSTDC'S Hotel Mayura Velapuri (☎ 22209, Temple Rd)* is the best place to stay in Belur. Large, comfortable sin-

Hoysala Architecture

The Hoysalas, who ruled this part of the Deccan between the 11th and 13th centuries, had their origins in the hill tribes of the Western Ghats and were, for a long time, feudatories of the Chalukyans. They did not become fully independent until about 1190 AD, though they first rose to prominence under their leader Tinayaditya (1047-78 AD), who took advantage of the waning power of the Gangas and Rashtrakutas. Under Bittiga (1110-52 AD), better known by his later name of Vishnuvardhana, they began to take off on a course of their own and it was during his reign that the distinctive temples at Belur and Halebid were built.

Typically, these temples are squat, star-shaped structures set on a platform to give them some height. They are more human in scale than the soaring temples found elsewhere in India, but what they lack in size they make up for in the sheer intricacy of their sculptures.

It's quickly apparent from a study of these sculptures that the arts of music and dance were highly regarded during the Hoysala period. As with Kathakali dancing in Kerala, the arts were used to express religious fervour, the joy of a victory in battle, or simply to give domestic pleasure. It's also obvious that these were times of a relatively high degree of sexual freedom and prominent female participation in public affairs.

The Hoysalas converted to Jainism in the 10th century, but then took up Hinduism in the 11th century. This is why images of Shaivite, Vaishnavite and Jain sects co-exist in Hoysala temples.

gles/doubles in the new wing cost Rs 168/200, though the upstairs rooms are the best (rooms in the old wing were being renovated at the time of writing). There's a fairly bland restaurant/bar serving veg/nonveg food and western breakfasts. The hotel is between the bus stand and the temple.

Swagath Tourist Home (☎ 22159, Temple Rd) is the cheapest place in town. Basic rooms with bath are good value at Rs 60. It's 50m before the temple.

Sri Vishnu Krupa (☎ 22263) is on the town's main road, a few minutes walk from the bus stand. It has reasonable but uninspiring doubles with bath for Rs 125 and Rs 250 (with TV) and grubby, dingy cheaper rooms with bath for Rs 50/75. It also has a veg restaurant.

Shri Raghavendra Tourist Home (☎ 22372), to the right of the temple entrance, near the massive temple chariot, has basic rooms with common bath and mattresses on the floor for Rs 75, or Rs 100 with bath. It's not good value.

Hotel Shankar, 200m before the temple, is the most popular of the town's handful of basic restaurants. There's also an *Indian Coffee House* near the temple entrance.

Halebid The only place to stay here is the peaceful *KSTDC'S Mayura Shantala (☎ 73224)*, set in a pleasant garden across the road from the Hoysaleswara Temple. There are four clean rooms with bath for Rs 150/200, or one cheaper room for Rs 100/150. There's a restaurant serving basic meals.

Getting There & Away

Belur and Halebid are only 16km apart. Crammed buses shuttle between the two towns every 30 minutes from around 6 am to 9 pm (Rs 5). See the previous Hassan section for details of buses to/from there. There are a few buses a day from Halebid to Mysore and many buses from Belur to Mysore. Belur is something of a transport hub, with direct buses to Bangalore, Mangalore, Dharmastala, Sravanabelagola (11.30 am) and Arsikere (for trains to Bangalore). If you're heading to Hampi, you'll need to catch a bus from Halebid to Shimoga (three hours) and pick up a bus to

KARNATAKA

Hospet (five hours), Hampi's access point, from there.

KSTDC offices in Bangalore and Mysore run tours that visit both Halebid and Belur. See the Organised Tours sections in those cities for details.

SRAVANABELAGOLA
☎ 08176 • pop 4000
This is one of the oldest and most important Jain pilgrimage centres in India, and the site of the huge 17m-high naked statue of Bahubali (Gomateshvara). Said to be the world's tallest monolithic statue, it overlooks the sedate country town of Sravanabelagola from the top of the rocky hill known as Indragiri. Its simplicity and serenity is in complete contrast to the complexity and energy of the sculptural work at the temples of Belur and Halebid. The word Sravanabelagola means the Monk of the White Pond.

History
Sravanabelagola has a long historical pedigree going back to the 3rd century BC when Chandragupta Maurya came here with his guru, Bhagwan Bhadrabahu Swami, after renouncing his kingdom. In the course of time Bhadrabahu's disciples spread his teachings all over the region, firmly establishing Jainism in the south. The religion found powerful patrons in the Gangas who ruled the southern part of what is now Karnataka between the 4th and 10th centuries, and it was during this time that Jainism reached the zenith of its influence.

Information
The helpful tourist office is as the foot of the stairway up Indragiri Hill and is open daily except Sunday 10 am to 5.30 pm. There's no entry fee to the site, but a donation is encouraged.

Gomateshvara Statue
The statue of Bahubali (Gomateshvara) was created during the reign of the Ganga king, Rachamalla. It was commissioned by a military commander in the service of Rachamalla and carved out of granite by the sculptor Aristenemi in 981 AD. Bahubali's father was the great Emperor Vrishabhadeva, who became the first Jain *tirthankar* (revered Jain teacher, literally ford crosser), Adinath. Bahubali and his brother Bharatha competed fiercely for the right to succeed their father but, on the point of victory, Bahubali realised the futility of the struggle and renounced his kingdom. He withdrew from the material world and entered the forest, where he began to meditate in complete stillness until he attained enlightenment.

The statue depicting Bahubali in this serene state stands atop Indragiri Hill and is reached by 614 rock-cut steps. You must leave your shoes at the foot of the hill, which is a problem in summer since the steps become scalding. Get there before the heat of the day, or wear socks.

Every 12 years, the statue of Bahubali is anointed with thousands of pots of coconut milk, yoghurt, ghee, bananas, jaggery, dates, almonds, poppy seeds, milk, saffron and sandalwood during the Mahamastakabhisheka ceremony. This will next occur in 2005.

Temples
In addition to the statue of Bahubali there are several interesting Jain (temples) and *mathas* (monasteries) in the town and on Chandragiri Hill, the smaller of the two hills between which Sravanabelagola nestles.

Two of these, the **Bhandari Basti** and the **Akkana Basti**, are in the Hoysala style, and a third, the **Chandragupta Basti**, is believed to have been built by Emperor Ashoka. The well-preserved paintings in one of the temples are like a 600-year-old comic strip of Jain stories.

Places to Stay & Eat
Nearly all of Sravanabelagola's accommodation is run by the local Jain organisation SDJMI, whose central accommodation office (☎ 57258) handles bookings for 21 guesthouses in town. Most are efficiently run and indistinguishable. They generally cost Rs 125, for a double, though the pick of the bunch, *Yatri Nivas*, costs Rs 150/200 for a double/triple. The accommodation office is behind

the Vidyananda Nilaya Dharamsala, just before the bus stand on the way into town.

The friendly *Hotel Raghu* (☎ *57238)*, 50m from the bottom of the stairway climbing Indragiri Hill, is the only privately owned establishment. Basic but decent singles/doubles/triples with bath and hot water in the mornings cost Rs 50/100/150. It also has a popular veg restaurant downstairs.

There are chai shops and basic vegetarian restaurants in the street leading to the foot of Indragiri Hill.

Getting There & Away
There are four buses a day to Hassan (Rs 13, one hour); three to Belur (Rs 26, 2½ hours); four to Bangalore (Rs 38, three hours); and one to Mysore (Rs 23, 2½ hours) at 7.30 am. Nearly all long-distance buses leave in the morning or at lunchtime; there's very little transport after 2 pm. If you miss one of the early buses, catch a local bus 10km northwest to Channarayapatna, which is on the main Bangalore-Mangalore road and has plenty of connections.

The KSTDC operates tours from Mysore and Bangalore to Sravanabelagola; see the Organised Tours sections in those cities for details.

Coast & Western Ghats

MANGALORE
☎ 0824 • pop 480,000
At one time Mangalore was the major seaport and shipbuilding centre of Hyder Ali's kingdom; today it's a centre for the export of coffee and cashew nuts. It has a languid tropical atmosphere and a strong Roman Catholic influence but no particular attractions. If you're passing this way, it can make a convenient overnight stop – otherwise you won't miss much by avoiding it.

Orientation
Mangalore is hilly and has winding, disorienting streets. Fortunately, all the hotels and restaurants, the city bus stand and the train station are in or around the hectic city centre. The KSRTC long-distance bus stand is 3km to the north; you'll need to take an auto-rickshaw (about Rs 12).

Information
The tourist office (☎ 442946) is in the Hotel Indraprastha, along with the KSTDC transport office (☎ 421692). It's open daily except Sunday 10.30 am to 5.30 pm.

Several banks have foreign exchange facilities; more efficient (for travellers cheques) is the Trade Wings travel agency on Lighthouse Hill Rd. The Bank of Baroda, nearby on Balmatta Rd, gives cash advances on Visa and MasterCard for the usual Rs 100 plus 1% commission.

The main post office is about 15 minutes walk downhill (south) of the city centre, just past Shetty Circle. For email and Internet access I-Net 107 Cyber Cafe on KS Rao Rd is a stylish setup charging Rs 65 per hour. It's open 10.30 am to 11 pm daily. Kohinoor Computer Zone on Lighthouse Hill Rd is cheaper at Rs 50 per hour, but it's hot and stuffy inside.

The Athree Book Centre on Balmatta Rd is full of books on a range of subjects.

Things to See
The main remnant of the past is the **Sultan's Battery**, 4km from the centre on the headland of the old port, but it hardly rates a special visit. A No 16 bus from the city centre will get you there.

The **Shreemanthi Bai Memorial Government Museum** is about 1km east of the KSRTC bus stand (take bus No 19). It's open daily except Monday 9 am to 5 pm. The Keralan-style **Kadri Temple**, whose Lokeshwara statue is reputed to be one of the best bronzes in India (bus Nos 3, 4 and 6), and the painted ceiling of **St Aloysius College Chapel** (open 8.30 to 10 am, 12.30 to 1 pm and 3.30 to 6 pm) are also worth a look. If you've still got time and energy to spare, try the **Rosario Cathedral**, **Sri Gokarnanatha Temple** or the **Mangladevi Temple**, which gave the town its name.

KARNATAKA

KARNATAKA

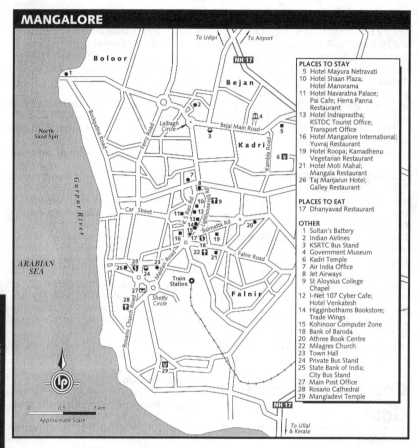

MANGALORE

PLACES TO STAY
5 Hotel Mayura Netravati
10 Hotel Shaan Plaza;
   Hotel Manorama
11 Hotel Navaratna Palace;
   Pai Cafe; Herra Panna
   Restaurant
13 Hotel Indraprastha;
   KSTDC Tourist Office;
   Transport Office
16 Hotel Mangalore International;
   Yuvraj Restaurant
19 Hotel Roopa; Kamadhenu
   Vegetarian Restaurant
21 Hotel Moti Mahal;
   Mangala Restaurant
26 Taj Manjarun Hotel;
   Galley Restaurant

PLACES TO EAT
17 Dhanyavad Restaurant

OTHER
1 Sultan's Battery
2 Indian Airlines
3 KSRTC Bus Stand
4 Government Museum
6 Kadri Temple
7 Air India Office
8 Jet Airways
9 St Aloysius College
   Chapel
12 I-Net 107 Cyber Cafe;
   Hotel Venkatesh
14 Higginbothams Bookstore;
   Trade Wings
15 Kohinoor Computer Zone
18 Bank of Baroda
20 Athree Book Centre
22 Milagres Church
23 Town Hall
24 Private Bus Stand
25 State Bank of India;
   City Bus Stand
27 Main Post Office
28 Rosario Cathedral
29 Mangladevi Temple

Places to Stay – Budget

Hotel Manorama (☎ 440306, KS Rao Rd) has large and clean single/double rooms with bathroom costing from Rs 145/231. Air-conditioned double rooms go for Rs 450.

Hotel Venkatesh (☎ 440793, KS Rao Rd) is not as good but rooms are reasonable at Rs 90/140.

Hotel Indraprastha (☎ 425750, Lighthouse Hill Rd) charges Rs 145/195 for big, old rooms with attached bathroom, and there are smaller singles for Rs 110. This place was being renovated at the time of writing.

Hotel Roopa (☎ 421271, Balmatta Rd) has OK rooms with bath for Rs 125/184 and air-con doubles for Rs 450. There are a couple of good restaurants here.

Hotel Mayura Netravati (☎ 211192, Kambla Rd), north of the centre in the Kadri Hills, sees relatively few guests but is worth a look. Dorm beds are Rs 45, and singles/doubles with bath are good value at Rs 105/135.

Places to Stay – Mid-Range & Top End

Hotel Shaan Plaza (☎ 440312, KS Rao Rd) has comfortable rooms for Rs 270/330, or air-con doubles for Rs 530.

The Hotel Mangalore International (☎ 444857, KS Rao Rd) is a new business class hotel with well-appointed rooms from Rs 450/550, or Rs 650/750 with air-con, including breakfast. There are a couple of restaurants and fast-food places in this complex but alcohol is not permitted. Checkout is 24 hours.

Hotel Moti Mahal (☎ 441411, fax 441011, Falnir Rd) is another good mid-range place with a bar, restaurant, coffee shop and swimming pool. Rooms cost Rs 550, or Rs 700 with air-con.

Taj Manjarun Hotel (☎ 420420, fax 420585, Old Port Rd) is the top hotel in town. Air-con rooms cost from US$30/40, up to US$95 for the suite. It has a good restaurant and a swimming pool.

Places to Eat

Despite its fishing port and the popularity of Mangalorean-style seafood in places such as Mumbai, you'll be hard-pressed to find a decent piece of seafood in the city. There are several fast-food places and ice cream parlours along KS Rao Rd.

Heera Panna (KS Rao Rd), in the basement of the Hotel Navaratna Palace, is a very popular veg restaurant with locals.

Janatha Deluxe at the Hotel Shaan Plaza is another excellent and cheap vegetarian restaurant.

Dhanyavad (cnr KS Rao and Lighthouse Hill Rds) is a popular veg restaurant serving snacks during the day and cheap 'meals' in the evening.

Yuvraj Restaurant, on the 1st floor of the Poonja International, serves good Indian and continental food in air-con comfort.

Galley Restaurant at the Taj Manjarun Hotel is one of the few places you can find Mangalore specialities such as lady fish. *Le Bistro*, at the same hotel, is a good place for a breakfast or lunchtime splurge.

Getting There & Away

Air Indian Airlines (☎ 455259) is about 3.5km out of town on Hathill Rd. The office is open Monday to Saturday from 9.25 am to 1 pm and 1.45 to 4 pm. The Jet Airways office (☎ 441181) is in the Ram Bhavan

Buffalo Surfing

Kambla, the Canaran sport of buffalo racing, first became popular in the early part of the 20th century, when farmers would race their buffalo home after a day in the fields. The event took off in the 1950s and 1960s, and today the best of the races are big business. At top events up to 50,000 spectators may attend, and one organiser in 1998 went to the trouble of procuring spotlighting and a photo finish. The racing buffaloes are extremely valuable, too, and are pampered and prepared like thoroughbreds for every race. A good animal can cost over Rs 300,000.

The events are held annually in the Dakshina Kannada region, between about October and March every year, when the paddy fields have enough water in them for racing. Although the racing 'season' is still observed, the exact timings are becoming less important as nowadays specially prepared tracks are often laid out. The 120m-long tracks are laid parallel to each other and the fastest pairs of buffalo can cover the distance through water and mud in around 14 seconds. There are two versions: in one the man runs alongside the buffalo, and in the other he rides on a board fixed to a ploughshare, literally surfing his way down the track behind the beasts. It's a truly awesome sight. For those who don't believe that these slow lumbering beasts can really move, look out!

KARNATAKA

Complex near KS Rao Rd. Air India (☎ 493875) has an office next to the Pancha Mahal Hotel in Kodialbail.

Indian Airlines flies daily to Mumbai (US$115) and three times a week to Chennai (US$95) via Bangalore (US$70). Jet Airways has two daily flights to Mumbai (US$115) and one to Bangalore (US$70).

Bus The KSRTC long-distance bus stand is about 3km north of the city centre. It's fairly orderly with daily deluxe departures to Bangalore (Rs 113/135, ordinary/deluxe, nine hours), Panaji (Rs 122, 10 hours), Hassan (Rs 45/54, four hours), Madikeri (Rs 36/44, four hours), Mysore (Rs 68/83, seven hours) and Kochi (Rs 190, 10 hours). There are also long-distance departures to Mumbai, Chennai and Hospet.

Private buses running to other destinations (including Udipi, Sringeri and Mudabridi) operate from the temporary bus stand opposite the city bus stand.

Several private bus companies, serving all the main destinations, have offices on Falnir Rd.

Train The Mangalore train station is on the southern fringe of the city centre. However, for the new Konkan Railway, most trains stop only at Kankanadi station, 5km east of the city. The *Mangalore-Kurla Express* is currently the only northbound train originating in Mangalore. It departs at 9 pm, arriving in Margao (Goa) at 1.45 am and Kurla (Mumbai) at 12.50 pm. For Goa, there are four expresses from Kankanadi to Margao. There are also numerous slow passenger trains on this route. Heading south, the *Malabar Express* departs Mangalore at 5 pm, arriving in Thiruvananthapuram at 9.25 am the next day.

At the time of writing, all rail services heading east (ie to Hassan, Mysore and Bangalore) had been suspended while the Mangalore-Hassan line is converted to broad gauge.

There are, however, two expresses from Mangalore to Chennai at 12.15 and 7.25 pm (Rs 245/862 sleeper/1st class, 18 hours), which loop south to avoid conversion work.

Getting Around

To/From the Airport The airport is 20km from the city centre. Bus Nos 47b and 47c from the city bus stand will get you there. The airport bus from the Indian Airlines office departs at 7 am on Tuesday, Thursday and Saturday and 9 am other days (Rs 20). A taxi costs around Rs 200.

Bus & Auto-Rickshaw The city bus stand is opposite the State Bank of India, close to the Taj Manjarun Hotel. There are plenty of auto-rickshaws and drivers should use their meters. Flagfall is Rs 7 and then Rs 4.20 per kilometre – trips around the city centre should cost no more than Rs 8. An auto-rickshaw to Kankanadi train station costs around Rs 40.

AROUND MANGALORE
Dharmastala

There are a number of Jain bastis in Dharmastala, 75km east of Mangalore, including the famous **Manjunatha Temple**. There's also a 14m-high statue of Bahubali, which was erected in 1973, and a **museum** (Rs 1). There are regular buses to Dharmastala from the KSRTC bus stand in Mangalore.

Venur

This town, approximately 50km north-east of Mangalore, has eight bastis and the ruins of a Mahadeva temple. An 11m-high **Bahubali statue**, dating back to 1604, stands on the southern bank of the Gurupur River.

Mudabidri

There are 18 bastis in Mudabidri, 35km north-east of Mangalore. The oldest of them is the 15th century **Chandranatha Temple**, known colloquially as the 1000-pillar hall.

Karkal

A farther 20km north of Mudabidri, at Karkal, are several important temples and a 13m-high **Bahubali statue**, which was completed in 1432. The statue is on a small, serene hillock on the outskirts of the town. There are good views of the Western Ghats from here.

SRINGERI
☎ 08265

The southern seat of the orthodox Hindu hierarchy is in Sringeri, a small, unspoilt town nestled among the lush coffee-growing hills of Chikmagalur, about 100km north-east of Mangalore. The interesting **Vidyashankar Temple** has zodiac pillars and a huge paved courtyard. A second temple is dedicated to Sharada, the goddess of learning. The Tunga River flows past the temple complex and hundreds of fish gather at the ghats to be hand-fed by pilgrims. The temple complex is open 6.15 am to 2 pm and from 5 to 9.30 pm.

Places to Stay

There's a range of pilgrim accommodation; report to the reception centre (☎ 50123) next to the temple entrance to be allocated a room. In the new accommodation block, good double rooms with bath cost Rs 75, or cheaper rooms are Rs 60 and Rs 25.

Getting There & Away

The bus stand is 200m to the right of the temple entrance. There are plenty of buses from Sringeri to virtually all points in Karnataka – private buses run to the destinations that the state buses don't cover. There are regular buses to Mangalore (five hours) and several services to Mysore (eight hours) via Hassan (4½ hours), and Bangalore (10 hours).

UDIPI
☎ 08252

The important Vaishnavaite town of Udipi (Udupi) is 58km north of Mangalore on the coastal road. It was here that the 13th century religious leader, Madhvacharya, lived and preached, and the town's Krishna Temple continues to draw many pilgrims. Udipi has another claim to fame since, according to local legend, the ubiquitous *masala dosa* was first created here.

The Canara Bank on Kanakadasa Rd will change cash and travellers cheques.

Things to See

The **Krishna Temple**, in the centre of town, is not too impressive to look at, but it's worth being around for the commotion when one of the daily ceremonies begins. There are 14 daily acts of worship by the swami in charge of the temple – pilgrims are herded out of the way, the temple elephants trumpet and a row of chanting monks pass through in procession to carry out the next ritual.

About 2km off the coast from Malpe (5km from Udipi) is **St Mary's Island**, supposed to have been the site of the first landfall that Vasco da Gama made when he arrived in India. The island is notable for the strange rock forms (columnar lava) in the shape of hexagonal pillars on the rocky outcrops around the shore. Boats go to the island from Malpe Harbour for Rs 30 per person if full (which may take a while), or it's Rs 900 to charter the boat. There's an average **beach** just west of Malpe Harbour.

Places to Stay

Hotel Vyavahar Lodge (☎ 22568, Kanakadas Rd), near the Krishna Temple, is excellent value. Large clean rooms with bath cost Rs 75/149.

Hotel Shaan (☎ 23901, Maque Rd), near the private bus stand, is another good budget place with rooms for Rs 140/180.

Hotel Sindhu Palace (☎ 20791, Court Rd) has small, basic but clean rooms with bath for Rs 100/140 and deluxe rooms for Rs 220.

Hotel Janardhan (☎ 23880), near the KSRTC bus stand, is a big place with a better standard of rooms for Rs 180/205.

Kediyoor Hotel (☎ 22381), also near the bus stand, is an upmarket place with excellent service. Large double rooms with TV and bath go for Rs 260/300, and air-con rooms start at Rs 600.

Places to Eat

Woodlands Restaurant, in the backstreets to the south-west of Car St, is a popular place with a good range of vegetarian food. The vegetarian restaurant in the *Kediyoor* is also good value, with excellent thalis and dosas from Rs 10 to Rs 20.

Classic Dining Bar, near Hotel Janardhan, is a modern place serving the usual range of Indian and Chinese dishes, plus a few local specialities that are worth trying, such as Crab Sukka (Rs 50). Next door is the modern **Wild Rain** pub, a dimly lit up-market bar with comfortable couches.

Getting There & Away

There are three bus stands in Udipi, all close together, but most travellers will only use two of them. The KSRTC bus stand is in the middle, just up from the Kediyoor Hotel. Services from here include Gokarna, Panaji, Mangalore and Bangalore. Private express buses to Mangalore also leave from here every 10 minutes (Rs 16). Buses to Malpe (Rs 2.75) and Manipal (Rs 2.25) leave from the City bus stand, 100m from the main (KSRTC) stand. There are numerous private operators running buses to destinations including Bangalore, Goa, Hospet, and Kochi.

The most convenient way to get to Gokarna, Goa or Mumbai is by rail on the Konkan Railway. At the time of writing there were four expresses running north to Margao at 12.40, 4.15 and 6.25 am and 10.05 pm, and a passenger service departing at 8.30 am. Heading south, the expresses depart at 12.52, 7.30 and 5.53 am and 12.07 pm. Udipi's train station is about 5km from the town centre.

JOG FALLS
☎ 08186

Jog Falls may be the highest in India, but they're not the most spectacular: the Linganamakki Dam further up the Sharavati River significantly limits the water flow. The falls are more voluminous during the monsoons, but the most comfortable time to visit is winter (December to February), when they may be obscured some of the time by mist. There are actually four falls; the longest drop of 253m is known as The Raja.

The setting here is superb and the countryside is perfect for gentle hiking. You can hike to the bottom of the falls by following the steps that start close to the bus stand; watch out for leeches during the wet season.

Places to Stay & Eat

There are two **forest resthouses** with rooms at Rs 75 per person. One is on the left, about

1km down the road to the coast from the falls; the other is 300m further down on the right and unsigned behind a blue and green fence.

It's worth trying for a room at the **PWD Bungalow**, perched precariously on the northern part of the falls, about 3km from the car park.

The **KSTDC'S Hotel Mayura Gerusoppa** (☎ 4732) is wonderfully situated overlooking the falls, about 150m from the car park. It offers spacious and quiet rooms for Rs 150/200 and has a dining room that is great for western breakfasts.

Tunga Tourist Home (☎ 4732), at the car park, is pretty ordinary although renovations may have improved things. Double rooms cost Rs 150, Rs 220 and Rs 330.

A **Youth Hostel** is a few hundred metres up from the car park, but several travellers have complained about unfriendly staff. Dorm beds cost Rs 100 per person, so it's not good value.

One side of the car park at the falls is lined with about a dozen **chai stalls**. Most serve cheap and tasty omelettes, thalis, fried noodles and fried rice, as well as hot and cold drinks.

Getting There & Away

Bus Jog Falls is surprisingly well connected by bus. The roads to/from the coast are fairly tortuous – the road from Manki is more spectacular, but also more likely to make you sick than the road from Bhatkal. For these trips, it's worth chartering a vehicle, so you can stop to admire the views and waterfalls along the way.

There are buses about every 45 minutes to Shimoga (2½ hours), three a day to Siddapur, two to Karwar and one to Gokarna (via Kumta) and Bhatkal.

Train The nearest train station is at Talguppa, between Sagar and Jog Falls. There are two trains a day to Shimoga.

GOKARNA
☎ 08386

The unspoilt town of Gokarna (Cow's Ear), 50km south of Karwar, attracts an unlikely mixture of Hindu pilgrims, Sanskrit scholars, beach-loving travellers and a hardcore hippy element who shifted here when things got way uncool in Goa. For Hindus, Gokarna is one of the most sacred sites in South India. It's a sleepy, charming town with a single ramshackle street composed entirely of Keralan-style wooden houses.

Information
You can change cash and travellers cheques at poor rates at the Om Lodge. The Pai STD shop on Main St gives slightly better rates but for a bank you'll need to go to Karwar. There's a small sub post office at the junction of Car and Main Sts, and you can make international calls from several STD/ISD places.

Temples
At the western end of Car St is the sacred **Mahabaleshwara Temple**, home to a revered Shiva lingam. Nearby is the **Ganapati Temple**, which honours the role that Ganesh played in rescuing the lingam. Near the temple are two enormous chariots, which are dragged along the main street amid much brouhaha on Shiva's birthday in February/March.

At the eastern end of the streets is the **Venkataraman Temple** and 100m south of this is **Koorti Teertha**, the large temple tank, where locals, pilgrims, and immaculately dressed Brahmins perform their ablutions next to *dhobi-wallahs* on the ghats.

Beaches
Travellers have been drifting into Gokarna for some time now, lured by stories of its deserted beaches that rival anything Goa has to offer. Although Gokarna village has its own beach, the closest decent stretch of sand is **Kudle Beach** (pronounced 'kood-lee'), a 20 minute walk to the south. To reach it, follow the footpath that begins on the southern side of the Ganapati Temple and heads southwards (if you reach the bathing tank, you've taken the wrong path).

The track soon climbs to the top of a barren headland with expansive sea views. On the southern side of the headland is the first in a series of four perfect half-moon beaches, hemmed in by headlands and backed by the foothills of the Western Ghats. There are four or five chai shops on Kudle Beach, all offering basic snacks, drinks and accommodation.

At the southern end of Kudle a track climbs over the next headland and a further 20 minute walk brings you to **Om Beach** – so named because of its distinctive shape. A dusty road now provides limited vehicle access to this beach but it's still almost deserted. Again, there's a handful of chai shops and beach shacks here. The other beaches – **Half-Moon Beach** and **Paradise Beach** – are a series of 30 minute walks to the south, each one more isolated. There's a couple of palm-thatch shelters for rent on Paradise Beach, but nothing permanent on Half Moon.

Places to Stay
The choice in Gokarna is between the rudimentary huts right on the beach or the basic but more comfortable options in town. The advantages of being on the beach are obvious and, since it's a decent hike from town, you're pretty much left to your own devices – highly appreciated by those travellers who like the odd *chillum* for breakfast.

Beaches The *huts* on the beach, mainly at Kudle and Om, cost from Rs 25 for flimsy palm-thatch shacks to Rs 50 for lockable mud huts in high season (December and January). They're mostly just a space to stash your gear and sleep on the floor at night, so bring a sleeping bag or a bedroll. Padlocks are provided and the huts are secure. Communal washing and toilet facilities are primitive but there is fresh water. The easiest way to find a place is to ask around at the chai shops along the beach.

The only exception to this basic beach accommodation is *Shiva Prasad*, at the south end of Kudle Beach. It has 10 rooms in a brick building set well back among the coconut groves. They're very basic for Rs 80 per person, but you get toilet and shower facilities and electricity.

KARNATAKA

If you want to sleep on the beach, it's best to leave your belongings at Vaibhav Niwas in town (see following) for a small fee. It's not a good idea to sleep alone on any of the beaches.

Gokarna There are a handful of good guesthouses in town.

Nimmu House (☎ 56730) is a very relaxed and recommended family-run place just back from the town beach (it's in the side streets near the Mahabaleshwara Temple). Simple doubles with common bath cost Rs 70 to Rs 100, and the upstairs doubles with bath are Rs 120; there are discounts in the low season.

Vaibhav Niwas (☎ 46714) is a cosy, relaxed guesthouse set back from the main road on the way into town. Small but acceptable singles/doubles with common bath cost Rs 30/50 and rooms with bath cost Rs 75 to Rs 100.

New Prasad Nilaya (☎ 56675) is a friendly modern hotel, in contrast with the others in Gokarna. It has plain, but clean and comfortable, rooms with bath for Rs 150. The hotel is on a small side road off the main street near the bus stand.

Om Lodge (☎ 56445), nearby on the same lane, has dreary, shabby rooms with bath for Rs 150, four-bed rooms for Rs 250 and air-con doubles for Rs 300.

Shastri Guest House (☎ 56220, Main St) is a slightly dingy but reasonable budget option near the bus stand. Small rooms with common bath are Rs 50 and doubles with bath are Rs 120.

Kinara Hotel, on the road leading to the town beach, has clean rooms with bath for Rs 150/200 and a small single with common bath for Rs 70. It's not the best value but it's well located and some rooms have balconies.

The *KSTDC'S Hotel Mayura Samudra (☎ 56236)* is a neglected hotel on a hilltop overlooking the sea, and is inconveniently located some 2km from town. Its three large rooms are cheap enough at Rs 75 for a double or Rs 125 for four people, all with bath.

Places to Eat

The *chai shops* on all of the beaches can rustle up basic snacks and meals.

Namaste Garden Cafe, at the northern end of Kudle Beach, is a popular and pleasant place for a meal or cold drink. There's another one at the start of Om Beach.

Vaibhav Niwas has an extensive menu of the usual travellers' fare and is a great place for breakfast, with porridge, toast and pancakes on offer, as well as things like pasta for dinner.

Pai Restaurant, halfway along Main St, has cheap vegetarian light meals and good masala dosas.

There are several cafes on the road leading to the town beach. *Vishwa Cafe* is popular with travellers in the evening, while *Sea Green Cafe,* a little further from the road, is quieter but also pleasant.

Kinara Hotel has a busy veg restaurant and an ice cream parlour.

Om Lodge is one of the few places to legally serve alcohol. It has a seedy bar and restaurant downstairs, but the 2nd floor terrace is a reasonable place to enjoy a cold beer.

Getting There & Away

Bus Gokarna has an oversized new bus stand just off Main St as you enter town.

Direct buses head to Karwar at 6.45 am and 4 pm (Rs 15, 1½ hours), but there are frequent private buses to Ankola where you can change to a local Karwar-bound bus. Karwar is also the place to pick up a bus for Goa. There are four buses to Hubli in the morning and one just after lunch. There's a direct 6.45 am bus to Mangalore. If you miss this, catch a local bus to Kumta (25km south), then one of the more-frequent Mangalore buses from there.

There's one bus to Bangalore (Rs 160, 12 hours), one to Hampi (Rs 90, 10 hours) at 7 am and one to Mysore (Rs 150, 12 hours).

Train The Konkan Railway is the best way to reach Goa and Mangalore and everywhere else along this line, even though only a couple of slow passenger trains currently stop at Gokarna Road station, 9km from town. A

KARNATAKA

bus from town runs out to the station at 11 am in time for the 11.30 am train to Margao. The south-bound train departs Gokarna Road at 4.25 pm. Auto-rickshaws want about Rs 75 to take you out to the station.

Express trains stop at Ankola and Kumta stations, both about 25km from Gokarna and accessible by local bus.

KARWAR
☎ 08382

Karwar is a dull, sleepy port town near the mouth of the Kali Nadi River, only a short distance south of Goa. While the town holds little of interest, the area immediately south is very picturesque since the foothills of the Western Ghats come right to the coast, forming headlands that are separated by sweeping sandy bays. Their peacefulness and beauty could change radically when work begins on a new naval base.

You can take a boat trip across the Kali Nadi to the Devbag Forest Beach Resort (Rs 50 per person), though the beach is nothing special, and the Kali Nadi bridge is a popular place to watch the sunset. The bridge is 3km north of town (Rs 20 in an auto-rickshaw).

Karwar's Indian Bank changes travellers cheques (but not cash).

Places to Stay & Eat

Anand Lodge (☎ 26156), a two minute walk from the bus stand, has acceptable doubles (only) with bath and balconies for Rs 100.

Hotel Navtara (☎ 20831, Kaikini Rd) is about a 10 minute walk from the bus stand, on the road in from the train station. Clean, bright rooms here cost Rs 90/130.

Hotel Bhadra (☎ 25212), just south of the Kali Nadi bridge, has modern doubles with bath for Rs 220, and air-con doubles for Rs 500 and Rs 550. It has a veg/nonveg restaurant and a bar.

Devbag Forest Beach Resort is administered by Jungle Lodges & Resorts (☎ 26596) from its office opposite the Hotel Bhadra. It's a peaceful resort (reached by a 10 minute boat ride – see above) with accommodation in comfortable timber huts on

stilts, but it's not cheap. A package including meals and use of recreational facilities is US$60 per night (Rs 1000 for Indians).

Udipi Hotel and its sister restaurant *Hotel Savita*, both on Main Rd, are clean, veg snack and 'meals' specialists.

Hotel Sitara, nearby, has a comfortable air-con restaurant upstairs serving a wide range of Indian, Chinese and continental dishes, and there's also a balcony dining area.

Getting There & Away

Karwar is a main station on the Konkan Railway so most expresses stop here. Heading south to Mangalore (Kankanadi) there's an express at 9.05 am, and north to Margao at 9.11 am and 7.30 pm.

The Karwar bus stand is on the southern edge of the town centre. There are numerous buses to Panaji (Rs 35, four hours) and Margao (Rs 22, three hours), Hubli (Rs 46, 3½ hours) and Mangalore (Rs 78). There are two buses to Jog Falls (Rs 49, five hours), one to Hassan and one direct to Hospet at 9.30 am (Rs 85, eight hours).

There are five direct KSRTC buses to Gokarna daily (Rs 15), but more-frequent private buses shuttle between Karwar and Ankola, where you can change for Gokarna. They depart from just outside the bus stand entrance.

Getting Around

The train station is 8km from town. A local bus meets incoming trains (Rs 3), but many more Karwar-bound buses pass along the main road about 50m from the station.

There are plenty of auto-rickshaws, but a good way to get to Kali Nadi bridge or the beaches around Karwar is by bicycle. They can be hired at several shops on Main St for Rs 2 an hour.

AROUND KARWAR

The nearest beaches to Karwar are **Binaga** and **Arga**, 3km and 5km south of the town respectively. They're both scimitar-shaped swathes of sand and are generally deserted.

Krishna Rest House (☎ 21613), set back from the beach at Binaga, is a great place to

KARNATAKA

stay if you want some peace and quiet. It's a basic family-run guesthouse with a few rooms with common bath and a small cottage, all for Rs 150. You can either self-cater or arrange food in advance with the owner. It's Rs 30 by auto-rickshaw or Rs 2 by bus from Karwar.

At the small town of **Ankola**, 37km south of Karwar, are the 15th century ruined walls of King Sarpamalika's fort and the equally old Sri Venkatraman Temple.

Central Karnataka

HAMPI

☎ 08394 • pop 930

The ruins of Vijayanagar, near the village of Hampi, are one of the most fascinating historical sites in South India. They're set in a strange and beautiful boulder-strewn landscape that has an almost magical quality.

Hampi is a thriving travellers' centre and most people stay at least a couple of days to soak up the atmosphere and explore the area. If you're in a hurry, it is possible to see the main sites in one day – either by bicycle or, if you start early, on foot – but this defeats the laid-back nature of Hampi. Signposting in some parts of the site is inadequate, but you can't really get lost. Unfortunately it's not safe to wander around the ruins alone at dawn or dusk, particularly on the climb up Matanga Hill. There have been reports in recent years of opportunistic thieves mugging lone travellers and stealing cameras and money, but local authorities are keen to clean up this situation.

Orientation

There are two main points of entry to the ruins: Hampi Bazaar and the small village of Kamalapuram to the south. Kamalapuram is a sleepy village with the KSTDC hotel and the site museum. The main travellers' scene is Hampi Bazaar, a bustling village with a burgeoning array of cheap lodges and restaurants, all dominated by the Virupaksha Temple. The ruins themselves can be divided into two main areas: the Sacred Centre, around Hampi Bazaar, and the Royal Centre, to the south around Kamalapuram.

Information

The tourist office (☎ 51339) is on the main street of Hampi Bazaar and is open 10 am to 5.30 pm daily except Sunday. It can arrange guides for Rs 350 per day or Rs 250 for half a day, and sells a map of the site. There are plenty of good books and better maps of Hampi available from Aspiration Stores, near the entrance to the Virupaksha Temple in Hampi Bazaar.

You can change travellers cheques and get cash advances on Visa and MasterCard (Rs 100 commission) at the Canara Bank in Hampi Bazaar from 11 am to 2 pm on weekdays (except Wednesday) and 11 am to 12.30 pm on Saturday. There are numerous authorised moneychangers offering slightly worse rates on the main street.

Hampi Bazaar & Virupaksha Temple

Now that locals are occupying the ancient buildings lining the main street, Hampi Bazaar is once more a bustling village. The Virupaksha Temple at the western end is one of the earliest structures in the city. The main gopuram, almost 50m high, was built in 1442, with a smaller one added in 1510. The main shrine is dedicated to Virupaksha, a form of Shiva.

Overlooking Virupaksha Temple to the south, **Hemakuta Hill** has a scattering of early ruins including Jain temples and a monolithic sculpture of Narasimha (Vishnu in his man-lion incarnation). It's worth the short walk up for the view over Hampi Bazaar.

Vittala Temple

From the eastern end of Hampi Bazaar an obvious track, navigable only on foot, leads left to the Vittala Temple, about 2km away. The undisputed highlight of the ruins, the 16th century Vittala Temple, is a World Heritage Monument. It's in a good state of preservation, though purists may have reservations about the cement-block columns erected to keep the main structure from falling down.

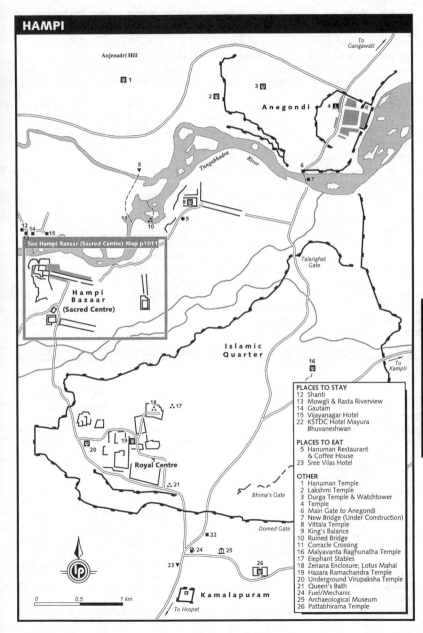

HAMPI

To Gangawati

Anjenadri Hill

🛕 1

2 🛕   3 🛕

Anegondi   4 🏛

Tungabhadra   River

5 ▼

6
●7

8 🛕

● 9

11
10

12 ■ ■ 14   ■ 15
13 ■

See Hampi Bazaar (Sacred Centre) Map p1011

**H a m p i
B a z a a r
(Sacred Centre)**

*Talarighat
Gate*

**I s l a m i c
Q u a r t e r**

16 🛕

To Kampli

18   ∴ 17
🏛
19
🛕
20

Royal Centre

∴ 21

Bhima's Gate

Domed Gate

■ 22

🏛 24   🏛 25

23 ▼   26
🛕

K a m a l a p u r a m

To Hospet

0   0.5   1 km

PLACES TO STAY
12 Shanti
13 Mowgli & Rasta Riverview
14 Gautam
15 Vijayanagar Hotel
22 KSTDC Hotel Mayura
    Bhuvaneshwari

PLACES TO EAT
 5 Hanuman Restaurant
    & Coffee House
23 Sree Vilas Hotel

OTHER
 1 Hanuman Temple
 2 Lakshmi Temple
 3 Durga Temple & Watchtower
 4 Temple
 6 Main Gate to Anegondi
 7 New Bridge (Under Construction)
 8 Vittala Temple
 9 King's Balance
10 Ruined Bridge
11 Corracle Crossing
16 Malyavanta Raghunatha Temple
17 Elephant Stables
18 Zenana Enclosure; Lotus Mahal
19 Hazara Ramachandra Temple
20 Underground Virupaksha Temple
21 Queen's Bath
24 Fuel/Mechanic
25 Archaeological Museum
26 Pattabhirama Temple

The Ruins of Vijayanagar

Vijayanagar (Hampi) was once the capital of one of the largest Hindu empires in Indian history. Founded by the Telugu princes Harihara and Bukka in 1336, it reached the height of its power under Krishnadevaraya (1509-29), when it controlled the whole of the peninsula south of the Krishna and Tungabhadra rivers, except for a string of commercial principalities along the Malabar Coast.

Comparable to Delhi in the 14th century, the city, which covered an area of 33 sq km, was surrounded by seven concentric lines of fortification and was reputed to have had a population of about half a million. It maintained a mercenary army of over one million according to the Persian ambassador, Abdul Razak, and ironically included Muslim mounted archers to defend it from the Muslim states to the north.

Vijayanagar's wealth was based on control of the spice trade to the south and the cotton industry of the south-east. Its busy bazaars, described by European travellers such as the Portuguese Nunez and Paes, were centres of international commerce.

The religion of Vijayanagar was a hybrid of current Hinduism, with the gods Vishnu and Shiva being lavishly worshipped in the orthodox manner. At the same time, Jainism was also prominent. Brahmins were privileged; *sati* (the burning of widows on the funeral pyres of their husbands) was widely practised and sacred prostitutes frequently worked from the city's temples. Brahmin inscriptions discovered on the site date the first Vijayanagar settlement back to the 1st century AD and suggest that there was a Buddhist centre nearby.

The empire came to a sudden end in 1565 after the disastrous battle of Talikota when the city was ransacked by the confederacy of Deccan sultans (Bidar, Bijapur, Golconda, Ahmednagar and Berar), thus opening up southern India for conquest by the Muslims.

Excavation at Vijayanagar was started in 1976 by the Archaeological Survey of India in collaboration with the Karnataka state government, and is still continuing.

Work is thought to have started on the temple in the reign of Krishnadevaraya (1509-29) and, although it was never finished or consecrated, the temple's incredible sculptural work is the pinnacle of Vijayanagar art. The outer pillars are known as the musical pillars as they reverberate when tapped, although this practice is now discouraged to avoid further damage. There's an ornate stone chariot in the temple courtyard containing an image of Garuda. The chariot's stone wheels used to be capable of turning. It costs Rs 5 to enter the temple complex (free on Friday).

Sule Bazaar & Achyutaraya Temple

Halfway along the path from Hampi Bazaar to the Vittala Temple, a track to the right leads to deserted Sule Bazaar, which gives you some idea of what Hampi Bazaar might have looked like if it hadn't been repopulated. At the southern end of this area is the Achyutaraya Temple, whose isolated location at the foot of Matanga Hill makes it even more atmospheric than the Vittala Temple.

Royal Centre

This area of Hampi is quite different from the northern section, since most of the rounded boulders that once littered the site have been used to create a mind-boggling proliferation of beautiful stone walls. It's a 2km walk from the Achyutaraya Temple on a poorly signposted track, so most people get to it from the Hampi Bazaar-Kamalapuram road. This area is easily navigable by bicycle since a decent dirt road runs through the heart of it.

Within various stone-walled enclosures here are the rest of Hampi's major attractions, including the **Lotus Mahal** and the **Elephant Stables**. The former is a delicately designed pavilion in a walled compound known as the Zenana Enclosure. It's an amazing synthesis of Hindu and Islamic style and it gets its name from the lotus bud carved in the centre of the domed and vaulted ceiling.

The Elephant Stables is a grand building with domed chambers, which once housed the state elephants. It costs Rs 5 to enter the Zenana Enclosure (free on Friday).

Further south is the Royal Enclosure area, with its various temples and elaborate waterworks, plus the **Underground Virupaksha Temple** and the impressive **Queen's Bath**.

Museum

The archaeological museum at Kamalapuram is open 10 am to 5 pm daily except Friday (free) and is worth a visit. It has some fine sculptures and a large floor model of the existing Vijayanagar ruins.

Anegondi

North of the river is the ruined fortified stronghold of Anegondi. There's not a lot to see here today, although much of the old defensive wall is intact and there are numerous small temples, including the tiny whitewashed **Hanuman Temple**, perched on top of a prominent rocky hill.

To get to Anegondi you need to take a coracle across the river then follow the dusty road north.

Places to Stay

Hampi Bazaar This is the best place to soak up Hampi's special atmosphere if you don't mind basic but adequate accommodation. Most of the lodges are north of the

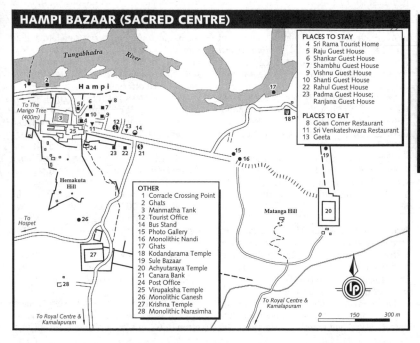

HAMPI BAZAAR (SACRED CENTRE)

PLACES TO STAY
4 Sri Rama Tourist Home
5 Raju Guest House
6 Shankar Guest House
7 Shambhu Guest House
9 Vishnu Guest House
10 Shanti Guest House
22 Rahul Guest House
23 Padma Guest House;
    Ranjana Guest House

PLACES TO EAT
8 Goan Corner Restaurant
11 Sri Venkateshwara Restaurant
13 Geeta

OTHER
1 Coracle Crossing Point
2 Ghats
3 Manmatha Tank
12 Tourist Office
14 Bus Stand
15 Photo Gallery
16 Monolithic Nandi
17 Ghats
18 Kodandarama Temple
19 Sule Bazaar
20 Achyutaraya Temple
21 Canara Bank
24 Post Office
25 Virupaksha Temple
26 Monolithic Ganesh
27 Krishna Temple
28 Monolithic Narasimha

Tungabhadra River
Hampi
To The Mango Tree (400m)
Hemakuta Hill
To Hospet
Matanga Hill
To Royal Centre & Kamalapuram
To Royal Centre & Kamalapuram
0   150   300 m

KARNATAKA

main road (follow one of the lanes behind the tourist office) and there are a couple of good places just south of the bus stand. Rates given here are for the high season (December/January).

Vishnu Guest House (☎ 41611) is a friendly family home. Singles/doubles with bath and bucket hot water are Rs 120/130.

Shanti Guest House (☎ 51368) is a popular travellers' haunt. Bare rooms with common bath are a bit overpriced at Rs 150 but there's a pleasant garden courtyard.

Raju Guest House, across the street, has clean simple rooms with common bath for Rs 60/80. It has a rooftop eating area where you can relax when your room gets claustrophobic.

Rahul Guest House (☎ 41648), south of the bus stand in the street running parallel to the bazaar, is a popular place with congenial common areas. Clean spartan rooms with mattresses on the floor and common bath cost Rs 70/100.

There are a couple of other good places in this street. **Ranjana Guest House** (☎ 41696) has very clean doubles with bathroom (and shower) for Rs 300 and **Padma Guest House** (☎ 41330) is a small friendly place with good-value rooms for Rs 80/100 with common bath.

Sri Rama Tourist Home (☎ 41219), to the right of the Virupaksha Temple, is popular with visiting Indians but it lacks atmosphere and charm. Doubles with bath cost Rs 100.

There are dozens more places to choose from: **Shankar Guest House** and **Shambhu Guest House** both have rooms for Rs 100/150 and the latter has a rooftop restaurant.

North of the River The most laid-back 'scene' in Hampi is across the river where a string of guesthouses cater for those who find even Hampi Bazaar too busy. To get across take a coracle (Rs 3) from the ghats north of the Virupaksha Temple.

Vijayanagar Hotel is the first place you come to. Basic rooms in a concrete building cost Rs 50/60 and there's a restaurant.

Gautam, further west, has rustic palm-thatched mud huts for Rs 40/50.

Mowgli & Rasta Riverview has the best rooms of the places along here. Newly built 'huts' with fan and common bath cost Rs 70/100 and there are cheaper huts closer to the river.

Shanti is the most basic of the lot with decrepit huts for Rs 30.

Kamalapuram The **KSTDC'S Hotel Mayura Bhuvaneshwari** (☎ 41574), on the northern outskirts of Kamalapuram, is modern and well maintained. Decent singles/doubles with bath and mosquito nets cost Rs 275/330, or Rs 400/495 with air-con (including tax). The hotel has a veg/nonveg restaurant and a basic bar.

Places to Eat

There are a few simple restaurants on the main street of Hampi Bazaar, but most of the newer places are among the guesthouses in the dusty streets behind the tourist office. There's very little to distinguish between them, since they all serve standard Indian fare and western standbys and all cater exclusively to the travelling community. Despite having extensive menus, most produce only limited offerings.

Sri Venkateswara, on the right as you near the Virupaksha Temple, is the most established restaurant. It serves tiffin and western snacks at lunch and thalis (Rs 15) in the evening. **Geeta** is a popular alternative. North of the bazaar, the **Goan Corner Restaurant** is popular. Many of the guesthouses have good rooftop restaurants.

The **Mango Tree** is away from the crowds, about 400m west of the ghats down a path through a banana plantation. Excellent thalis are served on mats on the earthen terrace.

There are a few humble eateries in Kamalapuram, the most notable being the **Sree Vilas Hotel**, opposite the bus stop. It closes at 7.30 pm.

Due to Hampi's religious significance, alcohol is not permitted – but that doesn't mean you can't get a discreet beer or two.

For a legal drink, there's a bar at the *KSTDC'S Hotel Mayura Bhuvaneshwari* in Kamalapuram.

Getting There & Away
While private buses from Goa and Bangalore will drop you in Hampi, you have to go to Hospet to catch a bus out (because local auto-rickshaw drivers complained about lost business). Local buses run roughly every hour from Hampi Bazaar to Hospet (Rs 10, 30 minutes). The first bus from Hospet is at 6.30 am, the last one back leaves Hampi at 8.30 pm. A rickshaw costs Rs 50, though the return journey will cost you 50% more.

If you're coming from Goa, the overnight sleeper bus (Rs 350) is a popular option. A couple of noisy stops along the way and some terrifying cornering that can fling you out of your 'bed' make sleep a bit erratic. There are several travel agents in Hampi Bazaar that can book onward bus, train and plane tickets or arrange a car and driver.

Getting Around
It makes a lot of sense to hire a bicycle to explore the ruins once you've seen the Vittala and Achyutaraya temples and Sule Bazaar. The road between Hampi Bazaar and Kamalapuram can be used to get to the ruins; key monuments are haphazardly signposted along its length. Bicycles cost around Rs 30 per day in Hampi Bazaar.

Walking is the only way to explore all the nooks and crannies of the site, but expect to cover at least 7km just to see the major ruins. Auto-rickshaws and taxis are available for sightseeing, and will drop you as close to each of the major ruins as they can. A five hour auto-rickshaw tour costs Rs 300, or Rs 150 for the Royal Centre only.

Organised tours depart from Hospet; see that section for details.

HOSPET
☎ 08394 • pop 151,900
Many people who come to see the Vijayanagar ruins at Hampi, 13km east, use Hospet as a base. It's a fairly typical Karnataka country town but has none of the ethereal atmosphere of Hampi. You'll need to come here to make transport connections though.

Information
The tourist office (☎ 28537) is open daily 7.30 am to 7.30 pm. It has maps and information on Hampi and sights in northern Karnataka. Malligi Tourist Home changes travellers cheques and the Andhra Bank on Station Rd gives cash advances on Visa and MasterCard.

Organised Tours
The daily KSTDC tour to the three main sites at Hampi (Hampi Bazaar, Vittala Temple and the Royal Centre) and to Tungabhadra Dam departs at 9.30 am and returns at 6 pm (Rs 60). Make bookings at the Hospet tourist office, Malligi Tourist Home or the Hotel Priyardarshini. Book a day in advance if possible.

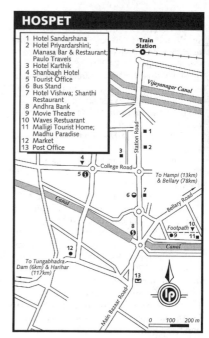

HOSPET

1 Hotel Sandarshana
2 Hotel Priyardarshini; Manasa Bar & Restaurant; Paulo Travels
3 Hotel Karthik
4 Shanbagh Hotel
5 Tourist Office
6 Bus Stand
7 Hotel Vishwa; Shanthi Restaurant
8 Andhra Bank
9 Movie Theatre
10 Waves Restuarant
11 Malligi Tourist Home; Madhu Paradise
12 Market
13 Post Office

Train Station

Vijayanagar Canal

Station Road

College Road

To Hampi (13km) & Bellary (78km)

Bellary Road

Canal

Footpath

Canal

To Tungabhadra Dam (6km) & Harihar (117km)

Main Bazaar Road

0   100   200 m

KARNATAKA

Firewalking in Hospet

For much of the year Hospet is not a particularly interesting place, but it comes alive during the festival of Muharram, which commemorates the martyrdom of Mohammed's grandson, Imam Hussain. If you're here at this time (the date varies from year to year) don't miss the firewalkers, who walk barefoot across the red-hot embers of a fire that's been going all day and night. Virtually the whole town turns out to watch or take part and the excitement reaches fever pitch around midnight. The preliminaries, which go on all day, appear to be a bewildering hybrid of Muslim and Hindu ritual. Those who are scheduled to do the firewalking must be physically restrained from going completely berserk just before the event.

Places to Stay

Hotel Vishwa (☎ 27171, Station Rd), opposite the bus stand, has large, clean rooms with bath that are good value at Rs 80/149, and four-bed rooms for Rs 290 including tax. The hotel is set back from the street so the rooms are quiet. There's hot water in the morning and some rooms have small balconies.

Hotel Sandarshan (☎ 28574, Station Rd) has acceptable doubles with bath for Rs 120.

Malligi Tourist Home (☎ 28101, 6/143 Jambunatha Rd) is an old favourite among travellers but is going downhill. Dingy doubles with bath and hot water start from Rs 140, up to Rs 550. The air-con rooms in the newer wing are better and range from Rs 350 to Rs 700. The hotel has a pleasant garden, a restaurant and a bookshop.

Hotel Priyardarshini (☎ 28838, Station Rd) is a better bet. Simple but clean rooms with bath start at Rs 140/195, deluxe doubles are Rs 270 and air-con doubles are Rs 440. All rooms have balconies and hot water in the morning. There's an office of Paulo Travels here (for overnight buses to Goa), and a veg/nonveg garden restaurant and bar.

Hotel Karthik (☎ 24938, Sardar Patel Rd) is a new place with spotless, well-appointed double rooms for Rs 250. Deluxe rooms are Rs 300 and air-con rooms are Rs 500.

Places to Eat

Madhu Paradise, at the Malligi Tourist Home, serves reasonably priced south and north Indian veg fare and western breakfasts. *Waves* 'multi-cuisine restaurant' is part of a new complex opposite the Malligi. The setting is upmarket and the food good, but there's little atmosphere.

Manasa Bar & Restaurant, in the Hotel Priyardarshini, serves nonveg Andhra-style dishes in a garden setting for lunch, and from 6 to 11 pm. The hotel also has an indoor veg restaurant open all day.

Shanthi Restaurant, in the Hotel Vishwa, does excellent vegetarian thalis at lunchtime, and snacks the rest of the day. *Shanbagh Hotel*, near the tourist office, is another recommended lunchtime vegetarian restaurant.

Getting There & Away

Bus The busy bus stand in Hospet is fairly well organised, though buses in this part of the state are generally crowded and you'll need to fight to get on. A large backpack can make this an uncomfortable experience.

Buses to Hampi depart from Bay No 10 every half an hour (Rs 10).

More than 10 express buses run daily to Bangalore (Rs 92/132 ordinary/deluxe, nine hours). They are nearly all morning or night departures: no Bangalore buses depart between 1 and 9.30 pm. The KSTDC runs its own overnight deluxe bus to Bangalore daily at 10 pm (Rs 160). There are regular public buses to Hubli (Rs 32, four hours).

There are three buses a day to Badami, or catch one of the many buses to Gadag or Ilkal and transfer to another bus there. The journey takes five hours via Gadag and close to six hours via Ilkal.

There are four buses to Bijapur (Rs 62, six hours); five buses to Hyderabad (Rs 113, nine hours); and also daily departures to Hassan, Mangalore and Shimoga. One bus heads to Gokarna (Rs 85, eight hours) daily at 1 am.

Train Hospet train station is a 20 minute walk or Rs 10 auto-rickshaw ride from the centre of town. There is one direct train daily to Bangalore at 8.20 pm (Rs 151/531 in sleeper/1st class, 10½ hours) or go to Guntakal (three hours), and get an express to Bangalore from here; and two expresses to Hubli (four hours). To get to Badami and Bijapur, catch a Hubli train to Gadag and pick up a connection from there.

HUBLI
☎ 0836 • pop 728,000

Hubli is important to the traveller principally as a major railway junction on the routes from Mumbai to Bangalore, Goa and northern Karnataka.

All the main services (hotels, restaurants, etc) are conveniently close to the train station. The bus stand is on Lamington Rd, a 15 minute walk from the train station.

Places to Stay

Ashoka Towers Hotel (☎ 362271, Lamington Rd), about 500m from the train station, has clean, good-value singles/doubles with bath for Rs 130/175. Air-con doubles cost Rs 350.

Hotel Kailash (☎ 352235, Lamington Rd), opposite the Ashoka, is more upmarket. Comfortable rooms with hot water and TV cost Rs 303/435 including tax. Air-con rooms are Rs 435/575.

Hotel Ajanta (☎ 362216) is a short distance off the main street and visible from the train station. It's a huge place so you'll always be able to find accommodation here. Average rooms cost Rs 60/100 with common bath or Rs 100/145 with bath. Check-out is 24 hours.

Hotel Ayodhya (☎ 351951, Station Rd) is the best of the hotels near the bus stand. Singles/doubles cost Rs 135/195.

Places to Eat

Parag Bar & Restaurant, on the street facing the train station, has a British pub-style restaurant and an open-air rooftop section serving passable veg and nonveg Indian and Chinese dishes.

Royal Palace, on a side street near the Ashoka Towers Hotel, is the best restaurant in this part of the city. North Indian mains cost around Rs 60.

There are plenty of late-night food stalls around the bus stand and train station.

Getting There & Away

Bus Hubli has a large and busy bus stand with a well-organised reservation and ticket hall in a separate building. The KSRTC has lots of deluxe buses to Bangalore (Rs 156, nine hours) and Hospet (Rs 41, four hours). There are also four buses daily to Mumbai (Rs 187, 15 hours); three to Mysore (Rs 156, 10 hours); two to Mangalore (Rs 124, 10 hours); and at least one daily departure to Bijapur, Gokarna and Jog Falls.

There are four KSRTC buses to Panaji (Rs 52, five hours), and Goa's Kadamba Transport Corporation also runs a number of services.

Opposite the bus stand are plenty of private companies operating deluxe buses to Bangalore, Bijapur, Goa, Mangalore, Mumbai and Pune.

Train The railway reservation office is open 8 am to 8 pm daily. If you're heading for Hospet (four hours), there are expresses at noon and 5 pm. To reach Bijapur, you'll have to catch one of these trains and change at Gadag (1½ hours). There are two to three expresses a day to Bangalore (10 hours) and usually two expresses to Mumbai (17 hours) via Londa (two hours). Londa is the closest junction with rail connections to Goa.

Northern Karnataka

BELGAUM
☎ 0831 • pop 453,000

On a rather bald plateau in the north-west corner of the state, Belgaum was a regional capital in the 12th and 13th centuries. The old oval-shaped stone **fort** near the bus stand is of no real interest. Mahatma Gandhi was locked up here once. Outside the fort gate, to the left, is the colourful and aromatic local **cattle market**. The **Masjid-Sata** mosque dates from 1519. There are also two interesting **Jain temples**, one with an extremely intricate roof, while the other has some fine carvings of musicians. Belgaum's **watchtower**, on Ganapath Galli in the town centre, provides a panorama of the flat countryside and distant hills. **Sunset Point**, on the old racetrack road, also offers fine views.

Places to Stay

Hotel Sheetal (☎ 429222, Khade Bazaar) is about three minutes walk from the bus stand. Clean, bright singles/doubles with bath cost Rs 110/190. It also has a veg restaurant.

KSTDC'S Hotel Mayura Mallaprabha (☎ 470781), on the NH4 bypass, just behind the lake, has cottages with bath for Rs 160/190 and there are dorm beds for Rs 40. There's also a tourist office here.

Hotel Sanman Deluxe (☎ 430777, College Rd) is slightly more upmarket with rooms from Rs 255/415 plus tax. There's a currency exchange service at reception.

Getting There & Away

The bus stand is close to the old town area and there are buses to Mumbai, Pune, Goa, and Hubli. Several express trains between Bangalore (15 hours) and Mumbai (14 hours) stop at the train station. You'll need to catch an auto-rickshaw here. These trains pass through Londa and Hubli. There's also a daily express to Delhi (37 hours).

BADAMI

☎ 08357 • pop 18,200

Set in beautiful countryside at the foot of a red sandstone ridge, the small rural town of Badami was once the capital of the Chalukyan empire, which covered much of the central Deccan between the 4th and 8th centuries AD. Here, and at nearby Aihole and Pattadakal, you can see some of the earliest and finest examples of Dravidian temples and rock-cut caves. The forms and sculptural work at these sites provided inspiration for the later Hindu empires that rose and fell in the southern part of the peninsula before the arrival of the Muslims.

Though principally promoters of the Vedic culture, the Chalukyans were tolerant of all sects, and elements of Shaivism, Vaishnavaism, Jainism and even Buddhism can be found in many of their temples.

History

Badami was the Chalukyan capital from about 540 AD until 757 AD when the Chalukyans were overthrown by the Rashtrakutas. The surrounding hills are dotted with temples, fortifications, carvings and inscriptions dating not just from the Chalukyan period, but from other times when the site was occupied as a fortress. After it fell to the Rashtrakutas, Badami was occupied successively by the Chalukyans of Kalyan (a separate branch of the Western Chalukyans), the Kalachuryas, the Yadavas of Devagiri, the Vijayanagar empire, the Adil Shahi kings of Bijapur and the Marathas.

All these various rulers have left their mark at Badami, and there's even a Pallava inscription dating back to 642 AD when their king, Narasimha Varman I, briefly overwhelmed the Chalukyans and occupied Badami for 13 years before being driven out.

Orientation & Information

The main street of Badami (Station Rd) has a few hotels and restaurants, and Badami village itself is squeezed between here and the hilltop caves. The tourist office (☎ 65414), open Monday to Saturday 10 am to 5.30 pm, is in the new wing of the KSTDC'S Hotel Mayura Chalukya.

It's best to change money before you get here, but if you're desperate, Mookambika Deluxe Lodge will change travellers cheques with a high commission charge.

Caves

Badami is best known for its beautiful cave temples, cut into the cliff face of a red sandstone hill. They display India's range of religious sects. The caves are open 6 am to 6 pm (Rs 2). Guides charge Rs 150 for a tour of the caves, or Rs 350 for the whole site.

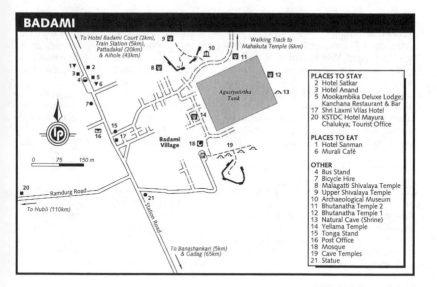

BADAMI

To Hotel Badami Court (2km),
Train Station (5km),
Pattadakal (20km)
& Aihole (43km)

Walking Track to
Mahakuta Temple (6km)

Agastyatirtha Tank

Badami Village

0 75 150 m

Ramdurg Road

To Hubli (110km)

Station Road

To Banashankari (5km)
& Gadag (65km)

PLACES TO STAY
2 Hotel Satkar
3 Hotel Anand
5 Mookambika Deluxe Lodge;
   Kanchana Restaurant & Bar
17 Shri Laxmi Vilas Hotel
20 KSTDC Hotel Mayura
   Chalukya; Tourist Office

PLACES TO EAT
1 Hotel Sanman
6 Murali Café

OTHER
4 Bus Stand
7 Bicycle Hire
8 Malagatti Shivalaya Temple
9 Upper Shivalaya Temple
10 Archaeological Museum
11 Bhutanatha Temple 2
12 Bhutanatha Temple 1
13 Natural Cave (Shrine)
14 Yellama Temple
15 Tonga Stand
16 Post Office
18 Mosque
19 Cave Temples
21 Statue

KARNATAKA

Cave One This cave, just above the entrance to the complex, is dedicated to Shiva. It is the oldest of the four caves, thought to have been carved during the 6th century. On the cliff wall to the right of the porch is a beautiful image of Nataraja striking 81 dances poses and whose 18 arms hold, among other things, a snake, a musical instrument and a *trishula* (trident).

On the right of the porch area is a huge figure of Ardhanarishvara. The right half of the figure shows features of Shiva, such as matted hair and a third eye, while the left half of the image has aspects of Parvati, including braided hair and ornaments. On the opposite wall is a large image of Harihara, the right half of which represents Shiva, and the left half Vishnu. A headless Nandi sits in the middle of the cave, facing a tiny sanctuary, which is carved into the back wall.

Cave Two This cave is simpler in design, and is dedicated to Vishnu. As with caves one and three, the front edge of the platform is decorated with images of pot-bellied dwarfs in various poses. Four pillars support the veranda, the top of each of which is carved with a bracket in the shape of a *yali*, or mythical beast. On the left wall of the porch is the pig-headed figure of Varaha, an incarnation of Vishnu and the emblem of the Chalukya empire. To his left is an image of Naga, the snake. On the right wall is a large sculpture of Trivikrama, another incarnation of Vishnu, booting out a demon while in his eight hands he holds a variety of weapons including a discus, a bow and a sword. The ceiling panels contain images of Vishnu riding Garuda, *gandharva* couples, swastikas and fish arranged in a wheel.

Between the second and third cave are two sets of steps to the right. The first gives access to a **natural cave**, the eastern wall of which contains a small Buddhist image of Padmapani (an incarnation of Buddha). The second set of steps leads up a narrow defile to the hilltop **South Fort**; sadly these steps are barred by a metal gate.

Cave Three This cave was carved under the orders of Mangalesha, the brother of King Kirtivarma, in 578. It is dedicated to

Vishnu and contains some of the best sculptures in the complex.

On the left-hand wall of the cave is a large carving of Vishnu, sitting on the coils of the snake; nearby is an image of Varaha with four hands. The pillars here have carved brackets in the shape of yalis, and the sides of the pillars are also carved. The ceiling panels contain images including Vishnu, Indra riding an elephant, Shiva on a bull, and Brahma on a swan.

Cave Four Dedicated to Jainism, Cave Four is the smallest of the set and was carved in the 7th to 8th centuries. The pillars, with their roaring yalis, are of a similar design to the other caves. The right wall of the cave has an image of Suparshvanatha (the 7th Jain *tirthankar*), surrounded by more than 20 Jain tirthankars. The sanctum contains an image of Adinath, the first Jain tirthankar.

Other Attractions

The caves overlook the picturesque 5th century **Agastyatirtha Tank** and the peaceful waterside **Bhutanatha temples**. On the other side of the tank is the **archaeological museum**, which houses superb examples of local sculpture, including remarkable Lajja-Gauri images of a fertility cult that flourished in the area. It's open 10 am to 5 pm daily except Friday (free). The stairway behind the museum climbs through a sandstone chasm and fortified gateways to reach the various temples and ruins of the **north fort**. The fort has expansive views and overlooks the rooftops of the small, friendly village of Badami.

It's definitely worth exploring Badami's narrow laneways, where you'll find old houses, tiny squares and the occasional Chalukyan ruin.

Places to Stay

Mookambika Deluxe Lodge (☎ 65067, Station Rd), opposite the bus stand, has gone upmarket with all its rooms now in the 'deluxe' category. They're not cheap in high season at Rs 300 for standard rooms, or Rs 600 with TV and bathtub. There's hot water in the morning.

Hotel Anand (☎ 65074, Station Rd), across the road, is better value with a wider range of rooms from dingy singles at the back for Rs 100 to new deluxe rooms with bathtub and TV for Rs 350/400. Ask to see a few rooms before deciding here.

Hotel Satkar (☎ 65417, Station Rd) has clean, basic rooms with bath and hot water in the morning from Rs 80/150. Checkout time is 24 hours.

Shri Laxmi Vilas Hotel (☎ 65077, Station Rd), near the tonga stand, has bland doubles (only) with bath and bucket shower for Rs 120.

KSTDC'S Hotel Mayura Chalukya (☎ 65046, Ramdurg Rd) is about 500m south of Station Rd. The neglected old section has tranquil gardens and doubles/triples for Rs 200/250. A new wing consisting of six deluxe air-con cottages was being completed at the time of writing.

Hotel Badami Court (☎ 65230, Station Rd), 2km from the town centre towards the train station, is Badami's top hotel. Impeccable air-con singles/doubles with bathtub and TV cost US$36/42.

Places to Eat

Kanchana Restaurant & Bar, attached to Mookambika Deluxe Lodge, is not the cheapest place around but it serves a good range of veg and nonveg food, western breakfasts and has a pleasant upstairs terrace.

Hotel Sanman, nearby, is popular with travellers and locals. It has cheap veg/nonveg food and cold beers.

Murali Cafe is a basic but atmospheric veg restaurant serving thalis at lunchtime.

Hotel Mayura Chalukya has the usual KSTDC veg restaurant and beer bar; the food available is limited.

Pulikeshi Dining Room in Hotel Badami Court is an upmarket, multicuisine, silver service restaurant where dinner costs around Rs 100 per head.

Getting There & Away

Bus The timetable at the bus stand in Badami is in English and Kannada but it's not particularly accurate. You'll also have

KARNATAKA

to cope with the usual rugby scrum to get on a bus when it arrives. There are six buses daily to Bijapur (four hours) and Hubli (three hours), and four buses to Bangalore (12 hours). The deluxe bus to Bangalore costs Rs 150. There are five buses direct to Hospet (five hours), or you can catch any of the buses to Gadag (two hours) or Ilkal (two hours) to pick up a connection.

Train Conversion work is still disrupting services to Bangalore, and the only trains stopping at Badami are those shuttling between Gadag and Bijapur – nearly all 2nd class passenger trains. Tickets for passenger trains go on sale about 30 minutes before the train arrives. Five trains head to Bijapur (Rs 22, four hours), and there are five to Gadag, where you can connect to Hospet and Hubli.

Getting Around

Badami train station is 5km from town. Tongas congregate outside to meet the trains. A private tonga from the station into town costs about Rs 25. You have the choice of a tonga, auto-rickshaw (Rs 35) or taxi (Rs 55) when heading from town out to the train station. You can hire bikes in Badami for Rs 3 per hour.

The best way to explore the surrounding area is by local bus, since they're fairly frequent and run pretty much to schedule. You can easily visit both Aihole and Pattadakal in one day from Badami if you start early. Start with Aihole since the last bus back from Aihole to Badami is around 4.30 pm; the last bus from Pattadakal to Badami is at 6 pm. There are plenty of buses from Badami to Aihole (Rs 12, two hours). From Aihole, there's a bus at 11.30 am and 1 pm to Pattadakal (30 minutes), from where there are hourly buses and minibuses back to Badami. It's a good idea to take food and water with you.

Taxi drivers in Badami quote around Rs 450 for a day trip taking in Pattadakal and Aihole. Mookambika Deluxe Lodge can arrange a car and driver to these two places and to other local sights on the way for Rs 150 per person (minimum three people).

AROUND BADAMI
Pattadakal

This village, 20km from Badami, was the second capital of the Badami Chalukyans and was used in particular for the royal coronations. While most of the temples here were built during the 7th and 8th centuries, the earliest remains date from the 3rd and 4th centuries, and the latest structure is a Jain temple of the Rashtrakuta period (9th century).

Pattadakal, like Aihole, was a developing ground for South Indian temple architecture. In particular, two main types of temple towers were tried out here. On the one hand there are the curvilinear shikharas of the Kasivisvesvara, Jambulinga and Galaganatha temples, while on the other, the Mallikarjuna, Sangamesvara and Virupaksha temples have a square roof and receding tiers.

The main **Virupaksha Temple** is a huge structure. The massive columns are covered with intricate carvings depicting episodes from the *Ramayana* and *Mahabharata*, and showing battle scenes, lovers and decorative motifs. Around the roof of the inner hall are sculptures of elephants' and lions' heads. To the east, and facing the temple, is a pavilion containing a massive Nandi. The exterior of the temple is covered with sculpture and ornamentation, some of it fairly eroded, but much of it still in good shape. The **Mallikarjuna Temple**, next to the Virupaksha Temple, is slightly more worn but almost identical in design. About 500m south of the main enclosure is the **Papanatha Temple**.

A classical dance festival is held at Pattadakal, normally at the end of January.

Aihole

Aihole was the Chalukyan regional capital between the 4th and 6th centuries. Here you can see Hindu temple architecture in its embryonic stage, from the earliest simple shrines, such as those in the Kontigudi Group and the Lad Khan Temple, to the later and more complex buildings such as the Meguti Temple.

In the centre of the village is a fenced enclosure (Rs 2) with the most impressive building in Aihole – the **Durga Temple**, which dates from the 7th century. The temple is notable for its semicircular apse, which was copied from Buddhist architecture, and for the remains of the curvilinear sikhara. Even more striking than the formal layout are the outstanding carvings crowding the colonnaded passageway around the sanctuary.

The small **museum** behind the Durga temple contains further examples of the Chalukyan sculptors' work, and is open 10 am to 5 pm (closed Friday).

To the south of the Durga temple are several other collections of buildings including some of the earliest structures in Aihole – the Gandar, Ladkhan, Kontigudi and Hucchapaya groups, which are of pavilion type with slightly sloping roofs. Six hundred metres to the south-east, on a low hilltop, is the Jain **Meguti Temple**.

Accommodation is available at the *Tourist Home* (☎ 74641), 1km from the village on the Amingad road. A large triple room with bath costs Rs 60 but the place is all but deserted.

Mahakuta Temple

About 10km east of Badami, this temple is easily visited en route to Aihole. Mahakuta was made sacred by the presence of the sage Agastya, who lived here, and the temple is still active as a pilgrimage site. Within the walled courtyard are two main temples on either side of an old tank. The first of these, nearest the entrance, is still in use but the other one is now deserted. A number of smaller shrines in various states of dilapidation are arranged around the outside of the courtyard.

Banashankari

This small village, about 5km south-east of Badami, is home to an attractive temple, with a huge tank surrounded by a pillared cloister. Banashankari is particularly worth visiting during the annual temple festival, which usually falls in January. For days on end the streets around the temple are taken over by a huge fair, which is best visited in the evening.

BIJAPUR
☎ 08352 • pop 217,500

Modern Bijapur is an undistinguished town blessed by the scattered ruins and still-intact gems of 15th to 17th century Muslim architecture. It is dotted with mosques, mausoleums, palaces and fortifications, including the famous Golgumbaz, whose vast dome is said to be the world's second largest. The austere grace of Bijapur's discoloured monuments is in complete contrast to the sculptural extravagance of the Chalukyan and Hoysala temples further south. The Ibrahim Roza mausoleum, in particular, is considered to be one of the most finely proportioned Islamic monuments in India.

Bijapur was the capital of the Adil Shahi kings (1489-1686), one of the five splinter states formed when the Bahmani Muslim kingdom broke up in 1482. The others, formed at roughly the same time, were Bidar, Golconda, Ahmednagar and Gulbarga. Bijapur is still strongly Muslim in character.

Orientation

The two main attractions, the Golgumbaz and the Ibrahim Roza, are at opposite ends of the town. Between them runs Station Rd (MG Rd) along which you'll find most of the major hotels and restaurants. The bus stand is a five minute walk from Station Rd; the train station is 2km east of the centre.

Information

The tourist office is behind the Hotel Mayura Adil Shahi Annexe on Station Rd, but there's not much information and they run no city tours. The post office, also on Station Rd, is open Monday to Saturday 8.30 am to 6 pm.

To change travellers cheques head to the Canara Bank, north of the market. You'll need to provide the bank with photocopies of the ID pages of your passport.

Golgumbaz

Bijapur's largest and most famous monument is the Golgumbaz. Built in 1659, it's an enormous, bulky, ill-proportioned building, containing an immense hall, buttressed

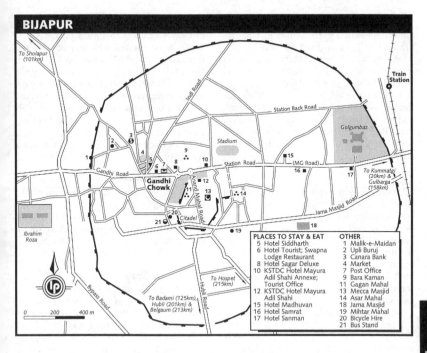

BIJAPUR

To Sholapur (101km)

Train Station

Indi Road

Station Back Road

Golgumbaz

Stadium

Station Road

(MG Road)

Gandhi Road

Gandhi Chowk

To Kummatgi (20km) & Gulbarga (158km)

Anand Mahal Road

Jama Masjid Road

Ibrahim Roza

To Hospet (215km)

Citadel

Bypass Road

Hubli Road

To Badami (125km), Hubli (201km) & Belgaum (213km)

0   200   400 m

PLACES TO STAY & EAT	OTHER
5 Hotel Siddharth	1 Malik-e-Maidan
6 Hotel Tourist; Swapna	2 Upli Buruj
Lodge Restaurant	3 Canara Bank
8 Hotel Sagar Deluxe	4 Market
10 KSTDC Hotel Mayura	7 Post Office
Adil Shahi Annexe;	9 Bara Kaman
Tourist Office	11 Gagan Mahal
12 KSTDC Hotel Mayura	13 Mecca Masjid
Adil Shahi	14 Asar Mahal
15 Hotel Madhuvan	18 Jama Masjid
16 Hotel Samrat	19 Mihtar Mahal
17 Hotel Sanman	20 Bicycle Hire
	21 Bus Stand

KARNATAKA

by octagonal seven storey towers at each of its corners. The structure is capped by an enormous dome, 38m in diameter, said to be the world's second largest after St Peter's in the Vatican City.

Around the base of the dome, high above the hall, is a gallery known as the 'whispering gallery'; if you speak into the wall a person listening on the opposite side of the gallery should hear you clearly. The acoustics here are such that any sound made is said to be repeated 10 times over. 'Bedlam gallery' would be a more appropriate name, since it is permanently full of yelling tourists and children running amok. Access to the gallery is via a narrow staircase in the south-eastern tower and there are views of Bijapur from the outside of the dome before you enter the gallery. The views are clearest in the early morning, which is also the best time to test the acoustics, before the school groups arrive.

The Golgumbaz is the mausoleum of Mohammed Adil Shah (1626-56), his two wives, his mistress (Rambha), one of his daughters and a grandson. Their caskets stand on a raised platform in the centre of the hall, though their actual graves are in the crypt, accessible by a flight of steps under the western doorway.

The mausoleum is open 6 am to 6 pm (Rs 2, free on Friday). Shoes should be left outside near the entrance to the hall and there's a Rs 25 video camera fee.

An **archaeological museum** in the ornamental gardens is open 10 am to 5 pm daily except Friday.

Ibrahim Roza

The beautiful Ibrahim Roza was built at the height of Bijapur's prosperity by Ibrahim Adil Shah II (1580-1626) for his queen. Unlike the Golgumbaz, which is impressive for its immensity, the emphasis here is on elegance and delicacy. Its 24m-high minarets are said to have inspired those of the Taj Mahal. It's also one of the few monuments in Bijapur with substantial stone filigree and other decorative sculptural work.

Interred here are Ibrahim Adil Shah, his queen, Taj Sultana, his daughter, two sons, and his mother, Haji Badi Sahiba. The entry fee is Rs 2; shoes should be left on the steps up to the platform on which the mausoleum stands.

Citadel

Surrounded by its own fortified walls and wide moat in the city centre, the citadel once contained the palaces, pleasure gardens and durbar hall of the Adil Shahi kings. Unfortunately, most of them are now in ruins, although some impressive fragments remain. The best is the **Gagan Mahal**, built by Ali Adil Shah I around 1561 to serve the dual purpose of a royal residence and a durbar hall.

Mohammed Adil Shah's seven storey palace, the **Sat Manzil**, is nearby, but substantially in ruins. Just across the road stands the delicate **Jala Manzil**, once a water pavilion surrounded by secluded courts and gardens. On the other side of Station Rd are the graceful arches of **Bara Kaman**, the ruined mausoleum of Ali Roza.

Jama Masjid

The finely proportioned Jama Masjid has graceful arches, a fine dome and a large inner courtyard with room for 2250 worshippers. Spaces for them are marked out in black on the polished floor of the mosque. The flat roof is accessible by several flights of stairs. It was constructed by Ali Adil Shah I (reigned 1557-80), who was also responsible for erecting the fortified city walls and the Gagan Mahal, and for installing a public water system.

Other Monuments

The **Asar Mahal**, to the east of the citadel, was built by Mohammed Adil Shah in about 1646 to serve as a Hall of Justice. The building was also used to house two hairs from the Prophet's beard. The rooms on the upper storey are decorated with frescoes and the front is graced with a square tank. Women are not allowed inside. The stained but richly decorated **Mihtar Mahal** to the south serves as an ornamental gateway to a small mosque.

Upli Buruj is a 16th century, 24m-high watchtower built on high ground near the western walls of the city. An external flight of stairs leads to the top, where there are a couple of hefty cannons and good views of the city and plains.

The **Malik-e-Maidan** (Monarch of the Plains) is a huge cannon measuring over 4m long, almost 1½m in diameter, and estimated to weigh 55 tonnes. It was cast in 1549 and brought to Bijapur as a war trophy thanks to the effort of 10 elephants, 400 oxen and hundreds of men.

Places to Stay

Hotel Sagar Deluxe (☎ 59234, Barakaman Rd), in the centre of town, is a new place with clean, comfortable rooms with bath for Rs 100/150 and 24 hour checkout.

Hotel Tourist (☎ 20655, Station Rd), further west, is not as good. Ordinary rooms are Rs 60/100.

KSTDC'S Hotel Mayura Adil Shahi (☎ 20934, Anand Mahal Rd) attracts a lot of travellers. Rooms are set around a leafy garden courtyard. Acceptable singles/doubles with mosquito nets, soggy bathrooms and hot water in the morning cost Rs 135/155, or deluxe doubles are Rs 175.

KSTDC'S Hotel Mayura Adil Shahi Annexe (☎ 20401, Station Rd) consists of four well-appointed air-con rooms with TV, bath and 24 hour hot water at Rs 504 including tax.

Hotel Samrat (☎ 21620, Station Rd) has large, airy doubles with bath for Rs 120, or deluxe doubles with TV and air-cooler for Rs 220.

Hotel Sanman (☎ 21866, Station Rd), opposite the Golgumbaz, has less presentable doubles/triples with bath for Rs 115/145.

Hotel Madhuvan (☎ 55571, Station Rd) is a modern and very comfortable hotel set back from the main road. Overpriced singles/doubles with TV and bath are Rs 650/850, or Rs 1080/1200 with air-con.

Places to Eat

Swapna Lodge Restaurant, on the 2nd floor of the building next to the Hotel Tourist, has good veg/nonveg food as well as cold beer. Its open-air terrace is perfect for evening dining.

Hotel Siddharth, in the busy market just north of Station Rd, is one of Bijapur's best veg places, and has a range of ice creams.

KSTDC'S Hotel Mayura Adhil Shahi has a reasonable restaurant, serving western breakfasts and Indian food, in the middle of its garden courtyard. Of all the bars in town, this one has the most pleasant setting for an evening beer.

Hotel Madhuvan, *Hotel Sanman* and *Hotel Samrat* all have restaurants and gloomy bars.

Getting There & Away

Bus There are daily services to Badami (Rs 35, four hours), Belgaum (Rs 56, five hours), Gulbarga (Rs 43, four hours), Bidar (Rs 70, seven hours), Hubli (Rs 55, 4½ hours) and Sholapur (Rs 32, two hours). There are six evening services to Bangalore (Rs 203, 12 hours in 'ultra-deluxe') via Hospet; four buses to Hyderabad and to Pune; and a couple to Bidar. There are also overnight buses to Hyderabad (Rs 151) and Mumbai (Rs 165).

There are private bus agencies near the bus stand with services to Bangalore and Mumbai.

Train Conversion to broad gauge line is complete between Bijapur and Sholapur, but is still continuing to Gadag. Once normal services resume it should be easy to get express connections to Sholapur and Gadag (via Badami). Sholapur has connections to Mumbai, Hyderabad and Bangalore; Gadag has connections to Hospet, Hubli and Bangalore. Bijapur station has a healthy quota of sleeping berths allotted to it on all major expresses. The 12.10 pm departure to Gadag connects with the *Hampi Express* to Bangalore.

Getting Around

The uncrowded local bus system has only one useful route: from the train station, along Station Rd to the gate at the western end of town. Buses run every 15 minutes.

Auto-rickshaw drivers charge what they think you will pay – intense haggling and Rs 20 should get you between the train station and the town centre. Between the Golgumbaz and Ibrahim Roza costs about Rs 25. Tonga drivers are eager for business but charge around the same.

You can rent bikes from the stall opposite the bus stand, or from outside Hotel Sanman for Rs 2 per hour.

THE NORTH-EAST
Gulbarga
☎ 08472 • pop 349,500

This dusty, scruffy town was the Bahmani capital from 1347 until its transfer to Bidar in 1428. Later the kingdom broke up into a number of smaller kingdoms – Bijapur, Bidar, Berar, Ahmednagar and Golconda. The last of these, Golconda, finally fell to Aurangzeb in 1687.

Gulbarga's **fort** is in a deteriorated state despite attempts to promote it as a tourist attraction – some locals say it's not safe to wander around the fort alone. It includes the **Jama Masjid**, reputed to have been built during the late 14th or early 15th century by a Moorish architect who is said to have imitated the great mosque in Cordoba in Spain. Gulbarga also has a number of imposing **tombs** of Bahmani kings, a shrine to an important Muslim saint and the **Sharana Basaveshwara Temple**.

Places to Stay & Eat The *KSTDC'S Hotel Mayura Bahamani* (☎ 20644, Station Rd) is a neglected place in what is considered to be a municipal garden. Rundown but clean rooms with mosquito nets, bath and hot water in the morning cost Rs 55/85. There's a bar and restaurant. The hotel is about 2km from the train station and 3km from the bus stand.

Hotel Aditya (☎ 24040, Station Rd) has well-appointed rooms with hot water in the morning for Rs 220/275, deluxe rooms for Rs 275/385 and air-con doubles for Rs 425. There's a clean restaurant (vegetarian) in the hotel.

Hotel Sanman (☎ *22801*), just off Station Rd, is friendly and the best value place in town. Clean rooms are Rs 130/190, or Rs 240/300 for deluxe rooms (with TV).

Getting There & Away There are plenty of government buses to Bijapur and Bidar (Rs 30, three hours), plus overnight buses to Bangalore. Four buses depart for Hyderabad, all of them in the evening.

An inordinate number of express trains pass through Gulbarga, giving it surprisingly good connections to Mumbai, Bangalore, Hyderabad and Kochi.

Bidar
☎ 08482

This little-visited, walled town in the extreme north-eastern corner of the state was the capital of the Bahmani kingdom from 1428, and later the capital of the Barid Shahi dynasty. It's a pleasant town with a relaxed atmosphere and a splendid 15th century **fort** containing the Ranjeenmahal, Chini Mahal and Turkish Mahal **palaces**.

The **Khwaja Mahmud Gawan Madrasa** in the middle of town has a few colourful remains of typical Islamic mosaics. The huge domed **tombs** of the Bahmani and Barid kings are also worth seeing. These abandoned structures, which dot the countryside to the west and east of town, have an enticingly desolate aura.

Bidar lent its name to the handicraft *bidriware* (for details see the Bidriware of Bidar boxed text).

Places to Stay & Eat Hotel standards in Bidar are mediocre and the choice is slim.

The Bidriware of Bidar

During its Islamic heyday, Persian craftsmen of Bidar came up with a form of damascening now known as bidriware. It involves moulding imaginative blends of blackened zinc, copper, lead and tin, which are then embossed, and overlaid or inlaid with pure silver. In both design and decoration, the artefacts are heavily influenced by the typically Islamic decorative motifs and features of the time. Finely crafted pieces such as hookahs, goblets, paan boxes and bangles are exquisitely embellished with interwoven creepers and flowing floral patterns, and occasionally framed by strict geometric lines. The effect of the delicate silver filigree against the ebony-toned background is striking. These days artists still tap away at their craft in the backstreets of Bidar, as well as in the neighbouring city of Hyderabad (Andhra Pradesh).

Hotel Ashoka (☎ *26249*), near Deepak Theatre, is the best place in town. Pleasant doubles start from Rs 130, or Rs 230 for deluxe. Air-con is Rs 410.

Hotel Ratna (☎ *27218*), *Sri New Venkateshwara Lodge* (☎ *26443*) and *Hotel Prince* (☎ *25747*) have barely acceptable singles/doubles with bath from Rs 50/80 to Rs 75/115. The first two are on the main street in the town centre, the last is on Udgir Rd, on the way into town from the bus stand.

Hotel Mayura Restaurant, opposite the bus stand, is a clean establishment where you can get reasonable Indian food and a cold beer.

Getting There & Away Bidar has plenty of bus connections to Gulbarga and Hyderabad, plus a few buses to Bijapur and Bangalore.

Top, left & middle right: The ruins of Vijayanagar (City of Victory), near the village of Hampi, Karnataka was once the capital of the largest Hindu empire in Indian history.
Bottom right: The lingam, a phallic symbol representing Shiva, and the trident, representing the trimurti of Brahma, Shiva and Vishnu, are enduring marks of Hinduism found countrywide.

Stalls are sometimes found at temple entrances, selling offerings of fruit and incense.

A young bride, Hampi.

Devarajah Market, Mysore.

Rickshaw passengers, Bijapur.

Taking a break from the daily routine, Bijapur.

Andhra Pradesh

Andhra Pradesh is situated on the Deccan (south) plateau – one of the oldest geological formations in India. The Godavari and Krishna rivers cut their way through the plateau, forming large deltas before entering the Bay of Bengal.

With its recent foray into information technology, through the new hi-tech centre on the outskirts of Hyderabad, Andhra Pradesh is promoting itself as the 'No 1 State'. Yet much of the state remains poor and undeveloped. Few travellers explore it, daunted by the long distances and poor tourist facilities. But it has plenty of interest nonetheless. The capital Hyderabad-Secunderabad is naturally a magnet due to its Muslim heritage. Warangal contains the ruins of Chalukyan-style architecture, while near Vijayawada there are ancient Hindu sites. Nagarjunakonda provides evidence of early Hindu-Buddhist societies and in the south, Tirumala and Puttaparthi are two of the most visited pilgrimage sites in the world.

History

By the 1st century AD the flourishing Satavahana dynasty reigned throughout the Deccan plateau. It had evolved from the Andhra people whose presence in southern India may date back as far as 1000 BC. In the 3rd century BC, the Andhras embraced Buddhism and built huge edifices in its honour.

From the 7th to the 10th centuries the Chalukyas established their Dravidian style of architecture especially along the coast. The Chalukya and Chola dynasties merged in the 11th century to be overthrown by the Kakatiyas who introduced pillared temples into south Indian religious architecture. Following the Kakatiya rule, the Vijayanagars rose to become one of the finest empires, not only of the region, but of India.

By the 16th century the Qutb Shahi dynasty, with its Islamic splendour, was established in Hyderabad. The Hyderabad rulers, known as the nizams, managed to re-

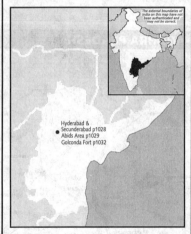

Andhra Pradesh at a Glance

Population: 76 million
Area: 276,754 sq km
Capital: Hyderabad
Main Language: Telugu
Best Time to Go: October to February

The external boundaries of India on this map have not been authenticated and may not be correct.

Hyderabad & Secunderabad p1028
Abids Area p1029
Golconda Fort p1032

- **Hyderabad –** wander the colourful bazaars, especially Laad bazaar

- **Golconda Fort –** picnic atop the ruins of this must-see 16th-century fortress

- **Tirumala's Venkateshwara Temple –** said to be the world's busiest holy site

tain relative control throughout the 17th and 18th centuries, as the British and French vied for trade. The region became part of the new independent India in 1947, and in 1956, the state of Andhra Pradesh was created – an amalgamation of the Telugu-speaking areas.

ANDHRA PRADESH

HYDERABAD & SECUNDERABAD

☎ 040 • pop 4.3 million

The twin city of Hyderabad-Secunderabad, the capital of Andhra Pradesh, combines Hindu and Islamic influences. It's a busy, noisy place, where narrow, ancient lanes meet large vehicle-choked roads. Centuries-old Islamic monuments stand alongside modern buildings. Known in some circles as Cyberabad, this city is embracing digital technology with a fervour. Hyderabad is unique among southern cities in that Urdu is the major spoken language. As capital to a 95% Hindu state, its population is almost 50% Muslim.

An important centre of Islamic culture, Hyderabad is central India's counterpart to the Mughal splendour of the northern cities of Delhi, Agra and Fatehpur Sikri.

History

Hyderabad owes its existence to a water shortage. Towards the end of the 16th cen-

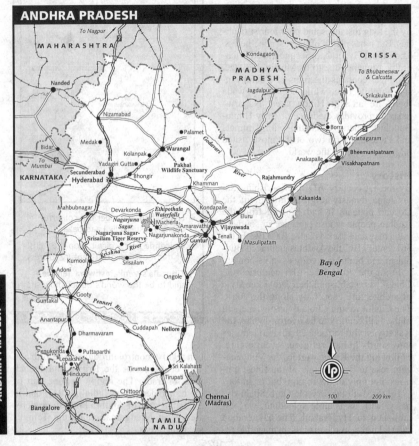

ANDHRA PRADESH

Festivals of Andhra Pradesh

festival	location	date	features
Samkranti Harvest Festival	statewide	Jan	harvest celebrations
Visakha Utsa	Visakhapatnam	Jan	cultural festival
Industrial Exhibition	Hyderabad	Jan/Feb	industrial exhibition
Deccan Festival	Hyderabad	25 Feb	cultural festival
Ugadi	statewide	Mar	Telugu new year
Mrigasira	Hyderabad	Jun/Jul	start of monsoon
Mahankali Jatra	statewide	Jun/Jul	Hindu festival to Kali
Rayalaseema Food & Dance Festival	Tirupathi	Oct	food & dance
Formation Day	statewide	1 Nov	public holiday
Pandit Motiram-Maniram Sangeet Samaroh	Hyderabad	last week of Nov	Hindu music

tury, the banks of the Musi River proved to be a preferable location for Mohammed Quli, of the Qutb Shahi dynasty. So the royal family moved from Golconda Fort to establish the new city of Hyderabad. In 1687, it was overrun by the Mughal emperor Aurangzeb. Subsequently the rulers of Hyderabad were viceroys, installed by the Mughal administration in Delhi.

In 1724 the Hyderabad viceroy, Asaf Jah, took advantage of waning Mughal power and declared Hyderabad an independent state with himself as its head. So began the dynasty of the nizams of Hyderabad, under which the traditions and customs of Islam flourished. Hyderabad developed into a focus for arts, culture and learning and the centre of Muslim India. Its abundance of rare gems and minerals furnished the nizams with enormous wealth.

In the early 1800s the British established a military barracks at Secunderabad, named after the nizam at the time, Sikander Jah. When Independence came in 1947, the then Nizam of Hyderabad, Osman Ali Khan, considered amalgamation with Pakistan, but the tensions between Muslims and Hindus increased and military intervention resulted in Hyderabad becoming part of the Indian union.

Orientation

Most of Hyderabad's places of interest are close to the Musi River. South of the river is the main landmark, the Charminar, surrounded by bustling bazaars. Nearby are the huge Mecca Masjid and the Salar Jung Museum. Just north of the river is the main bus stand (Imlibun), one of many in the city. The Hyderabad train station (known locally as Nampally station) and main post office are in the Abids and Nampally areas – a good place for budget accommodation.

Warning

Hyderabad is a city of many cultures and most of the time they live harmoniously. Occasionally, however, moments of tension and violence occur.

North of Hyderabad, and in the districts of Anantapur, Kurnool and Cuddapah, family feuds over land have resulted in violence and death. Such incidents are usually contained within the disputing parties. If you intend to travel in these areas ask locally about the current situation. Keeping informed of prevailing circumstances can assist your security.

ANDHRA PRADESH

HYDERABAD & SECUNDERABAD

OTHER
1 Hyderabad Airport
2 Hyderabad Film Club
3 Country Club
8 Book Selection
10 Central Cottage Industries
   Emporium; Lepakshi
   Handicrafts
11 Head Post Office (HPO)
12 Jubilee Bus Stand
15 Survey of India Map Sales
   Office
16 Osmania University
18 Buddha Statue
19 Lepakshi Emporium
23 Tombs of Qutb Shahi Kings
24 Golconda Fort
25 Mozamjahi Market
26 APSRTC Bus Stand
27 Imlibun Bus Stand
28 State Library
29 Osmania General Hospital
30 High Court
32 Salar Jung Museum
33 Laad Bazaar
34 Charminar
35 Mecca Masjid
36 Nehru Zoological Park

PLACES TO STAY
4 Yatri Nivas Hotel;
  Tourist Information;
  Tamarind Tree Restaurant;
  Hunter's Roost Restaurant
5 Hotel Deccan Continental
7 Hotel Karan
13 YMCA
14 Hotel Ramakrishna
17 Hotel Viceroy
20 Holiday Inn Krishna
21 Krishna Oberoi; Firdau
22 Taj Residency

PLACES TO EAT
6 Paradise Persis Restaurant
9 Kamat Hotel Restaurant
31 Qutub Shahi Dining Hall;
   Hotel Shadab

See Abids Area Map p1029

ANDHRA PRADESH

Farther north again and beyond the huge artificial lake, the Hussain Sagar, lies Secunderabad. The head post office is here and many trains terminate at Secunderabad train station. The Hyderabad airport is 8km north of the city.

Information

Tourist Offices The Andhra Pradesh Travel & Tourist Development Corporation (APTTDC) has two offices. The helpful Yatri Nivas Hotel office (☎ 460 1519), Sar-

dar Patel Rd, Secunderabad is open daily, 6.30 am to 7 pm.

The other APTTDC office (☎ 473 2554/2555) is at Gagan Vihar (5th and 11th floors), Mozamjahi Rd in Hyderabad and is open Monday to Saturday, 10.30 am to 5 pm. The small kiosk on the ground floor (6.30 am to 7 pm daily) has a basic map and brochure – sometimes. There are tourist information kiosks at Secunderabad train station and the airport. Information, at any of these offices, is scarce.

The Government of India tourist office (GITO, ☎ 763 0037) in the Sandozi Building (2nd floor) on Himayatnagar Rd is open Monday to Friday, 6 am to 7 pm.

The useful guides *Channel 6* for Rs 10 and *Hyderabad* for Rs 65 (published by Disha Books) are available from bookshops.

You can get guide maps from the Survey of India (☎ 701 8943) at Vigyan Chowk Na garik, Vinaya Kendra, Tarnaka, east of Secunderabad. If you want information on archaeological sites, visit the Archaeological

Survey of India (☎ 465 1012) 1-9-1113/30/1/C, Dayanandnagar, Vidyanagar

Money Thomas Cook (☎ 231988) is in the Nasir Arcade on the 1st floor, AG's Office Rd. Hours are Monday to Saturday, 9.30 am to 6 pm.

Banks open Monday to Friday, 10.30 am to 2.30 pm and until 12.30 pm on Saturday. Most are in the Abids area. The State Bank of India is here – down a passageway off Bank St; follow the 'do not spit' signs.

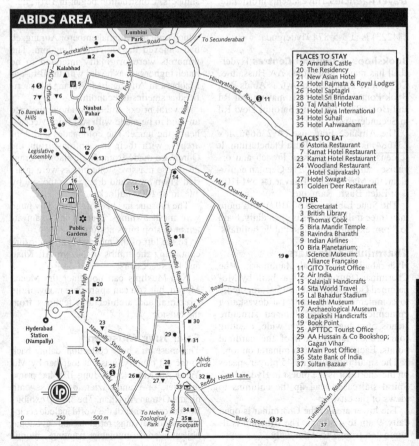

ABIDS AREA

PLACES TO STAY
2 Amrutha Castle
20 The Residency
21 New Asian Hotel
22 Hotel Rajmata & Royal Lodges
26 Hotel Saptagiri
28 Hotel Sri Brindavan
30 Taj Mahal Hotel
32 Hotel Jaya International
34 Hotel Suhail
35 Hotel Aahwaanam

PLACES TO EAT
6 Astoria Restaurant
7 Kamat Hotel Restaurant
23 Kamat Hotel Restaurant
24 Woodland Restaurant (Hotel Saiprakash)
27 Hotel Swagat
31 Golden Deer Restaurant

OTHER
1 Secretariat
3 British Library
4 Thomas Cook
5 Birla Mandir Temple
8 Ravindra Bharathi
9 Indian Airlines
10 Birla Planetarium; Science Museum; Alliance Française
11 GITO Tourist Office
12 Air India
13 Kalanjali Handicrafts
14 Sita World Travel
15 Lal Bahadur Stadium
16 Health Museum
17 Archaeological Museum
18 Lepakshi Handicrafts
19 Book Point
28 APTTDC Tourist Office
29 AA Hussain & Co Bookshop; Gagan Vihar
33 Main Post Office
36 State Bank of India
37 Sultan Bazaar

ANDHRA PRADESH

Post & Communications Post offices open 9.30 am to 5.30 pm Monday to Saturday. The main post office is on Abids Circle, Hyderabad, and is open for general business 9.30 am to 8 pm every day and for poste-restante collection Monday to Friday, 10 am to 3 pm (Saturday until 1 pm). In Secunderabad the head post office (HPO), in Rashtrapati Rd, has the same hours.

There are plenty of ISD/STD, fax and email kiosks around town, particularly in the Nampally and Abids districts.

Travel Agencies Travel agents proliferate. Prices and service vary markedly, so shop around. Sita World Travel (☎ 233638, fax 234223) is at 3-5-874 Hyderguda.

Bookshops & Cultural Centres Hyderabad has many bookshops: AA Hussain & Co is on MG Rd (also known as Abids Rd), Book Point is at 3-6 272 Himayatnagar Rd and Book Selection is in Sarojini Devi Rd in Secunderabad.

The Alliance Française (☎ 236646, fax 231684) is next to the Birla Planetarium. It screens weekly movies in French and organises cultural events. The German equivalent, the Max Mueller Bhavan (☎ 591410), is at Eden Bagh, Ramkote.

The State Library (☎ 500107) with more than three million books is open daily, 8 am to 8 pm, except Friday and public holidays.

Charminar & Bazaars

Hyderabad's principal landmark, the Charminar (four towers) was built by Mohammed Quli Qutb Shah in 1591, reputedly to commemorate the end of a devastating epidemic. This four-columned structure stands 56m high and 30m wide, creating four arches facing each of the cardinal points. Each column has a minaret on top.

The small mosque with 45 prayer spaces on the 2nd floor is the oldest in Hyderabad. Spiral staircases lead up the columns to views of the city.

The lower area of the Charminar is open daily, 9 am to 4.30 pm. The structure is illuminated from 7 to 9 pm daily.

West from the Charminar is the famous **Laad Bazaar** where you'll find just about everything (see the Laad Bazaar boxed text). Just north of the Charminar in Sardar Patel Rd is the centre of India's pearl trade, and you'll also find perfumeries, silk merchants, exquisite saris and maybe even antique books.

Mecca Masjid

Adjacent to the Charminar is the Mecca Masjid, one of the largest mosques in the world – accommodating up to 10,000 worshippers. Construction began in 1614, during the reign of Mohammed Quli Qutb Shah, but wasn't finished until 1687, by which time the Mughal emperor Aurangzeb had annexed the Golconda kingdom. The minarets were originally intended to be much higher but, as he did with the Bibi-qa-Maqbara in Aurangabad, Aurangzeb sacrificed aesthetics to economics.

Several bricks embedded above the gate are said to be made with soil from Mecca – hence the name. The colonnades and door arches, with their inscriptions from the Quran are made from single slabs of granite. These massive stone blocks were quarried 11km away and dragged to the site by a team of 1400 bullocks.

The mosque has been disfigured by huge wire mesh awnings, erected in a vain attempt to stop birds nesting.

To the left of the mosque is an enclosure containing the tombs of Nizam Ali Khan and his successors.

Non-Muslims can not enter the Mecca Masjid, but you can appreciate many of the structural and architectural features from the outside.

Salar Jung Museum

This museum's huge collection, dating back to the 1st century, was put together by Mir Yusaf Ali Khan (Salar Jung III), the prime minister, or grand vizier, of the seventh nizam, Osman Ali Khan. The 35,000 exhibits from every corner of the world include sculptures, woodcarvings, religious and devotional objects, Persian miniature paintings, illuminated manuscripts, weaponry, and over 50,000 books.

The museum is open daily except Friday, 10 am to 5 pm but avoid Sunday when it's bedlam. Entry is Rs 5. From Abids, bus No 7 will drop you at the Musi River bridge; just cross the river and take the first turn left.

Not far west of the Musi River bridge, facing each other across the river, are the spectacular **High Court** and **Osmania General Hospital** buildings, built in the Indo-Saracenic style.

Birla Mandir Temple & Planetarium

The Birla Mandir Hindu Temple, which was constructed of white Rajasthani marble in 1976, graces one of the twin rocky hills, Kalabahad, (black mountain) overlooking the southern end of Hussain Sagar. Dedicated to Lord Venkateshwara, the temple is a popular Hindu pilgrimage centre. There are excellent views over the city from the temple, especially at sunset. It's open to Hindus and non-Hindus, 7 am to noon and 3 to 9 pm.

On Naubat Pahar (drum rock), the hill adjacent to the Birla Mandir Temple, are the **Birla Planetarium & the Science Museum** (☎ 235081). The planetarium has daily sessions in Telugu, Hindi and English. Admission is Rs 10. The museum is open 10.30 am to 8.15 pm daily (closed on the last Tuesday of each month) and admission is Rs 6.

Buddha Statue & Hussain Sagar

Hyderabad boasts one of the largest stone Buddhas in the world. Work on the project began in 1985 at Raigir, 50km from Hyderabad, and was completed in early 1990. The 17.5m high, 350 tonne monolith was transported to Hyderabad and loaded onto a barge for ferrying across Hussain Sagar to be erected on the dam wall.

Unfortunately, disaster struck and the statue sank into the lake taking with it eight people. There languished for two years. Finally, in 1992, a Goan salvage company raised it (undamaged!) and it is now on a plinth in the middle of the lake.

Frequent boats make a 30 minute round trip to the statue from **Lumbini Park**, just north of Secretariat Rd, between 9 am and 6 pm for Rs 10 per head. You'll also need to pay the Rs 2 entrance fee for the park, which is a pleasant spot to enjoy Hyderabad's blood-red sunsets (open Tuesday to Sunday, 9 am to 9 pm).

The **Tankbund** skirts the eastern shore of Hussain Sagar. It has great views of the Buddha statue and is a popular promenade and jogging track.

Archaeological Museum

The Archaeological Museum contains a small collection of archaeological finds from the area, together with copies of paintings from the Ajanta caves in Maharashtra. Opening hours are 10.30 am to 5 pm daily, except Friday, and entry is Rs 0.50.

Also worth a quick visit is the nearby **Health Museum**, where you'll see a bizarre and eclectic collection of medical and public health paraphernalia. It's open 10.30 am to 1.30 pm and 2 to 5 pm; admission is free.

And there's an **aquarium** nearby in Jawahar Bal Bhavan. It's open daily, except Sunday, 10.30 am to 5 pm.

Nehru Zoological Park

One of the largest zoos in India, the Nehru Zoological Park is spread over 1.2 sq km of landscaped gardens. The 3000 animals and birds here live in large, open enclosures and don't look any less bored than animals in zoos elsewhere in the world. There's a prehistoric animal section, a toy train (Rs 1, every 15 minutes) a lion safari trip (Rs 5, every 15 minutes) and a nocturnal section.

The park is open daily except Monday from 9 am to 5 pm; entry costs Rs 1 (Rs 20 for cars). Once again, it's chaos on Sunday.

Golconda Fort

This 16th-century fortress is a must-see. Like many of the great forts in India, Golconda exudes a palpable sense of history.

It has experienced many waves of occupation and abandonment. Although the bulk of the fort dates from the time of the Qutb

Shah kings (16th to 17th centuries) its origins have been traced to the earlier Hindu periods when the Yadavas and, later, the Kakatiyas ruled this part of India.

For nearly 80 years Golconda was the capital of the independent state Telangana, but in 1590, Sultan Quli Qutb Shah abandoned the fort and moved to the new city of Hyderabad.

In the 17th century, Mughal armies from Delhi were sent against the Golconda kingdom to enforce payment of tribute. Abul Hasan, the last of the Qutb Shahi kings, held out at Golconda for eight months against the massive army of emperor Aurangzeb. The emperor finally succeeded via the treacherous actions of an insider, Abdullah Khan Pani.

Following Aurangzeb's death early in the next century, his viceroys (later the nizams) made Hyderabad their capital once again, and Golconda was abandoned.

When standing at the top of the fort, it's easy to see how the Mughal army came close to total defeat. The citadel is built on a granite hill 120m high and is surrounded by crenellated ramparts constructed of large masonry blocks. The massive gates are studded with large pointed iron spikes, intended to obstruct war elephants. Outside the citadel stands another crenellated rampart, surrounding the base of the hill, with a perimeter of 11km. Outside this wall is a third wall.

Survival within the fort was attributable not only to the walls, but also to water and sound. A complex series of concealed glazed earthen pipes ensured a reliable water supply and the acoustics guaranteed that even the smallest sound from the Grand Portico would echo across the fort complex, making anonymity impossible. Even today, silence only comes with stillness, and it is worth being still to consider the great tides that have moved through the fort.

Knowledgeable guides congregate at the entrance. They'll start asking Rs 250 for a 90 minute tour and rapidly lose interest in any offer below Rs 150. Alternatively, the *Guide to Golconda Fort & Qutb Shahi Tombs* (Rs 10) may be on sale.

The fort is open 8 am to 6.30 pm daily, and entrance costs Rs 2 (free on Friday). To get to the fort's main entrance, Balahisar Gate, take city bus No 119 or 142 from Nampally High Rd (Public Gardens Rd), outside the public gardens (Rs 3, 11km, one hour). An auto-rickshaw from Abids costs around Rs 150 return, including waiting charges. Early morning is best for relative peace and quiet – tour groups arrive from 11 am.

There's also a sound-and-light show here; for more information see Organised Tours, later in this section.

Tombs of Qutb Shahi Kings

These graceful domed tombs are about 1.5km north-west of Golconda Fort's Balahisar Gate. Surrounded by landscaped gardens, they are open daily except Friday, 9.30 am to 4.30 pm. Entrance is Rs 2. Most people walk from Golconda to the tombs, but there are usually a few auto-rickshaws willing to take you for a handsome price.

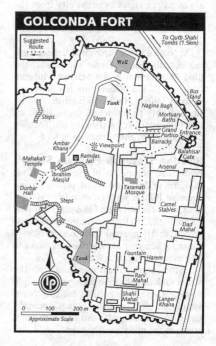

Organised Tours

The APTTDC (☎ 473 2554/2555, bookings ☎ 460 1519/1520) conducts daily tours of the city; pick up at 7.45 am from Yatri Nivas Hotel, 7.55 am from Secunderabad train station, 8.30 am from Gagan Vihar on Mozamjahi Rd, and finish at 5.15 pm at the Birla Mandir. The cost is Rs 100 (children over four, Rs 65) plus entry charges and includes a vegetarian lunch. The tours visit Buddha Statue, Qutb Shahi Tombs, Golconda Fort, Salar Jung Museum, Mecca Masjid, Charminar, Nehru Zoo, the inevitable handicrafts emporium, Birla Mandir Temple and the Planetarium. Brief stops are all you'll get, but if you're short of time, the tour is good value. Some tours do not include all sites.

Daily tours to Nagarjuna Sagar leave at 6.30 am and return at 9.30 pm; see Nagarjunakonda's Getting There & Away section for details. APTTDC also conducts weekend tours to the Venkateshwara Temple at Tirupathi (child/adult Rs 600/700); fare includes travel and accommodation.

The *Deccan by Dusk* tour, visits Lumbini Park and the Qutb Shahi tombs before going on to Golconda Fort for a quick tour and the sound-and-light show. This tour departs Yatri Nivas Hotel at 2 pm, returns at 8.45 pm and costs Rs 70 (including ticket for sound-and-light show). If you make your own way to the fort you can see the sound-and-light show for Rs 20. It starts at 6.30 pm (November to February) and 7 pm (March to October). Sessions are in Telugu, Hindi and English. No sessions on Monday.

Customised tours can be arranged at the APTTDC, as well as the many travel agents.

Places to Stay – Budget

The best of the cheap hotels are all in the Nampally/Abids area between Abids Circle and Hyderabad (Nampally) train station.

Royal Lodge, Royal Home, Royal Hotel, Neo Royal Hotel and *Gee Royal Lodge* are built around a courtyard opposite the station on Nampally High Rd (Public Gardens Rd). They're all similar – at Rs 100/180 for singles/doubles with not-very-clean bath and hot water in the morning only. All rooms have fans. The Royal Lodge claims to take only Indian residents.

New Asian Hotel (☎ 201275), across the road, is a typical, no-frills boarding house, but it's adequate at Rs 45/155 for older rooms and Rs 85/260 for newer rooms which look just as old. All rooms have bathrooms (though many have semi-detached plumbing) and fan.

Hotel Sri Brindavan (☎ 320 3970) near Abids Circle is good value. It offers singles/doubles with bath for Rs 220/280, with hot water from 4 to 7.30 am. Rooms are set around a quiet courtyard.

Hotel Suhail (☎ 510142) is clean and quiet with standard rooms for Rs 120/145, deluxe rooms for Rs 145/160 and air-con doubles for Rs 250. All rooms have TV and hot-water bath, and most have a balcony.

The *YMCA (☎ 756 4670)* accepts male and female guests and has six branches. The Secunderabad branch at the northern end of Station Rd has rooms for Rs 70/100. The branch of greater Hyderabad on Narayunguda Rd has rooms for Rs 85/120. Rooms don't have attached bath.

Only Secunderabad train station has *Retiring Rooms*. Air-con rooms are Rs 165/240 and non air-con rooms cost Rs 60/90. Dormitory rates are Rs 35 for 24 hours.

Places to Stay – Mid-Range

The *Yatri Nivas Hotel (☎ 840005, fax 867448, Sardar Patel Rd)* in Secunderabad has large, clean rooms for Rs 425/450 or Rs 550/600 with air-con. It has two good restaurants and a helpful tourist office.

Hotel Rajmata (☎ 320 1000) has 'deluxe' rooms (no air-con) with colour TV for Rs 300/380. There's a restaurant here with veg and nonveg food.

Hotel Saptagiri (☎ 460 3601, Nampally Station Rd), is clean. The rooms are small but good value at Rs 140/190, and Rs 350 for a double with air-con. All the rooms have a balcony and hot-water bath.

Hotel Aahwaanam (☎ 590301), opposite the noisy Ramakrishna Cinema, is huge with decent rooms for Rs 200/250 or Rs 300/350 with air-con. All the rooms have

ANDHRA PRADESH

bathrooms (bucket showers) with hot water and TV.

Hotel Jaya International (☎ 475 2929, fax 475 3919, Reddy Hostel Lane), off Bank St, has clean, comfortable rooms for Rs 210/320 or Rs 460/565 with air-con and TV.

Taj Mahal Hotel (☎ 237988), at the junction of MG and King Kothi Rds, is rambling and deservedly popular. Spacious rooms with bath, hot water and TV cost Rs 290/490, or Rs 420/570 with air-con. Facilities include two vegetarian restaurants and a coffee shop.

Hotel Ramakrishna (☎ 834567, 831133, fax 846609), opposite the Railway Reservation Complex in Secunderabad, is good value with clean rooms and piping hot water. Choose a back room, away from the noisy traffic. Non air-con single/double rooms are Rs 290/360, and air-con singles/doubles are Rs 370/450. The hotel has a good veg and nonveg restaurant. Alcohol is prohibited.

Places to Stay – Top End
Hotel Viceroy (☎ 753 8383, fax 753 8797), on the Tankbund towards Secunderabad, has comfortable, well-appointed singles/doubles for Rs 1500/1800 or Rs 1700/2000 with a lake view. All rates include a buffet breakfast. This centrally air-con hotel has the usual facilities, including email (for nonguests too).

Hotel Deccan Continental (☎ 840981, fax 840980, Sir Ronald Ross Rd, Secunderabad) has spotless rooms (some with splendid views) from Rs 800/900 with air-con, Rs 420/620, without. As well as two multicuisine restaurants, the hotel has a beer garden.

Hotel Karan (SD Rd, Secunderabad) has air-con single/doubles with bath from Rs 570/720 and suites between Rs 950 and Rs 1400. They have 24 hour hot water and a multicuisine restaurant (closed, 3 to 7 pm).

Amrutha Castle (☎ 598664, fax 241850, Secretariat Rd) is modelled on Mad King Ludwig's Bavarian folly, Neuschwanstein (by way of Disneyland and Camelot). Modern, well-appointed rooms start at Rs 1200/2300, and suites go for Rs 1800 to Rs 4000. Facilities include a fax in every room, a restaurant, coffee shop, gym and a rooftop pool.

The Residency (☎ 204060, fax 204040, Public Gardens Rd) lives up to its claim of providing five star comfort for three star prices. Standard rooms are Rs 950/1200. Executive and deluxe rooms are also available. Its numerous assets include plush (quiet) lobby and a 24 hour coffee shop.

Most of the five-star hotels are on Road No 1 at Banjara Hills. They're all centrally air-conditioned and have excellent restaurants and all facilities. All attract 20% tax.

Taj Residency (☎ 399999, fax 392218) is pleasantly situated on an artificial lake. Rates are from Rs 2200 to Rs 3030 in the executive rooms, including breakfast. *Holiday Inn Krishna (☎ 393939, fax 392682)*, just off Road No 1, has modern and luxurious rooms from Rs 2500 to Rs 4600. *Krishna Oberoi (☎ 392323, fax 393079)* is a palatial hotel with rooms costing from Rs 2500 to Rs 9000.

Places to Eat
The cuisine of Andhra Pradesh has two major influences. The northern Mughals and the former local nizam palaces brought the tasty *biryanis* of spiced meats, vegetables and rice, *haleem* (pounded spiced wheat with mutton) and kebabs. The Andhra styles combine vegetables with spices, particularly chilli and mustard. Andhra pickle, with chilli paste, lime peel and mango, is a particularly hot favourite. Mozamjahi Market at the corner of Mukkarramjahi and Jawaharlal Nehru Rds has alluring architecture and is a great place to buy fruits and vegetables.

Woodland, in the Hotel Saiprakash, Nampally Station Rd, does great south Indian veg breakfasts, snacks and meals.

Any *Kamat Hotel* dishes up good cheap meals. The main dishes are Rs 12 to Rs 25. There's one in Secunderabad on Sarojini Devi Rd, another in Abids on AG's Office Rd, and a third on Nampally Station Rd.

Astoria Restaurant, opposite Kamat Hotel on AG's Office Rd, is a popular open-air dinner spot. *Qutub Shahi Dining Hall* (downstairs) and *Hotel Shadab* (upstairs), at High Court Rd, Madina Circle, have sumptuous Andhran and north Indian meals from Rs 40.

Golden Deer on MG Rd, not far from Abids Circle, is more expensive, but a good choice for dinner. It's air-con and specialises in Chinese and Indian meals starting around Rs 45. *Hotel Ramakrishna* is also air-conditioned and has dosas from Rs 15 and biryanis from Rs 25.

Paradise Persis Restaurant, near the corner of Sardar Patel Rd and MG Rd, Secunderabad, is famous for its authentic Hyderabadi cuisine. This is *the* place to eat. It's a multilayered maze of eating venues with flashing fairy lights. At the sidewalk take-away try the juicy kababs for Rs 100.

The Hunter's Roost and the *Tamarind Tree* are relaxing and attractive outdoor venues attached to Yatri Nivas. The Hunter's Roost is multicuisine with a bar.

Top-end hotels all have excellent restaurants and coffee shops, in particular the *Dakhni* at the Taj Residency and the *Firdau* at the Krishna Oberoi. Expect to pay at least Rs 250 to Rs 500 per person. The Taj Residency's *Kabab-e-Bahar* is a less formal barbecue/kebab restaurant set outdoors on a small lake, with excellent veg and non-veg dishes for around Rs 150.

Entertainment

The *Ravindra Bharati Theatre* conducts nightly performances of music, drama and dance. Details are available from tourist offices and local papers. For discos try the *Gateway Hotel* at Banjara Hills (☎ 222222). Clubs may also have discos but usually for members only. An exception is the Country Club disco, *Pyramid* (☎ 312000). With the recent relaxation of liquor laws, many hotels are now providing music and dance venues.

There is a plethora of cinemas in Hyderabad showing Tamil and Telugu films. The *Hyderabad Film Club* (☎ 290265/290841) runs screenings of foreign films, sometimes in conjunction with the Alliance Française.

Hyderabad is a popular venue for cultural festivals, art exhibitions, forums, workshops, book fairs and car rallies. The city guide *Channel 6* or the daily papers will have details.

If you're into rocks, the *Save the Rocks Society* (☎ 238253) organises walks through the surreal Andhran landscape to raise awareness of the damage of intensive quarrying.

Shopping

The best place to buy arts and crafts from all over India is Kalanjali on Nampally High Rd. This shop has fixed prices and will send purchases anywhere around the world. It's open daily, 10 am to 8 pm. Central Cottage Industries Emporium is at 94 Minerva Complex on Sarojini Devi Rd, Secunderabad. Lepakshi, with a variety of crafts, has an outlet here and an emporium on Tankbund.

Silk and sari shops dominate the lower section of Nampally Station Rd. One of the biggest is Gianey's Silks and Saris, opposite Pulla Reddy Sweets. Fancy Silks, 21-2-28, Pathergatti, near the Charminar is also good.

Getting There & Away

Hyderabad has air, road and rail links to most major Indian cities and some overseas.

Air The Air India office (☎ 211804) is opposite the Legislative Assembly. International flights leave for Kuwait (twice weekly),

---

Laad Bazaar

Carts of colourful *lac* bangles line the street. Bright brocades hang outside shops, their silver and gold sequins glittering in the sun. In small boutiques, druggists sit and face their huge old scales and in old glass cases, incense sticks sit happily beside ointments for piles. Book stalls sell exam papers for the higher degree.

At intervals along the tiny street, men wash and carefully arrange betel leaf, dye merchants create mountains of coloured powders. Nearby tiny boys stand proudly by their trolley of pure plastic kitsch.

Traders are interspersed with craftspeople and camels drift slowly across the scene. Lacquer workers, silversmiths and drum makers; together they set a calm and continual vibration to which the entire market pulsates.

ANDHRA PRADESH

Muscat (three weekly) and Sharjah (three weekly). Air India also has flights to Mumbai and Chennai.

Indian Airlines (☎ 599333) is nearby and open daily, 10 am to 1 pm and 2 to 5.25 pm. There are Indian Airlines flights in both directions between Hyderabad and Bangalore (US$95, daily), Mumbai (US$105, three daily), Calcutta (US$190, daily except Tuesday and Sunday), Delhi (US$165, twice daily), Chennai (US$95, twice daily), Nagpur (US$95, twice weekly), Vizag (US$100, daily) and Tirupathi (US$75, twice weekly).

Jet Airways (☎ 3301222) flies daily to Bangalore, Mumbai and Calcutta.

Bus Of the several bus stands in Hyderabad, the main one is the Andhra Pradesh State Road Transport Corporation (AP-SRTC) Hyderabad/Imlibun complex at Gowliguda. Buses leave Imlibun bus stand (☎ 513955) for all parts of the state. They are well organised with timetables in Telugu and English. A computerised advance booking office is open 8 am to 9 pm daily. The Jubilee bus stand (☎ 780 2203), Secunderabad, operates a similar service with buses to destinations in the north and west.

Bus services from Hyderabad include:

destination	frequency (per day)	fare (Rs)
Aurangabad	3	140
Bangalore	11 (mainly evening)	198
Bidar	19	37
Chennai	1 (4.30 pm)	230
Gulbarga	6	97
Hospet	2	108
Kurnool	22	90
Mumbai	12	290
Nagpur	2	170
Nizamabad	32	50
Tirupathi	11	178
Vijayawada	32	100

Private bus companies have superdeluxe video services to Bangalore, Mumbai, Chennai, Nagpur and Tirupathi. Most of their offices are on Nampally High Rd near the entrance road to Hyderabad station. Daily departures are usually in the late afternoon. To Bangalore or Nagpur it's Rs 220 (12 hours); to Mumbai or Chennai it's Rs 250 (14 hours).

Train There are three train stations in Hyderabad – Secunderabad, Hyderabad (also known as Nampally) and Kacheguda. Secunderabad is the main station where you catch through trains (trains not originating in Hyderabad). Most stop at Kacheguda, a convenient set-down for Abids and the old city. Bookings for any train can be made at Hyderabad and Secunderabad stations, Monday to Saturday, 8 am to 8 pm, (4 pm on Sunday). Both stations have a tourist quota. For general inquiries ☎ 131; for reservations, cancellations and availability ☎ 135.

Trains leave for every part of the country. To Calcutta, you must first take a train to Vijayawada and then change to one of the east coast express trains such as the *Coromandel Express*. The fare to Calcutta is Rs 317/1209 in 2nd/1st class and the 1591km trip takes 30 hours.

Getting Around

The system of multinumbered addresses makes Hyderabad a confusing city to negotiate. Languages other than Telugu, Hindi and Urdu are rarely spoken or understood. However all this is more than compensated by the local cooperation and assistance.

To/From the Airport The airport is at Begampet, 8km north of Abids. There is no airport bus. An auto-rickshaw from Abids costs about Rs 40. Taxis ask about Rs 120.

Bus Buses you might find useful include:

No 2 – Secunderabad station to Charminar

No 7 – Secunderabad station to Afzalganj and return (this is the one to catch if you're heading for Abids, as it goes down Tankbund and Nehru Rd via the main post office)

No 8 & 8A – Secunderabad station to Hyderabad station

No 119 & 142 – Nampally High Rd to Golconda Fort

ANDHRA PRADESH

Major Trains from Hyderabad

destination	train no & name	departure time[1]	distance (km)	duration	fare (Rs) (2nd/1st)
Aurangabad	7664 *Manmad-Kacheguda Exp*	7.30 pm S	517	14 h	161/556
Bangalore	5092 *G/S-Bangalore Exp*[2]	6.20 pm S	790	15 h 50	214/766
Calcutta	7046 *East Coast Exp*	7.30 am S	1591	30 h	317/1209
Chennai	7054 *Hyderabad-Madras Exp*	3.30 pm H	794	14 h 25 min	214/766
Delhi	2723 *Andhra Pradesh Exp*	7.10 am H	1397	26 h 20 min	302/1102
	7021 *Dakshin Exp*	8.00 pm H		33 h 30 min	302/1102
Mumbai	7032 *Hyderabad-Mumbai Exp*	8.40 pm H	800	15 h	214/766
Tirupathi	7597 *Venkatadri Link Exp*	3.50 pm S	741	17 h 40 min	206/726

[1] S – Secunderabad, H – Hyderabad
[2] *Gorakhpur/Secunderabad-Bangalore Express*

There are several city bus stands and the main one, Hyderabad, is adjacent to the Imlibun (state service) in Gowliguda.

The 'Travel As You Like' ticket, available at any of the major bus stands or Secunderabad train station, permits unlimited bus travel anywhere within the city area for the day of purchase.

Car You can rent a car and driver from the APTTDC for Rs 450 for a half day within the city area. Outside the city, rates vary from Rs 4 to Rs 5 per kilometre, depending on the company (almost double if you want air-con). You can arrange car travel at many hotels. Hertz cars can be rented from Hotel Viceroy (☎ 618383) and Alpha Motors (☎ 201306), 17 Abids Shopping Centre. See also Organised Tours, earlier in this section.

Auto-Rickshaw & Taxi By the meter, auto-rickshaws cost Rs 6 for the first 2km plus Rs 3 for each additional kilometre. There's a minimum fee of Rs 5.60. Most drivers prefer a negotiated price rather than the metered one. Between 10 pm and 5 am you may have to pay a 50% surcharge. Taxis cost about twice as much as auto-rickshaws.

Around Hyderabad

There are several sites of interest near Hyderabad which can be visited in a day. Just 100km north of Hyderabad, is the **Medak** Christian church. Built in neo-Gothic style and famed for its stained glass, it can accommodate a congregation of 5000. The **fort** at Medak was built by the Kakatiyas and developed later by the Qutb Shahis. It's known for its huge gateway, Mubarek Mahal.

About 70km north-east of Hyderabad on the way to Warangal, **Kolanpak** has a beautifully sculptured, 2000-year-old Jain temple with a jade image of Mahavira.

NAGARJUNAKONDA
☎ 08680
Nagarjunakonda is 150km south-east of Hyderabad. Prehistoric remnants suggest that

ANDHRA PRADESH

human activity began here some 200,000 years ago. From the 2nd century BC until the early 3rd century AD, Nagarjunakonda and nearby Amaravathi became the sites of powerful Hindu and Buddhist empires.

Nagarjunakonda may be named after Nagarjuna, the revered Buddhist monk, who governed the *sangha* (Buddhist monastery) for nearly 60 years around the turn of the 2nd century AD. He founded the Madhyamika school, which studied and developed the teachings of Mahayana Buddhism.

The ancient remains at the site were discovered in 1926 by archaeologist AR Saraswathi. In 1950 the area was chosen as the site for a huge reservoir, the **Nagarjuna Sagar**, for irrigation and the generation of electricity. Before the flooding in 1960, excavations unearthed Buddhist ruins: *stupas*, *viharas*, *chaityas* and *mandapams*, as well as some outstanding examples of white marble depictions of the life of the Buddha. Many of these ancient monuments and structures were removed and rebuilt on an island in the middle of the dam.

The **Nagarjunakonda Museum** is also on the island. It's well laid out with information in Telugu, Hindi and English. Stone age picks, hoes and spears are on show. Impressive sculptures of large, voluptuous women stand next to exquisite Buddha statues.

The museum is open daily (except Friday), 9 am to 4 pm. Launches depart for the island from the village of Vijayapuri, on the banks of Nagarjuna Sagar, at 9.30 am and 1.30 pm each day (not Friday). The one-hour trip costs Rs 10/20 per child/adult.

The launch stays at the island for 30 minutes. To do the place justice take the morning launch out to the island and the afternoon one back. You may be told that you require a permit to do this – you don't. Weekends and holidays are crowded, so extra express launches may run for Rs 20/30. Light refreshments only are available on the island.

Places to Stay

Nagarjunakonda is popular and accommodation can be tight during May school holidays. It's also rather basic; sleeping sheet territory!

Vijay Vihar Complex (☎ 2125) is operated by the APTTDC. The beds in this spacious, crumbling hotel are in urgent need of replacements. Singles/doubles are Rs 320/470. The downstairs restaurant has a good range of veg and nonveg meals.

Project House (☎ 2040) is also APTTDC operated. Three kilometres from the jetty in a landscaped garden at Hill Colony, it offers basic rooms for Rs 220/330. The vegetarian restaurant is OK. There's a friendly tourist office with no maps, no brochures and no information.

There is also an OK *Youth Hostel* in Hill Colony; a bed costs Rs 15 to Rs 25, depending on the size of the room.

A number of basic, clean, and private *rooms* are available near Project House for around Rs 100 per room per day. For details check at the Suranthi Wine Shop.

Getting There & Away

The easiest way to visit Nagarjunakonda from Hyderabad is to take the APTTDC (☎ 040-816375) tour. It departs Hyderabad daily (if demand warrants it) at 6.30 am from Yatri Nivas Hotel, returns at 9.30 pm and costs Rs 150/200 per child/adult, lunch included. The tour includes visits to the Nagarjunakonda Museum (closed Friday), Nagarjuna Sagar and Ethipothala Waterfalls.

If you'd prefer to make your own way there, regular buses link Hyderabad, Vijayawada and Guntur with Nagarjuna Sagar. The nearest train station is 22km away at Macherla (a branch line running west from Guntur) from where buses leave regularly for Nagarjuna Sagar.

WARANGAL

☎ 08712 • pop 537,000

About 157km north-east of Hyderabad, Warangal was the capital of the Kakatiya kingdom which covered the greater part of present-day Andhra Pradesh from the late 12th to early 14th century until it was conquered by the Tughlaqs of Delhi. The Hindu Kakatiyas were great patrons of the arts, and during their reign the Chalukyan style of temple architecture reached its pinnacle.

If you have an interest in Hindu temple development then an outing to Warangal is worthwhile. Facilities are adequate for an overnight stop, or it can be visited in a long day trip from Hyderabad.

Warangal is a cotton market town. There's also a colourful **wool market** around the bus stand area in the cooler months.

Orientation & Information

The main locations of interest and information are Warangal, Hanamkonda (3km northwest of Warangal) and Kazipet (10km southwest of Warangal).

The Warangal train station and bus stand are opposite each other. Station Rd, running left as you leave the train station, is the main area for facilities including the post office and police station. Main Rd connects Warangal and Hanamkonda.

Kazipet, the train junction for northbound trains, has a tourist kiosk. The Regional Tourist Information Bureau is 3km north of here at the Tourist Resthouse and the Forest Department is nearby but all have very limited resources.

Bank hours are Monday to Friday, 10.30 am to 2.30 pm and until 12.30 pm on Saturday. For foreign exchange, go to the State Bank of Hyderabad (not weekends), opposite the Regional Tourist Information Bureau. Few places accept credit cards.

There's no shortage of local/STD/ISD booths; many open 24 hours.

Fort

Warangal's fort was a huge construction with three distinct circular strongholds surrounded by a moat. Four paths with decorative gateways, set according to the cardinal points, led to the centre where a huge Shiva temple once existed. The gateways are still obvious, but much of the fort is in ruins.

The fort is 5km from Warangal at Mantukonda and easily reached by bus or autorickshaw.

Hanamkonda

Built in 1163, the **1000-Pillared Temple** on the slopes of Hanamkonda Hill, 400m from the Hanamkonda crossroads, is a fine example of Chalukyan architecture. Dedicated to three deities – Shiva, Vishnu and Surya, it has been carefully restored with intricately carved pillars and a central, very impressive Nandi. It's open 6 am to 6 pm.

Down the hill and 3km to the right is the small **Siddheshwara Temple**. The **Bhadrakali Temple** featuring a stone statue of the goddess Kali, seated with a weapon in each of her eight hands, is high on a hill halfway between Hanamkonda and Warangal.

Places to Stay

Accommodation facilities are modest. In addition to room charges, several hotels have a once only guest charge of up to Rs 30.

Vijaya Lodge (☎ 61781/61782) on Station Rd, three minutes from the train station, is OK value at Rs 60/100 for rooms with bath, or Rs 110 for a double room with phone.

Vikas Lodge (☎ 24194), behind the bus stand and near the markets, has basic rooms with bath for Rs 55/75.

Ashok (☎ 85491, Main Rd) at Hanamkonda, is 7km from Warangal train station and has singles/doubles for Rs 180/255; with air-con it's Rs 340/420. It's spacious and noisy with occasional hot water. It has two good restaurants; one serves liquor.

Hotel Ratna (☎ 60645, fax 60096), newer than Ashok, has singles/doubles for Rs 200/270 and air-con doubles for Rs 450 and Rs 550. It accepts MasterCard and Visa.

Chariot, the AP tourist resthouse, is on the main road (3km before Kazipet bus stand) opposite the Regional Engineering College. The basic but spacious double rooms (no singles) are Rs 130. A dormitory of six beds costs Rs 300 (total). The resthouse has a good vegetarian restaurant. The Regional Tourist Information Bureau is also here.

Retiring Rooms at the Warangal train station are Rs 30/60 (non air-con) and Rs 50/100 (air-con). There are also *Retiring Rooms* at Kazipet train station.

Places to Eat

There are several small snack houses but few eating places in Warangal. *Ashok* and

ANDHRA PRADESH

Hotel Ratna have restaurants with good food. *Ruchi Restaurant* in central Station Rd serves nonveg dishes. *Kapila Restaurant* at the Hanamkonda crossroads has veg meals from Rs 20 and nonveg from Rs 95.

Getting There & Away

Regular buses run between Warangal and Hyderabad, Nizamabad and other major centres. Local buses connect Warangal with Kazipet and Hanamkonda.

Warangal is a major rail junction and there are regular trains to main cities such as Delhi and Chennai, as well as Hyderabad or Secunderabad (Rs 76/220 in 2nd/1st class, 152km, three hours) and Vijayawada (Rs 85/272, 209km, four hours). The three hour journey from Hyderabad makes a one day trip to Warangal and surrounds possible.

Getting Around

The bus stand is opposite the entrance to the train station. Bus No 28 will take you the 5km to the Warangal Fort at Mantukonda. Regular buses go to all the other sites. You can rent bikes (with crossbars) in Station St (Rs 2 an hour/Rs 12 a day). Auto-rickshaws and cycle-rickshaws are other alternatives.

AROUND WARANGAL
Palampet

Sixty kilometres north-east of Warangal the **Ramappa Temple**, built in 1234, provides another attractive example of Kakatiya architecture. Its pillars are ornately carved and its eaves shelter fine statues of female forms. The temple is open 6 am to 6.30 pm daily.

Just 1km south, the **Ramappa Cheruvu**, an artificial lake, now assumes a natural presence within the landscape. The *Vanavihar Guesthouse*, on the banks of the lake, has double rooms with bath for Rs 12 per person. You must book with the tourist information bureau in Kazipet and you'll need to bring all your own provisions.

VISAKHAPATNAM
☎ 0891 • pop 1.15 million
This coastal city is the commercial and industrial heart of Andhra Pradesh's isolated north-east corner, and is home to India's largest shipbuilding yard. Originally it was two separate towns – the northern and more urbane Waltair and the southern port town of Visakhapatnam (known as Vizag). However, as Vizag grew the pair gradually merged.

Orientation & Information

The train station and bus stand are about 1.5km apart. Both are about 2km from the city centre, which is based loosely around the Poorna Market area. The beach hotels are all in Waltair, which is the most pleasant place to stay. The tourist office in the train station has little information.

Things to See & Do

These days the twin towns have little to offer tourists. The best known sight is the rocky promontory known as the **Dolphin's Nose** (accessed only 3 to 5 pm daily) jutting into the harbour. Waltair, the hilly seaside area, is edged by long beaches affording views across the Bay of Bengal and the busy Calcutta-Chennai shipping lane.

At Simhachalam Hill, 16km north-east, is a fine 11th century **Vishnu Temple** in Orissan style. It's open daily for *puja* (worship) only (Rs 2, Rs 10 or Rs 30 – depending on the level of *darshan*, or viewing of the god). The best beach is **Rushikonda**, 10km north-east.

The APSRTC (☎ 546446) operates full-day city tours (including Vishnu Temple) for Rs 95 per person and day tours (weekends only) to Araku/Borra caves for Rs 165.

Places to Stay & Eat

There's no shortage of places to stay for any budget. The *Retiring Rooms* at the train station include men-only dorm beds for Rs 15 and comfortable doubles at Rs 160.

City Centre A good area for cheap hotels is Main Rd near the Poorna Market.

Hotel Poorna (☎ 502344) off Main Rd, has clean singles/doubles with bath from Rs 85/160, plus a once only guest charge of Rs 30. *Swagath Restaurant* nearby on Main Rd has a small rooftop garden and cheap vegetarian meals and snacks.

Sree Lekha Lodge (☎ 502693), in the quieter Dabagardens, is a good choice with rooms from Rs 58/120 to Rs 175/200.

Hotel Daspalla (☎ 564825, fax 562043) has rooms (air-con only) for Rs 510/625 or Rs 620/725 for executive style. The three star hotel has several restaurants serving Chinese, continental, tandoori and spicy local cuisine.

Dolphin Hotels Limited (☎ 567000, fax 567555) is a central four star place with a swimming pool and three restaurants – south Indian, multicuisine and a 24 hour coffee shop. Rooms range from Rs 595/795 to Rs 1025/1225, and breakfast is included in rooms priced above Rs 795.

Beach Area At the northern end of Beach Rd, *Palm Beach Hotel* (☎ 554026) is old and run-down, but it's OK if you just want to be close to the beach. Rooms are Rs 350/400 or Rs 550/750 with air-con.

Park Hotel (☎ 554488, fax 554181), next door, looks old and ugly from the outside but the rooms are modern and comfortable. Air-con rooms, all with a sea view, cost Rs 1200/2050. There's a swimming pool and three restaurants, and the staff are friendly.

Taj Residency (☎ 567756, fax 564370), Vizag's best, is a luxurious, tiered hotel that climbs the hill from Beach Rd. It has a swimming pool and a restaurant, and room prices range from Rs 1650 to Rs 4500 plus 20% tax.

Sai Priya Resorts (☎ 815284, fax 815344) at Rushikonda is excellent value with rooms and cottages with ocean views from Rs 300 to Rs 800.

Getting There & Away

Air Vizag's airport is 13km west of town; costing Rs 100 by auto-rickshaw. Indian Airlines (☎ 546501) flies to Calcutta (US$130) on Tuesday, Thursday and Saturday; to Chennai (US$105) on Sunday, Monday, Wednesday and Friday; and to Hyderabad (US$100) daily.

Train Visakhapatnam Junction station is on the main Calcutta-Chennai line. To Calcutta, the best train is the overnight *Coro-*

mandel Express (Rs 213/758 in 2nd/1st class, 879km, 15 hours). Heading south, it goes to Vijayawada (Rs 108/390, 352km, 5½ hours) and Chennai Central (Rs 198/772, 784km, 15 hours).

Bus From the well-organised bus stand, the APSRTC (☎ 546400) has services to destinations within Andhra Pradesh, as well as Puri in Orissa.

Boat A boat leaves once every two months for Port Blair, Andaman Islands. Bookings for the 56 hour journey can be made at the Shipping Office, which is on AV Bhanoji Row (☎ 565597, fax 566507), within the port complex. See Port Blair in the Andaman & Nicobar Islands chapter for more details.

AROUND VISAKHAPATNAM

About 25km north-east of Vizag, **Bheemunipatnam**, is one of the east coast's oldest Dutch settlements. Apart from a few tombs, little remains. A little way inland from here is **Hollanders Green**, the Dutch cemetery.

Some 90km north of Vizag are the million-year-old limestone **Borra caves** which are filled with stalagmite and stalactite formations. A farther 30km north is the **Araku Valley**, home to a number of isolated tribal communities.

VIJAYAWADA
☎ 0866 • pop 853,300

Vijayawada, at the head of the delta of the mighty Krishna river, has established itself as a major port and an important junction on the east coast train line from Calcutta to Chennai. About 265km east of Hyderabad and 70km inland from the sea, it's an important industrial centre and a hectic town.

For many, Vijayawada is the heart of Andhra culture and language. The main attractions here are the temples, including the ancient rock cave temples.

Tourist information is available from the kiosk at the train station (open 7 to 11 am and 2 to 6 pm – daily but not public holidays) and Krishnaveni Motel (see Places to Stay & Eat) in Seethanagaram, Tadepalli.

Lepakshi Handicrafts Emporium (☎ 573129) is in Ghandinagar.

Kanaka Durga Temple

This temple on Indrakila Hill is dedicated to the goddess and protector of the city. Legend has it that she eradicated the area of powerful demons. She now receives continual gratitude from her followers, who credit her with the prosperous development of Vijayawada.

Cave Temples

About 8km from Vijayawada, the 7th century Hindu cave temples of **Undavalli** house a huge statue of the reclining Vishnu. Find the man with the key to let you in and he'll light a candle to display the sculpture. Other shrines – the incomplete top section – are dedicated to the trimurti (the triad – Brahma, Vishnu and Shiva). The caves are well worth a visit. You can get there by bus from Vijayawada.

Amaravathi

Amaravathi, 30km west of Vijayawada, is a significant ancient Buddhist centre and former capital of the Andhras. Here you'll see the remnants of a 2000-year-old **stupa** – a grass hump and a few stones. In the nearby **museum**, you'll see a small replica. It's open daily, except Friday and public holidays, 10 am to 5 pm. Entry is free.

If you're into Buddhist history, you will no doubt wish to visit Amaravathi. But the best of the remaining sculptures are now in the Chennai Museum. There's no direct route from Vijayawada so it's necessary to travel 30km to Guntur and then a farther 30km to Amaravathi. Buses run from Vijayawada to Amaravathi (via Guntur) every hour, 6 am to 9 pm. The APTTDC organises bus tours for Rs 65, and also boat trips for Rs 80 return. Ask at the tourist offices in Vijayawada. There's no accommodation at Amaravathi and few places to get drinks and snacks.

Places to Stay & Eat

Hotel Swapna Lodge (☎ 575386, *Durgaiah St*), near the Navrang Theatre about 2km from the train station, offers the best value

among the cheapies. It's on a quiet backstreet and is friendly and clean. Rooms cost Rs 100/130.

The *Sree Lakshmi Vilas Modern Cafe* (☎ 572525, *Besant Rd*) at Governorpet, has rooms with common bath for Rs 90/100, or Rs 100/175 with bath and bucket shower. The hotel has a good vegetarian restaurant and a 'conveyance service' to the bus or train station.

Sree Nivas Hotel (☎ 573338), behind the UTI office off Bandar, Governorpet, is good value with singles/doubles at Rs 220/295 or with air-con for Rs 420/500.

Krishnaveni Motel (☎ 426382) is very good value with doubles (only) Rs 275 and air-con Rs 375. Set in pleasant gardens by the river, it's away from the chaos of the city. The staff are helpful, and boating facilities are available.

Hotel Raj Towers (☎ 571311, *Congress Office Rd*), Governorpet, 1.5km from the train station, has rooms with bath for Rs 275/375 and Rs 480/555 with air-con. The double deluxe rooms at Rs 650 are very good value. It also has a veg restaurant and bar.

Hanuman Dormitory (for men only) at the bus stand is Rs 25 for 24 hours. A hot shower is Rs 3 extra. The *Deluxe Lounge* next door provides a banana lounge environment with TV for men and women for Rs 5 per hour.

The well-maintained *Retiring Rooms* at the train station are Rs 80/135, air-con doubles Rs 230 and air-con suites Rs 350. Dormitories (for men only) cost from Rs 30 and Rs 125 for air-con.

Hotel Nandini, at the bus stand (upstairs), serves south Indian veg meals (10 am to 3 pm and 7 to 10 pm). The downstairs restaurant is open round the clock.

Getting There & Away

Air At the time of writing flights to Vijayawada had ceased.

Bus The enormous bus stand on Bandar Rd is 1.5km from the train station. It's well organised with dormitories, waiting rooms, a cloakroom and restaurant. Signs here are in

Telugu, but for non-Telugu speakers there is a helpful inquiry desk. From here, buses travel to all parts of Andhra Pradesh: every 30 minutes to Hyderabad (Rs 60, six hours), eight times daily to Warangal (Rs 48, six hours), seven times daily to Visakhapatnam (Rs 68, 10 hours) and twice daily to Chennai (Rs 88, 10 hours).

Train Vijayawada is on the main Chennai to Calcutta and Chennai to Delhi lines and all express trains stop here. The quickest train from Vijayawada to Chennai is the *Coromandel Express* (Rs 135/471 in 2nd/1st class, seven hours). The same train to Calcutta (20 hours) costs Rs 280/992.

There are plenty of trains via Warangal to Hyderabad (Rs 87/312, 6½ hours); one of the quickest is the *Godavari Express*. The *Tamil Nadu Express* to New Delhi (27 hours) costs Rs 308/1228.

To Tirupathi (nine hours), the daily *Howrah-Tirupathi Express* costs Rs 92/308. Heading north to Puri (Orissa), take the *Howrah-Tirupathi Express* to the junction, Khurda Rd (32 hours), then a passenger train or bus for the last 44km to Puri.

There are also weekly trains direct to Kanyakumari and Bangalore, trains four times weekly to Varanasi and daily to Thiruvananthapuram (Trivandrum).

TIRUMALA & TIRUPATHI
☎ 08574 • pop 191,000

The 'holy hill' of Tirumala in the extreme south-east of Andhra Pradesh is one of the most important pilgrimage centres in India, and the Venkateshwara Temple here is claimed to be the busiest in the world – eclipsing Jerusalem, Rome and Mecca in the sheer number of pilgrims.

The crowds are administered by the efficient Tirumala Tirupathi Devasthanams (TTD). Most pilgrims are housed in special pilgrims' *choultries* in both Tirumala and Tirupathi (the service town 20km away at the bottom of the hill). Buses constantly ferry pilgrims up and down the hill between Tirupathi and Tirumala from before dawn until well after dusk.

Tirumala is an engrossing place. It's one of the few places in India that allows non-Hindus into the sanctum. Despite this, the place sees few non-Hindu visitors. It's well worth a visit, even if you're not a pilgrim; see the Venkateshwara Temple boxed text. Down the hill from the main temple is **Sri Padmavathi Amma Vari Temple** dedicated to Lakshmi – the goddess of abundance.

Organised Tours
The APTTDC runs weekend tours to Tirupathi from Hyderabad. The tours leave at 3.30 pm on Friday and return at 7 am on Monday and include accommodation and 'special darshan'. The cost is Rs 600/700 a child/adult. It's also possible (but not advisable) to take the bus; this costs Rs 175 one way.

It's probably best to approach Tirupathi from Chennai; for more information see Organised Tours in the Chennai chapter.

Places to Stay
Hotel prices can vary, especially at festival times when there may be dramatic increases.

Tirupathi Tirupathi is the town and transport hub at the bottom of the hill. It has plenty of hotels and lodges, so there's no problem finding somewhere to stay. A number of hotels are clustered around the main bus stand, 500m from the centre of town, and there are *Retiring Rooms* at the train station.

Vasantha Vihar Lodge (☎ 20460, 141 G Car St) is a friendly place about a minute's walk from the train station. It has small, basic singles/double rooms for Rs 65/90 with fan and shower.

Hotel Bhimas Paradise (☎ 25747, fax 25568, Renigunta Rd) has double rooms only from Rs 450; Rs 750 to Rs 950 for air-con. As well as the 10% tax, there's a guest charge of Rs 100.

Hotel Bhimas (☎ 25744), a block away at 42 G Car St, has rooms for Rs 185/275 and doubles with air-con for Rs 600.

Bhimas Deluxe Hotel (☎ 25521, 34-38 G Car St), opposite, and apparently not associated with its namesakes, is a two star

ANDHRA PRADESH

Venkateshwara Temple

Pilgrims flock to Tirumala to visit the ancient temple of Venkateshwara, an *avataar* of Vishnu. This is the god whose picture graces the reception areas of most lodges and restaurants in South India. His eyes are covered since his gaze would scorch the world. His body is often garlanded in so many flowers that only his feet are visible.

Among the powers attributed to Venkateshwara is the granting of any wish that is made in front of the idol at Tirumala. It's considered auspicious to have your head shaved when visiting the temple. Hundreds of barbers attend the devotees.

There are never less than 5000 pilgrims here at any one time and, in a single day, the total is often as high as 100,000. The temple staff alone number 18,000. Such popularity makes the temple one of the richest in India, with an annual income of a staggering one billion rupees. This is administered by a temple trust which ploughs the bulk of the money back into hundreds of *choultries* and charities such as homes for the poor, orphanages, craft training centres, schools, colleges and art academies.

Special Darshan at Tirumala

For Rs 30 you can have 'special darshan' at Tirumala. This not only allows you to enter the Venkateshwara Temple, but it gives you priority – you get to go ahead of all those who have paid nothing for their ordinary *darshan* (viewing of a god) and who have to queue – often for 12 hours or more – in the claustrophobic wire cages that ring the outer wall of the temple.

Although special darshan is supposed to get you to the front of this immense queue in two hours, on weekends when the place is much busier it can take as long as five hours, and you still have to go through the cages. A signboard at the entrance keeps you briefed on the waiting time. To find the start of the queue, follow the signs to 'Sarvadarshanam', to the left of the temple entrance.

No matter which darshan you experience, once inside the temple, you'll have to keep shuffling along with everyone else and, before you know it, you'll have viewed Venkateshwara and will be back outside again.

You can however pay considerably more than Rs 30 and secure a position for other special darshans, some of which involve minimal waiting.

hotel with air-con rooms for Rs 540/650. All rooms have bath and TV, and also good views to the hills.

Hotel Mayura (☎ 25925, fax 25911, 209 TP Area) is a three star hotel close to the main bus stand. Rooms with bath cost Rs 475, or Rs 700/750 with air-con. There's a restaurant and some good views.

The newer *India Quality Inn Bliss* (☎ 21650, fax 29514), has singles/doubles for Rs 750/950 with air-con and Rs 395/475 without. All have TV. There are two restaurants – a veg and nonveg, a cake shop and a bar. It's a friendly place with great views.

Tirumala There's a huge variety of accommodation – from free dormitories to up-market apartments and cottages – on the Tirumala Hill close to the temple. It's well organised, pleasant and has all facilities, including a post office, several shopping complexes and a hospital.

Most pilgrims stay in the vast *dormitories* which ring the temple – beds here are free and open to anyone. If you want to stay, check in at the Central Reception Office and you'll be allocated a bed or a room. It's best to avoid weekends when the place becomes outrageously crowded.

Guesthouses and cottages range from Rs 250 for a suite to Rs 8000 for an entire guesthouse. Accommodation in these is organised through the Central Reception Office.

You can also make advance (up to 30 days) bookings for accommodation. To do this, you must write (not phone) giving all details of your requirements and including a bank draft for Rs 100 to the Assistant Executive Officer (Reception-I), TTD, Tirumala 517504. In the high season there are no reservations – it's first come, first served.

Places to Eat

Lakshmi Narayana Bhavan is a good vegetarian restaurant opposite the main bus stand in Tirupathi.

The *Bhimas Deluxe Hotel's* popular basement restaurant serves both north Indian and south Indian cuisine until late at night.

Huge *dining halls* in Tirumala serve thousands of free meals daily to keep the pilgrims happy. Other than that, there are numerous very good restaurants serving vegetarian meals.

Getting There & Away

It's possible to visit Tirupathi on a long day trip from Chennai, but staying overnight makes it far less rushed. If travelling by bus or train, it's possible to purchase 'link tickets' that cover the transport to Tirupathi and then up the mountain to Tirumala. These can save considerable time and confusion once you arrive.

Air The Indian Airlines office (☎ 22349) is in the Hotel Vishnupriya complex, opposite the main bus stand in Tirupathi. Flights come from Hyderabad (Tuesday and Saturday) for US$75.

Bus Tamil Nadu's state bus company has express buses (Nos 802, 848, 883 and 899) from the state express terminus in Chennai from 5.15 am. There are eight services daily. Ordinary buses are more frequent but much slower. The express buses take about four hours to do the 150km trip, cost Rs 40 and can be booked in advance in Chennai.

To Chennai, there are express buses from Tirupathi's main bus stand every 20 minutes from 2.30 am.

Buses to Hyderabad (Rs 195, 12 hours) leave in the late afternoon and evening. There are hourly buses to Vijayawada (Rs 140) as well as plenty of services to Vellore (Rs 185, 2½ hours) in neighbouring Tamil Nadu and most other major towns in Andhra Pradesh and Tamil Nadu.

Train Tirupathi is well served by express trains. There are three trains daily to Chennai (147km, three hours) which cost Rs 76/220 in 2nd/1st class.

The daily *Venkatadri Express* runs to Secunderabad (Rs 206/726, 741km, 17½ hours) and there are three daily express trains to Vijayawada (Rs 127/447, 389km, nine hours). There's also an express train to Madurai (Rs 190/662, 663km, 18 hours) via Vellore, Chidambaram and Tiruchirappalli, as well as a service to Mumbai (Rs 267/930, 1132km, 31 hours) twice weekly.

Getting Around

Bus Tirumala Link buses operate from two bus stands in Tirupathi: the main bus stand which is about 500m from the centre of town, and the Tirumala bus stand near the train station. The 20km trip takes 45 minutes and costs Rs 15/25 one way/return on an ordinary bus, or Rs 25/45 on an 'express' bus.

To get on a bus in either Tirupathi or Tirumala, you usually have to go through a system of crowd-control wire cages which are definitely not for the claustrophobic. At busy times (weekends and festivals), it can take up to two hours to file through and get on a bus. If you're staying in Tirupathi, buy a return ticket, which saves some queuing time. You can avoid the cages at Tirupathi by catching a bus from the main bus stand.

To find the bus queue at the Tirumala bus stand, walk through a choultry to reach the cages and ticket office – the choultry is about 200m from the entry to Tirupathi train station (turn to the right as you exit the station) opposite the bottom of the footbridge over the train line.

ANDHRA PRADESH

Taxi If you're in a hurry, or don't like the cages, there are share taxis available. Seats cost around Rs 55, depending on demand. A taxi of your own costs about Rs 350 one way.

Walking You can walk with the pilgrims up a pleasant 15km path in four to six hours. Deposit your luggage at the toll gate at Alipiri near the Hanuman statue. It will be transported for free to the reception centre. It's best to walk in the evening when it's cooler, but there are several rest points protected from the sun on the way, and even a canteen.

PUTTAPARTHI
☎ 08555
Prasanthi Nilayam, Abode of Highest Peace, the main ashram of Sri Sathya Sai Baba, is in the south-western corner of Andhra Pradesh at Puttaparthi. Sai Baba has a huge following in India and around the globe. He set up this ashram 40 years ago. He spends most of the year here but sometimes moves to Whitefields Ashram near Bangalore, or Kodaikanal in Tamil Nadu in the hot season.

The ashram sponsors numerous services including schools, a university, a planetarium, sports grounds and a state-of-the-art hospital that treats patients for free.

Places to Stay & Eat
Most people stay at the *ashram (☎ 87583)* – a small village with all amenities. Ashram accommodation, although basic, is well kept, comfortable and cheap. Advance bookings are not taken, but there is usually ample accommodation. Meal costs are low, starting from Rs 2 for breakfast of tiffin.

Accommodation outside the ashram is mostly run by Sai Baba devotees and rules (no alcohol, early to bed), similar to those in the ashram, apply.

Hotel Sai Sree Nivas (Main Rd), is typical of outside accommodation. It's basic with singles/doubles with bath for Rs 175/350. Prices fluctuate depending on demand.

Sri Sathya Sai Village, about 2km from the ashram on the road to the airport, is a new village with all facilities and a multicuisine restaurant. Prices range from Rs 750

(double room only) to Rs 1250 (double room with full board). Triple and quadruple rooms are also available. All rooms have air-con. Advance bookings can be made in Chennai (☎ 044-489 6060, fax 489 6069).

Big Pizza – Long Noodles Restaurant, in the Sai Jyothi Complex just off Chitravanthi Rd, has omelettes for Rs 24 and noodles for Rs 26. *Sai Bestways* has good paneers for about Rs 35 and dhal for Rs 15.

Getting There & Away
Puttaparthi is most easily reached by bus from Bangalore and there are regular departures to Bangalore from Puttaparthi.

From Bangalore or Hyderabad you can catch the train to Dharmavaram where regular buses connect to Puttaparthi. From Bangalore the train takes four hours (Rs 52/245 2nd/1st class, 180km). Many people take a taxi from Bangalore (Rs 800 to Rs 1000).

If you're coming from Chennai the overnight 'high-tech' bus handles the bumpy ride. It leaves Parry's Corner at 7 pm daily (Rs 185, 11 hours). Indian Airlines flies to Puttaparthi from both Chennai (US$65) and Mumbai (US$125) on Monday and Friday.

Getting Around
Puttaparthi is a well organised town and you should have no trouble finding your way. For travel farther afield, the large bus station has regular buses to surrounding areas such as Dharmavaram and Hindupur. The timetable is listed in Telugu, Hindi and English. There are many auto-rickshaws and cars can be hired from travel agencies, try Sri Sai Ravitheja (☎ 87429) opposite the ashram on Main Rd.

LEPAKSHI
If you're travelling between Puttaparthi and Bangalore, it's well worth detouring to the **Veerbhadra Temple** at Lepakshi.

At the town entrance is a huge, monolithic Nandi (Shiva's sacred bull). Just 500m on is the temple. Leave plenty of time to enjoy the splendour of this temple. Information booklets in Hindi and Telugu are available and there's a good English-speaking guide.

Kerala

Kerala, the narrow, fertile strip on the south-west coast of India, is sandwiched between the Lakshadweep Sea and the Western Ghats. The Western Ghats, with their dense forests and extensive ridges, have sheltered Kerala from many mainland invaders and the long coastline has encouraged maritime contact with the outside world. Such contact has resulted in an intriguing blend of cultures.

Kerala offers beautiful beaches, backwater trips along peaceful lagoons and canals, hill stations, wildlife sanctuaries and complex cultural customs.

HISTORY

People have been sailing to Kerala in search of spices, sandalwood and ivory for at least 2000 years. The coast had been known to the Phoenicians, then the Romans, and later the Arabs and Chinese. Kerala was also a transhipment point for spices from the Moluccas, and it was through Kerala that Chinese products and ideas found their way to the west.

The kingdom of the Cheras ruled much of present-day Kerala until the early Middle Ages. Its fortunes waxed and waned as it competed with kingdoms and small fiefdoms for territory and trade.

Vasco da Gama's arrival in 1498 heralded an era of European contact as Portuguese, Dutch and English interests fought the Arab traders and then each other for control of the spice trade.

The present-day state of Kerala was created in 1956 from the former states of Travancore, Cochin and Malabar. Traditional concern for the arts and education resulted in a post-Independence state that is one of the most progressive in India.

Kerala had the first freely elected communist government in the world, elected in 1957. The participatory political system has resulted in social policies that have produced relatively equitable distribution of land and income, low infant mortality and a

Kerala at a Glance

Population: 33 million
Area: 38,864 sq km
Capital: Thiruvananthapuram
Main Language: Malayalam
Best Time to Go: October to March

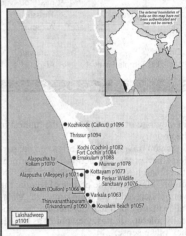

The external boundaries of India on this map have not been authenticated and may not be correct.

- **Kollam** – explore the backwaters aboard a *kettuvallam* (rice-barge houseboat)

- **Alappuzha** – home of the famous Nehru Cup Snake Boat race

- **Kovalam & Varkala** – sun, surf and seafood on busy beach resorts

- **Periyar Wildlife Sanctuary** – South India's most popular; jungle walks, boat trips and treks for the intrepid

- **Munnar** – beautiful mountain vistas and a chance to meet the rare Nilgiri tahr

- **Kochi** – an amalgam of Portuguese, Dutch and south Indian architecture

- **Lakshadweep** – a diver's paradise 300km off the Kerala coast

Festivals of Kerala

festival	location	date	features
Ashtamudi Craft & Art Festival of India	Kollam	26 Dec-10 Jan	artist workshops & demos
Natana Kairali Arts Festival	Irinjalakuda	Jan	puppetry, workshops & dance
Nehru Cup Snake Boat Race	Alappuzha	mid-Jan	boat race for tourists
Classical Music Festival	Thiruvananthapuram	27 Jan-3 Feb	music
Ettumanur Festival	Ettumanur, near Kottayam	Feb/Mar	elephant processions
Pooram Festival	Thrissur	Apr/May	elephant processions
Nehru Cup Snake Boat Race	Alappuzha	2nd Saturday of Aug	traditional boat race
Onam	statewide	Aug/Sep	harvest festival
Mullakal Temple Festival	Alappuzha	mid-Dec	music

literacy rate of around 95% – the highest in the country.

As you travel, you will often see the participatory process in action in the form of street marches. You may even be invited to join in. Malayalis (the people of Kerala; the word is derived from their language, Malayalam) enjoy political debate and are generally tolerant of most viewpoints as long as they make sense.

Southern Kerala

THIRUVANANTHAPURAM (Trivandrum)
☎ 0471 • pop 826,225

Built over seven hills, Thiruvananthapuram (City of the Sacred Serpent) retains some of the ambience characteristic of old Kerala: pagoda-shaped buildings with red-tiled roofs and narrow winding lanes. But this link is disappearing fast.

Many people prefer to stay in Kovalam and make day visits to Thiruvananthapuram. If, however, you want to escape the tourist scene and experience a different aspect of Keralan life, you could do worse than spend a few days in Thiruvananthapuram.

Orientation
MG Rd, the main street, runs north-south from the museums and zoo to the Sri Padmanabhaswamy Temple – about 4km. The Secretariat, halfway along MG Rd, is a handy landmark.

The Kerala State Road Transport Corporation (KSRTC) long-distance bus stand, train station and many of the budget hotels are all close together, while the municipal bus stand is close to the temple.

Information
Tourist Offices The Tourist Facilitation Centre (☎ 321132), Museum Rd, will stop at nothing to give you all the information you require. The Tourist Reception Centre (☎ 330031), in front of the KTDC Hotel Chaithram, arranges KTDC guided tours (see Organised Tours later in this section). There's a helpful tourist information desk at the airport.

The Alliance Française (☎ 327776, fax 327772), Mani Bhavan, Sasthamangalam, has a library and is about to set up a Web site for visitors.

Visa Extensions The office of the Commissioner of Police (☎ 320486) on Resi-

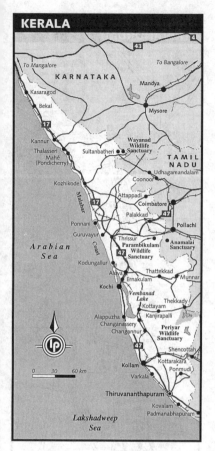

KERALA

Niranjan Towers, KP Elankath Rd, Vellayambalam, is super efficient and is open daily 9.30 am to 7.30 pm.

Post & Communications The main post office is on MG Rd; it's open Monday to Saturday 8 am to 8 pm.

There are numerous STD/ISD kiosks around town. Email is available during business hours at the central telegraph office and Multidata (☎ 321082), 3rd Floor, Kottarathil Buildings (behind the Bank of Baroda). There's a 24 hour service at Hotel Chaithram.

Travel Agencies Tourindia (☎ 330437, fax 331407), MG Rd, can organise treehouse stays near Wayanad – see the Wayanad section. Kerala Travels Interserve (☎ 324158, fax 323154), Vellayambalam Junction, organises trekking in Periyar (see the Periyar section).

Bookshops & Libraries The Victoria Diamond Jubilee Library (the state public library) is in a classic Victorian building on MG Rd. It's open daily 8 am to 8 pm.

The British Library (☎ 328716) is officially open to members only, but visitors are welcomed. It has British newspapers and a variety of magazines. It's open Tuesday to Saturday 11 am to 7 pm.

Along MG Rd you'll find many bookshops including Continental Books, Current Books, DC Books, Higginbothams, Modern Book Centre, CLS Books and Priya Books. Other bookshops include a second DC Books (Karimpanal, Statue Rd) and the Kerala Book Marketing Society, VJT Hall (near the mosque).

Medical Services The general hospital (☎ 443870) is on Statue Rd, about 1 km west of MG Rd.

Numerous places offer ayurvedic treatments. You can try Sreedhari Ayurveda Kendrum (☎/fax 331138), Narasimhavilasam Buildings, South Gate of the Secretariat, or at the CVN Kalari Sangham (see entry later in this section).

dency Rd issues visa extensions (daily except Sunday 10 am to 5 pm). The process may take a week and is not guaranteed. You don't have to leave your passport, and it speeds things up if you give a Thiruvananthapuram address rather than a Kovalam one.

Money Travellers cheques and credit card cash advances can be processed at the Canara Bank near the South Park hotel and at the Bank of India counter in the lobby of the Hotel Chaithram. TT Travels (☎ 332127),

Emergency Police ☎ 100; Fire ☎ 101; Ambulance ☎ 102; Hospital ☎ 443870.

Sri Padmanabhaswamy Temple

The 260-year-old Sri Padmanabhaswamy Temple covers an area of 2400 sq m. Its main entrance, the eastern *gopuram*, towers to over 30m and is devised, like those in Tamil Nadu, in the Dravidian style. In the inner sanctum, the deity, Padmanabha (an incarnation of Vishnu) reclines on the sacred serpent.

Although the temple is open to Hindus only, visitors are occasionally permitted entry if wearing a sari (women) or a dhoti (men).

Puthe Maliga Palace Museum

The Puthe Maliga Palace Museum is housed in wings of the 200-year-old palace of the maharajas of Travancore. Notable for its Keralan architecture, the palace took 5000 workers four years to complete. Many of the exhibits reflect the spice trade with China and Europe.

It's open daily except Monday 8.30 am to 12.30 pm and 3 to 5.30 pm; entry is Rs 10. Photography in the building is prohibited.

Name Changes

A number of places in Kerala have been stripped of their anglicised names and given Malayalam names, but these are far from universally used.

old name	new name
Alleppey	Alappuzha
Calicut	Kozhikode
Cannanore	Kannur
Changanacherry	Changanassery
Cochin	Kochi
Palghat	Palakkad
Quilon	Kollam
Sultan's Battery	Sulthanbatheri
Tellicherry	Thalasseri
Trichur	Thrissur
Trivandrum	Thiruvananthapuram

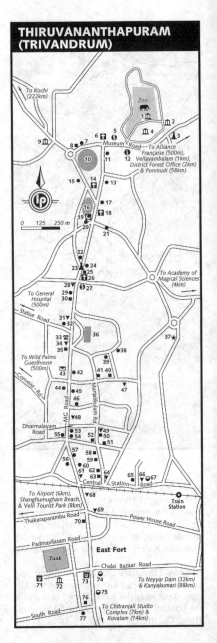

THIRUVANANTHAPURAM (TRIVANDRUM)

THIRUVANANTHAPURAM (TRIVANDRUM)

PLACES TO STAY		61	Hotel City Tower	24	Government
8	KTDC Mascot Hotel	63	Ambika Cafe; Prime Square		Sanskrit College
25	South Park	66	Maveli Cafe	26	St Georges Syria
30	YWCA International	68	Azad Restaurant		Orthodox Church
	Guesthouse	69	Rangoli	27	Canara Bank
35	Hotel Pankaj; Sandhya			29	Air Maldives
	Restaurant	**OTHER**		32	DC Books; Current Books
40	Hotel Residency Tower	1	Sri Chitra Art Gallery	33	Central Telegraph Office
41	Hotel Navaratna	2	Natural History Museum	36	Secretariat Building;
49	Sundar Tourist Home	3	C Kesavan Statue		Sreedhari Ayurvedi Kendrum
50	Hotel Regency	4	Napier Museum	37	Commissoner of Police
52	Sivada Tourist Home	5	State Bank of India;	38	SMSM Institute
58	Pravin Tourist Home		Kerala Travels	39	British Library
59	Manacaud Tourist Paradise	6	Mateer Memorial Church	42	Modern Book Centre
	& Hotel	7	Indian Airlines	43	Main Post Office
62	Hotel Highland;	9	Science & Technology	44	CLS Books
	City Queen Restaurant		Museum; Planetarium	45	Priya Books
63	Hotel Ammu	10	Stadium	46	Hastkala Indian
65	KTDC Hotel Chaithram;	11	Airtravel Enterprises		Arts & Crafts
	Gokulam; Tourist Reception	12	Tourist Facilitation Centre	53	Natesan's Antiqarts
	Centre	13	Victoria Diamond	54	Khadi Gramodyog Bhavan
70	Nalanda Tourist Home		Jubilee Library	55	Ayurveda College
76	Hotel Luciya Continental	14	Christ Church	56	KSRTC Long-Distance
		15	Kerala Legislative Assembly		Bus Stand
PLACES TO EAT		16	Stadium	71	Sri Padmanabhaswamy
28	Indian Coffee House;	17	Multidata		Temple
	Spencer's Store	18	St Joseph's Cathedral	72	Puthe Maliga Palace Museum
31	Ananda Bhavan	19	Mosque	73	Ganapathy Temple
34	Sree Arul Jyothi; New Arul	20	Kerala Book Marketing Society	74	Municipal Bus Stand
	Jyothi	21	Connemara Market	75	Bus Stand No 19
47	Snoozzer	22	Victoria Jubilee Town Hall		(Buses & Taxis to Kovalam)
48	Asok Veg Restaurant	23	Pattom A Thanu Pillai Statue	77	CVN Kalari Sangham

The palace hosts an annual **classical music festival** from 27 January to 3 February.

Velli Tourist Park

This well-designed park contains fine sculptures by local artist Canai Kunuram. The sculptures portray a distinctive sense of balance and harmony sometimes combined with the erotic. The park, well worth a visit, is open daily 10 am to 5.30 pm.

CVN Kalari Sangham

Near the Sri Padmanabhaswamy Temple, the CVN Kalari Sangham (☎ 474128) was built in 1956. Its founders played a significant role in the revival of *kalarippayat*, the traditional martial art of Kerala.

Training sessions can be viewed for free between 6.30 and 8.30 am daily except Sun-

day. Ayurvedic treatment for ailments (especially soft tissue injuries) is available 10 am to 1 pm and 5 to 7.30 pm Monday to Saturday, and 10 am to 1 pm on Sunday.

To join the combatants you must sign up for a course (three month minimum) at Rs 500 per month. You'll need to arrange your own accommodation, meals and transport.

Other Attractions

The zoo and a collection of museums are in a park in the north of the city. The museums are open Tuesday to Sunday 10 am to 4.45 pm (from 1 pm on Wednesday). A single Rs 5 entry ticket, purchased at the Natural History Museum, covers all the museums.

Housed in a Keralan-style building dating from 1880, the **Napier Museum** has an eclectic display of bronzes, temple carts, ivory carvings and life-size figures of Kathakali dancers in full costume.

The **Natural History Museum** has a rudimentary ethnographic collection as well as an interesting replica of a *tharawad* – a traditional wooden residence of the Nair family.

The **Sri Chitra Art Gallery** has paintings of the Rajput, Mughal and Tanjore schools, together with works by Ravi Varma, Svetoslav and Nicholas Roerich.

The **Zoological Gardens**, set among woodland and lakes, are open Tuesday to Saturday 9 am to 5.15 pm. Entry is Rs 4.

The **Science & Technology Museum** (10 am to 5 pm daily, Rs 2), with its interactive displays, is about 100m west of the Mascot Hotel. The nearby **Planetarium** (☎ 446976) has daily 40-minute shows for Rs 10 (in Malayalam at 10.30 am, 3 and 5 pm and English at noon). It's closed Monday.

Courses
Courses in Kathakali (see the Kathakali boxed text under Kovalam) and Kootiattam (traditional Sanskrit drama) are conducted for genuine students at the Margi Kathakali School, West Fort (☎ 434066). No experience is necessary; tuition is for beginners as well as advanced students. Fees must be organised with teachers. Accommodation is supplied for male students; female students may board outside the school. If you are interested write to or phone the treasurer, Mr Ramaiyer.

Organised Tours
KTDC offers a range of tours around the city and beyond. They're good value and will give you an overview of the attractions. All tours leave from the Tourist Reception Centre, in front of the Hotel Chaithram.

- Thiruvananthapuram city day tour to Sri Padmanabhaswamy Temple (non-Hindus not admitted), art gallery, zoo, Veli Lagoon & Kovalam Beach (Rs 95)
- Thiruvananthapuram half day tour to Kovalam Beach, aquarium & Veli Lagoon (Rs 60)
- Ponmudi day tour (Rs 160)
- Kanyakumari day tour to the Padmanabhapuram Palace, Suchindram Temple & Kanyakumari (Rs 180)

Other long-distance tours go to Munnar (three days, Rs 475) and Thekkady (two days, Rs 375), Rameswaram (four days, Rs 525), Bangalore (seven days, Rs 1575) and Kodaikanal (three days, Rs 630).

Places to Stay – Budget
The best hunting ground is Manjalikulam Rd, which runs parallel to MG Rd. Despite its central location, it's quiet and has a collection of cheap to mid-range hotels.

Pravin Tourist Home (☎ 330753) is a cheerful place with large singles/doubles/triples for Rs 90/160/225; tea and coffee is available.

Sundar Tourist Home (☎ 330532) has simpler rooms for Rs 40/75 with common bath; Rs 45/85 with bath.

Sivada Tourist Home (☎ 330320) has non air-con singles/doubles with bath for Rs 85/135 and air-con rooms for Rs 230/350.

Manacaud Tourist Paradise & Hotel (☎ 327578, Manjalikulam Rd) has large, clean rooms with bath for Rs 110/220.

Hotel Ammu (☎ 331937), nearby, is small and popular. Singles/doubles with bath are Rs 160/230, or with TV and air-con, Rs 450. There is a small air-con restaurant.

Nalanda Tourist Home (☎ 471864) is on busy MG Rd, but the rooms at the back are not too noisy and it's cheap at Rs 70/100.

The YWCA International Guesthouse (☎ 446518, MG Rd) has clean single/double/family rooms with bath for Rs 150/200/300.

Retiring rooms at the train station are Rs 25 for a dorm bed (men only).

Places to Stay – Mid-Range
The KTDC *Hotel Chaithram* (☎ 330977, fax 331446, Central Station Rd), next to the KSRTC long-distance bus stand, is efficient and noisy. Rooms cost Rs 475/575, or Rs 750/900 with air-con. Facilities include a bookshop, a Bank of India branch, a bright and friendly bar, a good air-con veg restaurant and an average nonveg restaurant.

Hotel Highland (☎ 333200, fax 332645, Manjalikulam Rd) is welcoming and has a good choice of rooms from Rs 230/295, or from Rs 450/550 with air-con – extra for a

TV. There's also an air-con multicuisine restaurant (no alcohol).

Hotel Regency (*☎ 331541, fax 331696, Manjalikulam Cross Rd*) has comfortable rooms for Rs 250/400, or Rs 750/950 with air-con. There's also a restaurant.

Hotel Residency Tower (*☎ 331661, fax 331311, Press Rd*) is clean and comfortable with friendly staff. Singles/doubles cost Rs 390/590, or Rs 790/990 with air-con. It has a bar and nonveg restaurant.

Hotel Navaratna (*☎ 331784, YMCA Rd*) is a favourite of business travellers, with rooms for Rs 220/250, or Rs 600 for an air-con suite. There's a reasonable restaurant and coffee shop.

Wild Palms Guest House (*☎/fax 454071, Puthen Rd*) offers a welcome break from the hotel environment. In a quiet backstreet, this clean and cosy guesthouse has spacious rooms for Rs 845, or Rs 1145 with air-con.

Places to Stay – Top End

Hotel Luciya Continental (*☎ 463443, fax 463347*), in East Fort, has rooms from Rs 1775/2250 and central air-con. There's a bar, restaurant, coffee shop, bookshop, business centre and pool.

South Park (*☎ 333333, fax 331861*), a swank, centrally air-conditioned hotel on MG Rd, has rooms from US$55/65 to US$100/110. It has one of the city's best restaurants, a coffee shop, a terrific cake shop and a bar.

The KTDC **Mascot Hotel** (*☎ 438990, fax 437745, Museum Rd*) is a pleasant place. Rooms all have air-con and start from Rs 1195/1395. There's a restaurant, coffee shop, and bar near the pool.

Hotel Pankaj (*☎ 464645, fax 465020, MG Rd*) has central air-con and rooms from Rs 1050/1450 up to Rs 2200 for a suite. There's a bar and two restaurants.

Places to Eat

Maveli Cafe is a bizarre, circular Indian Coffee House with good, cheap food.

Ambika Cafe, at the junction of Central Station and Manjalikulam Rds, is a good spot for a cheap breakfast.

Prime Square, adjacent to the Ambika Cafe, has good-value veg and nonveg restaurants and is deservedly popular.

Asok Veg Restaurant, further north along Manjalikulam Rd, is a typical good-value 'meals' restaurant.

Indian Coffee House is just off MG Rd, behind Spencer's Store.

Hotel City Tower (*MG Rd*), near the railway bridge, is another popular lunch spot; *thalis* are Rs 15.

There are several good, cheap vegetarian places opposite the Secretariat on MG Rd, including **Sree Arul Jyothi**, **New Arul Jyothi**, and **Ananda Bhavan**.

Rangoli, south of the railway line, on MG Rd, is reputedly the best place for Keralan breakfasts.

Azad Restaurant, a few doors north, is also clean, air-conditioned and good value.

There are restaurants in many of the hotels. **City Queen Restaurant,** in the Hotel Highland on Manjalikulam Rd, does good Indian, Chinese and western food. **Gokulam**, in the Hotel Chaithram, is a good air-con veg restaurant. **Mascot Hotel**, **Hotel Pankaj** and in particular the **South Park** all have popular lunchtime buffets.

The Hotel Regency has a top-floor restaurant.

The **Mascot** and the **Chaithram** have outdoor ice-cream parlours. Try the engagingly named **Snoozzer** (*Press Rd*); it's a great escape from the midday heat.

Entertainment

The **Academy of Magical Sciences** (*☎ 345910, fax 345920, Poojapurra*) was established in 1996 to revive some of the traditional magic of India. Under the directorship of Gopinath Muthukad, the academy holds regular shows and visitors are welcome. Telephone first for times.

Shopping

The SMSM Institute (*☎ 330298, fax 331582*), YMCA Rd, is a government-sponsored handicrafts outlet with the usual sandalwood carvings, textiles and bronzes. Natesan's Antiqarts (*☎ 331594, fax 330689*)

and Khadi Gramodyog Bhavan, opposite the
ayurvedic college on MG Rd, have collections of exquisite bronzes and fine Keralan
furniture. Hastkala Indian Arts & Crafts, off
MG Rd, is a Kashmiri shop with all the
usual artefacts. For nuts, tea and coffee try
Sankar's Tea & Coffee, MG Rd.

Getting There & Away

Air Airline offices (open Monday to Friday
10 am to 5.30 pm; closed 1 to 1.45 pm) in
Thiruvananthapuram include:

Air India
    (☎ 314837; airport ☎ 451426) Museum Rd,
    Vellayambalam
Air Lanka
    (☎ 328767), Geetanjali Bldg,
    Ganapathikoil Rd, Vazhuthacaud
Air Maldives
    (☎ 329557) MG Rd
British Airways
    (☎ 326604) Niranjan Towers,
    KP Elankath Rd, Vellayambalam
Gulf Air
    (☎ 328003) Gulf Air Bldg,
    KP Elankath Rd, Vellayambalam
Indian Airlines
    (☎ 318288) Mascot Square
Jet Airways
    (☎325367) Akshay Towers,
    Shastamangalam Junction
Kuwait Airways
    (☎ 323436) Panavila Junction

Indian Airlines has direct connections to
Bangalore (US$105, three flights weekly);
Mumbai (Bombay) (US$175, daily); Chen-
nai (Madras) (US$105, four weekly) and
Delhi (US$325, daily). Jet Airways has
daily flights to Mumbai and Chennai and
Air India also has daily flights to Mumbai.

There are connections to the Arabian
Gulf with Air India, Gulf Air and Kuwait
Airways. Air India also flies to Singapore
on Wednesday and Sunday.

For Colombo, Air Lanka flies daily and
Indian Airlines three times weekly (Rs
2190/4375 one way/return). Air Maldives
and Indian Airlines have four flights a week
to Malé for US$75/150 one way/return.

Bookings for all airlines can be made at
the friendly and efficient Airtravel Enter-

prises (☎ 327627, fax 331704), New Corporation Building, Palayam.

Bus From the somewhat chaotic KSRTC
bus stand (☎ 323886), opposite the train
station, regular buses operate to destinations north along the coast, including Kollam (Rs 17, 1½ hours), Alappuzha (Rs 49,
3¼ hours), Ernakulam (Rs 57, five hours)
and Thrissur (Rs 72, 6¾ hours). Buses depart hourly for the two hour trip to
Kanyakumari. There are two morning buses
daily for the eight hour trip to Thekkady (Rs
85) for Periyar Wildlife Sanctuary.

Most of the bus services to destinations in
Tamil Nadu are operated by the Tamil Nadu
state bus service – SETC, which has its office
at the eastern end of the long-distance bus
stand. It has services to Chennai (eight daily,
17 hours), Madurai (10 daily, seven hours),
Pondicherry (one daily, 16 hours), Coimbatore (one daily), as well as Nagercoil and
Erode. KSRTC also operates several services
daily to Coimbatore (Rs 68). Long-distance
buses operate to Bangalore (Rs 198), but it's
better to catch a train if you're going that far.

Bus No 111 goes to Kovalam Beach
every 30 minutes between 5.30 am and 9.30
pm from East Fort, Stand 19, on MG Rd.

Train The reservation office (8 am to 8 pm
daily, Sunday 8 am to 2 pm), on the 1st floor
of the station building, is efficient and computerised. Reservations should be made as
far in advance as possible because trains
out of Thiruvananthapuram are often heavily booked. If you're just making your way
up the coast in short hops or to Kochi,
there's no need to reserve a seat. The booking office where tickets can be bought just
prior to departure is open 24 hours.

Numerous trains run up the coast via Kollam and Ernakulam to Thrissur. Some trains
branch off east and north-east at Kollam and
head for Shencottah. Beyond Thrissur, many
others branch off east via Palakkad to Tamil
Nadu. It's 436km to Coimbatore (Rs 91/
141/490 for 2nd/sleeper/1st class, nine
hours). Coimbatore has connections to Mettupalayam and Ooty (Udhagamandalam).

Trains that go all the way up the coast as far as Mangalore in Karnataka include the daily *Parsuram Express* (departs 6 am; 15 hours) and *Malabar Express* (departs 5.40 pm). Both these trains travel via Ernakulam, and there are several additional daily expresses to Ernakulam (for Kochi) including the *Shoranur Venad Express* (departs 5 am and goes to Shoranur Junction) and the *Rajkot Express* (departs 2.10 pm).

It's about 42km (by train) from Thiruvananthapuram to Varkala (Rs 21/112 in 2nd/1st class, 55 minutes), 65km to Kollam (Rs 26/129, 1½ hours); 224km to Ernakulam (Rs 61/294, five hours); and 414km to Kozhikode (Rs 95/135/471 for 2nd/sleeper/1st class, 10 hours).

South of Thiruvananthapuram, it's 87km to Kanyakumari (Rs 30/159, two hours).

For long-haulers, there's the Friday-only *Himsagar Express* to Jammu Tawi, which goes via Delhi.

Getting Around

The airport is 6km from the city and 15km from Kovalam Beach. A No 14 local bus from the municipal bus stand will take you there for around Rs 2. Prepaid taxi vouchers from the airport cost Rs 90 to the city; Rs 190 to Rs 225 to Kovalam.

Auto-rickshaws are your best transport around the city. Standard rates are Rs 6 flagfall, then Rs 3 per kilometre.

Cars, with driver, may be hired from any number of travel agencies including Kerala Travels Interserve (☎ 324158, fax 323154), near Vellayambalam Junction. Prices average Rs 4 per kilometre for non air-con, Rs 7 with air-con and Rs 1100 per day to travel beyond the city limits.

AROUND THIRUVANANTHAPURAM
Chitranjali Studio Complex

These studios were established in 1980 to produce Malayalam films. If you have a genuine interest in film production and would like to look around you can organise a studio tour by contacting the studio manager (☎ 461450, fax 460946).

Ponmudi & The Cardamom Hills

Ponmudi, a small hill resort just 61km north-east of Thiruvananthapuram, makes for a pleasant day trip or overnight excursion. Accommodation in the *Government Guest House* is arranged by ringing the manager (☎ 0471-890230). The KTDC runs a restaurant/beer parlour.

The mix of lightly populated hills, carloads of young men, and a bar suggests that women travellers should exercise due care.

On the road to Ponmudi you will pass the turn-off to **Neyyar Dam** and the surrounding **Neyyar Wildlife Sanctuary**. The sanctuary has a lion park and a crocodile breeding park. These are popular for picnics and daytrips. Boats to view deer and other wildlife on an island in the dam are Rs 10 and Rs 40 (depending on the size of the boat).

Just near the Neyyar Dam the **Sivananda Yoga Vedanta Dhanwantari Ashram** (☎/fax 0472-273093), established in 1978, conducts hatha yoga courses for beginners as well as advanced students. Costs (donations) for a two week course range from Rs 150 to Rs 300 depending on the type of accommodation. Prices include tuition and all meals. Prior bookings (up to 15 days) are required. Write to PO Neyyar Dam, Thiruvananthapuram 695576.

Getting There & Away Six KSRTC buses daily go to Ponmudi from the long-distance bus stand. Change at Nedumangad for a smaller bus capable of negotiating the hairpin corners. A taxi will cost about Rs 950 for a day trip. The KTDC organises tours (Rs 180) that include Ponmudi and Neyyar Dam.

Padmanabhapuram Palace

The Padmanabhapuram Palace was once the seat of the rulers of Travancore, a princely state for more than 400 years that included a large part of present-day Kerala and the western coast of Tamil Nadu.

The palace is superbly constructed of local teak and granite, the oldest parts dating from 1550. The architecture is exquisite, with rosewood ceilings carved in floral patterns, windows laid with jewel-coloured mica, and floors finished to a high polish with a special compound of crushed shells, coconuts, egg white and the juices of local plants.

The 18th century murals in the *puja* (prayer) room on the upper floors have been beautifully preserved, and surpass even those at Mattancherry in Kochi.

Chinese traders sold tea and bought spices here for centuries and their legacy is evident throughout the palace. There are intricately carved rosewood chairs, screens and ceilings as well as large Chinese pickle jars. With its banqueting halls, audience chamber, women's quarters, and galleries, the palace shouldn't be missed.

The palace is open Tuesday to Saturday 9 am to 4.30 pm. Entry costs Rs 4.

Getting There & Away Padmanabhapuram is just inside Tamil Nadu, 65km southeast of Thiruvananthapuram. To get there, catch a local bus from Thiruvananthapuram (or Kovalam Beach) to Kanyakumari and get off at Thuckalay, from where it is a short rickshaw ride or 15 minute walk. Alternatively, take one of the tours organised by the KTDC (see Organised Tours in the Thiruvananthapuram section for details) or organise your own taxi (about Rs 850 return).

KOVALAM
☎ 0471

Thirty years ago Kovalam was a hippy idyll: a picture-perfect tropical beach; a traditional Keralan fishing village providing fresh fish, fruit and toddy (coconut beer); and about as far from decadent western civilisation as you could get and still hear Jim, Janis and Jimi. Today this tiny beach is the focus of a multimillion dollar business, drawing thousands of tourists for a two week dose of ozone, UV and a sanitised Indian 'experience'.

The result has been an influx of some get-rich-quick merchants, chaotic beachfront development, an avalanche of garbage, exorbitant prices and desperate souvenir sellers.

But while it's far from paradise, Kovalam retains a certain charm and is still popular

with travellers craving some rest from the long haul across the subcontinent. The beaches are generally safe and clean (although much of the rubbish is buried just under the surface), and the powerful Arabian Sea swells are inviting and invigorating. And each night local fishermen still row their boats out to sea.

Orientation
Kovalam consists of two palm-fringed coves (Lighthouse Beach and Hawah Beach) separated from less-populated beaches north and south by rocky headlands. The southern headland is marked by a prominent lighthouse; the northern headland is topped by the Ashok Beach Resort. It's a 15 minute walk from one headland to the other.

Information
There's a helpful tourist office inside the entrance to the Ashok Beach Resort and another (TOPIC) at Hawah Beach Restaurant.

There are numerous moneychangers along the beach. Wilson Tourist Home has official moneychanging facilities as does Pournami Handicrafts.

The post office is open daily 9 am to 5 pm and there are STD/ISD, fax and email facilities.

Visit India (☎/fax 481069), at the beach end of Lighthouse Rd, is a friendly travel agency that can arrange ticketing, tours, and car hire.

Dangers & Annoyances
Pit toilets result in unsafe drinking water. Stick to bottled water or use a purifying kit.

Theft does occur, from hotels and the beach. Ensure your room is locked (doors and windows). Keep an eye on your possessions at the beach.

Swim only between the flags, in the area patrolled by lifeguards. Strong rips at both ends of Lighthouse Beach carry away several swimmers every year.

Kovalam experiences electrical supply 'loadshedding' (blackouts) for 30 minutes every evening. Carry a torch (flashlight) after dark.

Top: Tea-growing estates surround the tiny hillside town of Munnar.
Middle: Cruising through Kerala's famous backwaters will take you past visually stimulating locations, including coconut groves and churches.
Bottom: Fishing and boat-building are traditional backwater activities.

Top: Traditional Chinese fishing nets are still used to pull in the catch at Cochin.
Middle: Though recent commercial development has threatened the ambience of Kovalam beach, there are still some untouched pockets to be found.
Bottom: A rice barge glides through the backwaters of Kerala.

KOVALAM BEACH

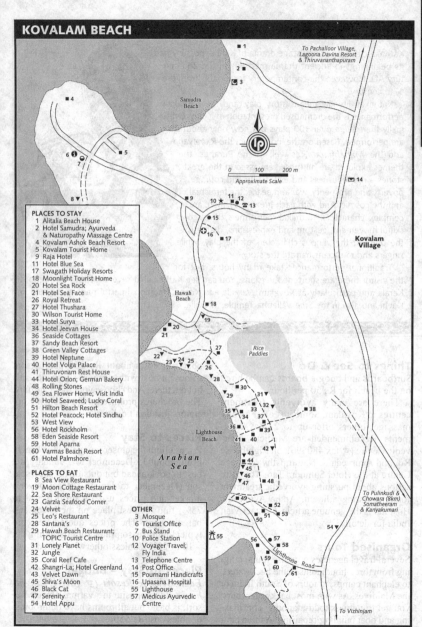

To Pachalloor Village,
Lagoona Davina Resort
& Thiruvananthapuram

Samudra
Beach

Kovalam
Village

Hawah
Beach

Rice
Paddies

Lighthouse
Beach

Arabian
Sea

To Pulinkudi &
Chowara (8km)
Somatheeram
& Kanyakumari

Lighthouse Road

To Vizhinjam

Approximate Scale
0   100   200 m

PLACES TO STAY
1 Alitalia Beach House
2 Hotel Samudra; Ayurveda
   & Naturopathy Massage Centre
4 Kovalam Ashok Beach Resort
5 Kovalam Tourist Home
9 Raja Hotel
11 Hotel Blue Sea
17 Swagath Holiday Resorts
18 Moonlight Tourist Home
20 Hotel Sea Rock
21 Hotel Sea Face
26 Royal Retreat
27 Hotel Thushara
30 Wilson Tourist Home
33 Hotel Surya
34 Hotel Jeevan House
36 Seaside Cottages
37 Sandy Beach Resort
38 Green Valley Cottages
39 Hotel Neptune
40 Hotel Volga Palace
41 Thiruvonam Rest House
44 Hotel Orion; German Bakery
48 Rolling Stones
49 Sea Flower Home; Visit India
50 Hotel Seaweed; Lucky Coral
51 Hilton Beach Resort
52 Hotel Peacock; Hotel Sindhu
53 West View
56 Hotel Rockholm
58 Eden Seaside Resort
59 Hotel Aparna
60 Varmas Beach Resort
61 Hotel Palmshore

PLACES TO EAT
8 Sea View Restaurant
19 Moon Cottage Restaurant
22 Sea Shore Restaurant
23 Garzia Seafood Corner
24 Velvet
25 Leo's Restaurant
28 Santana's
29 Hawah Beach Restaurant;
   TOPIC Tourist Centre
31 Lonely Planet
32 Jungle
35 Coral Reef Cafe
42 Shangri-La; Hotel Greenland
43 Velvet Dawn
45 Shiva's Moon
46 Black Cat
47 Serenity
54 Hotel Appu

OTHER
3 Mosque
6 Tourist Office
7 Bus Stand
10 Police Station
12 Voyager Travel;
   Fly India
13 Telephone Centre
14 Post Office
15 Pournami Handicrafts
16 Upasana Hospital
55 Lighthouse
57 Medicus Ayurvedic
   Centre

KERALA

Kathakali

Kathakali, the renowned stage drama of Kerala, possibly had its beginnings in ancient drama methods of the 2nd century AD. However, the contemporary form dates from the 17th century.

Kathakali literally means story play, and the Kathakali performance is the dramatised presentation of a play. Originally there were over 100 plays but now only about 30 are performed. Based on the Indian epics the *Ramayana* and the *Mahabharata*, as well as the Puranas, the themes explored are all those canvassed in the great stories – righteousness and evil, frailty and courage, poverty and prosperity, war and peace, the terrestrial and the cosmic. And with each great story there are complex characters. Kathakali performers, through skilful movement, gesture and expressions, dramatise the traits of the various characters of the play, while singers and musicians narrate the story.

Traditional performances take many hours, but for the visitor there are shortened versions. You can see Kathakali at several venues throughout Kerala and particularly at Kovalam, Varkala and Kochi. Traditional performances are held in Kochi and also in the Sree Vallabha Temple, Tiruvilla.

Things to See & Do

Surfboards and **boogie boards** can be hired on the beach for Rs 50 per hour.

There are many **ayurvedic treatment centres** in Kovalam. Some just offer an oily massage; others offer up to 21-day treatments. Recommended are Medicus Ayurvedic Centre (☎/fax 480596), on Lighthouse Rd, and Ayurveda & Naturopathy Massage Centre at the Hotel Samudra Tara. If you're serious about pursuing ayurvedic treatment for an existing ailment, Arsha Ayurvedic Hospital is the genuine article. Contact Visit India for details.

Organised Tours

Several travel agencies organise tours, ranging from three-hour jaunts in the backwaters, to elephant camps, to tours of South India or the Maldives. As with most backwater tours, you get to witness toddy tapping, coir making and boat building/repairing. A three hour boat trip costs about Rs 250 per person. Choose a boat with a proper sunshade – it's hot out there. And choose your tour carefully. The brochures promise much, but some operators just don't deliver.

Places to Stay

Prices climb the closer you get to the beach. From about 15 December to 7 January it's best to book ahead but outside the high season (December to January) it's a buyer's market and prices usually drop by 50 or 75%; find the best place on the beach and bargain hard. The prices quoted here are typical high-season rates (not including tax – 10 to 20%), unless otherwise stated.

Places to Stay – Budget

Eden Seaside Resort (☎ 481749, Lighthouse Rd), opposite the Varmas Beach Resort, is basic but all rooms have bathrooms; doubles cost Rs 550.

Green Valley Cottages (☎ 480636), in a wonderfully peaceful location next to the paddy fields, has clean, neat and colourful rooms with bath for Rs 500.

Hotel Greenland, also well back from the beach, is attached to the well-known Shangri-La restaurant. Simple but clean rooms cost Rs 330 (single or double occupancy).

Kovalam Tourist Home (☎ 480441), a long walk back from the beach, has simple rooms with bath for just Rs 350, or Rs 400/450 for singles/doubles with air-con.

Hotel Jeevan House (☎ 480662), right behind the Coral Reef Cafe, has a range of accommodation from Rs 230 to Rs 1400.

Sandy Beach Resort (☎ 480012) has refurbished rooms for Rs 560, and a restaurant.

Other places worth considering include the no-frills *Hotel Surya* (☎ 481012) just back from the beach with rooms from Rs 240, and the beachfront *Sea Flower Home* (☎ 480554), a touch close to the drain but friendly and clean with rooms for Rs 220 downstairs and Rs 440 with a balcony. *Hotel Paradise Rock* (☎ 480658), nearby, offers clean, small rooms for Rs 120/160.

Seaside Cottages (☎ 481937) has rooms for Rs 260 (single and double). *Thiruvonam Rest House* (☎ 480661) is a tad overpriced with rooms from Rs 420, up to Rs 550 (with a balcony) – an air-cooler is Rs 130. *Rolling Stones* has basic rooms for Rs 220 (single and double). Also worth a try is *West View*, a few minutes' stroll from the beach, with standard rooms from Rs 160 to Rs 260.

Hotel Samudra Tara (☎ 481608), further down Lighthouse Rd towards the beach, has clean and comfortable non air-con rooms for Rs 330 (Rs 450 with a balcony) and air-con rooms for Rs 800. There's an ayurvedic massage and naturopathy clinic here as well

Places to Stay – Mid-Range

Lighthouse Rd is the best place for mid-range hotels.

Hotel Seaweed (☎ 480391) is an excellent, friendly and secure place with sea breezes and bay views. Rooms are Rs 550 to Rs 1350, Rs 1050 to Rs 1400 with air-con (25% to 30% less in the low season).

Hilton Beach Resort (☎ 481476), nearby, has air-con singles/doubles for Rs 1000/1400.

Hotel Peacock (☎ 481395) has non air-con rooms for Rs 550 and air-con rooms with fridge for Rs 900 (including tax). There's a restaurant, the *Sea Bee*.

Hotel Rockholm (☎ 480306), further up Lighthouse Rd (ie away from the beach), is also an excellent choice. It has great views over the small cove beyond the lighthouse. Rooms cost Rs 1000/1100 with 25% discount in the low season.

Hotel Aparna (☎ 480950) has doubles for Rs 1150 (including tax). Credit cards and travellers cheques are not accepted.

Varmas Beach Resort (☎ 480478) has balconies overlooking a small cove. Doubles with air-con are Rs 1850, and without air-con, Rs 1390.

Hotel Palmshore (☎ 481481, fax 480495) fronts onto the private sandy cove south of the lighthouse headland. The pleasantly designed rooms, all with bath, cost US$60 (US$65 with air-con).

Hotel Neptune (☎ 480222) is set back from Lighthouse Beach and has standard rooms for Rs 550, balcony rooms for Rs 600 and air-con rooms for Rs 800.

Hotel Volga Palace (☎ 481663) is similar with rooms ranging from Rs 450 for the ground floor to Rs 850 for the gloomy palace suite on the top floor.

Wilson Tourist Home (☎ 480051) is large and friendly, with a range of non air-con rooms from Rs 450 during the high season, and air-con courtyard rooms for Rs 1000.

Hotel Sea Rock (☎ 480422, fax 480722), Hawah Beach, has overpriced doubles with bath for Rs 1250.

Hotel Thushara (☎/fax 481693), back in the coconut palms, has superbly built and beautifully furnished cottages and rooms for Rs 850.

Royal Retreat, next door, is a cluster of brand new air-con cottages from Rs 850 to Rs 1000 a double. There are also non air-con singles from Rs 350 to Rs 800.

Moonlight Tourist Home (☎ 480375, fax 481078), 300m south of the Upasana Hospital, is popular and squeaky clean. The spacious rooms have poster beds; doubles, some with small balconies, cost Rs 900, or Rs 1000/1400 with air-con. You can rent motorcycles here.

Hotel Orion (☎ 480999) is a friendly place overlooking Lighthouse Beach just 20m from the high-tide mark. Doubles are Rs 1290 and suites (with air-con and fridge) are Rs 2250.

Hotel Blue Sea (☎ 481401, fax 480401), in Keralan style, was originally the family home of the current managers – two affable brothers. Set in manicured gardens, rooms cost from Rs 700 for light, airy doubles, up to Rs 1500 for the penthouse (including breakfast and tax).

Raja Hotel (☎ 480355), well back from the beach, has sea-facing rooms with bath for Rs 800. Air-con rooms are Rs 1000 to Rs 2000. It also has a bar and a veg/nonveg restaurant.

Places to Stay – Top End
The *Kovalam Ashok Beach Resort* (☎ 480101, fax 481522) is superbly located on the headland of the second cove. The hotel has central air-con, a bar, restaurants, pool, sports and massage facilities, bank and bookshop. Room prices are Rs 4500/5000; uninspiring cottages are Rs 500 cheaper, while the Castle suite costs Rs 16,000.

Hotel Sea Face (☎ 481835, fax 481320) is right on Hawah Beach. Standard rooms are Rs 2250 (Rs 2650 with air-con), deluxe rooms are Rs 3500, and suites are Rs 5000. The pool overlooks the beach.

Swagath Holiday Resorts (☎ 481148, fax 330990) is set in well-tended gardens looking over the coconut palms to the lighthouse. Comfortable rooms cost Rs 900 to Rs 1800 (Rs 1000 to Rs 3500 with air-con); there are no low-season price reductions. There's an excellent multicuisine restaurant (lawn-service available), but no pool. Be warned: rooms with a lighthouse view are strafed with brilliant light all night long.

Places to Eat
Open-air restaurants line the beach area and are scattered through the coconut palms be-hind it. Almost all the restaurants offer a standard menu including porridge, muesli, eggs, toast, *idli* and *dosa* for breakfast, and curries or seafood with chips and salad for dinner.

At night, you stroll along the beachfront and select your fish – the range includes seer, barracuda, sea bass, catfish, king and tiger prawns, and crabs. You can also select the method of preparation: tandoor (delicious but on the dry side), sizzler (fried in garlic and other herbs) or grilled. Most preparations involve tasty spices. Always check the prices before you order. Fish and chips with salad typically costs between Rs 90 and Rs 110, depending on variety and portion size; tiger prawns will push the price beyond Rs 400.

There's plenty of competition so don't be afraid to negotiate. Quality can vary; ask other travellers for their recommendations. Beer is available, sometimes hot, in most restaurants – expect to pay Rs 70.

Santana's, *Hawah Beach*, *Coral Reef Cafe*, *Velvet Dawn*, *Garzia Seafood Corner*, *Velvet Restaurant*, *Leo's Restaurant* and the *Orion Cafe* (at the Hotel Orion) all have a reputation for quality and value. But almost without exception you'll have a long wait – 30 minutes – while the fish marinates.

Serenity, at the south end of the beach, turns out good travellers' breakfasts and recognisable 'spegatty'; nearby *Black Cat* and *Shiva's Moon* are similar. The *Sea View Restaurant* is popular all day long, and just beyond the headland the *Sea Shore Restaurant* is a good spot to sip beer at sunset. For cappuccino, apple strudel and croissants visit the rooftop *German Bakery*.

There are quite a few places back from the beach, although seafood is not the number one concern.

Lonely Planet vegetarian restaurant is nicely situated by a water lily pond. Excellent meals include south and north Indian as well as continental cuisine. (No, we have absolutely nothing to do with it and we are not planning to open a franchised chain!)

Jungle is run by a couple of Italian guys, so there's pasta as well as Indian and Chinese food. The *Shangri-La*, *Moon Cottage Restaurant* and *Hotel Sindhu* are also worth a look.

If you get tired of waiting for meals at the beachside places, try the mid-range hotels, which have better equipped kitchens and can turn out more consistent food with greater speed.

Lucky Coral rooftop restaurant at the Hotel Seaweed is ever-popular.

The *Rockholm's* celebrated restaurant includes a terrace overlooking the sea.

At the *Palmshore,* you can eat indoors or on the open balcony.

For a splurge, head to the *Ashok Beach Resort* or the *Swagath Holiday Resorts*, but don't expect a warm welcome if you haven't scrubbed up first.

Hotel Appu, well away from the beach, now has a well-earned reputation for the best cheap Indian food in Kovalam. It's packed with lunching locals from 1 to 1.30 pm.

On the beach, women sell fruit to sun worshippers. The ring of 'Hello. Mango? Papaya? Coconut?' will become a familiar part of your day. Once you establish the going rate, they'll remember you so you don't have to repeat the performance. They rarely have change, but they're reliable about bringing it later. Toddy (coconut beer) is also available.

Entertainment

During the holiday season, a shortened version of Kathakali is performed every night except Sunday: on Monday, Wednesday and Saturday you can see it at *Hotel Neptune*, and on Tuesday and Friday at *Ashok Beach Resort*. You can watch make-up and dressing from 5 to 6.45 pm. The performance is from 6.45 to 8.15 pm. Cost is Rs 100.

On weekends, cultural programs involving music and dance are sometimes performed on the beach. You'll see the flags notifying all the details.

For less cultural pursuits, western videos are shown twice a night in a few restaurants.

Shopping

Kovalam Beach has numerous craft and carpet shops (usually of Tibetan, Kashmiri and Rajasthani origin), clothing stores (ready to wear and made to order), book exchanges, general stores selling everything from cornflakes to sunscreen, travel agencies, and even yoga schools. Beach vendors sell batik *lungis* (sarongs), beach mats, sunglasses and leaf paintings, while others offer cheap (and illegal) Kerala grass.

Getting There & Away

Bus The local No 111 bus between Thiruvananthapuram and Kovalam Beach runs every 30 minutes between 5.30 am and 9.30 pm and costs Rs 4. The bus leaves Thiruvananthapuram, East Fort, Stand 19, on MG Rd, 100m south of the municipal bus stand. At Kovalam, the buses start and finish at the entrance to the Ashok Beach Resort.

There are also direct services to Ernakulam (Rs 63, 5½ hours) and Kanyakumari (Rs 22, 1½ hours, four daily) – good ways of avoiding the Thiruvananthapuram crush. Every morning a bus leaves for Thekkady in the Periyar Wildlife Sanctuary (Rs 95, 8½ hours). Direct buses go to Kollam (Rs 20, two hours).

Taxi & Auto-Rickshaw A taxi between Thiruvananthapuram and Kovalam Beach costs around Rs 250; auto-rickshaws are about Rs 100. It's best to arrive at the lighthouse (Vizhinjam) end of the beach because it's closer to the hotels and there are fewer touts. Prepaid taxis from Thiruvananthapuram airport to the beach cost around Rs 190 to Rs 225. Don't assume a rickshaw will be cheaper than a taxi – shop around.

Getting Around

It's easy to walk around Kovalam. For trips further afield take a bus from Ashok Beach Resort or you can hire your own two-wheeler transport from Voyager Travel (☎ 481993) or the next door Fly India (☎ 481763). Both have well-maintained machines. Prices per day (including helmet and insurance) are Rs 500 for an Enfield Bullet; Rs 350 for a Honda (100cc) and Rs 300 for a scooter. Discounts are available after five days. You'll need a current driver's licence and

KERALA

you'll be asked to surrender a passport or air ticket as security. Try to negotiate something less valuable as security.

AROUND KOVALAM
Vizhinjam
The fishing village of Vizhinjam (pronounced *Virinyam*), just 1km south of Kovalam Beach, is a sobering reminder of your geographic and cultural situation after the resort atmosphere of Kovalam. Once a capital of the Ay kingdom (600-1000 AD), its big artificial harbour is now dominated by a pink and green mosque on the northern end and a huge Catholic church to the south. Christian/Muslim relations have been tense, erupting in periodic violence in which several villagers have died. The peace is now maintained by a permanent police presence and a 'no-man's-land' between the two settlements.

Unless you have religious or other specific reasons for visiting Vizhinjam, it's possibly best not to go. Your presence can be intrusive and it would be easy to offend locals by wandering around in the same manner as you would at Kovalam Beach. If you do go, dress appropriately, be sensitive to the economic divide and take care in no-man's-land – its edges are well-used public toilets.

Pulinkudi & Chowara
Eight kilometres south of Kovalam are several interesting alternatives to Kovalam's crowded beaches. Prices quoted here are high season (and exclude 20% tax). Low-season rates may drop by 50%.

The Surya Samudra Beach Garden (☎ 480413, fax 481124) is a small and very select hotel with individual cottages, many of them constructed from transplanted traditional Keralan houses. There are private beaches, a fantastic natural rock swimming pool, and music, martial arts or dance performances at night. The food is superb. Room rates range from US$100 to US$360.

Somatheeram Ayurvedic Beach Resort (☎ 0471-481600, fax 480600), a little farther south at Chowara, combines beach life with ayurvedic medical treatment. Room prices range from US$45 to US$170. Various treatment packages are available. There is a sister resort, *Manaltheeram*, nearby.

Samudra Beach & Pozhikkara Beach
Samudra Beach, about 4km north of Kovalam, has a number of resorts competing for space with the local fishing villages. The steep and rough beach is not as amenable for swimming as the beaches further south and local resentment to tourism is discernible.

The KTDC *Hotel Samudra* (☎ 480089, fax 480242), a pleasant retreat from hectic Kovalam, has its own bar and restaurant. Air-con doubles cost Rs 3990.

Alitalia Beach House (☎ 480042), run by the amiable Shah Jahan, has singles for Rs 550 and doubles for Rs 1100. There's also a rooftop restaurant.

Lagoona Davina (☎ 480049, fax 450041), at Pachalloor village, behind Pozhikkara Beach, 5km north of Kovalam, is a small, exclusive resort with several tiny cabins that cost from Rs 3750 for room and breakfast.

VARKALA
☎ 0472 • pop 41,400
Varkala is a developing beach resort 41km north of Thiruvananthapuram. One look and it's apparent the mistakes of Kovalam are being repeated. Inappropriate developments already mar the beach, and garbage is piling up. Still, an Arabian Sea sunset viewed from the cliff-top is unlikely to be forgotten.

Orientation & Information
The town and the train station are 2km from the beach. The post office and police aid post are just before the helipad. Email exists in theory, but at the time of writing the server had been down for three months.

The Bureau de Change (☎ 602749) at Temple Junction cashes travellers cheques, has STD/ISD, and bus and train timetables. It's open daily 9 am to 10 pm.

The Tourist Helping Centre, at the beach end of Beach Rd, is friendly and organises elephant rides (full day, Rs 800) and backwater trips (full day, Rs 600). (See Beware the Middle Men of Varkala boxed text.)

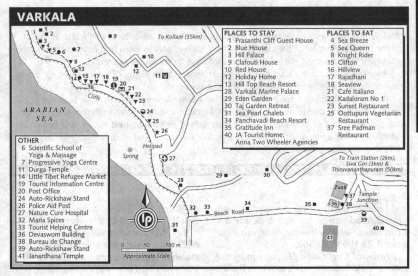

VARKALA

PLACES TO STAY	PLACES TO EAT
1 Prasanthi Cliff Guest House	4 Sea Breeze
2 Blue House	5 Sea Queen
3 Hill Palace	8 Knight Rider
9 Clafouti House	15 Clifton
10 Red House	16 Hillview
12 Holiday Home	17 Rajadhani
13 Hill Top Beach Resort	18 Seaview
28 Varkala Marine Palace	21 Cafe Italiano
29 Eden Garden	22 Kadaloram No 1
30 Taj Garden Retreat	23 Sunset Restaurant
31 Sea Pearl Chalets	25 Oottupura Vegetarian
34 Panchavadi Beach Resort	Restaurant
35 Gratitude Inn	37 Sree Padman
40 JA Tourist Home;	Restaurant
Anna Two Wheeler Agencies	

OTHER
6 Scientific School of
 Yoga & Massage
7 Progressive Yoga Centre
11 Durga Temple
14 Little Tibet Refugee Market
19 Tourist Information Centre
20 Post Office
24 Auto-Rickshaw Stand
26 Police Aid Post
27 Nature Cure Hospital
32 Maria Spices
33 Tourist Helping Centre
36 Devaswom Building
38 Bureau de Change
39 Auto-Rickshaw Stand
41 Janardhana Temple

To Kollam (35km)

ARABIAN
SEA

Cliffs

Helipad

Spring

To Train Station (2km),
Siva Giri (3km) &
Thiruvananthapuram (50km)

Beach Road

Temple
Junction

Tank

0   50   100 m
Approximate Scale

There is also a privately run tourist information centre just near the post office. The centre is primarily for ticketing and tour bookings.

Many small stores on the cliff-top have food items plus a few essentials such as soap and batteries.

Things to See & Do
Varkala is first and foremost a temple town and the **Janardhana Temple** is on Beach Rd. Non-Hindus may not enter but may be invited into the temple grounds where there is a huge banyan tree and shrines to Ayappa, Hanuman and Hindu deities.

Sivagiri Mutt is the headquarters of the Sree Narayana Dharma Sanghom Trust (☎ 602221, fax 550651), the ashram devoted to Sree Narayana Guru (1855-1928) who preached 'one caste, one religion, one god for people'. Inquiries are welcome.

There are numerous centres for **yoga** and **massage** and the quality of offering varies. Both the Progressive Yoga Centre and the Scientific School of Yoga & Massage offer courses and massage. Neither have phones,

so check with the Tourist Helping Centre to see if they are operating.

Places to Stay
Most places to stay are at the beach, which can disappear almost entirely during the monsoon, gradually reappearing in time for the tourist onslaught. Budget and mid-range accommodation is generally very good value as are the top-end places in the low season. Prices quoted here are high season (December to February); considerable discounts apply in low season.

Places to Stay – Budget
JA Tourist Home (☎ 602453) has basic accommodation ranging from Rs 75 to Rs 150.

Gratitude Inn (Beach Rd) has small, clean singles/doubles for Rs 100/150, and the expectation that you'll purchase handicrafts from the owner's Cottage Emporium!

Varkala Marine Palace (☎ 603204) has rooms from Rs 200 to Rs 500 with an open-air tandoor restaurant overlooking the beach.

On the cliffs, 10 minutes' walk north, accommodation is provided by small hotels

Beware the Middlemen of Varkala

Middlemen posing as travel agents and promoting bogus adventures proliferate in Varkala. Some travellers pay what they believe to be a full fee, only to learn that payment due at the other end has not been passed on. Then they have to cough up again.

Another trick is for the boat guide to ply passengers with plenty of 'complimentary' drinks and to present a massive drinks bill at the journey's end.

If you are planning a backwater trip or any other journey, choose your booking agent wisely. Ask many questions, shop around, take notes and don't pay a single rupee until you have clarified that all bookings have been confirmed and will be paid for on your behalf. As usual, seek the opinions of other travellers. Obtain advice and recommendations from the KTDC in Thiruvananthapuram before setting out.

and families. Some of these places haven't yet acquired names, so just look for the *Blue House* or *Red House*, with rooms at around Rs 100 to Rs 300.

Prasanthi Cliff Guest House, run by the folks at Cafe Italiano (make inquiries there), has three small, charmingly decorated rooms with common bath for Rs 250.

Hill Palace has very basic though acceptable rooms for Rs 75 with shared facilities or Rs 125 with bath.

Hill Top Beach Resort has simple rooms with bath for Rs 250 downstairs and Rs 450 upstairs. There's a restaurant.

Holiday Home (☎ 601054) is new, quiet and good value at Rs 200 for a double.

Places to Stay – Mid-Range & Top End

Eden Garden (☎ 603910, fax 481004) is delightfully situated, overlooking paddy fields. The 10 rather small, low-ceilinged rooms are Rs 350 for doubles. There's an in-house masseur.

Panchavadi Beach Resort (☎ 600200) has six small rooms for Rs 400 and two family rooms (each with two double beds) for Rs 700.

Clafouti House (☎ 601414) offers an intimate, homey atmosphere with the wafting smell of French pastries and clean double rooms for Rs 300.

Sea Pearl Chalets (☎ 605875) consists of 10 concrete wigwams on the headland south

of Beach Rd. Rooms overlooking the sea cost Rs 500 a double, the others are Rs 400.

Taj Garden Retreat (☎ 603000, fax 602296), a resort overlooking the beach has standard air-con rooms for US$80/90 to US$110/120. There's a restaurant, bar, pool, tennis courts and health club.

Places to Eat

Varkala's dry (no alcohol) status is somewhat remedied by the provision of 'special coffee'.

Sree Padman Restaurant, perched right at the edge of the tank at Temple Junction, is popular with locals and travellers alike.

Clafouti (☎ 601414) has delicious French pastries and coffee.

Many cliff-top places are seasonal, opening up at north Varkala Beach from November to February. They include *Sea Breeze*, *Sea Queen*, *Knight Rider*, *Clifton*, *Hilltop*, *Hillview*, *Seaview*, *Rajadhani*, *Cafe Italiano*, *Kadaloram No 1* and *Sunset Restaurant*. All offer similar standards (shaky tables and a diverse collection of rickety chairs), similar food (fresh fish on display out the front at night) and similar service (usually incredibly slow). A small tandoor tuna with rice or chips and salad costs about Rs 100.

For vegetarians, *Oottupura* serves a decent range of dishes.

Entertainment

Kathakali performances in the atmospheric surroundings of the old Devaswom building are held every Sunday, Wednesday and Friday during December and January for Rs 75. Make-up and dressing is from 5 to 6.45 pm and the performance with English commentary is from 6.45 to 8.15 pm.

Shopping

There are numerous craft places – try the Little Tibet Refugee Market. For spices there's Maria Spices.

Getting There & Away

Varkala is 41km north of Thiruvananthapuram by train (Rs 21/112 in 2nd/1st class, 55 minutes) and just 24km south of Kollam (Rs 18/100, 45 minutes). There are regular buses to/from Thiruvananthapuram and Kollam that stop at Temple Junction. From Varkala, it's easy to get to Kollam in time for the morning backwater boat to Alappuzha. A taxi from Thiruvananthapuram direct to Varkala costs about Rs 550 (Rs 650 from Kovalam).

Getting Around

Auto-rickshaws between the train station and Varkala's Temple Junction are Rs 20. A taxi to the beach costs about Rs 60. You can hire a 350cc Enfield Bullet (Rs 350 per day), and other bikes from Anna Two Wheeler Agencies, on the ground floor of JA Tourist Home on Beach Rd.

KOLLAM (Quilon)

☎ 0474 • pop 362,572

Surrounded by coconut palms and cashew plantations on the edge of Ashtamudi Lake, Kollam, still referred to as Quilon (pronounced 'koy-lon'), is a typical Keralan market town, with old wooden houses whose red-tiled roofs overhang winding streets.

The Malayalam era is calculated from the founding of Kollam in the 9th century.

Kollam is the southern gateway to the backwaters of Kerala, and is well known for the Kollam-Alappuzha backwater cruise (see The Backwaters boxed text).

Information

There's a very helpful District Tourism Promotion Council (DTPC) tourist information centre near the KSRTC bus stand (open daily 8 am to 7 pm), and another at the train station.

You can cash travellers cheques at the Bank of Baroda, or more quickly at the DTPC tourist information centre, between 10 am and 2 pm.

Email (Rs 100 per hour) is available at the very efficient Net 4 You (☎ 74126) in Bishop Jerome Nagar Complex and also at the DTPC Automation Centre (in the tourist centre).

Things to See & Do

In its efforts to promote Kollam as more than a stopping place for backwater tours, DTPC has developed a wide range of activities to suit all budgets. An example of its entrepreneurial acumen is the new monsoon package for Middle East visitors, desperate to experience rain. Other activities include the annual **Ashtamudi Craft & Art Festival of India,** from 26 December to 10 January, which involves artists from all over India. Workshops, demonstrations and exhibitions showcase the art at Asraman Maidan and entry is free. Plans are afoot to include centres that provide year-round yoga and ayurvedic treatments, water sports and performing arts.

Ayurvedic treatment including massage is available at Prince Health Club (☎ 749009) on Beach Rd.

There are several churches of interest. In town is the extraordinary **Shrine of Our Lady of Velamkanni** and at **Thangasseri,** 5km from Kollam's centre, there are 18th century sites.

Organised Tours

Guided tours (from Rs 250 per person) through the myriad paths and canals of **Monroe Island** in Ashtamudi Lake are organised by the DTPC. Tours include observation of prawn and fish farming, coir making, and even matchstick making, as well as opportunities for bird-watching.

Places to Stay – Budget

The *Government Guest House* (☎ 70356), 3km north of the centre on Ashtamudi Lake, is a forgotten relic of the Raj. Immense rooms, decorated with old willow pattern

KERALA

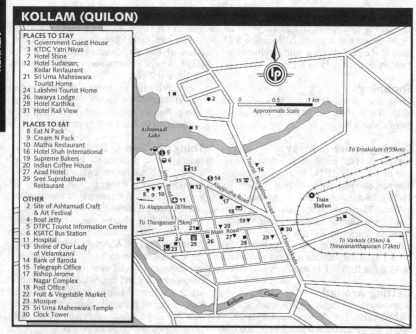

KOLLAM (QUILON)

PLACES TO STAY
1 Government Guest House
3 KTDC Yatri Nivas
7 Hotel Shine
12 Hotel Sudarsan;
    Kedar Restaurant
21 Sri Uma Maheswara
    Tourist Home
24 Lakshmi Tourist Home
26 Iswarya Lodge
28 Hotel Karthika
31 Hotel Rail View

PLACES TO EAT
8 Eat N Pack
9 Cream N Pack
10 Matha Restaurant
16 Hotel Shah International
19 Supreme Bakers
20 Indian Coffee House
27 Azad Hotel
29 Sree Suprabatham
    Restaurant

OTHER
2 Site of Ashtamudi Craft
    & Art Festival
4 Boat Jetty
5 DTPC Tourist Information Centre
6 KSRTC Bus Station
11 Hospital
13 Shrine of Our Lady
    of Velamkanni
14 Bank of Baroda
15 Telegraph Office
17 Bishop Jerome
    Nagar Complex
18 Post Office
22 Fruit & Vegetable Market
23 Mosque
25 Sri Uma Maheswara Temple
30 Clock Tower

Ashtamudi Lake

Approximate Scale
0   0.5   1 km

To Ernakulam (159km)

Train Station

To Alappuzha (87km)
To Thangasseri (5km)

Main Road

To Varkala (35km) &
Thiruvananthapuram (72km)

Kollam Canal

plates, are a bargain at Rs 55 per person but getting into town can be difficult because of the scarcity of auto-rickshaws.

Lakshmi Tourist Home (☎ 741067) is a no-frills lodge with clean singles/doubles for Rs 60/100 with bath.

Hotel Karthika (☎ 76241) is a large, popular place built around a central courtyard. Decent rooms are Rs 125/220 with bath or Rs 350 with air-con.

Iswarya Lodge (☎ 77801, Main Rd), nearby, is slightly cheaper at Rs 70/129.

Sri Uma Maheswara Tourist Home (☎ 743712) has doubles with bath for Rs 140. Staff are friendly and the premises clean.

Hotel Shine offers rooms for Rs 110/125 with bath.

Hotel Rail View (☎ 76918), opposite the train station, has rooms for Rs 70/100 and a bar and restaurant.

There are *retiring rooms* at the station.

Places to Stay – Mid-Range & Top End

Hotel Sudarsan (☎ 744322, fax 740480) is welcoming and good value at Rs 210/260 or from Rs 420/500 with air-con. Back rooms are quieter. All rooms have TV and there are restaurants and a bar.

The KTDC *Yatri Nivas* (☎ 745538) has a terrific riverside location and a touch of the grots. Rooms cost from Rs 120/175 to Rs 180/250, or Rs 400 for an air-con double. You can get across to the boat jetty in the hotel's speedboat or by auto-rickshaw for Rs 20.

Places to Eat

Matha Restaurant serves up a wickedly spicy chicken – a firm favourite with the rickshaw-drivers. Next door, *Eat N Pack* (thali Rs 10) and *Cream N Pack* (delicious ice cream), flank Hello Footwear.

Azad Hotel is bright, with veg and non-veg meals. The *Indian Coffee House* is on Main Rd.

Sree Suprabatham Restaurant, a typical 'meals' restaurant, serves lots of good, quick food.

Kedar Restaurant, in Hotel Sudarsan, is an air-con haven, with good, if somewhat bland, food.

Hotel Shah International's restaurant has good food and service.

Jala Subhiksa, a converted Keralan rice barge at the boat jetty, is Kollam's floating restaurant, serving multicuisine food.

Supreme Bakers, opposite the post office, is great for a treat – cakes, coffee and sweets.

Kollam is a cashew growing centre and nuts can be bought for Rs 10 to Rs 20.

Getting There & Away

Bus Kollam is on the well-serviced Thiruvananthapuram-Kollam-Alappuzha-Ernakulam bus route. The superexpress services (reservations possible) take 1½ hours to Thiruvananthapuram (Rs 30); 1¾ hours to Alappuzha (Rs 30); and 3½ hours to Ernakulam (Rs 65).

Train Kollam is 159km south of Ernakulam and the three to four hour trip costs Rs 47/224 in 2nd/1st class. The *Trivandrum Mail* from Chennai goes through Kollam, as does the *Mumbai-Kanyakumari Express* and the Mangalore-Thiruvananthapuram coastal service.

The *Quilon Mail* between Kollam and Chennai (Egmore station) via Madurai covers the 760km in 20 hours for Rs 211/737. The trip across the Western Ghats is a delight.

Boat See The Backwaters boxed text for information on backwater cruises to Alappuzha. There are public ferry services across Ashtamudi Lake to Guhanandapuram (one hour), Muthiraparam (2½ hours) or Perumon (2½ hours); fares are around Rs 6 return. The daily ATDC and DTPC tourist boats to Alappuzha can be booked at various hotels around town, but substantial discounts are given for direct bookings, with further discounts for students and pensioners. The tours either start by bus from the KSRTC bus stand or from one of the town jetties.

Getting Around

The KSRTC bus stand and the boat jetty are side by side, but the train station is on the opposite side of town. Auto-rickshaw drivers are reasonably willing to use their meters; expect to pay around Rs 10 from the train station to the boat jetty. The *Yatri Nivas* speedboat can be hired to explore the waterways for Rs 300 an hour.

AROUND KOLLAM
Krishnapuram Palace Museum

Two kilometres south of Kayankulam (halfway between Kollam and Alappuzha), the Krishnapuram Palace has been fully restored and is a fine example of Keralan architecture. Now a museum, the two storey palace houses paintings and antique furniture and sculptures. Its renowned mural, some 3m high, depicts the Gajendra Moksha, or liberation of Gajendra, the chief of the elephants, as told in the *Mahabharata*.

The palace is well worth a visit. Buses (Rs 12) leave Kollam every three minutes for Kayankulam. Get off at the bus stand near the temple gate, 2km before Kayankulam. From the bus stand it's a 600m very obvious walk to the palace. The palace is open 10 am to 1pm and to 2 pm to 5pm) daily except Monday. Entry is Rs 2.

ALAPPUZHA (Alleppey)
☎ 0477 • pop 264,969

Like Kollam, this is a pleasant, easy-going market town built on canals and surrounded by coconut trees. A walk through the streets will present many examples of Keralan architecture. If you arrive in mid-December you can enjoy the festivities at the **Mullakal Temple** when some of India's finest temple musicians perform in the main hall. In August, the annual **Nehru Cup Snake Boat Race** is not to be missed. And of course in this houseboat city, there are many opportunities for backwater tours (see The Backwaters boxed text following).

The Backwaters

Fringing the coast of Kerala and winding far inland is a vast network of lagoons, lakes, rivers and canals. These backwaters represent a unique geological formation and are the basis of a distinct lifestyle. Travelling the backwaters is one of the highlights of a visit to Kerala. The larger boats are motorised but there are numerous smaller boats propelled by punting with a long bamboo pole. The boats cross shallow, palm-fringed lakes studded with cantilevered Chinese fishing nets, and travel along narrow, shady canals where *coir* (coconut fibre), *copra* (dried coconut meat) and cashews are loaded onto boats. Along the way are small settlements where people live on narrow spits of reclaimed land only a few metres wide. Although practically surrounded by water, they still manage to keep cows, pigs, chickens and ducks and cultivate small vegetable gardens. Prawns and fish, including the prized *karimeen*, are also farmed, and shellfish are dredged by hand to be later burnt with coal dust to produce lime.

A comprehensive listing of backwater tours throughout Kerala is available in the brochure *The Backwaters of Kerala Tourist Guide*, available from tourist offices. The brochure includes prices and telephone booking contacts. More information is available on Kerala Tourism's Web site (www.keralatourism.org).

Backwater Ecology The backwaters are severely threatened by population growth, tourism, industry and agriculture. Kerala has 29 major lakes on the backwater system, seven of which drain to the sea. Land reclamation projects, legal and illegal, have reduced the area of these lakes from 440 sq km in 1968 to less than 350 sq km today (Only one-third of their mid-19th century levels). Pollution and destructive fishing (using dynamite, poison and very fine nets) has resulted in the extinction of mangroves, crocodiles and migratory fish. Many migratory birds no longer visit the backwaters. To the casual eye, the most visible danger is the spread of water hyacinth (African moss or Nile cabbage), which clogs many stretches of canal and causes difficulties for the boat operators.

Tourist Cruises The most popular backwater cruise is the eight hour trip between Kollam and Alappuzha.There are virtually identical daily cruises operated between Kollam and Alappuzha on alternate days by the Alleppey Tourism Development Cooperative (ATDC) and the state government District Tourism Promotion Council (DTPC). The ATDC office is in Komala Rd, Alappuzha, while the Alappuzha DTPC can be found at the Tourist Reception Centre. In Kollam, the DTPC is near the KSRTC bus station. Many hotels in Kollam and Alappuzha take bookings for one or other of these services. The cost is Rs 150 one way. Direct bookings with the DTPC in Kollam attract significant discounts. Discounts are even greater for students and pensioners. Cruises depart at 10.30 am and arrive at their destination at 6.30 pm.

Generally only two major stops are made along the way: a noon lunch stop and a brief afternoon chai stop. Ayiramthengu or the coir village of Thrikkunnappuha, and the island of Lekshmithuruthu are popular stops. Lekshmithuruthu is the lunch stop. Here you can witness a demonstration of Kathakali expressions and gestures. While this helps to understand a performance, at Rs 250 per person it is somewhat overpriced. A better option is to stay overnight and witness a performance which begins at 5.30 pm. Basic accommodation can be arranged for Rs 200 per double. You can then pick up the boat the following afternoon. To book, ring ☎ 0476-826449. The crew have an ice box full of fruit, soft drinks and beer to sell, although you might want to bring along additional refreshments and snacks. Bring sunscreen and a hat as well.

The Backwaters

Boats drop visitors off at the **Matha Amrithanandamayi Mission** (☎ 0476-621279) at Amrithapuri, the residence of Sri Sri Matha Amrithanandamayi Devi, one of India's very few female gurus, also known as The Hugging Mother. Visitors should dress conservatively and there is a strict code of behaviour to which all visitors are expected to adhere. You can stay at the ashram for Rs 100 per day (price includes meals), and you can pick up an onward or return cruise a day or two later. The trip also passes the **Kumarakody Temple**, where the noted Malayalam poet Kumaran Asan drowned. Close to Alappuzha, there's a glimpse of the 11th century **Karumadi Kuttan Buddha image** near the canal bank.

The cruise between Alappuzha and Kottayam is about 4½ hours (it follows a longer route than the public ferry, see below). The operator is the Bharath Tourist Service Society or BTSS (☎ 0477-262262), based in Alappuzha at the Raiban Shopping Complex on Boat Jetty Rd, and the cost is Rs 100 one way. Boats depart Alappuzha at 9.30 am, and Kottayam at 2.30 pm. The DTPC also runs a four hour cruise which departs Alappuzha at 10 am and returns at 2 pm. This cruise leaves daily during December and January, and on weekends during the rest of the year. The cost is Rs 100, or Rs 60 concession (students and children).

Houseboats & Charters A popular, but at times overpriced, option is to hire a houseboat, converted from a *kettuvallam*, or traditional rice barge. Boats can also be chartered through the DTPC in Kollam and Alappuzha. Houseboats cater for groups (up to eight bunks) or couples (one or two double bedrooms). They can be hired either on a day basis (Rs 3500 per boat) or overnight (Rs 5000), allowing you to make the Kollam-Alappuzha trip over two days, mooring in the backwaters overnight. Food can be provided (including a cook) for an extra Rs 400 per person. The DTPC also hires four-seat speedboats for Rs 300 per hour, and six-seaters for Rs 200 per hour. Between a group of people, this can be an economical proposition that allows you to plan your own itinerary. In Alappuzha, the tourist boats are moored across the North Canal from the boat jetty. Go directly to the boats if you don't want to deal with an intermediary tout. A one-way trip to Kottayam costs about Rs 500. Alternatively, there are boat operators like Penguin Tourist Boat Service (☎ 0477-261522) on Boat Jetty Rd, who have a long list of suggested trips from Alappuzha. Vembanad Tourist Services (☎ 0477-251395) and Blue Lagoon (☎ 0477-260103), both in Alappuzha, also have boats for hire.

Backwater Village Tours These usually involve small groups of less than 10 people, a knowledgeable guide and an open work boat or covered kettuvallam. The tours last from 2½ to six hours. You are taken to villages to watch coir making, boat building, toddy tapping and fish farming, and on the longer trips a traditional Keralan lunch is provided. These tours are more rewarding to the tourist and the villagers. Some of the best village tours operate out of Kochi, Kollam and Thiruvananthapuram (see Organised Tours in the relevant sections).

Public Ferries Most passengers on the eight hour Kollam-Alappuzha cruise will be western travellers. If you want the local experience or a shorter trip, there are State Water Transport boats between Alappuzha and Kottayam (Rs 6, 2½ hours, six boats daily) and Changanassery (Rs 9, three hours, two boats daily). The trip to Kottayam crosses Vembanad Lake and then runs along a fascinating canal. Changanassery is on the road and railway line, 18km south of Kottayam and 78km north of Kollam.

KERALA

ALAPPUZHA TO KOLLAM

Vembanad Lake

To Kottayam & Kochi

Alappuzha (Alleppey)

Changanassery

Karumadi
Kuttan
Ambalapuzha

Tiruvalla

Thrikkunnappuha
Haripad

Mavelikara

Kayankulam Kayal (Lake)

Kayankulam

ARABIAN SEA

Amrithapuh Ayiramthengu

47

Lekshmithuruthu Island

Karungapalli

Sasthankkota

Ashtamudi Kayal (Lake)

Panmana

Canal Entrance

Thirumullavaram
Thangasseri Prince Health Club Kollam (Quilon)

0   5   10 km

Orientation & Information
The bus stand and boat jetty are close to each other, and within easy walking distance of most of the cheap hotels. The train station is 4km south-west of the town centre. The DTPC Tourist Reception Centre and the Alleppey Tourism Development Cooperative (ATDC) are both very helpful. The Bank of India on Mullakal Rd cashes travellers cheques.

Alappuzha's water is notoriously unhealthy and it's advisable not to drink it.

Nehru Cup Snake Boat Race
This famous regatta on Vembanad Lake takes place on the second Saturday of August each year. Scores of long, low-slung *chundan vallams* (snake boats) compete for the Nehru Cup. Each boat is crewed by up to 100 rowers shaded by gleaming silk umbrellas. Watched avidly by thousands of spectators, the annual event celebrates the seafaring and martial traditions of ancient Kerala.

Tickets, available from numerous ticket stands, entitle you to seats on bamboo terraces, which are erected for the races. Ticket prices range from Rs 10 for standing room to Rs 250 for the Tourist Pavilion, which offers the best view at the finishing point.

The race is now repeated for tourists in mid-January.

Take food, drink and an umbrella to protect you from the monsoon rains or blistering sunshine.

Places to Stay – Budget
YMCA (☎ 245313) rents most of its rooms to students but visitors may get a place. There's a good restaurant and clean, basic double rooms are Rs 200, or Rs 300 with air-con.

Komala Hotel (☎ 243631), just north of the North Canal, has singles/doubles/triples/quads for Rs 100/140/200/230 and air-con singles/doubles for Rs 400/530 (taxes included).

Sheeba Lodge (☎ 244871), behind the Komala, is cheap and habitable at Rs 80/90, with doubles upstairs for Rs 140.

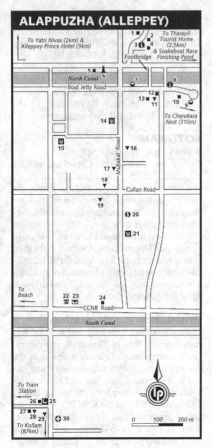

ALAPPUZHA (ALLEPPEY)

PLACES TO STAY
1 Hotel Karthika
2 Sheeba Lodge
4 Komala Hotel
5 YMCA
10 Hotel Arcadia
12 Hotel Raiban Annexe
13 Krishna Bhavan Lodge
24 St George's Lodging
26 Hotel Brothers
27 Hotel Raiban

PLACES TO EAT
11 Annapoorna
16 Hotel Aryas
17 Indian Coffee House
18 Hotel Rajas
19 Sree Durga Bhavan Restaurant
28 Annapoorna
29 Indian Coffee House

OTHER
3 Alappuzha Tourism Development Corporation (ATDC)
6 Mermaid Statue
7 Boat Jetty
8 DTPC Tourist Reception Centre & Restaurant
9 Bus Stand
14 Kidangamparamba Devi Temple
15 Temple
20 Bank of India
21 Mullakal Devi Temple
22 Telegraph Office
23 Post Office
25 Mosque
30 Hospital

Hotel Arcadia (☎ 251354), opposite the boat jetty, has quiet rooms which are good value at Rs 125/200. It has a restaurant and a bar.

St George's Lodging (☎ 251620, CCNB Rd), opposite South Canal, is the best of the cheapies. Clean rooms cost Rs 33/58 with common bath or Rs 45/83 with private bath.

Hotel Brothers (☎ 251653) has OK rooms for Rs 70/140/210 and musty air-con doubles for Rs 295. There's a veg/nonveg restaurant.

Places to Stay – Mid-Range & Top End

Hotel Raiban (☎ 251930), south of South Canal, and the **Hotel Raiban Annexe** (☎ 261017), opposite the jetty, have rooms for Rs 100/180, Rs 350 for an air-con double.

Yatri Nivas (☎ 244460), some 2km north of the town centre, offers clean, basic doubles with bath for Rs 150 or Rs 300 for deluxe air-con.

Alleppey Prince Hotel (☎ 243752, fax 243758, AS Rd), 3km north of the centre, has central air-con and is one of the best in town. It has a bar, an excellent restaurant (opens 7 pm) and an inviting pool. Rooms are Rs 780/880, or Rs 1250 for a suite.

KERALA

Guesthouses, in the form of converted private homes, are becoming a popular alternative to hotels. While children are welcome throughout India, this style of accommodation is particularly suitable for families.

Cherukara Nest *(☎ 251509, fax 243164)* is quiet, with several spacious rooms from Rs 400/550; deluxe rooms are Rs 800/950. Tasty and reasonably priced meals are provided.

Tharayil Tourist Home *(☎/fax 243543, Lake Punnamada Rd, Thathampally)* is 2.5km north-east of town, near the finishing point of the snake boat race. It's very popular, with clean, bright rooms for Rs 200 to Rs 350 (non air-con), up to Rs 750 for air-con.

Places to Eat
The restaurant at the DTPC ***Tourist Reception Centre*** on the North Canal is cheap, clean and offers a varied menu.

There's an ***Indian Coffee House*** branch on Mullakal Rd and another south of the South Canal.

Hotel Aryas *(Mullakal Rd)* serves good, cheap vegetarian meals. ***Hotel Rajas*** is a basic veg/nonveg restaurant.

Sree Durga Bhavan is a cheerful place where a good *masala dosa* is only Rs 8.

Komala Hotel and ***Hotel Raiban*** have OK restaurants, and there are two ***Annapoorna*** veg restaurants: one next door to the Hotel Raiban and the other on Book Jetty Rd.

Vembanad Restaurant at the Alleppey Prince Hotel is comfortable and air-conditioned (or you can elect to eat by the pool). It serves excellent veg/nonveg food.

Getting There & Away
Bus Buses operate frequently on the Thiruvananthapuram-Kollam-Alappuzha-Ernakulam route. From Thiruvananthapuram, it's about 3¼ hours and Rs 45/60 to Alappuzha by superfast/express bus. It takes 1¾ hours and costs Rs 20/27 to reach Ernakulam from Alappuzha. To Kottayam a superfast is Rs 18 and to Changanassery it's Rs 9.50.

Train The train station is about 4km south-west of the town centre. An auto-rickshaw

from town costs about Rs 25. The 57km journey to Ernakulam takes one hour and costs Rs 23/125 in 2nd/1st class. There are also plenty of trains to Kayankulam (Rs 18/105).

Boat Like Kollam, Alappuzha is another point from which to explore the backwaters. See The Backwaters Boxed text in the Around Thiruvananthapuram section.

KOTTAYAM
☎ 0481 • pop 166,552
Once a focus for Syrian Christians of Kerala, Kottayam is now a place of churches and seminaries and an important centre for rubber production. The citizens of Kottayam played an important role in the struggle to end caste injustice.

Kottayam is the headquarters of the daily newspaper *Malayala Manorama*. Published in Malayalam, with a circulation of 1.2 million (and a readership of around 8 million), it's second only to the English-language daily the *Times of India*.

Orientation & Information
The train station, boat jetty and KSRTC bus stand are all 2km to 3km from the centre. The Department of Tourism office is at the Collectorate – but there's no one there, no one knows where they are and the whisky bottle's empty. Instead, try the helpful tourist information office at the KSRTC. The tourist police are also here. The telegraph office, open 24 hours for STD/ISD and faxes, is quiet and very cooperative. Email is available from the efficient Base Station. You can cash travellers cheques and get Visa cash advances at the Canara Bank on KK Rd.

Things to See & Do
The **Thirunakkara Shiva Temple**, in typical Keralan style, is noted for its Kootiattam, traditional Sanskrit drama. Sometimes visitors are admitted. At the **Municipal Stage**, in the town centre, regular dramas are performed for free. About 3km north-west of the centre are two Syrian Christian churches. **Cheriapally**, St Mary's Orthodox Church, has an elegant facade with an interior noted

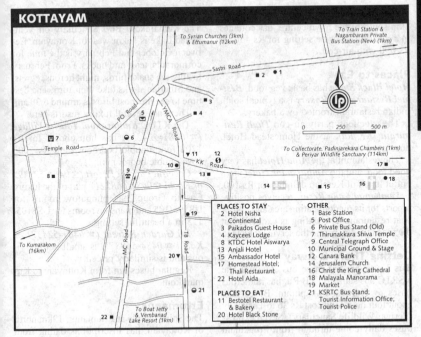

KOTTAYAM

To Syrian Churches (3km)
& Ettumanur (12km)

To Train Station &
Nagambaram Private
Bus Station (New) (1km)

Sastri Road

Temple Road

PO Road

YMCA Road

KK Road

To Collectorate, Padinjarekara Chambers (1km)
& Periyar Wildlife Sanctuary (114km)

0 250 500 m

MC Road

TB Road

To Kumarakom
(16km)

To Boat Jetty
& Vembanad
Lake Resort (1km)

PLACES TO STAY
2 Hotel Nisha
   Continental
3 Paikados Guest House
4 Kaycees Lodge
8 KTDC Hotel Aiswarya
13 Anjali Hotel
15 Ambassador Hotel
17 Homestead Hotel;
   Thali Restaurant
22 Hotel Aida

PLACES TO EAT
11 Bestotel Restaurant
   & Bakery
20 Hotel Black Stone

OTHER
1 Base Station
5 Post Office
6 Private Bus Stand (Old)
7 Thirunakkara Shiva Temple
9 Central Telegraph Office
10 Municipal Ground & Stage
12 Canara Bank
14 Jerusalem Church
16 Christ the King Cathedral
18 Malayala Manorama
19 Market
21 KSRTC Bus Stand;
   Tourist Information Office;
   Tourist Police

for its 400-year-old paintings. **Valiyapally**, another St Mary's church, is 100m away. Built in 1550, its guestbook dates from 1899, and was signed by (among others) Haile Selassie in 1956. An external plaque confirms the entry. **Backwater** trips are popular here (see The Backwaters boxed text earlier).

Places to Stay
Kaycees Lodge (☎ 563440, YMCA Rd) has OK rooms with bath for Rs 80/135. Women will find better options.

The KTDC *Hotel Aiswarya* (☎ 581254), just off Temple Rd, has singles/doubles for Rs 150/200, Rs 400/500 (deluxe) or Rs 600/750 with air-con. It has a multicuisine restaurant and a beer parlour.

The *Ambassador Hotel* (☎ 563293, KK Rd) is off the road – look for the driveway. Singles/doubles are Rs 110/137. There's a bakery and a good veg/nonveg restaurant.

Homestead Hotel (☎ 560467, KK Rd) has pleasant rooms from Rs 130/280, or Rs 600 for an air-con double. There's a vegetarian restaurant.

Hotel Nisha Continental (☎ 563984, Sastri Rd) has ordinary rooms for Rs 195/ 270, and a fairly ordinary restaurant too.

Paikados Guest House (☎ 584340) is very clean, very quiet and good value with rooms for Rs 100/160.

Hotel Aida (☎ 568391, fax 568399, MC Rd) has very comfortable rooms for Rs 300/500, or Rs 400/600 with air-con. It has a bar, a very good restaurant and currency exchange for guests.

Anjali Hotel (☎ 563661, fax 563669, KK Rd) is part of the excellent local Casino hotel chain, but it's somewhat gloomy and tatty here. Rooms range from Rs 675/975 to Rs 1150/1500. It has a bar, coffee shop and a restaurant.

Vembanad Lake Resort (☎ 564866), 2km south of the town centre, has cottages in a pleasant lakeside setting for Rs 450, or Rs 690 with air-con.

Places to Eat

Hotel Black Stone has basic veg food. *Bestotel Restaurant & Bakery* is a typical south Indian restaurant fronted by a bakery.

The excellent, partly air-con *Thali Restaurant (KK Rd)*, at the Homestead Hotel, does good thalis for Rs 20.

The restaurant at the *Aida Hotel* has very good food, and the *Ambassador Hotel* has a buffet lunch of Keralan delights for Rs 100.

Vembanad Lake Resort receives positive reports for its outdoor eating area and houseboat restaurant. The setting is exquisite but the food is ordinary and the service reluctant.

Getting There & Away

Bus Kottayam has three bus stations. The KSRTC bus stand, on TB Rd, has numerous buses to Thiruvananthapuram. Buses take about four hours and cost Rs 36 to Thekkady (Periyar Wildlife Sanctuary). Seven express buses daily come through from Ernakulam and either terminate at Thekkady, or continue to Madurai, a further three hours away.

The other two bus stations are private and mainly operate to local destinations within 10km to 30km – although you can get to Munnar and Kumily from the Nagambaram (new) bus station.

Train Kottayam is well served by express trains running between Thiruvananthapuram (Rs 48/233, three hours, 165km) and Ernakulam (Rs 26/129, two hours, 65km).

Boat The jetty is about 3km from the town centre. Six ferries daily make the 2½ hour trip to Alappuzha for Rs 6 or you can take the BTSS 4½ hour cruise for Rs 100 (see The Backwaters boxed text earlier).

Getting Around

An auto-rickshaw from the train station is Rs 35 to the ferry (ask for 'jetty') and Rs 20 to the KSRTC bus stand.

AROUND KOTTAYAM

The **Kumarakom Bird Sanctuary** on Vembanad Lake is 16km west of Kottayam. Between October and February is the time for cormorants, teals and ducks. From February to July the snake birds, night herons, egrets, and Siberian storks take their turn. The best time to see the most birds is around 6.30 am.

There are several luxury resorts here.

The KTDC *Kumarakom Tourist Village* (☎ 0481-524258) has houseboats for Rs 1200 (one double bedroom) and Rs 2000 (two double bedrooms).

Coconut Lagoon Resort (☎ 0481-524491 or Kochi ☎ 0484-668221), part of the luxury Casino Group, has bungalow rooms for US$95/105 and mansion rooms for US$105/115 in a beautiful setting.

Taj Garden Retreat (☎ 0481-524371 or Kochi ☎ 0484-668377) is small but luxurious and is similarly priced.

Regular buses run from Kottayam to Kumarakom.

Ettumanur

The Shiva temple at Ettumanur, 12km north of Kottayam, has inscriptions dating from 1542, but parts may be older than this. It's noted for its superb woodcarvings and murals similar in style to those at Mattancherry Palace in Kochi. The annual *festival,* involving exposition of the idol (Shiva in his fierce form) and elephant processions, is held in February/March.

Vijnana Kala Vedi Centre

The Vijnana Kala Vedi Cultural Centre at Aranmula, 12km from Changanassery (Changanacherry), offers courses in Indian arts under expert supervision. Subjects include Kathakali, Mohiniattam, Carnatic music, woodcarving, painting, Keralan cooking, languages, *kolams* (auspicious decorations), kalarippayat (Keralan martial art), ayurvedic medicine, astrology and religion.

You can customise your course and stay as long as you like, though a minimum commitment of one month is preferred. Fees, which include full board and two subjects of study, start at around US$200 a week – less for longer stays. For further details, write to The Director, Vijnana Kala Vedi Cultural Centre, Tarayil Mukku Junction, Aranmula 689533, Kerala.

Sree Vallabha Temple

Traditional, all-night **Kathakali** performances are staged almost every night at this temple, 2km from Tiruvilla. Non-Hindus may watch. Tiruvilla, 35km south of Kottayam, is on the rail route between Ernakulam and Thiruvananthapuram. The *DTPC Complex (no phone)*, 100m before the temple, has very basic double rooms for Rs 60.

The Western Ghats

PERIYAR WILDLIFE SANCTUARY
☎ 0486

Periyar is South India's most popular wildlife sanctuary. It encompasses an area of 777 sq km, with a 26 sq km artificial lake, created by the British in 1895. It's home to bison, antelopes, sambar, wild boar, monkeys, langur, a variety of birds, some 750 elephants and an estimated 35 tigers. But if you hope to see tigers, you're almost certain to be disappointed. If, on the other hand, you treat Periyar as a pleasant escape from the rigours of Indian travel, and an opportunity for a lake cruise and a jungle walk, then you'll probably find a visit quite enjoyable. Bring clothing that's warm and waterproof.

Orientation & Information

Kumily, 4km from the sanctuary and the closest town, is a small, tourist place with spice shops and Kashmiri emporiums. Thekkady is the centre inside the park with the KTDC hotels and the boat jetty. When people refer to the sanctuary, they tend to use Kumily, Thekkady and Periyar interchangeably, which can be confusing. 'Periyar' is used to refer to the whole park.

There's a Wildlife Information Centre in Thekkady and if you think you've come to terms with the DTPC, KTDC, ATDC etc, now try the IDTIO (Iddiki District Tourist Information Office) and the TTDC (Thekkady Tourist Development Council). DC Books (☎ 322548) has a wide selection of books and cassettes and the Nature Shop (☎ 322763) markets WWF merchandise. You can change money at Mukkadans Money Exchange, have an oily massage at the Ayurvedic Hospital or visit a spice garden.

The post office is near the park entrance and there are numerous STD/ISD kiosks. Faxes within the country are possible, but not overseas. Rissas Internet has email, but it's painfully slow.

Visiting the Park

Admission to the park enables multiple entries for three days and costs Rs 2 for Indians; Rs 50 for foreigners.

Two-hour **boat trips** on the lake are the usual way of touring the sanctuary. Entry to the park doesn't guarantee a place on the boat and since advance bookings are generally not possible you may be disappointed. If you miss out, hang around and pursue other possibilities – a place may miraculously appear. Boat tickets cost Rs 25/50 on the lower/upper deck in the larger KTDC craft, or Rs 15 in the sad-looking Forest Department craft. There are five KTDC cruises a day: at 7, 9.30 and 11.30 am and 2 and 4 pm and four Forest Department cruises (same times minus the 7am departure). The first and last departures offer the best wildlife-spotting prospects. It's better to get a small group together (the smaller the better) and charter your own boat. They're available in a variety of sizes from Rs 500 per cruise for a 12-person boat. Tickets for video cameras cost Rs 25 from the Wildlife Information Centre. Don't forget to get one; they're strictly policed.

Guided **jungle walks** depart daily at 7.30 am for about three hours and cost Rs 10 per person. Many visitors find these disappointing due to the lack of information and the often large and noisy groups. For walks further into the park the guides can be arranged from the Wildlife Information Centre. This activity isn't promoted because it's not official business – rather a sideline for the guides, so you must be insistent about it.

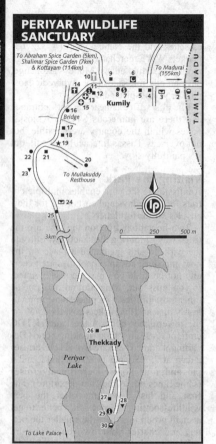

PERIYAR WILDLIFE SANCTUARY

To Abraham Spice Garden (5km), Shalimar Spice Garden (7km) & Kottayam (114km)

To Madurai (155km)

TAMIL NADU

Kumily

Bridge

To Mullakuddy Resthouse

3km

0   250   500 m

Thekkady

Periyar Lake

To Lake Palace

PERIYAR WILDLIFE SANCTUARY

PLACES TO STAY
4   Hotel Regent Tower; Maharani
5   Muckumkal Tourist Home;
    Little Chef Restaurant
9   Lake Queen Tourist Home;
    Lakeland Restaurant
12 Rolex Tourist Home; TTDC
17 Spice Village
18 Taj Garden Retreat
21 Hotel Ambadi
26 Periyar House
27 Aranya Nivas

PLACES TO EAT
23 Coffee Inn
28 Snack Bar

OTHER
1   Tamil Nadu Bus Station
2   Bus Stand & Tourist Taxis
3   Post Office
6   Mosque
7   Mukkadans Money Exchange
8   Rissas Internet
10 Lourdes Church
11 Iddiki District Tourist
    Information Office
13 Ayurvedic Hospital
14 St George Orthodox Church
15 Kumily Central Hospital
16 Ninja Tailoring & Spices
19 Tourist Police
20 Wildlife Preservation Office
22 Nature Shop – WWF
24 Post Office
25 Park Entry Post
29 Wildlife Information Centre
30 Boat Jetty

More serious **trekking** can be organised at the Nature Shop but it's best arranged in Thiruvananthapuram before leaving for Thekkady. Contact Kerala Travels Interserve (☎ 0471-324158, fax 323154) Mangala Saudham, Vellayambalam. Prices start at US$250 per person for two days.

Another way to see wildlife is to spend a night in an *observation tower* or *resthouse* (see Places to Stay). Elephant rides (Rs 30 for two people for 30 minutes) are for fun, not for serious wildlife-viewing.

The best time to visit the sanctuary is from September to May. Although the hot season (February to May) may be less comfortable, it offers more opportunities for wildlife sightings because, with other water resources drying up, the animals are forced to the lakeside. Avoid weekends and public holidays because of noisy day-trippers.

Spice Gardens
Spice Tours are organised by almost every spice shop and cost Rs 350 for about 3½

hours. They're good value if you get a knowledgeable guide. The Thekkady Tourism Development Council (TTDC) at Rolex Tourist Home and Ninja Tailoring & Spices are two possibilities.

At Abraham Organic Spice Garden, Kottayam Rd, opposite the Tropical Plantations, 5km from Kumily, the owners will show you around for Rs 50 per person.

Places to Stay & Eat

Prices quoted here are for the high season (21 December to 20 January). Discounts are available out of season.

Outside the Sanctuary *The Muckumkal Tourist Home* (☎ 322070) has its quieter rooms at the front, away from the generator. Rooms with bath are Rs 80/160; air-con doubles are Rs 500. The attached *Little Chef Restaurant* is OK.

Hotel Regent Tower, nearby, is run by the same folk. Rooms cost Rs 120/220, and there's a restaurant, the *Maharani*.

Lake Queen Tourist Home (☎ 322084) has 54 clean rooms from Rs 107/161. Run by the Catholic church, its profits go to charity. The *Lakeland Restaurant* is downstairs.

Rolex Tourist Home (☎ 322081) has clean, noisy singles/doubles with bath for Rs 100/250.

Taj Garden Retreat (☎ 322041, fax 22106) has rooms for US$95/105 for foreigners and Rs 3000 for Indians.

Spice Village (☎ 322314) has thoughtful service. Very attractive cottages in a pleasant garden are US$95/105, or US$145 for deluxe bungalows. Lunch and dinner buffets in the salubrious restaurant are Rs 300.

Hotel Ambadi (☎ 322193) has dank cottages (that some travellers find OK) for Rs 420 to Rs 690, and rooms for Rs 900 in a beautiful setting with a good multicuisine restaurant.

Coffee Inn is an indoor/outdoor cafe with travellers' fare (including home-made brown bread). There are also two small rooms with shared bath for Rs 150/175.

There are cheap meals places along Kumily's main drag.

Inside the Sanctuary The KTDC has three hotels in the park. It's a good idea to make reservations (at any KTDC office or hotel), particularly for weekends.

Periyar House (☎ 322026, fax 322526) is the cheapest of the three, with rooms starting at Rs 550/750, including breakfast and either lunch or dinner. There's bike hire, massage and money changing.

Aranya Nivas (☎ 322023, fax 322282) has pleasant rooms for Rs 1200/2100 and air-con suites for Rs 1250/2300. There's a bar, a good restaurant and a garden area.

Lake Palace (reservations Aranya Nivas ☎ 322023, fax 322282) is well away from the noise of day-trippers. Guests should arrive at the Thekkady boat jetty by 4 pm (the final trip of the day) for transport to the hotel. The six suites in the palace – once the maharaja's game lodge – cost Rs 5110/7268 including meals.

There are **resthouses** in the sanctuary at Manakavala (8km from Kumily), Mullakudy (39km) and Edappalayam (5km). Book at the Wildlife Preservation Office (☎ 322027) in Kumily. The resthouses cost Rs 200/300 and have a cook, although you must bring your own food.

There are also **observation towers** for Rs 100, which can be booked at the Wildlife Information Centre (☎ 322028). Although primitive (some are allegedly poorly maintained), and you must provide all your own food and bedding, to give you the best chance of seeing animals.

Getting There & Away

All buses originating or terminating at Periyar start and finish at Aranya Nivas, but they also stop at the Kumily bus stand, at the eastern edge of town.

At least 10 buses daily operate between Ernakulam and Kumily (Rs 50, six hours) and buses leave every half hour for the 114km trip to Kottayam (Rs 34, four hours).

At least two direct buses daily make the eight hour trip to Thiruvananthapuram (Rs 80). Another goes to Kovalam (nine hours), and another to Kodaikanal, in Tamil Nadu (6½ hours). Only private buses go to Munnar

KERALA

(Rs 36, 4½ hours). They all leave Kumily in the morning (from 6 to 9.45 am).

Getting Around

Although Kumily is 4km from Periyar Lake, you can catch the semi-regular bus (almost as rare as the tigers), take an auto-rickshaw (Rs 30 plus Rs 5 entrance for the auto), hire a bicycle (from Periyar House or Aranya Nivas for Rs 25 a day) or set off on foot; it's a pleasant, shady walk into the park.

AROUND PERIYAR

7km from Kumily, just 3km off the Kottayam road, the *Shalimar Spice Garden* (☎ 0486-322132) offers individually designed luxury cottages for US$60/70 to US$80/90. The restaurant serves Indian and Italian food. Ayurvedic packages are available.

Carmelia Haven (☎ 0486-370252, fax 370268), on the Munnar road, 20km from Kumily, has rooms from Rs 1350/1600, to Rs 3300/3600 for the treehouse.

MUNNAR
☎ 0486

Set amid dramatic mountain scenery in what was once known as the High Range of Travancore, the hill town of Munnar (1524m) is the commercial centre of some of the world's highest tea-growing estates.

The combination of the craggy peaks, manicured tea estates and crisp mountain air makes Munnar an ideal retreat.

Information

There are several tourist offices in town. They all arrange tours. For information head to the Tourist Information Service (☎ 530349), opposite the Gandhi statue, run by Joseph Iype, of Dervla Murphy fame. For Rs 50, he'll give you maps, copies of the various guidebooks and all the tourist goss.

STD/ISD booths are everywhere, but fax machines are rare and transmissions can only be made within India.

For changing money, the State Bank of Travancore is efficient and friendly.

The Wildlife Warden's Office is just beyond the PWD Guest House.

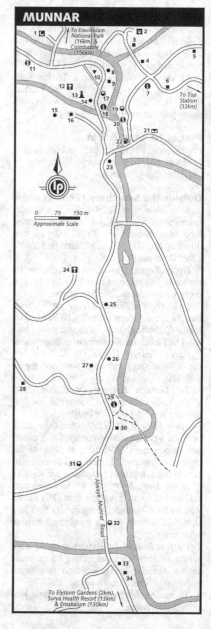

MUNNAR

MUNNAR

PLACES TO STAY & EAT
3   Hotel Brothers
4   Edassery Eastend
5   Government Guest House
6   Isaac's The Residency
9   Krishna Lodge
10 Rapsy Restaurant
16 PWD Guest House
28 Poopada Tourist Home
30 Sree Narayana (SN) Tourist Home
33 Hotel Hill View
34 Royal Retreat

OTHER
1   Mosque
2   Temple
7   Produce Market
8   Tourist Information Centre
11 State Bank of India
12 Mount Carmel Church
13 Gandhi Statue
14 St Anthony Shrine
15 Wildlife Warden's Office
17 Buses to Kumily & Ernakulam
18 Tourist Information Service
19 Buses to Top Station
20 State Bank of Travancore
21 Post & Telegraph Office
22 Petrol Station
23 Tata Tea Regional Office
24 Christ Church (Church of South India)
25 Anglo-Tamil Government Primary School
26 Raja Cycles
27 Sports Ground
29 DTPC
31 CTC & RMTC Buses to Tamil Nadu
32 KSRTC Bus Stand

Things to See & Do

The stone **Christ Church** (1910), now administered by the Church of South India, has fine stained glass. Inside, brass plaques honour the memory of the tea planters.

Walks around Munnar offer spectacular views. It's worth taking an auto-rickshaw (Rs 125 return) for the 16km to **Eravikulam National Park** (entry Rs 10/50 for Indian nationals/foreigners) where you can see the rare, but almost tame, Nilgiri tahr (a type of mountain goat), and walk around the Rajamala hills. Ten kilometres from Munnar on the way to Top Station, **Mudapetty Dam** is open daily for boating and very short horse rides.

From many places in Munnar you'll see **Anamudi** (2695m), South India's highest peak. Classified as a core forest area, it may not be climbed except for study purposes. See the Around Munnar section for more information on sights within the vicinity of the town.

Places to Stay

Most accommodation is in the middle to top-end range with the few budget options near the noisy bazaar. Generally, in all categories, the accommodation here is nothing to get excited about.

The **PWD Guest House** has some gloomy rooms for Rs 50.

Sree Narayana Tourist Home (☎ 530212, AM Rd), near the tourist information centre, is average with doubles from Rs 330.

Krishna Lodge (☎ 530669), in the bazaar, has rooms for Rs 85/160 with bath.

Hotel Brothers (☎ 530436) is a small, friendly place with doubles/triples for Rs 220/330. Two rooms have bathrooms, and there's a small restaurant.

The **Government Guest House** has spacious, clean doubles for Rs 550.

Poopada Tourist Home (☎ 530223), about 400m west of the DTPC, has doubles for Rs 550 and a good, cheap restaurant.

Isaac's The Residency (☎ 530501, fax 530265) has dismal rooms for Rs 600/700.

Hotel Hill View (☎ 530567, fax 530241), 3km from the town centre, is OK at Rs 300/600. All rooms have TV, telephone and hot water.

Edassery Eastend (☎ 530451, fax 530227) and **Royal Retreat** (☎ 530240, fax 530440) are comfortable with bright rooms ranging from about Rs 500/600 to Rs 1500.

Places to Eat

Early morning **food stalls** in the bazaar and near Isaac's serve breakfast snacks. In the evening, outdoor eating places set up near the Gandhi statue.

Rapsy Restaurant, in the arcade running off the bazaar, has excellent chicken *biryani*.

Hotel Brothers has one meal – 'Keralan dish' – fish curry and tapioca (Rs 15).

Edassery Eastend has two good restaurants: upstairs it's upmarket; downstairs it's simple, cheaper and incredibly slow.

The other middle and top-end hotels have good multicuisine restaurants.

Getting There & Away

The roads around Munnar are in poor condition and may be seriously affected by monsoons. Bus timings therefore may vary. Munnar, 130km east of Kochi, is best reached by direct bus from Kochi (4½ hours, eight daily), Kottayam (five hours, seven daily), Kumily (4½ hours, four daily), Thiruvananthapuram (nine hours, five daily), Coimbatore (six hours, two daily) or Madurai (six hours, one daily).

Getting Around

The DTPC hires out bikes (Rs 10 four hours), but they're quick to point out cheaper options. At Raja Cycles, rates are only Rs 5 for the same time.

AROUND MUNNAR

At Marayoor, east of the Eravikulam National Park and 42km from Munnar, you can experience the peace and beauty of a **sandalwood forest**. Some 10km past here is the **Chinnar Wildlife Sanctuary**, home to elephant, leopard and bear. There's a watchtower, but many visitors find the allocated viewing time – 10 minutes – insufficient. This may be extended for a 'small consideration'. Returning to Munnar at night is not advisable, and, contrary to official advice, you can't stay in the Forest Rest House. Instead try the *Marayoor Tourist Home* (☎ 04865-52231), with double rooms for Rs 125. The more upmarket *Chandana Residency* (☎ 04865-52222) is 5km east of town, and has rooms from Rs 500.

Top Station, on Kerala's border with Tamil Nadu, has spectacular views over the Western Ghats. Eight daily buses (from 7.30 am) from Munnar make the steep 32km climb in around an hour. Jeeps (Rs 600 per day) and rickshaws (Rs 300) can also be hired from along the main street in Munnar for the return trip.

The **Thattekkad Bird Sanctuary** is home to Malabar grey hornbills, woodpeckers, parakeets, and rarer species such as the Sri Lankan frogmouth and rose-billed roller. The 25 sq km sanctuary was established in 1983 by the renowned ornithologist, Salim Ali, and is an important research area. Entry is Rs 5. The best viewing time is from 5 to 6 am and the best visiting time is from October to March.

Thattekkad is 15km north-east of Kothamangalam, which is on the Ernakulam-Munnar road, roughly halfway between the two towns. There is an inspection bungalow and a dormitory at Thattekkad. The *Hornbill Bungalow* has double rooms for Rs 300 and beds in the dormitory are Rs 50. Very good food is available for Rs 15 per meal.

To get to Thattekkad, take a direct bus from Ernakulam to Kothamangalam or a more frequent bus to the larger town of Muvattupula, and change there for Kothamangalam – a further 8km. From Kothamangalam, you take the Thattekkad bus for the next 15km which will take about 30 minutes. Then you and the bus will be ferried along the Periyar River to Thattekkad.

PARAMBIKULAM WILDLIFE SANCTUARY

The Parambikulam Wildlife Sanctuary, 135km from Palakkad (via Pollachi), stretches around the Parambikulam, Thunakadavu and Peruvaripallam dams, and covers an area of 285 sq km. It's home to elephant, bison, gaur, sloth bear, wild boar, sambar, chital, crocodile and a few tigers and panthers. The sanctuary is open all year, but is best avoided from June to August due to the monsoon.

The sanctuary headquarters are at Thunakadavu, where the Forest Department has a *Forest Rest House* and a treetop hut (book through the Forest Inspection Bungalow (☎ 04253-7233) at Thunakadavu). At Parambikulam, there's a *PWD Rest House* and a *Tamil Nadu Government Inspection Bungalow* (book through the Junior Engineer, Tamil Nadu PWD, Parambikulam). There are also two **watchtowers**: one at

Anappadi (8km from Thunakadavu) and another at Zungam (5km from Thunakadavu).

The best access to the sanctuary is by bus from Pollachi (40km from Coimbatore and 49km from Palakkad). There are four buses in either direction between Pollachi and Parambikulam via Anamalai daily. The trip takes two hours.

WAYANAD WILDLIFE SANCTUARY

Also known as Muthanga Wildlife Sanctuary, Wayanad is a remote rainforest reserve connected to Bandipur National Park in Karnataka and Mudumalai Sanctuary in Tamil Nadu. Wayanad is not really geared up for visitors. The Forest Department staff are very helpful but you'll probably just get a short jeep trip on the outskirts of the sanctuary through plantations.

If chasing forest officers for permits gets too much you may like to try a treehouse experience at *Green Magic Nature Resort*, Vythiri, 65km north-east of Kozhikode. This genuine ecofriendly place is not for visitors used to regular creature comforts, but for those who seek a genuine forest experience with minimal environmental impact. All essentials must be carried in. Accommodation for two people is US$150 including all meals. Guided walks through the Wayanad forest are also available. All bookings must be made through Tourindia (☎ 0471-330437, fax 331407, MG Rd, Thiruvananthapuram).

Central Kerala

KOCHI (Cochin)
☎ 0484 • pop 1.1 million

With its wealth of historical associations and its setting on a cluster of islands and narrow peninsulas, the city of Kochi perfectly reflects the eclecticism of Kerala. Here you can see the oldest church in India, winding streets with mosques and 500-year-old Portuguese houses, cantilevered Chinese fishing nets, a Jewish community with ancient roots, a 16th century synagogue, and a palace built by the Portuguese and given to

the raja of Cochin. The palace, which was later renovated by the Dutch, contains some of India's most beautiful murals. Another must-see is a (world-famous) performance of Kathakali drama.

The older parts of Fort Cochin and Mattancherry are an unlikely blend of medieval Portugal, Holland and an English country village grafted onto the tropical Malabar Coast – a radical contrast to the bright lights of mainland Ernakulam.

Kochi is one of India's largest ports and a major naval base. The misty silhouettes of huge merchant ships can be seen anchored off Fort Cochin, waiting for a berth in the docks of Willingdon Island, an artificial island created with material dredged up when the harbour was deepened. All day, ferries scuttle back and forth between the various parts of Kochi. Dolphins can often be seen in the harbour.

Orientation
Kochi consists of mainland Ernakulam; the islands of Willingdon, Bolgatty and Gundu in the harbour; Fort Cochin and Mattancherry on the southern peninsula; and Vypeen Island, north of Fort Cochin. All these areas are linked by ferry; bridges also link Ernakulam to Willingdon Island and the Fort Cochin/Mattancherry peninsula. Most hotels and restaurants are in Ernakulam, where you'll also find the main train station, bus stand and the Tourist Reception Centre.

Almost all the historical sites are in Fort Cochin or Mattancherry, a more tranquil setting than Ernakulam. Two of the top hotels are on Willingdon Island. The new airport (domestic and international) is some 30km north-east of Kochi.

Information
Tourist Offices The KTDC Tourist Reception Centre (☎ 353234) on Ernakulam's Shanmugham Rd organises accommodation at the Bolgatty Palace Hotel and harbour cruises. The office is open 8 am to 7 pm daily. The very helpful Mr Varghese at the tourist desk (☎ 371761) at Ernakulam's main ferry jetty is a mine of information.

KERALA

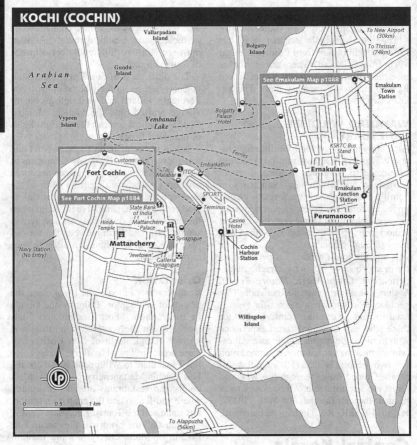

KOCHI (COCHIN)

Vallarpadam Island

To New Airport (30km)

To Thrissur (74km)

Bolgatty Island

Arabian Sea

Gundu Island

See Ernakulam Map p1088

Ernakulam Town Station

Vypeen Island

Vembanad Lake

Bolgatty Palace Hotel

KSRTC Bus Stand

Ferries

Ernakulam

Customs

Embarkation

Fort Cochin

Taj Malabar

ITDC

Ernakulam Junction Station

See Fort Cochin Map p1084

SPORTS

Perumanoor

State Bank of India

Terminus

Casino Hotel

Hindu Temple

Mattancherry Palace

Mattancherry

Synagogue

Cochin Harbour Station

Navy Station (No Entry)

'Jewtown'

Galleria Synagogue

Willingdon Island

0   0.5   1 km

To Alappuzha (56km)

Open daily 9 am to 7 pm, you can also book accommodation and tours.

There's also a DTPC on Park Ave, Ernakulam (☎ 381743).

The Government of India tourist office (☎ 668352) on Willingdon Island offers a range of leaflets and maps. The airport tourist information counter is staffed for flight arrivals.

Ernakulam's tourist police are specially trained to deal with visitor queries. You'll find them near the KTDC Tourist Reception

Centre (☎ 353234). They also maintain a presence at Fort Cochin at the palace, the airport and Ernakulam Junction station.

Visa Extensions Apply at the office of the Commissioner of Police (☎ 360700), at Shanmugham Rd, Ernakulam. Visa extensions can take up to 10 days and you have to leave your passport for processing.

Money In Ernakulam, there's a State Bank of India, and a very efficient Thomas Cook office on MG Rd. In Fort Cochin the State Bank of India is near Mattancherry Palace.

Post & Communications The main post office (including poste restante) is at Fort Cochin. Mail can be sent to the post office on Hospital Rd, Ernakulam if it's specifically addressed to that office. STD/ISD booths are all over town. Email is available in Ernakulam at Raiyaan Communication (☎ 351387, fax 380052), Raiyaan Complex, Padma Junction, MG Rd, and in Fort Cochin, at Rendez Vous Cyber Cafe, Burgher St.

Bookshops Bhavi Books is on Convent Rd, Ernakulam. A number of bookshops along Press Club Rd stock books in Malayalam while Cosmo Books and Current Books have titles in English. Higginbothams is on Chittoor Rd, and DC Books, with a collection of English-language classics, is on Banerji Rd.

In Mattancherry, Incy Bella has a range of reference books on India. Opposite there's the excellent Idiom Bookshop, with comprehensive sections on Indian art, culture, literature and religion. There's a second shop at Fort Cochin.

Film & Photography A knowledgeable supplier of photographic equipment is SP & Co on Convent Rd, Ernakulam.

Fort Cochin

St Francis Church, allegedly India's oldest European-built church, was constructed in 1503 by Portuguese Franciscan friars who accompanied the expedition led by Pedro Alvarez Cabral.

The original wooden structure was rebuilt in stone around the mid-16th century; the earliest Portuguese inscription in the church is dated 1562. The Protestant Dutch captured Kochi in 1663 and restored the

The Jews of Kochi

The Jewish diaspora extends all the way to Kochi (Cochin), home to a tiny Jewish community descended from those who fled Palestine 2000 years ago. The first Jewish settlement was at Kodungallur (Cranganore), north of Kochi. Like the Syrian Orthodox Christians, the Jews became involved in the trade and commerce of the Malabar Coast. Preserved in the Mattancherry synagogue are a number of copper plates bearing an ancient inscription granting the village of Anjuvannam (near Kodungallur) and its revenue to a Jewish merchant, Joseph Rabban, by King Bhaskara Ravi Varman I (962-1020). You can see these plates with the permission of the synagogue guardian.

Concessions given to Joseph Rabban by Ravi Varman I included permission to use a palanquin (carrying chair) and parasol. Given that palanquins and parasols were the prerogative of rulers, Ravi Varman I had in effect sanctioned the creation of a tiny Jewish kingdom. On Rabban's death, his sons fought each other for control of the 'kingdom' and this rivalry led to its break-up and the move to Mattancherry.

The community has been the subject of much research. One study by an American professor of ethnomusicology found that the music of the Cochin Jews contained strong Babylonian influences, and that their version of the Ten Commandments was almost identical to a Kurdish version housed in the Berlin Museum Archives. Of course, there has also been much local influence, and many of the hymns are similar to ragas.

Migration to Israel has reduced the community to a population of around 20. In spite of such low numbers, however, the community remains active with the synagogue as its focus. There has been no rabbi within living memory but all the elders are qualified to perform religious ceremonies and marriages.

church in 1779. After the occupation of Kochi by the British in 1795, it became an Anglican church and is presently being used by the Church of South India.

Having died in Cochin in 1524, Vasco da Gama was buried here for 14 years before his remains were taken to Lisbon. His tombstone can be seen in the church. Rope-operated *punkahs*, or fans, are one of this church's unusual features. Sunday services are in English at 8 am and Malayalam at 9.30 am.

The large, impressive Roman Catholic **Santa Cruz Basilica** dates from 1902, and has a fantastic pastel-coloured interior.

Strung out along the tip of Fort Cochin, the fixed, cantilevered **Chinese fishing nets** were introduced by traders from the court of Kublai Khan. You can also see them along many backwaters. They're mainly used at high tide, requiring at least four men to operate their system of counterweights.

Mattancherry Palace

Built by the Portuguese in 1555, Mattancherry Palace was presented to the raja

of Cochin, Veera Kerala Varma (1537-61), as a gesture of goodwill (and probably as a means of securing trading privileges).

The Dutch renovated the palace in 1663, hence its alternative name, the Dutch Palace. The two storey quadrangular building surrounds a courtyard containing a Hindu temple.

The central hall on the 1st floor was the coronation hall of the rajas. The astonishing **murals**, depicting scenes from the *Ramayana, Mahabharata* and Puranic legends, are one of the wonders of India. The ladies' bedchamber downstairs features a cheerful Krishna using his six hands and two feet to engage in foreplay with eight happy milkmaids.

The palace is open Saturday to Thursday 10 am to 5 pm; entry is free except for the 'donation'. Photography is prohibited but there's a good colour booklet for Rs 35.

Cochin/Mattancherry Synagogue

Originally constructed in 1568, the synagogue was destroyed by the Portuguese in 1662 and was rebuilt two years later when

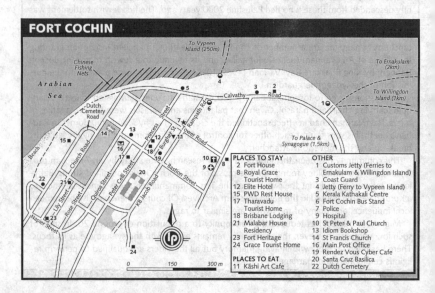

FORT COCHIN

PLACES TO STAY	OTHER
2 Fort House	1 Customs Jetty (Ferries to
8 Royal Grace	Ernakulam & Willingdon Island)
Tourist Home	3 Coast Guard
12 Elite Hotel	4 Jetty (Ferry to Vypeen Island)
15 PWD Rest House	5 Kerala Kathakali Centre
17 Tharavadu	6 Fort Cochin Bus Stand
Tourist Home	7 Police
18 Brisbane Lodging	9 Hospital
21 Malabar House	10 St Peter & Paul Church
Residency	13 Idiom Bookshop
23 Fort Heritage	14 St Francis Church
24 Grace Tourist Home	16 Main Post Office
	19 Rendez Vous Cyber Cafe
PLACES TO EAT	20 Santa Cruz Basilica
11 Kāshi Art Cafe	22 Dutch Cemetery

0   150   300 m

the Dutch took over Kochi. It features hand-painted willow pattern floor tiles brought from Canton in China in the mid-18th century by Ezekial Rahabi, who was also responsible for the erection of the building's clock tower.

A synagogue built at Kochangadi in 1344 has since disappeared, although a stone slab from this building, inscribed in Hebrew, can be found on the inner surface of the wall that surrounds the Mattancherry synagogue.

The area around the synagogue is known as **Jewtown** and is one of the centres of the Kochi spice trade. Scores of small firms huddle together in old, dilapidated buildings and the air is filled with the pungent aromas of ginger, cardamom, cumin, turmeric and cloves. Many Jewish names are visible on premises, and there are several curio shops on the street leading to the synagogue.

The synagogue is usually open Sunday to Friday, 10 am to noon and 3 to 5 pm. Entry is Rs 1. The synagogue's guardians are keen to talk about the building and the Jewish community.

Ernakulam
The **Parishath Thampuram Museum** contains 19th century oil paintings, old coins, sculptures and Mughal paintings, but apart from some interesting temple models, it's nothing special. Housed in a traditional Keralan building (previously the *durbar* hall) on Durbar Hall Rd, it's open Tuesday to Sunday 10 am to 12.30 pm and 2 to 4.30 pm; entry is free.

Vypeen & Gundu Islands
Ferries shuttle across the narrow strait from Fort Cochin to Vypeen Island. The island boasts a **lighthouse** at Ochanthuruth (open 3 to 5 pm daily), good **beaches** and the early 16th century **Pallipuram Fort** (open Thursday). Gundu, the smallest island in the harbour, belongs to the Taj Group and will no doubt be developed.

Organised Tours
The KTDC and tourist desk offer daily harbour and backwater cruises including:

- Dutch Palace, synagogue, Chinese fishing nets, St Francis Church and the Bolgatty Palace. This KTDC trip starts from Sea Lord boat jetty and takes 3½ hours (Rs 70 per person).
- Cochin village canal tour (three hours, Rs 315 with KTDC; half day, Rs 275 with the tourist desk)
- The tourist desk also offers a special 24 hour 'houseboat package' (Rs 3000 for two people).

All these tours are deservedly popular so book early to avoid disappointment.

Places to Stay
Ernakulam's range of accommodation is greater than Fort Cochin's and while it may appear frenetic it has many quiet possibilities. For the sake of Fort Cochin's environmental heritage, a stay in Ernakulam is preferable. Bolgatty Island has one unique top-end place and Willingdon Island has mid-range and two top-end places. During December/January hotel space is severely limited.

Places to Stay – Budget
Fort Cochin *Royal Grace Tourist Home* (☎ 223584) is a modern, concrete budget hotel with large double rooms with bath from Rs 150 (downstairs) to Rs 250 (upstairs, breezy and brighter), or Rs 550 with air-con. Under the same management is the smaller, but similarly priced, *Grace Tourist Home (KB Jacob Rd)*, south of the basilica. Checkout is 10 am.

Tharavadu Tourist Home (☎ 226897, *Quiros St*) is an airy, spacious traditional house with good views from the rooftop. Singles with bath are Rs 135, or there's two top floor double rooms for Rs 155 and Rs 205 that share a bathroom.

Elite Hotel (☎ 225733, *Princess St*) is a long-term favourite and has doubles with bath from Rs 150 to Rs 300. There's a popular but not especially good restaurant downstairs.

Brisbane Lodging (☎ 225962), a couple of doors away, has seven presentable rooms from Rs 150 to Rs 200.

PWD Rest House, near the waterfront, has two double rooms for Rs 110 each. The enterprising housekeeper organises village day trips using public transport, and acts as your personal guide.

Ernakulam Ernakulam's budget options include the following:

YMCA International House (☎ 353479, fax 364641, Chittoor Rd) is bright, clean and friendly. Rooms with bath are Rs 125/150 (economy), Rs 200/250 (executive) and Rs 350/450 (with air-con). There's also a multicuisine restaurant.

Basoto Lodge (☎ 352140, Press Club Rd) is small, simple, friendly and popular, so get there early. Singles with common bath cost Rs 55, and doubles with private bath are Rs 120.

Hotel Seaking (☎ 355341, fax 372608) is excellent value with singles/doubles for Rs 200/310, or Rs 495 with air-con. There's a restaurant.

Hotel Hakoba (☎ 369839, Shanmugham Rd), conveniently located on the busy waterfront, is another good choice. Doubles with bath start at Rs 194, or Rs 350 with air-con (including tax). There's a sad-looking restaurant, a noisy bar and a (not very reliable) lift.

Maple Tourist Home (☎ 355156, fax 371712, Canon Shed Rd) has good-value doubles from Rs 200 to Rs 300, or Rs 420 with air-con. The rooftop garden overlooks the jetty.

Bijus Tourist Home (☎ 381881, corner of Canon Shed and Market Rds) is a friendly place with good-value rooms for Rs 165/350, and air-con doubles for Rs 475.

Queen's Residency (☎ 365775, fax 352845) is a quaint hotel, airy and aesthetically pleasing, with rooms from Rs 175/220, or Rs 450 with air-con.

Hotel KK International (☎ 366010) is good value with rooms at Rs 160/290, or Rs 400 with air-con.

Geetha Lodge (☎ 352136, MG Rd) has simple rooms for Rs 160/280.

Anantha Bhavan (☎ 382071), nearby, has rooms from Rs 120/190 to Rs 180/280, and air-con doubles for Rs 650. Reports are that it accepts Indians only.

Hotel Luciya (☎ 381177), with efficient and friendly staff, has good-value rooms for

Rs 130/250, or Rs 285/435 with air-con. It has a restaurant and TV lounge.

Places to Stay – Mid-Range

Fort Cochin See some of the previous budget hotel listings that also have mid-priced rooms – they are the best choice in this price range.

The *Fort House (☎ 226103, fax 222066, Calvathy Rd)* is well located and good value with clean, comfortable doubles at Rs 695 (including breakfast and taxes).

Fort Heritage (☎/fax 225333, Napier St) has been run by the same family for many years. It's an old Dutch building, with spacious rooms furnished with antique rosewood furniture. It has a good restaurant including tandoori with lawn service in the back garden. Rooms, including breakfast, are US$30/45 (US$10 extra with air-con).

Ernakulam The *Paulson Park Hotel (☎ 382170, fax 370072)* has good-value rooms for Rs 250/480, or Rs 480/650 with air-con. There's a choice of multicuisine or tandoori restaurants.

Hotel Sangeetha (☎ 368487, fax 354261, Chittoor Rd) has a huge range of rooms with an even greater range of rates, from Rs 300/500 to Rs 680/790 with air-con; prices include breakfast.

Hotel Joyland (☎ 367764, fax 370645, Durbar Hall Rd) is well appointed and features a rooftop restaurant (Indian, Chinese and continental). Rooms are Rs 450/600, or Rs 520/800 with air-con.

Woodlands Hotel (☎ 368900, fax 382080, MG Rd) is a long-time favourite. Rooms are Rs 300/425, or Rs 475/650 with air-con. There's a vegetarian restaurant and a roof garden.

Hotel Aiswarya (☎ 364454) is a pleasant new hotel with good-value clean rooms for Rs 260/360, or Rs 800 with air-con. All rooms have hot water and TV, plus there's complimentary morning tea or coffee.

Hotel Excellency (☎ 374001, fax 374009, Nettipadam Rd), south of Jos Junction, is a three star place with rooms from US$12/15, or US$25/30 with air-con. It has good facilities, a restaurant, and even 'bed coffee'.

Bharat Hotel (☎ 353501, fax 370502, Durbar Hall Rd), next to the Indian Airlines office, is huge with rooms from Rs 550/650, or Rs 750/1000 with air-con. It has veg and nonveg restaurants, and a 24 hour coffee shop. Checkout is noon.

The Metropolitan (☎ 369931, fax 382227), friendly, quiet, efficient and centrally air-con, has good rooms from Rs 650/1150.

Places to Stay – Top End

The **Malabar House Residency** (☎/fax 221199, Parade Rd), across the playing field from St Francis Church in Fort Cochin, has beautifully furnished rooms for US$120 and suites for US$150.

Bolgatty Palace Hotel (☎ 355003, fax 354879), on Bolgatty Island, was built in 1744 by the Dutch, and later became a British Residency. Extensively renovated, it offers luxurious suites and cottages from Rs 1750. There's a pool, restaurant and bar and attractive landscaping enhances the magical location. Telephone first or inquire at the Tourist Reception Centre, Shanmugham Rd. Ferries (Rs 0.40) leave the High Court jetty in Ernakulam for Bolgatty Island every 20 minutes from 6 am to 10 pm; at other times, private launches are available.

Taj Malabar (☎ 666811) is a five star hotel wonderfully situated overlooking the harbour on Willingdon Island. The hotel boasts the full range of facilities, including a pool and ayurvedic massage. Rooms start at US$95/110; singles with harbour views are from US$115 to US$155; doubles from US$130 to US$170; deluxe suites US$250 to US$350.

Casino Hotel (☎ 668421, Willingdon Island) also has an excellent range of facilities, including a pool. Rates are a reasonable US$65/70, but its location near the train station and warehouses is no match for the Taj Malabar's.

Hotel Abad Plaza (☎ 381122, fax 370729, MG Rd, Ernakulam) is a modern, air-conditioned business hotel. Rooms start at Rs 1100/1450. It has restaurants, a coffee shop, a health club and a rooftop pool with great views over the city.

Taj Residency (☎ 371471, fax 371481, Marine Drive, Ernakulam), a more business-oriented sister to the Taj Malabar, is on the waterfront. It offers all mod cons (except a pool), boasts the Harbour View Bar, and charges US$80/90, or US$100/115 for rooms with a sea view.

Places to Eat

Fort Cochin **Badhariya** is a small nonveg restaurant with beef curry and paratha for around Rs 15.

Ramathula Hotel, near the junction of Irimpichi Rd and New Rd, is better known by the chef's name, Kayika. Excellent chicken or mutton biryanis are Rs 30.

Kāshi Art Cafe (☎ 221769, Burgher St) is the hip place in town. It opens at 8.30 am and serves a range of food including home-baked cakes. Filter coffee is Rs 30 (two cups). The cafe is keen to support contemporary art, and exhibitions, workshops and theatre performances are organised and held here. Interested artists can contact the cafe for possible residencies and networking.

Elite Hotel (Princess St), the travellers' stand-by, has a small range of fairly basic food including fish curries for around Rs 25.

The new top-end hotels have good quality restaurants. The biggest prices, smallest serves and longest waits are at the **Malabar House Residency**, which serves Indian and Italian dishes. The **Fort House** has already earned a good reputation for its preparation of seafood but two hours' notice is required.

Behind the Chinese fishing nets are a couple of **fishmongers**. The idea is you buy a fish (or prawns, scampi, lobster; Rs 50 to Rs 300 per kilogram), then take your selection to a kitchen where they will cook it and serve it to you (about Rs 30 for a large fish). Of course it's important to determine the freshness of the catch.

Willingdon Island In the Taj Malabar, the **Waterfront Cafe** offers a lunchtime buffet for Rs 275 (plus taxes). The Malabar's

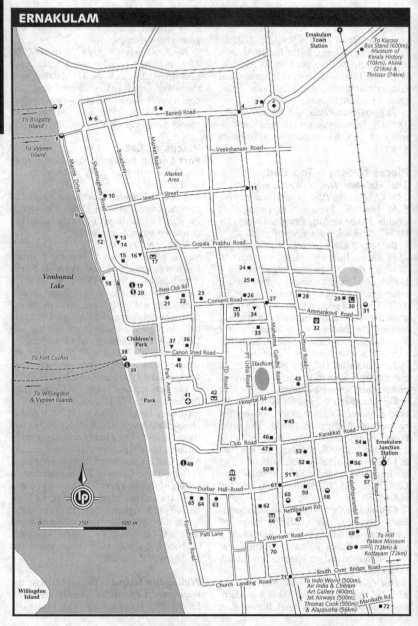

ERNAKULAM

Ernakulam Town Station

To Kacoor Bus Stand (600m),
Museum of Kerala History
(10km), Aluva (21km) &
Thrissur (74km)

1

To Bolgatty Island — 7
★ 6
5
Banerji Road
4 3

To Vypeen Island — 8
Veekshanam Road

Market Road
Market Area

Broadway
Shanmugham Road
Jews — Street 10
11

9
Gopala Prabhu Road

Vembanad Lake
12
13
14
15 16
17

18
19
20
Press Club Rd
21 22 23
Convent Road
26
27
24
25
28 29 30
31
Ammankovil Road
35 34
Mahatma Gandhi Road
Chittoor Road
32
33

Children's Park
37 36
Canon Shed Road
40

38
39
To Fort Cochin

To Willingdon & Vypeen Islands
Park Avenue
41
42
Hospital Rd
44
45

Park
PT Usha Road
Stadium
TD Road
43

Club Road
46
47
Karakkat Road
53 54
52 55 56
Ernakulam Junction Station

50
51
48
Durbar Hall Road
61
59
60
58
57
Kalathiparambil Rd
Caravara Road

65 64 63
62
66
Nettipadam Rd
67
68
To Hill Palace Museum (12km) & Kottayam (72km)
69

0   250   500 m

Palli Lane
Warriom Road
70

Foreshore Road
South Over Bridge Road
Church Landing Road
71
To Indo World (500m),
Air India & Chitram
Art Gallery (400m),
Jet Airways (500m),
Thomas Cook (550m)
& Alappuzha (56km)
72
Manikath Rd

Willingdon Island

ERNAKULAM

PLACES TO STAY
15 Hotel Hakoba
18 Taj Residency
22 Basoto Lodge
24 Hotel Abad Plaza;
   Regency Restaurant
25 Hotel Seaking
28 YMCA International House
29 Hotel Luciya
33 Queen's Residency
36 Bijus Tourist Home
40 Maple Tourist Home
46 Woodlands Hotel
47 Geetha Lodge
50 Anantha Bhavan
52 Hotel Sangeetha
54 The Metropolitan
55 Hotel KK International
56 Paulson Park Hotel;
   Moghul Hut
59 Hotel Joyland
62 Hotel Aiswarya
65 Bharat Hotel
67 Hotel Excellency

PLACES TO EAT
13 Bimbi's; South Star
14 Arul Jyoti
16 Bharath Coffee House

34 Chariot Restaurant
37 Indian Coffee House
45 Pandhal Restaurant
51 Indian Coffee House
70 Chinese Garden Restaurant

OTHER
1 Marikar Motors
2 Kacheripady Junction
3 Manuel Industries
4 Madhava Pharmacy Junction
5 DC Books
6 Commissioner of Police
7 High Court Jetty (Ferry to
   Bolgatty Island)
8 Private Ferry to Vypeen
   Island
9 Sealord Jetty
10 Sridhar Cinema
11 Padma Junction
12 Princy Tours
17 Post Office
19 KTDC Tourist Reception
   Centre
20 State Bank of India
21 Cosmo Books; Current Books
23 SP & Co
26 Bhavi Books
27 Shenoys Junction

30 Mosque
31 KSRTC Bus Terminal
32 Durga Temple
35 Ernakulam College Post
   Office; Ernakulam Public
   Library
38 Main Jetty
39 Tourist Desk
41 General Hospital
42 Main Post Office
43 Higginbothams
44 Curio & Antique Shop
48 DTPC Tourist
   Information Centre
49 Parishath Thampuram
   Museum
53 Galleria Mareecheka
58 Ernakulam South
   Bus Stand
57 South Bus Stand
60 Bus to Fort Cochin
61 Jos Junction
64 Indian Airlines
66 Post Office
63 TDM Hall
68 See India Foundation
69 Art Kerala
71 Pallimukku Junction
72 Cochin Cultural Centre

Chinese Jade Pavilion and the plush *Rice Boats* restaurants serve excellent seafood.

Ernakulam The *Indian Coffee House* on the corner of Canon Shed Rd and Park Ave has quaintly uniformed waiters in cummerbunds offering good snacks and breakfasts. It's popular and always busy, but women travellers report disturbing accounts of harassment.

Bimbi's (Shanmugham Rd) is a modern, self-serve restaurant with fast food (north and south Indian plus some western snacks) as well as sweets. An excellent masala dosa costs Rs 12. There's another branch near Jos Junction.

South Star (Shanmugham Rd) is an aircon restaurant above Bimbi's. It's good value with mains for around Rs 50.

Lotus Cascades/Jaya Cafe (MG Rd), in the Woodlands Hotel, turns out excellent vegetarian thalis for Rs 30.

Pandhal Restaurant (MG Rd) could easily be a western chain restaurant. It turns out excellent north Indian food and OK pizzas (Rs 90) but avoid the burgers.

Chinese Garden Restaurant (Warriom Rd) has good food and attentive service.

Arul Jyoti (Shanmugham Rd) is a straightforward 'meals' place with basic vegetarian meals for Rs 15. The *Bharath Coffee House* (Broadway) offers similar fare.

Sealord Hotel (Shanmugham Rd) has two restaurants: Chinese and Indian/continental. The reasonably priced food is consistently good. The choice is between air-con and live 'easy listening' rock, or the roof where conversation is accompanied by traffic noise wafting up on photochemical thermals.

The classy but reasonably priced *Regency Restaurant (MG Rd)*, in the Hotel Abad Plaza, offers good Indian, Chinese and western food.

The Paulson Park Hotel, near the Ernakulam Junction train station, has the *Moghul Hut* tandoori restaurant in its central atrium area.

Entertainment

The *Sridhar Cinema (Shanmugham Rd, Ernakulam)* screens films in Malayalam, Hindi, Tamil and English.

There are several places in Kochi where you can see Kathakali. (For more information see the earlier Kathakali boxed text).

Art Kerala (☎ 366238), near the See India Foundation, Ernakulam, stages rooftop performances for Rs 90. Make-up begins at 6 pm and the show runs from 7 to 8 pm.

Cochin Cultural Centre (☎ 367866), Souhardham, Manikath Rd, is south of Ernakulam Junction train station. The performance is held in a specially constructed air-conditioned theatre designed to resemble a temple courtyard. Make-up begins at 5.30 pm and the performance runs from 6.30 to 8 pm. The cost is around Rs 100.

Kerala Kathakali Centre stages performances at the Cochin Aquatic Club on River (Calvathy) Rd, Fort Cochin, near the bus stand. Enthusiastic performances from young Kathakali artists nicely balance the more formal introduction to the art at the See India Foundation. Make-up begins at 5 pm, and the performance runs from 6.30 to 7.30 pm. The last ferry from Fort Cochin to Ernakulam departs after the performance at 9.30 pm. Admission is Rs 85.

See India Foundation (☎ 369471), Devan Gurukulam, Kalathiparambil Rd, is near the Ernakulam Junction train station. The show features an extraordinary presentation by PK Devan, who explains the dance's history and makes a plucky attempt to simplify the main elements of Hinduism for visitors. Make-up begins at 6 pm, and the performance runs from 6.45 to 8 pm, with time for questions afterwards. It costs Rs 120, though you may be offered a discounted ticket from hotel staff in Ernakulam.

If, after viewing one of these performances, you wish to experience more of this fascinating art, you can attend a traditional all-night performance. Once a month the Ernakulam Kathakali Club hosts all-night performances by major artists at the TDM Hall on Durbar Hall Rd, Ernakulam. Programs covering the story in English are distributed from tourist offices a week in advance. The cost is Rs 100 (as donation).

Shopping

There are a number of handicraft and antique emporiums along MG Rd, Ernakulam, just south of Durbar Hall Rd. In Jew St, Mattancherry, there's a plethora of shops selling antiques and reproductions.

One of the more exciting developments in Kochi has been the encouragement of contemporary artists, including home-town talent. You can view and buy their work at Kāshi Art Cafe, Burgher St, Draavidia Art & Performance Gallery, Jew St, and Galleria Synagogue, also in Mattancherry.

In Ernakulam, Chitram Art Gallery, MG Rd and Galleria Mareecheka, Chittoor Rd, also exhibit works by well-known and emerging artists.

If you fancy picking up a sitar or set of tabla, head to Manuel Industries, Banerji Rd, Ernakulam. A sitar costs about Rs 3500, while a set of tabla is Rs 1500.

A new Enfield Bullet 350cc is yours for Rs 50,000 at Marikar Motors, on Lissie Junction. Second-hand models from its workshop are much cheaper.

Getting There & Away

Air The Indian Airlines office (☎ 352065) is in Ernakulam on Durbar Hall Rd, next to the Bharat Hotel. Air India (☎ 351295) is on MG Rd opposite Thomas Cook. Jet Airways (☎ 369212), MG Rd, has daily services to Mumbai (US$150).

Indian Airlines has daily flights to Bangalore (US$70), Mumbai (US$150), Delhi (via Goa, US$300), Goa (US$110) and four flights weekly to Chennai (US$105).

At the time of writing the new airport had not become operational so schedules are subject to change. The new airport with international and domestic flights should be in operation by June 1999.

Bus The KSRTC bus stand, also known as the central bus stand (☎ 372033) is by the railway line in Ernakulam, between the train stations. Because Kochi is in the middle of Kerala, many of the buses passing through Ernakulam originated in other cities. Although it's still possible to get a seat, you cannot make advance reservations; you simply have to join the scrum when the bus turns up. You can make reservations up to five days in advance for many of the buses that originate in Ernakulam. The timetable is in Malayalam and English, and the staff are very helpful.

There are also private bus stands: the Kaloor stand is north-east of Ernakulam Town train station, and the Ernakulam South stand is right outside the entrance of Ernakulam Junction train station.

The fares and times that follow are for superexpress buses from the KSRTC bus stand, unless otherwise noted. Superfast services are usually a few rupees cheaper and stop more often.

Southbound There are two routes to Thiruvananthapuram (221km): one via Alappuzha and Kollam, and the other via Kottayam. Over 60 KSRTC buses a day take the Alappuzha-Kollam route. Superexpress buses take 4½ hours to Thiruvananthapuram and cost Rs 85. The fares, times and intermediate distances for superexpress buses are: Alappuzha (Rs 30, 1½ hours, 62km), Kollam (Rs 60, three hours, 150km) and Kottayam (Rs 35, 1½ hours, 76km). There are also at least two direct buses a day to Kanyakumari, in Tamil Nadu (Rs 110, 8¾ hours, 302km).

Eastbound At least three direct buses a day run to Madurai (Rs 115, 9¼ hours, 324km). For those with phenomenal endurance, there are direct buses to Chennai (Rs 220, 16½ hours, 690km).

The Madurai buses pass through Kumily, near the Periyar Wildlife Sanctuary on the Kerala/Tamil Nadu border. They cost Rs 50 by fast passenger bus (six hours, 192km). Departure times are 6.30 am, 2 and 3.30 pm,

and you can book a seat on the morning departure. You will need to book your journey through to Kumbam (the end of a section) but disembark at Kumily.

There are several KSRTC buses a day to Munnar (Rs 44).

Northbound There are buses every half hour to Thrissur (Trichur) (Rs 32, two hours, 74km) and Kozhikode (Rs 78, five hours, 219km). Three daily buses run right up the coast beyond Kozhikode to Kannur (Cannanore), Kasaragod and across the Karnataka state border to Mangalore.

Half a dozen interstate express buses go to Bangalore (Rs 198, 15 hours, 565km) daily via Kozhikode, Sultan's Battery and Mysore.

In addition to the KSRTC state buses, there are a number of private bus companies that have superdeluxe video buses daily to Bangalore, Mumbai and Coimbatore. Check out Princy Tours (☎ 354712) in the GCDA Complex on Shanmugham Rd; Conti Travels (☎ 353080) at the Jos Junction of MG Rd; and Silcon A/C Coach (☎ 394596), Banerji Rd.

Train Ernakulam has two stations, Ernakulam Junction (the one you're most likely to use) and Ernakulam Town. Note that none of the through trains on the main trunk routes go to the Cochin Harbour station on Willingdon Island.

Trains regular run from Thiruvananthapuram via Kollam and Kottayam to Ernakulam; less frequently they continue on to Thrissur, Kozhikode, Thalasseri and Kasaragod. See the table Major Trains from Ernakulam.

Getting Around

To/From the Airport At the time of writing the new airport was not operational. It's likely taxis into town will be around Rs 250 and auto-rickshaws a little less.

Local Transport There are no convenient bus services between Fort Cochin and the Mattancherry Palace or the synagogue, but it's a pleasant 30 minute walk through the busy warehouse area along Bazaar Rd.

Major Trains from Ernakulam

destination	train no & name	departure time[1]	distance (km)	duration (hours)	fare (Rs) (2nd/1st)
Bangalore	6525 *Kanniya Kumari-Bangalore Express*	2.40 pm ET	637	13 h	187/650
Chennai	6320 *Chennai-Trivandrum Mail*	6.15 pm ET	697	13 h	196/687
Delhi	2625 *Kerala Express*	3.35 pm ET	2833	48 h	447/1933
Kozhikode	6307 *Cannanore Express*	4.50 pm EJ	190	4 h 15 min	53/258
Mangalore	6329 *Malabar Express*	10.53 pm ET	414	9 h 30 min	32/460
	6349 *Parsuram Express*	10.50 am ET		10 h	
Mumbai CST[2]	6332 *Kurla Express*	8.35 am EJ	1840	36 h 45 min	355/1385
Thiruvananthapuram	6305 *Guruvayur-Nagercoil Express*	11.27 pm ET	224	4 h 30 min	61/294
	6350 *Parsuram Express*	1.50 pm ET	224	5 h	61/294

[1] EJ – Ernakulam Junction; ET – Ernakulam Town
[2] CST – Chhatrapati Shivaji Terminus (Victoria Terminus)

Auto-rickshaws are available and you'll need to haggle hard – this is tourist territory.

In Ernakulam, auto-rickshaws are the most convenient mode of transport. The trip from the bus or train stations to the Tourist Reception Centre on Shanmugham Rd should cost about Rs 20.

Local buses are very good and economical. If you have to get to Fort Cochin after the ferries stop running, catch a bus in Ernakulam on MG Rd, south of Durbar Hall Rd. The fare is Rs 3. Auto-rickshaws will demand at least Rs 80 once the ferries stop running after about 10 pm.

Taxis charge round-trip fares between the islands, even if you only want to go one way. Ernakulam to Willingdon Island could cost up to Rs 150 late at night.

Boat Ferries are the main form of transport between the various parts of Kochi. Nearly all the ferry stops are named, making identification easy. The stop on the east side of Willingdon Island is Embarkation; the west one, opposite Mattancherry, is Terminus, and the main stop at Fort Cochin is Customs.

Getting a ferry at Ernakulam can sometimes involve scrambling across several ferries to get to the boat you want. Make sure you get the right ferry or you may find yourself heading for the wrong island – ask the skipper or deck hand.

Ferry fares are all Rs 2 or less.

From Ernakulam There are services to Fort Cochin every 45 minutes (around 6 am to 9.30 pm) from Main jetty. It's a pleasant 20 minute walk from the Fort Cochin pier to Mattancherry. There are also seven ferries a day direct to/from Mattancherry. The ticket office in Ernakulam opens 10 minutes before each sailing.

To Willingdon and Vypeen islands, ferries run every 20 minutes (6 am to 10 pm) from Main jetty. There are also ferries to Vypeen Island (sometimes via Bolgatty Island) from the High Court jetty on Shanmugham Rd.

Ferries for Bolgatty Island depart from the High Court jetty every 20 minutes between 6 am and 10 pm. It's a five minute walk from the public jetty to Bolgatty Palace Hotel.

From Fort Cochin Ferries operate between Customs jetty and the Taj Malabar/tourist office jetty on Willingdon Island about 30 times daily, except on Sunday, 6.30 am to 9 pm.

Ferries cross the narrow gap to Vypeen Island virtually nonstop from 6 am until 10 pm. There is also a vehicular ferry every half hour or so.

Hire Boats Motorised boats of various sizes can be hired from the Sealord jetty or from the small dock adjacent to the Main jetty in Ernakulam. They're an excellent way of exploring Kochi Harbour at your leisure and without the crowds; rates start at around Rs 300 an hour. Rowboats shuttle between Willingdon Island and Fort Cochin or Mattancherry on request for about Rs 40.

AROUND KOCHI
Tripunithura
The **Hill Palace Museum** at Tripunithura, 12km south-east of Ernakulam, en route to Kottayam, houses the collections of the Cochin and Travancore royal families. It's open Tuesday to Sunday 9 am to 12.30 pm and 2 to 4 pm; entry is Rs 1. Bus No 51 or 58 from MG Rd will take you there.

Edapally
The **Museum of Kerala History,** at Edapally, 10km north-east of Ernakulam en route to Aluva (Alwaye) and Thrissur, is open Tuesday to Sunday 10 am to noon and 2 to 4 pm; entry is Rs 2. Bus No 22 from MG Rd runs to Edapally.

Parur & Chennamangalam
About 35km north of Kochi, Parur encapsulates the cultural and religious medley of this region. There's a dusty synagogue, built around the same time as its famous counterpart in Mattancherry. Nearby is an *agraharam* (place of Brahmins), a small street of closely packed houses that was settled by Tamil Brahmins. Parur also boasts a Syrian Orthodox church, a Krishna temple and a temple to the goddess Mookambic.

Four kilometres from Parur is Chennamangalam, with the oldest **synagogue** in

Kerala – virtually in ruins and slowly disintegrating under the ineffectual guardianship of the Archaeological Survey of India.

There's a **Jesuit church** and the ruins of a Jesuit college. The Jesuits first arrived in Chennamangalam in 1577 and, soon after their arrival, the first book in Tamil (the written language used in this part of Kerala at this time) was printed here by John Gonsalves.

You can walk to the **Hindu temple** on the hill overlooking the Periyar River. On the way you'll pass a 16th century **mosque** as well as Muslim and Jewish **burial grounds**.

Whereas Parur is compact and locals can point you in the right direction, Chennamangalam is best visited with a guide. Indo World (☎ 0484-370127, fax 380968), 39/4155 Heera House, MG Rd, Ernakulam, can organise transport and a local retired history teacher to guide you.

To get to Parur, catch a bus from the KSRTC bus stand in Kochi. From Parur you can catch a bus, auto-rickshaw or taxi to Chennamangalam.

THRISSUR (Trichur)
☎ 0487 • pop 275,053
Thrissur has long been regarded as Kerala's cultural capital. Today it continues to assume the role with its numerous festivals, art schools and institutions that foster cultural activities.

Orientation & Information
Thrissur radiates from Vadakkunathan Kshetram with the encircling roads named after the four directions. The tourist information centre is useless.

The State Bank of India on Town Hall Rd cashes American Express and Thomas Cook travellers cheques but doesn't handle cards. Canara Bank on Round South can handle cash advances on Visa cards.

Email is available (sometimes) at IRS Computers & Communications.

Things to See & Do
In the centre of Thrissur, the Hindu-only **Vadakkunathan Kshetram** temple is famed for its artwork. To the west and east are the

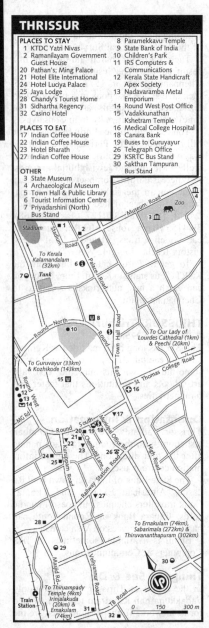

THRISSUR

PLACES TO STAY
1 KTDC Yatri Nivas
2 Ramanilayam Government
   Guest House
20 Pathan's; Ming Palace
21 Hotel Elite International
24 Hotel Luciya Palace
25 Jaya Lodge
28 Chandy's Tourist Home
31 Sidhartha Regency
32 Casino Hotel

PLACES TO EAT
17 Indian Coffee House
22 Indian Coffee House
23 Hotel Bharath
27 Indian Coffee House

OTHER
3 State Museum
4 Archaeological Museum
5 Town Hall & Public Library
6 Tourist Information Centre
7 Priyadarshini (North)
   Bus Stand

8 Paramekkavu Temple
9 State Bank of India
11 IRS Computers &
   Communications
12 Kerala State Handicraft
   Apex Society
13 Nadavaramba Metal
   Emporium
14 Round West Post Office
15 Vadakkunathan
   Kshetram Temple
16 Medical College Hospital
18 Canara Bank
19 Buses to Guruvayur
26 Telegraph Office
29 KSRTC Bus Stand
30 Sakthan Tampuran
   Bus Stand

lesser known Thiruampady and Para-mekkavu temples. Several festivals are celebrated at the temples. The annual April/May **Pooram Festival**, which includes colourful processions of decorated elephants, is one of the biggest.

There are several large churches, including **Our Lady of Lourdes Cathedral**. Skip the sad zoo, and the amazingly decrepit state museum in the zoo grounds. However, the **Archaeological Museum**, further along Museum Rd, is worth a visit. It has temple models, stone reliefs, Gandharan pieces and reproductions of some of the Mattancherry murals. It's open 10 am to 5 pm. The zoo and museums are closed Monday.

Places to Stay

The *Ramanilayam Government Guest House (☎ 332016)* is excellent value at Rs 45/50 for singles/doubles, or Rs 175/275 with air-con, but ring first as it's often full.

The KTDC *Yatri Nivas (☎ 332333, Stadium Rd)*, nearby, has rooms for Rs 100/150, or Rs 350/400 with air-con. There's a restaurant and bar.

Chandy's Tourist Home (☎ 421167, Railway Station Rd) has rooms for Rs 80 with shared bath or Rs 95/275 with private bath. There are several lodges nearby with similar standards and prices.

Jaya Lodge (☎ 423258, Kuruppam Rd), around the corner, is unexciting but cheap. Rooms are Rs 60/100; doubles with bath are Rs 110.

Pathan's (☎ 425620, Chembottil Lane) has rooms for Rs 150/230. The larger doubles for Rs 280 are good value.

Hotel Elite International (☎ 421033, fax 442057), across the road, has rooms for Rs 210/260, or Rs 410/480 with air-con. It has a bar and restaurant.

Hotel Luciya Palace (☎ 424731, fax 427290, Marar Rd) has comfortable rooms for Rs 350/475, or Rs 575/675 with air-con. There's an air-con restaurant, a garden restaurant and bar.

Sidhartha Regency (☎ 424773, fax 425116, corner of TB and Veliyannur Rds) is friendly, centrally air-conditioned and has pleasant rooms for Rs 600/750. There's also a good restaurant and a bar.

Casino Hotel (☎ 424699, fax 442037, TB Rd) is pleasant and friendly. Recently renovated, it has singles/doubles for Rs 400/450, or Rs 600/750 with air-con.

Places to Eat

A cluster of *snack stalls* sets up near the corner of Round South and Round East each evening.

Indian Coffee Houses are on Round South, PO Rd and Kuruppam Rd.

Upstairs in *Pathan's*, there's a good, basic vegetarian restaurant with an air-con section. A floor above Pathan's is the *Ming Palace* Chinese restaurant.

Hotel Bharath, further down Chembottil Lane, is good, busy and vegetarian.

The middle and top-end hotels have decent restaurants, usually with air-con. The *Luciya Palace* has a popular garden restaurant.

Shopping

Thrissur is the place for bell metal and there are a number of shops crammed with lamps, household appliances and images of deities. A good place is Nadavaramba Metal Emporium (☎ 421679) on Round West.

For typical Keralan handicrafts, try the Kerala State Handicraft Apex Society (☎ 420865) also on Round West. It's open Monday to Saturday 10 am to 7.30 pm.

Getting There & Away

Bus There are three bus stands in Thrissur: the KSRTC and Sakthan Tampuran stands in the south; and the Priyadarshini (also referred to as North) stand in the north.

Regular KSRTC buses go to Thiruvananthapuram (Rs 85, 7½ hours), Ernakulam (Rs 25, two hours), Kozhikode (Rs 38, 3½ hours) and Palakkad (Rs 21, 1½ hours). There are also buses to Ponnani, Kottayam and Perumpavoor (for connections to Munnar).

The large, private Sakthan Tampuran stand has buses bound for closer towns such as Kodungallor, Irinjalakuda and Guruvayur (Rs 8, one hour). The smaller, private Priyadarshini bus stand has many buses bound for Shoranur and Palakkad (Rs 15, two hours), Pollachi and Coimbatore.

Train Trains to Ernakulam, 74km south by rail, take about 1½ hours (Rs 28/149 2nd/1st class); trains to Kozhikode, 143km north, take about three hours (Rs 36/189). There are also several trains running to or through Palakkad (Rs 27/150) via Shoranur. The train station is 1km south-west of the town centre.

AROUND THRISSUR

The Hindu-only **Sri Krishna Temple** at Guruvayur, 33km north-west of Thrissur, is one of the most famous in Kerala and a popular pilgrim destination. The temple's elephants are kept at an old Zamorin palace, **Punnathur Kota** (the Zamorins were local rulers). It's definitely worth a visit.

Located 32km north-east of Thrissur at Cheruthuruthy, **Kerala Kalamandalam** (☎/fax 0492-622418) has made a significant contribution to the renaissance of the traditional art of Kerala. Students undergo intensive training in Kathakali, Mohiniattam, Kootiattam, percussion, voice and violin.

Visitors are welcome, 9 am to noon and 3 to 5 pm, when it's possible to stroll between the open-air buildings and watch classes in progress (special permission is required for video and photography).

Short courses (between six and 12 months) are available to foreigners for around Rs 950 per month (plus Rs 1000 for accommodation). For further information write to The Secretary, Kerala Kalamandalam, Cheruthuruthy, PO Thrissur, Kerala 679531.

The **Natana Kairali Research & Performing Centre for Traditional Arts** (☎ 0488-825559), 20km south of Thrissur near Irinjalakuda, offers training in traditional arts including rare forms of puppetry and dance. The centre hosts a 12 day **festival** in January. Short appreciation courses (usually about one month) are available to foreigners. For details of performances or enrolments, telephone or write to the Director, Natana Kairali Research & Performing Centre for Traditional Arts, Ammannu Thakyar, Mathom, Irinjalakuda, Thrissur District.

Northern Kerala

KOZHIKODE (Calicut)

☎ 0495 • pop 801,190

The landing of Vasco da Gama near Kozhikode in 1498 heralded the period of Portuguese colonisation in India. The Portuguese attempted to conquer Kozhikode and the local rulers, the Zamorins, but their attacks in 1509 and 1510 were repulsed. Tipu Sultan took control of the whole region in 1789, with British rule established in 1792.

Information

Money can be changed at the State Bank of India in Bank Rd or the faster PL Worldways, Lakhotia Computer Centre. The tourist office at the Hotel Malabar Mansion has closed. You'll be referred to Civil Station but don't waste your time.

There are numerous STD/ISD booths. International faxes and email can be difficult, even impossible.

Things to See

There are indicators in Kozhikode of its colourful past. **Mananchira Square** was the former courtyard of the Zamorins. Temples, mosques and churches illustrate the region's acquaintance with the major belief systems. Of note are the Tali Temple (non-Hindus prohibited), the Kuttichira Mosque and the Church of South India. The impressive **Mananchira Library** reflects the significance Kozhikode has always placed on it's literature.

Five kilometres north of town, at East Hill, archaeological displays at the **Pazhassirajah Museum** include copies of ancient murals, bronzes, coins and models of megalithic monuments – the earliest monuments of Ker-

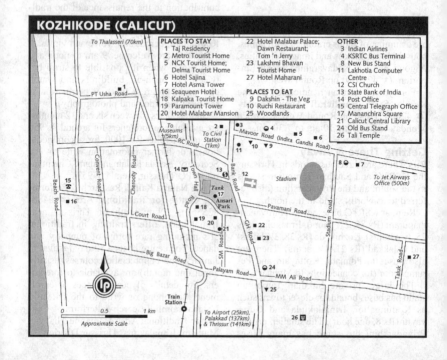

KOZHIKODE (CALICUT)

PLACES TO STAY
1 Taj Residency
2 Metro Tourist Home
5 NCK Tourist Home;
   Delma Tourist Home
6 Hotel Sajina
7 Hotel Asma Tower
16 Seaqueen Hotel
18 Kalpaka Tourist Home
19 Paramount Tower
20 Hotel Malabar Mansion

22 Hotel Malabar Palace;
   Dawn Restaurant;
   Tom 'n Jerry
23 Lakshmi Bhavan
   Tourist Home
27 Hotel Maharani

PLACES TO EAT
9 Dakshin - The Veg
10 Ruchi Restaurant
25 Woodlands

OTHER
3 Indian Airlines
4 KSRTC Bus Terminal
8 New Bus Stand
11 Lakhotia Computer
   Centre
12 CSI Church
13 State Bank of India
14 Post Office
15 Central Telegraph Office
17 Mananchira Square
21 Calicut Central Library
24 Old Bus Stand
26 Tali Temple

To Thalasseri (70km)
PT Usha Road
To Museums (5km)
To Civil Station (1km)
RC Road
Convent Road
Cherooty Road
Beach Road
Court Road
Big Bazar Road
Palayam Road
Town Hall
Prop
SM Road
Bank Road
Mavoor Road (Indira Gandhi Road)
Tank
Ansari Park
Pavamani Road
GH Road
Stadium
Stadium Road
MM Ali Road
Taluk Road
To Jet Airways Office (500km)
Train Station
To Airport (25km), Palakkad (137km) & Thrissur (141km)
Approximate Scale
0 0.5 1 km

ala. Next door, the **Krishna Menon Museum** has memorabilia of this former defence minister, while the **art gallery** has paintings of Raja Ravi Varma and Raja Raja Varma.

The three places are open Tuesday to Sunday 10 am to 5 pm, except on Wednesday when the Krishna Menon Museum and the art gallery open at noon.

Sixteen kilometres north, on the way to Kannur, there's a nondescript memorial for de Gama's landing at **Kappad Beach**.

Places to Stay – Budget

All of the following have bathrooms.

Metro Tourist Home (☎ 766029, corner of Mavoor and Bank Rds) has doubles only for Rs 250, or air-con rooms with TV for Rs 500.

Hotel Sajina (☎ 722975, Mavoor Rd) has basic rooms for Rs 100/140.

NCK Tourist Home has double rooms (no hot water) for Rs 165. Across the way the *Delma Tourist Home* charges Rs 170. Women travellers will find better options.

The Lakshmi Bhavan Tourist Home (☎ 722027, GH Rd) is a similar standard and costs Rs 95/170.

Hotel Maharani (☎ 722541, Taluk Rd) is slightly off the beaten track, and quiet. Rooms are Rs 150/185, or Rs 470 for an air-con double. There's a bar and a garden.

The KTDC *Hotel Malabar Mansion (☎ 722391, Mananchira Square)* rooms are Rs 185/235, Rs 370/420 with air-con. There's a restaurant, beer parlour and snack bar.

Kalpaka Tourist Home (☎/fax 720222, Town Hall Rd), with cockroaches, has singles/doubles for Rs 180/225, or air-con rooms for Rs 550. There is an OK restaurant.

Places to Stay – Mid-Range & Top End

The *Seaqueen Hotel (☎ 366604, fax 365854, Beach Rd)* is by the water. Rooms are Rs 385/520, or Rs 660/795 with air-con.

Paramount Tower (Town Hall Rd) was still undergoing extensive renovations at the time of writing.

Hotel Asma Tower (☎ 723560, Marvoor Rd) is friendly and good value. Rooms are Rs 250/300, or Rs 375/475 with air-con.

Hotel Malabar Palace (☎ 721511, fax 721794, GH Rd) has central air-con and rooms for Rs 1150/1475.

Taj Residency (☎/fax 766448, PT Usha Rd) has rooms starting at US$45/75.

Places to Eat

The glossy *Woodlands* vegetarian restaurant is in the easily spotted White Lines building on GH Rd.

Dakshin – The Veg and nearby *Ruchi Restaurant (Mavoor Rd)* both serve very good vegetarian food.

The restaurants in the *Metro*, *Kalpaka* and *Malabar Mansion* hotels are reasonably priced.

The air-con *Dawn Restaurant* at the Malabar Palace is good and there's an ice cream parlour, *Tom 'n' Jerry*, outside.

The restaurant at the *Seaqueen Hotel* has good food and warm beer.

Getting There & Away

Air Indian Airlines (☎ 766243, Eroth Centre, Bank Rd) flies daily to Mumbai (US$140) and Coimbatore (US$35), and three times weekly to Chennai (US$80). Jet Airways (☎ 356518, 29 Mavoor Rd) also connects daily with Mumbai.

Bus The KSRTC bus stand is on Mavoor Rd, close to the junction with Bank Rd. There's also the New bus stand, further east along Mavoor Rd, for long-distance private buses, and the Old bus stand, at the intersection of GH and MM Ali Rds, for local buses. There are regular buses to Bangalore, Mangalore, Mysore, Ooty, Madurai, Coimbatore, Pondicherry, Thiruvananthapuram, Alappuzha, Kochi and Kottayam.

Train The train station is south of Mananchira Square, about 2km from the New bus stand. It's 242km north to Mangalore (Rs 62/298 in 2nd/1st class, 4½ to 5½ hours), 190km south to Ernakulam (Rs 53/258, five hours) and 414km to Thiruvananthapuram (Rs 95/471, 9½ to 11 hours).

Heading south-east, there are trains to Coimbatore (Rs 50/313) via Palakkad

KERALA

(Palghat; Rs 40/195). These trains then head north to the centres of Bangalore, Chennai and Delhi.

Getting Around

There's no shortage of auto-rickshaws in Kozhikode, and the drivers will use their meters. It's about Rs 10 from the station to the KSRTC bus stand or most hotels.

MAHÉ
☎ 0497

Mahé, 60km north of Kozhikode, was a small French dependency handed over, with Pondicherry, to India at Independence. Except for Alliance Française (☎ 333029) there's little French influence left and Mahé's main function seems to be supplying truck drivers with cheap alcohol.

The first permanent English factory on the Malabar Coast was established here in 1683 by the Surat presidency to purchase pepper and cardamom. The East India Company also built a fort here in 1708. Today mosques, temples and sanitation shops are sandwiched between liquor shops.

There's also the interesting **Malayala Kalagramam Centre for Arts & Ideas** (☎ 332961) in Kochi House, founded in 1993 by well-known artist MV Devan. It offers courses in contemporary and classical art forms.

Visitors are welcome, particularly genuine artists interested in residency. To get to the centre, heading north, cross the bridge that leads into Mahé and turn right about 200m along the river.

It's far more pleasant to stay at Thalasseri, 8km north, though there are a few basic options in Mahé itself.

Government Tourist Home (☎ 332222), about 1km from the bridge, has singles/doubles for just Rs 12/20 with bath, but it's generally full. There is a very cheap 'meals' restaurant here as well.

Municipal Tourist Home (☎ 332233, Church Rd), beside the courthouse, is in the same price range with singles/doubles/family rooms for Rs 12/22/30.

Mahé is too small to warrant a bus stand, so buses stop at various places along Church Rd. There are regular buses to Thalasseri, Mangalore, Kozhikode and also a service to Pondicherry – inquire at the Government Tourist Home.

THALASSERI (Tellicherry)
☎ 0490

Thalasseri does not warrant a special detour but, if you are making your way along the coast, it's a pleasant place to stop for the night. You may even be lucky enough to catch an impromptu circus act in the street: Thalasseri is home to a circus school.

Near the waterfront, right behind the fire station, the East India Company's 1708 **fort** is neglected but relatively intact. There are at least two secret tunnels, one leading to the sea. The tunnels will be either 'closed', 'under repair' or 'inhabited by a cobra', but bring a torch (flashlight) and you may be offered a glimpse of a damp chamber.

Logan's Rd runs from Narangapuram, near the bus and train stations, to the town's main square near the fort.

Places to Stay

Hotel Pranam (☎ 220634) (turn left at Logan's Rd from the train station, then immediately right) has comfortable rooms for Rs 86/165, or Rs 335 with air-con. There's a restaurant.

For all other accommodation listed below take a right turn into Logan's Rd from the bus and train stations.

Brothers Tourist Home (☎ 21558), at the Narangapuram end of Logan's Rd, shares a courtyard with Shemy Hospital. It has rooms for Rs 50/85.

Paris Presidency Hotel (☎/fax 233666), close to the end of Logan's Rd, is welcoming and comfortable. It's good value at Rs 240/300, or Rs 390 for air-con doubles.

Paris Lodging House (☎ 231666), adjacent, is cheaper with rooms from Rs 70/115, up to Rs 288 for an air-con double.

Places to Eat

Parkview, near the railway crossing, is a simple nonveg eatery. Upstairs, *Kings Park* offers a greater choice.

Hotel New Westend, in the busy main square at the end of Logan's Rd, has good nonveg food, with excellent fish curry.

The *New Surya Restaurant*, a couple of doors away, has good food too.

The *Paris Presidency* has an air-con restaurant.

Getting There & Away
Frequent trains and buses head north to Mangalore and south to Mahé, Kozhikode and Kochi. An auto-rickshaw to any of the town's hotels should cost around Rs 10.

KANNUR (Cannanore)
☎ 0497 • pop 463,962
Kannur's days of glory were under the Kolathiri rajas, and its importance as a spice-trading port was mentioned by Marco Polo. From the 15th century various colonial powers exerted their influence, including the Portuguese, Dutch and British.

Information
Give the DTPC (☎ 706336) a miss. Opposite, the State Bank of Travancore, will cash American Express travellers cheques. For other brands and for cash advances on credit cards try the State Bank of India on Fort Rd.

Things to See
The Portuguese built St Angelo Fort in 1505 on the promontory north-west of town. Under the British it became a major military base and today the Indian army occupies the cantonment area beside the fort. The fort is a Rs 10 rickshaw ride from town (entry is free). The solid laterite fortifications were modified by the British who also remodelled many of the buildings within the walls.

At the Kanhirode Weavers Co-operative (☎ 0497-85259, fax 851865), 13km north-east of Kannur, you can see the 385 members turn out high-quality furnishing fabrics, saris, dhotis and fine silks. Visitors (by appointment only – phone the secretary) can buy direct for 20% below showroom prices.

The co-op on the Kannur-Mysore road, is easily reached by bus (or rickshaw, Rs 200) from Kannur. Ask to get off at Kudukkimotta.

Four kilometres from the weaving co-op, further along the road towards Mysore, you'll see the Dinesh Beedi Co-op – makers of the popular *beedi* cigarettes and a significant player in the Keralan economy. Visitors are welcome.

At the Parasinikadavu Temple, 18km north-east of Kannur, there are regular Teyyam (ritual temple dance) performances (October to February) usually 4 am to 9 am. Times and days vary so ask the locals (but not tourist officials – they're likely to give incorrect information).

Places to Stay & Eat
Accommodation here is seriously wanting. Mid-range prices are charged for accommodation with less than mid-range standards.

Government Guest House (☎ 706426) is for government ministers, but it's let to visitors if there's room. It's the best place to stay and at Rs 50 is very good value. Phone the manager first to make sure there's room.

Centaur Tourist Home (☎ 68270), directly across from the train station entrance, on MA Rd, has basic singles/doubles for Rs 100/160. There are plenty of similar lodges in the vicinity.

Kamala International (☎ 66910, fax 50189, SM Rd) has rooms for Rs 500/640, or Rs 700/850 with air-con and is overpriced for what it offers. At the time of writing the restaurants were closed.

Parkin's Chinese restaurant, New Subway, Thavakkara, serves huge, OK meals for reasonable prices.

Getting There & Away
There are direct buses to/from Mysore as well as regular buses to Mangalore and Kozhikode. Kannur is on the main train link between Mangalore and Kozhikode.

BEKAL
☎ 0499
Bekal, in the far north of the state, has long, palm-fringed beaches and a rocky headland topped by the huge Bekal Fort, built between 1645 and 1660. This fort, with views from the battlements north and south, has

an obscure early history but it has been under the control of the Kolathiri rajas and the Vijayanagar empire. The British East India Company occupied it for a period after the defeat of Tipu Sultan. There are slow-moving plans to establish resorts in this region, but the foreshore will remain relatively untouched save for a car park and gardens. The beach has fine sand and calm waters, but swimmers should beware of shifting sand bars. The Thanal Facility Centre opposite the fort is planning to provide information, a handicraft shop, restaurant and toilet facilities.

Places to Stay & Eat

You can stay inside the Bekal Fort walls at the *Tourist Bungalow*. There are just two rooms for Rs 40/60 with bath. To book, ring the District Collector, Kasaragod (☎ 430833). Cold mineral water and soft drinks are available but for food you'll have to head to the villages north of the fort – take a torch (flashlight).

Hotel Sri Sistha, nearby, is a fairly basic restaurant but one of the few open during Ramadan. Meals can be had for under Rs 10.

Fortland Tourist Home (☎ 736600, Main Rd) is a few kilometres further north at the village of Udma. Comfortable singles/doubles cost Rs 75/125, or Rs 350 with air-con. The attached *Sealord* restaurant serves good veg and nonveg food.

Getting There & Around

The train station for Bekal Fort is Kotikulum in the village of Palakunnu, and trains stop regularly. There are many buses to/from Kasaragod (Rs 3 to Rs 5.50), the nearest town of any size, and it's not too hard to find an auto-rickshaw or a bus at Bekal Junction to take you to/from Palakunnu and Udma.

KASARAGOD
☎ 0499

Kasaragod is about 20km north of Bekal and 47km south of Mangalore. There is a small 17th century fort nearby at Chandragiri built by Shivappa Nayaka.

The **Sri Gopalakrishna Yakshagana Bombeyata Sangha** performance troupe is based in Kasaragod. With one week's notice, they'll arrange a performance of their puppetry art, Yakshagana, for groups of five or more. If you're interested contact the founding director, Ramesh, after 8 pm (☎ 423927).

Places to Stay & Eat

There are a number of hotels along MG Rd, near the junction with National Highway 17.

Enay Tourist Home (☎ 421164) has single or double rooms for Rs 100 with shower. Of a similar standard are the *Ceeyel Tourist Home (☎ 430177)* and the *Aliya Lodge (☎ 430666)*, behind the post office.

Hotel City Tower (☎ 430562), the green-and-cream landmark at the bus stand end of MG Rd, has rooms, with the odd cockroach, for Rs 175/295, or Rs 545 with air-con.

Hotel Apsara Regency (☎ 430124), opposite the KSRTC bus stand, has good rooms (quieter at the back) for Rs 160/260, and Rs 360/400 with air-con. The attached *Sri Nivas* veg restaurant serves very good food – one dish is enough for two.

Getting There & Away

Private buses leave for Bekal and Mangalore from the Municipal bus stand near the Hotel City Tower. More regular buses leave from the KSRTC bus stand 1.5km south of the Municipal stand. Buses to Kahangad will drop you off at Udma, Palakunnu or Bekal.

The train station is a couple of kilometres south of town. It's only 1½ hours between Kasaragod and Mangalore by express train (Rs 21).

Lakshadweep

Located 300 to 400km off the Kerala coast, the Lakshadweep Islands make up India's smallest Union Territory. The total area of the 35 islands is only 32 sq km. Only 10 of them are inhabited. The population (nearly 52,000) is 93% Muslim, and Malayalam is the dominant language. Fishing and coir production are the main economic activities.

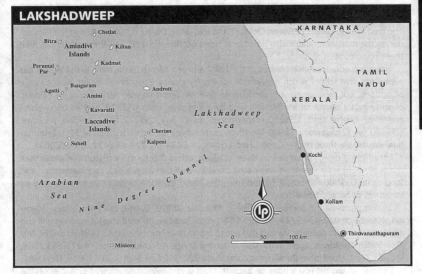

LAKSHADWEEP

Tourists require a special permit to visit the islands. Foreigners can only visit the resort on Bangaram Island and the tourist facilities on Kadmat. Indian nationals are allowed to visit other islands only as part of an organised cruise.

The expense and travel restrictions put Lakshadweep off limits for many travellers. However, with pristine lagoons, unspoiled coral reefs and average November to March temperatures of 24°C to 34°C, the islands are a diver's dream. (See the Diving boxed text for information about dive packages.)

History

A popular story is that the islands were discovered when the legendary ruler of Kerala, Cheraman Perumal, underwent a conversion to Islam and set off for Mecca. Relatives sent a search party to bring him back, but the ships were wrecked on Bangaram Island. Having made their repairs, the mariners sailed home to report what they had found, and were rewarded with the right to settle the islands.

While historians now agree that this legend has little factual basis, there's no con-

crete evidence to suggest who the first settlers really were.

Around the 12th century the islands came under the control of the mainland rulers, the Ali rajas of Cannanore. In 1525 the Portuguese began their brutal occupation. When their power waned the Ali rajas returned (with an equally brutal regime). In 1783 Hyder Ali assumed control. When the British defeated his son (Tipu Sultan) they took over the islands and in 1908 the entire region was ceded to the British government.

In 1956, nearly 10 years after Indian Independence, the islands became centrally administered by the government in Delhi as a Union Territory. In 1973 they became officially known as Lakshadweep.

Information

The Society for the Promotion of Recreational Tourism & Sports in Lakshadweep (SPORTS) is the main tourism organisation. Its office (☎ 0484-668387, fax 668155) is on IG Rd, Willingdon Island, Kochi, 682003.

The Lakshadweep tourist office in Delhi cannot provide Bangaram bookings, but may

Diving

The best time to dive is between October and mid-May. Diving is still possible in the lagoons during the monsoon, and is also possible at times outside the reefs, but the weather can limit these opportunities severely.

There are only two dive centres in the Lakshadweep Islands. Bangaram Island Resort has a well-run dive school which is available for use by guests. Experienced divers have a range of options, but newcomers are also able to dive. A 'resort course' package for a beginner, consisting of a couple of lessons followed by a reef dive, costs US$120, and an open-water certificate course costs US$250. Experienced divers pay US$222 for a six-dive package, US$420 for 12 dives or US$600 for 18 dives. No dives are permitted below 35m. Information is available through the Casino Hotel office (☎ 0484-668221, 668421, fax 668001).

Lacadives, a new dive school on Kadmat Island, offers slightly more reasonable prices than the costly Bangaram Resort. A week-long package with two dives a day, accommodation and food costs US$800. Transport to and from the island by plane or ship can be organised by Lacadives at an additional cost.

Bookings are via the company's office in Mumbai, at E20, Everest Building, Tardeo, Mumbai, 400034 (☎ 022-494 2723, fax 495 1644, email lacadives@hotmail.com). Lacadives will also arrange travel and permits. Visitors can opt to travel to or from the island by ship, on the MV *Tipu Sultan*. Lacadives' agent in the USA is Natural Mystic Adventure Travels (☎ 212-683 3989; fax 683 2831, email info@naturalmystic.com), Suite 320, 300 East 34th St, NY 10016, New York.

Because of weight restrictions on aircraft, most divers rely on equipment provided on the islands. Those who are going to Bangaram Island, however, can apply to the Casino Hotel office for an increased baggage allowance.

For a guide to environmentally friendly diving, see the Responsible Diving boxed text in the Facts for the Visitor chapter.

be able to provide other information. Contact the Liaison Office (☎ 011-338 6807, fax 378 2246), UTF Lakshadweep, F306, Kusum Road Hostel, Kasturba Gandhi Marg, New Delhi, 110001.

Places to Stay & Eat

The **Bangaram Island Resort** is run by Casino Hotels, and is administered from its hotel in Kochi (☎ 0484-668221, fax 668001).

There are 30 rooms, allowing a maximum of 60 guests. Double rooms with full board are US$240 (plus 10% tax) between mid-December and May; single occupancy is US$230. Prices drop in the low season. It's worth shopping around before you leave home – some operators book through Casino Hotels and can secure a better deal.

The resort has a restaurant and a bar. Activities include diving, snorkelling, deep-sea fishing and sailing. Casino Hotels will organise travel and permits for the islands but you should allow one month for the permit to be processed.

Getting There & Away

Indian Airlines has daily flights (except Sunday) from Kochi to Agatti (US$300 return). Flights from Goa have ceased. The plane used is tiny and passengers are restricted to 10kg of luggage. If staying on Bangaram Island, extra luggage can be left in the Casino Hotel on Willingdon Island (Kochi). The 1½ hour transfer by boat from Agatti to Bangaram costs an extra US$30 or, if seas are rough, US$80 by helicopter.

The MV *Tipu Sultan* operates five-day cruises for between Rs 6000 and Rs 10,000. Timetables are available from the SPORTS office on Willingdon Island.

Chennai (Madras)

The fourth largest city in India and the capital of Tamil Nadu, Chennai has grown from the merging of a number of small villages including its former namesake Madraspatnam. Though many still call it Madras, it is now officially known as Chennai. The city sprawls over more than 70 sq km and rather than claiming a centre, retains its former regional hubs.

Billboards are the most striking outward expressions of the city. These gargantuan icons of popular culture dwarf city buildings in their eagerness to promote everything from soap and shoes to power tools and blockbuster movies. In fact Chennai is the centre for Tamil film making.

Many of the Indian languages are spoken in Chennai, though the main language is Tamil. The Tamil people are zealous guardians of their language and culture and have been among the most vociferous opponents to Hindi becoming the national language.

With many esteemed educational institutes and a strong and sometimes volatile tradition of journalism and publishing, Chennai remains a focus for serious and diverse public discourse.

The pollution in Chennai can sometimes be horrendous and at times breathing feels positively dangerous. However, Chennai still seems to conveys a sense of spaciousness and ease.

For travellers with an interest in the colonial history of India, Chennai has much worth exploring and abundant transport options make other parts of the country readily accessible.

History

For more than 2000 years the area has been popular with seafarers, spice traders and cloth merchants. The 16th century saw the arrival of the Portuguese, followed by the Dutch. In 1639, the British East India Company established a settlement in the fishing village of Madraspatnam.

Chennai at a Glance

Population: 5.9 million
Main Language: Tamil
Area Code: 044
Best Time to Go: January to September

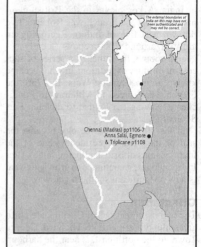

The external boundaries of India on this map have not been authenticated and may not be correct.

Chennai (Madras) pp1106-7
Anna Salai, Egmore
& Triplicane p1108

- **Kalakshetra Arts Village** – witness skilful performances of traditional dance
- **Valluvar Kottam** – experience the wisdom of the ancient poet, Thiruvalluvar
- **Film Studios** – try your luck at 'being discovered'

Fort St George was constructed over a period of 15 years and finally completed in 1653. George Town grew in the area of the fort and was granted its first municipal charter in 1688 by James II, making it the oldest municipality in India.

During the 18th and 19th centuries, French and British traders competed for supremacy

Festivals of Chennai

festival	date	features
Carnatic Music & Dance	mid-Dec to mid-Jan	cultural festival showcasing classical south Indian music & dance
Kalakshetra Arts Festival	Dec/Jan	cultural arts

in India. A key player in the British campaign against the French was Robert Clive (known as Clive of India). Recruiting an army of around 2000 sepoys (locally engaged troops), he launched a series of successful military expeditions in what became known as the Carnatic Wars. In 1756, the French were forced to withdraw to Pondicherry, leaving the British to develop Fort St George.

In the 19th century, the city became the seat of the Madras presidency, one of the four divisions of British imperial India. After Independence, it continued to grow into what is now a significant southern gateway.

Orientation

The two main sections of Chennai are north and south of Periyar EVR High Rd. George Town, to the north-east, is near the harbour. Its narrow streets contain shipping agencies, cheaper hotels, restaurants, bazaars and the main post office. The area's focal point is Parry's Corner – the intersection of Prakasam Rd (or Popham's Broadway) and NSC Bose Rd – where many city buses terminate. The two long-distance (SETC) bus stands are close by on Esplanade Rd.

The other main section of the city, south of Periyar EVR High Rd, is intersected by Chennai's main road, Anna Salai (Mount Rd), which is home to airline offices, tourist offices, top-end hotels and restaurants. It also contains Egmore and Central, Chennai's two main train stations. Many of the budget and mid-range hotels are clustered around Egmore station. Egmore is also the departure point for most destinations in Tamil Nadu. If you are going interstate, you'll probably leave from Chennai Central.

Nungambakkam, south-west of Egmore, houses the consulates and airline offices. Further south-west, the district of Theagaraya Nagar (also spelt Thyagaraya and Tyagaraja) is crammed with markets and shops, while south-east of Egmore, the Triplicane area includes the extensive Marina Beach as well as popular cheap hotels.

Travel around Chennai, particularly in auto-rickshaws, is easier if you know the PIN code of your destination. Although codes are six digits, they are commonly known by the last two or three digits. For example, Ashok Nagar is referred to as Chennai 83. See the Chennai Codes table for the main codes.

Information

Tourist Offices The Government of India tourist office (☎ 852 4295, fax 852 2193), 154 Anna Salai, is open Monday to Friday 9.15 am to 5.45 pm; Saturday and public holidays 9 am to 1 pm; closed Sunday. The

Chennai Codes

area	PIN code
Adyar	600020
Ashok Nagar	600083
Bessant Nagar	600090
Broadway	600108
C-in-C Rd	600105
Egmore	600008
Jafferkhanpet	600095
Kilpauk	600010
Mylapore	600004
Saidapet	600093
St Thomas Mount	600016
T Nagar	600017

friendly staff give free brochures, such as the monthly *Hallo! Madras* guide and can take bookings for Indian Tourism Development Corporation (ITDC) tours. Take bus No 11 or 18 from Parry's Corner or Central station.

There are also Government of India tourist information counters at the domestic and international airports.

The ITDC (☎ 827 8884), 29 Victoria Crescent (on the corner of C-in-C Rd) is open 5.30 am to 7 pm daily (mornings only on Sunday). This is not a tourist office as such, but all ITDC tours can be booked and start from here.

The Tamil Nadu Tourism Development Corporation or TTDC (☎ 830 3390), 143 Anna Salai, concentrates on selling tours and accommodation. You can book TTDC hotels and lodges from the office at the Hotel Tamil Nadu (☎ 582 916). There are also TTDC tourist booths at Central station and the State Express (SETC) bus stand.

The Automobile Association of South India (☎ 852 4061), 187 Anna Salai, is in the American Express administrative building (4th floor).

Foreign Consulates Foreign missions in Chennai are open Monday to Friday and are listed in the Facts for the Visitor chapter.

Visa Extensions & Permits The Foreigners' Registration Office or FRO (☎ 827 8210) is in the Shashtri Bhavan annexe (rear building, on the ground floor) at 26 Haddows Rd, Nungambakkam. Visa extensions (Rs 750 up to six months) are possible but can be very difficult to obtain. The office is open Monday to Friday, 10 am to 1 pm and 2 to 5 pm. Bus Nos 27J and 27RR, from opposite the Connemara Hotel, pass by.

If you're planning to visit the Andaman and Nicobar islands by boat, you'll need a permit before buying your ticket (air passengers obtain permits on arrival in Port Blair). Collect an application form from the Directorate of Shipping Services (☎ 522 6873) at 6 Rajaji Salai in George Town and submit the completed form, with two photos, to the FRO. If you apply in the morning, the permit

Street Name Changes

It's not only the city that's been renamed; many streets have had official name changes, so there's a confusing mixture of names used in the vernacular.

old name	new name
Adam's Rd	Swami Sivananda Salai
Broadway	NSC Chandra Bose Rd
Mount Rd	Anna Salai
Mowbray's Rd	TTK Rd
North Beach Rd	Rajaji Salai
Poonamallee High Rd	Periyar EVR High Rd
Popham's Broadway	Prakasam Rd
Pycroft's Rd	Bharathi Salai
South Beach Rd	Kamarajar Salai

may be ready on the same day between 4 and 5 pm. Permits are not issued for the next vessel, only for subsequent services.

Accommodation and access permits for national parks are issued at the Wildlife Warden's Office (☎ 413947), 4th floor, DMS Office, Teynampet.

Money American Express office (☎ 852 3638), G-17 Spencer Plaza, Anna Salai, exchanges cash and travellers cheques Monday to Saturday 9.30 am to 6.30 pm.

Thomas Cook charges a 1% fee (minimum Rs 20) to cash non-Thomas Cook travellers cheques. It has the following branches:

Egmore
   (☎ 855 1475) 45 Ceebros Centre, Montieth Rd – Monday to Saturday 9.30 am to 6 pm
George Town
   (☎ 534 2374) 20 Rajaji Salai – Monday to Saturday 9.30 am to 6 pm
International airport
   (☎ 233 2882) – 24 hours
Nungambakkam
   (☎/fax 827 4941) Eldorado Bldg, 112 Nungambakkam High Rd – Monday to Friday 9.30 am to 1 pm and 2 to 6.30 pm; Saturday 9.30 am to noon

CHENNAI

CHENNAI (MADRAS)

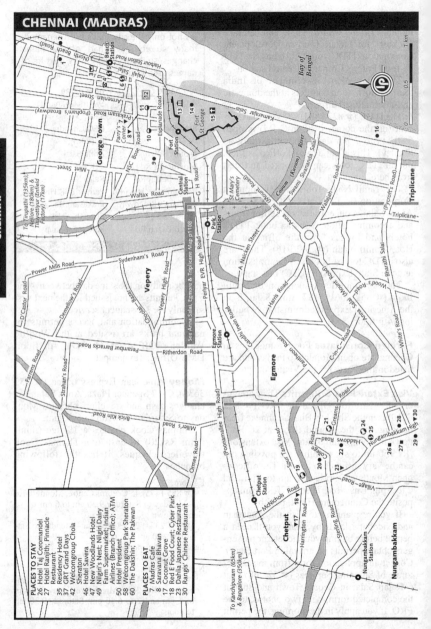

See Anna Salai, Egmore & Triplicane Map p1108

PLACES TO STAY
26 Hotel Taj Coromandel
27 Hotel Ranjith; Pinnacle Restaurant
35 Residency Hotel
42 GRT Grand Days; Welcongroup Chola
46 Sheraton
47 Hotel Savera
49 New Woodlands Hotel; Nilgir's Nest; Nilgiri Dairy Farm Supermarket; Indian Airlines (Branch Office); ATM
50 Hotel President
58 Welcongroup Park Sheraton
60 The Dakshin; The Pakwan

PLACES TO EAT
7 Madras Cafe
8 Saravana Bhavan
17 Coconut Grove
18 Red E Food Court; Cyber Park
23 Dahlia Japanese Restaurant
30 Rangis Chinese Restaurant

CHENNAI

CHENNAI (MADRAS)

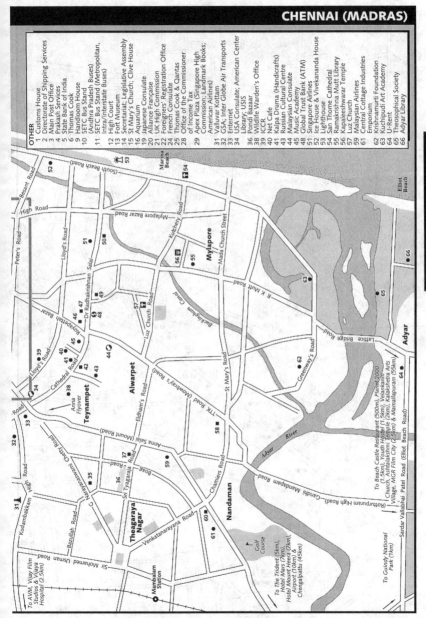

OTHER
1 Customs House
2 Directorate of Shipping Services
3 Main Post Office
4 Prakash Services
5 State Bank of India
9 Thomas Cook
9 Handloom House
10 SETC Bus Stand (Metropolitan, Intra/Interstate Buses)
11 SETC Bus Stand (Metropolitan, Andhra Pradesh Buses)
12 High Court
13 Fort Museum
14 Secretariat; Legislative Assembly
15 St Mary's Church; Clive House
16 Aquarium
19 Japanese Consulate
20 Alliance Française
21 UK High Commission
22 Foreigners' Registration Office
24 French Consulate
25 Thomas Cook & Qantas
28 Office of the Commissioner of Income Tax
29 Apex Plaza (Singapore High Commission; Landmark Books; American Airlines)
31 GSA; Inter Globe Air Transports
32 USA Consulate; American Center Library; USIS
33 Enternet
34 Wildlife Warden's Office
36 Pondi Bazaar
38 ICCR
39 Net Cafe
40 Kalpa Druma (Handicrafts)
41 Russian Cultural Centre
43 Malaysian Consulate
44 Music Academy
45 Global Trust Bank (ATM)
48 Singapore Airlines
51 Ice House & Vivekananda House
52 Lighthouse
53 San Thome Cathedral
54 Ramakrishna Mutt Library
55 Kapaleeshwarar Temple
57 Luz Church
59 Malaysian Airlines
61 Central Cottage Industries Emporium
62 Krishnamurti Foundation
63 Kuchipudi Art Academy
64 U-Rent
65 Theosophical Society
66 Adyar Library

CHENNAI

ANNA SALAI, EGMORE & TRIPLICANE

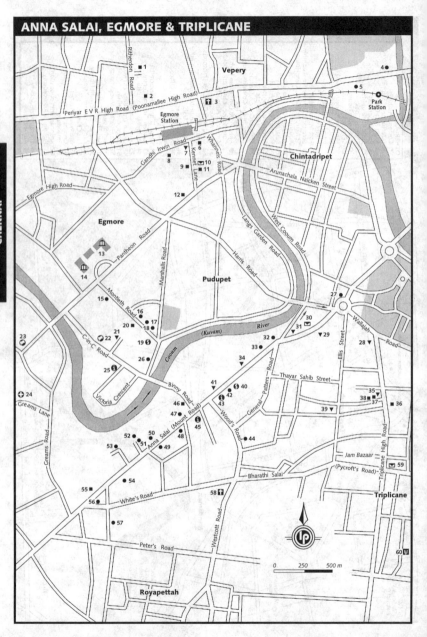

ANNA SALAI, EGMORE & TRIPLICANE

PLACES TO STAY
1 Salvation Army Red Shield Guest House
2 YWCA International Guest House
6 Hotel Chandra Towers; Vasanta Bhavan; Airport Bus
8 Tourist Home
9 Shri Lakshmi Lodge; Hotel Masa
11 Hotel Sri Durga Prasad; Hotel Pandian; Raj Restaurant
12 Dayal-De Lodge
20 Hotel Ambassador Pallava; The Other Room Restaurant
36 Hotel Himalaya
37 Paradise Guest House
38 Broadlands
46 Hotel Connemara; Raintree Restaurant; Giggles Bookshop; KLM
55 The Grand Orient

PLACES TO EAT
7 Bhoopathy Cafe
21 Ponnusamy Hotel
28 Hotel Tirumulai

29 Saravanaas; Devi Cinema Complex
31 Mathura Restaurant
34 Dasaprakash Restaurant
35 Maharaja Restaurant
39 Srinivasa Hotel
41 Annalakshmi

OTHER
3 St Andrew's Church
4 Train Reservation Complex
5 TTDC Booking Office
10 Kennet Lane Post Office
13 Government Museum
14 Art Gallery
15 British Airways
16 Thomas Cook
17 Jet Airways; Kuwait Airways; Air France
18 Gulf Air
19 Central Bank; Singapore Airlines
22 German Consulate
23 Sri Lanka High Commission
24 Apollo Hospital
25 ITDC
26 Indian Airlines/Air India

27 India Silk House
30 Anna Salai Post Office
32 Poomppuhar Emporium
33 Higginbothams
40 State Bank of India
42 Welcome Tours & Travels
43 TTDC Booking Office
44 Melody Cinema
45 Government of India Tourist Office
47 Spencer Plaza (American Express, The Bookshop, Cathay Pacific)
48 The Bookpoint
49 Lufthansa
50 Victoria Technical Institute
51 Development Centre for Musical Instruments
52 Air Lanka
53 British Council Library
54 Automobile Association of South India
56 Swissair
57 Sathyam Cinema
58 Wesley Church
59 Triplicane Post Office
60 Sri Parthasarathy Temple

CHENNAI

The State Bank of India's main branch is on Rajaji Salai in George Town. There are also branches on Anna Salai and at the international (open 24 hours) and domestic (open 5 am to 8 pm) airport terminals.

Several of the banks in Spencer Plaza give cash advances on MasterCard and Visa. Central Bank (Montieth Rd, Egmore) handles Visa cards.

There are ATMs at Nilgiri's Nest and the Global Trust Bank opposite the New Woodland's Hotel.

Post & Communications The main post office is on Rajaji Salai. There's also a post office in Kennet Lane, near Egmore station, and on Anna Salai. For poste restante it's more convenient to use the Anna Salai post office. The full address is Poste Restante, Anna Salai (Mount Rd) Post Office, Anna Salai, Chennai 600 002. Poste restante is open Monday to Saturday, 10 am to 6 pm; the post office itself is open Monday to Sat-

urday 8 am to 8.30 pm; Sunday 10 am to 5 pm. The Anna Salai post office is also the best place to post parcels. It's much less congested than the main post office and there's a super-efficient Professional Parcel Packer just inside (from 10 am).

Both the main and the Anna Salai post offices have 24 hour telegraph offices. Alternatively, you can make use of one of the many STD/ISD/fax booths around town. Prakash Services (☎ 534 0214, fax 534 1022, email mdsaaa53@giasmd01.vsnl.net.in), 146 Thambu Chetty St, George Town, is open 24 hours for faxes and phone calls. For email it's open Monday to Saturday, 10 am to 7 pm.

Internet Resources Email centres have mushroomed. The Net Cafe (☎ 826 3779), 101/1 Kanakasri Nagar, Cathedral Rd, opens daily 7 am to 10 pm, but give the coffee and cake a miss.

A cheaper internet cafe is Enternet at Kodambakkam (☎ 480 2956), 36/3 Taylors

Estate, Station View Rd. Another branch is at 225 SI Plaza Centre (☎ 822 2171), 2nd floor, 129 GN Chetty Rd. Both branches open daily 8 am to 10.30 pm.

Cyber Park (☎ 825 1790) at 107 Harrington Rd (adjacent to the Red E Food Court) opens daily 9 am to 11 pm.

Travel Agencies The American Express Travel Service (☎ 852 3628) in Spencer Plaza on Anna Salai and Thomas Cook (☎ 855 3276), 45 Ceebros Centre, Montieth Rd, Egmore, are both good.

Welcome Tourrs and Travels (☎ 852 0908, fax 858 6655), 150 Anna Salai, is approved by the Government of India Tourist Board and can organise everything from car hire and air or train tickets to customised individual or group tours. The drivers are well trained, good humoured and safety conscious. Further information is available on their Web site at www.sysprom.com/welcome.

Bookshops Landmark Books in Apex Plaza (3 Nungambakkam High Rd) has an excellent selection. It's open 9 am to 9 pm Monday to Friday, and noon to 9 pm Saturday and Sunday.

The popular Higginbothams is at 814 Anna Salai with kiosks at Central station and the domestic airport. The Bookpoint at 160 Anna Salai and The Bookshop in Spencer Plaza are both well stocked.

The tiny Giggles bookshop in the Connemara Hotel park is definitely worth a visit. The collection is excellent and so is the proprietor's knowledge.

Libraries & Cultural Centres The Indian Council for Cultural Relations or ICCR (☎ 827 4519, 201 Lloyd's Rd) facilitates cultural programs and visits from international artists. See the daily paper for details.

In Mylapore district, the Ramakrishna Mutt Library at 16 Ramakrishna Mutt Rd, specialises in philosophy, mythology and Indian classics. The Krishnamurti Foundation (☎ 493 7803) is further south, at 64 Greenway's Rd. The Adyar Library (☎ 491

3528), in the grounds of the Theosophical Society, has a huge collection on religion and philosophy.

The British Council Library (☎ 852 5412), 737 Anna Salai, offers temporary membership for Rs 100 a month. It's open Tuesday to Saturday 11 am to 7 pm.

The American Center Library (☎ 827 3040), attached to the US consulate, is open daily except Sunday 9.30 am to 6 pm. The Alliance Française de Chennai (☎ 827 2650) at 3/4A College Rd, Nungambakkam, is open Monday to Friday 9 am to 1 pm and 3.30 to 6.30 pm, and on Saturday morning.

Medical Services For 24 hour emergency services, head to Apollo Hospital (☎ 827 6566) at 21 Greams Lane, or the Vijaya Hospital (☎ 483 9166) at NSK Salai, Valapalani.

Emergency Police: ☎ 100; fire: ☎ 101; ambulance: ☎ 102.

High Court Building

This red Indo-Saracenic structure at Parry's Corner is the main landmark in George Town. Built in 1892, it is said to be the largest judicial building in the world after the Courts of London.

Fort St George

Built around 1653 by the British East India Company, the fort has undergone much alteration. It presently houses the Secretariat and the Legislative Assembly. The 46m-high flagstaff at the front is actually a mast salvaged from a 17th century shipwreck.

The **Fort Museum** has a fascinating collection of memorabilia from both the British and French East India Companies, as well as the Raj and Muslim administrations. Entry is Rs 2 and it's open 9 am to 5 pm; closed Friday.

St Mary's Church, built 1678-80, was the first English church in Madras, and is the oldest surviving British church in India. There are reminders in the church of Clive, who was married here in 1753, and of Elihu Yale, the early Governor of Madras who later founded the famous American university bearing his name. About a kilometre west of the church is the cemetery in Pallavan Salai.

St Andrew's Church

Near Egmore station, St Andrew's Church was completed in 1821 in the classical style. Inside, the impressive blue dome is decorated with gold stars. There are excellent views from the 55m steeple. Services are at 9 am and 6 pm on Sunday.

Government Museum

Well worth visiting, the Government Museum is on Pantheon Rd, between Egmore and Anna Salai. The buildings originally belonged to a group of eminent British citizens, known as the Pantheon Committee, who were charged with improving the social life of the British in Madras.

The main building has a fine **archaeological section** representing all the major south Indian periods including Chola, Vijayanagar, Hoysala and Chalukya. It also houses a good ethnology collection.

The **bronze gallery** has a superb collection of Chola art. One of the most impressive is the bronze of Ardhanariswara, the androgynous incarnation of Shiva.

The museum complex is open 9.30 am to 5 pm; closed Friday and public holidays. Entry costs Rs 3.

Development Centre for Musical Instruments

Ancient and modern Indian musical instruments are made and exhibited here. The centre is in the Tamil Nadu Handicrafts building at 759 Anna Salai and is open Monday to Friday, 9.30 am to 6 pm; Saturday 9.30 am to 1 pm.

Valluvar Kottam

The Valluvar Kottam, on the corner of Kodambakkam High Rd and Village Rd, honours the acclaimed Tamil poet, Thiruvalluvar, whose classic work, the *Kural*, is reputed to be about 2000 years old. Established in 1976, Valluvar Kottam replicates ancient Tamil architecture with the 1330

verse *Kural* inscribed on panels. It's open daily 8 am to 6 pm. Entry is Rs 2.

Sri Parthasarathy Temple

This temple off Triplicane High Rd is dedicated to Krishna. Built in the 8th century by the Pallavas, and renovated in the 16th century by the Vijayanagars, it's one of the oldest surviving temples in Chennai. It's open daily 6 am to noon and 4 to 8 pm.

Marina & Aquarium

The stretch of beach known as the Marina extends for 13km. South of the pitiful aquarium is the **Ice House**, once used to store massive ice blocks transported by ship from North America. It later became the venue from which Vivekananda preached his ascetic philosophy.

San Thome Cathedral

Built in 1504, then rebuilt in neo-Gothic style in 1893, this Roman Catholic church near Kapaleeshwarar Temple is said to house the remains of St Thomas the Apostle (Doubting Thomas). A crypt can be entered by a stairway just before the altar.

Kapaleeshwarar Temple

This ancient Shiva temple, off Kutchery Rd in Mylapore, is constructed in Dravidian style and displays the architectural elements – *gopurams, mandapams* and a tank – that are found in the famous temple cities of Tamil Nadu.

The temple is open for *puja* (worship) daily 4 am to noon and 4 to 8 pm. Bus No 21 runs here from Anna Salai or the High Court.

Luz Church

Dedicated to Our Lady of Light, this 16th century church is the oldest church in Chennai. It was built by Portuguese sailors who believed they owed their survival to Our Lady.

Little Mount

St Thomas is believed to have lived in this tiny cave when he came to India around 58 AD. Known locally as Chinnamalai, the cave is entered via the Portuguese church that was built in 1551.

Guindy National Park & Snake Park

These parks are adjacent to each other, just 1km from Guindy station. The Guindy National Park supposedly has much wildlife but it's a scraggy place and you're unlikely to see much.

The Snake Park with its lizards, crocodiles and turtles is more interesting. It is well maintained with generous enclosures. Information boards debunk many myths about reptiles. The hourly demonstration is truly pythonesque!

The parks are open daily, except Tuesday, 8.30 am to 5 pm. Entry is Rs 2.

The train from Egmore station will take you to Guindy station. It's then a 1km walk east or take an auto-rickshaw.

Film Studios

The film industry in Chennai now rivals Bollywood (Mumbai) for output, (see The Southern Cinema Invasion boxed text

below). One of the biggest studios is MGR Film City (☎ 235 2424). This is the only one routinely open to the public. If you have always fancied your chances as a film star, extras are occasionally needed. You can telephone the studios or simply try your luck and hang about waiting to be spotted (see My Life as an Extra boxed text in the Facts about India chapter).

MGR Film City is near Indira Nagar, about 10km south of Egmore. Bus 23C runs from Egmore station, bus 5C from Parry's Corner. The studios open daily 8 am to 8 pm and entry is Rs 15.

Elliot Beach

This beach near Adyar district is quieter than Marina Beach. At the southern end the **Velankanni Church** honours the Madonna of Health and the nearby **Ashtalakshmi Temple** is dedicated to the goddess Lakshmi.

Enfield Factory

Tiruvottiyur, 17km north of Chennai, is the site of the Enfield motorbike factory. Factory tours can be arranged by contacting the

---

The Southern Cinema Invasion

Chennai has long been the centre of the vibrant south Indian film industry. The studios are now so prolific that the city rivals Mumbai as the capital of the Indian film industry.

As with cinema the world over, the battles within south Indian cinema continue to be about art and integrity versus commercial viability. Many of the past films have been cliché ridden and much of the current output is a high-octane romp of sex (Indian style), violence and unadulterated melodrama. However, Tamil cinema has also been characterised by clever use of the medium for raising social awareness, and a number of writers and directors have made their mark with stories containing strong messages of justice and equality.

Like Tamil cinema, Telugu cinema has its fair share of pioneers who demonstrate a passion for their craft and a loyalty to their culture. When Boag Rd in Chennai was renamed BN Reddi Rd, one such pioneer was given his due recognition. Bommireddi Narasimha Reddi was born in 1908 in Andhra Pradesh. He died in 1977 after a life dedicated to quality films in his native Telugu.

The influence of screen culture upon political culture in Tamil Nadu is evidenced by the fact that two former movie stars have attained the position of state chief minister. The first was MG Ramachandran, a screen actor who cultivated enormous popularity during the 1960s and 1970s as a champion of the downtrodden. The vast government film studios in Chennai bear his name. More recently, Jayalalitha Jayaram moved from the celluloid to the political limelight.

product manager (☎ 543300, fax 54249, Web site www.royalenfield.com).

Organised Tours

TTDC and ITDC both conduct tours of Chennai and surrounds. For information on where to book, see Tourist Offices at the start of this chapter. TTDC tours can also be booked at the State Express bus stand on Esplanade Rd (☎ 534 1982) 6 am to 9 pm, or at Central station (☎ 535 3351).

Tours include:

City Sightseeing Tour This tour includes visits to Fort St George, the Government Museum, Valluvar Kottam, the Snake Park, Kapaleeshwarar Temple and Marina Beach. The daily tours are good value, although somewhat rushed. The morning tour is from 8 am to 1.30 pm, and the afternoon tour 1.30 to 6.30 pm; cost is Rs 95.

Kanchipuram & Mamallapuram (Mahabalipuram) This full-day tour costs Rs 210, or Rs 300 (air-con bus) including breakfast and lunch and a visit to a crocodile farm. It's good value if you're strapped for time, but otherwise it's a breathless dash.

Tirupathi This full-day tour to the famous Venkateshwara Temple at Tirumala in southern Andhra Pradesh includes 'special *darshan*' (see the Venkateshwara Temple boxed text in the Andhra Pradesh chapter). Darshan usually takes two hours, but can take five hours, which means you don't get back to Chennai until midnight. Daily tours leave at 6 am. The fare is Rs 280, or Rs 550 (air-con), and includes breakfast and lunch. This tour involves 12 hours on a bus.

Cultural & Spiritual Tours Window to the World specialises in cultural tours. Contact Faith Hawley (☎ 452-747022, fax 452-521979), Hotel Chentoor, 106 West Perumal Maistry, Madurai. There's an Australian office (☎/fax 612-6493 8595, Web site www.windowtotheworld.com. au), 36 Fieldbuckets Road, Quamma, NSW 2550.

Special Events

Chennai hosts a wide range of events from classical and contemporary concerts and theatre to art exhibitions and trade shows. See the daily papers for listings. The **Festival of Carnatic Music & Dance**, which takes place mid-December to mid-January, is one of the largest of its type in the world. See

the South Indian Music & Dance boxed text in this section.

At Kalakshetra (Temple of Arts) in Tiruvanmiyur, a special 10 day **arts festival** takes place over December and January. Tickets are available during the day at the Bharta Kalakshetra Auditorium and cost Rs 20 to Rs 100. Entry is through the main gate on the northern side opposite the auditorium. During the festival, some hotels run free shuttle buses between Kalakshetra and the city. Check with any tourist office.

Places to Stay

Egmore, on and around Kennet Lane, is the main budget and mid-range accommodation hub, but competition for rooms can be fierce. Book in advance or arrive early. Two other areas for cheap hotels are George Town, between Mint St, NSC Bose Rd and Rajaji Salai; and Triplicane, to the southeast of Anna Salai, which is less chaotic than Egmore. The top hotels are mainly along Anna Salai and the roads leading off it. If you'd like to stay in a private home, contact the Government of India tourist office for a list of home-stays. Prices range from Rs 100 to Rs 600 per person per week. At the time of writing new, low budget guesthouses were being planned for the city. Inquire at the tourist office for details.

Hotel tax in Tamil Nadu is currently among the highest in the country – 15% on rooms costing Rs 100 to Rs 199, and 20% for anything above. The top hotels add a further 5% to 10% service charge. Prices given in this section are *before* tax.

Places to Stay – Budget

Egmore The *Salvation Army Red Shield Guest House (☎ 532 1821, 15 Ritherdon Rd)*, a 20 minute walk from Egmore station, welcomes both men and women. It's a clean, quiet place in leafy surroundings. Dorm beds costs Rs 50, doubles/triples are Rs 195/220, all with common bath. Checkout is 9 am.

The *Tourist Home (☎ 825 0079, 21 Gandhi Irwin Rd)* fills up quickly. Singles/doubles with bath start at Rs 130/160; a double with air-con is Rs 250.

South Indian Music & Dance

The Festival of Carnatic Music & Dance is a celebration of the classical music of South India, with songs in all the main languages – Tamil, Telugu, Malayalam and Kannada. Most performances are preceded by a lecture and demonstration. Concerts usually start with a *varnam*, an uptempo introduction, followed by several songs, *kirtis*, or *kirtanas*, before the main number. The *raga* is the basis of Carnatic music: five six or seven notes arranged in ascending or descending scales.

The main instruments used are the violin, wooden flute, *veena* (a large stringed instrument), *gottuvadyam* (similar to the veena but without frets), *nagaswaram* (pipe), *thavil* (percussion instrument), *mridangam* (drum), and even a *ghatam* (mud pot). Daily papers and the Government of India tourist office can provide details.

During the rest of the year, at Tiruvanmiyur, near the temple of Marundeeswarar, the 40 hectare estate of Kalakshetra (Temple of the Arts) nurtures traditional arts, music, dance and craft.

Kalakshetra was founded in 1936 by Rukmini Devi, a remarkable woman born in 1904 and adopted at an early age by Annie Besant, president of the Theosophical Society. Rukmini married George Sydney Arundale, principal of the Theosophical School. In 1926 Rukmini and her husband travelled to Australia where she studied under the great Russian dancer, Anna Pavlova. A decade later she returned to India and founded Kalakshetra. She continued teaching, lecturing and writing until her death at the age of 82.

The atmosphere at Kalakshetra is decidedly creative. Described by the Indian media as a 'cultural empire', the centre has hosted many of India's finest musicians, dancers and artisans. In 1993, Kalakshetra was declared by the Indian Parliament to be an institution of national importance.

Shri Lakshmi Lodge (☎ 825 4576, 16 Kennet Lane) is clean and quiet and has singles/doubles with bath for Rs 155/320, or Rs 80/130 without air-con. The rooms face a quiet central courtyard. The nearby *Hotel Sri Durga Prasad (☎ 825 3881, 10 Kennet Lane)* is similarly priced and also often full.

Dayal-De Lodge (☎ 822 7328, 486 Pantheon Rd), at the southern end of Kennet Lane, has reasonable rooms from Rs 180/240; all have hot bath. Family rooms are Rs 330.

Hotel Masa (☎ 825 2966, 15 Kennet Lane) has singles/doubles/triples with bath from Rs 225/285/345. There are also air-con doubles/triples for Rs 420/475. This is a great place for those who can't tolerate silence.

The *retiring rooms* at the Central and Egmore stations have doubles from Rs 145 or Rs 260 with air-con. Dorm beds (men only) are Rs 80 for 12 hours and are quiet, clean and have air-con.

Triplicane You can reach this area on bus No 30, 31 or 32 from Esplanade Rd, outside the State Express bus stand in George Town. From Egmore station take bus No 29D, 22 or 27B.

Broadlands (☎ 854 5573, 16 Vallabha Agraharam St) is off Triplicane High Rd, opposite the Star Cinema. This travellers' institution is losing its edge. It has an unofficial policy of excluding Indians. The charm of the courtyard setting is offset by the basic and somewhat dingy rooms. Singles without/with bath cost Rs 170/175; doubles are Rs 350/390. Dorm beds are Rs 50.

Paradise Guest House (☎ 854 7542) next door has clean, basic rooms at Rs 160/220. A deluxe double is Rs 280.

Hotel Himalaya (☎ 854 7522, 54 Triplicane High Rd) is not a bad option, with singles/doubles/triples from Rs 330/390/510 and also some air-con rooms. There's a vegetarian restaurant and 24 hour hot water.

Indira Nagar The *Youth Hostel* (☎ *412882, 2nd Ave, Indira Nagar*) is about 10km south of Egmore in a peaceful residential area. Dorm beds cost Rs 40 for nonmembers, Rs 20 for members, and it's possible to camp in the garden. Phone in advance for a reservation and directions, and bring a padlock for your locker. Meals are available on request (Rs 10 for a *thali*). This is a good place for genuine shoestringers.

Places to Stay – Mid-Range

Egmore The *YWCA International Guest House* (☎ *532 4234, fax 532 4263, 1086 Periyar EVR High Rd, formerly Poonamallee High Rd*) has bright and spacious rooms. It's so popular you will need to book well in advance. In the low season (April/July and September/October) singles/doubles with clean bathrooms cost Rs 450/580; triples are Rs 800; and singles/doubles with air-con are Rs 630/750. The guesthouse accepts both men and women, but there's a transient membership fee of Rs 20 – valid for one month. The restaurant serves Indian, Chinese and western food. Because this is a service organisation, taxes do not apply. However, certain rules do: checkout is usually by noon, visitors are forbidden in the rooms, lunch and dinner in the restaurant must be ordered in advance, alcohol is not served and meals usually finish by 9 pm.

Hotel New Victoria (☎ *825 3638, fax 825 0070, 3 Kennet Lane*) has decent air-con rooms with bath and phone for Rs 870/1200.

Hotel Pandian (☎ *825 2901, fax 825 8459, 9 Kennet Lane*) is popular, clean, comfortable and friendly place. Ordinary singles/doubles are Rs 500/600; air-con rooms start at Rs 750/850. The hotel has an excellent veg/nonveg restaurant, and a bar.

Hotel Chandra Towers (☎ *823 3344, fax 825 1703, 9 Gandhi Irwin Rd*) has a lush lobby that belies the somewhat cramped singles/doubles for Rs 1150/1350. There's a good restaurant, 24 hour coffee shop, a bar and a Saturday and Sunday 'dance party'.

Mylapore The *New Woodlands Hotel* (☎ *827 3111, 72-75 Dr Radhakrishnan Salai*) is a sprawling complex with 170 rooms. Singles without air-con are Rs 250, doubles with air-con are Rs 600. Spacious deluxe rooms are Rs 800. The hotel has a billiard room, two vegetarian restaurants and a pool (Rs 60 for two swims a day). An ayurvedic masseur is also available. Advance bookings are essential.

Nilgiri's Nest (☎ *827 5222, fax 826 0214, 58 Dr Radhakrishnan Salai*) has singles/doubles for Rs 850/1200 including breakfast. Semideluxe rooms are Rs 1050/1550 and deluxe rooms are Rs 1400/2050. Nilgiri's Nest has a good restaurant and there's a supermarket next door. Advance bookings are essential.

Nungambakkam *Hotel Ranjith* (☎ *827 0521, fax 827 7688, 9 Nungambakkam High Rd*) is convenient for the consulates and airline offices. Rooms are Rs 800/950, or Rs 1250/1380 with air-con. There are two restaurants and a bar.

Airport *Hotel Mars* (☎ *840 2586*), at Pallavaram, has good-value singles/doubles from Rs 330/420. It's clean and tidy, and has hot water. Lone women travellers find the prevalence of female staff reassuring.

Hotel Mount Heera (☎ *234 9563, fax 233 1236, 287 MKN Rd, Alandur*) has pleasant staff and similar prices to Hotel Mars. Both are about 20 minutes by taxi from the airport.

Places to Stay – Top End

Unless otherwise stated, all the following hotels have central air-con, a swimming pool, multicuisine restaurants, and a bar.

The *Grand Orient* (☎ *852 4111, fax 852 3412, 693 Anna Salai*) has pleasant rooms from Rs 1195/1800.

Residency Hotel (☎ *825 3434, fax 825 0085, 49 GN Chetty Rd, Theagaraya Nagar*) is popular with middle-class Indian families. Singles/doubles start at Rs 1195/1800.

Hotel Savera (☎ *827 4700, fax 827 3475, 69 Dr Radhakrishnan Salai*) has well-appointed rooms for Rs 2350/2900.

Hotel President (☎ *853 2211, fax 853 2299, 16 Dr Radhakrishnan Salai*) is a big

CHENNAI

place with spacious rooms from Rs 1100/1575. It has a 24 hour coffee shop.

The Dakshin (☎ *433 0866, fax 432 2639, 35 Venkatanarayana Rd*) is a pleasant place with friendly staff. Standard singles/doubles start at Rs 1195/1500 and suites are Rs 2400. There's no pool but there's an excellent restaurant and a 24 hour coffee shop.

GRT Grand Days (☎ *822 0500, fax 823 0778, 120 Sir Theagaraya Rd, Pondy Bazaar*), one of Chennai's newest hotels, is amid the bustling Theagaraya markets. This serene hotel is well priced with quality rooms starting at Rs 2000/2600.

Chennai has no shortage of five-star hotels where rooms cost from US$150/200. Choices include:

Hotel Ambassador Pallava (☎ *855 4476, fax 855 4492, 53 Montieth Rd*) offers smart rooms from Rs 2650/3200 to Rs 6500.

Hotel Connemara (☎ *852 0123, fax 852 3361, Binny Rd, off Anna Salai*) it's lost a little of its charm since renovations. Singles/doubles cost Rs 3850/4250 to Rs 7000/7500. There's a shopping arcade and astrologer.

Hotel Taj Coromandel (☎ *827 2827, fax 825 7104, 17 Nungambakkam High Rd*) it's as luxurious as all the Taj Group hotels.

The Trident (☎ *234 4747, fax 234 6699, 1/24 GST Rd*) it's the closest luxury hotel to the airport (5km) but is a long haul from the city centre. Rooms cost Rs 5000 to Rs 7500.

Welcomgroup Chola Sheraton (☎ *828 0101, fax 827 8779, 10 Cathedral Rd*) it's closer to the centre than the Park Sheraton. Rooms cost Rs 3500/3800 to Rs 6500/6800.

Welcomgroup Park Sheraton (☎ *499 4101, 132 TTK Rd, Alwarpet*) it epitomises executive-class opulence. Rooms cost Rs 3500/3800 to Rs 6500/6800; suites are Rs 8500 to Rs 22,000.

Places to Eat

There are several vegetarian restaurants in Chennai, ranging from the simple 'meals' restaurants where a thali lunch is served on a banana leaf for under Rs 20 to sumptuous spreads for 20 times that amount in the major hotels. Breakfast at the simpler restaurants, which open shortly after dawn, consists of *dosa*, *idli*, curd and coffee.

For excellent vegetarian meals try the *Saravanaas/Saravana Bhavan* chain. These are clean and inexpensive self-service restaurants open 7 am to 11.30 pm. North Indian dishes are served, as well as Chinese food and pizzas. Pay for your meal first, then take the receipt to the serving area.

With the growing demand for meat, non-vegetarian restaurants are on the increase.

George Town In this old part of town there are many vegetarian restaurants, although few stand out. *Madras Cafe* (*Prakasam Rd*) dishes out good, cheap thalis. *Saravana Bhavan* has a large branch on NSC Bose Rd.

Egmore Most of the restaurants are along Gandhi Irwin Rd, in front of Egmore station. *Bhoopathy Cafe* is popular, and is directly opposite the station.

Vasanta Bhavan (*corner Gandhi Irwin Rd and Kennet Lane*) is bustling with waiters and features an upstairs dining hall.

Raj Restaurant at the Hotel Pandian serves good veg and nonveg dishes (Rs 55 to Rs 90).

Ponnusamy Hotel (*Wellington Estate, 24 C-in-C Rd*) is a nonveg restaurant serving meat and fish curry and biryani dishes starting from Rs 35. A few veg dishes are also on the menu.

Triplicane The *Maharaja Restaurant*, just around the corner from Broadlands, is popular with backpackers. The vegetarian menu is varied and available to midnight.

Hotel Tirumulai, further north, serves luscious banana-leaf thalis (Rs 30) and gigantic dosas.

The *Srinivasa Hotel* (*Ellis St*) is also a favourite.

Anna Salai A branch of *Saravanaas* is in the forecourt of the Shanti Theatre on Anna Salai. It's a great place for a quick meal.

Mathura Restaurant (*2nd floor, Tarapore Tower, Anna Salai*) is an excellent upmarket vegetarian restaurant. Its Madras thali (Rs 60) comes with ice cream for dessert and is served 11 am to 3 pm.

Dasaprakash Restaurant (*806 Anna Salai*), also known as AVM Dasa, is an excellent upmarket cafe-style restaurant. It serves vegetarian fare, with some interesting choices such as broccoli crepes.

The Other Room at the Hotel Ambassador Pallava serves pretty good western dishes. It also has pool-side buffets featuring various European cuisines for a set price of Rs 450.

Annalakshmi (☎ *855 0296, 804 Anna Salai*) is reputedly the best vegetarian restaurant in the city, with meals starting at Rs 150. This place is run by the devotees of Swami Shantanand Saraswati who established Shivanjali, an education trust. Annalakshmi is open noon to 3 pm and 7.30 to 10 pm daily except Monday. Should you have the need (and the money) you can even buy the furniture.

Hotel Connemara has a lunchtime buffet in the *coffee shop* for Rs 350. Its *Raintree* restaurant is open in the evening for meals (about Rs 500). The outdoor setting is superb, with live classical dancing and music some nights.

Nungambakkam & Chetput The *Welcomgroup Chola Sheraton* has an excellent dinner buffet for Rs 340 including taxes.

The restaurant at the *New Woodlands Hotel* (*Dr Radhakrishnan Salai*) is popular with locals. The dosas, tandoori and milk *burfis* (a delicious sweet made with coconut, nuts and sometimes eggs and fruit) all get rave reviews.

The Pinnacle (*9 Nungambakkam High Rd*) at Hotel Ranjith is a rooftop restaurant where one delicious tandoori platter is sufficient for two.

Rangis' (☎ *825 6041, 142 Uttamar Gandhi Salai*), across the road from Landmark Books, is an intimate Chinese restaurant with tasty dishes at reasonable prices (Rs 30 to Rs 60).

Dahlia (☎ *826 5240, Kaveri Complex, 96 & 104 Nungambakkam High Rd*) is one of the few Japanese restaurants in town. The food is good and you'll pay western prices – around Rs 450 per person.

Coconut Grove (☎ *826 8800, 95 Harrington Rd*) has an outdoor setting beneath leafy trees and a menu focusing on cuisine

from Kerala. Prices are reasonable (Rs 65 to Rs 80).

The Red E Food Court (☎ *827 2514, 107 Harrington Rd*) offers fast Indian, Chinese, Mexican and western dishes.

Elsewhere The *Beach Castle Restaurant* (☎ *491 6454, 34 Elliot Beach Rd*) offers excellent seafood right on the beach. Open for lunch 11 am to 3 pm and dinner 7 pm to midnight, it's worth the journey just for the fried crab in green pepper.

The Pakwan at the Dakshin hotel, 35 Venkatanarayana Rd, is just around the corner from the Central Cottage Industries Emporium. The multicuisine fare is very good. A two course meal is around Rs 200. The 24 hour coffee shop has less exciting offerings.

Hotel Runs is still South India's best-named restaurant. It's a cheap veg and non-veg place in Adyar, in the far south of the city, near ANZ Grindlays bank.

The *Nilgiri Dairy Farm* supermarket, next to the Nilgiri's Nest Hotel, is a good place to buy dairy products, boxed tea, coffee and other edibles (closed Tuesday).

If you're after fruit and vegetables or spices, head south along Ellis St to the junction of Bharathi Salai where you'll find the colourful *Jam Bazaar*.

Entertainment

Bars & Nightclubs Chennai is beginning to throb at night. The *Hotel Connemara* has a plush bar with plush prices and over-amplified music.

If you want to dance, there's the choice of *Gatsby* (☎ *499 4101*) at the Park Sheraton, or the *Cyclone* (☎ *853 2211*) at the Hotel President but only at weekends and it's best to ring first. The weekend dance party in the bowels of the *Hotel Chandra Towers* is popular with the hip set of Chennai. The music begins at 3 pm every Saturday and Sunday and continues until 10.30 pm. Tickets (per couple) cost Rs 200 and include a bottle of beer.

Planet 2000 (☎ *490 8702, 37/1 1st Main Rd, Gandhi Nagar*) is a nightclub with a dining room and a fitness centre. Reservations are essential.

Permit Rooms

Until the early 1990s, Tamil Nadu was a 'dry' state. Anyone who wanted an alcoholic drink had to obtain a liquor permit from the tourist office to buy a beer from a 'permit room' (bar). These permits were farcical, since they enabled patrons to purchase enough liquor to get cirrhosis of the liver.

Although prohibition has been abolished, the 'permit room' survives. Bars are usually in the basement of hotels, where the artificial lighting is so dim you could almost believe you're up to no good.

Tamil Nadu now boasts the highest per-capita consumption of alcohol in the country, and the prohibition lobby is stronger than ever. For this reason, you will find health warnings on beer labels, dry days (such as Gandhi's birthday) and draconian government taxes that ensure that the price of a beer in Tamil Nadu is one of the highest in India (over Rs 60).

If you're anywhere near Pondicherry it's worth knowing that part of the French legacy is a relaxed attitude towards alcohol, and beer costs around Rs 25 – but drink it there. You'll be in trouble if you try to leave with it.

Classical Music & Dance The *Music Academy* (☎ 827 5619, corner TTK Rd and Dr Radhakrishnan Salai) is Chennai's most popular public venue for Carnatic classical music and Bharat Natyam dance performances. Check *The Hindu* newspaper for details. Expect to pay about Rs 175 for a good seat.

Another concert venue is *Kalakshetra*, or the Temple of Art (☎ 491 1169, fax 491 4359), which was founded in 1936 and is committed to the revival of classical dance and music and of traditional textile design and weaving (see the South Indian Music & Dance boxed text). The college puts on regular public performances and visitors are encouraged to watch the classes that take place Monday to Friday 9 to 11.15 am and 1.25 to

4.45 pm (mornings only on Saturday, closed Sunday). For small groups, a lecture explaining the techniques and history is possible with prior arrangement. Bus No 19M from Parry's Corner will take you to Kalakshetra.

Kuchipudi Art Academy (☎ 493 7260, 105 Greenway's Rd) was founded in 1963 by the eminent teacher Dr Vempati Chinna Satyam. The vigorous and graceful Kuchipudi dance originated in northern Andhra Pradesh. The academy offers free teaching and accommodation to serious students, many of whom come from overseas.

Cinema There are 94 cinemas in Chennai – a reflection of the vibrant film industry here. Most cinemas screen Tamil films; some screen foreign-language movies. *Devi Complex* (☎ 855 5660, Anna Salai) and *Sathyam* (☎ 852 3813) often show English-language films. Check local papers for details.

British Council and *Alliance Française* have weekly film screenings. Film festivals are held at the *United States Information Service* or USIS (☎ 827 3040, 220 Anna Salai), and at the *Russian Cultural Centre* (☎ 499 0050, 27 Kasturi Ranga Rd). The *Madras Film Club* (☎ 854 0984) has regular screenings of Indian and foreign films.

Shopping

Chennai shopping is changing fast. New plazas are springing up while traditional stores are extending services.

Ready-made or tailored clothing, crafts from all corners of India, contemporary artworks, genuine antiques, jewellery, musical instruments and quality fabrics are all available.

For conventional souvenirs at fixed prices, including carvings and bronzes, head to the government emporiums along Anna Salai. These are usually open Monday to Friday 10 am to 6 pm, 10 am to 1 pm Saturday; closed Sunday.

Worth visiting are Poompuhar Emporium (☎ 852 0624), 818 Anna Salai; Victoria Technical Institute (☎ 852 3153), 765 Anna Salai (revenue from certain items supports various development groups); and the Central Cottage Industries Emporium in Temple Towers, 476 Anna Salai, Nandanam.

Private emporiums close at 9 pm. They negotiable prices but Kalpa Druma (☎ 826 7652), 61 Cathedral Rd (opposite Chola Sheraton), has an exquisite range of textiles, handicrafts and furniture at fixed prices.

For top-grade silks and cottons head to either the government-sponsored Handloom House (☎ 535 4840), 7 Rattan Bazaar, George Town (open daily except Sunday, 10 am to 1 pm and 3 to 8 pm) or the more expensive India Silk House on Anna Salai.

The Theagaraya Nagar district (known locally as T Nagar) is a great place to shop, especially in the bustling markets along Sir Mohamed Usman Rd and Pondy Bazaar. Numerous buses frequent this popular shopping area. From Parry's Corner you can take bus No 9, 9B, 10, 10C, 11, 11A, 11D or 11E.

For musical instruments, try AR Dawood & Sons, 286 Triplicane High Rd, not far from the Broadlands Hotel.

Getting There & Away

Air Anna international airport is efficient and not too busy, making Chennai a good entry or exit point. Next door is the relatively new domestic airport.

A departure tax of Rs 150 is payable for flights from Chennai to Sri Lanka and the Maldives, Rs 500 for other international destinations.

Domestic Airlines Addresses of domestic carriers that fly into Chennai include:

Indian Airlines
   (☎ 855 3039, fax 855 5208) 19 Marshalls Rd, Egmore – open Monday to Saturday 8 am to 8 pm
Jet Airways
   (☎ 855 5353) 43 Montieth Rd, Egmore

International Airlines Addresses of international airlines with offices in Chennai include:

Air France
   (☎ 855 4899) Thapa House, 43-44 Montieth Rd, Egmore

Air India
   (☎ 855 4477) 19 Marshalls Rd, Egmore
Air Lanka
   (☎ 852 4232) Mount Chambers, 758 Anna Salai
American Airlines
   (☎ 826 2409) GSA: Jetair, G 1/A Apex Plaza, 3 Nungambakkam High Rd
British Airways
   (☎ 855 4680) Alsamall, Khaleeli Centre, Montieth Rd, Egmore
Cathay Pacific Airways
   (☎ 852 2418) Spencer Plaza, 769 Anna Salai
Gulf Air
   (☎ 855 3091) Indian Red Cross Bldg, 52 Montieth Rd
KLM – Royal Dutch Airlines
   (☎ 852 0123) Hotel Connemara, Binney Rd
Kuwait Airways
   (☎ 855 4111) Thaper House, 43-44 Montieth Rd, Egmore
Lufthansa Airlines
   (☎ 852 5095) 167 Anna Salai
Malaysian Airlines
   (☎ 434 9291) Karumuthu Centre, 498 Anna Salai
Qantas Airways
   (☎ 827 8680) G3, Eldorado Bldg, 112 Nungambakkam High Rd
Saudia
   (☎ 434 9666)
Singapore Airlines (SIA)
   (☎ 852 1871) West Minster, 108 Dr Radhakrishnan Salai
Swissair
   (☎ 852 2541) 191 Anna Salai
Thai
   (☎ 822 6149) GSA: Inter Globe Air Transports, Malavikas Centre, 144 Kodambakkam High Rd, Nungambakkam

International Flights There are international flights to and from the following destinations:

Colombo (Air Lanka, Indian Airlines)
Dubai (Air India)
Frankfurt (Air India, Lufthansa)
Jakarta (Air India)
Kuala Lumpur (Malaysia Airlines, Air India, Indian Airlines)
London (British Airways)
Malé (Indian Airlines)
Penang (Malaysia Airlines)
Riyadh (Saudia)
Singapore (Singapore Airlines, Malaysia Airlines, Air India, Indian Airlines)

Domestic Flights from Chennai

destination	flight duration	flights per d[1]/w[2]	fare (US$)
Ahmedabad	3 h 5 min	3 w	220
Bangalore	45 min	5 d	65
Bhubaneswar	1 h 40 min	3 w	180
Calcutta	2 h 10 min	10 w	200
Coimbatore	1 h	10 w	80
Delhi	2 h 45 min	6 d	235
Goa	2 h 30 min	4 w	125
Hyderabad	1 h	2 d	95
Kochi (Cochin)	1 h 5 min	4 w	105
Kozhikode (Calicut)	2 h 10 min	3 w	80
Madurai	1 h	1 d	80
Mangalore	2 h	3 w	95
Mumbai (Bombay)	1 h 45 min	9 d	145
Port Blair	2 h	4 w	195
Pune	1 h 30 min	10 w	155
Puttaparthi	40 min	2 w	65
Thiruvan-anthapuram	1 h 10 min	11 w	105
Tiruchirappalli (Trichy)	45 min	3 w	70
Visakhapat-nam	1 h	4 w	105

[1]daily, [2]weekly

Bus Names of buses and terminals have changed, yet again. Bus services come under the auspices of the State Express Transport Corporation (SETC) and the bus terminals are on either side of Prakasam Rd in George Town, near the High Court building.

The eastern terminal is for most local, intrastate and interstate buses. The intrastate (☎ 534 1835) and interstate (☎ 534 1836) bus reservation offices are upstairs. They are computerised and open 7 am to 9 pm daily. There's a Rs 2 reservation fee, and you have to pay Rs 0.25 for the form! See the Bus Services from Chennai table for information on some of the SETC bus services.

The bus stand on the west side of Prakasam Rd is mainly for buses to Andhra Pradesh. Both terminals are fairly well organised; there are plenty of people to help you make sense of it all, and will, for a couple of rupees, find your bus.

There are also private bus companies with offices opposite Egmore station that run superdeluxe video buses daily to cities such as Bangalore, Coimbatore, Madurai and Trichy. Prices are similar to the state buses, although the private buses tend to be more comfortable.

Train The reservation office at Central station is on the 1st floor of the reservation complex next to the station (☎ 132 for general inquiries, ☎ 1361 for English, ☎ 1362 for Hindi and ☎ 1362 for Tamil). You can make reservations here for trains originating in most larger cities. The very helpful Foreign Assistance Tourist Cell deals with Indrail Pass and tourist-quota bookings.

The office is open Monday to Saturday, from 8 am to 2 pm and 2.15 to 8 pm; Sunday 8 am to 2 pm. At Egmore the booking office (☎ 535 3545) is in the station itself, and keeps the same hours as the office at Central station. See the Train Services from Chennai table for a selection of trains from Chennai.

Boat Services to the Andaman Islands are prone to change, so check the latest schedules. One boat, the MV *Nancowry*, sails from Chennai every 14 days to Port Blair (60 hours). For foreigners, there is no service between May and August. Once a month, the boat sails via Car Nicobar, but only residents may disembark here. This voyage takes an extra two days.

Cabin fares per person are Rs 3450 (deluxe cabin, two berth), Rs 2852 (1st class cabin, four berth) and Rs 2243 (2nd class cabin, six berth). 'Bunk class' costs Rs 955 per person. An additional Rs 2.10 toll tax is payable. Meals are available on board for about Rs 100 per day. Some bedding is supplied but you should carry at least a sleeping sheet.

Bus Services from Chennai

destination & bus no	frequency (daily)	distance (km)	travel time	fare (Rs)
Bangalore 628, 831, 863	30	351	8 h	120
Chidambaram 300	8	240	7 h	53
Kanyakumari 282	7	705	16 h	181
Kodaikanal 461	1	511	12 h	110
Madurai 135, 137	37	447	10 h	118
Mysore 863	2	497	11 h	150
Ooty 468, 860	2	565	15 h	150
Pondicherry 803, 803F	37	162	5 h	38
Rameswaram 166	1	570	13 h	148
Thanjavur 323	18	321	18 h	86
Thiruvananthapuram 794	6	752	17 h	200
Tiruchirappalli 123, 124	46	319	8 h	86
Tirupathi 902/911, 811, 848, 863	83	150	4 h	52
Vellore 831, 863	26	145	4 h	43

Tickets are issued at the Andaman Shipping Service Office, Directorate of Shipping Services (☎ 522 6873), 6 Rajaji Salai (opposite the Customs House, in the little office by Gate No 5) in George Town. Foreigners must get a permit for the islands before they buy a boat ticket (see Visa Extensions & Permits under Information at the start of this chapter).

If you need a shipping agent, try Hapag Lloyd (☎ 522 9282), 37 Rajaji Salai, George Town.

Getting Around

To/From the Airport The domestic and international terminals are 16km south of the city centre. The cheapest way to reach them is by suburban train from Egmore to Tirusulam, which is only about 500m across the road from the terminals. The trains run from 4.15 am until 11.45 pm, the journey into the city takes about 40 minutes, and the fare is Rs 6/80 in 2nd/1st class. These trains are not overly crowded, except during peak hours.

Public buses are not such a good bet, particularly if you've got a lot of luggage. Nos 18J, 52, 52A/B/C/D and 55A all start and finish at Parry's Corner and go along Anna Salai.

The purple airport bus leaves the Hotel Chandra Towers near Egmore station every 30 minutes and stops at both the domestic and international airports.

There's also a minibus service for Rs 60/100 during the day/night between the airport and the major hotels (including Broadlands) but it's a slow way to get into town. The booking counter is next to the taxi counters at the international terminal.

An auto-rickshaw to the airport costs about Rs 130/200 for a day/night trip.

A yellow-and-black taxi costs Rs 250. At the pre-paid taxi kiosk inside the international airport, you can buy a ticket into Chennai for Rs 200 to Rs 250 (depending on the distance). There's another pre-paid kiosk in the baggage collection area inside the domestic terminal – and this one is about 10% cheaper.

Bus The bus system in Chennai is run by the newly named Metropolitan Transport Corporation (MTC). It's less overburdened than those in the other large Indian cities, although peak hour is still best avoided.

CHENNAI

Some useful routes for getting around Chennai include:

Nos 16, 23C, 27, 27B, 27D, 29 & 29A – Egmore (opposite People's Lodge) to Anna Salai

Nos 31, 32 & 32A – Triplicane High Rd (Broadlands) to Central station and Parry's Corner. The No 31 continues on to Rajaji Salai (for the main post office and Directorate of Shipping Services)

Nos 22, 27B & 29A – Egmore to Wallajah Rd (for Broadlands)

Nos 9, 9A, 9B, 10, 17D, 17E & 17K – Parry's Corner to Central and Egmore stations

Nos 11, 11A, 11B, 11D, 17A, 18 & 18J – Parry's Corner to Anna Salai

Train The suburban train is an excellent way to get between Egmore and Central station (Rs 2), Egmore and George Town (Rs 2), to Guindy (Rs 4) or the airport (Rs 4). There are relatively uncrowded ladies' compartments.

Car Almost without exception, car hire means you hire the car and a driver. It's wise to use a travel agency approved by the Government of India tourist office or one of the many hotels that have travel desks. Rates can vary but a general guide for travelling within the city is Rs 800 per day (eight

Major Trains from Chennai

destination	train no & name	departure time[1]	distance (km)	duration	fare (Rs) (2nd/1st)
Bangalore	2007 *Shatabdi Exp*[2]	6.00 am MC	356	5 h	495/980
	6007 *Bangalore Mail*	10.10 pm MC		7 h 20 min	84/415
Calcutta	2842 *Coromandel Exp*	9.05 am MC	1669	28 h	337/1278
	6004 *Howrah Mail*	10.30 pm MC		32 h 20 min	
Coimbatore	2023 *Shatabdi Exp*[3]	3.10 pm MC	494	6 h 50 min	734/-
Delhi	2621 *Tamil Nadu Exp*	10.00 pm MC	2194	34 h	376/1545
Hyderabad	7059 *Charminar Exp*	6.10 pm MC	794	14 h 20 min	214/766
Kanyakumari	6119 *Nellai Kumari Exp*	6.00 pm ME	700	16 h 30 min	196/687
Kochi (Cochin)	6041 *Alleppey Exp*	7.35 pm MC	700	11 h	196/687
Madurai	6717 *Pandian Exp*[4]	7.05 pm ME	556	11 h	169/584
Mettup-palayam	6605 *Nilgiri Exp*	8.15 pm MC	630	10 h	187/650
Mumbai	1064 *Chennai Exp*	6.40 am MC	1279	30 h	289/1049
	6010 *Mumbai Mail*	9.50 pm MC		30 h	
Mysore	2007 *Shatabdi Exp*[2]	6.00 am MC	500	7 h 15 min	570/1150
Rameswaram	6713 *Kamban*	7.45 pm ME	656	12 h 30 min	190/662
Thanjavur	6153 *Cholan Exp*[3]	8.00 am ME	351	11 h	118/410
Thiruvan-anthapuram	6319 *Trivandrum Mail*	6.55 pm MC	921	12 h 30 min	235/805
Tiruchirappalli	2635 *Vaigai Exp*[3]	12.50 pm ME	337	5 h 50 min	115/398
Tirupathi	6057 *Saptagiri Exp*	6.25 am MC	147	3 h	43/220
Varanasi	6039 *Ganga Kaveri Exp*	5.30 pm MC	2144	39 h	376/1545

[1]MC – Madras Central; ME – Madras Egmore
[2]Not Tuesday; air-con only; fare includes meals and drinks
[3]Not Wednesday; air-con only; fare includes meals and drinks
[4]Services subject to significant alterations due to line work

hours). For travelling beyond the city limits costs are Rs 5 per kilometre (Rs 7 with aircon) with a minimum of 250km per day. Driver fees (for food and accommodation) are often additional, up to Rs 125 per day.

Motorbike Mopeds are available from U-Rent (☎ 491 0838), No 1 1st St, Main Rd, Gandhinagar (near the Traffic Jam Restaurant). Charges are Rs 150 per day but a year's membership of their rental scheme is also required (Rs 250). Helmets and insurance are mandatory and cost Rs 25 each per day. An international driving licence is generally needed but your home-country licence may be accepted. You'll also need your passport, two passport photos and two references from local residents.

Taxi Rates are Rs 25 for the first 1.5km and Rs 4.5 for each subsequent kilometre. Most drivers will quote you a fixed price rather than use the meter, so negotiate hard. Expect to pay more for travel at night and on Sunday and public holidays.

Auto-Rickshaw On the meter it's Rs 7 for the first kilometre, then Rs 3 per kilometre. Again, persuasion may be required before drivers will use the meter. Prices are at least 25% higher after 10 pm. There's a pre-paid booth outside the Central station. Auto-rickshaw drivers seem seriously underemployed and will compete vigorously for your custom. Consider walking some distance from your hotel and hailing one in the street to save the competitive hassle.

Tamil Nadu

In the southernmost part of India, Tamil Nadu is referred to as the cradle of Dravidian culture, an ancient culture distinguished by unique languages and customs. The cultural icons are everywhere – huge temples with their towering *gopurams* (gateways), intricate rock carvings, evocative music and, of course, the complex classical dance.

Throughout Tamil Nadu pilgrims pour into the ancient sites of Kanchipuram, Chidambaram, Kumbakonam, Tiruchirappalli, Thanjavur, Madurai, Kanyakumari and Rameswaram. These names are on the tourist map, but it is their significance as potent contours on the cultural map that guides pilgrims in their celebration of the land and its legends.

The coastline has resorts and delightful fishing villages. Mountain towns, such as Udhagamandalam (Ooty) and Kodaikanal, provide a cool haven from the hot summer while national parks offer unique flora and the chance to glimpse wildlife.

Tamil cuisine, traditionally vegetarian, consists of *dosas* (crispy pancakes) and *idlis* (steamed rice dumplings), delicately spiced vegetables and mounds of rice. Sweets are a favourite, and coffee is more popular than tea. Alcohol is more likely to be available in nonvegetarian restaurants (see the Permit Rooms boxed text in the Chennai chapter).

The Tamil Nadu Tourist Commission has a very good Web site (www.tamilnadutourism.com) covering the state which also allows you to make enquiries and reservations.

History

Tamil Nadu is the home of the Tamils and their Dravidian culture. It is not known exactly when the original Dravidians came or where they came from. Human activity in the area now known as Tamil Nadu may have begun as early as 300,000 years ago. There is speculation that the first Dravidians were part of early Indus civilisations and came south after invasions in the north, around 1500 BC.

Tamil Nadu at a Glance

Population: 55.8 million
Area: 130,058 sq km
Capital: Chennai (Madras)
Main Language: Tamil
Best Time to Go: December to February

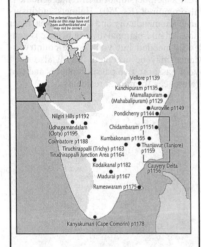

- **Madurai & Mamallapuram** – absorbing elements of ritual and sculpture

- **Mamallapuram** – discovering finely carved ancient monuments, combing beaches and watching sculptors ply their skills

- **Ooty** – revelling in the cool and peace of a hill station

- **Rural Life** – relaxing in the hospitality of village life

Festivals of Tamil Nadu

festival	location	date	features
Pongal (Harvest Festival)	statewide (especially Madurai)	mid-Jan	feasting, music & dance
Mamallapuram Dance Festival	Mamallapuram	mid-Jan	music & dance
Temple Car Festival	Kanchipuram/Tiruchirappalli	Jan	parade
Thaipusam Festival	Palani/Thanjuvar	Jan/Feb	ritual bathing
Thyagaraja Music Festival	Thiruvaiyaru	Jan	international music
Teppam (Float) Festival	Madurai	Jan/Feb	parade
Natyanjali Dance Festival	Chidambaram	Feb	dance
Feast of Our Lady of Lourdes	Tiruchirappalli	Feb	procession
Masi Magham	Swamimalai	Feb/Mar	parade
Temple Car Festival	Kanchipuram/Rameswaram	Feb/Mar	parade
Temple Car Festival	Chidambaram/Kanchipuram/Tiruvarur	Apr/May	parade
Chithrai	statewide (especially Madurai)	Apr/May	ritual bathing
Kumari Amman Temple Festival	Kanyakumari (Cape Comorin)	May/Jun	chariot processions
Drowpathiamman Temple Festival of Fire	Pondicherry	May/Jun	devotees walk across hot coals
Thiru Kalyana (Holy Marriage Festival)	Rameswaram	Jul/Aug	music, bathing & pageants
Feast of Our Lady of Good Health	Velanganni	Sep	procession
Avanimoolam	Madurai	Sep	15 day fair
Navrati	Madurai, Kanyakumari	Sep/Oct	Hindu offerings
Kamakshi's Birthday	Kanchipuram	Oct/Nov	processions & re-enactments
Karthikai Deepam Festival	Tiruvannamalai	Nov/Dec	Shiva worship
Vaikunta Ekadasi (Paradise Festival)	Tiruchirappalli	Dec	Vishnu festival with hymns
Temple Car Festival	Chidambaram	Dec/Jan	parade

By 1200 BC, a civilisation distinguished by huge stone sculptures existed in South India.

By the last centuries BC the region was controlled by three major dynasties – the Cholas in the east, Pandyas in the central area and Cheras in the west. This was the classical period of Tamil literature – the Sangam Age – that continued for some three centuries after the birth of Christ.

The domains of these three dynasties changed many times over the centuries. At times other sovereignties became powerful. The Pallava dynasty was influential particularly in the 7th and 8th centuries when it constructed many of the monuments at Mamallapuram. Although all these dynasties engaged in continual skirmishes, their steady patronage of the arts served to consolidate and expand Dravidian civilisation.

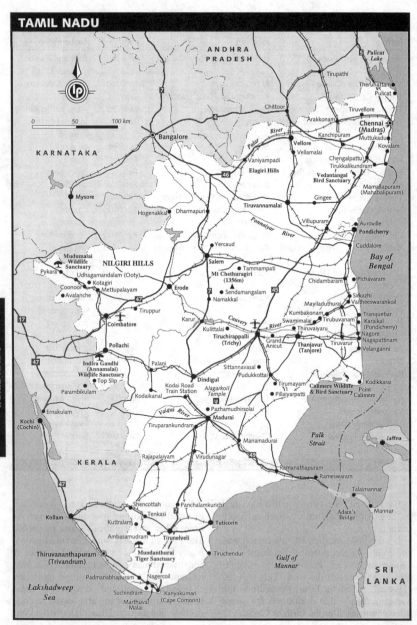

In the 13th century, with threats of Muslim invasions from the north, the southern Hindu dynasties combined and the empire of Vijayanagar, which incorporated all of South India, became firmly established. However, in the 16th century, the Vijayanagar empire began to weaken and by the 17th century, Southern India was ruled by various provincial leaders, most notably the Nayaks, who continued the development of monumental architecture.

In 1640, the British negotiated the use of Madraspatnam (now Chennai) as a trading post. Subsequent interest on the part of the French, Dutch and Danes led to continual conflict and finally, almost total domination by the British. Small pocketed areas including Pondicherry and Karaikal, remained under French control. Under British colonial rule most of South India was integrated into the region called the Madras Presidency.

Many Tamils played a significant part in the struggle for independence, which was finally won in 1947. In 1956, the Madras Presidency was disbanded and Tamil Nadu was established – an autonomous state based on linguistic lines.

Northern Tamil Nadu

The coast road from Chennai to Mamallapuram is dotted with beach resorts, recreation areas and artists' communities. **Cholamandal Artists' Village** (☎ 492 6092), 18km south of Chennai, has a gallery with fine contemporary paintings and sculptures.

Dakshinachitra (☎ 04114-45303), about 12km south of Cholamandal, showcases traditional art, craft and architecture from Tamil Nadu and Kerala (there are Andhra Pradesh and Karnataka displays scheduled for completion by 2001). Entry (including a tour) costs Rs 50 for locals (students Rs 25) and Rs 175 for foreigners (children/students Rs 10/70). The village is open daily except Tuesday and bus Nos 19 and 49 from Parry's Corner in Chennai will take you there.

Kovalam, which is also known as Covelong, is a fishing settlement with a fine beach, 38km south of Chennai. Here an ancient fort has been converted into the Taj Group's luxurious *Fisherman's Cove Resort* (☎ 04114-44304). Rooms are priced from US$125 with cottages from US$175 (all plus 30% tax).

Farther south and just 15km before Mamallapuram is the **Crocodile Bank**. This successful breeding farm augments the crocodile populations of India's wildlife sanctuaries.

You can get to the Crocodile Bank by bicycle from Mamallapuram or on the 119A bus from Chennai. It's open daily except Tuesday 8.30 am to 5.30 pm. The feeding frenzy is at 4.30 pm on Saturday and Sunday only. Entrance is Rs 10 plus Rs 20 to see the feeding. There's also a Snake Farm (Rs 4) open 9.30 am to 4.30 pm.

MAMALLAPURAM (Mahabalipuram)
☎ 04114 • pop 13,300

Mamallapuram, famous for its shore temple, was the second capital and seaport of the Pallava kings of Kanchipuram. Though the dynasty's origins are lost in the mists of legend, it was apparently at the height of its political power and artistic creativity from the 5th to 8th centuries AD. Most of the temples and rock carvings here were completed during the reigns of Narasimha Varman I (630-68) and Narasimha Varman II (700-28).

The early Pallava kings were followers of the Jain religion, but the conversion of Mahendra Varman I (600-30) to Shaivism explains why most temples at Mamallapuram (and Kanchipuram) are dedicated to either Shiva or Vishnu.

The sculptures here show scenes of everyday life – women milking buffaloes, pompous city dignitaries, young girls primping and posing at street corners or swinging their hips in artful come-ons. In contrast, other carvings throughout the state depict mostly gods and goddesses, with images of ordinary folk conspicuous by their absence. There is much to see at

TAMIL NADU

Mamallapuram. Even the ruins are worthy of lengthy exploration. Stone carving is still very much alive – approximately 200 sculptors line the streets and chisel their stone from dawn to beyond dusk.

Mamallapuram is especially popular with backpackers and weekenders from Chennai. As one of the more westernised towns in Tamil Nadu, it has prices to match. However, it does have an excellent combination of cheap accommodation, restaurants catering to all tastes, a good beach, handicraft shops *and* the remains of an ancient Indian kingdom. Accommodation is very tight in January during the Mamallapuram Dance Festival.

Orientation & Information

Some 50km south of Chennai, Mamallapuram covers an area of approximately 8 sq km. It's easy to visit the places of interest on foot.

The tourist office (☎ 42232) is in East Raja St (also known as Covelong Rd). Open 9.45 am to 5.45 pm, it has leaflets and transport schedules.

You can change most travellers cheques at the Indian Overseas Bank (Monday to Friday 10 am to 2 pm; Saturday until noon) on Tirukkalikundram Rd, and also at Prithvi Forexchequer (daily, 10 am to 6 pm, no commission) at 55A East Raja St, opposite Mamalla Bhavan Annexe.

The post office is down a lane just east of the tourist office.

For information on the regional sites visit the Archaeological Survey of India, next to the museum in East Raja St.

Dr Gladys Indhira has been recommended. Her surgery is behind Arafath Medicals, near the Indian Overseas Bank.

Shore Temple

This beautiful and romantic temple, ravaged by wind and sea, represents the final phase of Pallava art. Originally constructed around the middle of the 7th century, it was later rebuilt in the reign of Narasimha Varman II (also known as Rajasimha). The temple's two main spires contain shrines for

Shiva. Facing east and west the original linga captured the sunrise and sunset. A third and earlier shrine is dedicated to the reclining Vishnu. In 1996 further ruins, depicting Vishnu, were unearthed. A remarkable amount of temple carving remains, especially inside the shrines. The temple, with World Heritage listing, is now protected from further erosion by a huge rock wall. There's a helpful guide from the Archaeology Department.

The temple is open daily 9 am to 5 pm. Entry (Rs 5; free Friday) also allows you to visit the Five Rathas (see Five Rathas entry later in this section).

Arjuna's Penance

This relief carving on the face of a huge rock depicts animals, deities and other semidivine creatures as well as fables from the Hindu *Panchatantra* books. The panel (30m by 12m) is divided by a huge perpendicular fissure that's skilfully encompassed into the sculpture. Originally water flowed down the fissure, representing the waters of the Ganges.

Varying accounts relate the meaning of the Ajuna Penance relief. One of them is of Arjuna who does penance to Shiva in order to secure the weapon that will destroy his opponents.

Another account is of Bhagiratha, who wished to atone for his ancestor's crime – a crime that resulted in the deaths of 60,000 people. As there was not enough water in which to place the ashes of such a large number, Bhagiratha did penance to the goddess Ganga, beseeching her to deliver her waters from the heavenly realms to the earth below. Bhagiratha's request was granted and the waters of the Ganga flowed into the Himalaya and down onto the plains.

Many interpretations can be read into the stories, but whatever the carving depicts, it's one of the most realistic and unpretentious rock carvings in India.

The touts and hustlers here are persistent but once you move on, you'll be able to enjoy the remaining monuments in relative peace.

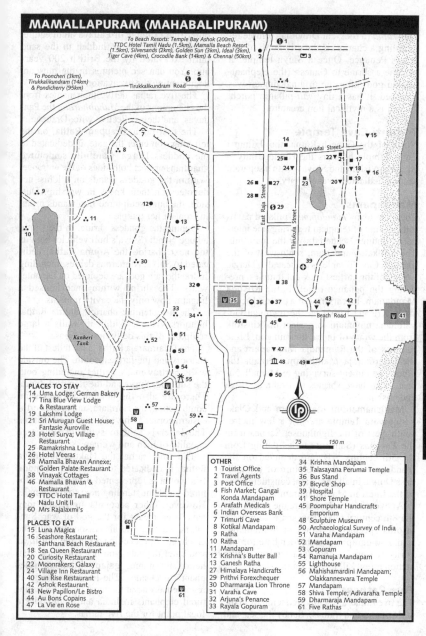

MAMALLAPURAM (MAHABALIPURAM)

To Beach Resorts: Temple Bay Ashok (200m),
TTDC Hotel Tamil Nadu (1.5km), Mamalla Beach Resort
(1.5km), Silversands (2km), Golden Sun (3km), Ideal (3km),
Tiger Cave (4km), Crocodile Bank (14km) & Chennai (50km)

To Pooncheri (3km),
Tirukkalikundram (14km)
& Pondicherry (95km)

Tiruukkalikundram Road

Othavadai Street

East Raja Street

Thirukula Street

Beach Road

Kanheri
Tank

TAMIL NADU

PLACES TO STAY
14 Uma Lodge; German Bakery
17 Tina Blue View Lodge
   & Restaurant
19 Lakshmi Lodge
21 Sri Murugan Guest House;
   Fantasie Auroville
23 Hotel Surya; Village
   Restaurant
25 Ramakrishna Lodge
26 Hotel Veeras
28 Mamalla Bhavan Annexe;
   Golden Palate Restaurant
38 Vinayak Cottages
46 Mamalla Bhavan &
   Restaurant
49 TTDC Hotel Tamil
   Nadu Unit II
60 Mrs Rajalaxmi's

PLACES TO EAT
15 Luna Magica
16 Seashore Restaurant;
   Santhana Beach Restaurant
18 Sea Queen Restaurant
20 Curiosity Restaurant
22 Moonrakers; Galaxy
24 Village Inn Restaurant
40 Sun Rise Restaurant
42 Ashok Restaurant
43 New Papillon/Le Bistro
44 Au Bons Copains
47 La Vie en Rose

0   75   150 m

OTHER
1 Tourist Office
2 Travel Agents
3 Post Office
4 Fish Market; Gangai
   Konda Mandapam
5 Arafath Medicals
6 Indian Overseas Bank
7 Trimurti Cave
8 Kotikal Mandapam
9 Ratha
10 Ratha
11 Mandapam
12 Krishna's Butter Ball
13 Ganesh Ratha
27 Himalaya Handicrafts
29 Prithvi Forexchequer
30 Dharmaraja Lion Throne
31 Varaha Cave
32 Arjuna's Penance
33 Rayala Gopuram

34 Krishna Mandapam
35 Talasayana Perumai Temple
36 Bus Stand
37 Bicycle Shop
39 Hospital
41 Shore Temple
45 Poompuhar Handicrafts
   Emporium
48 Sculpture Museum
50 Archaeological Survey of India
51 Varaha Mandapam
52 Mandapam
53 Gopuram
54 Ramanuja Mandapam
55 Lighthouse
56 Mahishamardini Mandapam;
   Olakkannesvara Temple
57 Mandapam
58 Shiva Temple; Adivaraha Temple
59 Dharmaraja Mandapam
61 Five Rathas

Ganesh Ratha

This *ratha* (a rock-cut Dravidian temple resembling a chariot) is directly north of Arjuna's Penance. Once a Shiva temple, it became a shrine to Ganesh (the elephant-headed god) after the original lingam was removed. It has a tiny *yali*-pillared porch. (A yali is a mythical lion creature.)

Trimurti Cave Temple

North of the Ganesh Ratha, the Trimurti Cave Temple honours the Hindu trinity – Brahma, Vishnu and Shiva – with a separate section dedicated to each deity.

Mandapams

There are many *mandapams* (pillared pavilions in front of temples) featuring fine internal sculptures, scattered over the main hill. The **Kotikal Mandapam**, south-west of the Trimurti Cave Temple, is dedicated to Durga.

One of the earliest rock-cut temples, pre-dating the penance relief, is the **Krishna Mandapam**. Its carvings of a pastoral scene show Krishna lifting up the mythical Govardhana mountain to protect his kinsfolk from the wrath of Indra, the rain god. Little remains of the **Ramanuja Mandapam** and the **Dharmaraja Mandapam**, perhaps the oldest monument surviving in Mamallapuram. Both have shrines to Brahma, Shiva and Vishnu.

Mahishamardini Mandapam and **Olakkannesvara Temple** are just a few metres south-west of the lighthouse. Scenes from the *Puranas* (Sanskrit stories dating from the 5th century AD) are depicted on the mandapam with the sculpture of the goddess Durga, in all her wrath, considered one of the finest in Mamallapuram.

Above this mandapam are the remains of the 8th century Olakkannesvara Temple. It affords spectacular views of Mamallapuram. Photography is forbidden here for 'security reasons' – there's a nuclear power station a few kilometres south.

Five Rathas

The five rathas are sculptured temples in the style of chariots (rathas). Set by the sea, and carved from solid rock, they provide another fine example of Pallava architecture. These structures were hidden in the sand until excavated by the British 200 years ago. You can see pictures in the museum documenting the excavation process.

The five rathas derive their names from the champions of the *Mahabharata,* the Pandavas, and their collective wife, Draupadi.

The first ratha, **Draupadi Ratha**, on the left after you enter the gate, is dedicated to the goddess Durga. Carefully sculptured guardians protect both sides of the entrance. Within, the goddess stands on a lotus, her devotees on their knees in worship. Outside, the huge sculptured lion stands proud in front of her temple.

Behind the goddess shrine, to the south, a huge Nandi (Shiva's bull vehicle) heralds the next chariot, the **Arjuna Ratha**, dedicated to Shiva. Numerous deities, including Indra, the rain god, are depicted on the outer walls. The shrine within once housed a lingam; now only the cavity remains.

The next temple chariot, **Bhima Ratha,** honours Vishnu. Within its walls a large sculpture of this deity lies in repose.

The **Dharmaraja Ratha** is the tallest of the chariots and the farthest south. The outside walls portray many deities including both the sun god, Surya and the rain god, Indra. There are also the notable Shiva/Vishnu combination, the Harihara, and at the north-eastern corner a Shiva/Parvati combination. The latter is said to symbolise the true equality of men and women.

The final ratha, the **Nakula-Sahadeva Ratha,** is dedicated to the rain god, Indra. His mount is represented in the fine sculptured elephant standing next to the temple. However, other accounts suggest it may have been meant for the god of war, Subrahmanya, who was also associated with the elephant. Approaching from the north, as you enter the gate, you'll see its back first, hence its name: **gajaprishthakara** (elephant's backside). The life-sized image is regarded as one of the most perfectly sculptured elephants in India and it provides a focal point for the five rathas.

Sculpture Museum

The Sculpture Museum, in East Raja St, contains more than 3000 sculptures by local artisans who work with wood, metal, brass and even cement. Some fine paintings are also on display. It's open daily 9 am to 6 pm. Entry is Rs 0.50.

Beach

The village is only a couple of hundred metres from the wide beach, north of the Shore Temple, where local fishers pull in their boats. Be warned – the local toilet is also here. Farther north, or south of the Shore Temple, it becomes cleaner.

Special Events

For four weeks each January, the **Mamallapuram Dance Festival** showcases dances from all over India, including the Bharata Natyam (Tamil Nadu), Kuchipudi (Andhra Pradesh) tribal dance, and performances including Kathakali (Kerala), puppet shows and classical music. Many events take place against the imposing backdrop of Arjuna's Penance. Pick up a leaflet at the tourist office or in Chennai. Local hotels can also assist with programs and tickets.

Courses

You can learn a traditional Indian musical instrument from K Saikumar on School St at Pooncheri Village, 3km from Mamallapuram, on the road to Chengalpattu. The New Papillon restaurant will give you all the details and arrange a translator.

Massage, Yoga & Ayurveda

There are numerous places offering massage, reiki, yoga and other ayurvedic practices. Sessions cost around Rs 350 for one hour. Krishna, at Sri Murugan Guest House, is recommended by male and female travellers.

Places to Stay

If you don't mind roughing it, you can stay in *home accommodation* with families near the Five Rathas, a 15 minute walk from the bus stand. Rooms are thatched huts, with electricity, fan and basic washing facilities.

Travellers' reports are positive. Touts will find you accommodation in the village but, of course, you'll pay more. The usual cost is around Rs 50 per day, Rs 250 per week (more if a tout takes you).

Hotel accommodation is abundant but can be tight during weekends, holidays and the high seasons – November to March and July/August. Be careful of the scams operating at the bus stand where auto-rickshaw drivers convince you that your desired hotel is full and whisk you to one where they receive a substantial commission that eventually comes out of your pocket. The best strategy is to check out places yourself and look as if you know what you're doing and where you're going.

Government hotel tax currently adds 20% to rooms priced at Rs 200 and above. Unless stated otherwise, all rooms have a bath.

Places to Stay – Budget

Mrs Rajalaxmi's place still rates well. Her rooms have fans and electricity, and there's a communal toilet and bucket shower. Meals are available on request.

Lakshmi Lodge (☎ 42463), near the beach, is popular with backpackers. There are airy rooms with fans from Rs 120/150 to Rs 250/300. Indian and western food is served on 'private terraces' or on the roof under the stars. A 'jealousy stone' hovers above the entrance; it will fall on anyone envious of this hotel's success at attracting foreign travellers!

Tina Blue View Lodge & Restaurant (☎ 42319), near Lakshmi Lodge, is run by the friendly Xavier and has a family-style atmosphere. Single/double rooms with bathroom cost from Rs 100/150 to Rs 250. There's also a four bed cottage. The breezy upstairs restaurant is a great place to eat, drink and linger.

Uma Lodge (☎ 42322, 15 Othavadai St) has clean doubles at Rs 100/150 without/with bath, and larger rooms with toilets are available from Rs 200 to Rs 300. There is no air-con and no hot water. The German Bakery is here.

Mamalla Bhavan (☎ 42250), opposite the bus stand, has simple doubles (no singles) with bath and mosquitoes for Rs 90.

Vinayak Cottages (☎ 42445), entered from either East Raja St or Thirukula St, boasts four garden cottages (all doubles). They're good value at Rs 200 for a square cottage, or Rs 250 for a larger round one. There are also clean double rooms in the main building for Rs 175.

Sri Murugan Guest House (☎ 42662, 42 Othavadai St) is close to the beach with clean, well-priced double rooms for Rs 175/280 downstairs/upstairs.

Ramakrishna Lodge (☎ 42431, 8 Othavadai St) is clean, friendly and justifiably popular. Rooms with bath and bucket hot water are from Rs 90/150 (more in high season). The roof terrace is a pleasant place to while away time.

Places to Stay – Mid-Range & Top End

Mamalla Bhavan Annexe (☎ 42260, 104 East Raja St) is very popular. Doubles (no singles) with bath start at Rs 300, Rs 525 with air-con, or Rs 650 for deluxe rooms. There's an excellent veg restaurant or you can eat on balconies or within the courtyard.

Hotel Veeras (☎ 42288, East Raja St), near (and similar) to the Mamalla Bhavan Annexe, has comfortable doubles for Rs 350, or Rs 550 to Rs 650 with air-con and fridge. There's a restaurant and bar.

La Vie en Rose (☎ 42068), better known as a restaurant, has a few pleasant, clean rooms (many face a courtyard) for Rs 350/550.

Hotel Surya (☎ 42292, Thirukula St) is friendly with a peaceful garden setting. The proprietor has good local knowledge. Rooms cost from Rs 175/275, double rooms with a balcony cost Rs 350/400, air-con rooms are Rs 500, deluxe are Rs 800.

TTDC Hotel Tamil Nadu Unit II (☎ 42287), which occupies pleasant shady grounds near the Shore Temple, has double cottages, all of which have bath and fan, from Rs 300 to Rs 500. Facilities available include a bar, a restaurant, a children's play area, and an invitation for a 'jolly walk in garden'.

The other mid-range and top-end hotels are scattered along the road north to Chennai. Each is positioned about 300m from the road and close to the beach. All these resorts offer a range of amenities usually including a swimming pool, bar, restaurant(s) and credit card facilities.

Temple Bay Ashok Beach Resort (☎ 42251, fax 42257) is 200m from town. Superdeluxe singles/doubles with air-con cost US$45/90 in either the main block or the detached cottages. Nonguests can use the small pool for Rs 100 per day.

TTDC Hotel Tamil Nadu Beach Resort (☎ 42235, fax 42268) is 1.5km north. This place has a splendid setting – a forested garden with swimming pool – but it's shabby. Doubles in sea-facing cottages with bath and balcony cost from Rs 550, Rs 850 with air-con.

Mamalla Beach Resort (☎ 42375, fax 42160) is farther north, but not as close to the sea. It's clean with doubles from Rs 360 downstairs and Rs 480 upstairs (air-con Rs 600). There's a veg/nonveg restaurant and staff are particularly friendly.

Silversands (☎ 42228) has a plethora of rooms and cottages, with the expensive suites and three-bed villas (Rs 2700) on the beachfront. It's overpriced, with seasonal rates ranging from Rs 300/400 to Rs 600/800 for normal singles/doubles.

Golden Sun Beach Resort (☎ 42245), 3km from Mamallapuram, has singles/doubles at Rs 600/700, Rs 800/1000 with air-con, or Rs 1300/1420 for sea-facing rooms. There's also a health club.

Ideal Beach Resort (☎ 42240, fax 42243), also located 3km from town, is one of the best places available. This small resort retains a warm and intimate atmosphere. It is popular with both expats and foreigners. Single/double rooms (all equipped with mosquito nets) cost Rs 1000/1100; air-conditioned cottages start from Rs 1300. The food is really quite good and nonguests can use the swimming pool for a fee of Rs 150.

Places to Eat

Mamallapuram caters to all tastes and budgets. Be sure to negotiate the seafood prices before ordering. Many restaurants help you 'customise' your meal according to budget and/or appetite. Beer usually costs Rs 60 at beach bars; Rs 35 in the wine shops.

Sea Shore Restaurant, on the beach, offers excellent seafood. Tiger prawns are Rs 250 and grilled prawns and salad cost Rs 40.

Santhana Beach Restaurant, next door, offers similar fare. For two people, fresh lobster is Rs 450 and king prawns Rs 400. The staff are helpful and they stay open late.

Luna Magica, also on the beach, has a tank full of live lobsters and prawns at prices similar to the Sea Shore. Coconut milk prawn curry is Rs 65; fried fish with chips and salad costs Rs 35.

Moonrakers (Othavadai St), run by three friendly brothers, is a late-night 'hang-out' that attracts travellers like moths to a lamp. The food is good – prawns in garlic sauce cost Rs 70 and there's muesli for breakfast.

Galaxy (☎ 43045, *Othavadai St*), next door, has similar fare, with good coffee and pancakes.

Village Inn Restaurant (Thirukula St) has an indoor section as well as an intimate garden terrace. Multicuisine food including fresh seafood is served. Meals start from a few rupees to Rs 450 for seafood.

Village Restaurant (Thirukula St) serves multicuisine fare and gets good reports.

Tina Blue View is good, especially in the heat of the day, when the shady upstairs area catches the breeze. Warm beer is Rs 60.

Sea Queen Restaurant, next to Tina Blue, is reliable for good seafood.

German Bakery (Othavadai St), at Uma Lodge, is run by Nepalese and is now also a Chinese and Italian restaurant. Excellent breads and pastries are available.

New Papillon/Le Bistro (Beach Rd) is a tiny place run by an enthusiastic crew. Cold beers are available, as well as early-morning breakfasts.

Au Bons Copains (Beach Rd) is friendly and the prawn fried rice is Rs 30.

Sun Rise Restaurant, behind the New Papillon and across the playing field, has a wide range of fish dishes that are good value.

Curiosity Restaurant opposite Lakshmi Lodge has good breakfasts but prices are still on the high side.

La Vie en Rose (East Raja St) is a lovely little place with good coffee and a different nonvegetarian menu each day – main courses are about Rs 70.

Mamalla Bhavan Restaurant is excellent for south Indian vegetarian food. Around the back, each day there's a different *thali* for Rs 20.

Golden Palate Restaurant in the Mamalla Bhavan Annexe is the top vegetarian restaurant in town. Eggplant masala fry with cashew gravy (Rs 25) is excellent.

Shopping

Mamallapuram has revived the ancient crafts of the Pallava sculptors, and the town wakes every day to the sound of chisels on granite. Sculptures are exported throughout the world. You can buy the work from the government Poompuhar Handicrafts Emporium (fixed prices – in theory) or from the craft shops that line the main roads (prices negotiable). Sculptures range from Rs 300 (for a small piece to fit in your baggage) to Rs 400,000 for a massive Ganesh that needs to be lifted with a mobile crane. Shipping to Europe or the USA costs around Rs 6000 and takes three months.

Soapstone images of Hindu gods, woodcarvings, jewellery and hammocks are all available. For book exchange, try Himalaya Handicrafts, East Raja St.

Fantasie Auroville, with its excellent crafts, is in the Sri Murugan complex. Near the shore temple you can buy stuffed mongoose!

Getting There & Away

The most direct route to/from Chennai (Rs 20, 50km, two hours, 20 daily) is on bus Nos 188 and 188A/B/D/K. Bus Nos 19C and 119A go to Chennai via Kovalam (21 daily). To Chennai via the airport you take No 108B (nine daily).

TAMIL NADU

To Pondicherry (Rs 18, 95km, 3½ hours, eight daily) take bus No 188 or 188A. There are five daily buses (No 212A/H) to Kanchipuram (Rs 10, 65km, two hours) via Tirukkalikundram and Chengalpattu (Chingleput). Alternatively, take a bus to Chengalpattu and then another bus from there to Kanchipuram.

To Madurai catch a bus to Chengalpattu (one hour) then a train from there (Rs 161/556 2nd/1st class, 15 hours).

Taxis are available from the bus stand. Long-distance trips may require haggling before the price becomes reasonable. It's about Rs 400 to Chennai airport.

Getting Around

The easiest way to get around is on foot. You can hire bikes from several places, including the bicycle shop opposite the bus stand, for around Rs 25 per day. Moped hire from Lakshmi Lodge is Rs 150 per day (petrol extra) or from Poornima Travels (☎ 42463) at 33 Othavadai St. Helmets are not available and you don't need a licence.

Auto-rickshaws are also available but, since this is a tourist town, negotiation is more cryptic than usual. Many travellers find that sharing a taxi is a good option to see places nearby.

AROUND MAMALLAPURAM
Tiger Cave

Almost 5km north of Mamallapuram this rock-cut shrine, possibly dating from the 7th century, is dedicated to Durga. It has a small mandapam featuring a crown of carved yali heads.

Tirukkalikundram

Fourteen kilometres from Mamallapuram, this pilgrimage centre has a hilltop temple dedicated to Shiva. According to legend two eagles come here each day at noon from Varanasi (Benares). But they often don't turn up!

Leading to the top are 550 steps and you must ascend bare-footed. The temple contains two tiny, beautiful shrines. Even if it's closed the custodian may let you in, for a small consideration. Views from the top encompass the larger Bhaktavatsaleshavra Temple, rocky hills and rice paddies.

You can get here from Mamallapuram by bus or bicycle. The temple is open 8.30 am to 1 pm and 5 to 7 pm. Entry is Rs 2.

KANCHIPURAM
☎ 04112 • pop 184,000

The temple town of Kanchipuram is one of the seven sacred cities of India. Of the original 1000 temples, there are about 200 left. Prices for Kanchipuram's handwoven silks are consistently higher than in Chennai so to get a bargain you need to know your silk. Check out prices in Chennai first. Other than temples and silks, Kanchipuram is a dusty and fairly nondescript town. It attracts many pilgrims and tourists, especially during the **temple car festivals** (January to May). Have plenty of small change handy to meet demands for 'small considerations' from temple caretakers, shoe minders, guides and assorted priests. All the temples close noon to 4 pm.

History

By the 3rd century AD Kanchipuram was reputedly a sophisticated city with diverse cultures and languages. It was significant for Buddhist scholarship, although Hinduism and Jainism were also prevalent.

When Kanchipuram became the Pallava capital (from the 6th to 8th centuries), the arts, especially literature, music and dance, prospered. The first south Indian stone temples were constructed. After their king, Mahendra Varman I, converted from Jainism, the inhabitants of Kanchipuram adopted Hinduism, and worshipped the god Shiva.

Subsequent dynasties, among them the Cholas and Pandyas, continued to support a prosperous Kanchipuram. New temples were built, old ones were renovated and extended, and Shaivism continued to be the major belief system.

Today Kanchipuram is not only a significant temple city and pilgrimage site, it is also an important centre of commerce and is famous for its handwoven silk fabrics.

Orientation & Information

Kanchipuram, also known as Kanchi, is on the main Chennai to Bangalore road, 76km south-west of Chennai.

The tourist information counter at the Hotel Tamil Nadu (☎ 22461) is little help, but guides are available at most temples. The post office is on Station Rd. The Indian Overseas Bank and the State Bank of India are in Gandhi Rd, but the State Bank (like most hotels) does not accept travellers cheques or Amex. Some hotels accept credit cards.

Kailasanatha Temple

Dedicated to Shiva, Kailasanatha is the oldest temple in Kanchi and for some, the most beautiful. Reflecting the freshness and simplicity of early Dravidian architecture, it was built by the Pallava king, Rayasimha, in the late 7th century, though its front was added later by his son, King Varman III.

Fragments of the 8th century murals are a visible reminder of how magnificent the original temple must have looked. Fifty-eight small shrines honour Shiva and Parvati and their sons, Ganesh and Murugan.

The temple is run by the Archaeology Department. Non-Hindus are allowed into the inner sanctum, where there is a prismatic lingam – the largest in Kanchi and third-largest in Asia. The guide and priest here are generous with information.

Sri Ekambaranathar Temple

The Sri Ekambaranathar Temple is dedicated to Shiva and is one of the largest temples in Kanchipuram, covering 12 hectares. Its 59m-high gopuram and massive outer stone wall were constructed in 1509 by Krishnadevaraya of the Vijayanagar empire, though construction was originally started by the Pallavas, with later Chola extensions.

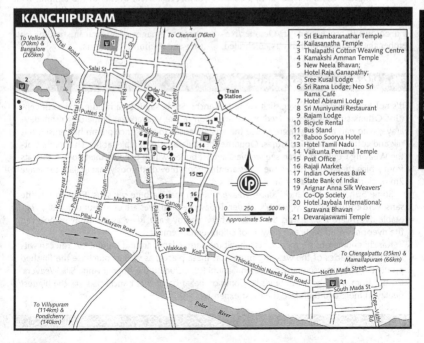

KANCHIPURAM

To Vellore (70km) & Bangalore (265km)

To Chennai (76km)

Pettai Road
Salai St
Odai St
Putteri St
Nellukkara St
Madam St
Gandhi Road
Pillai St
Palayam Road
Vilakkadi Koil
Thirukatchini Nambi Koil Road
North Mada Street
South Mada St
Palar River
Salai St
Santhiam Kutti Street
Krishnaiyar Street
Puthupallayam Street
Kolam Road
Reeva
Rajampet Street
Kossa St
Eerri Raja Vietthi
Station Rd
Train Station

To Chengalpattu (35km) & Mamallapuram (66km)

To Villupuram (114km) & Pondicherry (140km)

0   250   500 m
Approximate Scale

1 Sri Ekambaranathar Temple
2 Kailasanatha Temple
3 Thalapathi Cotton Weaving Centre
4 Kamakshi Amman Temple
5 New Neela Bhavan;
  Hotel Raja Ganapathy;
  Sree Kusal Lodge
6 Sri Rama Lodge; Neo Sri
  Rama Café
7 Hotel Abirami Lodge
8 Sri Muniyundi Restaurant
9 Rajam Lodge
10 Bicycle Rental
11 Bus Stand
12 Baboo Soorya Hotel
13 Hotel Tamil Nadu
14 Vaikunta Perumal Temple
15 Post Office
16 Rajaji Market
17 Indian Overseas Bank
18 State Bank of India
19 Arignar Anna Silk Weavers'
  Co-Op Society
20 Hotel Jaybala International;
  Saravana Bhavan
21 Devarajaswami Temple

Inside there is a 1000-pillared hall (which actually contains 540 decorated pillars).

The temple's name is said to derive from Eka Amra Nathar – Lord of the Mango Tree – and there is an old mango tree, with four branches representing the four *Vedas* (sacred Hindu texts). A plaque nearby claims that the tree is 3500 years old.

Non-Hindus cannot enter the sanctum. A 'camera fee' of Rs 10 goes towards the upkeep of the temple but the visit could cost you more, as this is undoubtedly one of the worst temples for hustlers.

Kamakshi Amman Temple

This imposing temple is dedicated to the goddess Parvati in her guise as Kamakshi, the goddess who accedes to all requests. To the right of the entrance is the marriage hall with its ornate pillars. Directly ahead the main shrine is topped with its more recent plating of gold.

The temple's Car Festival is in February/March. Wooden carriages housing statues of deities are hauled through the streets in a colourful procession. In October/November the goddess' birthday is celebrated.

Devarajaswami Temple

Dedicated to Vishnu, this enormous monument was built by the Vijayanagars. It has a beautifully sculptured pillared hall as well as a marriage hall commemorating the wedding of Vishnu and Lakshmi. One of the temple's most notable features is a huge chain carved from a single piece of stone.

Within the large temple tank a 10m statue of Vishnu is immersed. Every 40 years the waters of the tank are drained so that the statue may be viewed. In 1979, the last time such an event occurred, 10 million people reputedly visited. Entrance is Rs 2.

Vaikunta Perumal Temple

Dedicated to Vishnu, this temple was built shortly after the Kailasanatha Temple. The cloisters inside the outer wall consist of lion pillars and are representative of the first phase in the architectural evolution of the grand 1000-pillared halls. Wall sculptures depict historical events of the temple, with explanatory details given in 8th century script. The main shrine, on three levels, contains images of Vishnu in standing, sitting and reclining positions.

The Weavers of Kanchipuram

It's not known when weavers first came to Kanchi. Some say they arrived in the 12th century. Others suggest they arrived at the invitation of the Vijayanagar emperor, Krishnadevaraya, who had a strong desire to see the arts advance. Today Kanchipuram has prosperous silk and cotton weaving industries. Opposite the Kailasanatha Temple, at the Thalapathi Cotton Weaving Centre, you can see weavers almost buried within deep earthen holes – the pits from which they work. Above the holes are the looms they dexterously manipulate to weave 2m of cloth each, per day.

Some 50 years ago Kanchipuram weavers began making pure silk saris. Prior to this the saris were cotton with a woven silk border. Today chemical dyes are used, but originally, vegetable dyes were mixed with the waters of the nearby Palar River as the weavers believed the river possessed particular powers of colour-enhancement.

Kanchi's numerous silk merchants inhabit the narrow lanes around Gandhi Rd. You can witness the intricacies of the weaving process at these places, as well as purchase the finished product. There are also many places on Gandhi Rd, including the Arignar Anna Silk Weavers' Co-op, from where you can buy silk. Common belief has it that Kanchi silks are the highest quality in India and therefore the most expensive.

Places to Stay

Most of the cheap (and noisy) lodges are clustered in the town centre, a few minutes walk from the bus stand.

Rajam Lodge (☎ 22519, 9 Kamarajar St) is a friendly place with basic singles/doubles/triples with bath for Rs 70/100/200.

Hotel Abirami Lodge (☎ 20797, 109 Kamarajar St) has spotless rooms from Rs 100/160, but most have a claustrophobic feel as there are no outside windows. Those at the back are quietest. The hotel has a good 'meals' restaurant.

Sri Rama Lodge (☎ 22435, 20 Nellukkara St) is reasonably clean and friendly with rooms from Rs 90/150, or Rs 290/380 with air-con. All the rooms have bath with hot water. There's a good vegetarian restaurant, Neo Sri Rama Cafe.

Sree Kusal Lodge (☎ 23342, Nellukkara St) has clean, marble-lined rooms from Rs 100/160; air-con doubles are Rs 380. TV hire costs Rs 50.

Hotel Tamil Nadu (☎ 22553, fax 22552, Station Rd) is not one of the tourism department's best. Standard doubles are Rs 290, air-con doubles are Rs 480 and Rs 500. Deluxe air-con rooms (marginally bigger) are Rs 650. There's a bar and simple restaurant.

Baboo Soorya Hotel (☎ 22555, fax 22556, 85 East Raja Veethy) is the swankiest hotel in town. Staff are friendly and helpful. Clean and well-appointed singles/doubles cost Rs 290/350, or Rs 450/500 with effective air-con. There's a good vegetarian restaurant.

Hotel Jaybala International (☎ 24348, 504 Gandhi Rd) has spotless rooms from Rs 150/350 to Rs 450/500 with air-con. All major credit cards are accepted.

Places to Eat

The best and fastest meals are available from the *Saravana Bhavan* (part of the chain of vegetarian restaurants but with a different spelling here) at the Hotel Jayabala International.

Sri Muniyundi Restaurant (Kamarajar St) does reasonable nonveg food.

Baboo Soorya Hotel has a good vegetarian restaurant.

New Neela Bhavan and the popular *Hotel Raja Ganapathy* are next to Sree Kusal Lodge. Both offer cheap and good south Indian veg dishes.

You'll find many small vegetarian places (typical meal around Rs 15) near the bus stand.

Getting There & Away

Bus There's no problem finding a bus at the station. Look for direct, or 'Point-to-Point' buses; they're the fastest – No 76B runs to Chennai (Rs 12, 1½ hours). There are five direct No 212A buses daily to Mamallapuram (Rs 10, about two hours). Alternatively, take one of the more frequent buses to Chengalpattu and then catch another one from there to Mamallapuram.

There are direct State Express Transport Corporation (SETC) buses to Tiruchirappalli (No 122), Chennai (No 828) and Bangalore (No 828).

There are plenty of buses with the regional bus company, PATC, to Chennai, Vellore and Tiruvannamalai, as well as private ones to Pondicherry.

Train From Chennai Egmore change at Chengalpattu (Chingleput) for Kanchipuram (Rs 17, three hours). There are services from Chengalpattu to Kanchi at 8.20 am and 5.45 and 8.20 pm and from Kanchi to Chengalpattu at 6.05, 7 and 8.33 am and 6.13 pm (not on national public holidays – see the Public Holidays & Special Events section in the Facts for the Visitor chapter). It's possible to get to Kanchipuram from Chennai (or Tirupathi in Andhra Pradesh), and vice versa, via Arakkonam on the Bangalore to Chennai Central broad-gauge line, but there are only two connections per day in either direction: at 7.50 am and 5.30 pm from Arakkonam to Kanchipuram, and 9.23 am and 6.55 pm in the opposite direction.

Getting Around

Bicycles can be rented for Rs 2 per hour (Rs 20 for a day) from shops near the bus stand. Cycle-rickshaws should cost Rs 70 for a lightning temple tour (one to three hours). However, to fully appreciate the temples of Kanchi you'll need at least a day or preferably two. Auto-rickshaws are also available – even all the way to Mamallapuram for Rs 500.

VEDANTANGAL BIRD SANCTUARY
About 52km from Mamallapuram, this is an important breeding ground for waterbirds. Cormorants, egrets, herons, storks, ibis, spoonbills, grebes and pelicans come here from October to March, depending on the monsoons. At the height of the breeding season (December and January) there can be up to 30,000 birds here. The best viewing times are early morning and late afternoon. The sanctuary is open 6 am to 6 pm daily. Entry is Rs 1.

Basic accommodation is available at the *Forest Department Resthouse*, just 500m before the sanctuary. Charges are Rs 30 per person. Officially, advance reservations must be made with the Wildlife Warden (☎ 044-413947), 4th floor, DMS Office, Teynampet, Chennai. Unofficially, if you arrive and they happen to have a vacancy, you're in.

To get to Vedantangal you can take a bus from Chengalpattu to the Vedantangal bus stand, then walk the remaining 1km south. Often the buses will take you right there. An alternative is to get a bus from any of the major centres to Madurantakam, the closest town of any size, and then hire transport for the last 8km.

VELLORE
☎ 0416 • pop 330,200
Vellore, 145km west of Chennai, is a dusty, semi-rural bazaar town. For tourists, it is noteworthy for the Vijayanagar Fort and temple, which are in an excellent state of preservation.

The town has a modern central church built in an old British cemetery, which contains the tomb of a captain who died in 1799 'of excessive fatigue incurred during the

glorious campaign that ended in the defeat of Tipoo Sultaun'. Here, too, is a memorial to the victims of the little known 'Vellore Mutiny' of 1806. The mutiny was instigated by the second son of Tipu Sultan, who was incarcerated in the fort at that time, and was put down by a task force sent from Arcot.

Vellore is famed for its CMC Hospital – a leader in research and health care. The people who come here from all over India for medical care give this unassuming town a cosmopolitan feel.

Vellore Fort
Vellore Fort was built in the 16th century by a chieftain of the Vijayanagar empire. In 1676 the fort passed briefly into the hands of the Marathas. The British occupied the fort in 1760 following the fall of Srirangapatnam and the death of Tipu Sultan. Open daily, it now houses various public departments and private offices.

The small **museum** (closed Friday), inside the fort complex, contains sculptures dating back to Pallava and Chola times.

At the entrance to the fort the Archaeological Survey of India has a small information stall.

Jalakanteshwara Temple
This temple was built about 1550 and, although it doesn't compare with the ruins at Hampi, it is still a gem of late Vijayanagar architecture. During the invasions by the Adil Shahis of Bijapur, the Marathas and the Carnatic nawabs, the temple was occupied by a garrison and temple rituals ceased. However, it has reopened and is now a popular place of worship.

Within the temple, its pillared mandapam, famed for its sculptures of yali and other mythical creatures, is considered a masterpiece of its time. Large statues of Ganesh grace the entrance and mandapam. The temple is open daily, 6 am to 1 pm and 3 to 8 pm.

Places to Stay
Vellore's cheap hotels are concentrated along the roads south of and parallel to the hospital.

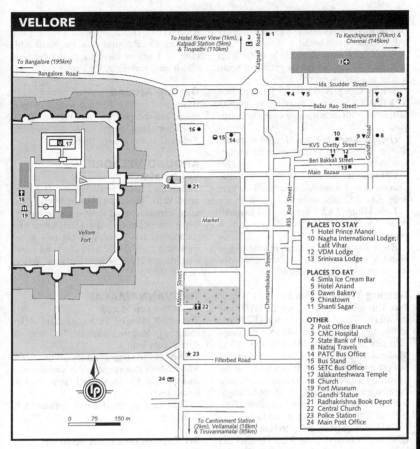

VELLORE

To Hotel River View (1km),
Katpadi Station (5km)
& Tirupathi (110km)

To Kanchipuram (70km) &
Chennai (145km)

To Bangalore (195km)

Bangalore Road

Ida Scudder Street

Babu Rao Street

KVS Chetty Street

Beri Bakkali Street

Main Bazaar

Katpadi Road

Gandhi Road

BSS Koil Street

Chunambukara Street

Minny Street

Vellore Fort

Market

Filterbed Road

PLACES TO STAY
1 Hotel Prince Manor
10 Nagha International Lodge;
     Lalit Vihar
12 VDM Lodge
13 Srinivasa Lodge

PLACES TO EAT
4 Simla Ice Cream Bar
5 Hotel Anand
6 Dawn Bakery
9 Chinatown
11 Shanti Sagar

OTHER
2 Post Office Branch
3 CMC Hospital
7 State Bank of India
8 Natraj Travels
14 PATC Bus Office
15 Bus Stand
16 SETC Bus Office
17 Jalakanteshwara Temple
18 Church
19 Fort Museum
20 Gandhi Statue
21 Radhakrishna Book Depot
22 Central Church
23 Police Station
24 Main Post Office

To Cantonment Station
(2km), Vellamalai (18km)
& Tiruvannamalai (85km)

0   75   150 m

Srinivasa Lodge (☎ 26389, 14 Beri Bakkali St) is a clean place run by friendly people. All rooms have bath and cost from Rs 100/130.

VDM Lodge (☎ 24008, 13 Beri Bakkali St) is a large place with ordinary rooms at Rs 80/110 and deluxe rooms with TV at Rs 200/220.

Nagha International Lodge (☎ 26731, 13 KVS Chetty St) is a large, modern hotel with rooms from Rs 100/160, to Rs 450 for an air-con double.

Hotel River View (☎ 25251, Katpadi Rd) is 1km north. It's modern and clean, but where's the view? Rooms cost Rs 370/420 with bathroom, Rs 550/650 with air-con; there are three restaurants, a bar and a garden.

Hotel Prince Manor (☎ 27726, Katpadi Rd) is an upmarket hotel with double rooms from Rs 550, or Rs 750 with air-con. There are three restaurants – veg, nonveg and a roof garden.

More hotels to suit a range of budgets are on Filterbed Rd in the south of town.

Places to Eat

Dawn Bakery (Gandhi Rd) has freshly baked biscuits and bread.

Simla Ice Cream Bar (Ida Scudder St) is not an ice cream bar but an excellent north Indian vegetarian cafe.

Shanti Sagar (Beri Bakkali St), next door to VDM Lodge, is a buzzing vegetarian restaurant with an attractive open-air courtyard.

Hotel Anand (Ida Scudder St) is an upmarket vegetarian restaurant with an aircon room.

Chinatown (Gandhi Rd), opposite Natraj Travels, does decent Asian meals. Tom yam soup is Rs 25, main dishes are about Rs 45.

Lalit Vihar (KVS Chetty St) has Gujarati meals for Rs 25 including all-you-can-eat *chapatis*.

River Room, one of three restaurants at Hotel River View, has fish and chips for Rs 70, pepper steak for Rs 80.

Getting There & Away

Bus This area is serviced by the PATC and the SETC. SETC bus Nos 139 and 280 run to Chennai (Rs 30), No 104 to Tiruchirappalli (Rs 55) and Nos 168, 866 and 983 to Madurai (Rs 68). All these buses originate in Vellore and can be booked in advance at the offices by the bus stands. Others, which pass through en route from Chennai and Bangalore (and may be full), go to Bangalore, Tirupathi (2½ hours), Thanjavur and Ooty.

PATC has 26 buses a day to Kanchipuram (Rs 10, 2½ hours) from 5 am. It also has buses to Chennai (Rs 30, 30 daily), Tiruchirappalli and Bangalore.

Train Vellore's main train station is 5km north at Katpadi. This is the junction of the broad-gauge line from Bangalore to Chennai, and the metre-gauge Tirupathi to Madurai line (which runs via Tiruvannamalai, Villupuram, Chidambaram, Thanjavur and Tiruchirappalli). The smaller Cantonment station, 2km south of town, is on the metre-gauge line only.

The 228km trip from Katpadi to Bangalore (4½ hours) costs Rs 88/294 in 2nd/1st

class. To Chennai (130km, two hours) it's Rs 39/196. The daily train to Tirupathi (105km, three hours) is at the unsociable hour of 1 am or there's a passenger train (5½ hours) leaving at 9.15 am.

Getting Around

Buses wait outside Katpadi station to meet trains and the journey into Vellore (Rs 2) takes anything from 15 to 30 minutes. Auto-rickshaws charge Rs 60.

AROUND VELLORE
Vellamalai

Vellamalai, 18km from Vellore, is named after Valli, Murugan's second wife. The main temple, carved from massive rock, is at the top of the hill. It's dedicated to Murugan, and has images of his two wives Devasena and Valli. There are good views from the top. The one hour trip from Vellore on bus No 20 (hourly) costs Rs 8.

TIRUVANNAMALAI
☎ 04175 • pop 100,000

The small town of Tiruvannamalai, 85km south of Vellore, sits at the base of Arunachala Hill.

This is an important Shaivite town, where Shiva is revered as Arunachaleswar, an aspect of fire (see The Lingam of Fire boxed text).

The temple is open 6 am to 1 pm and 5.30 to 10 pm.

Sri Ramanasramam Ashram

This small ashram, 2km south-west of Tiruvannamalai, draws devotees of Sri Ramana Maharishi, a guru who died in 1950 after nearly 50 years in contemplation. Day visits are permitted and *devotees only* may stay by applying in writing at least three months in advance to the President, Sri Ramanasramam, PO Tiruvannamalai. Office hours are 8 to 11 am and 2 to 5 pm (☎/fax 22491).

Places to Stay & Eat

There are several lodges near the temple with new upmarket ones about to open. At festival time (November/December) prices

The Lingam of Fire

Legend has it that Shiva appeared as a column of fire on Arunachala Hill in Tiruvannamalai, creating the original symbol of the lingam. Each November/December full moon, the Karthikai Deepam Festival celebrates this legend. A huge fire, lit from a 30m wick immersed in 2000L of ghee, blazes from the top of Arunachala Hill for several days.

Covering some 10 hectares, the Arunachaleswar Temple is one of the largest in India. It dates from the 11th century, with much of the structure being built from the 17th to 19th centuries. It has four large gopurams, one at each cardinal point, with the eastern one rising to 66m.

At festival time up to half a million people come to Tiruvannamalai. In honour of Shiva, they scale the mountain or circumnavigate its base (14km). On the upward path steps quickly give way to jagged and unstable rocks. There's no shade and the sun is relentless. And the journey must be undertaken in bare feet – a mark of respect to the deity (visitors are sometimes permitted shoes). None of this deters the thousands of pilgrims. If you're a visitor tempted to join in, it's a long, hot haul to the top. You'll be in the company of thousands of pilgrims who move with utmost calm and composure – a truly humbling experience.

Allow three to four hours one way, and take plenty of water and sun protection.

can rise by an astronomical 1000% and you'll need to haggle hard to get a reduction.

Park Lodge *(☎ 22471, 26 Kosamadam St)*, 1km north-east of the temple, has a good veg restaurant and basic singles/doubles for Rs 100/150.

Udupi Brindhavan Lodge *(☎ 22693, 57A Car St)*, 500m south-east of the temple, has simple rooms for Rs 100/150 and air-con rooms for Rs 350. Most have bath and bucket hot water.

Trishul Hotel *(☎ 22219, 6 Kanakaraya Mudali St)*, 500m east of the temple, has comfortable rooms for Rs 390/500, Rs 600/700 with air-con. There's a good veg restaurant. At festival time the hotel electrician turns on not only the room lights, but also *puja* lights for special rituals.

Getting There & Away

The train station is on the north-eastern side of town about 1.5km from the temple. The daily *Tirupati-Trichy Express* (No 6799, 6800) passes through Tiruvannamalai, southbound at 9.20 pm and northbound at 10.45 pm. Regular buses are available from Chennai and Pondicherry.

GINGEE (Senji)

Gingee Fort (pronounced 'shingee') is 37km east of Tiruvannamalai. Constructed mainly in the 16th century by the Vijayanagars (though some structures date from the 13th century), the fort has been occupied by various armies, including the forces of Adil Shah from Bijapur and the Marathas, who assumed control from 1677. In 1698 the Mughals took over. Then came the French, who remained until the British defeated them at Pondicherry.

Nowadays the fort is delightfully free of human activity. A walk around can take an entire day. Buildings within the fort include a granary, a Shiva temple, a mosque and the most prominent – the recently restored audience hall.

Open 9 am to 5 pm, the fort siren at 4.45 pm warns stragglers the gates are about to be locked. Entry is Rs 2.

Devi Lodge *(☎ 04145-2210)* is on the main road, 1.5km east of town. Clean rooms (some with a fort view) with hot water are Rs 50/70. A new upmarket place is being built and there are numerous cheap eating places nearby.

TAMIL NADU

Buses leave almost every hour from Tiruvannamalai. Ask to be let off at 'the fort'; it's 2km before Gingee. Day trips from Pondicherry are also possible.

PONDICHERRY
☎ 0413 • pop 789,416

Pondicherry (known in Tamil as Puducherry), the former French colony settled in the early 18th century, is a charming Indian town with a few enduring pockets of French culture, and an ashram set beside the sea. Together with the other former French enclaves of Karaikal (also in Tamil Nadu), Mahé (Kerala) and Yanam (Andhra Pradesh), it now forms the Union Territory of Pondicherry.

The French relinquished control of 'Pondy' some 50 years ago, but reminders of the colonial days remain, even though it is very much an Indian city: the Tricolour flutters over the grand French consulate, there's a *hôtel de ville* (town hall), and red *kepis* (caps) and belts are worn by the local police.

The French influence is reflected, as one might expect, in the food. Most of the restaurants serve authentic dishes, and bottled Pondicherry water is by far the best in India. Hotels are excellent value since Tamil Nadu's punitive taxes do not apply here. You'll be pleased to discover that as a result of this, beer is only Rs 40!

You may come here to see the Sri Aurobindo Ashram or to check up on ancestry, but you'll probably stay longer than you'd intended.

Orientation

Pondicherry is laid out on a grid plan. A north-south canal (now covered) divides the smaller eastern side from the larger western part. In colonial days the canal separated Pondicherry's European and Indian sections.

Navigating the town is easy, but there are some eccentricities with street names. Many have one name at one end and another at the other end. This is particularly so with east-west oriented streets.

The Sri Aurobindo Ashram as well as the French institutions and many restaurants are all on the eastern side, while most hotels are west of the canal. The train station is at the southern edge of town, while the bus stands are west along the main drag, Lal Bahabhur St.

Information

Tourist Offices The Pondy tourist office (☎ 339497), on Goubert Ave (Beach Rd), is open daily, 8 am to 1 pm and 2 to 6 pm. The office runs half-day city sightseeing tours (Rs 50) that take you to visit the ashram, Auroville, the handmade paper factory and the botanical gardens. Tours leave at 8 am and 2 pm.

Money The Indian Overseas Bank, in the courtyard of the *hôtel de ville*, accepts most travellers cheques. There's also a Canara Bank off Nehru St and the Andhra Bank in Mission St. All banks are open Monday to Friday, 10 am to 2 pm, and Saturday until noon.

Post & Communications The main post office, on Rangapillai St, is open 10 am to 7.30 pm, Monday to Saturday. Next door is the 24 hour telegraph office. There are numerous STD/ISD/fax booths. Email facilities are available at Raji Internet Corner (☎ 338609), 143A MG Rd. It's open between 9 am and 11 pm and access costs Rs 60 per hour.

Bookshops The Vak Bookshop, 15 Nehru St, specialises in religion and philosophy. The Kailash French Bookshop (☎ 331872, fax 343663) at 169 Lal Bahabhur St and the French Bookshop on Suffren St are also good. There's a branch of Higginbothams on Ambour Salai.

Libraries The library in Rangapillai St is open between 8.30 am to 8.30 pm. It is closed on Mondays.

Cultural Centres Alliance Française (☎ 338146), 38 Suffren St, runs French, English and Tamil classes and has a library and computer centre. Its small monthly newsletter, *Le Petit Journal*, details forthcoming events. The library (☎ 334351) is open daily, 9 am to noon and 4 to 7 pm. Temporary membership (valid for 15 days) is Rs 50.

Medical Services It is recommended that you visit Clinic Nallam (☎ 335463), 74 Iswaran (also known as ID) Koil St, if you need a doctor.

Sri Aurobindo Ashram
Founded by Sri Aurobindo in 1926, this ashram is one of the most popular with westerners in India. Its spiritual tenets represent a synthesis of yoga and modern science. After Aurobindo's death spiritual authority passed to a devotee known as The Mother, who died in 1973, aged 97. These days, the ashram underwrites many cultural and educational activities in Pondicherry, though there is a certain tension between it and locals who are concerned at its apparent reluctance to allow local participation in running the society.

The main ashram building is on Marine St. It's open daily, 8 am to noon and 2 to 6 pm. The flower-festooned *samadhi* (a tomb that is venerated as a shrine) of Aurobindo and The Mother is under the frangipani tree in the central courtyard. Their old black Humber sits rusting in the garage just off the courtyard.

Opposite the main building, in the educational centre, you can sometimes catch a film, slide show, play or lecture (a list of events is posted on the ashram's notice board). The centre is very well stocked with books written in almost every language.

There is no charge for entering the ashram (although children under three are prohibited) but a donation may be collected.

Things to See & Do
The **Pondicherry Museum** at Rangapillai St, next to the library, has a collection including everything from Pallava sculptures to a bed slept in by a peripatetic Dupleix, the colony's most famous governor. The

museum is open Tuesday to Sunday, 9.40 am to 1 pm and 2 to 5.30 pm.

Next to the old lighthouse on Goubert Ave is the **Jawahar Toy Museum**. It houses 120 dolls, dressed in costumes from various Indian states. Entry is free; hours are 10 am to 1 pm and 2 to 5 pm. It's closed Monday.

If you have an interest in 19th and 20th century police equipment, the **Police Museum** in the police station will appeal.

Pondy has several churches and temples. The **Church of our Lady of the Immaculate Conception** in Mission St was completed in 1791. Its medieval architecture is in the style of many of the Jesuit constructions of that time. The **Sacred Heart Church** on Subbayah Salai is an impressive sight with its Gothic architecture, stained glass and striking brown and white colours.

The **Sri Manakula Vinayagar**, Manakula Vinayagar Koil St, is dedicated to Ganesh. Recent renovations have furnished its sanctum with Rajasthan marble and its *vimana* (tower over the sanctum) with a gold roof. This small temple contains over 40 skilfully painted friezes.

The **Drowpathiamman Temple** (entrance in MG Rd) is dedicated to the goddess of the area and is noted for its 24 day fire festival in July/August.

The **Sri Aurobindo Handmade Paper Factory** produces quality paper and is a successful ashram enterprise. Visitors are welcome to wander through the factory at 50 SV Patel Salai (☎/fax 334763). A range of products is for sale. It's open daily except Sunday, 8.30 am to noon.

Established by the French in 1826, the **botanical gardens** is a peaceful place where you can meander down the many pathways and enjoy the extensive variety of plants.

The best **beaches** – Serenity, Quiet and Reppo (with lifeguards) are all within 2km of Pondy.

Places to Stay – Budget
Pondicherry Tourism Department Guest House (☎ 358276, *Dr Ambedkar Rd*), also called Tourist Home, is by far the cheapest option in town, with basic clean rooms.

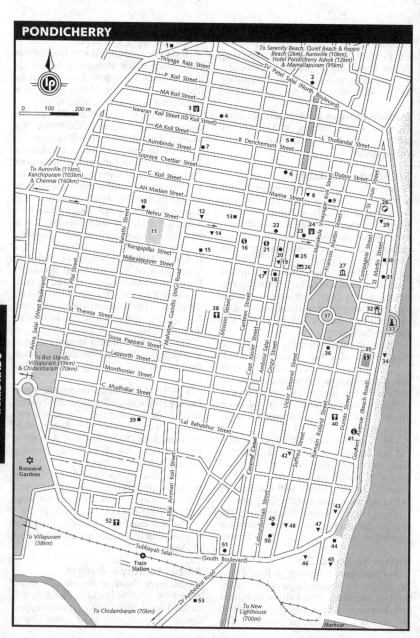

PONDICHERRY

PONDICHERRY

PLACES TO STAY					
1	Ananda; Hotel Surguru	45	Seagulls Restaurant	23	Vak Bookshop
5	Surya Swastika Guest House	46	La Terrasse	24	Sri Manakula Vinayagar
13	Aristo Guest House	47	Le Club		Temple
15	Amala Lodge	48	China Town	26	GPO; Telegraph Office
25	International Guest House			27	Library; Pondicherry
30	Sea Side Guest House	**OTHER**			Museum
36	Bar Qualithé Hotel &	2	Sri Aurobindo Handmade	28	French Consulate
	Restaurant		Paper Factory	31	Splendour
44	Park Guest House	3	Drowpathiamman	32	Old Lighthouse
53	Pondicherry Tourism Depart-		Temple	33	Gandhi Square
	ment Guest House	4	Clinic Nallam	35	Indian Overseas Bank;
		6	Vijay Arya Moped Rental		Hôtel de Ville (Town Hall)
PLACES TO EAT		7	Raji Internet Corner	37	Government Square
8	Bliss Restaurant	9	Sri Aurobindo Ashram	38	Church of Our Lady of the
12	Hotel Aristo	10	Handloom (Tamil Nadu)		Immaculate Conception
14	India Coffee House		Cooperative Shop	39	Kailash French Bookshop
17	Bamboo Hut	11	Market	40	Notre Dame des Anges
19	Hot Breads	16	Andhra Bank		Church
29	Le Cafe	18	Cottage Industries	41	Tourist Office
34	Le Cafe (Seafront)	20	Higginbothams	49	French Bookshop; Alliance
42	Rendezvous; Satsanga	21	Canara Bank		Francaise Library
43	Blue Dragon Chinese	22	La Boutique d'Auroville;	50	Alliance Française
	Restaurant		Police Station & Police	51	Bike Hire
			Museum	52	Sacred Heart Church

With bath they are Rs 25/35. There is also a restaurant (Le Cafe) serving veg and non-veg meals.

Amala Lodge (☎ 338910, 92 Rangapillai St) is clean, and run by a friendly family. Basic single/double rooms cost Rs 60/100 with common bath, Rs 70/120 with private bath.

Surya Swastika Guest House (☎ 343092, 11 Eswaran Koil St) is a small old-style guesthouse with pleasant staff. There are rooms for Rs 60/90 with common bath, Rs 70/100 with private bath. Additional bodies pay Rs 20 and a mat is provided. You must be in by 9.30 pm.

Aristo Guest House (☎ 336728, 50A Mission St) is clean and friendly and has singles/doubles with bath for Rs 80/120 as well as a few air-con doubles for Rs 650.

Bar Qualithé Hotel (☎ 334325, Government Square), predominantly a pub, has six 1st-floor rooms with a veranda overlooking the park. Four-bed rooms with bath cost Rs 400 and the one single room is Rs 150. The quality implied may eventuate when the long-awaited renovations are completed.

Railway retiring rooms are quiet and cost Rs 35/65.

Places to Stay – Mid-Range & Top End

The best places in Pondy are the guesthouses run by the Aurobindo Ashram. They're immaculately maintained and in the most attractive part of town. Although classified here as mid-range, some are cheaper than the budget hotels. As the accommodation is set up for ashram devotees, strict conditions apply – there's a 10.30 pm curfew, and smoking and alcohol are banned.

Park Guest House (☎ 334412, Goubert Ave) has the best facilities and position: all front rooms face the sea and have a balcony. Unlike many other ashram guesthouses, the proprietors here prefer devotees, rather than tourists, but unless they're full it's unlikely you'll be turned away. Doubles (concessions for singles) with private bath range

TAMIL NADU

from Rs 300 to Rs 400. There's a vegetarian restaurant.

International Guest House (☎ 336699, Gingy St) has single/double rooms from Rs 75/100 in the old wing. Doubles in the new wing cost Rs 110, or Rs 380 with air-con. All the rooms have bathrooms with hot water on request. Ashram rules apply here and so 'Drivers and servants are not allowed'.

Sea Side Guest House (☎ 221825, 14 Goubert Ave) has a far less institutional feel to it. This old house has eight very spacious rooms (all with bath) from Rs 275 to Rs 450, some with air-con.

Hotel Surguru (☎ 339022, fax 334377, SV Patel Salai) is popular. Bright, clean rooms from Rs 440/550, Rs 620/780 with air-con, all with bath and Star TV. Rear rooms are less noisy. The hotel also has a good friendly vegetarian restaurant.

Anandha (☎ 330711, fax 331241, SV Patel Salai), the top hotel in town, is a flashy neoclassical place. Air-con rooms are Rs 1100/1400, there's a bar, good non-veg and veg restaurants and an efficient travel desk.

Hotel Pondicherry Ashok (☎ 655160, fax 655140) is a Portuguese villa-style hotel 12km north of town. Rooms start at Rs 1350/2200. It's a great location but a little run down.

Places to Eat

Pondicherry has good places to eat, some open air, and most serve cheap beer. One of the cheapest places to eat is the ashram. For an advance purchase meal ticket (Rs 15) you can have lunch or dinner in mandatory silence.

West Side *The Hotel Aristo (Nehru St)* has a popular rooftop restaurant. Most main dishes range from Rs 40 to Rs 55. Interesting choices include walnut chicken with brown rice (Rs 55). Food is cheaper and faster in the ground floor restaurant (closed Friday).

India Coffee House (Nehru St) is good value for breakfast and snacks.

Bamboo Hut (3 Rangapillai St) serves well-priced Chinese dishes from its rooftop garden.

East Side Near the ashram, *Bliss Restaurant (Gingy St)*, serves straightforward thalis for Rs 20 (closed Sunday).

Le Cafe (Marine St), a snack bar opposite the French consulate (not to be confused with the seafront Le Cafe) offers good tea and samosas.

Le Cafe (Goubert Ave), is a crumbly old place, popular for popcorn and ice creams.

Bar Qualithé Hotel, overlooking Government Square, is an old place with comfy wicker chairs and bags of atmosphere. Have a plate of beef fry (Rs 30) with your beer (Rs 35). There's a range of more substantial dishes for around Rs 45.

Seagulls Restaurant (19 Dumas St) is right by the sea and serves quite good food. Alcohol is available.

Blue Dragon Chinese Restaurant (33 Dumas St) serves good Chinese food as does *China Town (Suffren St)*.

La Terrasse (5 Subbayah Salai), open air and multicuisine, is most popular for its pizzas. It's open 8.30 am to 10 pm daily except Wednesday.

Rendezvous (30 Suffren St) with decor straight out of rural France, including wicker chairs, gingham tablecloths and shutters, has bouillabaisse (Rs 70), grilled prawns (Rs 170) as well as good tandoori food. Open from 8 to 11 am, noon to 3 pm and 6 to 10.30 pm, you can have your meals on the attractive roof terrace.

Hot Breads (Ambour Salai), near Higginbothams, has great coffee, cakes and baguettes.

Satsanga (Suffren St) is just down the street from Rendezvous. French run, the food's as good as it sounds – *soupe de poisson* (Rs 55) and *terrine de lapin* (Rs 60). The coffee's superb, as is the crème caramel, and you can sit in the garden. There's an art gallery, and also a couple of rooms for rent. It's closed on Thursday.

Le Club (33 Dumas St) is a rambling old mansion in a pleasant garden. The cuisine is

French, the decor peachy and the service immaculate. Breakfast is from 7.30 to 9.30 am (best after 8.30 am when the baguettes have arrived). Lunch is from noon to 2 pm and dinner from 7 to around 10.30 pm daily except Monday. Expect to pay Rs 165 for a glass of wine, around Rs 80 for an entree, and Rs 250 for a main course. If your budget only extends to a coffee (which they don't seem to mind) it's well worth a visit. There's a cheaper tandoori restaurant, *Le Bistro*, in the garden.

Entertainment

By 10 pm at the latest, Pondy's a quiet, sleepy town. Residents do much of their entertaining at home. Unless you can secure an invite (or hang around Le Club – you may get lucky!) there's not a great deal to do in the evenings. The *Bar Qualithé Hotel* stays open until 10.30 pm.

Shopping

Fine handmade paper is sold from the Sri Aurobindo factory and jewellery, batiks, *kalamkari* drawings, carpets and woodcarvings may be purchased from La Boutique d'Auroville (Nehru St). Also on Nehru St is the Handloom (Tamil Nadu) Cooperative shop. Cottage Industries on Rangapillai St has a range of crafts while Splendour, at 16 Goubert Ave (closed Wednesday), has distinctive postcards and chic handbags.

Getting There & Away

Bus The SETC bus stand is west of the roundabout on the road to Villupuram. It's well organised with a computerised reservation service (Rs 2). There are hourly buses to Chennai (Rs 32, 4½ hours), and buses four times daily to Madurai (Rs 88, 7½ hours), Bangalore, Tirupathi and Coimbatore.

From the chaotic new bus stand, 500m to the west, there are regular buses to Villupuram and the following destinations.

destination	frequency
Bangalore	six daily
Chennai	20 daily
Chidambaram	every half hour
Kanchipuram	four daily
Karaikal	10 daily
Kumbakonam	five daily
Mamallapuram	four daily
Nagapattinam	three daily
Tiruchirappalli	four daily
Tiruvannamalai	nine daily
Vellore	seven daily

Train Pondicherry's train station is more popular with goats than people. There are four daily passenger trains to Villupuram (Rs 8, 38km, one hour) on the Chennai to Madurai line. They depart Pondicherry at 5.10 and 8 am, and 4.15 pm. From Villupuram timings tend to fluctuate so you'll need to check timetables before you leave. The computerised booking service located at the station covers all of the trains on the southern railway.

Taxi Taxis between Pondicherry and Chennai cost Rs 850 and to the airport they charge Rs 750.

Getting Around

One of the best ways to get around is by walking. Large three-wheelers shuttle between the bus stands and Gingy St for Rs 3, but they're so overcrowded you might not want to use them. Cycle and auto-rickshaws are plentiful. Although official fares for auto-rickshaws (Rs 6 for up to 2km) are posted near the main stands, you'll have to haggle hard to get something resembling these prices.

The most popular transport is bicycle – a good idea if you're going to Auroville. At the bike hire shops on MG Rd, Mission St and Subbayah Salai you may be asked for Rs 500 or your passport as a deposit. Details of your hotel (they may check proof of this) may forestall this request. Usual rental is Rs 3 per hour, or Rs 20 per day.

Mopeds can be rented from Vijay Arya (☎ 336179), 9 Aurobindo St, near the corner with Ambour Salai, for Rs 100 per day. You need to leave some ID (passport or driving licence) and a Rs 500 deposit.

TAMIL NADU

AUROVILLE
☎ 0413

Just over the border from Pondicherry in Tamil Nadu is the community of Auroville, whose international residents aim to develop a harmonious environment through the implementation of socially useful projects.

Auroville is the brainchild of The Mother, 'an experiment in international living where people could live in peace and progressive harmony above all creeds, politics and nationalities'. Designed by French architect Roger Anger, its opening ceremony on 28 February 1968 was attended by the president of India and representatives of 121 countries, who poured the soil of their lands into an urn to symbolise universal oneness.

The project has 80 settlements spread over 20km, and about 1200 residents (two-thirds of whom are foreigners). The settlements include: Forecomers, involved in alternative technology and agriculture; Certitude, working in sports; Aurelec, devoted to computer research; Discipline, an agricultural project; Fertile, Nine Palms and Meadow, all engaged in tree planting and agriculture; Fraternity, a handicrafts community working in cooperation with local Tamil villagers; and Aspiration, an educational, health care and village industry project.

To get a proper sense of the place you need to spend at least a few days here. Daytrippers and casual tourism are not encouraged, although visitors that do have a genuine interest will not be made unwelcome. As the Aurovillians put it: 'Auroville is very much an experiment that is in its early stages, and it is not at all meant to be a tourist attraction'.

Information
In Pondicherry, La Boutique d'Auroville (☎ 333855) has information on the community and it's worth dropping by here to organise accommodation before you head out. At Auroville itself, there is a visitor's centre (☎ 62239) near Bharat Nivas. This centre has a permanent exhibition of the community's activities and the helpful staff will address any queries. It's open daily 9.30 am to 5.30 pm. Next door is an Auroville handicrafts shop and a restaurant.

The monthly magazine, *Auroville Today*, available at the visitor's centre, has many articles that are refreshingly honest in their analysis and discourse. They certainly transcend the sort of public relations blurb common to so many ashrams. Extracts from particular issues are also available on the excellent Auroville Web site at www.auroville-india.org.

Matrimandir
The Matrimandir was designed to be the spiritual and physical centre of Auroville. Its construction has been very much a stop-start affair, due to erratic funding. However, the meditation chamber and the main structure are now finished with total completion expected early in the 21st century.

The meditation chamber is lined with white marble and houses a solid crystal (reputedly the largest in the world) 70cm in diameter and manufactured by the Zeiss company in Germany. Rays from the sun are beamed into this crystal from a tracking mirror located in the roof. On cloudy days, solar lamps do the job.

While the Matrimandir is undoubtedly a remarkable edifice and certainly the focal point of the community, many of the more pragmatic Aurovillians would have preferred the money spent on community infrastructure and on projects of a more tangible nature. Others claim that without any such physical manifestation of Auroville's (and, therefore, The Mother's) spiritual ideal, the community may have splintered long ago.

You can wander around the gardens between 9.30 am and 3.30 pm. Only between 3.30 and 4.30 pm are visitors allowed inside the Matrimandir, but you need to get a ticket (free) from the visitor centre, before 4 pm.

Places to Stay & Eat
Palms Beach Cottage Centre is at Chinna Mudaliarchavadi, on the way to Auroville

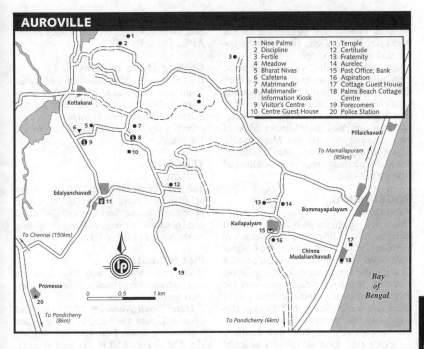

AUROVILLE

1 Nine Palms	11 Temple
2 Discipline	12 Certitude
3 Fertile	13 Fraternity
4 Meadow	14 Aurelec
5 Bharat Nivas	15 Post Office; Bank
6 Cafeteria	16 Aspiration
7 Matrimandir	17 Cottage Guest House
8 Matrimandir	18 Palms Beach Cottage
Information Kiosk	Centre
9 Visitor's Centre	19 Forecomers
10 Centre Guest House	20 Police Station

Kottakarai

Pillaichavadi

To Mamallapuram (85km)

Edaiyanchavadi

Bommayapalayam

Kuilapalyam

To Chennai (150km)

Chinna Mudaliarchavadi

Bay of Bengal

Promesse

0   0.5   1 km

To Pondicherry (8km)

To Pondicherry (6km)

from Pondy. Clean toilets and showers are shared, and there's an open-air gazebo for eating and relaxing in. Meals are around Rs 50. Singles/doubles cost Rs 90/160.

Cottage Guest House, a little further on, down the lane on the right opposite the turn-off to Auroville, offers basic singles/doubles in a thatched-roof, semi-concrete block for Rs 70/140 with shared bath. Doubles with bath in the new block are Rs 200. There's a communal dining area serving all meals.

People with a serious interest in the aims of Auroville can stay with virtually any one of the 40 community groups here; however, a stay – no shorter than a week and longer if possible – is preferred and although work isn't obligatory, it's very much appreciated. You come here, after all, to get involved in the purpose of Auroville. None of these community groups offer free accommodation in exchange for work. For most groups,

money is tight. Conditions, facilities and costs vary a great deal. Some places are quite primitive with minimal facilities; others have the lot. Prices range from Rs 100 to Rs 400, with some accommodation in the *Centre Guest House* (☎ 62155), very close to the Matrimandir. A list of accommodation places, complete with map and details, is available at the visitor's centre.

The only place in Auroville where casual visitors will find a meal – and it's a good one – is the brightly decorated cafeteria near the visitor's centre. It's open daily for lunch (Rs 30) and for dinner on Friday and Saturday. Savoury snacks, cakes, tea and coffee are also sold.

Getting There & Away

The best way to enter Auroville is from the coast road, at the village of Chinna Mudaliarchavadi. Ask around as it's not well signposted. It's also possible to enter from the main Pondicherry to Chennai road at Promesse. The turn-off, 1km after the police station, is signposted.

Once at Auroville, you'll need some form of transport as everything is very spread out. If you rent a bike or scooter in Pondicherry, you can count on cycling at least 30km there and back. It's mostly tarmac roads or good gravel tracks. Most of the community centres (eg Matrimandir, Bharat Nivas, etc) are signposted but the individual settlements tend to be hidden and difficult to locate.

HOGENAKKAL
☎ 043425

This quiet village, nestled in the forested Melagiri Hills, 170km south of Bangalore by road, is at the confluence of the Chinnar and Cauvery (Kaveri) rivers. From here the Cauvery develops into a series of impressive waterfalls that have recently provided the backdrop for some of Indian cinema's more tragic love scenes. Sadly, the falls have also at times attracted disconsolate real-life lovers who have actually jumped to their deaths.

Despite this, Hogenakkal is a peaceful respite and a popular day trip from Bangalore. It's most impressive in July/August, when the water is at its peak. Don't miss a ride in a coracle. These little round boats, known locally as *parisals*, are made from waterproof hides stretched over lightweight wicker frames. Another of Hogenakkal's treats is an oil massage – more than 100 masseurs ply their trade here.

Places to Stay & Eat
Private homes, near the police station (to the right just as you enter the village), have rooms to let. Stalls at the bus stand sell tasty fried fish.

Hotel Tamil Nadu (☎ 54447) has doubles for Rs 400, or Rs 600 with air-con, including tax, plus 30% on weekends. The large, airy rooms have monkey-proof balconies. Dorm beds (men only) in the attached youth hostel are Rs 70. There's a restaurant and food should be ordered a few hours in advance.

Tourist Resthouse and *Tourist Home* next to the bus stand both offer basic rooms for Rs 100 to Rs 150.

Getting There & Away
Hogenakkal straddles the border of Tamil Nadu and Karnataka. The nearest main town is Dharampuri, 45km east on the Salem-Bangalore road. From here, there are several daily buses to Hogenakkal (Rs 10, 1¼ hours).

YERCAUD
☎ 04281

This hill station (altitude 1500m) is 33km uphill from Salem. Surrounded by coffee plantations in the Servaroyan hills, it's a good place for relaxing, walking, or boating on the town's artificial lake.

Places to Stay
If you prefer solitude, stay away from the lake, which is continually blasted by raucous music.

Hotel Tamil Nadu (☎ 22273, Yercaud Ghat Rd), near the lake, is an OK place with double rooms from Rs 350 to Rs 500 (Rs 450 and Rs 650 in the high season). Dorm beds cost Rs 75. There's a restaurant and bar, but in spite of nearby coffee plantations, it's instant coffee here. There's a small playground for children as well as boating facilities.

Hotel Shevaroys (☎ 22288, fax 22387, Hospital Rd) has standard doubles/suites from Rs 475/675 in the low season and Rs 625/825 in the high season. It has two restaurants, offering Indian and Chinese food, and a bar. The hotel accepts credit cards and changes money.

Central Tamil Nadu

CHIDAMBARAM
☎ 04144

About 60km south of Pondicherry, Chidambaram's great temple complex of Nataraja, the dancing Shiva, is another Dravidian architectural highlight. Of the many festivals, the two largest are the 10-day car festivals which are celebrated in April/May and December/January. In February the Natyanjali Dance Festival attracts performers from all over the country.

The small town is developed around its temple with streets named after the cardinal points. This is an easy town for walking as most accommodation is close to the temple. The post offices are in North Car St and South Car St. They're open 10 am to 3 pm daily except Sunday. None of the banks provides foreign exchange.

The train and bus stands are close to town. The tourist office (☎ 22739) is at the TTDC Hotel Tamil Nadu, and is open 9 am to 5 pm Monday to Friday.

Nataraja Temple

Chidambaram was a Chola capital from 907 to 1310 and the Nataraja Temple was erected during the later time of the administration. The 22 hectare complex has four large gopurams with finely sculptured icons depicting Hindu myths facing each of the cardinal directions – the north and south ones tower 49m high. The temple is renowned for its prime examples of Chola artistry and has since been patronised by numerous dynasties.

The Nataraja Temple courtyard with its many shrines is open 4 am to noon and 4.30 to 9 pm daily. The daily puja (worship) is held about 5 pm. Although non-Hindus are not allowed into the inner sanctum, there are usually priests who will take you in for a fee. If you feel that way inclined, you may wish to support this magnificent building by way of donation, but don't be intimidated by priests who try to pressure you for big bucks.

Places to Stay

Most of the current accommodation is in lodges, which are well positioned away from the noise, with balconies and fine village views.

Railway retiring rooms are good value at Rs 70/100 for a double/triple with bath.

CHIDAMBARAM

To Cuddalore (50km), Pondicherry (71km) & Chennai (232km)

0   300   600 m
Approximate Scale

North Car Street
West Car Street
East Car Street
VOC Street
South Car Street
To Annamalai University (1.5km) & Pichavaram (15km)
Pillaiyar Koil Street

To Vaitheeswarankoil (25km) & Kumbakonam (69km)

Canal

Train Station

CHIDAMBARAM

PLACES TO STAY
4   Hotel Murugan
5   Hotel Akshaya; Aswini Restaurants
10 Star Lodge; Bakiya Lakshmi Restaurant
12 Shameer Lodge
13 Hotel Saradharam & Restaurant
16 TTDC Hotel Tamil Nadu; Tourist Office; Idli Shop

OTHER
1   Tillai Kali Amman Temple
2   North Car Street Post Office
3   Indian Overseas Bank
6   Nataraja Temple
7   Police Station
8   Bike Hire
9   State Bank of India
11 South Car Street Post Office
14 Bus Stand
15 Hospital

TAMIL NADU

Shiva's Cosmic Dance

Shiva in the form of Nataraja dances away evil and ignorance and is the human embodiment of apocalypse and creation. The circle of fire surrounding the dancer symbolises the eternal flux of the universe where nothing is permanent.

Creation is energised by the beat of the drum held in Shiva's upper right hand. His other right hand has the palm held out in a gesture of reassurance and protection.

Shiva's right foot tramples on a dwarf who symbolises ignorance, and his left hand pointing to his outstretched foot grants solace and balance.

The dance is a celebration of transcending the limitations of rigid thought and action. It is an invitation to broaden ideas and experience. As master of the cosmic dance, Shiva creates the master plan for life.

Book through the station master on platform one.

Star Lodge (☎ 22743, *South Car St*) has clean rooms for Rs 60/80 (four-bed rooms Rs 140) with bath. It's friendly and there's a good restaurant downstairs.

Shameer Lodge (☎ 22983, *Venugopal Pillai St*) is good value at Rs 60/90/120 for rooms with bath and clean sheets.

Hotel Murugan (☎ 20419, *West Car St*) is similar. You receive a hearty welcome and train and bus schedules are listed. Basic rooms with bath are Rs 60/120, and an air-con double is Rs 200. The dormitory (good value for a family) with five beds costs Rs 200.

TTDC Hotel Tamil Nadu (☎ 20056, *fax 20061, Railway Feeder Rd*) has basic rooms at Rs 140/200, or Rs 350 for a double with air-con, plus Rs 60 for Star TV. It has a multicuisine restaurant.

Hotel Akshaya (☎ 20192, *fax 22265, 17-18 East Car St*) has helpful staff, but it's not such good value for the standard that is offered. A double (no singles) is Rs 220, deluxe is Rs 350 and air-con is Rs 550 (including tax).

Hotel Saradharam (☎ 21337, *fax 22656, 19 VGP St*) is the best place in town. For Indians ordinary singles/doubles with fan and TV are Rs 300/450 and air-con rooms are Rs 500/575. For non-Indians it is 30% dearer.

Places to Eat

Bakiya Lakshmi Restaurant (formerly Babu Restaurant), on the ground floor of the Star Lodge, offers good vegetarian meals in south Indian style.

TTDC Hotel Tamil Nadu has veg and nonveg restaurants plus a very pleasant rooftop bar (beer is Rs 60).

Hotel Saradharam is an excellent place to eat; the veg and nonveg restaurants are inexpensive, service is good, there's a bar and the beer's really cold! You need to get there early for lunch or dinner as it's very popular.

The Idli Shop, next to the Hotel Tamil Nadu, serves idli-addicts from morning to evening.

The *Aswini* veg and nonveg restaurants at Hotel Akshaya offer good food and there's a multicuisine rooftop restaurant.

A Fortune Told, a Fortune Made

For millions of Indians, significant decisions about employment, home-buying or new relationships will not be made without astrological advice. Farmers sometimes consult astrologers over which crops to plant or which animals to purchase. Even everyday decisions, such as the most appropriate times to start work or leave home, can be astrologically determined. The few souls who claim to be nonbelievers may still avail themselves of the service. Astrological consultancy, they claim, gives them a broader perspective from which to consider and resolve problems. And it provides an intermediate phase for important transitions such as marriage.

There are several types of astrology and numerous variations in astrological practice. In South India, the astrologers of Vaitheeswarankoil, south of Chidambaram, engage in a practice called Nadi. These astrologers claim to be the custodians of ancient palm leaf manuscripts originally scribed by sages known as *rishis*. The rishis, 18 saints in all, professed to have divine powers that enabled them to record future events. Their language was Sanskrit and their material was palm leaf.

Centuries later, Tamil kings arranged for these rare manuscripts to be stored and translated into the Tamil language. During the British administration, the manuscripts were auctioned and bought by families living in the Vaitheeswarankoil area. Their descendants now study the manuscripts to deliver consultations. Their method is to obtain a thumbprint (right for a male, left for a female) of the person seeking information. The ancient palm leaves are then searched for a match with the thumbprint. Sometimes no match is found, and therefore no prediction made. However, if there is a match, and sometimes this is achieved only with intense questioning of the client, then the appropriate leaves will be located and read. The leaves are stored in bundles of 50 to 100. In some cases many bundles may be relevant to the client so the process may be ongoing for years, even a lifetime. All manner of advice and predictions are made, including matters relevant to education, family, marriage, residence, occupation, illness and longevity.

Knowledge of the palm leaves is passed on from father to son or from guru to disciple. Training can begin from the age of nine and can take many years. For Nadi practitioners, astrology is strictly a male domain. They claim women are prohibited from reading the leaves and assuming the profession because 'it is a sacred profession and women have natural aspects which prevent association with the sacred!'.

To believe or not to believe is a question faced by many who have considered seeking the services of the Nadi astrologers. They have a loyal and ever-growing number of satisfied clients. Others claim that these people invest more energy in making fortunes than in telling them. The fact remains that this is India, the astrologers are here, and your questions will be answered – in a manner of speaking.

Getting There & Away

The train station is a 20 minute walk southeast of the temple, or Rs 20 by cycle-rickshaw. Express and passenger trains leave for Chennai (six times daily), Kumbakonam, Thanjavur (twice daily), Tiruchirappalli and Madurai.

The bus stand, used by both SETC and local buses, is more central. Bus No 157 (seven per day) is the quickest bus to Chennai. Services for Pondicherry every half hour continue to Chennai (Nos 300, 324 and 326, Rs 38, seven hours). To Madurai take No 521 (Rs 55, eight hours).

Getting Around

There's a bike hire shop on South Car St (Rs 2 per hour). No deposit is required. Only bikes with bars are available.

AROUND CHIDAMBARAM

The seaside resort of **Pichavaram**, with its backwaters and mangroves, is 15km east of Chidambaram. Here you can navigate the 4000 canals and 1700 islands – with a guide so you don't get lost. The *TTDC Aringar Anna Tourist Complex* (☎ 04144-89232), on one of the small islands, charges Rs 50 for a dorm bed and Rs 150 for a two bedroom cottage.

About 25km south of Chidambaram, Vaitheeswarankoil is well known for its **Viadanatheeswarar Temple**, dedicated to Shiva and Parvati. People come to bathe in the tank waters in the belief that illnesses will be cured.

The town has another claim to fame – its **Nadi astrologers** who make predictions according to ancient palm leaf manuscripts (see the A Fortune Told, a Fortune Made boxed text). If you wish to see one avoid the touts, whose behaviour can be threatening.

There are two accommodation lodges: *Sri Abirami Lodge* (☎ 04364-79311, *Mayiladuthurai Rd*) and *Sri Bhakkiam Lodge* (☎ 04364-79460, *South Car St*). You can get to Vaitheeswarankoil by train from Chidambaram (Rs 2) or Thanjavur (Rs 13). Buses travel here from Bangalore, Tirupathi, Chennai and Tiruchirappalli and all points along the way.

KUMBAKONAM
☎ 0435

This busy, dusty commercial centre, nestled along the Cauvery river some 37km northeast of Thanjavur, is noted for its many temples with their colourful semi-erotic sculpture. According to legend, a *kumbh* (pitcher), that contained the 'seeds of creation' was brought here by flood waters. Shiva broke the pot, and its contents spilled and sprouted into linga all over the countryside. And this explains the large number of temples and shrines in the area.

Sarangapani Temple is the largest Vishnu temple in Kumbakonam, while **Kumbeshwara Temple** is the largest Shiva temple. **Nageshwara Temple**, also a Shiva temple, is dedicated to him in the guise of Nagaraja, the serpent king. Just 600m south-east of here is the palindromic **Mahamakham Tank**. The legend of the deluge, explained earlier, relates that much of the contents of the pitcher flowed into this tank. Current belief is that every 12 years, the waters of the Ganges flow into the tank and at this time a festival is held. The next festival will be in early 2004. All the temples are closed between noon and 4.30 pm.

Kumbakonam makes a good base from which to visit the very interesting nearby temples at Dharasuram and Gangakondacholapuram.

Places to Stay

New Diamond Lodge (☎ 30870, 93 Ayikulam Rd) has basic singles/doubles for Rs 50/75 with common bath, Rs 65/85 with private bath. It's fine but use your own padlock on the door. Rooms at the back have a great view over Nageshwara Temple.

Hotel Siva/VPR Lodge (☎ 21949, 104-105 TSR Big St) share the same reception. VPR Lodge offers excellent budget accommodation – Rs 75/100 for clean rooms. rooms. The Siva has huge, clean doubles with bath, and constant hot water for Rs 195, Rs 350 with air-con.

Pandiyan Hotel (☎ 30397, 52 Sarangapani East St) is popular and often full. All rooms have bath and cost Rs 65/110.

Femina Lodge (☎ 20369, 8 Post Office Rd) is a small place with excellent-value rooms: spotless doubles with bath are Rs 150, a room with four beds is Rs 250.

Hotel ARR (☎ 21234, 21 TSR Big St) is a large, friendly place with a bar. There are doubles for Rs 200 or Rs 450 with air-con.

Hotel Athitya (☎ 23262, Ayikulam Rd) has good rooms from Rs 300/325 to Rs 450/475 with air-con. There's a veg and nonveg restaurant.

Hotel Raya's (☎ 22545, 28-29 Head Post Office Rd), the swishest place in town, of-

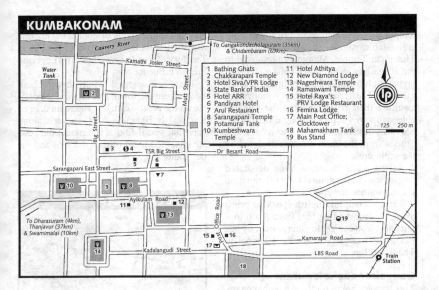

KUMBAKONAM

1 Bathing Ghats
2 Chakkarapani Temple
3 Hotel Siva/VPR Lodge
4 State Bank of India
5 Hotel ARR
6 Pandiyan Hotel
7 Arul Restaurant
8 Sarangapani Temple
9 Potamurai Tank
10 Kumbeshwara
   Temple
11 Hotel Athitya
12 New Diamond Lodge
13 Nageshwara Temple
14 Ramaswami Temple
15 Hotel Raya's;
   PRV Lodge Restaurant
16 Femina Lodge
17 Main Post Office;
   Clocktower
18 Mahamakham Tank
19 Bus Stand

fers well-furnished doubles/triples (no singles) from Rs 350/475, or Rs 450/600 with air-con. Room 101 (Rs 600) is the 'lovers' room' – with mirrors on every surface, including the ceiling above the bed.

Places to Eat
Arul Restaurant (Sarangapani East St), opposite Hotel Pandiyan, offers excellent vegetarian food with a range of thalis from Rs 10 to Rs 45 and an air-con dining hall which is upstairs.

PRV Lodge (Head Post Office Rd), next to Hotel Raya's and not to be confused with VPR Lodge, has good vegetarian food with meals from Rs 15, Rs 20 for specials. Breads are very good.

Hotel Raya's has a nonveg restaurant; main dishes are Rs 35 to Rs 45.

Getting There & Away
The bus stand and train station are about 2km east of the town centre.

SETC has four buses a day to Chennai (No 303, Rs 55, seven hours) and there are frequent departures to Thanjavur via Dha-

rasuram and to Gangakondacholapuram. Other buses pass through here on their way to Madurai, Coimbatore, Bangalore, Tiruvannamalai, Pondicherry and Chidambaram. Bus No 459 connects Kumbakonam with Karaikal.

Four daily express trains go to Chennai via Chidambaram, four go to Madurai and three to Thanjavur and Tiruchirappalli.

AROUND KUMBAKONAM
Not far from Kumbakonam are two Chola temples, Dharasuram and Gangakondacholapuram. Both have been restored by the Archaeological Survey of India. They have knowledgeable guides to show you around. Few visitors go to these temples, so you can appreciate their beauty in peace.

Dharasuram
The small town of Dharasuram is 4km west of Kumbakonam. Its **Airatesvara Temple**, built by Raja Raja II (1146-63), is a superb example of 12th century Chola architecture.

The temple is fronted by columns with unique miniature sculptures. In the 14th

TAMIL NADU

century, the row of large statues around the temple was replaced with brick and concrete statues similar to those found at the Thanjavur Temple. Many were removed to the art gallery in the raja's palace at Thanjavur, but have since been returned to Dharasuram. The remaining empty niches are awaiting their replacements. The remarkable sculptures depict, among other things, Shiva as Kankala-murti – the mendicant. Stories from the epics are also depicted by the sculptures.

At the main shrine, a huge decorated lingam stands, the natural light illuminating it from sunrise to sunset.

There's a helpful English-speaking priest available (for a small fee) from 8 am to 8 pm daily. You can get to Dharasuram by bus (Rs 2) or train (Rs 3) on the Chennai to Thanjavur line.

Gangakondacholapuram

This temple, 35km north of Kumbakonam, was built by the Chola emperor Rajendra I (1012-44) in the style of (and with the same name as) the Brihadishwara Temple at Thanjavur, built by his father. Later additions were made in the 15th century by the Nayaks. The ornate tower is almost 55m high and is said to weigh 80 tonnes. Opposite, to the east, a huge Nandi sits looking back towards the tower. Within the recesses of the temple walls stand many beautiful statues, including those of Ganesh, Nataraja and Harihara.

The temple has a knowledgeable guide and is open daily from 6 am to noon and 4 to 8 pm.

Next to the temple there's a small **museum** (closed Friday), which exhibits the excavated remains of the palace that once existed nearby.

There are buses from Kumbakonam bus stand to the temple (Rs 10).

KARAIKAL (Karikal)
☎ 04368

Karaikal is an important pilgrimage town with its Shiva **Darbaranyeswar Temple** and also the **Ammaiyar Temple**, dedicated to

Punithavathi, a Shaivite saint subsequently elevated to the status of goddess. This former French enclave, now part of the Union Territory of Pondicherry, has little lingering French influence.

There is a deserted, windy, **beach** about 1.5km from the town, and boating is possible on the nearby estuary. The main drag of Karaikal is Bharathiar Rd, and it's along here that you'll find accommodation, restaurants, the tourist office (☎ 2596) and the bus stand.

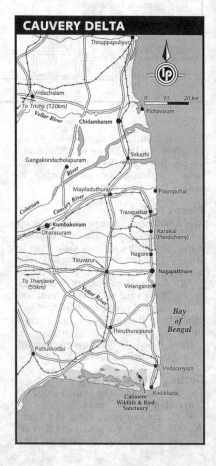

CAUVERY DELTA

AROUND KARAIKAL

Poompuhar
It was at Poompuhar, at the mouth of the Cauvery river, that the rulers of the Chola empire traded with Rome and other eastern centres. On the beach a monument provides a beautiful depiction of an ancient bathing scene. This place is popular with locals, but its black sands and rough surf make it unsuitable for swimming.

The *Department of Tourism Guesthouse* offers ordinary (very basic) rooms for Rs 25 and bizarre shell-shaped cottages (each with two beds) for Rs 50, or Rs 120 with air-con. There's also a restaurant. Book through the tourist office (☎ 04363-754439). You can get to Poompuhar by bus from Karaikal, or if you're approaching from the north, take a train to Sirkazhi, then continue by bus.

Tranquebar (Tharangambadi)
Fourteen kilometres north of Karaikal, Tranquebar was a Danish post, established in 1620. The **Danesborg Fort** was occupied by the British in 1801. Now it houses a small but fascinating museum (closed Friday) reflecting aspects of Danish history here.

Nagore (Nagur)
The village of Nagore, 12km south of Karaikal, has the *dargah* (tomb) of the revered Muslim saint, Hazat Mian (1491-1570), featuring beautiful domed arches and minarets. This pilgrimage centre is particularly important for Muslims but admits people of all faiths. Although most women are veiled this is not mandatory.

Velanganni (Vailankanni)
☎ 04365
Velanganni, near Nagapattinam, is the site of the Roman Catholic **Basilica of Our Lady of Good Health**. This impressive white neo-Gothic structure was elevated to the status of basilica in 1962 during the Pope's visit. The annual nine day festival culminates on 8 September.

Hotel Picnic (☎ 63510), on the main road near the basilica, offers basic but clean double rooms for Rs 140, or Rs 220 with air-con.

The Retreat (☎/fax 63534, 64 Nagapattinam Main Rd) is the best hotel with clean rooms and friendly service. High-season doubles are Rs 450, Rs 550 with air-con. Cottages are Rs 650, Rs 800 with air-con. Credit cards are not accepted.

CALIMERE WILDLIFE & BIRD SANCTUARY
☎ 614807
Also known as Kodikkarai, this 333 sq km sanctuary is 90km south-east of Thanjavur. It juts into the Palk Strait, which separates India and Sri Lanka by 28km. Noted for its vast flocks of migratory waterfowl, Calimere's tidal mud flats are home to teals, shovellers, curlews, gulls, terns, plovers, sandpipers, shanks and herons from November to January. In February/March, koels, mynas and barbets come here for the wild berries.

The easiest way to get to Calimere is by bus (Rs 3.50, every hour) or taxi from Vedaranyam, 12km away and the nearest town linked by frequent buses to Nagapattinam or Thanjavur.

The sanctuary is open daily, 6 am to 6 pm. Entry is Rs 5. There's a *Forest Department Resthouse* (☎ 72424) offering basic accommodation at only Rs 15 per person per night. Officially, reservations must be made with the Wildlife Warden in Nagapattinam (☎ 22349), but many travellers just turn up and get a room.

THANJAVUR (Tanjore)
☎ 04362 • pop 217,000
Thanjavur was the ancient capital of the Chola kings whose origins (like those of the Pallavas, Pandyas and Cheras with whom they shared the tip of the Indian peninsula) go back to the beginning of the Christian era. Power struggles between these groups were continual, with one or other gaining the ascendancy at various times. The Cholas' turn for empire building came between 850 and 1270 AD and, at the height of their power, they controlled most of the Indian peninsula, including parts of Sri Lanka and, for a while, the Srivijaya kingdom of the Malay Peninsula and Sumatra.

TAMIL NADU

Probably the greatest Chola emperors were Raja Raja (985-1014), who was responsible for building the Brihadishwara Temple (Thanjavur's main attraction), and his son Rajendra I (1014-44), whose navy competed with the Arabs for the Indian Ocean trade routes and who was responsible for bringing Srivijaya under Chola control. The Cholas also constructed the temples at Thiruvaiyaru, Gangakonda-cholapuram and Dharasuram and contributed to the enormous temple complex at

Srirangam near Tiruchirappalli – probably India's largest.

Thanjavur is famous also for its distinctive art style, which is usually a combination of raised and painted surfaces. Krishna is the most popular deity depicted, and in the Thanjavur school his skin is white, rather than the traditional blue-black.

Set on a fertile delta, agriculture is an important industry and makes Thanjavur a great place to be during Pongal (harvest) celebrations in January.

In 1995 Thanjavur hosted the World Tamil Congress. Many hotels received a face-lift and a price rise as a result.

Thanjavur's Distinctive Painting

Thanjavur is famous for its distinctive style of painting, known as Tanjore Painting. Opinions differ as to its origins, with Chola and later Vijayanagar times being cited. However, it was probably Serfoji, the 19th century Maharaja of Thanjavur, who developed the art. The paintings, which depict Vaisnavaite and Shaivite deities, are characterised by a slight relief, constructed from plaster, to emphasise aspects of the image. The positioning of glass, gold leaf and jewels adds a further dimension.

The process of painting is long and arduous. Having secured plywood or strong card, the artist covers it with cloth, using a thick paste. The cloth is then overlaid with a glue and powder solution. The picture is drawn onto the cloth and paint is applied, beginning with the larger sections, such as the sky. Then follows the decorative procedure, enabling artists to give full expression to their creativity. The final process is a light varnish.

The art almost died out, except for a few families in the Thanjavur district, who continued the work of their forbears. Modern materials have enabled contemporary artists to achieve similar results to their earlier colleagues in far less time. As such the art form has witnessed renewed interest from both artists and patrons, and now has an international profile.

Orientation

The Brihadishwara Temple is between the Grand Anicut Canal and the old town.

Gandhiji Rd, which runs north-south between the train station and the bus stations at the edge of the old town, has most of the hotels and restaurants, as well as the Poompuhar Arts & Crafts Emporium.

Information

The tourist office (☎ 23017), in Jawans Bhavan opposite the main post office, is open 10 am to 5.45 pm. There's also a counter at the TTDC Hotel Tamil Nadu. There's a small Government of India tourist office on Gandhiji Rd.

The Canara Bank on South Main Rd changes travellers cheques and the main post office, near the train station, is open daily, 10 am to 4 pm (Sunday from noon). The telegraph office next door is open 24 hours.

Brihadishwara Temple & Fort

Built by Raja Raja in 1010, the Brihadishwara Temple is the crowning glory of Chola temple architecture. This superb and fascinating monument is one of only a handful in India with World Heritage listing and is worth a couple of visits.

Constructed from a single piece of granite weighing an estimated 80 tonnes, the dome was hauled into place along a 4km earthwork ramp in a manner similar to that used for the Egyptian pyramids.

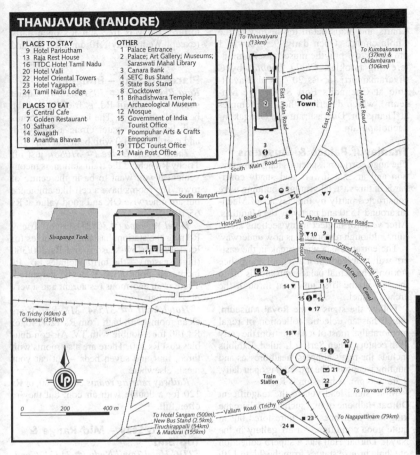

THANJAVUR (TANJORE)

PLACES TO STAY
9 Hotel Parisutham
13 Raja Rest House
16 TTDC Hotel Tamil Nadu
20 Hotel Valli
22 Hotel Oriental Towers
23 Hotel Yagappa
24 Tamil Nadu Lodge

PLACES TO EAT
6 Central Cafe
7 Golden Restaurant
10 Sathars
14 Swagath
18 Anantha Bhavan

OTHER
1 Palace Entrance
2 Palace; Art Gallery; Museums; Saraswati Mahal Library
3 Canara Bank
4 SETC Bus Stand
5 State Bus Stand
8 Clocktower
11 Brihadishwara Temple; Archaeological Museum
12 Mosque
15 Government of India Tourist Office
17 Poompuhar Arts & Crafts Emporium
19 TTDC Tourist Office
21 Main Post Office

The temple, set in spacious grounds, has several pillared halls and shrines and 250 linga are enshrined along the outer walls. Inscriptions record the names of dancers, musicians and poets – a reminder of the significance of this area to the development of the arts. A huge Nandi, 6m long by 3m high, faces the inner sanctum. Created from a single piece of rock, it weighs 25 tonnes and is one of India's largest Nandi statues.

Unlike most south Indian temples where the gopurams are the highest towers, here it is the 13 storey tower above the sanctum at 66m that reaches further into the sky. Its impressive gilded top is the original. The sanctum contains a 4m-high lingam with a circumference of 7m.

The temple now comes under the jurisdiction of the Archaeological Survey but worship here has recommenced. It's open daily, 6 am to 1 pm and 3 to 8 pm.

The **Archaeological Museum**, on the southern side of the courtyard, has some interesting sculptures and photographs that show the temple before restoration. Charts and maps detail the history of the Chola empire. Open daily, 9.30 am to 1 pm and 3 to 7 pm, the museum sells an interesting booklet, *Chola Temples* by C Sivaramamurti for Rs 20 (it's also available at Chennai's Fort St George Museum), which describes the three temples at Thanjavur, Dharasuram and Gangakondacholapuram.

Thanjavur Palace & Museums

The huge corridors, spacious halls, observation and arsenal towers and shady courtyards of this vast, labyrinthine building were constructed partly by the Nayaks of Madurai around 1550 and partly by the Marathas. After years of neglect many sections are in ruins, although restoration is now underway.

The entrance is a wide break in the eastern wall that leads past a school and police station. The actual palace entrance is off to the left at the first junction, through the arched tunnel.

Follow the signs to the **Royal Museum**, which has an eclectic collection of regal memorabilia, most of it dating from the early 19th century when Serfoji II ruled. Exhibits include the raja's slippers, head-dresses and hunting weapons. The museum is open daily, 9 am to 6 pm. Admission is Rs 1.

More signs lead you to the magnificent **Durbar Hall**, one of two such halls where the king held audiences. It's unrestored but in quite good condition. An **art gallery** in the Nayak Durbar Hall has a superb collection of Chola bronze statues from the 9th to 12th centuries. The gallery is open 9 am to 1 pm and 3 to 6 pm. Entry costs Rs 3. Nearby, the **Bell Tower**, reopened after some particularly unsympathetic restoration, is worth the climb (Rs 2) for the views.

The **Saraswati Mahal Library** is next to the gallery. Established around 1700, its collection includes over 30,000 palm leaf and paper manuscripts in Indian and European languages. The library is closed to the public but you can visit the interesting **museum**, where exhibits range from the whole *Ramayana* written on palm leaf to

explicit prints of prisoners under Chinese torture. Entry is free and it's open daily (except Wednesday), 10 am to 1 pm and 1.30 to 5.30 pm.

Places to Stay – Budget

Raja Rest House (☎ 30515), down a quiet street off Gandhiji Rd, is friendly and the best value in town. The large, basic rooms with bucket hot water circle a courtyard, and cost Rs 60/100 with bath and fan.

Tamil Nadu Lodge (☎ 31088), just off Trichy Rd behind the train station, is inconvenient if you want to be in the centre of town. The rooms have a cell-like ambience but are otherwise OK and good value at Rs 65/100.

Hotel Yagappa (☎ 30421), just off Trichy Rd near the station, has singles/doubles for Rs 150/195 (low season) and Rs 200/360 (high season) – the tariff includes tax. Its increased popularity is well warranted. There is an enormous restaurant and a very pleasant bar.

Hotel Valli (☎ 31584, MK Rd) offers clean rooms with bath from Rs 120/140, or Rs 180 for a double with TV. Air-con doubles cost Rs 320. There are also rooms with three, four and seven beds – but eat your meals elsewhere.

Railway retiring rooms cost Rs 60, or Rs 120 for a double with air-con, but they're often full.

Places to Stay – Mid-Range & Top End

TTDC Hotel Tamil Nadu (☎ 31421, Gandhiji Rd), with its quiet leafy courtyard, and helpful staff, is a good place. Rooms in this former raja's guesthouse are spacious and clean with constant hot water in the bathrooms. Doubles cost Rs 350, and Rs 500 with air-con. TV hire (for ordinary rooms) is Rs 50. There's a restaurant and a bar with cold beer.

Hotel Parisutham (☎ 31801, fax 30318, 55 Grand Anicut Canal Rd) is the most pleasant place to stay. It has a pool, manicured lawns, two restaurants and a bar. Unfortunately a number of the balconies have been enclosed to enlarge the rooms. Rooms cost US$46/86 (including breakfast).

Hotel Sangam (☎ *25151, fax 24895*) is a large, flashy hotel on Trichy Rd. Immaculate rooms (with bathtubs and showers) cost US$45/88. There's a pool, a hall for dancing, and a multicuisine restaurant.

Hotel Oriental Towers (☎ *30724, fax 30770, 2889 Srinivasam Pillai Rd*) has single/double central air-con rooms for US$37/47. It's a modern hotel that pays homage to an older style. It also has a handy supermarket.

Places to Eat

For self-caterers there's a supermarket in the Hotel Oriental Towers.

There are numerous vegetarian restaurants near the bus stand and on Gandhiji Rd.

Anantha Bhavan (*Gandhiji Rd*) is recommended for its good veg cuisine.

Central Cafe (*corner of Hospital & Gandhiji Rds*) is good for snacks, but closes at 4 pm.

Golden Restaurant (*Hospital Rd*) does good vegetarian meals for Rs 20.

Sathars (*Gandhiji Rd*) is a good veg (from Rs 20) and nonveg (from Rs 40) restaurant with great service and an extensive range of dishes. It's open until midnight.

Swagath (*Gandhiji Rd*), near the roundabout, does nonveg food that's good value; thalis are Rs 15.

Hotel Yagappa has a large restaurant with reasonable food including ginger chicken for Rs 45. The bar is very pleasant; beers are Rs 55.

Hotel Sangam offers a wide selection in its multicuisine restaurant, sometimes with classical music.

There are two restaurants at Hotel Parisutham. The nonveg *Les Repas* serves Indian and Chinese dishes (around Rs 60), and the *Geetham* offers vegetarian food but apparently the food is now middle-of-the-road having been adjusted to suit western tastes. The bar is a popular place for a late evening beer accompanied by complimentary peanuts.

Shopping

A stroll along Gandhiji Rd is a pleasant way to shop. Numerous places (including the ubiquitous Kashmiri emporiums) sell everything from quality crafts and ready-made clothes to inexpensive kitsch. For fixed prices and hassle free shopping, Poompuhar is the best bet.

Getting There & Away

Bus The SETC bus stand has a computerised reservation office open 7.30 am to 9.30 pm. There are 24 buses a day to Chennai, the fastest and most expensive being the No 323FP Bye-Pass Rider (Rs 80, 7½ hours). Other buses that can be booked here include No 851 to Tirupathi (Rs 90, daily), No 725 to Ooty (Rs 70) and No 928 to Pondicherry (daily at midnight, 177km). Numerous buses pass through on their way to Tiruchirappalli (Rs 12, 1½ hours) and Madurai.

Most state buses now use the new bus stand, 2.5km south of the centre, although those for Tiruchirappalli (Rs 9.50, 54km, 1½ hours) and Kumbakonam (37km, one hour) still stop at the old state bus stand near the SETC bus stand. Departures for both run every 15 minutes.

Train To Chennai (351km), the overnight *Rameswaram Express* takes nine hours and costs Rs 118/410 in 2nd/1st class. For the same prices, the *Cholan Express* travels by day. To Villupuram (for Pondicherry), the 192km trip takes six hours and costs Rs 53/258. To Tiruchirappalli (50km, one hour) the fare is Rs 22/122. It's one hour to Kumbakonam, and 2½ hours to Chidambaram.

AROUND THANJAVUR

Thirteen kilometres north of Thanjavur, Thiruvaiyaru hosts the January international **music festival** in honour of the saint and composer, Thyagaraja. The saint's birthplace is at **Tiruvarur**, 55km from Thanjavur. The Thyagararajaswami Temple here boasts the largest temple chariot in Tamil Nadu. With the deities inside it, the chariot is hauled through the streets during the 10 day car festival in April/May.

TIRUCHIRAPPALLI
(Trichy, Tiruchy)
☎ 0431 • pop 770,800

Trichy's long history goes back to before the Christian era when it was a Chola citadel. During the 1st millennium AD, both the Pallavas and Pandyas took power many times before the Cholas regained control in the 10th century. When the Chola empire finally decayed, Trichy came into the realm of the Vijayanagar emperors of Hampi until their defeat in 1565 AD by the forces of the Deccan sultans.

The town and its most famous landmark, the Rock Fort Temple, were built by the Nayaks of Madurai. Later in the 18th century Trichy witnessed much of the British-French struggle for supremacy in India.

Maybe it's the monuments; maybe it's the good range of hotels and the excellent local bus system; somehow Trichy has a different ambience about it.

Orientation
Trichy is scattered over a considerable area. Most of the hotels and restaurants, the bus stand, train station, tourist office and main post office are within a few minutes walk of each other in the junction (or cantonment) area. The Rock Fort Temple is 2.5km north of here, near the Cauvery River. The other temples are 5km to 7km farther north.

Information
The tourist office (☎ 460136), 1 Williams Rd, with branch offices at the station and airport, is open Monday to Friday only. It has a free leaflet but little else. The main post office on Dindigul Rd (State Bank Rd) is open Monday to Saturday 8 am to 7 pm. Money can be changed at the State Bank of India in Dindigul Rd.

Rock Fort Temple
The spectacular Rock Fort Temple is perched 83m high on a massive rocky outcrop. This smooth rock was first hewn by the Pallavas who cut small cave temples into the southern face, but it was the Nayaks who made use of its naturally fortified po-

sition. There are two main temples: **Sri Thayumanaswamy Temple**, dedicated to Shiva, halfway to the top, and one at the summit dedicated to Vinayaka (Ganesh).

It's a stiff climb to the top up the 437 stone-cut steps but well worth it.

Non-Hindus are not allowed into either temple but occasionally (for a small fee) temple priests waive this regulation. Open daily, 6 am until 8 pm, entry is Rs 1.

Sri Ranganathaswamy Temple (Srirangam)
The superb temple complex at Srirangam, about 3km north of the Rock Fort, is dedicated to Vishnu.

Although mentioned in *sangam* poetry by the early academy of Tamil poets (see under Madurai for more information on this academy), temple inscriptions date its existence from the 10th century. In the 12th century the philosopher, Ramanuja, became head of the temple school and his effective administrative practices continued until the 14th century Muslim invasion. With the Vijayanagar victory the temple was restored to the structure that exists today. Many dynasties have had a hand in its construction, including the Cheras, Pandyas, Cholas, Hoysalas, Vijayanagars and Nayaks – and work continues. The largest gopuram, the main entrance, was completed in 1987, and now measures an astounding 73m.

At 60 hectares, the Srirangam complex with its seven concentric walled sections and 21 gopurams is probably the largest in India. Non-Hindus may go to the sixth wall but are not allowed into the gold-topped sanctum.

Bazaars and Brahmins' houses fill the space between the outer four walls. You can buy the Rs 2 ticket to climb the wall for a panoramic view of the entire complex. It's worth engaging a guide (Rs 350 – somewhat negotiable!) as there is much to see.

A **Car Festival** is held here each January but the most important festival is the 21 day **Vaikunta Ekadasi** (Paradise Festival) in mid-December, when the celebrated Vaish-

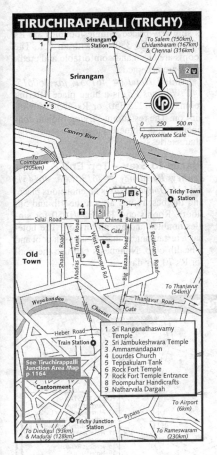

TIRUCHIRAPPALLI (TRICHY)

1 Srirangam Station

To Salem (150km), Chidambaram (167km) & Chennai (316km)

Srirangam

2 ♨

Cauvery River

0 250 500 m
Approximate Scale

To Coimbatore (205km)

Trichy Town Station

3

4 🏠
5
Chinna Bazaar
6 ♨
7

Salai Road

Old Town

Shastri Road
Madras Trunk Road
West Boulevard Rd
Big Bazaar Road
Le Boulevard Road

Gate

8
9

To Thanjavur (54km)

Woyakondan
Channel
Thanjavur Road
Gate

Heber Road
Train Station

See Tiruchirappalli Junction Area Map p 1164

Cantonment

Bypass

Trichy Junction Station

To Dindigul (93km) & Madurai (128km)

To Airport (6km)

To Rameswaram (230km)

1 Sri Ranganathaswamy Temple
2 Sri Jambukeshwara Temple
3 Ammamandapam
4 Lourdes Church
5 Teppakulam Tank
6 Rock Fort Temple
7 Rock Fort Temple Entrance
8 Poompuhar Handicrafts
9 Natharvala Dargah

five temples honouring the elements – in this case, water – the temple is built around a partly immersed Shiva lingam. Non-Hindus may not enter the sanctum, but the rule may be waived. A helpful guide will show you around. The temple is open daily, 6 am to 12.30 pm and 4 to 8.30 pm.

Churches

Completed in 1896, the **Lourdes Church** is modelled on the neo-Gothic Basilica in France. It was renovated in January 1998. An annual procession, the Feast of Our Lady of Lourdes, is held on 11 February for people of all faiths. Built in 1812, **St John's Church** has louvered side doors that open to turn the church into an airy pavilion. Rouse the doorkeeper to let you in. The surrounding cemetery reveals many stories.

Natharvala Dargah

This tomb of the popular Muslim saint, Nath-her, is an impressive building with a 20m-high dome with pinnacles. It's an important pilgrimage site for people of all faiths.

Places to Stay

Accommodation in Trichy is abundant and easy to find but places near the bus stand are noisy.

Places to Stay – Budget

Railway retiring rooms at Trichy Junction have dormitory beds for Rs 30 and double rooms without/with air-con for Rs 100/150.

Hotel Aristo (☎ 461818, 2 Dindigul Rd) is friendly, with a quiet leafy garden and a laid-back atmosphere. It's still popular with visitors, but gets mixed reports on cleanliness. Singles/doubles with bath cost Rs 100/150, quads are Rs 250, and air-con double cottages are Rs 350.

Hotel Arun (☎ 461421, 24 Dindigul Rd) is a good place set back from the road. Singles/doubles with bath are Rs 130/175; air-con rooms are Rs 250/350. A thali in the restaurant costs Rs 11.

Ashby Hotel (☎ 460652, 17A Junction Rd) has crumbling, old-world atmosphere

navaite text, *Tiruvaimozhi*, is recited before an image of Vishnu.

There's a small **museum** containing sculptures, bronze figures and plaques. The area within the fourth wall is closed daily 10 pm to 6 am.

Sri Jambukeshwara Temple

The nearby Sri Jambukeshwara Temple, dedicated to Shiva and Parvati, was built around the same time as the Sri Ranganathaswamy Temple. Being one of the though it's being renovated. The spacious rooms with bath are overpriced at Rs 150/270, or Rs 350/570 with air-con. There's a bar and an outdoor restaurant.

Hotel Ajanta (☎ *460501, Junction Rd*) has good at Rs 165/210, or Rs 350/450 with air-con. All have bathrooms and there's a good veg restaurant.

Hotel Aanand (☎ *460545, 1 Racquet Court Lane*) is one of the most attractive of the cheaper places. Rooms with bath cost Rs 200/230, or Rs 430 for a double with air-con. There's a good open-air restaurant.

Places to Stay – Mid-Range
Hotel Tamil Nadu (☎ *460383, McDonald's Rd*) offers reasonable rooms with air-con for Rs 310/410.

Hotel Mega (☎ *463092, 8 Rockins Rd*) has good doubles for Rs 170, or Rs 325/375 for a single/double with air-con.

Hotel Mathura (☎ *463737, Rockins Rd*) is similarly priced. Singles/doubles are Rs 150/195, or Rs 350/420 with air-con. The rooms are clean and comfortable and credit cards are accepted.

Femina Hotel (☎ *461551, fax 460615, 14C Williams Rd*) is a huge place offering rooms at Rs 225/350, or Rs 475/700 with air-con. The restaurant serving Indian, continental and Chinese cuisine is somewhat characterless.

Places to Stay – Top End
Jenneys Residency (☎ *461301, fax 461451, 3/14 McDonald's Rd*) is an enormous place, and the best rooms are on the 4th and 5th floors. Rooms cost Rs 1350/1650 for singles/doubles and are all air-con. The hotel has a restaurant, upmarket shops, a pool and a health club. Nonguests can use the pool for Rs 70 per day.

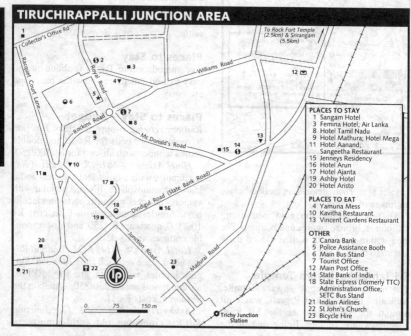

TIRUCHIRAPPALLI JUNCTION AREA

To Rock Fort Temple (2.5km) & Srirangam (5.5km)

PLACES TO STAY
1 Sangam Hotel
3 Femina Hotel; Air Lanka
8 Hotel Tamil Nadu
9 Hotel Mathura; Hotel Mega
11 Hotel Aanand; Sangeetha Restaurant
15 Jenneys Residency
16 Hotel Arun
17 Hotel Ajanta
19 Ashby Hotel
20 Hotel Aristo

PLACES TO EAT
4 Yamuna Mess
10 Kavitha Restaurant
13 Vincent Gardens Restaurant

OTHER
2 Canara Bank
5 Police Assistance Booth
6 Main Bus Stand
7 Tourist Office
12 Main Post Office
14 State Bank of India
18 State Express (formerly TTC) Administration Office; SETC Bus Stand
21 Indian Airlines
22 St John's Church
23 Bicycle Hire

0   75   150 m

Trichy Junction Station

Sangam Hotel (☎ *464700, Collector's Office Rd*) has all the facilities of a four star hotel. Rooms are US$45/88 but its restaurant is disappointing.

Places to Eat

Many of the hotels have restaurants providing a variety of good foods.

Yamuna Mess, an open-air 'diner' on a gravel parking lot behind the Guru Hotel, is a great place for cheap eats. In the evenings only it serves a limited number of veg or nonveg dishes. There's mellow music and friendly service.

Sangeetha Restaurant (*1 Racquet Court Lane*), at the Hotel Aanand, is also a good place for dinner. In the open-air restaurant most dishes, including chilli *gobi fry* (cauliflower fried with spices) are Rs 15.

Vincent Gardens Restaurant (*Dindigul Rd*) is a plush place with a multicuisine menu. It has a large, pleasant garden setting.

Kavitha Restaurant with excellent, elaborate thalis for Rs 15, has an air-con room.

The Peaks of Kunlun at Jenneys Residency gets mixed reports. It has a multicuisine menu and beer is Rs 70.

Shopping

Trichy has many craft shops. Poompuhar Handicrafts is on West Boulevard Rd and Heritage Arts Emporium at 5 Amma Mandapam Rd, Srirangam, is popular especially for quality bronzes.

Getting There & Away

Air The Indian Airlines office (☎ 462233), 4A Dindigul Rd, has daily flights (except Sunday) to Chennai for US$70. Air Lanka (☎ 460844), at the Femina Hotel, flies to Colombo on Wednesday, Thursday and Saturday.

Bus The SETC buses use the main bus stand, although a few buses still leave from the former TTC office on Junction Rd. Services to most places are frequent and tickets are sold by the conductor as soon as the bus arrives. Services include Thanjavur (Rs 12, 54km, 1½ hours, every 15 minutes) and

Madurai (Rs 28, 128km, four hours, every 10 minutes).

Other SETC buses can be computer-booked in advance. For Chennai the fastest bus is the Bye-Pass Rider (Rs 75, 7½ hours). Other destinations include: Bangalore (Rs 90, 10 daily), Coimbatore (Rs 38, every 30 minutes) and Tirupathi via Vellore (Rs 68, 9½ hours, two daily).

Private companies such as Jenny Travels, opposite the Hotel Tamil Nadu, or KPN Travels, below the Hotel Mathura, have super deluxe day/night services to Chennai for Rs 110/120 and Bangalore for Rs 130/150.

Train Trichy is on the main Chennai to Madurai and Chennai to Rameswaram lines. Some trains run directly to/from Chennai while others go via Chidambaram and Thanjavur. The quickest trains to Chennai (337km, 5¼ hours) are the *Vaigai Express* and the *Pallavan Express*, which cost Rs 115/398 in 2nd/1st class. The fastest service to Madurai (155km) is also on the *Vaigai Express*, which leaves at 11.56 am and 5.45 pm, takes 2¼ hours and costs Rs 46/223 in 2nd/1st class. The trip to Rameswaram (265km, seven hours) costs Rs 67/332 in 2nd/1st class.

For Mamallapuram, take a Chennai train as far as Chengalpattu and a bus from there.

Getting Around

To/From the Airport The ride into town is Rs 180 by taxi, Rs 80 by auto-rickshaw.

Bus Trichy's local bus service is excellent. Take a No 7, 59, 58 or 63 bus to the airport (7km, 30 minutes). The No 1 (A or B) bus from the SETC bus stand plies frequently between the train station, main post office, the Rock Fort Temple, the main entrance to Sri Ranganathaswamy Temple and close to Sri Jambukeshwara Temple.

Bicycle The town lends itself to cycling as it's dead flat. There are a couple of places on Junction Rd where you can hire bicycles for Rs 2 per hour. Note that the incredibly busy Big Bazaar Rd is a one-way road (heading north).

AROUND TIRUCHIRAPPALLI
Shantivanam Ashram

The Shantivanam (Forest of Peace) Ashram (☎ 04323-3060), at Thannirpalli, 35km west of Trichy, was established in keeping with the ideas of Father Bede Griffiths, who developed concepts around the merging of eastern and western philosophies. Dormitory (and some private) accommodation is available. It's best to write first to Shantivanam Ashram, Thannirpalli, PO Kulithalai, 639107.

Southern Tamil Nadu

MADURAI

☎ 0452 • pop 1.23 million

Madurai is an animated city packed with pilgrims, beggars, businesspeople, bullock carts and underemployed rickshaw drivers. It's one of South India's oldest cities, and has been a centre of learning and pilgrimage for centuries.

Madurai's main attraction is the famous Sri Meenakshi Temple in the heart of the old town, a riotously baroque example of Dravidian architecture with gopurams covered from top to bottom in a breathtaking profusion of multicoloured images of gods, goddesses, animals and mythical figures. The temple seethes with activity from dawn till dusk, its many shrines attracting pilgrims and tourists from all over the world. It's estimated that 10,000 visitors may come here on any one day!

Madurai resembles a huge, continuous bazaar crammed with shops, street markets, pilgrims' *choultries* (lodgings), hotels, restaurants and small industries. Although one of the liveliest cities in the south, it's small enough not to be overwhelming and is very popular with travellers.

History

Madurai is an ancient city. Tamil and Greek documents record its existence from the 4th century BC. The city was known to the Greeks via Megasthenes, their ambassador to the court of Chandragupta Maurya. It was popular for trade, especially in spices. It was also the site of the *sangam* – the academy of Tamil poets, whose poems celebrate Madurai's many attributes.

In the 10th century AD, Madurai was taken by the Chola emperors. It remained in their hands until the Pandyas briefly regained their independence in the 12th century, only to lose it again in 1310 to Muslim invaders under Malik Kafur, in the service of the Delhi Sultanate. Here, Malik Kafur established his own dynasty until 1364 when it was overthrown by the Hindu Vijayanagar kings of Hampi. After the fall of the Vijayanagars in 1565, the Nayaks ruled Madurai until 1781. During the reign of Tirumalai Nayak (1623-55), the bulk of the Meenakshi Temple was built, and Madurai became the cultural centre of the Tamil people, playing an important role in the development of the Tamil language.

Madurai then passed into the hands of the British East India Company. In 1840 the company razed the fort, which had previously surrounded the city, and filled in the moat. Four broad streets – the Veli streets – were constructed on top of this fill and to this day define the limits of the old city.

Orientation

Most places, including the main post office, tourist office, mid-range and budget hotels, restaurants, and some transport services, are near the temple.

Information

Tourist Offices The Madurai tourist office (☎ 734757), 180 West Veli St, is open Monday to Friday, 10 am to 5.45 pm. The staff are helpful and have brochures and maps for Rs 11. Tourist counters are also at the train station (☎ 742888) and airport.

For tourist complaints, the Foreigners' Reporting Office (☎ 744007) is at the Southern Tower, Sri Meenakshi Temple.

To cash travellers cheques go to the State Bank of India on West Veli St.

MADURAI

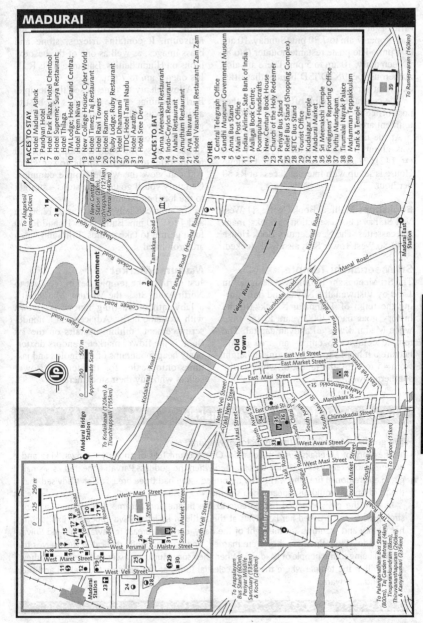

PLACES TO STAY
1 Hotel Madurai Ashok
2 Pandyan Hotel
7 Hotel Park Plaza; Hotel Chentool
8 Hotel Supreme; Surya Restaurant;
   Hotel Thilaga
10 TM Lodge; Hotel Grand Central;
   Hotel Prem Nivas
13 New College House; Cyber World
15 Hotel Times; Taj Restaurant
16 Hotel Ravi Towers
20 Hotel Ramson
22 Ruby Lodge; Ruby Restaurant
27 Hotel Dhanamani
30 TTDC Hotel Tamil Nadu
31 Hotel Aarathy
33 Hotel Sree Devi

PLACES TO EAT
9 Anna Meenakshi Restaurant
14 Indo-Ceylon Restaurant
17 Mahal Restaurant
18 Amutham Restaurant
21 Arya Bhavan
26 Hotel Vasanthani Restaurant; Zam Zam

OTHER
3 Central Telegraph Office
4 Gandhi Museum; Government Museum
5 Anna Bus Stand
6 Main Post Office
11 Indian Airlines; Sate Bank of India
12 Malligai Book Centre;
   Poompuhar Handicrafts
19 New Century Book House
23 Church of the Holy Redeemer
24 Periyar Bus Stand
25 Relief Bus Stand (Shopping Complex)
28 SETC Bus Stand
29 Tourist Office
32 Kudalagar Temple
34 Madurai Market
35 Sri Meenakshi Temple
36 Foreigners' Reporting Office
37 Puthu Mandapam
38 Tirumalai Nayak Palace
39 Mariamman Teppakkulam
   Tank & Temple

TAMIL NADU

Post & Communications The main post office is at the northern end of West Veli St and is open 7 am to 7.30 pm (Sunday, 10 am to 5 pm). The poste restante counter (No 8) is open daily, 10 am to 5 pm. There are also numerous local/STD/ISD booths that offer excellent service.

The central telegraph office and another post office are across the river in the Cantonment area.

At the time of writing the digital boom was about to hit Madurai. Cyber World (☎ 742162) on the 2nd floor of College House is set up with Internet access at Rs 60 per hour.

Bookshops Malligai Book Centre, 11 West Veli St, has a good selection of books, maps and cassettes. The New Century Book House at 79-80 West Tower St is also well stocked.

Sri Meenakshi Temple

The Sri Meenakshi Temple was designed in 1560 by Vishwanatha Nayak and built during the reign of Tirumalai Nayak. But its history goes back 2000 years to the time when Madurai was a Pandyan capital. The temple complex occupies an area of six hectares. It has 12 towers, ranging in height from 45 to 50m, the tallest of which is the southern tower.

Also within the temple complex, housed in the 1000 pillared hall, is the **Temple Art Museum**. It contains friezes, stone and brass images, as well as one of the best exhibits on Hindu deities. Entrance costs Rs 1. It's open 7 am to 7 pm.

Allow plenty of time to see this temple. Early mornings or late evenings are best to avoid crowds. 'Temple guides' charge negotiable fees rarely below Rs 200. They're usually a front for emporiums and tailor shops. Unless you want to shop, don't fall for the offer to take you up the tower where you can view the whole temple complex. Certainly you'll go up some steps – straight to the local emporium!

The temple usually opens 5 am to 12.30 pm and 4 to 9.30 pm. Entry is Rs 10 and Rs 30 for a permit to take photos. Film and video are prohibited.

Madurai Market

Just north of the temple, before you get to North Avani St, is the Madurai Market. It's a labyrinth of bustling laneways strewn with aromatic herbs. Adjacent, in a nondescript cement building upstairs on the 1st floor, is the flower market. Vendors dexterously heap mountains of marigolds and jasmine onto scales for the temple flower sellers who buy their stock here.

The Abode of the Goddess Meenakshi

The goddess Meenakshi is the protector of Madurai.

The story of Meenakshi is a major epic. One account tells of an early Pandyan king and queen, whose request for a child was granted when the goddess Parvati appeared as a small girl in a ceremonial fire. She was partly deformed – she had three breasts. Shiva advised that the third breast would disappear when she met her husband.

In time the girl succeeded her parents to the throne and became a celebrated military strategist. As she crushed her last rivals at the battle of Kailash, Shiva appeared. Exultant in her victory and wondrous at the sight of the deity, her third breast fell away. She and Shiva returned to Madurai, where they were married. They subsequently dedicated themselves to the wellbeing of the people of Madurai. When their son, Murugan, ascended the throne, they went within the temple where they took celestial forms as the goddess Meenakshi and the god Sundareshwara.

Tirumalai Nayak Palace

About 1.5km from the Meenakshi Temple, this Indo-Saracenic palace was built in 1636 by the ruler whose name it bears. Today, only the entrance gate, main hall and dance hall remain but these are well worth seeing. This rectangular courtyard, 75m by 52m, known as the Swargavilasa or Celestial Pavilion gives clues to the original grandeur of the building, regarded as one of the finest secular buildings in South India.

The palace was partially restored by Lord Napier, governor of Madras (1866-72). The entrance is on the far (eastern) side. It's open daily, from 9 am to 1 pm and 2 to 5 pm; entry costs Rs 1.

There's a daily sound-and-light show consisting of a few coloured lights and an audio presentation played at maximum volume and gross distortion – in English at 6.30 pm; Tamil at 8 pm. Tickets cost Rs 2 to Rs 5.

You can get to the palace on a No 11, 11A, 11B, 17 or 38 bus from the local bus stand (Shopping Complex section), or take the 20 minute walk from the Meenakshi Temple.

Museums

Housed in the old palace of the Rani Mangammal, the excellent **Gandhi Museum** is set in relaxing grounds and has a clear historical account of India's struggle for independence.

The Madurai **Government Museum** is in the same grounds, as is a small bookshop stocked with plenty of Gandhi reading matter.

To get there, take a No 2, 3, 4 or 23 bus from the local bus stand to the central telegraph office. From there, it's 500m along a shady street. Both museums (free entry) open daily, 10 am to 1 pm and 2 to 5.30 pm, although the latter closes Friday and the second Saturday of each month.

Mariamman Teppakkulam Tank

This tank, 5km east of the old city, covers an area almost equal to that of the Meenakshi Temple and is the site of the popular Teppam Festival (see Special Events). When it's empty (most of the year) it becomes a cricket ground for local kids. The tank was built by Tirumalai Nayak in 1646 and is connected to the Vaigai River by underground channels. Catch the No 4 bus (Rs 2) from the SETC bus stand to get there.

Other Attractions

The **Tiruparankundram** rock-cut temple, 8km south of town, is one of Murugan's six abodes. Take bus No 4A, 5 or 32 from Periyar bus stand.

The **Alagarkoil Temple**, 21km north of Madurai, is dedicated to Alagar, an aspect of Vishnu. Bus No 44 or 44D from Periyar bus stand will take you there.

Special Events

Madurai celebrates many festivals. Times and dates are determined by temple astrologers so check with the temple authorities or the tourist office for details. See the Tamil Nadu festivals table at the start of the chapter for other details.

During the 12 day **Teppam (Float) Festival** (January/February) adorned images of Meenakshi and Sundareshwara are mounted on floats on the Mariamman Teppakkulam Tank.

Madurai's main event is the 14 day **Chithrai Festival** (April/May), which celebrates the marriage of Meenakshi to Sundareshwara (Shiva). The deities are wheeled around the temple in massive chariots. The main chariot, 20m high, requires hundreds of people to haul it.

The 15 day 'harmony' festival **Avanimoolam** in September celebrates the coronation of Shiva.

The September/October **Navratri Festival** (nine nights) is held in honour of the goddess Durga. She is offered rice and flowers.

Places to Stay – Budget

In a pilgrim city of Madurai's size and importance, many of the cheap hotels are just flophouses that bear the scars of previous occupants' habits. The best places are mostly along Town Hall and Dindigul Rds.

TAMIL NADU

New College House (☎ 742971, 2 Town Hall Rd), with 200 rooms, almost guarantees you accommodation at any hour but the rooms are basic with toilet smells permeating some floors. Avoid top floor rooms if you want early-morning showers – it takes some time to pump the water up. Ordinary singles/doubles/triples cost Rs 130/210/20. A bookshop in the forecourt offers magazines and Indian music cassettes.

Hotel Ravi Towers (☎ 741961, 9 Town Hall Rd) is a good choice, with clean rooms with bath for Rs 135/250. A TV costs Rs 30 extra. There are also good air-con rooms for Rs 200/300.

The *Hotel Ramson* (☎ 740407, 9 Permal Tank St) looks expensive but isn't at Rs 90/120 for rooms with bath. In January the hotel is blasted with music from Pongal revellers.

Hotel Sree Devi (☎ 747431, 20 West Avani St) has spotlessly clean rooms (no singles) with bath starting at Rs 180, or Rs 450 with air-con. Avoid the room with no windows. The rooftop room has a spectacular view of the temple and costs Rs 700 including tax.

Ruby Lodge (☎ 742253, 92 West Perumal Maistry St) has rooms with bath and bucket showers for Rs 90/120. There's also a pleasant outdoor restaurant.

Hotel Grand Central (☎ 743940, 47 West Perumal Maistry St) is another hotel that looks more expensive than it is. It has good-sized rooms for Rs 150/200 and air-con doubles for Rs 450.

Hotel Dhanamani (☎ 742701, 20 Sunnambukara St) has singles with common bath for Rs 95, singles/doubles with attached bath for Rs 100/160, and good-value air-con doubles for Rs 300.

Hotel Times (☎ 742651, 15-16 Town Hall Rd) is a clean, friendly place and is excellent value with rooms for Rs 130/200 for singles/doubles or Rs 390 for a deluxe double with air-con.

Railway retiring rooms at Madurai station are noisy and cost Rs 50/95; dorm beds (men only) are just Rs 15.

Places to Stay – Mid-Range

Hotel Aarathy (☎ 537461, 9 Perumal Koil West Mada St) is popular with foreigners so book ahead. Rooms with bath cost Rs 200/280, or Rs 350/450 with air-con. They're comfortable and most have a small balcony with a great view over the temple. Rouse yourself for sunrise – it's superb! There's a pleasant open-air veg restaurant in the courtyard.

TTDC Hotel Tamil Nadu (☎ 537461, fax 627945, West Veli St) is good value with clean rooms with bath from Rs 150/195, Rs 260/400 with air-con and TV. There's a bar and a good restaurant.

The *Hotel Prem Nivas* (☎ 742532, fax 743618, 102 West Perumal Maistry St) is popular and has rooms with bath for Rs 190/270 and air-con doubles at Rs 420. Facilities are excellent and the hotel has its own air-con vegetarian restaurant.

TM Lodge (☎ 741651, 50 West Perumal Maistry St) is a reasonable place. Rooms with bath are Rs 175/250. An air-con double with TV is Rs 375. The upper rooms are lighter and airier.

Hotel Supreme (☎ 742637, 110 West Perumal Maistry St) has doubles (no singles) at Rs 360, or Rs 590 with air-con, plus more expensive suites. Although the rooms are dark, the facilities are good and there's an excellent rooftop veg restaurant.

Hotel Thilaga (☎ 740762, 111 West Perumal Maistry St) is clean and good value. Rooms with bath, 24 hour hot water and TV cost Rs 160/185. Air-con doubles are Rs 350.

The *Hotel Park Plaza* (☎ 742112, fax 743654, 114 West Perumal Maistry St) is similar to the Supreme, a little smarter, but somewhat overpriced for what it offers. It has comfortable rooms from Rs 775/1000 (including breakfast) with central air-con and a rooftop restaurant. It's an additional Rs 2500 if you steal the toilet!

Hotel Chentoor (☎ 747022, fax 521979, 106 West Perumal Maistry St) is new and good value with doubles for Rs 320, Rs 550 with air-con. Many of the rooms have excellent views of the temple including the gold vimana. There's also a rooftop restaurant and a branch of the Windows to the World tour operator.

Places to Stay – Top End

Madurai's three top hotels are well out of the town centre.

Hotel Madurai Ashok (☎ 537531, fax 537530, Alargakoil Rd) has rooms starting from Rs 1250/2000. The pool is Rs 75 for nonguests.

Pandyan Hotel (☎ 537090, fax 533424, Alargarkoil Rd) has rooms for Rs 1175/1700. Fully air-conditioned, it has a restaurant and bar. The manicured garden offers a respite from the city chaos but there's no pool.

Taj Garden Retreat (☎ 601020), 4km south-west of town, ranks as Madurai's best hotel. Rooms come in three varieties: standard for US$90/105 a single/double; old-world (part of the original colonial villa) at US$110/120; and deluxe (new cottages with private terraces and great views) costing US$125/140. Facilities include a multicuisine restaurant, pool (guests only), tennis court, gardens and bar.

Places to Eat

Idli lovers love Madurai – they can get idli here all day.

The *Indo-Ceylon Restaurant* (6 Town Hall Rd) is popular, as is the *Amutham Restaurant*, near the corner of West Masi St.

New College House has good-value thalis in its dining hall.

Arya Bhavan (corner of West Masi St & Dindigul Rd) does titanic dosas.

Ruby Restaurant (West Perumal Maistry St) is the only garden restaurant in Madurai and is deservedly popular. Delicious nonveg food is served; main meals cost Rs 40. It closes after midnight.

Anna Meenakshi Restaurant (West Perumal Maistry St) is large, bright and serves good, fast, vegetarian meals.

Hotel Vasanthani (West Perumal Maistry St) is good for cheap thalis and tiffin.

Zam Zam, nearby, is a popular shop for sweet or savoury snacks.

Taj Restaurant (10 Town Hall Rd) offers a varied cuisine including 'continentals', puddings and peach melba!

Mahal Restaurant (Town Hall Rd), a few doors along from the Taj Restaurant, is an excellent multicuisine restaurant that includes 'roast lamp'. Items from Rs 30 (none over Rs 60) are served in a comfortable aircon environment.

The *Surya Restaurant* (110 West Perumal Maistry St), on the roof of the Hotel Supreme, has a superb view and catches any breezes. It serves Indian, Chinese and continental vegetarian food (5 pm to midnight). Most items are around Rs 40. It's also open for breakfast 6 to 11 am; for lunch upmarket thalis are Rs 40.

Temple View Roof Top Restaurant, in the Hotel Park Plaza, serves nonveg dishes with the same view as the Surya. Chicken garlic fry is Rs 40, the tandoor chicken is especially succulent and there are good-value vegetarian dishes too.

Taj Garden Retreat is the place to go for a splurge. There are excellent à la carte meals in the multicuisine restaurant. On Saturday and Sunday evenings there's a deservedly popular buffet for Rs 250.

Shopping

Madurai, a textile centre from way back, teems with cloth stalls and tailors' shops. A great place for cottons and printed fabrics is Puthu Mandapam, the pillared former entrance hall at the eastern entrance to Sri Meenakshi Temple. Here you'll find tailors, all busily treadling away and capable of whipping up a good replica of whatever you're wearing in an hour or two.

Quality, designs and prices vary greatly. Touts are everywhere and their commissions will be added to the price of your garments.

If you want garments made, have your designs ready. It's also important to know a little about materials, quality and quantity required. Some merchants will talk you into buying way too much only to strike a deal with the tailor who makes your clothes to keep the leftovers. As always, take your time, look around carefully and bargain

TAMIL NADU

hard. It can be great fun and very satisfying to have clothes created to your own designs and specifications.

The government Poompuhar Handicrafts shop (☎ 740517) is at 12 West Veli St. Every tout, driver, 'temple guide' and tailor's brother will lead you to the shops in North Chitrai St – Cottage Arts Emporium and the Madurai Gallery. It's advisable to take your goods with you rather than shipping them, which can result in all kinds of convoluted hassles.

Getting There & Away
Air The Indian Airlines office (☎ 741234) is on West Veli St. It has one daily flight to Chennai (US$80), and four flights a week to Mumbai (US$170).

Bus At the time of writing, the entire Madurai bus system was being redesigned. The plan is that a New Central bus station (6km north-east) will handle intra/interstate services. The other five bus stands will offer local services only. For current information see the timekeeper in the glass booth near the Church of the Holy Redeemer. By the end of the encounter you'll probably need a holy redemption more than information!

At the time of writing, the bus stands were located as follows:

Periyar	West Veli St
Shopping Complex (also	West Veli St,
known as Relief bus stand)	opposite Periyar

SETC (to become	West Veli St,
local & renamed)	next to Periyar
Anna bus stand	north
Arapalayam	north-west
Palanganatham	south-west

All these city services are to be linked by a major ring road to the New Central bus station. City services cost from Rs 1.50 to Rs 2.

Services from the New Central bus station leave for Thanjavur, Tiruchirappalli (Trichy) and southern Kerala, as well as the following.

destination	price	frequency
Chidambaram	Rs 45	two daily
Coimbatore	Rs 31	30 daily
Kanyakumari	Rs 47	22 daily (No 556)
Kodaikanal	Rs 20	12 daily
Palani	Rs 18	11 daily
Rameswaram	Rs 27	30 daily
Tiruchendur	Rs 25,	20 daily
		(No 403/531)

During heavy monsoon rain, the road to Kodaikanal sometimes gets washed away and the buses go via Palani, adding an hour or two to the journey.

Private bus companies offer superdeluxe video services to Chennai and Bangalore. However, *beware* of buying a ticket for any destination. Many agencies will sell you a ticket to virtually anywhere, but you'll find yourself dumped on a state bus having paid substantially more than required.

Bus Services from Madurai Central Bus Station

destination & bus no	frequency (daily)	distance (km)	duration (hours)	fare (Rs)
Bangalore 846	12	450	15	103
Chennai 137, 491	32	447	10	90
Ernakulam 826	4	324	10	87
Mysore 837	2	450	12	95
Pondicherry 847	3	329	8	66
Thiruvananthapuram 865	1	305	7	61
Tirupathi	4	517	16	104

Major Trains from Madurai

destination	train no & name	departure time	distance (km)	duration	fare (Rs) (2nd/1st)
Coimbatore	6116 *Coimbatore-Rameswaram Exp*	9.45 pm	229	6 h 15 min	93/294
Chennai	6718 *Pandian Exp*	7.00 pm	490	12 h	157/531
	2636 *Vaigai Exp*	6.00 am		9 h 40 min	117/338
Rameswaram	6115 *Coimbatore-Rameswaram Exp*	6.00 am	164	5 h	27/198
Kanyakumari	6721 *Chennai-Kanniya Kumari Exp*	12.30 am	242	5 h 45 min	90/298

Train Madurai train station is on West Veli St. The 'Major Trains from Madurai' table lists the more frequent trains leaving Madurai.

If you're heading to Kollam (Quilon) in Kerala, you can take the No 721 passenger train from Madurai at 6.50 am to Virudunagar (one hour). The 6105 *Chennai-Quilon Mail* passes through Virudunagar at 9 am, reaching Kollam (225km) at 4.20 pm. The line crosses the Western Ghats through spectacular mountain terrain, passing the superb gopurams at Sriviliputur (between Sivakasi and Rajapalaiyam) and Sankarayinarkovil.

Getting Around
To/From the Airport The airport is 12km south of town and a taxi charges an extortionate Rs 250 to the town centre. Autorickshaws ask for around Rs 150 (even Rs 200). Alternatively, bus No 10A from the local bus stand goes to the airport but don't rely on it being on schedule.

Bus Some useful local buses include No 3 to the Anna bus stand, Nos 1 and 2 to near the Gandhi Museum, and Nos 4 and 4A to Mariamman Teppakkulam Tank – all depart from Periyar state bus stand.

Auto-Rickshaw Drivers are extremely reluctant to use meters and will quote whatever they think you will pay, but eventually they should settle on a reasonable rate.

Madurai is small enough to get around on foot.

RAMESWARAM
☎ 04573 • pop 35,750

Known as the Varanasi of the South, Rameswaram is a major pilgrimage centre for both Shaivites and Vaishnavaites. It was here that Rama (an incarnation of Vishnu and hero of the *Ramayana*) offered thanks to Shiva. At the town's core is the Ramanathaswamy Temple, one of the most important temples in South India.

Rameswaram is on an island in the Gulf of Mannar, connected to the mainland by Mandapam by rail, and by one of India's engineering wonders, the Indira Gandhi bridge, opened by Rajiv Gandhi in 1988.

The town lies on the island's eastern side. Although proximity to Sri Lanka results in a high security presence due to the conflict between a Tamil separatist movement in the north and government forces, Rameswaram has a decidedly laid-back atmosphere.

Orientation & Information
Most hotels and restaurants are clustered around the Ramanathaswamy Temple. The bus stand, 2km to the west, is connected by frequent shuttle buses to the town centre.

Staff at the tourist office (☎ 21371), East Car St, will happily recite the history and mythology of the island. The tourist counter at the train station has erratic times and is closed on Sunday. The temple information centre sells booklets and organises official guides.

Money can be changed at the State Bank of India near the temple. Take a good book to read – it's a lengthy process.

Don't be rushed into taking a boat trip. There are no officially approved tourist boat operators. Touts hang around the TTDC Hotel Tamil Nadu, promising a one hour 'luxury boat' trip with snorkel hire and a seafood meal which costs Rs 300. But this may mean a trip in a precarious fishing vessel with no snorkel equipment and where the only seafood is the flyblown leftovers of the morning catch! Check the boat before you make a deal, and then bargain hard. If boats venture too far they will be quickly spotted (and sometimes confiscated) by the military, which has the area under close surveillance.

Ramanathaswamy Temple
A fine example of late Dravidian architecture, this temple is most renowned for its four magnificent corridors lined with elaborately sculptured pillars. Spanning 1.2km, construction began in the 12th century AD. Later additions included a 53m high gopuram. Twenty-two *theerthams* (tanks) within the complex are believed by devotees to have particular powers. Only Hindus may enter the inner sanctum.

The temple opens 5 am to noon and 4 to 10 pm, but even when it's closed, it's possible to amble through the extensive corridors.

Kothandaraswamy Temple & Dhanushkodi
Twelve kilometres from town, this temple was the only structure to survive the 1964 cyclone that destroyed the rest of the village. Legend has it that Vibhishana, brother of Sita's kidnapper Ravana, surrendered to Rama at this spot.

Buses from the local bus stand on East Car St will bring you here. They continue 2km beyond the temple and then it's a 4km walk through fishing communities to Dhanushkodi. Local touts quote an exorbitant Rs 300. There's little here now but a few ruined houses (which make good sun shelters) and a lovely bathing pool. The walk to the tip of the peninsula is hot but well worth it.

Adam's Bridge
Adam's Bridge refers to the chain of reefs, sandbanks and islets that almost connect Sri Lanka with India. According to legend, these are the stepping stones used by Hanuman to follow Ravana, in his bid to rescue Sita.

Other Attractions
The **Gandamadana Parvatham**, 3km northwest of town, is a shrine reputedly containing Rama's footprints. Pilgrims visit at sunrise and sunset (the shrine is closed 11.30 am to 3.30 pm).

Dhanushkodi has the best **beach**. Closer to town, try the one in front of the Hotel Tamil Nadu. Most of the time it's deserted; the pilgrims prefer to do their auspicious wading at **Agni Theertham**, the seashore closest to the temple.

Special Events
There are many small festivals in Rameswaram. The main ones are the Temple Car Festival in February/March and the Marriage Festival in July/August. You can get all the details from the tourist office.

Places to Stay
Hotels, mainly geared towards pilgrims, are often completely booked out during festivals. There are no new hotels and existing ones are ageing quickly. Near the temple loud music blasts out daily from 4.30 am.

Temple Cottages (☎ 21223, Sannathi St), close to East Car St and the temple, provides basic accommodation for pilgrims keen to wake at 4 am. Singles/doubles with bucket bath are Rs 35/60.

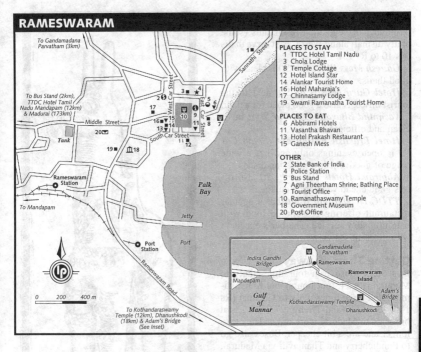

RAMESWARAM

PLACES TO STAY
1 TTDC Hotel Tamil Nadu
3 Chola Lodge
8 Temple Cottage
12 Hotel Island Star
14 Alankar Tourist Home
16 Hotel Maharaja's
17 Chinnasamy Lodge
19 Swami Ramanatha Tourist Home

PLACES TO EAT
6 Abbirami Hotels
11 Vasantha Bhavan
13 Hotel Prakash Restaurant
15 Ganesh Mess

OTHER
2 State Bank of India
4 Police Station
5 Bus Stand
9 Agni Theertham Shrine; Bathing Place
7 Tourist Office
10 Ramanathaswamy Temple
18 Government Museum
20 Post Office

Chola Lodge (☎ *21307, North Car St*) offers reasonable doubles (no singles) with bath for Rs 125. Family rooms (up to five beds) are Rs 220.

Alankar Tourist Home (☎ *21216, West Car St*) has basic double rooms with bath for Rs 90.

Swami Ramanatha Tourist Home (☎ *21217*), opposite the museum, has clean doubles with shower for Rs 160. The reception has a good display of local history.

Chinnasamy Lodge (☎ *21170, Middle St*) has clean but basic rooms from Rs 85. The front rooms are particularly noisy.

Hotel Maharaja's (☎ *21271, 7 Middle St*) is a good choice. Clean, pleasant and renovated doubles with bath and balcony cost Rs 220, or Rs 460 with air-con.

Hotel Island Star (☎ *21472, South Car St*) is clean and friendly. Doubles/triples are Rs 170/270; a triple with air-con is Rs 550.

Railway retiring rooms at the train station are large and airy. Their distance from the temple makes them reasonably peaceful. Doubles/triples with bath are Rs 85/100; dorm beds are Rs 20.

TTDC Hotel Tamil Nadu (☎ *21277, Sannathi St*) faces the sea. Although this is a good place to stay, it's often booked out and it's best to reserve a room in advance. Double/triple rooms are Rs 250/320 – Rs 550 for a double with air-con. There are also five and six-bed rooms that are sometimes let as dorms at Rs 45 per bed.

TTDC Hotel Tamil Nadu Mandapam (☎ *41512*) is 12km west of Rameswaram, over the bridge. If all the accommodation in Rameswaram is full, this is a good alternative, more for the sandy beach than the rooms. Basic doubles by the beach are Rs 260 in cement bunker-style cottages. A dorm bed is Rs 45.

Places to Eat

A number of vegetarian restaurants (some pretty dismal) along West Car St serve thalis (Rs 10 to Rs 15).

Ganesh Mess *(West Car St)* is clean with good thalis.

Hotel Guru *(East Car St)*, next to the tourist office, is also a good place for a thali.

Vasantha Bhavan *(East Car St)* is busy, clean and efficient.

Hotel Prakash Restaurant *(South Car St)* is open evenings only and has a wide range of good, cheap vegetarian dishes.

Abbirami Hotels *(Sannathi St)* also offers good cheap vegetarian cuisine.

TTDC Hotel Tamil Nadu has a popular restaurant offering reasonable food with painfully slow service. The bar's excellent with pleasant sea views.

Getting There & Away

Bus SETC buses run four times daily to Madurai (Rs 34, four hours) and Kanyakumari, and three times daily to Chennai (Rs 100, 13 hours) and Trichy (273km). Local buses go to Madurai more often. They take longer and are a bit cheaper. Buses also go to Pondicherry and Thanjavur via Madurai.

Train There are two daily express trains to/from Chennai – the *Sethu Express* and the *Rameswaram Express*. The 666km trip, costing Rs 190/660 in 2nd/1st class, takes 15 hours. Both take the direct route through Manamadurai and Trichy and therefore miss Madurai.

The direct train from Madurai to Rameswaram (Rs 27/48/233 in 3rd/2nd/1st class, 164km, five hours) departs at 6 am and returns at 4.10 pm.

Getting Around

Town buses (Rs 1) travel between the temple and the bus stand from early morning until late at night. In town, the buses stop at the west gopuram and opposite the tourist office. Auto and cycle-rickshaws are available at all hours; haggle hard!

Cycling is a good way to get around with many hire places charging just Rs 2 an hour.

Terracotta horses, mounts for the spirit soliders of Ayyana, can be seen guarding villages throughout south-east Tamil Nadu.

AROUND RAMESWARAM

Ramanathapuram, also known as Ramnad, is 36km west of Rameswaram and noted for its **Ramalinga Palace**. Built in the latter part of the 17th century, the palace belonged to the Setupati rajas, the traditional guardians of Rama's mythical bridge to Lanka. Following protracted struggles against the British, the Setupati dynasty finally capitulated at the end of the 18th century. It's the paintings in the palace that make the visit worthwhile. The huge murals depicting everything from business meetings, military conflicts and erotic encounters are well preserved. The palace is open daily (except Friday), 9 am to 1 pm and 2 to 5 pm.

Ramanathapuram is on the train line between Madurai and Rameswaram and buses from Madurai also stop here.

TIRUCHENDUR

On the coast south of Tuticorin, this impressive shore temple is one of the six abodes of Murugan. Dating from the 9th century, much of it was replaced early in the 20th century because of salt damage. Non-Hindus may enter the sanctum for a Rs 20 donation. The temple's open 5 am to 8 pm.

KANYAKUMARI (Cape Comorin)
☎ 04652 • pop 18,900

Kanyakumari is the 'Land's End' of the Indian subcontinent. Here, the Bay of Bengal meets the Indian Ocean and the Arabian Sea. Chaitrapurnima (Tamil for the April full moon day) is one of the best times to experience the sunset and moonrise over the ocean simultaneously.

Kanyakumari has great spiritual significance for Hindus. It's dedicated to the goddess Devi Kanya, an incarnation of Parvati, Shiva's wife. Pilgrims come here to visit the temple and bathe in the sacred waters.

For tourists Kanyakumari is a popular day trip from Kovalam in Kerala. However, it's best not to compare it with the Keralan beaches. It's essentially a pilgrimage town – a place where people fulfil their spiritual duties.

Orientation & Information

The temple is right on the point of Kanyakumari with all the facilities within 1km. The post office is on Main Rd near the Canara Bank (☎ 71276). The tourist office is open Monday to Friday, 10 am to 5.30 pm. The train station is almost 1km north of the temple, while the bus stand is 500m to the west. You can change money at the Canara Bank (next to the post office) and the State Bank of Travancore near the ferry jetty. There's a branch of the government emporium, Poompuhar, just near the temple.

Kumari Amman Temple

According to legend, Devi (the goddess) single-handedly conquered demons and secured freedom for the world. Pilgrims give her thanks for the safety and liberty she attained for them.

In May/June there is a car festival where an idol of the deity is taken in procession, and in September/October the Navratri Festival (nine nights), celebrates Devi's victory over the demons.

The temple is open daily, 4.30 to 11.45 am and 5.30 to 8.30 pm. Men must remove their shirts, and everyone their shoes (as always). Cameras are taken and safeguarded until you return.

Gandhi Memorial

This striking memorial stored some of the Mahatma's ashes until they were immersed in the sea. It resembles an Orissan temple and was designed so that on Gandhi's birthday (2 October), the sun's rays fall on the place where his ashes were kept. It's open daily, 7 am to 12.30 pm and 3 to 7 pm.

Vivekananda Puram – The Wandering Monk

This museum details the extensive journey across India made by the Indian philosopher, Swami Vivekananda. It's well worth a visit. The Swami developed a synthesis between the tenets of Hinduism and concepts of social justice.

The Wandering Monk is open daily, 8 am to noon and 4 to 8 pm. There's also a secure cloakroom available 6 am to 10 pm. Entry is Rs 1.

Vivekananda Memorial

This memorial is on two rocky islands about 400m offshore. Swami Vivekananda meditated here in 1892 before setting out as

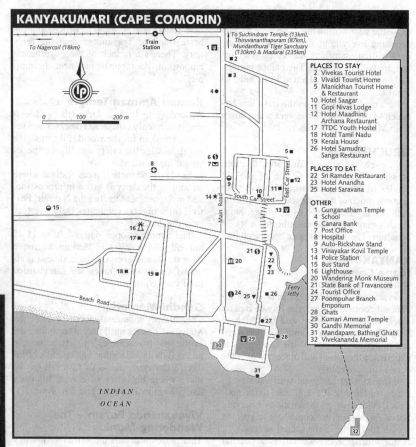

KANYAKUMARI (CAPE COMORIN)

To Nagercoil (18km)

Train Station

To Suchindram Temple (13km),
Thiruvananthapuram (87km),
Mundanthurai Tiger Sanctuary
(130km) & Madurai (235km)

0   100   200 m

East Car Street

South Car Street

Main Road

Beach Road

Ferry Jetty

INDIAN
OCEAN

PLACES TO STAY
2 Vivekas Tourist Hotel
3 Vivaldi Tourist Home
5 Manickhan Tourist Home
   & Restaurant
10 Hotel Saagar
11 Gopi Nivas Lodge
12 Hotel Maadhini;
   Archana Restaurant
17 TTDC Youth Hostel
18 Hotel Tamil Nadu
19 Kerala House
26 Hotel Samudra;
   Sanga Restaurant

PLACES TO EAT
22 Sri Ramdev Restaurant
23 Hotel Anandha
25 Hotel Saravana

OTHER
1 Gunganatham Temple
4 School
6 Canara Bank
7 Post Office
8 Hospital
9 Auto-Rickshaw Stand
13 Vinayakar Kovil Temple
14 Police Station
15 Bus Stand
16 Lighthouse
20 Wandering Monk Museum
21 State Bank of Travancore
24 Tourist Office
27 Poompuhar Branch
   Emporium
28 Ghats
29 Kumari Amman Temple
30 Gandhi Memorial
31 Mandapam; Bathing Ghats
32 Vivekananda Memorial

one of India's most important religious crusaders. The mandapam, built here in his memory in 1970, reflects architectural styles from all over India. The ferry to the island (half-hourly) costs Rs 6. It's a Rs 3 entry to the memorial, open 7 to 11 am and 2 to 5 pm.

Places to Stay

Although hotels are mushrooming in Kanyakumari, demand remains high especially at weekends and festivals. Some ho-

tels have seasonal rates so you may find during April/May and October to December, room prices are 100% up on what's quoted here. Few hotels have single rooms.

Gopi Nivas Lodge (East Car St) has basic singles/doubles at Rs 90/110.

Hotel Saagar (☎ 71325, South Car St) is a good place with doubles (no singles) from Rs 160 to Rs 220.

TTDC Youth Hostel, at the entrance to the Hotel Tamil Nadu, charges Rs 45 per dorm bed and is rarely full.

Railway retiring rooms at the train station include a six-bed dorm at Rs 15 per bed and singles/doubles for Rs 40/80.

Vivekas Tourist Hotel (☎ 71192, Main Rd) has clean, colourful rooms all with bath and shower from Rs 160/210 for a double/triple.

Manickhan Tourist Home (☎ 71387) has doubles for Rs 200, or Rs 280 with a sea view.

Vivaldi Tourist Home (☎ 71972, Main Rd) is clean and inexpensive at Rs 110/160 for doubles/triples. However, couples must be particularly slim to fit on the bed intended for two!

Hotel Maadhini (☎ 71787, fax 71657, East Car St), is a little upmarket with balconies virtually overhanging the village – fascinating for guests but probably a bit intrusive for villagers. The rooms are airy and clean. Doubles are Rs 360, or Rs 470/850 for ocean views without/with air-con. The Archana Restaurant here has excellent food in an open-air dining area with views of the hotel rather than the sea.

Kerala House (☎ 71229) claims to be the southernmost house on the subcontinent. Run by the Kerala Tourism Development Corporation (KTDC) it now caters for government officials but rooms are available to travellers who apply to the Political Department, State Secretariat, Thiruvananthapuram (Trivandrum) or who negotiate well with the manager. Large double rooms with sea views and bath are Rs 360 to Rs 420.

Hotel Tamil Nadu (☎ 71257) has basic doubles for Rs 100 with common bath, and much better doubles with bath for Rs 360 (Rs 500 with air-con). Clean rooms, most with a balcony, have great views of the Gandhi Memorial. Cottages and family rooms are also available.

Hotel Samudra (☎ 71162), near the temple, has doubles from Rs 360 to Rs 560, and a well-appointed air-con double with good views for Rs 850.

Places to Eat

Hotel Saravana, one of the town's most popular eateries, offers Chinese (of sorts) and south Indian cuisine from Rs 12. It has excellent dosas.

Hotel Anandha has a great ocean view and offers vegetarian cuisine from Rs 15.

Sri Ramdev Restaurant offers a mean range of north Indian vegetarian fare on its tiny open-air terrace.

Sanga Restaurant is an upmarket vegetarian place in Hotel Samudra.

Archana Restaurant at Hotel Maadhini has good veg and nonveg meals (from Rs 40). The outdoor restaurant is open only 7 to 10 pm; at lunchtime you'll be ushered to their indoor room, which has great ocean views.

Manickhan Tourist Home has perhaps the best restaurant in town with meals from Rs 40 but it's closed during the low season.

Getting There & Away

Bus The bus stand is a dusty five minute walk from the centre. It has timetables in Tamil and English, restaurants and waiting rooms. The reservation office is open 7 am to 9 pm.

SETC has buses to Madurai (Rs 55, 253km, six hours, hourly), Chennai (Rs 155, 679km, 16 hours, nine daily), Thiruvananthapuram (three hours, six daily) and Rameswaram (nine hours, seven daily).

Local buses go to Nagercoil, Padmanabhapuram (the palace of the former Travancore rulers – see the Kerala chapter for details), Thiruvananthapuram and Kovalam, among other places.

Train The daily *Nellai Kumari Express* departs for Chennai at 3.15 pm daily. It takes 15 hours and tickets are Rs 245/862 for 2nd/1st class.

The daily passenger train to Thiruvananthapuram leaves Kanyakumari at 5 pm and does the 87km in two hours (Rs 30 in 2nd class).

The *Kanyakumari Express* departs daily at 5 am and travels to Mumbai in 48 hours. The 2155km trip costs Rs 376/1545 in 2nd/1st class. This train will also take you to Thiruvananthapuram and Ernakulam (eight hours).

TAMIL NADU

For the real long-haulers, the weekly *Himsagar Express* runs all the way to Jammu Tawi (in Jammu & Kashmir), a distance of 3734km, in 74 hours. The longest single train ride in India, it leaves Kanyakumari on Friday at 12.50 am and from Jammu Tawi on Monday at 10.45 pm. This train also passes through Coimbatore (12 hours), Vijayawada (29 hours) and Delhi (60 hours).

AROUND KANYAKUMARI
Suchindram

Some 13km north-west of Kanyakumari, this impressive temple has ancient records inscribed in three languages – Tamil, Sanskrit and Pali. There's a 6m-high statue of Hanuman, the monkey god.

If you are non-Hindu you may be invited into the inner shrine, but this can be intrusive for devotees, so you may prefer to decline. The temple is open 3 am to 1 pm and 4 to 8 pm.

MUNDANTHURAI TIGER SANCTUARY

Mundanthurai, near the Kerala border, has had its pristine state altered by seven major dams and large hydroelectric pipes that intersect the landscape. It's principally a tiger sanctuary (apparently there are 17 left), though it's also noted for chital, sambar and the rare lion-tailed macaque.

Day visitors must leave the park by 6 pm. To stay on, you need a permit, obtainable from the Field Officer, Project Tiger, NGO 'A' Colony, Tirunelveli. The *Forest Department Resthouse* is Rs 12 per person per night and seriously basic.

The closest train station is Ambasamudram, about 25km north-west. Buses run from here to Papanasam (7km), the nearest village, from where you can catch another bus to the park.

KUTTRALAM (Courtallam)
☎ 04633

About 135km north-west of Kanyakumari, Kuttralam is popular for families who come to bathe at the waterfalls. Men wear sarongs; women full dress. Oil massages are available, but for men only.

In the high season, June to August, the place is impossibly crowded. In the low season the falls may dry up. Sadly, the scenic qualities are somewhat marred by litter.

Of the nine waterfalls, the only one in the village is the 60m-high **Main Falls**. Its sheer rock face is carved with old Hindu insignia, visible during the dry months of January and February. Other falls, mostly accessed by shuttle buses, are up to 8km away.

Kuttralam offers very basic lodging houses that aren't good value and are often full. Some people prefer to stay away from all the hype in Tenkasi, 5km north. *Krishna Tourist Home* (☎ 23125), next to the Tenkasi bus stand, has doubles for Rs 195, or Rs 450 with air-con. *Hotel Anandha Classic* (☎ 23303, 116-A/7 Courtallam Rd) has a similar tariff and a reasonable veg restaurant.

Tenkasi is the closest train station to Kuttralam. However, the main line from Madurai to Kollam does not pass here. To get to Tenkasi, catch the main train line to Shencottah (Sengottai), from where there's one express daily to take you the remaining 6km to Tenkasi. Faster and more frequent buses also ply these routes.

The Western Ghats

The Western Ghats stretch about 1400km from north of Mumbai, across Maharashtra, Goa, Karnataka and Kerala, to the southernmost tip of Tamil Nadu. The hills (average elevation of 915m) are covered with tropical and temperate evergreen forest, and mixed deciduous forest, and are the source of all major rivers in South India, including the Cauvery and Krishna.

The Western Ghats are home to a number of tribal groups. They also form a diverse biological and ecological haven: they have 27% of all India's flowering plants; 60% of all medicinal plants; and an incredible array of endemic wildlife. While parts of the

Ghats have suffered from development, naturalists regard this as one of the most important pristine forest and mountain areas left in Asia.

KODAIKANAL
☎ 04542 • pop 31,200

Kodaikanal – better known as Kodai – is on the southern crest of the Palani Hills, about 120km north-west of Madurai at an altitude of 2100m. It is surrounded by wooded (not so thickly any more) slopes, waterfalls and precipitous rocky outcrops. The journey up and down is breathtaking.

Kodai is the only hill station in India set up by Americans, though they were soon joined by the British. American missionaries established a school for European children here in the mid-1840s, the legacy of which is the Kodaikanal International School – one of the most prestigious private schools in the country.

Australian blue gums provide the eucalyptus oil sold in Kodai's street stalls and create numerous environmental problems. Plantations of exotic species together with rampant tourist development have resulted in local action to save Kodaikanal from further environmental damage.

The Kurinji shrub, unique to the Western Ghats, is found in Kodaikanal. This shrub has light, purple-blue coloured blossoms and flowers every 12 years (the next blossoming will be in 2004, though a few seem to have their natural clocks out of time).

Kodaikanal provides an escape from the heat and haze of the plains and the opportunity to hike in the quiet *sholas* (forests).

April to June (the main season) or August to October are certainly the best times to visit. The height of the wet season is November/December. The mild temperatures here range from 11°C to 20°C in summer and 8°C to 17°C in winter.

Orientation
Kodai is remarkably compact. The budget hotels, restaurants and the bus stand are all near the main street, Bazaar Rd (Anna Salai). Most of the better hotels are some distance from the bazaar, but usually not more than a 15 minute walk.

Information
The tourist office (☎ 41675), close to the bus stand, seems more interested in promoting friends than providing information. Open Monday to Saturday, it operates many local tours. For literature on Kodai visit the CLS Bookshop, opposite.

The State Bank of India, near the post office, is the best place to cash travellers cheques. And sending mail from the post office is a breeze!

Astrophysical Laboratory
Built in 1889, this laboratory stands on the highest point in the area, 3km along Observatory Rd uphill from Kodai's lake. It houses a small **museum**, open Friday, 10 am to noon and 3 to 5 pm. The buildings housing the instruments are off limits. It's a hard 45 minute uphill walk pushing a bicycle, but it only takes five minutes to coast down (you'll need good brakes).

Flora & Fauna Museum
Also worth a visit is the Flora & Fauna Museum at the Sacred Heart College at Shembaganur. It's a 6km hike and all uphill on the way back. The museum is open 10 am to noon and 3 to 5 pm; closed Sunday. Entry is Rs 1.

Parks & Falls
Near the start of Coaker's Walk is **Bryant Park**, a botanical park landscaped and stocked by the British officer after whom it is named. At **Chettiar Park**, about 3km uphill from town, 1.5km past the Kurinji Andavar Temple, you may be able to see some Kurinji flowers.

There are numerous waterfalls – the main one, **Silver Cascade**, is on the road up to Kodai.

Kurinji Andavar Temple
This tiny temple, 3km north-east of the lake, is dedicated to Murugan. It holds little interest for outsiders.

TAMIL NADU

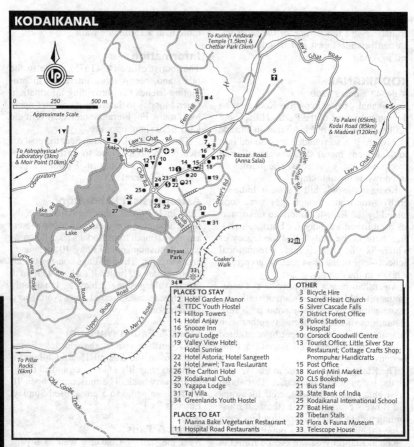

KODAIKANAL

0   250   500 m
Approximate Scale

To Kurinji Andavar
Temple (1.5km) &
Chettiar Park (3km)

To Astrophysical
Laboratory (3km)
& Moir Point (10km)

To Palani (65km),
Kodai Road (85km)
& Madurai (120km)

Bazaar Road
(Anna Salai)

Bryant
Park

Coaker's
Walk

To Pillar
Rocks
(6km)

PLACES TO STAY
2   Hotel Garden Manor
4   TTDC Youth Hostel
12 Hilltop Towers
14 Hotel Anjay
16 Snooze Inn
17 Guru Lodge
19 Valley View Hotel;
    Hotel Sunrise
22 Hotel Astoria; Hotel Sangeeth
24 Hotel Jewel; Tava Restaurant
26 The Carlton Hotel
29 Kodaikanal Club
30 Yagapa Lodge
31 Taj Villa
34 Greenlands Youth Hostel

PLACES TO EAT
1   Manna Bake Vegetarian Restaurant
11 Hospital Road Restaurants

OTHER
3   Bicycle Hire
5   Sacred Heart Church
6   Silver Cascade Falls
7   District Forest Office
8   Police Station
9   Hospital
10 Corsock Goodwill Centre
13 Tourist Office; Little Silver Star
    Restaurant; Cottage Crafts Shop;
    Promputhar Handicrafts
15 Post Office
18 Kurinji Mini Market
20 CLS Bookshop
21 Bus Stand
23 State Bank of India
25 Kodaikanal International School
27 Boat Hire
28 Tibetan Stalls
32 Flora & Fauna Museum
33 Telescope House

Activities

Walks The views at **Coaker's Walk**, which
has an observatory with telescope (Telescope House, entry Rs 1), and from **Pillar
Rocks**, a 7km hike (one way), are spectacular. There are also good walks from
Taj Villa.

For more serious trekking, head to the
District Forest Office (DFO), on a winding
road down (north) towards TTDC Youth
Hostel. For Rs 15 you can buy a pamphlet,
Sholas For Survival, which describes 17

local treks ranging from 8km ambles to
27km hikes. There's a rough map plus time
estimates and relative difficulty. This office
is open Monday to Friday, 10 am to 1 pm
and 2 to 6 pm.

Cycling Although the roads are rarely flat
there are some nice bike rides in the area.
One reader recommended going to Moir
Point (10km) via the Astrophysical Labora-
tory, then taking the Monnar Rd 14km to
Berijam Lake passing Silent Valley and

Caps Valley Viewpoint. From December to June the Monnar Rd is closed because of fire danger but you can get permission to cycle here from the DFO.

Boating & Horse Riding Kodai Lake has been wonderfully landscaped. Boats can be hired from the Kodaikanal Boat & Rowing Club (from Rs 30 for a two seater). The tourist department also has rowboats and pedal boats (Rs 35 for two people for 30 minutes). Around here you'll be accosted by people who want to rent horses for high prices. The prevailing rate is around Rs 100 per hour, accompanied or unaccompanied. Some of these horses should be retired.

Places to Stay
Hotel prices in high season (1 April to 30 June) jump by up to 300%, especially at the lower end of the market, and this is nothing but a blatant rip-off. During the season, it's worth staying in a mid-range hotel since their prices increase only marginally.

The majority of hotels here don't have single rooms and they're reluctant to discuss reductions for single occupancy in the high season. Most hotels in Kodai have a 9 or 10 am checkout time in the high season so don't get caught out. During the rest of the year it's usually, but not always, 24 hours.

Finally, beware of hotels with carpet (or floor covering referred to as carpet) – they may be stained with a sordid history!

Places to Stay – Budget
Unless otherwise stated all references to hot water mean piped water available 24 hours.

Greenlands Youth Hostel (☎ 41336, fax 41340), about 1km from the centre at the end of Coaker's Walk, has the best views and most of the budget travellers. But it can be suffocatingly crowded with double bunks arranged head to toe. A dorm (six to 15 beds) costs Rs 50/60 per person in the low/high season. There are also eight double rooms (four have fireplaces) with bath for Rs 190 to Rs 210 in the low season and Rs 240 to Rs 250 in the high season. There's hot water from 7 to 9 am for Rs 5.

Guru Lodge (Bazaar Rd) is one of several very basic hotels strung out along the steep Bazaar Rd. Doubles are Rs 80 (Rs 170 to Rs 290 in high season) with hot water is Rs 5 per bucket. Facilities are absolutely minimal – make sure you get blankets as it gets pretty chilly here.

Hotel Sunrise (☎ 40358), a few minutes walk from the bus stand, is a friendly place. There are doubles (no singles) with bath for Rs 160. The view from the front is excellent, and the rooms have hot-water heaters that work from 6 am to 6 pm.

Yagapa Lodge (☎ 41235), off Club Rd, is a peaceful place with doubles for Rs 170 with bath and hot water in buckets, or Rs 220 with constant hot water. Prices double in the high season. It's a friendly hotel with good views.

Places to Stay – Mid-Range
All places in this range have tap hot water available 24 hours, unless otherwise stated.

Taj Villa (☎ 40940, Coaker's Rd), off Club Rd, is an old stone-built group of houses in a small garden with sublime views from some rooms. Double rooms (no singles) cost Rs 450 and are 'subject to hike in season'. Most rooms have a bathroom.

Hotel Anjay (☎ 41089, Bazaar Rd) isn't a bad choice. Double rooms with bath start at Rs 200/440 in the low/high season.

Snooze Inn (☎ 40837) has clean economy doubles (no singles) with TV that cost Rs 280/560 in low/high season.

Hotel Sangeeth (☎ 40456) is good value at Rs 195/335 for a double in the low/high season. All rooms have bath but there are no views.

Hotel Astoria (☎ 40524), next door to the Sangeeth, has ordinary/deluxe doubles at Rs 300/400 in the low season and Rs 625/800 in the high season. Its restaurant serves north and south Indian dishes.

Hotel Jewel (☎ 41029, Hospital Rd) is good value at Rs 275/300 for ordinary/deluxe doubles in low season or Rs 450/650 in high season. The well-furnished rooms have carpet and colour TV.

TAMIL NADU

Hilltop Towers (☎ 40413, fax 40415, Club Rd), opposite the Kodai International School, is a flashy place with keen staff. Doubles/suites cost Rs 440/480 in low season and Rs 750/900 in high season.

Hotel Garden Manor (☎ 40461, Lake Rd) is set in terraced gardens overlooking the lake. Its spacious rooms are Rs 570 to Rs 800 (low season) and Rs 1100 to Rs 1450 (in season). Indoor and outdoor restaurants serve a variety of dishes.

Places to Stay – Top End

Kodaikanal Club (☎ 41341) is a colonial-style clubhouse with a library, video room, games tables, 'mud' tennis courts, a bar (with cheap beers) and a dining room. Double rooms are Rs 750/850 in the low/high season, plus 15% service charge. The room rate includes the obligatory temporary membership fee (Rs 50 per day, but definitely only available with a member's recommendation), breakfast (Indian or continental) and 'bed tea' (served in your room). The quaint rooms have adjoining sitting room, bathroom, TV, heater, wicker chairs and 24 hour hot water.

Valley View Hotel (☎ 40181, Post Office Rd), a large modern hotel, receives mixed reports. Rooms are a bargain in the low season at Rs 350/500. High-season rates are Rs 1400/1700 (including all meals). There's a good vegetarian restaurant.

The Carlton Hotel (☎ 40056, fax 41170, Lake Rd) is Kodai's most prestigious hotel with the formality associated with star hotels. Overlooking the lake, this hotel used to be a colonial-style wooden structure but was completely rebuilt a few years ago and is simply magnificent. Low-season rooms cost Rs 1690/2550 with breakfast and dinner; in the high season it's Rs 2000/4000 including all meals. There's an excellent restaurant and a bar.

Places to Eat

Hospital Rd, with a range of different cuisines, is the best place for cheap restaurants and it's here that you'll find most travellers congregating.

Tava Restaurant, below the Hotel Jewel, offers vegetarian Indian food.

Hotel Punjab does excellent tandoori food.

Ahaar is a little vegetarian place.

Silver Inn Restaurant is a good place for breakfasts and also does pizzas and other western dishes.

Wang's Kitchen has Chinese and western food at reasonable prices.

Tibetan Brothers Restaurant is a popular place serving westernised Tibetan food.

The Royal Tibet is a very popular place and serves veg and nonveg food. Its noodle soups make a filling meal on a cool night. Just give the coffee a miss!

Chefmaster has continental, Chinese and Keralan dishes, and also tempting handmade chocolates!

Hot Breads pretends to be a classy coffee shop. Apple pie is Rs 25, eclairs are Rs 12.

Eco Nut has a wide range of health food – brown bread, cheese, essential oils, etc. Try their Nutri Balls (Rs 10) – a mixture of jaggery, peanuts, coconut and *moong dhal*.

Little Silver Star (Bazaar Rd), upstairs in the building opposite the tourist office, does probably the best tandoori chicken in Kodai – Rs 75 for half a chicken.

Manna Bake Vegetarian Restaurant (Bear Shola Falls Rd) is run by Israel Booshi, who doubles as a chef and environmentalist. His brown bread is legendary, as is his apple pie (Rs 15). It's open 7.30 am until late.

Taj Villa (☎ 40940, Coaker's Rd) has a chef reputed to be turning out all manner of interesting dishes.

The Carlton Hotel (☎ 40056, fax 41170, Lake Rd) is the place for a splurge. There's an excellent buffet from 7.30 to 10 pm for Rs 270. Later you can relax in the bar.

Self-Catering Kodai is an orchard area and you'll find various fruits in season – pears, avocados, guavas, durians and grapefruit – in the street stalls around the bus stand. You can buy other food items at the small Kurinji Mini Market, a few metres up from the post office.

Shopping

The Cottage Crafts Shop on Bazaar Rd is run by Corsock, the Coordinating Council for Social Concerns in Kodai. This organisation, staffed by volunteers, supports the needy. Corsock also runs the Goodwill Centre, Hospital Rd, which sells clothing and rents books, with the proceeds again going to indigent causes. There's a branch of Poompuhar Handicrafts near the tourist office.

The road down to the lake (alongside the Kodaikanal Club) has Tibetan stalls selling warm clothing, shawls and fabrics at very reasonable prices.

Getting There & Away

Kodai is another one of those places where you'll be overwhelmed by persistent touts on arrival, with offers for transport and accommodation. As always, try to resist the onslaught, or you may end up in situations not to your liking.

Bus Kodai's bus stand is basically a patch of dirt opposite the Hotel Astoria. State buses run to Madurai (Rs 26, 121km, 3½ hours, eight daily), Tiruchirappalli (197km, three daily) and Kanyakumari (356km, one daily), and twice daily to both Coimbatore (244km) and Chennai (Rs 103, 513km). Frequent buses also go to Palani (Rs 20, 65km, three hours), Dindigul and Kodai Road train station. There's a KSRTC semideluxe bus daily to Bangalore for Rs 115 that leaves at 6 pm and takes 12 hours (480km).

Deluxe minibuses operate in the high season between Kodaikanal and Ooty. The all-day 332km trip costs Rs 200 to Rs 250. Mid-range hotels usually keep a list of the departure times.

Train The nearest train stations are Palani to the north (on the Coimbatore-Madurai-Rameswaram line), and Kodai Road on the Madurai-Trichy-Chennai line to the east. Both are about three hours by bus. Train bookings can be made at one of the many travel agencies.

Getting Around

Taxis are very expensive here. The minimum charge is Rs 50 and you won't be able to haggle – there are no rickshaws, so there's no competition.

The stall outside the Carlton Hotel rents mountain bikes for Rs 5/40 per hour/day. The bicycle stall near the Hotel Garden Manor has ordinary bikes for Rs 20 per day (negotiable). The hills present quite a challenge but, since you'd be walking up them anyway, you may as well push a bike and enjoy the coast down! Check the brakes before attempting any steep descents.

AROUND KODAIKANAL
Palani

There are fine views on the journey from Kodaikanal to Palani. Palani's hill temple, **Malaikovil**, dedicated to Murugan, has over 650 steps leading to the inner sanctum where the image of the deity is believed to have miraculous powers.

Some 200,000 pilgrims gather each year for Thaipusam in January. This temple is so popular that an electric winch has been installed to carry sick and aged devotees to the top.

There are several places to stay but *Hotel Modern Home (Railway Feeder Rd)* is far enough from the centre to be reasonably peaceful. Rooms are Rs 80/105 with bath. See Getting There & Away under Kodaikanal for information on getting to/from Palani.

INDIRA GANDHI WILDLIFE SANCTUARY (Annamalai Wildlife Sanctuary)

This is one of three wildlife sanctuaries in the Western Ghats along the Tamil Nadu/Kerala border. It covers almost 1000 sq km and is home to elephant, gaur, tiger, panther, spotted deer, wild boar, bear, porcupine and civet cat. The Nilgiri tahr, commonly known as the ibex, may also be spotted, as may many birds.

Six tribal groups engage in subsistence agriculture here – the Kadars, Malai, Malasars, Eravalars, Puliyars and Muthuvars.

TAMIL NADU

Information

Visitors are not discouraged here, but limitations are placed on their entry: wildlife takes priority and at least 90% of the park is closed to visitors.

The reception centre and most lodges are at Topslip, about 35km south-west of Pollachi. Day visitors may proceed directly to Topslip. Entrance is Rs 5.

Unless you have accommodation you may only be in the park between 6 am and 6 pm. The infrequent buses make accessibility difficult. However, if you come by private vehicle you cannot use this in the park and you'll be restricted to the tours conducted in the departmental vans that run 8 am to 5 pm (lunch break is 1 to 3 pm). These tours take one hour, cover about 14km and cost Rs 30 per person.

Along the route are two strategically placed domestic elephants. The bus will stop so you can have a better look and one of the elephants will perform various three-legged stunts and play a mouth organ. Sometimes there are elephant rides (Rs 100 per person per hour). In the little museum you'll see stuffed elephant legs, stuffed tigers and an elephant foetus preserved in formaldehyde!

Trekking in the park can be arranged at Topslip. However, you must be accompanied by a guide and the maximum length of trek is four hours for Rs 60 per person.

The sanctuary can be visited at any time of year, but there are several factors to consider. It's best to come Monday to Friday when there are staff to handle your inquiries and bookings. The time limitations for day and residential visitors mean you are unlikely to see many, if any, wild animals. The climate is cooler in January/February but you're more likely to see animals during the wet season in June/July and November/December. In March/April, with water shortages and fire risk, the sanctuary may be closed.

Once you get through the bureaucracy and arrive at the park, it's quiet, calm, cool and green. The staff are helpful and humorous. As they suggest, be content with the flora and the hope that, somewhere beyond it, wild animals may be living in sanctuary.

Places to Stay & Eat

Accommodation is available near Topslip and is usually limited to one night only, with a definite maximum of three nights. All accommodation *must* be booked in advance in Pollachi at the Wildlife Warden's Office (☎ 04259-25356) on Meenkarai Rd. The office is open 9 am to 5 pm Monday to Friday (no booking possible on weekends or holidays). Sometimes there is a screening process, where prospective visitors are interviewed to determine their suitability. Interviews are conducted 10 am to noon. Since accommodation availability and cost are constantly under review, it's a good idea to phone first to get the lowdown.

The accommodation near Topslip consists of two dormitories, a few suites, lodges and a small house.

Ambuli Illam, 2km from the reception centre, is the best. This has three 'suites' and costs Rs 45 per person. There's a canteen here, about the only place in the park where you'll get a decent meal.

Hornbill House has four beds and costs Rs 250.

At Parambikulam, the very basic *resthouse* has no catering facilities and only a few 'meals' places nearby.

For day visitors, although there is food and drink available, you may wish to bring your own.

Should you get stuck in Pollachi (a likely occurrence given the erratic hours of the Wildlife Warden's Office), you could stay at *Sakthi Hotels* (☎ 04259-23060, *Coimbatore Rd*) – the choice of the stars when they make their movies at Topslip. It offers doubles for Rs 230, or Rs 460 with air-con, and has a large (very noisy but very good) restaurant. A cheaper option on the same road, *Ramesh Lodge*, has doubles for Rs 125 (no singles).

Getting There & Away

Annamalai is between Palani and Coimbatore. Regular buses from both places stop at the nearest large town, Pollachi, which is also on the Coimbatore to Dindigul train line. From Pollachi, buses leave the bus stand for Topslip at 6 am and 3.30 pm and return at 8.30 am and 6 pm. A taxi from Pollachi is around Rs 500 one way.

COIMBATORE
☎ 0422 • pop 1.23 million

Coimbatore is a large industrial city often referred to as either the Manchester or Detroit of the south because of its production of textiles and engineering components. It's also full of 'suitings and shirtings' shops. It's organised, friendly and a pleasant place for an overnight stop.

Orientation & Information

The main bus station has three bus stands and is at Gandhipuram, 2km from the train station.

The main post office is open for poste restante collection 10 am to 3 pm, Monday to Saturday. For email and fax visit the efficient Best Business Centre (☎ 235538, fax 233894) in Kalingarayan St.

You can change money at the State Bank of India and Scotia Bank near the train station.

A tourist office can be found at the train station.

Places to Stay – Budget

Hotel Sivakami (☎ 210271, Dave & Co Lane) is friendly and helpful and has basic rooms with bath for Rs 130/150. There are several other similar places on this relatively peaceful street opposite the train station.

Hotel Shree Shakti (☎ 234225, 11/148 Sastri Rd) is a friendly place. Rooms have a fan and bathroom and cost Rs 150/190 for singles/doubles.

Zakir Hotel (Sastri Rd) has rooms for Rs 95/120, and cold water only.

Sri Ganapathy Lodge (☎ 230632, Sastri Rd) has reasonable rooms with bath for Rs 130/190.

Railway retiring rooms include doubles for Rs 120, or Rs 175 with air-con. The dorm beds (men only) are Rs 40. There's an electronic information board indicating occupied rooms.

Places to Stay – Mid-Range & Top End

Hotel Blue Star (☎ 230635, Nehru St) has well-appointed rooms for Rs 220/300 with bath. The back rooms are quieter. There's a basement bar and a veg and nonveg restaurant.

Hotel Tamil Nadu (☎ 236311), near the state bus stand, has ordinary rooms for Rs 200/320 with bath, and air-con rooms for Rs 360/450. The deluxe rooms (with grotty red carpet) are overpriced. The water is hot but the taps are hotter – take care!

The *Hotel City Tower (☎ 230681, fax 230103, Sivasamy Rd)* is a clean, modern place with singles/doubles for Rs 550/700, or Rs 900/1100 with air-con. All rooms have Star TV and bath. There are two excellent restaurants.

Nilgiri's Nest (☎ 217247, fax 217131, 739A Avanashi Rd) is a pleasant, well-run hotel. Bed and breakfast costs Rs 950/1100 in comfortable air-con rooms. The hotel has the same excellent restaurant and supermarket facility as its Chennai branch.

Hotel Surya International (☎ 217755, fax 216110, 105 Racecourse Rd) has luxurious standard rooms for Rs 1100/1300.

The Residency (☎ 201234, fax 201414, 1076 Avanashi Rd) is the swishest hotel in town. Singles/doubles start at Rs 1800/2000. A professional business centre offers email and fax facilities to guests and nonguests. The lobby has a coffee shop with tantalising goodies and a reasonable bookshop.

Places to Eat

There are numerous 'meals' restaurants in the train station area serving thalis from around Rs 30.

Royal Hindu Restaurant, about 100m north-east of the train station, is a huge place offering good vegetarian meals.

Hotel Top Form (Nehru St) serves nonvegetarian food at reasonable prices.

Hotel City Tower (☎ 230681, Sivasamy Rd) has a very pleasant rooftop restaurant – a good place for a splurge.

Annalakshmi (106 Racecourse Rd), next to the Hotel Surya International, is the top

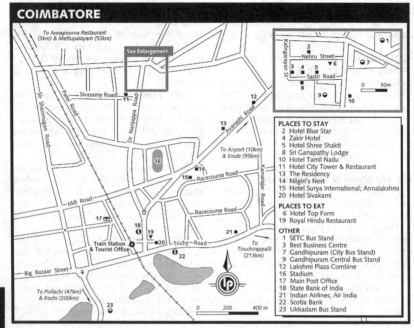

COIMBATORE

To Annapoorna Restaurant (3km) & Mettupalayam (53km)

See Enlargement

Kalingarayan St

Nehru Street

Sastri Road

0   50m

Sivasamy Road

Sir Shanmugam Road

Patel Road

Dr Nanjappa Road

Avanashi Road

To Airport (10km) & Erode (95km)

Kamarajar Road

Racecourse Road

Racecourse Road

Mill Road

Trichy Road

To Tiruchirappalli (213km)

Train Station & Tourist Office

Big Bazaar Street

To Pollachi (47km) & Kochi (200km)

0   200   400m

PLACES TO STAY
2 Hotel Blue Star
4 Zakir Hotel
5 Hotel Shree Shakti
8 Sri Ganapathy Lodge
10 Hotel Tamil Nadu
11 Hotel City Tower & Restaurant
13 The Residency
14 Nilgiri's Nest
15 Hotel Surya International; Annalakshmi
20 Hotel Sivakami

PLACES TO EAT
6 Hotel Top Form
19 Royal Hindu Restaurant

OTHER
1 SETC Bus Stand
3 Best Business Centre
7 Gandhipuram (City Bus Stand)
9 Gandhipuram Central Bus Stand
12 Lakshmi Plaza Combine
16 Stadium
17 Main Post Office
18 State Bank of India
21 Indian Airlines; Air India
22 Scotia Bank
23 Ukkadam Bus Stand

vegetarian restaurant. It's run by devotees of Swami Shantanand Saraswati who established Shivanjali, an education trust; the food is beautifully prepared. It's open daily for dinner, 6.45 to 9.45 pm; Monday to Saturday for lunch, noon to 3 pm. Set meals are Rs 230. There's another branch in Chennai.

Annapoorna vegetarian restaurant, Mettupalayam Rd, 3km north-west of town, is a favourite for thalis at Rs 25.

Getting There & Away

Air The airport is 12km to the east of town. Indian Airlines (☎ 399821) and Air India (☎ 213393) offices are on Trichy Rd. There are daily flights with Indian Airlines and/or Jet Airways to Mumbai (US$135), Chennai (US$83) and Kozhikode (Calicut) (US$35). Indian Airlines also has three flights a week to Bangalore (US$90).

Bus Coimbatore has two bus stations at Gandhipuram and Ukkadam.

The large Gandhipuram bus station has three bus stands all within 100m of each other. The northernmost stand (formerly TTC) is now the SETC bus stand. Buses from here leave for:

destination	frequency
Bangalore	10 daily
Chennai	15 daily
Ernakulam	11 daily
Kottayam	four daily
Pondicherry	five daily
Rameswaram	two daily
Thiruvananthapuram	eight daily

Bookings for these services can be made at the reservation office (open 9 am to 9 pm) at Bay 1 of the Gandhipuram bus station.

TAMIL NADU

The stand immediately south of this is known as Gandhipuram City bus stand. Buses from here are local city buses only.

The final bus stand at the Gandhipuram bus station is known as Gandhipuram Central bus stand. Buses from here travel to nearby destinations north and east of Coimbatore, including Mettupalayam (every five minutes) and Ooty (every 15 minutes).

The Ukkadam bus station has buses to destinations south of Coimbatore including:

destination	frequency
Dindigul	seven daily
Munnar	two daily
Madurai	every 30 minutes
Palani	every 20 minutes
Pollachi	every three minutes 6 am to 9 pm

There are also numerous private, long-distance 'sightseeing video buses'. You can get the details from travel agencies such as HM Travels (☎ 431839) at Bharathiyar Rd, Gandhipuram.

Train Coimbatore is a major rail junction. For Ooty, catch the daily *Nilgiri Express* at 6.25 am; it connects with the miniature railway at Mettupalayam. The whole trip takes 4½ hours and costs Rs 47/210 in 2nd/1st class.

There are numerous daily trains between Coimbatore and Chennai Central (494km), the fastest being the new *Shatabdi Express* service, which takes just under seven hours. Departure times are 7.25 am from Coimbatore and 3.10 pm from Chennai. An aircon chair car costs Rs 625. The *Kovai Express* takes 7½ hours and costs Rs 151/531 in 2nd/1st class. From Coimbatore it leaves at 2.20 pm; from Chennai it leaves at 6.15 am. Other trains take up to nine hours.

The *Coimbatore-Rameswaram Express* at 11.25 pm goes daily via Madurai (Rs 61/294 in 2nd/1st class, 229km, six hours) to Rameswaram (Rs 89/447, 393km, 12 hours). The *Kanniya Kumari Express* runs daily, departing Coimbatore at 1.20 am (Rs 161/556, 514km, 13½ hours).

To the Kerala coast, the daily *Hyderabad-Cochin Express* departs Coimbatore at 11.40 pm (Rs 76/184, 114km, 5½ hours).

The train for Pollachi leaves at 6.20 pm and costs Rs 20 (one hour; 2nd class only).

Getting Around

Many buses ply between the train station and the Gandhipuram bus station including bus Nos JJ, 24, 55 and 57. For the airport take No 20 from the Gandhipuram City bus stand or Nos 10 or 16 from the train station (Rs 27).

Auto-rickshaw drivers are rapacious. They'll charge Rs 50 between the bus and train stations and over Rs 200 for the airport.

The Nilgiri Hills

An integral part of the Western Ghats and the Nilgiri Biosphere Reserve, the Nilgiri Hills (also called Nilgiris) is the oldest and second-highest mountain range in India, after the Himalaya. The hills acquired the name Nilgiris (Blue Mountains) from local people some 1000 years ago because of their proclivity for blue haze. Covering an area of 2542 sq km, they consist of forested rolling hills, gentle and steep slopes, lakes and tea plantations. Several tribal groups still live here.

The Nilgiris present opportunities for trekking and other outdoor activities. The best time to visit is winter (November to February).

Flora & Fauna

The Nilgiris, with 40% of India's plant species, are home to ancient shola evergreen moist and mixed deciduous forests. There's also an impressive array of wildlife, such as gaur, mouse deer, muntjac (barking deer) and sambar, four-horned antelope, bonnet macaque, common langur, Malabar flying squirrel, rusty-spotted cat, and shy and endangered Nilgiri tahr – of the 2000 remaining in the world, 200 live here. A small number of leopards, elephants and tigers inhabit pockets of Mukurthi and

Hill Tribes of the Nilgiris

For centuries, the Nilgiris have been home to hill tribes who have lived together in relative peace and harmony. While retaining integrity in customs, dress, principal occupation and language, the tribes were interdependent economically, socially and culturally.

The Toda tribe lived on the western plateau in the area now called Ooty. Their social, economic and spiritual system centred on the buffalo. The dairy produce derived from the buffalo (mainly milk and ghee) was integral to their diet. It was used as currency – in exchange for grain, tools, pots and even medical services from other tribes. Perhaps most importantly, the dairy products were used as offerings to the gods and fuel for the funeral pyre. It was only at the ritual for human death that the strictly vegetarian Toda killed a buffalo. They killed not for food but to provide company for the deceased. Still today, the Toda believe that the soul of the dead buffalo accompanies the soul of a dead person to heaven and that the buffalo will continue to provide the valued dairy produce in heaven just as it did on earth. Other traditional customs that continue today include the division of labour: men care for the buffaloes; women embroider shawls used for ritual as well as practical purposes.

The Badaga migrated to the Nilgiri Hills in the wake of Muslim invasions in the north, and are thus not officially a tribal people. With knowledge of those outside the hills, they became effective representatives for the hill tribes. Their agricultural produce, particularly grain, added a further dimension to the hill diet, and they traded this for buffalo products from the Toda.

The Kotas lived in the Kotagiri area and were considered by other tribes to be lower in status. Artisans of leather goods and pots, the Kotas were also musicians. The Kotas still undertake ceremonies in which the gods are beseeched for rains and bountiful harvests.

The Kurumbas inhabited the thick forests of the south. They gathered bamboo, honey and materials for housing, some of which they supplied to other tribes. They also engaged in a little agriculture, and at sowing and harvest times, they employed the Badaga to perform rituals entreating the gods for abundant yields. Kurumba witchcraft was respected and sought after by the other tribes.

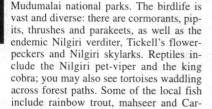

Mudumalai national parks. The birdlife is vast and diverse: there are cormorants, pipits, thrushes and parakeets, as well as the endemic Nilgiri verditer, Tickell's flowerpeckers and Nilgiri skylarks. Reptiles include the Nilgiri pit-viper and the king cobra; you may also see tortoises waddling across forest paths. Some of the local fish include rainbow trout, mahseer and Carnatic carp.

Environment

Environmental degradation in the Nilgiris is distressing. The capital, Ooty, strains under its permanent population and the colossal influx of tourists. In the countryside, some areas have been totally deforested; smuggling of teak and poaching of wildlife continue, sometimes with the connivance of forest rangers; tea plantations expand indiscriminately; dams are proliferating (there are 20 in this small district alone); unlicensed mines spring up; and there is unrestrained film production taking place in fragile environments.

If you'd like more information, contact the following organisations in Ooty:

Hill Area Development Programme
(☎ 43805) near the Wildlife Warden's Office – aims to 'conserve the fragile hill ecosystem' through reforestation and other conservation programs.

Nilgiri Wildlife & Environment Association
(☎ 43968) District Forest Officer (North), Mt

Hill Tribes of the Nilgiris

The Irulus, also from the southern slopes, produced tools and gathered honey and other forest products which they converted into brooms and incense. They are devotees of Vishnu and often performed special rituals for other tribes. Some Irulus are still practising these ancient rites at the Rangaswami Temple.

British settlement in the Ooty area from the early 19th century impacted significantly on tribal life. Some tribes adapted quickly, especially the Badaga. Being cultivators, they continued their traditional pursuits in untraditional ways: they cultivated the cash crops (tea and coffee) of the new settlers, but they were no longer able to provide the grains that were essential to the economy of the other tribes. Eventually tribal systems, especially economic and cultural ones, began to collapse.

Displaced tribes have been 'granted' land by the Indian government. But the cultivation of land is anathema to the Toda, who see themselves as caretakers of the soil – for them, to dig into the land is to desecrate it. To fulfil their traditional role and, at the same time, comply with government expectations, many have leased their land to others for cultivation. For this they have been labelled lazy and unwilling to work.

Today many tribal people have assimilated almost to the point of invisibility. Some have fallen into destructive patterns associated with displacement and alienation. Others remain straddled across two cultures, maintaining vestiges of their traditions while embracing customs and beliefs of the dominant culture.

It is in the hills beyond the town of Ooty that the strongest traditions remain. Irulas still live among the trees collecting their honey and fashioning products for others. Kotas work the tea plantations and their shrines can be seen amid the lucrative crop. The Kurumbas continue to practice their traditional medicine. And while some Toda practise Christianity or Hinduism (sometimes both), few leave this life without a tribal ceremony, a buffalo and a shawl. Next to their cement houses, cone-shaped shrines receive the daily dairy offerings. And outside on the grass, women still embroider shawls.

Steward Hill, Ooty – has a useful library and publishes the *Tahr* newsletter.

Save Nilgiris Campaign
(☎ 43082) Nilgiri Centre, Hospital Rd, Ooty – produces *A Greenprint for the Nilgiris.*

COONOOR
☎ 0423 • pop 48,000

At an altitude of 1850m, Coonoor is the first of the three Nilgiri hill stations – Udhagamandalam (Ooty), Kotagiri and Coonoor – that you come to when leaving behind the southern plains. Like Ooty, it's on the toy train line from Mettupalayam.

Coonoor is now a bustling town where tenacious touts can be overwhelming. It's only after climbing up out of the busy market area that you'll get a sense of what hill stations were originally all about. For this reason, most of the better accommodation is in Upper Coonoor 1km to 2km up the hill.

Things to See

The 12 hectare **Sim's Park** in Upper Coonoor has over 1000 plant species, which include magnolia, tree ferns, pines and camellia. Opposite Sim's Park, **Pasteur Institute** is renowned for its research on the treatment of rabies. **Dolphin's Nose** viewpoint, about 10km from town, exposes a vast panorama, which encompasses Catherine Falls. On the way to Dolphin's Nose, **Lamb's Rock** is another place for stunning views. Regular buses leave from the bus stand.

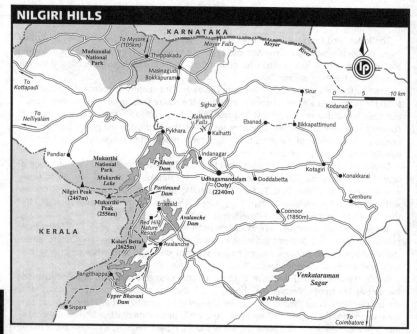

NILGIRI HILLS

Places to Stay & Eat

YWCA Guesthouse (☎ *34426*) in Upper Coonoor is the best budget option. Taxi and rickshaw drivers, as well as touts relate fantastic stories about it being full or overpriced. Phone first to check. This place continues to receive accolades from travellers. Open to men and women, it's a handsome old colonial house with two wooden terraces and views over Coonoor. Large, clean singles/doubles with bath cost Rs 200/370. Hot water and basic food are available. The one hour yoga class (Rs 120) is popular. To get there, take a town bus to Bedford; then it's a five minute walk.

Vivek Tourist Home (☎ *30658*), nearby, is a reasonable place. There are rooms from Rs 220/290 with bath; deluxe rooms with TV are more expensive.

Sri Lakshmi Tourist Home (☎ *31022*) offers basic rooms for Rs 160/210.

Blue Hills (☎ *30103, Mount Rd*) has a good nonveg restaurant; there are also rooms for Rs 160/330 with bath.

Taj Garden Retreat (☎ *30021*), on the hilltop, is an excellent hotel with a beautiful garden and a fine restaurant. Standard/deluxe rooms are in cottages and cost from US$70/80 in the low season, and from US$125/145 (doubles only with all meals) in the high season.

Ramachandra Restaurant (32 Mount Rd) has very good veg and nonveg food from Rs 10. Thalis are Rs 18 and breads are Rs 0.65.

Getting There & Away

Coonoor is on the toy train line between Mettupalayam (28km) and Ooty (18km) – for details see the Ooty Getting There & Away section. Buses to Kotagiri (Rs 8) leave every 15 minutes.

KOTAGIRI
☎ 0423 • pop 25,600

Kotagiri (Line of Houses of the Kotas) is a quiet village 28km east of Ooty. The oldest of the three Nilgiri hill stations, it's dusty and uninspiring but less frenetic than Ooty or Coonoor, and is surrounded by tea estates and tribal Kota settlements.

From Kotagiri you can visit **Catherine Falls**, 8km away near the Mettupalayam road (the last 3km is by foot only), **Elk Falls** (6km) and **Kodanad Viewpoint** (22km), where there's a panoramic view over the Coimbatore Plains and the Mysore Plateau. Buses and taxis (Rs 280 return to Ooty) will bring you here.

In town, a Women's Cooperative near Ramchand Square sells handicrafts like traditional Toda embroidery. Part of the profit is put towards the preservation of Toda culture.

Blue Mountain Railway

The Blue Mountain Railway, funded by Nilgiri citizens, was completed in 1898. Ten years later a link to Ooty was added. Along the 45km track, there are 13 tunnels, 19 bridges and 11 stations (some not operational).

Quite different to the toy trains found in places like Shimla and Darjeeling in northern India, the Blue Mountain train has a unique pinion rack system, with the locomotive pushing, rather than pulling, the carriages. Each of the three carriages has its own brakeman, who sits on a little platform and, when appropriate, waves a red or green flag.

The views of the Nilgiris (best from the left on the way up to Ooty) are spectacular. The train is often cancelled during or after the monsoons.

Maintenance costs are prohibitive so the future for the Blue Mountain Railway may be bleak.

For information on schedules, see the Getting There & Away section under Ooty in this chapter.

Places to Stay & Eat

There are very basic lodges such as the *Majestic Lodge*, the *Blue Star* and the *Hotel Ramesh Vihar*. Bring your own sheets. Double rooms with bath start at Rs 130. Until accommodation improves, it's preferable to visit Kotagiri as a day trip from Ooty.

The vegetarian *Kasturi Paradise Restaurant*, diagonally opposite the Women's Cooperative, is good value.

Getting There & Away

Buses stop at the edge of town, about 1km from the centre. From there you walk or get a taxi. Buses journey to Ooty every 40 minutes (crossing one of Tamil Nadu's highest passes) and cost Rs 14. The trip takes almost two hours. Buses to Mettupalayam leave every 30 minutes and to Coonoor every 15 minutes.

UDHAGAMANDALAM (Ooty)
☎ 0423 • pop 89,000

Historically, this is the area of the Toda, the tribal people whose belief systems and practices centre on the buffalo. Today only about 1500 Toda remain, their cone-shaped shrines prominent throughout the hills.

In the early 19th century, the British established Ooty to serve as the summer headquarters of the Madras (now Chennai) government. Until about two decades ago, Ooty (altitude 2240m) resembled an unlikely combination of southern England and Australia: single-storey stone cottages, bijou fenced flower gardens, leafy winding lanes, and tall eucalyptus stands. Other reminders of the British period include the stone churches, private schools, the Ooty Club, and the terraced botanical gardens. Maharaja summer palaces hark back to yet another time.

Now tourist development has totally transformed Ooty. The sewerage system, incapable of dealing with the demand, flows directly into the lake – important to remember, should you be thinking of boating.

In spite of this, Ooty retains a certain appeal. Life is relaxed here and touting and

TAMIL NADU

haranguing is less prevalent than elsewhere. Just a kilometre or two out of town you are in the peace of the hills, with their superb views and welcome silence. You can find accommodation that takes advantage of these aspects. You can even stay in one of the former palaces. The journey up on the toy train is stunning. Ooty's a great place at any time; from April to June it's a welcome relief from the hot plains and in winter – October to March – it's crisp and clear and the best time to come. You'll need warm clothing as the overnight temperature occasionally drops to 0°C.

Orientation

Ooty is spread over a large area among rolling hills and valleys. Between the lake and the racecourse are the train station and bus stand. From either of these it's a 10 minute walk to the bazaar area and 20 minutes to Ooty's real centre, Charing Cross, the junction of Coonoor, Kelso and Commercial roads.

Maps are available at the Survey of India, near the botanical gardens.

Information

The tourist office (☎ 43977), on Commercial Rd, is open Monday to Friday, 10 am to 1 pm and 2 to 5.45 pm. It mainly organises tours.

There is a confusing array of 'forest' departments in Ooty. They are generally open Monday to Friday, 10 am to 5.45 pm. There are two District Forest Officers (DFOs), both in the same complex, next to the police station near the roundabout at the top of Charing Cross. DFO North (☎ 43968) manages the northern and eastern areas including Coonoor, Kotagiri and Doddabetta. DFO South (☎ 44083) manages places in the south including Mukurthi National Park, Avalanche, Pykhara, Pandiar, Parsons Valley, Bangithappal and Sispara.

There's also a Wildlife Warden's Office (WWO; ☎ 44098) Mahalingam Buildings, Coonoor Rd, which manages most of Mukurthi National Park, Upper Bhavani, and Mudumalai National Park.

Money Money can be changed at the State Bank of India opposite the police station.

Post & Communications The post office in Ettines Rd is open Monday to Saturday, 9 am to 5 pm. The telegraph office (open 24 hours) is also here.

Email facilities for Rs 15 per page are available through the notary's office of Mr Kenneth Gonsalves (☎ 42224), in the Oriental Buildings near the court. He's a local advocate and his assistant, Mrs Xavier, is very helpful and will even ring your hotel when your email has arrived. The email address is: gonslaw@theoffice.net.

Bookshops Higginbothams has two bookshops – next to the tourist office and just near the Collector's Office. The staff are particularly helpful.

Library The Nilgiri Library (closed Friday), also close to the Collector's Office, is a quaint haven with a reading room and a collection of over 40,000 books, including rare titles on the Nilgiris and hill tribes. Temporary membership is Rs 20.

Emergency For Police call ☎ 100; Hospital ☎ 2212; Fire ☎ 2999.

Botanical Gardens

Established in 1848, these beautifully maintained gardens include numerous mature species as well as Italian and Japanese sections. There is also a fossilised tree trunk believed to be 20 million years old. At the eastern end of the gardens, there's a Toda *mund* (hill/village) where Toda people display aspects of their traditional culture to gawking tourists. Now a highly commercial show (described by one Toda activist as a human zoo), it is far removed from the reality of Toda life in the Nilgiri villages.

The gardens are open 8 am to 6.45 pm. Entry for children/adults is Rs 2/5.

St Stephen's Church

St Stephen's Church, on the hill in Club Rd, was built in 1829, consecrated in 1830, and

UDHAGAMANDALAM (OOTY)

PLACES TO STAY
2 Savoy Hotel & Restaurant
10 TTDC Youth Hostel
13 Hotel Tamil Nadu
16 Hotel Nahar & Restaurant;
 Naveen Tours & Travels
20 Hotel Khems
23 YWCA
25 Nilgiri Woodlands Hotel
26 Hotel Dasaprakash &
 Restaurant
31 Reflections Guest House
33 Fernhill Palace
34 Regency Villa

PLACES TO EAT
7 Shinkow's Chinese
 Restaurant
11 Ooty Bakers &
 Confectioners
12 Hotel Sanjay; Hills Travels
17 Tandoori Mahal

OTHER
1 Survey of India
3 Ooty Club
4 St Stephen's Church
5 Nilgiri Library
6 District Court; Collector's Office;
 Email Facility; Higginbothams
8 Police Station
9 State Bank of India
14 Tourist Office; MB Travels
15 Higginbothams
18 Main Post & Telegraph Office
19 U-Rent Motor Cycle Hire
21 Wildlife Warden's Office
22 Market
24 Racecourse
27 St Thomas Church
28 Bus Stand
29 Tourist Guides
 Association Office
30 Lake Park
32 Tourist Cafe (Boat & Horse Hire)

TAMIL NADU

is the oldest church in the Nilgiris. Its huge wooden beams came from the palace of Tipu Sultan in Srirangapatnam – hauled the 120km distance by a team of elephants. The attached cemetery contains the graves of many an Ooty pioneer, including John Sullivan, the founder of Ooty.

Activities

Ooty is a good place for outdoor activities.

Walking If you want a guide for walking, try the Ooty Tourist Guides Association opposite the bus stand, open daily, 7 am to 11 pm. There's no telephone but you can ring the kiosk next door on ☎ 45222. The price of the guides is negotiable (around Rs 200 per day, extra if you want overnight stays).

Horse Riding Alone or with a guide, there are two choices. You can hire horses at the Tourist Cafe on the north side of the lake. The rides here mostly consist of a circuit (up to one hour) of the lake area. Choose your animal carefully; some of these horses have clearly seen better years. Prices vary, so haggle hard. A fair price is about Rs 100 an hour.

For more serious riding, book at the reception of the Regency Villa. Each morning a pony man arrives with sturdy animals for a three hour trek through rolling hills and into a Toda village. The ride is exhilarating (not for beginners) and costs Rs 125 per hour. However, the encounter with the tribal people smacks of a beads and trinkets mentality.

Boating Rowboats can be rented from the Tourist Cafe by the lake. High-season crowds can make boating somewhat tortuous. Prices start from Rs 40 for a two seater pedal boat and up to Rs 200 for a 15 seater motor boat. Signs warn people to 'Avoid dancing on the boats'.

Horse Races The season for the Ooty horse races begins on April 14 and lasts till about June. Some consider the racecourse tatty and the betting tame, but the season creates considerable entertainment.

Organised Tours

The Tourist Office organises trips to Mudumalai Wildlife Sanctuary via the Pykhara Dam for Rs 200 (plus Rs 30 entrance to the park); and Coonoor taking in the Ooty botanical gardens, Doddabetta, Sim's Park and Dolphin's Nose for Rs 120. Naveen Tours & Travels (☎ 43747), near Hotel Nahar, and Hills Travels (☎ 42090), at Hotel Sanjay, are among several private operators who run a range of tours.

MB Travels (☎ 42604, fax 44912), adjacent to the tourist office, organises tours including camping, fishing and walking. Airline reservations can also be arranged here.

Places to Stay

Since Ooty is a sellers' market in the high season (1 April to 15 June), hoteliers double their prices, and these don't necessarily equate with quality. Note that checkout time is generally 9 am. In town, you'll be close to all amenities, noise and pollution. The peace and tranquillity can be found just a few kilometres out.

Places to Stay – Budget

TTDC Youth Hostel (☎ 43665, Charing Cross) offers dorm beds at Rs 80, and doubles for Rs 200/420 in the low/high season.

YWCA (☎ 42218, Ettines Rd) is reasonable value but it's often full. A dorm bed costs Rs 77 and doubles with bath are Rs 260 (low season) and Rs 330 (high season). There are also quiet cottages with private bathroom – worth booking ahead. Three-course veg meals are available (Rs 75) and there is a lounge with an open fire in winter. The YWCA is a good place to organise trekking.

Reflections Guest House (☎ 43834, North Lake Rd) has good views over the lake. Doubles rooms cost Rs 220 (Rs 330 in the high season). There are only six rooms, all with hot water, and the atmosphere is very homey and comfortable. The friendly owner, Mrs Dique, is a good source of information on the region's history. Be sure to confirm checkout time here.

Places to Stay – Mid-Range

Hotel Tamil Nadu (☎ 44370, fax 44369), on the hill above the tourist office, is a good place in this range. Set in a largish garden, doubles with bath cost Rs 450/800 in the low/high season. Cottages are available for Rs 550/950. There's a restaurant, coffee shop and bar.

Hotel Khems (☎ 44188, Shoreham Palace Rd) is very well appointed and good value. Standard/superior doubles are Rs 550/750 (low season) and Rs 900/1100 (high season). Hot water is available morning and evening. There's a restaurant.

Nilgiri Woodlands Hotel (☎ 42551, fax 42530, Ettines Rd) is a Raj-era hotel. Manicured gardens offer great views of Ooty. All rooms are clean with plumbing due for retirement. In the low season, doubles with bath cost Rs 300, cottages are Rs 600 and suites Rs 700. High-season rates are from Rs 500 to Rs 1100.

Hotel Dasaprakash (☎ 42434, Ettines Rd) is another long-established hotel. Doubles with bath range from Rs 180 to Rs 500 in the low season; Rs 360 to Rs 700 in the high season.

Regency Villa (☎ 42555, Fernhill), set within eight wooded hectares (along with Fernhill Palace) is owned by the Maharaja of Mysore. It's wonderfully atmospheric, although these days it's getting a little frayed around the edges. There are potted plants, wicker chairs and faded photographs of the Ooty Hunt, a popular pastime of the Raj. The best rooms are ultra spacious with bay windows, fully tiled Victorian bathrooms (with hot water) and a fireplace. In the main building doubles cost Rs 600 to Rs 1000; in the cottage they're Rs 270 to Rs 600. Budget doubles are particularly good value at Rs 180. And there's no price hike here – prices apply to both high and low season.

Hotel Nahar (☎ 42173, fax 45173, Commercial Rd) is a huge place at Charing Cross. Carpeted doubles with bath and TV cost Rs 650 to Rs 1100 (low season), and Rs 850 to Rs 1400 (high season). It's a 'teetotaller's paradise' with a multicuisine restaurant.

Places to Stay – Top End

Savoy Hotel (☎ 44142, fax 43318, 77 Sylks Rd) is very comfortable. Part of the Taj Group, this place has doubles for US$90 (low season) and US$145 (high season). It has manicured lawns, clipped hedges, rooms with bathtubs, wooden furnishings, working fireplaces, a 24 hour bar and an excellent multicuisine dining room.

Fernhill Palace (☎ 43910, Fernhill) is still closed for renovations. Owned by the Maharaja of Mysore and managed by the Taj Group, it was built in the days when expense was of no concern. For a small tip, the security guards will show you through the extensive ballroom. When it finally opens (current plans are for some time in the first half of the 21st century), its prices will be similar to the Savoy and it'll probably be the best place to stay in Ooty.

Places to Eat

Almost all hotels have restaurants. In addition there are plenty of basic vegetarian 'meals' places on Commercial Rd and Main Bazaar.

Hotel Nahar has two veg restaurants and a popular snack bar serving ice cream and milk shakes.

Hotel Sanjay is a big, bustling place with generous servings of veg and nonveg fare.

Tandoori Mahal (Commercial Rd) has tasty veg dishes for around Rs 40 and nonveg meals for around Rs 55. The service is good, and beer – not always cold – is available (Rs 70).

The *Shinkow's Chinese Restaurant (30 Commissioner's Rd)*, also known as the Zodiac Room, is a family-run business with some really good food. Dishes are around Rs 50.

Hotel Dasaprakash is well known for its lunch thalis for Rs 30. People crowd in, sit in ashram-style rows and are fed huge quantities of delicious items.

Savoy Hotel is the place for a splurge. Buffet lunch or dinner costs Rs 300 (plus tax) for all you can eat. The dining room fire takes the chill off the cool low-season nights.

Ooty Bakers & Confectioners (Wren Building, Charing Cross), has a gastronomical range of bread, 50 types of pastry and 35 different pies (veg and nonveg).

Getting There & Away

Air Coimbatore is the closest airport to Ooty. Flight reservations and confirmations for most airlines to domestic and international destinations can be made in Ooty at MB Travels (☎ 42604, fax 44912).

Bus The state bus companies all have reservation offices at the bus stand, open daily, 9 am to 5.30 pm. There are six buses daily to Mysore (Rs 55, five hours) and many continue to Bangalore (Rs 120, eight hours). There are buses every 10 minutes to Coimbatore (Rs 20, three hours), every 10 to 15 minutes to Mettupalayam (Rs 15, two hours), four buses to Chennai (Rs 120, 15 hours), and also direct services to Kanyakumari (14 hours), Thanjavur (10 hours) and Tirupathi (14 hours).

Most of the private companies are at Charing Cross. They're a little more expensive than the state buses, but worth it.

To get to Mudumalai Wildlife Sanctuary (Rs 22, 67km, 2½ hours), take one of the Mysore buses or one of the small buses that go via the narrow and twisting Sighur Ghat road. Most of these rolling wrecks travel only as far as Masinagudi, from where there are five buses a day to Theppakadu (at Mudumalai). Buses travelling via the sanctuary sometimes ask passengers for another Rs 30, which is the park entrance fee. Private services run to Mysore via Theppakadu for Rs 100.

Local buses leave every hour for Kotagiri (Rs 10, one to 1½ hours) and every 20 minutes to Coonoor (Rs 9, one hour). Buses to Doddabetta (Rs 12) depart about every 90 minutes.

Train The miniature train is the best way to get here. Departures and arrivals at Mettupalayam usually connect with those of the *Nilgiri Express*, which runs between Mettupalayam and Chennai. It departs Chennai at 8.15 pm and arrives in Mettupalayam at 8.30 am. From Mettupalayam, it leaves at 7.25 pm. Tickets cost Rs 223/767 in 2nd/1st class. If you're catching the miniature train from Ooty, and you want a seat, be at least 45 minutes early.

The miniature train leaves Mettupalayam for Ooty (Rs 22/114 in 2nd/1st class, 46km) at 7.45 am and arrives in Ooty at noon. From Ooty the train leaves at 3 pm. The trip down takes about 3½ hours. During the high season there's an extra departure in each direction daily; from Mettupalayam at 9.10 am and from Ooty at 2 pm. There are also two extra services between Ooty and Coonoor at this time – they leave Ooty daily at 9.30 am and 6 pm.

Getting Around

Plenty of unmetered auto-rickshaws hang around outside the bus stand. In the high season, the drivers quote outrageous fares. Taxis are also available.

You can hire a bicycle at the market but many of the roads are steep so you'll end up pushing it uphill (great on the way down though!). Motorcycles can be hired from U-Rent (☎ 42118) in the Hotel Sapphire Buildings on Ettines Rd. A 100cc machine will set you back Rs 380 per 24 hour period, including insurance but excluding petrol. A deposit of Rs 550 is required plus a current international or your home country driving licence (a car licence will suffice). Helmets are not supplied. U-Rent is open daily, 9 am to 7 pm.

MUDUMALAI WILDLIFE SANCTUARY
☎ 0423

In the foothills of the Nilgiris, this 321 sq km sanctuary is part of the Nilgiri Biosphere Reserve (3000 sq km) that includes Bandipur and Wayanad in neighbouring Karnataka and Kerala states. The larger reserve's vegetation ranges from grasslands to semi-evergreen forests. In Mudumalai, the mostly dense forest is home to chital (spotted deer), gaur, tiger, panther, wild boar and sloth bear. Otters and crocodiles inhabit the Moyar River. The sanctuary's wild elephant

TAMIL NADU

population, one of the largest in the country, supposedly numbers about 600; however, you're more likely to see their domesticated cousins carrying out logging duties.

The best time to visit Mudumalai is between December and June. Heavy rain is common in October and November and the sanctuary may be closed during the dry season, February to March.

Orientation & Information

The main service area in Mudumalai is Theppakadu, on the main road between Udhagamandalam (Ooty) and Mysore. Here you'll find the sanctuary's reception centre (☎ 56235), open daily 6.30 am to 6 pm. There is some accommodation and an elephant camp here.

Book sanctuary accommodation in advance with the Wildlife Warden's Office (WWO, ☎ 44098), Coonoor Rd, Ooty. Entry fees are Rs 2/5 for children/adults.

Jungle Tours & Travel (☎ 0423-56336), in the centre of Masinagudi, offers trekking and other adventure activities at reasonable rates.

Wildlife Tours

It's not possible to hike in the sanctuary and tours are limited to the sanctuary's minibuses, jeeps and elephants. Private vehicles are not allowed. Minibus tours (morning and afternoon) cost Rs 25 per person for 45 minutes, and they go about 15km into the 'jungle'. The one hour elephant rides (Rs 140) can be booked in advance at the WWO or direct at the Theppakadu reception centre.

Places to Stay & Eat

All budgets are catered for – there are cheap forest bungalows inside the park at Theppakadu; mid-range hotels in Masinagudi (8km from Theppakadu) and expensive resorts in Bokkapuram (4km south of Masinagudi).

Bungalows *Sylvan Lodge*, on the Moyar River in Theppakadu, has basic doubles for Rs 40, plus a reservation fee of Rs 2. Let staff know if you want meals (Rs 25 extra). Bookings must be made at WWO in Ooty.

There's a one night maximum stay, with extensions possible during slack periods. Beds at the dormitory at the back of the lodge, or at *Morgan Dormitory*, near the park reception centre, are a mere Rs 10.

You are unlikely to get into the nicer *Log House*, next to the Sylvan Lodge, because it's on permanent standby for VVIPs (very, *very* important people).

Hotels *Hotel Tamil Nadu* (☎ 56249), in the park, has large family rooms (with four beds) for Rs 450 and dorm beds for Rs 50 per person. The attached restaurant is the best place for a meal or cold drink. Please note that alcohol is banned in the park.

There are two hotels on the main road in Masinagudi.

The *Hotel Dreamland* (☎ 56127) is better than the outside suggests. It has clean but noisy rooms with TV and fan for Rs 250 a double.

Mountania Resthouse (☎ 56337), in a pretty garden and away from the main road, has doubles for Rs 420, and meals (for guests only) from Rs 35 to Rs 45.

Resorts Advance bookings, at any travel agency, are essential and you'll also require private transport from Masinagudi, although the resorts will usually arrange pick-up.

Bamboo Banks (☎ 56222) is 1.5km from Masinagudi. One of the region's oldest private lodges, it charges Rs 790 for a double (no singles), not including meals.

Forest Hills Guesthouse (☎ 56216) is a friendly, homestyle place. Spacious, clean rooms cost Rs 550/725/850 for a single/double/triple, with meals at Rs 75/125/150 for breakfast/lunch/dinner.

Jungle Hut Guesthouse (☎/fax 56240) is the most expensive place, and not particularly good value: Rs 980/1100/1300, and meals from Rs 100. It has a pleasant setting with a small pool.

Jungle Retreat (☎ 56470, fax 56469) is a newer place with rooms from Rs 850/1100 for doubles/triples (no singles), with buffet meals from Rs 100. You can pitch a tent in the grounds and use the facilities for Rs 250 per tent. The outdoor bar and restaurant is probably the highlight.

The ***Chital Walk*** *(☎ 56256; Jungle Trails Lodge)* has long been recognised as one of the more ecofriendly places. Set deeper in the forest, its rustic rooms are Rs 675 a double.

Getting There & Away

Buses from Ooty to Mysore, Bangalore or Hassan in Karnataka stop at Theppakadu, and it's not too difficult to wave them down.

An interesting 'short cut' to/from Ooty (36km, 1½ hours) involves taking one of the small government buses that make the trip up (or down) the tortuous Sighur Ghat road. The bends are so tight and the gradient so steep that large buses can't use it. In fact, there's a sign warning that 'you will have to strain your vehicle much to reach Ooty'. The longer route via Gudalur is equally interesting but not quite as steep (67km, 2½ hours).

Jeep Jeeps can be hired in Masinagudi for Rs 450 per half day.

Getting Around

Buses run daily every two hours between Theppakadu and Masinagudi. A local taxi-jeep charges Rs 200 for the same trip.

Andaman & Nicobar Islands

Take 300 mostly uninhabited tropical islands. Add unique fauna, lush forests, deserted beaches, exquisite coral, clear water, an extraordinary history – and you have the Andaman & Nicobar Islands. For weary mainland travellers, the Andamans offer opportunities for relaxation and/or activities such as trekking, snorkelling and diving.

Situated in the Bay of Bengal, 1000km off the east coast of India, the islands form the peaks of a vast submerged mountain range that extends for almost 1000km between Myanmar (Burma) and Sumatra. The total land area of the islands is 8248 sq km. The Andamans form about 6408 sq km with the highest point, Saddle Peak, at 732m, on North Andaman.

The Nicobar Islands begin 50km south of Little Andaman. While geographically and ethnically close to Myanmar, politically the islands belong to the Union Territory of India.

Until the beginnings of colonial rule the Andamans were populated mainly by Andamanese, indigenous tribes of the Negrito peoples. Patterns of traditional life still remain among the Jarawa and Onge tribes who live in the interior regions of South Andaman. However, the majority of the 300,000 people on the Andamans are mainlanders or their descendants who live in and around the capital of Port Blair on South Andaman.

The indigenous people of the Nicobars, the Nicobarese, are probably descended from people of Malaysia and Myanmar. Their dialects belong to the Mon-Khmer group.

The islands are accessible by boat and plane from Chennai and Calcutta (with an infrequent boat service from Visakhapatnam). International connections are expected with the completion of a new runway in 2001. However, significant travel restrictions apply. The maximum period of stay for foreigners is 30 days and access to the Nicobar Islands as well as some of the

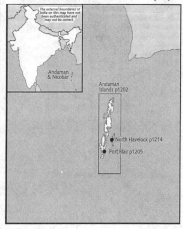

Andaman & Nicobar Islands at a Glance

Population: 340,000
Area: 8248 sq km on 319 islands
Capital: Port Blair
Main Languages: Hindi, Bengali, Tamil & tribal languages
Best Time to Go: December to early April

The external boundaries of India on this map have not been authenticated and may not be correct.

Andaman & Nicobar

Andaman Islands p1202

North Havelock p1214

Port Blair p1205

- **Deserted Beaches** – isolation is hard to find in India but on some island beaches it's there for the taking

- **World-Class Snorkelling** – the superb coral reefs are a major attraction

- **Cellular Jail** – a sobering reminder of the history of Port Blair

Andamans is denied to everyone except Indian nationals engaged in research, government business or trade.

History
The name Andaman is probably derived from the Malay, Handuman, a reference to

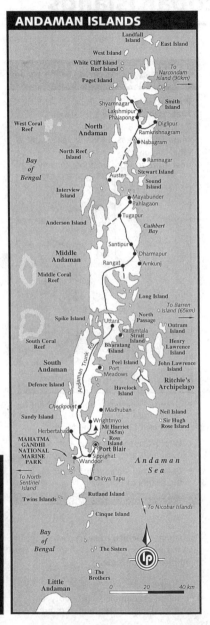

ANDAMAN ISLANDS

Landfall Island
East Island
West Island
White Cliff Island
Reef Island
To Narcondam Island (90km)
Paget Island
Shyamnagar
Smith Island
Lakshmipur
Phaiapong
Diglipur
North Andaman
Ramkrishnagram
Nabagram
West Coral Reef
North Reef Island
Ramnagar
Bay of Bengal
Austen
Stewart Island
Sound Island
Interview Island
Mayabunder
Bahlagaon
Tugapur
Anderson Island
Cuthbert Bay
Santipur
Middle Andaman
Dharmapur
Rangat
Amkunj
Middle Coral Reef
Long Island
To Barren Island (65km)
Spike Island
Uttara
North Passage
Outram Island
Kadamtala Strait Island
South Coral Reef
Bharatang Island
Henry Lawrence Island
South Andaman
Peel Island
Port Meadows
John Lawrence Island
Defence Island
Havelock Island
Ritchie's Archipelago
Checkpoint
Madhuban
Neil Island
Sandy Island
Wrightmyo
Sir Hugh Rose Island
Mt Harriet (365m)
Herbertabad
Ross Island
MAHATMA GANDHI NATIONAL MARINE PARK
Sippighat
Port Blair
Wandoor
Andaman Sea
To North Sentinel Island
Chiriya Tapu
Twins Islands
Rutland Island
To Nicobar Islands
Cinque Island
Bay of Bengal
The Sisters
Little Andaman
The Brothers
0   20   40 km
Andaman Trunk Rd

the Hindu monkey god, whereas the name Nicobar is believed to mean 'Land of the Naked'. Prior to European contact, the people lived healthily as hunters and gatherers.

The islands appeared in the 2nd century maps of the Roman geographer Ptolemy who referred to them as 'islands of cannibals'. Xuan Zang, the well-travelled 7th century Chinese Buddhist monk also noted the existence of the islands and Marco Polo named the islands 'the land of the head hunters' (although, contrary to popular belief, the great explorer never actually visited the islands).

In the late 17th century, the islands were annexed by the powerful Marathas whose empire swept across vast areas of India. In the 19th century the British annexed them for use as a penal colony. Initially the convicts were drawn from the ranks of 'regular thieves and criminals' on the mainland. Later the British transported dissidents – freedom fighters for independence.

Construction of the notorious Cellular Jail began in 1890 and was finished in 1908 (see The Penal Colony boxed text in the Port Blair section of this chapter). At this time the islands were referred to by locals as well as mainlanders as *Kali Pani* or Black Water, a reference to the fear and loathing that awaited the transported prisoners. During WWII, the islands were occupied by the Japanese. Some islanders initiated guerilla activities against the Japanese, but others regarded the Japanese as liberators from British colonialism. The debate on this issue still rages. With Independence in 1947, the islands were incorporated into the Indian Union.

Since Independence considerable development has occurred but in their effort to maximise island revenue, the government has disregarded the needs and land rights of the tribes and has encouraged massive transmigration from the mainland. The population has increased from 50,000 to over 300,000 in just 20 years, and the indigenous island cultures have been swamped. Massive destruction of native forests and rapid growth of plantation forests (teak and rubber) has changed the landscape.

The Indian navy patrols the islands (gun runners and drug smugglers frequently 'stray' into the Andaman Sea). Along with the increase in commercial shipping, these vessels cause significant coral damage, thereby destabilising an already very fragile ecosystem.

At present, administrators are appointed from Delhi on a two year 'hardship' posting. Some make a few nominal changes in the name of progress before they go home. Some of these 'inventive' schemes have included a velodrome (one of only four in India), a high-tech swimming pool (that is rarely used) and the Grand Trunk Rd (dubbed the Road to Nowhere), which cuts through a tribal reserve and links destinations already well served by sea.

Climate

Sea breezes keep temperatures within the 23°C to 31°C range and the humidity at around 80% all year. The south-west monsoons come to the islands between mid-May and June, and the north-east monsoons between November and December. The best time to visit is between December and early April. December and January are the high seasons.

Ecology & Environment

The Andaman and Nicobar islands epitomise a tension between tourism potential and environmental degradation. The major issues are indigenous rights, deforestation, and preservation of the coral reefs. With over 250 uninhabited islands, tourism has a potentially positive role. Looking to the Maldives, where a few uninhabited islands have been developed exclusively for tourism, the Indian government is considering following the same example. This could compensate for earnings lost from reduced tree-felling and would place a value on preservation of the environment. However, debate continues about the most appropriate development.

PERMITS

Foreigners need a permit to visit the Andaman Islands. The Nicobar Islands are off limits to all except Indian nationals engaged in research, government business or trade. The 30 day (maximum) permit allows foreigners to stay in South Andaman, Middle Andaman, Little Andaman (tribal reserves on these islands are out of bounds), Long, North Passage, Bharatang, Havelock and Neil islands. On North Andaman foreigners may stay only in Diglipur.

Day trips are permitted to Ross, Viper, Narcondam, Interview, Cinque, Brothers and Sisters islands, but currently there are regular boats only to Ross and Viper Islands near Port Blair. Boats are allowed to stop at Barren Island, but disembarkation is not allowed and, as yet, there are no regular services. All the islands of the Mahatma Gandhi National Marine Park are open except Boat, Hobday, Twin, Tarmugli, Malay and Pluto.

For air travellers, permits are issued on arrival in Port Blair. If you arrive with an unconfirmed return flight, you'll be given a permit of only 10 to 15 days, but this can be extended to allow a 30 day stay.

Travellers arriving by ship should obtain a permit before being issued with a ticket. The permit is available from the Foreigners' Registration Office in either Chennai or Calcutta (allow five hours – more if the application is submitted late in the day), or from any Indian embassy overseas. On arrival, ship passengers must immediately report to the deputy superintendent of police in Port Blair (in Aberdeen Bazaar). If you fail to do this you could encounter problems when departing since it will be difficult to prove that you have not been here longer than 30 days. Your permit will be stamped again when you depart.

PORT BLAIR

☎ 03192

The capital sprawls around a harbour on the east coast of South Andaman. The absence of touts and beggars adds to the relaxed ambience. Given the remoteness, infrastructure is surprisingly good. Most essentials, including bottled water and mosquito repellent are available and prices are only marginally higher than on the mainland. However, power and water are often restricted and the sewerage system is overstretched. Port Blair is operating at capacity and further growth without infrastructure development will have disastrous effects.

Even though close to mainland Myanmar (Burma), the Andamans still run on Indian time. This means that it's dark by 6 pm and light by 4 am.

Orientation

Most of the hotels, the bus station, passenger dock (Phoenix Bay jetty) and Shipping Corporation of India office are in the central Aberdeen Bazaar area. The airport is 5km south of town, and the nearest beach is at Corbyn's Cove, 7km south of Aberdeen Bazaar.

Information

Tourist Offices The Government of India tourist office (☎ 33006) advises on which islands are accessible and how. Open weekdays only, from 8.30 am to 5 pm, it's above Super Shoppe, about a kilometre from the centre of town on Junglighat Main Rd.

The ultramodern Andaman & Nicobar (A&N) Tourism office (☎ 32694) is diagonally opposite Indian Airlines. It's open 8.30 am to 5.30 pm. Staff are friendly but be aware that printed schedules and prices rarely reflect current reality.

The library, near the main post office, has a small collection of books on the history, geography, flora and fauna, and tribal people of the islands.

Money Travellers cheques and foreign currency can be converted at the State Bank of India (open 9 am to 1 pm during the week and 9 to 11 am on Saturday). A similar service is also available at Island Travels, near Sampat Lodge (open 2 to 4 pm daily except Sunday). Some larger hotels have foreign exchange facilities. Few places accept credit cards and some accept only Indian cards.

Post & Communications The main post office is 750m south of Aberdeen Bazaar. The cheapest place to send and receive faxes is at the telegraph office (fax 21318) next door, open 10 am to 5 pm Monday to Saturday. International telephone calls can be made from here, as well as from a number of places in Aberdeen Bazaar. At the time of writing public email facilities were not available.

Emergency Aberdeen police station (☎ 33077, 32100) is next to the State Bank of India in Aberdeen Bazaar. The GB Pant Hospital (☎ 32102) is next to the Cellular Jail.

Cellular Jail National Memorial

Built by the British over a period of 18 years from 1890, and preserved as a shrine to India's freedom fighters, the Cellular Jail is a major tourist attraction. Originally seven wings radiated from a central tower, but only three remain today. The others were destroyed by the Japanese during the war. The remnants however, give a fair impression of the 'hell on earth' that the prisoners endured.

Each evening (except Sunday) a sound and light show depicts the jail's brutal history. It's in Hindi at 6 pm; English at 7.15 pm and costs Rs 10. The show is sporadic during the rainy season.

Samudrika Marine Museum

Run by the Indian navy, this museum features displays of the history and geography of the islands. The museum is open Tuesday to Sunday 9 am to noon and 2 to 5.30 pm; entry is Rs 10.

Aquarium

This interesting aquarium and museum (formerly known as the Fisheries Museum) displays some of the 350 species found in the Andaman Sea. It's open daily 9 am to 1.30 pm and 2 to 5.30 pm daily (closed Monday and holidays).

Anthropological Museum

The small anthropological museum on MG Rd displays tools, clothing and photographs of the indigenous people of the islands. The

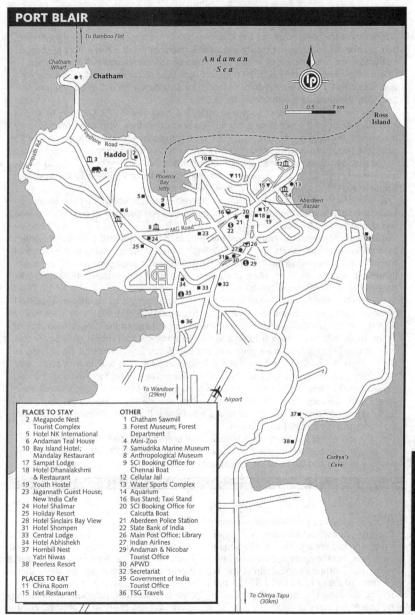

PORT BLAIR

Andaman Sea

To Bamboo Flat

Chatham Wharf

Chatham

Ross Island

Fireshore Road

Haddo

Panjpath Rd

Phoenix Bay Jetty

Aberdeen Bazaar

MG Road

To Wandoor (29km)

Airport

Corbyn's Cove

To Chiriya Tapu (30km)

0   0.5   1 km

PLACES TO STAY
2 Megapode Nest Tourist Complex
5 Hotel NK International
6 Andaman Teal House
10 Bay Island Hotel; Mandalay Restaurant
17 Sampat Lodge
18 Hotel Dhanalakshmi & Restaurant
19 Youth Hostel
23 Jagannath Guest House; New India Cafe
24 Hotel Shalimar
25 Holiday Resort
28 Hotel Sinclairs Bay View
31 Hotel Shompen
33 Central Lodge
34 Hotel Abhishekh
37 Hornbill Nest Yatri Niwas
38 Peerless Resort

PLACES TO EAT
11 China Room
15 Islet Restaurant

OTHER
1 Chatham Sawmill
3 Forest Museum; Forest Department
4 Mini-Zoo
7 Samudrika Marine Museum
8 Anthropological Museum
9 SCI Booking Office for Chennai Boat
12 Cellular Jail
13 Water Sports Complex
14 Aquarium
16 Bus Stand; Taxi Stand
20 SCI Booking Office for Calcutta Boat
21 Aberdeen Police Station
22 State Bank of India
26 Main Post Office; Library
27 Indian Airlines
29 Andaman & Nicobar Tourist Office
30 APWD
32 Secretariat
35 Government of India Tourist Office
36 TSG Travels

ANDAMAN & NICOBAR ISLANDS

The Penal Colony

The history of the penal colony on the Andaman Islands is a sorry tale of colonial oppression, bureaucratic ineptitude, abject cruelty and cultural displacement. It is also a story of courage, martyrdom and, ultimately, a triumph of the tactics of nonviolence and civil disobedience.

The colony began in 1858 with 200 convicts from India. Some were petty and some were violent criminals. Others were political prisoners, arrested during the Indian Uprising and sentenced by the British to transportation for life.

Within the first three months the convict population expanded to 773. Of these, 61 died in hospital, 140 escaped never to be captured (it was assumed they were either 'murdered by the natives' or died from starvation), and 87 were hanged for attempted escape. Within 15 years, the population reached 8000 males, 900 females and 578 children.

The shackled convicts endured extreme punishments such as floggings, as well as inadequate nutrition and rampant disease. It's no wonder the Indians referred to the Andaman Islands as *Kali Pani*, meaning Black Water, a place of no hope.

A surge of interest by the British establishment in the management of the penal colony followed the 1872 assassination of Lord Mayo, the viceroy and governor general of India who was stabbed in Port Blair by a convict.

Conditions were temporarily improved but news of this soon reached India and the British became concerned by reports that convicts in India preferred transportation to the Andaman Islands to incarceration in an Indian jail. This resulted in tighter management of the penal settlement, a reduction in the numbers of convicts transported and, between 1890 and 1908, the building of the infamous Cellular Jail.

Transportation of criminals would eventually be phased out but transportation of political prisoners continued. Brought in several waves between 1909 and 1937 they were mostly wealthy and educated and initiated hunger strikes in protest against their appalling treatment.

The death of Mahavir Singh in 1933, a popular participant in the Lahore Conspiracy (a plan to overcome British colonial rule), gave prisoners their first martyr. (He died in his cell following a hunger strike.) Significant pressure led to some reforms. The final turning point came with the hunger strike of 1937 involving 230 prisoners. Their claims for civil liberties across India received widespread support including a message from Mahatma Gandhi asking them to end their strike and renounce violence as a means of achieving social change. They eventually agreed to Gandhi's request and issued a statement that read 'Violence retards rather than advances the cause of our country'.

By the end of 1937 all the political prisoners had been repatriated to India. In 1945, when the British reclaimed the islands from Japanese occupation, 40,000 other prisoners were returned to India and the penal settlement was officially disbanded.

captions to some of the photos are poignant but telling. Above the museum is a small but well-stocked library. You are allowed to browse here, but the material cannot be borrowed. The anthropological museum is open from 10 am to 12.30 and 1.30 to 4 pm daily, except Sundays and holidays. There is no charge for entry.

Mini-Zoo & Forest Museum

Some of the 200 animal species unique to the islands can be seen at the mini-zoo. These include the Nicobar green imperial pigeon and Andaman pig, the staple diet of some tribal groups. The zoo's saltwater crocodile breeding program has been very successful and many have been returned to the wild. As with many zoos, the animals here seem jaded.

The zoo is open 8 am to 5 pm Tuesday to Sunday; entry is Rs 0.50 for adults, Rs 0.25 for children.

Nearby is the small Forest Museum, which has a display of locally grown woods, including padauk, with light and dark colours occurring in the same tree. Elephants are still used at some of the lumber camps. The museum is open 8 am to noon and 2.30 to 5 pm daily except Sunday; entry is free.

Chatham Sawmill

This government operation on Chatham island, 5km north-west of Aberdeen Bazaar, is the largest wood processor in Asia. Commenced in 1836 by the British, the mill employs about 2000 people around the clock in three shifts. Most of the timber goes to the mainland.

The sawmill is open for visitors from 6.30 am to 2.30 pm daily except Sunday.

Entry is free; the guide will be happy 'for a small consideration'.

Water Sports Complex

At the water sports complex, by the Fisheries Museum, you can rent rowboats, windsurfing equipment and sailing dinghies. Water-skiing costs Rs 60 for 15 minutes; windsurfing is Rs 35 for half an hour. You can rent snorkels here for Rs 20 per hour, but you can't take them anywhere else.

Organised Tours

A range of tours are offered by A&N Tourism at Andaman Teal House (☎ 32642); Shompen Travels (☎ 32360) in the Hotel Shompen and Island Travels (☎ 32358) in Aberdeen Bazaar. However, many tours will only operate once a minimum number of bookings have been made. This makes cancellations common which can be very frustrating for travellers who are on a tight schedule.

Snorkelling & Diving

The Andaman Islands offer some of the best snorkelling and diving in the world. However, organised diving is still in its infancy here and dive centres open and close each year. At present the choice is between three dive centres. Samudra (☎ 03192-33159, 32937, fax 32038, email manavi_th@hotmail.com) is very well run and based in an old Japanese bunker at the Hotel Sinclairs Bay View. It charges Rs 2000 for a couple of dives in the Port Blair area or Rs 3200 beyond (Wandoor etc). If you wish to dive in the national park there's an additional Rs 1000 charge (payable directly to the park). It offers the PADI Open Water Certificate course (four to five days) for Rs 14,000, and the advanced PADI course for Rs 8000. These courses lead to internationally recognised certification. It also offers a day's 'Discover Scuba Diving' for Rs 2500.

Prices are similar at the other professional outfit, Port Blair Underwater (☎ 03192-85389, 21358; fax 040-339 2718 in Chennai), which is also PADI registered. It is based at the Peerless Resort at Corbyn's Cove.

Slightly cheaper rates are available at Andaman Adventure Sports (☎/fax 03192-30295), near the Anthropological Museum in Port Blair. It has some reasonable equipment but the owner is not PADI registered (or recognised by any other diving organisation). This place is probably best only if you really know what you're doing.

Snorkelling equipment for hire from tour operators and hotels (around Rs 70 per day) is often substandard – it's best to bring your own, especially if you are travelling with children. The Jagannath Guest House rents snorkels for Rs 50.

For tips on how to 'step lightly' while underwater, see the Responsible Diving boxed text in the Facts for the Visitor chapter.

The Samudra Centre for Ocean Appreciation & Awareness (based at Hotel Sinclairs Bay View) offers all-inclusive diving and camping trips (see the Snorkelling & Diving boxed text for details).

KLM Tours & Travels (☎ 32111, fax 34255) is recommended for its environmental sensitivity and ability to customise an island experience for groups of two to 50 people.

Every afternoon at 3 pm, a boat leaves from the Phoenix Bay jetty for a 1½ hour harbour cruise. The trip costs Rs 25 and stops briefly at Viper Island where the remains of the gallows tower built by the British still stand.

Apart from visits to Jolly Buoy, Red Skin and Cinque islands, independent sightseeing is relatively easy.

Special Events

A 10 day Island Tourism Festival is held in Port Blair some time between December and February each year. Dance groups are imported from surrounding islands and the mainland. The festival also gives local tourism operators an opportunity to showcase their products. One of the festival's more bizarre aspects is the Andaman dog show.

Places to Stay

Most bottom end and mid-range hotels don't levy any additional taxes on their tariff. However a 10% service charge applies to some top hotels. Checkout time is usually 7 am.

Places to Stay – Budget

The *Youth Hostel* (☎ 32459) has dorm beds for Rs 30 (Rs 40 for nonmembers) and a few double rooms. There's a reasonable restaurant for guests.

Central Lodge (☎ 33632, *Middle Point*) is a basic wooden building set back from the road. It's popular among the cheapies, with singles/doubles from Rs 55/80 with common bath and Rs 100 for a double with attached bath. You can camp in the garden for Rs 30.

Sampat Lodge (☎ 33752, *Aberdeen Bazaar*) is very basic but friendly with clean

rooms for Rs 60/90 with common bath or Rs 110/160 with attached bath.

Jagannath Guest House (☎ 33140, *MG Rd*) is a good choice, with spotless singles/doubles/triples for Rs 90/135/220, all with attached bath. Run by a friendly manager, it's convenient for the bus station and Phoenix Bay jetty.

Places to Stay – Mid-Range

Most of the places in the mid-range bracket can be bargained down if they're not full. All rooms have attached bathrooms unless stated otherwise.

The *Holiday Resort* (☎ 30516, *Prem Nagar*) is very clean and a good place to stay. Rooms are Rs 220/300, or Rs 350/450 with air-con.

Hotel Abhishekh (☎ 33565) is quite good and has clean singles/doubles/triples for Rs 220/270/330; more for air-con.

Hotel Shalimar (☎ 33953) is on the road to Haddo. Rooms are Rs 160/200/270; Rs 320 for an air-con double. Discounts are available.

Hotel Dhanalakshmi (☎ 33953, *Aberdeen Bazaar*) has clean rooms for Rs 220/330, or Rs 450/550 with air-con (the rooms at the back are the quietest). It also has a restaurant.

Hotel Shompen (☎ 32360, fax 32425) is overpriced at the quoted rate of Rs 360 or Rs 780 with air-con. The hotel has a restaurant and a travel agency.

Hotel NK International (☎ 33066) is close to the Phoenix Bay jetty. Rooms cost Rs 230/340, or Rs 350/440 with air-con.

Hornbill Nest Yatri Niwas (☎ 32018) is run by A&N Tourism. It's about a kilometre north of Corbyn's Cove and has sea views. This is an excellent location but the service is painfully slow. Rooms with two/four/six beds are Rs 260/330/400. Mosquito nets are provided. There's a basic restaurant but some dishes need to be ordered in advance.

Andaman Teal House (☎ 32642) is also run by the tourist office, but is poorly located on the road to Haddo. Doubles cost Rs 260, or Rs 450 with air-con.

The *Megapode Nest Tourist Complex* (☎ 320207, fax 32702) at Haddo on the hill above the bay, is good value at Rs 550 for a large air-con double. Yurt-style air-con cottages are Rs 900 for a double.

Places To Stay – Top End

Hotel Sinclairs Bay View (☎ 32937) has rooms with some spectacular views for Rs 1400/1600, or Rs 1500/2000 with air-con and breakfast. Although it is right on the coast there's no beach. It's a pleasant though somewhat cavernous place and the restaurant is good but can be excruciatingly slow. The Samudra Diving Centre is based here. The Sinclairs chain of hotels has an office in Chennai (☎ 044-852 6296; fax 852 2506) through which bookings for Port Blair can be made. Major credit cards are accepted.

Peerless Resort (☎ 33462, fax 33463) at Corbyn's Cove is nicely located opposite the beach. Standard air-con singles/doubles are small and overpriced at Rs 1500/2500; rooms in the air-con cottages are Rs 2500/3000. There's a bar, restaurant, foreign exchange facilities and a boat for hire. Major credit cards are accepted.

Bay Island Hotel (☎ 20881, fax 33389), with sea views, is the top hotel in Port Blair. The rooms however don't quite match the aesthetics of the lobby and they're a little overpriced at Rs 3000/4500 – although this does include all meals. No singles are available in December and January. There's an excellent restaurant, bar and a seawater swimming pool.

Places to Eat

There are numerous small restaurants in Aberdeen Bazaar and most hotels have restaurants. Some seafood must be ordered in advance.

Dhanalakshmi Restaurant (☎ 20694), in the hotel of the same name, stays open late; main dishes are around Rs 50.

New India Cafe, adjacent to Jagannath Guest House, does good basic and cheap meals, including thalis for Rs 20. It opens around 7 am for breakfast.

Islet Restaurant, near the Cellular Jail, offers tasty inexpensive veg and nonveg dishes and has stunning bay views.

The *China Room* (☎ 30759), run by a Burmese-Indian couple, offers excellent seafood in what is really the front room of their house.

Mandalay Restaurant at the Bay Island Hotel is the place for a splurge. The open-air dining area catches the breeze and has bay views.

Getting There & Away

Air Jet Airways (☎ 36911) flies daily from Chennai (5.30 am) to Port Blair. Indian Airlines (☎ 33108) has four flights a week from Chennai to Port Blair and from Calcutta to Port Blair. These flights return to their city of origin on the same day. All flights take around two hours and cost around US$200 one way. The Indian Airline tickets can be included on the discount two or three week flight pass. The 25% youth discount is also applicable on Indian Airlines.

The daily connections should alleviate the long-standing difficulty of securing confirmed tickets.

Boat There are usually two to four sailings a month between Port Blair and Chennai or Calcutta on vessels operated by the Shipping Corporation of India or SCI (☎ 33347). A ship also sails between Visakhapatnam (Andhra Pradesh) and Port Blair although the frequency for this route is rarely more than once every two months. Contact SCI for the latest information on the erratic schedules. It's best to arrange return tickets when purchasing your outward ticket.

The length of the boat trip varies with the weather. On a good crossing it takes 60 hours to reach Port Blair from Chennai and 56 hours from Calcutta or Visakhapatnam.

The categories of accommodation includes deluxe cabin (two berth), A class cabin (usually two berth) and B class cabin (four to six berth). Prices are similar on all routes – Rs 3450 for deluxe, Rs 2852 for A class and Rs 2243 for B class. Deluxe or A class are usually reserved for government

VIPs. Some ships have an air-con dorm for Rs 1449. If you can get a ticket for bunk class, it will cost Rs 955. Prices are similar on all routes. For residents of the Andaman or Nicobar islands, fares are 40% cheaper. Food (thalis for breakfast, lunch and dinner) costs around Rs 120 per day. You may wish to bring something (fruit in particular) to supplement this.

The SCI will insist that you have a permit before selling you a ticket. On arrival you must register with the deputy superintendent of police in Port Blair.

The Port Blair SCI office is in Aberdeen Bazaar (☎ 33347), opposite Hotel Dhanalakshmi. For the Chennai boat, you may be directed to the office at Phoenix Bay. Bookings for the Calcutta boat open only a few days before the boat arrives; for the Chennai boat, you can book further in advance.

In Calcutta, the SCI office (☎ 033-284 2354) is on the 1st floor at 13 Strand Rd. In Chennai, the SCI (☎ 044-522 6873) is at Rajaji Salai (opposite the Customs House). In Visakhapatnam, the office is AV Bhanoji Row (☎ 0891-565597, fax 566507), within the port complex. It's essential to bring two passport-size photos and you'll need to be organised because bookings close at least four days before sailing.

Getting Around

Port Blair has buses, numerous taxis and a few auto-rickshaws. Taxi meters are rarely used. From the airport, the fare to Aberdeen Bazaar is around Rs 50, (less to Corbyn's Cove). The tourist office airport bus will take you to any hotel in Port Blair for Rs 20.

From the bus station in Port Blair, there are regular departures to key destinations. To Wandoor there are five buses a day (Rs 7, 90 minutes). To Chirya Tapu, there's an hourly bus between 5 am and 6 pm for Rs 8. The bus to Diglipur leaves Port Blair every day (except Sunday) at 5 am. The journey is supposed to take eight hours (often it's much longer) and costs Rs 145 return.

It's best to have your own transport to explore parts of the island. You can hire bicycles in Aberdeen Bazaar for Rs 35 per day. Mopeds, scooters or motorcycles can be hired from TSG Travels (☎ 32894) for Rs 150 per day. A deposit of Rs 1000 is required. Jagannath Guest House also has a few motorcycles for hire (Rs 150).

Private boats can be hired from the tour operators but charges are high – around Rs 10,000 per day.

AROUND PORT BLAIR
Viper Island

The moment you disembark on this tiny island you are confronted with a sign 'Way to the Gallows'. A path leads to the remains of the brick jail and the gallows built by the British in 1867. The stunning view from these gallows somehow accentuates the sheer horror of the place. The name Viper has nothing to do with snakes – it's the name of a 19th century British trading ship that was wrecked nearby.

Unless you have access to a private boat, the best way to see Viper Island is to take the afternoon harbour cruise that departs from Phoenix Bay jetty. Some of these boats only stop at the island for 15 minutes. If you want more time, negotiate with the captain.

Mt Harriet & Madhuban

Mt Harriet (365m) is across the inlet, north of Port Blair. There's a nature trail up to the top and, with Forest Department permits, it's possible to stay in the comfortable *Forest Guest House*. (Permits are theoretically available from the Forest Department in Port Blair, but not many travellers have been lucky enough to be granted one.)

To reach Mt Harriet, take the vehicle or passenger ferry from Chatham Wharf to Bamboo Flat (Rs 1, 10 minutes). From there, a road runs 7km along the coast and up to Mt Harriet. Jeep drivers, who charge an outrageous Rs 400 to take you to the top, insist that taxis can't make it to the top. They can, and a taxi costs only Rs 200. If you have time try walking up, but take plenty of water as there is none available en route.

To the north is Mt Harriet National Park and Madhuban, where elephants are sometimes trained for the logging camps. Madhuban is also accessible by boat; the tourist office and travel agencies organise occasional trips.

Ross Island

This eerie forlorn place was once the administrative headquarters for the British. Just 2km east of Port Blair, newspapers of the day called it the Paris of the East. However the manicured gardens and grand ballrooms were destroyed by an earthquake in 1941.

Six months later, after the Japanese entered WWII, the British transferred their HQ to Port Blair.

Ferries to Ross Island depart Phoenix Bay jetty at 8.30 and 10 am, 12.30 and 2 pm daily except Wednesday. From Ross Island, there are departures at 8.45 and 10.40 am, and 12.40, 2.10 and 4.40 pm. The journey takes 20 minutes and a return ticket costs Rs 15, plus Rs 10 entry fee. Ross Island is controlled by the navy and visitors must sign in on arrival. The museum near the jetty displays the opulence and decadence of a bygone era.

Corbyn's Cove

Corbyn's Cove, 4km east of the airport and 7km south of the town, is the nearest beach to Port Blair. It's a long, though pleasant and easy cliff-top stroll here from Port Blair.

Nearby **Snake Island** is surrounded by a coral reef. You can sometimes catch a ride to the island in a fishing boat, but swimming is not advised as the currents are particularly strong. If you do visit the island, watch out for snakes!

Sippighat Farm

On the road to Wandoor, 15km from Port Blair, research into spices such as cinnamon, pepper, nutmeg and cloves, is carried out at this government experimental farm. The staff here are particularly friendly and knowledgeable on local issues. The farm is open daily except Sunday, 8 am to 5.30 pm. Entry is free.

Wandoor

The Mahatma Gandhi National Marine Park at Wandoor covers 280 sq km and comprises 15 islands. The diverse scenery includes mangrove creeks, tropical rainforest and reefs supporting 50 types of coral. Boats leave from Wandoor village, 29km south-west of Port Blair, at around 10 am daily (except Monday) for visits to Jolly Buoy or Red Skin islands. Although it's well worth seeing the coral (there are usually a few snorkels for hire), only a couple of hours are spent at the islands. On Jolly Buoy, for the best coral go to the left of the landing spot, not to the right as directed. Watch out for powerful currents.

The trip costs Rs 85 (Rs 60 in the low season when boats go only as far as Red Skin). An entry permit (Rs 10) for the park is available at the kiosk by the Wandoor jetty.

You can reach Wandoor by bus from Port Blair (Rs 6.50, 1½ hours, five departures a day) or by joining a tour. There are a number of good, sandy beaches at Wandoor and some excellent snorkelling, but you should take care not to walk on the coral exposed at low tide. Much of this reef has already been damaged.

Chiriya Tapu

Chiriya Tapu, 30km south of Port Blair, is a tiny fishing village with beaches and mangroves. It's possible to arrange boats from here to Cinque Island. There's a beach a couple of kilometres south of Chiriya Tapu that has some of the best snorkelling in the area. There's a bus to the village every two hours from Port Blair (1½ hours, Rs 6.).

OTHER ISLANDS

A&N Tourism has targeted half a dozen beaches for development but the tourist infrastructure is currently very limited and you shouldn't expect too much. In 1997 Bharatang (between South and Middle Andaman) and nearby North Passage were added to the list of islands fully open to visitors. Narcondam, Interview, Brother and Sister islands are open for day visits only, but currently no regular boats visit these

Island Indigenes

The Andaman and Nicobar islands' indigenous people are victims of the Indian government's policy of colonisation and development. They now constitute less than 10% of the population and, in most cases, their numbers are falling. The Onge, Sentinelese, Andamanese and Jarawa are all resident in the Andaman Islands. The group on the Nicobar Islands includes the Shompen and Nicobarese.

Onge An anthropological study made in the 1970s suggested the Onge were declining because they were severely demoralised by loss of territory. Two-thirds of the Onges' island of Little Andaman was taken over by the Forest Department and 'settled' in 1977. The 100 or so remaining members of the Onge tribe are confined to a 100 sq km reserve at Dugong Creek. The Indian government has allowed further development – including the building of roads, jetties and a match factory – and has even built tin huts in an attempt to house these nomadic hunter-gatherers.

Sentinelese The Sentinelese, unlike the other tribes in these islands, have consistently repulsed any attempts by outsiders to make contact with them. Every few years, contact parties arrive on the beaches of North Sentinel Island with gifts of coconuts, bananas, pigs and red plastic buckets, only to be showered with arrows. About 120 Sentinelese remain, and North Sentinel Island is their territory. Perhaps they understand that their only hope of survival is to avoid contact with the outside world.

Andamanese Numbering only 30, it seems impossible that the Andamanese can escape extinction. There were almost 5000 Andamanese when the British arrived in the mid-19th century. Their friendliness to the colonisers was their undoing and, by the end of the century, most of the population had been swept away by measles, syphilis and influenza epidemics. They've been resettled on tiny Strait Island but their decline continues.

Jarawa The 250 remaining Jarawa occupy the 750 sq km reserve on South and Middle Andaman islands. Around them, forest clearance continues at a horrific rate and the Andaman Trunk Rd runs through part of their designated territory. Settlers are encroaching on their reserve, but the Jarawa are putting up a fight, killing one or two Indians each year. In 1996 they caught five loggers, killed two of them and cut off the hands of the other three. Considering that in 1953 the Chief Commissioner requested an armed sea plane bomb Jarawa settlements, the Jarawas' response seems comparatively more restrained than that of the Indian government. All Trunk Rd buses are now accompanied by an armed guard – though windows are still occasionally shattered by Jarawa arrows.

Shompen Only about 200 Shompen remain in the forests on Great Nicobar. They are hunter-gatherers who have resisted integration, tending to shy away from areas occupied by Indian immigrants.

Nicobarese The 30,000 Nicobarese are the only indigenous people whose numbers are not decreasing. They are fair-complexioned horticulturalists who have been partly assimilated into contemporary Indian society. Living in village units led by a headman, they cultivate coconuts, yams and bananas, and farm pigs. The Nicobarese inhabit a number of islands in the Nicobar group, centred on Car Nicobar. The majority of Nicobarese are Christians.

places. It's possible to charter a boat to visit volcanic Barren Island but disembarkation is forbidden.

Until the tourist complexes mooted for the islands are actually built, the only other accommodation is in Andaman PWD (APWD) or Forest Guest Houses (typically Rs 60 per bed in a double room). These should be reserved in advance in Port Blair, either at the APWD (near Hotel Shompen) or the Forest Department in Haddo (☎ 31371).

Some people bring tents or hammocks (made by tailors in Aberdeen Bazaar) and camp on the beaches. In Port Blair, you can rent two-person tents for Rs 40 per day from the Andaman Teal House. Other useful items include a bucket and a large knife. If you do camp, make sure you bury your rubbish. Fires are not allowed so bring a stove and kerosene with you. On the islands, kerosene supplies are usually reserved for locals.

Neil Island

Neil Island, 40km north-east of Port Blair, is populated by Bengali settlers. There's excellent snorkelling but some of the coral has been damaged by dynamiting for fish. Beaches are numbered: No 1 beach, a 40 minute walk west of the jetty and village, is popular with campers who set up hammocks under the trees. There's a well nearby for fresh water. The snorkelling is best around the point at the far end of the beach, where you may also see very large fish. At low tide it's difficult getting over the coral into the water from the beach.

Places to Stay & Eat In the village there's a market, a few shops and a couple of basic restaurants serving dosas, fried fish, veg and rice. The stalls and shops often run out of mineral water and soft drinks.

Hawabill Nest Yatri Niwas offers four-bed rooms for Rs 270 and air-con doubles for Rs 450. Reserve in advance at the A&N tourist office in Port Blair. The *APWD Guest House* has just two rooms.

Getting There & Away On Wednesday and Friday at 6.30 am, ferries leave Phoenix

Bay in Port Blair for Neil (Rs 10/15 for deck/upper class, three hours), continuing to Havelock. Occasionally they visit Havelock first.

Havelock Island

Fifty-four kilometres north-east of Port Blair, Havelock covers 100 sq km and is inhabited by Bengali settlers. There are picture-postcard white-sand beaches, turquoise waters and good snorkelling. Although there are coral reefs, it's the marine life here – dolphins, turtles and very large fish – that make it interesting. So do the elephants that were brought to the island for work but now earn their keep from tourism.

Only the northern third of the island is settled, and each village is referred to by a number. Boats dock at the jetty at No 1; the main bazaar is a couple of kilometres south at No 3.

Having your own transport is useful – bring a bike from Port Blair or rent one for Rs 40 per day in No 3 village or from the *paan* shop outside the entrance to the Dolphin Yatri Niwas. A few scooters (Rs 180) are available from the Narayan paan store in No 3 village. A local bus connects the villages on an hourly circuit and also runs out to No 7 beach. A tourist bus meets the ferry.

Places to Stay & Eat You need to make a reservation in advance at the A&N tourist office in Port Blair to stay in the Dolphin Yatri Niwas or the Tent Resorts.

Dolphin Yatri Niwas Complex offers pleasant accommodation in cottages beside a beautiful secluded beach, but there's no snorkelling here. Charges are Rs 200 for an ordinary double, Rs 300 for a deluxe room and Rs 800 for an air-con double, all with attached bath. Good but basic meals are served in the restaurant.

A&N Tourism's *Tent Resort*, beside No 7 beach, has eight roomy tents (twin beds) set up under the trees. They cost Rs 100 for a double and there's a maximum stay of four days. There's a couple of toilets but no washing facilities other than the wells. Basic fish thalis (Rs 25) and drinks (tea,

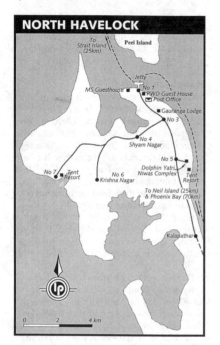

NORTH HAVELOCK

To Strait Island (25km)

Peel Island

Jetty

MS Guesthouse

No 1
PWD Guest House
Post Office

Gauranga Lodge

No 3

No 4
Shyam Nagar

No 5

No 7 Tent Resort

No 6
Krishna Nagar

Dolphin Yatri
Niwas Complex

Tent Resort

To Neil Island (25km)
& Phoenix Bay (70km)

Kalapathar

0   2   4 km

coffee, soft drinks and mineral water) are available. Some people bring their own tents or hammocks and camp by the beach. The police come by occasionally to check that people aren't making fires or stripping off and indulging in 'hippy behaviour'. There's good snorkelling and the idyllic beach stretches for several kilometres. The sandflies make sunbathing impossible.

A second **Tent Resort** opened recently near No 5 beach, and you can use the restaurant at the Dolphin Yatri Niwas if you stay here.

MS Guest House is 500m west of the jetty and has basic rooms with attached bath for Rs 100; Rs 40 for a dorm bed.

Gauranga Lodge is the green wooden building without a sign between village Nos 1 and 3. It has doubles for Rs 55.

Accommodation on Havelock can be difficult to find for foreigners because govern-

ment officials frequently assume the status of VIPs and book everything for themselves and their entourage.

Getting There & Away Ferries depart early in the morning usually on Tuesday, Wednesday, Friday and Saturday from Phoenix Bay in Port Blair. The four hour journey to Havelock costs Rs 10/15 on the lower/upper deck. The ferries return from Havelock to Port Blair the following day.

Long Island

This little island off the south-east coast of Middle Andaman has one small village and several sandy beaches that are perfect for camping. The only accommodation is the **Forest Rest House**.

On Wednesday and Saturday, the ferry from Port Blair and Havelock calls at Long Island (Rs 10/22 for lower/upper deck, eight hours) before reaching Rangat. Bicycles are the main form of transport on the island.

Middle Andaman

The Grand Trunk Rd runs north from Port Blair to Bharatang Island and Middle Andaman, which are linked by frequent ferries. Since this road runs beside Jarawa reserves on the west coasts of South and Middle Andaman, buses carry armed guards. Having lost land to Indian settlers, the Jarawa are hostile to any outsiders and independent travel is inadvisable. See the boxed text 'Island Indigenes' for more information. Motorbikes are forbidden beyond the checkpoint 40km outside Port Blair. There's tourist accommodation in Rangat and Mayabunder, but the entire island is now open to foreigners.

You can get to **Rangat** from Port Blair via the Havelock, Neil or Long island ferries (Rs 15/35 for lower/upper deck, nine hours) or by bus (Rs 50, six hours). There's basic rooms at the **Hare Krishna Lodge** (Rs 80/120), and the **PWD Guest House** (Rs 90). A bus runs to Cuthbert Bay for A&N Tourism's new **Hawksbill Nest** (Rs 80 per bed in a four bed dorm, Rs 400 for an air-con double). Bookings for the Hawksbill

Nest must be made in advance at the A& N tourist office in Port Blair.

Mayabunder, 71km north of Rangat, is linked by the daily bus from Port Blair (Rs 60, nine hours) and also by occasional ferries. There's an 18 bed *APWD Guest House* here. The recently completed *Swiftlet Nest* at Karmatang Bay, 13km north-east of Mayabunder charges Rs 75 per bed in a four bed dorm, Rs 400 for an air-con double.

North Andaman

Diglipur is the only place on North Andaman where foreigners can stay. To get there you can catch either the weekly ferry from Port Blair or one of the daily ferries from Mayabunder. There is also a bus departing daily at 5 am (except Tuesday) from Port Blair. The fare is Rs 140 and the journey is supposed to take eight hours but often takes 12. The 12 bed *APWD Guest House*, and the recently built *Turtle Resort* cost Rs 400 for an air-con double. Bookings should be made through the tourist office in Port Blair.

Cinque Island

The uninhabited islands of North and South Cinque are part of the national park south of Wandoor, just off Rutland Island. They are surrounded by pristine coral reefs, and are among the most beautiful islands in the Andamans. Visiting boats usually anchor off South Cinque and passengers transfer via dinghy to the beach. The snorkelling here is first class, however much of the coral close to the beach is dead and to see abundant marine life you need to swim out a few hundred metres.

Unless you are a VIP, only day visits are allowed. And unless you're going on one of the day trips occasionally organised by travel agents, you need to get permission from the Forest Department. The islands are two hours by boat from Chiriya Tapu or 3½ hours from Wandoor. The advantage of departing from Wandoor is that you access the boat by a jetty. At Chiriya Tapu you join the boat via a dinghy. This is OK in the morning light, but when returning after dark it can be precarious.

The Boy Who Fell from the Tree

In 1996, a 16 year old Jarawa boy was found semiconscious at the foot of a tree on South Andaman. He was 'picked up' by the police and taken to hospital in Port Blair. While some people believe the boy fell out of the tree, others claim he was frightened out by gunshot from angry settlers. In hospital he recovered with the help of medicines, bandages and food.

The authorities eventually returned him to his village. However, within a few weeks he was back among the Indian settlers, only this time he was not alone. He brought with him several members of his own tribe. He'd somehow convinced his people that within the settlement community, food, drink and medicine is freely available. Over the months, the boy would make several trips to the settlement areas, each time bringing new members of his tribe.

Local media hailed the boy's return to the settler community as a triumph of 'civilised life' over 'primitive life'. Indeed, many settlers believe that each 'contact' is a step towards complete integration. Others, however, have expressed grave concerns for the inevitable demise of the boy and his tribe. Staff at the Anthropology Museum are especially concerned that the expectations of free food and medicine will simply exacerbate the cultural displacement and result in a dependency on tobacco, alcohol and begging.

In their endless debate on the complex issues of appropriate development, the authorities continue to espouse the rhetoric of preservation, protection and sustainability. Meanwhile, each month, more tribal people move from a culture of independence and self-reliance into a culture of dependency.

ANDAMAN & NICOBAR ISLANDS

Little Andaman

The 100 remaining members of the Onge tribe are confined to a reserve in the south of this island. As the northern part of Little Andaman has been settled, and was opened to foreigners in 1997, time has probably run out for the Onge.

Ferries land at Hut Bay on the east coast. Basic supplies are available in the village 2km to the north. Another kilometre north is the *APWD Guest House*, which is the only accommodation (make reservations at the APWD in Port Blair). Just under 2km north of the guesthouse is the police station where you must register on arrival, then it's about 15km north to the main beach at Butler Bay, where some people camp. The beach is good for swimming but not for snorkelling.

The tribal reserve in the south is out of bounds to foreigners. Don't try to make contact with the Onge – you certainly won't help their cause by turning them into a tourist attraction.

Boats connect Port Blair with Hut Bay (Rs 16/35 for lower/upper deck, eight hours) once or twice a week.

Language

There is no one 'Indian' language as such. This is part of the reason why English is still widely spoken 50 years after the British left India and why it's still the official language of the judiciary.

Eighteen languages are recognised by the constitution, and these fall into two major groups: Indic, or Indo-Aryan, and Dravidian. Additionally, over 1600 minor languages and dialects were listed in the latest census. The scope for misunderstanding can be easily appreciated!

The Indic languages are a branch of the Indo-European group of languages (to which English belongs), and were the language of the Central Asian peoples who invaded what is now India. The Dravidian languages are native to south India, although they have been influenced by Sanskrit and Hindi over the years. Most of the languages have their own script, and these are used along with English. In some states, such as Gujarat, you'll hardly see a word of English, whereas in Himachal Pradesh virtually everything is in English. For a sample of the different scripts, look at a Rs 5 or larger banknote where 14 languages are represented. As well as Hindi and English there's a list of 12 other languages; from the top, they are: Assamese, Bengali, Gujarati, Kannada, Kashmiri, Malayalam, Marathi, Oriya, Punjabi, Sanskrit, Tamil, Telugu and Urdu. (See the India's Official Language boxed text opposite.)

Major efforts have been made to promote Hindi as the national language of India and to gradually phase out English. A stumbling block to this plan is that while Hindi is the predominant language in the north, it bears little relation to the Dravidian languages of the south; subsequently, very few people in the south speak Hindi. It is from here, particularly the state of Tamil Nadu, that the most vocal opposition to the adoption of Hindi comes, along with the strongest support for the retention of English.

For many educated Indians, English is virtually their first language, and for the large number of Indians who speak more than one language, English is often their second tongue. Thus it is very easy to get around India with English, but it's always good to know at least a little of the local language.

There are Hindi language schools in all the larger cities, but one place which has been recommended is Landour Language School (☎ 0135-631467), Mussoorie, Uttar Pradesh 248179. See India's Official Languages boxed text and for a far more comprehensive guide to Hindi get a copy of Lonely Planet's *Hindi & Urdu phrasebook*.

Strangely Familiar

Indian English is full of interesting everyday expressions. Whereas in New York you might get robbed by a mugger, in India it will be a *dacoit* who relieves you of your goods. Politicians may employ strong-arm heavies known in India as *goondas*. There is a plethora of Indian terms for strikes and lock-ins – Indians can have *bandhs*, *hartaals* and *gheraos*, for example. Then there are all those Indian servants – children get looked after by *ayahs*, your house and your godown (or warehouse) is guarded by a *chowkidar*, and when the toilet needs cleaning there is no way your bearer is going to do it.

It's surprising how many Indian terms have crept into English usage. We can sit on a veranda and drink chai, wear pyjamas or sandals and dungarees (which may well be khaki), shampoo our hair, visit the jungle, or worry about protecting our loot – they're all Indian words.

For definitions of everyday Indian terms see the Glossary which follows.

India's Official Languages

Assamese State language of Assam, and spoken by nearly 60% of that state's population. Dates back to the 13th century.

Bengali Spoken by nearly 200 million people (mostly in what is now Bangladesh), and the state language of West Bengal. Developed as a language in the 13th century.

Gujarati State language of Gujarat, it is an Indic language.

Kannada State language of Karnataka, spoken by about 65% of that state's population.

Hindi The most important Indian language, although it is only spoken as a mother tongue by about 20% of the population – mainly in the area known as the Hindi-belt, the cow-belt or Bimaru, which includes Bihar, Madhya Pradesh, Rajasthan and Uttar Pradesh. This Indic language is the official language of the Indian government, the states already mentioned, plus Haryana and Himachal Pradesh.

Kashmiri Kashmiri speakers account for about 55% of the population of Jammu & Kashmir. It is an Indic language written in the Perso-Arabic script.

Konkani Konkani is a Dravidian language spoken by people in the Goa region.

Malayalam A Dravidian language, and the state language of Kerala.

Manipuri An Indic language of the north-east region.

Marathi An Indic language dating back to around the 13th century, Marathi is the state language of Maharashtra.

Nepali Nepali is the predominant language of Sikkim, where around 75% of the people are ethnic Nepalis.

Oriya An Indic language, it is the state language of Orissa where it is spoken by 87% of the population.

Punjabi Another Indic language, this is the state language of the Punjab. Although based on Devanagari (the same script as Hindi), it is written in a 16th century script, known as Gurumukhi, which was created by the Sikh guru, Guru Angad.

Sanskrit One of the oldest languages in the world, and the language of classical India. All the *Vedas* and classical literature such as the *Mahabharata* and the *Ramayana* were written in this Indic language.

Sindhi A significant number of Sindhi speakers are found in what is now Pakistan, although the greater number are in India. In Pakistan, the language is written in a Perso-Arabic script, while in India it uses the Devanagari script.

Tamil An ancient Dravidian language at least 2000 years old, and the state language of Tamil Nadu. It is spoken by 65 million people.

Telugu The Dravidian language spoken by the largest number of people, it is the state language of Andhra Pradesh.

Urdu Urdu is the state language of Jammu & Kashmir. Along with Hindi, it evolved in early Delhi. While Hindi was largely adopted by the Hindu population, the Muslims embraced Urdu, and so the latter is written in the Perso-Arabic script and includes many Persian words.

HINDI

Hello/Goodbye.	*namaste.*
How are you?	*aap kaiseh hain?*
Very well,	*bahut acha,*
thank you.	*shukriya.*
Please.	*meharbani seh.*
Thank you.	*dhanyavaad/shukriyaa.*
You're welcome.	*koi baat nahin.*
Yes.	*haan.*
No.	*nahin.*
Excuse me/Sorry.	*kshamaa kijiyeh.*

Do you speak English?	*kya aap angrezi. samajhte hain?*
I don't understand.	*meri samajh men nahin aaya.*
Where is a hotel?	*hotal kahan hai?*
How far is ...?	*... kitni duur hai?*
How do I get to ...?	*... kojane ke liyeh kaiseh jaana parega?*
How much?	*kitneh paiseh?/ kitneh hai?*
This is expensive.	*yeh bahut mehnga hai.*
May I see the menu.	*mujheh minu dikhaiyeh.*
The bill please.	*bill de dijiyeh.*
What's your name?	*aapka shubh naam kya hai?*
My name is ...	*meraa naam ... hai.*
What's the time?	*kitneh bajeh hain?*

Beware of *acha*, that all-purpose word for 'OK'. It can also mean 'OK, I understand what you mean, but it isn't OK'.

big	*bherra*
small	*chhota*
today	*aaj*
day	*din*
night	*raat*
week	*haftah*
month	*mahina*
year	*saal*
medicine	*dava-ee*
egg	*aanda*
fruit	*phal*
vegetables	*sabzi*
sugar	*chini*
butter	*makkhan*
rice	*chaaval*
water	*paani*
tea	*chai*
coffee	*kaafi*
milk	*dudh*

TAMIL

Although Hindi is promoted as the 'official' language of India, it won't get you very far in the south, where Tamil reigns supreme (although English is also widely spoken). Tamil is a much more difficult language to master and the pronunciation is not easy.

Hello.	*vanakkam.*
Goodbye.	*sendru varugiren.*
How are you?	*neengal nalama?*
Very well, thank you.	*nandri, nandraga irukkindren.*
Excuse me.	*mannithu kollungal.*
Please.	*dhayavu seitu.*
Yes.	*aam.*
No.	*illai.*

Do you speak English?	*neengal aangilam pesuveergala?*
I don't understand.	*yenakku puriyavillai.*
Where is a hotel?	*hotel yenge irrukindradhu?*
How far is ...?	*yevallavu dhooram ...?*
How do I get to ...?	*haan yeppadi selvadhu ...?*
How much?	*yevvallvu?*
This is expensive.	*idhu vilai adhigam.*
Show me the menu.	*saapatu patiyalai kamiungal.*
The bill please.	*vilai rasidhai kodungal.*
What's your name?	*ungal peyar yenna?*
My name is ...	*en peyar ...*
What is the time?	*ippoludhu mani yevallavu?*

big.	*periyadhu.*
small.	*siriyadhu.*
today.	*indru.*
day.	*pagal.*
night.	*iravu/rathiri.*
week.	*vaaram.*
month.	*maadham.*
year.	*aandu.*
medicine.	*marundhu.*
ice.	*panikkatti.*
egg.	*muttai.*
fruit.	*pazhlam.*
vegetables.	*kaaikari.*
sugar.	*sarkarai/seeni.*
butter.	*vennai.*
rice.	*saadham/soru.*
water.	*thanner.*
tea.	*thenneer.*
coffee.	*kapi.*
milk.	*paal.*

NUMBERS

Whereas we count in tens, hundreds, thousands, millions and billions, the Indian numbering system goes tens, hundreds, thousands, hundred thousands, ten millions. A hundred thousand is a *lakh,* and 10 million is a *crore.*

These two words are almost always used in place of their English equivalents. Thus you will see 10 lakh rather than one million, and one crore rather than 10 million. The numbers are generally written that way too – three hundred thousand appears as 3,00,000 not 300,000, and ten million, five hundred thousand would appear as 1,05,00,000 (one crore, five lakh) not 10,500,000. If you say something costs five crore or is worth 10 lakh, it always means 'of rupees'.

The pattern of cardinal numbers from one to 100 in Hindi is less evident than that of English.

	Hindi	Tamil
1	*ek*	*onru*
2	*do*	*irandu*
3	*tin*	*moonru*
4	*char*	*naangu*
5	*panch*	*ainthu*
6	*chhe*	*aaru*
7	*saat*	*ezhu*
8	*aath*	*ettu*
9	*nau*	*onpathu*
10	*das*	*pathu*
11	*gyaranh*	*padhinondru*
12	*baranh*	*pannirendu*
13	*teranh*	*padhimundru*
14	*chodanh*	*padhinaangu*
15	*pandranh*	*padhinainthu*

	Hindi	Tamil
16	*solanh*	*padhinaaru*
17	*staranh*	*padhinezhu*
18	*aatharanh*	*padhinettu*
19	*unnis*	*patthonpathu*
20	*bis*	*irubadhu*
21	*ikkis*	*irubadhiondru*
22	*bais*	*irubadhirandu*
23	*teis*	*irubadhimoonru*
24	*chobis*	*irubadhinaangu*
25	*pachis*	*irubadhiainthu*
26	*chhabis*	*irubadhiaaru*
27	*sattais*	*irubadhiezhu*
28	*athais*	*irubadhiettu*
29	*unnattis*	*irubadhionpathu*
30	*tis*	*muppathu*
35	*paintis*	*muppathiainthu*
40	*chalis*	*narpathu*
45	*paintalis*	*narpathiainthu*
50	*panchas*	*aimbathu*
55	*pachpan*	*aimbathiainthu*
60	*saath*	*arubathu*
65	*painsath*	*arubathiainthu*
70	*sattar*	*ezhbathu*
75	*pachhattar*	*ezhubathiainthu*
80	*assi*	*enbathuS*
85	*pachasi*	*enabathiainthu*
90	*nabbe*	*thonooru*
95	*pachanabbe*	*thonootriainthu*
100	*so*	*nooru*
200	*do so*	*irunooru*
1000	*ek hazaar*	*aayiram*
2000	*do hazaar*	*irandaayiram*
100,000	*lakh*	*lacham*
10 million	*crore*	*kodi*

Glossary

The glossary that follows is a sample of the words and terms you may come across during your Indian wanderings. The definitions have been subdivided into General, Religion and Food & Drink sections.

General

abbi – waterfall.

acha – 'OK' or 'I understand'.

acharya – revered teacher; originally a spiritual guide.

adivasi – tribal person.

agarbathi – incense.

agni – fire; see also Religion glossary.

ahimsa – discipline of nonviolence.

AIR – All India Radio, the national broadcaster.

air-cooled rooms – rooms in guesthouses, generally with big, noisy fans built into the walls.

Amir – Muslim nobleman.

ananda – happiness; see also Religion glossary.

angrezi – foreigner.

anikut – dam.

anna – 16th of a rupee; no longer legal tender but occasionally referred to in marketplaces.

APSRTC – Andhra Pradesh State Road Transport Corporation.

APTTDC – Andhra Pradesh Travel & Tourist Development Corporation.

Aryan – Sanskrit word for 'noble'; refers to those who migrated from Persia and settled in northern India.

ashram – spiritual community or retreat.

ashrama – system. Essentially there are three stages in life recognised under this system: *brahmachari*, *grihastha* and *sanyasin*. This kind of merit is only available to the upper three castes.

attar – essential oil made from flowers and used as a base for perfumes.

auto-rickshaw – small, noisy, three-wheeled, motorised contraption for transporting passengers short distances. Found throughout the country they are cheaper than taxis.

ayah – children's nurse or nanny.

ayurveda – Indian herbal medicine.

babu – lower level clerical worker (derogatory).

bagh – garden.

bahadur – brave or chivalrous; an honorific title.

baksheesh – tip, bribe or donation.

bandar – monkey.

bandh – general strike.

banian – T-shirt or undervest.

baniya – moneylender.

banyan – Indian fig tree.

baoli – well, particularly a step-well with landings and galleries, more commonly found in Rajasthan and Gujarat.

baradari – summer house.

bazaar – market area. A market town is also called a bazaar.

bearer – rather like a butler.

begum – Muslim woman of high rank.

bhang – dried leaves and flowering shoots of the marijuana plant.

Bharat – Hindi for India.

bhavan – house, building.

bheesti – see *bhisti*.

bherra – big, important.

bhisti – water carrier.

bhojnalya – simple eatery.

beedi – see *bidi*.

bidi – small, hand-rolled cigarette; really just a rolled-up leaf.

bindi – forehead mark.

BJP – Bharatiya Janata Party

black money – undeclared, untaxed money. There's lots of it in India.

bodhi tree – tree under which the Buddha sat when he attained enlightenment.

brahmachari – chaste student stage of the *ashrama* system.

Brahmin – member of the priest caste, the highest Hindu caste.

BSTDC – Bihar State Tourist Development Corporation.

bugyal – high altitude meadow.

bund – embankment or dyke.

burkha – one-piece garment used by Muslim women to cover them from head to toe.

bustee – slum.

cantonment – administrative and military area of a Raj-era town.

caravanserai – traditional accommodation for camel caravans.

caste – one's hereditary station in life.

chalo, chalo, chalo – 'let's go, let's go, let's go'.

chance list – waitlist on Indian Airlines flights.

Chandragupta – important ruler of India in the 3rd century BC.

chappals – sandals.

charas – resin of the marijuana plant; also referred to as hashish.

charbagh – formal Persian garden, divided into quarters (literally 'four gardens').

charpoy – Indian rope bed.

chauri – fly whisk.

chela – pupil or follower, as George Harrison was to Ravi Shankar.

chhatri – a small, domed Mughal kiosk (literally 'umbrella').

chikan – embroidered cloth.

chillum – pipe of a *hookah*; commonly used to describe the pipes used for smoking ganja.

chinkara – gazelle.

chital – spotted deer.

choli – sari blouse.

choultry – *dharamsala* in southern India.

chowk – town square, intersection or marketplace.

chowkidar – night watchman.

chogyal – king.

chuba – dress worn by Tibetan women.

Cong (I) – Congress Party of India.

CPI – Communist Party of India.

CPI (M) – Communist Party of India (Marxist).

crore – 10 million.

cutcherry – office or building used for public business.

dacoit – robber, particularly armed robber.

dak – staging post, government-run accommodation.

Dalit – preferred term for India's *Untouchable* caste. Also see *Harijan*.

darwaza – gateway or door.

devadasi – temple dancer.

dharamsala – pilgrim's resthouse.

dharna – nonviolent protest.

dhobi – person who washes clothes.

dhobi ghat – place where clothes are washed.

dholi – covered litter. You may still see some elderly tourists being carried around Indian cities in them.

dhoti – like a *lungi*, but the cloth is then pulled up between the legs; worn by Hindu men.

dhurrie – rug.

diwan – principal officer in a princely state; royal court or council.

Diwan-i-Am – hall of public audience.

Diwan-i-Khas – hall of private audience.

dowry – money and goods given by a bride's parents to their son-in-law's family; it's illegal but no arranged marriage (most marriages are arranged) can be made without it.

Dravidian – member of one of the aboriginal races of India, pushed south by the Indo-Europeans and now mixed with them.

dun – valley.

dupatta – scarf worn by Punjabi women.

durbar – royal court; also used to describe a government.

elatalam – small hand-held cymbals.

election symbols – identifying symbols for the various political parties, used to canvas illiterate voters.

Emergency – period in the 1970s during which Indira Gandhi suspended many political rights.

Eve-teasing – sexual harassment.

filmee – music or other aspect of Indian movies.

firman – royal order or grant.

freaks – dropped-out westerners wandering India.

gabbas – Kashmiri rugs with appliqué.

gaddi – throne of a Hindu prince.

Ganga – River Ganges; see also Religion glossary.

ganj – market.

ganja – dried flowering tips of marijuana plant.

gaon – village.

garh – fort.

gari – vehicle; 'motor gari' is a car and 'rail gari' is a train.

gaur – Indian bison.

geyser – hot water heater.

ghat – steps or landing on a river; range of hills, or road up hills.

ghazal – Urdu songs derived from poetry; sad love themes.

gherao – industrial action where the workers lock in their employers.

giri – hill.

GITO – Government of India Tourist Office.

GMVN – Garhwal Mandal Vikas Nigam, Garhwal tourist organisation.

godown – warehouse.

Gonds – aboriginal Indian race, now mainly found in the jungles of central India.

goondas – ruffians or toughs. Political parties often employ them in gangs.

gopis – milkmaids. *Krishna* was very fond of them.

govinda – cowherd.

grihastha – householder stage of the *ashrama* system; discharge their duty to ancestors by having sons and making sacrifices to the gods.

gufa – cave.

hammam – Turkish bath.

Harijan – name (no longer considered acceptable) given by Gandhi to India's *Untouchables*, meaning 'children of god'.

hartaal – strike.

hashish – see *charas*.

hathi – elephant.

haveli – traditional ornately decorated residences, particularly in reference to those found in Rajasthan and Gujarat.

havildar – army officer.

hijra – eunuch.

hindola – swing.

hookah – water pipe.

howdah – seat for carrying people on an elephant's back.

HPTDC – Himachal Pradesh Tourist Development Corporation.

hypothecated – Indian equivalent of leased or mortgaged. You often see small signs on taxis or auto-rickshaws stating that the vehicle is 'hypothecated' to some bank or other.

idgah – open enclosure to the west of a town where prayers are offered during the Muslim Id-ul-Zuhara festival.

ikat – fabric made with thread which is tie-dyed before weaving.

Indo-Saracenic – style of colonial architecture that integrated western designs with Muslim, Hindu and Jain influences.

ishwara – lord; see also Religion glossary

jagamohan – assembly hall.

jali – carved marble lattice screen.

janata – literally 'people'. The Janata Party is the People's Party.

jauhar – ritual mass suicide by immolation, traditionally performed by *Rajput* women at times of military defeat to avoid being dishonoured by their captors.

jawan – policeman or soldier.

jheel – swampy area.

jhuggi – shanty settlement. Also called *bustee*.

jhula – bridge.

ji – honorific that can be added to the end of almost anything; thus 'Babaji', 'Gandhiji'.

JKLF – Jammu and Kashmir Liberation Front.

jootis – pointy-toed shoes.

juggernauts – huge, extravagantly decorated temple 'cars' dragged through the streets during Hindu festivals.

jumkahs – earrings.

kabaddi – traditional game (like tag).

kachairri – see *cutcherry*.

kameez – woman's shirt.

Kanishka – important king of the Kushana Empire who reigned in the early Christian era.

karmachario – workers.

khadi – homespun cloth; Mahatma Gandhi encouraged people to spin this rather than buy English cloth.

Khalistan – Sikh secessionists' name for an independent Punjab.

khan – Muslim honorific title.

kho-kho – traditional game (like tag).

khur – Asiatic wild ass.

kiangs – wild ass found in Ladakh.

KMVN – Kumaon Mandal Vikas Nigam, Kumaon tourist organisation.

kompu – C-shaped, metal trumpet.

kos minar – milestone.

kot – fort.

kothi – residence, house or mansion.

kotwali – police station.

kshatriyas – Hindu caste of soldiers or administrators.

kund – lake; Toda village.

kurta – shirt.

lakh – 100,000.

lathi – large bamboo stick; what Indian police

officers will hit you with if you get in the way of their charge.

lenga – long skirt with a waist cord.

lhamo – Tibetan opera.

lok – people.

loka – realm.

Lok Dal – political party; one of the components of the Janata Party.

Lok Sabha – lower house in the Indian parliament, comparable to the House of Representatives or House of Commons.

Losar – Tibetan new year; celebrated in late February/early March.

lungi – like a sarong.

machaan – observation tower.

madrasa – Islamic college.

mahal – house or palace.

maharaja, maharana, maharao – princely ruler or king.

maharani – wife of a princely ruler or a ruler in her own right.

mahatma – literally 'great soul'.

mahout – elephant rider/master.

Mahratta – see *Maratha*.

maidan – open grassed area in a city.

makara – crocodile; see also Religion glossary.

mali – gardener.

mandi – market.

Maratha – central Indian people who controlled much of India at various times and fought the Mughals.

marg – major road.

mata – mother.

maund – unit of weight now largely superseded (about 20kg).

mela – fair.

memsahib – married western lady (from 'madam-sahib'). More widely used than you'd think.

mendi – henna; ornate henna patterns painted on women's hands and feet for important festivals, particularly in Rajasthan. Beauty parlours and bazaar stalls will do it for you.

mithuna – pairs of men and women; often seen in temple sculpture.

Moghul – see *Mughal*.

monsoon – rainy season.

morcha – mob march or protest.

Mughal – Muslim dynasty of Indian emperors from Babur to Aurangzeb.

mund – village.

munshi – writer, secretary or teacher of languages.

nadi – river.

namaste – traditional Hindu greeting (hello or goodbye), often accompanied by a small bow, with the hands brought together at chest or head level, as a sign of respect.

natamandir – dancing hall.

nautch – dance.

nautch girls – dancing girls.

nawab – Muslim ruling prince or powerful landowner.

Naxalites – ultra-leftist political movement. Began in Naxal Village, West Bengal, as a peasant rebellion. Characterised by extreme violence. Still exists in Uttar Pradesh, Bihar and Andhra Pradesh.

nilgai – antelope.

niwas – house, building.

nizam – hereditary title of the rulers of Hyderabad.

NRI – Non-Resident Indian; of economic importance for modern India.

nullah – ditch or small stream.

numda – Rajasthani rug.

OTDC – Orissa Tourism Development Corporation.

pacha – green, pure.

padma – lotus; see also Religion glossary.

padyatra – 'foot journey' made by politicians to raise support at village level.

palanquin – box-like enclosure carried on poles on four men's shoulders; the occupant sits inside on a seat.

palia – memorial stone.

palli – village.

panchayat – village council.

pandals – marquees.

pandit – expert or wise person. Sometimes used to mean a bookworm.

Parsi – Persian; see also Religion glossary.

patachitra – Orissan cloth paintings.

PCO – public call office.

peepul – fig tree, especially a bo tree.

peon – lowest grade clerical worker.

pietra dura – marble inlay work characteristic of the Taj Mahal.

POK – Pakistan Occupied Kashmir.

pradesh – state.

pranayama – study of breath control.
pukkah – proper; very much a Raj-era term.
pukkah sahib – proper European gentleman.
punkah – cloth fan, swung by pulling a cord.
purdah – custom among some Muslims of keeping women in seclusion.

qila – fort.

raga – any of several conventional patterns of melody and rhythm that form the basis for freely interpreted compositions.
railhead – station or town at the end of a railway line; termination point.
raj – rule or sovereignty.
raja – king.
rajkumar – prince.
Rajya Sabha – Council of States.
Rajput – Hindu warrior castes, royal rulers of central India.
rakhi – amulet.
rangoli – chalk design.
rani – female ruler or wife of a king.
rasta roko – roadblock for protest purposes.
rath – temple chariot or car used in religious festivals.
rawal – nobleman.
rickshaw – small, two-wheeled passenger vehicle. Only in Calcutta and one or two hill stations do the old human-powered rickshaws still exist. Bicycle rickshaws are more widely used.
road – railway town which serves as a communication point to a larger town off the line, eg Mt Abu and Abu Road.

sadar – main.
sagar – lake, reservoir.
sahib – 'lord', title applied to any gentleman and most Europeans.
salai – road.
salwar – trousers worn by Punjabi women.
sambar – deer.
sangam – meeting of two rivers.
sardar – see *sirdar*.
satyagraha – non-violent protest involving a hunger strike, popularised by Mahatma Gandhi. From Sanskrit, literally meaning 'insistence on truth'.
Scheduled Castes – official term used for the *Untouchables* or *Dalits*.

sepoy – formerly an Indian solider in British service.
serai – accommodation for travellers.
shikar – hunting expedition.
shikara – gondola-like boat used on Srinagar's lakes in Kashmir.
shirting – material shirts are made from.
shola – virgin forest.
shree – see *shri*.
shri – honorific; these days the Indian equivalent of Mr or Mrs.
shruti – meaning heard.
shudras – caste of labourers.
singh – literally 'lion'; name of the Rajput caste and adopted by Sikhs as a surname.
sirdar – leader or commander.
sitar – Indian stringed instrument.
smriti – remembered.
sree – see *shri*.
sri – see *shri*.
sudra – low Hindu caste.
suiting – material suits are made from.
surya – sun; see also Religion glossary.
sutra – string; list of rules expressed in verse.
swaraj – independence.
sweeper – lowest caste servant, performs the most menial of tasks.
syce – groom.

tabla – pair of drums.
tal – lake.
taluk – district.
tank – reservoir.
tatty – woven grass screen soaked in water and hung outside windows to cool the air.
tempo – noisy three-wheeler public transport vehicle; bigger than an auto-rickshaw.
thakur – Hindu caste.
thangka – rectangular Tibetan painting on cloth.
thiru – holy.
tola – 11.6g.
tonga – two-wheeled horse or pony carriage.
tope – grove of trees, usually mangoes.
topi – pith helmet; widely used during the Raj era.
torana – architrave over a temple entrance.
toy train – narrow-gauge railway.
trekkers – jeeps.
tripolia – triple gateway.

uma – light; see also Religion glossary.

UNESCO – United Nations Educational, Scientific and Cultural Organization.
Untouchable – lowest caste or 'casteless', for whom the most menial tasks are reserved. The name derives from the belief that higher castes risk defilement if they touch one. Formerly known as *Harijan*, now *Dalit*.

varna – concept of caste.
veena – stringed instrument.
veranda – covered porch.
vihara – resting place, garden, cave with cells; see also Religion glossary.
vikram – large *tempo*.

wallah – man; added onto almost anything, eg *dhobi*-wallah, taxi-wallah, Delhi-wallah.
wazir – chief minister.

yagna – self-mortification.
yakshi – maiden.
yantra – geometric plan thought to create energy.
yatra – pilgrimage.
yatri – tourist.
yoni – vulva; see also the Religion glossary.

zakat – tax.
zamindar – landowner.
zenana – area in an upper-class Muslim house where women are secluded.

Religion

The multiplicity of religions in India provides a whole series of terms for temples, shrines, tombs or memorials. There are also many religious terms encompassing the numerous Hindu gods, their incarnations, attendants, consorts, vehicles and symbols.

Abhimani – eldest son of *Brahma*.
Abhimanyu – son of *Arjuna*.
Agasti – legendary Hindu sage, highly revered in the south as he is credited with introducing Hinduism and developing the Tamil language.
Agni – major deity in the *Vedas*; mediator between men and the gods.
amrita – immortality.
Ananda – Buddha's cousin and favourite disciple.
Ananta – snake on which *Vishnu* reclined.

Andhaka – 1000-headed demon, killed by *Shiva*.
Annapurna – form of *Durga*; worshipped for her power to provide food.
apsaras – heavenly nymphs.
Aranyani – Hindu goddess of forests.
Ardhanari – *Shiva* in half-male, half-female form.
Arishta – *daitya* who, having taken the form of a bull, attacked *Krishna* and was killed by him.
Arjuna – *Mahabharata* hero and military commander who married *Subhadra*, took up arms against and overcame all manner of demons, had the *Bhagavad Gita* related to him by *Krishna*, led Krishna's funeral ceremony at Dwarka and finally retired to the Himalaya.
Avalokitesvara – one of Buddha's most important disciples.
avataar – incarnation of a deity, usually *Vishnu*.
azan – Muslim call to prayer.

baba – religious master or father; term of respect.
Balarama – brother of *Krishna*.
basti – Jain temple.
bhakti – surrendering to the gods; faith.
Bhadrakali – another name for *Durga*.
Bhagavad Gita – Hindu Song of the Divine One; *Krishna's* lessons to *Arjuna*, the main thrust of which was to emphasise the philosophy of *bhakti*; part of the *Mahabharata*.
Bhairava – the Terrible; refers to the eighth incarnation of *Shiva* in his demonic form.
Bharata – half-brother of *Rama*; ruled while Rama was in exile.
Bhima – *Mahabharata* hero, brother of *Hanuman* renowned for his great strength.
bhoga-mandapa – Orissan hall of offering.
Bodhisattva – one who has almost reached *nirvana*, but who renounces it in order to help others attain it; literally 'one whose essence is perfected wisdom'.
Brahma – Hindu god; source of all existence and worshipped as the creator in the *trimurti*.
Brahmanism – early form of Hinduism which evolved from Vedism (see *Vedas*); named after Brahmin priests and *Brahma*.
Buddha – Awakened One; the originator of Buddhism; also regarded by Hindus as the ninth incarnation of *Vishnu*.

chaam – ritual masked dance performed by Buddhist monks in *gompas* to celebrate the victory of good over evil and of Buddhism over pre-existing religions.

Chamunda – form of *Durga*. A real terror, armed with a scimitar, noose and mace, and clothed in elephant hide. Her mission was to kill the demons Chanda and Munda.

chaitya – Buddhist temple, also prayer room or assembly hall.

chakra – focus of one's spiritual power; disc-like weapon of *Vishnu*.

chandra – moon, or the moon as a god.

char dham – four pilgrimage destinations of Badrinath, Kedarnath, Yamunotri and Gangotri.

chedi – see *pagoda*.

chomos – Tibetan Buddhist nuns.

chörten – Tibetan for *pagoda*.

dagoba – *see* pagoda.

daityas – demons and giants who fought against the gods.

Damodara – another name for *Krishna*.

dargah – shrine or place of burial of a Muslim saint.

darshan – offering or audience with someone; viewing of a deity.

Dasaratha – father of *Rama* in the *Ramayana*.

Dattatreya – *Brahmin* saint who embodied the *trimurti*.

deul – temple sanctuary.

Devi – *Shiva's* wife.

dham – holiest pilgrimage places of India.

dharma – the Hindu-Buddhist moral code of behaviour.

Digambara – Sky-Clad; a Jain sect whose followers demonstrate their disdain for worldly goods by going naked.

dikpalas – temple guardians.

Draupadi – wife of the five Pandava princes in the *Mahabharata*.

dukhang – Tibetan prayer hall.

Durga – the Inaccessible; a form of *Devi*, a beautiful but fierce woman riding a tiger; major goddess of the *Sakti* cult.

dwarpal – doorkeeper; sculpture beside the doorways to Hindu or Buddhist shrines.

export gurus – *gurus* whose followers are mainly westerners.

fakir – Muslim who has taken a vow of poverty; also applied to *sadhus* and other Hindu ascetics.

Ganesh – Hindu god of wisdom and prosperity. Popular elephant-headed son of *Shiva* and *Parvati*.

Ganga – Hindu goddess representing the sacred Ganges river; said to flow from the toe of *Vishnu*.

ganga aarti – river worship ceremony.

Garuda – man-bird vehicle of *Vishnu*.

Gayatri – sacred verse of *Rig-Veda*, repeated mentally by *Brahmins* twice a day.

Gita Govinda – erotic poem by Jayadeva relating *Krishna's* early life as *Govinda*.

godmen – commercially minded *gurus*; see also *export gurus*.

gompa – Tibetan Buddhist monastery.

Gopala – see *Govinda*.

gopuram – soaring pyramidal gateway tower of Dravidian temples.

Govinda – *Krishna* as a cowherd.

Granth Sahib – Sikh holy book.

gurdwara – Sikh temple.

guru – teacher or holy person (in Sanskrit, literally 'goe' – darkness – and 'roe' – to dispel).

gumbad – dome on a Muslim tomb or mosque.

haj – Muslim pilgrimage to Mecca.

haji – Muslim who has made the *haj*.

Hanuman – Hindu monkey god, prominent in the *Ramayana*, and a follower of *Rama*.

Hara – one of *Shiva's* names.

haram – prayer room in Muslim mosque.

Hari – another name for *Vishnu*.

Hinayana – small-vehicle of Buddhism.

Hiranyakasipu – *Daitya* king killed by *Narasimha*.

imam – Muslim religious leader.

imambara – tomb dedicated to a Shi'ite Muslim holy man.

Indra – most important and prestigious of the Vedic gods. God of rain, thunder, lightning and war.

Ishwara – another name given to *Shiva*.

Jagadhatri – Mother of the World; another name for *Devi*.

Jagannath – Lord of the Universe; a form of *Krishna*.

Jalasayin – literally 'sleeping on the waters'; name for *Vishnu* as he sleeps on his couch over water during the monsoon.

Janaka – father of *Sita*.

jatakas – tales from Buddha's various lives.

jyoti linga – most important shrines to *Shiva*, of which there are 12.

Kailasa – sacred Himalayan mountain; home of *Shiva*.

Kali – the Black; terrible form of *Devi* commonly depicted with black skin, dripping with blood, surrounded by snakes and wearing a necklace of skulls.

Kalki – White Horse; future (10th) incarnation of *Vishnu* which will appear at the end of Kali-Yuga, when the world ceases to be. Has been compared to *Maitreya* in Buddhist cosmology.

Kama – Hindu god of love.

Kanyakumari – Virgin Maiden; another name for *Durga*.

Kartikiya – Hindu god of war, *Shiva's* son.

kapali – sacred bowl made from a human skull.

karma – Hindu-Buddhist principle of retributive justice for past deeds.

kata – Tibetan prayer shawl, traditionally given to a *lama* when pilgrims are brought into his presence.

Kedarnath – name of *Shiva* and one of the 12 *jyotirlinga*.

kibla – direction in which Muslims turn in prayer, often marked with a niche carved into the mosque wall.

koil – Hindu temple.

Krishna – *Vishnu's* eighth incarnation, often coloured blue; he revealed the *Bhagavad Gita* to *Arjuna*.

Kusa – one of *Rama's* twin sons.

Lakshmana – half-brother and aide of *Rama* in the *Ramayana*.

Lakshmi – *Vishnu's* consort, Hindu goddess of wealth; she sprang forth from the ocean holding a lotus.

lama – Tibetan-Buddhist priest or monk.

Laxmi – see *Lakshmi*.

linga – plural of *lingam*.

lingam – phallic symbol; symbol of *Shiva*.

Mahabharata – Great Hindu *Vedic* epic poem of the Bharata dynasty; containing about 10,000 verses, describing the battle between the Pandavas and the Kauravas.

Mahabodhi Society – founded in 1891 to encourage Buddhist studies.

Mahadeva – Great God; *Shiva*.

Mahadevi – Great Goddess; *Devi*.

Mahakala – Great Time; *Shiva* and one of 12 *jyotirlinga*.

Mahayana – greater-vehicle of Buddhism.

Mahayogi – Great Ascetic; *Shiva*.

Maheshwara – Great Lord; *Shiva*.

Maitreya – future Buddha.

Makara – mythical sea creature and *Varuna's* vehicle.

Mahavir – last *tirthankar*.

Mahisa – Hindu demon.

mandal – shrine.

mandala – circle; symbol used in Hindu and Buddhist art to symbolise the universe.

mandapam – pillared pavilion in front of a temple.

mandir – Hindu or Jain temple.

mani stone – stone carved with the Tibetan-Buddhist mantra 'Om mani padme hum' or 'Hail to the jewel in the lotus'.

mani walls – Tibetan stone walls with sacred inscriptions.

mantra – sacred word or syllable used by Buddhists and Hindus to aid concentration; metrical psalms of praise found in the *Vedas*.

Mara – Buddhist god of death; has three eyes and holds the wheel of life.

Maruts – Hindu storm gods.

masjid – mosque.

math – monastery.

Meru – mythical mountain found in the centre of the earth; on it is *Swarga*.

mihrab – see *kibla*.

Mohini – *Vishnu* in his female incarnation.

moksha – salvation.

mudra – ritual hand movements used in Hindu religious dancing.

muezzin – one who calls Muslims to prayer from the minaret.

mujtahids – divines.

mullah – Muslim scholar, teacher or religious leader.

Naga – mythical snake with human face; person from Nagaland.

namaz – Muslim prayers.

Nanda – cowherd who raised *Krishna*.

Nandi – bull, vehicle of *Shiva*.

Narasimha – man-lion incarnation of *Vishnu*.

Narayan – incarnation of *Vishnu* the creator.

Narsingh – see *Narasimha*.

Nataraja – *Shiva* as the cosmic dancer.
Nilakantha – form of *Shiva*. His blue throat is a result of swallowing poison that would have destroyed the world.
nirvana – ultimate aim of Buddhists, final release from the cycle of existence.
noth – the Lord (Jain).

Om – sacred invocation representing the absolute essence of the divine principle. For Buddhists, if repeated often enough with complete concentration, it should lead to a state of emptiness.
Osho – Bhagwan Rajneesh, the guru who mixed Californian pop-psychology with Indian mysticism.

padma – lotus; another name for the Hindu goddess *Lakshmi*.
pagoda – Buddhist religious monument composed of a solid hemisphere topped by a spire, containing relics of the Buddha; also known as a *dagoba*, *stupa* or *chedi*.
Pali – derived from Sanskrit; the original language in which the Buddhist scriptures were recorded. Scholars still refer to the original Pali texts.
Panchatantra – series of traditional Hindu stories about the natural world, human behaviour and survival.
Parasurama – *Rama* with the axe; sixth incarnation of *Vishnu*.
Parsi – adherent of the Zoroastrian faith.
Parvati – another form of *Devi*.
pinjrapol – animal hospital maintained by Jains.
prasaad – food offering used in religious ceremonies.
puja – literally 'respect'; offering or prayers.
Puranas – set of 18 encyclopaedic Sanskrit stories, written in verse, relating to the three gods, dating from 5th century AD.

Radha – favourite mistress of *Krishna* when he lived as a cowherd.
Rama – seventh incarnation of *Vishnu*.
Ramayana – story of *Rama* and *Sita* and their conflict with *Ravana*. One of India's best-known legends; retold throughout almost all South-East Asia.
rathas – rock-cut *Dravidian* temples at Mahabalipuram.
Ravana – demon king of Lanka (modern-day Sri Lanka). He abducted *Sita*, and the titanic battle between him and *Rama* is told in the *Ramayana*.
Rig-Veda – original and longest of the four main *Vedas*, or holy Sanskrit texts.
rudraksh mala – strings of beads used in puja.
Rukmani – wife of *Krishna*; died on his funeral pyre.
rishi – any poet, philosopher, saint or sage; originally a sage to whom the hymns of the *Vedas* were revealed.

sadhu – ascetic, holy person, one who is trying to achieve enlightenment; usually addressed as 'swamiji' or 'babaji'.
Saivaite – follower of *Shiva*.
Saivism – worship of *Shiva*.
samadhi – ecstatic state, sometimes defined as 'ecstasy, trance, communion with God'. Also a place where a holy man has been cremated; usually venerated as a shrine.
samsara – Hindus believe earthly life is cyclical; you are born again and again, the quality of these rebirths being dependent upon your *karma* in previous lives.
sangha – community or order of Buddhist priests, or Buddhist monastery.
Sankara – *Shiva* as the creator.
sanyasin – like a *sadhu*; a wandering ascetic who has renounced all worldly things as part of the *ashrama* system.
Saraswati – wife of *Brahma*, goddess of speech and learning; usually sits on a white swan, holding a *veena*.
satsang – discourse by a *swami* or *guru*.
Sati – wife of *Shiva*. Became a sati ('honourable woman') by immolating herself. Although banned more than a century ago, the act of sati is occasionally performed.
satra – Hindu Vaishnavaite monastery and centre for art.
Shaivaite – see *Saivaite*.
shakti – creative energies perceived as female deities; devotees follow the cult of Shaktism.
Sheshnag – some believe that this snake is the one on which *Vishnu* reclines.
shahadah – Muslim declaration of faith ('there is no God but God; Mohammed is his prophet').
sikhara – Hindu temple-spire or temple.
Sita – Hindu goddess of agriculture. More commonly associated with the *Ramayana*.

Skanda – another name for *Kartikiya*.

Shiva – the destroyer; also the Creator, in which form he is worshipped as a *lingam*.

Siva – see *Shiva*.

sonam – *karma* accumulated in successive reincarnations.

stupa – *see* pagoda.

Subrahmanya – another name for *Kartikiya*.

Subhadra – *Krishna's* incestuous sister.

Surya – major deity in the *Vedas*.

sufi – ascetic Muslim mystic.

swami – title of respect meaning 'lord of the self'; given to initiated Hindu monks.

Swarga – heaven of *Indra*.

tandava – Hindu victory dance over *Mahisa*.

tantric Buddhism – Tibetan Buddhism with strong sexual and occult overtones.

theertham – temple tank.

Theravada – small-vehicle of Buddhism.

thug – follower of Thuggee; ritual murderers centred in Madhya Pradesh in the last century.

tika – mark devout Hindus put on their foreheads with tika powder.

tirthankars – the 24 great Jain teachers.

trimurti – triple form; the Hindu triad – *Brahma, Shiva* and *Vishnu*.

Tripitaka – classic *Theravada* Buddhist scriptures, divided into three categories, hence the name 'Three Baskets'.

Uma – *Shiva's* consort.

Upanishads – esoteric doctrine; ancient texts forming part of the *Vedas*; delving into weighty matters such as the nature of the universe and soul.

Valmiki – author of the *Ramayana*.

Vamana – fifth incarnation of *Vishnu*, as the dwarf.

varku – sacred flute made from a thigh bone.

vihara – part of monastery.

Varuna – supreme Vedic god.

Vedas – Hindu sacred books; collection of hymns composed in pre-classical Sanskrit during the second millennium BC and divided into four books: *Rig-Veda*, *Yajur-Veda*, *Sama-Veda* and *Atharva-Veda*.

vimana – principal part of Hindu temple.

vipassana – meditation style developed by Buddha.

Vishnu – third in the *trimurti*. Vishnu is the Preserver and Restorer, who so far has nine avataars: the fish Matsya; the tortoise Kurma; the wild boar Naraha; *Narasimha*; *Vamana*; *Parasurama*; *Rama*; *Krishna*; and *Buddha*.

yali – mythical lion creature.

yogini – female goddess attendants.

yoni – female fertility symbol.

Food & Drink

The following are some of the more common food and drink terms you will come across all over India. For more information see the Food and Drink sections in the Facts for the Visitor chapter.

arak – liquor distilled from coconut milk, potatoes or rice.

betel – nut of the betel tree; the leaves and nut are mildly intoxicating and are chewed as a stimulant and digestive.

bhang lassi – blend of *lassi* with *bhang* (a drink with a kick).

bhelpuri – crisp fried thin rounds of dough mixed with puffed rice, fried lentil, lemon juice, chopped onion, herbs and chutney.

biryani – fragrant steamed rice with meat or vegetables.

bombil – fish that are dried in the sun and deep fried to make Bombay Duck.

chaat – snack.

chai – tea.

chang – Tibetan rice or millet beer.

chapati – unleavened Indian bread.

cheiku – small brown fruit which looks like a potato, but it's sweet.

chota – small, spirit drink measure (as in 'chota peg').

country liquor – locally produced liquor.

curd – milk with acid or rennet added to solidify it.

dahin – yoghurt.

dhaba – hole-in-the-wall restaurant or snack bar; boxed lunches delivered to office workers.

dhal – lentil soup; the staple that most of India lives on.

dhal makhani – black lentils and red kidney beans with cream and butter.

dhansaak – meat with curried lentils and rice.

dosa – paper-thin pancakes made from lentil flour.

dum pukht – steam pressure cooking that uses a clay pot.

faluda – long chickpea-flour noodles.

feni – liquor distilled from coconut milk or cashews.

ghee – clarified butter.

gram – legumes.

gyarhcee – famous Tibetan hotpot.

haleen – pounded wheat with mutton sauce.

halwa – sugary dessert.

idli – south Indian rice dumpling.

IMFL – Indian Made Foreign Liquor; beer or spirits produced in India.

jaggery – hard, brown-sugar-like sweetener made from kitul palm sap.

kachauri – Indian-style breakfast of puris and vegetables.

khaja – popular Bihari puff-pastry sweet.

kheer – rice pudding.

korma – curry-like braised dish.

kulcha – charcoal-baked bread.

kulfi – pistachio-flavoured sweet similar to ice cream.

kumbh – pitcher.

lassi – refreshing yoghurt and iced-water drink.

masala – mix (often spices).

masala dosa – curried vegetables inside a *dosa*.

mattar paneer – peas and cheese in gravy.

momos – Tibetan fried dumplings with vegetables or meat.

Misthi dhoi – Bengali sweet; *curd* sweetened with *jaggery*.

namkin – prepackaged spicy nibbles.

paan – *betel* nut and leaves plus chewing additives such as lime.

pakoras – bite-size pieces of vegetable dipped in chickpea-flour batter and deep fried.

paratha – bread made with *ghee* and cooked on a hotplate.

pinda – funeral cake.

puri – flat dough that puffs up when deep fried.

rabri – milky confectionery.

ras gullas – sweet little balls of cream cheese flavoured with rose water.

ras malai – milk and sugar based sweet.

reshmi kabab – tender chicken kabab cooked in the tandoor.

rumali roti – huge paper-thin *chapatis*.

sabzi – curried vegetables.

soma – intoxicating drink derived from the juice of a plant.

sonf – aniseed seeds; come with the bill after a meal and used as a digestive.

thali – traditional south Indian and Gujarati 'all-you-can-eat' vegetarian meal.

thugpa – Tibetan noodle soup.

tiffin – snack, particularly around lunchtime.

toddy – alcoholic drink, tapped from palm trees.

tongba – Himalayan millet beer.

tsampa – Tibetan staple of roast barley flour.

Acknowledgements

THANKS

Many thanks to the travellers (apologies if we've misspelt your name) who used the last edition and wrote to us with helpful hints, useful advice and interesting anecdotes:

Marty & Veena, Trine & Sonny, Stephane & Kathy, Karin & Shai, Anna & Stella, Marie & Lise, Peter & Rikke, Kevin & Lisa, Leif & Blonda, Primo & Marcella, Yonni Abitbol, Dr Arun Abraham, Patrick Abraham, N Adler, Christine Agnith, G S Agral, Rakesh Agrawal, Bill Aitken, Daine & Alana Aitken, Laurie Alder, Mark Alder, TA Aldrin, Declan Alecner, Sofie Alen, R Alexander, Tim Alexander, Sascha Allen, Allison Allgaier, Anders Allgulin, Lasse Almeback, Nora Alterman, Nicholas Anchen, Moya Anchisi, Hakan Andekzen, David Anderson, Gail Anderson, Catherine Anderson, Beck Anderton, Andrej Andrejew, Giovannina M Anthony, I Anton, Vito Anzelmi, Herbert R Appell, Richard Appleton, Peter Apps, Yonat Arbel, Clare Arbuthnott, Gino Arduini, Luis Arevalogarcia, Matti Ariel, Guido Arlt, Leisa Armstrong, Verity Arnold, Perri Arnold Jnr, Cathy Arnquist, Tony Ashcroft, FA Ashcroft, Dorit & Chen Ashkenazi-Tzoref, Ulla Ashorn, Dan Asquiln, Jeanne van Asselt, Kristina Astrom, Michiel Aten, Nazir Athania, Laura Atkinson, Owen Atkinson, Andrew T Austin, Yaell Azaryahu

A Baan, Fons Baars, M Gina Bacalso, Mats Backlund, Karina Backstrom, Neelambar Badoni, Maarten van Baggum, K Bagram, Anthony Bailey, Sue Bailey, Bobbie Bailey, Horace Bailey, David Bain, S Bainbridge, llewellyn Baker, Fiona Baker, Jon Baldwin, Delyth Ball, Jemima Ball, Eve Ballenegger, Daniel Balogh, Helen Banks, S Bantz, Barbara Baracks, Marel Baran, Anita Barewal, Aviram Barhuim, Althea Barker, David Barker, Mike Barker, Rosie Barker, Lori Barkley, Leonie Barner, Spencer Barrett, Greg Barrett, Douglas Barrett, Elizabeth Barrett, Elaine Barritt, Giles Barroe, Marc Barthelemy, Keith D Barton, Anton Baser, Kevin Bateman, Larry Baumbach, Dr Richard H Beal, Emma Beal, Lucinda Beck, Dr Christine Becker, Dave Beedie, Jeff Bell, Michael Bell, Andrew Bell, Jeevan Belloappa, Anja Benesch, Alison Bennett, Michele Bennett, Abigail Bentall, Lizzie Benzimra, Trond Berg, John Erik Berganus, Simon Berger, Regina Berger, ME Van Der Bergh-Coumans, Marten Berglund, Heidi Bergsli, Erin Bernard, Paul Bernet, Camilla Berntsson, Dr Pradeep

Bery, Paul Bett, Vanesssa Bettes, Rohith Bhandary, RN Bhargana, Abhay Bharti, Kalyan Bhattacharjee, VP Bhavsar, Avan Z Bhumgara, Laurent Bianchi, Veronica Bielinski, Patrik Bifeldt, Shannon Biggins, Colin J Biggs, Dr Andrew Biggs, Inge Bilsen, Randi Bindra, Cheryl Binzen, Katoch Bipan, Geremy Birchard, Megan Bird, Rolf & Barbel Birk, DE Birmingham, Stephane Eric Bisson, Bob Blackham, James Blackstone, Geoffrey Blaisdell, Jody Marie Blaylock, Mirjam Blom, Mirka Blomme, Amanda Bloss, Patricia Blunt, William Boag, Johan Bockstael, Pamela Bode, Harry Bohm, Eckhard Bokamper, Frank Bolder, Talia Boltin, Cathryn E Boomer, Michael Tan Koon Boon, Joop Boonen, Claire Booth, Jordi Bosch, Robert Bough, Howard & Pearl Bourne, Nick Bourne, Els Bouw-Rijlaarsdam, John Bower, Heather Boyd, Thea Bracewell, Holly Brackenbury, Joel Bradley, Dan Brake, Jutta Brandt, Caroline Brandtner, J Braun, Bill Bray, Sarah Breen, Frank Breiting, Ian & Sarah Brenchley, Lynda Brenock, Jim Breret, Johannade Bresser, Jennifer Brewer, Valerie Bridjanovic, Jasper Van Den Brink, N Britton, L Britz, Joerg Broeker, Jeande Broima, Roel & Eric Brouwer, Meg Brown, Susan Brown, Nick Brown, Rhona Brown, Dr John W Brownbill, Tess Browne, Henry Browning, Bernhard Brummeir, Hakan Brusstrom, Michael Bruxner, Jim Bryant, Grant Buday, Robert Buerger, B Buetan, Tania Buffin, Jean Bullard, Claire Bungay, Chaowalit Bunyaphusit, Brandon Burg, Patricia Burke, Steven Burke, Elizabeth Grace Burkhart, Jeannie Burnett, A L Burnett, Jane Burns, El Burrell, Mark Burton, Sheridan Butler, Colin Butler, Alan Butterworth, Graham & Karen Bygate, John Byram

Donna Cabell, Charlotte Cain, Staurt Caldwell, Steve & Lisa Caliga, Rob Callen, Justine O Calverley, Francesca Camisoli, Tanya Campbell, Ursula Campbell, Sonja Candek, Naomi Canton, Andre ade Capoa, Shea Car, Ray Carey, Daniel & Ryan Carey, Hugo Cariss, M Carksun, Erin R Carlson, Cor Caroli, Sue Carpenter, Mike Carter, Radha Case, Lantuin Caskey, Franck Castegnaro-Wurtz, Rowan Castle, Isabelle De Castro, Gregory Cathcart, Gail Cathro, Eliane Cavalcante de Almeida, Luigi Cavaleri, Sandra Caville, Pat Celaya, Carrie Celloway, Chiara Cerutti, Bratin Chakravorty, Martin Chalcraft, Martin Chamberlain, K M Champs, Dweepl Chanana, Hari Chandra, Jacquie Chang, Dianna Chapman, Chris & Colin Charles, Liz & Guy Chasseloup, C Chatham, Sanjit Chatterjee, Dr JD Chaudhuri, Anjali Chauhan, UKS Chauhan, Sundar

Cheens, Carlo Cheric, Mr & Mrs Cherouvim, Louise Childs, Yvonne Christ, Douglas Christian, Teufel Christoph, Lneka Chromcova, Don Church, Tim Clael, Tom Claes, Ellen Claesdotter, Elizabeth Claridge, Tony Clark, Sarah Clark, Alan Clark, Alexander Clark, Mel Clark, Donna Clarke, Scott Clarke, Bruce Clarke, Sascha & Britter Clausen, Gareth Clayton, Richard Clayton, Paula Clegg, Ramon Clemente, Maria Kold Clemmensen, Leode Clercq, Miler Clevet, Laurence Cliché, Marc Clissen, Murray Clodagh, R & M Cobden, Irit Cohen, Ziv Cohen, Asaf Cohen, Orit Cohen, Laurie Cohn, LesleyJ Cole, Andrea Cole, David Coleman, Marina Collard, John Collier, Lyn Collins, Shanine Collinson, Jenny Collis, Caroline Coode, Kay Louise Cook, Bergendy Cooke, Stuart Cooke, Chris Cooper, Helen Cooper, Francoise Cooperman, Cynthia Benjamin Copper, Paul Corallot, Ann Corcoran, John M Cord, Dominic Corrigan, Juan I Costero, Diane Counsell, Alistair Cowan, Kerrianne Cowley, Joseph Cox, J & E Cox, Ben Coyne, Gabrielle Cozzolius, Debbie Craft, Michael R Crees, Marcia & John Crellin, Michael & Soonah Cribb, Ian Sid Crighton, Michael Crim, Thomas L Crisman, Alma Cristina, Kate Cromb, Howard W Crosthwaite, Yves Croteau, Dany Cuello, Bob Cullen, John & Wenche Cumming, Pauline Cummings, Aidan Michael Cunningham, John Cunningham, Caroline Cupitt, Clint Curé, Lucy Curry

Zoe D, Sophie Dackanbe, Yigal Dafne, John Dalby, Rod Daldry, Jan Dale, B Daly, Paul Daly, Irene Dam, Hansen & Mirjam Damen, Peter Damm, Sameer Dandage, Mark Daniel, Lizz Daniels, Russell Danrich, Shai Dariti, Pamela Darling, G Darmon, Victroia & Christopher Darue, John Darwin, Ayan Dasvarma, Raja David, Peter David, Jodie Davies, Denis Davies, Clive Davis, Des Davis, Nick Davis, Manisha Dayaram, Mary Ann D'Cruz, Sarah Deakin, Dorothy Dean, Bruce Deane, R & S DeCaroli, Joaclim Decker, Rita Deebest, Diane Defore, Santosh Dehadrai, Alex Deissenbeck, Rina Delafield, Philippe Deling, Sonja Demuth, CB Denning, Klaudia Deppisch, Susan Derby, Alex Derom, Utpal Desai, Marco Deterink, Andreas Deutscher, Baburao DH, Narinder Dhami, PM Dharmalingam, Dhawa Dhondup, Rosemary Di Benedetto, Miguel & Angel Diaz Matinez, Deborah Dickey, Martin Didler, Jan Auke Dijkstra, Giovanni Discenza, Wendy Dison, Andrew Dittfeld, Chris Ditzen, Barb Dodson, Melanie Doehler, K Doherty, WK Dolphin, Rob Donaldson, Jaap van Donkelaar, C Donnelly, Kate Donovan, Francois Donovan, Rene Doosje, Gunter Doppler, Vijay Doshi, Michael Doud, Chris Douglas, Peter Dowling, Lucinda Down, Lawrence & Matilda Dressman, Richard & Martina Drygas, Joseph D'Souza, Gloria & Ronald Duber, Dave Dubyne, Amy

Duckworth, Emmett Duffy, Monika Dukszta, Meldrum Duncan, Geoffrey Duncan, Rachel Duncan, Mick & Jo Dunican, Katherine Dunk, James Dunn, Orla Dunne, Hilary Dunne, Chris Dunning, Nandini Dutt, Diana Dwyer, Rachel Dwyer, Marge d'Wylde, Corey Dyer, J Dyer, Ian Dyus, Robert Dzexhage

Ken Eaton, Iwona Eberle, Michael Eckert, David Edwardes, R J Edwards, Nicky Efron, Jack Egerton, Maarten van Egmond, Gil Eiges, Kirsten & Leif Ekdahl, Kabid Ekonomi, Rayomand E Elavia, Wilfried Elfner, Joshua Eliezer, Alison Eliot, John Elklll, Jocelyn Elliot, Bethany Ellis, Gideon Ellwood, B Endicott, Dirk & Isabelle Engels, Simon Engemann, Chris England, Rachel Enright, Steve Enticknap, Livia Epps, Daniel Ericson, Linda Eriksson, Daniel Eschle, Offer Eshel, Marina Eskina, Pascal Esvan, Konoura Etsuko, Alex Evanov, Everlin Everz, Mats Exter, Wilna van Eyssen

Cath Fagan, Reg Fallah, Marianne Fallon, Linda Fane, Cindy Farina, Valerio Farinelli, Laura Farish, Yuval Farkash, Justin Farley, Michael Fasman, Heidi A Fassbind, Julie Faulk, Anne-Meike Fechter, Anja Feickert, Norman Feldman, Andi Feller, Chris Felstead, Kathryn Fenn, Benedetto Ferci, Mary Fernandez, Emilic Ferrcia, Wendy & Terry Fidgeon, Andrew Fincham, Genia Findeisen, Ciara Finn, Rachel Fisher, Steven Flanders, Caroline Fletcher, Sharon Flier, Pedro Flombaum, Lisa Flynn, Greg Flynn, Elizabeth Forbes, Anna K Ford, Dan Forrester, Gordon Forster, Helena Forsyth, Teresa Fowler, Vibhu-Irvin Fox, Elizabeth Fox-Wolfe, Boaz Franklin, Paul Fraser, Judy Frater, Lucille Frauenstein, Hilary Frazer, Charlesworth Frederick, Lucia Fresa, M Friday, Mary Ellen Leibheit, Frank Fried, Dr Annette Fried, Matt Friedman, Kevin Friesen, Christopher Frost, Lorraine Fry, Ben Fry

CG Gaanoo, Ms H Gae Sestero, Tony Galanides, Matt Galloway, Mahendra Gandhi, Indrani Ganguly, Julia Garcia, Ben Gardiner, Kate Gardner, Sunil Ji Garg, Bob Garner, Lucy Garrett, Hazel Garth, Robert Gasser, The Gebbett Family, Heike Geiselmann, Scott W Gentry, Kym Gentry, Stephen George, Sunil George, Sunil George, Matt Gerry, Yasmine Ghandour, Shami Ghosh, Massimo Giannini, Iain Gibbs, Julie Giblett, Serge Gielkens, Paul Gill, Sophie Gill, Susan Gillman, Katrien San Giorgi, Gaille Girod, Dawn Glaser, Roy Glasner, Melanie Glynn, Geoff Goats, Hilary Goldberg, Jill Golden, Lorne Goldman, Bernado Martin Gomez, Dean Gomsalves, Eduardo Gonzalea, Lisa Marie Gonzales, Kate Good, Shankan Goodall, KK Gopalakrishnan, Sharon Gorman, Kristina Gottwald, Raghuram Govindarajan, Stephen Gow, Anuj Goyal, Joanna Grabiak, Dean Gradon, Sabine Grafenstein, Orla Graham,

Breck A Graham, Dr Travers Grant, Laurie Graves, Hazel Gray, Peter Gray, Danielle Graysmark, Shira Green, Krischa Greenaway, H De Greeve, Herman Greeven, Dr Hans-Joachim Gregor, Cathryn Gregory, Luke Gregson, Clara Grein, Val Gretchev, David & Fiona Griffin Rudder, John Griffiths, Jan Grinberg, Nienke Groen, Richard Groom, Frankde Groot, Jamie & Rebecca Grover, Frank & Stephanie Gruson, Gster Guenero, Ashirvad Guesthouse, Alexandra Gulemeester, Nerajana Gunetilleke, David & Diana Gurney, Krishnan Guruswamy, Gote Gustafsson, Lode Hoo Gwendhoorn, Jacqueline Gygax

Jasonan Haard, J Van Haard, Kim Haas, Albert de Haas, Baro Haauardsholm, P Hackett-Jones, Annalisa Hainsome, Timothy Hall, Eric Hall, Joanna Hall, Niamh Hallissy, Jemma Halman, Kevin Halon, Georgina Hambert, Louise Hamer-Keijser, Stuart Hamilton, Kay Hammond, Davide Hanau, Susanne Hangaard Jensen, Bhavani Hannon, JL Hans, Paul Hansen, Helle Hansen, Brian Hansen, Charlotte & Lizette Hansen, Emma Hanson, Premiata Haralalka, Dr Marcus Harbord, Robert Harding, Maureen Hardinge, Dickon Hares, Csaba & Zsout Hargitai, Simon Harris, Shirley & Tim Harris, Simon Harris, Katrin Hartmann, Jane Harvey, Larissa & Kari Hass, AJ Hastak, Jim Hastings, James M Hastings, James Hatcher, Madri Haveli, Rachel Hawkes, Heather Hawkins, Natalie Hawkrigg, Vincent Hayes, Oliver Hayes, Julia Haywood, Trea & Kevin Heapes, Ashley Heath, Barbara Heatherley, Keely Hegarty, Petra Heitkamp, Judith Heitman, Richard Hemingway, Michiel A Hensema, Barbara Hersel, Johanna Hess, David Hewett, Tracey Hicks, Alain Hije, Susanne Hill, Karel Van Hilst, Jacinta Hingston, Richard Hinkson, Nina Hirst, Tony Hobbs, Martina Hodes, Phil Hoffer, Ursula Hoflin, S Hofstede, SA & DE Holbrook, Peter Holliger, Michael Holloway, Mark Holmes, Jon Holton, Spencer Home, Andrew Hood, Michael Hope, Jeff Hopewell, Siobhan Hopkins, Keith Hopper, Wee Keng Hor, Debbie Horbul, Bela Horvath, David Hothi, Eilish Hovengh, Peter Howe, G Howell, Franki Howes, Gunther Hsue, Andrew Hubbard, Heinrich Hubbert, Kirsti Hudson, John Hudson, Nadine & Mike Hudson, Jacques Huf, Becky Huges, David Hughes, Greeba Hughes, David Hughes, Heather Hughes, Paul Hughes-Smith, Frank van Hulsentop, Roelof vander Hulst, Bram Hulzebos, Richard Humble, Kelly Hunt, Bruce Hunter, Risto Huoso, Michael Huttner, Vicky Huyskens, Keith Hyams, Mair Hyman

Rebecca Ilott, Pasi Ilvesmaki, Susan Immergut, Wyn Ingham, Kati Inkinen, Trina Innes, Irina Innes, Gabriel Inoges, John Irvine, Rachel Irvine, John Irvine, Roland Ischanz, David Iser, Marko Istenic, Lara Iverson

Friederike Johnig, Abdeen Jabara, David Jackson, Ian Jackson, Mark Jackson, George Jackson, Irene Jackson, Gary Jacob, TN Jacobson, Dr RK Jaggi, Vivek Jain, Bett W James, Keith James, Jrh & AA James, Jeffy James, Nesta James, Andrew James, Tarja Janhuen, MN Jani, Ton Janusch, Liz Jason, Conny Jasperse, Nathan Jawblyn, Jaishankar Jayaraman, Helen Jeffreys, PR Jeffreys-Powell, Satja Jennings, Maria & Jesper Jensen, Knud Erik Jensen, Pia Jensen, Eom Jeong-Moo, Judy Jere, Bernard Jervis, Attul Jetha, Cameron Joe, Didomizio Joel, Obin Joelle, Kjaer Johansen, Per Kjaer Johansen, Karen John, Mary Johnson, Rebecca Johnson, Ewa Johnsson, Helen Johnston, Nagasha Jolob, Barry Jones, Ben Jones, Mark Jones, Craig Jones, Mr &Mrs DW Jones, Natalie Jones, Sally A Jones, Diana Jones, Brian Jones, Solveigog Jorgen Meyer, Rohit Joshi, Anne-Dorothee Jungblut, Gwendolyn Theresa Junod

Sumeet Kachwaha, Zoyab A Kadi, Bruno Kahn, Melita M Kalama, Hans Kalma, NN Kalpa, Chandrakant Kalyanpur, Juray Kaman, Haemish Kane, Gerhard Kanne, Rajiv Kapoor, George Karamanou, Jane Karlsson, Renko Karruppannan, Anita Kashyap, Lindsay Kassof, Easan Katir, Sergi Valle Kattendahl, Amrit Kaur, Rupinderjit Kaur Dhami, Abby Kaye, Allyson Keane, Ian Keefe, Dr Joachim Keller, Maurice Kellit, Brain Kelly, Liz Kelly, Emma Kempton, Tim Kendall, Mattias Kenig, Julie Kent, Julie Kepner, Miranda Kerklaan, Alistair Kernick, John Kerr, Stephen Kerr, Immelie Kesseler, M Ketterer, Gazi Khan, Priyanka Khanna, Kavi Khanna, Muninidra Khaund, Dayalji Kheta, Mark Kidd, H Kilday, Heather Kilday, Dave Kilsby, Mary Jo Kimbrough, JL Kinder, Stephen L King, Adi King, Catherine King, Ruth King, Nanne Kingma, Ivan Kirac, Hayley Kirkland, Andy Kirkwood, Sheila Kirwan, Esther Kleijer, Leslie Klein, Jette & Borge Klemmensen, Yechexkel Kling, Georg Klinghammer, Svenja Klotzbucher, Michael Knight, Julia Knop, Martin Knoth, Josef Koberl, Caroline Kobler, Antonin Kodet, Theo Koeten, Helmut Kolb, Arnold Kondijs, Iniva Konsas, Frits Koolschijn, Vimal Korstjens, Jan Koster, Gerta Koster, Rob Koster, Mieke-Ien Koster, Gerhard Kotschenruether, Stephanie Koutsaftis, Chris Koutsofrigas, Christopher Kowollik, Ursula Krahl, Uli Krause, Pauline Krebbers, Stefan Krenn, Sebastian Kresow, Vicky Krins, KP Krishan, G Krishnan, Jeroen Kroon, Mike Krosin, Hans-Lothar Kruger, Steve Krzystyniak, Rosie Kuhn, Jayant Kumar, N Anantha Kumar, Sanjay Kumar, Anand Kumar, Piyush Kumar, Ram Kumar, VS Kumar, Beksy Kurian, Igal Kutin, Anna Kwiecinska

Paiva Laakso-Marsh, Navroza Ladha, Pablo Alvarez Lago, Richard Lake, Raj Lalchandani, Gilbert Lamayo, Baylor Lancaster, Krishere Lants, John Larner, Mads Larsen, Matthias Larson, Leyre Lasa, Stefan Lasagna,

S & W De Lashmutt, Jodi Lathan, Fiona Law, Beth Lawrence, Gili Lazar, Duncan Leagh, Adam Leavesley, John leckie, Alison Lecky, Ken Lee, Andrew Lee, Chris Lee, Fred & Jackie Lee, Marc Leest, Marie-Jose Leferink, Donna Marcus Leffel, Barbara Lehndorf, Wendy Leighton, G Leiper, Jenni Leith, E Leomdeur, David Lepeska, Marie Lesaicherre, Meg Leug, Boris Levit, Hermes Liberty, Paul Lichstein, Anne Marie Ligtenberg, Julia Lilley, Yvonne Lin, Christian Lindquist, Lois Lindsay, Dr Hilde K Link, Heather Linson Lindberg, Corinna Lippe, Bobvon Liski, D Litchfield, Michael Livni, Malcolm Lloyd, Jasper Lloyd, Kenneth & Peggy Lloyd, Del Lloyd, Dr James G Lochtefeld, Ian Lockley, Jos & Ellen Lommerse, Judy Loney, Vincent Lonjon, Myrna Looise, Colin Loth, Dolly Loth, Chris Lovell, LG Lowe, John Ludwig, Nikita Lundin, Graham Lupp, Dr H Luthe, H Luthe, Roman Lysiah

Aileen A MacEwan, Rafael Macias-Giobbels, Selvaggia Macioti, Andrew Mack, John MacKay, Colin & Judi Mackie, Craig A Mackintosh, Dave Macmeekin, Donna MacRae, Emmanuel Madan, Kathy Madson, Tom Maes, Chilik Magal, Sarah Mahamed, Simone Maier, Larry J Maile, Geavauo Maio, Mirjam Malaika, Akhil Malaki, Elias Malamidis, Nischal Malarao, Douglas Malein, Aradhna Malik, Chris Malik, Jan Malik, Stefan Malmgren, Sarah Mann, Francis Mansbridge, Yvonne Mansell, Dan & Amy Marcus, Donna Marcus, Steve Marcus, Merau Marely, Cornelie Marks, Anita Marshall, Vicens Martf, Lisa Martin, Hager Martin, Luis F Martinez, Pier Paolo Martini, Isabelle Mas, Yubal Masalker, Vince Mash, Jane Masheder, Ardyn Hillary Masterman, RJ Mathers, Thomas Matros, Verity Maud, John Maude, Veri Mauro, Mira Maymon, Kellie McBride, Howard McCallum, Wendy McCarty, Frances McConnell, Mike McConnell, Jenny & David McDonald, Ruth McDonald, Rachel McEleney, David McGinniss, Caroline McGovern, Steve McIntosh, Isabel McIntosh, Dawn McKecmnie, C Mclain, Liz McMillan, E McMurray, Marion & Tony Meakin, Barbara Mears, Ony Meda, Nicola Medlik, Linda Medoff, Rita Meher, Ilka Mehlmann, Rsihad Mehta, Eric Meijer, A P Melgrave, Roberto Meliconi, Jonathon de Mello, Maux Meln, Vanessa Geneva Melter, Emanuela Mencaglia Martignoni, Anna Merimee, Wolfgang Messner, Jayne Metcalf, Richard Meury, Jeff, May & Grace Meyer, Ivano Michelazzi, David Middleton, Dr Kapil Midha, Karen Miiler, Karsten Mikkelsen, Xavier Millas Boixader, Ron Miller, Andy Miller, Claire Millhouse, Michael Mills, Richard Milton, Jan Min, Ariel Minkman, Imran Mirza, Kamal Mishra, Arvind Misra, Darshana Mistry, Paul Mitchell, Claire Mitchell, Mark & Audrea Moffat, Andrea Moffat, Rugyer Mohn, Phil Moir, Stine Moller Hansen, Lissen Moller, Truda

Money, Lisa Montague, Patina Monti, Tobias Moor, ArchieL Moore, Norman C Moore, Gary Moore, Damian Moore, Floripes Moraes, Shawn Moren, Tracey Morgan, Cindy Morgan, Elliotte & Lawrence Morgan-Persad, Salli Morita, Greg Morlow, Giulio Moroni, Peter Morris, Andreas Medin Mortensen, Lars Mortensen, S & B Moseley, Talma, Yaffa & Bruria Moshe, Davide Mosso, Jon Motchell, Tarn Mount, Dave Mountain, Dr Anuradha Mouree, Rita Mueller, Prachee Mukherjee, Fabienne Mulders, Uve Mullrich, Jason Mulrooney, Suchitra Mumford, Joss Munro, Casper Munter, Renee Murnain, Ronald Murphy, Michael Murphy, W Murphy, Joan Murphy, Musse Family, Jim Mydosh, Dean Myerson, Jenni Myllynen

Ghulam Nabi Jetha, Muhammad Nadeem, Yoseffa Naiman, Vinod G Nair, V Najran, Kaai Nakajima, John Nankervis, K Nazir, R Nazir, Robert Nelder, Adam Nelson, Saralie Nelson, Stephen Nelson, John D Neumaier, John Newbould, Judy Newsome, Michelle Newton, Mark Nicholls, Danell Nicholson, Trevor Nicklette, Viggo Bach Nielsen, Leif Nielsen, Henriette Nielsen, Camilla Nillson, Rebekka Ninan, Dr Nitinkumar, Herman R Noback, Brian Nomi, Gabriella Nonino, Dr Andy Nordin, Torbjorn Nordin, Anders Nordstrom, Helen Normand, Ola North, Voora & Anssi Nurmi, Richard Nutter, Massimo Nuvina, Erik Nyhus

Sue Oatley, Ciara O'Brien, Mike O'Connell, John O'Grady, Robert James Olajos, Gillian & Jean-Remy Olesen, Lisa Olier, Dr Charles Oliver, Elliot Olivestone, Mirjam Olsthoorn, Jean & Carole Olympio, Perry Omodei Zorini, Peter O'Neill, PG O'Neill, Stefan Orani, Mirta Oregna, Helen O'Riain, Andrew Orme, Alexandra Ornston, Nicolas & Sarah O'Rorke, Rebecca Osborne, Don Osborne, Lynn Osborne, Declan O'Sullivan, Miriam O'Sullivan Darcy, Surush Oswal, Eric Oving, Naama Ozer

Christabel Padmore, Vece Paes, Sandra Pagano, Caroline Pande, Santanu Panigrahi, Michael Papantoniou, Cathy Pardoe, Elizabeth Parker, Penelope Parkin, Kay Parkinson, Dave Parmar, Ange Parrish, Malcolm Part, Michael Pastroff, Lee & Helen Paterson, Kate Pattison, Stuart Pattullo, Werner Pauchli, Andrew Paull, Emma Pavey, Sharon Peake, CH Pearce, Sarah Pearce, Dominic Pearson, Chris Peck, Emily Peckham, Jannine Pedersen, Lars Pedersen, Chris Peers, Claire Pellit, Renate Pelzl, Yves Perisse, Steve Perlman, Jennifer Perrin, Janine Perry, Andrew Pestel, Ellie Peters, Jan Petranek, Haavard Petterson, Gail Petticrew, Andreas Philipp, Emma Phillips, Charlotte Phillips, Swanson Phung, Davide Piazza, Pauline & David Pickles, Nick Picton, Shirley Pierce, Franca Pieroni, Marele Pietsomis,

Rochelle Pilsworth, John Pinnington, Carolyn M Pione, Gergio Pisano, Vikki Pitcher, D Platt, Brad Platt, Lynn Plautz, Martin Plug, Yvonne Poelen, Sandra Polderman, Greg Pool, Claudia Poser, Hans-Joachim Possin, M Potrafke, Martin Potter, Stephen Poulson, Shalak Powale, Robert Powell, Marcelo Houacio Pozzo, Joelet Maria Teresa Prades, Atul Pradhan, V Prakaasha, Ashwin Prasad, Sanjay Prasad, N Prefontaine, Ian CH Prescott, Daryl Presswell, Claire Prest, Matthew Price, Leslie Price, Duncan Priestley, Nathan Prince, Pia Problemi, Helen Prosser, Shelley Pullan, Charlotte Pulver, Dheeraj Pun, Robert Purser, Adi Putra, Minna Pyhala

Andrew Quernmore, Alexis Quinlan, Tabish Qureshi

Petra Raddatz, Kieran Raftery, Rajen Raghavan, Gurdev Rai, Ash Raichura, Colleen Rains, Ganeve Rajkotia, Prabhat Raman, Prithy Rampersad, Nicola Ramplin, Helen Ranger, Michael Ranson, Jaliya Rasaputra, Babette Rasche, Solveg Rasmussen, Jamie Ratcliff, Jacqui Ratcliffe, Brett Raven, Tadeusz Rawa, Simon Rawson, M Rayappan, Shelley & Rachle Rayfield, Joy Rebello, Jeff Redding, Graeme & Janine Redfern, JF Reece, Alan Reed, David Reid, Douglas Reid, Manja Rekhi, Peter Renee, Luke Requa, Kim Restivo, Claudia Reuter, Tony Revel, Miriam Ribeiro, Heather Richards, A & MJ Richardson, David & Sue Richardson, Yann Richet, Oren Ridenour, Roger Ridsdill Smith, Ozarki Rie, Leovan Riemsdyke, John Riley, Laura-Maria Rinta, Claudia Riquelme, Isabella Riva, Eric Robbins, Norbert & An Robbrecht-De Graef, Kailas Roberts, Linda Roberts, Ben Roberts, Lisa Roberts, Simon Roberts, Carl Roberts, John Robertson, Nathan Robinson, Dave Robinson, Samuel Robinson Massey, Philip Robinson, Daniel Robinson, Angus Robinson, Malcolm Robinson, Bryan Roche, Sonya Rodgers, Hector Rodriguez, Claudia Rodriguez, David Rodriguez, Griffin Rodriguez, Sonya Rogers, Tamara Romahn, Anthony Romanidis, Robert Rome, Michael Rose, R Rose, Howard Rosenthal, Richard Rosow, Duncan Ross, Enrico Rossi, Felix Rotharmel, Sanjoy Roy, Anja Roza, Jay Ruchamkin, Amy Rucinski, Peter Ruebsamen, Wim Ruhe, Michael Ruland, Bruce Rumage, Goran & Annika Rumenius, L Russell, Lisa Ryan, Malin Rydeu, Ellyn & Andy Ryland, Watanabe Ryoko

Tanja Saarnio, Lawrence Saez, Wil Sahlman, Kengo Saito, Merja Salo, Francis Sanctis, Mark Sanderson, T Sandholdt, Adrian Sandhu, Brian Sands, Frida Sandstrom, Dr B Sanjeev, Mala Sanmugartnam, R V Sansom, Shanker Sanyal, P Saraswat, Brihas Sarathy, Dr Indrajit Sardar, Sanjay Sarma, Eugenia Sarsanedas, Josh Saunders, Mark Saunders, Wendy Saunt, Sharma Saurabh, Anthea Savage, Anne Savage, David, Louis & Nicholas Savage, DR Pereira Savid, Peter Saynt, Lisbeth Boye

Schack, Tbias Schade, Carmen & Stefan Schiene, Loren & Becky Schmidt, Stevie Schmiedel, Sebastian Schmitz, Eric Scholl, Ralp Schramm, Rolf Schrauwen, Hans & Rosi Schreck, Thomas Schrott, Olaf A Schulte, Walter Schultz, Anett Schwidrowski, Dede Schwidt-Pedersen, AT Scott, Rebecca Scott, Anna Scott, Wendy Seaky, Lorne Sederoff, Michelle Segal, Roland Seher, Lina Angelika Seifried, Seema Seiuastara, Frank Selbmann, Deb Serginson, Baily Seshagiri, Eric Seymour, Pravin Shah, Sameer Shah, Jinesh Shah, Yoram Shahak, Hasib Shakoor, S Shankaran, Bhavani Shanker, Bob Shannahan, Hariash Sharma, Rajiv Sharma, S Sharma, Frank A Sharman, S Shata, Steven Shaw, C Sheaf, Rajesh Shedde, Ajai Shekawat, Robyn Shelley, Rev Fr Baby Shepard, Rebecca Sheppard, Sham Shermiyas, Katie Shevlin, Dan Shingleton, Michael Shortland, Ian Shrier, Prakash Shukla, Victor Shum, Itay Sidat, Esther Siegrist, Merrick J Silberman, Barbara Siliquimi, Arianna Silvestri, Natalia Simanovsky, Peter Simpson, Clint Simpson, Lisa Simpson, Daniel & Ruth Sinclair, Paul Sinclair, Sukhjit Anand Singh, Randheer Geera Singh, Anraj Singh, Gurcharan Singh, Sohal Raghuvir Singh, Rama Khalsa Singh, Ramanpreet Singh, KB Singh, Ajai Singh, Alok Singhal, Michael Singleton, Capt R Sircar, Susan Skyrme, Rosemary Slark, Michael Slattery, Nathalie van der Slikke, Kirsten Slots, Catherine Sluggett, Phil Smart, Lois Smith, Alice Smith, Jay Smith, Cathy Smith, Louise Smith, John & Angela Smith, Lise Smith, Helena Smith, L Smith, Heather Smith, Vanessa Smith Holburn, Pamela Smith, A Smithee, Fenna Snater, Michael Snell, Alon Sobol, Ore Somolu, Nikki Sones, Anna Sophie, Jorg Spathelf, Derek Speirs, Stephen Spencer, Fred Spengler, Ian Spiller, Fank Sporkert, Martin Springer, Stephanie Springgay, Dr RC Squires, Krishnan Sridharan, K Srivatsa, KMR Srivatsa, Greta St John, Jenny Stainbank, Thomasina Stanford, Lee Stanning, Lieve Stassen, Craig Steed, IVD Steel, James Steele, Craig Stehn, Vanessa Stephen, Derek Stephen, D Stephen, Jules Stewart, Willemke Stilma, Catherine Stock, Leonie Stockwell, James Stoddart, Franka Stoepler, Greg Stone, Cato Stonex, Emman Stott, M Stout, Leon Strauss, Michael & Sue Streuli, Pamela Strivens, Gay Stuart, Julie Stuart-Smith, Dieter Stuckenberg, Brian Studd, KV Sudhakaran, Simona Sugoni, Ajit Sukhija, Nancy Sundberg, Eva Sunquist, Ritish Suri, Liam Swaffield, Peggy Swan, Brian Swanson, Royston Swarbrooke

Risa Tabatznik, Anita Taheer, Alex Tait, Jeanle Tallec, Jack Talman, Ariel Talmor, Bacci Tamara, Yael Tamir, Kim Tan, Carole Tapp, Sarah Tarkenton, Massimo Tarsia, Tsegyal Tashi, David Tayar, Bronwyn Taylor, S Taylor, Barb Taylor, Chris Taylor, Jeff Taylor, Lorraine Taylor, Hannah Taylor, Ben Taylor, James Taylor, Louise Teague, Ronna Temkin, Adrian Tempany, Jo Templey,

Beverly Terry, Henry Th, K Thavakumar, Claudia Theile, Susan Theron, Aaron Thieme, Dick Thoenes, Bob Thomas, Sarah Thomas, Sabina Thomas, Eileen Thompson, Martin Thompson, Neil Thompson, Richard Thomson, Jessica Thornelor, Jason Thornton, Sallie-Ann Thorp, A Throp, Premila Thurairatnam, David Thurlow, Elisabeth Thurn, Kokeny Tibor, Maria Tiguerola, Nick Todd, Celeste Tomkins, Stephen Tong, Jan Toohey, Georgina Topp, Nana Torii, Suzanne Tourvillle, Joanne Townsley, Ursula Trachsel, Michael Travers, Patrick Traynor, Tali Treibitz, Frances Trim, Manu Trivedi, Allan Trojan, Telita & John Trower, Tatyana Tsinberg, Inbul Tubi, Dr Mahesh Tunk Khatri, Wayne Tunnicliffe, Tzuk Turbovich

K Ujavari, Amy Urban, J Uzzeli

MS Vadiraja, Denis Vaillancourt, Jonathan Valdes, Jenny & Cor Valk, Jensen Helge Vandel, Iris Vandemoortele, Marc Vannoverbeke, John Vantlam, Ray Varnbuhler, Petr Vastl, Girish Vasudevan, Jerry van Veenendaal, Donald V Velsen, Mona Van Velson, Mike Venamore, S Vengadesh, Gert Venghaus, Suvir Ventataraman, Paul Venturino, Eveline Vermeersch, Monique Verschuren, Bart Versteijnen, Sonan Janzan Vertregt, Koen Vervacke, Klaus Viggers, M Vijaya, E K Vijayakumar, A Vincent, R Vinod, Narayan Vinodh, Arif Virani, Hans Visser, Krishna Vittaldev, Carol A Vitty, Paul & Marie Volkoff-Peschon, Claartje Vorstman, David Voss, Martyn de Vrier, Laurens de Vries

Sandi Wy Lai, Yonathon Wachsmann, Aron Wahl, Frank Wahner, Ali Wale, Chris Walker, Dean Wall, Max Wallenberg, Brian Wallis, Raymond Walsh, Megan Waltham, Mark Walton, Ong Beng Wan, Bernd Wanderl, JD Ward, Phillippa Ward, Richard Wareham, Satish Warier, Andrew Wasep, Zak Watson, Duncan Watson, Aaron Watt, Mark Watt, Paul Weaver, Cindy S Webb, Lawrence Webb, Robert Webster, Tanya Wegner, Anne Weiler, Mart Weiss, Vicki Weiss, Perry Weiss, Mart Weiss, Trudy van Wel, Des Wells, RE Wels, Carolyn Wetherby, Philippa Whalley, Andrea Wheatley, David Wheeler, June Wheeler, Kathleen White, Adeline White, Barry White, David Whitehead, Anthony Widdup, Andrew Wigglesworth, Jackie Wigh, Anthony Wight, Maria Wilkinson, W Will, Helmi Willems, Pierre Willems, Hans Willemsen, Anne Williams, Kathy Williams, Simon Rhys Williams, Amanda Williams, Deborah Williams, Sylvia Williamson, David Willis, Russell Willmoth, Stuart C Wilson, Joy Wilson, Tim Wilson, Charles Windsor, Phil Wingfield, Andy Winneke, Cameron Wiseman, Joanna Wiseman, Giles Wititarid, Dr Ludwig Witzani, C & J Woesthuis, Meera Wolfe, Becki Wood, Stephen Wood, Kevin Woodcock, Andrew Woolnough, Adrian Woolven, Stephen Wragg, Barrie Wraith, Richard Wright, Becky Wright, David Wright, Erik Wsppling, Mira Wuhr, Andreas & Heidi Wyder

Mark Yabsley, Melissa Yee, S & A Yorkhire, David Youna, Sandy Young, Alara Young, John & Gill Yudkin, Takebayashi Yuri

Allan Zanklusen, Bernard Zimmerman, David Ziringer, Mor Zohar, Marc U Zon, Tv Zuilen, Bostjan Zupancic, T Van Zuren, Arno Zuudwuk, Elizabeth Zvonar

Phrasebooks

LONELY PLANET

Phrasebooks

L onely Planet phrasebooks are packed with essential words and phrases to help travellers communicate with the locals. With colour tabs for quick reference, an extensive vocabulary and use of script, these handy pocket-sized language guides cover day-to-day travel situations.

- handy pocket-sized books
- easy to understand Pronunciation chapter
- clear & comprehensive Grammar chapter
- romanisation alongside script to allow ease of pronunciation
- script throughout so users can point to phrases for every situation
- full of cultural information and tips for the traveller

'... vital for a real DIY spirit and attitude in language learning'
– *Backpacker*

'the phrasebooks have good cultural backgrounders and offer solid advice for challenging situations in remote locations'
– *San Francisco Examiner*

Arabic (Egyptian) • Arabic (Moroccan) • Australian *(Australian English, Aboriginal and Torres Strait languages)* • Baltic States *(Estonian, Latvian, Lithuanian)* • Bengali • Brazilian • British • Burmese • Cantonese • Central Asia (Uyghur, Uzbek, Kyrghiz, Kazak, Pashto, Tadjik • Central Europe *(Czech, French, German, Hungarian, Italian, Slovak)* • Eastern Europe *(Bulgarian, Czech, Hungarian, Polish, Romanian, Slovak)* • Ethiopian (Amharic) • Fijian • French • German • Greek • Hebrew • Hill Tribes • Hindi & Urdu • Indonesian • Italian • Japanese • Korean • Lao • Latin American Spanish • Malay • Mandarin • Mediterranean Europe *(Albanian, Croatian, Greek, Italian, Macedonian, Maltese, Serbian, Slovene)* • Mongolian • Nepali • Pidgin • Pilipino (Tagalog) • Portugese • Quechua • Russian • Scandinavian Europe *(Danish, Finnish, Icelandic, Norwegian, Swedish)* • South-East Asia *(Burmese, Indonesian, Khmer, Lao, Malay, Tagalog Pilipino, Thai, Vietnamese)* • South Pacific Languages • Spanish (Castilian) *(also includes Catalan, Galician and Basque)* • Sri Lanka • Swahili • Thai • Tibetan • Turkish • Ukrainian • USA *(US English, Vernacular, Native American languages, Hawaiian)* • Vietnamese • Western Europe *(Basque, Catalan, Dutch, French, German, Greek, Irish, Italian, Portuguese, Scottish Gaelic, Spanish (Castilian), Welsh)*

Lonely Planet Journeys

JOURNEYS is a unique collection of travel writing – published by the company that understands travel better than anyone else. It is a series for anyone who has ever experienced – or dreamed of – the magical moment when they encountered a strange culture or saw a place for the first time. They are tales to read while you're planning a trip, while you're on the road or while you're in an armchair in front of a fire.

These outstanding titles explore our planet through the eyes of a diverse group of international writers. JOURNEYS books catch the spirit of a place, illuminate a culture, recount a crazy adventure or introduce a fascinating way of life. They always entertain, and always enrich the experience of travel.

IN RAJASTHAN
Royina Grewal

As she writes of her travels through Rajasthan, Indian writer Royina Grewal takes us behind the exotic facade of this fabled destination: here is an insider's perceptive account of India's most colourful state, conveying the excitement and challenges of a region in transition.

SHOPPING FOR BUDDHAS
Jeff Greenwald

In his obsessive search for the perfect Buddha statue in the backstreets of Kathmandu, Jeff Greenwald discovers more than he bargained for ... and his souvenir-hunting turns into an ironic metaphor for the clash between spiritual riches and material greed. Politics, religion and serious shopping collide in this witty account of an enlightening visit to Nepal.

BRIEF ENCOUNTERS
Stories of Love, Sex & Travel
edited by Michelle de Kretser

Love affairs on the road, passionate holiday flings, disastrous pick-ups, erotic encounters ... In this seductive collection of stories, 22 authors from around the world write about travel romances. A tourist in Peru falls for her handsome guide; a writer explores the ambiguities of his relationship with a Japanese woman; a beautiful young man on a train proposes marriage ... Combining fiction and reportage, *Brief Encounters* is must-have reading – for everyone who has dreamt of escape with that perfect stranger.

Includes stories by Pico Iyer, Mary Morris, Emily Perkins, Mona Simpson, Lisa St Aubin de Terán, Paul Theroux and Sara Wheeler.

Lonely Planet Travel Atlases

Lonely Planet has long been famous for the number and quality of its guidebook maps. Now we've gone one step further and produced a handy companion series: Lonely Planet travel atlases – maps of a country produced in book form.

Unlike other maps, which look good but lead travellers astray, our travel atlases have been researched on the road by Lonely Planet's experienced team of writers. All details are carefully checked to ensure the atlas corresponds with the equivalent Lonely Planet guidebook.

- full-colour throughout
- maps researched and checked by Lonely Planet authors
- place names correspond with Lonely Planet guidebooks
- no confusing spelling differences
- legend and travelling information in English, French, German, Japanese and Spanish
- size: 230 x 160 mm

Available now: Chile & Easter Island • Egypt • India & Bangladesh • Israel & the Palestinian Territories • Jordan, Syria & Lebanon • Kenya • Laos • Portugal • South Africa, Lesotho & Swaziland • Thailand • Turkey • Vietnam • Zimbabwe, Botswana & Namibia

---

Lonely Planet TV Series & Videos

Lonely Planet travel guides have been brought to life on television screens around the world. Like our guides, the programs are based on the joy of independent travel, and look honestly at some of the most exciting, picturesque and frustrating places in the world. Each show is presented by one of three travellers from Australia, England or the USA and combines an innovative mixture of video, Super-8 film, atmospheric soundscapes and original music.

Videos of each episode – containing additional footage not shown on television – are available from good book and video shops, but the availability of individual videos varies with regional screening schedules.

Video destinations include: Alaska • American Rockies • Australia – The South-East • Baja California & the Copper Canyon • Brazil • Central Asia • Chile & Easter Island • Corsica, Sicily & Sardinia – The Mediterranean Islands • East Africa (Tanzania & Zanzibar) • Ecuador & the Galapagos Islands • Greenland & Iceland • Indonesia • Israel & the Sinai Desert • Jamaica • Japan • La Ruta Maya • Morocco • New York • North India • Pacific Islands (Fiji, Solomon Islands & Vanuatu) • South India • South West China • Turkey • Vietnam • West Africa • Zimbabwe, Botswana & Namibia

The Lonely Planet TV series is produced by: Pilot Productions
The Old Studio
18 Middle Row
London W10 5AT, UK

Lonely Planet On-line

W hether you've just begun planning your next trip, or you're chasing down specific info on currency regulations or visa requirements, check out Lonely Planet On-line for up-to-the-minute travel information.

As well as mini guides to more than 250 destinations, you'll find maps, photos, travel news, health and visa updates, travel advisories, and discussion of the eco-logical and political issues you need to be aware of as you travel. You'll also find timely upgrades to popular guidebooks which you can print out and stick in the back of your book.

There's also an on-line travellers' forum where you can share your experience of life on the road, meet travel companions and ask other travellers for their recom-mendations and advice.

And of course we have a complete and up-to-date list of all Lonely Planet travel products including travel guides, diving and snorkeling guides, phrasebooks, atlases, travel literature and videos, and a simple on-line ordering facility if you can't find the book you want elsewhere.

Lonely Planet Diving & Snorkeling Guides

K nown for indispensible guidebooks to destinations all over the world, Lonely Planet's Pisces Books are the most popular series of diving and snorkeling titles available.

There are three series: **Diving & Snorkeling Guides**, **Shipwreck Diving** series and **Dive Into History**. Full colour throughout, the **Diving & Snorkeling Guides** combine quality photographs with detailed descriptions of the best dive sites for each location, giv-ing divers a glimpse of what they can expect both on land and in water. The **Dive Into History** series is perfect for the adven-ture diver or armchair traveller. The **Shipwreck Diving** series provides all the details for exploring the most interesting wrecks in the Atlantic and Pacific oceans. The list also includes under-water nature and technical guides.

Guides by Region

Lonely Planet is known worldwide for publishing practical, reliable and no-nonsense travel information in our guides and on our web site. The Lonely Planet list covers just about every accessible part of the world. Currently there are fifteen series: travel guides, Shoestrings, Condensed, Phrasebooks, Read This First, Healthy Travel, Walking guides, Cycling guides, Pisces Diving & Snorkeling guides, City Maps, Travel Atlases, Out to Eat, World Food, Journeys travel literature and Pictorials.

AFRICA Africa on a shoestring • Africa – the South • Arabic (Egyptian) phrasebook • Arabic (Moroccan) phrasebook • Cairo • Cape Town • Cape Town city map • Central Africa • East Africa • Egypt • Egypt travel atlas • Ethiopian (Amharic) phrasebook • The Gambia & Senegal • Healthy Travel Africa • Kenya • Kenya travel atlas • Malawi, Mozambique & Zambia • Morocco • North Africa • Read This First Africa • South Africa, Lesotho & Swaziland • South Africa, Lesotho & Swaziland travel atlas • Swahili phrasebook • Tanzania, Zanzibar & Pemba • Trekking in East Africa • Tunisia • West Africa • Zimbabwe, Botswana & Namibia • Zimbabwe, Botswana & Namibia Travel Atlas • World Food Morocco
Travel Literature: The Rainbird: A Central African Journey • Songs to an African Sunset: A Zimbabwean Story • Mali Blues: Traveling to an African Beat

AUSTRALIA & THE PACIFIC Auckland • Australia • Australian phrasebook • Bushwalking in Australia • Bushwalking in Papua New Guinea • Cycling New Zealand • Fiji • Fijian phrasebook • Healthy Travel Australia, NZ and the Pacific • Islands of Australia's Great Barrier Reef • Melbourne • Melbourne city map • Micronesia • New Caledonia • New South Wales & the ACT • New Zealand • Northern Territory • Outback Australia • Out To Eat – Melbourne • Out to Eat – Sydney • Papua New Guinea • Pidgin phrasebook • Queensland • Rarotonga & the Cook Islands • Samoa • Solomon Islands • South Australia • South Pacific • South Pacific Languages phrasebook • Sydney • Sydney city map • Sydney Condensed • Tahiti & French Polynesia • Tasmania • Tonga • Tramping in New Zealand • Vanuatu • Victoria • Western Australia
Travel Literature: Islands in the Clouds • Kiwi Tracks: A New Zealand Journey • Sean & David's Long Drive

CENTRAL AMERICA & THE CARIBBEAN Bahamas, Turks & Caicos • Bermuda • Central America on a shoestring • Costa Rica • Costa Rica Spanish phrasebook • Cuba • Dominican Republic & Haiti • Eastern Caribbean • Guatemala, Belize & Yucatán: La Ruta Maya • Jamaica • Mexico • Mexico City • Panama • Puerto Rico • Read This First Central & South America • World Food Mexico
Travel Literature: Green Dreams: Travels in Central America

EUROPE Amsterdam • Amsterdam city map • Amsterdam Condensed • Andalucía • Austria • Baltic States phrasebook • Barcelona • Barcelona Map • Berlin • Berlin city map • Britain • British phrasebook • Brussels, Bruges & Antwerp • Budapest • Budapest city map • Canary Islands • Central Europe • Central Europe phrasebook • Corfu & Ionians • Corsica • Crete • Crete Condensed • Croatia • Cyprus • Czech & Slovak Republics • Denmark • Dublin • Dublin Map • Eastern Europe • Eastern Europe phrasebook • Edinburgh • Estonia, Latvia & Lithuania • Europe on a shoestring • Finland • Florence • France • French phrasebook • Georgia, Armenia & Azerbaijan • Germany • German phrasebook • Greece • Greek Islands • Greek phrasebook • Hungary • Iceland, Greenland & the Faroe Islands • Ireland • Italian phrasebook • Italy • Krakow • Lisbon • The Loire • London • London city map • London Condensed • Mediterranean Europe • Mediterranean Europe phrasebook • Malta • Moscow • Munich • Norway • Paris • Paris city map • Paris Condensed • Poland • Portugal • Portugese phrasebook • Portugal travel atlas • Prague • Prague city map • Provence & the Côte d'Azur • Read This First Europe • Romania & Moldova • Rome • Russia, Ukraine & Belarus • Russian phrasebook • Scandinavian & Baltic Europe • Scandinavian Europe phrasebook • Scotland • Slovenia • Spain • Spanish phrasebook • St Petersburg • St Petersburg Map • Sweden • Switzerland • Trekking in Spain • Tuscany • Ukrainian phrasebook • Venice • Vienna • Walking in Britain • Walking in France • Walking in Ireland • Walking in Italy • Walking in Spain • Walking in Switzerland • Western Europe • Western Europe phrasebook • World Food Ireland • World Food Italy • World Food Spain
Travel Literature: The Olive Grove: Travels in Greece

INDIAN SUBCONTINENT Bangladesh • Bengali phrasebook • Bhutan • Delhi • Goa • Hindi & Urdu phrasebook • India • India & Bangladesh travel atlas • Indian Himalaya • Karakoram Highway • Kerala • Mumbai (Bombay) • Nepal • Nepali phrasebook • Pakistan • Rajasthan • Read This First: Asia & India • South India • Sri Lanka • Sri Lanka phrasebook • Trekking in the Indian Himalaya • Trekking in the Karakoram & Hindukush • Trekking in the

LONELY PLANET

Mail Order

Lonely Planet products are distributed worldwide. They are also available by mail order from Lonely Planet, so if you have difficulty finding a title please write to us. North and South American residents should write to 150 Linden St, Oakland CA 94607, USA; European and African residents should write to 10a Spring Place, London, NW5 3BH; and residents of other countries to PO Box 617, Hawthorn, Victoria 3122, Australia.

Nepal Himalaya
Travel Literature: In Rajasthan • Shopping for Buddhas • The Age Of Kali
ISLANDS OF THE INDIAN OCEAN Madagascar & Comoros • Maldives • Mauritius, Réunion & Seychelles

MIDDLE EAST & CENTRAL ASIA Bahrain, Kuwait & Qatar • Central Asia • Central Asia phrasebook • Dubai • Hebrew phrasebook • Iran • Israel & the Palestinian Territories • Israel & the Palestinian Territories travel atlas • Istanbul • Istanbul City Map • Istanbul to Cairo on a shoestring • Jerusalem • Jerusalem City Map • Jordan • Jordan, Syria & Lebanon travel atlas • Lebanon • Middle East • Oman & the United Arab Emirates • Syria • Turkey • Turkey travel atlas • Turkish phrasebook • World Food Turkey • Yemen
Travel Literature: The Gates of Damascus • Kingdom of the Film Stars: Journey into Jordan • Black on Black: Iran Revisited

NORTH AMERICA Alaska • Backpacking in Alaska • Boston • Boston Map • Baja California • California & Nevada • California Condensed • Canada • Chicago • Chicago city map • Deep South • Florida • Hawaii • Honolulu • Las Vegas • Los Angeles • Miami •Miami Map • New England • New Orleans • New York City • New York city map • New York Condensed • New York, New Jersey & Pennsylvania • Oahu • Pacific Northwest USA • Puerto Rico • Rocky Mountain • San Francisco • San Francisco city map • Seattle • Southwest USA • Texas • USA • USA phrasebook • Vancouver • Washington, DC & the Capital Region • Washington DC city map
Travel Literature: Drive Thru America

NORTH-EAST ASIA Beijing • Cantonese phrasebook • China • Hong Kong • Hong Kong city map • Hong Kong, Macau & Guangzhou • Japan • Japanese phrasebook • Japanese audio pack • Korea • Korean phrasebook • Kyoto • Mandarin phrasebook • Mongolia • Mongolian phrasebook • North-East Asia on a shoestring • Seoul • South-West China • Taiwan • Tibet • Tibetan phrasebook • Tokyo
Travel Literature: Lost Japan • In Xanadu

SOUTH AMERICA Argentina, Uruguay & Paraguay • Bolivia • Brazil • Brazilian phrasebook • Buenos Aires • Chile & Easter Island • Chile & Easter Island travel atlas • Colombia • Ecuador & the Galapagos Islands • Healthy Travel Central & South America • Latin American Spanish phrasebook • Peru • Quechua phrasebook • Rio de Janeiro • Rio de Janeiro city map • South America on a shoestring • Trekking in the Patagonian Andes • Venezuela
Travel Literature: Full Circle: A South American Journey

SOUTH-EAST ASIA Bali & Lombok • Bangkok • Bangkok city map • Burmese phrasebook • Cambodia • Hanoi • Healthy Travel Asia & India • Hill Tribes phrasebook • Ho Chi Minh City • Indonesia • Indonesia's Eastern Islands • Indonesian phrasebook • Indonesian audio pack • Jakarta • Java • Laos • Lao phrasebook • Laos travel atlas • Malay phrasebook • Malaysia, Singapore & Brunei • Myanmar (Burma) • Philippines • Pilipino (Tagalog) phrasebook • Read This First Asia & India • Singapore • South-East Asia on a shoestring • South-East Asia phrasebook • Thailand • Thailand's Islands & Beaches • Thailand travel atlas • Thai phrasebook • Thai audio pack • Vietnam • Vietnamese phrasebook • Vietnam travel atlas • World Food Thailand • World Food Vietnam

ALSO AVAILABLE: Antarctica • The Arctic • Brief Encounters: Stories of Love, Sex & Travel • Chasing Rickshaws • Lonely Planet Unpacked • Not the Only Planet: Travel Stories from Science Fiction • Sacred India • Travel with Children • Traveller's Tales

Index

Text

Bold indicates maps.
Italics indicates boxed text.

Bold indicates maps.
Italics indicates boxed text.

Bold indicates maps.
Italics indicates boxed text.

Boxed Text

MAP LEGEND

BOUNDARIES

.... International
.... State
.... Disputed

HYDROGRAPHY

.... Coastline
.... River, Creek
.... Lake
.... Intermittent Lake
.... Salt Lake
.... Canal
◎ ⤳ .... Spring, Rapids
⤙⊰ .... Waterfalls
.... Swamp

ROUTES & TRANSPORT

.... Freeway
.... Highway
.... Major Road
.... Minor Road
============ .... Unsealed Road
.... City Freeway
.... City Highway
.... City Road
.... City Street, Lane

⟯==== .... Tunnel
├──┼──●── .... Train Route & Station
══●══ .... Metro & Station
.... Pedestrian Mall
.... Tramway
╫──╫──╫──╫── .... Cable Car or Chairlift
──────── .... Walking Track
.... Walking Tour
━━━━━━━━ .... Ferry Route

AREA FEATURES

.... Building
❄ .... Park, Gardens
⁺ ⁺ × × .... Cemetery
.... Market
.... Beach, Desert
.... Urban Area

MAP SYMBOLS

⊙ **CAPITAL** .... National Capital
◉ **CAPITAL** .... State Capital
● **CITY** .... City
● **Town** .... Town
● **Village** .... Village
○ .... Point of Interest

■ .... Place to Stay
▲ .... Camping Ground
⚏ .... Caravan Park
⌂ .... Hut or Chalet

▼ .... Place to Eat
🍺 .... Pub or Bar

✈ .... Airport (International)
✛ .... Airport (Domestic)
∴ .... Archaeological Site
❸ .... Bank
🏖 .... Beach
⚠ .... Border Crossing
卍 .... Buddhist Temple
⛪ .... Church
☯ .... Embassy
⊕ .... Hammam
卐 .... Hindu Temple
✛ .... Hospital
⚔ .... Monument
☪ .... Mosque
🏛 .... Museum

🛟 .... National Park
🏰 .... Palace
)(............... Pass
⛽ .... Petrol Station
★ .... Police Station
✉ .... Post Office
❖ .... Shopping Centre
卍 .... Sikh Temple
🏊 .... Swimming Pool
☎ .... Telephone
🏛 .... Temple
◻ .... Tomb
❶ .... Tourist Information
● .... Transport
🐘 .... Zoo

Note: not all symbols displayed above appear in this book

LONELY PLANET OFFICES

Australia
PO Box 617, Hawthorn 3122, Victoria
tel: 03-9819 1877 fax: 03-9819 6459
e-mail: talk2us@lonelyplanet.com.au

USA
150 Linden St, Oakland, CA 94607
tel: 510-893 8555 TOLL FREE: 800 275-8555
fax: 510-893 8572
e-mail: info@lonelyplanet.com

UK
10a Spring Place, London, NW5 3BH
tel: 020-7428 4800 fax: 020-7428 4828
e-mail: go@lonelyplanet.co.uk

France
1 rue du Dahomey, 75011 Paris
tel: 01 55 25 33 00 fax: 01 55 25 33 01
e-mail: bip@lonelyplanet.fr

World Wide Web: www.lonelyplanet.com *or* AOL keyword: lp
Lonely Planet Images: lpi@lonelyplanet.com.au